COMMON ENGLISH BIBLE

a fresh translation to touch the heart and mind

HOLY BIBLE

www.CommonEnglishBible.com

Morehouse Publishing, 4775 Linglestown Road, Harrisburg, PA 17112

Morehouse Publishing, 19 East 34th Street, New York, NY 10016

Morehouse Publishing is an imprint of Church Publishing Incorporated.

www.churchpublishing.org

ISBN: 978-0-8192-2928-1

Printed in the United States of America

Philip Lee Montgomery
February 16, 2020

COMMON ENGLISH BIBLE

a fresh translation to touch the heart and mind

CONTENTS

OLD TESTAMENT

CONTENTS

NEW TESTAMENT

CONTENTS ALPHABETICAL

OLD TESTAMENT

CONTENTS ALPHABETICAL

NEW TESTAMENT

ABBREVIATIONS AND TERMS

Aram Aramaic
BCE Before the Common Era; traditionally BC: before Christ
CE Common Era; traditionally Anno Domini: year since the Lord's birth
cf compare
chap chapter
DSS Dead Sea Scrolls found at Qumran
- **(1QIsa^{a})** Isaiah scroll *a* in Cave 1 of the Dead Sea Scrolls
- **(1QDeut^{b})** Deuteronomy scroll *b* in Cave 1 of the Dead Sea Scrolls
- **(4QDeut^{b})** Deuteronomy scroll *b* in Cave 4 of the Dead Sea Scrolls
- **(4QDeut^{h})** Deuteronomy scroll *h* in Cave 4 of the Dead Sea Scrolls
- **(4QDeut^{j})** Deuteronomy scroll *j* in Cave 4 of the Dead Sea Scrolls
- **(4QDeut^{q})** Deuteronomy scroll *q* in Cave 4 of the Dead Sea Scrolls
- **(4QPhyl^{n})** Phylactery scroll *n* in Cave 4 of the Dead Sea Scrolls
- **(4QSam^{a})** Samuel scroll *a* in Cave 4 of the Dead Sea Scrolls
- **(4QSam^{b})** Samuel scroll *b* in Cave 4 of the Dead Sea Scrolls
- **(4QSam^{c})** Samuel scroll *c* in Cave 4 of the Dead Sea Scrolls
- **(4QTest)** Testimonia in Cave 4 of the Dead Sea Scrolls
- **(8QMez)** Mezuza scroll in Cave 8 of the Dead Sea Scrolls
- **(11QPs^{a})** Psalms scroll *a* in Cave 11 of the Dead Sea Scrolls

Eth Ethiopic translation of 2 Esdras in the Ge'ez language
Gk Greek
- **Gk uncertain** The meaning of the Greek text is uncertain.

Heb Hebrew
- **Heb uncertain** The meaning of the Hebrew text is uncertain.

Josephus *Ant.* Works of Flavius Josephus: Antiquities of the Jews
Kethib Aramaic term meaning what is written (the written consonantal text)
Lat Latin
LXX Septuagint; Greek translation of Hebrew Bible by seventy translators
- **LXX^{A}** In Samuel, the Greek uncial Alexandrinus
- **LXX^{B}** In Samuel, the Greek uncial Vaticanus
- **LXX^{L}** In Samuel, Lucianic Greek manuscripts
- **LXX^{M}** In Samuel, the Greek uncial Coislinianus
- **LXX^{N}** In Samuel, the Greek uncials Basilianus and Vaticanus
- **LXX^{1}** In Tobit, the Greek uncial Sinaiticus
- **LXX^{2}** In Tobit, the Greek uncials Alexandrinus and Vaticanus
- **LXX^{a}** in Sirach the Greek uncials Sinaiticus, Alexandrinus, and Vaticanus
- **LXX^{b}** In Sirach the Origenic and Lucianic Greek manuscripts

MT Masoretic Text; the Hebrew Bible
NT New Testament
OL Old Latin; manuscripts in Latin prior to the Vulgate
OT Old Testament
pl plural
Qere Aramaic term meaning what is read aloud (the vocalized text)
Sam Samaritan Hebrew text of the Old Testament
Selah Musical direction of uncertain meaning found in Psalms
Sym Greek version of the Old Testament translated by Symmachus
Syr Syriac, a translation known as the Peshitta in a dialect of the Aramaic language
Tg Targum; Aramaic translation of Hebrew Bible
Vulg Vulgate; standardized Latin version of the Bible

MEASURES

Capacity and linear measures

ammah *length of a forearm, standardized at eighteen inches; traditionally a cubit*
bath *a liquid measure equivalent to approximately twenty quarts*
ephah *a dry measure for flour or grains, approximately twenty quarts (five gallons)*
etsbah *length of the finger or thumb; traditionally a fingerbreadth*
hin *a liquid measure for wine or water, approximately one gallon*
homer *the largest dry measure, fifty gallons, equivalent to ten ephah*
issaron *one-tenth of an unknown weight; possibly an equivalent for omer*
kab *an unknown measure in 2 Kgs 6:25*
kor *a dry measure for grain, possibly equal to a homer; approximately fifty gallons as a liquid measure in Ezekiel*
litra *a Roman pound equal to approximately twelve ounces dry*
log *a liquid measure for oil in Leviticus, approximately two-thirds of a pint*
metretes *a liquid measure of approximately ten gallons*
milion *a mile; a Roman mile was 1,000 paces or approximately 4,855 feet*
omer *one-tenth of an ephah or two quarts dry*
pechon *approximately eighteen inches; traditionally a cubit*
pim *two-thirds of a shekel*
qaneh *a measuring rod in Ezekiel equivalent to six ammah or nine feet*
seah *a dry measure of grain, possibly seven and a half quarts but may be smaller amount in Genesis*
shearim *an unknown dry measure of grain*
stadion *a Roman linear measurement of approximately 607 feet*
tefakh or tofakh *width of the hand at the base of the fingers; traditionally a handbreadth or a palm*
tsimdo *traditionally an acre, the area that a team can plow in a day*
zereth *distance between tip of thumb to little finger; traditionally a span*

Monetary measures

beqa *one-half shekel, typically one-fifth of an ounce; ten or twelve gerahs*
daric *a gold Persian coin named after Darius 1, weighing one-third of an ounce*
denarion, denaria (pl) *a coin equivalent in value to one day's work*
drachme, drachmen (pl) *a silver coin equivalent in value to a denarion; also possibly a daric*
gerah *one-twentieth or one twenty-fourth of a shekel*
kikkar *a unit of weight in the common shekel system; traditionally a talent*
kodrantes *a coin equivalent to two lepta*
lepto *a coin equivalent to one-128th of a denarion*
maneh *in the Old Testament possibly fifty or sixty sanctuary shekels; in the New Testament a monetary unit equivalent to one hundred denaria*
shekel *basic measure, typically two-fifths of an ounce, for three monetary weight systems attested in the Old Testament: the royal shekel, the sanctuary shekel, and the common shekel*
talanta *a coin equivalent to six thousand denaria; traditionally a talent. In the Greek period, one talent is approximately 57 pounds of weight.*
qesitah *an unknown monetary weight*

PREFACE

The King James Version of the Bible was published in 1611. For two centuries the KJV competed for readership with the Geneva Bible. However, by the nineteenth century in America, the KJV would be described as the "common English Bible," because it was the most widely used translation of Christian scripture. Numerous translations have appeared since that time. However, it has proved difficult to combine concern for accuracy and accessibility in one translation that the typical reader or worshipper would be able to understand. Therefore, readers in the twenty-first century, four hundred years after the creation of the KJV, need and deserve a new translation that is suitable for personal devotion, for communal worship, and for classroom study.

The Common English Bible (CEB), completed in 2011, is a fresh translation of the Bible. Some editions include the books of the Apocrypha that are used in Anglican, Orthodox, and Catholic congregations. The translation is sponsored by the Common English Bible Committee, which is an alliance of denominational publishers, including Presbyterian (USA), Episcopalian, United Methodist, Disciples of Christ, and United Church of Christ representatives.

One hundred twenty biblical scholars from twenty-two faith traditions worked as translators for the CEB. In addition, members of seventy-seven reading groups from congregations throughout North America reviewed and responded to early drafts of the translation. As a result, more than five hundred individuals were integrally involved in the preparation of the CEB. These individuals represent the sorts of diversity that permit this new translation to speak to people of various religious convictions and different social locations.

The translators, reviewers, and editors represent the following faith communities: African Methodist Episcopal Church, American Baptist, Anglican, Baptist, Baptist General Conference, Church of the Nazarene, Disciples of Christ, Episcopal Church, Evangelical Free Church, Evangelical Lutheran Church, Free Methodist, Mennonite, Moravian, National Baptist, Presbyterian (USA), Progressive National Baptist, Quaker, Reformed Church in America, Reform Judaism, Roman Catholic Church, Seventh-day Adventist, United Churches of Christ, and United Methodist. The CEB is truly a Bible created by churches and for the Church.

Accuracy and clarity. The CEB translators balance rigorous accuracy in the rendition of ancient texts with an equally passionate commitment to clarity of expression in the target language. Translators create sentences and choose vocabulary that will be readily understood when the biblical text is read aloud. Two examples illustrate this concern for accuracy and clarity.

First, *ben 'adam* (Hebrew) and *huios tou anthrōpou* (Greek) are best translated as "human being" (rather than "son of man") except in cases of direct address, where CEB renders "human one" (instead of "son of man" or "mortal"; e.g., Ezek 2:1). When *ho huios tou anthrōpou* is used as a title for Jesus, the CEB refers to Jesus as "the Human One." People who have grown accustomed to hearing Jesus refer to himself in the Gospels as "the Son of Man" may find this jarring. Why "Human One"? Jesus' primary language would have been Aramaic, so he would have used the Aramaic phrase *bar enosha*. This phrase has the sense of "a human" or "a human such as I." This phrase was taken over into Greek in a phrase that might be translated woodenly as "son of humanity." However, Greek usage often refers to "a son of x" in the sense of "one who has the character of x." For example,

Luke 10:6 refers in Greek to "a son of peace," a phrase that has the sense of "one who shares in peace." In the Greek of Acts 13:10 Paul calls a sorcerer "a son of the devil." This is not a reference to the sorcerer's actual ancestry, but it serves to identify his character. He is devilish—or more simply in English "a devil." *Human* or *human one* represents accurately the Aramaic and Greek idioms and reflects common English usage. Finally, many references to Jesus as "the Human One" refer back to Daniel 7:13, where Daniel "saw one like a human being" (Greek *huios anthropou*). By using the title Human One in the Gospels and Acts, the CEB preserves this connection to Daniel's vision.

Second, the phrase "Lord of hosts" (*Yahweh sebaoth* in Hebrew; *Kyrios sabaoth* in Greek) appears hundreds of times in older Bibles and persists as an idiom in translations that preserve King James usage. This archaic translation is no longer meaningful to most English speakers. The CEB renders *Yahweh sebaoth* and *Kyrios sabaoth* as "Lord of heavenly forces," which conveys accurately the meaning of the Hebrew and Greek phrases by using contemporary English language.

English speakers, especially when telling a story, writing a letter, or engaging in conversation, make frequent use of contractions. As a result, translators have often used contractions, particularly in direct speech, in the CEB. However, formal genres of literature typically do not include contractions. As a result, translators did not include contractions in contexts such as (a) formal trials or royal interviews (socially formal situations), (b) much divine discourse (e.g., Hos 11:9; Exod 24:12), and (c) poetic and/or liturgical discourse (several types of psalms).

Texts. Translators of the Old Testament used as their base text the Masoretic Text (MT) as found in Biblia Hebraica Stuttgartensia and the published fascicles of Biblia Hebraica Quinta. For some books the Hebrew University Bible Project was consulted. Judicious departures from the Masoretic Text, based on ancient manuscript (e.g., reading with the Dead Sea Scrolls in 1 Sam 10:27*b* or Deut 32:8) and versional evidence (e.g., reading with the Septuagint in Gen 4:8), were sometimes necessary. In those situations, in which one may postulate two literary editions of a biblical book, or in which there are major or lengthy differences between the Masoretic Text and other texts or versions (e.g., 1 Sam 17), the CEB translated the edition that became canon in the Masoretic Text.

Translators of the New Testament used as their base text the eclectic Greek text known as Nestle Aland, the twenty-seventh edition, which was published in 1993.

Translators of the Apocrypha faced a more complicated set of choices. Translators generally used the base text presented in the Göttingen Septuagint. For those books not yet published in the fascicles of the Göttingen Septuagint, translators used the 2006 revised edition of Rahlfs' Septuaginta, edited by Robert Hanhart. However, in those instances in which Hebrew texts have survived and offer a better reading (e.g., in Sirach and Tobit), the translator noted alternative readings to the Greek Septuagint. Second Esdras presents a special problem, explained in a footnote about the Latin text.

Footnotes. Translators decided, in certain instances, that they should explain their translations or textual decisions. However, notes are kept to a minimum and are rendered with utmost concision. Such notes when present offer: (a) evidence from ancient texts and versions (e.g., LXX; MT *men of*); (b) brief philological comment (e.g., Heb uncertain); (c) explanations of anomalies in versification (e.g., Acts 8:37: Critical editions of the Gk New Testament do not include 8:37 *Philip said to him, "If you believe with your whole heart, you can be." The eunuch answered, "I believe that Jesus Christ is God's Son"*); (d) citations of the Old Testament in the New Testament; and rarely (e) alternative translations (e.g., Or *everyone*). In those instances in which the Old Testament is cited in the New Testament, the quoted text is set in italic font.

Measurements. When possible, the CEB converts linear and spatial dimensions to feet and inches. Thus archaic terms such as rods, cubits, spans, handbreadths, and fingerbreadths are replaced with feet and inches. For example, Genesis 6:15 gives the dimensions of Noah's ark in *'ammah* or "forearms." Most translations since the KJV use the archaic English cubit to translate *'ammah:* "the length of the ark three hundred cubits, its width fifty cubits, and its height thirty cubits." The CEB translates the dimensions of the ark as "four hundred fifty feet long, seventy-five feet wide, and forty-five feet high."

The CEB prefers to transliterate (rather than translate) measurements of capacity, both wet (e.g., bath) and dry (e.g., homer), as well as measurements of weight (e.g., talent; Gk *talanta*). When feasible, a footnote is allowed to calculate the rough equivalent in a U.S. English measurement, such as quarts.

Monetary values are inherently relative, and prices are constantly changing. Therefore, the CEB prefers to transliterate (rather than translate) monetary weights (e.g., shekel) and coins (e.g., denarion).

Months in the biblical lunar calendar are transliterated, with a footnote to indicate the approximate month or months in the Gregorian solar calendar (e.g., Nisan is March–April).

Pronouns. In ancient Hebrew and Greek a pronoun is often bound with the verb. If the translator is too literal, the English reader loses the antecedent of the pronoun so that one cannot tell who is speaking or acting in the sentence or paragraph. This problem occurs throughout much biblical literature. The CEB addresses this issue by substituting a noun for a pronoun, but only when the antecedent is clear. Because this problem and its resolution are so common, the CEB usually does not offer footnotes to identify these substitutions. CEB translators also use gender-inclusive or neutral syntax for translating pronouns that refer to humans, unless context requires otherwise.

Consistency. Although translators often try to use the same English word for a Hebrew or Greek word, many words in any language offer a breadth of meanings that do not readily correlate with a single word in the target language. For example, the Hebrew word *torah*, which has often been translated as Law, is often better translated as Instruction. The same could be said for *Sheol* (Hebrew) and *Hades* (Greek). The CEB translates these two terms as "grave" or "death" and "underworld" or "hell," respectively depending on context. A mechanical selection of any one term for words that involve semantic breadth would preclude a translation sensitive to the originating literary context.

The women and men who participated in the creation of the CEB hope that those who read and study it will find the translation to be an accurate, clear, and inspiring version of Christian scripture.

The Editorial Board of the Common English Bible
www.CommonEnglishBible.com

OLD TESTAMENT

GENESIS

World's creation in seven days

1 When God began to create[a] the heavens
and the earth—2the earth was without shape or form, it was dark over the
deep sea, and God's wind swept over the
waters—3God said, "Let there be light."
And so light appeared. 4God saw how good
the light was. God separated the light from
the darkness. 5God named the light Day
and the darkness Night.

There was evening and there was morning: the first day.

6God said, "Let there be a dome in the
middle of the waters to separate the waters
from each other." 7God made the dome and
separated the waters under the dome from
the waters above the dome. And it happened
in that way. 8God named the dome Sky.

There was evening and there was morning: the second day.

9God said, "Let the waters under the sky
come together into one place so that the
dry land can appear." And that's what happened. 10God named the dry land Earth,
and he named the gathered waters Seas.
God saw how good it was. 11God said, "Let
the earth grow plant life: plants yielding
seeds and fruit trees bearing fruit with
seeds inside it, each according to its kind
throughout the earth." And that's what
happened. 12The earth produced plant life:
plants yielding seeds, each according to its
kind, and trees bearing fruit with seeds inside it, each according to its kind. God saw
how good it was.

13There was evening and there was morning: the third day.

14God said, "Let there be lights in the
dome of the sky to separate the day from
the night. They will mark events, sacred seasons, days, and years. 15They will be lights in
the dome of the sky to shine on the earth."
And that's what happened. 16God made the
stars and two great lights: the larger light
to rule over the day and the smaller light
to rule over the night. 17God put them in
the dome of the sky to shine on the earth,
18to rule over the day and over the night,
and to separate the light from the darkness.
God saw how good it was.

19There was evening and there was morning: the fourth day.

20God said, "Let the waters swarm with
living things, and let birds fly above the earth
up in the dome of the sky." 21God created
the great sea animals and all the tiny living
things that swarm in the waters, each according to its kind, and all the winged birds, each
according to its kind. God saw how good it
was. 22Then God blessed them: "Be fertile
and multiply and fill the waters in the seas,
and let the birds multiply on the earth."

23There was evening and there was morning: the fifth day.

24God said, "Let the earth produce every
kind of living thing: livestock, crawling
things, and wildlife." And that's what happened. 25God made every kind of wildlife,
every kind of livestock, and every kind of
creature that crawls on the ground. God
saw how good it was. 26Then God said,
"Let us make humanity in our image to resemble us so that they may take charge of
the fish of the sea, the birds in the sky, the
livestock, all the earth, and all the crawling
things on earth."

27God created humanity
in God's own image,
in the divine image God created them,[b]
male and female God created them.

28God blessed them and said to them,
"Be fertile and multiply; fill the earth and
master it. Take charge of the fish of the sea,
the birds in the sky, and everything crawling on the ground." 29Then God said, "I now
give to you all the plants on the earth that
yield seeds and all the trees whose fruit
produces its seeds within it. These will be
your food. 30To all wildlife, to all the birds
in the sky, and to everything crawling on
the ground—to everything that breathes—
I give all the green grasses for food." And
that's what happened. 31God saw everything he had made: it was supremely good.

[a]Or *In the beginning, God created* [b]Heb has singular *him*, referring to *humanity*.

There was evening and there was morning: the sixth day.

2 The heavens and the earth and all who live in them were completed. 2 On the sixth[c] day God completed all the work that he had done, and on the seventh day God rested from all the work that he had done. 3 God blessed the seventh day and made it holy, because on it God rested from all the work of creation.[d] 4 This is the account of the heavens and the earth when they were created.

World's creation in the garden

On the day the LORD God made earth and sky— 5 before any wild plants appeared on the earth, and before any field crops grew, because the LORD God hadn't yet sent rain on the earth and there was still no human being[e] to farm the fertile land, 6 though a stream rose from the earth and watered all of the fertile land— 7 the LORD God formed the human[f] from the topsoil of the fertile land[g] and blew life's breath into his nostrils. The human came to life. 8 The LORD God planted a garden in Eden in the east and put there the human he had formed. 9 In the fertile land, the LORD God grew every beautiful tree with edible fruit, and also he grew the tree of life in the middle of the garden and the tree of the knowledge of good and evil.

10 A river flows from Eden to water the garden, and from there it divides into four headwaters. 11 The name of the first river is the Pishon. It flows around the entire land of Havilah, where there is gold. 12 That land's gold is pure, and the land also has sweet-smelling resins and gemstones.[h] 13 The name of the second river is the Gihon. It flows around the entire land of Cush. 14 The name of the third river is the Tigris, flowing east of Assyria; and the name of the fourth river is the Euphrates.

15 The LORD God took the human and settled him in the garden of Eden to farm it and to take care of it. 16 The LORD God commanded the human, "Eat your fill from all of the garden's trees; 17 but don't eat from the tree of the knowledge of good and evil, because on the day you eat from it, you will die!" 18 Then the LORD God said, "It's not good that the human is alone. I will make him a helper that is perfect for him." 19 So the LORD God formed from the fertile land all the wild animals and all the birds in the sky and brought them to the human to see what he would name them. The human gave each living being its name. 20 The human named all the livestock, all the birds in the sky, and all the wild animals. But a helper perfect for him was nowhere to be found.

21 So the LORD God put the human into a deep and heavy sleep, and took one of his ribs and closed up the flesh over it. 22 With the rib taken from the human, the LORD God fashioned a woman and brought her to the human being. 23 The human[i] said,

"This one finally is bone from my bones
and flesh from my flesh.
She will be called a woman[j]
because from a man[k] she was taken."

24 This is the reason that a man leaves his father and mother and embraces his wife, and they become one flesh. 25 The two of them were naked, the man and his wife, but they weren't embarrassed.

Knowledge, not eternal life

3 The snake was the most intelligent[l] of all the wild animals that the LORD God had made. He said to the woman, "Did God really say that you shouldn't eat from any tree in the garden?"

2 The woman said to the snake, "We may eat the fruit of the garden's trees 3 but not the fruit of the tree in the middle of the garden. God said, 'Don't eat from it, and don't touch it, or you will die.'"

4 The snake said to the woman, "You won't die! 5 God knows that on the day you eat from it, you will see clearly and you will be like God, knowing good and evil." 6 The woman saw that the tree was beautiful with delicious food and that the tree would provide wisdom, so she took some of its

[c] LXX, Sam, Syr; MT *seventh* [d] Or *from all his work, which God created to do* [e] Or *man* (Heb *adam*) [f] Heb *adam* [g] Heb *adamah* [h] Heb uncertain [i] Or *man* (Heb *adam*) [j] Or *wife* (Heb *ishshah*) [k] Or *husband* (Heb *ish*) [l] Heb sounds like *naked*.

fruit and ate it, and also gave some to her
husband, who was with her, and he ate it.
7Then they both saw clearly and knew that
they were naked. So they sewed fig leaves
together and made garments for themselves.
8During that day's cool evening breeze,
they heard the sound of the LORD God
walking in the garden; and the man and his
wife hid themselves from the LORD God in
the middle of the garden's trees. 9The LORD
God called to the man and said to him,
"Where are you?"
10The man[m] replied, "I heard your sound
in the garden; I was afraid because I was
naked, and I hid myself."
11He said, "Who told you that you were
naked? Did you eat from the tree, which I
commanded you not to eat?"
12The man said, "The woman you gave
me, she gave me some fruit[n] from the tree,
and I ate."
13The LORD God said to the woman,
"What have you done?!"
And the woman said, "The snake tricked
me, and I ate."
14The LORD God said to the snake,
"Because you did this,
you are the one cursed
out of all the farm animals,
out of all the wild animals.
On your belly you will crawl,
and dust you will eat
every day of your life.
15I will put contempt
between you and the woman,
between your offspring and hers.
They will strike your head,
but you will strike at their heels."
16To the woman he said,
"I will make your pregnancy very painful;
in pain you will bear children.
You will desire your husband,
but he will rule over you."
17To the man he said, "Because you listened to your wife's voice and you ate
from the tree that I commanded, 'Don't eat
from it,'
cursed is the fertile land because of you;
in pain you will eat from it
every day of your life.
18Weeds and thistles will grow for you,
even as you eat the field's plants;
19by the sweat of your face
you will eat bread—
until you return to the fertile land,
since from it you were taken;
you are soil,
to the soil you will return."
20The man named his wife Eve[o] because
she is the mother of everyone who lives.
21The LORD God made the man and his wife
leather clothes and dressed them. 22The
LORD God said, "The human being[p] has now
become like one of us, knowing good and
evil." Now, so he doesn't stretch out his hand
and take also from the tree of life and eat and
live forever, 23the LORD God sent him out of
the garden of Eden to farm the fertile land
from which he was taken. 24He drove out the
human. To the east of the garden of Eden, he
stationed winged creatures wielding flaming
swords to guard the way to the tree of life.

Cain and Abel

4 The man Adam knew his wife Eve intimately. She became pregnant and gave
birth to Cain, and said, "I have given life
to[q] a man with the LORD's help." 2She gave
birth a second time to Cain's brother Abel.
Abel cared for the flocks, and Cain farmed
the fertile land.
3Some time later, Cain presented an offering to the LORD from the land's crops
4while Abel presented his flock's oldest
offspring with their fat. The LORD looked
favorably on Abel and his sacrifice 5but
didn't look favorably on Cain and his sacrifice. Cain became very angry and looked
resentful. 6The LORD said to Cain, "Why are
you angry, and why do you look so resentful? 7If you do the right thing, won't you
be accepted? But if you don't do the right
thing, sin will be waiting at the door ready
to strike! It will entice you, but you must
rule over it."

[m]Or *He* [n]Heb lacks *some fruit.* [o]Heb sounds like *live.* [p]Or *man* (Heb *adam*) [q]Or *created;* Heb sounds similar to *Cain.*

8 Cain said to his brother Abel, "Let's go
out to the field."[r] When they were in the
field, Cain attacked his brother Abel and
killed him.
9 The LORD said to Cain, "Where is your
brother Abel?"
Cain said, "I don't know. Am I my brother's guardian?"
10 The LORD said, "What did you do? The
voice of your brother's blood is crying to
me from the ground. 11 You are now cursed
from the ground that opened its mouth to
take your brother's blood from your hand.
12 When you farm the fertile land, it will no
longer grow anything for you, and you will
become a roving nomad on the earth."
13 Cain said to the LORD, "My punishment is more than I can bear. 14 Now that
you've driven me away from the fertile land
and I am hidden from your presence, I'm
about to become a roving nomad on the
earth, and anyone who finds me will kill me."
15 The LORD said to him, "It won't
happen;[s] anyone who kills Cain will be paid
back seven times." The LORD put a sign on
Cain so that no one who found him would
assault him. 16 Cain left the LORD's presence, and he settled down in the land of
Nod, east of Eden.

Cain's descendants

17 Cain knew his wife intimately. She became pregnant and gave birth to Enoch.
Cain built a city and named the city after
his son Enoch.
18 Irad was born to Enoch. Irad fathered
Mehujael, Mehujael fathered Methushael,
and Methushael fathered Lamech. 19 Lamech
took two wives, the first named Adah and the
second Zillah. 20 Adah gave birth to Jabal; he
was the ancestor of those who live in tents
and own livestock. 21 His brother's name was
Jubal; he was the ancestor of those who play
stringed and wind instruments. 22 Zillah also
gave birth to Tubal-cain, the ancestor of[t]
blacksmiths and all artisans of bronze and
iron. Tubal-cain's sister was Naamah.
23 Lamech said to his wives,
"Adah and Zillah, listen to my voice;
wives of Lamech,
pay attention to my words:
I killed a man for wounding me,
a boy for striking me;
24 so Cain will be paid back seven times
and Lamech seventy-seven times."
25 Adam knew his wife intimately again,
and she gave birth to a son. She named him
Seth[u] "because God has given me another
child in place of Abel, whom Cain killed."
26 Seth also fathered a son and named him
Enosh. At that time, people began to worship in the LORD's name.

Adam's descendants

5 This is the record of Adam's descendants. On the day God created humanity,
he made them to resemble God 2 and created
them male and female. He blessed them
and called them humanity[v] on the day they
were created. 3 When Adam was 130 years
old, he became the father of a son in his
image, resembling him, and named him
Seth. 4 After Seth's birth, Adam lived 800
years; he had other sons and daughters. 5 In
all, Adam lived 930 years, and he died.
6 When Seth was 105 years old, he
became the father of Enosh. 7 After the
birth of Enosh, Seth lived 807 years; and
he had other sons and daughters. 8 In all,
Seth lived 912 years, and he died.
9 When Enosh was 90 years old, he
became the father of Kenan. 10 After Kenan's birth, Enosh lived 815 years; and
he had other sons and daughters. 11 In
all, Enosh lived 905 years, and he died.
12 When Kenan was 70 years old, he became the father of Mahalalel. 13 After the
birth of Mahalalel, Kenan lived 840 years;
and he had other sons and daughters. 14 In
all, Kenan lived 910 years, and he died.
15 When Mahalalel was 65 years old,
he became the father of Jared. 16 After
Jared's birth, Mahalalel lived 830 years;
and he had other sons and daughters.
17 In all, Mahalalel lived 895 years, and
he died.
18 When Jared was 162 years old, he became the father of Enoch. 19 After Enoch's

[r] LXX, Syr, Vulg, Sam; MT lacks *Let's go out to the field.* [s] LXX, Syr, Vulg; MT *therefore* [t] Heb lacks *the ancestor of.*
[u] Sounds like the Heb verb *gave* [v] Heb *adam*

birth, Jared lived 800 years; and he had other sons and daughters. 20 In all, Jared lived 962 years, and he died.

21 When Enoch was 65 years old, he became the father of Methuselah. 22 Enoch walked with God. After Methuselah's birth, Enoch lived 300 years; and he had other sons and daughters. 23 In all, Enoch lived 365 years. 24 Enoch walked with God and disappeared because God took him.

25 When Methuselah was 187 years old, he became the father of Lamech. 26 After Lamech's birth, Methuselah lived 782 years; and he had other sons and daughters. 27 In all, Methuselah lived 969 years, and he died.

28 When Lamech was 182 years old, he became the father of a son 29 and named him Noah, saying, "This one will give us relief[w] from our hard work, from the pain in our hands, because of the fertile land that the LORD cursed." 30 After Noah's birth, Lamech lived 595 years; and he had other sons and daughters. 31 In all, Lamech lived 777 years, and he died.

32 When Noah was 500 years old, Noah became the father of Shem, Ham, and Japheth.

Ancient heroes

6 When the number of people started to increase throughout the fertile land, daughters were born to them. 2 The divine beings saw how beautiful these human women were, so they married the ones they chose. 3 The LORD said, "My breath[x] will not remain in humans forever, because they are flesh. They will live one hundred twenty years." 4 In those days, giants[y] lived on the earth and also afterward, when divine beings and human daughters had sexual relations and gave birth to children. These were the ancient heroes, famous men.

Great flood

5 The LORD saw that humanity had become thoroughly evil on the earth and that every idea their minds thought up was always completely evil. 6 The LORD regretted making human beings on the earth, and he was heartbroken. 7 So the LORD said, "I will wipe off of the land the human race that I've created: from human beings to livestock to the crawling things to the birds in the skies, because I regret I ever made them." 8 But as for Noah, the LORD approved of him.

9 These are Noah's descendants. In his generation, Noah was a moral and exemplary man; he[z] walked with God. 10 Noah had three sons: Shem, Ham, and Japheth. 11 In God's sight, the earth had become corrupt and was filled with violence. 12 God saw that the earth was corrupt, because all creatures behaved corruptly on the earth.

13 God said to Noah, "The end has come for all creatures, since they have filled the earth with violence. I am now about to destroy them along with the earth, 14 so make a wooden ark.[a] Make the ark with nesting places and cover it inside and out with tar. 15 This is how you should make it: four hundred fifty feet long, seventy-five feet wide, and forty-five feet high. 16 Make a roof[b] for the ark and complete it one foot from the top.[c] Put a door in its side. In the hold below, make the second and third decks.

17 "I am now bringing the floodwaters over the earth to destroy everything under the sky that breathes. Everything on earth is about to take its last breath. 18 But I will set up my covenant with you. You will go into the ark together with your sons, your wife, and your sons' wives. 19 From all living things—from all creatures—you are to bring a pair, male and female, into the ark with you to keep them alive. 20 From each kind of bird, from each kind of livestock, and from each kind of everything that crawls on the ground—a pair from each will go in with you to stay alive. 21 Take some from every kind of food and stow it as food for you and for the animals."

22 Noah did everything exactly as God commanded him.

7 The LORD said to Noah, "Go into the ark with your whole household, because

[w] Heb resembles the sound of Noah's name. [x] Or *spirit* [y] Or *the Nephilim* [z] Heb *Noah* [a] Or *ark of gopher wood*, an unknown species of tree [b] Or *window* [c] Heb uncertain

among this generation I've seen that you are a moral man. 2 From every clean animal, take seven pairs, a male and his mate; and from every unclean animal, take one pair, a male and his mate; 3 and from the birds in the sky as well, take seven pairs, male and female, so that their offspring will survive throughout the earth. 4 In seven days from now I will send rain on the earth for forty days and forty nights. I will wipe off from the fertile land every living thing that I have made."

5 Noah did everything the LORD commanded him.

6 Noah was 600 years old when the floodwaters arrived on earth. 7 Noah, his sons, his wife, and his sons' wives with him entered the ark to escape the floodwaters. 8 From the clean and unclean animals, from the birds and everything crawling on the ground, 9 two of each, male and female, went into the ark with Noah, just as God commanded Noah. 10 After seven days, the floodwaters arrived on the earth. 11 In the six hundredth year of Noah's life, in the second month, on the seventeenth day—on that day all the springs of the deep sea erupted, and the windows in the skies opened. 12 It rained on the earth forty days and forty nights. 13 That same day Noah, with his sons Shem, Ham, and Japheth, Noah's wife, and his sons' three wives, went into the ark. 14 They and every kind of animal—every kind of livestock, every kind that crawls on the ground, every kind of bird[d]—15 they came to Noah and entered the ark, two of every creature that breathes. 16 Male and female of every creature went in, just as God had commanded him. Then the LORD closed the door behind them.[e]

17 The flood remained on the earth for forty days. The waters rose, lifted the ark, and it rode high above the earth. 18 The waters rose and spread out over the earth. The ark floated on the surface of the waters. 19 The waters rose even higher over the earth; they covered all of the highest mountains under the sky. 20 The waters rose twenty-three feet high, covering the mountains. 21 Every creature took its last breath: the things crawling on the ground, birds, livestock, wild animals, everything swarming on the ground, and every human being. 22 Everything on dry land with life's breath in its nostrils died. 23 God wiped away every living thing that was on the fertile land—from human beings to livestock to crawling things to birds in the sky. They were wiped off the earth. Only Noah and those with him in the ark were left. 24 The waters rose over the earth for one hundred fifty days.

8 God remembered Noah, all those alive, and all the animals with him in the ark. God sent a wind over the earth so that the waters receded. 2 The springs of the deep sea and the skies[f] closed up. The skies held back the rain. 3 The waters receded gradually from the earth. After one hundred fifty days, the waters decreased; 4 and in the seventh month, on the seventeenth day, the ark came to rest on the Ararat mountains. 5 The waters decreased gradually until the tenth month, and on the first day of the tenth month the mountain peaks appeared.

6 After forty days, Noah opened the window of the ark that he had made. 7 He sent out a raven, and it flew back and forth until the waters over the entire earth had dried up. 8 Then he sent out a dove to see if the waters on all of the fertile land had subsided, 9 but the dove found no place to set its foot. It returned to him in the ark since waters still covered the entire earth. Noah stretched out his hand, took it, and brought it back into the ark. 10 He waited seven more days and sent the dove out from the ark again. 11 The dove came back to him in the evening, grasping a torn olive leaf in its beak. Then Noah knew that the waters were subsiding from the earth. 12 He waited seven more days and sent out the dove, but it didn't come back to him again. 13 In Noah's six hundred first year, on the first day of the first month, the waters dried up from the earth. Noah removed the ark's hatch and saw that the surface of the fertile land had dried up. 14 In the second month, on the seventeenth day, the earth was dry.

[d] LXX; MT *every bird, every winged thing* [e] Heb lacks *the door.* [f] Or *the windows of the skies*

[15]God spoke to Noah, [16]"Go out of the ark, you and your wife, your sons, and your sons' wives with you. [17]Bring out with you all the animals of every kind—birds, livestock, everything crawling on the ground—so that they may populate the earth, be fertile, and multiply on the earth." [18]So Noah went out of the ark with his sons, his wife, and his sons' wives. [19]All the animals, all the livestock,[g] all the birds, and everything crawling on the ground, came out of the ark by their families.

God's promise for the earth

[20]Noah built an altar to the LORD. He took some of the clean large animals and some of the clean birds, and placed entirely burned offerings on the altar. [21]The LORD smelled the pleasing scent, and the LORD thought to himself, I will not curse the fertile land anymore because of human beings since the ideas of the human mind are evil from their youth. I will never again destroy every living thing as I have done.

[22]As long as the earth exists,
seedtime and harvest,
cold and hot,
summer and autumn,
day and night
will not cease.

God's covenant with all life

9

God blessed Noah and his sons and said to them, "Be fertile, multiply, and fill the earth. [2]All of the animals on the earth will fear you and dread you—all the birds in the skies, everything crawling on the ground, and all of the sea's fish. They are in your power. [3]Everything that lives and moves will be your food. Just as I gave you the green grasses, I now give you everything. [4]However, you must not eat meat with its life, its blood, in it.

[5]I will surely demand your blood
for a human life,
from every living thing I will demand it.
From humans, from a man for his brother,
I will demand something
for a human life.

[6]Whoever sheds human blood,
by a human his blood will be shed;
for in the divine image
God made human beings.

[7]As for you, be fertile and multiply. Populate the earth and multiply in it." [8]God said to Noah and to his sons with him, [9]"I am now setting up my covenant with you, with your descendants, [10]and with every living being with you—with the birds, with the large animals, and with all the animals of the earth, leaving the ark with you.[h] [11]I will set up my covenant with you so that never again will all life be cut off by floodwaters. There will never again be a flood to destroy the earth."

[12]God said, "This is the symbol of the covenant that I am drawing up between me and you and every living thing with you, on behalf of every future generation. [13]I have placed my bow in the clouds; it will be the symbol of the covenant between me and the earth. [14]When I bring clouds over the earth and the bow appears in the clouds, [15]I will remember the covenant between me and you and every living being among all the creatures. Floodwaters will never again destroy all creatures. [16]The bow will be in the clouds, and upon seeing it I will remember the enduring covenant between God and every living being of all the earth's creatures." [17]God said to Noah, "This is the symbol of the covenant that I have set up between me and all creatures on earth."

Shem's blessing and Canaan's curse

[18]Noah's sons Shem, Ham, and Japheth came out of the ark. Now Ham was Canaan's father. [19]These were Noah's three sons, and from them the whole earth was populated. [20]Noah, a farmer, made a new start and planted a vineyard. [21]He drank some of the wine, became drunk, and took off his clothes in his tent. [22]Ham, Canaan's father, saw his father naked and told his two brothers who were outside. [23]Shem and Japheth took a robe, threw it over their shoulders, walked backward, and covered their naked father without looking at him because they

[g]LXX; MT lacks *all the livestock.* [h]LXX; MT includes *for all the animals of the earth.*

turned away. 24 When Noah woke up from
his wine, he discovered what his youngest
son had done to him. 25 He said,

"Cursed be Canaan:
 the lowest servant
  he will be for his brothers."

26 He also said,

"Bless the LORD,
 the God of Shem;
Canaan will be his servant.
27 May God give space[i] to Japheth;
 he will live in Shem's tents,
  and Canaan will be his servant."

28 After the flood, Noah lived 350 years.
29 In all, Noah lived 950 years; then he died.

Noah's descendants

10 These are the descendants of Noah's
sons Shem, Ham, and Japheth, to
whom children were born after the flood.
2 Japheth's sons: Gomer, Magog, Madai,
Javan, Tubal, Meshech, and Tiras. 3 Gomer's
sons: Ashkenaz, Riphath, and Togarmah.
4 Javan's sons: Elishah, Tarshish, Kittim,
and Rodanim.[j] 5 From these the island-
nations were divided into their own countries, each according to their languages and
their clans within their nations.

6 Ham's sons: Cush, Egypt, Put, and
Canaan. 7 Cush's sons: Seba, Havilah,
Sabtah, Raamah, and Sabteca. Raamah's
sons: Sheba and Dedan. 8 Cush fathered
Nimrod, the first great warrior on earth.
9 The LORD saw him as a great hunter,
and so it is said, "Like Nimrod, whom the
LORD saw as a great hunter." 10 The most
important cities in his kingdom were
Babel, Erech, Accad, and Calneh in the
land of Shinar. 11 Asshur left that land
and built Nineveh, Rehoboth City, Calah,
12 and Resen, the great city between
Nineveh and Calah. 13 Egypt fathered
Ludim, Anamim, Lehabim, Naphtuhim,
14 Pathrusim, Casluhim, and Caphtorim,[k]
from which the Philistines came.

15 Canaan fathered Sidon his oldest
son, and Heth, 16 the Jebusites, the Amorites, the Girgashites, 17 the Hivites, the
Arkites, the Sinites, 18 the Arvadites, the
Zemarites, and the Hamathites. After
this the Canaanite clans were dispersed.
19 The Canaanite boundary extends from
Sidon by way of Gerar to Gaza and by way
of Sodom, Gomorrah, Admah, and Zeboiim to Lasha. 20 These are Ham's sons
according to their clans, their languages,
their lands, and their nations.

21 Children were also born to Shem the
father of all Eber's children and Japheth's
older brother.

22 Shem's sons: Elam, Asshur, Arpachshad, Lud, and Aram. 23 Aram's sons: Uz,
Hul, Gether, and Mash. 24 Arpachshad
fathered Shelah, and Shelah fathered
Eber. 25 To Eber were born two sons: The
first was named Peleg,[l] because during
his lifetime the earth was divided. His
brother's name was Joktan. 26 Joktan
fathered Almodad, Sheleph, Hazarmaveth, Jerah, 27 Hadoram, Uzal, Diklah,
28 Obal, Abimael, Sheba, 29 Ophir, Havilah,
and Jobab. All of these were Joktan's
sons. 30 Their settlements extended from
Mesha by way of Sephar, the eastern
mountains. 31 These are Shem's sons according to their clans, their languages,
their lands, and their nations.

32 These are the clans of Noah's sons
according to their generations and their
nations. From them the earth's nations
branched out after the flood.

Origin of languages and cultures

11 All people[m] on the earth had one language and the same words. 2 When
they traveled east,[n] they found a valley in
the land of Shinar and settled there. 3 They
said to each other, "Come, let's make bricks
and bake them hard." They used bricks for
stones and asphalt for mortar. 4 They said,
"Come, let's build for ourselves a city and a
tower with its top in the sky, and let's make
a name for ourselves so that we won't be
dispersed over all the earth."

5 Then the LORD came down to see the city
and the tower that the humans built. 6 And

[i] Heb sounds like *Japheth*. [j] LXX, Sam, 1 Chron 1:7; MT *Dodanim* [k] Or *Casluhim, from which the Philistines set out, and Caphtorim* [l] Or *separation* [m] Heb lacks *people*. [n] Or *from the east*

the LORD said, "There is now one people and they all have one language. This is what they have begun to do, and now all that they plan to do will be possible for them. 7Come, let's go down and mix up their language there so they won't understand each other's language." 8Then the LORD dispersed them from there over all of the earth, and they stopped building the city. 9Therefore, it is named Babel, because there the LORD mixed up[o] the language of all the earth; and from there the LORD dispersed them over all the earth.

Shem's descendants

10These are Shem's descendants.

When Shem was 100 years old, he became the father of Arpachshad, two years after the flood. 11After Arpachshad was born, Shem lived 500 years; he had other sons and daughters.

12When Arpachshad was 35 years old, he became the father of Shelah. 13After Shelah was born, Arpachshad lived 403 years; he had other sons and daughters.

14When Shelah was 30 years old, he became the father of Eber. 15After Eber was born, Shelah lived 403 years; he had other sons and daughters.

16When Eber was 34 years old, he became the father of Peleg. 17After Peleg was born, Eber lived 430 years; he had other sons and daughters.

18When Peleg was 30 years old, he became the father of Reu. 19After Reu was born, Peleg lived 209 years; he had other sons and daughters.

20When Reu was 32 years old, he became the father of Serug. 21After Serug was born, Reu lived 207 years; he had other sons and daughters.

22When Serug was 30 years old, he became the father of Nahor. 23After Nahor was born, Serug lived 200 years; he had other sons and daughters.

24When Nahor was 29 years old, he became the father of Terah. 25After Terah was born, Nahor lived 119 years; he had other sons and daughters.

26When Terah was 70 years old, he became the father of Abram, Nahor, and Haran.

27These are Terah's descendants. Terah became the father of Abram, Nahor, and Haran. Haran became the father of Lot. 28Haran died while with his father Terah in his native land,[p] in Ur of the Chaldeans. 29Abram and Nahor both married; Abram's wife was Sarai, and Nahor's wife was Milcah the daughter of Haran, father of both Milcah and Iscah. 30Sarai was unable to have children. 31Terah took his son Abram, his grandson Lot (son of Haran), and his son Abram's wife, Sarai his daughter-in-law. They left Ur of the Chaldeans for the land of Canaan, and arriving at Haran, they settled there. 32Terah lived 205 years, and he died in Haran.

Abram's family moves to Canaan

12 The LORD said to Abram, "Leave your land, your family, and your father's household for the land that I will show you. 2I will make of you a great nation and will bless you. I will make your name respected, and you will be a blessing.

3I will bless those who bless you,
those who curse you I will curse;
all the families of the earth
will be blessed because of you."[q]

4Abram left just as the LORD told him, and Lot went with him. Now Abram was 75 years old when he left Haran. 5Abram took his wife Sarai, his nephew Lot, all of their possessions, and those who became members of their household in Haran; and they set out for the land of Canaan. When they arrived in Canaan, 6Abram traveled through the land as far as the sacred place at Shechem, at the oak of Moreh. The Canaanites lived in the land at that time. 7The LORD appeared to Abram and said, "I give this land to your descendants," so Abram built an altar there to the LORD who appeared to him. 8From there he traveled toward the mountains east of Bethel, and

[o]Heb *balal*, wordplay on Babel [p]Or *birthplace* [q]Or *will bless themselves because of you;* or *will find a blessing because of you*

pitched his tent with Bethel on the west and Ai on the east. There he built an altar to the LORD and worshipped in the LORD's name. 9 Then Abram set out toward the arid southern plain, making and breaking camp as he went.

Abram and Sarai visit Egypt

10 When a famine struck the land, Abram went down toward Egypt to live as an immigrant since the famine was so severe in the land. 11 Just before he arrived in Egypt, he said to his wife Sarai, "I know you are a good-looking woman. 12 When the Egyptians see you, they will say, 'This is his wife,' and they will kill me but let you live. 13 So tell them you are my sister so that they will treat me well for your sake, and I will survive because of you."

14 When Abram entered Egypt, the Egyptians saw how beautiful his wife was. 15 When Pharaoh's princes saw her, they praised her to Pharaoh; and the woman was taken into Pharaoh's household. 16 Things went well for Abram because of her: he acquired flocks, cattle, male donkeys, men servants, women servants, female donkeys, and camels. 17 Then the LORD struck Pharaoh and his household with severe plagues because of Abram's wife Sarai. 18 So Pharaoh summoned Abram and said, "What's this you've done to me? Why didn't you tell me she was your wife? 19 Why did you say, 'She's my sister,' so that I made her my wife? Now, here's your wife. Take her and go!" 20 Pharaoh gave his men orders concerning Abram, and they expelled him with his wife and everything he had.

Abram and Lot separate

13 Abram went up from Egypt toward the arid southern plain with his wife, with everything he had, and with Lot. 2 Abram was very wealthy in livestock, silver, and gold. 3 Abram traveled, making and breaking camp, from the arid southern plain to Bethel and to the sacred place there, where he had first pitched his tent between Bethel and Ai, 4 that is, to the place at which he had earlier built the altar. There he worshipped in the LORD's name. 5 Now Lot, who traveled with Abram, also had flocks, cattle, and tents. 6 They had so many possessions between them that the land couldn't support both of them. They could no longer live together. 7 Conflicts broke out between those herding Abram's livestock and those herding Lot's livestock. At that time the Canaanites and the Perizzites lived in the land.

8 Abram said to Lot, "Let's not have disputes between me and you and between our herders since we are relatives. 9 Isn't the whole land in front of you? Let's separate. If you go north, I will go south; and if you go south, I will go north." 10 Lot looked up and saw the entire Jordan Valley. All of it was well irrigated, like the garden of the LORD, like the land of Egypt, as far as Zoar (this was before the LORD destroyed Sodom and Gomorrah). 11 So Lot chose for himself the entire Jordan Valley. Lot set out toward the east, and they separated from each other. 12 Abram settled in the land of Canaan, and Lot settled near the cities of the valley and pitched his tent close to Sodom. 13 The citizens of Sodom were very evil and sinful against the LORD.

14 After Lot separated from him, the LORD said to Abram, "From the place where you are standing, look up and gaze to the north, south, east, and west, 15 because all the land that you see I give you and your descendants forever. 16 I will make your descendants like the dust of the earth. If someone could count the bits of dust on the earth, then they could also count your descendants. 17 Stand up and walk around through the length and breadth of the land because I am giving it to you." 18 So Abram packed his tent and went and settled by the oaks of Mamre in Hebron. There he built an altar to the LORD.

Abram rescues Lot

14 While Amraphel was king of Shinar, Ellasar's King Arioch, Elam's King Chedorlaomer, and Goiim's King Tidal 2 declared war on Sodom's King Bera, Gomorrah's King Birsha, Admah's King Shinab, Zeboiim's King Shemeber, and the king of Bela, that is, Zoar. 3 These latter kings formed an alliance in the Siddim Valley

(that is, the Dead Sea[r]). 4For twelve years they had served Chedorlaomer, and in the thirteenth year they revolted. 5In the fourteenth year, Chedorlaomer and the kings of his alliance came and attacked the Rephaim in Ashteroth-karnaim, the Zuzim in Ham, the Emim in Shaveh-kiriathaim, 6and the Horites in the mountains of Seir as far as El-paran near the desert. 7Then they turned back, came to En-mishpat (that is, Kadesh), and attacked the territory of the Amalekites, as well as the Amorites who lived in Hazazon-tamar.

8Then the kings of Sodom, Gomorrah, Admah, Zeboiim, and Bera (that is, Zoar) took up battle positions in the Siddim Valley 9against King Chedorlaomer of Elam, King Tidal of Goiim, King Amraphel of Shinar, and King Arioch of Ellasar, four kings against five.

10Now the Siddim Valley was filled with tar pits. When the kings of Sodom and Gomorrah retreated, they fell into them; and the rest fled to the mountains. 11They took everything from Sodom and Gomorrah, including its food supplies, and left. 12They also took Lot, Abram's nephew who lived in Sodom, and everything he owned, and took off. 13When a survivor arrived, he told Abram the Hebrew, who lived near the oaks of the Amorite Mamre, who was the brother of Eshcol and Aner, Abram's treaty partners.

14When Abram heard that his relative had been captured, he took all of the loyal men born in his household, three hundred eighteen, and went after them as far as Dan. 15During the night, he and his servants divided themselves up against them, attacked, and chased them to Hobah, north of Damascus. 16He brought back all of the looted property, together with his relative Lot and Lot's property, wives, and people.

Abram blessed by Melchizedek

17After Abram returned from his attack on Chedorlaomer and the kings who were with him, the king of Sodom came out to the Shaveh Valley (that is, the King's Valley) to meet him. 18Now Melchizedek the king of Salem and the priest of El Elyon[s] had brought bread and wine, 19and he blessed him,

"Bless Abram by El Elyon,
 creator of heaven and earth;
20bless El Elyon,
 who gave you the victory
  over your enemies."

Abram gave Melchizedek one-tenth of everything. 21Then the king of Sodom said to Abram, "Give me the people and take the property for yourself."

22But Abram said to the king of Sodom, "I promised the LORD, El Elyon, creator of heaven and earth, 23that I wouldn't take even a thread or a sandal strap from anything that was yours so that you couldn't say, 'I'm the one who made Abram rich.' 24The only exception is that the young men may keep whatever they have taken to eat, and the men who went with me—Aner, Eshcol, and Mamre—may keep their share."

God's covenant with Abram

15 After these events, the LORD's word came to Abram in a vision, "Don't be afraid, Abram. I am your protector.[t] Your reward will be very great."

2But Abram said, "LORD God, what can you possibly give me, since I still have no children? The head of my household is Eliezer, a man from Damascus."[u] 3He continued, "Since you haven't given me any children, the head of my household will be my heir."

4The LORD's word came immediately to him, "This man will not be your heir. Your heir will definitely be your very own biological child." 5Then he brought Abram outside and said, "Look up at the sky and count the stars if you think you can count them." He continued, "This is how many children you will have." 6Abram trusted the LORD, and the LORD recognized Abram's high moral character.

7He said to Abram, "I am the LORD, who brought you out of Ur of the Chaldeans to give you this land as your possession."

8But Abram said, "LORD God, how do I know that I will actually possess it?"

[r]Or *Salt Sea* [s]Or *God Most High* [t]Or *shield* or *benefactor* [u]Heb uncertain

9 He said, "Bring me a three-year-old female calf, a three-year-old female goat, a three-year-old ram, a dove, and a young pigeon." 10 He took all of these animals, split them in half, and laid the halves facing each other, but he didn't split the birds. 11 When vultures swooped down on the carcasses, Abram waved them off. 12 After the sun set, Abram slept deeply. A terrifying and deep darkness settled over him.

13 Then the LORD said to Abram, "Have no doubt that your descendants will live as immigrants in a land that isn't their own, where they will be oppressed slaves for four hundred years. 14 But after I punish the nation they serve, they will leave it with great wealth. 15 As for you, you will join your ancestors in peace and be buried after a good long life. 16 The fourth generation will return here since the Amorites' wrongdoing won't have reached its peak until then."

17 After the sun had set and darkness had deepened, a smoking vessel with a fiery flame passed between the split-open animals. 18 That day the LORD cut a covenant with Abram: "To your descendants I give this land, from Egypt's river to the great Euphrates, 19 together with the Kenites, the Kenizzites, the Kadmonites, 20 the Hittites, the Perizzites, the Rephaim, 21 the Amorites, the Canaanites, the Girgashites, and the Jebusites."

Hagar and the Ishmaelites' origins

16 Sarai, Abram's wife, had not been able to have children. Since she had an Egyptian servant named Hagar, 2 Sarai said to Abram, "The LORD has kept me from giving birth, so go to my servant. Maybe she will provide me with children." Abram did just as Sarai said. 3 After Abram had lived ten years in the land of Canaan, Abram's wife Sarai took her Egyptian servant Hagar and gave her to her husband Abram as his wife. 4 He slept with Hagar, and she became pregnant. But when she realized that she was pregnant, she no longer respected her mistress. 5 Sarai said to Abram, "This harassment is your fault. I allowed you to embrace my servant, but when she realized she was pregnant, I lost her respect. Let the LORD decide who is right, you or me."

6 Abram said to Sarai, "Since she's your servant, do whatever you wish to her." So Sarai treated her harshly, and she ran away from Sarai.

7 The LORD's messenger found Hagar at a spring in the desert, the spring on the road to Shur, 8 and said, "Hagar! Sarai's servant! Where did you come from and where are you going?"

She said, "From Sarai my mistress. I'm running away."

9 The LORD's messenger said to her, "Go back to your mistress. Put up with her harsh treatment of you." 10 The LORD's messenger also said to her,

"I will give you many children,
so many they can't be counted!"

11 The LORD's messenger said to her,

"You are now pregnant
and will give birth to a son.
You will name him Ishmael[v]
because the LORD has heard about
your harsh treatment.
12 He will be a wild mule of a man;
he will fight everyone,
and they will fight him.
He will live at odds
with all his relatives."[w]

13 Hagar named the LORD who spoke to her, "You are El Roi"[x] because she said, "Can I still see after he saw me?"[y] 14 Therefore, that well is called Beer-lahai-roi;[z] it's the well between Kadesh and Bered. 15 Hagar gave birth to a son for Abram, and Abram named him Ishmael. 16 Abram was 86 years old when Hagar gave birth to Ishmael for Abram.

God's covenant with Abraham

17 When Abram was 99 years old, the LORD appeared to Abram and said to him, "I am El Shaddai.[a] Walk with me and be trustworthy. 2 I will make a covenant between us and I will give you many, many

[v] Or *God hears* [w] Or *He will reside near all his relatives.* [x] Or *God who sees* or *God whom I've seen* [y] Heb uncertain; or *Have I really seen God and survived?* [z] Or *the Well of the Living One who sees me* or *whom I've seen* [a] Or *God Almighty* or *God of the Mountain*

descendants." 3Abram fell on his face, and
God said to him, 4"But me, my covenant is
with you; you will be the ancestor of many
nations. 5And because I have made you the
ancestor of many nations, your name will
no longer be Abram[b] but Abraham.[c] 6I will
make you very fertile. I will produce nations
from you, and kings will come from you. 7I
will set up my covenant with you and your
descendants after you in every generation
as an enduring covenant. I will be your God
and your descendants' God after you. 8I will
give you and your descendants the land in
which you are immigrants, the whole land
of Canaan, as an enduring possession. And
I will be their God."

9God said to Abraham, "As for you, you
must keep my covenant, you and your descendants in every generation. 10This is my
covenant that you and your descendants
must keep: Circumcise every male. 11You
must circumcise the flesh of your foreskins,
and it will be a symbol of the covenant between us. 12On the eighth day after birth,
every male in every generation must be
circumcised, including those who are not
your own children: those born in your
household and those purchased with silver
from foreigners. 13Be sure you circumcise
those born in your household and those
purchased with your silver. Your flesh will
embody my covenant as an enduring covenant. 14Any uncircumcised male whose
flesh of his foreskin remains uncircumcised
will be cut off from his people. He has broken my covenant."

15God said to Abraham, "As for your wife
Sarai, you will no longer call her Sarai. Her
name will now be Sarah. 16I will bless her
and even give you a son from her. I will
bless her so that she will become nations,
and kings of peoples will come from her."

17Abraham fell on his face and laughed.
He said to himself, Can a 100-year-old man
become a father, or Sarah, a 90-year-old
woman, have a child? 18To God Abraham
said, "If only you would accept Ishmael!"

19But God said, "No, your wife Sarah
will give birth to a son for you, and you
will name him Isaac.[d] I will set up my covenant with him and with his descendants
after him as an enduring covenant. 20As
for Ishmael, I've heard your request. I will
bless him and make him fertile and give
him many, many descendants. He will be
the ancestor of twelve tribal leaders, and I
will make a great nation of him. 21But I will
set up my covenant with Isaac, who will
be born to Sarah at this time next year."
22When God finished speaking to him, God
ascended, leaving Abraham alone.

23Abraham took his son Ishmael, all
those born in his household, and all those
purchased with his silver—that is, every
male in Abraham's household—and he circumcised the flesh of their foreskins that
same day, just as God had told him to do.
24Abraham was 99 years old when he circumcised the flesh of his foreskin, 25and
his son Ishmael was 13 years old when
the flesh of his foreskin was circumcised.
26That same day Abraham and his son Ishmael were circumcised. 27All the men of his
household, those born in his household and
those purchased with silver from foreigners, were circumcised with him.

Isaac's birth announced

18 The LORD appeared to Abraham at
the oaks of Mamre while he sat at
the entrance of his tent in the day's heat.
2He looked up and suddenly saw three men
standing near him. As soon as he saw them,
he ran from his tent entrance to greet them
and bowed deeply. 3He said, "Sirs, if you
would be so kind, don't just pass by your
servant. 4Let a little water be brought so
you may wash your feet and refresh yourselves under the tree. 5Let me offer you a
little bread so you will feel stronger, and
after that you may leave your servant and
go on your way—since you have visited
your servant."

They responded, "Fine. Do just as you
have said."

6So Abraham hurried to Sarah at his tent
and said, "Hurry! Knead three seahs[e] of the
finest flour and make some baked goods!"

[b]Or *exalted ancestor* [c]Or *ancestor of a multitude* [d]Or *he laughs* [e]One seah is seven and a half quarts.

7 Abraham ran to the cattle, took a healthy young calf, and gave it to a young servant, who prepared it quickly. 8 Then Abraham took butter, milk, and the calf that had been prepared, put the food in front of them, and stood under the tree near them as they ate.

9 They said to him, "Where's your wife Sarah?"

And he said, "Right here in the tent."

10 Then one of the men said, "I will definitely return to you about this time next year. Then your wife Sarah will have a son!"

Sarah was listening at the tent door behind him. 11 Now Abraham and Sarah were both very old. Sarah was no longer menstruating. 12 So Sarah laughed to herself, thinking, I'm no longer able to have children and my husband's old.

13 The LORD said to Abraham, "Why did Sarah laugh and say, 'Me give birth? At my age?' 14 Is anything too difficult for the LORD? When I return to you about this time next year, Sarah will have a son."

15 Sarah lied and said, "I didn't laugh," because she was frightened.

But he said, "No, you laughed."

Abraham pleads for Sodom

16 The men got up from there and went over to look down on Sodom. Abraham was walking along with them to send them off 17 when the LORD said, "Will I keep from Abraham what I'm about to do? 18 Abraham will certainly become a great populous nation, and all the earth's nations will be blessed because of him. 19 I have formed a relationship with him so that he will instruct his children and his household after him. And they will keep to the LORD's path, being moral and just so that the LORD can do for Abraham everything he said he would." 20 Then the LORD said, "The cries of injustice from Sodom and Gomorrah are countless, and their sin is very serious! 21 I will go down now to examine the cries of injustice that have reached me. Have they really done all this? If not, I want to know."

22 The men turned away and walked toward Sodom, but Abraham remained standing in front of the LORD.[f] 23 Abraham approached and said, "Will you really sweep away the innocent[g] with the guilty?[h] 24 What if there are fifty innocent people in the city? Will you really sweep it away and not save the place for the sake of the fifty innocent people in it? 25 It's not like you to do this, killing the innocent with the guilty as if there were no difference. It's not like you! Will the judge of all the earth not act justly?"

26 The LORD said, "If I find fifty innocent people in the city of Sodom, I will save it because of them."

27 Abraham responded, "Since I've already decided to speak with my Lord, even though I'm just soil and ash, 28 what if there are five fewer innocent people than fifty? Will you destroy the whole city over just five?"

The LORD said, "If I find forty-five there, I won't destroy it."

29 Once again Abraham spoke, "What if forty are there?"

The LORD said, "For the sake of forty, I will do nothing."

30 He said, "Don't be angry with me, my Lord, but let me speak. What if thirty are there?"

The LORD said, "I won't do it if I find thirty there."

31 Abraham said, "Since I've already decided to speak with my Lord, what if twenty are there?"

The LORD said, "I won't do it, for the sake of twenty."

32 Abraham said, "Don't be angry with me, my Lord, but let me speak just once more. What if there are ten?"

And the LORD said, "I will not destroy it because of those ten." 33 When the LORD finished speaking with Abraham, he left; but Abraham stayed there in that place.

Lot leaves Sodom

19 The two messengers entered Sodom in the evening. Lot, who was sitting at the gate of Sodom, saw them, got up

[f] Some ancient manuscripts read *but the LORD remained standing in front of Abraham.* [g] Or *righteous* [h] Or *wicked*

to greet them, and bowed low. 2 He said, "Come to your servant's house, spend the night, and wash your feet. Then you can get up early and go on your way."

But they said, "No, we will spend the night in the town square." 3 He pleaded earnestly with them, so they went with him and entered his house. He made a big meal for them, even baking unleavened bread, and they ate.

4 Before they went to bed, the men of the city of Sodom—everyone from the youngest to the oldest—surrounded the house 5 and called to Lot, "Where are the men who arrived tonight? Bring them out to us so that we may have sex with them."

6 Lot went out toward the entrance, closed the door behind him, 7 and said, "My brothers, don't do such an evil thing. 8 I've got two daughters who are virgins. Let me bring them out to you, and you may do to them whatever you wish. But don't do anything to these men because they are now under the protection of my roof."

9 They said, "Get out of the way!" And they continued, "Does this immigrant want to judge us? Now we will hurt you more than we will hurt them." They pushed Lot back and came close to breaking down the door. 10 The men inside reached out and pulled Lot back into the house with them and slammed the door. 11 Then the messengers blinded the men near the entrance of the house, from the youngest to the oldest, so that they groped around trying to find the entrance.

12 The men said to Lot, "Who's still with you here? Take away from this place your sons-in-law, your sons, your daughters, and everyone else you have in the city 13 because we are about to destroy this place. The LORD has found the cries of injustice so serious that the LORD sent us to destroy it."

14 Lot went to speak to his sons-in-law, married to his daughters, and said, "Get up and get out of this place because the LORD is about to destroy the city." But his sons-in-law thought he was joking.

15 When dawn broke, the messengers urged Lot, "Get up and take your wife and your two daughters who are here so that you are not swept away because of the evil in this city." 16 He hesitated, but because the LORD intended to save him, the men grabbed him, his wife, and two daughters by the hand, took him out, and left him outside the city.

17 After getting them out, the men said, "Save your lives! Don't look back! And don't stay in the valley. Escape to the mountains so that you are not swept away."

18 But Lot said to them, "No, my lords, please. 19 You've done me a favor and have been so kind to save my life. But I can't escape to the mountains since the catastrophe might overtake me there and I'd die. 20 This city here is close enough to flee to, and it's small. It's small, right? Let me escape there, and my life will be saved."

21 He said to Lot, "I'll do this for you as well; I won't overthrow the city that you have described. 22 Hurry! Escape to it! I can't do anything until you get there." That is why the name of the city is Zoar.[i]

Sodom and Gomorrah destroyed

23 As the sun rose over the earth, Lot arrived in Zoar; 24 and the LORD rained down burning asphalt from the skies onto Sodom and Gomorrah. 25 The LORD destroyed these cities, the entire valley, everyone who lived in the cities, and all of the fertile land's vegetation. 26 When Lot's wife looked back, she turned into a pillar of salt.

27 Abraham set out early for the place where he had stood with the LORD, 28 and looked out over Sodom and Gomorrah and over all the land of the valley. He saw the smoke from the land rise like the smoke from a kiln.

Origin of Moab and Ammon

29 When God destroyed the cities in the valley, God remembered Abraham and sent Lot away from the disaster that overtook the cities in which Lot had lived. 30 Since Lot had become fearful of living in Zoar, he and his two daughters headed up from

[i] Or *small*

Zoar and settled in the mountains where he and his two daughters lived in a cave. 31 The older daughter said to the younger, "Our father is old, and there are no men in the land to sleep with us as is the custom everywhere. 32 Come on, let's give our father wine to drink, lie down with him, and we'll have children from our father." 33 That night they served their father wine, and the older daughter went in and lay down with her father, without him noticing when she lay down or got up. 34 The next day the older daughter said to the younger, "Since I lay down with our father last night, let's serve him wine tonight too, and you go in and lie down with him so that we will both have children from our father." 35 They served their father wine that night also, and the younger daughter lay down with him, without him knowing when she lay down or got up. 36 Both of Lot's daughters became pregnant by their father. 37 The older daughter gave birth to a son and named him Moab. He is the ancestor of today's Moabites. 38 The younger daughter also gave birth to a son and named him Ben-ammi.[j] He is the ancestor of today's Ammonites.

Abraham and Sarah visit Gerar

20 Abraham traveled from there toward the land of the arid southern plain, and he settled as an immigrant in Gerar, between Kadesh and Shur. 2 Abraham said of his wife Sarah, "She's my sister." So King Abimelech of Gerar took her into his household.

3 But God appeared to Abimelech that night in a dream and said to him, "You are as good as dead because of this woman you have taken. She is a married woman."

4 Now Abimelech hadn't gone near her, and he said, "Lord, will you really put an innocent nation to death? 5 Didn't he say to me, 'She's my sister,' and didn't she—even she—say, 'He's my brother'? My intentions were pure, and I acted innocently when I did this."

6 God said to him in the dream, "I know that your intentions were pure when you did this. In fact, I kept you from sinning against me. That's why I didn't allow you to touch her. 7 Now return the man's wife. He's a prophet; he will pray for you so you may live. But if you don't return her, know that you and everyone with you will die!"

8 Abimelech got up early in the morning and summoned all of his servants. When he told them everything that had happened, the men were terrified. 9 Then Abimelech summoned Abraham and said to him, "What have you done to us? What sin did I commit against you that you have brought this terrible sin to me and my kingdom, by doing to me something that simply isn't done?" 10 Abimelech said to Abraham, "What were you thinking when you did this thing?"

11 Abraham said, "I thought to myself, No one reveres God here and they will kill me to get my wife. 12 She is, truthfully, my sister—my father's daughter but not my mother's daughter—and she's now my wife. 13 When God led me away from my father's household, I said to her, 'This is the loyalty I expect from you: in each place we visit, tell them, "He is my brother."'"

14 Abimelech took flocks, cattle, male servants, and female servants, and gave them to Abraham; and Abimelech returned his wife Sarah. 15 Abimelech said, "My land is here available to you. Live wherever you wish." 16 To Sarah, he said, "I've given your brother one thousand pieces of silver. It means that neither you nor anyone with you has done anything wrong. Everything has been set right." 17 Abraham prayed to God; and God restored Abimelech, his wife, and his women servants to health, and they were able to have children. 18 Because of the incident with Abraham's wife Sarah, the LORD had kept all of the women in Abimelech's household from having children.

Isaac's birth

21 The LORD was attentive to Sarah just as he had said, and the LORD carried out just what he had promised her. 2 She became pregnant and gave birth to a son for Abraham when he was old, at the very

[j] *Or son of my people*

time God had told him. 3 Abraham named
his son—the one Sarah bore him—Isaac.[k]
4 Abraham circumcised his son Isaac when
he was eight days old just as God had commanded him. 5 Abraham was 100 years old
when his son Isaac was born. 6 Sarah said,
"God has given me laughter. Everyone who
hears about it will laugh with me."[l] 7 She
said, "Who could have told Abraham that
Sarah would nurse sons? But now I've given
birth to a son when he was old!"

Hagar and Ishmael evicted

8 The boy grew and stopped nursing. On
the day he stopped nursing, Abraham prepared a huge banquet. 9 Sarah saw Hagar's
son laughing, the one Hagar the Egyptian
had borne to Abraham. 10 So she said to
Abraham, "Send this servant away with her
son! This servant's son won't share the inheritance with my son Isaac."

11 This upset Abraham terribly because
the boy was his son. 12 God said to Abraham,
"Don't be upset about the boy and your servant. Do everything Sarah tells you to do
because your descendants will be traced
through Isaac. 13 But I will make of your
servant's son a great nation too, because he
is also your descendant." 14 Abraham got up
early in the morning, took some bread and
a flask of water, and gave it to Hagar. He
put the boy in her shoulder sling and sent
her away.

She left and wandered through the desert near Beer-sheba. 15 Finally the water in
the flask ran out, and she put the boy down
under one of the desert shrubs. 16 She walked
away from him about as far as a bow shot
and sat down, telling herself, *I can't bear to
see the boy die.* She sat at a distance, cried
out in grief, and wept.

17 God heard the boy's cries, and God's
messenger called to Hagar from heaven and
said to her, "Hagar! What's wrong? Don't be
afraid. God has heard the boy's cries over
there. 18 Get up, pick up the boy, and take
him by the hand because I will make of him
a great nation." 19 Then God opened her eyes,
and she saw a well. She went over, filled
the water flask, and gave the boy a drink.
20 God remained with the boy; he grew up,
lived in the desert, and became an expert
archer. 21 He lived in the Paran desert, and
his mother found him an Egyptian wife.

Abraham's treaty with the Philistines

22 At that time Abimelech, and Phicol
commander of his forces, said to Abraham,
"God is with you in everything that you do.
23 So give me your word under God that you
won't cheat me, my children, or my descendants. Just as I have treated you fairly, so
you must treat me and the land in which
you are an immigrant."

24 Abraham said, "I give you my word."
25 Then Abraham complained to Abimelech
about a well that Abimelech's servants had
seized.

26 Abimelech said, "I don't know who has
done this, and you didn't tell me. I didn't
even hear about it until today." 27 Abraham took flocks and cattle, gave them to
Abimelech, and the two of them drew up
a treaty.[m] 28 Abraham set aside, by themselves, seven female lambs from the flock.
29 So Abimelech said to Abraham, "What are
these seven lambs you've set apart?"

30 Abraham said, "These seven lambs that
you take from me will attest that I dug this
well." 31 Therefore, the name of that place
is Beer-sheba[n] because there they gave
each other their word. 32 After they drew
up a treaty[o] at Beer-sheba, Abimelech, and
Phicol commander of his forces, returned
to the land of the Philistines. 33 Abraham
planted a tamarisk tree in Beer-sheba, and
he worshipped there in the name of the
LORD, El Olam.[p] 34 Abraham lived as an immigrant in the Philistines' land for a long
time.

Binding of Isaac

22 After these events, God tested Abraham and said to him, "Abraham!"
Abraham answered, "I'm here."
2 God said, "Take your son, your only son

[k]Or *he laughs* [l]Or *God has made a joke of me. Everyone who hears about it will laugh at me.* [m]Or *covenant* [n]Or *Well of seven;* or *Well of giving one's word* [o]Or *covenant* [p]Or *the eternal God*

whom you love, Isaac, and go to the land of
Moriah. Offer him up as an entirely burned
offering there on one of the mountains that I
will show you." 3Abraham got up early in the
morning, harnessed his donkey, and took
two of his young men with him, together
with his son Isaac. He split the wood for the
entirely burned offering, set out, and went
to the place God had described to him.

4On the third day, Abraham looked up
and saw the place at a distance. 5Abraham
said to his servants, "Stay here with the
donkey. The boy and I will walk up there,
worship, and then come back to you."

6Abraham took the wood for the entirely
burned offering and laid it on his son Isaac.
He took the fire and the knife in his hand, and
the two of them walked on together. 7Isaac
said to his father Abraham, "My father?"

Abraham said, "I'm here, my son."

Isaac said, "Here is the fire and the wood,
but where is the lamb for the entirely burned
offering?"

8Abraham said, "The lamb for the entirely
burned offering? God will see to it,[q] my son."
The two of them walked on together.

9They arrived at the place God had described to him. Abraham built an altar there
and arranged the wood on it. He tied up his
son Isaac and laid him on the altar on top
of the wood. 10Then Abraham stretched out
his hand and took the knife to kill his son
as a sacrifice. 11But the LORD's messenger
called out to Abraham from heaven, "Abraham? Abraham?"

Abraham said, "I'm here."

12The messenger said, "Don't stretch
out your hand against the young man, and
don't do anything to him. I now know that
you revere God and didn't hold back your
son, your only son, from me." 13Abraham
looked up and saw a single ram[r] caught by
its horns in the dense underbrush. Abraham went over, took the ram, and offered it
as an entirely burned offering instead of his
son. 14Abraham named that place "the LORD
sees."[s] That is the reason people today say,
"On this mountain the LORD is seen."[t]

15The LORD's messenger called out to
Abraham from heaven a second time 16and
said, "I give my word as the LORD that because you did this and didn't hold back your
son, your only son, 17I will bless you richly
and I will give you countless descendants,
as many as the stars in the sky and as the
grains of sand on the seashore. They will
conquer their enemies' cities. 18All the nations of the earth will be blessed because of
your descendants, because you obeyed me."
19After Abraham returned to the young
men, they got up and went to Beer-sheba
where Abraham lived.

Abraham's nephews in Syria

20After these events, Abraham was told:
"Milcah has now also given birth to sons for
your brother Nahor. 21They are Uz his oldest
son, Buz his brother, Kemuel the father of
Aram, 22Chesed, Hazo, Pildash, Jidlaph, and
Bethuel." 23Bethuel became the father of Rebekah. These are the eight Milcah bore for
Nahor, Abraham's brother. 24His secondary
wife's name was Reumah, and she gave birth
to Tebah, Gaham, Tahash, and Maacah.

Sarah's death and burial site

23 Sarah lived to be 127 years old; this
was how long she lived. 2She died in
Kiriath-arba, that is, in Hebron, in the land
of Canaan; and Abraham cried out in grief
and wept for Sarah. 3After he got up from
embracing his deceased wife, he spoke with
the Hittites: 4"I am an immigrant and a
temporary resident with you. Give me some
property for a burial plot among you so that
I can bury my deceased wife near me."

5The Hittites responded to Abraham,
6"Listen to us, sir. You are an eminent man
of God among us. Bury your dead in one of
our own select burial sites. None of us will
keep our own burial plots from you to bury
your dead."

7Abraham rose, bowed to the local citizens the Hittites, 8and spoke with them:
"If you yourselves allow me to bury my
dead near me, listen to me and ask Ephron,

[q]Or *God will see*; or *God will provide* [r]LXX, Sam, Syr, Tg; MT *a ram behind* [s]Or *the* LORD *is seen*; or *the* LORD *provides* [t]Or *the* LORD *sees*; or *on the* LORD'S *mountain, it will be provided*

Zohar's son, 9to give me his own cave in Machpelah at the edge of his field. Let him give it to me for the full price, to be witnessed by you, as my own burial property."

10Now Ephron was a native Hittite. So Ephron the Hittite responded to Abraham publicly in order that the Hittites and everyone at his city's gate could hear: 11"No, sir. Listen, I will give you the field, and I will give you the cave in it. In front of my people's witnesses, I will give it to you. Bury your dead!"

12Abraham bowed before the local citizens 13and spoke to Ephron publicly in the presence of the local citizens: "If only you would accept my offer. I will give you the price of the field. Take it from me so that I can bury my dead there."

14Ephron responded to Abraham, 15"Sir, what is four hundred shekels of silver between me and you for the land so that you can bury your dead?" 16Abraham accepted Ephron's offer and weighed out for Ephron the silver he requested publicly before the Hittites: four hundred shekels of silver at the current rate of exchange.

17So the field of Ephron in Machpelah near Mamre—the field and the cave in it, and all the trees within the field's boundaries—was officially transferred 18to Abraham as his property in the presence of the Hittites and of everyone at his city's gate. 19After this, Abraham buried his wife Sarah in the cave in the field of Machpelah near Mamre, that is, Hebron, in the land of Canaan. 20The field and the cave in it were officially transferred from the Hittites to Abraham as his burial property.

Isaac marries Rebekah

24 As the days went by and Abraham became older, the LORD blessed Abraham in every way. 2Abraham said to the oldest servant of his household, who was in charge of everything he owned, "Put your hand under my thigh. 3By the LORD, God of heaven and earth, give me your word that you won't choose a wife for my son from the Canaanite women among whom I live. 4Go to my land and my family and find a wife for my son Isaac there."

5The servant said to him, "What if the woman doesn't agree to come back with me to this land? Shouldn't I take your son back to the land you left?"

6Abraham said to him, "Be sure you don't take my son back there. 7The LORD, God of heaven—who took me from my father's household and from my family's land, who spoke with me and who gave me his word, saying, 'I will give this land to your descendants'—he will send his messenger in front of you, and you will find a wife for my son there. 8If the woman won't agree to come back with you, you will be free from this obligation to me. Only don't take my son back there." 9So the servant put his hand under his master Abraham's thigh and gave him his word about this mission.

10The servant took ten of his master's camels and all of his master's best provisions, set out, and traveled to Nahor's city in Aram-naharaim. 11He had the camels kneel down outside the city at the well in the evening, when women come out to draw water. 12He said, "LORD, God of my master Abraham, make something good happen for me today and be loyal to my master Abraham. 13I will stand here by the spring while the daughters of the men of the city come out to draw water. 14When I say to a young woman, 'Hand me your water jar so I can drink,' and she says to me, 'Drink, and I will give your camels water too,' may she be the one you've selected for your servant Isaac. In this way I will know that you've been loyal to my master." 15Even before he finished speaking, Rebekah—daughter of Bethuel the son of Milcah wife of Nahor, Abraham's brother—was coming out with a water jar on her shoulder. 16The young woman was very beautiful, old enough to be married, and hadn't known a man intimately. She went down to the spring, filled her water jar, and came back up.

17The servant ran to meet her and said, "Give me a little sip of water from your jar."

18She said, "Drink, sir." Then she quickly lowered the water jar with her hands and gave him some water to drink. 19When she finished giving him a drink, she said, "I'll draw some water for your camels too, till

they've had enough to drink." 20She emptied her water jar quickly into the watering
trough, ran to the well again to draw water,
and drew water for all of the camels. 21The
man stood gazing at her, wondering silently
if the LORD had made his trip successful
or not.
22As soon as the camels had finished
drinking, the man took out a gold ring,
weighing a half shekel,[u] and two gold bracelets for her arms, weighing ten shekels. 23He
said, "Please tell me whose daughter you are.
Is there room in your father's house for us
to spend the night?"
24She responded, "I'm the daughter
of Bethuel, who is the son of Milcah and
Nahor." 25She continued, "We have plenty
of straw and feed for the camels, and a place
to spend the night."
26The man bowed down and praised the
LORD: 27"Bless the LORD, God of my master Abraham, who hasn't given up his loyalty and his faithfulness to my master. The
LORD has shown me the way to the household of my master's brother."
28The young woman ran and told her
mother's household everything that had
happened. 29Rebekah had a brother named
Laban, and Laban ran to the man outside
by the spring. 30When he had seen the ring
and the bracelets on his sister's arms, and
when he had heard his sister Rebekah say,
"This is what the man said to me," he went
to the man, who was still standing by the
spring with his camels. 31Laban said, "Come
in, favored one of the LORD! Why are you
standing outside? I've prepared the house
and a place for the camels." 32So the man
entered the house. Then Laban unbridled
the camels, provided straw and feed for
them and water to wash his feet and the
feet of the men with him, 33and set out a
meal for him.

But the man said, "I won't eat until I've
said something."

Laban replied, "Say it."
34The man said, "I am Abraham's servant.
35The LORD has richly blessed my master,
has made him a great man, and has given
him flocks, cattle, silver, gold, men servants, women servants, camels, and donkeys. 36My master's wife Sarah gave birth
to a son for my master in her old age, and
he's given him everything he owns. 37My
master made me give him my word: 'Don't
choose a wife for my son from the Canaanite women, in whose land I'm living. 38No,
instead, go to my father's household and to
my relatives and choose a wife for my son.'
39I said to my master, 'What if the woman
won't come back with me?' 40He said to me,
'The LORD, whom I've traveled with everywhere, will send his messenger with you
and make your trip successful; and you will
choose a wife for my son from my relatives
and from my father's household. 41If you go
to my relatives, you will be free from your
obligation to me. Even if they provide no
one for you, you will be free from your obligation to me.'
42"Today I arrived at the spring, and I
said, 'LORD, God of my master Abraham, if
you wish to make the trip I'm taking successful, 43when I'm standing by the spring
and the young woman who comes out to
draw water and to whom I say, "Please give
me a little drink of water from your jar,"
44and she responds to me, "Drink, and I will
draw water for your camels too," may she
be the woman the LORD has selected for
my master's son.' 45Before I finished saying
this to myself, Rebekah came out with her
water jar on her shoulder and went down to
the spring to draw water. And I said to her,
'Please give me something to drink.' 46She
immediately lowered her water jar and said,
'Drink, and I will give your camels something to drink too.' So I drank and she also
gave water to the camels. 47Then I asked
her, 'Whose daughter are you?' And she
said, 'The daughter of Bethuel, Nahor's son
whom Milcah bore him.' I put a ring in her
nose and bracelets on her arms. 48I bowed
and worshipped the LORD and blessed the
LORD, the God of my master Abraham, who
led me in the right direction to choose the
granddaughter of my master's brother for
his son. 49Now if you're loyal and faithful to

[u]Heb *beqa*

my master, tell me. If not, tell me so I will
know where I stand either way."
[50]Laban and Bethuel both responded,
"This is all the LORD's doing. We have nothing to say about it. [51]Here is Rebekah, right in
front of you. Take her and go. She will be the
wife of your master's son, just as the LORD
said." [52]When Abraham's servant heard what
they said, he bowed low before the LORD.
[53]The servant brought out gold and silver
jewelry and clothing and gave them to Rebekah. To her brother and to her mother he
gave the finest gifts. [54]He and the men with
him ate and drank and spent the night.

When they got up in the morning, the
servant said, "See me off to my master."
[55]Her brother and mother said, "Let the
young woman stay with us not more than
ten days, and after that she may go."
[56]But he said to them, "Don't delay me.
The LORD has made my trip successful. See
me off so that I can go to my master."
[57]They said, "Summon the young woman,
and let's ask her opinion." [58]They called Rebekah and said to her, "Will you go with
this man?"

She said, "I will go."
[59]So they sent off their sister Rebekah,
her nurse, Abraham's servant, and his men.
[60]And they blessed Rebekah, saying to her,

"May you, our sister, become
thousands of ten thousand;
may your children possess
their enemies' cities."

[61]Rebekah and her young women got up,
mounted the camels, and followed the man.
So the servant took Rebekah and left.
[62]Now Isaac had come from the region
of[v] Beer-lahai-roi and had settled in the arid
southern plain. [63]One evening, Isaac went
out to inspect the pasture,[w] and while staring he saw camels approaching. [64]Rebekah
stared at Isaac. She got down from the camel
[65]and said to the servant, "Who is this man
walking through the pasture to meet us?"

The servant said, "He's my master." So
she took her headscarf and covered herself.
[66]The servant told Isaac everything that
had happened. [67]Isaac brought Rebekah
into his mother Sarah's tent. He received
Rebekah as his wife and loved her. So Isaac
found comfort after his mother's death.

Abraham and Keturah's children

25 Abraham married another wife, named
Keturah. [2]The children she bore him
were Zimran, Jokshan, Medan, Midian, Ishbak, and Shuah. [3]Jokshan became the father
of Sheba and Dedan. Dedan's sons were
Asshurim, Letushim, and Leummim. [4]Mid-
ian's sons were Ephah, Epher, Enoch, Abida,
and Eldaah. All of these were Keturah's
sons. [5]Abraham gave everything he owned
to Isaac. [6]To the sons of Abraham's secondary wives, Abraham gave gifts and, while he
was still living, sent them away from his son
Isaac to land in the east.

Abraham's death

[7]Abraham lived to the age of 175. [8]Abra-
ham took his last breath and died after a
good long life, a content old man, and he
was placed with his ancestors. [9]His sons
Isaac and Ishmael buried him in the cave in
Machpelah, which is in the field of Zohar's
son Ephron the Hittite, near Mamre. [10]Thus
Abraham and his wife Sarah were both buried in the field Abraham had purchased
from the Hittites. [11]After Abraham's death,
God blessed his son Isaac, and Isaac lived in
Beer-lahai-roi.

Ishmael's descendants

[12]These are the descendants of Ishmael,
Abraham's son, whom Hagar the Egyptian,
Sarah's servant, bore for Abraham. [13]These
are the names of Ishmael's sons, by their
names and according to their birth order:
Nebaioth, Ishmael's oldest son; Kedar; Adbeel; Mibsam; [14]Mishma; Dumah; Massa;
[15]Hadad; Tema; Jetur; Naphish; and Kedemah. [16]These are Ishmael's sons. These
are their names by their villages and their
settlements: twelve tribal leaders according
to their tribes. [17]Ishmael lived to the age of
137. He took his last breath and died, and

[v]Heb uncertain; LXX *through the desert of* [w]Heb uncertain; possibly *to walk around in the pasture* or *to meditate in the pasture*

was placed with his ancestors. [18]He established camps[x] from Havilah to Shur, which is near Egypt on the road to Assyria. He died[y] among all of his brothers.

Jacob and Esau are born

[19]These are the descendants of Isaac, Abraham's son. Abraham became the father of Isaac. [20]Isaac was 40 years old when he married Rebekah the daughter of Bethuel the Aramean and the sister of Laban the Aramean, from Paddan-aram. [21]Isaac prayed to the LORD for his wife, since she was unable to have children. The LORD was moved by his prayer, and his wife Rebekah became pregnant. [22]But the boys pushed against each other inside of her, and she said, "If this is what it's like, why did it happen to me?"[z]

So she went to ask the LORD. [23]And the LORD said to her,

"Two nations are in your womb;
  two different peoples will emerge
    from your body.
One people will be stronger
  than the other;
  the older will serve the younger."

[24]When she reached the end of her pregnancy, she discovered that she had twins. [25]The first came out red all over, clothed with hair, and she named him Esau. [26]Immediately afterward, his brother came out gripping Esau's heel, and she named him Jacob. Isaac was 60 years old when they were born.

Jacob acquires the oldest son's rights

[27]When the young men grew up, Esau became an outdoorsman who knew how to hunt, and Jacob became a quiet man who stayed at home. [28]Isaac loved Esau because he enjoyed eating game, but Rebekah loved Jacob. [29]Once when Jacob was boiling stew, Esau came in from the field hungry [30]and said to Jacob, "I'm starving! Let me devour some of this red stuff." That's why his name is Edom.[a]

[31]Jacob said, "Sell me your birthright[b] today."

[32]Esau said, "Since I'm going to die anyway, what good is my birthright to me?"

[33]Jacob said, "Give me your word today." And he did. He sold his birthright to Jacob. [34]So Jacob gave Esau bread and lentil stew. He ate, drank, got up, and left, showing just how little he thought of his birthright.

Isaac and Rebekah visit Gerar

26 When a famine gripped the land, a different one from the first famine that occurred in Abraham's time, Isaac set out toward Gerar and toward King Abimelech of the Philistines. [2]The LORD appeared to him and said, "Don't go down to Egypt but settle temporarily in the land that I will show you. [3]Stay in this land as an immigrant, and I will be with you and bless you because I will give all of these lands to you and your descendants. I will keep my word, which I gave to your father Abraham. [4]I will give you as many descendants as the stars in the sky, and I will give your descendants all of these lands. All of the nations of the earth will be blessed because of your descendants. [5]I will do this because Abraham obeyed me and kept my orders, my commandments, my statutes, and my instructions."

[6]So Isaac lived in Gerar. [7]When the men who lived there asked about his wife, he said, "She's my sister," because he was afraid to say, "my wife," thinking, The men who live there will kill me for Rebekah because she's very beautiful. [8]After Isaac had lived there for some time, the Philistines' King Abimelech looked out his window and saw Isaac laughing together with his wife Rebekah.

[9]So Abimelech summoned Isaac and said, "She's your wife, isn't she? How could you say, 'She's my sister'?"

Isaac responded, "Because I thought that I might be killed because of her."

[10]Abimelech said, "What are you trying to do to us? Before long, one of the people would have slept with your wife; and you would have made us guilty." [11]Abimelech gave orders to all of the people, "Anyone

[x]LXX; MT *they established camps* [y]Or *He fell* [z]Heb uncertain [a]Or *red* [b]Or *oldest son's rights*

who touches this man or his wife will be put
to death!"

Isaac's treaty with the Philistines

[12]Isaac planted grain in that land and
reaped one hundred shearim[c] that year because the LORD had blessed him. [13]Isaac
grew richer and richer until he was extremely wealthy. [14]He had livestock, both
flocks and cattle, and many servants. As
a result, the Philistines envied him. [15]The
Philistines closed up and filled with dirt all
of the wells that his father's servants had
dug during his father Abraham's lifetime.
[16]Abimelech said to Isaac, "Move away from
us because you have become too powerful
among us."

[17]So Isaac moved away from there,
camped in the valley of Gerar, and lived
there. [18]Isaac dug out again the wells that
were dug during the lifetime of his father Abraham. The Philistines had closed
them up after Abraham's death. Isaac
gave them the same names his father had
given them. [19]Isaac's servants dug wells in
the valley and found a well there with fresh
water. [20]Isaac's shepherds argued with Gerar's shepherds, each claiming, "This is our
water." So Isaac named the well Esek[d] because they quarreled with him. [21]They dug
another well and argued about it too, so he
named it Sitnah.[e] [22]He left there and dug
another well, but they didn't argue about it,
so he named it Rehoboth[f] and said, "Now
the LORD has made an open space for us
and has made us fertile in the land."

[23]Then he went up from Gerar to Beer-
sheba. [24]The LORD appeared to him that
night and said, "I am the God of your father Abraham. Don't be afraid because I
am with you. I will bless you, and I will give
you many children for my servant Abraham's sake." [25]So Isaac built an altar there
and worshipped in the LORD's name. Isaac
pitched his tent there, and his servants dug
a well.

[26]But Abimelech set out toward him from
Gerar, with Ahuzzath his ally and Phicol
the commander of his forces. [27]Isaac said to
him, "Why have you come after me? You re-
sented me and sent me away from you."

[28]They said, "We now see that the LORD
was with you. We propose that there be a
formal agreement between us and that we
draw up a treaty[g] with you: [29]you must not
treat us badly since we haven't harmed you
and since we have treated you well at all
times. Then we will send you away peacefully, for you are now blessed by the LORD."
[30]Isaac prepared a banquet for them, and
they ate and drank. [31]They got up early
in the morning, and they gave each other
their word. Isaac sent them off, and they
left peacefully.

[32]That day Isaac's servants informed him
about the well that they had been digging
and said to him, "We found water." [33]He
called it Shibah;[h] therefore, the city's name
has been Beer-sheba[i] until today.

Esau's wives

[34]When Esau was 40 years old, he married Judith daughter of Beeri the Hittite,
and Basemath daughter of Elon the Hittite.
[35]They made life very difficult for Isaac and
Rebekah.

Jacob acquires his father's blessing

27 When Isaac had grown old and his
eyesight was failing, he summoned his
older son Esau and said to him, "My son?"

And Esau said, "I'm here."

[2]He said, "I'm old and don't know when
I will die. [3]So now, take your hunting gear,
your bow and quiver of arrows, go out to the
field, and hunt game for me. [4]Make me the
delicious food that I love and bring it to me so
I can eat. Then I can bless you before I die."

[5]Rebekah was listening when Isaac spoke
to his son Esau. When Esau went out to the
field to hunt game to bring back, [6]Rebekah
said to her son Jacob, "I just heard your father saying to your brother Esau, [7]'Bring
me some game and make me some delicious
food so I can eat, and I will bless you in the
LORD's presence before I die.' [8]Now, my

[c]An unknown measure of grain [d]Or *quarrel* [e]Or *accusation* [f]Or *open spaces* [g]Or *covenant* [h]Or *giving one's word* or *seven* [i]Or *Well of giving one's word* or *Well of seven*

son, listen to me, to what I'm telling you to do. [9]Go to the flock and get me two healthy young goats so I can prepare them as the delicious food your father loves. [10]You can bring it to your father, he will eat, and then he will bless you before he dies."

[11]Jacob said to his mother Rebekah, "My brother Esau is a hairy man, but I have smooth skin. [12]What if my father touches me and thinks I'm making fun of him? I will be cursed instead of blessed."

[13]His mother said to him, "Your curse will be on me, my son. Just listen to me: go and get them for me." [14]So he went and got them and brought them to his mother, and his mother made the delicious food that his father loved. [15]Rebekah took her older son Esau's favorite clothes that were in the house with her, and she put them on her younger son Jacob. [16]On his arms and smooth neck she put the hide of young goats, [17]and the delicious food and the bread she had made she put into her son's hands.

[18]Jacob went to his father and said, "My father."

And he said, "I'm here. Who are you, my son?"

[19]Jacob said to his father, "I'm Esau your oldest son. I've made what you asked me to. Sit up and eat some of the game so you can bless me."

[20]Isaac said to his son, "How could you find this so quickly, my son?"

He said, "The LORD your God led me right to it."[j]

[21]Isaac said to Jacob, "Come here and let me touch you, my son. Are you my son Esau or not?" [22]So Jacob approached his father Isaac, and Isaac touched him and said, "The voice is Jacob's voice, but the arms are Esau's arms." [23]Isaac didn't recognize him because his arms were hairy like Esau's arms, so he blessed him.

[24]Isaac said, "Are you really my son Esau?"

And he said, "I am."

[25]Isaac said, "Bring some food here and let me eat some of my son's game so I can bless you." Jacob put it before him and he ate, and he brought him wine and he drank.

[26]His father Isaac said to him, "Come here and kiss me, my son." [27]So he came close and kissed him. When Isaac smelled the scent of his clothes, he blessed him,

"See, the scent of my son
is like the scent of the field
that the LORD has blessed.
[28]May God give you
showers from the sky,
olive oil from the earth,
plenty of grain and new wine.
[29]May the nations serve you,
may peoples bow down to you.
Be the most powerful man
among your brothers,
and may your mother's sons
bow down to you.
Those who curse you will be cursed,
and those who bless you
will be blessed."

Esau receives a secondary blessing

[30]After Isaac had finished blessing Jacob, and just as Jacob left his father Isaac, his brother Esau came back from his hunt. [31]He too made some delicious food, brought it to his father, and said, "Let my father sit up and eat from his son's game so that you may bless me."

[32]His father Isaac said to him, "Who are you?"

And he said, "I'm your son, your oldest son, Esau."

[33]Isaac was so shocked that he trembled violently. He said, "Who was the hunter just here with game? He brought me food, and I ate all of it before you came. I blessed him, and he will stay blessed!"

[34]When Esau heard what his father said, he let out a loud agonizing cry and wept bitterly. He said to his father, "Bless me! Me too, my father!"

[35]Isaac said, "Your brother has already come deceitfully and has taken your blessing."

[36]Esau said, "Isn't this why he's called Jacob? He's taken me[k] twice now: he took my birthright, and now he's taken my blessing." He continued, "Haven't you saved a blessing for me?"

[j]Or *made something good happen for me* [k]Heb *ya'acob*, a wordplay on Jacob

37 Isaac replied to Esau, “I’ve already made him more powerful than you, and I’ve made all of his brothers his servants. I’ve made him strong with grain and wine. What can I do for you, my son?”

38 Esau said to his father, “Do you really have only one blessing, Father? Bless me too, my father!” And Esau wept loudly.

39 His father Isaac responded and said to him,

“Now, you will make a home
far away from the olive groves
of the earth,
far away from the showers
of the sky above.
40 You will live by your sword;
you will serve your brother.
But when you grow restless,[l]
you will tear away his harness
from your neck.”

Jacob sent away for protection

41 Esau was furious at Jacob because his father had blessed him, and Esau said to himself, When the period of mourning for the death of my father is over, I will kill my brother.

42 Rebekah was told what her older son Esau was planning, so she summoned her younger son Jacob and said to him, “Esau your brother is planning revenge. He plans to kill you. 43 So now, my son, listen to me: Get up and escape to my brother Laban in Haran. 44 Live with him for a short while until your brother’s rage subsides, 45 until your brother’s anger at you goes away and he forgets what you did to him. Then I will send for you and bring you back from there. Why should I suffer the loss of both of you on one day?”

46 Rebekah then said to Isaac, “I really loathe these Hittite women. If Jacob marries one of the Hittite women, like the women of this land, why should I go on living?”

28 So Isaac summoned Jacob, blessed him, and gave him these orders: “Don’t marry a Canaanite woman. 2 Get up and go to Paddan-aram, to the household of Bethuel, your mother’s father, and once there, marry one of the daughters of Laban, your mother’s brother. 3 God Almighty[m] will bless you, make you fertile, and give you many descendants so that you will become a large group of peoples. 4 He will give you and your descendants Abraham’s blessing so that you will own the land in which you are now immigrants, the land God gave to Abraham.” 5 So Isaac sent Jacob off, and he traveled to Paddan-aram, to Laban son of Bethuel the Aramean and brother of Rebekah, Jacob and Esau’s mother.

6 Esau understood that Isaac had blessed Jacob and sent him to Paddan-aram to marry a woman from there. He recognized that, when Isaac blessed Jacob, he had ordered him, “Don’t marry a Canaanite woman,” 7 and that Jacob had listened to his father and mother and gone to Paddan-aram. 8 Esau realized that his father Isaac considered Canaanite women unacceptable. 9 So he went to Ishmael and married Mahalath daughter of Abraham’s son Ishmael and sister of Nebaioth, in addition to his other wives.

Jacob’s dream at Bethel

10 Jacob left Beer-sheba and set out for Haran. 11 He reached a certain place and spent the night there. When the sun had set, he took one of the stones at that place and put it near his head. Then he lay down there. 12 He dreamed and saw a raised staircase, its foundation on earth and its top touching the sky, and God’s messengers were ascending and descending on it. 13 Suddenly the LORD was standing on it[n] and saying, “I am the LORD, the God of your father Abraham and the God of Isaac. I will give you and your descendants the land on which you are lying. 14 Your descendants will become like the dust of the earth; you will spread out to the west, east, north, and south. Every family of earth will be blessed because of you and your descendants. 15 I am with you now, I will protect you everywhere you go, and I will bring you back to this land. I will not leave you until I have done everything that I have promised you.”

[l] Heb uncertain [m] Heb *El Shaddai* or *God of the Mountain* [n] Or *beside it* or *beside him*

16When Jacob woke from his sleep, he thought to himself, The LORD is definitely in this place, but I didn't know it. 17He was terrified and thought, This sacred place is awesome. It's none other than God's house and the entrance to heaven. 18After Jacob got up early in the morning, he took the stone that he had put near his head, set it up as a sacred pillar, and poured oil on the top of it. 19He named that sacred place Bethel,[o] though Luz was the city's original name. 20Jacob made a solemn promise: "If God is with me and protects me on this trip I'm taking, and gives me bread to eat and clothes to wear, 21and I return safely to my father's household, then the LORD will be my God. 22This stone that I've set up as a sacred pillar will be God's house, and of everything you give me I will give a tenth back to you."

Jacob meets Rachel

29 Jacob got to his feet and set out for the land of the easterners. 2He saw a well in the field in front of him, near which three flocks of sheep were lying down. That well was their source for water because the flocks drank from that well. A huge stone covered the well's opening. 3When all of the flocks were gathered there, the shepherds would roll the stone from the well's opening, water the sheep, and return the stone to its place at the well's opening. 4Jacob said to them, "Where are you from, my brothers?"

They said, "We're from Haran."

5Then he said to them, "Do you know Laban, Nahor's grandson?"

They said, "We know him."

6He said to them, "Is he well?"

They said, "He's fine. In fact, this is his daughter Rachel now, coming with the flock."

7He said to them, "It's now only the middle of the day. It's not time yet to gather the animals. Water the flock, and then go, put them out to pasture."

8They said to him, "We can't until all the herds are gathered, and then we[p] roll the stone away from the well's opening and water the flock."

9While he was still talking to them, Rachel came with her father's flock since she was its shepherd. 10When Jacob saw Rachel the daughter of Laban his uncle, and the flock of Laban, Jacob came up, rolled the stone from the well's opening, and watered the flock of his uncle Laban. 11Jacob kissed Rachel and wept aloud. 12Jacob told Rachel that he was related to her father and that he was Rebekah's son. She then ran to tell her father. 13When Laban heard about Jacob his sister's son, he ran to meet him. Laban embraced him, kissed him, and invited him into his house, where Jacob recounted to Laban everything that had happened. 14Laban said to him, "Yes, you are my flesh and blood."

Jacob marries Leah and Rachel

After Jacob had stayed with Laban for a month, 15Laban said to Jacob, "You shouldn't have to work for free just because you are my relative. Tell me what you would like to be paid."

16Now Laban had two daughters: the older was named Leah and the younger Rachel. 17Leah had delicate eyes,[q] but Rachel had a beautiful figure and was good-looking. 18Jacob loved Rachel and said, "I will work for you for seven years for Rachel, your younger daughter."

19Laban said, "I'd rather give her to you than to another man. Stay with me."

20Jacob worked for Rachel for seven years, but it seemed like a few days because he loved her. 21Jacob said to Laban, "The time has come. Give me my wife so that I may sleep with her." 22So Laban invited all the people of that place and prepared a banquet. 23However, in the evening, he took his daughter Leah and brought her to Jacob, and he slept with her. 24Laban had given his servant Zilpah to his daughter Leah as her servant. 25In the morning, there she was—Leah! Jacob said to Laban, "What have you done to me? Didn't I work for you to have Rachel? Why did you betray me?"

26Laban said, "Where we live, we don't give the younger woman before the oldest.

[o]Or *God's house* [p]Or *they* [q]Heb uncertain; perhaps *Leah had poor eyesight*

27 Complete the celebratory week with this woman. Then I will give[r] you this other woman too for your work, if you work for me seven more years." 28 So that is what Jacob did. He completed the celebratory week with this woman, and then Laban gave him his daughter Rachel as his wife. 29 Laban had given his servant Bilhah to his daughter Rachel as her servant. 30 Jacob slept with Rachel, and he loved Rachel more than Leah. He worked for Laban seven more years.

Jacob's sons are born

31 When the LORD saw that Leah was unloved, he opened her womb; but Rachel was unable to have children. 32 Leah became pregnant and gave birth to a son. She named him Reuben[s] because she said, "The LORD saw my harsh treatment, and now my husband will love me." 33 She became pregnant again and gave birth to a son. She said, "The LORD heard that I was unloved, so he gave me this son too," and she named him Simeon.[t] 34 She became pregnant again and gave birth to a son. She said, "Now, this time my husband will embrace me,"[u] since I have given birth to three sons for him." So she named him Levi.[v] 35 She became pregnant again and gave birth to a son. She said, "This time I will praise the LORD." So she named him Judah.[w] Then she stopped bearing children.

30 When Rachel realized that she could bear Jacob no children, Rachel became jealous of her sister and said to Jacob, "Give me children! If you don't, I may as well be dead."

2 Jacob was angry at Rachel and said, "Do you think I'm God? God alone has kept you from giving birth!"

3 She said, "Here's my servant Bilhah. Sleep with her, and she will give birth for me. Because of her, I will also have children." 4 So Rachel gave her servant Bilhah to Jacob as his wife, and he slept with her. 5 Bilhah became pregnant and gave birth to a son for Jacob. 6 Rachel said, "God has judged in my favor, heard my voice, and given me a son." So she named him Dan.[x] 7 Rachel's servant Bilhah became pregnant again and gave birth to a second son for Jacob. 8 Rachel said, "I've competed fiercely with my sister, and now I've won." So she named him Naphtali.[y]

9 When Leah realized that she had stopped bearing children, she took her servant Zilpah and gave her to Jacob as his wife. 10 Leah's servant Zilpah gave birth to a son for Jacob, 11 and Leah said, "What good luck!" So she named him Gad.[z] 12 Leah's servant Zilpah gave birth to a second son for Jacob, 13 and Leah said, "I'm happy now because women call me happy." So she named him Asher.[a]

14 During the wheat harvest, Reuben found some erotic herbs[b] in the field and brought them to his mother Leah. Rachel said to Leah, "Give me your son's erotic herbs."

15 Leah replied, "Isn't it enough that you've taken my husband? Now you want to take my son's erotic herbs too?"

Rachel said, "For your son's erotic herbs, Jacob[c] may sleep with you tonight."

16 When Jacob came back from the field in the evening, Leah went out to meet him and said, "You must sleep with me because I've paid for you with my son's erotic herbs." So he slept with her that night.

17 God responded to Leah. She became pregnant and gave birth to a fifth son for Jacob. 18 Leah said, "God gave me what I paid for, what I deserved for giving my servant to my husband." So she named him Issachar.[d] 19 Leah became pregnant again and gave birth to a sixth son for Jacob, 20 and she said, "God has given me a wonderful gift. Now my husband will honor me since I've borne him six sons." So she named him Zebulun.[e] 21 After this, she gave birth to a daughter and named her Dinah.

22 Then God remembered Rachel, responded to her, and let her conceive. 23 She became pregnant and gave birth to a son and said, "God has taken away my shame."

[r] LXX, Sam, Syr, Tg, Vulg; MT *we will give* [s] Or *see, a son* [t] Sounds like the Heb verb *hear* [u] Or *be connected to me* [v] Sounds like the Heb verb *embrace,* or *connect* [w] Sounds like the Heb verb *praise* [x] Or *he judged* [y] Or *my competition* or *my wrestling* [z] Or *good fortune* [a] Or *happy* [b] Or *mandrakes* [c] Or *he* [d] Or *there is payment* [e] Or *honor*

24 She named him Joseph,[f] saying to herself, May the LORD give me another son.

God blesses Jacob and Laban

25 After Rachel gave birth to Joseph, Jacob said to Laban, "Send me off so that I can go to my own place and my own country. 26 Give me my wives and children whom I've worked for, and I will go. You know the work I've done for you."

27 Laban said to him, "Do me this favor. I've discovered by a divine sign that the LORD has blessed me because of you, 28 so name your price and I will pay it."

29 Jacob said to him, "You know how I've worked for you, and how well your livestock have done with me. 30 While in my care, what little you had has multiplied a great deal. The LORD blessed you wherever I took your livestock.[g] Now, when will I be able to work for my own household too?"

31 Laban said, "What will I pay you?"

Jacob said, "Don't pay me anything. If you will do this for me, I will take care of your flock again, and keep a portion.[h] 32 I will go through the entire flock today, taking out all of the speckled and spotted sheep, all of the black male lambs, and all of the spotted and speckled female goats. That will be my price. 33 I will be completely honest with you: when you come to check on our agreement, every female goat with me that isn't speckled or spotted and every male lamb with me that isn't black will be considered stolen."

34 Laban said, "All right; let's do it." 35 However, on that very day Laban took out the striped and spotted male goats and all of the speckled and spotted female goats—any with some white in it—and all of the black male lambs, and gave them to his sons. 36 He put a three-day trip between himself and Jacob, while Jacob was watching the rest of Laban's flock.

37 Then Jacob took new branches from poplar, almond, and plane trees; and he peeled white stripes on them, exposing the branches' white color. 38 He set the branches that he had peeled near the watering troughs so that they were in front of the flock when they drank, because they often mated when they came to drink. 39 When the flock mated in front of the branches, they gave birth to striped, speckled, and spotted young. 40 Jacob sorted out the lambs, turning the flock to face the striped and black ones in Laban's flock but keeping his flock separate, setting them apart from Laban's flock. 41 Whenever the strongest of the flock mated, Jacob put the branches in front of them near the watering troughs so that they mated near the branches. 42 But he didn't put branches up for the weakest of the flock. So the weakest became Laban's and the strongest Jacob's. 43 The man Jacob became very, very rich: he owned large flocks, female and male servants, camels, and donkeys.

Jacob's household leaves Laban

31 Jacob heard that Laban's sons were saying, "Jacob took everything our father owned and from it he produced all of this wealth." 2 And Jacob saw that Laban no longer liked him as much as he used to.

3 Then the LORD said to Jacob, "Go back to the land of your ancestors and to your relatives, and I will be with you."

4 So Jacob sent for Rachel and Leah and summoned them into the field where his flock was. 5 He said to them, "I am aware that your father no longer likes me as much as he used to. But my father's God has been with me. 6 You know that I've worked for your father as hard as I could. 7 But your father cheated me and changed my payment ten times. Yet God didn't let him harm me. 8 If he said, 'The speckled ones will be your payment,' the whole flock gave birth to speckled young. And if he said, 'The striped ones will be your payment,' the whole flock gave birth to striped young. 9 God took away your father's livestock and gave them to me. 10 When the flocks were mating, I looked up and saw in a dream that the male goats that mounted the flock were striped, speckled, and spotted. 11 In the dream, God's messenger said to me, 'Jacob!' and I said, 'I'm

[f] Or *he adds* [g] Or *them* [h] Heb uncertain

here.’ 12He said, ‘Look up and watch all the striped, speckled, and spotted male goats mounting the flock. I’ve seen everything that Laban is doing to you. 13I am the God of Bethel, where you anointed a sacred pillar and where you made a solemn promise to me. Now, get up and leave this country and go back to the land of your relatives.’ ”

14Rachel and Leah answered him, “Is there any share or inheritance left for us in our father’s household? 15Doesn’t he think of us as foreigners since he sold us and has even used up the payment he received for us? 16All of the wealth God took from our father belongs to us and our children. Now, do everything God told you to do.”

17So Jacob got up, put his sons and wives on the camels, 18and set out with all of his livestock and all of his possessions that he had acquired[i] in Paddan-aram in order to return to his father Isaac in the land of Canaan. 19Now, while Laban was out shearing his sheep, Rachel stole the household’s divine images that belonged to her father. 20Moreover, Jacob deceived Laban the Aramean by not sending word to him that he was leaving. 21So Jacob and his entire household left. He got up, crossed the river, and set out directly for the mountains of Gilead.

22Three days later, Laban found out that Jacob had gone, 23so Laban took his brothers with him, chased Jacob for seven days, and caught up with him in the mountains of Gilead. 24That night, God appeared to Laban the Aramean in a dream and said, “Be careful and don’t say anything hastily to Jacob one way or the other.”

25Laban reached Jacob after Jacob had pitched his tent in the mountains. So Laban and his brothers also pitched theirs in the mountains of Gilead. 26Laban said to Jacob, “What have you done? You have deceived me and taken off with my daughters as if they were prisoners of war. 27Why did you leave secretly, deceiving me, and not letting me know? I would’ve sent you off with a celebration, with songs and tambourines and harps. 28You didn’t even let me kiss my sons and my daughters good-bye. Now you’ve acted like a fool, 29and I have the power to punish you. However, your father’s God told me yesterday, ‘Be careful and don’t say anything hastily to Jacob one way or the other.’ 30You’ve rushed off now because you missed your father’s household so much, but why did you steal my gods?”

31Jacob responded to Laban, “I was afraid and convinced myself that you would take your daughters away from me. 32Whomever you find with your divine images won’t live. Identify whatever I have that is yours, in front of your brothers, and take it.” Jacob didn’t know that Rachel had stolen them. 33Laban went into Jacob’s tent, Leah’s tent, and her two servants’ tent and didn’t find them.

So he left Leah’s tent and went into Rachel’s. 34Now Rachel had taken the divine images and put them into the camel’s saddlebag and sat on them. Laban felt around in the whole tent but couldn’t find them. 35Rachel said to her father, “Sir, don’t be angry with me because I can’t get up for you; I’m having my period.” He searched but couldn’t find the divine images.

36Jacob was angry and complained to Laban, “What have I done wrong and what’s my crime that you’ve tracked me down like this? 37You’ve now felt through all of my baggage, and what have you found from your household’s belongings? Put it in front of our relatives, and let them decide between us. 38For these twenty years I’ve been with you, your female sheep and goats haven’t miscarried, and I haven’t eaten your flock’s rams. 39When animals were killed, I didn’t bring them to you but took the loss myself. You demanded compensation from me for any animals poached during the day or night. 40The dry heat consumed me during the day, and the frost at night; I couldn’t sleep. 41I’ve now spent twenty years in your household. I worked for fourteen years for your two daughters and for six years for your flock, and you changed my pay ten times. 42If the God of my father—the God of Abraham and the awesome one of

[i]LXX; MT includes *he had acquired, the livestock in his possession.*

Isaac—hadn't been with me, you'd have no
doubt sent me away without anything. God
saw my harsh treatment and my hard work
and reprimanded you yesterday."

Jacob and Laban's treaty

43 Laban responded and told Jacob, "The
daughters are my daughters, the children
are my children, and the flocks are my flocks.
Everything you see is mine. But what can I
do now about my daughters and about their
sons? 44 Come, let's make a treaty, you and
me, and let something be our witness."[j]

45 So Jacob took a stone, set it up as a
sacred pillar, 46 and said to his relatives,
"Gather stones." So they took stones, made
a mound, and ate there near the mound.
47 Laban called it Jegar-sahadutha,[k] but
Jacob called it Galeed.[l]

48 Laban said, "This mound is our witness
today," and, therefore, he too named it Galeed. 49 He also named it Mizpah,[m] because
he said, "The LORD will observe both of us
when we are separated from each other.
50 If you treat my daughters badly and if you
marry other women, though we aren't there,
know that God observed our witness."

51 Laban said to Jacob, "Here is this mound
and here is the sacred pillar that I've set up
for us. 52 This mound and the sacred pillar
are witnesses that I won't travel beyond this
mound and that you won't travel beyond this
mound and this pillar to do harm. 53 The God
of Abraham and the God of Nahor[n] will keep
order between us." So Jacob gave his word
in the name of the awesome one of his father Isaac. 54 Jacob offered a sacrifice on the
mountain, and invited his relatives to a meal.
They ate together and spent the night on the
mountain. 55[o] Laban got up early in the morning, kissed his sons and daughters, blessed
them, and left to go back to his own place.

Jacob prepares to meet Esau

32 Jacob went on his way, and God's
messengers approached him. 2 When
Jacob saw them, he said, "This is God's
camp," and he named that sacred place
Mahanaim.[p] 3 Jacob sent messengers ahead
of him to his brother Esau, toward the land
of Seir, the open country of Edom. 4 He gave
them these orders: "Say this to my master
Esau. This is the message of your servant
Jacob: 'I've lived as an immigrant with
Laban, where I've stayed till now. 5 I own
cattle, donkeys, flocks, men servants, and
women servants. I'm sending this message
to my master now to ask that he[q] be kind.'"

6 The messengers returned to Jacob and
said, "We went out to your brother Esau,
and he's coming to meet you with four hundred men."

7 Jacob was terrified and felt trapped, so
he divided the people with him, and the
flocks, cattle, and camels, into two camps.
8 He thought, If Esau meets the first camp
and attacks it, at least one camp will be left
to escape.

9 Jacob said, "LORD, God of my father
Abraham, God of my father Isaac, who said
to me, 'Go back to your country and your
relatives, and I'll make sure things go well for
you.' 10 I don't deserve how loyal and truthful you've been to your servant. I went away
across the Jordan with just my staff, but
now I've become two camps. 11 Save me from
my brother Esau! I'm afraid he will come
and kill me, the mothers, and their children.
12 You were the one who told me, 'I will make
sure things go well for you, and I will make
your descendants like the sand of the sea, so
many you won't be able to count them.'"

13 Jacob spent that night there. From
what he had acquired, he set aside a gift
for his brother Esau: 14 two hundred female
goats and twenty male goats, two hundred
ewes and twenty rams, 15 thirty nursing
camels with their young, forty cows and ten
bulls, and twenty female donkeys and ten
male donkeys. 16 He separated these herds
and gave them to his servants. He said to
them, "Go ahead of me and put some distance between each of the herds." 17 He ordered the first group, "When my brother
Esau meets you and asks you, 'Who are
you with? Where are you going? And whose

[j] Or *covenant* or *testimony* [k] Or *mound of witness* (Aram) [l] Or *mound of witness* [m] Or *observation* [n] LXX; MT includes *their father's God.* [o] 32:1 in Heb [p] Or *two camps* [q] Or *you*

herds are these in front of you?' 18 say, 'They are your servant Jacob's, a gift sent to my master Esau. And Jacob is actually right behind us.'" 19 He also ordered the second group, the third group, and everybody following the herds, "Say exactly the same thing to Esau when you find him. 20 Say also, 'Your servant Jacob is right behind us.'" Jacob thought, I may be able to pacify Esau with the gift I'm sending ahead. When I meet him, perhaps he will be kind to me. 21 So Jacob sent the gift ahead of him, but he spent that night in the camp.

Jacob wrestles with God

22 Jacob got up during the night, took his two wives, his two women servants, and his eleven sons, and crossed the Jabbok River's shallow water. 23 He took them and everything that belonged to him, and he helped them cross the river. 24 But Jacob stayed apart by himself, and a man wrestled with him until dawn broke. 25 When the man saw that he couldn't defeat Jacob, he grabbed Jacob's thigh and tore a muscle in Jacob's thigh as he wrestled with him. 26 The man said, "Let me go because the dawn is breaking."

But Jacob said, "I won't let you go until you bless me."

27 He said to Jacob, "What's your name?" and he said, "Jacob." 28 Then he said, "Your name won't be Jacob any longer, but Israel,[r] because you struggled with God and with men and won."

29 Jacob also asked and said, "Tell me your name."

But he said, "Why do you ask for my name?" and he blessed Jacob there. 30 Jacob named the place Peniel,[s] "because I've seen God face-to-face, and my life has been saved." 31 The sun rose as Jacob passed Penuel, limping because of his thigh. 32 Therefore, Israelites don't eat the tendon attached to the thigh muscle to this day, because he grabbed Jacob's thigh muscle at the tendon.

Esau forgives Jacob

33 Jacob looked up and saw Esau approaching with four hundred men. Jacob divided the children among Leah, Rachel, and the two women servants. 2 He put the servants and their children first, Leah and her children after them, and Rachel and Joseph last. 3 He himself went in front of them and bowed to the ground seven times as he was approaching his brother. 4 But Esau ran to meet him, threw his arms around his neck, kissed him, and they wept. 5 Esau looked up and saw the women and children and said, "Who are these with you?"

Jacob said, "The children that God generously gave your servant." 6 The women servants and their children came forward and bowed down. 7 Then Leah and her servants also came forward and bowed, and afterward Joseph and Rachel came forward and bowed.

8 Esau said, "What's the meaning of this entire group of animals that I met?"

Jacob said, "To ask for my master's kindness."

9 Esau said, "I already have plenty, my brother. Keep what's yours."

10 Jacob said, "No, please, do me the kindness of accepting my gift. Seeing your face is like seeing God's face, since you've accepted me so warmly. 11 Take this present that I've brought because God has been generous to me, and I have everything I need." So Jacob persuaded him, and he took it.

12 Esau said, "Let's break camp and set out, and I'll go with you."

13 But Jacob said to him, "My master knows that the children aren't strong and that I am responsible for the nursing flocks and cattle. If I push them hard for even one day, all of the flocks will die. 14 My master, go on ahead of your servant, but I've got to take it easy, going only as fast as the animals in front of me and the children are able to go, until I meet you in Seir."

15 Esau said, "Let me leave some of my people with you."

But Jacob said, "Why should you do this since my master has already been so kind to me?" 16 That day Esau returned on the road to Seir, 17 but Jacob traveled to Succoth. He

[r] Or *God struggles* or *one who struggles with God* [s] Or *face of God*

built a house for himself but made temporary shelters for his animals; therefore, he named the place Succoth.[t]

Dinah and the conflict at Shechem

[18]Jacob arrived safely at the city of Shechem in the land of Canaan on his trip from Paddan-aram, and he camped in front of the city. [19]He bought the section of the field where he pitched his tent from the sons of Hamor, Shechem's father, for one hundred qesitahs.[u] [20]Then he set up an altar there and named it El Elohe Israel.[v]

34 Dinah, the daughter whom Leah had borne to Jacob, went out to meet the women of that country. [2]When Shechem the son of the Hivite Hamor and the country's prince saw her, he took her, slept with her, and humiliated her. [3]He was drawn to Dinah, Jacob's daughter. He loved the young woman and tried to win her heart. [4]Shechem said to his father Hamor, "Get this girl for me as my wife." [5]Now Jacob heard that Shechem defiled his daughter Dinah; but his sons were with the animals in the countryside, so he decided to keep quiet until they got back. [6]Meanwhile, Hamor, Shechem's father, went out to Jacob to speak with him. [7]Just then, Jacob's sons got back from the countryside. When they heard what had happened, they were deeply offended and very angry, because Shechem had disgraced Israel by sleeping with Jacob's daughter. Such things are simply not done.

[8]Hamor said to them, "My son Shechem's heart is set on your daughter. Please let him marry her. [9]Arrange marriages with us: give us your daughters and take our daughters for yourselves. [10]Live with us. The land is available to you: settle down, travel through it, and buy property in it."

[11]Shechem said to Dinah's father and brothers, "If you approve of me, tell me what you want, and I will give it to you. [12]Make the bride price and marriage gifts as large as you like, and I will pay whatever you tell me. Then let me marry the young woman."

[13]Jacob's sons responded deviously to Shechem and his father Hamor because Shechem defiled their sister Dinah. [14]They said to them, "We can't do this, allowing our sisters to marry uncircumcised men, because it's disgraceful to us. [15]We can only agree to do this if you circumcise every male as we do. [16]Then we will give our daughters to you, and we will take your daughters for ourselves. We will live with you and be one people. [17]But if you don't listen to us and become circumcised, we will take our daughter and leave."

[18]Their idea seemed like a good one to Hamor and Hamor's son Shechem. [19]The young man didn't waste any time doing this because he liked Jacob's daughter so much. He was more respected than anyone else in his father's household. [20]Hamor and his son Shechem went to their city's gate and spoke to the men of their city: [21]"These men want peace with us. Let them live in the land and travel through it; there's plenty of land for them. We will marry their daughters and give them our daughters. [22]But the men will agree to live with us and become one people only if we circumcise every male just as they do. [23]Their livestock, their property, and all of their animals—won't they be ours? Let's agree with them and let them live with us." [24]Everyone at the city gate agreed with Hamor and his son Shechem, so every able-bodied male in the city was circumcised.

[25]On the third day, when they were still in pain, two of Jacob's sons and Dinah's brothers Simeon and Levi took their swords, came into the city, which suspected nothing, and killed every male. [26]They killed Hamor and his son Shechem with their swords, took Dinah from Shechem's household, and left. [27]When Jacob's other sons discovered the dead, they looted the city that had defiled their sister. [28]They took their flocks, their cattle, and their donkeys, whether in the city or in the fields nearby. [29]They carried off their property, their children, and their wives. They looted the entire place. [30]Jacob said to Simeon and Levi, "You've put me in

[t]Or *temporary shelters* [u]A monetary weight [v]Or *El, God of Israel*

danger by making me offensive to those who live here in the land, to the Canaanites and the Perizzites. I have only a few men. They may join forces, attack me, and destroy me, me and my household."

[31]They said, "But didn't he treat our sister like a prostitute?"

Jacob establishes worship at Bethel

35 God said to Jacob, "Get up, go to Bethel, and live there. Build an altar there to the God who appeared to you when you ran away from your brother Esau."

[2]Jacob said to his household and to everyone who was with him, "Get rid of the foreign gods you have with you. Clean yourselves and change your clothes. [3]Then let's rise and go up to Bethel so that I can build an altar there to the God who answered me when I was in trouble and who has been with me wherever I've gone." [4]So they gave Jacob all of the foreign gods they had, as well as the rings in their ears, and Jacob buried them under the terebinth at Shechem. [5]When they set out, God made all of the surrounding cities fearful so that they didn't pursue Jacob's sons. [6]Jacob and all of the people with him arrived in Luz, otherwise known as Bethel, in the land of Canaan. [7]He built an altar there and named the place El-bethel,[w] because God had revealed himself to him there when he ran away from his brother. [8]Rebekah's nurse Deborah died and was buried at Bethel under the oak, and Jacob named it Allon-bacuth.[x]

[9]God appeared to Jacob again, while he was on his way back from Paddan-aram, and blessed him. [10]God said to him, "Your name is Jacob, but your name will be Jacob no longer. No, your name will be Israel." And he named him Israel. [11]God said to him, "I am El Shaddai.[y] Be fertile and multiply. A nation, even a large group of nations, will come from you; kings will descend from your own children. [12]The land I gave to Abraham and to Isaac, I give to you; and I will give the land to your descendants after you." [13]Then God ascended, leaving him alone in the place where he spoke to him. [14]So Jacob set up a sacred pillar, a stone pillar, at the place God spoke to him. He poured an offering of wine on it and then poured oil over it. [15]Jacob named the place Bethel where God spoke to him.

Benjamin's birth and Rachel's death

[16]They left Bethel, and when they were still some distance from Ephrath, Rachel went into hard labor. [17]During her difficult labor, the midwife said to her, "Don't be afraid. You have another son." [18]As her life faded away, just before she died, she named him Ben-oni,[z] but his father named him Benjamin.[a] [19]Rachel died and was buried near the road to Ephrath, that is, Bethlehem. [20]Jacob set up a pillar on her grave. It's the pillar on Rachel's tomb that's still there today. [21]Israel continued his trip and pitched his tent farther on near the tower of Eder.

Jacob's family

[22]While Israel stayed in that place, Reuben went and slept with Bilhah his father's secondary wife, and Israel heard about it.

Jacob had twelve sons. [23]The sons of Leah were Reuben, Jacob's oldest son, and Simeon, Levi, Judah, Issachar, and Zebulun. [24]The sons of Rachel were Joseph and Benjamin. [25]The sons of Bilhah, Rachel's servant, were Dan and Naphtali. [26]The sons of Zilpah, Leah's servant, were Gad and Asher. These were Jacob's sons born to him in Paddan-aram.

Isaac's death

[27]Jacob came to his father Isaac at Mamre, that is, Kiriath-arba. This is Hebron, where Abraham and Isaac lived as immigrants. [28]At the age of 180 years, [29]Isaac took his last breath and died. He was buried with his ancestors after a long, satisfying life. His sons Esau and Jacob buried him.

Esau's descendants

36 These are the descendants of Esau, that is, Edom. [2]Esau married Canaanite

[w]Or *God of Bethel* [x]Or *oak of weeping* [y]Or *God Almighty* or *God of the Mountain* [z]Or *my suffering son*
[a]Or *right-hand son or strong son*

women: Adah the daughter of the Hittite Elon; Oholibamah the daughter of Anah son of the Hittite Zibeon,[b] 3 and Basemath the daughter of Ishmael and sister of Nebaioth. 4 Adah gave birth to Eliphaz for Esau, Basemath gave birth to Reuel, 5 and Oholibamah gave birth to Jeush, Jalam, and Korah. These are Esau's sons born to him in the land of Canaan.

6 Esau took his wives, his sons, his daughters, and everyone in his household, and his livestock, all of his animals, and all of the property he had acquired in the land of Canaan; and he moved away from the land of Canaan[c] and from his brother Jacob. 7 They had so many possessions that they couldn't live together. The land where they lived as immigrants couldn't support all of their livestock. 8 So Esau, that is, Edom, lived in the mountains of Seir.

9 These are the descendants of Esau, the ancestor of Edom, which lies in the mountains of Seir. 10 These are the names of Edom's sons: Eliphaz son of Esau's wife Adah, and Reuel son of Esau's wife Basemath. 11 Eliphaz's sons were Teman, Omar, Zepho, Gatam, and Kenaz. 12 Timna was the secondary wife of Eliphaz, Esau's son, and she gave birth to Amalek for Eliphaz. These are the sons of Esau's wife Adah. 13 These are Reuel's sons: Nahath, Zerah, Shammah, and Mizzah. These are the sons of Esau's wife Basemath. 14 These are the sons of Esau's wife Oholibamah, the daughter of Anah, Zibeon's son:[d] she gave birth to Esau, Jeush, Jalam, and Korah.

15 These are the tribal chiefs from Esau's sons. The sons of Eliphaz, Esau's oldest son: Chief Teman, Chief Omar, Chief Zepho, Chief Kenaz, 16 Chief Korah, Chief Gatam, and Chief Amalek. These are the tribal chiefs of Eliphaz in the land of Edom; they are Adah's sons. 17 These are the sons of Reuel, Esau's son: Chief Nahath, Chief Zerah, Chief Shammah, and Chief Mizzah. These are the tribal chiefs of Reuel in the land of Edom; they are the sons of Esau's wife Basemath. 18 These are the sons of Esau's wife Oholibamah: Chief Jeush, Chief Jalam, and Chief Korah. They are the tribal chiefs of Esau's wife Oholibamah the daughter of Anah. 19 These are the sons of Esau, who is Edom, and these are their tribal chiefs.

20 These are the sons of Seir, the Horite, who live in the land: Lotan, Shobal, Zibeon, Anah, 21 Dishon, Ezer, and Dishan. These are the Horite tribal chiefs, Seir's sons, in the land of Edom. 22 Lotan's sons are Hori and Heman, and Lotan's sister was Timna. 23 These are Shobal's sons: Alvan, Manahath, Ebal, Shepho, and Onam. 24 These are Zibeon's sons: Aiah and Anah. Anah is the one who found water[e] in the desert while pasturing his father Zibeon's donkeys.

25 These are Anah's children: Dishon and Anah's daughter Oholibamah. 26 These are Dishon's[f] sons: Hemdan, Eshban, Ithran, and Cheran. 27 These are Ezer's sons: Bilhan, Zaavan, and Akan. 28 These are Dishan's sons: Uz and Aran. 29 These are the Horite tribal chiefs: Chiefs Lotan, Shobal, Zibeon, Anah, 30 Dishon, Ezer, and Dishan. These are the Horite tribal chiefs, listed according to their chiefs in the land of Seir.

31 These are the kings who ruled in the land of Edom before a king ruled over the Israelites. 32 Bela, Beor's son, ruled in Edom; his city's name was Dinhabah. 33 After Bela died, Jobab son of Zerah from Bozrah became king. 34 After Jobab died, Husham from the land of the Temanites became king. 35 After Husham died, Hadad, Bedad's son who defeated Midian in the countryside of Moab, became king; his city's name was Avith. 36 After Hadad died, Samlah from Masrekah became king. 37 After Samlah died, Shaul from Rehoboth on the river became king. 38 After Shaul died, Baal-hanan, Achbor's son, became king. 39 After Baal-hanan, Achbor's son, died,

[b] LXX, Sam, Syr; MT *daughter* [c] LXX, Sam; MT *to a land* [d] LXX, Sam, Syr; MT *daughter* [e] Syr; Heb uncertain
[f] Sam, Syr; MT *Dishan's*

Hadar became king; his city's name was Pau and his wife's name was Mehetabel the daughter of Matred and granddaughter of Me-zahab.

[40]These are the names of Esau's tribal chiefs according to their families, their locations, and their names: Chief Timna, Chief Alvah, Chief Jetheth, [41]Chief Oholibamah, Chief Elah, Chief Pinon, [42]Chief Kenaz, Chief Teman, Chief Mibzar, [43]Chief Magdiel, and Chief Iram. These are Edom's tribal chiefs according to their settlements in the land they possessed. This is Esau, the ancestor of the Edomites.

Joseph dreams of power

37 Jacob lived in the land of Canaan where his father was an immigrant. [2]This is the account of Jacob's descendants. Joseph was 17 years old and tended the flock with his brothers. While he was helping the sons of Bilhah and Zilpah, his father's wives, Joseph told their father unflattering things about them. [3]Now Israel loved Joseph more than any of his other sons because he was born when Jacob was old. Jacob had made for him a long[g] robe. [4]When his brothers saw that their father loved him more than any of his brothers, they hated him and couldn't even talk nicely to him.

[5]Joseph had a dream and told it to his brothers, which made them hate him even more. [6]He said to them, "Listen to this dream I had. [7]When we were binding stalks of grain in the field, my stalk got up and stood upright, while your stalks gathered around it and bowed down to my stalk."

[8]His brothers said to him, "Will you really be our king and rule over us?" So they hated him even more because of the dreams he told them.

[9]Then Joseph had another dream and described it to his brothers: "I've just dreamed again, and this time the sun and the moon and eleven stars were bowing down to me."

[10]When he described it to his father and brothers, his father scolded him and said to him, "What kind of dreams have you dreamed? Am I and your mother and your brothers supposed to come and bow down to the ground in front of you?" [11]His brothers were jealous of him, but his father took careful note of the matter.

Joseph's brothers take revenge

[12]Joseph's brothers went to tend their father's flocks near Shechem. [13]Israel said to Joseph, "Aren't your brothers tending the sheep near Shechem? Come, I'll send you to them."

And he said, "I'm ready."

[14]Jacob said to him, "Go! Find out how your brothers are and how the flock is, and report back to me."

So Jacob sent him from the Hebron Valley. When he approached Shechem, [15]a man found him wandering in the field and asked him, "What are you looking for?"

[16]Joseph said, "I'm looking for my brothers. Tell me, where are they tending the sheep?"

[17]The man said, "They left here. I heard them saying, 'Let's go to Dothan.'" So Joseph went after his brothers and found them in Dothan.

[18]They saw Joseph in the distance before he got close to them, and they plotted to kill him. [19]The brothers said to each other, "Here comes the big dreamer. [20]Come on now, let's kill him and throw him into one of the cisterns, and we'll say a wild animal devoured him. Then we will see what becomes of his dreams!"

[21]When Reuben heard what they said, he saved him from them, telling them, "Let's not take his life." [22]Reuben said to them, "Don't spill his blood! Throw him into this desert cistern, but don't lay a hand on him." He intended to save Joseph from them and take him back to his father.

[23]When Joseph reached his brothers, they stripped off Joseph's long robe, [24]took him, and threw him into the cistern, an empty cistern with no water in it. [25]When they sat down to eat, they looked up and saw a caravan of Ishmaelites coming from Gilead, with camels carrying sweet resin,

[g]LXX *many-colored*

medicinal resin, and fragrant resin on their
way down to Egypt. 26 Judah said to his
brothers, "What do we gain if we kill our
brother and hide his blood? 27 Come on, let's
sell him to the Ishmaelites. Let's not harm
him because he's our brother; he's family."
His brothers agreed. 28 When some Midianite traders passed by, they pulled Joseph
up out of the cistern. They sold him to the
Ishmaelites for twenty pieces of silver, and
they brought Joseph to Egypt.

29 When Reuben returned to the cistern
and found that Joseph wasn't in it, he tore
his clothes. 30 Then he returned to his brothers and said, "The boy's gone! And I—where
can I go now?"

31 His brothers took Joseph's robe, slaughtered a male goat, and dipped the robe in the
blood. 32 They took the long robe, brought it
to their father, and said, "We found this. See
if it's your son's robe or not."

33 He recognized it and said, "It's my son's
robe! A wild animal has devoured him. Joseph must have been torn to pieces!" 34 Then
Jacob tore his clothes, put a simple mourning cloth around his waist, and mourned
for his son for many days. 35 All of his sons
and daughters got up to comfort him, but
he refused to be comforted, telling them,
"I'll go to my grave mourning for my son."
And Joseph's father wept for him. 36 Meanwhile the Midianites had sold Joseph to the
Egyptians, to Potiphar, Pharaoh's chief officer, commander of the royal guard.

Tamar's place in Judah's family

38 At that time, Judah moved away
from his brothers and settled near
an Adullamite named Hirah. 2 There Judah
saw the daughter of a Canaanite whose
name was Shua, and he married her. After
he slept with her, 3 she became pregnant
and gave birth to a son, whom she[h] named
Er. 4 She became pregnant again, gave birth
to a son, and named him Onan. 5 Then she
gave birth to one more son and named him
Shelah. She was in Chezib when she gave
birth to him.

6 Judah married his oldest son Er to
a woman named Tamar. 7 But the LORD
considered Judah's oldest son Er immoral,
and the LORD put him to death. 8 Judah
said to Onan, "Go to your brother's wife,
do your duty as her brother-in-law, and
provide children for your brother." 9 Onan
knew the children wouldn't be his so when
he slept with his brother's wife, he wasted
his semen on the ground, so he wouldn't
give his brother children. 10 The LORD considered what he did as wrong and put him
to death too. 11 Judah said to Tamar his
daughter-in-law, "Stay as a widow in your
father's household until my son Shelah
grows up." He thought Shelah would die
like his brothers had. So Tamar went and
lived in her father's household.

12 After a long time, Judah's wife the
daughter of Shua died. Then, after a period
of mourning, he and his neighbor Hirah the
Adullamite went up to Timnah, to those
who were shearing his sheep. 13 Tamar was
told, "Your father-in-law is now on his way
up to Timnah to shear his sheep." 14 So Tamar
took off the clothing she wore as a widow,
covered herself with a veil, put on makeup,[i]
and sat down at the entrance to Enaim on
the road to Timnah, since she realized that
although Shelah had already grown up, she
hadn't been given to him as a wife.

15 Judah saw her and thought she was a
prostitute because she had covered her face.
16 He turned to her beside the road and said,
"Let me sleep with you," because he didn't
know she was his daughter-in-law.

She said, "What will you give me for
sleeping with you?"

17 He said, "I will give you a kid goat from
my flock."

She said, "Only if you give me some deposit, as security to guarantee that you will
send it."

18 He said, "What kind of deposit should
I give you?"

And she said, "Your seal, its cord, and the
staff in your hand." He gave these to her, slept
with her, and she became pregnant by him.

19 Then she got up, left, and took off her
veil, dressing once again in the clothing she

[h] Sam, Tg; MT *he* [i] Or *perfumed herself* or *wrapped herself up*

wore as a widow. [20]Judah sent the kid goat with his neighbor the Adullamite so he could take back the deposits from the woman, but he couldn't find her. [21]He asked the locals of that place, "Where's the consecrated worker[j] who was at Enaim on the road?"

But they said, "There's no consecrated worker here."

[22]So he went back to Judah and said, "I couldn't find her. The locals even said, 'There's no holy woman here.' "

[23]Judah said, "Let her keep everything so we aren't laughed at. I did send this kid goat, but you couldn't find her."

[24]About three months later, Judah was told, "Your daughter-in-law Tamar has become a prostitute and is now pregnant because of it."

And Judah said, "Bring her out so that she may be burned."

[25]When she was brought out, she sent this message to her father-in-law, "I'm pregnant by the man who owns these things. See if you recognize whose seal, cord, and staff these are."

[26]Judah recognized them and said, "She's more righteous than I am, because I didn't allow her to marry my son Shelah." Judah never knew her intimately again.

[27]When she gave birth, she discovered she had twins in her womb. [28]At birth, one boy put out his hand, and the midwife took it and tied a red thread on his hand, saying, "This one came out first." [29]As soon as he pulled his hand back, his brother came out, and she said, "You've burst out on your own." So he was named Perez.[k] [30]Afterward, his brother with the red thread on his hand came out, and he was named Zerah.[l]

Joseph's rise and betrayal

39 When Joseph had been taken down to Egypt, Potiphar, Pharaoh's chief officer, the commander of the royal guard and an Egyptian, purchased him from the Ishmaelites who had brought him down there. [2]The LORD was with Joseph, and he became a successful man and served in his Egyptian master's household. [3]His master saw that the LORD was with him and that the LORD made everything he did successful. [4]Potiphar thought highly of Joseph, and Joseph became his assistant; he appointed Joseph head of his household and put everything he had under Joseph's supervision. [5]From the time he appointed Joseph head of his household and of everything he had, the LORD blessed the Egyptian's household because of Joseph. The LORD blessed everything he had, both in the household and in the field. [6]So he handed over everything he had to Joseph and didn't pay attention to anything except the food he ate.

Now Joseph was well-built and handsome. [7]Some time later, his master's wife became attracted to Joseph and said, "Sleep with me."

[8]He refused and said to his master's wife, "With me here, my master doesn't pay attention to anything in his household; he's put everything he has under my supervision. [9]No one is greater than I am in this household, and he hasn't denied me anything except you, since you are his wife. How could I do this terrible thing and sin against God?" [10]Every single day she tried to convince him, but he wouldn't agree to sleep with her or even to be with her.

[11]One day when Joseph arrived at the house to do his work, none of the household's men were there. [12]She grabbed his garment, saying, "Lie down with me." But he left his garment in her hands and ran outside. [13]When she realized that he had left his garment in her hands and run outside, [14]she summoned the men of her house and said to them, "Look, my husband brought us a Hebrew to ridicule us. He came to me to lie down with me, but I screamed. [15]When he heard me raise my voice and scream, he left his garment with me and ran outside." [16]She kept his garment with her until Joseph's master came home, [17]and she told him the same thing: "The Hebrew slave whom you brought to us, to ridicule me, came to me; [18]but when I raised my voice and screamed, he left his garment with me and ran outside."

[j]Traditionally *cultic prostitute* [k]Or *bursting out* [l]Or *dawn*

19When Joseph's master heard the thing that his wife told him, "This is what your servant did to me," he was incensed. 20Joseph's master took him and threw him in jail, the place where the king's prisoners were held. While he was in jail, 21the LORD was with Joseph and remained loyal to him. He caused the jail's commander to think highly of Joseph. 22The jail's commander put all of the prisoners in the jail under Joseph's supervision, and he was the one who determined everything that happened there. 23The jail's commander paid no attention to anything under Joseph's supervision, because the LORD was with him and made everything he did successful.

Joseph interprets dreams in prison

40 Some time later, both the wine steward and the baker for Egypt's king offended their master, the king of Egypt. 2Pharaoh was angry with his two officers, the chief wine steward and the chief baker, 3and he put them under arrest with the commander of the royal guard in the same jail where Joseph was imprisoned. 4The commander of the royal guard assigned Joseph to assist them. After they had been under arrest for some time, 5both of them—the wine steward and the baker for Egypt's king who were imprisoned in the jail—had dreams one night, and each man's dream had its own meaning. 6When Joseph met them in the morning, he saw that they were upset. 7He asked the officers of Pharaoh who were under arrest with him in his master's house, "Why do you look so distressed today?"

8They answered, "We've both had dreams, but there's no one to interpret them."

Joseph said to them, "Don't interpretations belong to God? Describe your dreams to me."

9The chief wine steward described his dream to Joseph: "In my dream there was a vine right in front of me, 10and on the vine were three branches. When it budded, its blossoms appeared, and its clusters ripened into grapes. 11Pharaoh's cup was in my hand, so I took the grapes, crushed them into Pharaoh's cup, and put the cup in Pharaoh's hand."

12Joseph said to him, "This is the dream's interpretation: The three branches are three days. 13After three days, Pharaoh will give you an audience and return you to your position. You will put Pharaoh's cup in his hand, just the way things were before when you were his wine steward. 14But please, remember me when you are doing well and be loyal to me. Put in a good word for me to Pharaoh, so he sets me free from this prison. 15I was stolen from the land of the Hebrews, and here too I've done nothing to be thrown into this dungeon."

16When the chief baker saw that the interpretation was favorable, he said to Joseph, "It was the same for me. In my dream, there were three baskets of white bread[m] on my head. 17In the basket on top there were baked goods for Pharaoh's food, but birds were eating them out of the basket on my head."

18Joseph responded, "This is the dream's interpretation: The three baskets are three days. 19After three days, Pharaoh will give you an audience and will hang you from a tree where birds will peck your flesh from you."

20The third day was Pharaoh's birthday, and he gave a party for all of his servants. Before all of his servants, he gave an audience to the chief wine steward and the chief baker. 21He returned the chief wine steward to his position, and he placed the cup in Pharaoh's hand. 22But the chief baker he hanged, just as Joseph had said would happen when he interpreted their dreams for them. 23But the chief wine steward didn't remember Joseph; he forgot all about him.

Joseph interprets Pharaoh's dreams

41 Two years later, Pharaoh dreamed that he was standing near the Nile. 2In front of him, seven healthy-looking, fattened cows climbed up out of the Nile and grazed on the reeds. 3Just then, seven other cows, terrible-looking and scrawny, climbed up out of the Nile after them and

[m] Heb uncertain

stood beside them on the bank of the Nile. [4]The terrible-looking, scrawny cows devoured the seven healthy-looking, fattened cows. Then Pharaoh woke up. [5]He went back to sleep and had a second dream, in which seven ears of grain, full and healthy, grew on a single stalk. [6]Just then, seven ears of grain, scrawny and scorched by the east wind, sprouted after them, [7]and the scrawny ears swallowed up the full and well-formed ears. Then Pharaoh woke up and realized it was a dream. [8]In the morning, he was disturbed and summoned all of Egypt's religious experts[n] and all of its advisors. Pharaoh described his dreams[o] to them, but they couldn't interpret them for Pharaoh.

[9]Then the chief wine steward spoke to Pharaoh: "Today I've just remembered my mistake. [10]Pharaoh was angry with his servants and put me and the chief baker under arrest with the commander of the royal guard. [11]We both dreamed one night, he and I, and each of our dreams had its own interpretation. [12]A young Hebrew man, a servant of the commander of the royal guard, was with us. We described our dreams to him, and he interpreted our dreams for us, giving us an interpretation for each dream. [13]His interpretations came true exactly: Pharaoh restored me to my position but hanged him."

[14]So Pharaoh summoned Joseph, and they quickly brought him from the dungeon. He shaved, changed clothes, and appeared before Pharaoh. [15]Pharaoh said to Joseph, "I had a dream, but no one could interpret it. Then I heard that when you hear a dream, you can interpret it."

[16]Joseph answered Pharaoh, "It's not me. God will give Pharaoh a favorable response."

[17]So Pharaoh said to Joseph, "In my dream I was standing on the bank of the Nile. [18]In front of me, seven fattened, stout cows climbed up out of the Nile and grazed on the reeds. [19]Just then, seven other cows, weak and frail and thin, climbed up after them. I've never seen such awful cows in all the land of Egypt. [20]Then the thin, frail cows devoured the first seven, fattened cows. [21]But after they swallowed them whole, no one would have known it. They looked just as bad as they had before. Then I woke up. [22]I went to sleep again[p] and saw in my dream seven full and healthy ears of grain growing on one stalk. [23]Just then, seven hard and thin ears of grain, scorched by the east wind, sprouted after them, [24]and the thin ears swallowed up the healthy ears. I told the religious experts,[q] but they couldn't explain it to me."

[25]Joseph said to Pharaoh, "Pharaoh has actually had one dream. God has announced to Pharaoh what he is about to do. [26]The seven healthy cows are seven years, and the seven healthy ears of grain are seven years. It's actually one dream. [27]The seven thin and frail cows, climbing up after them, are seven years. The seven thin ears of grain, scorched by the east wind, are seven years of famine. [28]It's just as I told Pharaoh: God has shown Pharaoh what he is about to do. [29]Seven years of great abundance are now coming throughout the entire land of Egypt. [30]After them, seven years of famine will appear, and all of the abundance in the land of Egypt will be forgotten. The famine will devastate the land. [31]No one will remember the abundance in the land because the famine that follows will be so very severe. [32]The dream occurred to Pharaoh twice because God has determined to do it, and God will make it happen soon.

Joseph's rise to power

[33]"Now Pharaoh should find an intelligent, wise man and give him authority over the land of Egypt. [34]Then Pharaoh should appoint administrators over the land and take one-fifth of all the produce of the land of Egypt during the seven years of abundance. [35]During the good years that are coming, they should collect all such food and store the grain under Pharaoh's control, protecting the food in the cities. [36]This food will be reserved for the seven years of famine to follow in the land of Egypt so that the land won't be ravaged by the famine."

[n]Or *magicians* [o]Sam; MT *dream* [p]LXX, Syr, Vulg; MT lacks *I went to sleep again.* [q]Or *magicians*

37 This advice seemed wise to Pharaoh
and all his servants, 38 and Pharaoh said to
his servants, "Can we find a man with more
God-given gifts[r] than this one?" 39 Then
Pharaoh said to Joseph, "Since God has
made all this known to you, no one is as
intelligent and wise as you are. 40 You will
be in charge of my kingdom,[s] and all my
people will obey[t] your command. Only as
the enthroned king will I be greater than
you." 41 Pharaoh said to Joseph, "Know this:
I've given you authority over the entire land
of Egypt." 42 Pharaoh took his signet ring
from his hand and put it on Joseph's hand,
he dressed him in linen clothes, and he put
a gold necklace around his neck. 43 He put
Joseph on the chariot of his second-in-
command, and everyone in front of him
cried out, "Attention!"[u] So Pharaoh installed
him over the entire land of Egypt. 44 Pharaoh said to Joseph, "I am Pharaoh; no one
will do anything or go anywhere in all the
land of Egypt without your permission."
45 Pharaoh renamed Joseph, Zaphenath-
paneah, and married him to Asenath,
the daughter of Potiphera the priest of
Heliopolis.[v]

Then Joseph assumed control of the land
of Egypt. 46 Joseph was 30 years old when
he began to serve Pharaoh, Egypt's king,
when he left Pharaoh's court and traveled
through the entire land of Egypt. 47 During
the seven years of abundance, the land produced plentifully. 48 He collected all of the
food during the seven years of abundance[w]
in the land of Egypt, and stored the food in
cities. In each city, he stored the food from
the fields surrounding it. 49 Joseph amassed
grain like the sand of the sea. There was so
much that he stopped trying to measure it
because it was beyond measuring. 50 Before
the years of famine arrived, Asenath the
daughter of Potiphera, priest of Heliopolis,[x]
gave birth to two sons for Joseph. 51 Joseph
named the oldest son Manasseh,[y] "because,"
he said, "God has helped me forget all of my
troubles and everyone in my father's household." 52 He named the second Ephraim,[z]
"because," he said, "God has given me children in the land where I've been treated
harshly."

53 The seven years of abundance in the
land of Egypt came to an end, 54 and the
seven years of famine began, just as Joseph
had said. The famine struck every country,
but the entire land of Egypt had bread.
55 When the famine ravaged the entire land
of Egypt and the people pleaded to Pharaoh
for bread, Pharaoh said to all of the Egyptians, "Go to Joseph. Do whatever he tells
you." 56 The famine covered every part of
the land, and Joseph opened all of the granaries[a] and sold grain to the Egyptians. In
the land of Egypt, the famine became more
and more severe. 57 Every country came to
Egypt to buy grain from Joseph, because in
every country the famine had also become
more severe.

Joseph's brothers arrive in Egypt

42 When Jacob learned that there was
grain in Egypt, he said to his sons,
"Why are you staring blankly at each other?
2 I've just heard that there's grain in Egypt.
Go down there and buy some for us so that
we can survive and not starve to death."
3 So Joseph's ten brothers went down to
buy grain in Egypt. 4 However, Jacob didn't
send Joseph's brother Benjamin along with
his brothers because he thought something
bad might happen to him. 5 Israel's sons
came to buy grain with others who also
came since the famine had spread to the
land of Canaan.

6 As for Joseph, he was the land's governor, and he was the one selling grain to
all the land's people. When Joseph's brothers arrived, they bowed down to him, their
faces to the ground. 7 When Joseph saw his
brothers, he recognized them, but he acted
like he didn't know them. He spoke to them
with a harsh tone and said, "Where have
you come from?"

And they said, "From the land of Canaan
to buy food."

8 Joseph recognized his brothers, but they

[r] Or *like this one, in whom is the spirit of God* [s] Or *house* [t] LXX; Heb uncertain, perhaps *submit themselves to your command* [u] An Egyptian loanword similar to the Heb word *kneel* [v] Heb *On* [w] LXX; MT lacks *of abundance.* [x] Heb *On* [y] Or *making forget* [z] Sounds like *has given me children* [a] LXX, Syr; MT *what was in them*

didn't recognize him. 9 Joseph remembered the dreams he had dreamed about them, and said to them, "You are spies. You've come to look for the country's weaknesses."

10 They said to him, "No, Master. Your servants have just come to buy food. 11 We are all sons of one man. We are honest men. Your servants aren't spies."

12 He said to them, "No. You've come to look for the country's weaknesses."

13 They said, "We, your servants, are twelve brothers, sons of one man in the land of Canaan. The youngest is now with our father, but one is gone."

14 Joseph said to them, "It's just as I've said to you. You are spies! 15 But here is how to prove yourselves: As Pharaoh lives, you won't leave here until your youngest brother arrives. 16 Send one of you to get your brother, but the rest of you will stay in prison. We will find out if your words are true. If not, as Pharaoh lives, you are certainly spies."

Joseph's brothers return to Canaan

17 He put them all in prison for three days. 18 On the third day, Joseph said to them, "Do this and you will live, for I'm a God-fearing man. 19 If you are honest men, let one of your brothers stay in prison, and the rest of you, go, take grain back to those in your households who are hungry. 20 But bring your youngest brother back to me so that your words will prove true and you won't die."

So they prepared to do this. 21 The brothers said to each other, "We are clearly guilty for what we did to our brother when we saw his life in danger and when he begged us for mercy, but we didn't listen. That's why we're in this danger now."

22 Reuben responded to them, "Didn't I tell you, 'Don't do anything wrong to the boy'? But you wouldn't listen. So now this is payback for his death." 23 They didn't know that Joseph was listening to them because they were using an interpreter. 24 He stepped away from them and wept. When he returned, he spoke with them again. Then he took Simeon from them and tied him up in front of them.

25 Then Joseph gave orders to fill their bags with grain, to put back each man's silver into his own sack, and to give them provisions for their trip, and it was done. 26 They loaded their grain onto their donkeys, and they set out. 27 When they stopped to spend the night, one of them opened his sack to feed his donkey, and he saw his silver at the top of his sack. 28 He said to his brothers, "My silver's been returned. It's right here in my sack." Their hearts stopped. Terrified, they said to each other, "What has God done to us?"

29 When they got back to their father Jacob in the land of Canaan, they described to him everything that had happened to them: 30 "The man, the country's governor, spoke to us with a harsh tone and accused us of being spies in the country. 31 We told him, 'We're honest men, not spies. 32 We are twelve brothers, all our father's sons. One of us is gone, but the youngest is right now with our father in the land of Canaan.' 33 The man, the country's governor, told us, 'This is how I will know you are honest men: Leave one of your brothers with me, take grain for those in your households who are hungry, and go. 34 But bring back your youngest brother to me. Then I will know that you are not spies but honest men. I will give your brother back to you, and you may travel throughout the country.'"

35 When they opened their sacks, each man found a pouch of his silver in his sack. When they and their father saw their pouches of silver, they were afraid. 36 Their father Jacob said to them, "You've taken my children from me. Joseph's gone. Simeon's gone. And you are taking Benjamin. All this can't really be happening to me!"

37 Reuben said to his father, "You may put both of my sons to death if I don't bring him back to you. Make him my responsibility, and I will make sure he returns to you."

38 But Jacob said to him, "My son won't go down with you because his brother's dead and he's been left all alone. If anything were to happen to him on the trip you are taking, you would send me—old as I am—to my grave in grief."

Joseph's brothers return with Benjamin

43 The famine was severe in the land, 2 and when they had eaten all the grain that they brought from Egypt, their father said to them, "Go back and buy us a little food."

3 Judah said to him, "The man was absolutely serious when he said, 'You may not see me again without your brother with you.' 4 If you agree to send our brother with us, then we will go down and buy you food. 5 But if you don't agree to send him, then we can't go down because the man said to us, 'You may not see me again without your brother with you.'"

6 Israel said, "Why have you caused me such pain by telling the man you had another brother?"

7 They said, "The man asked us pointedly about our family: 'Is your father still alive? Do you have a brother?' So we told him just what we've said. How were we to know he'd say, 'Bring your brother down here'?"

8 Judah said to his father Israel, "Send the young man with me. Let's get ready to leave so that we can stay alive and not die—we, you, and our children. 9 I will guarantee his safety; you can hold me responsible. If I don't bring him back to you and place him here in front of you, it will be my fault forever. 10 If we hadn't waited so long, we would've returned twice by now."

11 Their father Israel said to them, "If it has to be, then do this. Take in your bags some of the land's choice produce, and bring it down to the man as a gift: a little medicinal resin, a little honey, gum, resin, pistachios, and almonds. 12 Take twice as much silver with you, and take back the silver returned in the top of your sacks. It might have been a mistake. 13 And take your brother, get ready, and go back to the man. 14 May God Almighty[b] make the man compassionate toward you so that he may send back our other brother and Benjamin with you. But me, if I'm left childless, then I'm left childless."

15 So the men took this gift. They took twice as much silver with them, together with Benjamin. They left, traveled down to Egypt, and received an audience with Joseph. 16 When Joseph saw Benjamin with them, he said to the manager of his household, "Bring the men to the house and slaughter an animal and prepare it because the men will have dinner with me at noon." 17 The man did as Joseph told him and brought the men to Joseph's house.

18 When they were brought to Joseph's house, the men were frightened and said, "We've been brought here because of the silver put back in our sacks on our first trip so he can overpower us, capture us, make slaves of us, and take our donkeys."

19 They approached the man who was Joseph's household manager and spoke to him at the house's entrance: 20 "Please, Master, we came down the first time just to buy food, 21 but when we stopped to spend the night and opened our sacks, there was the exact amount of each man's silver at the top of his sack. We've brought it back with us, 22 and we've brought down with us additional silver to buy food. We don't know who put our silver in our sacks."

23 He said, "You are fine. Don't be afraid. Your God and your father's God must have hidden a treasure in your sacks. I received your money." Then he brought Simeon out to them.

24 The manager brought the men into Joseph's house and gave them water to wash their feet and feed for their donkeys. 25 They prepared the gift, anticipating Joseph's arrival at noon, since they had heard that they would have a meal there. 26 When Joseph came into the house, they presented him the gift they had brought with them into the house, and they bowed low in front of him. 27 He asked them how they were and said, "How is your elderly father, about whom you spoke? Is he still alive?"

28 They said, "Your servant our father is fine. He's still alive." And they bowed down again with deep respect.

29 Joseph looked up and saw his brother Benjamin, his own mother's son, and he said, "Is this your youngest brother whom

[b] Heb *El Shaddai* or *God of the Mountain*

you told me about? God be gracious to you,
my son." 30 Joseph's feelings for his brother
were so strong he was about to weep, so he
rushed to another room and wept there.
31 He washed his face, came back, pulled
himself together, and said, "Set out the dinner." 32 So they set out his food by himself,
their food by themselves, and the Egyptians' who ate with him by themselves because Egyptians don't allow themselves to
eat with Hebrews; the Egyptians think it
beneath their dignity. 33 They were seated
in front of him from the oldest to the
youngest in their exact birth order, and the
men looked at each other with amazement.
34 Portions of food from Joseph's table were
brought to them, but Benjamin's portion
was five times as large as theirs. So they
drank together and were at ease.

Joseph tests his brothers

44 Joseph gave commands to his household manager: "Fill the men's sacks
with as much food as they'll hold, and put
each man's silver at the top of his sack. 2 Put
my cup, the silver cup, on top of the youngest brother's sack, together with the silver
for his grain." So he did just as Joseph told
him to do.
3 At dawn, the men and their donkeys
were sent off. 4 They had left the city but
hadn't gone far when Joseph said to his
household manager, "Get ready, go after
the men and catch up with them! Ask them,
'Why have you repaid hospitality with
ingratitude?[c] 5 Isn't this the cup[d] my master drinks from and uses to discover God's
plans?[e] What you've done is despicable.'"
6 When he caught up to them, he repeated
these words. 7 They replied, "Why does my
master talk to us like this? Your servants
would never do such a thing. 8 The silver
that we found at the top of our sacks, we've
just brought back to you from the land of
Canaan. We didn't steal silver or gold from
your master's house. 9 Whoever of your servants is found with it will be put to death,
and we'll be my master's slaves."
10 He said, "Fine. We'll do just as you've
said. Whoever is found with it will be my
slave, and the rest of you will go free." 11 Everyone quickly lowered their sacks down to
the ground and each opened his sack. 12 He
searched the oldest first and the youngest
last, and the cup was found in Benjamin's
sack. 13 At this, they tore their clothing.
Then everyone loaded their donkeys, and
they returned to the city.
14 When Judah and his brothers arrived
at Joseph's house, he was still there, and
they fell to the ground in front of him.
15 Joseph said to them, "What's this you've
done? Didn't you know someone like me
can discover God's plans?"[f]
16 Judah replied, "What can we say to my
master? What words can we use? How can
we prove we are innocent? God has found
your servants guilty. We are now your
slaves, all of us, including the one found
with the cup."
17 Joseph said, "I'd never do such a thing.
Only the man found with the cup will be my
slave. As for the rest of you, you are free to
go back to your father."

Judah appeals for Benjamin

18 Judah approached him and said, "Please,
my master, allow your servant to say something to my master without getting angry
with your servant since you are like Pharaoh himself. 19 My master asked his servants, 'Do you have a father or brother?'
20 And we said to my master, 'Yes, we have
an elderly father and a young brother, born
when he was old. His brother is dead and
he's his mother's only child. But his father
loves him.' 21 You told your servants, 'Bring
him down to me so I can see him.' 22 And we
said to my master, 'The young man can't
leave his father. If he leaves, his father will
die.' 23 You said to your servants, 'If your
youngest brother doesn't come down with
you, you'll never see my face again.'
24 "When we went back to my father your
servant, we told him what you said. 25 Our
father told us, 'Go back and buy for us a little
food.' 26 But we said, 'We can't go down. We
will go down only if our youngest brother is

[c] LXX adds *Why have you stolen my silver cup?* [d] Syr; MT lacks *cup.* [e] Or *uses for divination* [f] Or *can practice divination*

with us. We won't be able to gain an audience with the man without our youngest brother with us.' 27Your servant my father said to us, 'You know that my wife gave birth to two sons for me. 28One disappeared and I said, "He must have been torn up by a wild animal," and I haven't seen him since. 29And if you take this one from me too, something terrible will happen to him, and you will send me—old as I am—to my grave in despair.' 30When I now go back to your servant my father without the young man—whose life is so bound up with his—31and when he sees that the young man isn't with us,[g] he will die, and your servants will have sent our father your servant—old as he is—to his grave in grief. 32I, your servant, guaranteed the young man's safety to my father, telling him, 'If I don't bring him back to you, it will be my fault forever.' 33Now, please let your servant stay as your slave instead of the young man so that he can go back with his brothers. 34How can I go back to my father without the young man? I couldn't bear to see how badly my father would be hurt."

Joseph reveals his identity

45 Joseph could no longer control himself in front of all his attendants, so he declared, "Everyone, leave now!" So no one stayed with him when he revealed his identity to his brothers. 2He wept so loudly that the Egyptians and Pharaoh's household heard him. 3Joseph said to his brothers, "I'm Joseph! Is my father really still alive?" His brothers couldn't respond because they were terrified before him.

4Joseph said to his brothers, "Come closer to me," and they moved closer. He said, "I'm your brother Joseph! The one you sold to Egypt. 5Now, don't be upset and don't be angry with yourselves that you sold me here. Actually, God sent me before you to save lives. 6We've already had two years of famine in the land, and there are five years left without planting or harvesting. 7God sent me before you to make sure you'd survive[h] and to rescue your lives in this amazing way. 8You didn't send me here; it was God who made me a father to Pharaoh, master of his entire household, and ruler of the whole land of Egypt.

9"Hurry! Go back to your father. Tell him this is what your son Joseph says: 'God has made me master of all of Egypt. Come down to me. Don't delay. 10You may live in the land of Goshen, so you will be near me, your children, your grandchildren, your flocks, your herds, and everyone with you. 11I will support you there, so you, your household, and everyone with you won't starve, since the famine will still last five years.' 12You and my brother Benjamin have seen with your own eyes that I'm speaking to you. 13Tell my father about my power in Egypt and about everything you've seen. Hurry and bring my father down here." 14He threw his arms around his brother Benjamin's neck and wept, and Benjamin wept on his shoulder. 15He kissed all of his brothers and wept, embracing them. After that, his brothers were finally able to talk to him.

Joseph's brothers return for Jacob

16When Pharaoh's household heard the message "Joseph's brothers have arrived," both Pharaoh and his servants were pleased. 17Pharaoh said to Joseph, "Give your brothers these instructions: Load your pack animals and go back to the land of Canaan. 18Get your father and your households and come back to me. Let me provide you with good things from the land of Egypt so that you may eat the land's best food. 19Give them these instructions too: Take wagons from the land of Egypt for your children and wives, and pick up your father and come back. 20Don't worry about your possessions because you will have good things from the entire land of Egypt."

21So Israel's sons did that. Joseph gave them wagons as Pharaoh instructed, and he gave them provisions for the road. 22To all of them he gave a change of clothing, but to Benjamin he gave three hundred pieces of silver and five changes of clothing. 23To his father he sent ten male donkeys carrying

[g] Sam, LXX; MT lacks *with us.* [h] Or *survive on earth*

End of Joseph

goods from Egypt, ten female donkeys carrying grain and bread, and rations for his
father for the road. 24 He sent his brothers
off; and as they were leaving, he told them,
"Don't be worried about the trip."[i]
25 So they left Egypt and returned to
their father Jacob in the land of Canaan.
26 They announced to him, "Joseph's still
alive! He's actually ruler of all the land of
Egypt!" Jacob's heart nearly failed, and he
didn't believe them.
27 When they told him everything Joseph had said to them, and when he saw
the wagons Joseph had sent to carry him,
Jacob recovered. 28 Then Israel said, "This is
too much! My son Joseph is still alive! Let
me go and see him before I die."

Jacob's household moves to Egypt

46 Israel packed up everything he owned
and traveled to Beer-sheba. There
he offered sacrifices to his father Isaac's
God. 2 God said to Israel in a vision at night,
"Jacob! Jacob!" and he said, "I'm here." 3 He
said, "I am El,[j] your father's God. Don't be
afraid to go down to Egypt because I will
make a great nation of you there. 4 I will go
down to Egypt with you, and I promise to
bring you out again. Joseph will close your
eyes when you die." 5 Then Jacob left Beer-
sheba. Israel's sons put their father Jacob,
their children, and their wives on the wagons Pharaoh had sent to carry him. 6 They
took their livestock and their possessions
that they had acquired in the land of Canaan, and arrived in Egypt, Jacob and all of
his children with him. 7 His sons and grandsons, his daughters and his granddaugh-
ters—all of his descendants he brought
with him to Egypt.
8 These are the names of the Israelites
who went to Egypt, including Jacob and
his sons. Jacob's oldest son was Reuben.
9 Reuben's sons were Hanoch, Pallu, Hezron, and Carmi. 10 Simeon's sons were
Jemuel, Jamin, Ohad, Jachin, Zohar, and
Shaul, whose mother was a Canaanite.
11 Levi's sons were Gershon, Kohath, and
Merari. 12 Judah's sons were Er, Onan,
Shelah, Perez, and Zerah. Er and Onan
both died in the land of Canaan. Perez's
sons were Hezron and Hamul. 13 Issachar's
sons were Tola, Puvah, Iob, and Shimron.
14 Zebulun's sons were Sered, Elon, and
Jahleel. 15 These are the sons Leah bore to
Jacob in Paddan-aram. Her daughter was
Dinah. All of these persons, including his
sons and daughters, totaled 33.
16 Gad's sons were Ziphion, Haggi,
Shuni, Ezbon, Eri, Arodi, and Areli.
17 Asher's sons were Imnah, Ishvah, Ishvi,
Beriah, and their sister Serah. Beriah's
sons were Heber and Malchiel. 18 These
are the sons of Zilpah, whom Laban gave
to his daughter Leah. She bore these to
Jacob, a total of 16 persons.
19 The sons of Jacob's wife Rachel were
Joseph and Benjamin. 20 To Joseph, in
the land of Egypt, were born Manasseh
and Ephraim. Asenath daughter of
Potiphera, priest of Heliopolis,[k] bore
them to him. 21 Benjamin's sons were
Bela, Becher, Ashbel, Gera, Naaman,
Ehi, Rosh, Muppim, Huppim, and Ard.
22 These are Rachel's sons who were born
to Jacob, a total of 14 persons.
23 Dan's son[l] was Hushim. 24 Naphtali's sons were Jahzeel, Guni, Jezer,
and Shillem. 25 These are the sons of Bilhah, whom Laban gave to his daughter
Rachel. She bore these to Jacob, a total
of 7 persons. 26 All of the persons going
to Egypt with Jacob—his own children,
excluding Jacob's sons' wives—totaled
66 persons. 27 Joseph's sons born to him
in Egypt were 2 persons. Thus, all of the
persons in Jacob's household going to
Egypt totaled 70.
28 Israel had sent Judah ahead to Joseph
so that Joseph could explain the way to
Goshen. Then they arrived in the land of
Goshen. 29 Joseph hitched up his chariot
and went to meet his father Israel in Goshen. When he arrived, he threw his arms
around his neck and wept, embracing him
for a long time. 30 Israel said to Joseph, "I
can die now after seeing your face. You are
really still alive!"

[i] Or *Don't quarrel during the trip.* [j] Or *God* [k] Heb *On* [l] Or *sons*

Jacob's household settles in Egypt

31 Joseph said to his brothers and to his father's household, "Let me go up and inform Pharaoh and tell him, 'My brothers and my father's household who were in the land of Canaan have arrived. 32 The men are shepherds, because they own livestock. They've brought with them their flocks and herds and everything they own.' 33 When Pharaoh summons you and says, 'What do you do?' 34 say, 'Your servants have owned livestock since we were young, both we and our ancestors,' so that you will be able to settle in the land of Goshen, since Egyptians think all shepherds are beneath their dignity."

47 Joseph went to inform Pharaoh and said, "My father and brothers with their flocks, herds, and everything they own have come from the land of Canaan and are now in the land of Goshen." 2 From all of his brothers, he selected five men and presented them before Pharaoh.

3 Pharaoh said to Joseph's brothers, "What do you do?"

They said to Pharaoh, "Your servants are shepherds, both we and our ancestors." 4 They continued, "We've come to the land as immigrants because the famine is so severe in the land of Canaan that there are no more pastures for your servants' flocks. Please allow your servants to settle in the land of Goshen."

5 Pharaoh said to Joseph, "Since your father and brothers have arrived, 6 the land of Egypt is available to you. Settle your father and brothers in the land's best location. Let them live in the land of Goshen. And if you know capable men among them, put them in charge of my own livestock."

7 Joseph brought his father Jacob and gave him an audience with Pharaoh. Jacob blessed Pharaoh, 8 and Pharaoh said to Jacob, "How old are you?"

9 Jacob said to Pharaoh, "I've been a traveler for 130 years. My years have been few and difficult. They don't come close to the years my ancestors lived during their travels." 10 Jacob blessed Pharaoh and left Pharaoh's presence. 11 Joseph settled his father and brothers and gave them property in the land of Egypt, in the best location in the land of Rameses, just as Pharaoh had ordered. 12 Joseph provided food for his father, his brothers, and his father's entire household, in proportion to the number of children.

Joseph centralizes power in Egypt

13 There was no food in the land because the famine was so severe. The land of Egypt and the land of Canaan dried up from the famine. 14 Joseph collected all of the silver to be found in the land of Egypt and in the land of Canaan for the grain, which people came to buy, and he deposited it in Pharaoh's treasury. 15 The silver from the land of Egypt and from the land of Canaan had been spent, and all of the Egyptians came to Joseph and said, "Give us food. Why should we die before your eyes, just because the silver is gone?"

16 Joseph said, "Give me your livestock, and I will give you food for your livestock if the silver is gone." 17 So they brought their livestock to Joseph, and Joseph gave them food for the horses, flocks, cattle, and donkeys. He got them through that year with food in exchange for all of their livestock.

18 When that year was over, they came to him the next year and said to him, "We can't hide from my master that the silver is spent and that we've given the livestock to my master. All that's left for my master is our corpses and our farmland. 19 Why should we die before your eyes, we and our farmland too? Buy us and our farms for food, and we and our farms will be under Pharaoh's control. Give us seed so that we can stay alive and not die, and so that our farmland won't become unproductive." 20 So Joseph bought all of Egypt's farmland for Pharaoh because every Egyptian sold his field when the famine worsened. So the land became Pharaoh's. 21 He moved the people to the cities[m] from one end of Egypt to the other. 22 However, he didn't buy the

[m] Sam, LXX *he made the people slaves*

farmland of the priests because Pharaoh allowed the priests a subsidy, and they were able to eat from the subsidy Pharaoh gave them. Therefore, they didn't have to sell their farmland.

23 Joseph said to the people, "Since I've now purchased you and your farmland for Pharaoh, here's seed for you. Plant the seed on the land. 24 When the crop comes in, you must give one-fifth to Pharaoh. You may keep four-fifths for yourselves, for planting fields, and for feeding yourselves, those in your households, and your children."

25 The people said, "You've saved our lives. If you wish, we will be Pharaoh's slaves." 26 So Joseph made a law that still exists today: Pharaoh receives one-fifth from Egypt's farmland. Only the priests' farmland didn't become Pharaoh's.

Jacob blesses Ephraim and Manasseh

27 Israel lived in the land of Egypt, in the land of Goshen. They settled in it, had many children, and became numerous. 28 After Jacob had lived in the land of Egypt for seventeen years, and after he had lived a total of 147 years, 29 Israel's death approached. He summoned his son Joseph and said to him, "If you would be so kind, lay your hand under my thigh, and be loyal and true to me. Don't bury me in Egypt. 30 When I lie down with my fathers, carry me from Egypt and bury me in their grave."

Joseph said, "I will do just as you say."

31 Israel said, "Give me your word!" and Joseph gave his word. Then Israel slumped down at the head of the bed.

48 After this happened, Joseph was told,[n] "Your father is getting weaker," so he took his two sons Manasseh and Ephraim with him. 2 When Jacob was informed,[o] "Your son Joseph is here now," he[p] pulled himself together and sat up in bed. 3 Jacob said to Joseph, "God Almighty[q] appeared to me in Luz in the land of Canaan. He blessed me 4 and said to me, 'I am about to give you many children, to increase your numbers, and to make you a large group of peoples. I will give this land to your descendants following you as an enduring possession.' 5 Now, your two sons born to you in the land of Egypt before I arrived in Egypt are my own. Ephraim and Manasseh are just like Reuben and Simeon to me. 6 Your family who is born to you after them are yours, but their inheritance will be determined under their brothers' names. 7 When I came back from Paddan-aram,[r] Rachel died, to my sorrow, on the road in the land of Canaan, with some distance yet to go to Ephrathah, so I buried her there near the road to Ephrathah,[s] which is Bethlehem."

8 When Israel saw Joseph's sons, he said, "Who are these?"

9 Joseph told his father, "They're my sons, whom God gave me here."

Israel said, "Bring them to me and I will bless them." 10 Because Israel's eyesight had failed from old age and he wasn't able to see, Joseph brought them close to him, and he kissed and embraced them.

11 Israel said to Joseph, "I didn't expect I'd see your face, but now God has shown me your children too." 12 Then Joseph took them from Israel's knees, and he bowed low with his face to the ground. 13 Joseph took both of them, Ephraim in his right hand at Israel's left hand, and Manasseh in his left hand at Israel's right hand, and brought them close to him. 14 But Israel put out his right hand and placed it on the head of Ephraim, the younger one, and his left hand on Manasseh's head, crossing his hands because Manasseh was the oldest son. 15 He blessed them[t] and said,

"May the God before whom my fathers
Abraham and Isaac walked,
may the God who was my shepherd
from the beginning until this day,
16 may the divine messenger
who protected me from all harm,
bless the young men.
Through them may my name be kept alive
and the names of my fathers
Abraham and Isaac.

[n] LXX, Syr, Tg, Vulg; MT *he told* [o] LXX; MT *he informed* [p] Heb *Israel* [q] Heb *El Shaddai* or *God of the Mountain*
[r] Sam, LXX, Syr; MT lacks *aram.* [s] Sam; MT *Ephrath* [t] LXX; MT *Joseph*

May they grow into a great multitude
throughout the land."
17 When Joseph saw that his father had
placed his right hand on Ephraim's head, he
was upset and grasped his father's hand to
move it from Ephraim's head to Manasseh's
head. 18 Joseph said to his father, "No, my
father! This is the oldest son. Put your right
hand on his head."
19 But his father refused and said, "I know,
my son, I know. He'll become a people too,
and he'll also be great. But his younger
brother will be greater than he will, and his
descendants will become many nations."
20 Israel blessed them that day, saying,
"Through you, Israel will pronounce
blessings, saying,
'May God make you
like Ephraim and Manasseh.'"
So Israel put Ephraim before Manasseh.
21 Then Israel said to Joseph, "I'm about to
die. God will be with you and return you to
the land of your fathers. 22 I'm giving you
one portion more than to your brothers,[u] a
portion that I took from the Amorites with
my sword and my bow."

Jacob reveals his sons' destinies

49 Jacob summoned his sons and said, "Gather around so that I can tell you what will happen to you in the coming days.

2 Assemble yourselves and listen,
sons of Jacob;
listen to Israel your father.

3 Reuben, you are my oldest son,
my strength and my first contender,[v]
superior in status and superior in might.
4 As wild as the waters, you won't endure,
for you went up to your father's bed,
you went up[w] and violated my couch.

5 Simeon and Levi are brothers,
weapons of violence their stock in trade.
6 May I myself never enter their council.
May my honor never be linked
to their group;
for when they were angry,
they killed men,
and whenever they wished,
they maimed oxen.
7 Cursed be their anger; it is violent,
their rage; it is relentless.
I'll divide them up within Jacob
and disperse them within Israel.

8 Judah, you are the one
your brothers will honor;
your hand will be
on the neck of your enemies;
your father's sons will bow down to you.
9 Judah is a lion's cub;
from the prey, my son, you rise up.
He lies down and crouches like a lion;
like a lioness—
who dares disturb him?
10 The scepter won't depart from Judah,
nor the ruler's staff
from among his banners.[x]
Gifts will be brought to him;
people will obey him.
11 He ties his male donkey to the vine,
the colt of his female donkey
to the vine's branches.
He washes his clothes in wine,
his garments in the blood of grapes.
12 His eyes are darker than wine,
and his teeth whiter than milk.

13 Zebulun will live at the seashore;
he'll live at the harbor of ships,
his border will be at Sidon.

14 Issachar is a sturdy donkey,
bedding down
beside the village hearths.[y]
15 He saw that a resting place was good
and that the land was pleasant.
He lowered his shoulder to haul loads
and joined the work gangs.

16 Dan[z] will settle disputes for his people,
as one of Israel's tribes.
17 Dan will be a snake on the road,
a serpent on the path,

[u] Heb uncertain [v] Or *first of my power* [w] LXX; MT *he went up* [x] Sam; MT *his feet*
[y] Or *stubbornly lying beneath its saddlebags* [z] Or *he judges*, or *settles disputes*

biting a horse's heels,
so its rider falls backward.

18 I long for your victory, LORD.

19 Gad[a] will be attacked by attackers,
but he'll attack their back.

20 Asher[b] grows fine foods,
and he will supply the king's delicacies.

21 Naphtali is a wild doe
that gives birth to beautiful fawns.[c]

22 Joseph is a young bull,[d]
a young bull by a spring,
who strides with oxen.[e]
23 They attacked him fiercely
and fired arrows;
the archers attacked him furiously.
24 But his bow stayed strong,
and his forearms were nimble,[f]
by the hands
of the strong one of Jacob,
by the name of the shepherd,
the rock of Israel,
25 by God, your father, who supports you,
by the Almighty[g] who blesses you
with blessings from the skies above
and blessings
from the deep sea below,
blessings from breasts and womb.
26 The blessings of your father exceed
the blessings
of the eternal mountains,[h]
the wealth of the everlasting hills.
May they all rest on Joseph's head,
on the forehead of the one
set apart from his brothers.

27 Benjamin is a wolf who hunts:
in the morning he devours the prey;
in the evening he divides the plunder."

28 These are the twelve tribes of Israel,
and this is what their father said to them.
He blessed them by giving each man his
own particular blessing.

Jacob's death and burial

29 Jacob ordered them, "I am soon to join
my people. Bury me with my ancestors in
the cave that's in the field of Ephron the
Hittite; 30 in the cave that's in the field of
Machpelah near Mamre in the land of Canaan that Abraham bought from Ephron the
Hittite as a burial property. 31 That is where
Abraham and his wife Sarah are buried, and
where Isaac and his wife Rebekah are buried,
and where I buried Leah. 32 It is the field and
the cave in it that belonged to the Hittites."
33 After he finished giving orders to his sons,
he put his feet up on the bed, took his last
breath, and joined his people.

50 Joseph fell across his father's body,
wept over him, and kissed him. 2 Joseph then ordered the physicians in his
service to embalm his father, and the physicians embalmed Israel. 3 They mourned for
him forty days because that is the period
required for embalming. Then the Egyptians mourned him for seventy days. 4 After
the period of mourning had passed, Joseph
spoke to Pharaoh's household: "If you approve my request, give Pharaoh this message: 5 My father made me promise, telling
me, 'I'm about to die. You must bury me in
the tomb I dug for myself in the land of Canaan.' Now, let me leave and let me bury my
father, and then I will return."
6 Pharaoh replied, "Go, bury your father
as you promised."
7 So Joseph left to bury his father. All of
Pharaoh's servants went with him, together
with the elder statesmen in his household
and all of the elder statesmen in the land
of Egypt, 8 Joseph's entire household, his
brothers, and his father's household. Only
the children, flocks, and cattle remained
in the land of Goshen. 9 Even chariots and
horsemen went with him; it was a huge
collection of people. 10 When they arrived
at the threshing floor of Atad on the other
side of the Jordan River, they observed a
solemn, deeply sorrowful period of mourning. He grieved seven days for his father.

[a] Or *he attacks* or *good fortune* [b] LXX, Syr, Vulg; MT *from Asher* [c] Or *who gives beautiful words*
[d] Heb uncertain [e] Heb uncertain [f] Heb uncertain; or *flexible* [g] Heb *Shaddai* or *the Mountain One*
[h] LXX; Heb uncertain

[11]When the Canaanites who lived in the land saw the observance of grief on Atad's threshing floor, they said, "This is a solemn observance of grief by the Egyptians." Therefore, its name is Abel-mizraim.[i] It is on the other side of the Jordan River. [12]Israel's sons did for him just as he had ordered. [13]His sons carried him to the land of Canaan and buried him in the cave in the field of Machpelah near Mamre, which Abraham had purchased as burial property from Ephron the Hittite. [14]Then[j] Joseph returned to Egypt, he, his brothers, and everyone who left with him to bury his father.

Joseph and his brothers in Egypt

[15]When Joseph's brothers realized that their father was now dead, they said, "What if Joseph bears a grudge against us, and wants to pay us back seriously for all of the terrible things we did to him?" [16]So they approached[k] Joseph and said, "Your father gave orders before he died, telling us, [17]'This is what you should say to Joseph. "Please, forgive your brothers' sins and misdeeds, for they did terrible things to you. Now, please forgive the sins of the servants of your father's God."'" Joseph wept when they spoke to him.

[18]His brothers wept[l] too, fell down in front of him, and said, "We're here as your slaves."

[19]But Joseph said to them, "Don't be afraid. Am I God? [20]You planned something bad for me, but God produced something good from it, in order to save the lives of many people, just as he's doing today. [21]Now, don't be afraid. I will take care of you and your children." So he put them at ease and spoke reassuringly to them.

[22]Thus Joseph lived in Egypt, he and his father's household. Joseph lived 110 years [23]and saw Ephraim's grandchildren. The children of Machir, Manasseh's son, were also born on Joseph's knees. [24]Joseph said to his brothers, "I'm about to die. God will certainly take care of you and bring you out of this land to the land he promised to Abraham, to Isaac, and to Jacob." [25]Joseph made Israel's sons promise, "When God takes care of you, you must bring up my bones out of here." [26]Joseph died when he was 110 years old. They embalmed him and placed him in a coffin in Egypt.

EXODUS

1 These are the names of the Israelites who came to Egypt with Jacob along with their households: [2]Reuben, Simeon, Levi, and Judah, [3]Issachar, Zebulun, and Benjamin, [4]Dan and Naphtali, Gad and Asher. [5]The total number in Jacob's family was seventy. Joseph was already in Egypt. [6]Eventually, Joseph, his brothers, and everyone in his generation died. [7]But the Israelites were fertile and became populous. They multiplied and grew dramatically, filling the whole land.

Israel is oppressed

[8]Now a new king came to power in Egypt who didn't know Joseph. [9]He said to his people, "The Israelite people are now larger in number and stronger than we are. [10]Come on, let's be smart and deal with them. Otherwise, they will only grow in number. And if war breaks out, they will join our enemies, fight against us, and then escape from the land." [11]As a result, the Egyptians put foremen of forced work gangs over the Israelites to harass them with hard work. They had to build storage cities named Pithom and Rameses for Pharaoh. [12]But the more they were oppressed, the more they grew and spread, so much so that the Egyptians started to look at the Israelites with disgust and dread. [13]So the Egyptians enslaved the Israelites. [14]They

[i]Or *the Egyptians' observance of grief* [j]LXX; MT includes *after he buried his father.* [k]LXX, Syr; MT *they commanded*
[l]Or *came*

made their lives miserable with hard labor, making mortar and bricks, doing field work, and by forcing them to do all kinds of other cruel work.

15 The king of Egypt spoke to two Hebrew midwives named Shiphrah and Puah: 16 "When you are helping the Hebrew women give birth and you see the baby being born, if it's a boy, kill him. But if it's a girl, you can let her live." 17 Now the two midwives respected God so they didn't obey the Egyptian king's order. Instead, they let the baby boys live.

18 So the king of Egypt called the two midwives and said to them, "Why are you doing this? Why are you letting the baby boys live?"

19 The two midwives said to Pharaoh, "Because Hebrew women aren't like Egyptian women. They're much stronger and give birth before any midwives can get to them." 20 So God treated the midwives well, and the people kept on multiplying and became very strong. 21 And because the midwives respected God, God gave them households of their own.

22 Then Pharaoh gave an order to all his people: "Throw every baby boy born to the Hebrews into the Nile River, but you can let all the girls live."

Moses' birth

2 Now a man from Levi's household married a Levite woman. 2 The woman became pregnant and gave birth to a son. She saw that the baby was healthy and beautiful, so she hid him for three months. 3 When she couldn't hide him any longer, she took a reed basket and sealed it up with black tar. She put the child in the basket and set the basket among the reeds at the riverbank. 4 The baby's older sister stood watch nearby to see what would happen to him.

5 Pharaoh's daughter came down to bathe in the river, while her women servants walked along beside the river. She saw the basket among the reeds, and she sent one of her servants to bring it to her. 6 When she opened it, she saw the child. The boy was crying, and she felt sorry for him. She said, "This must be one of the Hebrews' children."

7 Then the baby's sister said to Pharaoh's daughter, "Would you like me to go and find one of the Hebrew women to nurse the child for you?"

8 Pharaoh's daughter agreed, "Yes, do that." So the girl went and called the child's mother. 9 Pharaoh's daughter said to her, "Take this child and nurse it for me, and I'll pay you for your work." So the woman took the child and nursed it. 10 After the child had grown up, she brought him back to Pharaoh's daughter, who adopted him as her son. She named him Moses, "because," she said, "I pulled him out[a] of the water."

Moses runs away to Midian

11 One day after Moses had become an adult, he went out among his people and he saw their forced labor. He saw an Egyptian beating a Hebrew, one of his own people. 12 He looked around to make sure no one else was there. Then he killed the Egyptian and hid him in the sand.

13 When Moses went out the next day, he saw two Hebrew men fighting with each other. Moses said to the one who had started the fight, "Why are you abusing your fellow Hebrew?"

14 He replied, "Who made you a boss or judge over us? Are you planning to kill me like you killed the Egyptian?"

Then Moses was afraid when he realized: They obviously know what I did. 15 When Pharaoh heard about it, he tried to kill Moses.

But Moses ran away from Pharaoh and settled down in the land of Midian. One day Moses was sitting by a well. 16 Now there was a Midianite priest who had seven daughters. The daughters came to draw water and fill the troughs so that their father's flock could drink. 17 But some shepherds came along and rudely chased them away. Moses got up, rescued the women, and gave their flock water to drink.

18 When they went back home to their father Reuel,[b] he asked, "How were you able to come back home so soon today?"

19 They replied, "An Egyptian man rescued

[a] Heb *mashah* sounds like Moses *(moshe)*. [b] Also called Jethro

us from a bunch of shepherds. Afterward, he even helped us draw water to let the flock drink."

20 Reuel said to his daughters, "So where is he? Why did you leave this man? Invite him to eat a meal with us."

21 Moses agreed to come and live with the man, who gave his daughter Zipporah to Moses as his wife. 22 She gave birth to a son, and Moses named him Gershom, "because," he said, "I've been an immigrant[c] living in a foreign land."

23 A long time passed, and the Egyptian king died. The Israelites were still groaning because of their hard work. They cried out, and their cry to be rescued from the hard work rose up to God. 24 God heard their cry of grief, and God remembered his covenant with Abraham, Isaac, and Jacob. 25 God looked at the Israelites, and God understood.

Moses at the burning bush

3 Moses was taking care of the flock for his father-in-law Jethro,[d] Midian's priest. He led his flock out to the edge of the desert, and he came to God's mountain called Horeb. 2 The LORD's messenger appeared to him in a flame of fire in the middle of a bush. Moses saw that the bush was in flames, but it didn't burn up. 3 Then Moses said to himself, Let me check out this amazing sight and find out why the bush isn't burning up.

4 When the LORD saw that he was coming to look, God called to him out of the bush, "Moses, Moses!"

Moses said, "I'm here."

5 Then the LORD said, "Don't come any closer! Take off your sandals, because you are standing on holy ground." 6 He continued, "I am the God of your father, Abraham's God, Isaac's God, and Jacob's God." Moses hid his face because he was afraid to look at God.

7 Then the LORD said, "I've clearly seen my people oppressed in Egypt. I've heard their cry of injustice because of their slave masters. I know about their pain. 8 I've come down to rescue them from the Egyptians in order to take them out of that land and bring them to a good and broad land, a land that's full of milk and honey, a place where the Canaanites, the Hittites, the Amorites, the Perizzites, the Hivites, and the Jebusites all live. 9 Now the Israelites' cries of injustice have reached me. I've seen just how much the Egyptians have oppressed them. 10 So get going. I'm sending you to Pharaoh to bring my people, the Israelites, out of Egypt."

11 But Moses said to God, "Who am I to go to Pharaoh and to bring the Israelites out of Egypt?"

12 God said, "I'll be with you. And this will show you that I'm the one who sent you. After you bring the people out of Egypt, you will come back here and worship God on this mountain."

God's special name

13 But Moses said to God, "If I now come to the Israelites and say to them, 'The God of your ancestors has sent me to you,' they are going to ask me, 'What's this God's name?' What am I supposed to say to them?"

14 God said to Moses, "I Am Who I Am.[e] So say to the Israelites, 'I Am has sent me to you.'" 15 God continued, "Say to the Israelites, 'The LORD, the God of your ancestors, Abraham's God, Isaac's God, and Jacob's God, has sent me to you.' This is my name forever; this is how all generations will remember me.

16 "Go and get Israel's elders together and say to them, 'The LORD, the God of your ancestors, the God of Abraham, of Isaac, and of Jacob, has appeared to me. The LORD said, "I've been paying close attention to you and to what has been done to you in Egypt. 17 I've decided to take you away from the harassment in Egypt to the land of the Canaanites, the Hittites, the Amorites, the Perizzites, the Hivites, and the Jebusites, a land full of milk and honey." 18 They will accept what you say to them. Then you and Israel's elders will go to Egypt's king and say to him, "The LORD, the Hebrews' God, has met with us. So now let us go on a three-day

[c] Heb *ger* sounds like *Gershom*. [d] Also called Reuel [e] Or *I Will Be Who I Will Be*.

journey into the desert so that we can offer sacrifices to the LORD our God." 19However, I know that Egypt's king won't let you go unless he's forced to do it. 20So I'll use my strength and hit Egypt with dramatic displays of my power. After that, he'll let you go.

21"I'll make it so that when you leave Egypt, the Egyptians will be kind to you and you won't go away empty-handed. 22Every woman will ask her neighbor along with the immigrant in her household for their silver and their gold jewelry as well as their clothing. Then you will put it on your sons and daughters, and you will rob the Egyptians.'"

Signs of power

4 Then Moses replied, "But what if they don't believe me or pay attention to me? They might say to me, 'The LORD didn't appear to you!'"

2The LORD said to him, "What's that in your hand?"

Moses replied, "A shepherd's rod."

3The LORD said, "Throw it down on the ground." So Moses threw it on the ground, and it turned into a snake. Moses jumped back from it. 4Then the LORD said to Moses, "Reach out and grab the snake by the tail." So Moses reached out and grabbed it, and it turned back into a rod in his hand. 5"Do this so that they will believe that the LORD, the God of their ancestors, Abraham's God, Isaac's God, and Jacob's God has in fact appeared to you."

6Again, the LORD said to Moses, "Put your hand inside your coat." So Moses put his hand inside his coat. When he took his hand out, his hand had a skin disease flaky like snow. 7Then God said, "Put your hand back inside your coat." So Moses put his hand back inside his coat. When he took it back out again, the skin of his hand had returned to normal. 8"If they won't believe you or pay attention to the first sign, they may believe the second sign. 9If they won't believe even these two signs or pay attention to you, then take some water from the Nile River and pour it out on dry ground. The water that you take from the Nile will turn into blood on the dry ground."

10But Moses said to the LORD, "My Lord, I've never been able to speak well, not yesterday, not the day before, and certainly not now since you've been talking to your servant. I have a slow mouth and a thick tongue."

11Then the LORD said to him, "Who gives people the ability to speak? Who's responsible for making them unable to speak or hard of hearing, sighted or blind? Isn't it I, the LORD? 12Now go! I'll help you speak, and I'll teach you what you should say."

13But Moses said, "Please, my Lord, just send someone else."

14Then the LORD got angry at Moses and said, "What about your brother Aaron the Levite? I know he can speak very well. He's on his way out to meet you now, and he's looking forward to seeing you. 15Speak to him and tell him what he's supposed to say. I'll help both of you speak, and I'll teach both of you what to do. 16Aaron will speak for you to the people. He'll be a spokesperson for you, and you will be like God for him. 17Take this shepherd's rod with you too so that you can do the signs."

Moses goes back to Egypt

18Moses went back to his father-in-law Jethro and said to him, "Please let me go back to my family in Egypt and see whether or not they are still living."

Jethro said to Moses, "Go in peace."

19The LORD said to Moses in Midian, "Go back to Egypt because everyone there who wanted to kill you has died." 20So Moses took his wife and his children, put them on a donkey, and went back to the land of Egypt. Moses also carried the shepherd's rod from God in his hand.

21The LORD said to Moses, "When you go back to Egypt, make sure that you appear before Pharaoh and do all the amazing acts that I've given you the power to do. But I'll make him stubborn so that he won't let the people go. 22Then say to Pharaoh, 'This is what the LORD says: Israel is my oldest son. 23I said to you, "Let my son go so he could worship me." But you refused to let him go. As a result, now I'm going to kill your oldest son.'"

24During their journey, as they camped

overnight, the LORD met Moses[f] and tried to kill him. 25But Zipporah took a sharp-edged flint stone and cut off her son's foreskin. Then she touched Moses' genitals[g] with it, and she said, "You are my bridegroom because of bloodshed." 26So the LORD let him alone. At that time, she announced, "A bridegroom because of bloodshed by circumcision."

27The LORD said to Aaron, "Go into the desert to meet Moses." So he went, and Aaron met him at God's mountain and greeted him with a kiss. 28Moses told Aaron what the LORD had said about his mission and all the signs that the LORD had told him to do. 29Then Moses and Aaron called together all the Israelite elders. 30Aaron told them everything that the LORD had told to Moses, and he performed the signs in front of the people. 31The people believed. When they heard that the LORD had paid attention to the Israelites and had seen their oppression, they bowed down and worshipped.

First meeting with Pharaoh

5 Afterward, Moses and Aaron went to Pharaoh and said, "This is what the LORD, Israel's God, says: 'Let my people go so that they can hold a festival for me in the desert.'"

2But Pharaoh said, "Who is this LORD whom I'm supposed to obey by letting Israel go? I don't know this LORD, and I certainly won't let Israel go."

3Then they said, "The Hebrews' God has appeared to us. Let us go on a three-day journey into the desert so we can offer sacrifices to the LORD our God. Otherwise, the LORD will give us a deadly disease or violence."

4The king of Egypt said to them, "Moses and Aaron, why are you making the people slack off from their work? Do the hard work yourselves!" 5Pharaoh continued, "The land's people are now numerous. Yet you want them to stop their hard work?"

6On the very same day Pharaoh commanded the people's slave masters and supervisors, 7"Don't supply the people with the straw they need to make bricks like you did before. Let them go out and gather the straw for themselves. 8But still make sure that they produce the same number of bricks as they made before. Don't reduce the number! They are weak and lazy, and that's why they cry, 'Let's go and offer sacrifices to our God.' 9Make the men's work so hard that it's all they can do, and they can't focus on these empty lies."

10So the people's slave masters and supervisors came out and spoke to the people, "This is what Pharaoh says, 'I'm not giving you straw anymore. 11Go and get the straw on your own, wherever you can find it. But your work won't be reduced at all.'" 12So the people spread out all through the land of Egypt to gather stubble for straw. 13The slave masters drove them hard and said, "Make sure you make the same daily quota as when you had the straw." 14The Israelite supervisors, whom Pharaoh's slave masters had set over them, were also beaten and asked, "Why didn't you produce the same number of bricks yesterday and today as you did before?"

15Then the Israelite supervisors came and pleaded to Pharaoh, "Why do you treat your servants like this? 16 No straw is supplied to your servants, yet they say to us, 'Make bricks!' Look at how your servants are being beaten! Your own people are to blame!"

17Pharaoh replied, "You are lazy bums, nothing but lazy bums. That's why you say, 'Let us go and offer sacrifices to the LORD.' 18Go and get back to work! No straw will be given to you, but you still need to make the same number of bricks."

19The Israelite supervisors saw how impossible their situation was when they were commanded, "Don't reduce your daily quota of bricks." 20When they left Pharaoh, they met Moses and Aaron, who were waiting for them. 21The supervisors said to them, "Let the LORD see and judge what you've done! You've made us stink in the opinion of Pharaoh and his servants. You've given them a reason to kill us."

[f]Or *him* [g]Or *his feet*

22 Then Moses turned to the LORD and said, "My Lord, why have you abused this people? Why did you send me for this? 23 Ever since I first came to Pharaoh to speak in your name, he has abused this people. And you've done absolutely nothing to rescue your people."

God reassures Moses

6 The LORD replied to Moses, "Now you will see what I'll do to Pharaoh. In fact, he'll be so eager to let them go that he'll drive them out of his land by force."

2 God also said to Moses: "I am the LORD. 3 I appeared to Abraham, Isaac, and Jacob as God Almighty,[h] but I didn't reveal myself to them by my name 'The LORD.' 4 I also set up my covenant with them to give them the land of Canaan where they lived as immigrants. 5 I've also heard the cry of grief of the Israelites, whom the Egyptians have turned into slaves, and I've remembered my covenant. 6 Therefore, say to the Israelites, 'I am the LORD. I'll bring you out from Egyptian forced labor. I'll rescue you from your slavery to them. I'll set you free with great power and with momentous events of justice. 7 I'll take you as my people, and I'll be your God. You will know that I, the LORD, am your God, who has freed you from Egyptian forced labor. 8 I'll bring you into the land that I promised to give to Abraham, Isaac, and Jacob. I'll give it to you as your possession. I am the LORD.'" 9 Moses told this to the Israelites. But they didn't listen to Moses, because of their complete exhaustion and their hard labor.

10 Then the LORD said to Moses, 11 "Go and tell Pharaoh, Egypt's king, to let the Israelites out of his land."

12 But Moses said to the LORD, "The Israelites haven't even listened to me. How can I expect Pharaoh to listen to me, especially since I'm not a very good speaker?" 13 Nevertheless, the LORD spoke to Moses and Aaron about the Israelites and Pharaoh, Egypt's king, giving them orders to let the Israelites go from the land of Egypt.

Family line of Moses and Aaron

14 These were the leaders of their households.

The descendants of Reuben, Israel's oldest son: Hanoch, Pallu, Hezron, and Carmi. These were Reuben's clans. 15 The Simeonites: Jemuel, Jamin, Ohad, Jachin, Zohar, and Shaul, a Canaanite woman's son. These were Simeon's clans.

16 These were the Levites' names by their generations: Gershon, Kohath, and Merari. Levi lived 137 years. 17 The Gershonites: Libni and Shimei and their clans. 18 The Kohathites: Amram, Izhar, Hebron, and Uzziel. Kohath lived 133 years. 19 The Merarites: Mahli and Mushi. These were the Levite clans by their generations.

20 Amram married Jochebed, his father's sister. She gave birth to Aaron and Moses. Amram lived 137 years. 21 The Izharites: Korah, Nepheg, and Zichri. 22 The Uzzielites: Mishael, Elzaphan, and Sithri. 23 Aaron married Elisheba, Amminadab's daughter and Nahshon's sister. She gave birth to Nadab, Abihu, Eleazar, and Ithamar. 24 The Korahites: Assir, Elkanah, and Abiasaph. These were the Korahite clans. 25 Aaron's son Eleazar married one of Putiel's daughters. She gave birth to Phinehas. These were the leaders of Levite households by their clans.

26 It was this same Aaron and Moses whom the LORD commanded, "Bring the Israelites out of the land of Egypt in military formation." 27 It was also this same Moses and Aaron who spoke to Pharaoh king of Egypt to bring the Israelites out of Egypt.

28 At the time the LORD spoke to Moses in the land of Egypt, 29 the LORD said to him, "I am the LORD. Tell Pharaoh, Egypt's king, everything that I've said to you."

30 But Moses replied to the LORD, "Look, I'm not a very good speaker. How is Pharaoh ever going to listen to me?"

7 The LORD said to Moses, "See, I've made you like God to Pharaoh, and your brother Aaron will be your prophet. 2 You will say everything that I command you, and your brother Aaron will tell Pharaoh

[h] Heb *El Shaddai* or *God of the Mountain*

to let the Israelites out of his land. 3But I'll make Pharaoh stubborn, and I'll perform many of my signs and amazing acts in the land of Egypt. 4When Pharaoh refuses to listen to you, then I'll act against Egypt and I'll bring my people the Israelites out of the land of Egypt in military formation by momentous events of justice. 5The Egyptians will come to know that I am the LORD, when I act against Egypt and bring the Israelites out from among them." 6Moses and Aaron did just as the LORD commanded them. 7Moses was 80 years old and Aaron was 83 when they spoke to Pharaoh.

Turning rods into snakes

8The LORD said to Moses and Aaron, 9"When Pharaoh says to you, 'Do one of your amazing acts,' then say to Aaron, 'Take your shepherd's rod and throw it down in front of Pharaoh, and it will turn into a cobra.'"[i]

10So Moses and Aaron went to Pharaoh and did just as the LORD commanded. Aaron threw down his shepherd's rod in front of Pharaoh and his officials, and it turned into a cobra. 11Then Pharaoh called together his wise men and wizards, and Egypt's religious experts[j] did the same thing by using their secret knowledge. 12Each one threw down his rod, and they turned into cobras. But then Aaron's rod swallowed up each of their rods. 13However, Pharaoh remained stubborn. He wouldn't listen to them, just as the LORD had said.

Water into blood

14Then the LORD said to Moses, "Pharaoh is stubborn. He still refuses to let the people go. 15Go to Pharaoh in the morning. As he is going out to the water, make sure you stand at the bank of the Nile River so you will run into him. Bring along the shepherd's rod that turned into a snake. 16Say to him, The LORD, the Hebrews' God, has sent me to you with this message: Let my people go so that they can worship me in the desert. Up to now you still haven't listened. 17This is what the LORD says: By this you will know that I am the LORD. I'm now going to hit the water of the Nile River with this rod in my hand, and it will turn into blood. 18The fish in the Nile are going to die, the Nile will stink, and the Egyptians won't be able to drink water from the Nile." 19The LORD said to Moses, "Say to Aaron, 'Take your shepherd's rod and stretch out your hand over Egypt's waters—over their rivers, their canals, their marshes, and all their bodies of water—so that they turn into blood. There will be blood all over the land of Egypt, even in wooden and stone containers.'"

20Moses and Aaron did just as the LORD commanded. He raised the shepherd's rod and hit the water in the Nile in front of Pharaoh and his officials, and all the water in the Nile turned into blood. 21The fish in the Nile died, and the Nile began to stink so that the Egyptians couldn't drink water from the Nile. There was blood all over the land of Egypt. 22But the Egyptian religious experts did the same thing with their secret knowledge. As a result, Pharaoh remained stubborn, and he wouldn't listen to them, just as the LORD had said. 23Pharaoh turned and went back to his palace. He wasn't impressed even by this. 24Meanwhile, all the Egyptians had to dig for drinking water along the banks of the Nile River, because they couldn't drink the water of the Nile itself. 25Seven days went by after the LORD had struck the Nile River.

Invasion of frogs

8 [k]Then the LORD said to Moses, "Go to Pharaoh and tell him: This is what the LORD says: Let my people go so that they can worship me. 2If you refuse to let them go, then I'll send a plague of frogs over your whole country. 3The Nile will overflow with frogs. They'll get into your palace, into your bedroom and onto your bed, into your officials' houses, and among all your people, and even into your ovens and bread pans. 4The frogs will crawl up on you, your people, and all your officials." 5And[l] the LORD said to Moses, "Tell Aaron, 'Stretch out your

[i]Or *serpent* [j]Or *magicians* [k]7:26 in Heb [l]8:1 in Heb

hand with your shepherd's rod over the rivers, the canals, and the marshes, and make the frogs crawl up all over the land of Egypt.'" 6So Aaron stretched out his hand over the waters of Egypt. The frogs crawled up and covered the land of Egypt. 7However, the Egyptian religious experts were able to do the same thing by their secret knowledge. They too made frogs crawl up onto the land of Egypt.

8Then Pharaoh called for Moses and Aaron, and said, "If you pray to the LORD to get rid of the frogs from me and my people, then I'll let the people go so that they can offer sacrifices to the LORD."

9Moses said to Pharaoh, "Have it your way. When should I pray for you and your officials and your people to remove the frogs from your houses, courtyards, and fields? They'll stay only in the Nile."

10Pharaoh said, "Tomorrow!"

Moses said, "Just as you say! That way you will know that there is no one like the LORD our God. 11The frogs will leave you, your houses, your officials, and your people. They'll stay only in the Nile." 12After Moses and Aaron had left Pharaoh, Moses cried out to the LORD about the frogs that the LORD had brought on Pharaoh. 13The LORD did as Moses asked. The frogs died inside the houses, out in the yards, and in the fields. 14They gathered them together in big piles, and the land began to stink. 15But when Pharaoh saw that the disaster was over, he became stubborn again and wouldn't listen to them, just as the LORD had said.

Swarming lice

16Then the LORD said to Moses, "Tell Aaron, 'Stretch out your shepherd's rod and hit the land's dirt so that lice[m] appear in the whole land of Egypt.'" 17They did this. Aaron stretched out his hand with his shepherd's rod, hit the land's dirt, and lice appeared on both people and animals. All the land's dirt turned into lice throughout the whole land of Egypt.

18The religious experts[n] tried to produce lice by their secret knowledge, but they weren't able to do it. There were lice on people and animals. 19The religious experts said to Pharaoh, "This is something only God could do!" But Pharaoh was stubborn, and he wouldn't listen to them, just as the LORD had said.

Insects fill Egypt

20The LORD said to Moses, "Get up early in the morning and confront Pharaoh as he goes out to the water. Say to him, This is what the LORD says: Let my people go so that they can worship me. 21If you refuse to let my people go, I'll send swarms of insects[o] on you, your officials, your people, and your houses. All Egyptian houses will be filled with swarms of insects and also the ground that they cover. 22But on that day I'll set apart the land of Goshen, where my people live. No swarms of insects will come there so you will know that I, the LORD, am in this land. 23I'll put a barrier between my people and your people. This sign will happen tomorrow." 24The LORD did this. Great swarms of insects came into the houses of Pharaoh and his officials and into the whole land of Egypt. The land was ruined by the insects.

25Then Pharaoh called in Moses and Aaron and said, "Go, offer sacrifices to your God within the land."

26Moses replied, "It wouldn't be right to do that, because the sacrifices that we offer to the LORD our God will offend Egyptians. If we openly offer sacrifices that offend Egyptians, won't they stone us to death? 27We need to go for a three-day journey into the desert to offer sacrifices to the LORD our God as he has ordered us."

28So Pharaoh said, "I'll let you go to offer sacrifices to the LORD your God in the desert, provided you don't go too far away and you pray for me."

29Moses said, "I'll leave you now, and I'll pray to the LORD. Tomorrow the swarms of insects will leave Pharaoh, his officials, and his people. Just don't let Pharaoh lie to us again and not let the people go to offer sacrifices to the LORD."

[m]Heb uncertain [n]Or *magicians* [o]Heb uncertain

30 So Moses left Pharaoh and prayed to the LORD. 31 The LORD did as Moses asked and removed the swarms of insects from Pharaoh, from his officials, and from his people. Not one insect remained. 32 But Pharaoh was stubborn once again, and he wouldn't let the people go.

Animals sick and dying

9 Then the LORD said to Moses, "Go to Pharaoh and say to him, This is what the LORD, the Hebrews' God, says: Let my people go so that they can worship me. 2 If you refuse to let them go and you continue to hold them back, 3 the LORD will send a very deadly disease on your livestock in the field: on horses, donkeys, camels, cattle, and flocks. 4 But the LORD will distinguish Israel's livestock from Egypt's livestock so that not one that belongs to the Israelites will die." 5 The LORD set a time and said, "Tomorrow the LORD will do this in the land." 6 And the next day the LORD did it. All of the Egyptian livestock died, but not one animal that belonged to the Israelites died. 7 Pharaoh asked around and found out that not one of Israel's livestock had died. But Pharaoh was stubborn, and he wouldn't let the people go.

Skin sores and blisters

8 Then the LORD said to Moses and Aaron, "Take handfuls of ashes from a furnace and have Moses throw it up in the air in front of Pharaoh. 9 The ashes will turn to soot over the whole land of Egypt. It will cause skin sores that will break out in blisters on people and animals in the whole land of Egypt." 10 So they took ashes from the furnace, and they stood in front of Pharaoh. Moses threw the ash up in the air, and it caused skin sores and blisters to break out on people and animals. 11 The religious experts[p] couldn't stand up to Moses because of the skin sores, because there were skin sores on the religious experts as well as on all the Egyptians. 12 But the LORD made Pharaoh stubborn, and Pharaoh wouldn't listen to them, just as the LORD had said to Moses.

Hail and thunder

13 Then the LORD said to Moses, "Get up early in the morning and confront Pharaoh. Say to him, This is what the LORD, the God of the Hebrews, says: Let my people go so that they can worship me. 14 This time I'm going to send all my plagues on you, your officials, and your people so that you will know that there is no one like me in the whole world. 15 By now I could have used my power to strike you and your people with a deadly disease so that you would have disappeared from the earth. 16 But I've left you standing for this reason: in order to show you my power and in order to make my name known in the whole world. 17 You are still abusing your power against my people, and you refuse to let them go. 18 Tomorrow at this time I'll cause the heaviest hail to fall on Egypt that has ever fallen from the day Egypt was founded until now. 19 So bring under shelter your livestock and all that belongs to you that is out in the open. Every person or animal that is out in the open field and isn't brought inside will die when the hail rains down on them." 20 Some of Pharaoh's officials who took the LORD's word seriously rushed to bring their servants and livestock inside for shelter. 21 Others who didn't take the LORD's word to heart left their servants and livestock out in the open field.

22 The LORD said to Moses, "Raise your hand toward the sky so that hail will fall on the whole land of Egypt, on people and animals and all the grain in the fields in the land of Egypt." 23 Then Moses raised his shepherd's rod toward the sky, and the LORD sent thunder and hail, and lightning struck the earth. The LORD rained hail on the land of Egypt. 24 The hail and the lightning flashing in the middle of the hail were so severe that there had been nothing like it in the entire land of Egypt since it first became a nation. 25 The hail beat down everything that was in the open field throughout the entire land of Egypt, both people and animals. The hail also beat down all the grain in the fields, and it shattered every tree out in the field. 26 The only place where

[p] Or *magicians*

hail didn't fall was in the land of Goshen
where the Israelites lived.
27 Then Pharaoh sent for Moses and Aaron
and said to them, "This time I've sinned.
The LORD is right, and I and my people are
wrong. 28 Pray to the LORD! Enough of God's
thunder and hail! I'm going to let you go. You
don't need to stay here any longer."
29 Moses said to him, "As soon as I've
left the city, I'll spread out my hands to the
LORD. Then the thunder and the hail will
stop and won't return so that you will know
that the earth belongs to the LORD. 30 But I
know that you and your officials still don't
take the LORD God seriously." (31 Now the
flax and the barley were destroyed, because
the barley had ears of grain and the flax had
buds. 32 But both durum and spelt wheat
weren't ruined, because they hadn't come
up.) 33 Moses left Pharaoh and the city, and
spread out his hands to the LORD. Then
the thunder and the hail stopped, and the
rain stopped pouring down on the earth.
34 But when Pharaoh saw that the rain, hail,
and thunder had stopped, he sinned again.
Pharaoh and his officials became stubborn.
35 Because of his stubbornness, Pharaoh
refused to let the Israelites go, just as the
LORD had told Moses.

Invasion of locusts

10 Then the LORD said to Moses, "Go to
Pharaoh. I've made him and his officials stubborn so that I can show them my
signs 2 and so that you can tell your children
and grandchildren how I overpowered the
Egyptians with the signs I did among them.
You will know that I am the LORD."
3 So Moses and Aaron went to Pharaoh
and said to him, "This is what the LORD,
the Hebrews' God, says: How long will you
refuse to respect me? Let my people go so
that they can worship me. 4 Otherwise, if
you refuse to let my people go, I'm going to
bring locusts into your country tomorrow.
5 They will cover the landscape so that you
won't be able to see the ground. They will
eat the last bit of vegetation that was left
after the hail. They will eat all your trees
growing in the fields. 6 The locusts will fill
your houses and all your officials' houses
and all the Egyptians' houses. Your parents
and even your grandparents have never
seen anything like it during their entire
lifetimes in this fertile land." Then Moses
turned and left Pharaoh.
7 Pharaoh's officials said to him, "How
long will this man trap us in a corner like
this? Let the people go so that they can
worship the LORD their God. Don't you get
it? Egypt is being destroyed!"
8 So Moses and Aaron were brought back
to Pharaoh, and he said to them, "Go! Worship the LORD your God! But who exactly is
going with you?"
9 Moses said, "We'll go with our young
and old, with our sons and daughters, and
with our flocks and herds, because we all
must observe the LORD's festival."
10 Pharaoh said to them, "Yes, the LORD
will be with you, all right, especially if I let
your children go with you! Obviously, you are
plotting some evil scheme. 11 No way! Only
your men can go and worship the LORD, because that's what you asked for." Then Pharaoh had them chased out of his presence.
12 Then the LORD said to Moses: "Stretch
out your hand over the land of Egypt so
that the locusts will swarm over the land
of Egypt and eat all of the land's grain and
everything that the hail left." 13 So Moses
stretched out his shepherd's rod over the
land of Egypt, and the LORD made an east
wind blow over the land all that day and
all that night. When morning came, the
east wind had carried in the locusts. 14 The
locusts swarmed over the whole land of
Egypt and settled on the whole country.
Such a huge swarming of locusts had never
happened before and would never happen
ever again. 15 They covered the whole landscape so that the land turned black with
them. They ate all of the land's grain and all
of the orchards' fruit that the hail had left.
Nothing green was left in any orchard or in
any grain field in the whole land of Egypt.
16 Pharaoh called urgently for Moses and
Aaron and said, "I've sinned against the
LORD your God and against you. 17 Please
forgive my sin this time. Pray to the LORD
your God just to take this deathly disaster
away from me."

[18]So Moses left Pharaoh and prayed to the LORD. [19]The LORD turned the wind into a very strong west wind that lifted the locusts and drove them into the Reed Sea.[q] Not a single locust was left in the whole country of Egypt. [20]But the LORD made Pharaoh stubborn so that he wouldn't let the Israelites go.

Darkness covers Egypt

[21]Then the LORD said to Moses, "Raise your hand toward the sky so that darkness spreads over the land of Egypt, a darkness that you can feel." [22]So Moses raised his hand toward the sky, and an intense darkness fell on the whole land of Egypt for three days. [23]People couldn't see each other, and they couldn't go anywhere for three days. But the Israelites all had light where they lived.

[24]Then Pharaoh called Moses and said, "Go! Worship the LORD! Only your flocks and herds need to stay behind. Even your children can go with you."

[25]But Moses said, "You need to let us have sacrifices and entirely burned offerings to present to the LORD our God. [26]So our livestock must go with us. Not one animal can be left behind. We'll need some of them for worshipping the LORD our God. We won't know which to use to worship the LORD until we get there."

[27]But the LORD made Pharaoh stubborn so that he wasn't willing to let them go. [28]Pharaoh said to him, "Get out of here! Make sure you never see my face again, because the next time you see my face you will die."

[29]Moses said, "You've said it! I'll never see your face again!"

God announces the final disaster

11 The LORD said to Moses, "I'll bring one more disaster on Pharaoh and on Egypt. After that, he'll let you go from here. In fact, when he lets you go, he'll eagerly chase you out of here. [2]Tell every man to ask his neighbor and every woman to ask her neighbor for all their silver and gold jewelry." [3]The LORD made sure that the Egyptians were kind to the Hebrew people. In addition, Pharaoh's officials and the Egyptian people even came to honor Moses as a great and important man in the land.

[4]Moses said, "This is what the LORD says: At midnight I'll go throughout Egypt. [5]Every oldest child in the land of Egypt will die, from the oldest child of Pharaoh who sits on his throne to the oldest child of the servant woman by the millstones, and all the first offspring of the animals. [6]Then a terrible cry of agony will echo through the whole land of Egypt unlike any heard before or that ever will be again. [7]But as for the Israelites, not even a dog will growl at them, at the people, or at their animals. By this, you will know that the LORD makes a distinction between Egypt and Israel. [8]Then all your officials will come down to me, bow to me, and say, 'Get out, you and all your followers!' After that I'll leave." Then Moses, furious, left Pharaoh.

[9]The LORD said to Moses, "Pharaoh won't listen to you so that I can perform even more amazing acts in the land of Egypt." [10]Now Moses and Aaron did all these amazing acts in front of Pharaoh, but the LORD made Pharaoh stubborn so that he didn't let the Israelites go from his land.

First Passover

12 The LORD said to Moses and Aaron in the land of Egypt, [2]"This month will be the first month; it will be the first month of the year for you.[r] [3]Tell the whole Israelite community: On the tenth day of this month they must take a lamb for each household, a lamb per house. [4]If a household is too small for a lamb, it should share one with a neighbor nearby. You should divide the lamb in proportion to the number of people who will be eating it. [5]Your lamb should be a flawless year-old male. You may take it from the sheep or from the goats. [6]You should keep close watch over it until the fourteenth day of this month. At twilight on that day, the whole assembled Israelite community should slaughter their

[q]Or *Red Sea* [r]March–April; cf Exod 13:4

lambs. 7 They should take some of the blood
and smear it on the two doorposts and on
the beam over the door of the houses in
which they are eating. 8 That same night
they should eat the meat roasted over the
fire. They should eat it along with unleavened bread and bitter herbs. 9 Don't eat any
of it raw or boiled in water, but roasted over
fire with its head, legs, and internal organs.
10 Don't let any of it remain until morning,
and burn any of it left over in the morning.
11 This is how you should eat it. You should
be dressed, with your sandals on your feet
and your walking stick in your hand. You
should eat the meal in a hurry. It is the
Passover of the LORD. 12 I'll pass through
the land of Egypt that night, and I'll strike
down every oldest child in the land of
Egypt, both humans and animals. I'll impose judgments on all the gods of Egypt. I
am the LORD. 13 The blood will be your sign
on the houses where you live. Whenever I
see the blood, I'll pass over[s] you. No plague
will destroy you when I strike the land of
Egypt.

14 "This day will be a day of remembering
for you. You will observe it as a festival to
the LORD. You will observe it in every generation as a regulation for all time. 15 You
will eat unleavened bread for seven days.
On the first day you must remove yeast
from your houses because anyone who eats
leavened bread anytime during those seven
days will be cut off from Israel. 16 The first
day and the seventh day will be a holy occasion for you. No work at all should be
done on those days, except for preparing
the food that everyone is going to eat. That
is the only work you may do. 17 You should
observe the Festival of Unleavened Bread,
because on this precise day I brought you
out of the land of Egypt in military formation. You should observe this day in every
generation as a regulation for all time. 18 In
the first month, from the evening of the
fourteenth day until the evening of the
twenty-first day, you should eat unleavened
bread. 19 For seven days no yeast should be
found in your houses because whoever
eats leavened bread will be cut off from the
Israelite community, whether the person is
an immigrant or a native of the land. 20 You
should not eat anything made with yeast in
all your settlements. You should eat only
unleavened bread."

21 Then Moses called together all of Israel's elders and said to them, "Go pick
out one of the flock for your families, and
slaughter the Passover lamb. 22 Take a
bunch of hyssop, dip it into the blood that
is in the bowl, and touch the beam above
the door and the two doorposts with the
blood in the bowl. None of you should go
out the door of your house until morning. 23 When the LORD comes by to strike
down the Egyptians and sees the blood on
the beam above the door and on the two
doorposts, the LORD will pass over that
door. He won't let the destroyer enter your
houses to strike you down. 24 You should
observe this ritual as a regulation for all
time for you and your children. 25 When you
enter the land that the LORD has promised to give you, be sure that you observe
this ritual. 26 And when your children ask
you, 'What does this ritual mean to you?'
27 you will say, 'It is the Passover sacrifice
to the LORD, for the LORD passed over the
houses of the Israelites in Egypt. When he
struck down the Egyptians, he spared our
houses.'" The people then bowed down and
worshipped. 28 The Israelites went and did exactly what the LORD had commanded Moses
and Aaron to do.

Death of Egypt's oldest children

29 At midnight the LORD struck down
all the first offspring in the land of Egypt,
from the oldest child of Pharaoh sitting on
his throne to the oldest child of the prisoner in jail, and all the first offspring of the
animals. 30 When Pharaoh, all his officials,
and all the Egyptians got up that night, a
terrible cry of agony rang out across Egypt
because every house had someone in it who
had died. 31 Then Pharaoh called Moses and
Aaron that night and said, "Get up! Get
away from my people, both you and the

[s] Heb verb of the noun *Passover*

Israelites! Go! Worship the LORD, as you said! 32You can even take your flocks and herds, as you asked. Just go! And bring a blessing on me as well!"

Israel set free

33The Egyptians urged the people to hurry and leave the land because they thought, We'll all be dead. 34So the people picked up their bread dough before the yeast made it rise, with their bread pans wrapped in their robes on their shoulders. 35The Israelites did as Moses had told them and asked the Egyptians for their silver and gold jewelry as well as their clothing. 36The LORD made sure that the Egyptians were kind to the people so that they let them have whatever they asked for. And so they robbed the Egyptians.

37The Israelites traveled from Rameses to Succoth. They numbered about six hundred thousand men on foot, besides children. 38A diverse crowd also went up with them along with a huge number of livestock, both flocks and herds. 39They baked unleavened cakes from the dough they had brought out of Egypt. The dough didn't rise because they were driven out of Egypt and they couldn't wait. In fact, they didn't have time to prepare any food for themselves.

40The length of time that the Israelites had lived in Egypt was four hundred thirty years. 41At the end of four hundred thirty years, on that precise day, all the LORD's people in military formation left the land of Egypt. 42For the LORD, that was a night of intent watching, to bring them out of the land of Egypt. For all Israelites in every generation, this same night is a time of intent watching to honor the LORD.

Instructions for observing Passover

43The LORD said to Moses and Aaron: This is the regulation for the Passover. No foreigner may eat it. 44However, any slave who has been bought may eat it after he's been circumcised. 45No temporary foreign resident or day laborer may eat it. 46It should be eaten in one house. You shouldn't take any of the meat outside the house, and you shouldn't break the bones. 47The whole Israelite community should observe it. 48If an immigrant who lives with you wants to observe the Passover to the LORD, then he and all his males should be circumcised. Then he may join in observing it. He should be regarded as a native of the land. But no uncircumcised person may eat it. 49There will be one Instruction for the native and for the immigrant who lives with you.

50All the Israelites did just as the LORD had commanded Moses and Aaron. 51On that precise day, the LORD brought the Israelites out of the land of Egypt in military formation.

13 The LORD said to Moses: 2Dedicate to me all your oldest children. Each first offspring from any Israelite womb belongs to me, whether human or animal.

Unleavened bread

3Moses said to the people, "Remember this day which is the day that you came out of Egypt, out of the place you were slaves, because the LORD acted with power to bring you out of there. No leavened bread may be eaten. 4Today, in the month of Abib,[t] you are going to leave. 5The LORD will bring you to the land of the Canaanites, the Hittites, the Amorites, the Hivites, and the Jebusites. It is the land that the LORD promised your ancestors to give to you, a land full of milk and honey. You should perform this ritual in this month. 6You must eat unleavened bread for seven days. The seventh day is a festival to the LORD. 7Only unleavened bread should be eaten for seven days. No leavened bread and no yeast should be seen among you in your whole country. 8You should explain to your child on that day, 'It's because of what the LORD did for me when I came out of Egypt.'

9"It will be a sign on your hand and a reminder on your forehead so that you will often discuss the LORD's Instruction, for the LORD brought you out of Egypt with great power. 10So you should follow this regulation at its appointed time every year.

[t] March–April, named Nisan after the exile

Dedication of Israel's oldest offspring

[11]"When the LORD brings you into the land of the Canaanites and gives it to you as promised to you and your ancestors, [12]you should set aside for the LORD whatever comes out of the womb first. All of the first males born to your animal belong to the LORD. [13]But every first male donkey you should ransom with a sheep. If you don't ransom it, you must break its neck. You should ransom every oldest male among your children. [14]When in the future your child asks you, 'What does this mean?' you should answer, 'The LORD brought us with great power out of Egypt, out of the place we were slaves. [15]When Pharaoh refused to let us go, the LORD killed all the oldest offspring in the land of Egypt, from the oldest sons to the oldest male animals. That is why I offer to the LORD as a sacrifice every male that first comes out of the womb. But I ransom my oldest sons.' [16]It will be a sign on your hand and a symbol on your forehead that the LORD brought us out of Egypt with great power."

God leads the way

[17]When Pharaoh let the people go, God didn't lead them by way of the land of the Philistines, even though that was the shorter route. God thought, If the people have to fight and face war, they will run back to Egypt. [18]So God led the people by the roundabout way of the Reed Sea[u] desert. The Israelites went up out of the land of Egypt ready for battle. [19]Moses took with him Joseph's bones just as Joseph had made Israel's sons promise when he said to them, "When God takes care of you, you must carry my bones out of here with you." [20]They set out from Succoth and camped at Etham on the edge of the desert. [21]The LORD went in front of them during the day in a column of cloud to guide them and at night in a column of lightning to give them light. This way they could travel during the day and at night. [22]The column of cloud during the day and the column of lightning at night never left its place in front of the people.

Israel crossing the sea

14 Then the LORD said to Moses: [2]Tell the Israelites to turn back and set up camp in front of Pi-hahiroth, between Migdol and the sea in front of Baal-zephon. You should set up camp in front of it by the sea. [3]Pharaoh will think to himself, The Israelites are lost and confused in the land. The desert has trapped them. [4]I'll make Pharaoh stubborn, and he'll chase them. I'll gain honor at the expense of Pharaoh and all his army, and the Egyptians will know that I am the LORD. And they did exactly that.

[5]When Egypt's king was told that the people had run away, Pharaoh and his officials changed their minds about the people. They said, "What have we done, letting Israel go free from their slavery to us?" [6]So he sent for his chariot and took his army with him. [7]He took six hundred elite chariots and all of Egypt's other chariots with captains on all of them. [8]The LORD made Pharaoh, Egypt's king, stubborn, and he chased the Israelites, who were leaving confidently. [9]The Egyptians, including all of Pharaoh's horse-drawn chariots, his cavalry, and his army, chased them and caught up with them as they were camped by the sea, by Pi-hahiroth in front of Baal-zephon.

[10]As Pharaoh drew closer, the Israelites looked back and saw the Egyptians marching toward them. The Israelites were terrified and cried out to the LORD. [11]They said to Moses, "Weren't there enough graves in Egypt that you took us away to die in the desert? What have you done to us by bringing us out of Egypt like this? [12]Didn't we tell you the same thing in Egypt? 'Leave us alone! Let us work for the Egyptians!' It would have been better for us to work for the Egyptians than to die in the desert."

[13]But Moses said to the people, "Don't be afraid. Stand your ground, and watch the LORD rescue you today. The Egyptians you see today you will never ever see again. [14]The LORD will fight for you. You just keep still."

[15]Then the LORD said to Moses, "Why do

[u]Or *Red Sea*

you cry out to me? Tell the Israelites to get moving. 16 As for you, lift your shepherd's rod, stretch out your hand over the sea, and split it in two so that the Israelites can go into the sea on dry ground. 17 But me, I'll make the Egyptians stubborn so that they will go in after them, and I'll gain honor at the expense of Pharaoh, all his army, his chariots, and his cavalry. 18 The Egyptians will know that I am the LORD, when I gain honor at the expense of Pharaoh, his chariots, and his cavalry."

19 God's messenger, who had been in front of Israel's camp, moved and went behind them. The column of cloud moved from the front and took its place behind them. 20 It stood between Egypt's camp and Israel's camp. The cloud remained there, and when darkness fell it lit up the night. They didn't come near each other all night.

21 Then Moses stretched out his hand over the sea. The LORD pushed the sea back by a strong east wind all night, turning the sea into dry land. The waters were split into two. 22 The Israelites walked into the sea on dry ground. The waters formed a wall for them on their right hand and on their left. 23 The Egyptians chased them and went into the sea after them, all of Pharaoh's horses, chariots, and cavalry. 24 As morning approached, the LORD looked down on the Egyptian camp from the column of lightning and cloud and threw the Egyptian camp into a panic. 25 The LORD jammed their chariot wheels so that they wouldn't turn easily. The Egyptians said, "Let's get away from the Israelites, because the LORD is fighting for them against Egypt!"

26 Then the LORD said to Moses, "Stretch out your hand over the sea so that the water comes back and covers the Egyptians, their chariots, and their cavalry." 27 So Moses stretched out his hand over the sea. At daybreak, the sea returned to its normal depth. The Egyptians were driving toward it, and the LORD tossed the Egyptians into the sea. 28 The waters returned and covered the chariots and the cavalry, Pharaoh's entire army that had followed them into the sea. Not one of them remained. 29 The Israelites, however, walked on dry ground through the sea. The waters formed a wall for them on their right hand and on their left.

30 The LORD rescued Israel from the Egyptians that day. Israel saw the Egyptians dead on the seashore. 31 Israel saw the amazing power of the LORD against the Egyptians. The people were in awe of the LORD, and they believed in the LORD and in his servant Moses.

Moses' victory song

15 Then Moses and the Israelites sang this song to the LORD:

I will sing to the LORD,
for an overflowing victory!
Horse and rider he threw into the sea!
2 The LORD is my strength and my power;[v]
he has become my salvation.
This is my God, whom I will praise,
the God of my ancestors,
whom I will acclaim.
3 The LORD is a warrior;
the LORD is his name.

4 Pharaoh's chariots and his army he
hurled into the sea;
his elite captains were sunk
in the Reed Sea.[w]
5 The deep sea covered them;
they sank into the deep waters
like a stone.
6 Your strong hand, LORD,
is dominant in power;
your strong hand, LORD,
shatters the enemy!
7 With your great surge
you overthrow your opponents;
you send out your hot anger;
it burns them up like straw.
8 With the breath of your nostrils
the waters swelled up,
the floods surged up in a great wave;
the deep waters foamed
in the depths of the sea.
9 The enemy said, "I'll pursue, I'll overtake,
I'll divide the spoils of war.
I'll be overfilled with them.

[v] Or *song* [w] Or *Red Sea*

I'll draw my sword;
my hand will destroy them."
10 You blew with your wind;
the sea covered over them.
They sank like lead
in the towering waters.
11 Who is like you among the gods, LORD?
Who is like you, foremost in holiness,
worthy of highest praise,
doing awesome deeds?
12 You raised your strong hand;
earth swallowed them up.

13 With your great loyalty
you led the people you rescued;
with your power you guided them
to your sanctuary.
14 The peoples heard, they shook in terror;
horror grabbed hold
of Philistia's inhabitants.
15 Then Edom's tribal chiefs were terrified;
panic grabbed hold of Moab's rulers;
all of Canaan's inhabitants
melted in fear.
16 Terror and fear came over them;
because of your great power,
they were as still as a stone
until your people, LORD, passed by,
until the people you made your own
passed by.
17 You brought them in and planted them
on your own mountain,
the place, LORD,
that you made your home,
the sanctuary, LORD,
that your hand created.
18 The LORD will rule forever and always.

19 When Pharaoh's horses, chariots, and cavalry went into the sea, the LORD brought back the waters of the sea over them. But the Israelites walked through the sea on dry ground.

Miriam's victory song

20 Then the prophet Miriam, Aaron's sister, took a tambourine in her hand. All the women followed her playing tambourines and dancing.
21 Miriam sang the refrain back to them:

Sing to the LORD,
for an overflowing victory!
Horse and rider he threw into the sea!

Turning bitter water sweet

22 Then Moses had Israel leave the Reed Sea[x] and go out into the Shur desert. They traveled for three days in the desert and found no water.
23 When they came to Marah, they couldn't drink Marah's water because it was bitter. That's why it was called Marah.[y]
24 The people complained against Moses, "What will we drink?"
25 Moses cried out to the LORD, and the LORD pointed out a tree to him. He threw it into the water, and the water became sweet.

The LORD made a regulation and a ruling there, and there he tested them.
26 The LORD said, "If you are careful to obey the LORD your God, do what God thinks is right, pay attention to his commandments, and keep all of his regulations, then I won't bring on you any of the diseases that I brought on the Egyptians. I am the LORD who heals you."

27 Then they came to Elim, where there were twelve springs of water and seventy palm trees. They camped there by the water.

Wilderness food: manna and quail

16 The whole Israelite community set out from Elim and came to the Sin desert, which is located between Elim and Sinai. They set out on the fifteenth day of the second month[z] after they had left the land of Egypt.
2 The whole Israelite community complained against Moses and Aaron in the desert.
3 The Israelites said to them, "Oh, how we wish that the LORD had just put us to death while we were still in the land of Egypt. There we could sit by the pots cooking meat and eat our fill of bread. Instead, you've brought us out into this desert to starve this whole assembly to death."

4 Then the LORD said to Moses, "I'm going to make bread rain down from the sky for you. The people will go out each day and gather just enough for that day. In this way,

[x] Or *Red Sea* [y] Or *bitter* [z] April–May, Iyar

I'll test them to see whether or not they follow my Instruction. [5]On the sixth day, when they measure out what they have collected, it will be twice as much as they collected on other days." [6]So Moses and Aaron said to all the Israelites, "This evening you will know that it was the LORD who brought you out of the land of Egypt. [7]And in the morning you will see the LORD'S glorious presence, because your complaints against the LORD have been heard. Who are we? Why blame us?" [8]Moses continued, "The LORD will give you meat to eat in the evening and your fill of bread in the morning because the LORD heard the complaints you made against him. Who are we? Your complaints aren't against us but against the LORD."

[9]Then Moses said to Aaron, "Say to the whole Israelite community, 'Come near to the LORD, because he's heard your complaints.'" [10]As Aaron spoke to the whole Israelite community, they turned to look toward the desert, and just then the glorious presence of the LORD appeared in the cloud.

[11]The LORD spoke to Moses, [12]"I've heard the complaints of the Israelites. Tell them, 'At twilight you will eat meat. And in the morning you will have your fill of bread. Then you will know that I am the LORD your God.'"

[13]In the evening a flock of quail flew down and covered the camp. And in the morning there was a layer of dew all around the camp. [14]When the layer of dew lifted, there on the desert surface were thin flakes, as thin as frost on the ground. [15]When the Israelites saw it, they said to each other, "What[a] is it?" They didn't know what it was.

Moses said to them, "This is the bread that the LORD has given you to eat. [16]This is what the LORD has commanded: 'Collect as much of it as each of you can eat, one omer[b] per person. You may collect for the number of people in your household.'" [17]The Israelites did as Moses said, some collecting more, some less. [18]But when they measured it out by the omer, the ones who had collected more had nothing left over, and the ones who had collected less had no shortage. Everyone collected just as much as they could eat. [19]Moses said to them, "Don't keep any of it until morning." [20]But they didn't listen to Moses. Some kept part of it until morning, but it became infested with worms and stank. Moses got angry with them. [21]Every morning they gathered it, as much as each person could eat. But when the sun grew hot, it melted away.

[22]On the sixth day the people collected twice as much food as usual, two omers per person. All the chiefs of the community came and told Moses. [23]He said to them, "This is what the LORD has said, 'Tomorrow is a day of rest, a holy Sabbath to the LORD. Bake what you want to bake and boil what you want to boil. But you can set aside and keep all the leftovers until the next morning.'" [24]So they set the leftovers aside until morning, as Moses had commanded. They didn't stink or become infested with worms. [25]The next day Moses said, "Eat it today, because today is a Sabbath to the LORD. Today you won't find it out in the field. [26]Six days you will gather it. But on the seventh day, the Sabbath, there will be nothing to gather."

[27]On the seventh day some of the people went out to gather bread, but they found nothing. [28]The LORD said to Moses, "How long will you refuse to obey my commandments and instructions? [29]Look! The LORD has given you the Sabbath. Therefore, on the sixth day he gives you enough food for two days. Each of you should stay where you are and not leave your place on the seventh day." [30]So the people rested on the seventh day.

[31]The Israelite people called it manna. It was like coriander seed, white, and tasted like honey wafers. [32]Moses said, "This is what the LORD has commanded: 'Let an omer of it be kept safe for future generations so that they can see the food that I used to feed you in the desert when I brought you out of the land of Egypt.'"

[33]Moses said to Aaron, "Take a jar, and put one full omer of manna in it. Then set it in the LORD's presence, where it should be

[a]Heb *man* (= *What?*); cf Exod 16:31 [b]Two quarts

kept safe for future generations." [34]Aaron did as the LORD commanded Moses, and he put it in front of the covenant document for safekeeping. [35]The Israelites ate manna for forty years, until they came to a livable land. They ate manna until they came to the border of the land of Canaan. ([36]An omer[c] is one-tenth of an ephah.)

Water from a rock

17 The whole Israelite community broke camp and set out from the Sin desert to continue their journey, as the LORD commanded. They set up their camp at Rephidim, but there was no water for the people to drink. [2]The people argued with Moses and said, "Give us water to drink."

Moses said to them, "Why are you arguing with me? Why are you testing the LORD?"

[3]But the people were very thirsty for water there, and they complained to Moses, "Why did you bring us out of Egypt to kill us, our children, and our livestock with thirst?"

[4]So Moses cried out to the LORD, "What should I do with this people? They are getting ready to stone me."

[5]The LORD said to Moses, "Go on ahead of the people, and take some of Israel's elders with you. Take in your hand the shepherd's rod that you used to strike the Nile River, and go. [6]I'll be standing there in front of you on the rock at Horeb. Hit the rock. Water will come out of it, and the people will be able to drink." Moses did so while Israel's elders watched. [7]He called the place Massah[d] and Meribah,[e] because the Israelites argued with and tested the LORD, asking, "Is the LORD really with us or not?"

Israel defeats Amalek

[8]Amalek came and fought with Israel at Rephidim. [9]Moses said to Joshua, "Choose some men for us and go fight with Amalek. Tomorrow I'll stand on top of the hill with the shepherd's rod of God in my hand." [10]So Joshua did as Moses told him. He fought with Amalek while Moses, Aaron, and Hur went up to the top of the hill. [11]Whenever Moses held up his hand, Israel would start winning the battle. Whenever Moses lowered his hand, Amalek would start winning. [12]But Moses' hands grew tired. So they took a stone and put it under Moses so he could sit down on it. Aaron and Hur held up his hands, one on each side of him so that his hands remained steady until sunset. [13]So Joshua defeated Amalek and his army with the sword.

[14]Then the LORD said to Moses, "Write this as a reminder on a scroll and read it to Joshua: I will completely wipe out the memory of Amalek under the sky."

[15]Moses built an altar there and called it, "The LORD is my banner." [16]He said, "The power of the LORD's banner![f] The LORD is at war with Amalek in every generation."

Sharing the burden of leadership

18 Jethro, Midian's priest and Moses' father-in-law, heard about everything that God had done for Moses and for God's people Israel, how the LORD had brought Israel out of Egypt. [2]Moses' father-in-law Jethro took with him Zipporah, Moses' wife whom he had sent away, [3]along with her two sons. One was named Gershom because he said, "I have been an immigrant[g] living in a foreign land." [4]The other was named Eliezer[h] because he said, "The God of my ancestors was my helper who rescued me from Pharaoh's sword." [5]Jethro, Moses' father-in-law, brought Moses' sons and wife back to him in the desert where he had set up camp at God's mountain. [6]He sent word to Moses: "I, your father-in-law Jethro, am coming to you along with your wife and her two sons." [7]Moses went out to meet his father-in-law, and he bowed down and kissed him. They asked each other how they were doing, and then they went into the tent. [8]Moses then told his father-in-law everything that the LORD had done to Pharaoh and to the Egyptians on Israel's behalf, all the difficulty they had on their journey, and how the LORD had rescued them.

[c]Two quarts [d]Or *test* [e]Or *argument* [f]Heb uncertain [g]Heb *ger* sounds like *Gershom.* [h]Or *my God is a helper.*

9 Jethro was glad about all the good things that the LORD had done for Israel in saving them from the Egyptians' power.

10 Jethro said, "Bless the LORD who rescued you from the Egyptians' power and from Pharaoh's power, who rescued the people from Egypt's oppressive power. 11 Now I know that the LORD is greater than all the gods, because of what happened when the Egyptians plotted against them." 12 Then Jethro, Moses' father-in-law, brought an entirely burned offering and sacrifices to God. Aaron came with all of Israel's elders to eat a meal with Moses' father-in-law in God's presence.

13 The next day Moses sat as a judge for the people, while the people stood around Moses from morning until evening. 14 When Moses' father-in-law saw all that he was doing for the people, he said, "What's this that you are doing for the people? Why do you sit alone, while all the people are standing around you from morning until evening?"

15 Moses said to his father-in-law, "Because the people come to me to inquire of God. 16 When a conflict arises between them, they come to me and I judge between the two of them. I also teach them God's regulations and instructions."

17 Moses' father-in-law said to him, "What you are doing isn't good. 18 You will end up totally wearing yourself out, both you and these people who are with you. The work is too difficult for you. You can't do it alone. 19 Now listen to me and let me give you some advice. And may God be with you! Your role should be to represent the people before God. You should bring their disputes before God yourself. 20 Explain the regulations and instructions to them. Let them know the way they are supposed to go and the things they are supposed to do. 21 But you should also look among all the people for capable persons who respect God. They should be trustworthy and not corrupt. Set these persons over the people as officers of groups of thousands, hundreds, fifties, and tens. 22 Let them sit as judges for the people at all times. They should bring every major dispute to you, but they should decide all of the minor cases themselves. This will be much easier for you, and they will share your load. 23 If you do this and God directs you, then you will be able to endure. And all these people will be able to go back to their homes much happier."

24 Moses listened to his father-in-law's suggestions and did everything that he had said. 25 Moses chose capable persons from all Israel and set them as leaders over the people, as officers over groups of thousands, hundreds, fifties, and tens. 26 They acted as judges for the people at all times. They would refer the hard cases to Moses, but all of the minor cases they decided themselves. 27 Then Moses said good-bye to his father-in-law, and Jethro went back to his own country.

Arrival at Mount Sinai

19 On exactly the third-month anniversary of the Israelites' leaving the land of Egypt, they came into the Sinai desert. 2 They traveled from Rephidim, came into the Sinai desert, and set up camp there. Israel camped there in front of the mountain 3 while Moses went up to God. The LORD called to him from the mountain, "This is what you should say to Jacob's household and declare to the Israelites: 4 You saw what I did to the Egyptians, and how I lifted you up on eagles' wings and brought you to me. 5 So now, if you faithfully obey me and stay true to my covenant, you will be my most precious possession out of all the peoples, since the whole earth belongs to me. 6 You will be a kingdom of priests for me and a holy nation. These are the words you should say to the Israelites."

7 So Moses came down, called together the people's elders, and set before them all these words that the LORD had commanded him. 8 The people all responded with one voice: "Everything that the LORD has said we will do." Moses reported to the LORD what the people said.

Preparing for a divine encounter

9 Then the LORD said to Moses, "I'm about to come to you in a thick cloud in order that the people will hear me talking with you so that they will always trust you."

Moses told the LORD what the people
said, 10and the LORD said to Moses: "Go to
the people and take today and tomorrow
to make them holy. Have them wash their
clothes. 11Be ready for the third day, because
on the third day the LORD will come down
on Mount Sinai for all the people to see.
12Set up a fence for the people all around
and tell them, 'Be careful not to go up the
mountain or to touch any part of it.' Anyone who even touches the mountain must
be put to death. 13No one should touch
anyone who has touched it, or they must be
either stoned to death or shot with arrows.
Whether an animal or a human being, they
must not be allowed to live. Only when the
ram's horn sounds may they go up on the
mountain."

14So Moses went down the mountain to
the people. He made sure the people were
holy and that they washed their clothes.
15He told the men, "Prepare yourselves for
three days. Don't go near a woman."

16When morning dawned on the third
day, there was thunder, lightning, and a
thick cloud on the mountain, and a very
loud blast of a horn. All the people in the
camp shook with fear. 17Moses brought
the people out of the camp to meet God,
and they took their place at the foot of the
mountain. 18Mount Sinai was all in smoke
because the LORD had come down on it
with lightning. The smoke went up like the
smoke of a hot furnace, while the whole
mountain shook violently. 19The blasts of
the horn grew louder and louder. Moses
would speak, and God would answer him
with thunder. 20The LORD came down on
Mount Sinai to the top of the mountain.
The LORD called Moses to come up to the
top of the mountain, and Moses went up.
21The LORD said to Moses, "Go down and
warn the people not to break through to
try to see the LORD, or many of them will
fall dead. 22Even the priests who come
near to the LORD must keep themselves
holy, or the LORD will break loose against
them."

23Moses said to the LORD, "The people
aren't allowed to come up on Mount Sinai
because you warned us and said, 'Set
up a fence around the mountain to keep
it holy.'"

24The LORD said to him, "Go down,
and bring Aaron back up with you. But
the priests and the people must not break
through and come up to the LORD. Otherwise, the LORD will break loose against
them." 25So Moses went down to the people
and told them.

The Ten Commandments

20 Then God spoke all these words:
2I am the LORD your God who
brought you out of Egypt, out of the
house of slavery.

3You must have no other gods before[i] me.

4Do not make an idol for yourself—
no form whatsoever—of anything in
the sky above or on the earth below or in
the waters under the earth. 5Do not bow
down to them or worship them, because
I, the LORD your God, am a passionate
God. I punish children for their parents'
sins even to the third and fourth generations of those who hate me. 6But I am
loyal and gracious to the thousandth
generation[j] of those who love me and
keep my commandments.

7Do not use the LORD your God's
name as if it were of no significance; the
LORD won't forgive anyone who uses his
name that way.

8Remember the Sabbath day and
treat it as holy. 9Six days you may work
and do all your tasks, 10but the seventh
day is a Sabbath to the LORD your God.
Do not do any work on it—not you, your
sons or daughters, your male or female
servants, your animals, or the immigrant who is living with you. 11Because
the LORD made the heavens and the
earth, the sea, and everything that is in
them in six days, but rested on the seventh day. That is why the LORD blessed
the Sabbath day and made it holy.

12Honor your father and your mother

[i]Or *besides* [j]Or *to thousands*

so that your life will be long on the fertile
land that the LORD your God is giving you.
13 Do not kill.[k]
14 Do not commit adultery.
15 Do not steal.
16 Do not testify falsely against your
neighbor.
17 Do not desire your neighbor's house.
Do not desire and try to take your neighbor's wife, male or female servant, ox,
donkey, or anything else that belongs to
your neighbor.

18 When all the people witnessed the thunder and lightning, the sound of the horn,
and the mountain smoking, the people
shook with fear and stood at a distance.
19 They said to Moses, "You speak to us, and
we'll listen. But don't let God speak to us, or
we'll die."

20 Moses said to the people, "Don't be
afraid, because God has come only to test
you and to make sure you are always in
awe of God so that you don't sin." 21 The
people stood at a distance while Moses approached the thick darkness in which God
was present.

Instructions about worship

22 The LORD said to Moses: "Say this to
the Israelites: You saw for yourselves how I
spoke with you from heaven. 23 Don't make
alongside me gods of silver or gold for yourselves. 24 Make for me an altar from fertile soil on which to sacrifice your entirely
burned offerings, your well-being sacrifices,
your sheep, and your oxen. I will come to
you and bless you in every place where I
make sure my name is remembered. 25 But
if you do make for me an altar from stones,
don't build it with chiseled stone since
using your chisel on the stone will make it
impure. 26 Don't climb onto my altar using
steps: then your genitals won't be exposed
by doing so."

Instructions about slaves

21 These are the case laws that you
should set before them:
2 When you buy a male Hebrew slave,
he will serve you for six years. But in the
seventh year, he will go free without any
payment. 3 If he came in single, he will leave
single. If he came in married, then his wife
will leave with him. 4 If his master gave him
a wife and she bore him sons or daughters,
the wife and her children will belong to her
master. He will leave single. 5 However, if
the slave clearly states, "I love my master,
my wife, and my children, and I don't want
to go free," 6 then his master will bring him
before God. He will bring him to the door or
the doorpost. There his master will pierce
his ear with a pointed tool, and he will serve
him as his slave for life.

7 When a man sells his daughter as a
slave, she shouldn't be set free in the same
way as male slaves are set free. 8 If she
doesn't please her master who chose her
for himself, then her master must let her be
bought back by her family. He has no right
to sell her to a foreign people since he has
treated her unfairly. 9 If he assigns her to his
son, he must give her the rights of a daughter. 10 If he takes another woman for himself, he may not reduce her food, clothing,
or marital rights. 11 If he doesn't do these
three things for her, she will go free without
any payment, for no money.

Instructions about human violence

12 Anyone who hits and kills someone
should be put to death. 13 If the killing
wasn't on purpose but an accident allowed
by God, then I will designate a place to
which the killer can run away. 14 But if
someone plots and kills another person on
purpose, you should remove the killer from
my altar and put him to death.

15 Anyone who violently hits their father
or mother should be put to death.

16 Anyone who kidnaps a person, whether
they have been sold or are still being held,
should be put to death.

17 Anyone who curses their father or
mother should be put to death.

18 When two people are fighting and one
hits the other with a stone or with his fist
so that he is in bed for a while but doesn't

[k] Or *murder*

die—19if he recovers and is able to walk
around outside with a cane, then the one
who hit him shouldn't be punished, except
to pay for the loss of time from work and to
pay for his full recovery.
20When a slave owner hits a male or female slave with a rod and the slave dies immediately, the owner should be punished.
21But if the slave gets up after a day or two,
the slave owner shouldn't be punished because the slave is the owner's property.
22When people who are fighting injure a
pregnant woman so that she has a miscarriage but no other injury occurs, then the
guilty party will be fined what the woman's
husband demands, as negotiated with the
judges. 23If there is further injury, then you
will give a life for a life, 24an eye for an eye,
a tooth for a tooth, a hand for a hand, a foot
for a foot, 25a burn for a burn, a bruise for a
bruise, a wound for a wound.
26When a slave owner hits and blinds the
eye of a male or female slave, he should let
the slave go free on account of the eye. 27If
he knocks out a tooth of a male or female
slave, he should let the slave go free on account of the tooth.

Instructions about animals and property

28When an ox gores a man or a woman
to death, the ox should be stoned to death,
and the meat of the ox shouldn't be eaten.
But the owner of the ox shouldn't be punished. 29However, if the ox had gored people
in the past and its owner had been warned
but didn't watch out for it, and the ox ends
up killing a man or a woman, then the ox
should be stoned to death, and its owner
should also be put to death. 30If the owner
has to pay compensation instead, he must
pay the agreed amount to save his life. 31If
the ox gores a boy or a girl, this same case
law applies to the owner. 32If the ox gores
a male or female slave, the owner will pay
thirty silver shekels to the slave's owner,
and the ox will be stoned to death.
33When someone leaves a pit open or
digs a pit and doesn't cover it and an ox or a
donkey falls into the pit, 34the owner of the
pit must make good on the loss. He should
pay money to the ox's owner, but he may
keep the dead animal.
35When someone's ox hurts someone
else's ox and it dies, then they should sell
the live ox and divide its price. They should
also divide the dead animal between them.
36But if the ox was known for goring in the
past and its owner hadn't watched out for
it, the owner must make good the loss, an
ox for an ox, but may keep the dead animal.

22 [l]When someone steals an ox or a
sheep and then slaughters or sells it,
the thief must pay back five oxen for the
one ox or four sheep for the one sheep.
2[m]If the thief is caught breaking in and
is beaten and dies, the one who killed him
won't be guilty of bloodshed. 3However, if
this happens in broad daylight, then the
one who killed him is guilty of bloodshed.
For his part, the thief must make good on
what he stole. If he has nothing, he must
be sold to pay for his theft. 4If an animal
(whether ox, donkey, or sheep) is found
alive in the thief's possession, he must pay
back double.
5When someone lets an animal loose to
eat in another person's field and causes the
field or vineyard to be stripped of its crop,
the owner must pay them back with the
best from his own field or vineyard.
6When someone starts a fire and it
catches in thorns and then spreads to
someone else's stacked grain, standing
grain, or a whole field, the one who started
the fire must fully repay the loss.
7When someone entrusts money or
other items to another person to keep safe
and they are stolen from the other person's
house and the thief is caught, the thief
must pay back double. 8If the thief isn't
caught, the owner of the house should be
brought before God to determine whether
or not the owner stole the other's property.
9When any dispute of ownership over an
ox, donkey, sheep, piece of clothing, or any
other loss arises in which someone claims,
"This is mine," the cases of both parties

[l]21:37 in Heb [m]22:1 in Heb

should come before God. The one whom God finds at fault must pay double to the other.

[10]When someone gives a donkey, ox, sheep, or any other animal to another person to keep safe, and the animal dies or is injured or taken and no one saw what happened, [11]the person should swear a solemn pledge before the LORD in the presence of the owner that he didn't touch the other's property. The owner must accept that, and no payment needs to be made. [12]But if the animal was stolen, the person must make full payment to its owner. [13]If the animal was attacked and ripped apart and its torn body is brought as evidence, no payment needs to be made.

[14]When someone borrows an animal from another and it is injured or dies while the owner isn't present, full payment must be made. [15]If the owner was present, no payment needs to be made. If the animal was hired, only the fee for hiring the animal is due.

Instructions about social and religious matters

[16]When a man seduces a young woman who isn't engaged to be married yet and he sleeps with her, he must marry her and pay the bride-price for her. [17]But if her father absolutely refuses to let them marry, he must still pay the same amount as the bride-price for young women.

[18]Don't allow a female sorcerer to live.

[19]Anyone who has sexual relations with an animal should be put to death.

[20]Anyone who offers sacrifices to any god, other than the LORD alone, should be destroyed.

[21]Don't mistreat or oppress an immigrant, because you were once immigrants in the land of Egypt. [22]Don't treat any widow or orphan badly. [23]If you do treat them badly and they cry out to me, you can be sure that I'll hear their cry. [24]I'll be furious, and I'll kill you with the sword. Then your wives will be widows, and your children will be orphans.

[25]If you lend money to my people who are poor among you, don't be a creditor and charge them interest. [26]If you take a piece of clothing from someone as a security deposit, you should return it before the sun goes down. [27]His clothing may well be his only blanket to cover himself. What else will that person have to sleep in? And if he cries out to me, I'll listen, because I'm compassionate.

[28]Don't say a curse against God, and don't curse your people's chief.

[29]Don't delay offering the produce of your vineyards and winepresses. Give me your oldest son. [30]Do the same with your oxen and with your sheep. They should stay with their mother for seven days. On the eighth day, you should give them to me.

[31]You are holy people to me. Don't eat any meat killed by wild animals out in the field. Throw it to the dogs instead.

23 Don't spread false rumors. Don't plot with evil people to act as a lying witness. [2]Don't take sides with important people to do wrong. When you act as a witness, don't stretch the truth to favor important people. [3]But don't privilege unimportant people in their lawsuits either.

[4]When you happen to come upon your enemy's ox or donkey that has wandered off, you should bring it back to them.

[5]When you see a donkey that belongs to someone who hates you and it's lying down under its load and you are inclined not to help set it free, you must help set it free.

[6]Don't undermine the justice that your poor deserve in their lawsuits. [7]Stay away from making a false charge. Don't put an innocent person who is in the right to death, because I will not consider innocent those who do such evil. [8]Don't take a bribe, because a bribe blinds the clear-sighted and subverts the cause of those who are in the right.

[9]Don't oppress an immigrant. You know what it's like to be an immigrant, because you were immigrants in the land of Egypt.

Sabbaths and festivals

[10]For six years you should plant crops on your land and gather in its produce. [11]But in the seventh year you should leave it alone and undisturbed so that the poor among your people may eat. What they leave behind, the wild animals may eat. You should

do the same with your vineyard and your olive trees.

[12]Do your work in six days. But on the seventh day you should rest so that your ox and donkey may rest, and even the child of your female slave and the immigrant may be refreshed.

[13]Be careful to obey everything that I have said to you. Don't call on the names of other gods. Don't even mention them.

[14]You should observe a festival for me three times a year. [15]Observe the Festival of Unleavened Bread, as I commanded you. Eat unleavened bread for seven days at the appointed time in the month of Abib,[n] because it was in that month that you came out of Egypt.

No one should appear before me empty-handed. [16]Observe the Harvest Festival for the early produce of your crops that you planted in the field, and the Gathering Festival at the end of the year, when you gather your crop of fruit from the field. [17]All your males should appear three times a year before the LORD God.

[18]Don't offer the blood of my sacrifice with anything leavened. Don't let the fat of my festival offering be left over until the morning.

[19]Bring the best of your land's early produce to the LORD your God's temple.

Don't boil a young goat in its mother's milk.

God's promise: messenger and land

[20]I'm about to send a messenger in front of you to guard you on your way and to bring you to the place that I've made ready. [21]Pay attention to him and do as he says. Don't rebel against him. He won't forgive the things you do wrong because I[o] am with him. [22]But if you listen carefully to what he says and do all that I say, then I'll be an enemy to your enemies and fight those fighting you.

[23]When my messenger goes in front of you and brings you to the Amorites, the Hittites, the Perizzites, the Canaanites, the Hivites, and the Jebusites, and I wipe them out, [24]don't bow down to their gods, worship them, or do what they do. Instead, you should completely destroy them and smash their sacred stone pillars to bits. [25]If you worship the LORD your God, the LORD will bless your bread and your water. I'll take sickness away from you, [26]and no woman will miscarry or be infertile in your land. I'll let you live a full, long life. [27]My terrifying reputation will precede you, and I'll throw all the people that you meet into a panic. I'll make all your enemies turn their backs to you. [28]I'll send insect swarms in front of you and drive out the Hivites, the Canaanites, and the Hittites before you. [29]I won't drive them out before you in a single year so the land won't be abandoned and the wild animals won't multiply around you. [30]I'll drive them out before you little by little, until your numbers grow and you eventually possess the land. [31]I'll set your borders from the Reed Sea[p] to the Philistine Sea and from the desert to the River. I'll hand the inhabitants of the land over to you, and you will drive them out before you. [32]Don't make any covenants with them or their gods. [33]Don't allow them to live in your land, or else they will lead you to sin against me. If you worship their gods, it will become a dangerous trap for you.

Covenant at Sinai

24 Then the LORD said to Moses, "Come up to the LORD, you and Aaron, Nadab and Abihu, and seventy of Israel's elders, and worship from a distance. [2]Only Moses may come near to the LORD. The others shouldn't come near, while the people shouldn't come up with him at all."

[3]Moses came and told the people all the LORD's words and all the case laws. All the people answered in unison, "Everything that the LORD has said we will do." [4]Moses then wrote down all the LORD's words. He got up early in the morning and built an altar at the foot of the mountain. He set up twelve sacred stone pillars for the twelve tribes of Israel. [5]He appointed certain young Israelite men to offer entirely burned

[n]March–April, named Nisan after the exile [o]Or *my name* [p]Or *Red Sea*

offerings and slaughter oxen as well-being sacrifices to the LORD. 6Moses took half of the blood and put it in large bowls. The other half of the blood he threw against the altar. 7Then he took the covenant scroll and read it out loud for the people to hear. They responded, "Everything that the LORD has said we will do, and we will obey."

8Moses then took the blood and threw it over the people. Moses said, "This is the blood of the covenant that the LORD now makes with you on the basis of all these words."

Covenant meal with God

9Then Moses and Aaron, Nadab and Abihu, and seventy elders of Israel went up, 10and they saw Israel's God. Under God's feet there was what looked like a floor of lapis-lazuli tiles, dazzlingly pure like the sky. 11God didn't harm the Israelite leaders, though they looked at God, and they ate and drank.

12The LORD said to Moses, "Come up to me on the mountain and wait there. I'll give you the stone tablets with the instructions and the commandments that I've written in order to teach them."

13So Moses and his assistant Joshua got up, and Moses went up God's mountain. 14Moses had said to the elders, "Wait for us here until we come back to you. Aaron and Hur will be here with you. Whoever has a legal dispute may go to them."

15Then Moses went up the mountain, and the cloud covered the mountain. 16The LORD's glorious presence settled on Mount Sinai, and the cloud covered it for six days. On the seventh day the LORD called to Moses from the cloud. 17To the Israelites, the LORD's glorious presence looked like a blazing fire on top of the mountain. 18Moses entered the cloud and went up the mountain. Moses stayed on the mountain for forty days and forty nights.

Gifts offered for the dwelling

25 The LORD said to Moses: 2Tell the Israelites to collect gift offerings for me. Receive my gift offerings from everyone who freely wants to give. 3These are the gift offerings that you should receive from them: gold, silver, and copper; 4blue, purple, and deep red yarns; fine linen; goats' hair; 5rams' skins dyed red; beaded leather;[q] acacia wood; 6oil for the lamps; spices for the anointing oil and for the sweet-smelling incense; 7gemstones; and gems for setting in the priest's vest[r] and chest piece. 8They should make me a sanctuary so I can be present among them. 9You should follow the blueprints that I will show you for the dwelling and for all its equipment.

Instructions for building the chest containing the covenant

10Have them make an acacia-wood chest. It should be forty-five inches long, twenty-seven inches wide, and twenty-seven inches high. 11Cover it with pure gold, inside and out, and make a gold molding all around it. 12Cast four gold rings for it and put them on its four feet, two rings on one side and two rings on the other. 13Make acacia-wood poles and cover them with gold. 14Then put the poles into the rings on the chest's sides and use them to carry the chest. 15The poles should stay in the chest's rings. They shouldn't be taken out of them. 16Put the covenant document that I will give you into the chest.

17Then make a cover of pure gold, forty-five inches long and twenty-seven inches wide. 18Make two winged heavenly creatures of hammered gold, one for each end of the cover. 19Put one winged heavenly creature at one end and one winged heavenly creature at the other. Place the winged heavenly creatures at the cover's two ends. 20The heavenly creatures should have their wings spread out above, shielding the cover with their wings. The winged heavenly creatures should face each other toward the cover's center. 21Put the gold cover on top of the chest and put the covenant document that I will give you inside the chest. 22There I will meet with you. From there above the cover, from between the two

[q] Or *dolphin skins* [r] Heb *ephod*

winged heavenly creatures that are on top of the chest containing the covenant, I will deliver to you all that I command you concerning the Israelites.

Instructions for the table

[23]Make an acacia-wood table, three feet long, eighteen inches wide, and twenty-seven inches high. [24]Cover it with pure gold and make a gold molding all around it. [25]Make a frame around it that is four inches wide and a gold molding around the frame. [26]Make four gold rings for the table. Fasten the rings to the four corners at its four legs. [27]The rings that house the poles used for carrying the table should be close to the frame. [28]Make the poles from acacia wood and cover them with gold. The table should be carried with these poles. [29]Make its plates, dishes, jars, and bowls for pouring drink offerings. Make them of pure gold. [30]Set the bread of the presence on the table so it is always in front of me.

Instructions for the lampstand

[31]Make a lampstand of pure hammered gold. The lampstand's base, branches, cups, flowers, and petals should all be attached to it. [32]It should have six branches growing out from its sides, three branches on one side of the lampstand and three branches on the other side of the lampstand. [33]One branch will have three cups shaped like almond blossoms, each with a flower and petals, and the next branch will also have three cups shaped like almond blossoms, each with a flower and petals. So it will be for the six branches that grow out of the lampstand. [34]In addition, on the lampstand itself there will be four cups shaped like almond blossoms, each with its flower and petals. [35]There will be a flower attached under the first pair of branches, a flower attached under the next pair of branches, and a flower attached under the last pair of branches. So it will be for the six branches that grow out of the lampstand. [36]Their flowers and their branches will be permanently attached to it. The whole lampstand should be one piece of pure hammered gold. [37]Make its seven lamps and set up its lamps so that they direct their light in front of the lampstand. [38]You should also make its tongs and fire pans out of pure gold. [39]All these items should be made from pure gold weighing one kikkar. [40]See to it that you make them according to the blueprint for them that you were shown on the mountain.

Instructions for building the dwelling

26 Make the dwelling with ten curtains of fine twisted linen and blue, purple, and deep red yarns. Work figures of winged heavenly creatures into their design. [2]Each curtain should be forty-two feet long and each curtain six feet wide. All the curtains should be the same size. [3]Five curtains will be joined to each other as one set, while the other five curtains will be joined together as a second set. [4]Make loops of blue thread on the edge of the outer curtain in the first set. Do the same on the edge of the outer curtain in the second set. [5]Make fifty loops on the one curtain in the first set and fifty loops on the edge of the curtain that is in the second set. The loops should be opposite each other. [6]Then make fifty gold clasps. Join the curtains to each other with the clasps so that the dwelling becomes one whole structure.

[7]You should also make curtains of goats' hair for a tent over the dwelling. Make eleven curtains. [8]Each curtain should be forty-five feet long and each curtain six feet wide. The eleven curtains should all be the same size. [9]Join five of the curtains together, and join the six other curtains together. Double over the sixth curtain at the front of the tent. [10]Make fifty loops on the edge of the outer curtain in one set and fifty loops on the edge of the outer curtain in the second set.

[11]Make fifty copper clasps. Put the clasps into the loops and join the tent together so that it becomes one whole structure. [12]The extra cloth that is left over from the tent curtains, that is, the half curtain that remains, should hang over the back of the dwelling. [13]Eighteen inches on one side and eighteen inches on the other side of the leftover length of the tent's curtains will

hang over the two sides of the dwelling to cover it. [14]Then for the tent, make a covering of rams' skins dyed red and an outer covering of beaded leather.[s]

[15]Make acacia-wood boards to stand upright as a frame for the dwelling. [16]Each board will be fifteen feet long and twenty-seven inches wide. [17]Put two pegs on each board for joining them to each other. Do this for all the dwelling's boards. [18]Make twenty boards for the dwelling's southern side. [19]Then make forty silver bases to go under the twenty boards. There will be two bases under the first board for its two pegs, two bases under the next board for its two pegs, and so on. [20]For the dwelling's other side on the north, make twenty boards [21]and their forty silver bases, two bases under the first board, two bases under the next board, and so on. [22]For the back of the dwelling on the west, make six boards. [23]Make two additional boards for the dwelling's rear corners. [24]They should be spread out at the bottom but joined together at the top with one ring. In this way, these two boards will form the two corners. [25]And so there will be eight boards with their sixteen silver bases, two bases under the first board, two bases under the next board, and so on.

[26]You should also make acacia-wood bars: five for the boards on one side of the dwelling, [27]five bars for the boards on the other side of the dwelling, and five bars for the boards on the back wall of the dwelling on the west. [28]The middle bar, halfway up the boards, should run from one end to the other. [29]Cover the boards with gold. Make gold rings to house the bars. Cover the bars with gold. [30]Then set up the dwelling according to the plan for it that you were shown on the mountain.

[31]Make a veil of blue, purple, and deep red yarns and of fine twisted linen. Work figures of winged heavenly creatures into its design. [32]Hang it on four acacia-wood posts covered in gold. They should have gold hooks and stand on four silver bases. [33]Hang the veil under the clasps, and put the chest containing the covenant there behind the veil. The veil will separate for you the holy from the holiest space. [34]Place the gold cover on the chest containing the covenant in the holiest space. [35]Place the table outside the veil, and set the lampstand opposite the table by the south wall of the dwelling. Place the table by the north wall.

[36]Make a screen for the tent's entrance of blue, purple, and deep red yarns and of fine twisted linen, decorated with needlework. [37]Make five acacia-wood posts for the screen. Cover the posts with gold. Their hooks should be gold. Cast five copper bases for the posts.

Instructions for the altar

27 Make an acacia-wood altar. The altar should be square, seven and a half feet long and seven and a half feet wide. It should be four and a half feet high. [2]Make horns for the altar and attach them to it, one horn on each of its four corners. Cover it with copper. [3]Make pails for removing its ashes and its shovels, bowls, meat forks, and trays. Make all its equipment out of copper. [4]Make for the altar a grate made of copper mesh. Make four copper rings for each of the four corners of the mesh. [5]Slide the mesh underneath the bottom edge of the altar and then extend the mesh halfway up to the middle of the altar. [6]Make acacia-wood poles for the altar and cover them with copper. [7]Put the poles through the rings so that the poles will be on the two sides of the altar when it is carried. [8]Make the altar with planks but hollow inside. All these should be made just as you were shown on the mountain.

Instructions for the dwelling's courtyard

[9]You should also set up the dwelling's courtyard. The courtyard's south side should have drapes of fine twisted linen stretching one hundred fifty feet on that side, [10]with twenty posts, twenty copper bases, and silver hooks and bands for the posts. [11]Likewise along the north side the drapes should stretch one hundred fifty feet, with

[s]Or *dolphin skin*

twenty posts, twenty copper bases, and silver hooks and bands for the posts. 12 The courtyard's width on the west side should consist of seventy-five feet of drapes with their ten posts and their ten bases. 13 The courtyard's width on the front, facing east should be seventy-five feet. 14 There should be twenty-two and a half feet of drapes on one side with three posts and three bases for them. 15 There should be twenty-two and a half feet of drapes on the other side with three posts and three bases for them. 16 For the gate into the courtyard there will be a screen thirty feet long, made of blue, purple, and deep red yarns and of fine twisted linen, decorated with needlework. It will have four posts with their four bases. 17 All the posts around the courtyard will have silver bands, silver hooks, and copper bases. 18 The courtyard will be one hundred fifty feet long and seventy-five feet wide. Its walls' height will be seven and a half feet of fine twisted linen and its copper bases. 19 All the dwelling's equipment for any use and all its tent pegs and all the courtyard's tent pegs will be made of copper.

Olive oil for the lampstand

20 You must require the Israelites to bring you pure oil of crushed olives for the light so that the lamp may be set up to burn continually. 21 In the meeting tent, outside the veil that hangs in front of the covenant document, Aaron and his sons will tend the lamp from evening to morning in the LORD's presence. It will be a permanent regulation for the Israelites in every generation.

Instructions for the priests' clothing

28 Summon to you your brother Aaron and his sons from among the Israelites to serve me as priests—Aaron and Aaron's sons, Nadab and Abihu, and Eleazar and Ithamar. 2 Make holy clothing that will give honor and dignity to your brother Aaron. 3 Tell all who are skilled, to whom I have given special abilities, to make clothing for Aaron for his dedication to serve me as a priest. 4 These are the articles of clothing that they should make: a chest pendant, a vest, a robe, a woven tunic, a turban, and a sash. When they make this holy clothing for your brother Aaron and his sons to serve me as priests, 5 they should use gold, blue, purple, and deep red yarns and fine linen.

Priest's ornamental vest

6 They should make the vest of gold, of blue, purple, and deep red yarns and of fine twisted linen with embroidered designs. 7 The vest will have two shoulder pieces attached to its two edges so that they may be joined together. 8 The vest's belt should be attached to it and made in the same way of gold, of blue, purple, and deep red yarns and fine twisted linen. 9 Take two gemstones and engrave on them the names of Israel's sons, 10 six names on one stone and the other six names on the other stone, in the order of their birth. 11 Like a gem cutter who engraves official seals, you will engrave the two stones with the names of Israel's sons. Mount them in gold settings. 12 Attach the two stones to the vest's shoulder pieces as stones of reminder for the Israelites. Aaron will carry into the LORD's presence their names on his two shoulders as a reminder. 13 Then make gold settings 14 along with two chains of pure gold, twisted like cords. Attach the corded chains to the gold settings.

Priest's chest pendant used for making decisions

15 Make an embroidered chest pendant used for making decisions. Make it in the style of the vest, using gold, blue and purple and deep red yarns, and fine twisted linen. 16 It will be square and doubled, nine inches long and nine inches wide. 17 Set in it four rows of gemstone settings. The first row will be a row of carnelian, topaz, and emerald stones. 18 The second row will be a turquoise, a sapphire, and a moonstone. 19 The third row will be a jacinth, an agate, and an amethyst. 20 The fourth row will be a beryl, an onyx, and a jasper. Their settings will be made of decorative gold. 21 There will be twelve stones with names corresponding to the names of Israel's sons. They will be engraved like official seals, each with its name for the twelve tribes.

22 Make chains of pure gold twisted like cords for the chest pendant. 23 Make two gold rings for the chest pendant and attach the two rings to the two edges of the chest pendant. 24 Attach the two gold cords to the two rings at the edges of the chest pendant. 25 Then fasten the two ends of the cords to the two settings, which you should attach to the vest's two front shoulder pieces. 26 Make two gold rings and attach them to the two ends of the chest pendant on its inside edge facing the vest. 27 Make two gold rings and fasten them on the front of the lower part of the two shoulder pieces of the vest, at its seam just above the vest's belt. 28 The chest pendant should be held in place by a blue cord binding its rings to the vest's rings so that the chest pendant rests on the vest's belt and won't come loose from the vest. 29 In this way, Aaron will carry the names of Israel's sons on the chest pendant for making decisions over his heart when he goes into the sanctuary as a reminder before the LORD at all times. 30 Put into the chest pendant used for making decisions the Urim and the Thummim, so they will be over Aaron's heart when he goes into the LORD's presence. In this way, Aaron will carry the means to make decisions for the Israelites over his heart when in the LORD's presence at all times.

Instructions for other priestly clothing

31 You will make the robe for the vest all of blue. 32 The opening for the head should be in the middle of it. The opening should be reinforced by a woven binding, a strong border so that it doesn't tear. 33 On its lower hem add pomegranates made of blue, purple, and deep red yarns all around the lower hem, with gold bells between the pomegranates all around it. 34 A gold bell and a pomegranate should alternate all around the lower hem of the robe. 35 Aaron will wear the robe when he ministers as a priest. Its sound will be heard when he goes into the sanctuary in the LORD's presence and when he comes out, so that he will not die.

36 Make a flower ornament of pure gold and engrave on it like an official seal: "Holy to the LORD." 37 You should fasten it on the turban with a blue cord. It should be on the front of the turban. 38 It will be on Aaron's forehead, and Aaron will take on himself any guilt connected with the holy offerings that the Israelites give as their sacred donations. It will always be on his forehead so that the people may be remembered favorably in the LORD's presence.

39 Weave the tunic out of fine linen. Make the turban out of fine linen. Make a sash decorated with needlework. 40 For Aaron's sons, you should also make tunics, sashes, and turbans to mark their honor and dignity. 41 Put these garments on your brother Aaron and on his sons with him. Anoint them with oil, ordain them, and make them holy to serve me as priests. 42 You should also make linen undergarments for them to cover their naked skin from their hips to their thighs. 43 Aaron and his sons should wear this clothing when they go into the meeting tent or when they approach the altar to minister as priests in the sanctuary. Otherwise, they will bring guilt on themselves and die. This will be a permanent regulation for him and for his descendants after him.

Instructions for the priests' ordination

29 Now this is what you should do to make them holy in order to serve me as priests. Take a young bull and two flawless rams. 2 Take unleavened bread, unleavened flatbread made with oil, and unleavened wafers spread with oil. Make them out of high-quality wheat flour. 3 Put them all in one basket and present them in the basket along with the bull and the two rams. 4 Present Aaron and his sons at the entrance to the meeting tent and wash them with water. 5 Then take the priestly clothes and put them on Aaron: the tunic, the vest's robe, the vest itself, and the chest pendant. Put the vest on him with the vest's belt. 6 Set the turban on his head and place the holy crown on the turban. 7 Take the anointing oil and pour it on his head to anoint him. 8 Then present his sons and put the tunics on them. 9 Tighten the sashes on them, on both Aaron and his sons. Wrap

the turbans on their heads. It will be a permanent regulation that the duties of priesthood belong to them. In this way, you will ordain Aaron and his sons.

10 Present the bull at the front of the meeting tent. Aaron and his sons will lay their hands on the bull's head. 11 Then slaughter the bull in the LORD's presence at the meeting tent's entrance. 12 Take some of the bull's blood and smear it on the altar's horns with your finger. Pour out the rest of the blood at the altar's base. 13 Then take all the fat that covers the inner organs, the lobe of the liver, and the two kidneys along with the fat that is on them, and burn them up in smoke on the altar. 14 Burn the rest of the meat of the bull, its hide, and the intestines with their contents with a fire outside the camp. It is a purification offering.

15 Choose one of the rams, and have Aaron and his sons lay their hands on the ram's head. 16 Then slaughter the ram. Take its blood and throw it against all the altar's sides. 17 Cut up the ram into parts. Wash its inner organs and legs, and put them together with its parts and its head. 18 Then turn the entire ram into smoke by burning it on the altar. It is an entirely burned offering for the LORD, a soothing smell, a food gift for the LORD.

19 Take the second ram, and have Aaron and his sons lay their hands on the ram's head. 20 Slaughter the ram. Take some of its blood and smear it on the right earlobes of Aaron and his sons, on the thumbs of their right hands, and on the big toes of their right feet. Throw the rest of the blood against all the altar's sides. 21 Then take some of the blood on the altar and some of the anointing oil and sprinkle them on Aaron and on his clothes and on his sons and on his sons' clothes. In this way, Aaron, his sons, and all their priestly garments will be holy.

22 Take the fatty parts of the ram: the fat tail, the fat around the inner organs, the lobe of the liver, the two kidneys with the fat around them, and the right thigh (because it is a ram for ordination). 23 Add one loaf of bread, one flatbread made with oil, and one wafer from the basket of unleavened bread that was presented to the LORD. 24 Place all of these in the hands of Aaron and his sons, and lift them as an uplifted offering in the LORD's presence. 25 Then take them from their hands and turn them into smoke by burning them on the altar with the entirely burned offering as a soothing smell in the LORD's presence. It is a food gift for the LORD.

26 Take the breast of the ram for Aaron's ordination and lift it as an uplifted offering in the LORD's presence. It will be your portion. 27 Make holy the breast that was lifted for the uplifted offering and the thigh that was raised for the gift offering from the ram for the ordination. They belong to Aaron and his sons. 28 Those parts will be given to Aaron and his sons from the Israelites as a permanent provision, because they are a gift offering. They will be a gift offering from the Israelites, their gift offering to the LORD from their well-being sacrifices.

29 Aaron's holy clothes should be passed on to his sons after him. His sons should be anointed in them and ordained in them. 30 The son who is priest in his place should wear them seven days when he comes into the meeting tent to minister in the sanctuary.

31 Take the ram for the ordination and boil its meat in a holy place. 32 Aaron and his sons will eat the ram's meat and the bread that is in the basket at the meeting tent's entrance. 33 They alone should eat the food that was used to purify them, to ordain them, and to make them holy. No one else should eat it because it is holy. 34 If any meat for the ordination or any of the bread is left over until morning, then you should burn the leftovers with fire. It shouldn't be eaten because it's holy.

35 Treat Aaron and his sons just as I have commanded you. Ordain them for seven days. 36 Every day you should offer a bull as a purification offering for reconciliation. You should remove the sin from the altar through a ritual of reconciliation, and you should anoint the altar to make it holy. 37 Seven days you should perform the ritual of reconciliation for the altar and make it

holy. In this way, the altar will become most holy, and whatever touches the altar will also become holy.

Instructions for daily entirely burned offerings

38Now this is what you should offer on the altar: two one-year-old lambs regularly every day. 39Offer one lamb in the morning and offer the other lamb at twilight. 40With the first lamb, add one-tenth of a measure of the high-quality flour mixed with a quarter of a hin[t] of oil from crushed olives and a quarter of a hin of wine for a drink offering. 41With the second lamb offered at twilight, again include a grain offering and its drink offering as in the morning as a soothing smell, a gift offering for the LORD. 42This should be the regular entirely burned offering in every generation at the meeting tent's entrance in the LORD's presence. There I will meet with you, and there I will speak to you. 43I will meet with the Israelites there, and it will be made holy by my glorious presence. 44I will make the meeting tent and the altar holy. Likewise, I will make Aaron and his sons holy to serve me as priests. 45I will be at home among the Israelites, and I will be their God. 46They will know that I am the LORD their God, who brought them out of the land of Egypt so that I could make a home among them. I am the LORD their God.

Instructions for the incense altar

30 Make an acacia-wood altar for burning incense. 2The altar should be square, eighteen inches long and eighteen inches wide. It should be three feet high. Its horns should be permanently attached. 3Cover the altar with pure gold, including its top, all its sides, and its horns. You should also make a gold molding all around it. 4Make two gold rings and attach them under the molding on two opposite sides of the altar. They will house the poles used to carry the altar. 5Make acacia-wood poles and cover them with gold. 6Place the incense altar in front of the veil that hangs before the chest containing the covenant, in front of the cover that is on top of the covenant document where I will meet with you. 7Aaron will burn sweet-smelling incense on the incense altar every morning when he takes care of the lamps. 8And again when Aaron lights the lamps at twilight, he will burn incense. It should be a regular incense offering in the LORD's presence in every generation. 9Don't offer the wrong incense on the altar or an entirely burned offering or a grain offering. Don't pour a drink offering on it. 10Once a year Aaron should perform a ritual of reconciliation on its horns with the blood of the purification offering for reconciliation. Once a year in every generation he should perform a ritual of reconciliation at the altar. It is most holy to the LORD.

Census and compensation

11The LORD spoke to Moses: 12When you take a census of the Israelites to count them, each of them should pay compensation for their life to the LORD when they are counted. Then no plague will descend on them when they are counted. 13Every one who is counted should pay a half shekel according to the official shekel of the sanctuary (the shekel is twenty gerahs). The half shekel is a gift offering to the LORD. 14Every one who is counted, from 20 years old and above, should present a gift offering to the LORD. 15When you bring this gift offering to the LORD to pay compensation for your lives, the rich shouldn't give more and the poor shouldn't give less than the half shekel. 16Take the compensation money from the Israelites and use it to support the service of the meeting tent. It will serve for the Israelites as a reminder in the LORD's presence of the compensation paid for your lives.

Instructions for the washbasin

17The LORD spoke to Moses: 18Make a copper basin for washing along with its copper stand. Put it between the meeting tent and the altar, and put water in it. 19Aaron and his sons will use it to wash their hands and their

[t]One hin is approximately one gallon.

feet. [20]When they go into the meeting tent or approach the altar to minister and to offer a food gift to the LORD, they must wash with water so that they don't die. [21]They must wash their hands and their feet so that they don't die. This will be a permanent regulation for them, for Aaron and his descendants in every generation.

Instructions for oil and incense

[22]The LORD spoke to Moses: [23]Now take for yourself high-quality spices: five hundred weight of solid myrrh; half as much of sweet-smelling cinnamon, that is, two hundred fifty; two hundred fifty weight of sweet-smelling cane; [24]five hundred of cassia—measured by the sanctuary shekel—and a hin[u] of olive oil. [25]Prepare a holy anointing oil, blending them like a skilled perfume maker to produce the holy anointing oil. [26]Use it to anoint the meeting tent, the chest containing the covenant, [27]the table and all its equipment, the lampstand and its equipment, the incense altar, [28]the altar for entirely burned offerings and all its equipment, and the washbasin with its stand. [29]Make them holy so that they may be perfectly holy. Whatever touches them will become holy. [30]Then anoint Aaron and his sons and make them holy to serve me as priests. [31]Say to the Israelites: This will be my holy anointing oil in every generation. [32]Don't allow anyone else to use this oil. Don't make another oil like it by using the same formula. This oil is holy, and you should regard it as holy. [33]Whoever blends an oil like it or whoever uses the oil on someone else will be cut off from the people.

[34]The LORD said to Moses: Take an equal amount of each of these spices: gum resin, onycha, galbanum, and pure frankincense. [35]Like a skilled perfume maker, carefully blend them together and make incense, seasoned with salt, pure and holy. [36]Beat some of it into a fine powder and put part of it in front of the covenant document in the meeting tent where I will meet with you. You should regard it as perfectly holy. [37]When you make incense according to this formula, you shouldn't make any of it for your own use. You should regard it as holy to the LORD. [38]Whoever makes incense with this same formula to enjoy its fragrance will be cut off from the people.

Construction leaders: Bezalel and Oholiab

31 The LORD spoke to Moses: [2]Look, I have chosen Bezalel, Uri's son and Hur's grandson from the tribe of Judah. [3]I have filled him with the divine spirit, with skill, ability, and knowledge for every kind of work. [4]He will be able to create designs; do metalwork in gold, silver, and copper; [5]cut stones for setting; carve wood; and do every kind of work. [6]I have also appointed with him Oholiab, Ahisamach's son from the tribe of Dan. To all who are skillful, I have given the skill to make everything that I have commanded you: [7]the meeting tent, the chest containing the covenant, the cover that is on top of it, all the tent's furnishings, [8]the table and its equipment, the pure lampstand with all its equipment, the incense altar, [9]the altar for entirely burned offerings with all its equipment, the washbasin with its stand, [10]the woven clothing, the holy clothes for Aaron the priest and for his sons for their service as priests, [11]the anointing oil, and the sweet-smelling incense for the sanctuary. They will do just as I have commanded you.

Instructions for keeping the Sabbath

[12]The LORD said to Moses: [13]Tell the Israelites: "Be sure to keep my sabbaths, because the Sabbath is a sign between me and you in every generation so you will know that I am the LORD who makes you holy. [14]Keep the Sabbath, because it is holy for you. Everyone who violates the Sabbath will be put to death. Whoever does any work on the Sabbath, that person will be cut off from the people. [15]Do your work for six days. But the seventh day is a Sabbath of complete rest that is holy to the LORD. Whoever does any work on the Sabbath day

[u]One hin is approximately one gallon.

will be put to death. 16The Israelites should keep the Sabbath. They should observe the Sabbath in every generation as a covenant for all time. 17It is a sign forever between me and the Israelites that in six days the LORD made the heavens and the earth, and on the seventh day the LORD rested and was refreshed."

18When God finished speaking with Moses on Mount Sinai, God gave him the two covenant tablets, the stone tablets written by God's finger.

Worshipping the gold bull calf

32 The people saw that Moses was taking a long time to come down from the mountain. They gathered around Aaron and said to him, "Come on! Make us gods[v] who can lead us. As for this man Moses who brought us up out of the land of Egypt, we don't have a clue what has happened to him."

2Aaron said to them, "All right, take out the gold rings from the ears of your wives, your sons, and your daughters, and bring them to me." 3So all the people took out the gold rings from their ears and brought them to Aaron. 4He collected them and tied them up in a cloth.[w] Then he made a metal image of a bull calf, and the people declared, "These are your gods, Israel, who brought you up out of the land of Egypt!"

5When Aaron saw this, he built an altar in front of the calf. Then Aaron announced, "Tomorrow will be a festival to the LORD!" 6They got up early the next day and offered up entirely burned offerings and brought well-being sacrifices. The people sat down to eat and drink and then got up to celebrate.

7The LORD spoke to Moses: "Hurry up and go down! Your people, whom you brought up out of the land of Egypt, are ruining everything! 8They've already abandoned the path that I commanded. They have made a metal bull calf for themselves. They've bowed down to it and offered sacrifices to it and declared, 'These are your gods, Israel, who brought you up out of the land of Egypt!'" 9The LORD said to Moses, "I've been watching these people, and I've seen how stubborn they are. 10Now leave me alone! Let my fury burn and devour them. Then I'll make a great nation out of you."

11But Moses pleaded with the LORD his God, "LORD, why does your fury burn against your own people, whom you brought out of the land of Egypt with great power and amazing force? 12Why should the Egyptians say, 'He had an evil plan to take the people out and kill them in the mountains and so wipe them off the earth'? Calm down your fierce anger. Change your mind about doing terrible things to your own people. 13Remember Abraham, Isaac, and Israel, your servants, whom you yourself promised, 'I'll make your descendants as many as the stars in the sky. And I've promised to give your descendants this whole land to possess for all time.'" 14Then the LORD changed his mind about the terrible things he said he would do to his people.

15Moses then turned around and came down the mountain. He carried the two covenant tablets in his hands. The tablets were written on both sides, front and back. 16The tablets were God's own work. What was written there was God's own writing inscribed on the tablets. 17When Joshua heard the noise of the people as they shouted, he said to Moses, "It sounds like war in the camp."

18But Moses said,

"It isn't the sound of a victory song.
It isn't the sound of a song of defeat.
The sound of party songs is what I hear."

19When he got near the camp and saw the bull calf and the dancing, Moses was furious. He hurled the tablets down and shattered them in pieces at the foot of the mountain. 20He took the calf that they had made and burned it in a fire. Then he ground it down to crushed powder, scattered it on the water, and made the Israelites drink it.

21Moses said to Aaron, "What did these people do to you that you led them to commit such a terrible sin?"

22Aaron replied, "Don't get angry with me, sir. You know yourself that these

[v]*Or a god* [w]*Or formed them into a mold or engraved them with a stylus*

people are out of control.[x] 23They said to
me, 'Make us gods who can lead us. As for
this man Moses who brought us up out of
the land of Egypt, we don't have a clue what
has happened to him.' 24So I said to them,
'Whoever has gold, take it off!' So they gave
it to me, I threw it into the fire, and out
came this bull calf!"

25Moses saw that the people were out
of control because Aaron had let them get
out of control, making them an easy target for their enemies. 26So Moses stood at
the camp's gate and said, "Whoever is on
the LORD's side, come to me!" All the Levites gathered around him. 27Moses said to
them, "This is what the LORD, Israel's God,
says: Each of you, strap on your sword! Go
back and forth from one end of the camp
to the other. Each of you, kill your brother,
your friend, and your neighbor!" 28The
Levites did as Moses commanded. About
three thousand people were killed that day.
29Moses said, "Today you've been ordained
to the LORD, each one of you at the cost of
a son or a brother. Today you've gained a
special blessing for yourselves."

30The next day Moses said to the people,
"You've committed a terrible sin. So now
I will go up to the LORD. Maybe I can arrange reconciliation on account of your
sin." 31So Moses went back to the LORD and
said, "Oh, what a terrible sin these people
have committed! They made for themselves
gods[y] of gold. 32But now, please forgive
their sin! And if not, then wipe me out of
your scroll that you've written."

33But the LORD said to Moses, "The
ones I'll wipe out of my scroll are those
who sinned against me. 34Now go and lead
the people to the place I described to you.
My messenger here will go in front of you.
When the day of reckoning comes, I'll count
their sin against them." 35Then the LORD
sent a plague on the people because of what
they did with the bull calf that Aaron made.

The LORD: "I can't go"

33 The LORD said to Moses, "Go and
leave this place, you and the people
whom you brought up out of the land of
Egypt. Go to the land I promised to Abraham, Isaac, and Jacob when I said, 'I'll give
it to your descendants.' 2I'll send a messenger before you. I'll drive out the Canaanites,
the Amorites, the Hittites, the Perizzites,
the Hivites, and the Jebusites. 3Go to this
land full of milk and honey. But I won't go
up with you because I would end up destroying you along the way since you are a
stubborn people."

4When the people heard the bad news,
they were sorry. No one put on any jewelry,
5because the LORD had said to Moses, "Tell
the Israelites, 'You are a stubborn people. If I
were to go up with you even for a single moment, I would destroy you. So now take off
your jewelry, while I figure out what to do
with you.'" 6So after leaving Mount Horeb
the Israelites rid themselves of their jewelry.

Speaking with the LORD at the meeting tent

7Moses took the tent and pitched it outside the camp, far away from the camp. He
called it the meeting tent. Everyone who
wanted advice from the LORD would go
out to the meeting tent outside the camp.
8Whenever Moses went out to the tent, all
the people would rise and stand at the entrance to their tents and watch Moses until
he had gone into the tent. 9When Moses
entered the tent, the column of cloud would
come down and stand at the tent's entrance while the LORD talked with Moses.
10When all the people saw the column of
cloud standing at the tent's entrance, they
would all rise and then bow down at the
entrances to their tents. 11In this way the
LORD used to speak to Moses face-to-face,
like two people talking to each other. Then
Moses would come back to the camp. But
his young assistant Joshua, Nun's son,
wouldn't leave the tent.

Moses pleads with God

12Moses said to the LORD, "Look, you've
been telling me, 'Lead these people forward.'
But you haven't told me whom you will send

[x]Sam; MT *evil* [y]Or *a god*

with me. Yet you've assured me, 'I know you by name and think highly of you.' 13 Now if you do think highly of me, show me your ways so that I may know you and so that you may really approve of me. Remember too that this nation is your people."

14 The LORD replied, "I'll go myself, and I'll help you."

15 Moses replied, "If you won't go yourself, don't make us leave here. 16 Because how will anyone know that we have your special approval, both I and your people, unless you go with us? Only that distinguishes us, me and your people, from every other people on the earth."

17 The LORD said to Moses, "I'll do exactly what you've asked because you have my special approval, and I know you by name."

18 Moses said, "Please show me your glorious presence."

19 The LORD said, "I'll make all my goodness pass in front of you, and I'll proclaim before you the name, 'The LORD.' I will be kind to whomever I wish to be kind, and I will have compassion to whomever I wish to be compassionate. 20 But," the LORD said, "you can't see my face because no one can see me and live." 21 The LORD said, "Here is a place near me where you will stand beside the rock. 22 As my glorious presence passes by, I'll set you in a gap in the rock, and I'll cover you with my hand until I've passed by. 23 Then I'll take away my hand, and you will see my back, but my face won't be visible."

A deeper revealing of God's character

34 The LORD said to Moses, "Cut two stone tablets like the first ones. I'll write on these tablets the words that were on the first tablets, which you broke into pieces. 2 Get ready in the morning and come up to Mount Sinai. Stand there on top of the mountain in front of me. 3 No one else can come up with you. Don't allow anyone even to be seen anywhere on the mountain. Don't even let sheep and cattle graze in front of the mountain." 4 So Moses cut two stone tablets like the first ones. He got up early in the morning and climbed up Mount Sinai, just as the LORD had commanded him. He carried the two stone tablets in his hands. 5 The LORD came down in the cloud and stood there with him, and proclaimed the name, "The LORD." 6 The LORD passed in front of him and proclaimed:

"The LORD! The LORD!
a God who is
compassionate and merciful,
very patient,
full of great loyalty and faithfulness,
7 showing great loyalty
to a thousand generations,
forgiving every kind of sin
and rebellion,
yet by no means clearing the guilty,
punishing for their parents' sins
their children and their grandchildren,
as well as the third
and the fourth generation."

8 At once Moses bowed to the ground and worshipped. 9 He said, "If you approve of me, my Lord, please go along with us.[z] Although these are stubborn people, forgive our guilt and our sin and take us as your own possession."

Renewing the broken covenant

10 The LORD said: I now make a covenant. In front of all your people, I'll perform dramatic displays of power that have never been done before anywhere on earth or in any nation. All the people who are around you will see what the LORD does, because I will do an awesome thing with you.

11 Be sure to obey what I command you today. I'm about to drive out before you the Amorites, the Canaanites, the Hittites, the Perizzites, the Hivites, and the Jebusites. 12 Be careful that you don't make a covenant with the inhabitants of the land to which you are going, or it will become a dangerous trap for you. 13 You must tear down their altars, smash their sacred stone pillars, and cut down their sacred poles. 14 You must not bow down to another god, because the LORD is passionate: the LORD's name means "a passionate God." 15 Don't make a covenant

[z] LXX; MT adds *my Lord*.

with those who live in the land. When they prostitute themselves with their gods and sacrifice to their gods, they may invite you and you may end up eating some of the sacrifice. [16]Then you might go and choose their daughters as wives for your sons. And their daughters who prostitute themselves with their gods might lead your sons to prostitute themselves with their gods.

[17]Don't make metal gods for yourself.

[18]Observe the Festival of Unleavened Bread. You should eat unleavened bread for seven days, as I commanded you, at the set time in the month of Abib,[a] because it was in the month of Abib that you came out of Egypt.

[19]Every first offspring is mine. That includes all your male livestock, the oldest offspring of cows and sheep. [20]But a donkey's oldest offspring you may ransom with a sheep. Or if you don't ransom it, you must break its neck. You should ransom all of your oldest sons.

No one should appear before me empty-handed.

[21]You should do your work for six days, but on the seventh day you should rest. Even during plowing or harvesttime you should rest. [22]You should observe the Festival of Weeks, for the early produce of the wheat harvest, and the Gathering Festival at the end of the year. [23]All your males should appear three times a year before the LORD God, Israel's God. [24]I will drive out nations before you and extend your borders. No one will desire and try to take your land if you go up and appear before the LORD your God three times a year.

[25]Don't slaughter the blood of my sacrifice with anything leavened. The sacrifice of the Passover Festival shouldn't be left over until the morning.

[26]Bring the best of the early produce of your farmland to the LORD your God's temple.

Don't boil a young goat in its mother's milk.

[27]The LORD said to Moses: "Write down these words because by these words I hereby make a covenant with you and with Israel." [28]Moses was there with the LORD forty days and forty nights. He didn't eat any bread or drink any water. He wrote on the tablets the words of the covenant, the ten words.

Moses' brightly shining face

[29]Moses came down from Mount Sinai. As he came down from the mountain with the two covenant tablets in his hand, Moses didn't realize that the skin of his face shone brightly because he had been talking with God. [30]When Aaron and all the Israelites saw the skin of Moses' face shining brightly, they were afraid to come near him. [31]But Moses called them closer. So Aaron and all the leaders of the community came back to him, and Moses spoke with them. [32]After that, all the Israelites came near as well, and Moses commanded them everything that the LORD had spoken with him on Mount Sinai. [33]When Moses finished speaking with them, he put a veil over his face. [34]Whenever Moses went into the LORD's presence to speak with him, Moses would take the veil off until he came out again. When Moses came out and told the Israelites what he had been commanded, [35]the Israelites would see that the skin of Moses' face was shining brightly. So Moses would put the veil on his face again until the next time he went in to speak with the LORD.

35 Moses gathered together the whole Israelite community and said to them: These are the things that the LORD has commanded you to do:

Instructions for the Sabbath

[2]Do your work for six days, but the seventh day should be holy to you, a Sabbath of complete rest for the LORD. Whoever does any work on the Sabbath will be put to death. [3]Don't start a fire in any of your homes on the Sabbath day.

Preparing to build the dwelling

[4]Moses said to the whole Israelite community, This is what the LORD has commanded: [5]Collect gift offerings for the LORD

[a]March–April, named Nisan after the exile

from all of you. Whoever freely wants to give should bring the LORD's gift offerings: gold, silver, and copper; [6]blue, purple, and deep red yarns; fine linen; goats' hair; [7]rams' skins dyed red; beaded leather;[b] acacia wood; [8]the oil for the light; spices for the anointing oil and for the sweet-smelling incense; [9]gemstones; and gems for setting in the priest's vest[c] and in the priest's chest pendant.

[10]All of you who are skilled in crafts should come forward and make everything that the LORD has commanded: [11]the dwelling, its tent and its covering, its clasps, its boards, its bars, its posts, and its bases, [12]the chest with its poles and its cover, the veil for a screen, [13]the table with its poles and all its equipment, the bread of the presence, [14]the lampstand for light with its equipment and its lamps, the oil for the light, [15]the incense altar with its poles, the anointing oil and the sweet-smelling incense, the entrance screen for the dwelling's entrance, [16]the altar for entirely burned offerings with its copper grate, its poles, and all its equipment, the washbasin with its stand, [17]the courtyard's drapes, its posts, and its bases, and the screen for the courtyard gate, [18]the dwelling's tent pegs and the courtyard's tent pegs, and their cords, [19]the woven clothing for ministering in the sanctuary, and the holy clothes for Aaron the priest and his sons for their service as priests.

Gifts for building the dwelling

[20]The whole Israelite community left Moses. [21]Everyone who was excited and eager to participate brought the LORD's gift offerings to be used for building the meeting tent and all its furnishings and for the holy clothes. [22]Both men and women came forward. Everyone who was eager to participate brought pins, earrings, rings, and necklaces, all sorts of gold objects. Everyone raised an uplifted offering of gold to the LORD. [23]And everyone who had blue or purple or deep red yarn or fine linen or goats' hair or rams' skins dyed red or beaded leather brought them. [24]Everyone who could make a gift offering of silver or copper brought it as the LORD's gift offering. Everyone who had acacia wood that could be used in any kind of building work brought it. [25]All the skilled women spun cloth with their hands, and brought what they had spun in blue and purple and deep red yarns and fine linen. [26]All the women who were eager to use their skill spun the goats' hair. [27]The chiefs brought gemstones and gems to be set in the priest's vest and the chest pendant, [28]spices and oil for light and for the anointing oil, and for the sweet-smelling incense. [29]All the Israelite men and women who were eager to contribute something for the work that the LORD had commanded Moses to do brought it as a spontaneous gift to the LORD.

Moses introduces Bezalel and Oholiab

[30]Then Moses said to the Israelites: "Look, the LORD has chosen Bezalel, Uri's son and Hur's grandson from the tribe of Judah. [31]The LORD has filled him with the divine spirit that will give him skill, ability, and knowledge for every kind of work. [32]He will be able to create designs, do metalwork in gold, silver, and copper, [33]cut stones for setting, carve wood, do every kind of creative work, [34]and have the ability to teach others. Both he and Oholiab, Ahisamach's son from the tribe of Dan, [35]have been given the skill to do every kind of work done by a gem cutter or a designer or a needleworker in blue, purple, and deep red yarns and in fine linen or a weaver or anyone else doing work or creating designs.

36 "Let Bezalel, Oholiab, and every other skilled worker whom the LORD has given skill, ability, and knowledge for the work of building the sanctuary do all that the LORD has commanded."

[2]Moses then called together Bezalel, Oholiab, and every skilled person whom the LORD had given skill and who was eager to come and do the work. [3]Moses gave them all the gift offerings that the Israelites had contributed to the work on the sanctuary. They kept bringing him spontaneous gifts, morning after morning.

[b]Or *dolphin skins* [c]Heb *ephod*

4Finally, all the skilled workers building the sanctuary left their work that they
were doing one by one to come 5and say to
Moses, "The people are contributing way
too much material for doing the work that
the LORD has commanded us to do."
6So Moses issued a command that was
proclaimed throughout the camp: "Every
man and woman should stop making gift
offerings for the sanctuary project." So the
people stopped bringing anything more
7because what they had already brought
was more than enough to do all the work.

Construction of the dwelling

8All the skilled workers made the dwelling out of ten curtains of fine twisted
linen and blue, purple, and deep red yarns,
with figures of winged heavenly creatures
worked into their design. 9Each curtain was
forty-two feet long and six feet wide. All the
curtains were the same size.
10They joined five of the curtains to each
other and joined the other five curtains
to each other. 11They made loops of blue
thread on the edge of the outer curtain
of the first set. They did the same on the
edge of the outer curtain of the second set.
12They made fifty loops on the one curtain
and fifty loops on the outer curtain that
was in the second set. The loops were opposite each other. 13They also made fifty gold
clasps, and they used the clasps to join the
curtains to each other so that the dwelling
was one whole structure.
14They also made curtains of goats' hair
for a tent over the dwelling. They made
eleven curtains. 15Each curtain was forty-
five feet long and each curtain six feet wide.
All eleven curtains were the same size.
16They joined five curtains together and the
six other curtains together. 17They made
fifty loops on the edge of the outer curtain
of the one set and fifty loops on the edge
of the other set of curtains. 18They made
fifty copper clasps to join the tent together
so that it would be one whole structure.
19They also made a covering for the tent of
rams' skins dyed red and an outer covering
of beaded leather.
20Then they made acacia-wood boards
to stand upright as a frame for the dwelling. 21Each board was fifteen feet long and
twenty-seven inches wide. 22Each board
had two pegs for joining them to each other.
They did this for all the dwelling's boards.
23They made twenty boards for the dwelling's southern side. 24They made forty silver
bases under the twenty boards, with two
bases under the first board for its two pegs,
two bases under the next board for its two
pegs, and so on. 25For the dwelling's other
side on the north, they made twenty boards
26and forty silver bases, two bases under the
first board, two bases under the next board,
and so on. 27For the back of the dwelling on
the west, they made six boards. 28They made
two additional boards for the dwelling's rear
corners. 29They were spread out at the bottom but joined together at the top with one
ring. In this way, these two boards formed
the two corners. 30And so there were eight
boards with their sixteen silver bases, with
two bases under every board.
31They also made acacia-wood bars: five
for the boards on one side of the dwelling,
32five bars for the boards on the other side
of the dwelling, and five bars for the boards
on the back wall of the dwelling on the
west. 33They made the middle bar, which
was halfway up the boards, run from one
end to the other. 34They covered the boards
with gold. They made gold rings to house
the bars and covered the bars with gold.
35They made the veil of blue, purple,
and deep red yarns and fine twisted linen,
with figures of winged heavenly creatures
worked into its design. 36They made for
it four acacia-wood posts covered in gold
with gold hooks and cast four silver bases
for them. 37They made a screen for the entrance to the tent of blue, purple, and deep
red yarns and fine twisted linen, decorated
with needlework. 38They made its five posts
with hooks. They covered their tops and
bands with gold, but made their five bases
out of copper.

Building the chest containing the covenant document

37 Bezalel made the chest of acacia
wood. It was forty-five inches long,

twenty-seven inches wide, and twenty-seven inches high. [2]He covered the chest with pure gold inside and out, and made a gold molding all around it. [3]He cast four gold rings for it and put them on its four feet, two rings on one side and two rings on the other. [4]He made acacia-wood poles and covered them with gold. [5]He put the poles into the rings on the chest's sides to use to carry the chest. [6]He made a cover for the chest out of pure gold, forty-five inches long and twenty-seven inches wide. [7]He made two winged heavenly creatures of hammered gold for the two ends of the cover, [8]one winged heavenly creature at one end and one winged heavenly creature at the other. He placed the winged heavenly creatures at the cover's two ends. [9]The winged heavenly creatures spread out their wings above, shielding the cover with their wings. The winged heavenly creatures faced each other toward the cover's center.

Constructing the table and lampstand

[10]He also made the table of acacia wood, three feet long, eighteen inches wide, and twenty-seven inches high. [11]He covered it with pure gold and made a gold molding all around it. [12]He made a frame around it that was four inches wide and gold molding around the frame. [13]He made four gold rings for the table. He fastened the rings to the four corners at its four legs. [14]The rings that housed the poles used for carrying the table were close to the frame. [15]He made the poles used to carry the table out of acacia wood, and he covered them with gold. [16]He made the containers of pure gold that were to be on the table: its plates, dishes, bowls, and jars for pouring drink offerings.

[17]He also made the lampstand of pure, hammered gold. The lampstand's base, branches, cups, flowers, and petals were all attached to it. [18]It had six branches growing out from its sides, three branches on one side of the lampstand and three branches on the other side of the lampstand. [19]One branch had three cups shaped like almond blossoms, each with a flower and petals, and the next branch also had three cups shaped like almond blossoms, each with a flower and petals. A total of six branches grew out of the lampstand. [20]In addition, on the lampstand itself there were four cups shaped like almond blossoms, each with its flower and petals. [21]There was a flower attached under the first pair of branches, a flower attached under the next pair of branches, and a flower attached under the last pair of branches. [22]Their flowers and their branches were attached to it. The whole lampstand was one piece of pure hammered gold. [23]He made its seven lamps and its tongs and its fire pans out of pure gold. [24]He made the lampstand and all its equipment from pure gold weighing one kikkar.

Making the incense altar, incense, and oil

[25]He made the incense altar out of acacia wood. The altar was square, eighteen inches long by eighteen inches wide. It was three feet high, and its horns were permanently attached. [26]He covered it with pure gold, including its top, all its sides, and its horns. He also made a gold molding all around it. [27]He made two gold rings, and he attached them under the molding on two opposite sides of the altar. They housed the poles used to carry it. [28]He made the poles of acacia wood, and he covered them with gold.

[29]He also made the holy anointing oil and the pure sweet-smelling incense like a skilled perfume maker.

Making the altar for entirely burned offerings

38 He made the altar for entirely burned offerings out of acacia wood. The altar was square, seven and a half feet long and seven and a half feet wide. It was four and a half feet high. [2]He made horns for it, one horn on each of its four corners. Its horns were attached to the altar, and he covered it with copper. [3]He made all the altar's equipment: the pails, the shovels, the bowls, the meat forks, and the trays. He made all its equipment out of copper. [4]He made a grate for the altar of copper mesh underneath its bottom edge and extending halfway up to the middle of the altar. [5]He made four rings for each of the four cor-

ners of the copper grate to house the poles. [6]He made the poles out of acacia wood, and he covered them with copper. [7]He put the poles through the rings so that the poles were on the two sides of the altar when it was carried. He made the altar with planks but hollow inside.

[8]He made the copper washbasin with its copper stand from the copper mirrors among the ranks of women assigned to the meeting tent's entrance.

Constructing the dwelling's plaza

[9]He also set up the courtyard. The courtyard's south side had drapes of fine twisted linen stretching one hundred fifty feet [10]with twenty posts, twenty copper bases, and silver hooks and bands for the posts. [11]Likewise the north side stretched one hundred fifty feet, with twenty posts, twenty copper bases, and silver hooks and bands for the posts. [12]On the west side the drapes stretched seventy-five feet, with their ten posts, their ten bases, and silver hooks and bands for the posts. [13]The front side facing east was seventy-five feet. [14]There were twenty-two and a half feet of drapes on one side with three posts and three bases for them. [15]Likewise, there were twenty-two and a half feet of drapes on the other side of the plaza's gate with three posts and three bases for them. [16]All the drapes around the courtyard were made of fine twisted linen. [17]The bases for the posts were made of copper, but the hooks for the posts and their bands were made of silver. The tops of the posts were covered with silver, and all the posts surrounding the courtyard had silver bands. [18]The screen for the gate into the courtyard was made with blue, purple, and deep red yarns and fine twisted linen, decorated with needlework. It was thirty feet long and, along the width of it, seven and a half feet high, corresponding to the courtyard's drapes. [19]It had four posts, their four copper bases, their silver hooks, and their tops and bands covered with silver. [20]All the tent pegs for the dwelling and for the courtyard all around were made of copper.

A listing of materials used

[21]These are the accounts of the dwelling, the covenant dwelling, that were recorded at Moses' instructions. They are the work of the Levites, under the direction of Ithamar, Aaron the priest's son. [22]Bezalel, Uri's son and Hur's grandson from the tribe of Judah, made everything that the LORD had commanded Moses to make. [23]Working with Bezalel was Oholiab, Ahisamach's son from the tribe of Dan, who was a gem cutter, a designer, and a needleworker in blue, purple, and deep red yarns and in fine linen.

[24]The total amount of the gold that was used for construction of the whole sanctuary, gold from the uplifted offerings, was twenty-nine kikkars and seven hundred thirty shekels in weight, measured by the sanctuary shekel. [25]The silver from the community census totaled one hundred kikkars and one thousand seven hundred seventy-five shekels in weight, measured by the sanctuary shekel. [26]They gave a beqa per person (that is, half a shekel, measured by the sanctuary shekel) for everyone who was counted in the census, 20 years old and above, 603,550 men. [27]One hundred kikkars of silver were used to cast the bases for the sanctuary and the bases for the veil, one hundred bases from one hundred kikkars of silver, one kikkar for every base. [28]He used one thousand seven hundred seventy-five shekels of silver[d] to make the hooks for the posts, cover their tops, and make bands for them. [29]The amount of copper from the uplifted offering was seventy kikkars and two thousand four hundred shekels in weight. [30]He used it to make the bases for the meeting tent's entrance, the copper altar, its copper grate, and all the altar's equipment, [31]the bases all around the courtyard, and the bases for the courtyard's gate, all the dwelling's tent pegs, and all the tent pegs used around the courtyard.

Making the priests' clothing

39 They used the blue, purple, and deep red yarns to make the woven clothing for those ministering as priests in the

[d]Heb lacks *shekels of silver.*

sanctuary. They made the holy clothes for Aaron as the LORD had commanded Moses.

2 They made the vest[e] of gold, of blue, purple, and deep red yarns, and of fine twisted linen. 3 They beat out thin sheets of gold and cut them into threads to work into designs among the blue, purple, and deep red yarns and the fine linen. 4 They made shoulder pieces for it attached to its two edges so that they could be joined together. 5 The vest's belt was attached to it and made in the same way of gold, of blue, purple, and deep red yarns, and of fine twisted linen, just as the LORD had commanded Moses.

6 They prepared the gemstones by mounting them in gold settings and engraving on them the names of Israel's sons, like an official seal is engraved. 7 The stones were attached to the vest's shoulder pieces as reminder stones for the Israelites, just as the LORD had commanded Moses.

8 They made the embroidered chest pendant in the style of the vest, using gold, blue, purple, and deep red yarns, and fine twisted linen. 9 They made the chest pendant square and doubled, nine inches long and nine inches wide when doubled. 10 They set in it four rows of gemstones. The first row was a row of carnelian, topaz, and emerald stones. 11 The second row was a turquoise, a sapphire, and a moonstone. 12 The third row was a jacinth, an agate, and an amethyst. 13 The fourth row was a beryl, an onyx, and a jasper. The settings around them were decorative gold. 14 There were twelve stones with names corresponding to the names of Israel's sons. They were engraved like official seals, each with its name for the twelve tribes. 15 They made chains of pure gold, twisted like cords, for the chest pendant. 16 They made two gold settings and two gold rings. They attached the two rings to the two edges of the chest pendant. 17 They attached the two gold cords to the two rings at the edges of the chest pendant. 18 Then they fastened the two ends of the two cords to the two gold settings and attached them to the front of the vest's shoulder pieces. 19 They made two gold rings, and they attached them to the two edges of the chest pendant, on its inside edge facing the vest. 20 They made two gold rings and fastened them on the front of the lower part of the two shoulder pieces of the vest, at its seam just above the vest's belt. 21 The chest pendant was held in place by a blue cord binding its rings to the vest's rings so that the chest pendant rested on the vest's belt and didn't come loose from the vest, just as the LORD had commanded Moses.

22 They also made the vest's robe, woven completely in blue. 23 The opening of the robe in the middle of it was reinforced with a strong border so that it didn't tear. 24 On the robe's lower hem, they added pomegranates made of blue, purple, and deep red yarns and of fine twisted linen. 25 They also made pure gold bells and sewed the bells between the pomegranates, all around the robe's lower hem, 26 with a bell and a pomegranate alternating all around the lower hem of the robe that is used for ministering as a priest, just as the LORD had commanded Moses.

27 They also made the tunics woven out of fine linen for Aaron and his sons, 28 the turban of fine linen, the decorated turbans of fine linen, the linen undergarments of fine twisted linen, 29 the sashes of fine twisted linen, and of blue, purple, and crimson yarns, decorated with needlework, just as the LORD had commanded Moses.

30 They made the flower ornament for the holy crown out of pure gold. Like the engraving on an official seal, they engraved on it the saying "Holy to the LORD." 31 They fastened to it a blue cord to tie it to the top of the turban, just as the LORD had commanded Moses.

Completion of dwelling construction

32 In this way all the work of the meeting tent dwelling was finished. The Israelites did everything just exactly as the LORD had commanded Moses. 33 Then they brought to Moses the dwelling, the tent, and all its equipment:

[e] Heb *ephod*

its clasps, its boards, its bars, its posts, and its bases,

[34]the covering of rams' skins dyed red, the covering of beaded leather, and the veil for a screen,

[35]the chest containing the covenant with its poles and the cover,

[36]the table with all its equipment and the bread of the presence,

[37]the pure lampstand with its lamps set on it and all its equipment, and the oil for the light,

[38]the gold altar, the anointing oil, and the sweet-smelling incense,

the screen for the tent's entrance,

[39]the copper altar and its copper grate, its poles, and all its equipment,

the washbasin with its stand,

[40]the courtyard's drapes, its posts, and its bases,

the screen for the plaza's gate, its cords, and its tent pegs,

and all the other equipment for the service of the dwelling, for the meeting tent,

[41]the woven clothes for ministering as priests in the sanctuary, the holy clothes for the priest Aaron and the clothes for his sons to serve as priests.

[42]The Israelites did all of the work just as the LORD had commanded Moses. [43]When Moses saw that they in fact had done all the work exactly as the LORD had commanded, Moses blessed them.

Moses sets up the dwelling

40 The LORD spoke to Moses: [2]Set up the meeting tent dwelling on the first day of the first month.[f] [3]Place the chest containing the covenant inside the dwelling. Hide the chest from view with the veil. [4]Bring in the table and arrange its items. Bring in the lampstand and set up its lamps. [5]Place the gold altar for burning incense in front of the chest containing the covenant. Set up the screen at the dwelling's entrance. [6]Put the altar for entirely burned offerings in front of the entrance to the meeting tent dwelling. [7]Put the washbasin between the meeting tent and the altar and put water in it. [8]Set up the courtyard all around. Hang up the screen at the courtyard gate. [9]Then take the anointing oil and anoint the dwelling and everything in it. Make holy the dwelling and all its equipment, and it will be holy. [10]Anoint the altar for entirely burned offerings and all its equipment. Make the altar holy, and the altar will be most holy. [11]Anoint the washbasin with its stand and make it holy.

[12]Then bring Aaron and his sons to the meeting tent's entrance and wash them with water. [13]Dress Aaron in the holy clothes. Anoint him and make him holy so that he may serve me as priest. [14]Then bring his sons and dress them in tunics. [15]Anoint them like you anointed their father so that they may serve me as priests. Their anointing is to the priesthood for all time in every generation.

[16]Moses did everything exactly as the LORD had commanded him. [17]In the first month in the second year, on the first day of the month, the dwelling was set up. [18]Moses set up the dwelling. He laid out its bases. He set up its boards, inserted its bars, and raised up its posts. [19]He spread the tent out over the dwelling, and he put the covering of the tent over it, just as the LORD had commanded Moses. [20]He took the covenant document and placed it inside the chest. He put the poles on the chest, and he set the cover on top of the chest. [21]He brought the chest into the dwelling. He set up the veil as a screen to hide from view the chest containing the covenant, just as the LORD had commanded Moses. [22]He placed the table in the meeting tent, on the north side of the dwelling, outside the veil. [23]He set the bread in its proper place on the table in the LORD's presence, just as the LORD had commanded Moses. [24]He put the lampstand in the meeting tent, opposite the table on the south side of the dwelling. [25]He set up the lamps in the LORD's presence, just as the LORD had commanded Moses. [26]He put the gold altar in the meeting tent

[f]March–April, Abib

in front of the veil. 27He burned sweet-smelling incense on it, just as the LORD had commanded Moses. 28He also set up the screen at the entrance to the dwelling. 29He placed the altar for entirely burned offerings at the entrance to the meeting tent dwelling. He offered the entirely burned offering and the grain offering on it, just as the LORD had commanded Moses. 30He put the washbasin between the meeting tent and the altar, and put water in it for washing. 31Moses, Aaron, and his sons used it to wash their hands and their feet. 32Whenever they went into the meeting tent and whenever they approached the altar, they washed themselves, just as the LORD had commanded Moses. 33He set up the courtyard around the dwelling and the altar, and he hung up the screen at the courtyard's gate.

God's presence fills the dwelling!

When Moses had finished all the work, 34the cloud covered the meeting tent and the LORD's glorious presence filled the dwelling. 35Moses couldn't enter the meeting tent because the cloud had settled on it, and the LORD's glorious presence filled the dwelling. 36Whenever the cloud rose from the dwelling, the Israelites would set out on their journeys. 37But if the cloud didn't rise, then they didn't set out until the day it rose. 38The LORD's cloud stayed over the dwelling during the day, with lightning in it at night, clearly visible to the whole household of Israel at every stage of their journey.

LEVITICUS

1 Then the LORD called to Moses and said to him from the meeting tent, 2Speak to the Israelites and say to them: When any of you present a livestock offering to the LORD, you can present it from either the herd or the flock.

The entirely burned offering

3If the offering is an entirely burned offering from the herd, you must present a flawless male, bringing it to the meeting tent's entrance for its acceptance before the LORD. 4You must press your hand on the head of the entirely burned offering so that it will be accepted for you, to make reconciliation for you. 5Then you will slaughter the bull before the LORD. Aaron's sons the priests will present the blood and toss it against every side of the altar at the meeting tent's entrance. 6Then the entirely burned offering will be skinned and cut up into pieces. 7The sons of Aaron the priest[a] will light the altar and lay wood on the fire. 8Then Aaron's sons the priests will arrange the pieces, the head, and the fat on the wood that is on the altar fire, 9but the animal's insides and lower legs must be washed with water. The priest will then completely burn all of it on the altar as an entirely burned offering, a food gift[b] of soothing smell to the LORD.

10If the offering is an entirely burned offering from the flock—whether sheep or goat—you must present a flawless male. 11You must slaughter it on the north side of the altar before the LORD. Aaron's sons the priests will toss its blood against every side of the altar. 12Once it has been cut into pieces, including the head and the fat, the priest will arrange these out on the wood that is on the altar fire, 13but its insides and lower legs must be washed with water. Then the priest will present all of it and completely burn it on the altar. It is an entirely burned offering, a food gift of soothing smell to the LORD.

14If the offering for the LORD is an entirely burned offering from the birds, you can present your offering from the doves or pigeons. 15The priest will bring it to the altar. He will tear off its head and completely burn it on the altar. Its blood will be

[a]Some Heb sources, Sam, LXX, Syr, and some Tg sources have *Aaron's sons, the priests*, as in 1:5, 8. [b]Or (here and throughout Leviticus) *offering by fire* (cf 3:11)

drained against the side of the altar. [16]Then the priest will remove its throat along with its contents[c] and throw it by the east side of the altar, into the place for the ashes. [17]He will then tear the bird open by its wings, without splitting it. The priest will completely burn it on the altar, on the wood that is on the altar fire. It is an entirely burned offering, a food gift of soothing smell to the LORD.

The grain offering

2 When anyone presents a grain offering to the LORD, the offering must be of choice flour. They must pour oil on it and put frankincense on it, [2]then bring it to Aaron's sons, the priests. A priest will take a handful of its choice flour and oil, along with all of its frankincense, and will completely burn this token portion on the altar as a food gift of soothing smell to the LORD. [3]The rest of the grain offering belongs to Aaron and his sons as a most holy portion from the LORD's food gifts.

[4]When you present a grain offering baked in an oven, it must be of choice flour: unleavened flatbread mixed with oil or unleavened wafers spread with oil. [5]If your offering is grain prepared on a griddle, it must be of choice flour mixed with oil and it must be unleavened. [6]Crumble it into pieces and pour oil on it; it is a grain offering. [7]If your offering is grain prepared in a pan, it must be made of choice flour with oil. [8]You will bring the grain offering made in one of these ways to the LORD, presenting it to the priest, who will then bring it to the altar. [9]The priest will remove from the grain offering the token portion and completely burn it on the altar as a food gift of soothing smell to the LORD. [10]The rest of the grain offering belongs to Aaron and his sons as a most holy portion from the LORD's food gifts.

[11]No grain offering that you give to the LORD can be made with yeast. You must not completely burn any yeast or honey as a food gift for the LORD. [12]You can present those as first-choice offerings to the LORD, but they must not be entirely burned up on the altar as a soothing smell.

[13]You must season all your grain offerings with salt. Do not omit the salt of your God's covenant from your grain offering. You must offer salt with all your offerings.

[14]If you present a grain offering to the LORD from the first produce, you must make such an offering from the crushed heads of newly ripe grain, roasted with fire. [15]You must put oil and frankincense on it; it is a grain offering. [16]The priest will completely burn the token portion—some of the crushed new grain and oil along with all of the frankincense—as a food gift for the LORD.

The well-being sacrifice

3 If the offering is a communal sacrifice of well-being,[d] the one who offers the herd animal—whether it is male or female—must present a flawless specimen before the LORD. [2]You must press your hand on the head of the offering and slaughter it at the meeting tent's entrance. Aaron's sons the priests will toss the blood against every side of the altar. [3]Then you can offer a food gift to the LORD from the communal sacrifice of well-being: the fat that covers and surrounds the insides; [4]the two kidneys and the fat around them at the loins; and the lobe on the liver, which should be removed with the kidneys. [5]Aaron's sons will completely burn all of this on the altar—along with the entirely burned offering on the wood that is on the altar fire—as a food gift of soothing smell to the LORD.

[6]If the offering for a communal sacrifice of well-being for the LORD is from the flock—whether it is male or female—you must present a flawless specimen. [7]If you present a sheep as the offering, you must present it before the LORD. [8]You must press your hand on the head of the offering and slaughter it before the meeting tent. Aaron's sons will toss the blood against every side of the altar. [9]Then you may offer the fat from the communal sacrifice of well-being as a food gift for the LORD: the whole fat

[c]Heb uncertain [d]Or *peace offering*

tail, which should be removed close to the tailbone; the fat that covers and surrounds the insides; [10]the two kidneys and the fat around them at the loins; and the lobe on the liver, which should be removed with the kidneys. [11]The priest will then completely burn all of this on the altar as food—as a food gift for the LORD.

[12]If the offering is a goat, you must present it before the LORD. [13]You must press your hand on its head and slaughter it before the meeting tent. Aaron's sons will toss its blood against every side of the altar. [14]Then you may present as your offering—a food gift for the LORD—the fat that covers and surrounds the insides; [15]the two kidneys and the fat around them at the loins; and the lobe on the liver, which should be removed with the kidneys. [16]The priest will then completely burn all of this on the altar as food—as a food gift for a soothing smell.

All fat belongs to the LORD. [17]This is a permanent rule for your future generations, wherever you live: you must not eat any fat or blood.

The purification offering

4 The LORD said to Moses, [2]Say to the Israelites: Do the following whenever someone sins unintentionally against any of the LORD's commands, doing something that shouldn't be done:

[3]If it is the anointed priest who has sinned, making the people guilty of sin, he must present to the LORD a flawless bull from the herd as a purification offering[e] for the sin he has committed. [4]He will bring the bull before the LORD at the entrance to the meeting tent and press his hand on the bull's head. Then he will slaughter the bull before the LORD. [5]The anointed priest will take some of the bull's blood and take it into the meeting tent. [6]The priest will dip his finger into the blood and sprinkle some of it seven times before the LORD, toward the sanctuary's inner curtain. [7]Then the priest will put some of the blood on the horns of the altar of perfumed incense, which is in the meeting tent before the LORD. But he will pour out all the rest of the bull's blood at the base of the altar of entirely burned offerings, which is at the meeting tent's entrance. [8]Then he will remove all the fat from the bull for the purification offering: the fat that covers and surrounds the insides; [9]the two kidneys and the fat around them at the loins; and the lobe on the liver, which he will remove with the kidneys, [10]just as this is removed from the ox for the communal sacrifice of well-being. Then the priest will completely burn these on the altar of entirely burned offerings. [11]But the bull's hide and all of its flesh, along with its head, lower legs, entrails, and dung—[12]all that remains of the bull—will be taken to a clean location outside the camp, to the ash heap. It should be burned there at the ash heap on a wood fire.

[13]If it is the entire Israelite community that has done something wrong unintentionally and the deed escapes the assembly's notice—but they've done something that shouldn't be done in violation of the LORD's commands, becoming guilty of sin—[14]once the sin that they committed becomes known, the assembly must present a bull from the herd as a purification offering. They will bring it before the meeting tent. [15]The community elders will press their hands on the bull's head before the LORD and then slaughter it before the LORD. [16]The anointed priest will take some of the bull's blood into the meeting tent. [17]The priest will dip his finger into the blood and sprinkle it seven times before the LORD toward the inner curtain. [18]Then he will put some of the blood on the horns of the altar that is before the LORD in the meeting tent. But he will pour all the rest of the blood out at the base of the altar of entirely burned offerings that is at the meeting tent's entrance. [19]Then he will remove all the fat from it and completely burn it on the altar. [20]He will do the same with this bull as he did with the other bull for the purification offering; that is exactly what he must do. In this way, the priest will make reconciliation for them, and they will

[e]Or *sin offering* (Heb *hatta't*, which recurs frequently in Leviticus)

be forgiven. [21]Then the priest will take the bull outside the camp and burn it, just as the first bull was burned. It is the purification offering for the assembly.

[22]If a leader sins by unintentionally breaking any of the commands of the LORD his God, doing something that shouldn't be done, and becomes guilty of sin—[23]once the sin that he committed is made known to him—he must bring as his offering a flawless male goat. [24]He will press his hand on the goat's head. It will be slaughtered[f] at the place where an entirely burned offering would be slaughtered before the LORD. It is a purification offering. [25]The priest will take some of the blood from the purification offering and, using his finger, will put it on the horns of the altar of entirely burned offerings. But he will pour the rest of the blood out at the base of the altar of entirely burned offerings. [26]He will completely burn all of its fat on the altar just as the fat of the communal sacrifice of well-being is burned. In this way the priest will make reconciliation for the leader to remove his sin, and he will be forgiven.

[27]If any ordinary person[g] sins unintentionally by breaking one of the LORD's commands, doing something that shouldn't be done, and becomes guilty of sin—[28]once the sin they committed is made known to them—they must bring as their offering a flawless female goat because of the sin that was committed. [29]They will press their hand on the head of the purification offering. It will be slaughtered[h] at the place for the entirely burned offerings. [30]The priest will take some of its blood and, using his finger, will put it on the horns of the altar of entirely burned offerings. But he will pour all the rest of the blood out at the base of the altar. [31]He will remove all of its fat, just as the fat from a communal sacrifice of well-being is removed. Then the priest will completely burn it on the altar as a soothing smell to the LORD. In this way, the priest will make reconciliation for them, and they will be forgiven.

[32]If you offer a sheep as a purification offering, it must be a flawless female. [33]You must press your hand on the head of the purification offering. It will be slaughtered[i] as a purification offering in the place where the entirely burned offering is slaughtered. [34]Then the priest will take some of the blood from the purification offering and, using his finger, will put it on the horns of the altar of entirely burned offerings. But he will pour all the rest of the blood out at the base of the altar. [35]He will remove all of its fat, just as the fat of a sheep would be removed from the communal sacrifice of well-being. Then the priest will completely burn it on the altar along with the LORD's food gifts. In this way, the priest will make reconciliation for you for the sin you committed, and you will be forgiven.

Unintentional sin

5 If you sin:

by not providing information after hearing a public solemn pledge even though you are a witness, knowing something, or having seen something so that you become liable to punishment;

[2]or by touching some unclean thing—the dead body of an unclean wild animal, unclean livestock, or unclean swarming creature—but the fact goes unknown so that you become unclean and guilty of sin;

[3]or by touching human uncleanness—any uncleanness that makes one unclean—and the fact goes unknown, but you later learn of it and become guilty of sin;

[4]or by carelessly swearing to do something, whether bad or good—whatever one might swear carelessly—and the fact goes unknown, but you later learn of it and become guilty of sin concerning one of these things—

[5]at that point, when you have become guilty of sin in one of these ways, you must confess how you have sinned [6]and bring to

[f]Or *He will slaughter it . . . where he would slaughter* [g]Or *one of the people of the land* [h]Or *They will slaughter it.*
[i]Or *You will slaughter it.*

the LORD as compensation for the sin that was committed a female from the flock, either a sheep or goat, as a purification offering. The priest will then make reconciliation for you, to remove your sin.

Alternative offerings

7 If you can't afford an animal from the flock, you can bring to the LORD as compensation for your sin two doves or two pigeons, one as a purification offering and the other as an entirely burned offering. 8 You will bring them to the priest, who will first present the one for the purification offering. He will pinch off its head at the back of its neck without splitting it. 9 Then he will sprinkle some of the blood of the purification offering on the side of the altar. The rest of the blood will be drained out at the base of the altar. It is a purification offering. 10 Then, with the second bird, the priest will perform an entirely burned offering according to the regulation. In this way, the priest will make reconciliation for you because of the sin you committed, and you will be forgiven.

11 If you cannot afford two doves or two pigeons, you can bring as the offering for your sin a tenth of an ephah[j] of choice flour as a purification offering. You must not put any oil on it, nor any frankincense, because it is a purification offering. 12 You will bring it to the priest, and the priest will take a handful from it—the token portion—and will burn it completely on the altar along with the food gifts for the LORD. It is a purification offering. 13 In this way, the priest will make reconciliation for you for whichever one of the sins you committed, and you will be forgiven. The rest of the offering will belong to the priest like the grain offering.

The compensation offering

14 The LORD said to Moses, 15 Whenever you commit wrongdoing, unintentionally sinning against any of the LORD's holy things, you must bring to the LORD as your compensation a flawless ram from the flock, its value calculated in silver shekels according to the sanctuary's shekel, as a compensation offering. 16 You will make amends for the way you have sinned against the holy thing: you will add one-fifth to its value and give it to the priest. Then the priest will make reconciliation for you with the ram for the compensation offering, and you will be forgiven.

17 If you sin by breaking any of the LORD's commands, but without realizing it, doing something that shouldn't be done, and then become guilty and liable to punishment, 18 you must bring a flawless ram from the flock, at the standard value, as a compensation offering to the priest. The priest will make reconciliation for you for the unintentional fault that you committed, even though you didn't realize it, and you will be forgiven. 19 It is a compensation offering. You have definitely become guilty before the LORD.

6 [k]The LORD said to Moses, 2 If you sin:
by acting unfaithfully against the LORD;
by deceiving a fellow citizen concerning a deposit or pledged property;
by cheating a fellow citizen through robbery;
3 or, though you've found lost property, you lie about it;
or by swearing falsely about anything that someone might do and so sin,

4 at that point, once you have sinned and become guilty of sin, you must return the property you took by robbery or fraud, or the deposit that was left with you for safekeeping, or the lost property that you found, 5 or whatever it was that you swore falsely about. You must make amends for the principal amount and add one-fifth to it. You must give it to the owner on the day you become guilty. 6 You must bring to the priest as your compensation to the LORD a flawless ram from the flock at the standard value as a compensation offering. 7 The priest will make reconciliation for you before the LORD, and you will be forgiven for anything you may have done that made you guilty.

[j]Two quarts; one ephah is approximately twenty quarts dry. [k]5:20 in Heb

Priestly instructions
8[l]The LORD said to Moses: 9Command
Aaron and his sons: This is the Instruction for the entirely burned offering—the
entirely burned offering that must remain
on the altar hearth all night until morning,
while the fire is kept burning. 10The priest
will dress in his linen robe, with linen undergarments on his body. Because the fire
will have devoured the entirely burned offering on the altar, he must remove the
ashes and place them beside the altar. 11The
priest will then take off his clothes, dress in
a different set of clothes, and take the ashes
outside the camp to a clean location. 12The
altar fire must be kept burning; it must not
go out. Each morning the priest will burn
wood on it, will lay out the entirely burned
offering on it, and will completely burn the
fat of the well-being offering on it. 13A continuous fire must be kept burning on the
altar; it must not go out.
14This is the Instruction for the grain offering: Aaron's sons will present it before
the LORD in front of the altar. 15The priest
will remove a handful of the choice flour
and oil from the grain offering, and all of
the frankincense that is on it, and burn this
token portion completely on the altar as a
soothing smell to the LORD. 16Aaron and
his sons will eat the rest of it. It must be
eaten as unleavened bread in a holy place;
the priests must eat it in the meeting tent's
courtyard. 17It must not be baked with
leaven. I have made it the priests' share
from my food gifts. It is most holy like the
purification offering and the compensation
offering. 18Only the males from Aaron's
descendants can eat it as a permanent portion from the LORD's food gifts throughout
your future generations. Anything that
touches these food gifts will become holy.
19The LORD said to Moses, 20This is the
offering that Aaron and his sons must present to the LORD on the day of his anointment: one-tenth of an ephah[m] of choice
flour as a regular grain offering, half in the
morning and half in the evening. 21It must
be prepared on a griddle with oil. You must
bring it thoroughly mixed up and must present it as a grain offering of crumbled pieces[n]
as a soothing smell to the LORD. 22The priest
who is anointed from among Aaron's sons
to succeed him will prepare the offering as
a permanent portion for the LORD. It will
be completely burned as a complete offering. 23Every priestly grain offering must be
a complete offering; it must not be eaten.
24The LORD said to Moses, 25Say to Aaron
and his sons: This is the Instruction for the
purification offering: The purification offering must be slaughtered before the LORD at
the same place the entirely burned offering
is slaughtered; it is most holy. 26The priest
who offers it as a purification offering will
eat it. It must be eaten in a holy place, in
the meeting tent's courtyard. 27Anything
that touches the purification offering's
flesh will become holy. If some of its blood
splashes on a garment, you must wash the
bloodied part in a holy place. 28A pottery
container in which the purification offering
is cooked must be broken, but if it is
cooked in a bronze container, that must be
scrubbed and rinsed with water. 29Any male
priest can eat it; it is most holy. 30But no
purification offering can be eaten if blood
from it is brought into the meeting tent
to make reconciliation in the holy place; it
must be burned with fire.

7 This is the Instruction for the compensation offering: It is most holy. 2The compensation offering must be slaughtered at
the same place where the entirely burned
offering is slaughtered, and its blood must
be tossed against all sides of the altar. 3All
of its fat will be offered: the fat tail; the fat
that covers the insides; 4the two kidneys
and the fat around them at the loins; and
the lobe on the liver, which must be removed with the kidneys. 5The priest must
burn them completely on the altar as a food
gift for the LORD; it is a compensation offering. 6Any male priest can eat it. It must
be eaten in a holy place; it is most holy.
7The compensation offering is like the
purification offering—they share the same
Instruction: It belongs to the priest who

[l] 6:1 in Heb [m] Two quarts; an ephah is approximately twenty quarts dry. [n] Heb uncertain

makes reconciliation with it. [8]The hide of the entirely burned offering that a priest has offered belongs to the priest who offered it. [9]Any grain offering that is baked in an oven or that is prepared in a pan or on a griddle also belongs to the priest who offered it. [10]But every other grain offering, whether mixed with oil or dry, will belong to all of Aaron's sons equally.

[11]This is the Instruction for the communal sacrifice of well-being that someone may offer to the LORD: [12]If you are offering it for thanksgiving, you must offer the following with the communal sacrifice of thanksgiving: unleavened flatbread mixed with oil, unleavened thin loaves spread with oil, and flatbread of choice flour thoroughly mixed with oil. [13]You must present this offering, plus the leavened flatbread, with the communal thanksgiving sacrifice of well-being. [14]From this you will present one of each kind of offering as a gift to the LORD. It will belong to the priest who tosses the blood of the well-being offering.

[15]The flesh of your communal thanksgiving sacrifice of well-being must be eaten on the day you offer it; you cannot save any of it until morning. [16]But if your communal sacrifice of well-being is payment for a solemn promise or if it is a spontaneous gift, it may be eaten on the day you offer it as your communal sacrifice, and whatever is left over can be eaten the next day. [17]But whatever is left over of the flesh of the communal sacrifice on the third day must be burned with fire. [18]If any of it is eaten on the third day, it will not be accepted. It will not be credited to the one who offered it. It will be considered foul, and the person who eats of it will be liable to punishment.

[19]Flesh that touches any unclean thing must not be eaten; it must be burned with fire. Any clean person may eat the flesh, [20]but anyone who eats the flesh of a communal sacrifice of well-being that belongs to the LORD while in an unclean state will be cut off from their people. [21]Whenever anyone touches any unclean thing—whether it is human uncleanness, an unclean animal, or any unclean and disgusting creature—and then eats the flesh of a communal sacrifice of well-being that belongs to the LORD, that person will be cut off from their people.

[22]The LORD said to Moses: [23]Tell the Israelites: You must not eat the fat of an ox, sheep, or goat. [24]The fat of an animal that has died naturally or the fat of an animal that was killed by another animal may be put to any use, but you must definitely not eat it. [25]If anyone eats the fat of an animal from which a food gift could be offered to the LORD, that person will be cut off from their people. [26]You must not consume any blood whatsoever—whether bird or animal blood—wherever you may live. [27]Any person who consumes any blood whatsoever will be cut off from their people.

[28]The LORD said to Moses: [29]Say to the Israelites: If you wish to offer a communal sacrifice of well-being to the LORD, you are allowed to bring your offering to the LORD as your communal sacrifice of well-being.[o] [30]Your own hands must bring the LORD's food gifts. You will bring the fat with the breast so that the breast can be lifted as an uplifted offering before the LORD. [31]The priest will completely burn the fat on the altar, but the breast will go to Aaron and his sons. [32]You will give the right thigh of your communal sacrifice of well-being to the priest as a gift. [33]The right thigh will belong to the son of Aaron who offers the blood and fat of the well-being offering. [34]I have taken the breast of the uplifted offering and the thigh that is given by the Israelites from their communal sacrifices of well-being, and have given them to Aaron the priest and to his sons as a permanent portion from the Israelites.

[35]This is what Aaron and his sons are allotted from the LORD's food gifts once they have been presented to serve the LORD as priests. [36]The LORD commanded that these things be given to the priests by the Israelites, following their anointment. It is their permanent portion throughout their future generations.

[o]Heb uncertain

Conclusion concerning offerings

37This concludes the Instructions for the
entirely burned offering, the grain offering,
the purification offering, the compensation
offering, the ordination offering, and the
communal sacrifice of well-being, 38which
the LORD commanded Moses at Mount
Sinai on the day when he ordered the Israelites to present their offerings to the LORD,
in the Sinai desert.

The priests' ordination

8 The LORD said to Moses, 2Take Aaron
and his sons with him, the priestly clothing, the anointing oil, a bull for the purification offering, two rams, and a basket of
unleavened bread, 3and assemble the whole
community at the meeting tent's entrance.
4Moses did as the LORD commanded
him, and the community assembled at
the meeting tent's entrance. 5Moses said
to the community, "This is what the LORD
has commanded us to do." 6Then Moses
brought Aaron and his sons forward and
washed them in water. 7Moses put the
tunic on Aaron, tied the sash around him,
and dressed him in the robe. Moses then
put the priestly vest on Aaron, tied the
woven waistband of the vest around him,
and secured the vest to him with it. 8Then
Moses placed the chest piece on Aaron and
set the Urim and Thummim into the chest
piece. 9Moses placed the turban on Aaron's
head and put the gold flower ornament, the
holy crown, on the turban's front, just as
the LORD had commanded him.
10Moses then took the anointing oil
and anointed the dwelling[p] and everything
in it, making them holy by doing so. 11He
sprinkled some of the oil on the altar seven
times, and anointed the altar and all its
equipment, as well as the basin and its base,
to make them holy. 12He poured some of
the anointing oil on Aaron's head, thereby
anointing him to make him holy. 13Then
Moses brought Aaron's sons forward,
dressed them in tunics, tied sashes around
them, and wrapped headbands on them,
just as the LORD had commanded him.
14Next Moses brought forward the bull
for the purification offering. Aaron and
his sons pressed their hands on its head.
15Moses slaughtered it, then took the blood
and, using his finger, put it on all of the altar's horns, purifying the altar. He poured
the rest of the blood out at the altar's base.
Then he made the altar holy so that reconciliation could be performed on it.[q] 16Moses
removed all the fat that was around the insides, the lobe of the liver, the two kidneys
and their fat, and he completely burned it
on the altar. 17But the rest of the bull, including its hide, its flesh, and its dung, he
burned with fire outside the camp just as
the LORD had commanded him.
18Then Moses presented the ram for the
entirely burned offering, and Aaron and
his sons pressed their hands on its head.
19Moses slaughtered it, then tossed the
blood against all sides of the altar. 20He cut
up the ram into pieces, and then completely
burned the head, pieces, and fat. 21After
he washed the insides and lower legs with
water, Moses completely burned the whole
ram on the altar. It was an entirely burned
offering for a soothing smell; it was a food
gift for the LORD, as the LORD had commanded Moses.
22Moses then presented the second
ram, the ram for ordination, and Aaron
and his sons pressed their hands on its
head. 23Moses slaughtered it, then took
some of its blood and put it on Aaron's
right earlobe, on his right thumb, and on
his right big toe. 24Then Moses brought
forward Aaron's sons and put some of the
blood on their right earlobes, their right
thumbs, and their right big toes. Moses
tossed the rest of the blood against all
of the altar's sides. 25Then he took the
fat—the fat tail, all the fat that was around
the insides, the lobe of the liver, the two
kidneys and their fat—as well as the right
thigh. 26From the basket of unleavened
bread that was before the LORD, he took
one loaf of unleavened flatbread, one loaf
of flatbread made with oil, and one unleavened wafer, and he placed these on the fat

[p] Or *tabernacle* [q] Or *to make reconciliation for it* (i.e., the altar)

pieces and on the right thigh. [27]Moses set all of this in Aaron's and his sons' hands, then lifted them as an uplifted offering before the LORD. [28]Next Moses took this out of their hands and completely burned it on the altar, along with the entirely burned offering. This was an ordination offering for a soothing smell; it was a food gift for the LORD. [29]Next Moses took the breast from the ram for the ordination offering and lifted it as an uplifted offering before the LORD. It belonged to Moses as his portion, just as the LORD had commanded him. [30]Moses took some of the anointing oil and some of the blood that was on the altar and sprinkled it on Aaron and his clothes, and on his sons and their clothes as well. In this way, Moses made holy Aaron, his clothing, and Aaron's sons and their clothing.

[31]Moses said to Aaron and his sons: "Cook the meat at the meeting tent's entrance. You may eat it there along with the bread that is in the basket of the ordination offering, just as I was commanded,[r] 'Aaron and his sons can eat it.' [32]But you must burn whatever is left over of the meat and bread with fire. [33]You must not leave the meeting tent's entrance for seven days, until the period of your ordination is completed, because your ordination takes seven days. [34]What was done today was commanded by the LORD, to make reconciliation for you. [35]You must stay at the meeting tent's entrance for seven days, day and night, observing the LORD's requirement so you don't die, because that's what I was commanded."

[36]Aaron and his sons did everything the LORD commanded through Moses.

The priests' initiation

9 On the eighth day, Moses called for Aaron, Aaron's sons, and Israel's elders. [2]He said to Aaron, "Take a young bull from the herd as a purification offering and a ram as an entirely burned offering, both flawless animals, and bring them before the LORD. [3]Then tell the Israelites, 'Take a male goat as a purification offering; a young bull and a sheep—both one-year-old flawless animals—as an entirely burned offering; [4]an ox and a ram as a well-being sacrifice before the LORD; and a grain offering mixed with oil, because today the LORD will appear to you.'"

[5]They brought what Moses had commanded to the front of the meeting tent. Then the whole community came forward and stood before the LORD. [6]Moses said, "The LORD has ordered you to do this so that the LORD's glorious presence will appear to you." [7]Moses said to Aaron, "Come up to the altar and perform your purification offering and your entirely burned offering, making reconciliation for yourself and the people. Then perform the people's offering in order to make reconciliation for them, just as the LORD commanded."

[8]Aaron went to the altar and slaughtered the young bull for his purification offering. [9]Then Aaron's sons presented the blood to him, and he dipped his finger into the blood and put it on the altar's horns. He poured the rest of the blood out at the altar's base. [10]He completely burned on the altar the fat, kidneys, and lobe of the liver from the purification offering, just as the LORD commanded Moses. [11]But he burned the flesh and hide with fire outside the camp.

[12]Then Aaron slaughtered the entirely burned offering. Aaron's sons handed him the blood, and he tossed it against all sides of the altar. [13]They handed him the entirely burned offering in pieces, including the head, and he completely burned them on the altar. [14]Then he washed the insides and lower legs and completely burned them on the altar along with the rest of the entirely burned offering.

[15]Next, Aaron presented the people's offering. He took the male goat for the people's purification offering, slaughtered it, and offered it as a purification offering like the first purification offering. [16]He presented the entirely burned offering and did with it according to the regulation. [17]Then he presented the grain offering, took a

[r]LXX, Syr, Tg; cf 8:35; MT *as I commanded*

handful from it, and completely burned it
on the altar, in addition to the morning's
entirely burned offering.
[18]Aaron then slaughtered the ox and the
ram—the people's communal sacrifice of
well-being. Aaron's sons handed him the
blood, which he tossed against all sides
of the altar, [19]and the fat pieces of the ox
and ram—the fat tail, the covering fat, the
kidneys, and the lobe of the liver. [20]They
placed these fat pieces on the animals'
breasts, and Aaron completely burned
them on the altar. [21]But Aaron lifted up the
breasts and the right thigh as an uplifted
offering before the LORD, just as Moses had
commanded.
[22]Aaron then raised his hands toward
the people and blessed them. After performing the purification offering, the entirely burned offering, and the well-being
sacrifice, he came down. [23]Moses and Aaron
then entered the meeting tent. When they
came out, they blessed the people, and the
LORD's glorious presence appeared to all
the people. [24]Fire flew out from before the
LORD and devoured the entirely burned offering and the fat pieces on the altar. All the
people saw it. They shouted for joy and fell
facedown.

Nadab and Abihu

10 Now Nadab and Abihu, two of Aaron's
sons, each took an incense pan. They
put fire and incense on them and offered unauthorized fire before the LORD, which he
had not commanded them. [2]Then fire flew
out from before the LORD and devoured
them, and they died before the LORD.
[3]Moses said to Aaron, "When the LORD
said, 'I will show that I am holy among
those near me, and before all the people I
will manifest my glorious presence,' this is
what he meant!" But Aaron was silent.
[4]Then Moses called Mishael and Elzaphan the sons of Uzziel, Aaron's uncle, and
told them, "Go carry your relatives out from
the front of the sanctuary to a place outside
the camp." [5]So they went forward and carried Nadab and Abihu out by their tunics to
a place outside the camp, just as Moses had
ordered. [6]Moses then said to Aaron and his
sons, Eleazar and Ithamar, "Don't dishevel
your hair and don't rip your clothes into
pieces, or you will die and bring anger upon
the whole community. Your family—all of
Israel's house—will mourn the burning the
LORD has done. [7]But you must not leave
the meeting tent, or you will die because
the LORD's anointing oil is on you." So they
did what Moses ordered.

Priestly drinking and eating

[8]The LORD said to Aaron: [9]Both you
and your sons must not drink wine or beer
when you enter the meeting tent so that
you don't die—this is a permanent rule
throughout your future generations—[10]so
that you can distinguish between the holy
and the common, and between the unclean
and the clean, [11]and so that you can teach
the Israelites all the rules that the LORD
spoke to them through Moses.
[12]Moses then told Aaron and his remaining sons, Eleazar and Ithamar, "Take the
grain offering that is left over from the
LORD's food gifts and eat it unleavened
next to the altar, because it is most holy.
[13]You must eat it in a holy place because
it is your portion and your sons' portion
from the LORD's food gifts, as I have been
commanded. [14]You must eat the breast for
the uplifted offering and the thigh for the
gift offering in a clean place—both you and
your sons and daughters. These things are
designated as your portion and your children's portion from the Israelites' communal sacrifices of well-being. [15]The Israelites
must bring the thigh for the gift and the
breast for the uplifted offering along with
the food gifts of the fat pieces, to be lifted
up as an uplifted offering before the LORD.
These will belong to both you and your children as a permanent portion, just as the
LORD has commanded."
[16]Then Moses asked about the male
goat for the purification offering, and discovered that it had already been burned.
He was angry with Eleazar and Ithamar,
Aaron's remaining sons, and asked, [17]"Why
didn't you eat the purification offering in
the holy area? It's most holy, and it was assigned to you for bearing the community's

punishment by making reconciliation for them before the LORD. [18]Since its blood wasn't brought into the sanctuary's interior, you were to have eaten it in the sanctuary, just as I was commanded."[s]

[19]"Look," Aaron said to Moses, "today they offered their purification offerings and their entirely burned offerings before the LORD, but these things still happened to me! Would the LORD have approved if I had eaten a purification offering today?" [20]When Moses heard that, he approved.[t]

Dietary rules

11 The LORD said to Moses and Aaron: [2]Say to the Israelites: These are the creatures that you are allowed to eat from the land animals: [3]You can eat any animal that has divided hoofs, completely split, and that rechews food. [4]But of animals that rechew food and have divided hoofs you must not eat the following: the camel—though it rechews food, it does not have divided hoofs, so it is unclean for you; [5]the rock badger—though it rechews food, it does not have divided hoofs, so it is unclean for you; [6]the hare—though it rechews food, it does not have divided hoofs, so it is unclean for you; [7]the pig—though it has completely divided hoofs, it does not rechew food, so it is unclean for you. [8]You must not eat the flesh of these animals or touch their dead bodies; they are unclean for you.

[9]You are allowed to eat the following from all water animals: You may eat anything in the water that has fins and scales, whether in sea or stream. [10]But anything in the seas or streams that does not have fins and scales—whether it be any of the swarming creatures in the water or any of the other living creatures in the water—is detestable to you [11]and must remain so. You must not eat their flesh, and you must detest their dead bodies. [12]Anything in the water that does not have fins or scales is detestable to you.

[13]Of the birds, the following are the ones you must detest—they must not be eaten; they are detestable: the eagle, the black vulture, the bearded vulture, [14]the kite, any kind of falcon, [15]any kind of raven, [16]the eagle owl, the short-eared owl, the long-eared owl, any kind of hawk, [17]the tawny owl, the fisher owl, the screech owl, [18]the white owl, the scops owl, the osprey, [19]the stork, any kind of heron, the hoopoe, and the bat.[u]

[20]Any flying insect that walks on four feet is detestable to you, [21]but you can eat four-footed flying insects that have jointed legs above their feet with which they hop on the ground. [22]Of these you can eat the following: any kind of migrating locust, any kind of bald locust, any kind of cricket, and any kind of grasshopper. [23]But every other flying insect that has four feet is detestable to you.

Unclean animals

[24]You make yourself unclean by the following animals—whoever touches their dead bodies will be unclean until evening, [25]and anyone who carries any part of their dead bodies must wash their clothes and will be unclean until evening: [26]All animals that have divided hoofs, but they are not completely split, and that do not rechew food are unclean for you—whoever touches them will be unclean. [27]Of all the animals that walk on four feet, the ones that walk on their paws are unclean for you—anyone who touches their dead bodies will be unclean until evening. [28]Anyone who carries one of their dead bodies must wash their clothes and will be unclean until evening; these animals are unclean for you.

[29]The following are unclean for you among the small creatures that move about on the ground: the rat, the mouse, any kind of large lizard, [30]the gecko, the spotted lizard, the lizard, the skink, and the chameleon.[v] [31]Of all small moving creatures, these are unclean for you—anyone who touches them when they are dead will be unclean until evening. [32]Moreover, anything on which one of these creatures falls

[s]Syr, Tg, Vulg; MT *as I commanded;* cf 8:31 [t]Or *he was satisfied.* [u]Many of the species in 11:13-19 cannot be identified with certainty. [v]Many of the species in 11:29-30 cannot be identified with certainty.

when it is dead will be unclean, whether it is wood, cloth, skin, or funeral clothing—any such item that can be used to do work. It must be put into water and will be unclean until evening. Then it will be clean again. 33If any of these creatures fall into a pottery jar, everything inside it will be unclean; you must smash the pot. 34If water from such a jar gets on any edible food, it will be unclean; any drinkable beverage in such a jar will be unclean. 35Anything on which a part of these animals' dead bodies might fall will be unclean. If it is an oven or stove, it must be destroyed; they are unclean for you and must remain that way. 36Now, a spring or cistern that collects water is clean, but anyone who touches one of these animals' dead bodies in it will be unclean.[w] 37If any part of these animals' dead bodies falls on seed that is to be planted, the seed is still clean. 38But if water is poured on some seed and part of their dead bodies falls on it, it is unclean for you.

39If one of the animals that you are allowed to eat dies naturally, anyone who touches its dead body will be unclean until evening. 40Anyone who eats from the dead body must wash their clothes and will be unclean until evening. Anyone who carries such a dead body must wash their clothes and will be unclean until evening.

41Every creature that swarms on the earth is detestable; it must not be eaten. 42Among all such creatures that swarm on the earth, you must not eat anything that moves on its belly or anything that walks on four or more feet because they are detestable. 43Do not make yourselves detestable by means of any swarming creatures. Do not make yourselves unclean with them or be made unclean by them. 44I am the LORD your God. You must keep yourselves holy and be holy, because I am holy. You must not make yourselves unclean by any swarming creature that crawls on the ground. 45I am the LORD, who brought you up from the land of Egypt to be your God. You must be holy, because I am holy.

Conclusion concerning animals and diet

46This concludes the Instruction concerning animals, birds, all creatures that live in water, and all the creatures that swarm on the earth, 47in order to distinguish between the unclean and the clean and between creatures that can be eaten and those that cannot.

Purification after childbirth

12 The LORD said to Moses: 2Say to the Israelites: If a woman conceives a child and gives birth to a son, she will be unclean for seven days—just as she is during her menstrual period. 3On the eighth day, the flesh of the boy's foreskin must be circumcised. 4For thirty-three days the mother will be in a state of blood purification. She must not touch anything holy or enter the sacred area until her time of purification is completed. 5But if the woman gives birth to a daughter, she will be unclean for two weeks—just as she is during her menstrual period—and will be in a state of blood purification[x] for sixty-six days.

6When the time of purification is complete, whether for a son or a daughter, the mother must bring a one-year-old lamb as an entirely burned offering and a pigeon or turtledove as a purification offering to the priest at the meeting tent's entrance. 7The priest will present it before the LORD and make reconciliation for her. She will then be cleansed from her blood flow. This is the Instruction for any woman who has a child, male or female. 8But if the mother cannot afford a sheep, she can bring two turtledoves or two pigeons—one for the entirely burned offering and the other for the purification offering. The priest will then make reconciliation for her, and she will be clean.

Diagnosis of skin disease

13 The LORD said to Moses and Aaron, 2When a person has a swelling, a scab, or a shiny spot on their skin, and it becomes an infection of skin disease[y] on their

[w]Heb lacks *in it.* [x]Heb uncertain [y]The precise meaning is uncertain; traditionally *leprosy*—a term used for several different skin diseases.

skin, they will be brought to the priests, either to Aaron or one of his sons. [3]The priest will examine the infection on the skin. If hair in the infected area has turned white and the infection appears to be deeper than the skin, then it is an infection of skin disease. Once the priest sees this, he will declare the person unclean. [4]But if the shiny spot on the skin is white and does not appear to be deeper than the skin and the hair has not turned white, the priest will quarantine the infected person for seven days. [5]On the seventh day the priest will again examine the infection. If he sees that it has remained the same—the infection has not spread on the skin—the priest will quarantine the person for seven more days. [6]On the seventh day the priest will examine it again. If the infection has faded and has not spread over the skin, the priest will declare the person clean; it is just a rash. The person must wash their clothes, then they will be clean again. [7]But if the rash continues to spread over the skin after they appeared before the priest for purification, they must again show themselves to the priest. [8]If the priest sees that the rash has spread over the skin, the priest will declare the person unclean; it is a case of skin disease.

[9]Whenever someone has an infection of skin disease, they will be brought to the priest. [10]If the priest sees that there is a white swelling on the skin, it has turned the hair white, and there is a patch of raw flesh in the swelling, [11]then it is a case of chronic skin disease on their skin. The priest will declare the person unclean. The priest will not quarantine such persons, because they are already unclean. [12]But if the skin disease continues to break out so that the disease covers all of the infected person's skin from head to toe, as far as the priest can tell—[13]then the priest will make an examination. If the skin disease has covered the person's whole body, the priest will declare the infected person clean. The person has turned entirely white; he is clean. [14]But as soon as raw flesh appears in the swelling, they will be unclean. [15]When the priest sees the raw flesh, he will declare the person unclean. Raw flesh is unclean; it is a case of skin disease. [16]But if the raw flesh turns white again, the person will go back to the priest. [17]The priest will examine it. If the infection has turned white, the priest will declare the infected person clean; at that point, the person is clean.

[18]Whenever someone has a boil on their skin, it heals, [19]and in place of the boil there is a white swelling or reddish-white shiny spot, it must be shown to the priest. [20]If the priest sees that it appears to be lower than the skin, and its hair has turned white, the priest will declare the person unclean. It is an infection of skin disease that has broken out in the boil. [21]But if the priest examines it and there is no white hair in it, it is not lower than the skin, and it is faded, the priest will quarantine the person seven days. [22]If it continues to spread over the skin, the priest will declare the person unclean; it is an infection. [23]But if the shiny spot remains where it was and does not spread, it is just a scar from the boil. The priest will declare the person clean.

[24]Whenever there is a burn on someone's skin, and the raw patch of the burn becomes a reddish-white or white shiny spot, [25]the priest will examine it. If the hair has turned white in the shiny spot, and it appears to be deeper than the skin, it is a case of skin disease that has broken out in the burn. The priest will declare the person unclean; it is an infection of skin disease. [26]But if the priest examines it, and there is no white hair in the shiny spot, it is not lower than the skin, and it is faded, the priest will quarantine the person seven days. [27]On the seventh day the priest will again examine it. If it has continued to spread over the skin, the priest will declare the person unclean; it is an infection of skin disease. [28]But if the shiny spot remains where it was, has not spread over the skin, and is faded, it is just swelling from the burn. The priest will declare the person clean, because it is just the scar from the burn.

[29]Whenever a man or woman has an infection, whether on the head or in the beard, [30]the priest will examine it. If it

appears to be deeper than the skin, and
there is thin yellow hair in it, the priest
will declare the person unclean; it is a case
of scabies—a skin disease of the head or
beard. 31When the priest examines the scabies infection, if it does not appear to be
deeper than the skin, but there is no black
hair in it, the priest will quarantine the
person with the scabies infection for seven
days. 32On the seventh day the priest will
examine the infection again. If the scabies
has not spread, there is no yellow hair in it,
and it does not appear to be deeper than
the skin, 33the person must shave the area,
without shaving the scabies. The priest will
then quarantine that person another seven
days. 34On the seventh day the priest will
again examine the scabies. If it has not
spread over the skin and does not appear
to be deeper than the skin, the priest will
declare the person clean. They must wash
their clothes; then they will be clean again.
35But if the scabies continues to spread
over the skin after the person's purification, 36the priest must examine it again. If
the scabies has spread over the skin at all,
the priest does not need to look for the yellow hair; the person is unclean. 37But if the
priest sees that the scabies has remained
the same, and black hair has grown in it,
the scabies has healed. The person is clean,
and the priest will declare them to be so.

38Whenever a man or woman has many
white shiny spots on their skin, 39if the
priest sees that there are faded white shiny
spots on the skin of the body, it is just a
rash that has broken out on the skin; the
person is clean.

40If someone loses their hair, they are
bald, but they are clean. 41If the hair is lost
at the sides of the forehead, the person has
a receding hairline, but they are clean. 42But
whenever there is a reddish-white infection
in the bald spot or in the receding hairline,
it is a case of skin disease breaking out
there. 43The priest must examine it. If the
swelling of the infection is reddish white
in the bald spot or receding hairline and
resembles skin disease on the body, 44the
person is afflicted with skin disease; they
are unclean. The priest must declare them
unclean on account of the head infection.

45Anyone with an infection of skin disease must wear torn clothes, dishevel their
hair, cover their upper lip, and shout out,
"Unclean! Unclean!" 46They will be unclean as long as they are infected. They
are unclean. They must live alone outside
the camp.

Articles with skin disease

47Whenever there is an infection of skin
disease on clothing—on wool or linen clothing, 48in the weaving of the linen or wool, or
on a skin or skin item—49and the infection
is greenish or reddish on the clothing, the
weaving, or the skin or skin item, it is an
infection of skin disease. It must be shown
to the priest. 50The priest will examine the
infection and quarantine the infected item
seven days. 51On the seventh day he will examine the infection again. If the infection
has spread in the clothing, the weaving, or
the skin, whatever it is used for, the infection is a case of infectious skin disease; the
item is unclean. 52The priest will burn the
clothing, the weaving of the wool or linen,
or whatever skin item in which the infection was found, because it is an infectious
skin disease; it must be burned with fire.

53But if the priest sees that the infection
has not spread in the clothing, the weaving,
or on any skin item, 54the priest will order
that the infected piece be washed, and he
will quarantine it for another seven days.
55After it has been washed, if the priest
sees that the infection has not changed its
appearance, even though the infection has
not spread, it is unclean. You must burn it
with fire. It is a fungus,[z] whether it is on the
inside or outside.

56But if, after it is washed, the priest sees
that the infection has faded, he will tear the
infected part out of the cloth, the weaving, or the skin. 57If it appears again in the
cloth, the weaving, or any item of skin, it is
starting to break out. You must burn the infected item with fire. 58But if the infection

[z]Heb uncertain

disappears from the cloth, the weaving, or any item of skin that you washed, it must be washed again. Then it will be clean.

[59]This concludes the Instruction about the infection of skin disease in a woolen or linen cloth, weaving, or any skin item, in order to declare whether it is clean or unclean.

Persons with skin disease

14 The LORD said to Moses, [2]This will be the Instruction for anyone with skin disease[a] at the time of purification: When it has been reported to the priest, [3]he will go outside the camp. If the priest sees that the person afflicted with skin disease has been healed of the infection, [4]the priest will order that two birds—wild[b] and clean—and cedarwood, crimson yarn, and hyssop be brought for the person who needs purification. [5]The priest will order that one bird be slaughtered over fresh water in a pottery jar. [6]He will then take the other wild bird, along with the cedarwood, crimson yarn, and hyssop, and will dip all of this into the blood of the bird that was slaughtered over the fresh water. [7]He will sprinkle the person who needs purification from skin disease seven times and declare that they are clean. Then the priest will release the wild bird into the countryside. [8]The person who needs purification will then wash their clothes, shave off all of their hair, and bathe in water; at that point, they will be clean. After that, they can return to the camp, but they must live outside their tent for seven days. [9]On the seventh day, the person must shave off all their hair again: head, beard, and eyebrows—everything. They must wash their clothes and bathe in water; then they will be clean again.

[10]On the eighth day, that person must take two flawless male sheep, one flawless one-year-old ewe, a grain offering of three-tenths of an ephah[c] of choice flour mixed with oil, and one log[d] of oil. [11]The priest performing the purification will place these and the person needing purification before the LORD at the meeting tent's entrance.

[12]The priest will take one of the male sheep and present it as a compensation offering, along with the log of oil, and will lift them as an uplifted offering before the LORD. [13]The priest will slaughter the sheep at the same place where the purification offering and the entirely burned offering are slaughtered: in the holy area. The compensation offering, like the purification offering, belongs to the priest; it is most holy. [14]The priest will take some of the blood from the compensation offering and will put it on the right earlobe, the right thumb, and the right big toe of the person needing purification. [15]Then the priest will take some of the log of oil and pour it into his left palm. [16]The priest will then dip his right finger into the oil and sprinkle some of it with his finger seven times before the LORD. [17]Then the priest will put some of the oil that is left in his hand on the right earlobe, the right thumb, and the right big toe of the person needing purification—this oil will be placed on top of the blood of the compensation offering. [18]The priest will put whatever is left of the oil in his hand on the head of the person needing purification. In this way, the priest will make reconciliation for the person before the LORD.

[19]The priest will then perform the purification offering and make reconciliation for the person needing purification from their uncleanness. After that, the entirely burned offering will be slaughtered. [20]The priest will offer up the entirely burned offering and the grain offering on the altar. In this way, the priest will make reconciliation for the person, and they will be clean again.

[21]Now if the person is poor and cannot afford these things, they can bring one male sheep as a compensation offering, to be lifted up in order to make reconciliation for them; a grain offering of one-tenth of an ephah of choice flour mixed with oil; a log of oil; [22]and two turtledoves or two pigeons, whatever they can afford—one as a purification offering and the other as an entirely burned offering. [23]On the eighth day,

[a]The precise meaning is uncertain; traditionally *leprosy*—a term used for several different skin diseases.
[b]Or *live* or *healthy;* also in 14:6-7 [c]Heb lacks *ephah*; an *ephah* is approximately twenty quarts dry. [d]Heb *log*; two-thirds of a pint; also in 14:12, 15, 21, 24

they must bring these items for their purification to the priest at the meeting tent's entrance before the LORD.

24The priest will take the male sheep for the compensation offering and the log of oil, and will lift them as an uplifted offering before the LORD. 25The priest will slaughter the sheep for the compensation offering and will take some of its blood and put it on the right earlobe, the right thumb, and the right big toe of the person needing purification. 26The priest will pour some of the oil into his left palm. 27Next, the priest will sprinkle some of the oil seven times before the LORD using his right finger. 28The priest will then put some of the oil that is in his hand on the right earlobe, the right thumb, and the right big toe of the person needing purification—on top of the same places as the blood of the compensation offering. 29The priest will put whatever is left of the oil in his hand on the head of the person needing purification, to make reconciliation for them before the LORD.

30The person will then offer one of the turtledoves or pigeons, whatever they can afford—31one as a purification offering and the other as an entirely burned offering along with the grain offering.[e] In this way, the priest will make reconciliation before the LORD for the person needing purification.

32This is the Instruction concerning those who have an infection of skin disease but who cannot afford the normal means of purification.

Houses with skin disease

33The LORD said to Moses and Aaron: 34When you enter the land of Canaan, which I am giving to you as a possession, and I put an infection of skin disease on a house in the land you possess, 35the homeowner must come and tell the priest, "I think some sort of infection is in my house." 36The priest will order that the house be emptied before he comes to examine it so that nothing else in the house will become unclean. After that, the priest will come to examine the house. 37If he examines the infection, and the infection in the walls of the house consists of greenish or reddish depressions, which appear to be deeper than the surface of the wall, 38the priest will exit the house, go to the front door, and quarantine the house for seven days. 39On the seventh day, the priest will return. If he finds that the infection has spread over the walls of the house, 40the priest will order the stones in which the infection is found to be pulled out and discarded outside the city in an unclean area. 41The inside of the house will then be scraped on all sides, and the plaster that has been scraped off must be dumped outside the city in an unclean area. 42Then different stones will be used in place of the first ones, and new coating will be used to replaster the house.

43If the infection breaks out again in the house after the stones have been pulled out and the house scraped and replastered, 44the priest will return. If he finds that the infection has spread throughout the house, it is a case of infectious skin disease in the house; the house is unclean. 45The house must be destroyed—its stones, wood, and all the plaster in the house. All of it must be taken outside the city to an unclean area. 46Anyone who enters the house during the entire period when it is quarantined will be unclean until evening. 47Anyone who lies down in the house must wash their clothes. Anyone who eats in the house must also wash their clothes.

48But if the priest arrives and finds that the infection has not spread after the house was replastered, the priest will declare the house clean because the infection has been healed. 49To cleanse the house, the priest will take two birds, cedarwood, crimson yarn, and hyssop. 50He will slaughter one bird over fresh water in a pottery jar. 51He will then take the cedarwood, hyssop, and crimson yarn, along with the wild[f] bird, and will dip all of this into the fresh water and into the blood of the bird that was slaughtered. He will then sprinkle the house seven times. 52In this way, the priest will cleanse the house with the blood of the bird, the fresh

[e]LXX, Syr; MT repeats *whatever they can afford* at the beginning of 14:31. [f]Or *live* or *healthy*

water, the wild bird, the cedarwood, the hyssop, and the crimson yarn. 53Then he will release the wild bird outside the city into the countryside. In this way, he will make reconciliation for the house, and it will be clean.

Conclusion concerning skin disease

54This concludes the Instruction concerning every infection of surface disease: for scabies, 55for skin disease on clothing or in houses, 56and for swelling, scabs, or shiny spots, 57in order to determine when it is unclean or clean. This concludes the Instruction concerning skin disease.

Male genital emissions

15 The LORD said to Moses and Aaron: 2Speak to the Israelites and say to them: Whenever a man has a genital emission, that emission is unclean. 3This is the nature of the uncleanness brought about by his emission: regardless of whether his genital organ allows his emission to flow or blocks the flow, it is unclean to him. 4Any bed on which someone with an emission lies will be unclean, and any object on which that person sits will be unclean. 5Anyone who touches such a bed must wash their clothes, bathe in water, and will be unclean until evening. 6Anyone who sits on something that the one with the emission also sat on must wash their clothes, bathe in water, and will be unclean until evening. 7Anyone who touches the body of the one with the emission must wash their clothes, bathe in water, and will be unclean until evening. 8If the one with the emission spits on a clean person, the clean person must wash their clothes, bathe in water, and will be unclean until evening. 9Every saddle on which the person with the emission rode will be unclean. 10Anyone who touches anything that has been under such a person will be unclean until evening. Anyone who carries such items must wash their clothes, bathe in water, and will be unclean until evening. 11If the one with the emission touches someone without first rinsing his hands with water, that person must wash their clothes, bathe in water, and will be unclean until evening. 12Any pottery jar that the one with the emission touches must be broken, and any wooden tool must be rinsed with water.

13When the man with the emission is cleansed of his emission, he will count off seven days for his purification. He must wash his clothes and bathe his body in running water; then he will be clean again. 14On the eighth day he will take two turtledoves or two pigeons and come before the LORD to the meeting tent's entrance and give these to the priest. 15The priest will offer them, one as a purification offering and the other as an entirely burned offering. In this way, the priest will make reconciliation for him before the LORD because of his emission.

16If it is an emission of semen, the man must bathe his whole body in water and will be unclean until evening. 17Any clothing or skin on which there is an emission of semen must be washed in water and will be unclean until evening. 18If a man lies with a woman and has an emission of semen, both of them must bathe in water and will be unclean until evening.

Female genital emissions

19Whenever a woman has a discharge of blood that is her normal bodily discharge, she will be unclean due to her menstruation for seven days. Anyone who touches her will be unclean until evening. 20Anything on which she lies or sits during her menstruation will be unclean. 21Anyone who touches her bed must wash their clothes, bathe in water, and will be unclean until evening. 22Anyone who touches anything on which she has sat must wash their clothes, bathe in water, and will be unclean until evening. 23Whenever anyone touches something—whether it was on the bed or where she has been sitting—they will be unclean until evening. 24If a man has sexual intercourse with her and her menstruation gets on him, he will be unclean for seven days. Any bed he lies on will be unclean.

25Whenever a woman has a bloody discharge for a long time, which is not during her menstrual period, or whenever she has a discharge beyond her menstrual period, the duration of her unclean discharge will

be like the period of her menstruation;
she will be unclean. 26 Any bed she lies on
during the discharge should be treated like
the bed she uses during her menstruation;
and any object she sits on will be unclean,
as during her menstruation. 27 Anyone who
touches these things will be unclean. They
must wash their clothes, bathe in water,
and will be unclean until evening.

28 When the woman is cleansed of her
discharge, she will count off seven days;
after that, she will be clean again. 29 On the
eighth day she will take two turtledoves or
two pigeons and bring them to the priest
at the meeting tent's entrance. 30 The priest
will perform a purification offering with
one and an entirely burned offering with
the other. In this way, the priest will make
reconciliation for her before the LORD because of her unclean discharge.

31 You must separate the Israelites from
their uncleanness so that they don't die on
account of it, by making my dwelling[g] unclean, which is in their midst.

32 This concludes the Instruction concerning those with discharges: men with
emissions of semen that make them unclean, 33 women during their menstruation,
men or women with discharges, and men
who have had sexual intercourse with an
unclean woman.

The Day of Reconciliation

16 After the death of Aaron's two sons,
which happened when they approached the LORD and died, the LORD
spoke to Moses: 2 Tell your brother Aaron
that he cannot come whenever he wants
into the holy area inside the inner curtain,
to the front of the cover[h] that is on the chest,
or else he will die, because I am present[i] in
the cloud above the cover. 3 No, but Aaron
must enter the holy area as follows: with a
bull from the herd as a purification offering
and a ram as an entirely burned offering.
4 Aaron must dress in a holy linen tunic and
wear linen undergarments on his body. He
must tie a linen sash around himself and
wrap a linen turban around his head. These
are holy clothes—Aaron will first bathe his
body in water and then put them on. 5 He
will take from the Israelite community two
male goats for a purification offering and
one ram for an entirely burned offering.

6 Aaron will offer the bull as a purification offering to make reconciliation for
himself and his household. 7 He will take
the two male goats and place them before
the LORD at the meeting tent's entrance.
8 Aaron will cast lots over the two goats:
one lot labeled "the LORD's" and the other
lot labeled "Azazel's."[j] 9 Aaron will present
the goat selected by the LORD's lot and perform a purification offering with it. 10 But
the goat selected by Azazel's lot will be left
standing alive before the LORD in order to
make reconciliation upon it[k] by sending it
away into the wilderness to Azazel.

11 Aaron will offer the bull for his purification offering to make reconciliation for
himself and his household. He will slaughter the bull for his purification offering.
12 Then he will take an incense pan full of
burning coals from the altar, from before the LORD, and two handfuls of finely
ground perfumed incense and bring them
inside the inner curtain. 13 He will put the
incense on the fire before the LORD so that
the cloud of incense conceals the cover that
is on top of the covenant document, or else
he will die. 14 He will take some of the bull's
blood and sprinkle it with his finger on
the cover from the east side. He will then
sprinkle some of the blood with his finger
seven times in front of the cover. 15 Then
he will slaughter the goat for the people's
purification offering, bring the blood inside the inner curtain, and do with it as he
did with the bull's blood: he will sprinkle it
on the cover and in front of the cover. 16 In
this way, he will make reconciliation for the
inner holy area because of the pollution of
the Israelites and because of their rebellious sins, as well as for all their other sins.

Aaron must do the same for the meeting tent, which is with them among their

[g] Or *tabernacle* [h] Or *mercy seat* or perhaps *reconciliation cover* (Heb *kapporet*) [i] Or *I am seen* or *I appear*
[j] Or *scapegoat* [k] Or *over it* or *for it* or *with it*

pollution. [17]No one can be in the meeting tent from the time Aaron enters to make reconciliation in the inner holy area until the time he comes out. He will make reconciliation for himself, for his household, and for the whole assembly of Israel.

[18]Aaron will then go to the altar that is before the LORD and make reconciliation for it: He will take some of the bull's blood and some of the goat's blood and put it on each of the altar's horns. [19]He will sprinkle some of the blood on the altar with his finger seven times. In this way, he will purify it and make it holy again from the Israelites' pollution.

[20]When Aaron has finished reconciling the inner holy area, the rest of the meeting tent, and the altar, he will bring forward the live goat. [21]Aaron will press both his hands on its head and confess over it all the Israelites' offenses and all their rebellious sins, as well as all their other sins, putting all these on the goat's head. Then he will send it away into the wilderness with someone designated for the job.[l] [22]The goat will carry on itself all their offenses to a desolate region, then the goat will be released into the wild.

[23]After this, Aaron will enter the meeting tent, take off the linen clothes he was wearing when he entered the inner holy area, and will leave them there. [24]He will bathe his body in water in a holy place and dress in his priestly clothing. Then he will go out and perform the entirely burned offerings for himself and for the people. In this way, he will make reconciliation for himself and for the people. [25]He will completely burn the fat of the purification offering on the altar. [26]The one who set the goat free for Azazel must wash their clothes and bathe their body in water; after that they can return to the camp. [27]The bull and the goat for the purification offerings, whose blood was brought in to make reconciliation in the inner holy area, will be taken outside the camp. Their hides, flesh, and dung will be burned with fire. [28]The person who burns them must wash their clothes and bathe their body in water; after that, they can return to the camp.

[29]This will be a permanent rule for you: On the tenth day of the seventh month,[m] you must deny yourselves. You must not do any work—neither the citizen nor the immigrant who lives among you. [30]On that day reconciliation will be made for you in order to cleanse you. You will be clean before the LORD from all your sins. [31]It will be a Sabbath of special rest for you, and you will deny yourselves. This is a permanent rule.

Conclusion concerning the Day of Reconciliation

[32]The priest who is anointed and ordained to serve as priest after his father will perform the reconciliation, wearing the holy linen clothes. [33]He will reconcile the holiest part of the sanctuary and will do the same for the meeting tent and the altar. He will make reconciliation for the priests and for all the people of the assembly. [34]This will be a permanent rule for you, in order to make reconciliation for the Israelites from all their sins once a year.

It was done just as the LORD commanded Moses.

Sacrifice at the sanctuary

17 The LORD said to Moses, [2]Say to Aaron, to his sons, and to all the Israelites: This is what the LORD has commanded: [3]Anyone from the house of Israel who slaughters an ox, sheep, or goat inside or outside the camp [4]but does not bring it to the meeting tent's entrance to present it as an offering to the LORD in front of the LORD's dwelling[n] will be considered guilty of bloodshed; they have spilled blood. They will be cut-off from their people. [5]This will make the Israelites bring the communal sacrifices, which they are sacrificing in the countryside, to the LORD, to the priest at the meeting tent's entrance, and sacrifice them as communal sacrifices of well-being to the LORD. [6]The priest will toss the blood against the LORD's altar at the meeting tent's entrance and burn the fat completely as a soothing smell to the LORD. [7]The Israelites must no longer sacrifice their com-

[l]Heb uncertain [m]September–October, Tishrei [n]Or *tabernacle*

munal sacrifices to the goat demons that they follow so faithlessly.[o] This will be a permanent rule for them throughout their future generations. 8 You will also say to them: Anyone from Israel's house or from the immigrants who live with you who offers up an entirely burned offering or communal sacrifice 9 without bringing it to the meeting tent's entrance in order to offer it to the LORD will be cut off from their people.

Consuming blood forbidden

10 I will oppose the person who consumes blood—whether they are from Israel's house or from the immigrants who live with you—and I will cut them off from their people. 11 A creature's life is in the blood. I have provided you the blood to make reconciliation for your lives on the altar, because the blood reconciles by means of the life.[p] 12 That is why I have told the Israelites: No one among you can consume blood, nor can the immigrant who lives with you consume blood.

13 Anyone who hunts any animal or bird that can be eaten—whether the hunter is an Israelite or an immigrant who lives with you—must drain its blood out and cover it with dirt. 14 Again: for every creature's life, its blood is its life. That is why I have told the Israelites: You must not consume any creature's blood because every creature's life is its blood. Anyone who consumes it will be cut off.

Eating meat

15 Anyone, whether citizen or immigrant, who eats an animal that has died naturally or that was killed by another animal, must wash their clothes, bathe in water, and will be unclean until evening. At that time, they will be clean again. 16 If they do not wash or bathe their body, they will be liable to punishment.

Sexual conduct

18 The LORD said to Moses, 2 Speak to the Israelites and say to them: I am the LORD your God. 3 You must not do things like they are done in the land of Egypt, where you used to live. And you must not do things like they are done in the land of Canaan, where I am bringing you. You must not follow the practices[q] of those places. 4 No, my regulations and my rules are the ones you must keep by following them: I am the LORD your God. 5 You must keep my rules and my regulations; by doing them one will live; I am the LORD.

6 No one is allowed to approach any blood relative for sexual contact:[r] I am the LORD. 7 You must not uncover your father's nakedness, which is your mother's nakedness. She is your mother; you must not have sexual contact with her. 8 You must not uncover the nakedness of your father's wife; it is your father's nakedness. 9 You must not have sexual contact with your sister—regardless of whether she is your father's daughter or your mother's daughter, whether born into the same household as you or outside it. 10 You must not have sexual contact with your son's daughter or your daughter's daughter, because their nakedness is your own nakedness.[s] 11 You must not have sexual contact with the daughter of your father's wife, who was born into your father's family; she is your sister. 12 You must not have sexual contact with your father's sister; she is your father's blood relative. 13 You must not have sexual contact with your mother's sister because she is your mother's blood relative. 14 You will not uncover the nakedness of your father's brother—that is, you will not approach his wife for sex; she is your aunt. 15 You must not have sexual contact with your daughter-in-law; she is your son's wife. You must not have sexual contact with her. 16 You will not uncover the nakedness of your brother's wife; it is your brother's nakedness.

17 You must not have sexual contact with a woman and her daughter. You will not marry her son's daughter or her daughter's daughter, thereby uncovering her nakedness. They are her blood relatives; it is shameful. 18 You must not marry your

[o] Or *promiscuously* [p] Or *as life* [q] Or *rules* or *customs* [r] Or *to uncover nakedness* [s] Heb uncertain

wife's sister as a rival and have sexual contact with her while her sister is alive. [19]You
must not approach a woman for sexual
contact during her menstrual uncleanness.
[20]You must not have sexual relations with
the wife of your fellow Israelite, becoming
unclean by it.
[21]You must not give any of your children[t]
to offer them over to Molech so that you do
not defile your God's name: I am the LORD.
[22]You must not have sexual intercourse
with a man as you would with a woman; it
is a detestable practice. [23]You will not have
sexual relations with any animal, becoming unclean by it. Nor will a woman present
herself before an animal to mate with it; it
is a perversion.

Warning against uncleanness and moral pollution

[24]Do not make yourselves unclean in
any of these ways because that is how the
nations that I am throwing out before you
became unclean. [25]That is also how the
land became unclean, and I held it liable
for punishment, and the land vomited out
its inhabitants. [26]But all of you must keep
my rules and my regulations. You must not
do any of these detestable things, neither
citizen nor immigrant who lives with you
([27]because the people who had the land before you did all of these detestable things
and the land became unclean), [28]so that the
land does not vomit you out because you
have made it unclean, just as it vomited out
the nations that were before you. [29]Anyone
who does any of these detestable things will
be cut off from their people. [30]You must
keep my requirement of not doing any of
the detestable practices[u] that were done
before you arrived so that you don't make
yourselves unclean by them; I am the LORD
your God.

Living as holy people

19 The LORD said to Moses, [2]Say to the
whole community of the Israelites:
You must be holy, because I, the LORD your
God, am holy. [3]Each of you must respect
your mother and father, and you must keep
my sabbaths; I am the LORD your God. [4]Do
not turn to idols or make gods of cast metal
for yourselves; I am the LORD your God.
[5]When you sacrifice a communal sacrifice
of well-being to the LORD, offer it so that it
will be accepted on your account. [6]It must
be eaten on the day of your sacrifice or the
following day; whatever is left over on the
third day must be burned with fire. [7]If any
of it is eaten on the third day, it is foul; it
will not be accepted. [8]Anyone who eats it
will be liable to punishment, because they
defiled what is holy to the LORD. That person will be cut off from their people. [9]When
you harvest your land's produce, you must
not harvest all the way to the edge of your
field; and don't gather up every remaining
bit of your harvest. [10]Also do not pick your
vineyard clean or gather up all the grapes
that have fallen there. Leave these items for
the poor and the immigrant; I am the LORD
your God.
[11]You must not steal nor deceive nor lie
to each other. [12]You must not swear falsely
by my name, desecrating your God's name
in doing so; I am the LORD. [13]You must
not oppress your neighbors or rob them.
Do not withhold a hired laborer's pay overnight. [14]You must not insult a deaf person
or put some obstacle in front of a blind person that would cause them to trip. Instead,
fear your God; I am the LORD.
[15]You must not act unjustly in a legal
case. Do not show favoritism to the poor or
deference to the great; you must judge your
fellow Israelites fairly. [16]Do not go around
slandering your people.[v] Do not stand by
while your neighbor's blood is shed;[w] I am
the LORD. [17]You must not hate your fellow
Israelite in your heart. Rebuke your fellow
Israelite strongly, so you don't become responsible for his sin.[x] [18]You must not take
revenge nor hold a grudge against any of
your people; instead, you must love your
neighbor as yourself; I am the LORD.
[19]You must keep my rules. Do not cross-

[t]Or *seed* [u]Or *rules or customs* [v]Heb uncertain [w]Heb uncertain [x]Or *strongly, but don't become liable for punishment because of it*; Heb uncertain

breed your livestock, do not plant your field with two kinds of seed, and do not wear clothes made from two kinds of material. 20 If a man has sexual relations with a woman who is a slave engaged to another man, who hasn't yet been released or given her freedom, there must be a punishment.[y] But they will not be put to death because she had not yet been freed. 21 The man must bring as his compensation to the LORD at the meeting tent's entrance a ram for a compensation offering. 22 The priest will use the ram for the compensation offering to make reconciliation for him before the LORD on account of the sin he committed. Then he will be forgiven of the sin that he committed.

23 When you enter the land and plant any fruit tree, you must consider its fruit off-limits.[z] For three years it will be off-limits to you;[a] it must not be eaten. 24 In the fourth year, all of the tree's fruit will be holy, a celebration for the LORD. 25 In the fifth year you can eat the fruit. This is so as to increase its produce for you; I am the LORD your God.

26 You must not eat anything with its blood. You must not participate in divination or fortune-telling. 27 You must not cut off the hair on your forehead or clip the ends of your beard. 28 Do not cut your bodies for the dead[b] or put marks on[c] yourselves; I am the LORD. 29 Do not defile your daughter by making her sexually promiscuous or else the land will become promiscuous[d] and full of shame. 30 You must keep my sabbaths and treat my sanctuary with respect; I am the LORD. 31 Do not resort to dead spirits or inquire of spirits of divination—you will be made unclean by them; I am the LORD your God. 32 You must rise in the presence of an old person and respect the elderly. You must fear your God; I am the LORD.

33 When immigrants live in your land with you, you must not cheat them. 34 Any immigrant who lives with you must be treated as if they were one of your citizens. You must love them as yourself, because you were immigrants in the land of Egypt; I am the LORD your God. 35 You must not act unjustly in a legal case involving measures of length, weight, or volume. 36 You must have accurate scales and accurate weights, an accurate ephah[e] and an accurate hin.[f] I am the LORD your God, who brought you out of the land of Egypt. 37 You must keep all my rules and all my regulations, and do them; I am the LORD.

Worship of Molech forbidden

20 The LORD said to Moses, 2 You will also say to the Israelites: Any Israelite or any immigrant living in Israel who gives their children to Molech must be executed. The common people will stone such a person. 3 Moreover, I will set my own face against such a person, cutting them off from their people, because they gave their children to Molech, making my sanctuary unclean and degrading my holy name by doing so. 4 But if the common people choose to look the other way when someone gives their children to Molech and do not execute such a person, 5 I will set my own face against such a person and their extended family, cutting off from their people—both the guilty party and anyone with them who faithlessly followed Molech. 6 I will also oppose anyone who resorts to dead spirits or spirits of divination and faithlessly follows those things. I will cut such an individual off from their people.

Sexual prohibitions

7 You must be holy and keep yourselves holy because I am the LORD your God. 8 You will keep my rules and do them; I am the LORD, who makes you holy. 9 If anyone curses their father or mother, they must be executed. They have cursed their own father and mother; that person's blood is on their own heads. 10 If a man commits adultery with a married woman, committing adultery with a neighbor's wife, both the adulterer and the adulteress must be executed. 11 If a man has sexual intercourse with his father's wife, he has uncovered his father's nakedness. Both of them must be

[y] Or *an inquiry* [z] Or *treat its fruit as a foreskin* [a] Or *uncircumcised to you* [b] Or *for the living* [c] Or *tattoo*; Heb uncertain [d] Or *making her a prostitute so that the land won't become a prostitute* [e] Approximately twenty quarts [f] Approximately one gallon of liquid

executed; their blood is on their own heads. 12 If a man has sexual intercourse with his daughter-in-law, both of them must be executed. They have acted perversely; their blood is on their own heads. 13 If a man has sexual intercourse with a man as he would with a woman, the two of them have done something detestable. They must be executed; their blood is on their own heads. 14 If a man marries a woman and her mother as well, it is shameful. They will be burned with fire—the man and the two women—so that no such shameful thing will be found among you. 15 If a man has sexual relations with an animal, he must be executed and you must kill the animal. 16 If a woman approaches any kind of animal to mate with it, you must kill the woman and the animal. They must be executed; their blood is on their own heads. 17 If a man marries his sister—his father's daughter or his mother's daughter—and they have sexual contact with each other, it is a disgrace. They will be cut off in the sight of their people. Such a man has had sexual contact with his sister; he will be liable to punishment. 18 If a man sleeps with a woman during her menstrual period and has sexual contact with her, he has exposed the source of her blood flow and she has uncovered the same. Both of them will be cut off from their people. 19 You must not have sexual contact with your mother's sister or your father's sister, because that exposes your own close relative; both of you will be liable to punishment. 20 If a man has sexual intercourse with his aunt, he has uncovered his uncle's nakedness. The man and the aunt will be liable to punishment; they will die childless. 21 If a man marries his brother's wife, it is indecent. He has uncovered his brother's nakedness; the man and the woman will be childless.

Conclusion concerning conduct

22 You must keep all my rules and all my regulations, and do them so that the land I am bringing you to, where you will live, won't vomit you out. 23 You must not follow the practices[g] of the nations that I am throwing out before you, because they did all these things and I was disgusted with them. 24 But I have told you, "You will certainly possess their fertile land; I am giving it to you to possess. It is a land full of milk and honey." I am the LORD your God, who has separated you from all other peoples. 25 So you must separate between clean and unclean animals, and between clean and unclean birds. Do not become detestable through some animal, bird, or anything that moves on the fertile ground that I have separated from you as unclean. 26 You must be holy to me, because I the LORD am holy, and I have separated you from all other peoples to be my own. 27 If someone, whether male or female, is a medium with the dead or a diviner,[h] they must be executed. They will be stoned; their blood is on their own head.

Rules for priests

21 The LORD said to Moses, Say to the priests, Aaron's sons: None of you are allowed to make yourselves unclean by any dead person among your community 2 except for your closest relatives: for your mother, father, son, daughter, brother; 3 also for your unmarried sister, who is close to you because she isn't married—you may be polluted for her sake. 4 You must not make yourself unclean for in-laws, defiling yourself by doing so.

5 Priests must not shave bald patches on their heads or cut off the ends of their beards or make gashes in their bodies. 6 They must be holy to their God so that they do not make their God's name impure. They must be holy because they offer the LORD's food gifts, their God's food. 7 Priests must not marry a woman who is promiscuous and defiled, nor can they marry a woman divorced from her husband, because priests must be[i] holy to their God. 8 You will treat the priests as holy, because they offer your God's food. The priests will be holy to you, because I am the holy LORD, who makes you holy. 9 If the daughter of a priest defiles herself by being promiscuous, she defiles her father. She must be burned with fire.

[g] Or *rules or customs* [h] Or *has a spirit of the dead or a spirit of divination* [i] Or *are*

10 The high priest[j]—the one whose head
has been anointed with the anointing oil
and who is ordained to dress in the priestly
clothing—must not dishevel his hair or tear
his clothing. 11 He must not go near any dead
bodies and cannot make himself unclean
even for his father or mother. 12 He must
not exit the sanctuary, making his God's
sanctuary impure by doing so, because his
God's anointing oil, which separates,[k] is
upon him; I am the LORD. 13 The high priest
must marry a woman who is a virgin. 14 He
cannot marry a widow, a divorced woman,
or a woman defiled by promiscuity. He can
only marry a virgin from his own people
15 so that he doesn't make his children impure among his people, because I am the
LORD, who makes him holy.

16 The LORD said to Moses, 17 Say to Aaron:
None of your future descendants who have
some kind of imperfection are allowed to offer
their God's food. 18 No one who has an imperfection will be allowed to make an offering:
this includes anyone who is blind, crippled,
disfigured, or deformed; 19 anyone who has
a broken foot or hand; 20 anyone who is a
hunchback or too small; anyone who has an
eye disease, a rash, scabs, or a crushed testicle.[l]
21 No descendant of Aaron the priest who has
an imperfection will be allowed to offer the
LORD's food gifts; since he has an imperfection, he will not be allowed to offer his God's
food. 22 He may, of course, eat of his God's
most holy or holy food, 23 but since he has
an imperfection, he cannot enter toward the
inner curtain or officiate at the altar, making
these parts of my sanctuary impure by doing
so. I am the LORD, who makes them holy.

24 This is what Moses said to Aaron, his
sons, and to all the Israelites.

Priestly uncleanness

22 The LORD said to Moses: 2 Tell Aaron
and his sons to be very careful how
they treat the holy things that the Israelites
devote to me so that they do not make my
holy name impure: I am the LORD. 3 Say to
them: If any descendant of yours should
ever come near the holy things that the Israelites have dedicated to the LORD while
he is in an unclean state, he will be cut off
from before me; I am the LORD. 4 Any descendant of Aaron who is afflicted with
skin disease[m] or has a discharge cannot eat
of the holy things until he is clean. Anyone who touches anything made unclean
by a dead body, or who has an emission
of semen, 5 or who touches any swarming
creature or another person who makes
him unclean—whatever the uncleanness
might be—6 the person who touches these
things will be unclean until evening. He
must not eat of the holy things unless he
has bathed his body in water. 7 Once the sun
has set and he has become clean again, he
may eat of the holy things, for that is his
food. 8 He must not eat an animal that has
died naturally or that was killed by another
animal, becoming unclean by doing so; I am
the LORD. 9 The priests must keep my requirement so that they don't become liable
to punishment and die for having made it
impure.[n] I am the LORD, who makes them
holy.

Unauthorized eating

10 No layperson is allowed to eat the holy
offerings. No foreign guest or hired laborer
of a priest can eat it. 11 But if a priest pur-
chases a servant, that person can eat it, and
servants born into the priest's household
can also eat his food. 12 If a priest's daughter marries a layman, she is not allowed
to eat the holy offerings. 13 But if a priest's
daughter is a widow or divorced and has
no children and so returns to her father's
household as when she was young, she can
eat her father's food. But, again, no layperson is allowed to eat it. 14 If someone
eats a holy offering unintentionally, they
must provide the priest with an equal item,
plus one-fifth. 15 The Israelites must not
make the holy offerings impure that they
offer up to the LORD 16 or make themselves
liable to punishment requiring compensation by eating their own holy offerings. I am
the LORD, who makes them holy.

[j] Or *the priest who is greater than his brothers* [k] Or *consecrates* [l] The meaning of several words in 21:18-20 is uncertain. [m] The precise meaning is uncertain; traditionally *leprosy*—a term used for several different skin diseases. [n] Vulg; MT *and die in it*

Unacceptable animal offerings

[17]The LORD said to Moses: [18]Tell Aaron, his sons, and all the Israelites: Whenever someone from Israel's house or from the immigrants in Israel presents their offering to the LORD as an entirely burned offering—whether it is payment for a solemn promise or a spontaneous gift—[19]for it to be acceptable on your behalf, it must be a flawless male from the herd, the sheep, or the goats. [20]You must not present anything that has an imperfection, because it will not be acceptable on your behalf. [21]Whenever someone presents a communal sacrifice of well-being to the LORD from the herd or flock—whether it is payment for a solemn promise or a spontaneous gift—it must be flawless to be acceptable; it must not have any imperfection. [22]You must not present to the LORD anything that is blind or that has an injury, mutilation, warts, a rash, or scabs. You must not put any such animal on the altar as a food gift for the LORD. [23]You can, however, offer an ox or sheep that is deformed or stunted as a spontaneous gift, but it will not be acceptable as payment for a solemn promise. [24]You must not offer to the LORD anything with bruised, crushed, torn, or cut-off testicles. You must not do that in your land. [25]You are not allowed to offer such animals as your God's food even if they come from a foreigner. Because these animals have blemishes and imperfections in them, they will not be acceptable on your behalf.

Additional rules for sacrifice

[26]The LORD said to Moses: [27]When an ox or sheep or goat is born, it must remain with its mother for seven days. From the eighth day on it will be acceptable as an offering, a food gift for the LORD. [28]But you will not slaughter an ox or sheep and its offspring on the same day. [29]When you sacrifice a communal sacrifice of thanksgiving for the LORD, you must sacrifice it so that it will be acceptable on your behalf. [30]It must be eaten on the same day; you must not leave any of it until morning; I am the LORD. [31]You must keep my commands and do them; I am the LORD. [32]You must not make my holy name impure so that I will be treated as holy by the Israelites. I am the LORD—the one who makes you holy [33]and who is bringing you out of the land of Egypt to be your God; I am the LORD.

Sacred times

23 The LORD said to Moses: [2]Speak to the Israelites and say to them: These are my appointed times, the LORD's appointed times, which you will declare to be holy occasions: [3]Work can be done for six days, but the seventh day is a Sabbath of special rest, a holy occasion. You must not do any work on it; wherever you live, it is a Sabbath to the LORD. [4]These are the LORD's appointed times, holy occasions, which you will celebrate at their appointed times:

[5]The LORD's Passover is on the fourteenth day of the first month[o] at twilight. [6]The LORD's Festival of Unleavened Bread is on the fifteenth day of the same month. You must eat unleavened bread for seven days. [7]On the first day you will hold a holy occasion and must not do any job-related work. [8]You will offer food gifts to the LORD for seven days. The seventh day will be a holy occasion; you must not do any job-related work.

[9]The LORD said to Moses: [10]Speak to the Israelites and say to them: When you enter the land that I am giving you and harvest its produce, you must bring the first bundle of your harvest to the priest. [11]The priest will lift up the bundle before the LORD so that it will be acceptable on your behalf. The priest will do this on the day after the Sabbath. [12]On the day the bundle is lifted up for you, you must offer a flawless one-year-old lamb as an entirely burned offering to the LORD. [13]The accompanying grain offering must be two-tenths of an ephah[p] of choice flour mixed with oil, as a food gift for the LORD, a soothing smell. The accompanying drink offering must be a quarter of a hin of wine. [14]You must not eat any bread, roasted grain, or fresh grain until the exact day when you bring your God's offering.

[o]March–April, Nisan [p]Four quarts dry; also in 23:17

This is a permanent rule throughout your
future generations, wherever you live.
15You must count off seven weeks starting with the day after the Sabbath, the day
you bring the bundle for the uplifted offering; these must be complete. 16You will
count off fifty days until the day after the
seventh Sabbath. Then you must present
a new grain offering to the LORD. 17From
wherever you live, you will bring two loaves
of bread as an uplifted offering. These
must be made of two-tenths of an ephah
of choice flour, baked with leaven, as early
produce[q] to the LORD. 18Along with the
bread you must present seven flawless one-
year-old lambs, one bull from the herd, and
two rams. These will be an entirely burned
offering to the LORD, along with their grain
offerings and drink offerings, as a food gift
of soothing smell to the LORD. 19You must
also offer one male goat as a purification offering and two one-year-old lambs as a communal sacrifice of well-being. 20The priest
will lift up the two sheep, along with the
bread of the early produce, as an uplifted
offering before the LORD. These will be holy
to the LORD and will belong to the priest.
21On that very same day you must make a
proclamation; it will be a holy occasion for
you. You must not do any job-related work.
This is a permanent rule wherever you
live throughout your future generations.
22When you harvest your land's produce,
you must not harvest all the way to the
edge of your field; and don't gather every
remaining bit of your harvest. Leave these
items for the poor and the immigrant; I am
the LORD your God.
23The LORD said to Moses: 24Say to the
Israelites: On the first day of the seventh
month,[r] you will have a special rest, a holy
occasion marked by a trumpet signal. 25You
must not do any job-related work, and you
must offer a food gift to the LORD.
26The LORD said to Moses: 27Note that
the tenth day of this seventh month is the
Day of Reconciliation. It will be a holy occasion for you. You must deny yourselves and
offer a food gift to the LORD. 28You must
not do any work that day because it is a Day
of Reconciliation to make reconciliation for
you before the LORD your God. 29Anyone
who does not deny themselves on that day
will be cut off from their people. 30More-
over, I will destroy from their people anyone who does any work on that day. 31You
must not do any work! This is a permanent
rule throughout your future generations
wherever you live. 32This is a Sabbath of
special rest for you, and you must deny
yourselves. You will observe your Sabbath
on the ninth day of the month from evening to the following evening.
33The LORD said to Moses: 34Say to the
Israelites: The Festival of Booths to the
LORD will start on the fifteenth day of the
seventh month and will last for seven days.
35The first day is a holy occasion. You must
not do any job-related work. 36For seven
days you will offer food gifts to the LORD.
On the eighth day you will have a holy occasion and must offer a food gift to the LORD.
It is a holiday: you must not do any job-
related work.
37These are the LORD's appointed times
that you will proclaim as holy occasions,
offering food gifts to the LORD: entirely
burned offerings, grain offerings, communal sacrifices, and drink offerings—each
on its proper day. 38This is in addition to
the LORD's sabbaths and in addition to
your presents, all the payments for solemn
promises, and all the spontaneous gifts
that you give to the LORD.
39Note that on the fifteenth day of the
seventh month, when you have gathered
the land's crops, you will celebrate the
LORD's festival for seven days. The first day
and the eighth day are days of special rest.
40On the first day you must take fruit from
majestic trees,[s] palm branches, branches
of leafy trees,[t] and willows of the streams,
and rejoice before the LORD your God for
seven days. 41You will celebrate this festival
to the LORD for seven days each year; this
is a permanent rule throughout your future

[q]Or *firstfruits*; also in 23:20 [r]September–October, Tishrei; also in 23:27, 33, 39, 41 [s]Or *hadar trees*
[t]Heb uncertain

generations. You will celebrate it in the seventh month. [42]For seven days you must live in huts. Every citizen of Israel must live in huts [43]so that your future generations will know that I made the Israelites live in huts when I brought them out of the land of Egypt; I am the LORD your God.

[44]So Moses announced the LORD's appointed times to the Israelites.

The sanctuary's lamp and bread

24 The LORD said to Moses: [2]Command the Israelites to bring pure, pressed olive oil to you for the lamp, to keep a light burning constantly. [3]Aaron will tend the lamp, which will be inside the meeting tent but outside the inner curtain of the covenant document, from evening until morning before the LORD. This is a permanent rule throughout your future generations. [4]Aaron must continually tend the lights on the pure lampstand[u] before the LORD.

[5]You will take choice flour and bake twelve loaves of flatbread, two-tenths of an ephah[v] for each loaf. [6]You must place them in two stacks, six in a stack, on the pure table[w] before the LORD. [7]Put pure frankincense on each stack, as a token portion for the bread; it is a food gift for the LORD. [8]Aaron will always set it out before the LORD, Sabbath after Sabbath, on behalf of[x] the Israelites, as a permanent covenant. [9]It will belong to Aaron and his sons. They must eat it in a holy place because it is the most holy part of their share of the LORD's food gifts, a permanent portion.

Assault and blasphemy

[10]The son of an Israelite mother and an Egyptian father came out among the Israelites. A fight broke out between this half-Israelite[y] and another Israelite man in the camp, [11]during which the half-Israelite blasphemed the Lord's name and cursed. So he was brought to Moses. (His mother's name was Shelomith, Dibri's daughter from the tribe of Dan.) [12]He was put under guard until they could determine the LORD's verdict.

[13]Then the LORD said to Moses: [14]Take the one who cursed outside the camp. All who heard him will press their hands on his head. Then the whole community will stone him. [15]Tell the Israelites: Anyone who curses God will be liable to punishment. [16]And anyone who blasphemes the LORD's name must be executed. The whole community will stone that person. Immigrant and citizen alike: whenever someone blasphemes the Lord's name, that person will be executed.

[17]If anyone kills another person, they must be executed. [18]Someone who kills an animal may make amends for it: a life for a life. [19]If someone injures a fellow citizen, they will suffer the same injury they inflicted: [20]broken bone for broken bone, an eye for an eye, a tooth for a tooth. The same injury the person inflicted on the other will be inflicted on them. [21]Someone who kills an animal must make amends for it, but whoever kills a human being must be executed. [22]There is but one law on this matter for you, immigrant or citizen alike, because I am the LORD your God.

[23]Moses told this to the Israelites. So they took the one who had cursed outside the camp and stoned him. The Israelites did just as the LORD commanded Moses.

The sabbatical year

25 The LORD said to Moses on Mount Sinai, [2]Speak to the Israelites and say to them: Once you enter the land that I am giving you, the land must celebrate a sabbath rest to the LORD. [3]You will plant your fields for six years, and prune your vineyards and gather their crops for six years. [4]But in the seventh year the land will have a special sabbath rest, a Sabbath to the LORD: You must not plant your fields or prune your vineyards. [5]You must not harvest the secondary growth of your produce or gather the grapes of your freely growing vines. It will be a year of special rest for the land. [6]Whatever the land produces during its sabbath will be your food—for you, for your male and female servants, and for

[u]Perhaps *pure gold lampstand* [v]Approximately four quarts dry [w]Perhaps *pure gold table* [x]Or *from* or *as a gift of*; Heb uncertain [y]Or *Israelite woman's son*; also in 24:11

your hired laborers and foreign guests who live with you, [7]as well as for your livestock and for the wild animals in your land. All of the land's produce can be eaten.

The Jubilee year

[8]Count off seven weeks of years—that is, seven times seven—so that the seven weeks of years totals forty-nine years. [9]Then have the trumpet[z] blown on the tenth day of the seventh month.[a] Have the trumpet blown throughout your land on the Day of Reconciliation. [10]You will make the fiftieth year holy, proclaiming freedom throughout the land to all its inhabitants. It will be a Jubilee year[b] for you: each of you must return to your family property and to your extended family. [11]The fiftieth year will be a Jubilee year for you. Do not plant, do not harvest the secondary growth, and do not gather from the freely growing vines [12]because it is a Jubilee: it will be holy to you. You can eat only the produce directly out of the field. [13]Each of you must return to your family property in this year of Jubilee.

[14]When you sell something to or buy something from your fellow citizen, you must not cheat each other. [15]You will buy from your fellow citizen according to the number of years since the Jubilee; he will sell to you according to the number of years left for harvests. [16]You will raise the price if there are more years, or lower the price if there are less years because it is the number of harvests that are being sold to you. [17]You must not cheat each other but fear your God because I am the LORD your God. [18]You will observe my rules, and you will keep my regulations and do them so that you can live securely on the land.

Food during fallow years

[19]The land will give its fruit so that you can eat your fill and live securely on it. [20]Suppose you ask, "What will we eat in the seventh year if we don't plant or gather our crops then?" [21]I will send my blessing on you in the sixth year so that it will make enough produce for three years. [22]You can plant again in the eighth year and eat food from the previous year's produce until the ninth year. Until its produce comes, you will eat the food from the previous year.

Buying back family property

[23]The land must not be permanently sold because the land is mine. You are just immigrants and foreign guests of mine.

[24]Throughout the whole land that you possess, you must allow for the land to be bought back. [25]When one of your fellow Israelites faces financial difficulty and must sell part of their family property, the closest relative[c] will come and buy back what their fellow Israelite has sold. [26]If the person doesn't have someone to buy it back, but then manages to afford buying it back, [27]they must calculate the years since its sale and refund the balance to the person to whom they sold it. Then it will go back to the family property.[d] [28]If they cannot afford to make a refund to the buyer, whatever was sold will remain in the possession of the buyer until the Jubilee year. It will be released in the Jubilee year, at which point it will return to the family property.

[29]When a person sells a home in a walled city, it may be bought back until a year after its sale. The period for buying it back will be one year. [30]If it is not bought back before a full year has passed, the house in the walled city will belong to the buyer permanently and their descendants forever. It will not be released at the Jubilee. [31]But houses in settlements that are unwalled will be considered as if they were country fields. They can be bought back, and they must be released at the Jubilee.

[32]Levites will always have the right to buy back homes in the levitical cities that are part of their family property. [33]Levite property that can be bought back—houses sold in a city that is their family property—must be released at the Jubilee, because homes in levitical cities are the Levites'

[z]Heb *shofar* [a]September–October, Tishrei [b]Heb *yobel* [c]Or *next of kin*; traditionally *redeemer* [d]Or *they will go back to their family property;* also in 25:28.

family property among the Israelites. 34But
the pastureland around their cities cannot
be sold, because that is their permanent
family property.

Poor Israelites and slavery

35If one of your fellow Israelites faces
financial difficulty and is in a shaky situation with you,[e] you must assist them as
you would an immigrant or foreign guest
so that they can survive among you. 36Do
not take interest from them, or any kind of
profit from interest, but fear your God so
that your fellow Israelite can survive among
you. 37Do not lend a poor Israelite money
with interest or lend food at a profit. 38I am
the LORD your God, who brought you out
from the land of Egypt to give you Canaan's
land and to be your God.

39If one of your fellow Israelites faces
financial difficulty with you and sells themselves to you, you must not make him work
as a slave. 40Instead, they will be like a hired
laborer or foreign guest to you. They will
work for you until the Jubilee year, 41at
which point the poor Israelite along with
their children will be released from you. They
can return to their extended family and to
their family property. 42You must do this
because these people are my servants—I
brought them out of Egypt's land. They must
not be sold as slaves. 43You will not harshly
rule over them but must fear your God.

44Regarding male or female slaves that
you are allowed to have: You can buy a male
or a female slave from the nations that are
around you. 45You can also buy them from
the foreign guests who live with you and
from their extended families that are with
you, who were born in your land. These can
belong to you as property. 46You can pass
them on to your children as inheritance
that they can own as permanent property.
You can make these people work as slaves,
but you must not rule harshly over your
own people, the Israelites.

47If an immigrant or foreign guest prospers financially among you, but your fellow Israelite faces financial difficulty and
so sells themselves to the immigrant or
foreign guest, or to a descendant of a foreigner, 48the Israelite will have the right to
be bought back after they sold themselves.
One of their relatives can buy them back:
49their uncle or cousin can buy them back;
one of their blood relatives from their
family can buy them back; or they may be
able to afford their own purchase. 50The
Israelite will calculate with their owner the
time from the year they were sold until the
Jubilee year. The price of their release will
be based on the number of years they were
with the owner, as in the case of a hired laborer. 51If there are many years left before
the Jubilee, the Israelite will pay for their
purchase in proportion to their purchase
price. 52If only a few years are left, they will
calculate that and pay for their purchase
according to the years of service. 53Regard-
less, the Israelite will be to the buyer like a
yearly laborer; the buyer must not harshly
rule over them in your sight. 54If the Israelite is not bought back in one of these ways,
they and their children must be released
in the Jubilee year 55because the Israelites belong to me as servants. They are my
servants—I brought them out of Egypt's
land; I am the LORD your God.

Covenant blessings

26 You must not make any idols, and
do not set up any divine image or sacred pillar. You must not place any carved[f]
stone in your land, bowing down to it, because I am the LORD your God. 2You must
keep my sabbaths and respect my sanctuary; I am the LORD.

3If you live according to my rules, keep
my commands, and do them, 4I will give
you rain at the proper time, the land will
produce its yield, and the trees of the field
will produce their fruit. 5Your threshing
season will last until the grape harvest,
and the grape harvest will last until planting time. You will eat your fill of food and
live securely in your land. 6I will grant peace
in the land so that you can lie down without anyone frightening you. I will remove

[e] Heb uncertain [f] Heb uncertain

dangerous animals from the land, and no sword will pass through it. 7 You will chase your enemies, and they will fall before you in battle. 8 Five of you will chase away a hundred, and a hundred of you will chase away ten thousand, and your enemies will fall before you in battle. 9 I will turn my face to you, will make you fruitful and numerous, and will keep my covenant with you. 10 You will still be eating the previous year's harvest when the time will come to clear it out to make room for the new! 11 I will place my dwelling[g] among you, and I will not despise you. 12 I will walk around among you; I will be your God, and you will be my people. 13 I am the LORD your God, who brought you out of Egypt's land—who brought you out from being Egypt's slaves. I broke your bonds and made you stand up straight.

Covenant curses

14 But if you do not obey me and do not carry out all these commands—15 if you reject my rules and despise my regulations, not doing all my commands and breaking my covenant—16 then I will do the following to you:

I will bring horrific things:[h] wasting diseases and fevers that make the eyes fail and drain life away.

You will plant seed for no reason because your enemies will eat the food.

17 I will turn my face against you: you will be defeated by your enemies; those who hate you will rule over you; and you will run away even when no one is chasing you.

18 If, despite all that, you still do not obey me, I will punish you for your sins seven more times: 19 I will destroy your prideful power. I will turn your sky to iron and your land to bronze 20 so that your strength will be spent for no reason: your land will not produce its yield, and the trees of the land won't produce their fruit.

21 If you continue to oppose me and are unwilling to obey me, I will strike you for your sins seven more times: 22 I will send wild animals against you, and they will kill your children and destroy your livestock. They will make you so few in number that your roads will seem deserted.

23 If, despite these things, you still do not accept my discipline and continue to oppose me, 24 then I will continue to oppose you. I will strike you for your sins seven more times: 25 I will bring the sword against you, avenging the breaking of the covenant.[i] If you retreat into your cities, I will send a plague on you, and you will be handed over to the enemy. 26 When I destroy your food supply, ten women will bake bread in a single oven, and they will ration out bread by weight. You will eat but will never get full.

27 If, despite all this, you still do not obey me and continue to oppose me, 28 then I will continue to oppose you—with anger! I will punish you for your sins seven more times: 29 You will eat the flesh of your own sons and daughters. 30 I will eliminate your shrines, chop down your incense altars, and pile your dead bodies on the dead bodies of your idols. I will despise you. 31 I will turn your cities into ruins, I will devastate your sanctuaries, and I will not smell the soothing smells of your offerings. 32 I will personally devastate the land so much that your enemies who resettle it will be astonished by it. 33 I will scatter you among the nations. I will unsheathe my sword against you. Your land will be devastated and your cities will be ruins.

34 At that time, while it is devastated and you are in enemy territory, the land will enjoy its sabbaths. At that time, the land will rest and enjoy its sabbaths. 35 During the whole time it is devastated, it will have the rest it didn't have during the sabbaths you lived in it.

36 I will bring despair into the hearts of those of you who survive in enemy territory. Just the sound of a windblown leaf will put them to running, and they will run scared as if running from a sword! They will fall even when no one is chasing them! 37 They will stumble over each other as they would before a sword, even though no one is chasing them! You will have no power to stand before your enemies. 38 You will disappear

[g]Or *tabernacle* [h]Precise nature of the diseases uncertain [i]Or *executing covenant vengeance*

among the nations—the land of your enemies will devour you. 39 Any of you who do survive will rot in enemy territory on account of their guilty deeds. And they will rot too on account of their ancestors' guilty deeds.

Covenant and restoration

40 But if they confess their and their ancestors' guilt for the wrongdoing they did to me, and for their continued opposition to me—41 which made me oppose them, so I took them into enemy territory—or if their uncircumcised hearts are humbled and they make up for their guilt, 42 then I will remember my covenant with Jacob. I will also remember my covenant with Isaac. And my covenant with Abraham. And I will remember the land. 43 The land will be absent of them and will be enjoying its sabbaths while it lies devastated, free of them. They will be making up for their guilty deeds for no other reason than the fact that they rejected my regulations and despised my rules. 44 But despite all that, when they are in enemy territory, I will not reject them or despise them to the point of totally destroying them, breaking my covenant with them by doing so, because I am the LORD their God. 45 But for their sake I will remember the covenant with the first generation, the ones I brought out of Egypt's land in the sight of all the nations, in order to be their God; I am the LORD.

46 These are the rules, regulations, and instructions between the LORD and the Israelites that he gave through Moses on Mount Sinai.

Dedications

27 The LORD said to Moses, 2 Speak to the Israelites and say to them: When a person makes a solemn promise to the LORD involving the value of a person, 3 if it is the value for a male between 20 and 60 years old, his value is fifty silver shekels according to the sanctuary's shekel. 4 If the person is a female, her value is thirty shekels. 5 If the age of the person is between 5 and 20 years, the value for a male is twenty shekels, for a female ten shekels. 6 If the age of the person is between one month and 5 years, the value for a male is five silver shekels, for a female three silver shekels. 7 If the age of the person is 60 years or more, the value is fifteen shekels if the person is male, ten shekels for a female. 8 But if financial difficulty prevents the promise maker from giving the full value, they must set the person before the priest. The priest will assign the person a value according to what the promise maker can afford.

9 If a solemn promise involves livestock that can be offered to the LORD, any such animal given to the LORD will be considered holy. 10 The promise maker cannot replace or substitute for it, either good for bad or bad for good. But if one should substitute one animal for another, both it and the substitute will be holy. 11 If the solemn promise involves any kind of unclean animal that cannot be offered to the LORD, the promise maker must set the animal before the priest. 12 The priest will assign it a value, whether high or low.[j] Its value will be what the priest says. 13 If the promise maker wishes to buy it back, they must add one-fifth to its value.

14 When someone dedicates their house to the LORD as holy, the priest will assign a value to it, whether high or low. The value is fixed, whatever value the priest assigns to it. 15 If the one who dedicates the house wishes to buy it back, they must add one-fifth to its valued price, and it will be theirs again.

16 If a person dedicates part of the land from their family property to the LORD, the value will be set according to the seed needed to plant it: fifty silver shekels per homer of barley seed. 17 If the person dedicates the piece of land during the Jubilee year, its value will stay fixed. 18 But if the person dedicates the piece after the Jubilee year, the priest will calculate the price according to the years that are left until the next Jubilee year, and the value will be reduced. 19 If the one who dedicates the land wishes to buy it back, they must add one-fifth to its valued price, and it will be theirs again. 20 But if they do not buy it back or if

[j] Or *good or bad*; also in 27:14

it was sold to someone else, it is no longer able to be bought back. [21]When the piece of land is released in the Jubilee year, it will be holy to the LORD like a piece of devoted land; it will be the priest's property. [22]If the person dedicates land they purchased to the LORD—land that is not part of their family property—[23]the priest will calculate the amount of its value until the Jubilee year. The person must pay the value on that day as a holy donation to the LORD. [24]In the Jubilee year the piece of land will return to the seller, to the one who is the original owner of the family property. [25]Every value will be according to the sanctuary's shekel. The shekel will be twenty gerahs.

[26]But note that a person cannot dedicate any oldest offspring from livestock, which already belongs to the LORD because it is the oldest. Whether ox or sheep, it belongs to the LORD. [27]If it is an unclean animal, it may be bought back at its value plus twenty percent. If it is not bought back, it will be sold at its set value.

[28]Also note that everything someone devotes[k] to the LORD from their possessions—whether humans, animals, or pieces of land from their family property—cannot be sold or bought back. Every devoted thing is most holy to the LORD. [29]No human beings that have been devoted can be bought back; they must be executed.

[30]All tenth-part gifts[l] from the land, whether of seed from the ground or fruit from the trees, belong to the LORD; they are holy to the LORD. [31]If someone wishes to buy back part of their tenth-part gift, they must add one-fifth to it. [32]All tenth-part gifts from a herd or flock—every tenth animal that passes under the shepherd's staff—will be holy to the LORD. [33]The one bringing the tenth-part gift must not pick out the good from the bad, and cannot substitute any animal. But if one should substitute an animal, both it and the substitute will be holy and cannot be bought back.

[34]These are the commands that the LORD gave Moses on Mount Sinai for the Israelites.

NUMBERS

First census

1 The LORD spoke to Moses in the Sinai desert in the meeting tent on the first day of the second month,[a] in the second year after they left the land of Egypt: [2]Take a census of the entire Israelite community by their clans and their households, recording the name of every male, [3]20 years old and above, who is eligible for military service in Israel. These you and Aaron will enlist in their military units. [4]Take with you one man from each tribe who is the head of his household. [5]These are the names of the men who will assist you:

from Reuben, Elizur, Shedeur's son;
[6]from Simeon, Shelumiel,
Zurishaddai's son;
[7]from Judah, Nahshon,
Amminadab's son;
[8]from Issachar, Nethanel, Zuar's son;
[9]from Zebulun, Eliab, Helon's son;
[10]from Joseph's sons:
from Ephraim, Elishama,
Ammihud's son;
from Manasseh, Gamaliel,
Pedahzur's son;
[11]from Benjamin, Abidan, Gideoni's son;
[12]from Dan, Ahiezer,
Ammishaddai's son;
[13]from Asher, Pagiel, Ochran's son;
[14]from Gad, Eliasaph, Deuel's son;
[15]from Naphtali, Ahira, Enan's son.

[16]These are the ones appointed from the community, chiefs of their ancestral tribes and leaders of the divisions of Israel.

[17]Moses and Aaron took these men who were selected by name [18]and they assembled the entire community on the first day of the second month. They registered them by their clans and their households,

[k]Or *places under the ban* (also in 27:29), a technique of holy war, in which all is dedicated to the deity who helps in the battle; it often involved total destruction. [l]Or *tithes* [a]April–May, Iyar

recording the name of each male 20 years
old and above. 19 Moses enlisted them in
the Sinai desert just as the LORD commanded him.
20 There were the descendants of Reuben, Israel's oldest, registered by their
clans and their households. Every man
20 years old and above eligible for military service was individually recorded by
name. 21 Those enlisted from the tribe of
Reuben were 46,500.
22 There were the descendants of
Simeon, registered by their clans and
their households. Every male 20 years
old and above eligible for military service was individually recorded by name.
23 Those enlisted from the tribe of
Simeon were 59,300.
24 There were the descendants of
Gad, registered by their clans and their
households. The men 20 years old and
above eligible for military service were
recorded by name. 25 Those enlisted
from the tribe of Gad were 45,650.
26 There were the descendants of
Judah, registered by their clans and
their households. The men 20 years old
and above eligible for military service
were recorded by name. 27 Those enlisted
from the tribe of Judah were 74,600.
28 There were the descendants of Issachar, registered by their clans and
their households. The men 20 years old
and above eligible for military service
were recorded by name. 29 Those enlisted
from the tribe of Issachar were 54,400.
30 There were the descendants of Zebulun, registered by their clans and their
households. The men 20 years old and
above eligible for military service were
recorded by name. 31 Those enlisted from
the tribe of Zebulun were 57,400.
32 From Joseph's descendants there
were the descendants of Ephraim, registered by their clans and their households. The men 20 years old and above
eligible for military service were recorded by name. 33 Those enlisted from
the tribe of Ephraim were 40,500.
34 There were the descendants of
Manasseh, registered by their clans and
their households. The men 20 years old
and above eligible for military service
were recorded by name. 35 Those enlisted from the tribe of Manasseh were
32,200.
36 There were the descendants of Benjamin, registered by their clans and their
households. The men 20 years old and
above eligible for military service were
recorded by name. 37 Those enlisted from
the tribe of Benjamin were 35,400.
38 There were the descendants of Dan,
registered by their clans and their households. The men 20 years old and above
eligible for military service were recorded
by name. 39 Those enlisted from the tribe
of Dan were 62,700.
40 There were the descendants of
Asher, registered by their clans and their
households. The men 20 years old and
above eligible for military service were
recorded by name. 41 Those enlisted from
the tribe of Asher were 41,500.
42 There were the descendants of
Naphtali, registered by their clans and
their households. The men 20 years old
and above eligible for military service
were recorded by name. 43 Those enlisted
from the tribe of Naphtali were 53,400.
44 These are the ones who were enlisted
by Moses, Aaron, and the twelve chiefs of
Israel, each from his own household. 45 All
the Israelites 20 years old and above eligible
for military service in Israel were enlisted
by their households. 46 All those enlisted
were 603,550. 47 But the Levites, belonging
to their own ancestral tribe, weren't enlisted along with them.

The Levites' exclusion from the census

48 The LORD spoke to Moses: 49 You must
not enlist the tribe of Levi, nor should you
take their census along with the Israelites.
50 Rather, assign the Levites to the covenant dwelling, to all its equipment, and
to everything that belongs to it. They will
carry the dwelling and all its equipment,
perform its religious ceremonies, and camp
around the dwelling. 51 When it's time to
break camp, the Levites will take down the
dwelling; and when it's time to make camp,

the Levites will set up the dwelling. Any other person who approaches will be put to death. [52]The Israelites will camp each in their own place under the banner of their own military unit. [53]But the Levites will camp around the covenant dwelling so that God's anger will not strike the Israelite community. The Levites will guard the covenant dwelling.

[54]The Israelites did everything exactly as the LORD commanded Moses.

The wilderness camp's arrangement

2 The LORD spoke to Moses and Aaron: [2]The Israelites will camp each under the banner with the symbol of their household. They will camp around the meeting tent some distance from it.

The camp's east side

[3]On the east side toward the sunrise will be the banner of Judah's camp with its military units. The chief of the people of Judah is Nahshon, Amminadab's son. [4]His military unit and those enlisted in it are 74,600. [5]Those camping on one side of him are the tribe of Issachar. The chief of the people of Issachar is Nethanel, Zuar's son. [6]His military unit and those enlisted in it are 54,400. [7]On the other side, the tribe of Zebulun: the chief of the people of Zebulun is Eliab, Helon's son. [8]His military unit and those enlisted in it are 57,400. [9]All those enlisted in Judah's camp with their military units are 186,400. They will march first.

The camp's south side

[10]On the south side will be the banner of Reuben's camp with its military units. The chief of the people of Reuben is Elizur, Shedeur's son. [11]His military unit and those enlisted in it are 46,500. [12]Those camping on one side of him are the tribe of Simeon. The chief of the people of Simeon is Shelumiel, Zurishaddai's son. [13]His military unit and those enlisted in it are 59,300. [14]On the other side, the tribe of Gad: the chief of the people of Gad is Eliasaph, Reuel's son. [15]His military unit and those enlisted in it are 45,650. [16]All those enlisted in Reuben's camp with their military units are 151,450. They will march second.

The camp's center

[17]The meeting tent and the Levites' camp will march in the center of the camps. They will march in the same order as they camp: each in position under his banner.

The camp's west side

[18]On the west will be the banner of Ephraim's camp with its military units. The chief of the people of Ephraim is Elishama, Ammihud's son. [19]His military unit and those enlisted in it are 40,500. [20]On one side of him is the tribe of Manasseh. The chief of the people of Manasseh is Gamaliel, Pedahzur's son. [21]His military unit and those enlisted in it are 32,200. [22]On the other side, the tribe of Benjamin: the chief of the people of Benjamin is Abidan, Gideoni's son. [23]His military unit and those enlisted in it are 35,400. [24]All those enlisted in Ephraim's camp with their military units are 108,100. They will march third.

The camp's north side

[25]On the north will be the banner of Dan's camp with its military units. The chief of the people of Dan is Ahiezer, Ammishaddai's son. [26]His military unit and those enlisted in it are 62,700. [27]Those camping on one side of him are the tribe of Asher. The chief of the people of Asher is Pagiel, Ochran's son. [28]His military unit and those enlisted in it are 41,500. [29]On the other side, the tribe of Naphtali: the chief of the people of Naphtali is Ahira, Enan's son. [30]His military unit and those enlisted in it are 53,400. [31]All those enlisted in the camp of Dan are 157,600. They will march last under their banners.

[32]These are the enlisted Israelites by their households. The total enlisted in the camps with their military units is 603,550. [33]But the Levites weren't enlisted among the Israelites, as the LORD had commanded Moses. [34]The Israelites did everything exactly as the LORD had commanded Moses: they camped under their banners and they marched by their clans and by their households.

Aaron's sons

3 These are the descendants of Aaron and Moses at the time when the LORD spoke with Moses on Mount Sinai. [2]These are the names of Aaron's sons: Nadab the oldest, and Abihu, Eleazar, and Ithamar. [3]These are the names of Aaron's sons, who are the anointed priests and ordained to the priesthood. [4]Nadab and Abihu died before the LORD when they made an unauthorized offering to the LORD in the Sinai desert. They didn't have any sons. Eleazar and Ithamar served as priests during the lifetime of their father Aaron.

The Levites' first census

[5]The LORD spoke to Moses: [6]Bring near the tribe of Levi and place them before Aaron the priest. They will assist him. [7]They will perform duties for him and for the entire community before the meeting tent, doing the work of the dwelling. [8]They will be responsible for all the equipment of the meeting tent and the duties on behalf of the Israelites when they do the work of the dwelling. [9]You will give the Levites to Aaron and his sons. They have been assigned as a gift to him from the Israelites. [10]You will appoint Aaron and his sons to be responsible for the priesthood. Any other person who approaches will be put to death.

[11]The LORD spoke to Moses: [12]I claim the Levites from the Israelites in place of all the oldest males who open an Israelite womb. The Levites are mine [13]because all the oldest males are mine. When I killed all the oldest males in the land of Egypt, I reserved for myself all the oldest males in Israel, both humans and animals. They are mine; I am the LORD.

[14]The LORD spoke to Moses in the Sinai desert: [15]Enroll the Levites by their households and their clans. You will enroll all the males over one month old. [16]Moses enrolled them according to the LORD's word as he was commanded. [17]These were Levi's sons by name: Gershon, Kohath, and Merari. [18]These were the names of Gershon's sons by their clans: Libni and Shimei. [19]Kohath's sons by their clans: Amram, Izhar, Hebron, and Uzziel. [20]Merari's sons by their clans: Mahli and Mushi. These were the clans of Levi by their households.

[21]To Gershon belonged the clans of Libni and Shimei. These were the clans of the Gershonites. [22]Their enrollment, according to the number of males over one month old, was 7,500. [23]The clans of the Gershonites were to camp behind the dwelling on the west side. [24]The chief of the household of the Gershonites was Eliasaph, Lael's son. [25]In the dwelling, the Gershonites were responsible for the meeting tent, the tent with its covering, the screen for the entrance of the meeting tent, [26]the curtains of the courtyard, the screen for the entrance of the courtyard surrounding the meeting tent and the altar, and its cords—all these structures.

[27]To Kohath belonged the clans of the Amramites, Izharites, Hebronites, and Uzzielites. These were the clans of the Kohathites. [28]The number of males over one month old, who would perform duties for the sanctuary, was 8,600. [29]The clans of the Kohathites were to camp on the south side of the dwelling. [30]The chief of the household representing the clans of the Kohathites was Elizaphan, Uzziel's son. [31]They were responsible for the chest, the table, the lampstand, the altars, the equipment of the sanctuary with which they would minister, and the screen—all these furnishings. [32]The head chief over the chiefs of the Levites was Eleazar the son of Aaron the priest. He was supervisor over those performing the duties of the sanctuary.

[33]To Merari belonged the clans of Mahli and Mushi. These were the clans of the Merarites. [34]Their enrollment, according to the number of males over one month old, was 6,200. [35]The chief of the household representing the clans of the Merarites was Zuriel, Abihail's son. They were to camp on the north side of the dwelling. [36]The Merarites were assigned responsibility for the frames of the dwelling, its bars, pillars, bases, and all its equipment—all these items—[37]and the pillars of the courtyard all around, their bases, pegs, and cords.

[38]Those camping in front of the dwelling eastward (that is, before the meeting tent on the east side) were Moses, Aaron,

and his sons, who performed the duties of the sanctuary as service for the Israelites. Anyone else who approached would be put to death. [39]The total enrollment of the Levites, all the males over one month old whom Moses and Aaron enrolled by orders from the LORD, according to their clans, was 22,000.

Levites rescue the oldest male Israelites

[40]The LORD said to Moses: Enroll all the oldest males of the Israelites over one month of age and record their names. [41]Take the Levites for me, in place of all the oldest sons of the Israelites, for I am the LORD, and the cattle of the Levites in place of all the oldest cattle of the Israelites. [42]Moses enrolled all the oldest males of the Israelites as the LORD commanded. [43]All the oldest males over one month old, recorded by name according to their enrollment, were 22,273.

[44]Then the LORD spoke to Moses: [45]Take the Levites in place of all the oldest Israelites and the cattle of the Levites in place of their cattle. The Levites are mine; I am the LORD. [46]To rescue the 273 remaining oldest Israelites over and above the number of Levites, [47]you will receive five shekels each. You will receive them according to the sanctuary shekel of twenty gerahs to the shekel. [48]You will give the money for their rescue to Aaron and his sons.

[49]So Moses took the money from those rescued over and above the ones rescued by the Levites. [50]He took the money from the oldest of the Israelites, 1,365 shekels, according to the sanctuary shekel. [51]Moses gave the money for those rescued to Aaron and his sons according to the LORD's word, as the LORD commanded Moses.

Second census and the Levites' duties

The Kohathites' duties

4 The LORD spoke to Moses and Aaron: [2]Take a census of the Kohathites from among the Levites by their clans and their households, [3]from 30 to 50 years old, all who are eligible for service to do the work of the meeting tent. [4]These are the responsibilities of the Kohathites in the meeting tent: the most holy things.

[5]When it's time to break camp, Aaron and his sons will enter and take down the screening curtain, and they will cover the chest containing the covenant with it. [6]Then they will place a covering of fine leather[b] on it. They will spread a whole cloth of blue over it, and they will set its poles in place. [7]They will spread a blue cloth on the presentation table and place on it the plates, the dishes, the bowls, and the container for the drink offering. The usual bread will be on it. [8]They will spread on them a red cloth, cover it with fine leather, and set its poles in place. [9]They will take a blue cloth and cover the lampstand used for light, its lamps, its extinguishers, its trays, and all the containers for oil that are used in its service. [10]They will place it and its equipment in a covering of fine leather, and then place it on the carrying frame. [11]They will spread a blue cloth on the gold altar and cover it with fine leather. [12]They will take all the service equipment used in the sanctuary, place it in a blue cloth, and cover it with fine leather. Then they will place it on the carrying frame. [13]They will remove the ashes from the altar and spread a purple cloth on it. [14]They will place on it all the equipment used for servicing it, the censers, the meat fork, the shovels, the bowls, all the equipment of the altar. They will spread a covering of fine leather over it and then set its poles in place.

[15]Aaron and his sons will finish covering the sanctuary and all the equipment of the sanctuary when it is time to break camp. After that the Kohathites will enter to carry it, but they will not touch the sanctuary, lest they die. These are the objects in the dwelling that the Kohathites are to carry. [16]But Eleazar son of Aaron the priest will have oversight of the oil for lighting, the fragrant incense, the regular grain offering, and the anointing oil, as well as

[b]Or *dolphin skin*; see also 4:8, 10-12.

oversight of the entire dwelling and everything in it related to the sanctuary and its equipment.

[17]The LORD spoke to Moses and Aaron: [18]You must not let the tribe of the Kohathite clans be eliminated from the Levites. [19]This is what you must do for them so that they stay alive and don't die when they approach the most holy things. Aaron and his sons will enter and assign each of them his work and his load. [20]But they may not enter to look at the sanctuary even for a moment, lest they die.

The Gershonites' duties

[21]The LORD spoke to Moses: [22]Take a census of the Gershonites also, by their households and their clans. [23]You will enroll those from 30 to 50 years old, all who are eligible for service to do work in the dwelling. [24]This is the duty of the Gershonite clans for work and for carrying the load: [25]They will carry the fabric of the dwelling, the meeting tent with its covering, the outer covering of fine leather, the screen for the entrance of the meeting tent, [26]the curtains of the courtyard, the screen of the entrance at the gate of the courtyard that surrounds the meeting tent and the altar, their cords, and all their equipment for their work. They will do everything that needs to be done with these objects.

[27]All the duties of the Gershonites for carrying their load and for their work will be at the command of Aaron and his sons. You will assign to them the responsibility to carry their load. [28]This is the work of the Gershonite clans in the dwelling. Their responsibility will be under Ithamar son of Aaron the priest.

The Merarites' duties

[29]You will enroll the Merarites by their clans and their households. [30]You will enroll those from 30 to 50 years old, all who are eligible for service to do work in the meeting tent. [31]This is what they are responsible to carry as their work in the meeting tent: the frames of the meeting tent, its bars, pillars, and bases; [32]the pillars of the courtyard all around, with their bases, pegs, cords, and all the equipment used with them. You will list by name the objects they are required to carry. [33]This is the duty of the Merarite clans for all their work in the meeting tent under the supervision of Ithamar son of Aaron the priest.

Summary of the census

[34]So Moses, Aaron, and the chiefs of the community enrolled the Kohathites by their clans and their households, [35]those from 30 to 50 years old who were eligible for work in the meeting tent. [36]Their enrollment by their clans was 2,750. [37]These are the enrolled of the Kohathite clans, all who worked in the meeting tent and whom Moses and Aaron enrolled according to the LORD's command through Moses.

[38]The enrollment of the Gershonites by their clans and their households, [39]those 30 to 50 years old who were eligible for work in the meeting tent: [40]their enrollment by their clans and their households was 2,630. [41]These are the enrolled of the Gershonite clans, all who worked in the meeting tent, and whom Moses and Aaron enrolled according to the LORD's command.

[42]The enrollment of the Merarite clans by their clans and their households, [43]those 30 to 50 years old who were eligible for work in the meeting tent: [44]their enrollment by their clans was 3,200. [45]These are the enrolled of the Merarite clans, whom Moses and Aaron enrolled according to the LORD's command through Moses.

[46]All the enrolled Levites whom Moses, Aaron, and the chiefs of Israel enrolled by their clans and their households, [47]those 30 to 50 years old who were eligible to do the work and to carry the load of the meeting tent: [48]their enrollment was 8,580. [49]Each was enrolled by the LORD's command through Moses to work and to carry his load. Each was assigned just as the LORD had commanded Moses.

Instructions about purity in the camp

5 The LORD spoke to Moses: [2]Command the Israelites to send out from the camp anyone with a skin disease, an oozing discharge, or who has become unclean from con-

tact with a corpse. [3]You must send out both male and female. You must send them outside the camp so that they will not make their camp, where I live among them, unclean.

[4]The Israelites did so and sent them outside the camp. The Israelites did just what the LORD said to Moses.

[5]The LORD spoke to Moses: [6]Tell the Israelites: When a man or a woman commits any sin against anyone else, thus breaking faith with the LORD, that person becomes guilty. [7]Such persons will confess the sin they have done. Each will make payment for his guilt, add one-fifth more, and give it to the injured party. [8]If the person has no close relative to whom the payment can be made, then the compensation payment will go to the LORD for the priest. This is in addition to the ram of reconciliation by which the guilty party himself is reconciled. [9]Any gift offering from all the sacred donations that the Israelites offer will be the property of the priest. [10]The sacred donations belong to each person alone; whatever anyone gives to the priest will be his.

A woman accused of adultery

[11]The LORD spoke to Moses: [12]Speak to the Israelites and say to them: A man may suspect that his wife has had an affair[c] and has broken faith with him, [13]that a man has had intercourse with her unknown to her husband and that she has defiled herself in secret—even though there are no witnesses and she isn't caught. [14]If jealousy overcomes him and he is jealous of his wife who has defiled herself, or if jealousy overcomes him and he is jealous of his wife who hasn't defiled herself, [15]then the man will bring his wife to the priest. He will bring the offering required for her, one-tenth of an ephah[d] of barley flour. He will not pour oil on it, nor offer frankincense with it, because it is a grain offering for jealousy, a grain offering for recognition in order to recognize guilt.

[16]The priest will bring her close and make her stand before the LORD [17]The priest will take holy water in a clay jar, and taking dust from the floor of the dwelling, the priest will place it in the water. [18]The priest will make the woman stand before the LORD, let the hair of the woman hang down, and place the grain offering for recognition, that is, the grain offering for jealousy, in her hands. The water of bitterness that brings the curse will be in the hands of the priest.

[19]Then the priest will make her swear a solemn pledge, saying to the woman, "If no man has slept with you and if you haven't had an affair, becoming defiled while married to your husband, then be immune from the water of bitterness that brings these curses. [20]But if you have had an affair while married to your husband, if you have defiled yourself, and a man other than your husband has had intercourse with you"—[21]then the priest must make the woman utter the curse and say to the woman, "May the LORD make you a curse and a harmful pledge among your people, when the LORD induces a miscarriage and your womb discharges. [22]And may the water that brings these curses enter your stomach and make your womb discharge and make you miscarry."

And the woman will say, "I agree, I agree."

[23]The priest will write these curses in the scroll and wipe them off into the water of bitterness. [24]Then he will make the woman drink the water of bitterness that brings the curse. And the water that brings the curse will enter her, causing bitterness. [25]The priest will take the grain offering for jealousy from the woman's hands, elevate the grain offering before the LORD, and bring it to the altar. [26]The priest will take a handful of the grain offering as a token part of it and turn it into smoke on the altar. And afterward he will make the woman drink the water. [27]When he has made her drink the water, if she has defiled herself and has broken faith with her husband, then the water that brings the curse will enter her, causing bitterness, and her womb will discharge and she will miscarry. The woman will be a curse among her people. [28]But if the woman hasn't defiled herself and she is pure, then she will be immune and able to conceive.

[c]Or *goes astray*; see also 5:19-20, 29. [d]Two quarts; one ephah is approximately twenty quarts dry.

[29]These are the instructions about jealousy, when a wife has an affair while married to her husband and defiles herself, [30]or when jealousy overcomes a man and he is jealous of his wife. The priest will make the woman stand before the LORD and will follow all these instructions concerning her. [31]The man will be free from guilt, but the woman will bear her guilt.

Instructions for the nazirite

6 The LORD spoke to Moses: [2]Speak to the Israelites and say to them: If a man or a woman makes a binding promise to be a nazirite in order to be dedicated to the LORD, [3]that person must refrain from wine and brandy. He or she may not drink wine vinegar or brandy vinegar, nor drink any grape juice or eat grapes, whether fresh or dried. [4]While a nazirite, the person may not eat anything produced from the grapevine, not even its seeds or skin.

[5]For the term of the nazirite promise, no razor may be used on the head until the period of dedication to the LORD is fulfilled. The person is to be holy, letting his or her hair grow untrimmed. [6]The period of dedication to the LORD also requires that the person not go near a corpse, [7]whether father, mother, brother, or sister. Nazirites should not defile themselves because of the death of these people, because they bear the sign of their dedication to God on their heads.

[8]While a nazirite, the person is holy to the LORD. [9]If someone suddenly dies nearby, defiling the head of the nazirite, he or she will shave the head on the day of cleansing; they will shave it on the seventh day. [10]On the eighth day the person will bring two turtledoves or two young doves to the priest at the entrance of the meeting tent. [11]The priest will offer one for a purification offering and the other as an entirely burned offering. He will seek reconciliation for the person on account of the guilt acquired from the corpse, and he will make the head holy again on that same day. [12]The person will be rededicated to the LORD as a nazirite and bring a one-year-old male lamb for a compensation offering. The previous period will be invalid, because the nazirite promise was defiled.

[13]This is the Instruction for the nazirite. When the term as a nazirite is completed, the person will be brought to the entrance of the meeting tent [14]and offer a gift to the LORD, consisting of a flawless one-year-old male lamb as an entirely burned offering, a flawless one-year-old female lamb as a purification offering, one flawless ram as a well-being sacrifice, [15]and a basket of loaves of unleavened bread made with fine flour and mixed with oil, and unleavened wafers spread with oil, along with their grain offering and their drink offering. [16]The priest will come close to the LORD and offer the purification and entirely burned offerings. [17]The ram he will offer as a well-being sacrifice to the LORD with the basket of unleavened bread; then the priest will offer the grain offering and the drink offering. [18]The nazirite will shave his ordained head at the meeting tent's entrance, take the hair from his ordained head, and put it in the fire under the well-being sacrifice. [19]The priest will take the shoulder from the ram after it is boiled, one piece of unleavened bread from the basket, and one unleavened wafer, and place them in the hands of the nazirite after the ordained head is shaved. [20]Then the priest will raise them as an uplifted offering before the LORD; they are holy to the priest, with the breast of the uplifted offering and the thigh of the gift offering. After this the nazirite may drink wine.

[21]This is the instruction for the nazirite who takes the solemn promise. That person's offering to the LORD will be in accordance with the nazirite promise, in addition to whatever else the person may have offered. The person must do just as they have promised, in adherence with the nazirite promise.

Priestly blessing

[22]The LORD spoke to Moses: [23]Tell Aaron and his sons: You will bless the Israelites as follows. Say to them:

[24]The LORD bless you and protect you.
[25]The LORD make his face shine on you
and be gracious to you.

26 The LORD lift up his face to you
and grant you peace.
27 They will place my name on the Israelites, and I will bless them.

The dwelling's dedication

7 On the day when Moses finished setting
up the dwelling, he anointed and made it
holy. All its equipment, as well as the altar
and all its equipment, he also anointed
and made holy. 2 The chiefs of Israel, the
leaders of their households, made their
presentations. They were the tribal chiefs
and those who were in charge of the enlist-
ment. 3 They brought their offerings before
the LORD: six covered wagons and twelve
oxen—a wagon for every two chiefs, and an
ox for every chief. They brought them near
before the dwelling.
4 The LORD said to Moses: 5 Take these
from them and use them for service in the
meeting tent. Give them to the Levites according to their duties.
6 So Moses took the wagons and the oxen,
and he gave them to the Levites. 7 Two wagons and four oxen he gave to the Gershonites for their duty. 8 Four wagons and eight
oxen he gave to the Merarites for their duty
under the supervision of Ithamar, Aaron
the priest's son. 9 But to the Kohathites he
gave nothing because their duty concerned
the holy things that had to be carried on the
shoulders. 10 The chiefs made their presentations for the dedication of the altar on the
day it was anointed. The chiefs presented
their offerings before the altar.
11 The LORD said to Moses: One chief per
day will present their offering for the dedication of the altar.
12 The one presenting his offering on the
first day was Nahshon, Amminadab's son,
from the tribe of Judah. 13 His offering was
one silver dish weighing one hundred thirty
shekels, one silver basin weighing seventy
shekels according to the sanctuary shekel,
both of them full of fine flour mixed with oil
for a grain offering; 14 one gold bowl weighing ten shekels full of incense; 15 one bull
from the herd, one ram, and one year-old
male lamb for an entirely burned offering;
16 one male goat for a purification offering;
17 and for the well-being sacrifice two oxen,
five rams, five male goats, and five male
lambs a year old. This was the offering of
Nahshon, Amminadab's son.
18 On the second day Nethanel, Zuar's
son, the chief of Issachar, presented his offering. 19 He presented as his offering one
silver dish weighing one hundred thirty
shekels, one silver basin weighing seventy
shekels according to the sanctuary shekel,
both of them full of fine flour mixed with
oil for a grain offering; 20 one gold bowl
weighing ten shekels full of incense; 21 one
bull from the herd, one ram, and one year-
old male lamb for an entirely burned offering; 22 one male goat for a purification
offering; 23 and for the well-being sacrifice
two oxen, five rams, five male goats, and
five male lambs a year old. This was the offering of Nethanel, Zuar's son.
24 On the third day Zebulun's Chief Eliab,
Helon's son: 25 his offering was one silver dish
weighing one hundred thirty shekels, one
silver basin weighing seventy shekels according to the sanctuary shekel, both of them full
of fine flour mixed with oil for a grain offering; 26 one gold bowl weighing ten shekels full
of incense; 27 one bull from the herd, one ram,
and one year-old male lamb for an entirely
burned offering; 28 one male goat for a purification offering; 29 and for the well-being
sacrifice, two oxen, five rams, five male goats,
and five male lambs a year old. This was the
offering of Eliab, Helon's son.
30 On the fourth day Reuben's Chief Elizur, Shedeur's son: 31 his offering was one
silver dish weighing one hundred thirty
shekels, one silver basin weighing seventy
shekels according to the sanctuary shekel,
both of them full of fine flour mixed with
oil for a grain offering; 32 one gold bowl
weighing ten shekels full of incense; 33 one
bull from the herd, one ram, and one year-
old male lamb for an entirely burned offering; 34 one male goat for a purification
offering; 35 and for the well-being sacrifice
two oxen, five rams, five male goats, and
five male lambs a year old. This was the offering of Elizur, Shedeur's son.
36 On the fifth day Simeon's Chief Shelumiel, Zurishaddai's son: 37 his offering was

one silver dish weighing one hundred thirty
shekels, one basin weighing seventy shekels according to the sanctuary shekel, both
of them full of fine flour mixed with oil for
a grain offering; [38]one gold bowl weighing
ten shekels full of incense; [39]one bull from
the herd, one ram, and one year-old male
lamb for an entirely burned offering; [40]one
male goat for a purification offering; [41]and
for the well-being sacrifice two oxen, five
rams, five male goats, and five male lambs a
year old. This was the offering of Shelumiel,
Zurishaddai's son.

[42]On the sixth day Gad's Chief Eliasaph,
Deuel's son: [43]his offering was one silver dish
weighing one hundred thirty shekels, one silver basin weighing seventy shekels according
to the sanctuary shekel, both of them full of
fine flour mixed with oil for a grain offering;
[44]one gold bowl weighing ten shekels full of
incense; [45]one bull from the herd, one ram,
and one year-old male lamb for an entirely
burned offering; [46]one male goat for a purification offering; [47]and for the well-being
sacrifice two oxen, five rams, five male goats,
and five male lambs a year old. This was the
offering of Eliasaph, Deuel's son.

[48]On the seventh day Ephraim's Chief
Elishama, Ammihud's son: [49]his offering
was one silver dish weighing one hundred
thirty shekels, one silver basin weighing
seventy shekels according to the sanctuary
shekel, both of them full of fine flour mixed
with oil for a grain offering; [50]one gold
bowl weighing ten shekels full of incense;
[51]one bull from the herd, one ram, and one
year-old male lamb for an entirely burned
offering; [52]one male goat for a purification
offering; [53]and for the well-being sacrifice
two oxen, five rams, five male goats, and
five male lambs a year old. This was the offering of Elishama, Ammihud's son.

[54]On the eighth day Manasseh's Chief
Gamaliel, Pedahzur's son: [55]his offering
was one silver dish weighing one hundred
thirty shekels, one silver basin weighing
seventy shekels by the sanctuary scale, both
of them full of fine flour mixed with oil for
a grain offering; [56]one gold bowl weighing
ten shekels full of incense; [57]one bull from
the herd, one ram, and one year-old male
lamb for an entirely burned offering; [58]one
male goat for a purification offering; [59]and
for the well-being sacrifice two oxen, five
rams, five male goats, and five male lambs a
year old. This was the offering of Gamaliel,
Pedahzur's son.

[60]On the ninth day Benjamin's Chief
Abidan, Gideoni's son: [61]his offering was
one silver dish weighing one hundred thirty
shekels, one silver basin weighing seventy
shekels according to the sanctuary shekel,
both of them full of fine flour mixed with
oil for a grain offering; [62]one gold bowl
weighing ten shekels full of incense; [63]one
bull from the herd, one ram, and one year-
old male lamb for an entirely burned offering; [64]one male goat for a purification
offering; [65]and for the well-being sacrifice
two oxen, five rams, five male goats, and
five male lambs a year old. This was the offering of Abidan, Gideoni's son.

[66]On the tenth day Dan's Chief Ahiezer,
Ammishaddai's son: [67]his offering was one
silver dish weighing one hundred thirty
shekels, one silver basin weighing seventy
shekels according to the sanctuary shekel,
both of them full of fine flour mixed with oil
for a grain offering; [68]one gold bowl weighing ten shekels full of incense; [69]one bull
from the herd, one ram, and one year-old
male lamb for an entirely burned offering;
[70]one male goat for a purification offering;
[71]and for the well-being sacrifice two oxen,
five rams, five male goats, and five male
lambs a year old. This was the offering of
Ahiezer, Ammishaddai's son.

[72]On the eleventh day Asher's Chief Pagiel, Ochran's son: [73]his offering was one
silver dish weighing one hundred thirty
shekels, one silver basin weighing seventy
shekels according to the sanctuary shekel,
both of them full of fine flour mixed with
oil for a grain offering; [74]one gold bowl
weighing ten shekels full of incense; [75]one
bull from the herd, one ram, and one year-
old male lamb for an entirely burned offering; [76]one male goat for a purification
offering; [77]and for the well-being sacrifice
two oxen, five rams, five male goats, and
five male lambs a year old. This was the offering of Pagiel, Ochran's son.

[78]On the twelfth day Naphtali's Chief Ahira, Enan's son: [79]his offering was one silver dish weighing one hundred thirty shekels, one silver basin weighing seventy shekels according to the sanctuary shekel, both of them full of fine flour mixed with oil for a grain offering; [80]one gold bowl weighing ten shekels full of incense; [81]one bull from the herd, one ram, one year-old male lamb for an entirely burned offering; [82]one male goat for a purification offering; [83]and for the well-being sacrifice two oxen, five rams, five male goats, and five male lambs a year old. This was the offering of Ahira, Enan's son.

[84]This is what the Israelite chiefs provided for the dedication of the altar on the day it was anointed: twelve silver dishes, twelve silver basins, and twelve gold bowls; [85]each silver dish weighing one hundred thirty shekels and each basin seventy shekels—all the silver equipment weighed two thousand four hundred shekels according to the sanctuary shekel; [86]the twelve gold bowls full of incense weighing ten shekels each according to the sanctuary shekel—all the gold of the bowls weighed one hundred twenty shekels; [87]all the animals for the entirely burned offering were twelve bulls, twelve rams, twelve male lambs a year old, with their grain offering; twelve male goats for the purification offering; [88]and all the animals for the well-being sacrifice were twenty-four bulls, sixty rams, sixty male goats, and sixty male lambs a year old. This was the dedication offering for the altar after it was anointed.

Moses in the dwelling

[89]When Moses entered the meeting tent to speak with the LORD,[e] he would hear the voice speaking to him from above the cover[f] that was on the chest containing the covenant, from between the two winged creatures. In this way he spoke to Moses.

The lampstand

8 The LORD spoke to Moses: [2]Speak to Aaron and say to him: When you set them up, the seven lamps will give light in front of the lampstand.

[3]Aaron did so. He set up its lamps in front of the lampstand as the LORD commanded Moses. [4]This is how the lampstand was made: it was hammered gold; from its base to its flower it was hammered. Moses made the lampstand according to the vision that the LORD had shown Moses.

Dedication of the Levites

[5]The LORD spoke to Moses: [6]Separate the Levites from the Israelites and cleanse them. [7]This is what you will do to them to cleanse them: Sprinkle water of purification on them, have them shave their bodies, wash their clothes, and cleanse themselves. [8]They will take a bull from the herd, with its grain offering of fine flour mixed with oil. You will take a second bull from the herd for a purification offering. [9]You will bring the Levites before the meeting tent and gather the entire Israelite community. [10]Then you will bring the Levites into the LORD's presence, and the Israelites will lay their hands on the Levites. [11]Aaron will present the Levites as an uplifted offering in the LORD's presence from the Israelites so that they may do the LORD's service. [12]Then the Levites will lay their hands on the heads of the bulls, and Aaron will offer one as a purification offering and the other as an entirely burned offering to the LORD in order to seek reconciliation for the Levites.

[13]You will have the Levites stand before Aaron and his sons and you will present them as an uplifted offering to the LORD. [14]You will separate the Levites from the Israelites, and the Levites will be mine. [15]The Levites will enter to serve the meeting tent, after you have cleansed them and presented them as an uplifted offering. [16]They are given over to me from the Israelites in place of all the newborn, the oldest of all the Israelites. I take them for myself. [17]Every oldest male among the Israelites is mine, whether human or animal. When I killed all the oldest males in the land of Egypt, I dedicated them to myself. [18]I have taken

[e]Or *him* [f]Or *mercy seat* or perhaps *reconciliation cover* (Heb *kapporet*)

the Levites in place of all the oldest among the Israelites. [19]I have selected the Levites from the Israelites for Aaron and his sons to perform the service of the Israelites in the meeting tent and to seek reconciliation for the Israelites so that there will not be a plague when the Israelites approach the sanctuary.

[20]Moses, Aaron, and the entire Israelite community carried out for the Levites everything the LORD had commanded Moses. That is what the Israelites did for the Levites. [21]The Levites purified themselves and washed their clothes. Aaron presented them as an uplifted offering in the LORD's presence, and he sought reconciliation for them in order to cleanse them. [22]After this the Levites went in to perform their service in the meeting tent before Aaron and his sons. They did for the Levites just as the LORD had commanded Moses concerning them.

[23]The LORD spoke to Moses: [24]This rule applies[g] to the Levites: Everyone 25 years old and above will enter into service, performing the duties for the meeting tent. [25]At 50 years old each will retire from service. They will perform their duties no longer. [26]Each may assist his fellow Levites in the meeting tent with some responsibilities, but he may not perform service. This is how you should assign responsibilities to the Levites.

Passover

9 The LORD spoke to Moses in the Sinai desert in the first month[h] of the second year after they had left the land of Egypt: [2]Let the Israelites keep the Passover at its appointed time. [3]On the fourteenth day of this month at twilight you will keep it at its appointed time. Keep it according to all its regulations and its customary practices.

[4]Moses instructed the Israelites to keep the Passover. [5]At twilight on the fourteenth day of the first month[i] they kept the Passover in the Sinai desert. The Israelites did everything just as the LORD commanded Moses.

[6]But there were persons who were unclean from contact with a human corpse, and they were unable to keep the Passover on that day. They approached Moses and Aaron that day. [7]These persons said to him, "Although we are unclean from contact with a human corpse, why must we be prohibited from presenting the LORD's offering at its appointed time with the rest of the Israelites?"

[8]Moses said to them, "Wait while I listen for what the LORD will command concerning you."

[9]The LORD spoke to Moses: [10]Tell the Israelites: When any of you or your descendants are unclean from contact with a corpse or are on a long trip, they may still keep the Passover to the LORD. [11]They will keep it at twilight on the fourteenth day of the second month.[j] They will eat the Passover lamb with unleavened bread and bitter herbs. [12]They must not leave any of it until morning, nor break any of its bones. They will keep the Passover according to all its regulations. [13]But any persons who are clean and not on a trip, yet don't keep the Passover, those persons will be cut off from their people, because they didn't present the LORD's offering at its appointed time. Those persons will bear their sin. [14]If an immigrant resides among you and wishes to keep the Passover to the LORD, that one also will keep it according to its regulations and its customary practices. There will be one set of regulations for both of you, for the immigrant and for the native of the land.

Cloud over the dwelling

[15]On the day the dwelling was erected, the cloud covered the dwelling, the covenant tent. At night until morning, the cloud appeared with lightning over the dwelling. [16]It was always there. The cloud covered it by day,[k] appearing with lightning at night. [17]Whenever the cloud ascended from the tent, the Israelites would march. And the Israelites would camp wherever the cloud settled. [18]At the LORD's command, the Israelites would march, and at the LORD's command they would camp. As

[g]Heb lacks *rule applies.* [h]March–April, Nisan [i]March–April, Nisan [j]April–May, Iyar [k]LXX; MT lacks *by day.*

long as the cloud settled on the dwelling, they would camp. 19When the cloud lingered on the meeting tent for many days, the Israelites would observe the LORD's direction and they wouldn't march. 20Sometimes the cloud would be over the dwelling for a number of days, so they would camp at the LORD's command, marching again only at the LORD's command. 21Sometimes the cloud would settle only overnight, and they would march when the cloud ascended in the morning. Whether it was day or night, they would march when the cloud ascended. 22Whether it was two days, or a month, or a long time, the Israelites would camp so long as the cloud lingered on the dwelling and settled on it. They wouldn't march. But when it ascended, they would march. 23They camped at the LORD's command and they marched at the LORD's command. They followed the LORD's direction according to the LORD's command through Moses.

Trumpets

10 The LORD spoke to Moses: 2Make two silver trumpets and make them from hammered metalwork. Use them for summoning the community and for breaking camp. 3When both are blown, the entire community will meet you at the entrance of the meeting tent. 4When one is blown, the chiefs, the leaders of Israel's divisions, will meet you. 5When you blow a series of short blasts, the camp on the east side will march. 6And when you blow a second series of short blasts, the camp on the south side will march. You will blow a series of short blasts to announce their march.

7To gather the assembly, blow a long blast, not a series of short blasts. 8Aaron's sons the priests will blow the trumpets. This will be a permanent regulation for you throughout time.

9When you go to war in your land against an enemy who is attacking you, you will blow short blasts with the trumpets so that you may be remembered by the LORD your God and be saved from your enemies.

10On your festival days, your appointed feasts, and at the beginning of your months, you will blow the trumpets over your entirely burned offerings and your well-being sacrifices. They will serve as a reminder of you to your God. I am the LORD your God.

Organization of the wilderness march

11On the twentieth day of the second month in the second year, the cloud ascended from the covenant dwelling. 12The Israelites set out on their march from the Sinai desert, and the cloud settled in the Paran desert.

13They marched for the first time at the LORD's command through Moses. 14The banner of Judah's camp marched first with its military units. Nahshon, Amminadab's son, commanded its military. 15Nethanel, Zuar's son, commanded the military of the tribe of Issachar. 16Eliab, Helon's son, commanded the military of the tribe of Zebulun. 17The dwelling was taken down, and the Gershonites and the Merarites, who carried the dwelling, marched. 18The banner of Reuben's camp marched with its military units. Elizur, Shedeur's son, commanded its military. 19Shelumiel, Zurishaddai's son, commanded the military of the tribe of Simeon. 20Eliasaph, Deuel's son, commanded the military of the tribe of Gad. 21The Kohathites, who carried the holy things, marched. The dwelling would be set up before their arrival. 22The banner of Ephraim's camp marched with its military units. Elishama, Ammihud's son, commanded its military. 23Gamaliel, Pedahzur's son, commanded the military of the tribe of Manasseh. 24Abidan, Gideoni's son, commanded the military of the tribe of Benjamin. 25The banner of Dan's camp, at the rear of the whole camp, marched with its military units. Ahiezer, Ammishaddai's son, commanded its military. 26Pagiel, Ochran's son, commanded the military of the tribe of Asher. 27Ahira, Enan's son, commanded the military of the tribe of Naphtali. 28This was the order of departure of the Israelites with their military units when they set out.

The chest leads

29Moses said to Hobab the Midianite, Reuel's son and Moses' father-in-law,

"We're marching to the place about which
the LORD has said, 'I'll give it to you.' Come
with us and we'll treat you well, for the
LORD has promised to treat Israel well."
[30]Hobab said to him, "I won't go; I'd
rather go to my land and to my folk."
[31]Moses said, "Please don't abandon us,
for you know where we can camp in the
desert, and you can be our eyes. [32]If you go
with us, whatever good the LORD does for
us, we'll do for you."
[33]They marched from the LORD'S mountain for three days. The LORD's chest containing the covenant marched ahead of
them for three days to look for a resting
place for them. [34]Now the LORD's cloud
was over them by day when they marched
from the camp. [35]When the chest set out,
Moses would say, "Arise, LORD, let your enemies scatter, and those who hate you flee."
[36]When it rested, he would say, "Return,
LORD of the ten thousand thousands of Israel."

Complaint at Taberah

11 When the people complained intensely
in the LORD's hearing, the LORD heard
and became angry. Then the LORD's fire
burned them and consumed the edges of
the camp. [2]When the people cried out to
Moses, Moses prayed to the LORD, and the
fire subsided. [3]The name of that place was
called Taberah,[1] because the LORD's fire
burned against them.

Complaint over the lack of meat

[4]The riffraff among them had a strong
craving. Even the Israelites cried again and
said, "Who will give us meat to eat? [5]We remember the fish we ate in Egypt for free,
the cucumbers, the melons, the leeks, the
onions, and the garlic. [6]Now our lives are
wasting away. There is nothing but manna
in front of us."
[7]The manna was like coriander seed and
its color was like resin. [8]The people would
roam around and collect it and grind it with
millstones or pound it in a mortar. Then
they would boil it in pots and make it into
cakes. It tasted like cakes baked in olive oil.
[9]When the dew fell on the camp during the
night, the manna would fall with it.

Moses' complaint about leadership

[10]Moses heard the people crying throughout their clans, each at his tent's entrance.
The LORD was outraged, and Moses was
upset. [11]Moses said to the LORD, "Why have
you treated your servant so badly? And why
haven't I found favor in your eyes, for you
have placed the burden of all these people
on me? [12]Did I conceive all these people?
Did I give birth to them, that you would
say to me, 'Carry them at the breast, as a
nurse carries an unweaned child,' to the
fertile land that you promised their ancestors? [13]Where am I to get meat for all these
people? They are crying before me and saying, 'Give us meat, so we can eat.' [14]I can't
bear this people on my own. They're too
heavy for me. [15]If you're going to treat me
like this, please kill me. If I've found favor
in your eyes, then don't let me endure this
wretched situation."
[16]The LORD said to Moses, "Gather before me seventy men from Israel's elders,
whom you know as elders and officers of
the people. Take them to the meeting tent,
and let them stand there with you. [17]Then
I'll descend and speak with you there. I'll
take some of the spirit that is on you and
place it on them. Then they will carry the
burden of the people with you so that you
won't bear it alone. [18]To the people you will
say, 'Make yourselves holy for tomorrow;
then you will eat meat, for you've cried in
the LORD's hearing, "Who will give us meat
to eat? It was better for us in Egypt." The
LORD will give you meat, and you will eat.
[19]You won't eat for just one day, or two days,
or five days, or ten days, or twenty days,
[20]but for a whole month until it comes out
of your nostrils and nauseates you. You've
rejected the LORD who's been with you and
you have cried before him, saying, "Why did
we leave Egypt?" ' "
[21]Moses said, "The people I'm with are six
hundred thousand on foot and you're saying,

[1]Or *the place of burning*

'I will give them meat, and they will eat for a month.' [22]Can flocks and herds be found and slaughtered for them? Or can all the fish in the sea be found and caught for them?"

[23]The LORD said to Moses, "Is the LORD's power too weak? Now you will see whether my word will come true for you or not."

[24]So Moses went out and told the people the LORD's words. He assembled seventy men from the people's elders and placed them around the tent. [25]The LORD descended in a cloud, spoke to him, and took some of the spirit that was on him and placed it on the seventy elders. When the spirit rested on them, they prophesied, but only this once. [26]Two men had remained in the camp, one named Eldad and the second named Medad, and the spirit rested on them. They were among those registered, but they hadn't gone out to the tent, so they prophesied in the camp. [27]A young man ran and told Moses, "Eldad and Medad are prophesying in the camp."

[28]Joshua, Nun's son and Moses' assistant since his youth, responded, "My master Moses, stop them!"

[29]Moses said to him, "Are you jealous for my sake? If only all the LORD's people were prophets with the LORD placing his spirit on them!"

Quail from the sea

[30]Moses and Israel's elders were assembled in the camp. [31]A wind from the LORD blew up and brought quails from the sea. It let them fall by the camp, about a day's journey all around the camp and about three feet deep on the ground. [32]Then the people arose and gathered the quail all that day, all night, and all the next day. The least collected was ten homers,[m] and they laid them out around the camp. [33]While the meat was still between their teeth and not yet consumed, the LORD's anger blazed against the people. The LORD struck the people with a very great punishment. [34]The name of that place was called Kibroth-hattaavah,[n] because there they buried the people who had the craving.

Miriam and Aaron challenge Moses

[35]From Kibroth-hattaavah the people marched to Hazeroth.

12 When they were in Hazeroth, [1]Miriam and Aaron criticized Moses on account of the Cushite woman whom he had married—for he had married a Cushite woman. [2]They said, "Has the LORD spoken only through Moses? Hasn't he also spoken through us?" The LORD heard it. [3]Now the man Moses was humble, more so than anyone on earth.

The LORD defends Moses

[4]Immediately, the LORD said to Moses, Aaron, and Miriam, "You three go out to the meeting tent." So the three of them went out. [5]Then the LORD descended in a column of cloud, stood at the entrance of the tent, and called to Aaron and Miriam. The two of them came forward. [6]He said, "Listen to my words: If there is a prophet of the LORD among you,[o] I make myself known to him in visions. I speak to him in dreams. [7]But not with my servant Moses. He has proved to be reliable with all my household. [8]I speak with him face-to-face, visibly, not in riddles. He sees the LORD's form. So why aren't you afraid to criticize my servant Moses?" [9]The LORD's anger blazed against them, and they went back.

The LORD punishes Miriam

[10]When the cloud went away from over the tent, Miriam suddenly developed a skin disease flaky like snow. Aaron turned toward Miriam and saw her skin disease. [11]Then Aaron said to Moses, "Oh, my master, please don't punish us for the sin that we foolishly committed. [12]Please don't let her be like the stillborn, whose flesh is half eaten as it comes out of the mother's womb."

[13]So Moses cried to the LORD, "God, please heal her!"

[14]The LORD said to Moses, "If her father had spit in her face, would she not be shamed for seven days? Let her be shut out of the camp for seven days, and afterward she will be brought back." [15]So they

[m]Five hundred gallons; one homer is two hundred quarts [n]Or *graves of craving* [o]Heb uncertain; LXX *If there is a prophet of you for the LORD*

shut Miriam out of the camp seven days. And the people didn't march until Miriam was brought back. 16Afterward the people marched from Hazeroth, and they camped in the Paran desert.

Leaders explore the land of Canaan

13 The LORD spoke to Moses: 2Send out men to explore the land of Canaan, which I'm giving to the Israelites. Send one man from each ancestral tribe, each a chief among them. 3So Moses sent them out from the Paran desert according to the LORD's command. All the men were leaders among the Israelites. 4These are their names:

from the tribe of Reuben, Shammua, Zaccur's son;

5from the tribe of Simeon, Shaphat, Hori's son;

6from the tribe of Judah, Caleb, Jephunneh's son;

7from the tribe of Issachar, Igal, Joseph's son;

8from the tribe of Ephraim, Hoshea, Nun's son;

9from the tribe of Benjamin, Palti, Raphu's son;

10from the tribe of Zebulun, Gaddiel, Sodi's son;

11from the tribe of Joseph:

from the tribe of Manasseh, Gaddi, Susi's son;

12from the tribe of Dan, Ammiel, Gemalli's son;

13from the tribe of Asher, Sethur, Michael's son;

14from the tribe of Naphtali, Nahbi, Vophsi's son;

15from the tribe of Gad, Geuel, Machi's son.

16These are the names of the men whom Moses sent out to explore the land. Moses changed the name of Hoshea, Nun's son, to Joshua.

17When Moses sent them out to explore the land of Canaan, he said to them, "Go up there into the arid southern plain and into the mountains. 18You must inspect the land. What is it like? Are the people who live in it strong or weak, few or many? 19Is the land in which they live good or bad? Are the towns in which they live camps or fortresses? 20Is the land rich or poor? Are there trees in it or not? Be courageous and bring back the land's fruit." It was the season of the first ripe grapes.

21They went up and explored the land from the Zin desert to Rehob, near Lebo-hamath. 22They went up into the arid southern plain and entered Hebron, where Ahiman, Sheshai, and Talmai, the descendants of the Anakites, lived. (Hebron was built seven years before Tanis[p] in Egypt.) 23Then they entered the Cluster[q] ravine, cut down from there a branch with one cluster of grapes, and carried it on a pole between them. They also took pomegranates and figs. 24That place was called the Cluster ravine because of the cluster of grapes that the Israelites cut down from there.

Report about the land of Canaan

25They returned from exploring the land after forty days. 26They went directly to Moses, Aaron, and the entire Israelite community in the Paran desert at Kadesh. They brought back a report to them and to the entire community and showed them the land's fruit. 27Then they gave their report: "We entered the land to which you sent us. It's actually full of milk and honey, and this is its fruit. 28There are, however, powerful people who live in the land. The cities have huge fortifications. And we even saw the descendants of the Anakites there. 29The Amalekites live in the land of the arid southern plain; the Hittites, Jebusites, and Amorites live in the mountains; and the Canaanites live by the sea and along the Jordan."

30Now Caleb calmed the people before Moses and said, "We must go up and take possession of it, because we are more than able to do it."

31But the men who went up with him said, "We can't go up against the people because they are stronger than we." 32They started a rumor about the land that they had explored, telling the Israelites, "The

[p]Heb *Zoan* [q]Or *cluster of grapes*

land that we crossed over to explore is a
land that devours its residents. All the
people we saw in it are huge men. 33 We
saw there the Nephilim (the descendants
of Anak come from the Nephilim). We saw
ourselves as grasshoppers, and that's how
we appeared to them."

The Israelites' complaint

14 The entire community raised their
voice and the people wept that night.
2 All the Israelites criticized Moses and
Aaron. The entire community said to them,
"If only we had died in the land of Egypt or
if only we had died in this desert! 3 Why is
the LORD bringing us to this land to fall by
the sword? Our wives and our children will
be taken by force. Wouldn't it be better for
us to return to Egypt?" 4 So they said to each
other, "Let's pick a leader and let's go back
to Egypt."
5 Then Moses and Aaron fell on their
faces before the assembled Israelite community. 6 But Joshua, Nun's son, and Caleb,
Jephunneh's son, from those who had explored the land, tore their clothes 7 and said
to the entire Israelite community, "The land
we crossed through to explore is an exceptionally good land. 8 If the LORD is pleased
with us, he'll bring us into this land and
give it to us. It's a land that's full of milk
and honey. 9 Only don't rebel against the
LORD and don't be afraid of the people of
the land. They are our prey.[r] Their defense
has deserted them, but the LORD is with us.
So don't be afraid of them." 10 But the entire
community intended to stone them.

The LORD's anger and Moses' intercession

Then the LORD's glory appeared in the
meeting tent to all the Israelites. 11 The
LORD said to Moses, "How long will these
people disrespect me? And how long will
they doubt me after all the signs that I
performed among them? 12 I'll strike them
down with a plague and disown them. Then
I'll make you into a great nation, stronger
than they."
13 Moses said to the LORD, "The Egyptians
will hear, for with your power you brought
these people up from among them. 14 They'll
tell the inhabitants of this land. They've
heard that you, LORD, are with this people.
You, LORD, appear to them face-to-face.
Your cloud stands over them. You go before
them in a column of cloud by day and in a
column of lightning by night. 15 If you kill
these people, every last one of them, the
nations who heard about you will say, 16 'The
LORD wasn't able to bring these people to
the land that he solemnly promised to give
them. So he slaughtered them in the desert.'
17 Now let my master's power be as great as
you declared when you said, 18 'The LORD is
very patient and absolutely loyal, forgiving
wrongs and disloyalty. Yet he doesn't forgo
all punishment, disciplining the grandchildren and great-grandchildren for their ancestors' wrongs.' 19 Please forgive the wrongs
of these people because of your absolute
loyalty, just as you've forgiven these people
from their time in Egypt until now."
20 Then the LORD said, "I will forgive as
you requested. 21 But as I live and as the
LORD's glory fills the entire earth, 22 none
of the men who saw my glory and the signs
I did in Egypt and in the desert, but tested
me these ten times and haven't listened to
my voice, 23 will see the land I promised to
their ancestors. All who disrespected me
won't see it. 24 But I'll bring my servant
Caleb into the land that he explored, and
his descendants will possess it because he
has a different spirit, and he has remained
true to me. 25 Since the Amalekites and the
Canaanites live in the valley, tomorrow
turn and march into the desert by the route
of the Reed Sea."[s]

The Israelites' punishment

26 The LORD spoke to Moses and Aaron:
27 How long will this wicked community
complain against me? I've heard the Israelites' dissent as they continue to complain
against me. 28 Say to them, "As I live," says
the LORD, "just as I've heard you say, so I'll
do to you. 29 Your dead bodies will fall in

[r] Or *our bread* [s] Or *Red Sea*

this desert. None of you who were enlisted
and were registered from 20 years old and
above, who complained against me, 30will
enter the land in which I promised[t] to settle
you, with the exception of Caleb, Jephunneh's son, and Joshua, Nun's son. 31But your
children, whom you said would be taken by
force, I'll bring them in and they will know
the land that you rejected. 32Your bodies,
however, will fall in this desert, 33and your
children will be shepherds in the desert for
forty years. They will suffer for your unfaithfulness, until the last of your bodies
fall in the desert. 34For as many days as you
explored the land, that is, forty days, just
as many years you'll bear your guilt, that is,
forty years. This is how you will understand
my frustration." 35I the LORD have spoken.
I will do this to the entire wicked community who gathered against me. They will die
in this desert. There they'll meet their end.

36The men whom Moses sent out to explore the land had returned and caused the
entire community to complain against him
by starting a rumor about the land. 37These
men died by a plague in the LORD's presence on account of their false rumor. 38But
Joshua, Nun's son, and Caleb, Jephunneh's
son, survived from those men who went to
explore the land.

39Moses spoke these words to all the Israelites, and the people mourned bitterly.
40They rose early in the morning and went
up to the top of the mountain range, saying, "Let's go up to the place the LORD told
us to, for we have sinned."

41But Moses said, "Why do you disobey
the LORD's command? It won't succeed.
42Don't go up, for the LORD isn't with you.
Don't be struck down before your enemies. 43The Amalekites and the Canaanites will be there in front of you and you
will fall by the sword because you turned
away from the LORD, and the LORD is no
longer with you." 44Yet they recklessly[u] ascended toward the top of the mountains,
even though Moses and the LORD's chest
containing the covenant didn't depart from
the camp. 45Then the Amalekites and the
Canaanites, who lived in those mountains,
descended, struck them down, and beat
them all the way to Hormah.

Immigrants in the land of Canaan

15 The LORD spoke to Moses: 2Speak to
the Israelites and say to them: When
you enter the land where you will live, which
I am giving you, 3and you make a food gift[v]
to the LORD as a soothing smell for the
LORD from the herd or the flock—whether
an entirely burned offering, or a sacrifice to
fulfill a solemn promise, or a spontaneous
gift, or at your sacred seasons—4the one
presenting the offering to the LORD will
bring a grain offering of one-tenth of fine
flour mixed with one-fourth of a hin[w] of
oil. 5You will also offer one-fourth of a hin
of wine as a drink offering with either the
entirely burned offering or the sacrifice, for
each lamb. 6For a ram you will offer a grain
offering of two-tenths of a measure of fine
flour mixed with one-third of a hin of oil.
7You will also present one-third of a hin of
wine for a drink offering as a soothing smell
for the LORD. 8When you offer a bull for an
entirely burned offering, or a sacrifice to
fulfill a solemn promise, or a well-being sacrifice to the LORD, 9you will present[x] with
the bull a grain offering of three-tenths of
a measure of fine flour mixed with a half
hin of oil. 10You will present a half hin of
wine for a drink offering as a food gift that
is a soothing smell to the LORD. 11So will it
be done with each ox, each ram, or for any
sheep or goat. 12However many you offer,
you will do the same for each one.

13Every citizen will perform these rituals in bringing a food gift that is a soothing
smell to the LORD. 14If an immigrant lives
with you or has settled among you for many
years and would also like to offer a food gift
that is a soothing smell to the LORD, that
person must do just as you do. 15The assembly will have the same regulation for you and
for the immigrant. The regulation will be
permanent for all time. You and the immi-

[t]Or *raised my hand* [u]Heb uncertain [v]Or *offering by fire* (cf Lev 3:11) [w]One hin is approximately one gallon.
[x]Or *he will present*

grant will be the same in the LORD's presence. 16 There will be one set of instructions
and one legal norm for the immigrant and
for you.
17 The LORD spoke to Moses: 18 Speak to
the Israelites and say to them: When you
enter the land to which I'm bringing you,
19 whenever you eat the land's food you will
present a gift offering to the LORD. 20 You
will present a gift offering from the first
bread you bake just like you present a gift
offering from the threshing floor. 21 You will
give a gift offering from the first bread you
bake for all time.

Offerings for accidental sin

22 If by accident you don't obey all these
commands that the LORD spoke to Moses,
23 or everything that the LORD commanded
you through Moses from the day of the
LORD's command onward for all time,
24 then if it was done unintentionally without the knowledge of the community, the
entire community must offer one bull from
the herd as an entirely burned offering, a
soothing smell to the LORD, with its grain
and drink offering according to the specific
instruction, and one male goat for a purification offering. 25 The priest will seek reconciliation for the entire Israelite community.
They will be forgiven, because it was unintentional and because they brought their
food gift to the LORD, along with their purification offering in the LORD's presence
for their accidental error. 26 The entire
Israelite community and the immigrant
residing among them will be forgiven, because all the people acted unintentionally.
27 If an individual sins unintentionally,
that person must present a one-year-old female goat for a purification offering. 28 The
priest will seek reconciliation in the LORD's
presence for the person who sinned unintentionally, when the sin is an accident,
seeking reconciliation so that person will
be forgiven. 29 There will be one set of instructions for the Israelite citizen and the
immigrant residing with you for anyone
who commits an unintentional sin.

Punishment for intentional sin

30 But the person who acts deliberately,[y]
whether a citizen or an immigrant, and
insults the LORD, that person will be cut off
from the people 31 for despising the LORD's
word and breaking his commands. That
person will be completely cut off and bear
the guilt.

Instructions for Sabbath observance

32 When the Israelites were in the desert,
they found a man gathering wood on the
Sabbath day. 33 Those who found him gathering wood brought him to Moses, Aaron,
and the entire community. 34 They placed
him in custody, because it wasn't clear what
should be done to him. 35 Then the LORD
said to Moses: The man should be put to
death. The entire community should stone
him outside the camp. 36 The entire community took him outside the camp and stoned
him. He died as the LORD had commanded
Moses.

Fringes on garments

37 The LORD said to Moses: 38 Speak to
the Israelites and say to them: Make fringes
on the edges of your clothing for all time.
Have them put blue cords on the fringe on
the edges. 39 This will be your fringe. You
will see it and remember all the LORD's
commands and do them. Then you won't
go exploring the lusts of your own heart or
your eyes. 40 In this way you'll remember to
do all my commands. Then you will be holy
to your God. 41 I am the LORD your God,
who brought you out of the land of Egypt
to be your God. I am the LORD your God.

A challenge to the priesthood

16 Korah—Izhar's son, Kohath's grandson, and Levi's great-grandson—with
Dathan and Abiram, Eliab's sons, and On,
Peleth's son, descendants of Reuben, 2 rose
up against Moses, along with two hundred
fifty Israelite men, leaders of the community, chosen by the assembly, men of reputation. 3 They assembled against Moses and
Aaron and said to them, "You've gone too

[y] Or *with a high hand*

far, because the entire community is holy, every last one of them, and the LORD is with them. Why then do you exalt yourselves above the LORD's assembly?"

4When Moses heard this, he fell on his face. 5He spoke to Korah and all his community, "In the morning the LORD will make known who is his, who is holy, and who is able to approach him. The one he chooses for himself is the one who will be able to approach him. 6This is what must be done. Korah and your entire community: Take censers for yourselves. 7Tomorrow put fire in them and place incense on them in the LORD's presence. The man whom the LORD chooses, that one is holy. You Levites have gone too far!" 8Moses said to Korah, "Listen, you Levites, 9isn't it enough for you that Israel's God has separated you from the Israelite community to allow you to approach him, to perform the service of the LORD's dwelling, and to serve before the community by ministering for them? 10He has allowed you and all your fellow Levites with you to approach him. Yet you also seek the priesthood? 11Thus you and your entire community have assembled against the LORD. But Aaron, what is he that you complain about him?"

Test of priesthood

12Moses sent for Dathan and Abiram, Eliab's sons. But they said, "We won't come up! 13Isn't it enough that you've brought us up from a land full of milk and honey to kill us in the desert so that you'd also dominate us? 14Moreover, you haven't brought us to a land full of milk and honey, nor given us the inheritance of field and vineyard. Would you also gouge out the eyes of these men? We won't come up!"

15Moses became very angry and he said to the LORD, "Pay no attention to their offering. I haven't taken a single donkey from them, nor have I wronged any one of them."

16Moses said to Korah, "You and your entire community should appear before the LORD tomorrow, you, they, and Aaron. 17Every person should take his censer, place incense on it, and present it before the LORD. Each person will carry his censer, two hundred fifty censers in all, including you and Aaron." 18Then every person took his censer, placed fire on it, put incense on it, and stood at the entrance of the meeting tent with Moses and Aaron. 19Korah gathered the entire community with them to the entrance of the meeting tent.

Then the LORD's glory appeared to the entire community. 20The LORD spoke to Moses and Aaron, 21"Separate yourselves from this community so that I may consume them in a moment."

22They fell on their faces and said, "God, the God of all living things. If one person sins, should you become angry with the entire community?"

23The LORD said to Moses, 24"Speak to the community and say, 'Withdraw from around the dwellings of Korah, Dathan, and Abiram.'"

25Moses rose and went to Dathan and Abiram. Israel's elders followed him. 26He spoke to the community: "Move away from the tents of these wicked men and don't touch anything of theirs, lest you too be wiped out for all their sins." 27They withdrew from around the dwellings of Korah, Dathan, and Abiram. Then Dathan and Abiram came out and stood at the entrance of their tents with their wives, children, and little ones. 28Moses said, "By this you will know that the LORD sent me to do these deeds and that it wasn't my own desire. 29If all these people die a natural death, or if their fate be that of all humans, then the LORD hasn't sent me. 30But if the LORD performs an act of creation, and the ground opens its mouth and swallows them and everything that belongs to them, so that they descend alive to their graves, then you'll know that these men disrespected the LORD."

The rebels' punishment

31As soon as he finished speaking these words, the ground under them split open. 32The earth opened its mouth and swallowed them and their households, including every human that belonged to Korah and all their possessions. 33They along with all their possessions descended alive to their graves, and the earth closed over them. They perished in the middle of the assembly. 34All the Israelites who were around them fled at their cry, for they said, "The earth may swallow us." 35Then fire went out from the LORD and consumed the two hundred fifty men offering incense.

The reminder of the censers

36[z]The LORD spoke to Moses: 37Tell Eleazar, Aaron the priest's son, to raise the censers from the fire and scatter the ashes about, because they are holy. 38Hammer the censers of those who sinned and lost their lives into thin plates for the altar. Since they presented them in the LORD's presence, they had become holy. They will be a sign for the Israelites.

39Eleazar the priest took the bronze censers presented by those who had been consumed by fire and hammered them into a covering for the altar, 40just as the LORD instructed him through Moses. This was a reminder for the Israelites that no outsider who isn't one of Aaron's descendants should approach to burn incense in the LORD's presence, so as not to be like Korah and his community.

41On the next day the entire Israelite community complained to Moses and Aaron, "You killed the LORD's people." 42When the community assembled against Moses and Aaron, they turned toward the meeting tent. At that moment the cloud covered it, and the LORD's glory appeared. 43Moses and Aaron came to the front of the meeting tent, 44and the LORD spoke to Moses: 45Get away from this community, so that I may consume them in an instant.

They fell on their faces, 46and Moses said to Aaron, "Take the censer, put fire from the altar on it, place incense on it, go quickly to the community, and seek reconciliation for them. Indeed, the LORD's anger has gone out. The plague has begun." 47Aaron took it as Moses said and ran into the middle of the assembly, for the plague had already begun among the people. He burned incense and sought reconciliation for the people. 48He stood between the dead and the living, and the plague stopped. 49Those who died from the plague were fourteen thousand seven hundred, in addition to those who died because of Korah. 50Aaron returned to Moses at the entrance of the meeting tent once the plague stopped.

Aaron's budding staff

17 [a]The LORD spoke to Moses: 2Speak to the Israelites and take from them a staff from each household, from each of the chiefs of their households, twelve staffs. Write each person's name on his staff. 3Write Aaron's name on Levi's staff, for there will be one staff for the leader of each household. 4Then you will place them in the meeting tent in front of the chest containing the covenant, where I meet you. 5The staff of the person I choose will sprout. Then I will rid myself of the Israelites' complaints that they make against you.

6Moses spoke to the Israelites, and each of their chiefs gave him a staff, one staff for each chief and his household, twelve staffs, and the staff of Aaron was with their staffs. 7Moses placed the staffs before the LORD in the meeting tent. 8The next day Moses entered the covenant tent, and Aaron's staff of Levi's household had sprouted. It grew shoots, produced blossoms, and bore almonds. 9Moses brought out all the staffs from the LORD's presence to the Israelites. They saw what happened, and each person took back his staff.

10Then the LORD said to Moses, "Return Aaron's staff in front of the chest containing the covenant to serve as a sign to the rebels so that their complaints against me end and they don't die." 11Moses did exactly as the LORD commanded him.

12The Israelites said to Moses, "We are perishing. We are being destroyed. All of us are being destroyed. 13Anyone who approaches the LORD's dwelling will die. Are we doomed to perish?"

The priests' and Levites' duties

18 The LORD said to Aaron: You, your sons, and your household will bear

[z]17:1 in Heb [a]17:16 in Heb

the guilt of offenses connected with the sanctuary. You and your sons will bear the guilt of offenses connected with your priesthood. [2]Bring with you your brothers from the tribe of Levi, your father's tribe, so that they can assist you and serve you and your sons before the covenant tent. [3]They will perform their duties for you and the service for the entire tent. But they will not approach the holy equipment of the sanctuary or the altar, lest both they and you die. [4]They will assist you and they will perform the duties of the meeting tent with regard to all the work of the tent. But no outsider may accompany you. [5]You will perform the duties of the sanctuary and the altar. Then there will no longer be any anger against the Israelites. [6]I have taken your brothers, the Levites, from the Israelites. They are a gift to you, dedicated to the LORD to perform the service of the meeting tent. [7]You and your sons must perform the duties of your priesthood for all the matters of the altar and the area behind the curtain. I give you your priestly service as a gift. But an outsider who approaches will die.

The priests' compensation

[8]The LORD spoke to Aaron: I now place you in charge of my gifts, including all the Israelites' sacred offerings. I have given them to you and your sons as an allowance. This is a permanent regulation. [9]This is what belongs to you from the most holy offerings, from the offerings by fire: all their offerings, including their grain offerings, their purification offerings, and their compensation offerings. The most holy offerings that they bring to me will be yours and your sons'. [10]You will eat it as a most holy thing. Every male may eat it. It will be holy to you. [11]This will also belong to you, your sons, and your daughters: I'm giving you the gift offerings and all the Israelites' uplifted offerings. This is a permanent regulation. Anyone who is clean in your household may eat it. [12]All the choice oil, new wine, and the grain's first harvest that they give to the LORD, I'm giving to you. [13]The early produce of everything in their land, which they bring to the LORD, will be yours. Anyone who is clean in your household may eat it. [14]Everything that is devoted to the LORD in Israel will be yours. [15]Any oldest male from the womb of any living thing that is presented to the LORD, whether human or animal, will be yours. However, you will redeem the oldest males of humans and of unclean animals. [16]Their redemption price from one month of age you will calculate at five shekels of silver according to the sanctuary shekel, which is twenty gerahs. [17]But the oldest offspring of a cow, sheep, or goat you may not redeem. They are holy. You must dash their blood on the altar and turn their fat into smoke for a soothing smell to the LORD. [18]But their meat is yours. It will be yours just as the breast of the uplifted offering and the right thigh are yours. [19]All the holy gift offerings that the Israelites raise to the LORD I have given to you, your sons, and your daughters. This is a permanent regulation. It is a covenant of salt forever in the LORD's presence, for you and your descendants.

[20]The LORD said to Aaron: You will have no inheritance in their land, nor will you have a share among them. I am your share and your inheritance among the Israelites.

The Levites' compensation

[21]I have given all the one-tenth portions in Israel to the Levites as an inheritance. They are a reward for performing their service in the meeting tent. [22]The Israelites will no longer be able to approach the meeting tent, or they will be responsible for their sin and die. [23]The Levites will perform the service of the meeting tent, and they will be responsible for their own sins. This is a permanent regulation for all time. But they will not inherit land among the Israelites [24]because I've given the Israelites' one-tenth portion, which they have raised to the LORD as a gift offering, as an inheritance to the Levites. Therefore, I've said to them, "They won't inherit land among the Israelites."

[25]The LORD spoke to Moses: [26]Speak to the Levites and say to them: When you receive from the Israelites the one-tenth portion that I have given you from them as your inheritance, you also must present a gift

offering to the LORD from it, a tenth from
the one-tenth portion. [27]It will be considered your gift offering, like the grain of the
threshing floor and what fills the winepress.
[28]In this way you will also present a gift offering to the LORD from all the one-tenth
portions that you take from the Israelites.
You will provide from it a gift offering to
the LORD for Aaron the priest. [29]You will
present each gift offering to the LORD from
all your gifts, from its best portions and its
holiest parts.

[30]You will say to them: When you have
presented the best portion, it will be considered for the Levites equivalent to the
produce of the grain and the produce of
the winepress. [31]You and your household
may eat it anywhere, because it is payment
for your service in the meeting tent. [32]You
will not bear guilt after you have presented
the best portion. But you must not make
the sacred gifts of the Israelites impure, on
penalty of death.

Instructions about the red cow and the water of purification

19 The LORD spoke to Moses and Aaron:
[2]This is the regulation in the Instruction that the LORD commanded. Tell the
Israelites that they must bring you a red
cow without defect, which is flawless and
on which no yoke has been laid. [3]You will
give it to Eleazar the priest, and he will take
it outside the camp and slaughter it in front
of him. [4]Eleazar the priest will take some
of its blood with his finger and sprinkle it
seven times in front of the meeting tent.
[5]Then he will burn the cow in front of him,
its skin, flesh, and blood, with its dung.
[6]The priest will take cedarwood, hyssop,
and crimson cloth and throw them into
the fire where the cow is burning. [7]Then
the priest will wash his clothes and bathe
his body in water. Afterward the priest will
enter the camp, but he will be unclean until
evening. [8]The one who burned the cow will
wash his clothes in water and bathe his
body in water, but he will be unclean until
evening. [9]A person who is clean will gather
the ashes of the cow and place them outside
the camp in a clean place. They will be kept
for the water of purification for the Israelite
community as a purification offering. [10]The
one who gathers the ashes of the cow will
wash his clothes but will be unclean until
evening. This will be a permanent regulation for the Israelites and for the immigrant who lives among them.

Contact with a dead body

[11]The person who touches the dead body
of any human will be unclean for seven
days. [12]That person must be cleansed with
water on the third and seventh days to be
clean. If he fails to be cleansed with water
on the third and seventh days, he will not
be clean. [13]Anyone who touches the body of
a human who has died and doesn't cleanse
himself defiles the LORD's dwelling. Such
persons must be cut off from Israel because
the water of purification wasn't sprinkled
on them. They remain unclean.

[14]This is the instruction: When anyone
dies in a tent, all who go into the tent and
all who are in the tent are unclean for seven
days. [15]Any open jar without a sealed cover
on it is unclean. [16]Anyone in the open field
who touches a person slain by the sword, or
who died naturally, or a human bone or a
grave, will be unclean for seven days. [17]For
the unclean person, they will take some of
the ashes of the purification offering and
place fresh water with it in a jar. [18]Then a
clean person will take hyssop, dip it into
the water, and sprinkle it on the tent, on all
the jars, on the people who were there, and
on anyone who touched bone, the slain,
the dead, or the grave. [19]On the third day
and the seventh day the clean person will
sprinkle it on the unclean, so that he will
have purified him on the seventh day. He
will then wash his clothes, bathe in water,
and be clean at evening. [20]Any person who
is unclean and didn't cleanse himself will be
cut off from the assembly, because he has
defiled the LORD's sanctuary. He didn't have
the water of purification sprinkled on him.
He is unclean. [21]This will be a permanent
regulation for them. The one who sprinkles
the water of purification will wash his own
clothes. Anyone who touches the water of

purification will be unclean until evening.
[22]Whoever the unclean person touches will
be unclean, and the one who touches the
unclean will be unclean until evening.

Lawsuit over water and Moses' disobedience

20 In the first month,[b] the entire Israelite community entered the Zin
desert and the people stayed at Kadesh.
Miriam died and was buried there. [2]Now
there was no water for the community, and
they assembled against Moses and Aaron.
[3]Then the people confronted Moses and
said to him, "If only we too had died when
our brothers perished in the LORD's presence! [4]Why have you brought the LORD's
assembly into this desert to kill us and
our animals here? [5]Why have you led us
up from Egypt to bring us to this evil place
without grain, figs, vines, or pomegranates? And there's no water to drink!"
[6]Moses and Aaron went away from the
assembly to the entrance of the meeting
tent and they fell on their faces. Then the
LORD's glory appeared to them. [7]The LORD
spoke to Moses: [8]"You and Aaron your
brother, take the staff and assemble the
community. In their presence, tell the rock
to provide water. You will produce water
from the rock for them and allow the community and their animals to drink."
[9]Moses took the staff from the LORD's
presence, as the LORD had commanded
him. [10]Moses and Aaron gathered the assembly before the rock. He said to them,
"Listen, you rebels! Should we produce
water from the rock for you?" [11]Then Moses
raised his hand and struck the rock with his
staff twice. Out flooded water so that the
community and their animals could drink.
[12]The LORD said to Moses and Aaron,
"Because you didn't trust me to show my
holiness before the Israelites, you will not
bring this assembly into the land that I am
giving them." [13]These were the waters of
Meribah,[c] where the Israelites confronted
the LORD with controversy and he showed
his holiness to them.

The Israelites confront Edom

[14]Moses sent messengers from Kadesh
to the king of Edom: "This is what your
brother Israel says: 'You know all the adversity that has happened to us. [15]How our
ancestors went down to Egypt and lived in
Egypt for a long time. The Egyptians oppressed us as they had our ancestors, [16]and
we cried out to the LORD. He heard our
voice, sent a messenger, and brought us
out of Egypt. Now here we are in Kadesh,
a city on the edge of your border. [17]Please
let us cross through your land. We won't
pass through any field or vineyard, or drink
water from any well. We will walk on the
King's Highway and not turn to the right
or to the left until we have crossed your
border.'"
[18]Edom said to him, "You won't cross
through, or I will come out against you with
a sword."
[19]The Israelites said to him, "We'll go up
by the road. If we drink from your water,
either we or our livestock, we'll pay for it.
It's a small matter. We would only ask to
cross on foot."
[20]But he said, "You won't cross." Then
Edom came out against them with a powerful army and a strong hand. [21]Edom refused
to allow Israel to cross his border. And Israel turned away from him. [22]They marched
from Kadesh.

Aaron's death at Mount Hor

The entire Israelite community came to
Mount Hor. [23]The LORD said to Moses and
Aaron at Mount Hor on the border of the
land of Edom: [24]Aaron will join his ancestors, for he may not enter the land that I've
given to the Israelites, because you rebelled
against my command at the waters of Meribah. [25]Take Aaron and his son Eleazar, and
bring them up Mount Hor. [26]Strip Aaron
of his clothes and put them on Eleazar his
son. Then Aaron will die there.
[27]Moses did as the LORD commanded.
They went up Mount Hor in the sight of
the entire community. [28]Moses stripped
Aaron of his clothes and put them on

[b]March–April, Nisan [c]Or *confrontation*

Eleazar his son. Aaron died there at the top of the mountain. Then Moses and Eleazar descended from the mountain. 29 When the entire community saw that Aaron had died, the entire household of Israel wept thirty days for Aaron.

Defeat of the Canaanite king of Arad

21 When the Canaanite king of Arad, who ruled in the arid southern plain, heard that the Israelites were coming on the Atharim road, he fought against Israel and took some of them captive. 2 Then Israel made a solemn promise to the LORD and said, "If you give this people into our hands, we will completely destroy their city." 3 The LORD heard the voice of Israel and handed the Canaanites over. They completely destroyed them and their cities, so the name of the place is called Hormah.[d]

The bronze snake's healing power

4 They marched from Mount Hor on the Reed Sea[e] road around the land of Edom. The people became impatient on the road. 5 The people spoke against God and Moses: "Why did you bring us up from Egypt to kill us in the desert, where there is no food or water. And we detest this miserable bread!" 6 So the LORD sent poisonous[f] snakes among the people and they bit the people. Many of the Israelites died.

7 The people went to Moses and said, "We've sinned, for we spoke against the LORD and you. Pray to the LORD so that he will send the snakes away from us." So Moses prayed for the people.

8 The LORD said to Moses, "Make a poisonous snake and place it on a pole. Whoever is bitten can look at it and live." 9 Moses made a bronze snake and placed it on a pole. If a snake bit someone, that person could look at the bronze snake and live.

March around Moab

10 Then the Israelites marched and they camped at Oboth. 11 They marched from Oboth and camped at Iye-abarim in the desert on the border of Moab toward the east. 12 From there they marched and camped in the Zered ravine. 13 From there they marched and camped across the Arnon in the desert that extends from the border of the Amorites, for the Arnon was the border of Moab, between Moab and the Amorites. 14 For this reason the scroll of the LORD's wars says:

Waheb in Suphah and the ravines.
The Arnon 15 and the ravines
that extend to the settlement of Ar
and lie along the border of Moab.

16 From there they marched to Beer, the well where the LORD said to Moses, "Gather the people, and I'll give them water." 17 Then the Israelites sang this song:

"Well, flow up!
Sing about it!
18 The well that the officials dug,
that the officials of the people
hollowed out
with the ruler's scepter and their staffs."

They marched from the desert to Mattanah; 19 from Mattanah to Nahaliel; from Nahaliel to Bamoth; 20 from Bamoth to the valley in the Moabite countryside, to the top of Pisgah overlooking Jeshimon.[g]

Wars against Sihon and Og

21 Then the Israelites sent messengers to Sihon the Amorite king: 22 "Let us pass through your land. We won't turn aside into a field or vineyard. We won't drink water from a well. We will walk on the King's Highway until we cross your border."

23 But Sihon wouldn't allow the Israelites to cross his border. Sihon gathered all his people and went out to meet the Israelites in the desert. When he came to Jahaz, he attacked the Israelites. 24 The Israelites struck him down with their swords and took possession of his land from the Arnon to the Jabbok, as far as the Ammonites, for the border of the Ammonites was fortified. 25 The Israelites took all these cities. Then the Israelites settled in all the cities of the Amorites, in Heshbon and all its villages.

26 Now Heshbon was the city of Sihon the Amorite king who had fought against the former king of Moab. He had taken

[d] Or *destruction* [e] Or *Red Sea* [f] Heb uncertain [g] Or *wasteland*

all his land from him as far as the Arnon. 27 Therefore, the poets say:

"Come to Heshbon, let it be built.
Let the city of Sihon be established.
28 Fire went out from Heshbon,
flame from Sihon's city.
It consumed Ar of Moab
and swallowed up
the shrines of the Arnon.
29 You are doomed, Moab!
You are destroyed, people of Chemosh!
He gave his sons as fugitives,
and his daughters as captives
to the Amorite king Sihon.
30 Yet we have thrown them down,
destroying them[h]
from Heshbon to Dibon.
We brought ruin until Nophah,
which is by Medeba."

31 Israel settled in the land of the Amorites. 32 Moses sent spies to Jazer. They captured its villages and took possession of the Amorites who were there. 33 Then they turned and ascended the road of Bashan. Og, Bashan's king, came out at Edrei to meet them in battle, he and all his people. 34 The LORD said to Moses: Don't be afraid of him, for I have handed over all his people and his land. Do to him as you did to Sihon the Amorite king who ruled in Heshbon.

35 They slaughtered Og, his sons, and all his people until there were no survivors. Then they took possession of his land.

Balak summons Balaam to curse the Israelites

22 The Israelites marched and camped in the plains of Moab across the Jordan from Jericho. 2 Balak, Zippor's son, saw everything that the Israelites did to the Amorites. 3 The Moabites greatly feared the people, for they were so numerous. The Moabites were terrified of the Israelites. 4 The Moabites said to the elders of Midian, "Now this assembly will devour everything around us, as an ox eats up the grass in the field."

Balak, Zippor's son, was king of Moab at that time. 5 He sent messengers to Balaam, Beor's son, at Pethor, which is by the river in the land of his people,[i] to summon him: "A people has come out of Egypt, and they have now covered the land. They have settled next to me. 6 Now please come and curse this people for me because they are stronger than I am. Perhaps I'll be able to destroy them and drive them from the land, for I know that whomever you bless is blessed and whomever you curse is cursed."

7 So the elders of Moab and Midian went with the payment for divination in their hands. They came to Balaam and told him Balak's words. 8 He said to them, "Spend the night here and I'll bring back to you a word exactly as the LORD speaks to me." So the officials of Moab stayed with Balaam.

9 God came to Balaam and said, "Who are these men with you?"

10 Balaam said to God, "Moab's King Balak, Zippor's son, sent them to me with the message, 11 'A people has come out of Egypt and covered the land. Now come and curse them for me. Perhaps I'll be able to fight against them and drive them out.' "

12 God said to Balaam, "Don't go with them. Don't curse the people, because they are blessed."

13 Then Balaam arose in the morning and said to Balak's officials, "Go to your land, for the LORD has refused to allow me to go with you."

14 The officials of Moab arose, they went to Balak, and they said, "Balaam refused to come with us."

15 Balak continued to send other officials more numerous and important than these. 16 They came to Balaam and said to him, "This is what Balak, Zippor's son, says: 'Please let nothing hold you back from coming to me, 17 for I'll greatly honor you and I'll do anything you ask of me. Please come and curse this people for me.' "

18 Balaam answered and said to Balak's servants, "If Balak were to give me his house full of silver and gold, I wouldn't be able to do anything, small or great, to break the command of the LORD my God. 19 Now you also must remain the night here so

[h] Heb uncertain; LXX *their posterity has perished* [i] Sam, Syr, Vulg *the Ammonites*

that I may know what else the LORD may say to me."

20 God came to Balaam in the night and said to him, "If the men have come to summon you, arise and go with them. But you must do only what I tell you to do." 21 So Balaam arose in the morning, saddled his donkey, and went with the officials of Moab.

Balaam and the LORD's messenger

22 Then God became angry because he went. So while he was riding on his donkey accompanied by his two servants, the LORD's messenger stood in the road as his adversary. 23 The donkey saw the LORD's messenger standing in the road with his sword drawn in his hand, so the donkey turned from the road and went into the field. Balaam struck the donkey in order to turn him back onto the road. 24 Then the LORD's messenger stood in the narrow path between vineyards with a stone wall on each side. 25 When the donkey saw the LORD's messenger, it leaned against the wall and squeezed Balaam's foot against the wall, so he continued to beat it. 26 The LORD's messenger persisted and crossed over and stood in a narrow place, where it wasn't possible to turn either right or left. 27 The donkey saw the LORD's messenger and lay down underneath Balaam. Balaam became angry and beat the donkey with the rod. 28 Then the LORD opened the donkey's mouth and it said to Balaam, "What have I done to you that you've beaten me these three times?"

29 Balaam said to the donkey, "Because you've tormented me. If I had a sword in my hand, I'd kill you now."

30 The donkey said to Balaam, "Am I not your donkey, on whom you've often ridden to this day? Have I been in the habit of doing this to you?"

Balaam said, "No."

31 Then the LORD uncovered Balaam's eyes, and Balaam saw the LORD's messenger standing in the road with his sword drawn in his hand. Then he bowed low and worshipped. 32 The LORD's messenger said to him, "Why have you beaten your donkey these three times? I've come out here as an adversary, because you took the road recklessly in front of me. 33 The donkey saw me and turned away from me these three times. If it hadn't turned away from me, I would just now have killed you and let it live."

34 Balaam said to the LORD's messenger, "I've sinned, because I didn't know that you were standing against me in the road. Now, if you think it's wrong, I'll go back."

35 The LORD's messenger said to Balaam, "Go with the men. But don't say anything. Say only that which I tell you." So Balaam went with Balak's officials.

Balaam and Balak meet

36 When Balak heard that Balaam was coming, he went out to meet him at Ir-moab, which is on the border of the Arnon at the farthest point of the border. 37 Balak said to Balaam, "Didn't I send urgently and summon you? Why didn't you come to me? Am I really not able to honor you?"

38 Balaam said to Balak, "I've now come to you. But I'm only able to speak whatever word God gives me to say. That is what I will speak."

Balaam's first blessing of the Israelites

39 Then Balaam went with Balak and they came to Kiriath-huzoth. 40 Balak sacrificed oxen and sheep and sent them to Balaam and the officials who were with him. 41 In the morning Balak took Balaam and brought him up to Bamoth-baal, where he could see part of the people.

23 Balaam said to Balak, "Build me seven altars here and prepare for me seven bulls and seven rams." 2 Balak did as Balaam had said. Then Balak and Balaam offered a bull and a ram on each altar. 3 Balaam said to Balak, "Stay by your entirely burned offering. I will go and perhaps the LORD will grant me an appearance and speak. Whatever he shows me, I will tell you." Then he went off to a high outlook.

4 God granted Balaam an appearance. Balaam said to him, "I have arranged seven altars and I have sacrificed a bull and a ram on each altar."

5 The LORD gave Balaam something to say, and said to him, "Return to Balak and say this."

6 Balaam returned to him, while he and all the officials of Moab were standing next to his entirely burned offering. 7 Then he raised his voice and made his address:

"From Aram Balak led me;
the king of Moab,
from the eastern mountains.
Come, curse Jacob for me;
come, denounce Israel.
8 How can I curse
whom God hasn't cursed?
How can I denounce
whom God hasn't denounced?
9 From the top of the rocks I see him;
from the hills I gaze on him.
Here is a people living alone;
it doesn't consider itself
among the nations.
10 Who can count the dust of Jacob,
or number a fourth of Israel?
Let me die the death of those who do right,
and let my end be like his."

11 Then Balak said to Balaam, "What have you done to me? I took you to curse my enemy. But now you've blessed him."

12 He answered and said, "Don't I have to take care to speak whatever the LORD gives me to say?"

Balaam's second blessing of the Israelites

13 Then Balak said to Balaam, "Come with me, please, to another place where you'll see them. You'll see only part of them. You won't see all of them. Then curse them for
me from there." 14 He took him to the field of Zophim, to the top of Pisgah. He built seven altars and offered a bull and a ram on each altar.

15 Then Balaam said to Balak, "Stand here by your entirely burned offering, while I seek an appearance over there."

16 The LORD granted Balaam an appearance and gave him a message. He said, "Return to Balak and say this."

17 Balaam approached Balak, who was standing by his entirely burned offering with the officials of Moab. Balak said to him, "What did the LORD say?"

18 Then Balaam raised his voice and made his address:

"Arise, Balak, and listen;
hear me out, Zippor's son.
19 God isn't a man that he would lie,
or a human being that he would
change his mind.
Has he ever spoken and not done it,
or promised and not fulfilled it?
20 I received a blessing, and he blessed.
I can't take it back.
21 He hasn't envisioned misfortune
for Jacob,
nor has he seen trouble for Israel.
The LORD his God is with him,
proclaimed as his king.
22 God, who brought them out of Egypt,
is like a magnificent wild bull for him.
23 There is no omen against Jacob,
no divination against Israel.
Instantly it is told to Jacob,
and to Israel, what God performs.
24 A people now rises like a lioness,
like a lion it stands up.
It doesn't lie down until it eats the prey
and drinks the blood of the slain."

25 Then Balak said to Balaam, "Don't curse them or bless them."

26 But Balaam answered and said to Balak, "Didn't I say to you, 'I'll do whatever the LORD tells me to'?"

Balaam's third blessing of the Israelites

27 Balak said to Balaam, "Please come and I'll take you to another place. Perhaps God will prefer it, so that you could curse him for me from there."

28 So Balak took Balaam to the top of
Peor, which overlooks Jeshimon.[j] 29 Balaam
said to Balak, "Build me seven altars here and prepare for me seven bulls and seven
rams." 30 Balak did just as Balaam said. He offered a bull and a ram on each altar.

24 Balaam saw that it pleased the LORD to bless the Israelites, so he didn't go as the other times to seek omens. Instead,

[j] Or *wasteland*

he turned toward the desert. [2]Balaam
looked up and saw Israel camping by tribes.
Then God's spirit came on him. [3]He raised
his voice and made his address:

"The oracle of Balaam, Beor's son;
the oracle of a man whose eye is open.[k]
[4]The oracle of one
who hears God's speech,
who perceives the Almighty's[l] visions,
who falls down with eyes uncovered.
[5]How beautiful are your tents, Jacob,
your camps, Israel!
[6]Like palm groves that stretch out,
like gardens next to a river,
like eaglewood trees
that the LORD has planted,
like cedar trees next to water.
[7]Water will drip from his branches;
his seed will have plenty of water;
his king will be higher than Agag,
and his kingdom will be lifted up.
[8]God, who brought him from Egypt,
is like a magnificent wild bull for him.
He will devour enemy nations
and break their bones;
he will strike with his arrows.
[9]He crouched and lay down like a lion;
like a lioness, who can make her rise?
The one blessing you will be blessed,
and the one cursing you will be cursed."

[10]Balak was angry with Balaam. He
pounded his fists. Balak said to Balaam, "I
summoned you to curse my enemies, but
now you've given a blessing these three
times. [11]Now get out of here and go home. I
told you I'd greatly honor you, but the LORD
has denied you any honor."

Balaam predicts Moab's destruction

[12]Balaam said to Balak, "Didn't I tell your
messengers, whom you sent to me, [13]'If
Balak would give me his house full of silver
and gold, I wouldn't be able to break the
LORD's command for good or ill by my own
will. I'll say whatever the LORD says'? [14]So
now I'm going to my people. Let me advise
you what this people will do to your people
in the days to come." [15]He raised his voice
and made his address:

"The oracle of Balaam, Beor's son,
the oracle of a man whose eye is open.
[16]The oracle of one
who hears God's speech,
and understands
the Most High's[m] knowledge,
who perceives the Almighty's[n] visions,
who falls down with eyes uncovered.
[17]I see him, but not now;
I look at him, but not nearby.
A star comes from Jacob;
a scepter arises from Israel,
smashing Moab's forehead,
the head of all the Sethites.
[18]Edom will become a possession,
Seir a possession of its enemies.
But Israel acts powerfully.
[19]Someone from Jacob will rule
and destroy the survivors from Ir."

[20]He looked at Amalek
and raised his voice
and gave his address:
"Amalek is foremost
among the nations,
but its end is to perish forever."

[21]He looked at the Kenites
and raised his voice
and gave his address:
"Your dwelling is secure;
your nest is set in the rock.
[22]Yet Kain will burn
when Asshur takes you away captive."

[23]He raised his voice
and made his address:
"How terrible!
Who will live when God does this?
[24]Ships from Kittim will attack Asshur;
they will attack Eber,
and even he will perish forever."

[25]Then Balaam arose, set out, and returned home. Balak also went on his way.

Israelites and Moabites intermarry

25 When the Israelites lived at Shittim, the people made themselves impure by having illicit sex with Moabite women.

[k]Heb uncertain [l]Heb *Shaddai* or *Mountain One* [m]Heb *Elyon* [n]Heb *Shaddai* or *Mountain One*

[2]The Moabite women invited the people to the sacrifices for their god. So the people ate a meal, and they worshipped their god. [3]Israel became attached to the Baal of Peor, and the LORD was angry at the Israelites. [4]The LORD said to Moses: Take all the leaders of the people and kill them on behalf of the LORD in broad daylight, so that the LORD's anger turns away from Israel.

[5]Then Moses said to Israel's officials, "Each of you: kill your men who are attached to the Baal of Peor."

Israelites and Midianites intermarry

[6]An Israelite man brought a Midianite woman to his brothers in the sight of Moses and the entire Israelite community, who were weeping at the entrance of the meeting tent. [7]When Phinehas (Eleazar's son and Aaron the priest's grandson) saw this, he arose in the middle of the community, took a spear in his hand, [8]went after the Israelite man into the chamber, and stabbed the two of them, the Israelite man and the woman, through the stomach. Then the plague stopped spreading among the Israelites. [9]Yet those who died by the plague numbered twenty-four thousand.

[10]The LORD spoke to Moses: [11]Phinehas (Eleazar's son and Aaron the priest's grandson) has turned back my rage toward the Israelites. Because he was jealous for me among you, I didn't consume the Israelites due to my jealousy. [12]Therefore, say: I'm now giving him my covenant of well-being. [13]It will be for him and his descendants a covenant of permanent priesthood, because he was jealous for his God and sought reconciliation for the Israelites.

[14]The name of the slain Israelite man who was killed with the Midianite woman was Zimri the son of Salu, chief of Simeon's household. [15]The name of the slain Midianite woman was Cozbi the daughter of Zur, a tribal leader of a Midianite household. [16]The LORD spoke to Moses: [17]Go after the Midianites and destroy them [18]because they went after you by the deception they devised for you at Peor with Cozbi, the Midianite chief's daughter and their sister, who was killed on the same day as the plague during the events at Peor.

Second census of the Israelite tribes

26 [o]After the plague [p]the LORD said to Moses and Eleazar, Aaron the priest's son: [2]Take a census of the entire Israelite community, from 20 years old and above by their households, to determine everyone in Israel who is eligible for military service.

[3]Moses and Eleazar the priest spoke to the people on the plains of Moab by the Jordan opposite Jericho: [4]"Take a census of those 20 years old and above as the LORD commanded Moses." The Israelites who left the land of Egypt were:

[5]Reuben, Israel's oldest son.

Reuben's descendants: from Hanoch, the Hanochite clan; from Pallu, the Palluite clan; [6]from Hezron, the Hezronite clan; from Carmi, the Carmite clan. [7]These are the Reubenite clans. Their enrollment was 43,730.

[8]Pallu's descendants: Eliab.

[9]Eliab's descendants: Nemuel, Dathan, and Abiram. These are the Dathan and Abiram chosen by the community who fought against Moses and Aaron with the community of Korah, when they fought against the LORD. [10]The earth opened its mouth and swallowed them, along with Korah, when the community died and fire devoured 250 persons. They became a warning sign. [11]But Korah's descendants didn't die.

[12]Simeon's descendants according to their clans: from Nemuel, the Nemuelite clan; from Jamin, the Jaminite clan; from Jachin, the Jachinite clan; [13]from Zerah, the Zerahite clan; from Shaul, the Shaulite clan. [14]These are the Simeonite clans, 22,200.

[15]Gad's descendants according to their clans: from Zephon, the Zephonite clan; from Haggi, the Haggite clan; from Shuni, the Shunite clan; [16]from Ozni, the Oznite clan; from Eri, the Erite clan; [17]from Arod, the Arodite clan; from Areli,

[o]25:19 in Heb [p]26:1 in Heb

the Arelite clan. [18]These are the Gadite clans. Their enrollment was 40,500.

[19]Judah's descendants: Er and Onan. Er and Onan died in the land of Canaan. [20]Judah's descendants according to their clans: from Shelah, the Shelanite clan; from Perez, the Perezite clan; from Zerah, the Zerahite clan.

[21]Perez's descendants: from Hezron, the Hezronite clan; from Hamul, the Hamulite clan. [22]These are the Judahite clans. Their enrollment was 76,500.

[23]Issachar's descendants according to their clans: from Tola, the Tolaite clan; from Puvah, the Punite clan; [24]from Jashub, the Jashubite clan; from Shimron, the Shimronite clan. [25]These are the Issacharite clans. Their enrollment was 64,300.

[26]Zebulun's descendants according to their clans: from Sered, the Seredite clan; from Elon, the Elonite clan; from Jahleel, the Jahleelite clan. [27]These are the Zebulunite clans. Their enrollment was 60,500.

[28]Joseph's descendants according to their clans: Manasseh and Ephraim.

[29]Manasseh's descendants: from Machir, the Machirite clan. Machir fathered Gilead. From Gilead, the Gileadite clan. [30]These are Gilead's descendants: from Iezer, the Iezerite clan; from Helek, the Helekite clan; [31]from Asriel, the Asrielite clan; from Shechem, the Shechemite clan; [32]from Shemida, the Shemidaite clan; and from Hepher, the Hepherite clan. [33]But Zelophehad, Hepher's son, had no sons, only daughters. The names of Zelophehad's daughters were Mahlah, Noah, Hoglah, Milcah, and Tirzah. [34]These are the Manassehite clans. Their enrollment was 52,700.

[35]These are Ephraim's descendants according to their clans: from Shuthelah, the Shuthelahite clan; from Becher, the Becherite clan; from Tahan, the Tahanite clan. [36]These are Shuthelah's descendants: from Eran, the Eranite clan. [37]These are Ephraim's descendants. Their enrollment was 32,500. These are Joseph's descendants according to their clans.

[38]Benjamin's descendants according to their clans: from Bela, the Belaite clan; from Ashbel, the Ashbelite clan; from Ahiram, the Ahiramite clan; [39]from Shupham,[q] the Shuphamite clan; from Hupham, the Huphamite clan. [40]Bela's descendants were Ard and Naaman: from Ard, the Ardite clan; from Naaman, the Naamite clan. [41]These are Benjamin's descendants according to their clans. Their enrollment was 45,600.

[42]These are Dan's descendants according to their clans: from Shuham, the Shuhamite clan. These are the Danite clans according to their clans. [43]All the Shuhamite clans according to their enrollment were 64,400.

[44]Asher's descendants according to their clans: from Imnah, the Imnite clan; from Ishvi, the Ishvite clan; from Beriah, the Beriite clan. [45]From Beriah's descendants: from Heber, the Heberite clan; from Malchiel, the Malchielite clan. [46]The name of Asher's daughter was Serah. [47]These are the clans of Asher's descendants. Their enrollment was 53,400.

[48]Naphtali's descendants according to their clans: from Jahzeel, the Jahzeelite clan; from Guni, the Gunite clan; [49]from Jezer, the Jezerite clan; from Shillem, the Shillemite clan. [50]These are Naphtali's clans according to their clans. Their enrollment was 45,400.

[51]These are the ones enrolled as Israelites: 601,730.

[52]The LORD spoke to Moses: [53]The land will be apportioned to these as an inheritance according to the number of names. [54]To a large clan you will give a large inheritance, and to a small clan you will give a small inheritance. Each will be given its inheritance according to the number of its enrollment. [55]The land, however, will be apportioned by lot. They will inherit according to the names of their ancestral tribes. [56]Whether they are large or small, each tribe will inherit by means of the lot.

[q]LXX, Syr, Tg, Vulg; MT *Shephupham*

Second census of the Levites

[57]These are the ones enrolled as Levites according to their clans: from Gershon, the Gershonite clan; from Kohath, the Kohathite clan; from Merari, the Merarite clan.

[58]These are the Levite clans: the Libnite clan, the Hebronite clan, the Mahlite clan, the Mushite clan, and the Korahite clan. Now Kohath fathered Amram. [59]The name of Amram's wife was Jochebed, Levi's daughter, who was born to Levi in Egypt. She gave birth for Amram to Aaron, Moses, and Miriam their sister. [60]To Aaron were born Nadab, Abihu, Eleazar, and Ithamar. [61]Nadab and Abihu died when they made an unauthorized offering to the LORD. [62]Their enrollment was 23,000, consisting of every male one month old and above. They weren't enrolled with the Israelites because no inheritance of land was given to them among the Israelites.

Summary

[63]These are the ones whom Moses and Eleazar the priest enrolled. They enrolled the Israelites on the plains of Moab by the Jordan opposite Jericho. [64]There wasn't one person among these from those enrolled by Moses and Aaron the priest when they enrolled the Israelites in the Sinai desert. [65]The LORD had said to them, "They will die in the desert." Not one of them remained, except Caleb, Jephunneh's son, and Joshua, Nun's son.

Zelophehad's daughters' inheritance

27 The daughters of Zelophehad, Hepher's son, Gilead's grandson, Machir's great-grandson, and Manasseh's great-great-grandson, belonging to the clan of Manasseh and son of Joseph, came forward. His daughters' names were Mahlah, Noah, Hoglah, Milcah, and Tirzah. [2]They stood before Moses, Eleazar the priest, the chiefs, and the entire community at the entrance of the meeting tent and said, [3]"Our father died in the desert. He wasn't part of the community who gathered against the LORD with Korah's community. He died for his own sin, but he had no sons. [4]Why should our father's name be taken away from his clan because he didn't have a son? Give us property among our father's brothers."

[5]Moses brought their case before the LORD. [6]The LORD said to Moses: [7]Zelophehad's daughters are right in what they are saying. By all means, give them property as an inheritance among their father's brothers. Hand over their father's inheritance to them. [8]Speak to the Israelites and say: If a man dies and doesn't have a son, you must hand his inheritance over to his daughters. [9]If he doesn't have a daughter, you will give his inheritance to his brothers. [10]If he doesn't have any brothers, you should give his inheritance to his father's brothers. [11]If his father had no brothers, you should give his inheritance to his nearest relative from his clan. He will take possession of it. This will be a regulation and a case law for the Israelites, as the LORD commanded Moses.

Announcement of Moses' death

[12]The LORD said to Moses, "Go up this mountain, Abarim, and look at the land that I've given to the Israelites. [13]You will see it and then join your ancestors just as Aaron your brother has, [14]because in the Zin desert, when the community confronted you, you rebelled against my command to show them my holiness by means of the water." (These are the waters of Meribah[r] of Kadesh in the Zin desert.)

[15]Moses spoke to the LORD: [16]"Let the LORD, the God of all living things, appoint someone over the community [17]who will go out before them and return before them, someone who will lead them out and bring them back, so that the LORD's community won't be like sheep without their shepherd."

[18]The LORD said to Moses, "Take Joshua, Nun's son, a man who has the spirit, and lay your hand on him. [19]Place him before Eleazar the priest and the entire community and commission him before them. [20]You will give him some of your power so that the entire Israelite community may obey. [21]He will stand

[r] Or *confrontation*

before Eleazar the priest, who will determine for him the decision by lot before the LORD. At his command, he and all the Israelites with him, the entire community, will go out, and at his command they will return."

22Moses did as the LORD commanded him. He took Joshua and placed him before Eleazar the priest and the entire community. 23He laid his hands on him and commissioned him as the LORD had spoken through Moses.

Daily offering

28 The LORD spoke to Moses: 2Command the Israelites and say to them: Make sure to offer to me my offering, my food, my food gift as a soothing smell to me at its appointed time.

3You will say to them: This is the food gift that you must present to the LORD: two flawless one-year-old lambs as the regular entirely burned offering every day. 4One lamb you will offer in the morning and the second at twilight, 5with a tenth of an ephah[s] of fine flour for a grain offering mixed with a fourth of a hin[t] of beaten oil. 6It is the regular entirely burned offering begun at Mount Sinai, a food gift that is a soothing smell to the LORD. 7Their drink offering will be a fourth of a hin for each lamb. In the sanctuary a drink offering of brandy will be poured out for the LORD. 8The second lamb you will offer at twilight like the grain offering and the drink offering in the morning. You will offer a food gift that is a soothing smell to the LORD.

9On the Sabbath day: two flawless one-year-old male lambs and two-tenths of fine flour for a grain offering, mixed with oil, and its drink offering. 10This is the entirely burned offering for every Sabbath, in addition to the regular entirely burned offering and its drink offering.

Monthly offering

11At the beginning of every month you will present an entirely burned offering to the LORD: two bulls from the herd, one ram, and seven one-year-old male lambs, all flawless. 12Use three-tenths of fine flour for a grain offering mixed with oil for each bull, two-tenths of fine flour for a grain offering mixed with oil for each ram, 13and one-tenth of fine flour for a grain offering mixed with oil for each lamb. It is an entirely burned offering with a soothing smell, a food gift to the LORD. 14Their drink offerings will be half a hin of wine for a bull, a third a hin of wine for a ram, and a fourth a hin of wine for a lamb. This is the monthly entirely burned offering for every month through the months of the year. 15There will be one male goat for a purification offering to the LORD in addition to the regular entirely burned offering and its drink offering.

Yearly offerings

Passover and unleavened bread

16On the fourteenth day of the first month[u] there will be a Passover offering to the LORD. 17On the fifteenth day of this month there will be a festival. For seven days unleavened bread will be eaten. 18The first day will be a holy occasion. You will not do any job-related work. 19You will bring a food gift, an entirely burned offering to the LORD: two bulls from the herd, one ram, and seven male lambs one year old. They will be flawless. 20Their grain offering will be fine flour mixed with oil. You will offer three-tenths for the bull, two-tenths for the ram, 21and one-tenth for each of the seven lambs, 22along with one male goat for a purification offering to seek reconciliation for yourselves. 23You will offer these in addition to the entirely burned offering of the morning, which is the regular entirely burned offering. 24Like these, you will also offer each day for seven days a food gift as a soothing smell to the LORD. It will be offered in addition to the regular entirely burned offering and its drink offering. 25The seventh day will be a holy occasion for you. You will not do any job-related work.

Festival of Weeks

26The day of the early produce, when you present your new grain offering to the

[s]One ephah is approximately twenty quarts. [t]One hin is approximately one gallon. [u]March–April, Nisan

LORD at your Festival of Weeks, will be a holy occasion for you. You will not do any job-related work. [27]You will present an entirely burned offering as a soothing smell to the LORD: two bulls from the herd, one ram, and seven male lambs one year old. [28]Their grain offering will be fine flour mixed with oil: three-tenths for each bull, two-tenths for the one ram, [29]and one-tenth for each of the seven lambs. [30]Offer one male goat to seek reconciliation for yourselves. [31]You will offer these in addition to the regular entirely burned offering, its grain offering and drink offerings. They will be flawless.

Blowing of the trumpet

29 The first day of the seventh month[v] will be a holy occasion for you. You will not do any job-related work. It will be for you a day of the trumpet's sound. [2]You will offer an entirely burned offering as a soothing smell to the LORD: one bull from the herd, one ram, and seven male lambs one year old, all flawless. [3]Their grain offering will be fine flour mixed with oil, three-tenths for the bull, two-tenths for the ram, [4]and one-tenth for each of the seven lambs. [5]There will be one male goat for a purification offering to seek reconciliation for yourselves. [6]This is in addition to the monthly entirely burned offering with its grain offering, and the regular entirely burned offering with its grain offering and drink offerings as prescribed. It will be a soothing smell, a food gift to the LORD.

Day of Reconciliation

[7]The tenth day of this seventh month will be a holy occasion for you. You will deny yourselves and not do any work. [8]You will present an entirely burned offering to the LORD as a soothing smell: one bull from the herd, one ram, and seven male lambs one year old. They will be flawless. [9]Their grain offering will be fine flour mixed with oil, three-tenths for the bull, two-tenths for the one ram, [10]and one-tenth for each of the seven lambs. [11]There will be one male goat for a purification offering in addition to the purification offering of reconciliation, and the regular entirely burned offering with its grain offering and drink offerings.

Festival of Booths

[12]The fifteenth day of the seventh month[w] will be a holy occasion for you. You will not do any job-related work. You will celebrate a festival to the LORD for seven days. [13]You will present an entirely burned offering, a food gift as a soothing smell to the LORD: thirteen bulls from the herd, two rams, and fourteen male lambs one year old. They will be flawless. [14]Their grain offering will be fine flour mixed with oil: three-tenths for each of the thirteen bulls, two-tenths for each of the two rams, [15]and one-tenth for each of the fourteen lambs. [16]There will be one male goat for a purification offering in addition to the regular entirely burned offering with its grain offering and its drink offering.

[17]On the second day: twelve bulls from the herd, two rams, and fourteen male lambs one year old, all flawless. [18]The grain offering and drink offerings for the bulls, rams, and lambs will be as prescribed for their number. [19]There will be one male goat for a purification offering in addition to the regular entirely burned offering with its grain offering and drink offerings.

[20]On the third day: eleven bulls, two rams, and fourteen male lambs one year old, all flawless. [21]The grain offering and drink offerings for the bulls, rams, and lambs will be as prescribed for their number. [22]There will be one male goat for a purification offering in addition to the regular entirely burned offering with its grain offering and drink offering.

[23]On the fourth day: ten bulls, two rams, and fourteen male lambs one year old, all flawless. [24]The grain offering and drink offerings for the bulls, rams, and lambs will be as prescribed for their number. [25]There will be one male goat for a purification offering in addition to the regular entirely burned offering with its grain offering and drink offering.

[26]On the fifth day: nine bulls, two rams, and fourteen male lambs one year old, all flawless. [27]The grain offering and their

[v]September–October, Tishrei [w]September–October, Tishrei

drink offerings for the bulls, rams, and lambs will be as prescribed for their number. 28 There will be one male goat for a purification offering in addition to the regular entirely burned offering with its grain offering and drink offering.

29 On the sixth day: eight bulls, two rams, and fourteen male lambs one year old, all flawless. 30 The grain offering and their drink offerings for the bulls, rams, and lambs will be as prescribed for their number. 31 There will be one male goat for a purification offering in addition to the regular entirely burned offering with its grain offering and its drink offerings.

32 On the seventh day: seven bulls, two rams, and fourteen male lambs one year old, all flawless. 33 The grain offering and their drink offering for the bulls, rams, and lambs will be as prescribed for their number. 34 There will be one male goat for a purification offering in addition to the regular entirely burned offering with its grain offering and its drink offering.

35 On the eighth day you will have a holiday. You will not do any job-related work. 36 You will present an entirely burned offering, a food gift as a soothing smell to the LORD: one bull, one ram, and seven male lambs one year old, all without blemish. 37 The grain offering and their drink offerings for the bull, ram, and lambs will be as prescribed for their number. 38 There will be one male goat for a purification offering in addition to the regular entirely burned offering with its grain offering and its drink offering.

39 These you will offer to the LORD at your appointed times in addition to your payments for solemn promises, your spontaneous gifts, your entirely burned offerings, your grain offerings, your drink offerings, and your well-being sacrifices.

40[x] Moses told the Israelites everything that the LORD commanded Moses.

Solemn promises by men

30 Moses spoke to the leaders of the tribes of the Israelites: This is what the LORD has commanded: 2 When a man makes a solemn promise to the LORD or swears a solemn pledge of binding obligation for himself, he cannot break his word. He must do everything he said.

Solemn promises by women

3 When a woman makes a solemn promise to the LORD or a binding obligation while she is young and in her father's household, 4 and her father hears her solemn promise or her binding obligation for herself and keeps silent[y]—then all her solemn promises and any of her binding obligations for herself will stand. 5 But if her father expresses disapproval to her on the day that he hears her, none of her solemn promises nor any of her binding obligations for herself will stand. The LORD will forgive her, because her father expressed disapproval to her.

6 If she marries while her solemn promise is in effect or makes a statement by which she binds herself, 7 and her husband hears it and on the day he hears it keeps silent—her solemn promises will stand as well as her binding obligations for herself. 8 But if on the day that her husband hears it he expresses disapproval to her, he can break her solemn promise and the statement by which she bound herself. Then the LORD will forgive her.

9 Every solemn promise of a widow or a divorced woman who makes a binding obligation for herself will stand.

10 If a woman makes a solemn promise in her husband's household or makes a binding obligation for herself with a solemn pledge, 11 and her husband hears, keeps silent, and doesn't express disapproval to her—then all her solemn promises will stand and all her binding obligations for herself will stand. 12 If her husband breaks them on the day he hears them, then whatever she said with regard to her solemn promises or the binding obligations for herself will not stand. Her husband has broken them. The LORD will forgive her.

13 Her husband may allow any solemn promise or any binding pledge of self-denial

[x] 30:1 in Heb [y] Or *her father is deaf to her.*

to stand or be broken. [14]But if her husband keeps silent from one day to the next, he has upheld all her solemn promises, or all her binding obligations. He has upheld them because he remained silent on the day he heard them. [15]If he breaks them after he has heard them, he will assume her guilt.

[16]These are the regulations that the LORD commanded Moses concerning a husband and his wife and between a father and his daughter while she is young and in her father's household.

War against the Midianites

31 The LORD spoke to Moses: [2]Take just reparations for the Israelites from the Midianites. Afterward you will join your ancestors.

[3]Moses spoke to the people: "Equip some of your men for battle so that they may go against Midian and execute the LORD's just punishment against Midian. [4]You will send out for battle one thousand from each of the tribes of Israel."

[5]From the thousands of Israel, one thousand from each tribe were selected. Twelve thousand were equipped for battle. [6]Moses sent them to battle, one thousand from each tribe, along with Phinehas, Eleazar the priest's son, who carried the sanctuary equipment and the trumpets for sounding the alarm in his hand. [7]They battled against Midian as the LORD had commanded Moses, and they killed every male. [8]They killed the kings of Midian: Evi, Rekem, Zur, Hur, and Reba, the five kings of Midian, along with others slain. They also killed Balaam, Beor's son, with the sword. [9]The Israelites took captive the Midianite women, their little ones, all their cattle, their herds, and their possessions. [10]They burned all the cities where they lived and their encampments. [11]They took all the spoils of war and the valuable property, both human and animal, [12]and they brought the captives, the valuable property, and the spoils of war to Moses, Eleazar the priest, and the Israelite community, at the camp on the plains of Moab by the Jordan across from Jericho.

Purification from war

[13]Moses, Eleazar the priest, and the chiefs of the community went to meet them outside the camp. [14]Moses became angry with the commanders of the army, the officers of thousands and the officers of hundreds, who came back from the battle. [15]Moses said to them, "Have you let all the women live? [16]These very women, on Balaam's advice, made the Israelites break faith with the LORD in the affair at Peor, so there was a plague among the LORD's community. [17]Now kill every male child and every female who has known a man intimately by sleeping with him. [18]But all the young girls who have not known a man intimately by sleeping with him, spare for yourselves. [19]You will remain outside the camp for seven days. Everyone among you or your captives who has killed a person or touched a corpse must purify themselves on the third and seventh days. [20]You must also purify every garment, and everything made of leather, goats' hair, or wood."

Instructions about the spoils of war

[21]Eleazar the priest said to the men of battle who had gone out to war, "This is the regulation in the Instruction that the LORD commanded Moses: [22]Gold, silver, copper, iron, tin, and lead—[23]anything that can withstand fire—you will put through the fire and it will be clean. It will also be purified with the water of purification. Anything that isn't able to withstand fire, you will immerse in water. [24]You must wash your clothes on the seventh day and you will be clean. Afterward you may enter the camp."

[25]The LORD said to Moses: [26]You, Eleazar the priest, and the leaders of the community's households must take an inventory of the valuable property and the captives, both human and animals, [27]and divide the valuable property between the warriors who went into battle and the entire community. [28]You will offer as tribute to the LORD from each warrior who went into battle one living being in five hundred, whether human, oxen, donkeys, or flocks. [29]Take it from the warriors' half and give it to Eleazar the priest as a gift offering to

the LORD. [30]But from the Israelites' half you will take one out of every fifty, whether from human, oxen, donkeys, or flock—all the animals. You will give them to the Levites who carry out the duties of the LORD's dwelling.

[31]Moses and Eleazar the priest did as the LORD commanded Moses. [32]The valuable property remaining from the spoils of war that the people of the army had taken was 675,000 sheep, [33]72,000 oxen, [34]61,000 donkeys, [35]and 32,000 women who hadn't known a man intimately by sleeping with him. [36]The half-share of those who had gone out to battle numbered 337,500 sheep, [37]of which the LORD's tribute was 675. [38]The oxen were 36,000, of which the LORD's tribute was 72. [39]The donkeys were 30,500, of which the LORD's tribute was 61. [40]Humans were 16,000, of which the LORD's tribute was 32 persons. [41]Moses gave the tribute, a gift offering for the LORD, to Eleazar the priest as the LORD had commanded Moses.

[42]As for the half-share of the Israelites that Moses divided from those who had gone out to battle: [43]the community's half-share was 337,500 sheep, [44]36,000 oxen, [45]30,500 donkeys, [46]and 16,000 humans. [47]Moses took from the Israelites' half one out of every fifty, from humans and animals. He gave them to the Levites who carry out the duties of the LORD's dwelling, just as the LORD had commanded Moses.

[48]The commanders over the thousands of the army, officers over thousands and officers over hundreds, approached Moses [49]and said to Moses, "Your servants have counted the warriors in our charge and not one of us is missing. [50]We have brought the LORD's offering that each found, gold articles—anklets, bracelets, signet rings, earrings, and necklaces—to seek reconciliation for ourselves before the LORD." [51]Moses and Eleazar the priest took all the gold articles from them. [52]All the gold for the gift offering that was presented to the LORD from the officers of thousands and the officers of hundreds was sixteen thousand seven hundred fifty shekels. [53]Each of the men of battle took spoils of war for himself. [54]Yet Moses and Eleazar the priest also received the gold from the officers of thousands and of hundreds, and they brought it to the meeting tent as a memorial for the Israelites before the LORD.

Reuben and Gad request land

32 The livestock owned by the Reubenites and the Gadites were unusually vast and numerous. They saw that the land of Jazer and the land of Gilead were exactly the place for livestock. [2]So the Gadites and the Reubenites came and said to Moses, Eleazar the priest, and the chiefs of the community: [3]"Ataroth, Dibon, Jazer, Nimrah, Heshbon, Elealeh, Sebam, Nebo, and Beon is [4]the land that the LORD struck down before the Israelite community. It is a land for livestock, and your servants have livestock." [5]They said, "If you approve our request, give this land to your servants as property. Don't make us cross the Jordan."

[6]Moses said to the Gadites and the Reubenites, "Should your brothers go to war, while you stay here? [7]Why would you destroy the Israelites' resolve to cross into the land that the LORD gave them? [8]Your ancestors did this, when I sent them from Kadesh-barnea to inspect the land. [9]They went up to the Cluster ravine, saw the land, and destroyed the Israelites' resolve to enter the land that the LORD had given them. [10]The LORD became angry on that day and promised, [11]'None of the persons that went up from Egypt, those 20 years old and above, will see the fertile ground that I promised to Abraham, Isaac, and Jacob, because they didn't remain true to me, [12]except Caleb, Jephunneh the Kenizzite's son, and Joshua, Nun's son, because they remained true to the LORD.' [13]The LORD became angry with the Israelites and made them wander in the desert for forty years until the entire generation had died, which had done evil in the LORD's eyes. [14]Now you've taken the place of your ancestors, a group of sinful men, to intensify the LORD's anger against Israel. [15]If you turn away from him, he will turn away again to abandon Israel in the desert. Then you will destroy this entire people."

Conditions for possession of the land

16 So they approached him and said, "We will build walled enclosures here for our livestock and towns for our children. 17 Then we will eagerly fight in front of the Israelites until we have brought them into their place. Our children will live in the fortified cities because of the land's inhabitants. 18 And we won't return to our homes until each one of the Israelites takes possession of his property. 19 We won't inherit land with them there across the Jordan, because we've received our property on the east side of the Jordan."

20 Moses said to them, "Do this and fight before the LORD in war. 21 All of you who are equipped for war, cross the Jordan before the LORD until he has driven his enemies out before him 22 and the land is subdued in the LORD's presence. Then you may return innocently before the LORD and Israel, and this land will be your property before the LORD. 23 But if you don't do this, you've sinned against the LORD. Know that your sin will find you. 24 So build towns for your children and walled enclosures for your flocks, but do what you have promised."

25 The Gadites and the Reubenites said to Moses, "Your servants will do as my master has commanded. 26 Our children, wives, livestock, and all of our animals will remain in the cities of Gilead. 27 But your servants, everyone equipped for war before the LORD, will go over to do battle as my master said."

28 Moses made demands for them to Eleazar the priest, to Joshua, Nun's son, and to the leaders of the households of the Israelite tribes. 29 Moses said to them, "If the Gadites and the Reubenites cross the Jordan with you, each equipped for battle before the LORD, and the land is subdued before you, then you will give them the land of Gilead as a possession. 30 If, however, they don't cross with you, equipped for war, they will take possession of property with you in the land of Canaan."

31 The Gadites and the Reubenites answered, "We'll do just as the LORD has spoken to your servants. 32 We'll cross into the land of Canaan before the LORD, equipped for war. But the property we inherit will be across the Jordan."

Territory of Gad, Reuben, and half the tribe of Manasseh

33 So Moses gave to them—to the Gadites, the Reubenites, and half the tribe of Manasseh, Joseph's son—the kingdom of Sihon the king of the Amorites, and the kingdom of Og the king of Bashan, including the land, its cities, and the territory surrounding the land's cities. 34 The Gadites built Dibon, Ataroth, Aroer, 35 Atroth-shophan, Jazer, Jogbehah, 36 Beth-nimrah, and Beth-haran, fortified cities and walled enclosures for flocks. 37 The Reubenites built Heshbon, Elealeh, Kiriathaim, 38 Nebo, and Baal-meon (whose names were changed), and Sibmah. They named the cities that they built. 39 The descendants of Machir, Manasseh's son, went to Gilead, captured it, and drove out the Amorites who were there. 40 So Moses gave Gilead to Machir, Manasseh's son, and he lived there. 41 Manasseh's son Jair went and captured their villages and named them Havvoth-jair.[z] 42 Nobah went and captured Kenath and its surrounding villages. He renamed it Nobah after himself.

March out of Egypt and through the sea

33 These were the stages by which the Israelites marched when they left the land of Egypt, according to their military units under the leadership of Moses and Aaron. 2 Moses recorded the points of departure for each stage of the march at the LORD's command. These are the stages of their march according to their points of departure.

3 They marched from Rameses on the fifteenth day of the first month.[a] On the day after the Passover the Israelites went out defiantly[b] in the sight of all the Egyptians, 4 while the Egyptians were burying their oldest males, whom the LORD had

[z] Or *the villages of Jair* [a] March–April, Nisan [b] Or *with a high hand*

killed. The LORD also executed judgments
against their gods. [5]The Israelites marched
from Rameses and they camped at Succoth.
[6]They marched from Succoth and camped
at Etham on the edge of the desert. [7]They
marched from Etham and turned back to
Pi-hahiroth, which faces Baal-zephon, and
they camped before Migdol. [8]They marched
from Pi-hahiroth and they crossed through
the sea toward the desert.

March through the southern desert

Then they traveled three days in the
Etham desert and they camped at Marah.
[9]They marched from Marah and arrived at Elim. At Elim there were twelve
springs of water and seventy palm trees
and they camped there.

[10]They marched from Elim and camped by the Reed Sea.[c]

[11]They marched from the Reed Sea and camped in the Sin desert.

[12]They marched from the Sin desert and camped at Dophkah.

[13]They marched from Dophkah and camped at Alush.

[14]They marched from Alush and camped at Rephidim, where there was no water for the people to drink.

[15]They marched from Rephidim and camped in the Sinai desert.

[16]They marched from the Sinai desert and camped at Kibroth-hattaavah.

[17]They marched from Kibroth-hattaavah and camped at Hazeroth.

[18]They marched from Hazeroth and camped at Rithmah.

[19]They marched from Rithmah and camped at Rimmon-perez.

[20]They marched from Rimmon-perez and camped at Libnah.

[21]They marched from Libnah and camped at Rissah.

[22]They marched from Rissah and camped at Kehelathah.

[23]They marched from Kehelathah and camped at Mount Shepher.

[24]They marched from Mount Shepher and camped at Haradah.

[25]They marched from Haradah and camped at Makheloth.

[26]They marched from Makheloth and camped at Tahath.

[27]They marched from Tahath and camped at Terah.

[28]They marched from Terah and camped at Mithkah.

[29]They marched from Mithkah and camped at Hashmonah.

[30]They marched from Hashmonah and camped at Moseroth.

[31]They marched from Moseroth and camped at Bene-jaakan.

[32]They marched from Bene-jaakan and camped at Hor-haggidgad.

[33]They marched from Hor-haggidgad and camped at Jotbathah.

[34]They marched from Jotbathah and camped at Abronah.

[35]They marched from Abronah and camped at Ezion-geber.

[36]They marched from Ezion-geber and camped in the Zin desert (that is, Kadesh).

March through the Transjordan region

[37]They marched from Kadesh and
camped at Mount Hor, on the edge of the
land of Edom. [38]Aaron the priest ascended
Mount Hor at the LORD's command, and
he died there in the fortieth year on the
first day of the fifth month[d] after the Israelites left the land of Egypt. [39]Aaron was
123 years old when he died on Mount Hor.
[40]The Canaanite king of Arad, who ruled
in the arid southern plain in the land of
Canaan, heard of the Israelites' coming.

[41]They marched from Mount Hor and camped at Zalmonah.

[42]They marched from Zalmonah and camped at Punon.

[43]They marched from Punon and camped at Oboth.

[44]They marched from Oboth and camped at Iye-abarim in the territory of Moab.

[45]They marched from Iyim and camped at Dibon-gad.

[c]Or *Red Sea* [d]July–August, probably Av

46They marched from Dibon-gad and camped at Almon-diblathaim.

47They marched from Almon-diblathaim and camped in the Abarim mountains in front of Nebo.

48They marched from the Abarim mountains and camped in the plains of Moab by the Jordan across from Jericho.

49They camped by the Jordan from Beth-jeshimoth to Abel-shittim in the plains of Moab.

Divine instruction about the land

50The LORD spoke to Moses on the plains of Moab by the Jordan across from Jericho: 51Speak to the Israelites and say to them: When you cross the Jordan into the land of Canaan, 52you will drive out all the inhabitants of the land before you. You will destroy all their carved figures. You will also destroy all their cast images. You will eliminate all their shrines. 53You will take possession of the land and live in it, because I've given the land to you to possess. 54You will divide up the land by lot according to your clans. To the large you will make its inheritance large, and to the small you will make its inheritance small. To whomever the lot falls, that place will be his. You will inherit land according to your ancestral tribes. 55But if you don't drive out the inhabitants of the land before you, then those you allow to remain will prick your eyes and be thorns in your side. They will harass you in the land in which you are living. 56Then what I intended to do to them, I'll do to you.

Boundaries of the land of Canaan

34 The LORD said to Moses: 2Command the Israelites and say to them: When you enter the land of Canaan, this is the land that will fall to you as an inheritance. The land of Canaan according to its boundaries:

3Your southern boundary extends from the Zin desert alongside Edom. Your southern border extends from the edge of the Dead Sea on the east. 4Your border will turn south of the ascent of Akrabbim and cross toward Zin. Its limit will be south of Kadesh-barnea. It will go out to Hazar-addar and cross toward Azmon. 5The border will then turn from Azmon to the Egypt ravine. Its limit will be at the Mediterranean Sea.

6Your western border will be the Mediterranean Sea. This will be your western border.

7This will be your northern border: From the Mediterranean Sea you will mark out your boundary to Mount Hor. 8From Mount Hor you will mark out your boundary to Lebo-hamath. The limit of the border will be Zedad. 9The border will go out to Ziphron. Its limit will be Hazar-enan. This will be your northern border.

10You will mark out your eastern border from Hazar-enan to Shepham. 11The border will descend from Shepham to Riblah on the east side of Ain. The border will go down and meet the eastern slope of the Galilee Sea. 12The border will descend to the Jordan. Its limit will be the Dead Sea.

This will be your land with its borders all around.

13Moses commanded the Israelites: This is the land that you will inherit by lot, which the LORD has commanded to give to the nine and a half tribes, 14because the tribe of Reuben by their households and the tribe of Gad by their households, and half the tribe of Manasseh have taken their inheritance. 15The two and a half tribes have taken their inheritance across the Jordan at Jericho toward the east.

Appointment of leaders to assign the inheritance

16The LORD spoke to Moses: 17These are the names of the men who will assign the inheritance of the land: Eleazar the priest and Joshua, Nun's son. 18You will also take one chief from each tribe to apportion the land. 19These are the names of the men: from the tribe of Judah, Caleb, Jephunneh's son; 20from the tribe of the Simeonites, Shemuel, Ammihud's son; 21from the tribe of Benjamin, Elidad, Chislon's son; 22from the tribe of the Danites, a chief, Bukki, Jogli's son; 23from Joseph's descendants: of the tribe of the Manassites, a chief, Hanniel, Ephod's son; [24]and from the tribe of the Ephraimites, a chief, Kemuel, Shiphtan's son; [25]from the tribe of the Zebulunites, a chief, Elizaphan, Parnach's son; [26]from the tribe of the Issacharites, a chief, Paltiel, Azzan's son; [27]from the tribe of the Asherites, a chief, Ahihud, Shelomi's son; [28]from the tribe of the Naphtalites, a chief, Pedahel, Ammihud's son.

[29]These are the ones whom the LORD commanded to assign the inheritance of the Israelites in the land of Canaan.

Cities and pastures of the Levites

35 The LORD spoke to Moses in the Moab plains by the Jordan across from Jericho: [2]Command the Israelites that they give cities from their inherited property to the Levites in which to live. You will also give the Levites pastures around their cities. [3]The cities will be theirs in which to live. Their pastures will be for their cattle, their possessions, and all their animals. [4]The pastures of the cities that you must give to the Levites will extend from the wall of the city outward for one thousand five hundred feet in all directions. [5]You will measure outside the city on the east side three thousand feet, on the south side three thousand feet, on the west side three thousand feet, and on the north side three thousand feet, with the city in the middle. These will be their cities' pastures.

[6]Six of the cities that you give to the Levites will be refuge cities. You will allow the person who kills someone to flee there. In addition to these you will give them forty-two cities. [7]All the cities that you give to the Levites will total forty-eight, along with their pastures. [8]As for the cities that you give from the property of the Israelites, you will take more from the larger tribes and less from the smaller. Each in proportion to its inheritance will give cities to the Levites.

Refuge cities

[9]The LORD spoke to Moses: [10]Speak to the Israelites and say to them: When you cross the Jordan into the land of Canaan, [11]identify for yourselves cities to be refuge cities, where a person who kills someone by accident may flee. [12]The cities will be for you a place of refuge from the close relative of the dead. The person who killed someone may not be put to death until he stands before the community for judgment. [13]You will establish six refuge cities for yourselves. [14]You will establish three cities across the Jordan and three cities in the land of Canaan. They will be the refuge cities. [15]These six cities will be refuge for Israelites, immigrants, and temporary residents, as a place to flee for anyone who kills a person by accident.

[16]But if someone strikes a person with an iron object and he dies, he is a murderer. The murderer must definitely be put to death. [17]If someone strikes another with a stone in hand that could cause death and he dies, he is a murderer. The murderer must definitely be put to death. [18]Or if someone strikes with a wood object in hand that could cause death, he is a murderer. The murderer must definitely be put to death. [19]The close relative responsible for the blood[e] of the dead is the one who will put the murderer to death. When he meets him, he will execute him. [20]If in hatred someone hits another or throws something at him with premeditation, he will be put to death. [21]Or if in hostility someone strikes another with his hand and he dies, the one who struck is a murderer and he will be put to death. The close relative will put the murderer to death when he meets him.

[22]But if suddenly and without hostility someone hits another or throws any object at him without premeditation, [23]or accidentally drops any stone on him that could cause death and he dies—even though they weren't enemies and no evil was intended—[24]then the community must come to a verdict between the killer and the close relative in accordance with these case laws. [25]The community will protect the killer from the hand of the close relative and return him to the refuge city

[e]Or (here and throughout Num 36) *the close relative of the blood*

where he fled. He will live there until the death of the high priest who was anointed with holy oil. [26]But if the killer ever goes outside the boundaries of the refuge city where he fled [27]and the close relative finds him outside the boundary of his refuge city and kills him, he will not be responsible for his blood. [28]The killer must live in his refuge city until the high priest's death. After the high priest's death the killer may return to the land he owns.

[29]These will be the regulations and case laws for all time in all your settlements.

[30]Anyone who kills another will be executed on the evidence of witnesses. But one witness alone cannot testify against a person for a death sentence. [31]You may not accept a ransom for the life of a killer, who is guilty of a capital crime, for he must definitely be put to death. [32]You may not accept a ransom for someone who has fled to his refuge city so that he can return and live in the land before the priest's death. [33]You may not pollute the land in which you live, for the blood pollutes the land. There can be no recovery[f] for the land from the blood that is shed in it, except by the blood of the one who shed it. [34]You will not make the land in which you live unclean, the land in the middle of which I reside, for I the LORD reside among the Israelites.

Inheritance of Zelophehad's daughters

36 The leaders of the households of the clans of Gilead, Machir's son and Manasseh's grandson, of Joseph's clans, approached and spoke before Moses and the chiefs, who were the leaders of the Israelite households. [2]They said, "The LORD commanded my master to give the land as an inheritance by lot to the Israelites. But my master was also commanded by the LORD to give the inheritance of Zelophehad our brother to his daughters. [3]If they are married to someone from another Israelite tribe, their inheritance will be taken away from our household and given to another tribe into which they marry. Then it will be taken away from the lot of our inheritance. [4]At the Israelite Jubilee, their inheritance will be added to the inheritance of the tribe into which they married. Then their inheritance will be taken away from the inheritance of our ancestral tribe."

[5]Then Moses commanded the Israelites according to the LORD's word: "The tribe of Joseph's descendants are correct in what they're saying. [6]This is the word that the LORD commands to Zelophehad's daughters: They may marry whomever seems best to them, but they may only marry into one of the clans of their ancestral tribe, [7]so that the inheritance of the Israelites doesn't transfer from one tribe to another. The Israelites will each retain the tribal inheritance of his ancestral tribe. [8]Every daughter who inherits land from an Israelite tribe must marry into one of the clans of her father's tribe. In this way each Israelite will own the land of his ancestors. [9]An inheritance of land may not be transferred from one tribe to another, for the Israelite tribes will each retain its own inheritance."

[10]Zelophehad's daughters did as the LORD commanded Moses. [11]Mahlah, Tirzah, Hoglah, Milcah, and Noah, Zelophehad's daughters, married their cousins. [12]They married into the clan of Manasseh, Joseph's son. Their inheritance remained in the tribe of their father's clan.

Conclusion

[13]These are the commandments and the case laws that the LORD commanded the Israelites through Moses in the plains of Moab by the Jordan across from Jericho.

[f]Or *reconciliation*

DEUTERONOMY

The first heading: Introducing Deuteronomy

1 These are the words that Moses spoke
to all Israel across the Jordan River, in
the desert, on the plain across from Suph,
between Paran and Tophel, Laban, Hazeroth, and Di-zahab. (2 It is eleven days from
Horeb to Kadesh-barnea along the Mount
Seir route.) 3 It was in the fortieth year, on
the first day of the eleventh month, that
Moses spoke to the Israelites precisely what
the LORD had commanded him for them.
(4 This was after the defeat of Sihon, the
Amorite king who ruled in Heshbon, and
Og, Bashan's king, who ruled in Ashtaroth
and[a] Edrei.) 5 Beyond the Jordan, in the
land of Moab, Moses began to explain this
Instruction. He said the following:

Leaving Mount Horeb

6 At Horeb, the LORD our God told us:
You've been at this mountain long enough.
7 Get going! Enter the hills of the Amorites
and the surrounding areas in the desert, the
highlands, the lowlands, the arid southern
region, and the seacoast—the land of the
Canaanites—and the Lebanon range, all the
way to the great Euphrates River. 8 Look, I
have laid the land before you. Go and possess the land that I[b] promised to give to
your ancestors Abraham, Isaac, and Jacob,
as well as to their descendants after them.

9 At that same time, I told you: I can't
handle all of you by myself. 10 The LORD
your God has multiplied your number—you
are now as countless as the stars in the sky.
11 May the LORD, your ancestors' God, continue to multiply you—a thousand times
more! And may God bless you, just as he
promised. 12 But how can I handle all your
troubles, burdens, and disputes by myself?
13 Now, for each of your tribes, choose wise,
discerning, and well-regarded individuals. I
will appoint them as your leaders.

14 You answered me: "What you have proposed is a good idea."

15 So I took leading individuals from
your tribes, people who were wise and well-
regarded, and I set them up as your leaders.
There were commanders over thousands,
hundreds, fifties, and tens, as well as officials
for each of your tribes.

16 At that same time, I commanded your
judges: Listen to your fellow tribe members
and judge fairly, whether the dispute is between one fellow tribe member or between
a tribe member and an immigrant. 17 Don't
show favoritism in a decision. Hear both
sides out, whether the person is important
or not. Don't be afraid of anyone because
the ruling belongs to God. Any dispute that
is too difficult for you to decide, bring to me
and I will take care of it.

18 So at that time, I commanded you concerning everything you were to do.

The spy disaster

19 We left Horeb and journeyed through
that vast and terrifying desert you saw, on
the way to the hills of the Amorites, exactly as the LORD our God commanded us.
Then we arrived at Kadesh-barnea. 20 I said
to you: You have come to the hills of the
Amorites, which the LORD our God is giving to us. 21 Look! The LORD your God has
laid out the land before you. Go up and take
it, just as the LORD, your ancestors' God,
has promised you. Don't be afraid! Don't be
frightened!

22 Then all of you approached me, saying, "Let's send spies ahead of us—they can
check out the land for us. Then they can return with word about the route we should
use and bring a report about the cities that
we'll be entering."

23 This idea seemed good to me, so I selected twelve men, one from each tribe.
24 These set out and went up into the hills,
going as far as the Cluster[c] ravine. They
walked all around that area. 25 They took
some of the land's fruit and then came
back down to us. They reported to us: "The

[a] LXX, Syr, Vulg; MT lacks *and*. [b] Sam, LXX; MT *the* LORD [c] Heb *Eshcol* means *bunch, a cluster* (of grapes); cf Num 13:23-24; 32:9.

land that the LORD our God is giving to us is wonderful!" 26But you weren't willing to go up. You rejected the LORD your God's instruction. 27You complained in your tents, saying things like, "The LORD hates us! That's why he brought us out of Egypt—to hand us over to the Amorites, to destroy us! 28What are we doing? Our brothers have made our hearts sick by saying, 'People far stronger and much taller than we live there, and the cities are huge, with walls sky-high! Worse still, we saw the descendants of the Anakites there!'"

29But I said to you: Don't be terrified! Don't be afraid of them! 30The LORD your God is going before you. He will fight for you just as he fought for you in Egypt while you watched, 31and as you saw him do in the desert. Throughout your entire journey, until you reached this very place, the LORD your God has carried you just as a parent carries a child.

32But you had no faith in the LORD your God about this matter, 33even though he went ahead of you, scouting places where you should camp, in fire by night, so you could see the road you were taking, and in cloud during the daytime.

34The LORD heard what you said. He was angry and he swore: 35Not even one of these people—this wicked generation!—will see the wonderful land that I promised to give to your ancestors. 36The only exception is Caleb, Jephunneh's son. He will see it. I will give the land he walked on to him and his children for this reason: he was completely devoted to the LORD.

(37The LORD was even angry with me because of what you did. "You won't enter the land either," God said. 38"But Nun's son Joshua, your assistant, will enter it. Strengthen him because he's the one who will help Israel inherit the land.")

39Now as for your toddlers, those you said would be taken in war, and your young children who don't yet know right and wrong—they will enter the land. I will give it to them. They will possess it! 40But you all must now turn around. Head back toward the wilderness along the route of the Reed Sea.[d]

41You replied to me: "We've sinned against the LORD! We will go up! We will fight, just as the LORD our God commanded." Each one of you grabbed your weapons. You thought it would be easy[e] to go up into the hills. 42But the LORD told me: Tell them: Don't go up! Don't fight because I will not be with you. You will be defeated by your enemies.

43I reported this to you but you wouldn't listen. You disobeyed the LORD's instruction. Hotheadedly, you went up into the hills. 44And the Amorites who lived in those hills came out to meet you in battle. They chased you like bees give chase! They gave you a beating from Seir all the way to Hormah. 45When you came back, you cried before the LORD, but he wouldn't respond to your tears or give you a hearing.

46And so you stayed in Kadesh-barnea for quite some time.

Journeys in Transjordan

2 Next, we turned around and headed back toward the wilderness along the Reed Sea[f] road, exactly as the LORD instructed me. We traveled all around Mount Seir for a long time.

2Eventually the LORD said: 3You've been traveling around this mountain long enough. Head north. 4Command the people as follows: You are about to enter into the territory of your relatives who live in Seir: Esau's descendants. They will be afraid of you, so watch yourselves most carefully. 5Don't fight with them because I will not give the tiniest parcel of their land to you. I have given Mount Seir to Esau's family as their property. 6Of course you may buy food from them with money so you can eat, and also water with money so you can drink.

7No doubt about it: the LORD your God has blessed you in all that you have done. He watched over your journey through that vast desert. Throughout these forty years the LORD your God has been with you. You haven't needed a thing.

[d] Or *Red Sea* [e] Heb uncertain [f] Or *Red Sea*

[8]So we passed through the territory of our relatives who live in Seir, Esau's descendants, leaving the desert road from Elath and from Ezion-geber. Next we turned and went along the Moab wilderness route. [9]The LORD said to me: Don't aggravate Moab. Don't fight them in battle because I won't give any part of their land to you as your own. I have given Ar to Lot's descendants as their property.

([10]Now the Emim[g] had lived there before. They were big and numerous and tall—just like the Anakim. [11]Most people thought the Emim were Rephaim, like the Anakim were. But the Moabites called them "Emim." [12]Additionally, the Horim[h] had lived in Seir previously, but Esau's descendants took possession of their area, eliminating them altogether and settling in their place. That is exactly what Israel did in the land it took possession of, which the LORD gave to them.)

[13]"So then, get going. Cross the Zered ravine."

So we crossed the Zered ravine.

[14]It took us a total of thirty-eight years to go from Kadesh-barnea until we crossed the Zered ravine. It was at that point that the last of the previous generation, every one of fighting age in the camp, had died, just as the LORD had sworn about them. [15]In fact, the LORD's power was against them, to rid the camp of them, until they were all gone.

[16]Now as soon as all those of fighting age had died, [17]the LORD said to me: [18]Today you are crossing through the territory of Moab and Ar [19]and you will come close to the Ammonites. Don't aggravate them. Don't fight with them because I won't give any part of the Ammonites' land to you as your own. I've given it to Lot's descendants as their property.

[20]Now people thought that land was Rephaim territory as well. The Rephaim had lived there previously. But the Ammonites called them "Zamzummim."[i] [21]They were large, numerous, and tall, just like the Anakim. But the LORD completely destroyed the Zamzummim before the Ammonites, and they took possession of that area, settling in their place. [22]That is exactly what God did for Esau's descendants, who live in Seir, when he completely destroyed the Horites in their presence, and they took possession of the Horites' area, settling in their place to this very day. [23]The Avvim,[j] who had lived in settlements around Gaza, were completely destroyed by the Caphtorim, who had come from Caphtor. They replaced the Avvim there.

Victories in Transjordan

[24]"So get going. Cross the Arnon ravine. I have handed Sihon the Amorite king of Heshbon and his land over to you. It's time to possess the area! It's time to fight him in battle! [25]Starting right now, I am making everyone everywhere afraid of you and scared of you. Once they hear news of you, they will be shaking and worrying because of you."

[26]I then sent messengers from the Kedemoth desert to Sihon, Heshbon's king, with words of peace: [27]"Please let us[k] pass through your land. We promise to stay on the road. We won't step off it, right or left. [28]Please sell us food for money so we can eat; sell us water for money so we can drink. Let us pass through on foot—[29]just as Esau's descendants who live in Seir and the Moabites who live in Ar did for me—until we cross the Jordan River into the land that the LORD our God is giving to us."

[30]But Sihon, Heshbon's king, wasn't willing to let us pass through his land because the LORD your God had made his spirit hard and his heart inflexible so that God could hand him over to you, which is exactly how it happened. [31]The LORD said to me: Look! Right now I'm laying Sihon and his land before you. It's time to take possession of his land!

[32]Sihon and all his forces came out to meet us in battle at Jahaz. [33]But the LORD our God gave him to us. We struck him down, along with his sons, and all his forces. [34]At that time, we captured all of Sihon's cities,

[g]Or *Frighteners* [h]Or *Cave-dwellers* or *Hurrians* [i]Or *Mumblers* [j]Or *Ruiners* [k]Heb here and through 2:29*a* is singular *me, I.*

and we placed every town—men, women, and children—under the ban.[l] We left no survivors. 35 The only things we kept for ourselves were the animals and the plunder from the towns we had taken. 36 From Aroer, which is on the edge of the Arnon Ravine, to the town that is in the valley there,[m] even as far as Gilead, there wasn't a city that could resist us. The LORD our God laid everything out before us. 37 But you didn't go near the Ammonite lands or hillside cities alongside the Jabbok River, in compliance with all[n] that the LORD our God had commanded.

3 Next we turned and went up along the road to Bashan. Og, Bashan's king, came out with all his forces to meet us in battle at Edrei. 2 The LORD said to me: Don't be afraid of him! I have handed him, all his forces, and his land over to you. Do the same thing to him that you did to Sihon, the Amorite king who ruled in Heshbon.

3 And so the LORD our God also handed Og, Bashan's king, along with his forces, over to us. We struck them down until no survivor was left. 4 We also captured all of Og's towns at that time. There wasn't a single city that we didn't take from them—a total of sixty towns, the entire region of Argob, the whole kingdom of Og in Bashan. 5 Each of these towns was fortified with high walls, double gates, and crossbars. Outside the towns there were also a great number of villages.[o] 6 We placed them under the ban, just as we did with Sihon, Heshbon's king. Every town—men, women, and children—was under the ban.[p] 7 The only things we kept for ourselves were the animals and the plunder from the towns.

8 So at that time, we took the land that had belonged to the two Amorite kings beyond the Jordan, all the way from the Arnon Ravine to Mount Hermon (9 Sidonians call Hermon "Sirion," but the Amorites call it "Senir"), 10 including all the towns on the plateau, in the regions of Gilead and Bashan, and all the way to Salecah and Edrei—all the towns that belonged to Og's kingdom in Bashan.

(11 By the way, Bashan's King Og was the last of the Rephaim. His bed was made of iron. Isn't it still in the Ammonite town of Rabbah? By standard measurements, it was thirteen and a half feet long and six feet wide.)

12 So this is the land we possessed at that time. I gave some of it, from Aroer, which is beside the Arnon River, up through half of the Gilead highlands, along with its cities, to the Reubenites and the Gadites. 13 The rest of the Gilead region and all of Bashan, Og's kingdom, I gave to half the tribe of Manasseh.

(Now the whole Argob area, including all of Bashan, was often called Rephaim Country. 14 Jair, from the tribe of Manasseh, took possession of the entire Argob region, as far as the border with the Geshurites and the Maacathites. He named the Bashan area after himself, Jair's Settlement. That's what it's still called today.)

15 I also gave Gilead to Machir. 16 To the Reubenites and the Gadites, I gave land from the Gilead, as far as the Arnon River—the middle of the river being the boundary line—to the Jabbok River, which is the boundary line with the Ammonites. 17 Also the desert plain, with the Jordan River as the boundary, from the Galilee Sea[q] down to the desert sea (the Dead Sea[r]) below the slopes of Mount Pisgah on the east.

18 Then I commanded you: Although the LORD your God has given you this land to possess, you must now cross over before the rest of your Israelite relatives as a fighting force ready for battle! 19 However, your wives, children, and herds—I know you have lots of herds!—may remain in the towns that I have given to you. 20 Once the LORD settles your relatives, as you have been settled, and they also possess the land that the LORD your God is giving them across the Jordan River, each of you can return to the property that I have given to you.

21 It was at that same time that I commanded Joshua: You saw everything that

[l] A technique of holy war that often involves total destruction, in which everything that is destroyed is dedicated to the deity who helps in the battle [m] Heb uncertain [n] LXX, Tg Jonathan; MT *and all* [o] Heb uncertain [p] See note at 2:34. [q] Heb *Chinnereth* [r] Or *the Salt Sea*

the LORD your God did to these two kings. That is exactly what the LORD will do to all the kingdoms where you're going! [22]Don't be afraid of them because the LORD your God is the one who will be fighting for you.

Moses' prayer

[23]It was also at that same time that I begged the LORD: [24]Please, LORD God! You have only begun to show your servant your greatness and your mighty hand. What god in heaven or on earth can act as you do or can perform your deeds and powerful acts? [25]Please let me cross over the Jordan River so I can see the wonderful land that lies beyond it: those beautiful highlands, even the Lebanon region.

[26]But the LORD was angry with me because of you! He wouldn't listen to me. He said to me: That's enough from you! Don't ever ask me about this again! [27]Go up to the top of Mount Pisgah. Look west, north, south, and east. Have a good look, but you will not cross the Jordan River. [28]Instead, command Joshua, strengthen him, and encourage him because he's the one who will cross the river before this people. He's the one who will make sure they inherit the land you will see.

[29]After that, we stayed in the valley across from Beth-peor.

The events at Mount Horeb

4 Now, Israel, in light of all that, listen to the regulations and the case laws that I am teaching you to follow, so that you may live, enter, and possess the land that the LORD, your ancestors' God, is giving to you. [2]Don't add anything to the word that I am commanding you, and don't take anything away from it. Instead, keep the commands of the LORD your God that I am commanding all of you.

[3]You saw with your own eyes what the LORD did concerning the Baal of Peor. The LORD your God destroyed everyone who followed the Baal of Peor, [4]but all of you who stayed true to the LORD your God are alive today. [5]So pay attention! I am teaching all of you the regulations and the case laws exactly as the LORD my God commanded me. You must do these in the land you are entering to possess. [6]Keep them faithfully because that will show your wisdom and insight to the nations who will hear about all these regulations. They will say, "Surely this great nation is a wise and insightful people!" [7]After all, is there any great nation that has gods[s] as close to it as the LORD our God is close to us whenever we call to him? [8]Or does any great nation have regulations and case laws as righteous as all this Instruction that I am setting before you today?

[9]But be on guard and watch yourselves closely so that you don't forget the things your eyes saw and so they never leave your mind as long as you live. Teach them to your children and your grandchildren. [10]Remember that[t] day when you stood before the LORD your God at Horeb, when the LORD said to me: "Gather the people to me. I will declare my words to them so that they will learn to fear me every day of their lives on the fertile land, and teach their children to do the same." [11]Then you all came close and stood at the foot of the mountain. The mountain was blazing with fire up to the sky, with darkness, cloud, and thick smoke! [12]The LORD spoke to you out of the very fire itself. You heard the sound of words, but you didn't see any form. There was only a voice. [13]The LORD declared his covenant to you, which he commanded you to do—the Ten Commandments[u]—and wrote them on two stone tablets. [14]At that time, the LORD commanded me to teach you all the regulations and the case laws that you must keep in the land that you are entering to possess.

[15]So watch your conduct closely, because you didn't see any form on the day the LORD spoke to you at Horeb out of the very fire itself. [16]Don't ruin everything and make an idol for yourself: a form of any image, any likeness—male or female—[17]or any likeness whatsoever, whether of a land animal, a bird that flies in the sky, [18]an insect that crawls on the earth, or a fish that

[s]MT; LXX, Syr, Tg *a god so close* [t]Heb lacks *remember that.* [u]Or *the ten words*

lives in the sea. 19 Don't look to the skies, to the sun or the moon or the stars, all the heavenly bodies, and be led astray, worshipping and serving them. The LORD your God has granted these things to all the nations who live under heaven. 20 But the LORD took you and brought you out of that iron furnace, out of Egypt, so that you might be his own treasured people, which is what you are right now.

21 The LORD was angry with me because of your deeds and swore that I couldn't cross the Jordan River or enter the wonderful land that the LORD your God is giving you as an inheritance. 22 I will die here in this land. I won't cross the Jordan River. But you will, and you will take possession of that wonderful land. 23 So all of you, watch yourselves! Don't forget the covenant that the LORD your God made with you by making an idol or an image of any kind or anything the LORD your God forbids, 24 because the LORD your God is an all-consuming fire. He is a passionate God.

Warnings and teachings about future disobedience

25 Once you have had children and grandchildren and have grown old on the land, if you ruin things by making an idol, in any form whatsoever, and do what is evil in the eyes of the LORD your God and anger him, 26 I call heaven and earth as my witnesses against you today: You will definitely disappear—and quickly—from the land that you are crossing over the Jordan River to possess. You won't extend your time there but will instead be totally destroyed. 27 The LORD will scatter you among the nations. Only a very few of you will survive in the countries where the LORD will drag you. 28 There you will worship other[v] gods, made of wood and stone by human hands—gods that cannot see, listen, eat, or smell. 29 You will seek the LORD your God from there, and you will find him[w] if you seek him with all your heart and with all your being. 30 In your distress, when all these things happen to you in the future, you will return to the LORD your God and you will obey his voice, 31 because the LORD your God is a compassionate God. He won't let you go, he won't destroy you, and he won't forget the covenant that he swore to your ancestors.

32 Now look into it: into days long past, before your time—all the way back to the day God first created human beings on earth, from one end of heaven to the other. Has anything this amazing ever happened? Has anything like it ever been heard of before? 33 Has any people ever listened to a god's voice speaking out of fire, as each of you have, and survived? 34 Or has any god ever tried to take one nation out of another nation using tests, miracles, wonders, war, a strong hand and outstretched arm, or awesome power like all that the LORD your God did for you in Egypt while you watched? 35 You were shown these things so that you would know this: The LORD is the only God. There's no other god except him. 36 From heaven he made you hear his voice in order to discipline you. On earth he showed you his great fire. You heard his words from that very fire. 37 And because he loved your ancestors and chose their descendants after them, God brought you out of Egypt with his own presence, by his own great power, 38 in order to remove larger and stronger nations from before you and bring you into their land, giving it to you as an inheritance. That's where things stand right now. 39 Know then today and keep in mind that the LORD is the only God in heaven above or on earth below. There is no other. 40 Keep the Lord's regulations and his commandments. I'm commanding them to you today for your well-being and for the well-being of your children after you, so that you may extend your time on the fertile land that the LORD your God is giving you forever.

Cities of refuge

41 Then Moses set aside three cities on the eastern side of the Jordan River 42 so that anyone who killed someone accidentally and without prior hatred could flee to one of these cities and be safe: 43 Bezer in

[v] LXX; MT lacks *other*. [w] Heb lacks *him*.

the wilderness on the plateau for the Reubenites, Ramoth in Gilead for the Gadites, and Golan in Bashan for the Manassites.

The second heading: Recounting the Horeb covenant

[44]Now this is the Instruction that Moses set before the Israelites. [45]These are the laws and the regulations and the case laws that Moses spoke to the Israelites when they came out of Egypt. [46]This took place across the Jordan River, in the valley opposite Beth-peor, in the land of Sihon the Amorite king who ruled in Heshbon, whom Moses and the Israelites defeated when they came out of Egypt. [47]They took possession of his land and the land of Og, Bashan's king—the two Amorite kings across the Jordan River to the east—[48]from Aroer, which is on the banks of the Arnon River, all the way to Mount Sion,[x] also known as Hermon, [49]and all the desert regions across the Jordan River, on the east, down to the Dead Sea, beneath the slopes of Mount Pisgah.

Ten Commandments

5 Moses called out to all Israel, saying to them: "Israel! Listen to the regulations and the case laws that I'm recounting in your hearing right now. Learn them and carefully do them. [2]The LORD our God made a covenant with us at Mount Horeb. [3]The LORD didn't make this covenant with our ancestors but with us—all of us who are here and alive right now. [4]The LORD spoke with you face-to-face on the mountain from the very fire itself. [5]At that time, I was standing between the LORD and you, declaring to you the LORD's word, because you were terrified of the fire and didn't go up on the mountain."

The LORD said:

[6]I am the LORD your God, who brought you out of Egypt, out of the house of slavery.

[7]You must have no other gods before[y] me. [8]Do not make an idol for yourself—no form whatsoever—of anything in the sky above or on the earth below or in the waters under the earth. [9]Do not bow down to them or worship them because I, the LORD your God, am a passionate God. I punish children for their parents' sins—even to the third and fourth generations of those who hate me. [10]But I am loyal and gracious to the thousandth generation[z] of those who love me and keep my commandments.

[11]Do not use the LORD your God's name as if it were of no significance; the LORD won't forgive anyone who uses his name that way.

[12]Keep the Sabbath day and treat it as holy, exactly as the LORD your God commanded: [13]Six days you may work and do all your tasks, [14]but the seventh day is a Sabbath to the LORD your God. Don't do any work on it—not you, your sons or daughters, your male or female servants, your oxen or donkeys or any of your animals, or the immigrant who is living among you—so that your male and female servants can rest just like you. [15]Remember that you were a slave in Egypt, but the LORD your God brought you out of there with a strong hand and an outstretched arm. That's why the LORD your God commands you to keep the Sabbath day.

[16]Honor your father and your mother, exactly as the LORD your God requires, so that your life will be long and so that things will go well for you on the fertile land that the LORD your God is giving you.

[17]Do not kill.[a]

[18]Do not commit adultery.

[19]Do not steal.

[20]Do not testify falsely against your neighbor.

[21]Do not desire and try to take your neighbor's wife.

Do not crave your neighbor's house, field, male or female servant, ox, donkey, or anything else that belongs to your neighbor.

[22]Those are the words the LORD spoke to your entire assembly with a loud voice while on the mountain, from the midst of the fire, the cloud, and the thick smoke. He

[x]Syr *Sirion*; see 3:9. [y]Or *besides* [z]Or *to thousands* [a]Or *murder*

added no more. God wrote them on two
stone tablets, then gave them to me.

Moses' intercessory role

23Now once you heard the voice from the
darkness while the mountain was blazing
with fire, you came to me—more specifically, all the chiefs of your tribes and your
elders came—24and you said: "Look here!
The LORD our God has shown us his glory
and greatness. We've heard his voice come
out of the very fire itself. We've seen firsthand that God can speak to a human being
and they can survive! 25But why should we
die? Surely this massive fire will consume
us! If we hear any more of the LORD our
God's voice, we will die. 26Is there anyone
who has heard the living God's voice speaking out of the very fire itself, like we have,
and survived? 27You go and listen to all that
the LORD our God says. Then tell us all that
the LORD our God speaks to you. We'll listen and we'll do it."
28The LORD heard what you said, when
you said this to me. The LORD then told
me: I heard what the people said when they
spoke with you. Everything they suggest is
good. 29If only their minds were like this:
always fearing me and keeping all my commandments so that things would go well for
them and their children forever! 30Go and
tell them: You may go back to your tents.
31But you, Moses, must stay here with me.
I will tell you all the commandments,[b] the
regulations, and the case laws that you
must teach the Israelites to do in the land
that I am giving them to possess.
32So you must carefully do exactly what
the LORD your God commands you. Don't
deviate even a bit! 33You must walk the precise path that the LORD your God indicates
for you so that you will live, and so that things
will go well for you, and so you will extend
your time on the land that you will possess.

The great commandment

6 Now these are the commandments, the
regulations, and the case laws that the
LORD your God commanded me to teach
you to follow in the land you are entering
to possess, 2so that you will fear the LORD
your God by keeping all his regulations and
his commandments that I am commanding you—both you and your sons and
daughters—all the days of your life and
so that you will lengthen your life. 3Listen
to them, Israel! Follow them carefully so
that things will go well for you and so that
you will continue to multiply exactly as the
LORD, your ancestors' God, promised you,
in a land full of milk and honey.
4Israel, listen! Our God is the LORD!
Only the LORD![c]
5Love the LORD your God with all your
heart, all your being, and all your strength.
6These words that I am commanding you
today must always be on your minds. 7Re-
cite them to your children. Talk about them
when you are sitting around your house
and when you are out and about, when you
are lying down and when you are getting
up. 8Tie them on your hand as a sign. They
should be on your forehead as a symbol.[d]
9Write them on your house's doorframes
and on your city's gates.
10Now once the LORD your God has
brought you into the land that he swore
to your ancestors, to Abraham, Isaac, and
Jacob, to give to you—a land that will be
full of large and wonderful towns that you
didn't build, 11houses stocked with all kinds
of goods that you didn't stock, cisterns that
you didn't make, vineyards and olive trees
that you didn't plant—and you eat and get
stuffed, 12watch yourself! Don't forget the
LORD, who brought you out of Egypt, out
of the house of slavery. 13Revere the LORD
your God, serve him, and take your solemn
pledges in his name! 14Don't follow other
gods, those gods of the people around you—
15because the LORD your God, who is with
you and among you, is a passionate God. The
LORD your God's anger will burn against
you, and he will wipe you off the fertile land.
16Don't test the LORD your God the way
you frustrated him at Massah. 17You must

[b]Heb is singular, *commandment* (see 6:1). [c]Or *The LORD is our God, the LORD only;* or *The LORD is our God, the LORD alone;* or *The LORD our God is one LORD;* or *The LORD our God, the LORD is one;* or *The LORD is our God, the LORD is one.* [d]Heb uncertain; cf Exod 13:16; Syr *sign* or *mark*; Tg *phylacteries*

carefully follow the LORD your God's commands along with the laws and regulations he has given you. [18]Do what is right and good in the LORD's sight so that things will go well for you and so you will enter and take possession of the wonderful land that the LORD swore to your ancestors, [19]and so the LORD will drive out all your enemies from before you, just as he promised.

The next generation

[20]In the future, your children will ask you, "What is the meaning of the laws,[e] the regulations, and the case laws that the LORD our God commanded you?" [21]tell them: We were Pharaoh's slaves in Egypt. But the LORD brought us out of Egypt with a mighty hand. [22]Before our own eyes, the LORD performed great and awesome deeds of power[f] against Egypt, Pharaoh, and his entire dynasty. [23]But the Lord brought us out from there so that he could bring us in, giving us the land that he swore to our ancestors. [24]Then the LORD commanded us to perform all these regulations, revering the LORD our God, so that things go well for us always and so we continue to live, as we're doing right now. [25]What's more, we will be considered righteous if we are careful to do all this commandment before the LORD our God, just as he commanded us.

Dealing with foreign worship

7 Now once the LORD your God brings you into the land you are entering to take possession of, and he drives out numerous nations before you—the Hittites, the Girgashites, the Amorites, the Canaanites, the Perizzites, the Hivites, and the Jebusites: seven nations that are larger and stronger than you—[2]once the LORD your God lays them before you, you must strike them down, placing them under the ban.[g] Don't make any covenants with them, and don't be merciful to them. [3]Don't intermarry with them. Don't give your daughter to one of their sons to marry, and don't take one of their daughters to marry your son, [4]because they will turn your child away from following me so that they end up serving other gods. That will make the LORD's anger burn against you, and he will quickly annihilate you.

[5]Instead, this is what you must do with these nations: rip down their altars, smash their sacred stones, cut down their sacred poles,[h] and burn their idols [6]because you are a people holy to the LORD your God. The LORD your God chose you to be his own treasured people beyond all others on the fertile land. [7]It was not because you were greater than all other people that the LORD loved you and chose you. In fact, you were the smallest of peoples! [8]No, it is because the LORD loved you and because he kept the solemn pledge he swore to your ancestors that the LORD brought you out with a strong hand and saved you from the house of slavery, from the power of Pharaoh, Egypt's king. [9]Know now then that the LORD your God is the only true God! He is the faithful God, who keeps the covenant and proves loyal to everyone who loves him and keeps his commands—even to the thousandth generation! [10]He is the God who personally repays anyone who hates him, ultimately destroying that kind of person. The LORD does not waste time with anyone who hates him; he repays them personally. [11]So make sure you carefully keep the commandment, the regulations, and the case laws that I am commanding you right now.

[12]If you listen to these case laws and follow them carefully, the LORD your God will keep the covenant and display the loyalty that he promised your ancestors. [13]He will love you, bless you, and multiply you. He will bless the fruit of your wombs and the fruit of your fertile land—all your grain, your wine, your oil, and the offspring of your cattle and flocks—upon the very fertile land that he swore to your ancestors to give to you. [14]You will be more blessed than any other group of people. No one will be sterile or infertile—not among you or your animals. [15]The LORD will remove all sickness from you. As for all

[e]Or *What are the laws . . . ?* [f]Or *signs and wonders* [g]See note at 2:34. [h]Heb *asherim*, perhaps objects devoted to the goddess Asherah

those dreadful Egyptian diseases you experienced, the Lord won't put them on you but will inflict them on all who hate you. 16 You will destroy all the peoples that the LORD your God is handing over to you. Show them no pity. And don't serve their gods because that would be a trap for you.

Against power and lack of trust

17 If you happen to think to yourself, These nations are greater than we are; how can we possibly possess their land? 18 don't be afraid of them! Remember, instead, what the LORD your God did to Pharaoh and all Egypt: 19 the great trials that you saw with your own eyes, the signs and wonders, and the strong hand and outstretched arm the LORD your God used to rescue you. That's what the LORD your God will do to any people you fear. 20 The LORD your God will send terror[i] on them until even the survivors and those hiding from you are destroyed. 21 Don't dread these nations because the LORD your God, the great and awesome God, is with you and among you. (22 The LORD your God will drive out these nations before you bit by bit. You won't be able to finish them off quickly; otherwise, the wild animals would become too much for you to handle.) 23 The LORD your God will lay these nations before you, throwing them into a huge panic until they are destroyed. 24 He will hand their kings over to you, and you will wipe their names out from under the skies. No one will be able to stand before you; you will crush them.

25 Burn the images of their gods. Don't desire the silver or the gold that is on them and take it for yourself, or you will be trapped by it. That is detestable to the LORD your God. 26 Don't bring any detestable thing into your house, or you will be placed under the ban too, just like it is! You must utterly detest these kinds of things, despising them completely, because they are under the ban.

8 You must carefully perform all of the commandment that I am commanding you right now so you can live and multiply and enter and take possession of the land that the LORD swore to your ancestors. 2 Remember the long road on which the LORD your God led you during these forty years in the desert so he could humble you, testing you to find out what was in your heart: whether you would keep his commandments or not. 3 He humbled you by making you hungry and then feeding you the manna that neither you nor your ancestors had ever experienced, so he could teach you that people don't live on bread alone. No, they live based on whatever the LORD says.[j] 4 During these forty years, your clothes didn't wear out and your feet didn't swell up. 5 Know then in your heart that the LORD your God has been disciplining you just as a father disciplines his children. 6 Keep the commandments of the LORD your God by walking in his ways and by fearing him, 7 because the LORD your God is bringing you to a wonderful land, a land with streams of water, springs, and wells that gush up in the valleys and on the hills; 8 a land of wheat and barley, vines, fig trees, and pomegranates; a land of olive oil and honey; 9 a land where you will eat food without any shortage—you won't lack a thing there—a land where stone is hard as iron and where you will mine copper from the hills. 10 You will eat, you will be satisfied, and you will bless the LORD your God in the wonderful land that he's given you.

Against wealth and overconfidence

11 But watch yourself! Don't forget the LORD your God by not keeping his commands or his case laws or his regulations that I am commanding you right now. 12 When you eat, get full, build nice houses, and settle down, 13 and when your herds and your flocks are growing large, your silver and gold are multiplying, and everything you have is thriving, 14 don't become arrogant, forgetting the LORD your God:

the one who rescued you from Egypt,
from the house of slavery;
15 the one who led you through this
vast and terrifying desert of poisonous

[i] Heb uncertain; perhaps *wasp, plague,* or *pestilence* [j] Or *whatever comes out of the LORD's mouth*

snakes and scorpions, of cracked ground
with no water;
the one who made water flow for you
out of a hard rock;
16 the one who fed you manna in the
wilderness, which your ancestors had
never experienced, in order to humble
and test you, but in order to do good to
you in the end.

17 Don't think to yourself, My own
strength and abilities have produced all
this prosperity for me. 18 Remember the
LORD your God! He's the one who gives you
the strength to be prosperous in order to
establish the covenant he made with your
ancestors—and that's how things stand
right now. 19 But if you do, in fact, forget
the LORD your God and follow other gods,
serving and bowing down to them, I swear
to you right now that you will be completely destroyed. 20 Just like the nations
that the LORD is destroying before you,
that's exactly how you will be destroyed—
all because you didn't obey the LORD your
God's voice.

Against false piety and immodesty

9 Listen, Israel! Today you will cross the
Jordan River to enter and take possession of nations larger and more powerful than you, along with huge cities with
fortifications that reach to the sky. 2 These
people are large and tall—they are the Anakim. You know and have heard what people
say: "Who can stand up to the Anakim?"
3 Know right now that the LORD your God,
who is crossing over before you, is an all-
consuming fire! He will wipe them out! He
will subdue them before you! Then you will
take possession of their land, eliminating
them quickly, exactly as the LORD told you.

4 Once the LORD your God has driven
them out before you, don't think to yourself, It's because I'm righteous that the
LORD brought me in to possess this land.
It is instead because of these nations' wickedness that the LORD is removing them
before you. 5 You aren't entering and taking
possession of their land because you are
righteous or because your heart is especially virtuous; rather, it is because these
nations are wicked—that's why the LORD
your God is removing them before you, and
because he wishes to establish the promise
he made to your ancestors: to Abraham,
Isaac, and Jacob.

Gold calf

6 Know then that the LORD your God
isn't giving you this excellent land for you
to possess on account of your righteousness—because you are a stubborn people!
7 Remember—don't ever forget!—how you
made the LORD your God furious in the
wilderness. From the very first day you
stepped out of Egypt until you arrived at
this place, you have been rebels against
the LORD. 8 Even at Horeb you angered the
LORD! He was so enraged by you that he
threatened to wipe you out. 9 When I went
up on the mountain to get the stone tablets, the covenant tablets that the LORD
made with you, I was up there forty days
and forty nights. I ate no bread, drank no
water. 10 The LORD gave me the two stone
tablets, written by God's finger, and on
them were all the words that the LORD had
said to you on the mountain, out of the very
fire itself, on the day we assembled. 11 At
the end of those forty days and nights, the
LORD gave me the two stone tablets—the
covenant tablets. 12 Then the LORD said to
me, "Get going! Get down from here quickly
because your people, whom you brought
out of Egypt, have ruined everything! They
couldn't wait to turn from the path I commanded them! They've made themselves an
idol out of cast metal."

13 The LORD said more to me: "I have
seen this people. Look! What a stubborn
people they are! 14 Now stand back. I am
going to wipe them out. I will erase their
name from under heaven, then I will make
a nation out of you—one stronger and
larger than they were."

15 So I went down the mountain while
it was blazing with fire. The two covenant
tablets were in my two hands. 16 It was then
that I saw how you sinned against the LORD
your God: you made yourselves a calf, an
idol made of cast metal! You couldn't wait to
turn from the path the LORD commanded

you! 17 I grabbed the two tablets and threw them down with my own hands, shattering them while you watched. 18 Then I fell before the LORD as I had done the previous forty days and forty nights. I ate no bread and drank no water, all because of the sin that you had committed by doing such evil in the LORD's sight, infuriating him. 19 I was afraid of the massive anger and rage the LORD had for you—he was going to wipe you out! However, the LORD listened to me again in that moment.

20 But the LORD was furious with Aaron—he was going to wipe him out! So I also prayed hard for Aaron at that time. 21 And as for that sinful thing you made, that calf, I took it and I burned it with fire. Then I smashed it, grinding it thoroughly until it was as fine as dust. Then I dumped the dust into the stream that ran down the mountain.

22 Also at Taberah, again at Massah, and then again at Kibroth-hattaavah, you have been the kind of people who make the LORD angry. 23 And then, when the LORD sent you from Kadesh-barnea, telling you: "Go up and take possession of the land that I'm giving you," you disobeyed the LORD your God's command. You didn't trust him. You didn't obey God's voice. 24 You've been rebellious toward the LORD from the day I[k] met you.

Moses' intercessory prayer

25 But I fell on my knees in the LORD's presence forty days and forty nights, lying flat out, because the LORD planned on wiping you out. 26 But I prayed to the LORD! I said: LORD, my Lord! Don't destroy your people, your own possession, whom you saved by your own power, whom you brought out of Egypt with a strong hand! 27 Remember your servants: Abraham, Isaac, and Jacob! Don't focus on this people's stubbornness, wickedness, and sin. 28 Otherwise, that land out of which you brought us will say: The LORD wasn't strong enough to bring them into the land he'd promised them. Because he didn't care for them in the least, he brought them out to die in the desert. 29 But these are your people! Your own possession! The people you brought out by your great power and by your outstretched arm!

New tablets

10 At that time the LORD told me: Carve two stone tablets, just like the first ones, and hike up the mountain to me. Construct a wooden chest as well. 2 I will write on the tablets the words that were on the first tablets—the ones you smashed—then you will place them in the chest.

3 So I built a chest out of acacia wood and carved two stone tablets just like the first ones. Then I hiked up the mountain holding the two tablets in my hands. 4 God wrote on the new tablets what had been written on the first set: the Ten Commandments that the LORD spoke to you on the mountain, from the very fire itself, on the day we assembled there. Then the LORD gave them to me.

5 So I came back down the mountain. I put the tablets in the chest that I'd made, and that's where they are now, exactly as the LORD commanded me.

(6 Now, the Israelites had set out from Beeroth-bene-jaakan[l] to Moserah. It was there that Aaron died and was buried. His son Eleazar succeeded him in the priestly role. 7 From there the Israelites traveled to Gudgodah, then from Gudgodah to Jotbathah, which is a land with flowing streams. 8 At that time, the LORD selected the tribe of Levi to carry the chest containing the LORD's covenant, to minister before the LORD, to serve him, and to offer blessings in his name. That's the way things are right now. 9 That's why the Levites don't have a stake or inheritance with the rest of their relatives. The LORD is the Levites' inheritance, just as the LORD your God promised them.)

10 Just as the first time, I remained on the mountain forty days and nights. And the LORD listened to me again in this instance. The LORD wasn't willing to destroy you. 11 Then the LORD told me: Get going. Lead the people so they can enter and take

[k] LXX, Sam *he* (God) *met you* [l] Or *from the wells of the Jaakanites*

possession of the land that I promised I'd
give to their ancestors.

What the Lord requires

12 Now in light of all that, Israel, what
does the LORD your God ask of you? Only
this: to revere the LORD your God by walking in all his ways, by loving him, by serving
the LORD your God with all your heart and
being, 13 and by keeping the LORD's commandments and his regulations that I'm
commanding you right now. It's for your
own good!
14 Clearly, the LORD owns the sky, the
highest heavens, the earth, and everything
in it. 15 But the LORD adored your ancestors,
loving them and choosing the descendants
that followed them—you!—from all other
people. That's how things still stand now.
16 So circumcise your hearts[m] and stop being
so stubborn, 17 because the LORD your God
is the God of all gods and Lord of all lords,
the great, mighty, and awesome God who
doesn't play favorites and doesn't take
bribes. 18 He enacts justice for orphans and
widows, and he loves immigrants, giving
them food and clothing. 19 That means you
must also love immigrants because you were
immigrants in Egypt. 20 Revere the LORD
your God, serve him, cling to him, swear by
his name alone! 21 He is your praise, and he
is your God—the one who performed these
great and awesome acts that you witnessed
with your very own eyes. 22 Your ancestors
went down to Egypt with a total of seventy
people, but now look! The LORD your God
has made you as numerous as the stars in
the nighttime sky!

11 So love the LORD your God and follow
his instruction, his regulations, his
case laws, and his commandments always.
2 And know right now what your children
haven't known or yet witnessed:[n]

> The LORD your God's discipline,
> his power, his mighty hand and out-
> stretched arm;
> 3 the signs and the acts that he per-
> formed in the heart of Egyptian terri-
> tory, against Egypt's King Pharaoh and
> all his land;
> 4 what God did to the Egyptian army,
> to its horses and chariots—how he
> made the water of the Reed Sea[o] flow
> over their heads when they chased after
> you, but the LORD destroyed them, and
> that's how things stand right now;
> 5 what the Lord did for you in the des-
> ert, until you arrived at this place;
> 6 and what he did to Dathan and Abi-
> ram, the descendants of Eliab the Reu-
> benite, when the ground opened up its
> mouth and swallowed them, their fami-
> lies, their tents, and every living thing
> they possessed in the presence of all
> Israel.

7 Your own eyes witnessed each of these
powerful acts the LORD performed. 8 So keep
every part of the commandment that I am
giving you today so that you stay strong to
enter and take possession of the land that
you are crossing over to possess, 9 and so that
you might prolong your life on the fertile
land that the LORD swore to your ancestors
to give to them and their descendants—a
land full of milk and honey.
10 The land you are about to enter and
possess is definitely not like the land of
Egypt, where you came from, where you
sowed your seed and irrigated it by hand[p]
like a vegetable garden. 11 No, the land you
are entering to possess is a land of hills
and valleys, where your drinking water will
be rain from heaven. 12 It's a land that the
LORD cares for: the LORD's eyes are on it
constantly from the first of the year until
the very end of the year.
13 Now, if you completely obey God's[q]
commandments that I am giving you right
now, by loving the LORD your God and by
serving him with all your heart and all your
being, 14 then he[r] will provide rain for your
land at the right time—early rain and late
rain—so you can stock up your grain, wine,
and oil. 15 He[s] will also make your fields lush
for your livestock, and you will eat and be
satisfied. 16 But watch yourselves! Otherwise,

[m] Or *the foreskin of your hearts*; cf 30:6 [n] Heb uncertain [o] Or *Red Sea* [p] Or *foot* [q] LXX *his*; MT *my* [r] Sam, LXX, DSS (8QMez); Heb, Vulg, Syr, Tg, and several DSS *I*, in which case the text shifts to direct divine discourse.
[s] Sam, LXX, two DSS; Heb, four DSS, Syr, Tg *I*, in which case the text shifts to direct divine discourse.

your heart might be led astray so you stray away, serving other gods and worshipping them. 17 Then the LORD's anger would burn against you. He will close the sky up tight. There won't be any rain, and the ground won't yield any of its crops. You will quickly disappear off the wonderful land the LORD is giving to you.

18 Place these words I'm speaking on your heart and in your very being. Tie them on your hand as a sign. They should be on your forehead as a symbol.[t] 19 Teach them to your children, by talking about them when you are sitting around your house and when you are out and about, when you are lying down and when you are getting up. 20 Write them on your house's doorframes and on your city's gates. 21 Do all that so your days and your children's days on the fertile land the LORD swore to give to your ancestors are many—indeed, as many as the number of days that the sky's been over the earth!

22 It's true: if you carefully keep all this commandment that I'm giving you, by doing it, by loving the LORD your God, by walking in all his ways, and by clinging to him, 23 then the LORD will clear out all these nations before you. You will inherit what belonged to nations that are larger and stronger than you are. 24 Every place you set foot on will be yours: your territory will run from the wilderness all the way to the Lebanon range, and from the Euphrates River all the way to the Mediterranean Sea. 25 No one will be able to stand up to you. Just as he promised, the LORD your God will make the entire land deathly afraid of you wherever you advance in it.

Ceremony on Mount Gerizim and Mount Ebal

26 Pay attention! I am setting blessing and curse before you right now: 27 the blessing if you obey the LORD your God's commandments that I am giving you right now, 28 but the curse if you don't obey the LORD your God's commandments and stray from the path that I am giving you today by following other gods that you have not known. 29 Now when the LORD your God brings you into the land that you are entering to take possession of, put the blessing on Mount Gerizim and the curse on Mount Ebal. (30 Aren't both of these mountains across the Jordan River, down along the western road in the region of the Canaanites who live in the desert plain, across from Gilgal, next to the Moreh Oak Grove?)

31 So then, once you cross the Jordan River to enter and possess the land that the LORD your God is giving you, and you take possession of it, settling down in it, 32 you must carefully follow the regulations and the case laws that I am laying out before you right now.

Regulations and the case laws:

Worship at the location the LORD selects

12 These are the regulations and the case laws that you must carefully keep in the fertile land the LORD, your ancestors' God, has given to you to possess for as long as you live on that land:

2 You must completely destroy every place where the nations that you are displacing worshipped their gods—whether on high mountains or hills or under leafy green trees. 3 Rip down their altars and shatter their sacred stones. Burn their sacred poles[u] with fire. Hack their gods' idols into pieces. Wipe out their names from that place.

4 Don't act like they did toward the LORD your God!

5 Instead, you must search for the location the LORD your God will select from all your tribes to put his name there, as his residence, and you must go there. 6 You must bring your entirely burned offerings, your sacrifices, your tenth-part gifts, your contributions,[v] your payments for solemn promises, your spontaneous gifts, and the oldest offspring of your herds and flocks to that place. 7 You will have a feast there, each of you and your families, in the LORD your God's presence, and you will celebrate

[t] Heb uncertain; cf Exod 13:16; Syr *sign* or *mark*; Tg *phylacteries* [u] Heb *asherim*, perhaps objects devoted to the goddess Asherah [v] Or *the contribution of your hands;* also in 12:11, 17

all you have done because the LORD your
God has blessed you. 8Don't act like we've
been acting here lately—everyone doing
what seems right to them—9because up
to this point you haven't yet reached the
place of rest or the inheritance the LORD
your God is giving you. 10But you are about
to cross the Jordan River and will settle in
the land the LORD your God is giving you
as your inheritance. Then he will give you
rest from all your enemies on every side so
that you live safely and securely. 11At that
point, you must bring all that I am commanding you, your entirely burned offerings,
your sacrifices, your tenth-part gifts, your
contributions, and all your best payments
that you solemnly promised to the LORD, to
the location the LORD your God selects for
his name to reside. 12Then you will rejoice in
the LORD your God's presence: each of you,
your sons and daughters, your male and female servants, and the Levites who dwell in
your cities because they have no designated
inheritance.

13But watch yourself! Make sure you
don't offer up your entirely burned offerings in just any place you see. 14No, only at
the location the LORD selects from one of
your tribal areas—that's where you must
offer up your entirely burned offerings and
that's where you must perform everything
I'm telling you. 15However, whenever you
wish, you may slaughter and eat meat, as
the LORD your God sees fit to bless you
with such in your cities. People who are
polluted and people who are purified can
join in the feast, as they would if they were
eating gazelle or deer. 16But you must not
consume any of the animals' blood. Pour it
out on the ground, just like water.

17Within your cities you are not allowed
to eat any of the following: your tenth-part
gifts of grain, wine, and oil; the oldest offspring of your herds and flocks; any of the
payments you have solemnly promised; your
spontaneous gifts or your contributions.
18Only in the presence of the LORD your
God, at the location the LORD your God selects, can you eat these things—that holds
true for you, your son and daughter, your
male and female servant, and the Levite
who lives in your city. Then celebrate all you
have done in the LORD your God's presence.
19But watch yourself: as long as you are on
the land, don't forget about the Levites.

20Once the LORD your God has enlarged
your territory, as he promised you, and you
think to yourself, I'd like to eat some meat
(because you have the desire to do so), feel
free to do so whenever you want. 21But if
the location that the LORD your God will
choose to put his name is far away from
where you live, then slaughter an animal
from your herd or flock that the LORD has
given you, just as I have commanded you,
and eat it in your cities whenever you wish.
22But be sure to eat it as if it were gazelle
or deer. People who are polluted and people
who are purified can feast on it together.

23Furthermore, make sure that you don't
consume any of the blood, because blood is
life. You must not consume the life along
with the meat. 24You must not consume
any of it. Pour it out on the ground, just like
water. 25You must not consume any of it so
that things go well for you and for your children later because you did what was right in
the LORD's eyes.

26Note that you must bring your sacred
offerings and your payments for solemn
promises to the location the LORD selects,
27offering up your entirely burned sacrifices—both meat and blood—on the LORD
your God's altar. The blood from your sacrifices must be poured out on the LORD your
God's altar, but you are allowed to eat the
meat. 28Observe and obey all these words
that I am commanding you so that things
always go well for you and your children
later because you did what was good and
right in the LORD your God's eyes.

29Once the LORD your God has removed
from before you all the nations that you
are entering and taking possession of, and
you have displaced them and are living in
their land, 30then watch yourself! Don't be
trapped by following their practices after
they've been wiped out before you. Don't
go investigating their gods, thinking, How
did these nations worship their gods? I
want to do the very same thing!

31Don't act like they did toward the LORD

your God because they did things for their gods that are detestable to the LORD, which he hates. They even burned their own sons and daughters with fire for their gods!

32[w]Everything I'm commanding you, you must do it with utmost care! Don't add anything to it or take anything away from it.

False prophets and false gods

13 [x]Now if a prophet or a dream interpreter appears among you and performs a sign or wonder for you, 2 and the sign or wonder that was spoken actually occurs; if he says: "Come on! We should follow other gods"—ones you haven't experienced—"and we should worship them," 3 you must not listen to that prophet's or dream interpreter's words, because the LORD your God is testing you to see if you love the LORD your God with all your mind and all your being. 4 You must follow the LORD your God alone! Revere him! Follow his commandments! Obey his voice! Worship him! Cling to him—no other! 5 That prophet or dream interpreter must be executed because he encouraged you to turn away from the LORD your God who brought you out of Egypt, who redeemed you from the house of slavery; they tried to lead you away from the path the LORD your God commanded you to take. Remove[y] such evil from your community!

6 Similarly, if one of your relatives—even one of your own siblings—or your own son or daughter or your dear spouse or best friend entices you secretly, if someone like that says: "Come on! We should follow and worship other gods"—ones that neither you nor your ancestors have experienced, 7 gods from all the neighboring peoples, whether nearby or far away, from one end of the earth to the other—8 don't give in to them! Don't obey them! Don't have any mercy on them! Don't have compassion on them and don't protect them! 9 Instead, you must execute them. Your own hand must be against them from the beginning of the execution; the hand of all the people will be involved at the end. 10 Stone them until they are dead because they desired to lead you away from the LORD your God, the one who brought you out of Egypt, out of the house of slavery. 11 All Israel will hear about this and be afraid. They won't do that sort of evil thing among you again.

12 Or if you hear about one of your towns the LORD your God is giving you to inhabit, that 13 certain wicked people have gone out from your community and they've led the citizens of their town astray by saying: "Come on! We should follow and worship other gods"—ones you haven't experienced before; 14 at that point you must look into this situation very carefully to see if it's true. And if it's definitely true that this detestable thing was done in your community, 15 you must completely strike down the inhabitants of that city with the sword. Place it and all that is in it under the ban.[z] Put its animals to the sword. 16 Gather all the plunder into the middle of the town's square. Then burn the city and all of its plunder as an entirely burned offering to the LORD your God. It must remain a heap of rubble forever. It must not be rebuilt. 17 Don't hold on to any of the banned items—this will ensure that the LORD turns from his great anger and is compassionate to you, showing you mercy and multiplying you just like he swore to your ancestors. 18 You must definitely obey the LORD your God's voice, keeping all his commandments that I am giving you right now, by doing what is right in the LORD your God's eyes!

Complete devotion to the LORD

14 You are the LORD's children. Don't cut yourselves and don't shave your foreheads for the dead, 2 because you are a people holy to the LORD your God. You are the ones whom the LORD selected to be his own, to be a treasured people out of all other people on earth.

Dietary laws

3 Don't eat any detestable thing. 4 Here's a list of animals you are allowed to eat: ox, sheep, goat, 5 deer, gazelle, roebuck, wild goat, ibex, antelope, and mountain sheep.

[w]13:1 in Heb [x]13:2 in Heb [y]Or *burn* [z]See note at 2:34.

6You are also allowed to eat any animal with a divided hoof—the hoof being divided into two parts—and that rechews food among the various kinds of animals. 7However, here's a list of animals that either rechew food or have hooves divided in two parts that you are not allowed to eat:

the camel, the hare, and the rock badger—because these rechew food but don't have divided hoofs, they are off-limits for you;

8and the pig—because it has a divided hoof but doesn't rechew food, it's off-limits for you.

You may not eat these animals' meat, and you must not touch their carcasses.

9Here's a list of the water animals you are allowed to eat: you can eat anything that has fins and scales. 10But you aren't allowed to eat anything that lacks scales or fins. These are off-limits for you.

11You are allowed to eat any clean bird. 12Here's a list of those you are not allowed to eat: the eagle, the vulture, the osprey, 13the red kite, the black kite, and any kind of bird of prey, 14any kind of raven, 15the ostrich, the nighthawk, the seagull, any kind of hawk, 16the small owl and the large owl, the water hen, 17the desert owl, the carrion vulture, the cormorant, 18the stork, any kind of heron, the hoopoe, and the bat.[a]

19Also, all winged insects are off-limits for you. They are not to be eaten. 20Any clean winged creature can be eaten, however.

21You must not eat any decayed animal flesh because you are a people holy to the LORD your God. You can give decayed animal flesh to the immigrants who live in your cities, and they can eat it; or you can sell it to foreigners.

Don't cook a lamb in its own mother's milk.

Tenth part

22You must reserve a tenth part of whatever your fields produce each year. 23Eat the tenth part of your grain, wine, oil, oldest offspring of your herds and flocks in the presence of the LORD your God in the location he selects for his name to reside so that you learn to fear the LORD your God at all times. 24But if the trip is too long, because the location the LORD your God has selected to put his name is far away from where you live so that you can't transport the tenth part—because the LORD your God will certainly bless you—25then you can convert it to money. Take the money with you and go to the location the LORD your God selects. 26Then you can use the money for anything you want: cattle, sheep, wine, beer, or whatever else you might like. Then you should feast there and celebrate in the presence of the LORD your God, along with your entire household. 27Only make sure not to neglect the Levites who are living in your cities because they don't have a designated inheritance like you do.

28Every third year you must bring the tenth part of your produce from that year and leave it at your city gates. 29Then the Levites, who have no designated inheritance like you do, along with the immigrants, orphans, and widows who live in your cities, will come and feast until they are full. Do this so that the LORD your God might bless you in everything you do.

Year of canceled debts

15 Every seventh year you must cancel all debts. 2This is how the cancellation is to be handled: Creditors will forgive the loans of their fellow Israelites. They won't demand repayment from their neighbors or their relatives because the LORD's year of debt cancellation has been announced. 3You are allowed to demand payment from foreigners, but whatever is owed you from your fellow Israelites you must forgive. 4Of course there won't be any poor persons among you because the LORD will bless you in the land that the LORD your God is giving you to possess as an inheritance, 5but only if you carefully obey the LORD your God's voice, by carefully doing every bit of this commandment that I'm giving you right now. 6Once the LORD your God has blessed you, exactly as he said he would,

[a]The species of many of the birds in 14:12-18 is uncertain.

you will end up lending to many different peoples but won't need to borrow a thing. You will dominate many different peoples, but they won't dominate you.

[7]Now if there are some poor persons among you, say one of your fellow Israelites in one of your cities in the land that the LORD your God is giving you, don't be hardhearted or tightfisted toward your poor fellow Israelites. [8]To the contrary! Open your hand wide to them. You must generously lend them whatever they need. [9]But watch yourself! Make sure no wicked thought crosses your mind, such as, The seventh year is coming—the year of debt cancellation—so that you resent your poor fellow Israelites and don't give them anything. If you do that, they will cry out to the LORD against you, and you will be guilty of sin. [10]No, give generously to needy persons. Don't resent giving to them because it is this very thing that will lead to the LORD your God's blessing you in all you do and work at. [11]Poor persons will never disappear from the earth. That's why I'm giving you this command: you must open your hand generously to your fellow Israelites, to the needy among you, and to the poor who live with you in your land.

[12]If any of your fellow Hebrews, male or female, sell themselves into your service, they can work for you for six years, but in the seventh year you must set them free from your service. [13]Furthermore, when you set them free from your service, you must not let them go empty-handed. [14]Instead, provide for them fully from your flock, food, and wine. You must give to them from that with which the LORD your God has blessed you. [15]Remember how each of you was a slave in Egypt and how the LORD your God saved you. That's why I am commanding you to do this right now. ([16]Now if your male servant says to you: "I don't want to leave your service" because he loves you and your family and because life is good for him in your service, [17]then you may take a needle and pierce his ear with it into the doorframe. From that point on, he will be your permanent servant. Do the same thing for female servants.) [18]Don't consider it a hardship to set these servants free from your service, because they worked for you for six years—at a value double that of a paid worker. The LORD your God will bless you in everything that you do.

[19]You must devote every oldest male animal from your herds or flocks to the LORD your God. Don't plow with your oldest male ox and don't shear your oldest male sheep. [20]Year after year, you and your family are allowed to eat these animals in the presence of the LORD your God, in the location the LORD selects. [21]But if there is any defect in it, lameness, blindness, any flaw whatsoever, you must not sacrifice it to the LORD your God. [22]You are allowed to eat those in your own cities, whether you are polluted or purified, just as you would eat gazelle or deer. [23]Even so, don't consume any blood. Pour it out on the ground, like water.

Passover celebration

16 Wait for the month of Abib,[b] at which time you must perform the Passover for the LORD your God, because the LORD your God brought you out of Egypt at nighttime during the month of Abib. [2]Offer a Passover sacrifice from the flock or herd to the LORD your God at the location the LORD selects for his name to reside. [3]You must not eat anything containing yeast along with it.[c] Instead, for seven days you must eat unleavened bread, bread symbolizing misery, along with it because you fled Egypt in a great hurry. Do this so you remember the day you fled Egypt for as long as you live. [4]No dough with yeast should appear in any of your territory for seven days. Furthermore, none of the meat that you sacrificed on the first night should remain until morning. [5]You are not permitted to offer the Passover sacrifice in any of the cities that the LORD your God is giving you. [6]Instead, you must offer the Passover sacrifice at the location the LORD your God selects for his name to reside, at evening time, when the sun sets, which was the time

[b]March–April; called Nisan in post-exilic period [c]*It*, the Passover sacrifice

you fled Egypt. 7 Cook it and eat it in the location that the LORD your God selects. The next morning you can return to your tents. 8 For six days you will eat unleavened bread. The seventh day will be a celebration for the LORD your God. Don't do any work.

Festival of Weeks

9 Count out seven weeks, starting the count from the beginning of the grain harvest. 10 At that point, perform the Festival of Weeks for the LORD your God. Offer a spontaneous gift in precise measure with the blessing the LORD your God gives you. 11 Then celebrate in the presence of the LORD your God—you, your sons, your daughters, your male and female servants, the Levites who live in your cities, the immigrants, the orphans, and the widows who are among you—in the location the LORD your God selects for his name to reside. 12 Remember how each of you was a slave in Egypt, so follow these regulations most carefully.

Festival of Booths

13 Once you have collected the food and drink you need, perform the Festival of Booths for seven days. 14 Celebrate your festival: you, your sons, your daughters, your male and female servants, the Levites, the immigrants, the orphans, and the widows who live in your cities. 15 Seven days you must perform the festival for the LORD your God in the location the LORD selects because the LORD your God will bless you in all you do and in all your work. You will be overjoyed.

16 Three times a year every male among you must appear before the presence of the LORD your God in the location he will select: at the Festival of Unleavened Bread, the Festival of Weeks, and the Festival of Booths. They must not appear before the LORD's presence empty-handed. 17 Each one should have his gift in hand, in precise measure with the blessing the LORD your God gives you.

Judges and officials

18 Appoint judges and officials for each of your tribes in every city that the LORD your God gives you. They must judge the people fairly. 19 Don't delay justice; don't show favoritism. Don't take bribes because bribery blinds the vision of the wise and twists the words of the righteous. 20 Righteousness! Pursue righteousness so that you live long and take possession of the land that the LORD your God is giving you.

Rules for worship

21 Don't plant any tree to serve as a sacred pole[d] next to the altar you make for the LORD your God. 22 Don't set up any sacred stone either, because the LORD your God hates such things. **17** 1 Don't sacrifice to the LORD your God any oxen or sheep that have defects of any kind, because that is detestable to the LORD your God.

Capital punishment

2 If someone, whether male or female, is found in your community—in one of the cities the LORD your God is giving you—who does evil in the LORD your God's eyes, by breaking God's covenant, 3 by following and serving other gods, and by bowing down to them, to the sun or the moon or any of the heavenly bodies that I haven't permitted—4 and you hear news about it, then you must look into this situation very carefully. And if it's definitely true that this detestable thing was done in Israel, 5 then you must bring out the man or woman who has done this evil thing to the gates of the city. Stone that person until he or she is dead.

6 Capital punishment must be decided by two or three witnesses. No one may be executed on the basis of only one testimony. 7 In the execution, the hands of the witnesses must be against the guilty person from the start; the hand of all the people will be involved at the end. Remove[e] such evil from your community!

Legal disputes

8 If some legal dispute in your cities is too difficult for you to decide—say, between different kinds of bloodshed, different kinds of legal ruling, or different kinds of injury—

[d] Heb *asherah*, perhaps an object devoted to the goddess Asherah [e] Or *burn*

then take it to the location the LORD your God selects. [9]Go to the levitical priests and to the head judge in office at that time and look into things there. They will announce to you the correct ruling. [10]You must then act according to the ruling they announced to you from that location, the one the LORD selects. You must follow very carefully everything they instruct you to do. [11]Act precisely according to the instruction they give you and the ruling they announce to you. Don't deviate even a bit from the word they announce. [12]And whoever acts rashly by not listening to the priest who is in office serving the LORD your God or to the head judge will die. Remove[f] such evil from Israel! [13]All the people will hear about this and be afraid. They won't act arrogantly anymore.

Law of the king

[14]Once you have entered the land the LORD your God is giving you and you have taken possession of it and settled down in it, you might say: "Let's appoint a king over us, as all our neighboring nations have done." [15]You can indeed appoint over you a king that the LORD your God selects. You can appoint over you a king who is one of your fellow Israelites. You are not allowed to appoint over you a foreigner who is not one of your fellow Israelites. [16]That granted, the king must not acquire too many horses, and he must not return the people to Egypt in order to acquire more horses, because the LORD told you: "You will never go back by that road again." [17]The king must not take numerous wives so that his heart doesn't go astray. Nor can the king acquire too much silver and gold. [18]Instead, when he sits on his royal throne, he himself must write a copy of this Instruction on a scroll in the presence of the levitical priests. [19]That Instruction must remain with him, and he must read in it every day of his life so that he learns to revere the LORD his God by keeping all the words of this Instruction and these regulations, by doing them, [20]by not being overbearing toward his fellow Israelites, and by not deviating even a bit from the commandment. If the king does all that, he will ensure lasting rule in Israel for himself and for his successors.

Priests and Levites

18 Neither the levitical priests nor any Levite tribe member will have a designated inheritance in Israel. They can eat the sacrifices offered to the LORD, which are the LORD's portion,[g] [2]but they won't share an inheritance with their fellow Israelites. The LORD alone is the Levites' inheritance—just as God promised them.

[3]Now this is what the priests may keep from the people's sacrifices of oxen or sheep: They must give the priest the shoulder, the jaws, and the stomach. [4]You must also give the priest the first portions of your grain, wine, and oil, and the first of your sheep's shearing [5]because the LORD your God selected Levi from all of your tribes to stand and minister in the LORD's name—both him and his descendants for all time.

[6]Now if a Levite leaves one of your cities or departs from any location in Israel where he's been living and, because he wants to, comes to the location the LORD selects [7]and ministers in the LORD his God's name, just like his relatives—the other Levites serving there in the LORD's presence—[8]he is allowed to eat equal portions, despite the finances he has from his family.[h]

Communicating with God

[9]Once you enter the land that the LORD your God is giving you, don't try to imitate the detestable things those nations do. [10]There must not be anyone among you who passes his son or daughter through fire; who practices divination, is a sign reader, fortune-teller, sorcerer, [11]or spell caster; who converses with ghosts or spirits or communicates with the dead. [12]All who do these things are detestable to the LORD! It is on account of these detestable practices that the LORD your God is driving these nations[i] out before you.

[13]Instead, you must be perfect before the LORD your God. [14]These nations you

[f] Or *burn* [g] Heb uncertain [h] Heb uncertain [i] Or *them*

are displacing listened to sign readers and diviners, but the LORD your God doesn't permit you to do the same! 15 The LORD your God will raise up a prophet like me from your community, from your fellow Israelites. He's the one you must listen to. 16 That's exactly what you requested from the LORD your God at Horeb, on the day of the assembly, when you said, "I can't listen to the LORD my God's voice anymore or look at this great fire any longer. I don't want to die!"

17 The LORD said to me: What they've said is right. 18 I'll raise up a prophet for them from among their fellow Israelites—one just like you. I'll put my words in his mouth, and he will tell them everything I command him. 19 I myself will hold accountable anyone who doesn't listen to my words, which that prophet will speak in my name. 20 However, any prophet who arrogantly speaks a word in my name that I haven't commanded him to speak, or who speaks in the name of other gods—that prophet must die.

21 Now, you might be wondering, How will we know which word God hasn't spoken? 22 Here's the answer: The prophet who speaks in the LORD's name and the thing doesn't happen or come about—that's the word the LORD hasn't spoken. That prophet spoke arrogantly. Don't be afraid of him.[j]

Cities of refuge

19 Once the LORD your God has eliminated those nations—whose land the LORD your God is giving you—and you displace them, settling into their cities and their houses, 2 you must designate three cities for your use in the land the LORD your God is giving you to possess. 3 Mark out the roads to them[k] and divide the regions of the land the LORD your God is apportioning to you into three parts. These cities are the places to which a person who has killed can escape. 4 Here is the rule concerning a person who killed someone and is permitted to escape to one of these cities and live:

If it is someone who killed his neighbor accidentally, without having hated that person previously; 5 or if someone goes into the forest with a neighbor to chop some wood, and while swinging an ax to cut down the tree, the axhead flies off its handle and hits the neighbor, who subsequently dies—these kinds of killers may escape to one of these cities and live. 6 Otherwise, the blood avenger will chase after the killer out of rage and—especially if the distance to one of these cities[l] is too far—might catch and kill him, even though a death sentence was not in order because the killer didn't have prior malice toward the other. 7 This is why I am commanding you as follows: Designate three cities for your use.

8 Now if the LORD your God enlarges your territory, as he swore to your ancestors—and he will give you all the land he swore to give to them 9 as long as you keep all this commandment that I am giving you right now by doing it, by loving the LORD your God, and by always walking in his ways—you can add three more cities for your use along with the first three. 10 Innocent blood must not be spilled in the land the LORD your God is giving to you as an inheritance, or it will be bloodshed that will be required of you.

11 But if someone does hate a neighbor and ambushes him, rising up against him and attacking him so he dies, and then escapes to one of these cities, 12 elders from the killer's hometown will send word, and the killer will be sent back from there. They will then hand him over to the blood avenger, and he will be executed. 13 Show no mercy to such killers. Remove[m] innocent bloodshed from Israel so that things go well for you.

Property laws

14 Now in the land the LORD your God is giving you, in your allotted property that you will receive there, you must not tamper with your neighbor's property line, which has been previously established.

[j] Or *bothered by it* (the prophecy) [k] Heb uncertain and lacks *to them*. [l] Heb lacks *to one of these cities*.
[m] Or *burn*

Rules for testimony

[15]A solitary witness against someone in any crime, wrongdoing, or in any sort of misdeed that might be done is not sufficient. The decision must stand by two or three witnesses. [16]Now if a spiteful witness comes forward against someone, so as to testify against them falsely, [17]the two persons who have a legal suit must stand before the LORD, before the priests, and before the judges that are in office at that time. [18]The judges will look into the situation very carefully. If it turns out that the witness is a liar—that the witness has given false testimony against his fellow Israelite—[19]then you must do to him what he had planned to do to his fellow Israelite. Remove[n] such evil from your community! [20]The rest of the people will hear about this and be afraid. They won't do that sort of evil thing among you again. [21]Show no mercy on this point: life for life, eye for eye, tooth for tooth, hand for hand, foot for foot.

Rules for warfare

20 When you march out to battle your enemies and you see horses, chariots, and a fighting force larger than yours, don't be afraid of them, because the LORD your God, the one who brought you up from Egypt, is with you. [2]As you advance toward the war, the priest will come forward and will address the troops. [3]He will say to them: "Listen, Israel: Right now you are advancing to wage war against your enemies. Don't be discouraged! Don't be afraid! Don't panic! Don't shake in fear on account of them, [4]because the LORD your God is going with you to fight your enemies for you and to save you."

[5]The officials will also say to the troops: "Is there anyone here who has just built a new house but hasn't yet dedicated it? He can leave and go back to his house; otherwise, he might die in the war and someone else would dedicate the house. [6]Or is there anyone here who has planted a vineyard but hasn't yet put it to good use? He can leave and go back to his house; otherwise, he might die in the battle and someone else would use the vineyard. [7]Or is there anyone here who is engaged but not yet married? He may leave and go back to his house; otherwise, he might die in the battle and someone else would marry his fiancée."

[8]The officials will continue to address the troops, stating: "Is there anyone here who is afraid and discouraged? He can leave and go back to his house; otherwise, his comrades might lose courage just as he has." [9]Once the officials have completed their speech to the troops, the army commanders will assume leadership of the forces.

[10]When you approach a city to fight against it, you should first extend peaceful terms to it. [11]If the city responds with peaceful terms and surrenders to you, then all the people in the city will serve you as forced laborers. [12]However, if the city does not negotiate peacefully with you but makes war against you, you may attack it. [13]The LORD your God will hand it over to you; you must kill all the city's males with the sword. [14]However, you can take for yourselves the women, the children, the animals, and all that is in the city—all its plunder. You can then enjoy your enemies' plunder, which the LORD your God has given you.

[15]That's what you must do to all the cities that are located far away from you—specifically, those cities that don't belong to these nations here. [16]But in the case of any of the cities of these peoples—the ones the LORD your God is giving you as an inheritance—you must not spare any living thing. [17]Instead, you must place these under the ban:[o] Hittites, Amorites, Canaanites, Perizzites, Hivites, and Jebusites—just as the LORD your God commanded you. [18]Then they can't teach you to do all the detestable things they did for their gods, with the result that you end up sinning against the LORD your God.

[19]Now if you have been attacking a city for some time, fighting against it and trying to conquer it, don't destroy its trees by cutting them down with axes. You can eat from

[n]Or *burn* [o]See note at Deut 2:34.

those trees; don't cut them down! Do you think a tree of the field is some sort of warrior to be attacked by you in battle? [20]That said, if you know that a tree is not a food-producing tree, you are allowed to destroy it, cutting it down and using it in the siege against the city that is fighting against you until it falls.

Unsolved homicides

21 If a corpse is found on the ground the LORD your God is giving you to possess, lying in a field, and the identity of the killer is unknown, [2]your elders and judges must come out and measure the distances to the cities nearest the body. [3]Once it is determined which city is closest to the dead body, its elders must take a young cow that hasn't been used or yet pulled a plow, [4]and those elders will take the cow down to a ravine with a flowing stream—one that has not been plowed or planted—and they will break the cow's neck right there in the river valley. [5]Then the priests, the descendants of Levi, will step forward because the LORD your God selected them to minister for him and to bless in the LORD's name, and because every legal dispute and case of assault is decided by them. [6]All the elders of the city closest to the corpse will wash their hands over the cow whose neck was broken in the river valley. [7]They will then solemnly state: "Our hands did not shed this blood. Our eyes did not see it happen. [8]LORD, please forgive your people Israel, whom you saved. Don't put the guilt of innocent bloodshed on your people Israel."

Then the bloodguilt will be forgiven them. [9]But you must remove[p] innocent bloodshed from your community; do only what is right in the LORD's eyes.

Foreign wives

[10]When you wage war against your enemies and the LORD hands them over to you and you take prisoners, [11]if you see among the captives a beautiful woman, and you fall in love with her and take her as your wife, [12]bringing her into your home, she must shave her head, cut her nails, [13]remove her prisoner's clothing, and live in your house, mourning her father and her mother for one month. After that, you may consummate the marriage. You will be her husband, and she will be your wife. [14]But if you aren't pleased with her, you must send her away as she wishes. You are not allowed to sell her for money or treat her as a slave because you have humiliated her.

Right of the oldest son

[15]Now suppose a man has two wives—one of them loved and the other unloved. Both wives bear children, but the oldest male is the unloved wife's child. [16]On the day when the man decides what will go to each of his children as an inheritance, he isn't allowed to treat his loved wife's son as the oldest male rather than his unloved wife's son, who is the real oldest male. [17]Instead, he must acknowledge the unloved wife's son as the oldest male, giving to him two-thirds of everything that he owns, because that son is the earliest produce of his physical power. The oldest male's rights belong to that son.

Rebellious children

[18]Now if someone has a consistently stubborn and rebellious child, who refuses to listen to their father and mother—even when the parents discipline him, he won't listen to them—[19]the father and mother will take the son before the elders of that city at its gates. [20]Then they will inform the city's elders: "This son of ours is consistently stubborn and rebellious, refusing to listen to us. What's more, he's wild and a drunkard."

[21]Then all the people of that town will stone him until he dies.

Remove[q] such evil from your community! All Israel will hear about this and be afraid.

Hanging

[22]Now if someone is guilty of a capital crime, and they are executed, and you then hang them on a tree, [23]you must not leave the body hanging on the tree but must bury

[p]Or *burn* [q]Or *burn*

it the same day because God's curse is on those who are hanged.[r] Furthermore, you must not pollute the ground that the LORD your God is giving to you as an inheritance.

Rules for property and mixtures

22 Don't just watch your fellow Israelite's ox or sheep wandering around and do nothing about it. You must return the animal to its owner. 2If the owner doesn't live nearby, or you don't know who owns the animal, then you must take care of it. It should stay with you until your fellow Israelite comes looking for it, at which point you must return it to him.

3Do the same thing in the case of a donkey. Do the same thing in the case of a piece of clothing. Do the same thing in the case of anything that your fellow Israelite loses and you end up finding. You are not allowed to sit back and do nothing about it.

4Don't just watch your fellow Israelite's donkey or ox fall down in the road and do nothing about it. You must help your fellow Israelite get the animal up again.

5Women must not wear men's clothes, and men must not wear women's clothes. Everyone who does such things is detestable to the LORD your God.

6If you come across a bird's nest along your way, whether in a tree or on the ground, with baby birds or eggs, and the mother is sitting on the baby birds or eggs, do not remove the mother from her young.
7You must let the mother go, though you may take the young for yourself so that things go well for you and so you can prolong your life.

8Whenever you build a new house, you must build a railing for the roof so that you don't end up with innocent blood on your hands because someone fell off of it.

9Don't plant your vineyards with two types of seed; otherwise, the entire crop that you have planted and the produce of the vineyard will be unusable.[s]

10Don't plow with an ox and a donkey together.

11Don't wear clothes that mix wool and linen together.

12Make tassels for the four corners of the coat you wear.

Virgin bride

13Suppose a man gets married and consummates the marriage but subsequently
despises his wife. 14He then spreads false claims about her to the point that she has a bad reputation, because he said such things as, "I married this woman, but when I went to have sex with her, I couldn't find any proof that she was a virgin."

15At that point, the young woman's father and mother will bring proof of her virginity to the city's elders at the city
gate. 16The young woman's father will say to the elders: "I gave my daughter to this man to be his wife, but he doesn't like her
anymore. 17That's why he has spread false claims about her, saying, 'I couldn't find any proof that your daughter was a virgin.' But look! Here's proof of my daughter's virginity." At that point they will spread out the
blanket in front of the city's elders. 18The city's elders must then take that husband
and punish him. 19They will fine him one hundred silver shekels, giving that to the young woman's father, because that husband gave one of Israel's virgin daughters a bad reputation. Moreover, she must remain his wife; he is never allowed to divorce her.

20However, if the claim is true and proof of the young woman's virginity can't be produced,
21then the city's elders will bring the young woman to the door of her father's house. The citizens of that city must stone her until she dies because she acted so sinfully in Israel by having extramarital sex while still in her father's house.

Remove[t] such evil from your community!

Inappropriate sexual behavior

22If a man is found having sex with a woman who is married to someone else, both of them must die—the man who was having sex with the woman and the woman herself.

[r]LXX, Vulg, Tg Neofiti *God's curse is on those who are hanged;* Syr, Tg Onqelos *those who curse God are to be hanged;* Heb uncertain [s]Or *sanctified* [t]Or *burn*; so also 22:22, 24

Remove such evil from Israel!

[23]If a young woman who is a virgin is engaged to one man and another man meets up with her in a town and has sex with her, [24]you must bring both of them to the city gates there and stone them until they die—the young woman because she didn't call for help in the city, and the man because of the fact that he humiliated his neighbor's wife.

Remove such evil from your community!

[25]But if the man met up with the engaged woman in a field, grabbing her and having sex with her there, only the man will die. [26]Don't do anything whatsoever to the young woman. She hasn't committed any capital crime—rather, this situation is exactly like the one where someone attacks his neighbor and kills him.[u] [27]Since the man met up with her in a field, the engaged woman may well have called out for help, but there was no one to rescue her.

[28]If a man meets up with a young woman who is a virgin and not engaged, grabs her and has sex with her, and they are caught in the act, [29]the man who had sex with her must give fifty silver shekels to the young woman's father. She will also become his wife because he has humiliated her. He is never allowed to divorce her.

[30][v]A man cannot marry his father's former wife so that his father's private matters are not exposed.[w]

The LORD's assembly

23 [x]No man whose testicles are crushed or whose penis is cut off can belong to the LORD's assembly. [2]No one born of an illegitimate marriage[y] can belong to the LORD's assembly either. Not even the tenth generation of such children can belong to the LORD's assembly. [3]Ammonites and Moabites can't belong to the LORD's assembly. Not even the tenth generation of such people can belong to the LORD's assembly, as a rule, [4]because they didn't help you with food or water on your journey out of Egypt, and because they hired Balaam, Beor's son, from Pethor of Mesopotamia to curse you. [5]But the LORD your God wasn't interested in listening to Balaam. The LORD your God turned that curse into a blessing because the LORD your God loves you. [6]So don't be concerned with their health and well-being as long as you live.

[7]Don't detest Edomites, because they are your relatives. Don't detest Egyptians because you were immigrants in their land. [8]Children born to them are permitted to belong to the LORD's assembly starting with the third generation.

Rules for the war camp

[9]When you are camped in battle against your enemies, guard yourself from every possible evil. [10]If an individual in the camp becomes polluted due to a nighttime emission, he must exit the camp area and not reenter. [11]When the next evening arrives, he must wash with water; and when the sun sets, he can come back to the camp.

[12]The latrines[z] must be outside the camp. You will use them there, outside the camp. [13]Carry a shovel with the rest of your gear; once you have relieved yourself, use it to dig a hole, then refill it, covering your excrement.

[14]Do these things because the LORD your God travels with you, right in the middle of your camp, ready to save you and to hand your enemies over to you. For this reason your camp must be holy. The LORD must not see anything indecent among you, or he will turn away from you.

Escaped slaves

[15]Don't return slaves to owners if they've escaped and come to you. [16]They can stay with you: in your own community or in any place they select from one of your cities, whatever seems good to them. Don't oppress them.

Consecrated workers

[17]No Israelite daughter is allowed to be a consecrated worker.[a] Neither is any Israelite son allowed to be a consecrated worker.[b]

[u]See 19:11. [v]23:1 in Heb [w]Or *so that he doesn't uncover his father's skirt* [x]23:2 in Heb [y]Heb uncertain
[z]LXX, Syr, Vulg *place of the hand* (a euphemism); MT has only *hand.* [a]Traditionally *cultic prostitute*
[b]Traditionally *cultic prostitute*

18 Don't bring a female prostitute's fee or a male prostitute's[c] payment to the LORD your God's temple to pay a solemn promise because both of these things are detestable to the LORD your God.

Charging interest

19 Don't charge your fellow Israelites interest—whether on money, provisions, or anything one might loan. 20 You can charge foreigners interest, but not your fellow Israelite. Do this so that the LORD your God blesses you in all your work on the land you are entering to possess.

Solemn promise

21 When you make a promise to the LORD your God, don't put off making good on it, because the LORD your God will certainly be expecting it from you; delaying would make you guilty. 22 Now if you simply don't make any promises, you won't be guilty of anything. 23 But whatever you say, you should be sure to make good on, exactly according to the promise you freely made to the LORD your God because you promised it with your own mouth.

Neighbor's goods

24 If you go into your neighbor's vineyard, you can eat as many grapes as you like, until full, but don't carry any away in a basket. 25 If you go into your neighbor's grain field, you can pluck ears by hand, but you aren't allowed to cut off any of your neighbor's grain with a sickle.

Marriage and divorce

24 Let's say a man marries a woman, but she isn't pleasing to him because he's discovered something inappropriate about her. So he writes up divorce papers, hands them to her, and sends her out of his house. 2 She leaves his house and ends up marrying someone else. 3 But this new husband also dislikes her, writes up divorce papers, hands them to her, and sends her out of his house (or suppose the second husband dies). 4 In this case, the first husband who originally divorced this woman is not allowed to take her back and marry her again after she has been polluted in this way because the LORD detests that. Don't pollute the land the LORD your God is giving to you as an inheritance.

5 A newly married man doesn't have to march in battle. Neither should any related duties be placed on him. He is to live free of such responsibilities for one year, so he can bring joy to his new wife.

Pawning

6 Millstones or even just the upper millstone must not be pawned, because that would be pawning someone's livelihood.

Kidnapping

7 If someone is caught kidnapping their fellow Israelites, intending to enslave the Israelite or sell them, that kidnapper must die. Remove[d] such evil from your community!

Skin disease

8 Be on guard against outbreaks of skin disease[e] by being very careful about what you do. You must carefully do everything the levitical priests teach you, just as I have commanded them. 9 Remember, after all, what the LORD your God did to Miriam on your departure from Egypt!

Loans

10 When you make any type of loan to your neighbor, don't enter their house to receive the collateral. 11 You must wait outside. The person to whom you are lending will bring the collateral to you out there. 12 Moreover, if the person is poor, you are not allowed to sleep in their pawned coat. 13 Instead, be certain to give the pawned coat back by sunset so they can sleep in their own coat. They will bless you, and you will be considered righteous before the LORD your God.

Payment for workers

14 Don't take advantage of poor or needy workers, whether they are fellow Israelites

[c] Or *a dog* [d] Or *burn* [e] Heb uncertain; traditionally *leprosy*—a term used for several different skin diseases

or immigrants who live in your land or your cities. 15 Pay them their salary the same day, before the sun sets, because they are poor, and their very life depends on that pay, and so they don't cry out against you to the LORD. That would make you guilty.

Generational punishment

16 Parents shouldn't be executed because of what their children have done; neither should children be executed because of what their parents have done. Each person should be executed for their own guilty acts.

Rights of widows, orphans, and immigrants

17 Don't obstruct the legal rights of an immigrant or orphan. Don't take a widow's coat as pledge for a loan. 18 Remember how you were a slave in Egypt but how the LORD your God saved you from that. That's why I'm commanding you to do this thing.

19 Whenever you are reaping the harvest of your field and you leave some grain in the field, don't go back and get it. Let it go to the immigrants, the orphans, and the widows so that the LORD your God blesses you in all that you do. 20 Similarly, when you beat the olives off your olive trees, don't go back over them twice. Let the leftovers go to the immigrants, the orphans, and the widows. 21 Again, when you pick the grapes of your vineyard, don't pick them over twice. Let the leftovers go to the immigrants, the orphans, and the widows. 22 Remember how you were a slave in Egypt. That's why I am commanding you to do this thing.

Corporal punishment

25 Now two people have a disagreement and they enter into litigation and their case is decided, with the judges declaring one person legally right and the other legally liable. 2 If the guilty party is to be beaten, the presiding judge will have that person lie down and be punished in his presence—the number of blows in measure with the guilt determined. 3 Give no more than forty blows. If more than that is given, your fellow Israelite would be completely disgraced in your eyes.

Working oxen

4 Don't muzzle an ox while it is threshing grain.

The brother-in-law's duty

5 If brothers live together and one of them dies without having a son, the dead man's wife must not go outside the family and marry a stranger. Instead, her brother-in-law should go to her and take her as his wife. He will then consummate the marriage according to the brother-in-law's duty. 6 The brother-in-law will name the oldest male son that she bears after his dead brother so that his brother's legacy will not be forgotten in Israel. 7 If the brother does not want to marry his sister-in-law, she can go to the elders at the city gate, informing them: "My brother-in-law refuses to continue his brother's legacy in Israel. He's not willing to perform the brother-in-law's duty with me." 8 The city's elders will summon him and talk to him about this. If he doesn't budge, insisting, "I don't want to marry her," 9 then the sister-in-law will approach him while the elders watch. She will pull the sandal off his foot and spit in his face. Then she will exclaim: "That's what's done to any man who won't build up his own brother's family!" 10 Subsequently, that man's family will be known throughout Israel as "the house of the removed sandal."

Improper touching

11 If two men are fighting with each other—a man and his fellow Israelite—and the wife of one of them gets into the fight, trying to save her husband from his attacker and does so by reaching out and grabbing his genitals, 12 you must cut off her hand. Show no mercy.

Honest business practices

13 Don't have two different types of money weights in your bag, a heavy one and a light one. 14 Don't have two different types of ephahs in your house, a large one and a small one. 15 Instead, you must have only one weight, complete and correct, and only one ephah, also complete and correct, so that your life might be long in the fertile

land the LORD your God is giving you. [16]What's more, all who do such things, all who do business dishonestly, are detestable to the LORD your God. [17]Remember, after all, what Amalek did to you on your departure from Egypt: [18]how he met up with you on the way, striking from behind those who were lagging back because you were weak and tired, and because he didn't fear God. [19]So once the LORD your God gives you relief from all the enemies that surround you in the land the LORD your God is giving you as an inheritance to possess, you must wipe out Amalek's memory from under the heavens. Don't forget this!

The ceremony upon entering the land

26 Once you have entered the land the LORD your God is giving you as an inheritance, and you take possession of it and are settled there, [2]take some of the early produce of the fertile ground that you have harvested from the land the LORD your God is giving you, and put it in a basket. Then go to the location the LORD your God selects for his name to reside. [3]Go to the priest who is in office at that time and say to him: "I am declaring right now before the LORD my[f] God that I have indeed arrived in the land the LORD swore to our ancestors to give us."

[4]The priest will then take the basket from you and place it before the LORD your God's altar. [5]Then you should solemnly state before the LORD your God:

"My father was a starving Aramean. He went down to Egypt, living as an immigrant there with few family members, but that is where he became a great nation, mighty and numerous. [6]The Egyptians treated us terribly, oppressing us and forcing hard labor on us. [7]So we cried out for help to the LORD, our ancestors' God. The LORD heard our call. God saw our misery, our trouble, and our oppression. [8]The LORD brought us out of Egypt with a strong hand and an outstretched arm, with awesome power, and with signs and wonders. [9]He brought us to this place and gave us this land—a land full of milk and honey. [10]So now I am bringing the early produce of the fertile ground that you, LORD, have given me."

Set the produce before the LORD your God, bowing down before the LORD your God. [11]Then celebrate all the good things the LORD your God has done for you and your family—each one of you along with the Levites and the immigrants who are among you.

[12]When you have finished paying the entire tenth part of your produce on the third year—that is the year for paying the tenth-part—you will give it to the Levites, the immigrants, the orphans, and the widows so they can eat in your cities until they are full. [13]Then announce before the LORD your God: "I have removed the holy portion from my[g] house, and I have given it to the Levites, the immigrants, the orphans, and the widows—in full compliance with your entire commandment that you commanded me. I haven't broken your commandments. I haven't forgotten one! [14]I haven't eaten from the holy portion while mourning, nor did I remove it while I was polluted, nor have I dedicated any of it to the dead. I've obeyed the LORD my God's voice. I've done everything just as you commanded me. [15]Please look down from your holy home, from heaven itself, and bless your people Israel and the fertile land that you have given us—a land full of milk and honey—just like you promised our ancestors."

Conclusion to the regulations and case laws

[16]This very moment the LORD your God is commanding you to keep these regulations and case laws. So keep them and do them with all your mind and with your entire being! [17]Today you have affirmed that the LORD will be your God and that you will walk in his ways and follow his regulations, his commandments, and his case laws, and that you will obey his voice. [18]Today the LORD has gotten your agreement[h] that you will be his treasured people, just like he promised—by keeping his commandments—[19]in order

[f]LXX; MT and most versions read *your*. [g]LXX, Vulg; MT lacks *my*. [h]Heb uncertain

to set you high above all the other nations that he made in praise, fame, and honor; and so that you are a people holy to the LORD your God, just as he said you would be.

Stones of the Instruction

27 Then Moses and Israel's elders commanded the people:

Keep all of the commandment that I am giving you right now. 2 The same day you cross the Jordan River to enter the land the LORD your God is giving you, set up large stones and cover them with plaster. 3 Once you have crossed over, write on the stones all the words of this Instruction because you will have entered[i] the land the LORD your God is giving to you—a land full of milk and honey—exactly as the LORD, your ancestors' God, promised you. 4 Once you have crossed over the Jordan River, set up these stones that I'm telling you about right now on Mount Ebal. Cover them with plaster 5 and build an altar there for the LORD your God—an altar of stones that haven't been cut with iron tools. 6 (You must build the LORD your God's altar with uncut stones.) Then offer up on that altar entirely burned sacrifices to the LORD your God. 7 Offer up well-being sacrifices and eat them there, celebrating in the LORD your God's presence. 8 Make sure to write all the words of this Instruction on the stones plainly and clearly.

9 Then Moses and the levitical priests said to all Israel: Quiet down and listen, Israel! This very moment you have become the people of the LORD your God. 10 So obey the LORD your God's voice. Do his commandments and his regulations that I'm giving you right now.

Ceremony on Mount Gerizim and Mount Ebal

11 That same day Moses commanded the people: 12 Once you have crossed over the Jordan River, the following tribes will stand on Mount Gerizim to bless the people: Simeon, Levi, Judah, Issachar, Joseph, and Benjamin. 13 And these are the tribes that will stand on Mount Ebal for the cursing: Reuben, Gad, Asher, Zebulun, Dan, and Naphtali. 14 The Levites will address every individual Israelite with a loud voice:

15 "Cursed is anyone who makes an idol or an image—things detestable to the LORD, made by artisans—and sets it up secretly."

All the people will reply: "We agree!"[j]

16 "Cursed is anyone who belittles their father or mother."

All the people will reply: "We agree!"

17 "Cursed is anyone who tampers with their neighbor's property lines."

All the people will reply: "We agree!"

18 "Cursed is anyone who misleads a blind person on a road."

All the people will reply: "We agree!"

19 "Cursed is anyone who obstructs the legal rights of immigrants, orphans, or widows."

All the people will reply: "We agree!"

20 "Cursed is anyone who has sex with his father's wife, because that exposes his father's private matters."[k]

All the people will reply: "We agree!"

21 "Cursed is anyone who has sex with any kind of animal."

All the people will reply: "We agree!"

22 "Cursed is anyone who has sex with his sister, whether his father's daughter or his mother's daughter."

All the people will reply: "We agree!"

23 "Cursed is anyone who has sex with his mother-in-law."

All the people will reply: "We agree!"

24 "Cursed is anyone who kills his neighbor in secret."

All the people will reply: "We agree!"

25 "Cursed is anyone who accepts money to kill an innocent person."

All the people will reply: "We agree!"

26 "Cursed is anyone who doesn't support the words of this Instruction by carrying them out."

All the people will reply: "We agree!"

[i] Or *in order that you might enter*; Heb uncertain [j] Heb *Amen*; also in the following verses [k] Or *because that uncovers his father's skirt*

Future blessing

28 Now if you really obey the LORD
your God's voice, by carefully keeping all his commandments that I am giving
you right now, then the LORD your God will
set you high above all nations on earth. 2 All
these blessings will come upon you and find
you if you obey the LORD your God's voice:
3 You will be blessed in the city and blessed
in the field. 4 Your own fertility, your soil's
produce, and your livestock's offspring—
the young of both cattle and flocks—will
be blessed. 5 Your basket and your kneading
bowl will be blessed. 6 You will be blessed
when you are out and about and blessed
when you come back. 7 The LORD will defeat
any enemies who attack you. They will come
against you from one direction but will run
for their lives away from you in seven different directions. 8 The LORD will command
the blessing to be with you—in your barns
and on all the work you do—and he will
bless you on the land the LORD your God is
giving you. 9 The LORD will establish you as
his own, a holy nation, just as he swore to
you, if you keep the LORD your God's commandments and walk in his ways. 10 All the
earth's peoples will see that you are called
by the LORD's name, and they will be in awe
of you. 11 The LORD will make good things
abound for you—whether the fertility of
your womb, your livestock's offspring, or
your fertile soil's produce—on the very land
that the LORD swore to your ancestors to
give to you. 12 The LORD will open up for you
his own well-stocked storehouse, the heavens, providing your land with rain at just
the right time and blessing all your work.
You will lend to many nations, but you
won't have any need to borrow. 13 The LORD
will make you the head of things, not the
tail; you will be at the top of things, not the
bottom, as long as you obey the LORD your
God's commandments that I'm commanding you right now, by carefully doing them.
14 Don't deviate even a bit from any of these
words that I'm commanding you right now
by following other gods and serving them.

Future curses

15 But if you don't obey the LORD your
God's voice by carefully doing all his commandments and his regulations that I am
commanding you right now, all these curses
will come upon you and find you. 16 You will
be cursed in the city and cursed in the field.
17 Your basket and kneading bowl will be
cursed. 18 Your own fertility, your soil's produce, your cattle's young, and your flock's
offspring will be cursed. 19 You will be cursed
when you are out and about and cursed
when you come back. 20 The LORD will send
calamity, confusion, and frustration on you
no matter what work you are doing until
you are wiped out and until you disappear—
it'll be quick!—because of the evil acts by
which you have abandoned him.[l] 21 The
LORD will make a plague stick to you until
he has totally wiped you off the fertile land
you are entering to possess. 22 The LORD
will strike you with consumption, fever,
and inflammation; with scorching heat and
drought;[m] with destruction and disease for
your crops.[n] These things will chase you
until you are dead and gone. 23 The sky over
your head will be as hard as bronze; the
earth under your feet will be like iron. 24 The
LORD will turn the rain on your land into
dust. Only dirt will fall down on you from
the sky until you are completely wiped out.
25 The LORD will hand you over defeated to
your enemies. You will go out against them
by one direction, but you will run for your
life away from them in seven different directions. All the earth's kingdoms will be
horrified by you. 26 Your corpses will be
food for every bird in the sky and animal on
earth; no one will frighten them off. 27 The
LORD will afflict you with Egyptian inflammation, hemorrhoids,[o] rash, and itch. You
will be untreatable. 28 The LORD will make
you go crazy, make you blind, make your
mind confused. 29 You will fumble around
at high noon as blind people fumble around
in darkness. Your plans won't prosper. Instead, you will be constantly oppressed
and taken advantage of without any savior.

[l] Or *me*, in which case the text shifts to direct divine discourse. [m] Heb uncertain [n] Or *blight and mildew*
[o] Qere; Kethib *tumors*

30 You might get engaged to a woman, but
another man will have sex with her. You
might build a house, but you won't get to
live in it. You might plant a vineyard, but
you won't enjoy it. 31 Your ox will be slaughtered while you watch, but you won't get
to eat any of it. Your donkey will be stolen right out from under you, and it won't
come back. Your flocks will be given to your
enemies. No one will save you. 32 Your sons
and daughters will be given to another nation while you watch; you will long for them
constantly, but you won't have the power to
do anything about it. 33 The produce of your
land and all your hard work will be consumed by people you don't know. You will
be nothing but oppressed and mistreated
constantly. 34 The sights your eyes see will
drive you insane. 35 The LORD will strike
you with horrible inflammation in your
knees and legs, from the sole of your foot
to the top of your head. You will be untreatable. 36 The LORD will send you and the king
that you appoint over you far away to a nation that neither you nor your ancestors
have known. There you will worship other
gods made of wood and stone. 37 You will
become a horror, fit only for use in proverbs
and in insults by all the nations where the
LORD drives you. 38 You might scatter a lot
of seed on the field, but you will gather almost nothing because the locusts will eat it
all. 39 You might plant lots of vineyards and
work hard in them, but you won't drink any
wine or harvest the grapes because worms
will devour them. 40 You might have many
olive trees throughout your territories, but
you won't cover yourself with their oil because your olive trees will fail. 41 You might
have sons and daughters, but they won't be
yours for long because they will be taken
away as prisoners. 42 Crickets will take over
all your trees and your soil's produce. 43 The
immigrants who live among you will be promoted over you, higher and higher! But you
will be demoted, lower and lower! 44 They
will lend to you, but you will have nothing
to lend to them. They will be the head of
things; you will be the tail.

45 That's how all these curses will come
over you, pursuing you, reaching you until
you are completely wiped out, because you
didn't obey the LORD your God's voice by
keeping his commandments and his regulations that he gave you. 46 These things
will be a sign and a wonder on you and
your descendants forever. 47 Because you
didn't serve the LORD your God joyfully
and gladly above all else,[p] 48 you will serve
your enemies—the ones the LORD will
send against you—during famine, drought,
nakedness, and total depravation. God will
put an iron yoke on your neck until he has
wiped you out. 49 The LORD will bring a distant nation—one from the far ends of the
earth—against you as fast as the eagle flies:
a nation that speaks a language you can't
understand, 50 a stern nation that doesn't
go easy on the very old or show pity to the
very young. 51 That nation will devour your
livestock's offspring and your soil's produce
until you yourselves are destroyed because
you will have no grain, wine, or oil left—
nor any young from your cattle or offspring
from your flocks—that is, until that nation
annihilates you. 52 That nation will attack
you in all your cities until your high, reinforced walls that you thought were so safe
fall down across your entire countryside.
That nation will attack you in all your cities throughout the land the LORD your God
has given you. 53 You will eat the offspring
of your own womb—the flesh of your own
sons and daughters, whom the LORD your
God gave you—because of the desperate
and dire circumstances that your enemy
has brought on you.

54 Even the most gentle and refined man
among you will scowl at his brother or his
own dear wife, or the last of his surviving
children. 55 He won't want to give them any
of his children's flesh that he will be eating
because he has no other food due to the
desperate and dire circumstances that your
enemy has brought on you in all your cities.
56 Even the most gentle and refined woman
among you, who is so refined and gentle she
wouldn't stomp her foot on the ground, will

[p] Heb uncertain

scowl at her own dear husband, her son, or her daughter—[57]not wanting to give them any of the afterbirth she pushed out or the babies she bore, because she will be eating them secretly while starving due to the desperate and dire circumstances that your enemy will bring on you in your cities.

[58]If you don't carefully keep all the words of this Instruction that are written in this scroll, by fearing the awesome and glorious name of the LORD your God—[59]the LORD will overwhelm you and your descendants with severe and chronic afflictions, and with terrible and untreatable sicknesses. [60]He'll put on you all the Egyptian diseases about which you were so afraid; they will stick to you! [61]What's more, the LORD will bring on you all the other diseases and plagues that aren't written in this Instruction scroll until you are completely wiped out. [62]Once as countless as the stars in the night sky, only a few of you will be left alive—all because you didn't obey the LORD your God's voice. [63]And just as before, the LORD enjoyed doing good things for you and increasing your numbers, now the LORD will enjoy annihilating and destroying you. You will be torn off the very fertile land you are entering to possess. [64]The LORD will scatter you among every nation, from one end of the earth to the other. There you will serve other gods that neither you nor your ancestors have known—gods of wood and stone. [65]Among those nations you will have no rest and no place to call your own.[q] There the LORD will give you an agitated mind, failing eyes, and a depressed spirit. [66]Your life will seem to dangle before your very eyes. You will be afraid night and day. You won't be able to count on surviving for long. [67]In the morning you will say: "I wish it was nighttime," but at nighttime you will say, "I wish it was morning"—on account of your tortured mind, which will be terrified, and because of the horrible sights that your eyes will see. [68]Finally, the LORD will take you back to Egypt in ships, by the route I promised you would never see again. There you will try to sell yourselves as slaves—both male and female—but no one will want to buy you.

The third heading: The new covenant at Moab

29 [r]These are the words of the covenant the LORD commanded Moses to make with the Israelites in the land of Moab in addition to the covenant he had made with them at Horeb. [2][s]Moses summoned all Israel, saying to them:

You've seen with your own eyes everything the LORD did in Egypt, to Pharaoh, his servants, and all his land—[3]the great trials your eyes witnessed, those awesome signs and wonders! [4]But until this very moment, the LORD hasn't given you insight to understand, eyes to see, or ears to hear. [5]I've led you in the wilderness forty years now; neither the clothes on your back nor the sandals on your feet have worn out. [6]Neither have you eaten bread nor drunk wine or beer during this time—so that you would know that I am the LORD your God.[t] [7]When you arrived here, Sihon, Heshbon's king, and Og, Bashan's king, marched out to fight against us, but we defeated them. [8]We took possession of their land and gave it as an inheritance to the Reubenites, Gadites, and half of Manasseh's tribe. [9]So then keep the words of this covenant and do them so you can succeed in all you do.

[10]Right now, all of you are in the presence of the LORD your God—the leaders of your tribes,[u] your elders, and your officials, all the Israelite males, [11]your children, your wives, and the immigrants who live with you in your camp, the ones who chop your wood and those who draw your water—[12]ready to enter into the LORD your God's covenant and into the agreement that the LORD your God is making with you right now. [13]That means the Lord will make you his own people right now—he will be your God just as he promised you and just as he swore to our ancestors: to Abraham, Isaac, and Jacob. [14]But I'm not making this covenant and this

[q]Or *resting place for the sole of your foot* [r]28:69 in Heb [s]29:1 in Heb [t]Or *that I, the LORD, am your God.*
[u]LXX, Syr; MT *your leaders, your tribes*

agreement with you alone [15]but also with those standing here with us right now before the LORD our God, and also with those who aren't here with us right now.

[16]You know firsthand how we used to live in Egypt and how we passed right through the nations that you passed through. [17]You saw the horrific things, the filthy idols of wood and stone, silver and gold, that they had with them. [18]Make sure there isn't any one among you right now—male or female, clan or tribe—whose mind is turning from being with the LORD our God in favor of going to serve these nations' gods. Make sure there isn't any root among you that is sprouting poison and bitterness. [19]When that kind of person hears the words of this agreement, they congratulate themselves, thinking: I'll be fine even though I insist on being stubborn. This would cause something wet to dry up and become like something parched.[v] [20]The LORD won't be willing to forgive that kind of person; instead, the LORD's anger and passion will smolder against that person. Every curse written in this scroll will stretch out over them, and the LORD will wipe out their name from under the heavens. [21]Out of all Israel's tribes, the LORD will single them out for disaster in compliance with all the covenant curses that are written in this Instruction scroll.

[22]Future generations, your children after you, or foreigners from distant lands will say: Look[w] at all that land's plagues and the sicknesses that the LORD laid on it! [23]Look at all its land burned by sulfur and salt, unsuitable for planting, unable to grow or produce any vegetation, as devastated as Sodom and Gomorrah, Admah and Zeboiim, which the LORD devastated in anger and wrath! [24]Indeed, all nations will ask: Why did the LORD do this to this land? What led to this terrible display of anger? [25]They will deduce: It was because those people abandoned the covenant of the LORD, their ancestors' God, which he made with them when he brought them out of Egypt. [26]They followed other gods, serving them and worshipping them—other gods that they hadn't experienced before and that the Lord hadn't designated for them. [27]Then the LORD's anger burned against that land, and he brought against it every curse written in this scroll. [28]The LORD ripped them off their land in anger, wrath, and great fury. He threw them into other lands, and that's how things still stand today.

[29]The secret things belong to the LORD our God. The revealed things belong to us and to our children forever: to keep all the words of this covenant.

30 Now, once all these things happen to you, the blessing and the curse that I'm setting before you, you must call them to mind as you sit among the various nations where the LORD your God has driven you; [2]and you must return to the LORD your God, obeying his voice, in line with all that I'm commanding you right now—you and your children—with all your mind and with all your being. [3]Then the LORD your God will restore you as you were before and will have compassion on you, gathering you up from all the peoples where the LORD your God scattered you. [4]Even if he has driven you to the far end of heaven, the LORD your God will gather you up from there; he will take you back from there. [5]The LORD your God will bring you home to the land that your ancestors possessed; you will possess it again. And he will do good things for you and multiply you—making you more numerous even than your ancestors!

[6]Then the LORD your God will circumcise your hearts and the hearts of your descendants so that you love the LORD your God with all your mind and with all your being in order that you may live. [7]The LORD your God will put all these curses on your enemies and on those who hate you and chase you. [8]But you will change and obey the LORD's voice and do all his commandments that I'm commanding you right now. [9]The LORD your God will help you succeed

[v]Heb uncertain; perhaps the agricultural imagery of 29:18 is continued here or the terms are metaphors for human states. [w]Or *after they see*

in everything you do—in your own fertility, your livestock's offspring, and your land's produce—everything will be great! Because the LORD will once again enjoy doing good things for you just as he enjoyed doing them for your ancestors, [10]and because you will be obeying the LORD your God's voice, keeping his commandments and his regulations that are written in this Instruction scroll, and because you will have returned to the LORD your God with all your heart and all your being.

[11]This commandment that I'm giving you right now is definitely not too difficult for you. It isn't unreachable. [12]It isn't up in heaven somewhere so that you have to ask, "Who will go up for us to heaven and get it for us that we can hear it and do it?" [13]Nor is it across the ocean somewhere so that you have to ask, "Who will cross the ocean for us and get it for us that we can hear it and do it?" [14]Not at all! The word is very close to you. It's in your mouth and in your heart, waiting for you to do it.

Life and death

[15]Look here! Today I've set before you life and what's good versus death and what's wrong. [16]If you obey the LORD your God's commandments that[x] I'm commanding you right now by loving the LORD your God, by walking in his ways, and by keeping his commandments, his regulations, and his case laws, then you will live and thrive, and the LORD your God will bless you in the land you are entering to possess. [17]But if your heart turns away and you refuse to listen, and so are misled, worshipping other gods and serving them, [18]I'm telling you right now that you will definitely die. You will not prolong your life on the fertile land that you are crossing the Jordan River to enter and possess. [19]I call heaven and earth as my witnesses against you right now: I have set life and death, blessing and curse before you. Now choose life—so that you and your descendants will live—[20]by loving the LORD your God, by obeying his voice, and by clinging to him. That's how you will survive and live long on the fertile land the LORD swore to give to your ancestors: to Abraham, Isaac, and Jacob.

Moses announces his death

31 Then Moses said[y] these words to all Israel, [2]telling them:

I'm 120 years old today. I can't move around well anymore. Plus, the LORD told me "You won't cross the Jordan River." [3]But the LORD your God, he's the one who will cross over before you! He's the one who will destroy these nations before you so you can displace them. Joshua too will cross over before you just like the LORD indicated. [4]The LORD will do to these enemies the same thing he did to the Amorite kings Sihon and Og, and to their land, when he destroyed them. [5]The LORD will lay them out before you, and you will do to them exactly what the command I've given you dictates. [6]Be strong! Be fearless! Don't be afraid and don't be scared by your enemies, because the LORD your God is the one who marches with you. He won't let you down, and he won't abandon you.

[7]Then Moses called Joshua and, with all Israel watching, said to him: "Be strong and fearless because you are the one who will lead[z] this people to the land the LORD swore to their ancestors to give to them; you are the one who will divide up the land for them. [8]But the LORD is the one who is marching before you! He is the one who will be with you! He won't let you down. He won't abandon you. So don't be afraid or scared!"

Regular reading of the Instruction

[9]Then Moses wrote this Instruction down and gave it to the priests—the Levites who carry the chest containing the LORD's covenant—and to all of the Israelite elders. [10]Moses then commanded them:

At the end of seven years, at the appointed time in the year of debt cancellation, during the Festival of Booths, [11]when

[x]LXX; MT lacks *if you obey the LORD your God's commandments.* [y]LXX, DSS (1QDeut[b]) *When Moses had finished speaking* [z]Sam, Vulg, Syr; MT, Tg *accompany*

all Israel comes to appear before the LORD your God at the location he selects, you must read this Instruction aloud, in the hearing of all the people. 12 Gather everyone—men, women, children, and the immigrants who live in your cities—in order that they hear it, learn it, and revere the LORD your God, carefully doing all the words of this Instruction, 13 and so that their children, who don't yet know the Instruction, may hear it and learn to revere the LORD your God for as long as you live on the ground you are crossing the Jordan River to possess.

Joshua commissioned

14 Then the LORD said to Moses: "It's almost time for you to die. Summon Joshua. The two of you must present yourselves at the meeting tent so I can command him." So Moses and Joshua went and presented themselves at the meeting tent. 15 The LORD appeared in the tent in a pillar of cloud; the cloud pillar stood at the tent's entrance. 16 The LORD then said to Moses:

"Soon you will rest with your ancestors, and the people will rise up and act unfaithfully, going after strange gods of the land they are entering. They will abandon me, breaking my covenant that I made with them. 17 At that point my anger will burn against them, and I'll be the one who abandons them! I'll hide my face from them. They will become nothing but food for their enemies,[a] and all sorts of bad things and misfortunes will happen to them. Then they will say: 'Haven't these terrible things happened to us because our God is no longer with us?' 18 But I will hide my face at that time because of the many wrong things they have done, because they have turned to other gods! 19 So in light of all that, you must write down this poem and teach it to the Israelites. Put it in their mouths so that the poem becomes a witness for me against them. 20 When I bring the Israelites to the land I swore to their ancestors, which is full of milk and honey, and they eat, get full, then fat, and then turn toward other gods, serving them and disrespecting me and breaking my covenant, 21 then, when all kinds of bad things and misfortunes happen to them, this poem will witness against them, giving its testimony, because it won't be lost from the mouths of their descendants. Yes, I know right now what they are inclined to do, even before I've brought them into the land I swore."

22 So Moses wrote this poem down that very day, and he taught it to the Israelites.

23 Then the Lord commissioned Joshua, Nun's son: "Be strong and fearless because you are the one who will bring the Israelites to the land I swore to them. I myself will be with you."

Life after Moses

24 Once Moses had finished writing in their entirety all the words of this Instruction scroll, 25 he commanded the Levites who carry the chest containing the LORD's covenant as follows:

26 "Take this Instruction scroll and put it next to the chest containing the LORD your God's covenant. It must remain there as a witness against you 27 because I know how rebellious and hardheaded you are. If you are this rebellious toward the LORD while I'm still alive, it's bound to get worse once I'm dead! 28 Assemble all of your tribes' elders and your officials in front of me, so I can speak these words in their hearing, and so I can call heaven and earth as my witnesses against them, 29 because I know that after I'm dead, you will ruin everything, departing from the path I've commanded you. Terrible things will happen to you in the future because you will do evil in the LORD's eyes, aggravating him with the things your hands have made."

The poem of Instruction

30 Then Moses recited in their entirety the words of this poem in the hearing of the entire assembly of Israel:

32 Heaven! Pay attention
and I will speak;
Earth! Listen to the words
of my mouth.

[a] Heb lacks *for their enemies.*

[2] My teaching will fall like raindrops;
my speech will settle like dew—
like gentle rains on grass,
like spring showers
on all that is green—
[3] because I proclaim the LORD's name:
Give praise to our God!

[4] The rock: his acts are perfection!
No doubt about it: all his ways are right!
He's the faithful God, never deceiving;
altogether righteous and true is he.
[5] But children who weren't his own[b]
sinned against him with their defects;[c]
they are a twisted
and perverse generation.
[6] Is this how you thank the LORD,
you stupid, senseless people?
Isn't he your father, your creator?
Didn't he make you and establish you?

[7] Remember the days long past;
consider the years long gone.
Ask your father, he will tell you about it;
ask your elders,
they will give you the details:
[8] When God Most High
divided up the nations—
when he divided up humankind—
he decided the people's boundaries
based on the number of the gods.[d]
[9] Surely the LORD's property
was his people;
Jacob was his part of the inheritance.

[10] God found[e] Israel in a wild land—
in a howling desert wasteland—
he protected him, cared for him,
watched over him with his very own eye.
[11] Like an eagle protecting its nest,
hovering over its young,
God spread out his wings,
took hold of Israel,
carried him on his back.
[12] The LORD alone led Israel;
no foreign god assisted.
[13] God[f] made Israel[g] glide over the highlands;
he fed him[h] with food from the field,
nursed him with honey from a boulder,
with oil from a hard rock:
[14] curds from the herd,
milk from the flock,
along with the best of lambs,
rams from Bashan, he-goats too,
along with the finest wheat—
and for drink,
wine from the juiciest grapes!
[15] Jacob ate until he was stuffed;[i]
Jeshurun[j] got fat, then rebellious.[k]

It was you who got fat, thick, stubborn![l]

Jeshurun[m] gave up
on the God who made him,
thought the rock of his salvation
was worthless.
[16] They made God[n] jealous
with strange gods,
aggravated him with detestable things.
[17] They sacrificed to demons, not to God,
to deities of which
they had no knowledge—
new gods only recently on the scene,
ones about which your ancestors
had never heard.[o]
[18] You deserted[p] the rock that sired you;
you forgot the God
who gave birth to you!

[19] The LORD saw this and rejected
out of aggravation
his sons and his daughters.[q]
[20] He said: I will hide my face from them—
I will see what becomes of them—
because they are a confused generation;
they are children lacking loyalty.
[21] They provoked me with "no-gods,"
aggravated me with their pieces of junk.
So I am going to provoke them
with "No-People,"
aggravate them with a nation of fools.

[b] Heb uncertain [c] LXX, Vulg; Heb uncertain [d] DSS (4QDeut[j]), LXX; MT *the Israelites* [e] Vulg, Syr, and others; Sam, LXX, Tg Onkelos *sustained him* [f] Or *he* [g] Or *him* [h] Sam, Syr, LXX, Tg; MT *he ate* [i] DSS (4QPhyl[n]), Sam, LXX; MT lacks *Jacob ate until he was stuffed.* [j] A poetic name for Israel; see also 33:5, 26. [k] Or *kicked* [l] Heb uncertain [m] Or *he* [n] Or *him* [o] Heb uncertain [p] LXX, Vulg; Heb uncertain [q] Or, following LXX, DSS (4QPhyl[n]), and correcting *The LORD saw this and was jealous; he spurned his sons and daughters.*

22 A fire burns in me—
it will blaze to the depths of the grave;[r]
it will destroy the land and its crops;
it will blacken the base of the
mountains.
23 I'll throw[s] on them disaster
after disaster;
I'll destroy them with my arrows:
24 devastating hunger, consuming plague,
bitter sickness.
I'll send animal fangs after them,
venom from dust crawlers too.
25 Outside, in the streets,
the sword will bereave!
Inside, in the safest room,
there will be terror
for young men and women,
nursing baby and senior citizen.
26 I thought about it:
I could have struck them down,[t]
erased them from human memory,
27 but their enemies' rage concerned me;
their opponents might misunderstand.
They might say, "Our strong hands,
not the LORD's, did all this,"
28 because they are not
a thoughtful nation;
they lack any insight.
29 If they had any wisdom,
they would understand this;
they would discern
what will become of them.
30 How could one person
chase off a thousand in battle?
How could two people make ten
thousand flee for their lives?
Only because their rock sold them off,
only because the LORD
handed them over!
31 But, no, their rocks
can't compare to our rock!
Our enemies are completely stupid.[u]
32 Their roots run straight from Sodom—
from the fields of Gomorrah!
Their grapes are pure poison;
their grape clusters, nothing but bitter;
33 their wine is snake poison,
venom from a cruel cobra.

34 Don't I have this stored up,
sealed in my vaults?
35 Revenge is my domain,
so is punishment-in-kind,
at the exact moment their step slips up,
because the day of their destruction
is just around the corner;
their final destiny is speeding
on its way!

36 But the LORD will acquit his people,
will have compassion
on those who serve him,
once he sees that their strength
is all gone,
that both prisoners and free people
are wiped out.[v]
37 The Lord will ask, "Where are their gods—
the rocks they trusted in—
38 who ate up the fat of their sacrifices,
who drank their sacred wine?
They should stand up and help you!
They should protect you now!
39 Now, look here: I myself, I'm the one;
there are no other gods with me.
I'm the one who deals death
and gives life;
I'm the one who wounded,
but now I will heal.
There's no escaping my hand.
40 But now I'm lifting my hand to heaven—
I swear by my own eternity:
41 when I sharpen my blazing sword
and my hand grabs hold of justice,
I'll pay my enemies back;
I'll punish in kind
everyone who hates me.
42 I'll make my arrows drink much blood,
while my sword devours flesh,
the blood of the dead and captured,
flowing from the heads
of enemy generals."[w]

43 Heavens:[x] Rejoice with God![y]
All you gods: bow down to the Lord![z]
Because he will avenge
his children's[a] blood;
he will pay back his enemies;

[r]Heb *Sheol* [s]LXX [t]Heb uncertain; LXX *scattered them* [u]LXX; Heb uncertain [v]Heb uncertain [w]Heb uncertain [x]DSS (4QDeut[q]), LXX; MT *nations* [y]DSS (4QDeut[q]), LXX; MT *his people* [z]This line is missing in Heb; it is found in DSS (4QDeut[q]); LXX *him for the Lord.* [a]DSS (4QDeut[q]), LXX; MT *his servants*

he will punish in kind
those who hate him;[b]
he will cleanse his people's land.[c]

44 So Moses came and recited all the
words of this poem in everyone's hearing;
Joshua,[d] Nun's son, joined him. 45 When
Moses finished speaking all these words
to all Israel, 46 he told them: Set your mind
on all these words I'm testifying against
you right now, because you must command your children to perform carefully
all the words of this Instruction. 47 This is
no trivial matter for you—this is your very
life! It is by this means[e] alone that you will
prolong your life on the fertile land you are
crossing the Jordan River to possess.

Moses' death imminent

48 The LORD spoke to Moses that very
same day: 49 "Hike up the Abarim mountains, to Mount Nebo, which is in the land
of Moab opposite Jericho. Take a good
look at the land of Canaan, which I'm
giving to the Israelites as their property.
50 You will die on the mountain you have
hiked up, and you will be gathered to your
people just like your brother Aaron, who
died on Mount Hor and was gathered to
his people, 51 because the two of you were
unfaithful toward me in front of the Israelites at the waters of Meribath-kadesh,
in the Zin wilderness, because you didn't
treat me with proper respect before the
Israelites. 52 You can look at the land from
the other side of the river,[f] but you won't
enter there."[g]

The fourth heading: Moses' blessing

33 This is the blessing that Moses the
man of God gave the Israelites before he died. 2 He said:

The LORD came from Sinai:
from Seir he shone like the dawn on us,[h]
from Paran Mountain he beamed down.
Thousands of holy ones were with him;[i]
his warriors were next to him, ready.[j]
3 Yes, those who love[k] the nations—
all his holy ones—
were at your command;
they followed your footsteps;
they got moving when you said so.

4 Moses gave the Instruction to us—
it's the prized possession
of Jacob's assembly.
5 A king came to rule in Jeshurun,
when the people's leaders
gathered together,
when Israel's tribes were one.

6 "I pray that Reuben lives, doesn't die,
though his numbers are so few."

7 Moses said this to Judah:
"LORD, listen to Judah's voice!
Bring him back to his own people,
strengthen his hands;[l]
be his help against every enemy."

8 Then he told Levi:
"Give your Thummim to Levi,[m]
your Urim to your faithful one—
the one you tested at Massah,
the one you challenged
by Meribah's waters;
9 the one who said
of his own mother and father:
'I don't consider them as such';
of their siblings:
'I don't recognize them';
of their own children,
'I don't know them'—
but who obeyed your words
and who guarded your covenant!
10 They teach your case laws to Jacob,
your Instruction to Israel.
They hold sweet incense to your nose;
put the entirely burned offering
on your altar.

[b] DSS (4QDeut^{q}), LXX; MT lacks this line. [c] Sam, DSS (4QDeut^{q}), LXX, Vulg; MT *his land his people* or *his land for his people;* or, correcting, *he will wipe away his people's tears.* [d] Sam, Syr, Tg Neofiti; MT *Hoshea* [e] Or *word* [f] Heb lacks *of the river.* [g] LXX; MT, Sam, Vulg, Syr, Tg add *to the land that I am giving to the Israelites* [h] Correcting with LXX, Vulg, Syr, Tg Onkelos (see 33:4); MT and Sam *on them* [i] Correction; cf LXX, Sam, Syr, Vulg; MT *he came from Ribeboth-kodesh* [j] LXX *angels;* Heb uncertain [k] Correction; MT *lover of* [l] Or *with his hands he contended* [m] DSS (4QDeut^{h}, 4QTest) and LXX; MT lacks *Give to Levi.*

11 I pray that the LORD
blesses Levi's strength,
favors his hard work,
and crushes the insides of his enemies
so that those who hate him
can't fight anymore."

12 He said to Benjamin:
"The LORD's dearest one
rests safely on him.
The Lord always shields him;
he rests on God's chest."

13 Then he told Joseph:
"I pray that his land is blessed by God:
with heaven's gifts from above,[n]
with the deep waters
stretching out underneath;
14 with the gifts produced by the sun,
with the gifts generated by the moon;[o]
15 with the best fruit
from ancient mountains,
with the gifts of eternal hills;
16 with the gifts of the earth
and all that fills it,
and the favor of the one
who lives on Sinai.[p]
I pray that all these rest
on Joseph's head,
on the crown of that prince
among brothers.
17 A firstborn bull[q]—
that's how majestic he is!
A wild ox's horns—those are his horns!
With them he gores all peoples
completely, to the far ends
of the earth!
His horns[r] are Ephraim's
tens of thousands.
His horns are Manasseh's thousands."

18 Then he told Zebulun:
"Zebulun: celebrate
when you are out and about;
Issachar: celebrate when you are
at home in your tents!
19 They call all sorts of people
to the mountain,
where they offer right sacrifices.
It's true: They're nourished
on the sea's abundance;
they are nourished
on buried treasures in the sand."

20 Then he told Gad:
"May Gad's broad lands[s] be blessed!
He lives like a lion:
he rips an arm, even a head!
21 He chose the best part for himself
because there, where the commander's
portion was,
the leaders of the people
gathered together.[t]
Gad executed the LORD's justice
and the Lord's judgments for Israel."[u]

22 Then he told Dan:
"Dan is a lion cub.
He jumps up from Bashan."

23 Then he told Naphtali:
"Naphtali—you are full of favor,
overflowing with the LORD's blessing—
go possess the west and the south!"

24 Finally, he told Asher:
"Asher is the most blessed of sons.
I pray that he's his brothers' favorite—
one who dips his foot in fine oil.
25 I pray that your dead bolts
are iron and copper,
and that your strength
lasts all your days."[v]

26 Jeshurun! No one compares to God!
He rides through heaven to help you,
rides majestically through the clouds.
27 The most ancient God
is a place of safety;[w]
the eternal arms are a support.[x]
He drove out the enemy before you.
He commanded: "Destroy them!"

[n] Or *from the dew* [o] Or *moons* or *months* [p] Or *lives in a bush* [q] Sam, LXX, Vulg; DSS (4QDeut[h]) and Heb *the oldest offspring of his bull* [r] Or *they*; also in the next line [s] Or *the one who makes Gad large* [t] Cf LXX; MT *there the commander's portion was reserved; he came at the front of the people* or *there was the portion of the respected commander; the people's leaders came.* [u] Heb uncertain [v] Heb uncertain [w] Or *He humiliates the oldest gods.* [x] Or *He shatters the most ancient forces.*

28 So Israel now lives in safety—
Jacob's residence[y] is secure—
in a land full of grain and wine,
where the heavens drip dew.

29 Happy are you, Israel! Who is like you?
You are a people saved by the LORD!
He's the shield that helps you,
your majestic sword!
Your enemies will come crawling on
their knees to you,
but you will stomp on their backs![z]

Moses' death

34 Then Moses hiked up from the Moabite plains to Mount Nebo, the peak of the Pisgah slope, which faces Jericho. The LORD showed him the whole land: the Gilead region as far as Dan's territory; 2 all the parts belonging to Naphtali along with the land of Ephraim and Manasseh, as well as the entirety of Judah as far as the Mediterranean Sea; 3 also the arid southern plain, and the plain—including the Jericho Valley, Palm City—as far as Zoar.

4 Then the LORD said to Moses: "This is the land that I swore to Abraham, Isaac, and Jacob when I promised: 'I will give it to your descendants.' I have shown it to you with your own eyes; however, you will not cross over into it."

5 Then Moses, the LORD's servant, died—right there in the land of Moab, according to the LORD's command. 6 The Lord buried him in a valley in Moabite country across from Beth-peor. Even now, no one knows where Moses' grave is.

7 Moses was 120 years old when he died. His eyesight wasn't impaired, and his vigor hadn't diminished a bit.

8 Back down in the Moabite plains, the Israelites mourned Moses' death for thirty days. At that point, the time for weeping and for mourning Moses was over.

9 Joshua, Nun's son, was filled with wisdom because Moses had placed his hands on him. So the Israelites listened to Joshua, and they did exactly what the LORD commanded Moses.

10 No prophet like Moses has yet emerged in Israel; Moses knew the LORD face-to-face! 11 That's not even to mention all those signs and wonders that the LORD sent Moses to do in Egypt—to Pharaoh, to all his servants, and to his entire land— 12 as well as all the extraordinary power that Moses displayed before Israel's own eyes!

JOSHUA

Orders from the LORD

1 After Moses the LORD's servant died, the LORD spoke to Joshua, Nun's son. He had been Moses' helper. 2 "My servant Moses is dead. Now get ready to cross over the Jordan with this entire people to the land that I am going to give to the Israelites. 3 I am giving you every place where you set foot, exactly as I promised Moses. 4 Your territory will stretch from the desert and the Lebanon as far as the great Euphrates River, including all Hittite land, up to the Mediterranean Sea on the west. 5 No one will be able to stand up against you during your lifetime. I will be with you in the same way I was with Moses. I won't desert you or leave you. 6 Be brave and strong, because you are the one who will help this people take possession of the land, which I pledged to give to their ancestors.

7 "Be very brave and strong as you carefully obey all of the Instruction that Moses my servant commanded you. Don't deviate even a bit from it, either to the right or left. Then you will have success wherever you go. 8 Never stop speaking about this Instruction scroll. Recite it day and night so you can carefully obey everything written in it. Then you will accomplish your objectives and you will succeed. 9 I've commanded you to be brave and strong, haven't I? Don't be alarmed or terrified, because

[y] Or *fountain* [z] Or *their shrines*

the LORD your God is with you wherever you go."

Joshua gives orders

10 Then Joshua gave orders to the people's officers: 11 "Go through the camp and give orders to the people. Say, 'Get supplies ready for yourselves because in three days you will be crossing over the Jordan to enter the land and take it over. The LORD your God is going to give it to you as your possession.'"

12 Then Joshua addressed the Reubenites, the Gadites, and half the tribe of Manasseh: 13 "Remember the command that Moses the LORD's servant gave you: 'The LORD your God will give you rest and give you this land.' 14 Your wives, children, and cattle may remain in the land that Moses has given you on the east side of the Jordan. But all you brave fighters, organized for war, must cross over in front of your fellow Israelites. You must help them 15 until the LORD gives a rest like yours to your fellow Israelites and they too take possession of the land that the LORD your God is giving them. Then you may return and take over the land that belongs to you, which Moses the LORD's servant has given you on the east side of the Jordan."

16 They answered Joshua, "We will obey everything you have commanded us and go anywhere you send us. 17 We will obey you in the same way that we obeyed Moses. Just let the LORD your God be with you as he was with Moses! 18 Anybody who stubbornly opposes what you declare and doesn't obey any of your commands will be put to death. Be brave and strong!"

Joshua sends spies

2 Joshua, Nun's son, secretly sent two men as spies from Shittim. He said, "Go. Look over the land, especially Jericho." They set out and entered the house of a prostitute named Rahab. They bedded down there.

2 Someone told the king of Jericho, "Men from the Israelites have come here tonight to spy on the land."

3 So the king of Jericho sent word to Rahab: "Send out the men who came to you, the ones who came to your house, because they have come to spy on the entire land."

Rahab takes action

4 But the woman had taken the two men and hidden them. Then she said, "Of course the men came to me. But I didn't know where they were from. 5 The men left when it was time to close the gate at dark, but I don't know where the men went. Hurry! Chase after them! You might catch up with them." 6 But she had taken them up to the roof and hidden them under the flax stalks that she had laid out on the roof. 7 The men from Jericho[a] chased after them in the direction of the Jordan up to the fords. As soon as those chasing them went out, the gate was shut behind them.

Rahab sets terms

8 Before the spies bedded down, Rahab went up to them on the roof. 9 She said to the men, "I know that the LORD has given you the land. Terror over you has overwhelmed us. The entire population of the land has melted down in fear because of you. 10 We have heard how the LORD dried up the water of the Reed Sea[b] in front of you when you left Egypt. We have also heard what you did to Sihon and Og, the two kings of the Amorites on the other side of the Jordan. You utterly wiped them out. 11 We heard this and our hearts turned to water. Because of you, people can no longer work up their courage. This is because the LORD your God is God in heaven above and on earth below. 12 Now, I have been loyal to you. So pledge to me by the LORD that you in turn will deal loyally with my family. Give me a sign of good faith. 13 Spare the lives of my father, mother, brothers, and sisters, along with everything they own. Rescue us from death."

14 The men said to her, "We swear by our own lives to secure yours. If you don't reveal our mission, we will deal loyally and faithfully with you when the LORD gives us the land."

[a]Heb lacks *from Jericho.* [b]Or *Red Sea*

The spies escape

15So she lowered the spies on a rope through the window. Her house was on the outer side of the city wall, and she lived inside the wall. 16Then she said to them, "Go toward the highlands so that those chasing you don't run into you. Hide there for three days until those chasing you return. Then you may go on your way."

17The men said to her, "We won't be responsible for this pledge you made us swear 18unless, when we come into the land, you tie this red woven cord in the window through which you lowered us. Gather your father, your mother, your brothers, and your whole family into the house with you. 19Those who go outside the doors of your house into the street will have only themselves to blame for their own deaths. We won't be responsible. If anyone lays a hand on those who are with you in the house, we will take the blame for their death. 20But if you reveal our mission, we won't be responsible for this pledge you made us swear."

21She said, "These things will happen just like you said." She sent them away and they went off. Then she tied the red cord in the window.

Mission accomplished

22The spies went out and entered the highlands. They stayed there for three days until those chasing them came back. Those chasing them had searched all along the road but never found them. 23Then the two men came back down from the highlands. They crossed the Jordan and came to Joshua, Nun's son. They told him everything that had happened to them. 24They said to Joshua, "The LORD has definitely given the entire land into our power. In addition, all of the land's population has melted down in fear because of us."

Directions for crossing the Jordan

3 Joshua took down the camp early in the morning. He and all the Israelites marched out of Shittim and came to the Jordan, where they stayed overnight before crossing. 2At the end of three days the officers went through the middle of the camp. 3They commanded the people, "As soon as you see the LORD your God's chest containing the covenant and the levitical priests carrying it, you are to march out from your places and follow it. 4But let there be some distance between you and it, about three thousand feet. Don't come near it! You will know the way you should go, even though you've never traveled this way before."

5Joshua said to the people, "Make yourselves holy! Tomorrow the LORD will do wonderful things among you." 6Then Joshua said to the priests, "Lift up the covenant chest. Go along in front of the people." So they lifted up the covenant chest and went in front of the people.

7The LORD said to Joshua, "Today I will begin to make you great in the opinion of all Israel. Then they will know that I will be with you in the same way that I was with Moses. 8You are to command the priests who carry the covenant chest, 'As soon as you come to the bank of the Jordan, stand still in the Jordan.'"

9Joshua said to the Israelites, "Come close. Listen to the words of the LORD your God." 10Then Joshua said, "This is how you will know that the living God is among you and will completely remove the Canaanites, Hittites, Hivites, Perizzites, Girgashites, Amorites, and Jebusites before you. 11Look! The covenant chest of the ruler of the entire earth is going to cross over in front of you in the Jordan. 12Now pick twelve men from the tribes of Israel, one per tribe. 13The soles of the priests' feet, who are carrying the chest of the LORD, ruler of the whole earth, will come to rest in the water of the Jordan. At that moment, the water of the Jordan will be cut off. The water flowing downstream will stand still in a single heap."

Marching across the Jordan

14The people marched out from their tents to cross over the Jordan. The priests carrying the covenant chest were in front of the people. 15When the priests who were carrying the chest came to the Jordan, their feet touched the edge of the water. The Jordan had overflowed its banks completely, the way it does during the entire harvest season. [16]But at that moment the water of the Jordan coming downstream stood still. It rose up as a single heap very far off, just below Adam, which is the city next to Zarethan. The water going down to the desert sea (that is, the Dead Sea) was cut off completely. The people crossed opposite Jericho. [17]So the priests carrying the LORD's covenant chest stood firmly on dry land in the middle of the Jordan. Meanwhile, all Israel crossed over on dry land, until the entire nation finished crossing over the Jordan.

Twelve stones at Gilgal

4 When the entire nation had finished crossing over the Jordan, the LORD said to Joshua, [2]"Pick twelve men from the people, one man per tribe. [3]Command them, 'Pick up twelve stones from right here in the middle of the Jordan, where the feet of the priests had been firmly planted. Bring them across with you and put them down in the camp where you are staying tonight.'"

[4]Joshua called for the twelve men he had appointed from the Israelites, one man per tribe. [5]Joshua said to them, "Cross over into the middle of the Jordan, up to the LORD your God's chest. Each of you, lift up a stone on his shoulder to match the number of the tribes of the Israelites. [6]This will be a symbol among you. In the future your children may ask, 'What do these stones mean to you?' [7]Then you will tell them that the water of the Jordan was cut off before the LORD's covenant chest. When it crossed over the Jordan, the water of the Jordan was cut off. These stones will be an enduring memorial for the Israelites."

[8]The Israelites did exactly what Joshua ordered. They lifted twelve stones from the middle of the Jordan, matching the number of the tribes of the Israelites, exactly as the LORD had said to Joshua. They brought them over to the camp and put them down there. [9]Joshua also set up twelve stones in the middle of the Jordan where the feet of the priests had stood while carrying the covenant chest. They are still there today.

Crossing completed

[10]Meanwhile, the priests carrying the chest were standing in the middle of the Jordan. They stood there until every command that the LORD had ordered Joshua to tell the people had been carried out. This was exactly what Moses had commanded Joshua. The people crossed over quickly. [11]As soon as all the people had finished crossing, the LORD's chest crossed over. The priests then moved to the front of the people. [12]The people of Reuben, the people of Gad, and half the tribe of Manasseh crossed over, organized for war ahead of the Israelites, exactly as Moses had told them. [13]Approximately forty thousand armed for war crossed over in the LORD's presence to the plains of Jericho, ready for battle. [14]The LORD made Joshua great in the opinion of all Israel on that day. So they revered him in the same way that they had revered Moses during all of his life.

[15]The LORD said to Joshua, [16]"Command the priests carrying the chest containing the testimony to come up out of the Jordan."

[17]So Joshua commanded the priests, "Come up from the Jordan." [18]The priests carrying the LORD's covenant chest came up from the middle of the Jordan, and the soles of their feet touched dry ground. At that moment, the water of the Jordan started flowing again. It ran as before, completely over its banks. [19]The people came up out of the Jordan on the tenth day of the first month.[c] They camped at Gilgal on the east border of Jericho.

Stones at Gilgal

[20]Joshua set up at Gilgal those twelve stones they had taken from the Jordan. [21]He said to the Israelites, "In the future your children will ask their parents, 'What about these stones?' [22]Then you will let your children know: 'Israel crossed over the Jordan here on dry ground.' [23]This was because the

[c]March–April, Nisan

LORD your God dried up the water of the Jordan before you until you crossed over. This was exactly what the LORD your God did to the Reed Sea.[d] He dried it up before us until we crossed over. 24 This happened so that all the earth's peoples might know that the LORD's power is great and that you may always revere the LORD your God."

Enemy kings react

5 All the Amorite kings on the west side of the Jordan and all the Canaanite kings near the sea heard that the LORD had dried up the water of the Jordan before the Israelites until they had crossed over. Then their hearts melted. They lost all courage because of the Israelites.

Circumcision

2 At that time the LORD said to Joshua, "Make yourself flint knives. Circumcise the Israelites for a second time." 3 So Joshua made flint knives for himself. He circumcised the Israelites at Foreskins Hill. 4 This is the reason Joshua did so: All the people who went out of Egypt, that is, all the men who were soldiers, had died in the desert on the way after they left Egypt. 5 All the people who went out were circumcised. But none of the people born in the desert on the way after they had left Egypt had been circumcised. 6 This was because the Israelites journeyed forty years in the desert until the whole nation died off. These were the men old enough to fight who went out from Egypt and who hadn't obeyed the LORD. The LORD had pledged to them never to show them the land that the LORD had pledged to their ancestors to give us. It is a land full of milk and honey. 7 Joshua circumcised their children, the ones the LORD had set in their place. They were uncircumcised because they hadn't been circumcised on the way. 8 After the whole nation had undergone circumcision, they remained in the camp until they got well again. 9 Then the LORD said to Joshua, "Today I have rolled away from you the disgrace of Egypt." So the place was called Gilgal,[e] as it is today.

Passover

10 The Israelites camped in Gilgal. They celebrated Passover on the evening of the fourteenth day of the month[f] on the plains of Jericho. 11 On the very next day after Passover, they ate food produced in the land: unleavened bread and roasted grain. 12 The manna stopped on that next day, when they ate food produced in the land. There was no longer any manna for the Israelites. So that year they ate the crops of the land of Canaan.

Commander of the LORD's heavenly force

13 When Joshua was near Jericho, he looked up. He caught sight of a man standing in front of him with his sword drawn. Joshua went up and said to him, "Are you on our side or that of our enemies?"

14 He said, "Neither! I'm the commander of the LORD's heavenly force. Now I have arrived!"

Then Joshua fell flat on his face and worshipped. Joshua said to him, "What is my master saying to his servant?"

15 The commander of the LORD's heavenly force said to Joshua, "Take your sandals off your feet because the place where you are standing is holy." So Joshua did this.

Instructions about Jericho

6 Now Jericho was closed up tightly because of the Israelites. No one went out or came in. 2 The LORD said to Joshua, "Look. I have given Jericho and its king into your power, along with its mighty warriors. 3 Circle the city with all the soldiers, going around the city one time. Do this for six days. 4 Have seven priests carry seven trumpets made from rams' horns in front of the chest. On the seventh day, circle the city seven times, with the priests blowing the trumpets.

5 "Have them blow a long blast on the ram's horn. As soon as you hear that trumpet blast, have all the people shout out a loud war cry. Then the city wall will col-

[d] Or *Red Sea* [e] Gilgal sounds like the Heb verb *galal*, "to roll away." [f] March–April, Nisan

lapse, and the people will rise up, attacking straight ahead."

Israel destroys Jericho

6 So Joshua, Nun's son, called the priests. He said to them, "Lift up the covenant chest. Let seven priests carry seven trumpets made from rams' horns in front of the LORD's chest." 7 He said to the people, "Go forward. Circle the city. Let the armed soldiers go in front of the LORD's chest." 8 As soon as Joshua had spoken to the people, the seven priests carrying seven ram's horn trumpets moved forward in front of the LORD. They blew the trumpets. The LORD's covenant chest followed. 9 The initial group of soldiers was going in front of the priests who were blowing the trumpets. The rear guard was coming behind the chest, with trumpets blowing continuously. 10 Joshua ordered the people, "Don't shout. Don't let your voice be heard. Don't let a word come out of your mouth until the day I tell you, 'Shout!' Then shout!"

11 He made the LORD's chest circle the city, going around one time. They went back to the camp and stayed there overnight. 12 Joshua got up early in the morning. The priests lifted up the LORD's chest. 13 The seven priests carrying the seven trumpets made from rams' horns were going in front of the LORD's chest, blowing trumpets continuously. The armed soldiers were going in front of them. The rear guard was coming after the LORD's chest, blowing trumpets continuously. 14 They circled the city one time on the second day. Then they went back to the camp. They did this for six days.

15 On the seventh day, they got up at dawn. They circled the city in this way seven times. It was only on that day that they circled the city seven times. 16 The seventh time, the priests blew the trumpets. Then Joshua said to the people, "Shout, because the LORD has given you the city! 17 The city and everything in it is to be utterly wiped out as something reserved for the LORD. Only Rahab the prostitute is to stay alive, along with everyone with her in her house. This is because she hid the messengers we sent. 18 But you, keep away from the things set aside for God so that you don't desire[g] and take some of the things reserved. That would turn the camp of Israel into a thing doomed to be utterly wiped out and bring calamity on it. 19 All silver and gold, along with bronze and iron equipment, are holy to the LORD. They must go into the LORD's treasury." 20 Then the people shouted. They blew the trumpets. As soon as the people heard the trumpet blast, they shouted a loud war cry. Then the wall collapsed. The people went up against the city, attacking straight ahead. They captured the city. 21 Without mercy, they wiped out everything in the city as something reserved for God—man and woman, young and old, cattle, sheep, and donkeys.

Consequences

22 Joshua spoke to the two men who had scouted out the land. "Go to the prostitute's house. Bring out the woman from there, along with everyone related to her, exactly as you pledged to her." 23 So the young men who had been spies went and brought Rahab out, along with her father, her mother, her brothers, and everyone related to her. They brought her whole clan out and let them stay outside Israel's camp. 24 They burned the city and everything in it. But they put the silver and gold, along with the bronze and iron equipment, into the treasury of the LORD's house. 25 Joshua let Rahab the prostitute live, her family, and everyone related to her. So her family still lives among Israel today, because she hid the spies whom Joshua had sent to scout out Jericho.

26 At that time Joshua made this decree:

> "Anyone who starts to rebuild this city of Jericho will be cursed before the LORD.
> Laying its foundations will cost them their oldest child.
> Setting up its gates will cost them their youngest child."

27 The LORD was with Joshua. News about him spread throughout the land.

[g] LXX; Heb *wipe out as something reserved for God*

Israel defeated at Ai

7 The Israelites did a disrespectful thing concerning the items reserved for God. Achan was the son of Carmi, grandson of Zabdi, great-grandson of Zerah. He was from the tribe of Judah. He took some of the things reserved for God. So the LORD was furious with the Israelites.

2 Joshua sent men from Jericho to Ai, which is near Beth-aven to the east of Bethel. He said to them, "Go up. Scout out the land."

So the men went up and scouted out Ai. 3 They came back to Joshua and said to him, "There is no need for all of the people to go up. Two or three thousand men could go up and strike Ai. Don't make all of the people bother going there. There are just a few of them." 4 So about three thousand men from the people went up in that direction. But they fled from the men of Ai. 5 The men of Ai struck down approximately thirty-six of them. They chased them from outside the gate as far as Shebarim. They struck them down on the slope. Then the hearts of the people melted and turned to water.

Cause of Israel's defeat

6 Joshua ripped open his clothes. He, along with the elders of Israel, lay flat on their faces before the LORD's chest until evening. They put dust on their heads. 7 Then Joshua said, "Oh no, LORD God! Why did you ever bring this people across the Jordan? Was it to hand us over to the power of the Amorites, to destroy us? If only we had been prepared to live on the other side of the Jordan! 8 Please forgive me, LORD. What can I say now that Israel has retreated before its enemies? 9 The Canaanites and the whole population of the land will hear of it. They will surround us and make our name disappear from the earth. What will you do about your great name then?"

10 The LORD said to Joshua, "Get up! Why do you lie flat on your face like this? 11 Israel has sinned. They have violated my covenant, which I commanded them to keep. They have taken some of the things reserved for me and put them with their own things. They have stolen and kept it a secret. 12 The Israelites can't stand up to their enemies. They retreat before their enemies because they themselves have become a doomed thing reserved for me. I will no longer be with you unless you destroy the things reserved for me that are present among you. 13 Go and make the people holy. Say, 'Get ready for tomorrow by making yourselves holy. This is what the LORD, the God of Israel, says: "Israel! Things reserved for me are present among you. You won't be able to stand up to your enemies until you remove from your presence the things reserved for me."' 14 In the morning, come forward tribe by tribe. Whichever tribe the LORD selects must come forward clan by clan. Whichever clan the LORD selects must come forward family by family. Whichever family the LORD selects will come forward by individual soldiers. 15 The person selected, who has the things reserved for God, must be put to death by burning. Burn everything that belongs to him too. This is because he has violated the LORD's covenant and has committed an outrage in Israel."

Achan discovered and punished

16 Joshua got up early in the morning. He made Israel come forward tribe by tribe. The tribe of Judah was selected. 17 He made the clans of Judah come forward. He selected the clan of Zerah. He made the clan of Zerah come forward as individual soldiers. Zabdi was selected. 18 He made each soldier of his family come forward. Achan was selected. He was a son of Carmi, grandson of Zabdi, great-grandson of Zerah, and of the tribe of Judah. 19 Joshua said to Achan, "My son, give glory to the LORD the God of Israel. Tell me what you have done. Don't hide anything from me."

20 Achan answered Joshua, "It's true. I've sinned against the LORD, the God of Israel. This is what I have done: 21 Among the booty I saw a single beautiful robe in the Babylonian style, two hundred shekels of silver, and a single gold bar weighing fifty shekels. I desired them and took them. Now they are hidden in the ground inside my tent, with the silver on the bottom."

22 Then Joshua sent messengers. They
ran to the tent. There it was, hidden in his
tent, with the silver on the bottom. 23 They
took the things from inside the tent. They
brought them to Joshua and to all the Israelites and emptied them out before the
LORD. 24 Then Joshua seized Achan, Zerah's
son, along with the silver, the robe, the
gold bar, his sons and daughters, his cattle,
donkeys, flocks, tent, and everything that
belonged to him. All Israel joined Joshua.
They brought them up to Achor Valley.
25 Joshua said, "You have brought disaster
to us! May the LORD bring disaster to you
today!" Then all Israel stoned him. They
burned them with fire and stoned them
with stones. 26 They raised over him a great
pile of stones that is still there today. Then
the LORD turned away from his fury. So he
named that place Achor Valley.[h] It is still
called that today.

Plan to capture Ai

8 The LORD said to Joshua, "Don't be
afraid or terrified. Take the entire army
with you. Start to go up to Ai. Look! I have
given the king of Ai, his people, his city, and
his land into your power. 2 Do to Ai and its
king what you did to Jericho and its king.
But you may take its booty and cattle as
plunder. Set your ambush behind the city."
3 So Joshua and the whole army got ready
to go up to Ai. Joshua chose thirty thousand brave soldiers. He sent them out by
night. 4 He commanded them, "Look. You
are to ambush the city from behind. Don't
move too far away from the city. Be ready,
all of you. 5 I will approach the city with all
the people. When they come out against us
the same way as before, we will flee from
them. 6 They will come out after us until we
have drawn them away from the city. They
will think, They are fleeing from us as before. So we will flee from them. 7 But you
will rise up from the ambush and take over
the city. The LORD your God will give it into
your power. 8 As soon as you seize the city,
set it on fire. Act according to the LORD's
word. Indeed, I have given you an order!"
9 Joshua sent them off, and they went to
set the ambush. They stayed between Bethel
and Ai, to the west of Ai. Joshua spent that
night among the people. 10 Joshua got up
early in the morning and mustered the
people. Then he and the elders of Israel
went up in front of the people to Ai. 11 The
entire army that was with him went up.
They moved in close, in front of the city.
Then they camped north of Ai, with the valley between them and Ai. 12 He took about
five thousand men and positioned them as
an ambush between Bethel and Ai to the
west of the city. 13 The people positioned
the main camp on the north side of the
city and its rear guard on its west side. That
night, Joshua went into the middle of the
valley.

Israel's successful strategy

14 As soon as the king of Ai saw this,
he and all his troops, the men of the city,
hurried out early in the morning to meet
Israel in battle. They moved out to the
battleground on the slopes down toward
the Jordan.[i] He didn't know that there was
an ambush set against him behind the city.
15 Then Joshua and all Israel let themselves
be beaten before them. They fled in the direction of the desert. 16 Next, all the troops
who were still in the city were called out to
chase them. They chased after Joshua and
so let themselves be drawn away from the
city. 17 No one who hadn't gone out after Israel was left in either Ai or Bethel. They left
the city wide open and chased after Israel.
18 The LORD said to Joshua, "Point the
dagger in your hand toward Ai, because
I will give it into your power." So Joshua
pointed the dagger in his hand toward the
city. 19 The ambush quickly rose from its
place. As soon as he reached out his hand, it
charged. They entered the city and captured
it. They set the city on fire at once. 20 Then
the men of Ai turned around. They caught
sight of the smoke of the city rising toward
the sky. They had no chance to flee one way
or the other. The troops who were fleeing
toward the desert turned against the pursuit.

[h] Or *Calamity Valley* [i] Or *the Arabah*

21 Joshua and all Israel saw that the ambush had captured the city and that the smoke of the city was rising. So they turned and struck down the men of Ai. 22 When other Israelites came out of the city to confront them, the men of Ai were caught in the middle. Some Israelites were on one side of them and some on the other. The Israelites struck them down until there was no one left to escape. 23 But they seized the king of Ai alive and brought him to Joshua.

24 Israel finished killing the entire population of Ai that had chased them out into the open wasteland. All of them were finished off without mercy. Then all Israel went back to Ai and struck it down without mercy. 25 Twelve thousand men and women died that day, all the people of Ai. 26 Joshua didn't pull back the hand that was stretched out holding a dagger until he had wiped out the whole population of Ai as something reserved for God. 27 However, Israel did take the cattle and other booty of that city as plunder for themselves, in agreement with the command that the LORD had given Joshua. 28 Then Joshua burned Ai. He made it a permanently deserted mound. That is still the case today. 29 He hanged the king of Ai on a tree until evening. At sundown, Joshua gave an order, and they took his body down from the tree. They threw it down at the opening of the city gate. Then they raised over it a great pile of stones that is still there today.

Joshua reads the Instruction

30 Then Joshua built an altar on Mount Ebal to the LORD, the God of Israel. 31 This was exactly what Moses the LORD's servant had commanded the Israelites. It is what is written in the Instruction scroll from Moses: "an altar of crude stones against which no iron tool has swung."[j] On it they offered entirely burned offerings to the LORD and sacrificed well-being offerings. 32 There, in the presence of the Israelites, Joshua wrote on the stones a copy of the Instruction from Moses, which Moses had written earlier. 33 All Israel—with its elders, officers, and judges—were standing on either side of the chest. They were facing the levitical priests who carry the LORD's chest containing the covenant. They included both immigrants and full citizens. Half stood facing Mount Gerizim and half stood facing Mount Ebal. This was exactly what Moses the LORD's servant had initially commanded for the blessing of the Israelite people. 34 Afterward, Joshua read aloud all the words of the Instruction, both blessing and curse, in agreement with everything written in the Instruction scroll. 35 There wasn't a single word of all that Moses had commanded that Joshua failed to read aloud in the presence of the entire assembly of Israel. This assembly included the women and small children, along with the immigrants who lived among them.

The Gibeonites' trick

9 All the kings on the west side of the Jordan heard about this, including those in the highlands, the lowlands, and along the entire coast of the Mediterranean Sea toward Lebanon. They were Hittites and Amorites, Canaanites, Perizzites, Hivites, and Jebusites. 2 They formed an alliance to fight Joshua and Israel. 3 In contrast, when the population of Gibeon heard what Joshua had done to Jericho and Ai, 4 they acted cleverly. They set out pretending to be messengers.[k] They took worn-out sacks for their donkeys and worn-out wineskins that were split and mended. 5 They had worn-out, patched sandals on their feet and were wearing worn-out clothes. All the bread in their supplies was dry and crumbly.

6 They went to Joshua at the camp at Gilgal. They said to him and to Israel, "We have come from a distant country. So now, make a treaty with us."

7 Israel said to the Hivites, "Perhaps you live among us. How then could we make a treaty with you?"

8 Then they said to Joshua, "We are your servants."

Joshua said to them, "Who are you? Where have you come from?"

[j] Deut 27:5-6 [k] Heb uncertain

9 They said to him, "Your servants have
come from a very distant country because
of the reputation of the LORD your God.
We have heard a report about him and
everything he did in Egypt. 10 We heard
about everything he did to the two kings
of the Amorites on the east side of the Jordan, Heshbon's King Sihon and Bashan's
King Og, who was in Ashtaroth. 11 Our elders and all the population of our land said
to us, 'Take along supplies for the journey.
Go meet them and say to them, "We are
your servants. So now make a treaty with
us."' 12 This is our bread. On the day we left
to come to you we took it warm from our
houses as supplies. But now here it is, dried
up and crumbly. 13 These wineskins were
new when we filled them. But here they
are, split open. These clothes and sandals
of ours are worn out from the very long
journey." 14 The Israelites[l] took some of their
supplies, but they didn't ask for any decision from the LORD. 15 Joshua made peace
with them. He made a treaty with them to
protect their lives. The leaders of the community made a solemn pledge to them.

Israel discovers the trick

16 Three days after the Israelites made a
treaty with the Gibeonites, the Israelites
heard that they were actually their neighbors and were living among them. 17 So on
the third day the Israelites marched out and
came to their cities: Gibeon, Chephirah,
Beeroth, and Kiriath-jearim. 18 But the Israelites didn't strike at them. This was because
the leaders of the community had made a
solemn pledge to them by the LORD, the
God of Israel. The entire community grumbled against the leaders. 19 Then all the leaders said to the whole community, "We have
made a solemn pledge to them by the LORD,
the God of Israel. So we can't touch them
now. 20 This is what we'll do with them.
We'll let them live so that wrath won't come
down on us because of the solemn pledge
that we made to them." 21 The leaders went
on to say to them, "Let them live." So they
became woodcutters and water haulers for
the whole community, exactly as the leaders
had intended for them.

22 Joshua called for the Gibeonites and
spoke to them: "Why have you deceived us
by saying, 'We live very far away from you,'
when actually you live among us? 23 So now
you are cursed. Some of you will always
serve as woodcutters and water haulers for
my God's house."

24 They answered Joshua, "Your servants
had been told that the LORD your God had
commanded his servant Moses to give you
the entire land and to wipe out all its population on your account. So we feared for our
very lives because of you and did this thing.
25 Now, here we are in your power. Do to us
whatever seems good and proper to you."
26 So Joshua treated them in this way. He
spared them from the power of the Israelites, and they didn't kill them. 27 That day
Joshua assigned them as woodcutters and
water haulers for the community and for
the LORD's altar, located wherever God[m]
would choose. That is still the case today.

Gibeonites under attack

10 Jerusalem's King Adoni-zedek heard
that Joshua had captured Ai and had
wiped it out as something reserved for God.
Joshua did the same thing to Ai and its king
that he had done to Jericho and its king. He
also heard that the population of Gibeon
had made peace with Israel and were living
among them. 2 Adoni-zedek and his people[n]
were very afraid, because Gibeon was a
large city, like one of the royal cities. It was
larger than Ai. All its men were soldiers. 3 So
Jerusalem's King Adoni-zedek sent word
to Hebron's King Hoham, Jarmuth's King
Piram, Lachish's King Japhia, and Eglon's
King Debir: 4 "Come up and help me. We will
strike at Gibeon, because it has made peace
with Joshua and with the Israelites." 5 Then
the five kings of the Amorites gathered.
These were the kings of Jerusalem, Hebron,
Jarmuth, Lachish, and Eglon. They went
up with all their armies, camped against
Gibeon, and attacked it. 6 The people of
Gibeon sent word to Joshua in the camp at

[l] Or *men* [m] Or *he* [n] Or *they*

Gilgal: “Don’t desert your servants! Come
to us quickly. Rescue us! Help us! All the
Amorite kings from the highlands have assembled together against us.” 7So Joshua
went up from Gilgal with the entire army
and all the bravest soldiers.

The LORD fights for Israel

8Then the LORD said to Joshua, “Don’t
be afraid of them. I have given them into
your power. Not a single one of them can
stand up against you.” 9Joshua quickly attacked them, having come up overnight
from Gilgal. 10Then the LORD threw them
into a panic before Israel. Joshua struck a
mighty blow against them at Gibeon. He
chased them on the way up to Beth-horon
and struck them down as far as Azekah and
Makkedah. 11When they were fleeing from
Israel and were on the slope of Beth-horon,
the LORD threw down large stones from
the sky all the way to Azekah. So they died.
More died from the hailstones than the Israelites killed with the sword.

12On the day the LORD gave the Amorites
into the power of Israel, Joshua spoke to the
LORD in the presence of the Israelites:

“Sun, stand still at Gibeon!
  and Moon, at the Aijalon Valley!”
13The sun stood still
  and the moon stood motionless
    until a nation took revenge
      on its enemies.

Isn’t this written in the Jashar scroll? So
the sun stood motionless in the middle of
the sky. For a whole day, it was in no hurry
to go down. 14There hasn’t been a day like it
before or since, when the LORD responded
to a human voice. The LORD fought for
Israel. 15Then Joshua along with all Israel
came back to the camp at Gilgal.

Israel executes five kings

16Then those five kings fled and hid in
the cave at Makkedah. 17It was reported to
Joshua, “The five kings have been found,
hidden in the cave at Makkedah.”

18Joshua said, “Roll large stones over the
mouth of the cave. Station some men by it to
guard them, 19but don’t you stay there. Chase
after your enemies and attack them from the
rear. Don’t let them enter their cities, because
the LORD your God has given them into your
power.” 20Joshua and the Israelites finished
dealing them a stunning blow until they were
finished off. Some survivors among them
escaped into the fortified cities. 21Then the
whole people came back safely to Joshua in
the camp at Makkedah. Not a single person
threatened the Israelites.

22Joshua said, “Open up the mouth of
the cave. Bring those five kings out of the
cave to me.” 23They did so. They brought the
five kings out of the cave to him: the kings
of Jerusalem, Hebron, Jarmuth, Lachish,
and Eglon. 24When they brought these
kings out to Joshua, Joshua called for every
Israelite. He said to the military commanders who had gone out with him, “Come forward. Put your feet on the necks of these
kings.” So they went forward and put their
feet on their necks. 25Then Joshua said to
them, “Don’t be afraid or terrified. Be brave
and strong, because this is how the LORD
will deal with all the enemies you fight.”
26Next, Joshua struck them down. He put
them to death and then hanged them on five
trees. They were hanging on the trees until
evening. 27At sundown, Joshua gave an
order, and they took them down from the
trees. They threw them into the cave where
they had hidden themselves, and they set
large stones over the mouth of the cave. The
stones are still there to this very day.

Victories in the south

28On that day, Joshua captured Makkedah. With a sword, he struck it and its king
without mercy. He wiped them out, treating everyone in the city as something reserved for God. He left no survivors. He did
to the king of Makkedah exactly as he had
done to the king of Jericho.

29Then Joshua along with all Israel moved
on from Makkedah to Libnah. They attacked
Libnah. 30The LORD also gave it and its king
into the power of Israel. With a sword, he
struck it and everyone in it without mercy.
He left no survivors in it. He did to its king
exactly as he had done to the king of Jericho.

31Joshua along with all Israel moved on
from Libnah to Lachish. They camped near

it and attacked it. 32 The LORD gave Lachish
into the power of Israel. Joshua captured it
on the second day. With a sword, he struck
it and everyone in it without mercy, just
exactly as he had done to Libnah. 33 Then
Gezer's King Horam came up to help Lachish. But Joshua struck him and his people
down, until no survivors were left.

34 Joshua along with all Israel moved
on from Lachish to Eglon. They camped
against it and attacked it. 35 They captured
it on the same day and struck it down without mercy. On that day, he wiped out everyone in it as something reserved for God,
just exactly as he had done to Lachish.

36 Joshua along with all Israel went up
from Eglon to Hebron and attacked it.
37 They captured it and struck it down without mercy, along with its king, all its towns,
and everyone in it. He left no survivors, just
exactly as he had done to Eglon. He wiped
out the city and everyone in it as something
reserved for God.

38 Joshua along with all Israel turned
back to Debir and attacked it. 39 He captured it along with its king and all its cities. They struck them down without mercy
and wiped out everyone in it as something
reserved for God. He left no survivors. Exactly as he had done to Hebron, so he did to
Debir and its king—exactly as he had done
to Libnah and its king.

40 So Joshua struck at the whole land:
the highlands, the arid southern plains, the
lowlands, the slopes, and all their kings. He
left no survivors. He wiped out everything
that breathed as something reserved for
God, exactly as the LORD, the God of Israel,
had commanded. 41 Joshua struck them
down from Kadesh-barnea to Gaza, and
the whole land of Goshen as far as Gibeon.
42 Joshua captured all these kings and their
land all at the same time. This was because
the LORD, the God of Israel, fought for Israel. 43 Then Joshua along with all Israel
came back to the camp at Gilgal.

Victories in the north

11 King Jabin of Hazor heard about this.
So he sent word to Madon's King
Jobab, to the king of Shimron, and to the
king of Achshaph. 2 He sent word to the
kings from the north part of the highlands,
in the desert plain south of Chinneroth, in
the lowlands, and in Naphoth-dor on the
west. 3 He sent word to the Canaanites from
east and west, to the Amorites, Hittites,
Perizzites, and Jebusites in the highlands,
and to the Hivites at the foot of Hermon
in the land of Mizpah. 4 They went out with
all their battalions as a great army. They
were as numerous as the grains of sand on
the seashore. There were very many horses
and chariots. 5 All these kings came together.
They came and camped together at the waters of Merom to fight against Israel.

6 The LORD said to Joshua, "Don't be
afraid of them. By this time tomorrow, I
will make them all dead bodies in Israel's
presence. Cripple their horses! Burn their
chariots!"

7 Then Joshua along with the entire army
launched a surprise attack against them at
the waters of Merom. 8 The LORD gave them
into Israel's power. They struck them down.
They chased them as far as Great Sidon and
Misrephoth-maim, then to the east as far as
the Mizpeh Valley. They struck them down
until no survivors were left. 9 Joshua dealt
with them exactly as the LORD had told
him. He crippled their horses and burned
their chariots.

10 Joshua turned back at that time. He
captured Hazor and struck down its king
with the sword. Hazor had been the head
of all those kingdoms in the past. 11 They
struck down everyone there without mercy,
wiping them out as something reserved
for God. Nothing that breathed was left.
Hazor itself he burned. 12 Joshua captured
all these kings and their cities. He struck
them down without mercy. He wiped them
out as something reserved for God. This
was exactly as Moses the LORD's servant
had commanded. 13 But Israel didn't burn
any of the cities that still are standing on
their mounds. Joshua burned only Hazor.
14 The Israelites took all the valuable things
from those cities and the cattle as plunder
for themselves. But they struck down every
person without mercy until they had wiped
them out. They didn't let anything that

breathed survive. 15 What the LORD had commanded Moses his servant, Moses had commanded Joshua, and Joshua did exactly that. He didn't deviate a bit from any command that the LORD had given Moses.

Summary of Israel's victories

16 So Joshua took this whole land: the highlands, the whole arid southern plain, the whole land of Goshen, the lowlands, the desert plain, and both the highlands and the lowlands of Israel. 17 He took land stretching from Mount Halak, which goes up toward Seir, as far as Baal-gad at the foot of Mount Hermon in the Lebanon Valley. He captured all their kings. He struck them down and killed them. 18 Joshua waged war against all these kings for a long time. 19 There wasn't one city that made peace with the Israelites, except the Hivites who lived in Gibeon. They captured every single one in battle. 20 Their stubborn resistance came from the LORD and led them to wage war against Israel. Israel was then able to wipe them out as something reserved for God, without showing them any mercy. This was exactly what the LORD had commanded Moses.

21 At that time, Joshua went and wiped out the Anakim from the highlands. He wiped them out from Hebron, from Debir, and from Anab, from the whole highlands of Judah, and the whole highlands of Israel. Joshua wiped them out along with their cities as something reserved for God. 22 The Anakim no longer remained in the land of the Israelites. They survived only in Gaza, Gath, and Ashdod. 23 So Joshua took the whole land, exactly as the LORD had promised Moses. Joshua gave it as a legacy to Israel according to their tribal shares. Then the land had a rest from war.

Moses defeated two kings

12 The Israelites struck down these kings of the land and took over their land on the east side of the Jordan. This ran from the Arnon Valley as far as Mount Hermon and included the whole eastern part of the desert plain. 2 First there was the Amorites' King Sihon, who lived in Heshbon. He ruled from Aroer by the rim of Arnon Valley and then from the middle of the valley as far as the Jabbok Valley, the border of the Ammonites. This was half of Gilead. 3 He ruled the desert plain up to the east side of the Chinneroth Sea. This ran southward in the direction of Beth-jeshimoth at the foot of the Pisgah slopes as far as the east side of the desert plain (that is, the Dead Sea) and 4 the territory next to it.° Then there was Bashan's King Og. He was one of the last of the Rephaim. He lived in Ashtaroth and Edrei. 5 He ruled over Mount Hermon, Salecah, and all of Bashan as far as the border of the Geshurites and the Maacathites, and half of Gilead down to the border of Heshbon's King Sihon. 6 Moses the LORD's servant and the Israelites struck them down. Moses the LORD's servant gave their land as property to the Reubenites, Gadites, and half the tribe of Manasseh.

Kings west of the Jordan

7 Joshua and the Israelites struck down these kings of the land and took over their land on the west side of the Jordan. This ran from Baal-gad in the Lebanon Valley as far as Mount Halak, which goes up toward Seir. Joshua gave it to the tribes of Israel as shares of property. 8 This was in the highlands, in the lowlands, in the desert plain, in the slopes, in the desert, and in the arid southern plain. The land belonged to Hittites, Amorites, Canaanites, Perizzites, Hivites, and Jebusites. They were:

9 the king of Jericho	one
the king of Ai (which is near Bethel)	one
10 the king of Jerusalem	one
the king of Hebron	one
11 the king of Jarmuth	one
the king of Lachish	one
12 the king of Eglon	one
the king of Gezer	one
13 the king of Debir	one
the king of Geder	one
14 the king of Hormah	one
the king of Arad	one

° Heb lacks *next to it*.

15 the king of Libnah one
the king of Adullam one
16 the king of Makkedah one
the king of Bethel one
17 the king of Tappuah one
the king of Hepher one
18 the king of Aphek one
the king of Lasharon one
19 the king of Madon one
the king of Hazor one
20 the king of Shimron-meron one
the king of Achshaph one
21 the king of Taanach one
the king of Megiddo one
22 the king of Kedesh one
the king of Jokneam in Carmel one
23 the king of Dor in Naphath-dor one
the king of Goiim of Gilgal one
24 the king of Tirzah one
Total of all kings: thirty-one.

Land still unconquered

13 Now Joshua had reached old age. The
LORD said to him, "You have reached
old age, but much of the land remains to be
taken over. 2 This is the land that remains:
All the districts of the Philistines and all
those of the Geshurites. 3 (The land stretching from the Shihor near Egypt northward
as far as the Ekron territory is considered
to be Canaanite. There are five rulers of the
Philistines, for Gaza, Ashdod, Ashkelon,
Gath, and Ekron.) The land of the Avvites
4 in the south. The whole land of the Canaanites, along with Mearah, which belongs to the Sidonians, as far as Aphek and
as far as the Amorite border. 5 The land of
the Gebalites and the whole Lebanon eastward, stretching from Baal-gad at the foot
of Mount Hermon to Lebo-hamath.

6 "I myself will remove the entire population of the highlands from Lebanon to
Misrephoth-maim before the Israelites,
that is, all the Sidonians. You have only
to allot it to Israel as a legacy exactly as I
commanded you. 7 So now divide up this
land as a legacy for the nine tribes and half
the tribe of Manasseh. You will give it out
from the Jordan to the Mediterranean Sea
in the west. The Mediterranean Sea is the
border."[p]

Land east of the Jordan

8 As for the other half of the tribe of
Manasseh,[q] the Reubenites and Gadites together with it had already taken their legacy
that Moses had given them on the east side
of the Jordan. It was exactly what Moses the
LORD's servant had given them. 9 It ran from
Aroer by the rim of the Arnon Valley and the
city in the middle of the valley through the
whole Medeba plateau as far as Dibon. 10 It
included all the cities of the Amorites' King
Sihon, who ruled in Heshbon, as far as the
Ammonite border. 11 It also included Gilead
and the territory of the Geshurites and Maacathites, all Mount Hermon, and all Bashan
as far as Salecah—12 the entire kingdom
of Og in Bashan, who ruled in Ashtaroth
and in Edrei. He survived as the last of the
Rephaim. Moses had struck down and removed them. 13 But the Israelites didn't remove the Geshurites or the Maacathites. So
Geshur and Maacath still live among Israel
today. 14 It was only to the tribe of Levi that
he gave no legacy. Their legacy consists of
the fire offerings for the LORD, the God of
Israel, exactly as he had promised them.

For Reuben

15 Moses provided for the clans of the
Reubenite tribe. 16 Their territory ran from
Aroer by the rim of the Arnon Valley and
the city in the middle of the ravine, and the
whole plateau as far as Medeba. 17 It included
Heshbon and all its cities that are on the
plateau: Dibon, Bamoth-baal, Beth-baal-
meon, 18 Jahaz, Kedemoth, Mephaath,
19 Kiriathaim, Sibmah, the Zereth-shahar
highlands, 20 Beth-peor, the slopes of Pisgah,
and Beth-jeshimoth. 21 It included all the cities of the plateau and the whole kingdom
of Sihon king of the Amorites, who ruled
in Heshbon. Moses had struck him down,
along with Evi, Rekem, Zur, Hur, and Reba,
the leaders of Midian. They had lived in the

[p] LXX; MT lacks *You will give it out from the Jordan to the Mediterranean Sea in the west. The Mediterranean Sea is the border.* [q] LXX; MT lacks *As for the other half of the tribe of Manasseh.*

land as princes of Sihon. 22In addition to those others slain, the Israelites killed the fortune-teller Balaam, Beor's son, with the sword. 23The border of the people of Reuben was the Jordan and the territory next to it. This was the legacy of the people of Reuben—for their clans, their cities, and their settlements.

For Gad

24Moses provided for the clans of the Gadite tribe. 25Their territory was Jazer, all the cities of Gilead, and half the land of the Ammonites as far as Aroer near Rabbah. 26It also ran from Heshbon as far as Ramath-mizpeh and Betonim, and from Mahanaim as far as the territory of Lidebir. 27In the valley were Beth-haram, Beth-nimrah, Succoth, and Zaphon. This was the rest of the kingdom of Sihon king of Heshbon. It included the Jordan and the territory next to it up to the tip of the Chinnereth Sea on the east side of the Jordan. 28This was the legacy of the Gadites—for their clans, their cities, and their settlements.

For half of Manasseh

29Moses provided for half the tribe of Manasseh. It was for the clans in half the tribe of the people of Manasseh. 30Their territory ran from Mahanaim, all Bashan, the whole kingdom of Og king of Bashan, and all sixty of the tent villages of Jair that are in Bashan. 31Half of Gilead along with Ashtaroth and Edrei, cities of the kingdom of Og in Bashan, belonged to the people of Machir son of Manasseh. It belonged to the clans for half of the people of Machir.

32Moses assigned these territories when he was in the Moab plains on the other side of the Jordan, east of Jericho. 33But Moses gave no legacy to the tribe of Levi. The LORD God of Israel is their legacy, exactly as he promised them.

Dividing up Canaan

14 The Israelites received these inheritances in the land of Canaan. Eleazar the priest, Joshua son of Nun, and the heads of the families of the Israelite tribes assigned them. 2Their legacy was assigned by lot, exactly as the LORD had commanded the nine and a half tribes through Moses. 3In fact, Moses had given out the legacy of the two and a half tribes on the other side of the Jordan. But he gave no legacy among them to the Levites. 4The people of Joseph consisted of two tribes, Manasseh and Ephraim. The Levites weren't given any portion of the land, except cities to live in and pastureland for their cattle and flocks. 5The Israelites divided up the land exactly as the LORD had commanded Moses.

Caleb receives Hebron

6In Gilgal, the people of Judah approached Joshua. Caleb son of Jephunneh the Kenizzite said to him, "You know what the LORD said to Moses, man of God, about you and me when we were in Kadesh-barnea. 7I was 40 years old when Moses the LORD's servant sent me from Kadesh-barnea to scout out the land. I brought back a report to him of what I really thought. 8My companions who had gone up with me made the people's heart melt. But I remained loyal to the LORD my God. 9So Moses pledged on that day, 'The land on which you have walked will forever be a legacy for you and your children. This is because you remained loyal to the LORD my God.' 10Now look. The LORD has kept me alive, exactly as he promised. It is forty-five years since the LORD spoke about this to Moses. It was while Israel was journeying in the desert. Now look. Today I'm 85 years old. 11I'm just as strong today as I was the day Moses sent me out. My strength then was as my strength is now, whether for war or for everyday activities. 12So now, give me this highland that the LORD promised me that day. True, the Anakim are there with large fortified cities, as you yourself heard that day. But if the LORD is with me, I should be able to remove them, exactly as the LORD promised."

13So Joshua blessed him. He gave Hebron to Caleb, Jephunneh's son, as a legacy. 14So Hebron still belongs to Caleb son of Jephunneh the Kenizzite as a legacy today. This was because he remained loyal to the

LORD God of Israel. 15 (Hebron used to be called Kiriath-arba. Arba had been the greatest of the Anakim.) Then the land rested from war.

Border of Judah

15 The land determined by lot for the clans of the Judahite tribe ran southward to the border of Edom. The Zin wasteland was the southern limit. 2 Their south border ran from the end of the Dead Sea, from the bay that faces south. 3 It went south from the ascent of Akrabbim, passed on to Zin, and went up south of Kadesh-barnea. It passed on to Hezron, went up to Addar, and turned toward Karka. 4 It passed on to Azmon and went by the border[r] of Egypt. The border ended at the sea. This will be their south border.

5 The east border was the Dead Sea as far as the mouth of the Jordan.

The border on the north side ran from the bay of the sea at the mouth of the Jordan. 6 The border went up to Beth-hoglah and passed north of Beth-arabah. The border went up to the Stone of Bohan (Reuben's son). 7 The border went up to Debir from the Achor Valley, turning north to Gilgal. Gilgal was opposite the ascent of Adummim, which was south of the ravine. The border passed on to the waters of En-shemesh and ended at En-rogel. 8 The border went up by the valley of Ben-Hinnom to the slope of the Jebusite city, Jerusalem, on the south. The border went up to the top of the mountain that is opposite the Hinnom Valley on the west, which is at the north end of the Rephaim Valley. 9 The border turned from the top of the mountain to the waters of Nephtoah Spring and went to the cities of Mount Ephron. The border turned toward Baalah (that is, Kiriath-jearim). 10 The border turned westward from Baalah to Mount Seir. It passed on to the slope of Mount Jearim on the north (that is, Chesalon), went down to Beth-shemesh, and passed by Timnah. 11 The border went to the slope of Ekron on the north. The border turned toward Shikkeron, passed on to Mount Baalah, and went to Jabneel. The border ended at the sea.

12 The west border was the Mediterranean Sea and its shoreline. This was the border surrounding the clans of the Judahites.

Caleb and Achsah

13 In agreement with the LORD's command to him, Joshua gave a portion among the Judahites to Caleb, Jephunneh's son. It was Kiriath-arba, that is, Hebron (Arba was the father of Anak). 14 Caleb removed the three sons of Anak from there: Sheshai, Ahiman, and Talmai. They were the offspring of Anak. 15 Then he went up from there against the population of Debir. Debir used to be called Kiriath-sepher. 16 Caleb said, "I will give Achsah my daughter in marriage to whoever strikes Kiriath-sepher and captures it." 17 So Othniel son of Kenaz, Caleb's brother, captured it, and Caleb gave him Achsah his daughter in marriage.

18 Now when she arrived, she prodded Othniel into asking for a field from her father. After she got down off her donkey, Caleb asked her, "What do you want?"

19 She said, "Give me a blessing. Since the land you've given me is in the arid southern plain, you should also give me springs of water." So he gave her the upper springs and the lower springs.

Cities of Judah

20 This is the legacy for the clans of the tribe of the people of Judah. 21 The outlying cities of the tribe of the people of Judah ran down to the border of Edom.

In the arid southern plain: Kabzeel, Eder, Jagur, 22 Kinah, Dimonah, Adadah, 23 Kedesh, Hazor, Ithnan, 24 Ziph, Telem, Bealoth, 25 Hazor-hadattah, Kerioth-hezron (that is, Hazor), 26 Amam, Shema, Moladah, 27 Hazar-gaddah, Heshmon, Beth-pelet, 28 Hazar-shual, Beer-sheba and its dependent cities,[s] 29 Baalah, Iim, Ezem, 30 Eltolad, Chesil, Hormah, 31 Ziklag, Madmannah, Sansannah, 32 Lebaoth, Shilhim, Ain, and Rimmon. In total: twenty-nine cities and their surrounding areas.

[r] Or *Wadi*, traditionally Brook; LXX *their south border*; MT *your south border* [s] LXX and Neh 11:27; Heb *Biziothiah*

33In the lowlands: Eshtaol, Zorah, Ash-
nah, 34Zanoah, En-gannim, Tappuah, Enam,
35Jarmuth, Adullam, Socoh, Azekah,
36Shaaraim, Adithaim, Gederah, and Ged-
erothaim. In total: fourteen cities and their
surrounding areas.
37Zenan, Hadashah, Migdal-gad, 38Dilan,
Mizpeh, Jokthe-el, 39Lachish, Bozkath, Eglon,
40Cabbon, Lahmam, Chitlish, 41Gederoth,
Beth-dagon, Naamah, and Makkedah. In
total: sixteen cities and their surrounding
areas.
42Libnah, Ether, Ashan, 43Iphtah, Ash-
nah, Nezib, 44Keilah, Achzib, and Mareshah. In total: nine cities and their
surrounding areas.
45Ekron, its dependent cities and surrounding areas. 46From Ekron toward the
sea, everything that was near Ashdod and
its surrounding areas. 47Ashdod, its dependent cities and surrounding areas. Gaza, its
dependent cities and surrounding areas as
far as the border of Egypt and the Mediterranean Sea and its shoreline.
48In the highlands: Shamir, Jattir, Socoh,
49Dannah, Kiriath-sannah (that is, Debir),
50Anab, Eshtemoh, Anim, 51Goshen, Holon,
and Giloh. In total: eleven cities and their
surrounding areas.
52Arab, Dumah, Eshan, 53Janim, Beth-
tappuah, Aphekah, 54Humtah, Kiriath-arba
(that is, Hebron), and Zior. In total: nine
cities and their surrounding areas.
55Maon, Carmel, Ziph, Juttah, 56Jezreel,
Jokdeam, Zanoah, 57Kain, Gibeah, and
Timnah. In total: ten cities and their surrounding areas.
58Halhul, Beth-zur, Gedor, 59Maarath,
Beth-anoth, and Eltekon. In total: six cities
and their surrounding areas.
Tekoah, Ephrathah (that is, Bethlehem),
Peor, Etam, Koulon, Tatam, Sores, Karem,
Gallim, Bether, and Manahath. In total:
eleven cities and their surrounding areas.[t]
60Kiriath-baal (that is, Kiriath-jearim)
and Rabbah. In total: two cities and their
surrounding areas.
61In the desert: Beth-arabah, Middin,
Secacah, 62Nibshan (the Salt City), and
En-gedi. In total: six cities and their surrounding areas.
63But the people of Judah couldn't remove the Jebusites who lived in Jerusalem.
So today the Jebusites still live along with
the people of Judah in Jerusalem.

Ephraim

16 The land determined by lot for the
people of Joseph went out from the
Jordan near Jericho eastward to the waters
of Jericho. It went up by the desert from
Jericho to the Bethel highlands. 2It goes
from Bethel to Luz and passes on to the
border of the Archites at Ataroth. 3It goes
down westward to the border of the Japhle-
tites as far as the border of Lower Beth-
horon and as far as Gezer. It ends at the
sea. 4The people of Joseph, Manasseh and
Ephraim, received their legacy.
5This was the territory for the clans of
the people of Ephraim. The border of their
legacy ran from Ataroth-adar on the east as
far as Upper Beth-horon. 6The border goes
to the sea. Michmethath is on the north.
The border turns east of Taanath-shiloh
and passes along beyond it east of Janoah.
7It goes down from Janoah to Ataroth and
to Naarah, touches Jericho, and goes to the
Jordan. 8From Tappuah the border goes
westward by the Kanah Valley. It ends at
the sea. This is the legacy for the clans of
the Ephraimite tribe. 9It included cities set
apart for the people of Ephraim within the
legacy of the people of Manasseh, all the
cities and their surrounding areas. 10But
they didn't remove the Canaanites who
lived in Gezer. So today the Canaanites,
who were used for forced labor, still live
within Ephraim.

Manasseh

17 Land was determined by lot for the
tribe of Manasseh, who was actually
Joseph's oldest son. Gilead and Bashan
belonged to Machir, who was Manasseh's
oldest son and Gilead's father. This was
because he was a warrior. 2So an allotment
took place for the rest of the clans of the

[t]LXX; MT lacks *Tekoa, Ephrathah . . . surrounding areas.*

people of Manasseh—for the people of Abiezer, Helek, Asriel, Shechem, Hepher, and Shemida. These were the sons of Manasseh the son of Joseph, the male descendants by their clans.

3Zelophehad was Hepher's son, Gilead's grandson, Machir's great-grandson and Manasseh's great-great-grandson. Zelophehad had no sons, only daughters, who were named Mahlah, Noah, Hoglah, Milcah, and Tirzah. 4The daughters approached Eleazar the priest, Joshua, Nun's son, and the leaders. They said, "The LORD commanded Moses to give us a legacy along with our male relatives." So in agreement with the LORD's command, they were given a legacy along with their uncles. 5Manasseh had ten parcels in addition to the land of Gilead and Bashan on the other side of the Jordan. 6This was because the daughters of Manasseh received a legacy along with his sons. The land of Gilead belonged to the rest of the people of Manasseh.

7The border of Manasseh ran from Asher to Michmethath, which is opposite Shechem. The border went south to the population of En-tappuah. 8The land of Tappuah belonged to Manasseh. But Tappuah itself belonged to the people of Ephraim, even though it was on the border of Manasseh. 9The border went down by the Kanah Valley. South of the ravine are those cities that belong to Ephraim, even though they are located among the cities of Manasseh. The border of Manasseh lay on the north side of the ravine and ended at the sea. 10What lay south of the border belonged to Ephraim, and what lay north of it belonged to Manasseh. The sea was its border. The territory bordered Asher on the north and Issachar on the east.

11Belonging to Manasseh in Issachar and in Asher were Beth-shean and its dependent cities, Ibleam and its dependent cities, the population of Dor and its dependent cities, the population of En-dor and its dependent cities, the population of Taanach and its dependent cities, and the population of Megiddo and its dependent cities. (The third one is Naphath.)[u] 12The people of Manasseh couldn't take over these cities, and the Canaanites were determined to live in this land. 13When the Israelites grew strong, they subjected the Canaanites to hard labor but didn't remove them.

Future expansion for Joseph

14The tribe of Joseph spoke to Joshua: "Why have you only given us a single lot and a solitary parcel for a legacy? We are a numerous people whom the LORD has blessed so richly."

15Then Joshua said, "Yes, you are a numerous people. So go up to the forest and clear ground for yourselves there in the land of the Perizzites and Rephaim, because the Ephraimite highland is too small for you."

16The people of Joseph said, "The highland isn't enough for us. But all the Canaanites who live in the valley region have iron chariots, both those in Beth-shean and its dependent cities and those in the Jezreel Valley."

17Joshua then said to the house of Joseph, to Ephraim and to Manasseh, "You are a numerous people and possess great strength. You will have more than a single lot. 18The highland will belong to you. Because it is a forest, you can clear it. Its farthest limits will be yours. You will definitely remove the Canaanites, even though they have iron chariots and are strong."

Remainder of the land

18 The whole community of the Israelites assembled at Shiloh and set up the meeting tent there. The conquered land lay before them. 2Among the Israelites, seven tribes were left that had not yet received their legacy. 3Joshua said to the Israelites, "How long will you avoid going to take over the land that the LORD, the God of your ancestors, has given you? 4Pick out three men for each tribe. I will send them out, and they will go up and travel throughout the land. They will write a description of it as the basis for determining their legacy. Then they will come back to me. 5They will divide up the

[u]Heb uncertain

land among themselves into seven portions.
Judah will stay on its territory to the south.
The house of Joseph will stay on their territory to the north. 6But you will write a report in seven parts and bring the report back
here to me. Then I will cast the lot for you
here, before the LORD our God. 7However,
there won't be a portion among you for the
Levites because their legacy is the priesthood of the LORD. Gad, Reuben, and half
the tribe of Manasseh have already received
their legacy on the east side of the Jordan.
Moses the LORD's servant gave it to them."
8When the men had prepared to go,
Joshua gave orders to those going to write
a description of the land. "Go and travel
around the land, write about it, and return
to me. I will cast the lot for you before the
LORD here in Shiloh." 9So the men went
and passed through the land and wrote
about it in a document, city by city, in seven
sections. They came back to Joshua in the
camp at Shiloh. 10Then Joshua cast lots
for them in Shiloh before the LORD. There
Joshua divided up the shares of the land for
the Israelites.

Border of Benjamin

11The lot for the clans of the Benjaminite
tribe appeared first. The border of their allotment went out between the people of
Judah and the people of Joseph. 12Their
border on the north side ran from the Jordan. The border went up to the slope of
Jericho on the north. It went up westward
in the highlands and ended at the wasteland of Beth-aven. 13The border passed on
from there to Luz, to the slope of Luz on
the south (that is, Bethel). The border went
down to Ataroth-adar on the mountain that
is south of Lower Beth-horon. 14The border
turned and came around southward on
the west side, running from the mountain
that is opposite Beth-horon on the south.
It ended at Kiriath-baal (that is, Kiriath-
jearim), a city of the people of Judah. This
was its west side.
15The south side ran from the limits of
Kiriath-jearim. The border went out westward. It then proceeded to the waters of
Nephtoah Spring. 16The border went down
to the foot of the mountain that is opposite
the valley of the son of Hinnom, which is
in the north part of the Rephaim Valley. It
went down through the Hinnom Valley to
the slope of the Jebusite city on the south.
It then went down to En-rogel. 17It turned
northward. Then it went to En-shemesh
and then to Geliloth, which is opposite the
ascent of Adummim. It went down to the
Stone of Bohan (Reuben's son). 18It passed
on to the slope of Beth-arabah[v] on the
north and went down into the desert plain.
19The border passed on to the slope of Beth-
hoglah on the north. The border ended at
the north bay of the Dead Sea, at the southern mouth of the Jordan. This was the
southern border. 20The Jordan bordered it
on the east side. This is the legacy of the
Benjaminite clans according to its borders.

Cities of Benjamin

21The cities of the clans of the Benjaminite
tribe are Jericho, Beth-hoglah, Emek-keziz,
22Beth-arabah, Zemaraim, Bethel, 23Avvim,
Parah, Ophrah, 24Chephar-ammoni, Ophni,
and Geba. In total: twelve cities and their
surrounding areas.
25Gibeon, Ramah, Beeroth, 26Mizpeh,
Chephirah, Mozah, 27Rekem, Irpeel, Taralah,
28Zela, Haeleph, the Jebusite city (that is,
Jerusalem), Gibeath, and Kiriath. In total:
fourteen cities and their surrounding areas.
This is the legacy of the Benjaminite clans.

Simeon

19 The second lot fell to Simeon. The legacy of the clans of the Simeonite tribe
lay inside the legacy of the people of Judah.
2They had in their legacy: Beer-sheba, Sheba,
Moladah, 3Hazar-shual, Balah, Ezem, 4Elto-
lad, Bethul, Hormah, 5Ziklag, Beth-marcaboth, Hazar-susah, 6Beth-lebaoth, and
Sharuhen. In total: thirteen cities and their
surrounding areas. 7Ain, Rimmon, Ether,
and Ashan. In total: four cities and their
surrounding areas. 8In addition were all the
areas that surround these cities as far as

[v] LXX and Josh 15:6; MT *slope opposite the desert plain*

Baalath-beer and Ramah of the arid southern plain. This is the legacy of the clans of the Simeonite tribe. [9]Some of the portion of the people of Judah belonged to the legacy of the people of Simeon. This was because the portion of the people of Judah was too large for them. So the people of Simeon received a legacy inside Judah's legacy.

Zebulun

[10]The lot turned up third for the clans of Zebulun. The border of their legacy ran as far as Sarid. [11]Their border went up westward to Maralah, touched Dabbesheth, and touched the ravine that is opposite Jokneam. [12]It reversed from Sarid eastward toward the east to the border of Chisloth-tabor. It went to Daberath and then up to Japhia. [13]From there it passed on the east side, running eastward to Gath-hepher and Eth-kazin. Going to Rimmon, it bent toward Neah. [14]The border turned north of Hannathon and ended at the Iphtah-el Valley. [15]They also owned Kattath, Nahalal, Shimron, Idalah, and Bethlehem; in total: twelve cities and their surrounding areas. [16]These cities and their surrounding areas are the legacy of Zebulun's clans.

Issachar

[17]The lot went out fourth for the clans of Issachar. [18]Their border ran toward Jezreel. They also owned Chesulloth, Shunem, [19]Hapharaim, Shion, Anaharath, [20]Rabbith, Kishion, Ebez, [21]Remeth, En-gannim, En-haddah, and Beth-pazzez. [22]The border touched Tabor, Shahazumah, and Beth-shemesh. Their border ended at the Jordan; in total: sixteen cities with their surrounding areas. [23]These cities and their surrounding areas are the legacy for the clans of the Issachar tribe.

Asher

[24]The lot went out fifth for the clans of the tribe of Asher. [25]Their border included Helkath, Hali, Beten, Achshaph, [26]Allammelech, Amad, and Mishal. It touched Carmel on the west and Shihor-libnath. [27]The border reversed eastward to Beth-dagon. It touched Zebulun and the Iphtah-el Valley on the north, also Beth-emek and Neiel. It went to Cabul on the north, [28]as far as Great Sidon. They also owned Ebron, Rehob, Hammon, and Kanah. [29]The border turned around to Ramah as far as the fortified city of Tyre. The border turned around to Hosah and ended at the sea. They also owned Mahalab,[w] Achzib, [30]Ummah, Aphek, and Rehob; in total: twenty-two cities and their surrounding areas. [31]These cities and their surrounding areas are the legacy for the clans of the Asher tribe.

Naphtali

[32]For the people of Naphtali, the lot went out sixth. For the clans of Naphtali [33]their border ran from Heleph, from the oak in Zaanannim and Adami-nekeb and Jabneel as far as Lakkum. It ended at the Jordan. [34]The border reversed westward to Aznoth-tabor. It went from there to Hukkok. It touched Zebulun on the south, Asher on the west, and Judah at the Jordan on the east. [35]They also owned the fortified cities Ziddim, Zer, Hammath, Rakkath, Chinnereth, [36]Adamah, Ramah, Hazor, [37]Kedesh, Edrei, En-hazor, [38]Iron, Migdal-el, Horem, Beth-anath, and Beth-shemesh; in total: nineteen cities and their surrounding areas. [39]These cities and their surrounding areas are the legacy for the clans of the Naphtali tribe.

Dan

[40]The lot went out seventh for the clans of the Danite tribe. [41]The territory of their legacy was Zorah, Eshtaol, Ir-shemesh, [42]Shaalabbin, Aijalon, Ithlah, [43]Elon, Timnah, Ekron, [44]Eltekeh, Gibbethon, Baalath, [45]Jehud, Bene-berak, Gath-rimmon, [46]Me-jarkon, and Rakkon, along with the territory opposite Joppa. [47]But the territory of the people of Dan was lost to them. So the people of Dan went up and attacked Leshem and captured it. They struck it down without mercy. They took it over and settled it. Then they named Leshem as Dan, after the

[w]LXX; MT *Mehebel*

name of Dan their ancestor. 48 These cities and their surrounding areas are the legacy for the clans of the Danite tribe.

Legacy for Joshua

49 So when they finished assigning the borders of the land, the Israelites gave to Joshua, Nun's son, a legacy among them. 50 By the LORD's command, they gave him the city that he asked for. This was Timnath-serah in the highlands of Ephraim. He built a city and lived in it. 51 These are the legacies that Eleazar the priest, Joshua, Nun's son, and the heads of the families of the Israelite tribes assigned by lot at Shiloh. They did this before the LORD at the entrance of the meeting tent and finished dividing up the land.

Refuge cities

20 The LORD spoke to Joshua: 2 "Say to the Israelites, 'Set up refuge cities for yourselves. I spoke to you about these through Moses. 3 Anyone who kills by striking down someone unintentionally or by mistake may flee there. These places will be a refuge for you from any member of the victim's family seeking revenge. 4 The killer will flee to one of these cities, stand at the entrance of the city gate, and explain their situation to the elders of that city. The elders are to let the killer into the city and provide a place of refuge for the killer to live with them. 5 If a member of the victim's family follows, seeking revenge, they won't hand the killer over. This is because the killer struck down the neighbor by accident and hadn't been an enemy in the past. 6 The killer will live in that city until there can be a trial before the community or[x] until the death of the one who is high priest at that time. Then the killer may return home, back to the city from which the flight began.'"

7 So they set apart Kedesh in Galilee in the highlands of Naphtali, Shechem in the highlands of Ephraim, and Kiriath-arba (that is, Hebron) in the highlands of Judah. 8 On the other side of the Jordan east of Jericho, they set up Bezer in the wasteland on the plateau from the tribe of Reuben, Ramoth in Gilead from the tribe of Gad, and Golan in Bashan from the tribe of Manasseh. 9 These cities were the ones designated for all the Israelites and for immigrants residing among them. Anyone who struck down a person by mistake could flee there and escape death at the hand of some member of the victim's family seeking revenge, until there could be a trial before the community.

Cities for the Levites

21 The heads of the levitical families approached Eleazar the priest, Joshua, Nun's son, and the heads of the families of the Israelite tribes. 2 They spoke to them at Shiloh in the land of Canaan: "The LORD gave a command through Moses to give us cities to live in and their pasturelands for our cattle." 3 So the Israelites gave the Levites the following cities and their pasturelands out of their own legacy. This was in agreement with the LORD's command.

4 The lot went out for the clans of the Kohathites. The descendants of Aaron the priest from among the Levites acquired thirteen cities by lot from the tribes of Judah, Simeon, and Benjamin. 5 The rest of the descendants of Kohath acquired ten cities by lot from the clans of the tribes of Ephraim, Dan, and half of Manasseh. 6 The descendants of Gershon acquired thirteen cities by lot from the clans of the tribes of Issachar, Asher, Naphtali, and the half of Manasseh located in Bashan. 7 The descendants of Merari acquired twelve cities for their clans from the tribes of Reuben, Gad, and Zebulun. 8 So the Israelites gave these cities and their pasturelands to the Levites by lot, exactly as the LORD had commanded through Moses.

9 They gave the following cities, identified here by name, from the tribe of the Judahites and the tribe of the Simeonites. 10 The cities belonged to the descendants of Aaron, one of the Kohathite clans of the Levites, because the lot had fallen to them first. 11 They gave them Kiriath-arba (that

[x] Heb uncertain

is, Hebron) in the highlands of Judah and the pastures around it. (Arba was the father of Anak.) 12But they had already given the fields of the city and its surrounding areas to Caleb, Jephunneh's son, as his property. 13To the descendants of Aaron the priest they gave: Hebron, the refuge city for a killer, and its pastures; Libnah and its pastures; 14Jattir and its pastures; Eshtemoa and its pastures; 15Holon and its pastures; Debir and its pastures; 16Ain and its pastures; Juttah and its pastures; and Beth-shemesh and its pastures. Total from these two tribes: nine cities. 17From the tribe of Benjamin: Gibeon and its pastures, Geba and its pastures, 18Anathoth and its pastures, and Almon and its pastures. In total: four cities. 19This is the total of all the cities of the priests descended from Aaron: thirteen cities with their pastures.

20Other clans from the levitical descendants of Kohath still remained from among the descendants of Kohath. Some of their allotted cities were from the tribe of Ephraim. 21They gave them: Shechem, the refuge city for a killer, and its pastures in the highlands of Ephraim; Gezer and its pastures; 22Kibzaim and its pastures; and Beth-horon and its pastures; in total: four cities. 23From the tribe of Dan: Elteke and its pastures, Gibbethon and its pastures, 24Aijalon and its pastures, Gath-rimmon and its pastures; in total: four cities. 25From half the tribe of Manasseh: Taanach and its pastures, and Gath-rimmon and its pastures; in total: two cities. 26This is the total of all cities for the clans of the remaining descendants of Kohath: ten cities with their pastures.

27To the descendants of Gershon, one of the clans of the Levites, from half the tribe of Manasseh: Golan in Bashan, the refuge city for a killer, and its pastures; and Beeshterah and its pastures; in total: two cities. 28From the tribe of Issachar: Kishion and its pastures, Daberath and its pastures, 29Jarmuth and its pastures, En-gannim and its pastures; in total: four cities. 30From the tribe of Asher: Mishal and its pastures, Abdon and its pastures, 31Helkath and its pastures, and Rehob and its pastures; in total: four cities. 32From the tribe of Naphtali: Kedesh in Galilee, the refuge city for the killer, and its pastures; Hammoth-dor and its pastures; and Kartan and its pastures; in total: three cities. 33This is the total of all cities of the Gershonites for their clans: thirteen cities with their pastures.

34To the clans of the descendants of Merari, the rest of the Levites, from the tribe of Zebulun: Jokneam and its pastures, Kartah and its pastures, 35Dimnah and its pastures, Nahalal and its pastures; in total: four cities. 36From the tribe of Reuben: Bezer and its pastures, Jahaz and its pastures, 37Kedemoth and its pastures, and Mephaath and its pastures; in total: four cities.[y] 38From the tribe of Gad: Ramoth in Gilead, the refuge city for a killer, and its pastures; Mahanaim and its pastures; 39Heshbon and its pastures; Jazer and its pastures; in total: four cities. 40As for the cities of the descendants of Merari for their clans, the remaining clans of the Levites, their total allotment was twelve cities.

41This is the total of all the cities of the Levites within the property of the Israelites: forty-eight cities with their pastures. 42Each of these cities had its pastures around it. This was the case for all these cities.

Summary of the conquest

43The LORD gave to Israel all the land he had pledged to give to their ancestors. They took it over and settled there. 44The LORD gave them rest from surrounding danger, exactly as he had pledged to their ancestors. Not one of all their enemies held out against them. The LORD gave all their enemies into their power. 45Not one of all the good things that the LORD had promised to the house of Israel failed. Every promise was fulfilled.

Eastern tribes go home

22 Then Joshua summoned the Reubenites, the Gadites, and half the tribe

[y]LXX and 1 Chron 6:78-79 (Heb 6:63-64); some Heb manuscripts lack 21:36-37.

of Manasseh. 2 He said to them, “You obeyed everything that Moses the LORD’s servant commanded you. You have also obeyed me in everything that I have commanded you. 3 During these many years, you never once deserted your fellow Israelites. You faithfully obeyed the command of the LORD your God. 4 The LORD your God has now given rest to your fellow Israelites, exactly as he promised them. So turn around and go back home. Go to the land where you hold property, which Moses the LORD’s servant gave you on the other side of the Jordan. 5 Just be very careful to carry out the commandment and Instruction that Moses the LORD’s servant commanded you. Love the LORD your God. Walk in all his ways and obey his commandments. Hold on to him and serve him with all your heart and being.” 6 Then Joshua blessed them. He sent them away, and they went home.

7 Moses had provided for half of the tribe of Manasseh in Bashan. But Joshua provided for the other half on the west side of the Jordan along with their fellow Israelites. When he sent them back home, Joshua also blessed them. 8 He said to them, “Return home with great wealth and many cattle, with silver, gold, bronze, and iron, and with much clothing. Divide the spoil taken from your enemies among your own people.”

Disagreement about an altar

9 So the people of Reuben, the people of Gad, and half the tribe of Manasseh went back. They left the Israelites at Shiloh, which is in the land of Canaan. They went to the land of Gilead, to the land that they owned. They had settled there at the LORD’s command given by Moses. 10 They came to the districts[z] of the Jordan that are in the land of Canaan. The people of Reuben, the people of Gad, and half the tribe of Manasseh built an altar there by the Jordan, an altar that appeared to be immense. 11 Then the Israelites heard a report: “Look. The people of Reuben, the people of Gad, and half the tribe of Manasseh have built an altar at the far edge of the land of Canaan. It lies in the districts of the Jordan on the Israelite side!” 12 When the Israelites heard this, the entire Israelite community assembled at Shiloh to go up to war against them.

13 Then the Israelites sent Phinehas son of Eleazar the priest to the people of Reuben, the people of Gad, and half the tribe of Manasseh in the land of Gilead. 14 They sent with him ten leaders, one leader from each important family among the tribes of Israel. Each was the head of an important family among the military units of Israel. 15 They came to the people of Reuben, the people of Gad, and half the tribe of Manasseh in the land of Gilead and spoke with them. 16 They said, “Here is what the LORD’s entire community says: ‘What’s this disrespectful thing that you’ve done to the God of Israel? Today you’ve turned away from following the LORD by building yourselves an altar as an act of rebellion against the LORD. 17 Wasn’t the offense of Peor enough for us? Even today we still haven’t cleansed ourselves from that sin, when there was a plague on the LORD’s community! 18 Today you are turning away from following the LORD. If you rebel against the LORD today, he will be angry with the entire community of Israel tomorrow. 19 If your own property is unclean land, then cross over into the land of the LORD’s property and settle among us. That’s where the dwelling of the LORD stands. But don’t rebel against the LORD. And don’t involve us in rebellion[a] by building an altar for yourselves other than the altar of the LORD our God. 20 Didn’t Achan, Zerah’s son, do such a disrespectful thing with the items reserved for God? Wrath came on the entire community of Israel. And he wasn’t the only one to die for his crime.’ ”

21 Then the people of Reuben, the people of Gad, and half the tribe of Manasseh answered the heads of the military units of Israel: 22 “The LORD is God of gods! The LORD is God of gods! He already knows, and now let Israel also know it! If we acted in rebellion or in disrespect against

[z] Heb *Geliloth* [a] Or *rebel against us*

the LORD, don't spare us today. 23 If we've built ourselves an altar to turn away from following the LORD or to offer on it an entirely burned offering or gift offering, or to perform well-being sacrifices on it, let the LORD himself seek punishment. 24 No! The truth is we did this out of concern for what might happen. In the future your children might say to our children, 'What have you got to do with the LORD, the God of Israel? 25 The LORD has set the Jordan as a border between us and you people of Reuben and Gad. You have no portion in the LORD!' So your children might make our children stop worshipping the LORD. 26 As a result we said, 'Let's protect ourselves by building an altar. It isn't to be for an entirely burned offering or for sacrifice.' 27 But it is to be a witness between us and you and between our descendants after us. It witnesses that we too perform the service of the LORD in his presence through our entirely burned offerings, sacrifices, and well-being offerings. So in the future your children could never say to our children, 'You have no portion in the LORD.' 28 We thought, If in the future they ever say this to us or to our descendants, we could say, 'Look at this replica of the altar of the LORD that our ancestors made. It isn't for entirely burned offerings or for sacrifice but to be a witness between us and you.' 29 God forbid that we should rebel against the LORD and turn away today from following the LORD by building an altar for an entirely burned offering, gift offering, or sacrifice, other than the altar of the LORD our God that stands before his dwelling!"

30 Phinehas the priest, the leaders of the community, and the heads of the military units of Israel who were with him heard the words that the people of Reuben, Gad, and Manasseh spoke and approved them. 31 So Phinehas the son of Eleazar the priest said to the people of Reuben, Gad, and Manasseh, "Today we know that the LORD is among us, because you haven't done a disrespectful thing against the LORD. Now you've delivered the Israelites from the power of the LORD." 32 Then Phinehas the son of Eleazar the priest and the leaders left the people of Reuben and Gad in the land of Gilead and came back to the Israelites in the land of Canaan. They brought word back to them. 33 The Israelites agreed and blessed God. They no longer spoke of going to war against them to destroy the land where the people of Reuben and Gad were living. 34 The people of Reuben and Gad referred to the altar in this way: "It is a witness between us that the LORD is God."

Joshua's word of warning

23 A long time passed. The LORD had given rest to Israel from all their surrounding enemies, and Joshua had grown very old. 2 Joshua summoned all Israel, their elders, their heads, their judges, and their officers. He said to them, "I've grown very old. 3 You've seen all that the LORD your God has done to all these nations because of you. It is the LORD your God who fights for you. 4 Look. I've allotted to you these remaining nations as a legacy for your tribes, along with all the nations I have destroyed. They stretch from the Jordan to the Mediterranean Sea. 5 The LORD your God will force them out before you and remove them from you. Then you will take over their land, exactly as the LORD your God has promised you. 6 Be very strong. Carefully obey everything written in the Instruction scroll from Moses. Don't deviate a bit from it either to the right or to the left. 7 Don't have anything to do with these nations that remain with you. Don't invoke the names of their gods or take oaths by them. Don't serve them or worship them. 8 Hold on to the LORD your God instead, exactly as you've done right up to today.

9 "The LORD has removed great and powerful nations before you. To this day, no one has stood up to you. 10 A single one of you puts a thousand to flight. This is because the LORD your God fights for you, exactly as he promised you. 11 For your own sake, be very careful to love the LORD your God. 12 But if you should turn away and join the rest of these nations that remain with you, intermarry with them, and associate with each other, 13 then know for certain that the LORD your God won't keep on removing these nations before you. Instead, they will

be a snare and a trap for you. They will be a
whip on your sides and thorns in your eyes,
until you vanish from this fertile land that
the LORD your God has given you.
14“Look. I'm now walking on the road
to death that all the earth must take. You
know with all your heart and being that
not a single one of all the good things that
the LORD your God promised about you
has failed. They were all fulfilled for you.
Not a single one of them has failed. 15But
in the same way that every good thing
that the LORD your God promised about
you has been fulfilled, so the LORD could
bring against you every bad thing as well.
He could wipe you out from this fertile land
that the LORD your God has given you. 16If
you violate the covenant of the LORD your
God, which he commanded you to keep,
and go on to serve other gods and worship
them, then the LORD will be furious with
you. You will quickly vanish from the fertile
land that he has given you.”

What God has done

24 Joshua gathered all the tribes of Israel at Shechem. He summoned the
elders of Israel, its leaders, judges, and officers. They presented themselves before God.
2Then Joshua said to the entire people, “This
is what the LORD, the God of Israel, says:
Long ago your ancestors lived on the other
side of the Euphrates. They served other
gods. Among them was Terah the father of
Abraham and Nahor. 3I took Abraham your
ancestor from the other side of the Euphrates. I led him around through the whole land
of Canaan. I added to his descendants and
gave him Isaac. 4To Isaac I gave Jacob and
Esau. I gave Mount Seir to Esau to take over.
But Jacob and his sons went down to Egypt.
5Then I sent Moses and Aaron. I plagued
Egypt with what I did to them. After that
I brought you out. 6I brought your ancestors out of Egypt, and you came to the sea.
The Egyptians chased your ancestors with
chariots and horses to the Reed Sea.[b] 7Then
they cried for help to the LORD. So he set
darkness between you and the Egyptians.
He brought the sea down on them, and it
covered them. With your own eyes you saw
what I did to the Egyptians. You lived in the
desert for a long time.
8“Then I brought you into the land of the
Amorites who lived on the other side of the
Jordan. They attacked you, but I gave them
into your power, and you took over their
land. I wiped them out before you. 9Then
Moab's King Balak, Zippor's son, set out
to attack Israel. He summoned Balaam,
Beor's son, to curse you. 10But I wasn't
willing to listen to Balaam, so he actually
blessed you. I rescued you from his power.
11Then you crossed over the Jordan. You
came to Jericho, and the citizens of Jericho
attacked you. They were Amorites, Perizzites, Canaanites, Hittites, Girgashites,
Hivites, and Jebusites. But I gave them into
your power. 12I sent the hornet[c] before you.
It drove them out before you and did the
same to the two kings of the Amorites. It
wasn't your sword or bow that did this. 13I
gave you land on which you hadn't toiled
and cities that you hadn't built. You settled
in them and are enjoying produce from vineyards and olive groves that you didn't plant.

Challenge to be faithful

14“So now, revere the LORD. Serve him
honestly and faithfully. Put aside the gods
that your ancestors served beyond the Euphrates and in Egypt and serve the LORD.
15But if it seems wrong in your opinion to
serve the LORD, then choose today whom
you will serve. Choose the gods whom your
ancestors served beyond the Euphrates or the
gods of the Amorites in whose land you live.
But my family and I will serve the LORD.”
16Then the people answered, “God forbid
that we ever leave the LORD to serve other
gods! 17The LORD is our God. He is the one
who brought us and our ancestors up from
the land of Egypt, from the house of bondage. He has done these mighty signs in our
sight. He has protected us the whole way
we've gone and in all the nations through
which we've passed. 18The LORD has driven
out all the nations before us, including the

[b] Or *Red Sea* [c] Heb uncertain

Amorites who lived in the land. We too will serve the LORD, because he is our God."

19 Then Joshua said to the people, "You can't serve the LORD, because he is a holy God. He is a jealous God. He won't forgive your rebellion and your sins. 20 If you leave the LORD and serve foreign gods, then he will turn around and do you harm and finish you off, in spite of having done you good in the past."

21 Then the people said to Joshua, "No! The LORD is the one we will serve."

22 So Joshua said to the people, "You are witnesses against yourselves that you have chosen to serve the LORD."

They said, "We are witnesses!"

23 "So now put aside the foreign gods that are among you. Focus your hearts on the LORD, the God of Israel."

24 The people said to Joshua, "We will serve the LORD our God and will obey him."

Joshua makes a covenant

25 On that day Joshua made a covenant for the people and established just rule for them at Shechem. 26 Joshua wrote these words in God's Instruction scroll. Then he took a large stone and put it up there under the oak in the sanctuary of the LORD. 27 Joshua said to all the people, "This stone will serve here as a witness against us, because it has heard all the LORD's words that he spoke to us. It will serve as a witness against you in case you aren't true to your God." 28 Then Joshua sent the people away to each one's legacy.

Three important graves

29 After these events, Joshua, Nun's son, the LORD's servant, died. He was 110. 30 They buried him within the border of his own legacy, in Timnath-serah in the highlands of Ephraim north of Mount Gaash. 31 Israel served the LORD all the days of Joshua and all the days of the elders who outlived Joshua. They had known every act the LORD had done for Israel.

32 The Israelites had brought up the bones of Joseph from Egypt. They buried them at Shechem in the portion of field that Jacob had purchased for one hundred qesitahs from the descendants of Hamor the father of Shechem. They became a legacy of the descendants of Joseph.

33 Eleazar son of Aaron died. They buried him at Gibeah, which belonged to his son Phinehas. It had been given to him in the highlands of Ephraim.

JUDGES

The tribes and their military conflicts

1 After Joshua's death, the Israelites asked the LORD, "Who should go up first to fight for us against the Canaanites?"

2 The LORD said, "The tribe of Judah will go up. I've handed over the land to them."

3 So the tribe of Judah said to the tribe of Simeon, their brothers, "Come up with us into our territory, and let's fight against the Canaanites. Then we'll go with you into your territory too." So Simeon went with them.

4 When Judah went up, the LORD handed them the Canaanites and Perizzites. They defeated ten thousand men at Bezek. 5 There they found Adoni-bezek at Bezek, fought against him, and defeated the Canaanites and Perizzites. 6 Adoni-bezek fled, but they chased after him, captured him, and cut off his thumbs and big toes. 7 He said, "Seventy kings with severed thumbs and big toes used to pick up scraps under my table, so God has paid me back exactly for what I did." They brought him to Jerusalem, where he died. 8 The people of Judah fought against Jerusalem and captured it. They killed its people with their swords and set the city on fire.

9 Afterward, the people of Judah went down to fight against the Canaanites who lived in the highlands, the southern plain,[a] and the western foothills.[b] 10 Judah

[a]Heb *negeb* [b]Heb *shephelah*

moved against the Canaanites who lived in Hebron, known before as Kiriath-arba, and they defeated Sheshai, Ahiman, and Talmai. 11 From there they moved against those who lived in Debir, known before as Kiriath-sepher. 12 Caleb said, "I'll give my daughter Achsah as a wife to the one who defeats and captures Kiriath-sepher." 13 Othniel son of Kenaz, Caleb's younger brother, captured it; so Caleb gave him his daughter Achsah as a wife. 14 When she arrived, she convinced Othniel to ask her father for a certain piece of land. As she got down from her donkey, Caleb said to her, "What do you want?"

15 Achsah said to Caleb, "Give me a gift. Since you've given me land in the southern plain, give me springs of water." So Caleb gave her the upper and lower springs.

16 The descendants of Moses' father-in-law the Kenite went up with the people of Judah from Palm City into the Judean desert, which was in the southern plain near Arad. They went and lived with the Amalekites.[c] 17 Then the Judahites went with the Simeonites, their brothers, and they defeated the Canaanites who lived in Zephath, and they completely destroyed it. So the city was called Hormah.[d] 18 Judah also captured Gaza, Ashkelon, Ekron, and all their territories. 19 Thus the LORD was with the tribe of Judah, and they took possession of the highlands. However, they didn't drive out those who lived in the plain because they had iron chariots. 20 They gave Hebron to Caleb, just as Moses had commanded, and they drove out from there the three sons of Anak. 21 But the people of Benjamin didn't drive out the Jebusites who lived in Jerusalem. So the Jebusites still live with the people of Benjamin in Jerusalem today.

22 In the same way, Joseph's household went up against Bethel, and the LORD was with them. 23 When they sent men to spy on Bethel, previously named Luz, 24 the spies saw a man coming out of the city, and they said to him, "Show us the way into the city, and we'll be loyal to you in return." 25 So he showed them the way into the city. They killed the city's people with their swords, but they let that man and all his relatives go. 26 The man went to the land of the Hittites and built a city. He named it Luz, which is still its name today.

27 The tribe of Manasseh didn't drive out the people in Beth-shean, Taanach, Dor, Ibleam, Megiddo, or any of their villages. The Canaanites were determined to live in that land. 28 When Israel became stronger they forced the Canaanites to work for them, but they didn't completely drive them out. 29 The tribe of Ephraim didn't drive out the Canaanites living in Gezer, so the Canaanites kept on living there with them.

30 The tribe of Zebulun didn't drive out the people living in Kitron or Nahalol. These Canaanites lived with them but were forced to work for them. 31 The tribe of Asher didn't drive out the people living in Acco, Sidon, Ahlab, Achzib, Helbah, Aphik, or Rehob. 32 The people of Asher settled among the Canaanites in the land because they couldn't drive them out. 33 The tribe of Naphtali didn't drive out the people living in Beth-shemesh or Beth-anath but settled among the Canaanites in the land. The people living in Beth-shemesh and Beth-anath were forced to work for them.

34 The Amorites pushed the people of Dan back into the highlands because they wouldn't allow them to come down to the plain. 35 The Amorites were determined to live in Har-heres, Aijalon, and Shaalbim, but Joseph's household became strong, and the Amorites were forced to work for them. 36 The border of the Amorites ran from the Akrabbim pass, from Sela, and upward.

The LORD's messenger condemns

2 The LORD's messenger came up from Gilgal to Bochim and said, "I brought you up from Egypt and led you into the land that I had promised to your ancestors. I said, 'I will never break my covenant with you, 2 and you are not to make a covenant with those who live in this land. You should

[c] LXX (cf 1 Sam 15:6); MT *people* [d] Or *destruction*

break down their altars.' But you didn't obey me. What have you done? 3So now I tell you, I won't drive them out before you, but they'll be a problem[e] for you, and their gods will be a trap for you." 4When the LORD's messenger spoke these words to all the Israelites, they raised their voices and cried out loud. 5So they named that place Bochim,[f] and they offered a sacrifice to the LORD there.

Death of Joshua and his generation

6When Joshua dismissed the people, the Israelites each went to settle on their own family property in order to take possession of the land. 7The people served the LORD throughout the rest of Joshua's life and throughout the next generation of elders who outlived him, those who had seen all the great things that the LORD had done for Israel. 8Joshua, Nun's son and the LORD's servant, died when he was 110 years old. 9They buried him within the boundaries of his family property in Timnath-heres in the highlands of Ephraim north of Mount Gaash. 10When that whole generation had passed away, another generation came after them who didn't know the LORD or the things that he had done for Israel.

Israel's pattern of sin and punishment

11Then the Israelites did things that the LORD saw as evil: They served the Baals; 12and they went away from the LORD, their ancestors' God, who had brought them out of the land of Egypt. They went after other gods from among the surrounding peoples, they worshipped them, and they angered the LORD. 13They went away from the LORD and served Baal and the Astartes. 14So the LORD became angry with Israel, and he handed them over to raiders who plundered them. He let them be defeated by their enemies around them, so that they were no longer able to stand up to them. 15Whenever the Israelites marched out, the LORD's power worked against them, just as the LORD had warned them. And they were very distressed.

16Then the LORD raised up leaders[g] to rescue them from the power of these raiders. 17But they wouldn't even obey their own leaders because they were unfaithful, following other gods and worshipping them. They quickly deviated from the way of their ancestors, who had obeyed the LORD's commands, and didn't follow their example.

18The LORD was moved by Israel's groaning under those who oppressed and crushed them. So the LORD would raise up leaders for them, and the LORD would be with the leader, and he would rescue Israel from the power of their enemies as long as that leader lived.

19But then when the leader died, they would once again act in ways that weren't as good as their ancestors', going after other gods, to serve them and to worship them. They wouldn't drop their bad practices or hardheaded ways. 20So the LORD became angry with Israel and said, "Because this nation has violated my covenant that I required of their ancestors and hasn't obeyed me, 21I in turn will no longer drive out before them any of the nations that Joshua left when he died." 22As a test for Israel, to see whether they would carefully walk in the LORD's ways just as their ancestors had done, 23the LORD left these nations instead of driving them out immediately or handing them over to Joshua.

Nations remaining in the land

3 These are the nations that the LORD left to test all those Israelites who had no firsthand knowledge of the wars of Canaan. 2They survived only to teach war to the generations of Israelites who had no firsthand knowledge of the earlier wars: 3the five rulers of the Philistines, and all the Canaanites, Sidonians, and Hivites who lived in the highlands of Lebanon from Mount Baal-hermon to Lebo-hamath. 4They were to be the test for Israel, to find out whether they would obey the LORD's commands, which he had made to their ancestors through Moses. 5So the Israelites lived among the Canaanites, Hittites, Amorites, Perizzites, Hivites, and

[e]Heb uncertain [f]Or *weepers or weeping* [g]Or *judges*

Jebusites. [6]But the Israelites intermarried with them and served their gods.

Othniel, the model judge

[7]The Israelites did things that the LORD saw as evil, and they forgot the LORD their God. They served the Baals and the Asherahs.[h] [8]The LORD became angry with Israel and gave them over to King Cushan-rishathaim of Aram-naharaim. The Israelites served Cushan-rishathaim eight years. [9]But then they cried out to the LORD. So the LORD raised up a deliverer for the Israelites, Othniel, Kenaz's son, Caleb's younger brother, who rescued them. [10]The LORD's spirit was in Othniel, and he led Israel. When he marched out for war, the LORD handed over Aram's King Cushan-rishathaim. Othniel overpowered Cushan-rishathaim, [11]and the land was peaceful for forty years, until Othniel, Kenaz's son, died.

Ehud

[12]The Israelites again did things that the LORD saw as evil, and the LORD put Moab's King Eglon in power over them, because they did these things that the LORD saw as evil. [13]He convinced the Ammonites and Amalekites to join him, defeated Israel, and took possession of Palm City. [14]So the Israelites served Moab's King Eglon eighteen years.

[15]Then the Israelites cried out to the LORD. So the LORD raised up a deliverer for them, Ehud, Gera's son, a Benjaminite, who was left-handed. The Israelites sent him to take their tribute payment to Moab's King Eglon. [16]Now Ehud made for himself a double-edged sword that was about a foot and a half long, and he strapped it on his right thigh under his clothes. [17]Then he presented the tribute payment to Moab's King Eglon, who was a very fat man. [18]When he had finished delivering the tribute payment, Ehud sent on their way the people who had carried it. [19]But he himself turned back at the carved stones near Gilgal, and he said, "I have a secret message for you, King."

So Eglon said, "Hush!" and all his attendants went out of his presence. [20]Ehud approached him while he was sitting alone in his cool second-story room, and he said, "I have a message from God for you." At that, Eglon got up from his throne. [21]Ehud reached with his left hand and grabbed the sword from his right thigh. He stabbed it into Eglon's stomach, [22]and even the handle went in after the blade. Since he did not pull the sword out of his stomach, the fat closed over the blade, and his guts spilled out.[i] [23]Ehud slipped out to the porch, and closed and locked the doors of the second-story room behind him.

[24]After Ehud had slipped out, the king's servants came and found that the room's doors were locked. So they thought, He must be relieving himself in the cool chamber. [25]They waited so long that they were embarrassed, but he never opened the doors of the room. Then they used the key to open them, and there was their master lying dead on the ground!

[26]Ehud had gotten away while they were waiting and had passed the carved stones and escaped to Seirah. [27]When he arrived, he blew the ram's horn in the Ephraim highlands. So the Israelites went down from the highlands with Ehud leading them. [28]He told them, "Follow me, for the LORD has handed over your enemies the Moabites." So they followed him, and they took control of the crossing points of the Jordan in the direction of Moab, allowing no one to cross. [29]This time, they defeated the Moabites, about ten thousand big and strong men, and no one escaped. [30]Moab was brought down by the power of Israel on that day, and there was peace in the land for eighty years.

Shamgar

[31]After Ehud, Shamgar, Anath's son, struck down six hundred Philistines with an animal prod. He too rescued Israel.

Deborah, Barak, and Jael

4 After Ehud had died, the Israelites again did things that the LORD saw as evil. [2]So the LORD gave them over to King Jabin

[h]Heb *asherim*; perhaps objects or a pole devoted to the goddess Asherah [i]Heb uncertain

of Canaan, who reigned in Hazor. The commander of his army was Sisera, and he was stationed in Harosheth-ha-goiim. 3 The Israelites cried out to the LORD because Sisera[j] had nine hundred iron chariots and had oppressed the Israelites cruelly for twenty years.

4 Now Deborah, a prophet, the wife of Lappidoth,[k] was a leader of Israel at that time. 5 She would sit under Deborah's palm tree between Ramah and Bethel in the Ephraim highlands, and the Israelites would come to her to settle disputes. 6 She sent word to Barak, Abinoam's son, from Kedesh in Naphtali and said to him, "Hasn't the LORD, Israel's God, issued you a command? 'Go and assemble at Mount Tabor, taking ten thousand men from the people of Naphtali and Zebulun with you. 7 I'll lure Sisera, the commander of Jabin's army, to assemble with his chariots and troops against you at the Kishon River, and then I'll help you overpower him.'"

8 Barak replied to her, "If you'll go with me, I'll go; but if not, I won't go."

9 Deborah answered, "I'll definitely go with you. However, the path you're taking won't bring honor to you, because the LORD will hand over Sisera to a woman." Then Deborah got up and went with Barak to Kedesh. 10 He summoned Zebulun and Naphtali to Kedesh, and ten thousand men marched out behind him. Deborah marched out with him too.

11 Now Heber the Kenite had moved away from the other Kenites, the descendants of Hobab, Moses' father-in-law, and had settled as far away as Elon-bezaanannim, which is near Kedesh.

12 When it was reported to Sisera that Barak, Abinoam's son, had marched up to Mount Tabor, 13 Sisera summoned all of his nine hundred iron chariots and all of the soldiers who were with him from Harosheth-ha-goiim to the Kishon River. 14 Then Deborah said to Barak, "Get up! This is the day that the LORD has handed Sisera over to you. Hasn't the LORD gone out before you?" So Barak went down from Mount Tabor with ten thousand men behind him. 15 The LORD threw Sisera and all the chariots and army into a panic[l] before Barak; Sisera himself got down from his chariot and fled on foot. 16 Barak pursued the chariots and the army all the way back to Harosheth-ha-goiim, killing Sisera's entire army with the sword. No one survived.

17 Meanwhile, Sisera had fled on foot to the tent of Jael, the wife of Heber the Kenite, because there was peace between Hazor's King Jabin and the family of Heber the Kenite. 18 Jael went out to meet Sisera and said to him, "Come in, sir, come in here. Don't be afraid." So he went with her into the tent, and she hid him under a blanket.

19 Sisera said to her, "Please give me a little water to drink. I'm thirsty." So she opened a jug of milk, gave him a drink, and hid him again. 20 Then he said to her, "Stand at the entrance to the tent. That way, if someone comes and asks you, 'Is there a man here?' you can say, 'No.'"

21 But Jael, Heber's wife, picked up a tent stake and a hammer. While Sisera was sound asleep from exhaustion, she tiptoed to him. She drove the stake through his head and down into the ground, and he died. 22 Just then, Barak arrived after chasing Sisera. Jael went out to meet him and said, "Come and I'll show you the man you're after." So he went in with her, and there was Sisera, lying dead, with the stake through his head.

23 So on that day God brought down Canaan's King Jabin before the Israelites. 24 And the power of the Israelites grew greater and greater over Canaan's King Jabin until they defeated him completely.

Deborah's song

5 At that time, Deborah and Barak, Abinoam's son, sang:

2 When hair is long in Israel,
  when people willingly offer
    themselves—bless the LORD!

3 Hear, kings!
  Listen, rulers!

[j] Or *he* [k] Or *a woman of torches* [l] MT adds *before the edge of the sword.*

I, to the LORD,
I will sing.
I will make music to the LORD,
Israel's God.

4 LORD, when you set out from Seir,
when you marched out from Edom's fields,
the land shook,
the sky poured down,
the clouds poured down water.
5 The mountains quaked
before the LORD, the one from Sinai,
before the LORD, the God of Israel.

6 In the days of Shamgar, Anath's son,
in the days of Jael, caravans ceased.
Those traveling by road
kept to the backroads.
7 Villagers disappeared;
they disappeared in Israel,
until you,[m] Deborah, arose,
until you arose as a mother in Israel.
8 When they chose new gods,
then war came to the city gates.[n]
Yet there wasn't a shield
or spear to be seen
among forty thousand in Israel!
9 My heart is with Israel's commanders,
who willingly offered themselves
among the people—bless the LORD!

10 You who ride white donkeys,
who sit on saddle blankets,[o]
who walk along the road: tell of it.
11 To the sound of instruments[p]
at the watering places,
there they repeat the LORD's victories,
his villagers' victories in Israel.

Then the LORD's people marched
down to the city gates.
12 "Wake up, wake up, Deborah!
Wake up, wake up, sing a song!
Arise, Barak!
Capture your prisoners,
Abinoam's son!"
13 Then those who remained marched down
against royalty;
the LORD's people marched down[q]
against warriors.
14 From Ephraim they set out[r]
into the valley,[s]
after you, Benjamin,
with your people!
From Machir
commanders marched down,
and from Zebulun
those carrying the official's staff.
15 The leaders of Issachar came
along with Deborah;
Issachar was attached to Barak,
and was sent into the valley behind him.
Among the clans of Reuben
there was deep soul-searching.
16 "Why did you stay back
among the sheep pens,
listening to the music for the flocks?"
For the clans of Reuben
there was deep soul-searching.
17 Gilead stayed on the other side
of the Jordan,
and Dan, why did he remain
with the ships?
Asher stayed by the seacoast,
camping at his harbors.
18 Zebulun is a people
that readily risked death;
Naphtali too in the high countryside.

19 Kings came and made war;
the kings of Canaan fought
at Taanach by Megiddo's waters,
but they captured no spoils of silver.
20 The stars fought from the sky;
from their orbits
they fought against Sisera.
21 The Kishon River swept them away;
the advancing river, the Kishon River.
March on, my life, with might!

22 Then the horses' hooves pounded
with the galloping,
galloping of their stallions.
23 "Curse Meroz,"
says the LORD's messenger,
"curse its inhabitants bitterly,

[m] Or *I* [n] Heb uncertain [o] Heb uncertain [p] Heb uncertain [q] Heb adds *for me.* [r] Or *From Ephraim their root* [s] LXX; MT *in Amalek*

because they didn't come
to the LORD's aid,
to the LORD's aid against the warriors."

24 May Jael be blessed above all women;
may the wife of Heber the Kenite
be blessed above all
tent-dwelling women.
25 He asked for water, and she provided milk;
she presented him cream
in a majestic bowl.
26 She reached out her hand for the stake,
her strong hand
for the worker's hammer.
She struck Sisera;
she crushed his head;
she shattered and pierced his skull.
27 At her feet he sank, fell, and lay flat;
at her feet he sank, he fell;
where he sank, there he fell—dead.

28 Through the window she watched,
Sisera's mother looked longingly[t]
through the lattice.
"Why is his chariot taking
so long to come?
Why are the hoofbeats
of his chariot horses delayed?"
29 Her wisest attendants answer;
indeed, she replies to herself:
30 "Wouldn't they be finding
and dividing the loot?
A girl or two for each warrior;
loot of colored cloths for Sisera;
loot of colored, embroidered cloths;
two colored, embroidered cloths
as loot for every neck."

31 May all your enemies perish
like this, LORD!
But may your allies be like the sun,
rising in its strength.

And the land was peaceful for forty years.

Oppression by the Midianites

6 The Israelites did things that the LORD
saw as evil, and the LORD handed them
over to the Midianites for seven years.
2 The power of the Midianites prevailed
over Israel, and because of the Midianites, the Israelites used crevices and caves
in the mountains as hidden strongholds.
3 Whenever the Israelites planted seeds,
the Midianites, Amalekites, and other easterners would invade. 4 They would set up
camp against the Israelites and destroy the
land's crops as far as Gaza, leaving nothing
to keep Israel alive, not even sheep, oxen,
or donkeys. 5 They would invade with their
herds and tents, coming like a swarm of locusts, so that no one could count them or
their camels. They came into the land to
destroy it. 6 So Israel became very weak on
account of Midian, and the Israelites cried
out to the LORD.

7 This time when the Israelites cried out
to the LORD because of Midian, 8 the LORD
sent them a prophet, who said to them,
"The LORD, Israel's God, proclaims: I myself brought you up from Egypt, and I led
you out of the house of slavery. 9 I delivered
you from the power of the Egyptians and
from the power of all your oppressors. I
drove them out before you and gave you
their land. 10 I told you, 'I am the LORD your
God; you must not worship the gods of the
Amorites, in whose land you are living.' But
you have not obeyed me."

Gideon's commissioning

11 Then the LORD's messenger came and
sat under the oak at Ophrah that belonged
to Joash the Abiezrite. His son Gideon was
threshing wheat in a winepress to hide it
from the Midianites. 12 The LORD's messenger appeared to him and said, "The LORD is
with you, mighty warrior!"

13 But Gideon replied to him, "With all
due respect, my Lord, if the LORD is with
us, why has all this happened to us? Where
are all his amazing works that our ancestors
recounted to us, saying, 'Didn't the LORD
bring us up from Egypt?' But now the LORD
has abandoned us and allowed Midian to
overpower us."

14 Then the LORD turned to him and said,
"You have strength, so go and rescue Israel

[t] LXX; MT *cried*

from the power of Midian. Am I not personally sending you?"

[15]But again Gideon said to him, "With all due respect, my Lord, how can I rescue Israel? My clan is the weakest in Manasseh, and I'm the youngest in my household."

[16]The LORD replied, "Because I'm with you, you'll defeat the Midianites as if they were just one person."[u]

[17]Then Gideon said to him, "If I've gained your approval, please show me a sign that it's really you speaking with me. [18]Don't leave here until I return, bring out my offering, and set it in front of you."

The Lord replied, "I'll stay until you return."

[19]So Gideon went and prepared a young goat and used an ephah[v] of flour for unleavened bread. He put the meat in a basket and the broth in a pot and brought them out to him under the oak and presented them. [20]Then God's messenger said to him, "Take the meat and the unleavened bread and set them on this rock, then pour out the broth." And he did so. [21]The LORD's messenger reached out the tip of the staff that was in his hand and touched the meat and the unleavened bread. Fire came up from the rock and devoured the meat and the unleavened bread; and the LORD's messenger vanished before his eyes. [22]Then Gideon realized that it had been the LORD's messenger. Gideon exclaimed, "Oh no, LORD God! I have seen the LORD's messenger face-to-face!"

[23]But the LORD said to him, "Peace! Don't be afraid! You won't die."

[24]So Gideon built an altar there to the LORD and called it "The LORD makes peace." It still stands today in Ophrah of the Abiezrites.

[25]That night the LORD said to him, "Take your father's bull and a second bull seven years old. Break down your father's altar to Baal and cut down the Asherah[w] that is beside it. [26]Build an altar to the LORD your God in the proper way on top of this high ground. Then take the second bull and offer it as an entirely burned offering with the wood of the Asherah that you cut down." [27]So Gideon took ten of his servants and did just as the LORD had told him. But because he was too afraid of his household and the townspeople to do it during the day, he did it at night.

[28]When the townspeople got up early in the morning, there was the altar to Baal broken down, with the asherah image that had been beside it cut down, and the second bull offered on the newly built altar! [29]They asked each other, "Who did this?" They searched and investigated, and finally they concluded, "Gideon, Joash's son, did this!" [30]The townspeople said to Joash, "Bring out your son for execution because he tore down the altar to Baal and cut down the Asherah that was beside it."

[31]But Joash replied to all who were lined up against him, "Will you make Baal's complaint for him? Will you come to his rescue? Anyone who argues for him will be killed before morning. If he is a god, let him argue for himself, because it was his altar that was torn down." [32]So on that day Gideon became known as Jerubbaal, meaning, "Let Baal argue with him," because he tore down his altar.

Gideon seeks a sign

[33]Some time later, all the Midianites, Amalekites, and other easterners joined together, came over, and set up camp in the Jezreel Valley. [34]Then the LORD's spirit came over Gideon, and he sounded the horn and summoned the Abiezrites to follow him. [35]He sent messengers into all of Manasseh, and they were also summoned to follow him. Then he sent messengers into Asher, Zebulun, and Naphtali too, and they marched up to meet them.

[36]But then Gideon said to God, "To see if you really intend to rescue Israel through me as you have declared, [37]I'm now putting a wool fleece on the threshing floor. If there is dew only on the fleece but all the ground is dry, then I'll know that you are going to rescue Israel through me, as you have declared." [38]And that is what happened. When he got

[u]Or *each and every one of them* [v]An ephah is approximately twenty quarts. [w]Heb *asherim*; perhaps objects or a pole devoted to the goddess Asherah

up early the next morning and squeezed
the fleece, he wrung out enough dew from
the fleece to fill a bowl with water.
39Then Gideon said to God, "Don't be
angry with me, but let me speak just one
more time. Please let me make just one
more test with the fleece: now let only
the fleece be dry and let dew be on all the
ground." 40And God did so that night. Only
the fleece was dry, but there was dew on all
the ground.

Battle with Midian

7 Then Jerubbaal, that is, Gideon, and
all of the people with him rose early
and set up camp beside the Harod spring;
Midian's camp was north of theirs, in the
valley by the Moreh hill. 2The LORD said
to Gideon: "You have too many people on
your side. If I were to hand Midian over to
them, the Israelites might claim credit for
themselves rather than for me, thinking,
We saved ourselves. 3So now, announce in
the people's hearing, 'Anyone who is afraid
or unsteady may return home from Gideon's mountain.'"[x] At this, twenty-two thousand people went home, and ten thousand
were left.
4The LORD said to Gideon, "There are
still too many people. Take them down
to the water, and I will weed them out for
you there. Whenever I tell you, 'This one
will go with you,' he should go with you;
but whenever I tell you, 'This one won't
go with you,' he should not go." 5So he
took the people down to the water. And
the LORD said to Gideon, "Set aside those
who lap the water with their tongues, as
a dog laps, from those who bend down on
their knees to drink." 6The number of men
who lapped was three hundred, and all the
rest of the people bent down on their knees
to drink water, with their hands to their
mouths.[y] 7Then the LORD said to Gideon,
"With the three hundred men who lapped
I will rescue you and hand over the Midianites to you. Let everyone else go home."
8So the people gathered their supplies and
trumpets,[z] and Gideon sent all the Israelites home, but kept the three hundred.
Now Midian's camp was below Gideon
in the valley. 9That night the LORD said to
him, "Get up and attack the camp, because
I've handed it over to you. 10But if you're
afraid to attack, go down to the camp with
your servant Purah, 11and you'll hear what
they are saying. May you then get the
courage to attack the camp." So he went
down with his servant Purah to the outpost
of the armies that were in the camp. 12The
Midianites, Amalekites, and other easterners were spread across the valley like
a swarm of locusts; their camels were too
many to count, like the grains of sand on
the seashore.
13Just when Gideon arrived, there was
a man telling his friend about a dream. He
said, "Get this! I had a dream that a loaf of
barley bread was rolling into the Midianite
camp. It came to a tent and hit it, and the
tent collapsed. In fact, it rolled the tent
over upside down, so it fell flat."
14His friend replied, "Can this be anything other than the sword of the Israelite
Gideon, Joash's son? God has handed over
Midian and its entire camp to him!"
15When Gideon heard the telling of the
dream and its meaning, he worshipped.
Then he returned to the Israelite camp
and said, "Get up! The LORD has handed
over the Midianite camp to you." 16He divided the three hundred men into three
units and equipped every man with a
trumpet and an empty jar, with a torch
inside each jar. 17"Now watch me," he ordered them, "and do what I do. When I get
to the outpost of the camp, do just what
I do. 18When I blow the trumpet, along
with all who are with me, then you blow
the trumpets, all of you surrounding the
whole camp. And then shout, 'For the
LORD and for Gideon!'"
19Gideon and one hundred of his men
moved to the outpost of the camp at the
middle watch of the night, when they had
just changed the guards. Then they blew

[x] Or *Mount Gilead* [y] MT places the words *with their hands to their mouths* after the word *lapped*. [z] Or *the ones who lapped took the people's supplies and trumpets for themselves.*

the trumpets and smashed the jars that were in their hands. 20 So the three units blew their trumpets and broke their jars, holding the torches with their left hands and blowing the trumpets in their right hands. And they called out, "A sword for the LORD and for Gideon!" 21 Each man stood fast in his position around the camp, and the entire camp took off running, shouting, and fleeing. 22 When the three hundred trumpets sounded, the LORD turned the swords of fellow soldiers against each other throughout the whole camp. The camp fled as far as Beth-shittah toward Zererah, to the border of Abel-meholah, beside Tabbath.

23 The Israelites from Naphtali, Asher, and all of Manasseh were called out, and they chased after the Midianites. 24 Then Gideon sent messengers into all of the Ephraim highlands, saying, "Go down to meet the Midianites and take control of the Jordan's waters as far as Beth-barah." So all the Ephraimite men were called out, and they took control of the Jordan's waters as far as Beth-barah. 25 They also captured two Midianite officers, Oreb and Zeeb. They killed Oreb at Oreb's Rock, and killed Zeeb at Zeeb's Winepress. Then they went on chasing the Midianites, and they brought the heads of Oreb and Zeeb to Gideon on the other side of the Jordan.

Gideon's acts of vengeance

8 Then the Ephraimites said to him, "Why did you offend us this way by not calling us when you went to fight the Midianites?" And they argued with him fiercely.

2 But he said to them, "What have I done now, compared to you? Aren't Ephraim's leftovers better than Abiezer's main harvest? 3 God handed you the Midianite officers Oreb and Zeeb. What have I been able to do compared to you?" When he said this, their anger against him passed.

4 Then Gideon came to the Jordan. As he and the three hundred men with him crossed over, they were exhausted but still giving chase. 5 So he said to the people of Succoth, "Please give some loaves of bread to those who are on foot, because they're exhausted, but I'm chasing Zebah and Zalmunna, the kings of Midian."

6 But the officials of Succoth replied, "Haven't you already almost gotten your hands on Zebah and Zalmunna? Why should we give food to your army now?"

7 "Just for that," Gideon said, "when the LORD has handed over Zebah and Zalmunna to me, I'm going to beat your skin with desert thorns and briars!" 8 From there he went up to Penuel and made the same request. And the people of Penuel responded in the same way the people of Succoth had. 9 So he also told the people of Penuel, "When I return in victory,[a] I'll break down this tower!"

10 Now Zebah and Zalmunna were in Karkor with their camp, about fifteen thousand men, all the ones who were left from the easterners' entire camp. One hundred twenty thousand armed men had fallen. 11 Gideon marched up the caravan road[b] east of Nobah and Jogbehah, and attacked the camp while it was off-guard. 12 Zebah and Zalmunna fled, and he chased after them. He captured the two Midianite kings Zebah and Zalmunna and threw the entire army into panic.

13 Then Gideon, Joash's son, returned from the battle by the Heres Pass. 14 He captured a young man from the people of Succoth and interrogated him. He listed for Gideon the seventy-seven officials and elders of Succoth. 15 So Gideon went to the people of Succoth and said, "Here are Zebah and Zalmunna! You made fun of me because of them by saying, 'Haven't you already almost gotten your hands on Zebah and Zalmunna? Why should we give food to your exhausted men now?'" 16 Then he seized the city's elders, and he beat[c] the people of Succoth with desert thorns and briars. 17 He also broke down Penuel's tower, and killed the city's people.

18 Then he asked Zebah and Zalmunna, "What kind of men were those whom you killed at Tabor?"

They replied, "They were just like you; each one looked like a king's son."

[a]Or *in peace* [b]Or *the road of the tent dwellers* [c]Cf 8:7, cf LXX; MT *he taught a lesson to*

[19]"They were my brothers," Gideon said,
"my own mother's sons. As surely as the
LORD lives, I promise that if you had let
them live, I wouldn't kill you!" [20]So he ordered his oldest son Jether, "Stand up and
kill them." But the young man didn't draw
his sword because he was afraid, since he
was still young.
[21]So Zebah and Zalmunna said, "You
stand up and strike us yourself, because
as they say, 'A man is measured by his
strength!'" So Gideon stood up and killed
Zebah and Zalmunna, and took the cres-
cents that were on their camels' necks.

Gideon's request

[22]Then the Israelites said to Gideon,
"Rule over us, you and then your son and
then your grandson, because you've rescued us from Midian's power."
[23]Gideon replied to them, "I'm not the
one who will rule over you, and my son
won't rule over you either. The LORD rules
over you." [24]But Gideon said to them, "May
I make one request of you? Everyone give
me the earrings from their loot"; the Midianites had worn gold earrings because they
were Ishmaelites.
[25]"We'll gladly give them," they replied.
And they spread out a piece of cloth, and
everyone pitched in the earrings from their
loot. [26]The weight of the gold earrings that
he requested was one thousand seven hundred shekels of gold, not counting the cres-
cents, the pendants, and the purple robes
worn by the Midianite kings, or the collars
that were on their camels' necks. [27]Gideon
fashioned a priestly vest[d] out of it, and put
it in his hometown of Ophrah. All Israel became unfaithful there because of it, and it
became a trap for Gideon and his household.
[28]So Midian was brought down before
the Israelites and no longer raised its head.
The land was peaceful for forty years during
Gideon's time.

Gideon's death

[29]Jerubbaal, Joash's son, went home to
live with his own household. [30]Gideon had
seventy sons of his own because he had
many wives. [31]His secondary wife who was
in Shechem also bore him a son, and he
named him Abimelech. [32]Gideon, Joash's
son, died at a good old age and was buried
in the tomb of his father Joash in Ophrah
of the Abiezrites.
[33]Right after Gideon died, the Israelites once again acted unfaithfully by worshipping the Baals, setting up Baal-berith
as their god. [34]The people of Israel didn't
remember the LORD their God, who had
delivered them from the power of all their
enemies on every side. [35]Nor did they act
loyally toward the household of Jerubbaal,
that is, Gideon, in return for all the good
that he had done on Israel's behalf.

Abimelech becomes a king

9 Abimelech, Jerubbaal's son, went to
his mother's brothers in Shechem. He
spoke to them and to the entire clan of the
household to which his mother belonged:
[2]"Ask all the leaders of Shechem, 'Which do
you think is better to have ruling over you:
seventy men—all of Jerubbaal's sons—or
one man?' And remember that I'm your
flesh and blood!"
[3]So his mother's brothers spoke all these
words on his behalf to all the leaders of
Shechem. They decided to follow Abimelech because they said, "He's our relative."
[4]They gave him seventy pieces of silver
from the temple of Baal-berith, with which
Abimelech hired worthless and reckless
men, who became his posse. [5]He went
to his household in Ophrah and killed
all seventy of his brothers, Jerubbaal's
sons, on a single stone. Only Jotham the
youngest of Jerubbaal's sons survived, because he had hidden himself. [6]Then all the
leaders of Shechem and all Beth-millo assembled and proceeded to make Abimelech king by the oak at the stone pillar[e] in
Shechem.

Jotham's fable

[7]When Jotham was told about this, he
went and stood on the top of Mount Gerizim.

[d]Heb *ephod* [e]Heb uncertain

He raised his voice and called out, “Listen to
me, you leaders of Shechem, so that God may
listen to you!
8“Once the trees went out to anoint a
king over themselves. So they said to the
olive tree, ‘Be our king!’
9“But the olive tree replied to them,
‘Should I stop producing my oil, which is
how gods and humans are honored, so that
I can go to sway over the trees?’
10“So the trees said to the fig tree, ‘You
come and be king over us!’
11“The fig tree replied to them, ‘Should I
stop producing my sweetness and my delicious fruit, so that I can go to sway over the
trees?’
12“Then the trees said to the vine, ‘You
come and be king over us!’
13“But the vine replied to them, ‘Should
I stop providing my wine that makes gods
and humans happy, so that I can go to sway
over the trees?’
14“Finally, all the trees said to the thornbush, ‘You come and be king over us!’
15“And the thornbush replied to the
trees, ‘If you’re acting faithfully in anointing me king over you, come and take shelter
in my shade; but if not, let fire come out of
the thornbush and burn up the cedars of
Lebanon.’
16“So now, if you acted faithfully and innocently when you made Abimelech king,
and if you’ve done right by Jerubbaal and
his household, and have treated him as his
actions deserve—17my father fought for you
and risked his life to rescue you from Midian’s
power, 18but today you’ve risen up against
my father’s household, killed his seventy
sons on a single stone, and made Abimelech,
his female servant’s son, king over the leaders of Shechem, because he’s your relative—
19so if you’ve acted faithfully and innocently
toward Jerubbaal and his household today,
then be happy with Abimelech and let him
be happy with you. 20But if not, let fire come
out from Abimelech and burn up the leaders
of Shechem and Beth-millo; and let fire come
out from the leaders of Shechem and Beth-
millo and burn up Abimelech.”

21Then Jotham ran away. He fled to Beer
and stayed there for fear of his brother
Abimelech.

Abimelech’s monarchy fails

22Abimelech ruled over Israel for three
years. 23Then God stirred up ill will between
Abimelech and the leaders of Shechem, and
they acted like traitors toward Abimelech.
24This occurred because of the violence
done to Jerubbaal’s seventy sons. Their
blood came back on their brother Abimelech, who killed them, and on the leaders of Shechem, who supported him when
he killed his brothers. 25As an act against
him, the leaders of Shechem set ambushes
on the hilltops that robbed everyone who
passed by them on the road. This was reported to Abimelech.
26Then Gaal, Ebed’s son, and his relatives
came passing through Shechem, and the
leaders of Shechem shifted their allegiance
to him. 27They went out into the field, cut
off clusters from their vineyards, trampled
them out, and had a celebration. They entered their god’s temple and ate, drank,
and made fun of Abimelech. 28Gaal, Ebed’s
son, said, “Who is Abimelech, and who
are we of Shechem that we ought to serve
him? Didn’t this son of Jerubbaal and his
deputy Zebul once serve the men of Hamor,
Shechem’s father? Why should we of all
people serve him? 29If only this people were
under my command! I would push Abimelech aside! I[f] would tell Abimelech, ‘Build up
your army and march out for battle.’ ”
30When Zebul the city’s ruler heard
the words of Gaal, Ebed’s son, he became
angry. 31He sent messengers to Abimelech at Arumah[g] to say, “Watch out! Gaal,
Ebed’s son, and his relatives have come
to Shechem and are stirring up the city
against you. 32Now, you and the men who
are with you: Get up tonight and set an
ambush in the fields. 33Then in the morning, at sunrise, rise early and rush on the
city. Just as he and the men with him are
marching out to face you, you can do to
him whatever you wish.”

[f]LXX; MT *he* [g]Cf 9:41; Heb *Tormah*

[34]So Abimelech and all the men who were with him got up that night and set an ambush around Shechem in four companies. [35]When Gaal, Ebed's son, came out and stood in the entrance of the city's gate, Abimelech and the men with him sprang up from the ambush. [36]Gaal saw the men and said to Zebul, "Look! People are coming down from the hilltops."

Zebul replied to him, "The shadows on the hills just look like persons to you."

[37]But Gaal spoke up again, "Look! People are coming down from Tabbur-erez, and one company is coming from the direction of Elon-meonenim."[h]

[38]Then Zebul replied to him, "Where's all your talk now, you who said, 'Who is Abimelech that we ought to serve him?' Aren't these the men you despised? Now march out and fight them!" [39]So Gaal marched out at the head of the leaders of Shechem and fought with Abimelech. [40]Abimelech routed him, and he ran away. Many fell wounded, all the way up to the entrance of the gate. [41]Afterward, Abimelech stayed in Arumah, and Zebul drove away Gaal and his relatives so they couldn't stay in Shechem.

[42]The next day, the men of Shechem went out into the fields. When it was reported to Abimelech, [43]he took his men, divided them into three companies, and set an ambush in the fields. As soon as he saw the men coming from the city, he sprang upon them and attacked them. [44]Abimelech and his company charged forward and took a position at the entrance of the city's gate, while the other two companies charged at all those in the fields and attacked them. [45]Abimelech fought against the city that entire day. He captured the city and killed its people. Then he leveled the city and scattered salt over it.

[46]When all the leaders in the Tower of Shechem heard about this, they entered the side rooms in the El-berith temple. [47]It was reported to Abimelech that all the leaders from the Tower of Shechem had gathered in one place. [48]So Abimelech and all the men who were with him went up on Mount Zalmon. He grabbed an ax, cut off a bundle of branches, and hoisted them onto his shoulder. Then he ordered the men who were with him, "Hurry up and do what you've seen me do!" [49]Each one of the men cut off a bundle as well and followed Abimelech. They piled them up against the side rooms and set fire to the side rooms above them. So all the people in the Tower of Shechem died too, about one thousand men and women.

[50]Then Abimelech moved on to Thebez, set up camp against it, and captured it. [51]But there was a strong tower inside the city. All the men and women and all the city's leaders had fled there, shut themselves inside, and climbed to the tower's roof. [52]Abimelech came to the tower to storm it. But when he approached the tower's entrance to set it on fire, [53]a woman dropped an upper millstone on Abimelech's head and cracked his skull. [54]He quickly cried out to the servant who carried his armor, "Draw your sword and kill me. Don't let it be said of me, 'A woman killed him.'" So his servant stabbed him, and he died. [55]When the Israelites saw that Abimelech was dead, they all went home.

[56]Thus God paid back Abimelech for the evil he had done to his father by killing his seventy brothers. [57]God also paid back the people of Shechem for their evil. The curse of Jotham, Jerubbaal's son, had come upon them.

Tola and Jair

10 After Abimelech, Tola son of Puah and grandson of Dodo, a man of Issachar, arose to rescue Israel. He lived in Shamir in the Ephraim highlands. [2]For twenty-three years he led Israel; then he died and was buried in Shamir.

[3]After Tola, Jair from Gilead arose, and he led Israel for twenty-two years. [4]He had thirty sons who were mounted on thirty donkeys and controlled thirty towns in the land of Gilead—these are still known as Havvoth-jair today. [5]When Jair died, he was buried in Kamon.

[h]*Or the Diviners' Oak*

Israel's unfaithfulness and oppression by the Ammonites

6Then the Israelites again did things
that the LORD saw as evil. They served the
Baals and the Astartes, as well as the gods
of Aram, Sidon, Moab, the Ammonites,
and the Philistines. They went away from
the LORD and didn't serve him. 7The LORD
became angry with Israel and handed them
over to the Philistines and the Ammonites.
8Starting that year and for the next eighteen years, they beat and bullied the Israelites, especially all the Israelites who lived
on the east side of Jordan in the territory
of the Ammonites in Gilead. 9The Ammonites also crossed the Jordan to make
raids into Judah, Benjamin, and the households of Ephraim. So Israel was greatly
distressed.

10Then the Israelites cried out to the
LORD, "We've sinned against you, for we
went away from our God and served the
Baals."

11The LORD replied to the Israelites,
"When the Egyptians, Amorites, Ammonites, Philistines, 12Sidonians, Amalekites,
and Maonites oppressed you and you cried
out to me, didn't I rescue you from their
power? 13But you have gone away from
me and served other gods, so I won't rescue you anymore! 14Go cry out to the gods
you've chosen. Let them rescue you in the
time of your distress."

15The Israelites responded to the LORD,
"We've sinned. Do to us whatever you see as
right, but please save us this time." 16They
put away the foreign gods from among
them and served the LORD. And the LORD
could no longer stand to see Israel suffer.

17The Ammonites called out their army
and made camp in Gilead, while the Israelites gathered and set up their camp at
Mizpah. 18Gilead's rulers said to each other,
"Whoever is willing to launch the attack
against the Ammonites will become the
leader over all those living in Gilead."

Rise of Jephthah

11 Now Jephthah the Gileadite was a
mighty warrior. Gilead was his father,
but he was a prostitute's son. 2Gilead's
wife gave birth to other sons for him, and
when his wife's sons grew up, they drove
Jephthah away. They told him, "You won't
get an inheritance in our father's household
because you're a different woman's son."
3So Jephthah ran away from his brothers
and lived in the land of Tob. Worthless men
gathered around Jephthah and became his
posse.

4Sometime afterward, the Ammonites
made war against Israel. 5And when the
Ammonites attacked Israel, Gilead's elders
went to bring Jephthah back from the land
of Tob. 6They said to him, "Come be our
commander so we can fight against the
Ammonites."

7But Jephthah replied to Gilead's elders,
"Aren't you the ones who hated me and
drove me away from my father's household? Why are you coming to me now when
you're in trouble?"

8Gilead's elders answered Jephthah,
"That may be, but now we're turning back
to you, so come with us and fight the Ammonites. Then you'll become the leader
over us and everyone who lives in Gilead."

9And Jephthah said to Gilead's elders, "If
you bring me back to fight the Ammonites
and the LORD gives them over to me, I alone
will be your leader."

10Gilead's elders replied to him, "The
LORD is our witness; we will surely do what
you've said." 11So Jephthah went with Gilead's elders, and the people made him leader
and commander over them. At Mizpah before the LORD, Jephthah repeated everything he had said.

12Then Jephthah sent messengers to the
Ammonite king, saying, "What is the problem between us that you've come against
me to make war in my land?"

13The Ammonite king responded to
Jephthah's messengers, "When the Israelites were coming up from Egypt, they
seized my land from the Arnon to the Jabbok and all the way to the Jordan. Now give
it back peacefully!"

14Then Jephthah again sent messengers to the Ammonite king 15and said to
him, "Jephthah states: Israel didn't seize
the land of the Moabites or the land of the

Ammonites. 16When they were coming up from Egypt, the Israelites went through the desert to the Reed Sea[i] and came to Kadesh. 17Then the Israelites sent messengers to the king of Edom, saying, 'Please allow us to pass through your land'; but the Edomite king refused. They sent the same request to the king of Moab, and he was unwilling. So the Israelites stayed at Kadesh.

18"Later they journeyed into the desert but went around the lands of Edom and Moab, arriving on the east side of the land of Moab and setting up camp on the other side of the Arnon. They never entered Moabite territory, because the Arnon was the boundary of Moab. 19Then the Israelites sent messengers to Sihon king of the Amorites and king of Heshbon and said to him, 'Please allow us to pass through your land to our own place.' 20Yet Sihon didn't trust the Israelites to pass through his territory. He assembled his entire army, set up camp at Jahaz, and went to war with the Israelites. 21The LORD, Israel's God, handed over Sihon and his entire army to the Israelites, and they defeated Sihon. So the Israelites took possession of all the land of the Amorites who were living in that area. 22They took possession of all the Amorite territory from the Arnon to the Jabbok and from the desert to the Jordan.

23"So now that the LORD, Israel's God, has driven out the Amorites before his people Israel, will you take possession of their land? 24Shouldn't you possess what Chemosh your god has given you to possess? And shouldn't we possess everything that the LORD our God has given us to possess? 25Do you now have a better case than Moab's King Balak, Zippor's son? Did he make an accusation against the Israelites or go to war with them? 26Why didn't you take back this territory while the Israelites lived in Heshbon and its villages, in Aroer and its villages, and in all the towns along the branches of the Arnon for three hundred years? 27I haven't sinned against you, but you're doing me wrong by making war against me. Let the LORD, who is the judge, decide today between the Israelites and the Ammonites!"

28But the Ammonite king refused to listen to the message that Jephthah sent to him.

Jephthah's promise

29Then the LORD's spirit came on Jephthah. He passed through Gilead and Manasseh, then through Mizpah in Gilead, and from there he crossed over to the Ammonites. 30Jephthah made a solemn promise to the LORD: "If you will decisively hand over the Ammonites to me, 31then whatever comes out the doors of my house to meet me when I return victorious from the Ammonites will be given over to the LORD. I will sacrifice it as an entirely burned offering." 32Jephthah crossed over to fight the Ammonites, and the LORD handed them over to him. 33It was an exceptionally great defeat; he defeated twenty towns from Aroer to the area of Minnith, and on as far as Abel-keramim. So the Ammonites were brought down before the Israelites.

34But when Jephthah came to his house in Mizpah, it was his daughter who came out to meet him with tambourines and dancing! She was an only child; he had no other son or daughter except her. 35When he saw her, he tore his clothes and said, "Oh no! My daughter! You have brought me to my knees! You are my agony! For I opened my mouth to the LORD, and I can't take it back."

36But she replied to him, "My father, you've opened your mouth to the LORD, so you should do to me just what you've promised. After all, the LORD has carried out just punishment for you on your enemies the Ammonites." 37Then she said to her father, "Let this one thing be done for me: hold off for two months and let me and my friends wander the hills in sadness, crying over the fact that I never had children."

38"Go," he responded, and he sent her away for two months. She and her friends walked on the hills and cried because she would never have children.

39When two months had passed, she

[i]Or *Red Sea*

returned to her father, and he did to her
what he had promised. She had not known
a man intimately. But she gave rise to a
tradition in Israel where 40 for four days
every year Israelite daughters would go
away to recount the story of the Gileadite
Jephthah's daughter.

Jephthah defeats the Ephraimites

12 The Ephraimites were called up for
battle and crossed over to Zaphon.
They said to Jephthah, "Why did you cross
over to fight the Ammonites and not call us
to go with you? We're going to burn down
your house over you!"
2 Jephthah replied to them, "My people
and I were in a great conflict with the Ammonites. But when I cried out to you, you
didn't rescue me from their power. 3 When
I saw that you weren't going to rescue me, I
risked my own life and crossed over against
the Ammonites, and the LORD handed
them over to me. So why have you marched
against me today to fight me?"
4 So Jephthah gathered all the men of
Gilead and fought the Ephraimites. The
Gileadites defeated the Ephraimites, because they had said, "You are fugitives from
Ephraim! Gilead stands within Ephraim
and Manasseh."
5 The Gileadites took control of the Jordan's crossing points into Ephraim. Whenever one of the Ephraimite fugitives said,
"Let me cross," the Gileadites would ask
him, "Are you an Ephraimite?" If he said,
"No," 6 they would tell him, "Then say *shib-
boleth*." But he would say, "*sibboleth*," because he couldn't pronounce it correctly.
So they would seize him and kill him at the
Jordan's crossing points. Forty-two thousand of the Ephraimites fell at that time.
7 Jephthah led Israel for six years. Then
Jephthah the Gileadite died and was buried
in one of the towns in Gilead.

Ibzan, Elon, and Abdon

8 After Jephthah, Ibzan from Bethlehem
led Israel. 9 He had thirty sons and thirty
daughters. He married his thirty daughters
to those outside his clan, and brought in
thirty young women from outside for his
sons. He led Israel for seven years. 10 Then
Ibzan died and was buried in Bethlehem.
11 After Ibzan, Elon from Zebulun led Israel; he did so for ten years. 12 Then Elon the
Zebulunite died and was buried in Aijalon
in the land of Zebulun.
13 After Elon, Abdon, Hillel's son from
Pirathon, led Israel. 14 He had forty sons and
thirty grandsons mounted on seventy donkeys. He led Israel for eight years. 15 Then
Abdon, Hillel's son from Pirathon, died
and was buried in Pirathon in the land of
Ephraim, in the Amalekite highlands.

Samson's birth

13 The Israelites again did things that
the LORD saw as evil, and he handed
them over to the Philistines for forty years.
2 Now there was a certain man from
Zorah, from the Danite clan, whose name
was Manoah. His wife was unable to become pregnant and had not given birth to
any children. 3 The LORD's messenger appeared to the woman and said to her, "Even
though you've been unable to become pregnant and haven't given birth, you are now
pregnant and will give birth to a son! 4 Now
be careful not to drink wine or brandy or
to eat anything that is ritually unclean, 5 because you are pregnant and will give birth
to a son. Don't allow a razor to shave his
head, because the boy is going to be a nazirite for God from birth. He'll be the one
who begins Israel's rescue from the power
of the Philistines."
6 Then the woman went and told her husband, "A man of God came to me, and he
looked like God's messenger—very scary! I
didn't ask him where he was from, and he
didn't tell me his name. 7 He said to me, 'You
are pregnant and will give birth to a son, so
don't drink wine or brandy or eat anything
that is ritually unclean, because the boy is
going to be a nazirite for God from birth
until the day he dies.'"
8 Manoah asked the LORD, "Please, my
Lord," he said, "let the man of God whom
you sent come back to us once more, so he
can teach us how we should treat the boy
who is to be born."
9 God listened to Manoah, and God's

messenger came once more to the woman.
She was sitting in the field, but her husband
Manoah wasn't with her. 10So the woman
hurriedly ran and informed her husband.
She said to him, "The man who came to me
the other day has just appeared to me."
11Manoah got up and followed his wife.
He came to the man and said to him, "Are
you the man who spoke to this woman?"

"I am," he replied.

12Manoah said, "Now when your words
come true, what should be the rules for the
boy and how he should act?"
13The LORD's messenger answered Manoah, "The woman should be careful to do
everything that I told her. 14She must not
consume anything that comes from the
grapevine, drink wine or brandy, or eat
anything that is ritually unclean. She must
be careful to do everything I have commanded her."
15Manoah said to the LORD's messenger,
"Please let us persuade you to stay so we
can prepare a young goat for you."
16But the LORD's messenger replied to
Manoah, "If you persuaded me to stay, I
wouldn't eat your food. If you prepare an
entirely burned offering, offer it to the
LORD." Indeed, Manoah didn't know that
he was the LORD's messenger. 17Manoah
said to the LORD's messenger, "What's your
name, so that we may honor you when your
words come true?"
18The LORD's messenger responded to
him, "Why do you ask my name? You couldn't
understand it."
19So Manoah took a young goat and a
grain offering and offered them on a rock to
the LORD. While Manoah and his wife were
looking, an amazing thing happened: 20as
the flame from the altar went up toward the
sky, the LORD's messenger went up in the
altar's flame. When Manoah and his wife
saw this, they fell facedown on the ground.
21The LORD's messenger didn't reappear to
Manoah or his wife, and Manoah then realized that it had been the LORD's messenger.
22Manoah said to his wife, "We are certainly
going to die, because we've seen God!"
23But his wife replied to him, "If the
LORD wanted to kill us, he wouldn't have
accepted the entirely burned offering and
grain offering from our hands. He wouldn't
have shown us all these things or told us all
of this now."
24The woman gave birth to a son and
named him Samson. The boy grew up,
and the LORD blessed him. 25The LORD's
spirit began to move him when he was in
Mahaneh-dan, between Zorah and Eshtaol.

Samson's marriage to a Philistine woman

14 Samson traveled down to Timnah.
While he was in Timnah, a Philistine
woman caught his eye. 2He went back home
and told his father and mother, "A Philistine woman in Timnah caught my eye; now
get her for me as a wife!"
3But his father and mother replied to
him, "Is there no woman among your own
relatives or among all our people that you
have to go get a wife from the uncircumcised Philistines?"

Yet Samson said to his father, "Get her
for me, because she's the one I want!" 4His
father and mother didn't know that the
LORD was behind this. He was looking for
an opening with the Philistines, because
they were ruling over Israel at that time.
5Then Samson traveled down to Timnah
with his father and mother. When he came
to the vineyards in Timnah, suddenly a
lone young lion came roaring to meet him.
6The LORD's spirit rushed over him, and he
tore the lion apart with his bare hands as
one might tear apart a young goat. But he
didn't tell his father or mother what he had
done. 7Then he traveled down and talked
with the woman; she was the one Samson
wanted.
8After a while, he came back again to
marry her. He turned aside to look at the
lion's remains, and there was a swarm of
bees with honey inside the lion's skeleton.
9He scooped the honey into his hands, eating it as he continued along. When he got
to his father and mother, he gave some to
them, and they ate it too. But he didn't tell
them that he had scooped the honey from
the lion's skeleton.
10His father traveled down to the

woman, and Samson put on a feast there,
as was the custom for young men. 11When
the townspeople saw him, they selected
thirty companions to be with him. 12Then
Samson said to them, "Let me tell you a
riddle. If you can figure it out and tell me
the answer within the seven days of the
feast, I'll give you thirty linen robes and
thirty sets of clothes. 13But if you can't tell
me the answer, then it's you who have to
give me thirty linen robes and thirty sets
of clothes."

So they replied to him, "Tell your riddle;
let's hear it."

14He said to them,

"Out of the eater
 there came something to eat.
Out of the strong
 there came something sweet."

For three days they couldn't tell the
answer to the riddle. 15On the fourth[j] day
they said to Samson's wife, "Seduce your
husband so he'll tell us the answer to the
riddle, or else we'll set fire to you and your
household. Were we invited here just to become poor?"

16So Samson's wife cried on his shoulder
and said, "You hate me! You don't love me!
You told a riddle to my people but didn't tell
me the answer."

He replied to her, "Look, I haven't even
told the answer to my father and mother.
Why should I tell it to you?" 17But she cried
on his shoulder for the rest of the seven days
of the feast. Finally, on the seventh day, he
told her the answer, for she had nagged him.
And she told her people the answer to the
riddle. 18So on the seventh day, before the
sun set, the townspeople said to him,

"What's sweeter than honey?
 What's stronger than a lion?"

He replied to them,

"If you hadn't plowed with my heifer,
 you wouldn't have figured out
  my riddle!"

19Then the LORD's spirit rushed over
him, and he went down to Ashkelon. He
killed thirty of their men, stripped them of
their gear, and gave the sets of clothes to the
ones who had told the answer to the riddle.
In anger, he went back up to his father's
household. 20And Samson's wife married
one of those who had been his companions.

Samson attacks the Philistines

15 Later on, at the time of the wheat
harvest, Samson went to visit his
wife, bringing along a young goat. He said,
"Let me go into my wife's bedroom."

But her father wouldn't allow him to go
in. 2Her father said, "I was so sure that you
had completely rejected her that I gave her
in marriage to one of your companions.
Don't you think her younger sister is even
better? Let her be your wife instead."

3Samson replied, "No one can blame me
now for being ready to bring down trouble
on the Philistines!"

4Then Samson went and caught three
hundred foxes. He took torches, turned
the foxes tail to tail, and put a torch between each pair of tails. 5He lit the torches
and released the foxes into the Philistines'
grain fields. So he burned the stacked
grain, standing grain, vineyards, and olive
orchards.

6The Philistines inquired, "Who did this?"

So it was reported, "Samson the Tim-
nite's son-in-law did it, because his father-
in-law gave his wife in marriage to one of
his companions." So the Philistines went up
and burned her and her father to death.

7Samson then responded to them, "If
this is how you act, then I won't stop until
I get revenge on you!" 8He struck them
hard, taking their legs right out from under
them.[k] Then he traveled down and stayed in
a cave in the rock at Etam.

9The Philistines marched up, made camp
in Judah, and released their forces on Lehi.
10The people of Judah asked, "Why have
you marched up against us?"

"We've marched up to take Samson prisoner," they replied, "and to do to him just
what he did to us."

11So three thousand people from Judah
traveled down to the cave in the rock at
Etam and said to Samson, "Don't you real-

[j] LXX, Syr; MT *seventh* [k] Or *struck them hip and thigh*

ize that the Philistines rule over us? What have you done to us?”

But he told them, “I did to them just what they did to me.”

[12]Then the people of Judah said to him, “We’ve come down to take you prisoner so we can turn you over to the Philistines.”

Samson responded to them, “Just promise that you won’t attack me yourselves.”

[13]“We won’t,” they said to him. “We’ll only take you prisoner so we can turn you over to them. We won’t kill you.” Then they tied him up with two new ropes, and brought him up from the rock.

[14]When Samson arrived at Lehi, the Philistines met him and came out shouting. The LORD’s spirit rushed over him, the ropes on his arms became like burned-up linen, and the ties melted right off his hands. [15]He found a donkey’s fresh jawbone, picked it up, and used it to attack one thousand men. [16]Samson said,

“With a donkey’s jawbone,
stacks on stacks!
With a donkey’s jawbone,
I’ve killed one thousand men.”

[17]When he finished speaking, he tossed away the jawbone. So that place became known as Ramath-lehi.[l]

[18]Now Samson was very thirsty, so he called out to the LORD, “You are the one who allowed this great victory to be accomplished by your servant’s hands. Am I now going to die of thirst and fall into the hands of the uncircumcised?” [19]So God split open the hollow rock in Lehi, and water flowed out of it. When Samson drank, his energy returned and he was recharged. Thus that place is still called by the name En-hakkore[m] in Lehi today.

[20]Samson led Israel for twenty years during the time of the Philistines.

Samson and the prostitute

16 One day Samson traveled to Gaza. While there, he saw a prostitute and had sex with her. [2]The word spread[n] among the people of Gaza, “Samson has come here!” So they circled around and waited in ambush for him all night at the city gate. They kept quiet all night long, thinking, We’ll kill him at the first light in the morning. [3]But Samson slept only half the night. He got up in the middle of the night, grabbed the doors of the city gate and the two gateposts, and pulled them up with the bar still across them. He put them on his shoulders and carried them up to the top of the hill that is beside Hebron.

Samson and Delilah

[4]Some time after this, in the Sorek Valley, Samson fell in love with a woman whose name was Delilah. [5]The rulers of the Philistines confronted her and said to her, “Seduce him and find out what gives him such great strength and what we can do to overpower him, so that we can tie him up and make him weak. Then we’ll each pay you eleven hundred pieces of silver.”

[6]So Delilah said to Samson, “Please tell me what gives you such great strength and how you can be tied up and made weak.”

[7]Samson replied to her, “If someone ties me up with seven fresh bowstrings that aren’t dried out, I’ll become weak. I’ll be like any other person.” [8]So the rulers of the Philistines brought her seven fresh bowstrings that weren’t dried out, and she tied him up with them.

[9]While an ambush was waiting for her signal in an inner room, she called out to him, “Samson, the Philistines are on you!” And he snapped the bowstrings like a thread of fiber snaps when it touches a flame. So the secret of his strength remained unknown.

[10]Then Delilah said to Samson, “You made a fool out of me and lied to me. Now please tell me how you can really be tied up!”

[11]He replied to her, “If someone ties me up with new ropes that haven’t been used for work, I’ll become weak. I’ll be like any other person.”

[12]So Delilah took new ropes and tied him up with them. Then she called out to him, “Samson, the Philistines are on you!” Once again, an ambush was waiting in an inner

[l]Or *Jawbone Hill* [m]Or *Caller’s Spring* [n]LXX; MT lacks *spread.*

room. Yet he snapped them from his arms like thread.

13And Delilah said to Samson, "Up to now, you've made a fool out of me and lied to me. Tell me how you can be tied up!"

He responded to her, "If you weave the seven braids of my hair into the fabric on a loom and pull it tight with a pin, then I'll become weak. I'll be like any other person."[o]

14So she got him to fall asleep, wove the seven braids of his hair into the fabric on a loom,[p] and pulled it tight with a pin. Then she called out to him, "Samson, the Philistines are on you!" He woke up from his sleep and pulled loose the pin, the loom, and the fabric.

15Delilah said to him, "How can you say, 'I love you,' when you won't trust me? Three times now you've made a fool out of me and not told me what gives you such great strength!" 16She nagged him with her words day after day and begged him until he became worn out to the point of death.

17So he told her his whole secret. He said to her, "No razor has ever touched my head, because I've been a nazirite for God from the time I was born. If my head is shaved, my strength will leave me, and I'll become weak. I'll be like every other person."

18When Delilah realized that he had told her his whole secret, she sent word to the rulers of the Philistines, "Come one more time, for he has told me his whole secret." The rulers of the Philistines came up to her and brought the silver with them.

19She got him to fall asleep with his head on her lap. Then she called a man and had him shave off the seven braids of Samson's hair. He began to weaken,[q] and his strength left him. 20She called out, "Samson, the Philistines are on you!"

He woke up from his sleep and thought, I'll escape just like the other times and shake myself free. But he didn't realize that the LORD had left him. 21So the Philistines captured him, put out his eyes, and took him down to Gaza. They bound him with bronze chains, and he worked the grinding mill in the prison.

22But the hair on his head began to grow again right after it had been shaved.

Samson's death

23The rulers of the Philistines gathered together to make a great sacrifice to their god Dagon and to hold a celebration. They cheered, "Our god has handed us Samson our enemy!" 24When the people saw him, they praised their god, for they said, "Our god has handed us our enemy, the very one who devastated our land and killed so many of our people." 25At the height of the celebration,[r] they said, "Call for Samson so he can perform for us!" So they called Samson from the prison, and he performed in front of them. Then they had him stand between the pillars.

26Samson said to the young man who led him by the hand, "Put me where I can feel the pillars that hold up the temple, so I can lean on them." 27Now the temple was filled with men and women. All the rulers of the Philistines were there, and about three thousand more men and women were on the roof watching as Samson performed. 28Then Samson called out to the LORD, "LORD God, please remember me! Make me strong just this once more, God, so I can have revenge on the Philistines, just one act of revenge for my two eyes."[s] 29Samson grabbed the two central pillars that held up the temple. He leaned against one with his right hand and the other with his left. 30And Samson said, "Let me die with the Philistines!" He strained with all his might, and the temple collapsed on the rulers and all the people who were in it. So it turned out that he killed more people in his death than he did during his life.

31His brothers and his father's entire household traveled down, carried him back up, and buried him between Zorah and Eshtaol in the tomb of his father Manoah. He had led Israel for twenty years.

[o]LXX; MT lacks *and pull it . . . other person.* [p]LXX; MT lacks *so she got him . . . on a loom.* [q]LXX; MT *she began to torment him.* [r]Or *When their hearts were glad* [s]Or *so I can have revenge on the Philistines for one of my two eyes*

Micah's sanctuary and the Levite priest

17 Once there was a man named Micah who lived in the Ephraim highlands. 2 He said to his mother, "The eleven hundred pieces of silver that were taken from you led you to declare a curse and even to repeat it when I could hear. I have that silver. I'm the one who took it, and now I'll give it back to you."[t]

His mother replied, "May the LORD bless you, my son!" 3 When he gave the eleven hundred pieces of silver back to his mother, she said, "I wholeheartedly devote this silver to the LORD, to be made into a sculpted image and a molded image for my son." 4 So he gave the silver back to his mother, and she took two hundred pieces of silver and gave them to a silversmith, who used it for a sculpted image and a molded image. And they were placed in Micah's house. 5 This man Micah had his own sanctuary.[u] He made a priestly vest[v] and divine images[w] and appointed one of his sons to be his personal priest. 6 In those days there was no king in Israel; each person did what they thought to be right.

7 Now there was a young man from Bethlehem in Judah, from the area of the Judahite clan. He was a Levite residing there as an immigrant. 8 The man left the town of Bethlehem in Judah to settle as an immigrant wherever he could find a place. He came to Micah's house in the Ephraim highlands while he was making his way.[x]

9 "Where are you from?" Micah asked him.

He replied, "I'm a Levite from Bethlehem in Judah, and I'm looking to settle as an immigrant anywhere I can find a place."

10 So Micah said to him, "Stay with me and be a father and a priest to me, and I'll give you ten pieces of silver a year, a set of clothes, and your basic needs."[y] 11 The Levite agreed to stay with him; and the young man became like one of his own sons. 12 Micah appointed the Levite so that the young man became his personal priest and lived in Micah's sanctuary. 13 And Micah said to himself, Now I know that the LORD will give me good things, because a Levite has become my priest.

Dan's search for a land

18 In those days there was no king in Israel. Also in those days the tribe of Dan was searching for a territory of their own to live in, since no permanent territory had been assigned to them among the tribes of Israel up to that point. 2 The Danites sent five men from their whole clan, strong men from Zorah and Eshtaol, to spy on the land and explore it. They told them, "Go explore the land." So they went into the Ephraim highland as far as Micah's house, and they spent the night there. 3 When they were in the area of Micah's house, they recognized the accent of the young Levite. They turned in there and said to him, "Who brought you here? What are you doing in these parts? What is there for you here?"

4 "Micah has done a lot for me," he replied to them. "He hired me to be his personal priest."

5 They said to him, "Ask for an answer from God so we can know whether we'll be successful on this trip we've taken."

6 The priest replied to them, "Go in peace. The LORD is watching over you on this trip you've taken."

7 So the five men journeyed on until they reached Laish. There they saw that its people were living without worry in the same way as the Sidonians, undisturbed and secure. Nobody held back anything in the land, so no one had to hoard.[z] Yet they lived far away from the Sidonians and had no dealings with anyone else.[a]

8 When the men came back to their relatives at Zorah and Eshtaol, they asked them, "What did you find?"

9 "Come on," they replied, "let's march up against them! Indeed, we've seen the land, and it's very good. Right now you're doing nothing! Don't hold back from going and taking possession of the land. 10 When you arrive, you'll come upon a secure people

[t] The words *and now I'll give it back to you* are relocated from the end of 17:3 in Heb. [u] Or *god's house* [v] Heb *ephod* [w] Heb *terafim* [x] Or *to carry on his work* [y] Heb adds *and the Levite went.* [z] Heb uncertain [a] Or *with Aram*

and a wide-open land, because God has given to you a place where nothing on earth is lacking." [11]At this, six hundred men from the Danite clan at Zorah and Eshtaol set out armed for battle. [12]They marched up and made camp at Kiriath-jearim in Judah. This is why the place west of Kiriath-jearim is still known as Dan's Camp today. [13]From there they crossed into the Ephraim highlands and came to Micah's house.

Dan acquires a levitical priest

[14]Then the five men who had gone to spy on the land around Laish reported to their relatives, "Did you know that there is a priestly vest, divine images, a sculpted image, and a molded image in these buildings? Now think about what you should do!" [15]So they turned in there and went to the young Levite's house in Micah's compound and greeted him. [16]While the six hundred Danites armed for battle stood at the entrance of the gate, [17]the five men who had gone to spy on the land moved up, went inside, and took the sculpted image, the priestly vest, the divine images, and the molded image. The priest was standing at the entrance of the gate with the six hundred men armed for battle [18]when these five entered Micah's sanctuary and took the sculpted image, the priestly vest, the divine images, and the molded image.

The priest said to them, "What are you doing?"

[19]"Shut up!" they said to him. "Put your hand over your mouth! Come with us and be a father and a priest for us. Would you rather be a priest for one man's household or a priest for a tribe and a clan in Israel?" [20]The priest was convinced, so he took the priestly vest, the divine images, and the sculpted image and went along with the people.

[21]They headed back on their way, but they put the children, the livestock, and the prized possessions in front of them. [22]After they had gone a good distance away from Micah's house, the men who were in the houses around Micah's home were summoned for battle and caught up to the Danites. [23]They called out to the Danites, who turned around and said to Micah, "Why have you summoned men for battle?"

[24]Micah replied, "You've taken my gods that I made, and the priest, and have gone off! What do I have left? How can you ask me what is wrong?"

[25]But the Danites said to him, "Don't raise your voice with us or else hotheaded men will attack you, and you and your household will lose your lives." [26]Then the Danites went on their way. When Micah realized that they were too strong for him, he turned around and went home.

The Danites take possession of Laish

[27]The Danites took along the things that Micah had made, as well as the priest who had been with him, and came to Laish, to a people who were undisturbed and secure. They killed the people and burned down the city. [28]No one was there to rescue them because the city was far away from Sidon and had no dealings with anyone else.[b] It was in the Beth-rehob Valley.

They rebuilt the city and settled in it. [29]They renamed the city Dan, after their ancestor Dan who had been one of Israel's sons; but in fact, the original name of the city was Laish. [30]The Danites set up the sculpted image for themselves, and Jonathan son of Gershom and grandson of Moses,[c] and his sons became priests for the Danite tribe until the land went into exile. [31]They kept for themselves the sculpted image that Micah had made throughout the whole time that God's sanctuary was in Shiloh.

A Levite, a woman, and her father

19 In those days when there was no king in Israel, there was a certain Levite living as an immigrant in the far corners of the Ephraim highlands. He married a secondary wife from Bethlehem in Judah. [2]In an act of unfaithfulness toward him, his secondary wife left him and went back to her father's household at Bethlehem in

[b]*Or with Aram* [c]*Or Manasseh*

Judah. She stayed there four full months. 3Then her husband set out after her to convince her to come back. He had his servant and a couple of donkeys with him. She took him into her father's house, and when the young woman's father saw him, he was happy to welcome him. 4Since his father-in-law, the young woman's father, insisted, he stayed with him three days, eating, drinking, and spending the night there.

5On the fourth day, they got up early in the morning, and he got ready to set out. But the young woman's father said to his son-in-law, "Eat a little food to give you strength, and then you can go." 6So the two of them sat down and ate and drank together. The young woman's father said to the man, "Why not spend the night and enjoy yourself?" 7When the man got ready to set out, his father-in-law persuaded him, and he spent the night there again. 8On the fifth day, he got up early in the morning to set out, and the young woman's father said, "Have some food for strength." So the two of them ate, sitting around until late in the day. 9When the man got ready to set out with his secondary wife and servant, his father-in-law, the young woman's father, said, "Look, the day has turned to evening, so spend the night. Seriously, the day is over. Spend the night here and enjoy yourself. Then you can get up early tomorrow for your journey, and you can head home."

10But the man was unwilling to spend another night. He got up, set out, and went as far as the area of Jebus, that is, Jerusalem. He had a couple of saddled donkeys and his secondary wife with him. 11When they were near Jebus, the day was totally gone. The servant said to his master, "Come on, let's turn into this Jebusite city and spend the night in it."

12But his master replied to him, "We won't turn into a city of foreigners who aren't Israelites. We'll travel on to Gibeah. 13"Come on," he said to his servant, "let's reach Gibeah or Ramah and spend the night in one of those places." 14So they traveled on, and the sun set when they were near Gibeah in Benjamin. 15They turned in to enter there, so they could spend the night in Gibeah, and he went and sat down in the city square. But no one offered to take them home to spend the night.

Rape and murder at Gibeah

16Then in the evening, an old man was coming home from his daily work in the fields. This man was from the Ephraim highlands and was an immigrant in Gibeah, the people of that place being Benjaminites. 17He looked up and saw the traveler in the city square. "Where are you heading and where have you come from?" the old man asked.

18"We're traveling from Bethlehem in Judah to the far corners of the Ephraim highlands," he replied to the old man. "That's where I'm from. I went to Bethlehem in Judah, and I'm heading to my home.[d] But no one has offered to take me in tonight. 19We've got our own straw and feed for our donkeys, plus food and wine to provide for me, the woman, and my servant with us. We don't need anything."

20The old man answered, "You're welcome to stay with me,[e] but let me take care of all your needs. Just don't spend the night in the square." 21And he took him into his house. He mixed feed for the donkeys, and they washed their feet, ate, and drank.

22While they were relaxing, suddenly the men of the city, a perverse bunch, surrounded the house and started pounding on the door. They said to the old man, the owner of the house, "Send out the man who came to your house, so we can have sex with him!"

23The owner of the house went outside and said to them, "No, my friends, please don't commit such an evil act, given that this man has come to my home as a guest. Don't do this disgraceful thing! 24Here's my daughter, the young woman, and his secondary wife. Let me send them out, and you can abuse them and do whatever you want to them. But don't do such a disgraceful thing to this man!" 25But the men refused to listen to him.

[d] LXX; MT *to the* LORD*'s house* [e] Or *Peace be with you*

So the Levite grabbed his secondary wife and sent her outside to them. They raped her and abused her all night long until morning. They finally let her go as dawn was breaking.

26 At daybreak, the woman came and collapsed at the door of the man's house where her husband was staying, where she lay until it was daylight. 27 When her husband got up in the morning, he opened the doors of the house and went outside to set out on his journey. And there was his secondary wife, lying at the entrance of the house, with her hands clutching the doorframe. 28 "Get up," he said to her, "let's go." But there was no response. So he laid her across a donkey, and the man set out for home. 29 When he got home, he picked up a knife, took his secondary wife, and chopped her, limb by limb, into twelve pieces. Then he sent them into all the areas of Israel. 30 Everyone who saw it said, "Has such a thing ever happened or been seen since the time when the Israelites came up from the land of Egypt until today? Think about it, decide what to do, and speak out!"

Civil war between the Benjaminites and the Israelites

20 Then all the Israelites from Dan to Beer-sheba, as well as from the area of Gilead, marched out, and the group assembled as one body in the LORD's presence at Mizpah. 2 The commanders of the people and of all the tribes of Israel took their place in the assembly of God's people, four hundred thousand foot soldiers armed with swords. 3 And the Benjaminites got word that the Israelites had marched up to Mizpah.

The Israelites inquired, "Tell us how this evil act happened."

4 So the Levite, the husband of the murdered woman, answered, "My secondary wife and I came to Gibeah of Benjamin to spend the night, 5 and the leading citizens of Gibeah tried to attack me. They surrounded me in the house at night and were determined to kill me. They abused my secondary wife until she died. 6 I took her, chopped her up, and sent her pieces into every part of Israel's territory, because they had committed a disgraceful act in Israel. 7 All you Israelites, say what you think should be done here and now!"

8 At this, all the people stood as one to say, "Not a single one of us is going home or returning to our house! 9 This is what we're now going to do to Gibeah: We'll march up[f] against it as the lot determines. 10 From all the tribes of Israel, we'll get ten men for every hundred, one hundred for every thousand, and one thousand for every ten thousand to take supplies for the troops who are going to pay back[g] Gibeah of Benjamin for the disgraceful act they've done in Israel." 11 So all the Israelites joined together and were united as one against the city.

12 The Israelite tribes sent men throughout the whole tribe of Benjamin with this message: "What about this evil act that happened among you? 13 Now hand over those perverse men in Gibeah so that we can execute them and remove the evil from Israel." But the Benjaminites refused to comply with the demand of their own relatives the Israelites. 14 Instead, the Benjaminites from all the cities came together at Gibeah to march out for battle against the Israelites. 15 On that day, the Benjaminites called up from their cities twenty-six thousand men armed with swords, not counting those living in Gibeah.[h] 16 Out of this entire army, seven hundred specially chosen men were left-handed, and every one of them could sling a stone at a hair and not miss. 17 Not counting Benjamin, the Israelites called up four hundred thousand men armed with swords, and every one of them was a trained warrior.

18 Then the Israelites marched up to Bethel to ask for direction from God. They inquired, "Who should go up first to fight against the Benjaminites for us?"

And the LORD said, "Let the tribe of Judah be first."

[f] LXX; MT lacks *We'll march up.* [g] Cf LXX; Heb uncertain [h] LXX, Vulg, Syr; MT adds *seven hundred specially chosen men were called up.*

[19]So the next morning, the Israelites got up and camped near Gibeah. [20]They marched out to fight against the Benjaminites, lining up in battle formation against them at Gibeah. [21]But the Benjaminites marched out from Gibeah and cut down twenty-two thousand Israelite men that day.

[23][i]So the Israelites went back up and wept before the LORD until evening. They asked the LORD, "Should we move in again to fight our relatives the Benjaminites?"

And the LORD replied, "March out against them."

[22]The Israelite troops regrouped and lined up in battle formation again in the same place they had lined up the first day. [24]The Israelites moved in against the Benjaminites the second day. [25]But the Benjaminites marched out of Gibeah to meet them on that second day and cut down another eighteen thousand Israelite men, all of whom were armed with swords.

[26]Then all the Israelite troops went back up to Bethel and wept, just sitting there in the LORD's presence. They fasted that whole day until evening. Then they offered entirely burned offerings and well-being sacrifices to the LORD. [27]Now in those days the chest containing God's covenant was there, [28]and Phinehas, Eleazar's son and Aaron's grandson, was in charge of ministering before it. The Israelites asked the LORD, "Should we march out once again to fight our relatives the Benjaminites or should we give up?"

And the LORD replied, "March up, for I'll hand them to you tomorrow."

[29]So the Israelites set ambushes around Gibeah. [30]Three days later, the Israelites marched out against the Benjaminites. They lined up for battle against Gibeah as before. [31]When the Benjaminites came out to meet them, they were drawn away from the city. They began to strike down some of the troops just like the last time, about thirty Israelites along the main roads, one of which goes up to Bethel and one to Gibeah, as well as in the open fields. [32]The Benjaminites thought, *They're being wiped out before us like the first time.* But the Israelites had planned, *We'll retreat and draw them away from the city toward the main roads.* [33]The Israelites moved from their position and reformed their battle lines at Baal-tamar. Then the Israelites who had been set in ambush charged out from their positions west of Gibeah.[j] [34]Ten thousand specially chosen men from all the Israelites came against Gibeah. The fighting was fierce, and the Benjaminites didn't realize that disaster was almost on them. [35]The LORD wiped out the Benjaminites before Israel. The Israelites slaughtered twenty-five thousand one hundred Benjaminite men that day, all of them armed with swords. [36]Then the Benjaminites saw that they had been defeated.

The Israelites had given ground to the Benjaminites because they relied on the ambush that they had set around Gibeah. [37]Indeed, those in the ambush had dashed swiftly into Gibeah and killed all the people in the city with their swords. [38]The plan between the main force of the Israelites and those in the ambush was that when they sent up a big cloud of smoke from the city, [39]the Israelites would turn around in battle. The Benjaminites had begun to defeat some of the Israelites and had killed about thirty men, thinking, *They are definitely going to be wiped out before us, as in the first battle!* [40]But then the column of smoke began to rise from the city. When the Benjaminites looked back, there was the entire city going up in smoke to the sky. [41]The main force of the Israelites turned around, and the Benjaminites lost heart, because they recognized that disaster had fallen on them. [42]They turned back before the Israelites in the direction of the desert, but the fighting caught up with them, and those from the towns were slaughtering them there.[k] [43]They encircled the Benjaminites, chased them from Nohah,[l] and trampled them to the east of Gibeah. [44]Eighteen thousand Benjaminites fell, all of whom were strong warriors. [45]When they turned back and fled toward the desert to the rock of Rimmon,

[i]20:22 and 20:23 are reversed. [j]Heb *Geba* [k]Heb uncertain [l]LXX; MT *to a resting place*

the Israelites picked off another five thousand men on the main roads. And when they caught up with them at Gidom, they struck down two thousand more.

46 All in all, the total number of Benjaminites who fell that day was twenty-five thousand men, all of whom were armed with swords and were strong warriors. 47 Six hundred men turned back and fled toward the desert to the rock of Rimmon. They stayed at the rock of Rimmon for four months. 48 But the Israelites turned their attention to the rest of the Benjaminites and massacred them entirely—the city, the people, even the animals, and everything else they found. They also burned down every city they came across.

Wives for the Benjaminites

21 The Israelites had made a pledge at Mizpah, declaring, "None of us will allow his daughter to marry a Benjaminite." 2 But the people came to Bethel and sat there until evening before God, raising their voices and crying bitterly. 3 "LORD, God of Israel," they said, "why has this happened among us that as of today one tribe will be missing from Israel?" 4 And the next day, the people got up early and built an altar there. They offered entirely burned offerings and well-being sacrifices.

5 Then the Israelites asked, "Were there any out of all the tribes of Israel who didn't march up to the assembly before the LORD?" Indeed, they had made a solemn pledge that anyone who didn't march up before the LORD at Mizpah would be put to death. 6 The Israelites had a change of heart concerning their relatives the Benjaminites. They said, "Today one tribe has been cut off from Israel. 7 What can we do to provide wives for the ones who are left, since we ourselves have made a pledge before the LORD not to allow our daughters to marry them?" 8 So they asked, "Is there anyone from the tribes of Israel who didn't march up before the LORD at Mizpah?" There was! No one from Jabesh-gilead had come to the assembly at the camp. 9 When the people's attendance was taken, not one of those who lived in Jabesh-gilead had been there.

10 The community dispatched twelve thousand warriors there with these orders: "Go kill all the people in Jabesh-gilead, including women and children. 11 Here's what you should do: Exterminate every man and every woman who has slept with a man." 12 Among the people of Jabesh-gilead, they found four hundred young women who had not known a man intimately or slept with one, and they brought them to the camp at Shiloh in the land of Canaan. 13 The whole community then sent word to the Benjaminites who were at the rock of Rimmon and offered them a truce.[m] 14 So the Benjaminites returned at that time, and they gave them the women from Jabesh-gilead that they had allowed to live. Even so, there weren't enough for them.

15 Since the people had a change of heart concerning the Benjaminites because the LORD had caused a rupture in the tribes of Israel, 16 the community elders said, "What can we do to provide wives for the ones who are left, seeing that the Benjaminite women have been destroyed? 17 There must be a surviving line for those who remain from Benjamin," they continued, "so that a tribe won't be erased from Israel. 18 But we can't allow our daughters to marry them, for we Israelites have made this pledge: 'Let anyone who provides a wife for Benjamin be cursed!' 19 However," they said, "the annual festival of the LORD is under way in Shiloh, which is north of Bethel, east of the main road that goes up from Bethel to Shechem, and south of Lebonah." 20 So they instructed the Benjaminites, "Go and hide like an ambush in the vineyards 21 and watch. At the moment the women of Shiloh come out to participate in the dances, rush out from the vineyards. Each one of you, capture a wife for yourself from the women of Shiloh and go back to the land of Benjamin. 22 When their fathers or brothers come to us to object, we'll tell them, 'Do us a favor for their sake. We didn't capture enough women for every

m Or *peace*

man during the battle, and this way you
are not guilty because you didn't give them
anything willingly.'" 23And that is what the
Benjaminites did. They took wives for their
whole group from the dancers whom they
abducted. They returned to their territory,
rebuilt the cities, and lived in them. 24Like-
wise, the Israelites set out from there at
that time, heading home to their respec-
tive tribes and clans. They all left there for
their own territories.
25In those days there was no king in
Israel; each person did what they thought
to be right.

RUTH

The family in Moab

1 During the days when the judges ruled,
there was a famine in the land. A man
with his wife and two sons went from Bethlehem of Judah to dwell in the territory of
Moab. 2The name of that man was Elimelech, the name of his wife was Naomi, and
the names of his two sons were Mahlon and
Chilion. They were Ephrathites from Bethlehem in Judah. They entered the territory
of Moab and settled there.
3But Elimelech, Naomi's husband, died.
Then only she was left, along with her two
sons. 4They took wives for themselves,
Moabite women; the name of the first was
Orpah and the name of the second was Ruth.
And they lived there for about ten years.
5But both of the sons, Mahlon and Chilion, also died. Only the woman was left,
without her two children and without her
husband.
6Then she arose along with her daughters-
in-law to return from the field of Moab, because while in the territory of Moab she had
heard that the LORD had paid attention to his
people by providing food for them. 7She left
the place where she had been, and her two
daughters-in-law went with her. They went
along the road to return to the land of Judah.
8Naomi said to her daughters-in-law,
"Go, turn back, each of you to the household of your mother. May the LORD deal
faithfully with you, just as you have done
with the dead and with me. 9May the LORD
provide for you so that you may find security, each woman in the household of her
husband." Then she kissed them, and they
lifted up their voices and wept.
10But they replied to her, "No, instead we
will return with you, to your people."
11Naomi replied, "Turn back, my daughters. Why would you go with me? Will there
again be sons in my womb, that they would
be husbands for you? 12Turn back, my
daughters. Go. I am too old for a husband.
If I were to say that I have hope, even if I
had a husband tonight, and even more, if
I were to bear sons—13would you wait until
they grew up? Would you refrain from having a husband? No, my daughters. This is
more bitter for me than for you, since the
LORD's will has come out against me."
14Then they lifted up their voices and
wept again. Orpah kissed her mother-in-
law, but Ruth stayed with her. 15Naomi said,
"Look, your sister-in-law is returning to her
people and to her gods. Turn back after
your sister-in-law."
16But Ruth replied, "Don't urge me to
abandon you, to turn back from following
after you. Wherever you go, I will go; and
wherever you stay, I will stay. Your people
will be my people, and your God will be
my God. 17Wherever you die, I will die, and
there I will be buried. May the LORD do this
to me and more so if even death separates
me from you." 18When Naomi saw that
Ruth was determined to go with her, she
stopped speaking to her about it.
19So both of them went along until they
arrived at Bethlehem. When they arrived
at Bethlehem, the whole town was excited
on account of them, and the women of the
town asked, "Can this be Naomi?"
20She replied to them, "Don't call
me Naomi,[a] but call me Mara,[b] for the

[a]Naomi means *pleasant*. [b]Mara means *bitter*.

Almighty[c] has made me very bitter. [21]I went away full, but the LORD has returned me empty. Why would you call me Naomi, when the LORD has testified against me, and the Almighty has deemed me guilty?"

[22]Thus Naomi returned. And Ruth the Moabite, her daughter-in-law, returned with her from the territory of Moab. They arrived in Bethlehem at the beginning of the barley harvest.

Gleaning in Bethlehem

2 Now Naomi had a respected relative, a man of worth, through her husband from the family of Elimelech. His name was Boaz. [2]Ruth the Moabite said to Naomi, "Let me go to the field so that I may glean among the ears of grain behind someone in whose eyes I might find favor."

Naomi replied to her, "Go, my daughter." [3]So she went; she arrived and she gleaned in the field behind the harvesters. By chance, it happened to be the portion of the field that belonged to Boaz, who was from the family of Elimelech.

[4]Just then Boaz arrived from Bethlehem. He said to the harvesters, "May the LORD be with you."

And they said to him, "May the LORD bless you."

[5]Boaz said to his young man, the one who was overseeing the harvesters, "To whom does this young woman belong?"

[6]The young man who was overseeing the harvesters answered, "She's a young Moabite woman, the one who returned with Naomi from the territory of Moab. [7]She said, 'Please let me glean so that I might gather up grain from among the bundles behind the harvesters.' She arrived and has been on her feet from the morning until now, and has sat down for only a moment."[d]

[8]Boaz said to Ruth, "Haven't you understood, my daughter? Don't go glean in another field; don't go anywhere else. Instead, stay here with my young women. [9]Keep your eyes on the field that they are harvesting and go along after them. I've ordered the young men not to assault you. Whenever you are thirsty, go to the jugs and drink from what the young men have filled."

[10]Then she bowed down, face to the ground, and replied to him, "How is it that I've found favor in your eyes, that you notice me? I'm an immigrant." [11]Boaz responded to her, "Everything that you did for your mother-in-law after your husband's death has been reported fully to me: how you left behind your father, your mother, and the land of your birth, and came to a people you hadn't known beforehand. [12]May the LORD reward you[e] for your deed. May you receive a rich reward from the LORD, the God of Israel, under whose wings you've come to seek refuge." [13]She said, "May I continue to find favor in your eyes, sir, because you've comforted me and because you've spoken kindly to your female servant—even though I'm not one of your female servants."

[14]At mealtime Boaz said to her, "Come over here, eat some of the bread, and dip your piece in the vinegar." She sat alongside the harvesters, and he served roasted grain to her. She ate, was satisfied, and had leftovers. [15]Then she got up to glean.

Boaz ordered his young men, "Let her glean between the bundles, and don't humiliate her. [16]Also, pull out some from the bales for her and leave them behind for her to glean. And don't scold her."

[17]So she gleaned in the field until evening. Then she threshed what she had gleaned; it was about an ephah[f] of barley. [18]She picked it up and went into town. Her mother-in-law saw what she had gleaned. She brought out what she had left over after eating her fill and gave it to her. [19]Her mother-in-law said to her, "Where did you glean today? Where did you work? May the one who noticed you be blessed."

She told her mother-in-law with whom she had worked and said, "The name of the man with whom I worked today is Boaz."

[20]Naomi replied to her daughter-in-law, "May he be blessed by the LORD, who hasn't abandoned his faithfulness with the living or with the dead." Naomi said to her,

[c]Heb *El Shaddai* or *God of the Mountain* [d]Heb uncertain [e]LXX [f]An ephah is approximately twenty quarts of grain.

"The man is one of our close relatives; he's one of our redeemers."

21 Ruth the Moabite replied, "Furthermore, he said to me, 'Stay with my workers until they've finished all of my harvest.'" 22 Naomi said to Ruth her daughter-in-law, "It's good, my daughter, that you go out with his young women, so that men don't assault you in another field."

23 Thus she stayed with Boaz's young women, gleaning until the completion of the barley and wheat harvests. And she lived with her mother-in-law.

Encounter at the threshing floor

3 Naomi her mother-in-law said to her, "My daughter, shouldn't I seek security for you, so that things might go well for you? 2 Now isn't Boaz, whose young women you were with, our relative? Tonight he will be winnowing barley at the threshing floor. 3 You should bathe, put on some perfume, wear nice clothes, and then go down to the threshing floor. Don't make yourself known to the man until he has finished eating and drinking. 4 When he lies down, notice the place where he is lying. Then go, uncover his feet, and lie down. And he will tell you what to do."

5 Ruth replied to her, "I'll do everything you are telling me."

6 So she went down to the threshing floor, and she did everything just as her mother-in-law had ordered.

7 Boaz ate and drank, and he was in a good mood. He went over to lie down by the edge of the grain pile. Then she quietly approached, uncovered his legs, and lay down. 8 During the middle of the night, the man shuddered and turned over—and there was a woman lying at his feet. 9 "Who are you?" he asked.

She replied, "I'm Ruth your servant. Spread out your robe[g] over your servant, because you are a redeemer."

10 He said, "May you be blessed by the LORD, my daughter! You have acted even more faithfully than you did at first. You haven't gone after rich or poor young men. 11 And now, my daughter, don't be afraid. I'll do for you everything you are asking. Indeed, my people—all who are at the gate—know that you are a woman of worth. 12 Now, although it's certainly true that I'm a redeemer, there's a redeemer who is a closer relative than I am. 13 Stay the night. And in the morning, if he'll redeem you—good, let him redeem. But if he doesn't want to redeem you, then—as the LORD lives—I myself will redeem you. Lie down until the morning."

14 So she lay at his feet until morning. Then she got up before one person could recognize another, for he had said, "No one should know that the woman came to the threshing floor." 15 He said, "Bring the cloak that you have on and hold it out." She held it out, and he measured out six measures of barley and placed it upon her. Then she[h] went into town.

16 She came to her mother-in-law, who said, "How are you, my daughter?"

So Ruth told her everything the man had done for her. 17 She said, "He gave me these six measures of barley, for he said to me, 'Don't go away empty-handed to your mother-in-law.'"

18 "Sit tight, my daughter," Naomi replied, "until you know how it turns out. The man won't rest until he resolves the matter today."

A new family brings fulfillment

4 Meanwhile, Boaz went up to the gate and sat down there. Just then, the redeemer about whom Boaz had spoken was passing by. He said, "Sir, come over here and sit down." So he turned aside and sat down. 2 Then he took ten men from the town's elders and said, "Sit down here." And they sat down.

3 Boaz said to the redeemer, "Naomi, who has returned from the field of Moab, is selling the portion of the field that belonged to our brother Elimelech. 4 I thought that I should let you know and say, 'Buy it, in the presence of those sitting here and in the presence of the elders of my people.' If you

[g] Or *wing;* cf 2:12; Ps 91:4 [h] MT *he;* other Heb sources, Syr, Vulg *she*

will redeem it, redeem it; but if you[i] won't redeem it, tell me so that I may know. There isn't anyone to redeem it except you, and I'm next in line after you."

He replied, "I will redeem it."

[5]Then Boaz said, "On the day when you buy the field from Naomi, you also buy[j] Ruth the Moabite, the wife of the dead man, in order to preserve the dead man's name for his inheritance."

[6]But the redeemer replied, "Then I can't redeem it for myself, without risking damage to my own inheritance. Redeem it for yourself. You can have my right of redemption, because I'm unable to act as redeemer."

[7]In Israel, in former times, this was the practice regarding redemption and exchange to confirm any such matter: a man would take off his sandal and give it to the other person. This was the process of making a transaction binding in Israel. [8]Then the redeemer said to Boaz, "Buy it for yourself," and he took off his sandal.

[9]Boaz announced to the elders and all the people, "Today you are witnesses that I've bought from the hand of Naomi all that belonged to Elimelech and all that belonged to Chilion and Mahlon. [10]And also Ruth the Moabite, the wife of Mahlon, I've bought to be my wife, to preserve the dead man's name for his inheritance so that the name of the dead man might not be cut off from his brothers or from the gate of his hometown—today you are witnesses."

[11]Then all the people who were at the gate and the elders said, "We are witnesses. May the LORD grant that the woman who is coming into your household be like Rachel and like Leah, both of whom built up the house of Israel. May you be fertile in Ephrathah and may you preserve a name in Bethlehem. [12]And may your household be like the household of Perez, whom Tamar bore to Judah—through the children that the LORD will give you from this young woman."

[13]So Boaz took Ruth, and she became his wife.

He was intimate with her, the LORD let her become pregnant, and she gave birth to a son. [14]The women said to Naomi, "May the LORD be blessed, who today hasn't left you without a redeemer. May his name be proclaimed in Israel. [15]He will restore your life and sustain you in your old age. Your daughter-in-law who loves you has given birth to him. She's better for you than seven sons." [16]Naomi took the child and held him to her breast, and she became his guardian. [17]The neighborhood women gave him a name, saying, "A son has been born to Naomi." They called his name Obed.[k] He became Jesse's father and David's grandfather.

[18]These are the generations of Perez: Perez became the father of Hezron, [19]Hezron the father of Ram, Ram the father of Amminadab, [20]Amminadab the father of Nahshon, Nahshon the father of Salmon, [21]Salmon the father of Boaz, Boaz the father of Obed, [22]Obed the father of Jesse, and Jesse the father of David.

1 SAMUEL

Samuel's birth

1 Now there was a certain man from Ramathaim, a Zuphite[a] from the highlands of Ephraim, whose name was Elkanah. He was from the tribe of Ephraim, and he was the son of Jeroham son of Elihu son of Tohu son of Zuph. [2]Elkanah had two wives, one named Hannah and the other named Peninnah. Peninnah had children, but Hannah didn't.

[3]Every year this man would leave his town to worship and sacrifice to the LORD of heavenly forces in Shiloh, where Eli's two sons Hophni and Phinehas were the LORD's priests. [4]Whenever he sacrificed, Elkanah would give parts of the sacrifice to his wife

[i]MT *he;* LXX, Syr *you* [j]Vulg; MT *On the day that you buy the field from Naomi and from Ruth the Moabite*
[k]Obed means *one who serves (God).* [a]LXX; MT *Ramathaim-zophim*

Peninnah and to all her sons and daughters. [5]But he would give only one part of it to Hannah, though he loved her, because the LORD had kept her from conceiving.[b] [6]And because the LORD had kept Hannah from conceiving, her rival would make fun of her mercilessly, just to bother her. [7]So that is what took place year after year. Whenever Hannah went to the Lord's house, Peninnah would make fun of her. Then she would cry and wouldn't eat anything.

[8]"Hannah, why are you crying?" her husband Elkanah would say to her. "Why won't you eat? Why are you[c] so sad? Aren't I worth more to you than ten sons?"

[9]One time, after eating and drinking in Shiloh, Hannah got up and presented herself before the LORD.[d] (Now Eli the priest was sitting in the chair by the doorpost of the LORD's temple.) [10]Hannah was very upset and couldn't stop crying as she prayed to the LORD. [11]Then she made this promise: "LORD of heavenly forces, just look at your servant's pain and remember me! Don't forget your servant! Give her a boy! Then I'll give him to the LORD for his entire life. No razor will ever touch his head."

[12]As she kept praying before the LORD, Eli watched her mouth. [13]Now Hannah was praying in her heart; her lips were moving, but her voice was silent, so Eli thought she was drunk.

[14]"How long will you act like a drunk? Sober up!" Eli told her.

[15]"No sir!" Hannah replied. "I'm just a very sad woman. I haven't had any wine or beer but have been pouring out my heart to the LORD. [16]Don't think your servant is some good-for-nothing woman. This whole time I've been praying out of my great worry and trouble!"

[17]Eli responded, "Then go in peace. And may the God of Israel give you what you've asked from him."

[18]"Please think well of me, your servant," Hannah said. Then the woman went on her way, ate some food, and wasn't sad any longer.[e]

[19]They got up early the next morning and worshipped the LORD. Then they went back home to Ramah. Elkanah had sex with his wife Hannah, and the LORD remembered her. [20]So in the course of time, Hannah conceived and gave birth to a son. She named him Samuel, which means "I asked the LORD for him."[f]

Samuel's dedication

[21]When Elkanah and all his household went up to make the annual sacrifice and keep his solemn promise, [22]Hannah didn't go.

"I'll bring the boy when he is weaned," she told her husband, "so he can be presented to the LORD and stay there permanently. I will offer him as a nazirite forever."[g]

[23]"Do what seems best to you," said her husband Elkanah. "Stay here until you've weaned him. But may the LORD bring to pass what you've[h] promised." So the woman stayed home and nursed her son until she had weaned him.

[24]When he had been weaned and was still very young,[i] Hannah took him, along with a three-year-old bull,[j] an ephah[k] of flour, and a jar of wine, and brought him to the LORD's house at Shiloh. [25]They slaughtered the bull, then brought the boy to Eli.

[26]"Excuse me, sir!" Hannah said. "As surely as you live, sir, I am the woman who stood here next to you, praying to the LORD. [27]I prayed for this boy, and the LORD gave me what I asked from him. [28]So now I give this boy back to the LORD. As long as he lives, he is given to the LORD."

Then they worshipped there before the LORD.[l]

Hannah's song

2 Then Hannah prayed:
My heart rejoices in the LORD.

[b]Heb uncertain; Syr *But he would give a double portion to Hannah, because he loved her, though the LORD had kept her from conceiving.* [c]Or *your heart* [d]LXX; MT lacks *presented herself before the LORD.* [e]LXX; MT lacks *sad.* [f]Samuel means *God has heard* but here is connected to the Heb verb *to ask.* [g]DSS (4QSam[a]); MT lacks *I will offer . . . forever.* [h]LXX, DSS (4QSam[a]); MT *he* [i]Or *and the boy was a boy*; Heb uncertain [j]LXX, DSS (4QSam[a]), Syr; MT *three bulls* [k]An ephah was approximately twenty quarts. [l]Some Heb manuscripts, Syr, Vulg; MT he (Eli?) *worshipped*; DSS (4QSam[a]) *and she* (Hannah) *left him there and worshipped the LORD.*

My strength[m] rises up in the LORD!
My mouth mocks my enemies
because I rejoice in your deliverance.
2 No one is holy like the LORD—
no, no one except you!
There is no rock like our God!

3 Don't go on and on, talking so proudly,
spouting arrogance from your mouth,
because the LORD is the God
who knows,
and he weighs every act.

4 The bows of mighty warriors are shattered,
but those who were stumbling
now dress themselves in power!
5 Those who were filled full
now sell themselves for bread,
but the ones who were starving
are now fat from food!
The woman who was barren
has birthed seven children,
but the mother with many sons
has lost them all!
6 The LORD!
He brings death, gives life,
takes down to the grave,[n]
and raises up!
7 The LORD!
He makes poor, gives wealth,
brings low, but also lifts up high!
8 God raises the poor from the dust,
lifts up the needy
from the garbage pile.
God sits them with officials,
gives them the seat of honor!
The pillars of the earth
belong to the LORD;
he set the world on top of them!
9 God guards the feet of his faithful ones,
but the wicked die in darkness
because no one succeeds
by strength alone.

10 The LORD!
His enemies are terrified!
God thunders against them
from heaven!
The LORD!
He judges the far corners of the earth!

May God give strength to his king
and raise high the strength
of his anointed one.

11 Then Elkanah went home to Ramah,
but the boy served the LORD under Eli the
priest.

Corruption of Eli's sons

12 Now Eli's sons were despicable men
who didn't know the LORD. 13 This was how
the priest was supposed to act with the
people: Whenever anyone made a sacrifice,
while the meat was boiling, the priest's assistant would come with a three-pronged
fork in hand. 14 He would thrust it into the
cauldron or the pot.[o] Whatever the fork
brought up, the priest would take for himself. This is how it was done for all the Israelites who came to Shiloh.
15 But with Eli's sons,[p] even before the
fat was burned, the priest's assistant would
come and say to the person offering the sacrifice, "Give the priest some meat to roast.
He won't accept boiled meat from you."[q]
16 If anyone said, "Let the fat be burned
off first, as usual, then take whatever you
like for yourself," the assistant would reply,
"No, hand it over now. If not, I'll take it by
force." 17 The sin of these priestly assistants
was very serious in the LORD's sight because they were disrespecting the LORD's
own offering.
18 Now Samuel was serving the LORD. He
was a young boy, clothed in a linen priestly
vest.[r] 19 His mother would make a small robe
for him and take it to him every year when
she went up with her husband to offer the
annual sacrifice. 20 Eli would bless Elkanah
and his wife: "May the LORD replace[s] the
child of this woman that you gave back to
the LORD." Then they would return home.
21 The LORD paid attention to Hannah, and
she conceived and gave birth to three sons
and two daughters. Meanwhile, the boy
Samuel grew up in the LORD's service.

[m]Or *my horn*; also in 2:10 [n]Heb *Sheol* [o]Cf DSS (4QSam[a]); Heb has four different words for pots. [p]MT lacks *with Eli's sons*. [q]LXX; MT adds *only raw*. [r]Heb *ephod* [s]DSS (4QSam[a]); MT *give*

22 Eli was very old, but he heard everything his sons were doing to the Israelites,
and how they had sex with the women who
served at the meeting tent's entrance. 23 Eli
said to his sons, "Why are you doing these
terrible things that I'm hearing about from
everybody? 24 No, my sons. Don't do this.[t]
The report I hear spreading among God's
people isn't good. 25 If someone sins against
someone else, God can intercede; but if
someone sins against the LORD, who will
intercede then?" But they wouldn't obey
their father because the LORD wanted to
kill them. 26 Meanwhile, the boy Samuel
kept growing up and was more and more
liked by both the LORD and the people.
27 Now a man of God came to Eli and
said, "This is what the LORD says: I revealed myself very clearly to your father's
household when they were slaves[u] in Egypt
to the house of Pharaoh. 28 I chose your
father from all of Israel's tribes to be my
priest, to go up onto my altar, to burn incense, and to wear the priestly vest[v] in my
presence. I also gave all of the Israelites'
food offerings to your father's household.
29 Why then do you kick my sacrifices and
my offerings—the very ones I commanded
for my dwelling place? Why do you respect
your sons more than me, getting fat off the
best parts of every offering from my people
Israel? 30 Because of all that, this is what
the LORD, the God of Israel, declares: I had
promised that your household and your
father's household would serve me forever.
But now—this is what the LORD declares:
I'll do no such thing! No. I honor those
who honor me, and whoever despises me
will be cursed. 31 The days are coming soon
when I will eliminate both your children[w]
and the children of your father's household. There won't be an old person left in
your family tree. 32 You'll see trouble in my
dwelling place, though all will go well for
Israel.[x] But there will never be an old person
in your family tree. 33 One of your descendants whom I don't eliminate from serving
at my altar will cry his[y] eyes out and be full
of grief. Any descendants in your household
will die by the sword.[z] 34 And what happens
to your two sons Hophni and Phinehas will
be a sign for you: they will both die on the
same day. 35 Then I will establish for myself
a trustworthy priest who will act in accordance with my thoughts and desires. I will
build a trustworthy household for him, and
he will serve before my anointed one forever. 36 Anyone left from your household will
come and beg him for a bit of silver or a loaf
of bread, saying: 'Please appoint me to some
priestly duty so I can have a scrap of bread
to eat.'"

Samuel's call

3 Now the boy Samuel was serving the
LORD under Eli. The LORD's word was
rare at that time, and visions weren't widely
known. 2 One day Eli, whose eyes had grown
so weak he was unable to see, was lying
down in his room. 3 God's lamp hadn't gone
out yet, and Samuel was lying down in the
LORD's temple, where God's chest[a] was.
4 The LORD called to Samuel. "I'm here,"
he said.
5 Samuel hurried to Eli and said, "I'm
here. You called me?"
"I didn't call you," Eli replied. "Go lie
down." So he did.
6 Again the LORD called Samuel, so Samuel got up, went to Eli, and said, "I'm here.
You called me?"
"I didn't call, my son," Eli replied. "Go
and lie down."
(7 Now Samuel didn't yet know the
LORD, and the LORD's word hadn't yet been
revealed to him.)
8 A third time the LORD called Samuel.
He got up, went to Eli, and said, "I'm here.
You called me?"
Then Eli realized that it was the LORD
who was calling the boy. 9 So Eli said to Samuel, "Go and lie down. If he calls you, say,
'Speak, LORD. Your servant is listening.'" So
Samuel went and lay down where he'd been.
10 Then the LORD came and stood there,
calling just as before, "Samuel, Samuel!"

[t] LXX, DSS (4QSam[a]); MT lacks *Don't do this.* [u] DSS (4QSam[a]), LXX; MT lacks *slaves.* [v] Heb *ephod* [w] LXX; MT *arm* or *power* [x] Heb uncertain; LXX and DSS (4QSam[a]) omit 2:31*b*-32*a*. [y] DSS (4QSam[a]), LXX; MT *your* [z] LXX, DSS (4QSam[a]); MT *die by men* or *die as men* [a] Traditionally *ark*

Samuel said, "Speak. Your servant is
listening."
11The LORD said to Samuel, "I am about
to do something in Israel that will make the
ears of all who hear it tingle! 12On that day,
I will bring to pass against Eli everything
I said about his household—every last bit
of it![b] 13I told him that I would punish his
family forever because of the wrongdoing
he knew about—how his sons were cursing God,[c] but he wouldn't stop them. 14Be-
cause of that I swore about Eli's household
that his family's wrongdoing will never be
reconciled by sacrifice or by offering."
15Samuel lay there until morning, then
opened the doors of the LORD's house. Samuel was afraid to tell the vision to Eli. 16But
Eli called Samuel, saying: "Samuel, my son!"

"I'm here," Samuel said.

17"What did he say to you?" Eli asked.
"Don't hide anything from me. May God
deal harshly with you and worse still if you
hide from me a single word from everything he said to you." 18So Samuel told him
everything and hid nothing from him.

"He is the LORD," Eli said. "He will do as
he pleases."

19So Samuel grew up, and the LORD was
with him, not allowing any of his words to
fail. 20All Israel from Dan to Beer-sheba
knew that Samuel was trustworthy as the
LORD's prophet. 21The LORD continued
to appear at Shiloh because the LORD revealed himself to Samuel at Shiloh through
4 the LORD's own word. 1And Samuel's
word went out to all Israel.

The Philistines capture God's chest

In those days the Philistines gathered
for war against Israel,[d] so Israel went out
to engage the Philistines in war. Israel
camped at Ebenezer, while the Philistines
camped at Aphek. 2The Philistines readied
themselves to fight Israel. When the battle
was joined, Israel was defeated by the Philistines, who killed about four thousand
men on the battlefield. 3When the troops
returned to the camp, Israel's elders said,
"Why did the LORD defeat us today before
the Philistines? Let's bring the chest containing the LORD's covenant from Shiloh so
it can go with us and save us from our enemies' power." 4So the people sent to Shiloh
and brought from there the chest containing the covenant of the LORD of heavenly
forces, who sits enthroned on the winged
heavenly creatures.[e] Eli's two sons Hophni
and Phinehas were there with the chest
containing God's covenant.
5When the chest containing the LORD's
covenant entered the camp, all Israel let
out such a loud shout that the ground
shook. 6When the Philistines heard the
sound of that shout, they asked, "What
is that loud shouting in the Hebrew camp
about?" When they learned that the LORD's
chest had come into the camp, 7the Philistines were afraid and said, "A god has come
into that camp! We're doomed," they said,
"because nothing like this has ever happened before. 8We're doomed! Who will
deliver us from the grip of these powerful
deities? They are the same gods who struck
the Egyptians in the desert with every kind
of wound. 9Pull yourselves together and
act like men, Philistines! Otherwise, you'll
serve the Hebrews like they've been serving
you. Act like men and fight!"
10So the Philistines fought. Israel was
defeated, and everyone fled to their homes.
It was a massive defeat: thirty thousand
Israelite foot soldiers fell, 11God's chest
was taken, and Eli's two sons Hophni and
Phinehas died.
12That very day, a Benjaminite ran from
the battle to Shiloh. His clothes were torn,
and dirt was on his head. 13When he got
there, Eli was sitting in a chair beside the
road, waiting because he was nervous about
God's chest. The man arrived and gave the
news to the city, and the whole city cried out.
14Eli heard the sound of the cry and said,
"What's all this noise about?"

The man hurriedly went and told Eli the
news. (15Now Eli was 98 years old, and his
eyes stared straight ahead, unable to see.)

[b]Or *the beginning and the end* [c]LXX; MT *to themselves*, one of several intentional scribal corrections to avoid the phrase *cursing God* [d]LXX; MT lacks *In those days . . . against Israel.* [e]Heb *cherubim*

16 The man told Eli, "I'm the one who just came from the battle. I fled from the battle today."

"What's the report, my son?" Eli asked.

17 The messenger answered, "Israel has fled from the Philistines. The army has suffered a massive defeat. Also, your own two sons Hophni and Phinehas have died, and God's chest has been taken!" 18 At the mention of God's chest, Eli fell backward off the chair beside the gate. His neck broke, and he died because he was an old man and overweight. Eli had judged Israel for forty years.

19 Now Eli's daughter-in-law, Phinehas' wife, was pregnant and about to give birth. When she heard the news that God's chest had been captured and that her father-in-law and her husband had died, she doubled over and gave birth because her labor pains overwhelmed her. 20 As she was about to die, the women standing by helping her said, "Don't be afraid. You've given birth to a son!" But she didn't answer or pay them any attention. 21 She named the boy Ichabod,[f] saying, "The glory has left Israel," referring to the capture of God's chest and the death of her father-in-law and her husband. 22 "The glory has left Israel because God's chest has been taken," she said.

God's chest among the Philistines

5 After the Philistines took God's chest, they brought it from Ebenezer to Ashdod. 2 Then the Philistines took God's chest and brought it into Dagon's temple and set it next to Dagon. 3 But when the citizens of Ashdod got up early the next morning, there was Dagon, fallen facedown on the ground before the LORD's chest! So they took Dagon and set him back up where he belonged. 4 But when they got up early the next morning, there was Dagon again, fallen facedown on the ground before the LORD's chest—and this time Dagon's head along with both his hands were cut off and lying on the doorstep! Only Dagon's body[g] was left intact. 5 That's why to this day Dagon's priests or anyone else who enters his temple in Ashdod doesn't step on the threshold.

6 The LORD's hand was heavy on the people of Ashdod: God terrified them and struck them in Ashdod and its surroundings with tumors.[h] 7 When Ashdod's inhabitants saw what was happening, they said, "The chest of Israel's God must not stay here with us because his hand is hard against us and against our god Dagon." 8 So they summoned all the Philistine rulers to a meeting and asked, "What should we do with the chest of Israel's God?" The people of Gath said, "Let the chest of Israel's God be moved to us." So they moved the chest of Israel's God to Gath.[i] 9 But once they moved it, the LORD's hand came against the city, causing a huge panic. God struck the city's inhabitants, both young and old, and tumors broke out on them.

10 Then they sent God's chest to Ekron, but as soon as God's chest entered Ekron, the inhabitants cried out, "Why have you moved the chest of Israel's God to us? In order to kill us and our people?"[j]

11 So they summoned all the Philistine rulers to a meeting and said, "Send the chest of Israel's God away! Let it go back to its own home so it doesn't kill us and our people," because there was a deadly panic throughout the whole city. The hand of God was very heavy there. 12 The people who didn't die were struck with tumors, and the screams of the city went all the way up to heaven.

God's chest is returned

6 The LORD's chest was in Philistine territory for seven months. 2 The Philistines called for the priests and the diviners. "What should we do with the LORD's chest?" they asked. "Tell us how we should send it back to its own home."

3 They replied, "If you are returning the chest of Israel's God, don't send it back empty, but be sure to return a guilt offering to him.[k] Then you will be healed, and it will

[f] Meaning *Where is the glory?* [g] Cf LXX [h] Kethib; Qere *hemorrhoids* (cf Deut 28:27); also in 5:9, 12 [i] LXX
[j] DSS (4QSam[a]), LXX [k] Or *be sure to return it with a compensation offering.*

become clear to you why God's hand hasn't left you alone."

4 "What compensation offering should we return to him?" they asked.

The priests and diviners replied: "Five gold tumors[l] and five gold mice,[m] matching the number of the Philistine rulers, because the same plague came on all of you and your rulers. 5 You must make images of your tumors and the mice that have devastated the land. Honor Israel's God. Perhaps he will lighten the weight of his hand on you, your gods, and your land. 6 Why be stubborn like the Egyptians and Pharaoh? After God had dealt harshly with them, didn't they send the Israelites on their way? 7 So get a new cart ready along with two nursing cows that have never been yoked before. Harness the cows to the cart, but take any of their calves that are following back home. 8 Next, take the LORD's chest and put it in the cart. Set the gold items that you are giving God as a compensation offering in a box next to the chest. Then send it on its way. 9 Then watch what happens: If the cart goes up the road to its own territory toward Beth-shemesh, then Israel's God has brought this great disaster on us. If the cart goes another way, then we'll know that it wasn't God's hand that struck us. It happened to us randomly."

10 The rulers[n] did just that. They took two nursing cows and harnessed them to the cart, penning their calves up at home. 11 They put the LORD's chest on the cart along with the box containing the gold mice and the images of their tumors.[o] 12 The cows went straight ahead, following the road to Beth-shemesh. They kept to one route, mooing as they went, without turning right or left. The Philistine rulers followed them as far as the territory of Beth-shemesh.

13 Now the people of Beth-shemesh were harvesting wheat in the valley. When they looked up and saw the chest, they were overjoyed at the sight. 14 The cart entered the field belonging to Joshua of Beth-shemesh and stopped right by a large stone. They chopped up the wood of the cart and offered the cows as an entirely burned offering to the LORD. 15 The Levites unloaded the LORD's chest and the box that was with it that contained all the gold items, and they set them on the large stone. That very day the people of Beth-shemesh offered entirely burned offerings and made sacrifices to the LORD. 16 When the five Philistine rulers witnessed this, they went straight back to Ekron.

17 These are the gold tumors that the Philistines returned as a compensation offering to the LORD: one for Ashdod, one for Gaza, one for Ashkelon, one for Gath, and one for Ekron. 18 The gold mice matched the number of Philistine cities belonging to the five rulers, from fortified cities to country villages. And the large stone[p] they set the LORD's chest on is a witness even now in the field that belongs to Joshua of Beth-shemesh.

19 But God struck down some of the people from Beth-shemesh because they looked into the LORD's chest. God struck seventy people,[q] and the community grieved because the LORD had struck them so severely. 20 The people of Beth-shemesh said, "Who can stand before the LORD, this holy God? Where can he go that is away from us here?" 21 They sent messengers to the inhabitants of Kiriath-jearim. "The Philistines returned the LORD's chest!" they said. "Come down and take it back with you."

7 So the people of Kiriath-jearim came and took the LORD's chest. They brought it to Abinadab's house, which was on the hill. Then they dedicated Eleazar, Abinadab's son, to care for the LORD's chest.

Samuel leads Israel

2 Now a long time passed—a total of twenty years—after the chest came to stay in Kiriath-jearim, and the whole house of Israel yearned for[r] the LORD.

3 Then Samuel said to the whole house of Israel, "If you are turning to the LORD with all your heart, then get rid of all the foreign gods and the Astartes you have. Set your heart on the LORD! Worship him only! Then he will deliver you from the Phi-

[l]Kethib; Qere *hemorrhoids* (cf Deut 28:27); also in 6:5; see note at 6:11. [m]LXX lacks *and five gold mice.* [n]See 6:12; MT *men.* [o]Or *hemorrhoids;* also in 6:17, the Qere form for the Hebrew written form of *tumors* used in 6:4-5 [p]LXX [q]LXX; MT adds *fifty thousand people.* [r]Heb uncertain; LXX *searched for*

listines' power." 4So the Israelites got rid of
the Baals and the Astartes and worshipped
the LORD only.
5Next Samuel said, "Assemble all Israel
at Mizpah. I will pray to the LORD for you."
6So they assembled at Mizpah, and they
drew water and poured it out in the LORD's
presence. They fasted that same day and
confessed, "We have sinned against the
LORD." Samuel served as judge of the Israelites at Mizpah.
7When the Philistines heard that the
Israelites had assembled at Mizpah, the
Philistine rulers went up to attack Israel.
When the Israelites learned of this, they
were afraid of the Philistines. 8The Israelites said to Samuel, "Please don't stop praying to the LORD our God for us, so God will
save us from the Philistines' power!" 9So
Samuel took a suckling lamb and offered it
as an entirely burned offering to the LORD.
Samuel cried out in prayer to the LORD for
Israel, and the LORD answered him.
10While Samuel was offering the entirely
burned offering, the Philistines advanced
to attack Israel. But the LORD thundered
against the Philistines with a great blast
on that very day, throwing the Philistines
into such a panic that they were defeated
by Israel. 11The Israelite soldiers came out
of Mizpah and pursued the Philistines.
They struck them down until they reached
a place just below Beth-car. 12Then Samuel
took a stone and set it up between Mizpah
and Jeshanah.[s] He named it Ebenezer,[t] explaining, "The LORD helped us to this very
point."
13So the Philistines were defeated, and
they stopped coming into Israelite territory. The LORD's hand was against the
Philistines throughout Samuel's life. 14The
towns the Philistines had captured from
Israel, from Ekron to Gath, were returned
to Israel. Israel also recovered the territory
around those two cities from the Philistines. And there was peace between Israel
and the Amorites.
15Samuel served as Israel's judge his
whole life. 16Each year he traveled between Bethel, Gilgal, and Mizpah, serving
as Israel's judge in each of those locations.
17Then he would return to Ramah because
that's where his home was. In Ramah too
he served as Israel's judge, and that is also
where he built an altar to the LORD.

Israel demands a king

8 Now when Samuel got old, he appointed
his sons to serve as Israel's judges. 2The
name of his oldest son was Joel; the name
of the second was Abijah. They served as
judges in Beer-sheba. 3But Samuel's sons
didn't follow in his footsteps. They tried to
turn a profit, they accepted bribes, and they
perverted justice.
4So all the Israelite elders got together
and went to Samuel at Ramah. 5They said
to him, "Listen. You are old now, and your
sons don't follow in your footsteps. So appoint us a king to judge us like all the other
nations have." 6It seemed very bad to Samuel when they said, "Give us a king to judge
us," so he prayed to the LORD.
7The LORD answered Samuel, "Comply
with the people's request—everything they
ask of you—because they haven't rejected
you. No, they've rejected me as king over them.
8They are doing to you only what they've
been doing to me[u] from the day I brought
them out of Egypt to this very minute, abandoning me and worshipping other gods.
9So comply with their request, but give
them a clear warning, telling them how the
king will rule over them."[v]
10Then Samuel explained everything the
LORD had said to the people who were asking for a king. 11"This is how the king will
rule over you," Samuel said:
"He will take your sons, and will use
them for his chariots and his cavalry and
as runners for his chariot. 12He will use
them as his commanders of troops of one
thousand and troops of fifty, or to do his
plowing and his harvesting, or to make his
weapons or parts for his chariots. 13He will
take your daughters to be perfumers, cooks,

[s]LXX, Syr; MT *Ha-shen* (the tooth) [t]Meaning *stone of help* [u]LXX; MT lacks *to me*. [v]Or *telling them the lawful practice of the king*; also in 8:11; cf 10:25.

or bakers. 14 He will take your best fields, vineyards, and olive groves and give them to his servants. 15 He will give one-tenth of your grain and your vineyards to his officials and servants. 16 He will take your male and female servants, along with the best of your cattle[w] and donkeys, and make them do his work. 17 He will take one-tenth of your flocks, and then you yourselves will become his slaves! 18 When that day comes, you will cry out because of the king you chose for yourselves, but on that day the LORD won't answer you."

19 But the people refused to listen to Samuel and said, "No! There must be a king over us 20 so we can be like all the other nations. Our king will judge us and lead us and fight our battles."

21 Samuel listened to everything the people said and repeated it directly to the LORD. 22 Then the LORD said to Samuel, "Comply with their request. Give them a king."

Samuel then told the Israelite people, "Go back, each of you, to your own hometown."

Saul chosen to lead Israel

9 There was a wealthy man from the tribe of Benjamin named Kish. He was the son of Abiel son of Zeror son of Becorath son of Aphiah, a Benjaminite. 2 He had a son named Saul, who was a handsome young man. No one in Israel was more handsome than Saul, and he stood head and shoulders above everyone else.

3 When the donkeys belonging to Saul's father Kish were lost, Kish said to his son Saul, "Take one of the servant boys with you and go look for the donkeys." 4 So he traveled through the highlands of Ephraim and the land of Shalishah, but they didn't find anything. They traveled through the land of Shaalim, but still found nothing, so they crossed back into the land of Benjamin, but they still couldn't find the donkeys. 5 When they came to the territory of Zuph, Saul said to the boy who was with him, "Let's go back before my father stops worrying about the donkeys and starts worrying about us."

6 But the boy said to him, "Listen, there's a man of God in this town. He's famous—everything he says actually happens! So let's go there. Maybe he'll be able to tell us which way we should go."

7 Saul said to his young boy, "But if we go, what should we bring to the man? The food in our bags is all gone. We don't have any gift to offer the man of God. Do we have anything?"

8 "Here," the boy answered Saul, "I've got a quarter-shekel of silver. I'll give that to the man of God so he tells us which way to go." (9 Earlier in Israel, someone going to consult with God would say, "Let's go to the seer," because the people who are called prophets today were previously called seers.)

10 Saul said to the boy, "Great idea! Let's go." So they went into the town where the man of God lived. 11 They were going up the hill to the town when they met some young women coming out to draw water. "Is the seer here?" they asked them.

12 "He's just ahead of you," they answered. "Hurry up! He has just come to town because there is a sacrifice today for the people at the shrine. 13 You'll find him as soon as you enter the town, before he goes up to the shrine to eat. The people won't eat until he gets there, because he must bless the sacrifice. Only after that can the invited guests eat. Now get going because you'll find him momentarily."

14 So Saul and the boy went up to the town, and as they entered it, suddenly Samuel came toward them on his way up to the shrine. 15 Now the day before Saul came, the LORD had revealed the following to Samuel: 16 "About this time tomorrow I will send you a man from the Benjaminite territory. You will anoint him as leader of my people Israel. He will save my people from the Philistines' power because I have seen the suffering of[x] my people, and their cry for help has reached me." 17 When Samuel saw Saul, the LORD told him, "That's the man I told you about. That's the one who will rule[y] my people."

[w] LXX; MT *young men* [x] LXX; MT lacks *the suffering of.* [y] LXX; Heb uncertain, perhaps *restrain* or *gather (troops)*; cf 10:1

18 Saul approached Samuel in the city gate and said, "Please tell me where the seer's house is."

19 "I'm the seer," Samuel told Saul. "Go on ahead of me to the shrine. You can eat with me today. In the morning I'll send you on your way, and I will tell you everything you want to know. 20 As for the donkeys you lost three days ago, don't be worried about them because they've been found. Who owns all of Israel's treasures, anyway? Isn't it you and your whole family?"[z]

21 "I'm a Benjaminite," Saul responded, "from the smallest Israelite tribe, and my family is the littlest of the families in the tribe of Benjamin. Why would you say something like that to me?"

22 Then Samuel took Saul and his young servant and brought them to the banquet room. He gave them an honored place among the invited guests. There were about thirty total. 23 Samuel said to the cook, "Serve the portion I gave you—the one I told you to set aside." 24 So the cook took the thigh and what was on it,[a] and put it in front of Saul. Samuel said, "Look, what had been reserved is now in front of you. Eat up, because it was set apart for you for this specific occasion, ever since I invited the guests."[b] So Saul ate with Samuel that day. 25 When they came back from the shrine to the town, a bed was made for Saul on the roof, and he slept.[c]

26 Near dawn, Samuel called to Saul on the roof, "Wake up! I will send you on your way." So Saul got up, and the two of them, he and Samuel, went outside. 27 As they were nearing the edge of town Samuel said, "Tell the boy to go on ahead of us" (the servant did so) "but you stop for a bit so I can tell you God's word."

Samuel anoints Saul as king

10 Samuel took a small jar of oil and poured it over Saul's head and kissed him. "The LORD hereby anoints you leader of his people Israel," Samuel said. "You will rule the LORD's people and save them from the power of the enemies who surround them. And this will be the sign for you that the LORD has anointed you as leader of his very own possession:[d] 2 When you leave me today, you will meet two men near Rachel's tomb at Zelzah on the border of Benjamin. They will tell you, 'The donkeys you went looking for have been found. Now your father has stopped thinking about the donkeys and is worried about you. He's asking: What should I do about my son?' 3 Then, when you've gone on a bit farther, you will come to the oak at Tabor. Three men who are going to consult God at Bethel will meet up with you there, one carrying three young goats, one carrying three loaves of bread, and one carrying a jar of wine. 4 They will ask how you're doing and will offer you sacrificial bread,[e] which you should accept. 5 After that, you will come to Gibeath-elohim, which is a Philistine fort. When you enter the town, you will encounter a group of prophets coming down from the shrine preceded by harps, tambourines, flutes, and lyres. They will be caught up in a prophetic frenzy. 6 Then the LORD's spirit will come over you, and you will be caught up in a prophetic frenzy right along with them; it will be like you've become a completely different person. 7 Once these signs have happened to you, do whatever you would like to do, because God is with you. 8 Then go down to Gilgal ahead of me. I'll come down to meet you to offer entirely burned offerings and to make well-being sacrifices. Wait seven days until I get to you, then I'll tell you what you should do next."

9 And just as Saul turned to leave Samuel's side, God gave him a different heart, and all these signs happened that very same day. 10 When Saul and the boy got to Gibeah, there was a group of prophets coming to meet him. God's spirit came over Saul, and he was caught up in a prophetic frenzy right along with them. 11 When all the people who had known Saul saw him prophesying with the prophets, they said to each other, "What's happened to Kish's

[z] Or *But for whom does all Israel yearn if not for you and your whole family?* [a] Heb uncertain [b] Heb uncertain [c] LXX; MT *He* (Samuel?) *talked with Saul on the roof. Then they got up early.* [d] LXX; MT lacks *of his people Israel. . . . And this will be the sign for you that.* [e] LXX; DSS (4QSam[a]) *uplifted bread* (see Num 18:11); MT *two of bread*

son? Is Saul also one of the prophets?" [12]One of the locals then asked, "And who is their leader?"[f] So it became a proverb: "Is Saul also one of the prophets?" [13]When the prophetic frenzy was over, Saul went home.[g]

[14]Saul's uncle said to him and to his young servant, "Where did you go?"

"To look for the donkeys," Saul replied, "but when we couldn't find anything, we went to Samuel."

[15]"Please tell me what Samuel told you," Saul's uncle said.

[16]"He reassured us that the donkeys had been found," Saul answered. But Saul didn't tell his uncle what Samuel had said about the kingship.

Saul selected as king

[17]Samuel summoned the people to the LORD at Mizpah. [18]Then he told the Israelites: "This is what the LORD God of Israel says: I brought Israel up out of Egypt, and I delivered you from the Egyptians' power and from the power of all the kingdoms that oppressed you. [19]But today you've rejected your God who saved you from all your troubles and difficulties by saying, 'No! Appoint a king over us!' So now assemble yourselves before the LORD by your tribes and clans."

[20]Then Samuel brought all the Israelite tribes forward, and the tribe of Benjamin was selected. [21]Next Samuel brought the tribe of Benjamin forward by its families, and the family of Matri was selected. Samuel then brought the family of Matri forward, person by person,[h] and Saul, Kish's son, was selected. But when they looked for him, he wasn't to be found. [22]So they asked another question of the LORD: "Has the man come here yet?"

The LORD said, "Yes, he's hiding among the supplies." [23]They ran and retrieved Saul from there, and when he stood up in the middle of the people, he was head and shoulders taller than anyone else.

[24]"Can you see the one the LORD has chosen?" Samuel asked all the people. "He has no equal among the people."

Then the people shouted, "Long live the king!"

[25]Samuel then explained to the people how the monarchy should operate[i] and wrote it in a scroll and placed it in the LORD's presence. Then Samuel sent every person back to their homes. [26]Saul also went back to his home in Gibeah. Along with him went courageous men whose hearts God had touched. [27]But some despicable people said, "How can this man save us?" They despised Saul and didn't bring him gifts, but Saul didn't say anything.

Saul delivers Jabesh-gilead

[j]Nahash the Ammonite king had been severely oppressing the Gadites and the Reubenites. He gouged out everyone's right eye, thereby not allowing Israel to have a deliverer. There wasn't a single Israelite left across the Jordan River who hadn't had their right eye gouged out by the Ammonite king Nahash. But seven thousand people had escaped from the Ammonites' power and fled to Jabesh-gilead.

11 About a month later,[k] Nahash the Ammonite went up and laid siege to Jabesh-gilead. All the men of Jabesh said to Nahash, "Make a treaty with us, and we'll be your servants."

[2]"I will make a treaty with you on one condition: that everyone's right eye be gouged out!" Nahash the Ammonite said to them. "That's how I bring humiliation on all Israel."

[3]The elders of Jabesh replied to him, "Leave us alone for seven days so we can send messengers thoughout Israel's territory. If there's no one to save us, then we'll surrender to you."

[4]When the messengers reached Gibeah where Saul lived, they reported the news directly to the people there. Then they all wept aloud. [5]At just that moment, Saul was coming back from keeping the cattle in the fields. "What's wrong with everybody?" he asked.

[f]Or *father* [g]Correction; MT *Saul entered the shrine.* [h]LXX; MT lacks *Samuel then brought the family of Matri forward, person by person.* [i]Or *the lawful practices of the monarchy* [j]This paragraph is found in DSS (4QSam[a]) and is also attested in Josephus (*Ant.* 6.5.1 [68-71]), but is missing in MT. [k]DSS (4QSam[a]), LXX; MT lacks *About a month later.*

"Why are they crying?" Saul was then told what the men from Jabesh had said.

6 God's spirit came over Saul when he heard those words, and he burned with anger. 7 He took two oxen, cut them into pieces, and sent them by messengers throughout Israel's territory. "This is exactly what will be done to the oxen of anyone who doesn't come to the aid of Saul and Samuel," he said. Great fear of the LORD came over the people, and they came to Saul completely unified.[l] 8 When Saul counted them at Bezek, the soldiers from Israel totaled three hundred thousand and those from Judah thirty thousand.

9 The messengers who had come were then told, "Say this to the people of Jabesh-gilead: Tomorrow by the time the sun is hot, you will be saved." When the messengers returned and reported this to the people of Jabesh, they were overjoyed.

10 Then the people of Jabesh told the Ammonites, "We will surrender to you tomorrow. Then you can do whatever you want to us."

11 The next day Saul organized his troops into three formations. They attacked the Ammonite camp during the morning watch and slaughtered them until the heat of the day. The survivors were so scattered that not even two of them could be found together.

12 Then people asked Samuel, "Who was it who said, 'Will Saul rule over us?' Give us those people; we'll kill them!"

13 But Saul said, "No one will be executed because today the LORD has saved Israel."

14 "Let's go to Gilgal," Samuel told the people, "and renew the monarchy there." 15 So everyone went to Gilgal, and there at Gilgal they made Saul king in the LORD's presence. They offered well-being sacrifices in the LORD's presence, and Saul and all the Israelites held a great celebration there.

Samuel's last speech

12 Samuel said to all Israel: "Listen: I have done everything you asked of me and have placed a king over you. 2 The king will lead you now. I am old and gray, though my sons are still with you, and I've been your leader since I was young until now. 3 So I'm here: Tell the truth about me in the presence of the LORD and his anointed. Have I ever stolen someone's ox? Have I ever taken someone's donkey? Have I ever oppressed or mistreated anyone? Have I ever taken bribes from someone and looked the other way about something? Tell me the truth.[m] I will make it right."

4 "You haven't oppressed or mistreated us, and you've never taken anything from anyone," the people answered.

5 Samuel replied, "The LORD and his anointed one are witnesses against you today that you haven't found anything in my possession."

"Agreed," they said.

6 Then Samuel told the people: "The witness[n] is indeed the LORD, who appointed Moses and Aaron and brought your ancestors up from the land of Egypt. 7 So now stand here, and I will judge you in the LORD's presence because of all the LORD's righteous acts that he has done for you and your ancestors:

8 "When Jacob entered Egypt, the Egyptians oppressed them.[o] So your ancestors cried out to the LORD. The LORD then sent Moses and Aaron, who brought your ancestors out of Egypt and settled them here. 9 But your ancestors forgot the LORD their God, so he handed them over to Sisera the commander of Hazor's army, and to the Philistines, and to the Moabite king, all of whom fought against them. 10 Then your ancestors cried out to the LORD and said: 'We have sinned because we have abandoned the LORD and have worshipped the Baals and the Astartes. But now deliver us from the power of our enemies, and we will worship you.' 11 So the LORD sent Jerubbaal, Barak,[p] Jephthah, and Samson,[q] and he delivered you from the power of your enemies on every side. And you lived safe and secure. 12 But when you saw that Nahash the

[l] MT lacks *to Saul.* [m] LXX [n] LXX; MT lacks *witness.* [o] LXX; MT lacks *the Egyptians oppressed them.* [p] LXX, Syr; MT *Bedan* [q] Syr (cf Targ), LXX[L] *Samson*; MT, LXX[AB] *Samuel*

Ammonite king was coming against you, you said to me, 'No! There must be a king to rule over us.' But the LORD your God was already your king!

[13]"So now, here is the king you chose, the one you asked for. Yes, the LORD has put a king over you! [14]If you will fear the LORD, worship him, obey him, and not rebel against the LORD's command, and if both you and the king who rules over you follow the LORD your God—all will be well. [15]But if you don't obey the LORD and rebel against the LORD's command, then the LORD's power will go against you and your king to destroy you.[r]

[16]"So now take a stand! Look at this awesome thing the LORD is doing. [17]Isn't the wheat harvest today? I will call upon the LORD to send thunder and rain. Then you will know and will see for yourselves what great evil you've done in the LORD's eyes by asking for a king."

[18]Samuel called upon the LORD, and God sent thunder and rain on that very day. Then all the people were in awe of the LORD and Samuel.

[19]All of them said to Samuel, "Please pray for us, your servants, to the LORD your God so we don't die because we have added to our many sins the evil of asking for a king."

[20]But Samuel answered the people, "Don't be afraid. Yes, you've done all this evil; just don't turn back from following the LORD. Serve the LORD with all your heart. [21]Don't turn aside to follow useless idols that can't help you or save you. They're absolutely useless! [22]For the sake of his reputation, the LORD won't abandon his people, because the LORD has decided to make you his very own people. [23]But me? I would never sin against the LORD by failing to pray for you. I will teach you what is good and right. [24]Just fear the LORD and serve him faithfully with all your heart. Look at what great things he has done for you! [25]But if you continue to do evil, then both you and your king will be destroyed."

Samuel rejects Saul's dynasty

13 Saul was 30 years old[s] when he became king, and he ruled over Israel forty-two years.[t] [2]Saul selected three thousand men from Israel. Two thousand of those were with Saul at Michmash in the hills near Bethel, and one thousand were with Jonathan at Gibeah in Benjamin. He sent the remaining men home. [3]Jonathan attacked the Philistine fort at Geba, and the Philistines heard about it. So Saul sounded the alarm[u] throughout the land and said, "Hebrews! Listen up!" [4]When all Israel heard that Saul had attacked the Philistine fort and that Israel was hated by the Philistines, the troops were called to Saul's side at Gilgal. [5]The Philistines also were gathered to fight against Israel. They brought thirty thousand chariots with them, six thousand cavalry, and as many soldiers as there is sand on the seashore to fight Israel.[v] They marched up and camped at Michmash, east of Beth-aven. [6]When the Israelites saw that they were in trouble and that their troops were threatened, they hid in caves, in thickets, among rocks, in tunnels, and in cisterns. [7]Some Hebrews even crossed the Jordan River, going into the land of Gad and Gilead.

Saul stayed at Gilgal, and the troops followed him anxiously. [8]He waited seven days, the time appointed by Samuel, but Samuel didn't come to Gilgal, and his troops began to desert. [9]So Saul ordered, "Bring me the entirely burned offering and the well-being sacrifices." Then he offered the entirely burned offering.

[10]The very moment Saul finished offering up the entirely burned offering, Samuel arrived. Saul went out to meet him and welcome him. [11]But Samuel said, "What have you done?"

"I saw that my troops were deserting," Saul replied. "You hadn't arrived by the appointed time, and the Philistines were gathering at Michmash. [12]I thought, The Philistines are about to march against

[r]LXX[L]; MT *against you and against your ancestors* [s]LXX[L]; Syr *twenty-one*; MT lacks a number; 13:1 is omitted in LXX[B]. [t]Part of the number is missing in MT (. . . *and two years*) and all ancient witnesses. Acts 13:21 says Saul ruled forty years, as does Josephus (*Ant.* 6.14.9 [378]), though Josephus also says Saul ruled twenty years (*Ant.* 10.8.4 [143]). [u]Heb *shofar* [v]LXX; MT lacks *They brought, with them, and to fight Israel.*

me at Gilgal and I haven't yet sought the
LORD's favor. So I took control of myself[w]
and offered the entirely burned offering."
13"How stupid of you to have broken the
commands the LORD your God gave you!"
Samuel told Saul. "The LORD would have
established your rule over Israel forever,
14but now your rule won't last. The LORD
will search for a man following the Lord's
own heart,[x] and the LORD will commission
him as leader over God's people, because
you didn't keep the LORD's command."
15Samuel got up and went on his way from
Gilgal, but the rest of the people followed
Saul to join the army, and they went from
Gilgal[y] to Gibeah in Benjamin. Saul counted
about six hundred men still with him. 16Saul,
his son Jonathan, and the people who were
with him were staying at Geba in Benjamin,
while the Philistines camped at Michmash.
17Three raiding parties left the Philistine
camp. One took the road to Ophrah toward
the territory of Shual. 18Another took the
road to Beth-horon, and the last took the
border road that overlooks the Zeboim Valley toward the desert.

Philistine ironworking

19No metalworker was to be found anywhere in Israelite territory because the
Philistines had said, "The Hebrews must
not make swords and spears." 20So every Israelite had to go down to the Philistines to
sharpen their plowshares, mattocks, axes,
and sickles. 21The cost was two-thirds of a
shekel[z] for plowshares and mattocks, but
one-third of a shekel for sharpening axes
and for setting goads. 22So on the day of
the battle, no swords or spears were to be
found in the possession of any of the troops
with Saul and Jonathan, but Saul and his
son Jonathan had them.

Jonathan leads Israel to victory

23Now a group of Philistine soldiers had
marched out to the pass at Michmash.
14 One day Jonathan, Saul's son, said to
his young armor-bearer, "Come on!
Let's go over to the Philistine fort on the
opposite side." But he didn't tell his father.
2Saul was sitting on the outskirts of Gibeah
under the pomegranate tree at Migron. He
had about six hundred men with him, 3in-
cluding Ahijah, the son of Ahitub, who was
Ichabod's brother and the son of Phinehas
the son of Eli, who was the LORD's priest
at Shiloh. He was wearing a priestly vest.[a]
None of the troops knew that Jonathan
had gone.
4There were two stone outcroppings in
the pass where Jonathan planned on crossing over to the Philistine fort—one on each
side. One of these was named Bozez; the
other was named Seneh. 5One outcropping was on the north side, in front of
Michmash, and the other was on the south
side, in front of Geba. 6Jonathan said to
his young armor-bearer, "Come on, let's
go over to the fort of these uncircumcised
men. Maybe the LORD will act on our behalf. After all, nothing can stop the LORD
from saving, whether there are many soldiers[b] or few."
7"Go ahead with whatever you're planning," his armor-bearer replied. "I'm with
you, whatever you decide."
8"All right then," Jonathan said. "We'll
go over to the men and show ourselves. 9If
they say to us, 'Stay there until we get to
you,' then we'll stay where we are and won't
go up to them. 10But if they say, 'Come on
up,' then we'll go up because that will be the
sign that the LORD has handed them over
to us."
11So they showed themselves to the Philistine fort, and the Philistines said, "Look,
the Hebrews are coming out of the holes
they've been hiding in!" 12Then the troops in
the fort yelled to Jonathan and his armor-
bearer, "Come on up! We'll teach you a
lesson!"
So Jonathan said to his armor-bearer,
"Follow me, because the LORD has handed
them over to Israel!" 13So Jonathan scram-
bled up on his hands and feet with his armor-
bearer right behind him. The Philistines fell

[w]Or *forced myself*; Heb uncertain [x]Or *a man loyal to the Lord* [y]LXX; MT lacks much of this verse.
[z]Heb *pim*, which is two-thirds of a shekel [a]Heb *ephod* [b]MT lacks *soldiers*.

before Jonathan. His armor-bearer, coming behind him, would then finish them off. [14]In the first attack, Jonathan and his armor-bearer killed about twenty men in an area of about half an acre.[c] [15]Panic broke out in the camp, in the field, and among all the troops. Even those in the fort and the raiders shook with fear. The very ground shook! It was a terror from God.

[16]Now Saul's lookouts at Gibeah in Benjamin saw the Philistine camp running all over the place.[d] [17]Saul said to the troops with him, "Take a count and see who is missing." So they counted, and Jonathan and his armor-bearer were gone. [18]Saul said to Ahijah, "Bring the priestly vest!"[e] because at that time, Ahijah wore the priestly vest in Israel's presence.[f] [19]As Saul was talking to the priest, the confusion in the Philistine camp continued to grow. Saul said to the priest, "Withdraw your hand."[g]

[20]Then Saul called all his troops together, and they went into battle. The Philistines were completely confused; every soldier's sword was turned against his fellow soldier. [21]Even those Hebrews who had earlier joined up with the Philistines and moved into their camp changed sides to be with the Israelites who were with Saul and Jonathan. [22]Similarly, when all the Israelites who had been hiding in the highlands of Ephraim heard that the Philistines were on the run, they also joined the battle in hot pursuit of the Philistines. [23]The LORD saved Israel that day, and the fighting carried on beyond Beth-aven.

[24]Now the Israelite soldiers were in a difficult situation that day because Saul had bound the troops by a solemn pledge: "Anyone who eats anything before evening when I have taken revenge on my enemies is doomed." So none of the army ate anything. [25]The troops[h] came across a honeycomb with honey on the ground. [26]But even when they came across the honeycomb with the honey still flowing, no one ate any of it because the troops were afraid of the solemn pledge. [27]But Jonathan hadn't heard his father make the people swear the pledge, so he dipped the end of the staff he was carrying into the honeycomb. When he ate some his eyes lit up. [28]Then one of the soldiers spoke up: "Your father bound the troops by a solemn pledge: 'Anyone who eats food today is doomed.' That's why the troops are exhausted."

[29]Jonathan said, "My father has brought trouble to the land. Look how my eyes lit up when I tasted just a bit of that honey! [30]It would have been even better if the troops had eaten some of their enemies' plunder today when they found it! But now the Philistine defeat isn't as thorough as it might have been."

[31]That day, after they had fought the Philistines from Michmash to Aijalon, the troops were completely exhausted. [32]So the troops tore into the plunder, taking sheep, cattle, and calves. They slaughtered them right on the ground and devoured them with the blood still in them. [33]When it was reported to Saul, "The troops are sinning against the LORD by eating meat with blood in it," Saul said, "All of you are traitors! Roll a large stone over here right now. [34]Go among the troops and say to them, 'Everyone must bring their ox or sheep, and slaughter them here with me. Don't sin against the LORD by eating meat with blood still in it.'" So everyone brought whatever they had and slaughtered it there.[i] [35]And Saul built an altar to the LORD. It was the first altar he had built to the LORD.

[36]"Let's go after the Philistines tonight and plunder them until morning," Saul said. "We won't leave them a single survivor!"

"Do whatever you think is best," the troops replied.

But the priest said, "Let's ask God first."

[37]So Saul questioned God: "Should I go after the Philistines? Will you hand them over to Israel?" But God did not answer him that day.

[38]Then Saul said, "All you officers in the army, come forward! Let's find out what sin was committed today. [39]As surely as the LORD lives—the one who has saved

[c]Heb uncertain [d]LXX [e]LXX *ephod* [f]LXX; MT *"Bring out God's chest!" because at that time God's chest was with the Israelites;* cf 14:3. [g]That is, from the priestly vest (Heb *ephod*) or from the Urim and Thummim contained therein [h]MT *land* [i]LXX; MT *brought their ox and slaughtered it there that night.*

Israel—even if it's my own son Jonathan, that person will be executed." Not one of the soldiers answered him. 40 So Saul said to all Israel, "You be on one side, and my son Jonathan and I will be on the other."

"Do whatever you think is best," the troops said.

41 Then Saul asked the LORD God of Israel, "Why haven't you answered your servant today? If the wrongdoing is mine or my son Jonathan's, respond with Urim, but if the wrongdoing belongs to your people Israel, respond with Thummim."[j] Jonathan and Saul were taken by lot, and the troops were cleared.

42 Then Saul said, "Decide between me and my son Jonathan."[k] And Jonathan was selected.

43 "Tell me what you've done," Saul said to Jonathan.

So Jonathan told him. "I only took a very small taste of honey on the end of my staff," he said. "And now I'm supposed to die?"

44 "May God deal harshly with me and worse still if you don't die today!"[l] Saul swore.

45 But the troops said to Saul, "Why should Jonathan die when he has won this great victory for Israel? No way! As surely as the LORD lives, not one hair off his head will fall to the ground, because he did this today with God's help." So the troops rescued Jonathan, and he wasn't executed.

46 Then Saul stopped chasing the Philistines, and the Philistines went back to their own country.

Saul's wars

47 Saul secured his kingship over Israel. He fought against his enemies on every side: against Moab, the Ammonites, Edom, the king of Zobah,[m] and the Philistines. Wherever he turned, he was victorious.[n] 48 He acted heroically, defeating the Amalekites and rescuing Israel from the power of any who had plundered them.

49 Saul's sons were Jonathan, Ishvi, and Malchishua. The names of his two daughters were Merab, the oldest, and Michal, the younger daughter. 50 The name of Saul's wife was Ahinoam, Ahimaaz's daughter. The name of his general was Abner, Ner's son, Saul's uncle. 51 Kish, Saul's father, and Ner, Abner's father, were Abiel's sons.

52 There was fierce warfare against the Philistines throughout Saul's lifetime. So whenever Saul saw any strong or heroic man, he would add him to his troops.

Samuel rejects Saul's kingship

15 Samuel said to Saul, "The LORD sent me to anoint you king over his people Israel. Listen now to the LORD's words! 2 This is what the LORD of heavenly forces says: I am going to punish the Amalekites for what they did to Israel: how they attacked the Israelites as they came up from Egypt. 3 So go! Attack the Amalekites; put everything that belongs to them under the ban.[o] Spare no one. Kill men and women, children and infants, oxen and sheep, camels and donkeys."

4 Saul called out the troops and counted them at Telaim: two hundred thousand foot soldiers and ten thousand more troops from Judah. 5 Then Saul advanced on the Amalekite city and laid an ambush in the valley. 6 Saul told the Kenites, "Get going! Leave the Amalekites immediately because you showed kindness to the Israelites when they came out of Egypt. Otherwise, I'll destroy you right along with them." So the Kenites left the Amalekites. 7 Then Saul attacked the Amalekites from Havilah all the way to Shur, which is near Egypt. 8 He captured Agag the Amalekite king alive, but Saul placed all the people under the ban, killing them with the sword. 9 Saul and the troops spared Agag along with the best sheep, cattle, fattened calves,[p] lambs, and everything of value. They weren't willing to

[j] LXX, Vulg; MT *Saul asked the LORD God of Israel, "Give the right answer."* Urim and Thummim were sacred lots carried by the priest. [k] LXX adds *"Whoever the LORD selects will die." The army said to Saul, "Don't do this!" But Saul forced them, so they decided between him and Jonathan his son.* [l] LXX; MT *if you don't die, Jonathan* [m] LXX, DSS (4QSam[a]); MT *kings of Zobah* [n] LXX [o] A technique of holy war that often involves total destruction, in which everything that is destroyed is dedicated to the deity who helps in the battle; also in 15:8-9, 15, 18, 20-21. [p] LXX

put them under the ban; but anything that
was despised or of no value[q] they placed
under the ban.
10Then the LORD's word came to Samuel:
11"I regret making Saul king because he has
turned away from following me and hasn't
done what I said." Samuel was upset at this,
and he prayed to the LORD all night long.
12Samuel got up early in the morning
to meet Saul, and was told, "Saul went to
Carmel, where he is setting up a monument
for himself. Then he left and went down to
Gilgal."
13When Samuel reached Saul,[r] Saul
greeted him, "The LORD bless you! I have
done what the LORD said."
14"Then what," Samuel asked, "is this
bleating of sheep in my ears and mooing of
cattle I hear?"
15"They were taken from the Amalekites," Saul said, "because the troops spared
the best sheep and cattle in order to sacrifice them to the LORD your God. The rest
was placed under the ban."
16Samuel then said to Saul, "Enough! Let
me tell you what the LORD said to me last
night."
"Tell me," Saul replied.
17Samuel said, "Even if you think you are
insignificant, aren't you the leader of Israel's tribes? The LORD anointed you king
over Israel. 18The LORD sent you on a mission, instructing you, 'Go, and put the sinful Amalekites under the ban. Fight against
them until you've wiped them out.' 19Why
didn't you obey the LORD? You did evil in
the LORD's eyes when you tore into the
plunder!"
20"But I did obey the LORD!" Saul protested to Samuel. "I went on the mission
the LORD sent me on. I captured Agag the
Amalekite king, and I put the Amalekites
under the ban. 21Yes, the troops took sheep
and cattle from the plunder—the very best
items placed under the ban—but in order
to sacrifice them to the LORD your God at
Gilgal."
22Then Samuel replied,

"Does the LORD want
entirely burned offerings and sacrifices
as much as obedience to the LORD?
Listen to this:
obeying is better than sacrificing,
paying attention
is better than fat from rams,
23because rebellion is as bad
as the sin of divination;
arrogance is like the evil of idolatry.[s]
Because you have rejected
what the LORD said,
he has rejected you as king."

24Saul said to Samuel, "I have sinned because I disobeyed the LORD's command and
your instructions. I was afraid of the troops
and obeyed them. 25But now please forgive
my sin! Come back with me, so I can worship the LORD."
26But Samuel said to Saul, "I can't[t] return
with you because you have rejected what
the LORD said, and the LORD has rejected
you from being king over Israel."
27Samuel turned to leave, but Saul grabbed
at the edge of his robe, and it ripped. 28Then
Samuel told him, "The LORD has ripped the
kingdom of Israel from you today. He will
give it to a friend of yours, someone who
is more worthy than you. 29What's more,
the enduring one of Israel doesn't take back
what he says and doesn't change his mind.
He is not a human being who would change
his mind."
30"I have sinned," Saul said, "but please
honor me in front of my people's elders
and before Israel, and come back with me
so I can worship the LORD your God." 31So
Samuel went back with Saul, and Saul worshipped the LORD.
32"Bring me Agag the Amalekite king,"
Samuel said.
Agag came to him in chains, asking,
"Would death have been as bitter as this is?"[u]
33Samuel said, "Just as your sword left
women without their children, now your
mother will be childless among women."
Then Samuel cut Agag to pieces in the
LORD's presence at Gilgal.

[q]LXX; Heb uncertain [r]LXX adds *he was offering entirely burned sacrifices to the LORD, the best of the plunder that he had taken from Amalek. As Samuel approached Saul.* [s]Sym, LXX[B]; MT *evil and idolatry* [t]Or *won't*
[u]LXX; Heb uncertain

34 Then Samuel went to Ramah, but Saul went up to his home in Gibeah. 35 Samuel never saw Saul again before he died, but he grieved over Saul. However, the LORD regretted making Saul king over Israel.

Samuel anoints David

16 The LORD said to Samuel, "How long are you going to grieve over Saul? I have rejected him as king over Israel. Fill your horn with oil and get going. I'm sending you to Jesse of Bethlehem because I have found[v] my next king among his sons."

2 "How can I do that?" Samuel asked. "When Saul hears of it he'll kill me!"

"Take a heifer with you," the LORD replied, "and say, 'I have come to make a sacrifice to the LORD.' 3 Invite Jesse to the sacrifice, and I will make clear to you what you should do. You will anoint for me the person I point out to you."

4 Samuel did what the LORD instructed. When he came to Bethlehem, the city elders came to meet him. They were shaking with fear. "Do you come in peace?" they asked.

5 "Yes," Samuel answered. "I've come to make a sacrifice to the LORD. Now make yourselves holy, then come with me to the sacrifice." Samuel made Jesse and his sons holy and invited them to the sacrifice as well.

6 When they arrived, Samuel looked at Eliab and thought, That must be the LORD's anointed right in front.

7 But the LORD said to Samuel, "Have no regard for his appearance or stature, because I haven't selected him. God[w] doesn't look at things like humans do. Humans see only what is visible to the eyes, but the LORD sees into the heart."

8 Next Jesse called for Abinadab, who presented himself to Samuel, but he said, "The LORD hasn't chosen this one either." 9 So Jesse presented Shammah, but Samuel said, "No, the LORD hasn't chosen this one." 10 Jesse presented seven of his sons to Samuel, but Samuel said to Jesse, "The LORD hasn't picked any of these." 11 Then Samuel asked Jesse, "Is that all of your boys?"

"There is still the youngest one," Jesse answered, "but he's out keeping the sheep."

"Send for him," Samuel told Jesse, "because we can't proceed until he gets here."[x]

12 So Jesse sent and brought him in. He was reddish brown, had beautiful eyes, and was good-looking. The LORD said, "That's the one. Go anoint him." 13 So Samuel took the horn of oil and anointed him right there in front of his brothers. The LORD's spirit came over David from that point forward.

Then Samuel left and went to Ramah.

David is introduced to Saul

14 Now the LORD's spirit had departed from Saul, and an evil spirit from the LORD tormented him. 15 Saul's servants said to him, "Look, an evil spirit from God is tormenting you. 16 If our master just says the word, your servants will search for someone who knows how to play the lyre. The musician can play whenever the evil spirit from God is affecting you, and then you'll feel better."

17 Saul said to his servants, "Find me a good musician and bring him to me."

18 One of the servants responded, "I know that one of Jesse's sons from Bethlehem is a good musician. He's a strong man and heroic, a warrior who speaks well and is good-looking too. The LORD is with him."

19 So Saul sent messengers to Jesse to say, "Send me your son David, the one who keeps the sheep."

20 Jesse then took a donkey and loaded it with a homer of bread,[y] a jar of wine, and a young goat, and he sent it along with his son David to Saul. 21 That is how David came to Saul and entered his service. Saul liked David very much,[z] and David became his armor-bearer. 22 Saul sent a message to Jesse: "Please allow David to remain in my service because I am pleased with him." 23 Whenever the evil spirit from God affected Saul, David would take the lyre and play it. Then Saul would relax and feel better, and the evil spirit would leave him alone.

[v] Or *seen* [w] LXX; MT lacks *God.* [x] MT; LXX *we won't sit down* (that is, to eat) [y] LXX [z] Or *David liked Saul very much.*

David defeats Goliath

17 The Philistines assembled their troops for war at Socoh of Judah. They camped between Socoh and Azekah at Ephes-dammim. 2Saul and the Israelite army assembled and camped in the Elah Valley, where they got organized to fight the Philistines. 3The Philistines took positions on one hill while Israel took positions on the opposite hill. There was a valley between them.

4A champion named Goliath from Gath came out from the Philistine camp. He was more than nine feet tall.[a] 5He had a bronze helmet on his head and wore bronze scale-armor weighing one hundred twenty-five pounds.[b] 6He had bronze plates on his shins, and a bronze scimitar hung on his back. 7His spear shaft[c] was as strong as the bar on a weaver's loom, and its iron head weighed fifteen pounds.[d] His shield-bearer walked in front of him.

8He stopped and shouted to the Israelite troops, "Why have you come and taken up battle formations? I am the Philistine champion,[e] and you are Saul's servants. Isn't that right? Select one of your men, and let him come down against me. 9If he is able to fight me and kill me, then we will become your slaves, but if I overcome him and kill him, then you will become our slaves and you will serve us. 10I insult Israel's troops today!" the Philistine continued, "Give me an opponent, and we'll fight!" 11When Saul and all Israel heard what the Philistine said, they were distressed and terrified.[f]

12Now David was Jesse's son, an Ephraimite from Bethlehem in Judah who had eight sons. By Saul's time, Jesse was already quite old and far along in age.[g] 13Jesse's three oldest sons had gone with Saul to war. Their names were Eliab the oldest, Abinadab the second oldest, and Shammah the third oldest. 14(David was the youngest.) These three older sons followed Saul, 15but David went back and forth from Saul's side to shepherd his father's flock in Bethlehem.

16For forty days straight the Philistine came out and took his stand, both morning and evening. 17Jesse said to his son David, "Please take your brothers an ephah[h] of this roasted grain and these ten loaves of bread. Deliver them quickly to your brothers in the camp. 18And here, take these ten wedges of cheese to their unit commander. Find out how your brothers are doing and bring back some sign that they are okay. 19They are with Saul and all the Israelite troops fighting the Philistines in the Elah Valley."

20So David got up early in the morning, left someone in charge of the flock, and loaded up and left, just as his father Jesse had instructed him. He reached the camp right when the army was taking up their battle formations and shouting the war cry. 21Israel and the Philistines took up their battle formations opposite each other. 22David left his things with an attendant and ran to the front line. When he arrived, he asked how his brothers were doing. 23Right when David was speaking with them, Goliath, the Philistine champion from Gath, came forward from the Philistine ranks and said the same things he had said before. David listened. 24When the Israelites saw Goliath, every one of them ran away terrified of him. (25Now the Israelite soldiers had been saying to each other: "Do you see this man who keeps coming out? How he comes to insult Israel? The king will reward with great riches whoever kills that man. The king will give his own daughter to him and make his household exempt from taxes[i] in Israel.")

26David asked the soldiers standing by him, "What will be done for the person who kills that Philistine over there and removes this insult from Israel? Who is that uncircumcised Philistine, anyway, that he can get away with insulting the army of the living God?"

27Then the troops repeated to him what they had been saying. "So that's what will be done for the man who kills him," they said.

28When David's oldest brother Eliab

[a]LXX *over six feet tall* [b]Five thousand shekels [c]Qere, LXX, Syr (cf 2 Sam 21:19); Kethib *the point of his spear* [d]Six hundred shekels [e]MT *the Philistine* lacks *champion*. [f]The following verses are absent from LXX[B]: 17:12-31, 41, 48*b*, 50, 55-58. [g]LXX, Syr [h]One ephah is approximately twenty quarts. [i]Heb uncertain

heard him talking to the soldiers, he got very mad at David. "Why did you come down here?" he said. "Who is watching those few sheep for you in the wilderness? I know how arrogant you are and your devious plan: you came down just to see the battle!"

29"What did I do wrong this time?" David replied. "It was just a question!"

30So David turned to someone else and asked the same thing, and the people said the
same thing in reply. 31The things David had said were overheard and reported to Saul, who sent for him.

32"Don't let anyone[j] lose courage because of this Philistine!" David told Saul. "I, your servant, will go out and fight him!"

33"You can't go out and fight this Philistine," Saul answered David. "You are still a boy. But he's been a warrior since he was a boy!"

34"Your servant has kept his father's sheep," David replied to Saul, "and if ever a lion or a bear came and carried off one of
the flock, 35I would go after it, strike it, and rescue the animal from its mouth. If it turned on me, I would grab it at its jaw,
strike it, and kill it. 36Your servant has fought both lions and bears. This uncircumcised Philistine will be just like one of them because he has insulted the army of the living God.

37"The LORD," David added, "who rescued me from the power of both lions and bears, will rescue me from the power of this Philistine."

"Go!" Saul replied to David. "And may the LORD be with you!"

38Then Saul dressed David in his own gear, putting a coat of armor on him and
a bronze helmet on his head. 39David strapped his sword on over the armor, but he couldn't walk around well because he'd never tried it before. "I can't walk in this," David told Saul, "because I've never tried
it before." So he took them off. 40He then grabbed his staff and chose five smooth stones from the streambed. He put them in the pocket of his shepherd's bag and with sling in hand went out to the Philistine.

41The Philistine got closer and closer to David, and his shield-bearer was in front
of him. 42When the Philistine looked David over, he sneered at David because he was just a boy; reddish brown and good-looking.

43The Philistine asked David, "Am I some sort of dog that you come at me with sticks?" And he cursed David by his gods.
44"Come here," he said to David, "and I'll feed your flesh to the wild birds and the wild animals!"

45But David told the Philistine, "You are coming against me with sword, spear, and scimitar, but I come against you in the name of the LORD of heavenly forces, the God of Israel's army, the one you've
insulted. 46Today the LORD will hand you over to me. I will strike you down and cut off your head! Today I will feed your dead body and the dead bodies of the entire Philistine camp[k] to the wild birds and the wild animals. Then the whole world will know
that there is a God on Israel's side. 47And all those gathered here will know that the LORD doesn't save by means of sword and spear. The LORD owns this war, and he will hand all of you over to us."

48The Philistine got up and moved closer to attack David, and David ran quickly to
the front line to face him. 49David put his hand in his bag and took out a stone. He slung it, and it hit the Philistine on his forehead. The stone penetrated his forehead, and he fell facedown on the ground.
50And that's how David triumphed over the Philistine with just a sling and a stone, striking the Philistine down and killing him—and David didn't even have a sword!
51Then David ran and stood over the Philistine. He grabbed the Philistine's sword, drew it from its sheath, and finished him off. Then David cut off the Philistine's head with the sword.

When the Philistines saw that their hero
was dead, they fled. 52The soldiers from Israel and Judah jumped up with a shout and chased the Philistines all the way to Gath[l] and the gates of Ekron. The dead Philistines were littered along the Shaarim road all the

[j]LXX *my master* (the king) [k]LXX; MT lacks *your dead body.* [l]LXX; MT *Gai* or *a valley*

way to Gath and Ekron. 53 When the Israelites came back from chasing the Philistines, they plundered their camp. 54 David took the head of the Philistine and brought it to Jerusalem, but he put the Philistine's weapons in his own tent.

55 Now when Saul saw David go out to meet the Philistine, he asked Abner the army general, "Abner, whose son is that boy?"

"As surely as you live, Your Majesty, I don't know," Abner answered.

56 "Then find out whose son that young man is," the king replied.

57 So when David came back from killing the Philistine, Abner sent for him and presented him to Saul. The Philistine's head was still in David's hand. 58 Saul said to him, "Whose son are you, my boy?"

"I'm the son of your servant Jesse from Bethlehem," David answered.

Jonathan and David

18 As soon as David had finished talking with Saul, Jonathan's life[m] became bound up with David's life, and Jonathan loved David as much as himself.[n] 2 From that point forward, Saul kept David in his service[o] and wouldn't allow him to return to his father's household. 3 And Jonathan and David made a covenant together because Jonathan loved David as much as himself. 4 Jonathan took off the robe he was wearing and gave it to David, along with his armor, as well as his sword, his bow, and his belt. 5 David went out and was successful in every mission Saul sent him to do. So Saul placed him in charge of the soldiers, and this pleased all the troops as well as Saul's servants.

Saul jealous of David

6 After David came back from killing the Philistine, and as the troops returned home, women from all of Israel's towns came out to meet King Saul[p] with singing and dancing, with tambourines, rejoicing, and musical instruments. 7 The women sang in celebration:

"Saul has killed his thousands,
but David has killed
his tens of thousands!"

8 Saul burned with anger. This song annoyed him. "They've credited David with tens of thousands," he said, "but only credit me with thousands. What's next for him—the kingdom itself?" 9 So Saul kept a close eye on David from that point on.

10 The next day an evil spirit from God came over Saul,[q] and he acted like he was in a prophetic frenzy in his house. So David played the lyre as he usually did. Saul had a spear in his hand, 11 and he threw it, thinking, I'll pin David to the wall. But David escaped from him two different times.

12 Saul was afraid of David because the LORD was with David but no longer with Saul. 13 So Saul removed David from his service, placing him in command of a unit of one thousand men. David led the men out to war and back. 14 David was successful in everything he did because the LORD was with him. 15 Saul saw that he was very successful, and he was afraid of him. 16 Everyone in Israel and Judah loved David because he led them out in war and back again.

17 Saul said to David, "Look, here is my oldest daughter Merab. I will give her to you in marriage on this condition: you must be my warrior and fight the LORD's battles." I won't raise my hand against him, Saul thought; let the Philistines do that!

18 "I'm not worthy," David replied to Saul, "and neither is my family or my father's clan in Israel, to become the king's son-in-law." 19 And so when the time came for Saul's daughter Merab to be married to David, she was given to Adriel from Meholah instead.

20 Now Saul's younger daughter Michal loved David. When this was reported to Saul he was happy about it. 21 I'll give her to him Saul thought; she'll cause him problems, and the Philistines will be against him.

So Saul said to David a second time, "Become my son-in-law now."

22 Saul instructed his servants, "Tell

[m] Or *soul*; also twice more in this verse and in 18:3 [n] The following verses are absent from LXX[B]: 18:1-5, 10-11, 17-19, 29*b*-30. [o] MT lacks *in his service*. [p] MT; LXX *to meet David* [q] Or *to Saul*

David in private: 'Look, the king likes you, and all his servants love you. You should become the king's son-in-law.'"

23 Saul's servants whispered these things in David's ear. But David said, "Do you think it's a simple matter to become the king's son-in-law? I don't! I'm poor and insignificant."

24 Saul's servants reported what David said, 25 and Saul replied, "Tell David this: 'The king doesn't want any bridal gift, just a hundred Philistine foreskins as vengeance on the king's enemies.'" (Saul was hoping that David would die at the hands of the Philistines.) 26 When the servants reported this to David, he was happy to become the king's son-in-law. Even before the allotted time had expired,[r] 27 David got up and went with his soldiers and killed one hundred Philistines.[s] David brought their foreskins and counted them out for the king so he could become the king's son-in-law. Then Saul gave his daughter Michal to him in marriage.

28 When Saul knew for certain that the LORD was with David and that his daughter Michal loved him, 29 then Saul was even more afraid of David. Saul was David's enemy for the rest of his life.[t] 30 And whenever the Philistine commanders came out for battle, David would have more success than the rest of Saul's officers, so his fame spread widely.

David escapes Saul

19 Saul ordered his son Jonathan and all his servants to kill David, but Jonathan, Saul's son, liked David very much. 2 So Jonathan warned David, "My father Saul is trying to kill you. Be on guard tomorrow morning. Stay somewhere safe and hide. 3 I'll go out and stand by my father in the field where you'll be. I'll talk to my father about you, and I'll tell you whatever I find out."

4 So Jonathan spoke highly about David to his father Saul, telling him, "The king shouldn't do anything wrong to his servant David, because he hasn't wronged you. In fact, his actions have helped you greatly. 5 He risked his own life when he killed that Philistine, and the LORD won a great victory for all Israel. You saw it and were happy about it. Why then would you do something wrong to an innocent person by killing David for no reason?"

6 Saul listened to Jonathan and then swore, "As surely as the LORD lives, David won't be executed." 7 So Jonathan summoned David and told him everything they had talked about. Then Jonathan brought David back to Saul, and David served Saul as he had previously.

8 War broke out again. When David went out to fight the Philistines, he struck them with such force that they ran from him.

9 Then an evil spirit from the LORD came over Saul.[u] He was sitting in his house with his spear in hand while David was playing music. 10 Saul tried to pin David to the wall with his spear, but David escaped Saul. Saul drove the spear into the wall, but David fled and got away safely. That night 11 Saul sent messengers to David's house to keep watch on it and kill him in the morning. David's wife Michal warned him, "If you don't escape with your life tonight, you are a dead man tomorrow." 12 So Michal lowered David through a window. He took off and ran, and he got away. 13 Then Michal took the household's divine image and laid it in the bed, putting some goat's hair on its head and covering it with clothes.

14 Saul sent messengers to arrest David, but she said, "He's sick."

15 Saul sent the messengers back to check on David for themselves. "Bring him to me on his bed," he ordered, "so he can be executed." 16 When the messengers arrived, they found the idol in the bed with the goat's hair on its head. 17 Saul said to Michal, "Why could you betray me like this, letting my enemy go so that now he has escaped?"

Michal said to Saul, "David told me, 'Help me get away or I'll kill you!'"

18 So David fled and escaped. When he reached Samuel at Ramah, he reported to

[r] Heb uncertain [s] LXX, cf 2 Sam 3:14; MT *two hundred* [t] Or *Saul became David's constant enemy.* [u] Or *to Saul*

him everything Saul had done to him. Then he and Samuel went to stay in the camps.[v]

19When Saul was told that David was in the camps at Ramah, 20he sent messengers to arrest David. They saw a group of prophets in a prophetic frenzy, with Samuel standing there as their leader. God's spirit came over Saul's messengers, and they also fell into a prophetic frenzy. 21This was reported to Saul, and he sent different messengers, but they also fell into a prophetic frenzy. So Saul sent a third group of messengers, and they did the very same thing.

22At that point, Saul went to Ramah himself. He came to the well at the threshing floor that was on the bare hill there[w] and asked, "Where are Samuel and David?"

"In the camps at Ramah," he was told. 23So Saul went to the camps at Ramah, and God's spirit came over him too. So as he traveled, he was in a prophetic frenzy until he reached the camps at Ramah. 24He even took off all his clothes and fell into a prophetic frenzy in front of Samuel. He lay naked that whole day and night. That's why people say, "Is Saul also one of the prophets?"

Jonathan and David's friendship

20 David fled from the camps at Ramah. He came to Jonathan and asked, "What have I done? What is my crime? How have I wronged your father that he wants me dead?"

2Jonathan said to him, "No! You are not going to die! Listen: My father doesn't do anything big or small without telling me first. Why would my father hide this from me? It isn't true!"

3But David solemnly promised in response, "Your father knows full well that you like me. He probably said, 'Jonathan must not learn about this or he'll be upset.'[x] But I promise you—on the LORD's life and yours!—that I am this close to death!"

4"What do you want me to do?" Jonathan said to David. "I'll do it."

5"Okay, listen," David answered Jonathan. "Tomorrow is the new moon, and I'm supposed to sit with the king at the feast. Instead, let me go and I'll hide in the field until nighttime.[y] 6If your father takes note of my absence, tell him, 'David begged my permission to run down to his hometown Bethlehem, because there is an annual sacrifice there for his whole family.' 7If Saul says 'Fine,' then I, your servant, am safe. But if he loses his temper, then you'll know for certain that he intends to harm me. 8So be loyal to your servant, because you've brought your servant into a sacred covenant[z] with you. If I'm guilty, then kill me yourself; just don't take me back to your father."

9"Enough!" Jonathan replied. "If I can determine for certain that my father intends to harm you, of course I'll tell you!"

10"Who will tell me if your father responds harshly?" David asked Jonathan.

11"Come on," Jonathan said to David. "Let's go into the field." So both of them went out into the field. 12Then Jonathan told David, "I pledge by the LORD God of Israel that I will question my father by this time tomorrow or on the third day. If he seems favorable toward David, I will definitely send word and make sure you know. 13But if my father intends to harm you, then may the LORD deal harshly with me, Jonathan, and worse still if I don't tell you right away so that you can escape safely. May the LORD be with you as he once was with my father. 14If I remain alive, be loyal to me.[a] But if I die, 15don't ever stop being loyal to my household. Once the LORD has eliminated all of David's enemies from the earth, 16if Jonathan's name is also eliminated, then the LORD will seek retribution from David!"[b]

17So Jonathan again made a pledge to David[c] because he loved David as much as himself. 18"Tomorrow is the festival of the new moon," Jonathan told David. "You will be missed because your seat will be empty. 19The day after tomorrow, go all the way to the spot where you hid on the day of the incident, and stay close to that mound.[d] 20On the third day I will shoot an arrow to the side of the mound as if aim-

[v]Or *Naioth*, also in 19:19, 22-23 [w]LXX; MT *the large well at Secu* [x]LXX *or he'll tell David*; cf 20:34 [y]LXX; MT *until the third evening*; cf 20:12, 19-20 [z]MT *the LORD's covenant* [a]LXX; MT *show me the LORD's faithful love* [b]20:14-16 follows LXX. [c]LXX; MT *Jonathan made David pledge.* [d]LXX; MT *to the stone Ezel*; cf 20:41

ing at a target.[e] 21 Then I'll send the servant boy, saying, 'Go retrieve the arrow.' If I yell to the boy, 'Hey! The arrow is on this side of you. Get it!' then you can come out because it will be safe for you. There won't be any trouble—I make a pledge on the LORD's life. 22 But if I yell to the young man, 'Hey! The arrow is past you,' then run for it, because the LORD has sent you away. 23 Either way, the LORD is witness[f] between us forever regarding the promise we made to each other." 24 So David hid himself in the field.

When the new moon came, the king sat at the feast to eat. 25 He took his customary seat by the wall. Jonathan sat opposite him[g] while Abner sat beside Saul. David's seat was empty. 26 Saul didn't say anything that day because he thought, Perhaps David became unclean somehow. That must be it. 27 But on the next day, the second of the new moon, David's seat was still empty. Saul said to his son Jonathan, "Why hasn't Jesse's son come to the table,[h] either yesterday or today?"

28 Jonathan answered Saul, "David begged my permission to go to Bethlehem. 29 He said, 'Please let me go because we have a family sacrifice there in town, and my brother has ordered me to be present. Please do me a favor and let me slip away so I can see my family.' That's why David hasn't been at the king's table."

30 At that, Saul got angry at Jonathan. "You son of a stubborn, rebellious woman!" he said. "Do you think I don't know how you've allied yourself with Jesse's son? Shame on you and on the mother who birthed you![i] 31 As long as Jesse's son lives on this earth, neither you nor your dynasty will be secure. Now have him brought to me because he's a dead man!"

32 But Jonathan answered his father Saul, "Why should David be executed? What has he done?"

33 At that, Saul threw[j] his spear at Jonathan to strike him, and Jonathan realized that his father intended to kill David. 34 Jonathan got up from the table in a rage. He didn't eat anything on the second day of the new moon because he was worried about David and because his father had humiliated him.

35 In the morning, Jonathan went out to the field for the meeting with David, and a young servant boy went with him. 36 He said to the boy, "Go quickly and retrieve the arrow that I shoot." So the boy ran off, and he shot an arrow beyond him. 37 When the boy got to the spot where Jonathan shot the arrow, Jonathan yelled to him, "Isn't the arrow past you?" 38 Jonathan yelled again to the boy, "Quick! Hurry up! Don't just stand there!" So Jonathan's servant boy gathered up the arrow and came back to his master. 39 The boy had no idea what had happened; only Jonathan and David knew. 40 Jonathan handed his weapons to the boy and told him, "Get going. Take these back to town."

41 As soon as the boy was gone, David came out from behind the mound[k] and fell down, face on the ground, bowing low three times. The friends kissed each other, and cried with each other, but David cried hardest. 42[l] Then Jonathan said to David, "Go in peace because the two of us made a solemn pledge in the LORD's name when we said, 'The LORD is witness between us and between our descendants forever.'" Then David got up and left, but Jonathan went back to town.

David helped at Nob

21 [m]David came to Nob where Ahimelech was priest. Ahimelech was shaking in fear when he met David. "Why are you alone? Why is no one with you?" he asked.

2 David answered Ahimelech the priest, "The king has given me orders, but he instructed me, 'Don't let anyone know anything about the mission I'm sending you on or about your orders.' As for my troops, I told them to meet me at an undisclosed location. 3 Now what do you have here with you? Give me five loaves of bread or whatever you can find."

[e]Correction; MT *arrows* (plural here and in 20:21-22, 36, 38 Qere) [f]LXX; MT lacks *witness;* also in 20:42. [g]LXX; MT *Jonathan arose* [h]LXX, DSS (4QSam[b]); MT *to the feast* [i]Or *and shame on your mother's nakedness.* [j]MT; LXX *pointed* [k]LXX; MT *beside the south* [l]21:1 in Heb [m]21:2 in Heb

4“I don’t have any regular bread on hand,” the priest answered David, “just holy bread—but only if your troops have abstained from sexual activity.”

5“Definitely,” David answered the priest. “Whenever I go out to war, women are off-limits; that’s our standard operating procedure. Even on regular missions, the men’s gear is[n] kept holy. That’s even more true today, with the mission holy along with the gear.”[o] 6So the priest gave David holy bread, because there was no other bread except the bread of the presence, which is removed from the LORD’s presence and replaced by warm bread as soon as it is taken away.

7Now one of Saul’s servants was there that day, detained in the LORD’s presence. His name was Doeg. He was an Edomite and Saul’s head shepherd.

8David asked Ahimelech, “Do you have a spear or sword on hand? I didn’t bring my sword or gear with me because the king’s mission was urgent.”

9The priest said, “The sword of Goliath, the Philistine you killed in the Elah Valley, is here wrapped in a cloth behind a priestly vest.[p] If you want it, take it, because there are no other swords here.”

David said, “No sword is as good as that one! Give it to me!”

David pretends to be crazy

10So David got up and continued running from Saul. He went to Achish, Gath’s king. 11Achish’s servants said to him, “Isn’t that David, king of the land? He’s the one people sing about in their dances,

‘Saul has killed his thousands,
but David has killed
his tens of thousands!’ ”

12David took these words very seriously and became very frightened of Achish, Gath’s king. 13So he changed the way he acted with them, pretending to be insane while he was with them.[q] He scratched marks on the doors of the city gates[r] and let spit run down his chin.

14“Can’t you see he’s crazy?” Achish asked his servants. “Why bring him to me? 15Am I short on insane people that you’ve brought this person to go crazy right in front of me? Do you really think I’m going to let this man enter my house?”

David gathers support

22 David left Gath and escaped to Adullam’s fortress.[s] When David’s siblings and all his extended family learned of this, they went to join him there. 2Everyone who was in trouble, in debt, or in desperate circumstances gathered around David, and he became their leader. Approximately four hundred men joined him.

3From there David went to Mizpeh in Moab. He said to the Moabite king, “Please let my father and mother stay with you until I know what God will do to me.” 4So David left his parents with the Moabite king, and they stayed with him the whole time David was in the fortress.

5Then the prophet Gad told David, “Don’t stay in the fortress any longer. Leave now and go to the land of Judah.” So David left and went to Hereth forest.

Saul kills the priests of Nob

6Saul learned that David and his soldiers had been located. Saul was sitting under the tamarisk tree on the hill at Gibeah, spear in hand, with all his servants waiting on him. 7He said to them, “Listen up, Benjaminites! Will Jesse’s son give fields and vineyards to each and every one of you? Will he make each one of you commanders of units of one thousand men or commanders of units of one hundred? 8Is that why all of you have conspired against me? No one informed me when my son made a covenant with Jesse’s son! Not one of you is concerned about me or informs me when my own son sets my servant against me in an ambush—but that’s what has happened today!”

9Doeg the Edomite, who was standing with Saul’s servants, responded, “I saw Jesse’s son go to Ahimelech, Ahitub’s son, at Nob. 10Ahimelech questioned the LORD for

[n]MT; LXX *all the men are* [o]Heb uncertain [p]DSS (4QSam[b]); MT *behind the priestly vest* (Heb *ephod*) [q]Or *in their hand*; Heb uncertain [r]Or with correction *he spit on the doors of the city gate or he fell down at the doors of the city gate* (cf LXX). [s]Correction; cf 22:4-5; MT *cave*

David, and gave him provisions as well as
the sword of Goliath the Philistine."
11 The king then sent for the priest
Ahimelech, Ahitub's son, and all his extended family, who were the priests at Nob.
All of them came to the king.
12 "Listen here, son of Ahitub," Saul said.
"Yes sir," he replied.
13 Saul said to him, "Why have you
conspired against me—you with Jesse's
son—giving him food and a sword and
questioning God for him so that he is now
against me, waiting in ambush, which is
what has happened today?"
14 Ahimelech answered the king, "Out
of all your servants, who is as trustworthy
as David? He is the king's son-in-law, does
whatever you ask, and is well respected in
your house. 15 Was that the first time I questioned God for him? Of course not! But
please, the king shouldn't accuse me, his
servant, or anyone in my father's household of any wrongdoing, because your servant knew nothing whatsoever about this
matter."
16 But the king said, "You will be executed, Ahimelech—you and all of your father's household!"
17 The king ordered the guards waiting on
him: "Go ahead and kill the LORD's priests
because they've joined up with David too.
They knew he was on the run but didn't inform me."
But the king's servants were unwilling to
lift a hand to attack the LORD's priests.
18 The king then ordered Doeg, "Doeg!
You go attack the priests." So Doeg the
Edomite went and attacked the priests,
killing eighty-five men who wore the linen
priestly vest[t] that day. 19 He put the whole
priestly city of Nob to the sword: men and
women, children and infants, even oxen,
donkeys, and sheep.
20 But one of the sons of Ahimelech, Ahitub's son, escaped. His name was Abiathar,
and he fled to David. 21 Abiathar reported to
David that Saul had slaughtered the LORD's
priests.
22 David told Abiathar, "That day, when
Doeg the Edomite was there, I knew that he
would tell Saul everything. I am to blame[u]
for the deaths in your father's family. 23 Stay
with me, and don't be afraid. The one who
seeks my life now seeks yours too. But
you'll be safe with me."

Saul chases David

23 David was told, "The Philistines are
now attacking Keilah and looting
the threshing floors!"
2 David asked the LORD, "Should I go and
fight these Philistines?"
"Go!" the LORD answered. "Fight the
Philistines and save Keilah!"
3 But David's men said to him, "Look how
frightened we are here in Judah. It'll be
worse if we go to Keilah against Philistine
forces!"
4 So David asked the LORD again, and the
LORD reaffirmed, "Yes, go down to Keilah,
because I will hand the Philistines over
to you."
5 Then David and his soldiers went to
Keilah and fought the Philistines, driving
off their cattle and defeating them decisively. And that's how David saved the residents of Keilah.
6 Now after Abiathar, Ahimelech's son,
fled to David, he had accompanied David to
Keilah,[v] bringing a priestly vest[w] with him.
7 When Saul was told that David had gone to
Keilah, he said, "God has handed him over[x]
to me now because he has trapped himself
by entering a town with gates and bars!"
8 So Saul called up all his troops for war, to
go down to Keilah and attack David and his
soldiers.
9 When David learned that Saul was planning to harm him, he told the priest Abiathar, "Bring the priestly vest now."
10 Then David said, "LORD God of Israel,
I, your servant, have heard that Saul plans
on coming to Keilah and will destroy the
town because of me. 11 LORD God of Israel,
will Saul come down as your servant has
heard?[y] Please tell your servant."

[t]Heb *ephod* [u]LXX, Vulg; Heb uncertain [v]LXX; MT lacks *he had accompanied David to.* [w]Heb *ephod* [x]LXX, Targ; MT *made a stranger of him* [y]DSS (4QSam[b]), LXX; MT *LORD God of Israel, will the citizens of Keilah hand me over to him? Will Saul come down as your servant has heard?* Cf 23:12*a*.

"Yes, he will come down," the LORD answered.

12 Next David asked, "Will the citizens of Keilah hand me and my soldiers over to Saul?"

"Yes, they will hand you over," the LORD replied.

13 So David and his troops—approximately six hundred men—got up and left Keilah. They kept moving, going from one place to the next. When Saul was told that David had escaped from Keilah, he didn't go there.

14 David lived in the fortresses in the wilderness and in the hills of the Ziph wilderness. Saul searched for him constantly, but God did not hand David over to Saul. 15 While David was at Horesh in the Ziph wilderness he learned that Saul was looking to kill him. 16 Saul's son Jonathan came to David at Horesh and encouraged him with God. 17 Jonathan said to him, "Don't be afraid! My father Saul's hand won't touch you. You will be king over Israel, and I will be your second in command. Even my father Saul knows this." 18 Then the two of them made a covenant before the LORD. David stayed at Horesh, but Jonathan went back home.

19 Some Ziphites came to Saul at Gibeah. "David is hiding among us in the fortresses at Horesh on the hill of Hachilah, south of Jeshimon," they said. 20 "So whenever you want to come down, Your Majesty, do it! Leave it to us to hand him over to the king."

21 "The LORD bless you because you have shown this kindness to me!" Saul said. 22 "Go now and get everything ready. Find out everything you can: where he stays, where he goes, who has seen him. I am told he is very shrewd. 23 Find out every hiding place he uses there and come back to me when you know for certain. I will then go with you. If David is in the area, I will hunt him down among any of Judah's clans!" 24 So they got up and left for Ziph ahead of Saul.

Meanwhile, David and his soldiers were in the Maon wilderness in the desert plain south of Jeshimon. 25 When Saul and his troops went looking for him, David was told about it, so he went down to a certain rock there and stayed in the Maon wilderness. When Saul heard that, he went into the Maon wilderness after David. 26 Saul was going around one side of a hill there while David and his soldiers were going around the other. David was hurrying to get away from Saul while Saul and his troops were trying to surround David and his soldiers in order to capture them. 27 But a messenger suddenly came to Saul. "Come quick!" he said. "The Philistines have invaded the land!" 28 So Saul broke off his pursuit of David and went to fight the Philistines. That's why that place is called Escape Rock. 29[z] Then David went from there and lived at the En-gedi fortresses.

David spares Saul's life

24 [a]Even as Saul returned from pursuing the Philistines, he was informed that David was in the En-gedi wilderness. 2 So Saul took three thousand men selected from all Israel and went to look for David and his soldiers near the rocks of the wild goats. 3 He came to the sheep pens beside the road where there was a cave. Saul went into the cave to use the restroom.[b] Meanwhile, David and his soldiers were sitting in the very back of the cave.

4 David's soldiers said to him, "This is the day the LORD spoke of when he promised you, 'I will hand your enemy over to you, and you can do to him whatever you think best.'" So David snuck up and cut off a corner of Saul's robe. 5 But immediately David felt horrible that he had cut off a corner of Saul's robe.[c]

6 "The LORD forbid," he told his men, "that I should do something like that to my master, the LORD's anointed, or lift my hand against him, because he's the LORD's anointed!" 7 So David held his soldiers in check by what he said,[d] and he wouldn't allow them to attack Saul. Saul then left the cave and went on his way.

8 Then David also went out of the cave

[z] 24:1 in Heb [a] 24:2 in Heb [b] Or *to cover his feet* (a euphemism) [c] LXX, Syr, Targ; MT lacks *robe*. [d] Heb uncertain

and yelled after Saul, "My master the king!" Saul looked back, and David bowed low out of respect, nose to the ground.

9 David said to Saul, "Why do you listen when people say, 'David wants to ruin you'? 10 Look! Today your own eyes have seen that the LORD handed you over to me in the cave. But I refused[e] to kill you. I spared you, saying, 'I won't lift a hand against my master because he is the LORD's anointed.' 11 Look here, my protector! See the corner of your robe in my hand? I cut off the corner of your robe but didn't kill you. So know now that I am not guilty of wrongdoing or rebellion. I haven't wronged you, but you are hunting me down, trying to kill me. 12 May the LORD judge between me and you! May the LORD take vengeance on you for me, but I won't lift a hand against you. 13 As the old proverb goes, 'Evil deeds come from evildoers!' but I won't lift a hand against you. 14 So who is Israel's king coming after? Who are you chasing? A dead dog? A single flea? 15 May the LORD be the judge and decide between you and me. May he see what has happened, argue my case, and vindicate me against you!"

16 As soon as David finished saying all this to Saul, Saul said, "David, my son, is that your voice?" Then he broke down in tears, 17 telling David, "You are more righteous than I am because you have treated me generously, but I have treated you terribly. 18 Today you've told me the good you have done for me—how the LORD handed me over to you, but how you didn't kill me. 19 When someone finds an enemy, do they send the enemy away in peace? May the LORD repay you with good for what you have done for me today. 20 Now even I know that you will definitely become king, and Israel's kingdom will flourish in your hands. 21 Because of that, make a solemn pledge to me by the LORD that you won't kill off my descendants after I'm gone and that you won't destroy my name from my family lineage."

22 David made a solemn pledge to Saul. Then Saul went back home, but David and his soldiers went up to the fortress.

Abigail saves David

25 Now Samuel died, and all Israel gathered to mourn for him. They buried him at his home in Ramah. David then left and went down to the Maon wilderness.[f]

2 There was a man in Maon who did business in Carmel. He was a very important man and owned three thousand sheep and one thousand goats. At that time, he was shearing his sheep in Carmel. 3 The man's name was Nabal, and his wife's name was Abigail. She was an intelligent and attractive woman, but her husband was a hard man who did evil things. He was a Calebite.

4 While in the wilderness, David heard that Nabal was shearing his sheep. 5 So David sent ten servants, telling them, "Go up to Carmel. When you get to Nabal, greet him for me. 6 Say this to him: 'Peace to you,[g] your household, and all that is yours! 7 I've heard that you are now shearing sheep. As you know, your shepherds were with us in the wilderness.[h] We didn't mistreat them. Moreover, the whole time they were at Carmel, nothing of theirs went missing. 8 Ask your servants; they will tell you the same. So please receive these young men favorably, because we've come on a special day. Please give whatever you have on hand to your servants and to your son David.'"

9 When David's young men arrived, they said all this to Nabal on David's behalf. Then they waited. 10 But Nabal answered David's servants, "Who is David? Who is Jesse's son? There are all sorts of slaves running away from their masters these days. 11 Why should I take my bread, my water, and the meat I've butchered for my shearers and give it to people who came here from who knows where?" 12 So David's young servants turned around and went back the way they came. When they arrived, they reported every word of this to David.

13 Then David said to his soldiers, "All of you, strap on your swords!" So each of them strapped on their swords, and David did the same. Nearly four hundred men went up with David. Two hundred men remained back with the supplies.

[e]LXX; MT *Some said* [f]LXX; MT *Paran* [g]Heb uncertain [h]LXX, Syr; MT lacks *in the wilderness.*

14One of Nabal's servants told his wife Abigail, "David sent messengers from the wilderness to greet our master, but he just yelled at them. 15But the men were very good to us and didn't mistreat us. Nothing of ours went missing the whole time we were out with them in the fields. 16In fact, the whole time we were with them, watching our sheep, they were a protective wall around us both night and day. 17Think about that and see what you can do, because trouble is coming for our master and his whole household. But he's such a despicable person no one can speak to him."

18Abigail quickly took two hundred loaves of bread, two skins of wine, five sheep ready for cooking, five seahs[i] of roasted grain, one hundred raisin cakes, and two hundred fig cakes. She loaded all this on donkeys 19and told her servants, "Go on ahead of me. I'll be right behind you." But she didn't tell her husband Nabal.

20As she was riding her donkey, going down a trail on the hillside, David and his soldiers appeared, descending toward her, and she met up with them. 21David had just been saying, "What a waste of time—guarding all this man's stuff in the wilderness so that nothing of his went missing! He has repaid me evil instead of good! 22May God deal harshly with me, David,[j] and worse still if I leave alive even one single male[k] belonging to him come morning!"

23When Abigail saw David, she quickly got off her donkey and fell facedown before him, bowing low to the ground. 24She fell at his feet and said, "Put the blame on me, my master! But please let me, your servant, speak to you directly. Please listen to what your servant has to say. 25Please, my master, pay no attention to this despicable man Nabal. He's exactly what his name says he is! His name means fool,[l] and he is foolish![m] But I myself, your servant, didn't see the young men that you, my master, sent. 26I pledge, my master, as surely as the LORD lives and as you live, that the LORD has held you back from bloodshed and taking vengeance into your own hands! But now let your enemies and those who seek to harm my master be exactly like Nabal! 27Here is a gift, which your servant has brought to my master. Please let it be given to the young men who follow you, my master. 28Please forgive any offense by your servant. The LORD will definitely make an enduring dynasty for my master because my master fights the LORD's battles, and nothing evil will be found in you throughout your lifetime. 29If someone chases after you and tries to kill you, my master, then your life will be bound up securely in the bundle of life[n] by the LORD your God, but he will fling away your enemies' lives as from the pouch of a sling. 30When the LORD has done for my master all the good things he has promised you, and has installed you as Israel's leader, 31don't let this be a blot or burden on my master's conscience, that you shed blood needlessly or that my master took vengeance into his own hands. When the LORD has done good things for my master, please remember your servant."

32David said to Abigail, "Bless the LORD God of Israel, who sent you to meet me today! 33And bless you and your good judgment for preventing me from shedding blood and taking vengeance into my own hands today! 34Otherwise, as surely as the LORD God of Israel lives—the one who kept me from hurting you—if you hadn't come quickly and met up with me, there wouldn't be one single male left come morning." 35Then David accepted everything she had brought for him. "Return home in peace," he told her. "Be assured that I've heard your request and have agreed to it."

36When Abigail got back home to Nabal, he was throwing a party fit for a king in his house. Nabal was in a great mood and very drunk, so Abigail didn't tell him anything until daybreak. 37In the morning, when Nabal was sober, his wife told him everything. Nabal's heart failed inside him, and he became like a stone. 38About ten days later, the LORD struck Nabal, and he died.

[i]One seah is approximately seven and a half quarts. [j]LXX; MT *with David's enemies* [k]Or *who urinates on a wall*; also in 25:34 [l]Heb *nabal* [m]Heb *nebalah* [n]Or *bundle of the living*; Heb uncertain; perhaps a tied-up scroll (cf Exod 32:32-33; Ps 69:28; Isa 8:16)

39 When David heard that Nabal was dead,
he said, "Bless the LORD, who has rendered
a verdict regarding Nabal's insult to me and
who kept me, his servant, from doing something evil! The LORD has brought Nabal's
evil down on his own head." Then David sent
word to Abigail, saying that he would take
her as his wife.
40 When David's servants reached Abigail
at Carmel, they said to her, "David has sent
us to you so you can become his wife."
41 She bowed low to the ground and said,
"I am your servant, ready to serve and wash
the feet of my master's helpers." 42 Then
Abigail got up quickly and rode on her donkey, with five of her young women going
with her. She followed David's messengers
and became his wife.
43 David also married Ahinoam from Jezreel, so both of them were his wives. 44 But
Saul had given his daughter Michal, David's
wife, to Palti, Laish's son, from Gallim.

David spares Saul's life a second time

26 The Ziphites came to Saul at Gibeah.
"David is hiding on Hachilah's hill,
which faces Jeshimon," they said. 2 So Saul
got up and went down to the Ziph wilderness to look for David there. He had three
thousand handpicked soldiers from Israel
with him. 3 Saul camped on Hachilah's
hill opposite Jeshimon beside the road,
but David stayed in the wilderness. When
David learned that Saul had come after him
into the wilderness, 4 he sent spies and discovered that Saul had definitely arrived.
5 So David got up and went to the place
where Saul camped, and saw the place
where Saul and Abner, Ner's son and Saul's
general, were sleeping. Saul was sleeping
inside the camp with the troops camped all
around him. 6 David asked Ahimelech the
Hittite and Joab's brother Abishai, Zeruiah's son, "Who will go down into the camp
with me to Saul?"
"I'll go down with you," Abishai answered.
7 So David and Abishai approached the
troops at night and found Saul lying there,
asleep in the camp, with his spear stuck in
the ground by his head. Abner and the army
were sleeping all around him.
8 Abishai said to David, "God has handed
your enemy over to you today! Let me pin
him to the ground with my spear. One
stroke is all I need! I won't need a second."
9 But David said to Abishai, "Don't kill him!
No one can lift a hand against the LORD's
anointed and go unpunished. 10 As surely as
the LORD lives," David continued, "it will be
the LORD who will strike him down, or his
day will come and he will die, or he'll fall in
battle and be destroyed. 11 The LORD forbid that I lift my hand against the LORD's
anointed! But go ahead and take the spear
by Saul's head and the water jug and let's go!"
12 So David took the spear and the water jug
that were by Saul's head, and he and Abishai
left. No one saw them, no one knew they
were there, and no one woke up. All of them
remained asleep because a deep sleep from
the LORD had come over them.
13 David crossed over to the other side and
stood on top of a hill with considerable distance between them. 14 Then David shouted
to the army and to Abner, Ner's son, "Abner!
Aren't you going to answer me?"
"Who are you to shout to the king?"
Abner asked.
15 David answered Abner, "You are a man,
aren't you? And you have no equal in Israel,
right? Then why haven't you kept watch
over your master the king? One of the
soldiers came to kill your master the king.
16 What you've done is terrible! As surely as
the LORD lives, all of you are dead men because you didn't keep close watch over your
master, the LORD's anointed. Have a look
around! Where are the king's spear and the
water jug that were by his head?"
17 Saul recognized David's voice and said,
"David, my son, is that your voice?"
David said, "Yes it is, my master the
king. 18 Why," David continued, "is my master chasing me, his servant? What have I
done and what wrong am I guilty of? 19 My
master the king, please listen to what your
servant has to say. If it is the LORD who
has incited you against me, then let him accept an offering! But if human beings have
done it, then let them be cursed before the
LORD because they have now driven me
off, keeping me from sharing in the LORD's

inheritance. 'Go!' they tell me. 'Worship other gods!' [20]Don't let my blood spill on the ground apart from the LORD's presence, because the king of Israel has come out looking for a single flea[o] like someone hunting a partridge[p] in the mountains."

[21]Then Saul said, "I have sinned! David, my son, come back! Because you considered my life precious today, I won't harm you again. I have acted foolishly and have made a huge mistake."

[22]"Here is the king's spear," David answered. "Allow one of your servants to come over and get it. [23]Remember: The LORD rewards every person for their righteousness and loyalty, and I wasn't willing to lift a hand against the LORD's anointed, even though the LORD handed you over to me today. [24]And just as I considered your life valuable today, may the LORD consider my life valuable, and may he deliver me from all trouble."

[25]Then Saul said to David, "Bless you, David, my son! You will accomplish much and will certainly succeed." Then David went on his way, but Saul went back home.

David serves the Philistine Achish

27 David thought, One day I will be destroyed by Saul's power. The best thing for me to do is to escape to Philistine territory. Then Saul will give up looking for me in Israelite territory, and I will escape his power. [2]So David set out with his six hundred soldiers and went to Achish, Maoch's son and Gath's king. [3]David and his soldiers stayed there at Gath with Achish. Each man had his family with him, and David had his two wives, Ahinoam from Jezreel and Abigail, Nabal's widow from Carmel. [4]When Saul was told that David had fled to Gath, he didn't pursue him anymore.

[5]Then David said to Achish, "If you approve of me, please give me a place in one of the towns in the country so I can live there. Why should I, your servant, live in the capital city with you?" [6]So Achish gave the town of Ziklag to David at that time. That's why Ziklag has belonged to the kings of Judah until now. [7]David lived in the Philistine countryside for a total of one year and four months.

[8]David and his soldiers went out on raids against the Geshurites, the Girzites, and the Amalekites. They were the people who lived in the land from Telam[q] to Shur all the way to the land of Egypt. [9]When David attacked an area, he wouldn't leave anyone alive, man or woman. He would take the sheep, the cattle, the donkeys, the camels, and the clothes and would then go back to Achish. [10]When Achish asked, "Where did you raid today?"[r] David would say, "The southern plain of Judah," or "The southern plain of the Jerahmeelites," or "The southern plain of the Kenites." [11]David never spared a man or woman so they could be brought back alive to Gath. "Otherwise," he said, "they might talk about us, and say, 'David did this or that.'" So this was David's practice during the entire time he lived in the Philistine countryside.

[12]Achish trusted David, thinking, David has alienated himself so badly from his own people in Israel that he'll serve me forever.

28 At that time, the Philistines gathered their troops for war to fight against Israel. Achish said to David, "Count on you and your soldiers marching out with me in the army."

[2]"Excellent," David answered Achish. "Now you'll see for yourself what your servant can do."

"Excellent," Achish replied. "I will make you my permanent bodyguard."

Saul and the woman of En-dor

[3]Now Samuel had died, and all Israel mourned him and buried him in Ramah, his hometown. And Saul had banned all mediums and diviners from the land.

[4]The Philistines gathered their forces and advanced to camp at Shunem. Saul gathered all Israel, and they camped at Gilboa. [5]When Saul saw the Philistine army, he was so afraid that his heart beat wildly. [6]When

[o]Cf 24:14; LXX *my life* [p]Or *a caller*, Heb sounds like verb *to shout* or *call* in 26:14. [q]LXX; MT *from long ago* [r]DSS (4QSam[a]), LXX

Saul questioned the LORD, the LORD didn't answer him—not by dreams, not by the Urim, and not by the prophets. 7 So Saul said to his servants, "Find me a woman who communicates with ghosts! I'll then go to her and ask by using her techniques."[s]

"There is such a medium in En-dor," his servants replied.

8 So Saul disguised himself, dressing in different clothes. Then he and two men set out, going to the woman at nighttime.

"Please call up a ghost for me! Bring me the one I specify," Saul said.

9 "Listen," the woman said to him, "you know what Saul has done, how he has banned all mediums and diviners from the land. What are you doing? Trying to get me killed?"

10 But Saul promised to her by the LORD, "As surely as the LORD lives, you won't get into trouble for this."

11 So the woman said, "Who do you want me to bring up for you?"

"Bring up Samuel," he said.

12 When the woman saw Samuel, she screamed at Saul, "Why have you tricked me? You are Saul!"

13 "Don't be afraid!" the king said to her. "What do you see?"

The woman said to Saul, "I see a god[t] coming up from the ground."

14 "What does he look like?" Saul asked her.

"An old man is coming up," she said. "He's wrapped in a robe." Then Saul knew that it was Samuel, and he bowed low out of respect, nose to the ground.

15 "Why have you disturbed me by bringing me up?" Samuel asked Saul.

"I'm in deep trouble!" Saul replied. "The Philistines are at war with me, and God has turned away from me and no longer answers me by prophets or by dreams. So I have called on you to tell me what I should do."

16 "Why do you ask me," Samuel said, "since the LORD has turned away from you and has become your enemy?[u] 17 The LORD has done to you[v] exactly what he spoke through me: The LORD has ripped the kingdom out of your hands and has given it to your friend David. 18 The LORD has done this very thing to you today because you didn't listen to the LORD's voice and didn't carry out his fierce anger against the Amalekites. 19 The LORD will now hand over both you and Israel to the Philistines. And come tomorrow, you and your sons will be with me![w] The LORD will hand Israel's army over to the Philistines."

20 Saul immediately fell full length on the ground, utterly terrified at what Samuel had said. He was weak because he hadn't eaten anything all day or night. 21 The woman approached Saul, and after seeing how scared he was, she said, "Listen, your servant has obeyed you. I risked my life and did what you told me to do. 22 Now it's your turn to listen to me, your servant. Let me give you a bit of food. Eat it, then you'll have the strength to go on your way."

23 But Saul refused. "I can't eat!" he said. But his servants and the woman urged him to do so, and so he did. He got up off the ground and sat on a couch. 24 The woman had a fattened calf in the house, and she quickly butchered it.[x] She took flour, kneaded it, and baked unleavened bread. 25 She served this to Saul and his servants, and they ate. They got up and left that very night.

David sent home from fighting Saul

29 The Philistines assembled all their forces at Aphek, and the Israelites camped by the spring in Jezreel. 2 As the Philistine rulers went out marching in units of hundreds and thousands, David and his soldiers were in the rear with Achish.

3 "Who are these Hebrews?" the Philistine commanders asked.

"That's David," Achish told them, "the servant of Israel's King Saul. He's been with me a year or so now. I haven't found anything wrong with him from the day he defected until now."

4 But the Philistine commanders were angry with Achish. "Send the man home!" they told Achish. "He can go back to the

[s] Or *through her* or *by her* [t] Or *I see gods* or *I see divine figures* [u] LXX *is with your neighbor;* cf 15:28; 28:17
[v] LXX; MT *The LORD himself has done just what* [w] LXX *you and your sons will fall in battle.* [x] Or *sacrificed it*

place you gave him, but he won't go with us
into battle. Couldn't he turn against us in
the middle of the fight? How better to please
his former master than by taking the heads
of our soldiers? 5After all, this is the same
David people sing about in their dances,
'Saul has killed his thousands,
but David has killed
his tens of thousands!'"
6So Achish summoned David and told
him, "As surely as the LORD lives, you are an
upstanding individual. I would very much
like you to serve with me in the army because I haven't found anything wrong with
you from the day you came to me until now.
But the rulers don't approve of you. 7So go
back home now, and go in peace. Don't do
anything to upset the Philistine rulers."
8"But what have I done?" David asked
Achish. "What wrong have you found in
me, your servant, from the day I came to
you until now? Why shouldn't I go and fight
the enemies of my master the king?"
9"I agree," Achish answered David. "I
think you're as good as one of God's own
messengers. Despite that, the Philistine
commanders have ordered, 'He can't go
into battle with us.' 10So get up early in the
morning, both you and your master's servants who came with you, and return to
the place I gave you. Don't worry about this
negative report, because you've done well
before me.[y] Now get up early in the morning and leave as soon as it is light."
11So David and his soldiers got up early in
the morning to go back to Philistine territory, but the Philistines went up to Jezreel.

The Amalekite raid on Ziklag

30 Three days later, David and his
soldiers reached Ziklag. The Amalekites had raided the arid southern plain
and Ziklag. They had attacked Ziklag and
burned it down, 2taking the women and everyone in the city prisoner, whether young
or old.[z] They hadn't killed anyone but carried them off and went on their way. 3When
David and his soldiers got to the town and
found it burned down, and their wives,
their sons, and their daughters taken prisoner, 4David and the troops with him broke
into tears and cried until they could cry no
more. 5David's two wives had been captured as well: Ahinoam from Jezreel and
Abigail, Nabal's widow from Carmel.
6David was in deep trouble because the
troops were talking about stoning him.
Each of the soldiers was deeply distressed
about their sons and daughters. But David
found strength in the LORD his God.
7David said to the priest Abiathar, Ahimelech's son, "Bring the priestly vest[a] to me."
So Abiathar brought it to David.
8Then David asked the LORD, "Should
I go after this raiding party? Will I catch
them?"
"Yes, go after them!" God answered.
"You will definitely catch them and will
succeed in the rescue!"
9So David set off with six hundred men.
They came to the Besor ravine, where some
stayed behind. 10David and four hundred
men continued the pursuit, while two hundred men stayed there, too exhausted to
cross the Besor ravine.
11They found an Egyptian in the countryside and brought him to David. They gave
him bread, and he ate, and they gave him
water to drink. 12They also gave him a piece
of fig cake and two raisin cakes. He ate and
regained his strength because he hadn't
eaten any food or drunk any water for three
days and nights.
13Then David asked him, "Whose slave
are you? Where do you come from?"
"I'm an Egyptian servant boy," he said,
"and the slave of an Amalekite. My master
abandoned me when I got sick three days
ago. 14We had raided the arid southern plain
belonging to the Cherethites, the territory
belonging to Judah, and the southern plain
of Caleb. We also burned Ziklag down."
15"Can you guide me to this raiding
party?" David asked him.
"Make a pledge to me by God that you
won't kill me or hand me over to my master," the boy said, "and I will guide you to
the raiding party."

[y]LXX; MT lacks *and return to the place . . . done well before me.* [z]LXX; MT lacks *and everyone in the city.* [a]Heb *ephod*

[16]So the boy led David to them, and he found them scattered all over the countryside, eating, drinking, and celebrating over the large amount of plunder they had taken from Philistine and Judean territory.

[17]David attacked them from twilight until evening of the next day. He killed them all.[b] No one escaped except four hundred young men who got on camels and fled. [18]David rescued everything that the Amalekites had taken, including his own two wives. [19]Nothing was missing from the plunder or anything that they had taken, neither old nor young, son nor daughter. David brought everything back. [20]David also captured all the sheep and cattle, which were driven in front of the other livestock. The troops said, "This is David's plunder!"

[21]David reached the two hundred men who were too exhausted to follow him and had stayed behind at the Besor ravine. They came out to greet him and the troops who were with him. When David approached them, he asked how they were doing. [22]But then all the evil and despicable individuals who had accompanied David said, "We won't share any of the plunder we rescued with them because they didn't go with us. Each of them can take his wife and children and go—but that's it."

[23]"Brothers!" David said. "Don't act that way with the things the LORD has given us. He has protected us and handed over to us the raiding party that had attacked us. [24]How could anyone agree with you on this plan? The share of those who went into battle and the share of those who stayed with the supplies will be divided equally." [25]So from that day forward, David made that a regulation and a law in Israel, which remains in place even now.

[26]When David returned to Ziklag, he sent some of the plunder to the elders of Judah and to his friends. "Here is a gift for you from the plunder of the LORD's enemies," he said. [27]It went to those in Bethel, Ramoth of the arid southern plain, Jattir, [28]Aroer,[c] Siphmoth, Eshtemoa, [29]Racal, the towns of the Jerahmeelites, the towns of the Kenites, [30]Hormah, Bor-ashan, Athach, [31]Hebron, and all the places where David and his soldiers had spent time.

Saul dies in the battle of Gilboa

31 When the Philistines attacked the Israelites, the Israelites ran away from the Philistines, and many fell dead on Mount Gilboa. [2]The Philistines overtook Saul and his sons, and they killed his sons Jonathan, Abinadab, and Malchishua. [3]The battle was fierce around Saul. When the archers located him, they wounded him badly.[d]

[4]Saul said to his armor-bearer, "Draw your sword and kill me with it! Otherwise, these uncircumcised men will come and kill me or torture me." But his armor-bearer refused because he was terrified. So Saul took the sword and impaled himself on it. [5]When the armor-bearer saw that Saul was dead, he also impaled himself on his sword and died with Saul. [6]So Saul, his three sons, his armor-bearer, and all his soldiers died together that day.

[7]When the Israelites across the valley and across the Jordan learned that the Israelite army had fled and that Saul and his sons were dead, they abandoned their towns and fled. So the Philistines came and occupied the towns.

[8]The next day, when the Philistines came to strip the dead, they found Saul and his three sons lying dead on Mount Gilboa. [9]They cut off Saul's head and stripped off his armor, and then sent word throughout Philistine territory, carrying the good news to their gods' temples and to their people. [10]They put Saul's armor in the temple of Astarte, and hung his body on the wall of Beth-shan.

[11]But when all the people of Jabesh-gilead heard what the Philistines had done to Saul, [12]the bravest of their men set out, traveled all night long, and took the bodies of Saul and his sons off the wall of Beth-shan. Then they went back to Jabesh, where they burned them. [13]Then they took their bones and buried them under the tamarisk tree at Jabesh, and they fasted seven days.

[b]LXX; MT lacks *He killed them all.* [c]LXX *Ararah* [d]Correction; LXX *wounded in the belly*

Song of the Bow; 2 Samuel 1:19-27

2 SAMUEL

David learns of Saul's death

1 After Saul's death, when David had returned from defeating the Amalekites, he
stayed in Ziklag two days. 2 On the third day,
a man showed up from Saul's camp with his
clothes torn and dirt on his head. When he
reached David, he fell to the ground, bowing low out of respect.

3 "Where have you come from?" David
asked him.

"I've escaped from the Israelite army!" he
answered.

4 "What's the report?" David asked him.
"Tell me!"

The man answered, "The troops fled
from the battle! Many of the soldiers have
fallen and died. What's more, Saul and his
son Jonathan have also died!"

5 "How do you know," David asked the
young man who brought the news, "that
Saul and his son Jonathan are dead?"

6 The young man who brought the news
replied, "I just happened to be on Mount
Gilboa and Saul was there, leaning on his
spear, with chariots and horsemen closing
in on him. 7 He turned around and saw me,
then he called to me. 'Yes, sir,' I answered.
8 'Who are you?' he asked, and I told him,
'I'm an Amalekite.' 9 He said to me, 'Please
come over here and kill me, because convulsions have come over me but I'm still alive.'[a]
10 So I went over to him and killed him, because I knew he couldn't survive after being
wounded like that. I took the crown that
was on his head and the bracelet that was
on his arm, and I've brought them here to
you, my master."

11 Then David grabbed his clothes and
ripped them—and all his soldiers did the
same. 12 They mourned and cried and fasted
until evening for Saul, his son Jonathan,
the LORD's army, and the whole house
of Israel, because they had died by the
sword.

13 "Where are you from?" David asked the
young man who brought him the news.

"I'm the son of an immigrant," he answered. "An Amalekite."

14 Then David said to him, "How is it
that you weren't afraid to raise your hand
and destroy the LORD's anointed?" 15 Then
David called for one of the young servants.
"Come here!" he said. "Strike him down!"
So the servant struck the Amalekite down,
and he died.

16 "Your blood is on your own head,"
David said to the Amalekite, "because your
own mouth testified against you when you
admitted, 'I killed the LORD's anointed.'"

David mourns Saul and Jonathan

17 Then David sang this funeral song[b] for
Saul and his son Jonathan. 18 David ordered
everyone in Judah to learn the Song of the
Bow.[c] (In fact, it is written in the scroll from
Jashar.)

19 Oh, no, Israel! Your prince[d] lies dead
on your heights.[e]
Look how the mighty warriors
have fallen!
20 Don't talk about it in Gath;
don't bring news of it
to Ashkelon's streets,
or else the Philistines' daughters
will rejoice;
the daughters of the uncircumcised
will celebrate.
21 You hills of Gilboa!
Let there be no dew or rain on you,
and no fields yielding grain offerings.[f]
Because it was there
that the mighty warrior's[g] shield
was defiled—
the shield of Saul!—
never again anointed with oil.
22 Jonathan's bow never wavered
from the blood of the slain,
from the gore of the warriors.
Never did Saul's sword return empty.

23 Saul and Jonathan! So well loved,
so dearly cherished!

[a] Syr, Tg; Heb uncertain [b] Or *lament* [c] Heb lacks *Song.* [d] Or *gazelle* or *splendor* or *splendid one* [e] Correction [f] Heb uncertain, perhaps *bountiful fields*; alternatively, with LXX[L], *fields of death*, or with correction *and no springs from the deep* [g] Or *warriors'* (plural)

In their lives and in their deaths
they were never separated.
They were faster than eagles,
stronger than lions!
24 Daughters of Israel, weep over Saul!
He dressed you in crimson with jewels;
he decorated your clothes
with gold jewelry.
25 Look how the mighty warriors
have fallen in the midst of battle!
Jonathan lies dead on your heights.
26 I grieve for you, my brother Jonathan!
You were so dear to me!
Your love was more amazing to me[h]
than the love of women.
27 Look how the mighty warriors
have fallen!
Look how the weapons of war
have been destroyed!

David made king in Hebron

2 Some time later, David questioned the
LORD, "Should I go to one of the towns
in Judah?"
"Yes, go," the LORD told him.
"Which one should I go to?" David asked.
"To Hebron," the LORD replied.
2 So David went there, along with his two
wives: Ahinoam from Jezreel and Abigail,
Nabal's widow, from Carmel. 3 David also
took the soldiers who were with him, each
with his family, and they lived in the towns
around Hebron. 4 Then the people of Judah
came to Hebron and anointed David king
over the house of Judah.
When David was informed that it was
the people of Jabesh-gilead who had buried Saul, 5 he sent messengers to the people
of Jabesh-gilead. "The LORD bless you," he
said to them, "for doing this loyal deed for
your master Saul by burying him. 6 May the
LORD now show you loyal love and faithfulness. I myself will also reward you because
you did this. 7 So now take courage and be
brave—yes, your master Saul is dead, but
the house of Judah has anointed me king
over them."

Israel's King Ishbosheth

8 Meanwhile, Abner, Ner's son, the
commander of Saul's army, had taken
Ishbosheth,[i] Saul's son, and brought him
over to Mahanaim. 9 There he made him
king over Gilead, the Geshurites,[j] Jezreel,
Ephraim, and Benjamin—over all Israel.
10 Saul's son Ishbosheth was 40 years old
when he became king over Israel, and he
ruled for two years. The house of Judah,
however, followed David. 11 The amount of
time David ruled in Hebron over the house
of Judah totaled seven and a half years.

Conflict between Judah and Israel

12 Abner, Ner's son, along with the soldiers of Ishbosheth, Saul's son, left Mahanaim to go to Gibeon. 13 Joab, Zeruiah's
son, and David's soldiers also came out and
confronted them at the pool of Gibeon.
One group sat on one side of the pool; the
other sat on the opposite side of the pool.
14 Abner said to Joab, "Let's have the young
men fight in a contest[k] before us."
"All right," Joab said, "let's do it." 15 So
the men came forward and were counted
as they passed by: twelve for Benjamin and
Ishbosheth, Saul's son; and twelve of David's
soldiers. 16 Each man grabbed his opponent
by the head and stuck[l] his sword into his
opponent's side so that they both fell dead
together. That's why that place is called
The Field of Daggers,[m] which is located in
Gibeon. 17 A fierce battle took place that day,
and Abner and the Israelite troops were
defeated by David's soldiers.
18 Now Zeruiah's three sons were present at the battle: Joab, Abishai, and Asahel. Asahel was as fast as a gazelle in an
open field. 19 Asahel went after Abner, staying completely focused in his pursuit of
Abner.
20 Abner looked behind him and said, "Is
that you, Asahel?"
"Yes, it's me," Asahel answered.
21 "Break off your pursuit!" Abner told him.
"Fight one of the young warriors and take

[h] Or *your love* (or *care*; cf 1 Sam 18:1, 3; 20:17) *for me was more amazing* [i] Ishbosheth means *man of shame; shame* (Heb *bosheth*) may be a deliberate alteration from *Baal* (cf Esh-baal, *man of Baal* in 1 Chron 8:33; 9:39; see also 2 Sam 4:4); one manuscript of LXX[L] reads *Ishbaal.* [j] Syr, Vulg; MT *Ashurites* or *Assyrians;* cf Tg, LXX[L], Judg 1:32 *Asherites* [k] Or *come forward and play* or *compete* [l] Heb lacks *stuck.* [m] Heb *Helkath-hazzurim*

his gear for yourself!" But Asahel wouldn't
stop chasing him.
[22]So Abner repeated himself to Asahel:
"Stop chasing me. Why should I kill you?
How could I look your brother Joab in the
face?" [23]But Asahel wouldn't turn back,
so Abner hit him in the stomach with the
back end of his spear. But the spear went
through Asahel's back. He fell down and
died right there.
Everyone who came to the place where
Asahel had fallen and died just stood there,
[24]but Joab and Abishai went after Abner.
The sun was setting when they came to the
hill of Ammah, which faces Giah on the
road to the Gibeon wilderness. [25]The Benjaminites rallied behind Abner, forming a
single unit. Then they took their positions
on the top of a hill. [26]Abner yelled down to
Joab, "Must the sword keep killing forever?
Don't you realize that this will end bitterly?
How long before you order the troops to
stop chasing their brothers?"
[27]"As surely as God lives," Joab replied,
"if you hadn't just said that, the soldiers
would have continued after their brothers
until morning." [28]Joab blew the trumpet,[n]
and all the soldiers stopped. They didn't
pursue Israel anymore, nor did they continue to fight.
[29]Abner and his men then marched all
night through the wilderness, crossing the
Jordan River and marching all morning[o]
until they got to Mahanaim. [30]Joab, meanwhile, returned from pursuing Abner and
assembled the troops. Nineteen of David's
soldiers were counted missing in addition to Asahel. [31]But David's soldiers had
defeated the Benjaminites, killing three
hundred sixty of Abner's soldiers. [32]They
took Asahel and buried him in his father's
tomb in Bethlehem. Then Joab and his men
marched all night. When daylight came,
they were in Hebron.

3 The war between Saul's house and David's house was long and drawn out.
David kept getting stronger, while Saul's
house kept getting weaker.

David's family

[2]David's sons were born in Hebron. His
oldest son was Amnon, by Ahinoam from
Jezreel; [3]the second was Chileab, by Abigail, Nabal's widow from Carmel; the third
was Absalom, by Maacah,[p] who was the
daughter of Geshur's King Talmai; [4]the
fourth was Adonijah, by Haggith; the fifth
was Shephatiah, by Abital; [5]and the sixth
was Ithream, by David's wife Eglah. These
are David's sons that were born in Hebron.

Joab kills Abner

[6]Throughout the war between Saul's
house and David's house, Abner was gaining power in Saul's house. [7]Now Saul had
a secondary wife named Rizpah, Aiah's
daughter. Ishbosheth[q] said to Abner, "Why
have you had sex with my father's secondary wife?"
[8]Abner got very angry over what Ishbosheth had said.
"Am I some sort of dog's head?"[r] Abner
asked. "I've been nothing but loyal to the
house of your father Saul and to his brothers and his friends. I haven't handed you
over to David, but today you accuse me of
doing something wrong with this woman.
[9]May God deal harshly with me, Abner, and
worse still if I don't do for David exactly
what the LORD swore to him—[10]removing
the kingdom from Saul's house and securing David's throne over Israel and over
Judah, from Dan all the way to Beer-sheba!"
[11]Ishbosheth couldn't say a single word
in reply to Abner because he was afraid
of him.
[12]Abner sent messengers to represent
him to David and to say, "Who will own the
land?[s] Make a covenant with me, then I'll
help bring all Israel over to your side."
[13]"Good!" David replied. "I will make a
covenant with you, but on one condition:
don't show yourself in my presence unless
you bring Saul's daughter Michal when you
come to see me."
[14]Then David sent messengers to Saul's
son Ishbosheth. "Give me my wife Michal,

[n]Heb *shofar* [o]Heb uncertain [p]Or *son of*; also twice in 3:4 [q]Or *he*, supplied from 3:8; see note at 2:8 on *Ishbosheth*. [r]LXX; MT adds *that belongs to Judah*. [s]Heb uncertain; LXX lacks *Who will own the land?*

he demanded. "I became engaged to her at the cost of one hundred Philistine foreskins."

[15]Ishbosheth then sent for Michal and took her from her husband Paltiel, Laish's son. [16]Her husband went with her all the way to Bahurim, crying as he followed her.

"Go home!" Abner told him. So he went home.

[17]Abner then sent word to Israel's elders. "You've wanted David to be your king for some time now," he said. [18]"It's time to act because the LORD has said about David: I will rescue my people Israel from the power of the Philistines and all their enemies through my servant David."

[19]Abner also spoke directly to the Benjaminites. He then went to inform David in person at Hebron regarding everything that all Israel and the house of Benjamin were willing to do.

[20]When Abner, along with twenty others, reached David at Hebron, David threw a celebration for Abner and his men. [21]Then Abner said to David, "Please let me get going so I can assemble all Israel for my master the king. Then they can make a covenant with you, and you will rule over everything your heart[t] desires." At that, David sent Abner off in peace.

[22]Right then, David's soldiers and Joab returned from a raid, bringing a great deal of loot with them. Abner was no longer with David in Hebron because David had sent him off in peace. [23]When Joab and all the troops with him returned, Joab was told that Abner, Ner's son, had come to the king and that David had sent him off in peace.

[24]Joab went to the king and asked, "What have you done? Abner came to you here! Why did you send him off? Now he's gotten away! [25]Don't you know the evil ways of Abner, Ner's son?[u] He came to trick you, to find out where you come and go, and to learn everything you do!"

[26]Joab left David and sent messengers after Abner. They brought him back from the well at Sirah, but David didn't know anything of this. [27]When Abner returned to Hebron, Joab took him aside next to[v] the gate to speak with him in private. But instead Joab stabbed Abner in the stomach, and he died for shedding the blood of Asahel, Joab's brother.

[28]When David heard about this later, he said, "I and my kingdom are forever innocent before the LORD concerning the shedding of the blood of Abner, Ner's son. [29]May it fall upon the head of Joab and his entire family tree! May Joab's family never be without someone with a discharge or a skin disease,[w] someone who uses a crutch,[x] someone who dies by the sword, or someone who is hungry!"

[30]So that is how Joab and his brother Abishai murdered Abner, because he killed their brother Asahel in the battle at Gibeon.

[31]Then David ordered Joab and all the troops who were with him, "Tear your clothes and put on funeral clothes! Mourn for Abner!" King David himself walked behind the body. [32]They buried Abner in Hebron. The king wept loudly at Abner's grave. All the troops cried too. [33]Then the king sang this funeral song[y] for Abner:

"Should Abner have died
like a fool dies?
[34]Your hands weren't bound,
your feet weren't chained,
but you have fallen
like someone falls before the wicked."

Then the troops cried over Abner again.

[35]Then all the soldiers came to urge David to eat something while it was still day, but David swore, "May God deal harshly with me and worse still if I eat bread or anything else before the sun goes down." [36]All the troops took notice of this and were pleased by it. Indeed, everything that the king did pleased them. [37]So on that day all the troops and all Israel knew that it wasn't the king's idea to kill Abner, Ner's son.

[38]The king told his soldiers, "Don't you know that a prince and a great man in Israel has fallen today? [39]And today, though I am the anointed king, I am weak. These men,

[t]Or *soul* [u]LXX; MT *You know Abner, Ner's son.* [v]LXX; MT *to the middle of* [w]Traditionally *leprosy*, a term used for several different skin diseases [x]Or *who holds a spindle* [y]Or *lament*

Zeruiah's sons, are too strong for me.[z] May the LORD repay the one who does evil according to the evil they did!"

Ishbosheth murdered

4 When Ishbosheth,[a] Saul's son, heard that Abner had died in Hebron, he lost his courage,[b] and all Israel was alarmed. 2 Saul's son had two men who led the raiding parties—one was named Baanah and the other Rechab. Both were sons of Rimmon, a Benjaminite from Beeroth. (Beeroth was considered part of Benjamin. 3 The people of Beeroth had fled to Gittaim and even now live there as immigrants.)

4 Now Saul's son Jonathan had a boy whose feet were crippled. He was only 5 years old when the news about Saul and Jonathan came from Jezreel, and so his nurse snatched him up and fled. But as she hurried to get away, he fell and was injured. His name was Mephibosheth.[c]

5 Rechab and Baanah, the sons of Rimmon from Beeroth, set out and reached Ishbosheth's house at the heat of the day, right when he was lying down, taking an afternoon rest. 6 They went straight into his house, as if getting wheat,[d] and they stabbed him in the stomach. Then Rechab and his brother Baanah escaped. 7 They had entered the house while Ishbosheth was lying on the bed in his bedroom. After they stabbed him and killed him, they cut off his head, took it, and traveled all night through the wilderness.

8 They brought Ishbosheth's head to David at Hebron. "Here is the head of Ishbosheth," they told the king, "the son of Saul your enemy, who wanted you dead. Today the LORD has avenged our master[e] the king on Saul and his descendants."

9 David answered Rechab and his brother Baanah, the sons of Rimmon from Beeroth, "As surely as the LORD lives, who has rescued me[f] from all kinds of trouble," he told them, 10 "when someone told me Saul was dead back in Ziklag, thinking he was bringing good news, I grabbed him and killed him. That was the reward I gave him for his news! 11 What do you think I'll do when evil people kill a righteous person in his own house on his own bed? Why shouldn't I demand his blood from your hands and rid the earth of you both?"

12 So David gave the order to his servants, and they killed Rechab and Baanah, cutting off their hands and feet and hanging them up by the pool at Hebron. But they took Ishbosheth's head and buried it in the grave of Abner at Hebron.

David becomes king of Israel and Judah

5 All the Israelite tribes came to David at Hebron and said, "Listen: We are your very own flesh and bone. 2 In the past, when Saul ruled over us, you were the one who led Israel out to war and back. What's more, the LORD told you, You will shepherd my people Israel, and you will be Israel's leader."

3 So all the Israelite elders came to the king at Hebron. King David made a covenant with them at Hebron before the LORD, and they anointed David king over Israel.

4 David was 30 years old when he became king, and he ruled for forty years. 5 He ruled over Judah for seven and a half years in Hebron. He ruled thirty-three years over all Israel and Judah in Jerusalem.

Jerusalem is captured

6 The king and his troops marched on Jerusalem against the Jebusites, who inhabited the territory. The Jebusites said to David, "You'll never get us in here! Even the blind and the lame will beat you back!" "David will never enter here," they said to each other.[g] 7 But David did capture the fortress of Zion—which became David's City. 8 "On that day," David said, "whoever attacks the Jebusites should strike the windpipe because David hates the lame and the blind."[h] That is why people say, "The blind and the lame will not enter the temple."[i] 9 David occupied the fortress, so it

[z] Or *more ruthless than me;* DSS (4QSam[a]) lacks this clause. [a] Heb lacks *Ishbosheth*; LXX, DSS (4QSam[a]) *Mephibosheth*; cf 4:4 and the note at 2 Sam 2:8. [b] Or *his hands grew weak* [c] Called *Merib-baal* in 1 Chron 8:34; 9:40. See the note at 2 Sam 2:8. [d] Heb uncertain [e] Or *my master* [f] Or *my life or my soul* [g] Or *they thought*; Heb lacks *to each other.* [h] Or *take the water shaft against the lame and the blind who hate David;* Heb uncertain [i] Or *palace*

was renamed David's City. David built a city around it from the earthen terraces[j] inward.[k] 10 David grew increasingly powerful, and the LORD of heavenly forces was with him.

11 Tyre's King Hiram sent messengers to David with cedar logs, bricklayers, and carpenters to build David a palace. 12 Then David knew that the LORD had established him as king over Israel, and that his kingship was held in great honor for the sake of his people Israel. 13 After he left Hebron, David married more secondary wives in Jerusalem and fathered more sons and daughters. 14 The names of his children in Jerusalem were as follows: Shammua, Shobab, Nathan, Solomon, 15 Ibhar, Elishua, Nepheg, Japhia, 16 Elishama, Eliada, and Eliphelet.

David defeats the Philistines

17 When the Philistines heard that David had been anointed king over Israel, they all marched up to find him, but David heard of it and went down to the fortress. 18 The Philistines arrived and spread out over the Rephaim Valley. 19 David asked the LORD, "Should I attack the Philistines? Will you hand them over to me?"

"Attack them," the LORD replied, "because I will definitely hand the Philistines over to you."

20 So David arrived at Baal-perazim and defeated the Philistines there. He said, "The LORD has burst out against my enemies, the way water bursts out!" That is why that place is called Baal-perazim.[l] 21 The Philistines left their divine images behind, and David and his men carried them off.

22 Once again the Philistines came up and spread out across the Rephaim Valley. 23 When David asked the LORD, God replied, "Don't attack them directly. Circle around behind them and come at them from in front of the balsam trees. 24 As soon as you hear the sound of marching in the tops of the trees, then attack, for God has attacked in front of you to defeat the Philistine army." 25 David followed God's orders exactly, and they defeated the Philistine army from Gibeon all the way to Gezer.

God's chest is brought to Jerusalem

6 Once again David assembled the select warriors of Israel, thirty thousand strong. 2 David and all the troops who were with him set out for Baalah, which is Kiriath-jearim of Judah,[m] to bring God's chest up from there—the chest that is called by the name[n] of the LORD of heavenly forces, who sits enthroned on the winged creatures. 3 They loaded God's chest on a new cart and carried it from Abinadab's house, which was on the hill. Uzzah and Ahio, Abinadab's sons, were driving the new cart. 4[o] Uzzah was beside God's chest while Ahio was walking in front of it. 5 Meanwhile, David and the entire house of Israel celebrated in the LORD's presence with all their strength, with songs,[p] zithers, harps, tambourines, rattles, and cymbals.

6 When they approached Nacon's threshing floor, Uzzah reached out to God's chest and grabbed it because the oxen had stumbled.[q] 7 The LORD became angry at Uzzah, and God struck him there because of his mistake,[r] and he died there next to God's chest. 8 Then David got angry because the LORD's anger lashed out against Uzzah, and so that place is called Perez-uzzah today.[s]

9 David was frightened by the LORD that day. "How will I ever bring the LORD's chest to me?" he asked. 10 So David didn't take the chest away with him to David's City. Instead, he had it put in the house of Obed-edom, who was from Gath. 11 The LORD's chest stayed with Obed-edom's household in Gath for three months, and the LORD blessed Obed-edom's household and all that he had.

12 King David was told, "The LORD has blessed Obed-edom's family and everything

[j]Heb *Millo* [k]DSS (4QSam[a]); MT lacks *city.* [l]Baal-perazim means *the lord* (Heb *baal*) *of breaking out;* see note at 2 Sam 6:8. [m]DSS (4QSam[a]), 1 Chron 13:6; MT *from Baale-judah* [n]MT repeats *name,* but 1 Chron 13:6 omits one of these and LXX reads the first as *there.* [o]LXX, DSS (4QSam[a]), 1 Chron 13:7; MT repeats *they carried it from the house of Abinadab on the hill;* Uzzah has dropped out and must be restored. [p]LXX, DSS (4QSam[a]), 1 Chron 13:8; MT *with all sorts of pine instruments* [q]Heb uncertain [r]Heb uncertain; LXX lacks this phrase; cf Targ, Syr, 1 Chron 13:10 *because he had placed his hand on the chest.* [s]*Perez-uzzah* means *Uzzah-outbreak;* cf 2 Sam 5:20.

he has because of God's chest being there."[t]
So David went and brought God's chest up
from Obed-edom's house to David's City
with celebration. 13 Whenever those bearing the chest advanced six steps, David
sacrificed an ox and a fatling calf. 14 David,
dressed in a linen priestly vest,[u] danced
with all his strength before the LORD.
15 This is how David and the entire house
of Israel brought up the LORD's chest with
shouts and trumpet blasts.
16 As the LORD's chest entered David's
City, Saul's daughter Michal was watching
from a window. She saw King David jumping and dancing before the LORD, and she
lost all respect for him.[v]
17 The LORD's chest was brought in and
put in its place inside the tent that David
had pitched for it. Then David offered entirely burned offerings in the LORD's presence in addition to well-being sacrifices.
18 When David finished offering the entirely
burned offerings and the well-being sacrifices, he blessed the people in the name of
the LORD of heavenly forces. 19 He distributed food among all the people of Israel—
to the whole crowd, male and female—each
receiving a loaf of bread, a date cake, and a
raisin cake. Then all the people went back
to their homes.
20 David went home to bless his household, but Saul's daughter Michal came
out to meet him. "How did Israel's king
honor himself today?" she said. "By exposing himself in plain view of the female
servants of his subjects like any indecent
person would!"
21 David replied to Michal, "I was celebrating before the LORD, who chose me
over your father and his entire family, and
who appointed me leader over the LORD's
people, over Israel—and I will celebrate
before the LORD again! 22 I may humiliate
myself even more, and I may be humbled in
my own eyes, but I will be honored by the
female servants you are talking about!"
23 Michal, Saul's daughter, had no children to the day she died.

God's promise to David

7 When the king was settled in his palace,[w]
and the LORD had given him rest from
all his surrounding enemies, 2 the king said
to the prophet Nathan, "Look! I'm living in
a cedar palace, but God's chest is housed in
a tent!"[x]
3 Nathan said to the king, "Go ahead and
do whatever you are thinking, because the
LORD is with you."
4 But that very night the LORD's word
came to Nathan: 5 Go to my servant David
and tell him: This is what the LORD says:
You are not the one to build the temple for
me to live in. 6 In fact, I haven't lived in a
temple from the day I brought Israel out
of Egypt until now. Instead, I have been
traveling around in a tent and in a dwelling.
7 Throughout my traveling around with the
Israelites, did I ever ask any of Israel's tribal
leaders I appointed to shepherd my people:
Why haven't you built me a cedar temple?
8 So then, say this to my servant David:
This is what the LORD of heavenly forces
says: I took you from the pasture, from
following the flock, to be leader over my
people Israel. 9 I've been with you wherever
you've gone, and I've eliminated all your
enemies before you. Now I will make your
name great—like the name of the greatest
people on earth. 10 I'm going to provide a
place for my people Israel, and plant them
so that they may live there and no longer
be disturbed. Cruel people will no longer
trouble them, as they had been earlier,
11 when I appointed leaders over my people
Israel. And I will give you rest from all your
enemies.
And the LORD declares to you that the
LORD will make a dynasty for you. 12 When
the time comes for you to die and you lie
down with your ancestors, I will raise up
your descendant—one of your very own
children—to succeed you, and I will establish his kingdom. 13 He will build a temple
for my name, and I will establish his royal
throne forever. 14 I will be a father to him,
and he will be a son to me. Whenever he

[t]Heb lacks *being there.* [u]Heb *ephod* [v]Or *despised him for it* [w]Or *house*; the same Heb word (*beth*) appears with different nuances (*house, temple, palace, dynasty, family*) in 7:2, 5, 6, 7, 11, 13, 16, 18, 19, 25-26, 27, 29. [x]Or *among curtains*

does wrong, I will discipline him with a human rod, with blows from human beings. 15 But I will never take my faithful love away from him like I took it away from Saul, whom I set aside in favor of you. 16 Your dynasty and your kingdom will be secured forever before me.[y] Your throne will be established forever.

17 Nathan reported all of these words and this entire vision to David.

David's prayer

18 Then King David went and sat in the LORD's presence. He asked:

> Who am I, LORD God, and of what significance is my family that you have brought me this far? 19 But even this was too small in your eyes, LORD God! Now you have also spoken about your servant's dynasty in the future and the generation to come,[z] LORD God!
>
> 20 What more can David say to you? You know your servant, LORD God. 21 For the sake of your word and according to your own will, you have done this great thing so that your servant would know it.
>
> 22 That is why you are so great, LORD God! No one can compare to you, no god except you, just as we have always heard with our own ears.
>
> 23 And who can compare to your people Israel? They are the one nation on earth that God redeemed as his own people, establishing his name by doing great and awesome things for them,[a] by driving out nations and their gods before your people, whom you redeemed from Egypt.[b] 24 You established your people Israel as your own people forever, and you, LORD, became their God.
>
> 25 Now, LORD God, confirm forever the promise you have made about your servant and his dynasty. Do just as you have promised 26 so that your name will be great forever when people say, "The LORD of heavenly forces is Israel's God!" May your servant David's household be established before you, 27 because you, LORD of heavenly forces, Israel's God, have revealed to your servant that you will build a dynasty for him. That is why your servant has found the courage to pray this prayer to you.
>
> 28 LORD God, you are truly God! Your words are trustworthy, and you have promised this good thing to your servant. 29 So now willingly bless your servant's dynasty so that it might continue forever before you, because you, LORD God, have promised. Let your servant's dynasty be blessed forever by your blessing.

David's wars

8 Some time later, David defeated the Philistines and subdued them. David captured Metheg-ammah from Philistine control.

2 David also defeated the Moabites and made them lie on the ground, measuring them with a rope. He measured two rope lengths for those who were to be killed and one rope length for those who were to be spared. The Moabites became David's subjects and brought him tribute.

3 Next David defeated Zobah's King Hadadezer, Rehob's son, as Hadadezer was on his way to put[c] his monument along the Euphrates River.[d] 4 David captured one thousand chariots, seven hundred charioteers,[e] and twenty thousand foot soldiers. He cut the hamstrings of all but one hundred of the chariot horses. 5 When the Arameans of Damascus came to help Zobah's King Hadadezer, David killed twenty-two thousand of them. 6 David set up forts among the Arameans of Damascus. And the Arameans became David's subjects and brought him tribute. The LORD gave David victory wherever he went. 7 David took the gold shields carried by Hadadezer's servants and brought them to Jerusalem. 8 King David also took a large amount of bronze from Tebah[f] and Berothai, towns that belonged to Hadadezer.

[y] LXX (cf 7:26, 29); MT *you* [z] Correction; Heb uncertain *this is the law of humankind* [a] Or *you* (plural)
[b] LXX, 1 Chron 17:21; MT *for your land before your people whom you redeemed for yourself from Egypt, the nations and their gods* [c] Or *to restore* [d] DSS(4QSam^{a}), 1 Chron 18:3 [e] LXX, DSS(4QSam^{a}), 1 Chron 18:4; MT *seventeen hundred chariots* [f] Some LXX manuscripts and 1 Chron 18:8; MT *Betah*

9When Hamath's King Toi heard that
David had defeated the entire army of Hadadezer, 10he sent his son Joram to King
David to wish him well and congratulate
him on his battle and defeat of Hadadezer,
because Toi was an enemy of Hadadezer.
Joram brought silver, gold, and bronze
objects with him. 11King David dedicated
these to the LORD, along with the silver
and gold he had dedicated from all the nations that he had subdued: 12Edom, Moab,
the Ammonites, the Philistines, and Amalek, including the plunder of Zobah's King
Hadadezer, Rehob's son.

13So David made a name for himself.[g]
When he returned, he killed eighteen thousand Edomites[h] in the Salt Valley. 14He set
up forts in Edom,[i] and all the Edomites
became David's subjects. The LORD gave
David victory wherever he went.

David's administration

15David ruled over all Israel and maintained justice and righteousness for all
his people. 16Zeruiah's son Joab was in
command of the army; Ahilud's son Jehoshaphat was recorder; 17Ahitub's son
Zadok and Ahimelech's son[j] Abiathar were
priests; Seraiah was secretary; 18Jehoiada's
son Benaiah was in command of[k] the Cherethites and the Pelethites; and David's sons
were priests.

David and Mephibosheth

9 David asked, "Is there anyone from
Saul's family still alive that I could show
faithful love for Jonathan's sake?" 2There
was a servant from Saul's household named
Ziba, and he was summoned before David.

"Are you Ziba?" the king asked him.

"At your service!" he answered.

3The king asked, "Is there anyone left
from Saul's family that I could show God's
kindness to?"

"Yes," Ziba said to the king, "one of Jonathan's sons, whose feet are crippled."

4"Where is he?" the king asked.

"He is at the house of Ammiel's son
Machir at Lo-debar," Ziba told the king.

5So King David had him brought from
the house of Ammiel's son Machir at Lo-
debar. 6Mephibosheth, Jonathan's son and
Saul's grandson, came to David, and he fell
to the ground, bowing low out of respect.

"Mephibosheth?" David said.

"Yes," he replied. "I am at your service!"

7"Don't be afraid," David told him, "because I will certainly show you faithful love
for the sake of your father Jonathan. I will
restore to you all the fields of your grandfather Saul, and you will eat at my table
always."

8Mephibosheth bowed low out of respect
and said, "Who am I, your servant, that you
should care about a dead dog like me?"

9Then David summoned Saul's servant
Ziba and said to him, "I have given your
master's grandson everything belonging
to Saul and his family. 10You will work the
land for him—you, your sons, and your
servants—and you will bring food into
your master's house for them to eat.[l] But
Mephibosheth, your master's grandson,
will always be at my table." (Now Ziba had
fifteen sons and twenty servants.)

11Then Ziba said to the king, "Your servant will do whatever my master the king
commands."

So Mephibosheth ate at David's[m] table,
like one of the king's own sons. 12Me-
phibosheth had a young son named Mica.
All who lived in Ziba's household became
Mephibosheth's servants. 13Mephibosheth
lived in Jerusalem, because he always ate at
the king's table. He was crippled in both feet.

War with the Ammonites and Arameans

10 Some time later, the king of the Ammonites died, and his son Hanun
succeeded him as king. 2David said, "I'll
be loyal to Nahash's son Hanun, just as
his father was loyal to me." So David sent
his servants with condolences concerning
Hanun's father.

[g]Or *built a monument* [h]LXX; MT *he returned from killing eighteen thousand Arameans* [i]Cf 1 Chron 18:13; MT repeats *in all Edom he set up forts.* [j]MT *Abiathar's son Ahimelech*; cf 1 Sam 22:20; 23:6; 30:7; 2 Sam 20:25 [k]Syr, Tg, Vulg, 1 Chron 18:17; MT lacks *in command of.* [l]LXX[L]; MT *You will bring food for your master's son and he will eat it.* [m]LXX; MT *my*

But when David's servants arrived in Ammonite territory, [3]the Ammonite officials asked their master Hanun, "Do you really believe David is honoring your father because he has sent you condolences? Of course not! David has sent his servants to you to search the city, spy it out, and overthrow it." [4]So Hanun seized David's servants and shaved off their beards,[n] cut off half their garments, from their buttocks down, and sent them off.

[5]When this was reported to David, he sent men to meet them because they were completely ashamed. The king said, "Stay in Jericho until your beards have grown. Then you can come back."

[6]When the Ammonites realized that they had offended David, they sent for and hired the Arameans of Beth-rehob and the Arameans of Zobah, totaling twenty thousand foot soldiers; the king of Maacah with one thousand soldiers; and twelve thousand soldiers from Tob. [7]When David heard this, he sent Joab with the entire army of warriors. [8]The Ammonites marched out and formed a battle line at the entrance to the city. The Arameans of Zobah and Rehob and the soldiers from Tob and Maacah remained in the countryside.

[9]When Joab saw that the battle would be fought on two fronts, he chose some of Israel's finest warriors and deployed them to meet the Arameans. [10]The rest of the army Joab placed under the command of his brother Abishai. When they took up their positions to meet the Ammonites, Joab said, [11]"If the Arameans prove too strong for me, you must help me, and if the Ammonites prove too strong for you, I'll help you. [12]Be brave! We must be courageous for the sake of our people and the cities of our God. The LORD will do what is good in his eyes."

[13]When Joab and the troops who were with him advanced into battle against the Arameans, they fled from him. [14]When the Ammonites saw that the Arameans had fled, they also fled from Abishai and retreated to the city. Then Joab returned from fighting the Ammonites and went to Jerusalem.

[15]The Arameans saw that they had been defeated by Israel, so they regrouped. [16]Hadadezer sent for Arameans from beyond the Euphrates River. They came to Helam with Shobach leading them as commander of Hadadezer's army. [17]When this was reported to David he gathered all Israel, crossed the Jordan, and went to Helam. The Arameans formed battle lines against David and fought with him. [18]But the Arameans fled before Israel, and David destroyed seven hundred of their chariots and forty thousand horsemen. David wounded their army commander Shobach, and he died there. [19]When all the kings who served Hadadezer saw that they were defeated by Israel, they made peace with Israel and became their subjects. Never again would the Arameans come to the aid of the Ammonites.

David and Bathsheba

11 In the spring,[o] when kings[p] go off to war, David sent Joab, along with his servants and all the Israelites, and they destroyed the Ammonites, attacking the city of Rabbah. But David remained in Jerusalem.

[2]One evening, David got up from his couch and was pacing back and forth on the roof of the palace. From the roof he saw a woman bathing; the woman was very beautiful. [3]David sent someone and inquired about the woman. The report came back: "Isn't this Eliam's daughter Bathsheba, the wife of Uriah the Hittite?" [4]So David sent messengers to get her. When she came to him, he had sex with her. (Now she had been purifying herself after her monthly period.) Then she returned home. [5]The woman conceived and sent word to David.

"I'm pregnant," she said.

[6]Then David sent a message to Joab: "Send me Uriah the Hittite." So Joab sent Uriah to David. [7]When Uriah came to him, David asked about the welfare of Joab and the army and how the battle was going. [8]Then David told Uriah, "Go down to your house and wash your feet."

Uriah left the palace, and a gift from the king was sent after him. [9]However, Uriah

[n]LXX; MT *half their beard* [o]Or *At the turn of the year* [p]LXX, Tg, Vulg; MT *messengers*

slept at the palace entrance with all his
master's servants. He didn't go down to his
own house. 10David was told, "Uriah didn't
go down to his own house," so David asked
Uriah, "Haven't you just returned from a
journey? Why didn't you go home?"
11"The chest and Israel and Judah are all
living in tents," Uriah told David. "And my
master Joab and my master's troops are
camping in the open field. How[q] could I go
home and eat, drink, and have sex with my
wife? I swear on your very life,[r] I will not
do that!"
12Then David told Uriah, "Stay here one
more day. Tomorrow I'll send you back."
So Uriah stayed in Jerusalem that day. The
next day 13David called for him, and he ate
and drank, and David got him drunk. In
the evening Uriah went out to sleep in the
same place, alongside his master's servants,
but he did not go down to his own home.
14The next morning David wrote a letter
to Joab and sent it with Uriah. 15He wrote
in the letter, "Place Uriah at the front of the
fiercest battle, and then pull back from him
so that he will be struck down and die."
16So as Joab was attacking the city, he
put Uriah in the place where he knew there
were strong warriors. 17When the city's soldiers came out and attacked Joab, some of
the people from David's army fell. Uriah the
Hittite was also killed. 18Joab sent a complete report of the battle to David.
19"When you have finished reporting all
the news of the battle to the king," Joab instructed the messenger, 20"if the king gets
angry and asks you, 'Why did you go so close
to the city to fight? Didn't you know they
would shoot from the wall? 21Who killed Jerubbaal's son Abimelech?[s] Didn't a woman
throw an upper millstone on top of him from
the wall so that he died in Thebez? Why did
you go so close to the wall?' then say: 'Your
servant Uriah the Hittite is dead too.'"
22So the messenger set off, and when he
arrived he reported to David everything
Joab sent him to say.
23"The men overpowered us," the messenger told David. "They came out against us in
the open field, but we fought against them[t]
up to the entrance of the city gate. 24Archers
shot down on your servants from the wall.
Some of the king's servants died. And your
servant Uriah the Hittite is dead too."
25David said to the messenger, "Say this
to Joab: 'Don't be upset about this because
the sword is that way: taking the life of this
person or that person. Continue attacking
the city and destroy it!' Encourage Joab!"
26When Uriah's wife heard that her husband Uriah was dead, she mourned for her
husband. 27After the time of mourning was
over, David sent for her and brought her
back to his house. She became his wife and
bore him a son.
But what David had done was evil in the
LORD's eyes.

Nathan pronounces God's judgment

12 So the LORD sent Nathan to David.
When Nathan arrived he said, "There
were two men in the same city, one rich, one
poor. 2The rich man had a lot of sheep and
cattle, 3but the poor man had nothing—just
one small ewe lamb that he had bought. He
raised that lamb, and it grew up with him
and his children. It would eat from his food
and drink from his cup—even sleep in his
arms! It was like a daughter to him.
4"Now a traveler came to visit the rich
man, but he wasn't willing to take anything
from his own flock or herd to prepare for
the guest who had arrived. Instead, he took
the poor man's ewe lamb and prepared it
for the visitor."
5David got very angry at the man, and
he said to Nathan, "As surely as the LORD
lives, the one who did this is demonic![u]
6He must restore the ewe lamb seven times
over[v] because he did this and because he
had no compassion."
7"You are that man!" Nathan told David.
"This is what the LORD God of Israel says: I
anointed you king over Israel and delivered
you from Saul's power. 8I gave your master's
house[w] to you, and gave his wives into your

[q]LXX[L]; MT lacks *How.* [r]Or *I swear on your life and your soul's life;* cf LXX [s]LXX, Syr, Judg 7:1; MT *Jerub-besheth* [t]Or *we were upon them* [u]Or *as good as dead;* MT *a son of death* [v]LXX; MT *fourfold* (cf Exod 22:1) [w]Syr *daughters*

embrace. I gave you the house[x] of Israel and Judah. If that was too little, I would have given even more. [9]Why have you despised the LORD's word by doing what is evil in his eyes? You have struck down Uriah the Hittite with the sword and taken his wife as your own. You used the Ammonites to kill him. [10]Because of that, because you despised me and took the wife of Uriah the Hittite as your own, the sword will never leave your own house.

[11]"This is what the LORD says: I am making trouble come against you from inside your own family. Before your very eyes I will take your wives away and give them to your friend, and he will have sex with your wives in broad daylight. [12]You did what you did secretly, but I will do what I am doing before all Israel in the light of day."

[13]"I've sinned against the LORD!" David said to Nathan.

"The LORD has removed your sin," Nathan replied to David. "You won't die. [14]However, because you have utterly disrespected the LORD[y] by doing this, the son born to you will definitely die." [15]Then Nathan went home.

Bathsheba's child dies

The LORD struck the child that Uriah's wife had borne for David, and he became very sick. [16]David begged God for the boy. He fasted and spent the night sleeping on the ground. [17]The senior servants of his house approached[z] him to lift him up off the ground, but he refused, and he wouldn't eat with them either.

[18]On the seventh day, the child died. David's servants were afraid to tell him that the child had died. "David wouldn't listen to us when we talked to him while the child was still alive," they said. "How can we tell him the child has died? He'll do something terrible!"

[19]But when David saw his servants whispering, he realized the child had died.

"Is the child dead?" David asked his servants.

"Yes," they said, "he is dead."

[20]Then David rose from the ground, bathed, anointed himself, and changed his clothes. He entered the LORD's house and bowed down. Then he entered his own house. He requested food, which was brought to him, and he ate.

[21]"Why are you acting this way?" his servants asked. "When the child was alive, you fasted and cried and kept watch,[a] but now that the child is dead, you get up and eat food!"

[22]David replied, "While the child was alive I fasted and wept because I thought, Who knows? The LORD may have mercy on me and let the child live. [23]But he is dead now. Why should I fast? Can I bring him back again? No. I am going where he is, but he won't come back to me."

[24]Then David comforted his wife Bathsheba. He went to her and had sex with her. She gave birth to a son and named him Solomon.[b] The LORD loved him [25]and sent word by the prophet Nathan to name him Jedidiah[c] because of the LORD's grace.[d]

Defeat of the Ammonites

[26]Meanwhile, Joab fought the Ammonites at Rabbah and captured the royal city. [27]Joab then sent messengers to David, saying, "I have fought against Rabbah and captured the city's water supply.[e] [28]So gather the rest of the troops, attack the city, and capture it. Otherwise, I will capture the city myself, and it will be named after me."

[29]So David gathered all the troops, marched to Rabbah, fought against it, and captured it. [30]David took Milcom's[f] crown off his head. It weighed one kikkar of gold and was set with a valuable stone. It was placed on David's head. The amount of loot David took from the city was huge. [31]He brought out the people who were in the city and put them to work making bricks. David demolished the city with saws, iron picks, and axes;[g] he did this to all the Ammonite cities. Then David and all the troops returned to Jerusalem.

[x]Syr *daughters* [y]MT *the LORD's enemies*—a euphemism or ancient scribal correction (cf note at 1 Sam 25:22)
[z]LXX[L], DSS(4QSam[a]); MT *stood over* [a]LXX[L], OL; MT lacks *kept watch.* [b]Qere; Kethib *he* (David) *named*
[c]*Jedidiah* means *Loved by the LORD.* [d]Heb uncertain; some Heb and LXX manuscripts *by the LORD's word*
[e]Heb uncertain [f]LXX; MT *their king's crown* [g]Cf LXX[L], OL, Tg, 1 Chron 20:3

Amnon rapes Tamar

13 Some time later, David's son Amnon fell in love with Tamar the beautiful sister of Absalom, who was also David's son. 2 Amnon was so upset over his half sister that he made himself sick. She was a virgin, and it seemed impossible in Amnon's view to do anything to her. 3 But Amnon had a friend named Jonadab, Shimeah's son, David's brother, who was a very clever man.

4 "Prince," Jonadab said to him, "why are you so down, morning after morning? Tell me about it."

So Amnon told him, "I'm in love with Tamar, the sister of my brother Absalom."

5 "Lie down on your bed and pretend to be sick," Jonadab said to him. "When your father comes to see you, tell him, 'Please let my sister Tamar come and give me some food to eat. Let her prepare the food in my sight so I can watch and eat from her own hand.'"

6 So Amnon lay down and pretended to be sick. The king came to see him, and Amnon told the king, "Please let my sister Tamar come and make a couple of heart-shaped cakes in front of me so I can eat from her hand."

7 David sent word to Tamar at the palace: "Please go to your brother Amnon's house and prepare some food for him."

8 So Tamar went to her brother Amnon's house where he was lying down. She took dough, kneaded it, made heart-shaped cakes in front of him, and then cooked them. 9 She took the pan and served Amnon, but he refused to eat.

"Everyone leave me," Amnon said. So everyone left him. 10 Then Amnon said to Tamar, "Bring the food into the bedroom so I can eat from your hand." So Tamar took the heart-shaped cakes she had made and brought them to her brother Amnon in the bedroom. 11 When she served him the food, he grabbed her and said, "Come have sex with me, my sister."

12 But she said to him, "No, my brother! Don't rape me. Such a thing shouldn't be done in Israel. Don't do this horrible thing. 13 Think about me—where could I hide my shame? And you—you would become like some fool in Israel! Please, just talk to the king! He won't keep me from marrying you."

14 But Amnon refused to listen to her. He was stronger than she was, and so he raped her.

15 But then Amnon felt intense hatred for her. In fact, his hatred for her was greater than the love he had felt for her. So Amnon told her, "Get out of here!"

16 "No, my brother!"[h] she said. "Sending me away would be worse than the wrong you've already done."

But Amnon wouldn't listen to her. 17 He summoned his young servant and said, "Get this woman out of my presence and lock the door after her." (18 She was wearing a long-sleeved robe because that was what the virgin princesses wore as garments.)[i] So Amnon's servant put her out and locked the door after her.

19 Tamar put ashes on her head and tore the long-sleeved robe she was wearing. She put her hand on her head and walked away, crying as she went.

20 Her brother Absalom said to her, "Has your brother Amnon been with you? Keep quiet about it for now, sister; he's your brother. Don't let it bother you." So Tamar, a broken woman, lived in her brother Absalom's house.

21 When King David heard about all this he got very angry, but he refused to punish his son Amnon because he loved him as his oldest child.[j] 22 Absalom never spoke to Amnon, good word or bad, because he hated him for raping his sister Tamar.

Absalom kills Amnon

23 Two years later, Absalom was shearing sheep at Baal-hazor near Ephraim, and he invited all the king's sons. 24 Absalom approached the king and said, "Your servant is shearing sheep. Would the king and his advisors please join me?"

25 But the king said to Absalom, "No, my son. We shouldn't all go, or we would be a

[h]Correction; Heb uncertain; cf LXX, Vulg [i]Heb uncertain [j]LXX, DSS(4QSam[a]); MT lacks *but he refused . . . oldest child.*

burden on you." Although Absalom urged him, the king wasn't willing to go, although he gave Absalom a blessing.

26Then Absalom said, "If you won't come, then let my brother Amnon go with us."

"Why should he go with you?" they asked him. 27But Absalom urged him until he sent Amnon and all the other princes. Then Absalom made a banquet fit for a king.[k]

28Absalom commanded his servants, "Be on the lookout! When Amnon is happy with wine and I tell you to strike Amnon down, then kill him! Don't be afraid, because I myself am giving you the order. Be brave and strong men." 29So Absalom's servants did to Amnon just what he had commanded. Then all the princes got up, jumped onto their mules, and fled.

30While they were on the way, the report came to David: "Absalom has killed all of the princes! Not one remains." 31The king got up, tore his garments, and lay on the ground. All his servants stood near him, their garments torn as well. 32But Jonadab, the son of David's brother Shimeah, said, "My master shouldn't think that all the young princes have been killed—only Amnon is dead. This has been Absalom's plan ever since the day Amnon raped his sister Tamar. 33So don't let this bother you, my master; don't think that all the princes are dead, because only Amnon is dead, 34and Absalom has fled." Just then the young man on watch looked up and saw many people coming on the road behind him alongside the mountain. 35Jonadab told the king, "Look, the princes are coming, just as I, your servant, said they would."

36When Jonadab finished speaking, the princes arrived. They broke into loud crying, and the king and his servants cried hard as well.

37Meanwhile, Absalom had fled and gone to Geshur's King Talmai, Ammihud's son. David mourned for his son a long time. 38But Absalom, after fleeing to Geshur, stayed there for three years. 39Then the king's desire to go out after Absalom faded away because he had gotten over Amnon's death.[l]

Absalom is restored

14 Now Joab, Zeruiah's son, could see that the king's mind was on Absalom. 2So Joab sent someone to Tekoa and brought a wise woman from there. He said to her, "Pretend to be in mourning. Dress in mourning clothes. Don't anoint yourself with oil. Act like a woman who has spent a long time mourning over someone who has died. 3Go to the king and speak to him as follows." Then Joab told her what to say.

4When the woman from Tekoa came to the king, she fell facedown, bowing low out of respect. "King, help me!" she said.

5"What is wrong?" the king asked her.

"It's terrible!" she said. "I am a widow; my husband is dead. 6Your servant had two sons, but the two of them fought in the field. No one could separate them, and one struck the other and killed him. 7Now the entire clan has turned against your servant. They say, 'Hand over the one who killed his brother so we can execute him for murdering his brother, even though we would destroy the heir as well.' So they would snuff out the one ember I have left, leaving my husband without name or descendant on the earth."

8The king said to the woman, "Return home, and I will issue an order in your behalf."

9The woman of Tekoa said to the king, "My master and king, let the guilt be on me and on my father's household. The king and his throne are innocent."

10"If anyone speaks against you, bring him to me, and he will never trouble you again," the king replied.

11She said, "Please let the king remember the LORD your God so that the one seeking revenge doesn't add to the destruction and doesn't kill my son."

"As surely as the LORD lives," David said, "not one of your son's hairs will fall to the ground."

12Then the woman said, "May your female servant say something to my master the king?"

"Speak!" he said.

13The woman said, "Why have you planned

[k]LXX; MT lacks *Then Absalom . . . king.* [l]DSS(4QSam^a), LXX; Heb uncertain

the very same thing against God's people? In giving this order, the king has become guilty because the king hasn't restored his own banished son. [14]We all have to die—we're like water spilled out on the ground that can't be gathered up again. But God doesn't take life away; instead, he makes plans so those banished from him don't stay that way.[m]

[15n]"I have come to my master the king to talk about this because people have made me afraid. Your servant thought, I must speak with the king. Maybe the king will act on the request of his servant, [16]because the king will agree to deliver his servant from the power of anyone who would destroy both me and my son from the inheritance God gave. [17]Your servant thought, The word of my master the king will definitely comfort me, because my master the king is like one of God's messengers, understanding good and evil. May the LORD your God be with you!"

[18o]The king answered the woman, "I must ask you something—don't hide anything from me!"

The woman said, "Please, my master and king, speak."

[19]So the king said, "Has Joab put you up to this?"

The woman answered, "As surely as you live, my master and king, no one can deviate a bit from whatever my master and king says. Yes, it was your servant Joab who directed me, and it was Joab who told your female servant to say all these things. [20]Your servant Joab did this to change the way things look.[p] But my master's wisdom is like the wisdom of one of God's own messengers—he knows everything that takes place in the land."

[21]So the king said to Joab, "All right then. I will do it. Go and bring back my boy Absalom."

[22]Joab fell facedown, bowing low out of respect, and he blessed the king.

"Today your servant knows that you think well of me, my master and king," Joab said, "because the king has followed up on his servant's recommendation."

[23]So Joab got up, went to Geshur, and brought Absalom back to Jerusalem.

[24]The king said, "He must go straight to his own house. He must not see my face." So Absalom went straight to his own house and did not see the king.

[25]No man throughout Israel was as praised for his good looks as Absalom. From the soles of his feet to the crown of his head there was nothing wrong with him. [26]When he shaved his head—he had to shave his head at the end of each year because his hair was so heavy that he had to shave it—the weight of the hair from his head was two hundred shekels by the royal weight. [27]Absalom had three sons and one daughter. The daughter's name was Tamar. She was a beautiful woman.

[28]Absalom lived in Jerusalem two years without ever seeing the king's face. [29]Absalom called for Joab in order to send Joab to the king, but Joab refused to come. Absalom called for Joab a second time, but he still wouldn't come. [30]So Absalom said to his servants, "Look, Joab's property is next to mine. He has barley there. Go and set it on fire." So Absalom's servants set the property on fire. Then Joab's servants went to Joab with their clothes torn. "Absalom's servants set the property on fire," they said.[q]

[31]So Joab went straight to Absalom's house and said to him, "Why have your servants set my property on fire?"

[32]Absalom answered Joab, "Look, I sent you a message: Come here so I can send you to the king to ask, 'Why have I returned from Geshur? I would be better off if I were still there!' Please let me see the king's face. If I'm guilty, then the king can kill me."

[33]Joab went to the king and reported this to him. Then the king called for Absalom, and Absalom came to the king. He bowed low out of respect, nose to the ground before the king. Then the king kissed Absalom.

[m]Heb uncertain [n]14:15-17 may have originally followed 14:7. [o]14:18 may have originally followed 14:14.
[p]Heb uncertain [q]DSS(4QSam[c]) LXX; MT lacks *Then Joab's servants . . . said.*

Absalom plots rebellion

15 Some time later, Absalom got a chariot and horses for his own use, along with fifty men to run ahead of him. 2 Absalom would get up early and stand by the side of the road that went through the city gate. Whenever anyone had a lawsuit to bring before the king for judgment, Absalom would call to him, "What city are you from?" When the person said, "Your servant is from one of the tribes of Israel," 3 then Absalom would say to him, "No doubt your claims are correct and valid, but the king won't listen to you. 4 If only I were made a judge in the land," Absalom would continue, "then anyone with a lawsuit could come to me, and I would give them justice."

5 Whenever anyone came near to Absalom, bowing low out of respect, he would reach his hand out, grab them, and kiss them. 6 This is how Absalom treated every Israelite who came to the king seeking justice. This is how Absalom stole the hearts of the Israelites.

7 At the end of four[r] years, Absalom said to the king, "Please let me go to Hebron so I can fulfill a promise I made to the LORD. 8 Your servant made this promise when I lived in Geshur, in Aram. I promised that if the LORD would bring me back to Jerusalem, then I would worship the LORD in Hebron."[s]

9 "Go in peace," the king said. So Absalom left and went to Hebron.

10 But Absalom sent secret agents throughout the tribes of Israel with this message: "When you hear the sound of the trumpet, then say, 'Absalom has become king in Hebron!'" 11 Two hundred invited guests went with Absalom from Jerusalem. They were innocent and knew nothing of this matter when they went. 12 While Absalom was offering the sacrifices, he summoned David's advisor Ahithophel, who was from Giloh, to come from his hometown. So the conspiracy grew stronger, and Absalom's following grew.

David flees from Jerusalem

13 A messenger came to David, reporting, "The hearts of the Israelites have gone over to Absalom." 14 Then David told all the servants who were with him in Jerusalem, "Come on! We have to run for it, or we won't be able to escape Absalom. Hurry, or he will catch up with us in no time, destroy us,[t] and attack the city with the sword."

15 The king's servants said to him, "Your servants are ready to do whatever our master the king decides." 16 So the king left, with his entire household following him, but he left ten secondary wives behind to take care of the palace.

17 So the king left, with all his people following him, and they stopped at the last house. 18 All the king's servants marched past him, as did all the Cherethites, all the Pelethites, and the six hundred Gittites who had followed him from Gath. 19 The king said to Ittai the Gittite, "Why are you coming with us too? Go back! Stay with King Absalom.[u] You are a foreigner and an exile from your own country. 20 You just got here yesterday. So today should I make you wander around with us while I go wherever I have to go? No. Go back, and take your relatives with you. May the LORD show you loyal love and faithfulness."[v]

21 But Ittai answered the king, "As surely as the LORD lives and as surely as my master the king lives, wherever my master the king may be, facing death or facing life, your servant will be there too."

22 "Okay then," David replied to Ittai. "Keep marching!"

So Ittai the Gittite and all of his men and all the little children with him marched past. 23 The whole countryside cried loudly as all the troops marched past. The king crossed the Kidron Valley, and all the troops passed by on the Olive road[w] into the wilderness.

24 Zadok was there too, along with all the Levites carrying the chest containing God's covenant. They set God's chest down, and Abiathar offered sacrifices until all the troops had finished marching out of the city. 25 Then the king said to Zadok, "Carry God's chest back into the city. If the LORD thinks well of me, then he will bring me

[r] LXX, Syr, Vulg, Josephus; MT *forty* [s] LXX; MT lacks *in Hebron*. [t] Heb uncertain; LXX[L] *bring the city down on top of us* [u] Heb lacks *Absalom*. [v] LXX; MT lacks *may the LORD show you*. [w] LXX[L]; MT lacks *Olive*.

back and let me see it and its home again.
26 But if God says, 'I'm not pleased with
you,' then I am ready. Let him do to me
whatever pleases him."
27 "Do you understand?" the king said
to the priest Zadok. "Go back to the city in
safety—you and Abiathar[x] with your two
sons, your son Ahimaaz and Abiathar's son
Jonathan. 28 I will be waiting in the desert plains until you send word telling me
what to do." 29 So Zadok and Abiathar took
God's chest back to Jerusalem and stayed
there.
30 But David, his head covered, walked
barefoot up the slope of the Mount of Olives crying. All the people who were with
him covered their heads too and cried
as they went up. 31 David was told that
Ahithophel was also among the conspira-
tors with Absalom, so he prayed, "Please,
LORD, make Ahithophel's advice foolish."

David and Hushai

32 When David came to the summit
where people used to worship God, Hushai
from Erek met him. Hushai's clothes were
ripped, and dirt was on his head. 33 David
said to him, "If you come with me, you will
be a burden to me. 34 But if you return to
the city and say to Absalom, 'King, I am
your servant![y] Please spare my life! I was
your father's servant in the past, but now
I am your servant,' then you can help me
by countering Ahithophel's advice. 35 The
priests Zadok and Abiathar will be with
you there. So report everything you hear in
the king's palace to the priests Zadok and
Abiathar. 36 Their two sons, Zadok's son
Ahimaaz and Abiathar's son Jonathan, are
also there. Use them to report to me everything you hear."
37 So David's friend Hushai went into Jerusalem, just as Absalom was entering the city.

David and Ziba

16 When David had passed a short distance beyond the summit, Ziba, Mephibosheth's servant, met him with a pair of
saddled donkeys loaded with two hundred
loaves of bread, one hundred bunches of
raisins, one hundred figs,[z] and a jar of wine.
2 "What is all this for?" the king asked Ziba.
"The donkeys are for the royal family to
ride," Ziba explained. "The bread and summer fruit are for the young people to eat,
and the wine is for those who get exhausted
in the wilderness."
3 "Where is your master's grandson?" the
king asked.
"He is still in Jerusalem," Ziba answered
the king, "because he thinks that the Israelites are now going to give his grandfather's
kingdom back to him."
4 "Look here," the king said to Ziba.
"Everything that belonged to Mephibosheth
now belongs to you."
Ziba said, "I bow out of respect! Please
think well of me, my master and king."

Shimei curses David

5 When King David came to Bahurim, a
man from the same clan as Saul's family
came out from there. His name was Shimei; he was Gera's son. He was cursing as
he came out. 6 He threw rocks at David and
at all of King David's servants, even though
the entire army and all the warriors were on
either side of him.
7 This is what Shimei said as he cursed
David: "Get out of here! Get out of here! You
are a murderer! You are despicable! 8 The
LORD has paid you back for all the blood of
Saul's family, in whose place you rule, and
the LORD has handed the kingdom over to
your son Absalom. You are in this trouble
because you are a murderer!"
9 Zeruiah's son Abishai said to the king,
"Why should this dead dog curse my master the king? Let me go over and cut his
head off!"
10 But the king said, "My problems aren't
yours, you sons of Zeruiah. If he is cursing
because the LORD told him to curse David,
then who is to question, 'Why are you
doing this?'"
11 Then David addressed Abishai and all
his servants: "Listen! My own son, one of
my very own children, wants me dead. This

[x]Correction; MT lacks *and Abiathar.* [y]Correction, LXX; MT *King, I will be your servant.* [z]Or *summer fruit*

Benjaminite can only feel the same—only more! Leave him alone. And let him curse, because the LORD told him to. 12Perhaps the LORD will see my distress; perhaps the LORD will repay me with good for this cursing today."

13So David and his men kept walking, while Shimei went along on the hillside next to him, cursing as he went, throwing rocks and dirt at him. 14The king and all the people who were with him reached the Jordan River[a] exhausted, and he rested there.

Ahithophel's advice

15Now Absalom and all the Israelites entered Jerusalem, and Ahithophel was with him. 16Then David's friend Hushai, who was from Erek, approached Absalom and said to him, "Long live the king! Long live the king!"

17But Absalom said to Hushai, "Is this how you show loyal love to your friend? Why didn't you go with him?"

18"No," Hushai replied to Absalom, "I will belong to the one chosen by the LORD, by this people, and by all Israel, and I will stay with him. 19What's more, whom should I serve if not David's son? I served your father, and so I will serve you in the same way."

20Then Absalom said to Ahithophel, "Give your advice then. What should we do?"

21"Have sex with your father's secondary wives—the ones he left to take care of the palace," Ahithophel told Absalom. "Then all Israel will hear that you have alienated yourself from your father, and everyone who supports you will be encouraged."

22So they set up a tent for Absalom on the roof, and he had sex with his father's secondary wives in plain sight before all Israel. (23Now in those days, the advice Ahithophel gave was like asking for a word from God. That's why Ahithophel's advice was valued by both David and Absalom.)

17 Then Ahithophel said to Absalom, "Let me pick twelve thousand men, and I will go after David tonight. 2I will attack him while he is tired and weak, and I will throw him into a panic. All the troops with him will run off. I promise to kill the king alone, 3and I will bring all the people back to you like a bride comes back to her husband.[b] It's only one man's life you are seeking; everyone else can be at peace."

4This plan seemed excellent to Absalom and the Israelite elders.

Hushai's advice

5But Absalom said, "Call Hushai from Erek. Let's hear what he has to say as well." 6When Hushai from Erek arrived, Absalom said to him, "This is what Ahithophel has advised. Should we follow it or not? What do you say?"

7Hushai said to Absalom, "This time, the advice Ahithophel has given isn't right. 8You know that your father and his men are warriors," he continued, "and they are as desperate as a wild bear robbed of her cubs. Your father is a seasoned fighter. He won't spend the night with his troops. 9Even now he has probably hidden himself in one of the caves or some other place. When some of the troops[c] fall in the first attack, whoever hears it will say, 'The soldiers who follow Absalom have been defeated!' 10Then even the bravest soldier, whose heart is like a lion's, will melt in fear because all Israel knows that your father is a warrior and that those who are with him are brave. 11So I would advise that all the Israelites, from Dan to Beer-sheba—a group as countless as sand on the seashore—be summoned to join you, and that you yourself go into battle. 12When we attack him wherever he might be, we will fall on him like dew that falls on the ground. No one will survive—not him and not one of the soldiers who are with him! 13If he retreats into a city, all Israel will bring ropes to that city, and we will drag it into a valley until not even a pebble of it will be found."

14Then Absalom and everyone in Israel agreed, "The advice of Hushai from Erek is better than Ahithophel's advice." This was because the LORD had decided to counter Ahithophel's good advice so that the LORD could bring disaster on Absalom.

[a]LXX; MT lacks *at the Jordan River.* [b]LXX; Heb uncertain [c]LXX

Hushai warns David

15 Hushai told the priests Zadok and Abiathar, "Here is what Ahithophel advised Absalom and the Israelite elders, and here is what I advised. 16 Now send word immediately to David and tell him, 'Don't spend the night in the desert plains. You must cross over immediately. Otherwise, the king and all the troops who are with him will be swallowed up whole.'"

17 Jonathan and Ahimaaz were standing by at En-rogel. A female servant would come and report to them, and they would then travel and report to King David because they couldn't risk being seen entering the city. 18 But a boy saw them and reported it to Absalom. So the two of them left immediately and came to a man's house at Bahurim. He had a well in his courtyard, and they climbed down into it. 19 The man's wife took a covering and spread it over the well's opening, then scattered grain over it so no one would notice. 20 When Absalom's servants came to the woman at the house they demanded, "Where are Ahimaaz and Jonathan?"

The woman told them, "They crossed over the stream."[d] They looked for them but found nothing, so they returned to Jerusalem.

21 After they had left, Jonathan and Ahimaaz climbed out of the well. They went and reported to King David, "Get up! Cross the water immediately because Ahithophel has made plans against you!" 22 So David and all the troops who were with him got up and crossed the Jordan River. By daybreak there was no one left who hadn't crossed the Jordan.

23 Meanwhile, once Ahithophel saw that his advice hadn't been followed, he saddled his donkey and went home to his own town. He gave instructions to his household, then hanged himself and died. He was buried in his father's tomb.

24 David had reached Mahanaim by the time Absalom and all the Israelites who were with him crossed the Jordan River. 25 Absalom had put Amasa in charge of the army instead of Joab. Amasa was the son of a man named Ithra, an Ishmaelite[e] who had married Abigail, who was Nahash's daughter and the sister of Zeruiah, Joab's mother. 26 Israel and Absalom camped in the territory of Gilead.

27 When David arrived in Mahanaim, Nahash's son Shobi, who was from Rabbah of the Ammonites; Ammiel's son Machir, who was from Lo-debar; and Barzillai the Gileadite from Rogelim 28 brought couches, basins, and pottery, along with wheat, barley, flour, roasted grain, beans, lentils, 29 honey, curds, sheep, and cheese from the herd so that David and the troops who were with him could eat. They said, "The troops have grown hungry, tired, and thirsty in the wilderness."

Absalom's death

18 Then David gathered the troops who were with him and appointed unit commanders over thousands and hundreds. 2 David sent out the army—a third under Joab's command, a third under the command of Abishai, Zeruiah's son, and a third under the command of Ittai the Gittite. The king told the troops, "I will march out with you myself."

3 But the troops replied, "No! You must not march out! If we flee, they won't care about us. Even if half of us die, they won't care about us. But you are worth ten thousand of us. It is much better if you support us from the city."

4 The king said to them, "I will do whatever you think is best." So the king stood beside the gate as all the troops marched out by hundreds and thousands. 5 The king gave orders to Joab, Abishai, and Ittai: "For my sake, protect my boy Absalom." All the troops heard what the king ordered regarding Absalom to all the commanders.

6 So the troops marched into the field to meet the Israelites. The battle was fought in the Ephraim forest. 7 The army of Israel was defeated there by David's soldiers. A great slaughter of twenty thousand men took place that day. 8 The battle spread out over the entire countryside, and the forest

[d] Heb uncertain [e] LXX^{A} and 1 Chron 2:17; MT *an Israelite*; LXX^{M} *a Jezreelite*

devoured more soldiers than the sword that day.

[9]Absalom came upon some of David's men. Absalom was riding on a mule, and the mule went under the tangled branches of a large oak tree. Absalom's head got caught in the tree. He was left hanging in midair while the mule under him kept on going. [10]One of the men saw this and reported to Joab, "I just saw Absalom hanging from an oak tree."

[11]Joab said to the man who told him, "You saw this? Why didn't you kill him on the spot? I would have given you ten pieces of silver and a belt."

[12]But the man said to Joab, "Even if I had a thousand pieces of silver in my hand, I wouldn't touch the king's son! We heard what the king commanded you, Abishai, and Ittai—'For my sake, take care of my boy Absalom.'[f] [13]If I had taken Absalom's life behind the king's back then—though nothing is hidden from the king—you would have kept your distance from me."[g]

[14]Joab said, "I won't waste time like this with you!" He took three sticks in his hand and drove them into Absalom's chest while he was still alive in the oak. [15]Then ten young armor-bearers of Joab surrounded Absalom, struck him, and killed him. [16]Then Joab sounded the trumpet, and the troops stopped chasing the Israelites, because Joab held them back.

[17]They took Absalom and threw him into a big pit in the forest. They piled over him a huge heap of stones. Meanwhile, all the Israelites fled to their homes. [18]When he was alive, Absalom had raised a large pillar for himself in the King's Valley because he said, "I have no son to carry on the memory of my name." He named the pillar after himself. It is called Absalom's Monument to this day.

David mourns for Absalom

[19]Then Zadok's son Ahimaaz said, "Please let me run and take the news to the king that the LORD has vindicated him against his enemies' power."

[20]Joab said to him, "You aren't the one to bring the news today. You can bring news on another day, but not today, because the king's son is dead." [21]Then Joab said to a Cushite, "Go tell the king what you have seen." The Cushite bowed low before Joab, then ran off.

[22]But Zadok's son Ahimaaz again said to Joab, "I don't care what happens, just let me run after the Cushite too."

"Why do you want to go, son?" Joab asked. "You'll get no reward for going."[h]

[23]"I don't care what happens, I want to go," Ahimaaz said.[i]

So Joab said to him, "Run off then!"

Ahimaaz ran off, going by way of the plain, and passed the Cushite.

[24]Now David was sitting between the two gates. The watchman on duty went up on the roof of the gate by the wall. He looked out and saw a man running alone. [25]The watchman called out and reported this to the king. The king said, "If he's alone, it's good news."

The man got nearer and nearer, [26]and the watchman saw another man running and called down to the gatekeeper, "There's another man running alone."

The king said, "That one must be bringing good news too."

[27]The watchman said, "I can see that the first one runs like Zadok's son Ahimaaz."

"He's a good man," the king said, "and is coming with good news."

[28]Ahimaaz called out to the king, "Peace!" then bowed low before the king, his nose to the ground. He said, "Bless the LORD your God, who has delivered up the men who raised their hands against my master the king."

[29]The king said, "Is my boy Absalom okay?"

Ahimaaz said, "I saw a large crowd right when Joab, the king's servant, sent your servant off, but I don't know what it was about."

[30]"Step aside and stand right here," the king said. So Ahimaaz stepped aside and waited.

[f]LXX, Vulg, Syr; Heb uncertain [g]Or *Otherwise, I would have been dealing recklessly with my own life, because nothing is hidden from the king and you were stationed far from me*; Heb uncertain. [h]Heb uncertain [i]LXX; MT lacks *Ahimaaz said.*

[31]Then the Cushite arrived and said, "My master the king: Listen to this good news! The LORD has vindicated you this day against the power of all who rose up against you."

[32]The king said to the Cushite, "Is my boy Absalom okay?"

The Cushite answered, "May the enemies of my master the king and all who rise up against you to hurt you end up like that young man."

[33][j]The king trembled. He went up to the room over the gate and cried. As he went, he said, "Oh, my son Absalom! Oh, my son! My son Absalom! If only I had died instead of you! Oh, Absalom, my son! My son!"

19 [k]Joab was told that the king was crying and mourning Absalom. [2]So the victory that day was turned into mourning for all the troops because they heard that day that the king was grieving for his son. [3]So that day the troops crept back into the city like soldiers creep back ashamed after they've fled from battle. [4]The king covered his face and cried out in a loud voice, "Oh, my son Absalom! Oh, Absalom, my son! My son!"

[5]Joab came to the king inside and said, "Today you have humiliated all your servants who have saved your life today, not to mention the lives of your sons, your daughters, your wives, and your secondary wives, [6]by loving those who hate you and hating those who love you! Today you have announced that the commanders and their soldiers are nothing to you, because I know that if Absalom were alive today and the rest of us dead, that would be perfectly fine with you! [7]Now get up! Go out and encourage your followers! I swear to the LORD that if you don't go out there, not one man will stick with you tonight—and that will be more trouble for you than all the trouble that you've faced from your youth until now."

[8]So the king went and sat down in the city gate. All the troops were told that the king was sitting in the gate, so they came before the king.

David returns to Jerusalem

Meanwhile, the Israelites had fled to their homes. [9]Everyone was arguing throughout Israel's tribes, saying, "The king delivered us from our enemies' power, and he rescued us from the Philistines' power, but now he has fled from the land and from controlling his own kingdom.[l] [10]And Absalom, the one we anointed over us, is dead in battle. So why do you say nothing about bringing the king back?"

[11]When the things that all the Israelites were saying reached the king,[m] David sent a message to the priests Zadok and Abiathar: "Say the following to the elders of Judah: 'Why should you be the last to bring the king back to his palace?[n] [12]You are my relatives! You are my flesh and bones! Why should you be the last to bring the king back?' [13]And tell Amasa, 'Aren't you my flesh and bones too? May God deal harshly with me and worse still if you don't become commander of my army from now on instead of Joab!'"

[14]So he won over the hearts of everyone in Judah as though they were one person, and they sent word to the king: "Come back—you and all your servants." [15]So the king came back and arrived at the Jordan River. Judah came to Gilgal to meet the king and bring him across the Jordan.

[16]Gera's son Shimei, the Benjaminite from Bahurim, hurried down with the people of Judah to meet King David. [17]A thousand men from Benjamin were with him. Ziba too, the servant of Saul's house, along with his fifteen sons and twenty servants, rushed to the Jordan ahead of the king [18]to do the work of ferrying[o] over the king's household and to do whatever pleased him.

Gera's son Shimei fell down before the king when he crossed the Jordan. [19]He said to the king, "May my master not hold me guilty or remember your servant's wrongdoing that day my master the king left Jerusalem. Please forget about it, Your Majesty,[p] [20]because your servant knows that I have

[j]19:1 in Heb [k]19:2 in Heb [l]LXX; MT *from over Absalom* [m]LXX, OL; MT lacks *When . . . the king*, though a version of this clause appears in 19:12. [n]MT adds *The things that all the Israelites were saying reached the king in his home* (or *palace*). [o]LXX; MT *while the crossing was under way, to ferry* [p]19:18-19 Heb uncertain

sinned. But look, I am the first person from the entire family of Joseph to come down today and meet my master the king."

21 Zeruiah's son Abishai responded, "Shouldn't Shimei be put to death for that—for cursing the LORD's anointed?"

22 But David said, "My problems aren't yours, you sons of Zeruiah. Why are you becoming my enemy today? Should anyone in Israel be put to death today? Don't I know that today I am again king over Israel?"

23 Then the king told Shimei, "You will not die." And the king swore this to him.

24 Mephibosheth, Saul's grandson, also came down to meet the king. He hadn't taken care of his feet, trimmed his beard, or washed his clothes from the day the king left until the day he returned safely. 25 When he came from Jerusalem to meet the king, the king asked him, "Mephibosheth, why didn't you go with me?"

26 "My master and king," Mephibosheth answered, "my servant abandoned me! Because your servant is lame, I asked my servant, 'Saddle a donkey for me[q] so I can ride and go to the king.' 27 So Ziba has slandered your servant to my master and king, but my master and king is a messenger of God. So do whatever seems best to you. 28 Even though all the members of my grandfather's family were nothing short of demonic[r] toward my master and king, you still put your servant with those who eat at your table. So what right do I have to beg for still more from the king?"

29 "You don't need to talk any more about this," the king said to him. "I order you and Ziba to divide the property."

30 Mephibosheth said to the king, "Let him take all of it, since my master and king has come home safely."

31 Now Barzillai the Gileadite had come down from Rogelim. He accompanied the king to the Jordan River to send him off there. 32 Barzillai was very old, 80 years of age. He had supported the king during his stay at Mahanaim because Barzillai was a very wealthy man.

33 The king said to Barzillai, "Come over the Jordan with me. I will provide for you at my side in Jerusalem."

34 But Barzillai said to the king, "How many years do I have left that I should go up with the king to Jerusalem? 35 I am now 80 years old. Do I know what is good or bad anymore? Can your servant taste what I eat or drink? Can I even hear the voices of men or women singers? Why should your servant be a burden to my master and king? 36 Your servant will cross a short way over the Jordan with the king, but why should the king give me such a reward? 37 Let your servant return so I may die in my own town near the grave of my parents. But here is your servant Chimham. Let him cross over with my master and king, and treat him as you think best."

38 The king said, "Okay. Chimham will cross over with me, and I will treat him as I[s] think best. And I will do for you anything you desire from me."

39 So all the people crossed over the Jordan River, and the king stayed behind.[t] The king kissed Barzillai and blessed him, and then Barzillai went back to his home. 40 When the king crossed over to Gilgal, Chimham went with him. All the troops of Judah and half the troops of Israel escorted the king across.

41 Then everyone in Israel came and said to the king, "Why did our relatives the people of Judah steal you away, and bring the king and his household across the Jordan River, along with all of his soldiers?"

42 Then all the people of Judah answered the Israelites, "Because the king is our relative! Why are you angry at us about this? Have we taken any of the king's food? Has he given us any gifts?"

43 But the Israelites answered the people of Judah, "We have ten shares in the monarchy! What's more, we are the oldest offspring, not you![u] So why have you disrespected us? Weren't we the first to talk about bringing back our king?"

But the words of the people of Judah were even harsher than the words of the Israelites.[v]

[q]LXX, Syr, Vulg; MT *your servant said, I will saddle a donkey for myself* [r]Or *were doomed to death by my master the king*; MT *men of death* [s]LXX; MT *you* [t]LXX; MT *crossed over* [u]LXX, OL; MT *we have a greater claim on David than you do.* [v]19:39-43 Heb uncertain

Sheba's rebellion

20 Now a despicable man named Sheba, Bichri's son, from Benjamin, was also there. He sounded the trumpet and said:

"We don't care about David!
We have no stake in Jesse's son!
Go back to your homes, Israel!"

2 So all the Israelites left David to follow Bichri's son Sheba. But all the people of Judah stayed close to their king from the Jordan River all the way to Jerusalem.

3 When David arrived at his palace in Jerusalem, the king took the ten secondary wives he had left to take care of the palace and put them in a house under guard. He provided for them, but he didn't have sex with them. They were confined until the day they died, and lived like widows.

4 Then the king said to Amasa, "Call everyone in Judah here to me three days from now. You should be here too." 5 So Amasa went to call Judah together, but he took longer than the allotted time.

6 David told Abishai, "Bichri's son Sheba will cause more trouble for us than Absalom did. Take your master's servants and chase after him before he finds fortified cities and escapes from us." 7 So Joab's men marched out after Sheba—this included the Cherethites, the Pelethites, and all the warriors. They marched out of Jerusalem to pursue Bichri's son Sheba.

8 When they got to the great stone in Gibeon, Amasa came to meet them. Joab was dressed in his soldier's uniform. Over the tunic at his waist he wore a sword in its sheath. As Joab went forward it slipped out.

9 "How are you, my brother?" Joab asked Amasa, and with his right hand he took hold of Amasa's beard as if to kiss him. 10 But Amasa didn't notice the sword in Joab's hand. Joab struck him in the stomach with it so that Amasa's intestines spilled out on the ground. He died without Joab striking him a second time. Then Joab and his brother Abishai pursued Sheba, Bichri's son.

11 One of Joab's men stood by Amasa and said, "Whoever favors Joab, and whoever is for David, follow Joab!" 12 Amasa was writhing in blood in the middle of the road, and the man saw that everyone was stopping. When he saw this, he dragged Amasa from the road into a field and threw a robe over him. 13 Once Amasa was moved out of the road, everyone who followed Joab marched past in pursuit of Bichri's son Sheba.

14 Sheba went through all the Israelite tribes up to Abel of Beth-maacah. All the Bichrites[w] assembled and followed Sheba in. 15 Then Joab's men arrived and attacked Sheba at Abel of Beth-maacah. They piled up a ramp against the city, and it stood against the outer wall.[x] All of Joab's troops were hammering the wall, trying to bring it down.

16 Then a wise woman called from the city, "Listen! Listen! Tell Joab to come over here, so I can talk to him."

17 So Joab approached her, and the woman said, "Are you Joab?"

"I am," he answered.

"Pay close attention to the words of your female servant," she said.

"I'm listening," Joab replied.

18 She said, "People used to say long ago: 'Ask your question at Abel,' and that settled the matter. 19 I am one of the peaceful and faithful in Israel, but you are trying to kill a city that is one of Israel's mothers! Why would you annihilate the LORD's inheritance?"

20 Joab answered, "I would never, ever annihilate or destroy such a thing! 21 That's not the issue. A man named Sheba, Bichri's son, who is from the Ephraim highlands, has rebelled against King David. Just hand him over, and I'll leave the city alone."

The woman said to Joab, "His head will be thrown over the wall to you!"

22 When the woman went to everyone with her wise counsel, they cut off the head of Sheba, Bichri's son, and threw it out to Joab. Then Joab sounded the trumpet, and his troops left the city, returning to their homes. But Joab returned to the king in Jerusalem.

David's officials

23 Now Joab was in command of Israel's army; Jehoiada's son Benaiah commanded the Cherethites and the Pelethites; 24 Adoram

[w] Cf LXX, Vulg; MT *Berites* [x] Heb uncertain

was in charge of the forced labor; Ahilud's
son Jehoshaphat was the recorder; 25 Sheva
was secretary; Zadok and Abiathar were
priests; 26 and Ira from Jair was also a priest
for David.

Avenging the Gibeonites

21 There was a famine for three years in
a row during David's rule. David asked
the LORD about this, and the LORD said, "It
is caused by Saul and his household, who
are guilty of bloodshed because he killed
the people of Gibeon." 2 So the king called
for the Gibeonites and spoke to them.

(Now the Gibeonites weren't Israelites
but were survivors of the Amorites. The Israelites had sworn a solemn pledge to spare
them, but Saul tried to eliminate them in
his enthusiasm for the people of Israel and
Judah.)

3 David said to the Gibeonites, "What can
I do for you? How can I fix matters so you
can benefit from the LORD's inheritance?"

4 The Gibeonites said to him, "We don't
want any silver or gold from Saul or his
family, and it isn't our right to have anyone
in Israel killed."

"What do you want?"[y] David asked. "I'll
do it for you."

5 "Okay then," they said to the king. "That
man who opposed and oppressed[z] us, who
planned to destroy us, keeping us from
having a place to live anywhere in Israel—
6 hand over seven of his sons to us, and we
will hang them before the LORD at Gibeon[a]
on the LORD's mountain."

"I will hand them over," the king said.

7 But the king spared Mephibosheth,
Jonathan's son and Saul's grandson, because
of the LORD's solemn pledge that was between them—between David and Saul's son
Jonathan. 8 So the king took the two sons
of Aiah's daughter Rizpah, Armoni and Mephibosheth, whom she had birthed for Saul;
and the five sons of Saul's daughter Merab,[b]
whom she birthed for Adriel, Barzillai's son,
who was from Meholah, 9 and he handed
them over to the Gibeonites. They hanged
them on the mountain before the LORD. The
seven of them died at the same time. They
were executed in the first days of the harvest,
at the beginning of the barley harvest.

10 Aiah's daughter Rizpah took funeral
clothing and spread it out by herself on a
rock. She stayed there from the beginning of
the harvest until the rains poured down on
the bodies from the sky, and she wouldn't let
any birds of prey land on the bodies during
the day or let wild animals come at nighttime. 11 When David was told what Aiah's
daughter Rizpah, Saul's secondary wife, had
done, 12 he went and retrieved the bones of
Saul and his son Jonathan from the citizens of Jabesh-gilead, who had stolen the
bones from the public square in Beth-shan,
where the Philistines had hanged them on
the day the Philistines killed Saul at Gilboa.
13 David brought the bones of Saul and his
son Jonathan from there and collected the
bones of the men who had been hanged by
the Gibeonites. 14 The bones of Saul and his
son Jonathan were then buried in Zela, in
Benjaminite territory, in the tomb of Saul's
father Kish. Once everything the king had
commanded was done, God responded to
prayers for the land.

War with the Philistines

15 Once again war broke out between
the Philistines and Israel. David and the
soldiers who were with him went down
and fought the Philistines. When David
grew tired, 16 Ishbi-benob, a descendant of
the Raphah,[c] planned on killing David.[d]
The weight of his spear was three hundred
shekels of bronze, and he was wearing new
armor. 17 But Zeruiah's son Abishai came to
David's aid, striking the Philistine down
and killing him. Then David's men swore
a solemn pledge to him: "You will never
march out to battle with us again! You must
not snuff out Israel's lamp!"

18 Some time later, another battle with the
Philistines took place at Gob. Then Sibbecai
from Hushah killed Saph, a descendant of
the Raphah. 19 There was yet another battle

[y]LXX^{L}, OL; MT *What are you saying?* [z]LXX^{B}; MT *annihilated us* [a]Correction; cf LXX and 21:9; MT *at Gibeah of Saul, the LORD's chosen one* [b]LXX^{LN}; MT *Michal* (but cf 2 Sam 6:23) [c]Or *giants*; also in 21:18, 20, 22
[d]LXX *Joash's son Dodo, a descendant of the Raphah* (see previous note), *captured David.*

with the Philistines at Gob; and Elhanan,
Jair's son[e] from Bethlehem, killed Goliath
from Gath, whose spear shaft was as strong
as the bar on a weaver's loom. 20 In another
battle at Gath, there was a huge[f] man who
had six fingers on his hands and six toes
on his feet, twenty-four in all. He too was
descended from the Raphah. 21 When he insulted Israel, Jonathan, who was the son of
David's brother Shimei, killed him. 22 These
four Philistines were descended from the
Raphah in Gath, and they fell by the hands
of David and his servants.

David's thanksgiving psalm

22 [g]David spoke the words of this song
to the LORD after the LORD delivered
him from the power of all his enemies and
from Saul.

2 He said:
The LORD is my solid rock,
my fortress, my rescuer.
3 My God is my rock—
I take refuge in him!—
he's my shield and
my salvation's strength,
my place of safety and my shelter.
My savior! Save me from violence!
4 Because he is praiseworthy,[h]
I cried out to the LORD,
and I was saved from my enemies.
5 Death's waves were all around me;
rivers of wickedness terrified me.
6 The cords of the grave[i] surrounded me;
death's traps held me tight.
7 In my distress I cried out to the LORD;
I cried out to my God.
God heard my voice from his temple;
my cry for help reached his ears.

8 The earth rocked and shook;
the sky's foundations trembled
and reeled because of God's anger.
9 Smoke went up from God's nostrils;
out of his mouth came a devouring fire;
flaming coals blazed out in front of him!
10 God parted the skies and came down;
thick darkness was beneath his feet.
11 God mounted the heavenly creatures
and flew;
he was seen on the wind's wings.
12 God made darkness his covering;
water gathered in dense clouds!
13 Coals of fire blazed
out of the brightness before him.
14 The LORD thundered from heaven;
the Most High made his voice heard.
15 God shot arrows, scattering the enemy;
he sent the lightning
and whipped them into confusion.
16 The seabeds were exposed;
the earth's foundations were laid bare
at the LORD's rebuke,
at the angry blast of air
coming from his nostrils.

17 From on high God reached down
and grabbed me;
he took me out of deep waters.
18 God saved me from my powerful enemy,
saved me from my foes,
who were too much for me.
19 They came at me
on the very day of my distress,
but the LORD was my support.
20 He brought me out to wide-open spaces;
he pulled me out,
because he is pleased with me.
21 The LORD rewarded me
for my righteousness;
he restored me
because my hands are clean,
22 because I have kept the LORD's ways.
I haven't acted wickedly against my God.
23 All his rules are right in front of me;
I haven't turned away
from any of his laws.
24 I have lived with integrity before him;
I've kept myself from wrongdoing.
25 And so the LORD restored me
for my righteousness,
because I am clean in his eyes.

26 You deal faithfully with the faithful;
you show integrity toward the one
who has integrity.

[e]See 1 Chron 20:5, LXX[LMN] (cf 2 Sam 23:24); Heb *Jaare-oregim.* [f]See 1 Chron 20:6; MT *a Midianite* or *a combative man.* [g]This poem also occurs in Psalm 18 with some variations. [h]Heb uncertain [i]Heb *Sheol*

27 You are pure toward the pure,
but toward the crooked, you are tricky.
28 You are the one
who saves people who suffer,
but your eyes are against the proud.
You bring them down!
29 You are my lamp, LORD;
the LORD illumines my darkness.
30 With you I can charge into battle;
with my God I can leap over a wall.
31 God! His way is perfect;
the LORD's word is tried and true.
He is a shield for all who take refuge
in him.

32 Now really, who is divine
except the LORD?
And who is a rock except our God?
33 Only God! My mighty fortress,
who makes my way[j] perfect,
34 who makes my step[k]
as sure as the deer's,
who lets me stand securely
on the heights,
35 who trains my hands for war
so my arms can bend a bronze bow.
36 You've given me
the shield of your salvation;
your help has made me great.
37 You've let me walk fast and safe,
without even twisting an ankle.
38 I chased my enemies
and destroyed them!
I didn't come home until I finished
them off.
39 I ate them up! I struck them down!
They couldn't get up;
they fell under my feet.
40 You equipped me with strength for war;
you brought my adversaries
down underneath me.
41 You made my enemies turn tail from me;
I destroyed my foes.
42 They looked around,
but there was no one to save them.
They looked to the LORD,
but he wouldn't answer them.
43 I crushed them like dust on the ground;
I stomped on them,
trampled them like mud
dumped in the streets.
44 You delivered me from struggles
with many people;
you appointed me the leader
of many nations.
Strangers come to serve me.
45 Foreigners grovel before me;
after hearing about me, they obey me.
46 Foreigners lose their nerve;
they come trembling
out of their fortresses.[l]

47 The LORD lives! Bless God, my rock!
Let my God, the rock of my salvation,
be lifted high!
48 This is the God who avenges
on my behalf,
who subdues peoples before me,
49 who rescues me from my enemies.
You lifted me high above my adversaries;
you delivered me from violent people.
50 That's why I thank you, LORD,
in the presence of the nations.
That's why I sing praises to your name.
51 You are the one who gives
great victories to your king,
who shows faithful love
to your anointed one—
to David and to his descendants forever.

David's last words

23 These are David's last words:
This is the declaration
of Jesse's son David,
the declaration of a man raised high,
a man anointed by the God of Jacob,
a man favored
by the strong one of Israel.[m]
2 The LORD's spirit speaks through me;
his word is on my tongue.
3 Israel's God has spoken,
Israel's rock said to me:
"Whoever rules rightly over people,
whoever rules in the fear of God,
4 is like the light of sunrise
on a morning with no clouds,
like the bright gleam after the rain
that brings grass from the ground."

[j] Qere; Kethib *his way* [k] Qere; Kethib *his step* [l] Or *prisons* [m] Or *Israel's favorite singer* or *the favorite of Israel's songs*

5 Yes, my house is this way with God![n]
He has made an eternal covenant
with me,
laid out and secure in every detail.
Yes, he provides every one of my victories
and brings my every desire to pass.
6 But despicable people are like thorns,
all of them good for nothing,
because they can't be carried by hand.
7 No one can touch them,
except with iron bar or the shaft of a spear.
They must be burned up with fire
right on the spot!

David's warriors

8 These are the names of David's warriors: Jeshbaal[o] from Hachmon[p] was chief of the Three.[q] He raised his spear[r] against eight hundred, killing them on a single occasion.

9 Next in command was Eleazar, Dodo's son and Ahohi's grandson. He was among the three warriors with David when they insulted the Philistines who had gathered there for battle. The Israelites retreated, 10 but he stood his ground and fought the Philistines until his hand was weary and stuck to the sword. But the LORD accomplished a great victory that day. The troops then returned to Eleazar, but only to plunder the dead.

11 Next in command was Agee's son Shammah, who was from Harar. The Philistines had gathered at Lehi, where there was a plot of land full of lentils. The troops fled from the Philistines, 12 but Shammah took a position in the middle of the plot, defended it, and struck down the Philistines. The LORD accomplished a great victory.

13 At harvesttime, three of the thirty chiefs went down and joined David at the fortress[s] of Adullam, while a force of Philistines were camped in the Rephaim Valley. 14 At that time, David was in the fortress, and a Philistine fort was in Bethlehem. 15 David had a craving and said, "If only someone could give me a drink of water from the well by the gate in Bethlehem." 16 So the three warriors broke through the Philistine camp and drew water from the well by the gate in Bethlehem and brought it back to David. But he refused to drink it and poured it out to the LORD.

17 "The LORD forbid that I should do that," he said. "Isn't this the blood of men who risked their lives?" So he refused to drink it.

These were the kinds of things the three warriors did.

18 Now Zeruiah's son Abishai, the brother of Joab, was chief of the Thirty.[t] He raised his spear against three hundred men, killed them, and made a name for himself along with the Three. 19 He was the most famous of the Thirty.[u] He became their commander, but he wasn't among the Three.

20 Jehoiada's son Benaiah was a hero from Kabzeel who performed great deeds. He killed the two sons[v] of Ariel from Moab. He once went down into a pit and killed a lion on a snowy day. 21 He also killed a giant[w] Egyptian who had a spear in his hand. Benaiah went against him armed with a staff. He grabbed the spear out of the Egyptian's hand and killed him with his own spear. 22 These were the kinds of things Jehoiada's son Benaiah did. He made a name for himself along with the three warriors. 23 He was famous among the Thirty, but he didn't become one of the Three. David placed him in command of his own bodyguard.

24 Among the Thirty were:
Asahel, Joab's brother;
Elhanan, Dodo's son from Bethlehem;
25 Shammah from Harod;
Elika from Harod;
26 Helez from Pelet;
Ira, Ikkesh's son from Tekoa;
27 Abiezer from Anathoth;
Mebunnai the Hushathite;
28 Zalmon from Ahoh;
Maharai from Netophah;
29 Heleb, Baanah's son from Netophah;
Ittai, Ribai's son
from Gibeah in Benjamin;
30 Benaiah from Pirathon;
Hiddai from the Gaash ravines;

[n] Or *Yes, my house is surely with God!* [o] LXX^{L}, OL; MT *Josheb-bashebeth*; cf 1 Chron 11:11 [p] See 1 Chron 11:11. [q] LXX^{L}, Vulg; cf 1 Chron 11:11; MT *chief of the officers* [r] Cf 1 Chron 11:11; Heb uncertain [s] Or *cave*; cf 2 Sam 23:14 [t] Some Heb manuscripts, Syr; MT *third* or *three* [u] Syr; cf 1 Chron 11:25; MT *Wasn't he the most famous of the Three?* [v] LXX; MT lacks *sons*. [w] MT *handsome*; cf 1 Chron 11:23

31 Abi-albon from the desert plain;
Azmaveth from Bahurim;
32 Eliahba from Shaalbon;
Jashen the Gizonite;[x]
Jonathan, 33 Shammah's son[y]
from Harar;
Ahiam, Sharar's son from Harar;
34 Eliphelet, Ahasbai's son from Maacah;
Eliam, Ahithophel's son from Giloh;
35 Hezro from Carmel;
Paarai from Erab;
36 Igal, Nathan's son from Zobah;
Bani the Gadite;
37 Zelek the Ammonite;
Naharai from Beeroth, and the
armor-bearer for Zeruiah's son Joab;
38 Ira from Ither;
Gareb from Ither;
39 and Uriah the Hittite—
thirty-seven in all.

David's census

24 The LORD burned with anger against
Israel again, and he incited David
against them: Go and count the people of
Israel and Judah.
2 So the king said to Joab and the military commanders[z] who were with him,
"Go throughout all the tribes of Israel,
from Dan to Beer-sheba, and take a census
of the people so I know how many people
there are."
3 Joab said to the king, "May the LORD
your God increase the number of people a
hundred times while the eyes of my master
the king can still see it! But why does my
master the king want to do this?"
4 But the king's word overruled Joab and
the military commanders. So Joab and the
commanders left the king's presence to
take a census of the Israelites. 5 They crossed
the Jordan River and began from Aroer
and from[a] the town that is in the middle of
the valley of Gad, then on to Jazer. 6 They
continued to Gilead and on to Kadesh in
Hittite territory.[b] They came to Dan[c] and
went around to Sidon. 7 They went to the
fortress of Tyre and to all the towns of the
Hivites and the Canaanites. They went out
to Beer-sheba in the arid southern plain
of Judah. 8 At the end of nine months and
twenty days, after going through the entire country, they came back to Jerusalem.
9 Joab reported to the king the number of
the people who had been counted: in Israel
there were eight hundred thousand strong
men who could handle a sword; in Judah
the total was five hundred thousand men.
10 But after this David felt terrible that he
had counted the people. David said to the
LORD, "I have sinned greatly in what I have
done. Now, LORD, please take away the guilt
of your servant because I have done something very foolish."
11 When David got up the next morning,
the LORD's word came to the prophet Gad,
David's seer: 12 Go and tell David, This is
what the LORD says: I'm offering you three
punishments. Choose one of them, and
that is what I will do to you.
13 So Gad went to David and said to him,
"Will three[d] years of famine come on your
land? Or will you run from your enemies for
three months while they chase you? Or will
there be three days of plague in your land?
Decide now what answer I should take back
to the one who sent me."
14 "I'm in deep trouble," David said to
Gad. "Let's fall into the LORD's hands because his mercy is great, but don't let me
fall into human hands."
15 So the LORD sent a plague on Israel
from that very morning until the allotted
time. Seventy thousand people died, from
Dan to Beer-sheba. 16 But when the divine
messenger stretched out his hand to destroy Jerusalem, the LORD regretted doing
this disaster and said to the messenger who
was destroying the people, "That's enough!
Withdraw your hand." At that time the
LORD's messenger was by the threshing
floor of Araunah from Jebus.
17 When David saw the messenger who
was striking down the people, he said, "I'm
the one who sinned! I'm the one who has
done wrong. But these sheep—what have

[x]Cf 1 Chron 11:34; MT *Jashen's sons* [y]LXX; MT lacks *son.* [z]LXX and 2 Sam 24:4; MT *commander* [a]LXX; MT *camped in Aroer south of the city* [b]Hebrew uncertain; correction *on to the area beneath Hermon* [c]LXX[L]; MT *Dan-jaan* [d]LXX, 1 Chron 21:12; MT *seven*

they done wrong? Turn your hand against me and my household."

18 That same day Gad came to David and told him, "Go up and build an altar to the LORD on the threshing floor of Araunah from Jebus." 19 So David went up, following Gad's instructions, just as the LORD had commanded.

20 Araunah looked up and saw the king and his servants approaching him. Araunah rushed out and bowed low before the king, his nose to the ground. 21 Araunah said, "Why has my master and king come to his servant?"

David said, "To buy this threshing floor from you to build an altar to the LORD, so the plague among the people may come to an end."

22 Then Araunah said to David, "Take it for yourself, and may my master the king do what he thinks is best. Here are oxen for the entirely burned offering, and here are threshing boards and oxen yokes for wood. 23 All this, Your Majesty, Araunah gives to the king." Then he added, "May the LORD your God respond favorably to you!"

24 "No," the king said to Araunah. "I will buy them from you at a fair price. I won't offer up to the LORD my God entirely burned offerings that cost me nothing." So David bought the threshing floor and the oxen for fifty shekels of silver. 25 David built an altar there for the LORD and offered entirely burned offerings and well-being sacrifices. The LORD responded to the prayers for the land, and the plague against Israel came to an end.

1 KINGS

David and Abishag

1 King David had become very old. His servants covered him with blankets, but he couldn't stay warm. 2 They said to him, "Allow us to find a young woman for our master the king. She will serve the king and take care of him by lying beside our master the king and keeping him warm." 3 So they looked in every corner of Israel until they found Abishag from Shunem. They brought her to the king. 4 She was very beautiful. She cared for the king and served him, but the king didn't have sex with her.

Adonijah's rebellion

5 Adonijah, Haggith's son, bragged about himself and said, "I'll rule as king myself." He got his own chariot and horses with fifty runners to go in front. 6 Now Adonijah's father had never given him direction; he never questioned why Adonijah did what he did. He was very handsome and was born after Absalom. 7 He took advice from Joab, Zeruiah's son, and from the priest Abiathar. They assisted Adonijah. 8 But Zadok the priest, Jehoiada's son Benaiah, the prophet Nathan, Shimei and his friends, and David's veterans didn't join Adonijah. 9 So Adonijah prepared lamb, oxen, and fattened cattle at the Stone of Zoheleth, next to En-rogel. He invited his brothers (the royal princes) and all the citizens of Judah who were the royal servants to come. 10 But he didn't invite the prophet Nathan, Benaiah, David's veterans, or his brother Solomon.

11 Nathan said to Bathsheba, Solomon's mother, "Did you hear that Adonijah, Haggith's son, has become king, but our master David doesn't know about it? 12 Let me give you some advice on how you and your son Solomon can survive this. 13 Go to King David and say, 'Didn't my master the king swear to your servant, "Your son Solomon will certainly rule after me. He will sit on my throne"? Why then has Adonijah become king?' 14 While you are speaking there with the king, I'll come along and support your words."

15 So Bathsheba went to the king in his bedroom. The king was very old, and Abishag from Shunem was serving the king. 16 Bathsheba bowed down on her face before the king.

The king asked, "What do you want?"

17 She said to him, "Your Majesty, you swore by the LORD your God to your

servant, 'Your son Solomon will certainly rule after me. He will sit on my throne.' [18]But now, look, Adonijah has become king, and my master the king doesn't know about it. [19]He has prepared large quantities of oxen, fattened cattle, and lamb. He has invited all the royal princes as well as Abiathar the priest and Joab the general. However, he didn't invite your servant Solomon. [20]As for you, my master the king, the eyes of all Israel are upon you to tell them who will follow you on the throne of my master the king. [21]When my master the king lies down with his ancestors, then I and my son Solomon will become outlaws."

[22]While she was still speaking with the king, the prophet Nathan arrived. [23]The king was informed, "The prophet Nathan is here." Then Nathan came in before the king and bowed his face to the ground. [24]He said, "My master the king, you must have said, 'Adonijah will become king after me and will sit on my throne.' [25]Indeed, today he went down and prepared oxen, fattened cattle, and lamb in large numbers. He invited all the royal princes, the generals, and Abiathar the priest. They are eating and drinking with him, and they said, 'Long live King Adonijah!' [26]Adonijah didn't invite me, your servant, Zadok the priest, Jehoiada's son Benaiah, or your servant Solomon. [27]If this message was from my master the king, you didn't make it known to your servant. Who should follow you on the throne of my master the king?"

[28]King David answered, "Bring me Bathsheba." She came and stood before the king. [29]The king made a solemn pledge and said, "As surely as the LORD lives, who rescued me from every trouble, [30]regarding what I swore to you by the LORD, Israel's God, 'Your son Solomon will certainly succeed me; he will sit on the throne after me'—I'll see that it happens today."

[31]Bathsheba bowed down with her face to the ground. She honored the king and said, "May my master King David live forever!"

[32]King David said, "Bring me Zadok the priest, the prophet Nathan, and Benaiah, Jehoiada's son." They came to the king, [33]who said to them, "Take with you the servants of your masters. Put my son Solomon on my mule and bring him down to Gihon. [34]There Zadok the priest and the prophet Nathan will anoint him king over Israel. Blow the ram's horn and say, 'Long live King Solomon!' [35]You will follow him. He will enter and sit on my throne, and so he will succeed me as king. I have appointed him to become ruler over Israel and Judah."

[36]Benaiah, Jehoiada's son, responded to the king, "Yes, may it happen as the LORD, the God of my king, says. [37]Just as the LORD was with my master the king, so may he be with Solomon. May his throne be even greater than the throne of my master King David." [38]Zadok the priest, the prophet Nathan, Jehoiada's son Benaiah, and the Cherethites and the Pelethites went down and put Solomon on King David's mule. They led him to Gihon. [39]Zadok the priest took the horn of oil from the tent and anointed Solomon. They blew the ram's horn, and all the people said, "Long live King Solomon!" [40]All the people followed him playing flutes and celebrating. The ground shook at their noise.

[41]Adonijah and all his invited guests heard this when they had finished eating. When Joab heard the sound of the ram's horn, he said, "What's that noise coming from the city?" [42]While he was still speaking, Jonathan, Abiathar the priest's son, arrived.

Adonijah said, "Come on in! You are an honest man and will bring a good report."

[43]Jonathan replied to Adonijah, "No! Our master King David has made Solomon king! [44]To support him, the king sent along Zadok the priest; the prophet Nathan; Benaiah, Jehoiada's son; and the Cherethites and the Pelethites. They've put Solomon on the royal mule. [45]Zadok the priest and the prophet Nathan have anointed him king at Gihon. They went up from there celebrating so that the city was thrown into a commotion. That is the sound you heard. [46]There's more: Solomon has taken over the throne of the kingdom. [47]The royal attendants blessed our master King David: 'May your God make Solomon's name better than your name. May God elevate his throne above your throne.'"

The king then worshipped on his bed [48]and said, "Bless Israel's God, the LORD, who today has set my son[a] on my throne, and has allowed my eyes to see it."

[49]Trembling with fear, all of Adonijah's guests got up and fled, each going a different way. [50]Adonijah was afraid of Solomon, so he got up and went to grab hold of the horns of the altar. [51]Solomon was told, "Look! Adonijah is afraid of King Solomon and has grabbed the horns of the altar. He's saying, 'King Solomon must swear to me first that he won't execute his servant with the sword.'"

[52]Solomon said, "If he shows himself to be an honorable person, then not a hair of his head will be harmed. But if any evil is found in him, he will die." [53]King Solomon sent word and had him brought down from the altar. He came and bowed down to King Solomon. Solomon said to him, "Go home!"

David's last words

2 David's time was coming to an end. So he commanded Solomon his son, [2]"I'm following the path that the whole earth takes. Be strong and be a man. [3]Guard what is owed to the LORD your God, walking in his ways and observing his laws, his commands, his judgments, and his testimonies, just as it is written in the Instruction from Moses. In this way you will succeed in whatever you do and wherever you go. [4]So also the LORD will confirm the word he spoke to me: 'If your children will take care to walk before me faithfully, with all their heart and all their being, then one of your own children will never fail to be on the throne of Israel.' [5]You should know what Joab, Zeruiah's son, has done to me and what he did to the two generals of Israel, Abner, Ner's son, and Amasa, Jether's son. He murdered them, spilling blood at peacetime and putting the blood of war on the belt around his waist and on the sandals on his feet. [6]So act wisely: Don't allow him to die a peaceful death. [7]As for Barzillai's sons from Gilead, show them kindness. Let them eat with you. When I was running away from your brother Absalom, they came to me. [8]Now as for this Shimei, Gera's son—a Benjaminite from Bahurim—who is with you, he cursed me viciously when I went to Mahanaim. When he came down to meet me at the Jordan, I swore to him by the LORD, 'Surely I won't execute you with the sword.' [9]But you don't need to excuse him. You are wise and know what to do to him. Give him a violent death."

[10]Then David lay down with his ancestors and was buried in David's City. [11]He ruled over Israel forty years—seven years in Hebron and thirty-three years in Jerusalem.

Solomon secures his throne

[12]Solomon sat on the throne of his father David, and his royal power was well established. [13]Adonijah, Haggith's son, went to Bathsheba, Solomon's mother. She said, "Are you coming in peace?"

He said, "Yes. [14]I have something to say to you."

She said, "Say it."

[15]He said, "You know how the kingdom was mine. All Israel had appointed me as their king. Then suddenly the kingdom went to my brother as the LORD willed. [16]Now I have just one request of you. Don't refuse me!"

She said to him, "Go on."

[17]Adonijah continued, "Ask King Solomon to let me marry Abishag from Shunem—he won't refuse you."

[18]Bathsheba said, "Okay; I'll speak to the king for you."

[19]So Bathsheba went to King Solomon to talk with him about Adonijah. The king stood up to meet her and bowed low to her. Then he returned to his throne and had a throne set up for the queen mother. She sat to his right. [20]She said, "I have just one small request for you. Don't refuse me."

The king said to her, "Mother, ask me. I won't refuse you."

[21]"Let Abishag from Shunem be married to your brother Adonijah," she said.

[22]King Solomon replied to his mother, "Why ask only for Abishag from Shunem for Adonijah? Why not ask for the entire

[a]Heb lacks *my son*; other versions have it or something similar.

kingdom for him? After all, he is my older brother and has the support of Abiathar the priest and Joab, Zeruiah's son." 23King Solomon swore by the LORD, "May God do to me as he sees fit! Adonijah has made this request at the cost of his life! 24Now, as surely as the LORD lives—the one who supported me, put me on the throne of my father David, and provided a royal house for me exactly as he promised—Adonijah will be executed today." 25So King Solomon sent Benaiah, Jehoiada's son. He attacked Adonijah, and Adonijah died.

26The king said to the priest Abiathar, "Go to your fields at Anathoth, because you are a condemned man. However, I won't kill you today because you carried the LORD's chest in front of my father David and because you shared in all my father's sufferings." 27So Solomon expelled Abiathar from the LORD's priesthood in order to fulfill the LORD's word that was spoken against Eli's family at Shiloh.

28Now the news reached Joab because he had supported Adonijah, though he hadn't supported Absalom. Joab ran to the LORD's tent and grabbed the horns of the altar. 29King Solomon was told that Joab had fled to the LORD's tent and was now beside the altar. So Solomon sent Benaiah, Jehoiada's son, instructing him, "Go. Attack Joab!"

30Benaiah came to the LORD's tent and said to Joab, "The king says, 'Come out!'"

Joab said, "No! I'd rather die here."

Benaiah sent a report back to the king: "This is what Joab said and how he answered me."

31The king said to him, "Do as he said. Attack him and then bury him. In doing this, you will remove from me and from my father's royal house the guilt over the innocent blood that Joab shed. 32May the LORD return that bloodguilt back on his own head for attacking the two men who were better and more righteous than he was. He murdered those two with the sword: Abner, Ner's son and Israel's general, and Amasa, Jether's son and Judah's general. But my father David didn't know about it. 33May the bloodguilt for their deaths return on Joab's head and on the head of his family line forever. But may the LORD's peace be on David, his family, and his royal house forever." 34So Benaiah, Jehoiada's son, went and attacked Joab and killed him.

Joab was buried at his home in the wilderness. 35In his place, the king gave leadership of the army to Benaiah, Jehoiada's son. The king put the priest Zadok in Abiathar's position. 36Then he sent for Shimei and said, "Build a house for yourself in Jerusalem and stay in the city. Don't leave to go anywhere else. 37If you try to leave, be advised that on the day you cross the Kidron Valley you will most certainly die. Your bloodguilt will be on your own head."

38Shimei said to the king, "This is a good idea. Your servant will do just what my master the king said." So Shimei stayed in Jerusalem for a long time.

39After three years, two of Shimei's servants fled to the king of Gath, Achish, Maacah's son. Shimei was informed, "Your servants are now in Gath." 40Shimei saddled his donkey and went to Achish in Gath to look for his servants. Shimei then brought his servants back from Gath. 41Solomon was told that Shimei had left Jerusalem for Gath and then returned.

42The king sent for Shimei and asked him, "Didn't I make you swear a solemn pledge by the LORD? And didn't I swear to you, 'If you try to leave and go anywhere, be advised that on that very day you will most certainly die'? You said to me, 'This is a good idea. I agree to it.' 43Why didn't you keep your solemn promise to the LORD and the command that I gave you?" 44The king said further, "You know quite well all the evil that you did to my father David. May the LORD return your evil on your own head. 45However, may King Solomon be blessed and David's throne be secure before the LORD forever." 46Then the king commanded Benaiah, Jehoiada's son, who went and attacked Shimei, and he died.

In these ways royal power was handed over to Solomon.

Solomon first meets God

3 Solomon became the son-in-law of Pharaoh, Egypt's king, when he married

Pharaoh's daughter. He brought her to David's City until he finished building his royal palace, the LORD's temple, and the wall around Jerusalem. 2 Unfortunately, the people were sacrificing at the shrines because a temple hadn't yet been built for the LORD's name in those days. 3 Now Solomon loved the LORD by walking in the laws of his father David, with the exception that he also sacrificed and burned incense at the shrines.

4 The king went to the great shrine at Gibeon in order to sacrifice there. He used to offer a thousand entirely burned offerings on that altar. 5 The LORD appeared to Solomon at Gibeon in a dream at night. God said, "Ask whatever you wish, and I'll give it to you."

6 Solomon responded, "You showed so much kindness to your servant my father David when he walked before you in truth, righteousness, and with a heart true to you. You've kept this great loyalty and kindness for him and have now given him a son to sit on his throne. 7 And now, LORD my God, you have made me, your servant, king in my father David's place. But I'm young and inexperienced. I know next to nothing. 8 But I'm here, your servant, in the middle of the people you have chosen, a large population that can't be numbered or counted due to its vast size. 9 Please give your servant a discerning mind in order to govern your people and to distinguish good from evil, because no one is able to govern this important people of yours without your help."

10 It pleased the LORD that Solomon had made this request. 11 God said to him, "Because you have asked for this instead of requesting long life, wealth, or victory over your enemies—asking for discernment so as to acquire good judgment—12 I will now do just what you said. Look, I hereby give you a wise and understanding mind. There has been no one like you before now, nor will there be anyone like you afterward. 13 I now also give you what you didn't ask for: wealth and fame. There won't be a king like you as long as you live. 14 And if you walk in my ways and obey my laws and commands, just as your father David did, then I will give you a very long life."

15 Solomon awoke and realized it was a dream. He went to Jerusalem and stood before the chest containing the LORD's covenant. Then he offered entirely burned offerings and well-being sacrifices, and held a celebration for all his servants.

Solomon and the prostitutes

16 Sometime later, two prostitutes came and stood before the king. 17 One of them said, "Please, Your Majesty, listen: This woman and I have been living in the same house. I gave birth while she was there. 18 This woman gave birth three days after I did. We stayed together. Apart from the two of us, there was no one else in the house. 19 This woman's son died one night when she rolled over him. 20 She got up in the middle of the night and took my son from my side while I was asleep. She laid him on her chest and laid her dead son on mine. 21 When I got up in the morning to nurse my son, he was dead! But when I looked more closely in the daylight, it turned out that it wasn't my son—not the baby I had birthed."

22 The other woman said, "No! My son is alive! Your son is the dead one."

But the first woman objected, "No! Your son is dead! My son is alive!" In this way they argued back and forth in front of the king.

23 The king said, "This one says, 'My son is alive and your son is dead.' The other one says, 'No! Your son is dead and my son is alive.' 24 Get me a sword!" They brought a sword to the king. 25 Then the king said, "Cut the living child in two! Give half to one woman and half to the other woman."

26 Then the woman whose son was still alive said to the king, "Please, Your Majesty, give her the living child; please don't kill him," for she had great love for her son.

But the other woman said, "If I can't have him, neither will you. Cut the child in half."

27 Then the king answered, "Give the first woman the living newborn. Don't kill him. She is his mother."

28 All Israel heard about the judgment that the king made. Their respect for the king grew because they saw that God's wisdom was in him so he could execute justice.

Solomon's administration

4 King Solomon became king of all Israel.
2These were his officials: the priest
Azariah, Zadok's son; 3the scribes Elihoreph
and Ahijah, the sons of Shisha; Jehoshaphat,
the recorder, Ahilud's son; 4the general Benaiah, Jehoiada's son; the priests Zadok and
Abiathar; 5Azariah, Nathan's son, who was
in charge of the officials; Zabud, Nathan's
son, a priest and royal friend; 6Ahishar, who
was in charge of the palace; and Adoniram,
Abda's son, who was supervisor of the work
gangs.
7Solomon had twelve officers over all Israel. They supplied the king and his palace
with food. Each would provide the supplies
for one month per year. 8Here are their
names:

Ben-hur in the highlands of Ephraim;
9Ben-deker in Makaz, Shaalbim, Beth-
shemesh, and Elon-bethhanan;
10Ben-hesed in Arubboth, who had
Socoh and all the land of Hepher;
11Ben-abinadab in all of Naphath-dor
(Taphath, Solomon's daughter, was his
wife);
12Baana, Ahilud's son, in Taanach,
Megiddo, and all Beth-shean beside
Zarethan and below Jezreel, from Beth-
shean to Abel-meholah and over to the
region opposite Jokmeam;
13Ben-geber in Ramoth-gilead, who
controlled the villages of Jair, Manasseh's
son, which were in Gilead, and who had
the Argob region that was in Bashan—
sixty large walled cities with bronze bars;
14Ahinadab, Iddo's son, in Mahanaim;
15Ahimaaz in Naphtali, who also took
Solomon's daughter Basemath as his wife;
16Baana, Hushai's son, in Asher and
Bealoth;
17Jehoshaphat, Paruah's son, in
Issachar;
18Shimei, Ela's son, in Benjamin;
19Geber, Uri's son, in the land of Gilead, the land of the Amorite king Sihon
and of King Og of Bashan;
and there was a single officer who was
in the land of Judah.[b]

20Judah and Israel grew numerous like
the sand alongside the sea. They ate, drank,
and celebrated.
21[c]Solomon ruled over all the states
from the Euphrates River through the
Philistines' land and as far as the border
of Egypt. These areas brought tribute to
Solomon and served him all the days of
his life. 22Solomon's food requirements
for a single day included thirty kors[d] of
refined flour; sixty kors of flour; 23ten
head of grain-fattened cattle; twenty head
of pastured cattle; one hundred sheep; as
well as deer, gazelles, roebucks, and the
best of fowl. 24He ruled over all the lands
west of the Euphrates River, from Tiphsah
to Gaza, and over all the kings west of the
Euphrates. He had peace on all sides. 25The
people of Judah and Israel from Dan all
the way to Beer-sheba lived securely under
their vines and fig trees throughout the
days of Solomon.
26Solomon had forty thousand horse
stalls for his chariots and twelve thousand
additional horses. 27The officials provided
King Solomon and all who joined him at
the royal table with monthly food rations.
They left out nothing. 28Each brought their
share of barley and straw for the horses
and for the chariot horses, bringing it to
its proper place. 29And God gave Solomon
wisdom and very great understanding—insight as long as the seashore itself. 30Solo-
mon's wisdom was greater than all the
famous Easterners, greater even than all
the wisdom of Egypt. 31He was wiser than
anyone, more wise than Ethan the Ezrahite
or Mahol's sons: Heman, Calcol, and Darda.
His reputation was known throughout the
region. 32Solomon spoke three thousand
proverbs and one thousand five songs. 33He
described the botany of trees, whether the
cedar in Lebanon or the hyssop that grows
out of the wall. He also described cattle,
birds, anything that crawls on the ground,
and fish. 34People came from everywhere
to listen to Solomon's wisdom; even the
earth's kings who had heard about his wisdom came!

[b]LXX; MT lacks *of Judah*. [c]5:1 in Heb [d]One kor is possibly equal to fifty gallons.

Wood and stone for the temple

5 [e]Because King Hiram[f] of Tyre was loyal to David throughout his rule, Hiram sent his servants to Solomon when he heard that Solomon had become king after his father. 2 Solomon sent the following message to Hiram: 3 "You know that my father David wasn't able to build a temple for the name of the LORD my God. This was because of the enemies that fought him on all sides until the LORD put them under the soles of his feet. 4 Now the LORD my God has given me peace on every side, without enemies or misfortune. 5 So I'm planning to build a temple for the name of the LORD my God, just as the LORD indicated to my father David, 'I will give you a son to follow you on your throne. He will build the temple for my name.' 6 Now give the order and have the cedars of Lebanon cut down for me. My servants will work with your servants. I'll pay your servants whatever price you set, because you know we have no one here who is skilled in cutting wood like the Sidonians."

7 Hiram was thrilled when he heard Solomon's message. He said, "Today the LORD is blessed because he has given David a wise son who is in charge of this great people." 8 Hiram sent word back to Solomon: "I have heard your message to me. I will do as you wish with the cedar and pinewood. 9 My servants will bring the wood down the Lebanon Mountains to the sea. I'll make rafts out of them and float them on the sea to the place you specify. There I'll dismantle them, and you can carry them away. Now, as for what you must do for me in return, I ask you to provide for my royal house."

10 So Hiram gave Solomon all the cedar and pinewood that he wanted. 11 In return, Solomon gave an annual gift to Hiram of twenty thousand kors[g] of wheat to eat, and twenty thousand kors of pure oil for his palace use. 12 Now the LORD made Solomon wise, just as he had promised. Solomon and Hiram made a covenant and had peace.

13 King Solomon called up a work gang of thirty thousand workers from all over Israel. 14 He sent ten thousand to work in Lebanon each month. Then they would spend two months at home. Adoniram was in charge of the work gang. 15 Solomon had 70,000 laborers and 80,000 stonecutters in the highlands. 16 This doesn't include Solomon's 3,300 supervisors in charge of the work, who had oversight over the laborers. 17 At the king's command, they quarried huge stones of the finest quality in order to lay the temple's foundation with carefully cut stone. 18 The craftsmen of Solomon and Hiram, along with those of Byblos, prepared the timber and the stones for the construction of the temple.

Solomon builds the temple

6 In the four hundred eightieth year after the Israelites left Egypt, in the month of Ziv, the second month,[h] in the fourth year of Solomon's rule over Israel, he built the LORD's temple. 2 The temple that King Solomon built for the LORD was ninety feet long, thirty feet wide, and forty-five feet high. 3 The porch in front of the temple's main hall was thirty feet long. It ran across the whole width of the temple and extended fifteen feet in front of the temple. 4 He made recessed and latticed windows[i] for the temple 5 and built side rooms against the temple walls around both the main hall and the most holy place. 6 The lower walls were seven and a half feet wide. At the second floor the walls were nine feet wide, and at the third floor they were ten and a half feet wide. He made niches around the outside of the temple so the beams wouldn't be inserted into the temple walls.[j] 7 When the temple was built, they did all the stonecutting at the quarry. No hammers, axes, or any iron tools were heard in the temple during its construction. 8 The door to the stairs was at the south side of the temple. Winding stairs went up to the second floor and from there

[e]5:15 in Heb [f]Chronicles spells the king's name *Huram*; for example, 2 Chron 2:3, 11-12; but cf 1 Chron 14:1 Kethib. [g]One kor is possibly equal to fifty gallons. [h]April–May, Iyar; Ziv is a month from a Canaanite calendar. [i]Heb architectural and decorative terminology in 6:4-6 and elsewhere in chaps 6–7 is often uncertain. [j]Heb uncertain; Heb lacks *the beams*.

to the third floor. [9]He completed the temple with a roof of cedar beams and crossplanks.[k] [10]Then he built the side rooms all around the temple. They were seven and a half feet high. He attached them to the temple with cedarwood.

[11]The LORD's word came to Solomon, [12]Regarding this temple that you are building: If you follow my laws, enact my regulations, and keep all my commands faithfully, then I will fulfill for you my promise that I made to your father David. [13]I will live among the Israelites. I won't abandon my people Israel.

[14]So Solomon constructed the temple and completed it. [15]He built the walls within the temple with cedar planks, paneled from the floor to the ceiling. He overlaid the floor of the temple with pine planks. [16]At the back of the temple he built thirty feet of cedar panels from the floor to the ceiling. Solomon built the inner sanctuary, the most holy place. [17]In front of this, the main hall was sixty feet. [18]The cedar inside the temple was carved with gourds and blossoming flowers. The whole thing was cedar. No stone was seen. [19]He set up the inner sanctuary inside the temple so that he could put the chest containing the LORD's covenant there. [20]The inner sanctuary was thirty feet in length, width, and height. Solomon overlaid it with pure gold and covered the altar with cedar.[l] [21]Solomon covered the temple's interior with pure gold. He placed gold chains in front of the inner sanctuary and covered it with gold. [22]He overlaid the whole temple inside with gold until the temple was completely covered. He covered the whole altar that was in the inner sanctuary with gold. [23]He made two winged creatures of olive wood for the inner sanctuary, each fifteen feet high. [24]The wings of the first winged creature were each seven and a half feet long. It was fifteen feet from the end of one wing to the end of the other. [25]The second winged creature also measured fifteen feet. Both winged creatures had identical measurements and form. [26]The height of both winged creatures was fifteen feet. [27]Solomon placed the winged creatures inside the temple. Their wings spread out so that the wing of the one touched one wall and the wing of the other touched the other wall. In the middle of the temple, the wings of the two winged creatures touched each other. [28]He covered the winged creatures with gold.

[29]Solomon carved all the walls of the temple—inner and outer rooms—with engravings of winged creatures, palm trees, and blossoming flowers. [30]He also covered the floor of the temple with gold, in both the inner and the outer rooms. [31]He made the doors of the inner sanctuary from olive wood and carved the doorframes with five recesses.[m] [32]He overlaid the two olivewood doors with gold-plated carvings of winged creatures, palm trees, and blossoming flowers. [33]He made the door of the main hall with doorframes of olive wood with four recesses.[n] [34]The two doors of pinewood each pivoted on a socket. [35]Solomon carved winged creatures, palm trees, and blossoming flowers, and covered them with gold. [36]He built the inner courtyard with three rows of cut stone followed by one row of trimmed cedar.

[37]Solomon laid the foundation of the LORD's temple in the fourth year in the month of Ziv.[o] [38]He finished the temple in all its details and measurements in the eleventh year during the eighth month, the month of Bul.[p] He built it in seven years.

Solomon builds palaces

7 Now as for Solomon's palace, it took thirteen years for him to complete its construction. [2]He built the Forest of Lebanon Palace one hundred fifty feet in length, seventy-five feet in width, and forty-five feet in height. It had four rows of cedar columns with cedar engravings above the columns. [3]The palace's cedar roof stood above forty-five beams resting on the columns, fifteen beams to each row. [4]Three

[k]Heb uncertain [l]Heb uncertain [m]Heb uncertain [n]Heb uncertain [o]April–May, Iyar; Ziv is a month in the Canaanite calendar. [p]October–November, Heshvan; Bul is a month in the Canaanite calendar.

sets of window frames faced each other.
[5]All the doorframes were rectangular, facing each other in three sets. [6]He made a
porch with columns seventy-five feet long
and forty-five feet wide. Another porch was
in front of these with roofed columns in
front of them.[q] [7]He made the throne room
the Hall of Justice, where he would judge.
It was covered with cedar from the lower to
the upper levels. [8]The royal residence where
Solomon lived was behind this hall. It had a
similar design. Solomon also made a similar
palace for his wife, Pharaoh's daughter. [9]He
built all these with the best stones cut to
size, sawed with saws, back and front, from
the foundation to the highest points and
from the outer boundary to the great courtyard. [10]The foundation was laid with large
stones of high quality, some of fifteen feet
and some of twelve feet. [11]Above them were
high-quality stones cut to measure, as well
as cedar. [12]The surrounding great courtyard
had three rows of cut stones and a row of
trimmed cedar just like the inner courtyard
of the LORD's temple and its porch.

Solomon's temple equipment

[13]Then King Solomon sent a message
and brought Hiram from Tyre. [14]Hiram's
mother was a widow from the tribe of
Naphtali. His father was a Tyrian skilled in
bronze work. He was amazingly skillful in
the techniques and knowledge for doing all
kinds of work in bronze. He came to King
Solomon and did all his work.

[15]He[r] cast two bronze pillars. Each one
was twenty-seven feet high and required
a cord of eighteen feet to reach around it.[s]
[16]He made two capitals of cast bronze for
the tops of the columns. They were each
seven and a half feet high. [17]He made an
intricate network of chains for the capitals
on top of the columns, seven for each capital. [18]He made the pillars and two rows of
pomegranates for each network to adorn
each of the capitals. [19]The capitals on top
of the columns in the porch were made like
lilies, each six feet high. [20]Above the round-
shaped part and next to the network were
two hundred pomegranates. These were
placed in rows around both of the capitals
on top of the columns. [21]He set up the columns at the temple's porch. He named the
south column Jachin. The north column he
named Boaz. [22]After putting the lily shapes
on top of the columns, he was finished with
the columns.

[23]He also made a tank of cast metal
called the Sea. It was circular in shape, fifteen feet from rim to rim, seven and a half
feet high, forty-five feet in circumference.
[24]Under the rim were two rows of gourds
completely encircling it, ten every eighteen
inches, each cast in its mold. [25]The Sea
rested on twelve oxen with their backs toward the center, three facing north, three
facing west, three facing south, and three
facing east. [26]The Sea was as thick as the
width of a hand. Its rim was shaped like a
cup or an open lily blossom. It could hold
two thousand baths.[t]

[27]He also made ten bronze stands. Each
was six feet long, six feet wide, and four and
a half feet high. [28]This is how each stand
was made: There were panels connected between the legs. [29]Lions, bulls, and winged
otherworldly creatures appeared on the
panels between the legs. On the legs above
and below the lions and bulls were wreaths
on panels hanging off the stands. [30]There
were four bronze wheels with bronze axles
for each stand. There were four feet and
supports cast for each basin with wreaths
on their sides.[u] [31]Inside the bowl was an
opening eighteen inches deep. The opening was round, measuring twenty-seven
inches, with engravings. The panels of the
stands were square rather than round.
[32]There were four wheels beneath the panels. The axles of the wheels were attached
to the stand. Each wheel was twenty-seven
inches in height. [33]The construction of the
wheels resembled chariot wheels. The axles,
rims, spokes, and hubs were all made of cast
metal. [34]There was a handle on each of the
four corners of every stand, projecting from

[q]Heb uncertain [r]Or *he*, either Solomon or Hiram; this ambiguity continues in the following verses, but cf 1 Kgs 7:1, 8, 13; 1 Kgs 7:40. [s]Or *the second*; cf Jer 52:21 [t]One bath is approximately twenty quarts or five gallons.
[u]Heb uncertain

the side of the stand. [35]The top of the stand
had a band running around the perimeter
that was nine inches deep. The stand had
its own supports and panels. [36]On the sur-
faces of the supports and panels he carved
winged otherworldly creatures, lions, and
palm trees with wreaths everywhere.[v] [37]In
this manner he made ten stands, each one
cast in a single mold of the same size and
shape.

[38]He made ten bronze washbasins, each
able to hold forty baths.[w] Every washbasin
was six feet across, and there was one for
each of the ten stands. [39]He placed five
stands on the south of the temple and five
on the north of the temple. He placed the
Sea at the southeast corner of the temple.

[40]Hiram made the basins, shovels, and
bowls.

And so Hiram finished his work on the
LORD's temple for King Solomon:

[41]two columns;
two circular capitals on top of the columns;
two networks, adorning the two circular capitals on top of the columns;
[42]four hundred pomegranates for the
two networks, with two rows of pomegranates for each network that adorned
the two circular capitals on top of the
columns;
[43]ten stands with ten basins on them;
[44]one Sea;
twelve oxen beneath the Sea;
[45]and the pots, shovels, and bowls.

All the equipment that Hiram made for
King Solomon for the LORD's temple was
made from polished bronze. [46]The king
cast it in clay molds in the Jordan Valley
between Succoth and Zarethan. [47]Due to
the very large number of objects, Solomon
didn't even try to weigh the bronze.

[48]Solomon also made all the equipment
for the LORD's temple: the gold altar; the
gold table for the bread of the presence;
[49]the lampstands of pure gold, five on the
right and five on the left in front of the
inner sanctuary; the flowers, the lamps,
and the tongs of gold; [50]the cups, wick
trimmers, bowls, ladles, and censers of pure
gold; and the gold sockets for the doors to
the most holy place and for the doors to
the main hall. [51]When all King Solomon's
work on the LORD's temple was finished,
he brought the silver, gold, and all the objects his father David had dedicated and
put them in the treasuries of the LORD's
temple.

Solomon dedicates the temple

8 Then Solomon assembled Israel's elders,
all the tribal leaders, and the chiefs of
Israel's clans at Jerusalem to bring up the
chest containing the LORD's covenant from
David's City Zion. [2]Everyone in Israel assembled before King Solomon in the seventh month, the month of Ethanim,[x] during
the festival. [3]When all of Israel's elders had
arrived, the priests picked up the chest.
[4]They brought the LORD's chest, the meeting tent, and all the holy equipment that
was in the tent. The priests and the Levites
brought them up, [5]while King Solomon and
the entire Israelite assembly that had joined
him before the chest sacrificed countless
sheep and oxen. [6]The priests brought the
chest containing the LORD's covenant to
its designated spot beneath the wings of
the winged creatures in the inner sanctuary of the temple, the most holy place. [7]The
winged creatures spread their wings over
the place where the chest rested, covering
the chest and its carrying poles. [8]The carrying poles were so long that their tips could
be seen from the holy place in front of the
inner sanctuary, though they weren't visible
from outside. They are still there today.
[9]Nothing was in the chest except the two
stone tablets Moses had placed there while
at Horeb, where the LORD made a covenant
with the Israelites after they left Egypt.
[10]When the priests left the holy place, the
cloud filled the LORD's temple, [11]and the
priests were unable to carry out their duties
due to the cloud because the LORD's glory
filled the LORD's temple.

[v]Heb uncertain [w]One bath is approximately twenty quarts or five gallons. [x]September–October, Tishrei; Ethanim is a month from a Canaanite calendar.

12 Then Solomon said, "The LORD said
that he would live in a dark cloud, 13 but I
have indeed built you a lofty temple as a
place where you can live forever." 14 The
king turned around, and while the entire
assembly of Israel was standing there, he
blessed them, 15 saying, "Bless Israel's God,
the LORD, who spoke directly to my father David and now has kept his promise:
16 'From the day I brought my people Israel
out of Egypt I haven't selected a city from
any Israelite tribe as a site for the building
of a temple for my name. But now I have
chosen David to be over my people Israel.'
17 My father David wanted to build a temple
for the name of the LORD, Israel's God.

18 "But the LORD said to my father David,
'It is very good that you thought to build
a temple for my name. 19 Nevertheless, you
yourself won't build that temple. Instead,
your very own son will build the temple
for my name.' 20 The LORD has kept his
promise—I have succeeded my father David
on Israel's throne just as the LORD said,
and I have built the temple for the name
of the LORD, Israel's God. 21 There I've placed
the chest that contains the covenant that
the LORD made with our ancestors when he
brought them out of Egypt."

22 Solomon stood before the LORD's
altar in front of the entire Israelite assembly and, spreading out his hands toward
the sky, 23 he said:

> LORD God of Israel, there's no god
> like you in heaven above or on earth
> below. You keep the covenant and show
> loyalty to your servants who walk be-
> fore you with all their heart. 24 This is
> the covenant you kept with your ser-
> vant David, my father, which you prom-
> ised him. Today, you have fulfilled what
> you promised. 25 So now, LORD, Israel's
> God, keep what you promised my fa-
> ther David, your servant, when you
> said to him, "You will never fail to have
> a successor sitting on Israel's throne as
> long as your descendants carefully walk
> before me just as you walked before
> me." 26 So now, God of Israel, may your
> promise to your servant David, my fa-
> ther, come true.
>
> 27 But how could God possibly live
> on earth? If heaven, even the high-
> est heaven, can't contain you, how can
> this temple that I've built contain you?
> 28 LORD my God, listen to your ser-
> vant's prayer and request, and hear the
> cry and prayer that your servant prays
> to you today. 29 Constantly watch over
> this temple, the place about which you
> said, "My name will be there," and listen
> to the prayer that your servant is pray-
> ing toward[y] this place. 30 Listen to the
> request of your servant and your people
> Israel when they pray toward this place.
> Listen from your heavenly dwelling
> place, and when you hear, forgive!
>
> 31 If someone wrongs another and
> must make a solemn pledge assert-
> ing innocence before your altar in this
> temple,[z] 32 then listen from heaven, act,
> and decide which of your servants is
> right. Condemn the guilty party, repay-
> ing them for their conduct, but justify
> the innocent person, repaying them for
> their righteousness.
>
> 33 If your people Israel are defeated
> by an enemy because they have sinned
> against you, but then they change their
> hearts and lives, give thanks to your
> name, and ask for mercy before you at
> this temple, 34 then listen from heaven
> and forgive the sin of your people Israel.
> Return them to the land you gave their
> ancestors.
>
> 35 When the sky holds back its rain
> because Israel has sinned against you,
> but they then pray toward this place,
> give thanks to your name, and turn
> away from their sin because you have
> punished them for it,[a] 36 then listen
> from heaven and forgive the sin of your
> servants, your people Israel. Teach them
> the best way for them to follow, and
> send rain on your land that you gave to
> your people as an inheritance.
>
> 37 Whenever there is a famine or
> plague in the land; or whenever there is

[y] Or *for, regarding*; also used in several verses that follow [z] Heb uncertain [a] Or *answered them*

blight, mildew, locust, or grasshopper;
or whenever someone's enemy attacks
them in their cities;[b] or any plague or
illness comes; 38 whatever prayer or petition is made by any individual or by all
of your people Israel—because people
will recognize their own pain and spread
out their hands toward this temple—
39 then listen from heaven where you
live. Forgive, act, and repay each person
according to all their conduct, because
you know their hearts. You alone know
the human heart. 40 Do this so that they
may revere you all the days they live on
the land that you gave to our ancestors.
41 Listen also to the immigrant who
isn't from your people Israel but who
comes from a distant country because
of your reputation—42 because they
will hear of your great reputation, your
great power, and your outstretched
arm. When the immigrant comes and
prays toward this temple, 43 then listen
from heaven, where you live, and do
everything the immigrant asks. Do this
so that all the people of the earth may
know your reputation and revere you,
as your people Israel do, and recognize
that this temple I have built bears your
name.
44 When your people go to war against
their enemies, wherever you may send
them, and they pray to the LORD toward
the city you have chosen and toward
this temple that I have built for your
name, 45 then listen from heaven to their
prayer and request and do what is right
for them.
46 When they sin against you (for
there is no one who doesn't sin) and you
become angry with them and hand them
over to an enemy who takes them away
as prisoners to enemy territory, whether
distant or nearby, 47 if they change their
heart in whatever land they are held captive, changing their lives and begging for
your mercy,[c] saying, "We have sinned,
we have done wrong, we have acted
wickedly!" 48 and if they return to you
with all their heart and all their being in
the enemy territory where they've been
taken captive, and pray to you, toward
their land, which you gave their ancestors, toward the city you have chosen,
and toward the temple I have built for
your name, 49 then listen to their prayer
and request from your heavenly dwelling
place. Do what is right for them, 50 and
forgive your people who have sinned
against you. Forgive all their wrong that
they have done against you. See to it that
those who captured them show them
mercy. 51 These are your people and your
inheritance. You brought them out of
Egypt, from the iron furnace.
52 Open your eyes to your servant's request and to the request of your people
Israel. Hear them whenever they cry out
to you. 53 You set them apart from all the
earth's peoples as your own inheritance,
LORD, just as you promised through
your servant Moses when you brought
our ancestors out of Egypt.
54 As soon as Solomon finished praying
and making these requests to the LORD, he
got up from before the LORD's altar, where
he had been kneeling with his hands spread
out to heaven. 55 He stood up and blessed
the whole Israelite assembly in a loud voice:
56 "May the LORD be blessed! He has given
rest to his people Israel just as he promised. He hasn't neglected any part of the
good promise he made through his servant
Moses. 57 May the LORD our God be with
us, just as he was with our ancestors. May
he never leave us or abandon us. 58 May he
draw our hearts to him to walk in all his
ways and observe his commands, his laws,
and his judgments that he gave our ancestors. 59 And may these words of mine that
I have cried out before the LORD remain
near to the LORD our God day and night so
that he may do right by his servant and his
people Israel for each day's need, 60 and so
that all the earth's peoples may know that
the LORD is God. There is no other God!
61 Now may you be committed to the LORD
our God with all your heart by following his

[b] LXX *one of*; MT *in the land of their gates* [c] Heb adds *in the land they are held captive.*

laws and observing his commands, just as you are doing right now."

[62]Then the king and all Israel with him sacrificed to the LORD. [63]Solomon offered well-being sacrifices to the LORD: twenty-two thousand oxen and one hundred twenty thousand sheep when the king and all Israel dedicated the LORD's temple. [64]On that day the king made holy the middle of the courtyard in front of the LORD's temple. He had to offer the entirely burned offerings, grain offerings, and the fat of well-being sacrifices there, because the bronze altar that was in the LORD's presence was too small to contain the entirely burned offerings, the grain offerings, and the fat of the well-being sacrifices. [65]At that time Solomon, together with all Israel, held a celebration. It was a large assembly from Lebo-hamath to the border of Egypt. They celebrated for seven days and then for another seven days in the presence of the LORD our God: fourteen days in all. [66]On the eighth day,[d] Solomon dismissed the people. They blessed the king and went back to their tents happy and pleased about all the good that the LORD had done for his servant David and for his people Israel.

Solomon again meets God

9 Now once Solomon finished building the LORD's temple, the royal palace, and everything else he wanted to accomplish, [2]the LORD appeared to him a second time in the same way he had appeared to him at Gibeon. [3]The LORD said to him, "I have heard your prayer and your cry to me. I have set apart this temple that you built, to put my name there forever. My eyes and my heart will always be there. [4]As for you, if you walk before me just as your father David did, with complete dedication and honesty, and if you do all that I have commanded, and keep my regulations and case laws, [5]then I will establish your royal throne over Israel forever, just as I promised your father David, 'You will never fail to have a successor on the throne of Israel.' [6]However, if you or your sons turn away from following me and don't observe the commands and regulations that I gave you, and go to serve other gods, and worship them, [7]then I will remove Israel from the land I gave them and I will reject the temple that I dedicated for my name. Israel will become a joke, insulted by everyone. [8]Everyone who passes by this temple, so lofty now,[e] will be shocked and will whistle, wondering, Why has the LORD done such a thing to this land and this temple? [9]The answer will come: Because they deserted the LORD their God, who brought their ancestors out of Egypt's land. They embraced other gods, worshipping and serving them. That is why the LORD brought all this disaster on them."

Solomon's buildings and prosperity

[10]It took twenty years for Solomon to build the two structures, the LORD's temple and the royal palace. [11]King Hiram of Tyre gave Solomon all the cedar, pinewood, and gold that he wanted. Then King Solomon gave Hiram twenty towns in the region of Galilee. [12]Hiram went from Tyre to inspect the towns Solomon had given him. They didn't seem adequate in his view. [13]So Hiram remarked, "My brother, are these towns you've given me good for anything?" The cities are thus called the land of Cabul to this very day. [14]But Hiram sent the king one hundred twenty gold kikkars, nevertheless.

[15]This is the story of the labor gang that King Solomon put together to build the LORD's temple and his own palace, as well as the stepped structure, the wall of Jerusalem, Hazor, Megiddo, and Gezer: ([16]Pharaoh, Egypt's king, had attacked and captured Gezer, setting it on fire. He killed the Canaanites who lived in the city and gave it as a dowry to his daughter, Solomon's wife). [17]Solomon built Gezer, Lower Beth-horon, [18]Baalath, and Tamar in the wilderness (within the land), [19]along with all the storage cities that belonged to Solomon, as well as the cities used for storing chariots and

[d]The second seven-day celebration (see 2 Chron 7:8-9); but contrast LXX. [e]Or *will become high*; OL, Syr, Tg *will become a ruin*

cavalry and whatever he wanted to build in
Jerusalem, Lebanon, and throughout his
kingdom. 20 Any non-Israelite people who
remained of the Amorites, Hittites, Perizzites, Hivites, and Jebusites—21 that is, the
descendants of such people who were still in
the land because the Israelites weren't able
to wipe them out—Solomon forced into the
labor gangs that are still in existence today.
22 However, Solomon didn't force the Israelites to work as slaves; instead, they became
warriors, his servants, his leaders, his officers, and those in charge of his chariots and
cavalry.

23 These were the chief officers over Solomon's work: five hundred fifty had charge
of the people who did the work. 24 When
Pharaoh's daughter went up from David's
City to the palace he had built for her, Solomon built the stepped structure. 25 Three
times a year Solomon would offer entirely
burned offerings and well-being sacrifices
on the altar that he had built for the LORD.
Along with this he would burn incense to
the LORD. In this way, he completed the
temple.[f] 26 King Solomon built a fleet near
Eloth in Ezion-geber, on the coast of the
Reed Sea[g] in the land of Edom. 27 Hiram sent
his expert sailors on the fleet along with
Solomon's workers. 28 They went to Ophir
for four hundred twenty kikkars of gold,
which they brought back to King Solomon.

Queen of Sheba

10 When the queen of Sheba heard reports about Solomon, due to the
LORD's name,[h] she came to test him with
riddles. 2 Accompanying her to Jerusalem
was a huge entourage with camels carrying
spices, a large amount of gold, and precious
stones. After she arrived, she told Solomon
everything that was on her mind. 3 Solomon
answered all her questions; nothing was
too difficult for him to answer. 4 When the
queen of Sheba saw how wise Solomon was,
the palace he had built, 5 the food on his
table, the servants' quarters, the function
and dress of his attendants, his cupbearers, and the entirely burned offerings that
he offered at the LORD's temple, it took her
breath away.

6 "The report I heard about your deeds
and wisdom when I was still at home is
true," she said to the king. 7 "I didn't believe
it until I came and saw it with my own eyes.
In fact, the half of it wasn't even told to me!
You have far more wisdom and wealth than
I was told. 8 Your people and these servants
who continually serve you and get to listen
to your wisdom are truly happy! 9 Bless the
LORD your God because he was pleased to
place you on Israel's throne. Because the
LORD loved Israel with an eternal love, the
LORD made you king to uphold justice and
righteousness."

10 The queen gave the king one hundred
twenty kikkars of gold, a great quantity
of spice, and precious stones. Never again
has so much spice come to Israel as when
the queen of Sheba gave this gift to King
Solomon. 11 Hiram's fleet went to Ophir and
brought back gold, much almug wood, and
precious stones. 12 The king used the almug
wood to make parapets for the LORD's temple and for the royal palace as well as lyres
and harps for the musicians. To this day,
that much almug wood hasn't come into
or been seen in Israel. 13 King Solomon gave
the queen of Sheba everything she wanted
and all that she had asked for, in addition to
what he had already given her from his own
personal funds. Then she and her servants
returned to her homeland.

Solomon's wealth

14 Solomon received an annual income of
six hundred sixty-six kikkars of gold, 15 not
including income from the traders, the
merchants and their profits, all the Arabian
kings, and the officials of the land. 16 King
Solomon made two hundred body-sized
shields of hammered gold, using fifteen
pounds[i] of gold in each shield, 17 and three
hundred small shields of hammered gold,
using sixty ounces[j] of gold in each shield.
The king placed these in the Forest of Lebanon Palace.

18 The king also made a large ivory throne

[f] Heb uncertain [g] Traditionally *Red Sea* [h] Heb uncertain [i] Or *six hundred* (shekels) [j] *three manehs*

and covered it with pure gold. 19Six steps led up to the throne, and the back of the throne was rounded at the top. Two lions stood beside the armrests on both sides of the throne. 20Another twelve lions stood on both sides of the six steps. No other kingdom had anything like this. 21All of King Solomon's drinking cups were made of gold, and all the items in the Forest of Lebanon Palace were made of pure gold, not silver, since even silver wasn't considered good enough in Solomon's time! 22The royal fleet of Tarshish-style ships was at sea with Hiram's fleet, returning once every three years with gold, silver, ivory, monkeys, and peacocks.[k]

23King Solomon far exceeded all the earth's kings in wealth and wisdom, 24and so the whole earth wanted an audience with Solomon in order to hear his God-given wisdom. 25Year after year they came with tribute: objects of silver and gold, clothing, weapons, spices, horses, and mules.

26Solomon acquired more and more chariots and horses until he had fourteen hundred chariots and twelve thousand horses that he kept in chariot cities and with the king in Jerusalem. 27In Jerusalem, the king made silver as common as stones and cedar as plentiful as sycamore trees that grow in the foothills. 28Solomon's horses were imported from Egypt and Kue, purchased from Kue by the king's agents at the going price. 29They would import a chariot from Egypt for six hundred pieces of silver and a horse for one hundred fifty, and then export them to all the Hittite and Aramean kings.

Solomon meets God a third time

11 In addition to Pharaoh's daughter, King Solomon loved many foreign women, including Moabites, Ammonites, Edomites, Sidonians, and Hittites. 2These came from the nations that the LORD had commanded the Israelites about: "Don't intermarry with them. They will definitely turn your heart toward their gods." Solomon clung to these women in love. 3He had seven hundred royal wives and three hundred secondary wives. They turned his heart. 4As Solomon grew old, his wives turned his heart after other gods. He wasn't committed to the LORD his God with all his heart as was his father David. 5Solomon followed Astarte the goddess of the Sidonians, and Milcom the detestable god of the Ammonites. 6Solomon did what was evil in the LORD's eyes and wasn't completely devoted to the LORD like his father David. 7On the hill east of Jerusalem, Solomon built a shrine to Chemosh the detestable god of Moab, and to Molech the detestable god of the Ammonites. 8He did the same for all his foreign wives, who burned incense and sacrificed to their gods. 9The LORD grew angry with Solomon, because his heart had turned away from being with the LORD, the God of Israel, who had appeared to him twice. 10The LORD had commanded Solomon about this very thing, that he shouldn't follow other gods. But Solomon didn't do what the LORD commanded.

11The LORD said to Solomon, "Because you have done all this instead of keeping my covenant and my laws that I commanded you, I will most certainly tear the kingdom from you and give it to your servant. 12Even so, on account of your father David, I won't do it during your lifetime. I will tear the kingdom out of your son's hands. 13Moreover, I won't tear away the entire kingdom. I will give one tribe to your son on account of my servant David and on account of Jerusalem, which I have chosen."

Solomon and Hadad

14So the LORD raised up an opponent for Solomon: Hadad the Edomite from the royal line of Edom. 15When David was fighting against Edom, Joab the general had gone up to bury the Israelite dead, and he had killed every male in Edom. 16Joab and all the Israelites stayed there six months, until he had finished off every male in Edom. 17While still a youth, Hadad escaped to Egypt along with his father's Edomite officials. 18They set out from Midian and went

[k] Heb uncertain

to Paran. They took men with them from Paran and came to Egypt and to Pharaoh its king. Pharaoh assigned him a home, food, and land. 19 Pharaoh was so delighted with Hadad that he gave him one of his wife's sisters for marriage, a sister of Queen Tahpenes. 20 This sister of Tahpenes bore Hadad a son, Genubath. Tahpenes weaned him in Pharaoh's house. So it was that Genubath was raised in Pharaoh's house, among Pharaoh's children. 21 While in Egypt, Hadad heard that David had lain down with his ancestors and that Joab the general was also dead. Hadad said to Pharaoh, "Let me go to my homeland."

22 Pharaoh said to him, "What do you lack here with me that would make you want to go back to your homeland?"

Hadad said, "Nothing, but please let me go!"

Solomon and Rezon

23 God raised up another opponent for Solomon: Rezon, Eliada's son, who had escaped from Zobah's King Hadadezer. 24 Rezon recruited men and became leader of a band when David was killing them. They went to Damascus, stayed there, and ruled it. 25 Throughout Solomon's lifetime, Rezon was Israel's opponent and added to the problems caused by Hadad. Rezon hated Israel while he ruled as king of Aram.

Solomon and Jeroboam

26 Now Nebat's son Jeroboam was an Ephraimite from Zeredah. His mother's name was Zeruah; she was a widow. Although he was one of Solomon's own officials, Jeroboam fought against the king. 27 This is the story of why Jeroboam fought against the king:

Solomon had built the stepped structure and repaired the broken wall in his father David's City. 28 Now Jeroboam was a strong and honorable man. Solomon saw how well this youth did his work. So he appointed him over all the work gang of Joseph's house.

29 At that time, when Jeroboam left Jerusalem, Ahijah the prophet of Shiloh met him along the way. Ahijah was wearing a new garment. The two of them were alone in the country. 30 Ahijah tore his new garment into twelve pieces. 31 He said to Jeroboam, "Take ten pieces, because Israel's God, the LORD, has said, 'Look, I am about to tear the kingdom from Solomon's hand. I will give you ten tribes. 32 But I will leave him one tribe on account of my servant David and on account of Jerusalem, the city I have chosen from all the tribes of Israel. 33 I am doing this because they have abandoned me[1] and worshipped the Sidonian goddess Astarte, the Moabite god Chemosh, and the Ammonite god Milcom. They haven't walked in my ways by doing what is right in my eyes—keeping my laws and judgments—as Solomon's father David did. 34 But I won't take the whole kingdom from his hand. I will keep him as ruler throughout his lifetime on account of my servant David, who did keep my commands and my laws. 35 I will take the kingdom from the hand of Solomon's son, and I will give you ten tribes. 36 I will give his son a single tribe so that my servant David will always have a lamp before me in Jerusalem, the city that I chose for myself to place my name. 37 But I will accept you, and you will rule over all that you could desire. You will be king of Israel. 38 If you listen to all that I command and walk in my ways, if you do what is right in my eyes, keeping my laws and my commands just as my servant David did, then I will be with you and I will build you a lasting dynasty just as I did for David. I will give you Israel. 39 I will humble David's descendants by means of all this, though not forever.'"

40 Then Solomon tried to kill Jeroboam. But Jeroboam fled to Egypt and its king Shishak. Jeroboam remained in Egypt until Solomon died.

Solomon's remaining days

41 The rest of Solomon's deeds, including all that he did and all his wisdom, aren't they written in the official records of Solomon? 42 The amount of time Solomon ruled

[1] LXX, Syr, Vulg *he has abandoned me*

over all Israel in Jerusalem was forty years. 43 Then Solomon lay down with his ancestors. He was buried in his father David's City, and Rehoboam his son succeeded him as king.

How Rehoboam lost the kingdom

12 Rehoboam went to Shechem where all Israel had come to make him king. 2 When Jeroboam, Nebat's son, heard the news, he returned from Egypt where he had fled from King Solomon. 3 The people sent and called for Jeroboam, who along with the entire Israelite assembly went and said to Rehoboam, 4 "Your father made our workload[m] very hard for us. If you will lessen the demands your father made of us and lighten the heavy workload he demanded from us, then we will serve you."

5 He answered them, "Come back in three days." So the people left.

6 King Rehoboam consulted the elders who had served his father Solomon when he was alive. "What do you advise?" Rehoboam asked. "How should I respond to these people?"

7 "If you will be a servant to this people by answering them and speaking good words today," they replied, "then they will be your servants forever."

8 But Rehoboam ignored the advice the elders gave him and instead sought the counsel of the young advisors who had grown up with him and now served him. 9 "What do you advise?" he asked them. "How should we respond to these people who have said to me, 'Lighten the workload your father demanded of us'?"

10 The young people who had grown up with him said to him, "This people said to you, 'Your father made our workload heavy; lighten it for us!' Now this is what you should say to them: 'My baby finger[n] is thicker than my father's entire waist! 11 So if my father made your workload heavy, I'll make it even heavier! If my father disciplined you with whips, I'll do it with scorpions!'"

12 Jeroboam and all the people returned to Rehoboam on the third day, just as the king had specified when he said, "Come back to me in three days." 13 The king then answered the people harshly. He ignored the elders' advice 14 and instead followed the young people's advice. He said, "My father made your workload heavy, but I'll make it even heavier! My father disciplined you with whips, but I'll do it with scorpions!"

15 The king didn't listen to the people because this turn of events came from the LORD so that he might keep the promise he delivered through Ahijah from Shiloh concerning Jeroboam, Nebat's son. 16 When all Israel saw that the king wouldn't listen to them, the people answered the king:

"Why should we care about David?
We have no stake in Jesse's son!
Go back to your homes, Israel!
You better look
after your own house now, David!"

Then the Israelites went back to their homes, 17 and Rehoboam ruled over only the Israelites who lived in the cities of Judah.

18 When King Rehoboam sent Adoram to them (he was the leader of the work gang), all Israel stoned him to death. King Rehoboam quickly got into his chariot and fled to Jerusalem. 19 Israel has been in rebellion against the house of David to this day. 20 When all Israel heard that Jeroboam had returned, they sent for him. They called him to the assembly and crowned him king of all Israel.

Nothing was left to the house of David except the tribe of Judah. 21 When Rehoboam arrived at Jerusalem, he assembled the whole house of Judah and the tribe of Benjamin—one hundred eighty thousand select warriors—to fight against the house of Israel and restore the kingdom for Rehoboam, Solomon's son. 22 But God's word came to Shemaiah the man of God, 23 "Tell Judah's King Rehoboam, Solomon's son, and all the house of Judah and Benjamin, and the rest of the people, 24 'This is what the LORD says: Don't make war against your relatives the Israelites. Go home, every one of you, because this is my

[m] Or *our yoke*; also in the verses that follow [n] Or *pinky finger*, perhaps a euphemism

plan.'" When they heard the LORD's words,
they went back home, just as the LORD
had said.

Jeroboam I and the shrines

25 Jeroboam fortified Shechem at Mount
Ephraim and lived there. From there he
also fortified Penuel. 26 Jeroboam thought
to himself, The kingdom is in danger of
reverting to the house of David. 27 If these
people continue to sacrifice at the LORD's
temple in Jerusalem, they will again become loyal to their master Rehoboam, Judah's king, and they will kill me so they can
return to Judah's King Rehoboam. 28 So the
king asked for advice and then made two
gold calves. He said to the people, "It's too
far for you to go all the way up to Jerusalem. Look, Israel! Here are your gods who
brought you out from the land of Egypt."
29 He put one calf in Bethel, and the other
he placed in Dan. 30 This act was sinful. The
people went to worship before the one calf
at Bethel and before the other one as far
as Dan.[o] 31 Jeroboam made shrines on the
high places and appointed priests from
all sorts of people, but none were Levites.
32 Jeroboam set a date for a celebration on
the fifteenth day of the eighth month.[p] It
was just like the celebration in Judah. He
sacrificed on the altar. At Bethel he sacrificed to the calves he had made. There also
he installed the priests for the shrines he
had made. 33 On the fifteenth day of the
eighth month—the time he alone had
decided—Jeroboam went up[q] to the altar
he had built in Bethel. He made a celebration for the Israelites and offered sacrifices
on the altar by burning them up.[r]

Jeroboam I and the man of God

13 A man of God came from Judah by
God's command to Bethel. Jeroboam
was standing at the altar burning incense.
2 By the LORD's word, the man of God cried
out to the altar: "Altar! Altar! The LORD says
this: Look! A son will be born to the house
of David. His name will be Josiah. He will
sacrifice on you, Altar, the very priests of the
shrines who offer incense on you. They will
burn human bones on you." 3 At that time the
man of God gave a sign: "This is the sign that
the LORD mentioned: 'Look! The altar will be
broken apart, and its ashes will spill out.'"

4 When the king heard the word of the
man of God and how he cried out to the
altar at Bethel, Jeroboam stretched his
hand from the altar and said, "Seize him!"
But the hand that Jeroboam stretched out
against the man of God grew stiff. Jeroboam
wasn't able to bend it back to himself. 5 The
altar broke apart, and the ashes spilled
out from the altar, just like the sign that
the man of God gave by the LORD's word.
6 The king said to the man of God, "Plead
before the LORD your God and pray for me
so that I can bend my hand back again." So
the man of God pleaded before the LORD,
and the king's hand returned to normal
and was like it used to be. 7 The king spoke
to the man of God: "Come with me to the
palace and refresh yourself. Let me give you
a gift."

8 The man of God said to the king, "Even
if you gave me half your palace, I wouldn't
go with you, nor would I eat food or drink
water in this place. 9 This is what God commanded me by the LORD's word: Don't eat
food! Don't drink water! Don't return by
the way you came!"

10 So the man of God went by a different
way. He didn't return by the way he came
to Bethel. 11 Now there was an old prophet
living in Bethel. His sons came and told him
everything that the man of God had done
that day at Bethel. They also told their father the words that he spoke to the king.
12 "Which way did he go?" their father asked
them. His sons had seen the way the man
of God went when he came from Judah.
13 The old prophet said to his sons, "Saddle
my donkey." So they saddled his donkey,
and he got on it. 14 He went after the man
of God and found him sitting underneath a
terebinth tree. He said to him, "Are you the
man of God who came from Judah?"

[o] Cf LXX; MT lacks *before the one at Bethel.* [p] October–November [q] Or *offered sacrifices* [r] Or *went up on the altar to burn incense*

"I am," he replied.
15The old prophet then said to him,
"Come home with me and eat some food."
16But the man of God answered, "I can't
return or go with you, and I can't eat food or
drink water with you in this place 17because
of the message that came to me from the
LORD's word: Don't eat food! Don't drink
water! Don't return by the way you came!"
18The old prophet said to the man of
God, "I'm also a prophet like you. A messenger spoke to me with the LORD's word,
'Bring him back with you to your house so
that he may eat food and drink water.'"
But the old prophet was lying to him.
19So the man of God went back with the
old prophet. He ate food in his home and
drank water. 20Then as they were sitting
at the table, the LORD's word came to the
prophet who had brought him back. 21He
cried out to the man of God who had come
from Judah:

"The LORD says this:
You rebelled against the LORD's word!
You didn't keep the command
that the LORD your God gave you!
22You came back and ate food
and drank water in this place.

"But he had commanded you: 'Don't eat
food! Don't drink water!' Now your body
won't go to the grave of your ancestors."
23After he ate food and drank, the old
prophet saddled the donkey for the prophet
he had brought back. 24The man of God departed, and a lion found him on the road
and killed him. His body was thrown down
on the road. The donkey stood beside it,
and the lion also stood beside the body.
25Some people were traveling nearby, and
they discovered the body thrown down
on the road and the lion standing beside
it. They entered the town where the old
prophet lived and were talking about it.
26The prophet who brought the man of God
back from the road overheard. He thought:
That's the man of God who rebelled against
the LORD's command. The LORD has given
him to that lion that tore him apart, killing him in agreement with the LORD's word
that was spoken to him.
27The old prophet told his sons, "Saddle
the donkey." They did so, 28and he went
and found the body thrown down on the
road. The donkey and the lion were still
standing beside the body. The lion hadn't
eaten the body, nor had it torn the donkey apart. 29The prophet lifted the body
of the man of God and put it on the donkey. He brought it back, arriving in the
old prophet's town to mourn and bury the
man of God. 30He placed the body in his
own grave, and they mourned over him,
"Oh, my brother!" 31After the old prophet
buried him, he said to his sons, "When I
die, bury me in the grave where the man
of God is. Put my bones beside his bones.
32The message he gave by the LORD's word
concerning the altar of Bethel and all the
shrines in the towns of Samaria will most
certainly come true."
33Even after this happened, Jeroboam
didn't change his evil ways. Instead, he
continued to appoint all sorts of people as
priests of the shrines. Anyone who wanted
to be a priest Jeroboam made a priest for
the shrines. 34In this way the house of Jeroboam acted sinfully, leading to its downfall and elimination from the earth.

Abijah's illness

14 At that time, Jeroboam's son Abijah
became sick. 2Jeroboam said to his
wife, "Please go with a disguise so no one
will recognize you as Jeroboam's wife. Go to
Shiloh where the prophet Ahijah is. He told
me I would be king of this people. 3Take ten
loaves of bread, cakes, and a bottle of honey
with you. Go to him. He will tell you what
will happen to the boy." 4Jeroboam's wife
did precisely this. She left and went to Shiloh and came to Ahijah's house. Now Ahijah
had become blind in his old age.
5The LORD said to Ahijah, "Look! Jeroboam's wife has come seeking a word from
you about her son. He is sick. Say this and
that to her. When she comes, she will be
disguised."
6When Ahijah heard the sound of her
feet coming through the doorway, he said,
"Come in, Jeroboam's wife! Why have you
disguised yourself? I have hard news for
you. 7Tell Jeroboam: This is what the LORD,

Israel's God, says: When I lifted you up
from among the people, I appointed you as
a leader over my people Israel. 8 I tore the
kingdom from David's house and gave it to
you. But you haven't been like my servant
David, who kept my commands and followed me with all his heart by doing only
what is right in my eyes. 9 Instead, you have
done more evil than any who were before
you. You have made other gods and metal
images to anger me. You have turned your
back on me. 10 Therefore, I'm going to bring
disaster on Jeroboam's house! Because of
Jeroboam, I will eliminate everyone who
urinates on a wall, whether slave or free.
Then I will set fire to the house of Jeroboam, as one burns dung until it is gone.
11 Dogs will eat any of Jeroboam's family
who die in town. Birds will eat those who
die in the field. The LORD has spoken!

12 "As for you, get up and go back home.
When your feet enter the town, the boy
will die. 13 All Israel will mourn for him and
will bury him. Out of the whole line of Jeroboam, he alone will have a tomb, because
only in him did Israel's God, the LORD,
find something good. 14 For this reason the
LORD will raise up a king over Israel who
will eliminate the house of Jeroboam. This
begins today. What's that? Even now![s] 15 The
LORD will strike Israel so that it shakes like
a reed in water. He will uproot Israel from
this fertile land that he gave to their ancestors and their offspring, and he will scatter
them across the Euphrates River, because
they made the LORD angry by making their
sacred poles.[t] 16 Because of the sins Jeroboam committed, and because he made
Israel sin too, God will give Israel up."

17 Then Jeroboam's wife left and went to
Tirzah. When she stepped across the threshold of the house, the boy died. 18 All Israel
buried him and mourned him in agreement
with the LORD's word spoken through his
servant the prophet Ahijah. 19 The rest of
Jeroboam's deeds—how he fought and
how he ruled—are written in the official
records of Israel's kings. 20 Jeroboam ruled
twenty-two years and he lay down with his
ancestors. His son Nadab succeeded him
as king.

Rehoboam rules Judah

21 Rehoboam, Solomon's son, ruled over
Judah. Rehoboam was 41 years old when
he became king. He ruled for seventeen
years in Jerusalem, the city the LORD chose
from among all the tribes of Israel to set
his name. Rehoboam's mother's name was
Naamah from Ammon. 22 Judah did evil
in the LORD's eyes. The sins they committed made the LORD angrier than anything
their ancestors had done. 23 They also built
shrines, standing stones, and sacred poles[u]
on top of every high hill and under every
green tree. 24 Moreover, the consecrated
workers[v] in the land did detestable things,
just like those nations that the LORD had
removed among the Israelites.

25 During King Rehoboam's fifth year,
King Shishak of Egypt attacked Jerusalem.
26 He seized the treasures of the LORD's
temple and the royal palace. He took everything, even all the gold shields that Solomon had made. 27 King Rehoboam replaced
them with bronze shields and assigned
them to the officers of the guard who protected the entrance to the royal palace.
28 Whenever the king entered the LORD's
temple, the guards would carry the shields
and then return them to the guardroom.
29 The rest of Rehoboam's deeds and all that
he accomplished, aren't they written in the
official records of Judah's kings? 30 There
was continual warfare between Rehoboam
and Jeroboam. 31 When Rehoboam died,
he was buried with his ancestors in David's
City. His mother's name was Naamah from
Ammon. His son Abijam[w] succeeded him as
king.

Abijam rules Judah

15 Abijam[x] became king of Judah in the
eighteenth year of King Jeroboam, Nebat's son. 2 He ruled for three years in Jerusalem. His mother's name was Maacah, and

[s] Heb uncertain [t] Heb *asherim*, perhaps objects devoted to the goddess Asherah [u] Heb *asherim*, perhaps objects devoted to the goddess Asherah [v] Traditionally *cultic prostitutes* [w] Spelled *Abijah* in 2 Chron 12:16; LXX, Syr, Targ *Abijah* in 1 Kgs [x] Spelled *Abijah* in 2 Chron 12

she was Abishalom's daughter. 3Abijam followed all the sinful ways of his father before him. He didn't follow the LORD his God with all his heart like his ancestor David. 4Even so, on account of David, the LORD his God gave Abijam a lamp in Jerusalem by supporting his son who succeeded him and by preserving Jerusalem. 5This was because David did the right thing in the LORD's eyes. David didn't deviate from anything the LORD commanded him throughout his life—except in the matter of Uriah the Hittite. 6There was war between Rehoboam and Jeroboam as long as Abijam lived. 7The rest of Abijam's deeds and all that he did, aren't they written in the official records of Judah's kings? There was war between Abijam and Jeroboam. 8Abijam lay down with his ancestors; he was buried in David's City. His son Asa succeeded him as king.

Asa rules Judah

9In the twentieth year of Israel's King Jeroboam, Asa became king of Judah. 10He ruled in Jerusalem for forty-one years. His grandmother's[y] name was Maacah; she was Abishalom's daughter. 11Asa did the right things in the LORD's eyes, just like his father David. 12He removed the consecrated workers[z] from the land, and he did away with all the worthless idols that his predecessors had made. 13He even removed his grandmother Maacah from the position of queen mother because she had made an image of Asherah. Asa cut down her image and burned it in the Kidron Valley. 14Though the shrines weren't eliminated, nevertheless Asa remained committed with all his heart to the LORD throughout his life. 15He brought into the LORD's temple the silver and gold equipment that he and his father had dedicated. 16There was war between Asa and Israel's King Baasha throughout their lifetimes. 17Israel's King Baasha attacked Judah and fortified Ramah to prevent Judah's King Asa from moving into that area.

18Asa took all the silver and gold that remained in the treasuries of the LORD's temple and the royal palace, and he gave them to his officials. Then King Asa sent them with the following message to Aram's King Ben-hadad, Tabrimmon's son and Hezion's grandson, who ruled from Damascus: 19"Let's make a covenant similar to the one between our fathers. Since I have already sent you a gift of silver and gold, break your covenant with Israel's King Baasha so that he will leave me alone." 20Ben-hadad agreed with King Asa and sent his army commanders against the cities of Israel, attacking Ijon, Dan, Abel-beth-maacah, and all Chinneroth, along with all the land of Naphtali. 21As soon as Baasha learned this, he stopped building Ramah and stayed in Tirzah. 22King Asa issued an order to every Judean without exception: all the people carried away the stone and timber that Baasha was using to build Ramah, and King Asa used it to build Geba of Benjamin and Mizpah. 23The rest of Asa's deeds, his strength, and all that he did, as well as the towns that he built, aren't they written in the official records of Judah's kings? When he was old, Asa developed a severe foot disease. 24He died and was buried with his ancestors in David's City.[a] His son Jehoshaphat succeeded him as king.

Nadab rules Israel

25Jeroboam's son Nadab became king of Israel in the second year of Judah's King Asa. He ruled over Israel for two years. 26He did evil in the LORD's eyes by walking in the way of his father Jeroboam and the sin Jeroboam had caused Israel to commit. 27Baasha, Ahijah's son from the house of Issachar, plotted against him and attacked him at Gibbethon, which belonged to the Philistines. Nadab and all Israel were laying siege against Gibbethon. 28Baasha killed Nadab in the third year of Judah's King Asa and ruled in Nadab's place.

29When he became king, Baasha attacked the entire house of Jeroboam. He didn't allow any living person to survive in Jeroboam's family; he wiped them out according to the LORD's word spoken by the

[y]Or *mother*; also in 15:13; cf 2 Chron 13:2 [z]Traditionally *cultic prostitutes* [a]Heb adds *his father*.

LORD's servant Ahijah of Shiloh. 30 This
happened because of Jeroboam's sins that
he committed and that he caused Israel to
commit, and because he angered the LORD,
Israel's God. 31 The rest of Nadab's deeds and
all that he did, aren't they written in the official records of Israel's kings? 32 There was
war between Asa and Israel's King Baasha
throughout their lifetimes.

Baasha rules Israel

33 In the third year of Judah's King Asa,
Baasha, Ahijah's son, became king over all
Israel. He ruled in Tirzah for twenty-four
years. 34 He did evil in the LORD's eyes by
walking in Jeroboam's ways and the sin he
had caused Israel to commit.

16 The LORD's word came to Jehu, Hanani's son, against Baasha: 2 I raised
you up from the dust and made you a leader
over my people Israel, but you walked in
Jeroboam's ways, making my people Israel
sin, making me angry with their sins. 3 So
look, I am about to set fire to Baasha and
his household, and I will make your house
like the house of Jeroboam, Nebat's son.
4 Dogs will eat any of Baasha's family who
die in town. Birds will eat any who die in
the country.

5 Now the rest of Baasha's deeds, what
he did, and his powerful acts, aren't they
written in the official records of Israel's
kings? 6 Baasha lay down with his ancestors
and was buried in Tirzah. His son Elah succeeded him as king.

7 But the LORD's word came through the
prophet Jehu, Hanani's son, concerning
Baasha and his house. It concerned everything evil in the LORD's eyes that Baasha
had done, angering the Lord by his actions
so that he would end up just like the house
of Jeroboam. The message was also about
how the Lord attacked Baasha.[b]

Elah rules Israel

8 In the twenty-sixth year of Judah's
King Asa, Elah, Baasha's son, became king
over Israel. He ruled in Tirzah for two
years. 9 Zimri, his officer who led half the
chariots, plotted against him. Elah was at
Tirzah, getting drunk at the house of Arza,
who had charge over the palace at Tirzah.
10 Zimri came, attacked, and killed Elah in
the twenty-seventh year of Judah's King
Asa. Zimri succeeded him as king.

11 Once Zimri became king and sat on the
throne, he attacked all of Baasha's house.
He didn't spare anyone who urinates on
a wall, whether relative or friend. 12 Zimri
destroyed the entire house of Baasha in
agreement with the LORD's word that had
been spoken by the prophet Jehu to Baasha. 13 This happened because of all Baasha's
sins, as well as the sins of his son Elah and
because they caused Israel to sin. They angered Israel's God, the LORD, with their insignificant idols. 14 The rest of Elah's deeds
and all that he did, aren't they written in
the official records of Israel's kings?

Zimri rules Israel

15 In the twenty-seventh year of Judah's
King Asa, Zimri became king. He ruled
in Tirzah for seven days. The army was
camped at Gibbethon in Philistia. 16 They
heard the news: "Zimri has plotted against
the king and killed him." Right then, in the
camp, the whole Israelite army made their
general Omri king of Israel. 17 Omri and the
entire army then went up from Gibbethon
and laid siege to Tirzah. 18 When Zimri saw
that the city was captured, he went into the
fort of the royal palace and burned it down
on top of himself. So he died. 19 This happened because of the sins Zimri had committed by doing evil in the LORD's eyes and
by walking in Jeroboam's ways and the sin
he had done by causing Israel to sin. 20 The
rest of Zimri's deeds and the plot he carried out, aren't they written in the official
records of Israel's kings?

Omri rules Israel

21 At this time the people of Israel were
split in two. One half of the people followed
Tibni, Ginath's son, making him king; the
other half followed Omri. 22 Omri's side was
stronger than those who followed Tibni,

[b] *Or* and also about how he attacked him *or* and because Baasha had attacked Jeroboam

Ginath's son. So Tibni died and Omri became king. 23In the thirty-first year of Judah's King Asa, Omri became king of Israel. He ruled for twelve years, six of which were in Tirzah. 24He bought the hill of Samaria from Shemer for two kikkars of silver. He fortified the hill and named the town that he built there after Shemer, the previous owner of the hill of Samaria. 25Omri did evil in the LORD's eyes, more evil than anyone who preceded him. 26He walked in all the ways and sins of Jeroboam, Nebat's son, because he caused Israel to sin. They angered Israel's God, the LORD, with their worthless idols. 27The rest of Omri's deeds and his powerful acts, aren't they written in the official records of Israel's kings? 28Omri lay down with his ancestors and was buried in Samaria. His son Ahab succeeded him as king.

Ahab rules Israel

29In the thirty-eighth year of Judah's King Asa, Ahab, Omri's son, became king of Israel. He ruled over Israel in Samaria for twenty-two years 30and did evil in the LORD's eyes, more than anyone who preceded him. 31Ahab found it easy to walk in the sins of Jeroboam, Nebat's son. He married Jezebel the daughter of Ethbaal, who was the king of the Sidonians. He served and worshipped Baal. 32He made an altar for Baal in the Baal temple he had constructed in Samaria. 33Ahab also made a sacred pole[c] and did more to anger the LORD, the God of Israel, than any of Israel's kings who preceded him. 34During Ahab's time, Hiel from Bethel rebuilt Jericho. He set up its foundations at the cost of his oldest son Abiram. He hung its gates at the cost of his youngest son Segub. This fulfilled the LORD's word spoken through Joshua, Nun's son.

Elijah and the ravens

17 Elijah from Tishbe, who was one of the settlers in Gilead, said to Ahab, "As surely as the LORD lives, Israel's God, the one I serve, there will be neither dew nor rain these years unless I say so."

2Then the LORD's word came to Elijah: 3Go from here and turn east. Hide by the Cherith Brook that faces the Jordan River. 4You can drink from the brook. I have also ordered the ravens to provide for you there. 5Elijah went and did just what the LORD said. He stayed by the Cherith Brook that faced the Jordan River. 6The ravens brought bread and meat in the mornings and evenings. He drank from the Cherith Brook. 7After a while the brook dried up because there was no rain in the land.

Elijah and the widow from Zarephath

8The LORD's word came to Elijah: 9Get up and go to Zarephath near Sidon and stay there. I have ordered a widow there to take care of you. 10Elijah left and went to Zarephath. As he came to the town gate, he saw a widow collecting sticks. He called out to her, "Please get a little water for me in this cup so I can drink." 11She went to get some water. He then said to her, "Please get me a piece of bread."

12"As surely as the LORD your God lives," she replied, "I don't have any food; only a handful of flour in a jar and a bit of oil in a bottle. Look at me. I'm collecting two sticks so that I can make some food for myself and my son. We'll eat the last of the food and then die."

13Elijah said to her, "Don't be afraid! Go and do what you said. Only make a little loaf of bread for me first. Then bring it to me. You can make something for yourself and your son after that. 14This is what Israel's God, the LORD, says: The jar of flour won't decrease and the bottle of oil won't run out until the day the LORD sends rain on the earth." 15The widow went and did what Elijah said. So the widow, Elijah, and the widow's household ate for many days. 16The jar of flour didn't decrease nor did the bottle of oil run out, just as the LORD spoke through Elijah.

17After these things, the son of the widow, who was the matriarch of the household, became ill. His sickness got steadily worse unti he wasn't breathing anymore. 18She said tc Elijah, "What's gone wrong between us, mar

[c]Heb *asherah*, perhaps an object devoted to the goddess Asherah

of God? Have you come to me to call attention to my sin and kill my son?"

19 Elijah replied, "Give your son to me." He took her son from her and carried him to the upper room where he was staying. Elijah laid him on his bed. 20 Elijah cried out to the LORD, "LORD my God, why is it that you have brought such evil upon the widow that I am staying with by killing her son?" 21 Then he stretched himself over the boy three times and cried out to the LORD, "LORD my God, please give this boy's life back to him." 22 The LORD listened to Elijah's voice and gave the boy his life back. And he lived. 23 Elijah brought the boy down from the upper room of the house and gave him to his mother. Elijah said, "Look, your son is alive!"

24 "Now I know that you really are a man of God," the woman said to Elijah, "and that the LORD's word is truly in your mouth."

Elijah versus Baal's prophets

18 After many days, the LORD's word came to Elijah (it was the third year of the drought): Go! Appear before Ahab. I will then send rain on the earth. 2 So Elijah went to appear before Ahab.

Now the famine had become especially bad in Samaria. 3 Ahab had called Obadiah, who was in charge of the palace affairs. (Obadiah greatly feared the LORD. 4 When Jezebel killed the LORD's prophets, Obadiah took one hundred of them and hid them, fifty each in two caves. He supplied them with food and water.) 5 Ahab said to Obadiah, "Go throughout the land and check every spring of water and every brook. Perhaps we can find some grass to keep our horses and mules alive so we don't have to kill any of them." 6 To search, they divided the land between themselves. Ahab went one way by himself, while Obadiah went a different way by himself.

7 While Obadiah was out searching, suddenly Elijah met up with him. When Obadiah saw him, he fell on his face. "My master!" he said. "Are you Elijah?"

8 Elijah replied, "I am. Go and say to your master, 'Elijah is here!'"

9 Then Obadiah said, "How have I sinned that you are handing me, your servant, over to Ahab so he can kill me? 10 As surely as the LORD your God lives, there's no nation or kingdom where my master Ahab hasn't looked for you. They would insist, 'He's not here,' but Ahab would make them swear that they couldn't find you. 11 And now you are commanding me: 'Go and say to your master, "Elijah is here"?' 12 But here's what will happen: As soon as I leave you, the LORD's spirit will carry you off somewhere—I don't know where—then I'll report to Ahab, but he won't be able to find you. Then he will kill me! But your servant has feared the LORD from my youth. 13 Wasn't my master told what I did when Jezebel killed the LORD's prophets? I hid one hundred of the LORD's prophets, fifty each in two caves. I also supplied them with food and water. 14 But even after all that, you tell me, 'Say to your master, "Elijah is here!"' Ahab will kill me!"

15 Elijah said, "As surely as the LORD of heavenly forces lives, the one I serve, I will appear before Ahab today."

16 So Obadiah went to meet Ahab. He told him what had happened. Then Ahab went to meet Elijah. 17 When Ahab saw Elijah, Ahab said to him, "Is that you, the one who troubles Israel?"

18 Elijah answered, "I haven't troubled Israel; you and your father's house have! You did as much when you deserted the LORD's commands and followed the Baals. 19 Now send a message and gather all Israel to me at Mount Carmel. Gather the four hundred fifty prophets of Baal and the four hundred prophets of Asherah who eat at Jezebel's table."

20 Ahab sent the message to all the Israelites. He gathered the prophets at Mount Carmel. 21 Elijah approached all the people and said, "How long will you hobble back and forth between two opinions? If the LORD[d] is God, follow God. If Baal is God, follow Baal." The people gave no answer.

22 Elijah said to the people, "I am the last of the LORD's prophets, but Baal's prophets

[d] The contrast between the LORD's divine name (*YHWH*) and Baal's name is crucial throughout this passage.

number four hundred fifty. [23]Give us two bulls. Let Baal's prophets choose one. Let them cut it apart and set it on the wood, but don't add fire. I'll prepare the other bull, put it on the wood, but won't add fire. [24]Then all of you will call on the name of your god, and I will call on the name of the LORD. The god who answers with fire—that's the real God!"

All the people answered, "That's an excellent idea."

[25]So Elijah said to the prophets of Baal, "Choose one of these bulls. Prepare it first since there are so many of you. Call on the name of your god, but don't add fire."

[26]So they took one of the bulls that had been brought to them. They prepared it and called on Baal's name from morning to midday. They said, "Great Baal, answer us!" But there was no sound or answer. They performed a hopping dance around the altar that had been set up.

[27]Around noon, Elijah started making fun of them: "Shout louder! Certainly he's a god! Perhaps he is lost in thought or wandering or traveling somewhere.[e] Or maybe he is asleep and must wake up!"

[28]So the prophets of Baal cried with a louder voice and cut themselves with swords and knives as was their custom. Their blood flowed all over them. [29]As noon passed they went crazy with their ritual until it was time for the evening offering. Still there was no sound or answer, no response whatsoever.

[30]Then Elijah said to all the people, "Come here!" All the people closed in, and he repaired the LORD's altar that had been damaged. [31]Elijah took twelve stones, according to the number of the tribes of the sons of Jacob—to whom the LORD's word came: "Your name will be Israel." [32]He built the stones into an altar in the LORD's name, and he dug a trench around the altar big enough to hold two seahs[f] of dry grain. [33]He put the wood in order, butchered the bull, and placed the bull on the wood. "Fill four jars with water and pour it on the sacrifice and on the wood," he commanded. [34]"Do it a second time!" he said. So they did it a second time. "Do it a third time!" And so they did it a third time. [35]The water flowed around the altar, and even the trench filled with water. [36]At the time of the evening offering, the prophet Elijah drew near and prayed: "LORD, the God of Abraham, Isaac, and Israel, let it be known today that you are God in Israel and that I am your servant. I have done all these things at your instructions. [37]Answer me, LORD! Answer me so that this people will know that you, LORD, are the real God and that you can change their hearts."[g] [38]Then the LORD's fire fell; it consumed the sacrifice, the wood, the stones, and the dust. It even licked up the water in the trench!

[39]All the people saw this and fell on their faces. "The LORD is the real God! The LORD is the real God!" they exclaimed.

[40]Elijah said to them, "Seize Baal's prophets! Don't let any escape!" The people seized the prophets, and Elijah brought them to the Kishon Brook and killed them there. [41]Elijah then said to Ahab, "Get up! Celebrate with food and drink because I hear the sound of a rainstorm coming." [42]So Ahab got up to celebrate with food and drink. But Elijah went up to the top of Mount Carmel. He bowed down to the ground and put his face between his knees. [43]He said to his assistant, "Please get up and look toward the sea."

So the assistant did so. He said, "I don't see anything."

Seven times Elijah said, "Do it again."

[44]The seventh time the assistant said, "I see a small cloud the size of a human hand coming up from the sea."

Elijah said, "Go and tell Ahab, 'Pull yourself together, go down the mountain, and don't let the rain hold you back.'" [45]After a little while, the sky became dark with clouds, and a wind came up with a huge rainstorm. Ahab was already riding on his way to Jezreel, [46]but the LORD's power strengthened Elijah. He gathered up his clothes and ran in front of Ahab until he came to Jezreel.

[e]Heb uncertain [f]One seah is approximately seven and a half quarts. [g]Heb uncertain

Elijah runs to Mount Horeb

19 Ahab told Jezebel all that Elijah had done, how he had killed all Baal's prophets with the sword. 2 Jezebel sent a messenger to Elijah with this message: "May the gods do whatever they want to me if by this time tomorrow I haven't made your life like the life of one of them."

3 Elijah was terrified. He got up and ran for his life. He arrived at Beer-sheba in Judah and left his assistant there. 4 He himself went farther on into the desert a day's journey. He finally sat down under a solitary broom bush. He longed for his own death: "It's more than enough, LORD! Take my life because I'm no better than my ancestors." 5 He lay down and slept under the solitary broom bush.

Then suddenly a messenger tapped him and said to him, "Get up! Eat something!" 6 Elijah opened his eyes and saw flatbread baked on glowing coals and a jar of water right by his head. He ate and drank, and then went back to sleep. 7 The LORD's messenger returned a second time and tapped him. "Get up!" the messenger said. "Eat something, because you have a difficult road ahead of you." 8 Elijah got up, ate and drank, and went refreshed by that food for forty days and nights until he arrived at Horeb, God's mountain. 9 There he went into a cave and spent the night.

The LORD's word came to him and said, "Why are you here, Elijah?"

10 Elijah replied, "I've been very passionate for the LORD God of heavenly forces because the Israelites have abandoned your covenant. They have torn down your altars, and they have murdered your prophets with the sword. I'm the only one left, and now they want to take my life too!"

11 The LORD said, "Go out and stand at the mountain before the LORD. The LORD is passing by." A very strong wind tore through the mountains and broke apart the stones before the LORD. But the LORD wasn't in the wind. After the wind, there was an earthquake. But the LORD wasn't in the earthquake. 12 After the earthquake, there was a fire. But the LORD wasn't in the fire. After the fire, there was a sound. Thin. Quiet. 13 When Elijah heard it, he wrapped his face in his coat. He went out and stood at the cave's entrance. A voice came to him and said, "Why are you here, Elijah?"

14 He said, "I've been very passionate for the LORD God of heavenly forces because the Israelites have abandoned your covenant. They have torn down your altars, and they have murdered your prophets with the sword. I'm the only one left, and now they want to take my life too."

15 The LORD said to him, "Go back through the desert to Damascus and anoint Hazael as king of Aram. 16 Also anoint Jehu, Nimshi's son, as king of Israel; and anoint Elisha from Abel-meholah, Shaphat's son, to succeed you as prophet. 17 Whoever escapes from the sword of Hazael, Jehu will kill. Whoever escapes from the sword of Jehu, Elisha will kill. 18 But I have preserved those who remain in Israel, totaling seven thousand—all those whose knees haven't bowed down to Baal and whose mouths haven't kissed him."

19 So Elijah departed from there and found Elisha, Shaphat's son. He was plowing with twelve yoke of oxen before him. Elisha was with the twelfth yoke. Elijah met up with him and threw his coat on him. 20 Elisha immediately left the oxen and ran after Elijah. "Let me kiss my father and my mother," Elisha said, "then I will follow you."

Elijah replied, "Go! I'm not holding you back!" 21 Elisha turned back from following Elijah, took the pair of oxen, and slaughtered them. Then with equipment from the oxen, Elisha boiled the meat, gave it to the people, and they ate it. Then he got up, followed Elijah, and served him.

Ben-hadad's wars with Ahab

20 King Ben-hadad of Aram brought together all his army along with thirty-two kings plus horses and chariots. He went up, surrounded Samaria, and made war against it. 2 He sent messengers to Ahab, Israel's king, inside Samaria. 3 The message said, "This is what Ben-hadad says: 'Your silver and your gold are mine. Your good-looking wives and children are mine.'"

4 Israel's king answered, "Whatever you

say, my master, great king. I am yours and
so is everything I have."
5The messengers came back again: "This
is what Ben-hadad says: 'I sent you the
message: Give me your silver and gold, your
wives and your sons. 6However, at this time
tomorrow I will send my officers to you, and
they will search your palace and the houses
of your officers. Everything that you find
valuable they will seize and take away.'"
7Then Israel's king called all the elders of
the land and he said, "Please know and understand the evil this man wants to do! He
demanded from me my wives and sons, and
my silver and gold; and I didn't refuse him."
8All of the elders and the people said to
him, "Don't obey and don't give in!"
9So the king said to Ben-hadad's messengers, "Say to my master the king: 'Everything that you first ordered your servant, I
will do. But I can't comply with this new
command.'"

The messengers took this response to
Ben-hadad, 10who sent back this reply:
"May the gods do whatever they want to
me if there is even a handful of dust left in
Samaria for the armies under me!"
11Then Israel's king replied, "The one who
prepares for battle shouldn't brag like one
returning from battle."
12When Ben-hadad heard this message,
he and the other kings were drinking in
their tents. Ben-hadad said to his officers,
"Take your positions!" So they took up their
positions against the city.
13Suddenly a prophet approached Israel's
King Ahab. He said, "This is what the LORD
says: Do you see that great army? Today I
am handing it over to you. Then you will
know that I am the LORD."
14Ahab said, "Who will do it?"

The prophet answered, "This is what the LORD says: The servants of the district officials will do it."

"Who should start the battle?" Ahab asked.

"You should," the prophet replied.

15So Ahab assembled the servants of the
district officials. There were two hundred
thirty-two of them. Next he assembled the
entire Israelite army, seven thousand total.
16At noon they marched for battle. Meanwhile, Ben-hadad and the thirty-two kings
allied with him were getting drunk in their
tents. 17The servants of the district officials
were at the head of the march. Ben-hadad
sent for information and was told, "Some
men have marched out of Samaria."
18He said, "If they have come out in
peace, take them alive; if they have come
out for war, take them alive as well." 19So
the servants of the district governors with
the army behind them marched out from the
city. 20Each one struck down his opponent,
so that the Arameans fled. Israel chased
after them. Ben-hadad, Aram's king, escaped with some horses and chariots. 21Is-
rael's king went out and attacked the horses
and chariots. He attacked the Arameans
with a fierce assault.
22The prophet came to Israel's king and
said to him, "Maintain your strength! Know
and understand that at the turn of the coming year, Aram's king will attack you again."
23The officers of Aram's king said to him,
"Israel's god is a god of the mountains. That's
why they were stronger than us. But if we
fight them on the plains, we will certainly
be stronger than they are. 24This is what
you need to do: Remove the kings from
their military posts and appoint officials
in their place. 25Then raise another army like
the one that was destroyed, with horses like
those horses and chariots like those chariots. Then we will fight them on the plains, and
we will certainly be stronger than they are."
The king took their advice and followed it.
26So in the spring of the year, Ben-hadad
assembled the Arameans and marched up
to Aphek to fight with Israel. 27Now the
Israelites had already been assembled and
provisioned, so they went to engage the Arameans. The Israelites camped before them
like two small flocks of goats, but the Arameans filled the land.
28Then the man of God came forward
and said to Israel's king, "This is what the
LORD says: Because the Arameans said that
the LORD is a god of the mountains but
not a god of the valleys, I am handing this
whole great army over to you. Then you will
know that I am the LORD."

29The two armies camped opposite each other for seven days. On the seventh day, the battle began. The Israelites attacked and destroyed one hundred thousand Aramean foot soldiers in a single day. 30Those who were left fled to Aphek, into the city where a wall fell on twenty-seven thousand more of them. But Ben-hadad escaped and hid in an inner room within the city.

31Ben-hadad's officers said to him, "Listen, we have heard that the kings of Israel are merciful kings. Allow us to put mourning clothes on our bodies and cords around our heads. We will then go to Israel's king. Perhaps he will let you live." 32So they put mourning clothes on their bodies and cords around their heads. They went to Israel's king and said, "Ben-hadad is your slave. He begs, 'Please let me live!'"

Israel's king said, "Is he still alive? He is my brother."

33Taking this as a good sign, Ben-hadad's men quickly accepted this statement.[h] "Yes, Ben-hadad is your brother!" they said.

"Go and get him," the king ordered. So Ben-hadad came to him, and the king received him into his chariot.

34Ben-hadad said to the king, "I will return the towns that my father took from your father. Furthermore, you can set up markets for yourself in Damascus just as my father did in Samaria."

The king replied,[i] "On the basis of this covenant, I will let you go." So he made a covenant with Ben-hadad and set him free.

35At the LORD's command a certain man who belonged to a prophetic group said to his friend: "Please strike me." But his friend refused to hit him. 36So he said to his friend, "Because you didn't obey the LORD's voice, a lion will attack you as soon as you leave me." And as the friend left the prophet, a lion found him and attacked him. 37Then the prophet found another man and said, "Please strike me." He hit the prophet, and the attack left a wound. 38The prophet went and stood before the king by the road. He disguised himself by putting a bandage over his eyes. 39When the king passed by, the prophet called out to the king, "Your servant was in the middle of the battle when someone brought a prisoner. 'Guard this man,' he said. 'If he escapes it will be your life for his—that, or you will owe me a kikkar of silver.' 40Your servant got busy doing this and that, and the prisoner disappeared."

Israel's king replied, "It appears you have decided your own fate."

41The prophet quickly tore the bandage from over his eyes, and Israel's king recognized him as one of the prophets. 42Then the prophet said to the king, "This is what the LORD says: Because you freed a man I condemned to die, it will be your life for his life, and your people for his people." 43So Israel's king went to his palace at Samaria, irritated and upset.

Naboth's vineyard

21 Now it happened sometime later that Naboth from Jezreel had a vineyard in Jezreel that was next to the palace of King Ahab of Samaria. 2Ahab ordered Naboth, "Give me your vineyard so it can become my vegetable garden, because it is right next to my palace. In exchange for it, I'll give you an even better vineyard. Or if you prefer, I'll pay you the price in silver."

3Naboth responded to Ahab, "LORD forbid that I give you my family inheritance!"

4So Ahab went to his palace, irritated and upset at what Naboth[j] had said to him—because Naboth had said, "I won't give you my family inheritance!" Ahab lay down on his bed and turned his face away. He wouldn't eat anything.

5His wife Jezebel came to him. "Why are you upset and not eating any food?" she asked.

6He answered her, "I was talking to Naboth. I said, 'Sell me your vineyard. Or if you prefer, I'll give you another vineyard for it.' But he said, 'I won't give you my vineyard!'"

7Then his wife Jezebel said to him, "Aren't you the one who rules Israel? Get up! Eat some food and cheer up. I'll get

[h]Heb uncertain [i]Heb lacks *The king replied.* [j]Heb adds *from Jezreel;* also in 21:6-7, 15-16.

Naboth's vineyard for you myself." [8]So she wrote letters in Ahab's name, putting his seal on them. She sent them to the elders and officials who lived in the same town as Naboth. [9]This is what she wrote in the letters: "Announce a fast and place Naboth at the head of the people. [10]Then bring in two liars in front of him and have them testify as follows: 'You cursed God and king!' Then take Naboth outside and stone him so he dies."

[11]The elders and the officials who lived in Naboth's town did exactly as Jezebel specified in the letters that she had sent. [12]They announced a fast and placed Naboth at the head of the people. [13]Then the two liars came and sat in front of him. They testified against Naboth in front of the people, "Naboth cursed God and king!" So the people took Naboth outside the town and stoned him so that he died.

[14]It was then reported to Jezebel, "Naboth was stoned. He's dead." [15]As soon as Jezebel heard that Naboth had been stoned to death, she said to Ahab, "Get up and take ownership of the vineyard of Naboth, which he had refused to sell to you. Naboth is no longer alive; he's dead." [16]When Ahab heard that Naboth had died, he got up and went down to Naboth's vineyard to take ownership of it.

[17]The LORD's word came to Elijah from Tishbe: [18]Get up and go down to meet Israel's King Ahab in Samaria. He is in Naboth's vineyard. He has gone down to take ownership of it. [19]Say the following to him: This is what the LORD says: So, you've murdered and are now taking ownership, are you? Then tell him: This is what the LORD says: In the same place where the dogs licked up Naboth's blood, they will lick up your own blood.

[20]Ahab said to Elijah, "So you've found me, my old enemy!"

"I found you," Elijah said, "because you've enslaved yourself by doing evil in the LORD's eyes. [21]So I am now bringing evil on you! I will burn until you are consumed, and I will eliminate everyone who urinates on a wall that belongs to Ahab, whether slave or free. [22]I will make your household like that of Jeroboam, Nebat's son, and like the household of Baasha, Ahijah's son, because of the way you've angered me and because you've made Israel sin. [23]As for Jezebel, the LORD says this: Dogs will devour Jezebel in the area of Jezreel. [24]Dogs will eat anyone of Ahab's family who dies in town, and birds will eat anyone who dies in the country."

([25]Truly there has never been anyone like Ahab who sold out by doing evil in the LORD's eyes—evil that his wife Jezebel led him to do. [26]Ahab's actions were deplorable. He followed after the worthless idols exactly like the Amorites had done—the very ones the LORD had removed before the Israelites.)

[27]When Ahab heard these words, he tore his clothes and put mourning clothes on his body. He fasted, even slept in mourning clothes, and walked around depressed. [28]The LORD's word then came to Elijah from Tishbe: [29]Have you seen how Ahab has humbled himself before me? Because he has done so, I won't bring the evil during his lifetime. Instead, I will bring the evil on his household in the days of his son.

Jehoshaphat and Ahab

22 For three years there was no war between Aram and the Israelites. [2]In the third year, Judah's King Jehoshaphat visited Israel's king. [3]Israel's king said to his servants, "You know, don't you, that Ramoth-gilead is ours? But we aren't doing anything to take it back from the king of Aram." [4]He said to Jehoshaphat, "Will you go with me into battle at Ramoth-gilead?"

Jehoshaphat said to Israel's king, "I am with you, and my troops and my horses are united with yours. [5]But," Jehoshapat said to Israel's king, "first let's see what the LORD has to say."

[6]So Israel's king gathered about four hundred prophets, and he asked them, "Should I go to war with Ramoth-gilead or not?"

"Attack!" the prophets answered. "The LORD will hand it over to the king."

[7]But Jehoshaphat said, "Isn't there any other prophet of the LORD whom we could ask?"

8 “There is one other man who could ask the LORD for us,” Israel’s king told Jehoshaphat, “but I hate him because he never prophesies anything good about me, only bad. His name is Micaiah, Imlah’s son.”

“The king shouldn’t speak like that!” Jehoshaphat said.

9 So Israel’s king called an officer and ordered, “Bring Micaiah, Imlah’s son, right away.”

10 Now Israel’s king and Judah’s King Jehoshaphat were sitting on their thrones, dressed in their royal robes at the threshing floor beside the entrance to the gate of Samaria. All the prophets were prophesying in front of them. 11 Zedekiah, Chenaanah’s son, made iron horns for himself and said, “This is what the LORD says: With these horns you will gore the Arameans until there’s nothing left of them!”

12 All the other prophets agreed: “Attack Ramoth-gilead and win! The LORD will hand it over to the king!”

13 Meanwhile, the messenger who had gone to summon Micaiah said to him, “Listen, the prophets all agree that the king will succeed. You should say the same thing they say and prophesy success.”

14 But Micaiah answered, “As surely as the LORD lives, I will say only what the LORD tells me to say.”

15 When Micaiah arrived, the king asked him, “Micaiah, should we go to war with Ramoth-gilead or not?”

“Attack and win!” Micaiah answered. “The LORD will hand it over to the king!”

16 But the king said, “How many times must I demand that you tell me the truth when you speak in the name of the LORD?”

17 Then Micaiah replied, “I saw all Israel scattered on the hills like sheep without a shepherd! And then the LORD said: They have no master. Let them return safely to their own homes.”

18 Then Israel’s king said to Jehoshaphat, “Didn’t I tell you? He never prophesies anything good about me, only bad.”

19 Then Micaiah said, “Listen now to the LORD’s word: I saw the LORD enthroned with all the heavenly forces stationed beside him, at his right and at his left. 20 The LORD said, ‘Who will persuade Ahab so that he attacks Ramoth-gilead and dies there?’ There were many suggestions 21 until one particular spirit approached the LORD and said, ‘I’ll persuade him.’ ‘How?’ the LORD asked. 22 ‘I will be a lying spirit in the mouth of all his prophets,’ he said. The LORD agreed, ‘You will succeed in persuading him! Go ahead!’ 23 So now, since the LORD has placed a lying spirit in the mouths of every one of these prophets of yours, it is the LORD who has pronounced disaster against you!”

24 Zedekiah, Chenaanah’s son, approached Micaiah and slapped him on the cheek. “Just how did the LORD’s spirit leave me to speak to you?” he asked.

25 Micaiah answered, “You will find out on the day you try to hide in an inner room.”

26 “Arrest him,” ordered Israel’s king, “and turn him over to Amon the city official and to Joash the king’s son. 27 Tell them, ‘The king says: Put this man in prison and feed him minimum rations of bread and water until I return safely.’ ”

28 “If you ever return safely,” Micaiah replied, “then the LORD wasn’t speaking through me.” Then he added, “Pay attention, every last one of you!”

29 So Israel’s king and Judah’s King Jehoshaphat attacked Ramoth-gilead. 30 Israel’s king said to Jehoshaphat, “I will disguise myself when we go into battle,[k] but you should wear your royal attire.” When Israel’s king had disguised himself, they entered the battle.

31 Meanwhile, Aram’s king had commanded his thirty-two chariot officers, “Don’t bother with anyone big or small. Fight only with Israel’s king.”

32 As soon as the chariot officers saw Jehoshaphat, they assumed that he must be Israel’s king, so they turned to attack him. But Jehoshaphat cried out for help. 33 When the chariot officers realized that he wasn’t Israel’s king, they stopped chasing him. 34 But someone randomly shot an

[k] LXX, Tg; MT *Disguise yourself and go*

arrow that struck Israel's king between the
joints in his armor.[l]
"Turn around and get me out of the battle," the king told his chariot driver. "I've
been hit!"
35 While the battle raged all that day, the
king stood propped up in the chariot facing
the Arameans. But that evening he died after
his blood had poured from his wound into
the chariot. 36 When the sun set, a shout
spread throughout the camp: "Retreat to
your towns! Retreat to your land!" 37 Once
the king had died, people came from Samaria
and buried the king there. 38 They cleaned
the chariot at the pool of Samaria. The dogs
licked up the king's blood and the prostitutes
bathed in it, just as the LORD had spoken.

Ahab's last days

39 The rest of Ahab's deeds and all that he
did—including the ivory palace he built and
all the towns he constructed—aren't they
written in the official records of Israel's
kings? 40 Ahab lay down with his ancestors.
His son Ahaziah succeeded him as king.

Jehoshaphat rules Judah

41 Jehoshaphat, Asa's son, became king
over Judah in the fourth year of Israel's
King Ahab. 42 Jehoshaphat was 35 years
old when he became king, and he ruled for
twenty-five years in Jerusalem. His mother's
name was Azubah; she was Shilhi's daughter. 43 Jehoshapat walked in all the ways of
his father Asa, not deviating from it. He did
the right things in the LORD's eyes, with the
exception that he didn't remove the shrines.
The people continued to sacrifice and offer
incense at them. 44 Jehoshaphat made
peace with Israel's king. 45 The rest of Jehoshaphat's deeds, the great acts he did, and
how he fought in battle, aren't they written in the official records of Judah's kings?
46 Additionally, Jehoshaphat purged the land
of the consecrated workers[m] who remained
from the days of Asa.
47 Now Edom had no king; only a deputy
was ruler. 48 Jehoshaphat built Tarshish-
styled ships to go to Ophir for gold. But
the fleet didn't go because it was wrecked
at Ezion-geber. 49 Then Ahaziah, Ahab's son,
said to Jehoshaphat, "Let my sailors go
with your sailors on the ships." But Jehoshaphat didn't agree to this. 50 Jehoshaphat
died and was buried with his ancestors in
his ancestor David's City. His son Jehoram
succeeded him as king.

Ahaziah rules Israel

51 In the seventeenth year of Judah's King
Jehoshaphat, Ahaziah, Ahab's son, became
king over Israel in Samaria. He ruled over
Israel for two years. 52 He did evil in the
LORD's eyes. He walked in his father's ways
and his mother's ways—that is, in the ways
of Jeroboam, Nebat's son, who had caused
Israel to sin. 53 Ahaziah served Baal and
worshipped him. He angered the LORD, Israel's God, by doing all the same things his
father had done.

2 KINGS

Ahaziah's death

1 After Ahab died, Moab rebelled against
Israel.
2 Ahaziah fell out the window of his second-story room in Samaria and was hurt.
He sent messengers, telling them, "Go to
Ekron's god Baal-zebub, and ask if I will recover from this injury."
3 But the LORD's messenger said to Elijah
from Tishbe, "Go, intercept the messengers
of Samaria's king, and ask them, 'Is it because there's no God in Israel that you are
going to question Ekron's god Baal-zebub?
4 This is what the LORD says: You will never
get out of the bed you are lying in; you will
die for sure!'" So Elijah set off.
5 The messengers returned to Ahaziah. He
said to them, "Why have you come back?"
6 They said to him, "A man met us and
said, 'Go back to the king who sent you.

[l] Heb uncertain [m] Traditionally *cultic prostitutes*

Say to him, This is what the LORD says: Is it
because there's no God in Israel that you've
come to question Ekron's god Baal-zebub?
Because of this, you will never get out of the
bed you are lying in; you will die for sure!"
7 Ahaziah said to them, "Describe the
man who met you and said these things."
8 They said to him, "He wore clothes made
of hair[a] with a leather belt around his waist."
Ahaziah said, "That was Elijah from
Tishbe."
9 So Ahaziah sent out a commander with
fifty soldiers. The commander met up with
Elijah while he was sitting on a hilltop. The
commander said, "Man of God, the king
says, 'Come down!' "
10 Elijah replied to the commander of the
fifty soldiers, "If I really am a man of God,
may fire come down from the sky and burn
up you and your fifty soldiers." Then fire
came down from the sky and burned up the
commander and his fifty soldiers.
11 Ahaziah then sent another commander
with fifty soldiers. The commander said to
Elijah, "Man of God, this is what the king
says: 'Hurry and come down!' "
12 Elijah said to them, "If I really am a
man of God, may fire come down from the
sky and burn up you and your fifty soldiers." Then God's fire came down from the
sky and burned up the commander and his
fifty soldiers.
13 For a third time Ahaziah sent a commander with fifty soldiers. So the third
commander arrived. He kneeled before Elijah and begged him, "Man of God! Please
have some regard for my life and the lives of
these fifty soldiers who are your servants.
14 Look, fire came from the sky and burned
up the two earlier commanders and their
troops of fifty soldiers. Please have regard
for my life."
15 Then the LORD's messenger said to
Elijah, "Go down with him. Don't be afraid
of him." So Elijah set out to go with him to
the king.
16 Elijah said to the king: "This is what the
LORD says: Why did you send messengers to
question Ekron's god Baal-zebub? Is there
no God in Israel whose word you could seek?
Because of this, you won't ever get out of
the bed you are lying in; you'll die for sure!"
17 So Ahaziah died in agreement with the
LORD's word that Elijah had spoken.
Because Ahaziah had no son, Joram[b]
became king after him in the second year
of Judah's King Jehoram, who was Jehoshaphat's son. 18 The rest of Ahaziah's deeds,
aren't they written in the official records of
Israel's kings?

Elijah goes to heaven

2 Now the LORD was going to take Elijah
up to heaven in a windstorm, and Elijah
and Elisha were leaving Gilgal. 2 Elijah said
to Elisha, "Stay here, because the LORD has
sent me to Bethel."
But Elisha said, "As the LORD lives and
as you live, I won't leave you." So they went
down to Bethel.
3 The group of prophets from Bethel came
out to Elisha. These prophets said to Elisha,
"Do you know that the LORD is going to take
your master away from you today?"
Elisha said, "Yes, I know. Don't talk
about it!"
4 Elijah said, "Elisha, stay here, because
the LORD has sent me to Jericho."
But Elisha said, "As the LORD lives and
as you live, I won't leave you." So they went
to Jericho.
5 The group of prophets from Jericho approached Elisha and said to him, "Do you
know that the LORD is going to take your
master away from you today?"
He said, "Yes, I know. Don't talk about
it!"
6 Elijah said to Elisha, "Stay here, because
the LORD has sent me to the Jordan."
But Elisha said, "As the LORD lives and as
you live, I won't leave you." So both of them
went on together. 7 Fifty members from the
group of prophets also went along, but they
stood at a distance. Both Elijah and Elisha
stood beside the Jordan River. 8 Elijah then
took his coat, rolled it up, and hit the water.

[a] Or *He was a hairy man.* [b] Heb *Jehoram*; the king's name is variously spelled in either long *Jehoram* or short *Joram* form.

Then the water was divided in two! Both of them crossed over on dry ground. [9]When they had crossed, Elijah said to Elisha, "What do you want me to do for you before I'm taken away from you?"

Elisha said, "Let me have twice your spirit."

[10]Elijah said, "You've made a difficult request. If you can see me when I'm taken from you, then it will be yours. If you don't see me, it won't happen."

[11]They were walking along, talking, when suddenly a fiery chariot and fiery horses appeared and separated the two of them. Then Elijah went to heaven in a windstorm. [12]Elisha was watching, and he cried out, "Oh, my father, my father! Israel's chariots and its riders!" When he could no longer see him, Elisha took hold of his clothes and ripped them in two.

Elisha succeeds Elijah

[13]Then Elisha picked up the coat that had fallen from Elijah. He went back and stood beside the banks of the Jordan River. [14]He took the coat that had fallen from Elijah and hit the water. He said, "Where is the LORD, Elijah's God?" And when he hit the water, it divided in two! Then Elisha crossed over.

[15]The group of prophets from Jericho saw him from a distance. They said, "Elijah's spirit has settled on Elisha!" So they came out to meet him, bowing down before him. [16]"Look," they told him, "there are fifty strong men among us, your servants. Please let them go and search for your master. Perhaps the LORD's spirit has picked him up and put him down on some mountain or in some valley."

Elisha said, "Don't send them." [17]They insisted until he became embarrassed and said, "Okay, send them." So they sent fifty men who searched for three days. But they couldn't find Elijah. [18]When these men returned to Elisha, who was staying in Jericho, he said to them, "Didn't I tell you not to go?"

[19]The citizens said to Elisha, "As you can see, sir, this city is in a good location, but the water is bad, and the land causes miscarriages."

[20]He said, "Bring me a new bowl, and put some salt in it." They did so. [21]Elisha then went out and threw salt into the spring. He said, "This is what the LORD has said: I have purified this water. It will no longer cause death and miscarriage." [22]The water has stayed pure right up to this very day, in agreement with the word that Elisha spoke.

Elisha and the bears

[23]Elisha went up from there to Bethel. As he was going up the road, some young people came out of the city. They mocked him: "Get going, Baldy! Get going, Baldy!" [24]Turning around, Elisha looked at them and cursed them in the LORD's name. Then two bears came out of the woods and mangled forty-two of the youths. [25]From there Elisha went to Mount Carmel and then back to Samaria.

Moab's rebellion

3 Joram,[c] Ahab's son, became king of Israel in Samaria in the eighteenth year of Jehoshaphat, Judah's king. He ruled for twelve years. [2]He did what was evil in the LORD's eyes, but he wasn't as bad as his father and mother. He removed the sacred pillar of Baal that his father had made. [3]But he nevertheless clung to the sins that Jeroboam, Nebat's son, had caused Israel to commit. He didn't deviate from them.

[4]Now Moab's King Mesha kept sheep. He would pay Israel's king one hundred thousand lambs and the wool from one hundred thousand rams. [5]But when Ahab died, Moab's king rebelled against Israel's king. [6]So King Joram set out from Samaria at once. He prepared all Israel for war. [7]He sent word to Judah's King Jehoshaphat, "Moab's king has rebelled against me. Will you go with me to fight against Moab?"

Jehoshaphat responded, "Yes, I'll go. We'll fight as one: you and I, our troops and our horses."

[8]"Which road should we take?" Joram asked.

Jehoshaphat responded, "The road that goes through the Edomite wilderness."

[c]Heb *Jehoram* (also in 3:6); the king's name is variously spelled in either long *Jehoram* or short *Joram* form.

9So Israel's and Judah's kings set out with the king of Edom. They marched around for seven days until there was no water left for the army or for the animals with them. 10Israel's king said, "This is terrible! Has the LORD brought us three kings together only to hand us over to Moab?"

11Jehoshaphat said, "Isn't there any prophet of the LORD around, so we could question the LORD through him?"

One of the servants of Israel's king answered, "Elisha, Shaphat's son, is here. He used to pour water on Elijah's hands."

12Jehoshaphat said, "He has the LORD's word!" So Israel's king and Jehoshaphat and Edom's king went down to see Elisha.

13Elisha said to Israel's king, "What do we have to do with each other? Go to your father's or mother's prophets."

Then Israel's king said to him, "Don't say that, because it is the LORD who has brought us three kings together—but only to hand us over to Moab!"

14Elisha said, "I swear by the life of the LORD of heavenly forces, the one I stand before and serve, if I didn't care about Judah's King Jehoshaphat, I wouldn't notice you or even look at you! 15Now bring me a musician." While the musician played, the LORD's power came over Elisha. 16He said, "This is what the LORD says: This valley will be filled with pools.[d] 17This is what the LORD says: You won't see any wind or rain, but that valley will be full of water. Then you'll be able to drink—you, your cattle, and your animals. 18This is easy for the LORD to do. He will also hand Moab over to you. 19You will then attack every fort and every grand city, cutting down all the good trees, stopping up all the springs, and ruining the good fields with stones."

20The next morning, at the time to offer the grain offering, water came flowing from the direction of Edom. The land filled up with water.

21Now all the Moabites had heard how these kings had come to fight against them. So all who were able to fight were summoned, and they took up positions along the border. 22They got up early in the morning as the sun's rays shone on the water. The Moabites saw the water from a distance. It looked as red as blood. 23They said, "It's blood! The kings must have fought each other and killed themselves! Now get the plunder, Moab!"

24But when they entered Israel's camp, the Israelites rose up and attacked the Moabites. The Moabites fled from them. Israel moved forward, striking the Moabites down as they went.[e] 25Then the Israelites destroyed the Moabite cities. Each Israelite threw a stone on every piece of good land until it was covered. They stopped up every spring and cut down every good tree. Only Kir-hareseth remained with its stone wall intact,[f] but then stone throwers[g] surrounded it and attacked it.

26Moab's king saw that he was losing the battle. So he took seven hundred soldiers with him, each with sword in hand, to break through to Edom's king. But they failed. 27Then he took his oldest son, who was to succeed him as king, and he offered him on the wall as an entirely burned offering. As a result, outrage was expressed by Israel. So they pulled back from Moab's king and returned to their own country.

A poor widow

4 Now there was a woman who had been married to a member of a group of prophets. She appealed to Elisha, saying, "My husband, your servant, is dead. You know how he feared the LORD. But now someone he owed money to has come to take my two children away as slaves."

2Elisha said to her, "What can I do for you? Tell me what you still have left in the house."

She said, "Your servant has nothing at all in the house except a small jar of oil."

3He said, "Go out and borrow containers from all your neighbors. Get as many empty containers as possible. 4Then go in and close the door behind you and your sons. Pour oil into all those containers. Set each one aside when it's full."

[d]LXX, Vulg *Fill this valley with ditches.* [e]Heb uncertain [f]Heb uncertain [g]Heb uncertain

[5]She left Elisha and closed the door behind her and her sons. They brought her containers as she kept on pouring. [6]When she had filled the containers, she said to her son, "Bring me another container."

He said to her, "There aren't any more." Then the oil stopped flowing, [7]and she reported this to the man of God.

He said, "Go! Sell the oil and pay your debts. You and your sons can live on what remains."

A rich woman

[8]One day Elisha went to Shunem. A rich woman lived there. She urged him to eat something, so whenever he passed by, he would stop in to eat some food. [9]She said to her husband, "Look, I know that he is a holy man of God and he passes by regularly. [10]Let's make a small room on the roof. We'll set up a bed, a table, a chair, and a lamp for him there. Then when he comes to us, he can stay there."

[11]So one day Elisha came there, headed to the room on the roof, and lay down. [12]He said to his servant Gehazi, "Call this Shunammite woman." Gehazi called her, and she stood before him. [13]Elisha then said to Gehazi, "Say to her, 'Look, you've gone to all this trouble for us. What can I do for you? Is there anything I can say on your behalf to the king or to the commander of the army?'"

She said, "I'm content to live at home with my own people."

[14]Elisha asked, "So what can be done for her?"

Gehazi said, "Well, she doesn't have a son, and her husband is old."

[15]Elisha said, "Call her." So Gehazi called her, and she stood at the door. [16]Elisha said, "About this time next year, you will be holding a son in your arms."

But she said, "No, man of God, sir; don't lie to your servant."

[17]But the woman conceived and gave birth to a son at about the same time the next year. This was what Elisha had promised her.

[18]The child grew up. One day he ran to his father, who was with the harvest workers. [19]He said to his father, "Oh, my head! My head!"

The father said to a young man, "Carry him to his mother." [20]So he picked up the boy and brought him to his mother.

The boy sat on her lap until noon. Then he died. [21]She went up and laid him down on the bed for the man of God. Then she went out and closed the door. [22]She called her husband and said, "Send me one of the young men and one of the donkeys so that I can hurry to the man of God and come back."

[23]Her husband said, "Why are you going to him today? It's not a new moon or sabbath."

She said, "Don't worry about it." [24]She saddled the donkey, then said to her young servant, "Drive the donkey hard. Don't let me slow down unless I tell you." [25]So she went off and came to the man of God at Mount Carmel.

As soon as the man of God saw her from a distance, he said to Gehazi his servant, "Look, it's the Shunammite woman! [26]Run out to meet her and ask her, 'Are things okay with you, your husband, and your child?'"

She said, "Things are okay."

[27]When she got to the man of God at the mountain, she grabbed his feet. Gehazi came up to push her away, but the man of God said, "Leave her alone! She is distraught, but the LORD has hidden the reason from me and hasn't told me why."

[28]She said, "Did I ask you for a son, sir? Didn't I say, 'Don't raise my hopes'?"

[29]Elisha said to Gehazi, "Get ready, take my staff, and go! If you encounter anyone, don't stop to greet them. If anyone greets you, don't reply. Put my staff on the boy's face."

[30]But the boy's mother said, "I swear by your life and by the LORD's life, I won't leave you!" So Elisha got up and followed her.

[31]Gehazi went on ahead of them. He set the staff on the young boy's face, but there was no sound or response. So he went back to meet Elisha and told him, "The boy didn't wake up."

[32]Elisha came into the house and saw the boy lying dead on his bed. [33]He went in and closed the door behind the two of them. Then he prayed to the LORD. [34]He got up on the bed and lay down on top of the child, putting his mouth on the boy's mouth,

his eyes on the boy's eyes, his hands on the boy's hands. And as he bent over him, the child's skin grew warm. 35 Then Elisha got down and paced back and forth in the house. Once again he got up on the bed and bent over the boy, at which point the boy sneezed[h] seven times and opened his eyes. 36 Elisha called for Gehazi and said, "Call the Shunammite woman." Gehazi called her, and she came to Elisha. He told her, "Pick up your son." 37 She came and fell at his feet, facedown on the ground. Then she picked up her son and left.

Miracles with food

38 When Elisha returned to Gilgal, there was a famine in the land. A group of prophets was sitting before him. He said to his servant, "Put on the big pot and cook some stew for the prophets." 39 So one of them went out to the field to gather plants; he found a wild vine and gathered wild gourds from it, filling his garment. He came and cut them up into the pot of stew, but no one knew what they were.

40 The stew was served to the men, but as they started to eat it, they cried out and said, "There is death in that pot, man of God!" They couldn't eat it.

41 Elisha said, "Get some flour." He threw it into the pot and said, "Serve the people so they can eat." At that point, there was nothing bad left in the pot.

42 A man came from Baal-shalishah, bringing the man of God some bread from the early produce—twenty loaves of barley bread and fresh grain from his bag.[i] Elisha said, "Give it to the people so they can eat." 43 His servant said, "How can I feed one hundred men with this?"

Elisha said, "Give it to the people so they can eat! This is what the LORD says: 'Eat and there will be leftovers.'" 44 So the servant gave the food to them. They ate and had leftovers, in agreement with the LORD's word.

Naaman is healed

5 Naaman, a general for the king of Aram, was a great man and highly regarded by his master, because through him the LORD had given victory to Aram. This man was a mighty warrior, but he had a skin disease.[j] 2 Now Aramean raiding parties had gone out and captured a young girl from the land of Israel. She served Naaman's wife.

3 She said to her mistress, "I wish that my master could come before the prophet who lives in Samaria. He would cure him of his skin disease." 4 So Naaman went and told his master what the young girl from the land of Israel had said.

5 Then Aram's king said, "Go ahead. I will send a letter to Israel's king."

So Naaman left. He took along ten kikkars of silver, six thousand shekels of gold, and ten changes of clothing. 6 He brought the letter to Israel's king. It read, "Along with this letter I'm sending you my servant Naaman so you can cure him of his skin disease."

7 When the king of Israel read the letter, he ripped his clothes. He said, "What? Am I God to hand out death and life? But this king writes me, asking me to cure someone of his skin disease! You must realize that he wants to start a fight with me."

8 When Elisha the man of God heard that Israel's king had ripped his clothes, he sent word to the king: "Why did you rip your clothes? Let the man come to me. Then he'll know that there's a prophet in Israel."

9 Naaman arrived with his horses and chariots. He stopped at the door of Elisha's house. 10 Elisha sent out a messenger who said, "Go and wash seven times in the Jordan River. Then your skin will be restored and become clean."

11 But Naaman went away in anger. He said, "I thought for sure that he'd come out, stand and call on the name of the LORD his God, wave his hand over the bad spot, and cure the skin disease. 12 Aren't the rivers in Damascus, the Abana[k] and the Pharpar, better than all Israel's waters? Couldn't I wash in them and get clean?" So he turned away and proceeded to leave in anger.

13 Naaman's servants came up to him and spoke to him: "Our father, if the prophet had told you to do something difficult,

[h] Or *gasped*; Heb uncertain [i] Or *still on its stem* [j] Traditionally *leprosy*, a kind of scale skin disease [k] Or *Amana*

wouldn't you have done it? All he said to you was, 'Wash and become clean.'" 14 So Naaman went down and bathed in the Jordan seven times, just as the man of God had said. His skin was restored like that of a young boy, and he became clean.

15 He returned to the man of God with all his attendants. He came and stood before Elisha, saying, "Now I know for certain that there's no God anywhere on earth except in Israel. Please accept a gift from your servant."

16 But Elisha said, "I swear by the life of the LORD I serve that I won't accept anything."

Naaman urged Elisha to accept something, but he still refused. 17 Then Naaman said, "If not, then let me, your servant, have two mule loads of earth. Your servant will never again offer entirely burned offerings or sacrifices to any other gods except the LORD. 18 But may the LORD forgive your servant for this one thing: When my master comes into Rimmon's temple to bow down there and is leaning on my arm, I must also bow down in Rimmon's temple. When I bow down in Rimmon's temple, may the LORD forgive your servant for doing that."

19 Elisha said to him, "Go in peace."

But when Naaman had gone some distance from Elisha, 20 Gehazi (who was the servant of Elisha the man of God) thought, My master let this Aramean Naaman off the hook by not accepting the gift he brought! As surely as the LORD lives, I'll go after him and accept something from him. 21 So Gehazi pursued Naaman.

Naaman saw him running after him, so he got down off his chariot to meet him. He said, "Is everything okay?"

22 Gehazi answered, "Yes, but my master sent me to say, 'Two young men who are members of a group of prophets have just now come to me from the hills of Ephraim. Give them a kikkar of silver and two changes of clothing.'"

23 Naaman said, "By all means, take two kikkars!" He encouraged Gehazi to accept them. He tied two kikkars of silver up in two bags, along with two changes of clothes. Naaman gave them to two of his servants, and they carried them in front of Gehazi. 24 When Gehazi arrived at the elevated fortress,[l] he took the items from them and stored them in his house. Then he sent the servants away, and they left. 25 Gehazi then went and stood before his master.

Elisha said to Gehazi, "Where did you come from, Gehazi?"

"Your servant didn't go anywhere," Gehazi replied.

26 Elisha said to him, "Wasn't my heart going along with you[m] when the man got off his chariot to meet you? Is this the time to accept silver, clothes, olive trees, vineyards, sheep, cattle, or male and female servants? 27 Naaman's skin disease will now cling to you and to your descendants forever!" And Gehazi left Elisha's presence, flaky like snow with skin disease.

An ax head floats

6 The members of the group of prophets said to Elisha, "Look, the place where we now live under your authority is too small for us. 2 Let's go to the Jordan River and each get a log from there. Then we can make a place to live there."

Elisha said, "Do it!"

3 One of them said, "Please come with us, your servants."

Elisha said, "Okay, I'll go." 4 So he went with them. They came to the Jordan River and began cutting down trees. 5 One of them was cutting down a tree when his ax head fell into the water. He cried out, "Oh, no! Master, it was a borrowed ax!"

6 The man of God said, "Where did it fall?" He showed Elisha the place. Elisha then cut a piece of wood, threw it into the river there, and the ax head floated up. 7 "Lift it out," Elisha said. So the man then reached out and grabbed it.

Aramean attacks are stopped

8 Aram's king was fighting against Israel. He took counsel with his officers, saying "I'll camp at such-and-such a place."

9 The man of God sent word to Israel's king: "Beware of passing by this place be-

[l] Or *hillside*; Heb uncertain [m] LXX; MT lacks *along with you.*

cause the Arameans are going down there." 10Then Israel's king sent word to the place the man of God had mentioned to him. Time after time, Elisha warned the king, and the king stayed on the alert.

11Aram's king was extremely upset about this. He called his officers and said to them, "Tell me! Who among us is siding with Israel's king?"

12One of his officers said, "No one, Your Majesty! It's Elisha the Israelite prophet who tells Israel's king the words that you speak in the privacy of your bedroom."

13He said, "Go and find out where he is. Then I will send men to capture him."

They told him, "He is in Dothan." 14So the king sent horses and chariots there with a strong army. They came at night and surrounded the city.

15Elisha's servant got up early and went out. He saw an army with horses and chariots surrounding the city. His servant said to Elisha, "Oh, no! Master, what will we do?"

16"Don't be afraid," Elisha said, "because there are more of us than there are of them." 17Then Elisha prayed, "LORD, please open his eyes that he may see." Then the LORD opened the servant's eyes, and he saw that the mountain was full of horses and fiery chariots surrounding Elisha. 18The Arameans came toward him, so Elisha prayed to the LORD, "Strike this nation with blindness." And the LORD struck them blind, just as Elisha asked. 19Elisha said to them, "This isn't the right road or the right city. Follow me, and I'll lead you to the man you are looking for." But he took them to Samaria!

20When they arrived in Samaria, Elisha said, "LORD, open the eyes of these men so they can see." The LORD opened their eyes, and they saw that they were right in the middle of Samaria! 21When he saw them, Israel's king said to Elisha, "Should I kill them, my father? Should I?"

22He said, "No, don't kill them. Did you capture them with your own sword or bow? Do you have the right to kill them?[n] Put food and water in front of them so they can eat and drink and return to their master." 23So the king gave them a great feast, and they ate and drank. Then the king let them go, and they returned to their master. After that, Aramean raiding parties didn't come into Israel anymore.

Ben-hadad attacks Samaria

24Now it happened later that Aram's King Ben-hadad gathered all his forces and went up to attack Samaria. 25The siege lasted so long that there was a great famine in Samaria. A donkey's head sold for eighty shekels of silver and a quarter kab of doves' dung[o] for five shekels. 26Israel's king was passing by on the city wall when a woman appealed to him, "Help me, Your Majesty!"

27The king said, "No! May the LORD help you! Where can I find help for you? From the threshing floor or the winepress?" 28But then the king asked her, "What's troubling you?"

She answered, "A woman said to me, 'Give up your son so we can eat him today; we'll eat my son tomorrow.' 29So we cooked and ate my son. The next day I said to her, 'Hand over your son so we can eat him.' But she had hidden her son."

30When the king heard the woman's story, he ripped his clothes. And as he passed by along the wall, the people could see that he was wearing mourning clothes underneath. 31He said, "So may God do to me, and more, if the head of Elisha, Shaphat's son, remains on his shoulders today!"

32Elisha was sitting in his house, and the elders were sitting with him. The king sent a messenger on ahead, but before the man arrived, Elisha said to the elders, "Do you see that this murderer has sent someone to cut off my head? Watch for when the messenger comes, then close the door and hold it shut against him. The sound of his master's feet is right behind him, isn't it?"

33While Elisha was still speaking with them, the messenger[p] arrived and said, "Look, this disaster is the LORD's doing. Why should I trust the LORD any longer?"

7 Elisha said, "Hear the LORD's word! This is what the LORD says: At this time

[n]Heb uncertain [o]Or *wild onions* or *carob pods* [p]Or perhaps *the king*; cf 7:2

tomorrow a seah[q] of wheat flour will sell for a shekel at Samaria's gate, and two seahs of barley will sell for a shekel."

2 Then the officer, the one the king leaned on for support, spoke to the man of God: "Come on! Even if the LORD should make windows in the sky, how could that happen?"

Elisha said, "You will see it with your own eyes, but you won't eat from it."

The siege is broken

3 Now there were four men with skin disease[r] at the entrance to the city. They said to each other, "What are we doing sitting here until we die? 4 If we decide, 'Let's go into the city,' the famine is there, and we'll die in the city. But if we stay here, we'll die just the same. So let's go and surrender to the Aramean camp. If they let us live, we'll live. If they kill us, we'll die." 5 So they set out in the evening to the Aramean camp, and they came to the edge of the camp. But there was no one there because 6 the Lord had made the Aramean camp hear the sound of chariots, horses, and a strong army. They had said to each other, "Listen! Israel's king has hired the Hittite and Egyptian kings to come against us!" 7 So they had got up and fled in the evening, leaving their tents, horses, and donkeys. They left the camp exactly as it was and ran for their lives.

8 So these men with skin disease came to the edge of the camp. They entered a tent where they ate and drank. They carried off some silver, gold, and garments, and they hid them. Then they returned and went into another tent. They took more things from there, went away, and hid them. 9 But then they said to each other, "What we're doing isn't right. Today is a day of good news, but we're keeping quiet about it. If we wait until dawn, something bad will happen to us. Come on! Let's go and tell the palace." 10 So they went and called out to the gatekeepers, telling them, "We went to the Aramean camp, and listen to this: No one was there, not even the sound of anyone! The only things there were tied-up horses and donkeys, and the tents left just as they were." 11 The gatekeepers shouted out the news, and it was reported within the palace.

12 The king got up in the night. He said to his servants, "Let me tell you what the Arameans are doing to us. They know we are starving, so they've left the camp to hide in the fields. They are thinking, The Israelites will come out from the city, and then we'll capture them alive and invade the city."

13 But one of his servants answered, "Please let some men take five of the horses that are left, and let's send them out to see what happens. They are in the same situation as the large number of Israelites who are left here; they are no better off than the large number of Israelites who've already perished."[s] 14 So they chose two chariots with their horses.

The king sent them after the Aramean army, saying, "Go and see!" 15 So they went after the Arameans as far as the Jordan River. The road was filled the whole way with garments and equipment that the Arameans had thrown away in their rush. The messengers returned and reported this to the king.

16 Then the people went out and looted the Aramean camp. And so it happened that a seah of wheat flour did sell for a shekel, and two seahs of barley sold for a shekel, in agreement with the LORD's word. 17 But the king had put the officer whom he leaned on for support in charge of the city gate. The people trampled the officer at the gate, and he died. This was just what the man of God said when the king had come down to him. 18 Because when the man of God said to the king, "At this time tomorrow two seahs of barley will sell for a shekel at Samaria's gate, and one seah of wheat flour will sell for a shekel," 19 the officer had answered the man of God, "Come on! Even if the LORD should make windows in the sky, how could that happen?" Then Elisha had said, "You will see it with your own eyes, but you won't eat from it." 20 That's

[q] One seah is approximately seven and a half quarts. [r] Traditionally *leprosy*, a term used for several different skin diseases [s] Heb uncertain

exactly what happened to him. The people trampled him at the city gate, and he died.

The woman from Shunem

8 Elisha spoke to the woman whose son he had brought back to life: "You and your household must go away and live wherever you can, because the LORD has called for a famine. It is coming to the land and will last seven years."

2So the woman went and did what the man of God asked. She and her household moved away, living in Philistia seven years. 3When seven years had passed, the woman returned from Philistia. She went to appeal to the king for her house and her farmland. 4The king was speaking to Gehazi, the man of God's servant, asking him, "Tell me about all the great things Elisha has done." 5So Gehazi was telling the king how Elisha had brought the dead to life. At that very moment, the woman whose son he had brought back to life began to appeal to the king for her house and her farmland.

Gehazi said, "Your Majesty, this is the woman herself! And this is her son, the one Elisha brought to life!"

6The king questioned the woman, and she told him her story. Then the king appointed an official to help her, saying, "Return everything that belongs to her, as well as everything that the farmland has produced, starting from the day she left the country until right now."

Hazael becomes king

7Now Elisha had gone to Damascus when Aram's King Ben-hadad became sick. The king was told, "The man of God has come all this way."

8So the king said to Hazael, "Take a gift with you and go to meet the man of God. Question the LORD through him: 'Will I recover from this sickness?' "

9So Hazael went out to meet Elisha. He took along forty camel-loads of Damascus' finest goods as a gift. He came and stood before Elisha and said, "Your son Ben-hadad, the king of Aram, sent me to you to ask, 'Will I recover from this sickness?' "

10Elisha said to him, "Go and tell him, 'You will definitely recover,' but actually the LORD has shown me that he will die." 11Elisha stared straight at Hazael until he felt uneasy.[t] Then the man of God began to cry.

12Hazael said, "Master, why are you crying?"

"Because I know what violence you will do to the Israelites," Elisha said. "You will drive them from their forts with fire. You will kill their young men with the sword. You will smash their children and rip open their pregnant women."

13Hazael replied, "How could your servant, who is nothing but a dog, do such mighty things?"

Elisha said, "The LORD has shown me that you will be king over Aram." 14Then Hazael left Elisha and returned to his master.

"What did Elisha say to you?" Ben-hadad asked.

"He told me that you will certainly live," Hazael replied. 15But the next day he took a blanket, soaked it in water, and put it over Ben-hadad's face until he died. Hazael succeeded him as king.

Jehoram rules Judah

16In the fifth year of Israel's King Joram, Ahab's son Jehoram, the son of Judah's King Jehoshaphat, became king.[u] 17He was 32 years old when he became king, and he ruled for eight years in Jerusalem. 18He walked in the ways of Israel's kings, just as Ahab's dynasty had done, because he married Ahab's daughter. He did what was evil in the LORD's eyes. 19Nevertheless, because of his servant David, the LORD wasn't willing to destroy Judah. The LORD had promised to preserve a lamp for David and his sons forever. 20During Jehoram's rule Edom rebelled against Judah's power and appointed their own king. 21Jehoram[v] along with all his chariots crossed over to Zair. He got up at night to attack the Edomites who had surrounded him and his

[t]Heb uncertain [u]LXX, Syr; MT includes *Jehoshaphat had been Judah's king.* [v]Heb *Joram* (also in 8:23-24); the king's name is usually spelled in its long form *Jehoram* (cf 2 Chron 21:9).

chariot commanders,[w] but his army fled back home. 22 So Edom has been independent of Judah to this day. Libnah rebelled at the same time. 23 The rest of Jehoram's deeds and all that he accomplished, aren't they written in the official records of Judah's kings? 24 Jehoram died and was buried with his ancestors in David's City. His son Ahaziah succeeded him as king.

Ahaziah rules Judah

25 Ahaziah, the son of Judah's king Jehoram, became king in the twelfth year of Israel's King Joram,[x] Ahab's son. 26 Ahaziah was 22 years old when he became king, and he ruled for one year in Jerusalem. His mother's name was Athaliah; she was the granddaughter of Israel's King Omri. 27 He walked in the ways of Ahab's dynasty, doing what was evil in the LORD's eyes, just as Ahab's dynasty had done, because he had married into Ahab's family. 28 Ahaziah went with Joram, Ahab's son, to fight against Aram's King Hazael at Ramoth-gilead, where the Arameans wounded Joram. 29 King Joram returned to Jezreel to recover from the wounds the Arameans had given him at Ramah in his battle with Aram's King Hazael. Then Judah's King Ahaziah, the son of Jehoram, went down to visit Joram, Ahab's son, at Jezreel because he had been wounded.

Jehu rules Israel

9 The prophet Elisha called to a member of the group of prophets, "Get ready, take this jug of oil with you, and go to Ramoth-gilead. 2 When you arrive there, look for Jehu, Jehoshaphat's son and Nimshi's grandson. Go to him, then pull him away from his associates, taking him to a private room. 3 Take the jug of oil and pour it on his head. Then say, 'This is what the LORD has said: I anoint you king of Israel.' Then open the door, and run out of there without stopping."

4 So the young prophet went to Ramoth-gilead. 5 He came in, and the military commanders were sitting right there. He said, "Commander, I have a word for you."

"For which one of us?" Jehu asked.

The young prophet said, "For you, Commander."

6 So Jehu got up and went inside. The prophet then poured oil on his head and said to him, "This is what the LORD, Israel's God, says: I anoint you king over the LORD's people, over Israel. 7 You will strike down your master Ahab's family. In this way I will take revenge for the violence done by Jezebel to my servants the prophets and to all the LORD's servants. 8 Ahab's whole family will die. I will eliminate from Ahab everyone who urinates on a wall, whether slave or free, in Israel. 9 I will make Ahab's dynasty like the dynasty of Jeroboam, Nebat's son, and like the dynasty of Baasha, Ahijah's son. 10 And as for Jezebel: The dogs will devour her in the area of Jezreel. No one will bury her." Then the young prophet opened the door and ran.

11 Jehu went out to his master's officers. They said to him, "Is everything okay? Why did this fanatic come to you?"

Jehu said to them, "You know the man and the nonsense he talks."

12 "That's a lie!" they said. "Come on, tell us!"

Jehu replied, "This is what he said to me: 'This is what the LORD says: I anoint you king of Israel.'"

13 Then each man quickly took his cloak and put it beneath Jehu on the paved steps.[y] They blew a trumpet and said, "Jehu has become king!"

Jehu kills his enemies

14 Then Jehu, Jehoshaphat's son and Nimshi's grandson, plotted against Joram. Now Joram along with all of Israel had been guarding Ramoth-gilead against Aram's King Hazael, 15 but King Joram[z] had gone back to Jezreel to recover from wounds that the Arameans had given him when he fought Hazael. So Jehu said, "If this is the way you feel, then don't let anyone escape from the

[w] Heb uncertain [x] Heb *Jehoram* (also in 8:29); the king's name is variously spelled in either long *Jehoram* or short *Joram* form. [y] Heb uncertain [z] Heb *Jehoram* (also in 9:17, 21-24); the king's name is variously spelled in either long *Jehoram* or short *Joram* form.

city to talk about it in Jezreel." 16 Then Jehu
got on a chariot and drove to Jezreel because
Joram was resting there. Judah's King Ahaziah had also come to visit Joram.
17 The guard standing on the tower at
Jezreel saw a crowd of people coming with
Jehu. He said, "I see a crowd of people."
Joram said, "Take a chariot driver. Send
him out to meet them to ask, 'Do you come
in peace?'"
18 So the driver went to meet him and said,
"The king asks, 'Do you come in peace?'"
Jehu replied, "What do you care about
peace? Come around and follow me."
Meanwhile, the tower guard reported, "The
messenger met them, but he isn't returning."
19 The king sent a second driver. He came
to them and said, "The king asks, 'Do you
come in peace?'"
Jehu said, "What do you care about
peace? Come around and follow me."
20 The tower guard reported, "The messenger met them, but he isn't returning.
And the style of chariot driving is like Jehu,
Nimshi's son. Jehu drives like a madman."
21 Joram said, "Hitch up the chariot!" So
they hitched up his chariot. Then Israel's
King Joram and Judah's King Ahaziah—
each in his own chariot—went out to meet
Jehu. They happened to meet him at the
plot of ground that belonged to Naboth the
Jezreelite.
22 When Joram saw Jehu, he said, "Do
you come in peace, Jehu?"
He said, "How can there be peace as long
as the immoralities of your mother Jezebel
and her many acts of sorcery continue?"
23 Then Joram turned his chariot around
and fled. He shouted to Ahaziah, "It's a
trap, Ahaziah!"
24 Jehu took his bow and shot Joram in
the back. The arrow went through his heart,
and he fell down in his chariot. 25 Jehu said
to Bidkar his chariot officer, "Pick him up,
and throw him on the plot of ground belonging to Naboth the Jezreelite. Remember how
you and I were driving chariot teams behind
his father Ahab when the LORD spoke this
prophecy about him: 26 Yesterday I saw Naboth's blood and his sons' blood, declares
the LORD. I swear that I will pay you back
on this very plot of ground, declares the
LORD. Now pick him up, and throw him on
that plot of ground, in agreement with the
LORD's word."
27 Judah's King Ahaziah saw this and fled
on the road to Beth-haggan. Jehu chased
after him. "Do the same to him!" he commanded. They shot him[a] in his chariot on
the way up to Gur, near Ibleam. Ahaziah
fled to Megiddo and died there. 28 His servants carried him back in a chariot to Jerusalem. He was buried in his tomb with
his ancestors in David's City. 29 Ahaziah had
become Judah's king in the eleventh year of
Ahab's son Joram.
30 Jehu then went to Jezreel. When Jezebel heard of it, she put on her eye shadow
and arranged her hair. She looked down out
of the window. 31 When Jehu came through
the gate, she said, "Do you come in peace,
Zimri, you master murderer?"
32 Jehu looked up to the window and
said, "Who's on my side? Anyone?" Two
or three high officials looked down at him.
33 Then he said, "Throw her out!" So they
threw her out of the window. Some of her
blood splattered against the wall and on the
horses, and they trampled her. 34 Jehu then
went in to eat and drink. He said, "Deal
with this cursed woman and bury her. She
was, after all, a king's daughter." 35 They
went to bury her, but they couldn't find her
body. Only her skull was left, along with
her hands and feet. 36 They went back and
reported this to Jehu. He said, "This is the
LORD's word spoken through his servant
Elijah from Tishbe: Dogs will devour Jezebel's flesh in the area of Jezreel. 37 Jezebel's
corpse will be like dung spread out in a field
in that plot of land in Jezreel, so no one will
be able to say, This was Jezebel."

Jehu kills Ahab's family

10 Now Ahab had seventy sons in Samaria. So Jehu wrote letters and sent
them to Samaria, to the senior officers of the
city,[b] the elders, and the guardians of Ahab's

[a]LXX, Vulg; MT lacks *They shot him.* [b]Vulg, LXX; MT *Jezreel*

sons.[c] [2]The letters said: "Your master's sons are in your possession, along with horses and chariots, a fortified city, and weapons. Now when this letter reaches you, [3]look for the best and most capable of your master's sons. Place him on his father's throne. Then fight for your master's family."

[4]But they were frozen with fear. They said, "Not even two kings could resist him! How can we?" [5]So the palace administrator, the mayor, the elders, and the guardians sent a letter back to Jehu that read, "We are your servants. We will do whatever you tell us. We won't make anyone king. Do whatever seems right to you."

[6]Jehu wrote them a second letter: "If you are loyal to me and ready to obey me, take the heads of your master's sons and bring them to me at Jezreel at this time tomorrow."

Now the king's seventy sons were with the city leaders who were raising them. [7]So when the letter came to them, they took the king's sons and slaughtered all seventy of them. They placed their heads in baskets and sent them to Jehu at Jezreel.

[8]A messenger came and told Jehu, "They have brought the heads of the king's sons."

He responded, "Pile them in two stacks at the entrance of the gate where they will stay until morning." [9]In the morning he went out and stood there to address all the people. "You are innocent. I'm the one who plotted against my master and killed him, but who killed all these people? [10]Know this: Nothing that the LORD has said against Ahab's dynasty will fail to come true. The LORD has done what he said he would do, speaking through his servant Elijah." [11]Then Jehu struck down all those belonging to Ahab's family who were left in Jezreel, so that not one of his leaders, close acquaintances, or priests remained.

[12]Next Jehu set out for Samaria. Beth-eked of the Shepherds was on his way. [13]There Jehu met up with the brothers of Judah's King Ahaziah. "Who are you?" he asked.

"We're Ahaziah's relatives," they replied. "We've come down for a visit with the king's sons and the queen mother's sons."

[14]Jehu then commanded, "Take them alive!" His soldiers took them alive, then slaughtered them at the well of Beth-eked. There were forty-two of them, but not one was left.

Jehu kills Baal worshippers

[15]Jehu departed from there and encountered Rechab's son Jehonadab. Jehu greeted him, and asked, "Are you as committed to me as I am to you?"

Jehonadab responded, "Yes, I am."

"If so," said Jehu, "then give me your hand." So Jehonadab put out his hand, and Jehu pulled him up into the chariot.

[16]Jehu said, "Come with me and see my zeal for the LORD." So Jehu had Jehonadab ride with him in his chariot. [17]When Jehu arrived in Samaria, he killed all those belonging to Ahab who were left in Samaria until they were completely wiped out, in agreement with the LORD's word that was spoken to Elijah.

[18]Then Jehu gathered all the people, saying to them, "Ahab served Baal a little. Jehu will serve him a great deal! [19]So invite all of Baal's prophets, all his worshippers, and all his priests to come to me. Don't leave anyone out, because I have a great sacrifice planned for Baal. Anyone who doesn't show up won't survive." But Jehu was lying so that he could wipe out Baal's worshippers. [20]Jehu called for a holy assembly for Baal, and it was done. [21]Jehu then sent word throughout Israel. All Baal's worshippers came. No one stayed away. They entered Baal's temple until it was packed from one end to the other. [22]Then Jehu said to the person in charge of the vestments, "Bring out the special clothes for all Baal's worshippers." So he brought out robes for them. [23]Then Jehu and Jehonadab, Rechab's son, entered Baal's temple. They said to Baal's worshippers, "Make sure there are no worshippers of the LORD here with you. There should be only Baal worshippers." [24]Then they went in to offer sacrifices and entirely burned offerings. But Jehu had stationed eighty soldiers outside and told them, "I'm

[c] LXX; MT lacks *sons*.

handing these people over to you. Whoever
lets even one of them escape will pay for it
with his life." 25 So when Jehu finished offering the entirely burned offering, he said to
the guards and the officers, "Go in and kill
everyone! Don't let anyone escape!" They
killed the Baal worshippers without mercy.
The guards and the officers then disposed
of the bodies and entered the inner part
of Baal's temple. 26 They brought the sacred
pillar[d] out of Baal's temple and burned it.
27 They tore down Baal's sacred pillar and destroyed Baal's temple, turning it into a public restroom, which is what it still is today.

28 This is how Jehu eliminated Baal from Israel. 29 However, Jehu didn't deviate from the
sins that Jeroboam, Nebat's son, had caused
Israel to commit—specifically, the gold calves
that were in Bethel and Dan.

Jehu rules Israel

30 The LORD said to Jehu: Because you've
done well by doing what is right in my eyes,
treating Ahab's family as I wished, your descendants will sit on Israel's throne for four
generations. 31 But Jehu wasn't careful to
keep the LORD God of Israel's Instruction
with all his heart. He didn't deviate from
the sins that Jeroboam had caused Israel to
commit.

32 In those days the LORD began to reduce Israel's size. Hazael struck them down
in every region of Israel: 33 from the Jordan
River eastward, throughout the land of
Gilead (Gad, Reuben, and Manasseh), and
from Aroer by the Arnon Valley (that is, Gilead) and Bashan.

34 The rest of Jehu's deeds, all that he accomplished, and all his powerful acts, aren't
they written in the official records of Israel's
kings? 35 Jehu lay down with his ancestors.
He was buried in Samaria. His son Jehoahaz
succeeded him as king. 36 Jehu had ruled over
Israel for twenty-eight years in Samaria.

Queen Athaliah rules Judah

11 When Athaliah, Ahaziah's mother,
learned of her son's death, she immediately destroyed the entire royal family. 2 But
Jehosheba, King Jehoram's[e] daughter and
Ahaziah's sister, secretly took Ahaziah's son
Jehoash[f] from the rest of the royal children
who were about to be murdered and hid[g]
him in a bedroom along with his nurse. In
this way Jehoash was hidden from Athaliah
and wasn't murdered. 3 He remained hidden
with his nurse in the LORD's temple for six
years while Athaliah ruled the country.

4 But in the seventh year Jehoiada sent
for the commanders of the Carites and of
the guards and had them come to him at
the LORD's temple. He made a covenant
with them, and made them swear a solemn pledge in the LORD's temple. Then
he showed them the king's son. 5 He commanded them, "This is what you must do:
A third of you coming on sabbath duty will
guard the palace, 6 a second third will be at
the Sur Gate, and the final third will be at
the gate behind the guards. You will take
turns guarding the temple.[h] 7 You who are
in the first two groups that usually go off
duty on the Sabbath should also guard the
LORD's temple to protect the king. 8 Surround the king completely, each of you with
your weapons drawn. Whoever comes near
your ranks must be killed. Stay near the
king wherever he goes."

9 The unit commanders did everything
that Jehoiada the priest ordered. They each
took charge of those men reporting for
duty on the Sabbath as well as those going
off duty on the Sabbath. They came to the
priest Jehoiada. 10 Then the priest gave
the unit commanders King David's spears
and shields, which were kept in the LORD's
temple. 11 The guards, each with their weapons drawn, then took up positions near the
temple and the altar, stretching from the
south side of the temple to the north side to
protect the king. Everyone was holding his
weapons, surrounding the king. 12 Jehoiada
then brought out the king's son, crowned
him, gave him the royal law,[i] and made him
king and anointed him, as everyone applauded and cried out, "Long live the king!"

[d] LXX, Syr, Vulg; MT *pillars* [e] Heb *Joram*; the king's name is usually spelled in its long form *Jehoram* (cf 2 Chron 22:11). [f] Heb *Joash*; the king's name is variously spelled in either long *Jehoash* or short *Joash* forms. The latter is the form used in 2 Chron. [g] See 2 Chron 22:11; Heb lacks *hid*. [h] Heb uncertain [i] Heb lacks *royal*.

13When Athaliah heard the noise made by the guard and the people, she went to the people at the LORD's temple 14and saw the king standing by the royal pillar, as was the custom, with the commanders and trumpeters beside the king. All the people of the land were rejoicing and blowing trumpets. Athaliah ripped her clothes and screamed, "Treason! Treason!"

15Then the priest Jehoiada ordered the unit commanders who were in charge of the army: "Take her out under guard,"[j] he told them, "and kill anyone who follows her." This was because the priest had said, "She must not be executed in the LORD's temple." 16They arrested her when she reached the entrance of the Horse Gate at the royal palace. She was executed there.

17Jehoiada then made a covenant between the LORD, the king, and the people, that the people would belong to the LORD. The king and the people also made a covenant. 18Then all the people of the land went to Baal's temple and tore it down, smashing its altars and images into pieces. They executed Mattan, Baal's priest, in front of the altars. The priest Jehoiada posted guards at the LORD's temple. 19Then he took the unit commanders, the Carites, the guards, and all the people of the land, and they led the king down from the LORD's temple, processing through the Guards' Gate to the palace, where the king sat upon the royal throne. 20All the people of the land rejoiced, and the city was at peace now that Athaliah had been executed at the palace.

Jehoash rules Judah

21[k]Jehoash was 7 years old when he

12 became king.[l]He[l] became king in Jehu's seventh year, and he ruled for forty years in Jerusalem. His mother's name was Zibiah; she was from Beer-sheba.2Jehoash always did what was right in the LORD's eyes, because the priest Jehoiada was his teacher. 3However, the shrines were not removed. People kept sacrificing and burning incense at them. 4Jehoash said to the priests, "Collect all the currently available money relating to holy things that is brought to the temple—some is money people pay to redeem persons according to their assessed value. Collect all the money brought to the LORD's temple that people offer voluntarily.[m] 5The priests should take the money from their donors and use it to repair the temple wherever such a need for repair is discovered."

6But by the twenty-third year of King Jehoash, the priests still hadn't repaired the temple. 7So King Jehoash summoned Jehoiada the priest and the other priests together. "Why haven't you repaired the temple?" he asked them. "Stop taking money from your donors; instead, give it directly for temple repairs." 8The priests agreed that they wouldn't take any more money from the people nor be responsible for temple repairs. 9Then the priest Jehoiada took a box, made a hole in its lid, and placed it beside the altar, to the right as one enters the LORD's temple. The priests who stood watch at the door put all the money brought to the LORD's temple in the box. 10As soon as they saw that a large amount of money was in the box, the royal scribe and the high priest would come, count the money that was in the temple, and put it in a bag. 11They would then hand over the money that had been counted[n] to those who supervised the work on the temple. These supervisors then paid money to those who worked on the LORD's temple: carpenters, builders, 12masons, and stonecutters. The money was used to purchase wood and quarried stone to repair the LORD's temple and for every other cost involved in repairing it. 13But the money that was brought to the LORD's temple was not used to make silver basins, wick trimmers, sprinkling bowls, trumpets, or any gold or silver object for the LORD's temple. 14Instead, it was given directly to those who did the repair work; they used it to repair the LORD's temple. 15There was no need to check on those who received the money and paid the workers, because they acted honestly. 16Now as for the money for compen-

[j]Heb uncertain [k]12:1 in Heb [l]12:2 in Heb [m]Heb uncertain [n]Heb uncertain

sation and purification offerings, it wasn't brought to the LORD's temple. It belonged to the priests.

17About this same time, Aram's King Hazael came up, attacked Gath, and captured it. Next Hazael decided to march against Jerusalem. 18Judah's King Jehoash took all the holy objects that had been dedicated by his ancestors—Judah's kings Jehoshaphat, Jehoram, and Ahaziah—along with the holy objects he himself had dedicated, as well as all the gold in the treasure rooms of the LORD's temple and the palace, and he sent them to Aram's King Hazael. Hazael then pulled back from Jerusalem.

19The rest of Jehoash's[o] deeds and all that he accomplished, aren't they written in the official records of Judah's kings? 20Jehoash's officials plotted a conspiracy and killed him at Beth-millo on the road that goes down to Silla. 21It was Jozacar son of Shimeath and Jehozabad son of Shomer, his officials, who struck him so that he died. He was buried with his ancestors in David's City. His son Amaziah succeeded him as king.

Jehoahaz rules Israel

13 Jehoahaz, Jehu's son, became king of Israel in Samaria in the twenty-third year of Judah's King Jehoash,[p] who was Ahaziah's son. He ruled for seventeen years. 2He did what was evil in the LORD's eyes. He walked in the sins that Jeroboam, Nebat's son, had caused Israel to commit. He didn't deviate from them. 3So the LORD was angry at Israel. Time after time God handed them over to Aram's king Hazael, and to Hazael's son Ben-hadad.

4But Jehoahaz sought the LORD's presence, and the LORD listened to him because he saw how badly Aram's king was oppressing Israel. 5The LORD sent Israel a savior, and they escaped from Aram's power. Then the Israelites lived peacefully at home, just as they had in the past. 6But they didn't deviate from the sins that Jeroboam's dynasty had caused Israel to commit; they walked in them! Moreover, a sacred pole[q] stood in Samaria. 7No, nothing was left of Jehoahaz's army except fifty chariot riders, ten chariots, and ten thousand foot soldiers, because Aram's king had decimated them, trampling them as if they were dirt. 8The rest of Jehoahaz's deeds, all that he accomplished, and all his powerful acts, aren't they written in the official records of Israel's kings? 9Jehoahaz lay down with this ancestors. He was buried in Samaria. His son Joash succeeded him as king.

Joash rules Israel

10Joash,[r] Jehoahaz's son, became king of Israel in Samaria in the thirty-seventh year of Judah's King Jehoash. He ruled for sixteen years. 11He did what was evil in the LORD's eyes. He didn't deviate from all the sins that Jeroboam, Nebat's son, had caused Israel to commit, but he walked in them! 12The rest of Joash's deeds, all that he accomplished, and his powerful acts—how he fought against Judah's King Amaziah—aren't they written in the official records of Israel's kings? 13Joash lay down with his ancestors, and Jeroboam followed him on the throne. Joash was buried in Samaria with the kings of Israel.

Elisha's last days

14Now Elisha became sick with the illness that would kill him. So Israel's King Joash went down to see him. Joash cried over Elisha, saying, "Oh, my father, my father! Israel's chariots and its riders!"

15Elisha told Joash, "Get a bow and some arrows." So he brought Elisha a bow and some arrows. 16Elisha then said to Israel's king, "Put your hand on the bow." So Joash put his hand on the bow. Elisha then put his hands over the king's hands 17and said, "Open the window to the east." The king did so. "Now shoot!" Elisha told him.

[o]Heb *Joash* (also in 13:20); the king's name is variously spelled in either long *Jehoash* or short *Joash* form. The latter is the form used in 2 Chron. [p]Heb *Joash* (also in 13:10); the king's name is variously spelled in either long *Jehoash* or short *Joash* form. The latter is the form used in 2 Chron. [q]Heb *asherah*, perhaps an object devoted to the goddess Asherah [r]Heb *Jehoash* (also in 13:25); the king's name is variously spelled in either long *Jehoash* or short *Joash* form. The latter is the form used in 2 Chron.

Joash shot, then Elisha announced, "That's the LORD's rescue arrow! The rescue arrow against the Arameans! You will finish the Arameans off at Aphek." [18]Then Elisha said, "Take the arrows!" so Joash took them. Elisha then said to Israel's king, "Hit the ground with them!" Joash hit the ground three times and stopped. [19]The man of God became angry with him. He said, "If only you had struck five or six times, you would have finished the Arameans off. As it is, you will defeat them only three times."

[20]So Elisha died, and he was buried.

Sometimes Moabite raiding parties used to come into the land each spring. [21]Now it happened once that while a man was being buried, the people at the funeral suddenly saw a raiding party. They threw the body into Elisha's tomb and ran off. When the body touched Elisha's bones, the man came to life and stood up on his feet!

[22]Aram's King Hazael had oppressed Israel throughout Jehoahaz's rule. [23]But the LORD was gracious to Israel and had compassion on them, turning back to them because of his covenant with Abraham, Isaac, and Jacob; he didn't want to destroy them or throw them out of his presence until now. [24]Aram's King Hazael died. His son Ben-hadad succeeded him as king. [25]Then Jehoahaz's son Joash recaptured from Hazael's son Ben-hadad those cities that Hazael had won in battle from Joash's father Jehoahaz. Joash attacked Ben-hadad three times and took back these Israelite cities.

Amaziah rules Judah

14 Amaziah, the son of Judah's King Jehoash,[s] became king in the second year of Israel's King Joash, who was Jehoahaz's son. [2]Amaziah was 25 years old when he became king, and he ruled for twenty-nine years in Jerusalem. His mother's name was Jehoaddin; she was from Jerusalem. [3]He did what was right in the LORD's eyes, but not as well as his ancestor King David. He did everything his father Jehoash did. [4]However, the shrines weren't removed. People kept sacrificing and burning incense at them. [5]Once he had secured control over his kingdom, he executed the officials who had assassinated his father the king. [6]However, he didn't kill the children of the murderers, because of what is written in the Instruction scroll from Moses, where the LORD commanded, *Parents shouldn't be executed because of what their children have done; neither should children be executed because of what their parents have done. Each person should be executed for their own guilty acts.*[t]

[7]Next Amaziah struck down ten thousand Edomites in the Salt Valley and captured Sela in battle. He renamed it Joktheel, which is what it is still called today. [8]Then Amaziah sent messengers to Israel's King Joash[u] son of Jehoahaz son of Israel's King Jehu, saying, "Come on! Let's go head-to-head."

[9]But Israel's King Joash responded to Judah's King Amaziah, "Once upon a time, a thistle in Lebanon sent a message to a cedar, 'Give your daughter to my son as a wife.' But then a wild beast in Lebanon came along and trampled the thistle. [10]You have definitely defeated Edom and have now become conceited. Enjoy the honor, but stay home. Why invite disaster when both you and Judah will fall?"

[11]But Amaziah wouldn't listen, so Israel's King Joash moved against him, and he and Judah's King Amaziah went head-to-head in battle at Beth-shemesh in Judah. [12]Judah was defeated by Israel, and everyone ran home. [13]At Beth-shemesh, Israel's King Joash captured Judah's King Amaziah, Jehoash's son and Ahaziah's grandson. Joash then marched to Jerusalem and broke down six hundred feet of the Jerusalem wall from the Ephraim Gate to the Corner Gate. [14]Joash took all the gold and silver, and all the objects he could find in the LORD's temple and the treasuries of the palace, along with some hostages and returned to Samaria. [15]The rest of Joash's deeds and his powerful acts—how he fought against Ju-

[s]Heb *Joash* (also in 14:3, 17, 23); the king's name is variously spelled in either long *Jehoash* or short *Joash* form. The latter is the form used in 2 Chron. [t]Deut 24:16 [u]Heb *Jehoash* (also in 14:9, 11, 13, 15, 16-17); the king's name is variously spelled in either long *Jehoash* or short *Joash* form. The latter is the form used in 2 Chron.

dah's King Amaziah—aren't they written in the official records of Israel's kings? 16 Joash lay down with his ancestors. He was buried in Samaria with the kings of Israel. His son Jeroboam succeeded him as king.

17 Judah's King Amaziah, Jehoash's son, lived fifteen years after the death of Israel's King Joash, Jehoahaz's son. 18 The rest of Amaziah's deeds, aren't they written in the official records of Judah's kings? 19 Some people in Jerusalem plotted against him. When Amaziah fled to Lachish, they sent men after him to Lachish, and they murdered him there. 20 They carried him back on horses, and he was buried in Jerusalem with his ancestors in David's City.

21 Then all the people of Judah took Azariah and made him king after his father Amaziah. He was 16 years old. 22 He rebuilt Elath, restoring it to Judah after King Amaziah had lain down with his ancestors.

Jeroboam II rules Israel

23 Jeroboam, the son of Israel's King Joash, became king in Samaria in the fifteenth year of Judah's King Amaziah, Jehoash's son. He ruled for forty-one years. 24 He did what was evil in the LORD's eyes. He didn't deviate from all the sins that Jeroboam, Nebat's son, had caused Israel to commit. 25 He reestablished Israel's border from Lebo-hamath to the Dead Sea. This was in agreement with the word that the LORD, the God of Israel, spoke through his servant the prophet Jonah, Amittai's son, who was from Gath-hepher. 26 The LORD saw how brutally Israel suffered, whether slave or free, with no one to help Israel. 27 But the LORD hadn't said he would erase Israel's name from under heaven, so he saved them through Jeroboam, Joash's son. 28 The rest of Jeroboam's deeds, all that he accomplished, and his powerful acts—how he fought and how he restored Damascus and Hamath to Judah in Israel[v]—aren't they written in the official records of Israel's kings? 29 Jeroboam lay down with his ancestors the kings of Israel. His son Zechariah succeeded him as king.

Azariah rules Judah

15 Azariah, Amaziah's son, became king of Judah in the twenty-seventh year of Israel's King Jeroboam. 2 He was 16 years old when he became king, and he ruled for fifty-two years in Jerusalem. His mother's name was Jecoliah; she was from Jerusalem. 3 He did what was right in the LORD's eyes, just as his father Amaziah had done. 4 However, the shrines weren't removed. People kept sacrificing and burning incense at them. 5 Now the LORD afflicted the king with a skin disease that he had until his dying day, so he lived in a separate house.[w] The king's son Jotham supervised the palace administration and governed the people of the land. 6 The rest of Azariah's deeds and all he accomplished, aren't they written in the official records of Judah's kings? 7 Azariah died and was buried with his ancestors in David's City. His son Jotham succeeded him as king.

Zechariah rules Israel

8 Zechariah, Jeroboam's son, became king of Israel in Samaria in the thirty-eighth year of Judah's King Azariah. He ruled for six months. 9 He did what was evil in the LORD's eyes, just as his ancestors had done. He didn't deviate from the sins that Jeroboam, Nebat's son, had caused Israel to commit. 10 Shallum, Jabesh's son, plotted against Zechariah. He struck him down in public,[x] murdering him. Shallum then succeeded him as king. 11 The rest of Zechariah's deeds are written in the official records of Israel's kings. 12 This was exactly what the LORD spoke to Jehu: Your descendants will sit on Israel's throne for four generations. And that's exactly what happened.

Shallum rules Israel

13 Shallum, Jabesh's son, became king in the thirty-ninth year of Judah's King Uzziah. He ruled for one month in Samaria. 14 Menahem, Gadi's son, went up from Tirzah and came to Samaria. He struck down Jabesh's son Shallum in Samaria, murdering him.

[v]Heb uncertain [w]Heb uncertain [x]LXX *in Keblaam*; Heb uncertain

Menahem then succeeded him as king. [15]The rest of Shallum's deeds and the conspiracy he plotted are written in the official records of Israel's kings.

Menahem rules Israel

[16]Menahem then moved from Tirzah and attacked Tiphsah, all its citizens, and its neighboring areas. Because they wouldn't surrender, he attacked and ripped open all its pregnant women. [17]Menahem, Gadi's son, became king of Israel in the thirty-ninth year of Judah's King Azariah. He ruled for ten years in Samaria. [18]He did what was evil in the LORD's eyes. Throughout his life, he didn't deviate from the sins that Jeroboam, Nebat's son, had caused Israel to commit. [19]When Assyria's King Tiglath-pileser[y] marched against the land, Menahem gave Tiglath-pileser one thousand silver kikkars in order to become his ally and to strengthen his hold on the kingdom. [20]Menahem taxed Israel for this money. All the wealthy people had to give fifty silver shekels each to Assyria's king. So Assyria's king went home and didn't stay there in the land. [21]The rest of Menahem's deeds and all that he accomplished, aren't they written in the official records of Israel's kings? [22]Menahem lay down with his ancestors. His son Pekahiah succeeded him as king.

Pekahiah rules Israel

[23]Pekahiah, Menahem's son, became king of Israel in the fiftieth year of Judah's King Azariah. He ruled for two years in Samaria. [24]He did what was evil in the LORD's eyes. He didn't deviate from the sins that Jeroboam, Nebat's son, had caused Israel to commit. [25]Pekah, Remaliah's son and Pekahiah's officer, plotted against him. Pekah struck Pekahiah in Samaria at the palace fortress, along with Argob and Arieh.[z] Pekah had fifty Gileadites with him. He murdered Pekahiah and succeeded him as king. [26]The rest of Pekahiah's deeds and all that he accomplished are written in the official records of Israel's kings.

Pekah rules Israel

[27]Pekah, Remaliah's son, became king of Israel in the fifty-second year of Judah's King Azariah. Pekah ruled for twenty years in Samaria. [28]He did what was evil in the LORD's eyes. He didn't deviate from the sins that Jeroboam, Nebat's son, had caused Israel to commit. [29]In the days of Israel's King Pekah, Assyria's King Tiglath-pileser came and captured Ijon, Abel-beth-maacah, Janoah, Kedesh, and Hazor. He also captured Gilead, Galilee, and all the land of Naphtali. He sent the people into exile to Assyria. [30]Then Hoshea, Elah's son, plotted against Pekah, Remaliah's son. He struck Pekah down, murdering him. Hoshea became king after Pekah in the twentieth year of Uzziah's son Jotham. [31]The rest of Pekah's kingship and all that he accomplished are written in the official records of Israel's kings.

Jotham rules Judah

[32]Jotham, Uzziah's son, became king of Judah in the second year of Israel's King Pekah, Remaliah's son. [33]Jotham was 25 years old when he became king, and he ruled for sixteen years in Jerusalem. His mother's name was Jerusha; she was Zadok's daughter. [34]Jotham did what was right in the LORD's eyes, just as his father Uzziah had done. [35]However, he didn't remove the shrines. The people continued to sacrifice and burn incense at them. Jotham rebuilt the Upper Gate of the LORD's temple. [36]The rest of Jotham's deeds, aren't they written in the official records of Judah's kings? [37]It was in those days that the LORD began to send Aram's King Rezin and Pekah, Remaliah's son, against Judah. [38]Jotham died and was buried with his ancestors in David's City.[a] His son Ahaz succeeded him as king.

Ahaz rules Judah

16 Ahaz, Jotham's son, became king of Judah in the seventeenth year of Pekah, Remaliah's son. [2]Ahaz was 20 years old when he became king, and he ruled for

[y]Heb *Pul* [z]Heb uncertain [a]Heb adds *his ancestor.*

sixteen years in Jerusalem. He didn't do what was right in the LORD's eyes, unlike his ancestor David. [3]Instead, he walked in the ways of Israel's kings. He even burned his own son alive, imitating the detestable practices of the nations that the LORD had driven out before the Israelites. [4]He also sacrificed and burned incense at the shrines on every hill and beneath every shady tree. [5]Then Aram's King Rezin and Israel's King Pekah, Remaliah's son, came up to Jerusalem to fight. They surrounded Ahaz, but they weren't able to defeat him. [6]At that time Aram's King Rezin recovered Elath for the Arameans, driving the Judeans out of Elath. The Edomites[b] came to Elath and settled there, and that's still the case now.

[7]Ahaz sent messengers to Assyria's King Tiglath-pileser, saying, "I'm your servant and your son. Come up and save me from the power of the kings of Aram and Israel. Both of them are attacking me!" [8]And Ahaz took the silver and the gold that was in the LORD's temple and in the palace treasuries, and sent a gift to Assyria's king. [9]The Assyrian king heard the request and marched against Damascus. He captured it and sent its citizens into exile to Kir. He also killed Rezin.

[10]Then King Ahaz went to Damascus to meet up with Assyria's King Tiglath-pileser. King Ahaz noticed the altar that was in Damascus, and he sent the altar's plan and details for its construction to the priest Uriah. [11]Uriah built the altar, following the plans that King Ahaz had sent from Damascus; he had it finished before King Ahaz returned from Damascus.

[12]When the king arrived from Damascus, he inspected the altar. He came close to it, then went up on it, [13]burning his entirely burned offering and grain offering, pouring out his drink offering, and sprinkling the blood of his well-being sacrifices on the altar. [14]As for the bronze altar that used to stand before the LORD, Ahaz moved it away from the front of the temple where it had stood between the main altar and the LORD's temple. He put it on the north side of the new altar. [15]Then King Ahaz ordered the priest Uriah, saying, "Burn the following sacrifices on the main altar:

in the morning, the entirely burned offering;
in the evening, the grain offering;
the king's entirely burned offering and his grain offering;
the entirely burned offering for all the people of the land, their grain offering, and their drink offerings.

"Sprinkle all the blood of the entirely burned offerings and all the blood of the sacrifices on it. I will use the bronze altar for seeking guidance."[c] [16]Uriah the priest did everything that King Ahaz commanded. [17]King Ahaz cut off the side panels from the stands and removed the basins from them. He took the Sea down from the bronze bulls that were under it and put it on a stone pavement. [18]He also took away the sabbath canopy that had been built in the temple. He removed the royal entrance outside the LORD's temple. This was done because of the Assyrian king.

[19]The rest of Ahaz's deeds, aren't they written in the official records of Judah's kings? [20]Ahaz died and was buried with his ancestors in David's City. His son Hezekiah succeeded him as king.

Hoshea rules Israel

17 Hoshea, Elah's son, became king in Samaria in the twelfth year of Judah's king Ahaz. He ruled over Israel for nine years. [2]He did what was evil in the LORD's eyes, but he wasn't as bad as the Israelite kings who preceded him. [3]Assyria's King Shalmaneser marched against Hoshea, and Hoshea became Shalmaneser's servant, paying him tribute. [4]But the Assyrian king discovered that Hoshea was a traitor, because Hoshea sent messengers to Egypt's King So. Hoshea stopped paying tribute to the Assyrian king as he had in previous years, so the Assyrian king arrested him and put him in prison. [5]Then the Assyrian king invaded the whole country. He marched against Samaria and attacked it

[b]Qere; Kethib *Arameans* [c]Heb uncertain

for three years. 6In Hoshea's ninth year, the
Assyrian king captured Samaria. He sent Israel into exile to Assyria, resettling them in
Halah, in Gozan on the Habor River, and in
the cities of the Medes.

The northern kingdom falls

7All this happened because the Israelites
sinned against the LORD their God, who
brought them up from the land of Egypt,
out from under the power of Pharaoh,
Egypt's king. They worshipped other gods.
8They followed the practices of the nations
that the LORD had removed before the Israelites, as well as the practices that the
Israelite kings had done.[d] 9The Israelites
secretly did things against the LORD their
God that weren't right. They built shrines
in all their towns, from watchtowers to fortified cities. 10They set up sacred pillars and
sacred poles[e] on every high hill and beneath
every green tree. 11At every shrine they
burned incense, just as the nations did that
the LORD sent into exile before them. They
did evil things that made the LORD angry.
12They worshipped images about which the
LORD had said, Don't do such things! 13The
LORD warned Israel and Judah through all
the prophets and seers, telling them, Turn
from your evil ways. Keep my commandments and my regulations in agreement
with the entire Instruction that I commanded your ancestors and sent through
my servants the prophets.
14But they wouldn't listen. They were
stubborn like their ancestors who didn't
trust the LORD their God. 15They rejected
his regulations and the covenant he had
made with their ancestors, along with
the warnings he had given them. They
followed worthless images so that they
too became worthless. And they imitated
the neighboring nations that the LORD
had forbidden them to imitate. 16They
deserted all the commandments of the
LORD their God. They made themselves
two metal idols cast in the shape of calves
and made a sacred pole.[f] They bowed down
to all the heavenly bodies. They served
Baal. 17They burned their sons and daughters alive. They practiced divination and
sought omens. They gave themselves over
to doing what was evil in the LORD's eyes
and made him angry.
18So the LORD was very angry at Israel.
He removed them from his presence. Only
the tribe of Judah was spared. 19But Judah
didn't keep the commands of the LORD
their God either. They followed the practices of Israel. 20So the LORD rejected all
of Israel's descendants. He punished them,
and he handed them over to enemies who
plundered them until he finally threw them
out of his sight.
21When Israel broke away[g] from David's
dynasty, they made Nebat's son Jeroboam
the king. Jeroboam drove Israel away from
the LORD. He caused them to commit great
sin. 22And the Israelites continued walking in all the sins that Jeroboam did. They
didn't deviate from them, 23and the LORD
finally removed Israel from his presence. That
was exactly what he had warned through all
his servants the prophets. So Israel was exiled from its land to Assyria. And that's still
how it is today.

New settlers in Samaria

24The Assyrian king brought people
from Babylon, Cuth, Avva, Hamath, and
Sepharvaim, resettling them in the cities
of Samaria in place of the Israelites. These
people took control of Samaria and settled
in its cities. 25But when they began to live
there, they didn't worship the LORD, so
the LORD sent lions against them, and the
lions began to kill them. 26Assyria's king
was told about this: "The nations you sent
into exile and resettled in the cities of Samaria don't know the religious practices of
the local god. He's sent lions against them,
and the lions are killing them because none
of them know the religious practices of the
local god."
27So Assyria's king commanded, "Return one of the priests that you exiled from

[d]Heb uncertain [e]Heb *asherim,* perhaps objects devoted to the goddess Asherah [f]Heb *asherah,* perhaps an object devoted to the goddess Asherah [g]Or *When he* (God) *tore Israel away*

there. He[h] should go back and live there. He should teach them the religious practices of the local god." 28 So one of the priests who had been exiled from Samaria went back. He lived in Bethel and taught the people how to worship the LORD.

29 But each nationality still made its own gods. They set them up in the houses that the people of Samaria had made at the shrines. Each nationality did this in whichever cities they lived. 30 The Babylonian people made the god Succoth-benoth, the Cuthean people made Nergal, and the people from Hamath made Ashima. 31 The Avvites made Nibhaz and Tartak. The Sepharvites burned their children alive as a sacrifice to Adrammelech and Anammelech, the Sepharvite gods. 32 They also worshipped the LORD, but they appointed priests for the shrines from their whole population. These priests worked in the houses at the shrines. 33 So they worshipped the LORD, but they also served their own gods according to the religious practices of the nations from which they had been exiled.

34 They are still following their former religious practices to this very day. They don't really worship the LORD. Nor do they follow the regulations, the case laws, the Instruction, or the commandment that the LORD commanded the children of Jacob, whom he renamed Israel. 35 The LORD had made a covenant with them, commanding them, Don't worship other gods. Don't bow down to them or serve them. Don't sacrifice to them. 36 Instead, worship only the LORD. He's the one who brought you up from the land of Egypt with great strength and an outstretched arm. Bow down to him! Sacrifice to him! 37 You must carefully keep the regulations and case laws, the Instruction, and the commandment that he wrote for you. Don't worship other gods. 38 Don't forget the covenant that I made with you. Don't worship other gods. 39 Instead, worship only the LORD your God. He will rescue you from your enemies' power.

40 But they wouldn't listen. Instead, they continued doing their former religious practices. 41 So these nations worship the LORD, but they also serve their idols. The children and the grandchildren are doing the very same thing their parents did. And that's how things still are today.

Hezekiah rules Judah

18 Hezekiah, Ahaz's son, became king of Judah in the third year of Israel's King Hoshea, Elah's son. 2 He was 25 years old when he became king, and he ruled twenty-nine years in Jerusalem. His mother's name was Abi;[i] she was Zechariah's daughter. 3 Hezekiah did what was right in the LORD's eyes, just as his ancestor David had done. 4 He removed the shrines. He smashed the sacred pillars and cut down the sacred pole.[j] He crushed the bronze snake that Moses made, because up to that point the Israelites had been burning incense to it. (The snake was named Nehushtan.)

5 Hezekiah trusted in the LORD, Israel's God. There was no one like him among all of Judah's kings—not before him and not after him. 6 He clung to the LORD and never deviated from him. He kept the commandments that the LORD had commanded Moses. 7 The LORD was with Hezekiah; he succeeded at everything he tried. He rebelled against Assyria's king and wouldn't serve him. 8 He struck down the Philistines as far as Gaza and its territories, from watchtower to fortified city.

9 Assyria's King Shalmaneser marched against Samaria and attacked it in the fourth year of King Hezekiah, which was the seventh year of Israel's King Hoshea, Elah's son. 10 After three years the Assyrians captured the city. Samaria was captured in Hezekiah's sixth year, which was Hoshea's ninth year. 11 Assyria's king sent Israel into exile to Assyria. He settled them in Halah, in Gozan on the Habor River, and in the cities of the Medes. 12 All this happened because they wouldn't listen to the LORD their God. They broke his covenant—all that the LORD's servant Moses had commanded them. They didn't listen, and they didn't do it.

[h] LXX, Vulg, Syr; MT *They* [i] Cf 2 Chron 29:1 *Abijah* [j] Heb *asherah*, perhaps an object devoted to the goddess Asherah

13 Assyria's King Sennacherib marched against all of Judah's fortified cities and captured them in the fourteenth year of King Hezekiah. 14 Judah's King Hezekiah sent a message to the Assyrian king at Lachish, saying, "I admit wrongdoing. Please withdraw from me, and I'll agree to whatever you demand from me." Assyria's king required Judah's King Hezekiah to pay him three hundred kikkars of silver and thirty kikkars of gold. 15 So Hezekiah gave him all the silver that was in the LORD's temple and in the palace treasuries. 16 At that time King Hezekiah had to strip down the doors and doorposts of the LORD's temple, which he had covered with gold. He gave all of it to the Assyrian king.

17 Assryia's king sent his general, his chief officer, and his field commander from Lachish, together with a large army, to King Hezekiah at Jerusalem. They went up and arrived at Jerusalem. They stood at the water channel of the Upper Pool, which is on the road to the field where clothes are washed. 18 Then they called for the king. Hilkiah's son Eliakim, who was the palace administrator, Shebna the secretary, and Asaph's son Joah the recorder went out to them.

19 Then the field commander said to them, "Say to Hezekiah: This is what Assyria's Great King says: Why do you feel so confident? 20 Do you think that empty words are the same as good strategy and the strength to fight? Who are you trusting in that you now rebel against me? 21 It appears that you are trusting in a staff—Egypt—that's nothing but a broken reed! It will stab the hand of anyone who leans on it! That's all that Pharaoh, Egypt's king, is to anyone who trusts in him. 22 Now suppose you say to me, 'We trust in the LORD our God.' Isn't he the one whose shrines and altars Hezekiah removed, telling Judah and Jerusalem, 'You must worship before this altar in Jerusalem'?

23 "So now make a wager with my master, Assyria's king. I'll give you two thousand horses if you can supply the riders! 24 How will you drive back even the least important official among my master's servants when you are relying on Egypt for chariots and riders? 25 What's more, do you think I've marched against this place to destroy it without the LORD's support? It was the LORD who told me, March against this land and destroy it!"

26 Hilkiah's son Eliakim, Shebna, and Joah said to the field commander, "Please speak to your servants in Aramaic because we understand it. Don't speak with us in Hebrew, because the people on the wall will hear it."

27 The field commander said to them, "Did my master send me to speak these words just to you and your master and not also to the men on the wall? They are the ones who will have to eat their dung and drink their urine along with you." 28 Then the field commander stood up and shouted in Hebrew at the top of his voice, saying, "Listen to the message of the great king, Assyria's king. 29 This is what the king says: Don't let Hezekiah lie to you. He won't be able to rescue you from the power of Assyria's king. 30 Don't let Hezekiah persuade you to trust the LORD by saying, 'The LORD will certainly rescue us. This city won't be handed over to Assyria's king.'

31 "Don't listen to Hezekiah, because this is what Assyria's king says: Surrender to me and come out. Then each of you will eat from your own vine and fig tree, and drink water from your own well 32 until I come to take you to a land just like your land. It will be a land of grain and new wine, a land of bread and vineyards, a land of olive oil and honey. Then you will live and not die! Don't listen to Hezekiah, because he will mislead you by saying, 'The LORD will rescue us.' 33 Were any of the gods of the other nations able to rescue their lands from the power of Assyria's king? 34 Where are the gods of Hamath and Arpad? Where are the gods of Sepharvaim, Hena, and Ivvah? Have they rescued Samaria from my power? 35 Which one of any of the gods of those lands has rescued their country from my power? Why should the LORD rescue Jerusalem from my power?"

36 But the people kept quiet and didn't

answer him with a single word, because King Hezekiah's command was, "Don't answer him!" 37Hilkiah's son Eliakim, who was the palace administrator, Shebna the secretary, and Asaph's son Joah the recorder, came to Hezekiah with ripped clothes. They told him what the field commander had said.

Hezekiah and Isaiah

19 When King Hezekiah heard this, he ripped his clothes, covered himself with mourning clothes, and went to the LORD's temple. 2He sent Eliakim the palace administrator, Shebna the secretary, and the senior priests to the prophet Isaiah, Amoz's son. They were all wearing mourning clothes. 3They said to him, "This is what Hezekiah says: Today is a day of distress, punishment, and humiliation. It's as if children are ready to be born, but there's no strength to see it through. 4Perhaps the LORD your God has heard all the words of the field commander who was sent by his master, Assyria's king—how he insulted the living God—perhaps God will punish him for the words the LORD your God heard. Send up a prayer for those few people who still survive."

5When King Hezekiah's servants got to Isaiah, 6Isaiah said to them, "Say this to your master: 'This is what the LORD says: Don't be afraid at the words you heard, which the officers of Assyria's king have used to insult me. 7I'm about to put a spirit in him, so when he hears a rumor, he'll go back to his own country. Then I'll have him cut down by the sword in his own land.'"

8The field commander heard that the Assyrian king had left Lachish. So he went back to the king and found him attacking Libnah. 9Then the Assyrian king learned that Cush's King Tirhakah was on his way to fight against him. So he sent messengers to Hezekiah again, saying, 10"Say this to Judah's King Hezekiah: Don't let the God you trust in persuade you by saying, 'Jerusalem won't be handed over to the Assyrian king.' 11You yourself have heard what Assyrian kings do to other countries, wiping them out. Is it likely that you will be saved? 12Did the gods of the nations destroyed by my fathers—Gozan, Haran, Rezeph, or the people of Eden in Telassar—save them? 13Where now is Hamath's king, Arpad's king, or the kings of Lair, Sepharvaim, Hena, or Ivvah?"[k]

Hezekiah's prayer

14Hezekiah took the letters from the messengers and read them. Then he went to the temple and spread them out before the LORD. 15Hezekiah prayed to the LORD, saying, "LORD God of Israel, you sit enthroned on the winged creatures. You alone are God over all the earth's kingdoms. You made both heaven and earth. 16LORD, turn your ear this way and hear! LORD, open your eyes and see! Listen to Sennacherib's words. He sent them to insult the living God! 17It's true, LORD, that the Assyrian kings have destroyed many nations and their lands. 18The Assyrians burned the gods of those nations with fire because they aren't real gods. They are only man-made creations of wood and stone. That's how the Assyrians could destroy them. 19So now, LORD our God, please save us from Sennacherib's power! Then all the earth's kingdoms will know that you, LORD, are the only true God."

20Then Isaiah, Amoz's son, sent a message to Hezekiah: "This is what the LORD, Israel's God, says: I have heard your prayer about Assyria's King Sennacherib. 21This is the message that the LORD has spoken against him:

The young woman, Daughter Zion,
despises you and mocks you;
Daughter Jerusalem shakes her head
behind your back.
22Whom did you insult and ridicule?
Against whom did you raise your voice
and pridefully lift your eyes?
It was against the holy one of Israel!
23You've insulted the Lord
with your messengers;
you said, 'I, with my many chariots,

[k]Or *the king of the city of Sepharvaim* or *the king of the city of Sepharvaim, Hena, and Ivvah*

have gone up
to the highest mountains,
to the farthest reaches of Lebanon.
I have cut down its tallest cedars,
the best of its pine trees.
I have reached its most
remote lodging place,
its best forest.
24 I have dug wells,
have drunk waters in foreign lands.[l]
With my own feet, I dried up
all of Egypt's streams.'
25 Haven't you heard?
I set this up long ago;
I planned it in the distant past!
Now I have made it happen,
making fortified cities
collapse into piles of rubble.
26 Their citizens have lost their power.
They are frightened and ashamed.
They've become like plants in a field,
tender green shoots,
the grass on rooftops,
burned up before it matures.
27 I know where you live,
how you go out and come in,
and how you rage against me.
28 And because you rage against me
and because your pride
has reached my ears,
I will put my hook in your nose,
and my bit in your mouth.
I will make you go back
the same way you came.

29 "Now this will be the sign for you, Hezekiah: This year you will eat what grows by itself. Next year you will eat what grows from that. But in the third year, sow seed and harvest it; plant vineyards and eat their fruit. 30 The survivors of the house of Judah who have escaped will take root below and bear fruit above. 31 Those who remain will go out from Jerusalem, and those who survive will go out from Mount Zion. The zeal of the LORD of heavenly forces[m] will do this.

32 "Therefore, this is what the LORD says about Assyria's king: He won't enter this city. He won't shoot a single arrow there. He won't come near the city with a shield. He won't build a ramp to besiege it. 33 He will go back by the same way he came. He won't enter this city, declares the LORD. 34 I will defend this city and save it for my sake and for the sake of my servant David."

35 That night the LORD's messenger went out and struck down one hundred eighty-five thousand soldiers in the Assyrian camp. When people got up the next morning, there were dead bodies everywhere. 36 So Assyria's King Sennacherib departed, returning to Nineveh, where he stayed. 37 Later, while he was worshipping in the temple of his god Nisroch, his sons Adrammelech and Sharezer killed him with a sword. They then escaped to the land of Ararat. His son Esarhaddon succeeded him as king.

Hezekiah's illness

20 Around that same time, Hezekiah became deathly ill. The prophet Isaiah, Amoz's son, came to him and said, "This is what the LORD says: Put your affairs in order because you are about to die. You won't survive this."

2 Hezekiah turned his face to the wall and prayed to the LORD, saying, 3 "Please, LORD, remember how I have walked before you in truth and sincerity. I have done what is right in your eyes." Then Hezekiah cried and cried.

4 Isaiah hadn't even left the middle courtyard of the palace when the LORD's word came to him: 5 Turn around. Say to Hezekiah, my people's leader: This is what the LORD, the God of your ancestor David, says: I have heard your prayer and have seen your tears. So now I'm going to heal you. Three days from now you will be able to go up to the LORD's temple. 6 I will add fifteen years to your life. I will rescue you and this city from the power of the Assyrian king. I will defend this city for my sake and for the sake of my servant David.

7 Then Isaiah said, "Prepare a bandage made of figs." They did so and put it on the swelling, at which point Hezekiah started getting better.

8 Hezekiah said to Isaiah, "What is the sign that the LORD will heal me and that

[l] Heb uncertain [m] Qere, some Heb sources, and the parallel in Isa 32; Kethib lacks *of heavenly forces*.

I'll be able to go up to the LORD's temple in three days?"

[9]Isaiah said, "This will be your sign from the LORD that he will make his promise come true: Should the shadow go forward ten steps or back ten steps?"

[10]"It's easy for the shadow to go forward ten steps," Hezekiah said, "but not for the shadow to go back ten steps." [11]So the prophet Isaiah called on the LORD, who made the shadow go back ten steps, down the flight of stairs built by Ahaz.[n]

[12]At that time Merodach-baladan, son of Babylon's King Baladan, sent messengers to Hezekiah with letters and a gift. This was because he had heard that Hezekiah was sick. [13]Hezekiah granted them an audience and showed them everything in his treasury—the silver, the gold, the spices, and the fine oil. He also showed them his stock of weaponry and everything in his storehouses. There wasn't a single thing in his palace or his whole kingdom that Hezekiah didn't show them. [14]Then the prophet Isaiah came to King Hezekiah and said to him, "What did these men say? Where have they come from?"

Hezekiah said, "They came from a distant country: Babylon."

[15]"What have they seen in your palace?" Isaiah asked.

"They have seen everything in my palace," Hezekiah answered. "There's not a single thing in my storehouses that I haven't shown them."

[16]Then Isaiah said to Hezekiah, "Listen to the LORD's word: [17]The days are nearly here when everything in your palace and all that your ancestors collected up to now will be carried off to Babylon. Not a single thing will be left, says the LORD. [18]Some of your children, your very own offspring, will be taken away. They will become eunuchs in the palace of Babylon's king."

[19]Hezekiah said to Isaiah, "The LORD's word that you've spoken is good," because he thought: There will be peace and security in my lifetime.

[20]The rest of Hezekiah's deeds and all his powerful acts—how he made the pool and the channel and brought water inside the city—aren't they written in the official records of Judah's kings? [21]Hezekiah lay down with his ancestors. His son Manasseh succeeded him as king.

Manasseh rules Judah

21 Manasseh was 12 years old when he became king, and he ruled for fifty-five years in Jerusalem. His mother's name was Hephzibah. [2]He did what was evil in the LORD's eyes, imitating the detestable practices of the nations that the LORD had driven out before the Israelites. [3]He rebuilt the shrines that his father Hezekiah had destroyed, set up altars for Baal, and made a sacred pole,[o] just as Israel's King Ahab had done. He bowed down to all the stars in the sky and worshipped them. [4]He even built altars in the two courtyards of the LORD's temple—the very place the LORD was speaking of when he said: "I will put my name in Jerusalem." [5]Manasseh built altars for all the stars in the sky in both courtyards of the LORD's temple. [6]He burned his own son alive, consulted sign readers and fortune-tellers, and used mediums and diviners. He did much evil in the LORD's eyes and made him angry.

[7]Manasseh set up the carved Asherah image he had made in the temple—the very temple the LORD had spoken about to David and his son Solomon, saying, In this temple and in Jerusalem, which I have chosen out of all Israel's tribes, I will put my name forever. [8]I will never again remove Israel from the land I gave to their ancestors, provided they carefully do everything I have commanded them—keeping all the Instruction my servant Moses commanded them. [9]But they wouldn't listen. Manasseh led them into doing even more evil than the nations the LORD had wiped out before the Israelites.

[10]The LORD spoke through his servants the prophets: [11]Judah's King Manasseh has done detestable things, things more evil than the Amorites had done before his time. He has caused Judah to sin with his images. [12]Because of this, the LORD,

[n]Heb uncertain [o]Heb *asherah*, perhaps a pole devoted to the goddess Asherah

Israel's God, has said: I'm about to bring on Jerusalem and Judah such a great disaster that the ears of anyone who hears about it will ring. 13 I will stretch out over Jerusalem the same line that I used to measured Samaria and the same mason's level that I used on Ahab's family. I will wipe Jerusalem clean the same way someone wipes a plate clean, wiping it clean then turning it facedown. 14 Whatever survives of my inheritance, I'll leave behind, handing them over to their enemies. They will be nothing but plunder and loot for every one of their enemies. 15 This will happen because they have done what is evil in my eyes, making me angry from the day their ancestors left Egypt until this very moment.

16 Manasseh spilled so much innocent blood that he filled up every corner of Jerusalem with it. And this doesn't include the sins he caused Judah to commit so that they did what was evil in the LORD's eyes. 17 The rest of Manasseh's deeds, all that he accomplished, and the sin he committed, aren't they written in the official records of Judah's kings? 18 Manasseh lay down with his ancestors. He was buried in his palace garden, the Uzza Garden. His son Amon succeeded him as king.

Amon rules Judah

19 Amon was 22 years old when he became king, and he ruled for two years in Jerusalem. His mother's name was Meshullemeth; she was Haruz's daughter and was from Jotbah. 20 He did what was evil in the LORD's eyes, just as his father Manasseh had done. 21 He walked in all the ways his father had walked. He worshipped the same worthless idols his father had worshipped, bowing down to them. 22 He deserted his ancestors' God, the LORD—he didn't walk in the LORD's way.

23 Amon's officials plotted against him and assassinated the king in his palace. 24 The people of the land then executed all those who had plotted against King Amon and made his son Josiah the next king. 25 The rest of Amon's deeds, aren't they written in the official records of Judah's kings? 26 He was buried in his tomb in the Uzza Garden. His son Josiah succeeded him as king.

Josiah rules Judah

22 Josiah was 8 years old when he became king, and he ruled for thirty-one years in Jerusalem. His mother's name was Jedidah; she was Adaiah's daughter and was from Bozkath. 2 He did what was right in the LORD's eyes, and walked in the ways of his ancestor David—not deviating from it even a bit to the right or left.

3 In the eighteenth year of King Josiah's rule, he sent the secretary Shaphan, Azaliah's son and Meshullam's grandson, to the LORD's temple with the following orders: 4 "Go to the high priest Hilkiah. Have him carefully count[p] the money that has been brought to the LORD's temple and that has been collected from the people by the doorkeepers. 5 It should be given to the supervisors in charge of the LORD's temple, who in turn should pay it to those who are in the LORD's temple, repairing the temple—6 the carpenters, the builders, and the masons. It should be used to pay for lumber and quarried stone to repair the temple. 7 But there's no need to check on them regarding the money they receive, because they are honest workers."

8 The high priest Hilkiah told Shaphan the secretary: "I have found the Instruction scroll in the LORD's temple." Then Hilkiah turned the scroll over to Shaphan, who read it.

9 Shaphan the secretary then went to the king and reported this to him: "Your officials have released the money that was found in the temple and have handed it over to those who supervise the work in the LORD's temple." 10 Then Shaphan the secretary told the king, "Hilkiah the priest has given me a scroll," and he read it out loud before the king.

11 As soon as the king heard what the Instruction scroll said, he ripped his clothes. 12 The king ordered the priest Hilkiah, Shaphan's son Ahikam, Micaiah's son Achbor,

[p] Heb uncertain

Shaphan the secretary, and Asaiah the royal
officer as follows: 13 “Go and ask the LORD
on my behalf, and on behalf of the people,
and on behalf of all Judah concerning the
contents of this scroll that has been found.
The LORD must be furious with us because
our ancestors failed to obey the words of
this scroll and do everything written in it
about us.”
14 So Hilkiah the priest, Ahikam, Achbor,
Shaphan, and Asaiah went to the prophetess Huldah. She was married to Shallum,
Tikvah’s son and Harhas’ grandson, who
was in charge of the wardrobe. She lived in
Jerusalem in the second district. When they
spoke to her, 15 she replied, “This is what the
LORD, Israel’s God, says: Tell this to the
man who sent you to me: 16 This is what
the LORD says: I am about to bring disaster
on this place and its citizens—all the words
in the scroll that Judah’s king has read!
17 My anger burns against this place, never
to be quenched, because they’ve deserted
me and have burned incense to other gods,
angering me by everything they have done.[q]
18 But also say this to the king of Judah, who
sent you to question the LORD: This is what
the LORD, Israel’s God, says about the message you’ve just heard: 19 Because your heart
was broken and you submitted before the
LORD when you heard what I said about
this place and its citizens—that they will
become a horror and a curse—and because
you ripped your clothes and cried before
me, I have listened to you, declares the
LORD. 20 That’s why I will gather you to your
ancestors, and you will go to your grave in
peace. You won’t experience the disaster I
am about to bring on this place.”

Josiah’s reform

When they reported Huldah’s words to
23 the king, 1 the king sent a message,
and all of Judah’s and Jerusalem’s
elders gathered before him. 2 Then the king
went up to the LORD’s temple, together with
all the people of Judah and all the citizens
of Jerusalem, the priests and the prophets,
and all the people, young and old alike. There
the king read out loud all the words of the
covenant scroll that had been found in the
LORD’s temple. 3 The king stood beside the
pillar and made a covenant with the LORD
that he would follow the LORD by keeping
his commandments, his laws, and his regulations with all his heart and all his being in
order to fulfill the words of this covenant
that were written in this scroll. All of the
people accepted the covenant.
4 The king then commanded the high
priest Hilkiah, the second-order priests,
and the doorkeepers to remove from the
LORD’s temple all the religious objects made
for Baal, Asherah, and all the heavenly bodies. The king burned them outside Jerusalem in the Kidron fields and took the ashes
to Bethel. 5 He got rid of the pagan priests
that the Judean kings had appointed to
burn incense at the shrines in Judah’s cities and the areas around Jerusalem. He did
the same to those who burned incense to
Baal, to the sun, to the moon, to the constellations, and to all the heavenly bodies.
6 He removed the Asherah image[r] from the
LORD’s temple, taking it to the Kidron Valley outside Jerusalem. There he burned it,
ground it to dust, and threw the dust on the
public graveyard. 7 The king tore down the
shrines for the consecrated workers[s] that
were in the LORD’s temple, where women
made woven coverings[t] for Asherah.
8 Then Josiah brought all the priests out
of Judah’s cities. From Geba to Beer-sheba,
he defiled the shrines where the priests had
been burning incense. He also tore down
the shrines at the gates at the entrance
to the gate of Joshua the city’s governor,
which were on the left as one entered the
city gate. 9 Although the priests of these
shrines didn’t go up on the LORD’s altar in
Jerusalem, they did eat unleavened bread
with their fellow priests.
10 Josiah defiled the Topheth in the Ben-
hinnom Valley so no one could burn their
child alive in honor of the god Molech. 11 He
did away with the horses that Judah’s kings
had dedicated to the sun. They were kept
at the entrance to the LORD’s temple near

[q] Or *made* [r] Heb lacks *image*; perhaps a pole dedicated to the goddess. [s] Traditionally *cultic prostitutes* [t] Heb uncertain

a room in the annex[u] that belonged to an official named Nathan-melech. Josiah set fire to the chariots that were dedicated to the sun. 12 The king also tore down the altars that were on the roof of Ahaz's upper story, which had been made by the Judean kings, and he did the same with the altars that Manasseh had built in the two courtyards of the LORD's temple. He broke them up there[v] and threw their dust into the Kidron Valley. 13 The king then defiled the shrines facing Jerusalem, south of the Mountain of Destruction. Solomon the king of Israel had built these for Ashtoreth, the monstrous Sidonian god, for Chemosh, the monstrous Moabite god, and for Milcom, the detestable Ammonite god. 14 He smashed the sacred pillars and cut down the sacred poles,[w] filling the places where they had been with human bones.

15 Josiah also tore down the altar that was in Bethel. That was the shrine made by Jeroboam, Nebat's son, who caused Israel to sin. Josiah tore down that altar and its shrine. He burned the shrine, grinding it into dust. Then he burned its sacred pole.[x] 16 When Josiah turned around, he noticed tombs up on the hillside. So he ordered the bones to be taken out of the tombs. He then burned them on the altar, desecrating it. (This was in agreement with the word that the LORD announced by the man of God when Jeroboam stood by the altar at the festival.) Josiah then turned and saw the tomb of the man of God[y] who had predicted these things. 17 "What's this gravestone I see?" Josiah asked.

The people of the city replied, "That tomb belongs to the man of God who came from Judah and announced what you would do to the altar of Bethel."

18 "Let it be," Josiah said. "No one should disturb his bones." So they left his bones untouched, along with the bones of the prophet who came from Samaria.

19 Moreover, Josiah removed all the shrines on the high hills that the Israelite kings had constructed throughout the cities of Samaria. These had made the LORD angry. Josiah did to them just what he did at Bethel. 20 He actually slaughtered on those altars all the priests of the shrines who were there, and he burned human bones on them. Then Josiah returned to Jerusalem.

21 The king commanded all the people, "Celebrate a Passover to the LORD your God following what is instructed in this scroll containing the covenant." 22 A Passover like this hadn't been celebrated since the days when the judges judged Israel; neither had it been celebrated during all the days of the Israelite and Judean kings. 23 But in the eighteenth year of King Josiah's rule, this Passover was celebrated to the LORD in Jerusalem.

24 Josiah burned those who consulted dead spirits and the mediums, the household gods and the worthless idols—all the monstrous things that were seen in the land of Judah and in Jerusalem. In this way Josiah fulfilled the words of the Instruction written in the scroll that the priest Hilkiah found in the LORD's temple. 25 There's never been a king like Josiah, whether before or after him, who turned to the LORD with all his heart, all his being, and all his strength, in agreement with everything in the Instruction from Moses.

26 Even so, the LORD didn't turn away from the great rage that burned against Judah on account of all that Manasseh had done to make him angry. 27 The LORD said, "I will remove Judah from my presence just as I removed Israel. I will reject this city, Jerusalem, which I chose, and this temple where I promised my name would reside."

28 The rest of Josiah's deeds and all that he accomplished, aren't they written in the official records of Judah's kings? 29 In his days, the Egyptian king Pharaoh Neco marched against the Assyrian king at the Euphrates River. King Josiah marched out to intercept him. But when Neco encountered Josiah in Megiddo, he killed the king. 30 Josiah's servants took his body from Megiddo in a chariot. They brought him to

[u]Heb uncertain [v]Correction; MT *removed them quickly* or *ran from there* [w]Heb *asherim*, perhaps objects devoted to the goddess Asherah [x]Heb *asherah*, perhaps an object devoted to the goddess Asherah [y]LXX; MT lacks *when Jeroboam stood by the altar at the festival. Josiah then turned and saw the tomb of the man of God.*

Jerusalem and buried him in his own tomb.
The people of the land took Jehoahaz, Josiah's son, anointed him, and made him
king after his father.

Jehoahaz rules Judah

31Jehoahaz was 23 years old when he became king, and he ruled for three months
in Jerusalem. His mother's name was Hamutal; she was Jeremiah's daughter and
was from Libnah. 32He did what was evil
in the LORD's eyes, just as all his ancestors
had done. 33Pharaoh Neco made Jehoahaz
a prisoner at Riblah in the land of Hamath,
ending his rule in Jerusalem. Pharaoh Neco
imposed a fine on the land totaling one hundred kikkars of silver and one kikkar of gold.

Jehoiakim rules Judah

34Pharaoh Neco made Eliakim, Josiah's
son, king after his father Josiah. Neco
changed Eliakim's name to Jehoiakim. Neco
took Jehoahaz away; he later died in Egypt.
35Jehoiakim gave Pharaoh the silver and
gold, but he taxed the land in order to meet
Pharaoh's financial demands. Each person
was taxed appropriately. Jehoiakim exacted
silver and the gold from the land's people in
order to give it to Pharaoh Neco. 36Jehoia-
kim was 25 years old when he became king,
and he ruled for eleven years in Jerusalem.
His mother's name was Zebidah; she was
Pedaiah's daughter and was from Rumah.
37He did what was evil in the LORD's eyes,
just as all his ancestors had done.

24 In Jehoiakim's days, King Nebuchadnezzar of Babylon attacked. Jehoiakim had submitted to him for three years,
but then Jehoiakim changed his mind and
rebelled against him. 2The LORD sent Chaldean, Aramean, Moabite, and Ammonite
raiding parties against Jehoiakim, sending
them against Judah in order to destroy it.
This was in agreement with the word that
the LORD had spoken through his servants
the prophets. 3Indeed, this happened to
Judah because the LORD commanded them
to be removed from his presence on account
of all the sins that Manasseh had committed 4and because of the innocent blood that
he had spilled. Manasseh had filled Jerusalem with innocent blood, and the LORD
didn't want to forgive that.
5The rest of Jehoiakim's deeds and all
that he accomplished, aren't they written
in the official records of Judah's kings? 6Je-
hoiakim lay down with his ancestors. His
son Jehoiachin succeeded him as king.
7The Egyptian king never left his country again because the Babylonian king had
taken over all the territory that had previously belonged to him—from the border of
Egypt to the Euphrates River.

Jehoiachin rules Judah

8Jehoiachin was 18 years old when he
became king, and he ruled for three months
in Jerusalem. His mother's name was Ne-
hushta; she was Elnathan's daughter and
was from Jerusalem. 9He did what was evil
in the LORD's eyes, just as all his ancestors
had done. 10At that time, the officers of
Babylon's King Nebuchadnezzar attacked
Jerusalem and laid siege to the city. 11Baby-
lon's King Nebuchadnezzar himself arrived
at the city while his officers were blockad-
ing it. 12Judah's King Jehoiachin, along with
his mother, his servants, his officers, and
his officials, came out to surrender to the
Babylonian king. The Babylonian king took
Jehoiachin prisoner in the eighth year of
Jehoiachin's rule.
13Nebuchadnezzar also took away all
the treasures of the LORD's temple and of
the royal palace. He cut into pieces all the
gold objects that Israel's King Solomon
had made for the LORD's temple, which
is exactly what the LORD said would happen. 14Then Nebuchadnezzar exiled all of
Jerusalem: all the officials, all the military
leaders—ten thousand exiles—as well as
all the skilled workers and metalworkers.
No one was left behind except the poorest
of the land's people. 15Nebuchadnezzar exiled Jehoiachin to Babylon; he also exiled
the queen mother, the king's wives, the
officials, and the land's elite leaders from
Jerusalem to Babylon. 16The Babylonian
king also exiled seven thousand warriors—
each one a hero trained for battle—as well
as a thousand skilled workers and metalworkers to Babylon. 17Then the Babylonian

king made Mattaniah, Jehoiachin's uncle,
succeed Jehoiachin as king. Nebuchadnezzar changed Mattaniah's name to Zedekiah.

Zedekiah rules Judah

18 Zedekiah was 21 years old when he
became king, and he ruled for eleven years
in Jerusalem. His mother's name was Hamutal; she was Jeremiah's daughter and
was from Libnah. 19 He did what was evil
in the LORD's eyes, just as Jehoiakim had
done. 20 It was precisely because the LORD
was angry with Jerusalem and Judah that
he thrust them out of his presence.

The southern kingdom falls

Now Zedekiah rebelled against the
25 Babylonian king. 1 So in the ninth
year of Zedekiah's rule, on the tenth
day of the tenth month, Babylon's King Nebuchadnezzar attacked Jerusalem with his
entire army. He camped beside the city and
built a siege wall all around it. 2 The city was
under attack until King Zedekiah's eleventh
year. 3 On the ninth day of the month, the
famine in the city got so bad that no food
remained for the common people. 4 Then the
enemy broke into the city. All the soldiers
fled[z] by night using the gate between the
two walls near the King's Garden. The Chaldeans were surrounding the city, so the soldiers ran toward the desert plain. 5 But the
Chaldean army chased King Zedekiah and
caught up with him in the Jericho plains.
His entire army deserted him. 6 So the Chaldeans captured the king and brought him
back to the Babylonian king, who was at Riblah. There his punishment was determined.
7 Zedekiah's sons were slaughtered right
before his eyes. Then he was blinded, put
in bronze chains, and taken off to Babylon.
8 On the seventh day of the fifth month
in the nineteenth year of Babylon's King
Nebuchadnezzar, Nebuzaradan arrived at
Jerusalem. He was the commander of the
guard and an official of the Babylonian king.
9 He burned down the LORD's temple, the
royal palace, and all of Jerusalem's houses.
He burned down every important building. 10 The whole Chaldean army under
the commander of the guard tore down
the walls surrounding Jerusalem. 11 Then
Nebuzaradan the commander of the guard
exiled the people who were left in the city,
those who had already surrendered to Babylon's king, and the rest of the population.
12 The commander of the guard left some of
the land's poor people behind to work the
vineyards and be farmers. 13 The Chaldeans
shattered the bronze columns, the stands,
and the bronze Sea that were in the LORD's
temple. They carried the bronze off to Babylon. 14 They also took the pots, the shovels,
the wick trimmers, the dishes, and all the
bronze items that had been used in the
temple. 15 The commander of the guard took
the fire pans and the sprinkling bowls, which
were made of pure gold and pure silver. 16 The
bronze in all these objects—the two pillars,
the Sea, and the stands that Solomon had
made for the LORD's temple—was too heavy
to weigh. 17 Each pillar was twenty-seven feet
high. The bronze capital on top of the first
pillar was four and a half feet high. Decorative lattices and pomegranates, all made
from bronze, were around the capital. And
the second pillar was decorated with lattices
just like the first.
18 The commander of the guard also took
away Seraiah the chief priest, Zephaniah the
priest next in rank, and the three doorkeepers. 19 Of those still left in the city, Nebuzaradan took away an officer who was in
charge of the army and five royal advisors
who were discovered in the city. He also took
away the secretary of the officer responsible
for drafting the land's people to fight, as well
as sixty people who were discovered in the
city. 20 Nebuzaradan the commander of the
guard took all of these people and brought
them to the Babylonian king at Riblah. 21 The
king of Babylon struck them down, killing
them in Riblah in the land of Hamath.

So Judah was exiled from its land.

Gedaliah governs Judah

22 Babylon's King Nebuchadnezzar put
Gedaliah, Ahikam's son and Shaphan's

[z] LXX, cf Jer 52:7; MT lacks *fled*.

grandson, in charge of the people he had left behind in the land of Judah. 23 All the army officers and their soldiers heard that the Babylonian king had appointed Gedaliah as governor, so they came with their men to Gedaliah at Mizpah. The officers were Ishmael, Nethaniah's son; Johanan, Kareah's son; Seraiah, Tanhumeth's son who was a Netophathite; and Jaazaniah, Maacathite's son. 24 Gedaliah made a solemn pledge to them and their soldiers, telling them, "Don't be afraid of the Chaldean officials. Stay in the land and serve the Babylonian king, and things will go well for you."

25 But in the seventh month, Ishmael, Nethaniah's son and Elishama's grandson, who was from the royal family, came with ten soldiers, and they struck Gedaliah, and he died. They also killed the Judeans and the Chaldeans who were with him at Mizpah. 26 Then all the people, young and old, along with the army officers, departed for Egypt because they were afraid of the Chaldeans.

Jehoiachin in Babylon

27 In the year that Awil-merodach[a] became king of Babylon, he released Judah's King Jehoiachin from prison. This happened in the thirty-seventh year of the exile of King Jehoiachin, on the twenty-seventh day of the twelfth month. 28 Awil-merodach spoke kindly to Jehoiachin and seated him above the other kings who were with him in Babylon. 29 So Jehoiachin took off his prisoner clothes and ate regularly in the king's presence for the rest of his life. 30 At the king's command, a regular food allowance was given to him every day for the rest of his life.

1 CHRONICLES

Adam to Israel

1 Adam, Seth, Enosh; 2 Kenan, Mahalalel, Jared; 3 Enoch, Methuselah, Lamech; 4 Noah; Noah's family:[a] Shem, Ham, and Japheth.

5 Japheth's family: Gomer, Magog, Madai, Javan, Tubal, Meshech, and Tiras.

6 Gomer's family: Ashkenaz, Riphath,[b] and Togarmah.

7 Javan's family: Elishah, Tarshish, Kittim, and Rodanim.

8 Ham's family: Cush, Egypt, Put, and Canaan.

9 Cush's family: Seba, Havilah, Sabta, Raama, and Sabteca.

Raamah's family: Sheba and Dedan.

10 Cush was the father of Nimrod, the first warrior in the land.

11 Egypt was the father of Ludim, Anamim, Lehabim, Naphtuhim, 12 Pathrusim, Casluhim, from whom the Philistines came, and Caphtorim.

13 Canaan was the father of Sidon his oldest son, Heth, 14 the Jebusites, the Amorites, the Girgashites, 15 the Hivites, the Arkites, the Sinites, 16 the Arvadites, the Zemarites, and the Hamathites.

17 Shem's family: Elam, Asshur, Arpachshad, Lud, and Aram.

Aram's family:[c] Uz, Hul, Gether, and Meshech.

18 Arpachshad was Shelah's father, and Shelah was Eber's father. 19 Two sons were born to Eber: one was named Peleg,[d] because in his days the land was divided; and his brother's name was Joktan.

20 Joktan was the father of Almodad, Sheleph, Hazarmaveth, Jerah, 21 Hadoram, Uzal, Diklah, 22 Ebal, Abimael, Sheba, 23 Ophir, Havilah, and Jobab. All these were Joktan's family.

24 Shem, Arpachshad, Shelah; 25 Eber, Peleg, Reu; 26 Serug, Nahor, Terah; 27 and Abram, that is, Abraham.

28 Abraham's family: Isaac and Ishmael. 29 These were their descendants. Ishmael's oldest son was Nebaioth, then Kedar, Adbeel, Mibsam, 30 Mishma,

[a]*Awil-merodach* means Man of Marduk in Akkadian. [a]LXX; MT lacks *Noah's family.* [b]LXX; MT *Diphath*
[c]LXX; MT lacks *Aram's family.* [d]Or *division*

Dumah, Massa, Hadad, Tema, [31]Jetur, Naphish, and Kedemah. This was Ishmael's family. [32]Abraham's secondary wife Keturah's family: she gave birth to Zimran, Jokshan, Medan, Midian, Ishbak, and Shuah.

Jokshan's family: Sheba and Dedan.

[33]Midian's family: Ephah, Epher, Hanoch, Abida, and Eldaah. All these were members of Keturah's family.

[34]Abraham was Isaac's father. Isaac's family: Esau and Israel.

[35]Esau's family: Eliphaz, Reuel, Jeush, Jalam, and Korah.

[36]Eliphaz's family: Teman, Omar, Zephi, Gatam, Kenaz, Timna, and Amalek.

[37]Reuel's family: Nahath, Zerah, Shammah, and Mizzah.

[38]Seir's family: Lotan, Shobal, Zibeon, Anah, Dishon, Ezer, and Dishan.

[39]Lotan's family: Hori and Homam; Lotan's sister was Timna.

[40]Shobal's family: Alian, Manahath, Ebal, Shephi, and Onam.

Zibeon's family: Aiah and Anah.

[41]Anah's family: Dishon.

Dishon's family: Hamran, Eshban, Ithran, and Cheran.

[42]Ezer's family: Bilhan, Zaavan, and Jaakan.

Dishan's family:[e] Uz and Aran.

[43]These were the kings who ruled in the land of Edom before any king ruled over the Israelites: Bela, Beor's son, whose city was called Dinhabah. [44]When Bela died, Jobab, Zerah's son from Bozrah, succeeded him. [45]When Jobab died, Husham from the land of the Temanites succeeded him. [46]When Husham died, Hadad, Bedad's son who defeated Midian in the Moabite countryside, succeeded him; his city was called Avith. [47]When Hadad died, Samlah from Masrekah succeeded him. [48]When Samlah died, Shaul from Rehoboth on the river succeeded him. [49]When Shaul died, Baal-hanan, Achbor's son, succeeded him. [50]When Baal-hanan died, Hadad succeeded him; his city was called Pai. His wife's name was Mehetabel, Matred's daughter and Me-zahab's granddaughter. [51]When Hadad died, Edom's tribal chiefs were: Chief Timna, Chief Aliah, Chief Jetheth, [52]Chief Oholibamah, Chief Elah, Chief Pinon, [53]Chief Kenaz, Chief Teman, Chief Mibzar, [54]Chief Magdiel, and Chief Iram. These were Edom's tribal chiefs.

2 This was Israel's family: Reuben, Simeon, Levi, Judah, Issachar, Zebulun, [2]Dan, Joseph, Benjamin, Naphtali, Gad, and Asher.

Judah's line

[3]Judah's family: Er, Onan, and Shelah. These three were born to him with Bathshua the Canaanite. Although Er was Judah's oldest, the LORD considered him wicked and put him to death. [4]His daughter-in-law Tamar bore him Perez and Zerah. Judah had five sons in all.

[5]Perez's family: Hezron and Hamul.

[6]Zerah's family: Zimri, Ethan, Heman, Calcol, and Darda[f]—five in all.

[7]Carmi's family: Achar, who made trouble for Israel by disobeying the law dedicating war spoils to God.

[8]Ethan's family: Azariah.

[9]Hezron's family, who were born to him: Jerahmeel, Ram, and Chelubai. [10]Ram was the father of Amminadab, and Amminadab was the father of Nahshon, tribal chief of the Judeans. [11]Nahshon was the father of Salma, Salma was the father of Boaz, [12]Boaz was the father of Obed, and Obed was the father of Jesse. [13]Jesse was the father of Eliab his oldest son, Abinadab his second, Shimea his third, [14]Nethanel his fourth, Raddai his fifth, [15]Ozem his sixth, and David his seventh. [16]Their sisters were Zeruiah and Abigail.

Zeruiah's family: Abishai, Joab, and Asahel—three in all. [17]Abigail gave birth to Amasa, whose father was Jether the Ishmaelite.

[18]Caleb, Hezron's son, had children with his wife Azubah, and with Jerioth. These were her sons: Jesher, Shobab, and Ardon. [19]After Azubah died, Caleb married Ephrath, who gave birth to

[e] Cf 1:38; or *Dishon's family* [f] LXX, Syr; MT *Dara*

Hur for him. 20 Hur was the father of
Uri, and Uri was the father of Bezalel.
21 Later, Hezron had sexual relations
with the daughter of Machir, Gilead's
father, whom he married when he was
60 years old, and she gave birth to Segub
for him. 22 Segub was the father of Jair,
who owned twenty-three towns in the
land of Gilead, 23 but Geshur and Aram
took Havvoth-jair from them, as well as
Kenath and its villages, sixty towns.

All these were descendants of Machir,
Gilead's father. 24 After Hezron's death,
Caleb went to Ephrath.[g] Abijah, Hezron's wife, bore him Ashhur, Tekoa's
father.

25 The family of Jerahmeel, Hezron's
oldest son: Ram his oldest, Bunah,
Oren, Ozem, and Ahijah. 26 Jerahmeel
had another wife named Atarah; she was
the mother of Onam.

27 The family of Ram, Jerahmeel's oldest son: Maaz, Jamin, and Eker.

28 Onam's family: Shammai and Jada.

Shammai's family: Nadab and Abishur. 29 Abishur's wife's name was Abihail, and she gave birth to Ahban and
Molid for him.

30 Nadab's family: Seled and Appaim,
but Seled died without children.

31 Appaim's family: Ishi.

Ishi's family: Sheshan.

Sheshan's family: Ahlai.

32 The family of Jada, Shammai's
brother: Jether and Jonathan, but Jether
died without children.

33 Jonathan's family: Peleth and Zaza.
These were Jerahmeel's descendants.

34 Sheshan had no sons, only daughters; but Sheshan had an Egyptian servant whose name was Jarha. 35 Sheshan
gave his daughter in marriage to Jarha
his servant, and she gave birth to Attai
for him.

36 Attai was the father of Nathan,
Nathan was the father of Zabad, 37 Zabad
was the father of Ephlal, Ephlal was the
father of Obed, 38 Obed was the father
of Jehu, Jehu was the father of Azariah,
39 Azariah was the father of Helez, Helez
was the father of Eleasah, 40 Eleasah was
the father of Sismai, Sismai was the
father of Shallum, 41 Shallum was the
father of Jekamiah, and Jekamiah was
the father of Elishama.

42 The family of Caleb, Jerahmeel's
brother: Mesha his oldest son and Ziph's
father; and his second son[h] Mareshah,
Hebron's father.

43 Hebron's family: Korah, Tappuah,
Rekem, and Shema. 44 Shema was the
father of Raham, Jorkeam's father; and
Rekem was the father of Shammai.

45 Shammai's son: Maon; Maon was
Beth-zur's father. 46 Ephah, Caleb's second-
ary wife, gave birth to Haran, Moza, and
Gazez. Haran was the father of Gazez.

47 Jahdai's family: Regem, Jotham, Ge-
shan, Pelet, Ephah, and Shaaph. 48 Maacah, Caleb's secondary wife, gave birth
to Sheber and Tirhanah. 49 She also gave
birth to Shaaph, Madmannah's father;
and to Sheva, Machbenah and Gibea's
father. Caleb's daughter was Achsah.
50 These were Caleb's descendants.

The family of Hur, Ephrathah's oldest son: Shobal, Kiriath-jearim's father;
51 Salma, Bethlehem's father; and Hareph,
Beth-gader's father.

52 Shobal, Kiriath-jearim's father, had
a family: Haroeh, and the ancestor of
half of the Menuhoth.[i] 53 Kiriath-jearim's
clans: the Ithrites, the Puthites, the Shu-
mathites, and the Mishraites. From these
came the Zorathites and the Eshtaolites.

54 The family of Salma, Bethlehem's
father:[j] the Netophathites, Atroth-beth-
joab, half of the Manahathites, and the
Zorites.

55 The clans of the scribes who lived at
Jabez: the Tirathites, the Shimeathites,
and the Sucathites. They were Kenites
who descended from Hammath, Beth-
rechab's father.

David's line

3 This is David's family born to him
in Hebron: the oldest Amnon,

[g] LXX, Vulg; MT *in Caleb-ephrathah* [h] Or *the family of* [i] Heb lacks *the ancestor of.* [j] Cf 2:51; Heb lacks *father.*

with Ahinoam the Jezreelite; the second Daniel, with Abigail the Carmelite; 2the third Absalom son of Maacah, the daughter of Geshur's King Talmai; the fourth Adonijah, Haggith's son; 3the fifth Shephatiah, with Abital; the sixth Ithream, with his wife Eglah. 4Six were born to him in Hebron, where he reigned for seven and a half years. He also reigned in Jerusalem for thirty-three years. 5These were born to him in Jerusalem: Shimea, Shobab, Nathan, and Solomon—four from Bath-shua, Ammiel's daughter; 6Ibhar, Elishama, Eliphelet, 7Nogah, Nepheg, Japhia, 8Elishama, Eliada, and Eliphelet—nine in all. 9This was all of David's family, except for his secondary wives' children. Tamar was their sister.

10The descendants[k] of Solomon: Rehoboam, his son Abijah, his son Asa, his son Jehoshaphat, 11his son Joram, his son Ahaziah, his son Joash, 12his son Amaziah, his son Azariah, his son Jotham, 13his son Ahaz, his son Hezekiah, his son Manasseh, 14his son Amon, and his son Josiah.

15Josiah's family: the oldest Johanan, the second Jehoiakim, the third Zedekiah, and the fourth Shallum.

16Jehoiakim's family: his son Jeconiah and his son Zedekiah.

17The family of Jeconiah the prisoner: Shealtiel his son; 18Malchiram, Pedaiah, Shenazzar, Jekamiah, Hoshama, and Nedabiah.

19Pedaiah's family: Zerubbabel and Shimei.

Zerubbabel's family:[l] Meshullam, Hananiah, and their sister Shelomith; 20Hashubah, Ohel, Berechiah, Hasadiah, and Jushab-hesed—these five also.

21Hananiah's family:[m] Pelatiah, Jeshaiah, Rephaiah's family, Arnan's family, Obadiah's family, and Shecaniah's family.

22Shecaniah's family: Shemaiah and his family, Hattush, Igal, Bariah, Neariah, and Shaphat—six in all.

23Neariah's family: Elioenai, Hizkiah, and Azrikam—three in all.

24Elioenai's family: Hodaviah, Eliashib, Pelaiah, Akkub, Johanan, Delaiah, and Anani—seven in all.

Judah's line

4 Judah's family: Perez, Hezron, Caleb,[n] Hur, and Shobal.

2Shobal's son Reaiah was Jahath's father, and Jahath was the father of Ahumai and Lahad. These were the Zorathite clans.

3This was Etam's family:[o] Jezreel, Ishma, and Idbash. Their sister's name was Hazzelelponi. 4Penuel was Gedor's father, and Ezer was Hushah's father.

This was the family of Hur the oldest son of Ephrathah, Bethlehem's father: 5Ashhur, Tekoa's father, had two wives, Helah and Naarah. 6Naarah gave birth to Ahuzzam, Hepher, Temeni, and Haahashtari for him. This was Naarah's family.

7Helah's family: Zereth, Zohar,[p] and Ethnan. 8Koz was the father of Anub, Hazzobebah, and the clans of Aharhel, Harum's son.

9Jabez was more honored than his brothers. His mother had named him Jabez, saying, "I bore him in pain."[q] 10Jabez called on Israel's God: "If only you would greatly bless me and increase my territory. May your power go with me to keep me from trouble, so as not to cause me pain." And God granted his request.

11Chelub, Shuhah's brother, was the father of Mehir, who was Eshton's father. 12Eshton was the father of Beth-rapha, Paseah, and Tehinnah, Ir-nahash's father. These are the men of Recah.

13Kenaz's family: Othniel and Seraiah. Othniel's family: Hathath and Meonothai.[r] 14Meonothai was the father of Ophrah. Seraiah was the father of Joab the father of Ge-harashim,[s] so-called because they were skilled workers.

[k]LXX, Syr; MT *son* [l]LXX, Syr; MT *son* [m]LXX, Syr, Tg; MT *son* [n]Cf 1 Chron 2:19; MT *Carmi* [o]LXX; MT *father* [p]Qere, LXX; Kethib *Izhar* [q]Heb sounds like *Jabez.* [r]LXX, Vulg; MT lacks *Meonothai.* [s]Or *the valley of skilled workers*

15 The family of Caleb, Jephunneh's son: Iru, Elah, and Naam. This was Kenaz's family.[t]

16 Jehallelel's family: Ziph, Ziphah, Tiria, and Asarel.

17 Ezrah's family:[u] Jether, Mered, Epher, and Jalon. Jether was the father of[v] Miriam, Shammai, and Ishbah, Eshtemoa's father. 18 His Judean wife gave birth to Jered, Gedor's father; Heber, Soco's father; and Jekuthiel, Zanoah's father.

This is the family of Bithiah, Pharaoh's daughter, whom Mered married. 19 The family of his Judean wife,[w] the sister of Naham, Keilah's father the Garmite and Eshtemoa the Maacathite.

20 Shimon's family: Amnon, Rinnah, Ben-hanan, and Tilon.

Ishi's family: Zoheth and Ben-zoheth.

21 The family of Shelah, Judah's son: Er, Lecah's father; Laadah, Mareshah's father; the clans of the linen workers at Beth-ashbea; 22 Jokim; the men of Cozeba; Joash; and Saraph, who married into[x] Moab but returned to Bethlehem[y] (the records are ancient). 23 They were the potters who lived in Netaim and Gederah; they lived there with the king in his service.

Simeon's line

24 Simeon's family: Nemuel, Jamin, Jarib, Zerah, Shaul, 25 his son Shallum, his son Mibsam, and his son Mishma. 26 Mishma's family: his son Hammuel, his son Zaccur, and his son Shimei. 27 Shimei had sixteen sons and six daughters; but his brothers didn't have many children, and none of their clans became as numerous as the Judeans.

28 They lived in Beer-sheba, Moladah, Hazar-shual, 29 Bilhah, Ezem, Tolad, 30 Bethuel, Hormah, Ziklag, 31 Beth-marcaboth, Hazar-susim, Beth-biri, and Shaaraim. These were their towns until David became king. 32 Their villages were Etam, Ain, Rimmon, Tochen, and Ashan—five towns—33 as well as all their villages around these towns as far as Baal. These were their settlements, and they kept their own family records:

34 Meshobab, Jamlech, Joshah son of Amaziah, 35 Joel, Jehu son of Joshibiah son of Seraiah son of Asiel, 36 Elioenai, Jaakobah, Jeshohaiah, Asaiah, Adiel, Jesimiel, Benaiah, 37 and Ziza son of Shiphi son of Allon son of Jedaiah son of Shimri son of Shemaiah. 38 These mentioned by name were leaders in their clans, and their households increased greatly.

39 They went to the entrance of Gedor, as far as the east side of the valley, to find pasture for their flocks. 40 They found fertile pasture, and the land was spacious, quiet, and peaceful; the people of Ham used to live there. 41 These whose names were recorded, however, came in the days of Judah's King Hezekiah, attacked their tents and the Meunim[z] found there, and completely destroyed them, as can be seen today. They settled in their place, because there was pasture there for their flocks. 42 Some of them, five hundred Simeonites, went to Mount Seir, led by Pelatiah, Neariah, Rephaiah, and Uzziel, Ishi's sons. 43 They struck down those who were left of the Amalekites and have lived there ever since.

Lines of Reuben, Gad, and East Manasseh

5 The family of Reuben, Israel's oldest son: he was actually the oldest, but when he dishonored his father's bed his birthright[a] was given to the family of Joseph, Israel's son, so Reuben isn't listed as the oldest in the records. 2 Although Judah became the strongest among his brothers and a leader came from him, the birthright belonged to Joseph.

3 The family of Reuben, Israel's oldest son: Hanoch, Pallu, Hezron, and Carmi.

4 Joel's family: his son Shemaiah, his son Gog, his son Shimei, 5 his son Micah, his son Reaiah, his son Baal, 6 and his son Beerah, whom Assyria's King Tilgath-

[t] Cf 4:13; MT *the family of Elah and Kenaz* [u] LXX, Vulg; MT *son* [v] LXX; MT *and she conceived* [w] LXX; MT *the wife of Hodiah* [x] Or *ruled over* [y] Cf Tg, Vulg; MT *Lehem returned* [z] Qere; Kethib *Meinim* [a] Or *oldest son's rights*

pilneser carried away into exile. He was a chief of the Reubenites. [7]His relatives, by their[b] clans when their genealogy was listed in the records, were: Jeiel the first; Zechariah; [8]and Bela, Azaz's son, Shema's grandson, and Joel's great-grandson.

They lived in Aroer, as far as Nebo and Baal-meon. [9]They also settled in the east as far as the edge of the desert that stretches to the Euphrates River, because their livestock had increased in the land of Gilead. [10]In Saul's days they waged war on the Hagrites, whom they defeated. So they lived in their tents throughout the entire region east of Gilead.

[11]Gad's family lived opposite them in the land of Bashan as far as Salecah: [12]Joel was the first, Shapham the second, and Janai governed[c] Bashan.

[13]Their relatives according to their households: Michael, Meshullam, Sheba, Jorai, Jacan, Zia, and Eber—seven in all.

[14]This was the family of Abihail son of Huri son of Jaroah son of Gilead son of Michael son of Jeshishai son of Jahdo son of Buz. [15]Ahi, Abdiel's son and Guni's grandson, was the head of their household.

[16]They lived in Gilead, in Bashan and in its towns, and as far as the boundaries of all the open lands of Sharon. [17]They were all listed in the records in the days of Judah's King Jotham and Israel's King Jeroboam. [18]The Reubenites, the Gadites, and half the tribe of Manasseh were warriors who carried shield and sword, drew the bow, and were trained for war—44,760 ready for military service. [19]When they waged war on the Hagrites (the Jeturites, the Naphishites, and the Nodabites), [20]they received help against them. The Hagrites and all who were with them were handed over to them, because they cried out to God in battle. God granted their prayer because they trusted in him. [21]They seized their livestock: 50,000 of their camels, 250,000 sheep and goats, 2,000 donkeys, and 100,000 captives. [22]Many died, because God fought the battle. They lived there in place of the inhabitants until the exile.

[23]The members of half the tribe of Manasseh lived in the land from Bashan to Baal-hermon, Senir, and Mount Hermon. They were very numerous.

[24]These were the heads of their households:

Epher, Ishi, Eliel, Azriel, Jeremiah, Hodaviah, and Jahdiel—mighty warriors, famous men, heads of their households.

[25]But they were unfaithful to the God of their ancestors and faithlessly followed the gods of the peoples of the land, whom God had destroyed before them. [26]As a result, Israel's God stirred up the spirit of Assyria's King Pul, otherwise known as Assyria's King Tilgath-pilneser, who led the Reubenites, the Gadites, and half the tribe of Manasseh into exile, and brought them to Halah, Habor, Hara, and the Gozan River, where they remain to this day.

High priests

6 [d]Levi's family: Gershom, Kohath, and Merari.

[2]Kohath's family: Amram, Izhar, Hebron, and Uzziel.

[3]Amram's family: Aaron, Moses, and Miriam.

Aaron's family: Nadab, Abihu, Eleazar, and Ithamar.

[4]Eleazar was the father of Phinehas, Phinehas of Abishua, [5]Abishua of Bukki, Bukki of Uzzi, [6]Uzzi of Zerahiah, Zerahiah of Meraioth, [7]Meraioth of Amariah, Amariah of Ahitub, [8]Ahitub of Zadok, Zadok of Ahimaaz, [9]Ahimaaz of Azariah, Azariah of Johanan, [10]and Johanan of Azariah. He was the one who served as priest in the temple that Solomon built in Jerusalem.

[11]Azariah was the father of Amariah, Amariah of Ahitub, [12]Ahitub of Zadok, Zadok of Shallum, [13]Shallum of Hilkiah, Hilkiah of Azariah, [14]Azariah of Seraiah, and Seraiah of Jehozadak. [15]Jehozadak went away when the LORD caused Judah and Jerusalem to be exiled by Nebuchadnezzar.

[b]LXX[L], Syr; MT *his* [c]LXX, Tg; MT *Shaphatin* [d]5:27 in Heb

Levites

16[e]Levi's family: Gershom, Kohath, and Merari.

17These are the names of Gershom's family: Libni and Shimei.

18Kohath's family: Amram, Izhar, Hebron, and Uzziel.

19Merari's family: Mahli and Mushi.

These are the Levites' clans according to their fathers:

20Of Gershom: his son Libni, his son Jahath, his son Zimmah, 21his son Joah, his son Iddo, his son Zerah, and his son Jeatherai.

22Kohath's family: his son Amminadab, his son Korah, his son Assir, 23his son Elkanah, his son Ebiasaph, his son Assir, 24his son Tahath, his son Uriel, his son Uzziah, and his son Shaul.

25Elkanah's family: Amasai and Ahimoth, 26his son Elkanah,[f] his son Zophai, his son Nahath, 27his son Eliab, his son Jeroham, and his son Elkanah.

28Samuel's family: the oldest Joel,[g] and the second Abijah.

29Merari's family: Mahli, his son Libni, his son Shimei, his son Uzzah, 30his son Shimea, his son Haggiah, and his son Asaiah.

Levitical singers

31David put the following in charge of the music in the LORD's house after the chest was placed there. 32They ministered with song before the dwelling of the meeting tent, until Solomon built the LORD's temple in Jerusalem. They carried out their usual duties. 33Those who served and their families were:

Kohath's family: Heman the singer, son of Joel son of Samuel 34son of Elkanah son of Jeroham son of Eliel son of Toah 35son of Zuph son of Elkanah son of Mahath son of Amasai 36son of Elkanah son of Joel son of Azariah son of Zephaniah 37son of Tahath son of Assir son of Ebiasaph son of Korah 38son of Izhar son of Kohath son of Levi son of Israel. 39His relative was Asaph, who stood on his right, that is, Asaph son of Berechiah son of Shimea 40son of Michael son of Baaseiah son of Malchijah 41son of Ethni son of Zerah son of Adaiah 42son of Ethan son of Zimmah son of Shimei 43son of Jahath son of Gershom son of Levi.

44On the left were their relatives, Merari's family: Ethan son of Kishi son of Abdi son of Malluch 45son of Hashabiah son of Amaziah son of Hilkiah 46son of Amzi son of Bani son of Shemer 47son of Mahli son of Mushi son of Merari son of Levi. 48Their relatives the Levites were dedicated to all the services of the dwelling for God's house.

Priests from Aaron's line

49Aaron and his sons sacrificed on the altar for entirely burned offerings and on the altar for incense, doing all the work of the holiest place, to make reconciliation for Israel, just as Moses, God's servant, had commanded.

50This was Aaron's family: his son Eleazar, his son Phinehas, his son Abishua, 51his son Bukki, his son Uzzi, his son Zerahiah, 52his son Meraioth, his son Amariah, his son Ahitub, 53his son Zadok, and his son Ahimaaz.

Levitical cities

54These are the places they lived by their camps within their territory. To Aaron's family from the Kohathite clan, as chosen by lot, 55they gave Hebron in the land of Judah with its surrounding pasturelands. 56But the city's fields and its settlements they gave to Caleb, Jephunneh's son. 57To Aaron's family they gave the refuge cities: Hebron, Libnah with its pasturelands, Jattir, Eshtemoa with its pasturelands, 58Hilen[h] with its pasturelands, Debir with its pasturelands, 59Ashan with its pasturelands, Juttah with its pasturelands,[i] and Beth-shemesh with its pasturelands. 60From Benjamin's tribe: Gibeon with its

[e]6:1 in Heb [f]LXX; MT repeats *Elkanah.* [g]LXX, Syr; MT lacks *Joel.* [h]LXX, cf Josh 15:51; MT *Hilez*
[i]LXX, Syr, cf Josh 21:16; MT lacks *Juttah.*

pasturelands,[j] Geba with its pasturelands, Alemeth with its pasturelands, and Anathoth with its pasturelands. They had thirteen towns within their clan.

61 The remaining Kohathites were given ten towns by lot from the clan of half the tribe of Manasseh. 62 The Gershomites received by lot according to their clans thirteen towns from the tribes of Issachar, Asher, Naphtali, and Manasseh in Bashan. 63 The Merarites received by lot according to their clans twelve towns from the tribes of Reuben, Gad, and Zebulun. 64 In this way the Israelites gave the Levites the towns with their pasturelands. 65 They gave these towns, which they designated by name, by lot from the tribes of Judah, Simeon, and Benjamin.

66 Some of the Kohathite clans had towns of their territory from the tribe of Ephraim. 67 They gave them refuge cities: Shechem with its pasturelands in the Ephraimite highlands, Gezer with its pasturelands, 68 Jokmeam with its pasturelands, Beth-horon with its pasturelands, 69 Aijalon with its pasturelands, Gath-rimmon with its pasturelands; 70 and from half the tribe of Manasseh, Taanach[k] with its pasturelands, and Bileam with its pasturelands, for the Kohathite clans who remained.

71 To the Gershomites from the clan of half the tribe of Manasseh: Golan in Bashan with its pasturelands and Ashtaroth with its pasturelands; 72 from the tribe of Issachar: Kedesh with its pasturelands and Daberath with its pasturelands, 73 Ramoth with its pasturelands and Anem with its pasturelands; 74 from the tribe of Asher: Mashal with its pasturelands, Abdon with its pasturelands, and 75 Helkath[l] with its pasturelands and Rehob with its pasturelands; 76 and from the tribe of Naphtali: Kedesh in Galilee with its pasturelands, Hammon with its pasturelands, and Kiriathaim with its pasturelands. 77 To the remaining Merarites from the tribe of Zebulun: Jokneam with its pasturelands,[m] Rimmon[n] with its pasturelands, Tabor with its pasturelands, and Nahalal with its pasturelands;[o] 78 on the other side of the Jordan at Jericho, on the east side of the Jordan, from the tribe of Reuben: Bezer in the desert with its pasturelands, Jahzah with its pasturelands, 79 Kedemoth with its pasturelands, and Mephaath with its pasturelands; 80 and from the tribe of Gad: Ramoth in Gilead with its pasturelands, Mahanaim with its pasturelands, 81 Heshbon with its pasturelands, and Jazer with its pasturelands.

Issachar's line

7 Issachar's family: Tola, Puah, Jashub, and Shimron—four in all.

2 Tola's family: Uzzi, Rephaiah, Jeriel, Jahmai, Ibsam, and Shemuel—the heads of their households in Tola's line, mighty warriors of their generations. In David's time they numbered 22,600.

3 Uzzi's family: Izrahiah; and Izrahiah's family—Michael, Obadiah, Joel, and Isshiah—five in all, and all of them leaders. 4 According to the family records of their households, they had 36,000 troops in the units of their fighting force, since they had many wives and children. 5 Their relatives from all of Issachar's clans were 87,000 mighty warriors, all listed in the family records.

Lines of Benjamin and Naphtali

6 Benjamin's family:[p] Bela, Becher, and Jediael—three in all.

7 Bela's family: Ezbon, Uzzi, Uzziel, Jerimoth, and Iri—five heads of households, mighty warriors; 22,034 were listed in their family records.

8 Becher's family: Zemirah, Joash, Eliezer, Elioenai, Omri, Jeremoth, Abijah, Anathoth, and Alemeth. These were all Becher's family. 9 As listed in their family records by generation, as heads of their households, mighty warriors, there were 22,200.

10 Jediael's family: Bilhan.

Bilhan's family: Jeush, Benjamin, Ehud, Chenaanah, Zethan, Tarshish,

[j] Cf Josh 21:17; MT lacks *Gibeon.* [k] Cf Josh 21:25; MT *Aner* [l] Cf Josh 21:31; MT *Hukkok* [m] Cf Josh 21:34; MT lacks *Jokneam.* [n] LXX; MT *Rimmono* [o] Cf Josh 21:35; MT lacks *Nahalal.* [p] LXX; MT lacks *family.*

and Ahishahar. 11 All these were Jediael's family, heads of their households,
and mighty warriors. There were 17,200
ready for battle. 12 The Shuppites and
Huppites were Ir's family, and the Hush-
ites were Aher's family.
13 Naphtali's family: Jahziel, Guni,
Jezer, and Shallum. These were Bilhah's
family.

Manasseh's line

14 Manasseh's family: Asriel, to whom
his Aramean secondary wife gave birth.
She gave birth to Machir, Gilead's father.
15 Machir married Huppite and Shuppite
women. His sister's name was Maacah.
The second descendant's name was
Zelophehad, who had only daughters.
16 Machir's wife Maacah gave birth to a
son and named him Peresh. His brother's name was Sheresh, and his sons
were Ulam and Rekem.
17 Ulam's family: Bedan.
This was the family of Gilead, Machir's
son and Manasseh's grandson. 18 His
sister Hammolecheth gave birth to Ish-
hod, Abiezer, Mahlah, and Shemida.[q]
19 The members of Shemida's family were
Ahian, Shechem, Likhi, and Aniam.

Ephraim's line

20 Ephraim's family: Shuthelah, his
son Bered, his son Tahath, his son El-
eadah, his son Tahath, 21 his son Zabad,
his son Shuthelah, and Ezer and Elead.
The men of Gath, who were born in the
land, killed them when they came down
to take their cattle. 22 Ephraim their
father mourned many days, and his
brothers came to comfort him.
23 Ephraim had sex with his wife, and
she conceived and gave birth to a son.
He named him Beriah, because misfortune had come to his house. 24 His
daughter was Sheerah. She built both
Lower and Upper Beth-horon and Uzzen-
sheerah. 25 His son was Rephah, his son[r]
Resheph, his son Telah, his son Tahan,
26 his son Ladan, his son Ammihud, his
son Elishama, 27 his son Nun, and his son
Joshua. 28 Their possessions and settlements were Bethel and its towns, to the
east Naaran, and to the west Gezer and
its towns, and Shechem and its towns as
far as Ayyah and its towns. 29 Beth-shean
and its towns, Taanach and its towns,
Megiddo and its towns, and Dor and its
towns were under Manassite authority.
The family of Joseph, Israel's son, lived in
them.

Asher's line

30 Asher's family: Imnah, Ishvah, Ishvi,
Beriah, and their sister Serah.
31 Beriah's family: Heber and Malchiel, who was Birzaith's father. 32 Heber
was the father of Japhlet, Shomer, Hotham, and their sister Shua.
33 Japhlet's family: Pasach, Bimhal,
and Ashvath. This is Japhlet's family.
34 Shemer's family: Ahi, Rohgah, Je-
hubbah, and Aram.
35 His brother Helem's family: Zophah,
Imna, Shelesh, and Amal.
36 Zophah's family: Suah, Harne-
pher, Shual, Beri, Imrah, 37 Bezer, Hod,
Shamma, Shilshah, Ithran, and Beera.
38 Jether's family: Jephunneh, Pispa,
and Ara.
39 Ulla's family: Arah, Hanniel, and Rizia.
40 All these were Asher's family, heads
of households, select mighty warriors, the
heads of the princes. Those ready for battle listed in the records numbered 26,000.

Benjamin's line

8 Benjamin was the father of Bela his
oldest son, Ashbel his second son,
Aharah the third, 2 Nohah the fourth,
and Rapha the fifth.
3 Bela had a family: Addar, Gera, Abi-
hud, 4 Abishua, Naaman, Ahoah, 5 Gera,
Shephuphan, and Huram.
6 This was Ehud's family. They were
heads of households of the inhabitants of
Geba, who were sent into exile to Manahath. 7 Gera[s] sent them into exile and
was the father of Uzza and Ahihud.

[q] Cf 7:19, Josh 17:2; MT lacks *and Shemida.* [r] MT lacks *his son.* [s] MT *Naaman, Ahijah, and Gera*

8 Shaharaim had children in the country of Moab after he divorced his wives Hushim and Baara. 9 He had children with his wife Hodesh: Jobab, Zibia, Mesha, Malcam, 10 Jeuz, Sachia, and Mirmah. These were his sons, heads of households. 11 He also had children with Hushim: Abitub and Elpaal.

12 Elpaal's family: Eber, Misham, Shemed, who built Ono and Lod with its towns, 13 Beriah, and Shema. They were heads of households of the inhabitants of Aijalon, who drove out the inhabitants of Gath. 14 Their brothers[t] were Shashak and Jeremoth.

15 Beriah's family: Zebadiah, Arad, Eder, 16 Michael, Ishpah, and Joha.

17 Elpaal's family: Zebadiah, Meshullam, Hizki, Heber, 18 Ishmerai, Izliah, and Jobab.

19 Shimei's family: Jakim, Zichri, Zabdi, 20 Elienai, Zillethai, Eliel, 21 Adaiah, Beraiah, and Shimrath.

22 Shashak's family: Ishpan, Eber, Eliel, 23 Abdon, Zichri, Hanan, 24 Hananiah, Omri,[u] Elam, Anthothijah, 25 Iphdeiah, and Penuel.

26 Jeroham's family: Shamsherai, Shehariah, Athaliah, 27 Jaareshiah, Elijah, and Zichri.

28 These were the heads of households, in their generations. They were leaders who lived in Jerusalem. 29 Jeiel,[v] Gibeon's father, lived in Gibeon. His wife's name was Maacah; 30 his oldest son was Abdon, then Zur, Kish, Baal, Ner,[w] Nadab, 31 Gedor, Ahio, Zecher, and Mikloth.

32 Mikloth was the father of Shimeah. These also lived near their relatives in Jerusalem.[x]

33 Ner was the father of Kish, Kish was the father of Saul, and Saul was the father of Jonathan, Malchishua, Abinadab, and Esh-baal.

34 Jonathan's son was Merib-baal, and Merib-baal was Micah's father.

35 Micah's family: Pithon, Melech, Tarea, and Ahaz.

36 Ahaz was the father of Jehoaddah; Jehoaddah was the father of Alemeth, Azmaveth, and Zimri; and Zimri was the father of Moza. 37 Moza was the father of Binea; his son was Raphah, his son Eleasah, and his son Azel. 38 Azel had six sons, named Azrikam, his oldest,[y] Ishmael, Sheariah, Azariah,[z] Obadiah, and Hanan. All these were in Azel's family.

39 His brother Eshek's family: Ulam his oldest, Jeush the second, and Eliphelet the third. 40 Ulam's family were mighty warriors and archers, having many children and grandchildren—150 in all and all were Benjaminites.

9 So all Israel was listed in the official records of Israel's kings.

Restored Jerusalem community

Judah was carried into exile in Babylon because of their unfaithfulness. 2 The first to resettle their property in their towns were the Israelite people, the priests, the Levites, and the temple servants. 3 Those settling in Jerusalem included some from Judah, some from Benjamin, and some from Ephraim and Manasseh:

Judah and Benjamin

4 Uthai son of Ammihud son of Omri son of Imri son of Bani from the family of Perez, Judah's son.

5 From the Shilonites: Asaiah the oldest son and his family.

6 From Zerah's family: Jeuel and their relatives—690 in all.

7 From Benjamin's family: Sallu son of Meshullam son of Hodaviah son of Senaah;[a] 8 Ibneiah, Jeroham's son; Elah son of Uzzi son of Michri; Meshullam son of Shephatiah son of Reuel son of Ibnijah; 9 and their relatives in their line of descent—956 in all. All of these were heads of their households.

Priests and Levites

10 From the priests: Jedaiah, Jehoiarib, Jachin, 11 and Azariah son of

[t]LXX; MT *Ahio* [u]LXX; MT lacks *Omri.* [v]LXX; MT lacks *Jeiel.* [w]LXX; MT lacks *Ner.* [x]Syr; MT adds *with their relatives.* [y]LXX, Tg; MT *Bocheru* [z]LXX; MT lacks *Azariah.* [a]LXX; MT *Hassenuah*

Hilkiah son of Meshullam son of Zadok son of Meraioth son of Ahitub the leader of God's house; [12]Adaiah son of Jeroham son of Pashhur son of Malchijah; Maasai son of Adiel son of Jahzerah son of Meshullam son of Meshillemith son of Immer; [13]and their relatives, heads of their households, 1,760 capable men for the religious work of God's house.

[14]From the Levites: Shemaiah son of Hasshub son of Azrikam son of Hashabiah, from Merari's family; [15]Bakbakkar, Heresh, Galal, and Mattaniah son of Mica son of Zichri son of Asaph; [16]Obadiah son of Shemaiah son of Galal son of Jeduthun; and Berechiah son of Asa son of Elkanah, who lived in the settlements of the Netophathites.

Gatekeepers

[17]The gatekeepers: Shallum, Akkub, Talmon, and Ahiman. Their brother Shallum was the leader, [18]stationed until now in the King's Gate on the east side. These were the gatekeepers belonging to the Levites' camp.

[19]Shallum, Kore's son, Ebiasaph's grandson, and Korah's great-grandson, and his relatives belonging to his household, the Korahites, served as gatekeepers at the tent's entrances, as their ancestors had been gatekeepers at the entrance to the LORD's camp.

[20]Phinehas, Eleazar's son, the LORD be with him, was their leader in former times.

[21]Zechariah, Meshelemiah's son, was gatekeeper at the meeting tent's entrance.

[22]All those selected as gatekeepers at the entrances were two hundred twelve. They were listed in the family records by their settlements. David and Samuel the seer assigned them to their trusted position. [23]So they and their descendants were the gatekeepers guarding the LORD's house, that is, the tent.[b] [24]The gatekeepers were on the four sides: east, west, north, and south. [25]Their relatives came in from their settlements, from time to time, to assist them for a period of seven days. [26]Due to their trustworthiness, the four master gatekeepers, who were Levites, were in charge of the rooms and the treasuries of God's house. [27]They would spend the night patrolling God's house since they had guard duty and were responsible for unlocking it every morning. [28]Some of them were responsible for the worship objects; they counted them when they were brought in and taken out. [29]Others were appointed over the furniture, the holy equipment, the flour, wine, oil, incense, and spices. [30]Some of the priests blended the ointment for the spices; [31]and Mattithiah, one of the Levites, the oldest son of Shallum the Korahite, was entrusted with baking the flat cakes. [32]Also some of their Kohathite relatives were responsible for preparing the stacks of bread for each Sabbath. [33]The singers were the heads of the households of the Levites. They lived in temple rooms and were free from other service because they were on duty day and night. [34]These were the heads of the households of the Levites, according to descent. They lived in Jerusalem.

Saul's family

[35]Jeiel, Gibeon's father, lived in Gibeon. His wife's name was Maacah. [36]His oldest son was Abdon, followed by Zur, Kish, Baal, Ner, Nadab, [37]Gedor, Ahio, Zechariah, and Mikloth. [38]Mikloth was the father of Shimeam. They too lived near their relatives in Jerusalem.[c]

[39]Ner was the father of Kish, Kish of Saul, Saul of Jonathan, Malchishua, Abinadab, and Esh-baal.

[40]Jonathan's son was Merib-baal, and Merib-baal was the father of Micah.

[41]Micah's family were Pithon, Melech, Tahrea, and Ahaz.[d]

[42]Ahaz was the father of Jarah; and Jarah of Alemeth, Azmaveth, and Zimri.

Zimri was the father of Moza. [43]Moza was the father of Binea; Rephaiah was his son, Eleasah was his son, and Azel was his son. [44]Azel had six sons whose

[b] Or *house of the tent* [c] Heb adds *with their relatives.* [d] Cf 8:35; MT lacks *Ahaz.*

names were Azrikam, Bocheru, Ishmael, Sheariah, Obadiah, and Hanan. This was Azel's family.

Saul's death

10 When the Philistines attacked the Israelites, the Israelites ran away from the Philistines, and many fell dead on Mount Gilboa. 2The Philistines overtook Saul and his sons, and they killed his sons Jonathan, Abinadab, and Malchishua. 3The battle was fierce around Saul, and when the archers located him, he trembled in fear. 4Saul said to his armor-bearer, "Draw your sword and kill me with it! Otherwise, these uncircumcised men will come and kill me or torture me." But his armor-bearer refused because he was terrified. So Saul took the sword and impaled himself on it. 5When the armor-bearer saw that Saul was dead, he also impaled himself on his sword and died with Saul. 6So Saul and his three sons died; his whole household died together. 7When all the Israelites who were in the valley saw that the army had run away and that Saul and his sons were dead, they abandoned their towns and fled. So the Philistines came to live in them.

8The next day when the Philistines came to strip the dead, they found Saul and his sons lying dead on Mount Gilboa. 9They stripped him, carried off his head and armor, and sent messengers throughout the land of the Philistines to spread the news to their idols and to the people. 10They placed his armor in their god's temple and displayed his skull on a pole in the temple of Dagon.

11When all the people of Jabesh-gilead heard all that the Philistines had done to Saul, 12all their warriors arose and recovered the corpses of Saul and his sons. They brought them back to Jabesh, buried their bones under the oak in Jabesh, and fasted for seven days.

13Saul died because he was unfaithful to the LORD and hadn't followed the LORD's word. He even consulted a medium for guidance. 14He didn't consult the LORD, so the LORD killed him and gave the kingdom to David, Jesse's son.

All Israel makes David king

11 All the Israelites gathered around David at Hebron. "We're your own flesh and blood," they said. 2"In the past, even when Saul ruled over us, you were the one who led Israel. The LORD your God told you, 'You will shepherd my people Israel, and you will become a leader over my people Israel.'" 3So all of Israel's elders came to the king at Hebron, and David made a covenant with them before the LORD. They anointed David to make him king over Israel, just as the LORD had promised through Samuel.

David captures Jerusalem

4Then David and all Israel marched to Jerusalem, that is, Jebus, where the Jebusites lived. 5The people who lived in Jebus told David, "You'll never get in here!"

But David captured the mountain fortress of Zion, which became David's City. 6David had said, "The first one to kill a Jebusite will become commander in chief!" Joab, Zeruiah's son, was the first to attack and so became commander in chief. 7David occupied the fortress, so it was renamed David's City. 8He also built up the city on all sides, including its own foundations and the surrounding areas, while Joab restored the rest of the city. 9David grew increasingly powerful, and the LORD of heavenly forces was with him.

David and his warriors

10These are the commanders of David's warriors who continued to support him while he was king. Together with all Israel, they made him king, as the LORD had promised Israel. 11This is the list of David's warriors:

Jashobeam, a Hacmonite, was commander of the Thirty. He raised his spear against eight hundred, killing them on a single occasion.

12Next in command came Eleazar, Dodo's son the Ahohite, who was one of the three warriors. 13He was with David at Pasdammim. The Philistines were gathered there for battle, where part of a field was full of barley. When the people ran away from the Philistines, 14he and David stood in the middle of the field, held their ground, and defeated the Philistines. So the LORD achieved a great victory.

15 Three of the thirty commanders went down from the rock to David at the fortress[e] of Adullam, while the army of the Philistines camped in the Rephaim Valley.
16 At that time David was in the fortress, and a Philistine fort was in Bethlehem.
17 David had a craving and said, "If only someone could give me a drink of water from the well by the gate in Bethlehem."
18 So the three warriors broke through the Philistine camp and drew water from the well by the gate in Bethlehem and brought it back to David. But he refused to drink it and poured it out to the LORD.
19 "God forbid that I should do that," he said. "Isn't this the blood of men who risked their lives?" So he refused to drink it. Since they had brought it at the risk of their lives, David refused to drink it.

These were the kinds of things the three warriors did.

20 Abishai, Joab's brother, was chief of the Thirty.[f] He raised his spear against the three hundred men he had slain, but he wasn't considered one of the Three.
21 He was the most famous of the Thirty. He became their commander, but he wasn't among the Three.
22 Benaiah, Jehoiada's son from Kabzeel, was a hero who performed great deeds. He killed two of Moab's leaders,[g] and on a snowy day went down into a pit where he killed a lion.
23 He also killed an Egyptian seven and a half feet tall, who was holding a spear like a weaver's beam. Benaiah went down to him with a club, grabbed the spear from the Egyptian's hand, and killed him with it.
24 These were the exploits of Benaiah, Jehoiada's son; he wasn't considered one of the three warriors.
25 He was famous among the Thirty, but didn't become one of the Three. David placed him in command of his own bodyguard.

26 The mighty warriors:
Asahel, Joab's brother;
Elhanan, Dodo's son from Bethlehem;
27 Shammoth from Haror;
Helez from Pelon;
28 Ira, Ikkesh's son from Tekoa;
Abiezer from Anathoth;
29 Sibbecai the Hushathite;
Ilai from Ahoh;
30 Maharai from Netophah;
Heled, Baanah's son from Netophah;
31 Ithai, Ribai's son
from Gibeah of the Benjaminites;
Benaiah from Pirathon;
32 Hurai from the Gaash ravines;
Abiel the Arbathite;
33 Azmaveth from Baharum;
Eliahba from Shaalbon;
34 Hashem[h] the Gizonite;
Jonathan, Shagee's son
from Harar;
35 Ahiam, Sachar's son from Harar;
Eliphal, Ur's son;
36 Hepher the Mecherathite;
Ahijah the Pelonite;
37 Hezro from Carmel;
Naarai, Ezbai's son;
38 Joel, Nathan's brother;
Mibhar, Hagri's son;
39 Zelek the Ammonite;
Naharai from Beeroth, Zeruiah's son
and the armor-bearer for Joab;
40 Ira from Ither;
Gareb from Ither;
41 Uriah the Hittite;
Zabad, Ahlai's son;
42 Adina son of Shiza the Reubenite,
a leader of the Reubenites,
and thirty with him;
43 Hanan, Maacah's son;
Joshaphat the Mithnite;
44 Uzzia the Ashterathite;
Shama and Jeiel
the sons of Hotham the Aroerite;
45 Jediael, Shimri's son,
and his brother Joha the Tizite;
46 Eliel the Mahavite;
Jeribai and Joshaviah, Elnaam's sons;
Ithmah the Moabite;
47 Eliel, Obed, and Jaasiel the Mezobaite.

David's desert army

12 The following persons came to David at Ziklag while he was banished from

[e] Or *cave*; cf 2 Sam 23:14 [f] Syr; MT *three* [g] Heb *Ariel* [h] MT *the family of Hashem*

the presence of Saul, Kish's son. They were some of the warriors who helped him in battle, 2 armed with bows, and they could use either hand to shoot arrows or sling stones. They were Saul's relatives from Benjamin:

3 Ahiezer was the leader, then Joash, both Shemaah's sons from Gibeah; Jeziel and Pelet, Azmaveth's sons; Beracah; Jehu of Anathoth; 4 Ishmaiah from Gibeon, a warrior in the Thirty and a leader over the Thirty;[i] Jeremiah; Jahaziel; Johanan; Jozabad from Gederah; 5[j]Eluzai; Jerimoth; Bealiah; Shemariah; Shephatiah the Haruphite; 6 Elkanah, Isshiah, Azarel, Joezer, and Jashobeam the Korahites; 7 Joelah; and Zebadiah, Jeroham's son from Gedor.

8 Some left Gad to join David at the desert fortress, brave warriors trained for battle, armed with shield and spear, who looked like lions and who were swift as gazelles on the mountains: 9 Ezer the leader, Obadiah second, Eliab third, 10 Mishmannah fourth, Jeremiah fifth, 11 Attai sixth, Eliel seventh, 12 Johanan eighth, Elzabad ninth, 13 Jeremiah tenth, Machbannai eleventh.

14 These Gadites were military officers, the least of them ready to fight a hundred and the greatest a thousand. 15 These are the ones who crossed the Jordan in the first month, when it was overflowing all its banks, and chased away everyone living in the valleys to the east and the west.

16 Some Benjaminites and Judahites also came to David at the fortress. 17 David went out to meet them and said to them, "If you've come to me with good intentions in order to help me, then we will join forces. But if you've come to betray me to my enemies, though I've done no wrong, then may our ancestors' God see it and punish you."

18 Then a spirit took hold of Amasai, the leader of the Thirty:

David, we are yours;
  and on your side, Jesse's son!
May it go very well for you,
  and may it go well for whoever
    helps you!
  Yes, your God has helped you.

Then David received them, and put them at the head of his troops.

19 Some of the Manassites also joined David when he came with the Philistines for the battle against Saul. But he[k] didn't help them, because after considering the matter, the Philistine rulers sent him away. "He'll rejoin his master Saul," they said, "and it will cost us our heads." 20 When he went to Ziklag some joined him from Manasseh: Adnah, Jozabad, Jediael, Michael, Jozabad, Elihu, and Zillethai, leaders of units of a thousand in Manasseh. 21 They helped David against the raiding bands because they were all warriors and officers in the army. 22 Reinforcements came to David daily until there was an army as mighty as God's army.

23 These are the numbers of the commanders of those armed for battle who came to David in Hebron to make sure he took over Saul's kingdom, according to the LORD's word:

24 from Judah, carrying shield and spear,
  6,800 troops armed for battle;
25 from Simeon, mighty warriors, 7,100;
26 from Levi, 4,600;
27 also Jehoiada, leader of Aaron's line,
  and with him 3,700;
28 and Zadok, a young man, a mighty
  warrior, and 22 officers from his
  household;
29 from Benjamin, Saul's relatives, 3,000,
  most of whom had been loyal to
  Saul's household;
30 from Ephraim, 20,800, mighty
  warriors, famous in their households;
31 from half the tribe of Manasseh,
  18,000, designated by name to come
  and make David king;
32 from Issachar, those who understood
  the times and what Israel should do,
  200 chiefs, with all their relatives
  under their command;
33 from Zebulun, 50,000 experienced
  troops, armed for battle with all
  the weapons of war, to help with
  undivided loyalty;
34 from Naphtali, 1,000 officers,

[i] 12:5 in Heb [j] 12:6 in Heb [k] LXX; MT *they*

as well as 37,000 armed with shield
and spear;
35 from Dan, 28,600 armed for battle;
36 from Asher, 40,000 experienced troops
armed for battle;
37 from the other side of the Jordan,
the Reubenites, Gadites, and the
other half of the tribe of Manasseh,
120,000 armed with all the weapons
of war.

38 All these men of war, armed[l] for battle,
came to Hebron determined to make David
king over all Israel, and all the rest of Israel were fully agreed to make David king.
39 They were there with David for three
days, eating and drinking, while their relatives provided food for them. 40 Even their
neighbors from as far away as Issachar,
Zebulun, and Naphtali were bringing food
by donkeys, camels, mules, and oxen. There
was an abundance of flour, fig cakes, clusters of raisins, wine, oil, oxen, and sheep,
because Israel was joyful.

David's first attempt to move the chest

13 After consulting with the captains of
the units of a thousand and a hundred,
in fact with every leader, 2 David said to the
entire Israelite assembly: "If you approve,
and if the LORD our God agrees, let's spread
the word to the rest of our relatives in all the
regions of Israel, including the priests and
Levites in their cities with pasturelands. Let's
ask them to join us 3 so that we may bring the
chest of our God back to us, because we didn't
look for it in Saul's days." 4 The whole assembly agreed to do so, because all the people
thought it was the right thing to do.

5 So David assembled all Israel, from the
border[m] of Egypt to Lebo-hamath in order
to bring up God's chest from Kiriath-jearim.
6 Then David and all Israel went up toward
Baalah, to Kiriath-jearim, which belongs
to Judah, to bring up from there the chest
of God, the LORD, who sits enthroned on
the winged creatures, where he is called by
name.[n] 7 They moved God's chest on a new
cart from Abinadab's house. Uzzah and Ahio
were guiding the cart, 8 while David and all
Israel celebrated in God's presence with
all their strength, accompanied by songs,
zithers, harps, tambourines, cymbals, and
trumpets. 9 When they came to Chidon's
threshing floor, Uzzah reached out to the
chest and grabbed it because the oxen had
stumbled. 10 But the LORD became angry
with Uzzah and struck him because he had
placed his hand on the chest. He died right
there before God. 11 David was angry that the
LORD lashed out at Uzzah; and so that place
is still called Perez-uzzah today. 12 David was
frightened by God that day. "How will I ever
bring God's chest home to me?" he asked.
13 So David didn't take the chest away with
him to David's City. Instead, he had it put in
the house of Obed-edom the Gittite. 14 God's
chest stayed with Obed-edom's household
for three months, and the LORD blessed
Obed-edom's household and all that he had.

David's kingship established in Jerusalem

14 Tyre's King Hiram sent messengers to
David with cedar logs, bricklayers, and
carpenters to build David a palace. 2 Then
David knew that the LORD had established
him as king over Israel, and that his kingship was held in great honor for the sake
of his people Israel. 3 David married more
secondary wives in Jerusalem and fathered
more sons and daughters. 4 The names of
his children in Jerusalem were as follows:
Shammua, Shobab, Nathan, Solomon,
5 Ibhar, Elishua, Elpelet, 6 Nogah, Nepheg,
Japhia, 7 Elishama, Beeliada, and Eliphelet.

David defeats the Philistines

8 When the Philistines heard that David
had been anointed king over all Israel, they
all marched up to find him. David heard
this and went out to confront them. 9 The
Philistines had invaded and were plundering the Rephaim Valley. 10 David asked God
for advice: "Should I attack the Philistines,
and will you hand them over to me?"

The LORD answered, "Attack them, and
I'll definitely hand them over to you."

11 So they marched up to Baal-perazim, and

[l] LXX; MT *helpers* [m] Heb *Shikhor, river*; cf Josh 15:4; 1 Kgs 8:65; 2 Chron 7:8 [n] Heb uncertain

David defeated them there. "By my strength," David exclaimed, "God has burst out against my enemies, the way water bursts out." That's why the place is called Baal-perazim.[o] 12 The Philistines left their divine images behind, and David ordered them burned.

13 When the Philistines plundered the valley a second time, 14 David again asked God's advice, but God answered, "Don't attack them directly. Circle around behind them and come at them from in front of the balsam trees. 15 As soon as you hear the sound of marching in the tops of the trees, then attack, for God has attacked in front of you to defeat the Philistine army." 16 David followed God's orders exactly, and they defeated the Philistine army from Gibeon all the way to Gezer. 17 David's fame spread throughout all lands, and the LORD made all the nations fear him.

David prepares to bring the chest to Jerusalem

15 After he had built houses for himself in David's City, David prepared a place for God's chest and pitched a tent for it. 2 David said, "Only the Levites may carry God's chest, because the LORD has chosen them to carry the LORD's chest and to minister to him forever."

3 David assembled all Israel in Jerusalem to bring the LORD's chest to the place he had prepared for it. 4 David also gathered Aaron's family and the Levites:

5 Uriel, the leader of Kohath's family, and 120 of his relatives;
6 Asaiah, the leader of Merari's family, and 220 of his relatives;
7 Joel, the leader of Gershom's family, and 130 of his relatives;
8 Shemaiah, the leader of Elizaphan's family, and 200 of his relatives;
9 Eliel, the leader of Hebron's family, and 80 of his relatives;
10 and Amminadab, the leader of Uzziel's family, and 112 of his relatives.

11 David called for the priests Zadok and Abiathar, and the Levites Uriel, Asaiah, Joel, Shemaiah, Eliel, and Amminadab. 12 He said to them, "You are the household heads of the Levites. Make yourselves holy, you and your brothers, and then bring the chest of the LORD, Israel's God, to the place I've prepared for it. 13 When you weren't with us the first time, the LORD our God burst out against us because we didn't ask his advice properly." 14 So the priests and the Levites made themselves holy to bring up the chest of the LORD, Israel's God. 15 The Levites carried God's chest with poles on their shoulders, just as Moses had commanded according to the LORD's word.

16 Then David told the leaders of the Levites to appoint some of their relatives as singers to raise their voices joyfully, accompanied by musical instruments, including harps, lyres, and cymbals.

17 So the Levites appointed Heman, Joel's son; and from his relatives, Asaph, Berechiah's son; and from their Merarite relatives, Ethan, Kushaiah's son; 18 and second in rank with them their relatives: Zechariah, Jaaziel,[p] Shemiramoth, Jehiel, Unni, Eliab, Benaiah, Maaseiah, Mattithiah, Eliphelehu, Mikneiah, and Obed-edom and Jeiel the gatekeepers.

19 The singers Heman, Asaph, and Ethan were to make music with bronze cymbals.
20 Zechariah, Aziel, Shemiramoth, Jehiel, Unni, Eliab, Maaseiah, and Benaiah were to play harps tuned to the Alamoth.
21 Mattithiah, Eliphelehu, Mikneiah, Obed-edom, Jeiel, and Azaziah were to lead with lyres tuned to the Sheminith.
22 Chenaniah was leader of the Levites who provided transportation,[q] because he was skilled at it.
23 Berechiah and Elkanah were gatekeepers for the chest.
24 The priests Shebaniah, Joshaphat, Nethanel, Amasai, Zechariah, Benaiah, and Eliezer were to blow the trumpets before God's chest. Obed-edom and Jehiah also were to be gatekeepers for the chest.

David brings the chest to Jerusalem

25 Then David, along with Israel's elders and the captains of the thousands, went with rejoicing to bring up the chest contain-

[o] Or *master of outbursts* [p] LXX; MT *Jaaziel's* son [q] Heb uncertain

ing the LORD's covenant from Obed-edom's house. 26 Since God had helped the Levites who were carrying the chest containing the LORD's covenant, they sacrificed seven bulls and seven rams. 27 David wore a fine-linen robe, as did the singers, all the Levites who were carrying the chest, and Chenaniah, the leader of transportation.[r] David also wore a linen priestly vest.[s] 28 So all Israel brought up the chest containing the LORD's covenant with shouts of joy, accompanied by the blast of the ram's horn, by trumpets and cymbals, and playing on harps and lyres. 29 As the chest containing the LORD's covenant entered David's City, Michal, Saul's daughter, looked out the window. When she saw King David leaping and dancing, she lost all respect for him.

16 They brought in God's chest and placed it inside the tent David had pitched for it. Then they brought entirely burned offerings and well-being sacrifices before God. 2 When David had finished offering the entirely burned offerings and the well-being sacrifices, he blessed the people in the LORD's name 3 and distributed a loaf of bread, a piece of meat,[t] and a raisin cake to every Israelite man and woman.

David establishes worship

4 David appointed some of the Levites to serve before the LORD's chest in order to remember, to give thanks, and to praise the LORD, Israel's God: 5 Asaph was the leader, and Zechariah his assistant; also Jeiel, Shemiramoth, Jehiel, Mattithiah, Eliab, Benaiah, Obed-edom, and Jeiel with harps and lyres; Asaph sounding the cymbals; 6 and the priests Benaiah and Jahaziel blowing trumpets regularly before the chest containing God's covenant. 7 On the same day, for the first time, David ordered Asaph and his relatives to give thanks to the LORD.

David's song of praise

8 Give thanks to the LORD,
call on his name;
make his deeds known to all people!
9 Sing to God, sing praises to him;
dwell on all his wondrous works!
10 Give praise to God's holy name!
Let the hearts rejoice
of all those seeking the LORD!
11 Pursue the LORD and his strength;
seek his face always!
12 Remember the wondrous works
he has done,
all his marvelous works,
and the justice he declared—
13 you who are the offspring of Israel,
his servant,
and the children of Jacob,
his chosen ones.
14 The LORD—he is our God.
His justice is everywhere
throughout the whole world.
15 God remembers[u] his covenant forever,
the word he commanded
to a thousand generations,
16 which he made with Abraham,
the solemn pledge he swore to Isaac.
17 God set it up as binding law for Jacob,
as an eternal covenant for Israel,
18 promising, "I hereby give you
the land of Canaan
as your allotted inheritance."
19 When they[v] were few in number—
insignificant, just immigrants—
20 wandering from nation to nation,
from one kingdom to the next,
21 God didn't let anyone oppress them.
God punished kings for their sake:
22 "Don't touch my anointed ones;
don't harm my prophets!"
23 Sing to the LORD, all the earth!
Share the news of his saving work
every single day!
24 Declare God's glory among the nations;
declare his wondrous works
among all people
25 because the LORD is great
and so worthy of praise.
He is awesome beyond all other gods
26 because all the gods of the nations
are just idols,
but it is the LORD
who created heaven!

[r] MT adds *the singers.* [s] Heb *ephod* [t] Cf LXX, Syr, Vulg; Heb uncertain [u] LXX; MT *Remember* [v] LXX, Vulg; MT *when you were*

27 Greatness and grandeur
are in front of him;
strength and joy are in his place.
28 Give to the LORD,
all families of the nations—
give to the LORD glory and power!
29 Give to the LORD the glory
due his name!
Bring gifts! Enter his presence!
Bow down to the LORD
in his holy splendor!
30 Tremble before him, all the earth!
Yes, he set the world firmly in place;[w]
it won't be shaken.
31 Let heaven celebrate!
Let the earth rejoice!
Let the nations say, "The LORD rules!"
32 Let the sea and everything in it roar!
Let the countryside and
everything in it celebrate!
33 Then the trees of the forest
will shout out joyfully
before the LORD, because he is coming
to establish justice on earth!
34 Give thanks to the LORD
because he is good,
because his faithful love
endures forever.
35 Say: "Save us, God, our savior!
Gather us! Deliver us from among
the nations
so we can give thanks to your holy name
and rejoice in your praise."
36 Bless the LORD, Israel's God,
from forever in the past to forever always.
And let all the people say, "Amen!"
Praise the LORD!

37 Then David placed Asaph and his relatives, together with Obed-edom and sixty-
eight of his relatives, to minister there
continually before the chest containing the
LORD's covenant, following the routines
required on each day. 38 Obed-edom, Jeduthun's son, and Hosah served as gatekeepers. 39 David also placed the priest Zadok
and his other priestly relatives at the LORD's
dwelling at the shrine in Gibeon. 40 They
were to offer continually, both morning and
evening, entirely burned offerings to the
LORD on the altar for entirely burned offerings, following the written requirements
in the LORD's Instruction, which he had
given Israel. 41 With them were Heman and
Jeduthun and the rest of those chosen by
name to give thanks to the LORD, because
his faithful love lasts forever. 42 With them
were also[x] the trumpets and the cymbals
for the musicians and the instruments for
God's songs. Jeduthun's family was at the
gate. 43 Then all of the people left for their
homes. And David returned to bless his
household.

God's promise to David

17 When David was settled into his palace,[y] he said to the prophet Nathan,
"I'm living in a cedar palace while the chest
containing the LORD's covenant is under
curtains."

2 Nathan replied, "Go ahead and do
whatever you are thinking, because God is
with you."

3 But that very night God's word came to
Nathan: 4 Go to my servant David and tell
him, This is what the LORD says: You are not
the one to build the temple[z] for me to live
in. 5 In fact, I haven't lived in a temple from
the day I brought Israel out until this very
day. I've been traveling from tent to tent
and from dwelling to dwelling.[a] 6 Throughout
my traveling with the Israelites, did I ever
ask one of Israel's tribal leaders, whom I appointed to shepherd my people, Why haven't
you built me a cedar temple?

7 So then, say this to my servant David:
This is what the LORD of heavenly forces
says: I myself took you from the pasture,
from following the flock, to be leader over
my people Israel. 8 I've been with you wherever you've gone. I've eliminated all your
enemies before you. Now I will make your
name great—like the name of the greatest people on earth. 9 I'm going to provide
a place for my people Israel, and plant them
so that they may live there and no longer
be disturbed. Cruel people will no longer

[w]LXX; MT *the world is firmly established* [x]LXX; MT adds *Heman and Jeduthun.* [y]Or, here and elsewhere in this chapter, *house* [z]Or, here and elsewhere in this chapter, *house* [a]MT lacks *to dwelling.*

trouble them as they did earlier, [10]when I
appointed judges over my people Israel.
I'll subdue all your enemies and make you
great. As for a dynasty,[b] the LORD will build
one for you! [11]When the time comes for you
to die, I will raise up a descendant of yours
after you, one of your own sons, to succeed
you, and I will establish his kingship. [12]He
is the one who will build me a temple, and
I will establish his throne forever. [13]I will
become his father and he will become my
son, and I'll never withdraw my faithful
love from him as I did from the one before
you. [14]I'll install him in my house and in my
kingdom forever, and his throne will be established forever.
[15]Nathan faithfully reported all that he
had seen and heard to David.

David's prayer

[16]Then King David went and sat in the
LORD's presence. He asked:
Who am I, LORD God, and of what
significance is my family that you have
brought me this far? [17]But even this was
too small in your eyes, God. You have
spoken about the future of your servant's dynasty and have chosen me as
an important person, LORD God.
[18]What more can I say to you for honoring your servant? You yourself know
your servant. [19]LORD, for your servant's
sake and according to your will, you have
done this great thing in order to make
all these great things known.
[20]LORD, no one can compare to you,
no God except you, just as we have heard
with our own ears.
[21]Who is like your people Israel, a
unique nation on the earth, that God
redeemed as his own people, establishing
a name for yourself by doing great and
awesome things, by driving out nations
before your people whom you saved
from Egypt? [22]You established your
people Israel as your own people forever,
and you, LORD, became their God.
[23]Now, LORD, confirm forever the
promise you have made about your servant and his dynasty. Do as you have
promised [24]so that it may be established
and so that your name may be made
great forever when people say, "The
LORD of heavenly forces, the God of Israel, is Israel's God." May your servant
David's household be established before you. [25]You, my God, have revealed
to your servant that you will build him
a dynasty. That is why your servant has
found the courage to pray this prayer to
you. [26]LORD, you are truly God, and you
promised this good thing to your servant.
[27]So now willingly bless your servant's
dynasty so that it might continue forever
before you, because you, LORD God, have
promised. Let your servant's dynasty be
blessed forever by your blessing.

David's wars

18 Some time later, David defeated the
Philistines, subdued them, and took
Gath and its villages from Philistine control.
[2]He also defeated Moab, enslaving them and
requiring payment. [3]David defeated Zobah's
King Hadadezer at Hamath, as he continued
to establish his control along the Euphrates
River. [4]David captured one thousand chariots from him, seven thousand cavalry, and
twenty thousand foot soldiers. Then David
cut the hamstrings of all but one hundred
of the chariot horses. [5]When the Arameans
of Damascus came to help Zobah's King Hadadezer, David killed twenty-two thousand
of the Arameans. [6]David stationed soldiers[c]
in Aram of Damascus, enslaved them, and
required payment. The LORD gave David victory wherever he went.
[7]David took the gold shields carried by
Hadadezer's servants and brought them
to Jerusalem. [8]From Tibhath and Cun, Hadadezer's cities, David took large amounts
of bronze, with which Solomon made the
bronze basin,[d] the pillars, and the bronze
equipment.
[9]When Hamath's King Tou heard that
David had defeated the entire army of Zobah's King Hadadezer, [10]he sent his son Hadoram to King David to wish him well and to

[b]Or, here and elsewhere in this chapter, *house* [c]Cf 2 Sam 8:6; Heb lacks *soldiers*. [d]Or *sea*

congratulate him over his battle and defeat of Hadadezer, because Tou was an enemy of Hadadezer. Hadoram brought with him all kinds of gold, silver, and bronze objects. [11]King David dedicated these to the LORD along with the silver and the gold he had taken from all these nations: Edom, Moab, the Ammonites, the Philistines, and Amalek. [12]Abishai, Zeruiah's son, struck down eighteen thousand Edomites in the Salt Valley. [13]He stationed soldiers in Edom, and all the Edomites became David's slaves. The LORD gave David victory wherever he went.

David's administration

[14]David ruled over all Israel and maintained justice and righteousness for all his people. [15]Zeruiah's son Joab was in command of the army; Ahilud's son Jehoshaphat was recorder; [16]Ahitub's son Zadok and Abiathar's son Ahimelech[e] were priests; Shavsha was secretary; [17]Jehoiada's son Benaiah was in command of the Cherethites and the Pelethites; and David's sons were the king's chief personal advisors.

War with the Ammonites and Arameans

19 Some time later, the Ammonite King Nahash died, and his son succeeded him as king. [2]"I'll be loyal to Nahash's son Hanun," David said, "because his father was loyal to me." So David sent messengers with condolences about his father's death.

But when David's servants arrived in the Ammonite territory to express his sympathy to Hanun, [3]the Ammonite leaders asked Hanun, "Do you really believe David is honoring your father because he has sent you condolences? Of course not! His servants have come to search the city, spy it out, and overthrow it!" [4]So Hanun took David's servants, shaved them, cut off half their garments from their buttocks down, and sent them off.

[5]When this was reported to David, he sent messengers to the men because they were completely ashamed. The king said, "Stay in Jericho until your beards have grown. Then you can come back."

[6]When the Ammonites realized that they had offended David, Hanun and the Ammonites sent one thousand kikkars of silver to hire chariots and cavalry for themselves from Aram-naharaim, Aram-maacah, and Zobah. [7]They hired thirty-two thousand chariots, as well as King Maacah and his army, who came and camped in front of Medeba, while the Ammonites left their cities and came together ready for battle. [8]When David heard this, he sent Joab and the entire army of warriors. [9]The Ammonites marched out and formed a battle line at the entrance to the city, while the kings who had come remained in the countryside.

[10]When Joab saw that the battle would be fought on two fronts, he chose some of Israel's finest warriors and deployed them to meet the Arameans. [11]The rest of the army Joab placed under the command of his brother Abishai. When they took up their positions to meet the Arameans, [12]Joab said, "If the Arameans prove too strong for me, you must help me, and if the Ammonites prove too strong for you, I'll help you. [13]Be brave! We must be courageous for the sake of our people and the cities of our God. The LORD will do what is good in his eyes."

[14]When Joab and the troops who were with him advanced into battle against the Arameans, they fled from him. [15]When the Ammonites saw that the Arameans had fled, they also fled from his brother Abishai and retreated into the city. So Joab returned to Jerusalem.

[16]The Arameans saw that they had been defeated by Israel. They sent out messengers to bring Aramean reinforcements from the other side of the river, with Shophach the commander of Hadadezer's army at their head. [17]Upon hearing this, David gathered all Israel and crossed the Jordan. David advanced and took up positions against the Arameans to meet them in battle. After initiating the battle, [18]the Arameans fled before Israel, and David killed seven thousand Aramean chariot drivers and forty thousand foot soldiers. Shophach

[e]LXX, Syr; MT *Abimelech*

the commander of their army was killed too. 19 When the servants of Hadadezer saw that they had been defeated by Israel, they made peace with David and served him. Never again would the Arameans come to the aid of the Ammonites.

Defeat of the Ammonites

20 In the spring, the time when kings go to war, Joab marched out with the army, destroyed the land of the Ammonites, and besieged Rabbah. David stayed in Jerusalem while Joab attacked Rabbah and overthrew it. 2 David took Milcom's[f] crown from his head. He found that it weighed one kikkar of gold and was set with a valuable stone. It was placed on David's head. The amount of loot David took from the city was huge. 3 After removing the people who were in the city, David demolished the city with saws, iron picks, and axes,[g] as he did to all the Ammonite cities. Then David and all his troops returned to Jerusalem.

War with the Philistines

4 Once again war broke out at Gezer with the Philistines. At that time Sibbecai the Hushathite killed Sippai, one of the descendants of the Rephah,[h] and the Philistines were subdued. 5 In another war with the Philistines, Jair's son Elhanan killed Lahmi the brother of Goliath the Gittite. The shaft of his spear was like a weaver's beam. 6 At another war in Gath there was a huge man with six fingers on each hand and six toes on each foot, twenty-four in all, who was also descended from Raphah. 7 When he taunted Israel, Jonathan the son of David's brother Shimea killed him. 8 These were descended from the Raphah in Gath, and they fell by the hands of David and his servants.

David's census

21 A heavenly Adversary[i] arose against Israel and incited David to count Israel. 2 So David told Joab and the leaders of the people, "Go throughout all the tribes of Israel, from Dan to Beer-sheba, and take a census of the people so I know how many people there are."

3 But Joab replied, "May the LORD increase his people a hundred times! Sir, aren't you the king, and aren't they all your servants? Why do you want to do this? Why bring guilt on Israel?"

4 But the king overruled Joab, who left and traveled throughout all Israel. When he returned to Jerusalem, 5 he reported to David the total number: there were 1,100,000 men available for military service in all Israel, while Judah alone had 470,000. 6 He didn't include Levi and Benjamin among them, because Joab disagreed with the king's order.

7 God was offended by this census and punished Israel. 8 Then David said to God, "I have sinned greatly in what I have done! Now please take away the guilt of your servant because I have done something very foolish."

9 The LORD told Gad, David's seer: 10 Go and tell David, This is what the LORD says: I'm offering you three punishments. Choose one of them, and that is what I will do to you.

11 When Gad came to David, he said to him, "This is what the LORD says: Take your choice: 12 three years of famine, three months of fleeing[j] from your enemies while your enemies' sword overtakes you, or three days of the LORD's sword, that is, plague in the land and the LORD's messenger bringing disaster in every part of Israel. Decide now what answer I should take back to the one who sent me."

13 "I'm in deep trouble," David said to Gad. "I'd rather fall into the hands of the LORD, who is very merciful; don't let me fall into human hands." 14 So the LORD sent a plague throughout Israel, and seventy thousand Israelites fell dead.

15 Then God sent a messenger to Jerusalem to destroy it. But just as the messenger was about to destroy it, the LORD looked and changed his mind about the destruction. He said to the messenger who was destroying it, "That's enough! Withdraw your hand!" At that time the LORD's messenger

[f] LXX, Vulg; MT *their king* [g] Cf 2 Sam 12:31; MT *saws* [h] Or *giants;* also in 20:6-7 [i] Heb *satan* [j] LXX, cf 2 Sam 24:13; MT *being swept away*

was standing near the threshing floor of Ornan the Jebusite.

[16]When David looked up, he saw the LORD's messenger stationed between the earth and the sky with a drawn sword in his hand stretched out against Jerusalem. Then David and the elders, dressed in mourning clothes, fell on their faces; [17]and David said to God, "Wasn't it I who ordered the numbering of the people? I'm the sinner, the one responsible for this evil. But these sheep—what have they done? LORD, my God, turn your hand against me and my household, but spare your people from the plague."

[18]The LORD's messenger ordered Gad to tell David that he should go up to the threshing floor of Ornan the Jebusite in order to set up an altar for the LORD. [19]So David went up, following the instructions Gad had delivered in the LORD's name.

[20]Ornan turned around and saw the king.[k] His four sons who were with him hid themselves, but Ornan continued threshing wheat. [21]When David approached Ornan, Ornan looked up, recognized David, left the threshing floor, and bowed to David with his face to the ground. [22]David said to Ornan, "Give me the site of the threshing floor, charging me full price, so that I may build an altar to the LORD, and the plague among the people may come to an end."

[23]Ornan replied to David, "Take it for yourself, and may my master the king do what he thinks is best. I'll even provide the oxen for the entirely burned offerings, the threshing boards for wood, and the wheat for the grain offering—I'll provide everything!"

[24]But King David said to Ornan, "No, I will buy them from you at a fair price. I won't offer to the LORD what belongs to you nor offer an entirely burned offering that costs me nothing." [25]Then David gave Ornan six hundred shekels of gold by weight for the site. [26]David built an altar there for the LORD and offered entirely burned offerings and well-being sacrifices. He called on the LORD, who answered him with fire from heaven on the altar of the entirely burned offering, consuming the entirely burned offering.[l] [27]Then the LORD commanded the messenger to return his sword to its sheath.

Location of the future temple

[28]At that time, after David saw that the LORD had answered him at the threshing floor of Ornan the Jebusite, he offered sacrifices there. [29]The LORD's dwelling that Moses had made in the desert and the altar for entirely burned offerings were then at the shrine in Gibeon, [30]but David couldn't go there to seek God because he feared the sword of the LORD's messenger.

22 Then David said, "This is where the LORD God's temple will be, along with Israel's altar for entirely burned offerings."

David prepares to build the temple

[2]David gave orders to gather the immigrants living in the land of Israel, and he appointed masons who would cut stones for building God's temple. [3]David also provided a huge amount of iron for nails for the doors of the gates and for the braces, so much bronze that it couldn't be weighed, [4]and innumerable cedar logs from the Sidonians and the Tyrians, who gave them to David. [5]David thought, My son Solomon is too inexperienced to build the LORD's temple. It must be great beyond compare in order to win fame and glory throughout all lands, so I myself will prepare things for him. So David made extensive preparations before his death.

Instructions to Solomon

[6]David sent for his son Solomon and instructed him to build a temple for the LORD, the God of Israel. [7]David said to Solomon, "My son,[m] I had intended to build a temple for the name of the LORD my God. [8]But the LORD told me: You've shed much blood and waged great wars. You won't build a temple for my name because you've spilled so much blood on the ground before me. [9]A son has just been born to you. He'll be a man of peace, and I'll give him peace with all his surrounding enemies. In fact,

[k]LXX, cf 2 Sam 24:20; MT *messenger* [l]LXX; MT lacks *consuming the entirely burned offering.* [m]LXX, DSS; MT *his son*

his name will be Solomon,[n] and I'll give Israel peace and quiet during his reign. 10 He will be the one to build a temple for my name. He'll become my son, and I'll become his father, and I'll establish his royal throne over Israel forever.

11 "Now, my son, may the LORD be with you so that you may successfully build the temple of the LORD your God, as he promised you. 12 May the LORD be sure to give you insight and understanding so that when he appoints you over Israel, you will observe the Instruction from the LORD your God.[o] 13 Then, if you carefully follow the regulations and case laws that the LORD commanded Moses concerning Israel, you'll prosper. Be strong and brave. Don't be afraid or lose heart! 14 With great effort I've now provided for the LORD's temple one hundred thousand kikkars of gold, one million kikkars of silver, and so much bronze and iron that it can't be weighed, as well as wood and stone, though you may add to these. 15 You also have innumerable people to do the work: stonecutters, masons, and carpenters with every skill required for any task, 16 whether in gold, silver, bronze, or iron. So get to work, and may the LORD be with you."

Instructions to Israel's leaders

17 Then David ordered all of Israel's leaders to help his son Solomon: 18 "The LORD your God is with you! He's given you peace on every side. He's placed under my power the land's people, so that the land is under the control of the LORD and his people. 19 Now then, dedicate yourselves to seeking the LORD your God. Get to work and build the sanctuary of the LORD God, so that the chest containing the LORD's covenant together with God's holy equipment may be brought into the temple built for the LORD's name."

David appoints the Levites

23 When David had grown old after a long life, he made his son Solomon king over Israel. 2 He then gathered together all Israel's leaders along with the priests and the Levites. 3 When the Levites were counted, the head count of every male 30 and older totaled 38,000. 4 Of these, there were 24,000 to supervise the work on the LORD's temple, 6,000 officers and judges, 5 4,000 gatekeepers, and 4,000 praising the LORD with instruments made[p] for offering praise. 6 Then David divided them into three groups named after Levi's family members: Gershon, Kohath, and Merari.

Gershonites

7 The Gershonites included Ladan and Shimei.

8 Ladan's family: Jehiel the first, Zetham, and Joel—three in all. 9 Jehiel's[q] family: Shelomith, Haziel, and Haran—three in all. These were the heads of the households of Ladan.

10 Shimei's family: Jahath, Ziza,[r] Jeush, and Beriah. These four were Shimei's family: 11 Jahath was the first, and Ziza the second; since Jeush and Beriah didn't have many children, they became a single household.

Kohathites

12 Kohath's family: Amram, Izhar, Hebron, and Uzziel—four in all.

13 Amram's family: Aaron and Moses. Aaron, together with his sons, was set apart to make the holiest objects holy, to make offerings before the LORD, to serve him, and to give blessings in his name forever.

14 As for Moses the man of God, his sons were considered to be Levites. 15 Moses' family: Gershom and Eliezer.

16 Gershom's family: Shebuel the first.

17 Eliezer's family: Rehabiah the first; Eliezer had no other sons, but Rehabiah had many children.

18 Izhar's family: Shelomoth[s] the first.

19 Hebron's family: Jeriah the first, Amariah the second, Jahaziel the third, and Jekameam the fourth.

20 Uzziel's family: Micah the first and Isshiah the second.

[n] *Solomon* sounds like *peace* in Heb. [o] Heb uncertain [p] LXX, Vulg; MT *I made* [q] Cf 23:8, 10; MT *Shimei's*
[r] LXX; MT *Zina* [s] LXX, Syr, Aram; MT *Shelomith*

Merarites

21 Merari's family: Mahli and Mushi.
Mahli's family: Eleazar and Kish.
22 Eleazar died without sons, but he
did have daughters who married their
relatives from Kish's family.
23 Mushi's family: Mahli, Eder, and
Jeremoth—three in all.
24 These were the members of Levi's family
according to their households. The household heads were registered, along with a list-
ing of the names of each person 20 years old
and above who carried out assigned tasks in
the LORD's temple.

Levites' duties

25 David said, "Since the LORD, Israel's
God, has given his people peace and has made
his home in Jerusalem forever, 26 the Levites
need no longer carry the dwelling or any of
the equipment used in its service." 27 David's
last instructions were to count the Levites 20
years old and above. 28 Their assignment was
to be at the side of the Aaronites to serve in
the LORD's temple, maintaining the courtyards and side rooms and cleansing all of the
holy objects and doing whatever was needed
in the service of God's temple. 29 They were
responsible for the stacks of bread, the fine
flour for grain offerings, the wafers of unleavened bread, the cakes made on the griddle,
the offering mixed with oil, as well as all the
measuring. 30 They were to be present every
morning to thank and praise the LORD, and
to do the same every evening. 31 Whenever
entirely burned offerings were offered to the
LORD for the sabbaths, the new moons, and
festivals, a designated number were to serve
in the LORD's presence continuously. 32 In
this way they were to observe the instructions for the meeting tent, the instructions
for the sanctuary, and the instructions for
Aaron's family and relatives about serving in
the LORD's temple.

Divisions of the priests

24 The divisions of the Aaronites:
Aaron's family: Nadab, Abihu,
Eleazar, and Ithamar.
2 Nadab and Abihu died before their father did, without having sons, and so Eleazar
and Ithamar served as priests. 3 David, with
the help of Zadok from Eleazar's family and
Ahimelech from Ithamar's family, divided
them according to their appointed duties.
4 Since Eleazar's family was found to have
more male heads than Ithamar's family, they
divided them so that Eleazar's family had sixteen household heads and Ithamar's family
had eight. 5 They divided both groups by lots
because there were holy leaders, even outstanding leaders, among both Eleazar's and
Ithamar's descendants. 6 Shemaiah, Nethanel's son, the levitical scribe, recorded their
names in the presence of the king; the leaders; Zadok the priest; Ahimelech, Abiathar's
son; and the household heads of the priests
and Levites. One household was taken from
Eleazar followed by one from Ithamar.

7 The first lot fell to Jehoiarib,
the second to Jedaiah,
8 the third to Harim,
the fourth to Seorim,
9 the fifth to Malchijah,
the sixth to Mijamin,
10 the seventh to Hakkoz,
the eighth to Abijah,
11 the ninth to Jeshua,
the tenth to Shecaniah,
12 the eleventh to Eliashib,
the twelfth to Jakim,
13 the thirteenth to Huppah,
the fourteenth to Jeshebeab,
14 the fifteenth to Bilgah,
the sixteenth to Immer,
15 the seventeenth to Hezir,
the eighteenth to Happizzez,
16 the nineteenth to Pethahiah,
the twentieth to Jehezkel,
17 the twenty-first to Jachin,
the twenty-second to Gamul,
18 the twenty-third to Delaiah,
and the twenty-fourth to Maaziah.

19 These were to enter the LORD's temple
according to their appointed duty and by
the procedure established for them by their
ancestor Aaron, just as the LORD God of
Israel had instructed him.

Rest of the Levites

20 The rest of the Levites included:
from Amram's family: Shubael;

from Shubael's family: Jehdeiah;
21 from Rehabiah and his family: Isshiah the first;
22 from the Izharites: Shelomoth;
from Shelomoth's family: Jahath;
23 Hebron's family:[t] Jeriah the first,[u] Amariah the second, Jahaziel the third, Jekameam the fourth;
24 Uzziel's family: Micah;
from Micah's family: Shamir;
25 Micah's brother Isshiah;
from Isshiah's family: Zechariah;
26 Merari's family: Mahli, Mushi and his son Jaaziah's family;
27 Merari's family by his son Jaaziah: Shoham, Zaccur, and Ibri;
28 from Mahli: Eleazar, who had no sons;
29 from Kish and his family: Jerahmeel;
30 and Mushi's family: Mahli, Eder, and Jerimoth.

These were the Levites according to their
households. 31 Both the household head and
his youngest brother cast lots, just as their relatives, Aaron's descendants, had done in the presence of King David, Zadok, Ahimelech, and the heads of the priestly and levitical households.

Temple musicians

25 David and the army officers[v] set apart Asaph's family, Heman and Jeduthun, for service to prophesy[w] accompanied by lyres, harps, and cymbals.

This is the list of those who performed this special service:

2 From Asaph's family: Zaccur, Joseph, Nethaniah, and Asarelah. Asaph's family was under Asaph's direction and prophesied by order of the king.

3 From Jeduthun and his family: Gedaliah, Izri,[x] Jeshaiah, Shimei,[y] Hashabiah, and Mattithiah—six in all. They were under their father Jeduthun's direction, prophesying with the lyre and giving thanks and praise to the LORD.

4 From Heman and his family: Bukkiah, Mattaniah, Uzziel, Shebuel, Jerimoth, Hananiah, Hanani, Eliathah, Giddalti, Romamti-ezer, Joshbekashah, Mallothi, Hothir, and Mahazioth.

5 All these were the family of Heman the king's seer, according to God's promise to honor him. God gave Heman fourteen sons and three daughters.
6 They were all under their father's direction when singing in the LORD's temple with cymbals, harps, and lyres to provide service in God's temple, by order of the king.
As for Asaph, Jeduthun, and Heman,
7 the number of themselves and their relatives, who were trained in singing to the LORD and who were all skillful, was 288.
8 They cast lots for their assigned duties, small as well as great, teacher and pupil alike.

9 The first lot fell for Asaph to Joseph; the second to Gedaliah, his relatives, and his family, 12;
10 the third to Zaccur, his family, and his relatives, 12;
11 the fourth to Izri, his family, and his relatives, 12;
12 the fifth to Nethaniah, his family, and his relatives, 12;
13 the sixth to Bukkiah, his family, and his relatives, 12;
14 the seventh to Jesarelah, his family, and his relatives, 12;
15 the eighth to Jeshaiah, his family, and his relatives, 12;
16 the ninth to Mattaniah, his family, and his relatives, 12;
17 the tenth to Shimei, his family, and his relatives, 12;
18 the eleventh to Uzziel,[z] his family, and his relatives, 12;
19 the twelfth to Hashabiah, his family, and his relatives, 12;
20 the thirteenth to Shubael, his family, and his relatives, 12;
21 the fourteenth to Mattithiah, his family, and his relatives, 12;
22 the fifteenth to Jerimoth,[a] his family, and his relatives, 12;
23 the sixteenth to Hananiah, his family, and his relatives, 12;

[t] LXX; MT *my sons* [u] Cf 1 Chron 23:19; MT lacks *Jeriah.* [v] Or *liturgical officers* [w] DSS, LXX, Vulg; MT *the prophets* [x] Cf 25:11: MT *Zeri* [y] LXX, cf 25:17; MT lacks *Jeriah.* [z] LXX, Syr; MT *Azrael* [a] Cf 25:4; MT *Jeremoth*

24 the seventeenth to Joshbekashah, his family, and his relatives, 12;

25 the eighteenth to Hanani, his family, and his relatives, 12;

26 the nineteenth to Mallothi, his family, and his relatives, 12;

27 the twentieth to Eliathah, his family, and his relatives, 12;

28 the twenty-first to Hothir, his family, and his relatives, 12;

29 the twenty-second to Giddalti, his family, and his relatives, 12;

30 the twenty-third to Mahazioth, his family, and his relatives, 12;

31 and the twenty-fourth to Romamti-ezer, his family, and his relatives, 12.

Gatekeepers

26 The divisions of the gatekeepers: from the Korahites: Meshelemiah, Kore's son, one of Ebiasaph's[b] family.

2 Meshelemiah's family: Zechariah the oldest, Jediael the second, Zebadiah the third, Jathniel the fourth, 3 Elam the fifth, Jehohanan the sixth, and Eliehoenai the seventh.

4 Obed-edom's family: Shemaiah the oldest, Jehozabad the second, Joah the third, Sachar the fourth, Nethanel the fifth, 5 Ammiel the sixth, Issachar the seventh, and Peullethai the eighth. God truly blessed him. 6 To his son Shemaiah were born sons who ruled over their household, because they were valiant men. 7 Shemaiah's family: Othni, Rephael, Obed, Elzabad, and his relatives, Elihu and Semachiah, who were valiant men. 8 All these were members of Obed-edom's family, they, their sons, and their relatives. They were valiant and strong in their service, 62 men belonging to Obed-edom. 9 Meshelemiah's family and relatives, valiant men, numbered 18.

10 Hosah, one of Merari's family, also had a family: Shimri the first (though he wasn't the oldest, his father gave him that status), 11 Hilkiah the second, Tebaliah the third, and Zechariah the fourth. All of Hosah's family and relatives numbered 13.

12 These were the divisions of the gatekeepers with their leaders, who were responsible to minister in the LORD's temple, along with their relatives. 13 They cast lots for each gate in the same way, whether their household was small or large. 14 The lot for the East Gate fell to Shelemiah. They then cast lots for his son Zechariah, a wise counselor, and his lot indicated the North Gate. 15 Obed-edom was assigned the South Gate, and his sons were assigned the storehouses. 16 Hosah[c] was assigned the West Gate, that is, the chamber[d] gate on the upper road.

The guards had the same task: 17 each day[e] the East had six, the North four, and the South four, with two at each of the storehouses. 18 At the courtyard on the West, there were four at the road and two at the courtyard. 19 These were the divisions of the gatekeepers from Korah's family and Merari's family.

20 Their fellow[f] Levites were in charge of the treasuries of God's temple and the treasuries of the dedicated gifts: 21 from Ladan's family, the family of the Gershonites belonging to Ladan, and the heads of the households belonging to Ladan the Gershonite: Jehieli. 22 Jehieli's family: Zetham and Joel his brother were in charge of the treasuries of the LORD's temple. 23 From the Amramites, Izharites, Hebronites, and Uzzielites: 24 Shebuel, a descendant of Gershom, Moses' son, was the chief officer in charge of the treasuries. 25 His relatives through Eliezer included his son Rehabiah, his son Jeshaiah, his son Joram, his son Zichri, and his son Shelomoth. 26 This Shelomoth and his relatives were in charge of all the treasuries of the gifts dedicated by King David, by the household leaders, by the commanders[g] of the units of a thousand and a hundred, and by the army officers. 27 They had dedicated some of the valuable objects won in battle to repair the LORD's temple. 28 Everything that was dedicated by Samuel the seer, as well as by Saul, Kish's son; Abner,

[b] LXX; MT *Asaph* [c] MT *Shuppim and Hosah* [d] LXX; MT *Shallecheth* [e] LXX; MT *Levites* [f] LXX; MT *Ahijah*
[g] LXX; MT *to the commanders*

Ner's son; and Joab, Zeruiah's son—in fact, anything that had been dedicated—was under the supervision of Shelomoth[h] and his relatives.

29 From the Izharites: Chenaniah and his family had responsibilities over Israel outside the temple as officials and judges. 30 From the Hebronites: Hashabiah and his relatives, 1,700 capable men, were put in charge of Israel west of the Jordan concerning all of the LORD's affairs and the king's service. 31 From the Hebronites: Jerijah was the head of the Hebronites according to the family records of their households. In the fortieth year of David's rule, a search was made and capable men were found among them in Jazer in Gilead. 32 Jerijah's relatives, capable men, were 2,700 heads of households. King David put them in charge of Reuben, Gad, and half the tribe of Manasseh concerning all of God's and the king's affairs.

Divisions of the military

27 This is the list of the Israelites, the heads of households, the commanders of units of a thousand and a hundred, and their officers. They served the king in every way their divisions required, and they were on duty for a month at a time through all the months of the year. Each division numbered 24,000.

2 In charge of the first division for the first month was Jashobeam, Zabdiel's son. His division numbered 24,000. 3 He was a Perezite and the head of all the army officers for the first month.

4 In charge of the division for the second month was Dodai the Ahohite.[i] His division numbered 24,000.

5 The third army commander for the third month was Benaiah the chief priest Jehoiada's son. His division numbered 24,000. 6 This Benaiah was a warrior of the Thirty and in command of the Thirty. In command of his division was his son Ammizabad.

7 The fourth for the fourth month was Asahel, Joab's brother, and after him his son Zebadiah. His division numbered 24,000.

8 The fifth for the fifth month was the commander Shammoth the Zerahite.[j] His division numbered 24,000.

9 The sixth for the sixth month was Ira the Tekoite Ikkesh's son. His division numbered 24,000.

10 The seventh for the seventh month was Helez the Pelonite from Ephraim's family. His division numbered 24,000.

11 The eighth for the eighth month was Sibbecai the Hushathite from the Zerahites. His division numbered 24,000.

12 The ninth for the ninth month was Abiezer of Annathoth from the Benjaminites. His division numbered 24,000.

13 The tenth for the tenth month was Maharai the Netophathite from the Zerahites. His division numbered 24,000.

14 The eleventh for the eleventh month was Benaiah the Pirathonite from Ephraim's family. His division numbered 24,000.

15 The twelfth for the twelfth month was Heldai the Netophathite from Othniel. His division numbered 24,000.

Tribal leaders

16 In charge of the tribes of Israel:

for the Reubenites—the leader was Eliezer, Zichri's son;

for the Simeonites—Shephatiah, Maacah's son;

17 for the Levites—Hashabiah, Kemuel's son;

for Aaron—Zadok;

18 for Judah—Eliab,[k] one of David's relatives;

for Issachar—Omri, Michael's son;

19 for Zebulun—Ishmaiah, Obadiah's son;

for Naphtali—Jerimoth, Azriel's son;

20 for the Ephraimites—Hoshea, Azaziah's son;

for half the tribe of Manasseh—Joel, Pedaiah's son;

[h] LXX; MT *Shelomith* [i] LXX; MT adds *and his division, and Mikloth the leader.* [j] Cf 27:11, 13; MT *Izrahite*
[k] LXX; MT *Elihu*

[21]for half the tribe[l] of Manasseh in Gilead—Iddo, Zechariah's son;
for Benjamin—Jaasiel, Abner's son;
[22]for Dan—Azarel, Jeroham's son.

These were the leaders of the tribes of Israel. [23]But David didn't count those younger than 20 years of age, because the LORD had promised to make Israel as numerous as the stars in the sky. [24]Joab, Zeruiah's son, began to count them, but he never finished. Since Israel experienced wrath because of this, the number wasn't entered into the official records of King David.

Civil servants

[25]In charge of the king's treasuries—Azmaveth, Adiel's son;
in charge of the treasuries in the country, cities, villages, and towers—Jonathan, Uzziah's son;
[26]in charge of agricultural workers cultivating the fertile land—Ezri, Chelub's son;
[27]in charge of the vineyards—Shimei the Ramathite;
in charge of the vineyard's produce for the wine cellars—Zabdi the Shiphmite;
[28]in charge of the olive and sycamore trees in the western foothills—Baal-hanan the Gederite;
in charge of the stores of oil—Joash;
[29]in charge of the cattle that grazed in Sharon—Shitrai the Sharonite;
in charge of the cattle in the valleys—Shaphat, Adlai's son;
[30]in charge of the camels—Obil the Ishmaelite;
in charge of the female donkeys—Jehdeiah the Meronothite;
[31]in charge of the flocks of sheep and goats—Jaziz the Hagrite.
All these were stewards of King David's property.

Royal advisors

[32]Jonathan, David's uncle, was a counselor, a man of understanding, and a scribe. Jehiel, Hachmoni's son, took care of the king's sons. [33]Ahithophel was the king's counselor, and Hushai the Archite was the king's political advisor.[m] [34]After Ahithophel came Benaiah's son Jehoiada, and Abiathar. Joab was commander of the king's army.

David addresses Israel's leaders

28 David assembled all of Israel's leaders in Jerusalem, the leaders of the tribes, the leaders of the divisions that served the king, the commanders of units of a thousand and a hundred, the officials in charge of all the property and livestock of the king and his sons, as well as the officers, warriors, and all the valiant men. [2]Then King David stood up and said:

Listen to me, my relatives and my people. I wanted to build a temple as the permanent home for the chest containing the LORD's covenant, our God's footrest. But when I prepared to build it, [3]God said to me, You must not build a temple for my name, because you are a military man and you've shed blood. [4]The LORD, the God of Israel, chose me from my whole household to become king over Israel forever. He chose Judah as leader, and within Judah's family, my household, and among my father's family he was pleased with me, making me king over all Israel. [5]And from all the many sons the LORD has given me, he has chosen my son Solomon to sit on the throne of the LORD's kingdom over Israel. [6]He said to me: Your son Solomon will build my temple and my courtyards, for I've chosen him to become my son even as I myself will become his father. [7]I'll establish his kingdom forever if he remains committed to keeping my commands and case laws as he does now.

[8]So now, in the presence of all the LORD's assembly[n] and with God as our witness, carefully observe all the commands of the LORD your God, so that you may hold on to this good land and pass it on to your children forever. [9]As for you, Solomon, my son, acknowledge your father's God and serve him with enthusiastic devotion, because the LORD

[l]LXX, Vulg; MT lacks *for half the tribe.* [m]Or *friend* [n]LXX; MT *all Israel, the assembly of the LORD*

searches every mind and understands
the motive behind every thought. If you
seek him, he will be found by you; but
if you abandon him, he will reject you
forever. [10]Now then, since the LORD has
chosen you to build a temple for him[o] as
the sanctuary, work hard.
[11]Then David gave his son Solomon the
plan for the entrance hall, its buildings,
treasuries, upper and inner rooms, and the
room for the cover.[p] [12]He provided all of the
plans he had in mind: for the courtyards of
the LORD's temple, and for all its surrounding rooms where the treasures of God's
temple and the dedicated gifts would be
stored; [13]for the divisions of the priests and
Levites, for all their responsibilities within
the LORD's temple, and for all the equipment used in its service; [14]for the weight of
all the gold equipment used for every kind
of service, and the weight of all the silver
equipment used for every kind of service;
[15]for the weight of the gold lampstands and
their gold lamps—the weight of gold for
each lampstand with its lamps—and for
the weight of each silver lampstand and
its lamps depending on how each would be
used; [16]for the weight of gold for each table
with the stacks of bread, and the silver for
the silver tables; [17]for the forks, bowls, and
cups of pure gold; for the weight of each
gold dish and the weight of each silver dish;
[18]for the weight of the incense altar made
of refined gold; and for the construction
of the chariot—with the gold winged creatures spreading their wings and covering
the chest containing the LORD's covenant.
[19]All of this the LORD made clear to David[q]
directly in a document, including the plan
for all of the work.
[20]"Be strong and courageous," David said
to his son Solomon. "Get to work. Don't be
afraid or discouraged, because the LORD
God, my God, is with you. He'll neither
let you down nor leave you before all the
work for the service of the LORD's temple is
done. [21]Here are the divisions of the priests
and the Levites who will perform all the
service of God's temple. For all this work
you will have willing and able workers with
you to do it. The officials and all the people
are ready to follow your instructions."

Offerings for building the temple

29 Then King David said to the whole
assembly:
My son Solomon, the one whom
God chose, is too inexperienced for this
great task, since this temple won't be for
humans but for the LORD God. [2]Using
every resource at my disposal, I've provided everything for my God's temple:
gold for gold objects, silver for silver objects, bronze for bronze objects, iron for
iron objects, lumber for wooden objects,
carnelian stones for settings, antimony,
colorful stones, every kind of precious
stone, and a large amount of marble.
[3]What's more, because of my delight in
my God's temple, I have dedicated my
own private treasure of gold and silver
to my God's temple, in addition to all
that I've provided for the holy temple:
[4]three thousand kikkars of gold from
the gold of Ophir, seven thousand kikkars of refined silver for covering the
walls of the rooms,[r] [5]gold for gold objects, and silver for silver objects, to be
used for everything the skilled workers
will make. Who else, then, will volunteer, dedicating themselves to the LORD
today?
[6]Then the leaders of the households, the
leaders of the tribes of Israel, and the commanders of the units of a thousand and a
hundred, and the supervisors of the king's
work volunteered [7]to give five thousand
kikkars and ten thousand darics of gold,
ten thousand kikkars of silver, eighteen
thousand kikkars of bronze, and one hundred thousand kikkars of iron for the work
on God's temple. [8]Anyone who had precious stones donated them to the treasury
of the LORD's temple under the care of Jehiel the Gershonite. [9]The people rejoiced at
this response, because they had presented

[o]LXX; MT lacks *for him.* [p]Or *mercy seat* or perhaps *reconciliation cover* (Heb *kapporet*) [q]LXX; MT *to me*
[r]Or *houses*

their offerings to the LORD so willingly and
wholeheartedly. King David also rejoiced
greatly.
10 Then David blessed the LORD before
the whole assembly:

Blessed are you, LORD,
God of our ancestor Israel,
forever and always.
11 To you, LORD,
belong greatness and power,
honor, splendor, and majesty,
because everything in heaven
and on earth belongs to you.
Yours, LORD, is the kingship,
and you are honored as head of all.
12 You are the source of wealth and honor,
and you rule over all.
In your hand are strength and might,
and it is in your power to magnify
and strengthen all.
13 And now, our God, we thank you
and praise your glorious name.
14 Who am I,
and who are my people,
that we should be able to offer
so willingly?
Since everything comes from you,
we have given you
that which comes from your own hand.
15 To be sure, we are like all our ancestors,
immigrants without permanent homes.
Our days are like a shadow on the ground,
and there's no hope.

16 LORD, our God, all this abundance
that we have provided to build you a
temple for your holy name comes from
your hand and belongs to you. 17 Since
I know, my God, that you examine the
mind and take delight in honesty, I have
freely given all these things with the
highest of motives. And now I've been
delighted to see your people here offering so willingly to you.
18 LORD, God of our ancestors Abraham, Isaac, and Israel, keep these
thoughts in the mind of your people forever, and direct their hearts toward you.
19 As for Solomon my son, give him
the wholehearted devotion to keep your
commands, laws, and regulations—
observing all of them—and to build the
temple that I have prepared.

20 Then David said to the whole assembly,
"Bless the LORD your God," and the whole
assembly blessed the LORD, the God of their
ancestors, bowed down, and worshipped before the LORD and the king. 21 On the very
next day they offered sacrifices and entirely
burned offerings to the LORD—a thousand
bulls, a thousand rams, and a thousand
lambs, along with their drink offerings—
and many other sacrifices for all Israel's sake.
22 They ate and drank with great joy before
the LORD that day and made David's son
Solomon the king.[s] They anointed him[t] in
the LORD's presence as prince, and Zadok
as priest. 23 Thus Solomon sat on the LORD's
throne as king, succeeding his father David,
and he prospered. All Israel obeyed him,
24 and all the commanders and warriors, as
well as all of King David's sons, submitted to
King Solomon's authority. 25 Moreover, the
LORD magnified Solomon before all Israel,
giving him such royal majesty as no king before him[u] had enjoyed.

Summary of David's reign

26 David, Jesse's son, was king over all
Israel. 27 He reigned over Israel for forty
years: seven years in Hebron and thirty-
three in Jerusalem. 28 He died at a good old
age, having enjoyed a full life, wealth, and
honor; and his son Solomon followed him
as king. 29 The account of King David from
beginning to end is written in the records
of Samuel the seer, Nathan the prophet,
and Gad the visionary, 30 including everything concerning his powerful rule, and
what happened to him, to Israel, and to all
the kingdoms in other lands.

[s] LXX, Syr; MT adds *for the second time.* [t] LXX; MT lacks *him.* [u] LXX; MT adds *in Israel.*

2 CHRONICLES

Solomon first meets God

1 Solomon, David's son, was securely established over his kingdom because the LORD his God was with him and made him very great. 2Solomon summoned all Israel, including the officers of the army,[a] the judges, and every Israelite leader who was the head of a family. 3Then Solomon, accompanied by the whole assembly, went to the shrine at Gibeon because that is where God's meeting tent was, the tent that the LORD's servant Moses had made in the wilderness. 4Now David had already brought God's chest from Kiriath-jearim to the place he had prepared for it because he had pitched a tent for the chest in Jerusalem. 5But the bronze altar that Bezalel, Uri's son and Hur's grandson, had made was there in front of the LORD's dwelling, so that is where Solomon and the assembly worshipped. 6Solomon went there to the bronze altar in the LORD's presence at the meeting tent and offered a thousand entirely burned offerings upon it.

7That night God appeared to Solomon and said, "Ask whatever you wish, and I will give it to you."

8"You showed so much kindness to my father David," Solomon replied to God, "and you have made me king in his place. 9Now, LORD God, let your promise to my father David be fulfilled because you have made me king over a people as numerous as the earth's dust. 10Give me wisdom and knowledge so I can lead this people, because no one can govern this great people of yours without your help."

11God said to Solomon, "Since this is what you wish, and because you've asked for wisdom and knowledge to govern my people over whom I've made you king—rather than asking for wealth, riches, fame, victory over those who hate you, or even a long life—12your request for wisdom and knowledge is granted. But I will also give you wealth, riches, and fame beyond that of any king before you or after you." 13Then Solomon went from[b] the shrine in Gibeon, from the meeting tent to Jerusalem where he ruled over Israel.

Solomon's wealth

14Solomon acquired more and more chariots and horses until he had fourteen hundred chariots and twelve thousand horses, which he stationed in chariot cities and with the king in Jerusalem. 15In Jerusalem, the king made silver and gold as common as stones, and cedar as plentiful as sycamore trees that grow in the foothills. 16Solomon's horses were imported from Egypt and Kue, purchased from Kue by the king's agents at the going price. 17They would import a chariot from Egypt for six hundred pieces of silver and a horse for one hundred fifty, and then export them to all the Hittite and Aramean kings.

Solomon prepares to build the temple

2 [c]Solomon gave orders to build a temple for the LORD's name and to build a royal palace for himself. 2[d]To work in the highlands, Solomon drafted 70,000 laborers, 80,000 stonecutters, and 3,600 supervisors. 3Solomon sent the following message to King Huram[e] of Tyre:

> When my father David was building his palace, you sent him cedar logs. 4Now as his son[f] I am about to build a temple in the name of the LORD my God. I will dedicate it to him to burn fragrant incense before him, to set out the bread that is regularly displayed, and to offer entirely burned offerings every morning and evening, on the sabbaths, the first of every month, and the festivals of the LORD our God, as Israel has been commanded to do forever. 5The temple I am about to build must be magnificent, because our God is greater than all other gods. 6But who is able to build such a temple when even the highest heaven can't contain God?

[a]Or *officers over thousands and hundreds* [b]LXX, Vulg; MT *to* [c]1:18 in Heb [d]2:1 in Heb [e]1 Kings spells the king's name as Hiram. [f]LXX; MT lacks *his son.*

And who am I that I should build this
temple for God, except as a place to burn
incense in his presence? 7 So now send me
a craftsman skilled in gold, silver, bronze,
and iron, as well as in purple, crimson, and
violet yarn—someone also experienced
as an engraver. He will work with my
craftsmen in Judah and Jerusalem who
were provided by my father David. 8 Also
send me cedar, cypress, and sandalwood
logs from Lebanon. I know your servants
know how to cut Lebanese timber, so my
servants will work with your servants 9 to
prepare plenty of timber for me, because
the temple that I am about to build will be
magnificent and amazing. 10 I will pay the
woodcutters twenty thousand kors[g] of
crushed wheat, twenty thousand kors of
barley, twenty thousand baths[h] of wine,
and twenty thousand baths of olive oil.

11 Tyre's King Huram replied in a letter
that he sent to Solomon:

> The LORD must love his people Israel
> because he has made you their king!
> 12 Bless the LORD, Israel's God, who
> made heaven and earth. He gave King
> David a wise son who possesses the
> knowledge and understanding to build a
> temple for the LORD and a royal palace
> for himself. 13 I'm sending you a skilled
> and experienced craftsman, Huram-
> abi, 14 whose mother is from the tribe
> of Dan and whose father is from Tyre.
> He's skilled in working with gold, silver,
> bronze, iron, stone, and wood, as well
> as purple, violet, and crimson yarn, and
> fine linen. He can do any kind of engrav-
> ing and make any design given to him
> with the assistance of your craftsmen
> and the craftsmen of my master, your
> father David. 15 So once my master sends
> the wheat, barley, olive oil, and wine he
> has promised, 16 we will cut as much tim-
> ber as you need from Lebanon and bring
> it by raft on the sea to you at Joppa,
> where you can take it up to Jerusalem.

17 Then Solomon counted all the immigrants in the land of Israel, as his father
David had done, and the total was 153,600.
18 He made 70,000 of these immigrants laborers, 80,000 of them stonecutters in the
highlands, and 3,600 of them supervisors
to keep the people working.

Solomon builds the temple

3 Solomon began to build the LORD's
temple in Jerusalem on Mount Moriah, where the Lord[i] had appeared to his
father David, on the place David had prepared at the threshing floor of Ornan the
Jebusite. 2 He began building in the second
month[j] of the fourth year of his rule. 3 Solomon laid the foundations[k] for these structures in order to build the temple of God.
The length according to the old standard
of measurement was ninety feet and the
width thirty feet. 4 Across the front of the
temple[l] was a porch as long as the temple
was and thirty feet wide, and thirty feet[m]
high. He covered the inside walls with pure
gold. 5 He paneled the walls of the main
room with pine, covered them with fine
gold, and decorated them with palm trees
and chains. 6 He studded the room with
precious stones for beauty; the gold was
from Parvaim. 7 He covered the room, its
beams, doorframes, walls, and doors with
gold, and carved images of winged creatures on the walls. 8 Then he made the most
holy place. It was as long as the temple was
wide, thirty feet long and thirty feet wide.
He covered it with six hundred kikkars
of fine gold. 9 The gold nails weighed fifty
shekels.[n] He also covered the upper rooms
with gold.

10 In the most holy place he formed two
statues of winged creatures and covered
them with gold. 11 Together the wingspan
of these creatures was thirty feet. One of
the first creature's wings was seven and a
half feet long and touched the temple wall,
while the other wing was seven and a half
feet long, touching the wing of the other
creature. 12 Similarly, one wing of the other
creature was seven and a half feet long and
touched the temple wall, while the other

[g]One kor is equivalent to a homer and is possibly equal to fifty gallons of grain. [h]One bath is approximately twenty quarts or five gallons. [i]LXX; MT lacks *the* LORD. [j]LXX; MT adds *on the second (day)*. [k]Syr *the measurements* [l]LXX; cf 1 Kgs 6:3 [m]LXX, Syr; MT *one hundred eighty feet* [n]Or approximately thirty ounces

wing was seven and a half feet long and
touched the other creature. 13 The wings of
these creatures extended thirty feet. They
stood on their feet facing the main room.
14 Then he made the curtain out of fine
linen and violet, purple, and crimson yarn,
weaving winged creatures into it. 15 Then he
made two columns in front of the temple,
fifty-two and a half feet high, with a seven
and a half foot cap on top of each. 16 Then
he made chains like a necklace[o] and placed
them on the tops of the columns. He made
a hundred pomegranates and placed them
into the chains. 17 Then he set up the pillars in front of the sanctuary, one on the
south, the other on the north. The one on
the south he named Jachin, and the one on
the north he named Boaz.

Solomon's temple equipment

4 He[p] also made a bronze altar thirty feet
long, thirty feet wide, and fifteen feet
high. 2 Then he made a tank of cast metal
called the Sea. It was circular in shape, fifteen feet from rim to rim, seven and a half
feet high, and forty-five feet in circumference. 3 Under the rim were two rows of
oxlike figures completely encircling it, ten
every eighteen inches, each cast in its mold.
4 The Sea rested on twelve oxen with their
backs toward the center, three facing north,
three facing west, three facing south, and
three facing east. 5 The Sea was as thick as
the width of a hand. Its rim was shaped
like a cup or an open lily blossom. It could
hold three thousand baths.[q] 6 He also made
ten washbasins and put five on the south
and five on the north. The items used for
the entirely burned offerings were rinsed
in these. The priests washed in the Sea. 7 He
made ten gold lampstands as prescribed
and put them in the sanctuary, five on the
south and five on the north. 8 He also made
ten tables and put them in the sanctuary,
five on the south and five on the north, as
well as a hundred gold bowls. 9 He made
the courtyard of the priests and the great
courtyard, with doors covered with bronze
for the courtyard. 10 He placed the Sea at the
southeast corner.
11 Huram made the pots, the shovels, and
the bowls. So Huram finished all his work
on God's temple for King Solomon:

12 two columns;
two circular capitals on top of the
columns;
two networks adorning the two circular
capitals on top of the columns;
13 four hundred pomegranates for the
two networks, with two rows of
pomegranates for each network that
adorned the two circular capitals on
top of the columns;
14 ten[r] stands with ten[s] basins on them;
15 one Sea;
twelve oxen beneath the Sea;
16 and the pots, the shovels, and the meat
forks.

All the things that Huram-abi made for
King Solomon for the LORD's temple were
made of polished bronze. 17 The king cast
them in clay molds in the Jordan Valley between Succoth and Zarethan.[t] 18 Due to the
very large number of objects, Solomon didn't
even try to weigh the bronze. 19 Solomon also
made all the equipment for God's temple:
the gold altar; the tables for the bread of
the presence; 20 the lampstands with their
lamps, all of pure gold, to burn before the
inner sanctuary as prescribed; 21 the flowers,
the lamps, and the tongs of pure gold; 22 and
the wick trimmers, bowls, ladles, and censers
of pure gold. As for the temple entrance, the
inner doors to the most holy place as well as
the doors to the main hall were made of gold.

5 When all of Solomon's work on the
LORD's temple was finished, he brought
the silver, gold, and all the objects his
father David had dedicated and put them in
the treasuries of God's temple.

Solomon dedicates the temple

2 Then Solomon assembled Israel's elders,
all the tribal leaders, and the clan chieftains

[o]Heb adds *in the inner room.* [p]*Solomon* or *Huram*; this ambiguity with the pronoun continues in the following verses, but compare 2 Chron 3:1, 3; 4:11. If Huram is meant, this is a worker whose name is spelled Hiram in 1 Kgs 7:13-14. [q]One bath is approximately twenty quarts or five gallons. [r]LXX and 1 Kgs 7:43; MT *he made* [s]1 Kgs 7:43; MT *he made* [t]With 1 Kgs 7:46; Heb *Zeredah*

of Israel at Jerusalem to bring up the chest
containing the LORD's covenant from Zion,
David's City. 3Everyone in Israel assembled
before the king in the seventh month,[u] during the festival. 4When all Israel's elders had
arrived, the Levites picked up the chest.
5They brought the chest, the meeting tent,
and all the holy objects that were in the
tent. The priests and[v] the Levites brought
them up, 6while King Solomon and the entire Israelite assembly that had joined him
before the chest sacrificed countless sheep
and oxen. 7The priests brought the chest
containing the LORD's covenant to its designated spot beneath the wings of the winged
creatures in the inner sanctuary of the
temple, the most holy place. 8The winged
creatures spread their wings over the place
where the chest rested, covering the chest
and its carrying poles. 9The carrying poles
were so long that their tips could be seen
from the holy place[w] in front of the inner
sanctuary, though they weren't visible from
outside. They are still there today. 10Noth-
ing was in the chest except the two stone
tablets Moses placed there while at Horeb,
where the LORD made a covenant with the
Israelites after they left Egypt.

11Then the priests left the holy place. All
the priests who were present had sanctified themselves, regardless of their divisions. 12All the levitical musicians—Asaph,
Heman, Jeduthun, and their families and
relatives—were dressed in fine linen and
stood east of the altar with cymbals, harps,
and zithers, along with one hundred twenty
priests blowing trumpets. 13The trumpeters and singers joined together to praise
and thank the LORD as one. Accompanied
by trumpets, cymbals, and other musical
instruments, they began to sing, praising
the LORD:

Yes, God is good!
Yes, God's faithful love lasts forever!

Then a cloud filled the LORD's temple.[x]
14The priests were unable to carry out their
duties on account of the cloud because the
LORD's glory filled God's temple.

6 Then Solomon said, "The LORD said
that he would live in a dark cloud; 2but
God, I have built you a lofty temple—a
place where you can live forever."

3The king turned around, and while the
entire assembly of Israel was standing there,
he blessed them, 4saying:

Bless the LORD, the God of Israel,
who spoke directly to my father David
and now has kept his promise: 5"From
the day I brought my people out of the
land of Egypt, I haven't selected a city
from any Israelite tribe as a site for the
building of a temple for my name. Neither have I chosen anyone as prince over
my people Israel. 6But now I have chosen
Jerusalem as a place for my name, and
David as prince over my people Israel."

7My father David wanted to build a
temple for the name of the LORD, Israel's
God. 8But the LORD said to my father
David: "It is very good that you thought
to build a temple for my name. Nevertheless, 9you yourself won't build that temple. Instead, your very own son will build
the temple for my name." 10The LORD
has kept his promise—I have succeeded
my father David on Israel's throne, just
as the LORD said, and I have built the
temple for the name of the LORD, Israel's
God. 11There I've placed the chest that
contains the covenant that the LORD
made with the Israelites.

12Solomon stood before the LORD's altar
in front of the entire Israelite assembly and
spread out his hands. 13Now Solomon had
made a bronze platform seven and a half
feet long, seven and a half feet wide, and
four and a half feet high, and he set it in
the middle of the enclosure. He stood on it.
Then, kneeling before the whole assembly
of Israel and spreading his hands toward
the sky, 14he said:

LORD God of Israel, there is no god
like you in heaven or on the earth. You
keep the covenant and show loyalty to
your servants who walk before you with
all their heart. 15This is the covenant you

[u]September–October, Tishrei [v]LXX; MT *the levitical priests* [w]LXX; MT *the chest* [x]Cf LXX; MT *the temple, the LORD's temple*

kept with your servant David my father, which you promised him. Today you have fulfilled what you promised.

16 So now, LORD God of Israel, keep what you promised my father David your servant when you said to him, "You will never fail to have a successor sitting on Israel's throne as long as your descendants carefully walk according to my Instruction, just as you have walked before me." 17 So now, LORD God of Israel, may your promise to your servant David come true.

18 But how could God possibly live on earth with people? If heaven, even the highest heaven, can't contain you, how can this temple that I have built contain you? 19 LORD, my God, listen to your servant's prayer and request, and hear the cry and prayer that I your servant pray to you. 20 Constantly watch over this temple, the place where you promised to put your name, and listen to the prayer your servant is praying concerning this place. 21 Listen to the request of your servant and your people Israel when they pray concerning this place. Listen from your heavenly dwelling place, and when you hear, forgive!

22 If someone wrongs another and must take a solemn pledge asserting his innocence before your altar in this temple, 23 then listen from heaven, act, and decide which of your servants is right. Condemn the guilty party, repaying them for their conduct, but justify the innocent person, repaying them for their righteousness.

24 If your people Israel are defeated by an enemy because they have sinned against you, but then they change their hearts, give thanks to your name, and ask for mercy in your presence at this temple, 25 then listen from heaven and forgive the sin of your people Israel. Return them to the land you gave to them and their ancestors.

26 When the sky holds back its rain because Israel has sinned against you, but they then pray concerning this place, give thanks to your name, and turn away from their sin because you have punished them for it,[y] 27 then listen from heaven and forgive the sin of your servants, your people Israel. Teach them the best way for them to follow, and send rain on your land that you gave to your people as an inheritance.

28 Whenever there is a famine or plague in the land, or whenever there is blight, mildew, locusts, or grasshoppers, or whenever someone's enemies attack them in their cities, or any plague or illness comes, 29 whatever prayer or petition is made by any individual or by all of your people Israel—because people will recognize their own pain and suffering and spread out their hands toward this temple—30 then listen from heaven where you live. Forgive, act, and repay each person according to all their conduct because you know their hearts. You alone know the human heart! 31 Do this that they may revere you by following your ways all the days they live on the fertile land that you gave to our ancestors.

32 Listen also to the foreigner who isn't from your people Israel, but who comes from a distant country because of your great reputation, your great power, and your outstretched arm. When they come and pray toward this temple, 33 then listen from heaven where you live, and do everything the foreigner asks. Do this so that all the people of the earth may know your reputation and revere you, as your people Israel do, and recognize that this temple I have built bears your name.

34 When your people go to war against their enemies, wherever you may send them, and they pray to you toward this city that you have chosen and concerning this temple that I have built for your name, 35 then listen from heaven to their prayer and request and do what is right for them.

36 When they sin against you, for there is no one who doesn't sin, and you

[y] LXX, Vulg; MT *you have answered them*

become angry with them and hand them
over to an enemy who takes them away
as prisoners to enemy territory, whether
distant or nearby, 37 if they change their
heart in whatever land they are held
captive, turning back and begging for
your mercy,[z] saying, "We have sinned,
we have done wrong, and we have acted
wickedly!" 38 and if they return to you
with all their heart and all their being in
the enemy territory where they've been
taken captive, and pray concerning their
land, which you gave to their ancestors,
concerning the city you have chosen,
and concerning this temple I have built
for your name, 39 then listen to their
prayer and request from your heavenly
dwelling place. Do what is right for
them, and forgive your people who have
sinned against you.
40 Now, my God, may your eyes be
open and your ears attentive to the
prayers of this place. 41 And now go,
LORD God, to your resting place, you
and your mighty chest. May your
priests, LORD God, be clothed with salvation; may those loyal to you rejoice in
what is good. 42 LORD God, don't reject
your anointed one.[a] Remember your
faithful loyalty to your servant David.

7 As soon as Solomon finished praying,
fire came down from heaven and consumed the entirely burned offering and the
sacrifices, while the LORD's glory filled the
temple. 2 The priests were unable to enter
the LORD's temple because the LORD's
glory had filled the LORD's temple. 3 All the
Israelites were watching when the fire fell.
As the LORD's glory filled the temple, they
knelt down on the pavement with their
faces to the ground, worshipping and giving thanks to the LORD, saying, "Yes, God is
good! Yes, God's faithful love lasts forever!"
4 Then the king and all the people sacrificed to the LORD. 5 King Solomon sacrificed
twenty-two thousand oxen and one hundred twenty thousand sheep when the king
and all the people dedicated God's temple.
6 The priests stood at their posts, as did the
Levites with the LORD's musical instruments, which King David had made for giving thanks to the LORD, saying, "Yes, God's
faithful love lasts forever!" and which David
had used when he gave praise. Across from
them, the priests were blowing trumpets
while all Israel was standing.
7 Solomon also dedicated the middle of
the courtyard in front of the LORD's temple. He had to offer the entirely burned
offerings and the fat of the well-being sacrifices there because the bronze altar Solomon had made was too small to contain the
entirely burned offerings, the grain offerings, and the pieces of fat.
8 At that time Solomon, together with all
Israel, celebrated the festival for seven days.
It was a very large assembly that came from
Lebo-hamath to the border[b] of Egypt. 9 On
the eighth day there was a gathering. They
had dedicated the altar for seven days and
celebrated the festival for another seven
days. 10 On the twenty-third day of the seventh month,[c] Solomon dismissed the people
to their tents, happy and content because of
the goodness the LORD had shown to David,
to Solomon, and to his people Israel. 11 In this
way, Solomon finished the LORD's temple
and the royal palace. He successfully accomplished everything he intended for the
LORD's temple and his own palace.

Solomon again meets God

12 Then the LORD appeared to Solomon
at night and said to him: I have heard your
prayer and have chosen this place as my
house of sacrifice. 13 When I close the sky so
that there is no rain or I order the locusts to
consume the land or I send a plague against
my people, 14 if my people who belong to me
will humbly pray, seek my face, and turn
from their wicked ways, then I will hear from
heaven, forgive their sin, and heal their land.
15 From now on my eyes will be open and my
ears will pay attention to the prayers offered
in this place, 16 because I have chosen this
temple and declared it holy so that my name

[z] MT adds *in the land they are held captive.* [a] LXX; MT *anointed ones* [b] Or *Wadi*, traditionally *Brook*
[c] September–October, Tishrei

may be there forever. My eyes and my heart
will always be there. 17 As for you, if you will
walk before me just as your father David did,
doing all that I have commanded you and
keeping my regulations and case laws, 18 then
I will establish your royal throne, just as I
promised your father David: You will never
fail to have a successor ruling in Israel. 19 But
if any of you ever turn away from and abandon
the regulations and commands that I
have given you, and go to serve other gods
and worship them, 20 then I will uproot you[d]
from my land that I gave you, and I will reject
this temple that I made holy for my name.
I will make it a joke, insulted by everyone.
21 Everyone who passes by this temple—so
lofty now—will be shocked and will wonder,
Why has the LORD done such a thing to this
land and temple? 22 The answer will come,
Because they abandoned the LORD, the God
of their ancestors, who brought them out
of Egypt. They embraced other gods, worshipping
and serving them. This is why God
brought all this disaster on them.

Solomon's buildings and prosperity

8 After twenty years of building the
LORD's temple and his royal palace,
2 Solomon next rebuilt the cities Huram had
given him, and he settled Israelites there.
3 Solomon went to Hamath-zobah and
seized it. 4 He fortified Tadmor in the wilderness,
along with all the storage cities he
had built in Hamath. 5 Solomon also built
Upper Beth-horon and Lower Beth-horon
as fortress cities with walls, gates, and
crossbars; 6 Baalath; all the cities he used for
storage; and all the cities used for chariots
and cavalry—along with everything else
he wanted to build in Jerusalem, Lebanon,
and throughout his kingdom.
7 Any non-Israelite people who remained
of the Hittites, Amorites, Perizzites, Hivites,
and Jebusites—8 that is, the descendants
of such people who were still in the
land because the Israelites weren't able to
destroy them—Solomon forced into the
labor gangs that are still in existence today.
9 However, Solomon didn't force the Israelites
to work as slaves; instead, they became
warriors, chief officers, and the commanders
of his chariots and cavalry. 10 And Solomon
had two hundred fifty chief officers[e]
who were in charge of the people.
11 Solomon brought Pharaoh's daughter
from David's City to a palace he had built
for her, because he said, "My wife mustn't
live in the palace of Israel's King David, because
the places where the LORD's chest has
been are holy."
12 Then Solomon offered entirely burned
offerings to the LORD on the LORD's altar
that Solomon had built in front of the
porch, 13 as each day required, according to
the commandment of Moses for sabbaths,
new moon festivals, and the three annual
festivals—Unleavened Bread, Weeks, and
Booths. 14 Just as his father David had ordered,
Solomon set up the divisions of the
priests for their services and the Levites
to their posts for offering praise and ministering
in front of the priests, doing what
needed to be done each day; as well as the
gatekeepers in their divisions at each gate,
because this was what David the man of
God had commanded. 15 They didn't deviate
in any way from the king's commands concerning
the priests, the Levites, or the treasuries.
16 All Solomon's work was carried out
from the day the foundation of the LORD's
temple was laid until its completion. Then
the LORD's temple was completely finished.
17 Then Solomon went to Ezion-geber
and Eloth on the coast in the land of Edom.
18 Huram had his servants bring ships to
Solomon, along with crews of expert sailors.
They went with Solomon's servants
to Ophir and imported four hundred fifty
kikkars of gold, which they brought back to
King Solomon.

Queen of Sheba

9 When the queen of Sheba heard reports
about Solomon, she came to Jerusalem
to test Solomon with riddles. Accompanying
her was a huge entourage, with camels
carrying spices, large amounts of gold, and
precious stones. After she arrived, she told

[d] Or *Israel* (or *them*) [e] Qere; Kethib *officers of the troops*

Solomon everything that was on her mind. 2 Solomon answered all her questions; nothing was too difficult for him to answer. 3 When the queen of Sheba saw how wise Solomon was, the palace he had built, 4 the food on his table, his servants' quarters, the function and dress of his attendants, his cupbearers and their dress, and the entirely burned offerings he offered at the LORD's temple,[f] it took her breath away.

5 "The report I heard about your deeds and wisdom when I was still at home is true," she said to the king. 6 "I didn't believe it until I came and saw it with my own eyes. In fact, the half of it wasn't told to me! You have far more than I was told. 7 Your people and these servants who continually serve you and get to listen to your wisdom are truly happy! 8 Bless the LORD your God because he was pleased to put you on the throne as king for the LORD your God. Because your God loved Israel and wanted to establish them forever, he has made you their king to uphold justice and righteousness."

9 Then she gave the king one hundred twenty kikkars of gold, a great quantity of spices, and precious stones. Never again has such a quantity of spice come to Israel as when the queen of Sheba gave this gift to King Solomon.

10 In addition, Huram's servants and the servants of Solomon, who had brought gold back from Ophir, also brought algum wood and precious stones. 11 The king made steps[g] for the LORD's temple and for the royal palace with the algum wood, as well as lyres and harps for the musicians. Never before had anything like them been seen in the land of Judah. 12 King Solomon gave the queen of Sheba everything she wanted, even more than she had brought the king. Then she and her servants returned to her homeland.

Solomon's wealth

13 Solomon received an annual income of six hundred sixty-six kikkars of gold, 14 not including income from the traders and merchants. All the Arabian kings and the governors of the land also brought Solomon gold and silver. 15 King Solomon made two hundred body-sized shields of hammered gold, using fifteen pounds[h] of hammered gold in each shield; 16 and three hundred small shields of hammered gold, using seven and a half pounds[i] of hammered gold in each shield. The king placed these in the Forest of Lebanon Palace.

17 The king also made a large ivory throne and covered it with pure gold. 18 Six steps led up to the throne, which had a gold footrest attached. Two lions stood beside the armrests on both sides of the throne. 19 Another twelve lions stood on both sides of the six steps. No other kingdom had anything like this.

20 All King Solomon's drinking cups were made of gold, and all the items in the Forest of Lebanon Palace were made of pure gold, not silver, since even silver wasn't considered good enough in Solomon's time! 21 The royal fleet sailed to Tarshish with the servants of Huram, returning once every three years with gold, silver, ivory, monkeys, and peacocks.[j]

22 King Solomon far exceeded all the earth's kings in wealth and wisdom, 23 and kings of every nation wanted an audience with Solomon in order to hear his God-given wisdom. 24 Year after year they came with tribute: objects of silver and gold, clothing, weapons, spices, horses, and mules.

25 Solomon also had four thousand stalls for horses and chariots, together with twelve thousand horsemen that he kept in the chariot cities and with the king in Jerusalem. 26 He ruled all the kings from the Euphrates[k] to the Philistines' land and the border of Egypt. 27 In Jerusalem, the king made silver as common as stones and cedar as common as sycamore trees that grow in the foothills. 28 Solomon's horses were imported from Egypt and every land.

Solomon's remaining days

29 The rest of Solomon's deeds, from beginning to end, aren't they written in the

[f] LXX, Syr, Vulg, 1 Kgs 10:5; MT *how he processed* (or *went up*) *to the LORD's temple.* [g] LXX, Vulg; Heb uncertain [h] Or *six hundred shekels* [i] Or *three hundred shekels* [j] Or possibly *apes*; Heb uncertain [k] Or *the river*

records of the prophet Nathan, the prophecies of Ahijah from Shiloh, and the visions of the seer Iddo concerning Jeroboam, Nebat's son? 30 Solomon ruled over all Israel in Jerusalem for forty years. 31 Solomon lay down with his ancestors and was buried in David's City with his father. His son Rehoboam succeeded him as king.

How Rehoboam lost the kingdom

10 Rehoboam went to Shechem, where all Israel had come to make him king. 2 When Jeroboam, Nebat's son, heard the news, he returned from Egypt where he had fled from King Solomon. 3 The people sent and called for Jeroboam, who along with all Israel came and said to Rehoboam, 4 "Your father made our workload[l] very heavy; if you will lessen the demands your father made of us and lighten the heavy workload he demanded from us, then we will serve you."

5 He answered them, "Come back in three days." So the people left.

6 King Rehoboam consulted the elders who had served his father Solomon when he was alive. "What do you advise?" Rehoboam asked. "How should I respond to these people?"

7 "If you are kind to these people and try to please them by speaking gently with them," they replied, "they will be your servants forever."

8 But Rehoboam ignored the advice the elders gave him and instead sought the counsel of the young advisors who had grown up with him and now served him. 9 "What do you advise?" he asked them. "How should we respond to these people who said to me, 'Lighten the workload your father demanded from us'?"

10 The young people who had grown up with Rehoboam said to him, "This people said to you, 'Your father made our workload heavy. Lighten it for us!' Now this is what you should say to them, 'My baby[m] finger is thicker than my father's waist! 11 So if my father made your workload heavy, I'll make it even heavier! If my father disciplined you with whips, I'll do it with scorpions!'"

12 Jeroboam and all the people returned to Rehoboam on the third day, just as the king had specified when he said, "Come back in three days." 13 The king then answered the people harshly. He ignored the elders' advice, 14 and instead followed the young people's advice. He said, "My father made your workload heavy, but I'll make it even heavier; my father disciplined you with whips, but I'll do it with scorpions!"

15 The king didn't listen to the people because this turn of events came from God so that the LORD might keep his promise concerning Jeroboam, Nebat's son, which God delivered through Ahijah from Shiloh. 16 When all Israel saw[n] that the king wouldn't listen to them, the people answered the king,

"Why should we care about David?
We have no stake in Jesse's son!
Go back to your homes, Israel!
You better look after
your own house now, David!"

Then all Israel went back to their homes, 17 and Rehoboam ruled over only the Israelites who lived in the cities of Judah.

18 When King Rehoboam sent Hadoram to them (he was the leader of the work gang), the Israelites stoned him to death. King Rehoboam quickly got into his chariot and fled to Jerusalem. 19 And so Israel has been in rebellion against David's dynasty to this day.

11 When Rehoboam arrived at Jerusalem, he assembled the house of Judah and Benjamin, one hundred eighty thousand select warriors, to fight against Israel and to restore the kingdom to Rehoboam. 2 But the LORD's word came to Shemaiah the man of God: 3 Tell Judah's King Rehoboam, Solomon's son, and all Israel in Judah and Benjamin, 4 This is what the LORD says: Don't make war against your relatives. Go home, every one of you, because this is my plan. When they heard the LORD's words, they abandoned their attack against Jeroboam.

5 Rehoboam lived in Jerusalem, but he built cities for Judah's defense 6 in Bethlehem, Etam, Tekoa, 7 Beth-zur, Soco, Adullam,

[l] Or *our yoke* [m] Or *pinky*; perhaps a euphemism [n] Syr, OL, Tg; MT lacks *saw*.

8 Gath, Mareshah, Ziph, 9 Adoraim, Lachish,
Azekah, 10 Zorah, Aijalon, and Hebron.
These were the fortified cities in Judah
and Benjamin. 11 He made the fortifications
stronger, placed commanders in them, and
supplied them with food, oil, and wine.
12 He also stored shields and spears in each
of the cities, making them very strong.
This is how Judah and Benjamin remained
under his control.

13 The priests and the Levites from every
region throughout all Israel sided with Rehoboam. 14 The Levites left their pastures
and property to come to Judah and Jerusalem because Jeroboam and his sons had
refused to let them serve as the LORD's
priests, 15 having appointed his own priests
for the shrines and the goat and calf idols
he had made. 16 People from every tribe of
Israel who had made up their minds to seek
the LORD, Israel's God, came to Jerusalem to
sacrifice to the LORD, the God of their ancestors. 17 They strengthened the kingdom of
Judah and supported Rehoboam, Solomon's
son, for three years by following the way of
David and Solomon those three years.

18 Rehoboam married Mahalath daughter of Jerimoth, David's son, and Abihail
daughter of Eliab, Jesse's son. 19 The sons
she bore him were Jeush, Shemariah, and
Zaham. 20 Later he married Maacah, Absalom's daughter, who bore him Abijah, Attai,
Ziza, and Shelomith. 21 Rehoboam loved Absalom's daughter Maacah more than all his
wives and secondary wives. In all, he had
eighteen wives and sixty secondary wives,
twenty-eight sons, and sixty daughters.
22 Rehoboam named Abijah, Maacah's son,
as his successor in order to make him king.
23 He wisely placed some of his sons in every
region of Judah and Benjamin, in every fortified city, and gave them plenty of food and
sought many wives for them.

12

But as soon as Rehoboam had secured
his royal power, he, along with all
Israel, abandoned the LORD's Instruction.

Rehoboam rules

2 Egypt's King Shishak attacked Jerusalem in the fifth year of King Rehoboam
because Israel had been unfaithful to the
LORD. 3 Accompanying Shishak from Egypt
were twelve hundred chariots, sixty thousand horses, and countless Libyan, Sukkite,
and Cushite warriors. 4 He captured the fortified cities of Judah and came toward Jerusalem. 5 Then the prophet Shemaiah went
to Rehoboam and the leaders of Judah
who had gathered at Jerusalem because
of Shishak, and told them, This is what
the LORD says: Since you have abandoned
me, now I am abandoning you to Shishak's
power.

6 Then the leaders of Israel and the king
submitted. "The LORD is right," they said.

7 When the LORD saw that they had
submitted, the LORD's word came to Shemaiah: Since they have submitted, I won't
destroy them. I will deliver them in a little
while, and I won't use Shishak to pour out
my anger against Jerusalem. 8 Nevertheless, they will be subject to him so that they
learn the difference between serving me
and serving other nations.

9 Egypt's King Shishak attacked Jerusalem and seized the treasures of the LORD's
temple and the royal palace. He took everything, even the gold shields Solomon had
made. 10 King Rehoboam replaced them
with bronze shields and assigned them to
the officers of the guard who protected the
entrance to the royal palace. (11 Whenever
the king entered the LORD's temple, the
guards would carry the shields and then
return them to the guardroom.) 12 When
Rehoboam submitted, the LORD was no
longer angry with him, and total destruction was avoided. There were, after all,
some good things still in Judah.

13 So King Rehoboam was securely established in Jerusalem. Rehoboam was
41 years old when he became king, and
he ruled seventeen years in Jerusalem,
the city the LORD had chosen from all the
tribes of Israel to put his name. His mother's name was Naamah from Ammon. 14 But
Rehoboam did what was evil because he
didn't set his heart on seeking the LORD.
15 The deeds of Rehoboam, from beginning
to end, aren't they written in the records of
the prophet Shemaiah and the seer Iddo,
including the genealogical records? There

was continual warfare between Rehoboam and Jeroboam. 16 Rehoboam lay down with his ancestors and was buried in David's City. His son Abijah[o] succeeded him as king.

Abijah rules Judah

13 Abijah[p] became king over Judah in the eighteenth year of King Jeroboam. 2 He ruled for three years in Jerusalem. His mother's name was Micaiah; she was Uriel's daughter from Gibeah. When war broke out between Abijah and Jeroboam, 3 Abijah went to fight with an army of four hundred thousand select troops against Jeroboam's select forces numbering eight hundred thousand, who were arrayed in battle formation.

4 Abijah stood on the heights of Mount Zemaraim in Ephraim's highlands and said:

> "Listen to me, Jeroboam and all Israel! 5 Surely you know that the LORD, Israel's God, made an unbreakable covenant[q] with David and his descendants that they would rule Israel forever. 6 It was Jeroboam, Nebat's son, the servant of Solomon, David's son, who rebelled against his master. 7 When some useless, worthless people joined his cause, they overpowered Rehoboam, Solomon's son, who was too young and timid to resist them. 8 And now do you intend to challenge the LORD's royal rule, entrusted to David's descendants? You may have a numerical advantage, as well as the gold calves Jeroboam made for you as gods. 9 But you've banished the LORD's priests, Aaron's sons, along with the Levites, so that you could appoint your own priests as other countries do. Now anyone who shows up with a young bull and seven rams can become a priest of these phony gods!
>
> 10 "But us? The LORD is our God, and we haven't abandoned him. Aaron's descendants serve as the LORD's priests, assisted in the work by the Levites. 11 Every morning and every evening they offer entirely burned offerings and fragrant incense to the LORD, and set out bread in stacks upon a clean table. At night they light the lamps on the gold lampstand. Yes, while you are abandoning the LORD our God, we are doing what he requires. 12 Listen! God is on our side, at our head, along with his priests, who are ready to sound the battle trumpets against you. So, Israelites, don't fight against the LORD, the God of your ancestors, for you won't succeed!"

13 Meanwhile, Jeroboam had sent troops around behind them for an ambush so that the main force was in front of Judah while the ambush was behind. 14 When Judah looked around and suddenly realized that they were surrounded, they cried out to the LORD while the priests sounded the trumpets 15 and raised the battle cry. When they raised the battle cry, God defeated Jeroboam and all Israel before Abijah and Judah. 16 So the Israelites fled before Judah, and God gave Judah the victory. 17 Abijah and his people struck them severely: five hundred thousand select warriors were killed. 18 Israel was subdued on that occasion, and Judah succeeded because they relied on the LORD, the God of their ancestors. 19 Abijah pursued Jeroboam and took these cities away from him: Bethel, Jeshanah, and Ephron,[r] along with their villages. 20 Jeroboam failed to regain power during the time of Abijah. The LORD finally struck him down, and he died. 21 Abijah, however, grew strong. He married fourteen wives; he had twenty-two sons and sixteen daughters. 22 The rest of Abijah's deeds, what he did and what he said, are written in the

14 account of the prophet Iddo. 1 Abijah lay down with his ancestors and was buried in David's City. His son Asa succeeded him as king.

Asa rules Judah

[s]In Asa's time, the land had peace for ten years. 2[t]Asa did what was right and good in the LORD his God's eyes. 3 He removed the foreign altars and shrines, smashed the

[o]Spelled Abijam in 1 Kgs 14:31 [p]Spelled Abijam in 1 Kgs 15:1, 7-8 [q]Or *a covenant of salt* [r]Qere, LXX; Kethib *Ephrain* [s]13:23 in Heb [t]14:1 in Heb

sacred pillars, cut down the sacred poles,[u] [4]and urged Judah to seek the LORD, the God of their ancestors, by doing what the Instruction and the commandments required. [5]He also removed the shrines and incense altars from all the cities of Judah so that the kingdom was at peace under him. [6]When the land was at peace, he built fortified cities in Judah; there was no war in those years because the LORD had given him rest.

[7]"Let's build up these cities," Asa told Judah. "We'll surround them with walls, towers, gates, and crossbars while the land is still ours, because we sought the LORD our God and he sought us[v] and surrounded us with rest." As a result, the people successfully completed their building projects.

Judah defeats Cush

[8]Asa had an army of three hundred thousand Judeans armed with body-sized shields and spears and another two hundred eighty thousand from Benjamin armed with small shields and bows. All were brave warriors. [9]Zerah the Cushite marched against him with an army of one million men and three hundred chariots. When he got as far as Mareshah, [10]Asa marched against him, setting up for battle in a valley north[w] of Mareshah.

[11]Then Asa cried out to the LORD his God, "LORD, only you can help the weak against the powerful.[x] Help us, LORD our God, because we rely on you and we have marched against this multitude in your name. You are the LORD our God. Don't let a mere human stand against you!"

[12]So the LORD struck the Cushites before Asa and Judah, and the Cushites fled. [13]Asa and his troops chased them as far as Gerar. The Cushites fell until there were no survivors. They were completely crushed by the LORD and his army, who carried off a huge amount of loot, [14]and attacked all the cities surrounding Gerar who were terrified of the LORD. They plundered all these cities as well because there was a great amount of loot in them. [15]They also attacked the herdsmen's camps, taking many sheep and camels before returning to Jerusalem.

15 When God's spirit came upon Azariah, Oded's son, [2]he confronted Asa: "Listen to me, Asa and all Judah and Benjamin," he said. "The LORD is with you as long as you are with him. If you seek him, he will be found by you; but if you abandon him, he will abandon you. [3]For a long time Israel was without the true God, without a priest to teach them, and without the Instruction. [4]But in their time of trouble they turned to the LORD, Israel's God. They sought him and found him! [5]At that time, it wasn't safe to travel because great turmoil affected all the inhabitants of the area. [6]Nation was crushed by nation and city by city, as God troubled them with every kind of problem. [7]But as for you, be brave and don't lose heart, because your work will be rewarded!"

Asa's reforms

[8]As soon as Asa heard these words and the prophecy of Azariah, Oded's son,[y] he felt brave and removed the detestable idols from all of Judah and Benjamin, as well as from the cities he had captured in Ephraim's highlands, and he repaired the LORD's altar that stood before the LORD's entrance hall. [9]Then Asa gathered all Judah and Benjamin, along with those who were living among them as immigrants from Ephraim, Manasseh, and Simeon, because many people from Israel had joined up with him when they saw that the LORD his God was with him. [10]They gathered in Jerusalem in the third month of the fifteenth year of Asa's rule. [11]On that day they sacrificed to the LORD part of the loot they had taken: seven hundred oxen and seven thousand sheep. [12]They made a covenant to seek the LORD, the God of their ancestors, with all their heart and all their being. [13]They agreed that anyone who refused to seek the LORD, Israel's God, would be put to death, whether young or old, male or female. [14]They swore

[u]Heb *asherim*, perhaps objects devoted to the goddess Asherah; cf 1 Kgs 15:13 [v]LXX; MT lacks *and* and repeats *we sought*. [w]LXX; MT an otherwise unknown *Zephathah Valley* [x]Heb uncertain; or *it is not with you to help between the many and the powerless.* [y]Cf Syr, Vulg; MT *and the prophecy of the prophet Oded*

this to the LORD with a loud voice, shouts
of joy, and blasts from trumpets and horns.
15 All Judah was delighted with the solemn
pledge because they had sworn it with all
their hearts. When they enthusiastically
sought God, he was found by them, and the
LORD gave them peace on every side. 16 Asa
the king even removed his grandmother
Maacah from the position of queen mother
because she had made an image of Asherah.
Asa cut down her image, pulverized it, and
burned it in the Kidron Valley. 17 Although
the shrines weren't removed from Israel,
Asa nevertheless remained committed
with all his heart throughout his life. 18 He
brought into God's temple the various silver and gold objects that he and his father
had dedicated. 19 There was no war until the
thirty-fifth year of Asa's rule.

Aram invades Judah

16 In the thirty-sixth year of Asa's rule,
Israel's King Baasha attacked Judah
and fortified Ramah to prevent Judah's
King Asa from moving into that area. 2 Asa
took silver and gold from the treasuries
of the LORD's temple and the royal palace
and sent them to Aram's King Ben-hadad,
who ruled in Damascus, with the following
message: 3 "Let's make a covenant similar to
the one between our fathers. Since I have
already sent you silver and gold, break your
covenant with Israel's King Baasha so that
he will leave me alone." 4 Ben-hadad agreed
with King Asa and sent his army commanders against the cities of Israel, attacking
Ijon, Dan, Abel-maim, and all the store-
cities of Naphtali. 5 As soon as Baasha
learned of this, he stopped building Ramah
and abandoned his work. 6 Then King Asa
had all Judah carry away the stone and timber that Baasha was using to build Ramah,
and King Asa used it to build Geba and Mizpah. 7 At that time Hanani the seer came to
Judah's King Asa and said to him, "Because
you relied on Aram's king and not on the
LORD your God, the army of Aram's king
has slipped out of your grasp. 8 Weren't the
Cushites and the Libyans a vast army with
chariots and horsemen to spare? Still, when
you relied on the LORD, he delivered them
into your power, 9 because the LORD's eyes
scan the whole world to strengthen those
who are committed to him with all their
hearts. Your foolishness means that you
will have war on your hands from now on."
10 Asa was angry with the seer. Asa was so
mad he threw Hanani in jail and took his
anger out on some of the people.

Asa's disease and death

11 The rest of Asa's deeds, from beginning
to end, are written in the official records of
Israel's and Judah's kings. 12 In the thirty-
ninth year of his rule, Asa developed a severe foot disease. But even in his illness he
refused to seek the LORD and consulted
doctors instead. 13 In the forty-first year of
his rule, Asa lay down with his ancestors.
14 He was buried in the tomb he had prepared for himself in David's City, and was
laid on a bed filled with sweet spices and
various kinds of perfume, with a huge fire
made in his honor.

Jehoshaphat rules Judah

17 Asa's son Jehoshaphat succeeded him
as king. Jehoshaphat strengthened
his position against Israel 2 by stationing
troops in the fortified cities of Judah and
placing soldiers throughout the land of
Judah and in the cities of Ephraim that his
father Asa had captured. 3 The LORD was
with Jehoshaphat because he followed the
earlier ways of his father[z] by not seeking
Baal. 4 Instead, he sought the God of his
father, and unlike Israel, he followed God's
commandments. 5 The LORD gave him firm
control over the kingdom, and all Judah
brought Jehoshaphat tribute, so that he
had abundant riches and honor. 6 Jehoshaphat took pride in the LORD's ways and
again removed the shrines and the sacred
poles[a] from Judah.

7 In the third year of his rule, Jehoshaphat
sent his officials Ben-hail, Obadiah, Zechariah, Nethanel, and Micaiah to teach in the
cities of Judah. 8 They were accompanied

[z] LXX; MT *in the ways of his father David* [a] Heb *asherim*, perhaps objects devoted to the goddess Asherah

by the Levites Shemaiah, Nethaniah, Zebadiah, Asahel, Shemiramoth, Jehonathan, Adonijah, Tobijah, and Tob-adonijah, and by the priests Elishama and Jehoram. 9They taught throughout Judah. They brought with them the LORD's Instruction scroll as they made their rounds to all the cities of Judah, teaching the people.

10All the kingdoms surrounding Judah were afraid of the LORD and didn't wage war against Jehoshaphat. 11Some of the Philistines brought a load of silver as tribute to Jehoshaphat. The Arabians also brought flocks to Jehoshaphat: seventy-seven hundred rams and seventy-seven hundred goats. 12As Jehoshaphat grew increasingly powerful, he built fortresses and storage cities in Judah 13and had many supplies in the cities of Judah. He also had an army of mighty warriors in Jerusalem, 14registered by their clans as follows: Judah's officers over units of a thousand included Commander Adnah with three hundred thousand soldiers; 15next to him was Commander Jehohanan with two hundred eighty thousand soldiers; 16at his side was Amasiah, Zichri's son, who volunteered for the LORD with two hundred thousand soldiers. 17From Benjamin came a valiant warrior: Eliada, together with two hundred thousand armed with bow and shield; 18next to him was Jehozabad, together with one hundred eighty thousand soldiers. 19These were the individuals who served the king in addition to those the king placed in the fortified cities throughout Judah.

Jehoshaphat and Ahab

18 Even though Jehoshaphat already had great wealth and honor, he allied himself with Ahab through marriage. 2A few years later, while Jehoshaphat was visiting Ahab in Samaria, Ahab slaughtered many sheep and oxen for Jehoshaphat and those who were with him in order to persuade him to attack Ramoth-gilead. 3"Will you go with me to Ramoth-gilead?" Israel's King Ahab asked Judah's King Jehoshaphat.

Jehoshaphat replied, "I and my people will be united with you and your people in battle. 4But," Jehoshaphat said to Israel's king, "first, let's see what the LORD has to say." 5So Israel's king gathered four hundred prophets and asked them, "Should we go to war with Ramoth-gilead or not?"

"Attack!" the prophets answered. "God will hand it over to the king."

6But Jehoshaphat said, "Isn't there any other prophet of the LORD around whom we could ask?"

7"There's one other man who could ask the LORD for us," Israel's king told Jehoshaphat, "but I hate him because he never prophesies anything good about me, only bad. His name is Micaiah, Imlah's son."

"The king shouldn't speak like that!" Jehoshaphat said.

8So Israel's king called an officer and ordered, "Bring Micaiah, Imlah's son, right away."

9Now Israel's king and Judah's King Jehoshaphat were sitting on their thrones dressed in their royal robes at the threshing floor beside the entrance to the gate of Samaria. All the prophets were prophesying in front of them. 10Zedekiah, Chenaanah's son, made iron horns for himself and said, "This is what the LORD says: With these horns you will gore the Arameans until there's nothing left of them!"

11The other prophets agreed: "Attack Ramoth-gilead and win! The LORD will hand it over to the king!"

12Meanwhile, the messenger who had gone to summon Micaiah said to him, "Listen, the prophets all agree that the king will succeed. You should say the same thing they say and prophesy success."

13But Micaiah answered, "As surely as the LORD lives, I will say only what God tells me to say."[b]

14When Micaiah arrived, the king asked him, "Micaiah, should we go to war with Ramoth-gilead or not?"

"Attack and win!" Micaiah answered. "The LORD will hand it over to the king."

15But the king said, "How many times

[b]LXX, 1 Kgs 22:14; MT omits *me*.

must I demand that you tell me the truth when you speak in the LORD's name?"

16Then Micaiah replied, "I saw all Israel scattered on the hills like sheep without a shepherd! And then the LORD said: 'They have no master. Let them return safely to their own homes.'"

17Then Israel's king said to Jehoshaphat, "Didn't I tell you? He never prophesies anything good about me, only bad."

18Then Micaiah said, "Listen now to the LORD's word: I saw the LORD enthroned with all the heavenly forces stationed at his right and at his left. 19The LORD said, 'Who will persuade Israel's King Ahab so that he attacks Ramoth-gilead and dies there?' There were several suggestions, 20until one particular spirit approached the LORD and said, 'I will persuade him.' 'How?' the LORD asked. 21'I will be a lying spirit in the mouths of all his prophets,' he said. The LORD agreed: 'You will succeed in persuading him! Go ahead!' 22So now, since the LORD placed a lying spirit in the mouths of these prophets of yours, it is the LORD who has pronounced disaster against you!"

23Zedekiah, Chenaanah's son, approached Micaiah and slapped him on the cheek. "Just how did the LORD's spirit leave me to speak to you?" he asked.

24Micaiah answered, "You will find out on the day you try to hide in an inner room."

25"Arrest him," ordered Israel's king, "and turn him over to Amon the city governor and to Joash the king's son. 26Tell them, 'The king says: Put this man in prison and feed him minimum rations of bread and water until I return safely.'"

27"If you ever return safely," Micaiah replied, "then the LORD wasn't speaking through me." Then he added, "Mark my words, every last one of you!"

28So Israel's king and Judah's King Jehoshaphat attacked Ramoth-gilead. 29Israel's king said to Jehoshaphat, "I will disguise myself when we go into battle, but you should wear your royal attire." When the king of Israel had disguised himself, they entered the battle.

30Meanwhile, Aram's king had commanded his chariot officers, "Don't bother with anyone big or small. Fight only with Israel's king." 31When the chariot officers saw Jehoshaphat, they assumed that he must be Israel's king, so they turned to attack him. But when Jehoshaphat cried out, the LORD helped him, and God lured them away from him. 32When the chariot officers realized that he wasn't Israel's king, they stopped chasing him.

33Someone, however, randomly shot an arrow that struck Israel's king between the joints in his armor. "Turn around and get me out of the battle," the king told his chariot driver. "I've been hit!" 34While the battle raged all that day, Israel's king stood propped up in his chariot facing the Arameans. But that evening he died, just as the sun was going down.

19 Upon the safe arrival of Judah's King Jehoshaphat to his palace in Jerusalem, 2Jehu son of Hanani the seer came out to meet him and said, "Why did you help the wicked? Why have you loved those who hate the LORD? This is why the LORD is angry with you. 3Nevertheless, there is some good to be found in you, in that you have removed the sacred poles[c] from the land and set your mind to seek God."

Jehoshaphat's reforms

4Though Jehoshaphat lived in Jerusalem, he regularly went out among the people between Beer-sheba and Ephraim's highlands, and encouraged them to return to the LORD, the God of their ancestors. 5He appointed judges throughout the land in each of the fortified cities of Judah, 6instructing them, "Be careful when you pass judgment. You aren't dispensing justice by merely human standards but for the LORD, who is with you. 7Therefore, respect the LORD and act accordingly, because there can be no injustice, playing favorites, or taking bribes when it comes to the LORD our God."

8Jehoshaphat also appointed judges in Jerusalem from among the Levites, the

[c]Heb *asherot*, perhaps objects devoted to the goddess Asherah

priests, and the family heads of Israel to administer the LORD's Instruction and to settle disputes among those living[d] in Jerusalem. 9 He instructed them, "You must respect the LORD at all times, in truth, and with complete integrity. 10 In any case that comes before you from a fellow citizen in an outlying town, whether it involves bloodshed or is an issue of instruction, commandment, regulations, or case laws, you must warn them not to sin against the LORD, consequently making him angry with both you and your fellow citizen. Do this, and you won't sin. 11 Amariah the chief priest will be in charge of all religious matters, and Zebadiah, Ishmael's son, the leader of Judah's house, will be in charge of all civil matters. The Levites will serve as your officers of the court. Carry out your duties with confidence, and may the LORD be with those who do good."

Jehoshaphat's victory

20 Some time later, the Moabites and the Ammonites, along with some of the Meunites,[e] attacked Jehoshaphat. 2 Jehoshaphat was told, "A large army from beyond the sea, from Edom,[f] is coming to attack you. They are already at Hazazon-tamar!" (that is, En-gedi). 3 Frightened, Jehoshaphat decided to seek the LORD's help and proclaimed a fast for all Judah. 4 People from all of Judah's cities came to ask the LORD for help. 5 Then Jehoshaphat stood up in the congregation of Judah and Jerusalem in the LORD's temple in front of the new courtyard. 6 "LORD, the God of our ancestors, you alone are God in heaven. You rule all the kingdoms of the nations. You are so powerful that no one can oppose you. 7 You, our God, drove out the inhabitants of this land before your people Israel and gave this land to the descendants of your friend Abraham forever. 8 They have lived in it and have built a sanctuary in honor of your name in it, saying, 9 'If calamity, sword, flood,[g] plague, or famine comes upon us, we will stand before this temple, before you, because your name is in this temple. We will cry out to you in our distress, and you will hear us and save us.' 10 So look here! The Ammonites, the Moabites, and those from Mount Seir—the people you wouldn't let Israel invade when they came out of Egypt's land, so Israel avoided them and didn't destroy them—11 here they are, returning the favor by coming to drive us out of your possession that you gave to us! 12 Our God, won't you punish them? We are powerless against this mighty army that is about to attack us. We don't know what to do, and so we are looking to you for help."

13 All Judah was standing before the LORD, even their little ones, wives, and children. 14 Then the LORD's spirit came upon Jahaziel son of Zechariah son of Benaiah son of Jeiel son of Mattaniah, a Levite of the line of Asaph, as he stood in the middle of the assembly.

15 "Pay attention, all of Judah, every inhabitant of Jerusalem, and King Jehoshaphat," Jahaziel said. "This is what the LORD says to you: Don't be afraid or discouraged by this great army because the battle isn't yours. It belongs to God! 16 March out against them tomorrow. Since they will be coming through the Ziz pass, meet them at the end of the valley that opens into the Jeruel wilderness. 17 You don't need to fight this battle. Just take your places, stand ready, and watch how the LORD, who is with you, will deliver you, Judah and Jerusalem. Don't be afraid or discouraged! Go out tomorrow and face them. The LORD will be with you."

18 Then Jehoshaphat bowed down with his face to the ground, and all Judah and the inhabitants of Jerusalem fell before the LORD in worship. 19 Levites from the lines of Kohath and Korah stood up to loudly praise the LORD, the God of Israel.

20 Early the next morning they went into the Tekoa wilderness. When they were about to go out, Jehoshaphat stood and said, "Listen to me, Judah and every inhabitant of Jerusalem! Trust the LORD your God, and you will stand firm; trust his prophets and succeed!"

[d] LXX, Vulg; MT *they returned to Jerusalem* [e] LXX; MT *Ammonites* [f] OL; MT *Aram* [g] LXX; MT *judgment*

21 After consulting with the people, Jehoshaphat appointed musicians to play for the LORD, praising his majestic holiness. They were to march out before the warriors, saying, "Give thanks to the LORD because his faithful love lasts forever!" 22 As they broke into joyful song and praise, the LORD launched a surprise attack against the Ammonites, the Moabites, and those from Mount Seir who were invading Judah, so that they were defeated. 23 The Ammonites and the Moabites turned on those from Mount Seir, completely destroying them. Once they had finished off the inhabitants of Seir, they helped to destroy each other!

24 When Judah arrived at the point overlooking the wilderness, all they could see were corpses lying all over the ground. There were no survivors. 25 When Jehoshaphat and his army came to take the loot, they found a great amount of cattle,[h] goods, clothing,[i] and other valuables—much more than they could carry. In fact, there was so much it took three days to haul it away. 26 On the fourth day they assembled in Blessing Valley, where they blessed the LORD. That's why it is called Blessing Valley to this day. 27 Then everyone from Judah and Jerusalem, with Jehoshaphat at their head, joyfully returned home to Jerusalem because the LORD had given them reason to rejoice over their enemies. 28 They entered Jerusalem accompanied by harps, lutes, and trumpets, and they went to the LORD's temple.

29 The fear of God came on all the surrounding kingdoms when they heard how the LORD had fought against Israel's enemies. 30 As a result, Jehoshaphat's rule was peaceful because his God gave him rest on all sides.

Jehoshaphat's last days

31 Jehoshaphat ruled over Judah. He was 35 years old when he became king, and he ruled for twenty-five years in Jerusalem. His mother's name was Azubah; she was Shilhi's daughter. 32 Jehoshaphat walked in the way of his father Asa and didn't turn aside from it, doing what was right in the LORD's eyes, 33 with the exception that he didn't remove the shrines. The people were still not committed with all their hearts to the God of their ancestors. 34 The rest of Jehoshaphat's deeds, from beginning to end, are written in the records of Jehu, Hanani's son, which are included in the records of Israel's kings.

35 Sometime later, Judah's King Jehoshaphat formed an alliance with Israel's King Ahaziah, which caused him to sin. 36 They agreed to build a fleet of Tarshish-styled ships, and they built them in Ezion-geber. 37 Eliezer, Dodavahu's son from Mareshah, prophesied against Jehoshaphat: "Because you have formed an alliance with Ahaziah, the LORD will destroy what you have made." The ships were wrecked and couldn't sail to Tarshish.

21 Jehoshaphat died and was buried with his ancestors in David's City. His son Jehoram succeeded him as king.

Jehoram rules

2 Jehoram's brothers, the other sons of Jehoshaphat, were Azariah, Jehiel, Zechariah, Azariah, Michael, and Shephatiah. All of these were the sons of Israel's King Jehoshaphat. 3 Their father had given them many gifts of silver, gold, and other valuables, along with fortified cities in Judah, but he gave the kingdom to Jehoram because he was the oldest son.

4 When Jehoram had taken control of his father's kingdom, he established his rule by killing all his brothers, along with some other leaders of Israel. 5 Jehoram was 32 years old when he became king, and he ruled for eight years in Jerusalem. 6 He walked in the ways of Israel's kings, just as Ahab's dynasty had done, because he married Ahab's daughter. He did what was evil in the LORD's eyes. 7 Nevertheless, because of the covenant he had made with David, the LORD wasn't willing to destroy David's dynasty. He had promised to preserve a lamp for David and his sons forever. 8 During Jehoram's rule, Edom rebelled against Judah's power and appointed its own king.

[h]LXX; MT *among them* [i]Vulg; MT *corpses*

9Jehoram, along with all his chariots, crossed over to Zair.[j] The Edomites, who had surrounded him, attacked at night, defeating him[k] and his chariot officers. 10So Edom has been independent of Judah to this day. Libnah rebelled against Jehoram's rule at the same time because he had abandoned the LORD, the God of his ancestors. 11As if that wasn't enough, Jehoram constructed shrines throughout Judah's highlands, encouraged Jerusalem's citizens to be unfaithful, and led Judah astray.

12A letter from the prophet Elijah came to Jehoram that read, "This is what the LORD, the God of your ancestor David, says: Because you haven't walked in the ways of your father Jehoshaphat or the ways of Judah's King Asa, 13but have walked in the ways of Israel's kings and have encouraged Judah and Jerusalem's citizens to be unfaithful, just as the house of Ahab did, and because you have even murdered your own brothers, your father's family, who were better than you, 14the LORD will now strike your family, your children, your wives, and all your possessions with a heavy blow. 15You yourself will become deathly ill with a chronic disease that will cause your intestines to fall out."

16Then the LORD made the Philistines and the Arabs, who lived near the Cushites, angry with Jehoram. 17They attacked Judah, broke down its defenses, and hauled off all the goods that were found in the royal palace, along with the king's children and wives. Only Jehoahaz, Jehoram's youngest son, was spared. 18After all this, the LORD struck Jehoram with an incurable intestinal disease. 19For almost two years he grew steadily worse, until two days before his death, when his intestines fell out, causing him to die in horrible pain. His people didn't make a fire in his honor as they had done for his ancestors. 20He was 32 years old when he became king, and he ruled for eight years in Jerusalem. No one was sorry he died. He was buried in David's City but not in the royal cemetery.

22 The inhabitants of Jerusalem made his youngest son Ahaziah succeed him as king because the raiding party that had invaded the camp with the Arabs had killed all the older sons. So Ahaziah, Jehoram's son, became king of Judah.

Ahaziah rules

2Ahaziah was 22 years old[l] when he became king, and he ruled for one year in Jerusalem. His mother's name was Athaliah; she was the granddaughter of Omri. 3Ahaziah walked in the ways of Ahab's dynasty, encouraged in this wickedness by his mother. 4He did what was evil in the LORD's eyes, just as Ahab's dynasty had done, because after his father's death they gave him advice that led to his downfall. 5Ahaziah was following their advice when he went with Israel's King Joram,[m] Ahab's son, to fight against Aram's King Hazael at Ramoth-gilead, where the Arameans wounded Joram. 6Joram returned to Jezreel to recover from the wounds he suffered at Ramah in his battle with Aram's King Hazael. Then Judah's King Ahaziah,[n] Jehoram's son, went down to visit Joram, Ahab's son, at Jezreel because he had been wounded. 7But God used this visit to Joram to bring about Ahaziah's downfall. After his arrival, Ahaziah went with Joram to meet Jehu, Nimshi's son, whom the LORD had anointed to destroy Ahab's dynasty. 8While Jehu was executing judgment on Ahab's dynasty, he discovered the princes of Judah, Ahaziah's nephews, serving Ahaziah, and Jehu killed them. 9Jehu went looking for Ahaziah, who was captured while hiding in Samaria. He was then brought to Jehu and executed. He was given a decent burial, however, because people said, "He was the grandson of Jehoshaphat, who sought the LORD with all his heart."

There were now no members of Ahaziah's dynasty strong enough to rule the kingdom.

Queen Athaliah rules Judah

10When Athaliah, Ahaziah's mother, learned of her son's death, she immediately

[j]Correction with 2 Kgs 8:21; MT *with his officers* [k]Or *he defeated Edom* [l]LXX, Syr, 2 Kgs 8:26; MT 42
[m]Or *Jehoram* (also in 22:6-7); the king's name is variously spelled in either long *Jehoram* or short *Joram* form.
[n]LXX, Syr, Vulg; MT *Azariah*

destroyed the entire royal family of Judah's dynasty. [11]But Jehoshabeath the king's daughter secretly took Ahaziah's son Jehoash[o] from the rest of the royal children who were about to be murdered, and hid him in a bedroom, along with his nurse. In this way Jehoshabeath, the daughter of King Jehoram, the wife of the priest Jehoiada and the sister of Ahaziah, hid Jehoash from Athaliah so she couldn't murder him. [12]He remained hidden with them in God's temple for six years while Athaliah ruled the country.

23

But in the seventh year Jehoiada boldly formed a conspiracy with the following unit commanders: Jeroham's son Azariah, Jehohanan's son Ishmael, Obed's son Azariah, Adaiah's son Maaseiah, and Zichri's son Elishaphat. [2]They went throughout Judah recruiting the Levites from all the cities of Judah, as well as the family heads of Israel, who then came to Jerusalem. [3]The entire assembly made a covenant with the king in God's temple. Jehoiada said, "Look! Here is the king's son. He must be king, just as the LORD promised about David's descendants. [4]This is what you must do: A third of you priests and Levites coming on sabbath duty will guard the gates, [5]another third will be at the royal palace, and another third will be at the Foundation Gate. Meanwhile, all the people will be in the courtyards of the LORD's temple. [6]Don't enter the LORD's temple, because only the priests or Levites on duty can do that. They are allowed to enter because they are holy, but the rest of the people must follow the LORD's requirements. [7]The Levites must surround the king, each with his weapons drawn. Whoever comes near your ranks must be killed; stay near the king wherever he goes."

[8]The Levites and all Judah did everything that the priest Jehoiada ordered. They each took charge of those men reporting for duty on the Sabbath, as well as those going off duty, since Jehoiada hadn't released any divisions from duty. [9]Then the priest Jehoiada gave the unit commanders King David's spears and large and small shields that were kept in God's temple. [10]He positioned all the people, each with their weapons drawn, near the altar and the temple, stretching from the south side of the temple to the north side, so as to protect the king. [11]Then they brought out the king's son, crowned him, gave him the royal law,[p] and made him king. Jehoiada and his sons anointed him as everyone cried out, "Long live the king!"

[12]When Athaliah heard the noise made by the people running and cheering the king, she went to the people at the LORD's temple [13]and saw the king standing by the royal pillar at the entrance, with the commanders and trumpeters beside the king. All the people of the land were rejoicing and blowing trumpets, and singers accompanied by musical instruments were leading the praise. Athaliah ripped her clothes and screamed, "Treason! Treason!"

[14]Then the priest Jehoiada brought out the unit commanders who were in charge of the army. "Take her out under guard,"[q] he told them, "and kill anyone who follows her." This was because the priest had said, "She must not be executed in the LORD's temple." [15]They arrested her when she reached the entrance of the Horse Gate at the royal palace. She was executed there.

[16]Jehoiada then made a covenant between himself, all the people, and the king, that they would be the LORD's people. [17]Then all the people went to Baal's temple and tore it down, smashing its altars and images into pieces. They executed Baal's priest Mattan in front of the altars. [18]Jehoiada appointed the priests and[r] Levites in charge of the LORD's temple, and then appointed the divisions of the priests and Levites[s] that David had assigned to the LORD's temple to offer entirely burned sacrifices to the LORD, as written in the Instruction from Moses, with rejoicing and singing, just as David had ordered. [19]He posted guards at the gates of the LORD's

[o]Or *Joash*; the king's name is variously spelled in either long *Jehoash* or short *Joash* form in 2 Kgs.
[p]Or *testimony*; MT lacks *royal*. [q]Heb uncertain [r]LXX; MT *levitical priests* [s]LXX; MT lacks *and then appointed the divisions of the priests and the Levites.*

temple so that no one who was unclean in any way could enter. [20]Then he took the unit commanders, the officials, the rulers of the people, and all the people of the land, and they led the king down from the LORD's temple, processing through the Upper Gate to the palace, where the king sat upon the royal throne. [21]All the people of the land rejoiced, and the city was at peace now that Athaliah had been executed at the palace.

Jehoash rules

24 Jehoash[t] was 7 years old when he became king, and he ruled for forty years in Jerusalem. His mother's name was Zibiah; she was from Beer-sheba. [2]Jehoash did what was right in the LORD's eyes as long as Jehoiada the priest was alive. [3]Jehoiada had him marry two wives, and Jehoash fathered sons and daughters.

[4]Sometime later, Jehoash wanted to renovate the LORD's temple. [5]He gathered the priests and the Levites and said, "Go to the cities of Judah and collect the annual tax of silver due from all Israel for the upkeep of God's temple. Do it right away."

But the Levites procrastinated. [6]So the king summoned the chief priest Jehoiada and asked him, "Why haven't you required the Levites to bring in from Judah and Jerusalem the tax imposed by the LORD's servant Moses and the Israelite assembly for the covenant tent?" ([7]Now wicked Athaliah and her followers had broken into God's temple and used all the holy objects of the LORD's temple in their worship of the Baals.) [8]So at the king's command a box was made and placed outside the gate of the LORD's temple. [9]Then a proclamation was issued throughout Judah and Jerusalem requiring the people to bring to the LORD the tax that God's servant Moses had imposed on Israel in the wilderness. [10]This so pleased all the leaders and all the people that they gladly dropped their money in the box until it was full. [11]Whenever the box was brought by the Levites to the royal accountants, as soon as they saw that a large amount of money was in the box, the royal scribe and the representative of the high priest would come, empty the box, and return it to its place. This took place day after day, and a large amount of money was collected. [12]The king and Jehoiada would give it to those in charge of the work on the LORD's temple who in turn hired masons and carpenters to renovate the LORD's temple, as well as metalworkers for the iron and bronze to repair the LORD's temple. [13]The workers labored hard, and the restoration progressed smoothly under their control until they had brought God's temple back to its original state and reinforced it. [14]As soon as they finished, they brought the remaining money to the king and Jehoiada. They used it to make equipment for the LORD's temple, including what was used for the service and the entirely burned offerings, pans, and other objects made of gold and silver. As long as Jehoiada lived, the entirely burned offerings were regularly offered in the LORD's temple.

[15]Jehoiada grew old, and when he reached the age of 130, he died. [16]He was buried among the kings in David's City because of his exemplary service to Israel, God, and God's temple.

[17]After Jehoiada's death, however, the leaders of Judah came and bowed before the king, and the king listened to them. [18]They abandoned the temple of the LORD, their ancestors' God, and worshipped sacred poles[u] and idols. Anger came upon Judah and Jerusalem as a consequence of their sin, [19]and though God sent prophets to them to bring them back to the LORD and to warn them, they refused to listen. [20]Then the spirit of God enwrapped Zechariah the son of the priest Jehoiada. Standing before the people, he told them, "This is what God says: Why do you defy the LORD's commands and keep yourselves from prospering? Because you have abandoned the LORD, he has abandoned you!" [21]But the people plotted against Zechariah, and at the king's command stoned him to death in

[t]Heb *Joash* (see 24:2, 4, 22, 24); the king's name is variously spelled in either long *Jehoash* or short *Joash* form in 2 Kgs. [u]Heb *asherim*, perhaps objects devoted to the goddess Asherah

the courtyard of the LORD's temple. [22]King Jehoash failed to remember the loyalty that Jehoiada, Zechariah's father, had shown him and murdered Jehoida's son, who cried out as he lay dying, "May the LORD see and seek vengeance!"

[23]That spring the Aramean army marched against Jehoash. They attacked Judah and Jerusalem, destroyed all the people's leaders, and sent all the loot to the king of Damascus. [24]Although the Aramean forces were relatively small, the LORD handed over to them a very large army, because the people of Judah had abandoned the LORD, their ancestors' God. Jehoash was justly punished. [25]The Arameans left him badly wounded, but his own officials plotted against him for murdering the son[v] of the priest Jehoiada. So they killed him in his bed. He died and was buried in David's City but not in the royal cemetery. [26]Those who plotted against him were the Ammonite Zabad, Shimeath's son, and the Moabite Jehozabad, Shimrith's son. [27]The list of Jehoash's sons, the many prophecies against him, and the account of his restoration of God's temple are written in the comments on the records of the kings. His son Amaziah succeeded him as king.

Amaziah rules

25 Amaziah was 25 years old when he became king, and he ruled for twenty-nine years in Jerusalem. His mother's name was Jehoaddan; she was from Jerusalem. [2]He did what was right in the LORD's eyes but not with all his heart. [3]Once he had secured control over his kingdom, he executed the officials who had assassinated his father the king. [4]However, he didn't kill their children because of what is written in the Instruction scroll from Moses, where the LORD commanded, *Parents shouldn't be executed because of what their children have done; neither should children be executed because of what their parents have done. Each person should be executed for their own guilty acts.*[w]

[5]Amaziah gathered the people of Judah, organizing them into family units under captains of thousands and hundreds for all Judah and Benjamin. He summoned everyone 20 years old and older and found that there were three hundred thousand select troops, ready for service and able to handle spears and body-sized shields. [6]He also hired one hundred thousand warriors from Israel for one hundred kikkars of silver.

[7]But a man of God confronted him. "King," he said, "the troops from Israel must not go with you, because the LORD isn't on the side of Israel or any Ephraimite. [8]Should you go with them anyway, even if you fight fiercely, God will make you stumble before the enemy, because God has the ability to either help or make someone stumble."

[9]Amaziah asked the man of God, "What about the hundred kikkars I paid for the Israelite troops?"

"God can give you much more than that," the man of God replied.

[10]Amaziah released the Ephraimite troops who had joined him so they could go home, but this only infuriated them against Judah, and they left in a rage. [11]Amaziah courageously led his people to the Salt Valley, where they killed ten thousand people from Seir. [12]The Judean forces captured another ten thousand alive, brought them to the top of a cliff, and threw them off so that all were dashed to pieces. [13]Meanwhile, the troops Amaziah had released from fighting alongside him raided cities in Judah from Samaria to Beth-horon, killing three thousand people and carrying off a large amount of loot. [14]When Amaziah returned after defeating the Edomites, he brought the gods of the people of Seir. He set them up as his own gods, bowed down before them, and burned incense to them. [15]As a result, the LORD was angry with Amaziah and sent a prophet to him.

"Why do you seek the gods of this people?" the prophet asked. "They couldn't even deliver their own people from you!"

[16]"Since when do you give me advice?" Amaziah interrupted. "You better quit before you end up dead!"

[v]LXX, Vulg; MT *sons* [w]Deut 24:16

So the prophet stopped, but not until he said, "I know God plans to destroy you because you've done this and because you've refused to listen to my advice."

[17]After Judah's King Amaziah consulted with his advisors, he sent a challenge to Israel's King Joash, Jehoahaz's son and Jehu's grandson. "Come on," he said, "let's go head-to-head!"

[18]Israel's King Joash sent the following reply to Judah's King Amaziah: "Once upon a time, a thistle in Lebanon sent a message to a cedar: 'Give your daughter to my son as a wife.' But then a wild beast in Lebanon came along and trampled the thistle. [19]Do you think that because you've defeated Edom, you can arrogantly seek even more? Stay home! Why invite disaster when both you and Judah will fall?" [20]But Amaziah wouldn't listen, because God intended to use this to destroy them since they had sought Edom's gods. [21]So Israel's King Joash moved against Judah's King Amaziah and went head-to-head in battle at Beth-shemesh in Judah. [22]Judah was defeated by Israel, and everyone ran home. [23]At Beth-shemesh, Israel's King Joash captured Judah's King Amaziah, Jehoash's[x] son and Ahaziah's[y] grandson. Joash brought him to Jerusalem and broke down six hundred feet of the Jerusalem wall from the Ephraim Gate to the Corner Gate. [24]Joash took[z] all the gold and silver, and all the objects he could find in God's temple in the care of Obed-edom, and in the treasuries of the palace, along with some hostages. Then he returned to Samaria.

[25]Judah's King Amaziah, Jehoash's son, lived fifteen years after the death of Israel's King Joash, Jehoahaz's son. [26]The rest of Amaziah's deeds, from beginning to end, aren't they written in the official records of Israel's and Judah's kings? [27]From the time Amaziah turned away from the LORD, some people conspired against him in Jerusalem. When Amaziah fled to Lachish, they sent men after him, and they murdered him in Lachish. [28]They carried him back on horses and he was buried with his ancestors in David's City.[a]

Uzziah rules Judah

26 Then all the people of Judah took Uzziah,[b] who was 16 years old, and made him king after his father Amaziah. [2]He rebuilt Eloth, restoring it to Judah after King Amaziah had lain down with his ancestors.

[3]Uzziah was 16 years old when he became king, and he ruled for fifty-two years in Jerusalem. His mother's name was Jecoliah; she was from Jerusalem. [4]He did what was right in the LORD's eyes, just as his father Amaziah had done. [5]He sought God as long as Zechariah, who instructed him in the fear[c] of God, was alive. And as long as he sought the LORD, God gave him success. [6]He marched against the Philistines and broke down the walls of Gath, Jabneh, and Ashdod. Then he rebuilt towns near Ashdod and elsewhere among the Philistines. [7]God helped him against the Philistines, the Arabs who inhabited Gur,[d] and the Meunites. [8]The Meunites[e] paid taxes to Uzziah, whose fame spread even to Egypt because he had grown so powerful. [9]He built towers in Jerusalem, at the Corner Gate, the Valley Gate, and at the Angle, and reinforced them. [10]He also built towers in the wilderness and dug many wells for his large herds in the lowlands and the plain. He had many workers who tended his farms and vineyards, because he loved the soil. [11]Uzziah had a standing army equipped for combat whose units went to war according to the number determined by the scribe Jeiel and Maaseiah, an officer under the authority of Hananiah, one of the king's officials. [12]The grand total of family heads in charge of these courageous warriors was twenty-six hundred. [13]They commanded an army of three hundred seven thousand five hundred. They formed a powerful force that could support the king against the enemy. [14]Uzziah supplied the entire force with shields, spears, helmets, armor, bows, and sling stones. [15]He set up clever devices in

[x]Or *Joash* (see also 25:25); the king's name is variously spelled in either long *Jehoash* or short *Joash* form in 2 Kgs. [y]See 2 Kgs 14:13; MT *Jehoahaz*. [z]See 2 Kgs 14:14; Heb omits *took*. [a]LXX; MT *Judah* [b]Uzziah is usually named Azariah in 2 Kgs 14:21; 15:1, 6-7. [c]LXX; MT *visions* [d]Tg; MT *Gur-baal* [e]LXX; MT *Ammonites*

Jerusalem on the towers and corners of
the wall designed to shoot arrows and large
stones. And so Uzziah's fame spread far and
wide, because he had received wonderful
help until he became powerful.

[16]But as soon as he became powerful, he
grew so arrogant that he acted corruptly.
He was unfaithful to the LORD his God by
entering the LORD's sanctuary to burn incense upon the incense altar. [17]The priest
Azariah, accompanied by eighty other of
the LORD's courageous priests, went in
after him [18]and confronted King Uzziah.

"You have no right, Uzziah," he said,
"to burn incense to the LORD! That privilege belongs to the priests, Aaron's descendants, who have been ordained to burn
incense. Get out of this holy place because
you have been unfaithful! The LORD God
won't honor you for this."

[19]Then Uzziah, who already had a censer in his hand ready to burn the incense,
became angry. While he was fuming at the
priests, skin disease[f] erupted on his forehead in the presence of the priests before
the incense altar in the LORD's temple.
[20]When Azariah the chief priest and all the
other priests turned and saw the skin disease on his forehead, they rushed him out
of there. Uzziah also was anxious to leave
because the LORD had afflicted him. [21]King
Uzziah had skin disease until the day he
died. He lived in a separate house,[g] diseased
in his skin, because he was barred from the
LORD's temple. His son Jotham supervised
the palace administration and governed the
people of the land. [22]The rest of Uzziah's
deeds, from beginning to end, were written
down by the prophet Isaiah, Amoz's son.
[23]Uzziah died and was buried with his ancestors in a field belonging to the kings, because people said, "He had skin disease." His
son Jotham succeeded him as king.

Jotham rules

27 Jotham was 25 years old when he became king, and he ruled for sixteen
years in Jerusalem. His mother's name
was Jerushah; she was Zadok's daughter.
[2]Jotham did what was right in the LORD's
eyes, just as his father Uzziah had done.
Unlike Uzziah, Jotham didn't enter the
LORD's temple. But the people continued
their crooked practices. [3]Jotham rebuilt
the Upper Gate of the LORD's temple and
did extensive work on the wall of the elevated fortress.[h] [4]He built towns in Judah's
highlands and fortresses and towers in the
wooded areas. [5]He fought against the king
of the Ammonites and defeated the Ammonites. They paid him one hundred kikkars of
silver, ten thousand kors[i] of wheat, and ten
thousand kors of barley that year and for
the next two years. [6]Jotham was securely
established because he maintained a faithful life before the LORD his God. [7]The rest
of Jotham's deeds, including all his wars
and accomplishments, are written in the
official records of Israel's and Judah's kings.
[8]He was 25 years old when he became king,
and he ruled for sixteen years in Jerusalem.
[9]Jotham lay down with his ancestors and
was buried in David's City. His son Ahaz
succeeded him as king.

Ahaz rules

28 Ahaz was 20 years old when he became king, and he ruled for sixteen
years in Jerusalem. He didn't do what was
right in the LORD's eyes, unlike his ancestor David. [2]Instead, he walked in the ways
of Israel's kings, making images of the Baals
[3]and burning incense in the Ben-hinnom
Valley. He even burned his own sons alive,
imitating the detestable practices of the nations the LORD had driven out before the
Israelites. [4]He also sacrificed and burned
incense at the shrines on every hill and beneath every shady tree. [5]So the LORD his
God handed him over to Aram's king, who
defeated him and carried off many prisoners, bringing them to Damascus. Ahaz was
also handed over to Israel's king, who defeated him with a severe beating. [6]In Judah,
Pekah, Remaliah's son, killed one hundred
twenty thousand warriors in the course of

[f]The precise meaning is uncertain; traditionally *leprosy*—a term used for several different skin diseases. Also in 26:21-20, 23. [g]Heb uncertain [h]Or *hillside*; Heb uncertain [i]One kor is equivalent to a homer and is possibly equal to fifty gallons of grain.

a single day because they had abandoned the LORD, God of their ancestors. [7]An Ephraimite warrior named Zichri killed the king's son Maaseiah, the palace administrator Azrikam, and Elkanah, the king's second in command. [8]The Israelites took captive two hundred thousand women, boys, and girls from their Judean relatives and seized enormous amounts of plunder, which they took back to Samaria.

[9]One of the LORD's prophets named Oded lived in Samaria. When the army arrived there, he went to meet them and said, "Don't you see that the LORD God of your ancestors was angry with Judah and let you defeat them? But look what you've done! Your merciless slaughter of them stinks to high heaven! [10]And now you think you can enslave the men and women of Judah and Jerusalem? What about your own guilt before the LORD your God? [11]Listen to me! Send back the captives you took from your relatives, because the LORD is furious with you."

[12]At this, some of the Ephraimite leaders—Johanan's son Azariah, Meshillemoth's son Berechiah, Shallum's son Jehizkiah, and Hadlai's son Amasa—confronted those returning from battle. [13]"Don't bring the captives here," they told them. "Your plan will only add to our sin and guilt before the LORD. We're already guilty enough, and great anger is already directed at Israel." [14]So the warriors released the captives and brought the loot before the officers and the whole assembly. [15]Then people named for this task took charge of the captives and dressed everyone who was naked with items taken from the loot. They gave them clothing, sandals, food and drink, and bandaged their wounds. Everyone who couldn't walk they placed on donkeys, and they brought them to Jericho, Palm City, near their Judean relatives. Then they returned to Samaria.

[16]At that time King Ahaz sent for help from the king[j] of Assyria. [17]Once again, the Edomites had invaded Judah, defeating Judah and carrying off captives. [18]The Philistines had raided the towns in the lowlands and the arid southern plain of Judah, capturing Beth-shemesh, Aijalon, and Gederoth, along with Soco and its surrounding villages, Timnah and its surrounding villages, and Gimzo and its surrounding villages, and occupying all of these cities. [19]The LORD was humiliating Judah on account of Israel's King Ahaz, because he had exercised no restraint in Judah and had been utterly unfaithful to the LORD. [20]Assyria's King Tiglath-pileser[k] came to Ahaz, but he brought trouble, not support. [21]Even though Ahaz took items from the LORD's temple, the royal palace, and the officials to buy off the king of Assyria, it was of no help.

[22]It was during this troubled time that King Ahaz became even more unfaithful to the LORD [23]by sacrificing to the gods of Damascus, who had defeated him.

"Since the gods of Aram's kings are helping them," he said, "I'll sacrifice to them too, so that they will help me."

But they became the ruin of both him and all Israel. [24]Ahaz gathered the objects from God's temple, cut them up, shut the doors of the LORD's temple, and made himself altars on every corner in Jerusalem. [25]He made shrines in all the towns of Judah for burning incense to other gods. This made the LORD, the God of his ancestors, very angry.

[26]The rest of Ahaz's deeds, from beginning to end, are written in the official records of Israel's and Judah's kings. [27]Ahaz lay down with his ancestors and was buried in the city, in Jerusalem, but not in the royal cemetery of Israel's kings. His son Hezekiah succeeded him as king.

Hezekiah rules

29 Hezekiah became king when he was 25 years old, and he ruled for twenty-nine years in Jerusalem. His mother's name was Abijah; she was Zechariah's daughter. [2]He did what was right in the LORD's eyes, just as his ancestor David had done. [3]In the very first year of his rule, during the first

[j]LXX, Syr, Vulg; MT *kings* [k]MT *Tilgath-pilneser*

month, Hezekiah reopened the doors of the LORD's temple, having repaired them. 4Then he brought in the priests and Levites and assembled them in the eastern square.

5"Listen to me, you Levites!" he said. "Make yourselves holy so you can make holy the temple of the LORD God of your ancestors by removing from the sanctuary any impure thing. 6Our ancestors were unfaithful and did what was evil in the LORD our God's eyes. They abandoned him, they ignored the LORD's dwelling, and they defied him. 7They even closed the doors of the entrance hall, snuffed out the lamps, and stopped burning incense and offering entirely burned offerings in the sanctuary of the God of Israel. 8This angered the LORD so much that he made Judah and Jerusalem an object of terror and horror, something people hiss at, as you can see with your own eyes. 9That's why our ancestors died violent deaths, while our sons, daughters, and wives were taken captive. 10But now I intend to make a covenant with the LORD, Israel's God, so God will no longer be angry with us. 11Don't be careless, my sons! The LORD has chosen you to stand in his presence to serve him, so that you can be his servants and burn incense to him."

12Then the following Levites got up:
from the descendants of the
Kohathites: Mahath, Amasai's son, and Joel, Azariah's son;
from the descendants of Merari: Kish, Abdi's son, and Azariah, Jehallelel's son;
from the Gershonites: Joah, Zimmah's son, and Eden, Joah's son;
13from the descendants of Elizaphan: Shimri and Jeuel;
from the descendants of Asaph: Zechariah and Mattaniah;
14from the descendants of Heman: Jehuel and Shimei;
and from the descendants of Jeduthun: Shemaiah and Uzziel.

15These men gathered their relatives, made themselves holy, and went in to purify the LORD's temple by obeying the king's command as the LORD had told him. 16The priests went in to purify the inner portion of the LORD's temple. They brought out to the courtyard of the LORD's temple all the impurities they discovered inside. Then the Levites took them out to the Kidron Valley. 17They began to make things holy on the first day of the first month.[1] On the eighth day of the month they reached the LORD's entrance hall. They made holy the LORD's temple for eight days, finishing on the sixteenth day of the first month.

18Then they went before King Hezekiah. "We have purified the LORD's entire temple," they said, "and the altar for the entirely burned offering together with all its equipment, and the table for the stacks of bread together with all its equipment. 19We have also restored and made holy all the items King Ahaz threw out during his rule in his unfaithfulness. They are now before the LORD's altar."

Hezekiah rededicates the temple

20Early the next morning Hezekiah gathered the city leaders and went to the LORD's temple. 21They brought seven bulls, seven rams, and seven lambs, along with seven male goats, for a purification offering on behalf of the kingdom, the sanctuary, and Judah. Hezekiah ordered the priests, Aaron's sons, to offer them up on the LORD's altar. 22When they slaughtered the bulls, the priests took the blood and splashed it against the altar. Next they slaughtered the rams and splashed their blood against the altar, and also slaughtered the lambs, splashing their blood against the altar as well. 23Finally, they brought the goats for the purification offering before the king and the assembly. After laying their hands on them, 24the priests slaughtered them and smeared the blood on the altar as a purification offering to take away the sin of all Israel, because the king had specifically ordered that the entirely burned sacrifice and the purification offering should be on behalf of all Israel. 25Hezekiah had the Levites stand in

[1] March–April, Nisan

the LORD's temple with cymbals, harps,
and zithers, just as the LORD had ordered
through David, the king's seer Gad, and the
prophet Nathan. [26]While the Levites took
their places holding David's instruments,
and the priests their trumpets, [27]Hezekiah
ordered the entirely burned offering to
be offered up on the altar. As they began
to offer the entirely burned offering, the
LORD's song also began, accompanied by
the trumpets and the other instruments
of Israel's King David. [28]The whole congregation worshipped with singing choirs and
blaring trumpets until the end of the entirely burned offering. [29]After the entirely
burned offering was complete, the king
and all who were with him bowed down
in worship. [30]Then King Hezekiah and
the leaders ordered the Levites to praise
the LORD by using the words of David
and the seer Asaph. They did so joyously;
then they bowed down in worship too.
[31]"Now that you have dedicated yourselves to the LORD," King Hezekiah told
them, "bring sacrificial thank offerings to
the LORD's temple." So the assembly brought
sacrificial thank offerings, with some people
volunteering to provide entirely burned offerings. [32]All in all, the congregation brought
seventy bulls, a hundred rams, and two hundred lambs as entirely burned offerings for
the LORD, [33]as well as six hundred bulls
and three thousand sheep as holy offerings. [34]Unfortunately, there weren't enough
priests to skin all these entirely burned offerings. So their relatives the Levites (who
had been more conscientious about preparing themselves than the priests) stepped in
and helped them until the work was done
or additional priests had made themselves
holy. [35]In addition to the wealth of entirely
burned offerings, there was the fat of the
well-being sacrifices and drink offerings
accompanying the entirely burned offerings. In this way, the service of the LORD's
temple was restored, [36]and Hezekiah and
all the people rejoiced at what God had
done for them, since it had happened so
quickly.

Hezekiah's Passover

30 Then Hezekiah sent word to all Israel and Judah, and wrote letters
to Ephraim and Manasseh as well, inviting
them to the LORD's temple in Jerusalem to
celebrate the Passover of the LORD God of
Israel. [2]The king, his officials, and the entire
Jerusalem congregation had decided to celebrate Passover in the second month.[m] [3]They
had been unable to celebrate it at the usual
time because the priests had failed to make
themselves holy in sufficient numbers, and
the people hadn't gathered at Jerusalem.
[4]Since the plan seemed good to the king
and the entire congregation, [5]they made arrangements to circulate an announcement
throughout all Israel, from Beer-sheba to
Dan, to come to Jerusalem to celebrate the
Passover of the LORD God of Israel, because
they hadn't often kept it as written. [6]Under
the authority of the king, runners took letters from the king and his officials throughout all Israel and Judah, which read:

> People of Israel! Return to the LORD,
> the God of Abraham, Isaac, and Israel,
> so that he may return to those of you
> who remain, who have escaped capture
> by the Assyrian kings. [7]Don't be like
> your ancestors and relatives, who were
> unfaithful to the LORD, the God of
> their ancestors, so that he made them
> an object of horror as you can see for
> yourselves. [8]So don't be stubborn like
> your ancestors. Surrender to the LORD!
> Come to God's sanctuary, which he has
> made holy forever, and serve the LORD
> your God so that he won't be angry with
> you any longer. [9]When you return to the
> LORD, your relatives and your children
> will receive mercy from their captors
> and be allowed to return to this land.
> The LORD your God is merciful and
> compassionate. He won't withdraw his
> presence from you if you return to him.

[10]So the runners went from town to town
in Ephraim and Manasseh, all the way to
Zebulun. But they were laughed at and made
fun of. [11]Even so, some people from Asher,
Manasseh, and Zebulun were submissive

[m]April–May, Iyar

and came to Jerusalem. 12Moreover, God's power was at work in Judah, unifying them to do what the king and his officials had ordered by the LORD's command.

13A huge crowd gathered in Jerusalem to celebrate the Festival of Unleavened Bread in the second month. A very large congregation gathered. 14First, they removed the altars in Jerusalem, and hauled off the incense altars and dumped them in the Kidron Valley. 15They slaughtered the Passover lambs on the fourteenth day of the second month. Ashamed of themselves, the priests and the Levites made themselves holy and brought entirely burned offerings to the LORD's temple. 16They now took their places as laid out in the Instruction from Moses the man of God, and the priests splashed the blood they received from the Levites against the altar. 17Since many in the congregation hadn't made themselves holy, the Levites slaughtered the Passover lambs, making them holy to the LORD for all who weren't ceremonially clean. 18This included most of those who had come from Ephraim, Manasseh, Issachar, and Zebulun—people who hadn't purified themselves and so hadn't eaten the Passover meal in the prescribed way. But Hezekiah prayed for them: "May the good LORD forgive 19everyone who has decided to seek the true God, the LORD, the God of their ancestors, even though they aren't ceremonially clean by sanctuary standards." 20The LORD heard Hezekiah and healed the people. 21So the Israelites in Jerusalem joyfully celebrated the Festival of Unleavened Bread for seven days, with the Levites and the priests praising the LORD every day, accompanied by the LORD's mighty instruments. 22Hezekiah congratulated all the Levites who had performed so skillfully for the LORD. They feasted throughout the seven days of the festival, sacrificing well-being offerings and praising the LORD, the God of their ancestors.

23Then the whole congregation agreed to celebrate another seven days, which they joyfully did. 24Judah's King Hezekiah contributed one thousand bulls and seven thousand sheep for the congregation, while the officials provided another thousand bulls and ten thousand sheep, and great numbers of priests made themselves holy. 25Then the whole congregation of Judah rejoiced, as did the priests and the Levites, the whole congregation from Israel, the immigrants who had come from the land of Israel, and those who lived in Judah. 26There was great joy in Jerusalem. Nothing like this had taken place in Jerusalem since the days of Israel's King Solomon, David's son. 27Then the levitical priests blessed the people, and their voice was heard when their prayer reached God's holy dwelling in heaven.

31 When all of these things were finished, all of the Israelites who were present went out to the cities of Judah, smashed the sacred pillars, cut down the sacred poles,[n] and completely destroyed the shrines and altars throughout Judah as well as Benjamin, Ephraim, and Manasseh. Then all the Israelites returned to their individual homes in their own cities.

Hezekiah's reform

2Hezekiah reappointed the priests and the Levites, each to their divisions and their tasks, to make entirely burned offerings and well-being sacrifices, to serve, to give thanks, and to offer praise in the gates of the LORD's camp. 3As his portion, the king personally contributed the entirely burned offerings for the morning and evening sacrifices, as well as the entirely burned offerings for the Sabbaths, new moons, and festivals, as written in the LORD's Instruction. 4He ordered the people living in Jerusalem to provide the required portion for the priests and the Levites so they could devote themselves to the LORD's Instruction. 5As soon as the order was issued, the Israelites generously gave the best of their grain, new wine, oil, honey, and all their crops—a tenth of everything, a huge amount. 6The people of Israel and Judah, living in the cities of Judah, also brought

[n]Heb *asherim*, perhaps objects devoted to the goddess Asherah

in a tenth of their herds and flocks and a tenth of the items that had been dedicated to the LORD their God, stacking it up in piles. 7They began stacking up the piles in the third month[o] and finished them in the seventh.[p] 8When Hezekiah and the officials saw the piles, they blessed the LORD and his people Israel.

9When Hezekiah asked the priests and Levites about the piles, 10the chief priest Azariah, who was from Zadok's family, answered, "Ever since the people started bringing contributions to the LORD's temple we've had enough to eat with plenty to spare. The LORD has definitely blessed his people! There's a lot left over."

11So Hezekiah ordered them to prepare storerooms in the LORD's temple. When they finished preparing them, 12the priests conscientiously brought in the contributions, the tenth-part gifts, and the dedicated things. Conaniah, a Levite, was put in charge, assisted by his brother Shimei, 13while Jehiel, Azaziah, Nahath, Asahel, Jerimoth, Jozabad, Eliel, Ismachiah, Mahath, and Benaiah served as supervisors under them, as appointed by King Hezekiah and Azariah the official in charge of God's temple. 14The Levite Kore, Imnah's son, who was keeper of the east gate, was in charge of the spontaneous gifts to God. He was responsible for distributing the contribution reserved for the LORD and the dedicated gifts. 15Eden, Miniamin, Jeshua, Shemaiah, Amariah, and Shecaniah faithfully assisted him regarding[q] the priests by distributing the portions to their relatives, old and young alike, by divisions. 16Additionally, they also distributed daily rations to those males, registered by genealogy, three years old and older, all who entered the LORD's temple to carry out their daily duties as their divisions required. 17They also distributed to those priests registered by their families, and to Levites 20 years of age and older according to their divisional responsibilities. 18The official genealogy included all their small children, their wives, their sons, and their daughters—the entire congregation—for they had faithfully made themselves holy. 19As for Aaron's descendants, the priests who lived in the outskirts of the cities, men were assigned to distribute portions to every male among the priests and to every Levite listed in the genealogical records. 20This is what Hezekiah did throughout all Judah, doing what the LORD his God considered good, right, and true. 21Everything that Hezekiah began to do for the service of God's temple, whether by the Instruction or the commands, in order to seek his God, he did successfully and with all his heart.

Sennacherib's invasion

32 After these things and these faithful acts, Assyria's King Sennacherib invaded Judah and attacked its fortified cities, intending to capture them. 2When Hezekiah realized that Sennacherib also planned on fighting Jerusalem, 3he consulted with his officials and soldiers about stopping up the springs outside the city, and they supported him. 4A large force gathered to stop up all the springs and the streams that flowed through the land. "Why should the kings of Assyria come and find plenty of water?" they asked. 5Hezekiah vigorously rebuilt all the broken sections of the wall, erected towers, constructed another wall outside the first, reinforced the terrace of David's City, and made a large supply of weapons and shields. 6He appointed military officers over the troops, assembled them in the square of the city gate, and spoke these words of encouragement: 7"Be brave and be strong! Don't let the king of Assyria and all those warriors he brings with him scare you or cause you dismay, because our forces are greater than his.[r] 8All he has is human strength, but we have the LORD our God who will help us fight our battles!"

The troops trusted Judah's King Hezekiah.

9After this Assyria's King Sennacherib who was attacking Lachish with all his

[o]May–June, Sivan [p]September–October, Tishrei [q]Or *with the assistance of* cf LXX; MT *in the cities of* [r]Or *there is greater power with us than with him*

forces, sent his servants to Jerusalem with the following message for Judah's King Hezekiah and all the people of Judah who were in Jerusalem:

[10]This is what Assyria's King Sennacherib says: What makes you so confident that you stay put in Jerusalem while it is being attacked? [11]Obviously, Hezekiah has fooled you into surrendering yourselves to death by hunger and thirst when he says, "The LORD our God will rescue us from Assyria's king." [12]Isn't this the same Hezekiah who got rid of his shrines and altars, and then demanded of Judah and Jerusalem, "You must worship and burn incense before only one altar"? [13]Don't you know what I and my predecessors have done to the people of other nations? Were any of the gods of these other nations able to rescue their lands from my power? [14]Which one of any of the gods of these nations that my predecessors destroyed was able to rescue them from my power? So why should your god be able to rescue you from my power? [15]Don't let Hezekiah seduce you like fools. Don't believe him! No god of any other nation or kingdom has been able to rescue their people from me or from my predecessors. No, your gods won't rescue you from my power.

[16]The Assyrian king's servants continued to make fun of the LORD God and his servant Hezekiah. [17]He wrote other letters insulting the LORD God of Israel, defying him by saying, "Just as the gods of the nations in other countries couldn't rescue their people from my power, Hezekiah's god won't be able to rescue his people from my power." [18]Then they shouted loudly in Hebrew[s] at the people of Jerusalem gathered on the wall, in an attempt to frighten and demoralize them, in order to capture the city. [19]They spoke about the God of Jerusalem as though he were the work of human hands, like the gods of the other peoples of the earth. [20]King Hezekiah and the prophet Isaiah, Amoz's son, prayed about this, crying out to heaven. [21]Then the LORD sent a messenger who destroyed every warrior, leader, and officer in the camp of the Assyrian king. When Sennacherib went home in disgrace, he entered the temple of his god, and his own sons killed him with a sword. [22]This is how the LORD rescued Hezekiah and the citizens of Jerusalem from the power of Assyria's King Sennacherib, and all others, giving them rest[t] on all sides. [23]Many people brought offerings to the LORD in Jerusalem and costly gifts to Judah's King Hezekiah, who was highly regarded by all the nations from then on.

Hezekiah's illness

[24]Around that same time, Hezekiah became deathly ill and prayed to the LORD, who answered him with a miraculous sign. [25]But Hezekiah was too proud to respond appropriately to the kindness he had received, and he, along with Judah and Jerusalem, experienced anger. [26]However, Hezekiah and the citizens of Jerusalem humbled themselves in their pride, and so they didn't experience the LORD's anger for the rest of Hezekiah's reign.

[27]Hezekiah became very wealthy and greatly respected. He made storehouses for his silver, gold, precious stones, spices, shields, and other valuables. [28]He made barns to store the harvest of grain, wine, and olive oil; stalls for all kinds of cattle; and pens for flocks. [29]He acquired towns for himself and many flocks and herds because God had given him great wealth. [30]Hezekiah was the one who blocked the upper outlet of the waters of the Gihon Spring, channeling them down to the west side of David's City. Hezekiah succeeded in all that he did, [31]even in the matter of the ambassadors sent from Babylonian officials to find out about the miraculous sign that occurred in the land, when God had abandoned him in order to test him and to discover what was in his heart.

[32]The rest of Hezekiah's deeds, including his faithfulness, are written in the vision of the prophet Isaiah, Amoz's son, in the records of Israel's and Judah's kings.

[s]Or *the language of Judah* [t]LXX; MT *he led them*

[33]Hezekiah lay down with his ancestors and was buried in the upper area of the tombs of David's sons. All Judah and the inhabitants of Jerusalem honored him at his death. His son Manasseh succeeded him as king.

Manasseh rules

33 Manasseh was 12 years old when he became king, and he ruled for fifty-five years in Jerusalem. [2]He did what was evil in the LORD's eyes, imitating the detestable practices of the nations that the LORD had driven out before the Israelites. [3]He rebuilt the shrines that his father Hezekiah had destroyed, set up altars for the Baals, and made sacred poles.[u] He bowed down to all the stars in the sky and worshipped them. [4]He even built altars in the LORD's temple, the very place the LORD was speaking about when he said, "My name will remain in Jerusalem forever." [5]Manasseh built altars for all the stars in the sky in both courtyards of the LORD's temple. [6]He burned his own sons alive in the Ben-hinnom Valley, consulted sign readers, fortune-tellers, and sorcerers, and used mediums and diviners. He did much evil in the LORD's eyes and made him angry.

[7]Manasseh set up the carved image he had made in God's temple, the very temple God had spoken about to David and his son Solomon, saying: In this temple and in Jerusalem, which I have selected out of all Israel's tribes, I will put my name forever. [8]I will never again remove Israel from the fertile land I gave to your ancestors, provided they carefully do everything I have commanded them—keeping all the Instruction, the regulations, and the case laws given through Moses. [9]In this way Manasseh led Judah and the residents of Jerusalem into doing even more evil than the nations that the LORD had wiped out before the Israelites.

[10]The LORD spoke to Manasseh and his people, but they wouldn't listen. [11]So the LORD brought the army commanders of Assyria's king against them. They captured Manasseh with hooks, bound him with bronze chains, and carried him off to Babylon. [12]During his distress, Manasseh made peace with the LORD his God, truly submitting himself to the God of his ancestors. [13]He prayed, and God was moved by his request. God listened to Manasseh's prayer and restored him to his rule in Jerusalem. Then Manasseh knew that the LORD was the true God.

[14]After this, Manasseh rebuilt the outer wall of David's City, west of the Gihon Spring in the valley, extending as far as the entrance of the Fish Gate, enclosing the elevated fortress[v] and greatly increasing its height. He also installed military commanders in all the fortified cities of Judah. [15]He removed the foreign gods and the idol from the LORD's temple, as well as all the altars he had built on the hill of the LORD's temple and in Jerusalem, dumping them outside the city. [16]He restored the LORD's altar, offered well-being sacrifices and thank offerings on it, and ordered the people of Judah to worship the LORD, Israel's God. [17]The people, however, still sacrificed at the shrines, but only to the LORD their God. [18]The rest of Manasseh's deeds, including his prayer to God and what the seers told him in the name of the LORD, Israel's God, are found in the records of Israel's kings. [19]Manasseh's prayer and its answer, all his sin and unfaithfulness, and the locations of the shrines, sacred poles,[w] and idols he set up before he submitted are written in the records of Hozai.[x] [20]Manasseh lay down with his ancestors and was buried in his palace. His son Amon succeeded him as king.

Amon rules

[21]Amon was 22 years old when he became king, and he ruled for two years in Jerusalem. [22]He did what was evil in the LORD's eyes, just as his father Manasseh had done. He sacrificed to all the idols his father had made and worshipped them. [23]But unlike his father Manasseh, Amon didn't submit before the LORD; instead, Amon increased

[u]Heb *asherot*, perhaps objects devoted to the goddess Asherah [v]Or *hillside*; Heb uncertain [w]Heb *asherim*, perhaps objects devoted to the goddess Asherah [x]LXX *the seers*

his guilt. [24]His own officials plotted against him and killed him in his palace. [25]The people of the land then executed all those who had plotted against King Amon and made his son Josiah the next king.

Josiah rules

34 Josiah was 8 years old when he became king, and he ruled for thirty-one years in Jerusalem. [2]He did what was right in the LORD's eyes and walked in the ways of his ancestor David, not deviating from it even a bit to the right or left. [3]In the eighth year of his rule, while he was just a boy, he began to seek the God of his ancestor David, and in the twelfth year he began purifying Judah and Jerusalem of the shrines, the sacred poles,[y] idols, and images. [4]Under his supervision, the altars for the Baals were torn down, and the incense altars that were above them were smashed. He broke up the sacred poles, idols, and images, grinding them to dust and scattering them over the graves of those who had sacrificed to them. [5]He burned the bones of the priests on their altars, purifying Judah and Jerusalem. [6]In the cities of Manasseh, Ephraim, and Simeon, all the way up to Naphtali, he removed their temples,[z] [7]tore down the altars and sacred poles, ground the idols to dust, and smashed all the incense altars throughout the land of Israel. Then Josiah returned to Jerusalem.

Josiah repairs the temple

[8]In the eighteenth year of his rule, after he had purified the land and the temple, Josiah sent Azaliah's son Shaphan, Maaseiah the mayor of the city, and Joahaz's son Joah the secretary to repair the LORD his God's temple. [9]When they came to the high priest Hilkiah, they delivered the money that had been collected in God's temple by the levitical gatekeepers from Manasseh, Ephraim, and the rest of Israel, as well as from Judah, Benjamin, and the residents of Jerusalem. [10]They handed it over to the supervisors[a] in charge of the LORD's temple, who in turn paid it to those working on, repairing, and restoring the LORD's temple. [11]They then gave it to the carpenters and the builders to pay for quarried stone and lumber for rafters and beams in the buildings the kings of Judah had neglected. [12]The men worked conscientiously under the supervision of Jahath and Obadiah, who were Levites descended from Merari, and Zechariah and Meshullam from the Kohathites. The Levites, all of whom were accomplished musicians, [13]were also in charge of the laborers and all the workers, no matter what their jobs, while some of the Levites served as scribes, officials, and guards.

The Instruction scroll

[14]While they were bringing out the money that had been brought into the LORD's temple, Hilkiah the priest found the Instruction scroll that the LORD had given through Moses. [15]Hilkiah told the secretary Shaphan, "I have found the Instruction scroll in the LORD's temple."

Then Hilkiah turned the scroll over to Shaphan, [16]who brought it to the king with this report: "Your servants are doing everything you've asked them to do. [17]They have released the money that was found in the LORD's temple and have handed it over to the supervisors and the workers." [18]Then the secretary Shaphan told the king, "The priest Hilkiah has given me a scroll," and he read it out loud before the king.

[19]As soon as the king heard what the Instruction scroll said, he ripped his clothes. [20]The king ordered Hilkiah, Shaphan's son Ahikam, Micah's son Abdon, the secretary Shaphan, and the royal officer Asaiah as follows: [21]"Go and ask the LORD on my behalf, and on behalf of those who still remain in Israel and Judah, concerning the contents of this scroll that has been found. The LORD must be furious with us because our ancestors failed to obey the LORD's word and do everything written in this scroll."

[22]So Hilkiah and the royal officials went to the prophetess Huldah. She was married

[y]Heb *asherim*, perhaps objects devoted to the goddess Asherah; also in 34:4, 7 [z]Heb uncertain [a]LXX, Vulg; MT *supervisor*

to Shallum, Tokhath's son and Hasrah's grandson, who was in charge of the wardrobe. She lived in Jerusalem in the second district. When they spoke to her, 23 she replied, "This is what the LORD, Israel's God, says: Tell this to the man who sent you to me: 24 This is what the LORD says: I am about to bring disaster on this place and its citizens—all the curses written in the scroll that they have read to Judah's king. 25 My anger burns against this place, never to be quenched, because they've deserted me and have burned incense to other gods, angering me by everything they have done.[b] 26 But also say this to the king of Judah, who sent you to question the LORD: This is what the LORD, Israel's God, says about the message you've just heard: 27 Because your heart was broken and you submitted before the LORD when you heard what he said against this place and its citizens,[c] and because you ripped your clothes and cried before me, I have listened to you, declares the LORD. 28 I will gather you to your ancestors, and you will go to your grave in peace. You won't experience the disaster I am about to bring on this place and its citizens."

When they reported Huldah's words to the king, 29 the king sent a message and gathered together all the elders of Judah and Jerusalem. 30 Then the king went up to the LORD's temple, together with all the people of Judah and all the citizens of Jerusalem, the priests and the Levites, and all the people, young and old alike. There the king read out loud all the words of the covenant scroll that had been found in the LORD's temple. 31 The king stood in his place and made a covenant with the LORD that he would follow the LORD by keeping his commandments, his instructions, and his regulations with all his heart and all his being, in order to fulfill the words of the covenant that were written in this scroll. 32 Then he made everyone found in Jerusalem and Benjamin join in a similar promise. The citizens of Jerusalem lived according to the covenant made with God, the God of their ancestors. 33 Josiah got rid of all the detestable idols from all the regions that belonged to the Israelites, and he made everyone who lived in Israel serve the LORD their God. As long as Josiah lived, they didn't turn away from following the LORD God of their ancestors.

Josiah's Passover

35 Then Josiah celebrated the LORD's Passover in Jerusalem. They slaughtered the Passover lambs on the fourteenth day of the first month.[d] 2 He assigned the priests to their posts, encouraging them to fulfill their responsibilities in the LORD's temple.

3 Next Josiah ordered the Levites, who were holy to the LORD and who instructed all Israel: "Put the holy chest in the temple built by Israel's King Solomon, David's son. You don't need to carry it around on your shoulders anymore. Now serve the LORD your God and his people Israel. 4 Organize yourselves by families according to your divisions, as directed by Israel's King David and his son Solomon. 5 Stand in the sanctuary, according to the family divisions of your relatives the laypeople, so that there can be Levites for each family division.[e] 6 Slaughter the Passover lambs and prepare the holy sacrifices[f] for your relatives in order to celebrate according to the LORD's word through Moses."

7 On behalf of the laypeople, Josiah donated from his personal holdings thirty thousand lambs and young goats, and three thousand bulls, all for the Passover offerings. 8 His officials also provided spontaneous gift offerings for the people, the priests, and the Levites. Hilkiah, Zechariah, and Jehiel, the ones in charge of God's temple, gave two thousand six hundred Passover lambs and three hundred bulls for the priests. 9 Conaniah and his brothers Shemaiah and Nethanel, along with Hashabiah, Jeiel, and Jozabad, the leaders of the Levites, provided the Levites with five thousand lambs and five hundred bulls as Passover sacrifices. 10 When everything was ready, the priests and the

[b] Or *made*; perhaps a reference to idols [c] MT repeats *and because you humbled yourself before me.* [d] March–April, Nisan [e] Heb uncertain [f] Correction; cf 1 Esdr 1:6; MT *and sanctify yourselves*

Levites took their places as the king had ordered. [11]Then they slaughtered the Passover lambs, and the priests splashed the blood[g] while the Levites skinned the animals. [12]Next they divided the entirely burned offerings among the laypeople by their families to sacrifice to the LORD as written in the scroll from Moses, and they did the same with the bulls. [13]They roasted the Passover lambs in the fire as instructed, cooked the holy offerings in pots, kettles, and pans, and brought them quickly to all the laypeople. [14]Next they prepared food for themselves and for the priests. Since the priests, Aaron's descendants, were busy offering up the entirely burned offerings and fat pieces until nighttime, the Levites prepared food for themselves and for the priests, Aaron's descendants. [15]The Asaphite singers also remained at their stations as ordered by David, Asaph, Heman, and the king's seer Jeduthun, as did the guards at the various gates. They didn't need to leave their tasks because their fellow Levites prepared food for them. [16]So on that day all of the LORD's service was prepared for celebrating Passover and offering up entirely burned offerings on the LORD's altar, just as King Josiah had ordered. [17]The Israelites who were present celebrated the Passover at that time, and observed the Festival of Unleavened Bread for seven days. [18]Not since the days of the prophet Samuel had such a Passover been celebrated in Israel. And no other king of Israel had celebrated a Passover like the one Josiah celebrated with the priests, the Levites, all the people of Judah and Israel who were present, and the residents of Jerusalem. [19]This Passover was celebrated in the eighteenth year of Josiah's rule.

Josiah's death

[20]After all of these things, when Josiah had finished restoring the temple, Egypt's King Neco marched against Carchemish by the Euphrates, and Josiah marched out against him. [21]But Neco sent messengers to Josiah. "What do you want with me, king of Judah?" he asked. "I haven't come to attack you today. I'm after the dynasty that wars with me. God told me to hurry, and he is on my side. Get out of God's way, or he will destroy you."

[22]But Josiah wouldn't turn back. Instead, he camouflaged himself in preparation for battle, refusing to listen to Neco's words from God's own mouth, and went to fight Neco on the plain of Megiddo. [23]When archers shot King Josiah, he said to his servants, "Take me away; I'm badly wounded!" [24]So his servants took him out of his chariot, placed him in another one, and brought him to Jerusalem, where he died and was buried in the tombs of his ancestors. All Judah and Jerusalem mourned for Josiah. [25]Jeremiah composed a funeral song[h] for Josiah, and to this day every singer, man or woman, continues to remember Josiah in their funeral songs. They are now traditional in Israel and are written down among the funeral songs.

[26]The rest of Josiah's deeds, including his faithfulness in acting according to what is written in the LORD's Instruction, [27]and everything else he did, from beginning to end, are written in the official records of Israel's and Judah's kings.

Jehoahaz rules

36 The people of the land took Jehoahaz, Josiah's son, and made him the next king in Jerusalem. [2]Jehoahaz was 23 years old when he became king, and he ruled for three months in Jerusalem. [3]The king of Egypt removed him from office in Jerusalem. The Egyptian king imposed a fine on the land totaling one hundred kikkars of silver and one kikkar of gold. [4]Then the king of Egypt made Jehoahaz's brother Eliakim king of Judah and Jerusalem, and changed his name to Jehoiakim. Neco took his brother Jehoahaz prisoner and carried him off to Egypt.

Jehoiakim rules

[5]Jehoiakim was 25 years old when he became king, and he ruled for eleven years in Jerusalem. He did what was evil in the LORD's eyes. [6]Babylon's King

[g]LXX; MT *from their hand* [h]Or *lament*, twice more in this verse

Nebuchadnezzar attacked him, bound him with bronze chains, and took him to Babylon. [7]Nebuchadnezzar also took some equipment from the LORD's temple to Babylon and placed them in his own temple there. [8]The rest of Jehoiakim's deeds, including his detestable practices and all that was charged against him, are written in the official records of Israel's and Judah's kings. His son Jehoiachin succeeded him as king.

Jehoiachin rules

[9]Jehoiachin was 18[i] years old when he became king, and he ruled for three months[j] in Jerusalem. He did what was evil in the LORD's eyes. [10]In the springtime, King Nebuchadnezzar sent for him to be brought to Babylon, along with valuable equipment from the LORD's temple. Then he made Zedekiah his uncle the next king of Judah and Jerusalem.

Zedekiah rules

[11]Zedekiah was 21 years old when he became king, and he ruled for eleven years in Jerusalem. [12]He did what was evil in the LORD his God's eyes and didn't submit before the prophet Jeremiah, who spoke for the LORD. [13]Moreover, he rebelled against King Nebuchadnezzar, despite the solemn pledge Nebuchadnezzar had forced him to swear in God's name. He became stubborn and refused to turn back to the LORD, Israel's God. [14]All the leaders of the priests and the people also grew increasingly unfaithful, following all the detestable practices of the nations. They polluted the LORD's temple that God had dedicated in Jerusalem. [15]Time and time again, the LORD, the God of their ancestors, sent word to them through his messengers because he had compassion on his people and his dwelling. [16]But they made fun of God's messengers, treating God's words with contempt and ridiculing God's prophets to such an extent that there was no hope of warding off the LORD's rising anger against his people.

Jerusalem destroyed

[17]So God brought the Babylonian[k] king against them. The king killed their young men with the sword in their temple's sanctuary, and showed no pity for young men or for virgins, for the old or for the feeble. God handed all of them over to him. [18]Then the king hauled everything off to Babylon, every item from God's temple, both large and small, including the treasures of the LORD's temple and those of the king and his officials. [19]Next the Babylonians burned God's temple down, demolished the walls of Jerusalem, and set fire to all its palaces, destroying everything of value. [20]Finally, he exiled to Babylon anyone who survived the killing so that they could be his slaves and the slaves of his children until Persia came to power. [21]This is how the LORD's word spoken by Jeremiah was carried out. The land finally enjoyed its sabbath rest. For as long as it lay empty, it rested, until seventy years were completed.

Cyrus's decree

[22]In the first year of Persia's King Cyrus, to carry out the LORD's promise spoken through Jeremiah, the LORD moved Persia's King Cyrus to issue the following proclamation throughout his kingdom, along with a written decree:

> [23]This is what Persia's King Cyrus says: The LORD, the God of heaven, has given me all the earth's kingdoms and has instructed me to build a temple for him at Jerusalem in Judah. Whoever among you belong to God's people, let them go up, and may the LORD their God be with them!

[i]LXX, 2 Kgs 24:8; MT *eight* [j]2 Kgs 24:8; MT adds *and ten days.* [k]Heb *Chaldean*

EZRA

Permission to return to Jerusalem

1 In the first year of King Cyrus of Persia's
rule, to fulfill the LORD's word spoken by
Jeremiah, the LORD stirred up the spirit of
Persia's King Cyrus. The king issued a proclamation throughout his kingdom (it was
also in writing) that stated:

2 Persia's King Cyrus says: The LORD, the
God of heaven, has given me all the kingdoms of the earth. He has commanded
me to build him a house at Jerusalem in
Judah. 3 If there are any of you who are
from his people, may their God be with
them! They may go up to Jerusalem in
Judah and build the house of the LORD,
the God of Israel—he is the God who is
in Jerusalem. 4 And as for all those who
remain in the various places where they
are living, let the people of those places
supply them with silver and gold, and
with goods and livestock, together with
spontaneous gifts for God's house in
Jerusalem.[a]

Preparing to return

5 Then the heads of the families of Judah
and Benjamin, and the priests and the
Levites—everyone whose spirit God had
stirred up—got ready to go up and build
God's house in Jerusalem. 6 All their neighbors assisted them with silver equipment,
with gold, with goods, livestock, and valuable gifts, in addition to all that was freely
offered. 7 King Cyrus brought out the equipment of the LORD's house—those items
that Nebuchadnezzar brought from Jerusalem and placed in the house of his gods.
8 Persia's King Cyrus handed them over to
Mithredath the treasurer, who counted
them out to Sheshbazzar the prince of
Judah. 9 This was the count: thirty gold
dishes, one thousand silver dishes, twenty-
nine knives,[b] 10 thirty gold bowls, four
hundred ten larger[c] silver bowls, and one
thousand other objects. 11 The total of the
gold and silver objects numbered five thousand four hundred. Sheshbazzar brought
up all of these when the exiles went up from
Babylonia to Jerusalem.

List of the returnees

2 These were the people of the province
who went up from there—from among
those captive exiles whom Babylon's King
Nebuchadnezzar had deported to Babylonia. They returned to Jerusalem and Judah,
all to their own towns. 2 They came with
Zerubbabel, Jeshua, Nehemiah, Seraiah,
Reelaiah, Mordecai, Bilshan, Mispar, Bigvai, Rehum, and Baanah.

The number of the people of Israel

3 The family of Parosh	2,172
4 of Shephatiah	372
5 of Arah	775
6 of Pahath-moab, namely the family of Jeshua and Joab	2,812
7 of Elam	1,254
8 of Zattu	945
9 of Zaccai	760
10 of Bani	642
11 of Bebai	623
12 of Azgad	1,222
13 of Adonikam	666
14 of Bigvai	2,056
15 of Adin	454
16 of Ater, namely of Hezekiah	98
17 of Bezai	323
18 of Jorah	112
19 of Hashum	223
20 of Gibbar	95
21 of Bethlehem	123
22 The people of Netophah	56
23 of Anathoth	128
24 The family of Azmaveth	42
25 of Kiriatharim, Chephirah, and Beeroth	743
26 of Ramah and Geba	621
27 The people of Michmash	122
28 of Bethel and Ai	223
29 The family of Nebo	52
30 of Magbish	156
31 of the other Elam	1,254
32 of Harim	320

[a]Heb uncertain [b]Vulg; Heb uncertain [c]Heb *double*

[33] of Lod, Hadid, and Ono 725
[34] of Jericho 345
[35] of Senaah 3,630

[36] *The priests*
The family of Jedaiah,
namely the house of Jeshua 973
[37] of Immer 1,052
[38] of Pashhur 1,247
[39] of Harim 1,017
[40] The Levites: the family
of Jeshua and Kadmiel—
the family of Hodaviah 74

[41] *The singers*
The family of Asaph 128

[42] *The family of the gatekeepers*
of Shallum, Ater, Talmon,
Akkub, Hatita, and Shobai 139 in all

[43] *The temple servants*
The family of Ziha, Hasupha,
Tabbaoth, [44] Keros, Siaha,
Padon, [45] Lebanah, Hagabah,
Akkub, [46] Hagab, Shamlai,
Hanan, [47] Giddel, Gahar,
Reaiah, [48] Rezin, Nekoda,
Gazzam, [49] Uzza, Paseah,
Besai, [50] Asnah, Meunim,
Nephisim, [51] Bakbuk, Hakupha,
Harhur, [52] Bazluth, Mehida,
Harsha, [53] Barkos, Sisera,
Temah, [54] Neziah, and Hatipha

[55] *The family of Solomon's servants*
Sotai, Hassophereth, Peruda,
[56] Jaalah, Darkon, Giddel,
[57] Shephatiah, Hattil, Pochereth-hazzebaim, and Ami.
[58] All of the temple servants and
the family of Solomon's
servants 392

Exclusions

[59] The following came up from Tel-melah,
Tel-harsha, Cherub, Addan, and Immer, but
they were unable to demonstrate that their
family or their descent was from Israel:

[60] the family of Delaiah, Tobiah,
and Nekoda, 652
[61] and of the family of the priests:
the family of Habaiah, Hakkoz,
and Barzillai (who had married
one of the daughters of Barzillai
the Gileadite and was called by
their name).

[62] They looked for their entries in the
genealogical records, but they were not
found there, so they were excluded from
the priesthood as unclean. [63] The governor
ordered them not to eat of the most holy
food until a priest arose who could consult
Urim and Thummim.

Total

[64] The whole assembly together totaled
42,360, [65] not including their 7,337 male
and female servants; they also had 200
male and female singers, [66] 736 horses, 245
mules, [67] 435 camels, and 6,720 donkeys.

Arrival in Jerusalem

[68] When they arrived at the LORD's
house in Jerusalem, some of the heads of
the families brought spontaneous gifts for
the rebuilding of God's house on its site.
[69] According to their means, they gave to
the building fund 61,000 drachmen of gold,
5,000 manehs of silver, and 100 priestly
robes.

[70] The priests, the Levites, some of the
people, the singers, the gatekeepers, and
the temple servants settled in their own
towns, and all Israel in their towns.

Rebuilding the altar

3 When the seventh month[d] came and
the Israelites were in their towns, the
people gathered together as one in Jerusalem. [2] Then Jeshua, Jozadak's son along
with his fellow priests, and Zerubbabel,
Shealtiel's son along with his kin, started to
rebuild the altar of Israel's God so that they
might offer entirely burned offerings upon
it as prescribed in the Instruction from
Moses the man of God. [3] They set up the
altar on its foundations,[e] because they were

[d] September–October, Tishrei [e] A technical word meaning *pedestals*

afraid of the neighboring peoples,[f] and they offered entirely burned offerings upon it to the LORD, both the morning and the evening offerings.

4They celebrated the Festival of Booths, as prescribed. Every day they presented the number of entirely burned offerings required by ordinance for that day. 5After this, they presented the continual burned offerings, the offerings at the new moons, and at all the sacred feasts of the LORD, and the offerings of everyone who brought a spontaneous gift to the LORD. 6From the first day of the seventh month, they began to present entirely burned offerings to the LORD.

However, the foundation of the LORD's temple had not yet been laid. 7So they gave money to the masons and carpenters; and food, drink, and oil to the Sidonians and the Tyrians to bring cedarwood by sea from Lebanon to Joppa, according to the authorization given them by Persia's King Cyrus.

Laying the foundations of God's house

8In the second month of the second year after their arrival at God's house in Jerusalem, Zerubbabel, Shealtiel's son, and Jeshua, Jozadak's son, and the rest of their kin—the priests and the Levites and all who had come from the captivity to Jerusalem—made a beginning. They appointed Levites 20 years old and above to oversee the work on the LORD's house. 9Then Jeshua with his sons and his kin, Kadmiel and his sons, Binnui and his sons, the sons of Judah, along with the sons of Henadad, the Levites, and their sons and kin, collaborated to supervise the workers in God's house.

10When the builders laid the foundation of the LORD's temple, the priests clothed in their vests and carrying their trumpets, and the Levites the sons of Asaph with cymbals, arose to praise the LORD according to the directions of Israel's King David. 11They praised and gave thanks to the LORD, singing responsively, "He is good, his graciousness for Israel lasts forever."

All of the people shouted with praise to the LORD because the foundation of the LORD's house had been laid. 12But many of the older priests and Levites and heads of families, who had seen the first house, wept aloud when they saw the foundation of this house, although many others shouted loudly with joy. 13No one could distinguish the sound of the joyful shout from the sound of the people's weeping, because the people rejoiced very loudly. The sound was heard at a great distance.

Facing opposition

4 When the enemies of Judah and Benjamin heard that the returned exiles were building a temple for the LORD, the God of Israel, 2they came to Zerubbabel and the heads of the families and said to them, "Let's build with you, for we worship your God as you do, and we've been sacrificing to him ever since the days of Assyria's King Esarhaddon, who brought us here."

3But Zerubbabel, Jeshua, and the rest of the heads of the families in Israel replied, "You'll have no part with us in building a house for our God. We alone will build because the LORD, the God of Israel, and Persia's King Cyrus commanded us."

4The neighboring peoples[g] discouraged the people of Judah, made them afraid to build, 5and bribed officials to frustrate their plan. They did this throughout the rule of Persia's King Cyrus until the rule of Persia's King Darius.

Writing to King Artaxerxes

6In the rule of Ahasuerus, at the beginning of his rule, they composed an indictment against those who lived in Judah and Jerusalem. 7In the days of Artaxerxes, Bishlam, Mithredath, Tabeel, and the rest of their associates wrote to Persia's King Artaxerxes. The letter was written in Aramaic and translated.[h] 8Rehum the royal deputy and Shimshai the scribe wrote a letter concerning Jerusalem to King Artaxerxes as follows:

9From Rehum the royal deputy and Shimshai the scribe and the rest of their

[f] Or *peoples of the lands* [g] Or *peoples of the lands* [h] Heb adds *in Aramaic*, reporting that 4:8–6:18 is written in Aramaic.

colleagues, the judges, the administrators, the officials, the Persians, the people
of Erech, the Babylonians, the people of
Susa (that is, the Elamites), [10]and the
rest of the nations whom the great and
famous Osnappar deported and settled
in the cities of Samaria and in the rest of
the province Beyond the River.
([11]This is a copy of the letter they sent
to him.)
To King Artaxerxes from your servants, the people of the province Beyond
the River. [12]May it be known to the king
that the Jews who left you and came to
us have arrived in Jerusalem. They are
rebuilding the rebellious and wicked
city; they are completing the walls and
repairing the foundations. [13]May it be
known to the king that if this city is rebuilt and the walls completed, they will
not pay tribute or tax or dues, and the
royal revenue will be reduced.
[14]Since we receive our salary from the
palace,[i] and since it is not fitting for us
to witness the king's dishonor, we now
send this letter[j] and inform the king [15]so
that you may search the records of your
ancestors. You will discover in the records that this is a rebellious city, harmful to kings and provinces, and that it
has been in revolt over a long period of
time. As a result, this city was laid waste.
[16]We tell the king that if this city is rebuilt and its walls completed, you will
then have no possession in the province
Beyond the River.

Artaxerxes responds

[17]The king sent this answer:
Greetings to Rehum the royal deputy
and Shimshai the scribe and the rest of
their colleagues who live in Samaria and
elsewhere in the province Beyond the
River. [18]The entire letter that you sent to
us has been read in translation for me.
[19]I issued an order; they searched and
discovered that this city has revolted
against kings over a long period of time.
There has been much rebellion and revolt there. [20]However, there have been
mighty kings over Jerusalem who also
ruled over the whole province Beyond
the River. Tribute and taxes and dues
were paid to them.
[21]Therefore, issue an order to stop
these people: this city is not to be rebuilt
until I make a decree. [22]Be sure to carry
out this order! Why should danger grow
and threaten the king?
[23]When the copy of King Artaxerxes'
letter was read before Rehum and Shimshai the scribe and their colleagues, they
hurried to Jerusalem to oppose the Jews
and made them stop by force of arms.[k] [24]At
that time the work on God's house in Jerusalem stopped and was suspended until
the second year of the rule of Persia's King
Darius.

Work on God's house continues

5 Then the prophet Haggai and the
prophet Zechariah, Iddo's son, prophesied to the Jews who were in Judah and
Jerusalem in the name of Israel's God who
was over them. [2]Subsequently, Zerubbabel,
Shealtiel's son, and Jeshua, Jozadak's son,
began to rebuild God's house in Jerusalem.
God's prophets were with them, helping
them.
[3]At the same time, Tattenai, the governor of the province Beyond the River, and
Shethar-bozenai and their colleagues came
to them and spoke to them, asking, "Who
authorized you to build this house and finish preparing[l] this building material?"[m]
[4]They[n] also asked them, "What are the
names of the people who are building this
building?" [5]But their God looked after the
elders of the Jews, and they didn't stop
them until a report reached Darius and a
letter with his response had arrived.

Writing to King Darius

[6]This is a copy of the letter that Tattenai, the governor of the province Beyond
the River, and Shethar-bozenai and his

[i] Or *since we have salted the salt of the palace* [j] Heb lacks *this letter.* [k] Or *power and force* [l] Heb lacks *preparing.*
[m] Heb uncertain; so also 5:9 [n] LXX, Syr, Aram *We*

colleagues the officials who were in the province Beyond the River sent to King Darius. [7]In the message they sent him, the following was written:

To King Darius, all peace! [8]Let the king know that we went to the province of Judah, to the house of the great God. It is being built with dressed stone and with timber set into the walls. This work makes good progress and prospers in their hands. [9]We asked those elders, "Who authorized you to build this house and to complete the preparation of this material?" [10]We also asked them their names so that we could write down the names of the leaders for your information.

[11]This was their reply to us: "We are the servants of the God of heaven and earth. We are rebuilding the house that was built many years ago, which a great king of Israel built and completed. [12]But because our ancestors angered the God of heaven, he gave them over into the power of Babylon's King Nebuchadnezzar, the Chaldean, who destroyed this house and deported the people to Babylonia. [13]However, in the first year of his rule, Babylon's King Cyrus issued a decree to rebuild this house of God. [14]King Cyrus also took the gold and silver equipment from God's house out of the temple in Babylon (the ones that Nebuchadnezzar took from the temple in Jerusalem and placed in the temple in Babylon) and gave them to a man named Sheshbazzar, whom he had appointed governor. [15]Cyrus said to him, 'Take this equipment and go and put it in Jerusalem's temple, and let God's house be rebuilt on its original site.' [16]Then Sheshbazzar came and laid the foundations of God's house in Jerusalem. From then until now the rebuilding work has continued but is not yet complete."

[17]And now, if it seems good to the king, may a search be made in the royal archives in Babylon to see if King Cyrus had issued a decree to rebuild this house of God in Jerusalem. Then may the king be pleased to send us his decision about this matter.

Darius responds

6 Then King Darius made a decree, and they searched the archives where the documents were stored in Babylon. [2]But a scroll was found in Ecbatana, the capital of the province of Media, on which was written the following:

A memorandum—[3]In the first year of his rule, King Cyrus made a decree: Concerning God's house in Jerusalem: Let the house at the place where they offered sacrifices be rebuilt and let its foundations be retained. Its height will be ninety feet and its width ninety feet, [4]with three layers of dressed stones and one° layer of timber. The cost will be paid from the royal treasury. [5]In addition, the gold and silver equipment from God's house, which Nebuchadnezzar took out of the temple in Jerusalem and brought to Babylon, is to be restored, that is, brought back to Jerusalem and put in their proper place in God's house.

[6]Now you, Tattenai, governor of the province Beyond the River, Shethar-bozenai, and you, their colleagues, the officials in the province Beyond the River, keep away! [7]Leave the work on this house of God alone. Let the governor of the Jews and the elders of the Jews rebuild this house of God on its original site.

[8]I also issue a decree about what you should do to help these elders of the Jews as they rebuild this house of God: The total cost is to be paid to these people, and without delay, from the royal revenue that is made up of the tribute of the province Beyond the River. [9]And whatever is needed—young bulls, rams, or sheep for entirely burned offerings to the God of heaven, wheat, salt, wine, or oil, as requested by the priests in Jerusalem—let that be given to them day by day without fail [10]so that they may offer pleasing sacrifices to the God of heaven and pray for the lives of the king and his sons.

°LXX; Heb *new*

[11]I also decree that if anyone disobeys this edict, a beam is to be pulled out of the house of the guilty party, and the guilty party will then be impaled upon it. The house will be turned into a trash heap.

[12]May the God who has established his name there overthrow any king or people who try to change this order or to destroy God's house in Jerusalem. I, Darius, have decreed it; let it be done with all diligence.

God's house is completed and dedicated

[13]Then Tattenai, the governor of the province Beyond the River, Shethar-bozenai, and their colleagues carried out the order of King Darius with all diligence. [14]So the elders of the Jews built and prospered because of the prophesying of the prophet Haggai and Zechariah, Iddo's son. They finished building by the command of Israel's God and of Cyrus, Darius, and King Artaxerxes of Persia. [15]This house was completed on the third day of the month of Adar,[p] in the sixth year of the rule of King Darius.

[16]Then the Israelites, the priests and the Levites, and the rest of the returned exiles joyfully celebrated the dedication of this house of God. [17]At the dedication of this house of God, they offered one hundred bulls, two hundred rams, four hundred lambs, and as a purification offering for all Israel, twelve male goats, according to the number of the tribes of Israel. [18]They set the priests in their divisions and the Levites in their sections for the service of God in Jerusalem, as it is written in the scroll from Moses.

[19][q]On the fourteenth day of the first month,[r] the returned exiles celebrated the Passover. [20]All of the priests and the Levites had purified themselves; all of them were clean. They slaughtered the Passover animals for all the returned exiles, their fellow priests, and themselves. [21]The Israelites who had returned from exile, together with all those who had joined them by separating themselves from the pollutions of the nations of the land to worship the LORD, the God of Israel, ate the Passover meal.[s]

[22]They also joyfully celebrated the Festival of Unleavened Bread for seven days, because the LORD had made them joyful by changing the attitude of the king of Assyria toward them so that he assisted them in the work on the house of God, the God of Israel.

Introduction to Ezra

7 After this, in the rule of Persia's King Artaxerxes, Ezra son of Seraiah son of Azariah son of Hilkiah [2]son of Shallum son of Zadok son of Ahitub [3]son of Amariah son of Azariah son of Meraioth [4]son of Zerahiah son of Uzzi son of Bukki [5]son of Abishua son of Phinehas son of Eleazar son of Aaron the chief priest—[6]this Ezra came up from Babylon. He was a scribe skilled in the Instruction from Moses, which the LORD, the God of Israel, had given. Moreover, the king gave him everything he requested because the LORD his God's power was with him.

[7]Some of the Israelites and some of the priests and the Levites, the singers and gatekeepers and the temple servants also came up to Jerusalem in the seventh year of King Artaxerxes. [8]They reached Jerusalem in the fifth month, in the seventh year of the king. [9]The journey from Babylon began on the first day of the first month, and they came to Jerusalem on the first day of the fifth month, for the gracious hand of his God was upon him. [10]Ezra had determined to study and perform the LORD's Instruction, and to teach law and justice in Israel.

Letter from Artaxerxes

[11]This is a copy of the letter that Artaxerxes gave to Ezra the priest and scribe, a scholar of the text of the LORD's commandments and his requirements for Israel:

> [12][t]Artaxerxes, king of kings,
> to Ezra the priest, the scribe of the Instruction from the God of heaven.
> Peace![u]
>
> And now [13]I decree that any of the

[p]February–March [q]Heb resumes with this verse. [r]March–April, Nisan [s]Heb lacks *Passover meal.* [t]7:12-26 is written in Aramaic. [u]Syr, Vulg 1 Esdr 8:9; Aram *Perfect*

people of Israel or their priests or Levites in my kingdom who volunteer to
go to Jerusalem with you may go. [14]You
are sent by the king and his seven counselors to investigate Judah and Jerusalem according to the Instruction from
your God, which is in your hand.
[15]You should bring the silver and gold
that the king and his counselors have
freely offered to the God of Israel, whose
dwelling is in Jerusalem, [16]together with
any of the silver and gold that you find
in the entire province of Babylonia. You
should also bring the spontaneous gifts
of the people and the priests, given freely
for God's house in Jerusalem. [17]With this
money you will be careful to buy bulls,
rams, and lambs, as well as their grain offerings and their drink offerings. And you
will offer them on the altar of God's house
in Jerusalem. [18]As long as it is God's will,
you and your colleagues may do what you
think best with the rest of the silver and
gold. [19]You will deliver the equipment that
has been given to you for the service of
God's house to the God of Jerusalem. [20]If
anything else is required for God's house
that you are responsible to provide, you
may provide it from the royal treasury.
[21]I, King Artaxerxes, decree to all of
the treasurers in the province Beyond
the River: Whatever Ezra the priest and
scribe of the Instruction from the God
of heaven requires of you, it must be
provided precisely, [22]even up to one hundred kikkars of silver, one hundred kors
of wheat, one hundred baths[v] of wine,
one hundred baths of oil, and unlimited
salt. [23]Whatever the God of heaven
commands will be done carefully for the
house of the God of heaven, or wrath
will come upon the realm of the king
and his heirs. [24]You must also know that
it is illegal for you to charge tribute, custom, or dues on any of the priests and
Levites, the singers, the doorkeepers,
the temple servants, or other servants
of this house of God.

[25]And you, Ezra, based on the divine
wisdom that you have, appoint supervisors and judges to adjudicate among all
the people in the province Beyond the
River who know the laws of your God.
You will also teach those who do not
know them. [26]Let judgment be strictly
carried out upon anyone who does not
obey the Instruction from your God and
the law of your king, including death,
banishment, confiscation of property,
or imprisonment.

Ezra prepares to leave

[27]Bless the LORD, the God of our ancestors, who has moved the king to glorify the
LORD's house in Jerusalem, [28]and who has
demonstrated his graciousness for me before the king and his counselors and all the
king's mighty officers. I took courage because the LORD my God's power was with
me. I gathered leaders from Israel to go up
with me.

8 These are the heads of the families, and
this is the genealogy of those who went up
with me during the rule of King Artaxerxes:
[2]of the family of Phinehas, Gershom; of
Ithamar, Daniel; of David, Hattush, [3]Sheca-
niah's son;[w] of Parosh, Zechariah and with
him were registered 150 men;
[4]of Pahath-moab, Eliehoenai, Zerahiah's son and with him 200 men;
[5]of Zattu,[x] Shecaniah, Jahaziel's son
and with him 300 men;
[6]of Adin, Ebed, Jonathan's son and
with him 50 men;
[7]of Elam, Jeshaiah, Athaliah's son
and with him 70 men;
[8]of Shephatiah, Zebadiah, Michael's
son and with him 80 men;
[9]of Joab, Obadiah, Jehiel's son and
with him 218 men;
[10]of Bani,[y] Shelomith, Josiphiah's son
and with him 160 men;
[11]of Bebai, Zechariah, Bebai's son and
with him 28 men;
[12]of Azgad, Johanan, Hakkatan's son
and with him 110 men;

[v]One bath is approximately twenty quarts or five gallons. [w]LXX and 1 Esdr 8:29; Heb *of the descendants of Shecaniah* [x]LXX and 1 Esdr 8:32; Heb lacks *of Zattu.* [y]LXX and 1 Esdr 8:36; Heb lacks *of Bani.*

[13]of the last of Adonikam, namely Eliphelet, Jeuel, and Shemaiah and with them 60 men;

[14]of Bigvai, Uthai and Zaccur and with them were 70 men.

Voyage to Jerusalem

[15]I gathered them by the river that runs to Ahava, and there we camped for three days.

As I reviewed the people and the priests, I found no Levites there. [16]So I called for Eliezer, Ariel, Shemaiah, Elnathan, Jarib, Elnathan, Nathan, Zechariah, and Meshullam, all leaders, together with Joiarib and Elnathan, who were wise. [17]I sent them[z] to Iddo, the leader at the place named Casiphia, telling them what to say to Iddo and his colleagues the temple servants at Casiphia, namely, to send us ministers for God's house. [18]Because we were favored by God, they brought us Sherebiah, a skillful man of the family of Mahli, Levi's son and Israel's grandson, together with his sons and relatives so that there were eighteen in total. [19]They also brought us Hashabiah and with him Jeshaiah of the family of Merari, together with his relatives and their sons so that there were twenty in total. [20]In addition, there were two hundred twenty temple servants whom David and the princes had appointed to serve the Levites. These were all recorded by name.

[21]Then I called for a fast there at the Ahava River so that we might submit before our God and ask of him a safe journey for ourselves, our children, and all our possessions. [22]I had been ashamed to ask the king for a group of soldiers and cavalry to help us in facing enemies on the way, because we had told the king, "The power of God favors all who seek him, but his fierce wrath is against all who abandon him." [23]So we fasted and prayed to our God for this, and he responded to us.

[24]Then I selected twelve of the leading priests, Sherebiah and Hashabiah and ten of their relatives with them. [25]I weighed out to them the silver and the gold and the equipment, the offering for the house of our God that the king, his counselors, his officials, and all Israel present there had offered. [26]I weighed out into their keeping six hundred fifty kikkars of silver, one hundred silver containers weighing a certain number of kikkars, one hundred kikkars of gold, [27]twenty gold bowls worth one thousand darics, and two containers of highly polished copper, which were as precious as gold. [28]I said to them, "You are holy to the LORD, and the equipment is holy; the silver and the gold are a spontaneous gift to the LORD, the God of your ancestors. [29]Guard them carefully until you weigh them out in Jerusalem before the officials of the priests, the Levites, and the heads of the families of Israel, within the rooms of the LORD's house." [30]So the priests and the Levites received the silver and the gold and the utensils as they were weighed out, in order to bring them to Jerusalem, to our God's house.

[31]Then we left the Ahava River on the twelfth day of the first month[a] to go to Jerusalem. The power of our God was with us; he saved us from the power of the enemy and ambushes along the way.

Finishing the journey

[32]After arriving in Jerusalem, we rested there three days. [33]On the fourth day, the silver and the gold and the equipment were weighed out in our God's house into the care of the priest named Meremoth, Uriah's son, together with Eleazar, Phinehas' son; and the Levites, Jozabad, Jeshua's son, and Noadiah, Binnui's son. [34]Everything was counted and weighed, and the total weight was recorded.

[35]At that time, those who had come from the captivity, the returned exiles, offered as entirely burned offerings to the God of Israel twelve bulls for all Israel, ninety-six rams, seventy-seven lambs, and twelve male goats as a purification offering. All this was an entirely burned offering to the LORD. [36]They also delivered the king's orders to the royal chief administrators and governors of the province Beyond the River, who supported the people and God's house.

[z]Kethib *I ordered them* [a]March–April, Nisan

Facing a communal problem

9 When these tasks were finished, the officials approached me and said, "The people of Israel, the priests, and the Levites haven't kept themselves separate from the peoples of the neighboring lands with their detestable practices; namely, the Canaanites, the Hittites, the Perizzites, the Jebusites, the Ammonites, the Moabites, the Egyptians, and the Amorites. 2 They've taken some of their daughters as wives for themselves and their sons, and the holy descendants have become mixed with the neighboring peoples.[b] Moreover, the officials and leaders have led the way in this unfaithfulness."

3 When I heard this, I tore my clothes and cloak, pulled out hair from my head and beard, and sat down in shock. 4 Then all those who trembled at the words of the God of Israel gathered around me on account of the transgression of the returned exiles while I remained sitting in shock until the evening sacrifice.

Ezra prays

5 At the time of the evening sacrifice, I ended my penitential acts. While still wearing[c] my torn clothes and cloak, I fell upon my knees, spread out my hands to the LORD my God, 6 and said,

"My God, I'm too ashamed to lift up my face to you. Our iniquities have risen higher than our heads, and our guilt has grown to the heavens.

7 "From the days of our ancestors to this day, we've been deep in guilt. On account of our iniquities we, our kings, and our priests have been handed over to the kings of the lands, to the sword, to captivity, to plundering, and to utter shame, as is now the case.

8 "But now, for a brief while the LORD our God has shown favor in leaving us survivors and in giving us a stake in his holy place. Our God cheered us[d] and revived us for a little while in our slavery. 9 Even though we are slaves, our God hasn't abandoned us in our slavery. Instead, he's shown us his graciousness before Persia's kings by reviving us to set up our God's house, to repair its ruins, and to give us a wall in Judea and Jerusalem.

10 "And now, our God, what will we say after this? We have abandoned your commandments, 11 which you commanded through your servants the prophets, saying: 'The land which you are about to enter to possess is a land polluted by the impurity of the neighboring peoples.[e] Their detestable practices have filled it with uncleanness from end to end. 12 So now, do not give your daughters to their sons in marriage, do not take their sons for your daughters to marry, and never seek their peace or prosperity. This is so you may be strong, and eat the good of the land, and leave it for an inheritance to your children forever.'

13 "After all that has happened to us because of our evil deeds and our great guilt—although you, our God, have punished us less than our iniquities deserve and have allowed us to survive as we do— 14 will we once again break your commandments and intermarry with the peoples who practice these detestable things? Would you not be so angry with us that you leave us without remnant or survivor? 15 LORD, God of Israel, you are righteous, for we have survived and a few remain until now. Here we are before you in our guilt, though no one can face you because of this guilt."[f]

The community responds

10 While Ezra was praying and confessing, weeping and bowing down before God's house, a very large crowd of men, women, and children of Israel gathered around him. The people also wept in distress. 2 Then Shecaniah, Jehiel's son, from the family of Elam, spoke up and said to Ezra, "We've been unfaithful to our God by marrying foreign women from the neighboring peoples.[g] But even now, there is hope for Israel in spite of this. 3 Let's now make

[b] Or *peoples of the lands* [c] Heb uncertain [d] Or *brightened our eyes* [e] Or *peoples of the lands* [f] Heb lacks *guilt.* [g] Or *peoples of the lands*

a covenant with our God to send away all these wives and their children, according to the advice of my master and of those who tremble at the commandment of our God. Let it be done according to the Instruction. 4 Get up, for it is your duty to deal with this matter; we will support you. Be strong and act." 5 So Ezra got up and made the leading priests, the Levites, and all Israel take a solemn pledge that they would do as had been said. So they took a solemn pledge.

The assembly decides

6 Then Ezra got up from the area in front of God's house and went to the room of Jehohanan, Eliashib's son, where he spent[h] the night. He didn't eat food or drink water, for he was mourning because of the unfaithfulness of the exiles.

7 An order was then circulated throughout Judah and Jerusalem that all the returned exiles should gather in Jerusalem. 8 All those who failed to appear within three days, as mandated by the officials and elders, would have all their property taken away. They would be separated from the congregation of the exiles. 9 So within three days, all the people of Judah and Benjamin gathered in Jerusalem. It was the twentieth day of the ninth month.[i] All of the people sat in the area in front of God's house, trembling because of this order and because of the heavy rain.

10 Then Ezra the priest stood up and said to them, "You have been unfaithful by marrying foreign women and adding to Israel's guilt. 11 But now, make a confession to the LORD God of your ancestors and do his will. Separate yourselves from the neighboring peoples[j] and from the foreign wives."

12 The whole assembly shouted in reply, "Yes. We must do as you have said. 13 But there are many people, and it's the rainy season; we can't continue to stand outside. Nor can this task be completed in a day or two because many of us have sinned in this matter. 14 Let our leaders represent the entire assembly. Let all in our towns who have taken foreign wives come at appointed times, along with the elders and judges of every town, until God's great anger at us on account of this matter be averted." 15 Only Jonathan, Asahel's son, and Jahzeiah, Tikvah's son, opposed this; Meshullam and Shabbethai the Levites supported them.

Resolving the issue

16 Then the returned exiles did so. Ezra the priest chose[k] certain men, heads of families, each representing their family houses. Each of them was designated by name. On the first day of the tenth month[l] they sat down to examine the matter. 17 By the first day of the first month,[m] they had come to the end of all the men who had married foreign women.

18 Of the family of priests, there were found the following who had married foreign women—of the family of Jeshua, Jozadak's son and his brothers: Maaseiah, Eliezer, Jarib, and Gedaliah. 19 They promised to send their wives away, and their compensation offering was a ram of the flock for their guilt.

20 Of the family of Immer: Hanani and Zebadiah.

21 Of the family of Harim: Maaseiah, Elijah, Shemaiah, Jehiel, and Uzziah.

22 Of the family of Pashhur: Elioenai, Maaseiah, Ishmael, Nethanel, Jozabad, and Elasah.

23 Of the Levites: Jozabad, Shimei, Kelaiah (that is, Kelita), Pethahiah, Judah, and Eliezer.

24 Of the singers: Eliashib. Of the gatekeepers: Shallum, Telem, and Uri.

25 Of Israel: of the family of Parosh: Ramiah, Izziah, Malchijah, Mijamin, Eleazar, Hashabiah,[n] and Benaiah.

26 Of the family of Elam: Mattaniah, Zechariah, Jehiel, Abdi, Jeremoth, and Elijah.

27 Of the family of Zattu: Elioenai, Eliashib, Mattaniah, Jeremoth, Zabad, and Aziza.

28 Of the family of Bebai: Jehohanan, Hananiah, Zabbai, and Athlai.

29 Of the family of Bani: Meshullam,

[h] LXX, 1 Esdr 9:2; Heb *where he went* [i] November–December, Kislev [j] Or *peoples of the lands* [k] 1 Esdr 9:16; Syr; Heb *And there were separated* [l] December–January, Tevet [m] March–April, Nisan [n] 1 Esdr 9:26; LXX, Heb *Malchijah*

Malluch, Adaiah, Jashub, Sheal, and Jeremoth.
30 Of the family of Pahath-moab:
Adna, Chelal, Benaiah, Maaseiah, Mattaniah, Bezalel, Binnui, and Manasseh.
31 Of the family of Harim: Eliezer, Is-
shijah, Malchijah, Shemaiah, Shimeon,
32 Benjamin, Malluch, and Shemariah.
33 Of the family of Hashum: Mattenai, Mattattah, Zabad, Eliphelet, Jeremai, Manasseh, and Shimei.
34 Of the family of Bani: Maadai, Amram, Uel, 35 Benaiah, Bedeiah, Cheluhi,
36 Vaniah, Meremoth, Eliashib, 37 Mattaniah, Mattenai, and Jaasu.
38 Of the family of Binnui:[o] Shimei,
39 Shelemiah, Nathan, Adaiah, 40 Mach-
nadebai, Shashai, Sharai, 41 Azarel,
Shelemiah, Shemariah, 42 Shallum, Amariah, and Joseph.
43 Of the family of Nebu: Jeiel, Mattithiah, Zabad, Zebina, Jaddai, Joel, and
Benaiah.
44 All these men[p] had married foreign women, some of whom had borne
children.[q]

NEHEMIAH

Loss of Jerusalem

1 These are the words of Nehemiah, Hacaliah's son.
In the month of Kislev,[a] in the twentieth year,[b] while I was in the fortress city of
Susa, 2 Hanani, one of my brothers, came
with some other men from Judah. I asked
them about the Jews who had escaped
and survived the captivity, and about Jerusalem.
3 They told me, "Those in the province
who survived the captivity are in great
trouble and shame! The wall around Jerusalem is broken down, and its gates have been
destroyed by fire!"

Confession

4 When I heard this news, I sat down and
wept. I mourned for days, fasting and praying before the God of heaven. 5 I said:
"LORD God of heaven, great and awesome God, you are the one who keeps
covenant and is truly faithful to those
who love you and keep your commandments. 6 Let your ear be attentive and
your eyes open to hear the prayer of
your servant, which I now pray before
you night and day for your servants, the
people of Israel.
"I confess the sins of the people of Israel, which we have committed against
you. Both I and my family have sinned.
7 We have wronged you greatly. We
haven't kept the commandments, the
statutes, and the ordinances that you
commanded your servant Moses.
8 "Remember the word that you gave
to your servant Moses when you said,
'If you are unfaithful, I will scatter you
among the peoples. 9 But if you return
to me and keep my commandments by
really doing them, then, even though
your outcasts live[c] under distant skies,
I will gather them from there and bring
them to the place that I have chosen
as a dwelling for my name.' 10 They are
your servants and your people. They
are the ones whom you have redeemed
by your great power and your strong
hand.
11 "LORD, let your ear be attentive to
the prayer of your servant and to the
prayer of your servants who delight in
honoring your name. Please give success
to your servant today and grant him
favor in the presence of this man!"

Cupbearer's plea

At that time, I was a cupbearer to the king.
2 In the month of Nisan,[d] in the twentieth
year of King Artaxerxes, the king was
about to be served wine. I took the wine

[o]LXX, Heb *Bani, Binnui* [p]Heb lacks *men.* [q]Heb uncertain; 1 Esdr 9:36 *they sent them away with their children.*
[a]November–December [b]Of Artaxerxes [c]Heb lacks *live.* [d]March–April

and gave it to the king. Since I had never seemed sad in his presence, [2]the king asked me, "Why do you seem sad? Since you aren't sick, you must have a broken heart!"

I was very afraid [3]and replied, "May the king live forever! Why shouldn't I seem sad when the city, the place of my family's graves, is in ruins and its gates destroyed by fire?"

[4]The king asked, "What is it that you need?"

I prayed to the God of heaven [5]and replied, "If it pleases the king, and if your servant has found favor with you, please send me to Judah, to the city of my family's graves so that I may rebuild it."

[6]With the queen sitting beside him, the king asked me, "How long will you be away and when will you return?" So it pleased the king to send me, and I told him how long I would be gone.

[7]I also said to him, "If it pleases the king, may letters be given me addressed to the governors of the province Beyond the River to allow me to travel to Judah. [8]May the king also issue a letter to Asaph the keeper of the king's forest, directing him to supply me with timber for the beams of the temple fortress gates, for the city wall, and for the house in which I will live."

The king gave me what I asked, for the gracious power of my God was with me.

Inspecting Jerusalem

[9]So I went to the governors of the province[e] Beyond the River and gave them the king's letters. The king had sent officers of the army and cavalry with me.

[10]When Sanballat the Horonite and Tobiah the Ammonite official heard this, they were very angry that someone had come to seek the welfare of the people of Israel.

[11]When I reached Jerusalem and had been there for three days, [12]I set out at night, taking only a few people with me. I didn't tell anyone what my God was prompting me to do for Jerusalem, and the only animal I took was the one I rode. [13]I went out by night through the Valley Gate past the Dragon's Spring to the Dung Gate so that I could inspect the walls of Jerusalem that had been broken down, as well as its gates, which had been destroyed by fire.

[14]Then I went on to the Spring Gate and to the King's Pool. Since there was no room for the animal on which I was riding to pass, [15]I went up by way of the valley by night and inspected the wall. Then I turned back and returned by entering through the the Valley Gate.

Let's rebuild

[16]The officials didn't know where I had gone or what I was doing. I hadn't yet told the Jews, the priests, the officials, the officers, or the rest who were to do the work. [17]So I said to them, "You see the trouble that we're in: Jerusalem is in ruins, and its gates are destroyed by fire! Come, let's rebuild the wall of Jerusalem so that we won't continue to be in disgrace." [18]I told them that my God had taken care of me, and also told them what the king had said to me.

"Let's start rebuilding!" they said, and they eagerly began the work.[f]

[19]But when Sanballat the Horonite, Tobiah the Ammonite official, and Geshem the Arab heard about it, they mocked and made fun of us. "What are you doing?" they asked. "Are you rebelling against the king?"

[20]"The God of heaven will give us success!" I replied. "As God's servants, we will start building. But you will have no share, right, or claim in Jerusalem."

Rebuilding the gates and walls

3 Then Eliashib the high priest set to work with his fellow priests and built[g] the Sheep Gate. They dedicated it and set up its doors, then dedicated it as far as the Tower of the Hundred and as far as the Tower of Hananel.

[2]The people of Jericho built next to them, and Zaccur, Imri's son, built next to them. [3]The children of Hassenaah built the Fish Gate; they laid its beams and set up its doors, bolts, and bars. [4]Next to them Meremoth, Uriah's son and Hakkoz's grandson,

[e]Heb lacks *of the province.* [f]Or *they strengthened their hands for the good.* [g]Or *rebuild*

made repairs. Meshullam, Berechiah's son
and Meshezabel's grandson, made repairs
next to them, and Zadok, Baana's son,
made repairs next to them. 5 Next to them
the people from Tekoa made repairs, but
their officials wouldn't help with the work[h]
of their supervisors.[i]

6 Joiada, Paseah's son, and Meshullam,
Besodeiah's son, repaired the Mishneh Gate;[j]
they laid its beams and set up its doors,
bolts, and bars. 7 Next to them repairs were
made by Melatiah the Gibeonite, Jadon the
Meronothite, and[k] the people of Gibeon and
of Mizpah, who were ruled by the governor
of the province Beyond the River.

8 Uzziel, Harhaiah's son, one of the goldsmiths, made repairs next to them; and
Hananiah, one of the perfumers, made
repairs next to him. They restored Jerusalem as far as the Broad Wall. 9 Next to them
Rephaiah, Hur's son, ruler of half the district of Jerusalem, made repairs. 10 Next to
them Jedaiah, Harumaph's son, made repairs opposite his house, and Hattush, Hashabneiah's son, made repairs next to him.

11 Malchijah, Harim's son, and Hasshub,
Pahath-moab's son, repaired another section and the Tower of the Ovens. 12 Next
to them Shallum, Hallohesh's son, ruler of
half the district of Jerusalem, made repairs,
along with his daughters.

13 Hanun and the people of Zanoah repaired the Valley Gate; they built it and set
up its doors, bolts, and bars. They also repaired fifteen hundred feet of the wall, as
far as the Dung Gate.

14 Malchiah, Rechab's son, ruler of the
district of Beth-haccherem, repaired the
Dung Gate. He rebuilt it and set up its
doors, bolts, and bars.

15 And Shallum, Col-hozeh's son, ruler
of the Mizpah district, repaired the Spring
Gate. He rebuilt and covered it, and set up
its doors, bolts, and bars. He also built the
wall of the Pool of Shelah of the King's Garden, as far as the stairs that go down from
David's City.

16 After him, Nehemiah, Azbuk's son,
ruler of half the Beth-zur district, repaired
from the point opposite David's tombs as
far as the artificial pool and the Warriors'
House. 17 After him, the Levites made repairs:
Rehum, Bani's son, and next to him Hashabiah, ruler of half the district of Keilah, made
repairs for his district. 18 After him, their relatives made repairs: Binnui,[l] Henadad's son,
ruler of half the district of Keilah.

19 Next to him, Ezer, Jeshua's son, ruler
of Mizpah, repaired another section opposite the ascent to the armory at the Angle.
20 After him, Baruch, Zabbai's son, thoroughly repaired another section from the
Angle to the door of the house of the high
priest Eliashib. 21 After him, Meremoth,
Uriah's son and Hakkoz's grandson, repaired another section from the door to the
back of Eliashib's house.

22 After him, the priests from the surrounding area made repairs. 23 After them,
Benjamin and Hasshub made repairs opposite their house. After them, Azariah, Maaseiah's son and Ananiah's grandson, repaired
beside his house. 24 After him, Binnui,
Henadad's son, repaired another section
from the house of Azariah to the Angle and
to the corner. 25 Palal, Uzai's son, repaired[m]
from the point opposite the Angle and the
tower projecting from the upper house of
the king at the court of the guard. After
him, Pedaiah, Parosh's son, 26 and the temple servants living on Ophel made repairs[n]
up to the point opposite the Water Gate to
the east and the projecting tower. 27 After
them, the people of Tekoa repaired another
section opposite the great projecting tower
as far as the wall of Ophel. 28 From the
Horse Gate, the priests made repairs, each
one opposite his own house.

29 After them, Zadok, Immer's son, made
repairs opposite his own house. After him,
Shemaiah, Shecaniah's son, the keeper of
the East Gate, made repairs. 30 After him,
Hananiah, Shelemiah's son, and Hanun, Za-
laph's sixth son, repaired another section.
After them, Meshullam, Berechiah's son,
made repairs opposite his own room.

[h]Or *didn't bring their neck into the service of* [i]Or *lords* [j]Or *Old Gate* [k]Syr; Heb lacks *and.* [l]LXX, Syr; Heb *Bvvai*
[m]Heb lacks *repaired.* [n]Heb lacks *made repairs.*

31 After him, Malchiah, one of the goldsmiths, made repairs as far as the house of
the temple servants and the merchants, opposite the Parade Gate,[o] and as far as the
upper room at the corner. 32 And between
the upper room of the corner and the Sheep
Gate, the goldsmiths and the merchants
made repairs.

Opposition mounts

4 [p]When Sanballat heard that we were
building the wall, he became angry and
raged. He mocked the Jews, 2 saying in the
presence of his associates and the army
of Samaria: "What are those feeble Jews
doing? Will they restore things themselves?
Will they offer sacrifices? Will they finish it
in a day? Will they revive the stones from
the piles of rubble, even though they are
burned?"
3 Tobiah the Ammonite, who was beside
him, added: "If even a fox climbs on whatever they build, their wall of stones will
crumble."
4 Listen, God; we are despised! Turn their
insults to us[q] back on their heads and
make them like plunder in a captive land.
5 Don't forgive their iniquity or blot out
their sins from your sight. They have
thrown insults at the builders!
6 We continued to build the wall. All of
it was joined together, and it reached half
of its intended height because the people
were eager to work. 7 [r]But when Sanballat,
Tobiah, the Arabs, the Ammonites, and
the people of Ashdod heard that the work
on the walls was progressing and the gaps
were being closed, they were very angry.
8 They plotted together to come and fight
against Jerusalem and to create a disturbance in it.
9 So we prayed to our God and set a guard
as protection against them day and night.
10 But in Judah it was said,

"The carrier's strength is failing,
for there is too much rubble.
We are unable to rebuild the wall!"

11 Meanwhile, our enemies were saying:
"Before they know or see anything, we can
be in their midst and start to kill them.
We'll stop the work!"
12 Now the Jews who were living near
them came and said to us again and again,[s]
"You must return to us!"[t]

Armed guards protect the builders

13 So I took up a position in the lowest
parts of the space behind the wall in an
open area.[u] Then I stationed the people by
families, and they had their swords, spears,
and bows. 14 After reviewing this, I stood up
and said to the officials, the officers, and
the rest of the people, "Don't be afraid of
them! Remember that the LORD is great
and awesome! Fight for your families, your
sons, your daughters, your wives, and your
houses!"
15 Then our enemies heard that we had
found out and that God had spoiled their
plans. So we all returned to doing our own
work on the wall. 16 But from that day on,
only half of my workers continued in the
construction, while the other half held
the spears, shields, bows, and body armor.
Meanwhile, the leaders positioned themselves[v] behind the whole house of Judah,
17 who were building the wall. The carriers
did their work with a load in one hand and
a weapon in the other. 18 The builders built
with swords fastened in their belts, and the
trumpeter stayed by my side.
19 Then I said to the officials, the officers,
and the rest of the people, "The work is very
spread out, and we are far apart from each
other along the wall. 20 When you hear the
trumpet sound, come and gather where we
are. Our God will fight for us!" 21 So we continued the work, with half of them holding
spears from dawn until dusk.
22 I also said to the people at that time,
"Let every man and his servant spend the
night in Jerusalem so that we can guard
during the night and work during the
day." 23 Neither I nor my relatives, nor my
servants, nor my bodyguards took off our
clothes, even when they sent for water.[w]

[o]Or *Hammiphkad Gate* [p]3:33 in Heb [q]Heb lacks *to us.* [r]4:1 in Heb [s]Or *ten times from all sides* [t]Heb uncertain
[u]Heb uncertain [v]Heb lacks *positioned themselves.* [w]Heb uncertain

Internal unrest

5 Then there was a great protest of the people and their wives against their fellow Jews. [2]Some said, "With our sons and daughters we are many, and we all need grain to eat and stay alive."

[3]Others said, "We have to mortgage our fields, our vineyards, and our houses in order to get grain during the famine."

[4]Still others said, "We have had to borrow money against our fields and vineyards in order to pay the king's tax.

[5]"We are of the same flesh and blood as our kin, and our children are the same as theirs. Yet we are just about to force our sons and daughters into slavery, and some of our daughters are already slaves! There is nothing we can do since our fields and vineyards now belong to others."

[6]I was very angry when I heard their protest and these complaints. [7]After thinking it over, I brought charges against the officials and the officers. I told them, "You are all taking interest from your own people!" I also called for a large assembly in order to deal with them. [8]"To the best of our ability," I said to them, "we have bought back our Jewish kin who had been sold to other nations. But now you are selling your own kin, who must then be bought back by us!" At this they were silent, unable to offer a response.

[9]So I continued, "What you are doing isn't good! Why don't you walk in the fear of our God? This will prevent the taunts of the nations that are our enemies! [10]I myself, along with my family and my servants, am lending them money and grain. But let's stop charging this interest! [11]Give it back to them, right now. Return their fields, their vineyards, their olive orchards, and their houses. And give back the interest on money, grain, wine, and oil that you are charging them."

[12]They replied, "We'll return everything, and we won't charge anything else.[x] We'll do what you've asked."

So I called the priests and made them swear to do what they had promised. [13]I also shook out the fold of my robe, saying, "So may God shake out everyone from their house and property if they don't keep this promise. So may they be shaken out and emptied!"

The whole assembly said, "Amen," and praised the LORD. And the people did as they had promised.

Generous Governor Nehemiah

[14]In addition, from the time that I was appointed to be their governor in the land of Judah (that is, from the twentieth to the thirty-second year of King Artaxerxes for a total of twelve years), neither I nor my family ate from the governor's food allowance. [15]The earlier governors who had come before me laid heavy burdens on the people. They took food and wine from them as well as[y] forty shekels of silver. Even their servants oppressed the people. But because I was God-fearing, I didn't behave in this way. [16]Instead, I devoted myself to the work on this wall. We acquired no land, and all my servants were gathered there for the work. [17]One hundred fifty Jews and officials, along with those who came to us from the surrounding nations, gathered around my table. [18]One ox, six choice sheep, and birds were prepared each day. Every ten days there was a large amount of wine. Yet even with this I didn't ask for the governor's food allowance because of the heavy burden the people had to carry.

[19]Remember in my favor, my God, all that I've done for this people!

Nehemiah avoids his enemies

6 Now when Sanballat, Tobiah, Geshem the Arab, and the rest of our enemies heard that I had rebuilt the wall and that there were no gaps left in it (although I hadn't yet hung the doors in the gates), [2]Sanballat and Geshem sent me this message: "Come, let's meet together in one of the villages[z] in the plain of Ono."

But they wanted to harm me, [3]so I sent messengers to tell them, "I'm doing important work, so I can't come down. Why should the work stop while I leave it to come down to you?"

[x]Heb lacks *everything . . . anything else.* [y]Heb uncertain [z]LXX, Vulg; MT *at Hakkephirim*

[4]They sent me a message like this four times, and every time I gave them a similar reply. [5]But the fifth time, Sanballat sent his servant to me in the same way, except that now he carried an open letter. [6]It stated:

> It is reported among the nations and confirmed by Geshem[a] that you and the Jews intend to rebel. This is why you are rebuilding the wall. According to these reports, you intend to become their king. [7]You have also appointed prophets to make this announcement about you in Jerusalem: There is a king in Judah! Now, the king will hear of these reports, so come; let's talk together.

[8]So I sent him this reply: "Nothing that you say has happened. You are simply inventing this."

[9]All of them were trying to make us afraid, saying, "They will be discouraged, and the work won't get finished." But now, God, strengthen me!

[10]Later I went to see Shemaiah, Delaiah's son and Mehetabel's grandson, who was confined to his house, and he said:

"Let's meet together in God's house,
inside the temple itself.
Let's shut the doors of the temple,
for they are coming to kill you;
they are coming to kill you tonight!"

[11]But I replied, "Should someone like me run away? Who like me would go into the temple to save his life? I won't go in!" [12]Then I realized that God hadn't sent him at all but that he spoke this prophecy against me because Tobiah and Sanballat had hired him. [13]He was hired to frighten me and to make me sin by acting in this way. Then they could give me a bad name and discredit me. [14]My God, remember these deeds of Tobiah and Sanballat! Also remember Noadiah the prophetess and the rest of the prophets who have been trying to frighten me.

[15]So the wall was finished on the twenty-fifth day of the month of Elul.[b] It took fifty-two days. [16]When our enemies heard about this, all of the nations around us were afraid and their confidence was greatly shaken. They knew that this work was completed with the help of our God.

[17]In addition, in those days the officials of Judah sent many letters to Tobiah, and Tobiah's letters were coming to them. [18]Many in Judah were bound to him by solemn pledge because he was the son-in-law of Shecaniah, Arah's son, and his son Jehohanan had married the daughter of Meshullam, Berechiah's son. [19]They also kept talking about his good deeds in my presence and then reported back to him what I said. In addition, Tobiah sent letters to intimidate me.

The wall is complete

7 When the wall had been built and I had hung the doors, the gatekeepers, singers, and Levites were appointed. [2]Then I put my brother Hanani and Hananiah the commander of the fortress in charge of Jerusalem. Hananiah was a faithful man who revered God more than many.

[3]I[c] said to them, "The gates of Jerusalem aren't to be opened during the hottest time of the day. While the gatekeepers[d] are still on duty, have them shut and bar the doors. Also, appoint guards from among those who live in Jerusalem. Station some at their watch posts and some in front of their own houses."

Nehemiah registers the families

[4]Now although the city was wide and large, only a few people were living within it, and no[e] houses had been rebuilt. [5]My God then prompted me to assemble the officials, the officers, and the people so that they could be registered by families. I found the record of the families who were the first to return, and I found the following written in it:

> [6]These are the people of the province who returned from the captivity of those exiles whom Babylon's King Nebuchadnezzar had taken into exile. They all returned to Jerusalem and Judah, everyone to their own town.
>
> [7]They came with Zerubbabel, Jeshua, Nehemiah, Azariah, Raamiah, Naha-

[a]Or *Gashmu* [b]August–September [c]Or *He* [d]Or *while they* [e]Or *not enough*

mani, Mordecai, Bilshan, Mispereth,
Bigvai, Nehum, and Baanah.
The number of the people of Israel:

8 The family of Parosh	2,172
9 of Shephatiah	372
10 of Arah	652
11 of Pahath-moab, that is, of the descendants of Jeshua and Joab	2,818
12 of Elam	1,254
13 of Zattu	845
14 of Zaccai	760
15 of Binnui	648
16 of Bebai	628
17 of Azgad	2,322
18 of Adonikam	667
19 of Bigvai	2,067
20 of Adin	655
21 of Ater, that is, of the descendants of Hezekiah	98
22 of Hashum	328
23 of Bezai	324
24 of Hariph	112
25 of Gibeon	95
26 The people of Bethlehem and Netophah	188
27 of Anathoth	128
28 of Beth-azmaveth	42
29 of Kiriath-jearim, Chephirah, and Beeroth	743
30 of Ramah and Geba	621
31 of Michmas	122
32 of Bethel and Ai	123
33 of the other Nebo	52
34 the inhabitants of the other Elam	1,254
35 of Harim	320
36 of Jericho	345
37 of Lod, Hadid, and Ono	721
38 of Senaah	3,930
39 The priests: the descendants of Jedaiah, that is, of the house of Jeshua	973
40 of Immer	1,052
41 of Pashhur	1,247
42 of Harim	1,017
43 The Levites: the descendants of Jeshua, that is, of Kadmiel, of the descendants of Hodaviah	74
44 The singers: the descendants of Asaph	148
45 The descendants of gatekeepers: of Shallum, Ater, Talmon, Akkub, Hatita, and Shobai	138

46 The temple servants: the descendants of Ziha, Hasupha, Tabbaoth,
47 Keros, Sia, Padon,
48 Lebanah, Hagabah, Shalmai,
49 Hanan, Giddel, Gahar,
50 Reaiah, Rezin, Nekoda,
51 Gazzam, Uzza, Paseah,
52 Besai, Meunim, Nephushesim,
53 Bakbuk, Hakupha, Harhur,
54 Bazlith, Mehida, Harsha,
55 Barkos, Sisera, Temah,
56 Neziah, and Hatipha.

57 The descendants of Solomon's
servants: Sotai, Sophereth, Perida,
58 Jaala, Darkon, Giddel, 59 Shephatiah, Hattil, Pochereth-hazzebaim, and
Amon.

60 All of the temple servants and the
descendants of Solomon's servants totaled 392.

61 The following came up from Tel-
Melah, Tel-harsha, Cherub, Addon, and
Immer, but were unable to prove that
their family or their descent was from
Israel:

62 the descendants of Delaiah, Tobiah,
and Nekoda, 642.

63 And of the priests: the descendants
of Hobaiah, Hakkoz, and Barzillai (who
had married one of the daughters of Barzillai the Gileadite and was called by his[f]
name) 64 looked for their entries in the
genealogical records, but they weren't
found there, so they were excluded from
the priesthood as unclean.

65 The governor ordered that they
shouldn't eat of the most holy food until
a priest arose who could consult Urim
and Thummim.

66 The whole assembly together totaled 42,360. 67 This number doesn't
include their 7,337 male and female
servants; they also had 245 male
and female singers, 68 736 horses,

[f] Or *their*

245 mules,[g] 69[h]435 camels, and 6,720
donkeys.

70[i]Some of the heads of families made
a donation for the work. The governor
gave to the treasury 1,000 darics of gold,
50 bowls, and 530 priestly robes. 71Some
of the heads of families gave 20,000 darics of gold and 2,200 manehs of silver
to the treasury for the work. 72The rest
of the people gave 20,000 darics of gold,
2,000 manehs of silver, and 67 priestly
robes.

73So the priests, the Levites, the gatekeepers, the singers, some of the people,
the temple servants, and all Israel settled in
their towns.

Ezra reads the Instruction aloud

When the seventh month[j] came and the
people of Israel were settled in their towns,
8 all the people gathered together in the
area in front of the Water Gate. They
asked Ezra the scribe to bring out the Instruction[k] scroll from Moses, according to
which the LORD had instructed Israel.

2So on the first day of the seventh
month, Ezra the priest brought the Instruction before the assembly. This assembly was made up of both men and women
and anyone who could understand what
they heard. 3Facing the area in front of the
Water Gate, he read it aloud, from early
morning until the middle of the day. He
read it in the presence of the men and the
women and those who could understand,
and everyone listened attentively to the
Instruction scroll.

4Ezra the scribe stood on a wooden
platform that had been made for this purpose. And standing beside him were Mattithiah, Shema, Anaiah, Uriah, Hilkiah,
and Maaseiah on his righthand side; while
Pedaiah, Mishael, Malchijah, Hashum, Hash-
baddanah, Zechariah, and Meshullam
stood on his lefthand side.

5Standing above all of the people, Ezra
the scribe opened the scroll in the sight of
all of the people. And as he opened it, all of
the people stood up. 6Then Ezra blessed the
LORD, the great God, and all of the people
answered, "Amen! Amen!" while raising
their hands. Then they bowed down and
worshipped the LORD with their faces to
the ground.

7The Levites—Jeshua, Bani, Sherebiah,
Jamin, Akkub, Shabbethai, Hodiah, Maaseiah, Kelita, Azariah, Jozabad, Hanan, and
Pelaiah[l]—helped the people to understand
the Instruction while the people remained
in their places. 8They read aloud from the
scroll, the Instruction from God, explaining and interpreting it so the people could
understand what they heard.

9Then Nehemiah the governor, Ezra
the priest and scribe, and the Levites who
taught the people said to all of the people,
"This day is holy to the LORD your God.
Don't mourn or weep." They said this[m] because all the people wept when they heard
the words of the Instruction.

10"Go, eat rich food, and drink something sweet," he said to them, "and send
portions of this to any who have nothing
ready! This day is holy to our LORD. Don't
be sad, because the joy from the LORD is
your strength!"

11The Levites also calmed all of the people,
saying, "Be quiet, for this day is holy. Don't
be sad!" 12Then all of the people went to eat
and to drink, to send portions, and to have
a great celebration, because they understood
what had been said to them.

The people celebrate the Festival of Booths

13On the second day, the heads of the
families of all the people, along with the
priests and the Levites, gathered together
around Ezra the scribe in order to study the
words of the Instruction. 14And they found
written in the Instruction that the LORD
had commanded through Moses that the
Israelites should live in booths during the
festival of the seventh month.[n]

15They also found that they should
make the following proclamation and an-

[g]Ezra 2:66; MT lacks *they also . . . mules.* [h]7:68 in Heb [i]7:69 in Heb [j]September–October, Tishrei [k]Heb *Torah*
[l]Vulg 1 Esdr 9:48; MT *and the Levites* [m]Heb lacks *They said this.* [n]September–October, Tishrei

nounce it throughout their towns and in Jerusalem: "Go out to the hills and bring branches of olive, wild olive, myrtle, palm, and other leafy trees to make booths, as it is written."

16 So the people went out and brought them, and made booths for themselves, each on the roofs of their houses or[o] their courtyards, in the courtyards of God's house, in the area by the Water Gate, or in the area by the Gate of Ephraim.

17 The whole assembly of those who had returned from captivity made booths and lived in them. This was something that the people of Israel hadn't done since the days of Joshua,[p] Nun's son, and there was very great rejoicing.

18 He read from God's Instruction scroll every day, from the first until the last day of the festival.[q] They kept the festival for seven days and held a solemn assembly on the eighth day, just as the Instruction required.

Remembering the LORD's mighty deeds

9 On the twenty-fourth day of this month, the people of Israel were assembled. They fasted, wore funeral clothing,[r] and had dirt on their heads.[s] 2 After the Israelites separated themselves from all of the foreigners, they stood to confess their sins and the terrible behavior of their ancestors. 3 They stood in their place and read the Instruction scroll from the LORD their God for a quarter of the day. For another quarter of the day, they confessed and worshipped the LORD their God.

4 On the stairs of the Levites stood Jeshua, Bani, Kadmiel, Shebaniah, Bunni, Sherebiah, Bani, and Chenani. They cried out with a loud voice to the LORD their God. 5 Then the Levites—Jeshua, Kadmiel, Bani, Hashabneiah, Sherebiah, Hodiah, Shebaniah, and Pethahiah—said:

Stand up and bless the LORD your God.
From everlasting to everlasting
bless your glorious name,
which is high above
all blessing and praise.
6 You alone are the LORD.
You alone made heaven,
even the heaven of heavens,
with all their forces.
You made the earth and all that is on
it, and the seas and all that is in them.
You preserve them all,
and the heavenly forces worship you.
7 LORD God, you are the one
who chose Abram.
You brought him out
of Ur of the Chaldeans
and gave him the name Abraham.
8 You found him to be faithful
before you,
and you made a covenant with him.
You promised to give to his descendants
the land of the Canaanites, the Hittites,
the Amorites, the Perizzites,
the Jebusites, and the Girgashites.
And you have kept your promise
because you are righteous.

9 You saw the affliction
of our ancestors in Egypt
and heard their cry at the Reed Sea.[t]
10 You performed signs and wonders
against Pharaoh,
all his servants,
and the people of his land.
You knew that they had acted
arrogantly against our ancestors.
You made a name for yourself,
a name that is famous even today.
11 You divided the sea before them so that
they went through it on dry land.
But you cast their pursuers
into the depths,
as a stone into the mighty waters.
12 With a pillar of cloud
you led them by day
and with a column of lightning
by night;
they lit the way
in which the people should go.
13 You came down upon Mount Sinai
and spoke with them from heaven.
You gave them proper judgments
and true Instruction,
good statutes and commandments.

[o]Or *and* [p]Heb *Jeshua* [q]Heb lacks *of the festival.* [r]Or *sackcloth* [s]Or *on them* [t]Or *Red Sea*

14 You made known to them
your holy Sabbath,
and gave them commandments,
statutes, and Instruction
through your servant Moses.
15 When they were hungry,
you gave them bread from heaven;
when they were thirsty, you brought
water out of the rock for them.
You told them to go in to possess
the land that you had sworn
to give them.

16 But our ancestors acted arrogantly.
They were stubborn and wouldn't
obey your commandments.
17 They refused to obey,
and didn't remember the wonders
that you accomplished
in their midst.
They acted arrogantly and decided
to return to their slavery in Egypt.
But you are a God ready to forgive,
merciful and compassionate,
very patient, and truly faithful.
You didn't forsake them.
18 Even when they had cast
an image of a calf for themselves,
saying, "This is your God
who brought you up out of Egypt,"
and holding you in great contempt,
19 you, in your great mercy, didn't
abandon them in the wilderness.
The column of cloud continued
to guide them on their journey
during the day,
and the column of lightning
lit their path during the night.
20 You gave your good spirit
to teach them.
You didn't withhold your manna
from them,
and you gave them water
for their thirst.
21 You kept them alive for forty years—
they lacked nothing
in the wilderness!
Their clothes didn't wear out,
and their feet didn't swell.

22 You gave them kingdoms and peoples,
and assigned to them every side.[u]
They took possession of the land
of King Sihon of Heshbon
and the land of King Og of Bashan.
23 You multiplied their descendants
as the stars of heaven.
You brought them into the land
that you had told their ancestors
to enter and possess.
24 So the descendants went in
and possessed the land.
Before them, you subdued the
Canaanites who inhabited the land.
You also handed over to them their
kings and the neighboring peoples,
to do with as they wished.
25 They captured fortified cities
and productive land,
and took possession of houses filled
with all kinds of good things:
Excavated cisterns, vineyards,
olive orchards,
and a great many fruit trees.
They ate until they were satisfied
and grew fat,
and delighted themselves
in your great goodness.

26 But they were disobedient,
rebelled against you,
and turned their back
on your Instruction.
They killed your prophets
who had warned them
so that they might return to you.
They held you in great contempt.
27 Therefore, you handed them over
to the power of their enemies
who made them suffer.
But when they cried out to you
in their suffering,
you heard them from heaven.
Because you are merciful,
you gave them saviors
who saved them
from the power of their enemies.
28 But after they had rest from this, they
again started doing evil against you.

[u] Heb uncertain

So you gave them over
to the power of their enemies
who ruled over them.
Yet when they turned and cried to you,
you heard from heaven
and rescued them many times
because of your great mercy.
29 You also warned them
to return to your Instruction,
but they acted arrogantly
and didn't obey your commands.
They sinned against your judgments,
even though life comes
by keeping them.[v]
They turned a stubborn shoulder,
became headstrong,
and wouldn't obey.
30 You were patient with them
for many years
and warned them by your spirit
through the prophets.
But they wouldn't listen,
so you handed them over
to the neighboring peoples.
31 In your great mercy, however,
you didn't make an end of them.
Neither did you forsake them,
because you are a merciful and
compassionate God.

32 Now, our God,
great and mighty and awesome God,
you are the one who faithfully
keeps the covenant.
Don't treat lightly all of the hardship
that has come upon us,
upon our kings, our officials,
our priests, our prophets,
our ancestors, and all your people,
from the time of the kings of Assyria
until today.
33 You have been just in all
that has happened to us;
you have acted faithfully,
and we have done wrong.
34 Our kings, our officials, our priests,
and our ancestors
haven't kept your Instruction.
They haven't heeded your
commandments and the warnings
that you gave them.
35 Even in their own kingdom,
surrounded by the great goodness
that you gave to them,
even in the wide and rich land
that you gave them,
they didn't serve you or turn
from their wicked works.
36 So now today we are slaves,
slaves in the land
that you gave to our ancestors
to enjoy its fruit and its good gifts.
37 Its produce profits the kings whom you
have placed over us because of our sins.
They have power over our bodies and
do as they please with our livestock.
We are in great distress.

Commitment to follow the Instruction

38[w] Because of all this,[x] we are making a
firm agreement in writing, with the names
of our officials, our Levites, and our priests
on the seal.

10 [y]Upon the seals are the names of Governor Nehemiah, Hacaliah's son, and
Zedekiah;
2 Seraiah, Azariah, Jeremiah,
3 Pashhur, Amariah, Malchijah,
4 Hattush, Shebaniah, Malluch,
5 Harim, Meremoth, Obadiah,
6 Daniel, Ginnethon, Baruch,
7 Meshullam, Abijah, Mijamin,
8 Maaziah, Bilgai, Shemaiah;
these are the priests.

9 The Levites: Jeshua, Azaniah's son;
Binnui of the descendants of Henadad;
Kadmiel; 10 and their associates:
Shebaniah, Hodiah, Kelita,
Pelaiah, Hanan,
11 Mica, Rehob, Hashabiah,
12 Zaccur, Sherebiah, Shebaniah,
13 Hodiah, Bani, Beninu.

14 The leaders of the people: Parosh,
Pahath-moab, Elam, Zattu, Bani,
15 Bunni, Azgad, Bebai,
16 Adonijah, Bigvai, Adin,

[v] *Them* refers to judgments. [w] 10:1 in Heb [x] *This* refers to *great distress* in 9:37. [y] 10:2 in Heb

17 Ater, Hezekiah, Azzur,
18 Hodiah, Hashum, Bezai,
19 Hariph, Anathoth, Nebai,
20 Magpiash, Meshullam, Hezir,
21 Meshezabel, Zadok, Jaddua,
22 Pelatiah, Hanan, Anaiah,
23 Hoshea, Hananiah, Hasshub,
24 Hallohesh, Pilha, Shobek,
25 Rehum, Hashabnah, Maaseiah,
26 Ahiah, Hanan, Anan,
27 Malluch, Harim, Baanah.

28 The rest of the people, the priests, the Levites, the gatekeepers, the singers, the temple servants, and all who have separated themselves from the neighboring peoples to follow the Instruction from God, together with their wives, their sons, their daughters, and all who have knowledge and understanding. 29 They join with their officials and relatives, and make a solemn pledge to live by God's Instruction, which was given by Moses, God's servant, and to observe faithfully all the commandments, judgments, and statutes of our LORD God.

30 We won't give our daughters in marriage to the neighboring peoples, nor take their daughters in marriage for our sons.

31 If the neighboring peoples bring merchandise or any grain to sell on the Sabbath, we won't buy it from them on the Sabbath or on any holy day.

Every seventh year we won't plant crops, and we will return anything held in debt.

32 We pledge ourselves to keep the commandment and pay one-third of a shekel each year for the service of our God's house, 33 for the stacks of bread and the regular grain offering and the regular entirely burned offering, for the sabbaths and the new moons and the appointed festivals, for the holy offerings and the purification offerings to make reconciliation for Israel, and for all the work of our God's house.

34 We have also cast lots among the priests, the Levites, and the people so that we bring the wood offering into our God's house by families at the appointed times every year, to burn on the altar of the LORD our God, as it is written in the Instruction.

35 We will also bring the early produce of our soil and the early fruit from all trees every year to the LORD's house.

36 We will also bring the oldest offspring of our children and our cattle, as it is written in the Instruction, and the oldest males of our herds and flocks to our God's house, to the priests who serve in our God's house.

37 We will also bring the first of our dough, our contributions, the fruit of every tree, the wine, and the oil to the priests at the storerooms of our God's house. We will also bring one-tenth of the produce of our soil to the Levites, for it is the Levites who collect the tenth-part gifts in all the towns where we work.

38 A priest from the family of Aaron must be with the Levites when they collect the tenth-part gifts. Then the Levites must bring up one-tenth of the tenth-part gifts to our God's house, to the storerooms of the treasury. 39 The Israelites and the Levites must bring the contribution of grain, wine, and oil to the storerooms where the sanctuary equipment is kept, and where the priests on duty, the gatekeepers, and the singers reside. We won't neglect our God's house!

Inhabitants of Jerusalem

11 The leaders of the people lived in Jerusalem. The rest of the people cast lots to bring one out of ten to live in the holy city of Jerusalem, while the remaining nine stayed in the other towns. 2 The people blessed those who agreed to live in Jerusalem.

3 These are the leaders of the province who lived in Jerusalem; while the Israelites, the priests, the Levites, the temple servants, and the descendants of Solomon's servants lived in the towns of Judah on their own property in their towns. 4 Some of the descendants of Judah and Benjamin settled in Jerusalem.

From the family of Judah: Athaiah son of Uzziah son of Zechariah son of Amariah son of Shephatiah son of Mahalalel of the family of Perez; [5]and Maaseiah son of Baruch son of Col-hozeh son of Hazaiah son of Adaiah son of Joiarib son of Zechariah son of the Shilonite. [6]All of the family of Perez who lived in Jerusalem totaled 468 courageous people.

[7]From the family of Benjamin: Sallu son of Meshullam son of Joed son of Pedaiah son of Kolaiah son of Maaseiah son of Ithiel son of Jeshaiah. [8]And after him were Gabbai and Sallai: 928. [9]Joel son of Zichri was their supervisor, and Judah son of Hassenuah was second in charge of the city.

[10]Of the priests: Jedaiah son of Joiarib, Jachin, [11]Seraiah son of Hilkiah son of Meshullam son of Zadok son of Meraioth son of Ahitub the officer of God's house, [12]and their associates who carried out the work in the temple:[z] 822. There was also Adaiah son of Jeroham son of Pelaliah son of Amzi son of Zechariah son of Pashhur son of Malchijah, [13]and his associates, heads of families: 242. There was also Amashsai son of Azarel son of Ahzai son of Meshillemoth son of Immer [14]and their associates, for a total of 128 courageous people. Their supervisor was Zabdiel, Haggedolim's son.

[15]Of the Levites: Shemaiah son of Hasshub son of Azrikam son of Hashabiah son of Bunni; [16]as well as Shabbethai and Jozabad, who were some of the leaders of the Levites in charge of the outside work on God's house; [17]also Mattaniah son of Mica son of Zabdi son of Asaph the leader who began the thanksgiving with prayer, and Bakbukiah, who was the second among his associates; and Abda son of Shammua son of Galal son of Jeduthun. [18]All the Levites in the holy city totaled 284. [19]The gatekeepers: Akkub, Talmon, and their associates who guarded the gates totaled 172. [20]The rest of Israel, the priests, and the Levites were in all the towns of Judah, each of them in their own property. [21]But the temple servants lived in Ophel, with Ziha and Gishpa in charge of them. [22]The supervisor of the Levites in Jerusalem was Uzzi son of Bani son of Hashabiah son of Mattaniah son of Mica, from the family of Asaph, who were the singers in charge of the work of God's house.

[23]There was a command from the king setting out the daily requirements of the singers.

[24]Advising the king in all matters concerning the people was Pethahiah, Meshezabel's son, from the family of Zerah, Judah's son.

[25]As for the villages with their fields, some of the people of Judah lived in Kiriath-arba and its villages, in Dibon and its villages, in Jekabzeel and its villages, [26]in Jeshua, in Moladah and Beth-pelet, [27]in Hazar-shual, in Beer-sheba and its villages, [28]in Ziklag, in Meconah and its villages, [29]in En-rimmon, Zorah, Jarmuth, [30]Zanoah, Adullam, and their villages, Lachish and its fields, and Azekah and its villages. So they settled from Beer-sheba to the Hinnom Valley.

[31]The people of Benjamin also lived from beyond Geba, at Michmash, Aija, Bethel and its villages, [32]Anathoth, Nob, Ananiah, [33]Hazor, Ramah, Gittaim, [34]Hadid, Zeboim, Neballat, [35]Lod, and Ono, the valley of artisans. [36]Some divisions of the Levites in Judah were joined to Benjamin.

12 These are the priests and the Levites who came up with Zerubbabel son of Shealtiel and Jeshua: Seraiah, Jeremiah, Ezra, [2]Amariah, Malluch, Hattush, [3]Shecaniah, Rehum, Meremoth, [4]Iddo, Ginnethon,[a] Abijah, [5]Mijamin, Maadiah, Bilgah, [6]Shemaiah, Joiarib, Jedaiah, [7]Sallu, Amok, Hilkiah, Jedaiah.

These were the leaders of the priests and of their associates in the days of Jeshua. [8]The Levites: Jeshua, Binnui, Kadmiel, Sherebiah, Judah, and also Mattaniah, who was in charge of the thanksgiving songs along with his associates. [9]Bakbukiah and Unn and their associates stood opposite them in the service.

[10]Jeshua was the father of Joiakim, Joiakim the father of Eliashib, Eliashib the father of Joiada, [11]Joiada the father of Jonathan, and Jonathan the father of Jaddua.

[z]Or *house* [a]Heb *Ginnethoi*

12 These were the heads of the priestly families in the days of Joiakim: of Seraiah, Meraiah; of Jeremiah, Hananiah; 13 of Ezra, Meshullam; of Amariah, Jehohanan; 14 of Malluch,[b] Jonathan; of Shebaniah, Joseph; 15 of Harim, Adna; of Meraioth, Helkai; 16 of Iddo, Zechariah; of Ginnethon, Meshullam; 17 of Abijah, Zichri; of Miniamin, of Moadiah, Piltai; 18 of Bilgah, Shammua; of Shemaiah, Jehonathan; 19 of Joiarib, Mattenai; of Jedaiah, Uzzi; 20 of Sallai, Kallai; of Amok, Eber; 21 of Hilkiah, Hashabiah; of Jedaiah, Nethanel.

22 In the days of Eliashib, Joiada, Johanan, and Jaddua, the Levites and the priests were recorded as heads of families in the rule of[c] Darius the Persian.

23 The Levites who were heads of families were recorded in the official records until the time of Johanan, Eliashib's son. 24 These were the leaders of the Levites: Hashabiah, Sherebiah, and Jeshua, Kadmiel's son, and their associates who stood opposite them to praise and give thanks in turn according to the commandment of David, the man of God, namely, 25 Mattaniah, Bakbukiah, and Obadiah.

Meshullam, Talmon, and Akkub were gatekeepers standing guard by the storerooms of the gates. 26 These served in the days of Joiakim, Jeshua's son and Jozadak's grandson, and in the days of Governor Nehemiah and of Ezra the priest and scribe.

Dedication of the wall

27 When it was time for the dedication of Jerusalem's wall, they sought out the Levites in all the places where they lived in order to bring them to Jerusalem to celebrate the dedication with joy, with thanks and singing, and with cymbals, harps, and lyres.

28 The singers also gathered together both from the region around Jerusalem and from the villages of the Netophathites, 29 also from Beth-hagilgal and from the region of Geba and Azmaveth, because the singers had built themselves villages around Jerusalem. 30 After the priests and the Levites purified themselves, they purified the people, the gates, and the wall.

31 Then I[d] brought the leaders of Judah up onto the wall and organized two large groups to give thanks. The first group went in procession on the wall toward the right, in the direction of the Dung Gate. 32 Following them went Hoshaiah and half the officials of Judah, 33 along with Azariah, Ezra, Meshullam, 34 Judah, Benjamin, Shemaiah, and Jeremiah. 35 There were also some young priests with trumpets—Zechariah son of Jonathan son of Shemaiah son of Mattaniah son of Micaiah son of Zaccur son of Asaph— 36 along with his associates Shemaiah, Azarel, Milalai, Gilalai, Maai, Nethanel, Judah, and Hanani. They brought[e] the musical instruments of David the man of God. Ezra the scribe went in front of them.

37 When they reached the Fountain Gate they went straight up by the stairs of David's City, on the ascent to the wall, past the house of David to the Water Gate on the east. 38 The second group went in procession to the left.[f] I followed them with half of the people along the wall past the Tower of the Ovens to the Broad Wall, 39 past the Gate of Ephraim and over the Mishneh Gate,[g] the Fish Gate, the Tower of Hananel, and the Tower of the Hundred as far as the Sheep Gate. They came to stop at the Gate of the Guard.

In God's house

40 Then both groups of those who gave thanks stood in God's house. I was there too along with the half of the officials who were with me. 41 Also there were the priests Eliakim, Maaseiah, Miniamin, Micaiah, Elioenai, Zechariah, and Hananiah with trumpets. 42 Also there were Maaseiah, Shemaiah, Eleazar, Uzzi, Jehohanan, Malchijah, Elam, and Ezer. The singers sang with Jezrahiah as their leader.

43 They offered great sacrifices on that day and rejoiced, for God had made them rejoice with great joy. The women and children also rejoiced, and the sound of the joy in Jerusalem could be heard from far away.

[b]LXX; MT *Malluchi* [c]LXX, Vulg; MT *upon* [d]Or *I, Nehemiah* [e]Heb lacks *they brought.* [f]Or *opposite* [g]Or *Old Gate*

44 On that day, people were appointed
over the rooms for the things to be stored,
the contributions, the early produce, and
the tenth-part gifts. They were to gather
into them the portions required by the Instruction for the priests and for the Levites
from the fields belonging to the towns, for
the people of Judah were delighted with
the ministry of the priests and the Levites.
45 They performed the service of their God
and the service of purification, as did the
singers and the gatekeepers, according to the
command of David and his son Solomon.
46 Long ago, in the days of David and
Asaph, there was a leader of the singers,
and there were songs of praise and thanks
to God.
47 In the days of Zerubbabel and of Nehemiah all Israel gave the daily portions for
the singers and the gatekeepers. They also
set aside the portion for the Levites, and
the Levites set aside the portion for the
Aaronites.

Restoring the temple

13 On that day, when the scroll from
Moses was being read to the people,
they found written in it that no Ammonite
or Moabite should ever enter God's assembly. 2 This is because they hadn't met the
Israelites with food and water but instead
hired Balaam against them to curse them.
Yet our God turned the curse into a blessing. 3 When the people heard this law, they
separated out from Israel all those of mixed
descent.
4 Now before this, however, Eliashib the
priest, who was appointed to be in charge
of the storerooms of our God's house and
who was related to Tobiah, 5 prepared a
large room for Tobiah to use. This was the
room where they had previously kept the
grain offering, the incense, and the equipment, together with the tenth-part gifts
of grain, wine, and oil. These items were
for the Levites, singers, and gatekeepers as
well as the portions for the priests.
6 I wasn't in Jerusalem while this was happening because I had gone to Babylon's King
Artaxerxes in the thirty-second year of the
king. After some time, I asked the king's permission 7 and returned to Jerusalem. That
was when I saw the wrong that Eliashib had
done on behalf of Tobiah by preparing him
a room in the courtyards of God's house.
8 I was very angry and threw all of Tobiah's
household furniture out of the room. 9 Then
I gave orders that the rooms be purified, and
I put back the temple equipment, along with
the grain offering and the incense.
10 I also found out that the Levites hadn't
been given their portions, so they and the
singers who did the work had gone back to
their fields. 11 So I scolded the officials, asking, "Why is God's house being neglected?"
I gathered them together and set them in
their stations.
12 Then all Judah brought the tenth-part
gifts of the grain, wine, and oil into the
storehouses. 13 I appointed the priest Shelemiah, the scribe Zadok, and Pedaiah of the
Levites to be in charge over the storehouses.
I also appointed Hanan, Zaccur's son and
Mattaniah's grandson, as their assistant.
These men were considered trustworthy,
and their task was to hand out shares to
their colleagues.
14 Remember me, my God, concerning
this. Don't erase my good deeds that I have
done for my God's house and for its services.

Keeping the Sabbath

15 In those days I saw people in Judah
using the winepresses on the Sabbath.
They were also collecting piles of grain
and loading them on donkeys, as well as
wine, grapes, figs, and every kind of load,
and then bringing them to Jerusalem on
the Sabbath. I warned them at that time
against selling food.
16 In addition, people from Tyre who
lived in the city were bringing in fish and
all kinds of merchandise and selling them
to the people of Judah on the Sabbath. This
happened in Jerusalem itself!
17 So I scolded the officials of Judah: "What
is this evil thing that you are doing?" I asked.
"You are making the Sabbath impure! 18 This
is just what your ancestors did, and God
brought all this evil upon us and upon this
city. And now you are bringing more wrath
upon Israel by making the Sabbath impure!"

19 So when it began to grow dark at the gates of Jerusalem before the Sabbath, I gave orders that the doors should be shut. I also ordered that they shouldn't be reopened until after the Sabbath. To make sure that no load would come into the city[h] on the Sabbath, I stationed some of my own men at the gates. 20 Once or twice the traders and sellers of all kinds of merchandise spent the night outside Jerusalem. 21 But I warned them: "Why are you spending the night by the wall? If you do that again, I will lay hands on you!" At that point, they stopped coming on the Sabbath. 22 I also commanded the Levites to purify themselves and to come and guard the gates in order to keep the Sabbath day holy.

Remember this also in my favor, my God, and spare me according to the greatness of your mercy.

Marrying foreign women

23 Also in those days I saw Jews who had married women of Ashdod, Ammon, and Moab. 24 Half of their children spoke the language of Ashdod or the language of various peoples; they couldn't speak the language of Judah. 25 So I scolded them and cursed them, and beat some of them, and pulled out their hair. I also made them swear a solemn pledge in the name of God, saying, "You won't give your daughters to their sons in marriage, or take their daughters in marriage for your sons or yourselves. 26 Didn't Israel's King Solomon sin on account of such women? Among the many nations there was no king like him. He was well loved by his God, and God made him king over all Israel. Yet foreign wives led even him into sin! 27 Should we then listen to you and do all this great evil, acting unfaithfully toward our God by marrying foreign women?"

28 Now one of the sons of Joiada son of the high priest Eliashib was a son-in-law of Sanballat the Horonite. So I chased him away from me.

29 Remember them, my God, because they have defiled the priesthood and the covenant of the priests and the Levites!

30 So I purified them of everything foreign and established the services of the priests and Levites with specific duties for each person. 31 I also provided for the wood offering at appointed times as well as for the early produce.

Remember me, my God, for good.

ESTHER

Queen Vashti

1 This is what happened back when Ahasuerus lived, the very Ahasuerus who ruled from India to Cush—one hundred twenty-seven provinces in all. 2 At that time, Ahasuerus ruled the kingdom from his royal throne in the fortified part of Susa. 3 In the third year of his rule he hosted a feast for all his officials and courtiers. The leaders of Persia and Media attended, along with his provincial officials and officers. 4 He showed off the awesome riches of his kingdom and beautiful treasures as mirrors of how very great he was. The event lasted a long time—six whole months, to be exact! 5 After that the king held a seven-day feast for everyone in the fortified part of Susa. Whether they were important people in the town or not, they all met in the walled garden of the royal palace. 6 White linen curtains and purple hangings were held up by shining white and red-purple ropes tied to silver rings and marble posts. Gold and silver couches sat on a mosaic floor made of gleaming purple crystal, marble, and mother-of-pearl. 7 They served the drinks in cups made of gold, and each cup was different. The king made sure there was plenty of royal wine. 8 The rule about the drinks was "No limits!" The king had ordered everyone serving wine in the palace to offer as much as each guest wanted. 9 At the same time, Queen Vashti held a feast for women in King Ahasuerus' palace.

[h] Heb lacks *the city*.

10 On the seventh day, when wine had
put the king in high spirits, he gave an
order to Mehuman, Biztha, Harbona,
Bigtha, Abagtha, Zethar, and Carcas, the
seven eunuchs who served King Ahasuerus personally. 11 They were to bring
Queen Vashti before him wearing the royal
crown. She was gorgeous, and he wanted
to show off her beauty both to the general
public and to his important guests. 12 But
Queen Vashti refused to come as the king
had ordered through the eunuchs. The
king was furious, his anger boiling inside. 13 Now, when a need arose, the king
would often talk with certain very smart
people about the best way to handle it.
They were people who knew both the kingdom's written laws and what judges had
decided about cases in the past. 14 The ones
he talked with most often were Carsh-
ena, Shethar, Admatha, Tarshish, Meres,
Marsena, and Memucan. They were seven
very important people in Persia and Media
who, as the kingdom's highest leaders,
were in the king's inner circle. So the king
said to them, 15 "According to the law, what
should I do with Queen Vashti since she
didn't do what King Ahasuerus ordered
her through the eunuchs?"

16 Then Memucan spoke up in front of
the king and the officials. "Queen Vashti,"
he said, "has done something wrong not
just to the king himself. She has also done
wrong to all the officials and the peoples
in all the provinces of King Ahasuerus.
17 This is the reason: News of what the
queen did will reach all women, making
them look down on their husbands. They
will say, 'King Ahasuerus ordered servants
to bring Queen Vashti before him, but she
refused to come.' 18 This very day, the important women of Persia and Media who
hear about the queen will tell the royal officials the same thing. There will be no end
of put-downs and arguments. 19 Now, if the
king wishes, let him send out a royal order
and have it written into the laws of Persia
and Media, laws no one can ever change.
It should say that Vashti will never again
come before King Ahasuerus. It should
also say that the king will give her royal
place to someone better than she. 20 When
the order becomes public through the
whole empire, vast as it is, all women will
treat their husbands properly. The rule
should touch everyone, whether from an
important family or not."

21 The king liked the plan, as did the other
men, and he did just what Memucan said.
22 He sent written orders to all the king's
provinces. Each province received it written
in its own alphabet and each people received
it in its own language. It said that each husband should rule over his own house.

Finding a new queen

2 Sometime later when King Ahasuerus
was less angry, he remembered Vashti,
what she had done, and what he had decided about her. 2 So his young male servants said, "Let the king have a search made
for beautiful young women who haven't yet
married. 3 And let the king choose certain
people in all the royal provinces to lead
the search. Have them bring all the beautiful young women together to the fortified part of Susa, to the women's house,
to the care of Hegai the king's eunuch in
charge of the women so that he might provide beauty treatments for them. 4 Let the
young woman who pleases you the most
take Vashti's place as queen." The king liked
the plan and implemented it.

5 Now there was a Jew in the fortified
part of Susa whose name was Mordecai,
Jair's son. He came from the family line
of Shimei and Kish; he was a Benjaminite.
(6 Benjaminites had been taken into exile
away from Jerusalem along with the group,
which included Judah's King Jeconiah,
whom Babylon's King Nebuchadnezzar exiled to Babylon.) 7 Mordecai had been a father to Hadassah (that is, Esther), though
she was really his cousin, because she had
neither father nor mother. The girl had a
beautiful figure and was lovely to look at.
When her parents died, Mordecai had taken
her to be his daughter. 8 When the king's
order and his new law became public, many
young women were gathered into the fortified part of Susa under the care of Hegai.
Esther was also taken to the palace to the

care of Hegai, the one in charge of the women. [9]The young woman pleased him and won his kindness. He quickly began her beauty treatments and gave her carefully chosen foods. He also gave her seven servants selected from among the palace servants and moved her and her servants into the nicest rooms in the women's house. ([10]Esther hadn't told anyone her race and family background because Mordecai had ordered her not to.) [11]Each day found Mordecai pacing back and forth along the wall in front of the women's house to learn how Esther was doing and what they were doing with her. [12]According to the rules for women, the moment for each young woman to go to King Ahasuerus came at the end of twelve months. (She had six months of treatment with pleasant-smelling creams and six months with fragrant oils and other treatments for women.) [13]So this is how the young woman would go to the king: They gave her anything that she asked to take with her from the women's house to the palace. [14]In the evening she would go in, and the next morning she would return to the second women's house under the care of Shaashgaz. He was the king's eunuch in charge of the secondary wives. She would never go to the king again unless he was so pleased that he called for her by name. [15]Soon the moment came for Esther daughter of Mordecai's uncle Abihail, whom Mordecai had taken as his own daughter, to go to the king. But she asked for nothing except what Hegai the king's eunuch in charge of the women told her. (Esther kept winning the favor of everyone who saw her.)

[16]Esther was taken to King Ahasuerus, to his own palace, in the tenth month (that is, the month of Tevet)[a] in the seventh year of his rule. [17]The king loved Esther more than all the other women; she had won his love and his favor more than all the others. He placed the royal crown on her head and made her ruler in place of Vashti. [18]The king held a magnificent, lavish feast, "the feast of Esther," for all his officials and courtiers. He declared a public holiday[b] for the provinces and gave out gifts with royal generosity. [19]When they gathered the young women to the second women's house,[c] Mordecai was working for the king at the King's Gate. [20]Esther still wasn't telling anyone her family background and race, just as Mordecai had ordered her. She continued to do what Mordecai said, just as she did when she was in his care.

Mordecai saves the king

[21]At that time, as Mordecai continued to work at the King's Gate, two royal eunuchs, Bigthan and Teresh, became angry with King Ahasuerus. They were among the guards protecting the doorway to the king, but they secretly planned to kill him. [22]When Mordecai got wind of it, he reported it to Queen Esther. She spoke to the king about it, saying the information came from Mordecai. [23]The matter was investigated and found to be true, so the two men were impaled on pointed poles.[d] A report about the event was written in the royal record with the king present.

Haman plans to destroy Mordecai

3 Sometime later, King Ahasuerus promoted Haman, Hammedatha the Agagite's son,[e] by promoting him above all the officials who worked with him. [2]All the royal workers at the King's Gate would kneel and bow facedown to Haman because the king had so ordered. But Mordecai didn't kneel or bow down. [3]So the royal workers at the King's Gate said to Mordecai, "Why don't you obey the king's order?" [4]Day after day they questioned him, but he paid no attention to them. So they let Haman know about it just to see whether or not Mordecai's words would hold true.[f] (He had told them that he was a Jew.) [5]When Haman himself saw that Mordecai didn't kneel or bow down to him, he became very angry. [6]But he decided not to kill only Mordecai, for people had told him Mordecai's race. Instead, he planned to wipe out all the

[a]December–January [b]Or *remission of taxes* [c]Or *to the women's house a second time* [d]Or *hanged the two men on gallows* [e]Or *the braggart* [f]Or *stand*

Jews, Mordecai's people, throughout the whole kingdom of Ahasuerus. [7]In the first month (that is, the month of Nisan)[g] in the twelfth year of the rule of King Ahasuerus, servants threw pur, namely, dice, in front of Haman to find the best day for his plan. They tried every day and every month, and the dice chose the thirteenth[h] day of the twelfth month (that is, the month of Adar).

[8]Then Haman said to King Ahasuerus, "A certain group of people exist in pockets among the other peoples in all the provinces of your kingdom. Their laws are different from those of everyone else, and they refuse to obey the king's laws. There's no good reason for the king to put up with them any longer. [9]If the king wishes, let a written order be sent out to destroy them, and I will hand over ten thousand kikkars of silver[i] to those in charge of the king's business. The silver can go into the king's treasuries."

[10]The king removed his royal ring from his finger and handed it to Haman, Hammedatha the Agagite's son, enemy of the Jews. [11]The king said to Haman, "Both the money and the people are under your power. Do as you like with them." [12]So in the first month, on the thirteenth day, royal scribes were summoned to write down everything that Haman ordered. The orders were for the king's rulers and the governors in charge of each province, as well as for the officials of each people. They wrote in the alphabet of each province and in the language of each people. They wrote in the name of King Ahasuerus and sealed the order with the king's royal ring. [13]Fast runners were to take the order to all the provinces of the king. The order commanded people to wipe out, kill, and destroy all the Jews, both young and old, even women and little children. This was to happen on a single day—the thirteenth day of the twelfth month (that is, the month of Adar).[j] They were also to seize their property. [14]A copy of the order was to become law in each province and to be posted in public for all peoples to read. The people were to be ready for this day to do as the order commanded. [15]Driven by the king's order, the runners left Susa just as the law became public in the fortified part of Susa. While the king and Haman sat down to have a drink, the city of Susa was in total shock.

A crisis for the Jews

4 When Mordecai learned what had been done, he tore his clothes, dressed in mourning clothes, and put ashes on his head. Then he went out into the heart of the city and cried out loudly and bitterly. [2]He went only as far as the King's Gate because it was against the law for anyone to pass through it wearing mourning clothes. [3]At the same time, in every province and place where the king's order and his new law arrived, a very great sadness came over the Jews. They gave up eating and spent whole days weeping and crying out loudly in pain. Many Jews lay on the ground in mourning clothes and ashes. [4]When Esther's female servants and eunuchs came and told her about Mordecai, the queen's whole body showed how upset she was. She sent everyday clothes for Mordecai to wear instead of mourning clothes, but he rejected them.

[5]Esther then sent for Hathach, one of the royal eunuchs whose job it was to wait on her. She ordered him to go to Mordecai and find out what was going on and why he was acting this way. [6]Hathach went out to Mordecai, to the city square in front of the King's Gate. [7]Mordecai told him everything that had happened to him. He spelled out the exact amount of silver that Haman promised to pay into the royal treasury. It was in exchange for the destruction of the Jews. [8]He also gave Hathach a copy of the law made public in Susa concerning the Jews' destruction so that Hathach could show it to Esther and report it to her. Through him Mordecai ordered her to go to the king to seek his kindness and his help for her people. [9]Hathach came back and told Esther what Mordecai had said.

[10]In reply Esther ordered Hathach to tell Mordecai: [11]"All the king's officials and the people in his provinces know that there's

[g]March–April [h]See LXX and 3:13. [i]A kikkar weighed approximately seventy-five pounds. [j]February–March

a single law in a case like this. Any man or woman who comes to the king in the inner courtyard without being called is to be put to death. Only the person to whom the king holds out the gold scepter may live. In my case, I haven't been called to come to the king for the past thirty days."

12When they told Mordecai Esther's words, 13he had them respond to Esther: "Don't think for one minute that, unlike all the other Jews, you'll come out of this alive simply because you are in the palace. 14In fact, if you don't speak up at this very important time, relief and rescue will appear for the Jews from another place, but you and your family will die. But who knows? Maybe it was for a moment like this that you came to be part of the royal family."

15Esther sent back this word to Mordecai: 16"Go, gather all the Jews who are in Susa and tell them to give up eating to help me be brave. They aren't to eat or drink anything for three whole days, and I myself will do the same, along with my female servants. Then, even though it's against the law, I will go to the king; and if I am to die, then die I will." 17So Mordecai left where he was and did exactly what Esther had ordered him.

Esther acts

5 Three days later, Esther put on royal clothes and stood in the inner courtyard of the palace, facing the palace itself. At that moment the king was inside sitting on his royal throne and facing the palace doorway. 2When the king noticed Queen Esther standing in the entry court, he was pleased. The king held out to Esther the gold scepter in his hand, and she came forward and touched the scepter's tip.

3Then the king said to her, "What is it, Queen Esther? What do you want? I'll give you anything—even half the kingdom."

4Esther answered, "If the king wishes, please come today with Haman for the feast that I have prepared for him."

5"Hurry, get Haman," the king ordered, "so we can do what Esther says." So the king and Haman came to the feast that Esther had prepared. 6As they sipped wine, the king asked, "Now what is it you wish? I'll give it to you. What do you want? I'll do anything—even give you half the kingdom."

7Esther answered, "This is my wish and this is what I want: 8If I please the king, and if the king wishes to grant my wish and my desire, I'd like the king and Haman to come to another feast that I will prepare for them. Tomorrow I will answer the king's questions."

Haman boasts, complains, and acts

9That day Haman left Esther's place happy, his spirits high, but then he saw Mordecai in the King's Gate. Mordecai neither stood up nor seemed the least bit nervous around him, so Haman suddenly felt great rage toward Mordecai. 10But Haman held himself back and went on home. He sent word that his friends and his wife Zeresh should join him there. 11Haman boasted to them about his great wealth and his many sons. He told all about how the king had honored him by promoting him over the officials and high royal workers. 12"Best of all," Haman said, "Queen Esther has invited no one else but me to join the king for food and drinks that she has prepared. In fact, I've been called to join the king at her place tomorrow! 13But all this loses its meaning every time I see Mordecai the Jew sitting at the King's Gate."

14So his wife Zeresh and all his friends told him: "Have people prepare a pointed pole seventy-five feet high. In the morning, tell the king to have Mordecai impaled on it. Then you can go with the king to the feast in a happy mood." Haman liked the idea and had the pole prepared.

Honor for Mordecai

6 That same night, the king simply couldn't sleep. He had the official royal records brought in, and his young male servants began reading them to the king. 2They came to the report about Mordecai informing on Bigthan and Teresh. (They were the two royal eunuchs among the guards protecting the king's doorway, who secretly planned to kill King Ahasuerus.) 3"What was done to honor and reward Mordecai for this?" the king asked.

His young male servants replied, “Nothing was done for him, sir.”

4 “Who is that out in the courtyard?” the king asked. (Haman had just entered the outer courtyard of the palace. He had come to tell the king to impale Mordecai on the pole that he had set up for him.)

5 The king’s servants answered, “That’s Haman standing out in the courtyard, sir.”

So the king said, “Have him come in.”

6 When Haman entered, the king asked him, “What should be done for the man whom the king really wants to honor?”

Haman thought to himself, Whom would the king really want to honor more than me? 7 So Haman said to the king, “Here’s what should be done for the man the king really wants to honor. 8 Have servants bring out a royal robe that the king himself has worn and a horse on which the king himself has ridden. It should have a royal crest on its head. 9 Then hand over the robe and the horse to another man, one of the king’s officials. Have him personally robe[k] the man whom the king really wants to honor and lead him on the horse through the city square. As he goes, have him shout, ‘This is what the king does for the man he really wants to honor!’”

10 Then the king said to Haman, “Hurry, take the robe and the horse just as you’ve said and do exactly that for Mordecai the Jew, who works at the King’s Gate. Don’t leave out a single thing you’ve said!”

11 So Haman took the robe and the horse and put the robe on Mordecai. He led him on horseback through the city square, shouting as he went, “This is what the king does for the man he really wants to honor!” 12 Afterward, Mordecai returned to the King’s Gate, while Haman hurried home feeling great shame, his head covered.

13 Haman told his wife Zeresh and all his friends everything that had happened to him. Both his friends[l] and his wife said to him, “You’ve already begun to lose out to Mordecai. If he is of Jewish birth, you’ll not be able to win against him. You are surely going to lose out to him.”

Haman’s demise

14 They were still discussing this with him when several royal eunuchs arrived. They quickly hurried Haman off to the feast that Esther had prepared.

7 1 When the king and Haman came in for the banquet with Queen Esther, 2 the king said to her, “This is the second day we’ve met for wine. What is your wish, Queen Esther? I’ll give it to you. And what do you want? I’ll do anything—even give you half the kingdom.”

3 Queen Esther answered, “If I please the king, and if the king wishes, give me my life—that’s my wish—and the lives of my people too. That’s my desire. 4 We have been sold—I and my people—to be wiped out, killed, and destroyed. If we simply had been sold as male and female slaves, I would have said nothing. But no enemy can compensate the king for this kind of damage.”

5 King Ahasuerus said to Queen Esther, “Who is this person, and where is he? Who would dare do such a thing?”

6 Esther replied, “A man who hates, an enemy—this wicked Haman!” Haman was overcome with terror in the presence of the king and queen. 7 Furious, the king got up and left the banquet for the palace garden. But Haman stood up to beg Queen Esther for his life. He saw clearly that the king’s mood meant a bad end for him.

8 The king returned from the palace garden to the banquet room just as Haman was kneeling on the couch where Esther was reclining. “Will you even molest the queen while I am in the house?” the king said. The words had barely left the king’s mouth before covering Haman’s face with dread.[m]

9 Harbona, one of the eunuchs serving the king, said, “Sir, look! There’s the stake that Haman made for Mordecai, the man who spoke up and did something good for the king. It’s standing at Haman’s house—seventy-five feet high.”

“Impale him on it!” the king ordered. 10 So they impaled Haman on the very pole that he had set up for Mordecai, and the king’s anger went away.

[k]LXX sing *robe* and *lead*, cf Heb plural verbs [l]LXX; Heb *wise ones* [m]Or *the face of Haman was covered.*

Esther acts again

8 That same day King Ahasuerus gave Queen Esther what Haman the enemy of the Jews owned. Mordecai himself came before the king because Esther had told the king that he was family to her. 2The king took off his royal ring, the one he had removed from Haman, and gave it to Mordecai. Esther put Mordecai in charge of what Haman had owned.

3Esther again spoke before the king. She bowed at his feet, wept, and begged him to treat her kindly. She wanted him to overturn the evil plot of Haman the Agagite—his secret plan directed against the Jews. 4The king held out the gold scepter to Esther, and she got up and stood before him. 5She said, "If the king wishes, and if I please him—that is, if the idea seems right to the king, and if he still sees me as a good person—then have people write something to call back the order—the order that put into effect the plan of Haman, Hammedatha the Agagite's son, that he wrote to destroy the Jews in all the royal provinces. 6How can I bear to watch the terrible evil about to sweep over my people? And how can I bear to watch others destroy my own family?"

Mordecai writes a new law

7King Ahasuerus said to Queen Esther and to Mordecai the Jew, "Look, I've given Esther everything Haman owned. And Haman himself my servants have impaled on the pole because he planned to attack the Jews. 8So you yourselves write to the Jews whatever you like in the name of the king and seal the letters with the king's royal ring. Anything written in the name of the king and sealed with the king's royal ring can't be called back." 9So that was when the royal scribes were summoned—on the twenty-third day of the third month (that is, the month of Sivan).[n] They wrote exactly what Mordecai ordered to the Jews, rulers, governors, and officials of the provinces from India to Cush—one hundred twenty-seven in all. They wrote in the alphabet of each province and in the language of each people. 10They wrote in the name of King Ahasuerus and sealed the order with the king's royal ring. He sent letters with riders mounted on royal horses bred from mares known to run fast.[o] 11The order allowed Jews in each town to join together and defend their lives. The Jews were free to wipe out, kill, and destroy every army of any people and province that attacked them, along with their women and children. They could also take and keep anything their attackers owned. 12The one day in all the provinces of King Ahasuerus on which they could do so was the thirteenth day of the twelfth month (that is, the month of Adar). 13A copy of the writing was to become law in each province and be on public display for all its peoples to read. The Jews were to be ready on this day to get back at their enemies. 14The riders mounted on royal horses left Susa, spurred on by the king's order, and the law also became public in the fortified part of Susa.

15Mordecai went out from the king's presence in a blue and white royal robe wearing a large gold crown and a white and red-purple coat. The city of Susa greeted him with shouts of joy. 16For the Jews it was a day of light, happiness, joy, and honor. 17In every province and in every town—wherever the king's order and his law arrived—for the Jews it was a day of happiness and joy. For them it meant feasts and a holiday. Many people in the land became Jews themselves, out of fear of the Jews.

The fateful day

9 It was on the thirteenth day of the twelfth month (that is, the month of Adar)[p] that the king's order and his law were to be enforced. On the very day that the enemies of the Jews hoped to overpower them, the tables were turned against them. The Jews overpowered their enemies instead. 2The Jews joined together in their towns in all the provinces of King Ahasuerus to defend themselves against those who tried to harm them. No one was able to stand in their way because everyone

[n] May–June [o] Heb uncertain [p] February–March

was afraid of the Jews. 3All the leaders of the provinces, rulers, governors, and those in charge of the king's business helped the Jews because they were afraid of Mordecai. 4Because Mordecai was very important in the palace, news about him was sweeping through the provinces. Indeed, Mordecai was becoming more and more important every day. 5The Jews put down all their enemies with sword blows, killing, and destruction. They did whatever they wanted with those who hated them. 6In the fortified part of Susa, the Jews killed five hundred people. 7They also killed Parshandatha, Dalphon, Aspatha, 8Poratha, Adalia, Aridatha, 9Parmashta, Arisai, Aridai, and Vaizatha. 10These were the ten sons of Haman, Hammedatha's son, the enemy of the Jews. But the Jews didn't lay a hand on anything their enemies owned. 11That same day, a report concerning the number killed in the fortified part of Susa reached the king.

12So the king said to Queen Esther in the fortified part of Susa, "The Jews have killed five hundred people as well as the ten sons of Haman. What have they done in the rest of the royal provinces? What do you wish now? I'll give it to you. What is your desire? I'll do it this time too."

13Esther answered, "If the king wishes, let the Jews who are in Susa also have tomorrow to do what the law allows for today. And let them also impale the ten sons of Haman on pointed poles." 14The king ordered that this be done, and the law became public in Susa. They impaled the ten sons of Haman just as she said. 15The Jews in Susa joined together again, this time on the fourteenth day of the month of Adar. In Susa, they killed three hundred people, but they didn't lay a hand on anything the people owned.

16The Jews out in the royal provinces also joined together to defend their lives. They put to rest the troubles with their enemies and killed those who hated them. The total was seventy-five thousand dead, but the Jews didn't lay a hand on anything their enemies owned. 17They acted on the thirteenth day of the month of Adar. Then on the fourteenth day they rested, making it a day of feasts and rejoicing. (18The Jews in Susa joined together for self-defense on the thirteenth and fourteenth days of the month. But they rested on the fifteenth day of the month and made it a day of feasts and joyous events.) 19That is why Jews who live in villages make the fourteenth day of the month of Adar a day of rejoicing and feasts, a holiday. It is a day on which they send gifts of food to each other.

The new holiday of Purim

20Mordecai wrote these things down and sent letters to all the Jews in all the provinces, both near and far, of King Ahasuerus. 21He made it a rule that Jews keep the fourteenth and fifteenth days of the month of Adar as special days each and every year. 22They are the days on which the Jews finally put to rest the troubles with their enemies. The month is the one when everything turned around for them from sadness to joy, and from sad, loud crying to a holiday. They are to make them days of feasts and joyous events, days to send food gifts to each other and money gifts to the poor. 23The Jews agreed to continue what they had already begun to do—just what Mordecai had written to them. 24Indeed, Haman, Hammedatha the Agagite's son, the enemy of all the Jews, had planned to destroy the Jews. He had servants throw pur (that is, the dice) to find the best month and day to trouble greatly and destroy them. 25But when Esther came before the king, his written order said: The wicked plan that Haman made against the Jews should turn back on him instead. So they impaled him and his sons on pointed poles. 26That is why people call these days Purim, by using the ancient word *pur*. It all fit with what this letter said, with what they saw happen, and with what they themselves went through. 27The Jews agreed that they, their children, grandchildren, and great-grandchildren, as well as all non-Jews who become Jews, should always keep these two days. They agreed to follow the written rules—and at the proper time too—every year. 28So forever every family, province, and town remembers to keep these days. These days of Purim won't die out among the Jews. They will remember to keep them forever. [29]Queen Esther daughter of Abihail, along with Mordecai the Jew, wrote with her full royal power to show that this second letter about Purim was correct.[q] [30]Letters conveying good wishes and words of friendship were sent to all the Jews throughout the one hundred twenty-seven provinces in the kingdom of Ahasuerus. [31]Their aim was to make sure that the Jews kept these days of Purim at the proper time, following the rule that Mordecai the Jew and Queen Esther had made. The rule fit well with what they themselves had agreed to do forever and with other things they did—like fasting and lamenting. [32]Esther's order made these features of Purim part of the law, so it was written down.

The fame of Mordecai

10 King Ahasuerus taxed the entire kingdom, including the islands of the Mediterranean. [2]Now some may want to know about all the king's mighty, great deeds. They may also want a full report about how important Mordecai became after the king honored him. Are they not written in the official records of the kings of Media and Persia? [3]Certainly, Mordecai the Jew was second only to King Ahasuerus in importance. The Jews also admired him greatly, and his many brothers and sisters were proud of him. He always wanted to do good things for his Jewish people and to speak up for all his family whenever they needed help.

JOB

Job's piety and life of bliss

1 A man in the land of Uz was named Job. That man was honest, a person of absolute integrity; he feared God and avoided evil. [2]He had seven sons and three daughters, [3]and owned seven thousand sheep, three thousand camels, five hundred pairs of oxen, five hundred female donkeys, and a vast number of servants, so that he was greater than all the people of the east. [4]Each of his sons hosted a feast in his own house on his birthday. They invited their three sisters to eat and drink with them. [5]When the days of the feast had been completed, Job would send word[a] and purify his children.[b] Getting up early in the morning, he prepared entirely burned offerings for each one of them, for Job thought, Perhaps my children have sinned and then cursed[c] God in their hearts. Job did this regularly.

Job's motives questioned

[6]One day the divine beings[d] came to present themselves before the LORD, and the Adversary[e] also came among them. [7]The LORD said to the Adversary, "Where did you come from?"

The Adversary answered the LORD, "From wandering throughout the earth."

[8]The LORD said to the Adversary, "Have you thought about my servant Job; surely there is no one like him on earth, a man who is honest, who is of absolute integrity, who reveres God and avoids evil?"

[9]The Adversary answered the LORD, "Does Job revere God for nothing? [10]Haven't you fenced him in—his house and all he has—and blessed the work of his hands so that his possessions extend throughout the earth? [11]But stretch out your hand and strike all he has. He will certainly curse you to your face."

[12]The LORD said to the Adversary, "Look, all he has is within your power; only don't stretch out your hand against him." So the Adversary left the LORD's presence.

Job passes the test

[13]One day Job's sons and daughters were eating and drinking wine in their oldest

[q]Or *wrote a second time to show that this letter* [a]Heb lacks *word.* [b]Or *them* [c]Or *blessed.* The verb for *bless* is a euphemism for *curse* in 1:11; 2:5, 9; whereas in 1:10, 21 and 42:12 it has its usual meaning. [d]Or *children of God* [e]Heb *hassatan*

brother's house. 14A messenger came to Job
and said: "The oxen were plowing, and the
donkeys were grazing nearby 15when the
Sabeans took them and killed the young
men with swords. I alone escaped to tell
you."
16While this messenger was speaking,
another arrived and said: "A raging fire fell
from the sky and burned up the sheep and
devoured the young men. I alone escaped to
tell you."
17While this messenger was speaking,
another arrived and said: "Chaldeans set
up three companies, raided the camels and
took them, killing the young men with
swords. I alone escaped to tell you."
18While this messenger was speaking,
another arrived and said: "Your sons and
your daughters were eating and drinking wine in their oldest brother's house,
19when a strong wind came from the desert
and struck the four corners of the house. It
fell upon the young people, and they died. I
alone escaped to tell you."
20Job arose, tore his clothes, shaved his
head, fell to the ground, and worshipped.
21He said: "Naked I came from my mother's
womb; naked I will return there. The LORD
has given; the LORD has taken; bless the
LORD's name." 22In all this, Job didn't sin
or blame God.

Job's Adversary refuses to give up

2 One day the divine beings came to present themselves before the LORD. The
Adversary also came among them to present himself before the LORD. 2The LORD
said to the Adversary, "Where have you
come from?"
The Adversary answered the LORD,
"From wandering throughout the earth."
3The LORD said to the Adversary, "Have
you thought about my servant Job, for
there is no one like him on earth, a man
who is honest, who is of absolute integrity,
who reveres God and avoids evil? He still
holds on to his integrity even though you
incited me to ruin him for no reason."
4The Adversary responded to the LORD,
"Skin for skin—people will give up everything they have in exchange for their lives.
5But stretch out your hand and strike his
bones and flesh. Then he will definitely
curse[f] you to your face."
6The LORD answered the Adversary,
"There he is—within your power; only preserve his life."

The test intensifies

7The Adversary departed from the
LORD's presence and struck Job with severe sores from the sole of his foot to the
top of his head. 8Job took a piece of broken
pottery to scratch himself and sat down on
a mound of ashes. 9Job's wife said to him,
"Are you still clinging to your integrity?
Curse[g] God, and die."
10Job said to her, "You're talking like a
foolish woman. Will we receive good from
God but not also receive bad?" In all this,
Job didn't sin with his lips.

Job's three friends come to comfort him

11When Job's three friends heard about
all this disaster that had happened to him,
they came, each one from his home—
Eliphaz from Teman, Bildad from Shuah,
and Zophar from Naamah. They agreed to
come so they could console and comfort him.
12When they looked up from a distance
and didn't recognize him, they wept loudly.
Each one tore his garment and scattered
dust above his head toward the sky. 13They
sat with Job on the ground seven days and
seven nights, not speaking a word to him,
for they saw that he was in excruciating pain.

Job responds differently

3 Afterward, Job spoke up and cursed the
day he was born.
2Job said:
3Perish the day I was born,
the night someone said,
"A boy has been conceived."
4That day—let it be darkness;
may God above ignore it,
and light not shine on it.
5May deepest darkness claim it

[f] Or *bless* [g] Or *bless*

and a cloud linger over it;
may all that darkens the day terrify it.
6 May gloom seize that night;
may it not be counted
in the days of a year;
may it not appear in the months.
7 May that night be childless;
may no happy singing come in it.
8 May those who curse the day curse it,
those with enough skill
to awaken Leviathan.
9 May its evening stars stay dark;
may it wait in vain for light;
may it not see dawn's gleam,
10 because it didn't close
the doors of my mother's womb,[h]
didn't hide trouble from my eyes.

Job laments his misfortune

11 Why didn't I die at birth,
come forth from the womb and die?
12 Why did knees receive me
and breasts let me nurse?
13 For now I would be lying down quietly;
I'd sleep; rest would be mine
14 with kings and earth's advisors,
who rebuild ruins for themselves,
15 or with princes who have gold,
who fill their houses with silver.
16 Or why wasn't I
like a buried miscarried infant,
like babies who never see light?
17 There the wicked rage no more;
there the weak rest.
18 Prisoners are entirely at ease;
they don't hear a boss's voice.
19 Both small and great are there;
a servant is free from his masters.
20 Why is light given to the hard worker,
life to those bitter of soul,
21 those waiting in vain for death,
who search for it
more than for treasure,
22 who rejoice excitedly,
who are thrilled
when they find a grave?
23 Why is light given[i] to the person
whose way is hidden,
whom God has fenced in?
24 My groans become my bread;
my roars pour out like water.
25 Because I was afraid of something awful,
and it arrived;
what I dreaded came to me.
26 I had no ease, quiet, or rest,
and trembling came.

Eliphaz tries to comfort Job

4 Then Eliphaz, a native of Teman,
responded:
2 If one tries to answer you,
will you be annoyed?
But who can hold words back?
3 Look, you've instructed many
and given strength to drooping hands.
4 Your words have raised up the falling;
you've steadied failing knees.
5 But now it comes to you,
and you are dismayed;
it has struck you,
and you are frightened.
6 Isn't your religion
the source of[j] your confidence;
the integrity of your conduct,
the source of your hope?

Sinners don't live long

7 Think! What innocent person
has ever perished?
When have those who do the right
thing been destroyed?
8 As I've observed, those who plow sin
and sow trouble will harvest it.
9 When God breathes deeply, they perish;
by a breath of his nostril
they are annihilated.
10 The roar of a lion and snarl
of the king of beasts—
yet the teeth of lions are shattered;
11 the lion perishes without prey,
and its cubs are scattered.

A frightening dream

12 But a word sneaked up on me;
my ears caught a hint of it.
13 In profound thoughts,
visions of the night,
when deep sleep falls on people,

[h] Heb lacks *mother's*. [i] Heb lacks *is light given*. [j] Heb lacks *the source*.

14 fear and dread struck me;
all of my bones shook.
15 A breeze swept by my face;
the hair of my skin bristled.
16 It stopped. I didn't recognize
its visible form,
although a figure was
in front of my eyes.
Silence! Then I heard a voice:
17 "Can a human be more righteous
than God,
a person purer than their maker?"

Its interpretation

18 If he doesn't trust his servants and
levels a charge against his messengers,
19 how much less those who dwell
in houses of clay,
whose foundations are in dust,
and who are crushed like a moth?
20 They are smashed
between morning and evening;
they perish forever
without anyone knowing.
21 Isn't their tent cord pulled up?
They die without wisdom.[k]

Life's problems

5 Call out. Will anyone answer you?
To which holy one will you turn?
2 Surely anger can kill the foolish;
fury can kill the simple.
3 I've seen the foolish take root
and promptly curse their house.
4 Their children are far[l] from safety,
crushed in the gate without a deliverer.
5 The hungry devour[m] their crops;
it's taken even from the thorns,[n]
and the thirsty pant after their yield.
6 Surely trouble doesn't come from dust,
nor does distress sprout
from the ground.
7 Surely humans are born to distress,
just as sparks rise up.

The answer is God

8 But I would seek God,
put my case to God,
9 who does great things
beyond comprehension,
wonderful things without number;
10 who provides rain
over the earth's surface,
sends water to the open country,
11 exalts the lowly,
raises mourners to victory;
12 who frustrates the schemes
of the clever
so that their hands achieve no success,
13 trapping the wise in their cleverness
so that the plans of the devious
don't succeed.
14 They encounter darkness during the day,
and at noon they fumble about
as at night.
15 Yet he rescues the orphan[o]
from the sword of their mouth,
the needy from the grip of the strong;
16 so the poor have hope
and violence shuts its mouth.

Divine favor

17 Look, happy is the person
whom God corrects;
so don't reject the Almighty's
instruction.
18 He injures, but he binds up;
he strikes, but his hands heal.
19 From six adversities he will deliver you;
from seven harm won't touch you.
20 In famine he will ransom you
from death;
in war, from the power of the sword.
21 You will be hidden
from the tongue's sting,
and you won't fear destruction
when it comes.
22 You will laugh at destruction and hunger;
you won't be afraid of wild beasts;
23 for you will make an agreement with
the stones of the field;
and the beasts of the field
will be at peace with you.
24 You will know that your tent is secure.
You will examine your home
and miss nothing.

[k]Some interpreters end the quotation here rather than 4:17. [l]Or *May their children be far from safety.*
[m]Or *May the hungry devour their crops.* [n]Heb uncertain [o]Heb lacks *orphan.*

25 You will know that you'll have
many children.
Your offspring will be
like the grass of the earth.
26 You will come to your grave in old age
as bundles of grain stacked up
at harvesttime.
27 Look, we've searched this out, and so it is;
listen and find out for yourself.

Job defends his anger

6 Job responded:
2 Oh, that my grief
were actually weighed,
all of it were lifted up in scales;
3 for now it's heavier
than the sands of the sea;
therefore, my words are rash.[p]
4 The Almighty's arrows are in me;
my spirit drinks their poison,
and God's terrors
are arrayed against me.
5 Does a donkey bray over grass
or an ox bellow over its fodder?
6 Is tasteless food eaten without salt,
or does egg white[q] have taste?
7 I refuse to touch them;
they resemble food for the sick.

He wishes to die

8 Oh, that what I've requested would come
and God grant my hope;
9 that God be willing to crush me,
release his hand and cut me off.
10 I'd still take comfort,
relieved[r] even though in persistent pain;
for I've not denied
the words of the holy one.
11 What is my strength, that I should hope;
my end, that my life should drag on?
12 Is my strength that of rocks,
my flesh bronze?
13 I don't have a helper for myself;
success has been taken from me.

He accuses his friends

14 Are friends loyal
to the one who despairs,[s]
or do they stop fearing the Almighty?
15 My companions are treacherous
like a stream in the desert,
like channels that overrun
their streambeds,
16 like those darkened by thawing ice,
in which snow is obscured
17 but that stop flowing in dry times
and vanish from their channels in heat.
18 Caravans turn aside from their paths;
they go up into untamed areas
and perish.
19 Caravans from Tema look;
merchants from Sheba hope for it.
20 They are ashamed that they trusted;
they arrive and are dismayed.
21 That's what you are like;[t]
you see something awful and are afraid.

He appeals to his friends

22 Have I said, "Give me something?
Offer a bribe from your wealth for me?
23 Rescue me from the hand of my enemy?
Ransom me from
the grip of the ruthless?"
24 Instruct me and I'll be quiet;
inform me how I've erred.
25 How painful are truthful words,
but what do your condemnations
accomplish?
26 Do you intend to correct my words,
to treat the words of a hopeless man
as wind?
27 Would you even gamble over an orphan,
barter away your friend?
28 Now look at me—
would I lie to your face?
29 Turn! Don't be faithless.
Turn now! I am righteous.
30 Is there wrong on my tongue,
or can my mouth not
recognize disaster?

The human condition

7 Isn't slavery everyone's condition
on earth,
our days like those of a hired worker?
2 Like a slave we pant for a shadow,
await our task like a hired worker.
3 So I have inherited months of emptiness;

[p] Heb uncertain [q] Heb uncertain [r] Heb uncertain [s] Heb uncertain [t] Heb uncertain

nights of toil have been measured out
for me.
4 If I lie down and think—
When will I get up?—
night drags on,[u] and restless thoughts
fill me until dawn.
5 My flesh is covered with worms
and crusted earth;
my skin hardens and oozes.
6 My days are swifter
than a weaver's shuttle;
they reach their end without hope.[v]
7 Remember that my life is wind;
my eyes won't see pleasure again.
8 The eye that sees me now
will no longer look on me;
your eyes will be on me,
and I won't exist.
9 A cloud breaks apart and moves on—
like the one who descends to the grave[w]
and won't rise,
10 won't return home again,
won't be recognized in town anymore.

Job wants to be left alone

11 But I won't keep quiet;
I will speak in the adversity of my spirit,
groan in the bitterness of my life.
12 Am I Sea[x] or the Sea Monster[y]
that you place me under guard?
13 If I say, "My couch will comfort me,"
my bed will diminish my murmuring.
14 You scare me with dreams,
frighten me with visions.
15 I would choose strangling
and death instead of my bones.
16 I reject life;[z] I don't want to live long;
leave me alone,
for my days are empty.

A parody of Psalm 8

17 What are human beings,
that you exalt them,
that you take note of them,
18 visit them each morning,
test them every moment?
19 Why not look away from me;
let me alone until I swallow my spit?
20 If I sinned, what did I do to you,
guardian of people?
Why have you made me your target
so that I'm a burden to myself?
21 Why not forgive my sin,
overlook my iniquity?
Then I would lie down in the dust;
you would search hard for me,
and I would not exist.

Bildad defends God

8 Bildad from Shuah responded:
2 How long will you mouth such things
such that your utterances
become a strong wind?
3 Does God pervert justice,
or does the Almighty distort
what is right?
4 If your children sinned against him,
then he delivered them
into the power of their rebellion.
5 If you will search eagerly for God,
plead with the Almighty.
6 If you are pure and do the right thing,
then surely he will become
active on your behalf
and reward your innocent dwelling.
7 Although your former state was ordinary,
your future will be extraordinary.

Tradition

8 Ask a previous generation
and verify the findings
of your ancestors,
9 for we are only recently here
and don't know
because our days on earth
are a shadow.
10 Won't they instruct you and tell you;
will words not[a] proceed
from their hearts?

Examples from nature

11 Does papyrus grow apart from a marsh?
Does a reed flourish without water?
12 While still tender, uncut,
it will wither before every other grass.
13 So are the paths of all who forget God.
Hope perishes for the godless,

[u] Heb uncertain [v] Or *thread* [w] Heb *Sheol* [x] Heb *Yam*, a sea god [y] Heb *Tannin*, a sea dragon [z] Heb lacks *life*.
[a] Heb lacks *not*.

14 whose confidence is a fragile thing,[b]
their trust, a spider's web.
15 He leans on its web,
and it doesn't stand;
grasps it, and it can't remain in place.
16 It's like a well-watered plant in the sun;
its runners spread over its gardens.
17 Its roots are entwined
over a pile of rocks,
for it sees a home among stones.
18 If it's uprooted from its place,
it lies, saying, "I can't see you."
19 Surely its way is a joy,
for from the dust other plants[c] sprout.

God's faithfulness

20 Surely God won't reject integrity,
won't strengthen
the hand of the wicked.
21 He will still fill your mouth with joy,
your lips with a victorious shout.
22 Those who hate you
will be clothed with shame,
and the tent of the wicked will vanish.

Hymnic praise

9 Job responded:
2 I know for certain that this is so;
and how can anyone be innocent
before God?
3 If one wants to contend with him,
he won't answer one in a thousand.
4 He is wise[d] and powerful;
who can resist him and prosper?
5 Who removes mountains,
and they are unaware;
who overthrows them in anger?
6 Who shakes the earth from its place,
and its pillars shudder?
7 Who commands the sun,
and it does not rise,
even seals up the stars;
8 stretched out the heavens alone
and trod on the waves of the Sea;[e]
9 made the Bear and Orion, Pleiades
and the southern constellations;
10 does great and unsearchable things,
wonders beyond number?

A mismatch

11 If God goes by me, I can't see him;
he glides past,
and I can't perceive him.
12 If he seizes, who can bring back?
Who can say to him,
"What are you doing?"
13 God won't retract his anger;
the helpers of Rahab bow beneath him.
14 Yet I myself will answer him;
I'll choose my words
in a contest[f] with him.
15 Even if I'm innocent, I can't answer;
I must plead for justice.
16 If I were to call and he answered me,
I couldn't believe that he heard
my voice.
17 Who bruises me with a tempest
and multiplies my wounds
for no reason?
18 He doesn't let me catch my breath,
for he fills me with bitterness.
19 If the issue is strength—behold power!
If justice—who calls God to meet me?

There is no justice

20 If I'm innocent, my mouth condemns me;
I have integrity;
but God declares me perverse.
21 I'm blameless, yet don't know myself;
I reject my life.
22 It's all the same;
therefore, I say God destroys
the blameless and the sinners.
23 If calamity suddenly kills,
he mocks at the slaying[g] of innocents.
24 The earth is handed over to the wicked;
he covers the faces of its judges.
If not God, then who does?

Job wants an arbitrator

25 My days are swifter than a runner;
they flee and don't experience good.
26 They sweep by like ships made of reeds,
as an eagle swoops on prey.
27 If I say, "I'll forget my lament,
put on a different face so I can smile,"
28 I'm still afraid of all my suffering;

[b]Heb uncertain [c]Heb lacks *plants.* [d]Or *wise in heart*; cf 37:24 Heb *Yam*, a sea god [f]Heb lacks *in a contest.*
[g]Heb uncertain

I know that you
won't declare me innocent.
29 I myself am thought guilty;
why have I tried so hard in vain?
30 If I wash myself with snow,
purify my hands with soap,
31 then you'll hurl me into a slimy pit
so that my clothes detest me.
32 God is not a man like me—
someone I could answer—
so that we could come together in court.
33 Oh, that[h] there were a mediator
between us;
he would lay his hand on both of us,
34 remove his rod from me,
so his fury wouldn't frighten me.
35 Then I would speak—unafraid—
for I'm not that way.

Complaint to God

10 I loathe my life; I will let loose
my complaint;
I will speak out of my own bitterness.
2 I will say to God, Don't declare me guilty;
tell me what you are accusing me
of doing.
3 Does it seem good to you
that you oppress me,
that you reject the work of your hands
and cause the purpose of sinners
to shine?
4 Do you have physical eyes;
do you see like a human?
5 Are your days like those of a human,
your years like years of a human,
6 that you search for my wrongdoing
and seek my sin?
7 You know that I'm not guilty,
yet no one delivers me from your power.

Creator

8 Your hands fashioned and made me;
yet you want to destroy me utterly.
9 Remember that you made me from[i] clay,
and you will return me to dust.
10 Didn't you pour me out like milk,
curdle me like cheese?
11 You clothed me with skin and flesh,
wove me from bones and sinews.
12 Life and kindness you gave me,
and you oversaw and preserved
my breath.

No hiding place

13 These things you hid in your heart;
I know this is the case with you.
14 If I sin and you observe me,
you won't consider me innocent
of wrongdoing.
15 If I were guilty, doom to me;
I'm innocent, but can't lift my head,
full of shame and facing my misery.
16 I could boast like a lion,
and you would hunt me;
you would do awesome things
to me again.
17 You continue to send your witnesses
against me
and increase your anger toward me,
a swift army against me.[j]

Death wish

18 Why did you let me emerge
from the womb?
I wish I had died
without any eye seeing me.
19 Then I would be just as if
I hadn't existed,
taken from the belly to the grave.
20 Aren't my few days coming to an end?
Look away from me
so I can brighten up a little
21 before I go and don't return
to a land of deepest darkness,
22 a land whose light is like gloom,
utter darkness and confusion,
such that light shines like gloom.

Zophar's rebuke

11 Zophar from Naamah responded:
2 Should all these words
go unanswered
or a wordy man be justified?
3 Will your idle talk silence everyone;
will you mock
and not be put to shame?
4 You've said, "My teaching is pure,
and I'm clean in God's[k] eyes."

[h]Or *There is no* [i]Or *like* [j]Heb uncertain [k]Or *your*

Divine secrecy

5 But oh, that God would speak,
open his lips against you
6 and tell you secrets of wisdom;
for sound insight has two sides.
Know that God lets some of your sin
be forgotten.
7 Can you find the secret of God
or find the extent of the Almighty?
8 They are higher than the heavens—
what can you do?
Deeper than the underworld[l]—
what can you know?
9 Its measurement is longer
than the earth
and broader than the sea.
10 If God passes by, imprisons someone,
and calls a trial,
who can stop him?
11 He knows worthless people,
sees sin, and certainly[m] takes note.
12 A stupid person becomes intelligent
when a wild ass of a person
is born tame.[n]

Abiding hope

13 If you make your mind resolute
and spread your palms to him,
14 if you throw out the sin
in your hands
and don't let injustice
dwell in your tents,
15 then you will lift up your face
without blemish;
you will be secure and not fear.
16 You will forget trouble;
you will remember it
as water that flows past.
17 A life span will rise brighter than noon;
darkness will be like morning.
18 You will be secure, for there is hope;
you will look around and rest safely.
19 You will lie down
without anyone to scare you;
many will beg for your favor.
20 The eyes of the wicked will grow faint;
flight has vanished from them;
their hope is a dying gasp.

A living joke

12 Job responded:
2 Surely you are the people,
and wisdom will die with you.
3 I am also intelligent;
I'm not inferior to you.
Who isn't like these people?[o]
4 I'm a joke to friends
who called to God and he answered;
the innocent and blameless one
is a joke,
5 a torch[p] of contempt to one who is idle,
a fixed point for slipping feet.

Proverbial wisdom

6 Raiders' tents are prosperous
and God's provokers secure,
who carry God in their hands.[q]
7 But ask Behemoth, and he will teach you,
the birds in the sky,
and they will tell you;
8 or talk to earth, and it will teach you;
the fish of the sea will recount it for you.
9 Among all these, who hasn't known
that the LORD's hand did this?
10 In whose grasp is the life of every thing,
the breath of every person?
11 Doesn't the ear test words
and the palate taste food?
12 "In old age is wisdom;
understanding in a long life."

God's majesty

13 With him are wisdom and power;
counsel and understanding are his.
14 If he tears down, it can't be rebuilt;
if he ties a person up,
he can't be set free.
15 If he restricts water, they have drought;
if he lets it loose, it overturns the land.
16 With him are might and success;
the deceiver and the deceived are his.
17 He leads advisors away barefoot;
makes madmen of judges;
18 unties the belt of kings,
binds a garment around their loins;
19 leads priests away barefoot;
overthrows the well-established;

[l] Heb *Sheol* [m] Or *does not* [n] Or *a wild ass's colt can be born a man* [o] Heb lacks *people.* [p] Heb uncertain
[q] Heb uncertain

20 silences the talk of trusted people;
takes away elders' discernment;
21 pours contempt on royalty;
loosens the belt of the strong;
22 discloses deep secrets of darkness,
makes utter darkness enter the light;
23 makes nations prominent
and destroys them,
expands nations and leads them astray;
24 takes away the power to think
from earth's leaders,
making them wander
in untraveled wastelands.
25 They feel their way
in the dark without light;
he makes them stumble like drunks.

Self-defense

13 Look, my eye has seen it all;
my ear has heard and understood it.
2 Just as you know, I also know;
I'm not inferior to you.
3 But I want to speak to the Almighty;
I would gladly present my case to God.

Friends attacked

4 You, however, are plasterers of lies;
ineffective healers, all of you.
5 Would that you were completely quiet;
that would be your wisdom.
6 Hear my teaching
and pay attention to the arguments of
my lips.
7 Will you speak injustice for God,
speak deceit on his behalf?
8 Will you be partial
or contend for God?
9 Will it go well when he searches you,
or can you fool him as you fool people?
10 He will certainly correct you
if you've been secretly partial.
11 Wouldn't his majesty scare you
and dread of him fall on you?
12 Your old sayings are proverbs
made of ashes,
your sayings defenses made of clay.

Job will speak out

13 Be quiet and I will speak,
come what may.
14 For what reason will I take my flesh
in my teeth,
put my life in jeopardy?
15 He will slay me; I'm without hope;[r]
I will surely prove my way to his face.
16 Also this will be my vindication,
that a godless person
won't come before him.
17 Listen closely to my words
so that my remarks will be
in your ears.

Against God

18 Look, I have laid out my case;
I know that I'm innocent.
19 Who would dare contend with me,
for then I would be quiet and die.
20 Only don't do two things to me,
then I won't hide from your face.
21 Remove your hand far from me
and don't terrify me with your anger.
22 Then call and I'll answer,
or I'll speak and you can reply.
23 How many are my offenses and sins?
Inform me about my rebellions
and sins.
24 Why hide your face from me
and consider me your enemy?
25 Will you cause a wind-tossed leaf
to tremble,
or will you pursue dry straw?
26 You even write bitter things about me,
make me inherit
my youthful indiscretions.
27 You tie up my feet and restrict all actions;
you stamp marks
on the bottom of my feet.

Human destiny

28 Surely a person wastes away like refuse,
like clothing that a moth eats.
14 All of us[s] are born of women,
have few days, and are full of turmoil.
2 Like a flower, we[t] bloom, then wither,
flee like a shadow, and don't last.
(3 Yes, you open your eyes on this one;
you bring me into trial against you.)
4 Who can make pure from impure?
Nobody.

[r] Or *Though he slay me, yet I will trust him.* [s] Heb *adam* [t] Or *he;* also *he* in 14:5-6

5 If our days are fixed,
the number of our months with you,
you set a statute and we can't exceed it.
6 Look away from us that we may rest,
until we are satisfied
like a worker at day's end.

Trees versus humans

7 Indeed there is hope for a tree.
If it's cut down and still sprouting
and its shoots don't fail,
8 if its roots age in the ground
and its stump dies in the dust,
9 at the scent of water, it will bud
and produce sprouts like a plant.
10 But a human dies and lies there;
a person expires, and where is he?
11 Water vanishes from the sea;
a river dries up completely.
12 But a human lies down and doesn't rise
until the heavens cease;
they don't get up
and awaken from sleep.

Momentary hope

13 I wish you would hide me
in the underworld,[u]
conceal me until your anger passes,
set a time for me, and remember me.
14 If people die, will they live again?
All the days of my service I would wait
until my restoration took place.
15 You would call, and I would answer you;
you would long for your handiwork.
16 Though you now number my steps,
you would not keep a record of my sin.
17 My rebellion is sealed in a bag;
you would cover my sin.

God crushes hope

18 But an eroding mountain breaks up,
and rock is displaced.
19 Water wears away boulders;
floods carry away soil;
you destroy a people's hope.
20 You overpower them relentlessly,
and they die;
you change their appearance
and send them away.
21 Their children achieve honor,
and they don't know it;
their children become insignificant,
and they don't see it.
22 They only feel the pain of their body,
and they mourn for themselves.

Job's intelligence questioned

15 Eliphaz answered:
2 Will the wise respond
with windy knowledge
and fill their belly with the east wind?
3 Will they argue with a word
that has no benefit
and with unprofitable words?
4 You are truly making
religion ineffective
and restraining meditation
before God.
5 Your mouth multiplies your sins
a thousand times;
you opt for a clever tongue.
6 Your mouth condemns you, not I;
your lips argue against you.
7 Were you born the first Adam,
brought forth before the hills?
8 Did you listen in God's council;
is wisdom limited to you?
9 What do you know that we don't know;
what do you understand
that isn't among us?
10 Both the graybeard and the aged
are with us;
those much older than your father.
11 Are God's comforts not enough for you,
a word spoken gently with you?
12 Why has your mind seized you,
why have your eyes flashed,
13 so that you return your breath to God
and utter such words from your mouth?
14 What are humans
that they might be pure,
and those born of woman
that they might be innocent?
15 If he doesn't trust his holy ones
and the heavens aren't pure in his eyes,
16 how much less those who are
abominable and corrupt,
for they drink sin like water.

[u] Heb *Sheol*

The wicked's downfall

17 Listen to me; I will argue with you;
what I've seen, I will declare to you;
18 what the wise have told and have not
concealed from their family,
19 to whom alone the earth was given
and no stranger passed in their midst.
20 All the days of the wicked are painful;
the number of years reserved
for the hateful;
21 a sound of terror pierces[V] their ears;
when safe, raiders overtake them.
22 They can't count on turning away
from darkness;
they are destined for a sword.
23 They wander about for bread.
"Where is it?"
They know that their day of darkness
is fixed.
24 Adversity and stress scare them,
master them like a king ready
to strike;
25 for they raise a fist against God
and try to overpower the Almighty.
26 They run toward him aggressively,
with a massive and strong shield.
27 They cover their face with grease
and make their loins gross.
28 They lived in ruined cities,
unoccupied houses that turn to rubble.
29 They won't get rich;
their wealth won't last;
their property won't extend
over the earth.
30 They can't turn away from darkness;
a flame will dry out their shoots,
and they will be taken away
by the wind from his mouth.
31 They shouldn't trust
in what has no worth,
for their reward will be worthless.
32 Before their branch is formed,
before it is green,
33 like the vine, they will drop
early grapes
and cast off their blossoms
like the olive.
34 The ruthless gang is barren,
and fire consumes the tents of bribers.
35 They conceive toil
and give birth to sorrow;
their belly establishes deceit.

Job's response

16 Then Job answered:
2 I've heard many things like these.
All of you are sorry comforters.
3 Will windy talk ever cease;
what bothers you that you must argue?
4 In your situation I could speak like you;
I could put words together
to oppose you,
shake my head over you.
5 I could heap up words,
strengthen you with my speech;
my trembling lips would be held
in check.
6 If I speak, my pain is not eased;
if I hold back, what have I lost?

The innocent are God's targets

7 Now God has surely worn me out.
You have destroyed my entire group,
8 seized me, which became grounds
for an accusation.[W]
My leanness rises to bear witness
against me.
9 His anger tears me and afflicts me;
he slashes at me with his teeth.
My enemy pierces me with his eyes.
10 They open their mouths at me
and strike my cheek in a taunt;
they gang up on me.
11 God delivers me to a criminal
and forces me into the hands
of the wicked.
12 I was at rest, but he shattered me,
seized me by the back of my neck,
dashed me into pieces;
he raised me up for his target.
13 His archers surround me;
he cuts my kidneys open without pity
and doesn't care,
pours my gall on the ground,
14 bursts me open over and over,
runs against me like a strong man.
15 I've sewed rough cloth over my skin
and buried my dignity in the dust.

[V] Heb lacks *pierces*. [W] Heb uncertain

16 My face is red from crying,
and dark gloom hangs on my eyelids.
17 But there is no violence in my hands,
and my prayer is pure.

Lingering hope

18 Earth, don't cover my blood;
let my outcry never cease.
19 Surely now my witness stands in heaven;
my advocate is on high;
20 my go-between, my friend.[x]
While my eyes drip tears to God,
21 let him plead with God for a human being,
like a person pleads for a friend.
22 A number of years will surely pass,
and then I'll walk a path
that I won't return.

Another lament

17 My spirit is broken,
my days extinguished,
the grave,[y] mine.
2 Surely mockers are with me,
and my eye looks on their rebellion.
3 Take my guarantee.
Who else is willing
to make an agreement?
4 You've closed their mind to insight;
therefore, you won't be exalted.
5 He denounces his friends for gain,
and his children's eyes fail.
6 He makes me a popular proverb;
I'm like spit in people's faces.
7 My eye is weak from grief;
my limbs like a shadow—all of them.
8 Those who do the right thing
are amazed at this;
the guiltless become troubled
about the godless.
9 The innocent clings to his way;
the one whose hands are clean
grows stronger.
10 But you can bring all of them again,
and I won't find a wise one among you.
11 My days have passed;
my goals are destroyed,
my heart's desires.
12 They turn night into day;
light is near because of the darkness.
13 If I hope for the underworld[z]
as my dwelling,
lay out my bed in darkness,
14 I've called corruption "my father,"
the worm, "my mother and sister."
15 Where then is my hope?
My hope—who can see it?
16 Will they go down with me
to the underworld;[a]
will we descend together to the dust?

Attack from a friend

18 Bildad from Shuah answered:
2 How long?
Would you all stop talking.
Try to understand
and then we can speak.
3 Why are we considered beasts,
ignorant in your sight?
4 To you who tear yourself in rage—
will earth be forsaken for your sake,
a rock be dislodged from its place?

Evil people's fate

5 To be sure, the light of the wicked
goes out;
the blaze of their fire doesn't shine.
6 The light in their tent becomes dark,
and their lamp above doesn't shine.
7 Their strong strides slow down;
their plans trip themselves.
8 They are caught by their feet in a net;
they walk on mesh.
9 A trap grabs them by the heel;
a snare tightens on them.
10 A rope is hidden on the ground for them;
a trap for them along the path.
11 Terrors round about scare them;
they follow their steps.
12 Their offspring hunger;
calamity is ready for their spouses.
13 It eats some of their skin.
Death's firstborn consumes their limbs.
14 They are snatched from the safety
of their tent;
it parades them
before the king of terrors.
15 Nothing they own remains in their tent;
sulfur is scattered over their home.

[x] *Go-between* and *friend* are plural in Heb. [y] Or *graves* [z] Heb *Sheol* [a] Heb *Sheol*

[16]Their roots dry out below;
their branches wither above.
[17]The memory of them will perish
from the earth;
they will achieve
no recognition abroad.
[18]They are thrust from light into darkness,
banished from the world.
[19]They have no offspring or descendants
among their people,
no survivor in their dwelling place.
[20]Their successors are appalled
at what happens to them;
their predecessors pull their hair.
[21]These are surely the dwelling places
of the evil;
this is the place of the one
who doesn't know God.

Failed friendship

19 Then Job responded:
[2]How long will you harass me
and crush me with words?
[3]These ten times
you've humiliated me;
shamelessly you insult me.
[4]Have I really gone astray?
If so, my error remains
hidden inside me.
[5]If you look down on me
and use my disgrace to criticize me,
[6]know then that God has wronged me
and enclosed his net over me.

God's treatment of Job

[7]If I cry "Violence!" I'm not answered;
I shout—but there is no justice.
[8]He walled up my path so I can't pass
and put darkness on my trail,
[9]stripped my honor from me,
removed the crown from my head,
[10]tore me down completely so that I'll die,
and uprooted my hope like a tree.
[11]His anger burns against me;
he considers me his enemy.
[12]His troops come as one
and construct their siege ramp[b]
against me;
they camp around my tent.

Social ostracism

[13]He has distanced my family from me;
my acquaintances are also alienated
from me.
[14]My visitors have ceased;
those who know me have forgotten me.
[15]My guests and female servants
think me a stranger;
I'm a foreigner in their sight.
[16]I call my servant, and he doesn't answer;
I myself must beg him.
[17]My breath stinks to my wife;
I am odious to my children.
[18]Even the young despise me;
I get up, and they rail against me.
[19]All my closest friends despise me;
the ones I have loved turn against me.

Misery

[20]My bones cling to my skin and flesh;
I have escaped by the skin of my teeth.
[21]Pity me. Pity me. You're my friends.
God's hand has truly struck me.
[22]Why do you pursue me like God does,
always hungry for my flesh?

Brief hope

[23]Oh, that my words were written down,
inscribed on a scroll
[24]with an iron instrument and lead,
forever engraved on stone.
[25]But I know that my redeemer[c] is alive
and afterward he'll rise upon the dust.
[26]After my skin has been torn apart
this way—
then from my flesh[d] I'll see God,
[27]whom I'll see myself—
my eyes see,[e] and not a stranger's.
I am utterly dejected.

Warning

[28]You say, "How will we pursue him
so that the root of the matter can be
found in him?"[f]
[29]You ought to fear the sword yourselves,
for wrath brings punishment
by the sword.
You should know
that there is judgment.

[b]Or *their road* [c]Or *avenger* [d]Or *without my flesh* or *in my flesh* [e]Or *have seen* [f]Heb manuscripts; MT *in me*

Traditional belief

20 Zophar from Naamah said:
[2]Therefore, my troubled thoughts
make me turn back—
because of my inner turmoil.
[3]I hear teaching that insults me,
but I am forced to answer based
on my own understanding.[g]
[4]Do you know this from long ago—
from when humans were placed
on earth—
[5]that the rejoicing of the wicked is short,
the joy of the godless, brief?
[6]Though their height reaches heaven
and their heads touch the clouds,
[7]they will perish forever like their dung;
those who saw them will say,
"Where are they?"
[8]They will disappear like a dream,
and none will find them,
carried away like a nighttime vision.
[9]The eye that saw them
will do so no more;
they won't be seen again at home.
[10]Their children will repay the poor;
their hands will give back their wealth.
[11]Vigor filled their bones
and now sleeps with them in the dust.
[12]Though wickedness is sweet
in their mouths,
they hide it under their tongues;
[13]they like it, won't let it go;
they hold it in their cheeks.
[14]Food turns their stomachs,
becoming a cobra's poison inside.
[15]They swallow wealth and vomit it;
God dislodges it from their belly.
[16]They suck cobra's poison;
a viper's tongue kills them.
[17]They won't experience streams,
rivers of honey, and brooks of cream.
[18]They won't receive the reward
for their labor;
they won't enjoy the wealth
from their business.
[19]They crushed and abandoned the poor;
stole a house they didn't build;
[20]didn't know contentment in their belly;
couldn't escape with their treasure.
[21]Nothing remained of their food,
so their riches will not endure.
[22]Even in their plenty,
they are hard-pressed;
all sorts of trouble come on them.
[23]Let God[h] fill their belly,
unleash his burning anger on them,
rain punishing blows on them.
[24]If they flee an iron weapon,
a bronze bow pierces them.
[25]They pull it out,
but it sticks out from their backs;
its shaft in their liver brings terror.
[26]Complete darkness waits for their
treasured possessions;
fire that no one stoked
consumes them;
what's left in their tent is ruined.
[27]Heaven exposes their guilt;
earth opposes them.
[28]Their household wealth
will be carried off
by rushing streams on the day
of his anger.
[29]This is a wicked person's lot from God,
their heritage decreed by God.

Grant me a hearing

21 Then Job answered:
[2]Listen carefully to my remarks
and let that comfort you.
[3]Bear with me so I can speak, I myself;
and after my reply you can mock.
[4]Are my complaints against
another human;
why is my patience short?
[5]Turn to me and be appalled;
lay your hand over your mouth.
[6]If I recall it, I'm scared;
shaking seizes my body.

The success of the wicked

[7]Why do the wicked live,
grow old, and even become strong?
[8]Their children are always with them,
their offspring in their sight,
[9]their houses safe from dread,
God's punishing stick not upon them.
[10]Their bull always breeds successfully;

[g]Heb uncertain [h]Or *him*

their cows give birth
and never miscarry.
11 They send forth their little ones
like sheep;
their infants bounce around.
12 They raise drum and lyre,
rejoice at the sound of a flute.
13 They spend their days contentedly,
go down to the grave[i] peacefully.
14 They say to God, "Turn away from us;
we take no pleasure in
knowing your ways;
15 who is the Almighty[j]
that we should serve him,
and what can we gain
if we meet him?"
16 Look, isn't their well-being the work
of their own hands?
A sinner's logic is beyond me.

Desired vindication

17 How often does the lamp
of the wicked flicker
or disaster come upon them,
with its fury inflicting pain on them?
18 Let them be like straw in the wind,
like dry grass stolen by a storm.
19 God stores up his punishment
for his children.
Let him destroy them so they know.
20 Let their own eyes
witness their doom.
Let them drink
from the Almighty's wrath.
21 What do they care about their household
after they die,
when their numbered days are cut off?

A common fate

22 Will they instruct God—
he who judges the most powerful?
23 Someone dies in wonderful health,
completely comfortable and well,
24 their buckets full of milk,
their bones marrow-filled and sound.
25 Another dies in bitter spirit,
never having tasted the good things.
26 They lie together in the dust
and worms cover them.

Further disagreement

27 Look, I know your thoughts;
your plans harm me.
28 You say,
"Where is the official's house?
Where is the tent,
the dwelling of the wicked?"
29 Haven't you asked travelers
or paid attention to their reports?
30 On the day of disaster
the wicked are spared;
on the day of fury they are rescued.
31 Who can criticize their behavior
to their faces;
they act, and who can avenge them?
32 They are carried to their graves;
someone keeps guard over their tombs.
33 The soil near the desert streambed
is sweet to them;
everyone marches after them—
those before them, beyond counting.
34 How empty is your comfort to me;
only deceit remains in your responses.

Job's sins

22 Then Eliphaz from Teman answered:
2 Can a human being be useful to God?
Can an intelligent person bring profit?
3 Does the Almighty delight
in your innocence?
Does he gain
when you perfect your ways?
4 Does he rebuke you for your piety,
bring you in for judgment?
5 Isn't your wickedness massive,
your iniquity endless?
6 You have taken payments
from your family for no reason;
stripped the naked, leaving no clothes;
7 denied water to the thirsty,
withheld bread from the starving.
(8 The powerful own land;
the favored live in it.)
9 You have sent widows away empty;
crushed orphans' resources.
10 For this reason, snares surround you;
sudden dread brings panic to you
11 or a darkness that you can't see;
rushing water will cover you.

[i]Heb *Sheol* [j]Heb *Shaddai* or *Mountain One*

God's activity

12 Isn't God in the heights of heaven;
see how high the topmost stars are?
13 You say: "What does God know?
Can he judge through thick clouds?
14 Clouds conceal him so he can't see
while he walks on heaven's rim."
15 Will you keep the ancient way
traveled by sinful persons,
16 who were snatched prematurely
when a river flooded their foundations,
17 who say to God, "Turn away from us;
what can the Almighty do to us?"
18 Yet he filled their houses
with good things;
a sinner's logic is beyond me.
19 The righteous see and rejoice;
the innocent mock them:
20 our enemies are certainly cut off;
fire will devour what's left of them.

Turn to God

21 Get along well with God and be at peace;
from this something good
will come to you.
22 Receive instruction from his mouth;
put his words in your mind.
23 If you return to the Almighty,[k]
you will be restored;
if you keep wrongdoing
out of your tent.
24 Lay your prized possession in the dust,
your gold from Ophir on a rock
in a desert streambed.
25 The Almighty will be your
prized possession,
silver piled up for you.
26 Then you will take pleasure
in the Almighty;
lift up your face to God.
27 You will pray to him, and he will hear you;
you will fulfill your solemn promises.
28 If you decree something, it will stand;
light will shine on your ways.
29 When they're humbled, you will say:
"Cheer up;
God will rescue the lowly.
30 He will deliver the guilty;
they will be saved by your pure hands."

Grant me a trial

23 Job answered:
2 Today my complaint
is again bitter;[l]
my strength is weighed down
because of my groaning.
3 Oh, that I could know
how to find him—
come to his dwelling place;
4 I would lay out my case before him,
fill my mouth with arguments,
5 know the words
with which he would answer,
understand what he would say to me.
6 Would he contend with me
through brute force?
No, he would surely listen to me.
7 There those who do the right thing can
argue with him;
I could escape from my judge forever.

God's hiddenness

8 Look, I go east; he's not there,
west, and don't discover him;
9 north in his activity,
and I don't grasp him;
he turns south, and I don't see.
10 Surely he knows my way;
when he tests me,
I will emerge as gold.
11 My feet have stayed right in his tracks.
I have kept his way and not left it,
12 kept the commandments from his lips
and not departed,
valued the words from his mouth
more than my food.

Dread

13 He is of one mind; who can reverse it?
What he desires, he does.
14 He carries out what is decreed for me
and can do many similar things
with me.
15 Therefore, I am scared by his presence;
I think and become afraid of him.
16 God has weakened my mind;
the Almighty has frightened me.
17 Still I'm not annihilated by darkness;
he has hidden deep darkness from me.

[k] Heb *Shaddai* or *Mountain One*; also in 22:25 and 24:1 [l] Vulg, Syr, Tg; MT *my complaint is rebellious.*

Absence of justice

24 Why doesn't the Almighty establish
times for punishment?[m]
Why can't those who know him
see his days?
2 People move boundary stones,
herd flocks they've stolen,
3 drive off an orphan's donkey,
take a widow's ox as collateral,
4 thrust the poor out of the way,
make the land's needy hide together.
5 They are like the wild donkeys
in the desert;
they go forth at dawn
searching for prey;
the wasteland is food for their young.
6 They gather their food in the field,
glean in unproductive vineyards,
7 spend the night naked, unclothed,
in the cold without a cover,
8 wet from mountain rains,
with no refuge,
huddled against a rock.
9 The orphan is stolen from the breast;
the infant[n] of the poor
is taken as collateral.
10 The poor go around naked,
without clothes,
carry bundles of grain while hungry,
11 crush olives between millstones,[o]
tread winepresses, but remain thirsty.
12 From the city, the dying cry out;
the throat of the mortally wounded
screams, but God assigns no blame.

Sinners' conduct

13 They rebel against light,
don't acknowledge its direction,
don't dwell in its paths.
14 The murderer rises at twilight,
kills the poor and needy;
at night, they are like a thief.
15 The adulterer's eye watches for twilight,
thinking, No eye can see me,
and puts a mask over his face.
16 In the dark they break into houses;
they shut themselves in by day;
they don't know the light.
17 Deep darkness is morning to them
because they recognize the horror
of darkness.
18 They are scum on the water's surface;
their portion of the land is cursed;
no one walks down a path
in the vineyards.
19 Drought and heat steal melted snow,
just as the underworld[p] steals sinners.
20 The womb forgets them;
the worm consumes them;
they aren't remembered,
and so wickedness is shattered
like a tree.
21 They prey on the barren, the childless,
do nothing good for the widow.
22 They drag away the strong by force;
they may get up
but without guarantee of survival.
23 They make themselves secure;
they are at ease.
His[q] eyes are on their ways.
24 They are exalted for a short time,
but no longer.
They are humbled then gathered in
like everyone else;
cut off like heads of grain.
25 If this isn't so, who can prove me a liar
and make my words disappear?

Inferior humans

25 Bildad from Shuah replied:
2 Supreme power and awe
belong to God;
he establishes peace on his heights.
3 Can his troops be counted?
On whom does his light not rise?
4 How can a person be innocent before God;
one born of a woman be pure?
5 If even the moon is not bright
and the stars not pure in his eyes,
6 how much less a human, a worm,
a person's child, a grub.

Sarcasm

26 Then Job said:
2 How well you have helped the weak,
saved those with frail arms,
3 advised one lacking wisdom,
informed many with insight!

[m]Heb lacks *for punishment.* [n]Reading Heb *we'ul (infant)* for *we'al (against)* [o]Heb uncertain [p]Heb *Sheol* [q]Or *God's*

4 With whom have you spoken;[r]
whose breath was expelled from you?

Truth about God

5 The dead writhe,
the inhabitants beneath the waters
as well.
6 The grave[s] is naked before God;
the underworld[t] lacks covering.
7 He stretched the North[u] over chaos,
hung earth over nothing;
8 wrapped up water in his clouds,
yet they didn't burst out below;
9 hid the face of the full moon,[v]
spreading his cloud over it;
10 traced a circle on the water's surface,
at the limit of light and darkness.
11 Heaven's pillars shook,
terrified by his blast.
12 By his power he stilled the Sea;
split Rahab with his cleverness.
13 Due to his wind, heaven became clear;
his hand split the fleeing serpent.
14 Look, these are only the outer fringe
of his ways;
we hear only a whispered word
about him.
Who can understand
his thunderous power?

Job rejects Bildad's argument

27 Then Job took up his topic again:
2 As God lives,
who rejected my legal claim,
the Almighty, who made me bitter,
3 as long as breath is in me
and God's breath is in my nostrils—
4 my lips will utter no wickedness;
my tongue will mumble no deceit.
5 I will not agree that you are right.
Until my dying day,
I won't give up my integrity.
6 I will insist on my innocence,
never surrendering it;
my conscience will never blame me
for what I have done.[w]

Job curses his enemies

7 Let my enemy be like the wicked,
my opposition like the vicious.
8 For what hope has the godless
when God cuts them off,
when he takes them away.
9 Will God hear their cries
when distress comes to them;
10 will they delight in the Almighty,
call God at any time?

Job's view of his enemies' fate

11 I will teach you God's power,
not hide what pertains to the Almighty.
12 Look, those of you who recognize this—
why then this empty talk?
13 This is the wicked's portion with God,
the inheritance that the ruthless
receive from the Almighty.
14 If their children increase,
they belong to the sword;
their offspring
won't have enough bread.
15 Their survivors will be buried
with the dead;
their widows won't weep.
16 If they store up silver like dust,
amass clothing like clay,
17 they may amass,
but the righteous will wear it;
the innocent will divide the silver.
18 They built their houses like nests,
like a hut made by a watchman.
19 They lie down rich, but no longer;
open their eyes, but it's missing.
20 Terrors overtake them like waters;
a tempest snatches them by night;
21 an east wind lifts them,
and they are gone,
removes them from their places,
22 throws itself on them without mercy;
they flee desperately from its force.
23 It claps its hands over them,
hisses at them from their place.

Expertise in mining

28 There is a sure source of silver,
a place where gold is refined.
2 Iron is taken from the earth;
rock is smelted into copper.
3 Humans[x] put an end to darkness,
dig for ore to the farthest depths,
into stone in utter darkness,

[r] Or *told words* [s] Heb *Sheol* [t] Heb *Abaddon* [u] Heb *Zaphon* [v] Or *throne*; Heb uncertain [w] Or *for my days* [x] Or *they*

[4] open a shaft away from any inhabitant,
places forgotten by those on foot,
apart from any human
they hang and sway.
[5] Earth—from it comes food—
is turned over below ground as by fire.[y]
[6] Its rocks are the source for lapis lazuli;
there is gold dust in it.
[7] A path—
no bird of prey knows it;
a hawk's eye hasn't seen it;
[8] proud beasts haven't trodden on it;
a lion hasn't crossed over it.
[9] Humans thrust their hands into flint,
pull up mountains from their roots,
[10] cut channels into rocks;
their eyes see everything precious.
[11] They dam up the sources of rivers;
hidden things come to light.

Wisdom's value

[12] But wisdom, where can it be found;
where is the place of understanding?
[13] Humankind doesn't know its value;
it isn't found in the land of the living.
[14] The Deep[z] says, "It's not with me";
the Sea[a] says, "Not alongside me!"
[15] It can't be bought with gold;
its price can't be measured in silver,
[16] can't be weighed against
gold from Ophir,
with precious onyx or lapis lazuli.
[17] Neither gold nor glass
can compare with it;
she can't be acquired
with gold jewelry.
[18] Coral and jasper shouldn't be mentioned;
the price of wisdom
is more than rubies.
[19] Cushite topaz won't compare with her;
she can't be set alongside pure gold.
[20] But wisdom, where does she come from?
Where is the place of understanding?
[21] She's hidden from the eyes
of all the living,
concealed from birds of the sky.
[22] Destruction[b] and Death have said,
"We've heard a report of her."
[23] God understands her way;
he knows her place;
[24] for he looks to the ends of the earth
and surveys everything
beneath the heavens.
[25] In order to weigh the wind,
to prepare a measure for waters,
[26] when he made a decree for the rain,
a path for thunderbolts,
[27] then he observed it, spoke of it,
established it, searched it out,
[28] and said to humankind: "Look,
the fear of the LORD is wisdom;
turning from evil is understanding."

Job's previous blessing

29 Job took up his subject again:
[2] Oh, that life was like it used to be,
like days when God watched over me;
[3] when his lamp shone on my head,
I walked by his light in the dark;
[4] when I was in my prime;
when God's counsel was in my tent;
[5] when the Almighty was with me,
my children around me;
[6] when my steps were washed with cream
and a rock poured out
pools of oil for me.

Previous honor

[7] When I went out to the city gate,
took my seat in the square,
[8] the young saw me and drew back;
the old rose and stood;
[9] princes restrained speech,
put their hand on their mouth;
[10] the voices of officials were hushed,
their tongue stuck to their palate.

Job's implementation of justice

[11] Indeed, the ear that heard blessed me;
the eye that looked commended me,
[12] because I rescued the weak
who cried out,
the orphans who lacked help.
[13] The blessing of the perishing reached me;
I made the widow's heart sing;

[y] Heb uncertain [z] Heb *Tehom*, a reference to a divine being in the grave or underworld [a] Heb *Yam*, a sea god
[b] Heb *Abaddon*

14 I put on justice, and it clothed me,
righteousness as my coat and turban;
15 I was eyes to the blind,
feet to the lame.
16 I was a father to the needy;
the case I didn't know, I examined.
17 I shattered the fangs of the wicked,
rescued prey from their teeth.

Job's expected blessing

18 I thought, I'll die in my nest,
multiply days like sand,[c]
19 my roots opening to water,
dew lingering on my branches,
20 my honor newly with me,
my bow ever successful in my hand.

Previous honor

21 People listened to me and waited,
were silent for my advice.
22 After my speech, they didn't respond.
My words fell gently on them;
23 they waited for me as for rain,
opened their mouth
as for spring rain.
24 I smiled[d] on them;
they couldn't believe it.
They never showed me disfavor.
25 I decided their path, sat as chief.
I lived like a king with his troops,
like one who comforts mourners.

Mockers

30 But now
those younger than I mock me,
whose fathers I refused
to put beside my sheepdogs.
2 Their strength, what's it to me,
their energy having perished?
3 Stiff from want and hunger,
those who gnaw dry ground,
yesterday's desolate waste,
4 who pluck off the leaves on a bush,
the root of the broom—
a shrub is their food.
5 People banish them from society,
shout at them as if to a thief;
6 so they live in scary ravines,
holes in the ground and rocks.
7 Among shrubs, they make sounds
like donkeys;
they are huddled together
under a bush,
8 children of fools and the nameless,
whipped out of the land.

Specific mocking behavior

9 And now I'm their song;
I'm their cliché!
10 They detest me, keep their distance,
don't withhold spit from my face.
11 Because he loosened my bowstring
and afflicted me,
they throw off restraint
in my presence.
12 On the right, upstarts[e] rise
and target my feet,
build their siege ramps against me,
13 destroy my road,
profit from my fall,
with no help.
14 They advance as if through
a destroyed wall;[f]
they roll along beneath the ruin.
15 Terrors crash upon me;
they sweep away my honor like wind;
my safety disappears like a cloud.

Accusation against God

16 Now my life is poured out on me;
days of misery have seized me.
17 At night he bores my bones;
my gnawing pain won't rest.
18 With great force he grasps[g] my clothing;[h]
it binds me like the neck of my shirt.
19 He hurls me into mud;
I'm a cliché, like dust and ashes.
20 I cry to you, and you don't answer;
I stand up, but you just look at me.
21 You are cruel to me,
attack me with the strength
of your hand.
22 You lift me to the wind
and make me ride;
you melt me in its roar.
23 I know you will return me to death,
the house appointed
for all the living.

[c] Heb uncertain [d] Or *laughed at* [e] Heb uncertain [f] Or *a wide opening* [g] LXX [h] Heb uncertain

Job's agony

24 Surely he won't strike someone in ruins
if in distress he cries out to him,
25 if I didn't weep for those
who have a difficult day
or my soul grieve for the needy;
26 for I awaited good, but evil came;
I expected light, but gloom arrived.
27 My insides, churning, are never quiet;
days of affliction confront me.
28 I walk in the dark, lacking sunshine;
I rise in the assembly and cry out.
29 I have become a brother to jackals,
a companion to young ostriches.
30 My skin is charred;
my bones are scorched by the heat.
31 My lyre is for mourning,
my flute, a weeping sound.

Lust

31 I've made a covenant with my eyes;
how could I look at a virgin?
2 What is God's portion for me[i] from above,
the Almighty's inheritance
from on high?
3 Isn't it disaster for the wicked,
destruction for workers of iniquity?
4 Doesn't he see my ways,
count all my steps?

Deceit

5 If I have walked with frauds
or my feet have hurried to deceit,
6 let him weigh me on accurate scales;
let God know my integrity.
7 If my step has turned from the way,
if my heart has followed my eyes
or a blemish has clung to my hands,
8 then let me sow and another reap;
let my offspring be uprooted.

Adultery

9 If my heart has been drawn to a woman
and I have lurked
at my neighbor's door,
10 then may my wife grind for another
and others kneel over her;
11 for that's a crime;
it's a punishable offense;
12 indeed, it's a fire that consumes
to the underworld,[j]
uprooting all my harvest.

Slaves

13 If I've rejected the just cause
of my male or female servant
when they contended with me,
14 what could I do when God rises;
when he requires an account,
what could I answer?
15 Didn't the one who made me in the belly
make them;
didn't the same one fashion us
in the womb?

The defenseless

16 If I have denied what the poor wanted,
made a widow's eyes tired,
17 eaten my morsel alone,
and not shared any with an orphan
(18 for from my youth
I raised the orphan as a father,
and from my mother's womb
I led the widow);[k]
19 if I ever saw someone dying without
clothes, the needy naked;
20 if they haven't blessed me fervently,[l]
or if they weren't warmed
by the wool from my sheep;
21 if I have lifted my hand
against the orphans,
when I saw that I had help
in the city gate—
22 may my arm fall from my shoulder,
my forearm be broken at the elbow—
23 for God's calamity is terror to me;
I couldn't endure his splendor.

False worship

24 If I've made gold my trust,
said to fine gold: "My security!"
25 if I've rejoiced because
my wealth was great,
when my hand found plenty;
26 if I've looked at the sun when it shone,
the moon, splendid as it moved;
27 and my mind has been secretly enticed,
and threw a kiss with my hand,

[i] Heb lacks *for me.* [j] Heb *Abaddon* [k] Heb lacks *orphan . . . widow.* [l] Or *his loins*

[28] that also is a punishable offense,
because I would then be disloyal
to God above.

Other's misfortune

[29] If I have rejoiced over my foes' ruin
or was excited when evil found them,
[30] I didn't let my mouth sin
by asking for their life with a curse.
[31] Surely those in my tent never said:
"Who has been filled by Job's food?"
[32] A stranger didn't spend the night
in the street;
I opened my doors to the road.

Concealing sin

[33] If I have hidden my transgressions
like Adam,[m]
concealing my offenses inside me
[34] because I feared the large crowd;
the clan's contempt frightened me;
I was quiet and didn't venture outside.

Sealing the solemn pledge

[35] Oh, that I had someone to hear me!
Here's my signature;[n]
let the Almighty respond,
and let my accuser write an indictment.
[36] Surely I would bear it on my shoulder,
tie it around me like a wreath.
[37] I would give him an account
of my steps,
approach him like a prince.

Abuse of the land

[38] If my land has cried out against me,
its rows wept together;
[39] if I have eaten its yield
without payment
and caused its owners grief,
[40] may briars grow instead of wheat,
poisonous weeds instead of barley.

Job's words are complete.

Introduction of Elihu

32 These three men stopped answering Job because he thought he was
righteous.[o] [2] Elihu son of Barachel the Buzite from the clan of Ram was angry, angry
with Job because he considered himself
more righteous than God. [3] He was also
angry with his three friends because they
hadn't found an answer but nevertheless
thought Job wicked. [4] Elihu had waited
while Job spoke, for they were older than
he. [5] When Elihu saw that there had been no
response in the speeches of the three men,
he became very angry.

Elihu's justification for speaking

[6] Elihu son of Barachel the Buzite said:
I'm young and you're old,
so I held back, afraid to express
my opinion to you.
[7] I thought, Let days speak;
let multiple years
make wisdom known.
[8] But the spirit in a person,
the Almighty's breath,
gives understanding.
[9] The advanced in days aren't wise;
the old don't understand what's right.
[10] Therefore, I say: "Listen to me;
I'll state my view, even I."
[11] Look, I waited while you spoke,
listened while you reasoned,
while you searched for words.
[12] I was attentive to you,
but you offered no rebuke to Job,
no answer from you for his words.
[13] Be careful you don't say,
"We've found wisdom;
God, not a person, will defeat him."

[14] Now Job[p] hasn't addressed me,
and I won't quote you to him.
[15] They are troubled, no longer answer;
words now escape them.
[16] I waited, but they didn't speak,
for they stood but answered no more.
[17] I will answer.
Indeed, I will state[q] my piece;
I too will declare my view,
[18] for I'm full of words.
The spirit in my belly compels me.

[m] Or *like a human* [n] Heb *tau*, the last letter of the Hebrew alphabet [o] Or *was righteous in his own eyes*
[p] Or *he* [q] Heb lacks *will state.*

19 Look, my belly is like unopened wine;
like new wineskins it will burst.
20 I will speak and get relief;
I will open my lips and respond.
21 I won't be partial to anyone,
won't flatter a person;
22 for I don't know flattery;
otherwise my maker would quickly
whisk me away.

Elihu's appeal to be heard

33 But now, listen to me, Job;
pay attention to all my words.
2 Notice that I am opening my mouth;
my tongue is speaking in my mouth.[r]
3 My words come from a virtuous heart;
my lips speak knowledge clearly.
4 God's spirit made me;
the Almighty's breath enlivens me.
5 If you are able, answer me;
lay out your case[s] before me
and take a stand.
6 Notice that I'm just like you to God;
I also was pinched from clay.
7 Surely fear of me shouldn't scare you;
my pressure on you
shouldn't be heavy.

The argument

8 You certainly said in my hearing;
I heard the sound of your words:
9 "I'm pure, without sin;
I'm innocent, without offense.
10 Notice that he invents arguments
against me;
he considers me his enemy,
11 ties up my feet,
watches all my paths."
12 Now you're wrong about this;
I'll answer you,
for God is greater than anybody.
13 Why do you contend with him,
saying that he doesn't answer
all your words?[t]
14 God speaks in one way,
in two ways, but no one perceives it.
15 In the dream, a vision of the night,
when deep sleep falls upon humans,
during their slumber on a bed,
16 then he opens people's ears,
scares them with warnings,
17 to turn them from a deed
and to smother human pride.
18 He keeps one from the pit,
a life from perishing by the sword.
19 Or a person may be disciplined by pain
while in bed, bones ever aching
20 until a person loathes food,
an appetite rejects a delicacy;
21 the flesh wastes away,
no longer visible;
the bones, once hidden, protrude.
22 A life approaches the pit;
its very being draws near
the death dealers.
23 Surely there's a messenger
for this person,
a mediator, one out of a thousand
to declare one's integrity to another
24 so that God has compassion
on that person and says,
"Rescue this one from going down
to the pit;
I have found a ransom."
25 That person's flesh is renewed
like a child's;
they regain their youth.
26 They pray to God,
and God is pleased with them;
they behold God's presence
with a joyful shout.
God rewards a person's righteousness.
27 They sing before people and say:
"I have sinned, perverted justice,
but didn't experience the consequences.
28 He ransomed me
from crossing into the pit;
my life beholds light."
29 Look, God does all this,
twice, three times with persons
30 to bring them back from the pit,
to shine with life's light.
31 Listen, Job; hear me;
be quiet, and I will speak.
32 If you have words, answer me;
speak, for I want to be innocent.
33 If not, you must hear me;
be quiet, and I will teach you wisdom.

[r] Or *palate* [s] Heb lacks *your case.* [t] Or *his words*

34 Elihu continued:
2 Hear my words, wise ones;
knowledgeable ones, listen to me,
3 for the ear tests words
like the palate tastes food.
4 Let's choose for us what's right;
let's determine among ourselves
what's good;
5 for Job has said, "I'm innocent;
God has denied my just cause;
6 because of my cause I'm thought a liar;
my wound from an arrow is incurable,
even though I didn't rebel."
7 Who is a man like Job?
He drinks mockery like water
8 and travels a path with wrongdoers,
walking with evil persons.
9 Indeed he said, "No one is rewarded
for delighting in God."
10 Therefore, intelligent ones, hear me;
far be it from God to do evil
and the Almighty to sin,
11 for he repays people
based on what they do,
paying back everyone
according to their ways.
12 Surely God doesn't act wickedly;
the Almighty doesn't distort justice.
13 Who placed earth in his care,
and who gave him dominion
over the entire world?
14 If he were to decide to do it—
to gather his spirit and breath
back to himself—
15 all flesh would die together,
and humans would return to dust.

16 But if you have understanding, hear this;
pay attention to the sound of my words.
17 Will one who hates justice rule;
will you condemn
the most righteous one?
18 Will you say to a king, "Worthless!"
to royalty, "Evil!"
19 Who shows no favor to princes
nor regards the rich over the poor,
for they are all the work of God's
hands?
20 In the middle of the night
they suddenly die;
people are shaken and pass away.
The mighty are removed,
not by a human hand.
21 God's eyes are on human ways,
and he sees all their steps.
22 There's no darkness, no deep darkness,
where evildoers can hide themselves;
23 surely no time is set for a person
to appear before God in judgment.
24 He shatters the mighty
without examining them;
makes others take their place.
25 Thus he regards their deeds,
overturns them at night,
and they are crushed.
26 He strikes them
because of their wickedness
at a place where people can see it.
27 Because they turned from following him
and didn't value all his ways,
28 causing the cry of the poor to reach him,
he hears the cry of the afflicted.
29 Still, if he remains quiet,
who can condemn;
if he hides his face, who can see him?
30 He prevents a lawless person from ruling,
from capturing people.

31 Has Job said to God,
"I have borne punishment;
I won't sin again?
32 You teach me what I can't see;
if I've sinned, I won't do it again."
33 Will he repay you because you reject sin,
for you must choose, not I;
declare what you know.
34 Smart people say to me,
the wise who hear me,
35 "Job speaks without knowledge;
his words aren't astute."
36 I wish Job would be tested to the limit
because he responds like evil people.
37 He adds rebellion to his sin;
mocks us openly
and adds to his words against God.

Sin's impact

35 Elihu continued:
2 Do you think it right?
You say, "I'm more just than God."
3 Yet you ask, "What does it benefit you?
What have I gained by avoiding sin?"

[4]I'll answer you,
and your friends along with you.
[5]Look at the heavens and see;
scan the clouds high over you.
[6]If you've sinned,
how have you affected God?
Your offenses have multiplied;
what have you done to him?
[7]If you are righteous,
what do you give to him?
Or what does he receive
from your hand?
[8]Your evil affects others like you,
and your righteousness affects
fellow human beings.
[9]People cry out
because of heavy oppression;
shout under the power of the mighty.
[10]But no one says,
"Where is God my maker;
who gives songs in the night;
[11]who teaches us more than
the beasts of the earth,
makes us wiser than the birds in the sky?"
[12]Then they cry out;
but he doesn't answer,
because of the pride of the wicked.
[13]God certainly doesn't respond
to a deceitful cry;
the Almighty doesn't pay attention to it.
[14]Although you say that you don't see him,
the case is before him;
so wait anxiously for him.
[15]Even though his anger is now held back,
a person doesn't know it's only delayed.[u]
[16]So Job mouths emptiness;
he piles up ignorant words.

Reason for continuing

36 Continuing, Elihu said,
[2]Wait a little while
so I can demonstrate for you
that there is still something more
to say about God.
[3]I will draw from my broad knowledge,
attribute justice to my maker.
[4]My words are certainly truthful;
one with total knowledge
is present with you.

Divine discipline

[5]Look, God is mighty
and doesn't reject anyone;
he is mighty in strength and mind.
[6]He doesn't let the wicked live,
but grants justice to the poor.
[7]He doesn't avert his eyes
from the righteous;
he seats kings on thrones forever,
and they are lifted up.
[8]If they are tied with ropes,
caught in cords of affliction,
[9]he informs them about their offenses
and their grave sins.
[10]He opens their ears with discipline
and commands them
to turn from wrong.
[11]If they listen and serve,
they spend their days in plenty,
their years contentedly.
[12]But if they don't listen,
they perish by the sword,
breathe their last without understanding.
[13]Those with impious hearts
become furious;
they don't cry out
even though he binds them.
[14]They die young;
they are among the holy ones.
[15]He saves the weak in their affliction,
opens their ears through oppression.
[16]Surely he draws you up
from the brink of trouble
to a wide place without distress;
your table is set with rich food.
[17]You are overly concerned
about the case of the wicked;
justice will be upheld in it.
[18]Don't let them lure you with wealth;
don't let a huge bribe mislead you.
[19]Will he arrange your rescue from distress
or from all your exertions of strength?
[20]Don't wish for the night
when people vanish from their place.
[21]Take care; don't turn to evil
because you've chosen it over affliction.
[22]Look, God is inaccessible
due to his power;
who is a teacher like him?

[u]Heb uncertain

23 Who has repaid him for his action,
and who would ever say,
"You've done wrong"?
24 Remember to praise his work
that all of us have seen.
25 Every person has seen him;
people can observe at great distance.

God's control of the storm

26 Look, God is exalted and unknowable;
the number of his years
is beyond counting.
27 He draws up drops of water
that distill rain from his flood;
28 the clouds pour moisture
and drip continually on humans.
29 Even if one perceives a spreading cloud
and the thunder of his pavilion,[v]
30 look how he spreads lightning across it
and covers the seabed;
31 for by water[w] he judges peoples
and gives food in abundance.
32 He conceals lightning in his palms
and orders it to its target.
33 His thunder announces it;
even cattle proclaim its rising.

37 Oh, my mind is disturbed by this
and is more troubled than usual.
2 Listen closely to the rumble of his voice,
the roar issuing from his mouth.
3 He looses it under the whole sky,
his lightning on earth's edges.
4 After it, a voice roars;
he thunders with a mighty voice,
and no one can stop it
when his voice is heard.
5 God roars with his wondrous voice;
he does great things we can't know.
6 He says to the snow, "Fall to earth,"
and to the downpour of rain,
"Be a mighty shower."
7 He stamps the hand of every person
so all can know his work.[x]
8 The wild beast enters its lair,
lies down in its den.
9 The storm comes from its chamber,
the cold from the north wind.
10 By God's breath ice forms;
water's expanse becomes solid.
11 He also fills clouds with moisture;
his lightning scatters clouds.
12 He overturns the circling clouds;[y]
by his guidance they do[z] their work,
doing everything he commands
over the entire earth.
13 Whether for punishment, for his world,
or for kindness,
God makes it all happen.

14 Hear this, Job;
stop and ponder God's mighty deeds.
15 Do you realize that when God
commands them,
his clouds produce lightning?
16 Do you understand the positioning
of the clouds,
the amazing deeds of one
with perfect knowledge,
17 you whose clothes are hot
when earth is calmed
by the south wind?
18 Can you form the sky with him,
hard like a mirror made of metal?
19 Tell us what we should say to him;
we can't present our case
due to darkness.
20 Should someone inform him
that I wish to speak,
or would anyone say he wants
to be devoured?

Divine splendor

21 For now, no one can look at the sun;
it is bright in the sky;
the wind has passed and cleared away
the clouds.
22 From the north comes golden light,
the awesome splendor of God.
23 As for the Almighty,
we can't find him—
he is powerful and just,
abundantly righteous—
he won't respond.
24 Therefore, people fear him;
none of the wise[a] can see him.

[v]Or *canopy* [w]Or *them* [x]Or *that everyone he has made can know it* [y]Heb uncertain [z]Heb lacks *they do.*
[a]Or *wise in heart;* cf 9:4

The LORD answers from a whirlwind

38 Then the LORD answered Job from the whirlwind:

2 Who is this darkening counsel
with words lacking knowledge?
3 Prepare yourself like a man;
I will interrogate you,
and you will respond to me.

The establishing of order

4 Where were you
when I laid the earth's foundations?
Tell me if you know.
5 Who set its measurements?
Surely you know.
Who stretched a measuring tape on it?
6 On what were its footings sunk;
who laid its cornerstone,
7 while the morning stars sang in unison
and all the divine beings shouted?
8 Who enclosed the Sea[b] behind doors
when it burst forth from the womb,
9 when I made the clouds its garment,
the dense clouds its wrap,
10 when I imposed[c] my limit for it,
put on a bar and doors
11 and said, "You may come this far,
no farther;
here your proud waves stop"?

12 In your lifetime have you
commanded the morning,
informed the dawn of its place
13 so it would take hold of earth
by its edges
and shake the wicked out of it?
14 Do you turn it over like clay for a seal,
so it stands out
like a colorful garment?
15 Light is withheld from the wicked,
the uplifted arm broken.

The vast beyond

16 Have you gone to the sea's sources,
walked in the chamber of the deep?
17 Have death's gates been revealed to you;
can you see the gates of deep darkness?
18 Have you surveyed earth's expanses?
Tell me if you know everything about it.

19 Where's the road to the place
where light dwells;
darkness, where's it located?
20 Can you take it to its territory;
do you know the paths to its house?
21 You know, for you were born then;
you have lived such a long time![d]
22 Have you gone to snow's storehouses,
seen the storehouses of hail
23 that I have reserved for a time
of distress,
for a day of battle and war?
24 What is the way to the place
where light is divided up;
the east wind scattered over earth?

Meteorological facts

25 Who cut a channel for the downpours
and a way for blasts of thunder
26 to bring water to uninhabited land,
a desert with no human
27 to saturate dry wasteland
and make grass sprout?
28 Has the rain a father
who brought forth drops of dew?
29 From whose belly does ice come;
who gave birth to heaven's frost?
30 Water hardens like stone;
the surface of the deep thickens.
31 Can you bind Pleiades' chains
or loosen the reins of Orion?
32 Can you guide the stars
at their proper times,
lead the Bear with her cubs?
33 Do you know heaven's laws,
or can you impose its rule on earth?
34 Can you issue an order to the clouds
so their abundant waters cover you?
35 Can you send lightning so that it goes
and then says to you, "I'm here"?
36 Who put wisdom in remote places,
or who gave understanding
to a rooster?[e]
37 Who is wise enough
to count the clouds,
and who can tilt heaven's
water containers
38 so that dust becomes mud
and clods of dirt adhere?

[b] Heb *Yam*, a sea god [c] Heb uncertain [d] Or *the number of your days is many* [e] Heb uncertain

Lion and raven

39 Can you hunt prey for the lion
or fill the cravings of lion cubs?
40 They lie in their den,
lie in ambush in their lair.
41 Who provides food for the raven
when its young cry to God,
move about without food?

Mountain goat and doe

39 Do you know when mountain goats
give birth;
do you observe the birthing of does?
2 Can you count the months of pregnancy;
do you know when they give birth?
3 They crouch, split open for their young,
send forth their offspring.
4 Their young are healthy;
they grow up in the open country,
leave and never return.

Wild donkey

5 Who freed the wild donkey,
loosed the ropes of the onager
6 to whom I gave the desert as home,
his dwelling place in the salt flats?
7 He laughs at the clamor of the town,
doesn't hear the driver's shout,
8 searches the hills for food
and seeks any green sprout.

Wild ox

9 Will the wild ox agree to be your slave,
or will it spend the night in your crib?
10 Can you bind it with a rope
to a plowed row;
will it plow the valley behind you?
11 Will you trust it
because its strength is great
so that you can leave your work to it?
12 Can you rely on it to bring back your grain
to gather into your threshing floor?

Ostrich

13 The ostrich's wings flap joyously,
but her wings and plumage
are like a stork.
14 She leaves her eggs on the earth,
lets them warm in the dust,
15 then forgets that
a foot may crush them
or a wild animal trample them.
16 She treats her young harshly
as if they were not hers,
without worrying that her labor
might be in vain;
17 God didn't endow her with sense,
didn't give her some good sense.
18 When she flaps her wings high,
she laughs at horse and rider.

Horse

19 Did you give strength to the horse,
clothe his neck with a mane,
20 cause him to leap like a locust,
his majestic snorting, a fright?
21 He[f] paws in the valley, prances proudly,
charges at battle weapons,
22 laughs at fear, unafraid.
He doesn't turn away from the sword;
23 a quiver of arrows flies by him,
flashing spear and dagger.
24 Excitedly, trembling,
he swallows the ground;
can't stand still at a trumpet's blast.
25 At a trumpet's sound, he says, "Aha!"
smells the battle from afar,
hears[g] officers' shouting
and the battle cry.

Hawk and eagle

26 Is it due to your understanding
that the hawk flies,
spreading its wings to the south?
27 Or at your command does the eagle soar,
the vulture build a nest on high?
28 They dwell on an outcropping of rock,
their fortress on rock's edge.
29 From there they search for food;
their eyes notice it from afar,
30 and their young lap up blood;
where carcasses lie, there they are.

The LORD speaks and Job answers

40 The LORD continued
to respond to Job:
2 Will the one who disputes with the
Almighty correct him?
God's instructor must answer him.

[f] Or *they* [g] Heb lacks *hears*.

[3] Job responded to the LORD:
[4] Look, I'm of little worth.
What can I answer you?
I'll put my hand over my mouth.
[5] I have spoken once, I won't answer;
twice, I won't do it again.

A challenge from the LORD

[6] The LORD answered Job
from the whirlwind:
[7] Prepare yourself like a man;
I will interrogate you,
and you will respond to me.
[8] Would you question my justice,
deem me guilty so you can be innocent?
[9] Or do you have an arm like God;
can you thunder with a voice like him?
[10] Adorn yourself
with splendor and majesty;
clothe yourself with honor and esteem.
[11] Unleash your raging anger;
look on all the proud and humble them.
[12] Look on all the proud and debase them;
trample the wicked in their place.
[13] Hide them together in the dust;
bind their faces in a hidden place.
[14] Then I, even I, will praise you,
for your strong hand has delivered you.

Behemoth

[15] Look at Behemoth,
whom I made along with you;
he eats grass like cattle.
[16] Look, his strength is in his thighs,
his power in stomach muscles.
[17] He stiffens his tail like a cedar;
the tendons in his thighs
are tightly woven.
[18] His bones are like bronze tubes,
his limbs like iron bars.
[19] He is the first of God's acts;
only his maker can come near him
with a sword.
[20] Indeed, the hills bring him tribute,
places where all the wild animals play.
[21] He lies under the lotuses,
under the cover of reed and marsh.
[22] The lotuses screen him with shade;
poplars of the stream surround him.
[23] If the river surges, he doesn't hurry;
he is confident even though the Jordan
gushes into his mouth.
[24] Can he be seized by his eyes?
Can anyone pierce his nose by hooks?

Leviathan

41 [h] Can you draw out Leviathan
with a hook,
restrain his tongue with a rope?
[2] Can you put a cord through his nose,
pierce his jaw with a barb?
[3] Will he beg you at length
or speak gentle words to you?
[4] Will he make a pact with you
so that you will take him as a
permanent slave?
[5] Can you play with him like a bird,
put a leash on him for your girls?
[6] Will merchants sell him;
will they divide him among traders?
[7] Can you fill his hide with darts,
his head with a fishing spear?
[8] Should you lay your hand on him,
you would never remember
the battle.
[9] Such hopes[i] would be delusional;
surely the sight of him
makes one stumble.
[10] Nobody is fierce enough to rouse him;
who then can stand before me?
[11] Who opposes me that I must repay?
Everything under heaven is mine.
[12] I'm not awed by his limbs,
his strength, and impressive form.
[13] Who can remove his outer garment;
who can come with a bridle for him?
[14] Who can open the doors of his mouth,
surrounded by frightening teeth?
[15] His matching scales are his pride,
closely locked and sealed.
[16] One touches another;
even air can't come between them.
[17] Each clings to its pair;
joined, they can't be separated.
[18] His sneezes emit flashes of light;
his eyes are like dawn's rays.
[19] Shafts of fire shoot from his mouth;
like fiery sparks they fly out.

[h] 40:25 in Heb [i] Or *his hopes*

[20] Smoke pours from his nostrils
like a boiling pot over reeds.
[21] His breath lights coals;
a flame shoots from his mouth.
[22] Power resides in his neck;
violence dances before him.
[23] The folds of his flesh stick together;
on him they are tough and unyielding.
[24] His heart is solid like a rock,
hard like a lower millstone.
[25] The divine beings dread his rising;
they withdraw before his thrashing.
[26] The sword that touches him
won't prevail;
neither will the dart, spear, nor javelin.
[27] He treats iron as straw,
bronze as rotten wood.
[28] Arrows can't make him flee;
slingstones he turns to straw.
[29] He treats a club like straw;
he laughs at the lance's rattle.
[30] His abdomen is
like jagged pottery shards;
its sharp edges leave a trail in the mud.
[31] He causes the depths
to churn like a boiling pot,
stirs up the sea
like a pot of scented oils,
[32] leaves a bright wake behind him;
the frothy deep seems white-haired.
[33] None on earth can compare to him;
he is made to be without fear.
[34] He looks on all the proud;
he is king over all proud beasts.

Job's second response

42 Job answered the LORD:
[2] I know you can do anything;
no plan of yours
can be opposed successfully.
[3] You said,[j] "Who is this darkening counsel
without knowledge?"
I have indeed spoken about
things I didn't understand,
wonders beyond my comprehension.
[4] You said,[k] "Listen and I will speak;
I will question you
and you will inform me."
[5] My ears had heard about you,
but now my eyes have seen you.
[6] Therefore, I relent[l] and find comfort
on dust and ashes.

Epilogue

[7] After the LORD had spoken these words
to Job, he said to Eliphaz from Teman, "I'm
angry at you and your two friends because
you haven't spoken about me correctly as
did my servant Job. [8] So now, take seven
bulls and seven rams, go to my servant Job,
and prepare an entirely burned offering for
yourselves. Job my servant will pray for
you, and I will act favorably by not making
fools of you because you didn't speak correctly, as did my servant Job."
[9] Eliphaz from Teman, Bildad from Shuah,
and Zophar from Naamah did what the
LORD told them; and the LORD acted favorably toward Job. [10] Then the LORD changed
Job's fortune when he prayed for his friends,
and the LORD doubled all Job's earlier possessions. [11] All his brothers, sisters, and acquaintances came to him and ate food with
him in his house. They comforted and consoled him concerning all the disaster the
LORD had brought on him, and each one
gave him a qesitah[m] and a gold ring. [12] Then
the LORD blessed Job's latter days more
than his former ones. He had fourteen thousand sheep, six thousand camels, one thousand yoke of oxen, and one thousand female
donkeys. [13] He also had seven sons and three
daughters. [14] He named one Jemimah,[n] a second Keziah,[o] and the third Keren-happuch.[p]
[15] No women in all the land were as beautiful
as Job's daughters; and their father gave an
inheritance to them along with their brothers. [16] After this, Job lived 140 years and saw
four generations of his children. [17] Then Job
died, old and satisfied.

[j] Heb lacks *You said.* [k] Heb lacks *You said.* [l] The verse is capable of several translations: *I despise or relent,* no direct object; *repent of or concerning dust and ashes.* [m] A monetary unit [n] *Dove* [o] *Cinnamon* [p] *Jar for Dark Cosmetic*

PSALMS

BOOK I
(Psalms 1–41)

Psalm 1

1 The truly happy person
doesn't follow wicked advice,
doesn't stand on the road of sinners,
and doesn't sit with the disrespectful.
2 Instead of doing those things,
these persons
love the LORD's Instruction,
and they recite God's Instruction
day and night!
3 They are like a tree
replanted by streams of water,
which bears fruit at just the right time
and whose leaves don't fade.
Whatever they do succeeds.

4 That's not true for the wicked!
They are like dust
that the wind blows away.
5 And that's why the wicked
will have no standing
in the court of justice—
neither will sinners
in the assembly of the righteous.
6 The LORD is intimately acquainted
with the way of the righteous,
but the way of the wicked is destroyed.

Psalm 2

1 Why do the nations rant?
Why do the peoples rave uselessly?
2 The earth's rulers take their stand;
the leaders scheme together
against the LORD and
against his anointed one.
3 "Come!" they say.
"We will tear off their ropes
and throw off their chains!"
4 The one who rules in heaven laughs;
my Lord makes fun of them.
5 But then God speaks to them angrily;
then he terrifies them with his fury:
6 "I hereby appoint my king on Zion,
my holy mountain!"

7 I will announce the LORD's decision:
He said to me, "You are my son,
today I have become your father.
8 Just ask me,
and I will make the nations
your possession;
the far corners of the earth
will be your property.
9 You will smash them with an iron rod;
you will shatter them like a pottery jar."

10 So kings, wise up!
Be warned, you rulers of the earth!
11 Serve the LORD reverently—
trembling, 12 kiss his feet[a]
or else he will become angry,
and your way will be destroyed
because his anger ignites in an instant.

But all who take refuge in the LORD
are truly happy!

Psalm 3

A psalm of David,
when he fled from his son Absalom.

1 LORD, I have so many enemies!
So many are standing against me.
2 So many are talking about me:
"Even God won't help him." *Selah*[b]
3 But you, LORD, are my shield!
You are my glory!
You are the one who restores me.
4 I cry out loud to the LORD,
and he answers me
from his holy mountain. *Selah*
5 I lie down, sleep, and wake up
because the LORD helps me.
6 I won't be afraid of thousands of people
surrounding me on all sides.

7 Stand up, LORD!
Save me, my God!

[a] Correction; Heb uncertain; MT *rejoice with trembling, kiss the son* (but with *son* in Aram, not Heb)
[b] Heb uncertain; probably a musical term

In fact, hit all my enemies on the jaw;
shatter the teeth of the wicked!
8 Rescue comes from the LORD!
May your blessing be on your people!
Selah

Psalm 4

For the music leader. With stringed instruments. A psalm of David.

1 Answer me when I cry out,
my righteous God!
Set me free from my troubles!
Have mercy on me!
Listen to my prayer!

2 How long, you people,
will my reputation be insulted?
How long will you continue
to love what is worthless
and go after lies? *Selah*
3 Know this: the LORD takes
personal care of the faithful.
The LORD will hear me
when I cry out to him.
4 So be afraid, and don't sin!
Think hard about it in your bed
and weep over it! *Selah*
5 Bring righteous offerings,
and trust the LORD!

6 Many people say,
"We can't find goodness anywhere.
The light of your face has left us, LORD!"[c]
7 But you have filled my heart with more joy
than when their wheat and wine are
everywhere!
8 I will lie down and fall asleep in peace
because you alone, LORD,
let me live in safety.

Psalm 5

For the music leader. For the flutes. A psalm of David.

1 Hear my words, LORD!
Consider my groans!
2 Pay attention to the sound of my cries,
my king and my God,
because I am praying to you!
3 LORD, in the morning you hear my voice.
In the morning I lay it all out before you.
Then I wait expectantly.
4 Because you aren't a God
who enjoys wickedness;
evil doesn't live with you.
5 Arrogant people won't last long
in your sight;
you hate all evildoers;
6 you destroy liars.
The LORD despises people
who are violent and dishonest.

7 But me? I will enter your house
because of your abundant, faithful love;
I will bow down at your holy temple,
honoring you.
8 LORD, because of many enemies,
please lead me in your righteousness.
Make your way clear,
right in front of me.
9 Because there's no truth
in my enemies' mouths,
all they have inside them is destruction.
Their throats are open graves;
their tongues slick with talk.
10 Condemn them, God!
Let them fail by their own plans.
Throw them out for their many sins
because they've rebelled against you.
11 But let all who take refuge in you celebrate.
Let them sing out loud forever!
Protect them
so that all who love your name
can rejoice in you.
12 Because you, LORD, bless the righteous.
You cover them with favor like a shield.

Psalm 6

For the music leader. On stringed instruments. According to the eighth.[d] A psalm of David.

1 Please, LORD,
don't punish me when you are angry;
don't discipline me when you are furious.

[c]Correction; MT *Shine the light of your face on us, LORD!* [d]Perhaps a reference to an eight-string instrument; also in Ps 12

2 Have mercy on me, LORD,
because I'm frail.
Heal me, LORD,
because my bones
are shaking in terror!
3 My whole body[e] is completely terrified!
But you, LORD! How long will this last?
4 Come back to me, LORD! Deliver me!
Save me for the sake of your faithful love!
5 No one is going to praise you
when they are dead.
Who gives you thanks
from the grave?[f]

6 I'm worn out from groaning.
Every night, I drench my bed
with tears;
I soak my couch all the way through.
7 My vision fails because of my grief;
it's weak because of all my distress.
8 Get away from me, all you evildoers,
because the LORD has heard me crying!
9 The LORD has listened to my request.
The LORD accepts my prayer.
10 All my enemies will be ashamed
and completely terrified;
they will be defeated
and ashamed instantly.

Psalm 7

A shiggayon[g] of David, which he sang to the LORD about Cush, a Benjaminite.

1 I take refuge in you, LORD, my God.
Save me from all who chase me!
Rescue me!
2 Otherwise, they will rip me apart,
dragging me off
with no chance of rescue.
3 LORD, my God, if I have done this—
if my hands have done
anything wrong,
4 if I have repaid a friend with evil
or oppressed a foe for no reason—
5 then let my enemy
not only chase but catch me,
trampling my life into the ground,
laying my reputation in the dirt. *Selah*

6 Get up, LORD; get angry!
Stand up against the fury of my foes!
Wake up, my God;[h]
you command that justice be done!
7 Let the assembled peoples surround you.
Rule them from on high![i]
8 The LORD will judge the peoples.
Establish justice for me, LORD,
according to my righteousness
and according to my integrity.
9 Please let the evil of the wicked be over,
but set the righteous firmly in place
because you, the righteous God,
are the one who examines
hearts and minds.

10 God is my shield;
he saves those whose heart is right.
11 God is a righteous judge,
a God who is angry at evil[j]
every single day.
12 If someone doesn't change their ways,
God will sharpen his sword,
will bend his bow,
will string an arrow.
13 God has deadly weapons in store
for those who won't change;
he gets his flaming arrows ready!

14 But look how the wicked hatch evil,
conceive trouble, give birth to lies!
15 They make a pit, dig it all out,
and then fall right into the hole
that they've made!
16 The trouble they cause
will come back on their own heads;
the violence they commit
will come down on their own skulls.
17 But I will thank the LORD
for his righteousness;
I will sing praises
to the name of the LORD Most High.

Psalm 8

For the music leader. According to the Gittith.[k] A psalm of David.

1 LORD, our Lord, how majestic
is your name throughout the earth!

[e]Or *soul;* also in 6:4 [f]Heb *Sheol* [g]Perhaps *lament* [h]Or *for my sake* [i]Correction; MT *Come back to be exalted over them.* [j]Heb lacks *at evil.* [k]Perhaps the name of an instrument (Tg) or melody. LXX *About the winepresses;* or *About the Gittite;* also in Pss 81 and 84

You made your glory
higher than heaven![l]
[2] From the mouths of nursing babies
you have laid a strong foundation
because of your foes,
in order to stop vengeful enemies.
[3] When I look up at your skies,
at what your fingers made—
the moon and the stars
that you set firmly in place—
[4] what are human beings
that you think about them;
what are human beings
that you pay attention to them?
[5] You've made them only slightly
less than divine,
crowning them with glory and grandeur.
[6] You've let them rule
over your handiwork,
putting everything under their feet—
[7] all sheep and all cattle,
the wild animals too,
[8] the birds in the sky,
the fish of the ocean,
everything that travels
the pathways of the sea.
[9] LORD, our Lord, how majestic
is your name throughout the earth!

Psalm 9[m]

For the music leader. According to Muth-labben.[n] A psalm of David.

א [1] I will thank you, LORD,
with all my heart;
I will talk about
all your wonderful acts.
[2] I will celebrate and rejoice in you;
I will sing praises to your name,
Most High.

ב [3] When my enemies turn and retreat,
they fall down and die
right in front of you
[4] because you have established justice
for me and my claim,
because you rule from the throne,
establishing justice rightly.

ג [5] You've denounced the nations,
destroyed the wicked.
You've erased their names for all time.
[6] Every enemy is wiped out,
like something ruined forever.
You've torn down their cities—
even the memory of them is dead.

ה [7] But the LORD rules forever!
He assumes his throne
for the sake of justice.
[8] He will establish justice
in the world rightly;
he will judge all people fairly.
ו [9] The LORD is a safe place
for the oppressed—
a safe place in difficult times.
[10] Those who know your name trust you
because you have not abandoned
any who seek you, LORD.

ז [11] Sing praises to the LORD,
who lives in Zion!
Proclaim his mighty acts
among all people!
[12] Because the one who avenges bloodshed
remembers those who suffer;
the LORD hasn't forgotten
their cries for help.

ח [13] Have mercy on me, LORD!
Just look how I suffer
because of those who hate me.
But you are the one
who brings me back
from the very gates of death
[14] so I can declare all your praises,
so I can rejoice in your salvation
in the gates of Daughter Zion.

ט [15] The nations have fallen
into the hole they themselves made!
Their feet are caught
in the very net they themselves hid!

[l]Correction; Heb uncertain [m]Ps 9 is an alphabetic acrostic poem (cf Ps 119) in Heb, with successive letters of the alphabet beginning every few lines, with only a few exceptions. Only ten letters are found in Ps 9; the sequence may be continued in Ps 10, suggesting that Pss 9–10 are a single poem. [n]Or *Almuth labben*; Heb uncertain, perhaps a reference to the melody; cf Pss 46:1; 48:14

[16]The LORD is famous for the justice
he has done;
it's his own doing
that the wicked are trapped.
Higgayon.[o] *Selah*

י [17]Let the wicked
go straight to the grave,[p]
the same for every nation
that forgets God.

כ [18]Because the poor
won't be forgotten forever,
the hope of those who suffer
won't be lost for all time.

[19]Get up, LORD! Don't let people prevail!
Let the nations be judged before you.
[20]Strike them with fear, LORD.
Let the nations know
they are only human. *Selah*

Psalm 10[q]

ל [1]Why do you stand
so far away, LORD,
hiding yourself in troubling times?
[2]Meanwhile, the wicked are proudly
in hot pursuit of those who suffer.
Let them get caught
in the very same schemes
they've thought up!

[3]The wicked brag
about their body's[r] cravings;
the greedy reject the LORD, cursing.
[4]At the peak of their wrath,
the wicked don't seek God:
There's no God—
that's what they are always thinking.
[5]Their ways are always twisted.
Your rules are too lofty for them.
They snort at all their foes.
[6]They think to themselves,
We'll never stumble.
We'll never encounter
any resistance.

פ [7]Their mouths are filled
with curses, dishonesty, violence.
Under their tongues lie
troublemaking and wrongdoing.
[8]They wait in a place
perfect for ambush;[s]
from their hiding places
they kill innocent people;
ע their eyes spot those
who are helpless.
[9]They lie in ambush
in secret places,
like a lion in its lair.
They lie in ambush
so they can seize those who suffer!
They seize the poor, all right,
dragging them off in their nets.
[10]Their helpless victims are crushed;
they collapse, falling prey
to the strength of the wicked.
[11]The wicked think to themselves:
God has forgotten.
God has hidden his face.
God never sees anything!

ק [12]Get up, LORD!
Get your fist ready, God!
Don't forget the ones who suffer!
[13]Why do the wicked reject God?
Why do they think to themselves
that you won't find out?
ר [14]But you do see!
You do see troublemaking and grief,
and you do something about it!
The helpless leave it all to you.
You are the orphan's helper.

ש [15]Break the arms of those
who are wicked and evil.
Seek out their wickedness
until there's no more to find.
[16]The LORD rules forever and always!
The nations will vanish from his land.

ת [17]LORD, you listen to the desires
of those who suffer.
You steady their hearts;
you listen closely to them,

[o]Heb uncertain; or *recitation* (see Pss 1:2; 19:14) or *melody* (see Ps 92:3). [p]Heb *Sheol* [q]Pss 9 and 10 contain part of an acrostic poem and might originally be one poem in Heb. [r]Or *soul's* [s]Heb uncertain

18 to establish justice
for the orphan and the oppressed,
so that people of the land
will never again be terrified.

Psalm 11

For the music leader. Of David.

1 I have taken refuge in the LORD.
So how can you say to me,[t]
"Flee to the hills like a bird
2 because the wicked
have already bent their bows;
they've already strung their arrows;
they are ready to secretly shoot
those whose heart is right"?
3 When the very bottom of things falls out,
what can a righteous person
possibly accomplish?

4 But the LORD is in his holy temple.
The LORD! His throne is in heaven.
His eyes see—
his vision examines all of humanity.
5 The LORD examines
both the righteous and the wicked;
his very being[u] hates
anyone who loves violence.
6 God will rain fiery coals and sulfur
on the wicked;
their cups will be filled
with nothing but a scorching hot wind
7 because the LORD is righteous!
He loves righteous deeds.
Those whose heart is right
will see God's face.[v]

Psalm 12

For the music leader. According to the Sheminith.[w] A psalm of David.

1 Help, LORD,
because the godly are all gone;
the faithful have completely disappeared
from the human race!
2 Everyone tells lies to everyone else;
they talk with slick speech
and divided hearts.
3 Let the LORD cut off all slick-talking lips
and every tongue that brags and brags,
4 that says, "We're unbeatable
with our tongues!
Who could get the best of us
with lips like ours?"

5 But the LORD says,
"Because the poor are oppressed,
because of the groans of the needy,
I'm now standing up.
I will provide the help
they are gasping for."[x]
6 The LORD's promises are pure,
like silver that's been refined
in an oven,
purified seven times over!

7 You, LORD, will keep us,[y]
protecting us
from this generation forever.
8 The wicked roam all over the place,
while depravity is praised
by human beings.

Psalm 13

For the music leader. A song of David.

1 How long will you forget me, LORD?
Forever?
How long will you hide your face
from me?
2 How long will I be left to my own wits,
agony filling my heart? Daily?
How long will my enemy keep
defeating me?

3 Look at me!
Answer me, LORD my God!
Restore sight to my eyes!
Otherwise, I'll sleep the sleep of death,
4 and my enemy will say, "I won!"
My foes will rejoice over my downfall.

5 But I have trusted in your faithful love.
My heart will rejoice in your salvation.
6 Yes, I will sing to the LORD
because he has been good to me.

[t] Or *my soul* [u] Or *soul* [v] Heb lacks *heart*, but see 11:2 and Pss 7:10; 32:11; 36:10. [w] Perhaps a reference to an eight-string instrument; also in Ps 6 [x] Heb uncertain [y] LXX; MT *keep them*

Psalm 14

For the music leader. Of David.

1 Fools say in their hearts,
There is no God.
They are corrupt and do evil things;
not one of them does anything good.

2 The LORD looks down
from heaven on humans
to see if anyone is wise,
to see if anyone seeks God,
3 but all of them have turned bad.
Everyone is corrupt.
No one does good—
not even one person!

4 Are they dumb, all these evildoers,
devouring my people
like they are eating bread
but never calling on the LORD?

5 Count on it:[z] they will be in utter panic
because God is with
the righteous generation.
6 You evildoers may humiliate
the plans of those who suffer,
but the LORD is their refuge.

7 Let Israel's salvation come out of Zion!
When the LORD changes
his people's circumstances
for the better,
Jacob will rejoice;
Israel will celebrate!

Psalm 15

A psalm of David.

1 Who can live in your tent, LORD?
Who can dwell
on your holy mountain?
2 The person who
lives free of blame,
does what is right,
and speaks the truth sincerely;
3 who does no damage with their talk,
does no harm to a friend,
doesn't insult a neighbor;
4 someone who despises
those who act wickedly,
but who honors those
who honor the LORD;
someone who keeps their promise
even when it hurts;
5 someone who doesn't lend money
with interest,
who won't accept a bribe
against any innocent person.
Whoever does these things
will never stumble.

Psalm 16

A miktam[a] of David.

1 Protect me, God,
because I take refuge in you.
2 I say to the LORD, "You are my Lord.
Apart from you, I have nothing good."
3 Now as for the "holy ones" in the land,
the "magnificent ones"
that I was so happy about;
4 let their suffering increase because
they hurried after a different god.[b]
I won't participate
in their blood offerings;
I won't let their names
cross my lips.
5 You, LORD, are my portion, my cup;
you control my destiny.
6 The property lines have fallen
beautifully for me;
yes, I have a lovely home.

7 I will bless the LORD who advises me;
even at night I am instructed
in the depths of my mind.
8 I always put the LORD in front of me;
I will not stumble
because he is on my right side.
9 That's why my heart celebrates
and my mood is joyous;
yes, my whole body will rest in safety
10 because you won't abandon my life[c]
to the grave;[d]
you won't let your faithful follower
see the pit.

[z] Or *There they will be*; cf 53:5 [a] Perhaps *inscription* [b] Heb uncertain in 16:3-4; Heb lacks *because* and *god* in 16:4.
[c] Or *my soul* [d] Heb *Sheol*

11 You teach me the way of life.
In your presence is total celebration.
Beautiful things are always
in your right hand.

Psalm 17

A prayer of David.

1 Listen to what's right, LORD;
pay attention to my cry!
Listen closely to my prayer;
it's spoken by lips that don't lie!
2 My justice comes from you;
let your eyes see what is right!
3 You have examined my heart,
testing me at night.
You've looked me over closely,
but haven't found anything wrong.
My mouth doesn't sin.
4 But these other people's deeds?
I have avoided such violent ways
by the command from your lips.
5 My steps are set firmly on your paths;
my feet haven't slipped.

6 I cry out to you because you answer me.
So tilt your ears toward me now—
listen to what I'm saying!
7 Manifest your faithful love
in amazing ways
because you are the one
who saves those
who take refuge in you,
saving them from their attackers
by your strong hand.
8 Watch me with the very pupil of your eye!
Hide me in the protection
of your wings,
9 away from the wicked
who are out to get me,
away from my deadly enemies
who are all around me!
10 They have no pity;[e]
their mouths speak arrogantly.
11 They track me down—
suddenly, they surround me!
They make their plans
to put me in the dirt.
12 They are like a lion eager to rip its prey;
they are like a strong young lion
lying in wait.

13 Get up, LORD!
Confront them!
Bring them down!
Rescue my life from the wicked—
use your sword!
14 Rescue me from these people—
use your own hands, LORD!
Rescue me from these people
whose only possession
is their fleeting life.[f]
But fill the stomachs
of your cherished ones;
let their children be filled full
so that they have leftovers
enough for their babies.

15 But me? I will see your face
in righteousness;
when I awake, I will be filled full
by seeing your image.

Psalm 18[g]

For the music leader. Of David the LORD's servant, who spoke the words of this song to the LORD after the LORD delivered him from the power of all his enemies and from Saul.

1 He said: I love you, LORD, my strength.
2 The LORD is my solid rock,
my fortress, my rescuer.
My God is my rock—
I take refuge in him!—
he's my shield,
my salvation's strength,
my place of safety.
3 Because he is praiseworthy,[h]
I cried out to the LORD,
and I was saved from my enemies.
4 Death's cords were wrapped around me;
rivers of wickedness terrified me.
5 The cords of the grave[i] surrounded me;
death's traps held me tight.
6 In my distress I cried out to the LORD;

[e]Heb uncertain [f]Heb uncertain [g]This poem also occurs in 2 Sam 22 with some variations. [h]Heb uncertain
[i]Heb *Sheol*

I called to my God for help.
God heard my voice from his temple;
I called to him for help,
and my call reached his ears.

7 The earth rocked and shook;
the bases of the mountains
trembled and reeled
because of God's anger.
8 Smoke went up from God's nostrils;
out of his mouth came a devouring fire;
flaming coals blazed out in front of him!
9 God parted the skies and came down;
thick darkness was beneath his feet.
10 God mounted the heavenly creatures
and flew;
he soared on the wings of the wind.
11 God made darkness cloak him;
his covering was dark water
and dense cloud.
12 God's clouds went ahead
of the brightness before him;
hail and coals of fire went too.
13 The LORD thundered in heaven;
the Most High made his voice heard
with hail and coals of fire.
14 God shot his arrows, scattering the enemy;
he sent the lightning and threw them
into confusion.
15 The seabeds were exposed;
the earth's foundations were laid bare
at your rebuke, LORD,
at the angry blast of air coming
from your nostrils.

16 From on high God reached down
and grabbed me;
he took me out of all that water.
17 God saved me from my powerful enemy,
saved me from my foes,
who were too much for me.
18 They came at me on the very day
of my distress,
but the LORD was my support.
19 He brought me out to wide-open spaces;
he pulled me out safe
because he is pleased with me.
20 The LORD rewarded me
for my righteousness;
he restored me
because my hands are clean,
21 because I have kept the LORD's ways.
I haven't acted wickedly against my God.
22 All his rules are right in front of me;
I haven't turned away from
any of his laws.
23 I have lived with integrity before him;
I've kept myself from wrongdoing.
24 And so the LORD restored me
for my righteousness
because my hands are clean in his eyes.

25 You deal faithfully with the faithful;
you show integrity
toward the one who has integrity.
26 You are pure toward the pure,
but toward the crooked, you are tricky.
27 You are the one who saves
people who suffer
and brings down those with proud eyes.
28 You are the one who lights my lamp—
the LORD my God
illumines my darkness.
29 With you I can charge into battle;
with my God I can leap over a wall.
30 God! His way is perfect;
the LORD's word is tried and true.
He is a shield
for all who take refuge in him.

31 Now really, who is divine except the LORD?
And who is a rock but our God?
32 Only God! The God
who equips me with strength
and makes my way perfect,
33 who makes my step as sure as the deer's,
who lets me stand securely
on the heights,
34 who trains my hands for war
so my arms can bend a bronze bow.
35 You've given me the shield
of your salvation;
your strong hand has supported me;
your help has made me great.
36 You've let me walk fast and safe,
without even twisting an ankle.
37 I chased my enemies and caught them!
I didn't come home
until I finished them off.
38 I struck them down;
they couldn't get up again;
they fell under my feet.

39 You equipped me with strength for war;
you brought my adversaries down
underneath me.
40 You made my enemies turn tail from me;
I destroyed my foes.
41 They cried for help,
but there was no one to save them.
They cried for help to the LORD,
but he wouldn't answer them.
42 I crushed them
like dust blown away by the wind;
I threw them out
like mud dumped in the streets.
43 You delivered me from struggles
with many people;
you appointed me the leader
of many nations.
Strangers come to serve me.
44 After hearing about me, they obey me;
foreigners grovel before me.
45 Foreigners lose their nerve;
they come trembling
out of their fortresses.[j]

46 The LORD lives! Bless God, my rock!
Let the God of my salvation be lifted high!
47 This is the God who avenges on my behalf,
who subdues people before me,
48 who delivers me from my enemies.
Yes, you lifted me high
above my adversaries;
you delivered me from violent people.
49 That's why I thank you, LORD,
in the presence of the nations.
That's why I sing praises to your name.
50 You are the one who gives great victories
to your king,
who shows faithful love
to your anointed one—
to David and to his descendants forever.

Psalm 19

For the music leader. A psalm of David.

1 Heaven is declaring God's glory;
the sky is proclaiming his handiwork.
2 One day gushes the news to the next,
and one night informs another
what needs to be known.
3 Of course, there's no speech, no words—
their voices can't be heard—
4 but their sound[k] extends
throughout the world;
their words reach the ends
of the earth.

God has made a tent in heaven
for the sun.
5 The sun is like a groom
coming out of his honeymoon suite;
like a warrior,
it thrills at running its course.
6 It rises in one end of the sky;
its circuit is complete at the other.
Nothing escapes its heat.

7 The LORD's Instruction is perfect,
reviving one's very being.[l]
The LORD's laws are faithful,
making naive people wise.
8 The LORD's regulations are right,
gladdening the heart.
The LORD's commands are pure,
giving light to the eyes.
9 Honoring the LORD is correct,
lasting forever.
The LORD's judgments are true.
All of these are righteous!
10 They are more desirable than gold—
than tons of pure gold!
They are sweeter than honey—
even dripping off the honeycomb!
11 No doubt about it:
your servant is enlightened by them;
there is great reward in keeping them.
12 But can anyone know
what they've accidentally done wrong?
Clear me of any unknown sin
13 and save your servant
from willful sins.
Don't let them rule me.
Then I'll be completely blameless;
I'll be innocent of great wrongdoing.

14 Let the words of my mouth
and the meditations of my heart
be pleasing to you,
LORD, my rock and my redeemer.

[j] Or *prisons* [k] LXX, Vulg, Sym; MT *line* or *string* [l] Or *soul*

Psalm 20

For the music leader. A psalm of David.

1 I pray that the LORD answers you
whenever you are in trouble.
Let the name of Jacob's God protect you.
2 Let God send help to you
from the sanctuary
and support you from Zion.
3 Let God recall your many grain offerings;
let him savor your
entirely burned offerings. *Selah*
4 Let God grant what is in your heart
and fulfill all your plans.
5 Then we will rejoice
that you've been helped.
We will fly our flags
in the name of our God.
Let the LORD fulfill all your requests!

6 Now I know that the LORD saves
his anointed one;
God answers his anointed one
from his heavenly sanctuary,
answering with mighty acts of salvation
achieved by his strong hand.
7 Some people trust in chariots,
others in horses;
but we praise the LORD's name.
8 They will collapse and fall,
but we will stand up straight and strong.

9 LORD, save the king!
Let him answer us when we cry out!

Psalm 21

For the music leader. A psalm of David.

1 The king celebrates your strength, LORD;
look how happy he is
about your saving help!
2 You've given him what his heart desires;
you haven't denied
what his lips requested. *Selah*
3 You bring rich blessings right to him;
you put a crown of pure gold
on his head.
4 He asked you for life,
and you gave it to him, all right—
long days, forever and always!
5 The king's reputation is great
because of your saving help;
you've conferred on him
glory and grandeur.
6 You grant him blessings forever;
you make him happy
with the joy of your presence.
7 Because the king trusts the LORD,
and because of the Most High's
faithful love,
he will not stumble.

8 Your hand will catch all your enemies;
your strong hand will catch
all who hate you.
9 When you appear, LORD,
you will light them up
like an oven on fire.
God will eat them whole in his anger;
fire will devour them.
10 You will destroy their offspring
from the land;
destroy their descendants
from the human race.
11 Because they sought to do you harm,
they devised a wicked plan—
but they will fail!
12 Because you will make them turn and run
when you aim your bow
straight at their faces!

13 Be exalted, LORD, in your strength!
We will sing and praise your power!

Psalm 22

For the music leader. According to the "Doe of Dawn." A psalm of David.

1 My God! My God,
why have you left me all alone?
Why are you so far from saving me—
so far from my anguished groans?
2 My God, I cry out during the day,
but you don't answer;
even at nighttime I don't stop.
3 You are the holy one, enthroned.
You are Israel's praise.
4 Our ancestors trusted you—
they trusted you and you rescued them;

5 they cried out to you and they were saved;
they trusted you
and they weren't ashamed.

6 But I'm just a worm, less than human;
insulted by one person,
despised by another.
7 All who see me make fun of me—
they gape, shaking their heads:
8 "He committed himself to the LORD,
so let God rescue him;
let God deliver him
because God likes him so much."
9 But you are the one who pulled me
from the womb,
placing me safely at my mother's breasts.
10 I was thrown on you from birth;
you've been my God
since I was in my mother's womb.
11 Please don't be far from me,
because trouble is near
and there's no one to help.

12 Many bulls surround me;
mighty bulls from Bashan encircle me.
13 They open their mouths at me
like a lion ripping and roaring!
14 I'm poured out like water.
All my bones have fallen apart.
My heart is like wax;
it melts inside me.
15 My strength is dried up
like a piece of broken pottery.
My tongue sticks
to the roof of my mouth;
you've set me down in the dirt of death.
16 Dogs surround me;
a pack of evil people circle me like a lion—
oh, my poor hands and feet!
17 I can count all my bones!
Meanwhile, they just stare at me,
watching me.
18 They divvy up my garments
among themselves;
they cast lots for my clothes.

19 But you, LORD! Don't be far away!
You are my strength!
Come quick and help me!
20 Deliver me[m] from the sword.
Deliver my life from the power of the dog.
21 Save me from the mouth of the lion.
From the horns of the wild oxen
you have answered me!

22 I will declare your name
to my brothers and sisters;
I will praise you in the very center
of the congregation!
23 All of you who revere the LORD—
praise him!
All of you who are Jacob's descendants—
honor him!
All of you who are all Israel's offspring—
stand in awe of him!
24 Because he didn't despise or detest
the suffering of the one who suffered—
he didn't hide his face from me.
No, he listened when I cried out to him
for help.

25 I offer praise in the great congregation
because of you;
I will fulfill my promises
in the presence of those who honor God.
26 Let all those who are suffering
eat and be full!
Let all who seek the LORD praise him!
I pray your hearts live forever!
27 Every part of the earth
will remember and come back to the LORD;
every family among all the nations
will worship you.
28 Because the right to rule
belongs to the LORD,
he rules all nations.
29 Indeed, all the earth's powerful
will worship him;[n]
all who are descending to the dust
will kneel before him;
my being also lives for him.[o]
30 Future descendants will serve him;
generations to come will be told
about my Lord.
31 They will proclaim God's righteousness
to those not yet born,
telling them what God has done.

[m] Or *my soul*; also in 22:29 [n] Correction; MT *All the earth's powerful have eaten and will worship.* [o] Correction with LXX; Heb uncertain

Psalm 23

A psalm of David.

1 The LORD is my shepherd.
I lack nothing.
2 He lets me rest in grassy meadows;
he leads me to restful waters;
3 he keeps me[p] alive.
He guides me in proper paths
for the sake of his good name.

4 Even when I walk
through the darkest valley,
I fear no danger
because you are with me.
Your rod and your staff—
they protect me.

5 You set a table for me
right in front of my enemies.
You bathe my head in oil;
my cup is so full it spills over!
6 Yes, goodness and faithful love
will pursue me all the days of my life,
and I will live[q] in the LORD's house
as long as I live.

Psalm 24

A psalm of David.

1 The earth is the LORD's
and everything in it,
the world and its inhabitants too.
2 Because God is the one
who established it on the seas;
God set it firmly on the waters.

3 Who can ascend the LORD's mountain?
Who can stand in his holy sanctuary?
4 Only the one with clean hands
and a pure heart;
the one who hasn't made false promises,
the one who hasn't sworn dishonestly.
5 That kind of person receives blessings
from the LORD
and righteousness
from the God who saves.
6 And that's how things are
with the generation that seeks him—
that seeks the face of Jacob's God.[r]
Selah

7 Mighty gates: lift up your heads!
Ancient doors: rise up high!
So the glorious king can enter!
8 Who is this glorious king?
The LORD—strong and powerful!
The LORD—powerful in battle!
9 Mighty gates: lift up your heads!
Ancient doors: rise up high!
So the glorious king can enter!
10 Who is this glorious king?
The LORD of heavenly forces—
he is the glorious king! *Selah*

Psalm 25[s]

Of David.

א 1 I offer my life[t] to you, LORD.
ב 2 My God, I trust you.
Please don't let me be put to shame!
Don't let my enemies rejoice
over me!
ג 3 For that matter,
don't let anyone who hopes in you
be put to shame;
instead, let those who are treacherous
without excuse be put to shame.

ד 4 Make your ways known to me,
LORD;
teach me your paths.
ה 5 Lead me in your truth—
teach it to me—
because you are the God
who saves me.
ו I put my hope in you all day long.
ז 6 LORD, remember your compassion
and faithful love—
they are forever!
ח 7 But don't remember the sins
of my youth or my wrongdoing.
Remember me only
according to your faithful love
for the sake of your goodness, LORD.

[p] Or *my soul* [q] LXX; MT *I will return* [r] LXX, Syr; MT *seek your face, Jacob* [s] Ps 25 is an alphabetic acrostic poem; see the note at Pss 9–10. [t] Or *soul*; also in 25:13, 20

ט 8 The LORD is good and does the right thing;
he teaches sinners which way
they should go.
י 9 God guides the weak to justice,
teaching them his way.
כ 10 All the LORD's paths
are loving and faithful
for those who keep his covenant
and laws.
ל 11 Please, for the sake of your good name,
LORD, forgive my sins,
which are many!

מ 12 Where are the ones who honor the LORD?
God will teach them which path to take.
נ 13 They will live a good life,
and their descendants
will possess the land.
ס 14 The LORD counsels those who honor him;
he makes his covenant known to them.
ע 15 My eyes are always looking to the LORD
because he will free my feet from the net.

פ 16 Turn to me, God, and have mercy on me
because I'm alone and suffering.
צ 17 My heart's troubles
keep getting bigger—
set me free from my distress!
18 Look at my suffering and trouble—
forgive all my sins!
ר 19 Look at how many enemies I have
and how violently they hate me!
ש 20 Please protect my life! Deliver me!
Don't let me be put to shame
because I take refuge in you.
ת 21 Let integrity and virtue guard me
because I hope in you.

22 Please, God, save Israel
from all its troubles!

Psalm 26

Of David.

1 Establish justice for me, LORD,
because I have walked with integrity.
I've trusted the LORD without wavering.
2 Examine me, LORD; put me to the test!
Purify[u] my mind[v] and my heart.
3 Because your faithful love
is right in front of me—
I walk in your truth!
4 I don't spend time with people
up to no good;
I don't keep company with liars.
5 I detest the company of evildoers,
and I don't sit with wicked people.
6 I wash my hands—they are innocent!
I walk all around your altar, LORD,
7 proclaiming out loud my thanks,
declaring all your wonderful deeds!
8 I love the beauty[w] of your house, LORD;
I love the place where your glory resides.

9 Don't gather me[x] up with the sinners,
taking my life along with violent people
10 in whose hands are evil schemes,
whose strong hands are full of bribes.
11 But me? I walk with integrity.
Save me! Have mercy on me!

12 My feet now stand on level ground.
I will bless the LORD
in the great congregation.

Psalm 27

Of David.

1 The LORD is my light and my salvation.
Should I fear anyone?
The LORD is a fortress
protecting my life.
Should I be frightened of anything?
2 When evildoers come at me
trying to eat me up—
it's they, my foes and my enemies,
who stumble and fall!
3 If an army camps against me,
my heart won't be afraid.
If war comes up against me,
I will continue to trust in this:
4 I have asked one thing
from the LORD—
it's all I seek:
to live in the LORD's house
all the days of my life,
seeing the LORD's beauty
and constantly adoring his temple.

[u]LXX or *investigate* [v]Or *kidneys* [w]LXX; MT *the dwelling of your house* [x]Or *my soul*

5 Because he will shelter me
in his own dwelling
during troubling times;
he will hide me in a secret place
in his own tent;
he will set me up high, safe on a rock.
6 Now my head is higher
than the enemies surrounding me,
and I will offer sacrifices in God's tent—
sacrifices with shouts of joy!
I will sing and praise the LORD.

7 LORD, listen to my voice when I cry out—
have mercy on me and answer me!
8 Come, my heart says, seek God's face.[y]
LORD, I do seek your face!
9 Please don't hide it from me!
Don't push your servant aside angrily—
you have been my help!
God who saves me,
don't neglect me!
Don't leave me all alone!
10 Even if my father and mother
left me all alone,
the LORD would take me in.
11 LORD, teach me your way;
because of my opponents,
lead me on a good path.
12 Don't give me over
to the desires of my enemies,
because false witnesses
and violent accusers
have taken their stand against me.
13 But I have sure faith
that I will experience
the LORD's goodness
in the land of the living!

14 Hope in the LORD!
Be strong! Let your heart take courage!
Hope in the LORD!

Psalm 28

Of David.

1 I cry out to you, LORD.
You are my rock; don't refuse to hear me.
If you won't talk to me,
I'll be just like those
going down to the pit.
2 Listen to my request for mercy
when I cry out to you,
when I lift up my hands
to your holy inner sanctuary.
3 Don't drag me off with the wicked
and those who do evil;
the type who talk nice to their friends
while evil thoughts are in their hearts!
4 Pay them back for what they've done!
Pay them back for their evil deeds!
Pay them back for their handiwork!
Give back to them
exactly what they deserve!
5 Because they have no regard
for what the LORD has done,
no regard for his handiwork,
God will tear them down
and never rebuild!

6 Bless the LORD
because he has listened
to my request for mercy!
7 The LORD is my strength and my shield.
My heart trusts him.
I was helped, my heart rejoiced,
and I thank him with my song.
8 The LORD is his people's strength;
he is a fortress of protection
for his anointed one.
9 Save your people, God!
Bless your possession!
Shepherd them
and carry them for all time!

Psalm 29

A psalm of David.

1 You, divine beings! Give to the LORD—
give to the LORD glory and power!
2 Give to the LORD the glory due his name!
Bow down to the LORD
in holy splendor!

3 The LORD's voice is over the waters;
the glorious God thunders;
the LORD is over the mighty waters.
4 The LORD's voice is strong;

[y] Correction; MT *My heart says to/of you . . . see my face!*

the LORD's voice is majestic.
5 The LORD's voice breaks cedar trees—
yes, the LORD shatters
the cedars of Lebanon.
6 He makes Lebanon jump around
like a young bull,
makes Sirion jump around
like a young wild ox.
7 The LORD's voice unleashes fiery flames;
8 the LORD's voice shakes the wilderness—
yes, the LORD shakes
the wilderness of Kadesh.
9 The LORD's voice convulses the oaks,
strips the forests bare,
but in his temple everyone shouts,
"Glory!"
10 The LORD sits enthroned
over the floodwaters;
the LORD sits enthroned—king forever!

11 Let the LORD give strength to his people!
Let the LORD bless his people
with peace!

Psalm 30

A psalm. A song for the temple dedication. Of David.

1 I exalt you, LORD,
because you pulled me up;
you didn't let my enemies
celebrate over me.
2 LORD, my God, I cried out to you for help,
and you healed me.
3 LORD, you brought me[z] up
from the grave,[a]
brought me back to life from among
those going down to the pit.

4 You who are faithful to the LORD,
sing praises to him;
give thanks to his holy name!
5 His anger lasts for only a second,
but his favor lasts a lifetime.
Weeping may stay all night,
but by morning, joy!

6 When I was comfortable, I said,
"I will never stumble."
7 Because it pleased you, LORD,
you made me a strong mountain.
But then you hid your presence.
I was terrified.
8 I cried out to you, LORD.
I begged my Lord for mercy:
9 "What is to be gained by my spilled blood,
by my going down into the pit?
Does dust thank you?
Does it proclaim your faithfulness?
10 LORD, listen and have mercy on me!
LORD, be my helper!"

11 You changed my mourning
into dancing.
You took off my funeral clothes
and dressed me up in joy
12 so that my whole being
might sing praises to you
and never stop.
LORD, my God,
I will give thanks to you forever.

Psalm 31

For the music leader. A psalm of David.

1 I take refuge in you, LORD.
Please never let me be put to shame.
Rescue me by your righteousness!
2 Listen closely to me!
Deliver me quickly;
be a rock that protects me;
be a strong fortress that saves me!
3 You are definitely my rock
and my fortress.
Guide me and lead me
for the sake of your good name!
4 Get me out of this net
that's been set for me
because you are my protective fortress.
5 I entrust my spirit into your hands;
you, LORD, God of faithfulness—
you have saved me.
6 I hate those who embrace
what is completely worthless.
I myself trust the LORD.
7 I rejoice and celebrate
in your faithful love
because you saw my suffering—

[z] Or *my soul* [a] Heb *Sheol*

you were intimately acquainted
with my deep distress.
8 You didn't hand me over to the enemy,
but set my feet in wide-open spaces.

9 Have mercy on me, LORD,
because I'm depressed.
My vision fails because of my grief,
as do my spirit and my body.
10 My life is consumed with sadness;
my years are consumed with groaning.
Strength fails me
because of my suffering;[b]
my bones dry up.
11 I'm a joke to all my enemies,
still worse to my neighbors.
I scare my friends,
and whoever sees me in the street
runs away!
12 I am forgotten, like I'm dead,
completely out of mind;
I am like a piece of pottery, destroyed.
13 Yes, I've heard all the gossiping,
terror all around;
so many gang up together against me,
they plan to take my life!

14 But me? I trust you, LORD!
I affirm, "You are my God."
15 My future is in your hands.
Don't hand me over to my enemies,
to all who are out to get me!
16 Shine your face on your servant;
save me by your faithful love!
17 LORD, don't let me be put to shame
because I have cried out to you.
Let the wicked be put to shame;
let them be silenced in death's domain![c]
18 Let their lying lips be shut up
whenever they speak arrogantly
against the righteous
with pride and contempt!
19 How great is the goodness
that you've reserved
for those who honor you,
that you commit to those
who take refuge in you—
in the sight of everyone!
20 You hide them
in the shelter of your wings,[d]
safe from human scheming.
You conceal them in a shelter,
safe from accusing tongues.

21 Bless the LORD,
because he has wondrously revealed
his faithful love to me
when I was like a city under siege!
22 When I was panicked, I said,
"I'm cut off from your eyes!"
But you heard my request for mercy
when I cried out to you for help.

23 All you who are faithful, love the LORD!
The LORD protects those who are loyal,
but he pays the proud back
to the fullest degree.
24 All you who wait for the LORD,
be strong and let your heart take courage.

Psalm 32

A maskil[e] of David.

1 The one whose wrongdoing is forgiven,
whose sin is covered over,
is truly happy!
2 The one the LORD
doesn't consider guilty—
in whose spirit there is no dishonesty—
that one is truly happy!

3 When I kept quiet, my bones wore out;
I was groaning all day long—
every day, every night!—
4 because your hand was heavy upon me.
My energy was sapped as if in a
summer drought. *Selah*
5 So I admitted my sin to you;
I didn't conceal my guilt.
"I'll confess my sins to the LORD,"
is what I said.
Then you removed the guilt of my sin.
Selah
6 That's why all the faithful should pray to
you during troubled times,[f]

[b]LXX, Syr; MT *my sin* [c]Heb *Sheol* [d]Correction; see Ps 61:5; MT *in the hiding place of your face.* [e]Perhaps *instruction*; it also appears in Pss 42, 44–45, 52–55, 74, 78, 88–89, 142; cf 47:7; the root is used in Ps 32:8.
[f]Correction; MT *at a time of finding only*

so that a great flood of water
won't reach them.
7 You are my secret hideout!
You protect me from trouble.
You surround me with songs of rescue!
Selah

8 I will instruct you and teach you
about the direction you should go.
I'll advise you and keep my eye on you.
9 Don't be like some senseless
horse or mule,
whose movement must be controlled
with a bit and a bridle.[g]
Don't be anything like that![h]
10 The pain of the wicked is severe,
but faithful love surrounds
the one who trusts the LORD.
11 You who are righteous,
rejoice in the LORD and be glad!
All you whose hearts are right,
sing out in joy!

Psalm 33

1 All you who are righteous,
shout joyfully to the LORD!
It's right for those who do right
to praise God.
2 Give thanks to the LORD with the lyre!
Sing praises to him
with the ten-stringed harp!
3 Sing to him a new song!
Play your best with joyful shouts!
4 Because the LORD's word is right,
his every act is done in good faith.
5 He loves righteousness and justice;
the LORD's faithful love
fills the whole earth.
6 The skies were made by the LORD's word,
all their starry multitude
by the breath of his mouth.
7 He gathered the ocean waters into a heap;
he put the deep seas into storerooms.
8 All the earth honors the LORD;
all the earth's inhabitants
stand in awe of him.
9 Because when he spoke, it happened!
When he commanded, there it was!
10 The LORD overrules
what the nations plan;
he frustrates
what the peoples intend to do.
11 But the LORD's plan stands forever;
what he intends to do lasts
from one generation to the next.
12 The nation whose God is the LORD,
the people whom God has chosen
as his possession,
is truly happy!
13 The LORD looks down from heaven;
he sees every human being.
14 From his dwelling place God observes
all who live on earth.
15 God is the one who made
all their hearts,
the one who knows
everything they do.

16 Kings aren't saved by the strength
of their armies;
warriors aren't rescued
by how much power they have.
17 A warhorse is a bad bet for victory;
it can't save despite
its great strength.
18 But look here: the LORD's eyes watch
all who honor him,
all who wait for his faithful love,
19 to deliver their lives[i] from death
and keep them alive during a famine.

20 We put our hope in the LORD.
He is our help and our shield.
21 Our heart rejoices in God
because we trust his holy name.
22 LORD, let your faithful love surround us
because we wait for you.

Psalm 34[j]

Of David, when he pretended
to be crazy before Abimelech,
who banished him so that he left.

א 1 I will bless the LORD at all times;
his praise will always be in my mouth.

[g] Heb uncertain [h] Heb uncertain [i] Or *souls*; also in 33:20 [j] Ps 34 is an alphabetic acrostic poem; see the note at Pss 9–10 or Ps 111.

ב [2]I[k] praise the LORD—
let the suffering listen and rejoice.
ג [3]Magnify the LORD with me!
Together let us lift his name up high!

ד [4]I sought the LORD
and he answered me.
He delivered me from all my fears.
ה [5]Those who look to God will shine;
their faces are never ashamed.
ז [6]This suffering person cried out:
the LORD listened and saved him
from every trouble.
ח [7]On every side, the LORD's messenger
protects those who honor God;
and he delivers them.
ט [8]Taste and see
how good the LORD is!
The one who takes refuge in him
is truly happy!
י [9]You who are the LORD's holy ones,
honor him,
because those who honor him
don't lack a thing.
כ [10]Even strong young lions
go without and get hungry,
but those who seek the LORD
lack no good thing.

ל [11]Come, children, listen to me.
Let me teach you
how to honor the LORD:
מ [12]Do you love life;
do you relish the chance
to enjoy good things?
נ [13]Then you must keep your tongue
from evil
and keep your lips
from speaking lies!
ס [14]Turn away from evil! Do good!
Seek peace and go after it!

ע [15]The LORD's eyes
watch the righteous,
his ears listen to their cries for help.
פ [16]But the LORD's face is set against
those who do evil,
to eliminate even the memory of them
from the earth.

צ [17]When the righteous cry out,
the LORD listens;
he delivers them from all their troubles.
ק [18]The LORD is close
to the brokenhearted;
he saves those whose spirits
are crushed.

ר [19]The righteous have many problems,
but the LORD delivers them
from every one.
ש [20]He protects all their bones;
not even one will be broken.
ת [21]But just one problem
will kill the wicked,
and those who hate the righteous
will be held responsible.
[22]The LORD saves his servants' lives;
all those who take refuge in him
won't be held responsible for anything.

Psalm 35

Of David.

[1]LORD, argue with
those who argue with me;
fight with those who fight against me!
[2]Grab a shield and armor;
stand up and help me!
[3]Use your spear and ax[l]
against those who are out to get me!
Say to me:[m] "I'm your salvation!"
[4]Let those who want me dead
be humiliated and put to shame.
Let those who intend to hurt me
be thoroughly frustrated and disgraced.
[5]Let them be like dust on the wind—
and let the LORD's messenger
be the one who does the blowing!
[6]Let their path be dark and slippery—
and let the LORD's messenger
be the one who does the chasing!
[7]Because they hid their net for me
for no reason,
they dug a pit for me for no reason.
[8]Let disaster come to them
when they don't suspect it.
Let the net they hid
catch them instead!

[k]Or *my soul*; also in 34:22 [l]Correction [m]Or *my soul*; also in 35:4, 7, 9, 12, 13, 17, 24

Let them fall into it—
to their disaster!
9 But I will rejoice in the LORD;
I will celebrate his salvation.
10 All my bones will say,
"LORD, who could compare to you?
You rescue the weak
from those who overpower them;
you rescue the weak and the needy
from those who plunder them."

11 Violent witnesses stand up.
They question me about things
I know nothing about.
12 They pay me back evil for good,
leaving me stricken with grief.
13 But when they were sick,
I wore clothes for grieving,
and I kept a strict fast.
When my prayer came back unanswered,[n]
14 I would wander around
like I was grieving a friend or a brother.
I was weighed down, sad,
like I was a mother in mourning.
15 But when I stumbled,
they celebrated and gathered together—
they gathered together against me!
Strangers[o] I didn't know tore me
to pieces and wouldn't quit.
16 They ridiculed me over and over again,
like godless people would do,
grinding their teeth at me.

17 How long, my Lord,
will you watch this happen?
Rescue me from their attacks;
rescue my precious life
from these predatory lions!
18 Then I will thank you
in the great assembly;
I will praise you
in a huge crowd of people.
19 Don't let those who are my enemies
without cause celebrate over me;
don't let those who hate me
for no reason
wink at my demise.
20 They don't speak the truth;
instead, they plot false accusations
against innocent people in the land.
21 They speak out against me,
saying, "Yes! Oh, yes! We've seen it
with our own eyes!"

22 But you've seen it too, LORD.
Don't keep quiet about it.
Please don't be far from me, my Lord.
23 Wake up! Get up and do justice for me;
argue my case, my Lord and my God!
24 Establish justice for me
according to your righteousness,
LORD, my God.
Don't let them celebrate over me.
25 Don't let them say to themselves,
Yes! Exactly what we wanted!
Don't let them say, "We ate him up!"
26 Let all those who celebrate my
misfortune be disgraced
and put to shame!
Let those who exalt themselves over me
be dressed up in shame and dishonor!
27 But let those who want things
to be set right for me
shout for joy and celebrate!
Let them constantly say,
"The LORD is great—
God wants his servant to be at peace."
28 Then my tongue will talk
all about your righteousness;
it will talk
about your praise all day long.

Psalm 36

For the music leader.
Of the LORD's servant David.

1 I know the sinful utterance
of the wicked:[p]
No fear of God
confronts their own eyes,
2 because in their own eyes
they are slick with talk
about their guilt ever being
found out and despised.[q]
3 The words of their mouths
are evil and dishonest.

[n] Heb uncertain [o] Correction [p] Heb uncertain [q] Heb uncertain

They have stopped being wise
and stopped doing good.
4 They plot evil even while
resting in bed!
They commit themselves
to a path that is no good.
They don't reject what is evil.

5 But your loyal love, LORD,
extends to the skies;
your faithfulness reaches the clouds.
6 Your righteousness is
like the strongest mountains;
your justice is like the deepest sea.
LORD, you save both humans
and animals.
7 Your faithful love is priceless, God!
Humanity finds refuge
in the shadow of your wings.
8 They feast on the bounty
of your house;
you let them drink
from your river of pure joy.
9 Within you is the spring of life.
In your light, we see light.

10 Extend your faithful love
to those who know you;
extend your righteousness
to those whose heart is right.
11 Don't let the feet of arrogant people
walk all over me;
don't let the hands of the wicked
drive me off.
12 Look—right there is where
the evildoers have fallen,
pushed down, unable to get up!

Psalm 37[r]

Of David.

א 1 Don't get upset over evildoers;
don't be jealous of those who do wrong,
2 because they will fade fast, like grass;
they will wither
like green vegetables.
ב 3 Trust the LORD and do good;
live in the land, and farm faithfulness.
4 Enjoy the LORD,
and he will give what your heart asks.
ג 5 Commit your way to the LORD!
Trust him! He will act
6 and will make your righteousness
shine like the dawn,
your justice like high noon.
ד 7 Be still before the LORD,
and wait[s] for him.
Don't get upset when
someone gets ahead—
someone who invents evil schemes.

ה 8 Let go of anger and leave rage behind!
Don't get upset—it will only lead to evil.
9 Because evildoers will be eliminated,
but those who hope in the LORD—
they will possess the land.
ו 10 In just a little while
the wicked won't exist!
If you go looking around their place,
they won't be there.
11 But the weak will inherit the land;
they will enjoy a surplus of peace.
ז 12 The wicked plot against the righteous,
grinding their teeth at them.
13 But my Lord just laughs at them
because he knows
that their day is coming.
ח 14 The wicked draw their swords
and bend their bows
to bring down the weak and the needy,
to slaughter those whose way is right.
15 But the sword of the wicked
will enter their own hearts!
Their bows will be broken!

ט 16 Better is the little
that the righteous have
than the overabundant wealth
of the wicked.[t]
17 The arms of the wicked will be broken,
but the LORD supports the righteous.
י 18 The LORD is intimately acquainted
with the lives of the blameless;
their heritage will last forever.
19 They won't be ashamed
in troubling times,

[r] Ps 37 is an alphabetic acrostic poem; see the note at Pss 9–10 or Ps 111. [s] Correction with LXX, Vulg
[t] LXX, Vulg, Syr; MT *abundant wealth of many wicked*

and in a period of famine
they will eat their fill.

כ [20]But the wicked will die,
the LORD's enemies will disappear—
disappear like the beauty
of a meadow—in smoke.

ל [21]The wicked borrow
and don't pay it back,
but the righteous are generous and giving.
[22]Those blessed by God
will possess the land,
but those cursed by God will be cut off.

מ [23]A person's steps are made secure
by the LORD
when they delight in his way.
[24]Though they trip up,
they won't be thrown down,
because the LORD holds their hand.

נ [25]I was young and now I'm old,
but I have never seen
the righteous left all alone,
have never seen their children
begging for bread.
[26]They are always gracious and generous.
Their children are a blessing.

ס [27]Turn away from evil! Do good!
Then you will live in the land forever.
[28]The LORD loves justice.
He will never leave his faithful all alone.

ע They are guarded forever,
but the children of the wicked
are eliminated.
[29]The righteous will possess the land;
they will live on it forever.

פ [30]The mouths of the righteous
recite wisdom;
their tongues discuss justice.
[31]The Instruction of their God
is in their hearts;
they don't miss a step.

צ [32]The wicked, on the other hand,
target the righteous,
seeking to kill them.
[33]But the LORD won't leave the righteous
to the power of the wicked,
and won't let the righteous
be found guilty when they are judged.

ק [34]Hope in the LORD and keep his way!
He will lift you up
so you can possess the land.
When the wicked are eliminated,
you will see it for yourself!

ר [35]I myself have seen
wicked powerful people,
exalting themselves like a stately cedar.[u]
[36]But when I[v] came back, they were gone!
I looked all over for them,
but they couldn't be found!

ש [37]Observe those who have integrity
and watch those whose heart is right
because the future belongs
to persons of peace.
[38]But wrongdoers will be destroyed
all together;
the future of the wicked
will be cut short.

ת [39]The salvation of the righteous
comes from the LORD;
he is their refuge in times of trouble.
[40]The LORD will help them
and rescue them—
rescue them from the wicked—
and he will save them
because they have taken refuge in him.

Psalm 38

A psalm of David.
For the memorial offering.

[1]Please, LORD, don't punish me
when you are mad;
don't discipline me
when you are furious.
[2]Your arrows have pierced me;
your fist has come down hard on me.
[3]There's nothing in my body
that isn't broken
because of your rage;
there's no health in my bones
because of my sin.
[4]My wrongdoings are
stacked higher than my head;

[u]LXX [v]LXX, Syr, Vulg

they are a weight
that's way too heavy for me.
5 My wounds reek; they are all infected
because of my stupidity.
6 I am hunched over, completely down;
I wander around all day long, sad.
7 My insides are burning up;
there's nothing in my body
that isn't broken.
8 I'm worn out, completely crushed;
I groan because of my miserable heart.

9 Everything I long for
is laid out before you, my Lord;
my sighs aren't hidden from you.
10 My heart pounds;
my strength abandons me.
Even the light of my eyes is gone.
11 My loved ones and friends
keep their distance
from me in my sickness;
those who were near me
now stay far away.
12 Those who want me dead lay traps;
those who want me harmed utter threats,
muttering lies all day long.
13 But I'm like someone who is deaf,
who can't hear;
like someone who can't speak,
whose mouth won't open.
14 I've become like a person
who doesn't hear what is being said,
whose mouth has no good comeback.
15 But I wait for you, LORD!
You will answer, my Lord, my God!
16 Because I prayed:
"Don't let them celebrate over me
or exalt themselves over me
when my foot slips,"
17 because I'm very close to falling,
and my pain is always with me.
18 Yes, I confess my wrongdoing;
I'm worried about my sin.
19 But my mortal enemies are so strong;
those who hate me for no reason
seem countless.
20 Those who give, repay good with evil;
they oppose me for pursuing good.

21 Don't leave me all alone, LORD!
Please, my God, don't be far from me!
22 Come quickly and help me,
my Lord, my salvation!

Psalm 39

For the music leader. To Jeduthun.
A psalm of David.

1 I promised I would watch my steps
so as not to sin with my tongue;
promised to keep my mouth shut
as long as the wicked were
in my presence.
2 So I was completely quiet, silent.
I kept my peace, but it did no good.
My pain got worse.
3 My heart got hot inside me;
while stewing over it, the fire burned.
Then I spoke out with my tongue:
4 "Let me know my end, LORD.
How many days do I have left?
I want to know how brief my time is."
5 You've made my days so short;
my lifetime is like nothing in your eyes.
Yes, a human life
is nothing but a puff of air! *Selah*

6 Yes, people wander around like shadows;
yes, they hustle and bustle,
but pointlessly;
they don't even know who will get
the wealth they've amassed.
7 So now, Lord, what should I be waiting for?
My hope is set on you.
8 Deliver me from all my sins;
don't make me
some foolish person's joke.
9 I am completely silent;
I won't open my mouth
because you have acted.
10 Get this plague of yours off me!
I'm being destroyed by the blows
from your fist.
11 You discipline people for their sin,
punishing them;
like a moth, you ruin what they treasure.
Yes, a human life is just a puff of air!
Selah

12 Hear my prayer, LORD!
Listen closely to my cry for help!
Please don't ignore my tears!

I'm just a foreigner—
an immigrant staying with you,
just like all my ancestors were.
13 Look away from me
so I can be happy again
before I pass away and am gone.

Psalm 40

For the music leader. Of David. A psalm.

1 I put all my hope in the LORD.
He leaned down to me;
he listened to my cry for help.
2 He lifted me out of the pit of death,
out of the mud and filth,
and set my feet on solid rock.
He steadied my legs.
3 He put a new song in my mouth,
a song of praise for our God.
Many people will learn of this
and be amazed;
they will trust the LORD.
4 Those who put their trust in the LORD,
who pay no attention to the proud
or to those who follow lies,
are truly happy!

5 You, LORD my God!
You've done so many things—
your wonderful deeds
and your plans for us—
no one can compare with you!
If I were to proclaim
and talk about all of them,
they would be too numerous
to count!
6 You don't relish sacrifices
or offerings;
you don't require
entirely burned offerings
or compensation offerings—
but you have given me ears!
7 So I said, "Here I come!
I'm inscribed in the written scroll.
8 I want to do your will, my God.
Your Instruction is deep within me."
9 I've told the good news
of your righteousness
in the great assembly.
I didn't hold anything back—
as you well know, LORD!
10 I didn't keep your righteousness
only to myself.
I declared your faithfulness
and your salvation.
I didn't hide your loyal love
and trustworthiness
from the great assembly.

11 So now you, LORD—
don't hold back
any of your compassion from me.
Let your loyal love and faithfulness
always protect me,
12 because countless evils surround me.
My wrongdoings
have caught up with me—
I can't see a thing!
There's more of them
than hairs on my head—
my courage leaves me.
13 Favor me, LORD, and deliver me!
LORD, come quickly and help me!
14 Let those who seek my life,
who want me dead,
be disgraced and put to shame.
Let those who want to do me harm
be thoroughly frustrated
and humiliated.
15 Let those who say to me,
"Yes! Oh, yes!"[w]
be destroyed by their shame.
16 But let all who seek you
celebrate and rejoice in you.
Let those who love your salvation
always say,
"The LORD is great!"
17 But me? I'm weak and needy.
Let my Lord think of me.
You are my help and my rescuer.
My God, don't wait any longer!

Psalm 41

For the music leader.
A psalm of David.

1 Those who pay close attention
to the poor are truly happy!

[w] See Ps 35:21, 25.

The LORD rescues them
during troubling times.
2 The LORD protects them
and keeps them alive;
they are widely regarded throughout
the land as happy people.
You[x] won't hand them over to the will
of their enemies.
3 The LORD will strengthen them when
they are lying in bed, sick.
You will completely transform the place
where they lie ill.

4 But me? I said,
"LORD, have mercy on me!
Heal me because I have sinned
against you."
5 My enemies speak maliciously about me:
"When will he die
and his name disappear?"
6 Whenever they come to visit,
they say nothing of value.
Their hearts collect evil gossip;
once they leave,
they tell it to everybody.
7 All of those who hate me talk about me,
whispering to each other,
plotting evil against me:
8 "Some horrible thing
has been poured into him;
the next time he lies down,
he won't get up."
9 Even my good friend,
the one I trusted,
who shared my food,
has kicked me with his heel—
a betrayer!
10 But you, LORD, please have mercy on me
and lift me up
so I can pay them back!
11 Then I'll know you are pleased with me
because my enemy won't be shouting
in triumph over me.
12 You support me in my integrity;
you put me in your presence forever.

13 Bless the LORD, the God of Israel,
from forever to forever!
Amen and Amen!

BOOK II
(Psalms 42–72)

Psalm 42[y]

For the music leader.
A maskil[z] of the Korahites.

1 Just like a deer that craves
streams of water,
my whole being[a] craves you, God.
2 My whole being thirsts for God,
for the living God.
When will I come and see God's face?[b]
3 My tears have been my food
both day and night,
as people constantly questioned me,
"Where's your God now?"

4 But I remember these things
as I bare my soul:
how I made my way
to the mighty one's abode,[c]
to God's own house,
with joyous shouts
and thanksgiving songs—
a huge crowd celebrating the festival!
5 Why, I ask myself,
are you so depressed?
Why are you so upset inside?
Hope in God!
Because I will again give him thanks,
my saving presence and 6 my God.

My whole being is depressed.
That's why I remember you
from the land of Jordan and Hermon,
from Mount Mizar.
7 Deep called to deep
at the noise of your waterfalls;
all your massive waves surged over me.
8 By day the LORD commands
his faithful love;
by night his song is with me—
a prayer to the God of my life.

9 I will say to God, my solid rock,
"Why have you forgotten me?
Why do I have to walk around,
sad, oppressed by enemies?"

[x] LXX, Syr; Vulg *God won't* [y] Pss 42–43 form one single poem; cf the note at Pss 9–10. [z] Perhaps *instruction* [a] Or *soul*; also in 42:2, 4, 5, 6, 11; 43:5 [b] Syr, Tg; MT *and appear before God?* [c] Heb uncertain

10 With my bones crushed,
my foes make fun of me,
constantly questioning me:
"Where's your God now?"

11 Why, I ask myself, are you so depressed?
Why are you so upset inside?
Hope in God!
Because I will again give him thanks,
my saving presence and my God.

Psalm 43

1 Establish justice for me, God!
Argue my case against ungodly people!
Rescue me from the dishonest
and unjust!
2 Because you are my God,
my protective fortress!
Why have you rejected me?
Why do I have to walk around,
sad, oppressed by enemies?
3 Send your light and truth—
those will guide me!
Let them bring me
to your holy mountain,
to your dwelling place.
4 Let me come to God's altar—
let me come to God, my joy, my delight—
then I will give you thanks with the lyre,
God, my God!

5 Why, I ask myself, are you so depressed?
Why are you so upset inside?
Hope in God!
Because I will again give him thanks,
my saving presence and my God.

Psalm 44

For the music leader.
A maskil[d] of the Korahites.

1 We have heard it, God, with our own ears;
our ancestors told us about it:
about the deeds you did in their days,
in days long past.
2 You, by your own hand,
removed all the nations,
but you planted our ancestors.
You crushed all the peoples,
but you set our ancestors free.
3 No, not by their own swords
did they take possession of the land—
their own arms didn't save them.
No, it was your strong hand, your arm,
and the light of your face
because you were pleased with them.
4 It's you, God! You who are my king,
the one who orders salvation for Jacob.
5 We've pushed our foes away by your help;
we've trampled our enemies
by your name.
6 No, I won't trust in my bow;
my sword won't save me
7 because it's you who saved us
from our foes,
you who put those who hate us
to shame.
8 So we glory in God at all times
and give thanks to your name forever.
Selah

9 But now you've rejected and humiliated us.
You no longer accompany our armies.
10 You make us retreat from the enemy;
our adversaries plunder us.
11 You've handed us over
like sheep for butchering;
you've scattered us among the nations.
12 You've sold your people for nothing,
not even bothering to set a decent price.
13 You've made us a joke to all our neighbors;
we're mocked and ridiculed
by everyone around us.
14 You've made us a bad joke to the nations,
something to be laughed at
by all peoples.
15 All day long my disgrace confronts me,
and shame covers my face
16 because of the voices of those
who make fun of me and bad-mouth me,
because of the enemy who is out
for revenge.

17 All this has come upon us,
but we haven't forgotten you
or broken your covenant.
18 Our hearts haven't turned away,

[d] Perhaps *instruction*

neither have our steps
strayed from your way.
19 But you've crushed us in the place
where jackals[e] live,
covering us with deepest darkness.
20 If we had forgotten the name of our God
or spread out our hands
to some strange deity,
21 wouldn't God have discovered it?
After all, God knows every secret
of the heart.
22 No, God, it's because of you
that we are getting killed every day—
it's because of you that we are
considered sheep ready for slaughter.

23 Wake up! Why are you sleeping, Lord?
Get up! Don't reject us forever!
24 Why are you hiding your face,
forgetting our suffering
and oppression?
25 Look: we're going down to the dust;
our stomachs are flat on the ground!
26 Stand up! Help us!
Save us for the sake
of your faithful love.

Psalm 45

For the music leader. According to "The Lilies." Of the Korahites. A maskil.[f] A love song.

1 A marvelous word has stirred my heart
as I mention my works to the king.
My tongue is the pen
of a skillful scribe.

2 You are the most handsome of men;
grace has been poured out on your lips.
No wonder God has blessed
you forever!
3 Strap on your sword, great warrior,
with your glory and grandeur.
4 Go and succeed in your grandeur!
Ride out on behalf of truth,
humility, and righteousness!
Let your strong hand perform
awesome deeds.[g]
5 Let the peoples fall beneath you.
May your sharp arrows pierce the
hearts of the king's enemies.
6 Your divine throne
is eternal and everlasting.
Your royal scepter
is a scepter of justice.
7 You love righteousness
and hate wickedness.
No wonder God, your God,
has anointed you
with the oil of joy
more than all your companions!
8 All your clothes have the pleasing scent
of myrrh, aloes, and cinnamon.
The music of stringed instruments
coming from ivory palaces
entertains you.
9 The royal princess is standing
in your precious jewels;[h]
the queen stands at your right,
dressed in the gold of Ophir.

10 Listen, daughter; pay attention,
and listen closely!
Forget your people
and your father's house.
11 Let the king desire your beauty.
Because he is your master,
bow down to him now.
12 The city of Tyre, the wealthiest of all,
will seek your favor with gifts,
13 with riches of every sort
for the royal princess, dressed in pearls,[i]
her robe embroidered with gold.
14 In robes of many colors,
she is led to the king.
Her attendants,
the young women servants
following her,
are presented to you as well.
15 As they enter the king's palace,
they are led in with celebration and joy.

16 Your sons, great king,
will succeed your fathers;[j]
you will appoint them as princes
throughout the land.

[e] Or *the sea monster(s)* [f] Perhaps *instruction* [g] Heb uncertain [h] Syr; MT *royal princess is among your precious ones.*
[i] Correction; Heb lacks *for*; Heb uncertain in 45:12-13 [j] Heb lacks *great king.*

17 I will perpetuate your name
from one generation to the next
so the peoples will praise you
forever and always.

Psalm 46

For the music leader. Of the Korahites.
According to Alamoth.[k] *A song.*

1 God is our refuge and strength,
a help always near
in times of great trouble.
2 That's why we won't be afraid
when the world falls apart,
when the mountains crumble into the
center of the sea,
3 when its waters roar and rage,
when the mountains shake
because of its surging waves. *Selah*

4 There is a river whose streams
gladden God's city,
the holiest dwelling of the Most High.
5 God is in that city. It will never crumble.
God will help it when morning dawns.
6 Nations roar; kingdoms crumble.
God utters his voice; the earth melts.
7 The LORD of heavenly forces is with us!
The God of Jacob is our place of safety.
Selah

8 Come, see the LORD's deeds,
what devastation he has imposed
on the earth—
9 bringing wars to an end
in every corner of the world,
breaking the bow
and shattering the spear,
burning chariots with fire.

10 "That's enough!
Now know that I am God!
I am exalted among all nations;
I am exalted throughout the world!"

11 The LORD of heavenly forces is with us!
The God of Jacob is our place of safety.
Selah

Psalm 47

For the music leader.
A psalm of the Korahites.

1 Clap your hands, all you people!
Shout joyfully to God
with a joyous shout!
2 Because the LORD Most High is awesome,
he is the great king of the whole world.
3 He subdues the nations under us,
subdues all people beneath our feet.
4 He chooses our inheritance for us:
the heights of Jacob, which he loves.
Selah

5 God has gone up with a joyous shout—
the LORD with the blast
of the ram's horn.
6 Sing praises to God! Sing praises!
Sing praises to our king! Sing praises
7 because God is king of the whole world!
Sing praises with a song of instruction![l]

8 God is king over the nations.
God sits on his holy throne.
9 The leaders of all people are gathered
with the people of Abraham's God
because the earth's guardians
belong to God;
God is exalted beyond all.

Psalm 48

A song. A psalm of the Korahites.

1 In the city belonging to our God,
the LORD is great
and so worthy of praise!
His holy mountain 2 is a beautiful summit,
the joy of the whole world.
Mount Zion, in the far north,
is the city of the great king.
3 God is in its fortifications,
revealing himself as a place of safety.

4 Look: the kings assembled themselves,
advancing all together—
5 when they saw it, they were stunned;
they panicked and ran away frightened.
6 Trembling took hold of them right there—
like a woman giving birth,

[k]Heb uncertain; see note at Pss 9–10 or Ps 111. [l]Or *Sing praises with understanding* or *wisely* (cf LXX, Vulg); Heb *maskil*; see the note at Ps 32.

7 or like the east wind when it smashes
the ships of Tarshish.
8 Just like we had heard,
now we've seen it for ourselves
in the city of
the LORD of heavenly forces,
in the city of our God.
May God make it secure forever! *Selah*

9 We dwell on your faithful love, God,
in your temple.
10 Your praise, God,
just like your reputation,
extends to the far corners of the earth.
Your strong hand is filled
with righteousness.
11 Let Mount Zion be glad;
let the towns of Judah rejoice
because of your acts of justice!

12 Walk around Zion;
go all the way around it;
count its towers.
13 Examine its defenses closely;
tour its fortifications
so that you may tell future generations:
14 "This is God,
our God, forever and always!
He is the one who will lead us
even to the very end."[m]

Psalm 49

For the music leader.
A psalm of the Korahites.

1 Listen to this, all you people!
Listen closely,
all you citizens of the world—
2 people of every kind,
rich and poor alike!
3 My mouth speaks wisdom;
my heart's meditation is full of insight.
4 I will pay close attention to a proverb;
I will explain my riddle on the lyre.

5 Why should I be afraid in times of trouble,
when the wrongdoing of my bullies
engulfs me—
6 those people who trust
in their fortunes
and boast of their fantastic wealth?
7 Wealth? It can't save a single person!
It can't pay a life's ransom-price to God.
8 The price to save someone's life
is too high—
wealth will never be enough—
9 no one can live forever
without experiencing the pit.

10 Everyone knows that the wise die too,
just like foolish and stupid people do,
all of them leaving their fortunes
to others.
11 Their graves[n] are their eternal homes,
the place they live for all generations,
even if they had counties
named after them!
12 People won't live any longer
because of wealth;
they're just like the animals
that pass away.

13 That's how it goes
for those who are foolish,
as well as for those who follow their
lead, pleased with their talk. *Selah*
14 Like sheep, they're headed
straight for the grave.[o]
Death will be their shepherd—
but those who do right in their hearts
will rule over them come morning!—
their forms wasting away in the grave
rather than having
some dignified residence.[p]
15 But God will save my life
from the power of the grave,
because he will take me. *Selah*

16 Don't be overly impressed
when someone becomes rich,
their house swelling
to fantastic proportions,
17 because when they die,
they won't take any of it with them.
Their fantastic things
won't accompany them down under.

[m]LXX; Heb uncertain; Heb *al muth (unto death* or *against death),* but see the notes at Pss 9–10, 46—the words might belong in the heading of Ps 49. [n]Correction with LXX [o]Heb *Sheol;* also again in 49:7, 15
[p]Heb uncertain in 49:13-14

18 Though they consider themselves
blessed during their lives,
and even thank you
when you deal well with them,[q]
19 they too will join the ancestors
who've gone ahead;
they too will never see the light again.
20 Wealthy people?
They just don't understand;
they're just like the animals
that pass away.

Psalm 50

A psalm of Asaph.

1 From the rising of the sun to where it sets,
God, the LORD God, speaks,
calling out to the earth.
2 From Zion, perfect in beauty,
God shines brightly.
3 Our God is coming;
he won't keep quiet.
A devouring fire is before him;
a storm rages all around him.
4 God calls out to the skies above
and to the earth
in order to judge his people:
5 "Bring my faithful to me,
those who made a covenant with me
by sacrifice."
6 The skies proclaim his righteousness
because God himself is the judge. *Selah*

7 "Listen, my people, I will now speak;
Israel, I will now testify against you.
I am God—your God!
8 I'm not punishing you for your sacrifices
or for your entirely burned offerings,
which are always before me.
9 I won't accept bulls from your house
or goats from your corrals
10 because every forest animal
already belongs to me,
as do the cattle on a thousand hills.
11 I know every mountain bird;
even the insects in the fields are mine.
12 Even if I were hungry, I wouldn't tell you
because the whole world and
everything in it already belong to me.
13 Do I eat bulls' meat?
Do I drink goats' blood?
14 Offer God a sacrifice of thanksgiving!
Fulfill the promises
you made to the Most High!
15 Cry out to me
whenever you are in trouble;
I will deliver you, then you will honor me."

16 But to the wicked God says,
"Why do you talk about my laws?
Why do you even mention my covenant?
17 You hate discipline, and
you toss my words behind your back.
18 You make friends with thieves whenever
you see one;
you spend your time with adulterers.
19 You set your mouth free to do evil,
then harness your tongue to tell lies.
20 You sit around,
talking about your own siblings;
you find fault with the children
of your very own mother.
21 You've done these things
and I've kept quiet.
You thought I was just like you!
But now I'm punishing you;
I'm laying it all out,
right in front of your face.
22 So consider this carefully,
all you who forget God,
or I'll rip you to pieces
with no one to deliver you:
23 The one who offers
a sacrifice of thanksgiving
is the one who honors me.
And it is to the one who charts
the correct path that I will show
divine salvation."

Psalm 51

For the music leader. A psalm of David, when the prophet Nathan came to him just after he had been with Bathsheba.

1 Have mercy on me, God,
according to your faithful love!
Wipe away my wrongdoings
according to your great compassion!

q LXX, Syr

[2]Wash me completely clean of my guilt;
purify me from my sin!
[3]Because I know my wrongdoings,
my sin is always right in front of me.
[4]I've sinned against you—you alone.
I've committed evil in your sight.
That's why you are justified
when you render your verdict,
completely correct
when you issue your judgment.
[5]Yes, I was born in guilt, in sin,
from the moment my mother
conceived me.
[6]And yes, you want truth
in the most hidden places;
you teach me wisdom
in the most secret space.[r]

[7]Purify me with hyssop and I will be clean;
wash me and I will be whiter than snow.
[8]Let me hear joy and celebration again;
let the bones you crushed
rejoice once more.
[9]Hide your face from my sins;
wipe away all my guilty deeds!
[10]Create a clean heart for me, God;
put a new, faithful spirit deep inside me!
[11]Please don't throw me
out of your presence;
please don't take your holy spirit
away from me.
[12]Return the joy of your salvation to me
and sustain me with a willing spirit.
[13]Then I will teach wrongdoers your ways,
and sinners will come back to you.

[14]Deliver me from violence, God,
God of my salvation,
so that my tongue can sing
of your righteousness.
[15]Lord, open my lips,
and my mouth
will proclaim your praise.
[16]You don't want sacrifices.
If I gave an entirely burned offering,
you wouldn't be pleased.
[17]A broken spirit is my sacrifice, God.[s]
You won't despise a heart, God,
that is broken and crushed.

[18]Do good things for Zion by your favor.
Rebuild Jerusalem's walls.
[19]Then you will again want
sacrifices of righteousness—
entirely burned offerings
and complete offerings.
Then bulls will again be sacrificed
on your altar.

Psalm 52

For the music leader. A maskil[t] of David, when Doeg the Edomite came and told Saul, "David has gone to Ahimelech's house."

[1]Hey, powerful person!
Why do you brag about evil?
God's faithful love lasts all day long.
[2]Your tongue devises destruction:
it's like a sharpened razor,
causing deception.
[3]You love evil more than good;
you love lying more than speaking
what is right. *Selah*
[4]You love all destructive words;
you love the deceiving tongue.

[5]But God will take you down permanently;
he will snatch you up,
tear you out of your tent,
and uproot you from the land
of the living! *Selah*
[6]The righteous will see and be in awe;
they will laugh at those people:
[7]"Look at them! They didn't make God
their refuge.
Instead, they trusted in
their own great wealth.
They sought refuge in it—
to their own destruction!"

[8]But I am like a green olive tree
in God's house;
I trust in God's faithful love
forever and always.
[9]I will give thanks to you, God, forever,
because you have acted.
In the presence of your faithful people,
I will hope in your name
because it's so good.

[r]Heb uncertain [s]Correction [t]Perhaps *instruction*; it also appears in Pss 42, 44–45, 52–55, 74, 78, 88–89, 142; cf 47:7; the root is used in Ps 32:8.

Psalm 53

For the music leader, according to the mahalath. A maskil[u] *of David.*

1 Fools say in their hearts, There's no God.
They are corrupt and do horrible deeds;
not one of them does anything good.

2 God looks down from heaven on humans
to see if anyone is wise,
to see if anyone seeks God.
3 But all have turned away.
Everyone is corrupt.
No one does good—
not even one person!

4 Are they dumb—these evildoers—
devouring my people
like they are eating bread
but never calling on God?

5 There, where there was nothing to fear,
they will be in utter panic
because God will scatter the bones
of those who attacked you.
You will put them to shame
because God has rejected them.

6 Let Israel's salvation come out of Zion!
When God changes
his people's circumstances
for the better,
Jacob will rejoice;
Israel will celebrate!

Psalm 54

For the music leader. With stringed instruments. A maskil[v] *of David, when the Ziphites came and said to Saul, "Isn't David hiding among us?"*

1 God! Save me by your name;
defend me by your might!
2 God! Hear my prayer;
listen to the words of my mouth!

3 The proud have come up against me;
violent people want me dead.
They pay no attention to God. *Selah*
4 But look here: God is my helper;
my Lord sustains my life.
5 He will bring disaster on my opponents.
By your faithfulness, God, destroy them!

6 I will sacrifice to you freely;
I will give thanks to your name, LORD,
because it's so good,
7 and because God has delivered me
from every distress.
My eyes have seen
my enemies' defeat.[w]

Psalm 55

For the music leader. With stringed instruments. A maskil[x] *of David.*

1 God, listen to my prayer;
don't avoid my request!
2 Pay attention! Answer me!
I can't sit still while complaining.
I'm beside myself
3 over the enemy's noise,
at the wicked person's racket,
because they bring disaster on me
and harass me furiously.

4 My heart pounds in my chest
because death's terrors
have reached me.
5 Fear and trembling
have come upon me;
I'm shaking all over.
6 I say to myself,
I wish I had wings like a dove!
I'd fly away and rest.
7 I'd run so far away!
I'd live in the desert. *Selah*
8 I'd hurry to my hideout,
far from the rushing wind and storm.

9 Baffle them, my Lord!
Confuse their language
because I see violence and conflict
in the city.
10 Day and night they make their rounds
on its walls,
and evil and misery live inside it.

[u] Perhaps *instruction* [v] Perhaps *instruction*; it also appears in Pss 42, 44–45, 52–55, 74, 78, 88–89, 142; cf 47:7; the root is used in Ps 32:8. [w] Heb lacks *defeat.* [x] Perhaps *instruction*

11 Disaster lives inside it;
oppression and fraud
never leave the town square.

12 It's not an enemy that is insulting me—
I could handle that.
It's not someone who hates me
who is exalted over me—
I could hide from them.
13 No. It's you, my equal,
my close companion, my good friend!
14 It was so pleasant when
together we entered God's house
with the crowd.

15 Let death devastate my enemies;
let them go to the grave[y] alive
because evil lives with them—
even inside them!
16 But I call out to God,
and the LORD will rescue me.
17 At evening, morning, and midday
I complain and moan
so that God will hear my voice.
18 He saves me,[z] unharmed,
from my struggle,
though there are many
who are out to get me.
19 God, who is enthroned
from ancient days,
will hear and humble them *Selah*
because they don't change
and they don't worship God.

20 My friend attacked his allies,
breaking his covenant.
21 Though his talk is smoother
than butter,
war is in his heart;
though his words are more
silky than oil,
they are really drawn swords:
22 "Cast your burden on the LORD—
he will support you!
God will never let the righteous
be shaken!"

23 But you, God, bring the wicked
down to the deepest pit.
Let bloodthirsty
and treacherous people
not live out even half their days.
But me? I trust in you!

Psalm 56

For the music leader. According to "The Silent Dove of Distant Places." A miktam[a] of David, when the Philistines seized him in Gath.

1 God, have mercy on me
because I'm being trampled.
All day long the enemy oppresses me.
2 My attackers trample me all day long
because I have so many enemies.
Exalted one, 3 whenever I'm afraid,
I put my trust in you—
4 in God, whose word I praise.
I trust in God; I won't be afraid.
What can mere flesh do to me?

5 All day long they frustrate my pursuits;
all their thoughts are evil against me.
6 They get together and set an ambush—
they are watching my steps,
hoping for my death.
7 Don't rescue them for any reason!
In wrath bring down the people, God!

8 You yourself have kept track of my misery.
Put my tears into your bottle—
aren't they on your scroll already?
9 Then my enemies will retreat
when I cry out.
I know this because God is mine.
10 God: whose word I praise.
The LORD: whose word I praise.
11 I trust in God; I won't be afraid.
What can anyone do to me?

12 I will fulfill my promises to you, God.
I will present thanksgiving offerings
to you
13 because you have saved my life
from death,
saved my feet from stumbling
so that I can walk before God
in the light of life.

[y] Heb *Sheol* [z] Or *my life* or *soul* [a] Perhaps *inscription*

Psalm 57

For the music leader. Do not destroy.
A miktam[b] *of David, when he fled*
from Saul into the cave.

1 Have mercy on me, God;
have mercy on me
because I[c] have taken refuge in you.
I take refuge
in the shadow of your wings
until destruction passes by.
2 I call out to God Most High—
to God, who comes through for me.
3 He sends orders from heaven
and saves me,
rebukes the one who tramples me. *Selah*
God sends his loyal love
and faithfulness.

4 My life is in the middle
of a pack of lions.
I lie down
among those who devour humans.
Their teeth are spears and arrows;
their tongues are sharpened swords.
5 Exalt yourself, God,
higher than heaven!
Let your glory be over all the earth!
6 They laid a net for my feet
to bring me down;
they dug a pit for me,
but they fell into it instead! *Selah*

7 My heart is unwavering, God—
my heart is unwavering.
I will sing and make music.
8 Wake up, my glory!
Wake up, harp and lyre!
I will wake the dawn itself!
9 I will give thanks to you,
my Lord,
among all the peoples;
I will make music to you
among the nations
10 because your faithful love
is as high as heaven;
your faithfulness reaches the clouds.
11 Exalt yourself, God,
higher than heaven!
Let your glory be over all the earth!

Psalm 58

For the music leader. Do not destroy.
A psalm of David, a miktam.[d]

1 Do you really speak what is right, you gods?
Do you really judge humans fairly?
2 No: in your hearts you plan injustice;
your hands do violence on the earth.

3 The wicked backslide from the womb;
liars go astray from birth.
4 Their venom is like a snake's venom—
like a deaf cobra's—
one that shuts its ears
5 so it can't hear
the snake charmer's voice
or the spells of a skillful enchanter.

6 God, break their teeth out of their mouths!
Tear out the lions' jawbones, LORD!
7 Let them dissolve like water flowing away.
When they bend the bow,
let their arrows be like headless shafts.[e]
8 Like the snail that dissolves into slime,
like a woman's stillborn child,
let them never see the sun.
9 Before your pots feel the thorns,
whether green or burned up,
God will sweep them away![f]

10 But the righteous will rejoice
when they see vengeance done,
when they wash their feet
in the blood of the wicked.
11 Then it will be said:
"Yes, there is a reward for the righteous!
Yes, there is a God who judges people
on the earth."

Psalm 59

For the music leader. Do not destroy.
A miktam[g] *of David, when Saul sent men*
to watch the house in order to kill him.

1 Oh, my God, deliver me from my enemies;
put me out of reach from those
who rise up against me.
2 Deliver me from evildoers;
save me from the bloodthirsty.
3 Look at how they lie in ambush for my life!

[b] Perhaps *inscription* [c] Or *my soul* [d] Perhaps *inscription* [e] Heb uncertain [f] Heb uncertain [g] Perhaps *inscription*

Powerful people are attacking me,
LORD—
but not because of any error
or sin of mine.
4 They run and take their stand—
but not because of any fault of mine.

Get up when I cry out to you!
Look at what's happening!
5 You are the LORD God of heavenly forces,
the God of Israel!
Wake up and punish all the nations!
Grant no mercy to any wicked traitor! *Selah*

6 They come back every evening,
growling like dogs,
prowling around the city.
7 See what they belch out
with their mouths:
swords are between their lips!
Who can listen to them?[h]
8 But you, LORD, laugh at them.
You mock all the nations.
9 I keep looking for you, my strength,
because God is my stronghold.
10 My loving God will come to meet me.
God will allow me to look down
on my enemies.

11 Don't kill them,
or my people might forget;
instead, by your power
shake them up and bring them down,
you who are our shield and my Lord.
12 For the sin of their mouths,
the words that they speak,
let them be captured in their pride.
For the curses and lies they repeat,
13 finish them off in anger;
finish them off until they are gone!
Then let it be known
to the ends of the earth
that God rules over Jacob. *Selah*

14 They come back every evening,
growling like dogs,
prowling around the city.
15 They roam about for food,
and if they don't get their fill,
they stay all night.
16 But me? I will sing of your strength!
In the morning I will shout out loud
about your faithful love
because you have been my stronghold,
my shelter when I was distraught.
17 I will sing praises to you, my strength,
because God is my stronghold,
my loving God.

Psalm 60

For the music leader. According to "Lily." A testimony. A miktam[i] of David. For instruction, when he went to war with Aram-naharaim and Aram-sobah, and when Joab returned and defeated Edom, killing twelve thousand in the Salt Valley.

1 God, you have rejected us—
shattered us.
You've been so angry.
Now restore us!
2 You've made the ground quake,
splitting it open.
Now repair its cracks
because it's shaking apart!
3 You've made your people suffer hardship;
you've given us wine and we stagger.
4 Give a flag to those who honor you,
so they can rally around it,
safe from attack.[j] *Selah*
5 Save us by your power and answer us
so that the people you love might be
rescued.

6 God has spoken in his sanctuary:
"I will celebrate as I divide up Shechem
and portion out the Succoth Valley.
7 Gilead is mine;
Manasseh is mine;
Ephraim is my helmet;
Judah is my scepter.
8 But Moab is my washbowl;
I'll throw my shoe at Edom.
I shout in triumph over Philistia![k]
9 I wish someone would bring me
to a fortified city!
I wish someone would lead me
to Edom!"

[h] Heb uncertain [i] Perhaps *inscription* [j] Or *the bow*; Heb uncertain [k] Syr, Ps 108:9; MT *Celebrate over me, Philistia!*

10 But you have rejected us, God, haven't you?
God, you no longer accompany
our armies.
11 Give us help against the enemy;
human help is worthless.
12 With God we will triumph;
he's the one who will trample
our adversaries.

Psalm 61

For the music leader,
with stringed instruments. Of David.

1 God, listen to my cry;
pay attention to my prayer!
2 When my heart is weak,
I cry out to you
from the very ends of the earth.
Lead me to the rock
that is higher than I am
3 because you have been my refuge,
a tower of strength
in the face of the enemy.
4 Please let me live in your tent forever!
Please let me take refuge
in the shelter of your wings! *Selah*
5 Because you, God,
have heard my promises;
you've given me[l] the same possession
as those who honor your name.

6 Add days to the king's life!
Let his years extend
for many generations!
7 Let him be enthroned forever
before God!
Make it so love and faithfulness
watch over him!
8 Then I will sing praises
to your name forever,
and I will do what I promised
every single day.

Psalm 62

For the music leader. According to
Jeduthun. A psalm of David.

1 Only in God do I[m] find rest;
my salvation comes from him.
2 Only God is my rock and my salvation—
my stronghold!—
I won't be shaken anymore.

3 How long will all of you attack others;
how long will you tear them down[n]
as if they were leaning walls
or broken-down fences?
4 The only desire of this people
is to bring others down low;
they delight in deception.
With their mouths they bless,
but inside they are cursing. *Selah*

5 Oh, I[o] must find rest in God only,
because my hope comes from him!
6 Only God is my rock and my salvation—
my stronghold!—I will not be shaken.
7 My deliverance and glory depend on God.
God is my strong rock.
My refuge is in God.
8 All you people: Trust in him at all times!
Pour out your hearts before him!
God is our refuge! *Selah*

9 Human beings are nothing but a breath.
Human beings are nothing but lies.
They don't even register on a scale;
taken all together
they are lighter than a breath!
10 Don't trust in violence;
don't set false hopes in robbery.
When wealth bears fruit,
don't set your heart on it.
11 God has spoken one thing—
make it two things—
that I myself have heard:
that strength belongs to God,
12 and faithful love comes from you,
my Lord—
and that you will repay
everyone according to their deeds.

Psalm 63

A psalm of David,
when he was in the Judean desert.

1 God! My God! It's you—
I search for you!

[l]Heb lacks *me.* [m]Or *my soul* [n]Correction; MT *kill them* [o]Or *my soul*

My whole being[p] thirsts for you!
My body desires you
in a dry and tired land,
no water anywhere.
2 Yes, I've seen you in the sanctuary;
I've seen your power and glory.
3 My lips praise you
because your faithful love
is better than life itself!
4 So I will bless you as long as I'm alive;
I will lift up my hands in your name.

5 I'm fully satisfied—
as with a rich dinner.
My mouth speaks praise
with joy on my lips—
6 whenever I ponder you on my bed,
whenever I meditate on you
in the middle of the night—
7 because you've been a help to me
and I shout for joy in the protection
of your wings.
8 My whole being clings to you;
your strong hand upholds me.

9 But what about those people
who want to destroy me?
Let them go into the bowels
of the earth!
10 Let their blood flow by the sword!
Let them be food for wild jackals!
11 But the king should rejoice in God;
everyone who swears by God
should give praise
when the mouths of liars
are shut for good.

Psalm 64

For the music leader. A psalm of David.

1 Listen to me when I complain, God!
Protect my life
from the enemy's terror!
2 Hide me from the secret plots
of wicked people;
hide me from the schemes of evildoers
3 who sharpen their tongues
like swords.
They aim their arrow—a cruel word—
4 from their hiding places
so as to shoot an innocent person.
They shoot without warning
and without fear.
5 They encourage themselves
with evil words.
They plan on laying traps in secret.
"Who will be able to see them?"
they ask.
6 "Let someone try
to expose our crimes!
We've devised a perfect plot!
It's deep within
the human mind and heart."[q]

7 But God will shoot them
with an arrow!
Without warning,
they will be wounded!
8 The LORD will make them trip
over their own tongues;
everyone who sees them
will just shake their heads.
9 Then all people will honor God,
will announce the act of God,
will understand it was God's work.
10 Let the righteous rejoice in the LORD;
let them take refuge in him;
let everyone whose heart is
in the right place give praise!

Psalm 65

For the music leader. A psalm of David. A song.

1 God of Zion,
to you even silence is praise.
Promises made to you are kept—
2 you listen to prayer—
and all living things come to you.
3 When wrongdoings become
too much for me,
you forgive our sins.
4 How happy is the one you choose
to bring close,
the one who lives in your courtyards!
We are filled full
by the goodness of your house,
by the holiness of your temple.

[p]Or *my soul;* also in 63:5, 8 [q]Heb uncertain

5 In righteousness you answer us,
by your awesome deeds,
God of our salvation—
you, who are the security
of all the far edges of the earth,
even the distant seas.
6 You establish the mountains
by your strength;
you are dressed in raw power.
7 You calm the roaring seas;
calm the roaring waves,
calm the noise of the nations.
8 Those who dwell on the far edges
stand in awe of your acts.
You make the gateways
of morning and evening sing for joy.
9 You visit the earth
and make it abundant,
enriching it greatly
by God's stream, full of water.
You provide people with grain
because that is what you've decided.
10 Drenching the earth's furrows,
leveling its ridges,
you soften it with rain showers;
you bless its growth.
11 You crown the year
with your goodness;
your paths overflow with rich food.
12 Even the desert pastures drip with it,
and the hills are dressed in pure joy.
13 The meadowlands are covered
with flocks,
the valleys decked out in grain—
they shout for joy;
they break out in song!

Psalm 66

For the music leader. A song. A psalm.

1 Shout joyfully to God, all the earth!
2 Sing praises to the glory
of God's name!
Make glorious his praise!
3 Say to God:
"How awesome are your works!
Because of your great strength,
your enemies cringe before you.
4 All the earth worships you,
sings praises to you,
sings praises to your name!" *Selah*

5 Come and see God's deeds;
his works for human beings
are awesome:
6 He turned the sea into dry land
so they could cross the river on foot.
Right there we rejoiced in him!
7 God rules with power forever;
keeps a good eye on the nations.
So don't let the rebellious
exalt themselves. *Selah*

8 All you nations, bless our God!
Let the sound of his praise be heard!
9 God preserved us among the living;
he didn't let our feet slip a bit.

10 But you, God, have tested us—
you've refined us like silver,
11 trapped us in a net,
laid burdens on our backs,
12 let other people run
right over our heads—
we've been through fire and water.

But you brought us out to freedom!
13 So I'll enter your house
with entirely burned offerings.
I'll keep the promises I made to you,
14 the ones my lips uttered,
the ones my mouth spoke
when I was in deep trouble.
15 I will offer the best burned offerings
to you
along with the smoke
of sacrificed rams.
I will offer both bulls and goats. *Selah*

16 Come close and listen,
all you who honor God;
I will tell you
what God has done for me:
17 My mouth cried out to him
with praise on my tongue.
18 If I had cherished evil in my heart,
my Lord would not have listened.
19 But God definitely listened.
He heard the sound of my prayer.
20 Bless God! He didn't reject my prayer;
he didn't withhold
his faithful love from me.

Psalm 67

For the music leader, with stringed instruments. A psalm. A song.

1 Let God grant us grace and bless us;
let God make his face shine on us, *Selah*
2 so that your way becomes known
on earth,
so that your salvation becomes known
among all the nations.

3 Let the people thank you, God!
Let all the people thank you!
4 Let the people celebrate
and shout with joy
because you judge the nations fairly
and guide all nations on the earth. *Selah*
5 Let the people thank you, God!
Let all the people thank you!

6 The earth has yielded its harvest.
God blesses us—our God blesses us!
7 Let God continue to bless us;
let the far ends of the earth honor him.

Psalm 68

For the music leader. Of David. A psalm. A song.

1 Let God rise up;
let his enemies scatter;
let those who hate him
run scared before him!
2 Like smoke is driven away,
drive them away!
Like wax melting before fire,
let the wicked perish before God!
3 But let the righteous be glad
and celebrate before God.
Let them rejoice with gladness!
4 Sing to God! Sing praises to his name!
Exalt the one who rides the clouds!
The LORD is his name.
Celebrate before him!

5 Father of orphans
and defender of widows
is God in his holy habitation.
6 God settles the lonely in their homes;
he sets prisoners free with happiness,[r]
but the rebellious dwell
in a parched land.

7 When you went forth
before your people, God,
when you marched
through the wasteland, *Selah*
8 the earth shook!
Yes, heaven poured down
before God, the one from Sinai—
before God, the God of Israel!
9 You showered down abundant rain, God;
when your inheritance grew weary,
you restored it yourself,
10 and your creatures settled in it.
In your goodness, God,
you provided for the poor.

11 My Lord gives the command—
many messengers are
bringing good news:
12 "The kings of armies are on the run!
The women back home divide the spoil.
13 Even if you lie down
among the sheepfolds,
there are wings of a dove
covered with silver;
its pinions covered in precious gold."[s]
14 When the Almighty[t]
scattered the kings there,
snow fell on Mount Zalmon.

15 Mighty mountain, Mount Bashan;
many-peaked mountain, Mount Bashan!
16 You many-peaked mountain:
Why do you look with envy
at the mountain
God desired for his dwelling,
the mountain
where the LORD dwells forever?

17 God's chariots are twice ten thousand—
countless thousands!
My Lord came from Sinai[u]
into the sanctuary.

[r] Or *skillfully*; LXX, Vulg *with strength*; Heb uncertain [s] Heb uncertain [t] Heb *Shaddai* [u] Correction; MT *My Lord was among them, the one from Sinai, in holiness.*

18 You ascended the heights,
leading away your captives,
receiving tribute from people,
even from those who rebel
against the LORD God's dwelling there.
19 Bless the Lord!
The God of our salvation
supports us day after day! *Selah*
20 Our God is the God of salvation,
and escape from certain death
comes through God my LORD.

21 Yes, God will shatter
the heads of his enemies—
the very skulls of those who walk in guilt.
22 My Lord has spoken:
"From Bashan I will bring
those people back.
I will bring them back
from the ocean's depths
23 so that you can wash your feet
in their blood,
so that your dogs' tongues
can lap up their share of your enemies."

24 They saw your procession, God—
the procession of my God,
my king, into the sanctuary.
25 First came the singers,
then the musicians;
between them the young women
were playing hand drums:
26 "Bless God in the great congregation;
bless the LORD from Israel's fountain!"
27 There's Benjamin leading them,
though he's little;
then the princes of Judah,
their speaker;
then the princes of Zebulun
and the princes of Naphtali.

28 Summon your strength, God!
Show how strong you are, God,
just as you've done for us before,
29 from your temple above Jerusalem,
where kings bring you gifts.
30 Rebuke the wild animals
of the marshland,
the herd of bulls
among the calves of the peoples.
Trample those who delight in money;
scatter the peoples
who take pleasure in battles.
31 Let ambassadors come from Egypt;
let Cush stretch out its hands to God.

32 Sing to God, all kingdoms of the earth!
Sing praises to my Lord. *Selah*
33 Sing to the one
who rides through heaven,
the most ancient heaven.
Look! God sends forth his voice,
his mighty voice.
34 Recognize how strong God is!
His majesty extends over Israel;
his strength is in the clouds.
35 You are awesome, God,
in your sanctuaries—
the God of Israel who gives strength
and power to his people!

Bless God!

Psalm 69

For the music leader. According to "The Lilies." Of David.

1 Save me, God,
because the waters have reached my neck!
2 I have sunk into deep mud.
My feet can't touch the bottom!
I have entered deep water;
the flood has swept me up.
3 I am tired of crying.
My throat is hoarse.
My eyes are exhausted
with waiting for my God.

4 More numerous than the hairs
on my head
are those who hate me for no reason.
My treacherous enemies,
those who would destroy me,
are countless.
Must I now give back
what I didn't steal in the first place?
5 God, you know my foolishness;
my wrongdoings aren't hidden
from you.

6 LORD God of heavenly forces!—
don't let those who hope in you
be put to shame because of me.

God of Israel!—
don't let those who seek you
be disgraced because of me.
7 I am insulted because of you.
Shame covers my face.
8 I have become a stranger
to my own brothers,
an immigrant to my mother's children.
9 Because passion for your house
has consumed me,
the insults of those who insult you
have fallen on me!
10 I wept while I fasted—
even for that I was insulted.
11 When I wore funeral clothes,
people made fun of me.
12 Those who sit at the city gate
muttered things about me;
drunkards made up rude songs.

13 But me? My prayer reaches you, LORD,
at just the right time.
God, in your great and faithful love,
answer me with your certain salvation!
14 Save me from the mud!
Don't let me drown!
Let me be saved from those who hate me
and from these watery depths!
15 Don't let me be swept away
by the floodwaters!
Don't let the abyss swallow me up!
Don't let the pit close its mouth
over me!
16 Answer me, LORD,
for your faithful love is good!
Turn to me in your great compassion!
17 Don't hide your face from me,
your servant,
because I'm in deep trouble.
Answer me quickly!
18 Come close to me!
Redeem me!
Save me because of my enemies!

19 You know full well the insults
I've received;
you know my shame and my disgrace.
All my adversaries are right there
in front of you.
20 Insults have broken my heart.
I'm sick about it.
I hoped for sympathy,
but there wasn't any;
I hoped for comforters,
but couldn't find any.
21 They gave me poison for food.
To quench my thirst
they gave me vinegar to drink.

22 Let the table before them
become a trap,
their offerings a snare.
23 Let their eyes grow too dim to see;
make their insides tremble constantly.
24 Pour out your anger on them—
let your burning fury catch them.
25 Let their camp be devastated;
let no one dwell in their tents.
26 Because they go after those
you've already struck;
they talk about the pain
of those you've already pierced.
27 Pile guilt on top of their guilt!
Don't let them come
into your righteousness!
28 Let them be wiped out
of the scroll of life!
Let them not be recorded
along with the righteous!
29 And me? I'm afflicted.
I'm full of pain.
Let your salvation keep me safe, God!

30 I will praise God's name with song;
I will magnify him with thanks
31 because that is more pleasing to the
LORD than an ox,
more pleasing than a young bull
with full horns and hooves.
32 Let the afflicted see it and be glad!
You who seek God—
let your hearts beat strong again
33 because the LORD listens to the needy
and doesn't despise his captives.

34 Let heaven and earth praise God,
the oceans too, and all that moves
within them!
35 God will most certainly save Zion
and will rebuild Judah's cities
so that God's servants can live there
and possess it.

36 The offspring of God's servants
will inherit Zion,
and those who love God's name
will dwell there.

Psalm 70

For the music leader. Of David.
For the memorial offering.

1 Hurry, God, to deliver me;
hurry, LORD, to help me!
2 Let those who seek my life
be ashamed and humiliated!
Let them fall back and be disgraced—
those people who delight
in my downfall!
3 Let those who say, "Aha! Aha!"
stop because of their shameful
behavior.
4 But let all who seek you
rejoice and be glad in you,
and let those who love your saving help
say again and again:
"God is great!"
5 But me? I'm poor and needy.
Hurry to me, God!
You are my helper and my deliverer.
Oh, LORD, don't delay!

Psalm 71

1 I've taken refuge in you, LORD.
Don't let me ever be put to shame!
2 Deliver me and rescue me
by your righteousness!
Bend your ear toward me
and save me!
3 Be my rock of refuge
where I can always escape.
You commanded that my life be saved
because you are my rock
and my fortress.

4 My God, rescue me
from the power of the wicked;
rescue me from the grip of the
wrongdoer and the oppressor
5 because you are my hope, Lord.
You, LORD, are the one I've trusted
since childhood.
6 I've depended on you from birth—
you cut the cord when I came
from my mother's womb.
My praise is always about you.
7 I've become an example to many people
because you are my strong refuge.
8 My mouth is filled with your praise,
glorifying you all day long.
9 Don't cast me off in old age.
Don't abandon me when my strength
is used up!

10 Yes, my enemies have been
talking about me;
those who stalk me plot together:
11 "God has abandoned him!
Pursue him!
Grab him
because no one will deliver him!"
12 Don't be far from me, God!
My God, hurry to help me!
13 Let my accusers be put to shame,
completely finished off!
Let those who seek my downfall
be dressed in insults and disgrace!

14 But me? I will hope. Always.
I will add to all your praise.
15 My mouth will repeat
your righteous acts
and your saving deeds all day long.
I don't even know
how many of those there are!
16 I will dwell on your mighty acts,
my Lord.
LORD, I will help others remember
nothing but your righteous deeds.
17 You've taught me since my youth, God,
and I'm still proclaiming
your wondrous deeds!
18 So, even in my old age with gray hair,
don't abandon me, God!
Not until I tell generations
about your mighty arm,
tell all who are yet to come
about your strength,
19 and about your ultimate
righteousness, God,
because you've done awesome things!
Who can compare to you, God?
20 You, who have shown me
many troubles and calamities,

will revive me once more.[v]
From the depths of the earth,
you will raise me up one more time.
21 Please increase my honor
and comfort me all around.
22 Then I'll give you thanks with a harp—
I will thank you for your faithfulness,
my God.
I will make music for you
with the lyre, holy one of Israel.
23 My lips will rejoice aloud
when I make music for you;
my whole being,[w] which you saved,
will do the same.
24 My tongue, also, will tell of your
righteousness all day long,
because those who seek my downfall
have been put to shame and disgraced.

Psalm 72

Of Solomon.

1 God, give your judgments to the king.
Give your righteousness to the king's son.
2 Let him judge your people
with righteousness
and your poor ones with justice.
3 Let the mountains bring peace
to the people;
let the hills bring righteousness.
4 Let the king bring justice
to people who are poor;
let him save the children
of those who are needy,
but let him crush oppressors!
5 Let the king live[x] as long as the sun,
as long as the moon,
generation to generation.
6 Let him fall like rain upon fresh-cut grass,
like showers that water the earth.
7 Let the righteous flourish
throughout their lives,
and let peace prosper
until the moon is no more.
8 Let the king rule from sea to sea,
from the river to the ends of the earth.
9 Let the desert dwellers
bow low before him;
let his enemies lick the dust.
10 Let the kings of Tarshish
and the islands bring tribute;
let the kings of Sheba and Seba
present gifts.
11 Let all the kings bow down before him;
let all the nations serve him.

12 Let it be so, because he delivers the
needy who cry out,
the poor, and those who have no helper.
13 He has compassion on the weak
and the needy;
he saves the lives of those
who are in need.
14 He redeems their lives from oppression
and violence;
their blood is precious in his eyes.

15 Let the king live long!
Let Sheba's gold be given to him!
Let him be prayed for always!
Let him be blessed all day long!
16 Let there be abundant grain in the land.
Let it wave on the mountaintops.
Let its fruit flourish like Lebanon.
Let it thrive like grass on the land.
17 Let the king's name last forever.
Let his name endure as long as the sun.
Let all the nations be blessed
through him and call him happy.

18 Bless the LORD God, the God of Israel—
the only one who does wondrous things!
19 Bless God's glorious name forever;
let his glory fill all the earth!
Amen and Amen!

20 The prayers of David, Jesse's son,
are ended.

BOOK III

(Psalms 73–89)

Psalm 73

A psalm of Asaph.

1 Truly God is good to Israel,
to those who have a pure heart.
2 But me? My feet had almost stumbled;
my steps had nearly slipped

[v] Qere; Kethib *who have shown us . . . will revive us* [w] Or *soul* [x] LXX; MT *May they fear you.*

3 because I envied the arrogant;
I observed how the wicked are well off:
4 They suffer no pain;
their bodies are fit and strong.
5 They are never in trouble;
they aren't weighed down
like other people.
6 That's why they wear arrogance
like a necklace,
why violence covers them like clothes.
7 Their eyes bulge out
from eating so well;
their hearts overflow with delusions.
8 They scoff and talk so cruel;
from their privileged positions
they plan oppression.
9 Their mouths dare to speak
against heaven!
Their tongues roam the earth!
10 That's why people keep going back
to them,
keep approving what they say.[y]
11 And what they say is this:
"How could God possibly know!
Does the Most High
know anything at all!"
12 Look at these wicked ones,
always relaxed, piling up the wealth!

13 Meanwhile, I've kept my heart pure
for no good reason;
I've washed my hands
to stay innocent for nothing.
14 I'm weighed down all day long.
I'm punished every morning.
15 If I said, "I will talk about all this,"
I would have been unfaithful
to your children.
16 But when I tried to understand
these things,
it just seemed like hard work
17 until I entered God's sanctuary
and understood what would happen
to the wicked.
18 You will definitely put them
on a slippery path;
you will make them fall into ruin!
19 How quickly they are devastated,
utterly destroyed by terrors!
20 As quickly as a dream departs
from someone waking up, my Lord,
when you are stirred up,
you make them disappear.[z]

21 When my heart was bitter,
when I was all cut up inside,
22 I was stupid and ignorant.
I acted like nothing but an animal
toward you.
23 But I was still always with you!
You held my strong hand!
24 You have guided me with your advice;
later you will receive me with glory.
25 Do I have anyone else in heaven?
There's nothing on earth I desire
except you.
26 My body and my heart fail,
but God is my heart's rock
and my share forever.
27 Look! Those far from you die;
you annihilate all those
who are unfaithful to you.
28 But me? It's good for me to be near God.
I have taken my refuge in you,
my LORD God,
so I can talk all about your works!

Psalm 74

A maskil[a] of Asaph.

1 God, why have you abandoned us forever?
Why does your anger smolder
at the sheep of your own pasture?
2 Remember your congregation
that you took as your own long ago,
that you redeemed to be the tribe
of your own possession—
remember Mount Zion,
where you dwell.
3 March to the unending ruins,
to all that the enemy destroyed
in the sanctuary.

4 Your enemies roared
in your own meeting place;
they set up their own signs there!
5 It looked like axes raised
against a thicket of trees.[b]

[y] Heb uncertain [z] Heb uncertain [a] Perhaps *instruction*; the root is used in Ps 32:8. [b] Heb uncertain

6 And then all its carvings
they hacked down with hatchet
and pick.
7 They set fire to your sanctuary,
burned it to the ground;
they defiled the dwelling place
of your name.
8 They said in their hearts,
We'll kill all of them together!
They burned all of God's meeting places
in the land.
9 We don't see our own signs anymore.
No prophet is left.
And none of us know
how long it will last.

10 How long, God, will foes insult you?
Are enemies going to abuse
your name forever?
11 Why do you pull your hand back?
Why do you hold your strong hand
close to your chest?

12 Yet God has been my king
from ancient days—
God, who makes salvation happen
in the heart of the earth!
13 You split the sea with your power.
You shattered the heads
of the sea monsters on the water.
14 You crushed Leviathan's heads.
You gave it to the desert dwellers
for food!
15 You split open springs and streams;
you made strong-flowing rivers
dry right up.
16 The day belongs to you! The night too!
You established both the moon
and the sun.
17 You set all the boundaries of the earth
in place.
Summer and winter? You made them!

18 So remember this, LORD:
how enemies have insulted you,
how unbelieving fools
have abused your name.
19 Don't deliver the life of your dove
to wild animals!
Don't forget the lives
of your afflicted people forever!
20 Consider the covenant!
Because the land's dark places
are full of violence.
21 Don't let the oppressed live in shame.
No, let the poor and needy
praise your name!

22 God, rise up! Make your case!
Remember how unbelieving fools
insult you all day long.
23 Don't forget the voices of your enemies,
the racket of your adversaries
that never quits.

Psalm 75

For the music leader. Do not destroy.
A psalm of Asaph. A song.

1 We give thanks to you, God.
Yes, we give thanks!
Your name is near.
Your marvelous deeds are declared.

2 God says,[c]
"When I decide the time is right,
I will establish justice just so.
3 The earth and all its inhabitants will melt,
but I will keep its pillars steady." *Selah*

4 I said to the arrogant,
"Don't be arrogant!"
To the wicked I said,
"Don't exalt your strength!
5 Don't exalt your strength so highly.
Don't speak so arrogantly
against the rock."[d]
6 Because what exalts someone
doesn't come from the east or west;
it's not from the south either.
7 Rather it is God who is the judge.
He brings this person down,
but that person he lifts up.
8 Indeed, there's a cup
in the LORD's hand
full of foaming wine,
mixed with spice.
He will pour it out,

[c]Heb lacks *God says.* [d]LXX *against God*; MT *speak with an arrogant neck*

and all of the earth's wicked people
must drink it;
they must drink every last drop!

9 But I will rejoice[e] always;
I will sing praises to Jacob's God!
10 God says:[f]
"I will demolish every bit
of the wicked's power,
but the strength of the righteous
will be lifted up."

Psalm 76

For the music leader. With stringed instruments. A psalm of Asaph. A song.

1 God is known in Judah;
his name is great in Israel.
2 His dwelling place became Salem;
his habitation was Zion.
3 It was there that he broke
the fiery shafts of the bow,
the shield, the sword—
even the battle itself! *Selah*

4 You are ablaze with light,
mightier than the mountains
that give food.
5 The bravehearted lie plundered.
They sank into deep lethargy.
All the strong troops
couldn't even lift their hands!
6 At your rebuke, Jacob's God,
both chariot and horse
were stopped dead-still.

7 You! You are awesome!
Who can stand before you
when you are angry?
8 You have announced judgment
from heaven.
The earth grew afraid and fell silent
9 when God rose up to establish justice,
when God rose up to save
all of the earth's poor. *Selah*

10 Even human rage will turn to your praise
when you dress yourself
with whatever remains of your wrath.[g]
11 Make promises to the LORD your God
and keep them!
Let all around him bring gifts
to the awesome one.
12 He breaks the spirit of princes.
He is terrifying to all the kings
of the earth.

Psalm 77

For the music leader. According to Jeduthun. Of Asaph. A psalm.

1 I cry out loud to God—
out loud to God so that he can hear me!
2 During the day when I'm in trouble
I look for my Lord.
At night my hands are still
outstretched and don't grow numb;
my whole being[h] refuses
to be comforted.
3 I remember God and I moan.
I complain, and my spirit grows tired.
Selah

4 You've kept my eyelids from closing.
I'm so upset I can't even speak.
5 I think about days long past;
I remember years that seem an eternity
in the past.
6 I meditate with my heart at night;[i]
I complain, and my spirit keeps
searching:
7 "Will my Lord reject me forever?
Will he never be pleased again?
8 Has his faithful love
come to a complete end?
Is his promise over
for future generations?
9 Has God forgotten how to be gracious?
Has he angrily stopped up
his compassion?" *Selah*
10 It's my misfortune, I thought,
that the strong hand of the Most High
is different now.

11 But I will remember the LORD's deeds;
yes, I will remember your wondrous
acts from times long past.
12 I will meditate on all your works;

[e] LXX; MT *I will declare* [f] Heb lacks *God says.* [g] Heb uncertain [h] Or *soul* [i] LXX; MT *I remember my song in the night.*

I will ponder your deeds.
13 God, your way is holiness!
Who is as great a god as you, God?
14 You are the God who works wonders;
you have demonstrated your strength
among all peoples.
15 With your mighty arm
you redeemed your people;
redeemed the children of
Jacob and Joseph. *Selah*

16 The waters saw you, God—
the waters saw you and reeled!
Even the deep depths shook!
17 The clouds poured water,
the skies cracked thunder;
your arrows were flying all around!
18 The crash of your thunder
was in the swirling storm;
lightning lit up the whole world;
the earth shook and quaked.
19 Your way went straight through the sea;
your pathways went right through the
mighty waters.
But your footprints left no trace!
20 You led your people like sheep
under the care of Moses and Aaron.

Psalm 78

A maskil[j] of Asaph.

1 Listen, my people, to my teaching;
tilt your ears toward
the words of my mouth.
2 I will open my mouth with a proverb.
I'll declare riddles
from days long gone—
3 ones that we've heard
and learned about,
ones that our ancestors told us.
4 We won't hide them
from their descendants;
we'll tell the next generation
all about the praise due the LORD
and his strength—
the wondrous works God has done.
5 He established a law for Jacob
and set up Instruction for Israel,
ordering our ancestors
to teach them to their children.
6 This is so that the next generation
and children not yet born
will know these things,
and so they can rise up
and tell their children
7 to put their hope in God—
never forgetting God's deeds,
but keeping God's commandments—
8 and so that they won't become like
their ancestors:
a rebellious, stubborn generation,
a generation whose heart
wasn't set firm
and whose spirit
wasn't faithful to God.

9 The children of Ephraim,
armed with bows,
retreated on the day of battle.
10 They didn't keep God's covenant;
they refused to walk in his Instruction.
11 They forgot God's deeds
as well as the wondrous works
he showed them.
12 But God performed wonders
in their ancestors' presence—
in the land of Egypt,
in the field of Zoan.
13 God split the sea and led them through,
making the waters stand up like a wall.
14 God led them with the cloud by day;
by the lightning all through the night.
15 God split rocks open in the wilderness,
gave them plenty to drink—
as if from the deep itself!
16 God made streams flow from the rock,
made water run like rivers.

17 But they continued to sin against God,
rebelling against the Most High
in the desert.
18 They tested God in their hearts,
demanded food for their stomachs.
19 They spoke against God!
"Can God set a dinner table
in the wilderness?" they asked.
20 "True, God struck the rock
and water gushed and streams flowed,

[j] Perhaps *instruction*; the root is used in Ps 32:8.

but can he give bread too?
Can he provide meat for his people?"
21 When the LORD heard this,
he became furious.
A fire was ignited against Jacob;
wrath also burned against Israel
22 because they had no faith in God,
because they didn't trust
his saving power.
23 God gave orders to the skies above,
opened heaven's doors,
24 and rained manna on them
so they could eat.
He gave them the very grain of heaven!
25 Each person ate the bread
of the powerful ones;[k]
God sent provisions to satisfy them.
26 God set the east wind moving
across the skies
and drove the south wind
by his strength.
27 He rained meat on them
as if it were dust in the air;
he rained as many birds
as the sand on the seashore!
28 God brought the birds down
in the center of their camp,
all around their dwellings.
29 So they ate
and were completely satisfied;
God gave them exactly
what they had craved.
30 But they didn't stop craving—
even with the food
still in their mouths!
31 So God's anger came up against them:
he killed the most hearty of them;
he cut down Israel's youth
in their prime.
32 But in spite of all that, they kept sinning
and had no faith
in God's wondrous works.
33 So God brought their days to an end,
like a puff of air,
and their years in total ruin.
34 But whenever God killed them,
they went after him!
They would turn
and earnestly search for God.
35 They would remember that God
was their rock,
that the Most High was their redeemer.
36 But they were just flattering him
with lip service.
They were lying to him
with their tongues.
37 Their hearts weren't firmly set on him;
they weren't faithful to his covenant.
38 But God, being compassionate,
kept forgiving their sins,
kept avoiding destruction;
he took back his anger so many times,
wouldn't stir up all his wrath!
39 God kept remembering
that they were just flesh,
just breath that passes
and doesn't come back.

40 How often they rebelled
against God in the wilderness
and distressed him in the desert!
41 Time and time again they tested God,
provoking the holy one of Israel.
42 They didn't remember God's power—
the day when he saved them
from the enemy;
43 how God performed his signs in Egypt,
his marvelous works in the field of Zoan.
44 God turned their rivers into blood;
they couldn't drink
from their own streams.
45 God sent swarms against them
to eat them up,
frogs to destroy them.
46 God handed over their crops
to caterpillars,
their land's produce to locusts.
47 God killed their vines with hail,
their sycamore trees with frost.
48 God delivered their cattle
over to disease,[l]
their herds to plagues.
49 God unleashed his burning anger
against them—
fury, indignation, distress,
a troop of evil messengers.
50 God blazed a path for his wrath.
He didn't save them from death,

[k] Or *everyone ate the bread from heaven;* Heb uncertain [l] Correction; MT *to hailstones*

but delivered their lives over to disease.
51 God struck down
all of Egypt's oldest males;
in Ham's tents,
he struck their pride and joy.
52 God led his own people out like sheep,
guiding them like a flock
in the wilderness.
53 God led them in safety—
they were not afraid!
But the sea engulfed their enemies!
54 God brought them to his holy territory,
to the mountain that his own
strong hand had acquired.
55 God drove out the nations before them
and apportioned property for them;
he settled Israel's tribes in their tents.

56 But they tested and defied
the Most High God;
they didn't pay attention to his warnings.
57 They turned away, became faithless
just like their ancestors;
they twisted away like a defective bow.
58 They angered God
with their many shrines;
they angered him with their idols.
59 God heard and became enraged;
he rejected Israel utterly.
60 God abandoned the sanctuary
at Shiloh,
the tent where he had lived
with humans.
61 God let his power be held captive,
let his glory go to the enemy's hand.
62 God delivered his people
up to the sword;
he was enraged at his own possession.
63 Fire devoured his young men,
and his young women
had no wedding songs.
64 God's priests were killed by the sword,
and his widows couldn't even cry.
65 But then my Lord woke up—
as if he'd been sleeping!
Like a warrior shaking off wine,
66 God beat back his foes;
he made them an everlasting disgrace.

67 God rejected the tent of Joseph
and didn't choose the tribe of Ephraim.
68 Instead, he chose the tribe of Judah,
the mountain of Zion, which he loves.
69 God built his sanctuary
like the highest heaven
and like the earth,
which he established forever.
70 And God chose David, his servant,
taking him from the sheepfolds.
71 God brought him from shepherding
nursing ewes
to shepherd his people Jacob,
to shepherd his inheritance, Israel.
72 David shepherded them
with a heart of integrity;
he led them with the skill of his hands.

Psalm 79

A psalm of Asaph.

1 The nations have come
into your inheritance, God!
They've defiled your holy temple.
They've made Jerusalem
a bunch of ruins.
2 They've left your servants' bodies
as food for the birds;
they've left the flesh of your faithful
to the wild animals of the earth.
3 They've poured out the blood
of the faithful
like water all around Jerusalem,
and there's no one left to bury them.
4 We've become a joke to our neighbors,
nothing but objects of ridicule
and disapproval to those around us.

5 How long will you rage, LORD?
Forever?
How long will your anger burn like fire?
6 Pour out your wrath on the nations
who don't know you,
on the kingdoms
that haven't called on your name.
7 They've devoured Jacob
and demolished his pasture.
8 Don't remember the iniquities
of past generations;
let your compassion hurry to meet us
because we've been brought so low.
9 God of our salvation, help us
for the glory of your name!

Deliver us and cover our sins
for the sake of your name!
10 Why should the nations say,
"Where's their God now?"
Let vengeance for the spilled blood
of your servants
be known among the nations
before our very eyes!
11 Let the prisoners' groaning reach you.
With your powerful arm
spare those who are destined to die.
12 Pay back our neighbors seven times over,
right where it hurts,
for the insults they used on you, Lord.
13 We are, after all, your people
and the sheep of your very own pasture.
We will give you thanks forever;
we will proclaim your praises
from one generation to the next.

Psalm 80

For the music leader.
According to "Lotus Blossoms."
A testimony of Asaph. A psalm.

1 Shepherd of Israel, listen!
You, the one who leads Joseph
as if he were a sheep.
You, who are enthroned
upon the winged heavenly creatures.
Show yourself 2 before Ephraim,
Benjamin, and Manasseh!
Wake up your power!
Come to save us!
3 Restore us, God!
Make your face shine
so that we can be saved!

4 LORD God of heavenly forces,
how long will you fume
against your people's prayer?
5 You've fed them bread made of tears;
you've given them tears
to drink three times over!
6 You've put us at odds with our neighbors;
our enemies make fun of us.
7 Restore us, God of heavenly forces!
Make your face shine
so that we can be saved!

8 You brought a vine out of Egypt.
You drove out the nations and planted it.
9 You cleared the ground for it;
then it planted its roots deep,
filling the land.
10 The mountains were covered by its shade;
the mighty cedars were covered
by its branches.
11 It sent its branches
all the way to the sea;
its shoots went
all the way to the Euphrates River.[m]
12 So why have you now torn down its walls
so that all who come along
can pluck its fruit,
13 so that any boar from the forest
can tear it up,
so that the bugs can feed on it?

14 Please come back, God of heavenly forces!
Look down from heaven and perceive it!
Attend to this vine,
15 this root that you planted
with your strong hand,
this son whom you secured
as your very own.
16 It is burned with fire.
It is chopped down.
They die at the rebuke coming from you.
17 Let your hand be
with the one on your right side—
with the one whom you secured
as your own—
18 then we will not turn away from you!
Revive us
so that we can call on your name.
19 Restore us,
LORD God of heavenly forces!
Make your face shine
so that we can be saved!

Psalm 81

For the music leader.
According to the Gittith. Of Asaph.

1 Rejoice out loud to God, our strength!
Shout for joy to Jacob's God!
2 Take up a song and strike the drum!

[m] *Or the Great River*

Sweet lyre along with harp!
3 Blow the horn on the new moon,
at the full moon,
for our day of celebration!
4 Because this is the law for Israel;
this is a rule of Jacob's God.
5 He made it a decree for Joseph
when he went out
against the land of Egypt,
when I heard a language
I did not yet know:

6 "I lifted the burden off your shoulders;
your hands are free of the brick basket!
7 In distress you cried out, so I rescued you.
I answered you
in the secret of thunder.
I tested you
at the waters of Meribah. *Selah*
8 Listen, my people, I'm warning you!
If only you would listen to me, Israel.
9 There must be no foreign god among you.
You must not bow down
to any strange deity.
10 I am the LORD your God,
who brought you up from Egypt's land.
Open your mouth wide—I will fill it up!

11 "But my people wouldn't listen
to my voice.
Israel simply wasn't agreeable toward me.
12 So I sent them off
to follow their willful hearts;
they followed their own advice.
13 How I wish my people would listen to me!
How I wish Israel would walk in my ways!
14 Then I would subdue their enemies
in a second;
I would turn my hand against their foes.
15 Those who hate the LORD
would grovel before me,
and their doom would last forever!
16 But I would feed you with the finest wheat.
I would satisfy you with honey
from the rock."

Psalm 82

A psalm of Asaph.

1 God takes his stand in the divine council;
he gives judgment among the gods:
2 "How long will you judge unjustly
by granting favor to the wicked? *Selah*
3 Give justice to the lowly and the orphan;
maintain the right of the poor
and the destitute!
4 Rescue the lowly and the needy.
Deliver them
from the power of the wicked!"

5 They don't know; they don't understand;
they wander around in the dark.
All the earth's foundations shake.

6 I hereby declare, "You are gods,
children of the Most High—all of you!
7 But you will die like mortals;
you will fall down like any prince."

8 Rise up, God! Judge the earth
because you hold all nations
in your possession!

Psalm 83

A song. A psalm of Asaph.

1 God, don't be silent!
Don't be quiet or sit still, God,
2 because—look!—
your enemies are growling;
those who hate you
are acting arrogantly.
3 They concoct crafty plans
against your own people;
they plot against the people you favor.
4 "Come on," they say,
"let's wipe them out as a nation!
Let the name Israel
be remembered no more!"
5 They plot with a single-minded heart;
they make a covenant against you.
6 They are the clans
of Edom and the Ishmaelites,
Moab and the Hagrites,
7 Gebal, Ammon, Amalek,
Philistia along with the citizens of Tyre.
8 Assyria too has joined them—
they are the strong arm
for Lot's children. *Selah*

9 Do to them what you did to Midian,
to Sisera, and to Jabin at the Kishon River.

10 They were destroyed at Endor;
they become fertilizer for the ground.
11 Make their officials like Oreb and Zeeb,
all their princes
like Zebah and Zalmunna—
12 those who said, "Let's take God's
pastures for ourselves."
13 My God, make them like tumbleweeds,
like chaff blown by wind.
14 Just like a fire consumes a forest,
just like flames set mountains ablaze,
15 pursue them with your storm,
terrify them with your hurricane.
16 Cover their faces with shame,
LORD, so that they might
seek your name.
17 Let them be shamed and terrified forever.
Let them die in disgrace.
18 Let them know that you—
your name is the LORD!—
you alone are Most High
over all the earth.

Psalm 84

For the music leader. According to the Gittith. Of the Korahites. A psalm.

1 How lovely is your dwelling place,
LORD of heavenly forces!
2 My very being[n] longs, even yearns,
for the LORD's courtyards.
My heart and my body
will rejoice out loud to the living God!

3 Yes, the sparrow too
has found a home there;
the swallow has found herself a nest
where she can lay her young
beside your altars,
LORD of heavenly forces,
my king, my God!
4 Those who live in your house
are truly happy;
they praise you constantly. *Selah*

5 Those who put their strength in you
are truly happy;
pilgrimage is in their hearts.
6 As they pass through the Baca Valley,[o]
they make it a spring of water.
Yes, the early rain covers it
with blessings.
7 They go from strength to strength,
until they see the supreme God in Zion.[p]
8 LORD God of heavenly forces,
hear my prayer;
listen closely, Jacob's God! *Selah*
9 Look at our shield, God;
pay close attention
to the face of your anointed one!

10 Better is a single day in your courtyards
than a thousand days anywhere else!
I would prefer to stand outside
the entrance of my God's house
than live comfortably
in the tents of the wicked!
11 The LORD is a sun and shield;
God is favor and glory.
The LORD gives—doesn't withhold!—
good things
to those who walk with integrity.
12 LORD of heavenly forces,
those who trust in you are truly happy!

Psalm 85

For the music leader. Of the Korahites. A psalm.

1 LORD, you've been kind to your land;
you've changed Jacob's circumstances
for the better.
2 You've forgiven
your people's wrongdoing;
you've covered all their sins. *Selah*
3 You've stopped being furious;
you've turned away
from your burning anger.
4 You, the God who can save us, restore us!
Stop being angry with us!
5 Will you be mad at us forever?
Will you prolong your anger
from one generation to the next?
6 Won't you bring us back to life again
so that your people can rejoice in you?
7 Show us your faithful love, LORD!
Give us your salvation!

[n] Or *soul* [o] LXX; Vulg *Valley of Tears* [p] Correction; MT *the God of gods will be seen in Zion*

8 Let me hear what the LORD God says,
because he speaks peace to his people
and to his faithful ones.
Don't let them return to foolish ways.
9 God's salvation is very close
to those who honor him
so that his glory can live in our land.
10 Faithful love and truth have met;
righteousness and peace have kissed.
11 Truth springs up from the ground;
righteousness gazes
down from heaven.
12 Yes, the LORD gives what is good,
and our land yields its produce.
13 Righteousness walks before God,
making a road for his steps.

Psalm 86

A prayer of David.

1 LORD, listen closely to me and answer me,
because I am poor and in need.
2 Guard my life because I am faithful.
Save your servant
who trusts in you—you! My God!
3 Have mercy on me, Lord,
because I cry out to you all day long.
4 Make your servant's life[q] happy again
because, my Lord, I offer my life to you,
5 because, my Lord,
you are good and forgiving,
full of faithful love
for all those who cry out to you.
6 Listen closely to my prayer, LORD;
pay close attention to the sound
of my requests for mercy.
7 Whenever I am in trouble, I cry out to you,
because you will answer me.

8 My Lord! There is no one like you
among the gods!
There is nothing that can compare
to your works!
9 All the nations that you've made will come
and bow down before you, Lord;
they will glorify your name,
10 because you are awesome
and a wonder-worker.
You are God. Just you.

11 Teach me your way, LORD,
so that I can walk in your truth.
Make my heart focused
only on honoring your name.
12 I give thanks to you, my Lord, my God,
with all my heart,
and I will glorify your name forever,
13 because your faithful love toward me
is awesome
and because you've rescued my life
from the lowest part of hell.[r]

14 The arrogant rise up against me, God.
A gang of violent people want me dead.
They don't give a thought for you.
15 But you, my Lord,
are a God of compassion and mercy;
you are very patient
and full of faithful love.
16 Come back to me! Have mercy on me!
Give your servant your strength;
save this child of your servant!
17 Show me a sign of your goodness
so that those who hate me
will see it and be put to shame—
show a sign that you, LORD,
have helped me and comforted me.

Psalm 87

A psalm of the Korahites. A song.

1 God's foundation is set
on the holy mountains.
2 The LORD loves Zion's gates
more than all of Jacob's houses
combined.
3 Glorious things are said about you,
the city of God! *Selah*
4 I count Rahab and Babel
among those who know me;
also Philistia and Tyre, along with Cush—
each of these was born there.
5 And of Zion it is said:
"Each person was born in it,
but the one who will establish it
is the Most High."
6 The LORD makes a record
as he registers the peoples:
"Each one was born there." *Selah*

[q] Or *soul;* also in 86:4*b*, 13 [r] Heb *Sheol*

7 And while they dance, people sing:
"The source of my life comes from you."

Psalm 88

A song. A psalm of the Korahites.
For the music leader.
According to "Mahalath Leannoth."[s]
A maskil[t] *of Heman the Ezrahite.*

1 LORD, God of my salvation,
by day I cry out,
even at night, before you—
2 let my prayer reach you!
Turn your ear to my outcry
3 because my whole being[u]
is filled with distress;
my life is at the very brink of hell.[v]

4 I am considered as one of those
plummeting into the pit.
I am like those who are beyond help,
5 drifting among the dead,
lying in the grave, like dead bodies—
those you don't remember anymore,
those who are cut off from your power.
6 You placed me down in the deepest pit,
in places dark and deep.
7 Your anger smothers me;
you subdue me with it,
wave after wave. *Selah*
8 You've made my friends distant.
You've made me disgusting to them.
I can't escape. I'm trapped!
9 My eyes are tired of looking at my suffering.
I've been calling out
to you every day, LORD—
I've had my hands outstretched to you!

10 Do you work wonders for the dead?
Do ghosts rise up and give you thanks?
Selah
11 Is your faithful love
proclaimed in the grave,
your faithfulness in the underworld?[w]
12 Are your wonders known
in the land of darkness,
your righteousness
in the land of oblivion?
13 But I cry out to you, LORD!
My prayer meets you
first thing in the morning!
14 Why do you reject my very being, LORD?
Why do you hide your face from me?
15 Since I was young I've been afflicted,
I've been dying.
I've endured your terrors. I'm lifeless.
16 Your fiery anger has overwhelmed me;
your terrors have destroyed me.
17 They surround me all day long like water;
they engulf me completely.
18 You've made my loved ones
and companions distant.
My only friend is darkness.

Psalm 89

A maskil[x] *of Ethan the Ezrahite.*

1 I will sing of the LORD's loyal love forever.
I will proclaim your faithfulness
with my own mouth
from one generation to the next.
2 That's why I say,
"Your[y] loyal love is rightly built—forever!
You establish your faithfulness
in heaven."
3 You said,[z] "I made a covenant
with my chosen one;
I promised my servant David:
4 'I will establish your offspring forever;
I will build up your throne from one
generation to the next.'" *Selah*

5 Heaven thanks you
for your wondrous acts, LORD—
for your faithfulness too—
in the assembly of the holy ones.
6 Is there any in the sky
who could compare to the LORD?
Who among the gods
is equal to the LORD?
7 God is respected
in the council of the holy ones;
God is awesome and revered
more than all those around him.
8 Who is like you,
LORD God of heavenly forces?

[s]Heb uncertain [t]Perhaps *instruction*; the root is used in Ps 32:8. [u]Or *soul*, also in 88:14 [v]Heb *Sheol*
[w]Heb *Abaddon* [x]Perhaps *instruction*; the root is used in Ps 32:8. [y]Heb lacks *Your.* [z]Heb lacks *You said.*

Mighty LORD, your faithfulness
surrounds you!
9 You rule over the surging sea:
When its waves rise up,
it's you who makes them still.
10 It's you who crushed Rahab
like a dead body;
you scattered your enemies
with your strong arm.
11 Heaven is yours! The earth too!
The world and all that fills it—
you made all of it!
12 North and south—you created them!
The mountains Tabor and Hermon
shout praises to your name.
13 You have a powerful arm;
your hand is strong;
your strong hand is raised high!
14 Your throne is built
on righteousness and justice;
loyal love and faithfulness
stand in front of you.

15 The people who know the celebratory
shout are truly happy!
They walk in the light of your presence,
LORD!
16 They rejoice in your name all day long
and are uplifted
by your righteousness
17 because you are the splendor
of their strength.
By your favor you make us strong
18 because our shield is the LORD's own;
our king belongs
to the holy one of Israel!

19 Once you spoke in a vision
to your faithful servants:
I placed a crown on a strong man.
I raised up someone specially chosen
from the people.
20 I discovered my servant David.
I anointed him with my holy oil.
21 My hand will sustain him—
yes, my arm will strengthen him!
22 No enemy will oppress him;
no wicked person will make him suffer.
23 I will crush all his foes in front of him.
I will strike down
all those who hate him.
24 My faithfulness and my loyal love
will be with him.
He will be strengthened by my name.
25 I will set his hand on the sea.
I will set his strong hand on the rivers.
26 He will cry out to me:
"You are my father,
my God, the rock of my salvation."
27 Yes, I'll make him the one born first—
I'll make him the high king
of all earth's kings.
28 I will always guard my loyal love
toward him.
My covenant with him will last forever.
29 I will establish his dynasty for all time.
His throne will last
as long as heaven does.
30 But if his children ever
abandon my Instruction,
stop following my rules—
31 if they treat my statutes like dirt,
stop keeping my commandments—
32 then I will punish their sin with a stick,
and I will punish their wrongdoing
with a severe beating.
33 But even then I won't withdraw
my loyal love from him.
I won't betray my faithfulness.
34 I won't break my covenant.
I won't renege on what crossed my lips.
35 By my own holiness I've sworn one thing:
I will not lie to David.
36 His dynasty will last forever.
His throne will be like the sun,
always before me.
37 It will be securely established forever;
like the moon, a faithful witness
in the sky. *Selah*

38 But you, God, have rejected
and despised him.
You've become infuriated
with your anointed one.
39 You've canceled the covenant
with your servant.
You've thrown his crown in the dirt.
40 You've broken through all his walls.
You've made his strongholds
a pile of ruins.
41 All those who pass by plunder him.
He's nothing but a joke to his neighbors.

42 You lifted high his foes' strong hand.
You gave all his enemies
reason to celebrate.
43 Yes, you dulled the edge of his sword
and didn't support him in battle.
44 You've put an end to his splendor.
You've thrown his throne to the ground.
45 You've shortened the prime of his life.
You've wrapped him up in shame. *Selah*

46 How long will it last, LORD?
Will you hide yourself forever?
How long will your wrath burn like fire?
47 Remember how short my life is!
Have you created humans
for no good reason?
48 Who lives their life without seeing death?
Who is ever rescued
from the grip of the grave?[a] *Selah*
49 Where now are your loving acts
from long ago, my Lord—
the same ones you promised to David
by your own faithfulness?
50 Remember your servant's abuse, my Lord!
Remember how I bear in my heart
all the insults of the nations,[b]
51 the ones your enemies, LORD, use—
the ones they use to abuse
every step your anointed one takes.

52 Bless the LORD forever!
Amen and Amen!

BOOK IV

(Psalms 90–106)

Psalm 90

A prayer of Moses, the man of God.

1 Lord, you have been our help,
generation after generation.
2 Before the mountains were born,
before you birthed the earth
and the inhabited world—
from forever in the past
to forever in the future, you are God.

3 You return people to dust,
saying, "Go back, humans,"
4 because in your perspective
a thousand years
are like yesterday past,
like a short period
during the night watch.
5 You sweep humans away like a dream,
like grass that is renewed in the morning.
6 True, in the morning it thrives, renewed,
but come evening it withers, all dried up.
7 Yes, we are wasting away
because of your wrath;
we are paralyzed with fear
on account of your rage.
8 You put our sins right in front of you,
set our hidden faults
in the light from your face.
9 Yes, all our days slip away
because of your fury;
we finish up our years with a whimper.
10 We live at best
to be seventy years old,
maybe eighty, if we're strong.
But their duration brings
hard work and trouble
because they go by so quickly.
And then we fly off.
11 Who can comprehend
the power of your anger?
The honor that is due you
corresponds to your wrath.
12 Teach us to number our days
so we can have a wise heart.

13 Come back to us, LORD!
Please, quick!
Have some compassion
for your servants!
14 Fill us full every morning
with your faithful love
so we can rejoice and celebrate
our whole life long.
15 Make us happy for the same amount of
time that you afflicted us—
for the same number of years that we
saw only trouble.
16 Let your acts be seen by your servants;
let your glory be seen by their children.
17 Let the kindness of the Lord our God
be over us.

[a] Heb *Sheol* [b] Correction; MT *all of many peoples*

Make the work of our hands last.
Make the work of our hands last!

Psalm 91

1 Living in the Most High's shelter,
camping in the Almighty's[c] shade,
2 I say to the LORD, "You are my refuge,
my stronghold!
You are my God—the one I trust!"

3 God will save you from the hunter's trap
and from deadly sickness.
4 God will protect you with his pinions;
you'll find refuge under his wings.
His faithfulness is a protective shield.
5 Don't be afraid of terrors at night,
arrows that fly in daylight,
6 or sickness that prowls in the dark,
destruction that ravages at noontime.
7 Even if one thousand people
fall dead next to you,
ten thousand right beside you—
it won't happen to you.
8 Just look with your eyes,
and you will see the wicked punished.
9 Because you've made the LORD
my refuge,
the Most High, your place of residence—
10 no evil will happen to you;
no disease will come close to your tent.
11 Because he will order his messengers
to help you,
to protect you wherever you go.
12 They will carry you with their own hands
so you don't bruise your foot on a stone.
13 You'll march on top of lions and vipers;
you'll trample young lions
and serpents underfoot.

14 God says,[d]
"Because you are devoted to me,
I'll rescue you.
I'll protect you
because you know my name.
15 Whenever you cry out to me,
I'll answer.
I'll be with you in troubling times.
I'll save you and glorify you.
16 I'll fill you full with old age.
I'll show you my salvation."

Psalm 92

A psalm. A song for the Sabbath day.

1 It is good to give thanks to the LORD,
to sing praises to your name, Most High;
2 to proclaim your loyal love
in the morning,
your faithfulness at nighttime
3 with the ten-stringed harp,
with the melody of the lyre
4 because you've made me happy, LORD,
by your acts.
I sing with joy
because of your handiwork.
5 How awesome are your works, LORD!
Your thoughts are so deep!
6 Ignorant people don't know—
fools don't understand this:
7 though the wicked spring up like grass
and all evildoers seem to blossom,
they do so only to be destroyed forever.
8 But you, LORD, are exalted forever!

9 Look at your enemies, LORD!
Look at how your enemies die,
how all evildoers are scattered abroad!
10 But you've made me
as strong as a wild ox.
I'm soaked in precious ointment.
11 My eyes have seen my enemies' defeat;
my ears have heard
the downfall of my evil foes.

12 The righteous will spring up
like a palm tree.
They will grow strong
like a cedar of Lebanon.
13 Those who have been replanted
in the LORD's house
will spring up
in the courtyards of our God.
14 They will bear fruit
even when old and gray;
they will remain lush and fresh
15 in order to proclaim:
"The LORD is righteous.

[c]Heb *Shaddai* [d]Heb lacks *God says.*

He's my rock.
There's nothing unrighteous in him."

Psalm 93

1 The LORD rules!
He is robed in majesty—
the LORD is robed,
clothed with strength.
Yes, he set the world firmly in place;[e]
it won't be shaken.
2 Your throne is set firm
for a very long time.
You are eternal!

3 LORD, the floods have raised up—
the floods have raised up their voices;
the floods raise up a roar!
4 But mightier than the sound
of much water,
mightier than the sea's waves,
mighty on high is the LORD!
5 Your laws are so faithful.
Holiness decorates your house, LORD,
for all time.

Psalm 94

1 LORD, avenging God—
avenging God, show yourself!
2 Rise up, judge of the earth!
Pay back the arrogant
exactly what they deserve!
3 How long will the wicked—oh, LORD!—
how long will the wicked win?
4 They spew arrogant words;
all the evildoers are bragging.
5 They crush your own people, LORD!
They abuse your very own possession.
6 They kill widows and immigrants;
they murder orphans,
7 saying all the while,
"The LORD can't see it;
Jacob's God doesn't know
what's going on!"

8 You ignorant people better learn quickly.
You fools—
when will you get some sense?
9 The one who made the ear,
can't he hear?
The one who formed the eye,
can't he see?
10 The one who disciplines nations,
can't he punish?
The one who teaches humans,
doesn't he know?[f]
11 The LORD does indeed
know human thoughts,
knows that they are nothing
but a puff of air.

12 The people you discipline, LORD,
are truly happy—
the ones you teach
from your Instruction—
13 giving them relief from troubling times
until a pit is dug for the wicked.
14 The LORD will not reject his people;
he will not abandon
his very own possession.
15 No, but justice will once again
meet up with righteousness,
and all whose heart is right
will follow after.

16 Who will stand up for me
against the wicked?
Who will help me against evildoers?
17 If the LORD hadn't helped me,
I[g] would live instantly
in total silence.
18 Whenever I feel my foot slipping,
your faithful love steadies me, LORD.
19 When my anxieties multiply,
your comforting calms me down.

20 Can a wicked ruler be your ally;
one who wreaks havoc
by means of the law?
21 The wicked gang up
against the lives of the righteous.
They condemn innocent blood.
22 But the LORD is my fortress;
my God is my rock of refuge.
23 He will repay them
for their wickedness,

[e] LXX, Vulg; MT *the world is set firmly in place;* cf Ps 96:10
[g] Or *soul*; also in 94:19, 21
[f] Correction; MT *the one who teaches humans knowledge*

completely destroy them
because of their evil.
Yes, the LORD our God
will completely destroy them.

Psalm 95

1 Come, let's sing out loud to the LORD!
Let's raise a joyful shout
to the rock of our salvation!
2 Let's come before him with thanks!
Let's shout songs of joy to him!
3 The LORD is a great God,
the great king over all other gods.
4 The earth's depths are in his hands;
the mountain heights belong to him;
5 the sea, which he made, is his
along with the dry ground,
which his own hands formed.

6 Come, let's worship and bow down!
Let's kneel before the LORD, our maker!
7 He is our God,
and we are the people of his pasture,
the sheep in his hands.

If only you would listen to his voice
right now!
8 "Don't harden your hearts
like you did at Meribah,
like you did when you were at Massah,
in the wilderness,
9 when your ancestors tested me
and scrutinized me,
even though they had already seen
my acts.
10 For forty years I despised that generation;
I said, 'These people have twisted hearts.
They don't know my ways.'
11 So in anger I swore:
'They will never enter my place of rest!'"

Psalm 96

1 Sing to the LORD a new song!
Sing to the LORD, all the earth!
2 Sing to the LORD! Bless his name!
Share the news of his saving work
every single day!
3 Declare God's glory among the nations;
declare his wondrous works
among all people
4 because the LORD is great
and so worthy of praise.
He is awesome beyond all other gods
5 because all the gods of the nations
are just idols,
but it is the LORD
who created heaven!
6 Greatness and grandeur
are in front of him;
strength and beauty
are in his sanctuary.

7 Give to the LORD,
all families of the nations—
give to the LORD glory and power!
8 Give to the LORD the glory due his name!
Bring gifts!
Enter his courtyards!
9 Bow down to the LORD
in his holy splendor!
Tremble before him, all the earth!

10 Tell the nations, "The LORD rules!
Yes, he set the world firmly in place;[h]
it won't be shaken.
He will judge all people fairly."
11 Let heaven celebrate!
Let the earth rejoice!
Let the sea and everything in it roar!
12 Let the countryside
and everything in it celebrate!
Then all the trees of the forest too
will shout out joyfully
13 before the LORD because he is coming!
He is coming to establish justice
on the earth!
He will establish justice
in the world rightly.
He will establish justice
among all people fairly.

Psalm 97

1 The LORD rules! Let the earth rejoice!
Let all the islands celebrate!
2 Clouds and thick darkness surround God.

[h] LXX, Vulg; MT *the world is firmly established*; cf Ps 93:1

His throne is built
on righteousness and justice.
3 Fire proceeds before him,
burning up his enemies on every side.
4 His lightning lights up the world;
the earth sees it and trembles!
5 The mountains melt like wax
before the LORD,
before the Lord of the whole world!

6 Heaven has proclaimed
God's righteousness,
and all nations have seen his glory.
7 All those who worship images,
those who are proud of idols,
are put to shame.
All gods bow down to the Lord!
8 Zion has heard and celebrates,
the towns[i] of Judah rejoice,
because of your acts of justice, LORD,
9 because you, LORD, are the Most High
over all the earth,
because you are so superior
to all other gods.

10 Those of you who love the LORD,
hate evil!
God guards the lives of his faithful ones,
delivering them from
the power of the wicked.
11 Light is planted like seed
for the righteous person;
joy too for those whose heart is right.
12 Rejoice in the LORD, righteous ones!
Give thanks to his holy name!

Psalm 98

A psalm.

1 Sing to the LORD a new song
because he has done
wonderful things!
His own strong hand
and his own holy arm
have won the victory!
2 The LORD has made his salvation
widely known;
he has revealed his righteousness
in the eyes of all the nations.
3 God has remembered his loyal love
and faithfulness to the house of Israel;
every corner of the earth has seen
our God's salvation.

4 Shout triumphantly to the LORD,
all the earth!
Be happy!
Rejoice out loud!
Sing your praises!
5 Sing your praises to the LORD
with the lyre—
with the lyre and the sound of music.
6 With trumpets and a horn blast,
shout triumphantly before the LORD,
the king!
7 Let the sea and everything in it roar;
the world and all its inhabitants too.
8 Let all the rivers clap their hands;
let the mountains rejoice out loud
altogether 9 before the LORD
because he is coming to establish
justice on the earth!
He will establish justice
in the world rightly;
he will establish justice
among all people fairly.

Psalm 99

1 The LORD rules—
the nations shake!
He sits enthroned on the winged
heavenly creatures—
the earth quakes!
2 The LORD is great in Zion;
he is exalted over all the nations.
3 Let them thank your great
and awesome name.
He is holy!

4 Strong king[j] who loves justice,
you are the one
who established what is fair.
You worked justice and righteousness
in Jacob.
5 Magnify the LORD our God!
Bow low at his footstool!
He is holy!

[i] Or *daughters* [j] Correction; MT *A king's strength*

6 Moses and Aaron were among his priests,
Samuel too among those
who called on his name.
They cried out to the LORD,
and he himself answered them—
7 he spoke to them from a pillar of cloud.
They kept the laws and the rules
God gave to them.
8 LORD our God, you answered them.
To them you were a God who forgives
but also the one who avenged
their wrong deeds.
9 Magnify the LORD our God!
Bow low at his holy mountain
because the LORD our God is holy!

Psalm 100

A psalm of thanks.

1 Shout triumphantly to the LORD,
all the earth!
2 Serve the LORD with celebration!
Come before him with shouts of joy!
3 Know that the LORD is God—
he made us; we belong to him.[k]
We are his people,
the sheep of his own pasture.
4 Enter his gates with thanks;
enter his courtyards with praise!
Thank him! Bless his name!
5 Because the LORD is good,
his loyal love lasts forever;
his faithfulness lasts
generation after generation.

Psalm 101

Of David. A psalm.

1 Oh, let me sing
about faithful love and justice!
I want to sing my praises to you, LORD!
2 I want to study the way of integrity—
how long before it gets here?
I will walk with a heart of integrity
in my own house.
3 I won't set my eyes
on anything worthless.
I hate wrongdoing;
none of that will stick to me.
4 A corrupt heart will be far from me.
I won't be familiar with evil.
5 I will destroy anyone
who secretly tells lies about a neighbor.
I can't stomach anyone
who has proud eyes
or an arrogant heart.
6 My eyes focus on those
who are faithful in the land,
to have them close to me.
The person who walks without blame
will work for me.
7 But the person who acts deceitfully
won't stay in my house.
The person who tells lies
won't last for long before me.
8 Every morning I will destroy
all those who are wicked in the land
in order to eliminate all evildoers
from the LORD's city.

Psalm 102

A prayer of an oppressed person, when weak and pouring out grief to the LORD.

1 LORD, hear my prayer!
Let my cry reach you!
2 Don't hide your face from me
in my time of trouble!
Listen to me!
Answer me quickly as I cry out!
3 Because my days disappear like smoke,
my bones are burned up
as if in an oven;
4 my heart is smashed
like dried-up grass.
I even forget to eat my food
5 because of my intense groans.
My bones are protruding from my skin.
6 I'm like some wild owl—
like some screech owl in the desert.
7 I lie awake all night.
I'm all alone like a bird on a roof.
8 All day long my enemies make fun of me;
those who mock me
curse using my name!
9 I've been eating ashes instead of bread.
I've been mixing tears into my drinks

[k] Qere; Kethib *and not we ourselves*

10 because of your anger and wrath,
because you picked me up
and threw me away.
11 My days are like a shadow soon gone.
I'm dried up like dead grass.

12 But you, LORD, rule forever!
Your fame lasts
from one generation to the next!
13 You will stand up—
you'll have compassion on Zion
because it is time
to have mercy on her—
the time set for that has now come!
14 Your servants cherish Zion's stones;
they show mercy even to her dirt.
15 The nations will honor the LORD's name;
all the earth's rulers
will honor your glory
16 because the LORD will rebuild Zion;
he will be seen there in his glory.
17 God will turn
to the prayer of the impoverished;
he won't despise their prayers.

18 Let this be written down
for the next generation
so that people not yet created
will praise the LORD:
19 The LORD looked down
from his holy summit,
surveyed the earth from heaven,
20 to hear the prisoners' groans,
to set free those condemned to death,
21 that the LORD's name
may be declared in Zion
and his praise declared in Jerusalem,
22 when all people
are gathered together—
all kingdoms—to serve the LORD.

23 God broke my strength in midstride,
cutting my days short.
24 I said, "My God, don't take me away
in the prime of life—
your years go on
from one generation to the next!
25 You laid the earth's foundations long ago;
the skies are your handiwork.
26 These things will pass away,
but you will last.
All of these things will wear out
like clothing;
you change them like clothes,
and they pass on.
27 But you are the one!
Your years never end!
28 Let your servants' children live safe;
let your servants' descendants live
secure in your presence."

Psalm 103

Of David.

1 Let my whole being[1] bless the LORD!
Let everything inside me
bless his holy name!
2 Let my whole being bless the LORD
and never forget all his good deeds:
3 how God forgives all your sins,
heals all your sickness,
4 saves your life from the pit,
crowns you with faithful love
and compassion,
5 and satisfies you
with plenty of good things
so that your youth
is made fresh like an eagle's.

6 The LORD works righteousness;
does justice for all who are oppressed.
7 God made his ways known to Moses;
made his deeds known
to the Israelites.
8 The LORD is compassionate
and merciful,
very patient, and full of faithful love.
9 God won't always play the judge;
he won't be angry forever.
10 He doesn't deal with us
according to our sin
or repay us
according to our wrongdoing,
11 because as high as heaven
is above the earth,
that's how large God's faithful love
is for those who honor him.
12 As far as east is from west—

[1] Or *soul*; also in 103:2, 22

that's how far God has removed
our sin from us.
13 Like a parent feels compassion
for their children—
that's how the LORD feels compassion
for those who honor him.
14 Because God knows how we're made,
God remembers we're just dust.

15 The days of a human life are like grass:
they bloom like a wildflower;
16 but when the wind blows through it,
it's gone;
even the ground where it stood
doesn't remember it.
17 But the LORD's faithful love is from
forever ago to forever from now
for those who honor him.
And God's righteousness reaches
to the grandchildren
18 of those who keep his covenant
and remember to keep his commands.
19 The LORD has established his throne
in heaven,
and his kingdom rules over all.

20 You divine messengers,
bless the LORD!
You who are mighty in power
and keep his word,
who obey everything he says,
bless him!
21 All you heavenly forces,
bless the LORD!
All you who serve him and do his will,
bless him!
22 All God's creatures,
bless the LORD!
Everywhere, throughout his kingdom,
let my whole being
bless the LORD!

Psalm 104

1 Let my whole being[m] bless the LORD!
LORD my God, how fantastic you are!
You are clothed in glory and grandeur!
2 You wear light like a robe;
you open the skies like a curtain.
3 You build your lofty house on the waters;
you make the clouds your chariot,
going around on the wings of the wind.
4 You make the winds your messengers;
you make fire and flame your ministers.
5 You established the earth
on its foundations
so that it will never ever fall.
6 You covered it with the watery deep
like a piece of clothing;
the waters were higher
than the mountains!
7 But at your rebuke they ran away;
they fled in fear
at the sound of your thunder.
8 They flowed over the mountains,
streaming down the valleys
to the place you established for them.
9 You set a boundary they cannot cross
so they'll never again cover the earth.

10 You put gushing springs
into dry riverbeds.
They flow between the mountains,
11 providing water
for every wild animal—
the wild donkeys quench their thirst.
12 Overhead, the birds in the sky
make their home,
chirping loudly in the trees.
13 From your lofty house,
you water the mountains.
The earth is filled full
by the fruit of what you've done.
14 You make grass grow for cattle;
you make plants for human farming
in order to get food from the ground,
15 and wine,
which cheers people's hearts,
along with oil,
which makes the face shine,
and bread,
which sustains the human heart.
16 The LORD's trees are well watered—
the cedars of Lebanon,
which God planted,
17 where the birds make their nests,
where the stork has a home
in the cypresses.

[m] Or *soul*; also in 104:35

18 The high mountains
belong to the mountain goats;
the ridges are the refuge of badgers.
19 God made the moon for the seasons,
and the sun too,
which knows when to set.
20 You bring on the darkness and it is night,
when every forest animal prowls.
21 The young lions roar for their prey,
seeking their food from God.
22 When the sun rises, they gather together
and lie down in their dens.
23 Then people go off to their work,
to do their work until evening.

24 LORD, you have done so many things!
You made them all so wisely!
The earth is full of your creations!
25 And then there's the sea, wide and deep,
with its countless creatures—
living things both small and large.
26 There go the ships on it,
and Leviathan, which you made,
plays in it!
27 All your creations wait for you
to give them their food on time.
28 When you give it to them,
they gather it up;
when you open your hand,
they are filled completely full!
29 But when you hide your face,
they are terrified;
when you take away their breath,
they die and return to dust.
30 When you let loose your breath,
they are created,
and you make the surface of the
ground brand-new again.

31 Let the LORD's glory last forever!
Let the LORD rejoice in all he has made!
32 He has only to look at the earth,
and it shakes.
God just touches the mountains,
and they erupt in smoke.

33 I will sing to the LORD as long as I live;
I will sing praises to my God
while I'm still alive.
34 Let my praise be pleasing to him;
I'm rejoicing in the LORD!
35 Let sinners be wiped clean
from the earth;
let the wicked be no more.
But let my whole being bless the LORD!
Praise the LORD!

Psalm 105

1 Give thanks to the LORD;
call upon his name;
make his deeds known
to all people!
2 Sing to God;
sing praises to the Lord;
dwell on all his wondrous works!
3 Give praise to God's holy name!
Let the hearts rejoice of all those
seeking the LORD!
4 Pursue the LORD and his strength;
seek his face always!
5 Remember the wondrous works
he has done,
all his marvelous works,
and the justice he declared—
6 you who are the offspring of Abraham,
his servant,
and the children of Jacob,
his chosen ones.

7 The LORD—he is our God.
His justice is everywhere
throughout the whole world.
8 God remembers his covenant forever,
the word he commanded
to a thousand generations,
9 which he made with Abraham,
the solemn pledge he swore to Isaac.
10 God set it up as binding law for Jacob,
as an eternal covenant for Israel,
11 promising, "I hereby give you
the land of Canaan
as your allotted inheritance."

12 When they were few in number—
insignificant, just immigrants—
13 wandering from nation to nation,
from one kingdom to the next,
14 God didn't let anyone oppress them.
God punished kings for their sake:
15 "Don't touch my anointed ones;
don't harm my prophets!"

16 When God called for a famine in the land,
destroying every source of food,
17 he sent a man ahead of them,
who was sold as a slave:
it was Joseph.
18 Joseph's feet hurt in his shackles;
his neck was in an iron collar,
19 until what he predicted
actually happened,
until what the LORD had said
proved him true.[n]
20 The king sent for Joseph
and set him free;
the ruler of many people released him.
21 The king made Joseph master of his
house and ruler
over everything he owned,
22 to make sure his princes acted
according to his will,
and to teach wisdom to his advisors.
23 That's how Israel came to Egypt,
how Jacob became an immigrant in the
land of Ham.

24 God made his people very fruitful,
more powerful than their enemies,
25 whose hearts God changed
so they hated his people
and dealt shrewdly with his servants.
26 God sent Moses his servant
and the one he chose, Aaron.
27 They put God's signs on Egypt,[o]
his marvelous works
on the land of Ham.
28 God sent darkness, and it became dark,
but the Egyptians rejected his word.
29 God turned their waters into blood
and killed their fish.
30 God made their land swarm with frogs[p]—
even in the bedrooms of their king!
31 God spoke, and the insects came—
gnats throughout their whole country!
32 God turned their rain into hail
along with lightning flashes
throughout their land.
33 God destroyed their vines
and their fig trees;
shattered the trees of their countryside.
34 God spoke, and the locusts came—
countless grasshoppers came!
35 They devoured all the plants
in their land;
they devoured the fruit of their soil.
36 God struck down all the oldest sons
throughout their land;
struck down their very pride and joy.
37 Then God brought Israel out,
filled with silver and gold;
not one of its tribes stumbled.
38 Egypt celebrated when they left,
because the dread of Israel
had come upon them.

39 God spread out clouds as a covering;
gave lightning to provide light at night.
40 The people asked, and God brought quail;
God filled them full
with food from heaven.
41 God opened the rock
and out gushed water—
flowing like a river through the desert!
42 Because God remembered
his holy promise
to Abraham his servant,
43 God brought his people
out with rejoicing,
his chosen ones with songs of joy.
44 God gave them the lands
of other nations;
they inherited the wealth
of many peoples—
45 all so that they would keep his laws
and observe his instructions.

Praise the LORD!

Psalm 106

1 Praise the LORD!
Give thanks to the LORD
because he is good,
because his faithful love
endures forever.
2 Who could possibly repeat
all of the LORD's mighty acts
or publicly recount all his praise?

[n] Heb uncertain [o] Correction; MT *they put on them the words of God's signs* [p] Correction; DSS (11QPs[a]) *their land swarmed with frogs*

[3] The people who uphold justice,
who always do what is right,
are truly happy!
[4] Remember me, LORD, with the favor
you show your people.
Visit me with your saving help
[5] so I can experience the good things
your chosen ones experience,
so I can rejoice
in the joy of your nation,
so I can praise along
with your possession.

[6] We have sinned—
right along with our ancestors.
We've done what is wrong.
We've acted wickedly.
[7] Our ancestors in Egypt didn't
understand your wondrous works.
They didn't remember how much
faithful love you have.
So they rebelled by the sea—
at the Reed Sea.[q]
[8] But God saved them
for the sake of his good name,
to make known his mighty power.
[9] God scolded the Reed Sea,
and it dried right up;
he led them through the deeps
like they were a dry desert.
[10] God saved them from hostile powers;
he redeemed them
from the power of the enemy.
[11] But the waters covered over their foes—
not one of them survived!
[12] So our ancestors trusted God's words;
they sang God's praise.

[13] But how quickly they forgot
what he had done!
They wouldn't wait for his advice.
[14] They were overcome with craving
in the desert;
they tested God in the wastelands.
[15] God gave them what they asked for;
he sent food[r] to satisfy their appetites.

[16] But then they were jealous of Moses
in the camp,
jealous too of Aaron,
the LORD's holy one.
[17] So the earth opened up,
swallowing Dathan,
and covering over Abiram's crowd.
[18] Fire blazed throughout that whole group;
flames burned up the wicked.

[19] They made a calf at Horeb,
bowing down to a metal idol.
[20] They traded their glorious God[s]
for an image of a bull that eats grass.
[21] They forgot the God who saved them—
the one who had done
great things in Egypt,
[22] wondrous works in the land of Ham,
awesome deeds at the Reed Sea.
[23] So God determined that he would
destroy them—
except for the fact that Moses,
his chosen one,
stood in the way, right in front of him,
and turned God's destructive anger away.

[24] But then they rejected the land
that was so desirable.
They didn't trust God's promise.
[25] They muttered in their tents
and wouldn't listen to the LORD's voice.
[26] So God raised his hand against them,
making them fall in the desert,
[27] scattering their offspring
among the nations,
casting them across many lands.

[28] They joined themselves to Baal-peor
and ate sacrifices offered to the dead.
[29] They made God angry by what they did,
so a plague broke out against them.
[30] Then Phinehas stood up and prayed,
and the plague was contained.
[31] That's why Phinehas
is considered righteous,
generation after generation, forever.

[32] But they angered God at Meribah's waters,
and things went badly for Moses
because of them,
[33] because they made him bitter
so that he spoke rashly with his lips.

[q] Or *Red Sea*; also in 106:9, 22 [r] LXX [s] Or *their Glory*

34 They didn't destroy the nations
as the LORD had ordered them to do.
35 Instead, they got mixed up
with the nations,
learning what they did
36 and serving those false gods,
which became a trap for them.
37 They sacrificed their own
sons and daughters to demons!
38 They shed innocent blood,
the blood of their own
sons and daughters—
the ones they sacrificed
to Canaan's false gods—
so the land was defiled
by the bloodshed.
39 They made themselves unclean
by what they did;
they prostituted themselves
by their actions.

40 So the LORD's anger burned
against his people;
he despised his own possession.
41 God handed them over
to the nations;
people who hated them
ruled over them.
42 Their enemies oppressed them,
and they were humbled
under their power.
43 God delivered them numerous times,
but they were determined to rebel,
and so they were brought down
by their own sin.
44 But God saw their distress
when he heard their loud cries.
45 God remembered his covenant
for their sake,
and because of how much
faithful love he has,
God changed his mind.
46 God allowed them to receive compassion
from all their captors.

47 LORD our God, save us!
Gather us back together
from among all the nations
so we can give thanks
to your holy name
and rejoice in your praise!

48 Bless the LORD, the God of Israel,
from forever ago to forever from now!
And let all the people say, "Amen!"

Praise the LORD!

BOOK V
(Psalms 107–150)

Psalm 107

1 "Give thanks to the LORD
because he is good,
because his faithful love
lasts forever!"
2 That's what those who are redeemed
by the LORD say,
the ones God redeemed
from the power of their enemies,
3 the ones God gathered
from various countries,
from east and west, north and south.

4 Some of the redeemed had wandered
into the desert, into the wasteland.
They couldn't find their way
to a city or town.
5 They were hungry and thirsty;
their lives were slipping away.
6 So they cried out to the LORD
in their distress,
and God delivered them
from their desperate circumstances.
7 God led them straight
to human habitation.
8 Let them thank the LORD
for his faithful love
and his wondrous works for all people,
9 because God satisfied the one
who was parched with thirst,
and he filled up the hungry
with good things!

10 Some of the redeemed had been sitting
in darkness and deep gloom;
they were prisoners suffering in chains
11 because they had disobeyed
God's instructions
and rejected the Most High's plans.
12 So God humbled them with hard work.

They stumbled, and there was no one
to help them.
13 So they cried out to the LORD
in their distress,
and God saved them
from their desperate circumstances.
14 God brought them out
from the darkness and deep gloom;
he shattered their chains.
15 Let them thank the LORD
for his faithful love
and his wondrous works
for all people,
16 because God has shattered
bronze doors
and split iron bars in two!

17 Some of the redeemed were fools
because of their sinful ways.
They suffered because of
their wickedness.
18 They had absolutely no appetite for food;
they had arrived at death's gates.
19 So they cried out to the LORD
in their distress,
and God saved them
from their desperate circumstances.
20 God gave the order and healed them;
he rescued them from their pit.
21 Let them thank the LORD
for his faithful love
and his wondrous works for all people.
22 Let them offer thanksgiving sacrifices
and declare what God has done
in songs of joy!

23 Some of the redeemed had gone out
on the ocean in ships,
making their living on the high seas.
24 They saw what the LORD had made;
they saw his wondrous works
in the depths of the sea.
25 God spoke and stirred up a storm
that brought the waves up high.
26 The waves went as high as the sky;
they crashed down to the depths.
The sailors' courage melted
at this terrible situation.
27 They staggered and stumbled around
like they were drunk.
None of their skill was of any help.
28 So they cried out to the LORD
in their distress,
and God brought them out safe
from their desperate circumstances.
29 God quieted the storm to a whisper;
the sea's waves were hushed.
30 So they rejoiced because the waves
had calmed down;
then God led them to the harbor
they were hoping for.
31 Let them thank the LORD
for his faithful love
and his wondrous works for all people.
32 Let them exalt God
in the congregation of the people
and praise God
in the assembly of the elders.

33 God turns rivers into desert,
watery springs into thirsty ground,
34 fruitful land into unproductive dirt,
when its inhabitants are wicked.
35 But God can also turn the desert
into watery pools,
thirsty ground into watery springs,
36 where he settles the hungry.
They even build a city and live there!
37 They plant fields and vineyards
and obtain a fruitful harvest.
38 God blesses them,
and they become many.
God won't even let their cattle
diminish.
39 But when they do diminish—
when they're brought down
by oppression, trouble, and grief—
40 God pours contempt on their leaders,
making them wander aimlessly
in the wastelands.
41 But God raises the needy
from their suffering;
he makes their families
as numerous as sheep!

42 Those who do right see it and celebrate,
but every wicked person
shuts their mouth.
43 Whoever is wise will pay attention
to these things,
carefully considering
the LORD's faithful love.

Psalm 108[t]

A song. A psalm of David.

1 My heart is unwavering, God.
I will sing and make music—
yes, with my whole being!
2 Wake up, harp and lyre!
I will wake the dawn itself!
3 I will give thanks to you, LORD,
among all the peoples;
I will make music to you
among the nations,
4 because your faithful love
is higher than heaven;
your faithfulness reaches the clouds.
5 Exalt yourself, God, higher than heaven!
Let your glory be over all the earth!
6 Save me by your power and answer me
so that the people you love
might be rescued.

7 God has spoken in his sanctuary:
"I will celebrate as I divide up Shechem
and portion out the Succoth Valley.
8 Gilead is mine, Manasseh is mine;
Ephraim is my helmet,
Judah is my scepter.
9 But Moab is my washbowl;
I'll throw my shoe at Edom.
I shout in triumph over Philistia!
10 I wish someone would bring me
to a fortified city!
I wish someone would lead me to Edom!"

11 But you have rejected us, God,
haven't you?
You, God, no longer accompany
our armies.
12 Give us help against the enemy—
human help is worthless.
13 With God we will triumph:
God is the one who will trample
our adversaries.

Psalm 109

To the leader. Of David. A psalm.

1 God of my praise, don't keep quiet,
2 because the mouths of wicked liars
have opened up against me,
talking about me with lying tongues.
3 Hateful words surround me;
they attack me for no reason.
4 Instead of returning my love,
they accuse me—
but I am at prayer.
5 They repay me evil for good,
hatred in return for my love.

6 "Appoint a wicked person to be
against this person," they say,
"an accuser to stand right
next to him.
7 When the sentence is passed,
let him be found guilty—
let his prayer be found sinful!
8 Let his days be few;
let someone else assume his position.
9 Let his children become orphans;
let his wife turn into a widow.
10 Let his children wander aimlessly,
begging,
driven out of their ruined homes.
11 Let a creditor seize everything he owns;
let strangers plunder his wealth.
12 Let no one extend faithful love to him;
let no one have mercy on his orphans.
13 Let his descendants be eliminated;
let their names be wiped out
in just one generation!
14 Let his father's wrongdoing
be remembered before the LORD;
let his mother's sin never be wiped out.
15 Let them be before the LORD always,
and let God eliminate the very memory
of them from the land.
16 All because this person didn't remember
to demonstrate faithful love,
but chased after the poor and needy—
even the brokenhearted—
with deadly intent!
17 Since he loved to curse,
let it come back on him!
Since he didn't care much for blessing,
let it be far away from him!
18 Since he wore curses like a coat,
let them seep inside him like water,
seep into his bones like oil!
19 Let them be like the clothes he wears,
like a belt that is always around him."

[t] Ps 108:1-5 parallels Ps 57:7-11; Ps 108:6-13 parallels Ps 60:5-12.

20 But let all that be the reward my accusers
get from the LORD,
the reward for those
who speak evil against me!
21 But you, LORD, my Lord!—
act on my behalf
for the sake of your name;
deliver me
because your faithful love is so good;
22 because I am poor and needy,
and my heart is broken.
23 Like a lengthening shadow,
I'm passing away;
I'm shaken off, like some locust.
24 My legs are weak from fasting;
my body is skin and bones.
25 I've become a joke to my accusers;
when they see me,
they just shake their heads.

26 Help me, LORD my God!
Save me according to your faithful love!
27 And let them know
that this is by your hand—
that you have done it, LORD!
28 Let them curse—but you, bless me!
If they rise up, let them be disgraced,
but let your servant celebrate!
29 Let my accusers be dressed in shame;
let them wear their disgrace like a coat.
30 But I will give great thanks to the LORD
with my mouth;
among a great crowd I will praise God!
31 Because God stands
right next to the needy,
to save them from any
who would condemn them.

Psalm 110

Of David. A psalm.

1 What the LORD says to my master:
"Sit right beside me
until I make your enemies
a footstool for your feet!"

2 May the LORD make
your mighty scepter
reach far from Zion!
Rule over your enemies!
3 Your people stand ready
on your day of battle.
"In holy grandeur,
from the dawn's womb, fight![u]
Your youthful strength
is like the dew itself."
4 The LORD has sworn a solemn pledge
and won't change his mind:
"You are a priest forever
in line with Melchizedek."[v]
5 My master, by your strong hand,
God has crushed kings
on his day of wrath.[w]

6 God brings the nations to justice,
piling the dead bodies,
crushing heads throughout the earth.
7 God drinks from a stream along the way,
then holds his head up high.[x]

Psalm 111[y]

1 Praise the LORD!
א I thank the LORD with all my heart
ב in the company of those who do right,
in the congregation.
ג 2 The works of the LORD
are magnificent;
ד they are treasured
by all who desire them.
ה 3 God's deeds are majestic and glorious.
ו God's righteousness stands forever.
ז 4 God is famous for his wondrous works.
ח The LORD is
full of mercy and compassion.
ט 5 God gives food to those who honor him.
י God remembers his covenant forever.
כ 6 God proclaimed his powerful deeds
to his people
ל and gave them what had belonged
to other nations.
מ 7 God's handiwork is honesty and justice;
נ all God's rules are trustworthy—
ס 8 they are established always and forever:
ע they are fulfilled
with truth and right doing.

[u]Correction; or *Go!*; MT *to you* [v]*Or a rightful king by my decree* [w]*Or My Lord (God), because of your (the king's) strong hand, has crushed* or *The LORD is above your strong hand, crushing kings* [x]Heb uncertain [y]Ps 111 is an alphabetic acrostic poem; see the note at Pss 9–10.

פ 9 God sent redemption for his people;
צ God commanded
that his covenant last forever.
ק Holy and awesome is God's name!
ר 10 Fear of the LORD
is where wisdom begins;
ש sure knowledge
is for all who keep God's laws.
ת God's praise lasts forever!

Psalm 112[z]

א 1 Praise the LORD!
Those who honor the LORD,
ב who adore God's commandments,
are truly happy!
ג 2 Their descendants will be strong
throughout the land.
ד The offspring of those who do right
will be blessed;
ה 3 wealth and riches
will be in their houses.
ו Their righteousness stands forever.
ז 4 They shine in the dark
for others who do right.
ח They are merciful, compassionate,
and righteous.
ט 5 Those who lend generously
are good people—
י as are those who conduct
their affairs with justice.
כ 6 Yes, these sorts of people
will never be shaken;
ל the righteous
will be remembered forever!
מ 7 They won't be frightened at bad news.
נ Their hearts are steady,
trusting in the LORD.
ס 8 Their hearts are firm; they aren't afraid.
ע In the end, they will witness
their enemies' defeat.
פ 9 They give freely to those in need.
צ Their righteousness stands forever.
ק Their strength increases gloriously.
ר 10 The wicked see all this and fume;
ש they grind their teeth,
but disappear to nothing.
ת What the wicked want to see happen
comes to nothing!

Psalm 113

1 Praise the LORD!
You who serve the LORD—praise!
Praise the LORD's name!
2 Let the LORD's name be blessed
from now until forever from now!
3 From sunrise to sunset,
let the LORD's name be praised!
4 The LORD is high over all the nations;
God's glory is higher than the skies!

5 Who could possibly
compare to the LORD our God?
God rules from on high;
6 he has to come down
to even see heaven and earth!
7 God lifts up the poor from the dirt
and raises up the needy
from the garbage pile
8 to seat them with leaders—
with the leaders of his own people!
9 God nests the once barren woman
at home—
now a joyful mother with children!

Praise the LORD!

Psalm 114

1 When Israel came out of Egypt—
when the house of Jacob came out
from a people who spoke
a different language—
2 Judah was God's sanctuary;
Israel was God's territory.

3 The sea saw it happen and ran away;
the Jordan River retreated!
4 The mountains leaped away like rams;
the hills leaped away like lambs!
5 Sea, why did you run away?
Jordan, why did you retreat?
6 Mountains, why did you leap away
like rams?
Hills, why did you leap away
like lambs?

7 Earth: Tremble before the Lord!
Tremble before the God of Jacob,

[z] Ps 112 is an alphabetic acrostic poem; see the note at Pss 9–10.

8 the one who turned
that rock into a pool of water,
that flint stone into a spring of water!

Psalm 115

1 Not to us, LORD, not to us—
no, but to your own name give glory
because of your loyal love
and faithfulness!

2 Why do the nations say,
"Where's their God now?"
3 Our God is in heaven—
he can do whatever he wants!
4 Their idols are just silver and gold—
things made by human hands.
5 They have mouths, but they can't speak.
They have eyes, but they can't see.
6 They have ears, but they can't hear.
They have noses, but they can't smell.
7 They have hands, but they can't feel.
They have feet, but they can't walk.
They can't even make a noise
in their throats!
8 Let the people who made these idols
and all who trust in them
become just like them!

9 But you, Israel, trust in the LORD!
God is their help and shield.
10 Trust in the LORD, house of Aaron!
God is their help and shield.
11 You who honor the LORD,
trust in the LORD!
God is their help and shield.
12 The LORD remembers us and will bless us:
God will bless the house of Israel;
God will bless the house of Aaron;
13 God will bless those
who honor the LORD—
from the smallest to the greatest.

14 May the LORD add to your numbers—
both you and your children.
15 May you be blessed by the LORD,
the maker of heaven and earth!
16 The highest heaven belongs to the LORD,
but he gave the earth to all people.
17 The dead don't praise the LORD,
nor do those who go down to silence.
18 But us? We will bless the LORD
from now until forever from now!

Praise the LORD!

Psalm 116

1 I love the LORD because he hears
my requests for mercy.
2 I'll call out to him as long as I live,
because he listens closely to me.
3 Death's ropes bound me;
the distress of the grave[a] found me—
I came face-to-face
with trouble and grief.
4 So I called on the LORD's name:
"LORD, please save me!"[b]

5 The LORD is merciful
and righteous;
our God is compassionate.
6 The LORD protects simple folk;
he saves me
whenever I am brought down.
7 I tell myself, You can be at peace again,
because the LORD
has been good to you.
8 You, God, have delivered me from death,
my eyes from tears,
and my foot from stumbling,
9 so I'll walk before the LORD
in the land of the living.
10 I have remained faithful, even when I said,
"I am suffering so badly!"
11 even when I said, out of fear,
"Everyone is a liar!"

12 What can I give back to the LORD
for all the good things
he has done for me?
13 I'll lift up the cup of salvation.
I'll call on the LORD's name.
14 I'll keep the promises
I made to the LORD
in the presence of all God's people.
15 The death of the LORD's faithful
is a costly loss in his eyes.

[a] Heb *Sheol* [b] Or *my soul*; also in 116:7-8

16 Oh yes, LORD, I am definitely your servant!
I am your servant and the son
of your female servant—
you've freed me from my chains.
17 So I'll offer a sacrifice
of thanksgiving to you,
and I'll call on the LORD's name.
18 I'll keep the promises I made
to the LORD
in the presence of all God's people,
19 in the courtyards of the LORD's house,
which is in the center of Jerusalem.

Praise the LORD!

Psalm 117

1 Praise the LORD, all you nations!
Worship him, all you peoples!
2 Because God's faithful love toward us
is strong,
the LORD's faithfulness lasts forever!
Praise the LORD!

Psalm 118

1 Give thanks to the LORD
because he is good,
because his faithful love lasts forever.
2 Let Israel say it:
"God's faithful love lasts forever!"
3 Let the house of Aaron say it:
"God's faithful love lasts forever!"
4 Let those who honor the LORD say it:
"God's faithful love lasts forever!"

5 In tight circumstances,
I cried out to the LORD.
The LORD answered me
with wide-open spaces.
6 The LORD is for me[c]—I won't be afraid.
What can anyone do to me?
7 The LORD is for me—as my helper.
I look in victory on those who hate me.
8 It's far better to take refuge in the LORD
than to trust any human.
9 It's far better to take refuge in the LORD
than to trust any human leader.
10 All the nations surrounded me,
but I cut them down[d]
in the LORD's name.
11 Yes, they surrounded me
on every single side,
but I cut them down in the LORD's name.
12 They surrounded me like bees,
but they were extinguished
like burning thorns.
I cut them down in the LORD's name!
13 I was pushed so hard[e] I nearly died,
but the LORD helped me.
14 The LORD was my strength
and protection;
he was my saving help!
15 The sounds of joyful songs
and deliverance
are heard in the tents of the righteous:
"The LORD's strong hand is victorious!
16 The LORD's strong hand is ready to strike!
The LORD's strong hand is victorious!"

17 I won't die—no, I will live
and declare what the LORD has done.
18 Yes, the LORD definitely disciplined me,
but he didn't hand me over to death.

19 Open the gates of righteousness for me
so I can come in
and give thanks to the LORD!
20 This is the LORD's gate;
those who are righteous
enter through it.

21 I thank you because you answered me,
because you were my saving help.
22 The stone rejected by the builders
is now the main foundation stone!
23 This has happened because of the LORD;
it is astounding in our sight!
24 This is the day the LORD acted;
we will rejoice and celebrate in it!

25 LORD, please save us!
LORD, please let us succeed!

26 The one who enters in the LORD's name
is blessed;

[c] LXX *with me* or *mine*; also in 118:7 [d] Heb uncertain; LXX, Vulg *drove* or *warded off*; also in 118:11-12
[e] LXX, Vulg, Syr; MT *you pushed me*

we bless all of you
from the LORD's house.
27 The LORD is God!
He has shined a light on us!
So lead the festival offering with ropes
all the way to the horns of the altar.[f]
28 You are my God—
I will give thanks to you!
You are my God—I will lift you up high!
29 Give thanks to the LORD
because he is good,
because his faithful love lasts forever.

Psalm 119[g]

א ALEF

1 Those whose way is blameless—
who walk in the LORD's Instruction—
are truly happy!
2 Those who guard God's laws
are truly happy!
They seek God with all their hearts.
3 They don't even do anything wrong!
They walk in God's ways.
4 God, you have ordered that your decrees
should be kept most carefully.
5 How I wish my ways were strong
when it comes to keeping your statutes!
6 Then I wouldn't be ashamed
when I examine
all your commandments.
7 I will give thanks to you
with a heart that does right
as I learn your righteous rules.
8 I will keep your statutes.
Please don't leave me all alone!

ב BET

9 How can young people
keep their paths pure?
By guarding them
according to what you've said.[h]
10 I have sought you with all my heart.
Don't let me stray
from any of your commandments!
11 I keep your word close, in my heart,
so that I won't sin against you.
12 You, LORD, are to be blessed!
Teach me your statutes.
13 I will declare out loud
all the rules you have spoken.
14 I rejoice in the content of your laws
as if I were rejoicing over great wealth.
15 I will think about your precepts
and examine all your paths.
16 I will delight in your statutes;
I will not forget what you have said.

ג GIMEL

17 Be good to your servant
so I can go on living
and keeping your word.
18 Open my eyes so I can examine
the wonders of your Instruction!
19 I'm an immigrant in the land.
Don't hide your commandments
from me!
20 I'm worn out by longing
every minute for your rules!
21 You rebuke the arrogant,
accursed people
who stray from your commandments.
22 Take all their insults and contempt
away from me
because I've kept your laws!
23 Even if rulers gather and scheme
against me,
your servant will contemplate
your statutes!
24 Yes, your laws are my joy—
they are my most trusted advisors!

ד DALET

25 My life is stuck in the dirt.
Now make me live again
according to your promise!
26 I confessed my ways and you answered me.
Now teach me your statutes!
27 Help me understand
what your precepts are about
so I can contemplate
your wondrous works!
28 My spirit sags because of grief.
Now raise me up
according to your promise!

[f]Heb uncertain [g]Ps 119 is an alphabetic acrostic poem (cf Pss 9–10, 111) in Heb, with each line of Heb within the marked sections beginning with the same letter of the alphabet. [h]LXX

29 Remove all false ways from me;
show mercy to me
by means of your Instruction.
30 I've chosen the way of faithfulness;
I'm set on your rules.
31 I'm holding tight to your laws, LORD.
Please don't let me be put to shame.
32 I run the same path
as your commandments
because you give my heart insight.

ה HE

33 LORD, teach me what your statutes
are about,
and I will guard every part of them.
34 Help me understand
so I can guard your Instruction
and keep it with all my heart.
35 Lead me on the trail
of your commandments
because that is what I want.
36 Turn my heart to your laws,
not to greedy gain.
37 Turn my eyes away from looking at
worthless things.
Make me live by your way.
38 Confirm your promise to your servant—
the promise that is
for all those who honor you.
39 Remove the insults that I dread
because your rules are good.
40 Look how I desire your precepts!
Make me live by your righteousness.

ו WAW

41 LORD, let your faithful love come to me—
let your salvation come to me
according to your promise—
42 so I can have a response
for those who mock me
because I have trusted in your word!
43 Please don't take your true word
out of my mouth,
because I have waited for your rules.
44 I will always keep your Instruction,
always and forever!
45 I will walk around in wide-open spaces,
because I have pursued your precepts.
46 I will talk about your laws
before rulers with no shame
whatsoever.
47 I will rejoice in your commandments
because I love them.
48 I will lift up my hands
to your commandments
because I love them,
and I will contemplate all your statutes.

ז ZAYIN

49 Remember your promise
to your servant,
for which you made me wait.
50 My comfort during my suffering is this:
your word gives me new life.
51 The arrogant make fun of me to no end,
but I haven't deviated
from your Instruction.
52 When I remember your ancient rules,
I'm comforted, LORD.
53 But I'm seized with anger
because of the wicked—
because of those who abandon
your Instruction.
54 Your statutes have been
my songs of praise
wherever I lived as an immigrant.
55 LORD, I remember your name at nighttime,
and I keep your Instruction.
56 This has been my practice
because I guard your precepts.

ח KHET

57 The LORD is my possession.
I promise to do what you have said.
58 I've sought your favor with all my heart;
have mercy on me
according to your word.
59 I've considered my ways and turned
my feet back to your laws.
60 I hurry to keep your commandments—
I never put it off!
61 Though the wicked have surrounded me
with their ropes,
I haven't forgotten your Instruction.
62 I get up in the middle of the night
to give thanks to you
because of your righteous rules.
63 I'm a friend to everyone who honors you
and to all who keep your precepts.
64 LORD, the world is full
of your faithful love!
Teach me your statutes!

ט TET

65 You have treated your servant well,
LORD, according to your promise.
66 Teach me knowledge and good
judgment
because I've put my trust
in your commandments.
67 Before I suffered, I took the wrong way,
but now I do what you say.
68 You are good and you do good.
Teach me your statutes!
69 The arrogant cover me with their lies,
but I guard your precepts
with all my heart.
70 Their hearts are unfeeling, like blubber,
but I rejoice in your Instruction.
71 My suffering was good for me,
because through it
I learned your statutes.
72 The Instruction you've given to me
is better
than thousands of pieces
of gold and silver!

י YOD

73 Your hands have made me
and set me in place.
Help me understand
so I can learn your commandments.
74 Then those who honor you
will see me and be glad
because I have waited for your promise.
75 LORD, I know that your rules are right
and that you rightly made me suffer.
76 Please let your faithful love comfort me,
according to what you've said
to your servant.
77 Let your compassion come to me
so I can live again,
because your Instruction is my joy!
78 But let the arrogant be ashamed
because they oppressed me
with lies—
meanwhile, I will be contemplating
your precepts!
79 Let the people who honor you
come back to me;
let those who know your precepts
return to me.
80 Let my heart be blameless in your statutes
so that I am not put to shame.

כ KAF

81 My whole being yearns
for your saving help!
I wait for your promise.
82 My eyes are worn out
looking for your word.
"When will you comfort me?" I ask,
83 because I've become like a bottle
dried up by smoke,
though I haven't forgotten
your statutes.
84 How much more time
does your servant have?
When will you bring my oppressors
to justice?
85 The arrogant have dug pits for me—
those people who act
against your Instruction.
86 All your commandments are true,
but people harass me for no reason.
Help me!
87 They've almost wiped me
off the face of the earth!
Meanwhile, I haven't abandoned
your precepts!
88 Make me live again
according to your faithful love
so I can keep the law you've given!

ל LAMED

89 Your word, LORD,
stands firm in heaven forever!
90 Your faithfulness extends
from one generation to the next!
You set the earth firmly in place,
and it is still there.
91 Your rules endure to this day
because everything serves you.
92 If your Instruction hadn't been
my delight,
I would have died
because of my suffering.
93 I will never forget your precepts
because through them
you gave me life again.
94 I'm yours—save me
because I've pursued your precepts!
95 The wicked wait for me,
wanting to kill me,
but I'm studying your laws.
96 I've seen that everything,

no matter how perfect, has a limit,[i]
but your commandment is boundless.

מ MEM

97 I love your Instruction!
I think about it constantly.
98 Your commandment makes me wiser
than my enemies
because it is always with me.
99 I have greater insight
than all my teachers
because I contemplate your laws.
100 I have more understanding
than the elders
because I guard your precepts.
101 I haven't set my feet on any evil path
so I can make sure to keep your word.
102 I haven't deviated
from any of your rules
because you are the one
who has taught me.
103 Your word is so pleasing
to my taste buds—
it's sweeter than honey in my mouth!
104 I'm studying your precepts—
that's why I hate every false path.

נ NUN

105 Your word is a lamp before my feet
and a light for my journey.
106 I have sworn, and I fully mean it:
I will keep your righteous rules.
107 I have been suffering so much—
LORD, make me live again
according to your promise.
108 Please, LORD, accept my
spontaneous gifts of praise.
Teach me your rules!
109 Though my life is constantly in danger,
I won't forget your Instruction.
110 Though the wicked have set a trap for me,
I won't stray from your precepts.
111 Your laws are my possession forever
because they are my heart's joy.
112 I have decided to keep your statutes
forever, every last one.

ס SAMEK

113 I hate fickle people,
but I love your Instruction.
114 You are my shelter and my shield—
I wait for your promise.
115 Get away from me, you evildoers;
I want to guard
my God's commandments!
116 Sustain me according to your word
so I can live!
Don't let me be put to shame
because of hope.
117 Support me so I can be saved
and so I can focus constantly
on your statutes.
118 You discard everyone who strays
from your statutes
because they are dishonest
and false.
119 You dispose of all the wicked people on
earth like waste—
that's why I love your laws.
120 My body shudders because I fear you;
I'm in awe of your rules.

ע AYIN

121 I've done what is just and right.
Don't just hand me over
to my oppressors.
122 Guarantee good things
for your servant.
Please don't let the arrogant
oppress me.
123 My eyes are worn out
looking for your saving help—
looking for your word
that will set things right.
124 Act toward your servant
according to your faithful love.
Teach me your statutes!
125 I'm your servant!
Help me understand
so I can know your laws.
126 It is time for the LORD
to do something!
Your Instruction has been broken.
127 But I love your commandments
more than gold,
even more than pure gold.
128 That's why I walk straight by every
single one of your precepts.
That's why I hate every false path.

[i] Heb uncertain

פ PE

129Your laws are wonderful!
That's why I guard them.
130Access to your words[j] gives light,
giving simple folk understanding.
131I open my mouth up wide, panting,
because I long for your
commandments.
132Come back to me and have mercy on me;
that's only right
for those who love your name.
133Keep my steps steady by your word;
don't let any sin rule me.
134Redeem me from the people
who oppress me
so I can keep your precepts.
135Shine your face on your servant,
and teach me your statutes.
136Rivers of tears stream from my eyes
because your Instruction
isn't being kept.

צ TSADE

137LORD, you are righteous,
and your rules are right.
138The laws you commanded are righteous,
completely trustworthy.
139Anger consumes me
because my enemies have forgotten
what you've said.
140Your word has been tried and tested;
your servant loves your word!
141I'm insignificant and unpopular,
but I don't forget your precepts.
142Your righteousness lasts forever!
Your Instruction is true!
143Stress and strain have caught up with me,
but your commandments are my joy!
144Your laws are righteous forever.
Help me understand so I can live!

ק QOF

145I cry out with all my heart:
"LORD, answer me
so I can guard your statutes!"
146I cry out to you, "Save me
so I can keep your laws!"
147I meet the predawn light and cry for help.
I wait for your promise.
148My eyes encounter each hour of the night
as I think about your word.
149Listen to my voice,
according to your faithful love.
LORD, make me live again,
according to your justice.
150The people who love to plot wicked
schemes are nearby,
but they are so far
from your Instruction!
151But you, LORD, are nearby too,
and all your commandments are true.
152Long ago I learned from your laws
that you had established them forever.

ר RESH

153Look at my suffering and deliver me
because I haven't forgotten
your Instruction.
154Argue my case and redeem me.
Make me live again by your word.
155Salvation is far from the wicked
because they haven't pursued
your statutes.
156You have so much compassion, LORD—
make me live again,
according to your rules.
157My oppressors and enemies are many,
but I haven't turned away
from your laws.
158I look on the faithless, and I am disgusted
because they haven't kept your word.
159Look at how much I love your precepts.
Make me live again, LORD,
according to your faithful love!
160The first thing to know about your word
is that it is true
and that all your righteous rules
last forever.

שׂ SIN AND שׁ SHIN

161Rulers oppress me without cause,
but my heart honors what you've said.
162I'm overjoyed at your word,
like someone who finds great treasure.
163I hate, I absolutely despise, what is false,
but I'm in love with your Instruction.
164I praise you seven times a day
for your righteous rules.

[j] Vulg, Sym

165 The people who love your Instruction
enjoy peace—and lots of it.
There's no stumbling for them!
166 LORD, I wait for your saving help.
I do what you've commanded.
167 I keep your laws;
I love them so much!
168 I keep your precepts and your laws
because all my ways are seen by you.

ת TAV

169 Let my cry reach you, LORD;
help me understand
according to what you've said.
170 Let my request for grace
come before you;
deliver me according to your promise!
171 Let my lips overflow with praise
because you've taught me your statutes.
172 Let my tongue declare your word,
because all your commandments
are righteous.
173 Let your power help me
because I have chosen your precepts.
174 LORD, I long for your saving help!
Your Instruction is my joy!
175 Let me live again so I can praise you!
Let your rules help me!
176 I've wandered off like a sheep, lost.
Find your servant
because I haven't forgotten
your commandments!

Psalm 120

A pilgrimage song.[k]

1 I cried out to the LORD
when I was in trouble
(and he answered me):
2 "LORD, deliver me[l] from lying lips
and a dishonest tongue!"
3 What more will be given to you,
what more will be done to you,
you dishonest tongue?
4 Just this:[m]
a warrior's sharpened arrows,
coupled with burning coals
from a wood[n] fire!
5 Oh, I'm doomed
because I have been an immigrant
in Meshech,
because I've made my home
among Kedar's tents.
6 I've lived far too long
with people who hate peace.
7 I'm for peace,
but when I speak, they are for war.

Psalm 121

A pilgrimage song.

1 I raise my eyes toward the mountains.
Where will my help come from?
2 My help comes from the LORD,
the maker of heaven and earth.
3 God won't let your foot slip.
Your protector won't fall asleep
on the job.
4 No! Israel's protector
never sleeps or rests!
5 The LORD is your protector;
the LORD is your shade right beside you.
6 The sun won't strike you during the day;
neither will the moon at night.
7 The LORD will protect you from all evil;
God will protect your very life.[o]
8 The LORD will protect you
on your journeys—
whether going or coming—
from now until forever from now.

Psalm 122

A pilgrimage song. Of David.

1 I rejoiced with those who said to me,
"Let's go to the LORD's house!"
2 Now our feet are standing
in your gates, Jerusalem!

3 Jerusalem is built like a city
joined together in unity.
4 That is where the tribes go up—
the LORD's tribes!
It is the law for Israel
to give thanks there
to the LORD's name,

[k] Or *song of ascents* or *song of going up* (that is, to Jerusalem); cf Ps 122:4. The heading is found in every psalm from Ps 120 to Ps 134. [l] Or *my soul*; also in 120:6 [m] Heb lacks *this*. [n] Or *the gorse* or *broom tree* [o] Or *your soul*

[5] because the thrones of justice are there—
the thrones of the house of David!

[6] Pray that Jerusalem has peace:
"Let those who love you have rest.
[7] Let there be peace on your walls;
let there be rest on your fortifications."
[8] For the sake of my family and friends,
I say, "Peace be with you, Jerusalem."
[9] For the sake of the
LORD our God's house
I will pray for your good.

Psalm 123

A pilgrimage song.

[1] I raise my eyes to you—
you who rule heaven.
[2] Just as the eyes of servants attend
to their masters' hand,
just as the eyes of a female servant
attends to her mistress' hand—
that's how our eyes
attend to the LORD our God
until he has mercy on us.

[3] Have mercy on us, LORD! Have mercy
because we've had
more than enough shame.
[4] We've had more than enough mockery
from the self-confident,
more than enough shame
from the proud.

Psalm 124

A pilgrimage song. Of David.

[1] If the LORD hadn't been for us—
let Israel now repeat!—
[2] if the LORD hadn't been for us
when those people attacked us,
[3] then they would have swallowed
us up whole
with their rage burning against us!
[4] Then the waters would have drowned us;
the torrent
would have come over our necks;[p]
[5] then the raging waters
would have come over our necks!
[6] Bless the LORD
because he didn't hand us over
like food for our enemies' teeth!
[7] We escaped like a bird
from the hunters' trap;
the trap was broken so we escaped!

[8] Our help is in the name of the LORD,
the maker of heaven and earth.

Psalm 125

A pilgrimage song.

[1] The people who trust in the LORD
are like Mount Zion:
never shaken, lasting forever.
[2] Mountains surround Jerusalem.
That's how the LORD
surrounds his people
from now until forever from now!
[3] The wicked rod won't remain
in the land given to the righteous
so that they don't use their hands
to do anything wrong.[q]
[4] LORD, do good to people who are good,
to people whose hearts are right.
[5] But as for those people
who turn to their own twisted ways—
may the LORD march them off
with other evildoers!

Peace be on Israel!

Psalm 126

A pilgrimage song.

[1] When the LORD changed Zion's
circumstances for the better,
it was like we had been dreaming.
[2] Our mouths were suddenly filled
with laughter;
our tongues were filled
with joyful shouts.
It was even said, at that time,
among the nations,
"The LORD has done great things
for them!"
[3] Yes, the LORD has done great things for us,
and we are overjoyed.

[p] Or *soul*; also in 124:5, 7 [q] Heb uncertain

4 LORD, change our circumstances
for the better,
like dry streams in the desert waste!
5 Let those who plant with tears
reap the harvest with joyful shouts.
6 Let those who go out,
crying and carrying their seed,
come home with joyful shouts,
carrying bales of grain!

Psalm 127

A pilgrimage song. Of Solomon.

1 Unless it is the LORD
who builds the house,
the builders' work is pointless.
Unless it is the LORD
who protects the city,
the guard on duty is pointless.
2 It is pointless that you get up early
and stay up late,
eating the bread of hard labor
because God gives sleep
to those he loves.

3 No doubt about it:
children are a gift from the LORD;
the fruit of the womb
is a divine reward.
4 The children born when one is young
are like arrows in the hand
of a warrior.
5 The person who fills a quiver
full with them is truly happy!
They won't be ashamed
when arguing with their enemies
in the gate.

Psalm 128

A pilgrimage song.

1 Everyone who honors the LORD,
who walks in God's ways,
is truly happy!

2 You will definitely enjoy
what you've worked hard for—
you'll be happy;
and things will go well for you.
3 In your house, your wife will be
like a vine full of fruit.
All around your table,
your children will be like olive trees,
freshly planted.
4 That's how it goes for anyone
who honors the LORD:
they will be blessed!

5 May the LORD bless you from Zion.
May you experience Jerusalem's
goodness your whole life long.
6 And may you see your grandchildren.

Peace be on Israel!

Psalm 129

A pilgrimage song.

1 From youth, people have constantly
attacked me—
let Israel now repeat!—
2 from youth people have constantly
attacked me—
but they haven't beaten me!
3 They plowed my back like farmers;
they made their furrows deep.
4 But the LORD is righteous—
God cut me free
from the ropes of the wicked!

5 Let everyone who hates Zion be
ashamed, thoroughly frustrated.
6 Let them be like grass on a roof
that dies before it can be pulled up,
7 which won't fill the reaper's hand
or fill the harvester's arms.
8 Let no one who passes by say to them:
"May the LORD's blessing be on you!
We bless you in the LORD's name!"

Psalm 130

A pilgrimage song.

1 I cry out to you from the depths,
LORD—
2 my Lord, listen to my voice!
Let your ears pay close attention
to my request for mercy!
3 If you kept track of sins, LORD—
my Lord, who would stand a chance?
4 But forgiveness is with you—
that's why you are honored.

5 I hope, LORD.
My whole being[r] hopes,
and I wait for God's promise.
6 My whole being waits for my Lord—
more than the night watch
waits for morning;
yes, more than the night watch
waits for morning!

7 Israel, wait for the LORD!
Because faithful love is with the LORD;
because great redemption
is with our God!
8 He is the one who will redeem Israel
from all its sin.

Psalm 131

A pilgrimage song. Of David.

1 LORD, my heart isn't proud;
my eyes aren't conceited.
I don't get involved with things
too great or wonderful for me.
2 No. But I have calmed
and quieted myself[s]
like a weaned child on its mother;
I'm like the weaned child that is with me.

3 Israel, wait for the LORD—
from now until forever from now!

Psalm 132

A pilgrimage song.

1 LORD, remember David—
all the ways he suffered
2 and how he swore to the LORD,
how he promised
the strong one of Jacob:
3 "I won't enter my house,
won't get into my bed.
4 I won't let my eyes close,
won't let my eyelids sleep,
5 until I find a place for the LORD,
a dwelling place
for the strong one of Jacob."

6 Yes, we heard about it in Ephrathah;
we found it[t] in the fields of Jaar.
7 Let's enter God's dwelling place;
let's worship at the place
God rests his feet!
8 Get up, LORD, go to your residence—
you and your powerful covenant chest!
9 Let your priests be dressed
in righteousness;
let your faithful shout out with joy!
10 And for the sake of your servant David,
do not reject your anointed one.

11 The LORD swore to David
a true promise that God won't take back:
"I will put one of your own children
on your throne.
12 And if your children keep my covenant
and the laws that I will teach them,
then their children too
will rule on your throne forever."
13 Because the LORD chose Zion;
he wanted it for his home.
14 "This is my residence forever.
I will live here
because I wanted it for myself.[u]
15 I will most certainly
bless its food supply;
I will fill its needy full of food!
16 I will dress its priests in salvation,
and its faithful
will shout out loud with joy!
17 It is there that I will make David's
strength thrive.[v]
I will prepare a lamp
for my anointed one there.
18 I will dress his enemies in shame,
but the crown he wears will shine."

Psalm 133

A pilgrimage song. Of David.

1 Look at how good and pleasing it is
when families[w] live together as one!
2 It is like expensive oil
poured over the head,
running down onto the beard—
Aaron's beard!—
which extended over the collar
of his robes.

[r] Or *soul*; also in 130:6 [s] Or *my soul* [t] *It* may refer to the covenant chest (132:8*b*). [u] Heb lacks *for myself.*
[v] Or *make a horn sprout* [w] Or *brothers (and sisters)*; the term often encompasses extended family relationships.

3 It is like the dew on Mount Hermon
streaming down
onto the mountains of Zion,
because it is there that the LORD
has commanded the blessing:
everlasting life.

Psalm 134

A pilgrimage song.

1 All you who serve the LORD:
bless the LORD right now!
All you who minister in the LORD's
house at night: bless God!
2 Lift up your hands to the sanctuary
and bless the LORD!
3 May the LORD,
the maker of heaven and earth,
bless you from Zion.

Psalm 135

1 Praise the LORD!
Praise the LORD's name!
All you who serve the LORD, praise God!
2 All you who stand in the LORD's house—
who stand in the courtyards
of our God's temple—
3 praise the LORD,
because the LORD is good!
Sing praises to God's name
because it is beautiful!
4 Because the LORD chose Jacob as his own,
God chose Israel
as his treasured possession.

5 Yes, I know for certain
that the LORD is great—
I know our Lord is greater
than all other gods.
6 The LORD can do whatever he wants
in heaven or on earth,
in the seas and in every ocean depth.
7 God forms clouds at the far corners
of the earth.
God makes lightning for the rain.
God releases the wind
from its storeroom.
8 God struck down
the Egyptians' oldest offspring—
both human and animal!
9 God sent signs and wonders
into the very center of Egypt—
against Pharaoh and all his servants.
10 God struck down many nations
and killed mighty kings:
11 Sihon the Amorite king,
Og the king of Bashan,
and all the Canaanite kings.
12 Then God handed their land
over as an inheritance—
as an inheritance to Israel,
his own people.

13 LORD, your name is forever!
LORD, your fame extends
from one generation to the next!
14 The LORD gives justice to his people
and has compassion
on those who serve him.

15 The nations' idols
are just silver and gold—
things made by human hands.
16 They have mouths, but they can't speak.
They have eyes, but they can't see.
17 They have ears, but they can't listen.
No, there's no breath in their lungs!
18 Let the people who made these idols
and all who trust in them
become just like them!

19 House of Israel, bless the LORD!
House of Aaron, bless the LORD!
20 House of Levi, bless the LORD!
You who honor the LORD,
bless the LORD!
21 Bless the LORD from Zion—
bless the one who lives in Jerusalem!

Praise the LORD!

Psalm 136

1 Give thanks to the LORD
because he is good.
God's faithful love lasts forever!

2 Give thanks to the God of all gods—
God's faithful love lasts forever.
3 Give thanks to the Lord of all lords—
God's faithful love lasts forever.

4 Give thanks to the only one
who makes great wonders—
God's faithful love lasts forever.
5 Give thanks to the one
who made the skies with skill—
God's faithful love lasts forever.
6 Give thanks to the one
who shaped the earth on the water—
God's faithful love lasts forever.
7 Give thanks to the one
who made the great lights—
God's faithful love lasts forever.
8 The sun to rule the day—
God's faithful love lasts forever.
9 The moon and the stars
to rule the night—
God's faithful love lasts forever!

10 Give thanks to the one who struck down
the Egyptians' oldest offspring—
God's faithful love lasts forever.
11 Give thanks to the one
who brought Israel out of there—
God's faithful love lasts forever.
12 With a strong hand
and outstretched arm—
God's faithful love lasts forever!

13 Give thanks to the one
who split the Reed Sea[x] in two—
God's faithful love lasts forever.
14 Give thanks to the one
who brought Israel through—
God's faithful love lasts forever.
15 And tossed Pharaoh and his army
into the Reed Sea—
God's faithful love lasts forever!

16 Give thanks to the one
who led his people
through the desert—
God's faithful love lasts forever.
17 Give thanks to the one
who struck down great kings—
God's faithful love lasts forever.
18 And killed powerful kings—
God's faithful love lasts forever.
19 Sihon, the Amorite king—
God's faithful love lasts forever.
20 Og, king of Bashan—
God's faithful love lasts forever.
21 Handing their land over
as an inheritance—
God's faithful love lasts forever.
22 As an inheritance to Israel,
his servant—
God's faithful love lasts forever!

23 God remembered us
when we were humiliated—
God's faithful love lasts forever.
24 God rescued us from our enemies—
God's faithful love lasts forever.
25 God is the one who provides
food for all living things—
God's faithful love lasts forever!

26 Give thanks to the God of heaven—
God's faithful love lasts forever!

Psalm 137

1 Alongside Babylon's streams,
there we sat down,
crying because we remembered Zion.
2 We hung our lyres up
in the trees there
3 because that's where
our captors asked us to sing;
our tormentors requested songs of joy:
"Sing us a song about Zion!"
they said.
4 But how could we possibly sing
the LORD's song on foreign soil?

5 Jerusalem! If I forget you,
let my strong hand wither!
6 Let my tongue stick
to the roof of my mouth
if I don't remember you,
if I don't make Jerusalem
my greatest joy.
7 LORD, remember what the Edomites did
on Jerusalem's dark day:
"Rip it down, rip it down!
All the way to its foundations!"
they yelled.

[x] Or *Red Sea;* also in 136:15

8 Daughter Babylon, you destroyer,[y]
a blessing on the one who pays you back
the very deed you did to us!
9 A blessing on the one
who seizes your children
and smashes them against the rock!

Psalm 138

Of David.

1 I give thanks to you
with all my heart, LORD.[z]
I sing your praise before all other gods.
2 I bow toward your holy temple
and thank your name
for your loyal love and faithfulness
because you have made
your name and word
greater than everything else.[a]
3 On the day I cried out, you answered me.
You encouraged me with inner strength.[b]

4 Let all the earth's rulers
give thanks to you, LORD,
when they hear what you say.
5 Let them sing about the LORD's ways
because the LORD's glory is so great!
6 Even though the LORD is high,
he can still see the lowly,
but God keeps his distance
from the arrogant.

7 Whenever I am in deep trouble,
you make me live again;
you send your power
against my enemies' wrath;
you save me with your strong hand.
8 The LORD will do all this for my sake.

Your faithful love lasts forever, LORD!
Don't let go of what your hands
have made.

Psalm 139

For the music leader. Of David. A song.

1 LORD, you have examined me.
You know me.
2 You know when I sit down
and when I stand up.
Even from far away,
you comprehend my plans.
3 You study my traveling and resting.
You are thoroughly familiar
with all my ways.
4 There isn't a word on my tongue, LORD,
that you don't
already know completely.
5 You surround me—front and back.
You put your hand on me.
6 That kind of knowledge
is too much for me;
it's so high above me
that I can't fathom it.

7 Where could I go to get away
from your spirit?
Where could I go to escape
your presence?
8 If I went up to heaven,
you would be there.
If I went down to the grave,[c]
you would be there too!
9 If I could fly on the wings of dawn,
stopping to rest only
on the far side of the ocean—
10 even there your hand would guide me;
even there your strong hand
would hold me tight!
11 If I said,
"The darkness will definitely hide me;
the light will become night around me,"
12 even then the darkness
isn't too dark for you!
Nighttime would shine bright as day,
because darkness is the same
as light to you!

13 You are the one who created
my innermost parts;
you knit me together
while I was still in my mother's womb.
14 I give thanks to you
that I was marvelously set apart.
Your works are wonderful—
I know that very well.

[y] Sym, Tg, Syr; MT *the devastated* [z] LXX, Syr, Tg, DSS (11QPs[a]); MT lacks *Lord*. [a] Correction; Heb uncertain
[b] Heb uncertain [c] Heb *Sheol*

15 My bones weren't hidden from you
when I was being put together
in a secret place,
when I was being woven together
in the deep parts of the earth.
16 Your eyes saw my embryo,
and on your scroll every day was written
that was being formed for me,[d]
before any one of them
had yet happened.[e]
17 God, your plans are incomprehensible
to me!
Their total number is countless!
18 If I tried to count them—
they outnumber grains of sand!
If I came to the very end—
I'd still be with you.[f]

19 If only, God, you would kill the wicked!
If only murderers
would get away from me—
20 the people who talk about you,
but only for wicked schemes;
the people who are your enemies,
who use your name as if
it were of no significance.[g]
21 Don't I hate everyone who hates you?
Don't I despise those who attack you?
22 Yes, I hate them—
through and through!
They've become my enemies too.

23 Examine me, God! Look at my heart!
Put me to the test!
Know my anxious thoughts!
24 Look to see if there is any idolatrous
way[h] in me,
then lead me on the eternal path!

Psalm 140

For the music leader. A psalm of David.

1 Rescue me from evil people, LORD!
Guard me from violent people
2 who plot evil things in their hearts,
who pick fights every single day!
3 They sharpen their tongues like a snake's;
spider poison[i] is on their lips. *Selah*

4 Protect me from the power
of the wicked, LORD!
Guard me from violent people
who plot to trip me up!
5 Arrogant people have laid a trap
for me with ropes.
They've spread out a net
alongside the road.
They've set snares for me. *Selah*

6 I tell the LORD, "You are my God!
Listen to my request for mercy, LORD!"
7 My LORD God, my strong saving help—
you've protected my head
on the day of battle.
8 LORD, don't give the wicked
what they want!
Don't allow their plans to succeed,
or they'll exalt themselves
even more![j] *Selah*

9 Let the heads of the people
surrounding me
be covered with the trouble
their own lips caused![k]
10 Let burning coals fall on them!
Let them fall into deep pits
and never get out again!
11 Let no slanderer be safe in the land.
Let calamity hunt down violent people—
and quickly![l]

12 I know that the LORD
will take up the case of the poor
and will do what is right
for the needy.
13 Yes, the righteous will give thanks
to your name,
and those who do right
will live in your presence.

Psalm 141

A psalm of David.

1 I cry out to you, LORD:
Come to me—quickly!
Listen to my voice
when I cry out to you!

[d]Correction; Heb lacks *for me.* [e]Heb uncertain [f]Correction [g]Heb lacks *your name.* [h]Correction; cf Tg; LXX, Syr, Vulg *painful* or *wicked* or *hurtful way* [i]LXX *snake poison* [j]Heb uncertain [k]Heb uncertain [l]Heb uncertain

2 Let my prayer stand before you
like incense;
let my uplifted hands
be like the evening offering.

3 Set a guard over my mouth, LORD;
keep close watch over the door
that is my lips.
4 Don't let my heart turn aside
to evil things
so that I don't do wicked things
with evildoers,
so I don't taste their delicacies.

5 Instead, let the righteous discipline me;
let the faithful correct me!
Let my head never reject
that kind of fine oil,
because my prayers are always
against the deeds of the wicked.[m]
6 Their leaders will fall from jagged cliffs,
but my words will be heard
because they are pleasing.[n]
7 Our bones[o] have been scattered
at the mouth of the grave,[p]
just like when the ground
is broken up and plowed.[q]

8 But my eyes are on you,
my LORD God.
I take refuge in you; don't let me die!
9 Protect me from the trap
they've set for me;
protect me from the snares
of the evildoers.
10 Let the wicked fall into their own nets—
all together!—
but let me make it through safely.

Psalm 142

A maskil[r] of David, when he was in the cave. A prayer.

1 I cry out loud for help from the LORD.
I beg out loud
for mercy from the LORD.
2 I pour out my concerns before God;
I announce my distress to him.
3 When my spirit is weak inside me,
you still know my way.
But they've hidden a trap for me
in the path I'm taking.
4 Look right beside me: See?
No one pays attention to me.
There's no escape for me.
No one cares about my life.

5 I cry to you, LORD, for help.
"You are my refuge," I say.
"You are all I have
in the land of the living."
6 Pay close attention to my shouting,
because I've been brought down
so low!
Deliver me from my oppressors
because they're stronger than me.
7 Get me out of this prison
so I can give thanks to your name.
Then the righteous
will gather all around me
because of your good deeds to me.

Psalm 143

A psalm of David.

1 Listen to my prayer, LORD!
Because of your faithfulness,
hear my requests for mercy!
Because of your righteousness,
answer me!
2 Please don't bring your servant
to judgment,
because no living thing is righteous
before you.

3 The enemy is chasing me,[s]
crushing my life in the dirt,
forcing me to live in the dark
like those who've been dead forever.
4 My spirit is weak inside me—
inside, my mind is numb.

5 I remember the days long past;
I meditate on all your deeds;
I contemplate your handiwork.
6 I stretch out my hands to you;

[m]Heb uncertain [n]Heb uncertain [o]LXX manuscripts, Syr *their bones*; DSS (11QPs[a]) *my bones* [p]Heb *Sheol* [q]Heb uncertain [r]Perhaps *instruction*; it also appears in Pss 42, 44–45, 52–55, 74, 78, 88–89, 142; cf 47:7; the root is used in Ps 32:8. [s]Or *my soul*; also in 143:6, 8, 11-12

my whole being is like dry dirt,
thirsting for you.[t] *Selah*

7 Answer me, LORD—and quickly!
My breath is fading.
Don't hide your face from me
or I'll be like those going down to the pit!
8 Tell me all about your faithful love
come morning time,
because I trust you.
Show me the way I should go,
because I offer my life up to you.
9 Deliver me from my enemies, LORD!
I seek protection from you.[u]
10 Teach me to do what pleases you,
because you are my God.
Guide me by your good spirit
into good land.
11 Make me live again, LORD,
for your name's sake.
Bring me out of distress
because of your righteousness.
12 Wipe out my enemies
because of your faithful love.
Destroy everyone who attacks me,
because I am your servant.

Psalm 144

Of David.

1 Bless the LORD, my rock,
who taught my hands how to fight,
who taught my fingers how to do battle!
2 God is my loyal one, my fortress,
my place of safety, my rescuer,
my shield, in whom I take refuge,
and the one who subdues
people before me.

3 What are human beings, LORD,
that you know them at all?
What are human beings
that you even consider them?
4 Humans are like a puff of air;
their days go by like a shadow.

5 LORD, part your skies and come down!
Touch the mountains so they smoke!
6 Flash lightning and scatter the enemy!
Shoot your arrows and defeat them!
7 Stretch out your hand from above!
Rescue me and deliver me
from deep water,
from the power of strangers,
8 whose mouths speak lies,
and whose strong hand is
a strong hand of deception!

9 I will sing a new song to you, God.
I will sing praises to you
on a ten-stringed harp,
10 to you—the one
who gives saving help to rulers,
and who rescues his servant David
from the evil sword.
11 Rescue me and deliver me
from the power of strangers,
whose mouths speak lies,
and whose strong hand
is a strong hand of deception,
12 so that[v] our sons can grow up fully,
in their youth, like plants;
so that our daughters can be like pillars
carved to decorate a palace;
13 so that our barns can be full,
providing all kinds of food;
so that our flocks can be
in the thousands—
even tens of thousands—in our fields;
14 so that our cattle can be loaded
with calves;
so that there won't be any breach
in the walls,
no exile, no outcries in our streets!

15 The people who have it like this
are truly happy!
The people whose God is the LORD
are truly happy!

Psalm 145[w]

Praise. Of David.

א 1 I will lift you up high, my God,
the true king.
I will bless your name forever and always.

[t] Heb lacks *thirsting.* [u] Heb uncertain; MT *to you I have hidden* [v] Heb uncertain [w] Ps 145 is an alphabetic acrostic poem; see the note at Pss 9–10, 111, 119.

ב 2 I will bless you every day.
I will praise your name
forever and always.
ג 3 The LORD is great
and so worthy of praise!
God's greatness can't be grasped.
ד 4 One generation will praise
your works to the next one,
proclaiming your mighty acts.
ה 5 They will talk all about[x] the glorious
splendor of your majesty;
I will contemplate your wondrous works.
ו 6 They will speak of the power
of your awesome deeds;
I will declare your great
accomplishments.
ז 7 They will rave in celebration
of your abundant goodness;
they will shout joyfully
about your righteousness:
ח 8 "The LORD is merciful
and compassionate,
very patient, and full of faithful love.
ט 9 The LORD is good to everyone
and everything;
God's compassion extends
to all his handiwork!"
י 10 All that you have made
gives thanks to you, LORD;
all your faithful ones bless you!
כ 11 They speak of the glory of your
kingdom;
they talk all about your power,
ל 12 to inform all human beings
about God's power
and the majestic glory of God's
kingdom.
מ 13 Your kingdom is a kingship
that lasts forever;
your rule endures for all generations.
נ The LORD is trustworthy
in all that he says,
faithful in all that he does.[y]
ס 14 The LORD supports all who fall down,
straightens up all who are bent low.
ע 15 All eyes look to you, hoping,
and you give them their food
right on time,
פ 16 opening your hand
and satisfying the desire
of every living thing.
צ 17 The LORD is righteous in all his ways,
faithful in all his deeds.
ק 18 The LORD is close to everyone
who calls out to him,
to all who call out to him sincerely.
ר 19 God shows favor to those who honor him,
listening to their cries for help
and saving them.
ש 20 The LORD protects all who love him,
but he destroys every wicked person.
ת 21 My mouth will proclaim
the LORD's praise,
and every living thing
will bless God's holy name
forever and always.

Psalm 146

1 Praise the LORD!

Let my whole being[z] praise the LORD!
2 I will praise the LORD with all my life;
I will sing praises to my God
as long as I live.

3 Don't trust leaders;
don't trust any human beings—
there's no saving help with them!
4 Their breath leaves them,
then they go back to the ground.
On that very same day,
their plans die too.

5 The person whose help
is the God of Jacob—
the person whose hope
rests on the LORD their God—
is truly happy!
6 God: the maker of heaven and earth,
the sea, and all that is in them.
God: who is faithful forever,
7 who gives justice to people
who are oppressed,
who gives bread to people
who are starving!

[x] LXX, Syr, DSS (11QPs[a]); MT *and words of* [y] LXX, DSS (11QPs[a]), Syr; MT lacks these lines, but they correspond to the *nun* line in the alphabetic acrostic poem. [z] Or *soul*

The LORD: who frees prisoners.
8 The LORD: who makes the blind see.
The LORD: who straightens up
those who are bent low.
The LORD: who loves the righteous.
9 The LORD: who protects immigrants,
who helps orphans and widows,
but who makes the way of the wicked
twist and turn!

10 The LORD will rule forever!
Zion, your God will rule
from one generation to the next!

Praise the LORD!

Psalm 147

1 Praise the LORD!
Because it is good to sing praise
to our God!
Because it is a pleasure
to make beautiful praise!

2 The LORD rebuilds Jerusalem,
gathering up Israel's exiles.
3 God heals the brokenhearted
and bandages their wounds.
4 God counts the stars by number,
giving each one a name.
5 Our Lord is great and so strong!
God's knowledge can't be grasped!
6 The LORD helps the poor,
but throws the wicked down on the dirt!

7 Sing to the LORD with thanks;
sing praises to our God with a lyre!
8 God covers the skies with clouds;
God makes rain for the earth;
God makes the mountains
sprout green grass.
9 God gives food to the animals—
even to the baby ravens
when they cry out.
10 God doesn't prize the strength of a horse;
God doesn't treasure
the legs of a runner.
11 No. The LORD treasures the people
who honor him,
the people who wait
for his faithful love.

12 Worship the LORD, Jerusalem!
Praise your God, Zion!
13 Because God secures the bars
on your gates,
God blesses the children
you have there.
14 God establishes your borders peacefully.
God fills you full
with the very best wheat.

15 God issues his command to the earth—
God's word speeds off fast!
16 God spreads snow like it was wool;
God scatters frost like it was ashes;
17 God throws his hail down like crumbs—
who can endure God's freezing cold?
18 Then God issues his word
and melts it all away!
God makes his winds blow;
the water flows again.

19 God proclaims his word to Jacob;
his statutes and rules to Israel.
20 God hasn't done that
with any other nation;
those nations have no knowledge
of God's rules.[a]

Praise the LORD!

Psalm 148

1 Praise the LORD!

Praise the LORD from heaven!
Praise God on the heights!
2 Praise God, all of you
who are his messengers!
Praise God, all of you
who comprise his heavenly forces!
3 Sun and moon, praise God!
All of you bright stars, praise God!
4 You highest heaven, praise God!
Do the same, you waters
that are above the sky!
5 Let all of these praise the LORD's name

[a]LXX, Tg, DSS (11QPs[a]) *God hasn't let those nations know his rules.*

because God gave the command
and they were created!
6 God set them in place always and forever.
God made a law that will not be broken.

7 Praise the LORD from the earth,
you sea monsters
and all you ocean depths!
8 Do the same, fire and hail,
snow and smoke,
stormy wind that does what God says!
9 Do the same, you mountains,
every single hill,
fruit trees, and every single cedar!
10 Do the same, you animals—
wild or tame—
you creatures that creep along
and you birds that fly!
11 Do the same, you kings of the earth
and every single person,
you princes and every single ruler
on earth!
12 Do the same, you young men—
young women too!—
you who are old together
with you who are young!

13 Let all of these praise the LORD's name
because only God's name is high over all.
Only God's majesty
is over earth and heaven.
14 God raised the strength[b] of his people,
the praise of all his faithful ones—
that's the Israelites,
the people who are close to him.

Praise the LORD!

Psalm 149

1 Praise the LORD!

Sing to the LORD a new song;
sing God's praise
in the assembly of the faithful!
2 Let Israel celebrate its maker;
let Zion's children rejoice
in their king!
3 Let them praise God's name with dance;
let them sing God's praise
with the drum and lyre!
4 Because the LORD is pleased
with his people,
God will beautify the poor
with saving help.

5 Let the faithful celebrate with glory;
let them shout for joy on their beds.[c]
6 Let the high praises of God
be in their mouths
and a double-edged sword
in their hands,
7 to get revenge against the nations
and punishment on the peoples,
8 binding their rulers in chains
and their officials in iron shackles,
9 achieving the justice
written against them.
That will be an honor
for all God's faithful people.

Praise the LORD!

Psalm 150

1 Praise the LORD!

Praise God in his sanctuary!
Praise God in his fortress, the sky!
2 Praise God in his mighty acts!
Praise God as suits
his incredible greatness!
3 Praise God with the blast
of the ram's horn!
Praise God with lute and lyre!
4 Praise God with drum and dance!
Praise God with strings and pipe!
5 Praise God with loud cymbals!
Praise God with clashing cymbals!
6 Let every living thing praise the LORD!

Praise the LORD!

[b] Or *horn* [c] Heb uncertain

PROVERBS

Purpose of Proverbs

1 The proverbs of Solomon,
King David's son, from Israel:
2 Their purpose is to teach wisdom
and discipline,
to help one understand wise sayings.
3 They provide insightful instruction,
which is righteous, just,
and full of integrity.
4 They make the naive mature,
the young knowledgeable and discreet.
5 The wise hear them and grow in wisdom;
those with understanding
gain guidance.
6 They help one understand
proverbs and difficult sayings,
the words of the wise,
and their puzzles.
7 Wisdom begins with the fear of the LORD,
but fools despise wisdom
and instruction.

Avoid evil associations

8 Listen, my son,
to your father's instruction;
don't neglect your mother's teaching;
9 for they are a graceful wreath
on your head,
and beads for your neck.
10 My son, don't let sinners entice you.
Don't go 11 when they say:
"Come with us.
Let's set up a deadly ambush.
Let's secretly wait for the innocent
just for fun.
12 Let's swallow up the living
like the grave[a]—
whole, like those who go down
into the pit.
13 We'll find all sorts of precious wealth;
we'll fill our houses with plunder.
14 Throw in your lot with us;
we'll share our money."
15 My son, don't go on the path with them;
keep your feet from their way,
16 because their feet run to evil;
they hurry to spill blood.
17 It's useless to cast a net
in the sight of a bird.
18 But these sinners set up a deadly ambush;
they lie in wait for their own lives.
19 These are the ways of all
who seek unjust gain;
it costs them their lives.

Listen to "Woman Wisdom"

20 Wisdom shouts in the street;
in the public square she raises her voice.
21 Above the noisy crowd, she calls out.
At the entrances of the city gates,
she has her say:
22 "How long will you clueless people
love your naïveté,
mockers hold their mocking dear,
and fools hate knowledge?
23 You should respond when I correct you.
Look, I'll pour out my spirit on you.
I'll reveal my words to you.
24 I invited you, but you rejected me;
I stretched out my hand to you,
but you paid no attention.
25 You ignored all my advice,
and you didn't want me to correct you.
26 So I'll laugh at your disaster;
I'll make fun of you
when dread comes over you,
27 when terror hits you like a hurricane,
and your disaster comes in
like a tornado,
when distress and oppression
overcome you.
28 Then they will call me, but I won't answer;
they will seek me, but won't find me
29 because they hated knowledge
and didn't choose the fear of the LORD.
30 They didn't want my advice;
they rejected all my corrections.
31 They will eat from the fruit of their way,
and they'll be full of their own schemes.
32 The immature will die
because they turn away;
smugness will destroy fools.
33 Those who obey me will dwell securely,
untroubled by the dread of harm."

[a] Heb *Sheol*

Benefits of wisdom

2 My son, accept my words
and store up my commands.
2 Turn your ear toward wisdom,
and stretch your mind
toward understanding.
3 Call out for insight,
and cry aloud for understanding.
4 Seek it like silver;
search for it like hidden treasure.
5 Then you will understand
the fear of the LORD,
and discover the knowledge of God.
6 The LORD gives wisdom;
from his mouth come knowledge
and understanding.
7 He reserves ability for those with integrity.
He is a shield for those
who live a blameless life.
8 He protects the paths of justice
and guards the way of those
who are loyal to him.
9 Then you will understand righteousness
and justice,
as well as integrity, every good course.
10 Wisdom will enter your mind,
and knowledge will fill you with delight.
11 Discretion will guard you;
understanding will protect you.
12 Wisdom will rescue you from the evil path,
from people who twist their words.
13 They forsake the way of integrity
and go on obscure paths.
14 They enjoy doing evil,
rejoicing in their twisted evil.
15 Their paths are confused;
they get lost on their way.
16 Wisdom will rescue you
from the mysterious woman,
from the foreign woman
with her slick words.
17 She leaves behind the partner of her youth;
she even forgets her covenant with God.
18 Her house sinks down to death,
and her paths go down
to the shadowy dead.
19 All those who go to her will never return;
they will never again
reach the ways of the living.
20 So you should stay on the path
of good people,
guarding the road of the righteous.
21 Those who have integrity
will dwell in the land;
the innocent will remain in it.
22 But the wicked will be cut off
from the land,
and the treacherous will be ripped up.

Trust in the LORD

3 My son, don't forget my instruction.
Let your heart guard my commands,
2 because they will help you live
a long time
and provide you with well-being.
3 Don't let loyalty and faithfulness
leave you.
Bind them on your neck;
write them on the tablet of your heart.
4 Then you will find favor and approval
in the eyes of God and humanity.
5 Trust in the LORD with all your heart;
don't rely on your own intelligence.
6 Know him in all your paths,
and he will keep your ways straight.
7 Don't consider yourself wise.
Fear the LORD and turn away from evil.
8 Then your body[b] will be healthy
and your bones strengthened.
9 Honor the LORD with your wealth
and with the first of all your crops.
10 Then your barns will be filled
with plenty,
and your vats will burst with wine.
11 Don't reject the instruction of the LORD,
my son;
don't despise his correction.
12 The LORD loves those he corrects,
just like a father who treats his son
with favor.

Value of wisdom

13 Happy are those who find wisdom
and those who gain understanding.
14 Her profit is better than silver,
and her gain better than gold.
15 Her value exceeds pearls;
all you desire can't compare with her.

[b] Heb *navel*

16 In her right hand is a long life;
in her left are wealth and honor.
17 Her ways are pleasant;
all her paths are peaceful.
18 She is a tree of life
to those who embrace her;
those who hold her tight are happy.
19 The LORD laid the foundations
of the earth with wisdom,
establishing the heavens
with understanding.
20 With his knowledge,
the watery depths burst open,
and the skies drop dew.

Integrity of wisdom

21 My son, don't let them slip
from your eyes;
hold on to sound judgment
and discretion.
22 They will be life for your whole being,
and an ornament for your neck.
23 Then you will walk safely on your path,
and your foot won't stumble.
24 If you lie down, you won't be terrified.
When you lie down,
your sleep will be pleasant.
25 Don't fear sudden terror
or the ruin that comes to the wicked.
26 The LORD will be your confidence;
he will guard your feet
from being snared.
27 Don't withhold good
from someone who deserves it,
when it is in your power to do so.
28 Don't say to your neighbor,
"Go and come back;
I'll give it to you tomorrow,"
when you have it.
29 Don't plan to harm your neighbor
who trusts and lives near you.
30 Don't accuse anyone without reason,
when they haven't harmed you.
31 Don't envy violent people
or choose any of their ways.
32 Devious people are detestable to the LORD,
but the virtuous are his close friends.
33 The LORD's curse is on
the house of the wicked,
but he blesses the home
of the righteous.
34 He mocks mockers,
but he shows favor to the humble.
35 The wise gain respect,
but fools receive shame.

Love wisdom

4 Hear, children, fatherly instruction;
pay attention to gain understanding.
2 I'll teach you well.
Don't abandon my instruction.
3 When I was a son to my father,
tender and my mother's favorite,
4 he taught me and said to me:
"Let your heart hold on to my words:
Keep my commands and live.
5 Get wisdom; get understanding.
Don't forget and don't turn away
from my words.
6 Don't abandon her,
and she will guard you.
Love her, and she will protect you.
7 The beginning of wisdom:
Get wisdom!
Get understanding before anything else.
8 Highly esteem her,
and she will exalt you.
She will honor you if you embrace her.
9 She will place a graceful wreath
on your head;
she will give you a glorious crown."

Stay on the path of wisdom

10 Listen, my son, and take in my speech,
then the years of your life will be many.
11 I teach you the path of wisdom.
I lead you in straight courses.
12 When you walk, you won't be hindered;
when you run, you won't stumble.
13 Hold on to instruction; don't slack off;
protect it, for it is your life.
14 Don't go on the way of the wicked;
don't walk on the path of evil people.
15 Avoid it! Don't turn onto it;
stay off of it and keep going!
16 They don't sleep unless they do evil;
they are robbed of sleep unless
they make someone stumble.
17 They eat the bread of evil,
and they drink the wine of violence.
18 The way of the righteous
is like morning light

that gets brighter and
brighter till it is full day.
19 The path of the wicked
is like deep darkness;
they don't know where they will stumble.

Be careful about what you say

20 My son, pay attention to my words.
Bend your ear to my speech.
21 Don't let them slip from your sight.
Guard them in your mind.
22 They are life to those who find them,
and healing for their entire body.
23 More than anything you guard,
protect your mind, for life flows from it.
24 Have nothing to do with a corrupt mouth;
keep devious lips far from you.
25 Focus your eyes straight ahead;
keep your gaze on what is in front of you.
26 Watch your feet on the way,
and all your paths will be secure.
27 Don't deviate a bit to the right or the left;
turn your feet away from evil.

Avoid the mysterious woman

5 My son, pay attention to my wisdom.
Bend your ear to what I know,
2 so you might remain discreet,
and your lips might guard knowledge.
3 The lips of a mysterious woman drip honey,
and her tongue is smoother than oil,
4 but in the end she is bitter as gall,
sharp as a double-edged sword.
5 Her feet go down to death;
her steps lead to the grave.[c]
6 She doesn't stay on the way of life.
Her paths wander,
but she doesn't know it.

7 Now children, listen to me,
and don't deviate
from the words of my mouth.
8 Stay on a path that is far from her;
don't approach the entrance to her house.
9 Otherwise, you will give
your strength to others,
your years to a cruel person.
10 Otherwise, strangers
will sap your strength,
and your hard work will end up
in a foreigner's house.
11 You will groan at the end
when your body and flesh are exhausted,
12 and you say, "How I hated instruction!
How my heart despised correction!
13 I didn't listen to the voice of my instructor.
I didn't obey my teacher.
14 I'm on the brink of utter ruin
in the assembled community."

15 Drink water from your own cistern,
gushing water from your own well.
16 Should your fountains flood outside,
streams of water in the public squares?
17 They are yours alone,
not for you as well as strangers.
18 May your spring be blessed.
Rejoice in the wife of your youth.
19 She is a lovely deer, a graceful doe.
Let her breasts intoxicate you all the time;
always be drunk on her love.

20 Why, my son, should you lose
your senses with a mysterious woman
and embrace the breasts
of a foreign female?

21 The LORD's eyes watch
over every person's path,
observing all their ways.
22 The wicked will be caught
by their own evil acts,
grabbed by the ropes of their own sin.
23 Those without instruction will die,
misled by their own stupidity.

Wise advice

6 My son, if you guarantee a loan
for your neighbor
or shake hands in agreement
with a stranger,
2 you will be trapped by your words;
you will be caught by your words.
3 Do this, my son, to get out of it,
for you have come under the control
of your neighbor.
So go, humble yourself,[d]
and pester your neighbor.

[c] Heb *Sheol* [d] Heb uncertain

4 Don't give sleep to your eyes
or slumber to your eyelids.
5 Get yourself free like a gazelle
from a hunter,
like a bird from the hand of a fowler.
6 Go to the ant, you lazy person;
observe its ways and grow wise.
7 The ant has no commander, officer,
or ruler.
8 Even so, it gets its food in summer;
gathers its provisions at harvest.
9 How long, lazy person, will you lie down?
When will you rise from your sleep?
10 A little sleep, a little slumber,
a little folding of the arms to lie down—
11 and poverty will come on you
like a prowler,
destitution like a warrior.
12 Worthless people and guilty people
go around with crooked talk.
13 They wink their eyes,
gesture with their feet,
and point with their fingers.
14 Their hearts are corrupt
and determined to do evil;
they create controversies all the time.
15 Therefore, sudden disaster
will come upon them;
they will be quickly broken
beyond healing.
16 There are six things that the LORD hates,
seven things detestable to him:
17 snobbish eyes,
a lying tongue,
hands that spill innocent blood,
18 a heart set on wicked plans,
feet that run quickly to evil,
19 a false witness who breathes lies,
and one who causes conflicts
among relatives.

Danger of adultery

20 My son, keep your father's command;
don't abandon
your mother's instruction.
21 Bind them on your heart for all time;
fasten them around your neck.
22 When you walk around, they will lead you;
when you lie down, they will protect you;
when you awake,
they will occupy your attention.
23 The commandment is a lamp
and instruction a light;
corrective teaching is the path of life.
24 They guard you from the evil woman,
from the flattering tongue
of the foreign woman.
25 Don't desire her beauty in secret;
don't let her take you in
with her eyelashes,
26 for a prostitute costs a loaf of bread,[e]
but a married woman
hunts for a man's very life.
27 Can a man scoop fire into his lap
and his clothes not get burned?
28 If a man walks on hot coals,
don't his feet get burned?
29 So is the man who approaches
his neighbor's wife;
anyone who touches her will be punished.
30 People don't despise a thief if he steals
to fill his starving stomach.
31 But if he is caught, he must pay sevenfold;
he must give all the riches of his house.
32 He who commits adultery is senseless.
Doing so, he destroys himself.
33 He is wounded and disgraced.
His shame will never be wiped away.
34 Jealousy makes a man rage;
he'll show no mercy
on his day of revenge.
35 He won't accept compensation;
he'll refuse even a large bribe.

Avoid loose women

7 My son, keep my words;
store up my commands within you.
2 Keep my commands and live,
and my instruction
like the pupil of your eye.
3 Bind them on your fingers;
write them on the tablet of your heart.
4 Say to wisdom, "You are my sister";
call understanding "friend,"
5 so she might guard you
against the mysterious woman,
from the foreign woman
who flatters you.

[e] Heb uncertain

6 When from the window of my house,
from behind the screen, I gazed down,
7 I looked among the naive young men
and noticed among the youth,
one who had no sense.
8 He was crossing the street at her corner
and walked down the path to her house
9 in the early evening,
at the onset of night and darkness.
10 All of a sudden a woman approaches him,
dressed like a prostitute
and with a cunning mind.
11 She is noisy and defiant;
her feet don't stay long
in her own house.
12 She has one foot in the street,
one foot in the public square.
She lies in wait at every corner.
13 She grabs him and kisses him.
Her face is brazen as she speaks to him:
14 "I've made a sacrifice of well-being;
today I fulfilled my solemn promises.
15 So I've come out to meet you,
seeking you, and I have found you.
16 I've spread my bed with luxurious covers,
with colored linens from Egypt.
17 I've sprinkled my bed with myrrh,
aloes, and cinnamon.
18 Come, let's drink deep of love
until morning;
let's savor our lovemaking.
19 For my husband isn't home;
he's gone far away.
20 He took a pouch of money with him;
he won't come home till full moon."
21 She seduces him with all her talk.
She entices him with her flattery.
22 He goes headlong after her,
like an ox to the slaughter,
like a deer leaping into a trap,[f]
23 until an arrow pierces his liver,
like a bird hurrying to the snare,
not aware that it will cost him his life.

24 Now children, listen to me,
and pay attention to my speech.
25 Don't turn your heart to her ways;
don't wander down her paths.
26 She has caused many corpses to fall;
she has killed many people.
27 Her house is a path to the grave,[g]
going down to the chambers of death.

Wisdom's autobiography

8 Doesn't Wisdom cry out
and Understanding shout?
2 Atop the heights along the path,
at the crossroads she takes her stand.
3 By the gate before the city,
at the entrances she shouts:

4 I cry out to you, people;
my voice goes out to all of humanity.
5 Understand skill, you who are naive.
Take this to heart, you fools.
6 Listen, for I speak things that are correct;
from my lips comes what is right.
7 My mouth utters the truth;
my lips despise wickedness.
8 All the words of my mouth are righteous;
nothing in them is twisted or crooked.
9 All of them are straightforward
to those who understand,
and upright for the knowledgeable.
10 Take my instruction rather than silver,
knowledge rather than choice gold.
11 Wisdom is better than pearls;
nothing is more delightful than she.

12 I, Wisdom, dwell with prudence;
I have found knowledge and discretion.
13 To fear the LORD is to hate evil.
I hate pride and arrogance,
the path of evil and corrupt speech.
14 I have advice and ability,
as well as understanding and strength.
15 By me kings rule,
and princes issue righteous decrees.
16 By me rulers govern,
and officials judge righteously.[h]
17 I love those who love me;
those who seek me will find me.
18 Riches and honor are with me,
as well as enduring wealth
and righteousness.
19 My fruit is better than gold,
even fine gold;
my crops are better than choice silver.

[f] Heb uncertain [g] Heb *Sheol* [h] Heb uncertain

20 I walk on the way of righteousness,
on the paths of justice,
21 to provide for those who love me
and to fill up their treasuries.

22 The LORD created me
at the beginning of his way,
before his deeds long in the past.
23 I was formed in ancient times,
at the beginning, before the earth was.
24 When there were no watery depths,
I was brought forth,
when there were no springs
flowing with water.
25 Before the mountains were settled,
before the hills, I was brought forth;
26 before God[i] made the earth
and the fields
or the first of the dry land.
27 I was there when he established
the heavens,
when he marked out the horizon
on the deep sea,
28 when he thickened the clouds above,
when he secured the fountains
of the deep,
29 when he set a limit for the sea,
so the water couldn't go beyond
his command,
when he marked out
the earth's foundations.
30 I was beside him as a master of crafts.[j]
I was having fun,
smiling before him all the time,
31 frolicking with his inhabited earth
and delighting in the human race.

32 Now children, listen to me:
Happy are those who keep to my ways!
33 Listen to instruction, and be wise;
don't avoid it.
34 Happy are those who listen to me,
watching daily at my doors,
waiting at my doorposts.
35 Those who find me find life;
they gain favor from the LORD.
36 Those who offend me
injure themselves;
all those who hate me love death.

"Woman Wisdom's" invitation

9 Wisdom built her house;
she has carved out her seven pillars.
2 She slaughtered her animals,
mixed her wine,
and set her table.
3 She sends out her female servants;
she issues an invitation
from the top of the city heights:
4 "Whoever is naive turn aside here,"
she says to those who lack sense.
5 "Come, eat my food,
and drink the wine I have mixed.
6 Abandon your simplistic ways and live;
walk in the way of understanding."

Wise advice

7 Whoever instructs the cynic
gets insulted;
whoever corrects the wicked gets hurt.
8 Don't correct the impudent,
or they will hate you;
correct the wise,
and they will love you.
9 Teach the wise,
and they will become wiser;
inform the righteous,
and their learning will increase.
10 The beginning of wisdom
is the fear of the LORD;
the knowledge of the holy one
is understanding.
11 Through me your days will be many;
years will be added to your life.
12 If you are wise, it is to your benefit;
if you are cynical,
you will bear it all alone.

"Woman Folly's" invitation

13 Woman Folly is noisy;
she's stupid and doesn't even know it.
14 She sits at the doorway of her house,
on a seat at the city heights.
15 She invites those who pass by on the path,
those going straight on their way.
16 "Whoever is naive, come in here,"
she says to those who lack sense.
17 "Stolen water is sweet;
food eaten in secret is pleasant."

[i] Heb lacks *God.* [j] Heb uncertain

18 But they don't know that the dead
are there;
her guests are in the depths of the grave.[k]

Proverbs of Solomon

10 The proverbs of Solomon:
A wise child makes a father glad,
but a foolish child
brings sorrow to his mother.
2 The treasure of the wicked
won't profit them,
but righteousness rescues people
from death.
3 The LORD doesn't let
the righteous starve,
but he rejects the desires of the wicked.
4 Laziness brings poverty;
hard work makes one rich.
5 A wise son harvests in the summer;
a disgraceful son
sleeps right through the harvest.
6 Blessings cover the head of the righteous,
but the mouth of the wicked
conceals violence.
7 The memory of the righteous
is a blessing,
but the name of the wicked rots.
8 The skilled mind accepts commands,
but a foolish talker is ruined.
9 Those who walk in innocence
walk with confidence,
but those on crooked paths
will be found out.
10 Those who wink an eye bring trouble;
those who speak foolishly are ruined.
11 The mouth of the righteous
is a fountain of life,
but the mouth of the wicked
conceals violence.
12 Hate stirs up conflict,
but love covers all offenses.
13 Wisdom is found on the lips
of those who have understanding,
but there is a rod for the back
of those with no sense.
14 The wise store up knowledge,
but the mouth of a fool brings on ruin.
15 The riches of the wealthy
are their strong city;
the ruin of the poor is their poverty.
16 The wages of the righteous lead to life;
the earnings of the wicked lead to sin.
17 Those who heed instruction
are on the way to life,
but those who ignore correction
lose their way.
18 Lying lips conceal hate,
and those who spread slander are fools.
19 With lots of words comes wrongdoing,
but the wise restrain their lips.
20 The tongue of the righteous is choice silver,
but the heart of the wicked lacks value.
21 The lips of the righteous
nourish many people,
but fools who lack sense will die.
22 The LORD's blessing makes a person rich,
and no trouble is added to it.
23 Fools enjoy vile deeds,
but those with understanding
take pleasure in wisdom.
24 What the wicked dread will come on them,
but what the righteous desire
will be given to them.
25 After a whirlwind passes by,
the wicked are no more,
but the righteous stand firm forever.
26 Like vinegar to the teeth
and smoke to the eyes,
so are lazy people
to those who authorize them.
27 The fear of the LORD increases one's life,
but the years of the wicked
will be cut short.
28 The expectations of the righteous
result in joy,
but the hopes of the wicked will perish.
29 The path of the LORD is a refuge
for the innocent
and ruin for those who do evil.
30 The righteous will never be shaken,
but the wicked won't dwell in the land.
31 The mouth of the righteous
flows with wisdom,
but the twisted tongue will be cut off.
32 The lips of the wise
know what is acceptable,
but the mouth of the wicked knows
only what is perverse.

[k] Heb *Sheol*

11 The LORD detests dishonest scales,
but delights in an accurate weight.
2 When pride comes, so does shame,
but wisdom brings humility.
3 Integrity guides the virtuous,
but dishonesty ruins the treacherous.
4 Riches don't help in the day of wrath,
but righteousness rescues from death.
5 The righteousness of the innocent
makes their path straight,
but the wicked fall in their wickedness.
6 Those who do right
are saved by their righteousness,
but the untrustworthy
are caught by their own desires.
7 When the wicked die, their hope perishes.
Yes, any hope based on money perishes.
8 The righteous are saved from distress,
and the wicked take their place.
9 The godless destroy their neighbors
by their words,
but the righteous are saved
by their knowledge.
10 When the righteous succeed,
a city rejoices;
when the wicked perish,
there are shouts of joy.
11 A city is honored
by the blessing of the virtuous;
it is destroyed
by the words of the wicked.
12 Whoever despises their neighbor
lacks sense;
a sensible person keeps quiet.
13 A slanderer walks around
revealing secrets,
but a trustworthy person
keeps a confidence.
14 Without guidance, a people will fall,
but there is victory with many counselors.
15 Guaranteeing the debt of a stranger
brings big trouble,
but the one who refuses to shake hands
will be secure.
16 A gracious woman gains honor;
violent men gain only wealth.
17 Kind persons benefit themselves,
but cruel people harm themselves.
18 The wicked earn false wages,
but those who sow righteousness
receive a true reward.
19 The righteous are headed toward life,
but those who pursue evil, toward death.
20 The LORD detests a crooked heart,
but he favors those
whose path is innocent.
21 The evil person will surely not
go unpunished,
but the children of the righteous
will escape.
22 Like a gold ring in a pig's nose
is a beautiful woman
who lacks discretion.
23 The desires of the righteous end up well,
but the expectations of the wicked
bring wrath.
24 Those who give generously receive more,
but those who are stingy with
what is appropriate will grow needy.
25 Generous persons will prosper;
those who refresh others
will themselves be refreshed.
26 People curse those who hoard grain,
but they bless those[l] who sell it.
27 Those who look for good find favor,
but those who seek evil—
it will come to them.
28 Those who trust in their wealth
will wither,
but the righteous will thrive
like leafy trees.
29 Those who trouble their family
will inherit the wind.
The fool will be servant to the wise.
30 The fruit of the righteous is a tree of life,
and the wise gather lives.[m]
31 If the righteous receive their due on earth,
how much more the wicked and sinners?

12 Those who love discipline
love knowledge,
and those who hate correction
are stupid.
2 The LORD favors good people,
but he condemns schemers.
3 No one is established by wicked acts,
but the roots of the righteous
can't be disturbed.
4 A strong woman is a crown to her husband,

[l] Or *the heads of those* [m] Or LXX, Syr *violence takes lives away*

but a disgraceful woman
is like rot in his bones.
5 The plans of the righteous are just,
but the guidance of the wicked
is deceptive.
6 The words of the wicked are a deathtrap,
but the speech of those who do right
rescues them.
7 The wicked are destroyed
and are no more,
but the family of the righteous
will endure.
8 A person is praised for his insight,
but a warped mind leads to contempt.
9 Better to be held in low regard
and have a servant
than to be conceited and lack food.
10 The righteous care about
their livestock's needs,
but even the compassion of the wicked
is cruel.
11 Those who work their land
will have plenty to eat,
but those who engage
in empty pursuits have no sense.
12 Desiring evil is a trap for the wicked,
but the root of the righteous endures.[n]
13 The wicked are trapped
by the transgressions of their lips,
but the righteous escape from distress.
14 From the fruit of their speech,
people are well satisfied;
their work results in reward.
15 Fools see their own way as right,
but the wise listen to advice.
16 Fools reveal their anger right away,
but the shrewd hide their contempt.
17 Those who state the truth speak justly,
but a false witness deceives.
18 Some chatter on like a stabbing sword,
but a wise tongue heals.
19 Truthful lips endure forever,
but a lying tongue
lasts only for a moment.
20 Deceit is in the heart
of those who plan evil,
but there is joy
for those who advise peace.
21 No harm happens to the righteous,
but the wicked receive
their fill of trouble.
22 The LORD detests false lips;
he favors those who do what is true.
23 The shrewd conceal their knowledge,
but the heart of fools
proclaims their stupidity.
24 A hard worker is in charge,
while a lazy one will be sentenced
to hard labor.
25 Anxiety leads to depression,
but a good word encourages.
26 The righteous offer guidance
to their neighbors,[o]
but the path of the wicked
makes them wander.
27 The lazy don't roast[p] their prey,
but hard workers receive precious riches.
28 The way of the righteous leads to life,
but the detestable[q] path leads to death.

13 A wise son listens to[r]
the discipline of his father,
but a mocker doesn't listen to correction.
2 People eat well from the fruit
of their words,
but the treacherous have an appetite
only for violence.
3 People who watch their mouths
guard their lives,
but those who open their lips are ruined.
4 The lazy have strong desires
but receive nothing;
the appetite of the diligent
is satisfied.
5 The righteous hate false words,
but the wicked create disgust and scorn.
6 Righteousness guards the innocent
on the path,
but wickedness misleads sinners.
7 Some pretend to be rich but have nothing,
while others pretend to be poor,
but have great riches.
8 Wealth can ransom a person's life,
but the poor don't even receive threats.
9 The light of the righteous rejoices,
but the lamp of the wicked goes out.
10 The empty-headed cause conflict
out of pride;
those who take advice are wise.

[n] Or *gives* [o] Heb uncertain [p] Heb uncertain [q] LXX; MT *the path of the trail* [r] Heb lacks *listens to.*

11 Riches gotten quickly[s] will dwindle,
but those who acquire them
gradually become wealthy.
12 Hope delayed makes the heart sick;
longing fulfilled is a tree of life.
13 Trouble will come on those
who despise a word,
but those who respect
the commandment will be rewarded.
14 The teaching of the wise
is a fountain of life,
turning a person away from deathtraps.
15 Good insight brings favor,
but the way of the faithless is their ruin.[t]
16 The prudent all act intelligently,
but fools display their stupidity.
17 Wicked messengers fall into trouble,
but a reliable one brings healing.
18 Poverty and shame come to those
who don't care about instruction;
honor belongs to those
who heed correction.
19 A desire fulfilled is pleasant,
but fools find deviating
from evil disgusting.
20 Walk with wise people and become wise;
befriend fools and get in trouble.
21 Trouble pursues sinners,
but good things reward the righteous.
22 Good people leave their grandchildren
an inheritance,
but the wealth of sinners
is stored up for the righteous.
23 A poor person's land
might produce much food,
but it is unjustly swept away.
24 Those who withhold the rod
hate their children,
but the one who loves them
applies discipline.
25 The righteous eat their fill,
but the wicked have empty stomachs.

14 A wise woman builds her house,
while a foolish woman tears hers
down with her own hands.
2 Those who walk with integrity
fear the LORD,
but those who take a crooked path
despise him.
3 Pride sprouts in the mouth of a fool,[u]
but the lips of the wise protect them.
4 When there are no oxen, the stall is clean,
but when there is a strong bull,
there is abundant produce.
5 A truthful witness doesn't lie,
but a false witness spews lies.
6 A mocker searches for wisdom
and gets none,
but knowledge comes quickly
to the intelligent.
7 Stay away from fools,
for you won't learn wise speech there.
8 By their wisdom the prudent
understand their way,
but the stupidity of fools deceives them.
9 Fools mock a compensation offering,
but favor is with those who do right.
10 The heart knows its own distress;
another person can't share its joy.
11 The house of the wicked is destroyed,
but the tent flourishes
for those who do right.
12 There is a path that may seem straight
to someone,
but in the end it is a path to death.
13 The heart feels pain even in laughter,
and in the end, joy turns to sorrow.
14 Rebellious hearts receive satisfaction
from their ways;
the good receive the due reward
for their deeds.
15 The naive believe anything,
but the prudent give thought
to their steps.
16 The wise are careful and avoid evil,
but fools become excited
and overconfident.
17 Short-tempered people
make stupid mistakes,
and schemers are hated.
18 Stupidity is the lot of the naive,
but the prudent are crowned
with knowledge.
19 Evil people will bow down before the good;
wicked people are at the gates
of the righteous.
20 Even their neighbors hate the poor,
but many love the wealthy.

[s]LXX; MT *from meaninglessness* [t]LXX, Syr, Vulg; MT *endures* [u]Heb uncertain

[21]Those who despise their neighbors
are sinners,
but happy are those
who are kind to the needy.
[22]Don't those who plan evil go astray?
Those who plan good
receive loyalty and faithfulness.
[23]There is profit in hard work,
but mere talk leads to poverty.
[24]Wealth is the crown of the wise,
and the folly of fools is folly.
[25]A truthful witness saves lives,
but a deceiver proclaims lies.
[26]In the fear of the LORD
is strong confidence
and refuge for one's children.
[27]The fear of the LORD is a fountain of life,
turning people away from deathtraps.
[28]A king's glory is a large population,
but a dwindling people is a ruler's ruin.
[29]Patience leads to abundant understanding,
but impatience leads to stupid mistakes.
[30]A peaceful mind gives life to the body,
but jealousy rots the bones.
[31]Those who exploit the powerless
anger their maker,
while those who are kind to the poor
honor God.
[32]The wicked are thrown down
by their own evil,
but the righteous find refuge
even in death.
[33]Wisdom resides
in an understanding heart,
but it's not[V] known in fools.
[34]Righteousness dignifies a nation,
but sin disgraces a people.
[35]The king favors an insightful servant,
but is furious at a shameful one.

15 A sensitive answer turns back wrath,
but an offensive word stirs up anger.
[2]The tongue of the wise
enhances knowledge,
but the mouth of a fool
gushes with stupidity.
[3]The LORD's eyes are everywhere,
keeping watch on evil and good people.
[4]Wholesome speech is a tree of life,
but dishonest talk breaks the spirit.
[5]A fool doesn't like a father's instruction,
but those who heed correction
are mature.
[6]Great treasure is in the house
of the righteous,
but the gain of the wicked
brings trouble.
[7]The lips of the wise spread knowledge,
but the hearts of fools have none.
[8]The LORD detests the sacrifices
of the wicked,
but favors the prayers
of those who do right.
[9]The LORD detests the path of the wicked,
but loves those
who pursue righteousness.
[10]Discipline is severe for those
who abandon the way;
those who hate correction will die.
[11]The grave[W] and the underworld[X] lie open
before the LORD;
how much more the hearts
of human beings!
[12]Mockers don't like those
who correct them.
They won't go to the wise.
[13]A joyful heart brightens one's face,
but a troubled heart breaks the spirit.
[14]An understanding heart seeks knowledge;
but fools feed on folly.
[15]All the days of the needy are hard,
but a happy heart has a continual feast.
[16]Better a little with fear of the LORD
than a great treasure with turmoil.
[17]Better a meal of greens with love
than a plump calf with hate.
[18]Hotheads stir up conflict,
but patient people calm down strife.
[19]The path of the lazy
is like a hedge of thorns,
but the way of those who do right
is a clear road.
[20]A wise child brings joy to a father,
but fools despise their mothers.
[21]Folly is joy to those who lack sense,
but those with understanding
walk straight ahead.
[22]Plans fail with no counsel,
but with many counselors they succeed.

[V]LXX; MT lacks *not*. [W]Heb *Sheol* [X]Heb *Abaddon*

23 To give an appropriate answer is a joy;
how good is a word at the right time!
24 For those with insight,
life is an upward path,
avoiding the grave[y] below.
25 The LORD snatches away
the arrogant one's house,
but he preserves the widow's boundaries.
26 The LORD detests evil plans,
but gracious words are pure.
27 Those who acquire things unjustly
gain trouble for their house,
but those who hate bribes will live.
28 The righteous heart reflects
before answering,
but the wicked mouth blurts out evil.
29 The LORD is far from the wicked,
but he listens to the prayers
of the righteous.
30 Bright eyes give joy to the heart;
good news strengthens the bones.
31 The ear that listens to life-giving correction
dwells among the wise.
32 Those who refuse discipline
despise themselves,
but those who listen to correction
gain understanding.
33 The fear of the LORD is wise instruction,
and humility comes before respect.

16 To people belong the plans
of the heart,
but the answer of the tongue
comes from the LORD.
2 All the ways of people
are pure in their eyes,
but the LORD tests the motives.
3 Commit your work to the LORD,
and your plans will succeed.
4 The LORD made everything
for a purpose,
even the wicked for an evil day.
5 The LORD detests all who are arrogant;
they surely won't go unpunished.
6 Love and faithfulness reconcile guilt;
the fear of the LORD turns away evil.
7 When people draw favor
from the LORD,
even their enemies are at peace
with them.
8 Better a little with righteousness
than great profits without justice.
9 People plan their path,
but the LORD secures their steps.
10 A king's speech is like an oracle;
in a judgment,
one can't go against his words.
11 Honest balances and scales
are the LORD's;
all the weights in the bag are his doing.
12 Kings detest wicked deeds,
for their thrones are founded
on righteousness.
13 Kings favor those with righteous lips;
they love words of integrity.
14 The king's anger is a messenger of death;
the wise will calm him.
15 There's life in the light of the king's face.
His favor is like a cloud
that brings spring rain.
16 Acquiring wisdom
is much better than gold,
and acquiring understanding
is better than silver.
17 The road of those who do right
turns away from evil;
those who protect their path
guard their lives.
18 Pride comes before disaster,
and arrogance before a fall.
19 Better to be humble with the needy
than to divide plunder with the proud.
20 Those with insight find prosperity;
those who trust the LORD are blessed.
21 The skilled mind is called discerning,
and pleasant speech enhances teaching.
22 One who has insight is a fountain of life,
but the instruction of the foolish is folly.
23 The mind of the wise
makes their speech insightful
and enhances the teaching of their lips.
24 Pleasant words are flowing honey,
sweet to the taste
and healing to the bones.
25 There is a path that may seem straight
to someone,
but in the end it is the path of death.
26 The appetite of workers labors for them,
for their hunger presses them on.

[y] Heb *Sheol*

27 Worthless people dig up trouble;
their lips are like a scorching fire.
28 Destructive people produce conflict;
gossips alienate close friends.
29 Violent people entice their neighbors
and walk them down a path
that isn't good.
30 Those who wink their eye plot destruction;
those who purse their lips plan evil.
31 Gray hair is a crown of glory;
it is found on the path of righteousness.
32 Better to be patient than a warrior,
and better to have self-control
than to capture a city.
33 The dice are cast into the lap;
all decisions are from the LORD.

17 Better a dry crust with quiet
than a house full of feasting
with quarrels.
2 An insightful servant rules
over a disgraceful son
and will divide an inheritance
with the brothers.
3 A crucible is for silver
and a furnace for gold,
but the LORD tests the heart.
4 An evildoer pays attention to guilty lips;
a liar listens to a destructive tongue.
5 Those who mock the poor
insult their maker;
those who rejoice in disaster
won't go unpunished.
6 Grandchildren are the crown
of the elderly,
and the glory of children
is their parents.
7 Too much talking isn't right for a fool;
even less so false speech
for an honorable person.
8 A bribe seems magical in the eyes
of those who give it,
granting success to all who use it.
9 One who seeks love conceals an offense,
but one who repeats it divides friends.
10 A rebuke goes deeper
to an understanding person
than a hundred lashes to a fool.
11 Evil people seek only rebellion;
a cruel messenger
will be sent against them.
12 Safer to meet a bear robbed of her cubs
than fools in their folly.
13 Evil will never depart from the house
of those who return evil for good.
14 The start of a quarrel is like
letting out water,
so drop the dispute before it breaks out.
15 Judging the righteous wicked
and the wicked righteous—
the LORD detests both of these.
16 Why should a fool have money
to pay for wisdom? He has no mind.
17 Friends love all the time,
and kinsfolk are born
for times of trouble.
18 One with no sense shakes hands on a deal,
securing a loan for a friend.
19 Those who love an offense love a quarrel;
those who build a high doorway
invite a collapse.
20 Those with crooked hearts won't prosper,
and those with twisted tongues
will fall into trouble.
21 Having a fool for a son brings grief;
there's no joy for a scoundrel's father.
22 A joyful heart helps healing,
but a broken spirit dries up the bones.
23 The wicked take secret bribes
to twist the way of justice.
24 Wisdom is right in front of those
with understanding,
but the eyes of fools
are off to the edges of the earth.
25 A foolish son is irritating to his father
and bitter to her who gave birth to him.
26 It isn't good to punish the righteous,
to strike the honorable for their integrity.
27 Wise are those who restrain their talking;
people with understanding
are coolheaded.
28 Fools who keep quiet are deemed wise;
those who shut their lips are smart.

18 Unfriendly people look out
for themselves;
they bicker with sensible people.
2 Fools find no pleasure in understanding,
but only in expressing their opinion.
3 When the wicked arrive, so does contempt;
with shame comes insult.
4 The words of a person's mouth
are deep waters,
a bubbling stream, a fountain of wisdom.

5 Favoring the wicked isn't good;
it denies justice to the righteous.
6 The lips of fools make accusations;
their mouths elicit beatings.
7 The mouth of fools is their ruin;
their lips are a trap for their lives.
8 The words of gossips are like choice snacks;
they go down to the inmost parts.
9 Those who are lazy in their work
are brothers to thugs.
10 The LORD's name is a strong tower;
the righteous run to it and find refuge.
11 The riches of the wealthy are a strong city
and like a high wall in their imagination.
12 Pride comes before a disaster,
but humility comes before respect.
13 Those who answer before they listen
are foolish and disgraceful.
14 The human spirit sustains a sick person,
but who can bear a broken spirit?
15 An understanding mind gains knowledge;
the ear of the wise seeks knowledge.
16 A gift opens the way
for access to important people.
17 The first person to testify seems innocent,
until the other comes
and cross-examines him.
18 The dice settle conflicts
and keep strong opponents apart.
19 An offended ally
is more formidable than a city;
such quarreling
is like the bars of a castle.
20 The stomach is satisfied
by the fruit of the mouth;
one's lips can earn a satisfying income.
21 Death and life
are in the power of the tongue;
those who love it will eat its fruit.
22 He who finds a wife finds what is good,
gaining favor from the LORD.
23 The poor plead for help,
but the wealthy answer harshly.
24 There are persons for companionship,
but then there are friends
who are more loyal than family.

19 Better to be poor
and walk in innocence
than to have dishonest lips and be a fool.
2 Ignorant desire isn't good;
rushing feet make mistakes.
3 People's own folly corrupts their way,
but their hearts rage against the LORD.
4 Riches increase one's friends,
but the poor lose their friends.
5 A false witness won't go unpunished,
and a liar won't escape.
6 Many seek favor from rulers;
everyone befriends a gift giver.
7 All the relatives of the poor hate them;
even more, their friends
stay far from them.
When they pursue them with words,
they aren't there.
8 Those who acquire good sense
love themselves;
those who keep understanding
find success.
9 False witnesses won't go unpunished,
and liars will perish.
10 Luxury isn't fitting for a fool;
even less so for a servant
to rule over princes.
11 Insightful people restrain their anger;
their glory is to ignore an offense.
12 A raging king roars like a lion;
his favor is like the dew on the grass.
13 A foolish son is a disaster to his father;
a contentious wife
is like constant dripping.
14 House and riches are an inheritance
from one's ancestors,
but an insightful wife
is from the LORD.
15 Laziness brings on deep sleep;
a slacker goes hungry.
16 Those who keep the commandment
preserve their lives;
those who disregard their ways will die.
17 Those who are gracious to the poor
lend to the LORD,
and the Lord will fully repay them.
18 Discipline your children while there
is hope,
but don't plan to kill them.
19 Angry people must pay the penalty;
if you rescue them,
then you will have to do it again.
20 Listen to advice and accept instruction,
so you might grow wise in the future.
21 Many plans are in a person's mind,
but the LORD's purpose will succeed.

22 People long for trustworthiness;
it is better to be poor than a liar.
23 The fear of the LORD leads to life;
then one rests content,
untouched by harm.
24 Lazy people bury their hand in the bowl;
they won't even put it to their mouth.
25 Strike someone who scoffs,
and a naive person will become clever;
correct someone with understanding,
and they will gain knowledge.
26 Those who assault their father
and drive out their mother
are disgraceful children,
worthy of reproach.
27 If, my child, you stop listening
to discipline,
you will wander away from words
of knowledge.
28 A worthless witness mocks justice;
the wicked mouth gulps down trouble.
29 Punishments were made for mockers,
and blows for the backs of fools.

20 Wine is a mocker; beer a carouser.
Those it leads astray
won't become wise.
2 A king is as terrifying as a lion's growl.
Those who anger him may lose their life.
3 It is honorable to back off from a fight,
but fools jump right in.
4 The lazy don't plow during winter;
at harvest they look but find nothing.
5 Advice comes from the deep waters
of the heart;
those with understanding
can draw it out.
6 Many people will say that they are loyal,
but who can find a reliable person?
7 The righteous live with integrity;
happy are their children
who come after them.
8 A king who sits on his judgment throne
sifts out all evil with his eyes.
9 Who can say, "I'm innocent to the core;
I'm cleansed from my sin"?
10 False weights and measures—
the LORD detests them both.
11 Even young people are known
by their actions,
whether their conduct is pure
and upright.
12 Ears to hear and eyes to see—
the LORD made them both.
13 Don't love sleep or you will be poor;
stay alert and you will have plenty to eat.
14 The buyer says, "Bad, bad,"
but then goes away and brags.
15 Much gold and many pearls exist,
but wise speech
is the most precious jewel.
16 Take the garment of the person
who secures a loan for a stranger;
take his pledge for a foreigner.
17 Stolen bread is sweet,
but afterward the mouth is full of gravel.
18 Plans are firmed up by advice;
wage wars with good guidance.
19 Gossips reveal secrets;
don't associate with those
who talk too much.
20 Those who curse their father or mother—
their lamp will be snuffed out
when it becomes dark.
21 Inheritance gained quickly at first
won't bless later on.
22 Don't say, "I'll repay the evildoer!"
Wait for the LORD, and he will save you.
23 The LORD detests false weights;
deceptive scales aren't right.
24 A person's steps are from the LORD;
how then can people understand
their path?
25 It is a snare to say rashly, "It is holy,"
and only reflect after making the promise.
26 A wise king sifts out the wicked,
and runs them over with a wheel.
27 The breath of a person
is the lamp of the LORD,
searching all the inmost parts.
28 Kindness and faithfulness
protect the king;
he supports his throne by kindness.
29 Strength is the glory of young men;
gray hair is the splendor of old age.
30 Blows and bruises remove evil;
beatings cleanse the inner parts.

21 The king's heart is like channels of
water in the hand of the LORD;
he directs it wherever he wants.
2 Everyone's path is straight
in their own eyes,
but the LORD weighs the heart.

[3] Acting with righteousness and justice
is more valued by the LORD
than sacrifice.
[4] Prideful eyes, an arrogant heart, and
the lamp of the wicked are all sinful.
[5] The plans of the diligent end up in profit,
but those who hurry end up with loss.
[6] Those who gain treasure with lies
are like a drifting fog,
leading to death.
[7] The violence of the wicked
will sweep them away,
for they refuse to act with justice.
[8] The ways of some people
are twisted and strange,
but the behavior of those who do right
is pure.
[9] Better to live on the edge of a roof
than with a contentious woman
in a large house.
[10] Wicked people desire evil;
their neighbors receive
no mercy from them.
[11] When a mocker is punished,
the naive person gains wisdom;
when insight comes to the wise,
knowledge increases.
[12] The righteous one observes
the house of the wicked,
turning the wicked toward trouble.
[13] Those who close their ears
to the cries of the poor
will themselves call out
but receive no answer.
[14] A secret gift calms anger,
and a hidden bribe
removes[z] furious wrath.
[15] Acting justly is a joy to the righteous,
but dreaded by those who do evil.
[16] People who wander
from the path of insight
will rest in the company of the dead.
[17] Those who love pleasure end up poor;
lovers of wine and oil won't get rich.
[18] The wicked are a ransom
for the righteous;
the treacherous will be punished[a]
in the place of the virtuous.
[19] Better to live in a wilderness
than in a house
with a contentious and angry woman.
[20] Precious treasure and oil
stay in the home of the wise,
but fools swallow them up.
[21] Those who pursue righteousness
and kindness
will find life, righteousness, and honor.
[22] A wise person fought a city of warriors
and brought down the stronghold
in which they felt safe.
[23] Those who guard their mouths
and their tongues
guard themselves from trouble.
[24] Incredibly proud—
mockers are their name!
Their conduct involves excessive pride.
[25] The desires of the lazy will kill them,
because their hands refuse
to do anything.
[26] The lazy desire things constantly,
but the righteous give
without holding back.
[27] The LORD detests
the sacrifices of the wicked,
especially when brought
with devious motives.
[28] A lying witness will perish,
but one who listens
will testify successfully.
[29] The wicked person appears brash,
but the virtuous
think about the path ahead.
[30] No wisdom, understanding,
or advice
can stand up against the LORD.
[31] A horse is made ready
for the day of battle,
but victory belongs to the LORD.

22 A good reputation
is better than much wealth;
high esteem
is better than silver and gold.
[2] The rich and the poor
have this in common:
the LORD made them both.
[3] Prudent people see trouble and hide,
while the simpleminded
go right to it and get punished.

[z] Heb lacks *removes*. [a] Heb lacks *will be punished*.

4 The reward of humility
and the fear of the LORD
is wealth, honor, and life.
5 Thorns and nets are in the path
of the crooked;
those who guard their lives
keep their distance.
6 Train children in the way they should go;
when they grow old,
they won't depart from it.
7 The wealthy rule over the poor;
a borrower is a slave to a lender.
8 Those who sow injustice will harvest evil;
the rod of their fury
will come to an end.
9 Happy are generous people,
because they give some of their food
to the poor.
10 Remove the mocker
and conflict disappears;
judgment and shame also stop.
11 Those who love a pure heart—
their speech is gracious,
and the king is their friend.
12 The LORD's eyes protect knowledge,
but he frustrates the words
of the treacherous.
13 A lazy person says,
"There's a lion in the street!
I'll be killed in the town square!"
14 The mouth of a mysterious woman
is a deep pit;
those under the LORD's wrath
will fall in it.
15 Folly is bound up in a child's heart;
the rod of discipline removes it.
16 Oppressing the poor to get rich
and giving to the wealthy
lead only to poverty.

Thirty sayings of the wise

17 Turn your ear
and hear the words of the wise;
focus your mind on my knowledge.
18 It will be pleasant
if you keep the words in you,
if you have them ready on your lips.
19 So that your trust will be in the LORD,
I'm teaching you today—yes, you.
20 Haven't I written for you thirty[b] sayings
full of advice and knowledge?
21 Their purpose is to teach you true,
reliable words,
so you can report back reliably
to those who sent you.

22 Don't steal from the poor,
because they are poor.
Don't oppress the needy in the gate.
23 The LORD will take up their case
and press the life out of those
who oppress them.[c]

24 Don't befriend people controlled by anger;
don't associate with
hot-tempered people;
25 otherwise, you will learn their ways
and become trapped.

26 Don't shake hands to guarantee a loan.
27 If you can't repay,
why should they be able
to take your bed from you?

28 Don't remove
an ancient boundary marker
that your ancestors established.

29 Do you see people who work skillfully?
They will work for kings
but not work for lowly people.

23 When you sit down
to dine with a ruler,
carefully consider what is in front of you.
2 Place a knife at your throat
to control your appetite.
3 Don't long for the ruler's delicacies;
the food misleads.

4 Don't wear yourself out trying to get rich;
be smart enough to stop.
5 When your eyes fly to wealth
it is gone; it grows wings
like an eagle and flies heavenward.

6 Don't eat food with stingy people;
don't long for their delicacies,

[b] Heb uncertain [c] Heb uncertain

7 because they are like a hair
in the throat.[d]
They say to you, "Eat and drink!"
but they don't mean it.
8 You will eat scraps and vomit them out.
You will waste your pleasant words.
9 Don't speak in the ears of fools,
for they will scorn your insightful words.

10 Don't remove an ancient
boundary marker;
don't invade the fields of orphans,
11 for their redeemer is strong.
He will bring charges against you.

12 Bring your mind to instruction,
your ear to knowledgeable sayings.

13 Don't withhold instruction from children;
if you strike them with a rod,
they won't die.
14 Strike them with a rod,
and you will save their lives
from the grave.[e]

15 My child, if your heart is wise,
then my heart too will be happy.
16 My inner being will rejoice
when your lips speak with integrity.

17 Don't let your heart envy sinners,
but fear the LORD constantly;
18 then you will have a future,
and your hope won't be cut off.

19 Listen, my child, and be wise!
Keep your mind straight on the path.
20 Don't hang out with those
who get drunk on wine
or those who eat too much meat,
21 because drunks and gluttons
will be impoverished;
their stupor will clothe them in rags.

22 Listen to your father, who gave you life;
don't despise your elderly mother.
23 Buy truth and don't sell it;
buy wisdom, instruction,
and understanding.
24 The father of the righteous
will be very happy;
the one who gives life to the wise
will rejoice.
25 Your father and your mother will rejoice;
she who gave you birth will be happy.

26 My child, give your mind to me
and let your eyes keep to my path.
27 A prostitute is a deep pit,
and a foreign woman is a narrow well.
28 Indeed, she ambushes like a robber
and increases the number
of the faithless.

29 Who is suffering?
Who is uneasy?
Who has arguments?
Who has complaints?
Who has unnecessary wounds?
Who has glazed eyes?—
30 those who linger over wine;
those who go looking for mixed wine.
31 Don't look at wine when it is red,
when it sparkles in the cup,
going down smoothly.
32 In the end, it bites like a snake
and poisons like a viper.
33 Your eyes will see strange things,
and your heart will speak
distorted words.
34 You will be like one who lies down
while out on the sea[f]
or one who lies on top of a mast.
35 "Though hit, I feel no pain;
though beaten up,
I don't know anything about it.
When I wake up,
I'll look for wine again!"

24 Don't envy evil people,
and don't long to be with them.
2 Their hearts are focused on violence,
and their lips speak of trouble.

3 By wisdom a house is built;
by understanding it is established.
4 By knowledge rooms are filled
with all precious and pleasant wealth.

[d] LXX; Heb uncertain [e] Heb *Sheol* [f] Or *in the heart of the sea*

5 A wise person is mightier
than a strong one;[g]
a knowledgeable person
than a powerful one.
6 You should make war with guidance;
victory comes with many counselors.

7 Wisdom is beyond foolish people.
They don't open their mouths
in the gate.
8 Those who plot evil
will be called master schemers.
9 The scheming of fools is sin;
people detest mockers.

10 If you show yourself weak
on a day of distress,
your strength is too small.
11 Rescue those being taken off to death;
and from those staggering
to the slaughter, don't hold back.
12 If you say,
"Look, we didn't know about it,"
the one who weighs hearts—
doesn't he understand?
The one who protects your life—
he knows.
He makes people pay for their actions.

13 My child, eat honey, for it is good.
The honeycomb is sweet in your mouth.
14 Know that wisdom is like that
for your whole being.
If you find it, there is a future.
Your hope won't be cut off.

15 Wicked one, don't wait secretly
at the home of the righteous.
Don't destroy their dwelling.
16 The righteous may fall seven times
but still get up,
but the wicked will stumble
into trouble.

17 When your enemies fall, don't rejoice.
When they stumble,
don't let your heart be glad,
18 or the LORD will see it and be displeased,
and he will turn his anger from them.

19 Don't get fighting mad at evil people;
don't be envious of the wicked.
20 Indeed, there is no future for the evil;
the lamp of the wicked will be put out.

21 Fear the LORD, my child,
as well as the king.
Don't associate with those
who are rebellious.
22 Disaster comes suddenly from them.
Who can know the ruin
that both can bring?

More sayings of the wise

23 These are also the sayings of the wise:

Partiality in judgment isn't good.

24 Those who say to the guilty,
"You are innocent"—
the people will curse them.
Nations will condemn them.
25 But it will go well for those
who rebuke them.
A rich blessing will come to them.
26 Those who speak honestly
are like those who kiss on the lips.

27 Get your outside work done;
make preparations in the field;
then you can build your house.

28 Don't be a witness against your neighbor
without reason;
don't deceive with your lips.
29 Don't say, "I'll do to them
what they did to me.
I'll pay them back for their actions."

30 I happened upon the field
of a lazy person,
by the vineyard of one with no sense.
31 Thorns grew all over it;
weeds covered the ground,
and the stone wall was falling down.
32 I observed this and took it to heart;
I saw it and learned a lesson.
33 "A little sleep, a little slumber,
a little lying down with folded arms"—

[g] LXX; MT *A wise man is strong.*

34 and poverty will come on you
like a prowler,
deprivation like a man with a shield.

More proverbs of Solomon

25 These are also proverbs of Solomon, copied by the men of Hezekiah, king of Judah:

2 It is the glory of God to hide something
and the glory of kings
to discover something.
3 Like the high heavens
and the depths of the earth,
so the mind of a king is unsearchable.

4 Remove the dross from the silver,
and a vessel will come out for the refiner.
5 Remove the wicked
from the king's presence,
and his throne will be established
in righteousness.

6 Don't exalt yourself
in the presence of the king,
or stand in the place
of important people,
7 because it is better that he say to you,
"Come up here,"
than to be demoted before a ruler.

What your eyes see,
8 don't be quick to quarrel over;
what will you do in the future
when your neighbor shames you?
9 Argue it out with your neighbor,
and don't give away someone's secret.
10 Otherwise, the one who hears it
will vilify you;
the slander against you will never stop.

11 Words spoken at the right time
are like gold apples in a silver setting.
12 Wise correction to an ear that listens
is like a gold earring
or jewelry of fine gold.

13 Like the coolness of snow
on a harvest day
are reliable messengers to those
who send them;
they restore the life of their master.
14 People who brag about a gift never given
are like clouds and wind
that produce no rain.
15 A commander can be persuaded
with patience,
and a tender tongue can break a bone.
16 If you find honey,
eat just the right amount;
otherwise, you'll get full and vomit it up.
17 Don't spend too much time
in your neighbor's house.
Otherwise, they'll get fed up with you
and hate you.
18 People who testify falsely
against their neighbors
are like a club, sword,
and sharpened arrow.
19 Trusting a treacherous person
at a difficult time
is like having a bad tooth
or a wobbly foot.
20 Singing a song to a troubled heart
is like taking off a garment on a cold day
or putting vinegar on a wound.[h]
21 If your enemies are starving,
feed them some bread;
if they are thirsty,
give them water to drink.
22 By doing this, you will heap
burning coals on their heads,
and the LORD will reward you.
23 The north wind stirs up rain,
and a person who plots quietly
provokes angry faces.
24 Better to live on the edge of a roof
than to share a house
with a contentious woman.
25 Good news from a distant land
is like cold water for a weary person.
26 A righteous person giving in to the wicked
is like a contaminated spring
or a polluted fountain.
27 Eating too much honey isn't good,
nor is it appropriate to seek honor.
28 A person without self-control
is like a breached city, one with no walls.

[h] LXX; MT *vinegar on natron* (a detergent)

26 Like snow in the summer
or rain at harvest,
so honor isn't appropriate for a fool.
2 Like a darting sparrow,
like a flying swallow,
so an undeserved curse never arrives.
3 A whip for a horse, a bridle for a donkey,
and a rod for the back of fools.
4 Don't answer fools according to their folly,
or you will become like them yourself.
5 Answer fools according to their folly,
or they will deem themselves wise.
6 Sending messages with a fool
is like cutting off one's feet
or drinking down violence.
7 As legs dangle from a disabled person,
so does a proverb in the mouth of fools.
8 Like tying a stone in a sling,
so is giving respect to a fool.
9 Like a thorny bush in the hand of a drunk,
so is a proverb in the mouth of fools.
10 Like an archer who wounds
someone randomly,
so is one who hires a fool or a passerby.
11 Like a dog that returns to its vomit,
so a fool repeats foolish mistakes.
12 Do you see people
who consider themselves wise?
There is more hope for a fool
than for them.
13 A lazy person says,
"There's a lion in the path!
A lion in the plazas!"
14 As a door turns on its hinge,
so do lazy people in their beds.
15 Lazy people bury their hand into the bowl,
too tired to return it to their mouth.
16 Lazy people think they are wiser
than seven people who answer sensibly.

17 Like yanking the ears of a dog,
so is one who passes by and gets
involved in another person's fight.
18 Like a crazy person shooting deadly
flaming arrows
19 are those who deceive their neighbor
and say, "Hey, I was only joking!"
20 Without wood a fire goes out;
without gossips, conflict calms down.
21 Like adding charcoal to embers
or wood to fire,
quarrelsome people kindle strife.
22 The words of gossips
are like choice snacks;
they go down to the inmost parts.
23 Smooth[i] lips and an evil heart
are like silver coating on clay.
24 Hateful people mislead with their lips,
keeping their deception within.
25 Though they speak graciously,
don't believe them,
for seven horrible things
are in their heart.
26 They may cover their hatred with trickery,
but their evil will be revealed in public.
27 Those who dig a pit will fall in it;
those who roll a stone
will have it turn back on them.
28 A lying tongue hates those it crushes;
a flattering mouth causes destruction.

27 Don't brag about tomorrow,
for you don't know
what a day will bring.
2 Let another person praise you,
and not your own mouth;
a stranger, and not your own lips.
3 A stone is heavy and sand weighs much,
but the nuisance of fools
is heavier than both.
4 Wrath is cruel and anger is a flood,
but who can withstand jealousy?
5 A public correction
is better than hidden love.
6 Trustworthy are the bruises of a friend;
excessive are the kisses of an enemy.
7 Someone who is full refuses honey,
but anything bitter
tastes sweet to a hungry person.
8 Like a bird wandering from its nest,
so is one who wanders from home.
9 Oil and incense make the heart glad,
and the sweetness of friends
comes from their advice.[j]
10 Don't desert your friend
or a friend of your family;
don't go to your relative's house
when disaster strikes.

[i] LXX; Heb uncertain [j] Heb uncertain

Better a neighbor nearby
than a relative far away.
11 Be wise, my child, and make my heart glad,
so I can answer those who insult me.
12 Prudent people see evil and hide;
the simpleminded go right to it
and get punished.
13 Take the garment of the person
who secures a loan for a stranger;
take his pledge for a foreigner.
14 Greeting a neighbor with a loud voice
early in the morning
will be viewed as a curse.
15 The constant dripping on a rainy day
and a contentious woman are alike;
16 anyone who can control her
can control the wind
or pick up oil in his hand.
17 As iron sharpens iron,
so friends sharpen each other's faces.
18 Those who tend a fig tree will eat its fruit,
and those who look after their master
will be honored.
19 As water reflects the face,
so the heart reflects
one person to another.
20 The grave[k] and the underworld[l]
are never satisfied;
and people's eyes are never satisfied.
21 A crucible is for silver
and a furnace for gold,
so are people in the presence
of someone who praises them.
22 Even if you grind fools in a mortar,
even grinding them along with the grain,
their folly won't be driven from them.
23 Know your flock well;
pay attention to your herds,
24 for no treasure lasts forever,
nor a crown
generation after generation.
25 When the grass goes away,
new growth appears,
and the plants of the hills are gathered,
26 then the lambs will provide your clothes,
and the goats
will be the price of your fields.
27 There will be enough goat's milk
for your food,
for the food of your house,
and to nourish your young women.

28 The wicked run away even though
no one pursues them,
but the righteous
are as confident as a lion.
2 When a land rebels, there are many leaders;
but a person with understanding
brings order.
3 Poor people who oppress the needy
are rain that washes away food.
4 Those who abandon Instruction
praise the wicked,
but those who follow Instruction
battle them.
5 Evil people don't understand justice,
but those who seek the LORD
understand everything.
6 Better to be poor and walk in innocence
than to be on crooked paths and wealthy.
7 Intelligent children follow Instruction,
but those who befriend gluttons
shame their parents.
8 Those who become rich
through high interest rates
gather money for those
who are generous to the poor.
9 Those who turn their ears
from hearing Instruction—
even their prayers will be detested.
10 Whoever misleads those who do right
onto an evil path
will fall into their own pit,
but the blameless
will inherit good things.
11 Rich people think they are wise,
but an insightful poor person
sees through them.
12 When the righteous rejoice,
there is great respect,
but people hide when the wicked prosper.
13 Those who hide their sins won't succeed,
but those who confess
and give them up will receive mercy.
14 Happy are those
who are continually fearful,
but those whose hearts are hard
fall into trouble.

[k]Heb *Sheol* [l]Heb *Abaddon*

15 A wicked ruler over the poor
is like a growling lion or a prowling bear.
16 A prince without understanding
is a cruel oppressor,
but one who hates unjust gain
will live long.
17 If someone feels guilty about murder,
don't hold them back
from fleeing to the pit.
18 Those who walk in innocence will be saved,
but those who go on twisted paths
will fall into the grave.
19 Those who work the land
will have plenty to eat,
but those with worthless pursuits
will have plenty of poverty.
20 Reliable people
will have abundant blessings,
but those with get-rich-quick schemes
won't go unpunished.
21 Those who show favoritism aren't good;
people do wrong for a crust of bread.
22 The stingy try to get rich fast,
unaware that loss will come to them.
23 Those who correct someone will,
in the end, find more favor
than those with flattering tongues.
24 Those who steal from their father
and mother,
and say, "It's not a crime,"
are friends of vandals.
25 Greedy people stir up conflict,
but those who trust the LORD
become prosperous.
26 Those who trust in their own reasoning
are fools,
but those who walk in wisdom
will be kept safe.
27 Those who give to the poor
will lack nothing,
but those who turn a blind eye
will be greatly cursed.
28 When the wicked rise up, people hide,
but when they are destroyed,
the righteous multiply.

29 One who stays stubborn
after many corrections
will be suddenly broken, beyond healing.
2 When the righteous become numerous,
the people rejoice,
but when the wicked dominate,
the people moan.
3 A man who loves wisdom
makes his father rejoice,
but one who spends time
with prostitutes destroys riches.
4 A king gives stability to the land by justice,
but one who imposes heavy taxes
tears it down.
5 People who flatter their friends
spread out a net for their feet.
6 The wicked are snared by their own sin;[m]
the righteous sing and rejoice.
7 The righteous know the rights of the poor,
but the wicked don't understand.
8 Mockers set a city on fire,
but the wise turn back anger.
9 When the wise make a legal charge
against the foolish,
the fools shout, they laugh—
there is no calm.
10 Murderous people hate the innocent,
and they seek the lives of the virtuous.
11 Fools show all their anger,
but the wise hold it back.
12 If a ruler listens to lies,
those who serve him will be wicked.
13 The poor and their oppressors
have a common bond—
the LORD gives light to the eyes of both.
14 If a king judges the poor honestly,
his throne will be established forever.
15 The rod and correction lead to wisdom,
but children out of control
shame their mothers.
16 When the wicked become numerous,
so do crimes;
the righteous will see their downfall.
17 Instruct your children;
they will give you peace of mind
and bring delight into your life.
18 When there's no vision,
the people get out of control,
but whoever obeys instruction is happy.
19 Servants aren't disciplined by words;
they might understand,
but they don't respond.

[m] Tg, Syr; MT *In the sin of an evil man is a snare*

20 Do you see people
who are quick to speak?
There is more hope for fools
than for them.
21 Pamper servants from a young age,
and later on there will be trouble.
22 Angry people stir up conflict;
hotheads cause much offense.
23 Pride lays people low,
but those of humble spirit gain honor.
24 Those who share plunder with thieves
hate themselves;
even under oath, they don't testify.
25 People are trapped
by their fear of others;
those who trust the LORD are secure.
26 Many seek access to the ruler,
but justice comes from the LORD.
27 The unjust person is disgusting
to the righteous;
the straight path is disgusting
to the wicked.

Words of Agur

30 The words of Agur, Jakeh's son, from Massa.
The man declares: I'm tired, God;
I'm tired, God, and I'm exhausted.
2 Actually, I'm too stupid to be human,
a man without understanding.
3 I haven't learned wisdom,
nor do I have knowledge
of the holy one.

4 Who has gone up to heaven
and come down?
Who has gathered the wind
by the handful?
Who has bound up the waters
in a garment?
Who has established all the ends
of the earth?
What is this person's name
and the name of this person's child—
if you know it?

5 All God's words are tried and true;
a shield for those
who take refuge in him.
6 Don't add to his words,
or he will correct you
and show you to be a liar.

7 Two things I ask of you;
don't keep them from me before I die:
8 Fraud and lies—
keep far from me!
Don't give me either poverty or wealth;
give me just the food I need.
9 Or I'll be full and deny you,
and say, "Who is the LORD?"
Or I'll be poor and steal,
and dishonor my God's name.

More sayings of the wise

10 Don't slander a servant to his master;
otherwise, the servant will curse you,
and you will be guilty.

11 There are those who curse their father
and don't bless their mother.
12 There are those who think
they are clean,
but haven't washed off
their own excrement.
13 There are those—
how arrogant are their eyes;
how their eyebrows are raised!
14 There are those whose teeth are swords;
their jaw is a butcher's knife,
ready to devour the needy
from the earth,
and the poor from humanity.

15 The leech has two daughters:
"Give, give!"
There are three things
that are never satisfied,
four that never say, "Enough!":
16 the grave[n] and a barren womb,
a land never filled with water,
and fire that doesn't say, "Enough!"

17 An eye that mocks a father
and rejects obedience to a mother,
may the ravens of the river valley
peck it out,
and the eagle's young eat it.

[n] Heb *Sheol*

18 Three things are too wonderful for me,
four that I can't figure out:
19 the way of an eagle in the sky,
the way of a snake on the rock,
the way of a ship out on the open sea,
and the way of a man
with a young woman.

20 This is the way of an adulterous woman:
she eats and wipes her mouth,
and she says, "I've done nothing wrong!"

21 At three things the earth trembles,
at four it can't bear up:
22 at a servant when he becomes king
and fools when they are full of food;
23 at a detested woman
when she gets married
and a female servant
when she replaces her mistress.

24 Four things are among
the smallest on earth,
but they are extremely wise:
25 Ants as creatures aren't strong,
but they store away their food
in the summer.
26 Badgers as creatures aren't powerful,
but they make their homes
in the rocks.
27 Locusts don't have a king,
but they march together in ranks.
28 You can catch lizards in your hand,
but they are in kings' palaces.

29 There are three things
that are excellent in their stride,
four that are excellent as they walk:
30 a lion, a warrior among beasts,
which doesn't back down at anything;
31 the strut of a rooster or a male goat;
and a king with his army.

32 If you've been foolish and arrogant,
if you've been scheming,
put your hand to your mouth,
33 because churning milk makes curds,
squeezing the nose brings blood,
and stirring up anger produces strife.

Words of King Lemuel

31 The words of King Lemuel of Massa,
which his mother taught him:
2 No, my son!
No, son of my womb!
No, son of my solemn promises!
3 Don't give your strength to women,
your ways to those who wipe out kings.
4 It isn't for kings, Lemuel,
it isn't for kings to drink wine,
for rulers to crave[o] strong drink.
5 Otherwise, they will drink
and forget the law,
and violate the rights of the needy.
6 Give strong drink
to those who are perishing
and wine to those
whose hearts are bitter.
7 Let them drink and forget their poverty
and no longer remember their toil.
8 Speak out on behalf of the voiceless,
and for the rights of all
who are vulnerable.[p]
9 Speak out in order to judge
with righteousness
and to defend the needy and the poor.

The competent wife

10 A competent wife,
how does one find her?
Her value is far above pearls.
11 Her husband entrusts his heart to her,
and with her he will have all he needs.
12 She brings him good and not trouble
all the days of her life.
13 She seeks out wool and flax;
she works joyfully with her hands.
14 She is like a fleet of merchant ships,
bringing food from a distance.
15 She gets up while it is still night,
providing food for her household,
even some for her female servants.
16 She surveys a field and acquires it;
from her own resources,
she plants a vineyard.
17 She works energetically;
her arms are powerful.
18 She realizes that her trading is successful;
she doesn't put out her lamp at night.

[o] Or *where or or* [p] Or *all children who are passing away*

[19] She puts her hands to the spindle;
her palms grasp the whorl.
[20] She reaches out to the needy;
she stretches out her hands to the poor.
[21] She doesn't fear for her household
when it snows,
because they are all dressed
in warm[q] clothes.
[22] She makes bedspreads for herself;
fine linen and purple are her clothing.
[23] Her husband is known in the city gates
when he sits with the elders
of the land.
[24] She makes garments and sells them;
she supplies sashes to traders.
[25] Strength and honor are her clothing;
she is confident about the future.
[26] Her mouth is full of wisdom;
kindly teaching is on her tongue.
[27] She is vigilant over the activities
of her household;
she doesn't eat the food of laziness.
[28] Her children bless her;
her husband praises her:
[29] "Many women act competently,
but you surpass them all!"
[30] Charm is deceptive
and beauty fleeting,
but a woman who fears the LORD
is to be praised.
[31] Let her share in the results
of her work;
let her deeds praise her
in the city gates.

ECCLESIASTES

Opening motto

1 The words of the Teacher of the Assembly,[a]
David's son, king in Jerusalem:
[2] Perfectly pointless,[b] says the Teacher,
perfectly pointless.
Everything is pointless.

Some things are inevitable

[3] What do people gain
from all the hard work
that they work so hard at under the sun?
[4] A generation goes,
and a generation comes,
but the earth remains as it always has.
[5] The sun rises, the sun sets;
it returns panting to the place
where it dawns.
[6] The wind blows to the south,
goes around to the north;
around and around blows the wind;
the wind returns to its rounds again.
[7] All streams flow to the sea,
but the sea is never full;
to the place where the rivers flow,
there they continue to flow.
[8] All words[c] are tiring;
no one is able to speak.
The eye isn't satisfied with seeing,
neither is the ear filled up by hearing.
[9] Whatever has happened—
that's what will happen again;
whatever has occurred—
that's what will occur again.
There's nothing new under the sun.
[10] People may say about something: "Look
at this! It's new!" But it was already around
for ages before us. [11] There's no remembrance of things in the past, nor of things
to come in the future. Neither will there be
any remembrance among those who come
along in the future.

The Teacher's quest

[12] I am the Teacher. I was king over Israel
in Jerusalem.
[13] I applied my mind to investigate and to
explore by wisdom all that happens under
heaven. It's an unhappy obsession that God
has given to human beings.
[14] When I observed all that happens
under the sun, I realized that everything is
pointless, a chasing after wind.
[15] What's crooked can't be straightened;
what isn't there can't be counted.

[q] LXX; MT *red* [a] Or *Gatherer* or *Convener* or *Assembler* (Heb *Qoheleth*); see also 1:2, 12; 7:27; 12:8, 9, 10.
[b] Or *meaningless* or *vapor* or *puff of air* (Heb *hebel*, which often occurs in the book) [c] Or *things*

16 I said to myself, Look here, I have grown much wiser than any who ruled over Jerusalem before me. My mind has absorbed great wisdom and knowledge. 17 But when I set my mind to understand wisdom, and also to understand madness and folly, I realized that this too was just wind chasing.

18 Remember:

In much wisdom is much aggravation;
 the more knowledge, the more pain.

2 I said to myself,[d] Come, I will make you[e] experience pleasure; enjoy what is good! But this too was pointless! 2 Merriment, I thought, is madness; pleasure, of no use at all. 3 I tried cheering myself with wine and by embracing folly—with wisdom still guiding me—until I might see what is really worth doing in the few days that human beings have under heaven.

4 I took on great projects: I built houses for myself, planted vineyards for myself. 5 I made gardens and parks for myself, planting every kind of fruit tree in them. 6 I made reservoirs for myself to water my lush groves. 7 I acquired male servants and female servants; I even had slaves born in my house. I also had great herds of cattle and sheep, more than any who preceded me in Jerusalem. 8 I amassed silver and gold for myself, the treasures of kings and provinces. I acquired male and female singers for myself, along with every human luxury, treasure chests galore![f] 9 So I became far greater than all who preceded me in Jerusalem. Moreover, my wisdom stood by me. 10 I refrained from nothing that my eyes desired. I refused my heart no pleasure. Indeed, my heart found pleasure from the results of my hard work; that was the reward from all my hard work. 11 But when I surveyed all that my hands had done, and what I had worked so hard to achieve, I realized that it was pointless—a chasing after wind. Nothing is to be gained under the sun.

12 My reflections then turned to wisdom, madness, and folly. What can the king's heir do but what has already been done? 13 I saw that wisdom is more beneficial than folly, as light is more beneficial than darkness.

14 The wise have eyes in their head,
 but fools walk around in darkness.

But I also realized that the same fate happens to both of them. 15 So I thought to myself, What happens to the fool will also happen to me. So why have I been so very wise? I said to myself, This too is pointless. 16 There is no eternal memory of the wise any more than the foolish,[g] because everyone is forgotten before long. How can the wise die just like the fool? 17 So I hated life, because the things that happen under the sun were troublesome to me. Definitely, everything is pointless—just wind chasing.

18 I hated the things I worked so hard for here under the sun, because I will have to leave them to someone who comes after me. 19 And who knows whether that one will be wise or foolish? Either way, that person will have control over the results of all my hard work and wisdom here under the sun. That too is pointless. 20 I then gave myself up to despair, as I thought about all my laborious hard work under the sun, 21 because sometimes those who have worked hard with wisdom, knowledge, and skill must leave the results of their hard work as a possession to those who haven't worked hard for it. This too is pointless—it's a terrible wrong. 22 I mean, What do people get for all their hard work and struggles under the sun? 23 All their days are pain, and their work is aggravation; even at night, their hearts don't find rest. This too is pointless.

24 There's nothing better for human beings than to eat, drink, and experience pleasure in their hard work. I also saw that this is from God's hand— 25 Who can eat and find enjoyment otherwise?— 26 because God gives wisdom, knowledge, and joy to those who please God. But to those who are offensive,[h] God gives the task of hoarding and accumulating, but only so as to give it all to those who do please God. This too is pointless and a chasing after wind.

[d] Or *in my heart; mind* [e] Or *the self* (or *heart; mind*) [f] Or *many secondary wives* [g] Or *The wise and the foolish alike are never remembered.* [h] Or *to those who sin*

A season for everything

3 There's a season for everything
and a time for every matter
under the heavens:
2 a time for giving birth
and a time for dying,
a time for planting and a time for
uprooting what was planted,
3 a time for killing and a time for healing,
a time for tearing down
and a time for building up,
4 a time for crying and a time for laughing,
a time for mourning
and a time for dancing,
5 a time for throwing stones
and a time for gathering stones,
a time for embracing
and a time for avoiding embraces,
6 a time for searching
and a time for losing,
a time for keeping
and a time for throwing away,
7 a time for tearing
and a time for repairing,
a time for keeping silent
and a time for speaking,
8 a time for loving and a time for hating,
a time for war and a time for peace.

Hard work

9 What do workers gain from all their
hard work? 10 I have observed the task that
God has given human beings. 11 God has
made everything fitting in its time, but has
also placed eternity in their hearts, without
enabling them to discover what God has
done from beginning to end.

12 I know that there's nothing better for
them but to enjoy themselves and do what's
good while they live. 13 Moreover, this is
the gift of God: that all people should eat,
drink, and enjoy the results of their hard
work. 14 I know that whatever God does
will last forever; it's impossible to add to
it or take away from it. God has done this
so that people are reverent before him.[i]
15 Whatever happens has already happened,
and whatever will happen has already happened before. And God looks after what is
driven away.[j]

Enjoy what you do now

16 I saw something else under the sun: in
the place of justice, there was wickedness;
and in the place of what was right, there was
wickedness again! 17 I thought to myself,
God will judge both righteous and wicked
people, because there's a time for every
matter and every deed. 18 I also thought,
Where human beings are concerned, God
tests them to show them that they are but
animals 19 because human beings and animals share the same fate. One dies just like
the other—both have the same life-breath.
Humans are no better off than animals because everything is pointless.
20 All go to the same place:
all are from the dust;
all return to the dust.
21 Who knows if a human being's life-
breath rises upward while an animal's
life-breath descends into the earth? 22 So I
perceived that there was nothing better for
human beings but to enjoy what they do
because that's what they're allotted in life.
Who, really, is able to see what will happen
in the future?

Death is better than oppression

4 When I next observed all the oppres-
sions that take place under the sun, I
saw the tears of the oppressed—and they
have no one to comfort them. Their oppressors wield power—but they have no one to
comfort them. 2 So I declare that the dead,
who have already died, are more fortunate
than the living, who are still alive. 3 But happier than both are those who have never
existed, who haven't witnessed the terrible
things that happen under the sun.

Envy and loneliness

4 I also observed that people work hard
and become good at what they do only out
of mutual envy. This too is pointless, just
wind chasing.

[i] Or *to inspire awe before the divine* [j] Or *God seeks out what is pursued,* or *God seeks what has gone by,* or *God seeks the pursued;* Heb uncertain

5 Fools fold their hands
and eat their own flesh.
6 But better is resting with one handful
than working hard for two fistfuls
and chasing after wind.
7 Next, I saw under the sun something
else that was pointless: 8 There are people
who are utterly alone, with no companions,
not even a child or a sibling. Yet they work
hard without end, never satisfied with their
wealth. So for whom am I working so hard
and depriving myself of enjoyment? This
too is pointless and a terrible obsession.
9 Two are better than one because they
have a good return for their hard work. 10 If
either should fall, one can pick up the other.
But how miserable are those who fall and
don't have a companion to help them up!
11 Also, if two lie down together, they can
stay warm. But how can anyone stay warm
alone? 12 Also, one can be overpowered, but
two together can put up resistance. A three-
ply cord doesn't easily snap.
13 A poor but wise youth is better than
an old and foolish king, who no longer listens to advice. 14 He emerged from prison
to become king, even though during his
rule a poor child[k] is born. 15 I saw all who
live and walk under the sun following the
next youth who would rise to take his place.
16 There was no counting the number of
people he ruled, but those who came later
aren't happy with him. This too is pointless
and a chasing after wind.

Listen and speak carefully

5 Watch[l] your steps when you go to God's
house. It's more acceptable to listen
than to offer the fools' sacrifice—they have
no idea that they're acting wrongly. 2 Don't[m]
be quick with your mouth or say anything
hastily before God, because God is in
heaven, but you are on earth. Therefore, let
your words be few.
3 Remember:
Dreams come with many cares,
and the voice of fools
with many words.

4 When you make a promise to God, fulfill
it without delay because God has no pleasure in fools. Fulfill what you promise. 5 Better not to make a promise than to make a
promise without fulfilling it. 6 Don't let your
mouth make a sinner of you, and don't say
to the messenger: "It was a mistake!" Otherwise, God may become angry at such talk
and destroy what you have accomplished.
7 Remember:
When dreams multiply,
so do pointless thoughts
and excessive speech.
Therefore, fear God.

Hoarding wealth

8 If you witness the poor being oppressed
or the violation of what is just and right
in some territory, don't be surprised because a high official watches over another,
and yet others stand over them. 9 But the
land's yield should be for everyone if the
field is cultivated.[n] 10 The money lover isn't
satisfied with money; neither is the lover
of wealth satisfied with income. This too
is pointless. 11 When good things flow, so
do those who consume them. But what do
owners benefit from such goods, except
to feast their eyes on them? 12 Sweet is the
worker's sleep, whether there's a lot or little
to eat; but the excess of the wealthy won't
let them sleep.
13 I have seen a sickening tragedy under
the sun: people hoard their wealth to their
own detriment. 14 Then that wealth is lost in
a bad business venture so that when they
have children, they are left with nothing.
15 Just as they came from their mother's
womb naked, naked they'll return, ending
up just like they started. All their hard work
produces nothing—nothing they can take
with them. 16 This too is a sickening tragedy: they must pass on just as they arrived.
What then do they gain from working so
hard for wind? 17 What's more, they constantly eat in darkness, with much aggravation, grief, and anger.
18 This is the one good thing I've seen: it's

[k] Possibly the youth of 4:13; or *He emerged from prison to become king, even though he was born poor in the kingdom.*
[l] 4:17 in Heb [m] 5:1 in Heb [n] Correction; Heb uncertain; or *The land's advantage in everything is this: a king for a plowed field.*

appropriate for people to eat, drink, and find
enjoyment in all their hard work under the
sun during the brief lifetime that God gives
them because that's their lot in life. 19 Also,
whenever God gives people wealth and
riches and enables them to enjoy it, to accept
their place in the world[o] and to find pleasure
in their hard work—all this is God's gift.
20 Indeed, people shouldn't brood too much
over the days of their lives because God gives
an answer in their hearts' joy.

Controlled appetite

6 I saw a tragedy under the sun, and it
weighs heavily upon humanity. 2 God
may give some people plenty of wealth,
riches, and glory so that they lack nothing
they desire. But God doesn't enable them to
enjoy it; instead, a stranger enjoys it. This
is pointless and a sickening tragedy. 3 Some
people may have one hundred children and
live a long life. But no matter how long they
live, if they aren't content with life's good
things, I say that even a stillborn child with
no grave is better off than they are.[p] 4 Because that child arrives pointlessly, then
passes away in darkness. Darkness covers
its name. 5 It hasn't seen the sun or experienced anything. But it has more peace than
those 6 who live a thousand years twice
over but don't enjoy life's good things. Isn't
everyone heading to the same destina-
tion? 7 All the hard work of humans is for
the mouth, but the appetite is never full.
8 What advantage do the wise have over the
foolish? Or what do the poor gain by knowing how to conduct themselves before the
living? 9 It's better to enjoy what's at hand
than to have an insatiable appetite. This too
is pointless, just wind chasing.

10 Whatever happens has already been
designated, and human beings are fully
known. They can't contend with the one
who is stronger than they are. 11 Because
the more words increase, the more everything is pointless. What do people gain
by it? 12 Because who knows what's good
for human beings during life, during their
brief pointless life, which will pass away
like a shadow? Who can say what the future
holds for people under the sun?

Wisdom is better than wealth

7 A good name is better than fine oil,
and the day of death
better than the birthday.
2 It is better to go to a house in mourning
than to a house party,
because that is everyone's destiny;
and the living should take it to heart.
3 Aggravation is better than merriment
because a sad face may lead
to a glad heart.
4 The wise heart
is in the house that mourns,
but the foolish heart
is in the house that rejoices.
5 It is better to obey the reprimand
of the wise
than to listen to the song of fools,
6 because the fool's merriment
is like nettles crackling under a kettle.
That too is pointless.
7 Oppression turns the wise into fools;
a bribe corrupts the heart.
8 The end of something
is better than its beginning.
Patience is better than arrogance.
9 Don't be too quick to get angry
because anger lives in the fool's heart.
10 Don't ask, "How is it that the former
days were better than these?"
because it isn't wise to ask this.
11 Wisdom is as good as[q] an inheritance—
an advantage for those who see the sun.
12 Wisdom's protection is
like the protection of money;
the advantage of knowledge is that
wisdom preserves the lives
of its possessors.

Good times and bad

13 Consider God's work! Who can
straighten what God has made crooked?
14 When times are good, enjoy the good;
when times are bad, consider: God has

[o] Or *portion in life,* as in 5:18 [p] Correction; Heb puts the lack of burial site with those who do not enjoy life's good things. [q] Or *Wisdom is good with*

made the former as well as the latter so
that people can't discover anything that
will come to be after them.
15 I have seen everything in my pointless lifetime: the righteous person may die
in spite of their righteousness; then again,
the wicked may live long in spite of their
wickedness. 16 Don't be too righteous or too
wise, or you may be dumbfounded.[r] 17 Don't
be too wicked and don't be a fool, or you
may die before your time. 18 It's good that
you take hold of one of these without letting go of the other because the one who
fears God will go forth with both.
19 Wisdom makes a wise person stronger
than ten rulers who are in a city. 20 Remember: there's no one on earth so righteous as
to do good only and never make a mistake.[s]
21 Don't worry about all the things people
say, so you don't hear your servant cursing
you. 22 After all, you know that you've often
cursed others yourself!

Life is complicated

23 I tested all of this by wisdom. I thought,
I will be wise, but it eluded me.
24 All that happens is elusive and utterly unfathomable. Who can grasp it? 25 I
turned my mind to know, to investigate,
and to seek wisdom, along with an account of things, to know that wickedness
is foolishness and folly is madness.
26 I found one woman more bitter than
death: she who is a trap, her heart a snare,
her hands shackles. Anyone who pleases God
escapes her, but a sinner is trapped by her.
27 See, this is what I found, says the Teacher,
examining one matter after another to account for things. 28 But there's something
that I constantly searched for but couldn't
find: I found one man among a thousand, but
I couldn't find a woman among any of these.[t]
29 See, this alone I found: God made
human beings straightforward, but they
search for many complications.

8 Who is wise? And who knows
the meaning of anything?
A person's wisdom
brightens the expression;
it changes the hardness
of someone's face.

Watch out for power

2 Keep[u] the king's command
as you would keep a solemn pledge.
3 Don't be dismayed; leave his presence.
Don't linger in a harmful situation
because he can do whatever he wants!
4 Because the king's word has authority,
no one can say to him,
"What are you doing?"
5 Whoever keeps a command will meet no
harm, and the wise heart knows the right
time and the right way 6 because there's a
right time and right way for every matter.
But human misfortunes are overwhelming
7 because no one knows what will happen,
and no one can say when something might
happen. 8 No one has control over the life-
breath,[v] to retain it, and there's no control
over the day of death. There's no release
from war, and wickedness won't deliver
those who practice it.
9 I observed all of this as I paid attention
to all that happens under the sun. Sometimes people exercise power over each other
to their detriment. 10 Then I saw the wicked
brought to their graves, with people processing from a holy place,[w] while those who
had lived honestly were neglected in the
city. This too is pointless.
11 The condemnation for wicked acts isn't
carried out quickly; that's why people dare
to do evil. 12 Wrongdoers may commit a
hundred crimes but still live long lives. But
I also know that it will go well for those who
fear God, for those who are reverent before
God. 13 But it will not go well for the wicked;
they won't live long at all because they aren't
reverent before God. 14 Here's another thing
that happens on earth that is pointless: the
righteous get what the wicked deserve, and
the wicked get what the righteous deserve. I
say that this too is pointless.

Enjoy life

15 So I commend enjoyment because there's
nothing better for people to do under the sun

r Or *destroyed* s Or *and never sin* t Heb uncertain u Correction; Heb *I (say?) keep* v Or *wind* w Or *temple*

but to eat, drink, and be glad. This is what will
accompany them in their hard work, during
the lifetime that God gives under the sun.
16 Then I set my mind to know wisdom
and to observe the business that happens on earth, even going without sleep
day and night. 17 I observed all the work of
God—that no one can grasp what happens
under the sun. Those who strive to know
can't grasp it. Even the wise who are set on
knowing are unable to grasp it.

Everyone faces the same fate

9 So I considered all of this carefully, examining all of it: The righteous and the
wise and their deeds are in God's hand, along
with both love and hate. People don't know
anything that's ahead of them. 2 Everything
is the same for everyone. The same fate
awaits the righteous and the wicked, the
good and the bad,[x] the pure and the impure,
those who sacrifice and those who don't sacrifice. The good person is like the wrongdoer;
the same holds for those who make solemn
pledges and those who are afraid to swear.
3 This is the sad thing about all that happens
under the sun: the same fate awaits everyone. Moreover, the human heart is full of
evil; people's minds are full of madness while
they are alive, and afterward they die. 4 Whoever is among the living can be certain about
this. A living dog is definitely better off than
a dead lion, 5 because the living know that
they will die. But the dead know nothing at
all. There is no more reward for them; even
the memory of them is lost. 6 Their love and
their hate, as well as their zeal, are already
long gone. They will never again have a stake
in all that happens under the sun.
7 Go, eat your food joyfully and drink
your wine happily because God has already
accepted what you do. 8 Let your garments
always be white; don't run short of oil for
your head. 9 Enjoy life with your dearly loved
spouse all the days of your pointless life that
God[y] gives you under the sun—all the days
of your pointless life![z]—because that's your
part to play[a] in this life and in your hard work
under the sun. 10 Whatever you are capable of
doing, do with all your might because there's
no work, thought, knowledge, or wisdom in
the grave,[b] which is where you are headed.

Listen to common wisdom, not fools

11 I also observed under the sun that the
race doesn't always go to the swift, nor the
battle to the mighty, nor food to the wise,
nor wealth to the intelligent, nor favor to the
knowledgeable, because accidents can happen to anyone. 12 People most definitely don't
know when their time will come. Like fish
tragically caught in a net or like birds trapped
in a snare, so are human beings caught in a
time of tragedy that suddenly falls to them.
13 I also observed the following example
of wisdom under the sun—it impressed me
greatly: 14 There was a small town with only
a few residents. A mighty king came against
it, surrounded it, and waged a terrible war
against it. 15 Now there lived in that town a
poor but wise man who saved everyone by
his wisdom. But no one remembered that
poor man. 16 So I thought, Wisdom is better
than might, but the wisdom of commoners
is despised and their words aren't heeded.
17 The calm words of the wise are better
heeded than the racket caused by a ruler
among fools.
18 Wisdom is better than weapons of war,
but one incompetent person destroys much
good.

10 As dead flies spoil the perfumer's oil,
so a little folly outweighs
wisdom and honor.
2 The mind of the wise
tends toward the right,
but the mind of the fool toward the left.
3 Fools lack all sense
even when they walk down the street;
they show everyone that they are fools.
4 If a ruler's temper rises against you,
don't leave your post, because calmness
alleviates great offenses.

5 There's an evil that I have seen under
the sun: the kind of mistake that comes
from people in power. 6 Fools are appointed

[x] LXX [y] Or *he* or *that are given you* [z] This phrase is missing in some LXX sources, Syr, and Tg. [a] Or *portion*
[b] Or *underworld;* Heb *Sheol*

to high posts, while the rich sit in lowly positions. 7 I have seen slaves on horseback,
while princes walk on foot like slaves.

8 Whoever digs a pit may fall into it,
and whoever breaks through a wall
may be bitten by a snake.
9 Whoever quarries stones
may be injured by them;
whoever splits logs
may be endangered by them.
10 If an ax is dull
and one doesn't sharpen it first,
then one must exert more force.
It's profitable to be skillful and wise.
11 If a snake bites before it's charmed,
then there's no profit
for the snake charmer.

12 Words from a wise person's mouth are
beneficial, but fools are devoured by their
own lips.

13 Fools start out talking foolishness and
end up speaking awful nonsense.

14 Fools talk too much! No one knows
what will happen; no one can say what will
happen in the future.

15 The hard work of fools tires them out
because they don't even know the way to
town!

16 Too bad for you, land,
whose king is a boy
and whose princes feast in the morning.
17 Happy is the land
whose king is dignified
and whose princes feast
at the right time for energy,
not for drunkenness.
18 Through laziness, the roof sags;
through idle hands, the house leaks.
19 Feasts are made for laughter,
wine cheers the living,
and money answers everything.[c]

20 Don't curse a king even in private;
don't curse the rich in your bedroom, because a bird could carry your voice; some
winged creature could report what you said!

Take risks; life is short

11 Send your bread out on the water because, in the course of time, you may
find it again. 2 Give a portion to seven
people, even to eight: you don't know what
disaster may come upon the land. 3 If clouds
fill up, they will empty out rain on the
earth. If a tree falls, whether to the south
or to the north, wherever it falls, there it
will lie. 4 Those who watch the wind blow
will never sow, and those who observe the
clouds will never reap. 5 Just as you don't
understand what the life-breath does in the
fetus[d] inside a pregnant woman's womb, so
you can't understand the work of God, who
makes everything happen. 6 Scatter your
seed in the morning, and in the evening
don't be idle because you don't know which
will succeed, this one or that, or whether
both will be equally good.

7 Sweet is the light, and it's pleasant for
the eyes to see the sun. 8 Even those who
live many years should take pleasure in
them all. But they should be mindful that
there will also be many dark days. Everything that happens is pointless.

9 Rejoice, young person, while you are
young! Your heart should make you happy in
your prime. Follow your heart's inclinations
and whatever your eyes see, but know this:
God will call you to account for all of these
things. 10 Remove anxiety from your heart,
banish pain from your body, because youth
and the dawn of life are pointless too.

Troubling days to come

12 Remember your creator
in your prime,
before the days of trouble arrive,
and those years, about which you'll say,
"I take no pleasure in these"—
2 before the sun and the light grow dark,
the moon and the stars too,
before the clouds return after the rain;
3 on the day when the housekeepers
tremble and the strong men stoop;
when the women who grind
stop working because they're so few,
and those who look
through the windows grow dim;
4 when the doors to the street are shut,
when the sound of the mill fades,

[c] Or *money is everyone's answer.* [d] Correction with Tg; MT *like the bones*

the sound of the bird rises,
and all the singers come down low;
5 when people are afraid of things above
and of terrors along the way;
when the almond tree blanches,
the locust droops,
and the caper-berry comes to nothing;[e]
when the human goes
to the eternal abode,
with mourners all around in the street;
6 before the silver cord snaps
and the gold bowl shatters;
the jar is broken at the spring
and the wheel is crushed at the pit;
7 before dust returns to the earth
as it was before
and the life-breath returns to God
who gave it.

Motto and conclusion

8 Perfectly pointless, says the Teacher, everything is pointless.

9 Additionally: Because the Teacher was wise, he constantly taught the people knowledge. He listened and investigated. He composed many proverbs. 10 The Teacher searched for pleasing words, and he wrote truthful words honestly.

11 The words of the wise
are like iron-tipped prods;
the collected sayings of the masters
are like nails fixed firmly
by a shepherd.[f]
12 Be careful, my child,
of anything beyond them!

There's no end to the excessive production of scrolls. Studying too much wearies the body. 13 So this is the end of the matter; all has been heard. Worship God and keep God's commandments because this is what everyone must do. 14 God will definitely bring every deed to judgment, including every hidden thing, whether good or bad.

SONG OF SONGS

1 The Song of Songs, which is for Solomon.

Mutual admiration

[Woman][a]

2 If only he would give me
some of his kisses . . .

Oh, your loving is sweeter than wine!
3 Your fragrance is sweet;
your very name is perfume.
That's why the young women love you.
4 Take me along with you; let's run!

My king has brought me
into his chambers, saying,
"Let's exult and rejoice in you.
Let's savor your loving more than wine.
No wonder they all love you!"

5 Dark am I, and lovely,
daughters of Jerusalem—
like the black tents of the Kedar nomads,
like the curtains of Solomon's palace.
6 Don't stare at me because I'm darkened
by the sun's gaze.
My own brothers were angry with me.
They made me a caretaker
of the vineyards—
but I couldn't care
for my own vineyard.

7 Tell me, you whom I love
with all my heart—
where do you pasture your flock,
where do you rest them at noon?—
so I don't wander around with the
flocks of your companions.

[Man]

8 If you don't know your way,
most beautiful of women,
then follow the tracks of the herds
and graze your little goats
by the tents of the shepherds.

[e] Heb uncertain [f] Or *fixed by one shepherd* [a] Identification of speakers here and throughout the Song is hypothetical and in several cases uncertain.

9 I picture you, my dearest,
as a mare among Pharaoh's chariots!
10 Lovely are your cheeks,
adorned with ear hoops;
your neck, with beads.
11 Let's make hoops of gold
beaded with silver for you!

[Woman]

12 With my king close by,
my perfume filled the air.
13 A sachet of myrrh is my love to me,
lying all night between my breasts.
14 A cluster of henna flowers
is my love to me
in the desert gardens of En-gedi.

[Man]

15 Look at you—so beautiful, my dearest!
Look at you—so beautiful!
Your eyes are doves!

[Woman]

16 Look at you—so beautiful, my love!
Yes, delightful!
Yes, our bed is lush and green!
17 The ceilings of our chambers are cedars;
our rafters, cypresses.

Love in bloom

[Woman]

2 I'm a rose of the Sharon plain,
a lily of the valleys.

[Man]

2 Like a lily among thornbushes,
so is my dearest
among the young women.

[Woman]

3 Like an apple tree among the wild trees,
so is my lover among the young men.
In his shade I take pleasure in sitting,
and his fruit is sweet to my taste.
4 He has brought me to the house of wine;
his banner raised over me is love.

5 Sustain me with raisin cakes,
strengthen me with apples,
for I'm weak with love!
6 His left arm is beneath my head,
his right embraces me.

7 Make a solemn pledge,
daughters of Jerusalem,
by the gazelles or the wild deer:
Don't rouse, don't arouse love
until it desires.

8 Listen! It's my lover: here he comes now,
leaping upon the mountains,
bounding over the hills.
9 My lover is like a gazelle
or a young stag.
Here he stands now,
outside our wall,
peering through the windows,
peeking through the lattices.

10 My lover spoke and said to me,
"Rise up, my dearest,
my fairest, and go.
11 Here, the winter is past;
the rains have come and gone.
12 Blossoms have appeared in the land;
the season of singing[b] has arrived,
and the sound of the turtledove
is heard in our land.
13 The green fruit is on the fig tree,
and the grapevines in bloom
are fragrant.
Rise up,[c] my dearest,
my fairest, and go.
14 My dove—in the rock crevices,
hidden in the cliff face—
let me catch sight of you;
let me hear your voice!
The sound of your voice is sweet,
and the sight of you is lovely."

15 Catch foxes for us—
those little foxes
that spoil vineyards,
now that our vineyards are in bloom!

16 I belong to my lover
and he belongs to me—
the one grazing among the lilies.
17 Before the day breeze blows
and the shadows flee,

[b]Or *pruning* [c]LXX and Kethib add *go*; but Qere, DSS, Vulg, Syr, and Tg lack the verb; cf 2:10.

turn about, my love; be like a gazelle
or a young stag
upon the jagged mountains.[d]

The search

[Woman]

3 Upon my bed, night after night,
I looked for the one whom I love
with all my heart.
I looked for him but couldn't find him.[e]
2 "I will rise now
and go all around the city,
through the streets and the squares.
I will look for the one whom I love
with all my heart."
I looked for him but couldn't find him.
3 The guards found me,
those who make their rounds
in the city.
"The one whom I love
with all my heart—
have you seen him?"
4 No sooner did I depart from them
than I found the one whom I love
with all my heart.
I held on to him
and now I won't let him go,
until I've brought him
to my mother's house,
to the chamber of the one
who conceived me.
5 I place you under oath,
daughters of Jerusalem,
by the gazelles or the wild deer:
don't rouse, don't arouse love
until it desires.

Visions of grandeur

6 Who is this,
coming up from the wilderness,
like pillars of smoke?
She is perfumed
with myrrh and frankincense,
selected from all
the spice merchant's powders.

7 Picture Solomon's bed—
sixty heroic men round about it,
all from the heroes of Israel,
8 all of them skilled with the sword,
expert in warfare,
each with his sword ready at his thigh
against terrors that come by night.
9 King Solomon made a canopied couch
for himself
from the trees of Lebanon.
10 Its pillars he made of silver,
its covering, cloth of gold,
its cushions, royal purple;
its interior inlaid with love.
Daughters of Jerusalem, 11 go forth!
Look, daughters of Zion—
on King Solomon wearing the crown
with which his mother crowned him
on the day of his wedding,
on the day of his heart's joy.

In praise of her

[Man]

4 Look at you—so beautiful, my dearest!
Look at you—so beautiful!
Your eyes are doves
behind the veil of your hair!
Your hair is like a flock of goats
as they stream down Mount Gilead.
2 Your teeth are like newly shorn ewes
as they come up
from the washing pool—
all of them perfectly matched,
not one of them lacks its twin.
3 Like a crimson ribbon are your lips;
when you smile, it is lovely.
Like a slice of pomegranate
is the curve of your face
behind the veil of your hair.
4 Like David's tower is your neck,
splendidly built!
A thousand shields are hung upon it—
all the weapons of the warriors.
5 Your two breasts are like two fawns,
twins of a gazelle doe,
that graze among the lilies.
6 Before the day breeze blows
and the shadows flee,
I will be off to the mountain of myrrh,
to the hill of frankincense.
7 You are utterly beautiful, my dearest;
there's not a single flaw in you.

[d] Or *upon the mountains of Bether*; cf 8:14 *mountains of spice* [e] LXX adds *I called him, but he didn't answer me*; cf 5:6.

Garden of delight

[Man]

8 Come down with me from Lebanon,
my bride—
if only you would come down
with me from Lebanon.
Descend from the peak of Amana,
from the peaks of Senir and Hermon,
from the lions' dens,
from the mountain lairs of leopards.
9 You have captured my heart,
my sister,[f] my bride!
You have captured my heart
with one glance from your eyes,
with one strand of your necklace.
10 How beautiful is your loving,
my sister, my bride!
Your loving is so much better
than wine,
and your fragrance better
than any perfume!
11 Sweetness drops from your lips,
my bride;
honey and milk are
under your tongue,
and the fragrance of your garments
is like the fragrance of Lebanon.
12 An enclosed garden is
my sister, my bride;
an enclosed pool, a sealed spring.
13 Your limbs are
an orchard of pomegranates
with all kinds of luscious fruit,
henna, and spices:
14 nard and saffron,
sweet cane and cinnamon,
with all scented woods,
myrrh, and aloes,
with the very choicest perfumes!
15 You are a garden spring,
a well of fresh water,
streams from Lebanon.
16 Stir, north wind, and come,
south wind!
Blow upon my garden;
let its perfumes flow!

[Woman]

Let my love come to his garden;
let him eat its luscious fruit!

[Man]

5 I have come to my garden, my sister,
my bride!
I have gathered my myrrh and my spices.
I have eaten my honeycomb
with my honey;
I have drunk my wine and my milk.

Eat, dear friends!
Drink and get drunk on love!

A missed encounter

[Woman]

2 I was sleeping,
but my heart was awake.
A sound! My love is knocking:

[Man]

"Open for me, my sister, my dearest,
my dove, my perfect one!
My head is soaked with dew,
my hair, with the night mists."

[Woman]

3 "I have taken off my tunic—
why should I put it on again?
I have bathed my feet—
why should I get them dirty?"
4 My love put his hand in
through the latch hole,
and my body ached for him.
5 I rose; I went to open for my love,
and my hands dripped myrrh,
my fingers, liquid myrrh,
over the handles of the lock.
6 I went and opened for my love,
but my love had turned, gone away.
I nearly died when he turned away.
I looked for him but couldn't find him.
I called out to him,
but he didn't answer me.
7 They found me—the guards
who make their rounds in the city.
They struck me, bruised me.
They took my shawl away from me,
those guards of the city walls!
8 I place you under oath,
daughters of Jerusalem:
If you find my love,
what should you tell him?
That I'm weak with love!

[f] *Sister* here and below is a common term in ancient love poetry; it doesn't imply blood relation.

[Daughters of Jerusalem]

9 How is your lover different
from any other lover,
you who are the most beautiful
of women?
How is your lover different
from any other lover,
that you make us swear a solemn pledge?

In praise of him

[Woman]

10 My lover is radiant and ruddy;
he stands out among ten thousand!
11 His head is finest gold;
his wavy hair, black as a raven.
12 His eyes are like doves
by channels of water.
They are bathing in milk,
sitting by brimming pools.
13 His cheeks are like fragrant plantings,
towers of spices.
His lips are lilies
dripping liquid myrrh.
14 His arms are gold cylinders
studded with jewels.
His belly is smooth ivory
encrusted with sapphires.
15 His thighs are pillars of whitest stone
set on pedestals of gold.
His appearance—like Lebanon,
stately, like the cedars.
16 His mouth is everything sweet,
every bit of him desirable.

This is my love, this my dearest,
daughters of Jerusalem!

[Daughters of Jerusalem]

6 Which way did your lover go,
you who are the most beautiful
of women?
Which way did your lover turn,
that we may look for him
along with you?

[Woman]

2 My lover has gone down to his garden,
to the fragrant plantings,
to graze in the gardens,
to gather the lilies.
3 I belong to my lover
and my lover belongs to me—
the one grazing among the lilies.

An overwhelming sight

[Man]

4 You are as beautiful, my dearest,
as Tirzah,
as lovely as Jerusalem,
formidable as those lofty sights.
5 Turn your eyes away from me,
for they overwhelm me!

Your hair is like a flock of goats
as they stream down from Gilead.
6 Your teeth are like a flock of ewes
as they come up
from the washing pool—
all of them perfectly matched,
not one of them lacks its twin.
7 Like a slice of pomegranate
is the curve of your face
behind the veil of your hair.
8 There may be sixty queens
and eighty secondary wives,
young women beyond counting,
9 but my dove, my perfect one,
is one of a kind.
To her mother she's the only one,
radiant to the one who bore her.
Young women see her
and declare her fortunate;
queens and secondary wives praise her.

10 Who is this, gazing down
like the morning star,
beautiful as the full moon,
radiant as the sun,
formidable as those lofty sights?

Transported

[Man]

11 To the nut grove I went down
to look upon the fresh growth
in the valley,
to see whether the vine was in flower,
whether the pomegranates
had bloomed.
12 I hardly knew myself;
she had set me in an official's chariot![g]

[g]Or *I hardly knew what happened; my passion set me in an official's chariot!* LXX, Vulg *Aminadab's chariots*; Heb uncertain

Graceful dancer

[Man]

13 [h]Come back, come back, Shulammite![i]
Come back, come back,
so we may admire you.
How you all admire the Shulammite
as she whirls between
two circles of dancers!
7 How graceful are your sandaled feet,
willing woman!
The smooth curves of your thighs—
like fine jewelry,
the work of an artist's hands!
2 Your navel, cupped like the full moon—
may it never lack spiced wine!
Your belly is a mound
of winnowed wheat
edged with lilies.
3 Your two breasts are like two fawns,
twins of a gazelle doe;
4 your neck, like a tower of ivory;
your eyes, pools in Heshbon,
by the gate of that lordly city.[j]
Your profile is like
the tower of Lebanon,
looking out toward Damascus.
5 Your head crowns you
like Mount Carmel,
and your hair,
braided in royal purple—
a king is bound by the tresses!
6 You are so beautiful, so lovely—
my love, delightful one![k]
7 Your stately form resembles a date palm,
and your breasts
are like clustered fruit.
8 I say, "I will climb the palm tree;
I will hold its fruit!"
May your breasts be now
like grape clusters,
and the scent of your breath like apples!
9 Your palate is like excellent wine . . .

[Woman]

. . . flowing smoothly for my love,
gliding through the lips and teeth.[l]
10 I belong to my lover,
and his longing is only for me.

The ripeness of love

[Woman]

11 Come, my love:
Let's go out to the field
and rest all night
among the flowering henna.
12 Let's set out early for the vineyards.
We will see if the vines have budded
and the blossoms opened,
see if the pomegranates have bloomed.
There I'll give my loving to you.

13 The mandrakes give off their scent,
and at our doorways is every delicacy—
fresh or ripened—
my love, I have kept them
hidden for you.

Wishing

[Woman]

8 If only you were as my brother—
the one who nursed
at my mother's breast.
I would find you in the street and kiss you,
and no one would shame me for it.
2 I would lead you, I would bring you
to my mother's house;
she would teach me what to do.[m]
I would give you spiced wine to drink,
some of my fresh pomegranate juice.

3 His left arm is beneath my head,
and his right embraces me!

4 Make a solemn pledge,
daughters of Jerusalem,
never to rouse, never to arouse love
until it desires.

Love, strong and invaluable

[Daughters of Jerusalem]

5 Who is this coming up from the wilderness
leaning against her lover?

[Woman]

Under the apple tree I aroused you—
there, where your mother
labored with you,
there where, laboring, she bore you.

[h]7:1 in Heb [i]A name or title for the woman [j]Or *by the gate of Bath-rabbim* [k]With Syr and Aquila *daughter of delights;* MT *love in delights* or *love with every charm* [l]LXX, Syr, Vulg; MT *through the lips of those who sleep;* Heb uncertain [m]Or *you would teach me*; LXX, Syr *to my mother's house, and to the chamber of the one who conceived me* (cf 3:4)

6 Set me as a seal over your heart,
as a seal upon your arm,
for love is as strong as death,
passionate love unrelenting
as the grave.[n]
Its darts are darts of fire—
divine flame!
7 Rushing waters can't quench love;
rivers can't wash it away.
If someone gave
all his estate
in exchange for love,
he would be laughed
to utter shame.

[The Woman's Brothers]

8 Our sister is small;
she has no breasts.
What will we do for our sister
on the day that she
is spoken for?
9 If she is a city wall,
then we will build a turret of silver
on her.[o]
And if she is a door,
then we will barricade her[p]
with a panel of cedar.

[Woman]

10 I'm a city wall,
and my breasts are the towers.
So now I'm in his eyes
as one who brings peace.

[Man]

11 Solomon had a vineyard
in Baal-hamon.
He gave charge of the vineyard to keepers;
one would bring in exchange
for its fruit
a thousand pieces of silver.
12 My vineyard, my very own, is before me.
You can have the thousand, Solomon[q]—
with two hundred for those
who tend the fruit!

13 You who sit in the gardens,
my companions are listening
for your voice.
Let me hear it!

[Woman]

14 "Take flight, my love,
and be like a gazelle
or a young stag
on the mountains of spice!"

ISAIAH

1 The vision about Judah and Jerusalem that Isaiah, Amoz's son, saw in the days of Judah's kings Uzziah, Jotham, Ahaz, and Hezekiah.

Rebels condemned

2 Hear you heavens, and listen earth,
for the LORD has spoken:
I reared children; I raised them,
and they turned against me!
3 An ox knows its owner,
and a donkey its master's feeding trough.
But Israel doesn't know;
my people
don't behave intelligently.

4 Doom! Sinful nation,
people weighed down with crimes,
evildoing offspring, corrupt children!
They have abandoned the LORD,
despised the holy one of Israel;
they turned their backs on God.

5 Why do you invite further beatings?
Why continue to rebel?
Everyone's head throbs,
and everyone's heart fails.
6 From head to toe, none are well—
only bruises, cuts, and raw wounds,
not treated, not bandaged,
not soothed with oil.

7 Your country is deserted,
your cities burned with fire;
your land—strangers are devouring it
in plain sight.
It's a wasteland,
as when foreigners raid.

[n] Heb *Sheol* [o] Or *on it (the city wall)* [p] Or *it (the door)* [q] Cf 1 Kgs 11:3

8 Daughter Zion is left
like a small shelter in a vineyard,
like a hut in a cucumber field,
like a city besieged.[a]
9 If the LORD of heavenly forces
had not spared a few of us,
we would be like Sodom;
we would resemble Gomorrah.

Hands filled with bloodshed

10 Hear the LORD's word,
you leaders of Sodom.
Listen to our God's teaching,
people of Gomorrah!
11 What should I think
about all your sacrifices?
says the LORD.
I'm fed up with
entirely burned offerings of rams
and the fat of well-fed beasts.
I don't want the blood of bulls,
lambs, and goats.
12 When you come to appear before me,
who asked this from you,
this trampling of my temple's courts?
13 Stop bringing worthless offerings.
Your incense repulses me.
New moon, sabbath,
and the calling of an assembly—
I can't stand wickedness
with celebration!
14 I hate your new moons
and your festivals.
They've become a burden
that I'm tired of bearing.
15 When you extend your hands,
I'll hide my eyes from you.
Even when you pray for a long time,
I won't listen.
Your hands are stained with blood.
16 Wash! Be clean!
Remove your ugly deeds
from my sight.
Put an end to such evil;
17 learn to do good.
Seek justice:
help the oppressed;[b]
defend the orphan;
plead for the widow.

18 Come now, and let's settle this,
says the LORD.
Though your sins are like scarlet,
they will be white as snow.
If they are red as crimson,
they will become like wool.
19 If you agree and obey,
you will eat the best food of the land.
20 But if you refuse and rebel,
you will be devoured by the sword.
The LORD has said this.

Zion will be redeemed

21 This faithful town
has become a prostitute!
She was full of justice;
righteousness lived in her—
but now murderers.
22 Your silver has become impure;
your beer is diluted with water.
23 Your princes are rebels,
companions of thieves.
Everyone loves a bribe and pursues gifts.
They don't defend the orphan,
and the widow's cause
never reaches them.
24 Therefore, says the
LORD God of heavenly forces,
the mighty one of Israel:
Doom! I will vent my anger
against my foes;
I will take it out on my enemies,
25 and I will turn my hand against you.
I will refine your impurities as with lye,
and remove all your cinders.
26 Then I will restore your judges
as in earlier times,
and your counselors
as at the beginning.
After this you will be called
Righteous City, Faithful Town.

27 Zion will be redeemed by justice,
and those who change their lives
by righteousness.
28 But God will shatter
rebels and sinners alike;
those who abandon the LORD
will be finished.

[a]LXX, Vulg; MT *spared* [b]LXX, Vulg; MT *lead the oppressor*

29 You will be ashamed
of the oaks you once desired,
and embarrassed
by the gardens you once chose.
30 You will be like an oak
with withering leaves,
like a garden without water.
31 The strong will be like dry twigs,
their deeds like sparks;
the two will burn together,
with no one to extinguish them.

The LORD's mountain

2 This is what Isaiah, Amoz's son, saw concerning Judah and Jerusalem.
2 In the days to come
the mountain of the LORD's house
will be the highest of the mountains.
It will be lifted above the hills;
peoples will stream to it.
3 Many nations will go and say,
"Come, let's go up
to the LORD's mountain,
to the house of Jacob's God
so that he may teach us his ways
and we may walk in God's paths."
Instruction will come from Zion;
the LORD's word from Jerusalem.
4 God will judge between the nations,
and settle disputes of mighty nations.
Then they will beat
their swords into iron plows
and their spears into pruning tools.
Nation will not take up sword
against nation;
they will no longer learn
how to make war.

5 Come, house of Jacob,
let's walk by the LORD's light.

Everyone is brought low

6 You have abandoned your people,
house of Jacob.
They are full of sorcerers
from the east and fortune-tellers
like the Philistines;
they hold hands
with foreigners' children.[c]
7 Their land is full of silver and gold;
they have countless treasures.
Their land is filled with horses;
they have countless chariots.
8 Their land is filled with idols;
they worship their handiwork,
what their own fingers have made.

9 Humanity will be brought down;
each person laid low—
don't lift them up![d]
10 Go into the rocks,
and hide yourself in the dust
from the terror of the LORD,
from the splendor of God's majesty!
11 People's proud gazing will be stopped
and humanity's arrogance
brought down;
the LORD alone will be exalted
on that day.

12 The LORD of heavenly forces
has planned a day:
against all that is prideful
and haughty;
against all that is lofty,
and it will be laid low;[e]
13 against all the cedars of Lebanon,
high and lofty;
against all the oaks of Bashan;
14 against all the high mountains;
against all the lofty hills;
15 against every tall tower;
against every fortified wall;
16 against all the ships of Tarshish;
against all the wonderful boats.[f]
17 People's pride will be brought down
and human arrogance humiliated.
The LORD alone will be exalted
on that day;
18 the idols will completely pass away.

19 Go into caves in the rocks
and holes in the dust
before the terror of the LORD
and the splendor of God's majesty,
when he arises to terrify the earth.
20 On that day, people will toss
to the rodents[g] and to the bats

[c] Heb uncertain [d] Or *don't forgive them* [e] LXX *and high* [f] Heb uncertain [g] Heb uncertain

their idols of silver and idols of gold,
which they made for themselves
to worship.
21 They will hide in fissures of rocks
and in crevices of cliffs
before the terror of the LORD
and the splendor of God's majesty
when he arises to terrify the earth.

22 Quit admiring the human race,
who breathe through their nostrils.
Why should they be admired?

Your leaders mislead you

3 Now the LORD God of heavenly forces is removing from Jerusalem and from Judah every form of support:
all rations of food and water;
2 soldier and warrior;
judge and prophet;
fortune-teller and elder;
3 commander and celebrity;
counselor, clever craftsman,
and cunning charmer.
4 I will make youths their commanders;
mischief makers will rule over them.
5 The people will oppress each other,
each one against the other,
neighbor against neighbor.
The young will bully the old,
the rogue, and the respectable.

6 Someone will seize a family member,
saying, "You have clothing!
You be our leader!
This mess will be your responsibility!"
7 Someone else will cry out on that day,
"I'm no healer!
I have neither food nor clothing
in my house!
Don't make me the leader of the people!"

8 Yes, Jerusalem has stumbled
and Judah has fallen,
because the way they talk and act
in word and deed insults the LORD,
defying his brilliant glory.
9 Their bias in judgment gives them away;
like Sodom,
they display their sins in public.
Doom to them,
for they have done themselves in!
10 Tell the righteous how blessed they are;
they will eat the fruit of their labors.
11 Doom to the wicked; they are evil.
What they have done
will be done to them.
12 As for my people—
oppressors strip them
and swindlers[h] rule them.
My people—your leaders mislead you
and confuse your paths.

13 The LORD arises to accuse;
he stands to judge the peoples.
14 The LORD will enter into judgment
with the elders and princes
of his people:
You yourselves have devoured
the vineyard;
the goods stolen from the poor
are in your houses.
15 How dare you crush my people
and grind the faces of the poor?
says the LORD God of heavenly forces.

16 The LORD says:
Because Zion's daughters
applaud themselves,
walking with their chins in the air,
flirting with their eyes,
tiptoeing as they walk,
feet jingling—
17 the Lord will shave the heads
of Zion's daughters,
and will expose their scalps.
18 On that day, the LORD will remove:
the splendid ankle chains; headbands
and moon-shaped pendants;
19 the earrings, bracelets, and veils;
20 the hats, bangles, and sashes;
the amulets and charms;
21 the signet rings and nose rings;
22 the robes and capes;
the shawls and handbags;
23 the mirrors and linen garments;
the turbans and the veils.
24 Instead of perfume
there will be a disgusting odor;

[h] LXX; MT *women*

instead of a sash, a rope;
instead of styled hair, shaved heads;
instead of expensive clothes,
rags as mourning clothes;
instead of beauty, shame.[i]

25 Your men will fall by the sword,
your warriors in battle!
26 Her gates will lament and mourn;
desolate, she will sit on the ground.

4 Seven women will grab one man on that day, saying, "We will eat our own bread and wear our own clothes—only let us take your name; take away our disgrace."

Zion's glorious future

2 On that day, the LORD's branch will
become beautiful and glorious. The earth's
fruit will be the pride and splendor of Israel's survivors. 3 Whoever remains in Zion
and is left in Jerusalem will be called holy,
everyone who is on the list of those living in
Jerusalem. 4 When the Lord washes the filth
from Zion's daughters, and cleanses Jerusalem's bloodguilt from within it by means
of a wind of judgment and a searing wind,
5 then the LORD will create over the whole
site of Mount Zion and over its assembly a
cloud by day and smoke and the light of a
blazing fire by night. Over all the glory there
will be a canopy, 6 which will be a booth by
day for shade from the heat and a hiding
place and shelter from a stormy downpour.

Song of the vineyard

5 Let me sing for my loved one
a love song for his vineyard.
My loved one had a vineyard
on a fertile hillside.
2 He dug it,
cleared away its stones,
planted it with excellent vines,
built a tower inside it,
and dug out a wine vat in it.
He expected it to grow good grapes—
but it grew rotten grapes.
3 So now, you who live in Jerusalem,
you people of Judah,
judge between me
and my vineyard:
4 What more was there to do
for my vineyard
that I haven't done for it?
When I expected it to grow good grapes,
why did it grow rotten grapes?
5 Now let me tell you
what I'm doing to my vineyard.
I'm removing its hedge,
so it will be destroyed.
I'm breaking down its walls,
so it will be trampled.
6 I'll turn it into a ruin;
it won't be pruned or hoed,
and thorns and thistles will grow up.
I will command the clouds
not to rain on it.
7 The vineyard of
the LORD of heavenly forces
is the house of Israel,
and the people of Judah
are the plantings
in which God delighted.
God expected justice,
but there was bloodshed;
righteousness,
but there was a cry of distress!

Sayings of doom

8 Doom to those who acquire
house after house,
who annex field to field
until there is no more space left
and only you live alone in the land.
9 I heard the LORD of heavenly forces
say this:[j]
Many houses will become total ruins,
large, fine houses,
with no one living in them.
10 Ten acres of vineyard
will produce just one bath,[k]
and a homer of seed
will produce only an ephah.

11 Doom to those who wake up
early in the morning to run after beer,
to those who stay up late, lit up by wine.

[i] DSS (1QIsa[a]); MT lacks *shame.* [j] Heb lacks *say this.* [k] One bath is approximately twenty quarts, the same as an ephah; one homer contains ten ephahs (or baths) of grain.

[12]They party with lyre and harp,
tambourine, flute, and wine;
but they ignore the LORD'S work;
they can't see what God is doing.

[13]Therefore, my people go into exile
since they didn't understand—
their officials are dying of hunger;
so many of them
are dried up with thirst.
[14]Therefore, the grave[l] opens wide its jaws,
opens its mouth beyond all bounds,
and the splendid multitudes
will go down,
with all their uproar and cheering.
[15]Humanity will be humiliated;
each person laid low,
the eyes of the exalted laid low.
[16]But the LORD of heavenly forces
will be exalted in justice,
and the holy God will show himself
holy in righteousness.
[17]Lambs will graze as if in their pasture;
young goats[m] will feed
among the ruins of the rich.[n]

[18]Doom to those who drag guilt
along with cords of fraud,
and haul sin as if with cart ropes,
[19]who say, "God should hurry
and work faster so we can see;
let the plan of Israel's holy one come
quickly, so we can understand it."

[20]Doom to those who call evil good
and good evil,
who present darkness as light
and light as darkness,
who make bitterness sweet
and sweetness bitter.

[21]Doom to those
who consider themselves wise,
who think of themselves as clever.

[22]Doom to the wine-swigging warriors,
mighty at mixing drinks,
[23]who spare the guilty for bribes,
and rob the innocent of their rights.

[24]Therefore, as a tongue of fire
devours stubble,
and as hay shrivels in a flame,
so their roots will rot,
and their blossoms turn to dust,
for they have rejected the teaching of
the LORD of heavenly forces,
and have despised the word
of Israel's holy one.

God's powerful hand

[25]This is why the LORD's anger
burned against the people:
he extended his hand to strike them,
the mountains trembled,
and their corpses lay in the middle
of the streets like dung.
Even then God's anger didn't turn away;
God's hand was still extended.

[26]God will raise a signal
to a nation from far away
and whistle to them
from the end of the earth—
now look—hurrying, swiftly they come!
[27]Not one is tired; not one stumbles;
they don't rest or sleep;
no belt is loose; no sandal broken;
[28]their arrows are sharp;
all their bows drawn;
their horses' hooves are like flint;
their wheels like the whirlwind.
[29]Their roaring is like the lion;
they roar like young lions;
they growl, seize their prey,
and carry it off, with no one to rescue.
[30]On that day, they will roar over it
like the roaring of the sea.
And if one looks toward the land,
there's darkness.
Tyre and the Nile
will be darkened by the clouds.[o]

The divine throne room

6 In the year of King Uzziah's death, I
saw the Lord sitting on a high and exalted throne, the edges of his robe filling
the temple. [2]Winged creatures were stationed around him. Each had six wings: with

[l]Heb *Sheol* [m]Or *strangers* [n]Or *Calves and young goats will feed on the ruins*; Heb uncertain [o]Heb uncertain

two they veiled their faces, with two their feet, and with two they flew about. 3They shouted to each other, saying:

"Holy, holy, holy
is the LORD of heavenly forces!
All the earth
is filled with God's glory!"

4The doorframe shook at the sound of their shouting, and the house was filled with smoke.

5I said, "Mourn for me; I'm ruined! I'm a man with unclean lips, and I live among a people with unclean lips. Yet I've seen the king, the LORD of heavenly forces!"

6Then one of the winged creatures flew to me, holding a glowing coal that he had taken from the altar with tongs. 7He touched my mouth and said, "See, this has touched your lips. Your guilt has departed, and your sin is removed."

8Then I heard the Lord's voice saying, "Whom should I send, and who will go for us?"

I said, "I'm here; send me."

9God said, "Go and say to this people:
Listen intently, but don't understand;
look carefully,
but don't comprehend.
10Make the minds of this people dull.
Make their ears deaf
and their eyes blind,
so they can't see with their eyes
or hear with their ears,
or understand with their minds,
and turn, and be healed."

11I said, "How long, Lord?"

And God said, "Until cities lie ruined with no one living in them, until there are houses without people and the land is left devastated." 12The LORD will send the people far away, and the land will be completely abandoned. 13Even if one-tenth remain there, they will be burned again, like a terebinth or an oak, which when it is cut down leaves a stump. Its stump is a holy seed.

Reassurance to King Ahaz

7 In the days of Ahaz (Jotham's son and grandson of Judah's King Uzziah), Aram's King Rezin and Israel's King Pekah (Remaliah's son) came up to attack Jerusalem, but they couldn't overpower it.

2When the house of David was told that Aram had become allies with Ephraim, their hearts and the hearts of their people shook as the trees of a forest shake when there is a wind. 3But the LORD said to Isaiah, "Go out to meet Ahaz, you and your son Shear-jashub,[p] at the end of the channel of the Upper Pool, by the road to the field where laundry is washed, 4and say to him, 'Be careful and stay calm. Don't fear, and don't lose heart over these two pieces of smoking torches, over the burning anger of Rezin, Aram, and Remaliah's son. 5Aram has planned evil against you with Ephraim and Remaliah's son, saying, 6"Let's march up against Judah, tear it apart, capture it for ourselves, and install Tabeel's son as its king." 7But the LORD God says: It won't happen; it won't take place. 8The chief of Aram is Damascus; the chief of Damascus is Rezin (in sixty-five more years Ephraim will be shattered as a nation); 9the chief of Ephraim is Samaria; and the chief of Samaria is the son of Remaliah. If you don't believe this, you can't be trusted.' "

The sign of Immanuel

10Again the LORD spoke to Ahaz: 11"Ask a sign from the LORD your God. Make it as deep as the grave[q] or as high as heaven."

12But Ahaz said, "I won't ask; I won't test the LORD."

13Then Isaiah said, "Listen, house of David! Isn't it enough for you to be tiresome for people that you are also tiresome before my God? 14Therefore, the Lord will give you a sign. The young woman is pregnant and is about to give birth to a son, and she will name him Immanuel.[r] 15He will eat butter and honey, and learn to reject evil and choose good. 16Before the boy learns to reject evil and choose good, the land of the two kings you dread will be abandoned. 17The LORD will bring upon you, upon your people, and upon your families days unlike any that have come since the day Ephraim

[p]Or *the remaining few will return* [q]Heb *Sheol* [r]Or *God is with us*

broke away from Judah—the king of Assyria."

The devastated land

18 On that day, the LORD will whistle for the flies from the remotest streams of Egypt and for the bees that are in the land of Assyria. 19 They will come and settle in the steep ravines, in the cracks of the cliffs, in all the thornbushes, and in all the watering holes.

20 On that day, the Lord will shave with a razor hired from beyond the Euphrates—with the king of Assyria—the head and the pubic hair, and will cut off the beard as well.

21 On that day, one will raise a young cow and two sheep 22 and will eat butter because of the abundance of milk, for all who remain in the land will eat butter and honey.

23 On that day, there will be thorns and thistles in every place where a thousand vines worth a thousand silver shekels once grew. 24 Only those with bows and arrows will go there, because the entire land will become thorns and thistles. 25 As for the hills that were once farmed with hoes, you won't go there for fear of the thorns and thistles. They will become places where cattle are turned loose and sheep wander.

Isaiah's testimonies

8 The LORD said to me, "Take a large tablet, and write on it in ordinary letters,[s] For Maher-shalal-hash-baz.[t] 2 Summon trusted people, Uriah the priest and Zechariah, Jeberechiah's son, to witness it."

3 I then had sex with the prophetess, and she became pregnant and gave birth to a son. Then the LORD said to me, "Name him Maher-shalal-hash-baz. 4 Before the boy knows how to say 'my father' and 'my mother,' the wealth of Damascus and the spoil of Samaria will be carried away before the king of Assyria."

5 The LORD spoke again to me: 6 Since this people has rejected the waters of Shiloah that flow gently, and instead rejoices over[u] Rezin and Remaliah's son— 7 therefore, look, the Lord is raising up against them the powerful floodwaters of the Euphrates, the king of Assyria and all his glory. It will rise up over all its channels, overflowing all its banks, 8 and sweep into Judah, flooding, overflowing, and reaching up to the neck. But God is with us;[v] the span of his wings will cover the width of the land.

9 Unite[w] yourselves, peoples,
and be shattered!
Listen, all distant places of the earth!
Prepare to be shattered!
Prepare to be shattered!
10 Create a plan, but be frustrated!
Speak a word, but it won't stand,
for God is with us.[x]

11 The LORD spoke to me, taking hold of me and warning me not to walk in the way of this people: 12 Don't call conspiracy all that this people calls conspiracy. Don't fear what they fear, and don't be terrified. 13 It is the LORD of heavenly forces whom you should hold sacred, whom you should fear, and whom you should hold in awe.

14 God will become a sanctuary—
but he will be a stone to trip over
and a rock to stumble on
for the two houses of Israel;
a trap and a snare
for those living in Jerusalem.
15 Many of them will stumble and fall,
and be broken, snared, and captured.

16 Bind up the testimony; seal up the teaching among my disciples. 17 I will wait for the LORD, who has hidden his face from the house of Jacob, and I will hope in God. 18 Look! I and the children the LORD gave me are signs and wonders in Israel from the LORD of heavenly forces, who lives on Mount Zion.

19 If they say to you: "Consult the ghosts and the spirits that chirp and mutter. (Shouldn't a people consult its gods?) Consult the dead on behalf of the living 20 for instruction and for testimony"—they will surely say such things, but they will never see the dawn.[y]

[s] Heb uncertain [t] Or *spoil hastens, plunder hurries* [u] Or *melts before* [v] Heb *Immanuel* [w] Heb uncertain
[x] Heb *Immanuel* [y] Heb uncertain for 8:19-20

[21]They will pass through the land,[z] dejected and hungry, and when they are
hungry, they will be enraged and will curse
their king and God. They will turn toward
heaven [22]and look to the earth, but they
will see only distress and darkness, random
movement, and the anguish and doom of
banishment.[a]

A great light

9 [b]Nonetheless, those who were in distress won't be exhausted. At an earlier
time, God cursed the land of Zebulun and
the land of Naphtali, but later he glorified
the way of the sea, the far side of the Jordan, and the Galilee of the nations.[c]

[2][d]The people walking in darkness
have seen a great light.
On those living in a pitch-dark land,
light has dawned.
[3]You have made the nation great;
you have increased its joy.
They rejoiced before you
as with joy at the harvest,
as those who divide plunder rejoice.
[4]As on the day of Midian,
you've shattered the yoke
that burdened them,
the staff on their shoulders,
and the rod of their oppressor.
[5]Because every boot
of the thundering warriors,
and every garment rolled in blood
will be burned, fuel for the fire.
[6]A child is born to us,
a son is given to us,
and authority will be on his shoulders.
He will be named
Wonderful Counselor, Mighty God,
Eternal Father, Prince of Peace.
[7]There will be vast authority
and endless peace
for David's throne
and for his kingdom,
establishing and sustaining it
with justice and righteousness
now and forever.

The zeal of the LORD of heavenly forces
will do this.

God's hand still stretched out

[8]The Lord sent a word against Jacob;
it fell upon Israel;
[9]the people all knew it—
Ephraim and the one
who rules in Samaria.
But with a proud and arrogant heart
they said,
[10]"Bricks have fallen,
but let's rebuild with stones.
Sycamores were cut down,
but let's replace them with cedars."
[11]So the LORD raised up their foes
against them,[e]
and stirred up their enemies—
[12]Aram from the east and the Philistines
from the west—
and they devoured Israel
with an open mouth.
Even then God's anger
didn't turn away;
God's hand was still extended.

[13]But the people didn't turn
to the one who struck them.
They didn't seek
the LORD of heavenly forces.
[14]So the LORD cut off head and tail,
palm branch and reed
from Israel in one day.
[15](Elders and celebrities are the head;
prophets who teach lies are the tail.)
[16]But this people's leaders
were misleading,
and those being led were confused.
[17]So the Lord
showed their youth no pity,
and showed their orphans and widows
no mercy;
for everyone was godless and evil;
every mouth spoke nonsense.
Even then God's anger
didn't turn away;
God's hand was still extended.

[18]Wickedness burned like fire,
devouring thorn and thistle.
It kindled the thickets of the forest;
they swirled in rising smoke.

[z]Or *it* [a]Heb uncertain for 8:21-22 [b]8:23 in Heb [c]Heb uncertain [d]9:1 in Heb [e]Or *the enemies of Rezin*

19 The land was scorched by the rage of
the LORD of heavenly forces;
the people were like fuel for the fire.
Not one person pitied another:
20 they consumed on the right,
but remained hungry;
devoured on the left,
and weren't satisfied.
They devoured the flesh
of their own children.[f]
21 Manasseh devoured Ephraim
and Ephraim Manasseh;
together they turned against Judah.
Even then God's anger
didn't turn away;
God's hand was still extended.

Wicked laws

10 Doom to those
who pronounce wicked decrees,
and keep writing harmful laws
2 to deprive the needy of their rights
and to rob the poor among my people
of justice;
to make widows their loot;
to steal from orphans!
3 What will you do
on the day of punishment
when disaster comes from far away?
To whom will you flee for help;
where will you stash your wealth?
4 How will you avoid
crouching among the prisoners
and falling among the slain?
Even so, God's anger
hasn't turned away;
God's hand is still extended.

Assyria as God's punishing weapon

5 Doom to Assyria, rod of my anger,
in whose hand is the staff of my fury!
6 Against a godless nation I send him;
against an infuriating people
I direct him to seize spoil,
to steal plunder,
and to trample them
like mud in the streets.
7 But he has other plans;
he schemes in secret;
destruction is on his mind,
extermination of nation after nation.
8 He says:
Aren't my commanders all kings?
9 Isn't Calno like Carchemish?
Isn't Hamath like Arpad?
Isn't Samaria like Damascus?
10 Just as I took control
of idolatrous kingdoms
with more images
than Jerusalem and Samaria,
11 just as I did to Samaria
and her false gods,
won't I also do this to Jerusalem
and her idols?
12 But when the Lord has finished all this
work on Mount Zion and in Jerusalem, he
will punish[g] the Assyrian king's arrogant actions and the boasting of his haughty eyes.
13 He said, "By my own strength
I have achieved it,
and by my wisdom, since I'm so clever.
I disregarded national boundaries;
I raided their treasures;
I knocked down their rulers like a bull.
14 My hand found the wealth
of the peoples
as if it were in a nest.
Just as one gathers abandoned eggs,
I have gathered the entire earth;
no creature fluttered a wing
or opened a mouth to chirp."

15 Will the ax glorify itself
over the one who chops with it?
Or will the saw magnify itself
over its user?
As if a rod could wave the one who lifts it!
As if a staff could lift up
the one not made of wood!
16 Therefore,
the LORD God of heavenly forces
will make the well-fed people
waste away;
and among his officials,
a blaze will burn like scorching fire.
17 The light of Israel will become a fire,
its holy one a flame,
which will burn and devour

[f] Or *arm* [g] Or *I will punish*

its thorns and thistles
in a single day.
18 Its abundant forest and farmland
will be finished completely,[h]
as when a sick person wastes away;
19 its forest's remaining trees
will be no more than a child can count.

A few will return

20 On that day, what's left of Israel and
the survivors of the house of Jacob will no
longer depend on the one who beat them.
Instead, they will faithfully depend on the
LORD, the holy one of Israel. 21 A few will return, what's left of Jacob, to the mighty God.
22 Although your people, Israel, were like the
sand of the sea, only a few survivors will
return. The end is announced, overflowing
with justice. 23 Yes, destruction has been announced; the LORD God of heavenly forces
will carry it out against the entire land.
24 Therefore, the LORD God of heavenly
forces says: My people who live in Zion, don't
fear Assyria, which strikes you with the rod
and raises its staff against you as Egypt did.
25 In a very short time my fury will end, and
my anger at the world will be finished.[i]

26 Therefore, the LORD of heavenly forces
will crack a whip against Assyria,
as when he struck Midian
at the rock of Oreb.
He will raise a rod over the sea,
as he did in Egypt.
27 On that day, God will remove
the burden from your shoulder
and destroy the yoke on your neck.[j]

The exalted laid low

He has gone up from Samaria,
28 come against Aiath,
passed to Migron.
At Michmash he stored his equipment.
29 They crossed at the pass:
"We'll camp at Geba!"
Ramah trembles;
Gibeah of Saul has fled.
30 Cry aloud, Daughter Gallim!
Listen, Laishah!
Answer her, Anathoth!
31 Madmenah has flown.
Gebim's inhabitants sought refuge.
32 This very day he will stand at Nob
and shake his fist[k]
at Daughter Zion's mountain,
the hill of Jerusalem!
33 Look! The LORD God of heavenly forces
is chopping off the branches
with terrible power.
The loftiest ones
are about to be cut down
and the exalted laid low.
34 He will strike down the forest thickets
with an ax,
and mighty Lebanon will fall.

A shoot from Jesse's stump

11 A shoot will grow up
from the stump of Jesse;
a branch will sprout[l] from his roots.
2 The LORD's spirit will rest upon him,
a spirit of wisdom and understanding,
a spirit of planning and strength,
a spirit of knowledge
and fear of the LORD.
3 He will delight in fearing the LORD.
He won't judge by appearances,
nor decide by hearsay.
4 He will judge the needy
with righteousness,
and decide with equity
for those who suffer in the land.
He will strike the violent[m]
with the rod of his mouth;
by the breath of his lips
he will kill the wicked.
5 Righteousness will be
the belt around his hips,
and faithfulness
the belt around his waist.
6 The wolf will live with the lamb,
and the leopard will lie down
with the young goat;
the calf and the young lion
will feed[n] together,
and a little child will lead them.

[h] Syr, Vulg *body and soul* (that is, *completely*); MT *he will finish* [i] Heb uncertain [j] Or *and his yoke from your neck, and a yoke will be destroyed because of fatness* [k] Or *wave his hand* [l] LXX, Vulg; MT *bear fruit* [m] Or *land*
[n] Correction; MT *and the calf*

7 The cow and the bear will graze.
Their young will lie down together,
and a lion will eat straw like an ox.
8 A nursing child
will play over the snake's hole;
toddlers will reach
right over the serpent's den.
9 They won't harm or destroy
anywhere on my holy mountain.
The earth will surely be filled
with the knowledge of the LORD,
just as the water covers the sea.

A signal to the peoples

10 On that day, the root of Jesse will
stand as a signal to the peoples. The nations will seek him out, and his dwelling
will be glorious.
11 On that day, the Lord will extend his
hand a second time to reclaim the survivors
of God's people who are left from Assyria
and from Egypt, from Pathros, Cush, Elam,
Shinar, Hamath, and from the coastlands[o]
of the sea.

12 God will raise a signal for the nations
and gather the outcast men of Israel.
God will collect
the dispersed women of Judah
from the four corners of the earth.
13 Ephraim's jealousy will cease,
and Judah's harassment
will be eliminated.
Ephraim won't be jealous of Judah,
and Judah won't harass Ephraim.
14 But they will swoop down
on the slopes of Philistia to the west;
together they will plunder
the people to the east.
Edom and Moab
will be under their power,
and the Ammonites
will be their subjects.

15 The LORD will split the tongue of the
Egyptian sea. God will wave a hand over
the Euphrates with a powerful[p] wind and
break it into seven streams so that it can
be crossed in sandals. 16 Then there will be
a highway from Assyria for the survivors of
God's people who are left from Assyria, just
as there was for Israel on the day they went
up from the land of Egypt.

Hymn of trust

12 You will say on that day:
"I thank you, LORD.
Though you were angry with me,
your anger turned away
and you comforted me.
2 God is indeed my salvation;
I will trust and won't be afraid.
Yah, the LORD, is my strength
and my shield;
he has become my salvation."

3 You will draw water with joy
from the springs of salvation.
4 And you will say on that day:
"Thank the LORD; call on God's name;
proclaim God's deeds
among the peoples;
declare that God's name is exalted.
5 Sing to the LORD,
who has done glorious things;
proclaim this throughout
all the earth."
6 Shout and sing for joy, city of Zion,
because the holy one of Israel
is great among you.

Babylon falls

13 An oracle about Babylon, which Isaiah,
Amoz's son, saw.
2 On a bare mountain raise a signal;
cry aloud to them;
wave a hand;
let them enter the officials' gates.
3 I have commanded my holy ones;
I have called my warriors,
my proud, jubilant ones,
to execute my wrath.
4 Listen![q] A roar on the mountains
like that of a great crowd.
Listen! An uproar of kingdoms,
of nations coming together.
The LORD of heavenly forces
is mustering an army for battle.
5 They are coming from a distant land,
from the faraway heavens,

[o] Or *islands* [p] Heb uncertain [q] Heb lacks *Listen!*

the LORD and the instruments of his
fury, to destroy the whole land.

6 Wail, for the day of the LORD is near.
Like destruction from the Almighty[r]
it will come.
7 Then all hands will fall limp;
every human heart will melt,
8 and they will be terrified.
Like a woman writhing in labor,
they will be seized
by spasms and agony.
They will look at each other aghast,
their faces blazing.

9 Look, the day of the LORD is coming
with cruel rage and burning anger,
making the earth a ruin,
and wiping out its sinners.
10 Heaven's stars and constellations
won't show their light.
The sun will be dark when it rises;
the moon will no longer shine.
11 I will bring disaster
upon the world for its evil,
and bring their own sin
upon the wicked.
I will end the pride of the insolent,
and the conceit of tyrants
I will lay low.
12 I will make humans scarcer
than fine gold;
people rarer than the gold of Ophir.
13 I will rattle the heavens;
the earth will shake loose
from its place—because of the rage
of the LORD of heavenly forces
on the day his anger burns.
14 They will be like hunted gazelles,
like sheep without a shepherd;
all will turn to their own people
and flee to their own lands.
15 Whoever is found will be stabbed;
whoever is caught
will fall by the sword.
16 Their infants will be crushed
before their eyes;
their houses plundered,
their women raped.

17 Look! I'm rousing the Medes
against them;
the Medes pay no mind to silver,
no desire for gold.
18 Their bows will smash youths;
they will be merciless to newborns,
pitiless to children.
19 So Babylon,
a jewel among kingdoms,
the Chaldeans' splendor and pride,
will be like Sodom and Gomorrah,
destroyed by God.
20 No one will ever resettle
or live there for generations.
No Arab will camp there;
no shepherds will rest flocks there.
21 Wildcats will rest there;
houses will be filled with owls.
Ostriches will live there,
and goat demons will dance there.
22 Hyenas will howl in its strongholds,
and jackals in its luxurious palaces.
Babylon's[s] time is coming soon;
its days won't drag on.

Compassion for Jacob

14 The LORD will have compassion on
Jacob, will again choose Israel, and
will give them rest in their own land. Immigrants will join them, and attach themselves to the house of Jacob. 2 The peoples
will take them and will bring them to their
own place. The house of Israel will possess them as male and female slaves in the
LORD's land, making captives of their captors and ruling their oppressors.

Mockery of a tyrant

3 When the LORD has given you rest
from pain and trouble and from the hard
labor that you perform, 4 you will take up
this taunt against the king of Babylon:
How the oppressor[t] has ceased!
How the flood[u] has receded!
5 The LORD has broken
the staff of the wicked,
the rod of tyrants
6 that struck peoples in rage
with ceaseless blows,

[r] Heb *Shaddai* or *Mountain One* [s] Heb *Its* [t] Heb uncertain [u] DSS (1QIsa[a]), LXX, Syr, Tg; MT *fury*

that ruled nations with anger,
with relentless aggression.

[7]All the earth rests quietly,
then it breaks into song.
[8]Even the cypresses rejoice over you,
the cedars of Lebanon:
"Since you were laid low,
no logger comes up against us!"

[9]The underworld[v] beneath
becomes restless to greet your arrival.
It awakens the ghosts,
all the leaders of earth;
it makes the kings of the nations
rise from their thrones.
[10]All of them speak and say to you:
"Even you've become weak like we are!
You are the same as us!"
[11]Your majesty has been brought down
to the underworld,[w]
along with the sound of your harps.
Under you is a bed of maggots,
and worms are your blanket.

[12]How you've fallen from heaven,
morning star, son of dawn!
You are cut down to earth,
helpless on your back!
[13]You said to yourself,
I will climb up to heaven;
above God's stars,
I will raise my throne.
I'll sit on the mount of assembly,
on the heights of Zaphon.
[14]I'll go up to the cloud tops;
I'll be like the Most High!
[15]But down to the underworld[x]
you are brought,
to the depths of the pit.

[16]Those who see you will stare at you;
they will examine you closely:
"Is this the man who rattled the earth,
who shook kingdoms,
[17]who made the world a wasteland
and tore down its cities,
and wouldn't let his prisoners
go home?"

[18]All the kings of the nations
lie down honored,
all of them,
each in his own tomb.
[19]But you are cast away
from your own grave
like a rejected branch,
covered by the dead
and those pierced by the sword—
who go down to the stony pit—
like a trampled corpse.
[20]You won't join them in burial,
for you destroyed your own land;
you killed your own people.
Such evil offspring
will never be mentioned again!

[21]Prepare a place to slaughter his sons
for the guilt of their father. Don't let them
arise to take over the earth or fill the world
with cities.
[22]I will arise against them, says the LORD
of heavenly forces. I will cut off Babylon's
renown and remnant, offshoot and offspring. [23]I will make it the home of herons,
a swampland. I will sweep it away with the
broom of destruction, says the LORD of
heavenly forces.

Promise for oppressed Judah

[24]The LORD of heavenly forces
has promised:
As I intended, so it will be;
and as I have planned,
so it will happen:
[25]I will break Assyria in my land;
on my mountains I will trample it
and remove its yoke
from my people;[y]
his burden will be taken
from their shoulders.
[26]This is the plan that has been made
for all the earth;
this is the hand
extended over all the nations.
[27]The LORD of heavenly forces
has created a plan;
who can stop it?
God's hand is extended;
who will stop it?

[v]Heb *Sheol* [w]Heb *Sheol* [x]Heb *Sheol* [y]Or *them*

An oracle concerning the Philistines

28 This oracle came in the year of King Ahaz's death:

29 Don't rejoice, all you Philistines, that
the rod that struck you is broken,
because from the snake's root
a viper will grow,
and it will produce a winged creature.
30 The oldest offspring of the poor
will graze;
their needy will lie down secure.
But he will starve your offspring
to death,
and murder all who remain.
31 Wail, gate! Cry out, city!
Melt in terror, all you Philistines!
Smoke is coming from the north;
there is no straggler in its ranks.[z]
32 What will one say
to that nation's messengers?
The LORD has founded Zion;
the oppressed among God's people
will find refuge there.

Concerning Moab

15 An oracle about Moab.
Ar was devastated in a night;
Moab is ruined!
Kir was devastated in a night;
Moab is ruined!
2 Dibon has gone up to the temple,
to the shrines to weep.[a]
Moab wails over Nebo and over Medeba.
Every head is shaved,
every beard cut off.
3 In its streets
they wear mourning clothes;
on its rooftops and in its plazas,
everyone wails
and falls down weeping.
4 Heshbon and Elealeh cry out;
as far as Jahaz their voice is heard.
The armed men of Moab shout,
spirits trembling.
5 My heart cries out for Moab.
Its fugitives flee to Zoar,
to Eglath-shelishiyah.[b]
At the ascent of Luhith,
each will go up with weeping.
On the road to Horonaim,
they will raise a piercing cry.
6 The waters of Nimrim are used up.
Grass has withered;
vegetation is dead;
greenery is gone.
7 Therefore, they carry
what they had stored up,
all their provisions
to the Valley of the Willows.
8 An outcry sounds
within the borders of Moab,
as far as Eglaim, a cry of distress,
as far as Beer-elim, a cry of distress.
9 The waters of Dibon are full of blood.
But I will bring still more upon Dibon:
a lion for Moab's survivors,
for the remaining few in the land.

16 Send lambs to the ruler of the land,[c]
from Sela through the desert
to the mountain of Daughter Zion.
2 The daughters of Moab
at the fords of the Arnon
are like orphaned birds
pushed from the nest.
3 Consider carefully, act justly;
at high noon
provide your shade like night.
Hide the outcasts;
keep the fugitives hidden.
4 Let the outcasts of Moab
live among you.
Be a hiding place for them
from the destroyer.
When the oppressor is no more,
when destruction has ceased,
when the trampler has vanished
from the land,
5 a throne will be established
based on goodness,
and someone will sit faithfully on it
in David's dwelling[d]—
a judge who seeks justice
and timely righteousness.

6 We have heard of Moab's pride,
his great pride,
his outrageous pride and arrogance,
his empty boasting.

[z]Heb uncertain [a]Heb uncertain [b]Heb uncertain [c]Heb uncertain [d]Or *tent*

7 Therefore, let Moab wail;
let everyone wail for Moab.
Let them moan, utterly stricken,
for the raisin cakes of Kir-hareseth.
8 The fields of Heshbon languish.
The vines of Sibmah,
whose honored grapes
overpowered masters of nations,
had reached as far as Jazer
and strayed to the desert.
Their tendrils spread out
and crossed the sea.
9 Therefore,
I will weep with Jazer's weeping
for the vines of Sibmah.
I will drench you with my tears,
Heshbon and Elealeh.
Cheers have fallen silent
concerning your summer fruit
and your grain harvest.
10 Joy and happiness have been harvested
from the farmland,
and in the vineyards no one sings,
no one shouts.
No treader crushes grapes
in the wine vats;
I have brought the cheers to an end.
11 Therefore, my heart plays sadly
like a harp for Moab,
my inner being for Kir-heres.
12 Even if Moab presents himself,
and Moab wears himself out
going to the shrine,
and comes to his sanctuary to pray,
he won't prevail.

13 This is the word that the LORD had spoken concerning Moab long ago. 14 But now
the LORD has said: In three years, like the
years of a hired worker, the glory of Moab,
with all its great multitude, will dwindle.
The small remnant will be few and feeble.

Concerning Damascus and Ephraim

17 An oracle about Damascus.
Look! Damascus is finished as a city;
it will become a fallen ruin.
2 The villages of Aroer
are abandoned forever.[e]
They will be pastures for flocks,[f]
which will lie down undisturbed.
3 Ephraim's security will cease,
as will Damascus's rule.
What's left of Aram will resemble
the glory of the Israelites,
says the LORD of heavenly forces.

4 On that day, Jacob's glory will dwindle;
his sleek body will waste away.
5 It will be as when
harvesters gather grain.
God will harvest armfuls at a time,
like one who gathers grain
in the Rephaim Valley.
6 Only remaining bits are left,
like an olive tree that has been shaken:
two or three olives
on the highest branch;
four or five on a fruitful twig,
says the LORD God of Israel.

7 On that day, people will have regard
for their maker,
and their eyes will look
to the holy one of Israel.
8 They will have no regard for altars,
the work of their hands,
or look to what their fingers made:
sacred poles[g] and incense stands.

9 On that day, their strong cities will be
like those abandoned by the Hivites and
the Amorites;[h] abandoned because of the
Israelites. They will be a wasteland,
10 because you forgot the God
who saves you,
and didn't remember the rock
who shelters you.
Therefore, plant your pleasant plants,
and set out exotic sprouts;
11 make them grow the day you plant them,
and make them bloom
the morning you start them.
But the harvest will disappear on a day
of sickness and incurable pain.

12 Doom to the raging of many peoples;
like the thundering seas they thunder.

[e] Cf LXX; MT *The cities of Aroer are abandoned.* [f] Or *For flocks they will be* [g] Heb *asherim*, possibly objects devoted to the goddess Asherah [h] LXX; MT *like the abandonment of the forest and the bough*

Doom to the roar of nations,
like the roaring of mighty waters.
13 Nations roar
like the roaring of rushing waters.
But God will rebuke them,
and they will flee far away,
pursued like chaff
by wind in the mountains,
like tumbleweeds before a storm.
14 In the evening, there is terror;
but before morning it is gone.
This is the fate of those who loot us,
the destiny of those who rob us.

Concerning Cush

18 Doom to the land of winged ships,
beyond the rivers of Cush
2 that sends messengers by sea,
reed vessels on the water.
Go, swift messengers,
to a nation tall and clean-shaven,
to a people feared near and far,
a nation barbaric and oppressive,
whose land the rivers divide.

3 All you who inhabit the world,
who live on earth,
when a signal is raised
on the mountains, you will see!
When the trumpet blasts,
you will hear!
4 The LORD said to me:
I will quietly watch
from my own place,
like the shimmering heat of sunshine,
like a cloud's shade
in the harvest heat.
5 Before the harvest,
when the bloom is finished,
when the blossom is becoming
a ripening fruit,
God will cut the shoots
with a pruning knife,
and lop off the spreading branches.
6 They will all be left
to the mountain birds
and to the beasts of the land.
The birds will eat them in summer,
all the beasts of the land in winter.

7 At that time, gifts will be brought
to the LORD of heavenly forces
from a tall and clean-shaven people
and from a people feared near and far,
a nation barbaric and oppressive,
whose land the rivers divide,
to the place of the name of
the LORD of heavenly forces,
to Mount Zion.

Concerning Egypt

19 An oracle about Egypt.
Look! The LORD is riding
upon a swift cloud,
and is coming to Egypt.
Egypt's idols will tremble before God;
the Egyptians' hearts will melt
within them.
2 I will stir up Egyptian against Egyptian,
and they will fight,
one against another,
neighbor against neighbor,
city against city,
kingdom against kingdom.
3 Egypt's spirit will fail from within;
I will frustrate their plans.
They will consult the idols and spirits
and ghosts and fortune-tellers.
4 I will hand Egypt
over to a harsh master;
a strong king will rule them, says
the LORD God of heavenly forces.

5 The waters of the sea will dry up;
the river will be parched and bare.
6 The rivers will stink;
the streams will shrink and dry;
reeds and rushes will decay.
7 Grass around the Nile,
the grass at the mouth of the Nile,
and all the sown land of the Nile
will dry up, blow away, and be no more.
8 Those who fish will lament;
all who cast fishhooks in the Nile
will mourn,
and those who spread nets
on the water will pine away.
9 Workers with flax will be dismayed;
carders and weavers will grow pale.[i]

[i] DSS (1QIsa[a])

10 Makers of cloth will be crushed;
all who earn money
will become distressed.
11 The officials of Tanis are fools;
the wisest of Pharaoh's counselors
give stupid advice.
How can you say to Pharaoh,
"I'm a wise person,
one of the ancient kings"?
12 Where now are your wise ones?
Let them tell you,
let them inform you what
the LORD of heavenly forces
has planned concerning Egypt.
13 The officials of Tanis have become fools;
the princes of Memphis are deluded;
the tribal chiefs have led Egypt astray.
14 The LORD has poured into them
a spirit of confusion.
They will make Egypt stumble
in everything it does,
just as a drunk stumbles in his vomit.
15 Neither head nor tail,
palm branch nor reed
will be able to do anything for Egypt.

Bless God's people

16 On that day, the Egyptians will be like
women and will tremble with terror before
the hand that the LORD of heavenly forces
will raise against them. 17 Judah's land will
become what the Egyptians dread; whenever anyone mentions it, they will be terrified because of the plans that the LORD
of heavenly forces is making against them.
18 On that day, there will be five cities in
the land of Egypt that speak the language
of Canaan and swear loyalty to the LORD of
heavenly forces. One of them will be called
"the city of the sun."[j]
19 On that day, there will be an altar to
the LORD within the land of Egypt, and a
standing stone for the LORD at its border.
20 It will be a sign and a witness to the LORD
of heavenly forces in the land of Egypt.
When they cry out to the LORD because
of oppressors, God will send them a savior
and defender to rescue them. 21 The LORD
will make himself known to the Egyptians;
the Egyptians will know the LORD on that
day. They will worship with sacrifices and
offerings, making solemn promises to the
LORD and fulfilling them. 22 The LORD will
strike Egypt; striking and then healing.
They will return to the LORD, who will hear
their pleas and heal them.
23 On that day, there will be a highway
from Egypt to Assyria. The Assyrians will
come to Egypt, and the Egyptians to Assyria; and the Egyptians will worship with
the Assyrians.
24 On that day, Israel will be the third
along with Egypt and Assyria, a blessing
at the center of the world. 25 The LORD of
heavenly forces will pronounce this blessing: Bless Egypt my people, and Assyria my
handiwork, and Israel my inheritance.

Isaiah naked and barefoot

20 In the year that Assyria's King Sar-
gon sent his general to Ashdod, he
fought against Ashdod and captured it. 2 At
that time the LORD had spoken through
Isaiah, Amoz's son, "Go, take off the
mourning clothes from your waist, and remove the shoes from your feet." And Isaiah
did this, walking naked and barefoot.
3 The LORD said, "Just as my servant Isaiah has walked naked and barefoot three
years, as a sign and omen against Egypt and
Cush, 4 so will the king of Assyria lead the
captives of Egypt and the exiles of Cush, both
young and old, naked and barefoot, with buttocks bared, humiliating Egypt. 5 They will be
shattered and shamed because of Cush their
hope, and because of Egypt their glory.
6 "On that day, those who live on this
coast will say, 'Look at those in whom we had
hoped, to whom we fled for help and rescue
from the king of Assyria. How then will we
escape?'"

Fallen, fallen is Babylon

21 An oracle about the wilderness near
the sea.
Like whirlwinds sweeping
through the arid southern plain,

[j] DSS (1QIsa[a]), Tg, Vulg; Heb uncertain

it comes from the desert,
from a fearsome land.
2 A harsh vision
was proclaimed to me:
The betrayer betrays,
and the destroyer destroys.
Go up, Elam! Lay siege, Media!
Put an end to all her groaning.
3 Therefore, I'm shaken to my core
in anguish.
Pains have seized me
like the pains of a woman in labor.
I'm too bent over to hear,
too dismayed to see.
4 My heart pounds;
convulsions overpower me.
He has turned my evening of pleasure
into dread—
5 setting the table,
spreading the cloth,
eating, drinking.
"Arise, captains!
Polish the shields."

6 The Lord said this to me:
"Go, post a lookout
to report what he sees.
7 When he sees chariots,
pairs of horsemen,
donkey riders, camel riders,
he should listen carefully,
carefully, very carefully."

8 Then the seer[k] called out:
"Upon a watchtower, Lord,
I'm standing all day;
and upon my observation post
I'm stationed throughout the night.
9 Here they come:
charioteers, pairs of horsemen!"
One spoke up and said,
"Fallen, fallen is Babylon,
and all the images of her gods
are shattered on the ground!"
10 Oh, my downtrodden people,
threshed on my threshing floor,
what I heard from
the LORD of heavenly forces,
the God of Israel, I reported to you.

A mysterious dialogue

11 An oracle about Dumah.[l]
Someone is calling to me from Seir:
"Guard, how long is the night?
Guard, how long is the night?"
12 The guard said,
"Morning has come, but it is still night.
If you must inquire, inquire;
come back again."

13 An oracle about the desert.
In the woods,
in the desert where you camp,
caravans of the Dedanites
14 meet the thirsty with water;
inhabitants of the land of Tema
greet the refugees with bread.
15 They have fled from swords,
from the drawn sword,
from the bent bow
and from the intensity of battle.
16 So the Lord said to me: Within a
year, according to the number of years for
which a laborer is hired, all the glory of
Kedar will end; 17 there will be few Kedarite
archers remaining. The LORD God of Israel
has spoken.

Jerusalemites rebuked

22 An oracle about the Valley of Vision.
What is wrong with you,
that you have all gone up
to the rooftops,
2 you who are filled with noise,
you roaring city, you party town?
Your dead weren't slaughtered
by the sword;
they didn't die in battle.
3 All your leaders escaped together
but were captured
without a single bow shot.
All your escapees
were bound together,
even though they fled far away.[m]
4 Therefore, I said, "Don't look at me;
let me weep bitterly.
Don't try to comfort me
about the destruction
of my dearly loved people."

[k] DSS (1QIsa[a]), Syr; MT *a lion* [l] LXX *Edom* [m] Heb uncertain

5 The LORD God of heavenly forces
has a day of tumult and trampling
and turmoil in the Valley of Vision,
a breaking down of walls,
a cry for help to the mountains.
6 Elam carried the quiver
with chariots and horsemen,
and Kir uncovered the shield.
7 Your finest valleys
were filled with chariots,
and horsemen doggedly guarded
the gate.
8 Judah's covering
has been stripped away.

On that day, you trusted the weapons
in the Forest House.
9 You observed the many broken
defenses in David's City,
and you collected
the waters of the lower pool.
10 You counted Jerusalem's houses,
and you tore down houses
to fortify the wall.
11 You made a reservoir between the walls
for the water of the earlier pool.
But you didn't trust its maker;
you didn't consider the one
who planned it long ago.

12 The LORD God of heavenly forces
called on that day
for weeping and mourning,
and shaven heads,
and wearing of mourning clothes.
13 But instead there was
fun and frivolity,
killing of cattle
and slaughtering of sheep,
eating of meat and drinking of wine:
"Eat and drink! Tomorrow we will die!"
14 But the LORD of heavenly forces
has revealed in my hearing:
This iniquity won't
be forgiven you until you die, says
the LORD God of heavenly forces.

An administrator rebuked

15 The LORD God of heavenly forces says, Go
now to this official, to Shebna, who is in
charge of the house, and say to him:

16 What do you have here—
and whom do you have here—
that you have hewed out a tomb
for yourself,
you who cuts his grave on high and
carves himself a home in the cliff?
17 The LORD is about to hurl you down,
mighty man!

He is surely going to cover you
with darkness;
18 he will indeed
unroll your head wrapping,
rolling it like a ball
into the open country.
There you will die,
with your glorious chariots,
you disgrace to the house
of your master!
19 I will thrust you from your monument;
you will be pulled down
from your platform.
20 On that day, I will call my servant
Eliakim, Hilkiah's son.
21 I will give him your robe
and wrap him in your sash,
and I will hand over to him
your authority.
He will be a father
to the inhabitants of Jerusalem
and to the house of Judah.
22 I will place the key to David's house
on his shoulder;
what he opens no one will close,
and what he closes no one will open.
23 I will fasten him securely
like a tent peg,
and he will be a throne of honor
for his ancestors' house.

24 All the honor of his household will hang
on him, the offspring and the offshoots,
every little dish, every bowl, every jar.
25 On that day, says the LORD of heavenly
forces, the peg that is fastened securely will
give way; it will be cut down, and it will fall,
and all the load hanging on it will be lost.
The LORD has spoken.

Concerning Tyre

23 An oracle about Tyre.
Wail, ships of Tarshish,

because your port is destroyed![n]
When returning from Cyprus,
they heard about it.
2 Be still, inhabitants of the coast,
traders of Sidon,
whose messengers crossed over the sea,[o]
3 over the mighty waters.
The grain of Shihor, the Nile's harvest,
was her income;
she was the marketplace of nations.
4 Be ashamed, Sidon,
because the sea has spoken;
the fortress of the sea has said,
"I haven't been in labor;
I didn't give birth;
I never raised young men
or brought up young women."
5 When the Egyptians hear,
they will be in anguish
at the news about Tyre.
6 Cross over to Tarshish;
wail, inhabitants of the coast.
7 Is this your triumphant town,
whose origin is from ancient times,
whose feet carried her
to settle far away?
8 Who planned this concerning Tyre,
the one who gives crowns,
whose merchants were princes,
whose traders were the honored
of the earth?
9 The LORD of heavenly forces
planned it,
to defile the pride of all beauty,
to shame all the honored of the earth.

10 Go through your own land,
Daughter Tarshish,
for the harbor[p] is gone.
11 God's hand is extended over the sea,
shaking nations.
The LORD gave the command
to destroy Phoenicia's fortresses,
12 saying, You will no longer celebrate,
violated virgin Daughter Sidon.
Get up and head to Cyprus;
even there you will find no rest.
13 Look at the land of the Chaldeans,
the people who are no more.
Assyria destined it for wild animals:
they raised up their siege towers,
stripped its palaces,
and made it a ruin.
14 Wail, ships of Tarshish,
for your fortress is destroyed!
15 On that day, Tyre will be forgotten seventy years, the lifetime of one king. At the
end of seventy years, Tyre will become like
the prostitute in the song:
16 Take a harp, go around the city,
forgotten prostitute.
Play well, sing many songs,
so they'll remember you.
17 At the end of seventy years, the LORD
will visit Tyre. She will return to her trade
and will prostitute herself with all the kingdoms on the earth. 18 Her profits and wages
will be sacred to the LORD. They won't be
stored or saved. Her profits will go to those
living before the LORD, for plentiful food
and elegant clothes.

City of chaos falls

24 Look! The LORD will devastate
the earth and destroy it,
will twist its face
and scatter its inhabitants.
2 It will be the same for the people
and for the priest;
for the slave and for his master;
for the female servant
and for her mistress;
for the buyer and for the seller;
for the lender and for the borrower;
for the creditor and for the debtor.
3 The earth will be devastated,
totally devastated;
it will be destroyed, completely destroyed
because the LORD has said
it would be so.

4 The earth dries up and wilts;
the world withers and wilts;
the heavens wither away
with the earth.
5 The earth lies polluted
under its inhabitants,
for they have disobeyed instruction,

[n] Heb uncertain [o] Correction; MT *one crossing over the sea filled you* [p] Heb uncertain

swept aside law,
and broken the ancient covenant.
6 Therefore, a curse devours the earth;
its inhabitants suffer for their guilt.
Therefore, the earth's inhabitants
dwindle; very few are left.

7 The wine dries up;
the vine withers;
all the merry-hearted groan.
8 The joyous tambourines have ceased;
the roar of partyers has stopped;
the joyous harp has ceased.
9 No one drinks wine or sings;
beer is bitter to its drinkers.
10 The town is in chaos, broken;
every house is shut, without entrance.
11 There is a cry for wine in the streets.
All joy has reached its dusk;
happiness is exiled from the earth.
12 Ruin remains in the city,
and the gate is battered to wreckage.
13 It will be like this in the central part of
the land and among the peoples,
like an olive tree that has been shaken,
like remains from the grape harvest.

14 They raise their voice;
they sing with joy;
from the west they will shout
about the LORD's majesty.
15 Therefore, in the east honor the LORD;
in the islands of the sea,
the name of the LORD God of Israel!
16 From the ends of the earth
we have heard songs:
"Glory to the righteous one!"
But I say, "I waste away; I waste away;
I'm doomed!
Betrayers betray;
treacherously betrayers betray."

17 Terror, trench, and trap are upon you,
ruler of the earth!
18 Whoever flees from the sound of
terror will fall into the trench;
whoever climbs from the trench
will be caught in the trap.

Heaven's windows will open, and
the earth's foundations will quake.

19 The earth is shattering, shattering;
the earth is shaking, shaking;
the earth is teetering, tottering.
20 The earth trembles like a drunk
and shudders like a hut;
its rebellion weighs heavy upon it;
it will fall, no more to rise.
21 On that day, the LORD will punish the
forces of heaven in heaven, and the kings of
the earth on earth. 22 They will be gathered
together like prisoners in a pit, shut into
a prison, and punished after many days.
23 The moon will be diminished, and the sun
will fade, since the LORD of heavenly forces
will rule on Mount Zion and in Jerusalem,
glorious before his elders.

Rejoicing in God's salvation

25 LORD, you are my God.
I will exalt you;
I will praise your name,
for you have done wonderful things,
planned long ago, faithful and sure.
2 You have turned the city into rubble,
the fortified town into a ruin,
the fortress of foreigners
into a city no more,
never to be rebuilt.
3 Therefore,
strong people will glorify you;
the towns of tyrant nations
will fear you.
4 You have been a refuge for the poor,
a refuge for the needy in distress,
a hiding place from the storm,
a shade from the heat.
When the breath of tyrants
is like a winter[q] storm
5 or like heat in the desert,
you subdue the roar of foreigners.
Like heat shaded by a cloud,
the tyrants' song falls silent.

6 On this mountain,
the LORD of heavenly forces
will prepare for all peoples
a rich feast, a feast of choice wines,
of select foods rich in flavor,
of choice wines well refined.

[q]Or *wall*

7 He will swallow up on this mountain
the veil that is veiling all peoples,
the shroud enshrouding all nations.
8 He will swallow up death[r] forever.
The LORD God will wipe tears
from every face;
he will remove his people's disgrace
from off the whole earth,
for the LORD has spoken.
9 They will say on that day,
"Look! This is our God,
for whom we have waited—
and he has saved us!
This is the LORD,
for whom we have waited;
let's be glad
and rejoice in his salvation!"
10 The LORD's hand will indeed rest
on this mountain.

Moab will be trampled down
as straw is trampled into manure.
11 When in it they spread out their hands
as swimmers spread out
their hands to swim,
God will lay low their pride,
even by the efforts of their hands.
12 The fortified towers of their[s] walls
will be thrown down,
will be leveled,
will be brought down to the earth,
to the dust.

Trusting in God forever

26 On that day, this song
will be sung in the land of Judah:
Ours is a strong city!
God makes salvation
its walls and ramparts.
2 Open the gates
and let a righteous nation enter,
a nation that keeps faith.
3 Those with sound thoughts
you will keep in peace,
in peace because they trust in you.
4 Trust in the LORD forever,
for the LORD is a rock for all ages.
5 He has thrown down
those living on high,
and he will level the lofty town,
leveling it down to the earth;
he will bring it down to dust.
6 The feet trample it,
the feet of the poor,
the steps of the needy.

7 The way of the righteous is level;
you clear a path for the righteous.
8 In the path of your justice, LORD,
we wait for you;
with all our being, we long
for your name and your acclaim.
9 At night I long for you
with my whole being;
my spirit within me watches for you.
When your judgments
are at work in the earth,
those living in the world
learn righteousness.
10 When the wicked are favored,
they don't learn righteousness;
even among those who do right
they do wrong,
and they fail to see
the LORD's majesty.
11 LORD, your hand is lifted up,
but they don't see.
Let them see and shrink back
because of your zeal
for your people;
your burning anger
that consumes your enemies.

12 LORD, grant us peace,
because all that we have done
has been your doing.
13 LORD our God, other masters
besides you have ruled us,
but we will profess your name alone.
14 The dead don't live; ghosts don't rise.
Indeed, you have punished
and destroyed them,
and abolished all memory of them.
15 You've enlarged the nation, LORD.
You've enlarged the nation;
you are glorified.
You've expanded
all the land's boundaries.

[r] Heb *Maveth* [s] Or *your*

16 LORD, in distress they sought you out;
they poured out prayers to you
when you disciplined them.
17 As a pregnant woman close to
childbirth is in labor pains,
crying out in her pangs,
so were we because of you, LORD.
18 We were pregnant, we writhed,
but we gave birth to wind.
We have achieved no victories on earth;
the inhabitants of the earth never fall.

19 Your dead will live,
their[t] corpses will rise,
and those who dwell in the dust
will shout for joy.
Your shadow is a shadow of light,
but you will bring down
the ghosts into the underworld.
20 Go, my people, enter your rooms
and shut your doors behind you.
Take cover, for in a little while
the fury will be over.
21 Look! The LORD is going out
from his place
to bring the iniquity of the ruler
of the earth down upon him.
The earth will uncover its blood
and will conceal its slain no longer.

Scattered people return

27 On that day, the LORD will take a
great sword, harsh and mighty, and
will punish Leviathan the fleeing serpent,
Leviathan the writhing serpent, and will kill
the dragon that is in the sea. 2 On that day:
Sing about a delightful vineyard!
3 I, the LORD, am its guardian.
Every moment I water it;
night and day I guard it from attack.
4 I'm not angry,
but if it yields
thorns and thistles for me,
I will march to battle against it;
I will torch it completely.
5 Or let them[u] cling to me for refuge;
let them make peace with me;
let them make peace with me.
6 In coming days,[v]
Jacob will take root;
Israel will blossom and sprout
and fill the whole world with produce.

7 Did God strike Israel
as he struck those who struck him?
Was Israel killed
as his killers were killed?[w]
8 By frightening Jerusalem,
by sending her away,[x]
you contended with her,
expelling with a fierce blast
on the day of the east wind.
9 By this Jacob's guilt is reconciled,
and this was how his sins
were finally removed:
he made all the altar stones
like shattered chalk,
sacred poles[y] and incense altars
that couldn't stand.

10 The fortified city lies alone,
a hut forsaken,
abandoned like the desert.
Calves graze there;
they lie down there
and feed on its boughs.
11 When its branches are dry,
they are broken.
Women come and set fire to it.
These people have no understanding;
therefore, their maker
won't have compassion;
the one who formed them
won't be gracious.
12 On that day, the LORD will beat grain from
the channel of the Euphrates up to the Valley
of Egypt. You will be collected, Israelites, one
by one. 13 On that day, a great trumpet will be
played. Those who were lost in the land of Assyria and those who were scattered in the land
of Egypt will come. They will bow to the LORD
at his holy mountain in Jerusalem.

Judgment on Ephraim and Judah

28 Oh, the majestic garland of
Ephraim's drunks

[t]Or *my* [u]Or *it* [v]Or *those coming* [w]Heb uncertain [x]Heb uncertain [y]Heb *asherim*, perhaps objects devoted to the goddess Asherah

and the fading flower
of its splendid beauty
on the head that flows with perfume[z]
of those hammered with wine.
2 Look! The Lord has someone
who is powerful and strong;
like a hailstorm, a disastrous tempest,
like a downpour of mighty,
overflowing waters,
he can level them to the ground
with his hand.
3 The majestic garland of Ephraim's drunks
will be trampled underfoot.
4 The withered flower,
which is a thing of beauty[a]
as it sits on the head
of those bloated with fat,[b]
will be like an early fig
before the summer harvest:
whoever sees it
swallows it as soon as it is in hand.

5 On that day, the LORD of heavenly
forces will be a splendid garland and a beautiful wreath for the people who survive,
6 and a spirit of justice for the one who sits
in judgment, and a strength for those who
repel the assault at the gate.

7 These also stagger from wine
and stumble from beer:
priest and prophet stagger from beer;
they are confused by wine;
they stray on account of beer;
they err when receiving visions;
they stumble when making judgments.
8 All the tables are covered with vomit;
filth overruns the place.

9 To whom will God teach knowledge?
To whom will he explain the message?
To those just weaned from milk?
To those who have hardly
outgrown the breast?
10 It is "tsav letsav, tsav lestav;
qav leqav, qav leqav,"[c]
a little of this, a little of that.
11 With derisive speech
and a foreign tongue,
he will speak to this people.
12 He has said to them,
"This is the place of rest;
give rest to the weary;
this is the place of repose";
but they refused to listen.
13 So the LORD's word will be for them:
"tsav letsav, tsav letsav;
qav leqav, qav leqav,"
a little of this, a little of that.
So that they will go
and stagger backward,
they will be broken,
snared, and captured.

The covenant with death overturned

14 Therefore, hear the LORD's word,
you scoffers who rule this people
in Jerusalem.
15 You said, "We've cut a deal with death;[d]
with the underworld[e] we made a pact.
When the overflowing flood
passes through, it won't reach us;
for we have made lies our hiding place,
and in falsehood we take shelter."
16 Therefore, the LORD God says:
Look! I'm laying in Zion a stone,
a tested stone, a valuable cornerstone,
a sure foundation:
the one who trusts won't tremble.

17 I will make justice the measuring line
and righteousness the plumb line.
But hail will sweep away
the hiding place of lies,
and water will overflow the shelter.
18 Your deal with death[f] will be dissolved,
and your pact with the grave[g]
won't stand.
The rushing flood:
when it passes through,
you will be annihilated by it.
19 Every time it passes through
it will take you,
for morning by morning it will pass,
by day and by night.

It will be nothing but terror
to understand the message.

[z]DSS (1QIsa[a]) [a]Heb uncertain [b]Or *at the head of the fat valley* [c]A Hebrew version of baby talk or gibberish
[d]Heb *Maveth* [e]Heb *Sheol* [f]Heb *Maveth* [g]Heb *Sheol*

20 The bed is too short to stretch out,
and the shroud is too narrow
to cover oneself.

21 Just as on Mount Perazim,
the LORD will rise up;
as in the Gibeon Valley he will rage
to do his deed—strange is his deed!—
And to work his work—
foreign is his work!
22 So now stop your scoffing,
or your chains will be tightened,
because destruction has been ordered—
I have heard it!—
by the LORD God of heavenly forces
against the whole land.

Plowing and threshing

23 Listen and hear my voice;
pay attention and hear my word:
24 Does the plowman plow
without stopping for planting,
opening and harrowing their ground?
25 When he has smoothed its surface,
doesn't he scatter fennel,[h]
and sow cumin,
and plant wheat and barley
in their places,
and spelt as a border?
26 They are properly ordered;
their God directs them.[i]
27 Fennel[j] isn't threshed
with a threshing sledge,
nor is a cart wheel rolled over cumin,
but fennel[k] is beaten with a staff,
and cumin with a rod.
28 Bread grain is crushed,
but the thresher[l]
doesn't thresh it forever.
He drives the cart wheel over it;
he spreads it out but doesn't crush it.
29 This also comes from
the LORD of heavenly forces,
who gives wondrous counsel
and increases wisdom.

Ariel besieged but spared

29 Oh, Ariel, Ariel,
town where David encamped!
Year by year,
let the festivals come around—
2 but I will oppress Ariel.
There will be mourning and lamentation;
she will be like an Ariel to me.
3 I will surround you like a wall,
and I will lay a siege against you
with assault towers,
and I will raise up siegeworks
against you.
4 You will be brought down;
from the ground you will speak;
from low in the dust
your speech will come.
Your voice will be
like a ghost's from the earth;
from the dust
your words will whisper.
5 But your many enemies
will be like fine dust,
the terrible horde like passing chaff.
Suddenly, in an instant,
6 the LORD of heavenly forces
will come to you
with thunder, earthquake,
and a mighty voice,
with whirlwind, tempest,
and flames of devouring fire.
7 The horde of nations
fighting against Ariel,
and all who make war on her
and her fortress and besiege her,
will be like a dream,
a vision of the night.
8 It will be like when
a hungry person dreams of eating
but wakes up and the mouth is empty.
Or when a thirsty person
dreams of drinking
but wakes up and has a dry throat.
So will it be for all the horde of nations
who fight against Mount Zion.

9 Be shocked and stunned;
blind yourselves; be blind!
Be drunk, but not on wine;
stagger, but not on account of beer!
10 The LORD has poured on you
a spirit of deep sleep,

[h]Or *black cumin* [i]Or *waters them* [j]Or *black cumin* [k]Or *black cumin* [l]DSS (1QIsa[a])

and has shut your eyes, you prophets,
and covered your heads, you seers.
11 This entire vision has become for you
like the words of a sealed scroll. When they
give it to one who can read, saying, "Read
this," that one will say, "I can't, because it's
sealed." 12 And when the scroll is given to
one who can't read, saying, "Read this," that
one will say, "I can't read."

The wisdom of their wise

13 The Lord says:
Since these people turn toward me
with their mouths,
and honor me with lip service
while their heart is distant from me,
and their fear of me is just a human
command that has been memorized,
14 I will go on doing amazing things
to these people,
shocking and startling things.
The wisdom of their wise will perish,
and the discernment of their
discerning will be hidden.
15 Doom to those who hide
their plan deep, away from the LORD,
whose deeds are in the dark,
who say, "Who sees us?
Who knows us?"
16 You have everything backward!
Should the potter
be thought of as clay?
Should what is made say of its maker,
"He didn't make me"?
Should what is shaped
say of the one who shaped it,
"He doesn't understand"?

17 In just a little while won't Lebanon
become farmland once again,
and the farmland
be considered a forest?
18 On that day:
The deaf will hear
the words of a scroll and,
freed from dimness and darkness,
the eyes of the blind will see.
19 The poor will again
find joy in the LORD,
and the neediest of people
will rejoice in the holy one of Israel.
20 The tyrant will be no more,
the mocker will perish,
and all who plot evil will be eliminated:
21 all who incriminate others wrongly,
who entrap the judge in the gate,
and pointlessly postpone justice
for the innocent.

22 Therefore, proclaims the LORD,
the God of[m] the house of Jacob,
who redeemed Abraham:
Jacob won't be ashamed now,
and his face won't grow pale now.
23 When he sees his children
among them,
the work of my hands,
proclaiming my name holy,
they will make holy
the holy one of Jacob,
and stand in awe of Israel's God.
24 Those who wander in spirit
will have understanding,
and those who grumble
will gain insight.

Help from Egypt is futile

30 Doom to you, rebellious children,
says the LORD,
who make a plan, which is not mine;
who weave a plot,[n]
but not by my spirit,
piling up sin on sin;
2 setting out to go down to Egypt
without consulting me,
taking refuge in Pharaoh's refuge
and hiding in Egypt's shadow.
3 Pharaoh's refuge
will become your shame,
hiding in Egypt's shadow
your disgrace.
4 Though their officials are in Zoan,
and their messengers reach Hanes,
5 all will become shamed
because of a people
who can't assist them.
They are no help; they are no profit;
rather, shame and disgrace.

[m] Or *to* [n] Heb uncertain

6 An oracle about the beasts in the arid
southern plain.
Through a land of distress and danger,
lioness and roaring[o] lion,
viper and flying serpent,
they will carry their wealth
on donkeys' shoulders
and their treasures on camels' humps
to a people who won't profit,
7 for Egypt's help is utterly worthless.
Therefore, I call her
Rahab Who Sits Still.[p]

8 Now go, write it before them
on a tablet,
inscribe it on a scroll,
so in the future
it will endure as a witness.
9 These are rebellious people,
lying children,
children unwilling
to hear the LORD'S teaching,
10 who say to the seers, "Don't foresee,"
and to the visionaries,
"Don't report truthful visions;
tell us flattering things;
envision deceptions;
11 get out of the way;
step off the path;
let's have no more
'holy one of Israel.'"

12 Therefore, the holy one of Israel says:
Because you reject this word
and trust in oppression and cunning
and rely on them,
13 your sin will be like a crack
in a high wall; it bulges, about to fall:
suddenly, in an instant, it breaks!
14 Its breaking is like
the breaking of a storage jar
that is totally shattered.
No piece from among its fragments
will be large enough
to take fire from a hearth,
or to dip water from a cistern.

15 Therefore, the LORD God,
the holy one of Israel, says:
In return and rest you will be saved;
quietness and trust
will be your strength—
but you refused.
16 You said,
"No! We'll flee on horses"—
therefore, you will indeed flee—
"and we'll ride off;
on swift steeds we will ride"—
therefore, your pursuers will be swift.
17 One thousand will flee
at the threat of one,
and at the threat of five you will flee,
until you are left like a flagstaff
on a mountaintop,
like a flag on a hill.
18 Nonetheless, the LORD is waiting
to be merciful to you,
and will rise up to show you compassion.
The LORD is a God of justice;
happy are all who wait for him.

This is the way

19 People in Zion, who live in Jerusalem,
you will weep no longer. God will certainly
be merciful to you. Hearing the sound of
your outcry, God will answer you. 20 Though
the Lord gives you the bread of distress
and the water of oppression, your teacher
will no longer hide, but you will see your
teacher. 21 If you stray to the right or the
left, you will hear a word that comes from
behind you: "This is the way; walk in it."
22 You will defile your silver-plated idols and
your gold-covered priestly vest,[q] and you
will scatter them like menstrual rags. "Get
out," you will say to them.
23 God will provide rain for the seed you
sow in the ground, and the food the ground
produces will be rich and abundant. On that
day, your cattle will graze in large pastures.
24 The oxen and donkeys that are working
the ground will eat tasty feed spread for
them with shovel and fork.
25 On every lofty mountain, and on every
high hill, streams will run with water on the
day of the great massacre, when the towers
fall. 26 The light of the moon will be like the
light of the sun, and the light of the sun will

[o] Or *from them* [p] Or *Rahab the silent* [q] Correction; Heb *ephod*

be seven times brighter—like the light of seven days—on the day that the LORD bandages the people's brokenness and heals the wounds inflicted by his blows.

Assyria punished

27 Look there!
The LORD is coming from far away;
his anger blazing,
his smoke-cloud thick.
His lips are full of fury;
his tongue is like a devouring fire.
28 His breath is like a raging river
that reaches up to the neck,
to shake the nations
with a sieve of destruction,
and to put a misleading rein
on the people's jaws.
29 There will be singing for you
as on the night
that people celebrate a festival.
The heart will be joyful as it is
when one goes with a flute
to the LORD's mountain,
to the rock of Israel.
30 The LORD will unleash
his majestic voice
and display his crushing arm
in furious anger,
with a flame of consuming fire,
in stormy rain and hail.
31 The LORD's voice will terrify Assyria;
with a rod he will smite it.
32 And every crack that is made
in the foundation wall,
which the LORD will bring down
upon him,
will be accompanied
by timbrels and lyres.
The LORD will raise his arm
and fight against Assyria in battle.
33 His place for burning[r]
was arranged long ago;
it is indeed made ready for a king.
God has made its wood pile
wide and deep,
fire and wood in abundance.
The breath of the LORD, like a stream
of brimstone, ignites it.

Doom to those going to Egypt

31 Doom to those going down
to Egypt for help!
They rely on horses,
trust in chariots because they are many,
and on riders
because they are very strong.
But they don't look
to the holy one of Israel;
they don't seek the LORD.
2 But God also knows how to bring disaster;
he has not taken back his words.
God will rise up
against the house of evildoers
and against the help
of those who do wrong.
3 Egypt is human and not divine;
their horses are flesh and not spirit.
The LORD will extend his hand;
the helper will stumble,
those helped will fall,
and they will all die together.

4 The LORD has said to me:
When the lion growls,
the young lion, over its prey,
though a band of shepherds
is summoned against it,
isn't scared off by their noise
or frightened by their roar.
So the LORD of heavenly forces
will go down
to fight on Mount Zion and on her hill.
5 Like birds flying aloft,
so the LORD of heavenly forces
will shield Jerusalem:
shielding and saving,
sparing and rescuing.
6 People of Israel, return to the one
whom you have deeply betrayed! 7 On that
day, you will each reject the idols of silver
and the idols of gold, which you have sinfully made for yourselves.

8 Assyria will fall,
but not by a human sword—
a sword not made by humans
will devour them.
They will flee before the sword;

[r] Heb *Topheth*

their young men
will become forced laborers.
9 In horror they will flee
from their stronghold;
their officers will be terrified
at the signal,
says the LORD, whose fire is in Zion
and whose oven is in Jerusalem.

Righteous rule

32 See here: A king rules
to promote righteousness;
rulers govern to promote justice,
2 each like a shelter from the wind
and a refuge from a storm,
like streams of water in a wasteland,
like the shade of a massive cliff
in a worn-out land.
3 Then the eyes of those who can see
will no longer be blind,
the ears of those who can hear
will listen,
4 the minds of the rash
will know and comprehend,
and the tongues of those who stammer
will speak fluently and plainly.
5 Then a fool will no longer
be called honorable,
nor a villain considered respectable.
6 Fools speak folly;
their minds devise wickedness,
acting irreverently,
speaking falsely of the LORD,
leaving the hungry empty,
and depriving the thirsty of drink.
7 As for the villain, his villainies are evil.
He plans schemes
to destroy the poor with lying words,
even when the needy speak justly.
8 But an honorable person
plans honorable things
and stands up for what is honorable.

Warnings to the carefree

9 Women of leisure, stand up!
Hear my voice!
Carefree daughters,
listen to my word!
10 In a little over a year,
the carefree will shudder,
because the grape harvest will fail;
the vintage won't arrive.
11 Tremble, all of you who are at ease;
shudder, all of you who are secure!
Strip yourselves, bare your skin,
and tie mourning clothes
around your waist,
12 beating your breasts
for the pleasant fields,
for the fruitful vine,
13 for my people's soil
growing barbs and thorns,
for all the joyous houses
in the jubilant town.
14 The palace will be deserted,
the crowded city abandoned.
Stronghold and watchtower
will become empty fields forever,
suited for the pleasure of wild donkeys,
and a pasture for flocks—
15 until a spirit from on high
is poured out on us,
and the desert turns into farmland,
and the farmland
is considered a forest.
16 Then justice will reside in wild lands,
and righteousness
will abide in farmlands.
17 The fruit of righteousness
will be peace,
and the outcome of righteousness,
calm and security forever.
18 Then my people will live
in a peaceful dwelling,
in secure homes,
in carefree resting places.
19 Even if the forest falls[s]
and the humbled city is laid low,
20 those who sow beside any stream
will be happy,
sending out ox and donkey to graze.

Judgment and hope for the righteous

33 Doom to the destroyer
left undestroyed,
you traitor whom none have betrayed:
when you have finished destroying,
you will be destroyed;

[s] Or *it will hail when the forest falls*

and when you have stopped
betraying, they will betray you.

[2]LORD, show us favor;
we hope in you.
Be our strength every morning,
our salvation in times of distress.
[3]At the noise, peoples fled;
on account of your roar,
nations scattered.
[4]They gathered spoil like insects;
they rushed upon it
like a swarm of locusts.[t]
[5]The LORD is exalted; he lives on high,
filling Zion with
justice and righteousness.
[6]He will provide security
during a lifetime:[u]
a source of salvation,
wisdom, and knowledge—
fear of the LORD
will be Zion's treasure.[v]

[7]But then those in Ariel[w]
cried out in the streets;
messengers of peace wept bitterly.
[8]The highways were deserted;
travelers left the road.
The covenant was broken;
solemn pledges[x] were rejected;
no one cared for humanity.
[9]The land mourned; it wasted away;
Lebanon was ashamed; it withered.
Sharon became like the desert,
and Bashan and Carmel
were dropping their leaves.

[10]Now I will arise, says the LORD.
Now I will exalt myself;
now I will stand tall.
[11]You conceive straw, give birth to stubble;
your breath is a fire that devours you.
[12]Peoples will be burned to lime,
thorns cut up and set ablaze.
[13]You who are far away,
hear what I have done;
and you who are near,
know my strength!
[14]Sinners became terrified in Zion;
trembling seized the godless:
"Who among us can live
with the devouring fire?
Who among us can live
with the everlasting blaze?"
[15]The one who walks righteously
and speaks truthfully,
who rejects profit from extortion,
who waves away a bribe
instead of grabbing it,
who won't listen to bloody plots,
and who won't contemplate
doing something evil.
[16]He will live on the heights;
fortresses in the cliffs
will be his refuge.
His food will be provided,
his water guaranteed.
[17]When you gaze upon a king
in his glamour
and look at the surrounding land,
[18]in dismay you will think:
Where is the one who counts?
Where is the one who weighs?
Where is the one
who counts towers?
[19]You will no longer see
the defiant people,
the people of speech
too obscure to understand,
who stammer
in an incomprehensible language.
[20]Gaze upon Zion, our festival town.
Your eyes will see Jerusalem,
a carefree dwelling,
a tent that is not packed up,
whose stakes are never pulled up,
whose ropes won't snap.
[21]The LORD's majesty
will be there for us:
as a place of rivers, broad streams
where no boat will go,
no majestic ship will cross.
[22]The LORD is our judge;
the LORD is our leader;
the LORD is our king—
he will deliver us.

[t]Heb uncertain [u]Or *your times* [v]Or *his treasure* [w]Or *the valiant*; Heb uncertain [x]Correction; or *cities*; DSS (1QIsa[a]) *witnesses*

23 Your ropes are loosened;
they can't hold the mast firmly;
they can't spread the sail.
Then abundant spoil will be divided;
even the lame will seize spoil.
24 And no inhabitant will say,
"I'm sick."
The people living there
will be forgiven their sin.

Vengeance against Edom

34 Draw near, you nations, to hear;
and listen, you peoples.
Hear, earth and all who fill it,
world and all its offspring.
2 The LORD rages
against all the nations,
and is angry with all their armies.
God is about to wipe them out
and has prepared them for slaughter.
3 Their dead will be cast out,
the stench of their corpses will rise,
and the mountains
will melt from their blood.
4 All the stars of heaven will dissolve,
the skies will roll up like a scroll,
and all the stars will fall,
like a leaf withering from a vine,
like fruit from a fig tree.

5 When my sword has drunk its fill
in the heavens,
it will descend upon Edom for judgment,
upon a people
I have doomed for destruction.
6 The LORD has a sword
covered with blood;
it is soaked with fat
from the blood of lambs and goats,
from the kidney fat of rams,
for the LORD has a sacrifice in Bozrah,
a great slaughter in the land of Edom.
7 Wild oxen will fall with them,
steers with mighty bulls,
and their land will be drenched
with blood;
its soil soaked with fat.
8 The LORD has a day of vengeance,
a year of payback for Zion's cause.
9 Edom's streams will be turned into pitch,
its dust into sulfur,
and its land will become burning pitch.
10 Night and day won't be extinguished;
its smoke will go up forever.
From generation to generation
it will lie waste;
no one will ever pass through it again.
11 Screech owls and crows will possess it;
owls and ravens will live there.[y]
God will stretch over it
the measuring line of chaos
and the plummet stone of emptiness
over its officials.
12 No Kingdom There, they will call it,
and all its princes will disappear.
13 Thorns will grow up in its palaces,
weeds and brambles in its fortresses.
It will be a dwelling for jackals,
a home for ostriches.
14 Wildcats will meet hyenas,
the goat demon will call to his friends,
and there Lilith[z] will lurk
and find her resting place.
15 There the snake will nest and lay eggs
and brood and hatch in its shadow.
There too vultures will gather,
each with its mate.[a]
16 Consult the LORD's scroll and read:
Not one of these will be missing;
none will lack its mate.
God's own mouth has commanded;
God's own spirit has gathered them.
17 God has cast the lot for them;
God's hand allotted it to them
with the measuring line.
They will possess it forever;
they will live in it
from generation to generation.

Fertile wilderness

35 The desert and the dry land
will be glad;
the wilderness will rejoice
and blossom like the crocus.
2 They will burst into bloom,
and rejoice with joy and singing.
They will receive the glory of Lebanon,
the splendor of Carmel and Sharon.

[y]Species uncertain [z]Name of a demon [a]Species uncertain

They will see the LORD's glory,
the splendor of our God.

3 Strengthen the weak hands,
and support the unsteady knees.
4 Say to those who are panicking:
"Be strong! Don't fear!
Here's your God,
coming with vengeance;
with divine retribution
God will come to save you."

5 Then the eyes of the blind
will be opened,
and the ears of the deaf will be cleared.
6 Then the lame will leap like the deer,
and the tongue of the speechless
will sing.
Waters will spring up in the desert,
and streams in the wilderness.
7 The burning sand will become a pool,
and the thirsty ground,
fountains of water.
The jackals' habitat, a pasture;[b]
grass will become reeds and rushes.

8 A highway will be there.
It will be called The Holy Way.
The unclean won't travel on it,
but it will be for those walking
on that way.[c]
Even fools won't get lost on it;
9 no lion will be there,
and no predator will go up on it.
None of these will be there;
only the redeemed will walk on it.
10 The LORD's ransomed ones
will return and enter Zion
with singing,
with everlasting joy upon their heads.
Happiness and joy
will overwhelm them;
grief and groaning will flee away.

Sennacherib's message

36 Assyria's King Sennacherib marched
against all of Judah's fortified cities
and captured them in the fourteenth year
of King Hezekiah. 2 Assyria's king sent his
field commander from Lachish, together
with a large army, to King Hezekiah at Jerusalem. He stood at the water channel of the
Upper Pool, which is on the road to the field
where clothes are washed. 3 Hilkiah's son
Eliakim, who was the palace administrator,
Shebna the secretary, and Asaph's son Joah
the recorder went out to them.

4 Then the field commander said to them,
"Say to Hezekiah: Assyria's Great King
says this: Why do you feel so confident?
5 Do you think that empty words are the
same as good strategy and the strength to
fight? Who are you trusting that you now
rebel against me? 6 It appears that you are
trusting in a staff—Egypt—that's nothing
but a broken reed! It will stab the hand of
anyone who leans on it! That's all that Pharaoh, Egypt's king, is to anyone who trusts
in him. 7 Now suppose you say to me, 'We
trust in the LORD our God.' Isn't he the
one whose shrines and altars Hezekiah removed, telling Judah and Jerusalem, 'You
must worship only at this altar'?

8 "So now, make a wager with my master,
Assyria's king. I'll give you two thousand
horses if you can supply the riders! 9 How
will you drive back even the least important official among my master's servants
when you are relying on Egypt for chariots
and riders? 10 What's more, do you think
I've marched against this place to destroy
it without the LORD's support? It was the
LORD who told me, 'March against this
land and destroy it!' "

11 Eliakim, Shebna, and Joah said to the
field commander, "Please speak to your servants in Aramaic, because we understand
it. Don't speak with us in Hebrew,[d] because
the people on the wall will hear it."

12 The field commander said to them, "Did
my master send me to speak these words
just to you and your master and not also to
the men on the wall? They are the ones who
will have to eat their dung and drink their
urine along with you." 13 Then the field commander stood up and shouted in Hebrew at
the top of his voice: "Listen to the message
of the great king, Assyria's king. 14 The king

[b] Heb uncertain [c] Heb uncertain [d] MT *Judean*, so also 36:13

says this: Don't let Hezekiah lie to you. He won't be able to rescue you. 15Don't let Hezekiah persuade you to trust the LORD by saying, 'The LORD will certainly rescue us. This city won't be handed over to Assyria's king.'

16"Don't listen to Hezekiah, because this is what Assyria's king says: Surrender to me and come out. Then each of you will eat from your own vine and fig tree and drink water from your own well 17until I come to take you to a land just like your land. It will be a land of grain and new wine, a land of bread and vineyards. 18Don't let Hezekiah fool you by saying, 'The LORD will rescue us.' Did any of the other gods of the nations save their lands from the power of Assyria's king? 19Where are the gods of Hamath and Arpad? Where are the gods of Sepharvaim? Did they rescue Samaria from my power? 20Which one of the gods from those countries has rescued their land from my power? Will the LORD save Jerusalem from my power?"

21But they kept quiet and didn't answer him with a single word, because King Hezekiah's command was, "Don't answer him!" 22Hilkiah's son Eliakim, who was the palace administrator, Shebna the secretary, and Asaph's son Joah the recorder came to Hezekiah with ripped clothes. They told him what the field commander had said.

Hezekiah and Isaiah

37 When King Hezekiah heard this, he ripped his clothes, covered himself with mourning clothes, and went to the LORD's temple. 2He sent Eliakim the palace administrator, Shebna the secretary, and the senior priests to the prophet Isaiah, Amoz's son. They were all wearing mourning clothes. 3They said to him, "Hezekiah says this: Today is a day of distress, punishment, and humiliation. It's as if children are ready to be born, but there's no strength to see it through. 4Perhaps the LORD your God heard all the words of the field commander who was sent by his master, Assyria's king. He insulted the living God! Perhaps he will punish him for the words that the LORD your God has heard. Offer up a prayer for those few people who still survive."

5When King Hezekiah's servants got to Isaiah, 6Isaiah said to them, "Say this to your master: The LORD says this: Don't be afraid at the words you heard, which the officers of Assyria's king have used to insult me. 7I'm about to mislead him, so when he hears a rumor, he'll go back to his own country. Then I'll have him cut down by the sword in his own land."

8The field commander heard that the Assyrian king had left Lachish. So he went back to the king and found him attacking Libnah. 9Then the Assyrian king learned that Cush's King Tirhakah was on his way to fight against him. So he sent messengers to Hezekiah again: 10"Say this to Judah's King Hezekiah: Don't let the God you trust deceive you by saying, 'Jerusalem won't fall to the Assyrian king.' 11You yourself have heard what Assyrian kings do to other countries, wiping them out. Is it likely that you will be saved? 12Did the gods of the nations that my ancestors destroyed save them, the gods of Gozan, Haran, Rezeph, or the people of Eden in Telassar? 13Where now is Hamath's king, Arpad's king, or the kings of Lair, Sepharvaim, Hena, or Ivvah?"[e]

Hezekiah prays

14Hezekiah took the letters from the messengers and read them. Then he went to the temple and spread them out before the LORD. 15Hezekiah prayed to the LORD:

> 16"LORD of heavenly forces, God of Israel: you sit enthroned on the winged creatures. You alone are God over all the earth's kingdoms. You made both heaven and earth. 17LORD, turn your ear this way and hear! LORD, open your eyes and see! Listen to Sennacherib's words. He sent them to insult the living God! 18It's true, LORD, that the Assyrian kings have destroyed all the nations and their lands. 19The Assyrians burned the gods of those nations with fire because they aren't real gods. They are only

[e] Or *the king of the city of Sepharvaim;* or *the king of the city of Sepharvaim, Hena, and Ivvah*

man-made creations of wood and stone.
That's how the Assyrians could destroy
them. 20 So now, LORD our God, please
save us from Sennacherib's power! Then
all the earth's kingdoms will know that
you alone are LORD."
21 Then Isaiah, Amoz's son, sent a message
to Hezekiah: The LORD God of Israel says
this: Since you prayed to me about Assyria's
King Sennacherib, 22 this is the message that
the LORD has spoken against him:

The young woman, Daughter Zion,
despises you and mocks you;
Daughter Jerusalem shakes her head
behind your back.
23 Whom did you insult and ridicule?
Against whom did you raise your voice
and look on with disdain?
It was against the holy one of Israel!
24 With your servants,
you've insulted the Lord;
you said, "I, with my many chariots,
have gone up
to the highest mountains,
to the farthest reaches of Lebanon.
I have cut down its tallest cedars,
the best of its pine trees.
I have reached
its most remote lodging place,
its best forest.
25 I have dug wells,
have drunk water in foreign lands.[f]
With my own feet,
I dried up all of Egypt's streams."
26 Haven't you heard?
I set this up long ago;
I planned it in the distant past!
Now I have made it happen,
making fortified cities
collapse into piles of rubble.
27 Their citizens have lost their power;
they are frightened and dismayed.
They've become like plants in a field,
tender green shoots,
the grass on rooftops,
blasted by the east wind.
28 I know where you are,
how you go out and come in,
and how you rage against me.
29 Because you rage against me
and because your pride
has reached my ears,
I will put my hook in your nose
and my bit in your mouth.
I will make you go back
the same way you came.

30 Now this will be the sign for you, Hezekiah: This year you will eat what grows by
itself. Next year you will eat what grows
from that. But in the third year, plant seed
and harvest it; plant vineyards and eat their
fruit. 31 The survivors of Judah's family who
have escaped will put down roots and bear
fruit above. 32 Those who remain will go out
from Jerusalem, and those who survive will
go out from Mount Zion. The zeal of the
LORD of heavenly forces will do this.
33 Therefore, the LORD says this about
Assyria's king: He won't enter this city. He
won't shoot a single arrow here. He won't
come near the city with a shield. He won't
build a ramp to besiege it. 34 He'll go back by
the same way he came. He won't enter this
city, declares the LORD. 35 I will defend this
city and save it for my sake and for the sake
of my servant David.
36 The LORD's messenger went out and
struck down one hundred eighty-five thousand soldiers in the Assyrian camp. When
people got up the next morning, there were
dead bodies everywhere. 37 So Assyria's King
Sennacherib left and went back to Nineveh,
where he stayed. 38 Later, while he was worshipping in the temple of his god Nisroch, his
sons Adrammelech and Sharezer killed him
with a sword. Then they escaped to the land
of Ararat. His son Esarhaddon ruled after him.

Hezekiah's illness

38 At about that time Hezekiah became deathly sick. The prophet
Isaiah, Amoz's son, came to him and said:
"The LORD God says this: Put your affairs
in order because you are about to die. You
won't survive this."
2 Hezekiah turned his face to the wall and
prayed to the LORD: 3 "Please, LORD, remember how I've walked before you in truth

[f] Heb uncertain; DSS (1QIsa[a]) *in foreign lands*

and sincerity. I've done what you consider
to be good." Then Hezekiah cried and cried.
4 Then the LORD's word came to Isaiah:
5 "Go and say to Hezekiah: The LORD, the
God of your ancestor David, says this: I
have heard your prayer and have seen your
tears. I will add fifteen years to your life.
6 I will rescue you and this city from the
power of the Assyrian king. I will defend
this city. 7 This will be your sign from the
LORD that he will do what he promised:
8 once the shadow cast by the sun descends
on the steps of Ahaz, I will make it back up
ten steps." And the sun went back ten of the
steps that it had already descended.

9 A composition by Judah's King Hezekiah when he was sick and then recovered
from his sickness:

10 I thought, I must depart
in the prime of my life;
I have been relegated to the gates
of the underworld[g]
for the rest of my life.
11 I thought, I won't see the LORD.
The LORD is in the land of the living.
I won't look upon humans again
or be with the inhabitants
of the world.
12 My lifetime is plucked up
and taken from me
like a shepherd's tent.
My life is shriveled like woven cloth;
God cuts me off from the loom.
Between daybreak and nightfall
you carry out your verdict against me.
13 I cried out[h] until morning:
"Like a lion God crushes all my bones.
Between daybreak and nightfall
you carry out your verdict against me.
14 Like a swallow[i] I chirp;
I moan like a dove.
My eyes have grown weary
looking to heaven.
Lord, I'm overwhelmed; support me!"

15 What can I say?
God has spoken to me;
he himself has acted.
I will wander[j] my whole life
with a bitter spirit.
16 The LORD Most High is
the one who gives life to every heart,
who gives life to the spirit![k]
17 Look, he indeed exchanged my
bitterness for wholeness.[l]

You yourself have spared[m]
my whole being
from the pit of destruction,
because you have cast all my sins
behind your back.
18 The underworld[n] can't thank you,
nor can death[o] praise you;
those who go down to the pit
can't hope for your faithfulness.
19 The living, the living can thank you,
as I do today.
Parents will tell children
about your faithfulness.
20 The LORD has truly saved me,
and we will make music[p] at the LORD's
house all the days of our lives.

21 Then Isaiah said, "Prepare a salve made
from figs, put it on the swelling, and he'll
get better."
22 Hezekiah said to Isaiah, "What's the
sign that I'll be able to go up to the LORD's
temple?"

The Babylonian king's messengers

39 At that time, Babylon's King Merodach-
baladan, Baladan's son, sent letters
and a gift to Hezekiah, for he heard that
he had been ill and had recovered. 2 Hezekiah was pleased, and he showed them his
treasury—the silver and the gold, the spices
and fine oil—and everything in his armory,
all that was found in his storerooms. There
wasn't a thing in his house or in all his realm
that Hezekiah didn't show them.
3 Then Isaiah the prophet came to King
Hezekiah and said to him, "What did these
men say? Where did they come from?"
Hezekiah replied, "They came to me
from a distant land, from Babylon."

[g] Heb *Sheol* [h] Or *I lay down* [i] Heb uncertain [j] Heb uncertain [k] Heb uncertain [l] Heb uncertain [m] Cf LXX, Vulg; MT *loved* [n] Heb *Sheol* [o] Heb *Maveth* [p] Or *my stringed instruments*

[4]So Isaiah said, "What did they see in
your house?"

Hezekiah said, "They saw everything in
my house. There was nothing in my storerooms that I didn't show them."

[5]Isaiah said to Hezekiah, "Hear the word
of the LORD of heavenly forces: [6]Days are
coming when all that is in your house,
which your ancestors have stored up until
this day, will be carried to Babylon. Nothing
will be left, says the LORD. [7]Some of your
sons, your own descendants whom you
fathered, will be taken to become eunuchs
in the king of Babylon's palace."

[8]Hezekiah said to Isaiah, "The LORD's
word that you delivered is good," since he
thought, That means there will be peace
and security in my lifetime.

Comfort for God's people

40 Comfort, comfort my people!
says your God.
[2]Speak compassionately to Jerusalem,
and proclaim to her that her
compulsory service has ended,
that her penalty has been paid,
that she has received
from the LORD's hand
double for all her sins!

[3]A voice is crying out:
"Clear the LORD's way in the desert!
Make a level highway in the wilderness
for our God!
[4]Every valley will be raised up,
and every mountain and hill
will be flattened.
Uneven ground will become level,
and rough terrain a valley plain.
[5]The LORD's glory will appear,
and all humanity will see it together;
the LORD's mouth
has commanded it."

[6]A voice was saying:
"Call out!"
And another[q] said,
"What should I call out?"
All flesh is grass;
all its loyalty is
like the flowers of the field.
[7]The grass dries up
and the flower withers
when the LORD's breath blows on it.
Surely the people are grass.
[8]The grass dries up;
the flower withers,
but our God's word
will exist forever.

[9]Go up on a high mountain,
messenger Zion!
Raise your voice and shout,
messenger Jerusalem!
Raise it; don't be afraid;
say to the cities of Judah,
"Here is your God!"
[10]Here is the LORD God,
coming with strength,
with a triumphant arm,
bringing his reward with him
and his payment before him.
[11]Like a shepherd, God will tend the flock;
he will gather lambs in his arms
and lift them onto his lap.
He will gently guide
the nursing ewes.

The incomparable God

[12]Who has measured the waters
in the palm of a hand
or gauged the heavens with a ruler
or scooped the earth's dust up
in a measuring cup
or weighed the mountains on a scale
and the hills in a balance?
[13]Who directed the LORD's spirit
and acted as God's advisor?
[14]Whom did he consult for enlightenment?
Who taught him the path of justice
and knowledge
and explained to him
the way of understanding?
[15]Look, the nations are like a drop
in a bucket,
and valued as dust on a scale.
Look, God weighs the islands
like fine dust.

[q]MT; DSS (1QIsa^a), LXX *I*

16 Lebanon doesn't have enough fuel;
its animals aren't enough
for an entirely burned offering.
17 All the nations
are like nothing before God.
They are viewed as
less than nothing and emptiness.

18 So to whom will you equate God;
to what likeness will you compare him?
19 An idol? A craftsman pours it,
a metalworker covers it with gold,
and fashions silver chains.
20 The one who sets up an image
chooses wood that won't rot[r]
and then seeks a skilled artisan
to set up an idol that won't move.
21 Don't you know? Haven't you heard?
Wasn't it announced to you
from the beginning?
Haven't you understood
since the earth was founded?
22 God inhabits the earth's horizon—
its inhabitants are like locusts—
stretches out the skies like a curtain
and spreads it out
like a tent for dwelling.
23 God makes dignitaries useless
and the earth's judges into nothing.
24 Scarcely are they planted,
scarcely sown,
scarcely is their shoot
rooted in the earth
when God breathes on them,
and they dry up;
the windstorm
carries them off like straw.
25 So to whom will you compare me,
and who is my equal?
says the holy one.

Power for the weary

26 Look up at the sky and consider:
Who created these?
The one who brings out
their attendants one by one,
summoning each of them by name.
Because of God's great strength
and mighty power, not one is missing.
27 Why do you say, Jacob,
and declare, Israel,
"My way is hidden from the LORD
my God ignores my predicament"?
28 Don't you know? Haven't you heard?
The LORD is the everlasting God,
the creator of the ends of the earth.
He doesn't grow tired or weary.
His understanding
is beyond human reach,
29 giving power to the tired
and reviving the exhausted.
30 Youths will become tired and weary,
young men will certainly stumble;
31 but those who hope in the LORD
will renew their strength;
they will fly up on wings like eagles;
they will run and not be tired;
they will walk and not be weary.

Victor from the east

41 Be quiet before me, coastlands.
Let the nations renew their strength.
Let them approach and speak.
Let's draw near for a judgment.
2 Who has awakened one from the east
and has authority to summon him
to serve—
giving him nations,
conquering kings,
making them like dust with his sword,
like scattered straw with his bow?
3 He pursues them and passes untouched,
needing no path for his feet.
4 Who has acted and who has done this,
calling upon generation after
generation since the beginning?
I, the LORD, was first,
and I will be the last!

5 The coastlands see and fear;
the ends of the earth tremble;
they draw near and arrive.
6 Each helps the other,
each saying to the other,
"Take courage!"
7 The craftsman encourages
the metalworker;
the one who smoothes with the hammer

[r] Heb uncertain

encourages the one
who strikes the anvil,
saying of the welding, "That's good,"
and strengthening it with nails
so it won't move.

Israel as God's servant

8 But you, Israel my servant,
Jacob, whom I have chosen,
offspring of Abraham, whom I love,
9 you whom I took
from the ends of the earth
and called from its farthest corners,
saying to you, "You are my servant;
I chose you and didn't reject you":
10 Don't fear, because I am with you;
don't be afraid, for I am your God.
I will strengthen you,
I will surely help you;
I will hold you
with my righteous strong hand.
11 All who rage against you
will be shamed and disgraced.
Those who contend with you
will be as nothing and will perish.
12 You will look for your opponents,
and won't find them.
Those who fight you
will be of no account and will die.
13 I am the LORD your God,
who grasps your strong hand,
who says to you,
Don't fear; I will help you.
14 Don't fear, worm of Jacob,
people of Israel!
I will help you, says the LORD.
The holy one of Israel
is your redeemer.
15 Look, I've made you
into a new threshing tool
with sharp teeth.
You will thresh mountains
and pulverize them;
you will reduce hills to straw.
16 When you winnow them,
the wind will carry them off;
the tempest will scatter them.
You will rejoice in the LORD
and take pride in the holy one of Israel.
17 The poor and the needy
seek water, and there is none;
their tongues are parched with thirst.
I, the LORD, will respond to them;
I, the God of Israel,
won't abandon them.
18 I will open streams on treeless hilltops
and springs in valleys.
I will make the desert into ponds
and dry land into cascades of water.
19 I will plant in the desert cedar, acacia,
myrtle, and olive trees;
I will put in the wilderness cypress,
elm, and pine as well,
20 so that they will see and know
and observe and comprehend
that the LORD's hand has done this,
and the holy one of Israel
has created it.

Other gods challenged

21 Present your case, says the LORD.
Bring forward your evidence,
says Jacob's king.
22 Let the idols[s] approach
and tell us what will happen.
The prior things—what are they?
Announce them,
and we'll think about them
and know their significance.
Or proclaim to us what is to come!
23 Report things that will happen
in the future,
then we'll know that you are gods.
Do good! Or do bad!
Then we will all be afraid and fearful.
24 Look! You are nobody,
and your deeds are nothing.
Whoever chooses you is disgusting.
25 I woke up one from the north
and he came;
from the east,
one who calls my name.
He tramples governors like mud,
as a potter treads clay.
26 Who announced this from the start
so that we would know;
from an earlier time
so we would say, "That's right"?

[s] Or *them*

Truly, no one announced it,
no one proclaimed it,
and no one heard your words.
27 I first said it to Zion,
"Look, here they are";
to Jerusalem I now send a herald.
28 But I look, and there's no one
among them, no counselor;
and when I ask,
no one can answer.
29 Look, all of them are frauds;
their deeds amount to nothing;
their images are a total delusion.

God's servant described

42 But here is my servant,
the one I uphold;
my chosen, who brings me delight.
I've put my spirit upon him;
he will bring justice to the nations.
2 He won't cry out or shout aloud
or make his voice heard in public.
3 He won't break a bruised reed;
he won't extinguish a faint wick,
but he will surely bring justice.
4 He won't be extinguished or broken
until he has established justice
in the land.
The coastlands await his teaching.

5 God the LORD says—
the one who created the heavens,
the one who stretched them out,
the one who spread out the earth
and its offspring,
the one who gave breath to its people
and life to those who walk on it—
6 I, the LORD, have called you
for a good reason.
I will grasp your hand and guard you,
and give you as a covenant
to the people,
as a light to the nations,
7 to open blind eyes,
to lead the prisoners from prison,
and those who sit in darkness
from the dungeon.
8 I am the LORD;
that is my name;
I don't hand out my glory to others
or my praise to idols.
9 The things announced in the past—
look—they've already happened,
but I'm declaring new things.
Before they even appear,
I tell you about them.

Warrior and mother

10 Sing to the LORD a new song!
Sing his praise
from the ends of the earth!
You who sail the sea and all that fills it,
the coastlands and their residents.
11 Let the desert and its towns
shout aloud,
the villages that Kedar inhabits.
Let the cliff dwellers sing;
from the top of the mountains
let them shout.
12 Let them give the LORD glory
and declare God's praise
in the coastlands.
13 The LORD will go out like a soldier;
like a warrior God will stir up rage.
God will shout, will roar;
over enemies he will prevail.
14 I've kept still for a very long time.
I've been silent
and restrained myself.
Like a woman in labor I will moan;
I will pant, I will gasp.
15 I will wither mountains and valleys,
and I will dry up all their vegetation.
I will turn rivers into deserts,[t]
and I will dry up pools.
16 I will make the blind walk a road
they don't know,
and I will guide them
in paths they don't know.
But I will make darkness before them
into light
and rough places into level ground.
These things I will do;
I won't abandon them.

Blindness and deafness

17 Turned backward, utterly shamed
are those who trust in idols,

[t] Or *islands*

who say to a cast image,
"You are our god!"
18 Hear, deaf ones,
and blind ones, look and see!
19 Who is blind if not my servant
and deaf like my messenger
whom I send?
Who is blind like the restored one,[u]
blind like the servant of the LORD?
20 You have seen many things,
but don't keep watch.
With ears open, you don't hear.[v]
21 The LORD desired
for the sake of his righteousness
to expand and glorify the Instruction.
22 But this is a people
plundered and looted,
everyone trapped in holes
and hidden in dungeons.
They have become plunder
with no one to rescue,
loot with no one to say, "Give it back."

23 Which of you will listen to this,
will pay attention and respond
from now on?
24 Who gave Jacob to the looter,
and Israel to the plunderers?
Wasn't it the LORD,
the one we sinned against?
They were not willing to walk
in God's ways,
and wouldn't listen to his teaching.
25 So God poured out on Jacob
the heat of his anger
and the fury of battle.
It scorched him, and he didn't know it;
it burned him,
but he didn't give it much thought.

Don't fear

43 But now, says the LORD—
the one who created you, Jacob,
the one who formed you, Israel:
Don't fear, for I have redeemed you;
I have called you by name;
you are mine.
2 When you pass through the waters,
I will be with you;
when through the rivers,
they won't sweep over you.
When you walk through the fire,
you won't be scorched
and flame won't burn you.
3 I am the LORD your God,
the holy one of Israel, your savior.
I have given Egypt as your ransom,
Cush and Seba in your place.
4 Because you are precious in my eyes,
you are honored, and I love you.
I give people in your place,
and nations in exchange for your life.
5 Don't fear,
I am with you.
From the east I'll bring your children;
from the west I'll gather you.
6 I'll say to the north, "Give them back!"
and to the south, "Don't detain them."
Bring my sons from far away,
and my daughters
from the end of the earth,
7 everyone who is called by my name
and whom I created for my glory,
whom I have formed and made.

8 Bring out the blind people
who have eyes,
the deaf ones who have ears.
9 All the nations are gathered together;
the peoples are assembled.
Which of them announced this?
Who predicted to us the past events?
Let them bring their witnesses
as a defense;
let them hear and say, "It's true!"
10 You are my witnesses, says the LORD,
my servant, whom I chose,
so that you would
know and believe me
and understand that I am the one.
Before me no god was formed;
after me there has been no other.
11 I, I am the LORD,
and there is no savior besides me.
12 I announced, I saved, I proclaimed,
not some stranger among you.
You are my witnesses, says the LORD,
and I am God.

[u] Heb *Meshullam*, possibly a proper name [v] Or *he does not hear*

13 From the dawn of time, I am the one.
No one can escape my power.
I act, and who can undo it?

Don't remember

14 The LORD your redeemer,
the holy one of Israel, says,
For your sake,
I have sent an army[w] to Babylon,
and brought down all the bars,
turning the Chaldeans' singing
into a lament.[x]
15 I am the LORD, your holy one,
Israel's creator, your king!
16 The LORD says—
who makes a way in the sea
and a path in the mighty waters,
17 who brings out chariot and horse,
army and battalion;
they will lie down together
and will not rise;
they will be extinguished,
extinguished like a wick.
18 Don't remember the prior things;
don't ponder ancient history.
19 Look! I'm doing a new thing;
now it sprouts up;
don't you recognize it?
I'm making a way in the desert,
paths[y] in the wilderness.
20 The beasts of the field,
the jackals and ostriches, will honor me,
because I have put water in the desert
and streams in the wilderness
to give water to my people,
my chosen ones,
21 this people whom I formed for myself,
who will recount my praise.

22 But you didn't call out to me, Jacob;
you were tired of me, Israel.
23 You didn't bring me lambs
for your entirely burned offering;
you didn't honor me with your sacrifices.
I didn't make you worship with offerings;
I didn't weary you with frankincense.
24 You didn't buy spices for me
with your money,
or satisfy me with
the fat of your sacrifices.
Instead, you have burdened me
with your sins
and wearied me with your evil actions.
25 I, I am the one who wipes out
your rebellious behavior for my sake.
I won't remember your sin.
26 Summon me, and let's go to trial together;
you tell your story
so that you may be vindicated!
27 Your first ancestor sinned,
and your officials rebelled against me.
28 So I made the holy officials impure,
handed over Jacob to destruction
and Israel to abuse.

You are my witnesses

44 But now hear this, Jacob my servant,
and Israel, whom I have chosen.
2 The LORD your maker,
who formed you in the womb
and will help you, says:
Don't fear, my servant Jacob,
Jeshurun, whom I have chosen.
3 I will pour out water upon thirsty ground
and streams upon dry land.
I will pour out my spirit
upon your descendants
and my blessing upon your offspring.
4 They will spring up
from among the reeds
like willows by flowing streams.
5 This one will say, "I am the LORD's,"
and that one will be named after Jacob.
Another will write on his hand,
"The LORD's,"
and will take the name Israel.

6 The LORD, Israel's king and redeemer,
the LORD of heavenly forces, says:
I am the first, and I am the last,
and besides me there are no gods.
7 Who is like me?
Let them speak up, explain it,
and lay it out for me.
Who announced long ago what is to be?[z]
Let them tell us[a] what is to come.

[w]Heb lacks *an army.* [x]Heb uncertain [y]DSS (1QIsa[a]); MT *streams* [z]Or *Since I placed an ancient people and coming things* [a]Or *them*

8 Don't tremble; have no fear!
Didn't I proclaim it?
Didn't I inform you long ago?
You are my witnesses!
Is there a God besides me?
There is no other rock; I know of none.

Idol-makers mocked

9 Idol-makers are all as nothing;
their playthings do no good.
Their promoters
neither see nor know anything,
so they ought to be ashamed.
10 Who would form a god or cast an idol
that does no good?
11 All its worshippers will be ashamed,
and its artisans, who are only human.
They will all gather and stand,
tremble and be ashamed together.
12 A blacksmith with his tools
works it over coals,
and shapes it with hammers,
and works it with his strong arm.
He even becomes hungry and weak.
If he didn't drink water, he'd pass out.
13 A carpenter stretches out a string,
marks it out with a stylus,
fashions it with carving tools,
and marks it with a compass.
He makes it into a human form,
like a splendid human,
to live in a temple.
14 He cuts down cedars for himself,
or chooses a cypress[b] or oak,
selecting from all
the trees of the forest.
He plants a pine,[c]
and the rain makes it grow.
15 It becomes suitable to burn for humans,
so he takes some of the wood
and warms himself.
He kindles fire and bakes bread.
He fashions a god and worships it;
he makes an idol and bows down to it.
16 Half of it he burns in the fire;
on that half he roasts
and eats meat, and he is satisfied.
He warms himself and says,
"Ah, I'm warm, watching the fire!"
17 And the rest of it he makes into a god,
into his idol,
and he bows down, worships,
and prays to it, saying,
"Save me, for you are my god!"
18 They don't know or comprehend,
for their eyes can't see
and their minds can't comprehend.
19 He doesn't think,
and has no knowledge or
understanding to think:
Half of it I burned in the fire,
and I baked bread on its coals,
and roasted meat and ate.
Should I make the rest
into something detestable?
Should I bow down
to a block of wood?
20 He's feeding on ashes;
his deluded mind has led him astray.
He can't save himself and say,
"Isn't this thing in my hand a lie?"

Promises to Jacob and Jerusalem

21 Remember these things, Jacob;
Israel, for you are my servant.
I formed you; you are my servant!
I won't forget you, Israel.
22 I swept away your rebellions
like a cloud,
and your sins like fog.
Return to me,
because I have redeemed you.

23 Sing, heavens,
for the LORD has acted;
shout, depths of the earth!
Burst out with a ringing cry,
you mountains, forest,
and every tree in it.
The LORD has redeemed Jacob,
and will glorify himself
through Israel.

24 The LORD your redeemer
who formed you in the womb says:
I am the LORD, the maker of all,
who alone stretched out the heavens,
who spread out the earth by myself,

[b]Species uncertain [c]Species uncertain

25 who frustrates the omens of diviners
and makes a mockery of magicians,
who turns back the wise
and turns their knowledge into folly.
26 But who confirms the word
of my[d] servant,
and fulfills the predictions
of my messengers;
who says about Jerusalem,
"It will be resettled";
and who says about the cities of Judah,
"They will be rebuilt,
and I will restore their ruins";
27 who says to the ocean depths,
"Dry up; I will dry your streams";
28 who says about Cyrus,
"My shepherd—
he will do all that I want";
who says about Jerusalem,
"She will be rebuilt";
and who says about the temple,
"You will be founded
once again."

Cyrus as God's anointed

45 The LORD says to his anointed,
to Cyrus,
whom I have grasped by the strong hand,
to conquer nations before him,
disarming kings,
and opening doors before him,
so no gates will be shut:
2 I myself will go before you,
and I will level mountains.
I will shatter bronze doors;
I will cut through iron bars.
3 I will give you hidden treasures
of secret riches,
so you will know that I am the LORD,
the God of Israel, who calls you by name.
4 For the sake of my servant Jacob
and Israel my chosen,
I called you by name.
I gave you an honored title,
though you didn't know me.
5 I am the LORD, and there is no other;
besides me there is no God.
I strengthen you—
though you don't know me—
6 so all will know, from the rising
of the sun to its setting,
that there is nothing apart from me.
I am the LORD; there's no other.
7 I form light and create darkness,
make prosperity and create doom;
I am the LORD,
who does all these things.

8 Pour down, you heavens above,
and let the clouds flow
with righteousness.
Let the earth open for salvation
to bear fruit;
let righteousness sprout as well.
I, the LORD,
have created these things.

Potter and clay

9 Doom to the one
who argues with the potter,[e]
as if he were just another clay pot!
Does the clay say to the potter,
"What are you making?"
or "Your work has no handles"?
10 Doom to one who says to a father,
"What have you fathered?"
and to a woman,
"With what are you in labor?"
11 The LORD, the holy one of Israel
and its maker,[f] says:
Are you questioning me[g]
about my own children?
Are you telling me what to do
with the work of my hands?
12 I myself made the earth,
and created humans upon it.
My own hands
stretched out the heavens.
I commanded all their forces.
13 I have a right to awaken Cyrus;
I will smooth all his paths.
He will build my city
and set my exiles free,
not for a price and not for a bribe,
says the LORD of heavenly forces.

14 The LORD says:
Egypt will grow weary, Cush will be sold,[h]

[d]Or *his*; also in next line [e]Or *maker* [f]Or *potter* [g]Or *about future things ask me* [h]Heb uncertain

and the tall Sabeans
will cross over to you.
They will be yours,
and after you they will go.
In chains they will come;
to you they will bow down.
They will plead with you:
"Truly God is with you;
there's no other, no other God."
15 Surely you are a god who hides himself,
Israel's God and savior.

Idols contrasted with God

16 They will all be shamed and disgraced;
the makers of idols
will end up disgraced together.
17 Israel has been saved by the LORD
of everlasting salvation.
You won't be shamed,
and you won't be disgraced
forever and always.
18 For this is what the LORD said,
who created the heavens,
who is God,
who formed the earth and made it,
who established it,
who didn't create it a wasteland
but formed it as a habitation:
I, the LORD, and none other!
19 I didn't speak in secret
or in some land of darkness;
I didn't say to the offspring of Jacob,
"Seek me in chaos."
I am the LORD,
the one who speaks truth,
who announces what is correct.
20 Gather and come,
draw near together,
fugitives of the nations!
Those who carry their wooden idols
don't know;
those who pray to a god
who won't save.
21 Announce! Approach!
Confer together!
Who proclaimed this
from the beginning,
announced it from long ago?
Wasn't it I, the LORD?
There's no other God except me,
a righteous God and a savior;
there's none besides me!
22 Turn to me and be saved,
all you ends of the earth,
for I am God, and there's no other.
23 I have sworn a solemn pledge;
a word has left my mouth;
it is reliable and won't fail.
Surely every knee will bow
and every tongue will confess;
24 they will say, "Righteousness and
strength come only from the LORD.
All who are angry with him
will come to shame.
25 All the Israelites
will be victorious and rejoice."

Babylon's idols can't compare

46 Bel crouches down; Nebo cowers.
Their idols sit on animals, on beasts.
The objects you once carried about
are now borne as burdens
by the weary animals.
2 They crouch down and cower together.
They aren't able to rescue the burden,
but they themselves go into captivity.
3 Listen to me, house of Jacob,
all that remains from the house of Israel
who have been borne by me
since pregnancy,
whom I carried from the womb
4 until you grow old.
I am the one,
and until you turn gray
I will support you.
I have done it,
and I will continue to bear it;
I will support and I will rescue.
5 To whom will you liken me
and count me equal
and compare me so that we are alike?
6 Those who pour out gold from a bag
and weigh silver with a balance
hire a metalworker;
then he makes a god.
They bow down; they worship;
7 they carry the idol[i] on their
shoulders and support it;

[i] Or *it*

they set it down, and it stands still,
unable to move from its place.
If one cries out to it, it doesn't answer.
It can't save people from their distress.

Remember past events

8 Remember this and take courage;
take it to heart, you rebels.
9 Remember the prior things—
from long ago;
I am God, and there's no other.
I am God! There's none like me,
10 who tells the end at the beginning,
from ancient times
things not yet done,
saying, "My plan will stand;
all that I decide I will do,"
11 I call a bird of prey from the east,
a man from a distant land for my plan.
As surely as I have spoken,
I'll make it happen;
I have planned, and yes, I'll do it.
12 Listen to me, you bullheaded people
who are far from victory:
13 I'm bringing my victory near—
it isn't far,
and my salvation—it won't delay.
I will establish salvation in Zion
and grant my splendor to Israel.

Daughter Babylon dethroned

47 Go down and sit in the dust,
virgin Daughter Babylon!
Sit on the ground without a throne,
Daughter Chaldea,
because they will no longer call you
tender and pampered.
2 Take the millstones and grind flour!
Remove your veil, strip off your robe,
expose your thighs,
wade through the rivers!
3 Your nakedness will be exposed,
and your disgrace will be seen.
I will take vengeance;
no one will intervene.[j]
4 Our redeemer has spoken;
the LORD of heavenly forces
is his name,
the holy one of Israel.

5 Sit silent and go into darkness,
Daughter Chaldea,
because they will no longer call you
Queen of Kingdoms.
6 I was enraged with my people;
I made my inheritance impure
and put them under your power.
You took no pity on them.
You made your yoke heavy
even on the elderly.
7 You said, "I'm forever;
I'm the eternal mistress."
You didn't stop and think;
you didn't consider the outcome.
8 So listen to this,
luxuriant one who sits secure,
who says in her heart,
I'm utterly unique;
I'll never sit as a widow;
I'll never know childlessness:
9 Both of these will happen to you
at once, on a single day:
childlessness and widowhood
will envelop you in full measure,
despite your many sorceries,
despite your very powerful spells.
10 You felt secure in your evil;
you said, "No one sees me."
Your wisdom and knowledge
spun you around.
You thought to yourself,
I and no one else.
11 Now evil will come against you,
something you won't anticipate.
A curse will fall upon you,
something you won't be able to dispel.
Destruction will come upon you suddenly,
something you won't foresee.

12 Continue with your enchantments,
and with your many spells,
which you have practiced
since childhood.
Maybe you will be able to succeed.
Maybe you will inspire terror.
13 You are weary
from all your consultations;
let the astrologers stand up
and save you,

[j] Syr, cf Vulg; MT *I won't meet a man*

those who gaze at the stars,
and predict what will happen to you
at each new moon.
14 They are just like stubble;
the fire burns them.
They won't save themselves
from the powerful flames.
This is no warming ember
or fire to sit beside.
15 Those with whom you have
wearied yourself are like this,
those with whom you were
in business from your youth:
each has wandered off
on their own way;
none will save you.

New things from now on

48 Listen to this, house of Jacob,
who are known by the name of Israel,
descendants of Judah,[k]
who swear by the LORD's name
and invoke Israel's God
dishonestly and unrighteously.

2 They are known
as residents of the holy city,
those who depend
upon the God of Israel—
the LORD of heavenly forces
is his name.
3 Past things I announced long ago;
from my mouth I proclaimed them.
I acted suddenly, and they came about.
4 Because I know that you are stubborn,
your neck is made of iron,
and your forehead is bronze.
5 I informed you long ago;
before they came about
I proclaimed them to you
so you wouldn't say, "My idol did them;
my wood statue and metal god
commanded them."
6 You've heard and seen all this—
won't you admit it?
From now on I'll tell you new things,
guarded secrets that you don't know.
7 They are created now, not long ago;
before today you hadn't heard of them,
so you won't say,
"I already knew them."
8 You haven't heard,
nor have you known;
as in ages past your ears are closed,
because I knew
what a traitor you were;
you were known as a rebel from birth.
9 For the sake of my reputation
I control my anger;
for your sake
I restrain my powerful radiance
so as to not destroy you.
10 See, I have refined you,
but not like silver;
I have tested you[l]
in the furnace of misery.
11 For the sake of my reputation,
for my own sake, I will act,
for why will my name be made impure?
I won't give my glory to another.

12 Listen to me, Jacob;
Israel, whom I called:
I am the one;
I am the first and I am the last.
13 My hand founded the earth;
my strong hand
spread out the heavens.
When I call to them, they all stand up.
14 Gather yourselves,
all of you, and listen.
Who among you
announced these things?
"The LORD loves him.
He will do
what God wants with Babylon
and with the descendants[m]
of Chaldea."
15 I, I have spoken and told him
the things that will happen to him;
I will make him succeed.
16 Come close to me; listen to this:
Since the very beginning
I haven't spoken in secret.
Whenever anything happens,
I am there.
(And now the LORD God
has sent me with his spirit.)

[k] Or *came out from the waters of Judah* [l] Or *I have chosen* [m] LXX; MT *his arm*

17 The LORD your redeemer,
the holy one of Israel, proclaims:
I am the LORD your God
who teaches you for your own good,
who leads you in the way
you should go.
18 If you would pay attention
to my commands,
your well-being would be like a river,
and your righteousness
like the waves of the sea.
19 Your offspring would be
like the sand,
and your descendants like its grains.
Their name would never be eliminated,
never wiped out from before me.

20 Go out from Babylon;
flee from the Chaldeans!
Report this with a loud shout,
proclaim it;
broadcast it out
to the end of the earth.
Say, "The LORD has redeemed
his servant Jacob!"
21 They weren't thirsty when he led
them through the deserts.
God made water flow
from the rock for them;
split the rock, and water flowed out.
22 There is no well-being,
says the LORD, for the wicked.

The servant speaks up

49 Listen to me, coastlands;
pay attention, peoples far away.
The LORD called me before my birth,
called my name when
I was in my mother's womb.
2 He made my mouth like a sharp sword,
and hid me in the shadow
of God's own hand.
He made me a sharpened arrow,
and concealed me in God's quiver,
3 saying to me, "You are my servant,
Israel, in whom I show my glory."
4 But I said, "I have wearied myself in vain.
I have used up my strength
for nothing."
Nevertheless, the LORD
will grant me justice;
my reward is with my God.
5 And now the LORD has decided—
the one who formed me
from the womb as his servant—
to restore Jacob to God,
so that Israel might return to him.
Moreover, I'm honored
in the LORD's eyes;
my God has become my strength.
6 He said: It is not enough,
since you are my servant,
to raise up the tribes of Jacob
and to bring back
the survivors of Israel.
Hence, I will also appoint you
as light to the nations
so that my salvation may reach
to the end of the earth.

7 The LORD, redeemer of Israel
and its holy one,
says to one despised,
rejected by nations,
to the slave of rulers:
Kings will see and stand up;
commanders will bow down
on account of the LORD,
who is faithful,
the holy one of Israel,
who has chosen you.
8 The LORD said:
At the right time, I answered you;
on a day of salvation, I helped you.
I have guarded you,
and given you as a covenant
to the people, to restore the land,
and to reassign deserted properties,
9 saying to the prisoners,
"Come out,"
and to those in darkness,
"Show yourselves."
Along the roads animals[n] will graze;
their pasture will be
on every treeless hilltop.
10 They won't hunger or thirst;
the burning heat and sun
won't strike them,

[n] Heb lacks *animals.*

because one who has compassion
for them will lead them
and will guide them
by springs of water.
11 I will turn all my mountains
into roads;
my highways will be built up.
12 Look! These will come from far away.
Look! These from the north and west,
and these from the southland.[o]

13 Sing, heavens! Rejoice, earth!
Break out, mountains, with a song.
The LORD has comforted his people,
and taken pity on those who suffer.

Compassion for Zion

14 But Zion says,
"The LORD has abandoned me;
my Lord has forgotten me."
15 Can a woman forget
her nursing child,
fail to pity the child of her womb?
Even these may forget,
but I won't forget you.
16 Look, on my palms I've inscribed you;
your walls are before me continually.
17 Your builders[p] come quickly;
those who destroy and demolish you
will depart from you.
18 Look up all around and see:
they are all gathered;
they come to you.
As surely as I live, says the LORD,
you will put them all
on like ornaments,
bind them on like a bride.

19 As for your ruins and desolate places
and destroyed land—
you will soon be crowded with settlers,
and those who swallowed you
will be far away.
20 You will again hear the children
who were born bereaved say,
"The place is too crowded for me;
make room for me to settle."
21 And you will think to yourself,
Who bore me these?
I was bereaved and desolate,
exiled and sent off.
So who raised these?
I was left behind, I was alone;
where were these?

22 The LORD God says:
Look, I will raise my hand
to the nations,
and to the peoples
I will lift up my signal.
They will bring your sons in their arms,
and will carry your daughters
on their shoulders.
23 Kings will be your attendants,
and their queens your nursemaids.
With faces to the ground
they will bow down to you;
they will lick the dust from your feet.
You will know that I am the LORD;
the one who hopes in me
won't be ashamed.

24 Can loot be taken from warriors?
Can a tyrant's captives escape?
25 The LORD says:
Even the captives of warriors
will be taken,
and the tyrant's loot will escape.
I myself will oppose those
who oppose you,
and I myself will save your children.
26 I will make your oppressors
eat their own flesh;
and as with wine, with their own
blood they will be drunk,
so that all flesh will know that
I, the LORD, am your savior,
and the mighty one of Jacob
is your redeemer.

50 The LORD says:
Where's your mother's divorce decree,
with which I sent her away?
Or to which lender did I sell you?
On account of your sins
you were sold;
on account of your transgressions
your mother was sent away.

[o] Heb *Sinim* [p] Or *children*

2 Why did I come and find no one?
Why did I call when no one answered?
Is my hand too small to redeem you?[q]
Don't I have enough power to save?
With my rebuke I dry up the sea
and make the rivers into wilderness.
Their fish stink from lack of water;
they die of thirst.
3 I clothe the heavens with darkness
and cover them
with funeral clothing.

God's faithful servant

4 The LORD God
gave me an educated tongue
to know how to respond to the weary
with a word that will awaken them
in the morning.[r]
God awakens my ear
in the morning to listen,
as educated people do.
5 The LORD God opened my ear;
I didn't rebel; I didn't turn my back.
6 Instead, I gave my body to attackers,
and my cheeks to beard pluckers.
I didn't hide my face
from insults and spitting.
7 The LORD God will help me;
therefore, I haven't been insulted.
Therefore, I set my face like flint,
and knew I wouldn't be ashamed.
8 The one who will declare me innocent
is near.
Who will argue with me?
Let's stand up together.
Who will bring judgment against me?
Let him approach me.
9 Look! The LORD God will help me.
Who will condemn me?
Look, they will wear out like clothing;
the moth will eat them.

10 Who among you fears the LORD?
Who listens to the voice
of his servant,
who walks in darkness
and has no light?
They will trust in the LORD's name,
and rely upon their God.
11 Look! All of you are kindling fire,
igniting torches.
Walk by the light of your fire,
by the torches you have ignited.
This is what will happen
to you by my hand:
you will lie down in grief.

Look to Abraham and Sarah

51 Listen to me,
you who look for righteousness,
you who seek the LORD:
Look to the rock
from which you were cut
and to the quarry
where you were dug.
2 Look to Abraham your ancestor,
and to Sarah, who gave you birth.
They were alone when I called them,
but I blessed them
and made them many.
3 The LORD will comfort Zion;
he will comfort all her ruins.
He will make her desert like Eden
and her wilderness
like the LORD's garden.
Happiness and joy will be found in her—
thanks and the sound
of singing.

Salvation endures forever

4 Pay attention to me, my people;
listen to me, my nation,
for teaching will go out from me,
my justice, as a light to the nations.
5 I will quickly bring my victory.
My salvation is on its way,
and my arm will judge the peoples.
The coastlands hope for me;
they wait for my judgment.[s]
6 Look up to the heavens,
and gaze at the earth beneath.
The heavens will disappear
like smoke,
the earth will wear out
like clothing,
and its inhabitants will die like gnats.
But my salvation will endure forever,
and my righteousness will be unbroken.

[q] Heb lacks *you.* [r] Heb uncertain [s] Or *for my arm*

7 Listen to me,
you who know what is right,
people who carry my teaching
in your heart:
Don't fear human scorn,
and don't be upset
when they abuse you.
8 The moth will eat them
as if they were clothing,
and the worm will eat them like wool,
but my righteousness is forever,
and my salvation for all generations.

Awake, arm of the Lord

9 Awake, awake, put on strength,
arm of the LORD.
Awake as in times past,
generations long ago.
Aren't you the one who crushed Rahab,
who pierced the dragon?
10 Didn't you dry up the sea,
the waters of the great deep?
And didn't you make
the redeemed a road to cross
through the depths of the sea,
a road for the redeemed to pass?
11 Then let those
ransomed by the LORD return
and come to Zion with singing
and with everlasting joy
upon their heads.
Let happiness and joy overwhelm them;
let grief and groaning flee.

12 I, I am the one who comforts you.
Why should you fear humans
who will die,
mortals who are treated like grass?
13 You forgot the LORD your maker,
the one who stretched out the heavens
and founded the earth.
You were continually afraid,
all day long,
on account of the oppressor's wrath—
a fear by which they intend
to destroy you.
Where now is the oppressor's wrath?
14 The imprisoned ones
will soon be released;
they won't die in the pit
or even lack bread.
15 I am the LORD your God,
who stirs up the sea
so that its waves roar—
the LORD of heavenly forces
is his name.
16 I put my words in your mouth
and hid you in the shadow of my hand,
stretching out[t] the heavens,
founding the earth,
and saying to Zion,
"You are my people."

Wake yourself, Jerusalem

17 Wake yourself, wake yourself!
Rise up, Jerusalem,
who drank the cup of wrath
from the LORD's hand.
You drank;
you drained the goblet of reeling.
18 There's no one to guide her
among all the children she bore;
there's no one to take her
by the hand among all the children
she raised.
19 These two things
have happened to you—
Who will be sorry for you?[u]—
destruction and devastation,
famine and sword—
who will comfort you?[v]
20 Your children passed out;
they lay at the head of every street
like antelope in a net,
filled with the LORD's wrath,
with the rebuke of your God.

21 Therefore, hear this, suffering one,
who is drunk, but not from wine.
22 The LORD, your Lord and your God,
who contends for his people, says:
Look, I have taken the cup of reeling,
the goblet of my wrath,
from your hand.
You will no longer drink from it.
23 I will put it
in the hand of your tormentors,
who said to you,

[t] Or *planting* [u] DSS (1QIsa[a]), LXX, Vulg; MT *How will I* [v] Or *how will I comfort you?*

"Lie down so that we can walk on you.
Make your back like the ground,
like a street for those walking on it."

Awake, holy Zion

52 Awake, awake,
put on your strength, Zion!
Put on your splendid clothing,
Jerusalem, you holy city;
for the uncircumcised and unclean
will no longer come into you.
2 Shake the dust off yourself;
rise up; sit enthroned, Jerusalem.
Loose the bonds from your neck,
captive Daughter Zion!

3 The LORD proclaims:
You were sold for nothing,
and you will be redeemed
without money.
4 The LORD God proclaims:
Long ago my people went down
to reside in Egypt.
Moreover, Assyria
has oppressed them without cause.
5 And now what have I here?
says the LORD.
My people are taken away
for nothing.
Their rulers wail, says the LORD,
and continually all day long
my name is despised.
6 Therefore, my people
will know my name on that day;
I'm the one who promises it;
I'm here.

Your God rules

7 How beautiful upon the mountains
are the feet of a messenger
who proclaims peace,
who brings good news,
who proclaims salvation,
who says to Zion, "Your God rules!"
8 Listen! Your lookouts
lift their voice;
they sing out together!
Right before their eyes they see
the LORD returning to Zion.
9 Break into song together,
you ruins of Jerusalem!
The LORD has comforted his people
and has redeemed Jerusalem.
10 The LORD has bared his holy arm
in view of all the nations;
all the ends of the earth have seen
our God's victory.

11 Depart! Depart! Go out from there!
Unclean! Don't touch!
Get out of that place; purify yourselves,
carriers of the LORD's equipment!
12 You won't go out in a rush,
nor will you run away,
because the one going before you
is the LORD;
your rear guard is the God of Israel.

Suffering servant

13 Look, my servant will succeed.
He will be exalted
and lifted very high.
14 Just as many were appalled by you,
he too appeared disfigured, inhuman,
his appearance unlike that of mortals.
15 But he will astonish[w] many nations.
Kings will be silenced because of him,
because they will see
what they haven't seen before;
what they haven't heard before,
they will ponder.

53 Who can believe
what we have heard,
and for whose sake has
the LORD's arm[x] been revealed?
2 He grew up like a young plant before us,[y]
like a root from dry ground.
He possessed no splendid form
for us to see,
no desirable appearance.
3 He was despised and avoided by others;
a man who suffered,
who knew sickness well.
Like someone
from whom people hid their faces,
he was despised,
and we didn't think about him.

[w] Or *sprinkle* [x] Or *power* [y] Or *him*

4 It was certainly our sickness
that he carried,
and our sufferings that he bore,
but we thought him afflicted,
struck down by God and tormented.
5 He was pierced because of our rebellions
and crushed because of our crimes.
He bore the punishment
that made us whole;
by his wounds we are healed.
6 Like sheep we had all wandered away,
each going its own way,
but the LORD let fall on him
all our crimes.

7 He was oppressed and tormented,
but didn't open his mouth.
Like a lamb being brought to slaughter,
like a ewe silent before her shearers,
he didn't open his mouth.

8 Due to an unjust ruling
he was taken away,
and his fate—who will think about it?
He was eliminated
from the land of the living,
struck dead
because of my people's rebellion.
9 His grave was among the wicked,
his tomb with evildoers,[z]
though he had done no violence,
and had spoken nothing false.

10 But the LORD wanted to crush him
and to make him suffer.
If his life is offered[a] as restitution,
he will see his offspring;
he will enjoy long life.
The LORD's plans will come
to fruition through him.
11 After his deep anguish
he will see light,[b]
and he will be satisfied.
Through his knowledge,
the righteous one, my servant,
will make many righteous,
and will bear their guilt.
12 Therefore, I will give him a share
with the great,
and he will divide the spoil
with the strong,
in return for exposing his life to death
and being numbered with rebels,
though he carried the sin of many
and pleaded on behalf
of those who rebelled.

Sing, barren woman

54 Sing, barren woman
who has borne no child;
break forth into singing and cry out,
you who were never in labor,
for the children of the wife
who has been deserted
will be more numerous than the
children of the married,
says the LORD.
2 Enlarge the site of your tent,
and stretch out the drapes
of your dwellings;
don't hold back.
Lengthen your tent ropes
and strengthen your stakes.
3 To the right and to the left
you will burst out,
and your children will possess
the nations' land
and settle their desolate cities.

4 Don't fear,
because you won't be ashamed;
don't be dismayed,
because you won't be disgraced.
You will forget the shame of your youth;
you'll no longer remember
the disgrace of your widowhood.
5 The one marrying you
is the one who made you—
the LORD of heavenly forces
is his name.
The one redeeming you
is the holy one of Israel,
the one called the God of all the earth.
6 As an abandoned
and dejected woman
the LORD has summoned you;
as a young wife when she is rejected,
says your God.

[z] Cf Tg; MT *and with a rich one in his deaths* [a] Or *if you place his life* [b] DSS (1QIsa[a]); MT lacks *light*.

7 For a brief moment I abandoned you,
but with great mercy
I will bring you back.
8 In an outburst of rage,
I hid my face from you for a moment,
but with everlasting love
I have consoled you,
says your redeemer, the LORD.

9 These are like the days[c] of Noah for me,
when I promised that Noah's waters
would never again cover the earth.
Likewise I promise not to rage
against you or rebuke you.
10 The mountains may shift,
and the hills may be shaken,
but my faithful love
won't shift from you,
and my covenant of peace
won't be shaken,
says the LORD, the one who pities you.

11 Suffering one, storm-tossed,
uncomforted,
look, I am setting your gemstones
in silvery metal
and your foundations with sapphires.
12 I will make your towers of rubies,
and your gates of beryl,
and all your walls of precious jewels.
13 All your children will be disciples
of the LORD—
I will make peace abound
for your children.
14 You will be firmly founded
in righteousness.
You will stay far from oppression
because you won't fear,
far from terror
because it won't come near you.
15 If anyone attacks you,
it's none of my doing.
Whoever attacks you
will fall because of you.
16 Look, I myself created the metalworker
who blows the fire of coal
and who produces a tool for his work.
And I myself created the looter
to destroy.
17 No weapon fashioned against
you will succeed,
and you may condemn every tongue
that disputes with you.
This is the heritage
of the LORD's servants,
whose righteousness
comes from me, says the LORD.

Invitation to the feast

55 All of you who are thirsty,
come to the water!
Whoever has no money,
come, buy food and eat!
Without money, at no cost,
buy wine and milk!
2 Why spend money for what isn't food,
and your earnings
for what doesn't satisfy?
Listen carefully to me
and eat what is good;
enjoy the richest of feasts.
3 Listen and come to me;
listen, and you will live.
I will make
an everlasting covenant with you,
my faithful loyalty to David.
4 Look, I made him a witness
to the peoples,
a prince and commander of peoples.
5 Look, you will call a nation
you don't know,
a nation you don't know will run to you
because of the LORD your God,
the holy one of Israel,
who has glorified you.

6 Seek the LORD
when he can still be found;
call him while he is yet near.
7 Let the wicked abandon their ways
and the sinful their schemes.
Let them return to the LORD
so that he may have mercy on them,
to our God, because he is generous
with forgiveness.
8 My plans aren't your plans,
nor are your ways my ways,
says the LORD.

[c] Or *for the waters*

9 Just as the heavens
are higher than the earth,
so are my ways
higher than your ways,
and my plans than your plans.
10 Just as the rain and the snow
come down from the sky
and don't return there
without watering the earth,
making it conceive and yield plants
and providing seed to the sower
and food to the eater,
11 so is my word
that comes from my mouth;
it does not return to me empty.
Instead, it does what I want,
and accomplishes what I intend.

12 Yes, you will go out with celebration,
and you will be brought back in peace.
Even the mountains and the hills
will burst into song before you;
all the trees of the field
will clap their hands.
13 In place of the thorn
the cypress will grow;
in place of the nettle
the myrtle will grow.
This will attest to the LORD's stature,
an enduring reminder
that won't be removed.

Keepers of God's Sabbath

56 The LORD says:
Act justly and do what is righteous,
because my salvation is coming soon,
and my righteousness will be revealed.
2 Happy is the one who does this,
the person who holds it fast,
who keeps the Sabbath,
not making it impure,
and avoids doing any evil.

3 Don't let the immigrant
who has joined with the LORD say,
"The LORD will exclude me
from the people."
And don't let the eunuch say,
"I'm just a dry tree."

4 The LORD says:
To the eunuchs who keep my sabbaths,
choose what I desire,
and remain loyal to my covenant.
5 In my temple and courts,
I will give them
a monument and a name
better than sons and daughters.
I will give to them an enduring name
that won't be removed.
6 The immigrants who have joined me,[d]
serving me and loving my name,[e]
becoming my servants,[f]
everyone who keeps the Sabbath
without making it impure,
and those who hold fast
to my covenant:
7 I will bring them
to my holy mountain,
and bring them joy
in my house of prayer.
I will accept their entirely burned
offerings and sacrifices on my altar.
My house will be known as a house
of prayer for all peoples,
8 says the LORD God,
who gathers Israel's outcasts.
I will gather still others
to those I have already gathered.

Neglectful leaders

9 All you beasts of the field,
come and eat,
all you beasts of the forest!
10 The lookouts are blind;
they all lack sense.
They are all mute dogs that can't bark,
dreamers, loungers, loving to sleep.
11 But the dogs have monstrous appetites.
They never have enough.
They are shepherds
who don't understand.
All of them
have turned to their own ways,
every last one greedy for profit.
12 "Come! I'll get some wine!
Let's drink beer!
Tomorrow will be like today,
or even much better."

[d] Or *to the LORD* [e] Or *serving him and loving the LORD's name* [f] Or *becoming his servants*

57 The righteous person perishes,
and no one takes it to heart.
Loyal people are gathered together,
and no one understands
that because of evil
the righteous one passed away.
2 They will find peace;
those who walk in straight paths
will find rest on their burial beds.

Accusations against idolators

3 Come here, you children of sorcery,
offspring of adultery and prostitution!
4 Whom are you mocking?
Against whom do you
open your mouth wide
and stick out your tongue?
Aren't you children of rebellion,
offspring of lies,
5 who console yourselves with idols
under every green tree,
who slaughter children in the valleys,
under the rocky cliffs?
6 You belong with the smooth talkers[g]
in the valley;
they, they are your lot.
For them you poured out
a drink offering,
and presented a grain offering.
Should I condone these things?
7 On a very high mountain
you made your bed.
You went up there to offer a sacrifice.
8 Behind the door and the doorpost
you placed your symbols.
You abandoned me and lay down,
making room in your bed
and making deals for yourself
with them.[h]
You loved their bed;
you saw their nakedness.
9 You went down to Molech[i] with oil,
and you slathered on your ointments;
you sent your messengers far away,
sent them down to the underworld.[j]
10 Worn out by all your efforts,
yet you wouldn't say, "This is useless."
You found new strength;
therefore, you weren't tired.
11 Whom did you dread and fear
so that you lied,
didn't remember me
or give me a thought?
Isn't it because I was silent
and closed my eyes
that you stopped fearing me?
12 I will bring evidence about your
righteousness and your actions;
they won't help you.
13 When you cry out,
let those things you've gathered
save you!
The wind will lift them all;
one breath will take them away.
But those taking refuge in me
will inherit the land
and possess my holy mountain.

Peace for the remorseful

14 It will be said:
"Survey, survey; build a road!
Remove barriers
from my people's road!"
15 The one who is high and lifted up,
who lives forever,
whose name is holy, says:
I live on high, in holiness,
and also with the crushed[k]
and the lowly,
reviving the spirit of the lowly,
reviving the heart of those
who have been crushed.[l]
16 I won't always accuse,
nor will I be enraged forever.
It is my own doing
that their spirit is exhausted—
I gave them breath!
17 I was enraged about their illegal profits;
I struck them;
in rage I withdrew from them.
Yet they went on wandering
wherever they wanted.
18 I have seen their ways,
but I will heal them.
I will guide them,
and reward them with comfort.
And for those who mourn,
19 I will create reason for praise:[m]

[g]Or *smooth things* [h]Heb uncertain [i]Or *the king* [j]Heb *Sheol* [k]Or *contrite* [l]Or *contrite* [m]Heb uncertain

utter prosperity to those far and near,
and I will heal them, says the LORD.
20 But the wicked are like the churning sea
that can't keep still.
They churn up from their waters
muck and mud.
21 There is no peace, says my God,
for the wicked.

Fasting from injustice

58 Shout loudly; don't hold back;
raise your voice like a trumpet!
Announce to my people their crime,
to the house of Jacob their sins.
2 They seek me day after day,
desiring knowledge of my ways
like a nation that acted righteously,
that didn't abandon their God.
They ask me for righteous judgments,
wanting to be close to God.
3 "Why do we fast and you don't see;
why afflict ourselves
and you don't notice?"
Yet on your fast day
you do whatever you want,
and oppress all your workers.
4 You quarrel and brawl, and then you fast;
you hit each other violently
with your fists.
You shouldn't fast as you are doing today
if you want to make
your voice heard on high.
5 Is this the kind of fast I choose,
a day of self-affliction,
of bending one's head like a reed
and of lying down
in mourning clothing and ashes?
Is this what you call a fast,
a day acceptable to the LORD?

6 Isn't this the fast I choose:
releasing wicked restraints,
untying the ropes of a yoke,
setting free the mistreated,
and breaking every yoke?
7 Isn't it sharing your bread
with the hungry
and bringing the homeless poor
into your house,
covering the naked when you see them,
and not hiding from your own family?
8 Then your light
will break out like the dawn,
and you will be healed quickly.
Your own righteousness
will walk before you,
and the LORD's glory
will be your rear guard.
9 Then you will call,
and the LORD will answer;
you will cry for help,
and God will say, "I'm here."
If you remove the yoke from among you,
the finger-pointing, the wicked speech;
10 if you open your heart to the hungry,
and provide abundantly
for those who are afflicted,
your light will shine in the darkness,
and your gloom will be like the noon.
11 The LORD will guide you continually
and provide for you,
even in parched places.
He will rescue your bones.
You will be like a watered garden,
like a spring of water that won't run dry.
12 They will rebuild ancient ruins
on your account;
the foundations of generations past
you will restore.
You will be called Mender of Broken Walls,
Restorer of Livable Streets.

13 If you stop trampling the Sabbath,
stop doing whatever you want
on my holy day,
and consider the Sabbath a delight,
sacred to the LORD, honored,
and honor it
instead of doing things your way,
seeking what you want
and doing business as usual,
14 then you will take delight
in the LORD.
I will let you ride on the heights
of the earth;
I will sustain you with the heritage
of your ancestor Jacob.
The mouth of the LORD has spoken.

Alienation from God

59 Look! The LORD does not lack
the power to save,

nor are his ears too dull to hear,
2 but your misdeeds have separated you
from your God.
Your sins have hidden his face
from you
so that you aren't heard.
3 Your hands are stained with blood,
and your fingers with guilt.
Your lips speak lies;
your tongues mutter malice.
4 No one sues honestly;
no one pleads truthfully.
By trusting in emptiness
and speaking deceit,
they conceive harm
and give birth to malice.
5 They hatch adders' eggs,
and weave spiderwebs.
Whoever eats their eggs will die.
Moreover, the crushed egg
hatches a viper.
6 Their webs can't serve as clothing;
they can't cover themselves
with their deeds.
Their deeds are deeds of malice,
and the work of violence
is in their hands.
7 Their feet run to evil;
they rush to shed innocent blood.
Their thoughts are thoughts of malice;
desolation and destruction
litter their highways.
8 They don't know the way of peace;
there's no justice in their paths.
They make their roads crooked;
no one who walks in them
knows peace.

Injustice obscures vision

9 Because of all this,
justice is far from us,
and righteousness beyond our reach.
We expect light, and there is darkness;
we await a gleam of light,
but walk about in gloom.
10 We grope along the wall like the blind;
like those without eyes we grope.
We stumble at noonday
as if it were twilight,
and among the strong
as if we were dying.
11 All of us growl like bears,
and like doves we moan.
We expect justice, but there is none;
we await salvation, but it is far from us.
12 Our rebellions are numerous
in your presence;
our sins testify against us.
Our rebellions are with us;
we're aware of our guilt:
13 defying and denying the LORD,
turning away from our God,
planning oppression and revolt,
muttering lying words
conceived in our minds.
14 Justice is pushed aside;
righteousness stands far off,
because truth has stumbled
in the public square,
and honesty can't enter.
15 Truth is missing;
anyone turning from evil is plundered.

God will intervene

The LORD looked and was upset
at the absence of justice.
16 Seeing that there was no one,
and astonished that
no one would intervene,
God's arm brought victory,
upheld by righteousness,
17 putting on righteousness as armor
and a helmet of salvation on his head,
putting on garments of vengeance,
and wrapping himself in a cloak of zeal.
18 God will repay according to their actions:
wrath to his foes,
retribution to enemies,
retribution to the coastlands,
19 so those in the west
will fear the LORD's name,
and those in the east
will fear God's glory.
It will come like a rushing river
that the LORD's wind drives on.
20 A redeemer will come to Zion
and to those in Jacob
who stop rebelling,
says the LORD.

21 As for me, this is my covenant
with them, says the LORD.

My spirit, which is upon you,
and my words, which I have placed
in your mouth
won't depart from your mouth,
nor from the mouths
of your descendants,
nor from the mouths
of your descendants' children,
says the LORD,
forever and always.

Jerusalem's coming radiance

60 Arise! Shine! Your light has come;
the LORD's glory has shone
upon you.
2 Though darkness covers the earth
and gloom the nations,
the LORD will shine upon you;
God's glory will appear over you.
3 Nations will come to your light
and kings to your dawning radiance.

4 Lift up your eyes and look all around:
they are all gathered;
they have come to you.
Your sons will come from far away,
and your daughters
on caregivers' hips.
5 Then you will see and be radiant;
your heart will tremble
and open wide,
because the sea's abundance
will be turned over to you;
the nations' wealth will come to you.
6 Countless camels will cover your land,
young camels
from Midian and Ephah.
They will all come from Sheba,
carrying gold and incense,
proclaiming the LORD's praises.
7 All Kedar's sheep
will be gathered for you;
rams from Nebaioth
will be your offerings;
they will be accepted on my altar,
and I will glorify my splendid house.

8 Who are these who fly like a cloud,
like doves to their shelters?
9 I'm the hope of the coastlands.
Ships from Tarshish are in the lead
to bring your children from afar,
their silver and gold with them
for the name of the LORD your God
and for the holy one of Israel,
who has glorified you.
10 Foreigners will rebuild your walls,
and their kings will serve you.
Though in my rage
I struck you down,
in my favor I have consoled you.
11 Your gates will be open continually;
day and night they won't close,
to bring to you the wealth of nations,
and their kings led in procession.
12 The nation and the dynasty
that won't serve you will perish;
such nations will be devastated.
13 Lebanon's glory will come upon you,
cypress, elm, and pine,
to glorify the site of my sanctuary,
and I will honor my royal footstool.
14 The children of your tormenters
will come bending low to you;
all who despised you
will bow down at your feet.
They will call you The LORD's City,
Zion, of the holy one of Israel.
15 Instead of being abandoned,
hated, and forbidden,
I will make you majestic forever,
a joy for all generations.
16 You will suck the milk of nations,
and nurse at royal breasts.
You will know that I am the LORD,
your savior
and your redeemer,
the mighty one of Jacob.
17 Instead of bronze I will bring gold;
instead of iron I will bring silver;
instead of wood, bronze;
and instead of stones, iron.
I will make peace your governor
and righteousness your taskmaster.
18 Violence will no longer resound
throughout your land,
nor devastation or destruction
within your borders.
You will call your walls Salvation,
and your gates Praise.
19 The sun will no longer
be your light by day,

nor will the moon shine
for illumination by night.[n]
The LORD will be your everlasting light;
your God will be your glory.
20 Your sun will no longer set;
your moon will no longer wane.
The LORD will be
an everlasting light for you,
and your days of mourning
will be ended.
21 Your people will all be righteous;
they will possess the land forever.
They are the shoot that I planted,
the work of my hands, to glorify myself.
22 The least will become a thousand,
and the smallest a powerful people.
I am the LORD; at the right moment,
I will hurry it along.

Joyful proclamations

61 The LORD God's spirit is upon me,
because the LORD has anointed me.
He has sent me
to bring good news to the poor,
to bind up the brokenhearted,
to proclaim release for captives,
and liberation for prisoners,
2 to proclaim the year of the LORD's favor
and a day of vindication for our God,
to comfort all who mourn,
3 to provide for Zion's mourners,
to give them a crown in place of ashes,
oil of joy in place of mourning,
a mantle of praise
in place of discouragement.
They will be called Oaks of Righteousness,
planted by the LORD to glorify himself.
4 They will rebuild the ancient ruins;
they will restore
formerly deserted places;
they will renew ruined cities,
places deserted in generations past.

5 Foreigners will stay
and shepherd your sheep,
and strangers will be
your farmers and vinedressers.
6 You will be called The Priests of the LORD;
Ministers of Our God,
they will say about you.
You will feed on the wealth of nations,
and fatten[o] yourself on their riches.
7 Instead of shame,
their[p] portion will be double;
instead of disgrace,
they will rejoice over their share.
They will possess a double portion
in their land;
everlasting joy will be theirs.
8 I, the LORD, love justice;
I hate robbery and dishonesty.[q]
I will faithfully give them their wage,
and make with them
an enduring covenant.
9 Their offspring will be known
among the nations,
and their descendants
among the peoples.
All who see them will recognize
that they are a people
blessed by the LORD.

10 I surely rejoice in the LORD;
my heart is joyful because of my God,
because he has clothed me
with clothes of victory,
wrapped me in a robe of righteousness
like a bridegroom in a priestly crown,
and like a bride adorned in jewelry.
11 As the earth puts out its growth,
and as a garden grows its seeds,
so the LORD God will grow righteousness
and praise before all the nations.

Jerusalem redeemed

62 For Zion's sake I won't keep silent,
and for Jerusalem's sake
I won't sit still
until her righteousness
shines out like a light,
and her salvation blazes like a torch.
2 Nations will see your righteousness,
all kings your glory.
You will be called by a new name,
which the LORD's own mouth
will determine.

[n]Cf DSS (1QIsa[a]), LXX; MT lacks *by night.* [o]Heb uncertain [p]Or *your* [q]Heb manuscripts, LXX, Syr, Tg; MT *robbery with an entirely burned offering*

3 You will be a splendid garland
in the LORD's hand,
a royal turban in the palm of God's hand.
4 You will no longer be called Abandoned,
and your land will no longer be called
Deserted.
Instead, you will be called
My Delight Is in Her,
and your land, Married.
Because the LORD delights in you,
your land will be cared for once again.
5 As a young man
marries a young woman,
so your sons will marry you.
With the joy of a bridegroom
because of his bride,
so your God will rejoice because of you.

6 Upon your walls, Jerusalem,
I have appointed sentinels.
Continually, all day and all night,
they won't keep silent.
You who call on the LORD, don't rest,
7 and don't allow God to rest
until he establishes Jerusalem,
and makes it the praise of the earth.
8 The LORD has promised
with raised hand and strong arm:
I will never again give your grain
as food for your enemies.
Foreigners won't drink your wine
for which you labored.
9 Those who harvest will eat it
and will praise the LORD;
those who gather will drink it
in my holy courtyards.

10 Pass through, pass through the gates;
prepare the way for the people!
Build, build the road;
clear away the stones!
Raise up a signal for the peoples.
11 This is what the LORD announced
to the earth's distant regions:
Say to Daughter Zion,
"Look! Your deliverer arrives,
bringing reward and payment!"
12 They will be called The Holy People,
Redeemed By the LORD.
And you will be called Sought After—
A City That Is Not Abandoned.

Vengeance against the nations

63 Who is this coming from Edom,
from Bozrah in bright red garments,
this splendidly dressed one,
striding[r] with great power?
It is I, proclaiming righteousness,
powerful to save!
2 Why is your clothing red,
and your garments like those
of one who stomps on grapes?
3 I have pressed out in the vat by myself—
from the peoples, no one was with me.
I stomped on them in my anger,
trampled them in my wrath.
Their blood splashed on my garments,
and stained all my clothing,
4 because I intended a day of vengeance;
the year of my deliverance had arrived.
5 I looked and found no helper;
I was astonished to find no supporter.
But my arm brought victory for me;
my wrath helped me.
6 I trampled down nations in my anger
and made them drunk on my wrath;
I spilled their blood on the ground.

Prayer of yearning

7 I will recount the LORD's faithful acts;
I will sing the LORD's praises,
because of all the LORD did for us,
for God's great favor
toward the house of Israel.
God treated them compassionately
and with deep affection.
8 God said, "Truly, they are my people,
children who won't do what is wrong."
God became their savior.
9 During all their distress,
God also was distressed,
so a messenger who served him
saved them.
In love and mercy God redeemed them,
lifting and carrying them
throughout earlier times.
10 But they rebelled,
and made God's holy spirit terribly sad,

[r]Or *stooping*

so that he turned into their enemy—
he fought against them!
11 Then they remembered earlier times,
when he rescued his people.[s]
Where was the one
who drew them up from the sea,
the shepherd[t] of the flock?
Where was the one
who put within them his holy spirit;
12 the one who guided Moses' strong hand
with his glorious arm;
who split the water for them
to create an enduring reputation
for himself,
13 and who guided them through the depths?
Like a horse in the desert,
they didn't stumble.
14 Like cattle descending to the valley,
the LORD's spirit brought them to rest.
In this way you led your people
and made for yourself
a glorious reputation.

15 Look down from heaven and see,
from your holy and glorious perch.
Where are your energy and your might,
your concern and your pity?
Don't hold back![u]
16 You are surely our father,
even though Abraham doesn't know us,
and Israel doesn't recognize us.
You, LORD, are our father;
your reputation since long ago
is that of our redeemer.
17 Why do you lead us astray, LORD,
from your ways?
Why do you harden our heart
so we don't fear you?
Return for the sake of your servants
the tribes that are your heritage!
18 Why did the wicked
bring down your holy place?[v]
Why did our enemies
trample your sanctuary?
19 For too long we have been
like those you don't rule,
like those not known by your name.

64 [w]If only you would tear open
the heavens and come down!
Mountains would quake before you
2 like fire igniting brushwood
or making water boil.
[x]If you would make your name known
to your enemies,
the nations would tremble in your
presence.

3 When you accomplished wonders
beyond all our expectations;
when you came down,
mountains quaked before you.
4 From ancient times,
no one has heard,
no ear has perceived,
no eye has seen any god but you
who acts on behalf of
those who wait for him![y]
5 You look after those who gladly do right;
they will praise you for your ways.[z]
But you were angry when we sinned;
you hid yourself when we did wrong.[a]
6 We have all become like the unclean;
all our righteous deeds
are like a menstrual rag.
All of us wither like a leaf;
our sins, like the wind, carry us away.
7 No one calls on your name;
no one bothers to hold on to you,
for you have hidden yourself from us,
and have handed us over[b] to our sin.

8 But now, LORD, you are our father.
We are the clay, and you are our potter.
All of us are the work of your hand.
9 Don't rage so fiercely, LORD;
don't hold our sins against us forever,
but gaze now on your people, all of us:
10 Your holy cities
have become a wilderness;
Zion has become a wilderness,
Jerusalem a wasteland.
11 Our holy, glorious house,
where our ancestors praised you,
has gone up in flames;
all that we treasured has become a ruin.

[s]Or *Moses, his people* [t]LXX, Tg; MT *shepherds* [u]Heb uncertain [v]Cf LXX, Vulg; Heb uncertain [w]63:19*b* in Heb
[x]64:1 in Heb [y]Heb uncertain [z]Heb uncertain [a]Heb uncertain [b]LXX, cf Syr, Tg, Vulg; MT *melted*

12 After all this, will you hold back, LORD?
Will you keep silent
and torment us so terribly?

Judgment for idolators

65 I was ready to respond
to those who didn't ask.
I was ready to be found
by those who didn't look for me.
I said, "I'm here! I'm here!" to a nation
that didn't call on my name.
2 I extended my hands all day
to a rebellious people
walking in a way that isn't good,
following their own plans;
3 people who provoke me
to my face continually,
sacrificing in gardens
and burning incense on bricks,
4 who sit in tombs
and spend the night among rocks;[c]
who eat swine's flesh
with broth of unclean meat
in their bowls;
5 who say, "Keep to yourself!
Keep away from me!
I'm too holy for you."
These people ignite my anger
like a fire that burns all day.
6 Look, this stands written before me.
I won't be silent, but I will repay;
I will repay in full measure
7 your sins and the sins
of your ancestors as well,
says the LORD.
Since they burned incense
on the mountains,
and mocked me in the hills,
I will count out to them
full payment for their actions.

8 The LORD proclaims:
As new wine is found in the grape cluster,
and someone says, "Don't destroy it,
for there is a blessing in it,"
so I will do for the sake of my servants
and not destroy everything:
9 I will bring out offspring from Jacob,
and from Judah, heirs to my mountains.
My chosen ones will take possession;
my servants will dwell there.
10 Sharon will become a pasture for sheep,
and the Achor Valley
a resting place for cattle,
for my people who seek me.
11 But you who abandon the LORD,
who forget my holy mountain,
who set a table
for a god of good fortune,
and fill cups of mixed wine
for a god of fate:
12 I will offer you to the sword.
You will all bow down for slaughter,
because I called and you didn't answer;
I spoke and you wouldn't hear.
You did what I considered evil,
and chose what I didn't want.
13 Therefore, the LORD God says:
Look, my servants will eat,
but you will hunger.
My servants will drink,
but you will thirst.
My servants will rejoice,
but you will be ashamed.
14 My servants will sing
with contented hearts,
but you will cry out from heartache;
with broken spirits you will wail.
15 You will leave your name behind
for my chosen ones to curse:
"May the LORD God kill you!
May he call his servants
by a different name!"
16 Those who pronounce
a blessing in the land
will do so by the God called Amen;
those who make a solemn pledge
in the land will do so
by the God called Amen.[d]
Past troubles will be forgotten
and hidden from my sight.

New creation and new Jerusalem

17 Look! I'm creating
a new heaven and a new earth:
past events won't be remembered;
they won't come to mind.
18 Be glad and rejoice forever

[c] Or *in guarded places* [d] Or *so be it*

in what I'm creating,
because I'm creating Jerusalem as a joy
and her people as a source of gladness.
19 I will rejoice in Jerusalem
and be glad about my people.
No one will ever hear the sound
of weeping or crying in it again.
20 No more will babies live only a few days,
or the old fail to live out their days.
The one who dies at a hundred
will be like a young person,
and the one falling short of a hundred
will seem cursed.
21 They will build houses and live in them;
they will plant vineyards
and eat their fruit.
22 They won't build for others to live in,
nor plant for others to eat.
Like the days of a tree
will be the days of my people;
my chosen will make full use
of their handiwork.
23 They won't labor in vain,
nor bear children to a world of horrors,
because they will be people
blessed by the LORD,
they along with their descendants.
24 Before they call, I will answer;
while they are still speaking, I will hear.
25 Wolf and lamb will graze together,
and the lion will eat straw like the ox,
but the snake—its food will be dust.
They won't hurt or destroy
at any place on my holy mountain,
says the LORD.

Where God may be found

66 The LORD says:
Heaven is my throne,
and earth is my footstool.
So where could you build a house for me,
and where could my resting place be?
2 My hand made all these things
and brought them into being,
says the LORD.
But here is where I will look:
to the humble and contrite in spirit,
who tremble at my word.

3 The one who slaughters an ox
kills a person;
the one who sacrifices a sheep
breaks a dog's neck;
the one who makes a grain offering
offers swine's blood;
the one who burns incense
blesses an idol.
All these have chosen
their own ways,
and prefer their detestable things.
4 So I too will choose to punish them,
to bring horrors upon them,
since I called and no one answered.
I spoke and no one heard,
but they did evil in my eyes.
What I didn't want, they chose.

5 Listen to the LORD's word,
you who tremble at his word:
Your family members,
those who hate and exclude you
because of my name,
have said,
"Let the LORD be glorified;
let's see your joy."
But they will be ashamed.
6 The sound of an uproar from the city!
A sound from the temple!
The sound of the LORD repaying his
enemies what they have earned.

Mother Zion

7 Before she was in labor,
she gave birth.
Before her pangs came upon her,
she delivered a boy.
8 Whoever heard of such a thing?
Whoever saw such things as these?
Can a land come to birth in one day?
Can a nation be born all at once?
Yet as soon as birth pangs came,
Zion bore her children.
9 Will I open the womb
and not bring to birth?
says the LORD.
Will I, who create life,
close the womb? says your God.
10 Celebrate with Jerusalem;
be happy with her,
all you who love her!
Rejoice with her in joy,
all you who mourn over her,

11 so that you may nurse and be satisfied
from her comforting breasts,
that you may drink and be refreshed
from her full breasts.
12 The LORD says:
Look, I'm extending prosperity
to her like a river,
and the wealth of nations
like an overflowing stream.
You will nurse and be carried on the hip
and bounced upon the knee.

13 As a mother comforts her child,
so I will comfort you;
in Jerusalem you will be comforted.
14 When you see this,
your heart will rejoice;
your entire being
will flourish like grass.
The LORD's power will be known
among his servants,
but his fury among his enemies.
15 The LORD will come with fire,
God's chariots like a windstorm,
to repay in hot anger,
to rebuke with fiery flames.
16 With fire and with sword
the LORD will judge all humanity;
many will be slain by the LORD.

17 Those who became holy and purify
themselves, following their leader into the
gardens,[e] who eat pork, detestable animals,
and mice, will meet their end together, says
the LORD.

Worshippers gathered from the nations

18 Because of their actions and thoughts,
I'm coming to gather all nations and cultures. They will come to see my glory.
19 I will
put a sign on them, by sending out some of
the survivors to the nations, to Tarshish,
Libya, and Lydia, and to the archers of Cilicia
and Greece—distant coastlands that haven't
heard of my fame or seen my glory. They will
declare my glory among the nations.
20 They
will bring your family members from all nations as an offering to the LORD—on horses,
in chariots, in wagons, on mules, and on
camels—to my holy mountain Jerusalem,
says the LORD, like Israelites bringing an offering in purified containers to the LORD's
house.
21 I will select some of them as priests
and Levites, says the LORD.

22 As the new heavens
and the new earth that I'm making
will endure before me,
says the LORD,
so your descendants
and your name will endure.
23 From month to month
and from Sabbath to Sabbath,
all humanity will come
to worship me, says the LORD.
24 They will go out and see the corpses
of the people who rebelled against me,
where their worm never dies,
where their fire
is never extinguished.
They will be a horror to everyone.

JEREMIAH

Introduction

1 These are the words of Jeremiah, Hilkiah's son, who was one of the priests from
Anathoth in the land of Benjamin.
2 The
LORD's word came to Jeremiah in the thirteenth year of Judah's King Josiah, Amon's
son,
3 and throughout the rule of Judah's
King Jehoiakim, Josiah's son, until the
fifth month of the eleventh year of King
Zedekiah, Josiah's son, when the people of
Jerusalem were taken into exile.

Call of Jeremiah

4 The LORD's word came to me:
5 "Before I created you in the womb
I knew you;
before you were born I set you apart;
I made you a prophet to the nations."
6 "Ah, LORD God," I said,
"I don't know how to speak
because I'm only a child."
7 The LORD responded,
"Don't say, 'I'm only a child.'

[e] Heb uncertain

Where I send you, you must go;
what I tell you, you must say.
8 Don't be afraid of them,
because I'm with you to rescue you,"
declares the LORD.
9 Then the LORD stretched out his hand,
touched my mouth, and said to me,
"I'm putting my words in your mouth.
10 This very day I appoint you
over nations and empires,
to dig up and pull down,
to destroy and demolish,
to build and plant."

Jeremiah's mission confirmed

11 The LORD asked me, "What do you see,
Jeremiah?"
I said, "A branch of an almond[a] tree."
12 The LORD then said, "You are right, for
I'm watching over[b] my word until it is fulfilled." 13 The LORD asked me again, "What
do you see?"
I said, "A pot boiling over from the north."
14 The LORD said to me, "Trouble will erupt
from the north against the people of this
land."
15 I'm calling for all the tribes of great
nations from the north, says the LORD,
and they will set up their rulers by the
entrances of Jerusalem, on its walls, and
in every city of Judah. 16 I will declare my
judgment against them for doing evil: for
abandoning me, worshipping other gods,
and trusting in the works of their hands.
17 But you must prepare for battle and be
ready to utter every word I command you.
Don't be frightened before them, or I will
frighten you before them. 18 Today I have
made you an armed city, an iron pillar, and
a bronze wall against the entire land—the
kings of Judah, its princes, its priests, and
all its people. 19 They will attack you, but
they won't defeat you, because I am with
you and will rescue you, declares the LORD.

God's people abandon their God

2 The LORD's word came to me:
2 Go and proclaim
to the people of Jerusalem,
The LORD proclaims:
I remember your first love,[c]
your devotion as a young bride,
how you followed me in the wilderness,
in an unplanted land.
3 Israel was devoted to the LORD,
the early produce of the harvest.
Whoever ate from it became guilty;
disaster overtook them,
declares the LORD.
4 Listen to the LORD's word,
people of Judah,
all you families
of the Israelite household.
5 This is what the LORD says:
What wrong did your ancestors find in me
that made them wander so far?
They pursued what was worthless
and became worthless.
6 They didn't ask,
"Where's the LORD who brought us up
from the land of Egypt,
who led us through the wilderness,
in a land of deserts and ravines,
in a land of drought and darkness,
in a land of no return,
where no one survives?"
7 I brought you into a land of plenty,
to enjoy its gifts and goodness,
but you ruined my land;
you disgraced my heritage.
8 The priests didn't ask,
"Where's the LORD?"
Those responsible for the Instruction
didn't know me;
the leaders rebelled against me;
the prophets spoke in the name of Baal,
going after what has no value.
9 That is why I will take you to court
and charge even your descendants,
declares the LORD.
10 Look to the west
as far as the shores of Cyprus
and to the east
as far as the land of Kedar.
Ask anyone there:
Has anything this odd ever taken place?
11 Has a nation switched gods,
though they aren't really gods at all?

[a] Heb *shaqed* [b] Heb *shoqed* [c] Or *the love of your youth*

Yet my people have exchanged
their glory
for what has no value.
12 Be stunned at such a thing, you heavens;
shudder and quake,
declares the LORD.
13 My people have committed two crimes:
They have forsaken me,
the spring of living water.
And they have dug wells,
broken wells that can't hold water.

14 Is Israel a slave,
a servant by birth?
If not, why then has he become prey?
15 Lions roar at him; they growl.
They destroy his land
and make his towns desolate
until nothing is left.
16 As well, the people
of Memphis and Tahpanhes
lay open your scalp.
17 Haven't you brought this on yourself
by abandoning the LORD your God,
who has directed your paths?
18 So why take the path to Egypt
to drink water from the Nile?
Why travel the path to Assyria
to drink water from the Euphrates?
19 Your wrongdoing will punish you.
Your acts of unfaithfulness
will find you out.
Don't you understand how terribly bitter
it is to abandon the LORD your God
and not fear me?
declares the LORD of heavenly forces.
20 Long ago I broke your yoke;
I shattered your chains.
But even then you said,
"I won't serve you."
On every high hill
and under every lush tree,
you have acted like a prostitute.
21 Yet it was I who planted you,
a precious vine of fine quality;
how could you turn into a wild vine
and become good for nothing?
22 Even though you scrub yourself
with soap or strong powder,
the stain of your sin is still before me,
declares the LORD God.
23 How can you say,
"I'm not dirty;
I haven't gone after Baals."
Look what you have done in the valley;
consider what you have done there.
You are like a frenzied young camel,
racing around,
24 a wild donkey in the wilderness,
lustfully sniffing the wind.
Who can restrain such passion?
Those who desire her need not give up;
with little effort
they will find her in heat.
25 Don't run about
until your feet are blistered
and your throat is parched.
But you say, "What's the use?
I have fallen in love with foreign gods,
and I must pursue them."
26 As a thief is ashamed
when caught in his tracks,
so the people of Israel are ashamed—
their kings, officials,
priests, and prophets—
27 when they say to a piece of wood,
"You are my father,"
and to a stone, "You gave me birth."
They have turned their backs to me
and not their faces.
Yet in their time of trouble they say,
"Arise and save us!"
28 Where are the gods
you have made for yourselves?
Let's see if they will come through
for you in your time of trouble.
You have as many gods, Judah,
as you have towns.
29 Why would you bring charges against me?
You have all rebelled against me,
declares the LORD.
30 I have disciplined your children in vain;
they have rejected my correction.
You have devoured your prophets
like a hungry lion.
31 People of this generation,
listen closely to the LORD's word:
Have I been a wasteland to Israel
or a land of dense darkness?
Why then do my people say,
"We have wandered far away;
we'll come to you no longer"?

32 Does a young woman forget her jewelry
or a bride her wedding dress?
Yet you have forgotten me
days without end!
33 So skilled are you at pursuing lovers[d]
that you instruct
even the most wicked.[e]
34 Your garments are stained
with the blood of the innocent poor,
even though you didn't catch them
breaking and entering.
Yet, despite all this,[f] 35 you still insist,
"I'm innocent;
as a result he will turn his anger
away from me."
Because you claim not to have sinned,
I will pass judgment against you.
36 You change sides so casually!
But Egypt will shame you
no less than Assyria.
37 From there you will go out
with your hands on your heads,
because the LORD has rejected
those you rely on;
they won't help you.

Jeremiah's summons to change

3 If a man divorces his wife,
and after she leaves him
marries another,
can he return to her again?
Wouldn't such an act
completely corrupt the land?
Yet you have prostituted yourself
with many lovers.
Would you return to me?
declares the LORD.
2 Look to the well-traveled paths[g] and see!
Where haven't you committed adultery?
On the roadsides you sit in wait for lovers,
like a nomad in the wilderness.
You have corrupted the land
with your cheap and reckless behavior.
3 That's why the showers have failed
and the spring rains have ceased.
Still you act like a brazen prostitute[h]
who refuses to blush.
4 At the same time you say to me,
"My father, my friend since youth,
5 will you stay angry forever?
Will you continue to be furious?"
This is what you say
while you do as much evil
as you possibly can.
6 During the rule of King Josiah, the LORD
said to me: Have you noticed what unfaithful Israel has done? She's gone about looking for lovers on top of every high hill and
under every lush tree. 7 I thought that after
she had done all this she would return to me,
but she didn't. Her disloyal sister Judah saw
this. 8 She[i] also saw that I sent unfaithful Israel away with divorce papers because of all
her acts of unfaithfulness; yet disloyal sister
Judah was not afraid but kept on playing the
prostitute. 9 She didn't think twice about cor-
rupting the land and committing adultery
with stone and tree. 10 Yet even after all
this, disloyal sister Judah didn't return to
me with all her heart but only insincerely,
declares the LORD. 11 Then the LORD said
to me: Unfaithful Israel is less guilty[j] than
disloyal Judah.
12 Go proclaim these words to the north
and say:
Return, unfaithful Israel,
declares the LORD.
I won't reject you,
for I'm faithful,
declares the LORD;
I won't stay angry forever.
13 Only acknowledge your wrongdoing:
how you have rebelled
against the LORD your God,
and given yourself to strangers
under every lush tree
and haven't obeyed me,
declares the LORD.
14 Return, rebellious children,
declares the LORD,
for I'm your husband.
I'll gather you—
one from a city and two from a tribe—
and bring you back to Zion.
15 I will appoint shepherds with whom
I'm pleased, and they will lead you with

[d] Or *love* [e] Or *you have taught your ways to wicked women.* [f] Heb uncertain [g] Or *bare heights* [h] Or *You have a prostitute's forehead.* [i] LXX, Syr; MT *I* [j] Or *more righteous*

knowledge and understanding. 16 And in
those days, when your numbers have greatly
increased in the land, declares the LORD,
people will no longer talk about the LORD's
covenant chest; they won't recall or remember it; they won't even miss it or try to build
another one. 17 At that time, they will call Jerusalem the LORD's throne, and all nations
will gather there to honor the LORD's name.
No longer will they follow their own willful
and evil hearts. 18 In those days the people
of Judah and Israel will leave the north together for the land that I gave their ancestors as an inheritance.

19 I thought to myself,
How wonderful it would be
to treat you like children
and give you a beautiful land,
an inheritance unrivaled
among the nations.
And I thought, You will call me father,
and you won't turn away from me.
20 But as a woman betrays her lover,
so you, people of Israel,
have betrayed me,
declares the LORD.
21 A voice is heard
on the well-traveled paths;[k]
it's the crying and pleading
of the people of Israel,
who have lost their way
and forgotten the LORD their God.
22 Return, rebellious children,
and I will heal your rebellion.

"Here we are; we come to you,
for you are the LORD our God.
23 Surely what happens on the hills[l]
is a waste,
as is the uproar on the mountains.
Only in the LORD our God
is the salvation of Israel.
24 From our youth, shame[m] has devoured
the fruit of our parents' labor—
their flocks and herds,
as well as their sons and daughters.
25 Let's lie down in our shame.
Let our dishonor cover us,
for we have sinned
against the LORD our God,
both we and our ancestors,
from our youth to this very day.
We have disobeyed
the voice of the LORD our God."

4 If you return, Israel, return to me,
declares the LORD.
If you get rid of your disgusting idols
from my presence
and wander no more,
2 and if you swear by the living God
in truth, justice, and righteousness,
then the nations
will enjoy God's blessings;[n]
they will boast about him.

3 This is what the LORD says to the people
of Judah and to the residents of Jerusalem:
Break up your hard rocky soil;
don't plant among the thorns.
4 Dedicate[o] yourselves to the LORD;
don't be thick-skinned,[p]
people of Judah
and residents of Jerusalem,
or else my anger will spread
like a wildfire.
It will burn, with no one to put it out,
because of your evil deeds.

Disaster approaches

5 Announce in Judah,
in Jerusalem proclaim,
sound the alarm throughout the land,
cry out and say,
"Gather together!
Let's flee to the fortified towns!"
6 Set up a flag to Zion;
take cover, don't just stand there!
I'm bringing disaster from the north,
massive devastation.
7 A lion bursts out of the thicket;
a destroyer of nations advances.
He's gone forth from his place
to ravage your land,
to wipe out your towns,
until no one is left.
8 So put on funeral clothing.

[k]Or *bare heights* [l]LXX, Syr, Vulg; MT *from the hills* [m]Or *the shame* [n]Or *bless themselves in him* or *be blessed by him* or *will bless themselves* [o]Or *circumcise* [p]Or *remove the foreskins of your hearts*

Weep and wail,
for the LORD's fierce anger
hasn't turned away from us.
9 On that day, declares the LORD,
the courage of the king and his princes
will fail,
the priests will be stunned,
and the prophets will be shocked.
10 Then I said, "LORD God, no!
You have utterly deceived this people
and Jerusalem
by promising them peace
even though the sword is at their throats."
11 At that time, this people and Jerusalem
will be told:
A blistering wind
from the bare heights;
it rages in the desert toward my people,
not merely to winnow or cleanse.
12 This wind is too devastating for that.
Now I, even I, will pronounce
my sentence against them.
13 Look! He approaches like the clouds;
his chariots advance like a tempest,
his horses swifter than eagles.
How horrible! We're doomed!
14 Cleanse your heart of evil, Jerusalem,
that you may be saved.
How long will you entertain
your destructive ideas?
15 A voice declares from Dan;
someone proclaims disaster
from the highlands of Ephraim.
16 Warn the nations,
proclaim it to Jerusalem!
Armies are approaching
from a far-away country,
raising their war cries
against the towns of Judah.
17 They hem her in
like those guarding a field,
because she has rebelled against me,
declares the LORD.
18 Your own conduct, your own deeds
have done this to you.
This is your payment and how bitter it is,
piercing into the depths of your heart.

Anguish over looming disaster

19 Oh, my suffering, my suffering!
My pain is unbearable;
my heart is in turmoil;
it throbs nonstop.
I can't be silent,
because I hear the blast
of the trumpet
and the roar of the battle cry!
20 Disaster follows disaster;
the whole land is ruined.
Suddenly, my tents are destroyed,
my shelter in a moment.
21 How long must I see the battle flags
and hear the blast of the trumpet?
22 My people are foolish.
They don't even know me!
They are thoughtless children
without understanding;
they are skilled at doing wrong,
inept at doing right.
23 I looked at the earth,
and it was without shape or form;
at the heavens
and there was no light.
24 I looked at the mountains
and they were quaking;
all the hills were rocking back and forth.
25 I looked and there was no one left;
every bird in the sky had taken flight.
26 I looked and the fertile land was a desert;
all its towns were in ruins
before the LORD,
before his fury.
27 The LORD proclaims:
The whole earth
will become a desolation,
but I will not destroy it completely.
28 Therefore, the earth will grieve
and the heavens grow dark
because I have declared my plan
and will neither change my mind
nor cancel the plan.
29 As the horsemen and archers approach,
the people take flight.
They hide in the bushes
and escape to the cliffs.
Every city is deserted;
no one remains.
30 And you, devastated one,
why dress up in scarlet,
deck yourself in gold jewelry,
and color your eyes with paint?
In vain you get all decked out;

your lovers have rejected you
and now seek your life.
31 I hear the cry of a woman in labor,
the distress of one delivering
her first child.
It is the cry of Daughter Zion,
gasping for breath,
her arms stretched out,
and moaning,
"I'm about to fall
into the hands of murderers!"

Futile search for a good person

5 Search every street in Jerusalem,
comb the squares,
look far and wide
for one person,
even one who acts justly
and seeks truth that I may pardon her!
2 Even when making a pledge—
"As the LORD lives"—
they swear falsely.
3 LORD, don't you look for integrity?
You have struck them down,
but they didn't even cringe.
You have crushed them,
but they have ignored your discipline.
They make their faces harder than rock
and refuse to return.
4 Then I thought to myself,
These are the poor
who don't know better!
They don't understand the LORD's way
or the justice of their God.
5 Let me go and speak
to the powerful people,
for they will surely know
the LORD's way
and the justice of their God.
But they too have broken their yoke
and shattered the chains.
6 Therefore, a lion from the forest
will attack them;
a wolf from the desert will destroy them;
a leopard prowling around their towns
will tear to pieces
anyone venturing out—
because of their many crimes
and countless acts of unfaithfulness.
7 How can I pardon you?
Your children have forsaken me
and swear by gods that are not gods.
Although I could have satisfied them,
they committed adultery,
dashing off to the prostitution house.
8 They are lusty stallions roving about,
snorting for another's wife.
9 The LORD declares:
Shouldn't I confront these acts?
Shouldn't I take revenge
on such a nation?

Contempt for God

10 Climb through her vineyards
and ravage them,
although not completely.
Prune back her branches,
because they aren't the LORD's.
11 The people of Israel and Judah
have been utterly faithless to me,
declares the LORD.
12 They have lied about the LORD
and said, "He'll do nothing![q]
Disaster won't come upon us;
we won't see war or famine."
13 The prophets are so much wind;
the word isn't in them.
Thus and so may it be done to them.
14 Therefore, the LORD God of heavenly
forces proclaims:
Because you have spoken this way,
I will put my words
in your mouth as a fire;
it will consume the people,
who are but kindling.
15 I am about to bring a distant nation
against you,
people of Israel,
declares the LORD.
It is an established nation,
an ancient nation,
a nation whose language
you don't know,
whose speech you won't understand.
16 Its weapons are deadly;[r]
its warriors are many.
17 It will devour your harvest and food;
it will devour your sons and daughters;

[q] *Or not he* [r] *Or Its quiver is like an open grave*

it will devour your flocks and herds;
it will devour your vines and fig trees;
it will shatter your fortified towns
in which you trust—
with the sword!
18 Yet even in those days, declares the
LORD, I won't completely destroy you.
19 And when they ask, "Why has the LORD
our God done all these things to us?" you
must reply, "Just as you have abandoned me
and served foreign gods in your land, so you
will serve strangers in a land not your own."

Shouldn't you fear me?

20 Declare this to the people of Jacob,
announce it in Judah:
21 Listen, you foolish
and senseless people,
who have eyes but don't see
and ears but don't hear.
22 Shouldn't you fear me,
declares the LORD,
and tremble before me,
the one who set the shoreline
for the sea,
an ancient boundary that it can't pass?
Though its waves may rise and roar,
they can't pass the limits I have set.
23 And yet the people have stubborn
and rebellious hearts;
they turn and go their own way.
24 They don't say in their hearts,
Let's fear the LORD our God,
who provides rain in autumn and spring
and who assures us of a harvest
in its season.
25 Your wrongdoing has turned
these blessings[s] away.
Your sin has robbed you of good.
26 Criminals are found among my people;
they set traps to catch people,
like hunters lying in wait.[t]
27 Like a cage full of birds,
so their houses are full of loot.
No wonder they are rich and powerful
28 and have grown fat and sleek!
To be sure, their evil deeds
exceed all limits,
and yet they prosper.
They are indifferent
to the plight of the orphan,
reluctant to defend the rights of the poor.
29 Shouldn't I punish such acts?
declares the LORD.
Shouldn't I repay that nation
for its deeds?
30 An awful, a terrible thing
has happened in the land:
31 The prophets prophesy falsely,
the priests rule at their sides,[u]
and my people love it this way!
But what will you do when the end comes?

Prepare for war

6 Escape, people of Benjamin,
get out of Jerusalem!
Blow the trumpet in Tekoa,
sound the alarm in Beth-haccherem;
for disaster looms from the north,
massive devastation.
2 You are like a lovely pasture,
Daughter Zion.[v]
3 Shepherds come to her
with their flocks.
They pitch their tents around her
and graze in their place.
4 "Prepare for battle against her;
get ready; let's attack by noon!
Oh, no! Daylight is fading,
and the evening shadows lengthen.
5 Get ready, let's attack by night
and destroy her fortresses!"
6 The LORD of heavenly forces proclaims:
Cut down her trees,
and build siege ramps
against Jerusalem.
This city must be held accountable,[w]
for there's nothing but oppression
in her midst.
7 As a well brings forth fresh water,
she brings forth evil.
Violence and destruction
are heard within her;
injury and wounds are ever before me.
8 Hear me out,[x] Jerusalem,
or else I'll turn away from you
and reduce you to ruins,
a land unfit to live in.

[s] Heb lacks *blessings*. [t] Heb uncertain [u] Or *by their hands* [v] Heb uncertain [w] Heb uncertain [x] Or *Accept correction*

Unresponsive people

9 This is what the LORD of heavenly forces
says:
From top to bottom, let them harvest
the remaining few in Israel.
Pick clean every
last grape on the vine!
10 To whom can I speak and warn?
How can I get someone's attention?
Their ears are shut tight,[y]
so they won't hear.
They are ashamed of the LORD's word
and take no pleasure in it.
11 But I'm filled with the LORD's rage
and am tired of holding it in.

Pour it out on the children
in the streets
and on the youths gathered together;
husband with wife will be trapped,
as will those old and gray.
12 Their homes will be turned
over to others,
their fields and wives as well.
I will stretch out my hand
against the people of this land,
declares the LORD.
13 From the least to the greatest,
each is eager to profit;
from prophet to priest,
each trades in dishonesty.
14 They treat the wound of my people
as if it were nothing:
"All is well, all is well," they insist,
when in fact nothing is well.
15 They should be ashamed
of their detestable practices,
but they have no shame;
they don't even blush!
Therefore, they will fall among the fallen
and stumble when I bring disaster,
declares the LORD.
16 The LORD proclaims:
Stop at the crossroads and look around;
ask for the ancient paths.
Where is the good way?
Then walk in it
and find a resting place for yourselves.
But you[z] said, "We won't go!"
17 Still, I have appointed watchmen
to warn you.
But you[a] said, "We won't listen!"
18 Therefore, pay attention, nations;
take notice, assembly,
what is ahead of them.[b]
19 Pay attention, earth:
I'm bringing disaster upon my people,
the fruit of their own devices,
because they have ignored my words
and they have rejected my teaching.
20 What use to me is incense from Sheba
or sweet cane from a faraway land?
Your entirely burned offerings
won't buy your pardon;
your sacrifices won't appease me.
21 Therefore, the LORD proclaims:
I'm putting obstacles before this people,
and both parents and children
will stumble over them;
neighbor and friend alike will perish.

Panic-stricken Zion

22 The LORD proclaims:
An army is on the move
from the northern regions;
a great nation is roused
from the ends of the earth.
23 Equipped with bow and spear,
they are cruel;
they show no mercy.
Their horsemen sound
like the roaring sea,
arrayed in battle formation
against you, Daughter Zion.
24 We have heard reports of them
and are panic-stricken;
distress overwhelms us,
pain like that of a woman in labor.
25 Don't go out into the field!
Don't walk on the road!
The enemies' sword
terrorizes at every turn.
26 My people,
put on funeral clothes
and roll in ashes;
weep and wail as for an only child,
because the destroyer
will suddenly descend upon us.

[y]Or *uncircumcised* [z]Or *they* [a]Or *they* [b]Heb uncertain

Prophet as tester

27 I have made you a tester of metals,
to examine my people[c]
to know and prove their ways.
28 They are tin[d] and iron;
they are headstrong and rebellious.
They live to slander.
They act corruptly—every last one!
29 The bellows roar;
the lead is consumed.[e]
Yet the refining fails;
the impurities[f] remain.
30 They are called "rejected silver,"
for the LORD has rejected them.

The LORD's temple

7 Jeremiah received the LORD's word:
2 Stand near the gate of the LORD's temple and proclaim there this message: Listen
to the LORD's word, all you of Judah who
enter these gates to worship the LORD.
3 This is what the LORD of heavenly forces,
the God of Israel, says: Improve your conduct and your actions, and I will dwell with
you[g] in this place. 4 Don't trust in lies: "This
is the LORD's temple! The LORD's temple!
The LORD's temple!" 5 No, if you truly reform
your ways and your actions; if you treat
each other justly; 6 if you stop taking advantage of the immigrant, orphan, or widow;
if you don't shed the blood of the innocent
in this place, or go after other gods to your
own ruin, 7 only then will I dwell with you[h]
in this place, in the land that I gave long ago
to your ancestors for all time.

8 And yet you trust in lies that will only
hurt you. 9 Will you steal and murder, commit adultery and perjury, sacrifice to Baal
and go after other gods that you don't know,
10 and then come and stand before me in this
temple that bears my name, and say, "We
are safe," only to keep on doing all these detestable things? 11 Do you regard this temple,
which bears my name, as a hiding place for
criminals? I can see what's going on here,
declares the LORD. 12 Just go to my sanctuary[i] in Shiloh, where I let my name dwell at
first, and see what I did to it because of the
evil of my people Israel. 13 And now, because
you have done all these things, declares the
LORD, because you haven't listened when I
spoke to you again and again or responded
when I called you, 14 I will do to this temple
that bears my name and on which you rely,
the place that I gave to you and your ancestors, just as I did to Shiloh. 15 I will cast you
out of my sight, just as I cast out the rest of
your family, all the people of Ephraim.

16 As for you, don't pray for these people,
don't cry out or plead for them, and don't
intercede with me, for I won't listen to you.
17 Can't you see what they are doing in the
towns of Judah and in the streets of Jerusalem? 18 The children gather wood, the fathers light the fire, and the women knead
dough to make sacrificial cakes for the
queen of heaven. And to offend me all the
more, they pour out drink offerings to foreign gods. 19 But am I the one they are really
offending? declares the LORD. Aren't they
in fact humiliating themselves? 20 Therefore, this is what the LORD God says: I'm
going to pour out my fierce anger on this
place, on humans and beasts, on the trees
of the field and the crops of the fertile land.
It will burn and not go out.

21 This is what the LORD of heavenly
forces, the God of Israel, says: Add your entirely burned offerings to your sacrifices and
eat them yourselves! 22 On the day I brought
your ancestors out of the land of Egypt, I
didn't say a thing—I gave no instructions—
about entirely burned offerings or sacrifices. 23 Rather, this is what I required of
them: Obey me so that I may become your
God and you may become my people. Follow
the path I mark out for you so that it may go
well with you. 24 But they didn't listen or pay
attention. They followed their willful and
evil hearts and went backward rather than
forward. 25 From the moment your ancestors left the land of Egypt to this day, I have
sent you all my servants the prophets—day
after day. 26 But they didn't listen to me or
pay attention; they were stubborn and did
more harm than their ancestors. 27 When
you tell them all this, they won't listen to
you. When you call to them, they won't

[c] Heb uncertain [d] Or *bronze* [e] Heb uncertain [f] Or *wicked* [g] Or *I will let you dwell* [h] Or *I will let you dwell* [i] Or *place*

respond. [28]Therefore, say to them: This
nation neither obeys the LORD its God nor
accepts correction; truth has disappeared; it
has vanished from their lips.
[29]Cut off your hair and cast it away;
grieve on the well-traveled paths.
The LORD has rejected you
and has cast off a generation
that provokes his anger.
[30]The people of Judah have done what
displeases me, declares the LORD. They
have corrupted the temple that bears my
name by setting up their disgusting idols.
[31]They have built shrines at Topheth in
the Ben-hinnom Valley to burn their sons
and daughters in the fire, although I never
commanded such a thing, nor did it ever
cross my mind. [32]So now the time is coming, declares the LORD, when people will
no longer speak of Topheth or the Ben-
hinnom Valley, but the Carnage Valley. They
will bury in Topheth until no space is left.
[33]The corpses of this people will be food
for birds and wild animals, with no one to
drive them off. [34]I will silence the sound of
joy and delight as well as the voice of bride
and bridegroom in the towns of Judah and
in the streets of Jerusalem, for the country
will be reduced to a wasteland.
8 [1]At that
time, declares the LORD, the bones of
the kings of Judah and its officers, the
bones of the priests and the prophets, and
the bones of the people of Jerusalem will
be taken from their graves [2]and exposed to
the sun, the moon, and the whole heavenly
forces, which they have loved and served
and which they have followed, consulted,
and worshipped. Their bones won't be gathered for reburial but will become like refuse
lying on the ground. [3]The survivors of this
evil nation will prefer death to life, wherever I have scattered them, declares the
LORD of heavenly forces.

Depth of Judah's wrongdoing

[4]Say to them, The LORD proclaims:
When people fall down, don't they get up?
When they turn aside,
don't they turn back?
[5]Why then does this people,
rebellious Jerusalem,
persistently turn away from me?
They cling to deceit
and refuse to return.
[6]I have listened carefully
but haven't heard a word of truth
from them.
No one regrets their wrongdoing;
no one says, "What have I done?"
Everyone turns to their own course,
like a stallion dashing
into the thick of battle.
[7]Even the stork in the sky
knows the seasons,
and the dove, swallow,[j] and crane[k]
return in due time.
But my people
don't know the LORD's ways.
[8]How can you say, "We are wise;
we possess the LORD's Instruction,"
when the lying pen of the scribes
has surely distorted it?
[9]The wise will be shamed and shocked
when they are caught.
Look, they have rejected the LORD's word;
what kind of wisdom is that?
[10]Therefore, I will give their wives to others
and their fields to their captors.
From the least to the greatest,
all are eager to profit.
From prophet to priest,
all trade in falsehood.
[11]They treat the wound of my people
as if it were nothing:
"All is well, all is well," they insist,
when in fact nothing is well.
[12]They should be ashamed
of their detestable practices,
but they have no shame;
they don't even blush!
Therefore, they will fall among the fallen
and stumble when disaster arrives,
declares the LORD.
[13]I will put an end to them,[l]
declares the LORD;
there are no grapes on the vine,
no figs on the tree,
only withered leaves.

[j]Heb uncertain [k]Heb uncertain [l]Heb uncertain

They have squandered
what I have given them![m]

A lament for God's people

14 Why are we sitting here?
Come, let's go to the fortified towns
and meet our doom there.
The LORD our God has doomed us
by giving us
poisoned water to drink,
because we have sinned
against the LORD!
15 We longed for relief,
but received none;
for a time of healing,
but found only terror.
16 The snorting of their horses
can be heard as far as Dan;
the neighing of their stallions
makes the whole land tremble.
They come to devour the land
and everything in it,
towns and people alike.
17 See, I'm sending serpents against you,
vipers that you can't charm,
and they will bite you,
declares the LORD.
18 No healing,
only grief;
my heart is broken.[n]
19 Listen to the weeping of my people
all across the land:
"Isn't the LORD in Zion?
Is her king no longer there?"
Why then did they anger me
with their images,
with pointless foreign gods?
20 "The harvest is past,
the summer has ended,
yet we aren't saved."
21 Because my people are crushed,
I am crushed;
darkness and despair overwhelm me.

What to do with God's people

22 Is there no balm in Gilead?
Is there no physician there?
Why then have my people
not been restored to health?

9 [o]If only my head were a spring of water,
and my eyes a fountain of tears,
I would weep day and night
for the wounds of my people.
2 [p]If only I could flee for shelter in the desert,
to leave my people
and forget them—
for they are all adulterers,
a bunch of crooks.
3 They bend their tongues like bows
to spew out lies;
they are renowned in the land,
but not for truth.
They go from bad to worse.
They don't know me!
declares the LORD!
4 Be wary of your friends!
Don't trust your sibling![q]
Every sibling is a cheater,
and every friend traffics in slander.
5 One cheats the other;
no one tells the truth;
they train themselves to lie;
they wear themselves out
by doing wrong.
6 You live in a world of deceit,
and in their deceit
they refuse to know me,[r]
declares the LORD.
7 Therefore, the LORD of heavenly forces
proclaims:
I'm going to refine and test them,
for what else can I do with my people?
8 Their tongue is a lethal arrow;
their words are deceitful.
They wish their neighbors well,
but in their hearts plot their ruin.
9 Shouldn't I punish them for this?
declares the LORD;
shouldn't I avenge such a nation?
10 I will weep and wail for the mountains,
and lament for the grazing lands
in the wilderness.
They are dried up and deserted;
no sound of the flocks is heard;
no sign of birds or animals is seen;
all have vanished.
11 I will reduce Jerusalem to ruins,
a den for wild dogs.

[m]Heb uncertain [n]Heb uncertain [o]8:23 in Heb [p]9:1 in Heb [q]Or *brother* [r]Heb uncertain

I will make the towns of Judah
a wasteland, without inhabitant.
[12]Who is wise enough to understand this?
Who has been taught by the LORD
and can therefore explain it?
Why has the land been reduced to rubble
and laid waste like a desert,
with no one passing through?
[13]The LORD says: It is because they have
abandoned my Instruction that I gave them,
and haven't obeyed or followed it. [14]Instead,
they have followed their own willful hearts
and have gone after the Baals, as their ancestors taught them. [15]Therefore, this is what
the LORD of heavenly forces, the God of Israel, says: I'm going to feed this people bitter
food and give them poison to drink. [16]I will
scatter them among nations about whom
neither they nor their ancestors have ever
heard. I will pursue them with the sword
until all are gone.
[17]The LORD of heavenly forces proclaims:
Pay attention!
Summon the women who mourn,
let them come;
send for those best trained,
let them come.
[18]Hurry!
Let them weep for us
so that our eyes fill up with tears
and water streams down.
[19]The sound of sobbing
is heard from Zion:
"We're devastated!
We're so ashamed!
We have to leave the land
and abandon our homes!"
[20]Women, hear the LORD's word.
Listen closely to the word
from his mouth:
teach your daughters to mourn;
teach each other to grieve.
[21]Death has climbed through our windows;
it has entered our fortresses
to eliminate children from the streets,
the youth from the squares.
[22]Declare what the LORD says:
Dead bodies will lie
like dung on the fields,
like bundles of grain after the harvest,
with no one to pick them up.
[23]The LORD proclaims:
the learned should not boast
of their knowledge,
nor warriors boast of their might,
nor the rich boast of their wealth.
[24]No, those who boast should boast in this:
that they understand and know me.
I am the LORD who acts with kindness,
justice, and righteousness in the world,
and I delight in these things,
declares the LORD.
[25]The time is coming, declares the LORD,
when I will deal with everyone who is physically circumcised: [26]whether they are Egyptians or Judeans, Edomites or Ammonites,
Moabites or the desert dwellers who cut the
hair on their foreheads. All these nations
are really uncircumcised; even the people of
Israel are uncircumcised in heart.

Living God or human handiwork

10 Listen to the word that the LORD has spoken to you, people of Israel!
[2]The LORD proclaims:
Don't follow the ways of the nations
or be troubled by signs in the sky,
even though the nations
are troubled by them.
[3]The rituals of the nations are hollow:
a tree from the forest is chopped down
and shaped by the craftsman's tools.
[4]It's overlaid with silver and gold,
and fastened securely
with hammer and nails
so it won't fall over.
[5]They are no different than a scarecrow
in a cucumber patch:
they can't speak;
they must be carried
because they can't walk.
Don't be afraid of them,
because they can't do harm or good.
[6]LORD, no one is like you!
You are great,
and great is your mighty name.
[7]Who wouldn't fear you,
king of the nations?
That is your due;
among all the wise of the nations
and in all their countries,
there is no one like you!

8 But they are both foolish and silly;
they offer nothing
because they are mere wood.
9 Covered with silver from Tarshish
and gold from Uphaz,
they are the work of a craftsman
and the hands of a goldsmith.
Clothed in blue and purple,
all of them nothing more than the
work of artisans.
10 But the LORD is the true God!
He's the living God
and the everlasting king!
When he's angry, the earth quakes;
the nations can't endure his rage.
11 Tell them this: The gods who didn't
make the heavens and the earth will perish
from the earth and from under the heavens.[s]
12 But God made the earth by his might;
he shaped the world by his wisdom,
crafted the skies by his knowledge.
13 At the sound of his voice,
the heavenly waters roar.
He raises the clouds
from the ends of the earth.
He sends the lightning with the rain,
the wind from his treasuries.
14 Everyone is too foolish to understand;
every goldsmith is dishonored
by his idols,
for their images are shams;
they aren't alive.
15 They are a delusion, a charade;
at the appointed time they will vanish!
16 Jacob's portion is utterly different
because God has formed all things,
including Israel, his very own people—
the LORD of heavenly forces
is his name!

Get ready for exile!

17 Pack your bags and get ready to leave,
you who live under siege.[t]
18 The LORD proclaims:
I'm going to eject those who live
in the land at this time;
I will badger them until they leave.[u]

19 How terrible for me, due to my injury;
my wound is terrible.
Yet I said to myself:
This is my sickness,
and I must bear it.
20 But now my tent is destroyed;
all its ropes are cut,
and my children are gone for good.
There's no one left
to set up my tent frame
and to attach the fabric.
21 The shepherd kings have lost
their senses
and don't seek answers from the LORD.
That is why they have failed
and their flock is scattered.
22 Listen! The sound is getting louder,
a mighty uproar
from the land of the north;
it will reduce the towns of Judah to ruins,
a den for wild dogs.
23 I know, LORD, that our lives
are not our own,
that we're not able to direct our paths.
24 So correct me, LORD, but with justice,
not in your anger,
or else you will reduce me to nothing.
25 Pour out your wrath on the nations
that ignore you
and on the people
who don't call on you,
since they have devoured Jacob;
they have devoured him completely
and ruined his country.

Judah's broken covenant with God

11 Jeremiah received the LORD's word:
2 Listen to the terms of this covenant
and proclaim them to the people of Judah
and the citizens of Jerusalem. 3 Say to them:
This is what the LORD, the God of Israel,
says: Cursed are those who don't heed the
terms of this covenant 4 that I commanded
your ancestors when I bought them out of
the land of Egypt, that iron crucible, saying, Obey me and observe all that I instruct
you. Then you will be my people and I, even
I, will be your God. 5 I will fulfill my solemn
pledge that I made to your ancestors to give
them a land full of milk and honey, as is the
case today.

[s] 10:11 is written in Aramaic. [t] Heb uncertain [u] Or *find it*

And I replied, "As you say, LORD!"
6The LORD said to me: Announce all
these words in the towns of Judah and on
the streets of Jerusalem: Obey the terms
of this covenant and perform them. 7I repeatedly and tirelessly warned your ancestors when I brought them out of the land
of Egypt to this very day, saying, Obey
me. 8But they didn't listen or pay attention; they followed their own willful am-
bitions. So I brought upon them all the
punishments I prescribed for violating this
covenant—for refusing to obey.
9The LORD said to me: A conspiracy is
taking place among the people of Judah and
residents of Jerusalem. 10They have returned
to the sins of their ancestors who refused to
obey my words. They too are following other
gods and serving them. The people of Israel
and the people of Judah have broken my
covenant that I made with their ancestors.
11Therefore, the LORD proclaims: I will
bring upon them a disaster from which
they won't be able to escape. They will
cry out to me, but I won't listen to them.
12Then the people of Judah and those living
in Jerusalem will call upon the gods they
worship,[v] but they won't save them when
disaster strikes. 13You have as many gods
as you have towns, Judah, and you have as
many shameful altars for worshipping Baal
as you have streets in Jerusalem.
14As for you, don't pray for these people,
don't cry out or plead for them, for I won't
listen when they cry out to me on account
of their distress.

15What are my loved ones doing
in my temple
while working out
their many evil schemes?
Can sacred offerings cancel your sin
so that you revel in your evil deeds?[w]
16The LORD named you,
"A blossoming olive tree,
fair and fruitful";
but with the blast of a powerful storm
he will set it ablaze,
until its branches
are completely consumed.[x]

17The LORD of heavenly forces who
planted you has announced disaster for
you, because the people of Israel and Judah
have done evil and made me angry by worshipping Baal.

Jeremiah's lament

18The LORD informed me and I knew.
Then he helped me see
what they were up to.
19I was like a young lamb
led to the slaughter;
I didn't realize that they were planning
their schemes against me:
"Let's destroy the tree with its fruit;
let's cut him off from the land
of the living
so that even any knowledge of him
will be wiped out."
20LORD of heavenly forces, righteous judge,
who tests the heart and mind,
let me see your revenge upon them,
because I have committed
my case to you.

21This is what the LORD says concerning the men from Anathoth who seek your
life and say, "Don't prophesy in the LORD's
name or else you will die at our hands."
22Therefore, the LORD of heavenly forces
proclaims, I'm going to punish them. Their
young men will die in war, and their sons
and daughters will die by famine. 23No one
will be left because I will bring disaster
upon the men of Anathoth when their time
comes.

12 If I took you to court, LORD,
you would win.
But I still have questions
about your justice.
Why do guilty persons enjoy success?
Why are evildoers so happy?
2You plant them, and they take root;
they flourish and bear fruit.
You are always on their lips
but far from their hearts.
3Yet you, LORD, you know me.
You see me.
You can tell that I love you.[y]
So drag them away

[v]Or *to whom they burn incense* [w]Heb uncertain [x]Vulg; MT *broken* [y]Or *You test my heart.*

and butcher them like sheep.
Prepare them for the slaughterhouse.
4 How long will the land mourn
and the grass in the fields dry up?
The animals and birds are swept away
due to the evil of those in the land.
The people say,
"God doesn't see what we're up to!"

5 If you have raced with people
and are worn out,
how will you compete with horses?
If you fall down in an open field,[z]
how will you survive in the forest
along the Jordan?
6 Even your relatives, your very family,
are planning to trap you.
They are out to get you.
So don't trust them,
even if they appear to be on your side.

God's lament over Judah's destruction

7 I have abandoned my house;
I have deserted my inheritance.
I have given the one I love
into the power of her enemies.
8 My inheritance has turned against me
like a lion in the forest;
she growls at me;
therefore, I have rejected her.
9 My inheritance has become
like a bird of prey,
surrounded and attacked.[a]
Go, gather all the wild animals
for the feast.
10 Many shepherds have destroyed
my vineyard;
they have trampled down my field;
they have reduced my treasured field
to a desolate wilderness.
11 They have devastated her;
desolate, she cries out to me in distress:
"The whole land is desolate,
and no one seems to care."
12 Over all the desert roads
destroyers march;
for the sword of the LORD devours
from one end of the land to the other;
no one is safe.
13 They have sown wheat and reaped weeds;
they have worn themselves out
for nothing.
They will be ashamed of their[b] harvest
on account of the LORD's fierce anger.
14 The LORD proclaims: The evil nations
have seized the land[c] that I gave my people
Israel. I'm going to dig them up from their
own lands, and I will dig up the people of
Judah from among them. 15 And after I have
dug them up, I will again have compassion
on them and restore their inheritance and
their land. 16 And then, if they will learn the
ways of my people, to make a solemn pledge
in my name, "As the LORD lives," just as
they once taught my people to swear to
Baal, then they will be built up in the midst
of my people. 17 But if they don't listen, I will
dig up that nation; yes, I will dig up and destroy, declares the LORD.

Jeremiah's symbolic acts

13 The LORD proclaimed to me: Go and
buy a linen undergarment. Wear it for
a while without washing it. 2 So I bought a
linen undergarment, as the LORD told me,
and I put it on. 3 The LORD spoke to me
again: 4 Take the undergarment that you
are wearing and go at once to the Euphrates and put it under a rock. 5 So I went and
buried it at the Euphrates,[d] as the LORD instructed. 6 After a long time, the LORD said
to me: Return to the Euphrates and dig up
the undergarment that I commanded you
to bury there. 7 So I went to the Euphrates
and I dug up the linen undergarment from
the place I had buried it. But it was ruined
and good for nothing.
8 Then the LORD's word came to me: 9 The
LORD proclaims: In the same way I will ruin
the brazen pride of Judah and Jerusalem!
10 Instead of listening to me, this wicked
people follow their own willful hearts and
pursue other gods, worshipping and serving them. They will become like this linen
garment—good for nothing! 11 Just as a
linen undergarment clings to the body, so
I created the people of Israel and Judah to
cling to me, declares the LORD, to be my

[z] Or *If you are at ease only when in a peaceful land* [a] Heb uncertain [b] Or *your* [c] Or *inheritance* [d] Heb *Perath*

people for my honor, praise, and grandeur.
But they wouldn't obey.
12 So deliver this word to them: The
LORD the God of Israel proclaims: Every
wine jug should be filled with wine. And
they will answer you, "Don't we already
know that? Obviously every wine jug
should be filled with wine!" 13 Then you
should say to them: The LORD proclaims:
I'm going to fill everyone who lives in
this country with wine that makes them
drunk, including the kings on David's
throne, the priests, the prophets, and
all those living in Jerusalem. 14 And I
will shatter every one of them, even parents and children, declares the LORD. I
won't take pity; I won't have compassion;
I will show no mercy when I destroy them.

15 Listen closely, don't be arrogant,
for the LORD has spoken.
16 Honor the LORD your God,
before it's too late,
before you stumble
on the mountain paths
in the evening shadows.
Then you will hope for light,
only to find darkness and gloom.
17 If you are too proud to listen,
I will go off alone
and cry my eyes out.
I will weep uncontrollably
because the LORD's flock
will be dragged off into exile.
18 Tell the king and the queen mother:
Come down from your lofty place,
because your glorious crowns
will soon be removed
from your heads.
19 The towns of the arid southern plain
will be surrounded;
no one will get in or out;
all Judah will be taken into exile;
everyone will be led away.

20 Lift up your eyes
and see who is approaching
from the north.
Where is the flock entrusted to you,
your beautiful flock?
21 What will you say when he appoints
someone as head over you:
your defenders, your trusted allies?[e]
Won't pain grip you
like that of a woman in labor?
22 And when you ask yourself,
Why have all these things
happened to me?
it is because of your many sins
that you have been stripped
and violated.
23 Can a Cushite change his skin
or a leopard its spots?
Neither can you do good
when doing evil comes so naturally.
24 So I will scatter you[f] like straw
that is blown away
by the desert winds.
25 This is the future
that I have prepared for you,
declares the LORD,
because you have forgotten me
and trusted in lies.
26 I myself will pull up your skirt
over your face
and expose your shame.
27 I have seen your adultery and lust,
your disgusting idols and shameless
prostitution
on the hills and in the fields.
How terrible for you, Jerusalem!
How long will you remain dirty?

Destruction on the horizon

14 The LORD's word to Jeremiah concerning the droughts:

2 Judah mourns;
her gates wither away.
The people fall to the ground in sorrow,
as sobs of Jerusalem ascend.
3 The rich send their servants for water,
but the wells run dry.
They return with empty jars,
ashamed, bewildered, and in despair.
4 Because the ground is cracked
due to lack of rain,
the farmers too are ashamed;
they cover their heads.
5 Even the doe in the field

[e] Heb uncertain [f] Or *them*

abandons her newborn,
for there's no grass.
6 The wild donkeys stand
on the well-traveled paths,
panting like thirsty dogs;
they go blind
since there's nothing to eat.

7 Even though our sins testify against us,
help us, LORD, for your name's sake.
We have turned away from you
and sinned against you time and again.
8 You are the hope of Israel,
its savior in times of trouble.
Why are you like a stranger in the land,
like a tourist spending only the night?
9 Why are you like one taken by surprise,
like a warrior unable to act?
Yet you are in our midst, LORD;
we are called by your name.
Don't give up on us.

10 This is what the LORD proclaims about
this people:
Since they have loved to wander off
and haven't restrained themselves,
I[g] won't accept them.
Now I will recall their wrongdoing
and punish their sin.
11 The LORD said to me: Don't pray for the
safety of these people. 12 When they fast, I
won't pay attention to their pleas, and when
they offer entirely burned offerings and grain
offerings, I won't accept them. Instead, I will
devour them with war, famine, and disease.
13 I replied, "LORD God, the prophets are
telling them: 'You won't see war or famine,
for I will give you lasting peace in this place.'"
14 Then the LORD said to me: The prophets are telling lies in my name. I haven't
sent them. I haven't commanded them. I
haven't spoken to them. They are prophesying to you false visions, worthless predictions, and deceit they have made up
on their own. 15 Therefore, this is what the
LORD proclaims concerning the prophets
who are speaking in my name when I didn't
send them, and who are telling you that
war or famine will never come to this land:
Those very prophets will die in war and by
famine! 16 And the people they are prophesying to will be thrown into the streets
of Jerusalem, victims of famine and war.
There will be no one to bury them or their
wives and children. I will pour out on them
their own wickedness.
17 So deliver this word to them:
My eyes well up with tears;
I can't stop weeping—day and night,
because my virgin daughter, my people,
has suffered a crushing blow
and is mortally wounded.
18 If I go into the fields,
I see only the slain in battle.
If I enter the city,
I see only those suffering from famine.
Even both prophet and priest
wander about aimlessly in ignorance.
19 Have you completely rejected Judah?
Do you hate Zion?
Why then have you
mortally wounded us?
We look for peace,
but nothing good comes of it;
for a time of healing,
only to be terrorized.
20 We acknowledge our sin, LORD,
the wrongdoing of our ancestors,
because we have sinned against you.
21 For your name's sake, don't reject us,
don't scorn your glorious throne.
Remember your covenant with us;
don't break it.
22 Can any of the false gods of the nations
make it rain?
Can the sky by itself bring showers?
Aren't you the LORD, our God?
You are our hope,
since only you can do such things.

Lamenting Jerusalem's dire circumstances

15 The LORD said to me: Even if Moses
and Samuel stood before me, I wouldn't
change my mind about these people. Send
them away from me. Let them go! 2 And if
they say, "Go where?" tell them, This is what
the LORD proclaims:

[g] Or *the Lord*

Those marked for death—to death,
those marked for war—to war,
those marked for famine—to famine,
and those marked for exile—to exile.
3 I will appoint over them four agents[h] of
death, declares the LORD: soldiers to kill,
dogs to drag off, and vultures and wild animals to devour and destroy. 4 Because of what
Judah's King Manasseh, Hezekiah's son, has
done in Jerusalem, I will make them an object of horror to all nations on earth.
5 Who will pity you, Jerusalem?
Who will shed tears over you?
Who will stop and ask how you're doing?
6 You have deserted me,
declares the LORD.
You have turned your back on me.
So I will turn my hand against you
and destroy you.
I'm tired of holding back.
7 I will winnow them
with a winnowing fork
at the gates of their country.
I will bereave and destroy my people
because they haven't changed
their ways.
8 Their widows will outnumber
the sand on the shore.
I will bring a destroyer in broad daylight
against the mothers of young men.[i]
Suddenly I will bring distress
and terror upon them.
9 The mother of seven
will grow weak and gasp for air;
her sun will set while it is yet day;
she will be ashamed and disgraced.
I will deliver the survivors
to the sword,
to the power of their enemies,
declares the LORD.
10 I wish I had never been born! I have become a source of conflict and dissension in
my own country. Even though I haven't lent
or borrowed, still everyone curses me.
11 The LORD said:
Haven't I taken care of you?
Haven't I helped you with your enemies
in time of trouble and distress?[j]
12 Can a person shatter iron,
iron from the north, or bronze?
13 Your wealth and belongings
I will deliver as plunder,
without a fee,
because of all your sins
throughout your territory.
14 I will make you serve your enemies
in a land you don't know,
for my anger blazes like a fire
that won't go out.

15 You understand, LORD!
Remember me and act on my behalf.
Bring judgment on those who torment me.
In your mercy, spare my life.[k]
Consider how I'm insulted
on your account.
16 When your words turned up,
I feasted on them;
and they became my joy,
the delight of my heart,
because I belong to you,
LORD God of heavenly forces.
17 I didn't join the festive occasions;
I took no delight in them.
I sat alone
because your hand was upon me
and you had filled me with curses.
18 Why am I always in pain?
Why is my wound incurable,
so far beyond healing?
You have become for me as unreliable
as a spring gone dry!

19 Therefore, the LORD proclaims:
If you return to me, I will take you back
and let you stand before me.
If you utter what is worthwhile,
not what is worthless,
you will be my spokesman.
They will turn to you,
not you to them!
20 I will make you a sturdy bronze wall
against these people.
They will attack you,
but they won't triumph,
because I am with you
to protect and rescue you,
declares the LORD.

[h] Or *families* [i] Heb uncertain [j] Heb uncertain [k] Heb uncertain

21 I will rescue you
from the hand of the wicked;
I will redeem you
from the grasp of the violent.

Loss of hope

16 The LORD's word came to me: 2 Don't
marry or have children in this place.
3 This is what the LORD proclaims concerning children who are born in this place and
their mothers and fathers who give birth to
them in this place:

4 They will die of horrible diseases.
No one will mourn for them
or bury them.
They will be like refuse
lying on the ground.
They will die from the sword
and by famine,
and their corpses will be food
for birds and wild animals.

5 This is what the LORD says:
Don't enter a house
where there is mourning;
don't grieve or lament for them,
for I have taken away my blessing,
kindness, and mercy from this people,
declares the LORD.
6 From the least to the greatest,
all will die in this land,
and there will be no funerals
or time of mourning.
No one will gash themselves in grief
or shave their heads in sorrow.
7 No one will bring food[1] for the mourner
as comfort for the dead.
No one will offer a cup of consolation
for the loss of father or mother.

8 Don't enter a house where there is
feasting and sit down to eat and drink.
9 This is what the LORD of heavenly forces,
the God of Israel, proclaims:
Before your very eyes and in your own
lifetime, I will silence in this place the
sounds of joy and gladness and the voices of
the bridegroom and the bride.
10 When you proclaim all these things to
the people, and they ask you, "Why has the
LORD pronounced such massive devastation against us? What have we done wrong?
How have we sinned against the LORD our
God?" 11 then you should tell them: It's because your ancestors have deserted me and
followed other gods, declares the LORD.
They have served and worshipped them,
while abandoning me and refusing to keep
my Instruction. 12 And you, you have acted
worse than your ancestors, each of you following your own willful, evil hearts and
paying no attention to me. 13 So I will banish you from this land to a place that neither you nor your ancestors have known,
and there you will serve other gods day and
night, for I will show you no mercy.
14 But the time is coming, declares the
LORD, when no one will say, "As the LORD
lives who brought up the Israelites from the
land of Egypt"; 15 instead, they will say, "As
the LORD lives who brought up the Israelites
from the land of the north and from all the
lands where he has banished them." I will
bring them back to the land that I gave to
their ancestors.
16 I'm going to send hordes of fishermen
to catch them, declares the LORD. Afterward I will send a party of hunters to hunt
them down on every mountain, hill, and
cave. 17 I am watching their every move;
not one is hidden from me. Nor is their
sin concealed from my sight. 18 I will initially pay them back double for their evil
and sin, because they have corrupted my
land with their disgusting, lifeless idols
and have filled my inheritance with their
detestable practices.

19 LORD, you are my strength
and my stronghold;
you are my refuge in time of trouble.
The nations will flock to you
from the ends of the earth,
and they will say:
"Our ancestors have inherited utter lies,
things that are hollow and useless."
20 Can humans make their own gods?
If so, they are not gods at all!
21 Therefore, I will teach them;
this time I will teach them
my power and my might.

[1] LXX; Heb *break for them*

They will understand
that I am the LORD.

17 Judah's sin is engraved
with an iron pen.
It's etched with a diamond point
on the tablets of their hearts
and on the horns of their altars.
2 Their children remember their altars
and sacred poles[m]
by the lush trees and high hills.

3 Because you have committed such sins
throughout your country,
I will give to your enemies
my mountain in the land,
as well as your wealth
and all that you treasure.[n]
4 You will lose the inheritance
that I gave you.
I will make you slaves of your enemies
in a land you don't know,
for my anger blazes like a fire
that won't go out.

5 The LORD proclaims:
Cursed are those who trust
in mere humans,
who depend on human strength
and turn their hearts from the LORD.
6 They will be like a desert shrub
that doesn't know when relief comes.
They will live in the parched places
of the wilderness,
in a barren land where no one survives.
7 Happy are those who trust in the LORD,
who rely on the LORD.
8 They will be like trees
planted by the streams,
whose roots reach down to the water.
They won't fear drought when it comes;
their leaves will remain green.
They won't be stressed
in the time of drought
or fail to bear fruit.

9 The most cunning heart—
it's beyond help.
Who can figure it out?
10 I, the LORD, probe the heart
and discern hidden motives,
to give everyone what they deserve,
the consequences of their deeds.

11 Like a partridge gathering a brood
that is not its own,
so are those who acquire
their wealth corruptly.
By midlife it will be gone;
afterward they will look like fools.

12 Splendid and exalted throne,
the place of our sanctuary
from the beginning!
13 LORD, the hope of Israel,
all who forsake you
will suffer disgrace;
those who turn away from you[o]
in the land
will be written off,[p]
for they have abandoned the LORD,
the fountain of living water.

14 Heal me, LORD, and I'll be healed.
Save me and I'll be saved,
for you are my heart's desire.
15 See how they harass me:
"Where's the LORD's word?
Let it come now!"
16 Yet I didn't urge you to bring disaster;[q]
I didn't want the calamity to happen.
You know what comes out of my mouth;
it's always before you.
17 Don't terrorize me;
you are my refuge in time of disaster.
18 Let my tormentors be disgraced,
but not me;
let them be terrorized, but not me.
Bring on them the time of disaster,
as they deserve; destroy them
repeatedly.

19 The LORD proclaimed to me: Go and
stand by the People's Gate where Judah's
kings go in and out, and then by all the gates
of Jerusalem, 20 and say to them: Listen to
the LORD's word, you kings of Judah, all
you people of Judah, and anyone living in

[m] Heb *asherim*; perhaps objects devoted to the worship of Asherah [n] Heb uncertain [o] Or *me* [p] Heb uncertain
[q] LXX; Heb uncertain

Jerusalem who passes through these gates.
[21]The LORD says: Be on guard not to carry
a load on the Sabbath day or conduct business at the gates of Jerusalem. [22]Don't carry
a load from your houses or do any kind of
work on the Sabbath day. Rather, keep the
Sabbath day holy as I commanded your ancestors, [23]although they didn't listen or pay
attention. They were stubborn and wouldn't
obey or accept correction. [24]If you are careful to obey me, declares the LORD, and don't
conduct business at the gates of this city on
the Sabbath day, if you keep the Sabbath
day holy by not working, [25]then through
the gates of this city will come kings who
occupy the throne of David and their officers, all riding on chariots and horses. They
will be accompanied by the people of Judah
and those living in Jerusalem. And this city
will always be inhabited. [26]Others will come
from the towns of Judah and Benjamin,
from all around Jerusalem, and from the
western foothills, the highlands, and the
arid southern plain—they will come bringing entirely burned offerings, sacrifices,
grain offerings, incense, and thanksgiving
offerings to the LORD's temple. [27]But if you
don't obey me by keeping the Sabbath day
holy, if you carry your loads and conduct
your business at the gates of Jerusalem as
usual, then I will set fire to those gates that
will completely engulf the fortresses of Jerusalem; it will not be put out.

God the potter

18 Jeremiah received the LORD's word:
[2]Go down to the potter's house, and
I'll give you instructions about what to
do there. [3]So I went down to the potter's
house; he was working on the potter's
wheel. [4]But the piece he was making was
flawed while still in his hands, so the potter
started on another, as seemed best to him.
[5]Then the LORD's word came to me: [6]House
of Israel, can't I deal with you like this potter, declares the LORD? Like clay in the
potter's hand, so are you in mine, house of
Israel! [7]At any time I may announce that I
will dig up, pull down, and destroy a nation
or kingdom; [8]but if that nation I warned
turns from its evil, then I'll relent and not
carry out the harm I intended for it. [9]At
the same time, I may announce that I will
build and plant a nation or kingdom; [10]but
if that nation displeases and disobeys me,
then I'll relent and not carry out the good
I intended for it. [11]Now say to the people of
Judah and those living in Jerusalem: This
is what the LORD says: I am a potter preparing a disaster for you; I'm working out
a plan against you. So each one of you, turn
from your evil ways; reform your ways and
your actions. [12]But they said, "What's the
use! We will follow our own plans and act
according to our own willful, evil hearts."
[13]Therefore, the LORD proclaims:

Ask among the nations:
Have you ever heard anything like this?
Virgin Israel has done
the most horrible thing.
[14]Does the snow on the mountains of
Lebanon ever melt entirely
off their rocky cliffs?
Do the cool mountain streams
ever dry up?[r]
[15]Yet my people have forgotten me;
they have offered sacrifices to a lie.
And so they have stumbled
along the way,
even along the ancient paths.
They have taken side roads,
not the main roads.[s]
[16]They have ruined their country
and brought utter shame on it.
All who pass by are shocked
and shake their heads.
[17]Like a strong east wind,
I will scatter them before their enemy.
When disaster strikes them,
I will show them my back,
not my face.

[18]Then they said, "Come, let's unite against
Jeremiah, for the priest's instruction won't
fail, nor will the sage's counsel, nor the prophet's word. Come, let's silence him and pay no
attention to his words."

[19]Pay attention to me, LORD;
listen to what my enemies are saying.

[r]Heb uncertain; or *be dug up* [s]Heb uncertain

20 Should evil be returned for good?
Yet they have set traps for me.
Remember that I stood before you,
begging you to be merciful
and not to punish them.
21 Enough! Let their children starve;
let them die by the sword.
Let their wives be barren widows;
let their men be slaughtered
and their youth struck down in battle.
22 Let screams be heard from their homes
when you suddenly bring armies
against them.
They have dug a pit to capture me,
set traps for my feet.
23 But you, LORD, you know
all their sinister plots to kill me.
Don't overlook their wrongdoing;
don't cleanse their sin from before you.
May they stumble before you;
when you become angry,
do something about them.

Broken beyond repair

19 The LORD proclaims: Go buy a clay
jar from a potter in the presence of
the elders of the people and the priests.
2 Then go out to the Ben-hinnom Valley at
the entrance of the gate called Broken Pots
and proclaim there the words I will tell
you. 3 Listen to the LORD's word, you kings
of Judah and those of you living in Jerusalem: This is what the LORD of heavenly
forces, the God of Israel, says: I'm going
to bring such disaster upon this place that
it will shock all who hear of it. 4 They have
deserted me and degraded this place into a
shrine for other gods, which neither they
nor their ancestors nor Judah's kings have
ever known. And they have filled this place
with the blood of the innocent. 5 Yes, they
have built shrines to Baal, to burn their
sons and daughters in the fire, although I
never commanded or ordered such a thing,
nor did it ever cross my mind.
6 So now the time is coming, declares
the LORD, when people will no longer call
this place Topheth or Ben-hinnom Valley
but Carnage Valley. 7 I will foil the plans of
Judah and Jerusalem in this place and will
have them fall in battle before their enemies, before those who seek their lives. I
will give their corpses as food to the birds
and the wild animals. 8 I will make this city
something that sounds horrible; all who
pass by it will be shocked at its pain. 9 And
when their enemies lay siege to the city,
seeking their lives, they will resort in des-
peration to eating the flesh of their sons
and daughters, and to devouring the flesh
of their neighbors.
10 Then you should shatter the clay jar in
the sight of the people who are with you,
11 and you should say to them: This is what
the LORD of heavenly forces says: Just as
one smashes the potter's piece beyond repair, so I will smash this people and this
city. And they will bury the dead in Topheth
until there's no room left. 12 That is what I will
do to this place and its residents, declares
the LORD: I will make this city like Topheth.
13 The houses of Jerusalem and those of Judah's kings will become as foul as Topheth—
all the houses on whose roofs they made
offerings to the heavenly force and poured
out drink offerings to other gods.
14 When Jeremiah returned from Topheth
where the LORD had sent him to prophesy, he stood in the court of the LORD's
temple and said to all the people: 15 The
LORD of heavenly forces, the God of Israel, proclaims: I am about to bring upon
this city and its surrounding towns every
disaster that I have pronounced against
them, because they have been stubborn and
wouldn't obey my words.

20 When the priest Pashhur, Immer's
son, the officer in charge of the
LORD's temple, heard Jeremiah prophesying these words, 2 he beat the prophet and
detained him in confinement at the upper
Benjamin Gate in the LORD's temple. 3 The
next day, when Pashhur released Jeremiah
from confinement, Jeremiah said to him,
"The LORD has changed your name from
Pashhur to Panic Lurks Everywhere. 4 The
LORD proclaims: I'm going to strike panic
into your heart and into the hearts of
your friends. You will watch as they fall in
battle to their enemies. I will hand over
all Judah to the king of Babylon, who will
exile some to Babylon and slaughter oth-

ers. [5]I will hand over all the wealth of this city, all its goods and valuables, including the treasures of the kings of Judah, to their enemies, who will ransack and pillage and carry it all off to Babylon. [6]And you, Pashhur, and all those in your household, will go into captivity. You will be deported to Babylon where you will die. There you will be buried with all your friends to whom you prophesied falsely."

Total despair

[7]LORD, you enticed me, and I was taken in.
You were too strong for me,
and you prevailed.
Now I'm laughed at all the time;
everyone mocks me.
[8]Every time I open my mouth, I cry out
and say, "Violence and destruction!"
The LORD's word has brought me
nothing but insult and injury,
constantly.
[9]I thought, I'll forget him;
I'll no longer speak in his name.
But there's an intense fire in my heart,
trapped in my bones.
I'm drained trying to contain it;
I'm unable to do it.
[10]I hear many whispering—
"Panic Lurks Everywhere!—
proclaim, yes, let's proclaim it
ourselves!"
All my friends are waiting
for me to stumble:
"Perhaps he can be enticed.
Then we'll prevail against him
and get our revenge on him!"
[11]But the LORD is with me
like a strong defender.
Therefore, my oppressors
will stumble and not prevail.
They will be disgraced
by their own failures.
Their dishonor will never be forgotten.
[12]The LORD of heavenly forces
tests the righteous
and discerns the heart and the mind.
Let me see your retribution upon them,
for I have committed my case to you.
[13]Sing to the LORD,
praise the LORD,
for he has rescued the needy
from the clutches of evildoers.
[14]Cursed be the day that I was born.
May the day my mother
gave birth to me not be blessed.
[15]Cursed be the one
who delivered the news to my father,
"You have a son!"—
filling him with joy.
[16]May the bearer of that news
be like the cities
that the LORD destroyed without mercy.
May he hear screams in the morning,
and the battle cries at noon,
[17]because he didn't kill me in the womb
and let my mother become my grave,
her womb pregnant forever.
[18]Why was I ever born
when all I see is suffering and misery,
and my days are filled with shame?

Verdict against king and city

21 Jeremiah received the LORD's word when King Zedekiah sent Pashhur, Malchiah's son, and the priest Zephaniah, Maaseiah's son, to him with an appeal: [2]"Speak to the LORD on our behalf because Babylon's King Nebuchadnezzar[t] is attacking us. Perhaps the LORD will perform one of his mighty deeds and force him to withdraw from us."

[3]Jeremiah answered them: This is what you should tell Zedekiah: [4]"The LORD, the God of Israel, says: I'm going to turn your own weapons against you, yes, the weapons you are using to fight the king of Babylon and the Babylonians[u] who have surrounded you! I will round them up in the center of the city. [5]Then I myself will fight against you with an outstretched hand and strong arm in fierce anger and rage. [6]I will strike down those within this city—both people and animals—and they will die of a terrible plague. [7]Afterward, declares the LORD, I will deliver Judah's King Zedekiah, his servants, and those in this city who have survived plague, war, and famine to

[t]Heb *Nebuchadrezzar* [u]Heb *Chaldeans*

Babylon's King Nebuchadnezzar[v] and to
their enemies who seek to do them harm.
He will put them to the sword without pity,
mercy, or compassion.
8 This is what you should tell this people:
The LORD says: I'm setting before you the
way of life and the way of death. 9 Whoever
stays in the city will die by the sword, famine, and disease. But whoever leaves the
city and surrenders to the Babylonians[w]
will live; yes, their lives will be spared. 10 I
have set my face against this city for harm
and not for good, declares the LORD; it will
be delivered to the king of Babylon, who
will set it on fire.

Judah: Hear the LORD's word

11 House of Judah! This is what the LORD
says:
12 House of David! The LORD proclaims:
Begin each morning
by administering justice,
rescue from their oppressor those
who have been robbed
or else my anger
will spread like a wildfire,
with no one to put it out,
because of your evil deeds.
13 I am against you,
you who live in the valley,[x]
like a rock of the plain,
declares the LORD,
and who say, "Who will come down
to attack us?
Who will breach our fortresses?"
14 I will punish you
based on what you have done,
declares the LORD.
I will set your[y] forests on fire;
the flames will engulf
everything around you.[z]

Oracles against the kings

22 The LORD proclaims: Go down to
the palace of the king of Judah and
declare this message: 2 Listen to the LORD's
word, king of Judah, you who sit on David's throne—you and your attendants,
and all those who go through these gates.
3 The LORD proclaims: Do what is just and
right; rescue the oppressed from the power
of the oppressor. Don't exploit or mistreat
the refugee, the orphan, and the widow.
Don't spill the blood of the innocent in
this place. 4 If you obey this command, then
through the gates of this palace will come
kings who occupy the throne of David, riding on chariots and horses along with their
entourage and subjects. 5 But if you ignore
these words, I swear by myself, declares the
LORD, that this palace will become a ruin.
6 The LORD proclaims concerning the palace
of the king of Judah:

Though you are like Gilead to me,
like the summit of Lebanon,
I will turn you into a desert—
uninhabited cities.
7 I will summon destroyers against you,
who will use their weapons
to cut down your finest cedars
and hurl them into the fire.

8 People from many nations will pass by
this city and ask each other: "Why has the
LORD treated that great city like this?" 9 And
the answer will be, "Because they abandoned
the covenant with the LORD their God and
worshipped and served other gods."

10 Don't weep or lament for the dead king.[a]
Weep instead for the one
who has gone away,
for he will never return
to see his native soil.

11 This is what the LORD says about Shallum son of Judah's King Josiah, who succeeded his father Josiah as king but who
is now gone from this place: He will never
return! 12 He will die where he's been exiled
and never see this land again.

13 How terrible for Jehoiakim,
who builds his house with corruption
and his upper chambers with injustice,
working his countrymen for nothing,
refusing to give them their wages.
14 He says, "I'll build myself a grand palace,
with huge upper chambers,
ornate windows,
cedar paneling,
and rich red decor."

[v]Heb *Nebuchadrezzar* [w]Heb *Chaldeans* [x]Heb uncertain [y]Or *its* [z]Or *it* [a]Heb lacks *king*.

15 Is this what makes you a king,
having more cedar than anyone else?
Didn't your father eat and drink
and still do what was just and right?
Then it went well for him!
16 He defended the rights
of the poor and needy;
then it went well.
Isn't that what it means to know me?
declares the LORD.
17 But you set your eyes and heart
on nothing but unjust gain;
you spill the blood of the innocent;
you practice cruelty;
you oppress your subjects.
18 Therefore, this is what the LORD says
to Jehoiakim son of Judah's King Josiah:
They won't grieve for him, saying,
"My brother, my sister!"
They won't grieve for him, saying,
"My master, my majesty!"
19 They will give him a donkey's burial,
dragging him outside
the gates of Jerusalem
and dumping him there.

20 Go up to Lebanon and cry out,
lift up your voice in Bashan,
cry out from Abarim,
because all your lovers
have been ravished.
21 I spoke to you
when you felt safe and secure,
but you said, "I won't listen."
You have been that way since your youth:
not listening to a word I say.
22 Your shepherds will be tossed to the wind,
your lovers taken off to exile.
Then you will be embarrassed
and humiliated
by all your wickedness.
23 You who live in Lebanon,
nestled in cedar,
who will pity you[b]
when you are overcome in pain,
like that of childbirth?
24 As surely as I live, declares the LORD,
even if Coniah,[c] King Jehoiakim's son from
Judah were a signet ring on my right hand, I
would still remove you from there. 25 I would
hand you over to those who seek to kill you,
those you dread, even Babylon's King Nebuchadnezzar and his army.[d] 26 I will banish
you and your mother who bore you to a land
far from your native soil, and there the two
of you will die. 27 You[e] will never return to
the land you[f] long to go back to.
28 Is this man Coniah
merely a defiled and broken
pottery jar
that no one wants?
Why then have he and his children
been hurled out
and cast into an unfamiliar land?
29 Land, land, land,
hear the LORD's word:
30 The LORD proclaims:
Mark this man as childless;
he will not prosper during his lifetime.
None of his children
will sit on David's throne
and rule again in Judah.

Promise of restoration

23 Watch out, you shepherds who destroy and scatter the sheep of my
pasture, declares the LORD. 2 This is what
the LORD, the God of Israel, proclaims
about the shepherds who "tend to" my
people: You are the ones who have scattered my flock and driven them away. You
haven't attended to their needs, so I will
take revenge on you for the terrible things
you have done to them, declares the LORD.
3 I myself will gather the few remaining
sheep from all the countries where I have
driven them. I will bring them back to their
pasture, and they will be fruitful and multiply. 4 I will place over them shepherds who
care for them. Then they will no longer be
afraid or dread harm, nor will any be missing, declares the LORD.

Promise of a righteous and just king

5 The time is coming, declares the LORD,
when I will raise up a righteous descendant[g] from David's line, and he will rule as a
wise king. He will do what is just and right

[b]Heb uncertain [c]Cf *Jeconiah* in Jer 24:1 [d]Or *the Babylonians* [e]Or *They* [f]Or *they* [g]Or *branch*

in the land. 6During his lifetime, Judah
will be saved and Israel will live in safety.
And his name will be The LORD Is Our
Righteousness.[h]
7So the time is coming, declares the
LORD, when no one will say, "As the LORD
lives who brought up the Israelites from the
land of Egypt." 8Instead, they will say, "As
the LORD lives who brought up the descendants of the people of Israel from the land
of the north and from all the lands where
he[i] has banished them so that they can live
in their own land."

Oracles against the prophets

9 As for the prophets:
My heart inside me is broken;
my body aches.[j]
I stagger like a drunk
who has had too much wine to drink,
because of the LORD
and because of God's holy words.
10 Because the country teems
with adulterers,
because of them,[k]
yes, because their might isn't right
and their way is evil,
the land dries up,
and the grazing areas
in the wilderness wither.[l]
11 Both prophet and priest are godless;
I even find their evil in my temple,
declares the LORD.
12 Therefore, they will find themselves
on slippery ground
and will be thrust into darkness,
where they will collapse.
I will bring disaster upon them,
when their time comes,
declares the LORD.
13 In the prophets of Samaria
I saw something shocking:
They prophesied by Baal
and led astray my people Israel.
14 In the prophets of Jerusalem
I saw something horrible:
They commit adultery and tell lies.
They encourage evildoers
so that no one turns
from their wickedness.
In my eyes,
they are no better than Sodom;
its people are like Gomorrah.

15 Therefore, this is what the LORD of heavenly forces proclaims concerning the prophets:

I'm going to feed them bitter food
and give them poison to drink.
Wickedness has spread
from the prophets of Jerusalem
throughout the land.

16 The LORD proclaims:
Don't listen to the prophets
who are speaking to you;
they are deceiving you.
Their visions come
from their own hearts,
not from the LORD's mouth.
17 They keep saying to those
who scorn God's message,
"All will go well for you,"
and to those who follow
their own willful hearts,
"Nothing bad will happen to you."
18 But who has stood in the LORD's council
to listen to God's word?
Who has paid attention
to his word and announced it?
19 Look! The LORD's angry storm
breaks out;
it whirls around the heads of the wicked.
20 The LORD's fierce anger
won't turn back
until it accomplishes
all that he has planned.
In the days to come,
you will understand what this means.

21 I didn't send the prophets,
yet they ran anyway.
I didn't speak to them,
yet they prophesied anyway.
22 If they had stood in my council,
they would have proclaimed
my words to my people;

[h]Or *of Our Righteousness*, possibly a play on the name *Zedekiah* [i]Or *I* [j]Heb uncertain; or *my bones shake*
[k]LXX; MT *a curse* [l]Heb uncertain

they would have turned them
from their evil ways and deeds.
23 The LORD declares, Am I a God
who is only nearby and not far off?
24 Can people hide themselves
in secret places
so I might not see them?
Don't I fill heaven and earth?
25 I have heard the prophets prophesying lies in my name. They claim, "I've had
a dream; I've had a dream!" 26 How long will
deceitful prophecies dominate the minds of
the prophets? Those prophets are treacherous. 27 They scheme to make my people
forget me by their dreams that people tell
each other, just as their ancestors forgot me
because of Baal. 28 Let the prophet who has
a dream declare it, but let the one who has
my word proclaim it faithfully.
What a difference
between straw and wheat!
declares the LORD.
29 Isn't my word like fire
and like a hammer that shatters rock?
declares the LORD.
30 Therefore, I'm against the prophets
who steal my words from each other,
declares the LORD.
31 I'm against the prophets
who carelessly deliver oracles,[m]
declares the LORD.
32 I'm against the prophets
who dream up lies
and then proclaim them,
declares the LORD.
With their reckless lies,
they lead my people astray.
I didn't send them;
I didn't commission them.
They are completely useless
to these people,
declares the LORD.
33 When these people or a prophet or a
priest asks you, "What is the LORD's message?"[n] say to them, "What message? I will
cast you off, declares the LORD." 34 I will
punish anyone, including prophet or priest,
who says, "This is the LORD's message."
35 This is what you should ask each other:
"What has the LORD said?" "What has the
LORD declared?" 36 But you are no longer
to mention the LORD's message, because
everyone thinks they have received a message from the LORD. You destroy the very
word of the living God, the LORD of heavenly forces, our God. 37 So this is what you
should say to the prophet: "What has the
LORD said to you?" "What has the LORD
declared?" 38 But if you insist on saying,
"This is the LORD's message," the LORD
says to you: Because you have made this
claim—this is the LORD's message—when
I told you not to proclaim the LORD's message, 39 I will lift you up[o] and cast you out of
my presence, together with the city that I
gave to your ancestors. 40 I will make you an
object of disgrace and enduring shame that
no one will ever forget.

Good and bad figs

24 After Babylon's King Nebuchadnezzar had deported Judah's King Jeconiah, King Jehoiakim's son, and the Judean
officials, as well as the craftsmen and
metalworkers from Jerusalem to Babylon,
the LORD showed me two baskets of figs set
in front of the LORD's temple. 2 One basket
was filled with fresh and ripe figs; the other
basket was filled with rotten figs—too rotten to eat. 3 And the LORD asked me: "What
do you see, Jeremiah?"
I replied: "Figs! Some good ones and
others very bad—so bad that they can't be
eaten."
4 Then the LORD said to me: 5 The LORD,
the God of Israel, proclaims: Just as with
these good figs, I will treat kindly the Judean exiles that I have sent from this place
to Babylon. 6 I regard them as good, and I
will bring them back to this land. I will build
them up and not pull them down; I will plant
them and not dig them up. 7 I will give them
a heart to know me, for I am the LORD. They
will be my people, and I will be their God, for
they will return to me with all their heart.
8 And just like the rotten figs that are so bad
that they can't be eaten, the LORD says, I
will do to Judah's King Zedekiah and his

[m] Heb uncertain [n] Or *burden* [o] LXX, Syr, Vulg; MT *forget you*

officials, as well as the remaining few in Jerusalem and those who are living in Egypt. [9]I will make them an object of horror and evil to all the kingdoms of the earth. Wherever I scatter them, they will be disgraced and insulted, mocked and cursed. [10]I will send the sword, famine, and disease against them until they vanish from the fertile land that I gave to their ancestors.

A summary of Jeremiah's message

25 Jeremiah received the LORD's word concerning all the people of Judah in the fourth year of Judah's King Jehoiakim, Josiah's son. This was the first year of Babylon's King Nebuchadnezzar. [2]The prophet Jeremiah addressed all the people of Judah and all those living in Jerusalem. [3]From the thirteenth year of Judah's King Josiah, Amon's son, to this very day—twenty-three years—the LORD's word has come to me. I have delivered it to you repeatedly, although you wouldn't listen. [4]In fact, the LORD has tirelessly sent you all his servants, the prophets, but you wouldn't listen or pay attention. [5]They said, "Each one of you, turn from your evil ways and deeds and live in the fertile land that the LORD gave you and your ancestors for all time. [6]Don't follow or worship other gods and don't anger me by what you make with your hands. Then I won't bring disaster upon you." [7]But you wouldn't listen to me, making me angry by what you do and bringing disaster upon yourselves, declares the LORD.

[8]Therefore, this is what the LORD of heavenly forces says: Because you haven't listened to my words, [9]I am going to muster all the tribes of the north and my servant King Nebuchadnezzar of Babylon, declares the LORD, and I will bring them against this country and its residents as well as against all the surrounding nations. I will completely destroy them and will make them an object of horror, shock, and ruins for all time. [10]I will silence the sounds of joy and laughter and the voices of the bride and the bridegroom. Yes, I will silence the millstones and snuff out the lamplight. [11]This whole country will be reduced to a wasteland, and these nations will serve the king of Babylon for seventy years. [12]When the seventy years are over, I will punish the king of Babylon and his nation for their wrongdoing, declares the LORD. I will reduce the land of the Babylonians to a wasteland for all time. [13]I will unleash upon that land everything I decreed, all that is written in this scroll, which Jeremiah prophesied against all the nations. [14]Yes, many great nations and powerful kings will enslave them, and I will pay them back in full for what they have done and made with their hands.

[15]This is what the LORD, God of Israel, said to me: Take this seething cup of wine from my hand and make all the nations gulp it down where I'm sending you. [16]They will drink and stagger about half-crazed because of the sword that I am sending against them.

[17]So I took the cup from the LORD's hand, and I made all the nations drink from it where the LORD had sent me: [18]Jerusalem and the towns of Judah, its kings and officials. This was to make them a wasteland, an object of horror, shock, and cursing, as it is today; [19]Pharaoh, Egypt's king, his attendants and officials, and all his people, [20]including the foreigners[p] living there; all the kings of the land of Uz; all the kings of the land of the Philistines—Ashkelon, Gaza, Ekron, and what's left of Ashdod; [21]Edom, Moab, and the Ammonites; [22]all the kings of Tyre and Sidon, and the kings of the coastlands across the sea; [23]Dedan, Tema, Buz, and all those who cut the hair of their foreheads;[q] [24]all the kings of Arabia and the nomadic tribes,[r] [25]all the kings of Zimri,[s] Elam, and Media; [26]all the kings of the north, those nearby and those faraway, one after another, all the empires on the earth will drink from this cup.[t] And after them the king of Sheshach[u] will drink from it.

[27]Then say to them: The LORD of heavenly forces, the God of Israel, proclaims: Drink this seething cup of wine and get

[p]Heb uncertain [q]Heb uncertain [r]Heb uncertain [s]Heb uncertain [t]Heb lacks *will drink from this cup.*
[u]*Sheshak* is a name for Babylon.

drunk. Vomit and collapse and don't get up
again because of the sword that I'm thrust-
ing into you. 28 If they refuse to take the cup
in your hand and drink from it, tell them:
This is what the LORD of heavenly forces
says: You must drink! 29 Look! I'm bringing
disaster upon the city that bears my name;
how then will you escape unpunished? You
will not! I'm summoning the sword against
everyone on earth, declares the LORD of
heavenly forces.
30 Now prophesy all these things
and say to them:
The LORD roars on high;
from his holy place he thunders.
He roars fiercely against his flock,
like the shouting of those
who tread on grapes,
against everyone on earth.
31 The uproar is heard far and wide,
because the LORD is bringing
a lawsuit against the nations.
He's entering into judgment
with all people,
sentencing the guilty to death,
declares the LORD.
32 The LORD of heavenly forces proclaims:
Look! Disaster travels
from nation to nation.
A terrible storm comes
from the far ends of the earth.
33 At that time, those struck down by the
LORD will fill the earth. And no one will
mourn for them or prepare their bodies for
burial. They will become like refuse lying on
the ground.
34 Wail, you shepherds, cry out.
Roll in the dust,
you masters of the flock!
The day of your slaughter has arrived.
You will fall and shatter
like a fragile vase.
35 The shepherds have no place to hide;
the masters of the flock can't escape.
36 Hear the cry of the shepherds
and the sobbing of the masters
of the flock,
because the LORD
is ravaging their pasture.
37 There's an eerie silence
in the peaceful meadows,
because of the LORD's fierce anger.
38 The lion is on the prowl,
and the land is reduced to nothing,
because of the fierce sword,[v]
because of his fierce anger.

Jeremiah arrested and sentenced to death

26 Early in the rule of Judah's King
Jehoiakim, Josiah's son, this word
came from the LORD: 2 The LORD proclaims:
Stand in the temple courtyard and speak to
all the people of the towns of Judah who
have come to the temple to worship. Tell
them everything I command you; leave
nothing out. 3 Perhaps they will listen and
each will turn from their evil ways. If they
do, I will relent and not carry out the harm
I have in mind for them because of the
wrong they have done. 4 So tell them, The
LORD proclaims: If you don't listen to me or
follow the Instruction I have set before
you—5 if you don't listen to the words of
the prophets that I have sent to you time
and again, though you haven't listened,
6 then I will make this temple a ruin like Shiloh, and this city I will make a curse before
all nations on earth.
7 The priests, the prophets, and all the
people heard Jeremiah declare these words
in the LORD's temple. 8 And when Jeremiah
finished saying everything the LORD told
him to say, the priests and the prophets
and all the people seized him and said,
"You must die! 9 Why do you prophesy in
the LORD's name that 'this temple will become a ruin like Shiloh, and this city will be
destroyed and left without inhabitant'?"
Then all the people joined ranks against
Jeremiah in the LORD's temple.
10 When the officials of Judah heard
these things, they went up from the royal
palace to the LORD's temple and took their
places at the entrance of the New Gate
of the LORD's temple. 11 The priests and
the prophets said to the officials and all
the people: "This man deserves to die for

[v] LXX, Heb manuscripts; Heb uncertain

prophesying against this city as you have all heard firsthand."

[12]Jeremiah said to all the officials and to all the people, "The LORD sent me to prophesy to this temple and this city everything you have heard. [13]So now transform your ways and actions. Obey the LORD your God, and the LORD may relent and not carry out the harm that he's pronounced against you. [14]But me? I'm in your hands. Do whatever you would like to me. [15]Only know for certain that if you sentence me to death, you and the people of this city will be guilty of killing an innocent man. The LORD has in fact sent me to speak everything I have said to you."

[16]Then the officials and all the people said to the priests and the prophets, "This man doesn't deserve to die, for he has spoken to us in the name of the LORD our God."

[17]A few of the community elders got up and addressed the whole crowd: [18]"Micah of Moresheth, who prophesied during the rule of Judah's Hezekiah, said to all the people of Judah, 'The LORD of heavenly forces proclaims:

Zion will be plowed down like a field,
Jerusalem will become piles of rubble,
and the temple mount will become
an overgrown mound.'

[19]"Did King Hezekiah or anyone else in Judah execute him? Didn't he instead fear the LORD and plead for his mercy? Then the LORD relented of the harm that he had pronounced against them. We are about to commit a huge mistake that will cost us our lives."

[20]There was another man who prophesied in the LORD's name: Uriah, Shemaiah's son from Kiriath-jearim. He prophesied the same things that Jeremiah did about this city and against this land. [21]When King Jehoiakim and all his warriors and officials heard his words, the king sought to kill him. Uriah heard of this and fled in fear to Egypt. [22]But King Jehoiakim dispatched Elnathan, Achbor's son, and others to Egypt. [23]They brought Uriah back from Egypt to the king who had him killed, and his body was thrown into the common burial ground.

[24]But Ahikam, Shaphan's son, protected Jeremiah and wouldn't let the people execute him.

Submit to the king of Babylon and live

27 Early in the rule of Judah's King Zedekiah,[w] Josiah's son, this word came to Jeremiah from the LORD: [2]This is what the LORD said to me: Make a yoke of straps and bars and wear it on your neck. [3]Then send word[x] to the kings of Edom, Moab, Ammon, Tyre, and Sidon through their representatives who have come to Jerusalem to Judah's King Zedekiah. [4]Tell them to say to their masters: The LORD of heavenly forces, the God of Israel, proclaims: Say this to your masters:

[5]By my great power and outstretched arm, I have made the earth and the people and animals that are on it. I can give it to anyone I please. [6]Now I hand over all these countries to my servant King Nebuchadnezzar of Babylon. I even give him the wild animals as subjects. [7]All nations will serve him, his son and grandson, until the time for his land arrives; then many nations and great kings will conquer him.

[8]As for the nation or country that won't serve Babylon's King Nebuchadnezzar and won't put its neck under his yoke, I will punish it with sword, famine, and disease until I have destroyed it by his hand, declares the LORD. [9]As for you, don't listen to your prophets, diviners, dreamers,[y] mediums, or your sorcerers who say to you, "Don't serve the king of Babylon." [10]They are lying to you, and their lies will lead to banishment from your land. I will drive you out, and you will perish. [11]But any nation that puts its neck under the yoke of the king of Babylon and serves him, I will let stay in its land to till it and live on it, declares the LORD.

[12]I delivered the same message to Judah's King Zedekiah: If you want to live, put your necks under the yoke of the king of Babylon and serve him and his people. [13]Why should

[w]Heb manuscripts, Syr; MT *Jehoiakim* [x]Or *them* (the yokes) [y]Or *dreams*

you and your people die by sword, famine, and disease, as the LORD pronounced against any nation that won't serve the king of Babylon? [14]Pay no attention to the words of the prophets who encourage you not to serve the king of Babylon, for they are lying to you. [15]I haven't sent these prophets, declares the LORD; they are prophesying falsely in my name. If you listen to them, I will drive you out, and you will perish, both you and your prophets!

[16]Then I spoke to the priests and all this people: This is what the LORD says: Don't listen to the words of the prophets who are prophesying to you, "In a short while, the temple equipment will be brought back from Babylon." They are prophesying a lie to you. [17]Don't listen to them; serve the king of Babylon and live. Otherwise, this city will be reduced to ruin. [18]If they are really prophets and have the LORD's word, let them intercede with the LORD of heavenly forces not to let the equipment left in the LORD's temple and in the royal palace of Judah and Jerusalem be carted off to Babylon.

[19]This is what the LORD of heavenly forces proclaims about the pillars, the Sea, the stands, and the rest of the equipment left in this city, [20]which Babylon's King Nebuchadnezzar didn't plunder when he deported Jeconiah the son of Judah's King Jehoiakim from Jerusalem to Babylon, along with all the officials of Judah and Jerusalem. [21]Yes, this is what the LORD of heavenly forces, the God of Israel, proclaims about the equipment that is left in the LORD's temple and in the royal palace in Judah, and in Jerusalem: [22]They will be carted off to Babylon where they will remain until the day I come looking for them, declares the LORD; then I will bring them back and restore them to this place.

Prophet against prophet

28 That same year, early in the rule of Judah's King Zedekiah, in the fifth month of his fourth year, the prophet Hananiah, Azzur's son from Gibeon, spoke to me in the LORD's temple before the priests and all the people. [2]He said: "The LORD of heavenly forces, the God of Israel, proclaims: I have broken the yoke of the king of Babylon. [3]In two years I will restore to this place all of the temple equipment that Babylon's King Nebuchadnezzar carted off to Babylon. [4]I will also restore to this place Judah's King Jeconiah, Jehoiakim's son, along with all the exiles from Judah who were deported to Babylon, for I will break the yoke of the king of Babylon, declares the LORD."

[5]Then the prophet Jeremiah responded to Hananiah in the presence of the priests and all the people who were standing in the LORD's temple. [6]The prophet Jeremiah said: "Indeed. May the LORD do just as you have said! May the LORD fulfill the words that you have prophesied and bring back from Babylon the equipment of the LORD's temple and all the exiles to this place. [7]However, listen closely to what I have to say to you and all the people: [8]The prophets who came before you and me long ago prophesied war, disaster, and disease against many lands and great kingdoms. [9]So the prophet who prophesies peace is recognized as one who is actually sent by the LORD only when that prophet's message is fulfilled."

[10]Then the prophet Hananiah took hold of the yoke that was on the prophet Jeremiah's neck and broke it. [11]He said before all the people, "This is what the LORD says: Just as this yoke has been broken, I will break the yoke of Babylon's King Nebuchadnezzar from the neck of all the nations within two years." Then the prophet Jeremiah walked away.

[12]Sometime after Hananiah had broken the yoke that was on Jeremiah's neck, the LORD told him: [13]Go, say to Hananiah, The LORD proclaims: You have broken a wooden yoke,[z] but I[a] will replace it with an iron one. [14]The LORD of heavenly forces, the God of Israel, proclaims: I will put iron yokes on the necks of all these nations, and they will serve Babylon's King Nebuchadnezzar; even the wild animals will be subject to him!

[15]Then the prophet Jeremiah said to the

[z]Or *yokes* [a]Heb uncertain

prophet Hananiah: "Listen, Hananiah! The LORD hasn't sent you. All you are doing is persuading these people to believe a lie. 16 Therefore, the LORD proclaims: I'm going to send you somewhere—right off the face of the earth! Before the year ends, you will die since you have incited rebellion against the LORD." 17 The prophet Hananiah died in the seventh month[b] of that year.

Disturbing hope: Settle down in Babylon

29 The prophet Jeremiah sent a letter from Jerusalem to the few surviving elders among the exiles, to the priests and the prophets, and to all the people Nebuchadnezzar had taken to Babylon from Jerusalem. 2 The letter was sent after King Jeconiah, the queen mother, the court officials, the government leaders of Judah and Jerusalem, and the craftsmen and smiths had left Jerusalem. 3 It was delivered to Babylon by Elasah, Shaphan's son, and Gemariah, Hilkiah's son—two men dispatched to Babylon's King Nebuchadnezzar by King Zedekiah.

4 The LORD of heavenly forces, the God of Israel, proclaims to all the exiles I have carried off from Jerusalem to Babylon: 5 Build houses and settle down; cultivate gardens and eat what they produce. 6 Get married and have children; then help your sons find wives and your daughters find husbands in order that they too may have children. Increase in number there so that you don't dwindle away. 7 Promote the welfare of the city where I have sent you into exile. Pray to the LORD for it, because your future depends on its welfare.

8 The LORD of heavenly forces, the God of Israel, proclaims: Don't let the prophets and diviners in your midst mislead you. Don't pay attention to your dreams. 9 They are prophesying lies to you in my name. I didn't send them, declares the LORD.

10 The LORD proclaims: When Babylon's seventy years are up, I will come and fulfill my gracious promise to bring you back to this place. 11 I know the plans I have in mind for you, declares the LORD; they are plans for peace, not disaster, to give you a future filled with hope. 12 When you call me and come and pray to me, I will listen to you. 13 When you search for me, yes, search for me with all your heart, you will find me. 14 I will be present for you, declares the LORD, and I will end your captivity. I will gather you from all the nations and places where I have scattered you, and I will bring you home after your long exile,[c] declares the LORD.

15 Yet you say, The LORD has raised up prophets for us in Babylon:

16 This is what the LORD proclaims concerning the king sitting on David's throne and all the people who live in this city, that is, those among you who didn't go into exile: 17 The LORD of heavenly forces proclaims: I'm going to send the sword, famine, and disease against them. I will make them like rotten figs that are too spoiled to eat. 18 I will pursue them with the sword, famine, and disease; and I will make them an object of horror to all nations on earth and an object of cursing, scorn, shock, and disgrace among all the countries where I have scattered them, 19 because they wouldn't listen to my words, declares the LORD, which I sent them time and again through my servants the prophets. They[d] wouldn't listen, declares the LORD.

20 But now, all you exiles I deported from Jerusalem to Babylon, listen to the LORD's word. 21 This is what the LORD of heavenly forces, the God of Israel, proclaims concerning Ahab, Kolaiah's son, and Zedekiah, Maaseiah's son, who are prophesying lies to you in my name: I will hand them over to Babylon's King Nebuchadnezzar, and he will slay them before your very eyes. 22 Because of them, all the Judean exiles in Babylon will use this curse: "The LORD make you like Zedekiah and Ahab, who were burned alive by the king of Babylon." 23 They committed a horrible scandal in Israel—adultery with their neighbors' wives and deceit spoken in my name, with which I had nothing to do. Yet I'm still aware of it and am witness to it, declares the LORD.

24 Tell Shemaiah the Nehelamite, 25 This is what the LORD of heavenly forces, the

[b] September–October, Tishrei [c] Or *I will restore you to the place from which I exiled you.* [d] Syr; MT *you*

God of Israel, proclaims: [e]You sent letters on your own accord to all the people in Jerusalem, to the priest Zephaniah, Maaseiah's son, and to the rest of the priests.
26 You said to Zephaniah:[f] The LORD has appointed you priest in charge of the LORD's temple instead of Jehoiada. You are responsible for putting every madman who prophesies into stocks and neck irons.
27 So why haven't you threatened Jeremiah of Anathoth, who pretends to be a prophet among you?
28 He has sent a letter telling those of us in Babylon: "You are going to be there a long time, so build houses and settle down, plant gardens and eat what they produce."

29 The priest Zephaniah read this letter to the prophet Jeremiah.
30 Then the LORD's word came to Jeremiah:
31 Send word to all the exiles: The LORD proclaims concerning Shemaiah the Nehelamite: Because Shemaiah prophesied to you when I didn't send him, and because he convinced you to believe a lie,
32 I will punish Shemaiah the Nehelamite and his descendants, declares the LORD. Not one member of this people will be around to see the good that I have in store for my people, declares the LORD, for he incited rebellion against me.

THE SCROLL OF COMFORT

Healing and restoration for my people

30 Jeremiah received the LORD's word:
2 The LORD, the God of Israel, proclaims: Write down in a scroll all the words I have spoken to you.
3 The time is coming, declares the LORD, when I will bring back my people Israel and Judah from captivity,[g] says the LORD. I will bring them home to the land that I gave to their ancestors, and they will possess it.
4 Here are the words that the LORD spoke concerning Israel and Judah:

5 The LORD proclaims:
I[h] hear screams of panic and terror;
no one is safe.
6 Ask and see:
Can men bear children?
Then why do I see every man
bent over in pain,[i] as if he's in labor?
Why have all turned pale?
7 That day is awful, beyond words.
A time of unspeakable pain
for my people Jacob.
But they will be delivered from it.

8 At that time, I will break the yoke off their[j] necks and remove their[k] shackles. Foreigners will no longer enslave them, declares the LORD of heavenly forces.
9 They will serve the LORD their God and the king whom I will raise up for them from David's family.

10 So don't be afraid, my servant Jacob,
declares the LORD,
Don't lose hope, Israel.
I will deliver you from faraway places
and your children
from the land of their exile.
My people Jacob
will again be safe and sound,
with no one harassing them.
11 I am with you and will rescue you,
declares the LORD.
I will put an end to all the nations
where I have scattered you.
But I won't put an end to you.
I won't let you remain unpunished:
I will discipline you as you deserve.

12 This is what the LORD says:
Your injury is incurable;
your illness is grave.
13 No one comes to your aid;
no one attends to your wound;
your disease is incurable.
14 All your lovers disregard you;
they write you off as a lost cause,
because I have dealt harshly with you
as an enemy would,
because your guilt is great
and your sins are many.
15 Why cry out for relief
from your pain?
Your wound is incurable.
I have done these things to you,
because your guilt is great
and your sins are many.

[e]Or *because you sent* [f]Heb lacks *You said to Zephaniah.* [g]Or *restore the fortunes* [h]Or *We* [i]Or *with his hands on his groin* [j]Or *your* [k]Or *your*

[16]Yet all who ravage you will be ravaged;
all who oppress you will go into exile.
Those who rob you will be robbed,
and all who plunder you
will be plundered.
[17]I will restore your health,
and I will heal your wounds,
declares the LORD,
because you were labeled an outcast,
"Zion, the lost cause."

[18]The LORD proclaims:
I will restore Jacob's tents
and have pity on their birthplace.
Their city will be rebuilt on its ruins
and the palace in its rightful place.
[19]There will be laughter
and songs of thanks.
I will add to their numbers
so they don't dwindle away.
I will honor them
so they aren't humiliated.
[20]Their children will thrive
as they did long ago,
and their community will be
established before me.
I will punish their oppressors.
[21]They will have their own leader;
their ruler will come from among them.
I will let him approach me,
and he will draw near.
Who would dare approach me
unless I let them come?
declares the LORD.
[22]You will be my people,
and I will be your God.

[23]Look! The LORD's anger breaks out
like a violent storm,
a fierce wind that strikes
the heads of the wicked.
[24]The LORD's fierce anger won't turn back
until God's[l] purposes
are entirely accomplished.
In the days to come,
you will understand what this means.

31 At that time, declares the LORD,
I will be the God
of all the families of Israel,
and they will be my people.

[2]The LORD proclaims:
The people who survived the sword
found grace in the wilderness.
As Israel searched for a place of rest,
[3]the LORD appeared to them[m]
from a distance:[n]
I have loved you with a love
that lasts forever.
And so with unfailing love,
I have drawn you to myself.[o]
[4]Again, I will build you up,
and you will be rebuilt, virgin Israel.
Again, you will play your tambourines
and dance with joy.
[5]Again, you will plant vineyards
on the hills of Samaria;
farmers will plant
and then enjoy the harvests.
[6]The time will come when
the watchmen shout from
the highlands of Ephraim:
"Get ready! We're going up to Zion
to the LORD our God!"
[7]The LORD proclaims:
Sing joyfully for the people of Jacob;
shout for the leading nation.
Raise your voices with praise
and call out:
"The LORD has saved his people,[p]
the remaining few in Israel!"

[8]I'm going to bring them back
from the north;
I will gather them
from the ends of the earth.
Among them will be
the blind and the disabled,
expectant mothers and those in labor;
a great throng will return here.
[9]With tears of joy they will come;
while they pray, I will bring them back.
I will lead them by quiet streams
and on smooth paths
so they don't stumble.
I will be Israel's father,
Ephraim will be my oldest child.

[10]Listen to the LORD's word, you nations,
and announce it to the distant islands:

[l]Or *his or its* [m]Or *to me* [n]Or *a long time ago* [o]Heb lacks *myself.* [p]LXX; MT *Save your people, LORD*

The one who scattered Israel
will gather them
and keep them safe,
as a shepherd his flock.
11 The LORD will rescue the people of Jacob
and deliver them from the power
of those stronger than they are.
12 They will come shouting for joy
on the hills of Zion,
jubilant over the LORD's gifts:
grain, wine, oil, flocks, and herds.
Their lives will be like a lush garden;
they will grieve no more.
13 Then the young women
will dance for joy;
the young and old men will join in.
I will turn their mourning into laughter
and their sadness into joy;
I will comfort them.
14 I will lavish the priests with abundance
and shower my people with my gifts,
declares the LORD.

15 The LORD proclaims:
A voice is heard in Ramah,
weeping and wailing.
It's Rachel crying for her children;
she refuses to be consoled,
because her children are no more.
16 The LORD proclaims:
Keep your voice from crying
and your eyes from weeping,
because your endurance
will be rewarded,
declares the LORD.
They will return
from the land of their enemy!
17 There's hope for your future,
declares the LORD.
Your children will return home!

18 I hear, yes, I hear Ephraim lamenting:
"You disciplined me,
and I learned my lesson,
even though I was as stubborn as a mule.
Bring me back, let me return,
because you are the LORD my God.
19 After I turned away from you,
I regretted it;
I realized what I had done,
and I have hit myself[q]—
I was humiliated and disgraced,
and I have carried this disgrace
since I was young."

20 Isn't Ephraim my much-loved child?
Don't I utterly adore him?
Even when I scold him,
I still hold him dear.
I yearn for him and love him deeply,
declares the LORD.

21 Set up markers,
put up signs;
think about the road you have traveled,
the path you have taken.
Return, virgin Israel;
return to these towns of yours.
22 How long will you hem and haw,
my rebellious daughter?
The LORD has created
something new on earth:
Virgin Israel will once again
embrace her God![r]

23 The LORD of heavenly forces, the God
of Israel, proclaims: When I bring my people[s]
back from captivity, they will once again utter
these words in the land and towns of Judah:
The LORD bless you,
righteous dwelling place,
holy mountain.
24 Those who live in Judah and its towns
will dwell together with farmers and shepherds. 25 I will strengthen the weary and
renew those who are weak.
26 Then I woke up and looked around.
What a pleasant sleep I had!
27 The time is coming, declares the LORD,
when I will plant seeds in Israel and Judah,
and both people and animals will spring up.
28 Just as I watched over them to dig up and
pull down, to overthrow, destroy, and bring
harm, so I will watch over them to build and
plant, declares the LORD. 29 In those days,
people will no longer say:
Sour grapes eaten by parents
leave a bitter taste
in the mouths of their children.

[q]Or *struck my thigh* [r]Or *a woman surrounds a man* [s]Or *them*

30 Because everyone will die
for their own sins:
whoever eats sour grapes
will have a bitter taste
in their own mouths.

31 The time is coming, declares the LORD, when I will make a new covenant with the people of Israel and Judah. 32 It won't be like the covenant I made with their ancestors when I took them by the hand to lead them out of the land of Egypt. They broke that covenant with me even though I was their husband, declares the LORD. 33 No, this is the covenant that I will make with the people of Israel after that time, declares the LORD. I will put my Instructions within them and engrave them on their hearts. I will be their God, and they will be my people. 34 They will no longer need to teach each other to say, "Know the LORD!" because they will all know me, from the least of them to the greatest, declares the LORD; for I will forgive their wrongdoing and never again remember their sins.

35 The LORD proclaims:
The one who established the sun
to light up the day
and ordered[t] the moon and stars
to light up the night,
who stirs up the sea
into crashing waves,
whose name is
the LORD of heavenly forces:
36 If the created order should vanish
from my sight,
declares the LORD,
only then would Israel's descendants
ever stop being a nation before me.
37 The LORD proclaims:
If the heavens above could be measured
and the foundation of the earth below
could be fathomed,
only then would I reject
Israel's descendants
for what they have done,
declares the LORD.

38 The time is coming, declares the LORD, when the city will be rebuilt for the LORD from the Tower of Hananel to the Corner Gate. 39 Its boundaries will extend to the Gareb Hill and around to Goah. 40 The entire valley defiled by corpses and ashes, and all the fields as far as the Kidron Valley and the Horse Gate on the east, all this will be set apart for the LORD. And the city will never again be dug up or overthrown.

Nothing is too hard for the LORD

32 Jeremiah received the LORD's word in the tenth year of Judah's King Zedekiah, which was the eighteenth year of Nebuchadnezzar's rule. 2 At that time, the army of the Babylonian king had surrounded Jerusalem, and the prophet Jeremiah was confined to the prison quarters in the palace of Judah's king. 3 Judah's King Zedekiah had Jeremiah sent there after questioning him: "Why do you prophesy, 'This is what the LORD says: I'm handing this city over to the king of Babylon, and he will occupy it; 4 and Judah's King Zedekiah will be captured and handed over to the king of Babylon; he will speak to the king of Babylon personally and see him with his very own eyes. 5 And Zedekiah will be carried off to Babylon to live out his days until I punish him, declares the LORD. If you make war against the Babylonians, you will fail.'"

6 Jeremiah said, The LORD's word came to me: 7 Your cousin Hanamel, Shallum's son, is on his way to see you; and when he arrives, he will tell you: "Buy my field in Anathoth, for by law you are next in line to purchase it." 8 And just as the LORD had said, my cousin Hanamel showed up at the prison quarters and told me, "Buy my field in Anathoth in the land of Benjamin, for you are next in line and have a family obligation to purchase it." Then I was sure this was the LORD's doing.

9 So I bought the field in Anathoth from my cousin Hanamel, and weighed out for him seventeen shekels of silver. 10 I signed the deed, sealed it, had it witnessed, and weighed out the silver on the scales. 11 Then I took the deed of purchase—the sealed copy, with its terms and conditions, and

[t] Or *orders of*

the unsealed copy—12 and gave it to Baruch,
Neriah's son and Mahseiah's grandson, before my cousin Hanamel and the witnesses
named in the deed, as well as before all the
Judeans who were present in the prison
quarters. 13 I charged Baruch before all of
them: 14 "The LORD of heavenly forces,
the God of Israel, proclaims: Take these
documents—this sealed deed of purchase
along with the unsealed one—and put them
into a clay container so they will last a long
time. 15 The LORD of heavenly forces, the
God of Israel, proclaims: Houses, fields, and
vineyards will again be bought in this land."
16 After I had given the documents to Baruch, Neriah's son, I prayed to the LORD:
17 LORD God, you created heaven and earth
by your great power and outstretched arm;
nothing is too hard for you! 18 You act with
mercy toward thousands upon thousands,
but you also bring the consequences of the
fathers' sins on their children after them.
Great and mighty God, whose name is the
LORD of heavenly forces, 19 marvelous are
your purposes, and mighty are your deeds.
You are aware of all the ways of humanity,
and you reward us for how we live and what
we do even now. 20 You have performed
signs and wonders in the land of Egypt as
you do to this very day in Israel and everywhere else. That's why you are so renowned.
21 With a strong hand, an outstretched arm,
and with awesome power, yes, with signs
and wonders, you brought your people Israel out of the land of Egypt. 22 You gave
them this land that you promised to their
ancestors, a land full of milk and honey.
23 They entered and took possession of it,
but they didn't obey you or follow your Instruction. In fact, they didn't do anything
you commanded them. So you brought
upon them this disaster. 24 Now the siege
ramps are in place to take the city. And the
Babylonians are about to capture it by war,
famine, and disease. What you have pronounced is now happening, as you can see.
25 So why tell me, LORD God, Buy the field
for money and make sure there are witnesses, when the city is under Babylonian
control?
26 Then the LORD's word came to Jeremiah: 27 I am the LORD, the God of all living things! Is anything too hard for me?
28 Therefore, the LORD proclaims: I'm handing this city over to the Babylonians and
King Nebuchadnezzar, who will capture
it. 29 They will enter the city, set it on fire,
and burn it down—including the houses
on whose roofs offerings have been made
to Baal and drink offerings to other gods,
which made me especially angry. 30 The
people of Israel and Judah have done nothing but evil in my eyes since their youth;
the people of Israel and Judah have done
nothing but anger me by the work of their
hands, declares the LORD. 31 This city has
enraged me from the day it was built to this
very day, and so it must be removed from
my sight—32 because of all the evil done by
the people of Israel and Judah to make me
angry—they, their kings and officials, their
priests and prophets, the men of Judah,
and those who live in Jerusalem. 33 They
turned their backs to me and not their
faces; and though I taught them over and
over, they wouldn't accept my correction.
34 They set up their disgusting idols in the
temple that bears my name and violated it;
35 and they built shrines to Baal in the Ben-
hinnon Valley, where they sacrifice their
sons and daughters to Molech, though I
never commanded them—nor did it even
cross my mind—that they should do such
detestable things, leading Judah to sin.
36 You have been saying, "This city will
be handed over to the king of Babylon
through sword, famine, and disease." But
this is what the LORD, the God of Israel,
says: 37 I will gather them from all the countries where I have scattered them in my
fierce anger and rage. I will bring them back
to this place to live securely. 38 They will be
my people, and I will be their God. 39 I will
give them one heart and one mind so that
they may worship me all the days of their
lives, for their own good and for the good
of their children after them. 40 I will make
an everlasting covenant with them, never
to stop treating them graciously. I will put
into their hearts a sense of awe for me so
that they won't turn away from me. 41 I will
rejoice in treating them graciously, and I

will plant them in this land faithfully and with all my heart and being.

42 The LORD proclaims: Just as I brought this great disaster on this people, so I will bring on them all the good I promised them. 43 Fields will be bought in this land, a land you have said is bleak and uninhabited and in the possession of the Babylonians. 44 Fields will be bought, and deeds will be signed, sealed, and witnessed in the land of Benjamin and in the outlying areas of Jerusalem, in the towns of Judah and in the highlands, in the towns of the western foothills and the arid southern plain; for I will bring them back from their captivity, declares the LORD.

Restoration of Judah and Israel

33 While he was still confined to the prison quarters, the LORD's word came to Jeremiah a second time: 2 The LORD proclaims, the LORD who made the earth,[u] who formed and established it, whose name is the LORD: 3 Call to me and I will answer and reveal to you wondrous secrets that you haven't known.

4 This is what the LORD, the God of Israel, proclaims about the houses of this city and the palaces of the kings of Judah that were torn down to defend against the siege ramps and weapons 5 of the invading Babylonians.[v] They will be filled with the corpses of those slain in my fierce anger. I hid my face from the people of this city because of all their evil deeds, 6 but now I will heal and mend them. I will make them whole and bless them[w] with an abundance of peace and security. 7 I will bring back the captives of Judah and Israel, and I will rebuild them as they were at first. 8 I will cleanse them of all the wrongdoing they committed against me, and I will forgive them for all of their guilt and rebellion. 9 Then this city[x] will bring me great joy, praise, and renown before all nations on earth, when they hear of all the good I provide for them. They will be in total awe at all the good and prosperity I provide for them.

10 The LORD proclaims: You have said about this place, "It is a wasteland, without humans or animals." Yet in the ravaged and uninhabited towns of Judah and the streets of Jerusalem, 11 the sounds of joy and laughter and the voices of the bride and the bridegroom will again be heard. So will the voices of those who say, as thank offerings are brought to the LORD's temple, "Give thanks to the LORD of heavenly forces, for the LORD is good and his kindness lasts forever." I will bring back the captives of this land as they were before, says the LORD.

12 The LORD of heavenly forces proclaims: This wasteland, without humans or animals—and all its towns—will again become pastures for shepherds to care for their flocks. 13 Shepherds will again count their flocks in the towns of the highlands, the western foothills and the arid southern plain, in the land of Benjamin, as well as in the outlying areas of Jerusalem and the towns of Judah, says the LORD.

14 The time is coming, declares the LORD, when I will fulfill my gracious promise with the people of Israel and Judah. 15 In those days and at that time, I will raise up a righteous branch from David's line, who will do what is just and right in the land. 16 In those days, Judah will be saved and Jerusalem will live in safety. And this is what he will be called: The LORD Is Our Righteousness. 17 The LORD proclaims: David will always have one of his descendants sit on the throne of the house of Israel. 18 And the levitical priests will always have someone in my presence to make entirely burned offerings and grain offerings, and to present sacrifices.

19 Then the LORD's word came to Jeremiah: 20 This is what the LORD says: If one could break my covenant with the day and my covenant with the night so that they wouldn't come at their proper time, 21 only then could my covenant with my servant David and my covenant with the levitical priests who minister before me be broken; only then would David no longer have a descendant to rule on his throne. 22 And just as the stars in the sky can't be numbered and the sand on the shore can't be counted,

[u] LXX *the earth;* MT *it* [v] Heb uncertain [w] Heb uncertain [x] Or *it*

so I will increase the descendants of my servant David and the Levites who minister before me.

23 Then the LORD's word came to Jeremiah: 24 Aren't you aware of what people are saying: "The LORD has rejected the two families that he had chosen"? They are insulting my people as if they no longer belong to me.[y] 25 The LORD proclaims: I would no sooner break my covenant with day and night or the laws of heaven and earth 26 than I would reject the descendants of Jacob and my servant David and his descendants as rulers for the children of Abraham, Isaac, and Jacob. I will restore the captives and have compassion on them.

Lessons on obedience and disobedience

34 Jeremiah received the LORD's word when Babylon's King Nebuchadnezzar and his army, and all the countries and people he ruled, were attacking Jerusalem and all its towns. 2 The LORD, the God of Israel, proclaims, Go and speak to Judah's King Zedekiah and say to him: The LORD proclaims, I'm handing this city over to the king of Babylon, and he will burn it down. 3 You won't escape but will be captured and handed over to him. You will see the king of Babylon with your very own eyes and speak to him personally, and you will be taken to Babylon. 4 Even so, hear the LORD's word, King Zedekiah of Judah: This is what the LORD proclaims about you: You won't die in battle; 5 you will die a peaceful death. As burial incense was burned to honor your ancestors, the kings who came before you, so it will be burned to honor you as people mourn, "Oh, master!" I myself promise this, declares the LORD.

6 The prophet Jeremiah delivered this message to Judah's King Zedekiah in Jerusalem 7 when the army of the king of Babylon was attacking Jerusalem and all the remaining Judean towns, Lachish and Azekah—the only fortified towns still standing in Judah.

8 Jeremiah received the LORD's word after King Zedekiah had made a covenant with all the people in Jerusalem to proclaim liberty for their slaves: 9 everyone was to free their male and female Hebrew slaves and no longer hold a Judean brother or sister in bondage. 10 So all the officials and people who entered into this covenant agreed to free their male and female slaves and no longer hold them in bondage; they obeyed the king's command[z] and let them go. 11 But afterward they broke their promise, took back the men and women they had freed, and enslaved them again.

12 Then the LORD's word came to Jeremiah: 13 The LORD, the God of Israel, proclaims: I made a covenant with your ancestors when I brought them out of the land of Egypt, out of the house of slavery. 14 I said that every seventh year each of you must free any Hebrews who have been sold to you. After they have served you for six years, you must set them free. But your ancestors didn't obey or pay any attention to me. 15 Recently you turned about and did what was right in my sight; each of you proclaimed liberty for the other and made a covenant before me in the temple that bears my name. 16 But then you went back on your word and made my name impure; each of you reclaimed the men and women you had set free and forced them to be your slaves again.

17 Therefore, the LORD proclaims: Since you have defied me by not setting your fellow citizens free, I'm setting you free, declares the LORD, free to die by the sword, disease, and famine! And I will make you an object of horror for all nations on earth. 18 I will make those who disregarded my covenant, violating its terms that they agreed to in my presence, like the calf they cut in two and then walked between the halves of its carcass. 19 The officials of Judah and Jerusalem, the eunuchs and priests, and all the people who passed through the pieces of the calf 20 I will hand over to their enemies who seek to kill them. And their corpses will become food for birds and wild animals. 21 I will hand over Judah's King Zedekiah and his officials to their enemies who seek to

[y] Heb uncertain [z] Heb lacks *the king's command.*

kill them: namely, the army of Babylon's king, which has just withdrawn from you. [22]I'm about to issue orders, declares the LORD, that the army of Babylon return to this city. They will wage war against it, capture it, and burn it down along with other Judean cities. I will make Judah a wasteland, without inhabitants.

35 Jeremiah received the LORD's word during the rule of Judah's King Jehoiakim, Josiah's son: [2]Go to the Rechabite family and invite them to come to one of the rooms of the LORD's temple. When they arrive, offer them some wine to drink. [3]So I took Jaazaniah, Jeremiah's son and Habazziniah's grandson, and his brothers and all his sons, and the whole Rechabite family. [4]I brought them to the room in the LORD's temple assigned to the sons of Hanan, Igdaliah's son, the man of God. The room was next to the one used by the chief officers and right above the room of Maaseiah, Shallum's son, the temple doorkeeper.[a] [5]Then I set bowls full of wine before the Rechabites, along with several cups, and I said to them, "Have some."

[6]But they refused: "We don't drink wine because our ancestor Jonadab, Rechab's son, commanded us, 'You and your children are never to drink wine; [7]nor are you to build or own houses or plant gardens and vineyards; rather, you are always to dwell in tents so you may live a long time in the fertile land you pass through.' [8]We have obeyed everything our ancestor Jonadab, Rechab's son, commanded us. No one in our household, including our wives and children, has ever had wine. [9]And we haven't built houses to live in or had vineyards, fields, or crops. [10]We have lived in tents and done everything our ancestor Jonadab commanded us. [11]But when Babylon's King Nebuchadnezzar invaded the country, we said, 'We better go to Jerusalem to escape the Babylonian and Aramean armies.' That's why we're here in Jerusalem."

[12]Then the LORD's word came to Jeremiah: [13]The LORD of heavenly forces, the God of Israel, proclaims: Go and tell the people of Judah and those who live in Jerusalem: Can't you learn a lesson about what it means to obey me? declares the LORD. [14]Jonadab, Rechab's son, commanded his descendants not to drink wine, and to this very day they have not drunk wine, obeying their ancestor's instruction. But I have spoken to you again and again, and you haven't listened to me. [15]I have sent you all my servants, the prophets, time and again, saying, "Each of you, turn from your evil ways and reform your actions; don't worship or serve other gods. Then you may live in the fertile land I gave to you and your ancestors." But you haven't paid attention or listened to me. [16]The descendants of Jonadab, Rechab's son, have thoroughly obeyed their ancestor, but this people have not listened to me. [17]Therefore, this is what the LORD of heavenly forces, the God of Israel, says: I'm going to bring upon the people of Judah and all those who live in Jerusalem the disaster I pronounced against them, because they wouldn't listen to me or respond when I called.

[18]Then Jeremiah said to the Rechabite family: The LORD of heavenly forces, the God of Israel, proclaims: Because you have obeyed all Jonadab's instructions and you have done everything he commanded you, [19]the LORD of heavenly forces, the God of Israel proclaims: Jonadab, Rechab's son, will always have a descendant that stands before me.

Enduring word of God

36 In the fourth year of Judah's King Jehoiakim, Josiah's son, this word came to Jeremiah from the LORD: [2]Take a scroll and write in it all the words I have spoken to you concerning Israel, Judah, and all the nations from the time of Josiah until today. [3]Perhaps when the people of Judah hear about every disaster I intend to bring upon them, they will turn from their evil ways, and I will forgive their wrongdoing and sins. [4]So Jeremiah sent for Baruch, Neriah's son. As Jeremiah dictated all the words that the LORD had spoken to him, Baruch wrote them in the scroll. [5]Then

[a]Or *keeper of the threshold*

Jeremiah told Baruch, "I'm confined here and can't go to the LORD's temple. [6]So you go to the temple on the next day of fasting, and read the LORD's words from the scroll that I have dictated to you. Read them so that all the people in the temple can hear them, as well as all the Judeans who have come from their towns. [7]If they turn from their evil ways, perhaps the LORD will hear their prayers. The LORD has threatened them with fierce anger." [8]Baruch, Neriah's son, did everything the prophet Jeremiah instructed him: he read all the LORD's words from the scroll in the temple.

[9]In the ninth month of the fifth year of Judah's King Jehoiakim, Josiah's son, all the people in Jerusalem and all those who had come from Judean towns observed a fast for the LORD in Jerusalem. [10]Then Baruch read Jeremiah's words from the scroll to all the people in the LORD's temple; he read them in the chamber of Gemariah, Shaphan the scribe's son, in the upper courtyard near the entrance of the New Gate of the LORD's temple. [11]When Micaiah, Gemariah's son and Shaphan's grandson, heard all the LORD's words from the scroll, [12]he went down to the scribes' chamber in the royal palace. There he found all the officials meeting together: Elishama the scribe; Delaiah, Shemaiah's son; Elnathan, Achbor's son; Gemariah, Shaphan's son; Zedekiah, Hananiah's son, and all the other officials. [13]Micaiah told them all the words he heard Baruch read from the scroll before the people.

[14]Then all the officials sent Jehudi, Nethaniah's son and Shelemiah's grandson, and Cushi's great-grandson, to Baruch: "Take the scroll you read to the people and come with me."

So Baruch, Neriah's son, took the scroll and went to the officials. [15]They said to him, "Sit down and read it to us." So Baruch read it to them. [16]When they heard all its words, they were alarmed and said to Baruch: "We must at once report all this to the king!" [17]Then they asked Baruch, "Tell us, how did you write all these words? Did they come from Jeremiah?"

[18]Baruch replied, "He dictated all the words to me, and I wrote them with ink in the scroll."

[19]The officials then said to Baruch, "You and Jeremiah had better go and hide. And don't let anyone know where you are."

[20]After leaving the scroll in the room of Elishama the scribe, they went to the king's court and told him everything. [21]The king sent Jehudi to take the scroll, and he retrieved it from the room of Elishama the scribe. Then Jehudi read it to the king and all his royal officials who were standing next to the king. [22]Now it was the ninth month,[b] and the king was staying in the winterized part of the palace with the firepot burning near him. [23]And whenever Jehudi read three or four columns of the scroll, the king would cut them off with a scribe's knife and throw them into the firepot until the whole scroll was burned up. [24]Neither the king nor any of his attendants who heard all these words were alarmed or tore their clothes. [25]Elnathan, Delaiah, and Gemariah begged the king not to burn the scroll, but he wouldn't listen to them.

[26]The king commanded Jerahmeel, the king's son, along with Seraiah, Azriel's son, and Shelemiah, Abdeel's son, to arrest the scribe Baruch and the prophet Jeremiah. But the LORD hid them.

[27]The LORD's word came to Jeremiah after the king had burned the scroll containing the words written by Baruch at Jeremiah's dictation: [28]Get another scroll and write in it all the words that were in the first scroll that Judah's King Jehoiakim burned. [29]Then say to Judah's King Jehoiakim: The LORD proclaims: You burned that scroll because it declared that the king of Babylon will come and destroy this land and eliminate every sign of life from it. [30]Therefore, this is what the LORD proclaims about Judah's King Jehoiakim: He won't have any heirs to occupy the throne of David, and his dead body will be cast out and exposed to the heat of the day and the frost of the night. [31]I will punish him and his family and his attendants for their wrongdoing. I will

[b]November–December, Kislev

bring upon them, as well as the residents of Jerusalem and the people of Judah, every disaster I pronounced against them. But they wouldn't listen.

[32]So Jeremiah took another scroll and gave it to the scribe Baruch, Neriah's son, who wrote at Jeremiah's dictation all the words in the scroll burned in the fire by Judah's King Jehoiakim. Many similar words were added to them.

Jeremiah falsely accused and imprisoned

37 Babylon's King Nebuchadnezzar appointed Zedekiah, Josiah's son, to succeed Coniah, Jehoiakim's son, as king of Judah. [2]Neither Zedekiah, his attendants, nor the people of the land listened to the LORD's words spoken by the prophet Jeremiah.

[3]Nevertheless, King Zedekiah sent Jehucal, Shelemiah's son, and the priest Zephaniah, Maaseiah's son, to Jeremiah the prophet with this plea: "Please pray for us to the LORD our God." ([4]Now Jeremiah hadn't been imprisoned yet, so he was free to come and go among the people. [5]Pharaoh's army had recently[c] set out from Egypt; when the Babylonians who were attacking Jerusalem learned of the Egyptian advance, they withdrew from Jerusalem.)

[6]Then the LORD's word came to Jeremiah the prophet: [7]The LORD, the God of Israel, proclaims: Tell the king of Judah who sent his emissaries to seek advice from me: "Pharaoh's army that came to assist you is heading back to Egypt. [8]The Babylonians will return and attack this city. They will capture it and burn it down."

[9]The LORD proclaims: Don't let yourself be deceived into thinking that the Babylonians will withdraw for good.[d] They won't! [10]Even if you were to crush the entire Babylonian army that's attacking you and only the wounded in their tents remained, they would rise up and burn this city down.

[11]Now when the Babylonian army had withdrawn from Jerusalem due to Pharaoh's advance, [12]Jeremiah set out for the land of Benjamin to secure his share of the family property.[e] [13]He got as far as the Benjamin Gate in Jerusalem when the guard there named Irijah, Shelemiah's son and Hananiah's grandson, arrested the prophet Jeremiah, saying, "You are deserting to the Babylonians."

[14]"That's a lie," Jeremiah replied. "I'm not deserting to the Babylonians." But Irijah wouldn't listen to him. He arrested Jeremiah and brought him to the officials, [15]who were furious with him. They beat him and threw him into the house of the scribe Jonathan, which had been turned into a prison. [16]So Jeremiah was put in a cistern, which was like a dungeon, where he remained a long time.

[17]Later King Zedekiah sent for him and questioned Jeremiah secretly in the palace: "Is there a word from the LORD?"

"There is," Jeremiah replied. "You are going to be handed over to the king of Babylon." [18]Then Jeremiah asked King Zedekiah, "What have I done wrong to you or your attendants or this people that you should throw me into prison? [19]Where are your prophets now who prophesied that the king of Babylon wouldn't attack you and this land? [20]Now, my master and king, I beg you, don't send me back to the house of Jonathan the scribe, or I'll die there." [21]So King Zedekiah gave orders that Jeremiah be held in the prison quarters and that he receive a loaf of bread daily from the street vendors[f]—until all the bread in the city was gone. So Jeremiah remained in the prison quarters.

38 Shephatiah, Mattan's son; Gedaliah, Pashhur's son; Jucal, Shelemiah's son; and Pashhur, Malchiah's son heard what Jeremiah had been telling the people: [2]The LORD proclaims: Whoever stays in this city will die by the sword, famine, and disease. But whoever surrenders to the Babylonians will live; yes, their lives will be spared. [3]The LORD proclaims: This city will certainly be handed over to the army of Babylon's king, who will capture it.

[4]Then the officials said to the king: "This

[c]Heb lacks *recently.* [d]Heb lacks *for good.* [e]Heb uncertain [f]Or *from the street of the bakers*

man must be put to death! By saying such
things, he is discouraging the few remaining troops left in the city, as well as all the
people. This man doesn't seek their welfare
but their ruin!"
5 "He's in your hands," King Zedekiah
said, "for the king can do nothing to stop
you." 6 So they seized Jeremiah, threw him
into the cistern of the royal prince Malchiah, within the prison quarters, and lowered him down by ropes. Now there wasn't
any water in the cistern, only mud, and Jeremiah began to sink into the mud.
7 Ebed-melech the Cushite, a court official in the royal palace, got word that they
had thrown Jeremiah into the cistern. Since
the king was sitting at the Benjamin Gate,
8 Ebed-melech left the palace and said to
the king: 9 "My master the king, these men
have made a terrible mistake in treating the
prophet Jeremiah the way they have; they
have thrown him into the cistern where he
will die of starvation, for there's no bread
left in the city."
10 Then the king commanded Ebed-melech
the Cushite, "Take thirty men from here
and take Jeremiah the prophet out of the
cistern before he dies." 11 So Ebed-melech
took the men and returned to the palace,
to an underground supply room, where he
found some old rags and scraps of clothing.
Ebed-melech lowered them down the cistern by the ropes 12 and called to Jeremiah,
"Put these old rags and scraps of clothing
under your arms and hold on to the ropes."
When Jeremiah did this, 13 they pulled him
up by the ropes and got him out of the cistern. After that Jeremiah remained in the
prison quarters.
14 King Zedekiah ordered that the prophet
Jeremiah be brought to him at the third entrance of the LORD's temple, where the king
said to Jeremiah, "I want to ask you something, and don't hide anything from me."
15 Jeremiah replied, "If I do, you'll kill me!
And if I tell you what to do, you won't listen
to me!"
16 So King Zedekiah swore to Jeremiah
behind closed doors, "As the LORD lives,
who has given us this life, I won't put you
to death and I won't hand you over to those
who seek to kill you."
17 So Jeremiah said to Zedekiah: "The
LORD of heavenly forces, the God of Israel,
proclaims: If you surrender to the officers of
the king of Babylon, you and your family will
live, and this city will not be burned down.
18 If you don't surrender to the officers of the
king of Babylon, the city will be handed over
to the Babylonians, who will burn it down,
and you won't escape from them."
19 King Zedekiah said to Jeremiah, "I'm
afraid that I will fall into the hands of the
Judeans who have defected to the Babylonians, and they will torture me."
20 "That won't happen," Jeremiah replied,
"if you obey the LORD, whose message I
bring. You will survive, and all will go well
for you. 21 But if you refuse to surrender,
this is what the LORD has shown me: 22 All
the women left in the palace of the king of
Judah will be led out to the officers of the
king of Babylon. And they will say:

'Your trusted friends
 have betrayed you;
 they have deceived you;
 now that your feet are stuck in the mud,
 they are nowhere to be found.'

23 "All your wives and children will be led
out to the Babylonians, and you yourself
won't escape from them. The king of Babylon will capture you, and this city will be
burned down."
24 Zedekiah said to Jeremiah, "No one is
to know about these matters or else you will
die. 25 If the officials find out that we met,
and they come and say to you, 'Tell us what
you said to the king. Don't hide anything
from us; otherwise, we'll kill you. So what
did the king say to you?' 26 you should say to
them, 'I was begging the king not to send me
back to the house of Jonathan to die there.'"
27 Then all the officials approached Jeremiah to question him. And he responded
exactly as the king had instructed him. So
they stopped interrogating him because
the conversation between the king and Jeremiah[g] hadn't been overheard. 28 Jeremiah

[g] Heb lacks *between the king and Jeremiah.*

remained in the prison quarters until Jerusalem was captured.

Fall of Jerusalem

39 In the ninth year and the tenth month of Judah's King Zedekiah, Babylon's King Nebuchadnezzar and his entire army came against Jerusalem and surrounded it. 2 In the eleventh year of Zedekiah, on the ninth day of the fourth month, they broke through the city walls. 3 Then all the commanding officers of the king of Babylon—Nergal-sharezer, Samgar-nebo,[h] Sarsechim the chief officer, Nergal-sharezer the field commander—entered it and took their places at the middle gate with the rest of the officials of the king of Babylon.

4 When Judah's King Zedekiah and his troops saw them, they tried to escape at night through the royal gardens and the gate between the two walls, toward the desert plain. 5 But the Babylonian[i] army chased them down and caught Zedekiah in the plains of Jericho. They arrested him and brought him before Babylon's King Nebuchadnezzar at Riblah in the land of Hamath. There the king put him on trial. 6 The king of Babylon slaughtered Zedekiah's children at Riblah before his very own eyes, and the king of Babylon slaughtered all the officials of Judah. 7 Then he gouged out Zedekiah's eyes, bound him in chains, and dragged him off to Babylon.

8 The Babylonians burned down the royal palace and the houses of the people, and they destroyed the Jerusalem walls. 9 Nebuzaradan the captain of the special guard rounded up the rest of the people who were left in the city, including those who had defected to the Babylonians, and deported them to Babylon. 10 But Nebuzaradan the captain of the special guard left some of the poorest people in the land of Judah. He gave them vineyards and fields at that time.

11 Babylon's King Nebuchadnezzar gave orders concerning Jeremiah to Nebuzaradan the captain of the special guard: 12 "Find Jeremiah and look after him; don't harm him but do whatever he asks from you." 13 So Nebuzaradan the captain of the special guard, Nebushazban the chief officer, Nergal-sharezer the field commander, and all the commanders of the king of Babylon 14 sent orders[j] to release Jeremiah from the prison quarters. They entrusted him to Gedaliah, Ahikam's son and Shaphan's grandson, so that Jeremiah could move about freely[k] among the people.

15 The LORD's word came to Jeremiah when he was still confined to the prison quarters: 16 Go and say to Ebed-melech the Cushite that the LORD of heavenly forces, the God of Israel, proclaims: I'm about to fulfill my words concerning this city, for harm and not for good. You will witness it for yourself on that day. 17 But on that day, declares the LORD:

I will rescue you;
  you won't be handed over
    to those you dread.
18 I will defend you;
  you won't die in battle.
You will escape with your life,
  because you have trusted in me,
    declares the LORD.

Jeremiah's release

40 Jeremiah received the LORD's word after Nebuzaradan the captain of the special guard had released him from Ramah. He had been bound in chains there along with all the other detainees from Jerusalem and Judah who were being sent off to Babylon. 2 The captain of the special guard located Jeremiah and said to him, "The LORD your God declared that a great disaster would overtake this place. 3 Now the LORD has made it happen. He has done just as he warned because all of you have sinned against the LORD and haven't obeyed him. That's why this has happened to you. 4 But I'm setting you free from the chains on your hands. If you would like, come with me to Babylon, and I'll take care of you. If you would rather not come with me, that's fine too. Now, the whole land lies

[h] Or *Nergal-sharezer the Simmagir* [i] Heb *Chaldean* and hereafter through Jeremiah [j] Heb lacks *orders*.
[k] Heb uncertain

before you; go wherever you want. [5]If you decide to remain here,[l] stay with Gedaliah, Ahikam's son and Shaphan's grandson—the Babylonian appointee in charge of the cities of Judah. Stay with him and the people he rules or go wherever you want." Then the captain of the special guard gave him ample provisions and let him go. [6]Jeremiah went to Gedaliah, Ahikam's son at Mizpah, and he stayed with him and the people who remained in the land.

Gedaliah's provisional government

[7]Some of the army officers and their troops were still hiding out in the countryside when they heard that the king of Babylon had appointed Gedaliah, Ahikam's son, over the region, responsible for the men, women, and children who were the poorest in the land and who hadn't been deported to Babylon. [8]So they went out to meet Gedaliah at Mizpah: Ishmael, Nethaniah's son; Johanan and Jonathan, Kareah's sons; Seraiah son of Tanhumeth; the sons of Ephai the Netophathite; Jezaniah son of the Maacathite; and their troops. [9]Gedaliah, Ahikam's son and Shaphan's grandson, firmly assured them all: "Don't be afraid of serving the Babylonians. Remain in the land, serve the king of Babylon, and all will go well for you. [10]But me? I will stay at Mizpah so I can speak on your behalf when the Babylonians arrive. But you? Settle down in the towns you have taken; harvest the grapes, the summer fruits and figs, and then store them in your containers."

[11]In the same way, all the Judeans living in Moab, Ammon, Edom, and in other countries heard that the king of Babylon had left a few people in the land and that he had put Gedaliah, Ahikam's son and Shaphan's grandson, in charge of them. [12]So they left the places where they had been scattered and returned to the land, to Gedaliah at Mizpah. There they gathered large amounts of grapes and summer fruits.

[13]Johanan, Kareah's son, and all the army officers in the countryside approached Gedaliah at Mizpah [14]and said to him, "Are you aware that King Baalis of Ammon has sent Ishmael, Nethaniah's son, to kill you?" But Gedaliah, Ahikam's son, wouldn't believe them. [15]Still Johanan, Kareah's son, met with Gedaliah secretly at Mizpah and said to him, "Let me go and kill Ishmael, Nethaniah's son; no one needs to knows about this matter. Otherwise, he'll kill you, and all the Judeans who have gathered around you will be scattered, and the few who are left will perish."

[16]But Gedaliah son of Ahikam told Johanan, Kareah's son, "Don't do such a thing, for what you are saying about Ishmael is wrong."

Mutiny and murder

41 In the seventh month,[m] Ishmael, Nethaniah's son and Elishama's grandson, who was from a royal family and who was one of the chief officers of the king, came with ten men to Gedaliah, Ahikam's son, at Mizpah. While they were eating a meal together, [2]Ishmael, Nethaniah's son, and the ten men got up and struck down Gedaliah, Ahikam's son and Shaphan's grandson, with the sword. They murdered him because he had been appointed over the region by the king of Babylon. [3]Ishmael also murdered all the Judeans who had rallied around Gedaliah at Mizpah as well as the Babylonian soldiers who were posted there.

[4]The day after Gedaliah was killed, before anyone knew of it, [5]eighty men with shaved beards, torn clothes, and gashed bodies arrived from Shechem, Shiloh, and Samaria. They were bringing grain offerings and incense to present at the LORD's temple. [6]Ishmael, Nethaniah's son, left Mizpah to meet them, weeping as he went. When he reached them, he said, "Come to Gedaliah, Ahikam's son!" [7]When they arrived in the middle of the town, Ishmael, Nethaniah's son, and the men with him slaughtered them and threw their bodies[n] into a cistern.

[8]But there were ten men among them who begged Ishmael, "Don't kill us; we have wheat, barley, oil, and honey hidden in a field." So he stopped and didn't kill them along with the rest.

[l]Heb uncertain [m]September–October, Tishrei [n]Heb lacks *and threw their bodies;* cf 41:9.

(9 Now the cistern that Ishmael used to
discard the bodies of the men he had killed
because of their association with Gedaliah°
was the one that King Asa had made to defend against Israel's King Baasha. Ishmael,
Nethaniah's son, filled it with the dead.)
10 Ishmael captured the rest of the people
who were at Mizpah, including the daughters of the king and all those assigned to
Gedaliah, Ahikam's son, at Mizpah by Nebuzaradan the captain of the special guard.
Then Ishmael, Nethaniah's son, set out to
cross over to the Ammonites with the hostages.
11 Johanan, Kareah's son, and all the army
officers at his side heard of the terrible acts
committed by Ishmael, Nethaniah's son.
12 So they mustered all their forces and went
to fight him. They found Ishmael, Nethaniah's son, at the great pool in Gibeon.
13 When all those taken by Ishmael at Mizpah saw Johanan, Kareah's son, and all his
army officers with him, they were delighted.
14 They rallied around Johanan, Kareah's son,
and returned home with him. 15 But Ishmael, Nethaniah's son, and eight of his
men eluded Johanan and went to the Ammonites.
16 Then Johanan, Kareah's son, and all the
army officers with him took the small group
they had rescued in Gibeon, including the
soldiers, women, children, and commanding
officers that Ishmael, Nethaniah's son, had
captured at Mizpah after killing Gedaliah,
Ahikam's son. 17 They set out for Egypt, stopping on the way at Geruth Chimham near
Bethlehem, 18 because they were afraid of
what the Babylonians would do when they
found out that Ishmael, Nethaniah's son,
had killed Gedaliah, Ahikam's son, whom
the king of Babylon had appointed over the
region.

Don't go to Egypt!

42 Then all the army officers, including
Johanan, Kareah's son, and Jezaniah, Hoshaiah's son, and the rest of the
people, from the least to the greatest, approached 2 Jeremiah the prophet and said
to him, "We have something to ask you:
Please pray to the LORD your God for us,
this small group, for as you can see we were
once many but now are very few. 3 May the
LORD your God show us where we should
go and what we should do."
4 The prophet Jeremiah replied, "Yes,
I'll pray to the LORD your God as you have
asked. And I'll tell you whatever the LORD
says; I won't hide anything from you."
5 Then they said to Jeremiah, "May the
LORD be a true and faithful witness against
us if we fail to do everything that the LORD
your God tells us through you. 6 Whether
we like it or not, we will obey all that the
LORD our God says. We will obey the LORD
our God, to whom we're sending you, so it
may go well for us."
7 Ten days later Jeremiah received the
LORD's word. 8 So he called Johanan, Kareah's son, and all the army officers with
him and the rest of the people, from the
least to the greatest, 9 and he said to them:
You have sent me to present your plea to
the LORD, and this is what the LORD, the
God of Israel, says: 10 If you live in this land,
I will build you up and not pull you down. I
will plant you and not dig you up because
I grieve over the disaster I have brought
upon you. 11 You don't have to be afraid of
the king of Babylon, whom you now fear.
You don't have to be afraid of him anymore,
declares the LORD, for I will be with you to
save you and rescue you from his hand. 12 I
will be merciful to you, and he will be merciful and return you to your land.
13 But if you say, "We won't live in this
land," you will disobey the LORD your God.
14 And if you insist, "No, we're going to
live in Egypt, where there's no war, battle
alarms, or hunger, and there we will stay,"
15 then listen to the LORD's word, you remaining Judeans. The LORD of heavenly
forces, the God of Israel, proclaims: If you
are determined to go to Egypt and you then
go and live there, 16 then the war you fear
will seize you in the land of Egypt; and the
famine you dread will hunt you down in
Egypt, and there you will die. 17 Every one

°Or *by the hand of Gedaliah*

of you who is determined to go and live in Egypt will die by the sword, famine, and disease. No one will escape the disaster that I will bring upon them there.

18 The LORD of heavenly forces, the God of Israel, proclaims: Just as my fierce anger was poured out on the people of Jerusalem, so it will be poured out on you if you go to Egypt. You will become an object of cursing, scorn, shock, and disgrace. And you will never see this place again. 19 You who survive from Judah, the LORD has told you: Don't go to Egypt. Know without a doubt that I have warned you this day. 20 You are putting your lives at risk[p] by sending me to the LORD your God, saying, "Pray for us to the LORD our God; tell us everything the LORD our God says, and we'll do it." 21 Today I have told you, but you still haven't obeyed all that the LORD your God has sent me to tell you. 22 So know without a doubt that you will die by war, famine, and disease in the place you yearn to go and live.

Off to Egypt with Jeremiah and Baruch

43 When Jeremiah finished telling the people all the words of the LORD their God—he didn't omit anything the LORD sent him to convey—2 Azariah, Hoshaiah's son, and Johanan, Kareah's son, and all the arrogant men said to Jeremiah, "You're lying to us! The LORD our God didn't send you to tell us not to go to Egypt to live. 3 It's Baruch, Neriah's son, who put you up to it so that we end up in the hands of the Babylonians, who will either kill us or deport us to Babylon."

4 So Johanan, Kareah's son, and all the army officers and the rest of the people disobeyed the LORD's command to stay in the land of Judah. 5 Johanan, Kareah's son, and all the army officers took the remaining Judeans who had returned to the land of Judah after being scattered among the nations—6 men, women, children, the king's daughters, everyone Nebuzaradan the captain of the special guard had left with Gedaliah, Ahikam's son and Shaphan's grandson, including Jeremiah the prophet and Baruch, Neriah's son. 7 They went to the land of Egypt, as far as Tahpanhes, for they wouldn't obey the LORD.

8 The LORD's word came to Jeremiah in Tahpanhes: 9 Take some large stones and set them in the clay pavement[q] in front of Pharaoh's palace in Tahpanhes while the people of Judah are watching. 10 After that, say to the people: The LORD of heavenly forces, the God of Israel, proclaims: I'm sending for my servant King Nebuchadnezzar of Babylon, who[r] will set his throne over these stones and will spread his canopy over them. 11 He will come and ravage the land of Egypt:

those marked for disaster, to disaster,
and those marked for exile, to exile,
and those marked for war, to war.

12 He will set on fire[s] the temples of the Egyptian gods. He will burn them down and carry off their gods. He will wrap the land of Egypt around himself, just as a shepherd wraps[t] his garment around himself, and he will move on unharmed.[u] 13 He will shatter the sacred pillars in the temple of the sun in Egypt and burn down the temples of the Egyptian gods.

Jeremiah's final words to Judeans in Egypt

44 Jeremiah received the LORD's word for the Judeans living in the land of Egypt, those living in Migdol, Tahpanhes, and Memphis and in the land of Pathros. 2 The LORD of heavenly forces, the God of Israel, proclaims: You have seen the disaster I brought on Jerusalem and the towns of Judah. They are now a wasteland with no one left 3 because of their evil ways. They have angered me by making offerings and worshipping other gods that neither they nor you nor your ancestors knew. 4 Yet time and again I sent you all my servants the prophets, saying, "Don't do these detestable things that I hate." 5 But they wouldn't listen or pay attention or turn from their evil ways. They continued making offerings to other gods. 6 So my fierce anger poured out and blazed against the towns of Judah and the

[p]Or *to do evil* [q]Heb uncertain [r]LXX; MT *I* [s]LXX, Syr; MT *I will set on fire* [t]Or *picks clean* [u]Heb uncertain

streets of Jerusalem. And they were reduced
to an utter wasteland, as they are today.
7 Now the LORD of heavenly forces, the
God of Israel, proclaims: Why are you committing this huge mistake that will cost you
your lives? Every man, woman, child, and
infant will be eliminated from the midst of
Judah, and no one will be left. 8 Why do you
anger me by what you do: by burning incense
to other gods in the land of Egypt where you
have come to live? You will be eliminated and
become an object of cursing and disgrace
among all the nations of the earth. 9 Have you
forgotten the sins of your ancestors and the
sins of the kings of Judah and their wives?[v]
Have you forgotten the sins that you and
your wives committed in the land of Judah
and in the streets of Jerusalem? 10 To this day
you[w] haven't shown any sorrow for what you
have done. And you haven't revered me or
followed my Instruction and my laws that I
set before you and your ancestors.
11 Therefore, the LORD of heavenly forces,
the God of Israel, proclaims: I'm determined
to bring disaster on you, to eliminate all of
Judah. 12 I will take the few remaining Judeans who were determined to go to the
land of Egypt to live. They will all perish
there. They will fall by the sword and perish
due to famine. The least to the greatest will
die by the sword and by famine. They will become an object of cursing, scorn, contempt,
and disgrace. 13 I will punish those who live
in the land of Egypt, just as I punished Jerusalem with war, famine, and disease. 14 From
the few remaining in Judah, no fugitive or
survivor who came to live here in the land
of Egypt will be able to return to the land of
Judah. Even though they want to return and
live there, they won't be able to return, except for some fugitives.
15 Then all the men who knew that their
wives had made offerings to other gods,
along with the great crowd of women who
were present, as well as the people living in
Pathros in the land of Egypt, all answered
Jeremiah: 16 "We're not going to listen to
a word you have said to us in the LORD's
name! 17 No, we're going to do exactly what
we want: We're going to burn incense to the
queen of heaven and pour out drink offerings to her, as we and our ancestors, our
kings and our officials, have done in the
towns of Judah and in the streets of Jerusalem. Then we had plenty to eat and we were
thriving; we didn't have any troubles. 18 But
ever since we stopped burning incense to
the queen of heaven and pouring drink offerings to her, we have been destroyed by
the sword and by famine."
19 And the women added,[x] "Do you
think that we burn incense to the queen of
heaven and pour drink offerings to her
without our husbands' support when we
make cakes in her image and pour drink offerings to her?"
20 Jeremiah said to all the people, men
and women alike, in fact everyone who had
spoken this way: 21 "Do you really think the
LORD was unaware of what you were up to
in the towns of Judah and the streets of Jerusalem? Don't you think the LORD knew
that you and your ancestors were making
offerings to other gods[y]—along with your
kings and officials, and the people of the
land? 22 It got so bad that the LORD could no
longer bear your evil and shameless acts; it
was at that point that your land was reduced
to an utter wasteland and a curse, as it is
today. 23 The current dire situation occurred
because you made offerings to other gods[z]
and sinned against the LORD—because
you wouldn't obey the LORD or follow the
LORD's instruction, laws, or warnings."
24 Then Jeremiah said to all the people,
including the women: Listen to the LORD's
word, all you Judeans in the land of Egypt.
25 The LORD of heavenly forces, the God
of Israel, proclaims: You and your wives
have done exactly what you said you would
do. You said, "We will definitely fulfill our
promise to burn incense to the queen of
heaven and pour out drink offerings to
her." Go ahead and keep your promises!
26 But listen to the LORD's word, all you Judeans who live in the land of Egypt. I swear
by my great name, says the LORD, that no
one from Judah living in Egypt will utter

[v] Heb *his wives* [w] Or *they* [x] Syr; MT lacks *and the women added.* [y] Heb lacks *to other gods.* [z] Heb lacks *to other gods.*

my name again, even in the solemn pledge: "As surely as the LORD God lives." 27 I'm watching over them for harm and not for good. Everyone from Judah who is living in the land of Egypt will die by the sword and by famine, until all are gone. 28 Those who actually survive war and return from Egypt to the land of Judah will be very few. Then the few remaining Judeans living in Egypt will know for certain whose word is true—mine or theirs! 29 And this will be a sign for you, declares the LORD: I will punish you here so that you know my threats against you will surely be fulfilled. 30 The LORD proclaims: I will hand Pharaoh Hophra, Egypt's king, over to his enemies who seek to kill him, just as I delivered Judah's King Zedekiah over to his enemy King Nebuchadnezzar of Babylon, who sought to kill him.

A final word for Baruch

45 In the fourth year of Judah's King Jehoiakim, Josiah's son, Baruch was writing in a scroll the words that Jeremiah was dictating to him. Jeremiah the prophet told Baruch, Neriah's son: 2 This is what the LORD the God of Israel proclaims about you, Baruch: 3 You have said, "I can't take it anymore! The LORD has added sorrow to my pain. I'm worn out from groaning and can find no rest." 4 This is what you should say to him: "The LORD proclaims: I'm breaking down everything I have built up. I'm digging up that which I have planted—the entire land. 5 You seek great things for yourself, but don't bother. I'm bringing disaster on all humanity, declares the LORD, but wherever you go I will let you escape with your life."

ORACLES CONCERNING THE NATIONS

46 This is what the LORD told the prophet Jeremiah concerning the nations.

Prophecy against Egypt

2 About Egypt! A message for the army of Pharaoh Neco, Egypt's king, which was defeated by Babylon's Nebuchadnezzar at Carchemish near the Euphrates River in the fourth year of Judah's King Jehoiakim, Josiah's son:

3 Grab your shields
and prepare for war!
4 Saddle the horses;
mount the stallions!
Take your positions
with helmets on!
Polish your spears;
put on your armor!
5 Why do I see them terrified,
retreating in haste?
Their soldiers are crushed,
running for cover,
and they don't turn back.
Panic lurks at every turn,
declares the LORD.
6 The swift can't flee;
the mighty can't escape.
Up north by the Euphrates River,
they stagger and fall.

7 Who is this that rises like the Nile,
whose banks overflow?[a]
8 It's Egypt that rises like the Nile,
whose banks overflow,[b]
who declares, "I will arise
and cover the earth
and destroy cities and inhabitants."
9 Charge, you horses;
advance, you chariots!
Attack, you soldiers
with your shield in hand,
you people of Cush and Put[c]
with your bow drawn,
you archers from Lud.

10 But that day belongs to the
LORD God of heavenly forces;
it's a day of reckoning,
settling scores with enemies.
The sword will devour
until it has had its fill of blood.
The LORD God of heavenly forces
is preparing a sacrifice in the north
by the Euphrates River.
11 Go up to Gilead and seek balm,
virgin Daughter Egypt.

[a] Or *like rivers whose waters roar* [b] Or *like rivers whose waters roar* [c] Traditionally *Ethiopia and Libya*

You search out remedies in vain,
for your disease is incurable.
12 Nations hear of your shame;
the earth is filled with your sobs.
Soldier stumbles over soldier;
together they go down.
13 This is the word that the LORD spoke
to the prophet Jeremiah about the military
offensive of Babylon's King Nebuchadnezzar against the land of Egypt:
14 Tell Egypt, warn Migdol,
alert Memphis and Tahpanhes!
Say: "Brace yourselves for what's coming.
War is breaking out from every side!"
15 Why have your mighty fallen?
Why haven't they stood their ground?
Because the LORD
has struck them down.
16 He's tripped them up;
they fall over each other and say,
"Let's get out of here
and go home to our people,
where we were born,
far away from the oppressor's sword."[d]
17 There they call Pharaoh, Egypt's king,
Loudmouth—Nothing But Hot Air!
18 As I live, declares the king,
whose name is
the LORD of heavenly forces,
one is coming
just as surely as Tabor is
in the mountains
and Carmel is by the sea.[e]
19 Get what you need for deportation,
you inhabitants of Egypt.[f]
Memphis will be reduced
to a wasteland,
a ruin with no one left.
20 Egypt is a beautiful, yes, beautiful heifer,
but a horsefly from the north
is coming to bite her.[g]
21 Even her mercenaries
are like well-fed calves;
they too will retreat and run for cover;
they won't survive.
The day of disaster
has come to haunt them,
the time of their punishment.
22 Like the sound of a snake hissing
as it slithers away
is Egypt[h] as armies approach in force;
they come against her with axes,
like woodcutters.
23 They destroy her dense forest,
though it is vast,
because they outnumber locusts
and can't be counted,
declares the LORD.
24 Daughter Egypt will be humiliated,
handed over to people from the north.
25 This is what the LORD of heavenly forces,
the God of Israel, proclaims: I'm going to punish Amon of Thebes, Egypt and its gods and
kings, as well as Pharaoh and all who rely
on him. 26 I will hand them over to those
who seek to kill them, namely Babylon's
King Nebuchadnezzar and his servants. But
afterward Egypt will dwell like it did a long
time ago, declares the LORD.
27 But don't be afraid, my servant Judah;
don't lose heart, Israel.
I will deliver you from a faraway place
and your children
from the land of their exile.
My people Jacob will again
be safe and sound,
with no one harassing them.
28 So don't be afraid, my servant Jacob,
declares the LORD.
I'm with you;
I will put an end to all the nations
where I have scattered you.
But I won't put an end to you.
I won't let you avoid punishment;
I will discipline you as you deserve.

Prophecy against Philistia

47 The LORD's word to the prophet Jeremiah concerning the Philistines before Pharaoh conquered Gaza.
2 The LORD proclaims:
Waters are rising from the north
and turning into a raging flood.
They will engulf the land
and everything in it,
the towns and those living in them.
The people cry out;
all who live there scream.

[d] Heb uncertain [e] Heb uncertain [f] Or *inhabitant, Daughter Egypt* [g] Heb uncertain [h] Heb lacks *is Egypt*.

3 At the pounding
of the stallions' hooves,
at the deafening roar
of the chariots' wheels,
parents abandon children,
so paralyzed are they with fear.
4 Because the time is coming
for the Philistines' destruction,
for cutting off from Tyre and Sidon
anyone who might try to save Gaza,[i]
because the LORD will destroy
the Philistines,
the few left from the island of Caphtor.
5 Mourning[j] will come upon Gaza;
silence will cover Ashkelon,
the few left in their valley.
How long will you gash yourselves
in grief?[k]
6 You sword of the LORD,
how long until you are silent?
Return to your sheath;
rest and be still!
7 How can you be silent
when the LORD has directed you[l]
to attack Ashkelon and the coast line?

Prophecy against Moab

48 Concerning Moab:
The LORD of heavenly forces,
the God of Israel, proclaims:
How awful for Nebo;
it lies in ruins.
Kirathaim is captured and shamed;
the fortress is disgraced,
reduced to rubble.
2 No one sings Moab's praise any longer!
In Heshbon they are hatching
a plot against her:
"Come, let's bring down the nation!"
You too, madmen, will be silenced;
the sword will pursue you.
3 Listen to the cries for help
from Horonaim:
"Destruction and massive devastation!"
4 Moab is shattered;
its young cry for help.
5 On the way up to Luhith,
there is uncontrollable weeping.
On the way down to Horonaim,
they hear sobs of anguish.
6 Run for your lives!
Be like Aroer[m] in the desert.
7 Because you have relied
on your own strength and treasures,
you also will be captured.
Chemosh will go into exile,
together with his priests and officials.
8 The destroyer will sweep
through every town;
no town will escape.
The valleys will be ravaged;
the plateaus will be destroyed,
because the LORD has declared it so.
9 Give wings to Moab,
and it would fly away[n]
because its towns lie in ruins,
with no one left in them.

10 Cursed is the one who is halfhearted
in doing the LORD's work.
Cursed is the one who restrains
the sword from bloodshed.

11 From early on Moab has been at ease,
like wine[o] left to settle
on its sediment.
It hasn't been poured into jars;
nor has Moab been taken into exile.
Therefore, its taste is still pleasant,
and its aroma is the same.

12 But the time is coming, declares the
LORD, when I will send to him someone to
spill it—to pour out his wine and to smash
his jars. 13 And Moab will be put to shame
on account of Chemosh, just as the people
of Israel were put to shame on account of
Bethel, in which they trusted.[p]
14 How can you claim,
"We're soldiers; we're war heroes"?
15 Moab is doomed;
its towns will surrender;[q]
its elite forces will go down in defeat,
declares the king whose name
is the LORD of heavenly forces.
16 Moab's destruction is near;
its downfall approaches rapidly.

[i] Or *a helper* [j] Or *baldness* [k] Heb lacks *in grief.* [l] Or *it* [m] Heb uncertain [n] Heb uncertain [o] Heb lacks *like wine.*
[p] Or *And Moab will be ashamed of Chemosh just as the people of Israel were ashamed of Bethel, in which they trusted.*
[q] Heb uncertain

17 Grieve for this nation,
you neighbors of Moab,
all you who know his name.
Proclaim how its mighty scepter
and magnificent staff are shattered!

18 Come down from your lofty place
and sit in the dust,[r]
you inhabitants of Daughter Dibon;[s]
because Moab's destroyer
has arrived to level your fortresses.
19 Stand by the roads and watch,
you inhabitants of Aroer.
Ask the men who flee
and the women who run off,
"What's happened?"
20 Moab is shamed and shocked;
weep and wail!
Tell it by the Arnon River:
Moab's been destroyed!

21 Judgment has come
to the towns of the plateau—
to Holon, Jahzah, and Mephaath,
22 to Dibon, Nebo, and Beth-diblathaim,
23 to Kiriathaim, Beth-gamul,
and Beth-meon,
24 to Kerioth and Bozrah,
to all the towns of Moab, far and near.

25 Moab's horn is cut off;
its arm is broken,
declares the LORD.
26 Get Moab drunk,
because it has exalted itself
above the LORD.
Moab will collapse in its vomit
and become the butt of every joke.
27 Wasn't Israel the butt of your jokes?
Didn't you shake your head
as if they were thieves
caught in the act?
28 Leave your towns, head for the cliffs,
you people of Moab.
Hide like a dove
that nests in the mouth of a cave.

29 We have heard of Moab's pride:
arrogant, puffed up, exalted,
high and mighty, boastful!
30 I myself know about its arrogance,
declares the LORD,
the idle talk, the empty deeds.
31 But I'll still wail for Moab;
I'll cry out for all Moab;
I'll[t] sob for the people of Kir-heres.
32 I'll weep for you, vine of Sibmah,
more than I would for Jazer.
Though your branches
extended to the sea
and reached the coast of Jazer,
now the destroyer has come
to harvest your grapes
and summer fruits.
33 Joy and gladness have been taken
from the orchards and farms of Moab.
I have stopped making wine
in the presses.
No one shouts with joy
while treading the grapes.
Though there are shouts,
they are not shouts of joy![u]
34 Screams are heard from Heshbon
to Elealeh and Jahaz;
their cries resound from Zoar
to Horonaim and Eglath-shelishiyah.
Even the waters of Nimrim are dried up.
35 I'll put an end to Moab,
declares the LORD,
for making offerings on the shrines,
and worshipping their gods.

36 Therefore, my heart wails for Moab
like a mournful[v] flute
that plays the dirge;
my heart wails for the people
of Kir-heres,
like a mournful flute.
Their abundance is now gone.
37 Every head is shaved,
every beard is cut off,
every hand is slashed,
and everyone wears mourning clothes.
38 On every housetop of Moab
and in all its streets,
there's nothing but mourning.
I have shattered Moab
like a pottery vessel no one wants,
declares the LORD.

[r] Or *thirst* [s] Heb uncertain, or *residing Daughter Dibon* [t] Or *He* [u] Heb uncertain [v] Heb lacks *mournful*.

39 How it's shattered! Go wail!
How Moab turns away!
What shame!
Moab has become the butt of every joke,
horrific to all its neighbors.

40 The LORD proclaims:
Look! One who soars like an eagle
and spreads its wings over Moab.
41 The towns will be captured;
the strongholds will be seized.
On that day,
the heart of every soldier from Moab
will be like that of a woman
in the throes of labor.
42 Moab will be destroyed once and for all
because it has exalted itself
above the LORD.

43 Terror, traps, and trackers[w]
are upon you, people of Moab,
declares the LORD.
44 Those who flee from terror
will fall into a pit;
those who escape the pit
will be captured by the trap.
I will bring upon Moab
the year of its punishment,
declares the LORD.
45 In Heshbon tired refugees seek shelter.
But fire is raging in Heshbon,
flames from the house[x] of Sihon.
It has burned up part of Moab,
including the leader
of this rebellious nation.[y]
46 How terrible for you, Moab;
the people of Chemosh have perished.
Your sons have been carried off;
your daughters have been taken
captive.
47 But in the days to come
I'll bring back Moab from captivity,
declares the LORD.
Such is the judgment on Moab.

Prophecy against the Ammonites

49 Concerning the Ammonites,
the LORD proclaims:
Doesn't Israel have children?
Aren't there heirs to his land?
Why then has Milcom
taken over Gad?
Why have his people
settled in its towns?
2 Therefore, the time is coming,
declares the LORD,
when I will sound the battle alarm
against Rabbah,
the capital city of the Ammonites.
The city will be demolished,
and its neighboring villages
will be burned to the ground.
Then Israel will repossess
the land seized by its captors,
says the LORD.
3 Weep, you people of Heshbon;
Ai has been destroyed.
Wail, you daughters of Rabbah;
put on funeral clothing,
cry your eyes out,
run for shelter.[z]
Milcom will surely go into exile,
together with his priests and ministers.

4 Why do you brag about your strength?
Your strength is exhausted,[a]
you rebellious daughter.
You trust in your treasures,
never imagining who would attack you.
5 I'm the one who will terrify you
from every side,
declares the LORD of heavenly forces.
Every one of you
will be scattered about;
no one will gather those who fled.
6 Afterward, though, I will bring back
the Ammonites from captivity,
declares the LORD.

Prophecy against Edom

7 Concerning Edom,
the LORD of heavenly forces proclaims:
Is wisdom no longer in Teman?
Has good sense vanished
from the perceptive?
Are they no longer wise?
8 Turn, flee, and run for cover,
you inhabitants of Dedan.

[w]Or *terror, pit, and trap* [x]Heb manuscripts; MT *from among* [y]Heb uncertain [z]Heb uncertain; or *run back and forth in the sheepfolds* [a]Heb uncertain

I'm bringing disaster on Esau:
its day of reckoning.
9 If workers would come to you
to pick grapes,
they would at least leave
a few on the vine.
If thieves would come in the night,
they would take only what they needed.
10 But me? I will strip Esau bare.
I will expose his hiding places,
and he will find no place to take cover.
His offspring, family, and acquaintances
will perish,
and there will be no one left to say,[b]
11 "Leave me your orphans,
and I'll look after them;
trust your widows into my care."
12 The LORD proclaims: If the innocent
must drink the cup, why do you expect to
escape punishment? You won't! You will
drink it! 13 I myself swear, declares the
LORD, that Bozrah will become an object of
horror and scorn, a wasteland and a curse.
And all of its towns will lie in ruins forever.
14 I have heard a report from the LORD
that a messenger is sent
among the nations:
Join forces and come against her;
prepare for war!
15 I'm about to cut you down to size
before the nations;
you will be scorned by everyone.
16 The terror you have inflicted on others
has deceived you,
as has your own pride.
Though you live in a fortress
and occupy the high ground;
though you nest on high
like the eagles,
I will bring you down,
declares the LORD.
17 Then Edom will become a wasteland.
All who pass by will be shocked
by its injuries.
18 It will be like the destruction
of Sodom and Gomorrah
and their surrounding towns,
says the LORD.
No one will live there;
no human will dwell in it.
19 Like a lion coming up
from the jungle of the Jordan
to a well-watered meadow,[c]
so I will suddenly chase down Edom
and single out its choicest of rams.[d]
Who is like me?
Who can direct me?
What shepherd can withstand me?
20 Therefore, listen to the counsel
that the LORD has for Edom
and the plans he's devised
against the people of Teman:
The little ones of the flock
will be dragged off,
as their pasture watches
in utter disbelief.[e]
21 The earth quakes
as the Edomites go down;
their screams echo
as far as the Reed Sea.[f]
22 Look! One who mounts up
and soars like an eagle,
who swoops down and spreads
his wings over Bozrah.
On that day, the heart
of every soldier from Edom
will be like that of a woman
in the throes of labor.

Prophecy against Damascus

23 Concerning Damascus:
Hamath and Arpad lose heart
when they hear the bad news.
They are trembling with fear,
like the raging sea,
which can't become quiet.
24 Damascus staggers about;
she tries to flee,
but panic overwhelms her.
She's gripped by anguish and pain,
like a woman in labor.
25 Forsaken[g] is the renowned city,
city of my delight.
26 Yes, her young men will fall in the streets,
and her soldiers will be silent on that day,
declares the LORD of heavenly forces.

[b]LXX; MT *and there will (or he will) be no more* [c]Heb uncertain [d]Heb uncertain [e]Heb uncertain [f]Or *Red Sea*
[g]Vulg; MT *Not forsaken*

27 I will set fire to the walls of Damascus;
it will burn up the fortresses
of Ben-hadad.

Prophecy against Kedar and Hazor

28 Concerning Kedar and the kingdoms
of Hazor, which Babylon's King Nebuchadnezzar defeated, the LORD proclaims:
Get ready to attack Kedar;
destroy the people from the east!
29 Seize[h] their tents and their flocks,
their belongings and all their goods.
Take off with their camels
and shout as you go:
"Panic Lurks Everywhere!"
30 Run away; take cover,
you people of Hazor,
declares the LORD.
Babylon's King Nebuchadnezzar
has taken counsel and devised a plan
against you.
31 Get ready to attack a nation
that feels safe and secure,
declares the LORD,
one without barred gates
that lives by itself.
32 Their camels will become plunder;
their many cattle will be pillaged.
I will scatter to the winds those
who are clean-shaven,[i]
and I will bring disaster on them
from every side,
declares the LORD.
33 Hazor will become a den for wild dogs,
a wilderness forever.
No one will live there;
no human will dwell in it.

Prophecy against Elam

34 This is what the LORD told the prophet
Jeremiah concerning Elam at the beginning
of the rule of Judah's King Zedekiah. 35 The
LORD of heavenly forces proclaims:
I'm going to break the bow of Elam,
the backbone of its military might.
36 I will bring against Elam four winds
from the four corners of heaven,
and I will scatter them to the winds.
Those banished from Elam
will migrate to every nation.
37 I will terrify Elam before their enemies,
before those who seek to kill them.
I will bring disaster upon them,
my fierce anger,
declares the LORD.
I will send the sword to attack them
until I have destroyed them all.
38 I will establish my rule in Elam
and dispose of its king and officials,
declares the LORD.
39 But in the days to come
I will bring back the captives of Elam,
declares the LORD.

Prophecy against Babylon

50 This is what the LORD said concerning Babylon and the land of the
Babylonians through the prophet Jeremiah:
2 Tell the nations;
proclaim it far and wide!
Set up a flag;
proclaim it far and wide!
Hold nothing back;
just shout it:
"Babylon is captured;
Bel is shamed;
Marduk is panic-stricken.
Her images are shamed;
her idols are panic-stricken."
3 A nation from the north
has risen up against her.
It will decimate her land,
and no one will live in it.
Every living thing will flee.

4 In those days and at that time,
declares the LORD,
the people of Israel and Judah
will come out of Babylon[j] together;
with weeping they will leave
as they seek the LORD their God.
5 They will search for Zion,
turning their faces toward it.
They will come[k] and
unite with the LORD,
in an everlasting covenant
that will never be forgotten.

[h] Or *They will seize . . . they will take off* [i] Or *those who have temples that are shaved* [j] Heb lacks *of Babylon*.
[k] Heb uncertain

6 My people were lost sheep;
their shepherds led them astray;
they deserted them on the mountains,
where they wandered off among
the hills,
forgetting their resting place.
7 All who found them devoured them;
and their attackers said,
"It's not our fault,
because they have sinned against
the LORD,
the true pasture,[l]
the hope of their ancestors—
the LORD."
8 Now wander far from Babylon.
Get out of that country.
Like rams of the flock,
lead the way home.
9 I'm stirring up against Babylon
a coalition of mighty nations.
It will mobilize in the north,
and from there she will be captured.
Their arrows are like
those of an expert archer
who does not return empty-handed.
10 Babylon will be defeated;
its attackers will carry off
all that they want,
declares the LORD.

11 Sure, you gloat and rejoice,
you plunderers of my possession.
Sure, you dance around like a calf
and neigh like a stallion.
12 But Mother Babylon[m] will be humiliated;
the one who bore you will be disgraced.
She will become the least of the nations:
a wilderness, a desert, and parched land.
13 Because of the LORD's anger,
no one will live there;
she will be reduced to total ruin.
All who pass by Babylon will be shocked;
they will gasp at all her injuries.
14 Take up your positions around Babylon,
all you archers;
now shoot at her;
save none of your arrows,
because she's sinned
against the LORD.
15 Raise a victory shout
against her on every side!
She's surrendered;
her towers have collapsed;
her walls are destroyed.
This is the LORD's retribution;
now pay her back:
do to her what she's done to others!
16 Cut Babylon off from those who plant
and those who harvest the crops,
because of its ruthless sword.[n]
Now return, all of you, to your people;
flee to your homeland!

17 Israelites are scattered sheep,
driven away by lions.
First the king of Assyria devoured them,
and now Babylon's King Nebuchadnezzar
has ravaged them.[o]
18 Therefore, the LORD of heavenly
forces, the God of Israel, proclaims:
I'm going to punish the king of Babylon
and his land,
just as I punished the king of Assyria.
19 But I will restore Israel to their pasture;
they will graze on Carmel and Bashan;
they will eat their fill
in the highlands of Ephraim and Gilead.
20 In those days and at that time,
declares the LORD,
if one searches for the sin of Israel,
they will find nothing;
if one seeks out
the wrongdoing of Judah,
they will look in vain.
I will forgive those I have spared.

21 Attack the land of Merathaim;[p]
crush those living in Pekod.
Ruin and destroy them,
declares the LORD;
do all I have commanded you.
22 There's the sound of war in the land
and enormous devastation.
23 How the hammer of the whole earth
has been broken and shattered
into pieces!
How Babylon has become a wasteland
among the nations!

[l] Or *righteous dwelling place* [m] Or *your mother* [n] Heb uncertain [o] Or *gnawed their bones* [p] Or *Double rebellion*

24 You set a trap for others, Babylon,[q]
but you yourself were caught
in it unaware;
you have been found and captured
because you have defied the LORD.
25 The LORD has opened his arsenal
and brought out his brutal weapons.
The LORD God of heavenly forces
has a job to do
in the land of the Babylonians.
26 Come against her from every side;
throw open her granaries;
pile her up like stalks of grain;
totally destroy her;
leave nothing intact.
27 Destroy all her bulls;
prepare them for slaughter.
How terrible for them!
Their time has come,
the day of reckoning.
28 A voice of fugitives and refugees,
from the land of Babylon,
declaring in Zion
the retribution of the LORD our God
because of what has been done
to his temple.
29 Send the archers against Babylon,
all who draw the bow!
Surround her
and let no one escape.
Pay her back for her deeds;
do to her what she's done to others.
She has acted arrogantly
toward the LORD,
the holy one of Israel!

30 Therefore, her soldiers will fall
in the streets;
all her warriors will be silenced
on that day,
declares the LORD.
31 I'm against you, you arrogant one!
declares the LORD God
of heavenly forces.
Your day has come,
your time of reckoning.
32 The arrogant one will stumble and fall,
and no one will help her up.
I'll set your cities on fire,
and it will consume all that's around her.
33 The LORD of heavenly forces proclaims:
The people of Israel were oppressed,
together with the people of Judah.
Their captors held them
and refused to let them go.
34 Yet their redeemer is strong;
the LORD of heavenly forces is his name.
He will surely defend their cause
and give them rest in the land.
But he will unsettle
the people of Babylon.

35 A sword against Babylon and its people,
declares the LORD,
along with its officials and sages.
36 A sword against its diviners
so that they become fools.
A sword against its warriors
so that they are terrified.
37 A sword against its horses and chariots,
and the mercenaries[r] in its midst
so that they lose courage.[s]
A sword against its treasures
so that they are looted.
38 A sword[t] against the water supplies
so that they dry up.
It is truly the land of idols,
idols about which they have gone
utterly mad!
39 Therefore, Babylon
will become a ghost town,
a place for desert animals,
hyenas, and ravenous birds.[u]
No one will live there again;
no one will make it their home.
40 Just as God destroyed Sodom
and Gomorrah and their neighbors,
declares the LORD,
so no one will live in Babylon
or settle there again.

41 Look! An army is on the move
from the northern regions.
A powerful nation
and many kings are coming
from the ends of the earth.

[q]Or *I set a trap for you, Babylon, and you were* [r]Or *foreigners* [s]Or *become like women* [t]Or *drought* or *A drought*
[u]Heb uncertain

42 Equipped with bow and spear,
they are cruel
and show no mercy.
Their horsemen sound
like the roaring sea,
arrayed in battle formation against you,
Daughter Babylon.
43 The king of Babylon has heard
reports of them
and is panic-stricken;
distress overwhelms him,
pain like that of a woman in labor.

44 Like a lion coming up from
the jungle of the Jordan
to a well-watered meadow,[v]
so I will suddenly chase down Babylon
and single out its choicest of rams.
Who is like me?
Who can direct me?
What shepherd can withstand me?
45 Therefore, listen to the counsel
that the LORD has for Babylon
and the plans he's devised
against the land of Babylon:
The little ones of the flock
will be dragged off,
as their pasture watches
in utter disbelief.[w]
46 The earth quakes
at the sound of Babylon's capture;
its screams echo throughout the world.

51

The LORD proclaims:
I'm stirring up a violent wind
against Babylon
and those who live in Leb-qamai.[x]
2 I will send mercenaries[y] to Babylon
who will sift her and clear out her land.
They will surround her
on the day of disaster.
3 Let the archers draw their bows;
let them prepare their armor.
Show no mercy to her young men;
wipe out her entire company!
4 They will fall wounded
in the land of Babylon,
struck down in her streets.
5 God, the LORD of heavenly forces,
hasn't abandoned Israel and Judah,
even though they live
in a land filled with guilt
before the holy one of Israel.
6 Escape from Babylon;
each of you run for your lives!
Don't perish because of her guilt,
because this is the time
for the LORD's retribution,
a day of reckoning
for all that Babylon[z] has done.

7 Babylon was a gold cup
in the LORD's hand;
it made the whole earth drunk.
The nations drank her wine
and went mad.
8 But suddenly Babylon fell
and shattered into pieces.
Wail for her!
Bring medicine for her pain;
perhaps she will recover.

9 We tried to cure Babylon,
but she was beyond help.
Let's depart from her
and return to your own country,
each of you.
Her punishment reaches to heaven
and extends to the clouds.
10 The LORD has come to our defense,
so let's declare in Zion
what the LORD our God has done!

11 Sharpen your arrows;
prepare your shields.
The LORD is stirring up
the spirit of kings from Media.
He intends to destroy Babylon;
this is the LORD's retribution,
a day of reckoning for his temple.
12 Set up a flag on the walls of Babylon,
fortify the guards,
post watchmen,
prepare an ambush,
because the LORD has a plan
against the inhabitants of Babylon.

[v] Heb uncertain [w] Heb uncertain [x] Or *the inhabitants of Leb qamai*, a reference to Chaldea (Babylonia); or *those who rise up against me* [y] Or *foreigners* [z] Or *she or it*

He will accomplish it,
just as he said he would.
13 You live beside a great river,
and you are rich in treasures.
But your time has come;
your cruelty has caught up with you.[a]
14 The LORD of heavenly forces
has sworn by his own name:
I'm going to fill your cities[b]
with soldiers like a swarm of locusts;
they will celebrate their victory over you.

15 God made the earth by his might,
shaped the world by his wisdom,
and crafted the skies by his knowledge.
16 At the sound of God's voice,
the heavenly waters roar.
God raises the clouds
from the ends of the earth.
He makes lightning for the rain
and sends the wind from his treasuries.
17 Everyone is too foolish to understand;
every smith is shamed by his idols,
for their images are shams;
they aren't alive.
18 They are a delusion, a charade;
at the appointed time they will be ruined!
19 But the portion of Jacob
is utterly different,
for he has formed all things,
including his very own tribe;
the LORD of heavenly forces
is his name!

20 You are my hammer,
my weapon of war.
With you I will crush the nations.
With you I will destroy kingdoms.
21 With you I will crush horse and rider.
With you I will crush chariot and driver.
22 With you I will crush men and women.
With you I will crush old and young.
With you I will crush
young men and young women.
23 With you I will crush
shepherds and flocks.
With you I will crush farmers and oxen.
With you I will crush
governors and officials.
24 I will repay Babylon
and all its inhabitants
for the terrible things
they have done to Zion in your sight,
declares the LORD.
25 I'm against you,
you mountain of destruction,
declares the LORD,
you destroyer of the whole earth!
I will reach out against you;
I will topple you from your heights;
I will turn you into a rubbish heap.
26 They will never remove a cornerstone
or a foundation stone from you.
You will be a wasteland forever,
declares the LORD.

27 Set up a flag in the land;
sound the alarm among the nations!
Prepare them for war against her;
summon kingdoms against her—
Ararat, Minni, and Ashkenaz.
Appoint a commander against her;
call up the troops,
like swarms of locusts!
28 Prepare the nations for war against her,
the kings of Media,
its governors, all its officials,
and all the countries they rule.

29 The earth quakes and trembles
because the LORD's plans
against Babylon are fulfilled:
to reduce Babylon to a wasteland,
with no one left in it.
30 Babylon's warriors quit fighting;
they hide in their fortifications.
Their strength is worn out;
their courage is gone!
Babylon's houses are burned down,
and its gates are smashed.
31 Courier joins courier,
messenger joins messenger
to relate the news
to the king of Babylon
that his entire city has fallen.
32 The river crossings are blocked;
the marshes are on fire;
the soldiers are terrified.

[a]Heb uncertain [b]Heb lacks *cities*.

33 The LORD of heavenly forces, the God of Israel, proclaims:
Daughter Babylon is like a threshing floor
ready to be trampled down.
In a little while her harvest will come.

34 Babylon's King Nebuchadnezzar
has eaten us alive;
he's drained us of strength;
he's left us for dead.[c]
He's gobbled us up
like a great sea monster;
he's filled his belly with our treasures;
and he's spit us out.
35 May Babylon be violated
as our bodies were,
say the inhabitants of Zion.
May our blood be on the Babylonians,
say those from Jerusalem.
36 Therefore, the LORD proclaims:
I'm going to defend your cause;
I'll turn the tables on your attacker.
I'll dry up her sea;
I'll shut up her springs.
37 Babylon will become a heap of ruins,
a den of wild dogs, a wasteland
with no one left in it.

38 Like lions they will roar together;
they will growl like lions' cubs.
39 They are ready to devour,
so I'll prepare the feast
and mix the drinks!
But after their noisy drunkenness,
they will fall fast asleep.
They will sleep forever,
never to get up,
declares the LORD.
40 I'll lead them off
like lambs for slaughter,
like rams and goats.

41 How Sheshach[d] has been defeated,
the pride of the whole earth
taken captive!
How Babylon has become a wasteland
among the nations!
42 The sea has risen over Babylon;
its pounding waves overwhelm her.
43 Her towns are devastated;
her land is scorched and barren,
a place where no one lives
or dares to pass through.
44 I will punish Bel in Babylon;
I will force him to vomit
what he's consumed.
Then nations will no longer
stream to him,
and Babylon's walls will collapse!

45 Get out of Babylon, my people!
Run for your lives
from the LORD's fierce anger.
46 Don't be distracted or frightened
by the rumors you hear in the land.
Sometimes you hear one thing
and another time something else:
rumors of violence and uprisings.
47 The time is coming
when I will deal with Babylon's idols;
the whole land will be disgraced,
and her wounded will fall in her midst.
48 Then all creation will rejoice over Babylon,
because out of the north
destroying armies will come to attack her,
declares the LORD.
49 Babylon must fall
for the dead in Israel,
as the dead of all the earth
have fallen to Babylon.

50 You survivors of war,
leave now; don't delay!
Remember the LORD,
from a faraway land.
Keep Jerusalem alive in your hearts.

51 We're humiliated by their taunts;
we're disgraced that strangers
have violated the sacred places
of the LORD's temple.

52 The time is coming,
declares the LORD,
when I will deal with her idols,
and the wounded in her land will groan.
53 Even if Babylon scales the heavens
and strengthens its towering defenses,

[c] Or *He's made us an empty container.* [d] *Sheshach* is a name for Babylon.

the destroying armies will still come
against her, at my command,
declares the LORD.
54 Listen to the cries for help from Babylon,
signs of massive devastation in the land,
declares the LORD.
55 The LORD is destroying Babylon
and silencing her outcry,
whose roar is like the crushing waves,
a deafening crash.
56 He certainly comes against her;
the destroyer comes against Babylon.
Her warriors are captured;
their bows are broken.
The LORD is an exacting God
who repays in full.
57 I'll make her leaders and sages drunk,
her governors, officials,
and warriors as well.
They will sleep forever, never to get up,
declares the king,
whose name is
the LORD of heavenly forces.
58 The LORD of heavenly forces proclaims:
Babylon's massive walls will come down,
down to the ground;
and its high gates will be burned
to the ground.

People labor in vain;
nations toil for nothing but ashes!

59 This is what the prophet Jeremiah
instructed the staff officer[e] Seraiah, Neriah's son and Mahseiah's grandson, when
Seraiah went to Babylon with Judah's
King Zedekiah in the fourth year of his
rule. 60 Jeremiah wrote down in a single
scroll all the disasters that would happen
to Babylon—all these things concerning
Babylon. 61 Jeremiah said to Seraiah: When
you get to Babylon, see to it that you read
all these words. 62 Then say, "LORD, you
declared that this place will be destroyed
and nothing will remain in it—neither
human nor animal; that it will forever be a
wasteland!" 63 When you finish reading the
scroll, tie a stone to it and throw it into
the Euphrates River. 64 Then say, "In the
same way, Babylon will sink and never rise
again because of the disaster I'm bringing
against it."

Jeremiah's words end here.

Rule of Zedekiah and the fall of Jerusalem

52 Zedekiah was 21 years old when he
became king, and he ruled for eleven
years in Jerusalem. His mother's name was
Hamutal; she was a daughter of Jeremiah
from Libnah. 2 He did evil in the LORD's
eyes just as Jehoiachin had done. 3 It was
because the LORD was angry against Jerusalem and Judah that he thrust them out of
his presence. Zedekiah rebelled against the
king of Babylon.

4 In the ninth year, the tenth month,
and the tenth day of the month, Babylon's
King Nebuchadnezzar attacked Jerusalem
with all of his army. He camped beside the
city and built a siege wall around it. 5 The
city was under siege until the eleventh
year of King Zedekiah. 6 On the ninth day
of the fourth month, the famine in the city
reached a point that no food remained for
the people. 7 The enemy entered the city,
and all the soldiers fled by night along the
gate between the two walls by the royal
gardens. So the Babylonians surrounded
the city while the soldiers fled toward the
desert plain. 8 However, the Babylonian
army chased down Zedekiah and caught
him in the plains of Jericho. (His entire
army had fled from him.) 9 They arrested
the king and brought him before the king
of Babylon at Riblah in the land of Hamath. And he pronounced sentence on
him. 10 The king of Babylon slaughtered
Zedekiah's children before his very own
eyes, and he slaughtered all Judah's officers at Riblah. 11 Then he gouged out
Zedekiah's eyes and bound him in chains.
The king of Babylon dragged him off to
Babylon and put him in prison, where he
remained until he died.

12 In the tenth day of the fifth month,
which was the nineteenth year of Babylon's King Nebuchadnezzar, Nebuzaradan

[e] Or *officer of rest*, often translated as *quartermaster*

commander of the guard came to Jerusalem on behalf of his king. 13 He burned down the LORD's temple, the royal palace, all the houses of Jerusalem, and all the important buildings. 14 The entire Babylonian army and the commander of the guard destroyed the walls surrounding Jerusalem. 15 Nebuzaradan commander of the guard deported some of the poorest people, the rest of the people left in the city, a few skilled workers, and those who had joined the king of Babylon. 16 But Nebuzaradan commander of the guard left some of the poor to tend the vineyards and till the land.

17 The Babylonians broke apart the bronze columns, the stands, and the bronze Sea in the LORD's temple. They carried the bronze to Babylon. 18 They took the pots, the shovels, the wick trimmers, the sprinkling bowls, the incense dishes, and all the bronze equipment used for the temple services. 19 The commander of the guard took whatever gold or silver he could find as well: the small bowls, the fire pans, the sprinkling bowls, the pots, the lampstands, the basins, and the offering bowls. 20 There was too much bronze to be weighed: two columns, the bronze Sea and the twelve bronze bulls that held it up, and the stands, all of which Solomon had made for the LORD's temple. 21 Each column was about twenty-seven feet high and eighteen feet around. They were hollow, but the bronze was about three inches thick. 22 Each had a capital of bronze above it that towered seven and a half feet high, and each had an ornate design of bronze pomegranates around it. The second column was the same, also with pomegranates. 23 There were ninety-six pomegranates on the sides, a total of one hundred pomegranates around the ornate design.

24 The commander of the guard also took Seraiah the high priest, Zephaniah the deputy priest, and the three doorkeepers. 25 From the city, he took a eunuch who was appointed over the army and the seven royal advisors who remained in the city. He also took the scribe of the commander of the army in charge of military conscription and sixty military personnel[f] who were found in the city. 26 Nebuzaradan the commander of the guard took them and brought them to the king of Babylon at Riblah. 27 The king of Babylon struck them and put them to death at Riblah in the land of Hamath. And Judah went away from its land into exile.

28 This is the number of people whom Nebuchadnezzar deported: In the seventh year, 3,023 Judeans. 29 In the eighteenth year of Nebuchadnezzar, he took 832 people from Jerusalem. 30 In the twenty-third year of Nebuchadnezzar, he dispatched Nebuzaradan commander of the guard, who deported 745 Judeans. Altogether, 4,600 were taken captive.

31 Judah's King Jehoiachin had been in exile for thirty-seven years when Awil-merodach[g] became king in Babylon. He took note of Jehoiachin's plight and released him from prison on the twenty-fifth day of the twelfth month[h] of that very year. 32 Awil-merodach treated Jehoiachin kindly and gave him a throne higher than those of the other kings with him in Babylon. 33 So Jehoiachin discarded his prison clothes and ate his meals at the king's table for the rest of his life. 34 The Babylonian king provided him daily provisions for the rest of his life, right up until he died.

[f] Or *from the people of the land* [g] Or *Evil-merodach* [h] February–March, Adar

LAMENTATIONS[a]

Jerusalem's suffering

א 1 Oh, no!
She sits alone,
the city that was once full of people.
Once great among nations,
she has become like a widow.
Once a queen over provinces,
she has become a slave.

ב 2 She weeps bitterly in the night,
her tears on her cheek.
None of her lovers comfort her.
All her friends lied to her;
they have become her enemies.

ג 3 Judah was exiled after suffering
and hard service.
She lives among the nations;
she finds no rest.
All who were chasing her caught her—
right in the middle of her distress.

ד 4 Zion's roads are in mourning;
no one comes to the festivals.
All her gates are deserted.
Her priests are groaning,
her young women grieving. She is bitter.

ה 5 Her adversaries have become rulers;
her enemies relax.
Certainly the LORD caused her grief
because of her many wrong acts.
Her children have gone away,
captive before the enemy.

ו 6 Daughter Zion lost all her glory.
Her officials are like deer
that can't find pasture.
They have gone away, frail,
before the hunter.

ז 7 While suffering and homeless,
Jerusalem remembers all her treasures
from days long past.
When her people fell by the enemy's
hand, there was no one to help her.
Enemies saw her, laughed at her defeat.

ח 8 Jerusalem has sinned greatly;
therefore, she's become a joke.[b]
All who honored her now detest her,
for they've seen her naked.
Even she groans and turns away.

ט 9 Her uncleanness shows on her clothing;
she didn't consider
what would happen to her.
She's gone down shockingly;
she has no comforter.
"LORD, look at my suffering—
the enemy has definitely triumphed!"

י 10 The enemy grabbed all her treasures.
She watched nations
enter her sanctuary—
nations that you, God,[c] commanded:
They must not enter your assembly.

כ 11 All her people are groaning, seeking bread.
They give up their most precious things
for food to survive.
"LORD, look and take notice: I am most
certainly despised."

ל 12 Is this nothing to all you who pass by?[d]
Look around: Is there any suffering like
the suffering inflicted on me,
the grief that the LORD caused
on the day of his fierce anger?

מ 13 From above he sent fire into my bones;
he trampled them.
He spread a net for my feet;
he forced me backward.
He left me devastated, constantly sick.

נ 14 My steps[e] are being watched;[f]
by his hand they are tripped up.

[a]Four of the five chaps of Lamentations are alphabetically structured (acrostic) poems. Each verse in chaps 1, 2, and 4 begins with a consecutive letter of the Hebrew alphabet. Chap 3 is a triple acrostic: three verses in a row use the same letter before moving to the next letter. The acrostic form is not used in chap 5, though it does contain twenty-two verses, the same number as chaps 1, 2, and 4. [b]Or *she's become unclean*. [c]Heb lacks *God*. [d]Heb uncertain [e]Correction; or *my wrong acts* [f]Or *a yoke is bound to my wrong acts*; Heb uncertain

His yoke is on my neck;
he makes my strength fail.
My Lord has handed me over
to people I can't resist.

ס 15 My Lord has despised my mighty warriors.
He called a feast for me—
in order to crush my young men!
My Lord has stomped on the winepress
of the young woman Daughter Judah.

ע 16 Because of all these things I'm crying.
My eyes, my own eyes pour water
because a comforter who might
encourage me is nowhere near.
My children are destroyed because the
enemy was so strong.

פ 17 Zion spreads out her hands;
she has no comforter.
The LORD commanded Jacob's enemies
to surround him.
Jerusalem is just a piece of garbage
to them.

צ 18 The LORD is right,
because I disobeyed his word.
Listen, all you people;
look at my suffering.
My young women and young men
have gone away as prisoners.

ק 19 I called to my lovers, but they deceived me.
My priests and my elders
have perished in the city;
they were looking for food to survive.

ר 20 Pay attention, LORD, for I am in trouble.
My stomach is churning;
my heart is pounding inside me
because I am so bitter.
In the streets the sword kills;
in the house it is like death.

ש 21 People heard that I was groaning,
that I had no comforter.
All my enemies heard about my distress;
they were thrilled
that you had done this.
Bring the day you have announced
so they become like me!

ת 22 Let all their evil come before you.
Then injure them like you've injured me
because of all my wrong acts;
my groans are many,
my heart is sick.

God's anger toward Jerusalem

2 Oh, no!
In anger, my Lord put Daughter Zion
א under a cloud;[g]
he threw Israel's glory from heaven
down to earth.
On that day of wrath,
he didn't consider his own footstool.

ב 2 Showing no compassion, my Lord
devoured each of Jacob's meadows;
in his wrath he tore down the walled
cities of Daughter Judah.
The kingdom and its officials,
he forced to the ground, shamed.

ג 3 In his burning rage,
he cut off each of Israel's horns;
right in front of the enemy,
he withdrew his strong hand;
he burned against Jacob like a flaming
fire that ate up everything nearby.

ד 4 He bent his bow as an enemy would;
his strong hand was poised
like an adversary.
He killed every precious thing in sight;
he poured out his wrath
like fire on Daughter Zion's tent.

ה 5 My Lord has become like an enemy.
He devoured Israel;
he devoured all her palaces; he made
ruins of her city walls.
In Daughter Judah
he multiplied mourning
along with more mourning!

ו 6 He wrecked his own booth like a garden;
he destroyed his place for festivals.

[g] Heb uncertain

The LORD made Zion forget
both festival and sabbath;
in his fierce rage, he scorned
both monarch and priest.

ז 7 My Lord rejected his altar,
he abandoned his sanctuary;
he handed Zion's palace walls
over to enemies.
They shouted in the LORD's own house
as if it were a festival day.

ח 8 The LORD planned to destroy
Daughter Zion's wall.
He stretched out a measuring line,
didn't stop himself from devouring.
He made barricades and walls wither—
together they wasted away.

ט 9 Zion's gates sank into the ground;
he broke and shattered her bars;
her king and her officials are now
among the nations.
There is no Instruction![h]
Even her prophets couldn't find
a vision from the LORD.

י 10 Daughter Zion's elders
sit on the ground and mourn.
They throw dust on their heads;
they put on mourning clothes.
Jerusalem's young women bow
their heads all the way to the ground.

כ 11 My eyes are worn out from weeping;
my stomach is churning.
My insides are poured on the ground
because the daughter of my people
is shattered,
because children and babies
are fainting in the city streets.

ל 12 They say to their mothers,
"Where are grain and wine?"
while fainting like the wounded
in the city streets,
while their lives are draining away
at their own mothers' breasts.

מ 13 What can I testify about you,
Daughter Jerusalem?[i]
To what could I compare you?
With what could I equate you?
How can I comfort you,
young woman Daughter Zion?
Your hurt is as vast as the sea.
Who can heal you?

נ 14 Your prophets gave you worthless
and empty visions.
They didn't reveal your sin
so as to prevent your captivity.
Instead, they showed you
worthless and incorrect prophecies.

ס 15 All who pass by on the road
clap their hands about you;
they whistle, shaking their heads
at Daughter Jerusalem:
"Could this be the city called Perfect
Beauty, the Joy of All the Earth?"

פ 16 All your enemies open wide their mouths
against you;
they whistle, grinding their teeth.
They say, "We have devoured!
This is definitely the day
we've been waiting for.
We've seen it come to pass."

ע 17 The LORD did what he had planned.
He accomplished the word
that he had commanded long ago.
He ripped down,
showing no compassion.
He made the enemy rejoice over you;
he raised up your adversaries' horn.

צ 18 Cry out to my Lord from the heart,[j]
you wall of Daughter Zion;
make your[k] tears run down like a flood
all day and night.
Don't relax at all;
don't rest your eyes a moment.

ק 19 Get up and cry out at nighttime,
at the start of the night shift;

[h]Heb *Torah* [i]Or *How can I warn you?* or *To what could I liken you?*; Heb uncertain [j]Correction; or *their heart cried out to my Lord* [k]Heb lacks *your*.

pour out your heart
before my Lord like water.
Lift your hands up to him
for the life of your children—
the ones who are fainting from hunger
on every street corner.

ר 20 LORD, look and see to whom
you have done this!
Should women eat their own offspring,
their own beautiful babies?
Should priest and prophet be killed
in my Lord's own sanctuary?

ש 21 Young and old alike
lie on the ground in the streets;
my young women and young men
fall dead by the sword.
On the day of your anger, you killed;
you slaughtered,
showing no compassion.

ת 22 You invited—as if to a festival!—
terrors[l] from every side.
On the day of the LORD's anger,
no one escaped, not one survived.
The children that I nurtured,
that I raised myself,
my enemy finished them off.

An individual's complaint

3 I am someone[m] who saw the suffering
caused by God's[n] angry rod.
א 2 He drove me away, forced me to walk
in darkness, not light.
3 He turned his hand even against me,
over and over again, all day long.

ב 4 He wore out my flesh and my skin;
he broke my bones.
5 He besieged me, surrounding me
with bitterness and weariness.
6 He made me live in dark places
like those who've been dead
a long time.

ג 7 He walled me in so I couldn't escape;
he made my chains heavy.
8 Even though I call out and cry for help,
he silences my prayer.
9 He walled in my paths with stonework;
he made my routes crooked.

ד 10 He is a bear lurking for me,
a lion in hiding.
11 He took me from my path[o]
and tore me apart;
he made me desolate.
12 He drew back his bow, made me
a shooting target for arrows.

ה 13 He shot the arrows of his quiver
into my inside parts.
14 I have become a joke to all my people,
the object of their song of ridicule
all day long.
15 He saturated me with grief,
made me choke on bitterness.

ו 16 He crushed my teeth into the gravel;
he pressed me down into the ashes.
17 I've[p] rejected peace;
I've forgotten what is good.
18 I thought: My future is gone,
as well as my hope from the LORD.

ז 19 The memory of my suffering and
homelessness is bitterness and poison.
20 I[q] can't help but remember
and am depressed.
21 I call all this to mind—
therefore, I will wait.

ח 22 Certainly the faithful love
of the LORD hasn't ended;[r]
certainly God's compassion
isn't through!
23 They are renewed every morning.
Great is your faithfulness.
24 I think:[s] The LORD is my portion!
Therefore, I'll wait for him.

ט 25 The LORD is good to those who hope in
him, to the person[t] who seeks him.
26 It's good to wait in silence
for the LORD's deliverance.

[l]Correction; or *my attackers* [m]Or *the man*; also in 3:27, 35, 39 [n]Or *his* [o]Heb uncertain [p]Or *my spirit*; also in 3:20, 24, 25, 51, 58 [q]Or *My spirit can't help but remember and is depressed* [r]Tg, Syr, and other ancient sources; MT *we aren't finished.* [s]Or *My spirit thinks* [t]Or *spirit*

27 It's good for a man to carry a yoke
in his youth.
י 28 He should sit alone and be silent
when God lays it on him.
29 He should put his mouth in the dirt—
perhaps there is hope.
30 He should offer his cheek for a blow;
he should be filled with shame.

כ 31 My Lord definitely[u]
won't reject forever.
32 Although he has caused grief,
he will show compassion in measure
with his covenant loyalty.
33 He definitely doesn't enjoy affliction,[v]
making humans suffer.

ל 34 Now crushing underfoot
all the earth's prisoners,
35 denying someone justice
before the Most High,
36 subverting a person's lawsuit—
doesn't my Lord see all this?

מ 37 Who ever spoke and it happened if my
Lord hadn't commanded the same?
38 From the mouth of the Most High
evil things don't come,
but rather good!
39 Why then
does any living person complain;
why should anyone complain
about their sins?

נ 40 We must search and examine our ways;
we must return to the LORD.
41 We should lift up our hearts and hands
to God in heaven.
42 We are the ones who did wrong;
we rebelled.
But you, God, have not forgiven.

ס 43 You wrapped yourself up in wrath
and hunted us;
you killed, showing no compassion.
44 You wrapped yourself up in a cloud;
prayers can't make it through!
45 You made us trash and garbage
in front of all other people.

פ 46 All our enemies have opened
their mouths against us.
47 Terror and trap have come upon us,
catastrophe and collapse!
48 Streams of water pour from my eyes
because of the destruction of the
daughter of my people.

ע 49 My eyes flow and don't stop.
There is no relief
50 until the LORD looks down
from the heavens and notices.
51 My eyes hurt me[w] because of what's
happened to my city's daughters.

צ 52 My enemies hunted me down like a bird,
relentlessly, for no reason.
53 They caught me alive in a pit
and threw stones at me;
54 water flowed over my head.
I thought: I'm finished.

ק 55 I call on your name, LORD,
from the depths of the pit.
56 Hear my voice. Don't close your ear[x]
to my need for relief,
to my cry for help.[y]
57 Come near to me on the day I call to you.
Say to me, "Don't be afraid."

ר 58 My Lord! Plead my desperate case;[z]
redeem my life.
59 LORD, look at my mistreatment;
judge my cause.
60 Look at all of my enemies' vengeance,
all of their scheming against me.

ש 61 Hear their jeering, LORD,
all of their scheming against me,
62 the speech of those
who rise up against me,
their incessant gossiping about me.
63 Whether sitting or standing,
look at how I am the object
of their song of ridicule.

[u]Or *Because my Lord won't reject forever* [v]Heb *He does not afflict from his heart.* [w]Or *my spirit* [x]Or *You didn't close your ear.* [y]Or *You have heard my voice.* [z]Or *my spirit's case* or *my spirit's grievance*

ת [64]Pay them back fully, LORD,
according to what they have done.
[65]Give them a tortured mind—
put your curse on them!
[66]Angrily hunt them down; wipe them out
from under the LORD's heaven.

The people's suffering

4 Oh, no!
Gold is tarnished;[a]
א even the purest gold is changed.
Sacred jewels are scattered
on every street corner.

ב [2]Zion's precious children,
once valued as pure gold—
oh no!—now they are worth no more
than clay pots made by a potter.

ג [3]Even jackals offer the breast;
they nurse their young.
But the daughter of my people
has become cruel, like desert ostriches.

ד [4]The baby's tongue sticks to the roof
of its mouth, thirsty.
Children ask for bread, beg for it—
but there is no bread.

ה [5]Those who once ate gourmet food
now tremble in the streets.
Those who wore
the finest purple clothes
now cling to piles of garbage.

ו [6]Greater was the punishment[b]
of the daughter of my people
than Sodom's penalty,[c]
which was quickly overthrown
without any hand-wringing.[d]

ז [7]Her nazirites were purer than snow;
they were more dazzling than milk.
Their limbs were redder than coral;
their bodies were sapphire.

ח [8]But their appearance grew darker
than soot;
they weren't recognized in the streets.
Their skin shriveled on their bones;
it became dry like wood.

ט [9]Things were better for those stabbed
by the sword
than for those stabbed by famine—
those who bled away, pierced,
lacking food from the field.

י [10]The hands of loving women
boiled their own children
to become their food during
the destruction of the daughter of
my people.

כ [11]The LORD let loose his fury;
he poured out his fierce anger.
He started a fire in Zion;
it licked up its foundations.

ל [12]The earth's rulers didn't believe it—
neither did any
who inhabit the world—
that either enemy or adversary
could enter Jerusalem's gates.

מ [13]It was because of her prophets' sins,
her priests' iniquities,
those who shed righteous blood
in the middle of the city.

נ [14]People wandered blindly in the streets,
polluted with blood.
No one would even touch their clothing.

ס [15]"Go away! Unclean!" was shouted at
them, "Go away! Away! Don't touch!"
So they fled and wandered around.
The nations said,
"They can't stay here anymore."

פ [16]It was the LORD's presence
that scattered them;[e]
he no longer notices them.
They didn't honor the priests' presence;
they didn't favor the elders.

ע [17]Our eyes continually failed,
looking for some help, but for nothing.

[a]Heb uncertain [b]Or *iniquity* [c]Or *sin* [d]Heb uncertain [e]Heb uncertain

From our watchtower we watched
for a nation that doesn't save.

צ 18 Our steps were tracked;
we could no longer walk
in our streets.
Our end had drawn near;
our days were done—
our end had definitely come.

ק 19 Our hunters were faster
than airborne eagles.
They chased us up the mountains;
they ambushed us in the wilderness.

ר 20 The LORD's chosen one,
the very breath in our lungs,
was caught in their traps—
the one we used to talk about, saying,
"Under his protection we will live
among the nations."

ש 21 Rejoice and be happy, Daughter Edom,
you who live in the land of Uz.
But this cup will pass over to you too.
You will get drunk on it.
You will be stripped naked.

ת 22 Your punishment[f] is over,
Daughter Zion;
God won't expose you anymore.
But he will attend to your punishment,
Daughter Edom;
he will expose your sins.

The people's complaint

5 LORD, consider what has become of us;
take notice of our disgrace. Look at it!
2 Our property has been turned
over to strangers;
our houses belong to foreigners.
3 We have become orphans,
having no father;
our mothers are like widows.
4 We drink our own water—but for a price;
we gather our own wood—
but pay for it.
5 Our hunters have been at our necks;[g]
we are worn out, but have no rest.
6 We held out a hand to Egypt
and to Assyria, to get sufficient food.
7 Our fathers have sinned and are gone,
but we are burdened
with their iniquities.
8 Slaves rule over us;
there is no one to rescue us
from their power.
9 We get our bread at the risk of our lives
because of the desert heat.[h]
10 Our skin is as hot as an oven
because of the burning heat of famine.
11 Women have been raped in Zion,
young women in Judah's cities.
12 Officials have been hung up
by their hands;
elders have been shown no respect.
13 Young men have carried grinding stones;
boys have stumbled
under loads of wood.
14 Elders have left the city gate;
young people stop their music.
15 Joy has left our heart;
our dancing has changed
into lamentation.
16 The crown has fallen off our head.
We are doomed
because we have sinned.
17 Because of all this our heart is sick;
because of these things
our glance is dark.
18 Mount Zion, now deserted—
only jackals walk on it now!
19 But you, LORD, will rule forever;
your throne lasts from one generation
to the next.
20 Why do you forget us continually;
why do you abandon us
for such a long time?
21 Return us, LORD, to yourself.
Please let us return![i]
Give us new days,
like those long ago—
22 unless you have completely rejected us,
or have become too angry with us.[j]

[f]Or *iniquity* [g]Heb uncertain [h]Or *sword;* Heb uncertain [i]Or *and we will return* or *so that we can return* [j]Or *But instead you have completely rejected us, become too angry with us,* or *Because if you have completely rejected us, have become too angry with us.*

EZEKIEL

First vision

1 In the thirtieth year, on the fifth day of
the fourth month, I was with the exiles at
the Chebar River when the heavens opened
and I saw visions of God. (2 It happened on
the fifth day of the month, in the fifth year
after King Jehoiachin's deportation. 3 The
LORD's word burst in on the priest Ezekiel,
Buzi's son, in the land of Babylon at the
Chebar River. There the LORD's power overcame him.)

4 As I watched, suddenly a driving storm
came out of the north, a great cloud flashing fire, with brightness all around. At its
center, in the middle of the fire, there was
something like gleaming amber. 5 And inside that were forms of four living creatures. This was what they looked like: Each
had the form of a human being, 6 though
each had four faces and four wings. 7 Their
feet looked like proper feet, but the soles
of their feet were like calves' hooves,
and they shone like burnished bronze.
8 Human hands were under their wings on
all four sides. All four creatures had faces
and wings, and 9 their wings touched each
other's wings. When they moved, they
each went straight ahead without turning.
10 As for the form of their faces: each of the
four had a human face, with a lion's face on
the right and a bull's face on the left, and
also an eagle's face. 11 The pairs of wings[a]
that stretched out overhead touched each
other, while the other pairs covered their
bodies. 12 Each moved straight ahead wherever the wind propelled them; they moved
without turning. 13 Regarding the creatures' forms: they looked like blazing coals,
like torches. Fire darted about between
the creatures and illuminated them, and
lightning flashed from the fire. 14 The creatures looked like lightning streaking back
and forth.

15 As I looked at the creatures, suddenly
there was a wheel on the earth corresponding to all four faces of the creatures. 16 The
appearance and composition of the wheels
were like sparkling topaz. There was one
shape for all four of them, as if one wheel
were inside another. 17 When they moved
in any of the four directions, they moved
without swerving. 18 Their rims were tall
and terrifying, because all four of them
were filled with eyes all around. 19 When
the creatures moved, the wheels moved
next to them. Whenever the creatures
rose above the earth, the wheels also rose
up. 20 Wherever the wind would appear to
go, the wind would make them go there
too. The wheels rose up beside them, because the spirit[b] of the creatures was in the
wheels. 21 When they moved, the wheels[c]
moved; when they stood still, the wheels
stood still; and when they rose above the
earth, the wheels rose up along with them,
because the spirit[d] of the creatures was in
the wheels.

22 The shape above the heads of the creatures[e] was a dome; it was like glittering ice
stretched out over their heads. 23 Just below
the dome, their outstretched wings touched
each other. They each also had two wings to
cover their bodies. 24 Then I heard the sound
of their wings when they moved forward. It
was like the sound of mighty waters, like
the sound of the Almighty,[f] like the sound
of tumult or the sound of an army camp.
When they stood still, their wings came to
rest. 25 Then there was a sound from above
the dome over their heads. They stood still,
and their wings came to rest.

26 Above the dome over their heads,
there appeared something like lapis lazuli
in the form of a throne. Above the form
of the throne there was a form that looked
like a human being. 27 Above what looked
like his waist, I saw something like gleaming amber, something like fire enclosing
it all around. Below what looked like his
waist, I saw something that appeared to be
fire. Its brightness shone all around. 28 Just
as a rainbow lights up a cloud on a rainy
day, so its brightness shone all around.
This was how the form of the LORD's glory

[a] LXX; MT adds *and their faces.* [b] Or *wind* [c] Or *they* [d] Or *wind* [e] LXX; MT *creature* [f] Heb *Shaddai* or *Mountain One*

appeared. When I saw it, I fell on my face. I heard the sound of someone speaking.

Ezekiel's commissioning

2 The voice said to me: Human one, stand on your feet, and I'll speak to you. 2As he spoke to me, a wind[g] came to me and stood me on my feet, and I heard someone addressing me. 3He said to me: Human one, I'm sending you to the Israelites, a traitorous and rebellious people. They and their ancestors have been rebelling against me to this very day. 4I'm sending you to their hardheaded and hard-hearted descendants, and you will say to them: The LORD God proclaims. 5Whether they listen or whether they refuse, since they are a household of rebels, they will know that a prophet has been among them.

6And as for you, human one, don't be afraid of them or their words. Don't be afraid! You possess thistles and thorns that subdue scorpions.[h] Don't be afraid of their words or shrink from their presence, because they are a household of rebels. 7You'll speak my words to them whether they listen or whether they refuse. They are just a household[i] of rebels!

8As for you, human one, listen to what I say to you. Don't become rebellious like that household of rebels. Open your mouth and eat what I give you. 9Then I looked, and there in a hand stretched out to me was a scroll. 10He spread it open in front of me, and it was filled with writing on both sides, songs of mourning, lamentation, and doom.

3 Then he said to me: Human one, eat this thing that you've found. Eat this scroll and go, speak to the house of Israel. 2So I opened my mouth, and he fed me the scroll. 3He said to me: Human one, feed your belly and fill your stomach with this scroll that I give you. So I ate it, and in my mouth it became as sweet as honey.

4Then he said to me: Human one, go! Go to the house of Israel and speak my words to them. 5You aren't being sent to a people whose language and speech are difficult and obscure but to the house of Israel. 6No, not to many peoples who speak difficult and obscure languages, whose words you wouldn't understand. If I did send you to them, they would listen to you. 7But the house of Israel—they will refuse to listen to you because they refuse to listen to me. The whole house of Israel is hardheaded and hard-hearted too. 8I've now hardened your face so that you can meet them head-on. 9I've made your forehead like a diamond, harder than stone. Don't be afraid of them or shrink away from them, because they are a household of rebels.

10He said to me: Human one, listen closely, and take to heart every word I say to you. 11Then go to the exiles, to your people's children. Whether they listen or not, speak to them and say: The LORD God proclaims! 12Then a wind lifted me up, and I heard behind me a great quaking sound from his place. Blessed is the LORD's glory! 13The sound was the creatures' wings beating against each other and the sound of the wheels beside them; it was a great rumbling noise. 14Then the wind picked me up and took me away. With the LORD's power pressing down against me I went away, bitter and deeply angry, 15and I came to the exiles who lived beside the Chebar River at Tel-abib. I stayed there among them for seven desolate days.

16At the end of the seven days, the LORD's word came to me: 17Human one, I've made you a lookout for the house of Israel. When you hear a word from me, deliver my warning. 18If I declare that the wicked will die but you don't warn them, if you say nothing to warn them from their wicked ways so that they might live, they will die because of their guilt, but I will hold you accountable for their deaths. 19If you do warn the wicked and they don't turn from their wickedness or their wicked ways, they will die because of their guilt, but you will save your life.

20Or suppose righteous people turn away from doing the right thing. If they act dishonestly, and I make them stumble because of it, they will die because you didn't warn

[g]Or *spirit* [h]Or *thistles and thorns are with you, and you sit on scorpions.* [i]LXX, Syr, Tg; MT lacks *household*.

them of their sin. Their righteous deeds won't be remembered, and I will hold you accountable for their deaths. 21But if you do warn the righteous not to sin, and they don't sin, they will be declared righteous. Their lives will be preserved because they heeded the warning, and you will save your life.

22The LORD'S power overcame me, and he said to me: Get up! Go out to the valley, and I'll speak to you there. 23So I got up and went out to the valley. Suddenly, the LORD's glory stood there, like the glory that I had seen at the Chebar River, and I fell on my face. 24When a wind came to me and stood me on my feet, he spoke to me and said: Go, shut yourself up inside your house. 25Look at you, human one! They've now put cords on you and bound you up so that you can't go out among them. 26I'll make your tongue stick to the roof of your mouth and take away your ability to speak. You won't be able to correct them, because they are a household of rebels. 27But whenever I speak to you, I'll open your mouth, and you will say to them: The LORD God proclaims. Those who hear will understand, but those who refuse will not. They are just a household of rebels.

Jerusalem's siege

4 You, human one, take a brick. Put it in front of you and draw the city of Jerusalem on it. 2Prepare the siege: Build a wall, construct ramps, set up army camps, and place battering rams all around. 3Take an iron plate and set it up as an iron wall between you and the city. Face it directly. When it is under siege like this, press hard against it. This is a sign for the house of Israel.

4Now, lie on your left side, and set the guilt of the house of Israel on it. For the length of time that you lie on your side, you will bear their punishment. 5I appoint to you three hundred ninety days, one day for each year of their guilt. So you will bear the punishment of the house of Israel. 6When you have completed these days, lie on your right side to bear the guilt of the house of Judah. I appoint forty days to you, one day for each year. 7With your arm stretched out, face the siege of Jerusalem directly and prophesy against it. 8I've now bound you with cords so that you can't turn from one side to the other until you have completed the days of your siege.

9You, gather some wheat and barley, beans and lentils, and millet and spelt. Put them in a bowl and make your bread from them. Eat it during the three hundred ninety days that you lie on your side. 10At fixed times you will eat your food by weight, fourteen ounces a day.[j] 11You will also ration your water by measure, drinking a sixth of a hin[k] at fixed times each day. 12Eat it like barley bread, and bake it on human excrement while they watch. 13The LORD says: In this same way the Israelites will eat their unclean bread among the nations where I am scattering them.

14And I said: "Ah, LORD God! I've never been unclean! From my childhood until now I've never eaten anything that wasn't properly slaughtered,[l] and no unclean meat has ever entered my mouth!"

15He answered me: "Then I'll let you use cow dung instead of human excrement. You can make your bread over that."

16Then he said to me: Human one, I'm destroying the food supply in Jerusalem. They will anxiously ration and eat their food, and in dismay they will dole out and drink their water. 17When their food and water dwindles away, everyone will be horrified, and they will waste away because of their guilt.

5 You, human one, take a sharp sword. Use it like a razor and shave your head and beard. Then use scales to divide the hair. 2At the end of the siege, burn one-third of it in the city. Strike another third with the sword left and right. Then scatter one-third to the wind and let loose[m] the sword after it. 3From that third, take a few strands and hide them in your garment. 4From that hair, take yet another batch and throw it into the fire and burn it up. From there, fire will spread to the whole house of Israel.

[j]Or *twenty shekels* [k]A hin is approximately one pint. [l]Or *what died of itself* or *was torn by wild beasts* [m]Or *I will let loose*

5 The LORD God proclaims: This is Jerusalem! I have set her in the middle of the nations and surrounding countries. 6 But she
rebelled against my case laws and my regulations with greater treachery than these
nations and surrounding countries, who
also rejected my case laws and didn't follow
my regulations. 7 Therefore, the LORD God
proclaims: You have become more turbulent than these nations around you because
you haven't obeyed my regulations or followed my case laws. You haven't even followed the case laws of the nations around
you! 8 So now the LORD God proclaims: I
myself am now against you! I will impose
the case law penalties on you in the sight
of the nations. 9 Because of you, I will do
what I've never done before and will never
do again—all because of your detestable
practices. 10 Therefore, parents among you
will eat their children, and children will eat
their parents. I will impose penalties from
case laws on you and scatter all that is left
of you to the winds. 11 Therefore, as surely as
I live, this is what the LORD God says: Because you made my sanctuary unclean with
all your disgusting practices and detestable
things, I myself will shave you. I will not
shed a tear. You will have no compassion,
even from me. 12 One-third of you will die
of plague and waste away by famine among
you. One-third will fall by the sword all
around you. And one-third I will scatter to
all the winds, letting loose a sword to pursue them. 13 My anger will be complete. I will
exhaust my wrath against them and take
my revenge. Then they will know that I, the
LORD, have spoken against them in my zeal
and consumed them in my wrath. 14 I will
turn you into a desolation to the ridicule
of the nations all around you, in the sight
of all who pass by. 15 You will become an object of ridicule, a mockery, and a horrifying
lesson to the nations all around you, when
I impose penalties from case laws against
you in anger, wrath, and overflowing fury.
I, the LORD, have spoken. 16 When I launch
my deadly arrows of famine against you, I
have released them for your destruction! I
will add to your famine and completely cut
off your food supply. 17 I will send famine
and wild animals against you, and they will
leave you childless. Plague and bloodshed
will come to you, and I will bring the sword
against you. I, the LORD, have spoken.

Against the mountains of Israel

6 The LORD's word came to me: 2 Human
one, face Israel's mountains, and prophesy to them. 3 Say:

Hear the LORD God's word,
  mountains of Israel!
The LORD God proclaims
  to the mountains and hills,
  to the valleys
    and their deepest ravines:
I'm about to bring a sword against you
  and destroy your shrines.
4 Your altars will be destroyed,
  your incense altars broken.
  And I'll make your slain
    fall in front of your idols.
5 I'll throw the Israelites' corpses
  in front of their idols,
  and I'll scatter your bones
    all around your altars.
6 Wherever you live,
  cities will be in ruins,
    shrines made desolate,
  turned into utter ruin.
Your altars will be punished
  and then broken down.
Your idols will be demolished,
  your incense altars shattered,
  and all your works wiped out.
7 The slain will fall among you,
  and you will know that I am the LORD.

8 But I will spare a few.
  Some of you will escape
    the nations' swords
  when you are scattered
    throughout the lands.
9 Your fugitives will remember me
  in the nations
    to which they've been banished,
  how I was crushed
    when their roving hearts
    turned away from me,
  and their roving eyes
    went after their idols.
They will loathe themselves

for their treacherous acts
and detestable practices,
10 and they will know that I am the LORD.
Not in vain have I threatened
to bring this evil against them.
11 The LORD God proclaims: Clap your
hands, stamp your feet, and cry "Horror"
over all the detestable practices of the
house of Israel. They will fall by the sword,
famine, and plague.
12 Whoever is far off will
die of plague, whoever is nearby will fall to
the sword, and whoever finds refuge will
die of famine. I'll satisfy my wrath against
them!
13 They will know that I am the LORD
when their slain appear among their idols
and around their altars, wherever they
offered up pleasing aromas for all their
idols, on every high hill and mountaintop,
and under every lofty tree and leafy oak.
14 Wherever they live, I will direct my power
against them. I will turn the land into a
greater wasteland than the Riblah desert.
Then they will know that I am the LORD.

The end

7 The LORD's word came to me:
2 You,
human one, this is what the LORD God
proclaims to the land of Israel:
An end! The end has come
to the four corners of the earth!
3 Even now the end is upon you!
I'll send my anger against you,
I'll judge you according to your ways,
and I'll turn
all your detestable practices against you.
4 I won't shed a tear for you
or show any pity.
Instead, I'll turn your ways against you,
and your detestable practices
will stay with you.
Then you will know that I am the LORD.

5 The LORD God proclaims:
Disaster! A singular disaster!
Look, it comes!
6 The end has come!
Oh, yes, it has come!
It has come to you!
Look, it's here!
7 You who live on the earth,
you are finally caught in your own trap!
The time has come;
the day draws near.
On the hills panic, not glory.
8 And now it's near!
Against you I will pour out my wrath,
and my anger will be satisfied.
I'll judge you according to your ways,
and turn all your detestable practices
against you.
9 I won't shed a tear or show any pity
when I turn your ways against you,
and your detestable practices
stay with you.
Then you will know that I, the LORD, am
the one who strikes you!

10 Look, the day! Look, it comes!
Doom has arrived!
The staff blossoms,
and pride springs up!
11 Violence rises up as a wicked master.[n]
It isn't from others
or their armies or their violence.
It hasn't loomed up because of them.
12 The time is coming!
The day draws near!
No buyer should rejoice,
and no seller should mourn,
because wrath overcomes
the whole crowd.
13 The seller will never get back
what was sold,
even if both of them survive.
The vision concerns the whole crowd.
It won't be revoked.
And the guilty ones—
they won't even be able
to hang on to their lives.
14 They have blown the horn,
and everything is ready,
but no one goes to battle,
because my wrath
overcomes the whole crowd.
15 Outside, the sword!
Inside, plague and famine!
Whoever is out in the field
will die by the sword.

[n] Or *wicked staff*

Whoever is in the city,
plague and famine will consume them.
16 And those who flee?
They will turn up on the hills
like valley doves,
all of them moaning, those guilty ones.
17 Every hand will hang limp;
urine will run down every leg.
18 They will put on mourning clothes,
and horror will cover them.
On every face, shame;
on all their heads, baldness.
19 They will hurl their silver into the street,
and their gold will seem unclean.
Their silver and their gold
won't deliver them
on the day of the LORD's anger.
They won't satisfy their appetites
or fill their bellies.
Their guilt will bring them down.

20 From their beautiful ornament,
in which they took pride,
they have made horrible
and detestable images!
Therefore, I've declared it
an unclean thing for them.
21 I'll hand it over to foreigners
as loot taken in war,
to the earth's wicked ones as plunder—
they will defile it!
22 When I hide my face from my people,
foreigners will defile my treasured place.
Violent intruders will invade it;
they will defile it!

23 Make a chain!
The earth is full of perverted justice,
the city full of violence.
24 I'll bring up the cruelest nations,
and they will seize their houses.
I'll break their proud strength,
and their sanctuaries will be defiled.

25 Disaster! It has come!
They seek peace, but there is none.
26 One disaster comes after another,
and rumor follows rumor.

They seek a vision from the prophet.
Instruction disappears from the priest,
and counsel from the elders.
27 The king will go into mourning,
the prince will clothe himself in despair,
and the hands of the land's people
will tremble.
When I do to them as they have done
and judge them by their own justice,
they will know that I am the LORD.

Temple vision

8 In the sixth year, on the fifth day of the
sixth month, I was sitting in my house,
and Judah's elders were sitting with me,
when the LORD God's power overcame me.
2 I looked, and there was a form that looked
like fire. Below what looked like his waist
was fire, but above his waist it looked like
gold, like gleaming amber. 3 He stretched
out the form of a hand and picked me up
by the hair of my head. A wind lifted me up
between earth and heaven, and in a divine
vision it brought me to Jerusalem, to the
north-facing entrance of the gate to the
inner court. That was where the pedestal
was for the outrageous image that incites
outrage. 4 There I saw the glory of Israel's
God, exactly like what I had seen in the
valley. 5 He said to me: Human one, look
toward the north. So I looked north, and
there, north of the altar gate, was this outrageous image in the entrance. 6 He said to
me: Human one, do you see what they are
doing, the terribly detestable practices that
the house of Israel is doing here that drive
me far from my sanctuary? Yet you will see
even more detestable practices than these.
7 Then he brought me to the court entrance. When I looked, I saw a hole in the
wall. 8 He said to me: Human one, dig
through the wall. So I dug through the wall,
and I discovered a doorway. 9 And he said to
me: Go in and see what wicked and detestable things they are doing in there. 10 So I
went in and looked, and I saw every form of
loathsome beasts and creeping things and
all the idols of the house of Israel engraved
on the walls all around. 11 The seventy elders
of the house of Israel were standing in front
of them, and all of them were holding censers in their hands. Jaazaniah, Shaphan's
son, was standing right there with them,
and the scent of the incense cloud rose up.

[12]He said to me: Human one, do you see what the elders of the house of Israel are doing in the dark, every one of them in their rooms full of sculptured images? They say, "The LORD doesn't see us; the LORD has abandoned the land." [13]He said to me: You will see them performing even more detestable practices. [14]He brought me to the entrance of the north gate of the temple, where women were sitting and performing the Tammuz lament.

[15]He said to me: Human one, do you see? Yet you will see even more detestable practices than these. [16]He brought me to the inner court of the LORD's temple. There, at the entrance to the LORD's temple, between the porch and the altar, were twenty-five men facing toward the east with their backs to the LORD's temple. They were bowing to the sun in the east. [17]He said to me: Do you see, human one? Isn't it enough that the house of Judah has observed here all these detestable things? They have filled the land with violence, and they continue to provoke my fury. Look at them! They even put the branch to their noses! [18]I will certainly respond with wrath. I won't spare or pity anyone. Even though they call out loudly to me in my hearing, I won't listen to them.

9 Then in my hearing he called out loudly: Draw near, you guardians of the city, and bring your weapons of destruction! [2]Suddenly, six men came from the Upper Gate that faces north. All of them were holding weapons of destruction. Among them was another man who was dressed in linen and had a writing case at his side. When they came in and stood beside the bronze altar, [3]the glory of Israel's God rose from above the winged creatures[o] where he had been and moved toward the temple's threshold. The LORD called to the man who was dressed in linen with the writing case at his side: [4]Go through the city, through Jerusalem, and mark the foreheads of those who sigh and groan because of all the detestable practices that have been conducted in it. [5]To the others he said in my hearing: Go through the city after him, and attack. Spare no one! Be merciless! [6]Kill them all, old men, young men and women, babies and mothers. Only don't touch anyone who has the mark. Begin at my sanctuary. So they began with the men, the elders in front of the temple. [7]He said to them: Make the temple unclean! Fill the courts with the slain! Go! And they went out and attacked the city.

[8]While they were attacking, I was left alone. I fell on my face, and I cried out, "Oh, LORD God! When you pour out your wrath on Jerusalem, will you destroy all that is left of Israel?"

[9]He said to me: "Judah and the house of Israel are very, very guilty. The land is filled with blood, and the city is full of injustice. They have said, 'The LORD has forsaken the land; the LORD sees nothing.' [10]I most definitely won't spare or pity anyone! I will hold them accountable for their ways."

[11]Just then the man who was dressed in linen with the writing case at his side returned and said, "I've done just as you commanded."

10 At that moment I saw a form of a throne in the dome above the heads of the winged creatures. It appeared above them, and it looked like lapis lazuli. [2]He said to the man clothed in linen: Go in between the wheels under the winged creatures.[p] Fill your hands with fiery coals from between the winged creatures, and scatter them over the city. As I watched, he went in. [3]Now the winged creatures were standing to the right of the temple when the man went in, and the cloud filled the inner courtyard. [4]Then the LORD's glory rose from above the winged creatures[q] and moved toward the temple's threshold. The temple was filled with the cloud, and the courtyard was filled with the brightness of the LORD's glory. [5]The sound of the winged creatures' wings could be heard as far as the outer courtyard. It was like the sound of God Almighty[r] when he speaks. [6]When he instructed the man clothed in linen to take fire from between the winged creatures and their wheels, the man went and stood next to the wheel. [7]Then one of the winged creatures

[o]LXX; MT *creature* [p]LXX; MT *creature* [q]LXX; MT *creature* [r]Heb *El Shaddai* or *God of the Mountain*

stretched a hand between the winged creatures into the fire that was between them, and he drew out some of it and set it in the palm of the one clothed in linen. He took it and went out. 8 It appeared that the winged creatures had the form of a human hand under their wings.

9 Suddenly, I saw four wheels next to the winged creatures. There was a wheel next to each winged creature, and the appearance of the wheels was like sparkling topaz. 10 It appeared that there was one shape for all four of them, as if one wheel were inside another. 11 When they moved in any of the four directions, they moved without swerving. Whichever way the leading one faced, they moved in that direction without swerving. 12 Their whole body—backs, hands, and wings—as well as their wheels, all four of them, were covered with eyes all around. 13 It was these wheels that were called "the wheels" in my hearing. 14 Each winged creature had four faces. The first face was that of a winged creature, the second face was that of a human being, the third that of a lion, and the fourth that of an eagle. 15 The winged creatures rose up, the same creatures that I had seen at the Chebar River. 16 When the winged creatures moved, the wheels moved beside them. When the winged creatures lifted their wings to ascend above the earth, the wheels remained beside them without swerving. 17 When they stood still, the wheels stood still; when they rose up, they rose up with them, because the spirit[s] of the living creatures was in them. 18 Then the LORD's glory went out from above the temple's threshold and it stood over the winged creatures. 19 While I watched, the winged creatures raised their wings and rose from the ground to leave, with their wheels beside them. They stopped at the entrance to the east gate of the temple, and the glory of Israel's God was up above them. 20 These were the same living creatures that I saw underneath Israel's God at the Chebar River, and I realized that they were winged creatures. 21 Each had four faces and four wings, with the form of a human hand under their wings. 22 The forms of their faces were the same faces that I saw at the Chebar River. Their appearance was also the same. All four of them moved straight ahead.

11 A wind lifted me up and brought me to the east gate of the LORD's temple. There at the entrance to the gate were twenty-five men, and I saw that two officials of the people, Jaazaniah, Azzur's son, and Pelatiah, Benaiah's son, were with them.

2 He said to me: Human one, these men devise evil plans and give wicked advice in this city. 3 They are the ones who say, "The nearest relatives aren't building houses.[t] The city is the cooking pot, and we are the meat." 4 Therefore, prophesy against them, human one, prophesy! 5 The LORD's spirit took hold of me, and he said to me: Say, This is what the LORD God proclaims: So you have said, house of Israel! But I know what you really mean. 6 You continue to commit murder in this city, and you fill its streets with the slain.

7 Therefore, the LORD God proclaims: The city is the cooking pot, and the ones you have slain in it are the meat. But you will be taken out of it. 8 You fear the sword, so I will bring the sword against you. This is what the LORD God says! 9 I will lead you out of the city, hand you over to foreigners, and execute judgments against you. 10 You will fall by the sword! At Israel's borders I will judge you, and you will know that I am the LORD. 11 The city won't be your cooking pot, and you won't be the meat in it. At Israel's borders, I will judge you. 12 You will know that I am the LORD, whose regulations you didn't observe and whose case laws you didn't follow. Instead, you followed the case laws of the nations around you.

13 While I was prophesying, Benaiah's son Pelatiah dropped dead. I fell on my face, and I wailed and said, "Oh, LORD God! Are you finishing off even the Israelites who are left?"

14 The LORD's word came to me: 15 Human one, when the people living in Jerusalem said, "They've gone far from the LORD,

[s] Or *wind* [t] Or *it is not time to build houses*

and we've been given the land as an inheritance," they were talking about your family,
your nearest relatives, the whole house of
Israel, all of it.
16Therefore, say, The LORD God proclaims: Even though I made them go far
away among the nations and caused them
to scatter throughout the earth, I've provided some sanctuary for them in the countries to which they've gone.
17Therefore, say, The LORD God proclaims: I will gather you from the nations,
assemble you from the countries where you
were scattered, and I will give you Israel's
fertile land. 18They will enter the land, and
they will remove from it all its disgusting
and detestable things. 19I will give them a
single heart, and I will put a new spirit in
them. I will remove the stony hearts from
their bodies and give them hearts of flesh
20so that they may follow my regulations
and carefully observe my case laws. They
will be my people, and I will be their God.
21As for those whose hearts continue to go
after their disgusting and detestable things,
I will hold them accountable for their ways.
This is what the LORD God says!
22Then the winged creatures raised their
wings. The wheels were next to them, and
the glory of Israel's God was above them.
23The LORD's glory ascended from the
middle of the city, and it stopped at the
mountain east of the city. 24And a wind
lifted me up and brought me to the exiles
in Chaldea, through a vision with a divine
wind.[u] When the vision I had seen left me,
25I spoke to the exiles about everything the
LORD had shown to me.

Baggage for exile

12 The LORD's word came to me: 2Human
one, you live in a household of rebels.
They have eyes to see but they don't see,
ears to hear but they don't hear, because
they are a household of rebels. 3But you,
human one, prepare a backpack for going
into exile. In the daytime while they watch,
go into exile; while they watch, go out from
your place to another. Even though they
are a household of rebels, perhaps they will
understand. 4In the daytime while they
watch, carry your backpack as if for exile.
At twilight while they watch, go out like
those who are led out to exile. 5While they
watch, dig a hole through the wall and take
your backpack out through it. 6While they
watch, shoulder your backpack and carry it
out in the dark. Cover your face so that you
can't see the land, because I'm making you
a sign for the house of Israel. 7So I did as I
was commanded. I carried out my backpack
like an exile's backpack in the daytime. At
night I dug a hole through the wall with
my hands. In the darkness, I shouldered
my backpack and carried it out while they
watched.
8In the morning, the LORD's word came
to me: 9Human one, has the house of Israel,
that household of rebels, asked you, "What
are you doing?" 10Say to them, The LORD
God proclaims: This concerns the prince in
Jerusalem, along with the entire house of
Israel in it.[v] 11Say: I'm your sign. Just as I
have done, so it will be done to them. They
will go into captivity in exile. 12Their prince
will shoulder his backpack at night and go
out. They will dig through the wall to lead
him out through it, and he will cover his
face so that his eyes won't see the land.
13But I will spread my net over him, catch
him in my trap, and bring him to Babylon,
to the land of the Chaldeans. He won't see
it, but he will die there. 14As for all those
who are in league with him, I will scatter his
helpers and all his troops to the winds and
let the sword loose after them. 15They will
know that I am the LORD when I disperse
them among the nations and scatter them
throughout the lands. 16But I will preserve
a few of their number from the sword, famine, and plague, so that they may confess
all their detestable practices among the nations where they go. Then they will know
that I am the LORD.
17The LORD's word came to me: 18Human
one, eat your bread in trembling, and drink
your water in anxious agitation. 19Say to the
land's people, The LORD God proclaims to

[u]Or *spirit* [v]Or *them*

those living in Jerusalem regarding Israel's
fertile land: As they anxiously eat up their
bread and drink up their water in dismay,
the land will be emptied of everything in it
because of the violence of all who live there.
[20]The inhabited cities will be laid waste, the
land left desolate, and you will know that I
am the LORD.

Fulfillment of prophecy

[21]The LORD's word came to me: [22]Human
one, what is this proverb of your people
concerning Israel's fertile land? They say,
"The days go by, and every vision vanishes."
[23]Therefore, say to them, The LORD God
proclaims: I'll put an end to this proverb!
It will never again be uttered in Israel. Tell
them instead: The days are coming soon for
the fulfillment of every vision. [24]Never again
will there be any worthless vision or deceptive divination in the house of Israel. [25]I
am the LORD! The word that I speak is the
word that I will speak! It will happen and be
delayed no longer. In your own days, household of rebels, I speak a word and make it
happen. This is what the LORD God says!

[26]The LORD's word came to me: [27]Human
one, the house of Israel is now saying, "The
vision that he sees is for distant days; he
prophesies about future times." [28]There-
fore, say to them, The LORD God proclaims:
It will be delayed no longer. Every word of
mine that I've spoken is certain, and it will
happen. This is what the LORD God says.

Against the prophets

13 The LORD's word came to me: [2]Human
one, prophesy to Israel's prophets
who prophesy from their own imaginations. Say, Hear the LORD's word! [3]The
LORD God proclaims: Doom to the foolish
prophets who follow their own whims but
see nothing. [4]Israel, your prophets have
been like jackals among ruins. [5]You haven't
gone up into the breach or reinforced the
wall of the house of Israel, so that it might
withstand the battle on the day of the
LORD. [6]They saw worthless visions and performed deceptive divinations. Even though
the LORD didn't send them, they said, "This
is what the LORD says" and expected their
word to stand. [7]Didn't you see worthless
visions? And didn't you report deceptive
divinations and say, "This is what the LORD
says," even though I didn't speak?

[8]Therefore, the LORD God proclaims: Because you spoke worthless things and had
false visions, I'm against you. This is what
the LORD God says! [9]I'll wield my power
against the prophets, those seers of noth-
ingness and diviners of lies. They won't be
included in my people's council, or recorded
in the house of Israel's official records, or
enter Israel's fertile land. Then you will
know that I am the LORD.

[10]Without a doubt, they led my people
astray, saying "Peace" when there was no
peace, and "He is building a wall" when they
were the ones who laid on the plaster. [11]Say
to those who laid on the plaster that it will
fall. When the flooding rains appear and I
send hailstones, it will collapse, and the
storm winds will break it apart. [12]The wall
will certainly fall. Won't it be said about
you, "Where is your plaster now?"

[13]Therefore, the LORD God proclaims: In
my fury I will make a storm wind break out,
and in my anger there will be flooding rains
and hailstones in consuming wrath. [14]I will
tear down the wall on which you laid plaster. I will raze it to the ground and expose
its foundation. When it falls, you will be
destroyed with it, and you will know that I
am the LORD. [15]I will exhaust my fury on the
wall and on those who laid plaster on it. Then
I will say to you, "Where is the wall?"[w] and
"Where are those who plastered it, [16]those
prophets of Israel who prophesied to Jerusalem and envisioned peace when there was
no peace?" This is what the LORD God says!

[17]You, human one, face the daughters of
your people, those women who prophesy
from their imaginations. Prophesy against
them [18]and say, The LORD God proclaims:
Doom to the women who sew bands on
every wrist and make veils for heads of
all sizes to entrap human lives. Will you
ensnare my people's lives but preserve

[w] Syr, cf 13:12; MT *There is no wall.*

your own? 19When you degrade me to my people for handfuls of barley and bread crumbs, you mislead my gullible people, and you bring about the death of those who shouldn't die and keep alive those who shouldn't live.

20Therefore, the LORD God proclaims: I'm against the bands that you use to trap human lives.[x] I will tear them from your arms, and I will set free the lives that you've trapped like birds. 21I will tear off your veils and snatch my people out of your clutches. They will be prey in your clutches no longer. Then you will know that I am the LORD. 22You hurt the righteous with slander—I didn't wound them!—and you strengthened the hands of the wicked so that they survived without changing their evil ways! 23Therefore, you will no longer see empty visions or perform divinations. I will rescue my people from your clutches, and you will know that I am the LORD.

False devotion

14 When some of the elders of the house of Israel came to sit in my presence, 2the LORD's word came to me: 3Human one, these men decide on their own to set up their idols, so the cause of their downfall is right in front of them. Why should I allow them to ask me anything? 4Therefore, speak to them and tell them, The LORD God proclaims: If anyone from the house of Israel decides on his own to set up his idols and puts the cause of his downfall right in front him, but then comes to the prophet, I, the LORD, will require an answer from him through his many idols. 5So I'll seize the hearts of the house of Israel, whose idols have made them all strangers to me.

6Therefore, say to the house of Israel, The LORD God proclaims: Come back! Turn away from your idols and from all your detestable practices. Turn away! 7Or anyone of the house of Israel or any immigrant in Israel who becomes estranged from me by deciding on their own to set up their idols and puts the cause of their downfall right in front of them, but then comes to the prophet to ask me something through him, I, the LORD, will require an answer. 8I will confront that one. I will set them up as a sign and an object lesson, and I will cut them off from my people. Then you will know that I am the LORD.

9As for the prophet who was seduced into speaking a word, even though it was I, the LORD, who seduced that prophet, I will use my power against him and cut him off completely from my people Israel. 10The prophet and the inquirer alike will bear their guilt, 11so that the house of Israel won't stray away from me again or make themselves impure with any of their sins. They will be my people, and I will be their God. This is what the LORD God says!

Failed request

12The LORD's word came to me: 13Human one, suppose a land sins against me by acting faithlessly, so that I use my power against it, break off its food supply, let famine run rampant, and eliminate both humans and animals. 14If these three men, Noah, Daniel, and Job, lived there, their lives alone would be saved because they were righteous. This is what the LORD God says. 15Or suppose I allow wild animals to roam through the land, and it becomes so wild that no one can live there or even travel through it on account of the wild animals. 16If these three men lived there, as surely as I live, proclaims the LORD God, they wouldn't be able to rescue even their sons or daughters. They alone would be rescued, but the land would become a ruin. 17Or suppose I bring a sword against that land and command the sword to pass through and eliminate both humans and animals. 18If these three men lived there, as surely as I live, proclaims the LORD God, they wouldn't be able to rescue even their sons or daughters. They alone would be rescued. 19Or suppose I send a plague against that land and pour out my fury on it. With great bloodshed I would eliminate both humans and animals. 20If Noah, Daniel, and Job lived there, as surely as I live, proclaims

[x]LXX; MT adds *like birds.*

the LORD God, they wouldn't be able to rescue either sons or daughters. But they would save their lives because they were righteous.

21 The LORD God proclaims: How much more if I send all four of these terrible acts of judgment—sword, famine, wild animals, and plague—against Jerusalem, to eliminate both humans and animals? 22 Yet a few survivors will be left. Sons and daughters will be brought out to you. When you see their ways and their deeds, you will be consoled for the evil that I inflicted on Jerusalem, for all that I brought against it. 23 Seeing their ways and their deeds will bring you some consolation, because then you will understand what I've done, and that I didn't do any of these things without cause. This is what the LORD God says.

The vine's wood

15 The LORD's word came to me: 2 Human one, how is the vine's wood better than the wood of all the trees in the forest? 3 Can you make anything useful from its wood? Can you make a peg from it and hang objects on it? 4 If not, can it be used as firewood? Fire would consume its two ends, but its middle part would only get charred. So is it useful for anything? 5 Look, even when it was whole, it was worthless. Now that the fire has consumed it, and it is charred, it's even more useless.

6 Therefore, the LORD God proclaims: Of all the trees in the forest, I have decreed that the vine's wood is destined to be consumed by fire. So also have I decreed for those who live in Jerusalem, 7 and I have confronted them. They may try to go out from the fire, but the fire will consume them. You will know that I am the LORD, because I confronted them. 8 I will turn the land into a ruin because they acted faithlessly, proclaims the LORD God.

Jerusalem's unfaithfulness

16 The LORD's word came to me: 2 Human one, show Jerusalem her detestable practices. 3 Say, The LORD God proclaims to Jerusalem: By origin and birth you are from the land of Canaan. Your father was an Amorite, your mother a Hittite. 4 This is how you were treated on the day you were born: Your umbilical cord wasn't cut, you weren't washed clean with water or rubbed with salt, and you weren't wrapped in blankets. 5 No one took pity or cared enough to do any of these things for you. You were despised on the day of your birth and thrown out on the open field. 6 When I happened to come by, I saw you flailing about in your blood. I said to you while you were still bloody, "Live!" 7 I helped you to flourish like a young plant in the field, and you grew tall and became wonderfully endowed. Your breasts were firm, your hair beautifully thick. And you were completely naked.

8 When I passed by you, I realized that you were ready for love. So I spread my cloak over you and covered your nakedness. I made a solemn promise and entered into a covenant with you, and you became mine. This is what the LORD God says. 9 Then I washed you with water, rinsed off your blood, and poured oil on you. 10 I clothed you with colorful garments, put fine sandals on you, wrapped your head in linen, and covered you with jewels. 11 I adorned you with fine jewelry, and put bracelets on your wrists and a necklace around your neck. 12 I put a ring in your nose, earrings in your ears, and a beautiful crown on your head. 13 I adorned you with gold and silver, and your garments were made of the finest linen and brocade. You ate the finest flour, honey, and oil. You became very beautiful, fit for royalty. 14 Among the nations you were famous for your beauty. It was perfect because of the splendor that I had given you. This is what the LORD God says.

15 But you trusted in your beauty and traded on your fame. At every opportunity, you seduced all who came by. 16 You took some of your clothing to make colorful shrines and prostituted yourself in them. 17 You took the beautiful gold and silver jewelry that I had given to you, and you made male images for yourself and prostituted yourself with them. 18 You took your fine garments and clothed them. You set my oil and incense before them. 19 You set my food that I had given you to eat—fine wheat,

oil, and honey—before them as a pleasing aroma. This is what the LORD God says. [20]You took your sons and daughters, which you had borne to me, and you sacrificed these to them so they could consume them. Was this promiscuity of yours a small thing? [21]You slaughtered my sons and placed them in the fire for them! [22]In all your detestable practices and promiscuities, you didn't remember the days of your infancy when you lay completely naked, flailing about in your blood.

[23]After all your wickedness—doom, doom to you, proclaims the LORD God—[24]you built a pavilion for yourself and set up platforms in every square. [25]At every crossroad you built your platform and degraded your beauty by spreading your legs to all comers. And so you encouraged even more promiscuity. [26]You prostituted yourself with the Egyptians, your neighbors with the large sexual organs, and as you added to your seductions, you provoked me to anger. [27]So I used my power against you, cut off your allowance, and gave you up to the passions of the Philistine women who had been confounded by your infamous ways and had rejected you. [28]Still not satisfied, you prostituted yourself to the Assyrians, but they weren't enough for you either. [29]So you prostituted yourself with the Babylonians, the land of traders, but again you weren't satisfied. [30]How sick was your heart—the LORD God proclaims—that you could do all these things, the deeds of a hardened prostitute. [31]But you weren't like an ordinary prostitute! When you built your pavilion at the head of every street and made your platform in every square, you refused to be paid. [32]You are like an adulterous wife: you take in strangers instead of your husband. [33]Ordinary prostitutes are given gifts, but you gave your gifts to all your lovers. From every direction you even bribed them to come to you for your sexual favors. [34]As a prostitute, you were more perverse than other women. No one approached you for sexual favors, but you yourself gave gifts instead of receiving them. You are perversion itself! [35]Therefore, you prostitute, hear the LORD's word!

[36]The LORD God proclaims: You were in a constant state of arousal[y] and exposed yourself when you acted like a prostitute with your lovers and with the idols to which you gave your children's blood. [37]Therefore, I will now gather all of your lovers whom you pleased, the ones you loved and the ones you rejected. I will gather them against you from all around, and I will expose you to them. They will see it all. [38]I will convict you of adultery and murder, and I will hand you over in bloody fury and zeal. [39]I will hand you over to them, and they will tear down your pavilion and destroy your platforms. They will strip you of your garments, take your beautiful jewels, and they will leave you completely naked. [40]They will bring an army against you, pelt you with stones, and slaughter you with their swords. [41]They will burn down your houses and execute judgments against you in the sight of many women. I will bring an end to your prostitution; indeed, you will never again give payment. [42]When I've satisfied my anger, and my rage has turned away from you, I will be calm and no longer angry. [43]Because you didn't remember your youthful days, and infuriated me with all these things, I will hold you accountable for what you've done. This is what the LORD God says.

Have you not added bad reputation to all your detestable acts? [44]Now everyone who speaks in proverbs will say this about you: "Like mother, like daughter." [45]You are your mother's daughter! She loathed her husband and also her children. You are just like your sisters too! They also loathed their husbands and children. Your mother was a Hittite, and your father was an Amorite. [46]Your older sister is Samaria, who lives with her daughters in the north. Your younger sister is Sodom, who lives with her daughters in the south. [47]You didn't follow in their ways or engage in their detestable practices in any small way. You were far more destructive. [48]As surely as I live, says the LORD God, not even your sister Sodom and her daughters

[y]Heb uncertain

did what you and your daughters have done!
[49]This is the sin of your sister Sodom: She
and her daughters were proud, had plenty
to eat, and enjoyed peace and prosperity;
but she didn't help the poor and the needy.
[50]They became haughty and did detestable
things in front of me, and I turned away
from them as soon as I saw it.

[51]Samaria didn't sin even half as much as
you did. You've so outstripped her in multiplying your detestable practices, with all the
detestable things you've done, that you've
even made your sisters seem innocent.
[52]Bear your disgrace, which has actually im-
proved your sisters' position. Because your
sins and detestable acts were greater than
theirs, they are now more righteous than
you. Be ashamed, and bear the disgrace
of making your sisters righteous! [53]I will
improve the circumstances of Sodom and
her daughters and the circumstances of Samaria and her daughters. And what's left of
your fortune will go to them, [54]so that you
will bear your disgrace and be humiliated
by all that you've done to make them feel
better. [55]Then your sister Sodom and her
daughters will return to their former state,
and your sister Samaria and her daughters
will return to their former state. You and
your daughters will return to your former
state, [56]but you will no longer talk about
your sister Sodom as in your haughty days
[57]before your wickedness was exposed. You
are now the reproach of all the daughters of
Edom[z] and all those around her, including
the daughters of the Philistines. They mock
you on every side. [58]You alone must bear
your bad reputation and your detestable
ways. This is what the LORD says.

[59]The LORD God proclaims: I will do to
you just as you have done, despising solemn
pledges and breaking covenants. [60]Never-
theless, I will remember my covenant with
you when you were young, and I will establish an everlasting covenant with you.
[61]And you will remember your ways and be
ashamed, when in spite of your covenant I[a]
take your big sisters and little sisters from
you and give them back to you as daughters. [62]I myself will establish my covenant
with you, and you will know that I am the
LORD. [63]Then you will remember and be
ashamed, and you won't even open your
mouth because of your shame, after I've
forgiven you for all that you've done. This is
what the LORD God says.

Transplanted cedar

17 The LORD's word came to me: [2]Human
one, compose a riddle and a parable
about the house of Israel. [3]Say, The LORD
God proclaims: The great eagle with great
wings, long feathers, and full, colorful
plumage came to Lebanon and took the
top branch of the cedar. [4]He plucked a twig
from the cedar's crown, brought it to the
land of traders, and set it down in a city
of merchants. [5]He took a native seed and
planted it in a prepared field, placing it like
a willow beside plentiful water. [6]It grew and
became a low-spreading vine. Its foliage
turned toward him, and its roots developed
under him. And so it became a vine, and it
produced branches and sent out its shoots.

[7]Now there was another great eagle with
great wings and much plumage. This vine
bent its roots and turned its branches toward
him so that it might draw more water from
him than from its own bed, [8]a good field with
plentiful water where it was planted to grow
branches, bear fruit, and become a splendid
vine. [9]Say, The LORD God proclaims: Will it
thrive? Won't he tear out its roots, strip its
fruit, and cause all the leaves of its branches
to wither? It will dry up, and no one will need
a strong arm or a mighty army to uproot it.
[10]Though it is planted, will it thrive? When
the east wind touches it, won't it completely
wither? On the bed in which it was planted, it
will wither away.

[11]The LORD's word came to me: [12]Say
now to the rebellious household: Don't you
know what these things mean? Say: The
king of Babylon came to Jerusalem and carried its king and its officers away with him
to Babylon. [13]Then he took a prince from
the royal line, made an agreement with
him, and made him take a solemn pledge

[z]Syr; MT *Aram* [a]LXX; MT *you*

of loyalty. He also took away the land's officials. 14 Thus it would be a lowly kingdom, not asserting its own interests but observing the agreement so that it would survive. 15 But the prince rebelled against him and sent messengers to Egypt to supply him with horses and a great army. Can such a person succeed? Can one who does these things escape? Can he overturn the agreement and escape capture? 16 As surely as I live, says the LORD God, he will die in Babylon, in the place of the king who gave him the authority to rule, whose solemn pledge he scorned and whose agreement he overturned. 17 Pharaoh won't help him. There will be no strong force or mighty army in battle when siege ramps are set up and towers are built to eliminate many lives. 18 He scorned the solemn pledge and overturned the agreement! Even though he made a promise, he did all these things, and he won't escape capture. 19 So now the LORD God proclaims: As surely as I live, it was my solemn pledge that he scorned and my agreement that he overturned, and I will hold him accountable. 20 I will spread my net over him, and he will be caught in my trap. I will bring him to Babylon, and I myself will enter into judgment with him there for rebelling against me. 21 All his elite fighters[b] along with all his troops will fall by the sword, and those who are left will be scattered to the winds. Then you will know that I, the LORD, have spoken.

22 The LORD God proclaims: I myself will take one of the top branches from the tall cedar. I will pluck a tender shoot from its crown, and I myself will plant it on a very high and lofty mountain. 23 On Israel's mountainous highlands I will plant it, and it will send out branches and bear fruit. It will grow into a mighty cedar. Birds of every kind will nest in it and find shelter in the shade of its boughs. 24 Then all the trees in the countryside will know that I, the LORD, bring down the tall tree and raise up the lowly tree, and make the green tree wither and the dry tree bloom. I, the LORD, have spoken, and I will do it.

Sins of parents and children

18 The LORD's word came to me: 2 What do you mean by this proverb of yours about the land of Israel: "When parents eat unripe grapes, the children's teeth suffer"? 3 As surely as I live, says the LORD God, no longer will you use this proverb in Israel! 4 All lives are mine; the life of the parent and the life of the child belong to me. Only the one who sins will die.

5 People are declared innocent when they act justly and responsibly. 6 They don't eat on the hills or give their attention to the idols of the house of Israel. They don't defile the wives of their neighbors or approach menstruating women. 7 They don't cheat anyone, but fulfill their obligations. They don't rob others, but give food to the hungry and clothes to the naked. 8 They don't impose interest or take profit. They refrain from evil and settle cases between people fairly. 9 They follow my regulations, keep my case laws, and act faithfully. Such people are innocent, and they will live, proclaims the LORD God.

10 But suppose one of them has a violent child who sheds blood or does any one of these things, 11 even though his parents didn't do any of them. He eats on the mountains, defiles his neighbor's wife, 12 oppresses the poor and needy, robs others and doesn't fulfill his obligations, pays attention to the idols and does detestable things, 13 and takes interest and profit. Should he live? He should not. He engaged in all these detestable practices. He will surely die, and his blood will be on him.

14 But suppose he has a child who sees all the sins that his father committed. He becomes alarmed and doesn't do them. 15 He doesn't eat on the mountains or pay attention to the idols of the house of Israel. He doesn't defile his neighbor's wife. 16 He doesn't cheat anyone, either by seizing collateral for loans or committing robbery. He gives his food to the hungry and clothes to the naked. 17 He refrains from oppressing the poor by taking neither interest nor profit. He observes my case laws and follows

[b] LXX, Syr, Tg; MT *his fugitives*

my regulations. He won't die because of
his father's guilt. He will surely live. 18As
for his father: If he exploited the weak or
committed robbery, or did anything else
that wasn't good for the people, he will die
because of his own guilt.
19You will say, "Why doesn't the child
bear his parent's guilt?" The child has acted
justly and responsibly. The child kept all my
regulations and observed them. The child
will surely live. 20Only the one who sins will
die. A child won't bear a parent's guilt, and a
parent won't bear a child's guilt. Those who
do right will be declared innocent, and the
wicked will be declared guilty.
21But if the wicked turn away from all the
sins that they have committed, keep all my
regulations, and act justly and responsibly,
they will surely live and not die. 22None of
the sins that they committed will be held
against them, but they will live because
they do the right things. 23Do I take pleasure in the death of the wicked? says the
LORD God. Certainly not! If they change
their ways, they will live.
24If those who do the right thing turn
from righteousness and engage in the
same detestable practices that the wicked
committed, can they do these things and
live? None of their righteous deeds will
be remembered. They will die because of
their treacheries and sins. 25But you say,
"My Lord's way doesn't measure up." Listen, house of Israel, is it my ways that
don't measure up? Isn't it your ways that
don't measure up? 26When those who do
the right thing turn from their responsible ways and act maliciously, they will
die because of it. For their malicious acts
they will die. 27And when the wicked turn
from their wicked deeds and act justly and
responsibly, they will preserve their lives.
28When they become alarmed and turn
away from all their sins, they will surely
live; they won't die. 29Yet the house of
Israel says, "My Lord's way doesn't measure up." Is it my ways that don't measure
up? Isn't it your ways that don't measure
up, house of Israel? 30Therefore, I will
judge each of you according to your ways,
house of Israel. This is what the LORD God
says. Turn, turn away from all your sins.
Don't let them be sinful obstacles for you.
31Abandon all of your repeated sins. Make
yourselves a new heart and a new spirit.
Why should you die, house of Israel? 32I
most certainly don't want anyone to die!
This is what the LORD God says. Change
your ways, and live!

A mother's sons

19 You, raise a lament for Israel's
princes. 2Say:

What a lioness among lionesses
was your mother!
She bedded down among the strong
young lions and reared her cubs.
3She singled out one of her cubs,
and he became a strong young lion;
he learned to tear flesh
and devour humans.
4When the nations heard about him,
they caught him in their trap
and carried him with hooks
to the land of Egypt.
5When she realized that she waited in vain,
her hope faded.
So she took another of her cubs
and set him up as a strong young lion.
6He went on the prowl with the other
lions and became a strong young lion.
He learned to tear flesh
and devour humans;
7he ravaged[c] their widows
and laid waste to their cities.
When the earth and everything in it
became horrified by the sound
of his raging,
8the nations from the surrounding
regions allied against him.
They cast their nets over him
and caught him in their trap.
9They put a collar on him
and brought him with hooks.
They brought him with nets
to the king of Babylon
so that his voice would no longer be
heard on the mountains of Israel.

[c] Or *knew*

The proud mother

10 Your mother was like a vine in a
vineyard[d] planted beside the waters;
she bore lush fruit and foliage
because of the plentiful water,
11 and she produced mighty branches,
fit for rulers' scepters.
She grew tall, and her crown
went up between the clouds.
Because of her height and thick growth,
she became conspicuous.
12 So she was struck down in anger,
thrown down to the ground.
The east wind dried her out
and destroyed her fruit;
it sapped the branch of its strength,
and fire consumed it.
13 So now she is planted in the desert,
in a parched and thirsty land,
14 and fire has gone out from her branch
and consumed her foliage and fruit,
leaving her no strong branch
or ruler's scepter.

This is a lamentation, and it will serve as a lamentation.

History of rebellion

20 In the seventh year, on the tenth day of the fifth month, some of Israel's elders came to inquire of the LORD. As they were sitting with me, 2 the LORD's word came to me: 3 Human one, speak to Israel's elders and say to them, The LORD God proclaims: Have you come to petition me? As surely as I live, I reject your petitions. This is what the LORD God says! 4 Will you judge them, human one, will you judge them? Then expose to them the detestable practices of their ancestors. 5 Say to them, The LORD God proclaims: On the day I chose Israel, I swore a solemn pledge to the descendants of Jacob's household. When I made myself known to them in the land of Egypt, I swore a solemn pledge: I am the LORD your God. 6 On that day I swore that I would lead them out of the land of Egypt to a land that I would show them, a land full of milk and honey, the most splendid of all lands. 7 And I said to them, Every one of you must cast away your disgusting things. Don't let yourselves be defiled by Egypt's idols. I am the LORD your God. 8 But they rebelled against me and refused to listen to me. No one cast off their disgusting things or abandoned their Egyptian idols. So I declared that I would pour out my wrath on them and satisfy my anger against them in the land of Egypt. 9 But I acted for my name's sake, so that it wouldn't be degraded in the sight of the nations among whom they lived, and in whose sight I made it known that I would lead them out of the land of Egypt.

10 So I led them out of the land of Egypt and brought them into the desert. 11 I gave them my regulations and made known to them my case laws, which bring life to all who observe them. 12 I also gave them my sabbaths as a sign between us that I, the LORD, have set them apart for my purpose.[e] 13 But the house of Israel rebelled against me in the desert. They didn't follow my regulations and rejected my case laws, which bring life to all who observe them. They completely degraded my sabbaths. So I declared that I would pour out my anger against them and destroy them in the desert. 14 But instead, I acted for the sake of my name so that it wouldn't be degraded in the sight of the nations who saw me lead them out of Egypt. 15 So in the desert I swore another solemn pledge, that I wouldn't bring them to the land that I had given to them, a land full of milk and honey, a land more splendid than any other, 16 because they rejected my case laws, didn't follow my regulations, and degraded my sabbaths. They had their hearts set on their idols. 17 But I had too much compassion to destroy them, so I didn't put an end to them in the desert.

18 In the desert, I said to their children, Don't follow your parents' regulations or observe their case laws or become defiled by their idols. 19 I am the LORD your God! Follow my regulations! Observe my case laws and do them! 20 Make my sabbaths holy, and let them be a sign between us that

[d] Or *in your blood* [e] Or *to make them holy*

I am the LORD your God. 21But the children rebelled against me. They didn't follow my regulations or observe my case laws, which bring life to all who observe them. They also degraded my sabbaths. So I declared that I would pour out my wrath on them and satisfy my anger against them in the desert. 22But I restrained myself and acted for the sake of my name so that it wouldn't be diminished in the sight of the nations who saw me lead them out of Egypt. 23And I swore yet another solemn pledge in the desert, that I would disperse them among the nations and scatter them throughout the earth, 24because they didn't observe my case laws, they rejected my regulations, and they degraded my sabbaths while they kept looking to their parents' idols. 25I also issued regulations that were not good and case laws by which they could not live. 26I defiled them with their very gifts when they offered up all their oldest children. They were supposed to be so horrified that they would acknowledge that I am the LORD.

27Therefore, human one, speak to the house of Israel and say to them, The LORD God proclaims: Yet again your ancestors defamed me by rebelling against me! 28I brought them into the land that I swore to give to them. But when they saw all the high hills and lofty trees, there they made their sacrifices: irksome offerings here, pleasing aromas there, and drink offerings elsewhere! 29I said to them, What shrine are you going to now? So it's called Shrine[f] to this very day.

30So now say to the house of Israel, The LORD God proclaims: Will you defile yourselves as your ancestors did, and will you prostitute yourself after their disgusting things? 31When you offer up your gifts and make your children pass through the fire, you defile yourselves with all your idols to this very day. Should I let you seek me out, house of Israel? This is what the LORD God says: As surely as I live, I won't let you seek me. 32What is in your minds will never happen! You've been saying, "Let's be like the nations and the clans of the lands in the service of wood and stone." 33This is what the LORD God says: As surely as I live, with a strong hand, an outstretched arm, and with wrath poured out, I will be your king! 34I will lead you out from the peoples and gather you from the countries where you've been scattered—yes, with a strong hand and an outstretched arm and with wrath poured out! 35I will march you out to the wilderness nations, and there I will judge you face-to-face. 36Just as I judged your ancestors in the desert of the land of Egypt, so will I judge you. This is what the LORD God says. 37I will make you walk under the rod, and I will bring you into the covenant bond. 38I will remove from among you those who rebel and transgress against me. I will lead them out from the land where they lived as immigrants, but they won't enter Israel's fertile land. Then you will know that I am the LORD.

39But to you, house of Israel, the LORD God proclaims: Go ahead and serve your idols, all of you! But afterward, if any of you are left to listen to me,[g] you will no longer make my holy name impure with your gifts or your idols! 40On my holy mountain, on the high mountain in Israel, the whole house of Israel will serve me there—every one of them in the land! This is what the LORD God says. There I will accept them, and there I will ask for their offerings, their finest gifts, and all their holy things. 41When I bring you out from the nations and gather you from the countries where you are scattered, I will accept you as a pleasing aroma. Through you I will be made holy in the sight of the nations. 42Then you will know that I am the LORD, when I bring you to Israel's fertile land, to the land that I swore to give to your ancestors. 43There you will remember how your ways and all your wicked deeds defiled you, and you will loathe yourselves for all the wicked things that you've done. 44Then, house of Israel, you will know that I am the LORD, when I deal with you for the sake of my name and not according to your wicked ways and ruinous deeds. This is what the LORD God says.

[f]Heb sounds like *Where are you going?* [g]Heb uncertain

Fire in the southern plain

45 [h]The LORD's word came to me: 46 Human one, face Teman, preach against the south, and prophesy against the thicket in the arid southern plain. 47 Say to the thicket in the arid southern plain: Hear the LORD God's word. This is what the LORD God says: I'm about to set a fire in you, and it will consume every green and every dry tree in you. Its blazing flame won't be put out, and everything from south to north will be scorched. 48 Everyone will see that I, the LORD, have set it on fire. It won't be quenched. 49 Then I said, "Oh, LORD God! They say about me, 'Isn't he one for making metaphors?'"

The sword

21 [i]The LORD's word came to me: 2 Human one, face Jerusalem, preach against their sanctuary, and prophesy against Israel's fertile land. 3 Say to Israel's fertile land, The LORD proclaims: I'm now against you! I will draw my sword from its sheath and cut off both the righteous and the wicked from you. 4 In order to cut off the righteous and wicked from you, my sword will go out from its sheath against everyone from south to north. 5 And everyone will know that I, the LORD, have taken my sword out of its sheath. It won't be put away again.

6 You, human one, groan in their sight; groan bitterly with trembling knees. 7 If they ask you why you're groaning, say to them, "Because of the news." When it comes, every heart will despair, every hand will hang lifeless, every spirit will be listless, and urine will run down every leg. It's coming! It will happen! This is what the LORD God says.

The sword dance

8 The LORD's word came to me: 9 Human one, prophesy! Say, The Lord proclaims! Say:

A sword! A sharp and polished sword!
10 For utter slaughter it is sharpened,
polished to flash like lightning.
Let's not rejoice,
because no one will escape the purge.[j]
11 He appoints it for polishing,
to seize in the hand.
The sword is sharpened, it is polished;
it is ready for the destroyer's hand.
12 Human one, cry aloud, and wail,
for it comes against my people,
against all of Israel's princes,
handed over to the sword
along with my people.
Therefore, strike your thigh.
13 He's testing.
When even the rod rejects,
will it not certainly happen?[k]
This is what the LORD God says.
14 And you, human one, prophesy!
Strike hand to hand.
Let the sword strike twice, three times!
It's a deadly sword,
a great deadly sword.
It whirls around them
15 to make hearts shudder,
to make many stumble and fall.
I've set the slaughtering sword
against all their gates.
Oh! It's crafted to flash like lightning,
polished for slaughter!
16 Stab again and again! Plunge right,
plunge left, wherever your edge goes.
17 It is I who strike hand to hand!
I'll satisfy my wrath!
I, the LORD, have spoken.

Guilt remembered

18 The LORD's word came to me: 19 You, human one, mark two roads for the coming of the sword of the king of Babylon. They should diverge from a single country. Where the road to the city begins, set up a sign, 20 and point out the way for the sword to come: "To Rabbah of the Ammonites" or "To Judah in its stronghold Jerusalem." 21 The king of Babylon stands at the fork in the road where the two roads begin and performs his divinations. He shakes the arrows, consults the divine images, and inspects the liver. 22 On his right side appeared the omen for Jerusalem: to put battering rams in place, to proclaim war and raise the alarm, to place battering rams against the gates, and to set up siege ramps and build

[h]21:1 in Heb [i]21:6 in Heb [j]Heb uncertain [k]Heb uncertain

towers. 23 It seems to them like a lying divination, because solemn pledges had been
sworn to them. But he will remind them of
their guilt, and they will be captured.
24 So the LORD God proclaims: Now that
you have remembered your guilt and your
treacheries are exposed, your sins can be
seen in everything you do. Because you
have brought your guilt to light, you will
be captured! 25 But you vile, wicked prince
of Israel whose day has come, the time of
final punishment, 26 this is what the LORD
God says: Remove the turban, take off the
crown! Nothing will be as it was. Bring
down the exalted, and exalt the lowly. 27 A
ruin, ruin, ruin, I'll make it! Such a thing
has never happened! Even before the rightful judge comes, I've handed it over to him.

Avenging Ammon's disgrace

28 You, human one, prophesy and say,
The LORD God proclaims to the Ammonites concerning their disgrace. Say,
Sword! Sword unsheathed for slaughter,
burnished, battle-ready,[l] flashing like lightning: 29 False visions and lying divinations
set you against the necks of vile, wicked
men whose day had come, the time of final
punishment. 30 Return it to its sheath. In
the place where you were created, in the
land of your origin, I will judge you. 31 I will
pour out my wrath against you. With a raging fire I will blow against you, and I will
hand you over to those who burn and forge
destruction. 32 Fire will consume you, your
blood will sink into the earth, and you will
no longer be remembered. I, the LORD, have
spoken.

Bloody city

22 The LORD's word came to me: 2 You,
human one, will you judge? Will you
judge the bloody city? Then explain all her
detestable practices to her. 3 Say, The LORD
God proclaims: City, self-destructive blood-
letter, self-defiling idol maker: 4 All the blood
that you've shed is your punishment, and
all the idols that you've made are your defilement. This is how you've shortened your
days and hastened the end[m] of your years!
For this reason I've given you over to the
ridicule of nations and the derision of every
land. 5 Those from near and far will mock
your infamous name and great chaos. 6 Look,
Israel's princes, every one of them, have
joined forces to shed blood in you. 7 In you
they treat father and mother with contempt.
In you they oppress immigrants and deny the
rights of orphans and widows. 8 You despise
my holy things and degrade my sabbaths.
9 In you slanderers show up to shed blood. In
you they eat on the mountains. In you they
do obscene things. 10 In you a father's nakedness is uncovered. In you menstruating
women are violated. 11 Every man engages in
detestable practices with his neighbor's wife,
every man defiles his daughter-in-law with
obscene acts, and every man violates his sister, his own father's daughter. 12 In you they
take bribes to shed blood. You collect interest and fees, you profit by extorting your
neighbor, and you neglect even me! This is
what the LORD God says.
13 I now strike my hands over your ill-
gotten gain and blood that's been shed
in you. 14 Will your strength and courage
endure when I deal with you? I am the
LORD: I speak, and I act! 15 I will scatter
you among the nations and disperse you
throughout the lands, and so I will remove
your uncleanness from you. 16 When you
are degraded[n] like this in the sight of the
nations, then you will know that I am the
LORD.
17 The LORD's word came to me: 18 Human
one, the house of Israel has become a waste
product for me. They are all copper, tin,
iron, and lead. In the furnace, they've become the waste product of silver. 19 So this is
what the LORD God says: Because you've all
become a waste product, I'm now gathering
you into the middle of Jerusalem. 20 Just
as silver, copper, iron, lead, and tin are collected and placed in a furnace to fan the
flames under them and melt them down, so
in my anger and rage I will collect you, put
you in, and melt you down. 21 I will gather
you, fan the flames of my wrath under you,

[l] Or *to take in the hand* [m] LXX, Syr; Vulg *time*; MT *until* [n] MT adds *in you.*

and melt you down in the middle of it. [22]As silver is melted in a furnace, so you will be melted in it. You will know that I, the LORD, have poured out my rage on you.

[23]The LORD's word came to me: [24]Human one, say to her, You are an unclean land without rain on the day of reckoning. [25]The conspiracy of princes° in her is like a roaring lion ripping up prey. They've piled up wealth and precious goods and made many widows in her. [26]Her priests have done violence to my instructions and made my holy things impure. They have not clearly separated the holy from the ordinary, and they have not taught the difference between unclean and clean things. They've disregarded my sabbaths. So I've been degraded among them. [27]The officials in her are like wolves ripping up prey. They shed blood and destroy lives for unjust riches. [28]Her prophets have whitewashed everything for them, seeing false visions and making wrong predictions for them, saying, "This is what the LORD God says," when the LORD hasn't spoken. [29]The important people of the land have practiced extortion and have committed robbery. They've oppressed the poor and mistreated the immigrant. They've oppressed and denied justice. [30]I looked for anyone to repair the wall and stand in the gap for me on behalf of the land, so I wouldn't have to destroy it. But I couldn't find anyone. [31]So I've poured out my anger on them. With my furious fire I've finished them off. I've held them accountable. This is what the LORD God proclaims.

Two sisters

23 The LORD's word came to me: [2]Human one, there were two women, daughters of one woman. [3]When they were girls in Egypt, they began to prostitute themselves by allowing their young and nubile breasts to be touched and fondled. [4]The older sister was named Oholah, and the younger sister was named Oholibah. They became mine and gave birth to sons and daughters. Now Oholah is Samaria, and Oholibah is Jerusalem. [5]But Oholah became unfaithful to me and lusted after her lovers the Assyrians: [6]warriors dressed in fine blue cloth, governors and officers, charioteers and horsemen, all of them the most handsome of men. [7]She sought them out to seduce them, all of them men of the highest rank of Assyria. She defiled herself by everyone she lusted after and also by all their idols. [8]But she never gave up her promiscuities with the Egyptians, who had slept with her in her girlhood and fondled her nubile breasts, and who continued to seduce her. [9]Therefore, I handed her over to her lovers, to the Assyrians for whom she lusted. [10]They stripped her naked, took her sons and daughters, and killed her with the sword. And she became notorious among women for the punishments they enacted against her.

[11]Her sister Oholibah saw it, and she proceeded to outdo her sister in her lust and in her seductions. [12]She lusted after the Assyrians, governors and officers, warriors richly clothed, charioteers and horsemen, all of them the most handsome of men. [13]I saw that she too defiled herself. Both had the same tendencies, [14]but she was even more promiscuous. She saw men carved in wall reliefs, images of Chaldeans outlined in vermilion, [15]wearing only loincloths around their hips and flowing headbands on their heads. All of them had the appearance of warriors of the third rank, the likeness of Babylonians whose native land is Chaldea. [16]Aroused just by looking at them, she sent messengers to them in Chaldea. [17]The Babylonians came to her to lie down and make love with her, defiling her with their seductions. But once she had defiled herself with them, she recoiled from them in disgust. [18]When her seductions became known and her nakedness exposed, I recoiled from her just as I had recoiled from her sister. [19]But she added to her promiscuities, bringing to mind her youthful days when she was a prostitute in the land of Egypt. [20]She lusted after their male consorts, whose sexual organs were like those of donkeys, and whose ejaculation was like that of horses.

°LXX; MT *prophets*

[21]She relived the wicked days of her youth, when the Egyptians touched and fondled her young and nubile breasts.

[22]So Oholibah, the LORD God proclaims: I'm now inciting your lovers against you, all those from whom you recoiled, and I will bring them against you from all around— [23]Babylonians and all the Chaldeans, Pekod and Shoa and Koa, all the Assyrians with them, the most handsome young men, all of them governors and officers, career officers and conscripts, all of them on horseback. [24]They will come against you with weapons,[p] chariots, and wagons, and with a great army, with shield, buckler, and helmet; and they will surround you. I will hand your punishment over to them, and they will judge you according to their laws. [25]I will direct my passion against you, and they will deal with you in wrath. They will cut off your nose and ears, and those who are left will fall by the sword. They will seize your sons and daughters, and those who are left will be burned with fire. [26]They will strip your clothing from you and remove your beautiful crown. [27]That's how I will put an end to your lewdness and your Egyptian-styled promiscuity. Never again will you stare at them, and you won't remember Egypt anymore. [28]The LORD God proclaims: I'm now handing you over to those whom you hate and from whom you recoil. [29]They will deal hatefully with you: They will seize your pay and leave you completely naked. Your promiscuity, betrayal, and seductions will be exposed. [30]This will be done to you because you sold yourself to the nations and became defiled by their idols. [31]You followed in your sister's path, so I have put her cup into your hand.

[32]The LORD God proclaims:

Deep and wide is your sister's cup. Drink!
  Appointed for abuse and scorn,
    it overflows.
[33]You will be filled with drunken sadness.
  A cup of devastation and dismay
    is the cup of your sister Samaria.
[34]Drink it, drain it dry,
  break it into pieces,
  and tear off your breasts,
    for I have spoken.
This is what the LORD God says.

[35]So now the LORD God proclaims: Because you forgot me and turned your back on me, you alone will bear the consequences of your betrayal and promiscuities.

[36]Then the LORD said to me, Human one, judge Oholah and Oholibah, and make known their detestable practices to them. [37]They committed adultery, so now blood is on their hands. They committed adultery with their idols, and they even took their children whom they had borne to me and offered them up to be consumed for them. [38]They also did this to me: On the same day, they made my sanctuary unclean and made my sabbaths impure. [39]When they slaughtered their children for their idols, they came into my sanctuary and made it impure on that very same day. They actually did this inside my temple. [40]They even sent for men who came from a great distance. No sooner than a messenger was sent, they arrived! For these men you bathed, you painted your eyes, and you put on your jewelry. [41]You took your place on a splendid couch with a richly set table in front of it, and you set my incense and my oil on it. [42]The sound of a noisy crowd was around her. Men from the common multitude, drinkers of wine, were brought from the desert. They put bracelets on their wrists and beautiful crowns on their heads. [43]Then I thought, For a foolish woman they become adulterers! Incited by her seduction, they prostitute themselves—for her![q] [44]They come as if coming to a prostitute, first to Oholah, and then to Oholibah, those traitorous women. [45]But men who do the right thing will judge them, and they will be punished as adulterers and murderers, because they are in fact adulterers, and blood is on their hands.

[46]The LORD God proclaims: Bring up an assembly against them, and decree terror and plunder for them. [47]Let the assembly stone them! Let them carve them up with their swords, slay their sons and daughters, and burn their houses with fire! [48]So I will

[p]Heb uncertain [q]Heb uncertain

put an end to betrayal in the land. Taking warning, no woman will betray as you have done. [49]You will be held accountable for your betrayals, and you will bear the sins of your idols. Then you will know that I am the LORD God.

The useless pot

24 In the ninth year, on the tenth day of the tenth month, the LORD's word came to me: [2]Human one, write down today's date, because today the king of Babylon has set up camp at Jerusalem—today! [3]Compose a parable for the rebels' household and say to them, The LORD God proclaims:

Put on the pot, set it on,
and fill it with water.
[4]Add meat to it,
every good piece.
With shoulder and thigh,
the meatiest bones, fill it up.
[5]Take the flock's best animal;
arrange the wood[r] beneath it.
Bring it to a rolling boil,
and cook its bones in it.

[6]The LORD God proclaims: Horror! You bloody city, you corroded pot; pot whose corrosion can't be removed! Empty it piece by piece. She is rejected[s] [7]because her blood is still with her. She didn't pour it out on the ground so that it could be covered with dirt, but she spread it out on a bare rock. [8]In order to arouse wrath, to guarantee vengeance, I will spread her blood on a bare rock, never to be covered.

[9]So now the LORD God proclaims:
Horror! You bloody city!
I myself will add fuel to the fire!
[10]Pile on the wood, light the fire,
and cook the meat.
Season it well and let the bones be charred.
[11]Let the pot stand empty on its coals
until it's so hot that its copper glows,
its impurities melt in it,
and its corrosion is consumed.
[12]It's a worthless task.
Even by fire its great corrosion
isn't removed.

[13]How your betrayals defile you! I cleansed you, but you didn't come clean from your impurities. You won't be clean again until I have exhausted my anger against you. [14]I, the LORD, have spoken! It's coming, and I'll do it. I won't relent or have any pity or compassion. Your punishments will fit your ways and your deeds! This is what the LORD God says.

Ezekiel's wife dies

[15]The LORD's word came to me: [16]Human one, I am about to take the delight of your eyes away from you in a single stroke. Don't mourn or weep. Don't even let your tears well up. [17]Sigh inwardly; be deathly still. Don't perform mourning rites, but bind on your turban and put your shoes on your feet. And don't cover your upper lip or eat in human company.

[18]I spoke with the people in the morning, and by evening my wife was dead. The next morning I did as I was commanded. [19]The people asked, "Won't you tell us what your actions mean for us?"

[20]So I said to them, The LORD's word came to me: [21]Say to the house of Israel, the LORD God proclaims: I'm about to make my sanctuary impure, the pride of your strength, the delight of your eyes. Your heart's desire, the sons and daughters you left behind, will fall by the sword. [22]You will do as I have done. You will neither cover your upper lip nor eat in human company. [23]Your turbans will be on your heads, your sandals on your feet. You won't mourn or weep. You will waste away in your guilt, all of you groaning to each other. [24]Ezekiel is your sign. You will do everything that he has done. When this happens, you will know that I am the LORD God.

[25]And you, human one: On the day that I take from them their proud stronghold—their crowning joy, the delight of their eyes—and their sons and daughters, whose fate weighs on them, [26]on that day, a refugee will come to you so that you yourself will hear the news. [27]On that day your mouth will be opened to the refugee, and you will speak and no longer be silent. You will be their sign, and they will know that I am the LORD.

[r]Or *bones* [s]Or *the lot did not fall to her*

Against the neighboring nations

25 The LORD's word came to me:
2 Human one, face the Ammonites
and prophesy against them. 3 Say to the Ammonites: Hear the LORD God's word! The
LORD God proclaims: You laughed when
my sanctuary was degraded, when Israel's
fertile land was laid waste, and when the
house of Judah went into exile; 4 therefore,
I'm handing you over to people in the east
for them to take possession. They will set
up their encampments against you, establish residence, devour your fruit, and drink
your milk. 5 I'll make Rabbah into pastureland for camels and Ammon a resting place
for flocks. Then you will know that I am the
LORD.

6 The LORD God proclaims: Because you
clapped your hands and stamped your feet
when you rejoiced with utter contempt for
Israel's fertile land, 7 I'm about to overpower
you. Nations will plunder you. I will cut you
off from the peoples, remove you from the
lands, and utterly destroy you. Then you
will know that I am the LORD.

8 The LORD God proclaims: Because
Moab and Seir say, "Aha! The house of
Judah has become like all the nations," 9 I'll
open up the flank of Moab from the cities at
its border, the land's splendid cities, Beth-
jeshimoth, Baal-meon, and Kiriathaim.
10 I'll hand it over, along with the Ammonites, to people in the east for them to take
possession. And so Ammon will no longer
be remembered among the nations. 11 I'll
execute judgments in Moab, and they will
know that I am the LORD.

12 The LORD God proclaims: Edom acted
with excessive force against the house of
Judah. The Judeans were guilty, but Edom's
vengeance was excessive. 13 So the LORD
God now proclaims: I'll overpower Edom,
eliminate all living creatures, and make it a
wasteland from Teman to Dedan. They will
fall by the sword. 14 I will execute my vengeance in Edom through my people Israel's
power. They will act in Edom according to
my anger and fury, and they will know my
vengeance. This is what the LORD God says.

15 The LORD God proclaims: When the
Philistines set out to right the wrongs done
to them, they enacted revenge with utter
contempt and old hatreds. 16 So now the
LORD God proclaims: I will overpower the
Philistines, eliminate the Cherethites, and
obliterate all who are left along the coast-
line. 17 I will act against them with great
vengeance and with wrathful punishments.
When I execute my vengeance against
them, they will know that I am the LORD.

Against Tyre

26 In the eleventh year, on the first day
of the month, the LORD's word came
to me:

2 Human one,
because Tyre laughed at Jerusalem:
"The gate of the peoples is broken,
she lies open before me,
she is destroyed, but I will succeed!"

3 The LORD God now proclaims:
Tyre, I'm now against you!
Just as the sea hurls up its waves,
I will bring many nations
up against you.
4 When they destroy the walls of Tyre
and throw down its towers,
I will scrape off all its dirt
and make it into a bare rock,
5 a place for drying nets
in the middle of the sea.
I have spoken!
This is what the LORD God says.
It will become prey for the nations,
6 and its towns around it
will be put to the sword.
Then they will know
that I am the LORD.

7 The LORD God proclaims:
I'm bringing Nebuchadrezzar
against Tyre,
the king of Babylon from the north,
the greatest of all kings,
with horses, chariots, and charioteers,
an assembly, a great army.
8 The towns around you
he will destroy with the sword.
Then he will build towers against you,
erect siege ramps against you,
and set up shields.

9 He will pound his battering ram
against your walls;
with crowbars he will tear down
your towers.
10 The dust from all his horses will cover you
when he enters your gates
as one who enters a breached city.
Your walls will quake
at the thundering of the charioteers
and chariot wheels.
11 His horses' hooves will trample
all your courtyards;
he will cut down your people
with the sword,
and the monuments to your strength
he will bring down[t] to the ground.
12 They will destroy your wealth,
plunder your goods,
tear down your walls,
and raze your fine houses.
Your stone, lumber, and rubble
they will dump into the sea.

13 I will bring an end
to your cacophonous songs;
the sound of your lyres
will never be heard again.
14 I will make you into a bare rock,
a place for drying nets,
and you will never be rebuilt.
I, the LORD, have spoken.
This is what the LORD God says.

A lament for Tyre

15 The LORD God proclaims to Tyre: Won't the coastlands quake at the news of your downfall, when the wounded groan, and when the slaughter in your midst goes on and on?
16 All the princes of the sea will come down from their thrones, remove their royal robes, and strip off their fine garments. They will be clothed only in terror as they sit on the ground. They will be so terrified, they won't stop shuddering because of you.
17 They will sing a lament for you, and they will say:

How you have perished, queen of the sea,
city once praised,
who once dominated the sea,
she and her rulers,
who spread their terror abroad,
every one of them.
18 Now the wastelands tremble
on the day of your fall.
Your expulsion horrifies
the islands of the sea.

19 The LORD God proclaims: When I turn you into ruins like uninhabitable cities, when the deep sea washes over you and the raging seas cover you,
20 I will lead you down into the pit, to the everlasting people. I will install you in the world below,[u] in the everlasting ruins, with those who go down to the pit. And so you will neither rule nor radiate splendor in the land of the living.
21 I will terrify you, and you will disappear. You will be sought but never found again. This is what the LORD God says.

Tyre, the ship of state

27 The LORD's word came to me:
2 You, human one, sing a lament for Tyre.
3 Say this about Tyre, who sits enthroned at the entrance to the sea, the people's agent for trade throughout the coastlands. The LORD God proclaims:

Tyre, you say,
"I'm perfectly beautiful!"
4 But your territory is
in the depths of the sea,
and it's your builders
who made you beautiful.
5 For you they made your deck
of cypress from Senir.
To make your mast,
they took cedar from Lebanon.
6 For your oars,
they used the oaks of Bashan.
They made your hull, inlaid with ivory,
of boxwood from the coasts of Cyprus.
7 Fine embroidered linen from Egypt
was your sail;
it became your emblem.
Your awning was made of blue and
purple cloth from the coasts of Elishah.

8 The princes of Sidon and Arvad were your oarsmen. Your own wise men were in you as your helmsmen.
9 The elders and wise men of Gebal were in you, patching up your

[t] LXX; MT *it will fall* [u] Or *the land of the lowest places*

leaks. Every seagoing ship and its sailors came to do business with you. [10]Paras, Lud, and Put were the warriors in your army. By hanging their shields and helmets on you, they made you radiant. [11]The men of Arvad and Helech were stationed on your walls all around; the men of Gamad were in your towers. They hung their weapons on your walls all around. They were the ones who completed your beauty.

[12]Tarshish was your procurer of great wealth. For your wares, they exchanged silver, iron, tin, and lead. [13]Javan, Tubal, and Meshech were your agents in human trafficking. They gave you bronze vessels for these wares of yours. [14]Beth-togarmah traded horses, warhorses, and mules for your wares. [15]Islanders from Rhodes[v] were your agents. By contract they procured ebony and ivory for you from many coastlands. [16]Aram was your agent for many products. They traded turquoise, purple cloth, colorful brocades, linen, coral, and rubies for your wares. [17]Judah and the land of Israel were your agents, trading the finest wheat,[w] millet,[x] honey, oil, and balm for your wares. [18]For many of your finished products, Damascus traded out of its great wealth the wine of Helbon and white wool. [19]Vedan and Javan from the region of Uzal traded with you. They exchanged wrought iron, cinnamon, and spices for your wares. [20]Dedan was your agent for saddle blankets. [21]Arabia and all the princes of Kedar traded for you. They procured lambs, rams, and goats for you. [22]They were your agents in Sheba and Raamah. For your wares they exchanged the finest spices, every kind of precious stone, and gold. [23]Haran, Canneh, and Eden were your agents,[y] and also Assyria and Chilmad. [24]They procured fine finished goods for you, garments of purple and brocade, and plush carpets rolled up and securely tied with ropes, among your acquisitions. [25]The ships of Tarshish carried your goods.

You were filled to capacity
and heavily laden
in the middle of the sea.

[26]Your oarsmen brought you out
onto the high seas;
an east wind sank you
into the sea's depths.
[27]Your goods, your wares, your wealth,
your sailors, your helmsmen,
those patching your leaks,
your merchants, all your warriors in you,
and all the company that is with you—
they also sank into the sea's depth
on the day of your demise.
[28]At your helmsmen's cries for help,
the troubled waters seethe.
[29]Those entrusted with the oars
desert their posts.
All sailors and helmsmen
seek footing on the shore.
[30]Loudly they cry,
bitterly they wail,
and they put dust on their heads
and cover themselves with ashes.
[31]They cut off all their hair
and put on mourning clothes.
In despair they weep for you,
and bitterly perform
the mourning rites.
[32]In their lamentation
they raise a lament for you;
they sing lamentions over you:
"Who was like Tyre,
silenced in the middle of the sea?"

[33]When your wares came out from the seas,
you satisfied many people.
Your abundant wealth and merchandise
enriched the kings of the earth.
[34]Now you are shattered by the seas;
your cargoes,
as well as everyone in your company,
are sunk into the water's depths.
[35]Now the inhabitants of the coastlands
shudder on account of you.
And as for their kings,
their hair stands on end;
their faces betray their horror.
[36]The merchants for the peoples
hiss because of you.
You have become a terror;
from now on you are nothing.

[v]Heb *Dedan* [w]Or *wheat from Minnith* [x]Heb uncertain [y]LXX; MT adds *Sheba*.

Prince of Tyre

28 The LORD's word came to me: [2]Human one, say to the prince of Tyre, The LORD God proclaims: In your arrogance, you say, "I am God, and as God I rule the seas!" Though you claim to have the mind of a god, you are mortal, not divine. [3]You are certainly wiser than Daniel; no secrets are hidden from you. [4]By your wisdom and discernment, you made yourself rich, and you filled your storehouses with silver and gold. [5]Through your shrewd trading you multiplied your riches. But then you became proud of your riches.

[6]So now the LORD God proclaims: Because you claim to have the mind of a god, [7]I'll bring foreigners, the most ruthless nations, against you. They will let loose their swords against your fine wisdom, and they will degrade your splendor. [8]They will hurl you to destruction, and you will die, murdered, on the high seas. [9]When you face your murderers, will you still say, "I'm God"? In your killers' hands, you are mortal, not divine. [10]You will die as the uncircumcised do, at the hands of foreigners. I have spoken. This is what the LORD God has said.

[11]The LORD's word came to me: [12]Human one, sing a lament for the king of Tyre. Say to him, The LORD God proclaims: You were full of wisdom and beauty, the image of perfection. [13]You were in Eden, God's garden. You were covered with gold and every precious stone: carnelian, topaz, and moonstone; beryl, onyx, and jasper; lapis lazuli, turquoise, and emerald. On the day that you were created, finely crafted pendants and engravings were prepared. [14]You, a winged creature, were installed as a guardian. I placed you in God's holy mountain where you walked among the stones of fire. [15]From the day you were created until injustice was found in you, your ways were assured. [16]But because of your trade, your oppressive business practices piled up, and you became impure. So I expelled you from God's mountain. I removed you, winged creature, guardian, from among the stones of fire. [17]You exalted yourself because of your beauty and corrupted your wisdom for the sake of your splendor. I will cast you down to the earth in the sight of kings, and I will make a spectacle of you. [18]Because of your corrupt trade, which surpassed your many other sins, you made your sanctuaries impure. Therefore, I will bring fire from your midst. When it has consumed you, I will turn you into dust on the earth in the sight of all who see you. [19]Everyone among the peoples who knows you will be appalled because of you. You will become a terror. From that time on, you will be nothing.

Against Sidon

[20]The LORD's word came to me: [21]Human one, face Sidon, prophesy against it, [22]and say, The LORD God proclaims: I'm against you, Sidon, and I will manifest my glory in you. When I've executed judgment against it and through it have manifested my holiness, they will know that I am the LORD. [23]I will hurl plague against it, and blood will run in its streets. When the sword comes against it from all sides, the slain will fall within it. Then they will know that I am the LORD. [24]The house of Israel will no longer suffer from the pricking thorn or painful briar of any of its neighbors who hold it in contempt. And they will know that I am the LORD God.

[25]The LORD God proclaims: When I gather the house of Israel from the peoples among whom they've scattered, and I demonstrate my holiness through them in the sight of the nations, they will live on their fertile land, which I gave to my servant Jacob. [26]They will live on it in safety. They will build houses, plant vineyards, and live in safety. When I execute judgments against all who hold them in contempt on every side, they will know that I, the LORD, am their God.

Against Egypt

29 In the tenth year, on the twelfth day of the tenth month, the LORD's word came to me: [2]Human one, face Pharaoh, Egypt's king, and prophesy against him and against all of Egypt. [3]Speak and say, The LORD God proclaims:

I'm against you,
  Pharaoh, Egypt's king,
  great crocodile lurking
  in the Nile's canals,

who says, "The Nile is all mine;
I made it for myself!"
4 I will set hooks in your jaws;
I will make the fish
from the Nile's canals
cling to your scales.
I will drag you out of the Nile's canals,
and also all the fish
from the Nile's canals
clinging to your scales.
5 I will fling you out into the desert,
and also all the fish
from the Nile's canals.
You will fall on the open ground,
and won't be gathered or retrieved.

I've given you to the beasts of the earth
and the birds in the sky for food.
6 Everyone living in Egypt
will know that I am the LORD.

Because they were a flimsy crutch for
the house of Israel—7 when they took you
in hand, you would splinter and make their
shoulders sore; when they leaned on you, you
would break, bringing them to their knees—
8 now the LORD God proclaims: I'm bringing
a sword against you, and I will cut off from
you human and beast. 9 The land of Egypt will
be turned into a wasteland and ruins. Then
they will know that I am the LORD.

Because you[z] said, "The Nile is mine;
I made it," 10 I'm against you and against
the Nile's canals. I will make the land of
Egypt into an utter ruin, a wasteland, from
Migdol to Syene and as far as its boundary
with Cush. 11 No foot, animal or human, will
walk across it, and it won't be inhabited for
forty years. 12 I will make the land of Egypt
the most desolate of wastelands and its cities the most devastated of ruined cities. It
will be a wasteland for forty years, and the
Egyptians will be scattered among the nations and dispersed throughout the lands.

13 The LORD God proclaims: At the end of
forty years, I will gather the Egyptians from
among the nations where they are scattered.
14 I will improve their circumstances and bring
them back to the land of Pathros, the land of
their origin. Egypt will be a lowly kingdom
there. 15 Out of all the kingdoms, it will be the
lowliest. It will never again exalt itself over
the nations, and I will make it small to keep it
from ruling the nations. 16 The house of Israel
will never again bring guilt on itself by faithlessly turning to Egypt for help, for they will
know that I am the LORD God.

17 In the twenty-seventh year, on the first
day of the first month, the LORD's word
came to me: 18 Human one, Babylon's King
Nebuchadrezzar made his army labor very
hard against Tyre. Every head was scraped
bald, and every shoulder was rubbed raw,
yet he got nothing from Tyre for himself or
for his army for any of his efforts against
it. 19 So now the LORD God proclaims: I'm
going to give the land of Egypt to Babylon's
King Nebuchadnezzar. He will carry off its
wealth, he will plunder and loot it, and it
will be the wages for his army. 20 I will give
him the land of Egypt as payment for his
laboring for me. This is what the LORD
God says.

21 On that day I will give new strength[a]
to the house of Israel, and I will open your
mouth among them. Then they will know
that I am the LORD.

30 The LORD's word came to me:
2 Human one, prophesy and say, The
LORD God proclaims:
Howl! Horror for the day!
3 The day is coming,
the day of the LORD comes,
a day of clouds:
the nations' time has come.
4 A sword will come into Egypt,
and trembling will overcome Cush,
when the slain fall in Egypt,
its wealth carried away,
and its foundations razed.
5 Cush, Put, and Lud,
all Arabia and Cub,
and the people from
the allied country[b] with them
will fall by the sword.

6 The LORD proclaims:
When Egypt's helpers fall,
its proud strength will decline.

[z] Or *he* [a] Or *make a horn sprout* [b] Or *land of the covenant*

From Migdol to Syene
they will fall by the sword.
This is what the LORD God says.
7Of all the lands laid waste, it will be the
most desolate; of all cities, the most ruined.
8They will know that I am the LORD. On the
day that I set fire to Egypt and all its helpers are broken, 9messengers in ships will
go out from me to startle the complacent
Cushites. Anguish will overcome them on
Egypt's day. It's certainly coming.
10The LORD God proclaims:
I will bring an end to the hordes of Egypt
through the power
of Babylon's King Nebuchadrezzar.
11He and his people with him,
the most terrible of the nations,
will be brought in to destroy the land.
They will draw their swords
against Egypt
and fill the land with the slain.
12I will dry up the Nile canals;
I will sell the land to evildoers.
With the help of foreigners
I will lay waste to the land
and everything in it.
I, the LORD, have spoken.
13The LORD God proclaims:
I will destroy the idols
and bring an end to the images
in Memphis.
Never again will there be
a prince from the land of Egypt;
so I will kindle fear in the land of Egypt.
14I will turn Pathros into a desolation,
set fire to Zoan,
and execute judgments in Thebes.
15I will pour out my anger on Pelusium,
the stronghold of Egypt,
and I will cut down pompous Thebes.
16I will set Egypt on fire;
Pelusium will writhe in travail,
Thebes will be split open,
Memphis assaulted in broad daylight.
17The elite troops of On and Pi-beseth
will fall by the sword,
and the cities themselves
will go into captivity.
18At Tehaphnehes the day will go dark
when I break Egypt's yoke and bring an end
to its proud strength. A cloud will cover it,
and the towns around it will go into captivity. 19I will execute judgments in Egypt, and
they will know that I am the LORD.
20In the eleventh year, on the first day of
the seventh month, the LORD's word came
to me: 21Human one, I've broken the arm
of Pharaoh, Egypt's king, and it hasn't been
set so that it might heal, nor has it been
braced or wrapped up so that it might be
strong enough to grasp a sword.
22So now the LORD God proclaims: I'm
against Pharaoh, and I will break his arms,
both the sound one and the broken one, and
I'll make the sword fall out of his hand. 23I
will scatter the Egyptians among the nations
and disperse them throughout the earth. 24I
will strengthen the arms of the king of Babylon, and I will put my sword into his hand.
When I break the arms of Pharaoh, he will
groan like a dying man in his presence. 25I
will strengthen the arms of the king of Babylon, but the arms of Pharaoh will fall. They
will know that I am the LORD, when I put
my sword into the hand of the king of Babylon and he uses it against the land of Egypt.
26When I scatter the Egyptians among the
nations and disperse them throughout the
earth, they will know that I am the LORD.

Egypt is not Assyria

31 In the eleventh year, on the first day
of the third month, the LORD's word
came to me: 2Human one, say to Pharaoh,
Egypt's king, and his troops:
With whom do you compare
in your greatness?
3Consider Assyria, a cedar of Lebanon:
beautiful branches, dense shade,
towering height;
indeed, its top went up
between the clouds.
4Waters nourished it; the deep raised it up,
because its streams flowed around
the place where it was planted.
From there, water trickled down
to all the other trees of the field.
5And so it became higher than
all the trees of the field.
Its branches became abundant;
its boughs grew long.

Because of the plentiful water,
it grew freely.
6 All the birds in the sky
made nests in its branches;
all the beasts of the field
gave birth under its boughs,
and in its shade,
every great nation lived.
7 It became beautiful in its greatness
and in its lush foliage,
because it took root in plentiful water.
8 No cedar was its equal in God's garden.
The fir trees didn't have anything
like its branches,
and the plane trees had nothing
like its boughs.
None of the trees in God's garden
could compare to it in its beauty.
9 As for its beauty—
I made it so,
with its abundant foliage.
All the trees of Eden envied it,
all that were in God's garden.

10 So now the LORD God proclaims:
Consider the fate
of those who tower high!
When it allowed its branches to reach up
among the clouds,
it became arrogant.
11 So I handed it over
to the most powerful nation,
who continually
acted treacherously against it.
I banished it!
12 Foreigners, the worst of the nations,
cut it down
and left it to lie among the hills.
All its branches fell among the valleys,
and its boughs were broken off
in the earth's deep ravines.
All the earth's peoples departed
from its shade and abandoned it.
13 On its trunk roost all the birds in the sky,
and on its boughs lie
all the beasts of the field.
14 All this has happened so that no other
well-watered tree would tower high or allow
its branches to reach among the clouds.
Nor would their leaders achieve the towering stature of such well-watered trees. Certainly, all of them are consigned to death,
to the world below,[c] among human beings
who go down to the pit.
15 The LORD God proclaims: On the day
that it went down to the underworld,[d] I
caused mourning. I blocked off the deep
sea against it. I dried up its rivers and restrained the mighty waters. I made Lebanon go into mourning for it, and all the
trees of the field languished on its account.
16 When it was felled, the nations quaked at
the sound. When I cast it down into the underworld, with those who go down to the
pit, all the trees of Eden were comforted in
the world below, the choicest and the best
of Lebanon, all the trees that depended on
water. 17 His allies,[e] those among the nations who lived under his shade, these also
went down with him to the underworld, to
those who are slain by the sword.
18 Are you like any of these in glory or
greatness among Eden's trees? Then you
too will go down with Eden's trees to the
world below. You will lie among the uncircumcised, with those who are slain by the
sword. This is Pharaoh and his entire horde.
This is what the LORD God says.

Egypt the crocodile

32 In the twelfth year, on the first day
of the twelfth month, the LORD's
word came to me: 2 Human one, sing a lament for Pharaoh, Egypt's king. Say to him:
You consider yourself a young lion
among the nations,
but you are like the sea monster!
You thrash about in your rivers,
you roil the waters with your feet,
and you muddy your[f] rivers.
3 The LORD God proclaims:
In the company of many peoples
I will spread my net over you,
and I will haul you up in my dragnet.
4 I will cast you out on the earth
and throw you on the open ground.
I will cause all the birds in the sky
to settle on you,

[c] Or *the land of the lowest places* [d] Heb *Sheol* [e] Or *his arms* [f] LXX; MT *their*

and all the beasts of the earth
to devour you.
5 Your flesh I will set upon the mountains,
and I will fill the valleys with your gore.
6 With your blood I will soak
your irrigated land,[g]
and the streambeds
will be filled with you.
7 When you are snuffed out,
I will cover the sky,
and I will darken the stars.
I will cover the sun with a cloud,
and the moon won't radiate its light.
8 As for the shining lights of the heavens,
I will make them dark over you,
and set darkness over your land.
This is what the LORD God says.

9 I will trouble the hearts of many peoples
when I bring about your destruction
with nations from lands
you didn't know.
10 I will make many peoples appalled
because of you.
Their kings will shudder violently
on your account
when I brandish my sword before them.
They will tremble for their lives
again and again
on the day of your downfall.

11 The LORD God proclaims: The sword of
the king of Babylon is coming against you!
12 I will make your hordes fall by the swords
of mighty men, the most terrifying of the
nations, all of them. They will bring an end
to Egypt's pride, and all of its hordes will
be destroyed. 13 I will remove all its livestock
from beside the plentiful waters so that
neither human foot nor livestock's hoof
will trouble it again. 14 At that time, I will
allow the waters to run clear, and make its
rivers flow like oil. This is what the LORD
God says. 15 When I turn the land of Egypt
into a wasteland and the land is deprived of
all that fills it, and when I strike down those
who live there, then they will know that I
am the LORD. 16 This is a lament, and it will
be sung as a lament. The daughters of the
nations will lament for Egypt, and they will
also lament for Egypt's hordes. This is what
the LORD God says.

17 In the twelfth year, on the fifteenth day
of the first month,[h] the LORD's word came
to me: 18 Human one, mourn for Egypt's
hordes.

Send Egypt down
with the mighty nations subject[i] to it,
to the world below,[j]
among those who go down to the pit.
19 Whom do you surpass in beauty?
Go down and take your bed
with the uncircumcised,
20 among those who fall slain by the sword.

A sword is appointed, and all his hordes
will carry him off. 21 The mighty chieftains,
those who once came to his aid, will speak
to him from the middle of the underworld,[k]
for the uncircumcised have gone down and
have lain down, slain by the sword.

Vanished glory

22 Assyria is there, and all its assembly
round about his grave,
all of them slain, fallen by the sword,
23 who were assigned graves
in the deepest region of the pit.
His assembly surrounded his grave,
all of them slain, fallen by the sword,
who caused terror
in the land of the living.

24 Elam is there, her entire horde
round about her grave,
all of them slain, fallen by the sword,
who went down uncircumcised
to the world below,[l]
who caused terror
in the land of the living.
They bore their shame
like those who go down to the pit.
25 Among the slain they made a bed for her,
with all her hordes round about her grave,
all of them uncircumcised,
slain by the sword,
for they caused terror
in the land of the living.

[g] MT adds *to the mountains.* [h] LXX; MT lacks *the first month.* [i] Or *daughter nations* [j] Or *the land of the lowest places*
[k] Heb *Sheol* [l] Or *the land of the lowest places*

They bore their shame
like those who go down to the pit;
in the midst of the slain
she[m] was placed.

26 Meshech and Tubal are there,
and all their hordes
around their graves,
all of them uncircumcised,
slain by the sword,
for they caused terror
in the land of the living.

27 They don't lie with the mighty men
fallen among the uncircumcised. When they
went down to the underworld[n] with their
weapons of war, they put their swords under
their heads and their shields[o] over their
bones. The terror of the mighty men is in the
land of the living.

28 But you, you will be broken among the
uncircumcised, and you will lie with those
who are slain by the sword.

29 Edom is there,
its kings and all its princes,
who, though strong,
were put with those slain
by the sword.
They lie with the uncircumcised,
like those who go down to the pit.

30 All the princes of the north are there,
and all the Sidonians
who went down with the slain;
in spite of the terror of their strength,
they were disgraced.
They lie uncircumcised with
those slain by the sword.
They bore their shame
like those who go down to the pit.

31 When Pharaoh sees them,
he will be sorry for all his hordes
who are slain by the sword—
Pharaoh and all his army.
This is what the LORD God says,
32 Though it was I who put his terror
in the land of the living,
he will be laid out
among the uncircumcised,
with those slain by the sword,
Pharaoh and all his horde.
This is what the LORD God says.

The lookout

33 The LORD's word came to me:
2 Human one, speak to your people
and say to them: Suppose I bring a sword
against a country, and the people of the
land take a certain person from their assembly and make him their lookout. 3 When
he sees the sword coming against the land,
he blows the trumpet and warns the people.
4 If they hear the sound of the trumpet but
don't heed the warning, when the sword
comes and they are taken away, they are responsible for their blood. 5 They heard the
sound of the trumpet but didn't heed the
warning, so their blood is on them. If they
had paid attention to the warning, they
would have saved their lives. 6 If the lookout sees the sword coming but doesn't blow
the trumpet to warn the people, when the
sword comes and takes away any of them,
they are taken away in their sin, but I'll hold
the lookout responsible for their blood.
7 You, human one, I've made you a lookout for the house of Israel. Whenever you
hear me speaking, you must give them
warning from me. 8 If I pronounce a death
sentence on wicked people, and you don't
warn them to turn from their way, they will
die in their guilt, but I will hold you responsible for their blood. 9 But suppose you do
warn the wicked of their ways so that they
might turn from them. If they don't turn
from their ways, they will die in their guilt,
but you will save your life.
10 You, human one, say to the house of Israel: This is what all of you are saying: "How
our transgressions and our sins weigh on
us! We waste away because of them. How
can we live?" 11 Say to them, This is what the
LORD God says: As surely as I live, do I take
pleasure in the death of the wicked? If the
wicked turn from their ways, they will live.
Turn, completely turn from your wicked
ways! Why should you die, house of Israel?
12 You, human one, say to your people:

[m] Or *he* [n] Heb *Sheol* [o] Or *sin*

The righteousness of the righteous doesn't rescue them when they begin to sin. Nor does the wickedness of the wicked make them stumble if they turn from their wickedness. If the righteous sin, their righteousness won't protect them. [13]Even if I've told the righteous they will live, none of their righteous deeds will be remembered if they trust in their righteousness and do wrong. They will die because of their evil deeds. [14]And even if I have pronounced a death sentence on the wicked, if they turn from sin and do what is just and right—[15]if they return pledges, make restitution for robbery, and walk in life-giving regulations in order not to sin—they will live and not die. [16]None of the sins they've committed will be remembered against them. They've done what is just and right, and they will live.

[17]Yet your people say, "My Lord's way doesn't measure up." Isn't it their ways that don't measure up? [18]When the righteous turn from their righteousness to do wrong, they will die because of it. [19]And when the wicked turn from their wickedness to do what is just and right, it is for that reason they will live. [20]Yet you say, "My Lord's way doesn't measure up." I judge each one of you according to your ways, house of Israel!

News from Jerusalem

[21]In the twelfth year, on the fifth day of the tenth month of our exile, a survivor from Jerusalem came to me and reported, "The city has fallen!" [22]The LORD's power was with me in the evening before the survivor arrived, and just before he arrived in the morning, God opened my mouth. So my mouth was opened, and I was no longer speechless.

[23]The LORD's word came to me: [24]Human one, those who live among those ruins in Israel's fertile land are saying, "Abraham was just one man, and he inherited the land. We are many, so certainly the land has been given to us as an inheritance."

[25]So say to them, The LORD God proclaims: You eat with the blood, you lift your eyes to the idols, and you shed blood. Should you inherit the land? [26]You live by the sword, you observe detestable practices, and every one of you commits adultery.[p] Should you inherit the land?

[27]Say to them, The LORD God proclaims: As surely as I live, those in the ruins will fall by the sword, those in the countryside I will give to the wild beasts to consume, and those in the strongholds and caves will die of plague. [28]I will make the land an uninhabitable waste. Its proud strength will come to an end, and Israel's highlands will become so deserted that no one will cross through them. [29]They will know that I am the LORD when I make the land an uninhabitable waste because of all their detestable practices.

A fickle audience

[30]As for you, human one, your people talk about you beside the walls and in their doorways. One by one, they say to each other, "Let's go hear what sort of message has come from the LORD." [31]So they come to you as people do, and they sit before you as my people. They listen to your words, but they refuse to do them. Though they speak of their longing[q] for me, they act out of their own interests and opinions. [32]To them you are like a singer of love songs with a lovely voice and skilled technique. They listen to your words, but no one does them. [33]When this comes—and it is certainly coming—they will know that a prophet has been among them.

The good shepherd

34 The LORD's word came to me: [2]Human one, prophesy against Israel's shepherds. Prophesy and say to them, The LORD God proclaims to the shepherds: Doom to Israel's shepherds who tended themselves! Shouldn't shepherds tend the flock? [3]You drink the milk, you wear the wool, and you slaughter the fat animals, but you don't tend the flock. [4]You don't strengthen the weak, heal the sick, bind up the injured, bring back the strays, or seek out the lost;

[p]Or *defiles his neighbor's wife* [q]Or *love songs*

but instead you use force to rule them with
injustice. [5]Without a shepherd, my flock
was scattered; and when it was scattered, it
became food for all the wild animals. [6]My
flock strayed on all the mountains and on
every high hill throughout all the earth. My
flock was scattered, and there was no one to
look for them or find them. [7]So now shepherds, hear the LORD's word! [8]This is what
the LORD God says: As surely as I live, without a shepherd, my flock became prey. My
flock became food for all the wild animals.
My shepherds didn't seek out my flock. They
tended themselves, but they didn't tend
my flock.

[9]So, shepherds, hear the LORD's word!
[10]The LORD God proclaims: I'm against the
shepherds! I will hold them accountable for
my flock, and I will put an end to their tending the flock. The shepherds will no longer
tend them, because I will rescue my flock
from their mouths, and they will no longer
be their food.

[11]The LORD God proclaims: I myself will
search for my flock and seek them out.
[12]As a shepherd seeks out the flock when
some in the flock have been scattered, so
will I seek out my flock. I will rescue them
from all the places where they were scattered during the time of clouds and thick
darkness. [13]I will gather and lead them out
from the countries and peoples, and I will
bring them to their own fertile land. I will
feed them on Israel's highlands, along the
riverbeds, and in all the inhabited places.
[14]I will feed them in good pasture, and their
sheepfold will be there, on Israel's lofty
highlands. On Israel's highlands, they will
lie down in a secure fold and feed on green
pastures. [15]I myself will feed my flock and
make them lie down. This is what the LORD
God says. [16]I will seek out the lost, bring
back the strays, bind up the wounded, and
strengthen the weak. But the fat and the
strong I will destroy, because I will tend my
sheep[r] with justice.

[17]As for you, my flock, the LORD God
proclaims: I will judge between the rams
and the bucks among the sheep and the
goats. [18]Is feeding in good pasture or drinking clear water such a trivial thing that you
should trample and muddy what is left with
your feet? [19]But now my flock must feed
on what your feet have trampled and drink
water that your feet have muddied.

[20]So the LORD God proclaims to them:
I will judge between the fat and the lean
sheep. [21]You shove with shoulder and
flank, and with your horns you ram all the
weak sheep until you've scattered them
outside. [22]But I will rescue my flock so that
they will never again be prey. I will even
judge between the sheep! [23]I will appoint
for them a single shepherd, and he will feed
them. My servant David will feed them. He
will be their shepherd. [24]I, the LORD, will
be their God, and my servant David will
be their prince. I, the LORD, have spoken.
[25]I will make a covenant of peace for them,
and I will banish the wild animals from
the land. Then they will safely live in the
desert and sleep in the forest. [26]I will give
them and those around my hill a blessing
by sending the rain in its season. They will
be rains of blessing. [27]The trees in the field
will bear fruit, and the earth will yield its
harvest. They will be safe on their fertile
land, and they will know that I am the
LORD when I break the bars of their yoke
and deliver them from those who enslaved
them. [28]The nations will no longer prey on
them, and wild animals will no longer devour them. They will live in safety, with no
one to trouble them. [29]I will establish for
them a place famous for what it grows. No
longer will they experience famine in the
land, nor will they bear the disgrace of the
nations. [30]They will know that I, the LORD
their God, am with them, and they, the
house of Israel, are my people. This is what
the LORD God says. [31]You are my flock,
the flock of my pasture. You are human,
and I am your God. This is what the LORD
God says.

Against Edom

35 The LORD's word came to me:
[2]Human one, face Mount Seir, and

[r]Or *them*

prophesy against it. 3 Say to it, The LORD God proclaims:

I'm against you, Mount Seir!
  I will use my power against you.
I will make you
  into a desolate wasteland,
4 I will turn your cities into ruins,
  and you will become a desolation.
Then you will know
  that I am the LORD.

5 Because you nursed an ancient grudge, you handed the Israelites over to the sword in the time of their distress, during their final punishment. 6 So now the LORD God proclaims: As surely as I live, I will prepare you for blood, and blood will pursue you. Because you don't hate bloodshed, bloodshed will pursue you. 7 I will turn Mount Seir into a desolate wasteland, when I cut off from it both passerby and homecomer. 8 I will fill its highlands—your hills and your valleys, and all your ravines—with its slain. Those who are slain by the sword will fall on them. 9 I will turn you into an eternal desolation. Your cities won't be inhabited, and you will know that I am the LORD.

10 You said, "These two nations and these two territories are mine. We will take possession of them even if the LORD is there." 11 Therefore, the LORD God proclaims: As surely as I live, I will act according to the anger and zeal you displayed when you dealt with them so hatefully. When I judge you, I will make myself known to them, 12 and you will know that I am the LORD. I've heard the lies and libels that you uttered against Israel's highlands when you said, "They are laid waste. They've been given to us to consume." 13 With your mouths you exalted yourselves against me and spoke your words against me. I myself heard it!

14 The LORD God proclaims: As the whole world rejoices, I will turn you into a desolation. 15 Just as you rejoiced over the house of Israel's inheritance because it became desolate, so I will deal with you. Mount Seir, you will become a desolation, with all of Edom, all of it. Then they will know that I am the LORD.

Mountains of Israel

36 You, human one, prophesy to Israel's mountains and say, Hear the LORD's word, mountains of Israel! 2 The LORD God proclaims: The enemy mocked you and said, "The ancient heights belong to us." 3 Therefore, prophesy and say, The LORD God proclaims: When the surviving nations pressed in and ravaged you from all around to lay claim to you, you became an object of the people's slander and derision. 4 Hear the LORD God's word, mountains of Israel! The LORD God proclaims to the mountains and the hills, the watercourses and the valleys, the desolate ruins and the abandoned cities that were contemptuously looted by the surviving nations all around you.

5 So now, says the LORD God, I will speak in my fiery passion against the surviving nations and against Edom, all those who gleefully and spitefully took my land for themselves as a possession only for plunder.[s] 6 Prophesy concerning Israel's fertile land, and say to the mountains and to the hills, to the ravines and to the valleys, The LORD God proclaims: Because you endured the ridicule of the nations, my passion and fury lead me to speak. 7 So now the LORD God proclaims: I myself swear that the nations round about you will themselves suffer ridicule. 8 But you, mountains of Israel, will extend your branches and bear your fruit for my people Israel, because they will come home very soon. 9 Look, I'm here for you, and I will turn toward you, and you will be farmed and sown. 10 I will populate you with human beings, the whole house of Israel, all of them. The cities will be inhabited, the ruins rebuilt. 11 When I make people and animals increase on you, they will multiply and be fruitful. I will cause you to be inhabited as you were before. I will do more good for you than in the beginning, and you will know that I am the LORD. 12 I will let people walk through you, my people Israel! They will lay claim to you, you will be their inheritance, and you will no longer deprive them of anything.

[s] MT adds *to drive it out.*

13The LORD God proclaims: Because
people say, "You are a devourer of human
beings" and "You are depriving your nation," 14therefore, you will no longer devour
human beings or deprive your nation of
anything. This is what the LORD God says.
15You won't have to listen anymore to the
taunts of the nations or endure the scorn of
the peoples. And you will no longer deprive
your nation of anything. This is what the
LORD God says.

A new heart

16The LORD's word came to me: 17Human
one, when the house of Israel lived on their
fertile land, they polluted it with their ways
and deeds. Their ways before me were polluted like the blood of menstruation, 18and
so I poured out my fury on them for all
the blood they had poured out on the land
and for all the defilement of their idols.
19When I scattered them to the nations and
dispersed them into other lands, I judged
them according to their ways and deeds.
20But then when they entered the other nations, they degraded my holy name because
it was said of them, "These are the LORD's
people, yet they had to leave his land." 21So
I had compassion on my holy name, which
the house of Israel degraded among the nations where they had gone.

22Therefore, say to the house of Israel,
The LORD God proclaims: House of Israel,
I'm not acting for your sake but for the
sake of my holy name, which you degraded
among the nations where you have gone.
23I will make my great name holy, which
was degraded among the nations when you
dishonored it among them. Then the nations will know that I am the LORD. This is
what the LORD God says.

When I make myself holy among you in
their sight, 24I will take you from the nations, I will gather you from all the countries, and I will bring you to your own
fertile land. 25I will sprinkle clean water on
you, and you will be cleansed of all your pollution. I will cleanse you of all your idols.
26I will give you a new heart and put a new
spirit in you. I will remove your stony heart
from your body and replace it with a living
one, 27and I will give you my spirit so that
you may walk according to my regulations
and carefully observe my case laws. 28Then
you will live in the land that I gave to your
ancestors, you will be my people, and I will
be your God. 29I will save you from all your
uncleanness, and I will summon the grain
and make it grow abundantly so that you
won't endure famine. 30I will make abundant the orchards' fruit and the fields' produce so that you will never again endure the
shame of famine among the nations. 31Then
you will remember your evil ways and no-
good deeds, and you will feel disgust for
yourselves because of your sinful and detestable practices. 32Not for your sake do I
act. This is what the LORD God proclaims.
Let that be known to you! Be ashamed and
be humiliated because of all your ways,
house of Israel.

33The LORD God proclaims: On the day
that I cleanse you of all your guilt, I will
cause the cities to be inhabited, and the
ruins will be rebuilt. 34The desolate land will
be farmed, and it won't be like it was when
it seemed a wasteland to all who passed
by. 35They will say, "This land, which was
a desolation, has become like the garden
of Eden." And the cities that were ruined,
ravaged, and razed are now fortified and
inhabited. 36The surviving nations around
you will know that I, the LORD, have rebuilt
what was torn down and have planted what
was made desolate. I, the LORD, have spoken, and I will do it.

37The LORD God proclaims: I will also
allow the house of Israel to ask me to do
this for them: that I increase them like a
human flock. 38Like the holy flock, like the
flock of Jerusalem at its festivals, the ruined cities will be filled with a human flock.
Then they will know that I am the LORD.

Valley of dry bones

37 The LORD's power overcame me, and
while I was in the LORD's spirit, he
led me out and set me down in the middle
of a certain valley. It was full of bones. 2He
led me through them all around, and I saw
that there were a great many of them on
the valley floor, and they were very dry.

3He asked me, "Human one, can these bones live again?"

I said, "LORD God, only you know."

4He said to me, "Prophesy over these bones, and say to them, Dry bones, hear the LORD's word! 5The LORD God proclaims to these bones: I am about to put breath in you, and you will live again. 6I will put sinews on you, place flesh on you, and cover you with skin. When I put breath in you, and you come to life, you will know that I am the LORD."

7I prophesied just as I was commanded. There was a great noise as I was prophesying, then a great quaking, and the bones came together, bone by bone. 8When I looked, suddenly there were sinews on them. The flesh appeared, and then they were covered over with skin. But there was still no breath in them.

9He said to me, "Prophesy to the breath; prophesy, human one! Say to the breath, The LORD God proclaims: Come from the four winds, breath! Breathe into these dead bodies and let them live."

10I prophesied just as he commanded me. When the breath entered them, they came to life and stood on their feet, an extraordinarily large company.

11He said to me, "Human one, these bones are the entire house of Israel. They say, 'Our bones are dried up, and our hope has perished. We are completely finished.' 12So now, prophesy and say to them, The LORD God proclaims: I'm opening your graves! I will raise you up from your graves, my people, and I will bring you to Israel's fertile land. 13You will know that I am the LORD, when I open your graves and raise you up from your graves, my people. 14I will put my breath[t] in you, and you will live. I will plant you on your fertile land, and you will know that I am the LORD. I've spoken, and I will do it. This is what the LORD says."

Divided kingdom united

15The LORD's word came to me: 16You, human one, take a stick, and write on it, "Belonging to Judah and to the Israelites associated with him." Take another stick and write on it, "Stick of Ephraim belonging to Joseph and everyone of the house of Israel associated with him." 17Join them to each other to make a single stick so that they become one stick in your hand. 18When your people ask you, "Why won't you tell us what these sticks mean to you?" 19say to them, The LORD God proclaims: I'm taking Joseph's stick, which has been in Ephraim's hand, and the tribes of Israel associated with him, and I'm putting it with Judah's stick, and I'm making them into a single stick so that they will be one stick in my hand. 20When the two sticks that you've written on are in your hand in their sight, 21speak to them, This is what the LORD God says: I will take the Israelites from among the nations where they've gone, I will gather them from all around, and I will bring them to their fertile land. 22I will make them into a single nation in the land on Israel's highlands. There will be just one king for all of them. They will no longer be two nations, and they will no longer be divided into two kingdoms. 23They will no longer defile themselves with their idols or their worthless things or with any of their rebellions. I will deliver them from all the places where they sinned, and I will cleanse them. They will be my people, and I will be their God. 24My servant David will be king over them. There will be just one shepherd for all of them. They will follow my case laws and carefully observe my regulations. 25They will live on the land that I gave to my servant Jacob, where their ancestors lived. They will live on it, they and their children and their grandchildren, forever. My servant David will be their prince forever. 26I will make a covenant of peace for them. It will be their covenant forever. I will grant it to them and allow them to increase. I will set my sanctuary among them forever. 27My dwelling will be with them, and I will be their God, and they will be my people. 28The nations will know that I, the LORD, make Israel holy, when my sanctuary is among them forever.

[t]Or *spirit*

Attack of Gog

38 The LORD's word came to me:
2 Human one, face Gog in the land
of Magog, chief prince of Meshech and
Tubal. Prophesy concerning him 3 and say,
The LORD God proclaims: I challenge you,
Gog, chief prince of Meshech and Tubal! 4 I
will turn you about, set hooks in your jaws,
and lead you out, you and all your army,
horses and riders, handsomely dressed, all
of them, a great assembly, with buckler and
shield, all of them wielding swords. 5 Persia,
Cush, and Put are with you,[u] all of them
equipped with shield and helmet. 6 Gomer
and all his troops, Beth-togarmah from the
far north and all his troops; many peoples
are with you. 7 Stand ready and be prepared,
you and all your assembly. You will watch
out for those who gather against you.
8 After many days you will be called out.
In future years you will enter a country that
has been freed from the sword, a gathering
from many peoples on the mountains of
Israel, which had become a perpetual ruin.
This country was brought out from the peoples, and all of them live securely. 9 You will
invade like a sudden storm. You and all your
troops, and the many peoples with you, will
be like clouds covering the earth.
10 The LORD God proclaims: On that day,
thoughts will come into your mind, and you
will devise an evil plan. 11 You will say, "I will
go up against the open country and come
against a quiet people who all live securely
without walls, bars, or doors 12 to take
plunder and seize loot, to use my[v] power
against the resettled waste places, against
a people gathered from the nations, who
are acquiring goods and cattle, and who live
at the center[w] of the earth." 13 Sheba and
Dedan and the merchants and officials of
Tarshish will say to you, "Have you come to
take plunder and seize loot? Have you assembled your army to take silver and gold,
to take goods and cattle, to engage in great
looting?"
14 So now, prophesy, human one, and
say to Gog, The LORD God proclaims: Isn't
that what you will decide to do[x] on that day,
when my people Israel live securely? 15 You
will come up from your place from the far
north, you and many peoples with you, all
of them riding horses, a great assembly, a
mighty army. 16 You will go up against my
people Israel like a cloud covering the earth.
But when this happens in future days, I will
be the one who brings you up against my
land, so that the nations may know me,
Gog, when through you I show my holiness
in their sight!
17 The LORD God proclaims: Are you the
one about whom I spoke in former times
through my servants, Israel's prophets,
the ones who prophesied for years in those
days to bring you against them? 18 On that
day, the day when Gog comes against Israel's fertile land, my wrath will be aroused.
This is what the LORD God says. 19 In my
jealousy and blazing anger I declare: On
that day, a great quaking will come over Israel's fertile land. 20 The fish of the sea, the
birds in the sky, the beasts of the field, all
the creatures crawling on the ground, and
every living human being will quake in my
presence. Mountains will be thrown down
and cliffs will crumble; every wall will fall
to the ground. 21 I will summon a sword
against Gog on all my mountains. This is
what the LORD God says! The swords of the
warriors will be against each other, 22 and
I will enter into judgment with him, with
plague and blood. I will pour out flooding
rain, hailstones, fire, and sulfur on him,
on all his troops, and on the many peoples
with him. 23 So I will display my greatness,
show my holiness, and make myself known
in the sight of many nations. And they will
know that I am the LORD.

39 You, human one, prophesy about
Gog and say, The LORD God pro-
claims: I challenge you, Gog, chief prince of
Meshech and Tubal! 2 I will turn you about,
drag you out, and bring you out of the far
north, and I will bring you to Israel's mountains. 3 I will strike your bow from your left
hand, and make your arrows fall from your
right. 4 You will fall on Israel's mountains,
you, all your troops, and the peoples who

[u] Cf 38:6; MT *them* [v] LXX; MT *your* [w] Or *navel* [x] Or *you will know*

are with you. I will give you to the birds of prey, to every kind of bird and wild animal as food. 5 You will fall on the open field, for I have spoken! This is what the LORD God says! 6 I will send fire on Magog and on those who live securely in the coastlands, and they will know that I am the LORD. 7 I will make known my holy name among my people Israel. They will never again degrade my holy name, and the nations will know that I, the LORD, am holy in Israel. 8 Look, it has come! It has happened! This is what the LORD God says. This is the day that I spoke about.

9 Those who live in Israel's cities will go out and kindle a fire with the weapons—shield and buckler, bow and arrow, spear and lance. They will burn them with fire for seven years. 10 They won't gather wood from the field or chop down trees from the forest, because they will be able to keep the fire burning with the weapons. So they will take plunder and seize loot. This is what the LORD says.

11 On that day, I will assign Gog a place for burial in Israel in the Travelers' Valley east of the sea. It will block the travelers' way, because Gog and all of his horde will be buried there. It will be called Hamon-gog[y] Valley. 12 For seven months, the house of Israel will bury them in order to cleanse the land. 13 All the people of the land will take part in the burial, so they will make a name for themselves on the day that I glorify myself. This is what the LORD God says. 14 They will appoint people who will continually cross through the land and bury[z] the human remains that are left on the surface of the ground in order to purify it. They will begin their search at the end of seven months. 15 As the travelers cross through the land, when they see a human bone, they will set up a marker next to it until the gravediggers bury it in Hamon-gog Valley 16 (the name of the city is Hamonah). So they will purify the land.

17 And you, human one, the LORD God proclaims: Say to the birds of prey, to every kind of bird and every wild animal: Assemble and come! Come together from all around for the sacrifice that I make for you, a great sacrifice on Israel's mountains! You will eat flesh and drink blood. 18 You will eat the flesh of warriors and drink the blood of the princes of the earth: rams, lambs, goats, bulls, all fattened animals from Bashan. 19 Gorge yourselves on their fat, and get drunk on their blood, from the sacrifice that I have made for you. 20 Satisfy yourselves at my table with horses and riders, mighty men and every warrior. This is what the LORD God says! 21 When I glorify myself among the nations, all the nations will understand the judgments that I executed and the power that I used among them. 22 And the house of Israel will know that I, the LORD, am their God, from that day on. 23 The nations will know that the house of Israel went into exile because of their guilt. Because they rebelled against me, I hid my face from them. When I handed them over to their enemies, all of them fell by the sword. 24 I dealt with them according to their uncleanness and their transgressions and hid my face from them.

25 So the LORD God proclaims: Now I will bring back the captives of Jacob. I will have compassion on the whole house of Israel and defend my holy name. 26 They will forget their humiliation and all their rebellions against me when they live securely on their fertile land with no one to frighten them. 27 When I bring them back from the peoples and gather them from the lands of their enemies, I will be made holy through them in the sight of the many nations. 28 They will know that I am the LORD their God when, after I made them go into exile among the nations, I gathered them to their land. I won't leave any of them behind. 29 When I pour my Spirit upon the house of Israel, I won't hide my face from them again. This is what the LORD God says.

Vision of restoration

40 In the beginning of the twenty-fifth year of our exile, on the tenth day of the month, exactly fourteen years after

[y] Or *horde of Gog* [z] LXX; MT adds *the travelers.*

the city was struck down, on that very day, the LORD's power was on me, and he took me there. [2]In God's visions, he brought me to the land of Israel and set me down on a very high mountain, where there was a city structure to the south. [3]When he brought me there, I saw a man standing in the gate. He appeared to be bronze, and he had a linen cord and a measuring rod in his hand. [4]The man spoke to me, "Human one, look and listen well, and take seriously everything I show you, because you were brought here so that these things could be revealed to you. Describe everything you see to the house of Israel."

Temple compound

[5]Now there was an outer wall that went all the way around the temple compound. The measuring rod in the man's hand was ten and a half feet[a] (based on a standard eighteen inches[b] plus three inches[c]). When he measured the wall's height and width it was ten and a half feet high and ten and a half feet wide. [6]He entered the gate facing east. He went up its steps, and he measured the plaza[d] at the gate. It was ten and a half feet wide: the plaza was ten and a half feet wide. [7]The rooms were ten and a half feet long and ten and a half feet wide, with a space of seven and a half feet between them. The plaza next to the porch at the gate opposite the temple was ten and a half feet. [8]He measured the porch of the gate opposite the temple: it was ten and a half feet. [9]Then he measured the porch of the gate: it was twelve feet,[e] and its arches were three feet. The porch of the gate was opposite the temple. [10]Inside the east gate, there were three rooms on each side. Each was the same size, and the arches on each side were the same size also. [11]Then he measured the width of the gate opening, which was fifteen feet, and the gate's length, which was nineteen and a half feet. [12]A border running along the front of the rooms on each side was eighteen inches wide, and each of the rooms was nine feet square. [13]He measured the gate through the room openings that faced each other. From the outer ceiling edge of one room to the outer ceiling edge of the other, the gate was thirty-seven and a half feet wide. [14]Next he made out the perimeter of the hallway, defined by the arches inside the gate: it was ninety feet. [15]It was seventy-five feet from the front of the outer gate to the front of the inner porch of the gate. [16]Inside the gate, all of the rooms and their arches had closed windows; there were also niches inside the porch all the way around. The arches were decorated with palm trees.

[17]Then he brought me to the outer courtyard, which consisted of chambers and a pavement all the way around. Thirty chambers came up to the pavement, [18]and the pavement came up to the facades of the gates along their entire length. That was the lower pavement. [19]When he measured the width from the inside of the lower gate to the outer edge of the inner courtyard, it was one hundred fifty feet.

After he measured the east gate, he measured the north gate, [20]the one facing north at the outer courtyard. He measured its length and width, [21]its three inner rooms on each side, its arches, and its porch. Its measurements were the same as the first gate: seventy-five feet long and thirty-seven and a half feet wide. [22]The windows, porch, and palm decorations had the same measurements as those of the east gate. Seven steps led up to the entrance, and the porch was at the other end. [23]There were also gates to the inner courtyard opposite the north and east gates. When he measured from gate to gate, it was one hundred fifty feet.

[24]Then he had me walk toward the south, where there was a gate facing south. He

[a]Heb *shesh ammoth ba'ammah* traditionally *six long cubits,* which is defined as six times a standard *ammah* of eighteen inches plus a *topha* (traditionally *handbreadth*) of three inches. So the measuring rod has six segments of twenty-one inches each, which equals ten and a half feet. It is unclear whether the measurements with the rod continue past 40:8, when standard *ammah* appear, though the longer *ammah* do continue briefly in 43:13-17 for the altar. [b]Or *a standard cubit* [c]Or *a handbreadth* [d]Or *threshold*; Heb architectural and decorative terminology in Ezek 40–48 is often uncertain. [e]Or *eight cubits*

measured its arches and porch using the same measurements. 25Its windows and its porch all around were like the others, and the gate also was seventy-five feet long and thirty-seven and a half feet wide. 26Its stairway had seven steps, and its porch was at the other end. On its arches, one on either side, were palm decorations. 27There was a gate to the inner courtyard on the south. When he measured from gate to gate on the south side, it was one hundred fifty feet.

28When he brought me to the inner courtyard by way of the south gate, he took the same measurements of the south gate. 29Its rooms, arches, and porch, as well as its windows and porch all the way around, measured the same as the others. It was seventy-five feet long and thirty-seven and a half feet wide. 30There were porches all around, thirty-seven and a half feet long and seven and a half feet wide. 31Its porch faced the outer courtyard. Palms decorated its arches, and its stairway had eight steps.

32Then he brought me to the inner courtyard on the east side, and again he took the same measurements of the gate. 33Its rooms, arches, and porch measured the same as the others, as well as its windows and porch all the way around. It was seventy-five feet long and thirty-seven and a half feet wide. 34Its porch faced the outer courtyard. Palm trees decorated its arches on both sides, and its stairway had eight steps. 35Then he brought me to the north gate and took the same measurements of the 36rooms, arches, and porch, and also its windows all around. It was seventy-five feet long and thirty-seven and a half feet wide. 37Its porch[f] faced the outer courtyard. Palm trees decorated its arches on both sides, and its stairway had eight steps.

38At that gate, there was a room with an entrance in the arches for washing the entirely burned offering, 39and inside the porch on each side of the gate were two tables where the entirely burned offerings, the purification offerings, and the compensation offerings were slaughtered. 40Outside, two pairs of tables flanked the entrance of the north gate at both ends, at the steps on one end and the porch on the other. 41There were four tables on each side of the gate, eight tables in all, for preparing the animal offerings. 42The four tables that were used for the entirely burned offering as well as for the communal sacrifices were made of hewn stone. Each was twenty-seven inches square and eighteen inches high. Equipment used in the ritual slaughter was set on them. 43Hooks,[g] three inches wide, were securely fixed all the way around. The tables were for the flesh of the offerings.

44Outside the inner gate there were two[h] chambers in the inner courtyard. The one beside the north gate faced south, and the one beside the east gate faced north. 45He spoke to me: "The chamber facing south is for the priests who keep watch over the temple, 46and the chamber facing north is for the priests who keep watch over the altar. Of all the Levites, only the Zadokites may draw near to serve the LORD." 47Then he measured the courtyard. It was square, one hundred fifty feet long and one hundred fifty feet wide. The altar was in front of the temple.

The temple

48Then he brought me to the porch of the temple and measured its arches. They were seven and a half feet on each side, and the width of the gate was four and a half feet on each side. 49The porch was thirty feet long and eighteen feet wide. Steps led up into the porch, and there were columns for the arches, one on each side.

41 He brought me to the main hall, and he measured the arches. They were nine feet deep on both sides, so that was also the depth of the tent. 2The entrance was fifteen feet wide, and the facades on either side of the entrance were seven and a half feet. When he measured its length, it was sixty feet, and its width was thirty feet. 3Then he went into the inner room, and he measured the arches on both sides of the entrance; they were each three feet. The

[f]LXX; MT *arches* [g]Heb uncertain [h]LXX; MT *singing*

entrance was nine feet wide, and its depth was ten and a half feet. 4 When he measured the length of the inner room, it was thirty feet, and the width of the side adjoining the main hall was also thirty feet. He said to me, "This is the most holy place."

5 When he measured the wall of the temple, it was nine feet, and the side chambers that went all the way around the temple were six feet. 6 Now these side chambers adjoined each other, thirty chambers in three stories. The side chambers had a ledge in the temple wall all the way around to serve as supports, but these supports were not inserted into the temple wall itself. 7 A wide ramp ascended stage by stage to the side chambers all the way around the temple. In this way, the ascent stage by stage all around the temple added to the temple's width. One ascended from the foundation to the top by way of the middle story. 8 Then I looked at the temple: Its roof all around rested on the side chambers. Each raised section was ten and a half feet, and the indentations between them were nine feet.[i] 9 The width of the outer wall of the side chambers was seven and a half feet. The space left free between the temple's side chambers and 10 the other chambers was thirty feet wide all the way around the temple. 11 There were two entrances from the side chambers to the free space, one facing north, the other facing south. And the width of the place that was left free was seven and a half feet all the way around. 12 The structure facing the yard on the west was one hundred five feet wide. The structure's wall was seven and a half feet wide all the way around, and its length was one hundred thirty-five feet.

13 Then he measured the temple. It was one hundred fifty feet long. The yard, the structure, and its walls were also one hundred fifty feet. 14 The area in front of the house and the yard to the east was one hundred fifty feet also. 15 Then he measured the length of the structure along the side of the yard, including its promenades on both sides: one hundred fifty feet.

Now the interior of the main hall as well as the porches in the courtyard 16 were paneled all around, including the ceilings,[j] closed windows, and its three courses of promenades adjoined the ceiling. From the ground up to the windows was covered. 17 Above the entrance, from the interior to the exterior of the temple, and on every interior and exterior wall, 18 there were carved winged creatures and palm trees. The palm trees were positioned between the winged creatures, and each winged creature had two faces. 19 A human face turned toward one palm tree, and the face of a lion turned toward another. They were carved on the temple all the way around. 20 From the ground to above the entrance, the walls of the main hall were carved with winged creatures and palm trees. 21 In the main hall itself, there were square doorposts in front of the holy place, where there was the appearance of 22 the altar. It was four and a half feet high and three feet wide. It was made of wood, and its corners, base, and sides were also wood. He said to me, "This is the table that stands before the LORD."

23 The main hall and the holy place each had two doors, 24 and each door had two turning panels, two for one door and two for the other. 25 Like the walls, the doors of the main hall were carved with winged creatures and palm trees. A single luxuriant[k] tree stood outside, in front of the porch, 26 while closed windows and palm trees decorated both sides of the facade of the porch, the temple's side chambers, and the beams.

Chambers and promenades

42 Then he led me north to the outer courtyard and brought me into the set of chambers opposite the yard and the structure to the north. 2 The length of the facade at the north entrance was one hundred fifty feet, its depth seventy-five feet. 3 It was next to the twenty chambers that belonged to the inner courtyard and next to the pavement of the outer courtyard, and it had three courses of promenades. 4 In front of the chambers there was a passage

Heb uncertain [j]Or *thresholds* [k]Heb uncertain

fifteen feet wide, and to the inside, a passage eighteen inches wide. The entrance to the chambers was on the north. 5 The upper chambers were smaller, because the promenades took up more space from them than from the first and second stories. 6 This was because the promenades were arranged in three levels, but they didn't have columns like those in the courtyards. For this reason, the top story was narrower than the first and second stories. 7 A stone wall ran parallel to the chambers facing the outer courtyard. It was seventy-five feet long, 8 the same length, seventy-five feet, as the chambers facing the outer courtyard. Those facing the temple were one hundred fifty feet. 9-10 These chambers were entered from the outer courtyard at the end of the courtyard wall, because the entrance was at the end of the chambers at the east. South of the yard and the building, there were more chambers with a passage 11 in front of them. The design of the chambers resembled the ones to the north in length and width, as well as in all their exits. The arrangement of the entrances 12 to the chambers on the south side was identical as well. One entered from the east at the beginning of the corresponding wall.

13 Then he said to me, "The north and south chambers that face the building and the yard are the holy chambers where the priests eat the offerings that have been brought to the LORD. They are most holy. Here they will place the most holy things, the grain offering, the purification offering, and the compensation offering. The place is holy. 14 When the priests enter, they won't go out of the sanctuary to the outer courtyard. There they will place the priestly vests that they wore when they were ministering, because these garments are also holy. They will put on other garments when they go out to the people's area."

15 When he finished making the interior measurements of the temple, he led me out toward the east gate, and he measured all the way around. 16 He used the same measuring rod on all four sides. He measured the east side, seven hundred fifty feet; 17 the north side, seven hundred fifty feet; and 18 the south side, seven hundred fifty feet. 19 He turned to the west side, seven hundred fifty feet. 20 On all four sides he measured the wall all the way around. Its length was seven hundred fifty feet, and its width seven hundred fifty feet. So he made a division between the holy and the ordinary.

Return of the divine glory

43 Then he led me to the east gate, 2 where the glory of Israel's God was coming in from the east. Its sound was like the sound of a mighty flood, and the earth was lit up with his glory. 3 What appeared when I looked was like what I had seen when he[l] came to destroy the city, and also like what I saw at the Chebar River, and I fell on my face. 4 Then the LORD's glory came into the temple by way of the east gate. 5 A wind picked me up and brought me to the inner courtyard, and there the LORD's glory filled the temple. 6 A man was standing next to me, but the voice that I heard came from inside the temple. 7 He said to me, Human one, this is the place for my throne and the place for the soles of my feet, where I will dwell among the Israelites forever. The house of Israel will never again defile my holy name, neither they nor their kings, with their disloyalties[m] and with their kings' corpses at the shrines. 8 When they set their plazas[n] with mine and their doorposts next to mine, the wall was between us. They defiled my holy name with their detestable practices, so I consumed them in my anger. 9 Now let them remove their disloyalties and their kings' corpses from me, and I will dwell among them forever.

10 You, human one, describe the temple to the house of Israel. Let them be humiliated because of their guilt when they think about its design. 11 When they feel humiliated by all that they have done, make known to them the shape of the temple and its adornment, its exits and its entrances, its entire plan and all of its regulations.[o]

[l] Vulg; MT *I* [m] Or *prostitution* [n] Or *thresholds* [o] LXX; MT adds *and all of its structures and all of its instructions.*

Write them down in their sight so that they may observe all of its entire plan and all its regulations and perform them.

[12]These are the instructions for the temple: the top of the mountain, as well as its boundaries all around, are most holy. These are the instructions for the temple.

The altar

[13]These are the dimensions of the altar, according to a twenty-one-inch unit of measure.[p] The base is twenty-one inches high and twenty-one inches wide, with an outer curb measuring one and a half inches all around. This is the altar's height. [14]From the base at ground level to the lower ledge is forty-two inches; the lower ledge is twenty-one inches wide. The distance from the lower to the upper ledge is seven feet; the upper ledge is twenty-one inches wide. [15]The hearth is seven feet high, with four horns projecting upward from the hearth. [16]The hearth is twenty-one feet square; each side is equal to the others. [17]The ledge around the hearth is twenty-four and a half feet long by twenty-four and a half feet wide, a square. Its outer rim is ten and a half inches, and its base all around is twenty-one inches. Its ramp faces east.

Purification of the altar

[18]He said to me, Human one, the LORD God proclaims: These are the regulations established for the altar on the day when it is prepared for making entirely burned offerings and dashing blood on it. [19]You will provide a young bull as a purification offering to the levitical priests who are descendants of Zadok, the ones who may draw near to minster to me. This is what the LORD God says. [20]You will take some of its blood and set it on the four horns of the altar and on the four sides of the ledge and on the curb all around. So you will purify it and purge it. [21]Then you will take the bull selected as the purification offering, and the priests will burn it in a designated place of the temple outside of the sanctuary. [22]On the second day, you will present a flawless male goat as a purification offering. The priests will purify the altar just as they purified the altar with the bull. [23]When you have completed the purification, you will present a flawless bull from the herd and a flawless ram from the flock. [24]You will present them to the LORD. The priests will throw salt on them and offer them as entirely burned offerings to the LORD. [25]Daily, for seven days, you will present a male goat for a purification offering. You will also present a bull from the herd and a ram from the flock, both flawless. [26]For seven days the priests will purge the altar in order to purify it and to dedicate it. [27]When the seven days are completed, the priests will offer your entirely burned offerings and your well-being sacrifices on the altar from the eighth day on, and I will accept you with pleasure. This is what the LORD God says.

The closed gate

44 He brought me back to the outer sanctuary gate that faces east. It was closed. [2]The LORD said to me, This gate remains closed. It shouldn't be opened. No one should come in through it because the LORD, Israel's God, has entered through it. It will remain closed. [3]As for the prince, he may sit in it to eat bread in the LORD's presence. He may come in and go out by way of the gate's porch.

Foreigners, Levites, Zadokites

[4]Then he brought me by way of the north gate to the front of the temple. I looked, and suddenly the LORD's glory filled the LORD's temple, and I fell on my face. [5]Then the LORD said to me: Human one, pay close attention! Use your eyes and ears and listen to all that I say to you concerning the regulations of the LORD's temple and all its instructions. Pay close attention to the access to the temple through all the sanctuary portals.[q] [6]Speak to the rebels, to the house of Israel, The LORD God proclaims: Enough of your detestable practices, house of Israel! [7]You made my temple unclean because you brought into my sanctuary foreigners who were physically and spiritually uncircumcised. When

[p]Heb *ammah ammah*, traditionally *a long cubit* [q]Or *exits*

you offered my food of fat and blood to me, you[r] broke my covenant with all your detestable practices. [8]You didn't keep charge of my holy things. On the contrary, you appointed them[s] to keep charge in my sanctuary for you.

[9]The LORD God proclaims: Foreigners who are spiritually and physically uncircumcised must not enter my sanctuary; that is, all foreigners among the Israelites. [10]But the Levites, who went far from me when Israel went astray, who went astray from me after their idols, will bear their guilt. [11]They will keep charge in my sanctuary, and they will oversee the temple gates and keep charge of the temple. They will slaughter the entirely burned offerings and the sacrifices for the people, and they will stand before them to minister to them. [12]Because they ministered to them before their idols, they brought about the downfall of the house of Israel. For that reason I made a solemn pledge against them—this is what the LORD God says—and they will bear their guilt. [13]They won't approach me to officiate for me as priests or approach any of my holy things or the most holy place. Though they will bear their humiliation and the consequences of their detestable practices, [14]I will appoint them to keep charge of the temple, all its work, and all that is done in it.

[15]As for the priests of the levitical family of Zadok who did keep charge of my sanctuary when the Israelites strayed away from me, they will draw near to me to serve me. They will stand in my presence to present fat and blood to me. This is what the LORD God says. [16]They will come into my sanctuary, and they will approach my table to minister to me. They will keep my charge. [17]When they come through the gates to the inner courtyard, they will wear linen garments. They won't wear any wool when they minister at the gates of the inner courtyard or in the temple. [18]They will have linen turbans on their heads and linen undergarments around their waists. They won't wear anything that makes them sweat. [19]When they go out to the outer courtyard to the people, they will remove the garments in which they were ministering. They will lay them aside in the holy chambers and wear other clothing. They must not transfer holiness to the people through their clothing. [20]They must neither shave their heads nor let their hair grow long, but they will trim the hair on their heads. [21]None of the priests should drink wine when they come into the inner courtyard. [22]They must not marry widows or divorced women, but only Israelite virgins. Priests may, however, marry the widows of other priests. [23]They must teach my people the difference between the holy and the ordinary, and show them the difference between clean and unclean. [24]They must execute judgments according to my case laws in cases of civil conflict. They must observe my instructions and my regulations regarding all my festivals. They must keep my sabbaths holy. [25]In order to avoid uncleanness, they must not approach the dead. They may, however, become unclean for their father or mother, son or daughter, brother or unmarried sister. [26]Once the priest is clean again, he must count off seven days. [27]On the day that he comes into the holy place, the inner courtyard, to minister in the holy place, he will present his purification offering. This is what the LORD God says. [28]As for their inheritance, I am their inheritance. They won't be given family property in Israel; I am their family property. [29]They will eat the grain offerings, the purification offerings, and the compensation offerings. Every dedicated thing in Israel belongs to them. [30]The best of the early produce of every kind, and every contribution, all of them, belong to the priests. You will give the best of your bread dough to the priest so that a blessing may come to rest on your household. [31]The priests must not eat any bird or animal that dies naturally or is torn apart by prey.

The holy portion

45 When you distribute the land as an inheritance, you will set aside a holy portion of land for the LORD. It will be 7.1 miles long and 5.68 miles[t] wide. It will be

[r]LXX, Syr, Vulg; MT *they* [s]Heb lacks *them.* [t]LXX *twenty thousand* (*pechon*, standard cubit); MT *ten thousand* (*ammah*); see note at Ezek 40:5.

holy throughout the entire area. 2Out of this portion, an area seven hundred fifty feet by seven hundred fifty feet square will be for the sanctuary. All around it will be an open space seventy-five feet wide. 3Beginning with this measurement, you will measure out an area 7.1 miles long and 2.84 miles wide. The sanctuary, the most holy place, will lie on it. 4It is holy, set apart from the land, and it belongs to the priests who draw near to minister in the LORD's sanctuary. It will be a place for their houses, and a holy place for the sanctuary. 5The area 7.1 miles long and 2.84 miles wide will be for the Levites who minister in the temple. Twenty chambers are theirs as their property. 6As the property for the city, you will set aside an area 1.42 miles wide and 7.1 miles long next to the holy portion. It will be for the whole house of Israel. 7The territory for the prince will be on both sides of the holy portion and the city property, alongside the holy portion and alongside the city property, from their western boundaries westward and from their eastern boundaries eastward. Its length will equal one tribal portion, from the western border to the eastern border. 8The land will be his property in Israel, and my princes will no longer oppress my people. They will give the land to the house of Israel according to their tribes.

9The LORD God proclaims: Enough, princes of Israel! Turn aside from violence and oppression. Establish justice and righteousness. Cease your evictions of my people! This is what the LORD God says: 10You must use fair scales, a fair ephah,[u] and a fair bath.[v] 11The ephah and the bath must be the same size. Both should be calibrated to the homer: each will contain one-tenth of a homer. 12The shekel must weigh twenty gerahs. Twenty shekels, twenty-five shekels, and fifteen shekels will equal one maneh for you.

Sacrificial offerings and gifts

13These are your prescribed contributions: one-sixth of an ephah for each homer of wheat, and one-sixth of an ephah for each homer of barley; 14a regular amount of oil,[w] one-tenth of a bath for each kor[x] (each kor[y] contains ten baths); 15and one sheep from the flock for every two hundred from Israel's pastureland, for grain offerings, for entirely burned offerings, and for well-being sacrifices to make reconciliation for them. This is what the LORD God says. 16All the people will make this contribution on behalf of the prince in Israel. 17The prince will be responsible for the entirely burned offerings, grain offerings, and drink offerings for the festivals, new moons, and sabbaths, all the appointed festivals of the house of Israel. He will offer the purification offering, the grain offering, the entirely burned offering, and the well-being sacrifice to make reconciliation on behalf of the house of Israel.

Festivals

18The LORD God proclaims: On the first day of the first month,[z] you will take a flawless young bull from the herd, and you will purify the sanctuary. 19The priest will take some of the blood from the purification offering, and he will set it on the doorposts of the temple and on the four corners of the ledge of the altar and on the doorposts of the gate to the inner courtyard. 20You will do the same on the seventh day of the month for anyone who sins through inadvertence or ignorance. So you will purge the temple. 21Your Passover will be on the fourteenth day of the first month. Unleavened bread will be eaten during the seven days of the festival. 22On that day, the prince will provide a young bull as the purification offering for himself and for the people of the land. 23For the seven days of the festival, he will provide seven flawless bulls and seven flawless rams, one for each day of the festival, as the entirely burned offering for the LORD, and, for the purification offering, one male goat for each day. 24He will also provide the grain offerings, one ephah[a] for each bull, and one ephah for each ram, with one hin[b] of oil for each ephah. 25For the

[u]One ephah is approximately twenty quarts of grain. [v]One bath is approximately twenty quarts of liquid.
[w]Syr, Tg; MT adds *a bath of oil.* [x]MT adds *each homer contains ten baths.* [y]Vulg; MT *homer* [z]March–April, Nisan
[a]One ephah is approximately twenty quarts of grain. [b]One hin is approximately equal to one gallon.

festival that begins on the fifteenth day of the seventh month,[c] he will make the same provisions for the purification offerings, entirely burned offerings, grain offerings, and oil, for all seven days of the festival.

Sabbaths and gift offerings

46 The LORD God proclaims: The east-facing gate of the inner courtyard will remain closed for the six days of the workweek. But on the Sabbath and on the day of the new moon it will be opened, 2and the prince will come in from outside by way of the porch of the gate and stand at the gate's doorposts. The priests will present the prince's entirely burned offerings and well-being sacrifices, and then he will bow down on the threshold of the gate and go out. The gate won't be closed until evening 3so that the people of the land may bow in the presence of the LORD on sabbaths and new moons at the opening of that gate. 4On the Sabbath day, the prince will offer to the LORD an entirely burned offering of six flawless lambs and a flawless ram, 5a grain offering of one ephah for the ram, and a grain offering at his discretion for the lambs, with one hin of oil for each ephah. 6For the day of the new moon, the offering will be a flawless young bull from the herd, six lambs, and a flawless ram, 7and he will provide a grain offering of one ephah each for the bull and the ram, and for the lambs as much as he likes, with one hin of oil for each ephah.

8When the prince enters, he comes in by way of the porch of the gate and goes out in the same direction. 9When the people of the land come into the LORD's presence for the festivals, those who enter through the north gate to worship should go out through the south, and those who come in through the south gate should go out through the north gate. They shouldn't turn around and go out the same way they came in. Instead, they should go out the opposite gate. 10The prince should accompany them: when they come in, he comes in, and when they go out, he goes out. 11At the festivals and appointed gatherings, the grain offering is one ephah for each bull, one ephah for each ram, and whatever one is able to give for each lamb, with one hin of oil for each ephah.

12Whenever the prince makes a spontaneous gift to the LORD, whether it is an entirely burned offering or a well-being sacrifice, the gate facing east will be opened for him, and he will present his entirely burned offering and well-being sacrifices, just as he does on the Sabbath day. When he leaves, the gate will be closed after he has gone out.

Daily offerings

13As a daily entirely burned offering for the LORD, you will provide a flawless year-old lamb. You will make the offering every morning. 14You will provide a grain offering along with it every morning, one-sixth of an ephah along with one-third of a hin of oil to moisten the choice flour. This is a permanent and perpetual regulation for the grain offering to the LORD. 15So the lamb, the grain offering, and the oil are provided every morning as a perpetual entirely burned offering.

Royal land grants

16The LORD God proclaims: When the prince gives a gift to each of his sons, it becomes their inheritance. It becomes their family property as an inheritance. 17And if he gives one of his servants a gift from his inheritance, it will belong to the servant only until the year of release, and then it will revert to the prince. It is his children's inheritance; it belongs to them. 18The prince won't take the people's inheritance by evicting them from their family property. He will bequeath only his own property to his sons, lest any of my people be deprived of their rightful property.

Kitchens

19Then he brought me through the passage beside the gate next to the priests' quarters, the holy chambers facing north. There was a place hidden away on the western side. 20He said to me, "Rather than

[c] September–October, Tishrei

taking these offerings out into the outer courtyard and transferring holiness to the people, this is the place where the priests will boil the compensation offerings and the purification offerings, and where they will bake the grain offerings."

[21]Then he took me to the outer courtyard, and he had me pass through its four corners, and I saw that there were additional courtyards in each of the corners. [22]In all four corners of the courtyard, these courtyards were constructed to handle smoke. All four were the same size, sixty feet long by forty-five feet wide. [23]All four had stone masonry all the way around, and hearths were built under this masonry all the way around. [24]He said to me, "These are the kitchens where those who minister in the temple cook the people's sacrifices."

The river

47 When he brought me back to the temple's entrance, I noticed that water was flowing toward the east from under the temple's threshold (the temple faced east). The water was going out from under the temple's facade toward the south, south of the altar. [2]He led me out through the north gate and around the outside to the outer east gate, where the water flowed out under the facade on the south side. [3]With the line in his hand, the man went out toward the east. When he measured off fifteen hundred feet, he made me cross the water; it was ankle-deep. [4]He measured off another fifteen hundred feet and made me cross the water; it was knee-deep. He measured off another fifteen hundred feet and made me cross the water, and it was waist-high. [5]When he measured off another fifteen hundred feet, it had become a river that I couldn't cross. The water was high, deep enough for swimming but too high to cross. [6]He said to me, "Human one, do you see?" Then he led me back to the edge of the river. [7]When I went back, I saw very many trees on both banks of the river. [8]He said to me, "These waters go out to the eastern region, flow down the steep slopes,[d] and go into the Dead Sea.[e] When the flowing waters enter the sea, its water becomes fresh. [9]Wherever the river flows, every living thing that moves will thrive. There will be great schools of fish, because when these waters enter the sea, it will be fresh. Wherever the river flows, everything will live. [10]People will stand fishing beside it, from En-gedi to En-eglayim, and it will become a place for spreading nets. It will be like the Mediterranean Sea,[f] having all kinds of fish in it. [11]Its marshes and swamps won't be made fresh (they are left for salt), [12]but on both banks of the river will grow up all kinds of fruit-bearing trees. Their leaves won't wither, and their fruitfulness won't wane. They will produce fruit in every month, because their water comes from the sanctuary. Their fruit will be for eating, their leaves for healing."

[13]The LORD God proclaims: These[g] are the boundaries of the portions of land that will be distributed as an inheritance to the twelve tribes of Israel. Joseph will receive two portions. [14]What I swore to give to your ancestors, you will distribute as an inheritance equally. This land is given to you as an inheritance. [15]This is the boundary of the land. The northern limit begins at the Mediterranean Sea and goes in the direction of Hethlon toward Lebo-hamath, Zedad,[h] [16]Berothah, Sibraim (which is between the boundary of Damascus and the boundary of Hamath), and Hazer-hatticon (that is on the boundary of Hauran). [17]So the boundary from the Mediterranean Sea[i] to Hazar-enon will run north of the boundary of Damascus, with the boundary of Hamath to the north. This is the northern limit. [18]For the eastern limit, you will measure continuously between Hauran and Damascus and between Gilead and the land of Israel, along the Jordan River as far as the Dead Sea.[j] This is the eastern limit. [19]The southern limit runs from Tamar to the waters of Meribath-kadesh and from there along the border[k] of Egypt to the

[d]Or *Arabah* [e]Or *sea* [f]Or *great sea* [g]LXX, Tg, Vulg; Heb uncertain [h]LXX; MT transposes *Hamath* and *Zedad*. [i]Or *the sea* [j]Or *eastern sea* [k]Or *Wadi*; traditionally *Brook*

Mediterranean Sea. This is the southern limit. [20]For the western limit, the Mediterranean Sea is the boundary up to Lebo-hamath. This is the western limit. [21]You will apportion this land among yourselves according to the tribes of Israel. [22]When you distribute the land as an inheritance, the immigrants who reside with you and raise families among you are considered full citizens along with the Israelites. They will receive an inheritance along with you among the tribes of Israel. [23]You will assign the immigrants' inheritance with the tribe with whom they reside. This is what the LORD God says.

48 These are the tribes' names: Beginning at the north, along the Hethlon road from Lebo-hamath to Hazar-enon, the boundary of Damascus with Hamath to the north, from the eastern border to the western border: Dan, one portion. [2]Along the boundary of Dan from the eastern border to the western border: Asher, one portion. [3]Along the boundary of Asher from the eastern border to the western border: Naphtali, one portion. [4]Along the boundary of Naphtali from the eastern border to the western border: Manasseh, one portion. [5]Along the boundary of Manasseh from the eastern border to the western border: Ephraim, one portion. [6]Along the boundary of Ephraim from the eastern border to the western border: Reuben, one portion. [7]Along the boundary of Reuben from the eastern border to the western border: Judah, one portion.

[8]Along the boundary of Judah from the eastern border to the western border will be the portion that you will set aside, 7.1 miles wide and the length of a tribal portion from the eastern border to the western border. The sanctuary is in its center. [9]The portion that you will set aside for the LORD will be 7.1 miles long and 5.68 miles[1] wide. [10]These measurements define the holy portion for the priests: along the north, a length of 7.1 miles; along the west, a width of 2.84 miles; along the east, a width of 2.84 miles; and along the south, a length of 7.1 miles. The LORD's sanctuary is in its center. [11]This holy area is for the Zadokite priests who kept my charge and didn't stray as the Levites did when the house of Israel strayed away from me. [12]It belongs to them as a most special portion of the land, a most holy place, up to the border of the Levites. [13]The Levites' allotment is next to the boundary of the priests, a length of 7.1 miles and a width of 2.84 miles. The entire length is 7.1 miles and the width 2.84 miles. [14]None of it will be sold, exchanged, or transferred. It is the choicest land, because it is holy to the LORD. [15]The remaining area, 1.42 miles wide and 7.1 miles long, is for ordinary use for the city, for residences, and for pastures. The city will be in the middle of it. [16]It measures 1.28 miles on its northern border, 1.28 miles on its southern border, 1.28 miles on its eastern border, and 1.28 miles on its western border. [17]There will be pastures for the city, three hundred seventy-five feet on the north side, three hundred seventy-five feet on the south side, three hundred seventy-five feet on the east side, and three hundred seventy-five feet on the west side. [18]The remaining area alongside the holy portion is 2.84 miles on the east and 2.84 miles on the west. These areas that adjoin the holy portion will produce the food for the city's workers. [19]The city's workers from every tribe of Israel will farm it. [20]The entire portion that you will set aside is 7.1 miles by 7.1 miles, a square; it includes the holy portion in addition to the city property. [21]What is left on both sides of the holy portion and the city property belongs to the prince. The land from the edge of the portion of 7.1 miles, to the eastern boundary, and on the western edge of the 7.1 miles to the western boundary, belongs to the prince. It corresponds to one tribal portion. The holy portion and the temple sanctuary are in the middle of it, [22]but what belongs to the prince is separate from both the levitical property and the city property. The prince's territory will be between the boundary of Judah and the boundary of Benjamin.

[1]Cf LXX and Ezek 45:1; MT *ten thousand ammah* equals 2.84 miles.

23 Now for the rest of the tribes: From the eastern border to the western border: Benjamin, one portion. 24 Along the boundary of Benjamin from the eastern border to the western border: Simeon, one portion. 25 Along the boundary of Simeon from the eastern border to the western border: Issachar, one portion. 26 Along the boundary of Issachar from the eastern border to the western border: Zebulun, one portion. 27 Along the boundary of Zebulun from the eastern border to the western border: Gad, one portion. 28 Along the boundary of Gad to the southern border, the boundary will run from Tamar to the waters of Meribath-kadesh and from there to the border of Egypt[m] and to the Mediterranean Sea.[n] 29 This is the land that you will distribute as an inheritance for the tribes of Israel. These are their portions. This is what the LORD God says.

30 These are the city exits. The north side is measured at 1.28 miles. 31 The gates of the city go by the names of the tribes of Israel. There are three gates on the north side: one gate for Reuben, one gate for Judah, and one gate for Levi. 32 There are three gates on the east side along its 1.28 miles: one gate for Joseph, one gate for Benjamin, and one gate for Dan. 33 There are three gates on the south side measuring 1.28 miles: one gate for Simeon, one gate for Issachar, and one gate for Zebulun. 34 There are three gates on the west side along its 1.28 miles: one gate for Gad, one gate for Asher, and one gate for Naphtali. 35 The circumference of the city is 5.1 miles. As of today, the name of the city is The LORD Is There.

DANIEL

Jerusalem taken by the Babylonians

1 In the third year of the rule of Judah's King Jehoiakim, Babylon's King Nebuchadnezzar came to Jerusalem and attacked it. 2 The Lord handed Judah's King Jehoiakim over to Nebuchadnezzar, along with some of the equipment from God's house. Nebuchadnezzar took these to Shinar, to his own god's temple, putting them in his god's treasury.

Training for royal service

3 Nebuchadnezzar instructed his highest official Ashpenaz to choose royal descendants and members of the ruling class from the Israelites—4 good-looking young men without defects, skilled in all wisdom, possessing knowledge, conversant with learning, and capable of serving in the king's palace. Ashpenaz was to teach them the Chaldean language and its literature. 5 The king assigned these young men daily allotments from his own food and from the royal wine. Ashpenaz was to teach them for three years so that at the end of that time they could serve before the king. 6 Among these young men from the Judeans were Daniel, Hananiah, Mishael, and Azariah. 7 But the chief official gave them new names. He named Daniel "Belteshazzar," Hananiah "Shadrach," Mishael "Meshach," and Azariah "Abednego."

Test

8 Daniel decided that he wouldn't pollute himself with the king's rations or the royal wine, and he appealed to the chief official in hopes that he wouldn't have to do so. 9 Now God had established faithful loyalty between Daniel and the chief official; 10 but the chief official said to Daniel, "I'm afraid of my master, the king, who has mandated what you are to eat and drink. What will happen if he sees your faces looking thinner than the other young men in your group? The king will have my head because of you!"

11 So Daniel spoke to the guard whom the chief official had appointed over Daniel, Hananiah, Mishael, and Azariah: 12 "Why not test your servants for ten days? You could give us a diet of vegetables to eat and water to drink. 13 Then compare our appearance

[m] Or *Wadi*; traditionally *Brook*, MT lacks *of Egypt*. [n] Or *Great Sea*

to the appearance of the young men who eat the king's food. Then deal with your servants according to what you see."

14The guard decided to go along with their plan and tested them for ten days. 15At the end of ten days they looked better and healthier than all the young men who were eating the king's food. 16So the guard kept taking away their rations and the wine they were supposed to drink and gave them vegetables instead. 17And God gave knowledge, mastery of all literature, and wisdom to these four men. Daniel himself gained understanding of every type of vision and dream.

Result of the training

18When the time came to review the young men as the king had ordered, the chief official brought them before Nebuchadnezzar. 19When the king spoke with them, he found no one as good as Daniel, Hananiah, Mishael, and Azariah. So they took their place in the king's service. 20Whenever the king consulted them about any aspect of wisdom and understanding, he found them head and shoulders above all the dream interpreters and enchanters in his entire kingdom. 21And Daniel stayed in the king's service until the first year of King Cyrus.

An impossible challenge

2 In the second year of Nebuchadnezzar's rule, he had many dreams. The dreams made him anxious, but he kept sleeping. 2The king summoned the dream interpreters, enchanters, diviners, and Chaldeans to explain his dreams to him. They came and stood before the king.

3Then the king said to them: "I had a dream, and I'm anxious to know its meaning."

4The Chaldeans answered the king in Aramaic:[a] "Long live the king! Tell your servants the dream, and we will explain its meaning."

5The king answered the Chaldeans: "My decision is final: If you can't tell me the dream and its meaning, you will be torn limb from limb, and your houses will be turned into trash dumps. 6But if you do explain the dream and its meaning, you'll receive generous gifts and glorious honor from me. So explain to me the dream as well as its meaning."

7They answered him again: "The king must tell his servants the dream. We will then explain the meaning."

8The king replied: "Now I definitely know you are stalling for time, because you see that my decision is final 9and that if you can't tell me the dream, your fate is certain. You've conspired to make false and lying speeches before me until the situation changes. Tell me the dream now! Then I'll know you can explain its meaning to me."

10The Chaldeans answered the king: "No one on earth can do what the king is asking! No king or ruler, no matter how great, has ever asked such a thing of any dream interpreter, enchanter, or Chaldean. 11What the king is asking is impossible! No one could declare the dream to the king but the gods, who don't live among mere humans."

12At this, the king exploded in a furious rage and ordered that all Babylon's sages be wiped out. 13So the command went out: The sages were to be killed. Daniel and his friends too were hunted down; they were to be killed as well.

God reveals the mystery

14Then Daniel, with wisdom and sound judgment, responded to Arioch the king's chief executioner, who had gone out to kill Babylon's sages. 15He said to Arioch the king's royal officer, "Why is the king's command so unreasonable?" After Arioch explained the situation to Daniel, 16Daniel went and asked the king to give him some time so he could explain the dream's meaning to him. 17Then Daniel went to his house and explained the situation to his friends Hananiah, Mishael, and Azariah 18so that they would ask the God of heaven for help about this mystery, in hopes that Daniel and his friends wouldn't die with the rest of Babylon's sages. 19Then, in a vision by night, the mystery was revealed to Daniel! Daniel praised the God of heaven:

[a] The book switches into Aramaic at this point, returning to Hebrew in 8:1.

20 God's name be praised
from age to eternal age!
Wisdom and might are his!
21 God is the one who changes
times and eras,
who dethrones one king,
only to establish another,
who grants wisdom to the wise and
knowledge to those with insight.
22 God is the one who uncovers
what lies deeply hidden;
he knows what hides in darkness;
light lives with him!
23 I acknowledge and praise you,
my fathers' God!
You've given me wisdom and might,
and now you've made known to me
what we asked of you:
you've made known to us
the king's demand.

Daniel recounts the dream

24 So Daniel went to Arioch, the man the king had appointed to wipe out Babylon's sages. Daniel said to him, "Don't wipe out the sages of Babylon! Bring me before the king, and I will explain the dream's meaning to him." 25 Wasting no time, Arioch brought Daniel before the king, telling him, "I have found someone from the Judean exiles who will tell the dream's meaning to the king."

26 In reply the king said to Daniel (whose name was Belteshazzar), "Can you really tell me the dream that I saw, as well as its meaning?"

27 Daniel answered the king, "Sages, enchanters, dream interpreters, and diviners can't explain to the king the mystery he seeks. 28 But there is a God in heaven, a revealer of mysteries, who has shown King Nebuchadnezzar what will happen in the days to come! Now this was your dream—this was the vision in your head as you lay in your bed:

29 "As you lay in bed, Your Majesty, your thoughts turned to what will happen in the future. The revealer of mysteries has revealed to you what will happen. 30 Now this mystery was revealed to me, not because I have more wisdom than any other living person but so that the dream's meaning might be made known to the king, and so that you might know the thoughts of your own mind.

31 "Your Majesty, you were looking, and there, rising before you, was a single, massive statue. This statue was huge, shining with dazzling light, and was awesome to see. 32 The statue's head was made of pure gold; its chest and arms were made from silver; its abdomen and hips were made of bronze. 33 Its legs were of iron, and its feet were a mixture of iron and clay. 34 You observed this until a stone was cut, but not by hands; and it smashed the statue's feet of iron and clay and shattered them. 35 Then all the parts shattered simultaneously—iron, clay, bronze, silver, and gold. They became like chaff, left on summer threshing floors. The wind lifted them away until no trace of them remained. But the stone that smashed the statue became a mighty mountain, and it filled the entire earth.

The dream's meaning: four future rulers

36 "This was the dream. Now we will tell the king its meaning: 37 You, Your Majesty, are the king of kings. The God of heaven has given kingship, power, might, and glory to you! 38 God has delivered into your care human beings, wild creatures, and birds in the sky—wherever they live—and has made you ruler of all of them. You are the gold head. 39 But in your place, another kingdom will arise, one inferior to yours, and then a third, bronze kingdom will rule over all the earth. 40 Then will come a fourth kingdom, mighty like iron. Just as iron shatters and crushes everything; so like an iron that smashes, it will shatter and crush all these others. 41 As for the feet and toes that you saw, which were a mixture of potter's clay and iron, that signifies a divided kingdom; but it will possess some of the unyielding strength of iron. Even so, you saw the iron mixed with earthy clay 42 so that the toes were made from a mixture of iron and clay. Part of the kingdom will be mighty, but part of it will be fragile. 43 Just as you saw the iron mixed with earthy clay, they will join together by intermarrying,

but they will not bond to each other, just as
iron does not fuse with clay.
44“But in the days of those kings, the God
of heaven will raise up an everlasting kingdom that will be indestructible. Its rule will
never pass to another people. It will shatter
other kingdoms. It will put an end to all of
them. It will stand firm forever, 45just like
you saw when the stone, which was cut
from the mountain, but not by hands, shattered the iron, bronze, clay, silver, and gold.
A great God has revealed to the king what
will happen in the future. The dream is certain. Its meaning can be trusted.”

Nebuchadnezzar honors Daniel

46Then King Nebuchadnezzar bowed
low and honored Daniel. The king ordered
that grain and incense offerings be made
to Daniel. 47The king declared to Daniel,
“No doubt about it: your God is God of
gods, Lord of kings, and a revealer of mysteries because you were able to reveal this
mystery!” 48Then the king exalted Daniel
and lavished gifts on him, making him
ruler over all the province of Babylon and
chief minister over all Babylon’s sages.
49At Daniel’s urging, the king appointed
Shadrach, Meshach, and Abednego to
administer the province of Babylon, but
Daniel himself remained at the royal court.

Gold statue

3 King Nebuchadnezzar made a gold
statue. It was ninety feet high and nine
feet wide. He set it up in the Dura Valley
in the province of Babylon. 2King Nebuchadnezzar then ordered the chief administrators, ministers, governors, counselors,
treasurers, judges, magistrates, and all the
provincial officials to assemble and come
for the dedication of the statue that he had
set up. 3So the chief administrators, ministers, governors, counselors, treasurers,
judges, magistrates, and all the provincial
officials assembled for the dedication of
the statue that King Nebuchadnezzar had
set up. They stood in front of the statue
the king had set up. 4The herald proclaimed
loudly: “Peoples, nations, and languages!
This is what you must do: 5When you hear
the sound of the horn, pipe, zither, lyre,
harp, flute, and every kind of instrument,
you must bow down and worship the gold
statue that King Nebuchadnezzar has set
up. 6Anyone who will not bow down and
worship will be immediately thrown into a
furnace of flaming fire.” 7So because of this
order as soon as they heard the sound of
the horn, pipe, zither, lyre, harp, flute,[b] and
every kind of instrument, all the peoples,
nations, and languages bowed down and
worshipped the gold statue that King Nebuchadnezzar had set up.

Plot against Shadrach, Meshach, and Abednego

8At that moment some Chaldeans came
forward, seizing a chance to attack the
Jews. 9They said to King Nebuchadnezzar:
“Long live the king! 10Your Majesty, you
gave a command that everyone who hears
the sound of the horn, pipe, zither, lyre,
harp, flute, and every kind of instrument
should bow down and worship the gold
statue. 11Anyone who wouldn’t bow and worship would be thrown into a furnace of flaming fire. 12Now there are some Jews, ones
you appointed to administer the province of
Babylon—specifically, Shadrach, Meshach,
and Abednego—who have ignored your
command. They don’t serve your gods, and
they don’t worship the gold statue you’ve
set up.”
13In a violent rage Nebuchadnezzar ordered them to bring Shadrach, Meshach,
and Abednego. They were brought before
the king.
14Nebuchadnezzar said to them:
“Shadrach, Meshach, and Abednego: Is it
true that you don’t serve my gods or worship the gold statue I’ve set up? 15If you are
now ready to do so, bow down and worship
the gold statue I’ve made when you hear
the sound of horn, pipe, zither, lyre, harp,
flute, and every kind of instrument. But if
you won’t worship it, you will be thrown
straight into the furnace of flaming fire.

[b] Identification of the instruments is not certain; several of the Aramaic terms are Greek loanwords.

Then what god will rescue you from my power?"

[16]Shadrach, Meshach, and Abednego answered King Nebuchadnezzar: "We don't need to answer your question. [17]If our God—the one we serve—is able to rescue us from the furnace of flaming fire and from your power, Your Majesty, then let him rescue us.[c] [18]But if he doesn't, know this for certain, Your Majesty: we will never serve your gods or worship the gold statue you've set up."

Inside the furnace

[19]Nebuchadnezzar was filled with rage, and his face twisted beyond recognition because of Shadrach, Meshach, and Abednego. In response he commanded that the furnace be heated to seven times its normal heat. [20]He told some of the strongest men in his army to bind Shadrach, Meshach, and Abednego and throw them into the furnace of flaming fire. [21]So Shadrach, Meshach, and Abednego were bound, still dressed in all their clothes, and thrown into the furnace of flaming fire. ([22]Now the king's command had been rash, and the furnace was heated to such an extreme that the fire's flame killed the very men who carried Shadrach, Meshach, and Abednego to it.) [23]So these three men, Shadrach, Meshach, and Abednego, fell, bound, into the furnace of flaming fire.

[24]Then King Nebuchadnezzar jumped up in shock and said to his associates, "Didn't we throw three men, bound, into the fire?"

They answered the king, "Certainly, Your Majesty."

[25]He replied, "Look! I see four men, unbound, walking around inside the fire, and they aren't hurt! And the fourth one looks like one of the gods." [26]Nebuchadnezzar went near the opening of the furnace of flaming fire and said, "Shadrach, Meshach, and Abednego, servants of the Most High God, come out! Come here!" Then Shadrach, Meshach, and Abednego came out of the fire. [27]The chief administrators, ministers, governors, and the king's associates crowded around to look at them. The fire hadn't done anything to them: their hair wasn't singed; their garments looked the same as before; they didn't even smell like fire!

Nebuchadnezzar praises God

[28]Nebuchadnezzar declared: "May the God of Shadrach, Meshach, and Abednego be praised! He sent his messenger[d] to rescue his servants who trusted him. They ignored the king's order, sacrificing their bodies, because they wouldn't serve or worship any god but their God. [29]I now issue a decree to every people, nation, and language: whoever speaks disrespectfully about Shadrach, Meshach, and Abednego's God will be torn limb from limb and their house made a trash heap, because there is no other god who can rescue like this."

[30]Then the king made Shadrach, Meshach, and Abednego prosperous in the province of Babylon.

Nebuchadnezzar's testimony

4 [e]King Nebuchadnezzar's message to all the peoples, nations, and languages inhabiting the entire earth: "I wish you much peace. [2]I'm delighted to share the signs and miracles that the Most High God has worked in my life.

[3]His signs are superb!
His miracles so powerful!
His kingdom is everlasting.
His rule is for all time.

[4][f]"While I, Nebuchadnezzar, was safe in my house, content in my palace, [5]I had a terrifying dream. My thoughts while I was lying in bed and the vision in my mind overwhelmed me. [6]I ordered all Babylon's sages to come before me, so they might tell me the dream's meaning. [7]So the dream interpreters, enchanters, Chaldeans, and diviners came. I told them the dream, but they couldn't interpret it for me. [8]Daniel, who is called Belteshazzar after the name of my god, was the last to come before me. In him is the breath[g] of the holy gods! I told Daniel the dream:

[c]Or *he will deliver us* [d]Or *angel* [e]3:31 in Aram [f]4:1 in Aram [g]Or *spirit*; also in 4:9, 18

Nebuchadnezzar's dream

9 “Belteshazzar, chief of the dream interpreters, I know the breath of the holy gods
is in you, and no mystery is too difficult for
you. Tell me the meaning of the visions I
had in my dream. 10 In my mind, as I lay in
bed, I saw a vision:

At the center of the earth
was a towering tree.
11 The tree grew in size and strength;
it was as high as the sky;
it could be seen
from every corner of the earth.
12 Its leaves were beautiful,
its fruit abundant;
it had enough food for everyone.
Wild animals took shade under it;
birds nested in its branches.
All living things lived off that tree.

13 “In my mind, as I lay in bed, I saw another vision: A holy watcher came down
from heaven. 14 He proclaimed loudly:

‘Cut down the tree
and shear off its branches!
Strip its leaves and scatter its fruit!
The creatures should flee
from its shelter;
the birds should take flight
from its branches.
15 But leave its deepest root in the earth,
bound with iron and bronze
in the field grass.
Dew from heaven is to wash it,
and it must live with the animals
in the earth's vegetation.
16 Its[h] human mind is to be changed:
it will be given the mind of an animal.
Seven periods of time will pass
over it.
17 This sentence is by the watchers' decree;
this decision is the holy ones' word
so that all who live might know
that the Most High
dominates human kingship.
The Most High gives kingship
to anyone he wants
and sets over it the lowest of people.’

18 “This is the dream that I, King Nebuchadnezzar, had. So now Belteshazzar, tell
me the meaning because all the sages in my
kingdom were unable to interpret it for me.
But you are able to do it because the breath
of the holy gods is in you.”

Daniel interprets the visions

19 Daniel, who was called Belteshazzar,
was shocked for a bit. What he thought
about frightened him.

The king declared, “Don't let the dream
and its meaning scare you, Belteshazzar.”

Then Belteshazzar answered, “Sir, I wish
the dream to be for those who hate you and
its meaning to be for your enemies! 20 The
tree you saw that grew in size and strength,
that was as high as the sky, that could be
seen from every corner of the earth, 21 with
its beautiful leaves and its abundant fruit,
and that had enough food for everyone,
with wild animals living under it and birds
nesting in its branches— 22 Your Majesty,
that tree is you! You have grown large and
become powerful. Your greatness is as high
as the sky; your rule extends to the edge of
the earth!

23 “Your Majesty, the holy watcher you
saw coming down from heaven, who said,
‘Cut down the tree and destroy it, but leave
its deepest root in the earth, bound with
iron and bronze in the field grass, dew
from heaven is to wash it, and it must live
with the wild animals until seven periods
of time pass over it’— 24 Your Majesty, this
is the dream's meaning: It is the sentence
of the Most High, delivered to my master the king. 25 You will be driven away
from other humans and will live with the
wild animals. You will eat grass like cattle
and will be washed by dew from heaven.
Seven periods of time will pass over you,
until you acknowledge that the Most High
dominates human kingship, giving it to
anyone he wants. 26 And when he said to
leave the deepest root of the tree—that
means your kingship will again be yours,
once you acknowledge that heaven rules
all. 27 Therefore, Your Majesty, please accept my advice: remove your sins by doing
what is right; remove your wrongdoing

[h] Throughout 4:15-16 and later in this chap, *it* and *its* could also be translated *he* and *his*.

by showing mercy to the poor. Then your safety will be long lasting."

Visions come true

28 All this happened to King Nebuchadnezzar. 29 Twelve months later, he was walking on the roof of the royal palace in Babylon. 30 The king declared, "Isn't this Babylon, the magnificent city that I built as the royal house by my own mighty strength and for my own majestic glory?"

31 These words hadn't even left the king's mouth when a voice came from heaven: "You, King Nebuchadnezzar, are now informed: Kingship is taken away from you. 32 You will be driven away from other humans and will live with the wild animals. You will eat grass like cattle, and seven periods of time will pass over you until you acknowledge that the Most High dominates human kingship, giving it to anyone he wants."

33 Nebuchadnezzar's sentence was immediately carried out. He was driven away from other humans and ate grass like cattle. Dew from heaven washed his body until he grew hair like eagles' feathers and claws like a bird.

Nebuchadnezzar is restored

34 "At the end of that time, I, Nebuchadnezzar, raised my eyes to heaven. My reason returned to me, and I praised the Most High. I worshipped and glorified the one who lives forever because his rule is everlasting; his kingdom is for all time. 35 All of earth's inhabitants are nothing in comparison. The Most High does whatever he wants with heaven's forces and with earth's inhabitants. No one can contain his power or say to him, 'What do you think you are doing?' 36 So at that moment my reason returned to me. My honor and splendor came back to me for the glory of my kingdom. My associates and my princes wanted to be with me again. Not only was I reinstated over my kingdom, I received more power than ever before.

37 "Now I, Nebuchadnezzar, worship, magnify, and glorify the king of heaven. All his works are truth, all his paths are justice, and he is able to humble all who walk in pride."

Belshazzar's party

5 King Belshazzar threw a huge party for a thousand of his princes, and he drank a lot of wine in front of them. 2 While he was under the wine's influence, Belshazzar commanded that the gold and silver equipment that his father Nebuchadnezzar had taken from Jerusalem's temple be brought to the party so that the king, his princes, his consorts, and his secondary wives could drink wine out of them. 3 So the gold[i] equipment that had been carried out of the temple, God's house in Jerusalem, was brought in; and the king, his princes, his consorts, and his secondary wives drank out of it. 4 They drank a lot of wine; and they praised the gods of gold, silver, bronze, iron, wood, and stone.

Writing on the wall

5 Right then the fingers of a human hand appeared and wrote on the plaster of the king's palace wall in the light of the lamp. The king saw the hand that wrote. 6 The king's mood changed immediately, and he was deeply disturbed. He felt weak, and his knees were shaking. 7 The king yelled, calling for the enchanters, the Chaldeans, and the diviners.

The king told these sages of Babylon: "Anyone who can read this writing and tell me its meaning will wear royal robes, will have a gold chain around his neck, and will rule the kingdom as third in command."

8 Then all the king's sages arrived, but they couldn't read the writing or interpret it for the king. 9 At that point King Belshazzar was really frightened. All the color drained from his face, and his princes were also very worried.

10 Upon hearing the commotion coming from the king and his princes, the queen entered the banqueting hall and declared, "Long live the king! Don't be so disturbed.

[i] Vulg, Theodotion add *silver*.

Don't be so frightened. 11There is a man in your kingdom who has the breath[j] of holy gods in him! When your father was alive, this man was shown to possess illumination, insight, and wisdom like the very wisdom of the gods.[k] Your father King Nebuchadnezzar appointed this man as chief over the dream interpreters, enchanters, Chaldeans, and diviners. Yes, your father did this 12because this man—Daniel, the one the king named Belteshazzar—possesses an extraordinary spirit, knowledge, and insight into the meaning of dreams. He can explain ambiguities and resolve mysteries. Now in light of all that, summon Daniel! He will explain the meaning of this thing."

13So Daniel was brought before the king. The king said to him, "So you are Daniel, the Daniel from the exiles that my father the king brought from Judah? 14I have heard that the breath of the gods is in you and that you possess illumination, insight, and extraordinary wisdom. 15Now, the sages and the dream interpreters were brought before me to read this writing and interpret it for me, but they couldn't explain its meaning. 16But I've heard that you can explain meanings and solve mysteries. So if you can read this writing and interpret it for me, you will wear royal robes, have a gold chain around your neck, and will rule the kingdom as third in command."

Daniel interprets the writing

17Daniel answered the king: "Keep your gifts. Give the rewards to someone else. But I will still read the writing to the king and interpret it for him. 18Listen, Your Majesty: The Most High God gave kingship, power, glory, and majesty to your father Nebuchadnezzar. 19Because of the power God gave Nebuchadnezzar, all peoples, nations, and languages were terrified of him. He did whatever he wanted, whenever he wanted: killing or sparing, exalting or humbling. 20But when he became arrogant, acting in stubborn pride, he was pulled off his royal throne and the glory was taken from him. 21He was driven away from other humans, and his mind became like an animal's. He lived with wild donkeys, he ate grass like cattle, and dew from heaven washed his body until he realized that the Most High God dominates human kingship and sets over it anyone he wants.

22"But you who are his son, Belshazzar, you haven't submitted, even though you've known all this. 23Instead, you've set yourself up against the Lord of heaven! The equipment of God's house was brought to you; and you, your princes, your consorts, and your secondary wives drank wine out of it, all the while praising the gods of silver, gold, bronze, iron, wood, and stone—gods who can't see, hear, or know anything. But you didn't glorify the true God who holds your very breath in his hand and who owns every road you take.

24"That's why this hand was sent from God and why this message was written down. 25This is what was written down:

MENE, MENE, TEKEL, and PARSIN.[l]

26"This is the meaning of the word MENE: God has numbered[m] the days of your rule. It's over! 27TEKEL means that you've been weighed[n] on the scales, and you don't measure up. 28PERES[o] means your kingship is divided[p] and given to the Medes and the Persians."[q]

29Then Belshazzar commanded that Daniel be dressed in a purple robe, have a gold chain around his neck, and be officially appointed as third in command in the kingdom.

30That very same night, Belshazzar the Chaldean king was killed. 31Darius the Mede received the kingdom at the age of 62.

Plot against Daniel

6 Darius decided to appoint one hundred twenty chief administrators throughout the kingdom, 2and to set over them three main officers to whom they would report so that the king wouldn't have to be bothered with too much.[r] One of

[j]Or *spirit*; also in 5:14 [k]Or *wisdom of God* [l]Aram *Upharsin* [m]Aram *menah*, which is a wordplay with *Mene* [n]Aram *teqal*, which is a wordplay with *Tekel* [o]The singular form of the plural *Parsin* in 5:25 [p]Aram *peras*, which is a wordplay with *Parsin* [q]Aram *Paras*, another wordplay with *Parsin* [r]Aram uncertain

these main officers was Daniel. [3]Because of his extraordinary spirit, Daniel soon surpassed the other officers and the chief administrators—so much so that the king had plans to set him over the entire kingdom. [4]As a result, the other officers and the chief administrators tried to find some problem with Daniel's work for the kingdom. But they couldn't find any problem or corruption at all because Daniel was trustworthy. He wasn't guilty of any negligence or corruption.

[5]So these men said, "We won't find any fault in Daniel, unless we can find something to use against him from his religious practice."[s]

[6]So these officers and chief administrators ganged together and went to the king. They said to him, "Long live King Darius! [7]All the officers of the kingdom, the ministers, the chief administrators, the royal associates, and the governors advise the king to issue an edict and enforce a law, that for thirty days anyone who says prayers to any god or human being except you, Your Majesty, will be thrown into a pit of lions. [8]Now, Your Majesty, issue the law and sign the document so that it cannot be changed, as per the law of Media and Persia, which cannot be annulled." [9]Because of this, King Darius signed the document containing the law.

Daniel prays

[10]When Daniel learned that the document had been signed, he went to his house. Now his upper room had open windows that faced Jerusalem. Daniel knelt down, prayed, and praised his God three times that day, just like he always did. [11]Just then these men, all ganged together, came upon Daniel praying and seeking mercy from his God. [12]They then went and talked to the king about the law: "Your Majesty! Didn't you sign a law, that for thirty days any person who prays to any god or human being besides you, Your Majesty, would be thrown into a pit of lions?"

The king replied, "The decision is absolutely firm in accordance with the law of Media and Persia, which cannot be annulled."

[13]So they said to the king, "One of the Judean exiles, Daniel, has ignored you, Your Majesty, as well as the law you signed. He says his prayers three times a day!"

[14]When the king heard this report, he was very unhappy. He decided to rescue Daniel and did everything he could do to save Daniel before the sun went down. [15]But these men, all ganged together, came and said to the king, "You must realize, Your Majesty, that the law of Media and Persia, including every law and edict the king has issued, cannot be changed."

Daniel in the lions' pit

[16]So the king gave the order, and they brought Daniel and hurled him into the pit of lions.

The king said to Daniel: "Your God—the one you serve so consistently—will rescue you."[t]

[17]A single stone was brought and placed over the entrance to the pit. The king sealed it with his own ring and with those of his princes so that Daniel's situation couldn't be changed. [18]The king then went home to his palace and fasted through the night. No pleasures[u] were brought to him, and he couldn't sleep. [19]At dawn, at the first sign of light, the king rose and rushed to the lions' pit.

[20]As he approached it, he called out to Daniel, worried: "Daniel, servant of the living God! Was your God—the one you serve so consistently—able to rescue you from the lions?"

[21]Then Daniel answered the king: "Long live the king! [22]My God sent his messenger, who shut the lions' mouths. They haven't touched me because I was judged innocent before my God. I haven't done anything wrong to you either, Your Majesty."

[23]The king was thrilled. He commanded that Daniel be brought up out of the pit, and Daniel was lifted out. Not a scratch was found on him, because he trusted in his God. [24]The king then ordered that the men who had accused Daniel be brought and thrown

[s]Or *in the Instruction of his God* [t]Or *May your God—the one you serve so consistently—rescue you.* [u]Aram uncertain

into the lions' pit—including their wives and
children. They hadn't even reached the bottom of the pit before the lions overpowered
them, crushing all their bones.

New decree

25 Then King Darius wrote the following
decree:

To all the peoples, nations, and languages inhabiting the entire earth: I wish
you much peace. 26 I now issue this command: In every region of my kingdom, all
people must fear and revere Daniel's God
because:

He is the living God.
God stands firm forever.
His kingship is indestructible.
God's rule will last until the end of time.
27 He is rescuer and savior;
God performs signs and miracles
in heaven and on earth.
Here's the proof:
He rescued Daniel from the lions' power.

28 And so Daniel was made prosperous
during the rule of Darius and during the
rule of Cyrus the Persian.

Daniel's vision: four beasts

7 In the first year of Babylon's King
Belshazzar, Daniel had a dream—a vision in his head as he lay on his bed. He
wrote the dream down. Here is the beginning of the account:

2 I am Daniel. In the vision I had during
the night I saw the four winds of heaven
churning the great sea. 3 Four giant beasts
emerged from the sea, each different from
the others. 4 The first was like a lion with
eagle's wings. I observed it until its wings
were pulled off, and it was lifted up from
the ground. It was then set on two feet, like
a human being, and it received a human
mind. 5 Then I saw another beast, a second
one, like a bear. It was raised on one side.
It had three ribs in its mouth between its
teeth. It was told: "Get up! Devour much
flesh!" 6 I kept watching, and suddenly there
was another beast, this one like a leopard.
On its back it had four wings like bird
wings. This beast had four heads. Authority
was given to it.

7 After this, as I continued to watch this
night vision, I saw a fourth beast, terrifying and hideous, with extraordinary power
and with massive iron teeth. As it ate and
crushed, its feet smashed whatever was
left over. It was different from all the other
beasts before it, and it had ten horns. 8 I
was staring at the horns when, suddenly,
another small horn came up between them.
Three of the earlier horns were ripped out
to make room for it. On this new horn were
eyes like human eyes and a mouth that
bragged and bragged.

Throne of fire and the human figure

9 As I was watching,
thrones were raised up.
The ancient one took his seat.
His clothes were white like snow;
his hair was like a lamb's wool.
His throne was made of flame;
its wheels were blazing fire.
10 A river of fire flowed out
from his presence;
thousands upon thousands served him;
ten thousand times ten thousand
stood ready to serve him!
The court sat in session;
the scrolls were opened.

11 I kept watching. I watched from the
moment the horn started bragging until
the beast was killed and its body was destroyed, handed over to be burned with
fire. 12 Then the authority of the remaining
beasts was brought to an end, but they were
given an extension among the living for a
set time and season.

13 As I continued to watch this night vision of mine, I suddenly saw
one like a human being[v]
coming with the heavenly clouds.
He came to the ancient one
and was presented before him.
14 Rule, glory, and kingship
were given to him;

[v] Aram *kebar enash* (*like a son of man*) is an idiom that means *like a human being;* cf also 8:17; 10:16, 18 for Heb
approximations.

all peoples, nations, and languages
will serve him.
His rule is an everlasting one—
it will never pass away!—
his kingship is indestructible.

Beasts interpreted

15 Now this caused me, Daniel, to worry.[w]
My visions disturbed me greatly. 16 So I
went to one of the servants who was standing ready nearby. I asked him for the truth
about all this.

He spoke to me and explained to me the
meaning of these things. 17 "These four giant
beasts are four kings that will rise up from
the earth, 18 but the holy ones of the Most
High will receive the kingship. They will hold
the kingship securely forever and always."

19 Next I wanted greater clarity about
the fourth beast, the one that was different
from all the others and utterly terrifying
with its iron teeth and bronze claws. As it
ate and crushed, its feet smashed whatever
was left over. 20 I wanted greater clarity
about the ten horns on its head, and the
other horn that came up, along with the
three that fell out to make room for it—but
especially about the horn that had eyes and
a mouth that bragged, and that seemed
more important than the others. 21 As I
watched, this same horn waged war against
the holy ones and defeated them, 22 until
the Ancient One came. Then judgment was
given in favor of the holy ones of the Most
High. The set time arrived, and the holy
ones held the kingship securely.

23 This is what he said:
"The fourth beast means
that there will be a fourth kingship
on the earth.
It will be different
from all the other kingships.
It will devour the entire earth,
trample it, crush it.
24 The ten horns mean
that from this kingship
will rise ten kings,
and after them will rise yet another.
He will be different
from the previous ones.
He will defeat three kings.
25 He will say things against the Most High
and will exhaust the holy ones
of the Most High.
He will try to change times set by law.
And for a period of time,
periods of time,
and half a period of time,
they will be delivered into his power.
26 Then the court will sit in session.
His rule will be taken away—
ruined and wiped out for all time.
27 The kingship, authority, and power
of all kingdoms under heaven
will be given to the people,
the holy ones of the Most High.
Their kingship is an everlasting one;
every authority will serve them
and obey."

28 The account ends here.

Now as for how I, Daniel, felt about this:
My thoughts disturbed me greatly. My
mood darkened considerably, and I kept
thinking about this matter.

Vision of a ram and a goat

8 In the third year of King Belshazzar's
rule, a vision came to me, Daniel, some
time after the earlier vision I had. 2 I saw this
vision, and as I experienced it I was in the
walled city of Susa in the province of Elam,[x]
by the Ulai canal. 3 When I lifted my eyes, I
suddenly saw a ram with two horns standing in front of the canal. Both horns were
high, but one was higher than the other.
The higher one came up after the other
one. 4 I saw the ram goring west, north, and
south. No animal could resist the ram, and
no one could stop it, rescuing others from
its power. The ram did whatever it pleased.
It became powerful.

5 I was trying to understand this when
suddenly a he-goat came from the west,
crossing the entire earth but not touching
the ground. Between this goat's eyes was a
horn that was a sight to see. 6 The he-goat

[w] Or *my spirit was distressed in its sheath*; Aram uncertain

[x] Some LXX sources; MT repeats *I had this vision before I was by the Ulai canal.*

came to the ram that had two horns, the one I'd seen standing in front of the canal. The he-goat charged the ram in powerful anger. 7 I saw the he-goat approach the ram. It was enraged at the ram and attacked it, shattering the ram's two horns. The ram couldn't resist the he-goat. The he-goat threw the ram on the ground and trampled on it. No one could rescue the ram from the he-goat's power.

8 The he-goat became even greater, but at the height of its power, its large horn snapped. In its place, four horns, each a sight to see, came up toward the four winds of heaven. 9 A single, very small horn came out of one of the four horns. It grew bigger and bigger, stretching toward the south, the east, and the beautiful country. 10 It grew as high as the heavenly forces, until it finally threw some of them and some of the stars down to the earth. Then it trampled on them. 11 It grew as high as the very leader of those forces, taking the daily sacrifice away from him[y] and overturning his holy place. 12 In an act of rebellion, another force will take control of the daily sacrifice. It will throw truth to the ground and will succeed in everything it does.[z]

How long?

13 I then heard a certain holy one speaking. A second holy one said to the first one: "How long will this vision last—the one concerning the daily sacrifice, the desolating rebellion, and the handing over of the sanctuary and its forces to be trampled?"

14 He said to me, "For two thousand three hundred evenings and mornings. Then the sanctuary will be restored."

Vision interpreted

15 Now I, Daniel, needed help understanding the vision I saw. Suddenly standing in front of me was someone who looked like a man. 16 I then heard a human voice coming out of the center of the Ulai canal. It called out: "Gabriel, help this person understand what he has seen."

17 Gabriel approached me, and I was terrified when he came. I fell with my face to the ground. Gabriel said to me, "Know this, human one: the vision is for the end time." 18 As soon as he said this to me, I fell into a trance. My face was still on the ground. Then Gabriel touched me and set me up on my feet.

19 He said, "Now, I am going to tell you what will happen during the time of doom that is coming, because at the appointed time there will be an end. 20 The two-horned ram you saw represents the kings of Media and Persia. 21 The long-haired he-goat is the king of Greece, and the big horn between its eyes is the first king. 22 The horn that snapped so that four came up in its place means that four kingdoms will come from one nation, but these four won't have the strength of the first one.

23 When their kingship nears its end
and their sins[a] are almost complete,
a king will step forward.
He will be stern
and a master of deception.
24 At the height of his power,[b]
he will wreak
unbelievable destructions.
He will succeed in all he does.
He will destroy both the mighty
and the people of the holy ones.
25 Along with his cunning,
he will succeed by using deceit.
In his own mind, he will be great.
In a time of peace,
he will bring destruction on many,
opposing even the supreme leader.
But he will be broken—
and not by a human hand.

26 Now this vision of evening and morning, which has been announced, is true. But you must seal it up, because it is for days far in the future."

27 Then I, Daniel, was overwhelmed and felt sick for days. When I finally got up and went about the king's business, I remained troubled by the vision and couldn't understand it.

[y] Or *the daily sacrifice was taken away from him.* [z] Heb uncertain [a] LXX; MT *rebels* [b] LXX sources; MT *His power will grow strong, but not by his own power,* perhaps influenced by 8:22.

Daniel's prayer

9 In the first year of Darius' rule—Darius, who was Ahasuerus' son, a Median by birth and who ruled the Chaldean kingdom—2 I, Daniel, pondered the scrolls, specifically the number of years that it would take to complete Jerusalem's desolation according to the LORD's word to the prophet Jeremiah. It was seventy years. 3 I then turned my face to my Lord God, asking for an answer with prayer and pleading, and with fasting, mourning clothes, and ashes. 4 As I prayed to the LORD my God, I made this confession:

Please, my Lord—you are the great and awesome God, the one who keeps the covenant, and truly faithful to all who love him and keep his commands: 5 We have sinned and done wrong. We have brought guilt on ourselves and rebelled, ignoring your commands and your laws. 6 We haven't listened to your servants, the prophets, who spoke in your name to our kings, our leaders, our parents, and to all the land's people. 7 Righteousness belongs to you, my Lord! But we are ashamed this day—we, the people of Judah, the inhabitants of Jerusalem, all Israel whether near or far, in whatever country where you've driven them because of their unfaithfulness when they broke faith with you. 8 LORD, we are ashamed—we, our kings, our leaders, and our parents who sinned against you. 9 Compassion and deep forgiveness belong to my Lord, our God, because we rebelled against him. 10 We didn't listen to the voice of the LORD our God by following the teachings he gave us through his servants, the prophets. 11 All Israel broke your Instruction and turned away, ignoring your voice. Then the curse that was sworn long ago—the one written in the Instruction from Moses, God's servant—swept over us because we sinned against God. 12 God confirmed the words he spoke against us and against our rulers, bringing great trouble on us. What happened in Jerusalem hasn't happened anywhere else in the entire world! 13 All this trouble came upon us, exactly as it was written in the Instruction of Moses, but we didn't try to reconcile with the LORD our God by turning from our wrongdoing or by finding wisdom in your faithfulness. 14 So the LORD oversaw the great trouble and brought it on us, because the LORD our God has been right in every move he's made, but we haven't listened to his voice.

15 "But now, my Lord, our God—you who brought your people out of Egypt with a strong hand, making a name for yourself even to this day: We have sinned and done the wrong thing. 16 My Lord, please! In line with your many righteous acts, please turn your raging anger from Jerusalem, which is your city, your own holy mountain. Because of our sins and the wrongdoing of our parents, both Jerusalem and your people have become a disgrace to all our neighbors.

17 "But now, our God, listen to your servant's prayer and pleas for help. Shine your face on your ruined sanctuary, for your own sake, my Lord. 18 Open your ears, my God, and listen! Open your eyes and look at our devastation. Look at the city called by your name! We pray our prayers for help to you, not because of any righteous acts of ours but because of your great compassion. 19 My Lord, listen! My Lord, forgive! My Lord, pay attention and act! Don't delay! My God, do all this for your own sake, because your city and your people are called by your name.

Seventy weeks

20 While I was still speaking, praying, and confessing my sin and the sins of my people Israel—while I was still praying my prayer for help to the LORD my God about my God's holy mountain—21 while I was still speaking this prayer, the man Gabriel approached me at the time of the evening offering. This was the same Gabriel I had seen in my earlier vision. He was weary with exhaustion.[c]

[c] Or *approached me in swift flight at the time of the evening offering;* Heb uncertain

22 He explained as he spoke with me: "Daniel, here's why I've come: to give you insight and understanding. 23 When you began making your requests, a word went out, and I've come to tell it to you because you are greatly treasured. So now understand this word and grasp the meaning of this vision! 24 Seventy weeks are appointed for your people and for your holy city to complete the rebellion, to end sins, to cover over wrongdoing, to bring eternal righteousness, to seal up prophetic vision, and to anoint the most holy place.

25 "So you must know and gain wisdom about this: There will be seven weeks from the moment the word went out to restore and rebuild Jerusalem until a leader is anointed. And for sixty-two weeks the city will be rebuilt with a courtyard and a moat. But in difficult times, 26 after the sixty-two weeks, an anointed one will be eliminated. No one will support him.[d] The army of a future leader will destroy the city and the sanctuary. His[e] end will come in a flood, but devastations will be decreed until the end of the war.[f] 27 For one week, he will make a strong covenant with many people. For a half-week, he will stop both sacrifices and offerings. In their place[g] will be the desolating monstrosities until the decreed destruction sweeps over the devastator."

Vision of a man

10 In the third year of Persia's King Cyrus, a message was revealed to Daniel, who was called Belteshazzar. The message was true: there would be a great conflict. Daniel understood the message, having discerned the meaning of the vision.

2 During that time, I, Daniel, had been mourning for three weeks. 3 I didn't eat any rich foods. Neither meat nor wine passed my lips, and I didn't clean up at all until the three weeks were up. 4 Then, on the twenty-fourth day of the first month, as I was on the bank of the great Tigris River, 5 I looked up and suddenly saw a man clothed in linen in front of me. He had a brilliant gold belt around his waist, 6 and his body was like topaz. His face was like a flash of lightning, and his eyes were like burning torches. His arms and feet looked like polished bronze. When he spoke, it sounded like the roar of a crowd. 7 Only I, Daniel, saw this vision. The other people who were with me didn't see it. Despite that, they were terrified and ran away to hide.

8 So I was left alone to see this great vision all by myself. All my strength left me. My energy was sapped, and I couldn't stay strong. 9 Then I heard the sound of the man's words. When I heard it, I fell into a trance with my face on the ground. 10 But then a hand touched me, lifting me up to my hands and knees.

11 The man said to me, "Daniel, you are greatly treasured. Now grasp the meaning of what I'm saying to you. And stand up, because I've been sent to you."

As he said this to me, I stood up, shaking.

12 Then the man said to me, "Don't be afraid, Daniel, because from the day you first set your mind to understand things and to humble yourself before your God, your words were heard. I've come because of your words! 13 For twenty-one days the leader of the Persian kingdom blocked my way. But then Michael, one of the highest leaders, came to help me. I left Michael there with the leader of the Persian kingdom.[h] 14 But I've come to help you understand what will happen to your people in the future, because there is another vision concerning that time."

15 While he said this to me, I turned my face to the ground and kept quiet. 16 But then someone who looked like a human being[i] touched my lips. Then I opened my mouth and spoke, saying to the person standing in front of me: "My lord, the vision bothered me deeply, and I couldn't stay strong during it. 17 So how can I, my lord's servant, speak with you, my lord? Even now there's no strength in me, and I can barely breathe."

18 The one who looked like a human being

[d] Or *and will have nothing* or *and will disappear;* Heb uncertain [e] Or *Its* (the army's) [f] Heb uncertain
[g] Correction *on the wing;* Heb uncertain [h] LXX; Heb *after I was detained there with the kings of Persia*
[i] Heb *bene adam* (*a son of a man*) is an idiom that means *human being;* cf 7:13.

touched me again and gave me strength. 19 He
said, “Don’t be afraid. You are greatly treasured. All will be well with you. Be strong!”

As he spoke to me, I suddenly felt strong.
Then I said: “My lord can go on, because
you’ve made me strong.”

20 Then he said: “Do you know why I have
come to you? Now I must go back to fight
the leader of Persia. As I leave, the leader of
Greece will come! 21 But I will tell you what
is written in the Scroll of Truth. No one
stands strong with me against these leaders except your leader Michael.

A vast empire divided

11 “In the first year of Darius the Mede’s
rule, I took my stand to strengthen and
protect him. 2 I will now tell you the truth.
Persia will have three more kings, but the
fourth will be richer than all of them. Once
he has become strong through his great
riches, he will disturb everyone, including
the Greek kingdom. 3 Then a warrior-king
will come forward, ruling over a vast empire
and doing whatever he wants. 4 But even as
he takes control, his kingdom will be broken,
divided to the four winds of heaven. It won’t
pass to his descendants. No one will rule like
he did because his kingdom will be uprooted.
It will belong to others, not to these.

South and north

5 “Then the southern king will gain power,
but one of his princes will overpower him,
ruling in his place. His empire will be vast.
6 After some years, they will make an agreement together. The southern king’s daughter
will go to the northern king to finalize the
agreement, but she won’t retain her great
power. Neither will his power remain in
place. In those times she will be handed over,
along with her escort, the one who fathered
her, and the one who strengthened her.[j]

7 “A branch from her roots will rise up in
his place. Attacking the army, he will enter
the walled fortress of the northern king. He
will fight with them, and he will conquer.
8 He will even carry off their gods to Egypt,
along with their statues and their silver and
gold equipment. For years he will avoid the
northern king. 9 Then the northern king
will attack the kingdom of the southern
king, but will return to his own land. 10 His
sons will get ready for war, gathering massive forces. Their attack will be like an overwhelming flood. And they will attack again,
taking the battle as far as his walled fortress.

11 “The southern king, in a bitter rage,
will come out to battle the northern king.
He will muster a huge army, but the army
will be handed over to his enemy. 12 When
the army is carried off, he will become confident. He will kill tens of thousands, but he
will not stand strong. 13 The northern king
will then muster another army—this one
bigger than the first. After some years have
passed, he will attack with a large and well-
equipped army. 14 In those times, many will
oppose the southern king. Violent persons
from among your people also will rise up to
support the vision, but they will fail.

15 “When the northern king attacks, he
will throw up a siege ramp and occupy a
walled city. The southern forces will not be
able to resist—not even its elite forces. No
one will be strong enough to resist. 16 The
one who comes to attack will do whatever
he wants; no one will be able to oppose him.
He will take his place in the beautiful country, and he will hand out destruction. 17 He
will decide to occupy his entire kingdom
by force. He will make an agreement with
him and will give him a wife, intending to
destroy him,[k] but it won’t succeed and it
won’t happen.[l] 18 He will turn his face to the
coastlands, capturing many people. A commander will put an end to his disgrace,[m]
even though he won’t repay that disgrace.
19 Then he will turn his attention to the
walled fortresses of his own country but
will stumble, fall, and disappear.

20 “In his place one will arise who will
send his agent to exact a kingdom’s glory,
but in a few days he will be broken, though
not by anger and not by war. 21 A worthless
person will arise in his place. Royal majesty will not have been given to him, but
he will come in a time of security and seize

[j] Heb uncertain [k] DSS; MT *her* or *it* (the kingdom) [l] Heb adds *for him.* [m] Heb adds *for him.*

the kingdom by deceitful means. [22]Forces will be completely swept away and broken before him. The same is true for the leader of the covenant. [23]From the moment they make an agreement with him, he will act deceitfully. He will gain power at the expense of a small nation. [24]He will come into a province's richest places untroubled and will do what his fathers and grandfathers never could. He will hand out plunder, spoil, and wealth to them. He will make plans against fortresses, but only for a time.

[25]"Then with a large army he will gather his strength and courage against the southern king. The southern king, with a large and super powerful army, will prepare for war, but he won't endure because they will make plans against him. [26]Those who eat the king's provisions will destroy him. His army will be overrun. Many will die.

[27]"These two kings, with their minds set on evil, will sit at one table, telling lies, but with no success because the end will come at the set time. [28]He will return to his country with great wealth and set his mind against a holy covenant. He will do what he wants and then return to his country. [29]At the set time he will again battle against the south, but the second time will be different from the first. [30]Kittim ships will fight against him, and he will retreat in fear. He will rage against a holy covenant and will do what he wants. Then he will pay special attention to those who violate a holy covenant. [31]His forces will come and make the sanctuary fortress impure. They will stop the daily sacrifice and set up a desolating monstrosity. [32]By deceitful means he will corrupt those who violate a covenant, but the people who acknowledge their God will stand strong and will act.

[33]"The people's teachers will help many understand, but for a time they will fall by sword and by flame, by captivity and by plunder. [34]When they fall, they will receive a little help, but many will join them with deceitful plans. [35]Some of the teachers too will fall in order that they might be refined, purified, and cleansed—until an end time, because it is still not yet the set time.

An end to the arrogant king

[36]"The king will do whatever he wants. He will exalt himself, making himself greater than any god. He will say unbelievable things against the God of gods. He will succeed until the doom is completed, because what is decreed must take place. [37]He will give no thought to the gods of his fathers, nor to the god cherished by women. He will give no thought to any god, because he will make himself greater than all of them. [38]In their place, he will worship a god of walled fortresses. With gold and silver, rare stones and precious things, he will worship a god his fathers did not acknowledge. [39]He will deal with walled fortresses with the help of a foreign god. He will heap rewards on those who support him, making them rule over many and dividing up the land for a price. [40]At the end time, the southern king will attack him. The northern king will storm against him with chariots and horses and many ships. He will invade countries, sweeping over them like a flood. [41]He will invade the beautiful country, and tens of thousands will die. But Edom, Moab, and the best of the Ammonites will escape from his hand. [42]He will extend his power into other countries. Even Egypt won't escape. [43]He will take control of Egypt's hidden treasures of gold, silver, and all its precious things. Libyans and Cushites will follow at his feet. [44]But reports from the east and north will alarm him, and in a great rage he will set off to devastate and destroy many. [45]He will pitch his royal tents between the sea and the beautiful holy mountain. But he will come to his end, and no one will help him.

Eternal life or eternal disgrace

12 "At that time, Michael the great leader who guards your people will take his stand. It will be a difficult time—nothing like it has ever happened since nations first appeared. But at that time every one of your people who is found written in the scroll will be rescued. [2]Many of those who sleep in the dusty land[n] will wake up—

[n]Or *earthy soil* or *dust of the earth*

some to eternal life, others to shame and eternal disgrace. 3Those skilled in wisdom[o] will shine like the sky. Those who lead many to righteousness will shine like the stars forever and always. 4But you, Daniel, must keep these words secret! Seal the scroll until the end time! Many will stray far, but knowledge will increase."

Waiting for the end time

5I, Daniel, looked and suddenly saw two other figures—one standing on each side of the stream. 6One said to the man clothed in white linen, who was farther upstream: "When will these astonishing things be over?"

7I heard the man clothed in white linen, who was farther upstream, swear by the one who lives forever as he raised both hands to heaven: "For one set time, two set times, and half a set time. When the breaking of the holy people's power is over, all these things will be over."

8I heard it, but I didn't understand it. "My lord," I said, "what will happen after all this?"

9He said, "Get going now, Daniel, because these words must remain secret and sealed up until the end time. 10Many will purify, cleanse, and refine themselves, but the wicked will act wickedly. None of the wicked will understand, but those skilled in wisdom will understand. 11There will be one thousand two hundred ninety days from the time the daily sacrifice is stopped to the setting up of the desolating monstrosity. 12Happy is the one who waits and reaches one thousand three hundred thirty-five days. 13Now as for you, go on to the end. You will rest and will stand to receive your reward at the end of days."

HOSEA

1 The LORD's word that came to Hosea, Beeri's son, in the days of Judah's Kings Uzziah, Jotham, Ahaz, and Hezekiah, and in the days of Israel's King Jeroboam, Joash's son.

God commands Hosea to marry

2When the LORD first spoke through Hosea, the LORD said to him, "Go, marry a prostitute and have children of prostitution, for the people of the land commit great prostitution by deserting the LORD." 3So Hosea went and took Gomer, Diblaim's daughter, and she became pregnant and bore him a son. 4The LORD said to him, "Name him Jezreel; for in a little while I will punish the house of Jehu for the blood of Jezreel, and I will destroy the kingdom of the house of Israel. 5On that day I will break the bow of Israel in the Jezreel Valley." 6Gomer became pregnant again and gave birth to a daughter. Then the LORD said to Hosea, "Name her No Compassion, because I will no longer have compassion on the house of Israel or forgive them. 7But I will have compassion on the house of Judah. I, the LORD their God, will save them; I will not save them by bow, or by sword, or by war, or by horses, or by horsemen." 8When Gomer finished nursing No Compassion, she became pregnant and gave birth to a son. 9Then the LORD said, "Name him Not My People because you are not my people, and I am not your God."[a]

Hope for the future

10[b]Yet the number of the people of Israel will be like the sand of the sea, which can be neither measured nor numbered; and in the place where it was said to them, "You are not my people," it will be said to them, "Children of the living God." 11The people of Judah and the people of Israel will be gathered together, and they will choose one head. They will become fruitful in the land.[c] The day will be a wonderful one for Jezreel.

[o]See 1:4; or *The teachers;* see 11:33, 35; also in 12:10. [a]Or *I am not yours.* [b]1:10-11=Heb 2:12 [c]Or *They will go up from the land.*

Proclamation of wrongdoing

2 [d]Say to your brother, My People, and to
your sister, Compassion:
2 Level a charge against your mother;
plead with her!
She is not my wife,
and I am not her husband.
Let her remove prostitution
from her presence,
and adultery from between
her breasts,
3 or else I will strip her naked
and expose her
as on the day she was born.
I will make her like a desert,
and turn her into a dry land,
and make her die of thirst.
4 I will also have no compassion
on her children
because they are
children of prostitution.
5 Their mother has played the prostitute;
she who conceived them
has behaved shamefully.
She said, "I will seek out my lovers;
they give me my bread and my water,
my wool and my linen cloth,
my oil and my drink."

Divine correction

6 Therefore, I will line her path
with thorns;
and I will build a wall against her,
so that she can't find her paths.
7 She will go after her lovers,
but she won't catch up with them;
she will seek them,
but she won't find them.
Then she will say,
"I will return to my first husband,
for I had it better then than now."
8 She didn't know that I gave her
the corn, the new wine,
and the fresh oil,
and that I gave her much silver,
and gold that they used for Baal.
9 So now I will take back
my corn in its time,
and my wine in its season;
and I will take away my wool
and my linen cloth,
which were to cover her nakedness.
10 Now I will uncover her nakedness
in plain view of her lovers,
and no one will rescue her from me.
11 I will end all her religious celebrations,
her festivals, her new moons,
her Sabbath days,
and all her sacred seasons.
12 I will destroy her vines and her fig trees,
of which she said,
"These are my pay,
which my lovers have given to me."
I will change them into a forest,
and the wild animals will eat them.
13 I will punish her for the days
dedicated to the Baals,
when she offered sweet-smelling
sacrifices to them
and dressed herself up
with rings and jewelry,
and went after her lovers,
and forgot me, says the LORD.

Promises:
restoration and covenant love

14 Therefore, I will charm her,
and bring her into the desert,
and speak tenderly to her heart.
15 From there I will give her vineyards,
and make the Achor Valley
a door of hope.
There she will respond to me
as in the days of her youth,
like the time when she came out of
the land of Egypt.

16 On that day, says the LORD, you will
call me, "My husband," and no longer will
you call me, "My Lord." 17 I will take away
the names of the Baals from her mouth,
and they will not be mentioned by name
anymore. 18 On that day, I will make a covenant for them with the wild animals, the
birds in the sky, and the creeping creatures
of the fertile ground. I will do away with the
bow, the sword, and war from the land; I
will make you lie down in safety.

[d] 2:1-23=Heb 2:3-25

19 I will take you for my wife forever;
I will take you for my wife in
righteousness and in justice,
in devoted love, and in mercy.
20 I will take you for my wife
in faithfulness;
and you will know the LORD.

21 On that day I will answer, says the LORD.
I will answer the heavens
and they will answer the earth.
22 The earth will answer the corn,
the new wine, and the fresh oil,
and they will answer Jezreel;
23 I will sow him for myself in the land;
and I will have compassion on
No Compassion,
and I will say to Not My People,
"You are my people";
and he will say, "You are my God."

The lesson of infidelity

3 Then the LORD said to me again, "Go,
make love to a woman who has a lover
and is involved in adultery, just as the LORD
loves the people of Israel, though they turn
to other gods and love raisin cakes." 2 So I
bought her for fifteen pieces of silver, a large
amount of barley, and a portion of wine.[e]
3 I said to her, "You must stay with me for
many days; you won't act like a prostitute;
you won't have sex with a man, nor I with
you." 4 Similarly, the Israelites will remain
many days without king or prince, without
sacrifice or sacred standing stone, without a priestly vest or household divine images. 5 Afterward the Israelites will return
and seek the LORD their God and David
their king; they will come trembling to the
LORD and to the LORD's goodness in the
latter days.

Israel's sins and coming punishment

4 Hear the LORD's word,
people of Israel;
for the LORD has a dispute
with the inhabitants of the land.
There's no faithful love or loyalty,
and no knowledge of God in the land.
2 Swearing, lying, murder,
together with stealing and adultery
are common;
bloody crime followed by bloody crime.
3 Therefore, the earth itself becomes sick,
and all who live on it grow weak;
together with the wild animals
and the birds in the sky,
even the fish of the sea are dying.
4 Yet let no one protest,
and let no one complain.

Listen, priest,
I am angry with your people.[f]
5 You will stumble by day;
and at nighttime so will your prophet,
and I will destroy your mother.
6 My people are destroyed
from lack of knowledge.
Since you have rejected knowledge,
so I will reject you
from serving me as a priest.
Since you have forgotten the
Instruction of your God,
so also I will forget your children.
7 The more they increased,
the more they sinned against me;
they exchanged their glory for shame.
8 They feed on the sin of my people;
they set their hearts on evil things.
9 The priest will be just like the people;
I will punish them for their ways,
and judge them for their deeds.
10 They will eat but not be satisfied;
they will have sex like prostitutes,
but they will not have children,
because they have rejected the LORD
to devote themselves
to 11 false religious practices.

Description of Israel's idolatry

Wine and new wine
destroy understanding.
12 My people take advice
from a piece of wood,
and their divining rod
gives them predictions.
A spirit of prostitution
has led them astray;

[e] LXX [f] Heb uncertain

they have left God
to follow other gods.
13 They offer sacrifices on mountaintops,
and make entirely burned offerings
on hills;
they offer sacrifices
under various green trees,
because their shade is pleasant.
Therefore, your daughters
act like prostitutes,
and your daughters-in-law
commit adultery.
14 I will not punish your daughters
because they act like prostitutes,
nor your daughters-in-law
because they commit adultery;
for the men themselves visit prostitutes,
and offer sacrifices
with consecrated workers at temples;
so now the people without sense
must come to ruin.
15 Israel, even though you act
like a prostitute,
don't let Judah become guilty.
Don't enter into Gilgal,
or go up to Beth-aven,
and don't swear, "As the LORD lives."
16 Like a stubborn cow Israel is stubborn.
Now the LORD will tend them,[g]
as the LORD tends a lamb in a pasture.
17 Ephraim is associated with idols—
let him alone!
18 Though they have stopped drinking,
they continue to behave
like prostitutes;
indeed, they "love";
shame is their pride.
19 The wind has wrapped her in its wings;
they will be ashamed of their sacrifices.

Judgment on Israel and Judah

5 Hear this, priests!
Pay attention, house of Israel!
Listen, house of the king!
The judgment concerns you because
you have been a trap at Mizpah,
and a net spread out upon Tabor.
2 In their wicked condition,
they have sunk deep into corruption;
I will correct them through judgment.
3 I know Ephraim;
Israel doesn't escape my eye;
for now Ephraim
you have acted like a prostitute;
Israel is defiled.
4 Their deeds don't allow them
to return to their God,
because the spirit of prostitution
is within them,
and they don't know the LORD.
5 Israel's pride is a witness against him;
both Israel and Ephraim stagger
because of their guilt;
Judah staggers with them.
6 With their sheep and their cattle
they will go
to seek the LORD,
but they will not find him;
he has withdrawn from them.
7 They have acted faithlessly
against the LORD;
for their children have produced
illegitimate children.
Now the new moon will devour them[h]
along with their fields.

8 Blow a horn in Gibeah;
blow a trumpet in Ramah.
Sound the warning at Beth-aven:
"Look behind you, Benjamin!"
9 Ephraim will become a horrible place
on the Judgment Day.
Against the tribes of Israel
I will certainly announce
what is to take place.
10 The princes of Judah act like raiders
who steal the land;
I will pour out my anger
like water upon them.
11 Ephraim is under pressure
from its enemies;
Ephraim's rights aren't protected.
This is because Ephraim chose to
pursue worthless things.
12 Therefore, I am like a moth to Ephraim,
and like decay to the house of Judah.
13 When Ephraim saw his sickness,
and Judah his wound,

[g] Or *her* [h] Heb uncertain

then Ephraim went to Assyria,
and Ephraim sent for the great king.
But he could not heal them;
nor could he cure their wound.
14 I am like a lion to Ephraim,
like a young lion to the house of Judah.
I am the one who tears the prey
and goes forth;
no one can snatch it from me.
15 I will leave so that I can return
to my place
until they pay for their deeds,
until they seek me.
In their distress,
they will beg for my favor:
6 "Come, let's return to the LORD;
for it is he who has injured us
and will heal us;
he has struck us down,
but he will bind us up.
2 After two days he will revive us;
on the third day he will raise us up,
so that we may live before him.
3 Let's know, let's press on
to know the LORD;
whose appearing
is as certain as the dawn;
who will come to us like the showers,
like the spring rains
that give drink to the earth."

Infidelity and divine retribution

4 Ephraim, what will I do with you?
Judah, what will I do with you?
Your love is like a morning cloud,
like the dew that vanishes quickly.
5 Therefore, I have attacked them
by the prophets,
I have killed them
by the words of my mouth,
and my judgment goes forth
like a light.
6 I desire faithful love and not sacrifice,
the knowledge of God
instead of entirely burned offerings.
7 But like Adam[i]
they broke the covenant;
then they acted in bad faith
against me.
8 Gilead is a city of wicked people,
tracked with blood.
9 As robbers lie in wait for someone,
so the priests are in league
with each other;
they murder on the road to Shechem;
they have done evil things.
10 In the house of Israel I have seen
something horrible;
Ephraim acts like a prostitute;
Israel is defiled.
11 For you also, Judah,
a harvest is appointed,
when I would improve
the circumstances of my people.
7 When I would heal Israel,
the evil acts of Ephraim are exposed,
and the wicked deeds of Samaria;
for they deceive and steal,
a thief breaks in;
a group of bandits raid outside.
2 But they don't consider
within their hearts
that I remember all their wickedness.
Now their deeds show who they are,
right in front of my face.
3 By their wickedness
they make the king glad,
and give joy to the officials
with their lies.
4 They all act like adulterers;
they are like a heated oven,
whose baker doesn't need
to stoke the fire,
from the kneading of the dough
until it is leavened.
5 On the day of our king,
the officials became sick with the
heat of wine;
he stretched out his hand to those
who mocked him.
6 They approach like a hot oven,
their hearts burning.
Throughout the night,
their anger smolders;
in the morning, it continues
to burn like a flaming fire.
7 All of them are hot as an oven;
they devour their rulers.

[i] Or *at Adam*

All their kings have fallen;
none of them call upon me.
8 Ephraim mixes himself
among the people;
Ephraim is like flatbread that is
cooked on only one side.
9 Strangers have eaten up his strength,
yet he doesn't know it;
gray hairs are sprinkled
here and there upon him,
yet he doesn't know it.
10 Israel's pride is a witness against him;
yet they don't return
to the LORD their God,
or seek him because of all this.

Foolishness and God's wrath

11 Ephraim has become like a dove,
silly and without common sense;
they call upon Egypt; they go to Assyria.
12 As they go, I will spread my net
over them;
like birds in the sky,
I will bring them down;
I will judge them according to the
report made to their assembly.
13 Doom to them,
for they have strayed from me;
destruction will be their lot
because they have rebelled against me.
I would redeem them,
but they speak lies against me.
14 They don't cry to me from the heart,
but they sob upon their beds;
they fight[j] over grain and wine;
they resist me.
15 It was I who gave them their strength,
yet they plot evil against me.
16 They return, but not to the Most High;[k]
they have become like a worthless bow;
their officials will fall by the sword
because of the rage of their tongues;
in Egypt they will make fun of them.[l]

Divine proclamation about Israel's idolatry

8 Put a trumpet to your lips!
It's as if a bird of prey has flown over
the LORD's house,
because they have broken my covenant,
and have not kept my Instruction.
2 Israel cries to me,
"My God, we know you!"
3 Israel has turned away from the good;
the enemy will pursue him.
4 They set up kings, but not through me;
they chose princes,
but without my knowledge.
With silver and gold they crafted idols
for their own destruction.
5 Your calf is rejected, Samaria.
My anger burns against them.
How long will they remain guilty?
6 The calf is from Israel,
a person made it;
it is not God.
The calf of Samaria will be smashed.
7 Because they sow the wind,
they will get the whirlwind.
Standing grain, but no fresh growth;
it will yield no meal;
if it were to yield,
strangers would devour it.

Bargains, apostasy, and coming punishment

8 Israel is swallowed up;
among the nations, they are now
like a useless jar.
9 They have gone up to Assyria,
a wild ass wandering alone;
Ephraim has hired lovers.
10 Though they have bargained
with the nations,
I will now gather them up.
They will soon be diminished
due to the burden of kings and princes.
11 When Ephraim added more altars
to take away sin,
they became altars to him for sinning.
12 Even though I write out for him
a large number of my instructions,
they are regarded as strange.
13 Though they offer choice sacrifices,[m]
though they eat flesh,
the LORD doesn't accept them.
Now he will remember
their wickedness

[j] Or *cut themselves* [k] Heb uncertain [l] Or *they will be scorned in the land of Egypt.* [m] Correction; Heb uncertain

and punish their sins;
they will return to Egypt.
14 Israel has forgotten his maker,
and built palaces;
and Judah has multiplied
walled cities;
but I will send a fire upon his cities,
and it will devour his fortresses.

Arrival of divine judgment

9 Don't rejoice, Israel!
Don't celebrate as other nations do;
for as whores you have gone away
from your God.
You have loved a prostitute's pay
on all threshing floors of grain.
2 Threshing floor and wine vat
won't feed them;
the new wine will fail them.
3 They won't remain
in the land of the LORD;
but Ephraim will return to Egypt,
and in Assyria
they will eat unclean food.
4 They won't pour wine
as an offering to the LORD;
their sacrifices won't please him.
Such sacrifices will be like food
for those who touch the dead;
all who eat of it will be unclean;
their bread will be
for their hunger alone;
it will not come to the LORD's house.
5 What will you do
on the day of appointed festival,
on the day of the LORD's festival?
6 Even if they escape destruction,
Egypt will gather them,
Memphis will bury them.
Briars will possess
their precious things of silver;[n]
thorns will be in their tents.
7 The days of punishment have come;
the days of judgment have arrived;
Israel cries,
"The prophet is a fool,
the spiritual man is mad!"
Because of your great wickedness,
your rejection of me is great.

Tragic consequences

8 The prophet is God's watchman
looking over Ephraim,
yet a hunter's trap is set,
covering all his ways,
and rejection is in his God's house.
9 They have corrupted themselves terribly
as in the days of Gibeah;
he will remember their wickedness;
he will punish their sins.

10 Like grapes in the wilderness,
I found Israel.
In its first season,
like the first fruit on the fig tree,
I saw your ancestors.
But they came to Baal-peor,
and worshipped a thing of shame;
they became detestable
like the thing they loved.[o]
11 Ephraim's glory will fly away like a bird—
no birth, no pregnancy, no conception!
12 Though they bring up children,
I will make them childless
until no one is left.
Doom to them indeed when I leave them!
13 When I looked toward Tyre, Ephraim
was planted in a lovely meadow;
but now Ephraim must lead out his
children for slaughter.
14 Give them, LORD—
what will you give them?
Give them a womb that miscarries
and breasts that are dried up.
15 Every wickedness of theirs
began at Gilgal;
there I came to hate them.
Because of the wickedness of their deeds
I will drive them out of my house.
I will love them no more;
all their officials are rebels.
16 Ephraim is sick,
their root is dried up,
they will bear no fruit.
Even though they give birth,
I will put to death
their much-loved little ones.
17 Because they haven't listened to him,
my God will reject them;
they will wander among the nations.

[n] Or *the proud glory pertaining to their silver;* Heb uncertain [o] Heb uncertain

The folly of Israel's idolatry

10 Israel is a growing vine
that yields its fruit.
The more his fruit increased,
the more altars he built;
the richer his land became,
the more he set up
sacred standing stones.
2 Their heart is false;
now they must bear their guilt.
The LORD will break down
their altars
and destroy their standing stones.
3 For now they will say:
"We have no king,
because we don't love the LORD.
What then could a king do for us?"
4 They have spoken empty words,
swearing falsely
when making covenants;
so judgment springs up
like poisonous weeds
in the furrows of the field.
5 The inhabitants of Samaria shake
because of the calf of Beth-aven.
Its people will mourn over it,
just as its idolatrous priests
who rejoiced over its glory
that is now gone.

Shame and punishment

6 To Assyria it will be carried
as a gift for the great king.
Ephraim will be put to shame;
Israel will be ashamed
of his own idol.
7 Samaria will be cut off;
her king is like a chip of wood
on the surface of the water.
8 The sin of Israel, the shrines of Aven
will be torn down.
Thorn and thistle will sprout up
on their altars.
They will say to the mountains,
"Cover us,"
to the hills, "Fall on us."
9 Since the days of Gibeah,
you have sinned, Israel;
there they have continued.
Will not war overtake them in Gibeah?
10 I will come and punish them;
nations will be gathered against them
when they are punished
for their double crime.
11 Ephraim was a trained cow
that loved to pull a plow;
I spared her fair neck;
but I will make Ephraim
break through the ground;
Judah will plow;
Jacob will turn the soil for himself.
12 Sow for yourselves righteousness;
reap faithful love;
break up your unplanted ground,
for it is time to seek the LORD,
that he may come
and rain righteousness upon you.
13 You have plowed wickedness,
you have reaped depravity,
you have eaten the fruit of lies,
because you have trusted in your way
and in your many warriors.
14 Therefore, the noise of war
will rise against your people;
all your fortresses
will be destroyed,
as Shalman destroyed Beth-arbel
on the day of battle,
when mothers were dashed
into pieces with their children.
15 It will indeed happen to you, Bethel,
because of your great wickedness.
At dawn, the king of Israel
will be cut off completely.

Divine love

11 When Israel was a child, I loved him,
and out of Egypt I called my son.
2 The more I called them,
the further they went from me;
they kept sacrificing to the Baals,
and they burned incense to idols.
3 Yet it was I who taught Ephraim to walk;
I took them up in my arms,
but they did not know
that I healed them.
4 I led them
with bands of human kindness,
with cords of love.
I treated them like those
who lift infants to their cheeks;
I bent down to them and fed them.

Divine frustration

5 They will return to the land of Egypt,
and Assyria will be their king,
because they have refused
to return to me.
6 The sword will strike wildly in their cities;
it will consume the bars of their gates
and will take everything
because of their schemes.
7 My people are bent on turning
away from me;
and though they cry out
to the Most High,[p]
he will not raise them up.

Divine compassion

8 How can I give you up, Ephraim?
How can I hand you over, Israel?
How can I make you like Admah?
How can I treat you like Zeboiim?
My heart winces within me;
my compassion
grows warm and tender.

Israel's and Judah's responses

9 I won't act on the heat of my anger;
I won't return to destroy Ephraim;
for I am God and not a human being,
the holy one in your midst;
I won't come in harsh judgment.
10 They will walk after the LORD,
who roars like a lion.
When he roars,
his children will come trembling
from the west.
11 They will come trembling like a bird,
and like a dove
from the land of Assyria;
and I will return them to their homes,
says the LORD.
12 [q]Ephraim has surrounded me with lies,
the house of Israel with faithless acts;
but Judah still walks with God,
and is faithful to the holy one.

God's charge against Judah

12 [r]Ephraim herds the wind,
and pursues the east wind
all day long;
they multiply lies and violence;
they make a treaty with Assyria,
and oil is carried to Egypt.
2 The LORD has a charge against Judah,
and will punish Jacob
according to his ways,
and respond to him
according to his deeds.
3 From the womb he tried to be
the oldest of twin brothers;
as an adult he struggled with God.
4 He struggled with the messenger
and survived;
he wept and sought his favor;
he met him at Bethel,
and there he spoke with him.
5 The LORD God of heavenly forces,
the LORD is his name!
6 But you! Return to your God
with faithful love and justice,
and wait continually for your God.

7 He is a merchant;
the means to cheat are in his hands;
he loves to take advantage of others.
8 Ephraim has said,
"I'm rich,
I've gained wealth for myself;
in all of my gain
no offense has been found in me
that would be sin."
9 I am the LORD your God
from the land of Egypt;
I will make you live in tents again,
as in former days.
10 I spoke to the prophets;
and I multiplied visions,
and through them
I uttered parables.
11 In Gilead there is wickedness;
they will surely come to nothing.
In Gilgal they sacrifice bulls,
so their altars will be
like piles of stones
on the rows of the field.
12 Jacob fled to the land of Aram;
there Israel served for a wife,
and for a wife he kept watch
over livestock.

[p]Heb uncertain [q]12:1 in Heb [r]12:2 in Heb

13 By a prophet the LORD
brought Israel up from Egypt,
and by a prophet he was guarded.
14 Ephraim has given bitter offense;
so the LORD will bring his crimes
down on him
and pay him back for his wrongdoing.

Infidelity despite divine goodness

13 When Ephraim spoke,
there was excitement;
he was praised in Israel;
but he became guilty through Baal
and died.
2 And now they keep on sinning;
they have made metal images,
idols of silver,
as a result of their skill,
all of them the work of craftsmen.
"Sacrifice to these," they say.
People are kissing calves!
3 Therefore, they will be
like the morning mist,
like the dew that passes away early,
like husks that swirl
from the threshing floor,
or like smoke from a window.
4 Yet I have been the LORD your God
ever since the land of Egypt;
and you will know no other gods but me;
there is no savior besides me.
5 I knew you in the wilderness,
in the land of no rain.
6 When I fed them, they were satisfied;
and their hearts became proud;
therefore, they forgot me.

Consequences of infidelity

7 So I will become like a lion to them;
like a leopard I will lurk beside the road.
8 I will fall upon them
like a bear robbed of her cubs,
and I will tear open
the covering of their hearts.
I will devour them like a lion,
as a wild animal would eat them.
9 I will destroy you, Israel;
for you didn't realize
that I could help you.
10 Where is your king now,
so that he can save you?
Where in all your cities are your judges,
of whom you said,
"Give me a king and rulers"?
11 I gave you a king in my anger,
and I took him away in my wrath.
12 Ephraim's wickedness is bound up;
his sin is kept in store.
13 The pangs of a woman in childbirth
come for him,
but he is not aware
of the time to be born;
for at the proper time
he doesn't present himself
at the mouth of the womb.
14 Will I ransom them
from the power of the grave[s]?
Will I redeem them from death's hold?
Death, where are your diseases?
Grave,[t] where is your destruction?
Compassion is hidden from my eyes.
15 Although he may flourish among rushes,
the east wind will come—
the breath of God
rising from the wilderness;
and his spring will dry up;
his fountain will be dried up.
It will strip his household
of every cherished possession.
16 [u]Samaria will be desolate,
because she has rebelled
against her God;
by the sword they will fall—
their babies will be dashed,
and their pregnant women
ripped open.

A plea: Return to God

14 [v]Return, Israel, to the LORD your God;
you have stumbled
because of your wickedness.
2 Prepare to speak
and return to the LORD;
say to the LORD,
"Forgive all wickedness;
and receive the good.
Instead of bulls,
let us offer what we can say:

[s]Heb *Sheol* [t]Heb *Sheol* [u]14:1 in Heb [v]14:2 in Heb

3 Assyria won't save us;
we won't ride upon horses;
we will no longer say, 'Our God,'
to the work of our hands.
In you the orphan finds compassion."

Divine promise of healing

4 I will heal their faithlessness;
I will love them freely,
for my anger has turned from them.
5 I will be like the dew to Israel;
he will blossom like the lily;
he will cast out his roots
like the forests of Lebanon.[w]
6 His branches will spread out;
his beauty will be like the olive tree,
and his fragrance like that of Lebanon.
7 They will again live beneath my shadow,
they will flourish like a garden;
they will blossom like the vine,
their fragrance will be
like the wine of Lebanon.
8 Ephraim, what do idols
have to do with me?
It is I who answer and look after you.
I am like a green cypress tree;
your fruit comes from me.

Be careful

9 Whoever is wise
understands these things.
Whoever observes
carefully knows them.
Truly, the LORD's ways are right,
and the righteous will walk in them,
but evildoers will stumble in them.

JOEL

Song of lament

1 The LORD's word that came to Joel, Peth-
uel's son:
2 Hear this, elders;
pay attention, everyone in the land!
Has anything like this ever happened
in your days,
or in the days of your ancestors?[a]
3 Tell it to your children,
and have your children
tell their children,
and their children tell their children.
4 What the cutting locust left,
the swarming locust has eaten.
What the swarming locust left,
the hopping locust has eaten.
And what the hopping locust left,
the devouring locust has eaten.[b]
5 Wake up, you who drink too much,
and weep.
Scream over the sweet wine,
all you wine drinkers,
because it is snatched from your mouth;
6 because a nation,
powerful and beyond number,
has invaded my land.
Its teeth are like lions' teeth;
its fangs are like those of a lioness.
7 It has destroyed my vines,
splintered my fig trees,
stripped off their bark
and thrown it down;
their branches have turned white.
8 Lament like a woman
dressed in funeral clothing,
one who has lost
the husband of her youth.
9 The grain offering and the drink offering
are gone from the LORD's temple.
The priests
and the LORD's ministers mourn.
10 The fields are devastated,
the ground mourns;
for the grain is destroyed,
the new wine dries up,
the olive oil fails.
11 Be shocked, you farmers;
howl, you vinedressers,
over the wheat and the barley,
for the crops of the field are destroyed.
12 The grapevine is dried up;
the fig tree withers.

[w] Or *like Lebanon* [a] Or *your fathers* [b] The Heb uses several different words for *locust*; none of the meanings are identical.

Pomegranate, palm, and apple—
all the trees of the field are dried up.
Joy fades away from the people.[c]

Call to mourn

13 Dress for a funeral and grieve,
you priests;
lament, ministers of the altar.
Come, spend the night in funeral
clothing, servants of my God,
because the grain offering
and the drink offering
have gone from the temple
of your God.
14 Demand a fast,
request a special assembly.
Gather the elders
and all the land's people
to the temple of the LORD your God,
and cry out to the LORD.

Time of suffering

15 What a terrible day!
The day of the LORD is near;
it comes like chaos from the Almighty.[d]
16 Isn't the food cut off
right before our eyes?
Aren't joy and gladness
also gone from our God's house?
17 The grain shrivels under the shovels;[e]
the barns are empty.
The granaries are in ruin
because the grain has dried up.
18 How the animals groan!
Herds of cattle are in distress
because there is no pasture for them;
even the flocks of sheep pant.

The prophet's prayer

19 To you, LORD, I cry,
for fire has completely destroyed
the pastures of the wilderness;
and flames have burned
all the trees of the field.
20 Even the field's wild animals cry to you
because the streams have dried up;
the fire has completely destroyed
the meadows of the wilderness.

Announcement of alarm and peril

2 Blow the horn in Zion;
give a shout on my holy mountain!
Let all the people of the land tremble,
for the day of the LORD is coming.
It is near—
2 a day of darkness and no light,
a day of clouds and thick darkness!
Like blackness spread out
upon the mountains,
a great and powerful army[f] comes,
unlike any that has ever come
before them,
or will come after them
in centuries ahead.
3 In front of them a fire consumes;
and behind them a flame burns.
Land ahead of them
is like Eden's garden,
but they leave behind them
a barren wasteland;
nothing escapes them.
4 They resemble horses,
and like warhorses they charge,
5 like the rumbling of chariots.
They leap on the mountaintops—
like the crackling of a fire's flame,
devouring the stubble;
like a powerful army
ready for battle.
6 In their presence,
peoples shake with fear;
all faces turn red with worry.
7 Like warriors they charge;
like soldiers they climb the wall.
Each keeps to their own path;
they didn't change their course.
8 They don't crowd each other;
each keeps to their own path.
Even if they fall among the weapons,
they won't stop.
9 They rush upon the city;
they run upon the walls.
They climb into the houses;
they enter through the windows
like thieves.
10 The earth quakes before them;
the heavens shake.

[c] Or *from the sons of men*; cf 2:1 Heb *the people of the land* [d] Heb *Shaddai* [e] Heb uncertain [f] Or *a great and strong people*

The sun and the moon are darkened;
the stars have stopped shining,
11 because the LORD utters his voice
at the head of his army.
How numerous are his troops!
Mighty are those who obey his word.
The day of the LORD is great;
it stirs up great fear—
who can endure it?

Change your hearts

12 Yet even now, says the LORD,
return to me with all your hearts,
with fasting, with weeping,
and with sorrow;
13 tear your hearts
and not your clothing.
Return to the LORD your God,
for he is merciful
and compassionate,
very patient, full of faithful love,
and ready to forgive.
14 Who knows whether he will have
a change of heart
and leave a blessing behind him,
a grain offering and a drink offering
for the LORD your God?
15 Blow the horn in Zion;
demand a fast;
request a special assembly.
16 Gather the people;
prepare a holy meeting;
assemble the elders;
gather the children,
even nursing infants.
Let the groom leave his room
and the bride her chamber.
17 Between the porch and the altar
let the priests,
the LORD's ministers, weep.
Let them say, "Have mercy, LORD,
on your people,
and don't make your inheritance
a disgrace,
an example of failure
among the nations.
Why should they say
among the peoples,
'Where is their God?'"

Words of compassion and promise

18 Then the LORD became passionate
about this land,[g] and had pity on his people.
19 The LORD responded to the people:
See, I am sending you
the corn, new wine, and fresh oil,
and you will be fully satisfied by it;
and I will no longer make you
a disgrace among the nations.
20 I will remove the northern army
far from you
and drive it into a dried-up
and desolate land,
its front into the eastern sea,
and its rear into the western sea.
Its stench will rise up;
its stink will come to the surface.
The LORD is about to do great things!
21 Don't fear, fertile land;
rejoice and be glad,
for the LORD is
about to do great things!
22 Don't be afraid, animals of the field,
for the meadows of the wilderness
will turn green;
the tree will bear its fruit;
the fig tree and grapevine
will give their full yield.
23 Children of Zion,
rejoice and be glad
in the LORD your God,
because he will give you the early rain
as a sign of righteousness;
he will pour down abundant rain
for you,
the early and the late rain, as before.[h]
24 The threshing floors will be full of grain;
the vats will overflow with new wine
and fresh oil.
25 I will repay you for the years
that the cutting locust,
the swarming locust, the hopping
locust, and the devouring locust
have eaten—
my great army,
which I sent against you.
26 You will eat abundantly and be satisfied,
and you will praise the name
of the LORD your God,

[g] Or *then the LORD became jealous for his land* [h] Or *at the first*

who has done wonders for you;
and my people will never again
be put to shame.
27 You will know
that I am in the midst of Israel,
and that I am the LORD your God—
no other exists;
never again will my people
be put to shame.
28 After that I will pour out my spirit
upon everyone;
your sons and your daughters
will prophesy,
your old men will dream dreams,
and your young men will see visions.
29 In those days, I will also pour out my
spirit on the male and female slaves.

30 I will give signs in the heavens and on
the earth—blood and fire and columns of
smoke. 31 The sun will be turned to darkness, and the moon to blood before the
great and dreadful day of the LORD comes.
32 But everyone who calls on the LORD's
name will be saved; for on Mount Zion and
in Jerusalem there will be security, as the
LORD has promised; and in Jerusalem, the
LORD will summon those who survive.

Judgment on the nations

3 Truly, in those days and in that time, I
will bring back to Judah and Jerusalem
those who were sent away. 2 I will gather
all the nations, and I will bring them to
the Jehoshaphat Valley. There I will enter
into judgment with them in support of my
people and my possession, Israel, which
they have scattered among the nations.
They have divided my land, 3 and have cast
lots for my people. They have traded boys
for prostitutes, and sold girls for wine,
which they drank down. 4 What are you to
me, Tyre and Sidon, and all the regions of
Philistia? Are you paying me back for something? If you are paying me back, then in
a flash I will turn your deeds back upon
your own heads. 5 You have taken my silver and my gold, and have carried my rich
treasures into your temples. 6 You have sold
the people of Judah and Jerusalem to the
Greeks, removing them far from their own
border. 7 But now I am calling them from
the places where you have sold them, and
I will repay you for your deeds. 8 I will sell
your sons and your daughters as a possession of the people of Judah, and they will
sell them to the Sabeans, to a nation far
away; for the LORD has spoken.

Declaration of war

9 Announce this among the nations:
Prepare a holy war,
wake up the warriors;
let all the soldiers draw near,
let them come up!
10 Beat the iron tips of your plows
into swords
and your pruning tools into spears;
let the weakling say, "I am mighty."
11 Come quickly,
all you surrounding nations;
gather yourselves there;
bring your mighty ones, LORD.
12 Let the nations prepare themselves,
and come up
to the Jehoshaphat Valley;
for there I will sit to judge
all the surrounding nations.
13 Cut with the sickle,
for the harvest is ripe.
Go and crush grapes,
for the winepress is full.
The jars overflow with wine,
for their wickedness is great.
14 Crowd after crowd
fills the valley of judgment,
for the day of the LORD is near
in the valley of judgment.
15 The sun and the moon are darkened;
the stars have ceased shining.

Salvation for God's people

16 The LORD roars from Zion,
and utters his voice from Jerusalem;
the heavens and the earth quake.
But the LORD is a refuge
for his people,
a shelter for the people of Israel.
17 So you will know
that I am the LORD your God,
settle down in Zion,
my holy mountain.
Jerusalem will be holy,

and never again
will strangers pass through it.
18 In that day
the mountains will drip sweet wine,
the hills will flow with milk,
and all the streambeds of Judah
will flow with water;
a spring will come forth
from the LORD's house
and water the Shittim Valley.
19 Egypt will become desolate
and Edom a desolate wilderness.
This is because of the violence
done to the people of Judah,
in whose land they have shed
innocent blood.
20 But Judah will be inhabited forever,
and Jerusalem for all generations.
21 I will forgive their bloodguilt,
which I had not forgiven.
I will act on their account;
I will not pardon the guilty.

The LORD dwells in Zion.

AMOS

Introduction

1 These are the words of Amos, one of the shepherds of Tekoa. He perceived these things concerning Israel two years before the earthquake, in the days of Judah's King Uzziah and in the days of Israel's King Jeroboam, Joash's son.

Proclamation of divine judgment

2 He said:
The LORD roars from Zion.
He shouts from Jerusalem;
the pastures of the shepherds wither,
and the top of Carmel dries up.

A word to Damascus

3 The LORD proclaims:
For three crimes of Damascus,
and for four,
I won't hold back the punishment,
because they have harvested Gilead
with sharp iron tools.
4 I will send down fire
on the house of Hazael;
it will devour the palaces of Ben-hadad.
5 I will break the fortified
gates of Damascus,
and eliminate the people
from the Aven Valley,
including the one who rules
from Beth-eden;
the people of Aram will be forced
to live in Kir,
says the LORD.

A word to Gaza and Ashdod

6 The LORD proclaims:
For three crimes of Gaza,
and for four,
I won't hold back the punishment,
because they rounded up
entire communities,
to hand them over to Edom.
7 I will send down a fire
on the wall of Gaza;
it will devour Gaza's palaces.
8 I will eliminate the people
from Ashdod,
the one who rules from Ashkelon.
I will turn my hand against Ekron,
and the Philistines who remain
will perish,
says the LORD God.

A word to Tyre

9 The LORD proclaims:
For three crimes of Tyre,
and for four,
I won't hold back the punishment,
because they have delivered up
entire communities over to Edom,
and neglected
their covenantal obligations.
10 So I will send a fire on the wall of Tyre;
it will devour their palaces.

A word to Edom

11 The LORD proclaims:
For three crimes of Edom,

and for four,
I won't hold back the punishment,
because he chased after his brother
with the sword,
denied all compassion,
kept his anger alive,
and fueled his wrath forever.
12 So I will send a fire on Teman;
it will devour the fortresses
of Bozrah.

A word to Ammon

13 The LORD proclaims:
For three crimes of the Ammonites,
and for four,
I won't hold back the punishment,
because they have ripped open
pregnant women in Gilead
in order to possess more land.
14 So I will start a fire
at the wall of Rabbah;
the fire will devour its palaces,
with a war cry on the day of battle,
with strong wind
on the day of the storm.
15 Then their king will be taken away,
he and his officials together,
says the LORD.

A word to Moab

2 The LORD proclaims:
For three crimes of Moab,
and for four,
I won't hold back the punishment,
because he burned to lime
the bones of the king of Edom.
2 So I will send down a fire on Moab;
it will devour the palaces of Kerioth.
Moab will die in a great uproar,
with a war cry,
with the sound of the ram's horn.
3 I will remove their judge from them
and slay all their officials with him,
says the LORD.

A word to Judah

4 The LORD proclaims:
For three crimes of Judah,
and for four,
I won't hold back the punishment,
because they have rejected the
Instruction of the LORD,
and haven't kept his laws.
They have been led off the right path by
the same lies
after which their ancestors walked.
5 So I will send a fire on Judah,
and it will devour the palaces
of Jerusalem.

A word to Israel

6 The LORD proclaims:
For three crimes of Israel,
and for four,
I won't hold back the punishment,
because they have sold the innocent
for silver,
and those in need
for a pair of sandals.
7 They crush the head of the poor
into the dust of the earth,
and push the afflicted
out of the way.
Father and son have intercourse
with the same young woman,
degrading my holy name.
8 They stretch out beside every altar
on garments taken in loan;
in the house of their god they drink
wine bought with fines they imposed.
9 Yet I destroyed the Amorite
before them,
whose height was as tall
as cedar trees,
and whose strength
was as strong as oak trees.
I destroyed his fruit above
and his roots below.
10 Also I brought you up
out of the land of Egypt,
and led you forty years
in the wilderness,
to lay claim
to the land of the Amorite.
11 I raised up some of your children
to be prophets
and some of your youth
to be nazirites.
Isn't this so, people of Israel?
says the LORD.

12 But you made the nazirites drink wine,
and commanded the prophets,
saying, "You won't prophesy."
13 So now I will oppress you,
just like a cart is weighed down[a]
when it is full of harvested grain.
14 Fast runners will find no refuge;
the strong will lose their strength;
the mighty will be unable
to save their lives.
15 Those who shoot the bow won't survive.
Fast runners won't escape;
those who ride horses
won't save themselves.
16 The bravest warrior
will flee away naked in that day,
says the LORD.

Words of doom for Israel

3 Hear this word that the LORD has spoken against you, people of Israel, against the whole family that I brought out of the land of Egypt:
2 You only have I loved so deeply
of all the families of the earth.
Therefore, I will punish you
for all your wrongdoing.
3 Will two people walk together
unless they have agreed to do so?[b]
4 Does a lion roar in the forest
when it has no prey?
Does a young lion cry out from its den
if it has caught nothing?
5 Will a bird fall into a trap
on the ground
when there is no bait for it?
Will a trap spring up from the ground
when it has taken nothing?
6 If a ram's horn is blown in a city,
won't people tremble?
If disaster falls on a city,
is it the LORD who has done it?
7 Surely the LORD God does nothing
without revealing his secret
to his servants the prophets.

8 A lion has roared;
who will not fear?
The LORD God has spoken;
who can but prophesy?

9 Proclaim it to the palaces of Ashdod
and to the palaces in the land of Egypt.
Say, "Gather yourselves
on Mount Samaria,
and see the great turmoil in the city,
and what violent deeds are inside it."
10 They don't know how to do right,
says the LORD—
those who store up violence and
robbery in their palaces.
11 Therefore, the LORD my God proclaims:
An enemy will surround the land;
he will bring you down
from your protected places,
and your palaces will be robbed.

12 The LORD proclaims:
Just as the shepherd rescues two legs or
the piece of an ear from the mouth of the
lion, so will the people of Israel be rescued.
Those who live in Samaria will escape with
the corner of a bed, and those in Damascus
with a piece of a couch.[c]
13 Hear this and speak
against the house of Jacob,
says the LORD God,
the God of heavenly forces:
14 On the day I punish the crimes of Israel,
I will also visit the altars of Bethel;
the horns of the altar will be cut off
and will fall to the ground.
15 I will tear down the winter house
as well as the summer house;
the houses of ivory will perish;
the great houses will be swept away,
says the LORD.

Judgment on Israel's elite

4 Hear this word, you cows of Bashan,
who are on Mount Samaria,
who cheat the weak,
who crush the needy,
who say to their husbands,
"Bring drinks, so we can get drunk!"
2 The LORD God has solemnly promised
by his holiness:
The days are surely coming upon you,
when they will take you away
with hooks,

[a] Heb uncertain [b] Or *Will two walk together unless they have agreed?* [c] Heb uncertain

even the last one of you
with fishhooks.
3 You will go out through the broken wall,
each one after another;
and you will be flung out into Harmon,
says the LORD.

A divine taunt

4 Come to Bethel—and commit a crime;
multiply crimes at Gilgal.
Bring your sacrifices every morning,
your tenth-part gifts every three days.
5 Offer a thanksgiving sacrifice
of leavened bread,
and publicize your gifts to the LORD;
for so you love to do, people of Israel!
says the LORD God.

Israel's stubbornness

6 I have sent a famine in all your cities,
and not provided enough bread
in all your places,
yet you didn't return to me,
says the LORD.
7 I also withheld rain from you
when there were still three months
to the harvest.
I allowed no rain to fall on one city,
no rain to fall on another city.
One field was rained on,
and the field dried up
where it didn't rain.
8 So two or three thirsty towns went to
one city to drink water,
and weren't satisfied;
yet you didn't return to me,
says the LORD.

9 I struck you with disease and mildew.
I destroyed your gardens
and your vineyards.
The locust devoured your fig trees
and your olive trees;
yet you didn't return to me,
says the LORD.

10 I sent a plague against you
like the one in Egypt.
I killed your young men
with the sword.
I carried away your horses.
I made the stink of your camp
go up into your nostrils;
yet you didn't return to me,
says the LORD.

11 I destroyed some of you,
as when God destroyed
Sodom and Gomorrah.
You were like a burning coal
plucked out of the fire;
yet you didn't return to me,
says the LORD.
12 Truly, Israel,
I will act in this way toward you;
therefore, I will do this to you.
Prepare to meet your God, Israel!

13 The one who forms the mountains,
creates the wind,
makes known his thoughts
to humankind,
makes the morning darkness,
and moves over the heights
of the earth—
the LORD, the God of heavenly forces
is his name!

A song of lament

5 Hear this word—a funeral song—that I
am lifting up against you, house of Israel:
2 Fallen, no more to rise,
is virgin Israel,
deserted on her land,
with no one to raise her up.
3 The LORD God proclaims:
The city that marched out
one thousand people
will have one hundred left,
and the city that marched out
one hundred will have ten left
in the house of Israel.

Words of encouragement

4 The LORD proclaims
to the house of Israel:
Seek me and live.
5 But don't seek Bethel,
don't enter into Gilgal,
or cross over to Beer-sheba;
for Gilgal will go into exile,
and Bethel will come to nothing.

6 Seek the LORD and live,
or else God might rush like a fire
against the house of Joseph.
The fire will burn up Bethel,
with no one to put it out.

Words of doom

7 Doom to you who turn justice into poison,
and throw righteousness
to the ground!

8 The one who made
the Pleiades and Orion,
and turns deep darkness
into the morning,
and darkens the day into night;
who summons the waters of the sea,
and pours them out
on the surface of the earth—
this one's name is the LORD—
9 who causes destruction to flash out
against the strong,
so that destruction comes
upon the fortress.

10 They hate the one who judges
at the city gate,
and they reject the one
who speaks the truth.
11 Truly, because you crush the weak,
and because you tax their grain,
you have built houses of carved stone,
but you won't live in them;
you have planted pleasant vineyards,
but you won't drink their wine.
12 I know how many are your crimes,
and how numerous are your sins—
afflicting the righteous,
taking money on the side,
turning away the poor
who seek help.
13 Therefore, the one who is wise
will keep silent in that time;
it is an evil time.

Words of inspiration

14 Seek good and not evil,
that you may live;
and so the LORD,
the God of heavenly forces,
will be with you just as you have said.
15 Hate evil, love good,
and establish justice at the city gate.
Perhaps the LORD God of heavenly forces
will be gracious
to what is left of Joseph.

Divine wrath anticipated

16 Truly, the LORD proclaims,
the God of heavenly forces, the Lord:
Crying will be heard in all the squares.
In all the streets they will say,
"Oh no! Oh no!"
They will call upon the farmers to wail,
and those skilled in mourning
to lament.
17 In all the vineyards
there will be bitter crying because
I will pass through your midst,
says the LORD.

A statement of divine disgust

18 Doom to those who desire
the day of the LORD!
Why do you want the day of the LORD?
It is darkness, not light;
19 as if someone fled from a lion,
and was met by a bear;
or sought refuge in a house,
rested a hand against the wall,
and was bitten by a snake.
20 Isn't the day of the LORD darkness,
not light;
all dark with no brightness in it?

21 I hate, I reject your festivals;
I don't enjoy your joyous assemblies.
22 If you bring me your entirely burned
offerings and gifts of food—
I won't be pleased;
I won't even look at your offerings
of well-fed animals.
23 Take away the noise of your songs;
I won't listen to the melody
of your harps.
24 But let justice roll down like waters,
and righteousness
like an ever-flowing stream.
25 Did you bring me sacrifices
and offerings
during the forty years in the
wilderness, house of Israel?

26 You will take up Sakkuth your king,
and Kaiwan your star-god,
your images,
which you made for yourselves.
27 Therefore, I will take you away
beyond Damascus, says the LORD,
whose name is
the God of heavenly forces.

Warnings to the self-satisfied

6 Doom to those resting
comfortably in Zion
and those trusting in Mount Samaria,
the chiefs of the nations,
to whom the house of Israel comes!
2 Cross over to Calneh and see;
from there go to Hamath the great;
then go down to Gath
of the Philistines.
Are you better than these kingdoms?
Or is your territory greater
than their territory?

3 Doom to those who ignore the evil day
and make violent rule draw near:
4 who lie on beds of ivory,
stretch out on their couches,
eat lambs from the flock,
and bull calves from the stall;
5 who sing idle songs
to the sound of the harp,
and, like David, compose tunes
on musical instruments;
6 who drink bowls of wine,
put the best of oils on themselves,
but who aren't grieved
over the ruin of Joseph!
7 Therefore, they will now
be the first to be taken away,
and the feast of those who lounged
at the table will pass away.

8 The LORD God has solemnly sworn,
says the LORD,
the God of heavenly forces:
I reject the pride of Jacob.
I hate his fortresses.
I will hand over the city
and all that is in it.
9 If ten people remain in one house,
then they will die.
10 If a relative,
someone who burns the dead,
picks up the body to bring it out
of the house,
and says to someone
inside the house,
"Is anyone else with you?"
the answer will be, "No."
Then the relative will say,
"Hush! We mustn't mention
the name of the LORD."
11 Look, the LORD is giving an order;
he will shatter the great house into bits
and the little house into pieces.
12 Do horses run on rocks?
Does one plow the sea with oxen?
But you have turned justice
into poison
and the fruit of righteousness
into bitterness—
13 you who rejoice in Lo-debar,
who say, "Haven't we by our own strength
taken Karnaim for ourselves?"
14 Indeed, I will raise up against you
a nation, house of Israel,
says the LORD God of heavenly forces,
and they will oppress you from
Lebo-hamath to the desert ravine.

A vision of locusts

7 This is what the LORD God showed me:
The LORD God was forming locusts at
the time the late grass began to sprout. (It
was the late grass after the king's harvest.)
2 When they had finished eating the green
plants of the land, I said,

"LORD God, please forgive!
How can Jacob survive?
He is so small!"
3 The LORD relented concerning this:
"It won't take place,"
says the LORD.

A vision of fire

4 This is what the LORD God showed me:
The LORD God was calling for judgment with
fire, and it devoured the great deep and was
eating up part of the land. 5 Then I said,
"LORD God, I beg you, stop!
How can Jacob survive?
He is so small!"

[6]The LORD relented concerning this:
"This also won't take place,"
says the LORD God.

A vision of a plumb line

[7]This is what the LORD showed me: The
LORD was standing by a wall, with a plumb
line in his hand. [8]The LORD said to me,
"Amos, what do you see?"

"A plumb line," I said.
Then the LORD said,
"See, I am setting a plumb line
in the middle of my people Israel.
I will never again forgive them.
[9]The shrines of Isaac will be made desolate,
and the holy places of Israel
will be laid waste,
and I will rise against the house of
Jeroboam with the sword."

Exchange between Amaziah, Jeroboam, and Amos

[10]Then Amaziah, the priest of Bethel,
reported to Israel's King Jeroboam, "Amos
has plotted against you within the house
of Israel. The land isn't able to cope with
everything that he is saying. [11]Amos has
said, 'Jeroboam will die by the sword, and
Israel will be forced out of its land.'"

[12]Amaziah said to Amos, "You who see
things, go, run away to the land of Judah, eat
your bread there, and prophesy there; [13]but
never again prophesy at Bethel, for it is the
king's holy place and his royal house."

[14]Amos answered Amaziah, "I am[d] not
a prophet, nor am I a prophet's son; but I
am a shepherd, and a trimmer of sycamore
trees. [15]But the LORD took me from shepherding the flock, and the LORD said to me,
'Go, prophesy to my people Israel.'
[16]"Now then hear the LORD's word.
You say, 'Don't prophesy against Israel,
and don't preach
against the house of Isaac.'
[17]"Therefore, the LORD proclaims:
'Your wife will become a prostitute
in the city,
and your sons and your daughters
will fall by the sword,
and your land will be measured
and divided up;
you yourself will die in an unclean land,
and Israel will surely be taken away
from its land.'"

A vision of summer fruit

8 This is what the LORD God showed me:
a basket of summer fruit. [2]He said,
"Amos, what do you see?"
I said, "A basket of summer fruit."
Then the LORD said to me,
"The end has come upon my people Israel;
I will never again forgive them.
[3]On that day, the people
will wail the temple songs,"
says the LORD God;
"there will be many corpses,
thrown about everywhere.[e]
Silence."

Judgment on oppressors and hypocrites

[4]Hear this, you who trample
on the needy and destroy
the poor of the land, [5]saying,
"When will the new moon
be over so that we may sell grain,
and the Sabbath
so that we may offer wheat for sale,
make the ephah smaller,
enlarge the shekel,
and deceive with false balances,
[6]in order to buy the needy for silver
and the helpless for sandals,
and sell garbage as grain?"

[7]The LORD has sworn
by the pride of Jacob:
Surely I will never forget
what they have done.
[8]Will not the land tremble on this account,
and all who live in it mourn,
as it rises and overflows like the Nile,
and then falls again,
like the River of Egypt?[f]

[9]On that day, says the LORD God,
I will make the sun go down at noon,

[d]Or *was*; the verb is implied. [e]Heb uncertain [f]Heb uncertain

and I will darken the earth
in broad daylight.
10 I will turn your feasts into sad affairs
and all your singing into a funeral song;
I will make people
wear mourning clothes
and shave their heads;
I will make it like the loss
of an only child,
and the end of it like a bitter day.
11 The days are surely coming,
says the LORD God,
when I will send hunger and thirst
on the land;
neither a hunger for bread,
nor a thirst for water,
but of hearing the LORD's words.
12 They will wander from sea to sea,
and from north to east;
they will roam all around,
seeking the LORD's word,
but they won't find it.
13 On that day the beautiful young women
and the young men
will faint with thirst.
14 Those who swear by the guilt of Samaria,
and say, "As your god lives, Dan,"
and, "As the way of Beer-sheba lives"—
even they will fall
and never rise again.

Description of Israel's fate

9 I saw the Lord standing beside the
altar, and the Lord said:
Strike the pillars
until the foundations shake,
shatter them on the heads
of all the people.
With the sword,
I will kill the last of them;
not one of them will flee,
not one of them will escape.
2 If they dig through
into the underworld,[g]
from there my hand will take them.
If they climb up to the heavens,
from there I will bring them down.
3 If they hide themselves
on the top of Carmel,
I will search for them there
and remove them.
If they hide from my sight
at the bottom of the sea,
I will give an order to the sea serpent,
and it will bite them.
4 If they are forced from their homes
before their enemies,
there I will give an order to the sword,
and it will kill them.
I will fix my eyes on them
for harm and not for good.

A divine confession

5 The LORD, God of heavenly forces,
touches the earth and it melts,
and all who live in it are sick to death.
All of it[h] rises up like the Nile
and sinks again,
like the Nile of Egypt.
6 It is the LORD who builds
his upper rooms in the heavens
and establishes his residence
upon the earth;
who summons the waters of the sea,
and pours them out
upon the face of the earth—
the LORD is his name.

Divine address to the Israelites

7 Aren't you like the Cushites to me,
people of Israel?
says the LORD.
Haven't I brought Israel up
from the land of Egypt,
and the Philistines from Caphtor
and the Arameans from Kir?
8 Look, the LORD God is eyeing
the sinful kingdom,
and I will destroy it
from the face of the earth.
However, I won't destroy fully
the house of Jacob,
says the LORD.

Warning to the house of Israel

9 Look, I am giving orders,
and I will shake the house of Israel
among all the nations

[g] Heb *Sheol* [h] Or *the earth*

as one sifts dirt with a screen,
but no pebble will fall to the ground.
10 All the sinners of my people
will die by the sword,
those who say,
"Evil won't overtake or meet us."

Divine promise of restoration

11 On that day I will raise up
the meeting tent of David
that has fallen,
and repair its broken places.
I will raise up its ruins,
and I will rebuild it
like a long time ago;
12 so that they may possess
what is left of Edom,
as well as all the nations
who are called by my name,
says the LORD who will do this.
13 The days are surely coming, says the LORD,
when the one who plows
will overtake the one who gathers,
when the one who crushes grapes
will overtake the one
who sows the seed.
The mountains will drip wine,
and all the hills will flow with it.
14 I will improve the circumstances
of my people Israel;
they will rebuild the ruined cities
and inhabit them.
They will plant vineyards
and drink their wine;
and they will make gardens
and eat their fruit.
15 I will plant them upon their land,
and they will never again
be plucked up
out of the land
that I have given them,
says the LORD your God.

OBADIAH

Edom falls

1 The vision of Obadiah.
The LORD God proclaims
concerning Edom:
We have heard a message
from the LORD—
a messenger has been sent
among the nations:
"Rise up! Let us rise against her
for battle!"
2 Look now, I will make you of little
importance among the nations;
you will be totally despised.
3 Your proud heart has tricked you—
you who live in the cracks of the rock,
whose dwelling is high above.
You who say in your heart,
"Who will bring me
down to the ground?"
4 Though you soar like the eagle,
though your nest is set
among the stars,
I will bring you down from there,
says the LORD.

Edom is robbed

5 If thieves approach you,
if robbers by night—
how you've been devastated!—
wouldn't they steal
only what they wanted?
If those who gather grapes came to you,
wouldn't they leave some grapes?
6 How Esau has been looted,
his treasures taken away!
7 All those who were your allies
have driven you to the border.
Those who were on your side
tricked you
and triumphed over you.
They are setting your own bread
as a trap under you,[a]
but you don't see it coming.
8 Won't I on that day, says the LORD,
destroy the wise from Edom
and understanding from Mount Esau?
9 Your warriors will be shattered, Teman,
and everyone from Mount Esau
will be eliminated.

[a] Heb uncertain

Edom's misdeeds

10 Because of the slaughter and violence
done to your brother Jacob,
shame will cover you,
and you will be destroyed forever.
11 You stood nearby,
strangers carried off his wealth,
and foreigners entered his gates
and cast lots for Jerusalem;
you too were like one of them.
12 But you should have taken no pleasure
over your brother
on the day of his misery;
you shouldn't have rejoiced
over the people of Judah
on the day of their devastation;
you shouldn't have bragged
on their day of hardship.
13 You shouldn't have entered
the gate of my people
on the day of their defeat;
you shouldn't have even looked
on his suffering
on the day of his disaster;
you shouldn't have stolen
his possessions
on the day of his distress.
14 You shouldn't have waited on the roads
to destroy his escapees;
you shouldn't have handed over
his survivors
on the day of defeat.
15 The day of the LORD is near
against all the nations.
As you have done,
so it will be done to you;
your actions will make you suffer!
16 Just as you have drunk
on my holy mountain,
so will all the nations around you drink;
they will drink and swallow quickly,
and they will be like they've never
been before.

Edom's punishers

17 But on Mount Zion
there will be those who escape,
and it will be holy;
and the house of Jacob will drive out
those who drove them out.
18 The house of Jacob will be a fire,
the house of Joseph a flame,
and the house of Esau straw;
they will burn them up completely,
and there will be no one left
of the house of Esau,
for the LORD has spoken.
19 Those of the arid southern plain
will possess Mount Esau,
and those of the western foothills,
the land of the Philistines;
they will possess the land of Ephraim
and the land of Samaria,
and Benjamin will possess Gilead.
20 Those who remain of the Israelites
will possess the land of the
Canaanites as far as Zarephath;
and those left from Jerusalem
and who are now living in Sepharad
will possess the cities
of the arid southern plain.
21 The deliverers will go up to Mount Zion
to rule Mount Esau,
and the kingdom will be the LORD's.

JONAH

Commissioning of a reluctant prophet

1 The LORD's word came to Jonah, Amittai's
son: 2 "Get up and go to Nineveh, that
great city, and cry out against it, for their
evil has come to my attention."
3 So Jonah got up—to flee to Tarshish
from the LORD! He went down to Joppa and
found a ship headed for Tarshish. He paid
the fare and went aboard to go with them
to Tarshish, away from the LORD. 4 But the
LORD hurled a great wind upon the sea, so
that there was a great storm on the sea; the
ship looked like it might be broken to pieces.
5 The sailors were terrified, and each one cried
out to his god. They hurled the cargo that was
in the ship into the sea to make it lighter.
Now Jonah had gone down into the hold
of the vessel to lie down and was deep in

sleep. 6The ship's officer came and said to him, "How can you possibly be sleeping so deeply? Get up! Call on your god! Perhaps the god will give some thought to us so that we won't perish."

7Meanwhile, the sailors said to each other, "Come on, let's cast lots so that we might learn who is to blame for this evil that's happening to us." They cast lots, and the lot fell on Jonah. 8So they said to him, "Tell us, since you're the cause of this evil happening to us: What do you do and where are you from? What's your country and of what people are you?"

9He said to them, "I'm a Hebrew. I worship the LORD, the God of heaven—who made the sea and the dry land."

10Then the men were terrified and said to him, "What have you done?" (The men knew that Jonah was fleeing from the LORD, because he had told them.)

11They said to him, "What will we do about you so that the sea will become calm around us?" (The sea was continuing to rage.)

12He said to them, "Pick me up and hurl me into the sea! Then the sea will become calm around you. I know it's my fault that this great storm has come upon you."

13The men rowed to reach dry land, but they couldn't manage it because the sea continued to rage against them. 14So they called on the LORD, saying, "Please, LORD, don't let us perish on account of this man's life, and don't blame us for innocent blood! You are the LORD: whatever you want, you can do." 15Then they picked up Jonah and hurled him into the sea, and the sea ceased its raging. 16The men worshipped the LORD with a profound reverence; they offered a sacrifice to the LORD and made solemn promises.

No escape for the prophet

17[a]Meanwhile, the LORD provided a great fish to swallow Jonah. Jonah was in the belly of the fish for three days and three nights.

2 Jonah prayed to the LORD his God from the belly of the fish:

2"I called out to the LORD in my distress,
and he answered me.
From the belly of the underworld[b]
I cried out for help;
you have heard my voice.
3You had cast me into the depths
in the heart of the seas,
and the flood surrounds me.
All your strong waves and rushing
water passed over me.
4So I said, 'I have been driven
away from your sight.
Will I ever again look
on your holy temple?
5Waters have grasped me
to the point of death;
the deep surrounds me.
Seaweed is wrapped around my head
6at the base
of the undersea[c] mountains.
I have sunk down to the underworld;
its bars held me
with no end in sight.
But you brought me out of the pit.'
7When my endurance[d] was weakening,
I remembered the LORD,
and my prayer came to you,
to your holy temple.
8Those deceived by worthless things
lose their chance for mercy.[e]
9But me, I will offer a sacrifice to you
with a voice of thanks.
That which I have promised,
I will pay.
Deliverance belongs to the LORD!"

10Then the LORD spoke to the fish, and it vomited Jonah onto the dry land.

Nineveh hears God's word

3 The LORD's word came to Jonah a second time: 2"Get up and go to Nineveh, that great city, and declare against it the proclamation that I am commanding you." 3And Jonah got up and went to Nineveh, according to the LORD's word. (Now Nineveh was indeed an enormous city, a three days' walk across.)

4Jonah started into the city, walking one day, and he cried out, "Just forty days more

[a]2:1 in Heb [b]Heb *Sheol* [c]Heb lacks *undersea.* [d]*Endurance* here renders the same Heb word as *life* in 1:14 and *death* in 2:5. [e]Heb uncertain

and Nineveh will be overthrown!" 5 And the people of Nineveh believed God. They proclaimed a fast and put on mourning clothes, from the greatest of them to the least significant.

6 When word of it reached the king of Nineveh, he got up from his throne, stripped himself of his robe, covered himself with mourning clothes, and sat in ashes. 7 Then he announced, "In Nineveh, by decree of the king and his officials: Neither human nor animal, cattle nor flock, will taste anything! No grazing and no drinking water! 8 Let humans and animals alike put on mourning clothes, and let them call upon God forcefully! And let all persons stop their evil behavior and the violence that's under their control!" 9 He thought, Who knows? God may see this and turn from his wrath, so that we might not perish.[f]

10 God saw what they were doing—that they had ceased their evil behavior. So God stopped planning to destroy them, and he didn't do it.

Jonah balks at God's mercy

4 But Jonah thought this was utterly wrong, and he became angry. 2 He prayed to the LORD, "Come on, LORD! Wasn't this precisely my point when I was back in my own land? This is why I fled to Tarshish earlier! I know that you are a merciful and compassionate God, very patient, full of faithful love, and willing not to destroy. 3 At this point, LORD, you may as well take my life from me, because it would be better for me to die than to live."

4 The LORD responded, "Is your anger a good thing?" 5 But Jonah went out from the city and sat down east of the city. There he made himself a hut and sat under it, in the shade, to see what would happen to the city.

6 Then the LORD God provided a shrub,[g] and it grew up over Jonah, providing shade for his head and saving him from his misery. Jonah was very happy about the shrub. 7 But God provided a worm the next day at dawn, and it attacked the shrub so that it died. 8 Then as the sun rose God provided a dry east wind, and the sun beat down on Jonah's head so that he became faint. He begged that he might die, saying, "It's better for me to die than to live."

9 God said to Jonah, "Is your anger about the shrub a good thing?"

Jonah said, "Yes, my anger is good—even to the point of death!"

10 But the LORD said, "You 'pitied' the shrub, for which you didn't work and which you didn't raise; it grew in a night and perished in a night. 11 Yet for my part, can't I pity Nineveh, that great city, in which there are more than one hundred twenty thousand people who can't tell their right hand from their left, and also many animals?"

MICAH

The LORD is coming!

1 The LORD's word that came to Micah of Moresheth in the days of Judah's Kings Jotham, Ahaz, and Hezekiah, which he saw concerning Samaria and Jerusalem:

2 Listen, all you peoples!
Pay attention, earth,
and all that fills it!
May the LORD God
be a witness against you,
the Lord from his holy temple.
3 Look! The LORD is coming out
from his place;
he will go down and tread
on the shrines of the earth.
4 Then the mountains
will melt under him;
the valleys will split apart,
like wax yielding to the fire,
like waters poured down a slope.
5 All this is for the crime of Jacob
and the sins of the house of Israel.

[f] Heb lacks *For he thought*. [g] Botanists disagree about whether Heb *qiqayon* refers to a climbing gourd plant, a castor bean plant, or some other shrub.

Who is responsible
for the crime of Jacob?[a]
Isn't it Samaria?
Who is responsible
for[b] the shrines of Judah?
Isn't it Jerusalem?
6 So I will make Samaria
a pile of rubble in the open field,
a place for planting vineyards.
I will pour her stones into the valley;
her foundations I will lay bare.
7 All her images will be beaten to pieces;
all her wages will be burned;
I will make all her idols worthless.
Since she gathered them
from the wages of a prostitute,
they will again become
wages of a prostitute.
8 On account of this, I will cry out and howl;
I will go about barefoot and stripped.
I will cry out like the jackals,
and mourn like the ostriches.

Destruction looms

9 Indeed, Zion has been weakened
by her wounds!
It has come as far as Judah;
he has struck as far as the gate
of my people,
as far as Jerusalem.
10 In Gath tell it not; no need to weep there![c]
In Beth-le-aphrah,
roll yourself in the dust!
11 Pass by (for your sake),[d]
inhabitants of Shaphir!
In nakedness and shame
she will not go out,
inhabitants of Zaanan.
The cry of Beth-ezel
will take away from you[e]
any place to stand.
12 How she longs for good,
inhabitants of Maroth!
Calamity has come down from the LORD
to the gate of Jerusalem.
13 Harness the horses to the chariot,
inhabitants of Lachish!
It was the beginning of sin
for Daughter Zion;
the crimes of Israel
have been found in you.
14 Therefore, you will give good-bye gifts
to Moresheth-gath;
the houses of Achzib have become
a deception for the kings of Israel.
15 Again I will bring to you
the one who conquers,
inhabitants of Mareshah;
the glory of Israel
will come as far as Adullam.
16 Make yourself bald
and cut off your hair
because of your cherished children!
Make yourself as bald as the vulture,
for they have gone from you
into exile.

Oppressors will themselves be ruined

2 Doom to those
who devise wickedness,
to those who plan evil
when they are in bed.
By the light of morning they do it,
for they are very powerful.
2 They covet fields and seize them,
houses and take them away.
They oppress a householder
and those in his house,
a man and his estate.
3 Therefore, the LORD proclaims:
I myself am devising an evil
against this family
from which you will not be able
to remove your necks!
You will no longer be able
to go about arrogantly,
for it will be an evil time.
4 On that day, a taunt will be raised
against you;
someone will wail bitterly:
"We are utterly destroyed!
He exchanges the portion
of my people;
he removes what belongs to me;
he gives away our fields to a rebel."
5 Therefore, you will have no one
to set boundary lines
by lot in the LORD's assembly.

[a]Heb lacks *responsible for.* [b]Heb lacks *responsible for.* [c]Heb lacks *there.* [d]*You* (plural) [e]*You* (feminine singular)

Leaders unwilling to hear God's word

6 "They mustn't preach!"
so they preach.
"They mustn't preach of such things!
Disgrace won't overtake us."
7 (Should this be said, house of Jacob?)
"Is the LORD's patience cut short?
Are these his deeds?"
Don't my words help
the one who behaves righteously?
8 But yesterday, my people,
the LORD rose up as an enemy.[f]
You strip off the glorious clothes[g]
from trusting passersby,
those who reject war.
9 You drive out the women
of my people,
each from her cherished house;
from their young children
you take away my splendor forever.
10 Rise up and go! This can't be
the resting place;
because of its uncleanness,
it destroys and the destruction
is horrific.
11 If someone were to go about inspired
and say deceitfully:
"I will preach to you
for wine and liquor,"
such a one would be
the preacher for this people!

The false prophet's "peace" will be destruction

12 I'll surely gather Jacob—all of you!
I'll surely assemble you,
those who are left of Israel!
I'll put them together
like sheep in Bozrah,[h]
like a flock in its pen,
noisy with people.
13 The one who breaks out
will go before them;
they will break out
and pass through the gate;
they will leave by it.
They will pass on,
their king before them,
the LORD at their head.

Micah justifies the coming destruction

3 But I said:
Hear, leaders of Jacob,
rulers of the house of Israel!
Isn't it your job to know justice?—
2 you who hate good and love evil,
who tear the skin off them,
and the flesh off their bones,
3 who devour the flesh of my people,
tear off their skin,
break their bones in pieces,
and spread them out as if in a pot,
like meat in a kettle.
4 Then they will cry out to the LORD,
but he won't answer them.
He will hide his face from them
at that time,
because of their evil deeds.
5 The LORD proclaims
concerning the prophets,
those who lead my people astray,
those who chew with their teeth
and then proclaim "Peace!"
but stir up war against the one
who puts nothing in their mouths:
6 Therefore, it will become night for you,
without vision, only darkness
without divination!
The sun will set on the prophets;
the day will be dark upon them.
7 Those seeing visions will be ashamed,
and the diviners disgraced;
they will all cover their upper lips,[i]
for there will be no answer from God.
8 But me! I am filled with power,
with the spirit of the LORD,
with justice and might,
to declare to Jacob his wrongdoing
and to Israel his sin!
9 Hear this, leaders of the house of Jacob,
rulers of the house of Israel,
you who reject justice
and make crooked all that is straight,
10 who build Zion with bloodshed
and Jerusalem with injustice!
11 Her officials give justice for a bribe,
and her priests teach for hire.
Her prophets offer divination for silver,
yet they rely on the LORD, saying,

[f] Heb lacks *the LORD*. [g] Heb uncertain [h] See Isa 34:6; 63:1. [i] Or *mustache* or *beard*

"Isn't the LORD in our midst?
Evil won't come upon us!"
12 Therefore, because of you,
Zion will be plowed like a field,
Jerusalem will become piles of rubble,
and the temple mount will become
an overgrown mound.

A peaceable world

4 But in the days to come,
the mountain of the LORD's house
will be the highest of the mountains;
it will be lifted above the hills;
peoples will stream to it.
2 Many nations will go and say:
"Come, let's go up
to the mountain of the LORD,
to the house of Jacob's God,
so that he may teach us his ways
and we may walk in God's paths!"
Instruction will come from Zion
and the LORD's word
from Jerusalem.
3 God will judge between the nations
and settle disputes of mighty nations,
which are far away.
They will beat their swords
into iron plows
and their spears into pruning tools.
Nation will not take up sword
against nation;
they will no longer learn
how to make war.
4 All will sit underneath
their own grapevines,
under their own fig trees.
There will be no one to terrify them;
for the mouth of the LORD of
heavenly forces has spoken.

An assertion of enduring loyalty

5 Each of the peoples walks
in the name of their own god;
but as for us, we will walk
in the name of the LORD our God
forever and always.

Dominion in Zion

6 On that day, says the LORD,
I will gather the lame;
I will assemble those
who were driven away
and those whom I have harmed.
7 I will make the lame into survivors,
those driven away
into a mighty nation.
The LORD will rule over them
on Mount Zion
from now on and forever.
8 As for you, Tower of Eder,[j]
hill of Daughter Zion,
as for you it will come,
the former dominion will come,
the royal power
belonging to Daughter Zion.

God is in control

9 Now why do you cry out so loudly?
Isn't the king in you?
Or has your counselor perished,
so that pain has seized you
like that of a woman in labor?
10 Writhe and scream, Daughter Zion,
like a woman in labor!
Now you will leave the city
and dwell in the open field;
you will go to Babylon.
There you will be rescued;
there the LORD will redeem you
from the power of your enemies.
11 Now many nations
may gather against you;
they say, "Let her be defiled,"
or "Let our eyes look with desire
at Zion."
12 But they don't know
the plans of the LORD;
they can't understand his scheme,
namely, that he will bring them
like grain to the threshing floor!
13 Arise and thresh, Daughter Zion,
for I will make your horn out of iron;
your hooves I will make
out of bronze.
You will crush many peoples;
you will dedicate their ill-gotten gains
to the LORD,
their wealth to the LORD
of all the earth.

[j] Or *tower of the flock*

Call to arms; the future is secure

5 [k]Now muster your troops,
Daughter Troop![l]
They have laid siege against us;
with a rod they will strike the cheek
of the judge of Israel.
2 As for you, Bethlehem of Ephrathah,
though you are the least significant
of Judah's forces,
one who is to be a ruler in Israel
on my behalf will come out from you.
His origin is from remote times,
from ancient days.
3 Therefore, he will give them up
until the time when
she who is in labor gives birth.
The rest of his kin will return
to the people of Israel.
4 He will stand and shepherd his flock[m]
in the strength of the LORD,
in the majesty of the name
of the LORD his God.
They will dwell secure,
because he will surely become great
throughout the earth;
5 he will become one of peace.[n]
When Assyria invades our land
and treads down our fortresses,
then we will raise up against him
seven shepherds and
eight human princes.
6 They will shepherd the land of Assyria
with the sword,
the land of Nimrod
with the drawn sword.
He will rescue us from Assyria
when he invades our land
and treads within our territory.
7 Then the few remaining in Jacob
will be amid many peoples
like dew from the LORD,
like spring showers upon the grass,
which does not hope for humans
or wait for human ones.
8 Then the few remaining in Jacob
will be among the nations,
amid many peoples,
like a lion among the creatures
of the forest,
like a young lion among flocks
of sheep, which when it passes by,
tramples and tears to pieces
with no one to deliver.
9 Your hand will be lifted over your foes;
all your enemies will be cut off.

Doom for Israel's enemies

10 On that day—says the LORD—
I will cut down your horses
in your midst;
I will destroy your chariots!
11 I will cut down the cities of your land;
I will tear down your defenses!
12 I will demolish
the sorceries you perform;
you will have no more diviners!
13 I will cut down your images
and your sacred pillars in your midst.
You will no longer bow down
to the works of your hands!
14 I will tear down your sacred poles[o]
in your midst;
I will destroy your cities!
15 I will exact vengeance in anger
and in wrath
on the nations that don't obey!

God's dispute with Israel

6 Hear what the LORD is saying:
Arise, lay out the lawsuit
before the mountains;
let the hills hear your voice!
2 Hear, mountains, the lawsuit
of the LORD!
Hear, eternal foundations
of the earth!
The LORD has a lawsuit
against his people;
with Israel he will argue.
3 "My people, what did I ever do to you?
How have I wearied you? Answer me!
4 I brought you up out of the land of Egypt;
I redeemed you
from the house of slavery.
I sent Moses, Aaron, and Miriam
before you.
5 My people, remember what
Moab's King Balak had planned,

[k] 4:14 in Heb [l] Heb uncertain [m] Heb lacks *his flock.* [n] Or *this will ensure peace.* [o] Heb *asherim*

and how Balaam, Beor's son,
answered him!
Remember everything[p]
from Shittim to Gilgal,
that you might learn to recognize
the righteous acts of the LORD!"

What does the LORD require?

6 With what should I approach the LORD
and bow down before God on high?
Should I come before him
with entirely burned offerings,
with year-old calves?
7 Will the LORD be pleased
with thousands of rams,
with many torrents of oil?
Should I give my oldest child
for my crime;
the fruit of my body
for the sin of my spirit?
8 He has told you, human one,
what is good and
what the LORD requires from you:
to do justice, embrace faithful love,
and walk humbly with your God.

Punishment is near

9 The voice of the LORD
calls out to the city;
wisdom appears
when one fears your name.[q]
Hear, tribe, and who appointed her![r]
10 Are the treasures of wickedness
still in the house of wickedness,
while the shorted basket[s]
is denounced?[t]
11 Can I approve wicked scales
and a bag of false weights
12 in a city[u] whose wealthy
are full of violence
and whose inhabitants speak falsehood
with lying tongues in their mouths?
13 So I have made you sick by striking you!
I have struck you because of your sins.
14 You devour, but you aren't satisfied;
a gnawing emptiness is within you.
You put something aside,
but you don't keep it safe.
That which you do try to keep safe,
I will give to the sword.
15 You sow, but you don't gather.
You tread down olives,
but you don't anoint with oil;
you tread grapes,
but don't drink wine.
16 Yet you[v] have kept the policies of Omri,
all the practices of the house of Ahab;
you have followed their counsels.
Therefore, I will make you
a sign of destruction,
your[w] inhabitants an object of hissing!
You must bear the reproach of my people.

The prophet laments

7 I'm doomed!
I've become like one who,
even after the summer fruit
has been gathered,
after the ripened fruits
have been collected,
has no cluster of grapes to eat,
no ripe fig that I might desire.
2 Faithful ones have perished from the land;
there is no righteous one
among humanity.
All of them lie in wait for bloodshed;
they hunt each other with nets.
3 Their hands are skilled at doing evil.
Official and judge alike ask for a bribe;
the powerful speak however they like;
this is how they conspire.
4 The good among them are like a briar;
those who do the right thing are
like a thorny thicket.
(A day for your lookouts![x]
Your punishment has arrived.
The confusion of the wicked[y]
is nearby.)
5 Don't rely on a friend;
put no trust in a companion;
guard the doors of your mouth
from her who lies in your embrace.
6 Son disrespects father;
a daughter rises up against her mother,
a daughter-in-law against
her mother-in-law;

[p] Heb lacks *everything*. [q] Heb uncertain [r] Heb uncertain [s] Or *ephah*, approximately twenty quarts of grain
[t] Heb uncertain [u] Heb lacks *in a city*. [v] Or *he* [w] Or *her* [x] Heb uncertain [y] Heb lacks *the wicked*.

the enemies of a man
are those of his own household.
[7]But me! I will keep watch for the LORD;
I will wait for the God of my salvation;
my God will hear me.

Zion speaks

[8]Do not rejoice[z] over me, my enemy,
because when I fall, I will rise;
if I sit in darkness,
the LORD is my light.
[9]I must bear the raging of the LORD,
for I have sinned against him,
until he decides my case
and provides justice for me.
He will bring me out into the light;
I will see by means of his righteousness.
[10]Then my enemy will see;
shame will cover her who said to me:
"Where is the LORD your God?"
My eyes will see her ruin;[a]
now she will become something
to be trampled,
like mud in the streets.

Micah responds to Zion

[11]A day for the building of your walls!
On that day, the boundary
will be distant.
[12]On that day, they will come to you
from Assyria and the cities of Egypt,
from Egypt to the River,
from sea to sea,
and from mountain to mountain.
[13]And the earth will become desolate
because of her inhabitants,
because of the fruit of their actions.

Micah intercedes for the people

[14]Shepherd your people with your staff,
the sheep of your inheritance,
those dwelling alone in a forest
in the midst of Carmel.
Let them graze in Bashan and Gilead,
as a long time ago.

God agrees

[15]As in the days when you came
out of the land of Egypt,
I will show Israel wonderful things.

The prophet continues

[16]Nations will see and be ashamed
of all their strength;
they will cover their mouths;
their ears will be deaf.
[17]They will lick dust like the snake,
like things that crawl on the ground.
They will come trembling from their
strongholds to the LORD our God;
they will dread and fear you!
[18]Who is a God like you,
pardoning iniquity,
overlooking the sin of the few
remaining for his inheritance?
He doesn't hold on to his anger forever;
he delights in faithful love.
[19]He will once again have compassion on us;
he will tread down our iniquities.
You will hurl all our sins
into the depths of the sea.
[20]You will provide faithfulness to Jacob,
faithful love to Abraham,
as you swore to our ancestors
a long time ago.

NAHUM

1 An oracle about Nineveh: the scroll containing the vision of Nahum the Elkoshite.

Power of the creator

[2]The LORD is a jealous and vengeful God;
the LORD is vengeful
and strong in wrath.
The LORD is vengeful against his foes;
he rages against his enemies.
[3]The LORD is very patient
but great in power;
the LORD punishes.
His way is in whirlwind and storm;
clouds are the dust of his feet.
[4]He can blast the sea and make it dry up;
he can dry up all the rivers.

[z]*Rejoice* (feminine singular) [a]Heb lacks *ruin*.

Bashan and Carmel wither;
the bud of Lebanon withers.
5 The mountains quake because of him;
the hills melt away.
The earth heaves before him—
the world and all who dwell in it.
6 Who can stand before his indignation?
Who can confront the heat of his fury?
His wrath pours out like fire;
the rocks are shattered
because of him.
7 The LORD is good,
a haven in a day of distress.
He acknowledges those
who take refuge in him.
8 With a rushing flood,
he will utterly destroy her[a] place
and pursue his enemies
into darkness.

A challenge to God's enemies

9 What are you plotting against the LORD?
He is one who can annihilate!
Distress will not arise twice.
10 They are tangled up like thorns,
like drunkards in their cups.
They are consumed like stubble
that is entirely dried up.
11 From you[b] goes out
one who plots evil against the LORD—
a worthless counselor!

Reassurance for God's people

12 The LORD proclaims:
Though once they were a healthy
and numerous force,
they have been cut off
and have disappeared.
I have afflicted you;
I won't afflict you further, Zion.[c]
13 Now I will break off his yoke from you
and tear off your chains.

Assyrian king's future doom

14 The LORD has commanded
concerning you:
You will have no children
to carry on your name.
I will remove carved idol and cast
image from the house of your gods;
I will make your grave,
for you are worthless.
15 [d]Look, on the mountains: the feet of a
messenger who announces peace!
Celebrate your festivals, Judah!
Fulfill your solemn promises!
The worthless one
will never again invade you;
he has been completely cut off.

A city under attack

2 A scatterer has come up against you.
Guard the ramparts, watch the road,
protect your groin,
save your[e] strength!
2 The LORD will restore the pride of Jacob,
indeed, the pride of Israel,
because ravagers have destroyed
them and spoiled their branches.
3 The shields of his warriors are red;
his soldiers are dressed in crimson.
The ironwork of the chariots
flashes like fire
on the day he has prepared;
the horses quiver.
4 The chariots race wildly
through the streets;
they rush back and forth
through the squares.
They look like flaming torches;
they dart like bolts of lightning.
5 He musters his officers;
they stumble as they press forward.
They hurry to the city wall,
and the portable shield is set up.
6 The gates of the rivers are opened;
the palace melts.
7 It is decreed:[f]
She is sent into exile, carried away,
while her female servants moan
like doves, beating their breasts.
8 Nineveh has been like a pool of water.
Such are its waters,[g]
and others are fleeing.
"Stop, stop!"—but no one
can turn them back.

[a] *her;* likely Nineveh [b] *you* (feminine singular); likely Nineveh [c] Heb lacks *Zion.* [d] 2:1 in Heb [e] Heb lacks *your.*
[f] Heb uncertain [g] Heb uncertain

9 Plunder silver! Plunder gold!
There is no end to the supplies,
an abundance of precious objects!
10 Destruction and devastation;
the city is laid waste!
The heart grows faint and knees buckle;
there is anguish in every groin;
all the faces grow pale.

Cruel Nineveh will be destroyed

11 Where is the lions' den,
the meadow of the young lions,
where lion, lioness, even lion cub go
about with no one to terrify them?
12 The lion has torn enough prey
for his cubs and strangled enough
for his lionesses;
he has filled his lairs with prey,
his dens with torn flesh.
13 Look! I am against you, proclaims
the LORD of heavenly forces.
I will burn your[h] chariots in smoke;
the sword will devour
your young lions;
I will cut off your prey from the earth,
the voice of your messengers
will never again be heard!

3 Doom, city of bloodshed—all deceit,
full of plunder:
prey cannot get away.
2 Cracking whip and rumbling wheel,
galloping horse and careening chariot!
3 Charging cavalry, flashing sword,
and glittering spear;
countless slain, masses of corpses,
endless dead bodies—they stumble
over their dead bodies!
4 Because of the many whorings
of the whore,
the lovely graces
of the mistress of sorceries,
the one who sells nations
by means of her whorings
and peoples by means of her sorceries:
5 Look! I am against you, proclaims
the LORD of heavenly forces.
I will lift your skirts over your face;
I will show nations your nakedness
and kingdoms your dishonor.
6 I will throw disgusting things at you;
I will treat you with contempt
and make you a spectacle.
7 Then all who look at you
will recoil from you and say,
"Nineveh has been devastated!
Who will lament for her?"
Where could I possibly
seek comforters for you?
8 Are you better than Thebes,
situated by the Nile,
waters surrounding her,
whose fortress is sea
and whose city wall is waters?
9 Cush[i] and Egypt constituted
her strength, without limit;
Put and the Libyans were her[j] help.
10 Yet even she was destined for exile;
she went into captivity.
Indeed, her infants were dashed
to pieces at the head of every street.
They cast lots for her officials;
all of her powerful citizens
were bound in chains.
11 Yes, even you will become drunk;
you will have to hide!
Even you will have to seek refuge
from the enemy!
12 All your fortifications
are fig trees with ripe fruit;
when the trees are shaken, the fruit
falls into the mouth of the eater.
13 Look, your people are women
in your midst.
The gates of your land have been flung
wide open to your enemies.
Fire consumes the bars of your gates.
14 Draw water for yourself
to prepare for siege!
Strengthen your fortifications!
Tread the clay, trample the mortar,
grab the brick mold!
15 Fire will consume you there;
the sword will cut you down;
like the locust it will consume you.
Multiply like the locust;
multiply like the grasshopper!
16 You boasted more traders
than the heavens have stars.

[h]Or *her* [i]Traditionally *Ethiopia* [j]LXX; MT *your*

The locust sheds its skin
and flies away.
17 Your guards are like grasshoppers,
your marshals like swarms of cicadas
that encamp on stone fences
on a chilly day;
when the sun rises, they take flight;
no one knows where they have gone.
18 Your shepherds have fallen asleep,
king of Assyria!
Your officials are lying down.
Your people are scattered
across the mountains;
there is no one to gather them.
19 There is no remedy for your injury;
your wound is grievous.
All who hear the news about you
clap their hands over you.
Who has not suffered
from your continual cruelty?

HABAKKUK

1 The oracle that Habakkuk the prophet saw.

The prophet complains

2 LORD, how long will I call for help
and you not listen?
I cry out to you, "Violence!"
but you don't deliver us.
3 Why do you show me injustice
and look at anguish
so that devastation and violence
are before me?
There is strife, and conflict abounds.
4 The Instruction is ineffective.
Justice does not endure
because the wicked
surround the righteous.
Justice becomes warped.

The LORD responds

5 Look among the nations and watch!
Be astonished and stare
because something is happening
in your days
that you wouldn't believe even if told.
6 I am about to rouse the Chaldeans,
that bitter and impetuous nation,
which travels throughout the earth
to possess dwelling places
it does not own.
7 The Chaldean is dreadful and fearful.
He makes his own justice and dignity.[a]
8 His horses are faster than leopards;
they are quicker than
wolves of the evening.
His horsemen charge forward;
his horsemen come from far away.
They fly in to devour, swiftly,
like an eagle.[b]
9 They come for violence,
the horde with all their faces
set toward the desert.[c]
He takes captives like sand.
10 He makes fun of kings;
rulers are ridiculous to him.
He laughs at every fortress,
then he piles up dirt and takes it.
11 He passes through like the wind
and invades;
but he will be held guilty,
the one whose strength is his god.

The prophet questions the LORD

12 LORD, aren't you ancient,
my God, my holy one?
Don't let us die.[d]
LORD, you put the Chaldean here
for judgment.
Rock, you established him as a rebuke.
13 Your eyes are too pure to look on evil;
you are unable to look at disaster.
Why would you look at the treacherous
or keep silent when the wicked
swallows one who is more righteous?
14 You made humans like the fish of the sea,
like creeping things
with no one to rule over them.
15 The Chaldean brings all of them up
with a fishhook.
He drags them away with a net;

[a] Or *his justice and dignity come from him* [b] Or *vulture* [c] Heb uncertain [d] Heb uncertain

he collects them in his fishing net,
then he rejoices and celebrates.
16 Therefore, he sacrifices to his net;
he burns incense to his fishing nets,
because due to them
his portion grows fat
and his food becomes luxurious.
17 Should he continue to empty his net
and continue to slay nations
without sparing them?

2 I will take my post;
I will position myself on the fortress.
I will keep watch to see
what the Lord says to me
and how he[e] will respond
to my complaint.

The LORD *responds*

2 Then the LORD answered me and said,
Write a vision,
and make it plain upon a tablet
so that a runner can read it.[f]
3 There is still a vision
for the appointed time;
it testifies to the end;
it does not deceive.[g]
If it delays, wait for it;
for it is surely coming;
it will not be late.
4 Some people's desires are truly audacious;[h]
they don't do the right thing.
But the righteous person
will live honestly.
5 Moreover, wine betrays an arrogant man.
He doesn't rest.
He opens his jaws[i] like the grave;[j]
like death, he is never satisfied.
He gathers all nations to himself
and collects all peoples for himself.
6 Won't everyone tell parables about him
or mocking poems concerning him?
They will say:
Doom to the one who multiplies
what doesn't belong to him
and who increases his own burden.
How long?
7 Won't they suddenly rise up to bite you?
Those who frighten you will awaken;
you will become plunder for them.
8 Since you yourself
have plundered many nations,
all the rest of the peoples
will plunder you
because of the human bloodshed
and the violence done to the earth,
to every village,
and to all its inhabitants.

9 Doom to the one making evil gain
for his own house,
for putting his own nest up high,
for delivering himself
from the grasp of calamity.
10 You plan shame for your own house,
cutting off many peoples
and sinning against your own life.
11 A stone will cry out from a village wall,
and a tree branch will respond.

12 Pity the one building a city with bloodshed
and founding a village with injustice.
13 Look, isn't this from the LORD of
heavenly forces?
Peoples grow weary from making just
enough fire;
nations become tired for nothing.[k]
14 But the land will be full of the knowledge
of the LORD's glory,
just as water covers the sea.

15 Doom to the one
who makes his companions drunk,
pouring out your wrath
in order to see them naked.[l]
16 You have drunk your fill of dishonor
rather than glory.
So drink and stagger.[m]
The cup of the LORD's strong hand
will come around to you;
disgrace will engulf you.
17 Because of the violence done to
Lebanon, he will overwhelm you;
the destruction of animals
will terrify you,
as will human bloodshed and violence
throughout the land, the villages,
and all their inhabitants.[n]

18 Of what value is an idol,
when its potter carves it,

[e]Syr *he*; MT *I* [f]Or *a reader can run with it* [g]Heb uncertain; antecedants to pronouns in 2:3-6 are uncertain. [h]Heb uncertain [i]Or *throat* [j]Heb *Sheol* [k]Heb uncertain [l]Heb uncertain [m]DSS, LXX; MT *uncircumcised* [n]Heb uncertain

or a cast image that has been shaped?
It is a teacher of lies,
for the potter trusts the pottery,
though it is incapable of speaking.
19 Doom to the one saying to the tree,
"Wake up!"
or "Get up" to the silent stone.
Does it teach?
Look, it is overlaid with gold and silver,
but there is no breath within it.
20 But the LORD is in his holy temple.
Let all the earth be silent before him.

The LORD's victory

3 The prayer of Habakkuk the prophet, according to Shigionoth:
2 LORD, I have heard your reputation.
I have seen your work.
Over time, revive it.
Over time, make it known.
Though angry, remember compassion.
3 God comes from Teman
and the holy one
from the mountain of Paran. *Selah*
His majesty covers the heavens
and his praise fills the earth.
4 His radiance is like the sunlight,
with rays flashing from his hand.
That is the hiding place of his power.
5 Pestilence walks in front of him.
Plague marches at his feet.
6 He stops and measures the earth.
He looks and sets out
against the nations.
The everlasting mountains collapse;
the eternal hills bow down;
the eternal paths belong to him.
7 I saw the tents of Cushan under duress.
The curtains of the land of Midian
were quaking.

8 Was the LORD raging against the rivers?
Or was your anger directed
against the rivers?
Or was your fury directed
against the sea
when you rode on your horses
or rode your chariots to victory?
9 You raise up your empty bow,
uttering curses for the arrows.[o] *Selah*
With rivers you split open the earth.
10 The mountains see you and writhe.
A flood of water rushes through.
The deep utters its voice;
it raises its hands aloft.[p]
11 Sun and moon stand still high above.
With the light, your arrows shoot,
your spear at the flash of lightning.
12 In fury, you stride the earth;
in anger you tread the nations.
13 You go out to save your people.
For the salvation of your anointed
you smashed the head
of the house of wickedness,
laying bare the foundation
up to the neck. *Selah*
14 You pierce the head of his warrior
with his own spear.
His warriors are driven off,
those who take delight
in oppressing us,[q]
those who take pleasure
in secretly devouring the poor.
15 You make your horses tread on the sea;
turbulent waters foam.

The prophet responds

16 I hear and my insides tremble.
My lips quiver at the sound.
Rottenness enters my bones.
I tremble while I stand,[r]
while I wait for the day of distress
to come against the people
who attack us.
17 Though the fig tree doesn't bloom,
and there's no produce on the vine;
though the olive crop withers,
and the fields don't provide food;
though the sheep is cut off
from the pen,
and there is no cattle in the stalls;
18 I will rejoice in the LORD.
I will rejoice in the God
of my deliverance.
19 The LORD God is my strength.
He will set my feet like the deer.
He will let me walk upon the heights.[s]

To the director, with stringed instruments

[o] Heb uncertain [p] Heb uncertain [q] Or *me* [r] Or *I tremble beneath me.* [s] Or *my heights*

ZEPHANIAH

1 The LORD's word that came to Zephaniah, Cushi's son, Gedaliah's grandson, Amariah's great-grandson, and Hezekiah's great-great-grandson in the days of Judah's King Josiah, Amon's son.

Judgment on the world and Judah

2 I will wipe out everything
from the earth, says the LORD.
3 I will destroy humanity and the beasts;
I will destroy the birds in the sky
and the fish in the sea.
I will make the wicked
into a heap of ruins;
I will eliminate humanity
from the earth, says the LORD.

4 I will stretch out my hand against Judah
and against all the inhabitants
of Jerusalem.
I will eliminate what's left of Baal
from this place
and the names of the priests
of foreign gods,[a]
5 those bowing down to the
forces of heaven on the rooftops,
those swearing by the LORD along
with those swearing by Milcom,
6 those turning away from the LORD,
those who don't seek the LORD
and don't pursue him.

The day of the LORD

7 Hush before the LORD God,
for the day of the LORD is near!
The LORD has established a sacrifice;
he has made holy those
he has summoned.
8 On the day of the LORD's sacrifice,
I will punish the princes,
the king's sons,
and all those wearing foreign clothes.
9 I will punish the one leaping
on the threshold on that day,
those filling the house of their master
with violence and deceit.
10 On that day—says the LORD—
an outcry will resound
from the Fish Gate,
wailing from the second quarter,
a loud crash from the hills.
11 The ones who grind the grain[b] will wail;
all the merchants will be silenced.
I will eliminate all those
weighing out silver.
12 At that time,
I will search Jerusalem with lamps;
I will punish the men growing fat
on the sediment in their wine,
those saying to themselves,
The LORD won't do good or evil.
13 Their wealth will be looted
and their houses destroyed.
They will rebuild houses,
but not live in them;
they will plant vineyards,
but not drink the wine.
14 The great day of the LORD is near;
it is near and coming very quickly.
The sound of the day of the LORD
is bitter.
A warrior screams there.
15 That day is a day of fury,
a day of distress and anxiety,
a day of desolation and devastation,
a day of darkness and gloominess,
a day of clouds and deep darkness,
16 a day for blowing the trumpet
and alarm
against their invincible cities
and against their high towers.
17 I will make humanity suffer;
they will walk like the blind
because they sinned
against the LORD.
Their blood will be
poured out like dust
and their intestines like manure.
18 Moreover, their silver and their gold
won't be able to deliver them
on the day of the LORD's fury.
His jealousy will devour
the entire land with fire;
he will make an end,

[a] Or *the name of the priests of foreign gods along with the priests* [b] Or *keeper of the mortar*

a truly horrible one,
for all the inhabitants of the land.
2 Gather together and assemble
yourselves, shameless nation,
2 before the decision is made—
the day vanishes like chaff[c]—
before the burning anger
of the LORD comes against you,
before the day of the LORD's anger
comes against you.
3 Seek the LORD, all you humble
of the land who practice his justice;
seek righteousness;
seek humility.
Maybe you will be hidden
on the day of the LORD's anger.

Oracles against foreign nations

4 Gaza will certainly be abandoned;
and Ashkelon destroyed.
Ashdod will be driven out at noon;
Ekron will be uprooted.
5 Doom, inhabitants of the seacoast,
nation of Cretans.
The LORD's word is against you,
Canaan, land of the Philistines.
I will exterminate you,
leaving no inhabitant.
6 The seacoast will become pastureland,
with wells for shepherds
and pens for the flocks.
7 The coast will belong to the
survivors from the house of Judah;
they will pasture beside the sea;[d]
in the houses of Ashkelon
they will lie down in the evening.
The LORD their God will visit them
and restore their possessions.

8 I have heard the taunting of Moab
and the defamation
of the Ammonites;
they taunted my people
and enlarged their borders.
9 Therefore, as I live—
says the LORD of heavenly forces,
the God of Israel—
Moab will become like Sodom
and the Ammonites like Gomorrah:
a plot of weeds, salt pits,
and devastation forever.
The few remaining from my people
will plunder them;
the rest of my nation will possess them.
10 This will happen on account of their pride,
because they taunted and boasted
over the people
of the LORD of heavenly forces.
11 The LORD will terrify them;
he will make all the gods
of the earth disappear.
All the coastlands of the nations
will bow down to the LORD,
each one in its own place.

12 Moreover, you too, Cushites,
will be pierced by my sword.
13 He will stretch out his hand
against the north
and will cause Assyria to perish.
Let him make Nineveh a desolation,
a desolate place like the wilderness.
14 Flocks will lie down in its midst,
every living thing of the nation.
Moreover, the owl and the porcupine
will spend the night on its columns.
A bird's call will resound
from the window.
Desolation will be on the sill,
for the cedar will be stripped bare.
15 This is the jubilant city,
the one dwelling securely,
the one saying in her heart,
I, and no one else, will endure forever.
How she has become a desolation,
a resting place for the wild animals.
All those who pass through her
hiss and shake their fist.

Judgment against Jerusalem

3 Doom, obstinate one,
the defiled one,
the violent city.
2 She listened to no voice;
she accepted no discipline.
She didn't trust in the LORD,
nor did she draw near to her God.
3 The princes in her midst are roaring lions.

[c]Heb uncertain [d]Or *they will pasture by them.*

Her judges are wolves of the evening;
they leave nothing for the morning.
4 Her prophets are reckless,
men of treachery.
Her priests pollute that which is holy;
they do violence to the Instruction.
5 The LORD is righteous in her midst.
He does nothing unjust.
Morning by morning
he renders justice,
but the unrighteous one
knows no shame.
6 I will cut off nations;
their towers will be destroyed;
I will devastate their streets.
No one will pass through.
Their cities will be laid waste.
There will be no person,
no inhabitant left.
7 I said, "Surely, she will fear me;
she will take instruction
so that her habitation won't be cut off[e]
because of everything I did to her."
However, they rose early
to corrupt their deeds.
8 Therefore, wait for me, says the LORD,
wait for the day
when I rise up as a witness,[f]
when I decide to gather nations,
to collect kingdoms,
to pour out my indignation upon them,
all the heat of my anger.
In the fire of my jealousy,
all the earth will be devoured.

Restoration of the nations and Jerusalem

9 Then I will change the speech
of the peoples into pure speech,
that all of them will call on
the name of the LORD
and will serve him as one.[g]
10 From beyond the rivers of Cush,
my daughter, my dispersed ones,
will bring me offerings.
11 On that day, you won't be ashamed
of all your deeds
with which you sinned against me;
then I will remove from your midst
those boasting with pride.
No longer will you be haughty
on my holy mountain,
12 but I will cause a humble and powerless
people to remain in your midst;
they will seek refuge
in the name of the LORD.
13 The few remaining from Israel
won't commit injustice;
they won't tell lies;
a deceitful tongue
won't be found on their lips.
They will graze and lie down;
no one will make them afraid.

14 Rejoice, Daughter Zion! Shout, Israel!
Rejoice and exult with all your heart,
Daughter Jerusalem.
15 The LORD has removed your judgment;
he has turned away your enemy.
The LORD, the king of Israel,
is in your midst;
you will no longer fear evil.
16 On that day, it will be said to Jerusalem:
Don't fear, Zion.
Don't let your hands fall.
17 The LORD your God is in your midst—
a warrior bringing victory.
He will create calm with his love;
he will rejoice over you with singing.

18 I will remove from you those worried
about the appointed feasts.[h]
They have been a burden for her,
a reproach.
19 Watch what I am about to do
to all your oppressors at that time.
I will deliver the lame;
I will gather the outcast.
I will change their shame into praise
and fame throughout the earth.
20 At that time, I will bring all of you back,
at the time when I gather you.
I will give you fame and praise
among all the neighboring peoples
when I restore your possessions and
you can see them[i]—says the LORD.

[e] Heb uncertain [f] LXX; MT *it* [g] Or *with one shoulder* [h] Heb uncertain [i] Or *before your eyes*

HAGGAI

The challenge to rebuild

1 The LORD's word came through Haggai the prophet in the second year of King Darius, in the sixth month on the first day of the month, to Judah's governor Zerubbabel, Shealtiel's son, and to the high priest Joshua, Jehozadak's son:

2 This is what the LORD
of heavenly forces says:
These people say, "The time hasn't come,
the time to rebuild the LORD's house."

3 Then the LORD's word came through Haggai the prophet:

4 Is it time for you to dwell
in your own paneled houses
while this house lies in ruins?
5 So now, this is what
the LORD of heavenly forces says:
Take your ways to heart.
6 You have sown much,
but it has brought little.
You eat, but there's not enough
to satisfy.
You drink, but not enough to get drunk.
There is clothing, but not enough
to keep warm.
Anyone earning wages puts those
wages into a bag with holes.

7 This is what the LORD
of heavenly forces says:
Take your ways to heart.
8 Go up to the highlands
and bring back wood.
Rebuild the temple so that I may enjoy it
and that I may be honored,
says the LORD.
9 You expect a surplus,
but look how it shrinks.
You bring it home, and I blow it away,
says the LORD of heavenly forces,
because my house lies in ruins.
But all of you hurry to your own houses.
10 Therefore, the skies above you
have withheld the dew,
and the earth has withheld
its produce because of you.
11 I have called for drought on the earth,
on the mountains, on the grain,
on the wine, on the olive oil,
on that which comes forth
from the fertile ground,
on humanity, on beasts,
and upon everything that
handles produce.

12 Zerubbabel, Shealtiel's son, and the high priest Joshua, Jehozadak's son, along with all who remained among the people, listened to the voice of the LORD God and to the words of Haggai the prophet because the LORD their God sent him. Then the people feared the LORD.

13 Then Haggai, the LORD's messenger, gave the LORD's message to the people:
I am with you, says the LORD.

14 The LORD moved the spirit of Judah's governor Zerubbabel, Shealtiel's son, and the spirit of the high priest Joshua, Jehozadak's son, and the spirit of all the rest of the people. Then they came and did work on the house of the LORD of heavenly forces, their God,
15 on the twenty-fourth day of the sixth month in the second year of Darius the king.

Encouraging the people

2 On the twenty-first day of the seventh month, the LORD's word came through Haggai the prophet:
2 Say to Judah's governor Zerubbabel, Shealtiel's son, and to the chief priest Joshua, Jehozadak's son, and to the rest of the people:

3 Who among you is left who saw
this house in its former glory?
How does it look to you now?
Doesn't it appear as nothing to you?
4 So now, be strong, Zerubbabel,
says the LORD.
Be strong, High Priest Joshua,
Jehozadak's son,
and be strong, all you people
of the land, says the LORD.
Work, for I am with you,
says the LORD of heavenly forces.
5 As with our agreement
when you came out of Egypt,
my spirit stands in your midst.

Don't fear.
6 This is what the LORD
of heavenly forces says:
In just a little while,
I will make the heavens, the earth,
the sea, and the dry land quake.
7 I will make all the nations quake.
The wealth of all the nations will come.
I will fill this house with glory,
says the LORD of heavenly forces.
8 The silver and the gold belong to me,
says the LORD of heavenly forces.
9 This house will be more glorious
than its predecessor,
says the LORD of heavenly forces.
I will provide prosperity in this place,
says the LORD of heavenly forces.

Cleansing the work

10 On the twenty-fourth day of the ninth
month in the second year of Darius, the
LORD's word came to Haggai the prophet:
11 This is what the LORD
of heavenly forces says:
Go ahead and ask the priests for a ruling:
12 "If someone lifts holy meat
into the hem of one's garment
and that hem touches bread,
stew, wine, oil, or any kind of food,
will it be made holy?"
And the priests responded, "No."
13 Haggai said,
"If an unclean person touches any of
these things, will it become unclean?"
And the priests responded,
"It will be unclean."
14 Then Haggai responded:
Thus has this people and this nation
become to me, says the LORD,
and everything that they do
with their hands.
Whatever they offer is unclean.
15 So now, take it to heart
from this day forward.
Before stone was placed on stone
in the LORD's temple,
16 when one came to the granary
for twenty measures,
there were only ten;
and when one came to the wine vat
for fifty measures,
there were only twenty.
17 I struck you—
everything you do with your hands—
with blight and mildew and hail;
but you didn't return to me.[a]
18 So take it to heart
from this day forward,
from the twenty-fourth day
of the ninth month.
Take it to heart from the day when
the foundation for the LORD's
temple was laid.
19 Is the seed yet in the granary—
or the vine, the fig tree,
or the pomegranate—
or has the olive tree not borne fruit?
From this day forward, I will bless you.

Royal expectations

20 And the LORD's word came to Haggai
a second time on the twenty-fourth of the
month, saying:
21 Speak to Judah's governor Zerubbabel:
I am about to make the heavens
and the earth quake.
22 I will overthrow the thrones
of the kingdoms;
I will destroy the strength
of the nations.[b]
I will overthrow chariot and rider;
horses and riders will fall.
Each one will fall
by the sword of his companion.
23 On that day,
says the LORD of heavenly forces:
I will take you,
Zerubbabel, Shealtiel's son, my servant,
says the LORD;
I will make you like a signet ring
because I have chosen you,
says the LORD of heavenly forces.

[a] *Or but you weren't with me.* [b] *Or of the kingdoms of the nations*

ZECHARIAH

The people change

1 In the eighth month in the second year of Darius, the LORD's word came to Zechariah the prophet, Berechiah's son and Iddo's grandson:

2 The LORD was terribly angry
with your ancestors.
3 But you must say to the people,
The LORD of heavenly forces proclaims:
Return to me,
says the LORD of heavenly forces,
and I will return to you,
says the LORD of heavenly forces.
4 Don't be like your ancestors to whom
the former prophets preached:
The LORD of heavenly forces
proclaims:
Turn from your evil ways
and your evil deeds.
But they didn't listen;
they didn't draw near to me.
5 So where are your ancestors?
Do the prophets live forever?
6 In fact, didn't my words and laws,
which I gave to my servants,
the prophets,
pursue your ancestors?
And then the people changed their hearts,
and they said,
The LORD of heavenly forces
has treated us according to
what we have done,[a]
exactly as he planned.

First night vision

7 On the twenty-fourth day of the eleventh month (the month of Shebat[b]) in the second year of Darius, the LORD's word came to Zechariah the prophet, Berechiah's son and Iddo's grandson:

8 Tonight I looked and saw a man
riding on a red horse,
which was standing
among the myrtle trees in the valley;
and behind him were red, sorrel,
and white horses.
9 I said, "What are these, sir?"
The messenger speaking with me said,
"I will show you what they are."
10 The man standing
among the myrtles responded,
"These are the ones the LORD sent
to patrol the earth."
11 Then they responded
to the LORD's messenger,
who was standing among the myrtles,
"We have patrolled the earth.
The whole earth
is peaceful and quiet."
12 Then the LORD's messenger, who was
speaking with me, said:
"LORD of heavenly forces,
how long will you withhold
compassion from Jerusalem
and the cities of Judah,
with whom you have been angry
these seventy years?"
13 The LORD responded to the messenger
who was speaking with me
with kind and compassionate words.
14 The messenger speaking with me
called out,
"This is what
the LORD of heavenly forces says:
I care passionately
about Jerusalem and Zion.
15 And I am exceedingly angry
with those carefree nations.
Though I was somewhat angry,
they added to the violence."
16 Therefore, this is what the LORD says:
I have returned to Jerusalem
with compassion.
My house will be built in it,
says the LORD of heavenly forces.
Let a measuring line
be stretched over Jerusalem.
17 Call out again,
The LORD of heavenly forces proclaims:
My cities will again
overflow with prosperity.
The LORD will again
show compassion to Zion
and will again choose Jerusalem."

[a] Or *our ways and our actions* [b] January–February

Second night vision

18[c]Then I looked up and saw four horns.
19I said to the messenger speaking
with me,
"What are these?"
He said to me,
"These are the horns that scattered
Judah, Israel, and Jerusalem."
20Then the LORD showed me
four metalworkers.
21I said,
"What are they coming to do?"
And he said,
"These are the horns that scattered
Judah so that no one could raise
his head.
The metalworkers have come to terrify
them and to destroy the horns of the
nations, those who were attacking
the land of Judah with[d] their horns
to scatter it."

Third night vision

2 [e]Then I looked up and saw a man.
In his hand was a measuring line.
2I said, "Where are you going?"
He said to me,
"To measure Jerusalem to see how
wide and long it will be."
3As I watched, the messenger speaking
with me went ahead and another
messenger came to meet him.
4He said to him,
"Run! Say to this young man:
Jerusalem will be inhabited
like open fields
because of the throngs
of people and cattle inside it.
5But I will be a wall of fire around it,
says the LORD,
and I will be glorious inside it.
6Look out; look out!
Flee from the land of the north,
says the LORD,
for I will scatter you like the four
winds of heaven, says the LORD.
7Look out, Zion.
Flee, you who dwell
with Daughter Babylon!
8The LORD of heavenly forces proclaims
(after his glory sent me)[f]
concerning the nations plundering you:
Those who strike you
strike the pupil of my eye.
9But look, I am about to raise my hand
against them;
they will become prey
to their own slaves,
so you will know that the LORD of
heavenly forces sent me.
10Rejoice and be glad, Daughter Zion,
because I am about to come
and dwell among you, says the LORD.
11Many nations will be joined
to the LORD on that day.
They will become my people,
and I will dwell among you
so you will know that
the LORD of heavenly forces
sent me to you."
12The LORD will possess Judah as his
inheritance upon the holy land;
he will again choose Jerusalem.
13Be silent, everyone, in the LORD's
presence, because he has moved
from his holy habitation!

Fourth night vision

3 Then the LORD showed me the high
priest Joshua, standing before the
messenger from the LORD,
and the Adversary[g] was standing by
his right side to accuse him.
2And the LORD said to the Adversary:
"The LORD rebukes you, Adversary.
The LORD, the one choosing Jerusalem,
rebukes you.
Is this one not a log
snatched from the fire?"
3Joshua was wearing filthy clothes
and standing before the messenger.
4He responded
to those standing before him,
"Take off his filthy clothes."
And he said to Joshua,
"Look, I have removed your guilt
from you.
Put on priestly robes."

[c]2:1 in Heb [d]Or *those lifting their horns toward Judah* [e]2:5 in Heb [f]Heb uncertain [g]Heb *hassatan*; cf Job 1:6

5 He[h] said, "Put a clean turban
upon his head."
So they put the clean turban
upon his head,
and they dressed him in garments
while the LORD's messenger stood by.
6 Then the LORD's messenger admonished
Joshua:
7 "The LORD of heavenly forces
proclaims:
If you will walk in my paths,
if you will keep my charge,
then you will lead my house
and guard my courts,
and I will allow you to walk
among those standing here.
8 Now listen, High Priest Joshua,
you and your companions
sitting before you—
for these men are a sign—
look, I am about to bring
my servant, Branch.
9 See this stone
that I have put before Joshua.
Upon one stone,
there are seven facets.
I am about to engrave
an inscription on it,
says the LORD of heavenly forces.
I will remove the guilt of that land
in one day.
10 On that day,
says the LORD of heavenly forces,
everyone will invite their neighbors
to sit beneath their vines
and the fig trees."

Fifth night vision

4 The messenger speaking with me returned and woke me like one who awakens someone who is asleep.
2 Then he said to me,
"What do you see?"
I said, "I see a lampstand
made entirely of gold.
It has a bowl on top.
The bowl has seven lamps on top
and seven metal pipes
for those lamps.
3 It has two olive trees
beside the lampstand,
one to the right of its bowl
and one to the left."
4 I responded to the messenger speaking
with me,
"What are these, sir?"
5 The messenger responded to me:
"Don't you know what these are?"
I said, "No, sir. I don't."
6 He answered me:
"This is the LORD's word to Zerubbabel:
Neither by power, nor by strength,
but by my spirit,
says the LORD of heavenly forces."
7 Who are you, great mountain?
Before Zerubbabel
you will become a plain.
He will present the capstone
to shouts of great gratitude.

8 The LORD's word came to me:
9 The hands of Zerubbabel laid the
foundation of this house,
and his hands will finish it
so that you will know
that the LORD of heavenly forces
has sent me to you.
10 Those who despise a time
of little things will rejoice
when they see the plumb line[i]
in Zerubbabel's hand.
These are the seven eyes of the LORD,
surveying the entire earth.
11 I responded to him,
"What are these two olive trees
on the right and left sides
of the lampstand?"
12 Then I responded a second time,
"What are these two olive branches
that empty out golden oil
through the two gold pipes?"
13 He said to me,
"Don't you know what these are?"
I said, "No, sir."
14 He said,
"These are the two anointed ones[j]
standing beside the LORD
of all the earth."

[h]Or *I* [i]Or *stone, tin* [j]Or *sons of oil*

Sixth night vision

5 I looked up again and saw a flying scroll.
2 And he said to me, "What do you see?"
I said, "I see a flying scroll, thirty feet
long and fifteen feet wide."
3 He said to me,
"This is the curse
going out across all the land.
Anyone stealing will be purged
according to what's on one side
of the scroll,[k]
and anyone swearing lies[l]
will be purged according to
what's on the other side.
4 I sent it out,
says the LORD of heavenly forces.
It will come to the house of the thief
and the one swearing lies in my name.
It will lodge in their house and
destroy the wood and stones
of that house."

Seventh night vision

5 Then the messenger speaking with me
came forward and said,
"Look up and see what's approaching."
6 I said, "What's this?"
He said, "This is the basket[m]
that is going out.
This is how it appears[n]
throughout the entire land."[o]
7 Then a lead cover was lifted,
showing a woman sitting
in the middle of the basket.
8 He said, "This is wickedness."
He shoved her back into the basket,
and he put the lead stone
over its opening.
9 I looked up again and saw two women
going out.
There was a wind in their wings;
their wings were like
the wings of a stork.
They carried the basket
between the earth and the sky.
10 I said to the messenger
speaking with me,
"Where are they taking the basket?"
11 He said to me,
"To build a house for it
in the land of Shinar.
It will be firmly placed there
on its base."

Eighth night vision

6 I looked up again
and saw four chariots coming out
from between two mountains;
the mountains were made of bronze.
2 The first chariot had red horses,
and the second chariot
had black horses.
3 The third chariot had white horses,
and the fourth chariot
had horses that were heavily spotted.
4 I responded and said to the messenger
speaking with me,
"What are these, sir?"
5 The messenger answered and said to me,
"These are the four winds of heaven
that are going out
after presenting themselves
to the LORD of all the earth.
6 The one with the black horses
is going to the north country;
the white ones are going to the west;[p]
and the spotted ones are going south."
7 Then the powerful ones approached,
intent on going to patrol the earth.
He said, "Go! Patrol the earth!"
So they patrolled the earth.
8 Then he called out and said to me,
"Look, the ones going north
have provided rest for my spirit
in the north."

9 The LORD's word came to me:
10 Take silver and gold[q] from the exiles
who came from Babylon,
from Heldai, from Tobijah,
and from Jedaiah.
As for you, go that same day to the
house of Josiah son of Zephaniah.
11 Take silver and gold and make a crown.[r]
Place it on the head of the
high priest Joshua, Jehozadak's son.

[k]Heb lacks *of the scroll.* [l]Heb lacks *lies.* [m]Heb *ephah,* a basket measuring approximately twenty quarts
[n]Or *their eye* [o]Heb uncertain [p]Or *after them* [q]Heb lacks *silver and gold*; cf 6:11. [r]LXX; Heb *crowns,* so also 6:14

12 Say to him,
"The LORD of heavenly forces proclaims:
Here is a man.
His name is Branch, and he will
branch out from his place;
he will build the LORD's temple.
13 He will build the LORD's temple.
He will be majestic;
he will sit and rule on his throne.
There will be a priest on his throne,
and the two of them
will share a peaceable plan.
14 The crown will be a memorial
in the LORD's temple
for Helem, Tobijah, Jedaiah,
and for Hen, Zephaniah's son.
15 People from far away will come
and build the LORD's temple
so you might know that
the LORD of heavenly forces
has sent me to you.
It will happen if you truly obey
the voice of the LORD your God."

Answering the Bethel delegation

7 In the fourth year of Darius the king, the LORD's word came to Zechariah on the fourth day of the ninth month, Kislev.[s] 2 The people of[t] Bethel sent Sharezer and Regem-Melech,[u] along with his men, to seek the LORD's favor, 3 saying to the priests who were in the house of the LORD of heavenly forces and to the prophets: "Should I weep in the fifth month and abstain as I have done for a number of years?"

4 Then the word of the LORD of heavenly forces came to me: 5 Say to all the land's people and to the priests: When you fasted and lamented in the fifth month and the seventh month for these past seventy years, did you fast for me? 6 When you ate and drank, weren't you the ones eating and drinking? 7 Weren't these the words that the LORD proclaimed through the former prophets when Jerusalem was dwelling quietly along with the surrounding cities, and when the arid southern plain and the western foothills were inhabited?

8 The LORD's word came to Zechariah:
9 The LORD of heavenly forces proclaims:
Make just and faithful decisions; show kindness and compassion to each other! 10 Don't oppress the widow, the orphan, the stranger, and the poor; don't plan evil against each other! 11 But they refused to pay attention. They turned a cold shoulder and stopped listening.

12 They steeled their hearts against hearing the Instruction and the words that the LORD of heavenly forces sent by his spirit through the earlier prophets. As a result, the LORD of heavenly forces became enraged.

13 So just as he called and they didn't listen, when they called, I didn't listen, says the LORD of heavenly forces. 14 I scattered them throughout the nations whom they didn't know. The land was devastated behind them, with no one leaving or returning. They turned a delightful land into a wasteland.

8 The word from the LORD of heavenly forces came to me:[v]
2 The LORD of heavenly forces proclaims:
I care passionately about Zion; I burn with passion for her. 3 The LORD proclaims: I have returned to Zion; I will settle in Jerusalem. Jerusalem will be called the city of truth; the mountain of the LORD of heavenly forces will be the holy mountain.
4 The LORD of heavenly forces proclaims:
Old men and old women will again dwell in the plazas of Jerusalem. Each of them will have a staff in their hand because of their great age. 5 The city will be full of boys and girls playing in its plazas.
6 The LORD of heavenly forces proclaims:
Even though it may seem to be a miracle for the few remaining among this people in these days, should it seem to be a miracle for me? says the LORD of heavenly forces.
7 The LORD of heavenly forces proclaims:
I'm about to deliver my people from the land of the east and the land of the west. 8 I'll bring them back so they will dwell in Jerusalem. They will be my people, and I will be their God—in truth and in righteousness.

[s] November–December [t] Heb lacks *the people of.* [u] Heb uncertain [v] Heb lacks *to me.*

9 The LORD of heavenly forces proclaims:
Be strong, you who are now hearing
these words from the mouths of the prophets spoken on the day when the foundations for the house of the LORD of heavenly
forces were laid. 10 Before this time, there
were no wages for people or animals; there
was no relief from distress about going out
or coming in, because I set everyone against
their own neighbor. 11 But now, unlike those
earlier days, I'll be with the few remaining
among this people, says the LORD of heavenly forces.

12 The seed is healthy:
the vine will give its fruit.
The land will give its produce;
the heavens will give its dew.
I will give the remnant of
this people all these things.
13 Just as you were a curse
among the nations,
house of Judah and house of Israel,
so now I will deliver you;
you will be a blessing.
Don't fear, but be strong.

14 The LORD of heavenly forces proclaims:
Just as I planned evil against you when
your ancestors angered me, says the LORD
of heavenly forces, and did not relent, 15 so
now I have changed course and again plan
to do good to Jerusalem and the house of
Judah. Don't be afraid.
16 These are the things you should do:
Speak the truth to each other; make truthful, just, and peaceable decisions within
your gates. 17 Don't plan evil for each other.
Don't adore swearing falsely, for all of these
are things that I hate, says the LORD.

18 The word of the LORD of heavenly forces
came to me:
19 The LORD of heavenly forces proclaims:
The fasts of the fourth, fifth, seventh,
and tenth months will become times of joy
and gladness, pleasant feasts for the house
of Judah. Love truth and peace!
20 The LORD of heavenly forces proclaims:
Peoples will still come, the inhabitants
of many cities. 21 The inhabitants of one city
will go to another saying, "Let's go and seek
the favor of the LORD, and look for the LORD
of heavenly forces. I'm going too." 22 Many
peoples and mighty nations will come to
seek the LORD of heavenly forces in Jerusalem and to seek the favor of the LORD.
23 The LORD of heavenly forces proclaims:
In those days ten men from nations with
entirely different languages will grab hold
of a Judean's clothes and say, "Let's go with
you, for we have heard that God is with you."

Fate of the nations

9 A pronouncement. The LORD's word is
against the land of Hadrach,
and Damascus is its resting place,
for the city of Aram[W] and all the tribes
of Israel belong to the LORD.
2 Hamath also borders on it.
Tyre and Sidon, indeed,
each is exceedingly wise.
3 Tyre built a fortress for herself.
She piled up silver like dust
and gold like mud in the streets,
4 but the LORD will take
her possessions away
and knock her wealth into the sea.
She will be devoured with fire.

5 Ashkelon will look and be afraid.
Gaza will writhe in agony,
and also Ekron,
because her hope has dried up.
The king will perish from Gaza;
Ashkelon won't be inhabited.
6 An illegitimate child will dwell in Ashdod;
I will eliminate
the pride of the Philistines.
7 I will remove bloody food from his mouth
and pieces of unclean food
from between his teeth.
He will be a survivor
who belongs to our God.
He will be like a chieftain in Judah;
Ekron will be like a Jebusite.
8 I will encamp before my house as a guard
against anyone departing or returning.
A slave driver will no longer
pass through against them,
for I have seen you[X] with my eyes.

[W] Or *eyes of humanity* [X] Heb lacks *you.*

Joy and protection for Judah and Ephraim

9 Rejoice greatly, Daughter Zion.
Sing aloud, Daughter Jerusalem.
Look, your king will come to you.
He is righteous and victorious.
He is humble and riding on an ass,
on a colt, the offspring of a donkey.
10 He[y] will cut off the chariot from Ephraim
and the warhorse from Jerusalem.
The bow used in battle will be cut off;
he will speak peace to the nations.
His rule will stretch from sea to sea,
and from the river
to the ends of the earth.
11 Moreover,[z] by the blood of your covenant,
I will release your prisoners
from the waterless pit.
12 Return to the stronghold,
prisoners of hope.
Moreover, declare today
that I will return double to you.
13 Indeed, I myself will bend Judah as a bow;
I will fill it with Ephraim.
Zion, I will rouse your sons
against your sons.
Greece, I will make you
like a warrior's sword.
14 The LORD will appear above them;
his arrow will go forth like lightning.
The LORD God will blow the horn;
he will march forth on the stormy
winds of the south.
15 The LORD of heavenly forces
will protect them.
They will devour and subdue
like sling stones.[a]
They will drink,
mumbling like one having wine.
They will be filled like a bowl,
like the corners of the altar.
16 The LORD their God will deliver them
on that day as the flock of his people;
they will be the jewels
in a crown dotting his land.
17 What is his goodness,
and what is his beauty?
Grain will make his young men flourish;
so too wine his young women.

Fate of Judah and Ephraim

10 Ask the LORD for rain when it is
time for the spring rain.
The LORD is the one
who makes the thunderstorms.
He gives them rain showers.
He gives vegetation in the field
to each of them.[b]
2 The household divine images
speak idolatry, and diviners see lies.
They interpret dreams falsely
and provide empty comfort.
Therefore, they wander like sheep,
but they are oppressed
because there is no shepherd.
3 My anger burns hot
against the shepherds;
I will punish the goats.
The LORD of heavenly forces
will take care of his splendor,
the house of Judah.
He will make them
like his majestic horse in battle.
4 The cornerstone, the tent peg,
and the bow used in battle
will come from Judah.
Every oppressor
will leave Judah simultaneously.
5 Judah will be like warriors,
trampling through the muddy streets
during battle.
They will do battle
because the LORD is with them.
All the cavalry will be ashamed.
6 I will strengthen the house of Judah
and deliver the house of Joseph.
I will bring them back[c] because I have
compassion on them.
They will be as though
I hadn't rejected them,
for I am the LORD their God;
I will respond to them.

7 Ephraim will be like a warrior.
They will be as glad
as if they were drinking wine.
Their children will watch and be glad.
Their hearts will rejoice
in the LORD.

[y]LXX; MT *I* [z]Heb uncertain [a]Heb uncertain [b]Heb lacks *of them.* [c]Or *I will restore them*

8 I will whistle for them and gather them,
because I have ransomed them.
They will be as numerous
as they were previously.
9 Though I sowed them among the peoples,
they will remember me
in the distant places
where they are living with
their children until they return.
10 I will bring them back
from the land of Egypt;
I will collect them from Assyria.
I will bring them to the land
of Gilead and Lebanon
until there is no more room for them.
11 They[d] will pass through
the sea of distress
and strike the sea with waves.[e]
All the depths of the river will dry up.
The pride of Assyria
will be brought down;
the scepter of Egypt will turn away.
12 I will strengthen them in the LORD,
and they will walk in his name,
says the LORD.

11 Open your doors, Lebanon,
so that fire will devour your cedars.
2 Scream, cypress, for the cedar has fallen;
those majestic ones
have been devastated.
Scream, oaks of Bashan,
for the deep forest has fallen.
3 The sound of screaming
appears among the shepherds
because their majesty
has been devastated.
The sound of roaring can be heard
among the young lions
because the pride of the Jordan
has been devastated.

The shepherd's two staffs

4 This is what the LORD my God says:
Shepherd the flock
intended for slaughter.
5 Those who buy them will kill them,
but they will go unpunished.
Those who sell them will say,
"Blessed is the LORD,
for I have become rich."
And their own shepherds
won't spare them.
6 In fact, I will no longer spare
the inhabitants of the land,
says the LORD.
But look what I am about to bring
upon humanity,
upon each of them by their neighbor's
hand and by the hand of their king:
They will beat the land to pieces,
but I won't rescue anyone
from their hand.
7 So I shepherded the flock
intended for slaughter,
the afflicted of the flock.[f]
I took two staffs for myself.
I named one Delight;
the other I named Harmony.
I shepherded the flock.
8 I removed three shepherds in one month
when I grew impatient with them.
Moreover, they detested me.
9 Then I said, "I won't shepherd you.
Let the dying die,
and let what is to be removed
be removed.
Let those who are left
devour the flesh of their neighbor."

10 Then I took the staff Delight,
and I chopped it up
in order to break my covenant
that I had made with all the peoples.
11 It was broken on that day.
As a result, the afflicted[g] of the flock
knew that it was the LORD's word.
12 And I said to them,
"If it appears good to you,
give me my wages;
but if not, then stop."
So they weighed out my wages,
thirty shekels of silver.
13 The LORD said to me,
"Put it in the treasury.[h]
They value me
at too magnificent a price."
So I took the thirty shekels[i] of silver

[d]LXX; MT *he* [e]Heb uncertain [f]Heb uncertain [g]Cf Zech 11:7 [h]Syr; MT *to the potter* [i]Heb lacks *shekels.*

and put them in the treasury
of the LORD's house.

14 Then I chopped up
my second staff Harmony,
to break the alliance
between Judah and Israel.
15 Then the LORD said to me,
"Take for yourself again the equipment
of a foolish shepherd,
16 because I am about to appoint
a shepherd in the land.
He won't tend to those
who have been removed.
He won't seek the young
or heal the broken.
He won't sustain the one standing.
Instead, he will devour the flesh
of the fat ones,
even tearing off their hooves.
17 Doom, foolish shepherd
who forsakes the flock.
A sword will strike[j] his arm
and his right eye.
His arm will wither completely;
his right eye will become blind."

Jerusalem on that day

12 A pronouncement.
The LORD's word against Israel,
an utterance of the LORD
who stretches out the heavens,
who establishes the earth,
and who fashions the spirit
of humanity within it:
2 I am about to make Jerusalem a cup
that will stagger
all the surrounding nations.
There will be a siege against Judah
and against Jerusalem.

3 On that day I will make Jerusalem
into a heavy stone[k] for all the peoples.
All who carry it will hurt themselves;
nevertheless, the nations of the earth
will conspire against it.

4 On that day, says the LORD, I will strike
every horse with confusion
and its rider with madness.
I will keep my eyes open
for the house of Judah;
I will strike blind
every horse of the peoples.
5 The chieftains of Judah will say to
themselves, We are strong;
the inhabitants of Jerusalem will say,
The LORD their God of heavenly
forces is strong.[l]

6 On that day I will place
the chieftains of Judah like a pot
on a wood fire and like a burning torch
among the bundles of grain.
They will devour all the surrounding
nations to the right and the left.
Jerusalem will dwell again in its place,
in Jerusalem.
7 The LORD will first deliver
the tents of Judah
so that the splendor of David's house
and the splendor
of Jerusalem's inhabitants
won't overshadow Judah.

8 On that day the LORD will protect
the inhabitants of Jerusalem.
Anyone among them who stumbles
on that day will become like David,
and David's house will become like God,
like the LORD's messenger
in front of them.

9 On that day I intend to destroy all the
nations who come against Jerusalem,
10 but I will pour out a spirit of grace
and mercy on David's house
and on the inhabitants of Jerusalem.
They will look to me concerning
the one whom they pierced;
they will mourn over him
like the mourning for an only child.
They will mourn bitterly over him
like the bitter mourning
over the death of[m] an oldest child.

11 On that day, the mourning in Jerusalem
will be as great

[j]Heb lacks *will strike.* [k]Heb uncertain [l]Heb uncertain [m]Heb lacks *the death of.*

as the mourning of Hadad-Rimmon
in the Megiddo Valley.
12 The land will mourn,
each of the clans by itself:
the clan of David's house by themselves,
and their women by themselves;
the clan of Nathan's house
by themselves,
and their women by themselves;
13 the clan of Levi's house
by themselves,
and their women by themselves;
and the Shimeites' clan
by themselves,
and their women by themselves;
14 and all the remaining clans,
each clan by itself,
and their women by themselves.

13 On that day, a fountain will open
to cleanse[n] the sin and impurity
of David's house
and the inhabitants of Jerusalem.

2 On that day,
says the LORD of heavenly forces,
I will eliminate the names of the idols
from the land;
they will no longer be remembered.
Moreover, I will remove the prophets
and the sinful spirit from the land.
3 If anyone again prophesies,
then that person's
birth father and mother will say,
"You won't live, for you have told a lie
in the name of the LORD."
That person's own birth father and
mother will stab him
when he prophesies.

4 On that day each of the prophets
will be ashamed of his vision
when he prophesies
and won't put on a shaggy coat
in order to deceive.
5 Each will say, "I'm not a prophet.
I'm a man who works the ground,
for the soil has been my occupation
since I was young."
6 Someone will say to him,
"What are these wounds
between your hands?"
And he will say, "These happened
when I was hit in my friends' home."

7 Sword, arise against my shepherd,
against the man responsible for[o]
my community,
says the LORD of heavenly forces!
Strike the shepherd
in order to scatter the flock!
I will turn my hand
against the little ones.
8 Throughout all the land,
says the LORD,
two-thirds will be cut off and die;
but one-third will be left in it.
9 I will put the third part into the fire.
I will refine them like one refines silver;
I will test them like one tests gold.
They will call on my name,
and I will respond to them.
I will say, "They are my people."
And they will say,
"The LORD is our God."

The day of the LORD

14 A day is coming
that belongs to the LORD,
when that which has been plundered
from you will be divided among you.
2 I will gather all the nations to Jerusalem
for the battle,
the city will be captured,
the houses will be plundered,
and the women will be raped.
Half of the city will go forth into exile,
but what is left of the people
won't be eliminated from the city.
3 The LORD will go out and fight
against those nations
as when he fights on a day of battle.
4 On that day he will stand upon
the Mount of Olives,
to the east of Jerusalem.
The Mount of Olives will be split
in half by a very large valley
running from east to west.

[n] Heb lacks *to cleanse.* [o] Heb lacks *responsible for.*

Half of the mountain will move north,
and the other half will move south.
5 You will flee
through the valley of my mountain,
because the valley of the mountains
will reach to Azal.
You will flee just as you fled
from the earthquake in the days
of Judah's King Uzziah.
The LORD my God will come,
and all the holy ones with him.[p]
6 On that day, there will be no light.
Splendid things will disappear.[q]
7 On one day known to the LORD,
there will be neither day nor night,
but at evening time there will be light.
8 On that day, running water will flow
out from Jerusalem,
half of it to the Dead Sea[r]
and half of it to the Mediterranean;[s]
this will happen
during the summer and the fall.
9 The LORD will become king
over all the land.
On that day the LORD will be one,
and the LORD's name will be one.
10 The entire land will become
like the desert[t]
from Geba to Rimmon,
south of Jerusalem.
Jerusalem will be high up
and firmly in place
from the Benjamin Gate
to the place of the former gate,
to the Corner Gate, and from the
Hananel Tower to the king's wine vats.
11 People will dwell in it;
it will never again be destroyed.
Jerusalem will dwell securely.
12 This will be the plague with which the
LORD will strike all the peoples who
swarmed against Jerusalem:
their flesh will rot,
even while standing on their feet;
their eyes will rot in their sockets;
and their tongues will rot
in their mouths.
13 On that day, a great panic brought on
by the LORD will fall upon them;
they will all grasp at the hand
of their neighbors;
neighbors will attack each other.
14 Even Judah will fight in Jerusalem.
The wealth of all the surrounding
nations will be collected:
gold, silver, and a great abundance
of garments.
15 This[u] plague will also affect the horses,
mules, camels, donkeys, and any cattle
in those camps during this plague.

16 All those left from all the nations who
attacked Jerusalem will go up annually to pay
homage to the king, the LORD of heavenly
forces, and to celebrate the Festival of Booths.
17 Whoever among the families of the
earth doesn't go up to Jerusalem to pay
homage to the king, the LORD of heavenly
forces, upon them no rain will fall.
18 And if the family of Egypt doesn't go
up and doesn't present itself, then no rain[v]
will fall on them. There will[w] be a plague like
the one with which the LORD struck the nations that didn't go up to celebrate the Festival of Booths.
19 This would be the sin of Egypt and the
sin of all the nations who don't go up to
celebrate the Festival of Booths.

20 On that day, *Holy to the LORD* will be
inscribed[x] on the bells of the horses,
and the pots in the LORD's house will
be holy[y] like the bowls
before the altar.
21 Every pot in Jerusalem and in Judah will
be holy to the LORD of heavenly forces.
All those who sacrifice will come.
They will take some of the pots
and cook with them.
There will no longer be any merchants[z]
in the house of the LORD of heavenly
forces on that day.

[p] Or *you* [q] Heb uncertain [r] Or *eastern sea* [s] Or *western sea* [t] Heb *Arabah* [u] Heb lacks *this,* cf 14:12.
[v] Heb lacks *rain.* [w] Or *will not.* [x] Heb lacks *inscribed.* [y] Heb lacks *holy.* [z] Heb *Canaanite*

MALACHI

1 A pronouncement. The LORD'S word to Israel through Malachi.[a]

Love of Jacob

2 I have loved you, says the LORD;
but you say, "How have you loved us?"
Wasn't Esau Jacob's brother?
says the LORD.
I loved Jacob, 3 but I rejected Esau.
I turned Esau's mountains
into desolation,
his inheritance into a wilderness
for jackals.
4 Edom may say, "We are beaten down,
but we will rebuild the ruins";
but the LORD of heavenly forces
proclaims:
They may build,
but I will tear them down.
They will call themselves
a wicked territory,
the people against whom
the LORD rages forever.
5 Your eyes will see it and you will say,
"May the LORD be great
beyond the borders of Israel."

Honoring the LORD

6 A son honors a father,
and a servant honors his master.
But if I'm a father, where is my honor?
Or if I'm a master, where is my respect?
says the LORD of heavenly forces
to you priests who despise my name.
So you say,
"How have we despised your name?"
7 By approaching my altar
with polluted food.
But you say,
"How have we polluted it[b]?"
When you say,
"The table of the LORD can be
despised."
8 If you bring a blind animal to sacrifice,
isn't that evil?
If you bring a lame or sick one,
isn't that evil?
Would you bring it to your governor?
Would he be pleased with it
or accept you?
says the LORD of heavenly forces.

9 So now ask God to be gracious to us.
After what you have done,
will he accept you?
says the LORD of heavenly forces.
10 Who among you will shut
the doors of the temple[c]
so that you don't burn something
on my altar in vain?
I take no delight in you,
says the LORD of heavenly forces.
I won't accept a grain offering
from your hand.

11 Nevertheless, from sunrise to sunset,
my name will be great
among the nations.
Incense and a pure grain offering will be
offered everywhere in my name,
because my name is great
among the nations,
says the LORD of heavenly forces.
12 But you make my name impure
when you say,
"The table of the LORD is polluted.
Its fruit, its food, is despised."
13 But you say, "How tedious!"
And you groan about it,
says the LORD of heavenly forces.
You permit what is stolen, lame, or sick
to be brought for a sacrifice,[d]
and you bring the grain offering.
Should I accept such from your hands?
says the LORD.
14 I will curse the cheater
who has a healthy[e] male in his flock,
but who promises and sacrifices
to the LORD that which is corrupt.
I am truly a great king,
says the LORD of heavenly forces,
and my name is feared
among the nations.

2 But now, this command is for you,
priests:

[a]Or *my messenger* [b]Gk; Heb *you* [c]Heb lacks *of the temple.* [d]Heb lacks *for a sacrifice.* [e]Heb lacks *healthy.*

2 If you don't listen,
or don't intend to glorify my name,
says the LORD of heavenly forces,
then I will send a curse among you.
I will curse your blessings,
and I mean really curse them,
because none of you intend to do it.
3 I am about to denounce your offspring;
I will scatter feces on your faces,
the feces of your festivals.
Then I will lift you up to me,[f]
4 and you will know that I have sent
this command to you
so that my covenant with Levi
can continue to exist,
says the LORD of heavenly forces.
5 My covenant with him involved
life and peace, which I gave him,
and also fear so that he honored me.
He was in awe of my name.
6 True Instruction was in his mouth;
injustice wasn't found on his lips.
He walked with me in peace
and did the right thing;
he made many turn from iniquity.
7 The lips of the priest
should guard knowledge;
everyone[g] should seek Instruction
from his mouth,
for he is the messenger from
the LORD of heavenly forces.
8 But you have turned from the path.
You have caused many to stumble
by your instruction.
You have corrupted
the covenant of Levi,
says the LORD of heavenly forces.
9 Moreover, I have made you despised
and humiliated in the view
of all the people,
since none of you keep my ways
or show respect for Instruction.

Judah's dishonesty

10 Isn't there one father for all of us,
one God who created us?
Why does everyone cheat each other
to make the covenant
of our ancestors impure?
11 Judah cheated—
a detestable thing was done
in Israel and Jerusalem.
Judah made the LORD's
holy place impure, which God loved,
and married the daughter
of a foreign god.
12 May the LORD eliminate anyone
who does so from the tents of Jacob,
anyone awaking, testifying,[h]
and making an offering
to the LORD of heavenly forces.
13 You should do this as well:
cover the altar of the LORD
with tears, weeping, and groaning
because there is still no divine favor
for your offering
or favorable regard
for anything from your hand.
14 But you say, "Why?"
Because the LORD testifies about you
and the wife of your youth
against whom you cheated.
She is your partner,
the wife of your covenant.
15 Didn't he make her[i] the one[j]
and the remnant of his spirit?[k]
What is the one?
The one seeking godly offspring.
You should guard your own spirit.
Don't cheat on the wife of your
youth 16 because he hates divorce,
says the LORD God of Israel,
and he also hates the one covering
his garment with violence,[l]
says the LORD of heavenly forces.
Guard your own life, and don't cheat.

Purifying judgment

17 You have made the LORD tired
with your words.
You say,
"How have we made him tired?"
When you say:
"Anyone doing evil is good in the
LORD's eyes,"
or "He delights in those doing evil,"[m]
or "Where is the God of justice?"

[f] Heb uncertain; MT *He will carry you to it.* [g] Or *they* [h] Heb uncertain [i] Heb lacks *her.* [j] Heb uncertain; *her* refers to the *wife* in Mal 2:14. [k] Heb uncertain [l] Heb uncertain [m] Or *them*

3 Look, I am sending my messenger
who will clear the path before me;
suddenly the LORD whom you are
seeking will come to his temple.
The messenger of the covenant
in whom you take delight is coming,
says the LORD of heavenly forces.
2 Who can endure the day of his coming?
Who can withstand his appearance?
He is like the refiner's fire
or the cleaner's soap.
3 He will sit as a refiner
and a purifier of silver.
He will purify the Levites
and refine them like gold and silver.
They will belong to the LORD,
presenting a righteous offering.
4 The offering of Judah and Jerusalem
will be pleasing to the LORD
as in ancient days
and in former years.
5 I will draw near to you for judgment.
I will be quick to testify
against the sorcerers,
the adulterers, those swearing falsely,
against those who cheat
the day laborers out of their wages
as well as oppress the widow
and the orphan,
and against those who brush aside
the foreigner and do not revere me,
says the LORD of heavenly forces.
6 I am the LORD, and I do not change;
and you, children of Jacob,
have not perished.

Return to the LORD

7 Ever since the time of your ancestors,
you have deviated from my laws
and have not kept them.
Return to me and I will return to you,
says the LORD of heavenly forces.
But you say,
"How should we return?"
8 Should a person deceive God?
Yet you deceive me.
But you say,
"How have we deceived you?"
With your tenth-part gifts and offerings.
9 You are being cursed with a curse,
and you, the entire nation,
are robbing me.
10 Bring the whole tenth-part
to the storage house so there
might be food in my house.
Please test me in this,
says the LORD of heavenly forces.
See whether I do not open all the
windows of the heavens for you
and empty out a blessing
until there is enough.[n]
11 I will threaten the one
who wants to devour you
so that it doesn't spoil the fruit
of your fertile land,
and so that the vine doesn't abort
its fruit in your field,
says the LORD of heavenly forces.
12 All the nations
will consider you fortunate,
for you will be a desirable land,
says the LORD of heavenly forces.

13 You have spoken harshly about me,
says the LORD;
but you say,
"What have we spoken about you?"
14 You said,
"Serving God is useless.
What do we gain
by keeping his obligation
or by walking around as mourners
before the LORD of heavenly forces?
15 So now we consider the arrogant
fortunate.
Moreover, those doing evil are built up;
they test God and escape."

The scroll of remembrance

16 Then those revering the LORD,
each and every one,
spoke among themselves.
The LORD paid attention
and listened to them.
Then a scroll of remembrance
was written before the LORD
about those revering the LORD,
the ones meditating on his name.

[n] Or *Until what is required is lacking.*

17 On the day that I am preparing,
says the LORD of heavenly forces,
they will be my special possession.
I will spare them just as parents
spare a child who serves them.
18 You will again distinguish
between the righteous and the wicked,
between those serving God
and those not serving him.

The day of the LORD

4 [o]Look, the day is coming,
burning like an oven.
All the arrogant ones and
all those doing evil will become straw.
The coming day will burn them,
says the LORD of heavenly forces,
leaving them neither root nor branch.
2 But the sun of righteousness will rise
on those revering my name;
healing will be in its wings
so that you will go forth and jump
about like calves in the stall.
3 You will crush the wicked;
they will be like dust
beneath the soles of your feet
on the day that I am preparing,
says the LORD of heavenly forces.
4 Remember the Instruction from Moses,
my servant,
to whom I gave Instruction
and rules for all Israel at Horeb.
5 Look, I am sending
Elijah the prophet to you,
before the great and terrifying
day of the LORD arrives.
6 Turn the hearts of the parents
to the children
and the hearts of the children
to their parents.
Otherwise, I will come and
strike the land with a curse.

[o]3:19 in Heb

COMMON ENGLISH BIBLE

a fresh translation to touch the heart and mind

The Apocrypha

APOCRYPHA (DEUTEROCANONICAL BOOKS)

CONTENTS ALPHABETICAL

APOCRYPHA

BOOKS INCLUDED IN ROMAN CATHOLIC, GREEK, AND SLAVONIC BIBLES

TOBIT

Tobit and his background

1 This scroll is a story told by Tobit. He was
the son of Tobiel son of Hananiel son of
Aduel son of Gabael son of Raphael son of
Raguel, whose family came from Asiel, of
the Naphtali tribe. 2 In the days of Shalmaneser king of the Assyrians, he was captured in Thisbe, south of Kedesh-naphtali
in the upper hills of Galilee, northwest of
Hazor and north of Peor.

Tobit's piety

3 I, Tobit, was trustworthy and behaved
righteously during my entire life. I would
help support my relatives and others of
my country who were captured and taken
with me to Nineveh in the country of the
Assyrians.

4 While I was young and in my own
country of Israel, the tribe of my ancestor
Naphtali deserted the descendants of my
ancestor David and stayed away from Jerusalem, the city chosen from among all the
tribes of Israel for offering sacrifices on behalf of all the tribes of Israel. There God's
own dwelling place, the temple, was built
and dedicated for use by all future generations. 5 Instead, all my relatives and the
whole tribe of my ancestor Naphtali would
offer sacrifices on all the hills of Galilee to
the image of a calf that Israel's King Jeroboam had set up in Dan.

6 I would often go by myself to Jerusalem on religious holidays, as the Law commanded for every Israelite for all time.
I would hurry off to Jerusalem and take
with me the early produce of my crops, a
tenth of my flocks, and the first portion of
the wool cut from my sheep. 7 I would present these things at the altar to the priests,
the descendants of Aaron. I would give
the first tenth of my grain, wine, olive oil,
pomegranates, figs, and other fruit to the
Levites who served in Jerusalem. For six
out of seven years,[a] I also brought the cash
equivalent of the second tenth of these
crops to Jerusalem where I would spend it
every year. 8 I gave this to orphans and widows, and to Gentiles who had joined Israel.
In the third year, when I brought and gave
it to them, we would eat together according
to the instruction recorded in Moses' Law,
as Deborah my grandmother[b] had taught
me (for my father had died and left me an
orphan).

9 When I became an adult, I married a
woman from our clan.[c] Together we had
a son, whom I named Tobias.

Tobit rewarded for his piety

10 After I was taken captive to Assyria
and came to Nineveh,[d] all my relatives and
fellow Jews there were eating Gentile food.
11 I, however, avoided eating the Gentiles'
food. 12 Because I kept God in view with all
my heart, 13 the Most High gave me favor
and good standing before Shalmaneser, and
I would buy for him everything he needed.
14 I used to go to Media on business for him
until he died. While in the land of Media,
I entrusted 570 pounds of silver to Gabael
brother of Gabri.

15 When Shalmaneser died, Sennacherib his son ruled in his place. The roads to
Media became dangerous,[e] and I couldn't
travel there any longer.

Tobit is harassed for his pious acts

16 During the time of Shalmaneser, I gave
away a lot of money to my relatives, my
fellow Jews. 17 I gave a portion of my food
to the hungry and clothes to the naked.
Whenever I saw that the corpse of anyone
from my nation had been flung outside the
wall of Nineveh, I buried it.

18 I also buried anyone whom Sennacherib murdered after fleeing home from
Judea, at the time when the king of heaven
had punished him for all his insulting actions. In his rage Sennacherib killed many
Israelites. However, I would take their
bodies and bury them secretly. Sennach-

[a] Gk *For six years* [b] LXX² *the mother of our father Hananiel* [c] Or *ancestral kindred* [d] LXX² *After I was taken into captivity into Assyria and when I was taken captive, I went into Nineveh.* [e] Or *slipped from his control*

erib looked for them, but he didn't find them. 19 A native Ninevite went to the king and told him that I was the one burying the bodies. So I went into hiding. When I found out[f] that I was being hunted down to be put to death, I fled from the city in fear. 20 All my possessions were seized, and everything of mine became royal property except for my wife Anna and my son Tobias.

21 Within forty days Sennacherib was killed by two of his sons, who escaped to the mountains of Ararat. His son Esarhaddon became king in his place. He hired Ahikar, my brother Hanael's son, to be in charge of all the financial accounts of his kingdom and all the king's treasury records.

22 Ahikar petitioned the king on my behalf, and I returned to Nineveh. Ahikar had been the chief officer,[g] the keeper of the ring with the royal seal, the auditor of accounts, and the keeper of financial records under Assyria's King Sennacherib. And Esarhaddon promoted him to be second in charge after himself. Ahikar was my nephew and one of my family.

2 When I returned to my house in the time of King Esarhaddon, my wife Anna and my son Tobias were restored to me.

Tobit is blinded

During our Festival of Pentecost, which is the holy Festival of Weeks, a splendid meal was cooked for me, and I lay down to eat. 2 The table was set before me, and many fine foods were brought to me. Then I said to my son Tobias, "Go, my son, and find one of our poorer relatives captive here in Nineveh, someone who pays attention to God with all his heart. Bring him here to eat with me. I will wait here, son, until you return."

3 Tobias left to find some poor person among our relatives. When he returned, he said, "Father?"

I answered, "I'm here, my son."

He exclaimed, "Father, one of our people has been murdered and tossed into the marketplace; his strangled body is just lying there."

4 I got up and left the meal before tasting it. I removed the body from the street and placed it in one of the smaller houses until sunset when I would bury it. 5 Then, when I returned, I washed myself and ate my food in sadness. 6 I remembered the word that Amos the prophet pronounced against Bethel: *Your festivals will be transformed into sadness and all your songs*[h] *into sorrowful wailing.*[i] And I wept.

7 After sunset I went out, dug a hole, and buried him. 8 My neighbors made fun of me, saying, "Is he no longer afraid that he will be killed for doing this kind of thing? He ran away, but now look: he is burying the dead again!"

9 That night I washed myself and went into my courtyard and fell asleep alongside the courtyard wall, with my face uncovered because of the heat. 10 I didn't know that there were sparrows in the wall above me, and their warm droppings fell into my eyes, forming white spots. I went to doctors to be healed, but the more they applied their medicines on me, the worse the white spots became until I was completely blinded. I couldn't see with my eyes for four years. All my relatives felt sorry for me, and Ahikar took care of me for two years until he went to Elymais.

Tobit's plight worsens

11 At that time my wife Anna made a living by weaving cloth out of wool.[j] 12 She would send the cloth to the wool suppliers,[k] and they would pay her for it. On the seventh day of Dystrus,[l] she finished a piece on the loom for her employers. They gave her the full wages, along with a young goat from their herd for her home. 13 When it approached me, the kid began to bleat. So I called to Anna and said, "Where does this goat come from? It isn't stolen, is it? Return it to its owners, for we have no right to eat anything that is stolen!"

14 But she said to me, "It was given to me

[f] Gk adds *that the king was aware of me and* [g] Or *chief cupbearer* [h] Gk *paths* [i] Amos 8:10 [j] Gk *by doing women's work* [k] Or *to its owners* [l] March

as a bonus in addition to my pay." I didn't believe her and demanded that she return it to the owners. I grew red with anger at her. But she replied and said to me, "And what's become of your charitable donations? What's become of your righteous deeds? You have a reputation for that sort of thing, don't you?!"[m]

Tobit's prayer to die

3 Deeply upset in my heart, I sighed and wept and began to pray with sighs:

2 "You are just, Lord, and all your deeds are just; mercy and truth mark all your ways. You judge the world.

3 "Now, Lord, remember me and look upon me. Don't punish me for my sins and the mistakes I made in ignorance, nor for those of my ancestors. They sinned against you, 4 and I disregarded your commandments. So you have handed us over to plunder, captivity, and death. We have become a parable and the object of chatter and scorn among all the nations to which you have scattered us. 5 You are right in your many judgments, holding me responsible for my sins; for we didn't observe your commandments, and we haven't behaved faithfully toward you.

6 "And now, deal with me as you wish. Command that my spirit be taken from me so that I might be set free from the earth[n] and become dust. It is better for me to die than to live, for I have heard false insults, and I'm full of grief. Lord, command that I might be set free from this distress. Set me free to go to the eternal place. Don't turn your face from me, Lord, for it is better for me to die than to experience this distress in my life and to endure insults."

Sarah's plight and her prayer to die

7 On the same day in Ecbatana of Media, Sarah, Raguel's daughter, also heard insults from one of her father's female servants.

8 Sarah had been given in marriage to seven husbands; and Asmodeus, an evil demon, killed them before they could lie with her as newlyweds do.[o] And so the female servant said to her, "You are the one who keeps killing your husbands! See, you have already been given to seven husbands, and you haven't carried the name of any of them. 9 Are you beating us because they have all died? Go with them, and may we never see a son or daughter of yours!"

10 On that day Sarah was deeply upset in her heart and wept. She went upstairs to a room in her father's house, and planned to hang herself. But she had second thoughts and said, "They will never insult my father by saying to him, 'You had but one dearly loved daughter, and she hanged herself because of her troubles.' If I did this, I would bring my old father down to the grave in sorrow. It is better for me not to hang myself, but to beg of the Lord to let me die so that I no longer hear insults during my lifetime."

11 At that moment, she stretched her hands out toward the window and prayed:

"You are blessed, merciful God, and your name is blessed forever! May all your works forever praise you! 12 And now, Lord, I lift my face and my eyes toward you. 13 Speak the word, and set me free from the earth so that I don't have to hear insults anymore. 14 You know, Master, that I'm pure from any uncleanness from relations with a man. 15 You know that I haven't tarnished my name or my father's name in this country where we are captives. I'm my father's only child. He has no other child to be his heir, nor does he have a brother or near relative for whom I can keep myself as a wife. Seven have died on me already, so why should I go on living? And if you don't like the idea of killing me, take notice, at least, of how they insult me."

Raphael helps Tobit and Sarah

16 At that very moment, the prayers of both Sarah and Tobit were heard in God's glorious presence. 17 Raphael was sent to heal the two of them: Tobit, by remov-

[m] Gk *Where are your charitable donations now? Where are your righteous deeds? See, these things are known about you!* [n] DSS Heb; LXX[1,2] *land* [o] Gk *according to what is prescribed for wives*

ing the white spots from his eyes to see God's light with his eyes again, and Sarah, Raguel's daughter, by giving her as a wife to Tobias, Tobit's son, and by ridding her of the evil demon. It was Tobias' right to inherit her before all the others who wished to take her. At that very moment Tobit returned from the courtyard back into his house, and Sarah, Raguel's daughter, also came down from the upstairs room.

Tobit tells Tobias about the money

4 That day Tobit remembered the silver he had entrusted to Gabael in Rages of Media. 2He said to himself, I have asked for death; I should call my son Tobias and tell him about the money before I die.

3So he called for his son Tobias, and Tobias came to him. Tobit said to him: "Give me a proper burial. Honor your mother and take care of her[p] as long as she lives. Do what pleases her and don't grieve her spirit in any matter. 4Remember her, my son, because she went through many dangers while pregnant with you. And when she dies, bury her next to me in the same grave.

5"My child, pay attention to the Lord as long as you live, and don't make it your desire to sin or to disobey his commandments. Do what is just as long as you live, and don't follow the paths that lead to wickedness. 6Those who live in line with the truth will prosper in everything they do.

7"To everyone who practices righteousness, make donations based on what you have, and don't let your eye begrudge what you've given. Don't turn your face away from any poor person, and God's face will never turn away from you. 8Give aid, my child, according to what you have. If you have a lot, make a donation out of your riches. If you have only a little, don't be afraid to make a donation in proportion. 9In this way, you will store up a valuable treasure for a time of need. 10Giving assistance to the poor rescues a person from death and keeps a person from going down into darkness. 11For everyone who does it, donating money to the needy is a good gift in the sight of the Most High.

12"Child, keep yourself away from all inappropriate sex. First, take a wife from the descendants of your ancestors, and don't take a foreign woman who isn't from your ancestral tribe, for we are children of the prophets. Noah was first a prophet, and then Abraham, Isaac, and Jacob, our ancestors from earlier times. Remember, my child, that they all took wives from their relatives.[q] They were blessed through their children, and their descendants will inherit the land.

13"And now, my child, love your relatives and don't be too proud in your heart to take a daughter from the descendants of your people as your wife. In pride there is much ruin and instability, and laziness results in loss and great poverty, for laziness is the mother of hunger.

14"Pay the wages of any person who works with you that same day. Don't delay to pay a person's wages, and your own wages will certainly not be withheld if you truly serve God. Keep yourself under control, my child, in everything you do and be disciplined in every aspect of your behavior.

15"What you yourself hate, do that to no one. Don't get drunk with wine, and don't let drunkards[r] accompany you on your way.

16"Give some of your food to the one who is hungry and some of your clothing to those who are naked. Give away all your surplus to the poor, and don't let your eye be resentful when you give your things away.

17"Place your bread and wine on the tombs of the righteous, but don't give anything to sinners.

18"Get advice from everyone who is wise, and don't despise what they say, since all advice is useful.

19"At every opportunity praise God and ask him to make all your ways straight and all your activities prosper. No nation has good counsel, but the Lord himself gives good counsel. The Lord will bring down whomever he wishes, even as far as hell below. For this

[p]Gk *don't neglect her* [q]OL; LXX[1] *We are children of the prophets. Remember that Noah, Abraham, Isaac, and Jacob, our ancient ancestors, all took wives from among their families.* [r]Gk *drunkenness*

reason, my son, remember these instructions, and don't let them be erased from your heart.

[20]"And now, my child, I want you to know that I have placed 570 pounds of silver in trust with Gabael the son of Gabrias in Rages of Media. [21]So don't worry, my child, about the fact that we have been poor. You have many good things if you fear God, flee from every kind of sin, and do what the Lord your God thinks is right."

Azariah (Raphael) travels with Tobias to Media

5 Then Tobias said to his father Tobit, "I will do everything you have commanded me, Father. [2]But how am I going to get it from Gabael, since he doesn't know me and I don't know him? What proof can I give him so that he will recognize and trust me and give me the money? Moreover, I don't know the roads to take to get to Media."

[3]Then Tobit said to his son Tobias, "He gave me a signed receipt, and I gave him a handwritten document as well. I divided them in two, and we each took one part, and I deposited one with the money. And now it is twenty years since I deposited this money. So then go find a reliable man who will go with you, and we will pay him for his time until you return. Then you can retrieve this money from Gabael."

[4]Then Tobias went out to look for a man who knew the way to Media and would go with him. He went out and found the angel Raphael standing near him, but he didn't know that he was an angel from God. [5]Tobias said to him, "Where are you from, young man?"

He said to Tobias, "I am one of the Israelites, your relatives. I have come here to find work."

Tobias said to him, "Do you know the way to Media?"

[6]He replied, "Yes, I have been there many times; I'm familiar with all the roads and know them well. Often I have gone to Media and have spent the night with Gabael, our relative, who lives in Ecbatana[s] of Media. It is a good two days' journey from Ecbatana to Rages,[t] because it is located in a mountainous area while Ecbatana lies in the midst of a plain."

[7]Tobias said to him, "Wait here for me, young man, until I go and report this to my father, because I need you to go with me, and I'll pay your wages."

[8]Raphael replied, "All right, I'll wait. But don't delay!"

[9]So Tobias went in and reported to his father Tobit, saying, "Wow, I've found a man from among our relatives the Israelites."

Tobit said to Tobias, "Call the man in to me, my son,[u] so that I learn who his family is, from which tribe he is, and whether he can be trusted to go with you."

[10]So Tobias went out, called Raphael, and said to him, "Young man, my father is calling for you." Raphael went in, and Tobit was the first to greet him.

Raphael[v] said, "May joy be yours!"

Tobit responded, "What joy can there still be for me? My eyes are useless, and I can't see the light of heaven. Instead, I lie in darkness just like the dead who no longer see the light. I live among the dead, hearing the sound of human beings without seeing them."

Raphael said to him, "Take heart! The time is near when God will heal you. Take heart!"

Then Tobit said to him, "My son Tobias wants to go to Media. Brother, can you accompany and guide him? I will pay your wages."

Raphael said to him, "I'm able to go with him, for I know all the roads and have often traveled to Media and have passed through all its plains. So I'm familiar with its mountains and all its roads."

[11]Tobit said to him, "Brother, which family and which tribe do you come from? Tell me, brother!"

[12]The young man answered, "Why do you need to know about my tribe?"

[s]LXX^2; OL *Rages* [t]LXX^2 *Garras*; OL adds *a city of Phagar.* [u]Gk *child*, as generally throughout the book
[v]Gk *The young man*

Tobit replied, "I would like to know in all honesty, brother, who your father is and what your name is."

[13]Then he answered, "I'm Azariah, the great Hananiah's son, one of your relatives."

[14]Tobit said to him, "May you come in health and safety, brother! Don't be offended, brother, that I wanted to know the truth about your family. But you happen to be a relative, and you are from a good and honorable heritage. I knew Hananiah and Nathan, the two sons of the great Shemeliah. They used to go with me to Jerusalem. They used to worship with me there and weren't led astray. Your relatives are good men; you are of good stock, and may you feel welcome for coming here!"

[15]Then he added,[w] "I will pay you a drachme a day as well as provide for your expenses just as for those of my son. So do go with my son, [16]and I'll give you additional pay."

The young man replied, "I'll go with him. Don't be afraid; we'll depart safely and we'll return safely to you, because the road is secure."

[17]Tobit answered, "Bless you, brother!"

Then Tobit called his son and said to him, "My child, prepare provisions for the trip and head off with your brother. May God who is in heaven protect you on your way and restore you safely to me. May his angel travel with you and protect you, my child."

He went to begin his journey, and he kissed his father and mother. Tobit said to him, "Travel safely!"

[18]His mother began to weep and said to Tobit, "Why have you sent my child away? Isn't he the staff on which we lean[x] as he comes and goes in our presence? [19]Don't make money more important than it is;[y] instead, let it be ransom for our child's sake. [20]It's enough for us to live as the Lord has provided."

[21]Tobit said to her, "Don't make such an issue of it! Our child will go safely and will come safely back to us. Your eyes will see him on the day he returns to you safe and sound. Don't overreact, and don't be afraid for them, my sister! [22]A good angel will go with him, his journey will prosper, and he will return safely."

6 Then she calmed down and stopped crying.

Tobias and Raphael at the Tigris River

[2]So their son departed, with the angel alongside him. Tobias' dog also went with him and accompanied them on the journey. They both journeyed until the first night fell upon them, and they set up camp along the Tigris River.

[3]Now the lad went down to the Tigris River to wash his feet. Suddenly,[z] a massive fish leaped up out of the water and tried to swallow the lad's foot, and he cried out. [4]The angel said to him, "Grab the fish and hang on to it." So Tobias hung on to the fish and brought it up onto the dry ground. [5]The angel said to him, "Cut open the fish and remove its gallbladder, heart, and liver and keep them with you, and throw away the guts. Its gallbladder, heart, and liver are useful medicines."

[6]So Tobias cut open the fish and gathered up the gallbladder, heart, and liver. He cooked the fish and ate it; and the remaining part of it, which he salted, he put aside. Then they both journeyed together until they approached Media. [7]Tobias asked the angel, "Brother Azariah, what medicine is there in the fish's heart, liver, and gallbladder?"

[8]Raphael replied, "If you burn the fish's heart and liver in the presence of a man or woman under attack by a demon or evil spirit, the spirit will flee and never bother that person again. [9]As for the gallbladder, if you smear the gall on a person's eyes in which white spots have appeared, and then blow on the white spots, the eyes will heal."

Raphael instructs Tobias

[10]When he arrived in Media and was already coming within reach of Ecbatana, [11]Raphael said to the lad, "Tobias my brother!"

[w]OL; LXX[2] *he said to him* [x]Gk *staff of our hands* [y]Gk *don't pile up silver upon silver* [z]DSS Aram

He replied, "I'm here!"

Raphael said, "Tonight we must lodge with Raguel your relative. He has a daughter named Sarah. [12]Except for her, he has no other son or daughter. Of all men you are her closest relative. The right to inherit her and her father's estate is yours. The girl is sensible, courageous, and very beautiful; moreover, her father loves her and[a] is a good man."

[13]He continued, "It's right for you to marry her. So listen to me, brother: I'll speak to her father about the girl tonight so that we can take her as a bride for you. And when we return from Rages,[b] we will celebrate her wedding. I know that Raguel can't keep her from you, nor can he promise her to someone else without incurring the death penalty according to the ruling of the scroll from Moses. He knows that the regulation for inheritance makes it fitting that you, rather than any other man, should marry his daughter. So now listen to me, brother: We will speak about the girl tonight and arrange for her engagement to you. When we return from Rages, we will take her and bring her back with us to your home."

[14]Tobias said to Raphael, "Brother Azariah, I've heard that she has already been given to seven men and that they died in the bridal chamber. They dropped dead the very night they tried to have sex with her. I've heard people saying that a demon kills them. [15]Now I'm also afraid, because the demon loves her and[c] doesn't harm her but kills anyone who desires to approach her. I'm my father's only child, and I'm afraid[d] that I will die and bring my father and mother down to their graves with grief over me. Moreover, they don't have another son to bury them."

[16]Raphael said to him, "Don't you remember your father's instructions, that you should take a wife from among your father's relatives? Now listen to me, my brother: Don't worry about this demon. Take her, for I know that tonight she will be given to you as your wife. [17]When you enter into the bridal chamber, take some of the fish's liver and heart and lay them over the warm incense coals. This will let off an odor, [18]and the demon will smell it, flee, and never stalk her[e] again. And before you have sex with her, the two of you must rise and pray and plead with the Lord of heaven for mercy and deliverance. So don't be afraid; she has been assigned to you before the world came into being. You will save her, and she will go with you. I'm convinced that you will also have children by her, and they will be like brothers and sisters to you. So stop worrying."

When Tobias heard Raphael's words, and learned that she was his relative and descendant from his father's house, he fell deeply in love with her and his heart was united with her.

Tobias and Raphael arrive at Raguel's house

7 When they[f] entered Ecbatana, Tobias said to him, "Brother Azariah, bring me at once to Raguel our relative." So Azariah took him to Raguel's house. They found him sitting at the gate of the courtyard and greeted him first.

Raguel said to them, "Many greetings, brothers. You have come generously and in health!" Raguel brought them into his house [2]and said to his wife Edna, "This young man looks so much like my relative Tobit!"

[3]Then Edna asked them, "Where are you from, brothers?"

They answered her, "We are from the Naphtalites, who are captives in Nineveh."

[4]She asked them, "Do you know our relative Tobit?"

They replied, "We do indeed know him."

Then she asked them, "Is he well?"

[5]They answered, "He is alive and well." Tobias said, "He is my father."

[6]Raguel jumped up and kissed him. He began to cry [7]and say, "Bless you, young man, son of a good and generous father! What a terrible tragedy that such a righteous and

[a]DSS Aram, OL; LXX² omits *loves her and.* [b]OL; LXX² *Raguel* [c]DSS Aram, OL; LXX² omits *loves her and.*
[d]LXX¹; omitted in LXX², OL [e]LXX¹ *return* [f]Or *he*

charitable man has been made blind!" He embraced his relative Tobias and wept.

8 Raguel's wife Edna also wept for Tobit, as did Sarah their daughter.

Tobias marries Sarah

9 Raguel slaughtered a ram from his flock and eagerly entertained his guests. When they had bathed and washed, they reclined to eat dinner. Tobias said to Raphael, "Brother Azariah, tell Raguel that he should give me my relative Sarah as a wife."

10 Raguel overheard Tobias' comment and said to the young man, "Eat, drink, and be happy tonight! There is no other man except you, my brother, for whom it is proper to marry my daughter Sarah. What's more, I have no right to give her to any man except for you since you are my nearest relative.

"But, my lad, I must tell you the truth. 11 I have given her to seven men among our relatives, and they all died the night they tried to have sex with her. Now, however, eat and drink, my son, and may the Lord act on behalf of you both."

Tobias replied, "I won't eat or drink here until you resolve the matters that have to do with me."

Raguel said to him, "I will do it. She is given to you according to the ruling of the scroll from Moses, and it has been decided in heaven that she be given to you. Receive your sister! From now on you are her brother and she is your sister. She is given to you from today until eternity. And tonight may the Lord of heaven grant success to both of you, my son, and may he shower you both with mercy and peace."

12 Raguel sent for his daughter Sarah, and she came to him. He took hold of her hand, delivered her to Tobias, and said, "Take her to be your wife according to the Law and according to the ruling written in the scroll from Moses. Take her and lead her to your father safely. And may the God of heaven grant both of you success with peace."

13 Then Raguel called for her mother and told her to bring a scroll. He wrote a marriage contract, stating how he was giving her to him as a wife according to the ruling of the scroll from Moses. Then he sealed it.[g] 14 From that point on, they began to eat and drink.

15 Raguel called his wife Edna and said to her, "My sister, prepare the other bedroom and take Sarah there."

16 She went and got things ready in the bedroom, just as Raguel had told her. She brought Sarah there and cried for her. Then Edna dried her tears and said to her, "Take courage, my daughter! May the Lord of heaven give you joy in place of your pain. Take courage, my daughter!" Then she left.

Deliverance from the demon

8 When they had all finished eating and drinking, they wanted to go to bed. So the bride's parents led the young man away and brought him into the bride's bedroom. 2 Tobias remembered Raphael's words. He took the fish's liver and heart out of his bag and laid them upon the warm incense coals. 3 The odor from the fish drove off the demon, and he sped off to the region of Egypt. Raphael went after the demon, bound him there hand and foot, and immediately put him in chains.

4 Then the parents left and shut the door of the bedroom. Tobias got up from the bed and said to Sarah, "Get up, my sister! Let's pray and beg our Lord to show us mercy and give us deliverance."

5 She got up, and they began to pray and to ask that they might be delivered. Tobias then began to speak:

> "Blessed are you, God of our ancestors, and blessed is your name for all generations. May the heavens and all your creation bless you forever! 6 You created Adam and you created Eve his wife to help and support him, and from the two of them has come the human race. You said, 'It isn't good for the man to be alone; let's make for him a helper like himself.' 7 I'm not taking this sister

[g] DSS Aram, OL; LXX² omits *Then he sealed it.*

of mine now out of lust but with honest integrity.[h] Grant that she and I will be shown mercy and grow old together."

[8]Together they said, "Amen, amen." [9]Then they fell asleep for the night.

Upon getting up during the night,[i] Raguel summoned his servants, and they went with him and dug a grave. [10]He said, "Tobias might die as well, and people will laugh and jeer at us."

[11]When they had finished digging the grave, Raguel returned to his house, called his wife, [12]and said, "Send one of the female servants in to see if he's alive. If he's dead, let's bury him so that no one knows what has happened."

[13]So they sent for the female servant, lit a lamp, and opened the door. The female servant entered and found them fast asleep together. [14]Then she came out and told them, "He's alive, and there's nothing wrong."

[15]They praised the God of heaven, saying, "Blessed are you, God, with every pure blessing; may people bless you forever! [16]Blessed are you, because you have brought me joy. It didn't happen as I had expected. Instead, you have dealt with us according to your great mercy. [17]Blessed are you, because you have shown mercy to our only two children. Master, provide them with mercy and well-being,[j] and bring both their lives to fulfillment with joy and mercy."

[18]Then Raguel told his servants to fill up the grave with dirt before dawn, [19]and he told his wife to bake a lot of bread. From his herd he brought back two oxen and four rams. He gave instructions to have them slaughtered, and they began to make preparations.

[20]Raguel then called Tobias and said, "You will certainly not leave here for the next fourteen days. Instead, you will remain here to eat and drink with me, and you will bring joy to my daughter's troubled soul. [21]Take now half of whatever I own and go in health to your father. When my wife and I die, the other half will be yours. Take courage, my son! I'm your father and Edna is your mother. From now on and forever we will stand beside both you and your sister. Take courage, my son!"

Tobias sends Raphael to collect Tobit's money

9 Then Tobias called Raphael and said to him, [2]"Brother Azariah, take along four servants and two camels. Travel to Rages and go to Gabael's place. Give him the signed contract, get the money, and bring it with you back to the wedding feast. [3]You know that my father will be counting the days, and if I delay just one day, I will cause him a lot of grief. [4]You see what Raguel swore, and that I'm not in a position to go against his solemn pledge."

[5]So Raphael went with four servants and two camels to Rages of Media, and they spent the night at Gabael's place. Raphael gave him the receipt and told him that Tobias, Tobit's son, had taken a wife and was inviting Gabael to the wedding feast. Gabael got up and checked the sacks, which were still sealed, and they packed them up.

[6]They got up early in the morning together and went to the wedding feast. They came to Raguel's place and found Tobias reclining at a table. Tobias jumped up and greeted him, and Gabael wept and blessed him, saying, "Good and generous man, son of a good and generous man who is just and charitable! May the Lord grant a heavenly blessing to you and your wife, and to your wife's father and mother. May God be praised, for I have now seen in Tobias the image of Tobit my cousin!"

Tobias and Sarah leave Media for Nineveh

10 Meanwhile, each and every day Tobit would keep count of how many days Tobias would need in order to travel and return. And when that number of days was past and his son hadn't arrived, [2]he said, "Perhaps he was kept there, or perhaps Gabael died, and no one gave him the money." [3]So he began to worry.

[4]Moreover, his wife Anna was saying,

[h]Or *with truth* [i]OL; LXX[2] omits *during the night.* [j]Or *and salvation*

"My child has perished and no longer remains among the living." She began to cry and mourn for her son, saying, [5]"What misery is mine, my child, light of my eyes, because I let you go away!"

[6]Tobit would reply, "Be quiet! Don't get so upset, my sister! He's fine! Surely something has distracted them there. Moreover, the man traveling with him is trustworthy and one of our relatives. Don't grieve about him, my sister. He'll get here soon."

[7]"You be quiet!" she would say. "Don't lie to me! My son has perished."

Daily she hurried out to scan the road on which her son had gone and she wouldn't be persuaded by anyone. When the sun set, she would come inside, mourning and weeping the whole night without sleeping.

When the fourteen days of the wedding feast were finished, which Raguel had sworn to celebrate for his daughter, Tobias came to him and said, "Send me off, for I know that my father and my mother don't believe they will ever see me again. So now, father, I ask you to send me off to go to my father. I have already let you know how I left him."

[8]Raguel said to Tobias, "Stay, my child. Stay with me. I'll send messengers to Tobit your father, and they will report to him about you."

[9]Tobias replied, "Absolutely not! I ask that you allow me to return to my father."

[10]So Raguel arose and gave to Tobias his wife Sarah and half of all his possessions, including servants and female servants, oxen and sheep, donkeys and camels, clothes, money, and furnishings. [11]He sent them away safely and said farewell to Tobias. "Good-bye, my son. Have a safe trip! May the Lord of heaven cause you and your wife Sarah to prosper! May I see your children before I die!"

[12]Raguel said to his daughter Sarah, "Go to your father-in-law, since from now on they are your parents, just as if they had conceived you. Go in peace, my daughter! May I hear a good report about you as long as I'm alive!" Having said good-bye, he allowed them to go.

Then Edna said to Tobias, "My child and dearly loved brother, may the Lord bring you back, and may I see your children while I'm still alive and those of my daughter before I die! In the Lord's presence I entrust my daughter into your care. Don't ever be a cause of grief to her, not as long as you live. Go in peace, my child! From now on I'm your mother, and Sarah is your sister. May all our ways prosper together all the days of our lives!" Then she kissed them both and sent them safely[k] on their way.

[13]So Tobias parted from Raguel in good health, rejoicing and praising the Lord of heaven and earth, the king of all, for making his journey so successful. Raphael said to Tobias, "You enjoyed this success that you might honor them all the days of their lives."[l]

Tobias returns to Nineveh

11 When they approached Kaserin, which is across from Nineveh, [2]Raphael said, "You know how we left your father. [3]Let's run ahead of your wife and get the house ready while the rest are coming."

[4]So they both went on together, and Raphael said, "Get the gallbladder ready." The dog came with them, still following behind.

[5]Now Anna was sitting down and watching the road that her son had taken. [6]When she saw him coming, she said to her husband,[m] "Look! Your son is coming, along with the man who went with him!"

[7]Before Tobias reached his father, Raphael said to him, "I know that his eyes will be opened. [8]Smear the fish's gall on his eyes. The medicine will make the white spots shrink and peel away from his eyes. Then your father will regain his sight and see the light."

[9]Anna jumped up and embraced her son, saying, "I see you, my child! Now I'm ready to die." She began to cry.

[k]Or *in good health* [l]Gk uncertain; OL *and he blessed Raguel and Anna (!) and said, "I have been enjoined by the Lord to honor you all the days of your lives."* [m]Vulg; LXX² *his father*

Tobit's blindness is healed

10Then Tobit rose and stumbled through
the courtyard door. Tobias went to him
11with the fish's gallbladder in his hand.
Tobias sprinkled[n] some of the gall into
his father's eyes, saying, "Don't be afraid,
Father!"[o] He poured out the medicine on
him and applied it. 12–13Then with both his
hands, he peeled off the white spots from
the corners of Tobit's eyes.

Tobit embraced him and began to cry,
saying, "I see you, my child and light of
my eyes! 14May God be praised, and may
his great name be praised, and may all his
holy angels be praised forever! May his
great name be upon us, and may all the angels be praised for all eternity! 15Though he
has disciplined me, look now! I see my son
Tobias!"

Then Tobit came in rejoicing and praising God at the top of his lungs.[p] Tobias told
his father that his trip had been successful:
that he had brought the money; that he had
taken Sarah, Raguel's daughter, as his wife;
and that, indeed, she was arriving and was
near the gate of Nineveh.

16Then Tobit went out to meet Tobias'
bride at the gate of Nineveh, rejoicing and
praising God. The people of Nineveh were
amazed when they saw him walking and
moving along with all his strength without
anyone leading him by the hand. 17Tobit declared to them that God had shown mercy
on him and opened his eyes. Then Tobit approached Sarah, his son Tobias' wife, and
he blessed her, saying, "May you come in
good health, my daughter; may your God
who has brought you to us be praised. May
your father be blessed, may my son Tobias
be blessed, and may you be blessed, my
daughter. Come into your house in good
health, in blessing and joy. Come in, my
daughter!"

On this day joy came to all the Jews who
were in Nineveh. 18Ahikar and Nadab, Tobit's nephews, were also there, rejoicing
with Tobit. And Tobias' wedding feast was
celebrated joyfully for seven days.[q]

The angel reveals his identity

12 When the wedding feast was over,
Tobit called his son Tobias to him and
said, "My child, make sure to give the man
who went with you his wages, and give him
a bonus as well."

2Tobias asked him, "Father, how much
in wages should I give him? I wouldn't lose
anything if I give him half my possessions,
which he brought back with me. 3After all, he
has guided me safely, healed my wife,
brought the money with me, and healed you.
How much of a bonus should I give him?"

4Tobit answered, "It is right, my son, for
him to receive half of everything that he
had when he came back."

5So Tobit called Raphael in and said,
"Take as your wages half of everything you
had when you came, and go in good health."

6Then Raphael spoke to them privately,
saying, "Praise God and tell all living beings
about the good things he has done for you,
praising and singing to his name. Make
God's words known in an honorable way
to everyone, and don't fail to acknowledge
him. 7It's good to hide a king's secret from
view, and good to reveal God's works and
bear witness to them with due respect.

"Do what's good, and evil won't overtake
you. 8Prayer with fasting[r] is good, and so is
giving to the poor with righteousness. The
possession of a little with righteousness is
better than much with injustice.[s] Giving
to the poor is better than storing up gold.
9Giving to the poor saves from death, and
it washes away every sin. Those who give
to the poor will feel satisfied with life, 10but
those who commit sin and injustice are
their own worst enemies.

11"I will tell you the whole truth, and I will
keep nothing secret from you. I have already
said to you, 'It's good to hide a king's secret
from view, and good to reveal God's works
in an honorable way.' 12So when you and
Sarah prayed, it was I who brought the record of your prayer into God's glorious presence, and likewise when you used to bury
the dead, 13and when you didn't hesitate to

[n]DSS Heb; LXX[2] *blew* [o]DSS Heb; LXX[2] *Take courage, Father!* [p]Gk *with his whole mouth* [q]OL, LXX[1]; LXX[2] omits *And . . . days.* OL adds *And he was given many gifts.* [r]OL, LXX[1]; LXX[2] *sincerity* [s]LXX[1]; LXX[2] *and giving to the poor with righteousness is better than the possession of much with injustice.*

get up and leave your dinner to go and bury
the corpse. 14 I was sent to test you then, and
at the same time God sent me to heal you
and Sarah, your son's bride.[t] 15 I am Raphael,
one of the seven angels who stand ready and
who enter the Lord's glorious presence."

16 The two were shocked. They fell on
their faces in fear. 17 But Raphael said to
them, "Don't be afraid; be at peace! Praise
God for all time! 18 While I was with you,
it wasn't because I was showing you any
favor but because of God's will. Praise him
all your days and sing to him! 19 You were
observing me, but[u] I wasn't eating or drinking[v] anything. Instead, you were seeing a
vision. 20 Now praise the Lord here on earth
and acknowledge God. Notice that I'm
ascending to the one who sent me. So record everything that has happened to you."
Then Raphael ascended.

21 Tobit and Tobias got up and were no
longer able to see him. 22 They continued to
praise and sing to God, and acknowledged
him for these great works of his. They marveled at[w] how one of God's angels had appeared to them.

Tobit's thanksgiving song

13 Then Tobit spoke and wrote down a
psalm in praise, saying,[x]

Bless the God who lives forever,
and bless his kingdom,
2 because he punishes and shows mercy.
He brings people[y] down to the
underworld below the earth,
and he himself raises people
up from great destruction.
What is there that escapes
from his hand?[z]
3 Bear witness to him, Israelites,
in the presence of the nations,
because he has scattered you
among them,
4 and he has shown you
his greatness there.
Bring him honor in the presence
of everything that lives,
because he is our Lord:
he himself is our God;
he himself is our father,
and he is God forever and always.
5 He will punish you for your unjust acts,
but he will also show all of you mercy
and gather you together[a]
out of all the nations among which
you have been scattered.
6 When you turn to him
with all your heart and your all being
to act sincerely before him,
then he will turn to you and never
hide his face from you again.
And now, look at what
he has done for you,
and acknowledge him
in everything you say.[b]
Praise the Lord of righteousness,
and exalt the king of the ages!
I will acknowledge him in the land
where I am a captive
and make known his power
and greatness to a sinful nation.[c]
So turn around, you sinners,
and act justly before him.
Who knows?
Perhaps he will want you back
and show you mercy.
7 My soul exalts my God,
the king of heaven,
and my soul will rejoice
all the days of my life.
8 Praise the Lord, all you chosen ones,
and let everyone
praise his greatness.
Let them speak through psalms,[d]
use your days for rejoicing,
and acknowledge him.
9 He has punished you, Jerusalem, holy city,
because of the deeds of your hands.[e]
10 Acknowledge the Lord in goodness,
and praise the Lord of ages!

[t] Gk *your bride* [u] LXX^{2} *that* [v] DSS Aram; LXX^{2} omits *or drinking*; OL *for you used to see me eating*; LXX^{1} *all those days I merely appeared to you without actually eating or drinking.* [w] DSS Heb; LXX^{2} omits *they marveled at.* [x] LXX^{2} omits *and . . . saying.* [y] Gk lacks *people.* [z] DSS Heb; LXX^{1,2} *nothing will escape his hand.* [a] OL; LXX^{2} omits *and . . . together*; Vulg *and he will save us on account of his mercy.* [b] Gk *with your whole mouth* [c] OL; LXX^{1} *to a nation of sinners* [d] DSS Heb; OL omits line. [e] OL; LXX^{1} reads for 13:7-9 *I will exalt my God, and my whole being will exalt the king of heaven and rejoice on account of his greatness.* (8) *Let all speak and bear witness to him in Jerusalem.* (9) *Jerusalem, holy city, he will punish you because of the deeds of your children, but he will again show mercy to the children of those who are righteous.*

Then[f] your dwelling will be rebuilt
for you with joy.
He will bring joy to
all the captives among you,
and he will love for all eternity
all those who have been subjugated.
11 A bright light will shine forth
into the farthest corners of the earth.
Many nations will come to you
from afar,
and inhabitants from all the ends
of the earth will come
to your holy name.
They will bear gifts in their hands
for the king of heaven.
Generation after generation
will give joyful worship to you
and honor your name forever and always.
12 May all who have despised you
and slandered you be cursed!
Cursed are all who hate you and all who
speak a harsh word against you.[g]
But all who revere you
will be blessed for eternity.
13 Rejoice then and be glad[h]
for the children of the righteous,
for all will be gathered together
and praise the eternal Lord.
14 Favored by God are those who love you,
favored are those who rejoice
when you are at peace,
and favored are all the people
who grieve when you are afflicted,
for they will rejoice over you
and will see all your joy forever.
15 I praise the Lord, the great king!
16 Jerusalem will be built as a city,
God's house for all ages to come.
I will be greatly favored
when the few remaining from
my offspring see your glory
and acknowledge the king of heaven!
The gates of Jerusalem will be built
with sapphire and emerald,
and all your walls
will be made of precious stone.
The towers of Jerusalem
will be built with gold,
and their fortifications will be made of
pure gold.
17 The streets of Jerusalem will be paved
with garnet and stone from Ophir.
18 And the gates of Jerusalem will burst
into song with joyful hymns,
and all her houses will shout out,
"Hallelujah!
May the God of Israel be praised,
and may those who bless the holy
name be blessed forever and always!"

Tobit's final instructions and death

14 Thus the words of Tobit's thanks came
to an end. He died in peace at the age
of 112 and was given an honorable burial
in Nineveh. 2 He was 62 years old when he
went blind, and after regaining his sight,
he lived in wealth and gave to the poor.
He continued to praise God and tell about
God's greatness.
3 Now when Tobit was dying, he summoned Tobias his son and seven grandsons[i]
and gave him instructions, saying, "My
child, take your children 4 and hurry away
to Media. I trust God's word that Nahum[j]
spoke about Nineveh; everything will come
true and happen to Assyria and Nineveh.
Indeed, everything that the prophets of
Israel sent by God have said will actually
occur. None of their words will fail, and everything will happen in its own time. Thus
it will be safer in Media than in Assyria and
Babylon. I know then and believe that everything that God has said will be accomplished and come true. Not a single detail of
what they have spoken will fail to happen.
All our relatives who dwell in the land of Israel will be scattered, and they will be taken
away from that good land into captivity.
The entire land of Israel will be deserted.
Samaria and Jerusalem will be deserted,
and after a while even God's house, still in
mourning, will be destroyed by fire.
5 "But God will have mercy on them
again. God will bring them back to the
land of Israel, and they will rebuild the
house, though not like the first one, until

[f] Gk *and*; OL *so that* [g] OL, cf DSS Heb; LXX² *May everyone be cursed who speaks a harsh word. All who destroy you and tear down your walls, who topple your towers and set your homes on fire, will be cursed.* [h] DSS Heb, OL, LXX¹; LXX² *Go then and be joyful.* [i] OL, cf DSS Aram; LXX¹ *six*; LXX² omits *and seven grandsons.* [j] OL *he* (God); LXX¹ *Jonah*

the appointed time has been fulfilled. Afterward, they will all return from the places where they are captives and build Jerusalem in grandeur. God's house will be built in it, just as Israel's prophets have predicted about it. [6]Then all the nations of the whole earth will turn and genuinely revere God. They will all leave behind their idols that have deceived them and led them into error. [7]They will praise the eternal God in righteousness. All the Israelites who are delivered in those days, who are genuinely mindful of God, will be gathered together. They will come to Jerusalem and will live forever in the land of Abraham in security, and it will be given to them. Those who genuinely love God will rejoice, while those who commit sin and injustice will be wiped out entirely from the land.

[8–9]"So now, my children, I'm giving you this instruction: Serve God with sincerity, and do what pleases him. Teach your children to do what is just and to give to the poor so that they will keep God ever in mind and praise his name at all times in sincerity and with all their strength.

"Now, my child, get out of Nineveh and don't stay here. [10]On the very day when you bury your mother beside me, don't stay within its borders another night. I see that a lot of iniquity and deception are practiced here, and its people have no sense of shame. My child, take note of what Nadab did to Ahikar, who brought him up. Was he not, even while alive, brought down into the earth? God paid back the dishonorable thing that he did in his presence: Ahikar came back into the light, while Nadab entered into eternal darkness, because he sought to kill Ahikar. By giving to the poor, he escaped the death trap that Nadab laid down for him. Nadab fell into that death trap instead, and it destroyed him.

[11]"Now then, my children, see what giving to the poor does and what injustice does. It kills! Now—my life is departing." And they laid him down on the bed. He died and was buried honorably.

Anna's and Tobias' deaths

[12]When his mother died, Tobias buried her next to his father. Then he and his wife headed off to Media and lived in Ecbatana with Raguel his father-in-law. [13]Tobias took care of them honorably and buried them in Ecbatana of Media. He inherited Raguel's house as well as his father Tobit's house. [14]Tobias died honorably at the age of 117 years. [15]Before his death, he saw and heard about the destruction of Nineveh. He saw the Ninevite captives, who had been taken prisoner by King Cyaxares of Media being led away to Media. So he praised God for everything that God had done to the Ninevites and Assyrians. Before dying, he rejoiced over Nineveh and praised the Lord God forever and always.

JUDITH

Nebuchadnezzar goes to war against Arphaxad

1 It was the twelfth year of the rule of Nebuchadnezzar, who ruled the Assyrians in the great city of Nineveh. In those days, Arphaxad ruled the Medes in Ecbatana. 2 Arphaxad built walls around Ecbatana from cut stones that measured four and a half feet wide and nine feet long. The walls he built were one hundred five feet high and seventy-five feet wide. 3 He built towers at the gates one hundred fifty feet high, with foundations that were ninety feet wide. 4 He made its gates one hundred five feet high and sixty feet wide so that his mighty armies could march out in formation. 5 In those days King Nebuchadnezzar fought against King Arphaxad in the great plain that is on the border with Ragau. 6 And many people joined him—everyone who lived in the highlands, everyone who lived along the Euphrates, the Tigris, the Hydaspes, and on the plain of Arioch, king of the Elymeans. Many nations joined forces with the Assyrians.[a]

Nebuchadnezzar's ultimatum

7 King Nebuchadnezzar of the Assyrians sent a message to everyone who lived in Persia, to everyone who lived in the west—those who lived in Cilicia, Damascus, Lebanon, and Anti-Lebanon, and everyone who lived along the seashore, 8 and those among the nations of Carmel and Gilead, and upper Galilee and the great plain of Esdraelon, 9 and everyone in Samaria and its cities, and beyond the Jordan as far as Jerusalem and Bethany and Chelous and Kadesh, and the river of Egypt, and Tahpanhes and Raamses, and all the land of Goshen, 10 even beyond Tanis and Memphis, and everyone who lived in Egypt as far away as the border of Ethiopia. 11 But the people who lived in all those lands ignored the orders of King Nebuchadnezzar of the Assyrians. They didn't join him in the war because they weren't afraid of him and considered him to be nothing more than one man. So they sent away his messengers empty-handed and in disgrace.

Arphaxad defeated

12 Nebuchadnezzar was very angry with the whole region. He swore by his throne and his kingdom that he would get revenge upon the entire region of Cilicia, Damascus, and Syria. He would kill them with his sword, as well as everyone living in Moab, including the children of Ammon, all of Judea, and everyone in Egypt, as far as the shores of the two seas. 13 In the seventeenth year of his rule he marched his armies against King Arphaxad and defeated him in battle. He overpowered all of Arphaxad's armies, all of his cavalry, and all of his chariots. 14 He gained control of Arphaxad's cities, marched as far as Ecbatana, captured its towers, looted the marketplace, and turned its glory into disgrace. 15 He captured Arphaxad in the mountains of Ragau and stabbed him with spears, putting an end to him forever. 16 Then he returned to Nineveh with all of his combined forces, a very large group of fighting men, where he and his army rested and feasted for one hundred twenty days.

Nebuchadnezzar plans his revenge

2 In the eighteenth year of his rule, on the twenty-second day of the first month, a discussion took place in the palace of King Nebuchadnezzar of the Assyrians, about how to take revenge upon the whole region as he had promised. 2 After calling together all his attendants and all his officials, he laid out before them his secret plan and established, with his own mouth, all the wickedness of the region. 3 They determined to destroy everyone who hadn't obeyed his command.[b]

4 When he finished laying out his plan, King Nebuchadnezzar of the Assyrians called for Holofernes, the general of his army and next in charge after the king

[a] Or *Chaldeans* [b] Or *the word of his mouth*

himself. The king said to him, 5“The great
king, the master of all the earth, says that
you will leave my presence and take with
you men who are sure of their own strength,
one hundred twenty thousand infantry and
twelve thousand cavalry. 6You will lead
them out against all the lands in the west
because they disobeyed my command.

7“You will tell the people to prepare earth
and water, for I’m coming out against them
in my rage, and I will cover the entire earth
with the feet of my army. I will hand them
over as spoil. 8Their wounded will fill up
their valleys and every brook and river will
be filled, overflowing with their dead. 9Then
I will lead them as prisoners to the ends of
the earth. 10You will go ahead of me to seize
all of their territory. If they surrender to
you, keep them for me until the day of their
punishment. 11But show no mercy to any
who continue to resist. Hand them over to
be killed and plundered. Do this wherever
you go. 12As I live, and by the power of my
kingdom, I have spoken, and I will do this
with my own hand. 13Now don’t neglect
even one of your master’s commands, but
carry them out exactly as I have ordered
you and without delay.”

Holofernes destroys the rebels

14Holofernes left the presence of his
master and called together all the leaders,
captains, and commanders of the Assyrian
army. 15He assembled the chosen men in
divisions as his master commanded him,
one hundred twenty thousand infantry and
twelve thousand cavalry armed with bows.
16He arranged them as a great army prepared for war. 17He also took a great many
camels, donkeys, and mules to carry their
baggage, and countless sheep, oxen, and
goats as provisions. 18He took enough food
for everyone, as well as a large quantity of
gold and silver from the king’s palace.

19Then he and his whole army set out
ahead of King Nebuchadnezzar to cover
the whole face of the earth to the west with
their chariots, cavalry, and chosen infantry.
20Joining them was an assorted group of
people, so many that they couldn’t be numbered. They were like swarms of locusts,
like the dust of the earth.

21After marching for three days from
Nineveh to the plain of Bectileth, they
camped across from Bectileth near the
mountain to the north of Upper Cilicia.
22From there Holofernes took his whole
army—the infantry, the cavalry, and his
chariots—and he went up into the highlands. 23He cut through Put and Lud, and
looted all the people of Rassis and the Ishmaelites along the edge of the desert to the
south of the Chelleans. 24He traveled along
the Euphrates, passing through Mesopotamia, and destroyed every strategic city
along the brook of Abron until he reached
the sea. 25He seized the territory of Cilicia,
killing everyone who resisted him. Then he
went to the region of Japheth, to the south
along the edge of Arabia. 26He surrounded
all of the Midianites, burned their tents,
and plundered their sheep pens. 27Then
he went down onto the plain of Damascus during the wheat harvest and burned
all their fields, destroyed their flocks and
herds, and sacked their cities. He emptied
their fields and killed all their young men
with the sword.

People on the seacoast surrender

28Fear and dread of Holofernes fell
upon the people living along the seacoast,
in Sidon and Tyre, those living in Sur and
Ocina, and those living in Jamnia. The
people who lived in Azotus and Ascalon
were especially afraid of him. 1So they sent
3 messengers to Holofernes, requesting
peace: 2“Look, we are the servants of
the Great King Nebuchadnezzar, and we
present ourselves to you. Do with us whatever you think is best. 3Look, here are our
homes and all of our property, all the wheat
fields and flocks and herds. All of our tents[c]
lie before you. Do with them as you think
is best. 4Our cities and the people who live
there are your slaves. Come down and deal
with them as you see fit.”

5The men brought this message to

[c]Or *the sheepfolds of our tents*

Holofernes. 6Then he and his army went down to the seacoast and placed guards in strategic cities and chose men from among them to form a reserve army. 7Everyone in the surrounding countryside welcomed him with wreaths, dancing, and drums. 8Yet he still demolished all their shrines[d] and cut down their sacred groves. He had been commanded to destroy all the gods of the land so that all the nations would worship only Nebuchadnezzar, and so that those of every language and tribe would call upon him as their god.

9Then Holofernes approached Esdraelon near Dothan, which is opposite the great ridge of Judea, 10and set up camp between Geba and Scythopolis. He stayed there one whole month, waiting for all of his army's baggage to arrive.

The Israelites prepare for war

4 The Israelites living in Judea heard about everything that Holofernes the general of King Nebuchadnezzar, of the Assyrians, had done to all the other nations and how he had looted and destroyed all of their temples. 2They were especially terrified of his coming and were anxious about the safety of Jerusalem and the temple of the Lord their God. 3They had just recently returned from captivity in exile. All the people of Judea had only just gathered together again, and the temple together with its altar and equipment had been newly dedicated to God after being polluted. 4They sent word, therefore, to all the regions of Samaria and to Kona, Beth-horon, Belmain, Jericho, and to Choba, Aesora, and the Salem Valley. 5Preparing for war, they occupied all the high hilltops, reinforced the villages on them, and stockpiled the food recently harvested from their fields.

6Then Joakim, the high priest in Jerusalem at that time, wrote to the residents of Bethulia and Betomasthaim, which is opposite Esdraelon, facing the plain near Dothan, 7telling them to guard the mountain passes because they were the entrance to Judea. It would be easy to stop anyone trying to enter through them, because the passages were narrow and allowed for only two men at the most to pass through. 8So the Israelites did everything that they were told to do by Joakim the high priest and the council of the Israelites that was meeting in Jerusalem.

The Israelites seek help from God

9Every man in Israel humbled himself and cried out earnestly to God. 10They, along with their wives, their children, and their cattle, and every immigrant, hired worker, and slave put funeral clothing around their waists. 11And all the Israelite men, women, and children living in Jerusalem fell on their faces before the temple, putting ashes on their heads and stretching out their funeral clothing before the Lord. 12They even laid funeral clothing around the altar. They earnestly cried out in unison to the God of Israel not to let their children and women be carried off like stolen goods, nor the cities they inherited to be destroyed and the sanctuary polluted and defiled—giving the nations something to gloat over.

13The Lord heard their cries and looked kindly on their troubles, for the people fasted many days throughout all Judea and in Jerusalem in front of the sanctuary of the Lord Almighty. 14The high priest Joakim and all of the priests who stood before the Lord ministering to the Lord, wearing funeral clothing around their waists, offered the daily entirely burned offerings along with the prayers and spontaneous gifts of the people. 15With ashes on their turbans, they continued to cry out to the Lord with all their strength to look with favor upon the whole house of Israel.

Israel's resistance reported

5 Holofernes the general of the Assyrian army was told that the Israelites, in preparation for war, had closed off the mountain passes, fortified all the high hilltops, and set up roadblocks in the plains. 2Filled with anger, he called together all the rulers of Moab, the commanders of

[d]Syr; LXX *borders*

Ammon, and all the governors of the coastlands. 3He said to them, "Tell me, you Canaanites: Who are these people living in the highlands? In what cities do they dwell? How big is their army? Where does their strength and power lie? Who is set up as their king, leading their army? 4And why—unlike all those living in the west—have they refused to come and meet me?"

Achior relates the history of Israel

5Then Achior the leader of all the Ammonites said to Holofernes, "Please listen to the word of your servant, my master, and I will tell you the truth about this people who live in the highlands near you. I'm your servant and won't lie to you. 6These people are descended from the Chaldeans. 7In the past they lived as strangers in Mesopotamia because they weren't willing to follow the gods of their ancestors in the land of Chaldea. 8They broke with the customs of their parents and worshipped the God of heaven, the God whom they knew. So their ancestors sent them away from the presence of their gods, and they fled to Mesopotamia, where they lived as strangers for a long time. 9Then their God commanded them to leave there and go to the land of Canaan. They settled there and became very rich in gold, silver, and cattle. 10But when a famine spread through the land of Canaan, they went down to live as strangers in Egypt, where there was food. While they were there, their numbers increased so that they couldn't be counted. 11Then the king of Egypt turned against them and took advantage of them, enslaving them and forcing them to make bricks. 12They cried out to their God, and he sent incurable plagues upon the entire land of Egypt, so that the Egyptians drove them out of their sight. 13God dried up the Red Sea[e] before the Israelites, 14and led them by way of Sinai and Kadesh-barnea. They drove out all of the inhabitants of the desert. 15They lived in the land of the Amorites and destroyed all the Heshbonites with their strength. Once they had crossed the Jordan, they took possession of all the highlands. 16They drove out the Canaanites, the Perizzites, the Jebusites, the Shechemites, and all the Gergesites, and they lived there for a long time.

17"As long as they didn't sin against their God, they prospered, because the God who hates wrongdoing was with them. 18But when they neglected the way God had laid out for them, they were greatly defeated in many battles and taken as prisoners to a foreign land. The temple of their God was burned to the ground, and their enemies took possession of their cities. 19But now they have turned back to their God, having returned from the place where they were scattered. They have occupied Jerusalem, where their sanctuary is, and settled in the highlands, because it was desolate. 20Now, my lord and master, if this people should slip up and sin against their God, and if we find out about their offense, then we can go up and defeat them. 21But if they as a nation aren't guilty, it is better that my master just pass them by, for their Lord and God will protect them, and we will become a joke throughout all the land."

22As Achior finished relating these things, all the people standing around in the tent began to grumble. Holofernes' officers and everyone from the seacoast and Moab said that Achior should be executed. 23They said, "We aren't afraid of the Israelites. Indeed, these people don't have the power or strength for making war. 24Therefore, Lord Holofernes, let's go up and devour them with your entire army."

Achior is handed over to the Israelites

6 When the commotion of the men who surrounded the council quieted down, Holofernes the general of the Assyrian army said to Achior and all the Moabites in the presence of all the assembled foreigners: 2"Who are you, Achior, and you soldiers-for-hire from Ephraim, that you prophesy to us as you have today and say that we shouldn't attack the Israelites because their God will protect them? Who is god except

[e]Traditionally *Reed Sea* in Heb

Nebuchadnezzar? He will send his power and destroy them from the earth, and their God won't rescue them. [3]We, on the other hand, are Nebuchadnezzar's servants and will destroy them as if they were only a single man. They won't be able to resist the power of our cavalry, [4]which will wipe them out. Their hills will be drunk with their blood, and their fields will be filled with their dead. Not even their footprints will survive! They will be completely destroyed. So says King Nebuchadnezzar, master of all the earth, for he has spoken and none of his words will fail.

[5]"But as for you, Achior, you Ammonite mercenary, what you've said today comes from your own wickedness. You won't see me again from now until the day I take revenge on this race that came out of Egypt. [6]And when I return, the sword of my army and the spear[f] of my servants will pierce through your ribs, and you will fall among their wounded. [7]Now my servants will deliver you to the highlands and leave you in one of the cities near the mountain passes. [8]You won't die until you are destroyed along with them. [9]If in your heart you really do hope that they won't be conquered, cheer up! But I promise you, nothing I have spoken will fail to happen."

[10]Then Holofernes ordered the slaves who were waiting on him in the tent to seize Achior, deliver him to Bethulia, and hand him over to the Israelites. [11]So the slaves seized him and led him out of the camp to the plain and from the plain to the highlands, and they arrived at the springs below Bethulia. [12]When the men of the city[g] saw them, they grabbed their weapons and ran out of the city to the hilltop. They kept them off the mountain pass by throwing stones at them with their slings. [13]By finding shelter below the hill, the Assyrians tied up Achior and left him at the bottom of the hill, and then returned to their master.

[14]When the Israelites came down from their city, they found Achior. They untied him and led him into Bethulia, and presented him to the rulers of their city. [15]In those days the rulers were Uzziah, Micah's son, from the tribe of Simeon, and Chabris, Gothoniel's son, and Charmis, Melchiel's son. [16]They called together all the elders of the city, and all their young men and women ran to the assembly. They set Achior in the middle of all their people, and Uzziah questioned him about what had happened. [17]He answered and told them what was said in Holofernes' council—both what he had said among the Assyrian commanders and what Holofernes had boasted he would do to the house of Israel.

[18]Then the people fell down and worshipped God. They cried out: [19]"Lord God of heaven, look at their arrogance and have mercy on our nation in its humble state. Look favorably this day upon those who have been dedicated to you." [20]They comforted Achior and praised him greatly. [21]Uzziah took him from the assembly to his own house and made a feast for the elders, and all through the night they called on Israel's God for help.

Holofernes lays siege to Bethulia

7 The next day Holofernes ordered his entire army and all his allies to break camp and move out against Bethulia, occupy the mountain passes, and engage the Israelites in battle. [2]So the entire force broke camp that day. The strength of their forces was one hundred seventy thousand infantry and twelve thousand cavalry, not including the baggage and the men handling it—a very great multitude. [3]They positioned themselves in the valley near Bethulia, beside the spring, and they spilled over Dothan as far as Balbaim, extending from Bethulia as far as Cyamon, which is opposite Esdraelon.

[4]When the Israelites saw the great multitude, they were extremely frightened and said to each other: "These people will now devour the whole countryside! Neither the highlands nor the valleys nor the foothills will be able to support their weight!" [5]Nevertheless, they each grabbed their weapons and, after lighting fires on their towers, remained on guard all that night.

[6]On the second day, Holofernes led out

[f]Syr; LXX *people* [g]LXX adds *on the top of the hill.*

his entire cavalry in full view of the Israelites who were in Bethulia. [7]He examined the approaches to their city, inspected the springs of water, seized them, and placed guards around them. Then he returned to the camp.

[8]Then all the rulers of the Edomites, all the leaders of the Moabites, and the commanders of the coastland came to him and said: [9]"May our master listen to our advice, and your army won't suffer any losses. [10]These people, the Israelites, don't rely on their spears but on the height of the hills where they live, because it isn't easy to climb up to their hilltops. [11]Therefore, Master, don't fight them in the usual way, and not one of your men will fall. [12]Instead, wait in your camp, keeping all the men of your army there, and let your servants seize the spring of water that flows out from the base of the hill, [13]because this is the water source for all those who live in Bethulia. Thirst will be their undoing, and it will force them to surrender their city. In the meantime, we and our people will go up to occupy the tops of the nearby hills and set up guard, to make sure that no man leaves the city. [14]Then they, their wives, and their children will wither with hunger in the streets where they live before a sword even comes near them. [15]Thus you will repay them with evil because they rebelled and didn't welcome you peacefully."

[16]Their plan pleased Holofernes and his advisors, and he directed them to do as they had said. [17]So the Ammonites together with five thousand Assyrians moved their camp to the valley and seized the Israelite water supply and springs. [18]Meanwhile, the Edomites and the Ammonites went up and camped in the highlands opposite Dothan and sent some of their men to the south and the east to Egrebeh, which is near Chusi, beside the Mochmur ravine. The rest of the Assyrian army camped on the plain and covered the whole countryside, and their tents and baggage stretched out over a vast encampment. They were indeed a very great multitude.

The Israelites begin to weaken

[19]The Israelites cried out to the Lord their God, for their spirits were low, because their enemies had completely surrounded them, and no escape was in sight.

[20]The whole Assyrian army remained around them, the infantry and chariots and cavalry, for thirty-four days until the water supplies of everyone who lived in Bethulia ran dry. [21]Their reservoirs were nearly empty, and because drinking water was being rationed, on no day did anyone have enough to drink. [22]Their children were discouraged, and the women and young men fainted from thirst in the city streets, collapsing at the entrance to the gates. They had no strength left.

[23]Then all the people—the young men, the women, and the children—gathered around Uzziah and the rulers of the city. They cried out before all the elders with a loud voice, saying: [24]"Let God judge between you and us! You have done us great wrong by not making peace with the Assyrians. [25]Now there's no one to help us. Instead, God has handed us over to them to be scattered before them in thirst and great destruction. [26]Call them, therefore, and surrender the whole city as plunder to the people of Holofernes and his army. [27]It would be better for us to be captured by them.[h] Even though we would become slaves, we would save our lives and not have to see with our own eyes the deaths of our little ones, nor watch our wives and children losing their lives. [28]We testify against you by heaven and earth and our God, the Lord of our ancestors, who punishes us for our sins and the sins of our ancestors, if you don't do everything we have spoken today."

[29]The whole congregation was wailing aloud together as they cried out to the Lord with a loud voice. [30]Uzziah said to them, "Be brave, brothers and sisters. Let's wait five more days for the Lord our God to come to our aid. Surely he won't abandon us in the end. [31]But if the days pass by and help hasn't arrived, I'll do as you have said."

[h]Other sources add *than to die by thirst.*

[32]Then he dismissed the people. They went back to their various posts on the walls and towers of the city, and Uzziah sent the women and children home. They were in great misery throughout the city.

Judith is introduced

8 Now in those days Judith heard about these things. She was the daughter of Merari son of Ox son of Joseph son of Oziel son of Elkiah son of Ananias son of Gideon son of Raphain son of Ahitub son of Elijah son of Hilkiah son of Eliab son of Nathanael son of Salamiel son of Sarasadai son of Israel. [2]Her husband Manasseh, who was from her tribe and her family, had died during the barley harvest. [3]He suffered heat stroke while he was overseeing the workers in the fields, and died in his bed in Bethulia, his hometown. They buried him with his ancestors in the field between Dothan and Balamon. [4]Judith had lived as a widow in her house for three years and four months. [5]She pitched a tent for herself on the roof of her house, put funeral clothing around her waist, and wore widow's clothing. [6]She fasted all the days of her widowhood except for the day before the Sabbath and the Sabbath itself, the day before the new moon, the day of the new moon, and the feasts and celebration days of the house of Israel. [7]She was very beautiful and lovely to stare at. Her husband Manasseh left her gold and silver, male and female slaves, cattle, and fields, which she continued to oversee. [8]And no one had a bad word to say about her, for she revered God greatly.

Judith speaks to the elders

[9]Judith heard the people's harsh words against the ruler, for they were growing weak from the lack of water. Judith also heard everything that Uzziah told them, how he promised to surrender the city to the Assyrians in five days. [10]So she sent her most trusted servant, the one who managed her property, to call for Uzziah, Chabris, and Charmis, the elders of her city. [11]When they came to her, she said to them:

"Listen to me, rulers of the inhabitants of Bethulia. What you have said to the people today isn't right. What is this promise you have made? How can you bargain with God by saying that you'll surrender the city to our enemies if the Lord doesn't send help within a certain time? [12]So who are you to test God today and set yourselves up in the place of God in the midst of the people? [13]You can question the Lord Almighty, but you won't ever learn anything. [14]You can't sound the depths of a person's heart or comprehend the thoughts of that person's mind. How then will you search out God, who made all these things? How will you understand God's mind and comprehend God's thoughts?

"No, brothers, don't provoke the Lord our God, [15]even if he chooses not to help us in the next five days. God has the power to visit us in however many days he wishes or to destroy us in front of our enemies. [16]Don't attempt to block the plans of the Lord our God. God isn't like a human being who can be argued with, a person who can be threatened. [17]Therefore, while we're waiting for his rescue, we should call upon him for help, and he will hear our voice if it pleases him. [18]There hasn't been in our generation, nor is there today, a tribe, a family, a people, or a city among us who worships gods made with human hands as happened in times past. [19]This is the reason why our ancestors were handed over to the sword and to plunder, and they suffered greatly in the presence of our enemies. [20]But we have known no other gods except him.

"Therefore, we hope that he won't forget about us and our generation. [21]If we are captured, so also will the rest of Judea be captured. Then our sanctuary will be plundered, and God will hold us responsible for its ruin with our own blood. [22]He will bring the murder of our families, the captivity of the land, and the destruction of our inheritance down upon our heads, wherever we may be enslaved among the nations. Those who purchase us as slaves will consider us offensive and disgraceful. [23]Our slavery won't bring us favor. Rather, the Lord our God will turn it into a disgrace.

[24]"Now, brothers, let us be an example to those whose lives depend on us. The

sanctuary, the temple, and the altar depend on us as well. 25In the midst of all this, let us give thanks to the Lord our God, who is testing us just as he did our ancestors. 26Remember what he did with Abraham, how he tested Isaac, and what happened to Jacob while he was in Mesopotamia of Syria, tending his uncle Laban's sheep? 27He hasn't yet tested us with fire, as he did them to examine their hearts, nor has he taken vengeance upon us. Rather, the Lord afflicts those close to him in order to warn them."

28Uzziah said to her: "You have spoken all this from a genuine heart, and no one disagrees with your words. 29Today isn't the first time you have demonstrated your wisdom. Since your earliest days, all the people have observed your insight and the goodness of your heart. 30But the people are very thirsty, and they strongly urged us to do what we promised them, and to make a solemn promise that we can't break. 31You are a godly woman. So pray for us, and the Lord will send rain to fill our reservoirs, and we won't die."

32Judith said to them: "Listen to me. I'm going to do something that will be remembered for generations to come. 33Stand at the gate tonight, and I, along with my most trusted servant, will go out. By the deadline you set for surrendering the city to our enemies, the Lord will deliver Israel by my hand. 34Don't ask what I will do. I won't tell you until I'm finished."

35Then Uzziah and the rulers said to her: "Go in peace, and may the Lord God go before you to take vengeance on our enemies." 36So they left the tent[i] and returned to their posts.

Judith prays to God

9 Judith fell on her face, put ashes on her head, and uncovered the funeral clothing she was wearing. Then, at the time when the evening incense was being offered in God's house in Jerusalem, Judith cried out to the Lord with a loud voice and said:

2"Lord, God of my ancestor Simeon, you put a sword into his hand to take revenge on the strangers who opened up a virgin's womb to pollute her, who exposed her thighs to shame her, and who violated her womb to disgrace her. You said that such a thing shouldn't happen, and yet they did it anyway. 3So you handed over their rulers to be murdered. You stained with blood the beds that were ashamed of their owners' deceit. You struck down slaves along with princes, even princes upon their thrones. 4You handed over their women as booty and their daughters as prisoners. You gave all of their property to be divided up among your dearly loved children, who burned with holy zeal for you and hated the pollution of their blood, and called on you for help. God, my God, also hear me—a widow. 5You did those things in the past, and other things before these, and other things that have happened since. You intended the current situation and the things yet to come. What you planned has occurred. 6The things you considered stood ready and said, 'Here we are!' Indeed, all your ways are prepared in advance, and your judgment is known ahead of time.

7"Look, the Assyrians have increased their army—priding themselves on their cavalry and horses, boasting in the weapons of their infantry, hoping in their shields, spears, bows, and slings. They don't know that you are the Lord who crushes wars. 8The Lord is your name. Destroy their strength with your might, and break their power in your anger. For they plan to defile your sanctuary, to pollute the dwelling[i] where your glorious name resides, and to break off the horns of your altar with a sword. 9Look at their arrogance, and send your wrath upon their heads. Give my hand, the hand of a widow, the strength to do what I have planned. 10By using my lying lips, strike down the slave along with the ruler, the ruler along with his servant. Break their pride by

[i]Or *tabernacle*

the hand of a woman. 11 Your might isn't in numbers, and your power isn't in the strength of a human being. But you are the God of the humble. You are a helper of the underdog, defender of the weak, protector of those who despair, savior of those without hope. 12 I beg you, God of my ancestor, God of Israel's inheritance, ruler of heaven and earth, creator of the waters, king of all your creation, hear my prayer! 13 Make my lying words a wound and a bruise to those who have planned cruel things against your covenant, your sacred temple, Mount Zion, and the house your children possess. 14 Make your whole nation and every tribe understand and know that you are God, the God of all power and might, and that there is no one else who protects the people of Israel except you."

Judith enters the Assyrian camp

10 When she had finished crying out to Israel's God and had finished saying all these things, 2 she stood up from where she was lying, called her closest servant, and went down into her house where she would spend her sabbaths and feast days. 3 She took off the funeral clothing she had been wearing and removed her widow's garments. Then she washed her body with water, put on some expensive perfume, combed her hair, tied a headband around her head, and put on one of the festive dresses she used to wear when her husband Manasseh was still alive. 4 She slipped sandals on her feet, and adorned herself with bracelets on her ankles and wrists, rings, earrings, and all her jewelry. She made herself very beautiful in order to attract the eyes of any man who might see her. 5 She gave her servant a container of wine and a flask of olive oil. She filled a bag with grain, a fig cake, and fine bread.[j] She wrapped this up along with her tableware and gave it to her servant to carry.

6 Then they left the city of Bethulia through the gate and found Uzziah standing there with Chabris and Charmis the city elders. 7 They saw that she had transformed her appearance and changed her clothing, and they were astonished by her beauty. They said to her: 8 "May the God of our ancestors grant you favor and accomplish your plans for the glory of the Israelites and the exaltation of Jerusalem." And she worshipped God.

9 Then she said to them: "Order the city gate to be opened for me, and I will go out to accomplish what you have spoken to me." Then they ordered the young men to open the gate for her just as she had said. 10 When they did so, Judith went out, along with her servant. The men of the city watched her until she went down the hill and passed through the valley, until they could no longer see her.

11 Judith and her female servant continued to go straight through the valley until an Assyrian patrol met them. 12 They arrested her and asked, "Who are your people? Where did you come from? And where are you going?"

She replied, "I'm a daughter of the Hebrews, and I'm escaping from them because they are about to be handed over to you to be consumed. 13 I'm going to see Holofernes the general of your army, to bring to him a true report of the situation. Furthermore, I will show him a road he can use to control all of the highlands without losing the life of even one of his men."

14 When the men heard her words and saw her face (for they found her very beautiful), they said to her, 15 "You have saved your own life by hurrying down here to see our master. Now go to his tent, and some of us will escort you to deliver you to him personally. 16 When you stand before him, don't let your heart be afraid. Tell him everything you just told us, and he'll treat you well."

Judith meets Holofernes

17 The patrol chose one hundred of their men to accompany Judith and her servant, and they led them to Holofernes' tent. 18 The soldiers in the camp turned out in droves, for word of her arrival had spread from tent to tent. So they came and stood around her

[j] Other sources add *and cheese*.

as she waited outside Holofernes' tent while the patrol told him about her. [19]They were amazed by her beauty and admired the Israelites because of her. They said to each other, "Who will underestimate these people when they have such women? It wouldn't be good to leave even one of their men alive, for they could beguile the whole world."

[20]Then Holofernes' bodyguards and his attendants went out and brought her into the tent. [21]Holofernes was relaxing on his bed under a canopy made from purple and gold cloth woven with emeralds and precious stones. [22]When they told him about her, he went out to the front of the tent with silver lamps being carried before him. [23]As Judith came before him and his servants, they were all amazed by the beauty of her face. She fell to the ground before him and paid him respect, but his slaves raised her up.

11 Holofernes said to her, "Take courage, woman, and don't let your heart be afraid. I've never harmed anyone who chose to serve Nebuchadnezzar king of all the earth. [2]Even now, if your people who live in the highlands hadn't insulted me, I wouldn't have raised my spear against them. But they have brought this on themselves. [3]Now tell me why you escaped from them and came to us. You're safe now, so take courage. You will live tonight and from now on. [4]No one will harm you. They will treat you well, just like all the slaves of my master King Nebuchadnezzar."

Judith's speech

[5]Judith answered him, "Listen to the words of your slave and let your servant woman speak in your presence. I won't lie to you this night, my master. [6]If you follow the instructions of your female servant, God will accomplish something great through you, and my master's plans won't fail. [7]As Nebuchadnezzar king of the whole earth lives, and as his power that sent you to direct every living being endures—not only do humans serve him because of you, but even the animals of the field, the cattle, and the birds in the sky live under Nebuchadnezzar and all his house because of your power. [8]We've heard about your wisdom and your cunning spirit, and it was reported throughout all the land that, out of the entire kingdom, you alone are dignified, capable in intellect, and wonderful in military campaigns. [9]We heard what Achior told your council and his advice. The men of Bethulia spared him, and he told us everything he said to you. [10]Now, my master and lord, don't ignore what he told you, but keep it in mind because it's all true. Our nation can't be punished, and the sword won't succeed against the Israelites, unless they have sinned against their God. [11]But now, death will soon fall upon them, so that my master won't end up frustrated and defeated. A sin has overtaken them, and they will anger their God when they do what is wrong. [12]Their food supply is almost used up, and water is scarce. So they have determined to kill their cattle and to consume everything that God, by his laws, has commanded them not to eat. [13]They have decided to eat the early produce from the grain and one-tenth of the wine and olive oil that were set apart and reserved for the priests who serve in Jerusalem in the presence of our God—things it isn't lawful for the people even to touch with their hands. [14]Since even the people who live in Jerusalem have been doing the same thing, they sent messengers there to bring back permission from the council. [15]Whenever they receive this communication and act on it, that very same day they will be handed over to you for destruction.

[16]"Therefore, when I your slave woman learned of all this, I escaped from them. God sent me to accomplish things with you that will amaze the whole world, wherever people hear about these things. [17]Your slave woman is pious, and I serve the God of heaven, day and night. So I will stay with you, my master, and each night your slave woman will go out to the valley and pray to God. He will tell me when the people have committed their sins. [18]I'll come and report to you, and you'll go out with your whole army, and none of them will be able to resist you. [19]Then I will lead you through Judea to Jerusalem, and I will set your throne in her midst. You will drive them out like sheep without a shep-

herd, and not even a dog will growl at you. This was predicted to me and announced to me, and I was sent to tell you."

[20]Everything she said pleased Holofernes and all his attendants. They wondered at her wisdom and said to her, [21]"There isn't another woman anywhere in the whole world as lovely in appearance or as wise in speech."

[22]Holofernes said to her, "God did well by sending you ahead of the people to strengthen our hands and to bring destruction on those who despise my master. [23]You are beautiful in appearance and impressive in speech. If you do as you have said, your God will be my God. You will live in the house of King Nebuchadnezzar, and your name will be known throughout the entire world."

12 Then he commanded them to bring her in to where his table was set, and he ordered them to place before her some of his own food and wine to drink.

[2]But Judith said, "I won't eat this, or it will be an offense. I'll have enough to eat from what I brought with me."

[3]Holofernes said to her, "But if your supply runs out, where can we get similar food for you, since there is no one else here from your nation?"

[4]Judith said to him, "As surely as you live, my master, your slave woman won't use up what she brought, before the Lord accomplishes by my hand what he has determined."

[5]Then Holofernes' attendants led her into the tent, and she slept there until the middle of the night. She got up when it was the first watch of the morning [6]and sent word to Holofernes, saying, "Please, my master, issue an order permitting your servant to go out and pray." [7]So Holofernes ordered his bodyguards not to stop her. She remained in the camp for three days. Each night she went out to the Bethulia Valley and bathed in the spring of water near the camp. [8]When she came up from the water, she would pray to the Lord God of Israel to direct her way so as to uplift the children of her[k] people. [9]Then she returned purified to the tent and remained there until evening time, when her food was brought to her.

Holofernes throws a banquet

[10]On the fourth day Holofernes hosted a party for his closest attendants and didn't send an invitation to anyone besides them. [11]He said to Bagoas the eunuch, who looked after his property, "Go and persuade the Hebrew woman who is in your care to come join us and eat and drink with us. [12]It would be a shame for us to let such a woman go without having sex with her. If we don't reel her in, she'll laugh at us."

[13]So Bagoas left Holofernes and went to her and said, "Don't let this pretty female servant delay in coming to my master, to be honored in his presence, to enjoy drinking wine with us, and to become today like one of the Assyrian women who are present in Nebuchadnezzar's house."

[14]Then Judith said to him, "Who am I to argue with my master? Whatever pleases him I will do quickly, and it will be my joy until the day I die." [15]She arose and dressed in all of her woman's adornments. Her servant went out with the sheepskins that Bagoas had given to her for daily use while reclining and eating, and spread these out on the floor in front of Holofernes.

[16]When Judith entered the tent and lay down, Holofernes' heart was struck by her, he was shaken to the core, and he was very eager to have sex with her. He had been looking for an opportunity to seduce her since the day when he first saw her. [17]So Holofernes said to her, "Please, join us for a drink and enjoy yourself with us."

[18]Judith said, "I will certainly drink, my master, because today is the best day of my life since the day I was born." [19]Then she ate and drank before him the food prepared by her servant. [20]Holofernes was very pleased with her, and he drank a large amount of wine, more than he had ever drunk in any single day since the day he was born.

Judith kills Holofernes

13 When evening came, his slaves left quickly, and Bagoas closed up the tent from the outside and shut out those who had been waiting on his master. They

[k]Other sources read *his*.

all went to bed, for they were exhausted because the party had lasted a long time. [2]Judith was left alone in the tent with Holofernes sprawled out on his bed, dead drunk.

[3]Now Judith told her servant to stand outside of the bedroom and to watch for her to come out just as she had done on other days. She said that she would be going out to pray, and she told Bagoas the same thing. [4]So everyone went out, and there was no one left with them in the bedroom, either small or great. Then Judith stood next to his bed and said in her heart, Lord, God of all power, look at this hour upon the work of my hands for the glory of Jerusalem. [5]Now is the time to help your inheritance and to accomplish my plans to destroy the enemies who have risen up against us.

[6]Then she went to the bedpost near Holofernes' head and took down his sword. [7]When she came closer to the bed, she grabbed the hair on his head and said, "Give me strength today, Lord God of Israel." [8]She struck him in the neck twice with all her might and cut off his head. [9]Then she rolled his body off the bed and pulled down the canopy from the rods. After a little while she went out and handed Holofernes' head to her servant, [10]who placed it in her food bag.

Judith and her servant escape to Bethulia

The two of them went out to pray, as was their habit. They walked through the camp, circled around the valley, went up the hill to Bethulia, and arrived at the city gates. [11]From a distance Judith called out to the guards at the gate, "Open, open the gate! God, our God, is with us and is still demonstrating strength in Israel and power against our enemies! He has done so even today!"

[12]When the people in her city heard her voice, they hurried down to the city gate and called together the elders of the city. [13]They all ran together, from the youngest to the oldest, because it seemed impossible that she had returned safely. They opened the gate and welcomed them. After lighting a fire to give some light, they stood around them. [14]Then Judith said to them in a loud voice, "Praise God! Praise, praise God, who hasn't taken his mercy away from the house of Israel! Rather, he has destroyed our enemies by my hand this very night!"

[15]And with that she pulled the head out of the bag. Showing it to them, she said, "Look! Here's the head of Holofernes, the general of the Assyrian army, and here too is the canopy under which he was lying in a drunken stupor. The Lord struck him down by the hand of a woman! [16]As the Lord lives, who protected me on my mission, I deceived him with my appearance in order to kill him. But he committed no sin with me, to pollute or shame me."

[17]Everyone was completely amazed and bowed down, worshipping God. They said with one voice, "Blessed are you, our God, who has disgraced the enemies of your people this day."

[18]Then Uzziah said to her, "Daughter, you are blessed by the Most High God above all other women on the earth. And blessed is the Lord God, who made the heavens and the earth, who guided you to cut off the head of our enemy's leader. [19]Your hope[1] will never fade away from the hearts of the people who remember God's strength. [20]May God make these things a continual source of honor for you and give you good things. You risked your own life for our nation when it was being oppressed, and you prevented our destruction by walking a straight line before our God."

And all the people said, "Amen, amen."

Judith's instructions for victory

14 Judith said to them, "Listen well, my people! Take this head and hang it from the highest spot on your city walls. [2]At daybreak, when the sun rises upon the earth, take up your weapons, each one of you, and let every capable man go outside of the city. Place a captain over them as if you are preparing to go down to the plain

[1]Other sources read *Praise of you.*

against the Assyrian guard. Only don't go
down. 3 Then they will take up their armor
and rush to their camp to wake up the
Assyrian army officers. They will run together to Holofernes' tent, but they won't
find him. Then fear will fall on them, and
they'll run from the sight of you. 4 You and
all those who live within the borders of
Israel will take chase and lay them low on
their way. 5 But before this, call Achior the
Ammonite to me so that he can see and recognize the man who insulted the house of
Israel and sent him to us as if to his death."

Achior converts

6 They brought Achior from Uzziah's
house. When he came and saw Holofernes'
head in the hand of one of the men at the
assembly of the people, he fainted and fell
on his face. 7 After they raised him up, he
threw himself at Judith's feet, bowed before her, and said, "Blessed are you in every
dwelling of Judah! In every nation, whoever
hears your name will be terrified. 8 Now tell
me what you've been doing during these
last few days." So Judith told him in the
presence of the people everything she had
done since the day she left, up to the time
she began talking to them.
9 When she finished speaking, the people
gave a great shout and made a joyful noise
in their city. 10 When Achior saw all that the
God of Israel had done, he believed in God
wholeheartedly. So he was circumcised and
joined the house of Israel, remaining until
this day.

The Assyrians discover Holofernes' body

11 At dawn they hung Holofernes' head
on the wall, and all the men took up their
weapons and went out in groups to the
mountain passes. 12 When the Assyrians
saw them, they sent word to their leaders,
who went to the captains, the commanders, and all the other officers. 13 They came
to Holofernes' tent and said to the one who
looked after his property, "Wake up our
master, for the slaves have become so bold
as to come down to make war with us—
only to be completely destroyed."
14 Then Bagoas went in and knocked at
the entrance to the tent, for he assumed
that Holofernes was sleeping with Judith.
15 But when there was no answer, he entered
the bedroom and found him sprawled on
the floor, dead, with his head missing. 16 He
cried out with a loud voice, weeping, groaning, and shouting, and he tore his clothes.
17 Next he went into the tent where Judith
had been staying. Not finding her, he ran
out to the people and shouted, 18 "The slaves
have made fools of us! One Hebrew woman
has brought shame upon the house of King
Nebuchadnezzar. Look, Holofernes is lying
on the ground and his head is gone!" 19 When
the leaders of the Assyrian army heard this
news, they tore their clothes. They were
greatly disturbed, and their shouts and
cries rang throughout the camp.

The Israelites defeat the Assyrians

15 When those who were still in their
tents heard all this, they were shocked
at what had happened. 2 They were overcome
with fear and trembling. Without waiting for
anyone else, each and every person rushed
out and fled in every direction across the
plain and into the highlands. 3 Even those
who were camped in the hills around Bethulia turned and fled. Then every Israelite man
capable of fighting rushed out upon them.
4 Uzziah sent messengers to Betomasthaim,
Choba, Kola, and all the regions of Israel,
announcing what had happened and saying
that everyone should rush out upon their
enemies to destroy them. 5 When the Israelites heard about it, they joined together,
fell upon their enemies, and cut them down
as far as Choba. Similarly, those from Jerusalem and everyone in the highlands also
came, for they had been told what happened in the enemy camp. The Gileadites
and the Galileans outflanked the Assyrians,
inflicting heavy losses as far as Damascus
and its territories. 6 Meanwhile, the rest of
the people living in Bethulia entered the
Assyrian camp and plundered it, and they
became extremely rich. 7 When the Israelites returned from the slaughter, they took
what was left behind. Even the villages
and farms in the highlands and the plain

received large portions of the spoils, because there was plenty to go around.

[8]At that time Joakim the high priest and the council of the Israelites who lived in Jerusalem came to witness the good things that the Lord had done for Israel, to see Judith, and to wish her well. [9]When they came to her, they joined together in blessing her and said, "You are the glory of Jerusalem; you are the great pride of Israel; you are the high honor of our nation. [10]You've done all these things with your own hand. You've done well for Israel, and God is pleased with these things. May you be forever blessed by the Lord Almighty!"

And all the people said, "Amen!"

[11]The people plundered the camp for thirty days, and they gave Holofernes' tent to Judith, including the silver plates, the beds, the bowls, and all of his furniture. She took it all, loaded up her mule, then hitched up her carts and filled them up as well.

[12]All the women of Israel gathered together to see her. They blessed her, and some performed a dance for her. Then Judith took wands wrapped with ivy in her hands and gave them to the women who were with her. [13]They all crowned themselves with wreaths woven from olive branches. Then she went before all the people in a dance, leading all the women. All the men of Israel followed, carrying their weapons, wearing wreaths of victory, and singing hymns. [14]Judith began this thanksgiving song in front of all Israel, and all the people enthusiastically sang this hymn.

Song of Judith

16 Judith said:
Begin to praise my God with drums;
sing to the Lord with cymbals.
Adapt a psalm for him;
lift up your praise,
and call upon his name.
[2]The Lord is a God who crushes wars.
He rescued me
from the hand of my oppressors,
and brought me into his camp
in the midst of his people.
[3]The Assyrian came from the mountains
in the north;
he came with tens of thousands
of his warriors;
their crowd of people
blocked the ravines,
and their cavalry covered the hills.
[4]He bragged that he would
burn my territory,
kill my young men with the sword,
throw my infants to the ground,
take my children as slaves,
and rape my virgins.
[5]But the Lord Almighty overthrew them
by the hand of a woman.[m]
[6]Their leader didn't fall to his knees
because of young men,
nor did the sons of the Titans
strike him down,
nor did the tall giants assault him.
But Judith, Merari's daughter,
paralyzed him with her beauty.
[7]She took off her widow's clothing
to lift up the oppressed in Israel.
She put perfume on her face,
[8]tied a headband around her hair,
and put on a linen gown to trick him.
[9]Her sandal captured his eyes;
her beauty captured his heart,
and the sword sliced through his neck.
[10]The Persians trembled at her daring,
and the Medes were troubled
by her boldness.
[11]Then my humbled ones shouted loudly;
my weak ones cried out,[n]
they lifted up their voices,
and the enemies were overthrown.
[12]Sons of mere girls stabbed them
and wounded them
like the children of deserters.
They perished before
my Lord's army.
[13]I will sing to my God a new song.
Lord, you are great and glorious,
marvelous in strength,
never to be outdone.
[14]May all of your creation serve you;
you spoke,
and they came into being.

[m]Other sources add *and brought them to shame.* [n]Other sources read *were afraid.*

You sent forth your spirit
and it shaped them;
there is no one
who can resist your voice.
15 The mountains will be shaken from their foundations with the waters;
rocks will melt like wax before you.
Yet you will show mercy
to those who fear you.
16 The pleasant fragrance of all offerings
is a small thing to you,
and the fat of all entirely burned offerings means even less to you.
But those who fear the Lord
are great forever.
17 How terrible it will be for those nations
who rise up against my people.
The Lord Almighty will take vengeance
upon them on the Judgment Day.
He will send fire and worms
into their flesh,
and they will weep forever with the pain.

End of Judith's life

18 When they arrived in Jerusalem, they
worshipped God. Once the people were
purified, they offered their entirely burned
offerings and spontaneous gifts. 19 Judith
dedicated all of Holofernes' belongings that
the people had given her. The canopy that
she herself had taken from his bedroom,
she dedicated as an offering to God. 20 The
people continued to celebrate in Jerusalem
for three months in front of the sanctuary.
And Judith remained with them.

21 At the end of these days, everyone
returned to their homes. Judith went
back to Bethulia and lived on her estate.
She was honored for the rest of her life
all throughout the land. 22 There were
many men who desired her, but no man
had relations with her all the rest of her
life after her husband Manasseh died and
was buried with his people. 23 She became
increasingly famous and grew old in her
husband's house, reaching the advanced
age of 105. She set her trusted servant
free and died in Bethulia. They buried her
in her husband Manasseh's cave, 24 and
the house of Israel mourned her for seven
days. Before she died, she divided her
property among all the relatives of Manasseh her husband, and among her own
relatives. 25 No one terrified the Israelites
again during Judith's lifetime or for a long
time after her death.

ESTHER (GREEK)

Addition A

Mordecai's dream

A In the second year of the rule of Artaxerxes the Great, on the first day of Nisan,[a] Mordecai had a dream. He was Jair's son, Shimei's grandson, and Kish's great-grandson, from the tribe of Benjamin. 2 He was a Jew living in the city of Susa, an important man serving in the royal court. 3 He was one of the prisoners of war whom King Nebuchadnezzar of Babylon had brought from Jerusalem along with Judea's King Jeconiah.

4 This was his dream:

Look! Noise and confusion, thunder and earthquake, and chaos on the earth.

5 Look! Two mighty dragons came forward, both ready to fight, and they roared loudly. 6 At their roar every nation got ready for battle, to make war on the righteous nation.

7 Look! A day of darkness and gloom, misery and suffering, distress and chaos on the earth. 8 The entire righteous nation was thrown into a state of panic, dreading the evil that was coming against them.[b] They expected to die. 9 So they cried out to God. Their cry was small at first, like a little spring, but soon it became loud as a mighty river, an abundance of water. 10 Then the sun with its light shone, the lowly were raised up high, and it devoured those who were held in honor. 11 Then Mordecai, who had this dream and saw what God had planned to do, woke up and kept it secret. He wished to examine it in every detail before nightfall.

12 Mordecai was relaxing in the courtyard with Gabatha and Tharra, two castrated men,[c] attendants of King Artaxerxes who were guarding the courtyard. 13 He overheard their plans and investigated their intentions. He learned that they were preparing to attack King Artaxerxes, so he informed the king about them. 14 The king questioned the two eunuchs. Once they had confessed, they were taken away[d] to be executed. 15 The king wrote these matters down so they would be remembered, and Mordecai also wrote about them. 16 The king appointed Mordecai to serve in the court and gave him gifts for his service. 17 But Haman, Hammedatha's son, a Bougaean who was greatly respected by the king, sought to injure Mordecai and his people for the sake of the king's two eunuchs.

Queen Vashti

1 After these events, this is what happened back during the rule of Artaxerxes, the very one who ruled as far as India, one hundred twenty-seven provinces in all. 2 At that time, Artaxerxes ruled the kingdom from his royal throne in the city of Susa. 3 In the third year of his rule he hosted a feast for all his officials and those from other nations. The leaders of Persia and Media attended, along with his provincial dignitaries and officials. 4 He showed off the awesome riches and beautiful treasures of his kingdom as a reflection of how great he was. The event lasted a long time—six whole months, to be exact! 5 When the days of the wedding feast were over, the king held a six-day wine festival for everyone who remained in the city. They all met in the walled garden of the royal palace. 6 White linen and cotton curtains hung from shining white and red-purple ropes tied to gold and silver rings and marble posts. Gold and silver couches sat on a mosaic floor made of emerald, marble, and mother-of-pearl. 7 The cups were made of gold and silver. There was a miniature cup made of ruby, worth 1,710,000

[a] March–April [b] Or *dreading their own evils* [c] Gk *eunuchs;* also throughout Esther [d] Gk *led off*

pounds of silver.[e] The king made sure there was plenty of the best wine, which he himself also drank. [8]The wine festival had no established rules, so the king ordered everyone serving wine in the palace to offer as much as each guest wanted. [9]At the same time, Queen Vashti also held a wine festival of her own for women in King Artaxerxes' palace.

[10]On the seventh day, when wine had put the king in high spirits, the king gave an order to Mehuman, Biztha, Harbonah, Bigtha, Abagtha, Zethar, and Carkass,[f] the seven eunuchs who served King Artaxerxes personally. [11]They were to bring Queen Vashti before him so that he could introduce her as queen and place the royal crown upon her head. She was gorgeous, and he wanted to show off her beauty to his important guests and to the general public. [12]But Queen Vashti refused to come with the eunuchs. The king was furious, boiling with anger. [13]So he said to his political advisors, "This is what Vashti has said, so give your ruling and make a decision on this situation." [14]So Arkesaeus, Sarsathaeus, and Malesear, the rulers of the Persians and Medes who were closest to the king and his chief advisors, came to him. [15]They told him what was appropriate, according to the law, since the queen had disobeyed the king's order.

[16]Then Memucan[g] spoke up in front of the king and the officials. "Queen Vashti," he said, "has done something wrong not merely to the king himself. She has also done wrong to all the officials and the governors of the king." [17](The king had reported to them the queen's words and how she defied the king.) "Just as she defied King Artaxerxes, [18]after today the important women of Persia and Media who hear about the queen's actions will dare to dishonor their own husbands. [19]Now, if the king likes this suggestion, he might send out a royal order and have it written into the laws of Persia and Media. It shouldn't be applied differently for anyone. It should say that the queen should never again be allowed to come before the king. It should also say that King Artaxerxes will give Vashti's royal place to someone better than she. [20]When the king's order becomes public through the whole empire, however he decides to put it, all women will treat their husbands properly, whether from an important family or not."

[21]The king liked the plan, as did the governors, and he did just what Memucan[h] said. [22]He sent written orders throughout the kingdom. Each country received the orders written in its own language. Fear and respect were established in every home.

Finding a new queen

2 Sometime later when King Artaxerxes was less angry, he no longer remembered Vashti, what she had done, or what he had decided about her. [2]His servants said, "Perhaps the king could have a search made for beautiful young women who haven't yet had sex with a man. [3]Perhaps the king could choose certain people in all the royal provinces to lead the search. They could bring all the beautiful young women together to the city of Susa, to the women's house, under the care of the king's eunuch in charge of the women, and supply them with bath oils and anything else they might need. [4]Perhaps the young woman who pleases you the most could take Vashti's place as queen." The king liked the plan and put it in place.

[5]Now there was a Jew in Susa whose name was Mordecai, Jair's son. He came from the family line of Shimei and Kish; he was a Benjaminite. [6]He had been taken into exile away from Jerusalem by King Nebuchadnezzar of Babylon. [7]Mordecai had a foster child named Esther, a daughter of his uncle Aminadab. When her parents died, Mordecai had taken her and raised her to become his wife. The girl was lovely to look at. [8]When the king's order and his new law became public, many young women were gathered into the city of Susa under the care of Hegai.[i] Esther was also taken to Hegai, the one in charge of the women.

[e]Gk *talantas* [f]Gk *Haman, Bazan, Tharra, Boraze, Zatholtha, Abataza, and Tharaba* [g]Gk *Mouchaios* [h]Gk *Mouchaios* [i]Gk *Gai*

[9]The young woman pleased him and won his kindness. He eagerly began her beauty treatments and gave her carefully chosen foods. He also gave her seven female servants selected from among the palace servants and provided well for her and her female servants in the women's house. [10]Esther hadn't told anyone her race or family background because Mordecai had ordered her not to. [11]Each day Mordecai walked back and forth along the wall in front of the women's house to learn how Esther was doing.

[12]According to the rules for women, there were twelve months of preparation before the time arrived for each young woman to see the king. She had six months of rubbing treatment with oil from myrrh and six months with fragrant oils and cosmetics. [13]So this is how the young woman would go to the king: They gave her anything that she asked to take with her from the women's house to the palace. [14]In the evening she would go in, and the next morning she would return to the second women's house under the care of Shaashgaz.[j] He was the king's eunuch in charge of the secondary wives. She would never go to the king again unless she was called by name. [15]The time came for Esther daughter of Aminadab, Mordecai's uncle, to go to the king. She didn't refuse anything that Hegai, the king's eunuch in charge of the women, told her to take along. Esther kept winning the favor of everyone who saw her.

[16]Esther went in to see King Artaxerxes in the twelfth month, the month of Adar,[k] in the seventh year of his rule. [17]The king fell in love with Esther, and she gained more favor than all the other young women. He placed the royal crown on her head. [18]The king sponsored a wine festival for all his political advisors and important officials for seven days. He celebrated Esther's wedding ceremony and canceled debts for many under his rule.

Mordecai saves the king

[19]Meanwhile, Mordecai was working for the king in the court. [20]Esther still wasn't telling anyone her family background and race. As Mordecai had ordered her, she continued to worship God and obey God's commands just as when she was in his care. Esther didn't change the way she lived. [21]But two eunuchs, the king's two main bodyguards, became very upset because Mordecai was promoted. They secretly planned to kill King Artaxerxes. [22]When Mordecai got wind of it, he reported it to Esther, who spoke to the king about the plan. [23]The king questioned the two men and hanged them. Then the king ordered a record of the event to be placed in the royal archive to remember Mordecai's loyalty.

Haman plans to destroy Mordecai

3 Sometime later, King Artaxerxes honored Haman, Hammedatha's son, a Bougaean, by promoting him above all other political advisors. [2]Everyone at the court would kneel and bow down to Haman because the king had so ordered. But Mordecai didn't kneel or bow down. [3]So the people at the king's court said to him, "Mordecai, why don't you obey the king's command?" [4]Day after day they tried to speak to him, but he didn't listen to them. So they let Haman know that Mordecai was disregarding the king's order. Earlier Mordecai had explained to them that he was a Jew. [5]When Haman himself became aware that Mordecai didn't kneel or bow down to him, he became very angry. [6]So he planned to wipe out all the Jews throughout the whole kingdom of Artaxerxes. [7]He made a decision in the twelfth year of Artaxerxes' rule, and he threw lots to determine the day and month on which Mordecai's people would be destroyed in a single day. The lot fell on the fourteenth[l] day of the twelfth month, that is, the month of Adar.[m]

[8]Then Haman said to King Artaxerxes, "A certain group of people exist in pockets among the other peoples throughout your kingdom. Their laws are different from those of everyone else, and they refuse to obey the king's laws. It is against the king's interests to put up with them any longer.

[j]Gk *Gai* [k]February–March [l]MT *thirteenth day* [m]February–March

[9]If the king wishes, perhaps a written order could be sent out that they should be destroyed, and I will contribute ten thousand big sacks[n] of silver to the king's treasury."
[10]The king removed his royal ring from his finger and handed it to Haman to put a seal on the orders he would write against the Jews. [11]The king said to Haman, "Keep the silver. Do as you wish to the people."
[12]So in the first month, on the thirteenth day, royal scribes were summoned to write down everything that Haman ordered in the name of King Artaxerxes. The orders were sent out to the governors and rulers in charge of each province, from India to Ethiopia, to one hundred twenty-seven regions in their own language. [13]Fast runners carried the order throughout Artaxerxes' kingdom. The order commanded people to wipe out all the Jews on a single day of the twelfth month, the month called Adar, and to seize their property.

Addition B

Artaxerxes' decree

B The following is a copy of the letter: The Great King Artaxerxes writes as follows to the governors of the one hundred twenty-seven provinces from India to Ethiopia, and to the district governors subject to them:

[2]I rule over many nations and have conquered the whole world. Nevertheless, I am not carelessly driven by power; rather, I have always conducted my affairs with moderation and gentleness. I am committed to providing a calm and stable environment for my subjects, and to restore the peace that all people desire. In this way, the kingdom will be at peace and safe for travel throughout its borders.

[3]I have, therefore, asked my advisors how this might be accomplished. Haman stands out among us for his moderation. He has demonstrated goodwill and firm loyalty in equal measure, and has attained the second highest honor in the kingdom. [4]He pointed out to us that there is a certain hostile group scattered among all the peoples of the world. These people are at odds with every nation because of their peculiar laws. They constantly ignore the king's decrees, so that the government, although well managed by us, is never secure. [5]We see that this nation stands alone in its constant hostility toward everyone. They follow a strange manner of life because of their law code, and they don't think well of our actions. They carry out the worst evils so that the kingdom is not at peace.

[6]We have therefore commanded that this people—pointed out to you in the letters written by Haman, who has been appointed over the government and is like a second father to us—should be destroyed one and all by the swords of their enemies, without pity or restraint. Their wives and children should also be destroyed, all on the fourteenth day of the twelfth month, Adar,[o] in the current year. [7]In this way, these people who have always been hostile to us, and remain so, will all go straight to the grave in a single day. Then our affairs will be stable and peaceful.

3 [14]Copies of the order were posted in each region, and the people were to be ready for this day. [15]The matter proceeded quickly and became public in the city of Susa almost immediately. While the king and Haman got drunk together, the city of Susa was full of unrest.

A crisis for the Jews

4 When Mordecai learned what was going on, he tore his clothes, dressed in mourning clothes, and put ashes on his head. Then he went out into the heart of the city and cried out loudly, "An innocent

[n]Gk *talantas* [o]February–March

nation is being destroyed." [2]He went only
as far as the king's gate and stood there because it was against the law for anyone to
pass through it wearing mourning clothes
and ashes. [3]In every region wherever the orders were posted, the Jews gave themselves
over to crying and wailing out loud. They
clothed themselves in mourning clothes
and ashes. [4]When Esther's female servants
and eunuchs came and told her, the queen
was noticeably shaken after hearing the
news. She sent someone to clothe Mordecai in regular clothes instead of mourning
clothes, but he couldn't be persuaded.

[5]Esther then sent for Hathach[p] the royal
eunuch who served her. She sent him to
discover from Mordecai what was going
on.[q] [7]Mordecai told him everything that
had happened, how Haman had promised
to contribute ten thousand sacks[r] of silver to the royal treasury in exchange for
the destruction of the Jews. [8]He also gave
Hathach a copy of the king's order made
public in Susa concerning the Jews' destruction so that Hathach could show it
to Esther. Through him, Mordecai ordered
her to go to the king to beg his help for her
people: "Remember your more humble days
when I raised you. Haman, a leader second
to the king, has spoken against us to put us
to death. Call on the Lord now and speak to
the king about us. Deliver us from death!"

[9]Hathach came back and told Esther
what Mordecai had said. [10]In reply Esther
ordered Hathach to tell Mordecai: [11]"All the
nations of the empire know that there is no
deliverance for the man or woman who approaches the king in the inner court without an invitation. Only the person to whom
the king holds out the gold scepter will be
safe. In my case, I haven't been called to
come to the king for the past thirty days."

[12]When Hathach told Esther's words
to Mordecai, [13]he responded, "Go and tell
Esther, 'Don't think for one minute that,
unlike all the other Jews, you alone will be
safe. [14]If you don't speak up at this very important time, relief and protection will appear for the Jews from another place, but
you and your family will die. Who knows?
Maybe it was for a moment like this that
you were made queen.'"

[15]Esther sent back word to Mordecai:
[16]"Go, gather all the Jews who are in Susa
and tell them to fast from eating for my
sake. They aren't to eat or drink anything
for three whole days, and I myself will do
the same, along with my female servants.
Then, even though it's against the law, I will
go to the king, even if it means my death."
[17]So Mordecai left and did exactly what Esther had ordered him.

Addition C

Mordecai and Esther pray for deliverance

C Then, calling to mind all the works
of the Lord, Mordecai pleaded
with the Lord, [2]saying, "Lord, Lord,
you are the king who rules over all
things. The universe is in your power,
and there is no one to stop you when
you have resolved to save Israel. [3]You
made the heavens and the earth, and
everything that is wonderful under
heaven. [4]You are Lord of all, and there
is no one who will oppose you, Lord.

[5]"You know all things. You know,
Lord, that it wasn't out of disrespect,
pride, or self-importance that I didn't
bow down before proud Haman. [6]To
save Israel, I would have been glad to
kiss the soles of his feet. [7]Rather, I
did this to avoid setting the honor of
any human being above God's honor.
I won't bow down before anyone except you, my Lord. Nor will I do these
things out of pride.

[8]"Now, Lord God, King, God of
Abraham, spare your people, because
the enemy seeks our ruin. They desire
to destroy what has been your possession from the beginning. [9]Don't
neglect your people, whom you deliv-

[p]Gk *Hachratheus* [q]4:6 is absent from the LXX; MT *Hathach went out to Mordecai, to the city square in front of the king's gate.* [r]Gk *talantas*

ered out of Egypt. [10]Listen to my appeal, and have mercy on the people who are your lot. Turn our mourning into feasting, that we might live and sing praises to your name, Lord. Don't silence the voice of those who praise you."

[11]And all Israel cried out with all their might, for death was staring right at them.

[12]Queen Esther, overcome by this contest with death, turned to the Lord for protection. [13]She took off her royal garments and put on mourning clothes. Instead of the finest spices, she smeared her head and body with ashes and dung, and humbled herself. Each place she had once joyfully beautified, she now covered with her tangled hair.

[14]Then she begged the Lord God of Israel: "My Lord, you alone are our king. Help me! I have no one to help me but you, [15]and I am in great danger now. [16]From my birth, Lord, I have heard how you chose Israel from among the rest of the nations, and our fathers from their ancestors, to be an everlasting inheritance. I have heard how you did for them all that you had promised. [17]But now we have sinned before you, and you have delivered us into the power of our enemies [18]because we worshipped their gods. You are just, Lord. [19]Yet the enemies weren't satisfied with our bitter slavery, so they shook hands with their idols in partnership. [20]They plan to set aside the promises you made, to rob you of your inheritance, to silence those who praise you, and to stamp out the honor of your temple and your altar. [21]They want to open the mouths of the nations to praise the wonderful deeds of useless idols[s] so that a human king might be honored forever.

[22]"Don't surrender your scepter, Lord, to things that don't exist. Don't let them mock our downfall. Instead, turn their scheme against them and make an example of the one who started this against us. [23]Remember us, Lord, and reveal yourself in the time of our distress. Give me courage, king of the gods and ruler of every authority. [24]When I speak, let my words be persuasive before the lion, and turn the king's heart to hatred toward the one who is fighting against us, to bring his life to an end along with those who agree with him. [25]Deliver us by your actions, and help me, I who am alone and have no one except you, Lord.

"You know all things. [26]You know that I hate the honor of those who don't follow your Law. I detest sharing the bed of this uncircumcised king or indeed of any foreigner. [27]You know my trouble: I hate the crown[t] that is on my head when I appear in public. I despise it as I would a menstrual rag, and I don't wear it when I am in private. [28]I, your servant, didn't dine at Haman's table. Nor did I honor the king's banquet or drink wine that had been offered to the gods. [29]From the day of my crowning until now, your servant hasn't had any joy except in you, Lord, God of Abraham. [30]All-powerful God, listen to the voice of those who despair, and deliver us from the hands of those who do wrong, and deliver me from my fear!"

Addition D

Esther appears before the king

D On the third day, when she had finished praying, she removed her mourning clothes and put on her royal robes. [2]Calling on the all-seeing God and savior, she appeared in full view of the court. She took along with her two female servants, [3]delicately leaning on the one, [4]while the other followed behind, carrying her train.

[s]Gk *useless things* [t]Or *symbol of my pride*

5 She was blushing in the full bloom of her beauty, and her face was delightfully cheerful, but her heart was tense with fear.

6 When she had passed through all the doors, she stood in the presence of the king. He was seated on his royal throne, clothed in all his majesty—all in gold and precious stones—and was terrifying. 7 He lifted his face, which blazed gloriously, about to explode in anger, and looked at her. The queen collapsed. Her color turned pale, and she fell face forward onto the female servant who was walking ahead of her.

8 Then God changed the king's spirit to tenderness. He leaped anxiously from his throne, and took her up in his arms until she was calm. He tried to comfort her with reassuring words, 9 saying to her: "What is it, Esther? I'm your brother.[u] Take heart! 10 You won't die, for the order only holds for ordinary people. 11 Come with me!" 12 He then lifted his gold scepter and placed it on her neck. He embraced her and said: "Speak to me."

13 She said to him, "I saw you, Master, as if you were one of God's angels, and my heart was struck with terror at the sight of your glory. 14 You inspire awe, Master, and your face is full of divine grace."[v] 15 But while she was speaking, she collapsed again. The king was distressed, and all his servants tried to comfort her.

Esther acts

5 3[w] Then the king said to her, "What is it, Queen Esther? What do you want? I'll give you anything—even half the kingdom."

4 Esther answered, "Today is a special day for me. If the king wishes, please come today with Haman for a special dinner that I will prepare."

5 "Hurry, get Haman," the king ordered, "so we can do what Esther says." So the king and Haman came to the dinner that Esther spoke about. 6 As they sipped wine, the king asked, "Now, what is it you wish, Queen Esther? I'll give it to you, if you just ask."

7 Esther answered, "This is my wish and this is what I want: 8 If I have pleased the king, I'd like the king and Haman to come tomorrow to another special dinner that I will prepare for them. Tomorrow I will prepare the same things."

Haman boasts, complains, and acts

9 That day Haman left the king's court happy and in high spirits. But when he saw Mordecai in the king's gate, Haman became very angry. 10 Haman went on home and called for his friends and his wife Zeresh. 11 Haman told them about his wealth and the great honor the king had given him by promoting him to the highest office in the kingdom. 12 Haman said, "Queen Esther has invited no one else but me to join the king for dinner, and I'm supposed to go tomorrow! 13 But none of this gives me any pleasure as long as I see Mordecai the Jew sitting at the king's gate."

14 So his wife Zeresh and all his friends told him, "Order preparation of a pole that is seventy-five feet high. In the morning, speak with the king about having Mordecai impaled on it. Then you can go with the king to the feast in a happy mood." Haman liked the idea and had the pole prepared.

Honor for Mordecai

6 That same night, the king simply couldn't sleep. He told his secretary to bring the official records and to read them to him. 2 He came across the report about Mordecai, how he had informed the king about the two royal eunuchs who were planning to assault the king while on guard duty. 3 "What did we do to honor or show favor to Mordecai for this?" the king asked.

His servants replied, "You have done nothing for him."

4 While the king was asking about the goodwill that Mordecai had displayed,

[u] *Brother* is a term of endearment between married couples. [v] Gk *full of graces* [w] In LXX, Addition D replaces Heb 5:1-2.

Haman showed up in the courtyard. The
king asked, "Who is that out in the courtyard?" Haman had come to speak with the
king about impaling Mordecai on the pole
that he had set up for him.
5 The king's servants answered, "That's
Haman standing out in the courtyard."
So the king said, "Call him in."
6 The king asked Haman, "What should
I do for a person whom I really want to
honor?"
Haman thought to himself, Whom would
the king really want to honor, except me?
7 So Haman said to the king, "Regarding the
person whom the king really wants to honor,
8 have your servants bring out a fine linen
robe that the king himself has worn and a
horse on which the king himself has ridden.
9 Have one of your most honored officials
place the robe upon the person whom the
king so loves, and let him help that person
mount the horse. Have him shout through
the city streets, 'This is what the king does
for the person the king honors!'"
10 Then the king said to Haman, "Do all
that you said for Mordecai the Jew who
serves at the king's gate. Don't leave out a
single thing that you've said!"
11 So Haman took the robe and the horse
and put the robe on Mordecai. He led him
on horseback through the city square,
shouting, "This is what the king does for
the person the king really wants to honor!"
12 Then Mordecai returned to the king's
gate, while Haman hurried home, feeling
great shame, his head covered. 13 Haman
told his wife Zeresh and his friends about
everything that had happened to him.
Both his friends[x] and his wife said to him,
"You've begun to lose face to Mordecai. If
Mordecai belongs to the Judean people, and
you've been humiliated before him, you will
indeed fall. You will never be able to hold
your own against him, because the living
God is with him."

Haman's demise

14 They were still discussing this with
him when several royal eunuchs arrived.
They quickly hurried Haman off to the feast
7 that Esther had prepared. 1 The king and
Haman came in for the banquet with
the queen. 2 On the second day of the party
the king said to Esther, "What's the reason
for all this? What's your purpose and your
request? What do you want? I'll do it for
you, even to the point of giving you half the
kingdom."
3 Esther answered, "If I please the king,
grant my request that my life be spared—
and my petition that the lives of my people
be spared as well. That's my desire, 4 because
my people and I have been sold out to be
killed, plundered, and enslaved—we and
our children, to become slaves and female
servants. The man who accuses us is not
worthy to be in the king's court!"
5 The king said, "Who is this person who
dares to do such a thing?"
6 Esther replied, "The enemy is this wicked
Haman!"
Haman was overcome with terror in the
presence of the king and the queen. 7 The
king got up and left the banquet for the palace garden, and Haman began to plead with
Queen Esther, because he found himself in
dire straits.
8 When the king returned from the palace
garden, Haman had thrown himself upon
the couch, pleading with the queen. The
king said, "Will you even molest the queen
in my own house?" Upon hearing this,
Haman turned his face away in shame.
9 Bugathan, one of the eunuchs, said to
the king, "Look, sir! Haman even prepared
a pole for Mordecai, the man who gave information about the king. It's standing at
Haman's house—seventy-five feet high."
"Crucify Haman on it!" the king ordered.
10 So they hanged Haman on the pole that
he had set up for Mordecai, and the king's
anger went away.

Esther acts again

8 That same day King Artaxerxes gave
Queen Esther everything that had belonged to Haman the accuser. Mordecai
was summoned before the king because

[x] LXX; MT *wise ones*

Esther told the king that he was family to her. 2The king took the royal ring that he had removed from Haman and gave it to Mordecai. Esther put Mordecai in charge of what Haman had owned.

3Esther spoke further to the king. She bowed at his feet and asked him to overturn the evil plot of Haman and whatever evils he planned to do to the Jews. 4The king held out the gold scepter to Esther, and she got up and stood before him. 5Esther said, "If the idea seems right to the king, and if I still please him, revoke the written decrees sent out by Haman, ordering the destruction of the Jews living within your kingdom. 6How can I bear to watch the terrible evil about to sweep over my people? And how can I be delivered from the destruction of my people?"

Mordecai writes a new law

7The king said to Esther, "I've given you everything Haman owned: I've favored you and impaled him on a pole because he planned to attack the Jews. 8Write to the Jews in the king's name whatever seems best to you and seal the letters with my royal ring. Anything written in the name of the king and sealed with the king's royal ring can't be revoked."

9So the royal scribes were summoned on the twenty-third day of the first month (that is, the month of Nisan[y]). They wrote out Mordecai's orders regarding the Jews for the officials and governors of the provinces from India to Cush, one hundred twenty-seven in all. They wrote in the alphabet of each province and in the language of each people. 10They wrote in the name of the king and sealed the order with the king's royal ring. They sent the letters out by messengers on horseback. 11Mordecai ordered the Jews to live according to their own laws and to defend themselves. He allowed them to do as they wished to their attackers and opponents 12throughout Artaxerxes' entire kingdom, on the thirteenth day of the twelfth month (that is, the month of Adar[z]).

Addition E

Artaxerxes' second decree

E Written below is a copy of the letter: The Great King Artaxerxes writes to the governors in the one hundred twenty-seven provinces from India to Ethiopia, and to those who are loyal to us. Greetings!

2Many people who are greatly honored, owing to the immense generosity of their benefactors, become overly ambitious. 3Not only do they seek to harm our subjects, but they even attempt to scheme against their own benefactors since they are unable to manage their pride. 4Not only do they fail to exhibit gratitude among people, but encouraged by the boasts of people who know nothing of goodness, they even suppose they will escape the judgment of the God who sees all. 5Often, many people in positions of authority become accessories to the shedding of innocent blood because of the influence of friends they trusted to manage their affairs. They suffer terrible misfortunes 6as a result of the cruel lies of those who take advantage of the innocent goodwill of rulers.

7Now this can be seen, not so much from older accounts that we have inherited but from what is right before your eyes.[a] Consider the ungodly things that have been done as a result of the corruption of those not worthy to hold power. 8But looking to the future, we will make the kingdom peaceful and secure for all people, 9adopting changes and settling those matters that come to our attention with a fair reply.

10As for Haman, Hammedatha's son, a Macedonian, he was not Persian, and was far removed from us in kindness. Yet we warmly welcomed him. 11He gained the goodwill that we have for every nation to such an extent that he was publicly proclaimed

[y]March–April [z]February–March [a]Or *alongside your feet*

our father. All worshipped him as
the person second only to the royal
throne. [12]But when he could no longer
hold his pride in check, he made it his
business to rob us of our leadership
and our life. [13]With lies and tricks he
called for the destruction of Mordecai, our savior and constant benefactor, and Esther, our innocent partner
in the kingdom, together with their
whole nation. [14]He thought that, by
these methods, he could render us
helpless and turn the Persian Empire
over to the Macedonians.

[15]But we find that the Jews, whom
this accursed man wanted to destroy,
are not criminals but are governed by
just laws. [16]They are children of the
most high, most great, living God, who
has guided the kingdom on the best
course for us and for our ancestors.

[17]You would do well, therefore, not
to act on the letters sent by Haman,
Hammedatha's son. [18]Haman, who devised these things, has been impaled
at the gates of Susa together with his
entire household. The God who holds
power over all things swiftly passed
this fair judgment on him. [19]And you
should publish a copy of this letter in
every place for all to see, to allow the
Jews to live by their own customs, [20]and
to assist them so that they can defend
themselves against their attackers in
the time of distress, on the thirteenth
day of the twelfth month, Adar.[b] [21]God,
who rules over all things, has made this
a joyous day for his chosen line rather
than one of destruction. [22]As for you,
celebrate it with feasting [23]as a special
holiday among your festivals so that it
will be for us, and for all Persians of
goodwill, a memorial of deliverance,
both now and in the future. But for
those who plot against us, it will be a
memorial of destruction. [24]Any city or
region, without exception, that does
not act accordingly will be completely
destroyed by fire and spear. This city
will be made uninhabitable not only to
humans but also to wild animals and
birds for all time.

8 [13]Let copies of this decree be displayed
publicly throughout the kingdom so
that all the Jews may be ready on this day
to do battle with their enemies. [14]Messen-
gers on horses sped off to do as the king
said, and the law was made public in the
city of Susa.

[15]Mordecai went out dressed in a royal
robe, wearing a gold crown and a turban
made of purple linen. The people of Susa
rejoiced to see him, [16]and light and gladness came to the Jews. [17]In every city and
region—wherever the king's order was
posted and the decree proclaimed—the
Jews had happiness and joy, feasts and a
holiday. Many of the Gentiles had themselves circumcised and became Jews themselves, out of fear of the Jews.

The fateful day

9 On the thirteenth day of the twelfth
month (that is, the month of Adar[c]), the
letters written by the king were to be enforced. [2]On that day, the Jews' enemies perished. Out of fear for the Jews, no one stood
in their way. [3]All the leaders of the provinces, the governors, and those in charge of
the king's business respected the Jews. They
were afraid of Mordecai, [4]because the king
decreed that Mordecai's name was to be honored throughout the kingdom.[d] [6]In the city
of Susa, the Jews killed five hundred people.
[7]They also killed Parshandatha, Dalphon,
Aspatha, [8]Poratha, Adalia, Aridatha, [9]Par-
mashta, Arisai, Aridai, and Vaizatha, [10]and
they plundered their houses. These were the
ten sons of Haman the enemy of the Jews,
the son of Hammedatha, a Bougaean.

[11]That same day, a report concerning the
number killed in Susa reached the king that
it was five hundred people. [12]So the king said
to Esther in the city of Susa, "The Jews have

[b]February–March [c]February–March [d]Some manuscripts add as 9:5 *The Jews struck all their enemies with sword blows, killing, and destruction. They did whatever they wanted with those who hated them.*

killed five hundred people in Susa as well as the ten sons of Haman. What have they done in the rest of the royal provinces? What more do you wish now? I'll give it to you."

13 Esther said to the king, "Give the Jews leave to do likewise tomorrow so that they may hang Haman's ten sons." 14 The king ordered that this be done, and he allowed the Jews in the city to hang the bodies of Haman's ten sons.

15 The Jews in Susa joined together again on the fourteenth day of Adar.[e] They killed three hundred people, but they didn't take anything the people owned. 16 The rest of the Jews throughout the kingdom also came together and helped each other. They found rest from their enemies, for they had destroyed fifteen thousand of them on the thirteenth of Adar, and they didn't take anything their enemies owned. 17 They rested on the fourteenth day of the same month. They spent it as a day of rest, with joy and celebration. 18 The Jews in Susa joined together for self-defense on the fourteenth day and did not rest. But they rested on the fifteenth day with joy and celebration. 19 This is why Jews out in the country celebrate the fourteenth of Adar as a holiday, sending gifts of food to their neighbors, but those who live in the big cities celebrate the fifteenth of Adar as a holiday, sending gifts of food to their neighbors.

The new holiday of Purim

20 Mordecai wrote these things down in a scroll and sent copies to the Jews throughout Artaxerxes' kingdom, both near and far away. 21 He made it a rule that Jews keep the fourteenth and fifteenth days of Adar[f] as special days each and every year. 22 They are the days on which the Jews found rest from their enemies. The whole of Adar, the month in which sadness was turned into joy and mournful weeping into a holiday, was to be celebrated as a special time for weddings, for parties, and for sending gifts of food to friends and to the poor.

23 The Jews accepted what Mordecai had written to them—24 how Haman, Hammedatha's son, the Macedonian, declared war on the Jews, how he made an edict and cast lots to destroy them, 25 and how he went to the king to have Mordecai impaled. But whatever evils Haman tried to bring upon the Jews turned back on him instead, and he and his sons ended up impaled. 26 This is why people call these days Purim—on account of the lots, which are called *purim* in the Hebrew language. Mordecai established the festival on the basis of the contents of this letter, on the basis of what the Jews suffered because of all these events, and on the basis of how it all turned out for them. 27 The Jews took it upon themselves, their children, grandchildren, and great-grandchildren, as well as all non-Jews who become Jews, to celebrate these two days[g] and never do otherwise. These days are a commemoration to be observed generation after generation in every city, land, and region. 28 These days of Purim will be observed for all time, and the events they commemorate will never be forgotten.

29 Queen Esther, Aminadab's daughter, along with Mordecai the Jew, wrote about all they had done and confirmed the letter about Purim.[h] 31 Mordecai and Queen Esther established this ruling by their own authority, at the same time that they secured their own well-being and plan.[i] 32 Esther's order made this decree binding for all time, and it was written down for posterity.

The fame of Artaxerxes and Mordecai

10 The king instituted a toll on all the land and sea routes of his kingdom.[j] 2 His strength and courage, wealth and fame, are all recorded for posterity in the official records of the Persian and Median kings.

3 Mordecai was second only to King Artaxerxes, and he was a great man in the kingdom. He was held in honor by all the Jews and loved by his whole nation for his conduct.

[e] February–March [f] February–March [g] Gk lacks *to celebrate these two days.* [h] 9:30 in Heb is omitted in Gk *Peaceful and honest words were sent by letter to every Jew in one hundred twenty-seven provinces in Ahasuerus' kingdom.* [i] Gk uncertain [j] Or *The king levied a tax on his kingdom by land and by sea.*

Addition F

Mordecai interprets his dream

F Mordecai said, "These things came from God. [2]I remember the dream that I had about these things. Not one aspect of it failed to come true. [3]There was the little spring that became a great river, and there were light and the sun and an abundance of water. The river is Esther, whom the king married and made queen. [4]The two dragons are Haman and myself. [5]The nations are those who gathered to wipe out the very name of the Jews.

[6]"As for my nation Israel, it cried out to God and was saved. The Lord saved his people, and the Lord delivered us from all these evils. God has done signs and great wonders that have not happened among the nations. [7]For this reason God made two lots, one to represent God's people and one to represent the nations. [8]These two lots came before God for the hour and season and day of decision in the presence of all the nations. [9]God remembered his people and affirmed the just cause of his inheritance.

[10]"The fourteenth and fifteenth days of the month of Adar[k] will be observed among God's people Israel with a gathering, with joy and feasting in the presence of God, from generation to generation forever."

[11]In the fourth year of the rule of Ptolemy and Cleopatra, Dositheus, who affirmed that he was a priest and Levite, and his son Ptolemy brought the preceding letter concerning Purim. They verified its genuineness. Lysimachus, Ptolemy's son, a resident of Jerusalem, translated the letter.

[k]February–March

WISDOM OF SOLOMON

Seek wisdom and justice

1 You who judge the earth, love what is right. Set your mind on the Lord in goodness. Seek him with a sincere heart.

2 Those who don't put the Lord to the test will find him. He makes himself known to those who trust him. 3 Perverse reasoning separates people from God. His power exposes the foolish people who test him.

4 Wisdom will avoid a deceptive soul that plans evil. Wisdom won't make her home in a body that is devoted to sin. 5 A holy, instructive spirit will flee deceit and leave when ignorant people start to plot. It is ashamed to be found in the presence of wrongdoing. 6 Wisdom is a spirit that wants only what is best for humans.

Wisdom won't declare blasphemers to be innocent because their own words convict them. God is witness to their thoughts. Truth examines the heart and hears what is said. 7 The Lord's Spirit fills the whole world. It holds everything together and knows what everyone says. 8 Therefore, those who utter unjust words don't escape notice. Justice will expose them and not pass them by. 9 A proper inquiry will be made into the plots of ungodly people. News of their words will reach the Lord and make their lawless deeds known. 10 God's ear listens intently to everything anyone says. Murmurings can't be kept secret for long. 11 So guard against useless murmuring. Keep your tongue from speaking ill. Everything you say has some consequence, even if you think that you are speaking in private. A lying mouth destroys the soul.

12 Don't seek death through the error of your ways. Don't invite destruction on yourself by what you do. 13 God didn't make death. God takes no delight in the ruin of anything that lives. 14 God created everything so that it might exist. The creative forces at work in the cosmos are life-giving. There is no destructive poison in them. The underworld[a] doesn't rule on earth. 15 Doing what is right means living forever.

The deluded reasoning of unrighteous people

16 In spite of this, the ungodly called out to death by what they did and said. Thinking that death was their friend, they lost their resolve and made a treaty with death. Let them have each other: death and the ungodly belong together!

2 By reasoning in their twisted way, the ungodly said: Our lives are short and painful. There is no antidote for death; no one has come back from the grave. 2 All of us came into being by chance. When our lives are over, it will be just as if we had never been. The breath in our nostrils is mere smoke. Reason is just a spark in the beating of our hearts. 3 When that spark is extinguished, the body will be turned into ashes. The spirit will evaporate into thin air. 4 Over time, our names will be forgotten. No one will remember our deeds. Our lives will pass away like the last wisps of a cloud. Our lives will be dispersed like a morning mist chased away by the sun and weighed down by the day's heat. 5 Our time here is like a shadow passing by. There's no turning back from death. It has been sealed, and no one will alter it.

6 Come then! Let's enjoy all the good things of life now. Let's enjoy creation to the fullest as we did in our youth. 7 Let's drink our fill of expensive wines and enjoy fine perfumes. Let's pluck every fresh blossom of spring as we pass by. 8 Let's crown ourselves with rosebuds before they wither. 9 Let's make sure that no meadow is left untouched by our high-spirited fun. Let's leave evidence everywhere that we made the most of this life, because this life is all we have.

10 Let's take advantage of the day laborer who does what's right. Let's not be afraid to abuse the widow. Let's show that we couldn't care less for the gray hair of our elders. 11 May strength be our only law and determine what's right, for it's clear to us that what is weak is worthless.

[a] Gk *Hades*

12 Let's lie in ambush for the one who does what is right. He's a nuisance to us. He always opposes our actions. He blames us because we have failed to keep the Law. He condemns us for turning our backs on our upbringing. 13 He boasts of his knowledge of God. He even calls himself the Lord's servant.[b] 14 He exposes our secret plans. Just to look at him makes us sick. 15 His life isn't like the lives of others. His ways are completely different. 16 He thinks we're frauds. He avoids us and our actions as though we're unclean. Instead, he blesses the final days of those who do what's right. He even boasts that God is his Father.

17 Let's see if his words are true. Let's put him to the extreme test and see what happens. 18 If this man who does the right thing is indeed God's son, then God will assist him. God will rescue him from the hand of those who oppress him. 19 Let's test him by assaulting and torturing him. Then we will know just how good he really is. Let's test his ability to endure pain. 20 Let's condemn him to a disgraceful death: according to him, God should show up to protect him.

21 This was how the ungodly reasoned, but they were mistaken. Their malice completely blinded them. 22 They didn't know of God's secret plan. They didn't hope for the reward that holiness brings. They didn't consider the prize they would win if they kept their whole beings free from stain. 23 God created humans to live forever. He made them as a perfect representation of his own unique identity. 24 Death entered the universe only through the devil's envy. Those who belong to the devil's party experience death.[c]

Reward and punishment after death

3 The souls of those who do what is right are in God's hand. They won't feel the pain of torment. 2 To those who don't know any better, it seems as if they have died. Their departure from this life was considered their misfortune. 3 Their leaving us seemed to be their destruction, but in reality they are at peace. 4 It may look to others as if they have been punished, but they have the hope of living forever. 5 They were disciplined a little, but they will be rewarded with abundant good things, because God tested them and found that they deserve to be with him. 6 He tested them like gold in the furnace; he accepted them like an entirely burned offering. 7 Then, when the time comes for judgment, the godly will burst forth and run about like fiery sparks among dry straw. 8 The godly will judge nations and hold power over peoples, even as the Lord will rule over them forever. 9 Those who trust in the Lord will know the truth. Those who are faithful will always be with him in love. Favor and mercy belong to the holy ones. God watches over God's chosen ones.

10 The ungodly will get what their evil thinking deserves. They had no regard for the one who did what was right, and instead, they rose up against the Lord. 11 Those who have contempt for wisdom and instruction will be miserable. People like this have no hope. Their work won't amount to anything. Their actions will be worthless. 12 They will marry foolish people. Their children will be wicked. Their whole family line will be cursed.

13 What a contrast to the barren woman who has kept herself pure, who hasn't had sex with another in sin. She will be blessed. When God inspects entire lives, she will bear fruit. 14 Even the eunuch who doesn't break the Law with his hands and doesn't think evil thoughts against the Lord will receive a precious gift for his fidelity and a special place in the Lord's temple. 15 Everyone will praise the fruit of good work. Good sense is a root that never withers.

16 The children of adulterers, however, will come to nothing. The seed of people who have sex with others in violation of the Law will dry up. 17 Even if they live to old age, their lives won't amount to anything. In their old age they will have no honor. 18 If they die young, they will have no hope or comfort on Judgment Day. 19 The family line of those who don't do what is right will come to a bad end.

[b] Or *child* [c] Or *continue to test people*

4 It's better to be virtuous but childless. Virtue is what will be remembered, and this means immortality. Virtue is recognized by both God and humans. [2]When humans find virtue in their midst, they imitate it. When virtue is gone, they long for its return. In every age, virtue wins the contest in which the prizes are unstained. It wears the victory crown, riding in triumph in the victory parade.

[3]Even though the ungodly have many children, none of them will amount to anything. Those bastard saplings will never put their roots down deep or be firmly established. [4]They may shoot up for a time like trees with lots of new branches, but the wind will shake them with ease, and the wind's force will uproot the whole tree. [5]Even before the twigs have had a chance to bud, they will be broken off. Their fruit will be useless. It will never ripen and be fit to eat. It'll be good for absolutely nothing. [6]Children born of sex outside the bounds of the Law will be called as witnesses against their parents' illicit sex when the time for judgment comes.

[7]In contrast, those who have done what is right will be at rest, even if they die an early death. [8]Those who are old aren't honorable simply because time has passed. Old age isn't measured by counting up a person's years. [9]Wisdom and a spotless life are the marks of honorable maturity. [10]There was a man who pleased God, was loved by God, and was taken away from living in the midst of sinners. [11]He was snatched away so that evil didn't pervert his understanding and so that deception didn't corrupt his soul. [12]Envying what is worthless blinds people to what is good, and the whirlwind of desire undermines an innocent mind.

[13]Those who do what's right are quickly perfected and live a long life in a short span of time. [14]They are whisked away from the wickedness that surrounds them because their whole beings are pleasing to the Lord. People around them see this, but they don't understand. It doesn't sink in [15]that favor and mercy rest upon God's chosen ones, and that God watches over his holy ones.

[16]So the dead who did what's right will condemn the ungodly who are still alive, and someone who dies young will condemn the old person who has lived many years but hasn't done what is right. [17]People will see the death of the wise, but they won't understand the Lord's purposes for them, nor to what end the Lord kept them safe. [18]Instead, they will laugh at what they see. In the end, however, the Lord will have the last laugh on them. [19]Then they will be no better than mutilated corpses, a scandal to the rest of the dead forever. The Lord will crush them and leave them lying there speechless. He will shake them from their very foundations. They will waste away in agony. Their memory will be wiped out. [20]They will cower when their sins are counted up. Their lawless deeds will witness against them and convict them.

Final judgment

5 Then the one who did do what was right will stand up with full confidence in the very midst of those who caused his suffering and made light of his distress. [2]They will tremble with great fear when they see him. They will be amazed that he was delivered so unexpectedly. [3]They will sing a different tune as they gasp and say to themselves: [4]He's the one we mocked?! He's the one we insulted? What idiots we were! We thought his life was madness and his death a disgrace. [5]How is it that he's now counted among God's children? How is it that he's now considered one of the saints?

[6]Clearly we were the ones who missed the way to truth. The light that would have shown us the right thing to do hasn't shone for us. That sun didn't rise upon us. [7]We got entangled in lawlessness and destruction. We wandered through desolate wildernesses. We didn't know the Lord's way.

[8]What good did our pride do us? What good were our wealth and pretension? [9]These things have all passed away like a shadow. They're gone like old news. [10]They're gone like a ship passing through a storm-tossed sea: once it has passed, it leaves no trace of its passing; its keel leaves no lasting mark on the waves. [11]That's all disappeared in the way a bird

flies through the air and leaves no hint of its path: it beats its wings against the thin air, dives with a rush, uses its wings to circle round—yet afterward there's no sign in the air that the bird was ever there. 12It's all vanished like an arrow that's shot at its target: the air opens up as the arrow flies through it but immediately closes up behind the arrow, and no one can detect any trace of the arrow's path.

13That's us! We came into being, and almost immediately afterward, we died. We leave behind no evidence of virtue. We squandered what we had in bad living.

14The ungodly person's hope disappears like dust in the wind, like frost that is stripped away and scattered by a mighty wind, like smoke that rises and is immediately dispersed by the wind, like the memory of a stranger who spends the day and then is gone.

15In contrast, those who do the right thing live forever. Their reward comes from the Lord. The Most High takes care of them. 16For this reason, they will receive a lovely palace and a beautiful royal crown from the Lord himself. With his right hand he shelters them and with his right arm he protects them. 17For his weapon, the Lord will take his zeal. He will arm creation itself for the fight against his foes. 18He will put on justice as his body armor. He will strap on honest judgment as his helmet. 19He will take up holiness as a shield that can never be beaten down. 20He will sharpen his fierce anger into a sword.

The cosmos itself will join with him to defeat those who have wandered from reason. 21Shafts of lightning will strike with precision. They will leap from the clouds as if shot from a well-bent bow, and they will hit their target every time. 22Showers of hail will rain down upon them as if shot from a catapult that never stops firing. The sea's waters will rage against them, and rivers will rise up and wash over them in a fury. 23A powerful wind will blow against them and like a whirlwind, it will scatter them. Lawlessness will turn the whole earth into a desert. Evildoing will pull down the thrones of the powerful.

Rulers should seek wisdom and righteousness

6 So then listen, you rulers, and understand. Learn, you who judge the far reaches of the earth. 2Pay attention, you who have power over multitudes, you who take pride in having power over throngs of nations.

3The Lord gave you authority to rule. The Most High gave you your power. He will watch carefully what you do and examine everything that you are planning. 4You are merely stewards of his kingdom. If you don't judge rightly, if you don't keep the Law, or if you don't act according to God's plan, 5then he'll fall upon you very suddenly and very terribly. Judgment falls hard on those in high places. 6Those who aren't important may be pardoned out of compassion, but the powerful will be powerfully examined. 7The ruler of all won't back down from anyone. He won't show any special consideration to someone whom others consider great. The ruler of all made both the small and the great, and he regards them all in the same way. 8But a stern judgment will fall upon the ruthless.

9Yes, I'm speaking to you who rule with unbridled might so that you may learn wisdom and avoid going astray. 10Those who have treasured holy things in a holy way will themselves be made holy. Those who have been instructed in holy things will be able to offer a defense for what they have done. 11So desire my words with all your heart. Commit yourself to them, and you will be educated.

12Wisdom is bright and unfading. She readily appears to those who love her. She's found by those who keep seeking after her. 13She makes herself known even in advance to those who desire her with all their hearts. 14Someone who awakens before dawn to look for her will find her already sitting at the door. 15Taking wisdom to heart is the way to bring your thinking to maturity. The one who can't sleep at night because he's consumed with thinking about her will soon be free from worry.

16She herself goes about looking for those who are worthy of her. She graciously makes herself known to them as they travel. She comes to them in each of the ideas that they think. 17The real beginning of wisdom is to desire instruction with all your heart. 18Love for instruction expresses itself in careful reflection. If you love Wisdom, you will keep her laws. If you are attentive to her laws, you can be assured that you will live forever. 19If you live forever, you will be near to God. 20If you desire wisdom with all your heart, you will know what good leadership is. 21So if you, who take charge over peoples, want to keep enjoying the thrones and symbols of power that you presently possess, honor wisdom so that you may rule forever.

22I'll tell you what Wisdom is and how she came into being. I won't hide these secret matters from you. I'll show you her very origins. I'll lay all that I know of her in the open. I won't skip past the truth. 23I won't be selfish or allow jealousy to make me keep this to myself, for jealousy has nothing to do with wisdom. 24The more wise people there are in the world, the more likely it is that the world will be saved. A sensible ruler gives stability to his people. 25So it will do you good to be instructed by my words.

The ruler's need for wisdom

7 I'm just a human like everyone else. I'm a descendant of the first person who was created out of earth. My flesh was molded into shape during the time that I was in my mother's womb. 2Over the course of ten months, I took shape from her blood, built up out of a man's seed and a night of pleasure. 3When I was born, I gulped in the same air as everyone else. I dropped out onto the same earth that all people share. I let out my first cry that was just like the sound anyone else makes. 4I was nurtured by snug clothes and good care. 5No king has ever begun life any differently. 6There's only one way into life for everyone, and only one way out as well.

7Because of this, I prayed, and the ability to reason wisely was given to me. I called out, and Wisdom's spirit came to me. 8I chose wisdom above all the symbols of royalty and over any throne. In comparison to her, I counted riches as nothing. 9She was more precious to me than even a priceless jewel, since all the gold in the world would be nothing more than a little sand before her. All the silver would be just like clay in her presence. 10I loved her more than health or beauty. I chose her above sunlight itself, for her brightness never sets.

11Yet then I found that every other good thing also came with her, for in her hands were countless riches. 12I rejoiced in all this because Wisdom brings them all in tow. I didn't know that she had given birth to them. 13I learned in innocence, and I don't begrudge sharing it with you. I won't conceal her riches. 14She's a never-ending treasure for humans. Those who possess her are ready to be God's friends, commended for the gifts that come from instruction.

Wisdom's all-embracing excellence

15I pray that God will allow me to speak knowledgeably and to ponder well what God has taught me. God himself is the guide even of Wisdom, and God keeps those who already possess wisdom on the right course. 16We're in God's hands, as are our words, all our reasoning, and all our practical knowledge. 17He's given me accurate knowledge of all that is—of how the world is made and holds together, and of the forces at work in the world's essential elements. 18He's given me knowledge of the beginning, end, and middle of time; of the alternation of the solstices and the changes of seasons; 19of the cycle of the year and the positions of the stars; 20of the nature of animals, the temperaments of beasts, the extraordinary powers of spirits, the thoughts of humans, the different types of plants, and the healing powers of roots. 21I now know everything, visible and hidden, 22for Wisdom, the designer of everything that is, has taught me.

Her spirit is insightful, holy, unique, diverse, refined, kinetic, pure, spotless, transparent, harmless, delighting in what is good, sharp, 23unstoppable, overflowing with kindness, delighting in humans, steadfast, secure, not anxious, all-powerful, and all-seeing. Her spirit can be found in every spirit that is perceptive, pure, and refined.

24Wisdom is more mobile than anything
that moves. She pervades and embraces
everything because she is so pure. 25Wis-
dom is the warm breath of God's power.
She pours forth from the all-powerful
one's pure glory. Therefore, nothing impure
can enter her. 26She's the brightness that
shines forth from eternal light. She's a mirror that flawlessly reflects God's activity.
She's the perfect image of God's goodness.
27She can do anything, since she's one and
undivided. She never changes, and yet she
makes everything new. Generation after
generation, she enters souls and shapes
them into God's friends and prophets.
28God doesn't love anything as much as
people who make their home with Wisdom.
29She's more splendid than the sun and
more wonderful than the arrangement of
the stars. She's even brighter than sunlight,
30for night follows day, but evil can never
8 overcome Wisdom. 1She stands strong
from one end of the world to the other.
She is a marvelous governor over everything in between.

Solomon's love for wisdom

2From my youth, I loved her and sought
her out. I sought to make her my bride. I
burned within for her beauty. 3She honors her dignified birth by sharing her life
with God. The master of all loves her. 4She
knows God's secret ways and is a partner
in God's works. 5If wealth is a possession
to be desired with all one's heart, what
could be wealthier than Wisdom, who has
given form to everything? 6If thoughtful
planning accomplishes things, who could
possibly be wiser than she who designed
everything that is? 7If anyone loves to do
what is right, laboring with Wisdom will
produce every virtue. She trains persons
to learn moderation and practical wisdom.
She teaches them what is right and how to
exercise courage. Nothing is more advantageous than these when it comes to human
existence. 8If someone wants to gain experience, she's the one to teach it: She knows
what has been from the beginning and
sees what is yet to come. She can figure out
puzzles of language and resolve riddles. She
knows beforehand what signs and wonders
point to. She knows what will happen in
time and during the seasons of the year.

9For these reasons, I decided to bring
her to live with me. I knew that she would
be a good counselor. I knew that she would
be able to offer me advice when there were
concerns or suffering. 10I knew that crowds
would honor me because of her and that my
elders would esteem me, even though I was
just a young man. 11I knew that people would
say that I had good judgment because of
her. I knew that other leaders would admire
me. 12I knew that they would wait for me to
speak if I had not yet spoken, and that they
would praise what I had said after I had spoken. I also knew that, if I did have more to
say, they would put their hands over their
mouths until I had finished speaking. 13I
knew that because of her, I would gain everlasting life and that I would leave behind an
everlasting memorial for those who would
come after me. 14I knew that because of her,
I would be able to govern nations and that
the peoples of the world would obey me. 15I
knew that even terrible tyrants would fear
me once they had heard me. I knew that the
common people would see that I was a good
king and a courageous warrior. 16I knew
that when I entered my house, she would be
there, and I would be able to rest easy, for
life with her is sweet. I knew that sharing
my life with her would mean that I would
live a pain-free life, one full of celebration
and joy.

Solomon's prayer for wisdom

17I thought all these things to myself. I
reflected on them in my heart. I thought: If
immortality is to be found by becoming part
of Wisdom's family, 18if dignified delight is
to be found in being Wisdom's friend, if
unending wealth comes through the works
of her hands, if practical intelligence comes
through being well acquainted with her, if
fame comes through conversing with her,
then I will definitely make her mine. 19I was
a clever child and had been born with a dignified attitude—20or, better said, because
my soul was already dignified, it entered a
spotless body.

21 But I knew that there was no way I
could possess Wisdom unless God gave her
to me (and to know this was also a mark of
intelligence!). So I came before the Lord and
pleaded with him. I said with all my heart:

9 God of our ancestors and Lord of
mercy, you made everything by your
word. 2 You gave shape to humanity
through your wisdom so that humans
might rule the creatures that you made,
3 so that they might govern the world by
holiness and by doing what was right,
and so that they might be honest in
passing judgment. 4 Give me Wisdom,
who sits enthroned beside you. Don't
reject me, out of all your servants. 5 I'm
your servant and the son of one of your
servants. I'm just a weak human who
will live a short life as other humans do.
And I'm the least of all humans when it
comes to understanding judgment and
laws properly. 6 Indeed, even if somebody might be thought of as perfect,
this person is nothing without your wisdom. 7 But you chose me to be king over
your people and to be a judge of your
sons and daughters. 8 You told me to
construct a temple on your holy mountain and an altar in the city in which you
had taken up residence. It was to be a
copy of the holy tent that you had prepared from the beginning.

9 You have Wisdom with you. She
knows all your works. She was present
with you when you were making the
world. She knows what pleases you. She
knows what someone needs to do to follow your commandments. 10 Send her
out to me from your holy heavens. Send
her from your glorious throne so that
she may labor with me here and that I
may learn what is pleasing to you. 11 She
knows and understands everything.
She'll guide me wisely in all that I do.
Her great honor will guard me. 12 Then
my works will be acceptable. Then I'll be
able to judge your people rightly. Then
I'll be worthy of my father's great throne.

13 What human will ever know God's
counsel? Who can understand what
God wishes? 14 Mortals have only a weak
capacity for reasoning, and our intentions are uncertain. 15 The body that is
headed for destruction weighs down
the soul. Our earthly container burdens
our minds with cares and concerns.
16 At best, we can barely draw correct
inferences concerning things we find
on earth. Only after much thought and
work do we come to understand what
is right in front of us. Who among us
then is able to examine heavenly things?
17 Who's ever known your counsel, unless
you gave them wisdom and sent down
your Holy Spirit from on high? 18 Only
then did your ways become clear to us
on earth. Only then were humans able
to learn what pleases you, and were thus
rescued by wisdom.

Wisdom's purpose in history

10 Wisdom kept watch over the world's
first-formed parent, when he alone
had been created. She delivered him from
his grave misstep. 2 Wisdom gave him the
strength to have dominion over everything.

3 When a wicked man disregarded Wisdom in his anger, he perished along with his
desire to murder his brother. 4 Because of
him, the earth was flooded. Wisdom again
came to the rescue. She took a man who did
what was right and steered him straight on
a vessel made of cheap wood.

5 When the peoples of the world were
thrown into confusion by the combined
force of their wickedness, Wisdom found
one who did what was right and kept him
pure before God. She even kept him strong
when he would have been swayed by compassion for his child.

6 When the ungodly were about to be
wiped out, Wisdom saved a man who did
what was right. He was able to flee from
the fire that descended on the five cities. 7 A
smoking wasteland is all that remains, witnessing to their wickedness. Plants there
never produce fully formed fruit. A pillar
of salt still stands there as a reminder of a
faithless being. 8 By trying to get along without Wisdom, they didn't recognize what
was good. In doing so, they left a lasting
memorial of their foolishness for everyone

to see. They were unable to hide the things that led to their downfall.

9But Wisdom rescues her servants from their trials. 10When a man, who did what was right, fled from his brother's anger, Wisdom led him on straight paths. She showed him God's kingdom and gave him knowledge of holy things. She caused him to prosper through his handiworks and increased the fruit of his labors. 11When some, because of greed, sought to get the upper hand over him, she stood by him and made him even richer. 12She protected him from his enemies and kept him safe from those who set an ambush for him. She intervened on his behalf in a difficult contest so that he might know that godliness is more powerful than anything.

13When a man who did what was right was sold into slavery, she didn't abandon him. She rescued him from sin. 14She even went down into the pit with him. She didn't forsake him when he was in chains. In the end, she obtained for him the symbol of kingly rule and authority over those who would have ruled over him. She showed that those who had accused him were liars. She gave him eternal glory.

15Wisdom rescued a holy people and a pure generation from the grip of people who were crushing them. 16She entered the soul of a man who served the Lord. She enabled him to oppose terrifying kings by means of signs and wonders. 17She rewarded the holy ones for their labors and led them along a wonderful route. She became a shelter for them by day and a flaming shower of stars by night. 18She carried them across the Red Sea[d] and led them through deep waters. 19She drowned their enemies and caused the depths to boil up over them. 20The people who did what was right then stripped the ungodly of their weapons. All together they sang hymns to your holy name, Lord. They praised your hand, which had defended and fought for them. 21Wisdom opens the mouths of those who can't speak and puts clear words on the tongues of infants.

The Nile and water from the rock

11 She caused their works to prosper by the hand of the holy prophet. 2They wandered through a desert in which no one lived. They set up their tents in the midst of desolate surroundings. 3They opposed those who fought against them and defended themselves from their enemies. 4They thirsted and cried out to you. You gave them water from a sharp rock, and their thirst was quenched by liquid from that hard stone. 5When your people were in need, they were blessed with the very things that you used to punish their enemies. 6So instead of a source of fresh water, your enemies found their own flowing river to be polluted with blood and gore. It was a judgment on those who killed their own children. 7But you gave your people water in greater abundance than they could possibly imagine. 8You showed your people through their own experience of thirst how you punished their opponents.

9When your people were put to the test, you disciplined them, but you also showed mercy. But they learned from this how harshly the ungodly were tormented when you judged them. 10You disciplined your people in the same way that parents warn their children, but you examined and passed sentence on the ungodly like a strict ruler. 11Whether they were distant or close by, you still afflicted them. 12They groaned on account of their punishment and on account of the memory of the things that they had done. 13When they heard that the Hebrews were benefiting from their punishment, they perceived that it was the Lord's doing. 14They thirsted, but their thirst was so different from the thirst of those who do what is right! In the end, they stood in awe of the man they had mockingly rejected long ago because he had been set adrift and exposed.

Small animals and quail

15Because their foolish and wicked thoughts had led them astray to worship unthinking reptiles and worthless animals,

[d]Or traditionally *Reed Sea* in Hebrew Bible

you sent hordes of mindless creatures upon them as a punishment. [16]In this way they learned that people are punished by the very same things by which they sin. [17]Your all-powerful hand, which had brought the world into being out of formless matter, would have been more than able to send a host of bears and fierce lions against them. [18]Or they could have been met by newly created beasts that no one had ever seen before, full of rage, breathing fire, belching smoke, and shooting deadly sparks from their eyes. [19]The damage that these beasts would have been able to do would have been more than enough to wipe out your enemies. Just the sight of them would have been enough to make them die from fear! [20]Or without any of these, your enemies could have been cut down by a single breath—pursued by your justice and crushed by a powerful breath.

Digressions on divine justice

But you have set all things in right order by proportion: by measure, by number, and by weight. [21]You are indeed able at any time to carry out mighty deeds. Who could possibly withstand the strength of your arm? [22]Before you, the whole world is nothing but dust on the scale or but a drop of dew that falls to earth in the night. [23]Yet precisely because you can do all things, you show mercy to everyone. You overlook their sins, giving them a chance to change their hearts and minds. [24]You love everything that exists. You despise nothing that you have made. If you hated it, you wouldn't have created it. [25]Nothing could survive unless you had willed it. Nothing could remain unless you continued to call it into being. [26]You spare all things because all things are yours, ruler and lover of life.

12 Your imperishable spirit is present in all things. [2]Therefore, Lord, little by little you correct those who have gone astray. You warn them by reminding them of how they have sinned, so that they can be set free from their wickedness and believe in you. [3]You hated the people who once lived in your holy land because of the evil deeds they were doing. [4]They were casting spells and using drugs, and performed unholy rites. [5]They murdered their own children without pity! Those who were initiated into their secret rituals feasted on human flesh and blood. [6]You were determined to use our ancestors to destroy parents who kill helpless beings. [7]You did this so that the land you honored above all others might be settled in a way that God's children deserved.

[8]But you spared even these men and women when you sent wasps at the head of your army to destroy your enemies little by little. [9]It's not that you weren't able to hand the ungodly over to the righteous or because you weren't able to wipe out the ungodly from the face of the earth all at once by fierce beasts or with a powerful word. [10]You were judging them little by little to give them an opportunity to change their hearts and minds. You did so even though you knew full well that they were wicked from their birth, that their natural inclination was to evil, and that they would never change their minds. [11]Their genetic character[e] was cursed from the start. You didn't grant them immunity for their sins out of concern for anyone's opinion.

[12]After all, who will question what you have done? Who will oppose your decision? Who will accuse you of destroying peoples that you yourself created? Who will come and stand before you as the champion of those who have done wrong? [13]There's no god, other than you, caring for everyone. There's no one to whom you must prove that your judgments are right. [14]There's no king or ruler who's able to challenge you concerning those whom you punished. [15]You always do what's right. You've always governed all things correctly. You'd consider it a crime against yourself to destroy someone who didn't deserve to be cut down. [16]Your strength is the very origin of doing the right thing. Because you rule over all, you spare all. [17]You show your strength to those who doubt how powerful you really are. You condemn the pride of those who should know better than to doubt you.

[e]Or *seed* or *DNA*

[18]Still, though you rule absolutely, you exercise careful judgment. You govern us with amazing restraint. If you wanted to, you could do anything you wished. [19]By your actions, you taught your people that those who do what is right must always want what is best for others. Your sons and daughters saw that you give to those who have sinned a chance to change their hearts and minds. In this way you encouraged them. [20]They knew if you gave their enemies the opportunity to free themselves from evil, punishing them with such care, and even letting them go free when they clearly deserved death, [21]how much more care would you exercise in judging your children, to whose fathers you had given such rich promises by means of solemn pledges and covenants? [22]While you are disciplining us, you scourge our enemies ten thousand times as much, in order that we may keep your goodness in mind when we ourselves are passing judgment. And you teach us that when we ourselves are judged, we should expect your mercy.

[23]It was for this reason that you tortured those who lived foolish and unjust lives through their own disgusting offenses. [24]They wandered far even from the normal ways in which people err! They took horrible things to be gods, the worst forms of animal life. They were deceived like foolish children. [25]So you sent your judgment upon them to mock them, treating them as if they were in fact mindless children. [26]The ones who weren't brought back to their senses by this mocking judgment would experience the just judgment of God. [27]They were plagued by the very things they once took to be gods, and came to hate them.

In the end, they recognized that you, whom they had so long denied to be God, were in fact God. It was then that the full weight of judgment fell upon them.

13 All humans who don't know God are empty-headed by nature. In spite of the good things that can be seen, they were somehow unable to know the one who truly is. Though they were fascinated by what he had made, they were unable to recognize the maker of everything. [2]Instead, they thought that all these things—fire or wind or quickly moving air or a constellation of stars or rippling water or the sky's bright lights that govern the world—were all gods.

[3]They should have known that all these things—which they took to be gods and delighted in—were much less beautiful than the one who rules them all. The creator of beauty itself created them. [4]Those who fear the power and might of created things should know how much more powerful than these things is the one who fashioned them. [5]These people could have perceived something of the one who created all things as they thought about the power and beauty of the things that were created. [6]It is for this reason that they're not without guilt.

Yet perhaps we shouldn't blame them too much. They may have gone astray while they were looking for God, wanting to find him. [7]They spend a lot of time exploring his works. Something about their appearance leads them to wonder, for the things that they see are indeed wonderful. [8]Even so, these persons aren't excused. [9]After all, if they were indeed able to know so much that they could speculate about space and time, how is it that they weren't able to discover the ruler of space and time more quickly?

[10]How much more miserable, though, are those people who put their trust in things that are dead? These people call gods the works of human hands, objects of gold and silver that artisans practice on, artistic representations of animals, even worthless stones carved by someone long ago.

[11]Imagine this. A woodcutter with some skill cuts down a pliable shrub. He carefully strips the outside covering of the plant and then, because he has some skill, shapes it into a tool for daily use. [12]Afterward he picks up the leftover bark that he had stripped away and uses it to cook a meal for himself. He eats his fill and [13]then picks up one of the leftover pieces of wood, one that wasn't good for anything, a crooked hard piece with broken ends where the branches had been. Having nothing else to do, he takes this piece of wood and starts carving. By a process of trial and error, he's finally able to give it a human shape, [14]or

he fashions it into something that vaguely resembles some miserable creature. He covers it with red paint, giving it a rosy hue where the creature's flesh is supposed to be. He covers over every flaw in the wood. [15]Finally, he makes a perfect little shrine for it and fastens the shrine securely to the wall with a nail [16]so that it doesn't fall down. He knows full well that it can't do anything for itself. After all, it's only an image, and it requires help.

[17]In time he begins to pray to it: for his possessions, for his marriage, for his children. He's not ashamed to talk to this lifeless object. In fact, he begins to ask this fragile little creation to provide him with good health. [18]He begins to pray for his life to this lifeless object. He cries out for help to this thing that has no experience at all. He prays about a journey to a thing that can't even take a single step. [19]He asks it for wealth, for profit in his work, and for success in all he sets his hands to do—all this from something whose hands are powerless to do anything.

14 Or imagine this: A man is preparing for a trip. He's about to board a ship that must sail through rough waves. So the man cries out for protection to a little piece of wood that is even more flimsy than the boat that will carry him. [2]Desire for profit led to the ship's planning, and wisdom was the artisan who built it, [3]but your watchful guidance, Father, pilots the ship. You made a way in the sea, a sure path through strong waves. [4]You have shown us that you can rescue us from anything, so that even those who have no skill can put out to sea. [5]Your will is that the works of your wisdom be fruitful. This is the only reason in the end why humans can entrust their lives to cheap pieces of wood and can reach land safely by riding the breaking surf on a ship that is no more than a raft. [6]Near the beginning, at a time when proud giants were being destroyed, the hope of the world escaped on just such a raft. This was how the genetic character[f] of a new generation survived for the world to come. They were steered the whole way by your hand. [7]Praised be the wood by means of which it has now become possible for us to do what is right!

[8]But idols made by human hands are cursed, as are those who make them. Those who make them are cursed because they make them. The idols are cursed because, though made of corruptible material, people call them gods. [9]Both are equally hateful to God: the godless craftsmen and the products of their godlessness. [10]The thing that has been produced will be punished along with the one who produced it. [11]Therefore, God will come in judgment on the nation's idols, for they have turned a part of God's creation into something that God hates. They have produced stumbling blocks for the well-being of humans, a trap set to spring when the feet of the foolish step on it. [12]The very notion of idols was the beginning of immoral sexual activity. The invention of idols ruined human life. [13]In the beginning, idols didn't exist, and they won't last forever. [14]They came into the world through the empty-headed imaginings of humans. Therefore, they'll come to a quick end.

[15]Imagine a father overcome with grief at the untimely death of his child. In his grief, he makes an image of the child. The person who was once a corpse he now honors as a god. He passes it on to those under his authority, along with certain mysteries and special ceremonies. [16]As time goes by, his godless custom becomes tradition. Eventually, his custom becomes law, and rulers order the people to worship these carved images.

[17]These rulers, moreover, lived far away from most of their subjects. So because the people couldn't pay their respects in person, they imagined what the ruler looked like and made an image of their honored leader. By their diligent efforts, they were thus still able to shower the king with their flattery. [18]But the artist's desire to be recognized for his work also incited the fools to an ever greater intensity of worship.

[f]Or *seed* or *DNA*

19 Perhaps out of a desire to please the person in power, the artist makes the most of
his artistic skill to fashion an even more
beautiful and perfect image. 20 The masses,
charmed by the object's workmanship, now
begin to consider the object worthy of their
worship, where not long before they had
only honored the person as a human being.
21 In this way idolatry becomes a trap for
one's life. Whether it is because of a father's
misfortune or because people are ordered to
do so, stones and plants begin to be called
by the name that was never supposed to be
shared with anything or anyone else.
22 Then, as if it weren't enough that they
should err concerning the knowledge of
God, other things follow. When living ig-
norantly in the midst of great war, people
call such evil things peace. 23 Then, in the
celebration of secret religious ceremonies
involving the ritual murder of children or
in hidden mysteries or in the mad orgies
of strange worship practices, 24 people stop
keeping their lives and their marriages
pure. Instead, one person plots to kill another by lying in ambush. Another person
causes grief by becoming sexually involved
with another person's spouse. 25 Everything
becomes a confused mix of blood, murder,
theft, and deception. Corruption, breaking one's word, upheaval, false pledges—
all these things abound. 26 What is good is
shouted down. Favors are forgotten. Entire
beings are stained with guilt. Legitimate genealogy is lost. Marriage is thrown into confusion. Adultery and promiscuity abound.
27 The worship of nameless idols is the origin of all evil—its cause as well as its result.
28 People begin to party so wildly that they
all go mad. They prophesy lies. They live in
such a way that everything they do is wrong.
They bear false witness, 29 but because they
have entrusted themselves into the hands of
lifeless idols, they don't expect any harm to
come from swearing false pledges. 30 A double
judgment will hunt them down—first,
because they acted wickedly toward God
when they gave their attention to idols; and
second, because they made solemn pledges
falsely out of contempt for what was holy.
31 It isn't the power of the things by which
they made these solemn pledges but justice
that will pursue them until it punishes them
for doing wrong.

15 But you, our God, are good and true.
You are very patient. You govern
everything in your mercy. 2 Even if we sin,
we will still belong to you because we know
your power. But we won't sin, since you consider us as your own. 3 Perfection of life is to
know you. To recognize your power is the
root from which everlasting life grows. 4 The
misguided art of humans didn't deceive us,
nor did the fruitless labor of clever painters
even when they created an image that was
dazzling in its combination of colors.
5 The sight of idols, however, creates desire in fools. They begin to long for a dead
statue's lifeless image. 6 Those who make
them, those who want them, and those
who worship them are all lovers of wicked
things. They all deserve to have their hopes
misdirected in this way.
7 The potters take great pains to mold
the clay. They make each piece for our use.
They make some containers to be used
for holy purposes. Others will be used for
ordinary purposes. Both pieces are made
from the same clay, and both are made in
the same way. But the use to which each is
put is left up to the judgment of the potter. 8 The potters takes great care—but it is
an evil care!—to design a useless god from
the very same clay that only a moment
before had come from the same earth from
which the potters themselves also had
been taken. It is the same earth to which
the potters will one day return when their
entire being's debt has to be paid back. 9 Yet
the potters don't worry that they are going
to come down with some terrible disease
or even that they will have only a short life.
Rather, they spend all their time competing with the goldsmiths and the silver-
smiths, imitating the bronzeworkers, and
thinking it's the greatest honor imaginable
that they spend their lives making counterfeit gods.
10 Their hearts are nothing but rust. Their
hopes are more useless than dirt. Their
lives are worth less than the clay they mold.
11 Why? Because the potters don't know who

made them. They don't know who breathed life into them and made them move, who put a spirit in them to become a living being. [12]They think that life is just a game. They think that our day-to-day existence is just a profit-seeking carnival. As they say: "You must earn a living however you can, even if it means doing the wrong thing." [13]These people know better than anyone else that they are sinning when they give shape to equipment and images that are easily broken, because they are both fashioned from the same earthy material.

[14]But the people who are most foolish of all, and even more to be pitied than the soul of a little child, are the enemies who oppressed your people. [15]These enemies considered the nation's idols to be gods, even though these idols have no eyes for seeing, no nostrils for breathing air, no ears for hearing, no fingers for touching, and no feet for walking. [16]A mere human made them. A person who has been given his spirit on loan crafted them. But no human is ever able to fashion a god who is anything like God. [17]Being a human, a person can construct only a dead thing with lawless hands. These people are better than the things that they worship, for they have life and the things that they worship do not.

[18]On top of it all, the enemies of your people worship the most hateful animals, things that are less intelligent than any other creatures. [19]Even as animals, there's nothing appealing or beautiful about them. They have neither the praise nor the blessing of God.

Small animals and quail resumed

16 Therefore, the enemies of your people deserved to be punished and tormented by swarms of the very same monsters. [2]In contrast to their punishment, you blessed your people when they were famished. You prepared for them a tasty delicacy—a feast of quail! [3]You did so in order that the enemies of your people, who were also hungry, wouldn't be able to stomach food because of the ugliness of those creatures that you had sent against them. You also did so in order that your people, who were in need only for a little while, might share in a novel meal. [4]The enemies of your people, who oppressed them like tyrants, were fated to experience a famine that never seemed to end. But all that was necessary for your people was to show them how their enemies were to be tortured.

Insects and the bronze serpent

[5]Even when the terrible fury of beasts overwhelmed your people and they were perishing from the stings of coiled serpents, your anger didn't last long. [6]They were terrified only for a little while as a warning, since they had the sign of their salvation as a reminder of the command of your Law. [7]Those who turned to that sign were saved not by what they saw but by you, the savior of all. [8]In this way, you persuaded our enemies that you are the only one who rescues people from every evil. [9]Our enemies died when they were bitten by locusts and flies. There was no healing that was able to keep them alive. They deserved to be punished by those insects. [10]Yet not even the fangs of poisonous snakes were able to overcome your children, because your mercy traveled along with them and healed them. [11]You did sting them in order to remind them of the things that you had told them. But you came to their rescue quickly so that they might not fall into a deep forgetfulness of your goodwill toward them. [12]It wasn't any herb or ointment that healed them but your word alone, Lord, which heals everything. [13]You have power over life and death. You lead people down to the gates of hell, and you bring them back up again. [14]Humans can indeed kill by their evil, but they can't bring back the life that has expired or restore the spirit that has been taken away.

Storms and bread

[15]It is impossible to escape from your hand. [16]Even though the ungodly denied any knowledge of you, it was your strong arm that afflicted them. They were pursued by strange rainfalls that never stopped, and by hailstorms and downpours. They were pursued by a fire that consumed everything. [17]The most unusual thing about this

fire was that it showed that it was stronger than water, which normally quenches any fire. Yet the universe itself comes to the defense of those who do what is right. 18At one point the flame did die down, so that it might not destroy the creatures that had been sent but only punish them. The ungodly noticed and realized it was God's judgment that was hunting them down. 19Then suddenly the fire flared up again, right in the midst of water, with an even greater intensity than normal fire. It destroyed the crops in a land dominated by wrongdoing.

20In contrast, you fed your people with the food from angels. Again and again, you provided your people with a bread that had been prepared in heaven. It was a bread that was able to satisfy anyone's longing and please anyone's taste. 21You even showed your children your sweet side: when they ate, the bread was changed into whatever they wanted it to become! 22And though it was like snow and snowflakes, it endured the fire, which didn't melt it. In this way, they knew that their enemies' crops had been destroyed by an unusual fire, one that blazed even in the midst of the hail and let off sparks even in the midst of the rain. 23But in order that those who do the right thing might be fed, fire itself forgot how powerful it was. 24Creation, which serves you, the one who made it, tenses itself in preparation for the judgment of those who have done wrong and then relaxes itself again in order to benefit those who have put their trust in you.

25And so it was that what was created was changed. It became a minister of your gift, completely nourishing and fulfilling the desire of those in need. 26In this way your children, whom you love, Lord, would learn that it isn't the various kinds of crops that sustain humans, but it is your word that preserves those who trust in you. 27As proof, what wasn't destroyed by the fire simply melted away when it was warmed by a gentle sunbeam. 28In this way we learn that we too must arise before the sun to thank you and pray to you with the dawn of light. 29The hope of those who don't thank God, however, will melt away like winter frost and drain away like wastewater.

Darkness and fire

17 Your judgments are great and difficult to explain. This is why those who haven't been well-taught go astray. 2When lawless people tried to oppress your holy nation, in actual fact they were the prisoners who were being held in a dark place, bound in chains through a long night. They were confined to their own homes as they vainly tried to flee from a plan that had been prepared for all eternity. 3They thought that they could hide their sins by pulling a blanket of forgetfulness over themselves. But instead they were scattered in every direction, terrified by fear, and spooked by nightmarish visions.

4They hid themselves in the deepest corners of their houses, but couldn't escape from their fears. Even there they heard all around them sounds that terrified them. Mournful ghosts with gloomy faces appeared to them. 5No fire gave them any light, nor did the stars' light shine brightly enough to illumine that horrible night. 6Only once did anything shine through: it was a frightening fire that seemed to have a life of its own. But then, when they lost sight of that light, they were even more afraid than they had been before they had seen it! They began to realize that what they had seen was even worse than what they had thought. 7They realized that their mocking attempts at magic were too weak and that they had no real power. It became clear to them that they had given themselves far too much credit for understanding what was happening. 8Those who had thought they could dispel fears and free sick beings from terror became sick themselves with a laughable case of nerves. 9Even when there was nothing around to frighten them, they were scared by the simple sounds of animals' movements and hissing serpents. 10Trembling, they were dying with fright, shutting their eyes even against the empty air, as if they could thus avoid what was scaring them. 11Wickedness is cowardly, condemned by its own witness. Distressed by conscience, the wicked person thinks everything is worse than it is. 12 Fear betrays our ability to help ourselves by thinking clearly. 13 Expecting the worst, people prefer to remain ignorant of the cause of their torment.

14 The night itself was powerless, rising up from the darkest corners of a hell that didn't really exist. As they slept the same sleep, 15 monsters from their own imaginations rose up and hunted them down. They were paralyzed with fear as their spirits failed them. A sudden and unexpected fear drenched their whole being. 16 All who fell into that kind of place became like prisoners, locked up in cells without metal bars. 17 Whether they were farmers or shepherds or laborers toiling alone in the desert, the same fate overtook them all, and they were all bound in the darkness as by a single chain.

18 Whether it was the whispering of the wind, or the sound of birds singing in the thick branches of trees, or the rhythm of rushing water, 19 or the crashing down of rocks from a high cliff, or the unseen scurrying of little animals, or the howling of the most frightening of beasts, or an echo from the valleys between the hills; whatever it was, it frightened them so much that they were completely paralyzed. 20 So while bright sunlight lit up the rest of the world, and people and things went about their ordered, active lives, 21 an oppressive night lay all around them, and around them alone. It was a sign of the darkness that was going to receive them, but they were a heavier burden to themselves than even the darkness itself.

18 In contrast, an incredible light shone all around your holy ones. Their enemies heard their voices, but couldn't see their physical forms. They considered your holy ones fortunate, since they weren't suffering as their enemies were. 2 They were grateful that your holy ones didn't take advantage of them, even when they could have and even after they had been treated so badly. They asked forgiveness of your people for having been at odds.

3 You provided your people with a fiery pillar to lead them on their way on the unknown journey. That pillar was like a sun, and yet that sun didn't hurt them during their long journey to a foreign land. 4 The others deserved to be robbed of light and to be locked up in darkness. After all, they had kept your children locked up, even though it was through them that the never-ending light of the Law was to be given to the world.

Deliverance of the Israelites

5 So you swept away in judgment a huge number of the children of those who had sought to kill off your holy ones' children (though one child, who was exposed to die, was saved!). You destroyed the rest by overwhelming them with water.

6 You had already alerted our fathers to that night well in advance. You did so in order that our fathers might rejoice and put their whole trust in the promises they had been given. 7 Your people fully expected that those who always do what is right would be delivered, while their enemies would be destroyed. 8 In the same way that you punished those who opposed your people, in just this way you called your people out of that land and gave them great honor. 9 Your holy children offered secret sacrifice of the very best that they had. They were all of one mind as they carried out the Law, which had come from God, that the holy people were to share good things as well as experience dangers together, while already singing the praises of their ancestors.

10 In contrast, the loud moaning of their enemies was a jarring and miserable sound. It rose up and could be heard everywhere as they mourned their dead children. 11 The same judgment fell on both slave and ruler. Both were punished together. The lowest person and the king suffered the same thing. 12 Countless bodies lay around, united together by a common name: death. There weren't even enough of the living left to bury the dead! In one fleeting moment, their most valued children were destroyed. 13 Because of their misguided casting of spells and drug use, they didn't believe until it was too late.

As a result, all their oldest males were destroyed. It was only then that they acknowledged your people to be your children. [14]It was then, while everything was wrapped in a gentle silence, and half a night had already passed, [15]that your all-powerful word had leaped down from heaven, the royal throne. Like a fierce warrior, he had entered the land that was marked for destruction. [16]He carried with him your unchanging declaration like a sharp sword. He stood up and filled everything with death; he reached the sky while still standing on the ground. [17]Immediately the visions of their nightmares shook them. Unexpected fears assaulted them. [18]One here, then another there, fell to the ground half-dead. They shouted out to tell those around them why they were dying. [19]The dreams that had so bothered them had foretold that this was to happen. And so they perished knowing full well why they were suffering.

[20]Those who did what is right were also touched by a test of death when many fell in the desert. But that wrath didn't last long, [21]because a man in whom no blame could be found was already running to join the fight. He took up prayer and the reconciling incense as his weapons. He stood strong against the fury. In doing so, he limited the damage that was done. He showed that he was your servant. [22]He overcame divine anger not by bodily strength or by the power of weapons. He subdued the punisher by the word. He reminded him of the solemn pledges that had been made to our ancestors and of the covenants that had been given to them. [23]The dead already lay fallen one upon another in heaps when he stood between the punisher and the people and stopped the assault. He cut off the punisher's access to the living. [24]On his long robe could be seen the whole of the universe. On the four rows of carved stones were the glories of the patriarchs. On the royal crown upon his head was your majesty. [25]The destroyer yielded to all these, because he feared them.

Death and salvation at the Red Sea

This one experience of wrath was sufficient for them,

19 [1]but anger without mercy assaulted the ungodly right up to the very end. God knew before they did what was yet to come: how, [2]after agreeing to send your people away, and in fact sending them away in haste, their enemies would change their minds and pursue them. [3]And so, even as they still held in their arms those whom they mourned and even as they still raised up their laments at the graves of their dead, another thoughtless plan occurred to them. They decided to pursue those who had fled even after they had agreed to their request to send them away. [4]A fate they fully deserved drew them to this inevitable decision and made them forget about all the things that had so recently happened to them. All this took place so that they might complete the one punishment lacking in their sufferings.

[5]So at the same time as your people began an incredible journey, their enemies found a strange death. [6]The whole creation began to take on a new shape in its very nature. It once again submitted to your commands so that your children might be kept unharmed. [7]A cloud appeared, casting its shadow over their camp. Dry land appeared where before there had been only water. It presented them an open path through the Red Sea,[g] a grassy plain where before there had been only violent surf. [8]Those who were protected by your hand passed through as a single nation, seeing amazing wonders. [9]They were like horses ranging about and like lambs skipping along. They praised you, Lord, for you were rescuing them. [10]They remembered all that had happened in the foreign land in which they had lived so long. They remembered how the ground had brought forth insects instead of livestock. They remembered how the river had vomited up frogs instead of its normal wildlife. [11]Later, driven by hunger, they requested meat and found a new breed of bird. [12]Quail arose from the sea to nourish them.

[g]Or traditionally *Reed Sea* in the Hebrew Bible

[13]In contrast, punishments rained down upon the sinners, but not before they were given a clear warning through violent thunder. It was right for them to suffer for their evil deeds and for their hatred of the immigrants in their midst. [14]Some people have failed to welcome strangers who came into their midst to stay awhile. But these people went so far as to make slaves of people who were their guests and benefactors. [15]Judgment will come on those who greeted people who weren't like them as enemies. [16]But these people first gave feasts to welcome those who did right and shared with them the blessings of the land. But then they began to force the strangers to do hard labor. [17]Therefore, they were struck blind, just like those people who had gathered at the door of one who had also done what was right. A veil of darkness was cast around them, and each one of them groped for the entrance to his own gates.

[18]If we are careful to observe events, we can see just how the elements of the universe are transformed. It's the same transformation that happens when someone changes the sounds that a harp makes by changing the key while continuing to play the same melody. [19]In this way, land animals were changed into underwater creatures, while animals that swam in the waters now moved onto the land. [20]Fire was able to burn on the open water, while water forgot that it was supposed to put fire out. [21]Flames no longer burned the exposed flesh of living beings, who were able to walk through the flames. Flames didn't even melt the frost-like crystals that were a kind of food of everlasting life.

God is faithful

[22]In every way, Lord, you have made your people great and given them great honor. You never neglected them, but you stood by them in every time and place.

If we are careful to observe events we can see [illegible] the elements [illegible] [illegible] [illegible] saw [illegible] [illegible] [illegible] that happens when someone [illegible] the sounds that a harp makes by [illegible] key [illegible] the same [illegible]. In this way [illegible] changed into underwater creatures, while animals that [illegible] in the waters now moved onto the land. [illegible] able to [illegible] in the open [illegible] while [illegible] supposed to [illegible] no longer [illegible] [illegible] of living beings, who were able to walk through the flames [illegible] the [illegible] [illegible] of [illegible].

[illegible]

[illegible] [illegible] people [illegible] given them [illegible] you never neglected them, but you stood by them everywhere and in every place.

Immigrant peoples [illegible] into the mountains, but not before they were given a clear warning through [illegible] [illegible] it was right for them to suffer for their own deeds and for their hatred of the immigrants in their midst. Some people [illegible] welcomed strangers [illegible] [illegible] their [illegible] [illegible] But the people [illegible] [illegible] of people who were their guests and benefactors. [illegible] [illegible] those who [illegible] people who were [illegible] like them as enemies. But these people first gave feasts to welcome those who [illegible] and shared with them the [illegible] [illegible] the land, but then they began to force [illegible] strangers to do hard labor [illegible] [illegible] they were [illegible] [illegible] not like those people who [illegible] the [illegible] who had [illegible] one [illegible] [illegible] darkness [illegible] around them, and each one of them [illegible] for the [illegible] [illegible].

SIRACH

Prologue

1 Numerous and wonderful things have
been given to us through the Law, the
Prophets, 2 and the other writings that followed them. 3 For this reason, it is necessary
to praise Israel for education and wisdom.
4 It is also necessary not only for those who
read them to gain understanding 5 but also
for those who love learning to be of service
to strangers 6 when they speak and write.
7 Because of this, my grandfather, Jesus,
who had devoted himself more and more
8 to the reading of the Law, 9 the Prophets,
10 and the other ancestral scrolls, 11 and had
gained enough experience with them, 12 was
himself led to compose a work dealing with
education and wisdom. 13 His goal was that
lovers of learning who were committed to
education and wisdom[a] 14 should gain much
more by living according to the Law.

15 You are invited, therefore, 17 to read
16 with goodwill and attention 18 and to be
forgiving 19 in cases where we seem 20 less
than perfect in translating some expressions,
despite working hard on the translation.
21-22 What was originally expressed in Hebrew
does not have the same power when translated
into another language. 23 Not only in this case
24 but even in the case of the Law, the Prophets, 25 and the rest of the scrolls, 26 there's no
small difference between the translation and
their expression in their own language.

27 In the thirty-eighth year of the rule
of King Euergetes, 28 after I had arrived in
Egypt and stayed awhile, 29 having found
a copy of this scroll to contain no small
amount of practical advice, 30 I personally
made it a high priority to apply speed and
hard work to translating this very scroll.
31-32 I worked skillfully and stayed up many
nights 33 to bring the scroll to completion in
order to publish it 34 for those living abroad,
who want to become well educated, 35 preparing their character to live by the Law.

Wisdom's origins

1 All wisdom comes from the Lord.
It lives with him forever.
2 Who can count the grains of sand
in the seas,
the drops of rain,
or the days of eternity?
3 Who can discover heaven's height,
the earth's breadth,
the abyss,[b] or wisdom?
4 Wisdom was created before
everything else.
Right understanding
is as old as eternity.[c]
6 To whom was Wisdom's root revealed?
Who knew her wonderful feats?[d]
8 There is one who is wise, greatly feared,
seated upon his throne.
9 The Lord himself created her;
he saw her; he measured her.
The Lord poured her out
over everything he made,
to be with each person
to the extent that God grants,
and he supplied her abundantly
to those who love him.[e]

Fear of the Lord is Wisdom

11 Fear of the Lord is a person's glory,
boasting, gladness,
and crown of rejoicing.
12 Fear of the Lord will cheer the heart,
and it will give gladness, joy,
and a long life.[f]
13 Things will go well at the end
for those who fear the Lord.
They will be blessed
at the time of death.

14 Wisdom starts with fearing the Lord,
and she is joined to the faithful
even within the womb.
15 Wisdom built her nest among human
beings as an eternal foundation,

[a] Gk *these things* [b] Gk *abysson* [c] LXX[b] adds 1:5 *The source of wisdom is God's word in the highest places. She walks in accordance with eternal commandments.* [d] LXX[b] adds 1:7 *To whom has Wisdom's skill been shown? Who has understood her vast experience?* [e] LXX[b] adds to 1:10 *Love for the Lord is recognized as wisdom. He gives wisdom to the person to whom he appears as a vision of himself.* [f] LXX[b] adds to 1:12 *Fear of the Lord is the Lord's gift, because he also establishes paths for love.*

and they will entrust
their offspring to her.
16 Wisdom is fully satisfied
with fearing the Lord,
and she will make people drunk
with her fruits.
17 She will fill all their houses
with desirable things
and fill their storehouses
from her produce.
18 Fearing the Lord
is Wisdom's crowning garland,
sprouting forth peace
and restorative health.[g]
19 She rained down skill
and insightful knowledge,
and she raised up the reputation
of those who held on to her.
20 Fearing the Lord is Wisdom's root,
and her branches yield a long life.[h]

22 Unjust anger won't be justified,
for the tipping point of one's anger
is one's downfall.
23 Patient people will hold themselves back
until the right moment,
and afterward they will be paid back
with joy.
24 They will hide their words
until the right moment,
and many will talk about
their good judgment.

25 There are intelligent proverbs
in Wisdom's treasuries,
but sinners avoid godliness
like the plague.
26 If you want to find Wisdom,
then keep the commandments,
and the Lord will supply her to you
in vast quantities.
27 Fearing the Lord brings
wisdom and education.
He is pleased with faithfulness
and gentleness.
28 Don't disobey the fear of the Lord,
and don't approach him[i]
with a divided heart.
29 Don't give people reason
to call you a hypocrite,
and pay attention to what you say.
30 Don't exalt yourself,
or else you might fall
and bring dishonor to yourself.
The Lord will reveal your secrets,
and he will overthrow you
in the middle of the congregation,
because you didn't come
with proper regard for the Lord
and your heart was full of insincerity.

Trusting in God

2 My child, if you come to serve the Lord,
prepare yourself for testing.
2 Set your heart straight, be steadfast,
and don't act hastily in a time of distress.
3 Hold fast to God
and don't keep your distance from him,
so that you may find strength
at your end.
4 Accept whatever happens to you,
and be patient
when you suffer humiliation,
5 because gold is tested with fire,
and acceptable people are tested
in the furnace of humiliation.[j]
6 Trust him, and he will help you;
make your ways straight,
and hope in him.

7 You who fear the Lord, wait for his mercy,
and don't turn aside
or else you might fall.
8 You who fear the Lord, trust him,
and you won't lose your reward.
9 You who fear the Lord,
hope for good things,
for unending joy and mercy.[k]
10 Look at the people
from long ago and see:
Who trusted in the Lord
and was put to shame?
Or who remained firm in godly fear
and was left behind?
Or who called upon the Lord,
and the Lord overlooked him?

[g] LXX[b] adds to 1:18 and the beginning of 1:19 *Both are God's gifts for peace, and those who love God find more reason to boast. God saw Wisdom and measured her.* [h] LXX[b] adds 1:21 *Fear of the Lord drives sins away, and when it lasts, it will turn aside all wrath.* [i] Or *it* [j] LXX[b] adds to 2:5 *In sickness and in poverty trust in him.* [k] LXX[b] adds to 2:9 *God repays with a gift of unending joy.*

11 After all, the Lord is compassionate
and merciful;
he forgives sins and rescues people
in a time of hardship.

12 How terrible it will be
for cowardly hearts and idle hands
and for a sinner who sets foot
upon two paths.
13 How terrible it will be for the timid heart.
Because it doesn't trust,
therefore it won't be protected.
14 How terrible it will be for you
who have lost your stamina.
What will you do when the Lord comes
for his inspection?

15 Those who fear the Lord
won't disobey his words,
and those who love him
will keep his ways.
16 Those who fear the Lord
will try to please him,
and those who love him will be fully
occupied with observing the Law.
17 Those who fear the Lord
will prepare their hearts,
and they will humble themselves
before him.
18 May we fall into the hands of the Lord
and not into the hands of human beings,
because his mercy
is equal to his greatness.

Duties to parents

3 Listen to a father's warning, children,
and act accordingly
so that you may be safe.
2 The Lord gives pride of place
to a father above his children
and establishes a mother's judgment
above that of her offspring.
3 Those who honor their fathers
will make up for their own sins,
4 and those who praise their mother
are like people storing up treasure.
5 Those who honor their fathers
will be made happy
by their own children,
and they will be heard when they pray.
6 Those who praise their fathers
will live a long life,
and those who listen to the Lord
will give rest to their mothers,[l]
7 and they will serve their parents
as their masters.
8 Honor your father in action and word
so that a blessing will come
from him to you,
9 since a father's blessing
supports his children's families,
but a mother's curse
undermines their foundations.
10 Don't glorify yourself
in your father's disgrace,
because your father's disgrace
brings you no credit.
11 A father's honor is the starting point
for his children's reputation,
and a mother in disrepute
is a disgrace to her children.

12 My child, help your father in his old age,
and don't give him grief during his life.
13 And if his understanding fails,
be tolerant,
and don't shame him,
because you have all your faculties.
14 Taking care of one's father
won't be forgotten.
It will be credited to you
against your sins.
15 When you are in trouble,
this will be recalled about you;
like frost warmed by sunshine,
so your sins will melt away.
16 Those who abandon their fathers
are like blasphemers,
and those who anger their mothers
have been cursed by the Lord.

Humility and charity

17 My child, conduct your affairs
with gentleness,
and you will be loved
more than a person of good repute.[m]
18 However great you become,
humble yourself more,

[l] LXX[b] adds 3:7a *Those who fear the Lord will honor their father.* [m] Heb *a person who gives*

and you will find favor before the Lord,[n]
[20] because the Lord's power is great,
and he is glorified by the humble.
[21] Don't seek out things
that are too difficult for you,
and don't investigate matters
too perplexing for you.
[22] Think about what
you have been commanded,
because you have no need
for matters that are hidden.
[23] Don't meddle in things
beyond your own affairs
since you have already been shown
things beyond human understanding.
[24] Speculation has led many people astray,
and false conjectures have
weakened their thoughts.[o]
[26] A stubborn heart will come to misery,
and whoever loves danger
will be destroyed by it.
[27] A stubborn heart will be weighed down
by suffering,
and the sinner will keep on sinning.
[28] There's no healing for the distress
of arrogant people,
because an evil plant
has taken root in them.
[29] The hearts of intelligent people
will think about a proverb,
and the wise desire people
who are ready to listen.

[30] Water will put out a blazing fire,
and giving to those in need
will make up for sins.
[31] Those who repay favors
consider the future,
and at the moment when they fall,
they will find support.

4 Don't deprive a poor person's life,
and don't avoid looking
the needy in the eyes.
[2] Don't grieve a hungry person,
and don't make a person
in dire straits angry.
[3] Don't trouble an angry person,
and don't put off giving to the needy.
[4] Don't keep rejecting the plea
of someone in distress,
and don't turn your face
away from the poor.
[5] Don't turn your eyes
away from someone begging,
and don't give anyone an opportunity
to curse you.
[6] If some curse you
in their bitter circumstances,
the one who made them
will hear their prayer.

[7] Behave yourself pleasantly in the assembly,
and bow your head
to an influential person.
[8] Listen to the poor,
and reply with peaceful
and gentle speech.
[9] Set the wronged free
from the hand of the wrongdoer,
and don't be timid
when you give judgment.
[10] Be like a parent to orphans,
and take care of their mothers
as you would your own wife or husband.
Do this, and you will be like a child
of the Most High,
and God will love you
more than your own mother does.

Submission to Wisdom

[11] Wisdom will exalt[p] her children
and take hold of those who seek her.
[12] Whoever loves her loves life.
Those who wake early for her
will be filled with gladness.
[13] Those who possess her will inherit glory.
The Lord blesses the place
where they enter.[q]
[14] Those who serve her will serve
the holy one;
the Lord loves those who love her.
[15] Whoever obeys her will judge nations.
Whoever is devoted to her
will live with confidence.
[16] If they persevere in faith,
they will inherit her,

[n] LXX[b] adds 3:19 *Many are lofty and of high repute, but to the gentle he reveals his secrets.* [o] LXX[b] adds 3:25 *If you have no pupils, you will be at a loss for light, and if you are without knowledge, don't exult in it.* [p] Heb *teaches*
[q] Or perhaps *she enters*

and their descendants will possess her.
17 At first she will walk
in twists and turns with them.
She will bring fear and dread upon them,
and she will torture them
with her discipline
until she trusts them completely.
She will test them
with her commandments,
18 and again she will come straight back
to them, make them glad,
and reveal to them her secrets.
19 If they go astray,
she will leave them behind
and hand them over to their downfall.

Shame and speech

20 Watch closely for the right opportunity,
be on guard against evil,
and don't be ashamed of yourself.
21 There's a kind of shame
that brings about sin,
and there's a kind of shame
that brings good reputation and favor.
22 Don't show partiality to your own hurt,
and don't show respect
to your own downfall.
23 Don't keep from speaking
in a time of need,[r]
24 for wisdom will show itself
in one's speech,
and education through one's words.
25 Don't contradict the truth,
but don't be ashamed
when you don't know the answer.
26 Don't be ashamed to confess your sins,
and don't force the flow of a river.
27 Don't lower yourself before a fool,
and don't show partiality
toward the powerful.
28 Fight to the death on behalf of truth,
and the Lord God will fight for you.

29 Don't be bold to speak,
but sluggish and slack
when it comes to action.
30 Don't be like a lion in your house,
putting on airs
among your household slaves.
31 Don't stretch your hand out
to receive and withdraw it
when it is time to pay back.

Practical precepts

5 Don't be preoccupied with your money,
and don't say, "I'm self-sufficient."
2 Don't follow your inclination
or your strength,
in order to walk in the desires
of your heart.
3 And don't say,
"Who'll have power over me?"
When the Lord punishes,
he will punish.
4 Don't say, "Sure, I sinned,
but what happened to me?"
The Lord is patient indeed.
5 Don't be too confident
of being forgiven,
adding sin upon sin.
6 Don't say, "His compassion is great;
he will forgive the whole heap
of my sins."
Mercy and wrath are with him,
and his anger will rest on sinners.
7 Don't wait to turn back to the Lord.
Don't put it off day after day,
because the Lord's wrath
will come forth suddenly;
when the time for punishment comes,
you will be destroyed.
8 Don't be preoccupied
with ill-gotten gains;
it will be of no benefit
when you are in trouble.

9 Don't be blown about by every wind,
and don't take every shortcut.
This is how the devious[s] sinner acts.
10 Be firmly grounded
in your understanding,
and let your speech be consistent.
11 Listen carefully,
and utter a patient reply.
12 If you have understanding,
answer your neighbor,
but if you don't,
clap your hand over your mouth.

[r] Heb *at the right moment;* LXX[b] adds *and don't hide your wisdom in beauty.* [s] LXX *double-tongued*

[13] Speaking brings glory or dishonor.
Indeed, the tongue
can be a person's downfall.
[14] Don't get a reputation
for being a slanderer,
and don't set traps for people
with your speech,
because shame comes to the thief,
and terrible blame
comes upon the deceitful.[t]
[15] Don't be ignorant in matters
large or small.

6 Don't become an enemy
instead of a friend.
If you get a bad name, you will also
inherit shame and reproach,
as is the case with the
deceitful[u] sinner.

[2] Don't be enamored
of your own intelligence
lest your strength be taken captive
like a bull.
[3] You will devour your leaves,
destroy your fruit,
and leave yourself like a withered tree.
[4] If you have a bad soul, it will destroy you;
it will make you a joke to your enemies.

Friendship

[5] Pleasant speech gains more friends
for itself,
and a sweet-speaking tongue
will multiply pleasant exchanges.
[6] Let those who are at peace with you
be many,
but let only one in a thousand
be your advisor.
[7] If you make friends, test them thoroughly
and don't trust them quickly.
[8] Some are friends when it is convenient,
but they won't stay around
during hard times.
[9] There are friends who turn into enemies,
and they will reveal
your disgraceful arguments.
[10] There are friends who are companions
at your table,
but they won't stay during hard times.
[11] They will act as if your belongings
are theirs,
and they will be bold
toward your household slaves.
[12] If you are brought low,
they will be against you,
and they will abandon you.
[13] Stay away from your enemies,
and be careful with your friends.
[14] Trustworthy friends are a strong shelter;
whoever finds one
has found a treasure.
[15] Trustworthy friends have no price,
and no one can estimate their worth.
[16] Trustworthy friends are life's medicine,
and those who fear the Lord
will find them.
[17] Those who fear the Lord
will direct their friendships well,
because they will associate with people
of like mind.[v]

Submission to Wisdom

[18] My child, from your youth
welcome education, and you will
continue to discover Wisdom
until you are gray-haired.
[19] Approach her like one who plows
and one who sows,
and wait for her good fruits.
When cultivating her,
you will labor a little,
but you will eat her produce soon.
[20] Wisdom is rugged terrain
to the uneducated,
and the fainthearted
won't persevere with her.
[21] She will be like a heavy stone
that tests them,
and they won't hesitate
to throw her aside.
[22] Wisdom is like her name,
and she won't be visible to many.

[23] Listen, my child,
and welcome my opinion.
Don't reject my advice.
[24] Put your feet into her shackles
and your neck into her collar.

[t] LXX *double-tongued* [u] LXX *double-tongued* [v] LXX *because as they are, so are their neighbors*

25 Bend your shoulder down and carry her,
and don't chafe at her bonds.
26 Come to her with your whole being,
and keep to her ways
with all your strength.
27 Track her down and seek her,
and she will become known to you.
When you get possession of her,
don't let her go.
28 In the end, you will find rest in her,
and she will turn to you
and make you happy.
29 Her shackles will be
a strong shelter for you,
and her collar will be a glorious robe.
30 She bears[w] a gold ornament,
and her bonds
will be like blue embroidery.[x]
31 You will wear her like a glorious robe,
and you will put her on
like a crown of joy.
32 If you want, my child,
you will be instructed,
and if you devote your whole being,
you will be intelligent.
33 If you love to listen, you will receive,
and if you pay attention,
you will be wise.
34 Keep company with the elders,
and stick closely to their wisdom.
35 Desire to listen
to every godly conversation,
and don't let intelligent proverbs
escape you.
36 If you find individuals who are intelligent,
get up before dawn to see those people,
and let your foot
wear out their doorsteps.
37 Think about the Lord's decrees,
and meditate constantly
on his commandments.
He will make your heart steadfast,
and will grant your desire for wisdom.

Practical advice

7 Don't do evil things,
and evil will never catch up with you.
2 Keep your distance from anything
unjust, and it will turn away from you.
3 Don't sow in furrows of injustice,
and you won't reap
evil things sevenfold.
4 Don't seek political power from the Lord
or a seat of honor from the king.
5 Don't justify yourself
in the Lord's presence,
and don't make a show of your wisdom
with a king.
6 Don't aspire to become a judge;
you might not be strong enough
to get rid of injustice.
Perhaps you will be too cautious
in the presence of a powerful person
and bring a scandal on your good name.
7 Don't sin against a city's inhabitants,
and don't bring yourself down
in their estimation.[y]

8 Don't repeat a sin,
for you won't be innocent
even of committing it the first time.
9 Don't say,
"He will look at the heap of my gifts,
and when I make an offering
to the Most High, he will accept it."
10 Don't be timid in your prayer,
and don't neglect caring for those in need.
11 Don't mock a person
who is bitter in spirit;
for there's one who humbles
and who exalts.
12 Don't cultivate a lie against your relative
or do the same thing to a friend.
13 Don't desire to tell a lie;
continuing in a lie results in no good.
14 Don't babble when the elders
are assembled,
and don't repeat yourself when praying.

15 Don't hate hard work and farming,
which were created by the Most High.
16 Don't count yourself
among a group of sinners;
remember that God's anger won't delay.
17 Humble your whole being
as much as possible,
because fire and worms
are the punishment of the ungodly.

[w]Or *her yoke is* [x]LXX *thread* [y]LXX *in a crowd*

Household, priests, and the poor

18 Don't trade a friend for cash
or a genuine friend for the gold of Ophir.
19 Don't neglect[z] a wise and good wife,
for her grace is worth more than gold.
20 Don't abuse household slaves
who work hard
or laborers who devote themselves
to their work.
21 Cherish household servants
who are intelligent;
don't deprive them of freedom.

22 Do you have cattle? Look after them.
If they are useful to you, keep them.
23 Do you have children? Instruct them.
Train them to be obedient[a]
from their youth.
24 Do you have daughters?
Be attentive to their chastity,[b]
and don't be too cheerful with them.[c]
25 Give a daughter in marriage,
and you will have completed a great deed,
but present her
to an understanding husband.
26 Do you have a wife who is a soul mate?[d]
Don't divorce her,
and don't trust yourself to a woman
whom you hate.

27 Honor your father with all your heart,
and don't forget
your mother's labor pains.
28 Remember that you were born
because of your parents.
How will you pay them back
for what they have done for you?

29 Revere the Lord with your whole being,
and honor his priests.
30 With all your might
love the one who made you,
and don't neglect his ministers.
31 Fear the Lord and honor the priest.
Give the priest his portion,
just as you were commanded:
early produce, a sin offering,
the gift of the shoulders,
the dedicatory offering,
and the early produce
from the holy things.

32 Extend your hand to the poor
so that your blessing may be complete.
33 The kindness of a gift
stands before all who are alive;
moreover, don't withhold kindness
from the dead.
34 Walk beside those who weep,
and mourn with those who mourn.
35 Don't hesitate to visit the sick,
because you will be loved
on account of these acts.
36 In all of your words,[e]
remember your end,
and you will never sin.

Circumstances to avoid

8 Don't fight with powerful people,
or you might fall into their hands.
2 Don't argue with rich people,
since they might outmatch
your resources;
for gold has destroyed many,
and it has turned aside
the hearts of kings.
3 Don't fight with talkative people,
adding fuel to their fire.

4 Don't make fun of the uneducated,
or your ancestors might be insulted.
5 Don't reproach someone
turning away from sin;
remember that we are all
worthy of punishment.
6 Don't dishonor people in their old age;
some of us are growing old as well.
7 Don't celebrate
because someone has died;
remember that we all will pass away.
8 Don't neglect the conversation
of the wise,
but keep returning to their proverbs,
because you will learn instruction
from them,
how to minister to dignitaries.

[z]Or *reject* [a]LXX *Bend their necks* [b]LXX *body* [c]LXX *Don't brighten your face toward them.* [d]LXX *like your soul*; Heb *whom you abhor* [e]Heb *deeds*

9 Don't reject the words of the aged,
because they also learned
from their elders,
and you will learn understanding
from them
and how to give an answer
when it is necessary.

10 Don't stoke up the coals of a sinner,
and don't let his fire set you ablaze.
11 Don't rise out of your seat
in the presence of insolent persons,
because they might set a trap
for what you say.
12 Don't lend to people
who are more powerful than you,
but if you do lend,
treat it as though it were lost.
13 Don't guarantee a loan
beyond your ability,
and if you do guarantee one,
consider that you will need to pay.

14 Don't go to court with a judge;
people will judge him
according to his prestige.
15 Don't walk on the road
with reckless people,
or you will bear
the weight of your mistakes.
They will walk wherever they want,
and you will be destroyed
because of their foolishness.
16 Don't get in a fight
with hot-tempered people,
and don't travel through the desert
with them,
because spilling blood
is nothing to them,
and where there's no one to help,
they will strike you down.
17 Don't consult with fools,
because they can't keep a secret.
18 Don't do anything in front of strangers
that should be kept hidden,
for you don't know what they will reveal.
19 Don't open your heart to just anyone,
and don't accept a favor from just anyone.[f]

Women and friends

9 Don't be jealous
of your dearly loved wife
or teach her a bad lesson
that hurts you too.
2 Don't give yourself to a woman
so that she crushes your strength.
3 Don't meet up with a female escort,
since you might fall into her traps.
4 Don't hang around
with a female musician,
since you might get caught
in her advances.
5 Don't stare at a young woman,
since you might incur punishment
for her.
6 Don't give yourself to prostitutes,
since you might lose your inheritance.
7 Don't look around in the city streets,
and don't wander in its deserted areas.
8 Turn your eye away
from a shapely woman,
and don't stare at beauty
belonging to someone else.
Many have gone astray
because of a woman's beauty,
and out of it affection
flames up like a fire.
9 Don't ever sit[g] with a married woman,
and don't share meals
or indulge in wine with her,
since your soul
might be attracted to her
and you might slip into destruction
because of your passion.[h]

10 Don't abandon old friends,
because newer ones are not their equals.
New friends are like new wine;
when wine ages,
you will drink it with good cheer.

11 Don't envy the good reputation
of sinners,
since you don't know
how sudden their end will be.
12 Don't delight in the success
of the ungodly.

[f]LXX; Heb *and don't drive goodness away from yourself* [g]Or *Don't sit down at a meal.* [h]Heb *in your passion;* LXX *in your blood*

Remember that they won't
be considered righteous,
even in the grave.[i]

13 Keep far away from people
who have the authority to kill,
and you won't be worried
by the fear of death.
If you do approach them,
don't make a mistake,
or they might take away your life.
Be aware that you are stepping
among traps
and that you are walking
on the parapet of the city's walls.
14 As much as you can,
investigate your neighbor
and consult with wise people.
15 Converse with intelligent people,
and talk constantly about the Law
of the Most High.
16 Let righteous people
be your dinner companions,
and let your pride
be in the fear of the Lord.

On rulers

17 A handicraft is praised
because of the craftsperson's skill,
and the one who leads a people
is wise in speech.
18 Talkative people are feared in their city,
and people who are reckless in speech
will be hated.

10 Wise judges will instruct their people,
and an intelligent person's rule
will be orderly.
2 As the people's judges are,
so will their officials be,
and as the ruler of a city is,
so also are all of its inhabitants.
3 An uneducated king will ruin his people,
and a city is founded
on the intelligence of its rulers.
4 Authority over the earth
belongs to the Lord,
and he will identify the person
who is right for the time.
5 A people's success belongs to the Lord,
and he will give glory
to the legal expert.[j]

On pride

6 Don't become angry with your neighbor
over every wrong,
and don't do anything that offers
a flagrant insult.
7 Arrogance is hateful to God and people,
and injustice is wrong to both.
8 Sovereignty passes from
nation to nation
because of injustice, pride, and money.[k]
9 How can dust and ashes be arrogant?
Even when they are alive,
human bodies are decaying.[l]
10 A long illness mocks a doctor;
today's king will die tomorrow.
11 When people are dead,
they inherit maggots, vermin,[m]
and worms.
12 Human arrogance begins when people
rebel against the Lord,
and their hearts rebel
against the one who made them.
13 The beginning of arrogance is sin,
and those who cling to it
will pour out blasphemy.
For this reason
the Lord brings calamities upon them,
and he ruins them completely.
14 The Lord destroyed the thrones of rulers,
and he raised up the gentle
in their place.
15 The Lord plucked up the roots of nations,
and he planted the humble
in their place.
16 The Lord ruined the lands of the nations,
and he leveled them
to their very foundations.
17 He removed some people
and destroyed them,
and he erased their memory
from the earth.
18 Humans were not created to be arrogant,
nor were those born of women
made to indulge in anger.

[i]LXX *Hades* [j]Or *he will glorify the scribe.* [k]LXX[b] adds *For there is nothing more lawless than love of money, because such people put their own souls up for sale.* [l]Heb; LXX *I threw off its entrails.* [m]LXX *beasts*

Honor and humility

[19] What offspring are honorable?
Human offspring.
What offspring are honorable?
Those who fear the Lord.
What offspring are dishonorable?
Human offspring.
What offspring are dishonorable?
Those who violate
the commandments.
[20] Among brothers and sisters,
their leader is honored,
and those who fear the Lord
are honored in his sight.[n]
[22] The rich, the heroes, and the poor—
their pride is the fear of the Lord.
[23] It's not right to dishonor
someone who is intelligent but poor,
and it's not proper to give glory
to a sinful person.
[24] The official, the judge, and the ruler
will be glorified,
but none of them are greater
than the one who fears the Lord.
[25] Free people will serve the wise person
who has been enslaved,
and a knowledgeable person
won't complain.

[26] Don't show off your wisdom
when you do your work,
and don't magnify yourself
when you have difficulties.
[27] Those who work and have what they need
in abundance are better
than those who walk around
glorifying themselves but lack bread.
[28] My child, hold yourself in honor
with gentleness,
and give yourself honor as you deserve it.
[29] Who will justify those
who sin against themselves?
And who will honor those
who bring dishonor to their own lives?
[30] Poor people will be honored
because of their knowledge,
and rich people will be honored
because of their wealth.
[31] Whoever is honored in poverty,
how much more will he or she
be honored in wealth?
And whoever is disreputable in wealth,
how much more will he or she
be disreputable in poverty?

11 The wisdom of humble people
raises up their heads,
and it will seat them among officials.
[2] Don't praise people
for their beautiful looks,
and don't despise people
for their appearance.
[3] The bee is small among flying creatures,
but its produce is the origin
of everything sweet.
[4] Don't take pride in the way you dress,
and don't promote yourself
when you are being honored,[o]
because the Lord's works
are wonderful,
and his works are hidden
from humans.
[5] Many tyrants have sat on the ground,
and one who was never expected
to rule has worn a crown.
[6] Many rulers have been
completely dishonored,
and those once held in honor
have been handed over to others.

On deliberation

[7] Don't find fault before you investigate;
consider first, and then reprimand.
[8] Don't answer before you listen,
and don't interrupt someone
who is speaking.
[9] Don't argue about something
that doesn't matter to you,
and don't deliberate in a court case
between sinners.

[10] My child, don't be busy with many things;
if you multiply pursuits,
you won't be held guiltless.
If you pursue them,
you won't overtake them,
and when you flee, you won't escape.

[n] LXX[b] adds 10:21 *Fear of the Lord is the beginning of acceptance, but the beginning of rejection is stubbornness and arrogance.* [o] Heb *Don't mock someone wearing a linen undergarment, and don't make fun of someone in bitter circumstances.*

[11] Some people work hard, struggle,
and hurry—
and end up even more deeply in need.
[12] Others are sluggish and need support,
lacking strength
and immersed in poverty.
The Lord has looked upon them
with kindness,
and has restored them
from their low position.
[13] He has raised up their heads,
and many have been amazed at them.

[14] Good things and bad, life and death,
poverty and wealth come from the Lord.[p]
[17] The Lord's gift remains with the godly,
and his favor will always bring success.
[18] Some become rich from diligence
and greed,[q]
and this is part of their reward:
[19] When they say, "I've found rest,
and now I'll eat of my good things,"
they don't know when the time
will come
when they will leave these things
to others and die.

[20] Stand by your agreement,
devote attention to accomplishing it,
and grow old in your work.
[21] Don't be amazed at the works of sinners,
but trust in the Lord
and continue your work,
because it is easy in God's sight
to make the poor person
quickly and suddenly rich.
[22] The Lord's blessing is part
of the godly person's wages,
and God's good pleasure
causes a person to flourish very quickly.
[23] Don't say, "What do I need?
What good things will be mine
from now on?"
[24] Don't say, "I have enough.
What harm can come upon me
from now on?"
[25] At a time of prosperity,
adversity is forgotten,
and at a time of adversity,
prosperity is not remembered.
[26] It is easy for the Lord to pay back people
according to their ways
in the hour of death.
[27] An hour of misery
makes one forget luxury;
the end of a person's life
reveals his or her deeds.
[28] Don't call anyone happy
before their death;
people are known
through their children.[r]

Friends and associates

[29] Don't bring just anyone into your house,
because deceitful people
set many ambushes.
[30] The hearts of arrogant people
are like decoy birds in a cage;
and like spies
they will observe your downfall.[s]
[31] They set up ambushes
and turn good into bad;
they place blame
on praiseworthy actions.
[32] From a fire's spark come many coals,
and sinful people plot and connive
to shed blood.
[33] Beware of evildoers, for they plan
evil things, and they might bring
lasting disgrace upon you.
[34] If you allow strangers to live with you,
they will twist you around in confusion
and make you a stranger
to your own family.

12 If you do good,
know for whom you do it,
and there'll be gratitude
for your good deeds.
[2] Do good to the godly,
and you will find a reward,
and if not from them,
then from the Most High.
[3] There is nothing good
for those who continue to do evil
or for those who
don't freely offer charity.

[p] LXX[b] adds 11:15-16 *Wisdom and knowledge and understanding of the law are from the Lord; love and the ways of good works come from him. Error and darkness were created together with sinners, and evil grows old along with those who exult in evil.* [q] Heb *self-denial* [r] Heb *A person is known by the way he or she dies.* [s] Heb *weakness*

4 Give to the pious, but don't assist sinners.
5 Do good to the humble,
but don't give to the ungodly.
Hold back your bread,
and don't give it to them,
since by it they might gain power
over you.
You will encounter twice as much evil
for all the good things
that you have done for them.
6 The Most High also hated sinners,
and he will repay the ungodly
with punishment.[t]
7 Give to good people,
and don't assist sinners.
8 A friend is not avenged[u] in prosperity,
and an enemy is not hidden
in adversity.
9 When people are prosperous,
their enemies are in pain,
and when they meet with adversity,
even friends will keep away.
10 Don't ever trust your enemies;
for just as copper corrodes,
so their wickedness does as well.
11 If they are humbled
and walk away stooped over,
look after yourself,
and keep up your guard against them.
You will be to them
as one who polishes a mirror,
and you will know that it won't be
completely tarnished.
12 Don't put them next to you;
they might overthrow you
and take your place.
Don't sit them on your right side,
since they might seek your seat.
In the end you will understand my words,
and you will be pierced by what I've said.

13 Who pities a snake charmer
who gets bitten?
Or anyone who goes near wild beasts?
14 So it is with anyone
who goes near sinful people
and becomes involved in their sins.
15 They will remain with you for a time,
but if you waver, they won't be loyal.
16 Enemies speak sweetly with their lips,
but in their hearts,
they plan to throw you into a ditch.
Enemies cry tears with their eyes,
but if they find an opportunity,
they won't be able to
get enough blood.
17 If you meet up with trouble,
you will find them there ahead of you;
and appearing to help,
they will trip you.
18 They will shake their heads
and clap their hands,
and they will whisper many things
and change their faces.

13 Whoever touches tar will get dirty,
and those who associate with the
arrogant will become like them.
2 Don't lift something
that's too heavy for you,
and don't associate with people
who are more powerful and rich
than you are.
What does a clay pot have in common
with a metal cauldron?
The one will knock against the other
and be shattered.
3 Rich people inflict injury,
but then act as if they're the ones
who have been wronged;
the poor suffer injury,
but they're the ones
who must apologize.
4 If you are useful to the rich,
they will work with you,
but if you are in need,
they will abandon you.
5 If you own anything,
they will live with you;
they will exhaust what you have,
and they won't suffer.
6 If they need you, they will deceive you
and smile at you and give you hope;
they will speak nicely to you and say,
"What do you need?"
7 They will embarrass you
with their fine foods,
until they have cleaned you out
two or three times over.

[t] LXX[b] adds *and he is keeping them for the time of their punishment.* [u] Heb *is not recognized*

In the end they will mock you,
and after these things,
they will see you and abandon you
and shake their heads at you.

8 Take care that you don't go astray,
and don't be humiliated
by your own foolishness.
9 When powerful people invite you,
show yourself reluctant,
and they will invite you all the more.
10 Don't be forward,
or you might be rejected;
and don't stand far off,
or you might be forgotten.
11 Don't think that you can speak
with them as an equal,
and don't trust in their
lengthy conversations,
because they will test you
with a lot of talking;
and when they are smiling, they are
really examining you.
12 Those who won't guard your secrets
are cruel,
and they won't spare you
from mistreatment
and imprisonment.
13 Be on guard and pay attention,
because you are tiptoeing
around your own downfall.[v]

15 All living creatures love what is like them,
and all people their neighbors.
16 All beings gather together
with their own kind,
and people cling to those
who are like them.
17 What does a wolf have in common
with a lamb?
So sinners have nothing in common
with the godly.
18 What peace is there
between a hyena and a dog?
And what peace is there
between the rich and the poor?
19 Wild asses in the desert are prey for lions;
so the poor are feeding grounds
for the rich.
20 The arrogant detest humility;
so the rich detest the poor.
21 When rich people stumble,
they are supported by friends.
But when the humble fall,
their own friends push them away.
22 When the rich slip,
their helpers are many;
they speak things that shouldn't be
spoken, and people justify them.
The humble slip,
and people criticize them as well;
they utter something sensible,
and no one pays attention.
23 The rich speak, and everyone is silent,
and what they say is praised
to the heavens.
The poor speak, and they say,
"Who is this?"
And if the poor stumble,
others push them down all the more.
24 Wealth is good as long as it's free of sin;
the ungodly speak of poverty
as an evil in and of itself.

On happiness

25 A person's heart changes the disposition,
whether for good or for ill.
26 A cheerful face indicates
a heart full of good;
coming up with proverbs requires
conversation along with hard work.

14 Happy are those
who haven't slipped in their speech
and who haven't been stabbed
with pain for their sins.
2 Happy are those
whose spirit hasn't condemned them,
and who haven't given up their hope.

On wealth

3 Wealth isn't good for a mean person.
What use is money
to a begrudging person?
4 Those who deny themselves
collect for others,

[v]LXX[b] adds 13:14 *When you hear things in your sleep, wake up; love the Lord for all of your life, and call upon him for your deliverance.*

and others will live luxuriously
with their goods.
5 Those who are evil to themselves,
to whom will they be good?
They will never enjoy their money.
6 There are none worse than those
who begrudge themselves,
and this is the payback
for their wickedness:
7 If they do good,
they do it without being aware,
and in the end they reveal
their wickedness.
8 The miserly are evil;
they turn their face away
and disregard people.
9 Those who have greedy eyes
are never satisfied with their share,
and evil injustice withers their soul.
10 Envious people are even begrudging
when it comes to bread,
and it's lacking on their table.

11 My child, treat yourself well
according to what you have,
and bring offerings to the Lord
that are worthy.
12 Remember that death won't delay,
and the decree of the grave[w]
hasn't been shown to you.
13 Before you die, treat your friends well.
According to your ability, reach out,
and give to them.
14 Enjoy[x] a good day,
and don't let your share
of a good desire pass you by.
15 Won't you end up leaving behind
to another what you have worked
so hard for?
Won't the things you have toiled for
end up being divided by lot?
16 Give, take, and distract yourself,[y]
because you can't search for luxury
in the grave.[z]
17 All flesh grows old like a garment;
the ancient decree is,
"You will certainly die!"
18 Like a budding leaf on a leafy tree,
it sheds some and it puts forth others;
so is a generation of flesh and blood;
one dies, and another is born.
19 All deeds decay and cease,
and those who do them
will pass away with them.

Seeking Wisdom brings happiness

20 Happy are those who meditate
on Wisdom
and who reason intelligently.
21 Those who consider her ways
in their hearts
will also reflect on her secrets.
22 Pursue her like a hunter,
and lie in wait by her paths.
23 Those who peer into her windows
will also listen at her doorways.
24 Those who lodge near her house
will also fasten a tent peg in her walls.
25 They will pitch their tent close at hand
and will find accommodation
in a lodging place full of good things.
26 They will put their children
under her shelter,
and will encamp under her branches.
27 She will shelter them from the heat,
and they will dwell in her glory.

15 Whoever fears the Lord
will do these things,
and whoever has a firm hold
on the Law will possess Wisdom.
2 She will come to meet them like a mother,
and she will await them
like a young bride.
3 She will feed them bread
of understanding,
and will give them water of wisdom
to drink.
4 They will be supported by her
and not be undermined;
they will be intent upon her
and will never be put to shame.
5 She will raise them above their neighbors,
and allow them to speak
in the midst of the assembly.
6 They will inherit gladness,
a crown of rejoicing,
and an eternal name.

[w]LXX *Hades*; Heb *Sheol* [x]LXX *Don't hold back from* [y]Heb *treat yourself well* [z]LXX *Hades*; Heb *Sheol*

[7] People who lack sense will never
receive her,
and sinners will never see her.
[8] She keeps far away from the arrogant,
and liars will never remember her.
[9] Praise isn't proper in the mouth of sinners
because it hasn't been assigned
by the Lord.
[10] Praise must be spoken in wisdom,
and the Lord will cause it to prosper.

Free will and God's justice

[11] Don't say, "I fell away because of the Lord."
What the Lord hates, he won't do.
[12] Don't say, "The Lord made me go astray."
He has no use for sinful people.
[13] The Lord has hated every foul thing,
and those who fear him
have no love for such things.
[14] He created humanity at the beginning,
and he left them to the power
of their choices.
[15] If you choose to,
you will keep the commandments,
and keep faith out of goodwill.[a]
[16] He has put fire and water before you;
you can stretch out your hand
for whichever you choose.
[17] Life and death are in front
of human beings;
and they will be granted
whichever they please,
[18] because the wisdom
of the Lord is great;
he's mighty in authority,
he sees everything,
[19] his eyes are upon those who fear him,
and he knows every human action.
[20] He doesn't command anyone
to be ungodly,
and he doesn't give anyone
a license to sin.

16 Don't wish for a multitude
of worthless children,
and don't be glad about sons and
daughters if they are ungodly.
[2] If they have children,
don't rejoice over them
unless they respect the Lord.
[3] Don't be confident that they will live,
and don't rely on their great number.[b]
One is better than a thousand,
and it's better to die childless
than to have ungodly children.
[4] A city will be populated
through one intelligent person,
but a tribe of lawless people
can transform it into a desert.

[5] My eye has seen many such things,
and my ear has heard more
extraordinary matters than these.
[6] A fire will be kindled
in an assembly of sinners,
and wrath will flash forth
in a disobedient nation.
[7] The Lord didn't seek reconciliation
with the ancient giants[c]
who rebelled in their might.
[8] He didn't spare Lot's neighbors,
whom he detested
because of their arrogance.
[9] He showed no mercy on a nation
doomed to destruction,
on people who were driven off
because of their sins.[d]
[10] So also he showed no mercy
to the six hundred thousand
foot soldiers
who gathered together
in their stubbornness.[e]

[11] Even if there was one
stiff-necked person,
it would be amazing
if that one would go unpunished,
because mercy and wrath are with him,
the Lord who reconciles
and who pours out wrath.
[12] His scrutiny is as severe
as his mercy is abundant;
he will judge people
according to their deeds.

[a] Gk uncertain [b] LXX[b] adds *You will lament in untimely mourning; you will suddenly learn of their end.* [c] Heb *princes*
[d] LXX[b] adds *He did all these things to hard-hearted nations, and the multitude of his holy ones did not appease him.*
[e] Or *hardness of their hearts*; LXX[b] adds *By flogging, showing mercy, striking, healing, the Lord watched carefully with compassion and discipline.*

13 A sinner won't escape with plunder,
and the endurance of the godly
will never fail.
14 He will make allowance
for every act of charity;
everyone will receive their just reward.[f]

17 Don't say, "I'll be hidden from the Lord,"
and "Who from on high
will call me to mind?
Among a great many people,
I'll never be recognized;
for what am I in such a vast creation?
18 Look at the heavens,
indeed the highest heavens;
the abyss and the earth
will tremble at the Lord's visitation.[g]
19 All at once the mountains
and the foundations of the earth
will shake together, quaking,
when he looks upon them.
20 The mind cannot even think
about these things.
Who can ponder his ways?
21 Most of his deeds are hidden
like a hurricane that no one can see.[h]
22 Who will announce just actions?
Or who will endure,
since God's covenant is far off?"[i]
23 Those who lack sense think this way;
a foolish and misguided person
thinks foolish things.

Wisdom and the creation of humans

24 Listen to me, my child: gain knowledge
and apply your mind to my words.
25 I will disclose instruction accurately,[j]
and with precision
I will declare knowledge.

26 The Lord's works in creation
existed from the beginning,
and he defined their exact stations
when he made them.
27 He set their works in order forever,
and arranged their spheres of authority
for as long as they last.
They have never gotten hungry
or grown weary,
and they have never
abandoned their tasks.
28 None of them crowd out their neighbor,
and none will ever disobey his word.
29 Afterward, the Lord looked at the earth
and filled it with his good things.
30 He covered its surface
with every living being,
and they return into it.

17 The Lord created a human being
out of earth,
and he returned that human being
into it again.
2 God gave human beings a set number
of days and a fixed time,
and he gave them authority
over the things that are upon the earth.
3 God endowed them with strength like
his, and he made them according
to his image.
4 God made all living beings afraid of
them, so that they might exercise
dominion over the animals and birds.[k]
6 God gave them the capacity to plan,
a tongue and eyes,
ears and a mind[l] for thinking.
7 God filled them with common sense,
and he showed them
good things and bad.
8 God put awe for him in their hearts,
in order to show them the greatness
of his works.[m]
9 So that they might tell of the
magnificence of his works,
10 they will praise his holy name.
11 God placed knowledge before them,
and he gave them a code for living.[n]
12 God established an eternal covenant
with them,

[f]LXX[b] adds 16:15-16 *The Lord hardened Pharaoh so that he didn't know him, so that God's works would be known everywhere under heaven. His mercy is evident to all creation, and his light and darkness he allotted to Adam.* [g]LXX[b] adds *The entire world, past and present, is in his will.* [h]LXX uncertain; Heb *If I sin, no one will see me; if I tell lies in complete secrecy, who will know?* [i]LXX[b] adds: *and everyone will be scrutinized in the end.* [j]LXX *by weight* [k]LXX[b] adds 17:5 *They received the use of the Lord's five faculties, but he apportioned to them the gift of mind as a sixth, and the seventh, reason, the interpreter of his faculties.* [l]LXX *heart* [m]LXX[b] adds *He allowed them to boast about his wonders through the ages.* [n]LXX[b] adds *so that they are mindful that those who are alive now are mortal.*

and he showed them his decrees.
13 They saw the majesty of his glory
with their own eyes,
and they heard his glorious voice
with their own ears.
14 God said to them,
"Beware of every injustice,"
and he gave each of them
commandments concerning
their neighbor.

15 Their ways are always before him;
they won't be hidden from his sight.[o]
17 God appointed a leader for each nation,
and Israel is
the Lord's responsibility.[p]
19 All of their deeds are before him
as plain as the sun,
and his eyes are always on their ways.
20 Their wrongs are not hidden from him,
and all their sins are exposed
in the Lord's presence.[q]
22 A person's acts of charity
are like a seal with him,
and he will treasure a person's
generosity like the apple of his eye.[r]
23 Afterward God will rise up
and repay them;
he will deliver their repayment
upon their heads.
24 However, for those who changed their
hearts and minds, God granted a way
back, and he encouraged those
who were abandoning hope.

25 Turn back to the Lord
and leave sin behind;
offer prayers in his presence,
and reduce your offense.
26 Return to the Most High,
and turn from injustice,[s]
and hate what he detests.
27 Who will praise the Most High
in the grave[t]
instead of the living
and those who give thanks?
28 From the dead thanksgiving has
perished, since they are no longer alive;
those who are alive and healthy
will praise the Lord.
29 How great is the Lord's mercy!
How quickly is he reconciled
with those who turn back to him!
30 Human beings can't do all things,
because no person is immortal.
31 What shines brighter than the sun?
Even that fails.
Flesh and blood will hanker after evil.
32 The Lord examines the might
of heaven's height,
and all human beings are dust and ashes.

18 The one who lives forever
created everything
in a common fashion.
2 Only the Lord will be declared just.[u]
4 He has given no one the power
to proclaim his works.
Who can search out his majestic deeds?
5 Who will measure
the power of his greatness?
Who will continue to recount his mercy?
6 It's impossible to diminish
or to increase these things,
and it's impossible
to search out the wonders of the Lord.
7 When people finish,
then they are just beginning,
and when they pause,
then they are puzzled.
8 What are human beings,
and what use are they?
What's good about them,
and what's evil about them?
9 The length of a person's life
is as much as one hundred years.[v]
10 Like a drop of water from the sea
or a grain of sand,
so are a few years in the span of eternity.

[o]LXX[b] adds 17:16-17*a Their ways from youth led toward evil things, and they were not strong enough to make their hearts flesh instead of stone. When he divided up the nations of all the earth,* [p]LXX[b] 17:18 adds *whom, being the oldest male, he nurtures with instruction, and, apportioning the light of his love, he doesn't neglect Israel* (or *him*). [q]LXX[b] adds 17:21 *But the Lord, being kind and knowing how they are formed, neither neglected them nor stopped sparing them.* [r]LXX[b] adds *doling out changed lives to his sons and daughters.* [s]LXX[b] adds *because he will guide you out of darkness into the healthful light.* [t]LXX *Hades*; Heb *Sheol* [u]LXX[b] adds 18:2*b*-3 *and there is no other besides him. He steers the world with the palm of his hand, and all things obey his will. By his power, he is the king of all things, dividing the holy things from the ordinary among them.* [v]LXX[b] adds *but the death of any one of them cannot be calculated by anyone.*

[11]Therefore, the Lord was patient
with them,
and he poured out his mercy upon them.
[12]He saw and knew that their end
was terrible;
therefore, his willingness to be
reconciled increased.
[13]Neighbors display mercy
toward each other,
but the mercy of the Lord is for all beings:
he corrects, instructs, teaches,
and turns them back,
as a shepherd does his flock.
[14]He shows mercy to those
who accept discipline
and to those who passionately pursue
his judgments.

Speech and self-control

[15]My child, let the good you do
be without blemish,
and don't give harsh words
along with your gifts.
[16]Doesn't dew put an end
to scorching heat?
So a word is better than a gift.
[17]Look! Doesn't a word exceed a good gift?
And both come from a person
who is gracious.
[18]A fool reproaches ungraciously,
and a gift from a begrudging giver
becomes an eyesore.[w]

[19]Learn before you speak,
and attend to yourself
before you get sick.
[20]Examine yourself before judgment,
and you will be reconciled
when you are examined.
[21]Humble yourself before you get sick,
and when you commit sins
show a changed heart and mind.
[22]Don't be prevented from repaying
a solemn promise in a timely way,
and don't wait until death
to be vindicated.
[23]Prepare yourself before making
a solemn promise,
and don't be like someone
who tests the Lord.
[24]Be mindful of his wrath in times of death
and in times of vengeance
when he turns his face away.
[25]Remember a time of hunger
in a time of plenty,
a time of poverty and want
in times of wealth.
[26]From morning until evening
opportune times change,
and all things are fleeting
in the Lord's presence.

[27]Wise people exercise caution
in everything,
and in times of sin
they will take heed against error.
[28]All intelligent people
have recognized Wisdom,
and they will acknowledge[x]
anyone who finds her.
[29]Those who are intelligent with words
have become wise themselves,
and they have poured forth
fitting proverbs.[y]

Self-control[z]

[30]Don't go after your desires,
and restrain yourself
from your appetites.
[31]If you cater to your desires,
you will become a laughingstock
to your enemies.
[32]Don't be glad for great luxury,
and don't be made needy
by an encounter with it.
[33]Don't become poor
by feasting with borrowed money,
when you have nothing in your pocket.[a]

19 A drunken worker[b]
won't become rich,
and whoever neglects the little things
will fail little by little.
[2]Wine and women
will mislead an intelligent person,
and the one who has sex with
prostitutes will become more reckless.

[w]LXX *melts away eyes* [x]Or *she will acknowledge* [y]LXX[b] adds *Confidence in a single master is better than adhering with a dead heart to a dead one.* [z]The title appears in Gk manuscripts. [a]LXX[b] adds *because you will be plotting against your own life.* [b]Heb *Whoever does this*

3 Decay and worms will possess him,
and his reckless soul will be carried away.
4 Those who trust others too quickly
have empty heads,
and those who sin injure themselves.
5 Those who rejoice in wickedness
will be condemned.[c]
6 And those who are reticent to speak
diminish wickedness.
7 Never repeat something that you've heard,
and you will not lose anything.
8 Don't report it to a friend or an enemy,
and, as long as it wouldn't be a sin for
you, don't reveal it.
9 People might hear you or observe you,
and in time they will hate you.
10 Have you heard some word?
Let it perish along with you.
Have courage!
It won't make you burst.
11 Because of something spoken,
a fool will suffer labor pains
like those caused by a baby
about to be delivered.
12 Like an arrow stuck in a thigh,
so is a word in the belly of a fool.
13 Question a friend;
perhaps he didn't do it.
And if he did, question him
so he doesn't do it again.
14 Question a neighbor;
perhaps she didn't say it.
And if she did say it,
question her so that she doesn't
repeat it.
15 Question a friend, because it often
turns out to be a false accusation.
Don't trust everything that is said.
16 There are those who slip,
and it wasn't intentional.
Who hasn't sinned with the tongue?
17 Question your neighbor
before issuing a threat,
and give the Law of the Most High
its place.[d]

Wisdom and cleverness

20 Fearing the Lord is the whole of wisdom,
and all wisdom involves
doing the Law.[e]
22 The knowledge of wickedness
isn't wisdom,
and there is no prudence
in the advice that sinners give.
23 There is a kind of cleverness
that is detestable,
and there is a senseless person
who lacks wisdom.
24 Someone who fears God
but who has inferior intelligence
is better than someone
who abounds in intelligence
but who violates the Law.
25 There is cleverness that is precise
but unjust,
and there are people who abuse favors
in order to get a favorable decision.[f]
26 And there are people who act wickedly,
bowed down gloomily,
and their insides are full of treachery.
27 They hide their faces,
and they pretend they can't hear;
when you aren't paying attention,
they will outrun you.
28 If they are prevented from sinning,
it's because they lack the strength.
If they find an occasion,
they will do evil.
29 People are known by their appearance,
and sensible people are recognized
in a face-to-face meeting.
30 A person's clothing,
their vigorous laughter,
and the way they walk
will proclaim things about them.

On speech

20 There is a bad time
to rebuke someone.
Those who keep silent
are the prudent ones.

[c]LXX[b] adds 19:5*b*-6*a* *but those who withstand pleasures bring glory to their life. Those who control their tongue will live without conflict.* [d]LXX[b] adds 19:18-19 *The fear of the Lord is the beginning of acceptance, and wisdom secures affection from him. Knowledge of the Lord's commandments is education for life, and those who do things that are pleasing to him will harvest the fruit of the tree of immortality.* [e]LXX[b] adds 19:20*c*-21 *and there is knowledge of his omnipotence. When household slaves say to the master, "I won't do what pleases you," and if after this they do those things, they still anger the one who provides for them.* [f]LXX[b] adds *and whoever treats others justly is wise in judgment.*

2 How much better to investigate
than to be angry!
3 And those who confess openly
will be kept from loss.
4 Like eunuchs desiring to violate a girl,
so are those who make decisions
by force.
5 There are people who are silent
and are found to be wise,
and there are those who are hated
because they talk a lot.
6 There are those who keep silent
because they have nothing to say
in response,
and there are those who keep silent
because they know the right time.
7 Wise people keep silent
until the proper moment,
but those who swagger and are
senseless will miss the right moment.
8 Those who talk excessively will be loathed,
and those who pretend
to have authority will be hated.[g]

9 Some people have success
in bad circumstances,
and there's a windfall that results
in loss.
10 There's a gift that won't profit you,
and there's a gift that will bring
twice the return.
11 There are losses suffered
for the sake of one's reputation,
and there are people who have raised
their heads from humiliation.
12 There are those who buy a lot for a little,
and they pay for it seven times over.
13 Wise people make themselves
dearly loved by means of words,[h]
but fools pour out gifts.
14 Gifts from senseless people
won't profit you,[i]
because they look for a lot
rather than a little in return.[j]
15 They will give a little and reproach a lot,
and they will open their mouths
like a town crier.
Today they will lend
and tomorrow ask for it back;
such people are hateful.
16 Fools say, "I don't have a friend,
and there's no gratitude
for my good deeds."
Those who eat the bread of such people
have mean tongues.
17 How many will ridicule them,
and how often?[k]

18 A slip on the pavement is preferable
to a slip of the tongue;
so the downfall of evil people
will come quickly.
19 A disagreeable person, an untimely story—
it will always be
in the mouth of the uneducated.
20 Proverbs told by fools will be rejected,
because they'll never tell them
at their proper time.

21 Some are prevented from sinning
because of poverty,
and their conscience won't be pained
when they rest.
22 Some destroy their life through shame,
and they destroy it
because of foolish appearances.
23 Some promise a favor to a friend
out of shame,
and they create an enemy for no reason.

24 A lie is a bad blemish on a person;
ignorant people tell them incessantly.
25 A thief is preferable to someone
who continuously lies,
but both will inherit destruction.
26 The character of liars is dishonorable;
their shame is continuously
with them.

Proverbial sayings[l]

27 Wise people distinguish themselves
by their words,
and prudent people will please
the powerful.

[g]LXX[b] *How good it is when someone who is reproved shows a changed heart and mind! In this way, you will escape sinning voluntarily.* [h]Heb *a few things* [i]LXX[b] adds *and neither will the gift of a grudging person who's forced to give.* [j]LXX *for their eyes are many rather than one* [k]LXX[b] adds *They haven't received what they have with real feeling, and what they don't have is similarly indifferent to them.* [l]The title appears in Gk manuscripts.

[28]Those who work the soil
will pile up their harvest,
and those who please the powerful
will secure reconciliation for injuries.
[29]Friendly relationships and gifts
will blind the eyes of the wise;
like a muzzle on a mouth,
they turn away reproof.
[30]Hidden wisdom and unseen treasure—
of what benefit is either?
[31]Better are those who hide
their foolishness
than those who hide their wisdom.[m]

On sin

21 My child, if you have sinned,
don't do it any longer,
and pray concerning your previous sins.
[2]Run away from sin
like you would from a snake:
If you go near it, it will bite you.
Its teeth are lion's teeth,
destroying a person's life.
[3]All lawlessness is a two-edged sword,
and there's no healing for its wound.

[4]Alarm and insolence will strip away wealth;
thus will an arrogant person's house
be uprooted.
[5]The petition of the poor goes
from their mouth to God's ears,
and his judgment comes quickly.
[6]Anyone who hates reproof
walks in the footsteps of a sinner,
and those who fear the Lord
will turn back to him from the heart.
[7]Those who are powerful in speech
are widely known,
but those who are thoughtful
know when they slip.

[8]Those who build their houses
with another person's money
are like those who gather stones
for their own burial mound.
[9]A gathering of lawless people
is the same as bundled flax;
their end is a flaming fire.
[10]The path of sinners
is made level with stones,
but its end is the pit of hell.[n]

Wisdom and folly

[11]Those who keep the Law
become masters of their thoughts;
fearing the Lord
leads ultimately to wisdom.
[12]Those who aren't clever
won't receive instruction,
but there is a kind of cleverness
that makes troubles multiply.
[13]The knowledge of the wise
will increase like a flood,
and their counsel is like
a stream of life.
[14]The mind[o] of a fool is like a broken jar:
it can't hold knowledge.

[15]If those who understand
hear a wise word;
they will praise it and add to it.
Those who like to indulge themselves
hear it and are displeased,
and they turn their back on it.
[16]A fool's endless talk
is a burden while on a journey,
but grace will be found
on the lips of the intelligent.
[17]The speech of the prudent
will be sought out in an assembly,
and its members will take their words
to heart.

[18]Like a house in disrepair,
so is wisdom to the foolish,
and the knowledge of ignorant people
will not stand up to examination.
[19]Education is shackles
on the feet of the ignorant,
like manacles on their hand.
[20]Fools raise their voice in laughter,
but clever people will smile subtly
in silence.
[21]To the prudent,
education is like a gold ornament,
like a bracelet on the arm.

[m]LXX[b] adds 20:32 *Better is unmovable endurance when seeking the Lord than a charioteer of one's life that has no master.* [n]LXX *Hades*; Heb *Sheol* [o]LXX *entrails*

22 The foolish enter quickly into a house,
but experienced people
will be ashamed to do so.[p]
23 The senseless peer into a house
through the door,
but the educated will stand outside.
24 Ignorance causes people to listen
through a door,
but the prudent will be distressed
at the dishonor of doing so.

25 The lips of strangers
will report these things,
but the words of the prudent
will be placed on a balance.
26 Fools say whatever is on their minds,
but the wise remain mindful
of what they say.
27 When the ungodly
curse their enemies,[q]
they curse themselves.
28 Those who whisper stain themselves,
and they will be hated
by their neighbors.

22 People who are afraid to act
are like filthy stones;
everyone will hiss at their dishonor.
2 People who are afraid to act
are like clumps of cow manure;
those who pick it up
will shake off their hand.

3 An uneducated son is a disgrace
to a father,
and a daughter's birth is a liability.
4 A prudent daughter
will get a husband of her own,
and a daughter in disgrace
is a grief to her parents.
5 A disrespectful daughter
shames her father and her husband,
and both will despise her.
6 Ill-timed talk is like party music
during mourning,
but a whipping and discipline
are wisdom at any time.[r]

9 Whoever teaches a fool
is gluing together a broken pot
or waking up someone
out of a deep sleep.
10 Whoever talks with a fool
converses with someone who is drowsy;
when the conversation is over,
the fool will say, "What is it?"
11 Weep for the dead,
for they have left the light behind;
and weep for fools,
for they have
left understanding behind.
Weep sweetly over the dead,
because they are at rest,
but the life of a fool is worse
than death.
12 Mourn for the dead for seven days,
but mourn for the foolish and the
ungodly all the days of their lives.

13 Don't talk a lot with fools,
and don't go to the unintelligent.[s]
Be on guard against them
so that you don't have trouble
and don't get dirty
when they shake themselves off.
Stay away from them
and you will find rest,
and their senselessness
won't make you weary.
14 What's heavier than lead?
And what name does it have but "Fool"?
15 Sand, salt, and a lump of iron
are easier to bear
than an unintelligent person.

16 A wooden beam fastened into a building
won't be loosened by an earthquake.
So a heart firmly set
on thoughtful counsel
won't be afraid at any time.
17 A heart fixed on thoughtful understanding
is like an engraved ornament
on a smooth wall.
18 A protective barrier set on a high place
will never endure against the wind.

[p]Heb *An honorable person will stand outside.* [q]LXX *the satan* [r]LXX[b] adds 22:7–8 *Children who are brought up to live a good life mask the lowly birth of their parents. Children who take pride in contempt and lack of education pollute the honorable name of their own family.* [s]LXX[b] adds *When people are senseless, they will bring everything of yours to nothing.*

So a timid heart backed up
by a fool's plan
will never endure against any fear.

Preserving friendship

19 Whoever pricks an eye
will make tears flow,
and whoever pricks a heart
reveals its feelings.
20 Whoever throws a stone at birds
scares them off,
and whoever insults a friend
breaks up a friendship.
21 If you draw a sword on a friend,
don't despair,
because there can be a way back.
22 If you speak harshly to a friend,
don't be concerned,
because there can be reconciliation.
But in the case of reproach, arrogance,
the revealing of a secret,
or a treacherous blow,
any friend will flee.

23 Gain your neighbors' trust
while they are poor,
so that when they are prosperous,
you will be filled along with them.
In a time of distress remain with them
so that when they inherit,
you will be a joint heir.[t]
24 Before there's a fire,
a furnace has vapor and smoke;
so before bloodshed there are insults.
25 I won't be ashamed to shelter friends,
and I won't hide from them.
26 And if something bad happens to me
because of them,
everyone who hears of it
will be on guard against them.

Prayer for protection from sinning

27 Who will put a guard on my mouth
and an effective seal upon my lips
so that I don't fall
because of my speech
and so that my tongue
doesn't destroy me?

23 Lord, Father, and master of my life,
don't abandon me to their will,
and don't let me fall because of them.
2 Who will station whips
to keep my thoughts in line
and set the discipline of wisdom
over my heart,
so that I might not be spared my faults
due to ignorance
and my sins not go unnoticed?
3 Otherwise, my acts of ignorance
might multiply,
and my sins might increase,
and I'll fall before my adversaries,
and my enemy will rejoice over me.[u]
4 Lord, Father, God of my life,
don't let me have prideful eyes;
5 turn desire away from me.
6 Don't allow gluttony or sexual desire
to overtake me,
and don't hand me over
to a shameless spirit.[v]

Instruction about the mouth[w]

7 Listen, my children, to instruction
about your mouth;
whoever follows my instruction
will never succumb to it.
8 The lips of sinners will seize them
and make abusers
and the arrogant stumble.
9 Don't let your mouth
get used to making solemn pledges,
and don't get accustomed
to saying the name of the holy one.
10 Just as a household slave
who is constantly examined
won't be lacking bruises,
so also the person who always swears
and speaks the Lord's name
will never be cleansed from sin.
11 People who make many solemn pledges
will be full of lawlessness,
and a scourge won't depart
from their house.
If they break their solemn pledges,
their sin is on them,
and if they disregard it, they sin doubly,

[t] LXX[b] adds *One shouldn't always despise appearances, nor are the rich admirable when they have no sense.*
[u] LXX[b] adds *The hope of your mercy is far from them.* [v] LXX *soul* [w] The title appears in Gk manuscripts.

and if they swear falsely,
they won't be justified,
but their houses will be full of misery.

12 There is a way of speaking
that's comparable to death;
don't let it be found
among Jacob's descendants.
All these things will stay far away
from the godly,
and they will not wallow in their sins.
13 Don't grow accustomed
to saying coarse things,
because to do so is to engage
in sinful speech.
14 Remember your father and mother,
because you sit in the council
among officials.
This way, you won't forget yourself
in front of them
and act foolishly out of habit—
then you'd wish
that you hadn't been born,
and you'd curse the day of your birth.
15 People who are accustomed
to reproachful words
will never learn anything
their whole life.

On sex

16 Two types of people multiply sins,
and a third will bring wrath.
A hot temperament that burns like fire
will never be quenched until it is spent.
People who are promiscuous
with their kin
will never stop until the fire burns out.
17 To promiscuous people all bread is sweet;
they don't become weary until they die.
18 There are people
who violate their marriage bed,
saying to themselves, Who will see me?
Darkness envelops me;
the walls hide me;
no one will see me.
Why do I have a care?
The Most High
will never recall my sins.
19 They fear human eyes,
but they are unaware
that the eyes of the Lord
are ten thousand times brighter
than the sun;
they observe all the ways
of human beings
and look into hidden places.
20 Before all things were created,
God knew them;
so as well after they were finished.
21 These people will be punished
in the streets of the city,
and when they least expect it,
they will be seized.

22 So it is with a woman
when she is unfaithful to her husband
and she presents him with an heir
by another man.
23 First, she's disobeyed
the Law of the Most High;
second, she's wronged her husband;
third, she's committed adultery
by her illicit sexual behavior
and produced children
by another man.
24 She will be led into the assembly,
and her punishment
will be upon her children.
25 Her children won't take root,
and her branches won't bear fruit.
26 She will leave behind a cursed memory,
and her reproach won't be wiped clean.
27 And those who remain will know
that nothing is better
than fearing the Lord,
and nothing is sweeter than keeping
the Lord's commandments.[x]

Praise of Wisdom[y]

24 Wisdom will praise herself,
and she will boast in the midst of
her people.
2 In the assembly of the Most High,
she will open her mouth,
and in the presence of
his heavenly forces, she will boast:

[x] LXX[b] adds 23:28 *It is a great glory to follow God; to be received by him is to have a long life.* [y] The title appears in Gk manuscripts.

3 "I came forth from the mouth
of the Most High,
and I covered the earth like a mist.
4 I lived in the heights,
and my throne was in a pillar of cloud.
5 I alone encircled the vault of heaven
and walked in the depths of abysses.
6 In the waves of the sea and in every land,
and among every people and nation,
I led the way.
7 I sought a resting place
among all of these.
In whose allotted territory
should I make my home?

8 "Then the creator of all things
gave me a command;
the one who created me pitched my tent
and said, 'Make your dwelling in Jacob,
and let Israel receive your inheritance.'
9 Before the ages, from the beginning,
he created me,
and till eternity I will never fail.
10 I ministered before him in the holy tent,
and so I was established in Zion.
11 In the same way, he made
the dearly loved city my resting place
and established my authority
in Jerusalem.
12 I took root in a glorified people;
among the people the Lord chose
for his inheritance.

13 "I rose high like a cedar in Lebanon,
like a cypress on Mount Hermon.
14 I rose high like a palm in En-geddi,
and like rosebushes in Jericho,
like a fair olive tree in a field.
I rose high like a plane tree.
15 Like cinnamon and camel's thorn
used for spices,
I gave off a fine aroma.
Like choice myrrh,
I spread forth my fragrance,
like galbanum, onycha, and stacte,
and like the smell of frankincense
in the tent.
16 Like a terebinth oak
I spread out my branches,
and my branches were glorious
and graceful.
17 Gracious favor was the leaf
that I put forth like a vine,
and honor and wealth
were the fruit that my blossoms bore.[z]

19 "Come to me, you who desire me,
and take your fill of my produce.
20 Calling me to mind is sweeter
than honey,
and possessing me
is better than a dripping honeycomb.
21 Those who eat of me will hunger
for more,
and those who drink of me
will thirst for more.
22 Whoever obeys me won't be ashamed,
and those who work with me
won't sin."

Wisdom and the Law

23 All these things are in the covenant
scroll of the Most High God,
the Law that Moses commanded us,
the inheritance of the congregations
of Jacob.[a]
25 God supplies Wisdom comparable
to the fullness of the Pishon River,
even like the Tigris River
in the springtime.
26 God provides understanding
as deep as the Euphrates,
or like the Jordan at the time
of the harvest.
27 God pours forth understanding like light,
as does the Gihon Spring
at the time of the grape harvest.
28 The first human
didn't know Wisdom completely,
and so the last won't probe her fully.
29 Her thoughts are more plentiful
than the sea;
her counsel is deeper
than the great abyss.[b]

[z] LXX[b] adds 24:18 *I am the mother of beautiful love, of awe, of knowledge, and of devout hope, and I grant them, together with all things, to my children eternally generated gifts, to those whom God chooses.* [a] LXX[b] adds 24:24 *Don't stop being strong in the Lord, but cling to him so that he might strengthen you. The Lord Almighty alone is God, and there's no savior except for him.* [b] Or *Her thoughts grow from the sea, and her plan grows from the deep abyss.*

30 Like a canal from a river,
like an irrigation channel,
I went out into a garden.
31 I said, "I'll water my garden,
and I'll drench my flower bed.
And look! The canal
turned into a river for me,
and my river turned into a sea.
32 I'll continue to make instruction
shine forth like the dawn,
and I'll make things clear
to those who are far off.
33 I'll continue to pour out teaching
like prophecy,
and I'll leave it behind
for future generations.
34 See, I've not labored for myself alone,
but for all those who seek her."

Things to be praised

25 My whole being takes pleasure
in three things,
and these are beautiful to the Lord
and to human beings:
harmony among brothers and sisters,
friendship among neighbors,
and a wife and husband
who adapt to each other.
2 My whole being despises
three types of persons,
and I am angered by the way they live:
an arrogant poor person,
a rich liar,
an old adulterer who never learns.

3 If you have gathered nothing
in your youth,
how then will you find anything
in your old age?
4 How beautiful is sound judgment
in gray-haired women
and finding good advice in elderly men!
5 How beautiful is wisdom in the aged
and thought and counsel
in those who are respectable!
6 Experience is the crown of the aged
and respecting the Lord
is their claim to fame.
7 In my heart, I would consider
nine conditions to be happy,
and I'll name a tenth with my tongue—
people who are made glad
by their children,
and who live to see the downfall
of their enemies.
8 Happy are those
who live with sensible wives,[c]
who don't slip with their tongue,
and who haven't been a servant to one
inferior to themselves.
9 Happy is the one
who has gained good sense
and who is passing this along
to listening ears.
10 How great is one who finds Wisdom,
but no one does better
than the one who fears the Lord.
11 Fear of the Lord surpasses everything;
those who possess it are incomparable.[d]

Evil and good women

13 Any wound, but not a wound to the heart;
and any wickedness,
but not a woman's wickedness!
14 Any attack,
but not an attack by those who hate;
and any vengeance,
but not the vengeance of enemies.
15 No poison is worse than a snake's poison,[e]
and no anger is worse
than an enemy's anger.

16 I would rather live with a lion or a serpent
than live with a wicked woman.
17 A woman's wickedness
changes her appearance,
and it darkens her face like that of a bear.
18 Her husband sits down among
his neighbors
and unintentionally groans bitterly.
19 Any evil is small
when compared to a woman's evil;
may she experience a sinner's fate.
20 A talkative wife for a quiet husband
is like a sand dune
beneath the feet of an elderly person.

[c]Heb adds *and who does not plow with an ox and an ass together. Happy are those who;* LXX lacks this phrase and the prior line. [d]LXX[b] adds 25:12 *Fear of the Lord is the start of loving him, and faith is the start of clinging to him.* [e]In both cases, LXX has *head.*

[21] Don't fall for a woman's beauty,
and don't long for a woman.
[22] There will be anger, shamelessness,
and utter disgrace
when a wife provides for her husband.
[23] A wicked wife causes a humiliated heart,
a gloomy face,
and a wounded heart.
Drooping hands and weakened knees
come from a woman
who doesn't make her husband happy.
[24] Sin began with a woman,
and because of her all of us die.
[25] Don't allow an outlet for water,
and don't give a wicked wife
freedom to speak.
[26] If she doesn't do as you say,
divorce her.[f]

26 The husband of a good wife
is favored,
and the length of his life will be doubled.
[2] A courageous wife
will make her husband happy,
and he will complete his years in peace.
[3] A good wife is a great blessing.
The one who fears the Lord will receive
her as part of his God-given portion.
[4] Whether in poverty or in wealth,
his heart is happy;
at every moment he has a cheerful face.

[5] My heart was cautious about three things,
and I was fearful
in the face of a fourth—
slander in a city,
the gathering of a mob,
and a false accusation—
all of these are more miserable
than death.
[6] Women who are rivals
bring heartache and grief,
and a tongue-lashing shares it
with everyone.
[7] A wicked wife is like a chafing ox yoke;
the one who holds her
is like one who grasps a scorpion.
[8] A drunken wife is the same as rage;
she won't hide her disgraceful conduct.
[9] A wife's promiscuity is seen
in the arrogance of her eyes,
and her eyelids make it known.

[10] Keep a strict watch
over a disobedient daughter,
or else, if she finds you off guard,
she will take advantage of it.
[11] Beware of her shameless eye,
and don't be surprised
if she wrongs you.
[12] Just as thirsty travelers
will open their mouths
and drink from water that is near,
she will sit in front of every peg,
and she will open her quiver
to an arrow.

[13] A wife's charm will delight her husband,
and her skill will put fat on his bones.
[14] A silent wife is a gift from the Lord,
and nothing can be traded
for her self-discipline.
[15] A modest wife adds charm upon charm,
and there is no balance that can weigh
the full value of her self-control.
[16] As the sun rising in the Lord's
high heavens,
so is the beauty of a good wife
in her well-ordered home.
[17] As a lamp shines on the holy lampstand,
so also is a beautiful face
along with steady maturity.
[18] Like gold pillars upon a silver base,
so also are shapely legs
on steadfast feet.

[19] [g]My child, keep the vitality
of your prime of life safe and sound,
and don't give your strength
over to strangers.
[20] After you have chosen a fertile plot
out of every field,
sow your own seed,
being confident of your
excellent descent.
[21] Thus your offspring who surround you
and who have confidence

[f] LXX *separate her from your flesh* [g] LXX[b] adds 26:19–27.

in their excellent descent,
will become great.
22 A hired woman will be considered
the same as spit,
but a married woman will be
considered a tower of death to those
who associate too closely with her.
23 An ungodly woman will be bestowed
on a lawless man as his portion,
but a godly woman is granted
to the man who fears the Lord.
24 A shameless woman will always be
in disgrace,
but a dignified daughter will show
modesty even with her husband.
25 An unruly wife will be thought of
as a dog,
but the wife who feels shame
will fear the Lord.
26 A wife who honors her own husband
will appear wise to everyone,
but the wife who dishonors her
husband with arrogance
will be known to all as ungodly.
The husband of a good wife is happy,
for the number of his years will double.
27 A loudmouthed and talkative wife
is like a battle trumpet
sounding an attack.
The spirit of the man
who lives under such conditions
lives perpetually in the chaos
of the battlefield.

On integrity

28 My heart has been saddened
by two things,
and I was made angry because of a third:
a warrior who is needy
and impoverished,
intelligent people who are treated
with contempt,
and people who are turned
from righteousness to sin—
the Lord will prepare them
for the sword.

29 A merchant will scarcely be kept
from wrongdoing,
and a retailer won't be innocent of sin.

27 Many have sinned because of
money,
and whoever seeks to get more
will turn a blind eye.
2 A stake is driven
between cracks in stones,
and sin will be wedged
between selling and buying.
3 If people don't remain mindful
of the respect due the Lord,
their houses will be quickly overthrown.

4 When a sieve is shaken,
rubbish remains behind;
so in the process of reasoning,
a person's flaws appear.
5 A kiln tests a potter's jars,
and decision making tests a person.
6 A tree's fruit reveals
how well it has been cultivated.
In the same way, reasoning makes plain
a person's thoughts.
7 Don't praise people
until after they present an argument,
for this is how people are tested.

8 If you pursue what's just,
you will possess it
and wear it like a glorious robe.
9 Birds will nest with their own kind,
and truth comes back
to those who practice it.
10 A lion lies in wait for prey
just as sin lies in wait
for those who practice injustice.

11 The godly always speak wisdom,
but the fool changes like the moon.
12 Limit the time you spend
with unintelligent people,
but linger with the thoughtful.
13 The conversation of fools is offensive,
as is their laughter
over sinful pleasures.
14 Their speech, full of profanity,
makes a person's hair stand on end,
and their conflicts make people
stop up their ears.
15 The conflict of the arrogant
ends in bloodshed,
and their abuse is miserable to hear.

Relations with associates

16 Those who reveal secrets
have destroyed trust,
and they will never find a friend
for themselves.
17 Show affection to friends
and be loyal to them,
but if you reveal their secrets,
don't follow after them.
18 Just as people destroy an enemy,[h]
so you have destroyed your friendship
with your neighbors.
19 And as you set a bird free from your hand,
so too you have let your neighbors go,
and you won't catch them.
20 Don't pursue them,
because they have withdrawn
far away from you,
and they have escaped
like a gazelle from a trap.
21 In the same way that it's possible
to bandage a wound,
there's also reconciliation for insult,
but the one who has let a friend's
secrets slip out has no hope.

22 Those who wink their eye plan evil,
and whoever recognizes them
will keep their distance.
23 To your face their speech will be sweet,
and they will express amazement
at your words.
But later they will distort what they said,
and they will use your own words
against you.
24 I've hated many things,
but nothing compares with them.
Even the Lord will hate them.
25 Those who throw stones up high
throw them on their own heads,
and a deceitful blow
will open up wounds.
26 Whoever digs a hole will fall into it,
and whoever sets a trap
will get caught in it.
27 Evil will roll back upon those
who practice evil,
and they will never know
where it came from.
28 Mocking and blaming
belong to the arrogant,
and vengeance, like a lion,
will lie in wait for them.
29 Those who rejoice when godly people fall
will get caught in a trap,
and pain will consume them
before their death.

30 Wrath and anger—
these also are detestable,
and they will possess the sinful person.

28 Those who are vengeful
will suffer the Lord's vengeance,
because the Lord keeps strict count
of their sins.
2 Forgive your neighbor a wrong,
and then, when you pray,
your sins will be forgiven.
3 Can people hold on to their anger
against others, and then look for
healing from the Lord?
4 Can they refuse to have mercy
on people like themselves,
and then pray about their own sins?
5 If they, who are just flesh,
hold on to anger,
who will secure pardon
for their own sins?
6 Be mindful of the end that awaits you,
and put an end to enmity;
be mindful of decay and death,
and be faithful to the commandments.
7 Be mindful of the commandments,
and don't be irate at your neighbor;
be mindful of the covenant of the
Most High, and overlook a mistake.

8 Keep away from conflict,
and you will reduce your sins;
for hot-tempered people spark conflict.
9 Sinful people will stir up trouble for friends,
and they spread slander
among people who are at peace.
10 A fire burns in proportion to its fuel,
and conflict increases
the longer it continues.
The more powerful individuals are,
the stronger their anger will be;

[h] Some manuscripts *a corpse*

and the wealthier they are,
the more their wrath will increase.
11 A hasty quarrel sparks a fire,
and hasty conflict sheds blood.

12 If you blow on a spark, it will flame up,
and if you spit on it, it will go out;
nonetheless, both come out
of your mouth.

13 A curse on slanderers and the deceitful,[i]
because they have destroyed many
who are at peace.
14 Slander[j] has shaken up many people,
scattered them from nation to nation,
demolished mighty cities,
and overthrown the houses
of dignitaries.
15 Slander[k] has driven out
courageous women,
and it has deprived them
of the rewards of their work.
16 Those who pay attention to slander
will never find rest,
nor will they live in peace.
17 The blow of a whip leaves a welt,
but the blow of the tongue
will break bones.
18 Many have fallen by the edge
of the sword,
but many more have fallen
because of the tongue.
19 Happy is the person
who is protected from the tongue,
who hasn't endured its anger,
who hasn't pulled its yoke
or been bound by its shackles.
20 Its yoke is made of iron,
and its shackles are made of bronze.
21 The death it inflicts is a wicked death,
and the grave[l] is preferable to it.
22 It will never conquer the godly,
and they won't be burned by its flame.
23 Those who abandon the Lord
will fall to it;
it will burn within them,
and it will never go out.
It will be sent against them like a lion,
and like a leopard it will mangle them.
24a Watch out! Fence in your property
with thorns,
25b and make a door
and a bolt for your mouth.
24b Lock up your silver and gold;
25a make a balance and a weight
for your words.[m]
26 Pay attention, and don't slip
by your tongue;
don't fall in front of those
who are just waiting to attack you.

Lending and borrowing

29 Those who show compassion
will lend to a neighbor,
and those who lend a helping hand
keep the commandments.
2 Lend to neighbors in their time of need,
and pay your neighbor back again
on time.
3 Keep your word,
and be trustworthy in your dealings,
and you will find what you need
every time.
4 Many think of a loan as a windfall,
and they have caused trouble
for those who have helped them.
5 Until they receive the loan,
they will kiss the hands of those
who can help,
and they will speak with deference
about their neighbor's money,
but when it's time for repayment,
they will put it off,
offer weak excuses,
and say it is a bad time.
6 If they can repay, their creditors
will barely recover half the amount,
and the creditors will consider
that much a windfall;
but if they can't pay,
they have defrauded their creditors
of their money,
and they have made enemies
out of them needlessly.
They will repay their creditors
with curses and insults,

[i] LXX *double-tongued* [j] LXX *a third tongue* [k] LXX *a third tongue* [l] LXX *Hades*; Heb *Sheol* [m] The lines of these verses have suffered transposition in some manuscripts.

and they will repay them with dishonor
rather than glory.
7 Many have refused to make a loan,
not because they were vicious
but because they were cautious
about being needlessly cheated.

8 Even so, be patient with those
in humble circumstances,
and don't make them wait for assistance.
9 Help the needy for the
commandment's sake,
and in proportion to their need
don't turn them away empty-handed.
10 Part with silver for a relative's
or friend's sake,
and don't let it corrode under a stone
and be destroyed.
11 Invest your treasure
according to the commandments
of the Most High,
and it will profit you more than gold.
12 Store up acts of charity in your treasuries,
and it will deliver you
from every distress.
13 More than a sturdy shield
and more than a hefty spear,
it will fight for you against an enemy.

14 Good people will guarantee a loan
for neighbors,
and those who have lost any
sense of shame will abandon them.
15 Don't forget the kindness of those
who have guaranteed a loan,
since they gave their life
on your behalf.
16 Sinners will ruin
their guarantor's property,
17 and ungrateful persons
intentionally abandon their rescuers.
18 Guaranteeing a loan
has ruined many prosperous people
and tossed them about
like a wave on the sea.
It has led to the exile of the powerful,
and they have wandered
among foreign nations.
19 Sinners will fall into guaranteeing loans,
and when they chase profits,
they will fall into lawsuits.
20 Help your neighbor as much as you can,
but keep yourself from ruin.

Home and children

21 Life's foundations are water,
bread, clothing,
and a house for ensuring privacy.
22 Better is the life of the poor
under a shelter of rafters
than magnificent food
in foreign countries.
23 Be content with a little or a lot,
and you will never be put down
for being a sojourner.
24 Going from house to house
is a miserable life,
and wherever you are an immigrant,
don't open your mouth.
25 You will entertain and provide drink
without thanks,
and you will hear bitter words
such as these:
26 "Come here, foreigner, prepare a table;
and if there's something in your hand,
feed it to me.
27 Go away, foreigner,
I have a reputable guest;
my brother has come to visit,
and I need the house."
28 These are difficult things
for a person of intelligence:
criticism for being an immigrant
and rebuke from a moneylender.

Concerning children[n]

30 The person who loves his sons
will discipline them often
so that he may be glad
about how they turn out.
2 Whoever instructs his sons
will benefit from them,
and he will boast about them
among his acquaintances.
3 The person who teaches his sons
will make his enemy jealous,
but among his friends
he will rejoice over them.

[n] The title appears in Gk manuscripts.

4 When their father passes away,
it is as if he hadn't died,
because he left behind sons
who are like him.
5 When he was alive,
he saw them and was glad,
and at his end, he wasn't grieved.
6 He was survived by those
who would avenge him
against his enemies
and who would repay kindness
to his friends.

7 A parent who spoils children now
will end up tending to their wounds,
and will experience heartache
at every outcry.
8 A horse that is unbroken
turns out stubborn,
and a child, when given free rein,
turns out reckless.
9 Indulge children,
and they will terrorize you;
play with them,
and they will grieve you.
10 Don't laugh together with them,
so that you don't suffer together
and in the end
grind your teeth in regret.
11 Don't give them free rein in their youth.[o]
12 Bruise their sides
while they are still young,
or else they will become stubborn
and disobey you.
13 Educate your children, and work on them,
so that you don't end up offended
by their shameful behavior.

Food and health

14 It is better to be poor,
but healthy and strong,
than a rich person
whose body is afflicted.
15 Being healthy and fit
is better than any gold,
and a strong spirit
is better than untold riches.
16 No wealth is better than a healthy body,
and no gladness is better than
happiness in one's heart.
17 Death is better than a bitter life,
and eternal rest is
better than chronic illness.

Concerning foods[p]

18 Good things that are poured out
on a closed mouth
are the same as food offerings
placed on a grave.
19 Of what use is an offering of fruit
to an idol?
It can't eat or smell.
The person whom the Lord punishes
is like this,
20 looking with the eyes and groaning
like a eunuch who embraces
a young woman and groans.[q]

21 Don't let grief take you over,
and don't distress yourself on purpose.
22 A joyful heart means life
for a human being,
and a person's rejoicing
provides long life.
23 Distract yourself, cheer yourself up,
and keep grief far away from you
because grief has destroyed many,
and there's no benefit in it.
24 Jealousy and anger
shorten a person's life,
and anxiety brings old age
before its time.
25 Those who are cheerful
and contented at meals
will attend well to their food.[r]

On wealth

31 Sleeplessness over wealth
makes the body waste away,
and anxiety about wealth
keeps sleep away.
2 Worrying will keep you awake,
and serious illness
will chase sleep away.
3 Rich people have worked
to accumulate money,

[o]LXX[b] adds 30:11*b*-12*a* *and don't overlook his mistakes. In his youth, bow down his neck.* [p]The title appears in Gk manuscripts. [q]LXX[b] adds 30:20*c* *So is the one who makes judgments under pressure.* [r]Gk and Heb uncertain

and when they rest,
they fill themselves with their luxuries.
4 Poor people have worked
to eke out a living,
and when they rest,
they become needy again.

5 Whoever loves gold won't be declared just,
and whoever pursues profits
will be led astray by them.
6 Many have been ruined because of gold,
and their destruction has met them
head-on.[s]
7 It's a stumbling block for those
who are possessed by it,
and it will take
every senseless person captive.
8 Happy are the rich
who are without blame
and who don't follow after gold.
9 Who are they,
so that we might praise them?
They have done wonders
among the people.
10 Who has been tested by wealth[t]
and been found perfect?
For them it will be a reason to boast.
Who had the power to sin and didn't,
and could do evil but didn't?
11 The possessions of such people
will be secure,
and the congregation will tell
of their acts of charity.

Behavior at meals

12 Have you been seated
at a magnificent table?
Don't be greedy as you sit there,
and don't say,
"Look how much food there is!"
13 Remember, a greedy eye is a bad thing.
What has been created more greedy
than the eye?
For this reason, every face sheds tears.
14 Don't reach out your hand
for whatever you see,
and don't crowd your dinner companion
by reaching into the same bowl.
15 Put yourself in your companion's place,
and be considerate in everything.
16 Eat what's put in front of you
like a normal human being,[u]
and don't chew rudely,
or you will be hated.
17 Be the first to stop
to show your good breeding,
and don't be gluttonous;
otherwise, you will offend.
18 If you have been seated
with a lot of people,
don't help yourself before they do.

19 A little food is more than enough
for well-educated people!
They won't gasp for breath
when they lie down to sleep.
20 Healthy sleep depends
on not stuffing yourself.
Such people arise early and feel good.[v]
The gluttons suffer the pains of
insomnia, nausea, and colic.
21 If you've overstuffed yourself,
get up, vomit far away,
and you will feel better.
22 Listen to me, my child,
and don't show me contempt,
and in the end you will understand
what I'm saying;
be careful[w] in everything you do,
and you will never fall sick.
23 People will bless those
who are generous with bread;
they give reliable testimony
to the excellence of such people.
24 The city will murmur about those
who are stingy with bread,
giving accurate witness
to the wickedness of such people.

25 Don't demonstrate your bravado
in wine drinking,
because wine has destroyed many.
26 A furnace tests the hardening of steel
when it's dipped,[x]
so wine tests the heart
when the arrogant quarrel.

[s] Heb *and who have trusted in jewels.* [t] Gk *it* [u] Heb *like a well-mannered person* [v] LXX *and their spirit with them*
[w] Heb *moderate* [x] Heb *tests the work of the smith*

27 If taken in moderation,
wine makes people's lives better.
What's life to those who
don't have wine?
It was created from the beginning
to bring merriment.
28 The right amount of wine
consumed at the right time
makes for a joyful heart
and a light spirit.
29 Too much wine drunk
in the midst of strife and conflict
makes for a bitter spirit.
30 Getting drunk causes fools to lose
their temper and do themselves harm,
reducing their strength,
and adding injuries as well.
31 Don't correct your neighbors
at a wine banquet,
and don't show them contempt
when they are partying;
don't say any reproachful word
to them,
and don't trouble them
with any demands.

32 If they have appointed you
as the banquet leader,
don't think too much of yourself;
behave toward them
as if you were one of them.
Take care of their needs
and then sit down.
2 When you have done
everything necessary, recline,
so that you can have fun with them,
and because of your excellent behavior
you will receive a wreath.

3 Speak, you who are older,
for it's your privilege.
But know what you're talking about,
and don't interrupt the music.
4 Where there's a performance,
don't talk too much,
and don't be clever at the wrong time.
5 A musical performance at a wine party
is like a ruby seal on a gold ornament.
6 Melodic music accompanying sweet wine
is like an emerald seal
in a setting of gold.
7 Speak, you who are young,
if it's necessary,
but only twice,
and only if you are asked.
8 Sum up what you have to say;
much can be said in few words.
Be like one who knows
but who can keep silent.
9 When you are among the more
influential, don't presume authority;
and where elders are present,
don't talk idly about many things.
10 Lightning comes before thunder,
and good favor walks
in front of a modest person.
11 Rise up to leave in time,
and don't be the last person out;
go back to your own home,
and don't miss your work
the next day.
12 Enjoy yourself there,
and do what you please,
but don't sin with arrogant words.
13 More than this,
bless the one who made you
and who lets you drink freely
from his good bounty.

On divine providence

14 Whoever fears the Lord
will accept instruction;
those who rise early
will find approval.
15 Whoever seeks the Law
will be filled with it,
but the hypocrite will stumble over it.
16 Those who fear the Lord
will discover his decree,
and they will kindle righteous deeds
like a lamp.
17 Sinful people turn away from correction;
they will look for a judgment
that suits them.

18 A well-advised person
won't overlook an intelligent thought;
the stranger and the arrogant
won't cower out of fear.
19 Do nothing without deliberation,
and when you have acted,
don't feel regret.

[20]Don't walk on a hazardous path,
and don't stumble on stony ground.[y]
[21]Don't trust an unexplored road,
[22]and be on guard
concerning your children.[z]
[23]Trust yourself[a] in every action,
because this also means
keeping the commandments.

[24]Whoever has faith in the Law
pays attention to the commandments;
whoever trusts the Lord
won't suffer loss.

33 Those who fear the Lord
won't encounter evil,
but when they are tested
they will be delivered again and again.
[2]Wise people won't hate the Law,
but those who are hypocrites about it
are like a boat in a storm.
[3]Sensible people will trust the Lord's word;[b]
for them, the Law is as trustworthy
as divine oracles.

[4]Prepare your speech,
and then you will be heard;
draw upon your training,
and give an answer.
[5]The emotions of the foolish
are like a wagon wheel,
and their arguments are like
a turning axle.
[6]A friend who mocks is like a stallion
that whinnies underneath
anyone who rides him.

[7]Why is one day more significant
than another,
when all the daylight in a year
is from the sun?
[8]The Lord, in his knowledge,
classified them,
and he distinguished between
different seasons and festivals.
[9]He lifted out some days
and made them holy,
and some he made regular days.
[10]All people come from the ground,
and Adam[c] was created out of earth.
[11]In the fullness of his knowledge
the Lord made distinctions
between them,
and he made their ways different.
[12]Some of them he blessed and lifted up,
and some he made holy
and brought them near to himself;
some of them he cursed, brought low,
and expelled them from their place.
[13]Like clay in the potter's hand,
shaped according to the
potter's pleasure,
so are human beings
in the hand of the one
who made them,
whom he repays according
to his judgment.

[14]Good is the opposite of evil,
and life is the opposite of death;
so the sinner is the opposite
of the godly.
[15]Observe, then,
all the works of the Most High,
two by two, one opposite the other.

[16]I was the last to keep vigil,
as one who gathered the leftovers
after the grape pickers.
[17]By the blessing of the Lord,
I was first on the scene,
and like the grape pickers,
I filled up a wine vat.
[18]Understand that I haven't labored
for myself alone,
but for all those who are seeking
instruction.

On independence

[19]Listen to me, you who are great
among the people;
pay attention,
you leaders in the congregation.
[20]Don't give son or wife, sibling or friend,
authority over you in your lifetime,
and don't give your property
to someone else,

[y]Heb *don't stumble twice on an obstacle* [z]Heb *Be careful of your paths* [a]Heb *be careful of yourself*
[b]LXX lacks *Lord's.* [c]Heb *humankind*

since you might change your mind
and ask for it back.
21 While you still live
and have breath in you,
don't exchange places with anyone else.
22 It's better for your children
to make requests of you
than that you should look to them
for generosity.
23 Excel in everything you do;
don't bring a stain on your reputation.
24 On the last day of your life,
at the moment of death,
distribute your inheritance.

On slaves

25 Fodder, a rod, and burdens for donkeys;
bread, discipline,
and work for household slaves.
26 Set them to work with discipline,
and you will have leisure;
let their hands be idle,
and they will seek freedom.
27 A yoke and a strap will bend a neck,
and there are racks and tortures
for a wicked household slave.
28 Put them to work so that they aren't idle,
29 because idleness teaches many evils.
30 Set them to work, as is proper for them,
and if they don't obey,
make their shackles heavy.
Don't overburden a person
made of flesh,
and don't do anything
without exercising good judgment.

31 If you have household slaves,
treat them like yourself,
because you purchased them with blood.
If you have household slaves,
treat them like siblings,
because you will need them
as you go through life.
32 If you mistreat them,
and they leave and run away,
33 on which road will you search for them?

On dreams

34 Senseless people
have empty and false hopes,
and dreams excite fools.
2 Those who pay attention to dreams
are just like people who grasp
at a shadow or pursue the wind.
3 What one sees in a dream is a reflection,
a face looking at its own likeness.
4 What will be made clean
from something unclean?
And what will be true
of something false?
5 Divinations, omens,
and dreams are empty.
The mind has fantasies,
just like a woman in labor does.
6 Unless the Most High sends a dream
by means of a visitation,
don't pay any attention to it.
7 Dreams have misled many,
and those who have placed hope in
them have fallen.
8 The Law will be fulfilled without lies;
wisdom in a faithful person's mouth
is fulfillment.

Experience and fear of the Lord

9 People who have traveled know a lot,
and those who are experienced
will speak sense.
10 People with no experience know little,
11 but those who have traveled
have become more clever.
12 I have seen a lot in my wandering,
and I understand more than I can tell.
13 I've often been in danger,
close to death,
and I was saved
because of these experiences.

14 The spirit of those who fear the Lord
will live,
15 because their hope is in the one
who saves them.
16 Those who fear the Lord
won't be timid about anything;
they will never turn coward,
because the Lord is their hope.
17 The souls of those who fear the Lord
are favored.
18 To whom do they look?
And who is their support?
19 The Lord's eyes
are upon those who love him.

The Lord is a powerful shield,
a strong support,
a shelter from the heat,
a shade from the midday sun,
a guard against stumbling,
and a help against falling;
20 one who lifts up the spirit,
one who gives light to the eyes,
and one who gives healing
for life and blessing.

On sacrifice and worship

21 When someone sacrifices something
unjustly gotten,
the offering is flawed;
22 the gifts of those who don't follow
the Law are not acceptable.
23 The Most High is not pleased
with the offerings of the ungodly,
nor will he forgive sins
for a multitude of sacrifices.
24 Someone who brings a sacrifice that
comes from the property of the needy
is like someone who slaughters a son
in the presence of his father.
25 The needy person's bread
means life for that poor person;
whoever withholds it is a murderer.
26 Whoever takes away a neighbor's living
commits murder,
27 and whoever deprives a worker
of wages sheds blood.

28 One person builds,
and another tears down;
what have they gained
other than hard work?
29 One person prays,
and another person curses;
to whose voice will the master listen?
30 When people bathe after touching
a corpse and touch it again,
what have they gained by washing?
31 So when people fast because of their sins,
and then go and do the same
things again,
who will listen to their prayer,
and what did they gain
by humbling themselves?

35 Whoever keeps the Law
gives many offerings;
2 whoever obeys the commandments
makes a sacrifice of well-being.
3 Whoever repays a kindness
offers the finest flour,
4 and whoever does an act of charity
makes a sacrifice of praise.
5 Staying away from wickedness
pleases the Lord,
and keeping away from injustice
means reconciliation.
6 Don't come into the Lord's presence
empty-handed,
7 since fulfilling the commandments
means making offerings.
8 The righteous person's offering
enriches the altar,
and its pleasing odor comes
before the Most High.
9 A righteous person's offering
is acceptable,
and its memory will last forever.
10 Honor the Lord generously,
and don't skimp
on the early produce you present.[d]
11 Every time you give, have a cheerful face,
and dedicate your tithe gladly.
12 Give to the Most High as he has given,
and give with generosity
from what you have,
13 because the Lord is the one who repays,
and he will repay you seven times over.

14 Don't offer a bribe,
because the Lord won't accept it.
15 Don't present an unrighteous sacrifice,
because the Lord is a judge,
and he shows no partiality.
16 God will not be partial to the poor,
but he will listen to the complaint
of those who are wronged.
17 God will never ignore an orphan's plea,
nor that of a widow
when she pours out a complaint.
18 Don't a widow's tears fall down
on her cheek,
19 and isn't her plea against the one
who caused her tears?

[d] LXX *of your hands*

20 Those who serve with goodwill
will be accepted,
and their prayer will reach to the clouds.
21 The prayer of the humble passes
through the clouds,
and it will never stop
until it draws near to God.[e]
It will never withdraw
until the Most High takes notice,
22 gives justice for the righteous,
and executes judgment.
Indeed, the Lord will never delay,
nor will he be patient with them
until he crushes the power[f]
of the unmerciful,
23 until he exacts vengeance
on the nations,
until he removes the multitude
of abusive people
and shatters the authority
of the unrighteous,
24 until he repays individuals
according to their deeds
and the works of human beings
according to their thoughts,
25 until he decides the case of his people
and makes them glad by his mercy.
26 His mercy is timely in a period
of distress,
like rain clouds in a dry season.

Prayer for Israel's deliverance

36 Have mercy on us, Lord God of all;
2 and teach all nations to stand
in awe of you.
3 Raise up your hand
against foreign nations,
and let them see your power.
4 Just as they saw your holiness
made visible in our midst,
so let us see your power
made visible in their midst.
5 Let them know you,
just as we also have known, Lord,
that there's no God except you.
6 Renew the signs,
and work different wonders;
7 make your strong hand and arm glorious.
8 Arouse your anger;
pour out your wrath;
9 remove the adversary;
destroy the enemy.
10 Act quickly,
remember what you have sworn,
and let people tell of your mighty acts.
11 Let those who survive
be consumed in a fiery wrath,
and may those who harm your people
come to destruction.
12 Crush the heads of hostile rulers,
who say, "We're all that matters."
13 Gather all the tribes of Jacob,[g]
16 and give them their inheritance,
as you did at the beginning.
17 Have mercy, Lord, on the people
who have been called by your name;
on Israel, whom you made like
an oldest child.
18 Take pity on the city
where your sanctuary is;
on Jerusalem,
the place where you live.[h]
19 Fill Zion with the celebration
of your mighty deeds,[i]
and fill your temple with your glory.
20 Bear witness to those
whom you created at the beginning,
and fulfill the prophecies
that were given in your name.
21 Give a reward to those
who wait for you,
and let your prophets
be found trustworthy.
22 Hear, Lord, the prayer
of your household slaves
according to your goodwill
toward your people,
and all those
who live upon the earth
will know that you are the Lord,
the God of the ages.

Wives, friends, and counselors

23 The stomach will accept any food,
but one kind of food
is better than another.

[e]LXX lacks *to God*. [f]LXX *testicles* [g]Due to a mistaken transposition in chapter and verse order in every Gk manuscript, no text is missing, but verses 36:14-15 are not used for chap 36. [h]Heb *the place where your dwelling is* [i]Heb *your splendor*

24 As the palate tastes different
types of game,
so an intelligent mind tests[j] false words.
25 A perverse heart will cause grief,
but an experienced person
will know how to give payback.
26 A woman will accept any male
as a husband,[k]
but some daughters are preferable
to other ones.
27 A woman's beauty brightens a man's face,
and she surpasses a man's every desire.
28 If her speech is characterized
by mercy and gentleness,
her husband is unlike anyone else.
29 Whoever acquires a wife
takes his first step toward success.[l]
She will be a fit helper for him
and a pillar of rest.[m]
30 Where no fence exists,
the property is carried off,
and where there's no wife,
a man sighs as he wanders about.[n]
31 Who will trust a well-equipped robber
who travels from city to city?
Likewise, who will trust a man
who does not have a nest
and who lodges wherever night falls?

37 Every friend will say,
"I too have been a friend,"
but there's a friend who is one
in name only.
2 Doesn't the pain bring a person
close to death
when a companion and friend
turns into an enemy?
3 Evil inclination,
how did you get involved
in covering the land with deceit?
4 Some companions take delight
in a friend's happiness,
but they turn against them
in a time of distress.
5 Some companions work alongside
a friend for their stomach's sake,
but in the heat of battle,
they will shield themselves.[o]
6 Don't forget friends in your heart,
and don't neglect them
when it comes to your money.[p]
7 Every counselor spews out advice,
but some give advice
for their own benefit.
8 Guard yourself against counselors,
and know beforehand
where their interest lies,
since they too
will give advice for their own benefit
and might cast the lot against you.
9 They might say to you, "Your way is good,"
but they will stand aside
to see what will happen to you.
10 Don't consult with people
who view you with suspicion;
hide your plans from those
who are jealous of you.
11 Don't consult with a woman
about her rival,
or with the cowardly about war;
or with a merchant about business,
or with a buyer about a sale;
or with a slanderer about gratitude,
or with the unmerciful about kindness;
or with the idle about anything
involving work,
or with an annual laborer about
finishing a job;
or with a lazy household slave
about a large task.
Don't look to these persons
for any advice.
12 Consult[q] instead with a godly person
whom you know
keeps the commandments,
who thinks the same way you do
and will empathize with you if you fail.
13 Listen carefully to what
your own heart tells you,
since nothing is more faithful
to you than it.
14 At times a person's intuition
keeps them informed
better than seven sentries
sitting high up on a lookout.

[j]LXX lacks *tests.* [k]LXX lacks *as a husband.* [l]Heb *gets his best possession* [m]Heb *pillar of support* [n]Heb *he becomes a fugitive and a wanderer* [o]Heb *Good friends will fight with you against a stranger, and against your enemies they will be a strong shield.* [p]Heb *Don't forget friends in battle, and don't neglect them when you divide the spoil.* [q]LXX *persevere*

[15] But above everything else,
pray to the Most High,
so that he may make your path straight
in truth.

Speech and moderation

[16] Speech is the beginning of every deed,
and planning comes before
every action.
[17] The key to change is the heart;
[18] it poses four possibilities:
good and evil, life and death,
and their continual master
is the tongue.
[19] Some people instruct many,
but they are useless to themselves.
[20] Some skilled speakers are hated;
they will be deprived of any luxuries.
[21] The Lord hasn't granted them
any refinement,
because they are deprived
of any wisdom.
[22] Some people are wise to their
own benefit,
and the fruits of their understanding
are evident to all.
[23] The wise will instruct their own people,
and the fruits of their understanding
are trustworthy.
[24] Wise people will be highly praised,
and everyone who sees them
will consider them to be favored.
[25] A person's life is a limited time,
but Israel's days cannot be numbered.
[26] Those who are wise among their people
will inherit honor,
and their names will live forever.

[27] My child, test yourself during your life.
See what's bad for you,
and don't give in to it.
[28] All things aren't beneficial to everybody,
and all things aren't pleasing
to every person.
[29] Don't be greedy for every delicacy,
and don't be unrestrained with food.
[30] Eating a lot of food will make one sick,
and gluttony will lead to nausea.
[31] Many have died because of gluttony,
but those who are on guard against it
will prolong life.

On physicians

38 Honor doctors for their services,[r]
since indeed the Lord created them.
[2] Healing comes from the Most High,
and the king will reward them.
[3] The skill of doctors will make
them eminent,
and they will be admired
in the presence of the great.
[4] The Lord created medicines
out of the earth,
and a sensible person
won't ignore them.
[5] Wasn't water made sweet
by means of wood
so that the Lord's[s] strength
might be known?
[6] And he endowed human beings
with skill
so that he would be glorified
through his marvelous deeds.
[7] With those medicines,
the doctor cures and takes away pain.
[8] Those who prepare ointments
will make a compound out of them,
and their[t] work will never be finished,
and well-being spreads
over the whole world from them.

[9] My child, when you are sick,
don't look around elsewhere,
but pray to the Lord,
and he will heal you.
[10] Stay far from error,
direct your hands rightly,
and cleanse your heart from all sin.
[11] Offer a sweet-smelling sacrifice
and a memorial of fine flour,
and pour an offering of oil,
using what you can afford.[u]
[12] And give doctors a place,
because the Lord created them also,
and don't let them leave you,
because you indeed need them.

[r] Heb *Make friends with a physician before you need one*. [s] LXX *his*; possibly *its* [t] The referent of the pronouns in these two clauses and the next could possibly be God. [u] Heb; LXX uncertain

13 There's a time when success
is in their hands as well.
14 They will also ask the Lord
so that he might grant them rest[v]
and healing in order to preserve life.
15 May those who sin against their creator
fall into the hands of a doctor.

On mourning

16 My child, let your tears flow for the dead;
as one who is suffering terribly,
give voice to your sorrow.
Lay out their bodies in accordance
with their wishes,
and don't neglect their burial.
17 Let your crying be bitter
and express your sorrow fervently,
and make your mourning
worthy of them.
Mourn for one day or two
so that there can be no criticism,
and then be comforted from your grief.
18 Too much grief can lead to death,
and grief in one's heart
will sap one's strength.
19 Grief also lingers in misery,
and the life of the poor
is a curse upon the heart.
20 Don't give your heart over to grief;
stay away from it,
remembering your own end.
21 Don't forget that there's no coming back;
you won't do them any good,
and you will hurt yourself.
22 Remember their sentence,
because it's yours also:
"Yesterday it was I, and today it's you!"
23 When the dead are at rest,
put their memory to rest,
and be comforted for them
when their spirit has left.

The scribe's superiority

24 The scribe's wisdom depends
on the opportunity for leisure,
and whoever lacks busyness
will become wise.
25 How will people become wise
when they take hold of a plow
or pride themselves
in how well they handle an ox prod,
when they drive cattle
and are absorbed with their work,
and their conversation is about bulls?
26 Their hearts are given over
to plowing furrows,
and they lose sleep
because they're concerned
about supplying heifers with food.
27 So it is also with every craftsperson
and master artisan
who carries over the day's work
into the night,
who carves figures on seals
and works diligently
to make diverse ornamentations.
They will devote themselves
to producing a lifelike painting,
and they lose sleep
in order to finish their work.
28 So it is with smiths who sit near an anvil
and who closely examine works of iron.
The blast of the fire
will melt their flesh,
and they will struggle
with the heat of the furnace.
The sound of the hammer
will strike their ears again and again,
and their eyes are focused
on the pattern of the object.
They will devote themselves
to finishing the work,
and they lose sleep
in order to complete its decoration.
29 So it is with potters sitting at their work,
turning the wheel at their feet.
They lie down always feeling anxiety
about their work,
and every product of theirs is valued.
30 They will mold the clay with their hands
and work the wheel with their feet.
They will devote themselves
to finishing the glazing,
and they lose sleep
in order to clean the kiln.
31 All of these have relied on their hands,
and each one is skilled in their work.

[v] Heb *a diagnosis*

32 Without them a city can't be inhabited,
and they neither go abroad to live
as immigrants nor travel about.
However, they aren't sought out
when the people hold a council,
33 and they won't gain prominence
in the assembly.
They won't sit in the judge's seat,
and they won't understand
the disposition of a legal case.
They will never shed light
on instruction and judgment,
and their words
won't be memorialized in proverbs.[w]
34 But they support the world
from its foundations,
and their prayer is concerned
with their craft.

But those who devote themselves
and think about the Law of the
Most High are the exception.
39 They will seek out the wisdom
of all the ancestors,
and they will be occupied
with prophecies.
2 They will preserve the stories
of famous people,
and they will penetrate
the subtle turns of parables.
3 They will seek out
the hidden meanings of proverbs,
and will live with the puzzles of parables.
4 They will serve among the great
and appear before rulers.
They will travel in foreign lands,
because they will test what's good
and what's evil in people.
5 They will commit themselves to rise early,
to seek the Lord who made them,
and to pray to the Most High.
They will open their mouth in prayer
and ask forgiveness for their sins.
6 If the great Lord is willing,
they will be filled
with a spirit of understanding;
they will pour forth words of wisdom,
and they will give thanks
to the Lord in prayer.
7 Their reasoning and knowledge
will remain on course,
and they will ponder God's mysteries.
8 They will bring to light
the learning of their instruction,
and they will make the laws
of the Lord's covenant their boast.
9 Many will praise their understanding,
and it will never be forgotten.
The remembrance of them
will never disappear,
and their name will live
for generations upon generations.
10 The nations will speak of their wisdom,
and the congregation
will proclaim their praise.
11 If they live a long time,
they will leave behind a name
greater than a thousand names,
and if they find rest,
it will be enough for them.

Praise of the creator

12 I'll speak of other things
I've been thinking,
since I was filled like the full moon.
13 Listen to me, faithful children,
and blossom
like a rose growing near
a running stream.
14 Send forth a fragrant aroma like incense,
and bloom with blossoms like a lily.
Raise your voice, give praise together,
and bless the Lord for all his works.
15 Tell of the greatness of his name,
and give thanks when you praise him
with songs on your lips and with harps.
And this is what you will say
when you give thanks:

16 All the works of the Lord are very good.
Every command of his
will be carried out in its proper time.
17 It's not for us to say,
"What's this?" or
"For what purpose is that?"
Everything will be examined
at its proper time.
At his command water piled up in a heap,

[w] LXX *among parables*

and by his spoken word
reservoirs of water stood erect.
18 His command accomplishes
his good pleasure,
and no one can diminish
the deliverance he intends.
19 The works of all living beings
are before him;
nothing can hide from his eyes.
20 He sees from one end of eternity
to the other,
and nothing is too wondrous for him.
21 It's not for us to say,
"What's this?" or
"For what purpose is that?"
All things were created
for their own purpose.

22 His blessing covers like a river
and soaks the dry land like a flood.
23 Similarly, his anger will overtake
the nations,
as he changed fresh waters into brine.
24 For the godly, his paths are straight,
but for the lawless,
there are obstacles.
25 From the beginning, good things
have been made for good people,
but bad things for sinners.[x]
26 Basic to all the necessities of human life
are water, fire, iron, salt,
fine flour, milk, honey,
wine,[y] oil, and clothing.
27 For the godly,
all these things are for good,
but for sinners, they will turn into evil.

28 There are winds that have been created
for vengeance,
and they whip with strength
in their wrath.
At the moment of consummation,
they will pour out their strength,
and they will calm the wrath
of their maker.
29 Fire, hail, famine, and death—
all have been created for vengeance—
30 the teeth of wild beasts, scorpions,
vipers, and a sword
punishing the ungodly
with destruction.
31 These things gladly do
what he commands.
They will be ready for his service
on the earth,
and they won't violate his word
when their time comes.

32 Because of this,
I've been steadfast from the beginning:
I've thought things out
and left them in writing.
33 All the works of the Lord are good,
and he will supply every need in its time.
34 It's not for us to say,
"This is worse than that,"
since everything will prove its worth
at the proper moment.
35 And now, sing hymns
with all your heart and voice,
and bless the Lord's name.

Life's joys and miseries

40 Hard work was created
for every person,
and a heavy yoke lies upon
human beings,
from the day when they leave
their mother's womb
until the day when they return
to the mother of all.
2 Anxious expectation—the day of death—
fills their inner musings
and plants fear in their hearts.[z]
3 From the person who sits
upon a glorious throne
down to the person brought low
in dust and ashes,
4 from the person who wears purple
and a crown
down to the person dressed
in rough linen—
5 there exists anger, envy, confusion,
unrest, fear of death,
fury, and conflict.
Even when they rest in bed,
nighttime dreams disturb their mind.
6 They get little or no rest;

[x]Heb *good things and bad* [y]LXX *blood of the grape* [z]Gk uncertain

they even toil in their dreams,
just as they do in the day,
being troubled by images in their mind,
as one who escapes from war.
7 They wake up at the most
desperate moment
and are astonished
that they were afraid for nothing.
8 To all flesh, both human and animal,
but to sinners seven times more so,
9 come death, blood, strife, sword,
catastrophes, famine, ruin,
and disease.[a]
10 All these things were created
for the lawless,
and because of such people
the flood happened.
11 Everything that's from earth;
returns to the earth;
everything that's from water
returns to the sea.[b]

12 All bribery and injustice
will be wiped out,
but good faith will last forever.
13 The money of the unjust
will dry up like a river,
and it will crash like loud thunder
in a rainstorm.
14 Generous people will rejoice,
but those who sin will ultimately fail.
15 The offspring of the ungodly
won't produce many branches,
and they are polluted roots
on sheer rock.
16 A reed by any water or riverbank
will be pulled up before any grass.
17 Kindness is like an orchard of blessings,
and an act of charity will last forever.

18 Life will be sweet for the self-reliant
and the hardworking,
but better than both
is the person who finds a treasure.
19 Children and building a city
establish one's name,
but better than both
is a wife who is considered blameless.
20 Wine and music make the heart glad,
but better than both
is the love of wisdom.[c]
21 A flute and a harp make sweet melodies,
but better than both is a pleasant voice.
22 The eye will desire grace and beauty,
but better than both
are the first shoots of a crop.
23 A friend and a companion encounter
each other at an opportune moment,
but better than both
is a woman with her husband.
24 Relatives and help
in a time of distress are good,[d]
but acts of charity
will rescue one better than both.
25 Gold and silver make one stand firm,
but more highly esteemed than both
is good advice.
26 Money and strength will lift up
one's heart,
but fearing the Lord is better than both.
If you fear the Lord,
you'll lack nothing;
if you have it,
there's no reason to look for help.
27 Fear of the Lord
is like an orchard of blessing,
and it covers a person
more fully than any glory.

28 My child, don't live the life of a beggar;
it's better to die than to beg.
29 When people look
to another person's table,
their way of life
cannot be considered a life.
They pollute themselves
by eating someone else's food,
but a person who is intelligent
and educated will guard
against that.
30 In the mouth of the shameless,
begging is sweet,
but a fire will burn inside of them.

41 How bitter, death,
is the thought of you
to those who are at peace
among their possessions,

[a]Gk *scourge* [b]Heb *what's from above returns above* [c]Heb *friends* [d]Gk lacks *are good.*

to those who aren't anxiously
distracted, who prosper at everything
and still have the strength
to enjoy good food.
2 Your sentence looks good, death,
to a person who is needy
and lacks strength,
who is extremely old and anxious
about everything,
who is not compliant
and whose endurance has failed.
3 Don't fear death's judgment;
remember those who came before you
and those who will come after you.
4 This is the Lord's judgment for all beings:
Why should you reject
the good pleasure of the Most High?
Whether ten or one hundred
or one thousand years,
there's no arguing about life
in the grave.[e]

5 The children of sinners are detestable,
and they live together
in the neighborhoods of the ungodly.
6 The inheritance of sinners' children
will be destroyed,
and their offspring
will always live in disgrace.
7 Children will blame an ungodly father,
because they will be disgraced
because of him.
8 How terrible it will be for you
who are ungodly,
who have abandoned the Law
of the Most High![f]
9 When you are born,
you are born to a curse,
and when you die,
you will leave a curse as your legacy.[g]
10 Everything that's from the earth
will go back to the earth;
so the ungodly come from a curse
and go to destruction.

11 Human beings show their grief
in their bodies,
but the no-good name of sinners
will be erased.[h]
12 Guard your reputation,
for it will continue after you
longer than one thousand
great treasures of gold.
13 A good life has a limited number of days,
but a good name will continue forever.

On shame

14 Hold on to your education in peace,
my children.
Hidden wisdom
and an invisible treasure—
of what use is either?
15 People who hide their foolishness
are better than people
who hide their wisdom.
16 Therefore, respect my judgment,
because it isn't good to guard
against every shame,
and not everyone, in good faith,
holds all the same things
in good repute.

17 Be ashamed:
of sexual immorality
before your father and mother,
of lying before a prince or leader,
18 of error before a judge and an official,
of lawlessness before the assembly
and the people,
of injustice before a partner and friend,
19 of theft in the neighborhood
where you are staying.

Be ashamed:
before the Lord's truth and covenant,[i]
of leaning on your elbow at meals,
of showing contempt
when receiving or giving,
20 of silence when people greet you,
of looking at a female escort,
21 of turning away a relative,
of depriving someone of a share
or a gift,
of staring at another man's wife,

[e] LXX *Hades*; Heb *Sheol* [f] LXX[b] adds 41:9a *If you multiply, it is only to be destroyed.* [g] Heb *If you have children, harm will be at hand, and if you become a parent, you will sigh. If you stumble, it will evoke lasting joy, and if you die, you will be allotted a curse.* [h] Heb *The bodies of human beings are vapor, but a virtuous name will never be cut off.* [i] Heb *of breaking a solemn pledge or an agreement*

22 of fooling around with his
female servant—
(and don't get near her bed),
of reproachful words before friends
(and don't criticize after you give),
42 of repeating gossip;
and of revealing secrets—
then you will be truly modest
and find favor with every human being.

Don't be ashamed of these things,
and don't show favoritism
so that you sin.
2 Don't be ashamed:
of the Law of the Most High
or the covenant,
of a just verdict
in favor of an ungodly person,
3 of keeping a record of expenses with a
partner or a traveling companion,
of distributing an inheritance
to others,
4 of accuracy with scales and weights,
of acquiring a lot or a little,
5 of profit from business with merchants,
of frequent discipline of children,
and of whipping wicked
household slaves until they bleed.
6 In the case of a wicked wife,
using your seal on your documents and
supplies[j] is an excellent idea,
and lock up things
anywhere there are lots of hands.
7 Whatever you deposit,
whether by number and weight,
and whatever you give or receive,
put everything in writing.
8 Don't be ashamed of discipline
for the stupid and foolish
and for the old codger
who is guilty of sexual immorality.
Then you will have been truly educated
and approved by everyone alive.

On daughters

9 A daughter is a hidden source
of sleeplessness for her father,
and anxiety about her deprives him
of sleep:
in her youth, that she doesn't pass
her prime,
and when she's married,
that she not be hated;
10 while she's a virgin,
that she not be seduced
and become pregnant
while still living at home;
when she's married,
that she not go straying;
or having married,
that she not be infertile.
11 Keep a strict watch over
an unruly daughter
so that she doesn't make you
an object of ridicule to your enemies,
a topic of talk in the city
and the assembly of the people,
and she shame you before the crowd.
12 Don't consider the beauty
of any person,[k]
and don't spend time among women.
13 Moths come out of clothes,
and a woman's wickedness
comes from a woman.
14 A man's wickedness
is better than a woman who does good
and a disgraced woman
who brings shame.

God's created order

15 Now I'll call to mind the works
of the Lord,
and I'll tell about what I've seen.
The Lord's works came into being
by his words.[l]
16 The shining sun looked down
on everything,
and the Lord's work is radiant
with his glory.
17 The Lord has not allowed his holy ones
to describe all of his wonders,
which the Lord Almighty established
so that the universe would stand firm
in his glory.

[j]Gk lacks *on your documents and supplies.* [k]Heb *Don't allow any latticework in her room nor a place that overlooks the entrance to the house; don't let her display her beauty before any man.* [l]Heb adds *and they agree to do his will*; LXX[b] *and judgment comes about by his good will.*

18 He has searched the abyss and the heart,
and he took their great achievements
into consideration,
because the Most High
knew everything to be known.
He saw the sign of the age,[m]
19 explaining what has passed
and what will be,
and revealing the clues to things
that are hidden.
20 No thought escaped him,
and not a single word
was hidden from him.
21 He ordered the splendors of his wisdom.
He remains the same[n]
from the beginning of time
all the way to eternity.
Nothing can be added to him
nor be taken away,
and he needed no one to give him advice.
22 How desirable are all of his works,
and how brilliant they are to look upon.
23 All these things live and remain forever
in every circumstance,
and everything obeys him.[o]
24 All things exist in pairs,
one opposite the other,
and he made nothing that
was incomplete.
25 Each thing strengthens the good parts
of the other;
who can get enough of seeing
God's glory?

43 The pride of the heights
is the clear heavenly vault,
the appearance of the sky
in a vision of glory.
2 The sun, when it appears,
announces at its rising
what an amazing thing it is,
a work of the Most High.
3 At noon it dries up the land,
and who can endure its burning heat?
4 A person blows on a furnace,
working in its burning heat,
but the sun is three times hotter
when it burns up mountains.
When it breathes out fiery vapors,
and shines forth its rays, it blinds eyes.
5 Great is the Lord who made it;
it speeds on its course by his command.

6 The moon stands at its proper time,[p]
a notification of times
and an everlasting sign.
7 The sign for a feast comes from the moon,
a luminous body that wanes
when it completes its course.
8 The new moon shares the character
of its name,[q]
increasing wonderfully as it changes,
a signal on high for armies,[r]
shining in the vault of the sky.

9 The stars' glory is the sky's beauty,
shining ornaments
in the heights of the Lord.
10 They stand at the words of the holy one,
just as he orders,
and they will never grow tired
as they keep watch.
11 Look at the rainbow,
exceedingly beautiful in its brightness,
and bless the one who made it.
12 It encircled the sky with a glorious ring;
the Lord's hands stretched it out.

13 He drives the snow forward
by his command,
and he speeds the lightning bolts
of his judgment on their way.
14 To this end, the storehouses are opened,
and clouds fly out like birds.
15 In his might he subdues clouds,
and stones are broken apart for hail.
17a The sound of his thunder
scolds the earth,
16 and mountains will be shaken
when he appears.
The south wind blows by his will,
17b as do storms from the north
and whirlwinds.
He sprinkles the snow
like birds flying down,
and its descent is like locusts alighting.

[m]Heb *and he saw what was to come forever* [n]Gk *He is one* [o]Heb *and all things are maintained for every need.* [p]Heb *The moon indicates the seasons* [q]Heb *The new moon, like its name, renews itself.* [r]Heb *a military beacon for the clouds on high*

18 The eye marvels at its beautiful whiteness,
and the heart is amazed
at its showering down.
19 He pours frost, like salt, upon the earth,
and when it freezes it has pointy thorns.
20 A cold north wind will blow,
and ice will freeze on the water;
it will settle on every pool of water,
and the water will put it on like armor.
21 He will consume mountains,
burn up the wilderness,
and extinguish grass like a fire.
22 A mist hastens the healing of all things;
the dew that appears
will give relief from the heat.

23 By his calculations, he stilled the deep,
and he planted islands in it.
24 Those who sail the sea
describe its danger,
and we are amazed at what we hear.
25 Incredible and amazing works are there,
all sorts of living things,
great sea monsters.
26 Because of him, each messenger succeeds,
and all things hold together by his word.

27 We could say many things
and never say enough.
The final word is: The Lord is "the All."
28 Where will we find the strength
to glorify him?
For God is great beyond all his works.
29 The Lord is awesome and very great,
and his power is marvelous.
30 Glorify the Lord,
and exalt him as much as you can:
he surpasses even that.
Exalt him, increase your strength,
and don't grow tired:
you will never say enough.
31 Who has seen him and will describe him?
Whose praises of him
will match what he really is?
32 There are many hidden things
greater than these,
for we have seen only
a few of his works.
33 The Lord made everything,
and he gave wisdom to the godly.

Hymn to the ancestors[s]

44 Now allow us to praise
famous people and our ancestors,
generation by generation.[t]
2 The Lord created[u] great glory,
his majesty from eternity.
3 They ruled in their kingdoms,
and made a name with their power,
some giving counsel
by their intelligence;
some making pronouncements
in prophecies;
4 some leading the people
by their deliberations,
and by their understanding
of the people's learning,
giving wise words in their instruction;
5 others devising musical melodies,
and composing poems;
6 rich people endowed with strength,
living in peace in their dwellings—
7 all of these were honored
in their generation,
a source of pride in their time.
8 Some of them left behind a name
so that their praises might be told.
9 For some there is no memory,
and they perished as though
they hadn't existed.
These have become as though
they hadn't been born,
they and even their children after them.
10 But these were compassionate people
whose righteous deeds
haven't been forgotten.
11 This will persist with their children;
their descendants
will be a good legacy.[v]
12 Their descendants stand
by the covenants,
and their children also, for their sake.
13 Their descendants will last forever,
and their glory will never be erased.
14 Their bodies were buried in peace,
but their name lives for generations.

[s]The title appears in Gk manuscripts. [t]Heb *in their generations* [u]Heb *measured out* [v]Heb *Their goods will remain with their descendants, and their inheritance will be for their grandchildren.*

15 The people will tell of their wisdom,
and the congregation
will proclaim their praise.

Enoch

16 Enoch pleased the Lord
and was transferred,[w]
an example of a changed heart
and mind for generations.

Noah

17 Noah was found perfect and righteous;
in a time of anger,
he was selected in exchange
for the ungodly.[x]
Because of him,
a few survivors remained on the earth
when the flood happened.
18 Eternal covenants were made with him
so that all living things would not be
wiped out by a flood again.

Abraham, Isaac, and Jacob

19 Abraham was the great father
of a multitude of nations,
and there was no smudge on his glory.[y]
20 He kept the laws of the Most High,
and he entered into a covenant with him.
He established a covenant in his flesh,
and when he was tested,
he proved faithful.
21 Therefore, the Lord certified for Abraham
with a solemn pledge
that he would bless nations
through his descendants,
that he would make him increase
like the dust of the earth,
exalt his descendants like the stars,
and give them an inheritance
from sea to sea
and from the river to the end
of the earth.

22 He made the same commitment to Isaac
because of Abraham his father.
He made a blessing for all humanity
and a covenant
23 to rest on Jacob's head.
The Lord acknowledged him
with his blessings;
he gave him an inheritance,
divided his shares,
and allotted them
among the twelve tribes.

Moses

The Lord brought forward out of Jacob[z]
a man of mercy,
who found favor with all living beings,
45 dearly loved by God
and human beings—
Moses, who is remembered
with blessing.
2 The Lord made Moses' glory
equal to that of the holy ones,
and he made Moses great
so that Moses' enemies would fear him.
3 By Moses' words,
he brought signs to a halt;[a]
the Lord glorified Moses
in the presence of kings.
The Lord gave Moses commandments
for his people,
and he showed Moses his glory.
4 The Lord ordained Moses
because of his faithfulness
and gentleness;
he chose him out of all human beings.
5 The Lord let Moses hear his voice;
he led him into the deep darkness,
and he gave Moses commandments
face-to-face,
an instruction for life,
and knowledge to teach the covenant
to Jacob and his laws to Israel.

Aaron

6 The Lord exalted Aaron,
a holy person like Moses,
his brother from the tribe of Levi.
7 The Lord established
an eternal covenant with him
and gave him the priesthood
of the people.
He blessed Aaron with dignity,
and wrapped him in a glorious cloak.

[w] Heb *was taken* [x] Gk lacks *for the ungodly*; Heb *he continued the human race.* [y] Some Gk manuscripts *He had no equal in glory.* [z] Gk *him* [a] LXX; Heb *he brought forth signs*

8 The Lord clothed him
with unrivaled praise,[b]
and honored him
with objects of power—
leggings, a full-length robe,
and the priestly vest.
9 He encircled Aaron with pomegranates,
with a great number of gold bells
all around,
in order to create a sound
when he stepped,
to make a sound that would be heard
in the temple,
as a reminder for the children
of the Lord's people.
10 He clothed Aaron with the priestly vest,
with gold, blue, and purple,
the work of an embroiderer,
with the oracle of judgment
for making the truth known;
11 with braided scarlet,
the work of a craftsperson;
with the precious stones
of an engraved seal
in a gold setting,
the work of a jeweler,
as a memorial in engraved writing
according to the number
of the tribes of Israel.
12 He set a gold crown
upon his turban,
carved with a sacred seal,
an item worthy of praise,[c]
a work of strength,
desirable objects to look at,
richly adorned.
13 Before Aaron, such beautiful things
had not existed.
No stranger will ever wear them,
but only his sons and his descendants
for all time.
14 His sacrifices will be entirely burned up
twice daily, for all time.
15 Moses ordained Aaron
and anointed him with holy oil;
it became an everlasting covenant
for him
and for his descendants
for as long as heaven lasts,
to minister to God,
to be a priest at the same time,
and to bless his people in his name.
16 Moses chose him
out of all who were alive
to offer fruitful sacrifices to the Lord,
incense and a pleasing aroma
as a remembrance,
to secure reconciliation for the people.
17 By his commandments,
the Lord gave him authority
over covenants for judgment,
to teach Jacob the testimonies,
and to enlighten Israel with his Law.
18 Strangers conspired against Aaron,
and they were jealous of him
in the wilderness;
those who were with
Dathan and Abiram
and the company of Korah
assembled in anger and fury.
19 The Lord saw it and wasn't pleased,
and they were destroyed
in his furious anger;
he performed wonders among them,
consuming them in a blazing fire.
20 He added to Aaron's glory
and gave him an inheritance;
he gave him as his share
the initial portion of the early produce;
he prepared in abundance
bread from the early produce.
21 They also will eat the sacrifices
of the Lord,
which he gave to him
and to his descendants.
22 But he has no inheritance
in the land of the people,
and he has no portion among the people;
for the Lord is your portion
and inheritance.

Phinehas

23 Phinehas, Eleazar's son,
comes third in glory,
since he was on fire
with the fear of the Lord,
and since he stood firm
when the people turned away,

[b]Heb *complete splendor* [c]Heb *majesty, glory;* LXX *a boast of honor*

in the goodness and readiness
of his spirit;
thus he secured reconciliation for Israel.
24 Therefore, a covenant of peace
was established with Phinehas,
that he should preside
over the holy places
and over his people,
so that he and his descendants
might have the splendor
of the priesthood forever.
25 The Lord also made a covenant
with David,
Jesse's son, from the tribe of Judah;
the king's inheritance
that passes from son to son only;
Aaron's inheritance
is also for his descendants.

26 May the Lord grant you peace
in your heart,[d]
to judge his people justly,
so that the good things they have
might not vanish
and so that their glory might extend
to generations to come.

Joshua and Caleb

46 Joshua, Nun's son,
was powerful in battle,
and he was Moses' successor
in prophecy.
As his name suggests,
he was mighty
to deliver the Lord's chosen ones,
and to take revenge on enemies
when they rose against them,
so that he might give Israel
an inheritance.
2 How glorious he was
when he raised his hands
and when he extended his sword
against cities!
3 Who among those who came before
stood as he did?
Indeed, he fought the Lord's wars.
4 Wasn't the sun restrained by his hand,
and one day lasted for two?
5 He called upon the Most High,
the mighty one,
when his enemies pressed in on him
from every side,
and the great Lord responded to him
with hailstones of mighty power.
6 He rushed headlong against a nation
in battle,
and on a hill he destroyed those
who opposed him,
so that the nations might know
how well-equipped he was,
because his war was fought
in the Lord's presence.
Indeed, he was a follower
of the mighty one.
7 In the days of Moses
he performed acts of mercy,
he and Caleb, Jephunneh's son.
They opposed the congregation,
restrained the people from sin,
and put an end
to their wicked grumbling.
8 So out of six hundred thousand soldiers,
the two were spared to lead the people
into their inheritance,
into a land full of milk and honey.
9 The Lord gave Caleb strength,
and it remained with him
until he was old,
so that he went up to the highlands,
and his descendants had it
as an inheritance.
10 In this way, all the Israelites
could see that it is a good thing
to follow the Lord.

Judges

11 May the memories of the judges
bring blessings,
each with their own name,
whose hearts remained faithful
and who didn't turn away from the Lord.
12 May their bones send forth new shoots
of life from their burial places,
and their names,
honored by all humanity,
continue in their descendants.[e]

[d]Heb begins *And now bless the good Lord who has crowned you with glory.* [e]Heb *may their names be renewed in their descendants.*

Samuel

[13] Samuel was dearly loved by his Lord.
As a prophet from the Lord,
he established a kingdom
and anointed rulers over his people.
[14] He judged the congregation
by the Lord's law,
and the Lord watched over Jacob.
[15] He proved to be a reliable prophet
because of his faithfulness,
and through his words
he became known as a trustworthy seer.
[16] He called upon the Lord, the mighty one,
with an offering of a nursing lamb
when his enemies pressed on him
from every side.
[17] The Lord thundered from heaven,
and he made his voice loudly heard.
[18] He destroyed the leaders
of the people of Tyre[f]
and all the rulers of the Philistines.
[19] Before the time of his eternal sleep,
Samuel testified
before the Lord and his anointed one,
"No property, not even a pair of sandals,
have I taken from anyone!"
And not one person accused him.
[20] Samuel prophesied
after he had fallen asleep,[g]
and he showed the king
what his end would be.
He made his voice heard from the ground
in prophecy to wipe out
the people's lawless behavior.

Nathan

47 After him, Nathan rose up
to prophesy at the time of David.

David

[2] Just as the fat is separated
from the offering of well-being,
so David was set apart
from the Israelites.
[3] He played with lions
as if they were young goats,
and with bears
as if they were lambs from the flock.
[4] Didn't he kill a giant in his youth
and take away disgrace from the people,
when he raised his hand
with a stone shot from a sling
and struck down
the arrogant Goliath?
[5] David called upon the Lord Most High,
and the Lord gave strength
to his strong arm
to do away with a mighty warrior,
to assert the power[h] of his people.
[6] For this, they glorified him
in throngs of thousands.
They praised him,
calling down the Lord's blessings,
when they brought him
a glorious crown.
[7] David destroyed his enemies
on every side,
and he despised the Philistines,
his adversaries;
he shattered their power,
which has never recovered.[i]
[8] In everything he did, he gave thanks
to the holy one, the Most High,
with glorious words.
He sang hymns with all his heart,
and he loved his maker.
[9] He appointed singers with harps
before the altar
to make sweet melody with their sounds.[j]
[10] He brought dignity to the festivals,
and he adorned the whole cycle
of sacred seasons,[k]
as they were praising God's holy name,
and from early morning
the sanctuary resounded.
[11] The Lord took away David's sins,
and he exalted his power[l] forever.
He established his kingdom by agreement;
and a glorious throne in Israel.

Solomon

[12] After David a well-instructed son arose,
and because of David,
he enjoyed a large kingdom.[m]
[13] Solomon reigned at a time of peace.
God gave him tranquillity on every side,

[f] Heb *he subdued the deputies of the enemy* [g] Heb *after he died* [h] LXX *horn* [i] LXX *shattered their horn to this very day*
[j] LXX[b] adds *and every day they offer praise with their songs.* [k] Gk *he adorned the times until their completion* [l] LXX *horn*
[m] Gk *he lived in broad places*; Heb *he lived in security.*

so that he might build a house
for God's name
and prepare a sanctuary
that would last forever.
14 How wise you were in your youth!
You were filled
like a river with understanding.
15 Your spirit filled the earth,
and you were full of puzzling proverbs.
16 Your name reached faraway islands,
and you were dearly loved
because of your peaceful rule.
17 Countries marveled at you
on account of your songs, parables,
proverbs, and teachings.
18 In the Lord God's name,
who is called God over Israel,
you collected gold like tin,
and you amassed silver like lead.
19 You gave yourself to women,[n]
and you were subdued
by your own body.
20 You brought disgrace on your honor,
and you polluted your offspring,
so that you brought punishment
upon your children
and caused pain
because of your foolishness.
21 Your empire became divided,
and a rival kingdom sprang up
out of Ephraim.
22 But the Lord will never
abandon his mercy,
and none of his words will perish.
He will never wipe out
the descendants of his chosen one,
and never take away the descendants
of the one who loved him.
Therefore, he gave a remnant to Jacob
and a root to David from his family.

Establishment of the northern kingdom

23 Solomon rested with his ancestors,
and he left behind one of his offspring—
Rehoboam, a foolish man among the
people,[o] one lacking understanding.
He caused the people to rebel
because of his policy,
led by Jeroboam, Nebat's son,
who made Israel sin
and set Ephraim on its sinful path.
24 Their sins increased greatly
until they were removed from their land.
25 They explored every kind of wickedness
until vengeance overtook them.

Elijah

48 Then Elijah the prophet
rose up like fire,
and his word burned like a torch.
2 He brought a famine upon them,
and he reduced their number by his zeal.
3 By the Lord's word he shut up the sky,
and in the same way
he brought down fire three times.
4 How glorious you were, Elijah,
in your amazing deeds!
Who will boast like you can?
5 You raised a corpse from death,
from the grave[p] by a word
of the Most High.
6 You brought kings down to destruction
and dragged the famous
from their beds.
7 You heard a rebuke at Sinai
and decrees of punishment at Horeb.
8 You anointed kings to bring retribution
and prophets to succeed you.
9 You were taken up in a whirlwind of fire
and in a chariot of fiery horses.
10 It is recorded that you are ready
for the designated times,
to calm anger before it turns to wrath,
to turn the heart of a father to his son,
and to restore the tribes of Jacob.
11 Happy are those who saw you
and who have fallen asleep[q]
in your love,
for we will surely live as well.

Elisha

12 Elijah was covered by the whirlwind,
and Elisha was filled with his spirit.[r]
In his time, he didn't tremble
before any ruler,
and no one oppressed him.

[n] LXX *You bent your sides for women*; Heb *You gave your genitals to women.* [o] Heb *extensive in folly* to form a pun on the name *Rehoboam* [p] LXX *Hades*; Heb *Sheol* [q] Heb *died* [r] Heb (with help of Syr) adds *He performed twice as many signs and marvels with every word from his mouth.*

13 Nothing was too great for him,
and in death his body prophesied.[s]
14 During his life,
he performed wonders,
and in death his accomplishments
were marvelous.

15 In spite of these things,
the people didn't change
their hearts and lives,
and they didn't turn from their sins
until they were torn away
from their land and scattered
over the whole earth.
The people who remained
were few in number,
but they had a ruler
from the house of David.
16 Some of them did what pleased God,
but others sinned even more.

Hezekiah and Isaiah

17 Hezekiah strengthened
the city's defenses,
and he provided a water supply.
He tunneled through rock
with iron tools,
and he constructed storage tanks
for water.
18 During his rule,
Sennacherib moved on Jerusalem,[t]
commissioned the field commander,
and departed.
The field commander attacked Zion,
and made great boasts
in his arrogance.
19 Then the people's hearts and hands
were shaken,
and they were in agony
like a woman who is in labor.
20 They called upon the Lord
who is merciful,
reaching out their hands to him.
The holy one at once heard them
from heaven,
and he rescued them through Isaiah.
21 The Lord struck down
the camp of the Assyrians,
and his messenger destroyed them.

22 Hezekiah did what was pleasing
to the Lord,
and he kept to the ways of David
his ancestor,
as Isaiah the prophet, who was great
and whose visions were reliable,
had commanded.

23 In Isaiah's time, the sun moved backward,
and he extended the king's life.
24 By his great spirit,
he saw what was to come,
and he comforted those
who mourned in Zion.
25 He revealed forever what would be
and hidden things even before
they happened.

Josiah

49 The memory[u] of Josiah
is like a blend of incense,
prepared with skill by a perfumer.
It will be sweet in the mouth, like honey,
like music at a wine-drinking party.
2 He succeeded in turning around
the people,
and he removed unlawful displays
of idolatry.
3 He directed his heart toward the Lord;
at a time of lawlessness,
he made devotion to God stronger.

Destruction of Jerusalem

4 Except for David, Hezekiah, and Josiah,
all of them struck a bad chord,
because they abandoned
the Law of the Most High.
The kings of Judah came to an end.
5 They gave their power[v] to others
and their glory to a foreign nation,
6 which set fire to Jerusalem, the chosen
city, and its sanctuary
and made its streets desolate,
as Jeremiah said.
7 They mistreated him,
even though he had been set apart
from the womb to be a prophet
to uproot, ruin, destroy,
and likewise to build and plant.

[s] Heb *he did wonders* [t] Gk *came up* [u] Heb *name* [v] LXX *horn*

Ezekiel

8 Ezekiel saw a vision of glory,
when God showed him
the chariot of the winged creatures.
9 He remembered the enemies
in the storm,
and favored those keeping
to a righteous path.[w]
10 May the bones of the twelve prophets
sprout new life from their
burial places,
because they comforted Jacob
and rescued them
with hopeful confidence.

Zerubbabel, Joshua, and Nehemiah

11 How should we praise Zerubbabel?
He also was like a signet ring
on the right hand,
12 as was Joshua, Jozadak's son.
In their time, they built a house
and raised a holy temple to the Lord,
prepared for everlasting glory.

13 Nehemiah's memory is lasting;
he who raised our fallen walls,
set up gates and bars,
and rebuilt our buildings.

Miscellaneous ancestors

14 No one was created on the earth
who was like Enoch,
for he was taken up from the earth.
15 Nor has any man been born like Joseph,
a leader of his brothers,
a support for the people.[x]
They took special care
even of his bones.
16 Shem and Seth were honored
among human beings,[y]
and above every living thing in creation
was Adam.

High Priest Simon

50 Simon, Onias' son, was
a great high priest.[z]
During his life, he repaired the house
and, in his time,
strengthened the temple's defenses.
2 He made the foundation
for the courtyard wall,
a high fortification for the
temple enclosure.
3 In his time, he dug out a storage basin
for water,
a reservoir with a circumference
like a lake's.
4 He gave forethought to keeping
his people from disaster,
and he strengthened the city
against sieges.
5 How glorious he was as the people
thronged around him
when he came out from behind
the curtain and left the temple![a]
6 Like a morning star
in the midst of a cloud,
like the full moon at the time of a feast,
7 like the sun shining
on the temple of the Most High,
like a rainbow gleaming
in glorious clouds,
8 like a rose blossom in springtime,
like lilies by streams of water,
like a fresh shoot of the incense tree
in the summertime,
9 like fire and incense
in an incense burner,
like an object of hammered gold
adorned with all sorts
of precious stones,
10 like an olive tree sprouting fruit,
and like a cypress towering
to the clouds.
11 When he put on his glorious robe
and clothed himself
with perfect splendor,[b]
when he stepped up to the holy altar,
he brought glory to the courts
of the temple.

12 When he received the portions
of the sacrificial animals[c]
from the priests' hands,

[w]Heb *God also remembered Job, a prophet, who held fast to all the ways of righteousness.* [x]Heb lacks *a support for the people.* [y]Heb adds *Enosh* to the list. [z]Heb *Distinguished among his brothers and the glory of his people was the high priest Simon son of Onias.* [a]Heb *when he gazed out of the temple* [b]Heb *and when he put on splendid clothes* [c]Gk lacks *of the sacrificial animals.*

standing beside the altar's hearth,
surrounded by a wreath of brothers,
he was like a new cedar of Lebanon,
and they surrounded him
like palm-tree trunks.
13 All Aaron's sons were in their glory,
and they held the Lord's offering
in their hands
in front of the entire assembly
of Israel.
14 When he was finishing his service
at the altar,
after he had arranged an offering
to the Most High, the almighty,
15 he stretched out his hand
for the cup used for drink offerings
and he poured a libation of wine.[d]
He poured it out at the base
of the altar,
a pleasing aroma to the Most High,
the king of all.
16 Then Aaron's sons cheered;
they blew trumpets
made of hammered metal
and caused a great sound to be heard
as a reminder before the Most High.
17 Then all at once, all the people
put their faces to the ground,
bowing down to worship their Lord,
the almighty, God Most High.

18 The singers, accompanied by harps,
sang praises with their voices;
they made a sweet melody
with a full-bodied sound.
19 The people of the Lord Most High
offered prayers before the merciful one
until the order of the Lord's service
was completed,
and they finished their
worship duties to him.
20 Then Simon came down
and raised his hands
over the entire assembly
of the Israelites
to give the Lord's blessing from his lips
and to glorify his name.
21 And they bowed down to worship
a second time,
to receive the blessing
from the Most High.

22 Now bless the God of all
who everywhere does great things,
who raises us up from our birth
and deals mercifully with us.
23 May he give us gladness in our hearts,
and may there be peace in our time,
in Israel as in times past.
24 May he grant us his mercy,
and may he rescue us in our lifetime.[e]

Epilogue

25 My spirit takes offense at two nations,
and the third is not even a nation:
26 those who settled on Samaria's hills,[f]
the Philistines,
and the foolish people
who dwell in Shechem.

27 Instruction in understanding
and knowledge
were inscribed in this scroll
by Jesus, Sirach's son and grandson
of Eleazar the Jerusalemite.[g]
He poured forth wisdom from his heart.
28 Favored are those who devote their time
to these things;
when they take them to heart,
they will be wise.
29 Indeed, if they do these things,
they will be up to any task,
because the fear of the Lord
is their path.[h]

Prayer of Jesus, Sirach's son[i]

51 I will give thanks to you,
Lord and King,
and I will praise you, God my savior.
I give thanks to your name,
2 because you have been
my protector and helper.
You have rescued my body
from destruction,

[d] LXX *blood of the grape* [e] Heb in 50:24 *May his kindness to Simon endure, and may he fulfill the covenant of Phineas, so that it won't be cut off from him or his descendants as long as the heavens last.* [f] Heb *the ones settling in Seir* [g] LXX lacks *grandson*; Heb *Jesus, Eleazar's son and Sirach's grandson.* [h] LXX[b] adds *and he gave wisdom to the godly. Bless the Lord forever. Amen. Amen.* [i] The title appears in Gk manuscripts.

from the trap set
by a slanderous tongue,
from lips that fabricate lies.
In the presence of those who stood
around me,
3 you were my helper.
In line with your abundant mercy
and your great name,
you rescued me from grinding teeth
prepared to devour me,
from the power of those
who wanted to take my life,
from the many troubles that I have had,
4 from choking fire all around me,
from the midst of a fire
that I didn't start,
5 from the depths of the belly
of the grave,[j]
and from a polluted tongue
and lying words,
6 as well as the arrowlike
tongue of the unrighteous.
My soul approached death,
and my life was
on the edge of the grave[k] below.
7 People surrounded me on every side,
and no one helped;
I looked for assistance from human
beings, and there was none.
8 Then I remembered your mercy, Lord,
and your charity[l] from long ago,
that you raise up those who wait for you
and save them from the hands
of the wicked.
9 I sent up my prayer from the earth,
and I begged to be rescued from death.
10 I called out to the Lord,
the father of my master:[m]
"Don't desert me in the time
of my distress,
when I am helpless before the arrogant.
11 I will praise your name continually,
and I will sing thanksgiving hymns."
My prayer was heard,
12 because you saved me from destruction
and you rescued me from an evil time.
For this, I will give thanks, praise you,
and bless the Lord's name.[n]

Search for Wisdom

13 When I was still young,
before I had traveled,
I sought Wisdom openly in my prayer.
14 In front of the temple, I asked for her,
and I will search for her until I die.
15 From the first blossom
to the ripening of the grape clusters,
my heart delighted in her;
I walked in straight paths;
I chased her down from my youth.

16 I paid a little attention, and I received her
and found much instruction for myself.
17 I made progress with her;
I will give glory to the one
who gives me Wisdom.

18 I made up my mind
to put Wisdom into practice;
I sought the good,
and I will never be ashamed.
19 My whole being grappled with her,
and I was brought to perfection
in my performance of the Law.
I spread out my hands
toward heaven,
and I kept in mind[o]
my ignorance of her.
20 I directed my whole being toward her,
and in purity I found her.

I had a heart for her[p]
from the beginning.
For this reason
I will never be abandoned.
21 My guts were stirred to seek her;
for this reason I gained
a desired possession.
22 The Lord gave me the power
to speak well, as my reward,
and I will praise him with it.

23 Draw near to me,
you who lack education,
and stay in my school.
24 Why are you still lacking in these things;
why do you[q] thirst for this?

[j]LXX *Hades* [k]LXX *Hades* [l]Some Gk manuscripts *work*; Heb *faithful loyalty* [m]Heb *I cried out to the Lord, "You are my father."* [n]Between 51:12 and 13, Heb adds a long doxology. [o]Some Gk manuscripts *I mourned because of* [p]Or *I acquired a heart with her* [q]Or *your soul*

25 I opened my mouth and said,
"Acquire[r] her for yourselves
without money.

26 Place your neck under her yoke,
and let your soul
receive instruction.
It is found close at hand."

27 See for yourselves that I have labored
a little,
and I have found much rest for myself.
28 Invest in your education
with a great amount of silver,
and with it you will acquire much gold.[s]
29 May your whole being take delight
in God's mercy,
and may you never be ashamed
when you praise him.
30 Accomplish your work in good time,
and he will give you your reward
in his time.

[r]Heb adds *Wisdom.* [s]Heb *Listen to a little of my instruction, and you will acquire silver and gold through me.*

BARUCH

Writing from Babylon

1 These are the words of the scroll that Baruch—son of Neriah son of Mahseiah son of Zedekiah son of Hasadiah son of Hilkiah—wrote in Babylon 2 in the fifth year on the seventh day of the month at the time when the Chaldeans took Jerusalem and burned it down.

3 Baruch read the words of this scroll aloud to Judah's King Jeconiah, Jehoiakim's son, and to all the people who came to hear the reading of the scroll, 4 and to the powerful ones, the rulers' sons, the elders, and all the people, from the least important to the greatest, and to all the ones who lived in Babylon by the Sud River. 5 They wept, fasted, and prayed before the Lord. 6 They collected silver from everyone able to give, and 7 they sent it to Jerusalem to the priest Jehoiakim, Hilkiah's son, Shallum's grandson, and to the other priests, and to all the people who were with Jehoiakim in Jerusalem. 8 During the same time, on the tenth day of Sivan,[a] Baruch took the equipment from the Lord's house that had been removed from the temple—the silver equipment that Judah's King Zedekiah, Josiah's son, had made—to return it to Judah. (9 This occurred after Babylon's King Nebuchadnezzar removed Jeconiah, the leading officials, the prisoners, the powerful ones, and the land's people from Jerusalem, and brought them[b] to Babylon.)

Response to Jerusalem

10 And the people in exile said:

We have sent you silver. Buy what is needed for entirely burned offerings and sin offerings. Buy incense and prepare grain as well, and offer them on the Lord our God's altar.

11 Pray for the lives of King Nebuchadnezzar of Babylon and his son Belshazzar that their days on earth may be like the days of heaven. 12 The Lord will give us strength and clear vision. We'll live under the protection of King Nebuchadnezzar and his son Belshazzar, and we'll serve them many days and find favor with them.

13 Pray for us to the Lord our God because we have sinned against the Lord our God. Even now, the Lord's wrath and anger haven't turned away from us. 14 Read aloud this scroll that we sent to you to make it public in the Lord's house on every festival day and appointed time.

Sins of the community

15 You will say:

Justice is on the side of the Lord God, but public shame is upon us today, upon everyone in Judah, upon those living in Jerusalem, 16 and upon our rulers, leading officials, priests, prophets, and ancestors, 17 upon all of us who have sinned against the Lord.

18 We have disobeyed the Lord. We have not listened to the Lord God's voice so as to keep the commandments that he gave to us. 19 From the day when the Lord brought our ancestors from the land of Egypt until today, we have been disobedient to the Lord our God and have acted carelessly by not listening to his voice. 20 Therefore, to this day horrible things have come upon us, even the curse that the Lord ordered through Moses his servant in the day when he brought our ancestors out of Egypt to give us a prosperous land full of milk and honey. 21 But we didn't listen to the Lord God's voice through the prophets whom he sent to us. 22 All of us went off in the direction of our own evil hearts, serving other gods and doing horrible things in the presence of our Lord God.

2 The Lord carried out the word that he spoke against us, against Israel's judges, rulers, leading officials, and every person of Israel and Judah. 2 What God did in Jerusalem hadn't been done anywhere under heaven, just as was written in the Law from Moses. 3 Some of us ate the flesh of our sons and daughters. 4 God handed them over to be subjects of all the kingdoms around us—objects of insult and outcasts wherever the

[a] May–June [b] Or *him*

Lord scattered them. 5 They were brought down and not lifted up, because we sinned against the Lord our God by not listening to his voice. 6 Justice is on the side of the Lord our God, but public shame is upon us and upon our ancestors to this very day. 7 All these horrible things that the Lord had spoken came on us. 8 But we didn't plead with the Lord so as to turn each one of us from the designs of our wicked hearts. 9 Thus has the Lord kept watch over our wicked deeds and brought this upon us. The Lord is just in every action that he commanded us to do, 10 but we didn't listen to the Lord's voice to walk by the commandments that the Lord gave to us.

Prayer for deliverance

11 Now Lord God of Israel, you brought your people from Egypt by a powerful hand, by signs and wonders, with great power and an extended arm, and you have made your name famous to this very day.

12 Lord our God, we have sinned. We were ungodly. We have broken all of your commandments. 13 Turn your anger away from us, for only a few of us remain among the nations where you have scattered us. 14 Lord, listen to our prayer and our pleading. For your own sake, set us free and give us favor with those who have brought us into exile 15 so that all the earth might know that you are the Lord our God, since Israel and her children carry your name.

16 Lord, look down on us from your holy house and think of us. Lord, bend your ear and listen. 17 Lord, open your eyes and look upon us. Surely the dead who are in the grave,[c] whose spirit has been taken from their bodies, won't acknowledge the Lord's glory and justice! 18 But Lord, the one who is grieved, who goes about weak and bent over, whose eyes are failing and whose spirit is hungering—that one will acknowledge your glory and righteousness.

19 Lord our God, we are not basing our prayer for mercy on any righteous actions of our ancestors and rulers. 20 You've sent your anger and wrath on us just as you spoke through your servants the prophets. You said: 21 "The Lord says: 'Bend your shoulders and serve the king of Babylon, and then you'll reside in the land that I gave to your ancestors. 22 But if you don't listen to the Lord's voice and serve the king of Babylon, 23 I'll bring an end to the sound of joy and gladness and the celebration of marriage from the cities of Judah and around Jerusalem. The whole land will be a wasteland without life.'"

24 But we didn't listen to your voice, to serve the king of Babylon, so you have carried out the words that you spoke through your servants the prophets. The bones of our rulers and ancestors were brought out of their tombs. 25 Look, their bones have been thrown out into the heat of the day and the frost of the night. They died by many horrors, from famine, sword, and exile. 26 Because of Israel's and Judah's evil, you have made the house that carries your name what it is today.

Hope for restoration

27 Lord our God, you have acted toward us in line with your great kindness and your great compassion, 28 just as you spoke through your servant Moses on the day when you commanded him to write your Law in the presence of the Israelites.

You said:

29 If you don't listen to my voice, this great buzzing crowd will certainly turn into a small one among the nations where I'll scatter them. 30 I knew that they wouldn't listen to me, because they are stubborn. But they will change their hearts while in the land of captivity. 31 They will know that I am the Lord their God, and I'll give them a heart and ears that listen. 32 They will praise me in the land of their captivity, and they will remember my name. 33 They will turn away from their stubborn side and their wicked actions, because they will remember what happened to their ancestors who sinned in the Lord's presence. 34 I'll bring them back to the land that I promised in a solemn pledge to their ancestors—to Abraham,

[c] Gk *Hades*

Isaac, and Jacob—and they will rule it. And
I'll repopulate the land, and they will never
decrease. 35 I'll make an eternal covenant
with them that I will be their God and they
will be my people. I'll never again remove
my people Israel from the land that I have
given them.

3 Lord Almighty, God of Israel, a soul
under great stress and a wearied spirit
cry out to you. 2 Lord, listen and have
mercy, because we've sinned in your presence, 3 because you are enthroned for all
time, and we are perishing for all time.
4 Lord Almighty, God of Israel, listen now
to the prayers of those who have died in Israel and the prayers of the children of those
who kept sinning before you, who didn't listen to the Lord their God. Horrible things
continue to trouble us. 5 Don't remember
our ancestors' unjust actions, but remember your power and your reputation at this
time, 6 because you, Lord, are our God, and
we'll praise you. 7 You have planted respect
for you in our hearts so that we'll call on
your name. We'll praise you in this land far
from home, for we have put away from our
hearts all the injustice of our fathers who
sinned before you. 8 Today we are far from
home, where you have scattered us as an
insult, a curse, and a penalty due to all the
unjust actions of our ancestors, who deserted the Lord our God.

The glory of wisdom

9 Hear, Israel, the commandments of life.
Listen carefully, and you'll come to
know Wisdom.
10 Why is it, Israel, that you are in the
enemies' land,
growing old in a foreign land,
11 polluted by the dead,
and counted as people
already in the grave?[d]
12 You have abandoned the fountain
from which wisdom flows.
13 If you had walked in the way of God,
you would be living in peace forever.
14 Learn where there are wisdom, strength,
and understanding
so that you may know at the same time
where there are longevity, life,
understanding,[e] and peace.
15 Who has found her place of residence,[f]
and who has entered
her storehouses?
16 Where are the leading officials
of the nations
and the masters of the animals
that are on the earth?
17 Where are those who entrap
the birds in the sky,
and those who store up silver and gold,
in which humans have trusted?
There is no end to their attempts
to acquire more.
18 Where are those who anxiously schemed
to acquire silver?
There is no trace of their actions.
19 They have all vanished
and gone to the grave,[g]
and others have risen up in their place.
20 New generations have seen the light
and lived on the earth,
but they didn't know
the way of knowledge.
21 They didn't understand her paths
or take hold of her.
Their children also went far off course.
22 She hadn't been heard of in Canaan
or seen in Teman.
23 Hagar's children,
who seek earthly understanding,
the traders of Merran and Teman,
the storytellers
and knowledge seekers,
haven't learned the way of Wisdom,
nor have they remembered her paths.
24 Israel, how great is God's house
and spacious is God's domain!
25 It is great and has no end;
it is high and immeasurable!
26 The giants were born there,
the famous ones
from the beginning of time,
who were very large
and experts in war.
27 God didn't select them or give them
the way of true knowledge.

[d] Gk *Hades* [e] Or *light for the eyes* [f] Gk lacks *of residence.* [g] Gk *Hades*

28 So they perished
because they didn't have Wisdom;
they perished
through their carelessness.
29 Who went into heaven, took Wisdom,
and brought her down from the clouds?
30 Who crossed over to the other side of
the sea and found her,
and who will bring her back
with choice gold?
31 No one knows the road she takes
or thinks much about
the path she travels.
32 But the one who knows all things
knows her;
God found her by his understanding;
the one who made the earth
for time eternal,
and filled it with four-footed animals;
33 the one who sends the light
and it shines forth;
who called it
and it obeyed him with trembling.
34 The stars shone at their appointed posts
and were delighted.
God called them,
and the stars said, "Here we are."
They shone joyfully
for the one who made them.
35 This is our God.
No other will be compared to him.
36 God discovered every way of knowledge
and gave her to his child[h] Jacob,
to Israel, whom he loved.
37 After this, she appeared on the earth
and lived among humans.

4 She is the scroll containing God's
commandments,
the Law that exists forever.
All who hold on to her will live,
but those who desert her will die.
2 Jacob, turn and grab on to her.
Travel toward the rays
coming from her light.
3 Don't give your honor to another
or your advantages to a foreign nation.
4 Israel, we are blessed
because we know
what is pleasing to God.

Poem of encouragement

5 Be confident, my people,
you who are the legacy of Israel!
6 You weren't sold to the nations
for complete destruction,
but you were handed over
to your opponents
because you made God angry.
7 You upset your creator
when you sacrificed to demons
and not to God.
8 You forgot the eternal God
who raised you;
and you caused pain to Jerusalem,
who nurtured you.
9 Jerusalem saw the wrath of God
that came on you and said:
Neighbors of Zion, listen!
God has brought me great grief.
10 I have watched my sons and daughters
taken captive,
the action of the eternal one.
11 I nursed them joyfully,
but I sent them away
with tears and mourning.

12 Don't any of you rejoice over me,
a widow deserted by many.
My children avoided God's Law,
so I was stripped bare
because of their sins.
13 They didn't acknowledge
God's requirements,
walk in the ways of
God's commandments,
or follow the paths in which
his righteousness trained them.
14 Neighbors of Zion, come!
Remember the exile
my sons and daughters suffered,
brought on them by the eternal one.
15 God brought a nation
from far away against them,
a nation that is shameless
and speaks a strange language,
that showed no respect for the elderly
or pity for the child.
16 It[i] took away the widow's
dearly loved sons

[h]Or *servant* [i]Or *they*

and deprived the lonely woman
of her daughters.
17 But how am I able to help you?
18 The one who brought
the horrible things on you
will rescue you
from your enemies' grasp.
19 Go, children, go,
for I have been left desolate.
20 I've stripped off the robe of peace and
put on the rough cloth of mourners.
I'll spend my days crying out
to the eternal one.
21 Children, be confident! Cry out to God!
God will rescue you from your enemies'
authority and grip.
22 I have placed hope in the eternal one
for your salvation;
the holy one has sent me joy,
because your eternal savior
will soon have mercy on you.
23 I sent you away
with mourning and wailing,
but God will restore you to me
with gladness and joy forever.
24 Just as Zion's neighbors
have now seen your exile,
they'll also soon see
God's deliverance of you;
it will come to you with all the glory
and splendor of the eternal one.
25 Children, bear up patiently
under God's anger,
which has come on you.
Your enemy has hunted you down,
but you'll soon see their destruction.
Then you'll step on their throats.
26 My delicate children
have traveled rough roads.
They were taken as a flock
snatched away by enemies.
27 Children, be confident!
Cry out to God,
for the one who brought this on you
will remember you.
28 Just as you plotted
to stray away from God,
return with ten times as much effort
to seek him out.
29 The one who brought
these horrible things on you
will bring you eternal joy
along with your deliverance.

Comfort for Jerusalem

30 Jerusalem, be confident!
The one who named you will comfort you.
31 Misery will fall upon those
who mistreated you
and celebrated your fall.
32 Misery will fall upon the cities
that enslaved your young.
Misery will fall upon the cities[j]
that received your children.
33 Just as the enemy[k] celebrated your fall
and rejoiced at your misfortune,
she herself will feel the pain
of being left desolate.
34 I'll strip away the pride
she has in her great population,
and turn her arrogance into grief.
35 The eternal one will send fire on her
for many days,
and demons will inhabit her
for a long time.
36 Jerusalem, look to the east
and see the joy that is coming
to you from God.
37 The children you sent away are coming.
By the holy one's word,
they are coming from the east
and the west,
rejoicing in God's glory.

5 Take off your mourning clothes
and oppression, Jerusalem!
Dress yourself in the dignity
of God's glory forever.
2 Wrap the justice that comes from God
around yourself like a robe.
Place the eternal one's glory
on your head like a crown.
3 God will show your brilliance everywhere
under heaven.
4 God will give you this name
by which to be called forever:
The Peace That Comes from Justice,
The Honor That Comes
from Reverence for God!

[j] Or *the city* [k] Or *he*

[5] Get up, Jerusalem!
Stand on the high place,
and look around to the east!
See your children gathered
from the west to the east
by the holy one's word,
as they rejoice that God has
remembered them.
[6] They went out from you on foot,
driven along by their enemies,
but God will bring them back to you,
carried aloft with glory
as on a royal throne.
[7] God has ordered every high mountain
and the eternal hills
to be brought down,
and the valleys to be filled in
to level the ground
so that Israel may walk safely
in God's glory.
[8] The woods and every fragrant tree
have shaded Israel
with God's command.
[9] God will lead Israel with gladness
by the light that shines forth
from his glory,
with the mercy and righteousness
that come from him.

LETTER OF JEREMIAH

Introduction

This is a copy of the letter that Jeremiah
sent to those who would be taken as prisoners to Babylon by the Babylonian king.
Jeremiah wrote to give them the instructions that God imposed upon him.

God's exile of Israel into Babylon

1 Nebuchadnezzar, Babylon's king, will
bring you as prisoners to Babylon because
of the sins that you committed in the presence of God. 2 When you enter Babylon, you
will be there a long time, as long as seven
generations. Afterward, I will bring you out
from there peacefully. 3 In Babylon you will
see gods of silver, gold, and wood paraded
on the Babylonians' shoulders. These gods
inspire awe among the people. 4 Be careful
that you don't become like the Gentiles,[a]
letting fear of these gods grip you, 5 especially when you see large crowds of people
walking in front of and behind them, worshipping them. But say to yourself, Lord,
we want to worship you. 6 For God's[b] angel
is with you, examining your souls.

Inability of the idols to do anything

7 A carpenter smooths out the tongues of
the idols. They are covered in gold and silver, but they are fake and unable to speak.
8 The Gentiles take gold and place crowns on
their gods' heads, like a young girl playing
dress up. 9 Sometimes the priests secretly
take away the gold and silver from their
gods to spend on themselves and give to
prostitutes in the brothels. 10 The Gentiles
dress these gods of silver, gold, and wood
with clothing just like people. But these
idols can't be rescued from rust and rotting.[c]
11 Even though the idols are dressed in rich
purple clothing, the Gentiles have to wipe
off the idols' faces because of the dust in
the temple that thickly covers them. 12 One
idol has a royal staff, like a person who is
a regional judge, but the idol can't destroy
the person who offends it. 13 Another one
has a dagger or an ax in its right hand, but
it can't defend itself from war or robbers.
14 Clearly they are no gods, so don't be afraid
of them.

15 Just as a person's utensil is useless
after it's broken, so are the Gentiles' gods
after they have been placed in their temples.
16 Their eyes are full of dust from the feet of
visitors. 17 Even as the courtyards are locked
up on every side when one is sentenced to
death for doing wrong against a king, so
the priests secure their temples with doors,
bolts, and bars from robbers and thieves.
18 The priests light more lamps for the idols
than for themselves, but their gods can't
see them. 19 The idols are just like the beams
that support a house, but people say that
their hearts melt before them.[d] They don't
notice when vermin from the earth have
eaten them and their clothing. 20 Their faces
have been darkened by the smoke that is
in the temple. 21 Bats, swallows, birds, and
cats land on their bodies and heads. 22 From
this you will know that they aren't gods. So
don't be afraid of them.

23 As for the gold they wear beautifully, the
idols won't shine unless someone else wipes
away the rust. They didn't have any feeling
when they were made. 24 They are purchased
at great cost, but there is no breath in them.
25 Since they have no feet, others carry them
on their shoulders, demonstrating their
worthlessness to people. Their servants are
ashamed, since the idols fall to the ground
unless they steady them and hold them
up. 26 If anyone stands an idol up, it can't
move by itself. If one is tilted over, it can't
straighten itself up. Yet gifts are placed in
front of them—just as people place gifts in
front of the dead!

Worthlessness of the idols

27 Their priests misuse the sacrifices
by selling them and using the money for
themselves. Their wives also preserve some
of the meat,[e] but they don't share it with
the poor or disabled. Menstruating[f] women
and others who have just given birth have

[a] Or *foreigners* [b] Or *my* [c] Or *food* [d] Gk uncertain; Gk lacks *before them.* [e] Or *of them* [f] Or *Sitting apart*

handled their sacrifices. 28Since you know from these things that they aren't gods, don't be afraid of them.

29Why call them gods? Because women place food before these gods of silver, gold, and wood? 30Or because the priests sit in their temples with their garments torn, with their heads and beards shaved, and their heads uncovered? 31They howl and shout in front of their gods as some do at a funeral feast for the dead. 32Yet the priests take the gods' clothing to dress their wives and children.

33Whether one treats them badly or well, the gods aren't able to repay in kind. They aren't able to install or remove a ruler. 34They can't give either wealth or money. If someone makes a solemn promise and doesn't keep it, they can't enforce it. 35They can't save a person from death or rescue a weak person from a strong one. 36They can't restore sight to the blind or rescue a person in an emergency. 37They can't show mercy to a widow, nor can they do any good for an orphan. 38These wooden things covered in gold and silver are like stones from a mountain. Their servants will be humiliated. 39So why should anyone consider or call them gods?

40In addition, even the Chaldeans dishonor them. When they see a person who is unable to speak, they bring out Bel and expect Bel to make a sound as if he were able to understand. 41Even after observing this, the Chaldeans themselves are unable to abandon the idols because they have no sense. 42The women, with cords wrapped around them, sit along the streets and burn corn husks as incense. 43When one of these women is dragged away by someone to have sex, she makes fun of the one nearest her by saying that the other woman wasn't as worthy as she, nor has the woman's cord been broken. 44Everything that is done for the gods is phony. So why should anyone consider or call them gods?

45Carpenters and goldsmiths make them. They can be only what these designers want them to be. 46Their creators won't live long themselves, so how can the things they have made be gods? 47These designers leave behind something fake and disgraceful for those who come after them. 48When war or disasters come, the priests consult with each other about where they may hide along with the idols. 49So how can one not grasp that they aren't gods? They can't save themselves from war or other disasters. 50After such events as this, the idols, made of wood and covered in gold and silver, will be recognized as fake. It will be clear to the nations and to the rulers that they aren't gods but human creations. There's nothing divine about them. 51Who then doesn't realize that they aren't gods?

52They could never raise up a ruler over a country or provide rain for people. 53They can't render a verdict in their own cases, nor can they save those falsely accused, because the idols are powerless. They are like crows between the sky and the earth. 54When a fire breaks out in the home of their wooden gods covered in gold and silver, their priests will run and save themselves, but the gods will be destroyed like the supporting beams. 55The idols can't stand up against kings or enemies in war. 56So why should anyone consider or call them gods?

57The wooden gods covered in gold and silver can't be saved from thieves and robbers, who will take away the gold, silver, and clothing that the idols wear. They won't be able to protect themselves. 58It's better to be a ruler who has courage or a household utensil that the owner can actually use than to be fake gods. The door of a house, which keeps safe the things that are in it, is better than fake gods. A wooden column in a palace is better than these fake gods.

The power of Israel's God

59The sun, moon, and stars are bright, and they willingly obey when given an order. 60Also lightning is widely seen when it flashes and draws attention. The wind also blows in every land. 61When God commands the clouds to move across the whole world, they carry out the order. When the fire is sent out from above to destroy mountains and forests, it accomplishes what it is ordered to do. 62But the idols can't be compared with such forces of nature in appearance or ability. [63]There's no reason at all to believe in them or call them gods. They aren't able to judge anyone's case or do good for anyone. [64]Since you know they aren't gods, don't be afraid of them.

[65]They can't curse or bless rulers. [66]They can't show signs in the sky among the nations or shine like the sun or give light like the moon. [67]The animals are better off than the idols, for they are able to run for shelter and help themselves. [68]It is obvious to us that the idols aren't gods. So don't be afraid of them.

[69]As a scarecrow in a cucumber field offers no protection, so do[g] their wooden gods covered in gold and silver. [70]In the same way, their wooden gods covered in gold and silver could be compared to a briar patch where every bird perches or to a dead body thrown out into the darkness. [71]From the purple cloth—and the marble that decays and crumbles[h] on them—you will know they aren't gods. Later they themselves will be devoured, and it will be a disgrace in the land.

[72]So it is better to be a righteous person without any idols. That person will be far removed from disgrace.

[g]Or *are* [h]Gk lacks *and crumbles.*

PRAYER OF AZARIAH (AND HYMN OF THE THREE YOUNG MEN)

Azariah's prayer for reconciliation

1[a]Shadrach, Meshach, and Abednego[b]
walked around in the flames, singing
hymns to God, blessing the Lord. 2While
standing and praying in the middle of the
fire, Azariah spoke like this:

3 Blessed are you,
Lord God of our ancestors.
You deserve to be praised
and honored forever!
4 Everything you've done to us is fair.
All your actions are right,
your ways consistent;
all your decisions are sound.
5 You judged us fairly
in all the things you've done to us
and to Jerusalem,
our ancestors' holy city.
You were honest and fair
in doing all these things
to us because of our sins.
6 We sinned and broke the law
by turning from you;
we sinned in everything we did.
7 We didn't obey your commands;
we didn't keep them or do as you
ordered us,
although the orders were
for our own good.
8 All that you've brought upon us,
all that you've done to us,
has been fair.
9 You handed us over to our enemies,
immoral rebels who hate God's laws,
and to an unjust king, the most evil
one in the whole world.
10 Now there's nothing that we can say.
Shame and blame cover your servants
and those who worship you.
11 For the sake of your own reputation,
please don't hand us over permanently!
Don't set aside your covenant!
12 Don't turn your mercy away from us!
Hold to it
for the sake of Abraham,
whom you loved,
and Isaac, your servant,
and Israel, your holy one.
13 You told them
you would give them descendants,
as many as the stars of the sky
and the grains of sand beside the sea.
14 Look, Lord, we have become smaller
than any other nation.
We are disgraced now in front of
everybody because of our sins.
15 In this time we have no ruler
or prophet or leader,
no entirely burned offering or sacrifice,
no special gift or incense,
no place to bring gifts to you
and find mercy.
16 Accept us, please, with our crushed souls
and humble spirits,
as if we brought entirely burned
offerings of rams and bulls,
as if we brought tens of thousands
of fat lambs.
17 May this be the kind of offering we make
in your presence today,
and may we follow you completely,[c]
since no shame will come to those who
come to terms with you.
18 Now we follow you with our hearts,
honor you, and seek your presence.
19 Don't put us to shame!
Instead, deal with us in line
with your kindness and great mercy.

[a]Appears in Gk between Dan 3:23 and 3:24 [b]Shadrach, Meshach, and Abednego equal Hananiah, Mishael, and Azariah (Dan 1:7). [c]Gk uncertain

[20]As you have worked wonders before,
so rescue us now!
Build up your reputation, Lord!
[21]Let all who mistreat your servants
be humiliated.
Let them be put to shame
and lose all their authority;
may their strength be smashed.
[22]Let them know that you alone
are the Lord God,
more honored
than anyone else in the world.

Heating the fire

[23]Now the king's aides, who had thrown
them into the furnace, were constantly feeding the fire with petroleum, tar, kindling,
and dry sticks. [24]Flame shot out of the furnace to a height of more than seventy feet,
[25]spreading out and burning the Babylonians who stood near the furnace. [26]But the
Lord's angel came down among Azariah and
his friends and waved the fiery flames out
of the furnace. [27]He made the middle of the
furnace seem like a cool breeze was blowing
through it. The fire didn't touch them at all;
it didn't hurt or upset them.

Hymn of the three young men

[28]Then with one voice the three began
singing hymns, praising and blessing God
right there in the furnace. They said:
[29]Blessed are you,
Lord God of our ancestors.
You are worthy of praise and raised
high above all others forever.
Blessed is your glorious
and holy reputation,
worthy of praise and raised high above
all others forever.
[30]Blessed are you in your glorious,
holy temple,
worthy of hymns and honored
above all others forever.
[31]Blessed are you,
sitting on the winged creatures,
looking down into the farthest depths,
worthy of praise and raised high
above all others forever.
[32]Blessed are you on your royal throne,
worthy of hymns and raised high
above all others forever.
[33]Blessed are you in the dome of the sky,
worthy of hymns
and honored forever.

[34]All works of the Lord, bless the Lord,
sing hymns, and lift God high
above all others forever.
[35]Heavens, bless the Lord,
sing hymns, and lift God high
above all others forever.
[36]Angels serving the Lord, bless the Lord,
sing hymns, and lift God high
above all others forever.
[37]All you waters above the sky,
bless the Lord,
sing hymns, and lift God high
above all others forever.
[38]All you heavenly powers,[d] bless the Lord,
sing hymns, and lift God high
above all others forever.
[39]Sun and moon, bless the Lord,
sing hymns, and lift God high
above all others forever.
[40]Stars of the sky, bless the Lord,
sing hymns, and lift God high
above all others forever.
[41]Rainstorms and dew, bless the Lord,
sing hymns, and lift God high
above all others forever.
[42]All you winds, bless the Lord,
sing hymns, and lift God high
above all others forever.
[43]Fire and burning, bless the Lord,
sing hymns, and lift God high
above all others forever.
[44]Cold and heat, bless the Lord,
sing hymns, and lift God high
above all others forever.
[45]Dew drops and falling snow,
bless the Lord,
sing hymns, and lift God high
above all others forever.
[46]Nights and days, bless the Lord,
sing hymns, and lift God high
above all others forever.
[47]Light and darkness, bless the Lord,

[d]Gk lacks *heavenly*.

sing hymns, and lift God high
above all others forever.
48 Ice and winter, bless the Lord,
sing hymns, and lift God high
above all others forever.
49 Frost and snow, bless the Lord,
sing hymns, and lift God high
above all others forever.
50 Lightning and clouds, bless the Lord,
sing hymns, and lift God high
above all others forever.

51 Let the earth bless the Lord.
Let it sing hymns and lift God high
above all others forever.
52 Mountains and hills, bless the Lord,
sing hymns, and lift God high
above all others forever.
53 All you things that grow in the earth,
bless the Lord,
sing hymns, and lift God high
above all others forever.
54 Oceans and rivers, bless the Lord,
sing hymns, and lift God high
above all others forever.
55 Running waters, bless the Lord,
sing hymns, and lift God high
above all others forever.
56 Sea monsters and all you things that
swarm in the water, bless the Lord,
sing hymns, and lift God high
above all others forever.
57 All birds of the sky, bless the Lord,
sing hymns, and lift God high
above all others forever.
58 Wild and tame animals, bless the Lord,
sing hymns, and lift God high
above all others forever.
59 You human beings, bless the Lord,
sing hymns, and lift God high
above all others forever.
60 Israel, bless the Lord,
sing hymns, and lift God high
above all others forever.
61 Priests, bless the Lord,
sing hymns, and lift God high
above all others forever.
62 You who serve the Lord, bless the Lord,
sing hymns, and lift God high
above all others forever.
63 Spirits and souls of good people,
bless the Lord,
sing hymns, and lift God high
above all others forever.
64 You people who are holy and have
humble hearts, bless the Lord,
sing hymns, and lift God high
above all others forever.

65 Hananiah, Azariah, and Mishael,
bless the Lord,
sing hymns, and lift God high
above all others forever,
because he rescued us from
the grave,[e]
and saved us from death.
God pulled us out of the middle
of the scorching furnace,
and pulled us out
of the middle of the fire.
66 Tell people that the Lord is good,
because his mercy lasts forever.
67 All you who worship the Lord,
the God of gods, bless him,
sing hymns, and tell people
that God's mercy lasts forever!

[e] Gk *Hades*

SUSANNA[a]

1 A man named Joakim once lived in Babylon. 2 His wife Susanna, Hilkiah's daughter, was very beautiful and honored the Lord. 3 Her parents were good people, and they taught their daughter according to the Law from Moses.

4 Joakim was very rich, and he had a large private garden next to his home. The Jews came to him because he was the most honored among them. 5 Two elders among the people had been appointed as judges that year. It was about them that the Lord had spoken: "Lawless disorder[b] has come out of Babylon, from elders, from judges who were supposed to guide the people." 6 These men spent a lot of time at Joakim's house, and all the people with lawsuits came to them.

7 When the people went away in the middle of the day, Susanna would walk around her husband's private garden. 8 Every day the two elders would see her coming in and walking around, and they desired her sexually. 9 They ceased thinking clearly, neither looking to heaven nor caring about justice. 10 Both of them thought about her and nothing else, but they didn't tell each other their craving, 11 because they were ashamed to admit how they desired her and wanted to be with her. 12 But they were on the lookout every day, eager to get a glimpse of her.

13 One said to the other, "It's time for lunch. Let's go home." They split up and left, 14 but doubling back, they met again at the same place. They started asking each other for an explanation, and so each confessed his desire. Then they plotted together for a time when they would be able to find her alone.

15 When they were watching closely for the right moment, Susanna came by, just as she had the day before and the day before that, alone with her two female servants. She wanted to bathe in the privacy of the garden, since it was hot. 16 No one was there except the two elders, who were hidden and spying on her. 17 She said to her female servants, "Please bring me some olive oil and lotion and lock the gates so I can bathe." 18 They did just what she said. They locked the gates to the garden and went through the side doors into the house to fetch the things she had wanted. They didn't see the elders, since they were hiding.

19 When the female servants went out, the two elders stood up and ran at her. 20 They said, "Look, the gates are locked, and nobody can see us. We desire you, so do what we want and have sex with us. 21 If you don't, we'll swear that you were meeting with a young man, and that's why you sent your female servants away."

22 Susanna groaned. "I'm trapped! If I do this, it's death; but if I don't, I still won't escape your plotting.[c] 23 But I'd rather not do this and fall into your hands, than sin in the Lord's sight." 24 So Susanna screamed, and at the same time the two elders called out. 25 One of them ran and opened the gates to the garden.

26 When people in the house heard the shouting in the garden, they ran out through the side doors to see what had happened to Susanna. 27 When the two elders had their say, the servants were very ashamed because nothing like this had ever been said about Susanna.

28 The next day when the people came to her husband Joakim, the two elders came too, full of their immoral scheme to have Susanna killed. They said in front of the people, 29 "Call Susanna, Hilkiah's daughter, who is married to Joakim." So they called her in. 30 She came with her parents, her children, and all her relatives.

31 Now Susanna was elegant, beautiful in appearance. 32 The criminals ordered the veil that she was wearing to be removed so they could soak in her beauty. 33 But her household and all who saw her were crying. 34 Upon tak-

[a]This translation is based on Theodotion's edition, which displaced the older Septuagint edition in the usage of the Christian church by the late third century. All major codices of the Septuagint actually contain the Theodotion edition of Daniel. Other ancient versions (the Vulgate, the Peshitta, the Ethiopic, Coptic, Arabic, and Armenian) are based on Theodotion. [b]Or *lawlessness* [c]Or *hands*

ing the stand in front of everybody, the elders laid their hands on Susanna's head to give testimony.[d] 35But she looked up to heaven while crying because she trusted the Lord.

36The elders said, "While we were walking around the large garden by ourselves, this woman came in with two female servants. She locked the gates of the garden and sent away the female servants. 37Then a young man, who had been hiding, came and lay with her. 38We were in a corner of the garden, and when we saw this lawless act, we went running to them. 39We saw them having sex, but we couldn't hold on to the man because he was stronger than we were. He opened the gates and ran away. 40So we grabbed this woman and asked who the young man was, 41but she wouldn't tell us. To this we swear."

The assembly believed them because they were the people's elders and judges. So they sentenced Susanna to death.

42Susanna screamed out: "Eternal God, you know what is hidden; you see everything before it happens. 43You know they've lied in this court about me! Look, I'm going to die, although I didn't do any of the things these men accuse in their malice!"

44The Lord heard her cry. 45As she was being led away to die, God stirred up the holy spirit of a young man named Daniel. 46He shouted out loud, "I'm innocent of this woman's blood!"

47All the people turned to him and asked, "What are you saying?!"

48He stood among them and said, "Are you so stupid, Israelites, that you've sentenced an Israelite woman to death without cross-examining or finding the facts? 49Go back to court: these men have given false testimony against her."

50Everyone rushed back. The other elders said to Daniel, "Sit here with us and advise us, since God has given you the status of an elder."

51Daniel told them, "Separate them from each other, and I'll cross-examine them."

52When they had been separated from each other, he called in one of the judges and said to him, "The sins you did earlier are catching up to you now at the end of a long evil life. 53You judged unfairly, sentencing the innocent to death, and letting the guilty go, even though the Lord says, 'You will not sentence innocent and good people to death.' 54Now then, if you really saw this woman, tell me this. Under what tree did you see them having sex?" He said, "Under a clove tree."

55Daniel said, "Right! You lied! It's on your own head! Already God's angel has orders to cleave you down the middle!"

56Then setting that one aside, he ordered them to bring in the other judge. He said to him, "You're a Canaanite and not from Judah. Beauty seduced you, and sexual desire twisted your mind. 57You treated women from Israel this way, and they had sex with you because they were afraid of you. But this woman from Judah wouldn't tolerate your lawless immorality. 58So tell me now: Under what tree did you catch them having sex with each other?" He said, "Under a yew."[e]

59Daniel said to him, "Right! You lied too! It's on your own head. God's angel waits with his sword to hew you down the middle, to destroy both of you."

60Then the whole assembly started shouting out praises to the God who saves those who hope in him. 61They rose up against the two elders, because Daniel had shown from their own words that they were false witnesses. They treated them in the same way that they had plotted to treat their neighbor. 62By following the Law from Moses, they killed them. Innocent blood was saved that day. 63Hilkiah and his wife gave thanks that their daughter Susanna had not been found guilty of a shameful crime. Her husband Joakim and all their relatives also gave thanks. 64From that day Daniel was honored among the people.

[d]Gk lacks *to give testimony*. [e]Or *evergreen oak*

BEL AND THE SNAKE[a]

Bel's secret

1 When King Astyages was buried with his ancestors, Cyrus the Persian took over his kingdom. 2 Daniel was a companion of the king, honored above all Cyrus' political advisors.[b] 3 Now the Babylonians had an idol named Bel. Each day they supplied it with twelve bushels of fine flour, forty sheep, and sixty gallons[c] of wine. 4 The king honored Bel and worshipped it daily, but Daniel worshipped his own God. So the king said to him, "Why don't you worship Bel?"

5 He said, "I don't honor idols made by humans, rather the living God who created heaven and earth and has authority over all living things."

6 The king said to him, "You believe Bel is a living god, don't you? Haven't you seen how much he eats and drinks every day?"

7 Daniel laughed and said, "Don't be taken in, Your Majesty! This is clay on the inside and brass on the outside. It hasn't eaten or drunk anything, ever!"

8 Furious, the king called for his priests. He said to them, "If you don't tell me who eats these provisions, you die! But if you can prove that Bel eats them, Daniel will die for insulting Bel."

9 Daniel said to the king, "That's fair enough."

Now Bel had seventy priests plus their wives and children. 10 The king went with Daniel to Bel's temple. 11 Bel's priests said, "We're going outside now. Your Majesty, you set out the food and mix the wine. Lock the door and seal it with your own seal. Early tomorrow, if you don't find that Bel has eaten everything, you can kill us. Otherwise, kill Daniel for lying about us!" (12 The priests weren't worried because they had made a hidden entrance under the table, which they regularly used to enter to eat everything.)

13 When the priests went out, the king set out Bel's food. 14 But Daniel ordered his servants to bring ashes and sprinkle the whole temple, with only the king watching. Then everyone went out, locked the door, sealed it with the king's seal, and left.

15 The priests came that night, as usual, with their wives and children, and ate and drank everything. 16 The king and Daniel got up very early the next morning. 17 The king said, "Are the seals unbroken, Daniel?"

He answered, "Unbroken, Your Majesty."

18 As soon as the doors were opened, the king looked at the table and yelled, "You are great, Bel! There's nothing fake about you!"

19 But Daniel laughed and held the king back from going in. He said, "Look at the floor. Whose tracks are these?"

20 The king said, "I see the footprints of men, women, and children!" 21 Then the king became angry. He arrested the priests, their wives, and children. They showed him the hidden doors through which they regularly entered to eat what was on the table. 22 The king killed them and handed Bel over to Daniel, who tore it and its temple down.

A living god?

23 Now there was a big snake that the Babylonians worshipped. 24 The king said to Daniel, "You can't say that this one isn't a living god. So worship it!"

25 Daniel said, "I will keep worshipping the Lord my God, because he is a living God. But, Your Majesty, just give me permission, and I'll kill the snake without using a sword or stick!"

26 The king said, "I give you permission."

27 Then Daniel took tar and cooking grease and hair. He boiled them down, made patties, and put them into the snake's mouth. The snake swallowed them and burst open. Daniel said, "Look at what you have been worshipping!"

Daniel in the lions' pit

28 When the Babylonians heard what happened, they were very angry. They came

[a] This translation is based on Theodotion's edition, which displaced the older Septuagint edition in the usage of the Christian church by the late third century. All major codices of the Septuagint actually contain the Theodotion edition of Daniel. Other ancient versions (the Vulgate, the Peshitta, the Ethiopic, Coptic, Arabic, and Armenian) are based on Theodotion. [b] Or *Friends* [c] Gk *metretai*, a liquid measure of approximately ten gallons

together as a mob and started toward the king, saying, "The king has become a Jew! He's torn down Bel, killed the snake, and murdered the priests!"
29 When they reached the king, they said, "Hand Daniel over to us! If you don't, we'll kill you and your family!"

30 The king saw that he was in a bind and was forced to hand Daniel over to them.
31 They threw Daniel into a pit of lions. He was there six days.
32 There were seven lions in the pit. Usually they were fed two bodies and two sheep daily, but now they were fed nothing so that they would devour Daniel.

33 At the same time, the prophet Habakkuk was in Judah. He had boiled a stew, put some bread in a bowl, and was carrying it to the people harvesting the field.
34 But the Lord's angel said to Habakkuk, "Take this lunch to Babylon, to Daniel in the lions' pit."

35 Habakkuk said, "Lord, I've never seen Babylon, and I'm not familiar with that pit."
36 So the Lord's angel lifted Habakkuk by his hair and brought him in a rush of wind[d] to Babylon, right above the pit.
37 Habakkuk yelled, "Daniel! Daniel! Take the lunch that God has sent to you!"

38 Daniel said, "God, you remembered me! You don't abandon the people who love you."
39 Daniel got up and ate, while God's angel took Habakkuk instantly back to his own place.

40 On the seventh day the king came to the pit to grieve for Daniel. He looked in, and there was Daniel, sitting there!
41 Then the king shouted out loud, "You are great, Lord, Daniel's God! There's no other but you!"
42 He pulled Daniel out. But he threw the ones who had planned Daniel's destruction into the pit, and they were eaten instantly, right in front of him.

[d] Or *in the rush of his spirit*

1 MACCABEES

Alexander the Great

1 Alexander was Philip's son, a Macedonian, one of the western peoples known as the Kittim. After Alexander became king of Greece, he defeated King Darius, who ruled the Persians and the Medes. By doing so, Alexander greatly enlarged his realm.
2 He successfully fought many battles, conquered fortresses, and put to death many kings. 3 He advanced to the very ends of the known earth, plundering nation after nation. Finally, his battles reached an end, and he was widely recognized as supreme king, which made him proud. 4 He built a very strong army and ruled countries, nations, and princes; and they all owed allegiance to him.

5 But eventually Alexander fell sick and was confined to bed. He knew that he was dying. 6 He therefore called for his most esteemed officers, those who had been raised with him; and he divided his kingdom among them while he was still alive.
7 Then Alexander died, having ruled for twelve years.[a]

8 Subsequently, his officers began to rule, each in his own territory. 9 They ruled as kings, and after them their descendants ruled for many years. Together they caused much suffering across the earth.

Antiochus Epiphanes and renegade Jews

10 From these descendants sprouted a sinful root—Antiochus Epiphanes. He was a son of King Antiochus, and he had been brought up in Rome as a hostage. Antiochus Epiphanes began to rule in the year 137[b] according to the calendar of the Greek kingdom.

11 At that time, some renegade Israelites emerged. These people went against their ancestral laws and encouraged many other Jews to join them. They spoke up, saying, "Let's make an agreement with the Gentiles around us, because many horrible things have happened to us since we separated ourselves from them." 12 The proposal pleased their fellow Jews. 13 Some of them eagerly went to King Antiochus, who gave them permission to start living by the laws of the Gentiles. 14 Consequently, they built a gymnasium in Jerusalem, following Gentile custom. 15 They even took steps to remove the marks of circumcision, utterly abandoning the holy covenant. They joined with Gentiles and gave themselves over to an evil course.

Antiochus in Egypt

16 When Antiochus felt that his own kingdom was fully established, he determined also to take control of the land of Egypt so that he could rule over both kingdoms. 17 He invaded Egypt with a very strong force, including soldiers in chariots and on elephants, as well as cavalry and a large fleet.
18 When Antiochus met the Egyptian king Ptolemy in battle, Ptolemy and his forces hastily retreated. Many were wounded and killed. 19 Antiochus and his forces were able to capture the fortified cities in Egypt and plunder the land.

Oppression of the Jews

20 After he conquered Egypt, Antiochus returned in the year 143.[c] He went up to Israel and entered Jerusalem with a strong force. 21 With arrogance he went into the sanctuary. He took the gold altar, the lampstand for the light, and all its equipment.
22 He also took the table that was used for the sacred bread, drink-offering cups, bowls, gold censers, a curtain, crowns, and the gold decoration on the front of the temple. He stripped it all. 23 He took silver, gold, and costly equipment. He took every hidden treasure he could find. 24 Taking it all, he went back to his own land. He committed murder and spoke very arrogantly.

25 Every community in Israel
grieved deeply.
26 Rulers and elders groaned;
young women and men became faint.

[a] 323 BCE [b] 175 BCE [c] 169 BCE

The women's beauty faded.
27 Every bridegroom was saddened,
and intended brides sat
mourning in their chambers.
28 Even the land shook for its people,
and all of Jacob's house
was clothed with shame.

Occupation of Jerusalem

29 Two years later,[d] to collect tribute from
the Judean cities, King Antiochus sent his
chief officer, who came to Jerusalem with
a large army. 30 The agent spoke peaceably
and the Jews believed him, but he was deceitful. Without warning, he attacked the
city, dealt it a brutal blow, and killed many
Israelites. 31 He plundered the city. He set
fires within it, destroyed its houses, and
tore down its protective walls. 32 His forces
took women and children as prisoners and
seized livestock. 33 After all of this, the
agent's forces fortified David's City with a
very strong wall and powerful towers, and
it became their fortress. 34 They stationed
sinful, immoral people there, and these
soldiers held down their position. 35 They
stocked up with weapons and food, collected the spoils of Jerusalem, and stored
them there. They were a great menace.
36 They[e] ambushed the sanctuary.
They were an evil opponent of Israel
at all times.
37 Its inhabitants shed innocent blood
all around the sanctuary,
and they even polluted
the sanctuary itself.
38 Because of them,
those who lived in Jerusalem fled.
The city became
a dwelling place for strangers.
She was like a stranger to her offspring,
and her children abandoned her.
39 Her sanctuary was as barren as a desert.
Her feasts turned into mourning,
her sabbaths into shame,
her honor into contempt.
40 Her dishonor became as great
as her glory had been.
Her joy turned into sadness.

Installation of Gentile worship

41 Then King Antiochus sent word throughout his entire kingdom that everyone
should act like one people, 42 giving up their
local customs. The Gentile nations all readily accepted the king's command. 43 Many
Jews also willingly adopted the king's religion. They sacrificed to idols and violated
the Sabbath. 44 The king sent messengers
carrying letters to Jerusalem and the surrounding towns of Judah. He directed Jews
to follow customs that had been unknown
in the land. 45 He banned the regular practices of entirely burned offerings, sacrifices, and drink offerings in the sanctuary.
He banned the observance of sabbaths and
feast days. 46 The sanctuary and its priests
were to be defiled. 47 They should build new
altars, together with sacred precincts and
shrines for idols. They should sacrifice pigs
and other ritually impure animals. 48 Jews
were no longer to circumcise their sons.
They were supposed to make themselves
repulsive to God by doing unclean and improper acts. 49 All of this was intended to
make them forget the Law and change its
regulations. 50 Whoever didn't obey the
king would die.

51 In this way, Antiochus wrote to his
whole kingdom. He appointed inspectors
over all the people, and commanded the
Jewish communities to offer pagan sacrifices, town by town. 52 Many Jewish people,
those who abandoned the Law, followed
suit and did evil in the land. 53 The king's
inspectors[f] drove Israel into hiding in every
place of refuge they had available.

54 Now on the fifteenth day of Kislev,[g] in
the year 145, they set up a disgusting and
destructive thing on the altar for entirely
burned offerings in the sanctuary. The inspectors[h] built other altars in the surrounding Judean towns. 55 They burned incense
at the doors of houses and in the streets.
56 When they found the Law scrolls, they
tore them to pieces and burned them. 57 If
anyone was caught in possession of a copy
of the covenant scroll or if anyone kept to
the Law, that person was condemned to

[d] 167 BCE [e] Or *It* [f] Or *They* [g] November–December [h] Or *They*

death by royal decree. 58They were unrelenting in attacking Israelites, all those who
were identified as law-observant month
after month throughout the towns. 59On
the twenty-fifth day of the month they offered sacrifice on the altar built over the
altar for entirely burned offerings. 60In
keeping with the decree, they killed women
who had circumcised their sons. 61They
hanged the infant boys from their mothers' necks. The king's agents also killed the
families of the women as well as those who
had performed the circumcisions.

62But many in Israel stood strong, and
they resolved in their hearts not to eat impure food. 63They chose to die rather than
to be defiled by the food or to dishonor the
holy covenant. And they did die. 64A great
anger came against Israel.

Mattathias and his sons

2 In those days a priest from Joarib's family named Mattathias, the son of John
and grandson of Simeon, moved from Jerusalem and settled in Modein. 2He had five
sons: John, who had the surname Gaddi;
3Simon, called Thassi; 4Judas, called Maccabeus; 5Eleazar, called Avaran; and Jonathan, called Apphus.

6Mattathias saw the offensive actions
against God that were taking place in Judah
and Jerusalem. 7He said:

"Horrible! Why was I born to see this—
the ruin of my people,
the ruin of the holy city?
Why was I born to live there when it
was given over to the enemy,
and when the sanctuary
was given over to strangers?
8Her temple has become
like a person stripped of honor.
9Her glorious equipment
has been taken away into exile.
Her babies have been killed
in her streets,
her young people
by the enemy's sword.
10Is there a nation that hasn't
taken away some part of her majesty
and seized upon her loot?
11All her adornment has been taken away.
She is no longer free,
but is instead a slave.
12Look! Our holy place, our beauty,
and our glory have all been destroyed.
The Gentiles have trampled them.
13Why should we live any longer?"

14Then Mattathias and his sons tore their
clothes and put on mourning clothes, and
they lamented.

Pagan worship refused

15At that time, the king's officers were
enforcing the decrees to give up Jewish
practice. They came to the town of Modein
to make its people offer pagan sacrifice.
16Many from Israel came out to them, including Mattathias and his sons. 17Then the
king's officers spoke to Mattathias: "You're
a leader, honored and important in this
town, and supported by sons and brothers.
18Be the first to come and do what the king
has commanded, as have all the Gentiles,
the people of Judah, and those who are
left in Jerusalem. Then you and your sons
will be counted among the king's closest
political advisors; you and your sons will be
honored with silver, gold, and many gifts."

19But Mattathias answered loudly, "Even
if all the nations that live under the king's
rule obey him and have chosen to follow
his orders, departing from their ancestral
religion, 20My sons and brothers and I will
continue to live according to our ancestors'
covenant. 21We will never abandon the Law
and its commands! 22We won't obey the
king's orders by turning aside from our religion to either the right or the left."

23When he finished speaking, a Jew
came forward in plain sight to offer sacrifice on the altar in Modein, in keeping with
the king's command. 24When Mattathias
saw this action, he burned with zeal, and
his spirit was stirred up. He gave way to his
righteous anger, and he ran over and killed
the man on the altar. 25He also killed the
king's officer who was overseeing the sacrifice at that time, and he tore down the altar.
26He burned with zeal for the Law, just like
Phinehas did against Zimri, Salu's son.

27Then Mattathias shouted loudly in the
town, "Everyone who is zealous for the Law

and supports the covenant should come with me!" [28]So he and his sons fled to the hills and left behind all that they had in the town.

[29]At that time, many who sought righteousness and justice went to live in the desert. [30]They were there with their sons, their wives, and their livestock because troubles pressed heavily on them. [31]The king's officers and the troops in Jerusalem, David's City, learned that those who had rejected the king's command had gone down to hiding places in the wilderness. [32]Many pursued and overtook them. The king's military forces camped opposite them and prepared for battle against them on the Sabbath. [33]They said to them: "Enough of this! Come out and do what the king commands, and you will live."

[34]But the Israelites replied: "We won't come out, and we won't do what the king commands and so violate the Sabbath." [35]So the enemy immediately attacked them. [36]Still they didn't answer or throw a rock at them or even block up their hiding places. [37]They said, "Let's all die in our innocence. Heaven and earth testify on our behalf that you are killing us unjustly." [38]So the troops attacked them on the Sabbath. They died, with their wives and children and livestock, as many as one thousand people.

[39]When Mattathias and his friends learned about this, they deeply mourned for the dead. [40]They said to each other: "If we all do as our people have done and refuse to fight against the Gentiles for our lives and our commandments, they will soon eliminate us from the earth." [41]So they decided that day: "We will fight against anyone who comes to attack us on the Sabbath. Let's not all die as our people did in their hiding places."

Counterattack

[42]At that time a company of Hasideans,[i] mighty warriors of Israel, united with them. They offered their lives willingly for the Law. [43]Others who became fugitives to escape their troubles joined them as well and reinforced them. [44]Together they organized an army. In their fury, they struck down sinners and renegades. Survivors fled to the Gentiles for safety.

[45]Mattathias and his friends went around tearing down the altars to other gods.[j] [46]They forcibly circumcised boys whom they found uncircumcised within the borders of Israel. [47]They hunted down arrogant people, and their missions were successful. [48]They rescued the Law from the power of the Gentiles and kings, and they never let the sinner regain power.

Last words of Mattathias

[49]Now the days drew near for Mattathias to die, and he spoke to his sons: "Arrogance and contempt are present everywhere. It is a time of ruin and raging anger. [50]Now, my children, demonstrate zeal for the Law, and give your lives for our ancestors' covenant.

[51]"Remember the deeds of the ancestors, which they did in their day, and you will inherit great honor and everlasting remembrance.

[52]Wasn't Abraham found faithful
when he was tested, and it was considered righteousness?
[53]Joseph kept the commandment in
the time of his distress, and he became ruler of Egypt.
[54]Our ancestor Phinehas received
the covenant of everlasting priesthood because he was deeply zealous.
[55]Joshua became a judge in Israel
because he fulfilled the command.
[56]Caleb received an inheritance in
the land because he testified in the assembly.
[57]David inherited the throne of
the kingdom forever because he was merciful.
[58]Elijah was taken up into heaven because he had great zeal for the Law.
[59]Hananiah, Azariah, and Mishael believed, and were rescued from the flame.
[60]Daniel was delivered from the lions'
mouths because of his innocence.

[61]"So you see that from generation to generation, no one who continues to

[i]Or *the pious ones* [j]Gk lacks *to other gods*.

trust God will lack strength. 62 Don't fear the words of sinners, for their glory will turn into dung and worms. 63 Today they may be exalted, but tomorrow they can't be found, because they will have returned to the dust and their plans will have vanished. 64 My children, show courage and grow strong in the Law, because this will bring you honor.

65 "Look, here is your brother Simon, who I know is a man with purpose. Always listen to him. He will be your father. 66 Judas Maccabeus has been a powerful fighter since he was a boy. He will command the army for you and lead the battle against the peoples. 67 Rally around yourselves all who observe the Law, and avenge wrong done to your people. 68 Pay the Gentiles back in full, and obey what the Law commands."

69 Then he blessed them and joined his ancestors. 70 He died in the year 146[k] and was buried in an ancestral tomb at Modein. All Israel mourned for him with sorrow.

Early victories of Judas

3 Then his son Judas, known as Maccabeus, took command in his place. 2 Every one of his brothers and all who had joined his father helped him, and they gladly fought for Israel.

3 He advanced the honor of his people.
He put on his breastplate like a giant.
He strapped on his war armor
and waged battles,
protecting the camp with his sword.
4 He was like a lion in his actions,
like a lion's cub roaring after prey.
5 He hunted and pursued
those who broke the Law.
He burned up
those who troubled his people.
6 Lawbreakers were afraid of him
and retreated.
All evildoers were in turmoil.
His hand successfully
brought deliverance.
7 He angered many kings,
but he brought joy to Jacob by his deeds.
His memory is blessed forever.
8 He went through the cities of Judah
and destroyed the ungodly
out of the land.
As a result, he turned wrath
away from Israel.
9 His fame extended
to the ends of the earth.
He gathered together
those who were perishing.

10 Apollonius gathered Gentiles and a large force from Samaria to fight against Israel. 11 When Judas found out about it, he went out to meet him in battle, then defeated and killed him. Judas wounded and killed many, while the rest fled. 12 Then the Israelites seized their spoils. Judas took Apollonius' sword and used it in battle for the rest of his life.

13 At this point, Seron the commander of the Syrian army heard that Judas had gathered a large company, including a group of faithful soldiers who stayed with him and went out to battle. 14 He said, "I will make a name for myself and win honor in the kingdom. I will make war on Judas and his companions who reject the king's command."
15 Once more, a strong army of godless men went up with Seron to help him take vengeance on the Israelites.

16 When he approached the ascent to go up to Beth-horon, Judas went out to meet him with a small group. 17 When they saw Seron's army that was coming against them, they said to Judas, "How can we, who are so few, fight against so large and strong a multitude? What's more, we feel faint because we haven't eaten today."

18 Judas answered, "It's easy for many to be trapped by a few. In the sight of heaven, it makes no difference to win by many or by few. 19 It's not the size of the army that brings victory in battle, because strength comes from heaven. 20 They're coming against us with a lot of pride and evil. They want to destroy us, along with our wives and children. They want to ruin us. 21 But we are fighting for our lives and for our laws.
22 The heavenly one himself will crush them before us. Don't be afraid of them."

k 166 BCE

23After Judas said these words, his soldiers rushed suddenly against Seron's army, and they crushed them. 24Judas's soldiers pursued Seron's army down the hill from Beth-horon to the plain below. Eight hundred of them died. The rest fled into the land of the Philistines. 25After this, Judas and his brothers were feared. Terror fell on all the Gentiles around them. 26Even the king heard about his reputation, and the Gentiles talked about the battles waged by Judas.

Policy of Antiochus

27When King Antiochus heard about these matters, he became very angry. So he gathered together all the forces of his empire, a mighty army. 28He opened up his treasury and gave his soldiers a year's pay in advance, and he ordered them to be ready for anything. 29Then he realized that the money in his treasury was all used up. The revenues from the country were small because of the turmoil and disaster that he had brought about in the land by abolishing the laws that had existed from early days. 30He became afraid that he might not have enough funds to provide for his expenses as well as for the gifts that he granted more abundantly than previous kings. 31He was very troubled by this. Then he decided to go to Persia and collect revenues there and raise a large sum of money.

32The king appointed Lysias, a distinguished man from a royal family, to be in charge of his affairs from the Euphrates River to the Egyptian border. 33He also wanted Lysias to take care of his young son Antiochus until he returned. 34So he gave Lysias authority over half of his armed forces and war elephants. He gave him orders regarding what he wanted him to do, including the matter of the inhabitants of Judea and Jerusalem. 35He wanted Lysias to send an army against them to wipe out and destroy Israel's strength and the few remaining in Jerusalem. He ordered that their memory should be completely erased from the place. 36Lysias was to settle strangers in all their territory and divide up their lands by lot. 37Then the king took the other half of his forces and left his capital Antioch in the year 147.[l] He crossed the Euphrates River and went through the upper provinces.

Preparations for battle

38Lysias selected Ptolemy, Dorymenes' son, as well as Nicanor and Gorgias, two able men who were among the king's chief political advisors. 39He sent them with forty thousand infantry and seven thousand cavalry to go into Judah and destroy it, as the king had commanded. 40So they headed out with their whole force. When they arrived, they set up camp in the plain near Emmaus. 41When traders in the region heard about their plan, they took a great amount of silver and gold, together with shackles, and went to the camp intending to obtain some Israelites for slaves. A force from Idumea[m] and the land of the Philistines also joined them.

42Judas and his brothers saw that the situation was becoming increasingly difficult, as the military forces were encamped in their territory. They learned also that the king had commanded their complete destruction. 43But they spoke to each other, "Let's restore our people after all they've suffered, and fight for our people and the sanctuary." 44So the congregation gathered to prepare for battle, and to pray and ask for mercy and compassion.

45 Jerusalem was deserted
    like a wilderness.
    None of her children moved around.
The sanctuary was trampled,
    and strangers held the elevated fortress.
        Gentiles lodged there.
Joy was taken from Jacob.
    The flute and the harp
        were no longer heard.

46Then they assembled and went to Mizpah, across from Jerusalem, because Israelites used to have a place of prayer there. 47They fasted for a day and put on mourning clothes, sprinkled ashes on their heads,

[l]166 BCE [m]Correction; LXX *Syria*

and tore their garments. 48In addition, they
opened up the Law scroll to find answers
to the kinds of questions Gentiles would
ask of their idols. 49They also brought out
the priestly garments as well as early produce and tenth-part gifts. They stirred up
nazirites, who had completed the duration
of their solomn promises. 50Then they cried
aloud to heaven:

"What should we do with these people?
Where should we take them?
51Your sanctuary is trampled and degraded.
Your priests mourn in humiliation.
52The Gentiles are gathered here against us,
planning to destroy us.
You know what they are plotting.
53How will we be able to withstand them
if you don't help us?"

54Then they blew the trumpets and gave
a loud shout. 55Judas appointed leaders
of the people in charge of thousands and
hundreds and fifties and tens. 56In keeping
with the Law, he told all who were building
houses or were about to get married or were
planting a vineyard or were fainthearted
to go home. 57Then the army went on the
march and camped south of Emmaus.

58Judas said: "Arm yourselves and be
fearless. Be ready early in the morning to
fight these Gentiles who have gathered here
against us to destroy us and our sanctuary.
59It would be better for us to die fighting than
to see the misfortunes of our nation and the
sanctuary. 60Whatever may be heaven's will,
that's what the heavenly one will do."

Battle at Emmaus

4 Gorgias took five thousand infantry and
one thousand select cavalry, and this
division moved out secretly at night. 2He
wanted to come to the Jewish camp and
attack without warning. Men from the elevated fortress served as his guides. 3But
Judas heard about it, and he and his warriors moved out to attack the king's forces
in Emmaus 4while the division was absent
from the camp. 5So when Gorgias entered
Judas' camp during the night, there was no
one there. He started looking for them in
the hills, because he said, "These men are
running away from us."

6At daybreak, Judas appeared in the plain
with three thousand men. But they didn't
have armor and swords such as they would
have liked. 7They saw the Gentile camp,
strongly fortified, surrounded by cavalry
clearly trained in warfare. 8Judas said to
those who were with him: "Don't fear their
numbers or be afraid when they charge. 9Re-
member how our ancestors were saved at
the Red Sea,[n] when Pharaoh was pursuing
them with his forces. 10So let's cry to heaven
to see if the heavenly one will favor us and
remember his covenant with our ancestors
and crush this army in front of us today.
11Then all the Gentiles will know that there is
someone who redeems and saves Israel."

12The foreigners looked up and saw the
Israelites coming against them. 13They
went out from their camp to engage them
in battle. The men with Judas blew their
trumpets, and the battle began. 14The Gentiles were crushed and fled into the plain.
15All those who were in the rear were killed
by the sword. The Israelites pursued them
to Gazara, to the plains of Idumea, and to
Azotus and Jamnia. Three thousand Gentiles died. 16Judas and his forces stopped
pursuing them. 17He said to everyone:
"Don't be greedy to plunder, for there is
still a battle ahead of us. 18Gorgias and his
force are still near us in the hills. Stand now
against our enemies and fight them. Then
afterward boldly seize the spoils."

19Just as Judas said this, a detachment
of Gentiles cautiously appeared, coming
out of the hills. 20They saw that their army
had been put to flight and that the Jews
were burning the camp, as evident from
the smoke over the area. 21When they saw
the devastation and noticed Judas's army
in the plain ready for battle, they were
terrified. 22They ran away into the land of
the Philistines. 23So Judas went back to
plunder the camp. His army took a great
amount of gold and silver, cloth that was
dyed blue and purple, and great riches. 24As
they returned, they sang hymns and songs

[n]Traditionally *Reed Sea* in the Hebrew Bible

of praise to heaven: "God is good, because
his mercy endures forever." 25That day Israel
had a great deliverance.

First campaign of Lysias

26The foreigners who escaped went and
told Lysias about all that had happened.
27When he heard it, he was perplexed and discouraged. Things hadn't happened to Israel
as he had intended, and they hadn't turned
out the way that the king commanded. 28The
next year he gathered together sixty thousand select men and five thousand cavalry,
intending to subdue the Israelites. 29They
came to Idumea and camped at Beth-zur.
Judas, on the other hand, went out to meet
them with ten thousand men.

30When Judas saw how numerous their
army was, he prayed:

Blessed are you, Savior of Israel,
  who crushed the attack
    of the mighty warrior
    through the power
      of your servant David.
You handed over the camp
  of the Philistines
  to Saul's son Jonathan
    and the man who carried his armor.
31So surround this army
  by the power of your people Israel,
  and let them be disappointed
    by their troops and cavalry.
32Fill them with cowardice.
  Melt away the boldness
    of their strength.
  Let them quake in their destruction.
33Strike them down with the sword
  of those who love you,
  and let all who know your name
    praise you with hymns.

34Then both sides attacked each other.
Five thousand men from Lysias' army died
in the fighting. 35Lysias saw his troops being
defeated and took note of the boldness that
inspired Judas's troops—how ready they
were to live or die bravely. So he withdrew
to Antioch and enlisted mercenaries so that
he could invade Judea again with an even
bigger army.

Cleansing and dedication of the temple

36At that time Judas and his brothers said, "Look, our enemies have been
crushed. Let's go up to cleanse and re-
dedicate the sanctuary." 37All the army
gathered together and went up to Mount
Zion. 38They found the sanctuary deserted,
the altar treated with disrespect, and the
gates burned. In the courts, bushes had
sprung up like in an open field or on one of
the mountains. They saw that the priests'
chambers were in ruins as well. 39So they
tore their clothes and mourned with great
sorrow. They sprinkled their heads with
ashes 40and fell facedown on the ground.
When the trumpets sounded a signal, they
cried out to heaven.

41Then Judas chose some soldiers to
fight against those stationed in the elevated fortress until he completed cleansing
the sanctuary. 42He selected priests who
were blameless and devoted to the Law.
43They cleansed the sanctuary and took the
polluted stones to a ritually unclean place.
44They discussed what to do about the altar
for entirely burned offerings, since it had
been polluted. 45They decided it was best to
tear it down so that it wouldn't be a lasting shameful reminder to them that the
Gentiles had defiled it. So they tore down
the altar. 46They stored the stones in a convenient place on the temple mount until a
prophet should arise who could say what to
do with them. 47They then took unfinished
stones, in keeping with the Law, and built a
new altar like the former one.

48They also restored the sanctuary and
the temple interior, and dedicated the courtyards. 49They fashioned new holy equipment
and brought the lampstand, the incense
altar, and the table into the temple. 50Then
they offered incense on the altar and lit the
lamps on the lampstand, which illuminated
the temple. 51They placed bread on the table
and hung curtains. Finally, they completed
all the work that they had started.

52They rose early in the morning of the
twenty-fifth day of the ninth month, the
month of Kislev.° It was the year 148. 53They

°November–December, 164 BCE

offered sacrifice, following the Law, on the
new altar for entirely burned offerings that
they had made. 54 In the very season, on the
exact day that the Gentiles had polluted it,
it was dedicated with songs, harps, lutes,
and cymbals. 55 All the people bowed to the
ground and worshipped and blessed heaven,
which had given them success.

56 So they celebrated the rededication of
the altar for eight days and joyfully made
entirely burned offerings. They offered a
sacrifice of deliverance and praise. 57 They
decorated the front of the temple with gold
crowns and small shields. They restored the
gates and the priests' chambers, furnishing
them with doors. 58 The people were extremely glad, and the disgrace the Gentiles
brought was lifted.

59 Then Judas, with his brothers and all
the assembly of Israel, laid down a law that
every year at that season the dedication of
the altar should be observed with joy and
happiness for eight days, beginning with
the twenty-fifth day of Kislev.[p]

60 At that same time the Israelites built
high walls and strong towers all around
Mount Zion so that the Gentiles did not
come and trample them as they had done
previously. 61 Judas stationed an occupying
force there as guards. He also built up Beth-
zur to protect it so that the people might
have a fortress that faced in the direction
of Idumea.

Wars with neighboring peoples

5 When the Gentiles living nearby learned
that the altar had been rebuilt and the
sanctuary had been dedicated just as it
was before, they became very angry. 2 They
sought to wipe out Jacob's descendants
who lived among them. So they started to
kill and destroy the people.

3 But Judas waged war on the descendants of Esau in Idumea at Akrabattene
because they kept ambushing Israelites. He
dealt them a heavy blow, humbling them
and taking their goods. 4 He also took note
of the wickedness of Baean's sons, who were
trapping, catching, and ambushing people
on the highways. 5 Judas shut them up in
their towers. He camped against them, and
by promising their complete destruction,
he burned their towers and all who were in
them. 6 Then he moved against the Ammonites. He found a strong group with many
people and a man named Timothy as their
leader. 7 Judas had many battles with them,
beat them severely, and struck them down.
8 He also captured Jazer and its villages.
Then he went back to Judea.

Liberation of Galilean Jews

9 Then the Gentiles in Gilead gathered
together against the Israelites who lived in
their territory, planning to destroy them. So
the Jews fled to the fortress of Dathema.
10 They sent a letter to Judas and his brothers:

> The Gentiles around us have gathered to
> destroy us. 11 They are making prepara-
> tions to come and capture the fortress
> to which we've escaped, and Timothy is
> leading them. 12 Please, come and rescue
> us from them because many of us have
> died already. 13 Our people who were in
> the land of Tob have been killed. The
> enemy captured their wives, children,
> and goods. They killed nearly a thousand
> people there.

14 While the letter was still being read,
other messengers from Galilee, with torn
clothing, said similar things. 15 They related
that the people of Ptolemais, Tyre, Sidon,
and all Galilee of the Gentiles had gathered
together "to annihilate us." 16 When Judas
and the people heard all this, a great assembly was called to decide what they should do
to assist their people who were in distress
and were being attacked by enemies. 17 Then
Judas said to Simon his brother: "Choose
your men and go rescue your people in Galilee. My brother Jonathan and I will go to
Gilead." 18 He left Joseph, Zechariah's son,
and Azariah, a leader of the people, with
the rest of the forces in Judea to guard it.
19 He commanded them, "Take charge of
this people, but don't engage in battle with
the Gentiles before we return." 20 Three
thousand men were assigned to Simon to

[p] November–December

go to Galilee, and eight thousand were to go with Judas to Gilead.

21So Simon went to Galilee, fought several battles with the Gentiles, and crushed them. 22He pursued them to the gate of Ptolemais. As many as three thousand Gentiles died, and he plundered their possessions. 23Then he took the Jews of Galilee and Arbatta, together with their wives and children and all they owned, and led them to Judea with great rejoicing.

Judas and Jonathan in Gilead

24Judas Maccabeus and his brother Jonathan crossed the Jordan and traveled for three days into the wilderness. 25They encountered the Nabateans, who greeted them in peace and related all that had happened to their people in Gilead: 26"Many of them have been cornered inside Bozrah and Bosor, in Alema and Chaspho, in Maked and Carnaim." These were strong and large towns. 27"Some have been confined in other towns in Gilead. The enemy is getting ready to attack the fortresses tomorrow. They intend to capture and destroy all these people in a single day."

28So Judas and his army turned back quickly to Bozrah by the wilderness road. He took the town and killed every male by the sword. He seized all their goods and burned down the town. 29He left there by night and went all the way to the fortress. 30At daybreak they looked around and saw a large company, too many to count, carrying ladders and war engines to use to capture the fortress. They were attacking those inside. 31So Judas saw that the battle had already begun and that the cries of the townspeople went up to heaven. There were trumpet blasts and loud shouts. 32He said to his forces: "Fight today for your people!" 33He came up behind them in three companies. They sounded their trumpets and cried out in prayer. 34When Timothy's army realized that it was Maccabeus, they ran away. But Judas dealt them a heavy blow. As many as eight thousand of the enemy died that day.

35Judas turned next to Maapha. He fought against it and took it. He killed every male in it, plundered it, and burned it with fire. 36After that he marched ahead and took Chaspho, Maked, Bosor, and the other towns of Gilead.

37Following this, Timothy assembled another army and encamped opposite Raphon, on the other side of the stream. 38Judas sent spies to observe the camp, and they reported: "All the Gentiles around us have gone over to him—it's a very large force. 39They have also hired Arabs to help them. They're camped across the stream, and they're ready to come and fight against you." So Judas went out to meet them.

40As Judas and his army were drawing near to the stream of water, Timothy told the officers of his forces, "If Judas crosses the water first, we won't be able to resist him, and he'll surely defeat us. 41But if he hesitates out of fear and camps on the other side of the river, then we'll cross over and defeat him."

42When Judas came to the stream of water, he stationed the scribes of the people there and issued this command: "Don't let anyone start to make camp. Instead, force them all to enter the battle." 43He then crossed over against them first, and the whole army followed him. All the Gentiles were defeated. They threw down their weapons and ran away into the sacred grounds at Carnaim. 44But Judas took the town and burned the sacred grounds with fire, together with all who were hiding there. Even Carnaim was conquered, and they couldn't oppose Judas any longer.

Return to Jerusalem

45Then Judas gathered all the Israelites in Gilead to go to the land of Judah. It was a very large group, both small and great, with all their wives, children, and goods. 46They came to Ephron, a large and secure town along the way. They couldn't go around it on either side. They had to go through it. 47But the townspeople shut them out and blocked up the gates with rocks.

48Judas sent them a peaceful message: "Let us pass through your land to get to ours. We won't do you any harm. We'll just pass through by foot." But they still refused to open to him. 49So Judas ordered that

the army camp wherever they were, 50 and
the forces did so. All that day and night he
fought against the town, and it was handed
over to him. 51 He killed every male by the
edge of the sword, and he demolished
and plundered the town. Then he passed
through it, walking over the dead bodies.

52 After that they crossed the Jordan and
came into the large plain in front of Beth-
shan. 53 Judas kept rallying those who fell
behind and encouraged the people all along
the way until he came to the land of Judah.
54 They went up to Mount Zion with joy and
gladness. They made entirely burned offerings, because they had returned safely. Not
one of them had died.

Joseph and Azariah defeated

55 Now this is what happened while
Judas and Jonathan were in Gilead and
their brother Simon was in Galilee in
front of Ptolemais. 56 Joseph, Zechariah's
son, and Azariah (the commanders of the
forces that had remained behind) heard
about their brave deeds and the war they
had fought. 57 So they said, "Let's make a
name for ourselves too. Let's go and make
war on the Gentiles around us." 58 They gave
orders to the troops who were with them
and marched against Jamnia. 59 Gorgias
and his troops came out from the town to
engage them in battle. 60 Joseph and Azariah were decisively defeated, and they
were pursued to the borders of Judea. As
many as two thousand Israelites died that
day. 61 As a result, the people of Israel suffered a great defeat because, wanting to do
a brave thing, they didn't obey Judas and
his brothers. 62 Furthermore, they didn't
belong to the family of those men through
whom deliverance was given to Israel.

63 All Israel and all the Gentiles greatly
esteemed Judas and his brothers, wherever
their name was heard. 64 People gathered to
them and praised them.

Success at Hebron and Philistia

65 At that time, Judas and his brothers
headed out and fought Esau's descendants
in the land to the south. He struck Hebron
and its villages, tore down its fortress, and
burned its towers all around. 66 He then set
out to enter the land of the Philistines and
passed through Marisa. 67 That day some
priests who wished to do a brave deed died
in battle because they had gone out to battle
unwisely. 68 But Judas turned aside to Azotus in the land of the Philistines. Judas tore
down their altars, and he burned the carved
images of their gods with fire. He plundered
the towns and returned to Judah.

Last days of Antiochus Epiphanes

6 King Antiochus was traveling through
the upper provinces when he heard that
Elymais, a city in Persia, was famous for
its great quantities of silver and gold. 2 Its
temple was very rich and contained gold
shields, breastplates, and weapons that Alexander (the son of Philip, the first Macedonian king to rule over the Greeks) left
there. 3 So he went and tried to take the city
by force and plunder it. But he was unsuc-
cessful because the city's inhabitants knew
about his plan. 4 They resisted him in battle,
and he fled. With great disappointment, he
planned to return to Babylon.

5 While King Antiochus was in Persia,
someone came to him and reported that
the armies that had gone into the land
of Judah had been thoroughly defeated.
6 Lysias, who had gone first with a strong
force, had turned and run from the Jews.
The Jews then grew stronger when they
took weapons, supplies, and abundant
spoils from the armies they defeated. 7 They
had taken down the disgusting thing that
he had set up on the altar in Jerusalem.
Furthermore, they had surrounded the
sanctuary and also Lysias' town Beth-zur
with high walls like before.

8 When the king heard this news, he was
stunned and badly shaken. He took to his
bed, sick from grief. Things hadn't turned
out for him as he had planned. 9 He lay there
for many days because he was deeply depressed. He realized that he was dying. 10 He
called his closest political advisors[q] and

[q] Or *Friends*

said to them, "Sleep has left my eyes. I'm depressed from worrying. [11]I say to myself, What distress I've come to! What a great flood I've now been plunged into! Once I was kind and was loved in my power. [12]But now I recall the wrongs I did in Jerusalem. I seized all its silver and gold equipment. I ordered the destruction of the inhabitants of Judah without good reason. [13]I know it's because of all this that these misfortunes have come on me. I'm here, dying of bitter disappointment, in a foreign land."

[14]Then he called for one of his advisors named Philip and made him ruler over all of his kingdom. [15]He gave him the crown, his robe, and the seal so that he might guide his son Antiochus and prepare him to be king. [16]Then King Antiochus died there in the year 149. [17]When Lysias found out that the king had died, he arranged for the king's son Antiochus, whom he had brought up from childhood, to rule. Lysias named him Eupator.

Renewed attacks from Syria

[18]Meanwhile, the inhabitants of the elevated fortress kept surrounding the Israelites in the sanctuary. They were trying every way they could to harm them and strengthen the Gentiles. [19]Judas decided to destroy them. He brought all the people together to besiege them. [20]They assembled together, built siege towers and other war engines, and attacked the Gentiles in the year 150. [21]However, some of the enemy forces escaped from the blockade, joined by a number of sinful Israelites. [22]They went to the king and said: "How long will you hold back from acting justly to avenge our people? [23]We happily served your father. We did what he said, obeying his commands. [24]Because of this, some of our people have laid siege to the citadel and are hostile to us. Furthermore, they've killed as many of us as they could catch. Now they've taken our wealth. [25]Judas and his forces haven't lifted their hands against us alone. They've also attacked all the neighboring lands. [26]Look, today they've camped against the elevated fortress in Jerusalem to capture it. They've fortified both the sanctuary and Beth-zur. [27]Unless you do something soon to prevent them, they'll do even worse things. Then you won't be able to stop them."

[28]The king was enraged when he heard this. He gathered all his chief political advisors,[r] the commanders of his troops, and those with authority. [29]Mercenary forces from other kingdoms and the Mediterranean islands also joined him. [30]The total number of his forces was one hundred thousand army troops and twenty thousand cavalry, with thirty-two elephants trained for war. [31]They came through Idumea and camped against Beth-zur. For many days, they fought and constructed war engines. But the Jews would go out and burn the war engines with fire and continued to fight bravely.

Battle at Beth-zechariah

[32]Then Judas marched away from the elevated fortress and camped at Beth-zechariah, opposite the king's camp. [33]Early in the morning the king marched out, taking his army on a forced march along the road to Beth-zechariah. His troops readied themselves for battle, and they sounded their trumpets. [34]They aroused the elephants using grape and mulberry juices, to get them ready for battle. [35]They distributed the animals among groups of soldiers. With each elephant, they stationed one thousand infantry wearing armor and brass helmets. Five hundred select cavalry were also assigned to each animal. [36]The troops positioned themselves wherever the animal was. Wherever it went, they went; and they never left it. [37]Strong covered wooden towers were set on top of the elephants. Special harnesses were fastened on each animal. On each were four armed men who fought from there, and an Indian driver also. [38]The remaining cavalry were stationed on either side of the elephants, to harass the enemy while being protected inside the two flanks of the army. [39]When the sun shone on the gold and brass shields, the hills looked like

[r]Or *Friends*

they were on fire from their reflection and glowed like burning torches.
40Part of the king's army was spread out on the high hills, and some troops were on the plain. They held their ranks and steadily moved forward. 41Everyone who heard the noise of marching feet and clanking arms trembled because the army was very large and powerful. 42Nevertheless, Judas and his army went forth to do battle. Six hundred of the king's soldiers died. 43Eleazar, called Avaran, saw that one of the animals was taller than all the others and was equipped with royal armor. He figured that the king must be on it. 44So he gave his life to save his people and to secure an everlasting name for himself. 45He ran courageously into the midst of a group of soldiers to reach it, killing men right and left so that they had to give way to him on both sides. 46He got under the elephant and stabbed it from underneath. He killed it, but it fell to the ground on top of him, and he died there. 47As the Jews experienced the might and the fierce attack of the king's forces, they turned away and fled.

Siege of the temple

48The king's army went up to Jerusalem against them. The king camped in Judea and at Mount Zion. 49He made peace with the people of Beth-zur. They evacuated the town because they lacked sufficient resources there to withstand a siege (it was a sabbatical year for the land). 50So the king took Beth-zur and positioned a guard unit there to hold it. 51Then he camped in front of the sanctuary for many days. He set up siege towers, war engines that threw fire and rocks, machines to shoot darts, and catapults. 52The Jews made war engines to match theirs, and they battled for many days. 53But they had no food in storage since it was the seventh year. Those people who had found safe haven in Judea from the Gentiles had eaten the last of the food. 54Only a few people remained in the sanctuary. The famine was so intense that the others had scattered to their own homes.

Syria offers terms

55Then Lysias heard that King Antiochus, before he died, had appointed Philip to bring up Antiochus his son to be king. 56Philip had returned from Persia and Media with the forces that had gone with the king, and he was trying to seize control of the government. 57So Lysias quickly gave orders to withdraw and told the king, the commanders of the forces, and the troops, "We're growing weaker every day because our food supply is scarce. The place we're fighting against is strong, and the affairs of the kingdom are pressing urgently on us. 58Let's come to terms now with these people and make peace with them and their nation. 59Let's agree to let them live by their laws like they used to do. It was because of their laws, which we abolished, that they got angry and did all these things."
60This speech pleased the king and the commanders, so he sent the Jews an offer of peace, which they accepted. 61The king and his commanders gave their word, so the Jews left the fortress. 62However, when the king went into Mount Zion and saw how securely the place was built, he went back on his word and ordered that the wall be torn down all around. 63Then he set off in a hurry to return to Antioch. He found that Philip was in control of the city, so he fought against him and took the city by force.

Expedition of Bacchides and Alcimus

7 In the year 151,[s] Demetrius the son of Seleucus set out from Rome. He sailed with a small group to a town by the sea and claimed the kingship there. 2As he entered the royal palace of his ancestors, the army seized Antiochus and Lysias, intending to bring them to him. 3But when he learned about this act, he said, "Don't let me see their faces!" 4So the soldiers killed them. Demetrius then took his seat on the throne of the kingdom.
5All the immoral and sinful Israelites came to him. Alcimus, who wanted to be high priest, led them. 6They made an accusation

[s]161 BCE

to King Demetrius against the people, "Judas
and his brothers have destroyed all your political advisors[t] and have driven us out of our
land. 7Now send someone that you trust to
go and see all the ruin that Judas has brought
on us and on the king's land. Let that person
punish them and all who help them."

8The king selected Bacchides, one of the
king's chief political advisors and governor
of the province called Beyond the River. He
was a powerful man in the kingdom and
was loyal to the king. 9The king sent him
and sent the wicked Alcimus along with
him. He made Alcimus high priest and
authorized him to take vengeance on the
Israelites. 10So they marched forward and
came with a large force into the land of
Judah. Bacchides sent messengers to Judas
and his brothers using peaceful but deceitful words. 11But they ignored the messengers because they saw that they had come
with a large military force.

12Then a group of legal experts came
before Alcimus and Bacchides to ask for
just terms. 13The Hasideans were the first
among the Israelites to seek peace with
them. 14They said, "A priest who is descended from Aaron has come with the
army, and he won't harm us."

15Alcimus spoke peaceably to them and
made a pledge to them: "We won't seek to
injure you or your friends." 16So they trusted
him. But he seized sixty of them and killed
them in one day. This was in keeping with
the written word:

17*The flesh of your faithful ones . . .*
and their blood they poured out
all around Jerusalem;
there was no one to bury them.[u]

18Then fear and dread came over all the
people. They said, "They are not truthful or
just, because they broke the promise they
made."

19Bacchides retreated from Jerusalem
and camped in Beth-zaith. He captured
many of the soldiers and some of the people
who had deserted to his side. He killed them
and threw them into a great pit. 20He put
Alcimus in charge of the country and left
a force to assist him. Then Bacchides went
back to the king.

21Alcimus struggled to maintain the high
priesthood. 22All the troublemakers joined
him. They gained control of Judah and did
great damage in Israel. 23Judas saw all the
wrongs that Alcimus and those with him
had done among the Israelites, exceeding
what the Gentiles had done. 24So Judas
went into the surrounding Judean highlands and took vengeance on those who had
deserted. He prevented them from going
out into the country. 25When Alcimus saw
that Judas and his companions had grown
strong, he knew he couldn't resist them. So
he returned to the king and brought spiteful charges against them.

Nicanor in Judea

26Then the king sent for Nicanor, one
of his honored princes who hated and despised Israel, and the king commanded him
to destroy the people. 27So Nicanor went
to Jerusalem with a large force. He deceitfully sent a peaceful message to Judas and
his brothers: 28"Let there be no fighting between you and me. I'll come with a few men
to see you personally in peace."

29So he came to Judas, and they greeted
each other peaceably. But the enemy was
preparing to kidnap Judas. 30Judas found
out that Nicanor had come to him with
treacherous intentions. He was afraid of
him and wouldn't meet with Nicanor again.
31When Nicanor learned that his plan had
been discovered, he went out to meet Judas
in battle near Caphar-salama. 32About five
hundred of Nicanor's soldiers died. The rest
fled into David's City.

Nicanor threatens the temple

33After these events, Nicanor went up to
Mount Zion. Some priests from the sanctuary and some of the elders of the people
came out to greet him peacefully. They
pointed out to him the entirely burned offering that was being offered on behalf of
the king. 34But he mocked, ridiculed, and
defiled them, and spoke in an arrogant way.

[t]Or *Friends* [u]Ps 79:2-3

[35]Angrily, he swore, "Unless Judas and his army are handed over to me this time, I will burn down this house if I return safely in the future." And he departed in great fury.

[36]Then the priests went inside and stood before the altar and the temple. They wept out loud and said:

[37]You, heavenly one, chose this house
to be called by your name
and to be a house of prayer
and petition for your people.
[38]Take vengeance on this man
and on his army!
Make them die by the sword.
Remember their evil slander.
Don't let them live any longer.

Death of Nicanor

[39]Now Nicanor, along with the Syrian army, left Jerusalem and camped in Beth-horon. [40]Judas camped in Adasa with three thousand men. Then Judas prayed:

[41]When the messengers
from the king of the Assyrians
insulted us with words,
your angel went out and struck down
one hundred eighty-five thousand.
[42]So crush this army before us today.
Let the rest learn
that he has spoken against
your sanctuary in an evil way,
and judge him for this wickedness.

[43]So the armies met in battle on the thirteenth day of the month of Adar.[v] Nicanor's army was crushed, and he himself was the first to die in the battle. [44]When his army saw that Nicanor had died, they threw down their weapons and fled. [45]The Jews pursued them a day's journey, from Adasa to Gazara. As they followed them, they kept blasting the battle call on the trumpets. [46]People came out of the surrounding Judean villages. They outflanked the enemy and drove them back toward their pursuers so that they all died by the sword. Not a single one of them was left alive. [47]Then the Jews seized the spoils and the goods left behind. They cut off Nicanor's head and his right hand, which he had arrogantly stretched out. They brought them and displayed them just outside Jerusalem. [48]The people rejoiced greatly and celebrated that day as a day of great happiness. [49]They established this day as a day of annual celebration on the thirteenth day of Adar.[w] [50]And the land of Judah enjoyed peace for a while.

Praise for the Romans

8 Now Judas heard about the Romans' reputation for being strong and loyal to all who made an alliance with them. They pledged friendship to those who came to them. [2]They were very powerful. Judas had been told of their wars and of the brave deeds that they were doing among the Gauls—how they had defeated them and forced them to pay tribute. [3]He was told what they had done in Spain to get control of the silver and gold mines there. [4]They gained control over the entire region through their planning and patience, even though the place was a great distance from them. They also subdued the kings from the ends of the earth who fought against them, until they crushed them and inflicted heavy casualties on them. The rest paid annual fines to them. [5]They crushed in battle and conquered Philip and King Perseus of the Macedonians,[x] as well as others who rose up against them. [6]They also defeated Antiochus the Great, king of Asia, who went to fight against them with one hundred twenty elephants, with cavalry, chariots, and a very large army. They crushed him, [7]but they took him alive. They declared that he, and those who succeeded him, should pay a heavy fine and turn over hostages as well as some of their best territories. [8]These included the countries of India, Media, and Lydia. They took them from Antiochus and gave them to King Eumenes.

[9]The Greeks thought about coming to destroy them. [10]But the Romans became aware of this, so they sent a general against the Greeks and attacked them. Many Greeks were wounded and died. The Romans took

[v]February–March, 160 BCE [w]February–March [x]Or *Kittim*

their wives and children captive. They plundered them, conquered their land, tore down their fortresses, and enslaved them to this day. [11]They destroyed and enslaved many of the remaining kingdoms and islands that opposed them. [12]But the Romans have kept friendship with their allies and those who rely on them. They have subdued kings far and near, and as many as have heard of their reputation have feared them. [13]Those whom they wish to help come to power, they make kings. Those whom they wish, they bring down. The Romans have been greatly exalted. [14]Yet even with all this, not one of them has put on a crown or worn purple as a mark of pride. [15]Instead, they built for themselves a senate chamber. Daily, three hundred twenty senators plan constantly concerning their people in order to govern them well. [16]They trust one man each year to rule over them and to control all their land. All listen to this one man, and there is no envy or jealousy among the Romans.

An alliance with Rome

[17]So Judas chose Eupolemus son of John and grandson of Accos, and also Jason, Eleazar's son. He sent them to Rome to establish friendship, alliance, [18]and also to free the Jewish people from oppression. They observed that the Greek kingdom was completely enslaving Israel.

[19]They took the long journey to Rome. They entered the senate chamber, and they spoke: [20]"Judas, called Maccabeus, along with his brothers and the Jewish people, has sent us to you to establish alliance and peace with you. We seek to be enrolled as your allies and friends." [21]This proposal pleased the Romans. [22]This is a copy of the letter that they wrote in reply on bronze tablets, which they sent to Jerusalem to remain with them there as a memorial of peace and alliance:

> [23]May all go well with the Romans and with the nation of the Jews at sea and on land forever. May sword and enemy stay away from them. [24]If war comes first to Rome or to any of their allies throughout their territory, [25]the Jewish nation should act as their allies wholeheartedly, as the occasion may indicate to them. [26]They will not give or supply grain, weapons, money, or ships to an enemy that makes war on them. This is Rome's decision. And they will keep their obligations without compensation. [27]In the same way, if war comes first to the nation of the Jews, the Romans will willingly act as their allies, as the occasion may indicate to them. [28]They will not give to their enemies any grain, weapons, money, or ships, just as Rome has decided. And they will keep these obligations and do so without deceit. [29]On these terms, the Romans make a treaty with the Jewish people. [30]If after these terms are in effect and either party determines to add or delete anything, they will do so at their discretion. Any addition or deletion that they may make will be valid.
>
> [31]Regarding the bad things that King Demetrius is doing to them, we have written to him, "Why have you made your yoke so heavy on our friends and allies the Jews? [32]If they appeal now again for help against you, we will defend their rights and fight you on both sea and land."

Bacchides returns to Judea

9 When Demetrius heard that Nicanor and his army had been defeated in battle, he sent Bacchides and Alcimus into the land of Judah a second time. The right wing of the army was with them. [2]They went by the road that leads to Gilgal[y] and prepared for battle against Mesaloth in Arbela. They captured it and killed many people. [3]In the first month[z] of the year 152,[a] they camped against Jerusalem. [4]Then they marched off and went to Berea with twenty thousand infantry and two thousand cavalry.

[5]Now Judas was camped at Elasa with three thousand handpicked soldiers. [6]When they saw the huge number of enemy forces,

[y]Or *Galilee* [z]March–April, Nisan [a]160 BCE

they became afraid. Many of them slipped away from the camp, until no more than eight hundred of them remained.

7When Judas saw that members of his army had slipped away and the battle was coming close, he was dejected because he had no time to assemble more troops. 8He felt weak, but he said to those who stayed, "Let's get up and move against our enemies. We may be able to fight them."

9They tried to change his mind: "We don't have the strength. Let's save ourselves now and come back later with our people to fight them. We are too few."

10But Judas replied, "Don't even consider running from them. If our time has come, then let's die bravely for our people. Let's leave no reason to question our honor."

Final battle of Judas

11Then the enemy army marched out from the camp and took its positions to fight. The cavalry was divided into two companies. The slingers and the archers went ahead of the army, as did all the best warriors. 12Bacchides was on the right wing. Flanked by the two companies, the military force advanced to the sound of the trumpets. Those with Judas also blew their trumpets. 13The earth shook from the noise of the armies. And the battle raged from morning till evening.

14Judas saw that Bacchides and the strength of his army were on the right. Then Judas' most courageous soldiers went with him. 15They crushed the right wing and pursued them as far as Mount Azotus. 16When those on the left wing saw that the right wing had been crushed, they turned and followed close behind Judas and his men. 17The battle became frantic, and many on both sides were wounded and died. 18Judas himself died, and the rest fled.

19Then Jonathan and Simon took their brother Judas, buried him in their ancestral tomb at Modein, 20and wept for him. All Israel expressed deep sorrow for him and mourned for many days. They said, 21"What a mighty one has fallen, saving Israel!" 22Now the rest of Judas's achievements—his wars, the brave things that he did, his greatness—haven't been recorded, but they were many.

Jonathan succeeds Judas

23After Judas's death, renegades appeared throughout Israel. All the immoral people reappeared. 24There was also a very great famine at that time, and the country went over to the enemy's side. 25Bacchides chose the godless and put them in charge of the country. 26They hunted down Judas' friends and brought them to Bacchides. He took vengeance on them and treated them terribly. 27So there was great distress in Israel, the worst since the time when prophets ceased to appear among them.

28Then the other friends of Judas assembled and said to Jonathan, 29"Since your brother Judas died, there hasn't been anyone like him to fight against our enemies and Bacchides, and to deal with those among our people who hate us. 30So we've chosen you today to take his place as our ruler and leader to fight our battle." 31Jonathan accepted the leadership at that time in place of his brother Judas.

Campaigns of Jonathan

32When Bacchides learned about this development, he tried to kill Jonathan. 33But Jonathan, his brother Simon, and all those with him heard about it and fled into the Tekoa wilderness. They camped beside the water of the pool of Asphar. 34Bacchides found out about this on a Sabbath day, and he and his army crossed the Jordan River.

35Jonathan sent his brother John, as leader of a large contingent, to beg his friends the Nabateans for permission to store with them the large amount of baggage that they had. 36But the family of Jambri from Medeba came out and captured John and everything he had. And they left with it.

37After this Jonathan and his brother Simon were told, "The family of Jambri is celebrating a great wedding. They are bringing the bride, a daughter of one of the great officials of Canaan, from Nadabath with a large escort." 38Remembering how their

brother John had been killed, they went
out and hid under cover of the mountain.
[39]They looked out and saw a rowdy procession with a large amount of baggage.
The bridegroom came out with his friends
and his brothers to meet them with tambourines, musicians, and many weapons.
[40]Then those who were with Jonathan
ambushed them and began killing them.
They wounded and killed many. The rest
fled to the mountain, and the Jews took all
their goods. [41]So the wedding turned into
mourning, and the sound of their musicians into a funeral hymn. [42]After they had
fully avenged their brother's death, they returned to the marshes of the Jordan.

[43]When Bacchides heard about this, he
came with a large force to the banks of the
Jordan on the Sabbath. [44]Jonathan said to
his companions, "Let's get up now and fight
for our lives. Today things are not like they
were before. [45]Look! The battle is in front
of us and behind us. The water of the Jordan is on this side and on that, with marsh
and thicket. There's no place to turn. [46]Cry
out now to heaven so that you may be rescued from our enemies." [47]So the battle
began. Jonathan reached out his hand to
strike Bacchides, but he escaped and went
to the rear. [48]Then Jonathan and his forces
jumped into the Jordan and swam to the
other side. The enemy didn't cross the Jordan to attack them. [49]About one thousand
of Bacchides' soldiers died that day.

Bacchides builds fortifications

[50]Then Bacchides returned to Jerusalem
and built strong cities in Judea: the fortress
in Jericho, Emmaus, Beth-horon, Bethel,
Timnath, Pharathon, and Tephon, all with
high walls and gates and bars. [51]He placed
soldiers in each of them to harass Israel.
[52]He also fortified Beth-zur, Gazara, and
the elevated fortress. He put soldiers and
stores of food in them. [53]He took hostage
the sons of the leading citizens and put
them under guard in the elevated fortress
at Jerusalem.

[54]In the second month of the year 153,[b]
Alcimus gave orders to tear down the wall
of the inner court of the sanctuary—to tear
down the work of the prophets. But he only
initiated the project. [55]Right at that moment Alcimus had a stroke, and his work
was stalled. He was paralyzed and couldn't
speak or give commands concerning his
house. [56]Alcimus died a painful death
shortly thereafter. [57]When Bacchides saw
that Alcimus was dead, he returned to the
king. The land of Judah was quiet for two
years.

End of the war

[58]Then all the people who did not live by
the Law developed a plan and said, "Look!
Jonathan and his people are living in quiet
and confidence. Now let's bring Bacchides
back—he'll capture them all in one night."
[59]They went and talked it over with him.
[60]He came with a large military force. Secretly, he sent letters to all his allies in
Judea. He told them to seize Jonathan
and his followers. But they weren't able to
do it because their plan was discovered.
[61]Instead, Jonathan's followers captured
approximately fifty people who were leaders in this treachery and killed them.

[62]Then Jonathan, his followers, and
Simon withdrew to Bethbasi in the wilderness. He rebuilt the parts of it that had been
demolished and fortified it. [63]When Bacchides found out about this, he assembled all
his forces and gave orders to the Judeans.
[64]Then he came and camped against Bethbasi. He made war machines and fought
against it for many days.

[65]But Jonathan left his brother Simon in
the town while he went out into the country. He took only a few men and [66]struck
down Odomera and his people, as well as
the people of Phasiron in their tents. Then
he began to attack and went into battle
with his forces. [67]Simon and his group
left the town and set fire to the war machines. [68]They fought Bacchides, and he
was crushed by them. They put so much
pressure on him that his plan and invasion
came to nothing. [69]So he was very angry

[b]April–May, Iyar, 159 BCE

at the renegade Jews who had advised him to return to the country. He killed many of them before he decided to go back to his own land.

70When Jonathan learned about this, he sent ambassadors to make peace with him and to gain release of captives. 71Bacchides agreed and kept his word. He swore to Jonathan that he wouldn't try to harm him for the rest of his life. 72He returned the captives he had taken previously from the land of Judah. Then he turned and went back to his own land and didn't come again into their territory. 73So war had ended for Israel. Jonathan settled in Michmash and began to govern the people. He destroyed the godless who were in Israel.

Revolt of Alexander Epiphanes

10 In the year 160,[c] Alexander Epiphanes, Antiochus' son, landed and occupied Ptolemais. They welcomed him there, and he began to rule.

2When King Demetrius heard about it, he assembled a very large army. He marched out to meet Alexander in battle. 3Demetrius sent a friendly letter to Jonathan to honor him. 4Demetrius thought to himself, We should make peace with Jonathan before he aligns with Alexander against us. 5If we don't do so, he will recall all the wrongs that we did to him, his brothers, and his nation.

6So Demetrius gave Jonathan authority to recruit troops, to arm them, and to become his ally. He ordered that the hostages in the elevated fortress be released to Jonathan.

7Then Jonathan came to Jerusalem and read the letter in front of all the people and those inside the elevated fortress. 8These people were very concerned when they heard that the king had given him authority to recruit troops. 9The inhabitants in the elevated fortress released the hostages to Jonathan, and he returned them to their parents.

10Jonathan took up residence in Jerusalem and began to rebuild and restore the city. 11He directed the workers to build the walls and encircle Mount Zion with squared stones for better reinforcement, which they did.

12Then from the fortress that Bacchides had built, the foreigners fled. 13All of them left their places and returned to their own lands. 14Only in Beth-zur did some Jews remain who had neglected the Law and the commandments, because Beth-zur was a place of refuge.

Jonathan becomes high priest

15Now King Alexander heard about all the promises that Demetrius made to Jonathan. He also heard about the battles that Jonathan and his brothers had fought, the brave deeds they had done, and the troubles they had endured. 16He said to himself, Will we find another man like this? We should make him our friend and ally. 17So he wrote a letter to Jonathan:

> 18King Alexander to his brother Jonathan. Greetings!
>
> 19We have heard about you—that you are a mighty warrior and worthy to be our friend. 20So we have appointed you today to be the high priest of your nation. You are to be named the king's political advisor.[d] You should take our side and keep friendship with us.

He sent also a purple robe and a gold crown.

21So Jonathan put on the sacred garments in the seventh month of the year 160[e] at the Festival of Booths. He recruited troops and equipped them with abundant weapons.

Demetrius' letter to Jonathan

22When Demetrius heard about these things he was distressed. He said, 23"What have we done? Alexander has moved more quickly in forming a friendship with the Jews to strengthen himself. 24I'll also write them words of encouragement and promise them honor and gifts so that I may gain their help." 25So he sent a message to them:

> King Demetrius to the nation of the Jews. Greetings!

[c]152 BCE [d]Or *Friend* [e]September–October, Tishrei, 152 BCE

[26]We have heard and rejoice that you have kept your agreement and have continued your friendship with us, and have not sided with our enemies. [27]Now continue to keep faith with us, and we will repay you in kind according to the good you do for us. [28]We will grant you many exemptions and give you gifts.

[29]I now free you and excuse all the Jews from payment of tribute as well as salt and royal taxes. [30]Instead of collecting a third of the grain and half of the fruit of the trees as I should, I release you from payment from now on. I will not collect them from the land of Judah or from the three districts added to it from Samaria and Galilee, from this day on and for all time. [31]Jerusalem and its surroundings, its tenth-part gifts and its revenues, will be holy and free from tax.

[32]I will also give up my control of the elevated fortress in Jerusalem and give it to the high priest. He may station people of his own choice to guard it. [33]I set free, without payment, all of the Jews who have been taken captive from Judah into any part of my kingdom. Furthermore, let all officials also cancel taxes on their livestock.

[34]All the festivals will be days of immunity and release for all the Jews who are in my kingdom, including sabbaths, new moons, appointed days, and the three days before and after a festival. [35]No one will have authority to demand anything from them or annoy any of them about anything.

[36]Let Jews be enrolled in the king's forces to the number of thirty thousand. And let the privileges be given them that are due to all the forces of the king. [37]Let some of them be stationed in the king's great fortress. Let some of them be placed in trustworthy positions in the kingdom. Let their officers and leaders come from their own people, and let them live by their own laws, just as the king has commanded in the land of Judah.

[38]As for the three districts that have been added to Judea from the country of Samaria, let them be annexed to Judea so that they may be considered under one ruler and obey no other authority than the high priest. [39]I give Ptolemais as a gift and the land adjoining it to the sanctuary in Jerusalem, to provide the necessary expenses of the sanctuary. [40]I also grant fifteen thousand silver shekels annually out of the king's revenues from appropriate places. [41]All the additional funds that the government officials haven't paid as they used to, they will give from now on for the service of the temple. [42]Moreover, the five thousand silver shekels that my officials have received annually from the income of the services of the temple, this too is canceled, because it belongs to the priests who minister there. [43]As for all who have taken refuge on the grounds of the temple in Jerusalem because they owe money to the king or are in debt, they are released from debt and I will restore all their property in my kingdom.

[44]Let the cost of rebuilding and restoring the structures of the sanctuary be paid from the king's revenues. [45]And let the cost of rebuilding the walls of Jerusalem and revitalizing it all round, and the cost of rebuilding the walls in Judea, also be paid from the king's revenues.

Death of Demetrius

[46]When Jonathan and the people heard these words, they didn't believe or accept them. They remembered vividly the great wrongs Demetrius had done in Israel and how much he had oppressed them. [47]They preferred Alexander because he had been the first to speak peaceful words to them. So they remained his allies all of his days.

[48]Now King Alexander assembled large forces and camped opposite Demetrius. [49]The two kings met in battle, and the army of Demetrius fled. Alexander pursued him and outmaneuvered them. [50]He pressed the battle hard until sunset, and on that day Demetrius died.

Treaty of Ptolemy and Alexander

[51]Then Alexander sent ambassadors to
Egypt's King Ptolemy, and they delivered
the following message:

> [52]I have returned to my kingdom and
> taken my seat on the throne of my an-
> cestors. I have established my rule by
> crushing Demetrius to gain control of
> our country. [53]I met him in battle, and
> we crushed him and his army. I have
> taken my seat on the throne of his
> kingdom. [54]Therefore, let us establish
> friendship with each other. Give me
> your daughter to be my wife, and I will
> become your son-in-law. I will give gifts
> to you and to her in keeping with your
> position.

[55]Ptolemy the king replied,

> Happy was the day on which you re-
> turned to the land of your ancestors and
> took your seat on the throne of their
> kingdom. [56]Now I will do for you as you
> wrote, but meet me at Ptolemais so that
> we may see each other, and I will become
> your father-in-law, as you have said.

[57]So Ptolemy set out from Egypt—he and
his daughter Cleopatra—and came to Ptolemais in the year 162.[f] [58]King Alexander met
Ptolemy, who gave him his daughter Cleopatra in marriage. He celebrated her wedding at
Ptolemais with much ceremony, as kings do.

[59]King Alexander then wrote to Jonathan to come and meet him. [60]So he went
with majestic apparel to Ptolemais and met
the two kings. He gave silver and gold and
many other gifts to them and their chief
political advisors,[g] and he found favor
with them. [61]A group of troublemakers
from Israel gathered together to slander
him, but the king paid no attention to
them. [62]Instead, he gave orders to take off
Jonathan's garments and to clothe him in
purple. And they did so. [63]The king also
seated him at his side, and he spoke to his
officers: "Go with him into the middle of
the city and announce that no one should
bring charges against him about any matter. Furthermore, let no one annoy him for
any reason." [64]His accusers saw the honor
that was paid Jonathan in keeping with the
proclamation. They saw him clothed in purple, so they all fled. [65]In this way, the king
honored him and enrolled him among his
chief political advisors, and made him general and governor of the province. [66]And
Jonathan returned to Jerusalem in peace
and gladness.

Apollonius is defeated by Jonathan

[67]In the year 165,[h] Demetrius the son
of Demetrius came from Crete to the land
of his ancestors. [68]When King Alexander
heard, he was greatly distressed and returned to Antioch. [69]Demetrius appointed
Apollonius the governor of Coele-Syria, who
assembled a large force and camped against
Jamnia. Then Apollonius sent the following
message to the high priest Jonathan:

> [70]You are the only one to oppose us. I
> have fallen into ridicule and disgrace
> because of you. Why do you assume
> authority against us in the highlands?
> [71]Now if you have confidence in your
> military forces, come down to the plain
> to meet us. Let's match strength against
> strength there, because I have with me
> the forces of the cities. [72]Discover who
> I am and who the others are that are
> helping us, and you will learn that you
> cannot stand before us. Twice before,
> your ancestors were forced to flee in
> their own land. [73]Now you will not be
> able to stand up against my cavalry and
> my army in the plain, where there is no
> stone or pebble, or place to escape.

[74]When Jonathan heard Apollonius'
words, a fire was lit under him. He chose ten
thousand men and set out from Jerusalem.
His brother Simon met him to assist. [75]He
camped in front of Joppa. But the people of
the city closed its gates because Apollonius
had a defense force there. So they fought
against it. [76]And the people of the city became frightened and opened the gates. So
Jonathan gained possession of Joppa.

[77]When Apollonius heard the news, he
assembled three thousand cavalry and a
large army. He went to Azotus and acted as

[f]150 BCE [g]Or *Friends* [h]147 BCE

if he were going farther. At the same time, he advanced into the plain, because he had a large troop of cavalry and had confidence in it. 78 Jonathan pursued him to Azotus, and their armies engaged in battle. 79 Apollonius had secretly left one thousand cavalry to the rear. 80 Jonathan found out that there was an ambush behind him. They surrounded his army and shot arrows at his soldiers from early in the morning until late in the afternoon. 81 But his soldiers stood steady, as he had commanded. Eventually, the horses of the enemy got tired.

82 Simon led his force forward and engaged the foreign enemy in battle since the cavalry was exhausted. He overwhelmed them, and they fled. 83 The cavalry was dispersed in the plain. They fled to Azotus and entered Beth-dagon, the temple of their idol, to seek safety. 84 But Jonathan burned Azotus and the surrounding towns and plundered them. He burned down the temple of Dagon and those who had taken refuge in it. 85 The number of those who died, either by the sword or by fire, came to eight thousand.

86 Then Jonathan left there and camped against Ashkelon, and the people of the city came out to meet him with great ceremony.

87 He and his companions returned to Jerusalem with a large treasure. 88 When King Alexander heard about all this, he honored Jonathan even more. 89 He sent to him a gold buckle, such as is the custom to give to the king's kindred. He also gave him Ekron and all its surroundings as his possession.

Ptolemy invades Syria

11 Then King Ptolemy of Egypt gathered a great army, numbering like the sand by the seashore, and many ships. He tried to gain possession of Alexander's kingdom by trickery to add it to his own kingdom. 2 Ptolemy set out for Syria, speaking peaceful words. The people of the towns opened their gates to him. They went to meet him because King Alexander had commanded them to do so, since Ptolemy was his father-in-law. 3 But when Ptolemy entered the towns, he stationed forces as a garrison in each one.

4 When he approached Azotus, they showed him that Dagon's temple had been burned. Azotus and its suburbs had been destroyed. Corpses were lying about, the charred bodies of those whom Jonathan had burned in the war. They had piled them in heaps along his route. 5 They also told the king what Jonathan had done, throwing blame on him. But the king kept silent. 6 Jonathan met the king at Joppa with great ceremony. They greeted each other and spent the night there. 7 Jonathan went with the king as far as the Eleutherus River, and then he returned to Jerusalem.

8 So King Ptolemy gained control of the coastal cities as far as Seleucia by the sea. He kept devising evil plans against Alexander. 9 He sent envoys to King Demetrius to say, "Come, let's make an agreement with each other. I'll give you my daughter to marry, Alexander's wife. Then you will rule over your father's kingdom. 10 I now regret having given him my daughter since he tried to kill me." 11 He cast blame on Alexander because he desired to take his kingdom. 12 So he took his daughter away from Alexander and gave her to Demetrius. Ptolemy was estranged from Alexander, and their hostility was obvious to all.

13 Then Ptolemy entered Antioch and put on the crown of Asia. Thus he claimed two crowns for his head, those of Asia and Egypt. 14 King Alexander was in Cilicia at the time, because the people of that region were in revolt.

15 When Alexander heard about it, he came against Ptolemy in battle. Ptolemy marched out and met him with a strong force and caused him to retreat. 16 So Alexander fled into Arabia to seek protection there. King Ptolemy was triumphant. 17 Zabdiel the Arab cut off Alexander's head and sent it to Ptolemy. 18 But King Ptolemy died three days later, and his troops in the fortress were killed by the inhabitants of the towns. 19 So Demetrius became king in the year 167.[i]

[i] 145 BCE

Jonathan's diplomacy

[20]In those days, Jonathan assembled the Judeans to attack the elevated fortress in Jerusalem. They built many engines of war to use against it. [21]Certain renegades who hated their nation went to King Demetrius and told him that Jonathan was attacking the elevated fortress. [22]When he heard this, he was angry and set out immediately to go to Ptolemais. He sent an order to Jonathan not to continue the attack but to meet him instead for a conference at Ptolemais as soon as possible.

[23]When Jonathan heard this, he gave orders to continue the siege. He chose some of the elders of Israel and some of the priests and put himself in danger [24]because he went to the king at Ptolemais. He took silver and gold as well as clothing and numerous other gifts. Fortunately, he won his favor. [25]Certain renegades from Israel kept making complaints against Jonathan. [26]But the king treated him as those before him had done. He praised Jonathan in the presence of all his chief political advisors.[j] [27]He confirmed him in the high priesthood and in as many other honors as he formerly had. He made him one of his leading political advisors.

Demetrius' letter to Jonathan

[28]So Jonathan asked the king to free Judea and the three Samaritan districts from the payment of taxes. And he promised him 17,100 pounds of silver. [29]The king agreed. He wrote a letter to Jonathan about all these things:

[30]King Demetrius to his brother Jonathan and to the nation of the Jews. Greetings!

[31]This is a copy of the letter that we wrote about you to our advisor Lasthenes. We're sending it to you also so that you may know what it says.

[32]Greetings from King Demetrius to his father Lasthenes. [33]We have decided to treat the nation of the Jews well. They are our friends and keep their obligations to us. They show goodwill toward us. [34]We have confirmed, as their possession, the territory of Judea and the three districts of Aphairema, Lydda, and Rathamin. The latter districts, with the entire region bordering them, were added to Judea from Samaria. To all those who offer sacrifice in Jerusalem, we have granted release from the royal taxes the king formerly received from them each year, from the crops of the land and the fruit of the trees. [35]Furthermore, we grant them release from all other payments due to us from the tenth-part gifts, the taxes, the salt pits, and the crown taxes from now on. [36]These exemptions are never to be canceled. [37]Therefore, be sure to make a copy of this letter. Give it to Jonathan and display it in a prominent place on the holy mountain.

Intrigue of Trypho

[38]King Demetrius saw that the land was quiet and that there was no opposition to him. So he dismissed his troops and sent them back to their homes. He kept only the foreign troops that he had recruited from the island nations. All the troops who had served under his predecessors hated him.

[39]Now Trypho had formerly been one of Alexander's supporters. He realized that the troops were grumbling against Demetrius. So he went to Imalkue the Arab, who was bringing up Antiochus the young son of Alexander. [40]Imalkue watched over Antiochus carefully until he might hand him over to become king in place of his father. Trypho also reported to Imalkue what Demetrius had done and told him about the hatred of the troops toward Demetrius. He remained there many days.

[41]Now Jonathan sent to King Demetrius the request that he remove the troops in the elevated fortress from Jerusalem, as well as the troops in the fortress, because they continued fighting against Israel. [42]Demetrius sent this message back to Jonathan: "Not only will I do these things for

[j]Or *Friends*

you and your nation, but I will confer great honor on you and your nation if I get an opportunity. [43]In return, you would do well to send me some soldiers to help me, because my troops are in revolt." [44]Jonathan sent three thousand strong men to him at Antioch. When they came to the king, he rejoiced at their arrival.

[45]At that time, the people of the city assembled, one hundred twenty thousand in number, and they wanted to kill the king. [46]But he fled into the palace. Then the people took control of the main streets of the city and began to fight. [47]So the king called the Jews to his aid. They rallied around him and spread out through the city. They killed about one hundred thousand people that day. [48]They set fire to the city, ravaged many goods, and saved the king. [49]When the people saw that the Jews had gained control of the city as they pleased, their courage failed. They made a request of the king: [50]"Give us peace, and make the Jews stop fighting against us." [51]They threw down their weapons and made peace. So the Jews received honor from the king and all the people in his kingdom. They returned to Jerusalem with a large amount of treasure.

[52]So King Demetrius sat on the throne of his kingdom, and the land was peaceful before him. [53]But he broke his word about all that he had said. He became estranged from Jonathan and didn't repay the favors that Jonathan had done him. Instead, he treated him harshly.

Trypho seizes power

[54]After this, Trypho returned, accompanied by the young boy Antiochus, who put on the crown and began to rule. [55]The troops that Demetrius had dismissed gathered to fight against Demetrius and routed him, so he fled. [56]Trypho captured the elephants and gained control of Antioch. [57]Then the young Antiochus wrote to Jonathan, "I confirm you in the high priesthood, set you over the four districts, and make you one of the king's chief political advisors."[k] [58]He also sent him gold plates and table utensils, and granted him the right to drink from gold cups, dress in purple, and wear a gold buckle. [59]He appointed Jonathan's brother Simon governor from the peaks of Tyre to the borders of Egypt.

Campaigns of Jonathan and Simon

[60]Jonathan traveled through Beyond the River and among the towns. All the Syrian army gathered to him as allies. When he came to Ashkelon, the people of the city met him and honored him. [61]From there, he went to Gaza, but the people shut him out. So he attacked Gaza and burned and plundered the areas surrounding the city. [62]Then the people of Gaza pleaded with Jonathan, and he made peace with them. He took the sons of their rulers as hostages and sent them to Jerusalem. And he passed through the country as far as Damascus.

[63]Then Jonathan heard that Demetrius' officers had come to Kadesh in Galilee with a large army, intending to remove him from office. [64]He went to meet them but left his brother Simon in the country. [65]Simon camped before Beth-zur and fought against it for many days, hemming it in. [66]Then they asked Simon to grant them terms of peace, and he did so. He removed them from there and took possession of the town. He appointed troops to guard it.

[67]Jonathan and his army camped by the waters of Gennesaret. Early in the morning they marched to the plain of Hazor, [68]where the foreign army met him. They had set an ambush against him in the mountains, but they themselves met him face-to-face. [69]Then the men waiting to ambush emerged from their places and joined the battle. All the men with Jonathan fled. [70]Not one of them was left except Mattathias, Absalom's son, and Judas, Chalphi's son, commanders of the army forces. [71]Jonathan tore his clothes, put dust on his head, and prayed. [72]Then he turned back to the battle against the enemy, routed them, and they fled. [73]When his men who were running away saw this, they returned to him. They joined

[k]Or *Friends*

him in the pursuit as far as Kadesh, where
they camped. 74As many as three thousand
foreigners died that day. Finally, Jonathan
returned to Jerusalem.

Alliances with Rome and Sparta

12 When Jonathan felt that the time
was favorable, he chose envoys and
sent them to Rome in order to confirm
and renew friendship with them. 2He also
sent letters in the same vein to the Spartans and to others. 3The envoys went to
Rome and entered the senate chamber.
They said, "Jonathan the high priest and
the Jewish nation have sent us to renew
our former friendship and alliance." 4The
Romans provided letters for them to give
to various people to ask them to assure the
envoys safe passage back to Judah. 5This is
a copy of the letter that Jonathan wrote to
the Spartans:

6The high priest Jonathan, the senate
of the nation, the priests, and the rest of
the Jewish people. To their brothers the
Spartans. Greetings!

7In the past, your king Arius sent a letter to the high priest Onias, stating that
you are our relatives as the appended
copy shows. 8Onias welcomed the envoy
with honor and received the letter, which
contained a clear declaration of alliance
and friendship. 9Generally, we have no
need of these things, since we have the
holy scrolls as encouragement. 10Yet we
have desired to renew our family ties
and friendship with you so that we may
not become estranged from you, because
considerable time has passed since you
sent your letter to us. 11We remember
you constantly on every occasion—at
our festivals and on other appropriate
days, at the sacrifices that we offer, and
in our prayers—as it is right and proper
to remember relatives. 12Furthermore,
we rejoice at your success.

13As for us, we have experienced many
trials and many wars. The kings around
us have waged war against us. 14We have
not wanted to bother you and our other
allies and friends about these wars 15be-
cause we have the help that comes from
heaven. So we have been delivered from
our enemies, and they have been humbled. 16Therefore, we chose Numenius,
Antiochus' son, and Antipater, Jason's
son, and sent them to Rome to renew
our former friendship and alliance with
them. 17We have told them to go to you
as well and greet you and deliver to you
this letter from us concerning the re-
newal of our family ties. 18So please send
us a reply.

19This is a copy of the letter that they
sent to Onias:

20King Arius of the Spartans.

To the high priest Onias. Greetings!

21It has been discovered in a written
record that the Spartans and the Jews
are relatives and are both of the family
of Abraham. 22Since we have learned
this, please let us know how you are.
23On our part, we write to let you know
that what is yours—your livestock and
property—belongs to us, and ours belongs to you. We therefore command
that our envoys report to you in keeping
with this.

Further campaigns of Jonathan and Simon

24Jonathan heard that Demetrius' commanders had returned with a larger force
than before to wage war against him. 25So
he marched away from Jerusalem and met
them in the region of Hamath. He didn't
allow them any opportunity to invade his
country. 26He sent spies to their camp.
They returned and reported to him that the
enemy was lining up in battle formation to
attack the Jews at night. 27When the sun
had set, Jonathan commanded his troops
to be on alert. They were to keep their weapons at hand so they could be ready through
the night for battle. He also stationed guard
posts around the camp. 28When the enemy
heard that Jonathan and his troops were
prepared for battle, they were extremely
terrified. So they lit fires in their camp and
retreated. 29Jonathan and his troops didn't
know about this until morning because
they saw the fires burning. 30Then Jonathan tried to pursue them, but he couldn't

catch them since they had already crossed the Eleutherus River. 31 So Jonathan turned aside against the Arabs, who are called Zabadeans, and he crushed and plundered them. 32 Then he broke camp and went to Damascus and marched throughout that region.

33 Simon also marched through the country as far as Ashkelon and the fortresses in the area. He turned aside to Joppa and took it by surprise, 34 because he had heard that they were ready to hand over the fortress to people that Demetrius had sent. So he stationed a force there to occupy and guard it.

35 When Jonathan returned to Jerusalem, he assembled the elders of the people and planned with them how to build fortresses in Judea. 36 They also discussed how to build the walls of Jerusalem still higher, and to erect a high barrier between the elevated fortress and the city to separate them. This was to isolate the elevated fortress so that its troops couldn't buy or sell things. 37 So they gathered together to rebuild the city. Part of the wall toward the valley to the east had fallen, and he repaired the section called Chaphenatha. 38 Simon also built Adida in the western foothills. He secured it and installed gates with bolts.

Trypho captures Jonathan

39 At that time, Trypho attempted to rise up against King Antiochus, put on the crown, and become king in Asia. 40 He feared that Jonathan might not permit him to do this, making war on him. So he kept trying to capture and kill him. He marched out and came to Beth-shan. 41 Jonathan went out to meet him with forty thousand select warriors. He also came to Beth-shan. 42 When Trypho saw that he had come with a large army, he was afraid to lift a hand against him. 43 So he received Jonathan with honor and commended him to all his chief political advisors.[1] He gave him gifts and told his advisors and troops to obey him as they would himself. 44 Then he said to Jonathan, "Why have you put all these people to so much trouble when we're not at war? 45 Tell them to go back to their homes. Pick for yourself a few men to stay with you, and come with me to Ptolemais. I'll hand it over to you as well as the other fortresses and the remaining troops and officials. Then I'll turn around and go home. That's why I'm here."

46 Jonathan trusted him and did what he said. He sent away his troops, and they returned to Judah. 47 He kept with himself three thousand troops—two thousand of whom he left in Galilee, while one thousand accompanied him. 48 But when Jonathan entered Ptolemais, the people there closed the gates and captured him, and killed with their swords all those who had entered with him.

49 Trypho then sent infantry and cavalry into Galilee and the great plain to destroy Jonathan's soldiers. 50 But Jonathan's forces believed that Jonathan had been seized and had died along with his troops. They encouraged each other and kept marching in tight formation, ready for fighting. 51 When their pursuers saw that they would fight for their lives, they turned back. 52 So they all reached the land of Judah safely. They mourned for Jonathan and his companions, and they were very anxious. All Israel mourned deeply. 53 All the nations around them tried to destroy them, saying, "They have no leader or helper now. Let's make war against them and blot out their memory from humanity."

Simon takes command

13 Simon heard that Trypho had assembled a large army to invade the land of Judah and destroy it. 2 He saw that the people were trembling and afraid, so he went up to Jerusalem and gathered the people together. 3 He encouraged them by saying, "You yourselves know what great things my brothers and I, and our father's family, have done for the laws and the sanctuary. You also know about the wars and the difficulties that we have seen. 4 Because of this, all my brothers have died for Israel's sake. I alone am left. 5 Now, far be it from me to spare my own life at any time of distress. I'm not better than

1 Or *Friends*

my brothers. [6]Instead, I will avenge my
nation and the sanctuary, your wives and
children. All the nations have gathered to
destroy us out of hatred."

[7]The spirit of the people was renewed
when they heard these words. [8]They answered loudly, "You are our leader in place
of Judas and Jonathan your brothers.[m]
[9]Fight our battles, and all that you tell us
we will do." [10]So he assembled the warriors
and rushed to complete the walls of Jerusalem and secured it on every side. [11]He sent
Jonathan, Absalom's son, to Joppa with a
sufficient army. He drove out its occupants
and remained there.

Trypho's deceit and treachery

[12]Then Trypho left Ptolemais with a
large army to invade the land of Judah,
taking Jonathan with him under guard.
[13]Simon camped in Adida, facing the plain.
[14]Trypho learned that Simon had taken
the place of his brother Jonathan and that
he was about to battle against him. So he
sent envoys to Simon who said, [15]"We are
detaining your brother Jonathan because
of the money he owes the royal treasury in
connection with the offices he held. [16]Send
now 5,700 pounds of silver and two of his
sons as hostages, to ensure that when he is
released he won't revolt against us, and we
will release him."

[17]Simon knew that they were speaking deceitfully to him, but he sent for the
money and the sons so that he wouldn't
arouse hostility among the people. [18]He
was concerned that they might say, "Jonathan died because Simon didn't send the
money and his sons." [19]So he sent the sons
and 5,700 pounds of silver. But Trypho
broke his word and didn't release Jonathan.

[20]After this, Trypho came to invade and
destroy the country. He circled around by
the way to Adora. But Simon and his army
kept marching opposite him, every place
he went. [21]Now the men in the elevated
fortress kept sending messengers to Trypho, urging him to come to them by way
of the wilderness and to send them food.
[22]So Trypho got all his cavalry ready to
go, but that night a very heavy snow fell
so he didn't go. Instead, he marched into
the land of Gilead. [23]When he approached
Baskama, he killed Jonathan and buried
him there. [24]Then Trypho returned to his
own land.

Jonathan's tomb

[25]Simon sent someone to get the bones
of Jonathan his brother, and he buried him
in Modein, the city of his ancestors. [26]All
Israel mourned Jonathan with great expressions of grief for many days. [27]Simon
built a monument over the tomb of his
father and his brothers. He made it high so
that all might see it. It had polished stone
at the front and back. [28]He also set up
seven pyramids, opposite each other, for his
father and mother and four brothers. [29]He
devised an elaborate site for the pyramids,
setting up great columns around them. On
the columns, he put suits of armor for a
permanent memorial. Beside the suits of
armor, he carved ships so that all who sail
the sea might see them. [30]This is the tomb
that he built in Modein, which remains
to this day.

Judea gains independence

[31]Trypho dealt dishonestly with the
young king Antiochus and killed him.
[32]He put on the crown of Asia and became
king in his place. He brought great disaster on the land. [33]But Simon built up the
fortresses of Judea and put protection all
around them with high towers, great walls,
gates, and bolts. In addition, he stored food
in the fortresses. [34]Simon also sent messengers to King Demetrius with a request
to grant relief to the country, because Trypho had stolen many of their goods. [35]King
Demetrius sent a reply to this request, and
wrote him a letter:

> [36]King Demetrius. To Simon, the high
> priest and advisor of kings, and to the el-
> ders and nation of the Jews. Greetings!
>
> [37]We have received the gold crown
> and the palm branch that you sent. We

[m]Or *brother*

are ready to make a general peace with
you and to write to our officials to grant
you release from tribute. [38]All the exemptions that we have made to you remain valid. Let the fortresses that you
have built be in your possession. [39]We
pardon any errors and offenses committed to this day. Plus, we cancel the
crown tax that you owe. Whatever other
tax has been collected in Jerusalem will
not be collected any longer. [40]If any of
you are qualified to be enrolled in our
bodyguard, let them be enrolled. Finally,
let there be peace between us.
[41]In the year 170,[n] the yoke of the Gentiles was removed from Israel. [42]The people
of Israel began to write in their documents
and contracts, "In the first year of Simon
the great high priest, commander and
leader of the Jews."

Simon captures Gazara

[43]In those days, Simon camped against
Gazara and surrounded it with troops. He
made a siege engine and brought it up to the
city. He battered and captured one tower.
[44]The men in the siege engine leaped out
into the city, and a great tumult arose. [45]To-
gether with their wives and children, the
men went up on the wall with their clothes
torn. They cried out loudly, asking Simon to
make peace with them. [46]They said, "Don't
treat us according to our wicked acts but according to your mercy." [47]So Simon reached
an agreement with them and stopped fighting. But he expelled them from the city and
cleansed the houses in which the idols were
located. He then entered it with hymns and
praise. [48]He removed all pollution from it
and settled people there who observed the
Law. He also strengthened its defenses and
built a house for himself there.

Simon regains the elevated fortress at Jerusalem.

[49]Those who were in the elevated fortress
at Jerusalem were prevented from moving
around to buy and sell in the country. So
they were very hungry, and many perished
from famine. [50]They appealed to Simon to
make peace with them, and he did. But he
expelled them from there and cleansed the
elevated fortress from its pollutions. [51]On
the twenty-third day of the second month,[o]
in the year 171, the Jews entered it with
praise and palm branches, with harps and
cymbals and stringed instruments, and with
hymns and songs. A great enemy had been
crushed and removed from Israel. [52]Simon
declared that they should celebrate this day
annually with rejoicing. He strengthened
the defenses of the temple hill alongside
the elevated fortress, and he and his soldiers lived there. [53]Simon saw that his son
John had become a man, and so he made
him commander of all the forces. And John
lived at Gazara.

Capture of Demetrius

14 In the year 172,[p] King Demetrius gathered together his military forces. He
marched into Media to find help, in order to
wage war against Trypho. [2]When Arsaces,
the king of Persia and Media, heard that
Demetrius had invaded his territory, he sent
one of his generals to capture him alive. [3]The
general went and defeated the army of Demetrius. He arrested Demetrius and took
him to Arsaces, who put him under guard.

Eulogy of Simon

[4]The land of Judah enjoyed peace all the
days of Simon.
He sought what was good for his nation.
His rule was agreeable to them,
as was the honor shown him
all his days.
[5]His crowning achievement
was to take Joppa for a harbor,
opening the way to the sea
with its islands.
[6]He also extended his country's borders.
He gained full control of the land;
[7]he took a great number of captives.
He ruled over Gazara, Beth-zur,
and the elevated fortress.
He removed the impurities
from the elevated fortress.

[n]142 BCE [o]April–May, Iyar, 141 BCE [p]140 BCE

There were none to oppose him.
[8] People worked their farmland in peace.
The ground was fertile,
and the trees of the plains
were fruitful.
[9] Old men sat along the sides of the
streets and talked about good things.
The young put on
impressive military uniforms.
[10] Simon supplied the towns with food
and with the means for defense.
His fame spread to the ends of the earth.
[11] He established peace
throughout the land,
and Israel had great joy.
[12] All the people sat under their own vines
and fig trees.
No one made them afraid.
[13] No one was left in the land to fight them,
because foreign kings had been crushed
in those days.
[14] He gave help to all the humble ones
among his people.
He sought lawful ways.
He did away with evil people
and those who sinned against the Law.
[15] He made the sanctuary glorious,
and added to its holy equipment.

Diplomacy with Rome and Sparta

[16] The people in Rome, and those who
were as far away as Sparta, learned that Jonathan had died, and they were all very sad.
[17] They also heard that Simon his brother had
become high priest in his place and that he
was ruling over the country and its towns.
[18] So they wrote to him on bronze tablets
to renew with him the friendly alliance
that they had established with his brothers
Judas and Jonathan. [19] The tablets were read
before the assembly in Jerusalem.

[20] This is a copy of the letter that the
Spartans sent:

The rulers of the Spartans, with the city.
To the high priest Simon, the elders, the
priests, and the rest of the Jewish people, our brothers and sisters. Greetings!
[21] The envoys who were sent to our people have told us about your glory and
honor, and we rejoiced when they came.
[22] We made this record in our public decrees concerning what they said: "Numenius, Antiochus' son, and Antipater,
Jason's son, Jewish representatives,
have come to renew their friendship
with us. [23] Our people were pleased to
receive them with respect and to maintain a copy of their words in the public
archives so that Spartans may have a
record of them. They have also sent a
copy of this to Simon, the high priest.

[24] Following this exchange, Simon sent
Numenius to Rome with a large gold shield
weighing one thousand manehs, to confirm
the alliance with the Romans.

Official honors for Simon

[25] When the people heard these things
they said, "How should we thank Simon
and his sons? [26] He and his brothers, and his
father's family, have stood firm. They have
fought and repelled Israel's enemies and
established our freedom." So they made a
written record on bronze plaques and put it
on pillars on Mount Zion. [27] This is a copy of
the document:

On the eighteenth day of Elul,[q] in the
year 172, the third year of the great high
priest Simon. [28] In the great assembly of
the priests, the people, and the rulers
and elders of the country, the following
was proclaimed to us.

[29] Wars occurred often in our country.
Simon, Mattathias' son, a priest of the
sons of Joarib, and his brothers bravely
faced danger and fought against the enemies of their nation. They preserved the
sanctuary and the Law, and they brought
great honor to their nation. [30] Jonathan
rallied the nation and became their high
priest, and was gathered to his people.
[31] Their enemies decided to invade their
country and take hold of their sanctuary. [32] Then Simon rose up and fought
for his nation. He spent great amounts
of his own money to arm soldiers of his
nation and give them pay. [33] He fortified
the towns of Judea and Beth-zur on the

[q] August–September, 140 BCE

borders of Judea, where enemy weapons had been stored in the past, and placed a group of Jewish soldiers there. [34]He also fortified Joppa by the sea, along with Gazara on the borders of Azotus, where enemies formerly lived. He settled Jews there and provided whatever was needed to restore the towns.

[35]The people saw Simon's faithfulness and the honor that he had resolved to win for his nation. So they made him their leader and high priest, because he had done all these things and had acted toward his nation with justice and loyalty. He sought in every way to lift up his people. [36]In his days, things prospered under his leadership so that the Gentiles were driven out of the country, as well as those in David's City in Jerusalem, who had built themselves an elevated fortress. Gentiles used to leave the elevated fortress and defile the sanctuary area, doing great damage to its purity. [37]He settled Jewish troops in the elevated fortress and fortified it for the safety of the country and of the city, and built the walls of Jerusalem higher.

[38]In light of all these things, King Demetrius confirmed him as high priest. [39]He also made him one of the leading political advisors,[r] and paid him other high honors. [40]For he had heard that the Jews were considered friends, allies, and brothers by the Romans, and that the Romans had welcomed the ambassadors of Simon with honor.

[41]The Jews and their priests have resolved that Simon should be their leader and high priest forever, until a trustworthy prophet should arise. [42]He should govern them and take charge of the sanctuary, appointing officials to oversee its tasks and the weapons and the fortresses of the country. [43]Everyone should obey him. All contracts in the land should bear his name. In addition, he should be clothed in royal purple and wear gold.

[44]None of the people or the priests can annul these decisions or oppose what he says. They cannot convene an assembly without his permission. No one else can be clothed in purple or put on a gold buckle. [45]Whoever fails to follow all of these decisions or acts contrary to them will be punished.

[46]All the people agreed to give Simon the power to act in keeping with these decisions. [47]Simon accepted and agreed to be high priest, to command and rule the Jews and the priests, and to protect them all. [48]Also they gave orders to write this decision on bronze plates and to set them up in a public place in the sanctuary grounds. [49]Finally, they were to place copies in the treasury so that Simon and his sons would have access to them.

Letter of Antiochus VII

15 Antiochus the son of King Demetrius sent a letter from the sea islands to Simon, the priest and ruler of the Jews, and to all the nation:

[2]King Antiochus to Simon the high priest and ruler, and to the nation of the Jews. Greetings!

[3]Some troublemakers have gained control of our ancestors' kingdom. I intend to take command of the kingdom so that I may restore it to the way it used to be. I have recruited a large number of foreign troops and have equipped warships. [4]I am going to come to the country so that I can move against the people who have destroyed our country and devastated many cities in my kingdom. [5]Therefore, I confirm all of the favorable tax exemptions that previous kings have given you. Also, I consent to any agreements you had with them to release you from other payments. [6]You have my permission to mint your own coins to use in your country. [7]Furthermore, I give freedom to Jerusalem and the sanctuary. All the weapons you made and the fortress you built will remain in your possession. [8]I cancel any debts you owe to the royal treasury now or in the future. [9]When I

[r]Or *Friends*

gain control of the kingdom, I will give you great rewards. I will honor you, your nation, and the temple. Your reputation will become evident in all the earth.

10In the year 174,[s] Antiochus invaded the land of his ancestors. All the troops went over to his side. Trypho had only a few remaining. 11Antiochus pursued him, and Trypho fled to Dor, which is by the sea. 12He knew that things looked bad for him and that his troops had deserted him. 13Antiochus camped against Dor with one hundred twenty thousand warriors and eight thousand cavalry. 14He surrounded the town, and ships joined the battle from the sea. He pressured the town from land and sea, and he didn't let anyone leave or enter it.

Rome supports the Jews

15Then Numenius and his companions arrived from Rome with letters to the kings and countries:

16Lucius, consul of the Romans. To King Ptolemy. Greetings!

17Jewish messengers came to us as our friends and allies to renew our ancient friendship and alliance. The high priest Simon and the Jewish people sent them. 18They have brought us a gold shield weighing one thousand manehs. 19Because of this, we have decided to write to the kings and countries to tell them that they should not seek their harm or make war against them, their cities, or their country, or make alliance with those who war against them. 20We are pleased to accept the shield. 21Therefore, if any troublemakers have run away to your lands from their country, hand them over to the high priest Simon. Then he can punish them according to Jewish law.

22The consul wrote the same thing to King Demetrius and to Attalus, Ariarathes, and Arsaces. 23He also wrote it to all the countries—to Sampsames, the Spartans, Delos, Myndos, Sicyon, Caria, Samos, Pamphylia, Lycia, Halicarnassus, Rhodes, Phaselis, Cos, Side, Aradus, Gortyna, Cnidus, Cyprus, and Cyrene. 24They also sent a copy of these things to Simon the high priest.

Antiochus VII threatens Simon

25King Antiochus besieged Dor for a second time, continually making war engines and throwing his forces against it. He forced Trypho to stay inside and restricted his movement. 26Simon sent two thousand select troops to fight for Antiochus. He also sent silver, gold, and a large amount of military equipment. 27But Antiochus wouldn't accept them. He broke all the agreements that he had made with Simon in the past and became like a stranger to him. 28He sent Athenobius, one of his leading political advisors,[t] to talk with Simon: "You hold control of Joppa and Gazara and the elevated fortress in Jerusalem. They are cities of my kingdom. 29You have devastated their territory. You have done great damage in the land. You have taken possession of many places in my kingdom. 30Now hand over the cities that you have captured and the money you have received from the places you have conquered beyond Judea's borders. 31Or you can pay me 28,500 pounds of silver for the destruction you have caused and another 28,500 pounds for the tribute money of the cities. Otherwise, I will come and make war on you."

32So the king's advisor Athenobius came to Jerusalem. When he saw the magnificence of Simon, including his special cupboard that had gold and silver on it, all representing his considerable position, he was amazed. But he delivered the king's message. 33Simon replied, "We haven't taken foreign land or property. We've taken only our ancestors' inheritance, which was unjustly stolen by our enemies. 34Now that we have the opportunity, we will hold on firmly to their inheritance. 35As for Joppa and Gazara, which you demand, they were causing a lot of problems for our people and land. But we'll give you 5,700 pounds of silver for them." Athenobius didn't say a word.

[s]138 BCE [t]Or *Friends*

[36]Instead, he returned with great anger and told the king what Simon had said. He also reported on Simon's wealth and all that he had seen, and the king was enraged.

Victory over Cendebeus

[37]Meanwhile, Trypho escaped on a ship and went to Orthosia. [38]The king made Cendebeus supreme commander of the coastal lands, and he gave him infantry and cavalry. [39]He commanded him to camp against Judea, to secure Kedron and its gates, and to wage war against the people. Then the king went to hunt down Trypho. [40]Cendebeus came to Jamnia and bothered the people. He invaded Judea and killed the prisoners of war. [41]Following the king's orders, he fortified Kedron. He stationed cavalry and troops there so that they could go out and raid along the roads of Judea.

16 John went up from Gazara and reported to his father Simon what Cendebeus had done. [2]Simon summoned his two oldest boys, Judas and John. He said to them, "My brothers and I, and my father's family, have fought Israel's wars from our youth until this day. We have prospered and have delivered Israel many times. [3]But now I've become old. By heaven's mercy, you are mature in years. Take my place and that of my brothers, and go out and fight for our nation. May the help that comes from heaven be with you!"

[4]So John chose twenty thousand warriors and cavalry from across the country. They marched against Cendebeus, camping overnight in Modein. [5]They started out early in the morning and marched into the plain, where a large force of infantry and cavalry was advancing to meet them. A stream lay between them. [6]Then John and his army lined up against them. He saw that his soldiers were afraid to cross the stream, so he crossed it first. When his troops saw his action, they crossed over after him. [7]Then he divided up the army, placing the cavalry in the middle of the infantry, because the enemy had a large number of cavalry. [8]They sounded the trumpets and decisively defeated Cendebeus and his army. Many of them were killed, and the rest headed into the fortress. [9]During the battle, John's brother Judas was wounded, but John pursued them until Cendebeus reached Kedron, which he had built. [10]Some also fled into the towers that were in the fields of Azotus. John burned them down, killing about two thousand. Then he safely returned to Judea.

Murder of Simon and his sons

[11]Now Ptolemy, Abubus' son, had been appointed governor over Jericho. He had a large amount of silver and gold [12]because he was the high priest's son-in-law. [13]He became arrogant and was determined to gain control of the country. He made devious plans against Simon and his sons to do away with them.

[14]Now Simon was out visiting the towns in the countryside and attending to their needs. He went down to Jericho with his sons Mattathias and Judas. It was the eleventh month, the month of Shevat,[u] in the year 177. [15]Abubus' son welcomed them deceitfully in the little fortress called Dok, which he had built. He threw a great banquet for them, but he hid men in the hall. [16]When Simon and his sons became drunk, Ptolemy and his men took their weapons. They rushed forward against Simon, and killed him and his two sons in the banquet hall, as well as some of his servants. [17]So he committed an act of great treachery, returning evil for good.

John succeeds Simon

[18]Ptolemy wrote a report about these matters and sent it to the king. He asked him to send troops to aid him and to turn over the towns and country to him. [19]He sent other soldiers to Gazara to kill John. And he sent letters to the captains asking them to come to him so that he could give them silver and gold and gifts. [20]He sent other troops to capture Jerusalem and the temple mount. [21]But someone ran ahead

[u]January–February, 134 BCE

and told John at Gazara that his father and brothers had died, and also said, "He has sent men to kill you also." 22When he heard this news, he was greatly shocked. He detained the men who had come to destroy him and killed them because he had learned about their intentions.

23The rest of John's actions, his wars, the brave deeds that he did, his achievements, and the building of the walls that he completed—24these are written in the records of his high priesthood, dating from the time when he became high priest after his father.

2 MACCABEES

The first letter

1 To our Jewish brothers and sisters in Egypt.

Greetings! Your Jewish brothers and sisters in Jerusalem and in the country of Judea wish you prosperous peace.

[2]May God do good for you and remember the covenant with Abraham, Isaac, and Jacob, his faithful servants.

[3]May God give to all of you the passion to worship him and to do his will with a whole heart and a willing spirit.

[4]May God open your heart to his Law and commands, and give you peace.

[5]May God listen to your prayers and be reconciled with you and not abandon you in an evil time. [6]We are praying for you here.

[7]In the year 169,[a] during the rule of Demetrius, we Jews wrote to you during a critical period of suffering that happened to us in the years after Jason and his followers revolted from the holy land and the kingdom. [8]They burned down the gate and murdered innocent people. We pleaded to the Lord, and the Lord heard us. We offered sacrifices and fine flour, lit the lamps, and set out the sacred loaves. [9]So now you should keep the Festival of Booths in the month of Kislev, [10]in the year 188.[b]

The second letter

The citizens of Jerusalem and Judea, the council of elders, and Judas send greetings and wishes of good health to Aristobulus, teacher of King Ptolemy and a member of the family of the anointed priests, and to the Jews in Egypt. [11]God saved us from great danger when we were battling against the king. So we greatly praise God [12]because he forced those fighting in the holy city to leave.

[13]The ruler and his armed forces that went into Persia seemed invincible. But they were slain in the goddess Nanea's temple, when Nanea's priests tricked them. [14]Since Antiochus came in order to marry the goddess, he and his political advisors[c] came into the temple[d] to take the great wealth as payment for her dowry. [15]When the priests of Nanea had set it out, the king entered with a few men into the enclosed space of the shrine. After closing off the temple as Antiochus entered, [16]and opening the hidden door of the ceiling, they threw stones that struck down the ruler like a bolt of lightning. After dismembering and beheading the bodies, they tossed the heads to those outside.

[17]May our God who gave up the immoral to death be praised in every way!

[18]Since we are about to celebrate the cleansing of the temple on the twenty-fifth of Kislev, we thought it right to notify you so that you yourselves might also celebrate the Festival of Booths and Fire, when Nehemiah offered sacrifices after he had built the temple and the altar. [19]When our ancestors were taken as captives into Persia, the holy priests secretly took the fire of the altar and hid it in a dry pit. They were careful that no one knew the place. [20]Many years later, when it seemed good to God, Nehemiah, who was commissioned by the king of Persia, sent the descendants of the priests who had hidden the fire to retrieve it. After they explained to us that they didn't find the fire, but rather a thick liquid, he ordered them to bring the liquid. [21]When they brought up the provisions for the sacrifice, Nehemiah commanded the priests to sprinkle the liquid on the wood and on the items lying there. [22]Some time after they did this, as the sun shone brightly from behind the clouds, a great fire flared up and astonished everyone. [23]While the sacrifices were burning, the priests prayed, the priests and all the people. Jonathan took the lead while the others, including Nehemiah, responded. [24]The prayer went like this:

Lord, Lord God, creator of all,
  you are fearsome, mighty,
    just, and merciful.
  You are the only king
    and only generous one.

[a]143 BCE [b]November–December, 124 BCE [c]Or *Friends* [d]Or *place*

25 You are the only provider,
the only just, almighty, and eternal one.
You save Israel from all evil.
You chose the patriarchs
and made them holy.
26 Receive this sacrifice on behalf of
all your people Israel. Guard your portion and make it holy.
27 Gather together our scattered people,
free the ones enslaved among the nations,
watch over those who are despised and
loathed, and let the nations know that
you are our God. 28 Punish the oppressors
and those who commit arrogant acts of
violence. 29 Plant your people in your holy
place, just as Moses said.[e]

30 The priests sang the hymns. 31 When
the elements of the sacrifice were consumed, Nehemiah commanded them to
pour the remaining liquid on larger stones.
32 When this happened, a flame flared up on
these stones. But it went out in the presence of the light shining from the altar.
33 When this situation became known, it
was reported to the king of the Persians
that in the place where the exiled priests
hid the fire, a liquid appeared from which
Nehemiah's followers purified the elements
of the sacrifice. 34 After fencing off the place
and declaring it holy, the king examined the
matter. 35 The king showed favor to those
involved and presented many excellent
gifts to them. 36 Nehemiah's circle called
this liquid *nephthar*, which means "purification," but most people call it nephthai.

2 One finds in the records that the prophet
Jeremiah commanded those who were
deported to take some of the fire, which
is the story I've just related. 2 Having given
them the Law, the prophet commanded
those who were deported not to forget
the Lord's commands or to be led astray
in their thoughts when they saw gold and
silver idols and how they were decorated.
3 With these kinds of words, he urged them
not to forget the Law. 4 The same document
also states that the prophet commanded,
with a solemn divine pronouncement,
that the meeting tent and the chest containing the covenant should go with him.
The documents reported that he went to
the mountain that Moses ascended to
see the inheritance that God promised.

5 When Jeremiah arrived, he discovered
a cave where he deposited the meeting tent,
the covenant chest, and the incense altar.
He blocked up the opening. 6 Some who
had accompanied him went along to mark
the way but couldn't find it again. 7 When
Jeremiah found out, he rebuked them and
said: "The place will remain unknown until
God gathers the people together again and
shows mercy. 8 Then the Lord will disclose
these things. The Lord's glory will appear
with the cloud, as they were revealed in the
time of Moses and when Solomon prayed
that the place might be made holy."

9 It was also made clear that, since Solomon possessed wisdom, he offered up a sacrifice for the inauguration and completion
of the temple. 10 Just as Moses prayed to the
Lord and fire came down from heaven and
consumed the components of the sacrifice,
so also Solomon prayed and fire came down
to consume the entirely burned offerings.
11 Moses said, "Because the purification offering had not been eaten, it was destroyed
by fire." 12 Likewise, Solomon observed the
eight days.[f]

13 Nehemiah also narrated the same
things in his writings and journals. He
also told how, when Solomon established
a library, he gathered the scrolls concerning the kings and prophets and the scrolls
of David and letters of kings regarding offerings for solemn promises. 14 In the same
way, Judas also gathered together all the
scrolls that went missing because of the
war, so that those documents are now in
our possession. 15 So if you need them, send
messengers to carry them back.

16 Now as we are about to celebrate the
Purification Festival, we write to you. Act
honorably by observing the days. 17 God has
saved all of his people and restored to all the
inheritance, even the kingdom, the priesthood, and the holy place, 18 as he promised
through the Law. We have hope in God that

[e] Cf Exod 15:17 [f] Cf 1 Kgs 8:65-66

he will quickly extend mercy and gather us
from everywhere under heaven into the
holy place. He has brought us out of great
evils and purified the place.

Author's preface

19This scroll is about the stories of
Judas the Maccabee and his brothers, the
purification of the great temple, and the
restoration of the altar. 20It will tell of the
wars against Antiochus Epiphanes and his
son Eupator, 21and the appearances from
heaven to those who had gloriously performed brave deeds for Judaism. Though
they were few in number, they took back
the whole country, chased off the barbaric
hordes, 22regained the temple renowned
throughout the whole inhabited world,
freed the city, and restored the laws that
were almost abolished—because the Lord
with all kindness was merciful to them.

23Jason of Cyrene recorded all of these
things in five scrolls, which we will attempt
to condense into one.

24Jason's scrolls contain an abundance
of material and pose serious difficulty for
those wanting to plunge into the historical
accounts because of the amount of detail.
25We aimed, therefore, to provide something amusing for those who want to read,
to make it easy for those inclined to commit
facts to memory, and to offer something
useful to all those who happen to pick up
the scroll. 26For those of us who engage in
the strenuous task of abbreviation, it isn't
easy but involves sweat and loss of sleep,
27just as it isn't easy to prepare a banquet
for the enjoyment of others. Nevertheless,
in order to gain the praise of many, we endure the task cheerfully.

28Leaving the responsibility for accuracy in the details to the original writer, we
must follow the guidelines for preparing
a summary. 29Just as the builder of a new
house must give thought to the foundation
of the whole, so also the one attempting to
paint and decorate must investigate what is
suitable for its own decoration. This I think
also applies to us. 30The duty of the first author of the history is to occupy the ground,
to explore the subject fully, and to inquire
closely into the details in particular. 31The
one retelling the shorter version should be
allowed to pursue conciseness of expression and to be excused from an exhaustive
treatment of the matter. 32From this point
then we will begin the narrative, not adding
further to what was already said. After all,
it would be absurd to prolong the preface
but then cut short the history.

The story of Heliodorus

3 When the holy city was living in harmony, and people observed the laws
rigorously because of Onias the high priest,
who was devoted to God and hated evil,
2the kings used to honor the place and glorify the temple by sending the best gifts.
3Seleucus the king of Asia even supplied all
expenses for the sacrificial service from his
own revenues. 4But a certain Simon from
the tribe of Benjamin, who had been appointed administrator of the temple, had
a difference of opinion with the high priest
about the management of the city market.
5Since he wasn't able to overcome Onias,
he went to Thraseas' son Apollonius, who
was governor of Coele-Syria and Phoenicia at that time. 6Simon told him that the
treasury in Jerusalem was filled with untold riches and that it was full of uncounted
cash, which didn't belong to the accounts
for the sacrifices, but potentially fell under
the king's authority. 7Apollonius met with
the king and told him about the funds.

The king chose his chief administrator
Heliodorus and sent him with orders to
confiscate the funds in question. 8Helio-
dorus immediately made the journey, supposedly to inspect the cities of Coele-Syria
and Phoenicia but actually to put the king's
plan into effect. 9When he arrived in Jerusalem and was received in a friendly manner
by the high priest of the city, he revealed
the information that had been reported
and stated plainly why he had come. Then
he asked whether these things were true.
10The high priest informed him that these
were the deposits of widows and orphans,
11and also some deposits of Hyrcanus the
Tobiad, an exceedingly prominent man.
He also said that there were only 22,800

pounds of silver and 11,400 pounds of gold, and that the ungodly Simon had given a false report. 12It was wholly unthinkable, he added, to commit such an injustice against those who trusted in the holiness of the place and in the dignity and sacredness of the temple that is honored throughout the whole world. 13But Heliodorus, because of the royal commands, was firm that in any case the king could take these funds. 14So he set a date and proceeded to inspect these funds. This caused great agony throughout the whole city. 15But the priests threw themselves down before the altar in their priestly robes and called to heaven to the one who had given the laws about such deposits, that he should keep the deposits safe. 16Anyone seeing the outward appearance of the high priest would have been heartbroken, because his expression and changed color revealed his inner anguish. 17Fear and trembling seized the man, making the grief lodged in his heart clear to observers. 18People burst from their houses in crowds to plead for help because the temple[g] was about to be dishonored. 19With mourning clothes wrapped beneath their breasts, women filled the streets. The virgins, who usually remained indoors, ran together to the gates and some to the walls, while others peeped through their windows. 20But all raised up their hands to heaven and pleaded for help. 21To see the whole crowd on its knees and faces and the great suffering and dread of the high priest was a pitiful sight. 22So they called on the almighty Lord to protect the deposits for those who had entrusted them.

23But Heliodorus carried on with what had been decided. 24When he and his spearmen approached the treasury, however, the ruler of all spirits and all authority made an awesome display, so that all those daring to come with Heliodorus fainted, terrified and awestruck by God's power. 25A horse appeared to them with a fearsome rider and decked out with a beautiful saddle. While running furiously, the horse attacked Heliodorus with its front hooves. The rider appeared to be clothed in full body armor made of gold. 26Two young men also appeared before him—unmatched in bodily strength, of superb beauty, and with magnificent robes. They stood on either side of Heliodorus and beat him continuously with many blows. 27When he suddenly fell to the ground unconscious, his men grasped him and placed him on a stretcher. 28This was the same man who had just entered the treasury with a large group of men and a full bodyguard. Now they carried him away helpless, despite his weapons, and they publicly acknowledged God's power. 29While he was being cut down and left speechless through the divine power and deprived of all hope of recovery, 30the people were praising the Lord for acting miraculously on behalf of his holy place. And the temple, which had been weighed down with fear and disturbance a short time earlier, was now filled with delight and joy because the almighty Lord had publicly appeared.

31Some of Heliodorus' companions rushed to ask Onias to pray to the Most High to give life to the one who was about to draw his last breath. 32The high priest, fearful that perhaps the king might think that the Jews had done something evil to Heliodorus, offered a sacrifice for the man's recovery.

33While the high priest was making the sacrifice for reconciliation, the same two[h] young men, dressed in the same clothing, appeared again to Heliodorus. They stood by him and said, "You owe Onias the high priest your gratitude. Because of him the Lord has graciously given life to you. 34But you who suffered a beating from heaven must proclaim the great power of God to all." Once they said these things, they disappeared.

35Heliodorus offered a sacrifice to the Lord and made many solemn promises to the savior for sparing his life. After thanking Onias, he took his military force back to the king. 36He testified to everyone about the works of the great God that he had seen with his own eyes. 37When the king asked Heliodorus who would be the right sort

[g]Or *place* [h]Gk lacks *two*.

of person to send again to Jerusalem, he said: 38“If you have an enemy or someone plotting against your government, send him, and he will come back badly beaten if he should come back at all, because some divine power truly surrounds the temple.[i] 39The one who lives in heaven watches over that place and will strike and destroy anyone coming with evil intent.” 40So this is how matters turned out concerning Heliodorus and the guarding of the treasury.

4 This Simon, who had informed about the wealth of the temple and acted as an informer against his native land, slandered Onias. 2He accused the latter of threatening Heliodorus and becoming a perpetrator of evil. He dared to label the benefactor of the city, the protector of his fellow citizens, and a passionate advocate for the laws, as a traitor against the government. 3His hatred was so intense that one of Simon’s men had even attempted to commit murders. 4Seeing the danger of the dispute—including how Menestheus’ son Apollonius, the governor of Coele-Syria and Phoenicia, encouraged Simon’s evil—5Onias went to the king not to accuse his fellow citizens but to safeguard the public and private welfare of the people. 6He recognized that without royal attention pubic affairs would not return to a peaceful state, and Simon would not cease from his madness.

Jason as high priest

7After Seleucus died and Antiochus (who was called Epiphanes) received the kingdom, Jason the brother of Onias gained the high priesthood by corruption. 8He offered the king, in private communication, 20,520 pounds of silver, and an additional 4,560 pounds from another source of revenue. 9He also promised to pay another 8,550 pounds of silver if he were permitted to set up, under his own authority, a gymnasium and a place for training the young people, and to enroll those living in Jerusalem as citizens of Antioch. 10When the king had granted this and Jason had taken possession of his office, he immediately made his fellow citizens change to the Greek way of life. 11He set aside the customs established for the Jews by royal generosity, negotiated through John the father of Eupolemus (the one who had made the official journey to secure friendship and alliance with the Romans). He abolished the lawful government and introduced customs contrary to the law. 12He eagerly founded a gymnasium right below the elevated fortress[j] and induced the most honorable of the trainees to wear the traditional Greek hat. 13So the Greek way of life caught on very quickly, and the adoption of foreign customs increased because of Jason—an excessively wicked and ungodly man who was no high priest. 14Even the priests were no longer devoted to the service of the altar, but they treated the temple with contempt. By neglecting the sacrifices, they hurried to participate in the lawless wrestling spectacles in the arena as soon as the discus-throwing event was announced. 15They ignored their ancestral honors and sought after Greek status symbols instead. 16For this reason a dangerous situation engulfed them. Those same people to whom they were devoted and whose way of life they wished to imitate became their enemies and inflicted punishment on them. 17To be ungodly in the face of the divine laws isn’t a light matter, as the following events would reveal.

18Once when the king was present at the athletic games they held every five years in Tyre, 19the evil Jason sent residents of Jerusalem who were now citizens of Antioch as his envoys, carrying three hundred silver drachmen[k] for the sacrifice to Hercules. Because it was inappropriate, the envoys didn’t think it was right to use these funds for sacrifice. Instead, they applied the expense to something else. 20So although Jason designated this sum for a sacrifice to Hercules, the envoys spent it on equipping warships.

21After Menestheus’ son Apollonius was sent to Egypt for the coronation of Ptolemy Philometor as king, Antiochus thought

[i]Or *place* [j]Gk *acropolis* [k]A drachme is equivalent in value to a typical day’s wage.

about his own security because he had received a report that the Egyptian king was
hostile toward his government. So after
sailing to Joppa, he came to Jerusalem.
22 Jason received him magnificently, and
the people of the city welcomed him with
torches and shouts. Then Antiochus took
his army to Phoenicia.

Menelaus as high priest

23 Three years later, Jason sent Menelaus (brother of the previously mentioned
Simon) to bring funds to the king and settle
the accounts of some urgent business matters. 24 When he was introduced to the king,
he honored him with an air of authority
and bought the high priesthood for himself, outbidding Jason by 17,100 pounds
of silver. 25 When he received the king's
assent, he turned up holding no qualifica-
tions of the high priesthood but instead
displaying the temper of a cruel tyrant and
the wrath of a savage beast. 26 So Jason,
who had replaced his brother in an unjust
manner, was now displaced by another and
forced to escape to Ammonitis. 27 Menelaus
took authority but didn't send any of the
promised money to the king. 28 Sostratus
the commander of the elevated fortress[l]
demanded settlement of the debt, for he
had the responsibility of collecting payment. Finally, the two were summoned by
the king. 29 Menelaus left behind as deputy
of the high priesthood his own brother
Lysimachus, and Sostratus left Crates,
who was commander of the troops from
Cyprus.

30 While these things were happening,
the people of Tarsus and Mallus rebelled
when their cities were given as a gift to
Antiochis, the king's secondary wife. 31 The
king swiftly set off to restore order to
the situation, leaving Andronicus, one of
his high-ranking officials, as his deputy.
32 Menelaus recognized an opportunity,
seized some of the temple's gold equipment, and made them a gift to Andronicus,
though he had already sold some of them
in Tyre and the surrounding cities. 33 When
he became aware of what was happening,
Onias made accusations against Menelaus
after arriving at a safe and scared place in
Daphne near Antioch. 34 So Menelaus took
Andronicus aside and urged him to do away
with Onias. Andronicus came to Onias and
[m]persuaded him by deception, extending
his strong hand with solemn pledges,[n] to
come out of safety despite his fear. Then
with no regard for justice, he did away with
him on the spot. 35 For this reason, not
only Jews but also many other people were
grieved and angry over the wicked murder
of this man. 36 When the king had returned
from the region of Cilicia, the Jews in the
city and some Greeks, feeling hatred for
the senseless killing of Onias, obtained an
audience with him. 37 Antiochus was deeply
grieved, moved to pity and tears, because of
the modest behavior and good conduct of
the dead man. 38 Burning with anger, he immediately stripped off Andronicus' purple
robe, tore off his clothes, and dragged him
around the whole city to the place where he
had wrongfully killed Onias. There he rid
the world of the murderer, giving him the
punishment he deserved from the Lord.

39 With Menelaus' approval, Lysimachus
committed many sacrilegious acts against
the city. There was a report that he had
smuggled much of the temple's gold equipment abroad, so the populace gathered
together against Lysimachus. 40 Because
the crowds were aroused and furious, Lysimachus armed three thousand men and
incited cruel force under the leadership of
a certain Auranus, a man as senseless as
he was old. 41 When the people saw Lysimachus' assault, they grabbed stones and
blocks of wood—some even took handfuls
of ashes—and they hurled these at Lysimachus' men, causing great confusion. 42 In
the end, they wounded many, killed some,
and forced all of them to flee. They overpowered and killed the temple plunderer
Lysimachus near the treasury.

43 The people brought charges against
Menelaus regarding these matters. 44 When
the king arrived in Tyre, the council of el-

[l]Gk *acropolis* [m]Correction; Gk uncertain [n]Correction; Gk uncertain

ders sent three men to present the case
before him. 45 But Menelaus, without an
ally, promised enough money to Ptolemy,
Dorymenes' son, to gain the king's support. 46 So Ptolemy took the king aside into
a royal porch area, as though to get some
fresh air. He convinced the king to change
his mind. 47 So Menelaus, the cause of all
the evil, was allowed to leave court acquit-
ted of all charges, but the wretched envoys,
who would have been found innocent even
had they pleaded their case before Scythians, were falsely condemned to death.
48 As a result, these men, who had spoken
in defense of the city, the people, and the
temple equipment, were abruptly subjected
to an unjust penalty. 49 For this reason, to
show their hatred at such twisted justice,
even the Tyrians gave generously so that
the men could have an impressive funeral.
50 But, through the greed of those in power,
Menelaus remained in office and persisted
in evil as a great conspirator against the
citizens.

Antiochus robs the temple

5 At about this time, Antiochus made his
second invasion of Egypt. 2 For about
forty days, there were visions of soldiers
on horses running through the air around
the city. They wore gold garments and were
armed with spears and 3 with drawn swords.
They organized companies of cavalry, each
attacking and counterattacking, wielding shields and spears and shooting arrows. Gold ornaments and armor gleamed
brightly. 4 As a result, everyone hoped that
the visions were a good sign. 5 When a false
rumor spread that Antiochus had died,
Jason took no fewer than a thousand soldiers and made an unexpected assault on
the city. When the troops on the wall had
been defeated, and the city had been seized
at last, Menelaus fled into the elevated
fortress.[o] 6 Jason mercilessly slaughtered
his own citizens. He failed to realize military success against one's own people is the
greatest misfortune but thought that he
was winning trophies from his enemies and
not from his fellow citizens. 7 But he didn't
gain the government; instead, he received
shame as a result of his plot and again fled
as a fugitive into Ammonite country. 8 Finally, he came to a miserable end. Brought
up on charges before Aretas the Arab tyrant, he fled from city to city, chased by everyone. Hated as a traitor to the laws and
loathed as the murderer of his native land
and citizens, he was cast ashore in Egypt.
9 He, who had exiled many from their homeland, died in a foreign land after he sailed
to the Spartans to seek protection because
of their kinship. 10 So the one who had cast
out a crowd of corpses to lie unburied died
without mourning and received no funeral
or place in his ancestral burial plot.

11 When the news of these events reached
the king, he thought Judea was in revolt.
So he broke camp and marched from Egypt
while wild with emotion, and took the city
by force. 12 He commanded his soldiers to
cut down without mercy anyone they met
and to slaughter those fleeing into their
houses. 13 They killed young and old, murdered adolescents, women and children, and
slaughtered virgins and infants. 14 Over a
three-day period, eighty thousand people's
lives were ruined. Forty thousand were
killed in hand-to-hand fighting, and no
fewer than those slaughtered were sold as
slaves. 15 Not content with these measures,
he dared to enter into the holiest temple of
all the earth, guided by Menelaus, who had
become a traitor to the laws and to his native land. 16 Clutching the holy equipment
with polluted and unclean hands, Antiochus
made off with them and the things donated
by other kings to increase the prestige, glory,
and honor of the holy place. 17 Antiochus was
really pleased with himself, not realizing the
Lord had become angry for a short time because of the sins of those who lived in the
city. For this reason, he had shut his eyes to
the holy temple.[p] 18 If they hadn't previously
been involved in so many sins, Antiochus
would have been forced to abandon his
rashness and been defeated at once when
he attacked, just like Heliodorus (the one

[o] Gk *acropolis* [p] Or *place*

King Seleucus sent to inspect the treasury). [19]But the Lord didn't choose the nation because of the place, but the place because of the nation. [20]So the temple[q] also shared the misfortunes of the nation, but afterward it also shared in its good fortunes. That which the almighty abandoned in his wrath would again be restored with all glory when the nation was reconciled to the great Lord.

[21]Antiochus carried away 102,600 pounds of silver from the temple and hurried back to Antioch, imagining in his pride and arrogance that it was possible to sail across the land and march across the sea. [22]He left governors who mistreated the people. In Jerusalem there was Philip of the Phrygians, who had a manner more barbarous than that of the man who appointed him. [23]In Mount Gerizim there was Andronicus, and in addition there was Menelaus, who treated the citizens worse than the others. In his hostility against the Jewish citizens, [24]Antiochus sent Apollonius, a Mysian leader of twenty-two thousand soldiers, with the command to slaughter all adult men but to sell the women and children into slavery. [25]When Apollonius arrived in Jerusalem, he pretended to be peaceable. He waited until the holy Sabbath day to take advantage of the Jewish rest from work, and then he led an armed parade of his troops. [26]He suddenly killed with swords all those who had come out to see the spectacle. While running into the city with his foot soldiers, he slaughtered a large number of the crowd. [27]But Judas, also known as the Maccabee, and about ten men with him, fled into the highlands where he (along with those accompanying him) managed to avoid defiling themselves by living like wild animals: they ate grass for food.

Judaism is outlawed

6 Shortly afterward the king sent out an Athenian elder[r] to force the Jews to turn away from their ancestral laws and stop living according to God's laws. [2]He was also ordered to defile the temple in Jerusalem and to rename it for Zeus Olympus, and to rename the temple in Mount Gerizim for Zeus, Friend of Strangers,[s] just as the people living there requested. [3]The onslaught of this evil was severe and hard for all to bear. [4]The Gentiles filled the temple with wild partying and sexual indulgence. They were entertaining themselves with prostitutes and having sex with women in the priestly chambers. In addition, they carried in unfit things, [5]and the altar was illegally covered with offerings forbidden by the laws. [6]It was impossible to keep the Sabbath or the ancestral festivals, or even simply to profess to be a Jew. [7]Instead, out of bitter necessity, they had to observe the birthday of the king each month by eating the organs of sacrificial animals. When the Festival of Dionysus arrived, they were forced to take part in a procession honoring Dionysus, holding ivy wreaths. [8]At Ptolemais' suggestion,[t] a decision was announced to the neighboring Greek cities that they should adopt the same policy against the Jews and that they should be made to eat the sacrificial portions, [9]and that those who refused to change to Greek practices should be slaughtered. At that point it was easy to see the miserable state that had arrived. [10]For instance, they brought forward two women who had circumcised their sons, with their infants hanging from their breasts. They dragged them around the city publicly, then hurled them down from the city wall. [11]Others gathered secretly into caverns nearby to keep the seventh day, but they were betrayed to Philip. They were all burned together because they were reluctant to defend themselves, out of respect for the most sacred day.

[12]So I urge those stumbling upon this scroll not to shrink back because of these misfortunes but to understand that these punishments weren't for the destruction of our people but for their discipline. [13]It is a sign of great kindness that those Jews who acted immorally weren't left alone for very long but experienced punishments immediately. [14]With other nations the Lord patiently delays punishment until they fill up

[q]Or *place* [r]Or *Geron*, an Athenian [s]Gk *Xenios* [t]Or *At the suggestion of the people of Ptolemais*

the full measure of their sins, but with us
he decided to deal differently, and is exacting retribution on us before [15]our sins reach
their peak. [16]Therefore, he never withdraws
his mercy from us. Although disciplining us
with misfortunes, God doesn't forsake his
own people. [17]Only let this be said to us as
a reminder. After this brief digression, it is
necessary to go on with the narrative.

Martyrs for the faith

[18]A certain Eleazar, one of the leading scribes, elderly in age and with a most
dignified outward appearance, was being
compelled to open his mouth and eat pork.
[19]But preferring death with honor to life
with religious defilement, he proceeded
voluntarily to the torture instrument,
[20]spitting out the meat. In this he showed
how everyone ought to stand fast and reject what isn't lawful to taste despite the
intense desire to live.

[21]But those in charge of the unlawful sacrifice, because they had known the man for
a long time, took him aside in private and
urged him to bring meat that was lawful,
prepared beforehand by himself, and then
pretend to eat the meat from the sacrifice
that the king commanded. [22]By doing this
he might escape death and attain friendly
treatment because of his old friendship
with them. [23]But adopting a dignified perspective worthy of his seniority, his distinguished old age and the gray hair he had
acquired, and worthy of his excellent conduct from childhood, and, moreover, worthy of the holy and God-created laws, he
declared to them to send him to the grave[u]
immediately: [24]"It's not worthy of our old
age to act out such a role. Otherwise, many
of the young would assume wrongly that Eleazar the 90-year-old had changed to a foreign way of life. [25]If I acted out this charade
for the sake of living a moment longer, I
would mislead them, and I would be defiled
and dishonored in my old age. [26]Even if I
escaped the punishment of human beings
for the moment, I would certainly not escape the hands of the almighty—whether
alive or dead. [27]So I give up my life courageously now to show myself worthy of my
old age, [28]and to leave a fine example for
the young people of how to die a good death
with eagerness and dignity for the revered
and sacred laws." After he spoke he immediately approached the torture instrument.
[29][v]Those who had shown goodwill toward
him earlier now felt hostility toward him,[w]
because the words he had spoken seemed
insane to them. [30]When his life was about
to end from the beating, he groaned, "It is
clear to the Lord with his sacred knowledge
that, although I could have been saved from
death, I endure in my body harsh pain from
this beating, yet in my soul I cheerfully suffer these things because I respect him." [31]In
this manner he died, and his own death left
behind a most noble and memorable example of virtue not only for the youth but also
for the majority of his nation.

7 There were also seven brothers who
were arrested along with their mother.
The king was trying to compel them to eat
the forbidden pork by torturing them with
whips and cords. [2]One of them, speaking
on behalf of the others, said, "What do
you hope to ask and learn from us? We are
prepared to die rather than sin against our
ancestral laws." [3]The king became angry
and commanded frying pans and caul-
drons to be heated. [4]As soon as they were
hot, he commanded that the one acting
as spokesman have his tongue cut out, be
scalped, and have his hands and feet cut
off while the rest of his brothers and his
mother watched. [5]After the brother was
maimed and utterly helpless, the king commanded him to be brought to the fire and
fried alive. Although the smoke from the
pan had spread widely, the brothers and
their mother encouraged each other to die
honorably, saying, [6]"The Lord God truly
watches over us and will come to our aid.
Moses testified to this in his song against
them, saying, 'God will have compassion on
his servants.'"[x]

[7]After the first brother died in this manner, they led forward the second one with

[u]Gk *Hades* [v]Correction; Gk uncertain [w]Correction; Gk uncertain [x]See Deut 32:36.

mockery. They ripped off the skin of his
head along with the hair and demanded,
"Will you eat before every part of your body
is punished limb by limb?"
[8]But he answered in his native language,
"Not at all." Therefore, this brother also received in turn the same punishment as the
first. [9]With his last breath he said, "You,
who are marked out for vengeance, may
take our present life, but the king of the
universe for whose laws we die will resur-
rect us again to eternal life."
[10]After this, the third one was mocked.
When it was demanded, he put out his
tongue quickly, extended his hands courageously, [11]and stated with dignity, "I have
received these limbs from heaven, and I
give them up for the sake of God's laws. But
I hope to recover them from God again."
[12]The king and those with him marveled at
the young man's spirit, since he considered
his agonies nothing.
[13]After this one had died, the tormenters
tortured the fourth brother as well. [14]When
the end was approaching, he said, "Death at
the hands of humans is preferable, since we
look forward to the hope that God gives of
being raised by him. But for you there will
be no resurrection to life."
[15]Immediately afterward, they led the
fifth brother forward and began to torture
him. [16]While looking at the king he said,
"You, though human, have power among
human beings and do what you want. But
don't think that God has abandoned our
people. [17]Just wait and observe his great
strength, when God will torture you and
your children."
[18]After him they brought forward the
sixth brother. As he was about to die, he
said, "Don't deceive yourself in vain. We
suffer these things because of our own sins
against our God. Things worthy of wonder
have happened. [19]But don't think you will
escape unpunished after trying to fight
against God."
[20]The mother was particularly amazing
and worthy of an honorable memory. She
watched her seven sons die in the course
of a single day but accepted it with a stout
heart because of her hope in the Lord.
[21]She encouraged each of them in their native language. Filled with noble thoughts,
she fired up her womanly reasoning with
manly courage, saying to them, [22]"I don't
know how you grew in my womb, nor did
I grant the breath of life to you or arrange
what makes you who you are. [23]For this reason, the creator of the world—who brought
about the beginning of humanity and
searched out the origin of all things—will
again mercifully give you both spirit and
life, since you disregard yourselves because
of his laws."
[24]Antiochus thought that he was being
treated with contempt and was suspicious
of the tone of her voice. So he appealed to
the youngest son, since he was still alive,
not only through words but also through
solemn pledges. If the young man turned
from his ancestral practices, Antiochus
promised him, he would make him both
rich and prosperous, he would be considered a political advisor,[y] and he would be
entrusted with public affairs. [25]When the
young man wouldn't accept the offer by any
means, the king appealed to the mother to
counsel the boy to save himself. [26]After a
great deal of urging, she agreed to try to
persuade her son. [27]By leaning toward her
son and mocking the savage tyrant, she
spoke in their native language: "Son, pity
me who carried you in the womb nine
months, nursed you for three years, nurtured you, and brought you into this stage
of life with care. [28]I beg you, child, to look at
heaven and earth. See everything that is in
them and know that God made these things
from nothing, and created humankind in
the same way. [29]Don't fear this killer but
prove worthy of your brothers. Accept
death so that in God's mercy I should recover you with your brothers."
[30]Just at the moment when she finished
speaking,[z] the young man said, "What are
you all waiting for? I don't intend to obey
the king's order, but I hear the command
of the Law given to our ancestors through

[y]Or *Friend* [z]Correction; Gk uncertain

Moses. 31 But you, King, who have invented all sorts of evil against the Hebrews, will by no means escape God's power. 32 We are suffering because of our own sins. 33 If our living Lord is angry for a short time in order to rebuke and discipline us, he will again be reconciled with his own servants. 34 But you, unholy man, the most bloodstained of all people, don't be so proud without having cause. Bloated by futile hope, you raise up your hand against the children of heaven. 35 You haven't at all escaped the judgment of the almighty God, who oversees all. 36 Now our brothers, who endured pain for a short time, have been given eternal life under God's covenant, but you will suffer the penalty of your arrogance by the righteous judgment of God. 37 Just like my brothers, I give up both body and life for the ancestral laws. I call upon God to be merciful to the nation without delay, and to make you confess, after you suffer trials and diseases, that only he is God. 38 Also I hope through me and my brothers to stop the anger of the almighty, who is justly punishing our entire nation." 39 Bitterly annoyed at the young boy's contempt, the king grew angry and treated him worse than the others. 40 And this brother then died with integrity, trusting entirely in the Lord. 41 Last, after her sons, the mother died.

42 So then with regard to the eating of sacrificial meats and the extreme tortures they suffered, let this account be sufficient.

Judas the Maccabee revolts

8 Judas, also named the Maccabee, and his companions went secretly into the villages and called together their relatives and those who continued to follow Judaism, enlisting a force of about six thousand soldiers. 2 They called on the Lord to look on the people who were oppressed by all, to take pity on the temple that was degraded by ungodly people, 3 and to have mercy on the city that was being destroyed and about to be leveled. They called on the Lord to listen to the shed blood of those who had appealed to God for help, 4 to remember the needless massacre of innocent infants, and to show his hatred of the evil things said against his name. 5 Once he organized his army, the Maccabee couldn't be stopped by the Gentiles, because the Lord's wrath had turned into mercy. 6 He would come suddenly into towns and villages, set them ablaze, capture a number of the strategically important places, and put many of the enemy to flight. 7 He especially found the night advantageous for such attacks. Talk of his good courage spread everywhere.

8 Philip saw how Judas was progressing little by little and gaining ground with each success, so he wrote to Ptolemy the governor of Coele-Syria and Phoenicia to come to the aid of the royal government. 9 Nicanor, Patroclus' son, one of the king's most important political advisors,[a] was immediately chosen and sent with a military unit of no fewer than twenty thousand men of various nationalities to eliminate Judea's entire population. He also sent with him Gorgias, a general experienced in military affairs. 10 Nicanor agreed to raise the payment that the king owed the Romans—114,000 pounds of silver—by selling the Jewish prisoners of war. 11 Immediately, he sent a message into the coastal cities, summoning them to purchase Jews as slaves, setting the price at fifty-seven pounds of silver for every ninety persons. But he didn't anticipate the judgment that was coming from the almighty.

12 When news of Nicanor's plan reached Judas, he told those with him about the imminent appearance of the military force. 13 The cowardly and those who didn't trust God's judgment ran away and hid themselves. 14 Some were selling all they possessed while at the same time calling on the Lord to rescue those whom Nicanor had sold even before they met. 15 They asked that God do this, if not for their sake then for the sake of the covenants with their ancestors, and because he had called them by his revered and glorious name.

16 The Maccabee gathered around him approximately six thousand men. He encouraged them not to be terrified by their

[a]Or *Friends*

enemies nor to fear the great number of
Gentiles coming at them unjustly. Rather,
they were to fight honorably 17and keep
before their eyes the outrage committed
unlawfully in the holy place, the torture
of the scorned city, and the overthrow
of their ancestral way of life. 18"They rely
on weapons and daring," he said, "but we
trust in the almighty God, who is able to
strike down with a single nod those coming against us—and even the whole world."
19He also gave them examples of when God
helped their ancestors, such as when one
hundred eighty-five thousand of the enemy
died during the time of Sennacherib, 20or
the battle with the Galatians in Babylonia. A
total of eight thousand Jewish troops went
into action along with four thousand Macedonians, who got into severe difficulty, yet
the eight thousand Jewish forces, with the
assistance they received from heaven, killed
one hundred twenty thousand of the enemy
and took the spoils of war.

21With such words he so encouraged them
that they were prepared to die for their laws
and homeland. He divided the army into
four parts and 22appointed his brothers as
commanders of each unit. Simon, Joseph,
and Jonathan each commanded fifteen
hundred men, 23while Eleazar was publicly
to read aloud the holy scroll.

Giving the watchword of "God's help,"
Judas took command of the first military
unit and attacked Nicanor. 24With the almighty as their ally, they slaughtered more
than nine thousand of the enemy, wounding and disabling many of Nicanor's army
and driving them all to flight. 25They seized
the funds of those who came to buy them.
After pursuing them a long way, they returned while there was still time 26because
it was the day before the Sabbath. For that
reason they didn't continue to pursue
them. 27After collecting the arms of the
enemy and stripping them of their spoils,
they kept the Sabbath, praising and giving
thanks to the Lord for saving them that
day and for giving them this initial sign
of mercy. 28When the Sabbath had ended,
they shared the loot with those who had
suffered torture, with the widows, and with
the orphans. They divided up the rest with
their children. 29When they had completed
these final tasks, they made a common appeal and prayed for the merciful Lord to be
reconciled finally with his servants.

30In close combat with the supporters
of Timothy and Bacchides, they killed more
than twenty thousand men and easily took
control over some high fortresses. The war
spoils that they took they divided equally
between themselves and those suffering
torture: the orphans, the widows, and also
the elderly. 31They carefully placed the captured armor all together in strategic places,
but the rest of the spoils they carried into
Jerusalem. 32They killed the commander of
Timothy's troops, a most ungodly man who
had caused grief to many Jews. 33While
celebrating victory in their homeland, they
burned alive those who had set on fire the
sacred gates, including Callisthenes, who
had fled into a small house, so that he received the just reward for his sin.[b] 34But the
utterly corrupt Nicanor, who had invited
one thousand merchants for the sale of the
Jews, 35was humiliated with the Lord's help
by those he despised the most. He stripped
off his stately uniform and traveled into
Antioch by the inland road like a lone fugitive, having succeeded only in destroying his own army. 36The one who accepted
the mission to collect the tribute for the
Romans from the Jerusalem prisoners of
war announced publicly that the Jews had
a defender and that, as a result, the Jews
couldn't be defeated because they followed
God's ordained laws.

Antiochus retreats and dies

9 About this time Antiochus retreated in
confusion out of the region of Persia.
2When he had come into Persepolis, he attempted to loot the temple and take over
the city. However, he was decisively beaten
when the populace took up arms. Antiochus
fled from the inhabitants and had to make
a shameful retreat. 3News reached him at

[b]Correction; Gk uncertain

Ecbatana of what happened to Nicanor and to Timothy's forces. 4 Swelling with rage, he planned to make the Jews pay for his own calamity when he was recently forced to flee. So he ordered his chariot driver to keep driving without stopping in order to complete the journey, but the judgment of heaven was already on him. He had said in his arrogance, "When I get to Jerusalem, I will turn it into a mass grave for the Jews."

5 But the all-seeing Lord God of Israel struck him with a deadly and invisible blow. As soon as he had uttered this statement, he developed a pain in his stomach and a cruel torment in his internal organs from which he could find no relief. 6 This was altogether just, since he had tortured the inner organs of others with many extraordinary torments. 7 By no means, however, did it put a stop to his arrogance. In his contempt, a fiery anger against the Jews still filled him, and he issued a command to increase the speed of the journey. Then he fell from the chariot as it rushed along, and he suffered a severe accident that caused him pain all over his body. 8 Only a short time earlier, he had thought in his superhuman arrogance to command the waves of the sea and to be able to place the mountain peaks in a pair of scales. Now he was thrown down to the ground and was carried in a stretcher[c] for the remainder of his journey, demonstrating God's power to all. 9 Worms issued from the eyes[d] of this ungodly man. While he was living in pain and in agony, his flesh was rotting away, and the whole camp stank of rottenness from his smell. 10 The one who had formerly thought that he could touch the stars of heaven couldn't be transported by anyone because of the intense, unbearable stench.

11 From this point on, he began to lose arrogance. He felt devastated and became aware of the divine punishment, suffering intense pain every moment. 12 Unable to put up with his own odor, he said, "It is fair to submit to God and for humans to stop thinking that they are God's equals." 13 This repulsive individual solemnly promised to the Lord (although God no longer had mercy on him), declaring that 14 the holy city, to which he was rushing to knock down to the ground and turn into a mass cemetery, was now free. 15 And he would make all Jews equal to the Athenians, even though previously he had considered them unworthy of burial but fit only for bird food, and their infants fit for animals to prey upon. 16 He would adorn the holy temple, which he had formerly looted, with the most beautiful offerings. He would restore the temple equipment many times over and would give liberally from his own revenues to the expenses for the sacrifices. 17 In addition, he would become a Jew and would visit every inhabited place, announcing publicly God's power. 18 When his pains didn't diminish in any way—for God's judgment had come upon him justly—and he had given up hope, he wrote to the Jews a letter of appeal. This was the content:

19 To the worthy Jewish citizens, from the king and governor Antiochus. Greetings and health and prosperity.

20 If you are in good health and your children and affairs are prospering, I give thanks to God with great joy, having hope in heaven, 21 remembering with affection your honor and goodwill.[e] After returning from Persia and falling ill, which created a serious situation, I regarded it as necessary to think of the common safety of all the people. 22 I haven't abandoned my situation as hopeless but rather hold on to hope that I might recover from the illness. 23 I have also considered, however, that my father (on the occasions when he fought in the upper regions) used to appoint a successor to rule. 24 He did this so that if anything should happen contrary to expectation or even if there should be some unwelcome news, people throughout the country would know that someone was left behind to govern and wouldn't be deprived of their peace of mind. 25 Moreover, observing how neighboring dynasties and kingdoms wait for

[c] Gk *litter* [d] Or *body* [e] Correction 9:20-21; Gk uncertain

the right moment and look forward with anticipation to what might happen next, I appoint my son Antiochus as king. Many times when I had to hurry to the upper provinces, I entrusted and commended him to most of you. I have written these orders to him as well. 26 I call on you then, and request each one of you—remembering my benefits both public and private—to be faithful toward me and my son. 27 I firmly believe he will follow my example closely, acting with kindness and generosity, with the intention of accommodating himself to you.

28 Then the murderer, who also showed God the greatest disrespect, suffered the worst things, just as he had treated others. His life ended pitifully in a foreign area in the mountains. 29 Philip, who was his close friend, transported his body home. But he was suspicious of the king's son Antiochus, so he fled to Ptolemy Philometor in Egypt.

10 The Maccabee and his companions, with the Lord leading them, recovered the temple and the city. 2 They demolished the altars that the foreigners built near the marketplace, as well as the sacred precincts. 3 They cleansed the temple and made another altar. Then they struck flints to make fire and they offered up sacrifices after a lapse of two years, and they prepared incense, lamps, and the sacred loaves. 4 After they had done these things, they bowed to the ground and pleaded with the Lord that they would not experience such misfortunes again, but if they should ever sin, they would be disciplined by him with fairness and not turned over to slanderous and barbaric nations. 5 On the anniversary of the temple's defilement by foreigners, on that very day, the sanctuary was purified, on the twenty-fifth of the month, which is Kislev.[f] 6 They celebrated eight days with cheer in a manner like the Festival of Booths, remembering how during the previous Festival of Booths they had been roaming about in mountains and caverns like animals. 7 So they held ivy wands, beautiful branches, and also palm leaves, and offered hymns to the one who had made the purification of his own temple[g] possible. 8 They voted and issued a public decree that all Jews should celebrate these days each year. 9 And so the matters concerning Antiochus called Epiphanes came to an end.

Wars of Antiochus Eupator

10 We will now report about what occurred under Antiochus Eupator, that ungodly man's son, summarizing the distressful events of the dreadful wars. 11 When this man received the kingdom, he appointed a certain Lysias as supreme governor of Coele-Syria and Phoenicia. 12 Ptolemy, called Macron, took the lead in showing justice to the Jews because of the wrongs done to them, and he tried to handle matters concerning them peacefully. 13 Because of this, the king's political advisors[h] accused him before Eupator and branded him a traitor. They accused him of abandoning Cyprus after Philometor had entrusted him with it, and of going back to Antiochus Epiphanes. Because Ptolemy no longer commanded the respect of his high office,[i] he poisoned himself and died.

14 Gorgias, who became governor of the region, maintained a mercenary army and waged constant war against the Jews. 15 In addition to him, the Idumeans who controlled some strategic fortresses harassed the Jews. They gave safe harbor to those who were driven from Jerusalem and tried to keep the war going. 16 The Maccabee and his followers were praying and calling on God to help them. They rushed against the Idumean fortresses. 17 After mounting a vigorous attack, they gained control of all the sites and held off those fighting on the wall. They slaughtered all those they encountered, killing at least twenty thousand. 18 When no fewer than nine thousand fled into two towers well equipped for a siege, 19 the Maccabee departed to other places that needed his urgent attention, leaving Simon, Joseph, and Zacchaeus with a sufficient force for the siege of these towers. 20 Some men in the towers bribed

[f] November–December [g] Or *place* [h] Or *Friends* [i] Correction; Gk uncertain

greedy people around Simon. These people in turn, after receiving seventy thousand drachmen,[j] allowed some of the enemy to slip away. 21When the Maccabee found out what happened, he gathered the leaders of the people and accused them of selling their brothers for silver by setting free the enemy. 22He executed the traitors and then quickly took the two towers. 23He was successful in all things relating to war and killed more than twenty thousand men in the two towers.

24Timothy, who was defeated by the Jews earlier, assembled a large number of foreign troops and brought many horses from Asia. He arrived intending to fight against Judea. 25As he approached, the Maccabee's followers prayed to God for help. Sprinkling their heads with dust, wrapping themselves with mourning clothes, 26and falling down opposite the foundation of the altar, they begged God to be gracious to them, to be hostile to those hostile to them, and to be an opponent of their opponents, just as the Law promises.[k] 27After praying, they took up arms and moved out some distance from the city. They drew near to their enemies and then halted. 28At dawn, each side attacked. As an assurance of success and victory, the Jews had their courage and their trust in the Lord, but the Greeks made rage the driving force of their struggles. 29When the battle became fierce, five magnificent men from heaven appeared to the enemy, riding on horses with gold bridles and leading the Jews. 30Two of them took the Maccabee between them, completely protecting him against harm with their own armor, and they shot arrows and thunderbolts into the ranks of their opponents. Thrown into confusion by blindness, the enemy then ran off in different directions, filled with terror. 31Twenty thousand five hundred foot soldiers and six hundred cavalry were cut down.

32But Timothy himself fled into a fortress called Gazara, a secured area commanded by Chaereas. 33The followers of the Maccabee eagerly attacked the area for four days. 34Because the place was strongly fortified, those inside verbally insulted the enemy, uttering unlawful words. 35As the fifth day began, twenty of the young men among the Maccabee's followers burned with anger because of the verbal insults, and they bravely attacked the wall. In savage fury, they cut down anyone they found. 36As this destruction occurred, others also went up after them against those inside, set the towers on fire, stoked the flames, and burned the offenders alive. When others tore down the gates, letting in the rest of the army, they took the city. 37They slaughtered Timothy, who had hidden himself in a cistern, as well as his brother Chaereas and also Apollophanes. 38With these things accomplished, they praised the Lord with hymns and thanks for showing kindness to Israel and giving victory to them.

Lysias and the Jews

11 Lysias, the guardian and relative of the king, was in charge of the government. After a very short time he became extremely displeased at what happened. 2He led eighty thousand troops and all his cavalry against the Jews. He intended to make the city a Greek territory, 3to make the temple subject to tribute like the sacred sites of other nations, and to put the high priesthood on sale every year. 4He gave no thought whatsoever to the power of God but was inflated by his tens of thousands of foot soldiers, his thousands of cavalry, and his eighty elephants. 5He entered Judea, drew near to Beth-zur (a strongly fortified town about a half mile[l] from Jerusalem), and attacked it. 6When the Maccabee's followers received information that Lysias was surrounding the fortresses, they and all the people begged the Lord with laments and tears to send a good angel to save Israel. 7The Maccabee was himself the first to take up arms, and he urged the others to run risks as he did and to come to the aid of their brothers. They dashed out at once, ready for action. 8While they were still near Jerusalem, a horseman

[j]A drachme is equivalent in value to a typical day's wage. [k]See Exod 23:22. [l]Or *five stades* or 3,021 feet; a stadion is a linear measure of approximately 607 feet.

in white garments and wearing full body
armor made of gold appeared to them
and led them. 9All together they praised
the merciful God, and their souls were
strengthened. They prepared themselves to
attack not only men but also the most fierce
animals and even the iron walls. 10They
proceeded in battle order, having a heavenly ally thanks to the Lord's mercy toward
them. 11Charging like lions against their
enemies, they took down eleven thousand
foot soldiers and sixteen hundred horses,
and they put all the rest to flight. 12Most of
them escaped wounded and naked, while
Lysias himself escaped by disgracefully running away. 13Showing intelligence, Lysias
pondered the reality of this defeat and realized that the Hebrews, assisted by God's
power, couldn't be defeated. So he sent a
messenger 14and persuaded them to come
to a just settlement in all issues concerning
civil rights. He also persuaded[m] them that
he would convince the king to become their
friend. 15The Maccabee consented to Lysias'
proposals, thinking it was best for all involved. Whatever the Maccabee presented
in writing to Lysias concerning the Jews,
the king granted.
16This is what Lysias' letter[n] to the Jews said:

> 17Lysias to the Jewish community.
> Greetings!
>
> John and Absalom, the men you sent,
> gave me the administrative document
> copied below and made a request con-
> cerning its contents. 18Whatever needed
> to be presented in person to the king,
> I stated plainly; and whatever was fea-
> sible, he has granted. 19If then you will
> preserve goodwill toward the govern-
> ment, in the future I will attempt to pro-
> mote your well-being. 20But concerning
> the details, I commanded these men to
> confer with you, along with my repre-
> sentatives. 21Farewell!
>
> Year 148, the twenty-fourth day of
> the month of Dios Korinthos.[o]

22This is what the king's letter said:

> 23King Antiochus to his brother
> Lysias. Greetings!
>
> After our father joined the gods, it
> was my desire that those who want calm
> be left alone to tend to their own busi-
> ness. 24We heard that the Jews haven't
> agreed to change to the Greek way of
> life, as our father wanted, but preferred
> their own way of life and asked to be
> permitted to have their own law. 25Since
> we would choose for this nation to be
> free from unrest, we have decided to
> restore to them their temple and to let
> them conduct their life according to the
> customs of their ancestors. 26You would
> do well, then, to send a message to them
> and assure them of friendship, so that
> they might know our policy and be at
> ease and live cheerfully, achieving their
> own goals.

27This is what the king's letter to the nation
said:

> King Antiochus to the Jewish council
> of elders and to all other Jews. Greetings!
>
> 28If you are well, it is what we wish.
> We are also in good health. 29Menelaus
> has informed us that you want to return
> home to take care of your own affairs.
> 30Those who return by the thirtieth
> of Xanthicus[p] will have our pledge of
> friendship with no need for fear. 31We
> will allow the Jews to follow their own
> dietary laws and other laws just as they
> used to do, and not let anyone bother
> them concerning any crime committed
> in ignorance. 32I have also sent Mene-
> laus to comfort you. 33Be well!
>
> Year 148, the fifteenth day of the
> month of Xanthicus.

34Also the Romans sent a letter to the Jews
that said:

> Quintus Memmius, Titus Manius, am-
> bassadors of the Romans, to the people
> of the Jews. Greetings!
>
> 35Lysias the king's relative has handed
> rights over to you, and we agree. 36But
> give consideration immediately to what-
> ever he decided to bring to the attention
> of the king; you should consider and then
> send someone immediately concerning
> your views, so that we might make sug-

[m]Correction; Gk uncertain [n]Or *letters* [o]December, 164 BCE [p]March–April; also in 11:33, 38

gestions to you, as is appropriate. We are
approaching Antioch, 37so hurry and send
someone so that we might also know of
your opinion. 38Be in good health!

Year 148, the fifteenth day of the
month of Xanthicus.

Judas' victories

12 Having reached these agreements,
Lysias returned to the king while
the Jews went back to farming. 2But some
of the regional governors—Timothy and
Apollonius (Gennaeus' son), Hieronymous
and Demophon, as well as Nicanor the
commander from Cyprus—wouldn't permit them to live in peace. 3Some men from
Joppa committed a horrible act. After calling together the Jews living among them
with their wives and children, they invited
them to go sailing in boats that they provided. They acted as if they had no hostility
against them at all. 4This was a decision
made by the city as a whole. The Jews accepted the invitation because they desired
to live together with them peaceably, and
the Jews had no suspicions. But they took
them out to sea and drowned them—no
fewer than two hundred people. 5When
Judas received news of the cruelty that had
happened to his fellow Jews, he gave orders
to his troops. 6After calling out to God the
righteous judge, he moved against the murderers of their brothers, setting fire to the
harbor by night, burning the boats, and killing those who took refuge there. 7Because a
large area of the city was secured against
his attack, he departed, intending to return
and root out the entire citizen community
of Joppa. 8He learned that the people of
Jamnia were also planning to finish off the
Jews living among them in the same way.
9So Judas mounted a night attack against
Jamnia and set its harbor and fleet on fire,
so that the gleams of light shone in Jerusalem twenty-eight miles[q] away.

10When Judas withdrew about a mile[r]
away from Jamnia, in pursuit of Timothy,
Arabs attacked him with no fewer than five
thousand men and five hundred cavalry.
11A fierce battle took place, but Judas' followers were successful because of God's
help. The defeated nomads asked Judas for
a pledge of friendship, promising to give
them some livestock and to be of service to
them in other ways. 12Judas agreed to make
peace because he thought that they might
truly be useful to them in many ways. After
pledging friendship to each other, the Arabs[s] departed into their tents.

13Judas also made an attack on a city
named Caspin, whose defenses included
a fortified bridge and surrounding walls.
It was inhabited by people from many nations. 14Because the walls had been solidly
secured and there was plenty of food for future use, the inhabitants acted disrespectfully. They not only spoke in an insulting
way to Judas' men, they were even uttering
unlawful insults against God. 15Calling out
to the great mighty one of the universe who
caused Jericho to fall in Joshua's time even
without battering rams or war engines,
Judas' forces attacked the wall furiously.
16They took the city by God's will and killed
so many men that a nearby lake a quarter
of a mile[t] wide appeared to be filled with
blood.

17Withdrawing from there, they made a
journey of ninety-four miles[u] to Charax, to
those Jews who are called Toubians. 18They
didn't find Timothy in the area because he
left the region without any success, except
that he left behind one military force in a
well-secured place. 19But the Maccabee's
commanders Dositheus and Sosipater
marched out and destroyed those Timothy left in the fortified place, killing more
than ten thousand men. 20The Maccabee,
dividing the army around him in units, set
men in command over the units and moved
quickly against Timothy, who had with him
one hundred twenty thousand foot soldiers
and twenty-five hundred horses. 21After receiving information about Judas' approach,
Timothy sent the wives and children and
their belongings ahead to a village called

[q]Or *two hundred forty stades*; a stadion is a linear measure of approximately 607 feet. [r]Or *nine stades*
[s]Or *they* [t]Or *two stades* [u]Or *seven hundred fifty stades*

Carnaim. He did this because the place was difficult to surround or attack on account of the narrowness of the approaches. [22]After Judas' first tactical unit appeared, the enemy was afraid, especially when the "one who sees all things" appeared to them. They took flight, running here and there, so that many were injured by their own comrades and pierced by the tips of their own swords. [23]Judas pursued them vigorously. Stabbing sinners left and right, he killed as many as thirty thousand men. [24]Timothy himself fell into the hands of Dositheus, Sosipater, and their men. He skillfully argued that he should be set free, persuading them that he held many parents and other relatives as prisoners who might not receive any consideration. [25]After he promised repeatedly to return them unharmed, they released him for the benefit of the safety of their relatives.

[26]Next Judas attacked Carnaim and the temple of Atargatis, killing twenty-five thousand people. [27]After overturning and destroying these places, he made war also on Ephron, a fortified city with a mixed population, where Lysias made his home. Strong young men fought bravely, however, in front of the walls where there were also many war engines and arrows. [28]Calling on the Lord who crushes the strength of the enemy, the Jews took control of the city and killed about twenty-five thousand people. [29]Then breaking camp and marching from there, they moved swiftly against Scythopolis, seventy-five miles[v] from Jerusalem. [30]But the Jews who lived there reported that the citizens of Scythopolis showed kindness and a civil attitude toward them even in times of misfortune. [31]They thanked them and encouraged them also to be well-disposed toward their people in the future as well. Then they returned to Jerusalem since the Festival of Weeks was about to begin.

[32]After the Festival of Pentecost they moved against Gorgias, the governor of Idumea. [33]He came out with three thousand foot soldiers and four hundred horses. [34]A small number of Jews fell during the battle. [35]Dositheus, one of Bacenor's men, a strong man on horseback, had seized Gorgias. Holding on to the governor's robe, he dragged him down roughly, trying to take the horrible man alive. But one of the Thracian cavalry men assaulted Dositheus, crushed his shoulder, and Gorgias escaped into Marisa. [36]The men around Esdris were fighting fiercely but became weary. Judas called out to the Lord to show himself as their ally and to lead the battle. [37]Beginning to sing hymns in the native language with a loud voice, he suddenly made an attack against Gorgias' men and defeated them.

[38]Judas took his army and came into the city of Adullam. When the seventh day arrived, they purified themselves according to custom and observed the Sabbath. [39]On the next day, it was necessary for Judas and his men to recover the bodies of the fallen and to bury them with their relatives in the ancestral tombs. [40]They found sacred charms, idols from Jamnia that the Law forbids Jews to wear, under the clothing of each of the dead. It became clear to all why these men had fallen. [41]Then they all praised the Lord, the righteous judge who makes hidden things visible. [42]They appealed to God and prayed for the sin that had been committed to be completely wiped out. The honorable Judas called on the people to keep themselves free from sin, since everyone had seen what had happened because of the sin of those who fell. [43]After taking a collection from each man, he sent the sum of two thousand silver drachmen[w] to Jerusalem to provide for a sin offering. He was acting honorably and appropriately, thinking about the resurrection. [44]If he hadn't been looking forward to the resurrection of the dead, then it would have been unnecessary and frivolous to pray for them. [45]He was looking, however, to that best reward laid up for those who die in godliness, and so this was a pious and holy thought. Thus he made an offering of reconciliation so that the dead would be forgiven of their sin.

[v]Or *six hundred stades* [w]A drachme is equivalent in value to a typical day's wage.

Events in Modein and Beth-zur

13 In year 149[x] the news reached Judas' followers that Antiochus Eupator was moving against Judea with a large army. [2]With him was Lysias, Antiochus' guardian and head of the government. Each one had a Greek force of one hundred ten thousand foot soldiers, fifty-three hundred cavalry, and twenty-two elephants, as well as three hundred chariots armed with scythes. [3]Menelaus also joined them and encouraged Antiochus with many lies, not out of a concern for the safety of his homeland but because he expected that he would be set over the government. [4]The king of kings, however, aroused Antiochus' anger against the sinner. When Lysias informed the king that this man was the cause of all the evils, Antiochus commanded that Menelaus be brought to Beroea and executed according to the custom there. [5]That place has a tower seventy-five feet tall and full of ashes with a steep rim on all sides leading into the ashes. [6]Here anyone guilty of temple robbery or other similar crimes is thrown down to their death. [7]In this manner the lawless Menelaus died. He didn't receive a proper burial. [8]This was completely just, since he had committed many sins against the altar whose fire and ashes were holy, so in ashes he died.

[9]The king became barbaric in his thoughts and intended to show the Jews far worse things than his father did. [10]When Judas learned of these things, he commanded the community to call on the Lord day and night—now if ever—to help those soon to be deprived of the Law, the homeland, and the holy temple. [11]They were to pray that the people who had recently enjoyed temporary relief not be permitted again to come under the control of slanderous nations. [12]After everyone had prayed in the same manner together—pleading with the merciful Lord with weeping and fasting and lying facedown for three days—Judas called them together and commanded them to report for duty. [13]In consultation with the elders, Judas decided to march out to determine the matter by God's help before the army of the king could enter Judah and take control of the city. [14]He left the decision to the creator of the universe and called on his men to fight to the death for the laws, temple, city, country, and citizenship. He made the region of Modein his headquarters [15]and gave his men the watchword "God's Victory." He chose the best of the young men, and attacked the king's quarters in the enemy camp at night. They killed nearly two thousand men as well as the lead elephant, stabbing its rider. [16]After they filled the camp with fear and panic, they departed in good spirits. [17]This had happened just as the day was dawning because the Lord's protection had come to Judas' aid.

[18]Having received a taste of the Jews' courage, the king made an attempt on their military positions through other tricks. [19]He moved against a well-protected watchpost of the Jews at Beth-zur, but he was pushed back. He struck again, but this time he was defeated. [20]Judas sent necessary supplies to those inside. [21]But Rhodocus from the Judean ranks gave military secrets to the enemies. When it was discovered, he was caught and imprisoned. [22]The king negotiated again with those in Beth-zur. They shared tokens of friendship. Then he went away, mounted an attack against Judas' men, and was defeated. [23]Meanwhile, he received news that Philip (left in charge of the government in Antioch) had rebelled. He was entirely caught off guard, and so offered reconciliation to the Jews, accepted their terms, swore to respect all their rights, and reached a settlement. He also offered a sacrifice, honored the temple, and was generous toward the place. [24]He welcomed the Maccabee and made Hegemonides governor from Ptolemais to Gerar. [25]Then he went to Ptolemais. The people of Ptolemais found it hard to accept the agreement. They became very angry and wanted to annul the terms of the treaty. [26]In defense Lysias spoke publicly as well as he could and convinced and appeased them. After gaining their support, he marched into Antioch. So

[x]163 BCE

this is how the advance and withdrawal of the king occurred.

Alcimus and Nicanor

14 Three years later it was reported to Judas' followers that Demetrius, Seleucus' son, had sailed into the harbor at Tripolis with a strong army and a fleet. 2It was also reported that he had taken possession of the country, killing Antiochus and his guardian Lysias. 3A certain Alcimus, who had become high priest earlier but had willingly defiled himself during the revolt, became aware that he was no longer safe and that he would no longer have access to the holy altar. 4He approached King Demetrius in the year 151,[y] bringing him a gold crown, a palm tree, and some customary gifts of olive branches from the temple. He kept quiet that day 5but waited for the right opportunity to accomplish his folly. Finally, Demetrius called him into the council to ask him about the condition of the Jews and their frame of mind. He replied, 6"The Jews called Hasideans, whose leader is Judas the Maccabee, maintain a warlike policy and rebel frequently, not permitting the kingdom to have peace. 7Deprived of my ancestral glory—I speak of course of the high priesthood—I have now come here, 8first out of a sincere concern for the king's interests and second out of regard for my fellow citizens. Through the recklessness of those mentioned earlier, the entire nation is in a state of misfortune. 9But, King, since you have knowledge of these things, take thought for both the country and our oppressed nation with the same generosity you have had for all. 10As long as Judas lives, the government is powerless to establish peace."

11Alcimus had no sooner finished speaking when the rest of the political advisors,[z] who strongly disliked Judas, further enraged Demetrius. 12Immediately choosing Nicanor the commander of the elephants and appointing him governor of Judea, the king sent him out 13with written orders to kill Judas and scatter those with him, and to install Alcimus as high priest of the greatest temple. 14The Judean Gentiles who had fled from Judas joined Nicanor in large numbers, thinking that they would benefit from the misfortunes and calamities of the Jews.

15When they heard about Nicanor's advance and the support he had from the Gentiles, the Jews sprinkled themselves with earth. They prayed to the one who had established his own people forever and who always helped them by intervening on their behalf. 16At the command of their leader Judas, they immediately broke camp, marched from there, and met the enemy at the village of Dessau. 17Simon, Judas' brother, met Nicanor in battle but was slowly losing ground because of the unexpected confusion caused by their enemies. 18Nevertheless, when Nicanor heard that Judas' troops were fighting bravely and courageously as they struggled for their homeland, he was somewhat afraid to decide the matter through bloodshed. 19So he sent Posidonius, Theodotus, and Mattathias to develop a peace agreement. 20When the Jews had carefully inspected the proposal, and their leader Judas had informed the community, who appeared to give unanimous consent, they accepted the terms of the agreement. 21They set a day on which the leaders from each side would come to the same place in private, a chariot coming from each side, with chairs set out for the meeting. 22Judas placed armed men in appropriate places, in order to prevent unexpected treachery from the enemies. So they held successful negotiations.

23Nicanor lived for a time in Jerusalem and did nothing improper. He dismissed the crowds of ordinary people who gathered there. 24He kept Judas continually in his presence since he became strongly attached to the man. 25He encouraged him to marry and to have children. So Judas married, enjoyed tranquillity, and began to live a normal life.

26When Alcimus noted the goodwill that Nicanor and Judas had toward each

[y] 161 BCE [z] Or *Friends*

other, he obtained the documents of agreement drawn up between them and went to Demetrius. He claimed that Nicanor was disloyal to the government because he had appointed Judas, who plotted against the king, as his successor. 27The king was furious and, provoked by the accusations of the thoroughly depraved Alcimus, wrote to Nicanor. He forcefully asserted that he was displeased with the terms of agreement and ordered him to send the Maccabee as a prisoner to Antioch immediately. 28When this order reached Nicanor, he was upset and found it difficult to revoke the agreements, seeing how the man had done no wrong. 29But he couldn't defy the king, so he watched for an opportune time to set a trap. 30But the Maccabee noticed that Nicanor was becoming more reserved toward him, conducting customary meetings in a less courteous manner. Sensing that this new rudeness wasn't for the best, he gathered a large number of men and hid from Nicanor. 31When Nicanor realized that Judas had completely outwitted him, he went to the great and holy temple where priests were offering up the appropriate sacrifices and ordered them to hand over the man. 32When they asserted with solemn pledges that they didn't know where he was, 33he stretched out his strong hand against the temple and made the following pronouncement: "If you don't turn Judas over to me as a prisoner, I will level the sacred area of God, tear down the altar to the ground, and build here a great temple to Dionysus." 34With these words, he left. But the priests, stretching out their hands to heaven, called on the one who always fights in defense of our nation, saying, 35"You, Lord, who need nothing, made the temple your dwelling among us. 36Now, holy one, Lord of all holiness, keep your newly purified house free from all defilement forever."

37A Jerusalem elder named Razis was denounced to Nicanor as someone who loved the citizens, was well spoken of, and was called "Father of the Jews" because of his kindness. 38Early on in the revolt, he had been put on trial for Judaism and risked body and soul for its cause. 39Wanting to make public the hatred he had toward the Jews, Nicanor sent a group of more than five hundred soldiers to take him, 40because he thought that by arresting him, he would create a problem for the Jewish people.[a] 41When the mob was about to take the tower, forcing open the door of the courtyard, they commanded that the door be set on fire. Razis was surrounded on every side, so he fell on his own sword. 42He wanted to die bravely rather than fall into the hands of sinners and suffer outrages unworthy of his own high birth. 43But the blow didn't strike its mark because of the haste of the struggle and the surge of the mob through the doors. Running with honor out onto the wall, he courageously threw himself down into the mob. 44When they suddenly drew back, a space opened up, and he landed in the middle of it. 45While still breathing and burning with anger, he rose up, ignoring the gushing blood and the terrible injuries, and made his way through the crowd to stand on a pile of rubble. 46Entirely drained of blood, he tore out his intestines, took them in both hands, and threw them at the mob. As he did this, he called out to the one with authority over life and spirit to return his insides to him, and in this manner he died.

Nicanor's defeat

15 Nicanor learned that Judas' forces were in the region of Samaria, so he wanted to attack them on the day of rest when there would be no risk. 2But the Jews who were compelled to follow him said, "No! Don't destroy with such cruelty and savagery, but respect the day that is honored with holiness above all others by the one who observes all."

3The repeat offender asked if there was in heaven some mighty one who commanded the keeping of the Sabbath day.

4They declared, "The living Lord himself, the ruler in heaven, commands us to keep the seventh day."

5Nicanor replied, "And I am the ruler on

[a]Or *them*

earth who commands you to take up arms
and to carry out the royal orders." Nevertheless, he didn't succeed in carrying out
his terrible plan.
[6]Nicanor, holding his head high with all
his boasting, decided to build a public monument marking the defeat of Judas' forces.
[7]But the Maccabee was fully confident in
his hope of obtaining the Lord's help. [8]So
he encouraged his troops not to fear the
Gentiles' attack but to remember the aid
they had previously received from heaven
and to look for victory from the almighty
now. [9]Reassuring them with words from
the Law and the Prophets, and reminding
them of the struggles they had overcome,
he made them even more eager. [10]Stirring
up their spirits, he gave them orders and
pointed out at the same time the treachery
of the Gentiles and their violation of solemn pledges. [11]He armed each of them not
so much with the security of shields and
spears as with the encouragement of good
words. He also told them about a trustworthy dream—a kind of waking vision—
which raised everyone's morale.
[12]In his vision, Judas saw Onias, who
had been high priest and was virtuous,
good, modest in all things, gentle of man-
ners, and well-spoken. From childhood he
had learned all things that properly belong
to a good moral life. This man had his hands
extended to pray for the entire nation of
the Jews. [13]Then in the same manner, another man, noteworthy for his gray hair
and dignity, appeared with astonishing and
splendid glory. [14]Onias said, "This man is
one who loves his brothers and sisters and
prays many prayers for the people and the
holy city: God's prophet Jeremiah."
[15]Jeremiah extended his strong hand and
gave to Judas a gold sword, saying, [16]"Take
this holy sword as a gift from God, and with
it you will destroy your enemies."
[17]Judas' eloquent and powerful words
urged them on to courage and made the
young men's spirits brave. They determined
not to prepare for a long campaign but to attack honorably and fight hand-to-hand with
all courage. In this way the matter would be
decided, as danger faced their city, the holy
things, and the temple. [18]They weren't as
concerned for their women and children, or
their brothers and relatives, as they were for
the holy temple. [19]Those trapped in the city
were also very anxious, fearful of an attack
in the open. [20]Everyone was waiting for
the upcoming conflict, with fighting units
already formed, soldiers drawn up in battle
order, beasts sent to strategic positions,
and cavalry arranged on either side. [21]The
Maccabee saw the masses that were before
him, the diverse sorts of equipped military
arms, and the fierceness of the elephants, so
he extended his hands to heaven and called
on the wonder-working Lord. He knew that
it isn't through arms that God decides to
award victory but he gives it to those who
deserve it. [22]He prayed like this: "You, my
Lord, sent your angel to Hezekiah king of
Judah and he killed one hundred eighty-five
thousand from Sennacherib's camp. [23]Now
ruler of the heavens, send a good angel in
front of us to cause fear and trembling.
[24]May your mighty arm terrify those who
come with verbal insults against your holy
people." With that he stopped speaking.
[25]Nicanor's forces advanced with trumpet calls and battle cries. [26]But Judas' men
battled against their enemies with appeals
and prayers. [27]Fighting with their hands but
praying to God with their hearts and rejoicing in God's appearance, they killed no fewer
than thirty-five thousand soldiers. [28]When
they returned from the battle to their camp
with joy, they found Nicanor lying dead in
full armor. [29]With shouts and excitement,
they praised the ruler in their native language. [30]Their leader, who had always fought
for the citizens with body and soul and had
carefully preserved the goodwill toward his
fellow citizens from his youth, commanded
that Nicanor's head and arm be cut off
and carried to Jerusalem. [31]After arriving
there, Judas called together his fellow citizens, stationed the priests at the altar, and
sent for those from the elevated fortress.[b]
[32]He displayed the head of the repulsive

[b] Gk *acropolis*

Nicanor and the slanderer's hand, which he had extended against the almighty's holy house while uttering great boasts. 33 He cut out the tongue of the ungodly Nicanor and ordered that it be given to the birds in pieces, and he hung the rewards of his stupidity in front of the temple. 34 Looking to heaven, everyone praised the Lord, who had made himself known, saying, "Blessed is the one who kept his own holy place pure." 35 Judas hung Nicanor's head from the elevated fortress in plain sight of all, as a clear sign of the Lord's help. 36 The people decided to issue a regulation forbidding anyone to forget this day but reminding all to celebrate the thirteenth day of the twelfth month, called Adar[c] in the Syrian language, the day before Mordecai's day.

37 After things turned out this way with Nicanor, the Hebrews controlled the city from that time on. So at this point I will stop. 38 If the story was told effectively, this is what I wanted. But if it was told in a poor and mediocre fashion, this was the best I could do. 39 Just as it is harmful to drink wine or water alone while wine mixed with water is delightful and produces joy, so also may the writing of this story delight the ears of those who encounter this work.

The end.

[c] February-March

BOOKS INCLUDED IN GREEK AND SLAVONIC BIBLES

1 ESDRAS[a]

Josiah revives the Passover

1 Josiah celebrated the Passover to the Lord in Jerusalem. He sacrificed the Passover lamb on the fourteenth day of the first month.[b] [2]He gave the priests, dressed in religious robes, their daily assignments in the Lord's temple. [3]He said to the Levites serving in Israel's temple: "Dedicate yourselves to the Lord for placing the Lord's holy chest in the house that David's son King Solomon built. You don't need to carry it on your shoulders anymore. [4]Now worship the Lord your God and serve Israel, God's people. Prepare yourselves according to your families and tribes, and according to the plan of King David and the greatness of his son Solomon. [5]Take your positions in the temple according to your inherited priestly[c] groups, serving before your people the Israelites. [6]Sacrifice the Passover lamb and prepare sacrifices for your people, and conduct the Passover ceremony according to the rules that the Lord gave to Moses."

[7]Josiah gave to the people a gift of thirty thousand lambs and kid goats and three thousand calves. These came as promised from the king's own possessions to the people, priests, and Levites. [8]Hilkiah, Zechariah, and Jehiel[d] (the chief officials of the temple) gave to the priests for the Passover twenty-six hundred sheep and three hundred calves. [9]Jeconiah, Shemaiah and his brother Nethanel, Hashabiah, Ochiel, and Joram, military commanders, gave to the Levites five thousand sheep and seven hundred calves for the Passover.

[10]This is what happened. Early in the morning the priests and Levites, [11]holding the unleavened bread, stood in the proper order of their tribes [12]and by their inherited groups. They brought the offerings to the Lord according to the scroll from Moses. [13]They roasted the Passover lamb over fire as required. They boiled the sacrifices, with a sweet aroma, in copper pots and kettles and carried them over to all the people. [14]Later on, the Levites prepared the Passover meal for themselves and for their fellow priests, Aaron's sons, since the priests were offering the fat of the sacrifices until late into the night. [15]The temple singers, Asaph's sons, were in their designated positions according to the instructions set down by David and by Asaph, Zechariah, and Eddinus, the king's advisors. The city gatekeepers were at each gate. No one needed to change his daily routine, because the Levites had prepared the Passover meal for them. [16]Everything for the Lord's sacrifice was accomplished on that day. They celebrated the Passover and offered sacrifices on the Lord's altar according to King Josiah's command.

[17]The Israelites celebrated the Passover and the Festival of Unleavened Bread for seven days. [18]No Passover like it had been celebrated in Israel since the time of the prophet Samuel. [19]Nor had any of the kings of Israel ever celebrated a Passover like that celebrated by Josiah, the priests, the Levites, the Judeans, and all of Israel who were living in Jerusalem. [20]In the eighteenth year of the rule of Josiah this Passover was celebrated.

[21]Josiah did the right thing in the Lord's presence, because his heart was devoted to God. [22]The story of his rule was officially recorded in ancient times. The records include those who sinned and committed ungodly acts toward the Lord, beyond those of any other nation and kingdom. Their acts intentionally grieved the Lord, so that the Lord spoke against Israel.

Death of Josiah

[23]Sometime after Josiah's actions, Pharaoh, Egypt's king, went to start a war at Carchemish on the Euphrates. Josiah went out against him.

[24]The king of Egypt sent a message to Josiah: "What do you want with me, King

[a]The versification of this translation follows the standard Greek text. [b]March–April, Nisan [c]Or *levitical* [d]Gk *Esyelus*

of Judea? [25]I haven't been sent out by the Lord God against you; rather, my war is at the Euphrates. Now the Lord is with me and urges me on. So stand aside and don't oppose the Lord."

[26]Josiah, however, didn't return to his chariot but resolved to fight. He didn't pay attention to the words of the prophet Jeremiah, which came from the Lord. [27]He went to war with Pharaoh in the plain of Megiddo, and Pharaoh's commanders came against King Josiah. [28]The king said to his attendants, "Take me away from the battle, for I'm severely wounded." His attendants immediately took him away from the line of battle. [29]Josiah got into a second chariot. After he was brought back to Jerusalem, he died and was buried in his family tomb.

[30]The whole land of Judea mourned for Josiah. The prophet Jeremiah also grieved for Josiah. The leading citizens, with the women, grieve over him until this day. This has become a tradition for the whole nation of Israel to observe. [31]These events have been written in the official records of the Judean kings. All of Josiah's actions—including his honor, his understanding of the Law of the Lord, all that he did previously, and these things that are now told—are described in the official records of the kings of Israel and Judea.

[32]Then the leaders of the nation appointed Jeconiah, Josiah's son, who was 23 years old, as king to succeed his father. [33]He ruled in Judea and Jerusalem for three months. Then the king of Egypt removed him from his rule in Jerusalem [34]and fined the nation 5,700 pounds of silver and fifty-seven pounds of gold.

[35]The king of Egypt appointed his own brother Jehoiakim as king of Judea and Jerusalem. [36]Jehoiakim put the officials in prison. He seized his other brother Zarius and took him from Egypt. [37]Jehoiakim was 25 years old when he began to rule over Judea and Jerusalem; he did what was evil in the Lord's presence.

[38]Then Babylon's King Nebuchadnezzar went up against him, bound him with bronze chains, and took him away to Babylon. [39]Nebuchadnezzar also seized some of the Lord's holy equipment, carried it off to Babylon, and placed it in his temple. [40]But the things reported about Jehoiakim,[e] his impurity and godlessness, have been written in the scroll about the times of the kings.

[41]His son Jehoiachin[f] ruled in his place. When he was appointed king, he was 18 years old. [42]He ruled in Jerusalem for three months and ten days, and he did evil things in the Lord's presence.

[43]After a year, Nebuchadnezzar removed Jehoiachin to Babylon, along with the Lord's holy equipment. [44]He appointed Zedekiah king of Judea and Jerusalem when Zedekiah was 21 years old. He ruled for eleven years. [45]He also did evil things in the Lord's presence and paid no attention to the words Jeremiah the prophet spoke, which came from the Lord. [46]Although King Nebuchadnezzar had made him swear a solemn pledge in the Lord's name, he swore falsely and rebelled. He was stubborn and broke the laws of the Lord, the God of Israel.

[47]The leaders of the people and the priests committed godless and immoral acts far beyond the impure ones of the nations. They even corrupted the Lord's temple that had been made holy in Jerusalem. [48]The God of their ancestors sent his messenger to call them back, because he was trying to spare them and his dwelling place. [49]But they mocked the messengers and made fun of the prophets on the day that the Lord spoke.

Finally, God, with divine anger, brought the Chaldean kings against his chosen nation because of their godless acts. [50]The Chaldeans killed the young people around the holy temple. They spared neither man nor woman, young nor old, for God handed over all of them. [51]They seized and carried off to Babylon all the Lord's holy equipment, great and small, the treasure chests of the Lord, and the royal stores. [52]They set fire to the Lord's house. They smashed the

[e] Or *him* [f] Gk *Jehoiakim*

walls of Jerusalem. They burned its towers
with fire. [53]They utterly ruined all of its radiance. King Nebuchadnezzar led away the
survivors to Babylon under guard. [54]They
became servants to him and to his sons
until the rise of the Persian kingdom, which
fulfilled the Lord's word through Jeremiah,
[55]who said, "Until the land has enjoyed its
sabbath rest, it will remain untouched,[g]
after its destruction, for seventy years."

Exiles return to Jerusalem

2 In the first year of Cyrus as king of the
Persians the Lord motivated the spirit
of King Cyrus to fulfill the Lord's word spoken through Jeremiah. He made a royal announcement throughout the whole of his
kingdom that he also put into writing. [2]This
is what Persia's King Cyrus says:

> The Lord of Israel, the Most High Lord,
> has appointed me king of the entire
> world. The Lord has commissioned me
> to build God's house in Jerusalem in
> Judea. [3]Therefore, if you are from this
> nation, may your Lord be with you.[h] Go
> up to Jerusalem in Judea and build the
> house of the Lord of Israel—for this is
> the Lord who dwells in Jerusalem. [4]As
> many of you live in other places, help the
> Lord with gold and silver, with horses
> and cattle, in addition to pledging other
> things dedicated for the Lord's temple in
> Jerusalem.

[5]Then the heads of the families of Judah
and Benjamin rose up. The priests and the
Levites, and everyone whose spirit the Lord
aroused, went up to build a house for the
Lord in Jerusalem. [6]Their neighbors helped
them with everything, with silver and gold,
with horses and cattle, and with many other
things pledged by those whose minds were
inspired to do so.

[7]King Cyrus also brought out the Lord's
holy equipment that Nebuchadnezzar had
carried away from Jerusalem and placed in
his temple of idols. [8]When King Cyrus of the
Persians brought these out, he handed them
over to Mithridates, his own treasurer, and
through him they were given over to Governor Sheshbazzar[i] of Judea. [9]The number
of these was one thousand gold cups, one
thousand silver cups, twenty-nine silver
censers, [10]thirty gold bowls, twenty-four
hundred ten silver bowls, and one thousand other objects. [11]They handed over all
five thousand four hundred sixty-nine gold
and silver objects. So Sheshbazzar, with
the help of war prisoners returning from
Babylon, carried the equipment back to
Jerusalem.

Opposition to rebuilding Jerusalem

[12]Then during the time of King Artaxerxes of the Persians, Bishlam, Mithridates,
Tabeel, Rehum, Beltethmus, Shimshai the
scribe, and others associated with them
living in Samaria and other places nearby
wrote the king a letter, opposing those who
were living in Judea and Jerusalem:

> [13]To Your Majesty, King Artaxerxes,
> your servants Rehum the reporter and
> Shimshai the scribe, and the rest of their
> council, and the judges in Coele-Syria
> and Phoenicia:
>
> [14]Our master the king, may you know
> that the Judeans who came up to us have
> come to Jerusalem and are rebuilding
> that rebellious and evil city, restoring its
> marketplaces and walls, and laying the
> foundations for a temple. [15]If this city
> is rebuilt and the walls are completed,
> not only will they refuse to pay foreign
> taxes, but they will also be able to resist
> kings. [16]Since the work on the temple is
> in progress, we didn't think we should
> overlook such an act but should call it to
> the attention of our master the king so
> that if it concerns you, a search may be
> made in the records of your ancestors.
> [17]You will discover in the records what
> has been written about them. You will
> learn that this city was rebellious, an-
> noying to both kings and other cities.
> The Judeans were rebels and would reg-
> ularly set up huge barriers around the
> city. That is why this city was destroyed.
> [18]So we now advise you, Master and
> King, that if this city is rebuilt and if its

[g]Or *it will keep sabbath* [h]Or *with him* [i]Gk *Sanabassaros*

walls are erected, you will no longer have secure lines of access to Coele-Syria and Phoenicia.

[19]The king wrote back to the recorder Rehum, Beltethmus, the scribe Shimshai, and their associates living in Samaria, Syria, and Phoenicia, as follows:

[20]I have read the letter that you sent to me. [21]Consequently, I ordered a search to be made. It was discovered that this city has indeed rallied against kings in the past, that the people in it revolted frequently and started wars, [22]and that powerful and cruel kings have ruled in Jerusalem and exacted taxes from Coele-Syria and Phoenicia. [23]Therefore, I issued orders to prevent these people from rebuilding the city [24]and to take care in advance that nothing more be done and that such wicked designs go no further to upset the kings.

[25]After King Artaxerxes' letter was read, Rehum and the scribe Shimshai and their associates marched on Jerusalem immediately, with cavalry and a large group of armed troops, in order to stop the builders. [26]So the building of the temple in Jerusalem ceased until the second year of the rule of Persia's King Darius.

Contest of the bodyguards

3 Now King Darius gave a great banquet for all his subjects, everyone born in his house, all the officials of Media and Persia, [2]and all the chief administrators, generals, and district governors who were under him in the one hundred twenty-seven administrative districts from India to Ethiopia. [3]They ate and drank, and they left after they had enough. King Darius retired to his bedroom and went to sleep, but he eventually woke up again.

[4]Then the three young men, the bodyguards who protected the king, said to each other: [5]"Let's each offer one word that we think is the most superior thing in the world. To the one whose statement seems wisest, King Darius will give expensive gifts and great prizes as a reward. [6]He should be clothed in purple, drink from gold cups, and sleep on a gold bed. He should have a chariot with gold-studded bridles, a turban of fine linen, and a gold necklace around his neck. [7]He will sit next to Darius on account of his wisdom and will be called Darius' confidant." [8]Then each bodyguard composed his own statement and sealed it. They placed them under the pillow of King Darius. They said, [9]"When the king wakes up, his servants will give him the written statements; and whoever's statement the king and the three officials of Persia judge to be wisest will be given the victory according to Persian law."

[10]The first wrote, "Wine is superior."

[11]The second wrote, "The king is superior."

[12]The third wrote, "Women are superior, but truth conquers all."

[13]When the king woke up, they gave the written statements to him, and he read them.

[14]Then he sent for all the officials of Persia and Media and the administrators, generals, district governors, and civil authorities. He sat in the council room, and the written statements were read before them all. [15]He said, "Call in the young men to explain their statements."

So they were called together. [16]He said to them, "Give us an explanation for what you wrote."

Superiority of wine

[17]So the first young man, who had spoken of the strength of wine, started: [18]"Gentlemen, how is it that wine is so superior? It misleads the minds of all who drink it. [19]It makes the mind of the king the same as that of the orphan, likewise of the slave and the free, of the poor and the rich. [20]It changes every thought to feasting and cheerfulness, and forgets all grief and every obligation. [21]It fattens all hearts, makes one remember neither kings nor administrators, and makes everyone talk in outrageous sums. [22]When drinking, people forget to be civil even with their friends and relatives, and after a while they draw their swords. [23]When they recover from the wine, they don't even remember what they did. [24]Gentle-

men, isn't wine superior, since it forces people to behave like this?" With that, he stopped speaking.

Superiority of the king

4 Then the second young man, who had spoken of the strength of the king, spoke: 2"Gentlemen, aren't people superior who control land and sea and all that's in them? 3But the king is most superior, because he is their ruler and master, and whatever he might say to them they obey as soon as they hear it. 4If he tells them to make war on each other, they do so; and if he sends them out against the enemy, they march and overcome mountain fortresses, walls, and towers. 5They murder and are murdered, but they don't disobey the king's word. If they win a battle, they bring everything to the king—whatever plunder they take and everything else. 6Similarly, for those who don't serve in the army or make war but farm the land, whenever they sow and reap, they bring some to the king. They force each other to pay taxes to the king. 7Yet the king is only one man! If he tells them to kill, they kill. If he tells them to set someone free, they set someone free. 8If he tells them to strike, they strike. If he tells them to destroy or build something, they destroy it or they build it. 9If he tells them to cut down something, they cut it down. If he tells them to plant, they plant. 10All his people and his military powers obey him. Furthermore, he reclines, eats, drinks, and sleeps; 11but they keep watch around him, and no one can go away to take care of his own matters, nor do they disobey him. 12Gentlemen, isn't the king superior, since he is to be completely obeyed in this manner?" Then he stopped speaking.

Superiority of women

13Then the third young man, Zerubbabel, who had spoken of women and truth, began to speak: 14"Gentlemen, isn't the king great, aren't men abundant, and isn't wine strong? Who is it, though, that masters them or rules over them? Isn't it women? 15Women give birth to the king and to all the people who rule over the sea and land. 16From women they all are born. It was women who brought up those men who plant the vineyards from which wine is produced.

17"Women make men's clothes. They bring men honor. Without women, men aren't even able to exist. 18If men gather gold and silver or any valuable thing, and then see a desirable and beautiful woman, 19they forget everything to gaze at her. With mouths wide open, they stare at her. All choose her over gold, silver, or any other valuable thing. 20A man leaves his own father, who raised him, and his own country, and clings to his own wife. 21With his wife he departs this life, with no memory of his father or mother or country. 22Therefore, surely you must recognize that women rule over you!

"Don't you work and labor, yet you bring everything and give it to women? 23A man takes his sword, goes out to travel abroad to raid, steal, and sail the sea and rivers. 24He faces lions; he walks in darkness; when he steals and robs and plunders, he carries it back to the woman he loves. 25A man loves his own wife much more than his father or mother. 26Many men have lost their heads over women, and have become slaves on account of them. 27Many have perished, stumbled, or sinned because of women.

28"Now don't you believe me? Isn't the king great in his authority? Don't all countries fear to touch him? 29I once saw the king and Apame his mistress, the daughter of the eminent Bartacus, sitting by his right side. 30She took the crown from the king's head and put it on her own head, and slapped the king with her left hand. 31At this the king would stare at her with his mouth wide open. If she smiles at him, he laughs; but if she should get angry with him, he humors her so that she may be reconciled to him. 32Gentlemen, aren't women powerful, since they can do such things?"

Superiority of truth

33The king and the officials looked at each other, and the third young man began to speak about truth: 34"Gentlemen, aren't women strong? The earth is great, heaven

is high, and the sun is swift in its course,
for it circles the heavens and returns again
to its place in a single day. 35 Isn't the one
who does these things great? Yet truth is
also great and superior still to all of these
things. 36 The whole earth calls on truth,
and heaven praises it. All of heaven's works[j]
move and tremble at the sight of it, and
there's nothing wrong with truth. 37 You
can't trust wine; you can't trust the king;
you can't trust women. No human beings
are trustworthy. Everything they do is
wrong. There is no truth in them. They will
perish in their lies. 38 But truth endures and
is valid for all time; it lives and succeeds forever. 39 With it there's no charade or pref-
erence, but it does what is right instead of
what is wrong or evil. Everyone approves
of its deeds. There's nothing unjust in its
judgment. 40 To it belongs the strength, the
royalty, the authority, and the greatness of
all ages. Bless God's truth!" 41 He stopped
speaking, and all the people cried out,
"Great is truth and superior to all!"

Darius rewards Zerubbabel

42 Then the king said to Zerubbabel,
"Ask for whatever you like, even more than
what was proposed, and we'll give it to
you, for you've been found to be the wisest
one. You may sit next to me and be called
my confidant."

43 Zerubbabel said to the king, "Remember
the promise that you made to rebuild Jerusalem on the day that you became king. 44 You
promised to send back all the holy equipment that was taken from Jerusalem, which
Cyrus set apart when he promised to destroy
Babylon and also promised to send it back
there. 45 You also solemnly swore to rebuild
the temple, which was burned down by the
Edomites when Judea was devastated by the
Chaldeans. 46 Now, Master and King, this is
what I ask and request of you, something that
is fitting for your greatness. I beg you to fulfill
the pledge you solemnly swore to the king of
heaven with your own mouth."

47 Then King Darius stood up and kissed
him. He wrote letters for him to all the
treasurers, district governors, generals, and
administrators so that they would send him
out and all those who were going up with
him to rebuild Jerusalem. 48 He wrote letters
to all the district governors in Coele-Syria
and Phoenicia and to those in Lebanon, to
bring cedar timber from Lebanon to Jerusalem and to help him rebuild the city. 49 He
wrote on behalf of all the Judeans who were
going up from the kingdom to Judea, for the
benefit of their freedom, that no administrator, district governor, or treasurer should
break down their doors. 50 He wrote that all
the territory they forcibly took was for them
to live in without taxation, and that the Idumeans should leave behind the villages of
the Judeans that they had seized. 51 He wrote
that 1,140 pounds of silver a year should be
given for the building of the temple until it
was completely rebuilt. 52 In addition, 570
pounds of silver a year should be given for
entirely burned offerings that are provided
daily on the altar, in keeping with the commandment that they make seventeen offerings in all. 53 He wrote that all who depart
from Babylon to rebuild the city should have
their freedom, both they and their children
and all the priests who depart as well. 54 He
wrote about the expenses and the priests'
holy garments in which they were to serve.
55 He wrote that the expenses for the Levites
should be supplied until the day when the
temple would be completed and Jerusalem
rebuilt. 56 He wrote that all who guarded
the city should be supplied with land and
wages. 57 He sent back from Babylon all the
holy equipment that Cyrus had set aside.
Everything that Cyrus had said he would
do, Darius himself commanded to do them
and to send them to Jerusalem.

58 When the young man Zerubbabel
went outside, he lifted up his face to heaven
toward Jerusalem and praised the king of
heaven: 59 "From you come the victory and
wisdom. To you belongs the glory. I'm your
household servant. 60 You are worthy of
praise, you who have given wisdom to me. I
praise you, Lord of our ancestors."

61 So he took the letters, went to Babylon,

[j] Or *God's works*

and reported this to all of his people. 62 They
praised the God of their ancestors, because
he had given them amnesty and permission
63 to go up and rebuild Jerusalem and the
temple that is called by God's name. They
celebrated with music and enthusiasm for
seven days.

Those returning from captivity

5 After this the leaders of the family
houses were chosen to go up, according to their tribes, with their wives, sons,
daughters, their male and female servants,
and their farm animals. 2 Darius sent with
them one thousand cavalry to restore them
back in Jerusalem in peace. With the music
of drums and flutes, 3 all of their Jewish relatives were celebrating. Darius commanded
them to go along with them.

4 These are the names of the men in
charge of their assigned groups, who went
up according to their families in the tribes:
5 the priests, the sons of Phinehas son of
Aaron; Jeshua son of Jozadak son of Seraiah, and Joakim son of Zerubbabel son
of Shealtiel, from the house of David, from
the family line of Phares, and from the tribe
of Judah, 6 who spoke wise words to Persia's
King Darius, in the second year of his rule,
in the first month, the month of Nisan.[k]

7 These are the ones from Judea who came
up out of their captivity in exile, whom King
Nebuchadnezzar of Babylon had taken to
Babylon 8 and who returned to Jerusalem
and Judea, each to their own city. They
came with their leaders Zerubbabel, Jeshua,
Nehemiah, Seraiah, Resaiah, Eneneus, Mordecai, Beelsarus, Aspharasus, Reelaiah,[l] Rehum, and Baanah.

9 The number of those of the nation and
their leaders:

The family of Parosh	2,172
10 The family of Shephatiah	472
The family of Arah	756
11 The family of Pahath-moab of the family of Jeshua and Joab	2,812
12 The family of Elam	1,254
The family of Zattu	945
The family of Chorbe	705
The family of Bani	648
13 The family of Bebai	623
The family of Azgad	1,322
14 The family of Adonikam	667
The family of Bigvai	2,066
The family of Adin	454
15 The family of Ater descended from Hezekiah	92
The family of Kilan and Azetas	67
The family of Azaru	432
16 The family of Annias	101
The family of Arom.	
The family of Bezai	323
The family of Arsiphurith	112
17 The family of Baiterus	3,005
The family of Bethlomon	123
18 Those from Netophah	55
Those from Anathoth	158
Those from Bethasmoth	42
19 Those from Kiriatharim	25
Those from Chephirah and Beeroth	743
20 The Chadiasans and Ammidians	422
Those from Kirama and Geba	621
21 Those from Macalon	122
Those from Betolio	52
The family of Niphish	156
22 The family of the other Calamolalus and Ono	725
The family of Jerechus	345
23 The family of Senaah	3,330
24 The priests—the family of Jedaiah, Jeshua's son, of the family of Anasib	972
The family of Immer	1,052
25 The family of Pashhur	1,247
The family of Charme	1,017
26 The Levites—the family of Jeshua, Kadmiel, Bannas, and Sudias—	74
27 The temple singers—the family of Asaph—	128

28 The city gatekeepers:
the family of Shallum,
the family of Ater,
the family of Talmon,
the family of Akkub,
the family of Hatita,
the family of Shobai, in all 139.

[k] March–April [l] Cf Ezra 2:1; Gk *Borolias*

29The temple servants: the family of Esau, the family of Hasupha, the family of Tabbaoth, the family of Keros, the family of Suah, the family of Padon, the family of Lebanah, the family of Hagabah, 30the family of Akkub, the family of Uthai, the family of Ketab, the family of Hagabah, the family of Subai, the family of Hana, the family of Cathua, the family of Geddur, 31the family of Jairus, the family of Daisan, the family of Noeba, the family of Chezib, the family of Gazera, the family of Uzza, the family of Phinoe, the family of Hasrah, the family of Basthai, the family of Asnah, the family of Maani, the family of Nephisim, the family of Acuph, the family of Hakupha, the family of Asur, the family of Pharakim, the family of Bazluth, 32the family of Mehida, the family of Cutha, the family of Charea, the family of Barkos, the family of Serar, the family of Temah, the family of Neziah, the family of Hatipha.

33The family of Solomon's servants—the family of Assaphioth, the family of Peruda, the family of Jaalah, the family of Lozon, the family of Isdael, the family of Shephatiah, 34the family of Agia, the family of Pochereth-hazzebaim, the family of Sarothie, the family of Masiah, the family of Gas, the family of Addus, the family of Subas, the family of Apherra, the family of Barodis, the family of Shaphat, the family of Allon.

35All the temple servants and the family of Solomon's servants numbered 372. 36These following persons are those who went up from Tel-melah and Tel-harsha, under the leadership of Cherub, Addan, and Immer, 37who weren't able to prove by their family houses or by their lineage that they had descended from Israel: the family of Delaiah, Tobiah's son, and the family of Nekoda, 652.

38Also from the priests, the following persons had assumed the priestly office but were found to be unqualified: the family of Habaiah, the family of Hakkoz, and the family of Jaddus, who had married Agia, one of the daughters of Barzillai, and was called by his name. 39When they inspected the registry and didn't find the lineage of these men, they excluded them from the service of the priesthood. 40Nehemiah and Attharias told them not to share in the holy things until a high priest arrives wearing Clarity and Truth.[m]

41All those who were from Israel, 12 or more years old, excluding male and female servants, were 42,360; their male and female servants were 7,337; there were 245 harpists and singers. 42There were 435 camels, 7,036 horses, 245 mules, and 5,525 donkeys.

43Some of the leaders of the family houses, when they came to God's temple in Jerusalem, solemnly pledged that they would erect the house on its site, 44and that they would give to the sacred treasury for the work one thousand manehs of gold, five thousand manehs of silver, and one hundred priests' robes. 45The priests, the Levites, and some of the people took up residence in Jerusalem and the surrounding area. The temple singers, the gatekeepers, and the rest of Israel settled in the villages.

Work on the temple is delayed

46When the seventh month[n] came and the Israelites were all in their own homes, they gathered together in the square near the first gate on the eastern side. 47Then Jeshua, Jozadak's son with his fellow priests, and Zerubbabel, Shealtiel's son with his group, took their positions and prepared the altar of the God of Israel 48to offer up entirely burned offerings, according to the stipulations in the scroll from Moses, the man of God.

49Some from the other neighboring peoples gathered with them. They erected the altar in its proper place (even though all the other neighboring peoples were hostile to them and were stronger than they were). They offered sacrifices and entirely burned offerings to the Lord at the proper morning and evening times. 50They celebrated the Festival of Booths, as it is commanded

[m]Urim and Thummim in Neh 7:65 [n]September–October, Tishrei

in the Law, and offered sacrifices daily as expected, [51]in addition to the continual offerings and sacrifices on sabbaths, at new moons, and at all the sacred feasts.

[52]All who made a solemn promise to God began to offer sacrifices to God, from the new moon of the seventh month,[o] even though God's temple wasn't yet rebuilt. [53]They gave money to the stonemasons and the carpenters, along with daily meals. They gave gifts[p] to the Sidonians and the Tyrians, to deliver cedar logs from Lebanon and ferry them in rafts to the harbor of Joppa, according to the written orders they had from Persia's King Cyrus.

[54]In the second month of the second year,[q] after they came to God's temple in Jerusalem, Zerubbabel, Shealtiel's son, and Jeshua, Jozadak's son, made a new start, together with their associates and the levitical priests and all who had returned to Jerusalem from captivity. [55]They then laid the foundation of God's temple on the new moon of the second month in the second year of their arrival in Judea and Jerusalem. [56]They appointed the Levites who were 20 years old or more in charge of the Lord's work.

Rising up were Jeshua, his sons and associates; his brother Kadmiel and Jeshua's sons; Emadabun and Joda's sons; and Iliadun's son with their sons and brothers. With them, all the Levites worked with a common purpose doing the work in God's house. [57]So the builders built God's temple. The priests stood dressed up in their robes, with musical instruments and trumpets, and the Levites, Asaph's sons, with cymbals, singing to the Lord and praising him, according to the directions of King David of Israel. [58]They sang hymns, praising the Lord, "God's goodness and glory are on Israel forever." [59]The people blew trumpets and shouted loudly, singing to the Lord on the occasion of the construction of the Lord's house. [60]Some of the levitical priests and leaders of family houses, the elderly who had seen the former house, came to this building with much weeping and wailing. [61]Many others came with trumpets and joy, with a tremendous uproar. [62]But the people couldn't hear the trumpets because of the people's weeping, even though the crowd was blowing the trumpets so loudly that the noise was heard far away.

[63]When the enemies of the tribe of Judah and Benjamin heard it, they came to investigate what the sound of the trumpets meant. [64]They discovered that those who had returned from captivity were building the temple to the Lord God of Israel. [65]So they came before Zerubbabel and Jeshua and the leaders of the family houses and said to them, "We will build with you. [66]We also obey your Lord, and we have been giving offerings to him ever since the days of Assyria's King Esarhaddon,[r] who transported us here." [67]Zerubbabel, Jeshua, and the leaders of the family houses in Israel, however, said to them, "We will have nothing to do with each other in building the house for the Lord our God. [68]We alone will build it for the Lord of Israel, just as Persia's King Cyrus commanded us." [69]But the neighboring peoples harassed the Judeans and hindered their rebuilding. [70]By scheming, spreading lies among the people, and stirring up trouble, they prevented the completion of the rebuilding as long as King Cyrus lived. [71]They were kept from building for two years, until Darius' rule.

Work on the temple is finished

6 In the second year of Darius' rule, the prophets Haggai and Zechariah (Iddo's son) prophesied to the Judeans who were in Judea and in Jerusalem in the name of the Lord God of Israel, who is ruler over them. [2]Then Zerubbabel, Shealtiel's son, and Jeshua, Jozadak's son, went up and began to build the Lord's house in Jerusalem, assisted by the Lord's prophets.

[3]At the same time, Sisinnes, the commander of Syria and Phoenicia, and Sathrabuzanes and their associates came to them and said, [4]"By whose order are you building this house and this roof and finishing all the other things? Who are the

[o]September–October, Tishrei [p]Gk uncertain [q]April–May, Iyar [r]Gk *Asbasareth*

builders who are doing all of these things?" 5 Yet the elders of the Judeans enjoyed the gracious protection of the Lord on the exiles, 6 and they weren't prevented from building until Darius could be informed about them and return an answer. 7 Here is a copy of the letter that Sisinnes, the commander of Syria and Phoenicia, Sathrabuzanes, and their associates, the local officials in Syria and Phoenicia, wrote to Darius:

8 To King Darius. Greetings.

Our master the king, may you know that when we came to the country of Judea and entered the city of Jerusalem, we found the elders of the Jews, who had been in captivity, building in the city of Jerusalem a large new house for the Lord, of polished stone with costly beams set in the walls. 9 These projects are proceeding swiftly, and the overall work is succeeding. They are completing it with brillance and precision. 10 So we asked these elders, "By whose command are you building this house and laying the foundations of this project?" 11 In order that we might inform you, we questioned them about who the leaders are and demanded a list of the names of the troublemakers. 12 They told us, "We are the servants of the Lord who created the heaven and the earth. 13 The house was built many years before by a great and mighty king of Israel, and it was finished. 14 But when our ancestors angrily sinned against the Lord of Israel who is in heaven, God gave them over into the hands of King Nebuchadnezzar of Babylon, king of the Chaldeans; 15 and they tore down the house and burned it, and led the people away as prisoners to Babylon. 16 But in the first year of Cyrus' rule over the country of Babylonia, King Cyrus wrote that this house should be rebuilt. 17 King Cyrus took out the holy gold and silver equipment from the temple in Babylon, which Nebuchadnezzar had removed from the house in Jerusalem and deposited in his own temple. Cyrus handed it over to Zerubbabel and the governor Sheshbazzar 18 with the order that they[s] take all of this equipment back and place it in the temple in Jerusalem, and that the Lord's temple be rebuilt on its site. 19 After coming here, Sheshbazzar laid the foundations of the Lord's house in Jerusalem. It has been under construction until now, although it isn't finished." 20 Now, King, if it seems right, please search the royal archives that are in Babylon. 21 If it is discovered that the building of the Lord's house in Jerusalem was done with King Cyrus' consent, and if it seems right to our master the king, please direct us concerning these things.

22 Then King Darius commanded a search of the royal archives that were kept in Babylon. In Ecbatana, within the palace of Medea, a scroll was found that recorded the following words:

23 In the first year of Cyrus's rule, King Cyrus commissioned the rebuilding of the Lord's house in Jerusalem, where they offer sacrifices with continuous fire. 24 Its height should be ninety feet and its width ninety feet, with three layers of polished stone and one layer of new native wood. The expenses should come out of the treasury of King Cyrus. 25 Also the holy silver and gold equipment from the Lord's house, which Nebuchadnezzar removed from the house in Jerusalem and transported to Babylon, should be restored to the house in Jerusalem, to be kept where it used to be.

26 So he commanded Sisinnes the governor of Syria and Phoenicia, and Sathrabuzanes, and their associates, and those who were appointed as local officials in Syria and Phoenicia to stay away from the place and to let Zerubbabel, the Lord's servant and Judea's governor, and the elders of the Jews rebuild the Lord's house on its site.

27 I hereby command that it be built completely and that close attention

[s] Or *he*

be paid to helping those who have returned from the exile of Judea, until
the Lord's house is finished. [28]A sum
of money, out of the tribute of Coele-
Syria and Phoenicia, should be carefully arranged to be given to these
persons, specifically to Zerubbabel the
governor, for offerings to the Lord, for
bulls, rams, and lambs. [29]Also money
should be given for wheat, salt, wine,
and oil, continually every year, without
arguing, for daily use as the Jerusalem
priests may indicate [30]so that drink offerings may be made to the Most High
God for the king and his children, and
prayers be offered for their lives.

[31]He further commanded that if anyone
should disobey any of the things previously mentioned or previously written, or
attempt to cancel them, a beam should be
taken out of the house of the guilty, who
then should be hung on it, and all their possessions forfeited to the king.

[32]May the Lord, on whose name they
called, destroy every king and nation
that will stretch out their hands to prevent or damage the Lord's house in Jerusalem.

[33]I, King Darius, have declared that it be
done with the necessary care described
here.

7 Following the king's announcements,
Sisinnes, the commander of Coele-Syria
and Phoenicia, Sathrabuzanes, and their
associates [2]supervised the holy work, carefully assisting the Judean elders and the
temple officials. [3]The holy work flourished,
while the prophets Haggai and Zechariah
prophesied. [4]They finished it by the command of the Lord God of Israel. [5]So with
the consent of Cyrus, Darius, and Artaxerxes, the kings of the Persians, the holy
house was finished by the twenty-third day
of the month of Adar,[t] in the sixth year of
King Darius.

[6]The Israelites, the priests, the Levites,
and the rest of those who returned from
exile acted according to what was written
in the scroll from Moses. [7]For the dedication of the Lord's temple, they brought offerings of one hundred bulls, two hundred
rams, four hundred lambs, [8]and twelve
male goats for the sin of all Israel, according to the number of the twelve leaders of
the tribes of Israel. [9]The priests and the
Levites stood dressed in their robes, according to their tribes, for the services of
the Lord God of Israel according to the
scroll from Moses; and the gatekeepers
stood at each gate.

[10]The Israelites who came from exile celebrated the Passover on the fourteenth day
of the first month,[u] after the priests and the
Levites were purified together. [11]Not everyone returning from exile was purified, but
the Levites were all purified together. [12]The
Levites sacrificed the Passover lamb on behalf of the returned exiles, for their brothers
the priests, and for themselves. [13]The Israelites who had returned from exile, those who
had separated themselves from the scandal
of the neighboring peoples and sought the
Lord, ate the Passover meal. [14]They also celebrated the Festival of Unleavened Bread
for seven days, rejoicing before the Lord,
[15]because he had changed the attitude of
the king of the Assyrians toward them, to
prepare them for the service of the Lord
God of Israel.

Ezra leads more exiles out of Babylon

8 Sometime later, during Artaxerxes'
rule as the king of the Persians, Ezra
arrived. He was the son of Seraiah son of
Azariah son of Hilkiah son of Shallum
[2]son of Zadok son of Ahitub son of Amariah son of Uzzi son of Bukki son of Abishua son of Phinehas son of Eleazar son of
the high priest Aaron. [3]Ezra came up from
Babylon as a legal expert well trained in
the Law from Moses, a gift from the God
of Israel. [4]The king showed him honor because he found favor with the king[v] in all
of his requests. [5]Going up to Jerusalem
with him were some of the Israelites and
some of the priests, Levites, temple singers, gatekeepers, and temple servants, in
the seventh year of Artaxerxes' rule, in the

[t]February–March [u]March–April, Nisan [v]Or *him*

fifth month.[w] 6They left Babylon on the
new moon of the first month[x] and arrived
in Jerusalem on the new moon of the fifth
month,[y] since the Lord gave them a safe
journey. 7Ezra had such a great understanding that he left out nothing from the Law
that came from the Lord or the commandments, but he taught Israel all the regulations and decisions.

8The following is a copy of the written
decree from King Artaxerxes that he gave to
Ezra the priest and reader of the Law from
the Lord:

9King Artaxerxes to Ezra the priest
and reader of the Law from the Lord.
Greetings.

10In accordance with my humane policies, I have given orders that those who
are mindful of the Judean people and
of the priests, Levites, and others in our
kingdom, those who wish to do so, may
accompany you to Jerusalem. 11Therefore,
let all who wish to do so join with you, just
as I and my seven advisors have agreed,
12so that they might take an interest in
matters in Judea and in Jerusalem, according to the Law from the Lord. 13They
might bring to Jerusalem the gifts for the
Lord of Israel that I and my advisors have
solemnly promised. They might acquire
for the Lord in Jerusalem all the gold and
silver that may be found in the country of
Babylonia, together with what the nation
gives them for the Lord's temple in Jerusalem. 14Gold and silver for bulls, rams,
lambs, and what goes with them should
be collected 15so that sacrifices may be offered on their Lord's altar in Jerusalem.
16Whatever you and your people wish to
do with the gold and silver, do it according to God's will. 17Deliver the Lord's holy
equipment that is given to you for use in
your God's temple in Jerusalem. 18What-
ever else you think of that is needed in
your God's temple, pay for it out of the
royal treasury.

19I, King Artaxerxes, have commanded
the treasurers of Syria and Phoenicia so
that whatever Ezra the priest and reader of
the Law of the Most High God sends for,
they should give to him completely, up to
5,700 pounds of silver, 20up to one hundred kors[z] of wheat, one hundred baths[a] of
wine, and a lot of salt. 21Let everything be
carried out for the Most High God strictly
according to God's Law, so that God's
wrath may not come on the king's empire
and his family. 22Also no foreign tax or any
other fine should be placed on any of the
priests, Levites, temple singers, gatekeepers, temple servants, or people working on
this temple. No one has authority to impose anything on them.

23You, Ezra, according to God's wisdom, should appoint judges and justices
to have jurisdiction over all those who
know the Law from your God, throughout all Syria and Phoenicia. You should
teach it to those who don't know it. 24All
who disobey the Law from your God or
the royal law will be strictly punished,
whether by death or some other punishment, either fine or arrest.

25[b]Bless the Lord alone, who put this
into the king's heart, to glorify his house in
Jerusalem, 26and who honored me before
the king, the counselors, all of his political
advisors,[c] and officials. 27I was encouraged
by my God's help, and I gathered people
from Israel to go up with me.

28These are the leaders, according to
their families and their divisions, who went
up with me from Babylon, in King Artaxerxes' rule:

29From the family of Phinehas, Gershom.
From the family of Ithamar, Gamael.
From the family of David, Hattush,
Shecaniah's son.
30From the family of Parosh, Zechariah,
and with him 150 men registered.
31From the family of Pahath-moab,
Eliehoenai, Zerahiah's son and with
him 200 men.
32From the family of Zattu, Shecaniah,
Jahaziel's son and with him 300 men.

[w]July–August, Av [x]March–April, Nisan [y]July–August, Av [z]A kor is equivalent to one hundred gallons dry in volume. [a]A bath is approximately equivalent to twenty gallons wet in volume. [b]Some manuscripts add *Then Ezra the scribe said.* [c]Or *Friends*

From the family of Adin, Obed,
Jonathan's son and with him 250 men.
33 From the family of Elam, Jeshaiah,
Gotholiah's son and with him 70 men.
34 From the family of Shephatiah, Zeraiah,
Michael's son and with him 70 men.
35 From the family of Joab, Obadiah,
Jehiel's son and with him 212 men.
36 From the family of Bani, Shelomith,
Josiphiah's son and with him 160 men.
37 From the family of Bebai, Zechariah,
Bebai's son and with him 28 men.
38 From the family of Azgad, Johanan,
Hakkatan's son and with him 110 men.
39 From the family of Adonikam, the
last ones, their names were Eliphelet,
Jeuel, and Shemaiah, and with them
70 men.
40 From the family of Bigvai, Uthai,
Istalcurus' son and with him 70 men.

41 I assembled them at the Theras River,
where I inspected them. We camped at
that place for three days. 42 When I found
no families from the priests or the Levites
there, 43 I sent word to Eleazar, Iduel, Maas-
mas, Elnathan, Shemaiah, Jarib, Nathan,
Elnathan, Zechariah, and Meshullam, who
were the leaders and persons of great learning. 44 I told them to go to Iddo, who was
the official in charge at the residence of the
treasury, 45 and ordered them to ask Iddo
and his relatives and the treasurers at that
place to send us some persons to serve as
priests in the Lord's house. 46 By the Lord's
direction, they brought us knowledgeable
persons from the family of Mahli, Levi's
son, and grandson of Israel, namely Sherebiah[d] with eighteen members of his family;
47 also Hashabiah, Annunus, and a brother
Jeshaiah, from the family of Hananiah, and
their family, twenty persons in all. 48 Of the
temple servants, whom David and the leaders had given for the service of the Levites,
they brought us two hundred twenty temple servants. All their names were listed in
the register.

49 Then I announced a fast for the young
people before our Lord, 50 to seek from him
a safe journey for ourselves, for those with
us, our children and our farm animals. 51 I
was ashamed to ask the king for infantry,
cavalry, and an escort for safety from our
enemies, 52 because we told the king, "The
Lord's guidance will be with those who diligently seek after him, until everything is
put right again." 53 So we prayed to our Lord
about these things, and we obtained mercy.

54 I chose twelve of the leaders of the
priestly families, Sherebiah and Hashabiah,
and ten of their companions. 55 I weighed
out for them the silver, the gold, and the
holy equipment from the Lord's house,
which the king himself, his advisors, the
officials, and all Israel had contributed. 56 I
presented to them 37,050 pounds of silver, silver equipment worth 5,700 pounds,
5,700 pounds of gold, twenty gold bowls,
and twelve bronze objects of such fine
quality that it glittered like gold. 57 I told
them, "You are holy to the Lord, and the
equipment is holy, and the silver and the
gold are solemnly committed to the Lord,
the Lord of our ancestors. 58 Be alert and
careful until you hand them over to the
leaders of the priestly families, to the Levites, and to the heads of the family houses
of Israel, in Jerusalem, in the inner rooms
of the Lord's house." 59 So the priests and
the Levites carried the silver, the gold, and
the equipment, which was in Jerusalem,
and brought them to the Lord's temple.

60 On the twelfth day of the first month,[e]
we left the Theras River and arrived in
Jerusalem by the Lord's guidance. The Lord
rescued us from every enemy on the way,
and we arrived in Jerusalem. 61 After being
there for three days, the silver and gold
were weighed and handed over to the Lord's
house, to the priest Meremoth, Uriah's son.
62 With him was Eleazar, Phinehas' son,
and with them were the Levites Jozabad,
Jeshua's son, and Moeth, Binnui's[f] son.The
whole collection was counted and weighed,
and the total weight was recorded at that
very moment. 63 All those who had returned
from exile offered sacrifices to the Lord God
of Israel, twelve bulls for all Israel, ninety-
six rams, seventy-two lambs, and twelve

[d] Gk *Asbebias* [e] March–April, Nisan [f] Gk *Sabannus*

male goats as a well-being offering—all as a sacrifice to the Lord. 64 They delivered the king's orders to the royal managers and to the commanders of Coele-Syria and Phoenicia. These officials honored the people and the Lord's temple.

Problem of mixed marriages in Judah

65 After these things happened, the leaders came to me and said, 66 "The people of Israel, the rulers, the priests, and the Levites haven't separated themselves from the impurities in the foreign neighboring peoples: the Canaanites, the Hittites, the Perizzites, the Jebusites, the Moabites, the Egyptians, and the Edomites. 67 They and their families have intermarried with their daughters, and the holy nation has been intermixed with the land's foreigners. The leaders and the officials have been sharing in this unlawful practice right from the start."

68 As soon as I heard about these things, I tore my clothes and my priest's robe. I pulled out hair from my head and beard, and I sat down depressed and very sad. 69 Everyone who was moved by the word of the Lord of Israel gathered around me as I mourned over this unlawful deed, and I sat there depressed until the evening sacrifice. 70 After rising from my fast, with my clothes and priest's robe still torn, I knelt down, stretching out my hands to the Lord, and spoke:

71 Lord, I'm ashamed and disgraced before you. 72 Our sins are greater than what we imagined. Our ignorant deeds have reached heaven. 73 From the times of our ancestors, we exist in great sin to this very day. 74 Because of our sin and our ancestors' sin, we were handed over—with our brothers, sisters, kings, and priests—to the kings of the earth for death, exile, and plunder. We continue to bear the shame until today.

75 But you, Lord, have shown to us a measure of mercy, to leave for us a descendant and honor in your holy place, 76 to uncover a light for us in the Lord's house, and to give us nourishment in the time of our slavery. 77 Even in our servitude we weren't forgotten, but the Lord showed us favor among the kings of the Persians 78 so that they've given us provisions, honored the Lord's temple, and rebuilt the ruins of Zion, to give us a solid place in Judea and Jerusalem.

79 Now that we have these things, what will we say, Lord? We have violated your commandments, which you gave by your servants the prophets: 80 "The land that you are about to possess is a land polluted with the foreigners of the land. The foreigners have filled it with their impurity. 81 So don't give your daughters in marriage to their sons, and don't take their daughters for your sons. 82 Don't seek at any time to make a peace treaty with them, so that you may be strong and eat the good things of the land and pass it on as an inheritance to your children forever." 83 All that has happened to us has resulted from our evil deeds and our great sins. 84 For you, Lord, removed our sins, and you gave us such a root as this. Yet we again turned away to disobey your Law by intermixing with the impure of the neighboring peoples. 85 Weren't you angry enough with us to destroy us without leaving a root or a descendant or our honor?

86 Lord of Israel, you are true. We are left as a root this very day. 87 Look! We are now before you in our immorality.[g] We can't stand in your presence anymore because of these things.

88 While Ezra was praying and offering up his confession, weeping in the dust before the temple, a very large crowd of men, women, and youth from Jerusalem gathered around him. There was great weeping among the people. 89 Then Shecaniah, Jehiel's son, one of the men of Israel, shouted to Ezra, "We have sinned against the Lord, and we have married foreign women from the neighboring peoples. Yet there is hope for Israel. 90 Let's swear a pledge to the Lord about this matter, to divorce all of our foreign wives, with their children, as it seems just to you and to as many who follow the Lord's Law.

[g] Or *lawlessness*

91 Stand up and take part, for it is your duty,
and we are with you to act with resolve."
92 Then Ezra stood up and made the leaders of the priests and Levites of all Israel
swear to do as was said, and they swore
9 that they would. 1 Ezra went out from
the temple court to the inner room of
Jehohanan, Eliashib's son, 2 and stayed the
night there. He neither ate bread nor drank
water, as he was mourning for the great
immoral deeds of the multitude.
3 An announcement was issued throughout Judea and Jerusalem to all who had returned from exile that they should gather
at Jerusalem. 4 Whoever didn't meet there
within two or three days, according to the
order of the leading elders, their animals
would be used for sacrifice and the people
themselves cut off from the company of
those who had returned from the exile.
5 Then everyone from the tribe of Judah
and the tribe of Benjamin gathered together
at Jerusalem within three days; this was the
twentieth day of the ninth month.[h] 6 The
whole crowd sat in the square of the temple, shivering because it was winter. 7 Then
Ezra stood up and said, "You have broken
the Law and married foreign women, and
thus have increased the sin of Israel. 8 So
confess and give glory to the Lord God of
our ancestors. 9 Do God's will and separate
yourselves from the neighboring peoples
and from the foreign women."
10 The whole crowd cried out, "We will do
what you have said. 11 But it's a big crowd,
and it's winter, and we aren't strong enough
to keep standing outside. This isn't something we can do in one or two days, because
we have sinned too greatly in these matters. 12 So let the leaders of the crowd remain, and let all those in our settlements
who have foreign wives come at a specific
time, 13 with the local elders and judges,
until we are free from the Lord's wrath that
is against us in this affair."
14 Jonathan, Asahel's son, and Jahzeiah,
Tikvah's[i] son, accepted these terms, and
Meshullam and Levi and Shabbethai supported them as moderators. 15 Those who
had returned from exile followed these rec-
ommendations in every respect. 16 Ezra the
priest chose for himself the leading men of
their families, each by name. On the new
moon of the tenth month[j] they convened
their investigation of this affair. 17 The cases
of the men who had married foreign wives
were completed by the new moon of the
first month.[k]
18 Those who were found to have married
foreign wives from the priesthood were:
19 Of the family of Jeshua, Jozadak's son,
and his brothers Maaseiah, Eleazar, Jarib,
and Jodan. 20 They pledged to divorce their
wives and to offer rams as reconciliation
for their error in judgment. 21 Of the family of Immer: Hanani, Zebadiah, Maaseiah,
Shemaiah, Jehiel, and Azariah. 22 Of the
family of Pashhur: Elioenai, Maaseiah, Ishmael, Nathanael, Gedaliah, and Salthas.
23 And of the Levites: Jozabad, Shimei,
Kelaiah who was Kelita, Pethahiah, Judah,
and Jonah. 24 Of the temple singers: Eliashib and Zaccur.[l] 25 Of the gatekeepers:
Shallum and Telem.[m]
26 Of Israel: of the family of Parosh: Ramiah, Izziah, Malchijah, Mijamin, Eleazar,
Asibias, and Benaiah. 27 Of the family of
Elam: Mattaniah, Zechariah, Jezrielus,
Abdi, Jeremoth, and Elijah. 28 Of the family
of Zamoth: Eliadas, Eliashib, Othoniah, Jeremoth, Zabad and Zerdaiah. 29 Of the family of Bebai: Jehohanan, Hananiah, Zabbai,
and Emathis. 30 Of the family of Mani: Ola-
mus, Mamuchus, Adaiah, Jashub, Sheal, and
Jeremoth. 31 Of the family of Addi: Naathus,
Moossias, Laccunus, Naidus, Bescaspasmys,
Sesthel, Belnuus, and Manasseas. 32 Of the
family of Annan: Elionas, Asaias, Melchias,
Sabbaias, and Simon Chosamaeus. 33 Of the
family of Hashum: Mattenai, Mattattah,
Zabad, Eliphelet, Manasseh, and Shimei.
34 Of the family of Bani: Jeremai, Momdius,
Maerus, Joel, Mamdai, Bedeiah, Vaniah,
Carabasion, Eliashib, Mamitanemus, Elia-
sis, Binnui, Elialis, Shimei, Shelemiah,
and Nethaniah. Of the family of Ezora:

[h] November–December, Kislev [i] Gk *Thocanos* [j] December–January, Tevet [k] March–April, Nisan [l] Gk *Bacchurus* [m] Gk *Tolbanes*

Shashai, Azarel, Azael, Samatus, Zambris,
and Joseph. 35 Of the family of Nooma: Ma-
zitias, Zabad, Iddo, Joel, and Benaiah. 36 All
these had married foreign women, and they
divorced them, along with their children.

37 The priests, the Levites, and the Israelites lived in Jerusalem and in the countryside. On the new moon of the seventh
month,[n] after the people of Israel were
settled in their homes, 38 the whole crowd
gathered together in the courtyard near
the east gate of the temple. 39 They told
Ezra the chief priest and reader to bring
the Law from Moses that had been given
by the Lord God of Israel. 40 On the new
moon of the seventh month, Ezra the chief
priest brought the Law before the whole
crowd, both men and women, as well as
the priests, to hear the Law. 41 He read from
dawn until noon in the courtyard near the
temple gate, before men and women. The
whole crowd gave full attention to the Law.
42 Ezra the priest and reader of the Law
stood on the wooden podium that had been
prepared. 43 Next to him stood Mattathiah,
Shema, Ananias, Azariah, Uriah, Hezekiah,
and Baalsamus at his right; 44 and at his left
were Pedaiah, Mishael, Malchijah, Lothasu-
bus, Nabariah, and Zechariah. 45 Ezra took
up the Law scroll in front of the large crowd
(for he was in charge in the place of honor
before everyone). 46 When he opened the
Law, everyone stood up. Ezra blessed the
Lord God Most High, the God of heavenly
forces, the almighty, 47 and the whole crowd
responded, "Amen." They lifted up their
hands. They fell to the ground and worshipped the Lord. 48 The Levites (Jeshua,
Anniuth, Sherebiah, Jadinus, Akkub, Shabbethai, Hodiah, Maiannas, Kelita, Azariah,
Jozabad, Hanan, and Pelaiah) taught and
read the Law from the Lord to the crowd,
explaining the meaning.

49 Then Attharates said to Ezra the chief
priest and reader, and to the Levites who
were teaching the people, and to everyone,
who were all weeping as they listened to the
Law: 50 "This day is holy to the Lord. 51 Go
your way, eat the rich food and drink the
sweet wine, and send some of it to those
who have nothing, 52 because the day is
holy to the Lord. Don't be sad, because the
Lord will honor you." 53 The Levites ordered
all the people, "This day is holy; don't be
sad." 54 They all went their way, to eat and
drink and to rejoice, and to share with
those who had none, and to enjoy themselves. 55 They were excited by the words
that they had been taught. And they came
together.

[n] September–October, Tishrei

PRAYER OF MANASSEH

[1]Lord Almighty, God of our ancestors,
God of Abraham, Isaac, Jacob,
and their righteous children,
[2]you made heaven and earth
with all their beauty.
[3]You set limits for the sea
by speaking your command.
You closed the bottomless pit,
and sealed it by your powerful
and glorious name.
[4]All things fear you and tremble
in your presence,
[5]because no one can endure
the brightness of your glory.
No one can resist the fury
of your threat against sinners.

[6]But your promised mercies
are beyond measure and imagination,
[7a]because you are the highest, Lord,
kind, patient, and merciful,
and you feel sorry over human troubles.

Syriac
[7b]You, Lord, according to
your gentle grace,
promised forgiveness to those
who are sorry for their sins.
In your great mercy,
you allowed sinners to turn
from their sins and find salvation.

[8]Therefore, Lord,
God of those who do what is right,
you didn't offer
Abraham, Isaac, and Jacob,
who didn't sin against you,
a chance to change
their hearts and lives.
But you offer me, the sinner,
a chance to change my heart and life,
[9a]because my sins outnumbered
the grains of sand by the sea.
My sins are many, Lord; they are many.
I am not worthy to look up,
to gaze into heaven
because of my many sins.

Syriac
[9b]Now, Lord, I suffer justly.
I deserve the troubles I encounter.
Already I'm caught in a trap.

[10]I'm held down by iron chains
so that I can't lift up my head
because of my sins.
There's no relief for me,
because I made you angry,
doing wrong in front of your face,
setting up false gods
and committing offenses.

[11]Now I bow down before you
from deep within my heart,
begging for your kindness.
[12]I have sinned, Lord, I have sinned,
and I know the laws I've broken.
[13]I'm praying, begging you:
Forgive me, Lord, forgive me.

Don't destroy me along with my sins.
Don't keep my bad deeds
in your memory forever.
Don't sentence me to the earth's depths,
for you, Lord, are the God
of those who turn from their sins.
[14]In me you'll show how kind you are.
Although I'm not worthy,
you'll save me according
to your great mercy.

[15]I will praise you continuously
all the days of my life,
because all of heaven's forces praise you,
and the glory is yours
forever and always. Amen.

PSALM 151[a]

151A [Hebrew]

A hallelujah of David, Jesse's son.

1 I was the smallest of my brothers,
the youngest of my father's sons.
He made me shepherd of his flock,
ruler over their young.

2 My hands made a flute,
my fingers a lyre.
Let me give glory to the LORD,
I thought to myself.

3 The mountains
cannot witness to God;
the hills cannot proclaim him.
But the trees have cherished
my words,
the flocks my deeds.

4 Who can proclaim,
who can announce,
who can declare the LORD's deeds?
God has seen everything;
God has heard everything;
God has listened.

5 God sent his prophet to anoint me;
Samuel to make me great.
My brothers went out to meet him,
handsome in form and appearance:

6 Their stature tall,
their hair beautiful,
but the LORD God
did not choose them.

7 Instead, he sent and took me
from following the flock.
God anointed me with holy oil;
God made me leader for his people,
ruler over the children
of his covenant.

151B [Hebrew and Syriac][b]

At the beginning of David's power
after the prophet of God anointed him.

1 I went out to attack the Philistine,
who cursed me by his idols.

2 But after I uncovered his own sword,
I cut off his head.
So I removed the shame
from the Israelites.[c]

Psalm 151 [Greek]

This additional psalm is said to have been
written by David when he fought Goliath
in single combat.

1 I was small among my brothers,
and the youngest of my father's sons.
I was shepherd of my father's sheep.

2 My hands made a musical instrument;
my fingers strung a lap harp.

3 Who will tell my Lord?
The Lord himself, the Lord hears me.

4 The Lord himself sent his messenger,
and took me away
from my father's sheep.
He put special oil on my forehead
to anoint me.

5 My brothers were good-looking and tall,
but the Lord didn't take
special pleasure in them.

6 I went out to meet the Philistine,
who cursed me by his idols.

7 But I took his own sword out of its sheath
and cut off his head.
So I removed the shame
from the Israelites.[d]

[a]The oldest tradition indicates that Psalm 151 was originally two psalms. [b]The Heb manuscript is damaged. The translation here follows the Syriac. [c]Or *children of Israel* [d]Or *children of Israel*

3 MACCABEES

Battle of Raphia

1 [a]Now Ptolemy Philopator learned from those who had returned that Antiochus had captured some of Ptolemy's territory. Ptolemy gave orders to all his forces, foot soldiers and mounted soldiers, to break camp. Along with all his forces, and accompanied by his sister Arsinoë, he set out for the region of Raphia where Antiochus' troops had set up camp.

2 Now a certain Theodotus made up his mind to carry out a plot to kill Ptolemy. He took the best of the weapons that had been assigned to him from Ptolemy's own arsenal. He crossed over by night to Ptolemy's tent, intending to put an end to the
war by killing him single-handedly. 3 But
Dositheus, known as Drimylus' son, had led Ptolemy away and arranged for an unimportant person to sleep in the king's tent. This person then met the fate intended for Ptolemy. (Now this Dositheus was a Jew by birth, but he had changed his mind about their customs and had turned away from the teachings of his ancestors.)

4 When a fierce battle arose, and things were going rather well for Antiochus, Arsinoë went out to Ptolemy's army with pathetic cries and with her hair all in disarray. She urged them to rescue themselves and their children and wives, and bravely promised to give to each man two manehs
of gold if they won the battle. 5 And so
it turned out that the enemies were destroyed in hand-to-hand combat, and many
were taken prisoner. 6 After overcoming the
plot, Ptolemy decided to visit the neighboring cities to encourage them. 7 By doing this
and by distributing gifts for their sacred shrines, he reassured his subjects.

Ptolemy Philopator at the temple

8 The Jews had sent elders and members of the council to greet him, to bring gifts of friendship, and to congratulate him on recent events. As a result he was even more eager to come to them as soon as possible.
9 So he traveled to Jerusalem, sacrificed to the supreme God, made thank offerings, and did what was appropriate for the temple. As he entered the temple, he was struck with amazement at its brilliance and
beauty. 10 And as he admired the orderly
arrangement of the temple, he conceived
a notion to enter into the holy place. 11 But
they said that it wasn't right to do this since even those of their own nation weren't permitted to enter it. Not even all the priests were allowed, but only the chief priest, who was in charge over all, and he could do so only once a year. But Philopator wasn't at
all persuaded. 12 Even after the law was read
to him, he continued to claim that it was necessary for him to enter, saying, "Even if those persons are denied this honor, I
shouldn't be." 13 He asked why, when he was
entering every other sacred place, none of
those present prevented him. 14 And someone said (without thinking) that he was
wrong to speak of this as a sign. 15 "But even
if for some reason this were true," Philopator replied, "why should I, of all people, not enter, whether they are willing or not?"

The Jews' reaction

16 But the priests fell to the ground, still in their sacred robes. They filled the temple with crying and tears, praying to the supreme God to help them and to change the mind of the one who was wrongly impos-
ing himself. 17 Those who were left in the
city were troubled and hurried out, thinking something mysterious was happening.
18 The young girls who had been kept secluded at home rushed out with their mothers. They sprinkled their hair with dust and began to fill the streets with weeping and
groaning. 19 Even the young women who
had just been adorned for their weddings left the bridal bedrooms that had been prepared for the marriage night. Neglecting all proper modesty, they came together in
the city in a wild rush. 20 Mothers and nurses
left newborn children here and there, some

[a]The opening paragraph or paragraphs of the book have been lost.

in houses, some in the streets, and crowded together into the most high temple without looking back. 21The people who assembled offered all kinds of prayers on account of the evil plot of the king. 22Some of the bolder citizens weren't going to put up with his intended plan or fulfill what he had in mind. 23They rallied each other to attack with weapons and to die courageously for the sake of the law of their ancestors, creating a great uproar in the holy place. The old men and the elders were barely able to restrain them, but turned them at last to the same stance of prayer.

24Now the crowd in front of the temple was occupied in praying, 25but the elders standing near the king tried in many ways to turn his arrogant mind from the scheme that he had conceived. 26But he, being made bold and ignoring all their arguments, began to make his approach, determined to carry out his plan. 27So when those who were near him saw this, they turned together with the people to appeal to the one who was fully able to come to their aid and not to overlook this insolent transgression. 28An immense roar went up from the intensity and passion of the crowd's concerted shouting. 29Indeed it seemed that not only the people but also the walls and the entire land were echoing, because at that time all were prepared to accept death instead of making the holy place impure.

Prayer of Simon

2 [b]Then the high priest Simon knelt in front of the temple, extended his hands, and offered this prayer in a dignified manner:

2"Lord, Lord, king of the heavens and master of all creation, holy among the holy ones, only ruler, almighty: Pay attention to us. We are being crushed by an evil and impure man, caught up in his own arrogance and power. 3You are the creator of all things and the just master who rules over all. You judge those who act with violence and arrogance. 4You destroyed those who did evil in the past, even giants. The giants trusted in their bodily strength and boldness, but you destroyed them in a great flood. 5The people of Sodom acted arrogantly and were notorious for their wicked deeds.[c] You destroyed them with fire and sulfur, making them an example to others for all time. 6When the arrogant ruler of Egypt enslaved your holy people Israel, you tested him with many, varied punishments. You made your power known; indeed, you made known your great strength. 7When the ruler of Egypt pursued Israel with chariots and a multitude of people, you overwhelmed him with the depth of the sea. But those who trusted in you, the one who holds power over all creation—these people you brought safely through the sea. 8And when they saw your powerful work, they praised you, the almighty.

9"Although you, King, created the whole wide earth, you chose this city and set this place apart for your name, though you don't need anything. You made it wonderful, giving it a splendid appearance, and established its order for the reputation of your great and honored name. 10Because you love the house of Israel, you promised that you would hear our prayer if we came to this holy place and prayed whenever we experienced a setback or were overwhelmed with distress. 11Indeed, you are faithful and true. 12Whenever our ancestors were hard-pressed or humiliated, you helped them and rescued them from great hardships. 13See now, Holy King, how we are being afflicted and have been subjected to our enemies and are weakened to the point of helplessness because of our many and great sins. 14But in the midst of our calamity this arrogant and unholy man is determined to insult the holy place dedicated on earth to your glorious name. 15For human beings can't enter your dwelling place, the heaven of heavens. 16But since you were pleased for your glory to rest among your people Israel, you set this place apart. 17Don't take vengeance on us

[b]Some manuscripts lack 2:1. [c]Some manuscripts read *secretive in their wicked deeds*.

because of the impurity of these people.
Don’t call us to account because of their
pollution, so that the lawless don’t boast
in their hearts or rejoice in the arrogance
of their tongues, saying, 18“We trampled
the house of holiness just as the houses of
idols are trampled.” 19Wipe away our sins
and scatter our faults to the winds, and
reveal your compassion in this hour.
20Let your mercies quickly overtake us.
Put praises in the mouths of those who
are downcast and crushed in their spirits,
granting us peace.

Punishment of Ptolemy Philopator

21Then the God who watches over all
things, the first father of all, holy among
the holy ones, heard this lawful prayer
and scourged the one who had claimed too
much for himself in his violence and arrogance. 22God shook him this way and that
as a reed is shaken by the wind, with the
result that he lay helpless on the ground.
His limbs were paralyzed, and he was unable to speak, since he was struck by a just
judgment. 23His friends and bodyguards
saw that the punishment that had seized
him was severe. Fearing that even his life
might fail, they quickly dragged him out,
since they were terror-stricken. 24After a
while, the king recovered, and even though
he had been punished, he didn’t change his
heart and mind at all, but went away issuing bitter threats.

Ptolemy Philopator and the Alexandrian Jews

25When he had returned to Egypt, he
added to his evil deeds with the assistance
of his drinking companions and friends,
who were strangers to everything just.
26He wasn’t satisfied with his innumerable
indecent acts, but he also advanced to such
a degree of impudence that he circulated
false reports in the various districts. Many
of his friends took note of the king’s purpose and followed his lead. 27He proposed
to spread blame publicly against the Jewish
nation. He set up a stone near the tower in
the courtyard with the following inscription carved upon it:

> 28None who refuse to sacrifice are to
> enter into their sanctuaries. In addi-
> tion all the Jews are to be registered and
> their property cataloged. Those who ob-
> ject are to be taken by force and put to
> death. 29Those who are registered are to
> be branded on the body by fire with the
> ivy leaf sign of Dionysus and are also to
> be assigned to their former, limited civic
> status.

30But so as not to seem hateful to all, he
added:

> But if any of them should prefer to join
> those who have been initiated into the
> mysteries, these are to enjoy political
> rights equal to the Alexandrians.

31Now some Jews, while pretending to
detest the steps to be undertaken for the
city’s religion, readily surrendered themselves to share in great fame through the
association they would have with the king.
32But the honorable majority were strong
and didn’t depart from their religion. They
bravely tried to save themselves from being
registered by resorting to bribes in exchange
for their lives. 33They remained hopeful of
obtaining help, and they looked with contempt on those Jews who had deserted
them. They considered those who gave in
to be enemies of the Jewish nation, and no
longer associated with them or offered them
assistance.

Genocide, slander, and neighborly advocates

3 When the godless Philopator learned
of this, he became so enraged that not
only was he angry at those Jews in Alexandria but he also was very bitterly opposed
to those living in the countryside. He gave
an order that they should all be gathered
together at once into one place and killed
by the most brutal means possible. 2While
these plans were being put into action,
some people plotted to injure the Jewish nation by circulating a hostile report
against them on the pretext that the Jews
were hindering others from practicing their
own customs. 3But the Jews were maintaining goodwill and unswerving loyalty toward
the royal house. 4While they worshipped

God and conducted their lives according to God's Law, they kept themselves separate in the matter of foods. For this reason they appeared hostile to some people. [5]But they had established a good reputation with everyone through their lifestyle of doing the right thing. [6]Now even though the Jews' good deeds on behalf of the nation were commonly talked about by everyone, those of other races didn't take these into account. [7]Instead, they kept harping on the differences in worship and diet, and claimed that the Jewish people were loyal neither to the king nor to the authorities, but were hostile and strongly opposed to the royal administration. And so they placed significant blame on the Jews.

[8]But the Greeks in the city, who hadn't been injured in any way, saw the unexpected turmoil surrounding these people and the purposeless mobs that were forming. Although they didn't have the power to offer assistance, for they lived under tyranny, they tried to encourage the Jews. They were grieved and assumed that these circumstances would change for the better, [9]because so great a community shouldn't be left to its fate in this way, since it had done nothing wrong. [10]Already some neighbors and friends and business associates secretly drew them aside and promised that they would fight by their side and make every effort to assist them.

Ptolemy Philopator's decree

[11]But the king took pride in his present success and disregarded the authority of the supreme God. Assuming that he would continue in the same plan without hindrance, he wrote this letter against the Jews:

> [12]King Ptolemy Philopator to his generals and soldiers in Egypt and in every place. Greetings and good health.
>
> [13]Both I myself and our affairs prosper. [14]After our campaign against Asia Minor came to a successful conclusion, as you yourselves are aware, with the gods fighting alongside us, [15]we thought that we should care for the nations inhabiting Coele-Syria and Phoenicia, not with the violence of the spear but with fairness and much kindness, eagerly treating them well. [16]After we had distributed generous funds to the temples in every city, we proceeded also to Jerusalem. We went up to honor the temple of those wretched people who never cease from their folly. [17]They spoke as if they welcomed our presence, but in fact they acted in a way that was dishonest. When we wanted to enter their sanctuary and to honor it with the most extraordinary and beautiful gifts, [18]they were carried away by their traditional arrogance and prevented us from entering. They were spared a display of our power because of the kindness that we have toward all people. [19]But they made clear their ill will toward us, as the only one of the nations showing such stiff-necked defiance to kings and to their own benefactors. They aren't willing to receive anything as sincere.
>
> [20]But we showed indulgence toward the folly of these people and returned to Egypt in triumph. We treated all the nations in a kindly way and acted in a manner that was proper. [21]Among other things, we made known to everyone our policy of amnesty toward their fellow Jews here because of our alliance with them and the countless matters sincerely entrusted to them from the beginning. We bravely decided to make a change, to consider them worthy of Alexandrian citizenship and to make them partners in the regular religious rites.[d] [22]But they received it in a disagreeable manner and rejected what is good in line with their natural, spiteful character. Turning continually to what is worthless, [23]they not only rejected the priceless offer of citizenship but also showed their contempt, by what they said and by their silence, for those few Jews among them who favored us with honor. In every case they suspected, in keeping with their most shameful way

[d]Other manuscripts read *partners with the regular priests.*

of life, that we would swiftly reverse the policy. 24 We were fully persuaded indeed by such proofs that these people were ill-disposed toward us in every way.

Therefore, we took care so that, if a sudden rebellion should arise against us later, we won't find that we have these evil people at our backs as traitors and uncivilized enemies. 25 We have given an order that as soon as this letter arrives, you are immediately to send to us those Jews who live among you, together with their wives and children, to suffer a certain and shameful death appropriate for enemies. Treat them harshly and abusively, and bind them on all sides in iron chains. 26 We are sure that, when these people have all been punished, the affairs of our state will be established more securely and in a more excellent condition for the future. 27 But whoever shelters any of the Jews, from an elderly person to a child to nursing infants, will be tortured, household and all, with the most horrible punishments. 28 But the one who is willing to give information will receive the property of the person falling under judgment. They will also be given two thousand drachmen[e] from the royal treasury, and will be rewarded with their freedom. 29 But every place, without exception, where a Jew is discovered to be sheltered, will be laid waste and burned with fire. It will become utterly useless to every living creature for all time.

30 And so the form of the letter was committed to writing.

Rounding up the Jews

4 Wherever this decree was read, a feast was arranged for the Gentiles at public expense with shouts of joy. Their deep, long-standing hatred was now openly being revealed. 2 But among the Jews, there were constant grief, lament, and crying. Everywhere their hearts were on fire as they groaned and bewailed the unexpected destruction that the king had suddenly inflicted on them. 3 What district or city, or what inhabited place of any kind, or what streets weren't filled with grieving and weeping for them? 4 They were being sent off together by the generals in every city in a merciless and cruel manner. At the sight of these unusual punishments, even some of the Jews' enemies wept over their most miserable expulsion, for they saw their pitiable state and reflected on the uncertain outcome of life. 5 A multitude of gray-haired, elderly men were being led away, bent over with age, their feet plodding along under the distress of a forced, swift march, with no consideration given to their age. 6 Young women, who had just entered the bridal bedroom for the sharing of life, exchanged joy for weeping and sprinkled dust on their hair that was still wet with perfume. They were led away with their heads bare and began to sing a funeral song together in place of a wedding song, as they were roughly handled by the cruel treatment of a foreign nation.[f] 7 These captives were violently dragged away in public view to be put on board ship. 8 Their husbands, in the prime of their youth, had ropes tied around their necks instead of festive garlands. They spent the remaining days of their wedding festivities weeping rather than celebrating and enjoying youthful amusements, seeing the grave already yawning at their feet. 9 They were driven like animals, constrained by the power of iron chains. Some were fastened by the neck to the ship's benches; some were secured by their feet with unbreakable shackles. 10 Moreover, they were plunged into total darkness due to thick planks positioned above them so that they would receive the treatment due traitors throughout the entire voyage.

11 When these people had been brought to the place called Schedia, and the voyage was finished, just as the king had decreed, Ptolemy ordered the captives to be encamped on the outskirts of the city in the racecourse. This stadium had been built with an im-

[e] A drachme was equivalent to a typical day's wage. [f] Some manuscripts read *as though torn asunder by the lion's whelps of a foreign nation.*

mense perimeter and was very well placed for providing a public spectacle to all those returning home to the city and to those setting out from the city into the country for a trip abroad. The captives had no communication at all with the king's forces, nor were they considered worthy of the protection of the city wall. [12]When this was done, the king heard that their fellow Jews were frequently going forth from the city in secret to express sympathy for the shameful misery of their kindred. [13]He became very angry and gave an order to deal with these people in exactly the same thorough fashion as the others, not leaving out any part of their punishment. [14]The entire tribe was to be registered by name—no longer for the service of hard labor described earlier, but to be tortured with the prescribed punishments and, in the end, to be killed within a single day. [15]So the process of drawing up a list of these people was carried out with cruel eagerness and intense diligence from the rising of the sun until its setting, coming to an end, though still incomplete, after forty days.

[16]Filled with constant joy, the king organized banquets at the sites of all his idols. With a mind that had strayed far from the truth and with a polluted mouth, he praised objects that were deaf and unable to speak or give aid, but he spoke improper words against the supreme God. [17]At the end of the forty days, the clerks reported to the king that they were no longer able to complete the task of drawing up a list of all the Jews because of their countless number. [18]Though the majority were still in the country, some still in their homes, and some even on-site,[g] the job had become impossible for all the generals in Egypt. [19]After the king had threatened the clerks severely, claiming that they had accepted money to arrange a plan of escape, he came to be convinced [20]when they explained and offered proof that both the paper supply and the reed pens that they were using had already run out. [21]But this happened by the invincible providence of the one who was giving the Jews help from heaven.

Sleep foils the king's plan

5 Then the king, completely stubborn and filled with extreme rage and bitterness, called for Hermon the elephant keeper. [2]He ordered him to drug all the elephants—five hundred in number—with heaping handfuls of frankincense and much unmixed wine on the following day. When the abundant quantity of drink had driven them wild, Hermon was to bring them in so that the Jews might meet their doom. [3]When Ptolemy had given these commands, he went back to his partying, having gathered those of his friends and of the army who were especially hostile toward the Jews. [4]But Hermon the elephant keeper promptly began to carry out the orders. [5]The servants in charge of the Jews went out in the evening, bound the hands of those enduring this distress, and arranged for their continued custody through the night. They expected that the entire race would come to a ruinous end. [6]To the Gentiles it seemed that the Jews were entirely without refuge, since in their chains, distress surrounded them on every side. [7]But with persistent cries and tears they all called upon their almighty Lord and merciful God and father, who rules over every power. They continued to pray [8]that he would turn away the evil plot against them and rescue them with a glorious display of power from their impending fate. [9]So their prayer rose earnestly to heaven.

[10]Now when Hermon had made the savage elephants drunk so that they were full of a great quantity of wine and drugged with frankincense, he came to the palace courtyard early in the morning to report to the king. [11]But God sent to the king a portion of sleep, the precious creation from before recorded time, granted night and day by the one who gives it generously to whomever he wishes. [12]By the Lord's doing, the king was overcome by a most pleasant and deep sleep,[h] such that he utterly failed in his unlawful purpose and was completely cheated out of his stubborn plan. [13]And the Jews, having escaped the announced hour,

[g]Other manuscripts have *on the way*. [h]Some manuscripts read *deep sleep from evening until the ninth hour.*

praised their holy God and again prayed that the one who is quickly reconciled to his people would show the might of his exceedingly strong hand to the arrogant Gentiles.

14 When it was almost the middle of the tenth hour, the person in charge of the invitations, seeing that the guests were gathered, approached the king and nudged him. 15 After waking him with some difficulty, he informed him that the time of the banquet was already slipping by, and gave him an account concerning the matter. 16 The king, after considering this, returned to his drinking and commanded those who were present at the banquet to recline across from him. 17 When this had been done, he urged the guests to give themselves over to feasting and to make up for the lost time by celebrating all the more now. 18 After the party had been going on for some time, the king called Hermon in and asked him, with angry threats, why the Jews had been permitted to remain alive through the present day. 19 But Hermon pointed out that he had fully carried out the orders at night, and his friends confirmed his story. 20 So the king, with a savagery worse than the tyrant Phalaris, said that the Jews could be grateful for today's sleep, but "Tomorrow," he said, "without delay, prepare the elephants in the same way for the destruction of the unseemly Jews." 21 So the king spoke, and when all those present gave their unanimous approval readily and joyfully, they all departed for their own homes. 22 But they didn't spend their night sleeping so much as devising all kinds of insults for those who seemed to be doomed.

Forgetfulness foils the king's plan

23 By dawn, when the roosters began to crow, Hermon had outfitted the beasts and started them moving along in the great colonnade. 24 Crowds of people from throughout the city gathered for the most sorry spectacle and were eagerly awaiting the early morning. 25 The Jews were at their last gasp, since time was short. With tearful prayer and mournful sounds, they stretched out their hands to heaven and begged the supreme God to help them again quickly. 26 Before the rays of the sun were scattered across the sky, while the king was receiving his friends, Hermon approached him and invited him to come out, indicating that the king's desire was ready to be put into action. 27 When he heard this, the king was surprised at the unusual invitation to come out from the palace. He was completely overcome by confusion, and he asked what it was that they had worked so hard to prepare for him. 28 Now this was God's doing, the God who is Lord over all things, who had placed in the king's mind forgetfulness of the schemes that he had previously devised. 29 Hermon and all the king's friends pointed out, "The beasts and the forces have been prepared, Your Majesty, according to your careful plan."

30 But at these words the king was filled with extreme wrath because the providence of God had scattered every thought of his concerning these matters. He glared threateningly at Hermon and said, 31 "If your parents or children were here, I would have them prepared[i] as a lavish meal for wild animals instead of the Jews. They are blameless as far as I'm concerned, and have demonstrated constant loyalty above all others toward my ancestors. 32 Indeed, if it weren't for the affection of our common upbringing and your service, you would've been deprived of life instead of them." 33 So Hermon endured an unexpected and dangerous threat, and his eyes and face showed his dismay. 34 One by one the king's friends slipped away sullenly, and the guests were dismissed, each to his own business. 35 Now when the Jews heard about what the king had said, they praised God, the Lord, the king of kings, who had made his power apparent in giving them this assistance.

36 Now the king resumed the entire banquet, according to the same rules, and began inviting the guests to return to their celebration. 37 He summoned Hermon and said with a threat, "How often, you sorry creature, must I command you concern-

[i] Some manuscripts read *they would have prepared* or *you would have prepared.*

ing these same matters? [38]Equip the elephants yet again for the destruction of the Jews tomorrow." [39]But the king's officials, who were reclining at the table with him, were taken aback by his unstable mind and began to protest as follows: [40]"Your Majesty, how long will you test us, as though we were fools, giving an order a third time to destroy the Jews and again reversing your decisions? [41]As a result, the city is in an uproar because of its expectation. It is already swarming with mobs and is very much at risk of being plundered." [42]At that point the king, a Phalaris in every way, was filled with madness and gave no thought at all to the change of heart that had come about in him concerning the punishment of the Jews. He firmly swore an irrevocable pledge that he would send these people to the grave[j] without delay, mangled by the knees and feet of the beasts. [43]He swore he would march against Judea and swiftly burn it to the ground with fire and spear. Their temple, which he hadn't been allowed to enter, he would level with fire, ridding it forever of those who performed sacrifices there. [44]Then the friends and officials departed with joy and confidently assigned the armed forces to the places in the city that were best for keeping watch.

Horror at the racecourse

[45]Now the elephant keeper drove the beasts almost to a state of madness with the most fragrant drinks, namely, wine mixed with incense, and he equipped them with frightful trappings. [46]Around dawn, when the city was already filled with countless crowds moving toward the racecourse, he entered the palace and urged the king on to the matter at hand. [47]So the king, filled with rage, rushed out with all fierceness to join the beasts. He wanted to witness with steely heart and with his own eyes the painful and miserable destruction of the previously mentioned people. [48]The Jews saw the dust cloud created by the elephants going out at the gate, the armed force following them, and the marching of the crowd, and they heard the noisy ruckus. [49]Thinking that this was their final moment of life, the fulfillment of their most wretched fear, they gave themselves over to pitiful wailing and weeping. They began to kiss each other, embracing their families and throwing themselves upon each other's shoulders, parents to children and mothers to daughters. Other women had their newborn infants at their breasts drawing their last milk. [50]Nevertheless, when they took into consideration the assistance that they had previously received from heaven, they took their infants away from their breasts and all together bowed down. [51]They cried out with a very loud voice, pleading with the Lord of all power to have mercy on them by intervening, since they now stood at the gates of death.

Prayer of Eleazar

6 Now a certain Eleazar was a distinguished person among the priests from the country. He had attained an advanced age, and throughout his life he had displayed every virtue. He restrained the elders around him from calling on the holy God, while he prayed as follows:

[2]Dear King, mighty in power, almighty God Most High, you govern the whole creation with mercy. [3]Look upon the descendants of Abraham, upon the children of sacred Jacob, father, a people set apart as your inheritance, who are strangers perishing in a strange land. [4]Pharaoh, the former ruler of this land of Egypt, with his multitude of chariots, showed great presumption with his arrogant actions and proud boasts. But you destroyed him along with his arrogant army. You drowned them in the sea and showed forth the light of your mercy to your people Israel. [5]Sennacherib, the cruel king of the Assyrians, prided himself in his innumerable forces and had already subdued the entire earth by the spear. He rose up against your holy city, speaking fierce words with arrogant boasting, and you, Lord, shattered him, displaying your power openly to many nations. [6]Daniel's three friends in Babylon voluntarily gave their

[j]Gk *Hades*

lives to the fire in order not to serve worthless things. You rescued them, sprinkling the fiery furnace with dew, such that not a hair on their heads was harmed, while you sent the flames forth upon all their enemies. 7Because Daniel was envied and slandered, he was thrown down into the earth to lions as food for the beasts. But you led him back up into the light unhurt. 8And you, Father, looked upon Jonah, when he was wasting away in the belly of a sea monster from the depths, and you restored him unharmed to all his family.

9So you who hate arrogance, most merciful defender of all things, reveal yourself quickly to those of the people of Israel who are being spitefully mistreated by vile and lawless Gentiles. 10If we've gotten tangled up in sins during our exile, rescue us from the hand of our enemies, Lord, and destroy us by whatever fate you choose. 11Don't let these empty-headed people praise their empty gods for the destruction of your dearly loved people, saying, "Not even their God rescued them!" 12But you, who have all might and all power, eternal one, look upon us now. Have mercy on us who, by the senseless arrogance of lawless people, are being deprived of life as if we were traitors. 13Let the Gentiles tremble in fear today at your matchless power, honored one, you who possess the power to rescue the people of Jacob. 14The entire multitude of infants and their parents is begging you with tears. 15Let it be shown to all the Gentiles that you are with us, Lord, and you haven't turned your face away from us. But just as you have said, "Not even when they were in the land of their enemies did I neglect them,"[k] so bring it to pass, Lord.

God delivers the Jews

16Now as Eleazar was concluding his prayer, the king arrived at the racecourse with the beasts and all the arrogance of his power. 17When the Jews saw this, they cried out to heaven so loudly that even the nearby valleys echoed, putting the army into a panic. 18Then the most glorious, almighty, and true God showed forth his holy face and opened the heavenly gates. Two glorified angels of frightful appearance descended, visible to all except the Jews. 19They opposed the power of the enemies, filled them with confusion and dread, and made them freeze in their tracks as with shackles. 20Even the body of the king gave a slight shudder, and he forgot his sullen arrogance. 21The elephants turned back on the armed forces that were following them, and they began to trample and destroy them.

22The king's anger was changed into pity and tears because of the schemes that he had previously devised. 23When he heard the loud cry and saw the Jews all lying on the ground awaiting destruction, he wept and violently threatened his friends, saying, 24"You have used your power badly and acted more savagely than tyrants. You are now attempting to rob even me, your benefactor, of my rule and my life. Secretly you devise things that are of no advantage to the kingdom. 25Who has driven from their homes those who have faithfully commanded the fortresses of our country? Who has senselessly gathered them all in this place? 26Who has so unjustly rewarded those who from the beginning differed from all the nations in their goodwill toward us in every way, and who often have taken upon themselves the worst human dangers by mistreating them on every side? 27Release them from those undeserved chains! Send them in peace back to their homes, and seek forgiveness for the deeds that have been done. 28Free the children of the almighty, living God of heaven, who from the days of our ancestors until now has given our kingdom constant and notable stability." 29So the king said these things, and the Jews, who were released immediately, praised their holy God and savior, since they had just now escaped death.

[k] Lev 26:44

Celebration of deliverance

[30]Then the king went back into the city and called for the official in charge of the treasury. He ordered him to supply the Jews with wines and everything else needed for a seven-day festival. The king decided that the Jews should celebrate their rescue with all joy in the same place where they thought they would meet destruction. [31]So the people who previously had been disgraced and stood near death—at its very brink!—prepared for a festival of deliverance instead of a bitter and most mournful fate. The place that had been prepared for their ruin and burial was joyfully divided up among people in celebration. [32]They stopped singing their sad songs of lament and took up an ancient hymn in praise of their rescuer, the wonder-working God.[l] They threw aside all weeping and wailing and instead sang songs in organized groups as a sign of peaceful joy. [33]The king also assembled a huge banquet because of these events. He kept giving generous praise to heaven for the remarkable rescue that he[m] had experienced. [34]Those who had previously believed that the Jews would be destroyed and would become food for the birds, and who had drawn up the lists of their names and goods with delight, now groaned. For they were clothed with shame, and the fire of their boldness had been thoroughly doused.

[35]The Jews, as we said before, organized singing groups and spent their time in celebration with cheerful thanksgiving psalms. [36]They decided that this would be a holiday to be observed for generations to come by the Jewish community living in exile there. The festival would be kept in a spirit of celebration, not as an excuse for overeating and getting drunk but because of the rescue that God had accomplished for them. [37]They appealed to the king, asking for his permission to return to their homes.

[38]The drawing up of the lists of names was conducted from the twenty-fifth of Pachon[n] to the fourth of Epiphi,[o] over a period of forty days; and their destruction was planned for the fifth of Epiphi until the seventh, a period of three days. [39]But also during those days the Lord of all gloriously displayed his mercy and brought them through without harm, each and every one. [40]So being well supplied by the king, they feasted until the fourteenth day, on which day they made the petition concerning their return.

Ptolemy Philopator's letter

[41]The king granted it to them and wrote the following letter on their behalf to the generals in every city, generously stating his deep concern:

7 King Ptolemy Philopator to the generals throughout Egypt and to all those put in charge of affairs. Greetings and good health.

[2]We ourselves and our children also enjoy good health since the great God guides our affairs, as is our desire. [3]Certain of our friends, by frequently urging us out of spite, persuaded us to gather the Jews from throughout the kingdom together in one place and to torment them with unusual punishments as traitors. [4]They insisted that our government would never be stable until this was accomplished, due to the hostility that these people were said to have toward all the nations. [5]These friends also drove them along in chains, treating them harshly as slaves, or rather, as traitors. Without any investigation or trial they attempted to destroy them, displaying a cruelty more savage than the barbarians from Scythia. [6]Now we threatened them sternly for these actions, but we granted them their lives (but just barely!) in keeping with the patience that we show toward all people. Because we have learned that the heavenly God surely shields the Jews and fights alongside them as a father for his children, [7]and because we have considered the constant goodwill that they have shown

[l]Some manuscripts read *praising Israel and the wonder-working God.* [m]Some manuscripts read *they had experienced.* [n]Possibly May, Egyptian calendar [o]Possibly June, Egyptian calendar

toward us and our ancestors, we rightly hold them innocent of every charge of whatever kind.

[8]We have ordered them all to return, each and every one, to their homes. No one anywhere is to harm them at all, or cast any blame on them regarding these senseless events. [9]You should be aware that, if we ever devise any evil against these people or trouble them in any way, we won't have a human being as our enemy but rather the Most High God, who is Lord over every power. It is he who will enforce the punishment for our actions in every way, and from him there is no escape. Farewell.

Punishment of Jewish lawbreakers

[10]When the Jews received this letter, they didn't rush to depart. Instead, they petitioned the king that they might carry out the punishment deserved by those Jews who had voluntarily turned aside from the holy God and God's Law. [11]They insisted that those who had broken divine laws for the sake of the belly would never be reliable subjects under the king's government either. [12]The king recognized and agreed that they were speaking the truth. So he gave them a free hand to utterly destroy those who had violated God's Law in every place within his kingdom, and to do so with confidence and without needing royal approval or supervision. [13]Then they applauded him, as was fitting, and their priests and all the crowd shouted the Hallelujah joyously and departed. [14]On their way they punished and killed any fellow Jews they came upon who had polluted themselves, making a public example of them. [15]On that day they killed more than three hundred persons, a day that they also observed as a joyous festival since they had subdued the renegades. [16]But those who had held fast to God to the point of death, having obtained the complete reward of deliverance, set out from the city crowned with all kinds of the most fragrant flowers, celebrating and shouting, giving thanks with praises and beautiful hymns to the God of their ancestors, the eternal savior of Israel.

The Jews return home

[17]The Jews arrived at Ptolemais, named "Rose-bearing" because of a distinctive feature of the place, where the fleet waited for them for seven days in line with their common desire. [18]There they toasted their rescue, since the king had generously supplied them, each and every one, with all things they needed until their arrival at their own homes. [19]When they had reached their land in peace, there too, in like manner with appropriate expressions of thanks, they decided to observe these days as a festival for as long as they lived in Egypt. [20]They inscribed the record of these events on a pillar and dedicated a place of prayer at the site of the festival. Then they departed unharmed, free, and overjoyed, being safely returned by land, sea, and river to their own homes, by the king's command. [21]They gained more influence among their enemies than they had had previously, and were held in honor and awe. No one at all kept back their possessions from them. [22]The Jews recovered all their property in keeping with the lists that had been previously drawn up, with the result that those who held anything of theirs returned it to them with the greatest deference, for the supreme God had perfectly performed mighty deeds for their salvation. [23]Bless the rescuer of Israel from now to eternity! Amen.

BOOKS INCLUDED IN SLAVONIC BIBLES AND IN AN APPENDIX TO THE VULGATE OR IN AN APPENDIX TO THE GREEK BIBLE

2 ESDRAS[a]

1 The second scroll of the prophet Ezra son of Saraiah son of Azariah son of Hilkiah son of Shallum son of Zadok son of Ahitub [2]son of Ahijah son of Phinehas son of Eli son of Amariah son of Aziah son of Maraimoth son of Arna son of Uzziah son of Borith son of Abishua son of Phinehas son of Eleazar [3]son of Aaron from the tribe of Levi. Ezra was a captive in the region of the Medes during the rule of King Artaxerxes of the Persians.

Rejection of Israel as God's people

[4]The Lord's word came to Ezra, Chusi's son, in the days of King Nebuchadnezzar: [5]Go and announce to my people their crimes. Tell their children about the sins they committed against me. Let their children also announce this to their own children, [6]because the children have added to their parents' sins. They forgot me and offered sacrifices to foreign gods! [7]Didn't I bring them out of the land of Egypt where they lived in slavery? Why then have they angered me and rejected my advice?

[8]Therefore, the Lord says: Tear out your hair and hurl every kind of disaster at them, because they haven't obeyed my Law. Undisciplined people! [9]How long will I put up with them—and after I granted them so many favors? [10]I have overthrown many kings for their sakes. I plunged Pharaoh together with his servants and his whole army into the sea!

[11]Didn't I destroy the city of Bethsaida for your sake? Didn't I burn up two cities south of you, Tyre and Sidon, with fire and kill those opposing you?[b] [13]Didn't I bring you through the sea, and make walls to your right and left? I gave Moses and Aaron to you as leaders. [14]I gave you a column of lightning for light. These are the many wonderful deeds that I performed among you, but you have forgotten me, says the Lord.

[15]The Lord says this: The quails were a sign for you. I gave you safe places to camp, and there you grumbled. [16]I sank your pursuer along with his army, and yet the people grumble about their own destruction. [17]What kind of return is this for the favors I granted you?[c]

When you were hungry and thirsty in the wilderness, you called out to me, [18]"Why did you lead us into this wilderness to kill us? It would have been better for us to serve the Egyptians than to die in this desert." [19]Therefore, I felt sorry for your groans. I gave you manna, and you ate. [20]When you were thirsty, I split open the rock so that water flowed in abundance. Because of the hot sun,[d] I created trees covered with leaves for you.

[21]I gave you fertile lands. I drove out Canaanites, Hittites, Perizzites, and their children before you. What more can I do for you?! says the Lord.

[22]The Lord says this: In the desert when you were thirsty at the bitter river and insulting my name, [23]I didn't become angry. Instead, I cast wood into the water and made the river sweet.

[24]What will I do to you, Jacob?
Judah, you wouldn't obey me.
I will turn to another nation
and give them my name.
They will certainly keep my ordinances.
[25]When those who abandoned me
beg for mercy,
I won't have mercy on them.
[26]When they call upon me,
I won't hear them

[a]2 Esdras 1–2 (or Fifth Ezra) and 2 Esdras 15–16 (or Sixth Ezra) are translated from the eclectic Latin text reconstructed by Theodore A. Bergren, *Fifth Ezra: The Text, Origin and Early History.* Septuagint and Cognate Studies 25 (University Press, Atlanta: Scholars Press, 1990) and Bergren, *Sixth Ezra: The Text and Origin* (New York: Oxford, 1998), with reference to the edition of Robert L. Bensly, *The Fourth Book of Ezra:* Texts and Studies 3 (Cambridge: Cambridge University Press, 1895). 2 Esdras 3–14 (or Fourth Ezra) is translated from the edition of A. F. J. Klijn, *Der Lateinische Text der Apokalypse des Esra:* Texte und Untersuchungen zur Geschichte der Altchristlichen Literatur (Berlin: Akademie Verlag, 1983), with use of the text-critical notes of M. E. Stone, *Fourth Ezra.* Hermeneia (Minneapolis: Fortress Press, 1990). [b]1:12, Bensly's edition *But you speak to them, saying: The Lord says this"* [c]Lat *Where are the favors I granted you?* [d]Lat *heat*

because they have stained their souls,
and have hands stained with blood.
Your feet aren't slow to commit murder.
27You haven't abandoned me;
rather, you have abandoned
yourselves, says the Lord.

28The Lord says this: Didn't I plead with you like a father with his sons, like a mother with her daughters, and like a nurse who loves her little one, 29that you should be my people and I your God, and that you should be my children and I your Father? 30I gathered you as a hen gathers her chickens under her wings. But what will I do with you?

I will throw you out of my presence. 31When you bring me offerings, I will turn my eyes away from you. I didn't command you to observe[e] festival days, new moons, sabbaths, and circumcisions. 32I sent my servants the prophets to you. You took them, mangled them, and slaughtered those who had been sent.[f] But I will make you pay for their deaths, says the Lord.

33The almighty Lord says this: Your house is left empty. I will scatter you as the wind scatters straw. 34Your children will have no children, because they have neglected my commandment, and have done evil in front of me.

35I will hand over your houses to a people who will come from far away. Those who didn't know me will believe me, and those to whom I showed no signs will do what I commanded. 36They didn't see prophets but are mindful of the prophets' antiquity. 37The apostles will joyfully testify to the coming people. Those who didn't see me with their physical eyes believe in their spirit. They have heard the things I said and believe me.

38Now, Father, look with pride and see the people coming from the east. 39I will give them authority, together with Abraham, Isaac, and Jacob, Elijah and Enoch, Zechariah and Hosea, Amos, Joel, Micah, Obadiah, Zephaniah, 40Nahum, Jonah, Malachi, Habakkuk, and twelve angels carrying flowers.

2 The Lord says this: I led forth a people to whom I gave commandments. But they were unwilling to listen, and they ignored my advice 2The mother who bore them says to them: "Go, children, because I am widowed and abandoned. 3I brought you up with joy, but I will send you away with mourning and sadness, because you have sinned in the presence of the Lord God and have done bad things in his sight. 4But now what will I do for you? I am a widow and abandoned by my children. Go, children, and seek mercy from the Lord, 5for I am left all alone."

I call upon you, Father, concerning the mother of those who were unwilling to keep your covenant: 6Throw them into confusion and their mother into ruin. May they leave no descendants, 7but be scattered among the nations! May their names be wiped out from the earth because they despised my covenant!

8How terrible it will be for you, Assyria—you who are hiding the wicked in your midst! Evil city, remember what I did to Sodom and Gomorrah, 9whose land was dragged down all the way to hell. I will do the same to those who haven't obeyed me, says the almighty Lord.

The church as God's people

10The Lord said this to Ezra: Announce to my people that I have prepared a feast for them, and I will give them the kingdom of Jerusalem, which I was about to give to Israel. 11I will take Israel's glory for them and give to them the eternal dwelling places I had prepared for Israel. 12The tree of life will provide them with fragrant ointment, and they won't labor or grow tired.

13Ask and you will receive; ask for yourselves just a few days so that your days may be shortened. Already my kingdom is prepared to come, so be watchful in spirit. 14I call heaven and earth as witnesses: I have dismissed evil and created good, because I live, says the Lord.

15Good mother, embrace your children. Give them joy, like a dove that brings up its

[e] Lat lacks *to observe.* [f] Lat *the apostles*

children. Make their feet steady, for I have chosen you, says the Lord. 16 I will raise the dead from their places and from their tombs, for I have recognized that my name is in them.

17 Don't fear, mother of the children: I have chosen you, says the Lord. 18 I will send my servants Jeremiah, Isaiah, and Daniel to help you. It was on their advice that I have made you holy. I will prepare twelve trees with various kinds of fruit for you, 19 and seven springs full of milk and honey, and huge mountains bearing roses and lilies, which I have prepared for you and your children. I will fill your children with joy.

20 Defend the widow's rights. Judge in favor of the fatherless. Provide for those who are in need. Protect the orphan. Clothe the naked. 21 Care for the broken and the weak. Don't mock the lame, but protect them instead. Help the blind to see a vision of my glory. 22 Gather the old and the young within your walls. Watch over your infants. Let your servants and employees rejoice, and your whole community will have good morale.

23 When I find your dead, I will raise them. I will watch for signs, and I will give them the front seat at the resurrection I will bring about.[g] 24 Wait a little; your rest will come.

25 Good nurse, nourish your children. Strengthen those whom you bore and make their feet steady, 26 because none of those whom I have given you will perish. I will require them from your number. 27 Give it your all![h] Strengthen them! Days of pressure and anguish will come; others will weep and be sad, but you will be happy and have plenty. 28 All the nations will be jealous of you, but they won't be able to do anything against you, says the Lord. 29 All things tremble before me; my eyes see the pit of hell.[i]

30 Rejoice, mother, with your children, and I will rescue you, says the Lord. 31 I will remember your children who sleep, because I will seek them out from the breadth of the earth. Strengthen them in the abundance of your glory and show mercy, because I am merciful, says the Lord. 32 Embrace those born from you until I come, and show mercy to the others, because my springs will overflow and my favor won't fail.

33 I, Ezra, received a command from the Lord on Mount Horeb for Israel, but they rejected this commandment. 34 I say to you who hear and understand: Wait for your shepherd. I will give you your eternal rest, because the end of the age and the decline of humankind are near. 35 Be prepared for the kingdom's rewards, for everlasting light will shine on you, and eternity is prepared for you. 36 Run away from this world's shadow that holds your glory captive. I testify that my savior has been commissioned by the Lord.

37 Receive the joy that comes from your glory, all of you, giving thanks to him who has called you to heavenly kingdoms. 38 Rise, stand, and see the number of those sealed at the feast, 39 those who have transferred themselves from the shadow of this world and received bright garments from the Lord.

40 Welcome your full number, Mount Zion. Receive the full tally of your white-robed people who serve you in obedience, because they have fulfilled the Lord's Law. 41 Since you have long wished for your children to come, fill up their number. Ask the Lord's sovereign power that your people may be honored as holy, since they were called from the beginning.

42 I, Ezra, saw on Mount Zion a great crowd, which I couldn't number. They were all praising the Lord together with songs. 43 In their midst was a tall young man, standing above all the rest. He placed crowns on each of their heads, and they were further honored.

I began to wonder, 44 and I asked an angel, "Who are these people?"

45 The angel answered me, "These are the ones who took off the mortal garment and put on the immortal and confessed the name of God. Now they are being crowned, and they are receiving palms."

46 I said to the angel, "Who is that young man who gives them crowns and palms?"

[g] Lat *at my resurrection* [h] Lat *Be unwilling to just do enough* [i] Lat *Gehennam*

47 The angel answered, "That is God's Son, whom they confessed in the mortal world."

I began to praise and celebrate the Lord. 48 The angel said to me, "Go announce to his people how many wonders the Lord God has shown you."

First dialogue

3 [j]In the thirtieth year after our city was destroyed, I, Salathiel, who am also Ezra, was in Babylon. I was disturbed as I lay on my bed, and my thoughts kept welling up inside me, 2 because I saw how Zion lay in ruins and how those who lived in Babylon enjoyed abundance. 3 I was deeply disturbed, and I began to speak reverently to the Most High: 4 "Supreme Lord, didn't you speak in the beginning, when you fashioned the earth, and did this alone? Didn't you command the earth,[k] 5 and it gave you[l] Adam, a lifeless body? But it was the work of your hands, and so you breathed into him the breath of life, and he came to life in your presence. 6 You led him into paradise, which your strong hand had planted before earth came to be. 7 You gave him one command, and he disobeyed it, and so you immediately appointed death for him and for his descendants. Nations, tribes, peoples, and families without number were born from him. 8 Each nation lived by its own will, and people acted without giving you a thought. They acted with scorn, and you didn't prevent them. 9 But again, in time you brought the flood over the world and upon those who live in it[m] and destroyed them. 10 Their fate was all the same: as death came upon Adam so the flood came upon them. 11 But you left one of them, Noah, with his household, and all the righteous descended from him.

12 "When those who lived on earth began to multiply (and multiply they did—children, peoples, and many nations), they began again to act wickedly, even more so than the previous ones. 13 When they committed iniquity before you, you chose one from among them whose name was Abraham. 14 You loved him and showed him alone the end of times, secretly by night. 15 You made an eternal covenant with him, and you told him that you would never abandon his family line. You gave him Isaac, and you gave Jacob and Esau to Isaac. 16 You set Jacob apart for yourself, but you set Esau aside, and Jacob became a great multitude. 17 When you brought his descendants out of Egypt, you led them to Mount Sinai. 18 You bent down the heavens; you shook[n] the earth; you moved the world; you made the abyss tremble; you made the whole cosmos shudder. 19 Your glory passed through the four gates of fire, earthquake, wind, and ice so that you would give the Law to Jacob's descendants, the rules to be observed to Israel's offspring.

20 "But you didn't take away from them the inclination to do evil[o] so that your Law might bear fruit in them. 21 The first Adam, burdened with this inclination, disobeyed you and was overcome, but so were all those descended from him. 22 The disease became permanent; the Law was in the people's heart along with the wicked root, and that which was good departed and the wickedness remained. 23 Times passed and years were completed, and you raised up for yourself a servant named David. 24 You told him to build a city to your name and to bring you offerings in it from what is yours. 25 This was done for many years. But those who inhabited the city sinned, 26 doing in every matter just as Adam and all his descendants had done, for they too exercised their inclination to do evil. 27 So you handed your city over to your enemies.

28 "I said then in my heart, Are the lives of Babylon's inhabitants any better? Is that why Babylon has gained dominion[p] over Zion? 29 But when I came here, I saw their countless godless acts. I have seen many sinners during these thirty years.[q] Then my heart failed, 30 because I saw how you sustain these sinners and have spared those who act without giving you a thought. I saw how you destroyed your people and pre-

[j]Chaps 3–14 = Fourth Ezra [k]Syr, Eth *dust* [l]Correction; Lat *you gave* [m]Syr, Eth; Lat *those inhabiting the age* [n]Syr; Lat *you established* [o]Lat *wicked heart* [p]Correction; Lat *will gain dominion* [q]Eth; Lat *in this thirtieth year*

served your enemies, 31 and haven't given anyone any clue as to how to make sense of these ways.[r] Does Babylon do better than Zion? 32 Has any other nation known you besides Israel? What tribes have believed your covenants as have these tribes of Jacob, 33 whose reward hasn't appeared and whose labor hasn't borne fruit? I have traveled widely among the nations and seen them enjoying abundance while not giving your commandments a thought. 34 Now then put our sins on one side of a pair of scales, and put the sins of those who live in the world on the other side. Let's see then which way the scales tip. 35 When have those who live on earth not sinned in your sight, or what other nation has observed your commandments as has ours? 36 You will find individuals who have kept your laws, but nations you will not find."

4

Then the angel who had been sent to me, whose name was Uriel, replied: 2 "Your mind[s] has utterly failed with regard to this world, and do you think you can understand the way of the Most High?"

3 I said, "Yes, my Lord."

He answered: "I am sent to show you three ways and to set three problems before you. 4 If you can say anything to me about one of these, I will show you the way you want to see, and I will teach you why the heart leans toward evil."

5 I said, "Speak, my Lord."

He said to me, "Go, weigh for me the weight of fire, or measure for me a blast of wind, or call back for me the day that is past."

6 I answered, "Who alive can do this? How can you ask me these things?"

7 Uriel said to me: "If I had asked you, 'How many dwellings are in the depths of the sea, or how many springs are in the source of the abyss, or how many paths are there above the dome, or which are the exits of paradise,'[t] 8 you would perhaps have said to me: 'I haven't descended into the abyss nor as yet into hell, nor have I ever ascended to heaven.' 9 But I've only asked you here about fire and wind and the day you have passed through, things you can't exist without, and you haven't answered me about them."

10 He said to me: "You can't even understand the things that are yours, which you have grown up with. 11 How then can your mind[u] contain the way of the Most High? How can a person who is already corrupted by the corrupt world understand the realm beyond corruption?"

I fell on my face 12 and said to him, "It would have been better not to have come into being than to come here, live in the middle of wickedness, suffer, and not understand why."

13 He answered me: "I went forth to a forest of trees on the plain,[v] and they devised a plan 14 and said: 'Come, let's go and make war on the sea so that it may recede before us, and let's make for ourselves more forests.' 15 And likewise, the waves of the sea also formed a plan and said, 'Come, let's go up and subdue the forest on the plain so that there too we may complete another region for ourselves.' 16 But the plan of the forest came to naught, for fire came and consumed it. 17 Likewise also the plan of the waves of the sea, for the sand stood firm and prevented it. 18 If then you were judge of these, which would you begin to justify and which to condemn?"

19 I answered, "Each made a stupid plan, for land is given to the forest, and the sea is the appointed place for its waves."

20 Uriel answered me: "You have judged well. So why haven't you judged well in your own case? 21 As the land is given to the forest and the sea to the waves, so also only those who live on earth can understand the things that are on earth, and only those who live above the heavens can understand the things that are above the height of the heavens."

22 I answered, "I beg you, Lord, why has the sense of understanding been given to me? 23 It wasn't my purpose to ask about the ways above but about the things that we

[r] Syr; Lat *how to abandon this way* [s] Lat *heart* [t] Lat; other versions have *exits of the netherworld and entrances of paradise*. [u] Lat *cup* [v] Lat; Syr *Once upon a time the forests of trees on the plain set forth*

see every day. Why has Israel been handed over to the Gentiles to our shame? Why has the people you loved been given over to godless tribes? Why has the Law of our ancestors been invalidated and the written ordinances come to nothing? [24]Why do we pass from the world like locusts and our life like a mist? Why aren't we worthy to obtain mercy? [25]What will God do for the sake of his name, which is bestowed on us? About these things I have asked."

[26]He answered me: "If you remain alive, you'll see. If you live, you will often be amazed, because the world is indeed rushing to its end. [27]Indeed, it can't bring the things that are promised to the just during this age, because this world is full of sadness and sickliness. [28]The evil about which you asked me has been sown, and its full harvest hasn't yet come. [29]If that which was sown isn't reaped, and the place where evil has been sown hasn't departed, the field where good is sown won't come. [30]A grain of evil seed was sown in the heart of Adam from the beginning, and how much godlessness it has produced until now and will produce until the time for threshing comes! [31]Calculate for yourself how much godless fruit the grain of evil seed will have produced! [32]When the innumerable ears of grain are sown, how great a threshing floor will they begin to make!"

[33]I answered: "Where and when will these things be? Why are our years few and evil?"

[34]He answered: "Don't be in a greater hurry than the Most High. You hurry only for yourself, but the Most High on behalf of many. [35]Didn't the souls of the just in their resting places ask about these things, saying, 'How long are we to remain here,[w] and when will the harvest of our reward come?' [36]Then Jeremiel the angel answered them, 'When the number of those like you[x] is complete, for God has weighed the world in a balance [37]and measured the times by measure and numbered the times by number, and he won't move or arouse himself until the prescribed measure is fulfilled.'"

[38]I answered: "Supreme Lord, we all are also full of impiety. [39]Is it perhaps because of us, and because of the sins of those who live on earth, that the harvest of the just is delayed?"

[40]He answered me, "Go ask a pregnant woman whether her womb can keep the baby inside her when she has completed her nine months."

[41]I said, "It can't, Lord."

He said to me: "The underworld[y] and the resting places of the souls are like the womb. [42]As the one who gives birth hastens to escape the distress of giving birth, so these also hasten to give back those things that were entrusted to them from the beginning. [43]Then you will be shown the things you want to see."

[44]I answered, "If I have found favor with you, if it is possible, if I am worthy, [45]show me this also, whether there is more time yet to come than has past or whether the greater times have passed over us, [46]for I know what has passed, but I don't know what is to come."

[47]He answered me: "Stand off to the right, and I will show you the interpretation of a parable."

[48]I stood aside and looked, and right there a burning furnace passed before me, and when the flame had passed, I looked and the smoke remained. [49]And after this a cloud full of water passed before me, and it poured down much rain with force, and when the rainstorm had passed there remained drops in the cloud.[z]

[50]He said to me, "Consider for yourself: as the rain is greater than the drops and the fire is greater than the smoke, so the measure that has passed is greater, but drops and smoke remain."

[51]I prayed and said, "Do you think I will live until those days? Who will be alive in those days?"

[52]He answered me: "I can tell you in part concerning the signs you ask about, but about your own life I'm not sent to tell you. I don't know.

[w]Syr, Aram; Lat *How long must I hope for this?* [x]Syr; Lat *when the number of seeds is completed for you*
[y]Lat *inferno* [z]Lat *in it*

5 "But about the signs: Look, the days
will come when those who live on earth
will be seized with great terror.[a] The way of
truth will be hidden, and the land will be
barren and devoid of faith. 2Injustice will
be multiplied beyond what you yourself
see and beyond what you have heard of
formerly. 3The land that you now see holding sway will have no one left to walk upon
it, and people[b] will see it desolate. 4But if
the Most High grants that you live, you
will see it thrown into confusion after the
third period of time.[c] The sun will suddenly
start shining by night and the moon by day.
5Blood will drip from wood, and stones will
speak out. Peoples will be troubled, and
natural courses will be changed. 6A person no one on earth expected will come to
power, and birds will migrate together. 7The
sea of Sodom will cast up fish; it will utter
sounds in a voice that many don't know, but
all will hear its voice. 8Chasms will open up
in many places, and fire will be shot forth
frequently. Wild beasts will roam beyond
their territory, and women will give birth
to monsters. 9Salt waters will be found in
sources of freshwater. Friends everywhere
will begin to fight each other. Reason will
be hidden, and intelligence will go into hiding. 10Many will look for it, but they won't
find it, and injustice and lust will be multiplied on earth. 11One country will ask its
neighbor, 'Has justice passed through you,
doing what is right?' and the answer will be
no. 12At that time people will hope but not
get what they hoped for; they will labor, but
they will make no progress. 13I am permitted to tell you these signs, and if you pray
again and continue to weep as you are now
doing and fast for seven days, you will again
hear greater things than these."

14I awoke, my body shuddered greatly,
and my spirit labored so that it fainted.
15The angel who came and talked to me held
me, comforted me, and set me on my feet.

16On the second night, Phaltiel a leader
of the people came to me and said, "Where
were you, and why is your face sad? 17Don't
you realize that Israel has been entrusted to
you while it is in exile in this land? 18Arise
then, and take some food so that you may
not abandon us like a shepherd who leaves
his flock in the power of cruel wolves."

19I said to him, "Leave me and don't
come near me again for seven days. After
that, you will come to me." He heard how I
spoke and withdrew from me.

Second dialogue

20I didn't eat food for seven days, wailing
and weeping, as the angel Uriel had commanded me. 21After seven days, my deepest thoughts were again very troubling to
me. 22Then I recovered my wits and I began
again to speak words before the Most High:

23Supreme Lord, you chose one vine
from every forest on earth and from
all its trees, 24and from all this world's
lands you chose for yourself one region,[d]
and from all the world's flowers you
chose for yourself one lily, 25and from all
the ocean's depths you filled for yourself
one river, and from all cities that have
been built you dedicated for yourself
Zion, 26and from all the created birds you
named for yourself one dove, and from
all the flocks that have been made you
provided for yourself one sheep, 27from
all the peoples that have multiplied you
acquired for yourself one people, and to
this people that you desired you gave
the Law celebrated by all. 28Now, Lord,
why did you give the one to the many?
Why dishonor[e] the one root above all the
rest, and scatter your only one among
the many? 29Those who have denied
your promises have trampled those who
believed in your covenants! 30If you really hate your people, they should be
punished with your own hands.

31When I had said these words, the angel
who had come to me on the previous night
was sent to me. 32He said to me: "Listen to
me, and I will instruct you; pay attention to
me, and I will tell you more."

33I said, "Speak, my Lord."

[a]Syr; Lat uncertain [b]Lat *they* [c]Lat uncertain [d]Syr, Eth; Lat *pit* [e]Lat *prepare*, apparently because of a corruption in the Gk

He said to me, "Are you really more deeply
disturbed over Israel, or do you love him
more than the one who made him does?"
34 I said: "No, Lord, but I spoke in grief.
My heart torments me every hour while I
try to make sense of the Most High's ways
and investigate his decisions."
35 He said to me, "You can't."
And I said: "Why, Lord? Or else why was
I born, and why did my mother's womb not
become my tomb so that I might not see
the toil of Jacob and the exhaustion of the
line of Israel?"
36 He said to me: "Count for me those
who haven't yet been born, gather for me
the scattered raindrops, make the withered
flowers bloom again for me, 37 open for me
the closed warehouses and bring forth for
me the winds shut up in them, or show me
what a voice looks like. Then I will show you
what you ask to see."
38 I said: "Supreme Lord, who can know
these things except one who doesn't live
among human beings? 39 But I'm ignorant.
How can I speak of these things that you
asked me about?"
40 He said to me: "As you can't do one
of these things that were mentioned, so
you can't comprehend my judgment or
the goal[f] of the love I have promised to my
people."
41 I said: "Look, Lord, you've made promises concerning these who are alive at the
end, but what will those who are before us
do, or we, or those who come after us?"
42 He said to me, "I will compare my judgment to a crown.[g] Just as there is no delay
for those who come last, so there is no rushing for those who come before."
43 I replied, "Couldn't you have created all
at once those who have been and those who
are and those who will be so that you might
show your judgment more quickly?"
44 He replied to me, "The creation can't
run ahead of its creator, nor can the world
sustain all at one time those who are created in it."
45 I said: "How then could you say to your
servant that you will certainly give life to
the creation created by you at one time? If,
therefore, they will live at one time[h] and the
creation will sustain them then, couldn't it
sustain them at one time now?"
46 He said to me: "Ask a woman's womb:
If you bear ten children,[i] why do you only
do it over time? Ask it then to produce ten
at once."
47 I said, "Surely it can't, but only over time."
48 He said to me: "I also have given the
earth's womb for those who have been
sown on it over time. 49 As an infant doesn't
give birth and a woman who has become
old doesn't give birth any longer, so I have
set in order the world I created."
50 I asked: "Since you have given me
opportunity, let me speak before you. Is
our mother, of whom you spoke to me,
still young? Or is she already approaching
old age?"
51 He responded to me: "Ask one who
gives birth, and she will tell you. Say to her,
52 'Why are those you have borne now not
like those whom you bore before, but are
smaller in stature?' 53 She herself will tell
you, 'Those who are born in youth's vigor
are different from those who are born in
the time of old age, when the womb is failing.' 54 Therefore, consider that you yourself
are smaller in stature than those who were
before you, 55 and those who come after you
will be even smaller than you, as born of a
creation that is already aging and past the
strength of youth."
56 I said: "I ask, Lord, if you look favorably on me, show your servant through
whom you will visit your creation."

6 He said to me: "In the beginning of the
earthly world—[j]

before the world's exits were made,
before the gathered winds blew,
2 before the voices
of the thunders sounded,
before the flashes of lightning shone,
before paradise's foundations
were made firm,
3 before beautiful flowers were seen,

[f] Lat *limit* [g] Lat, Syr; some versions *circle* [h] Lat omits *if, therefore, they will live at one time.* [i] Latin omits *ten.*
[j] Lat *in the beginning, the earthly world*; Syr and other versions *The beginning is through man and the end is through me.*

before the powers of movement
were established,
before the innumerable heavenly armies
of angels were assembled,
4 before the heights of the air
were lifted up,
before the measures
of the firmament were named,
before Zion's footstool was established,
5 before the present years
were reckoned,
before the imaginations of those
who now sin were alienated,
before those who stored up faith
as a treasure were sealed—
6 then I planned these things. As they
were done by me and not by another, so also
the end will come by me and not through
another."
7 I answered, "What separates the times?
When is the end of the first and the beginning of that which follows?"
8 He said to me: "From Abraham to Abraham, because Jacob and Esau were born
from him, but Jacob's hand held Esau's heel
from the outset. 9 Esau represents the end
of this age, and Jacob represents the beginning of the following. 10 The beginning of
the one man is his hand, and the end of the
other man is his heel.[k] Don't look for anything else between heel and hand, Ezra."
11 I answered: "Supreme Lord, if only you
looked so favorably upon me 12 that you would
show your servant your final signs,[l] which you
showed me in part on a previous night."
13 He answered: "Get up on your feet.
You'll hear a loud, echoing voice. 14 Don't
be afraid if the place on which you stand is
greatly moved 15 while the voice is speaking.
Since the word concerns the end, and since
the foundations of the earth will understand
16 that the speech is about them, the place
will tremble and shake, because it knows
that it is destined to be transformed."
17 When I heard, I rose on my feet and
listened. There was a voice speaking,
and its sound was like the sound of deep
waters. 18 It said: "Look! The days are coming
when I will begin to come near to visit those
who live on earth, 19 when I will begin to examine those who unjustly inflicted harm
in their cruelty. When the humiliation of
Zion is complete, 20 when the seal is placed
on the age that begins to pass away, I will
perform these signs: Scrolls will be opened
in view of the firmament, and all will see
together. 21 Infants a year old will speak
with their voices, and pregnant women will
give birth to premature babies of three and
four months, but they will live and dance.
22 Fields that were not sown will suddenly
appear sown,[m] and full warehouses will suddenly be found empty. 23 A trumpet will
sound with a blast; when all hear it they will
suddenly be terrified. 24 In that time friends
will make war on friends like enemies, the
earth along with those who live on it will
be terrified, and the sources of rivers will
stand still so that they don't run for three
hours. 25 Then everyone who is left after all
these things that I have foretold to you will
be saved. These will see my deliverance and
the end of my age. 26 They will see[n] the people
who have been taken up and who haven't
tasted death from their birth. The hearts
of those who live on earth[o] will be changed
and converted to a different spirit, 27 for
evil will be erased and grief extinguished.
28 Faith will flourish, and corruption will be
overcome. Truth that was without fruit for
so long will be displayed."
29 While he was still speaking with me, the
place on which I stood was shaken,[p] little by
little. 30 He said to me: "I came to show you
these things this night.[q] 31 If you ask further
and fast again for seven days, I will again
declare daily[r] to you greater things than
these, 32 because the Most High has listened
to your voice. The mighty one has seen your
virtue and perceived the humility you have
had from your youth. 33 Because of this he
sent me to show you all these things and
to say to you: Trust confidently, and don't
be afraid. 34 Don't be hasty to think empty
thoughts about the former times, lest you
be hasty about the last times."

[k] Syr; Lat uncertain [l] Lat *the end of your signs* [m] Or *the reverse*; Lat uncertain [n] Antecedent unclear; or the verb should be passive *and those who were taken up will be seen.* [o] Lat omits *on earth.* [p] Correction of Lat by other versions [q] Syr, Eth; Lat uncertain [r] Lat; other versions lack *daily.*

Third dialogue

35 After all this I wept again and abstained from food for another seven days,
to complete the three weeks that had been
prescribed for me. 36 Then on the eighth
night my heart was disturbed within me
again, and I began to speak before the Most
High. 37 My spirit was greatly agitated, and
my soul was troubled.

38 Then I said: "Lord, you spoke from the
beginning of creation on the first day, 'Let
heaven and earth be made,' and your word
accomplished the deed. 39 Then the spirit
was hovering, darkness was spread around,
and there was silence. There was as yet no
sound of a human voice.[s] 40 Then you commanded that a ray of light be brought forth
from your treasuries so that your works
might be seen.

41 "Then on the second day you created
the spirit of the firmament and commanded that it divide and make a division
between the waters so that a certain part
might recede upward and another part remain below.

42 "On the third day you commanded the
waters to be gathered together in a seventh
part of the earth, but you made six parts
dry and preserved them so that some of
these might be sown and cultivated, to be
of service before you. 43 Your word went
forth, and the work was immediately accomplished. 44 Suddenly, fruit blossomed
in great abundance in an infinite variety of
flavors, and flowers with matchless color
and scents of unspeakable fragrance. These
things were done on the third day.

45 "On the fourth day you commanded
the sun's splendor to be made, the moon's
light, and the arrangement of the stars.
46 You commanded them to serve the
human being who was about to be formed.

47 "On the fifth day you commanded the
seventh part where the water was gathered
to produce animals, birds, and fish. 48 The
silent and lifeless water, as it was commanded, brought forth animals so that
peoples might recount your wonders. 49 You
kept two living creatures[t] in reserve; one
you named Behemoth, and the second you
named Leviathan. 50 You separated them
from each other, for the seventh part where
the water was gathered couldn't contain
them. 51 You gave Behemoth one part of the
land that had been dried on the third day,
where there are a thousand mountains so
that he might live there. 52 To Leviathan,
however, you gave the watery seventh part.
You kept them to be eaten by whomever
you wish, and whenever you wish.

53 "On the sixth day you commanded
the earth that it create before you cattle,
beasts, and reptiles, 54 and over these you
set Adam, the leader over all the things
you had made. From him we all, the people
you have chosen, have been brought forth.

55 "I have said all these things before
you, Lord, because you have said that you
created the oldest age[u] for our sake. 56 You
have said that the other nations born of
Adam are nothing, that they are like spit,
and you have compared their abundance to
a drop from a pitcher. 57 But look now, Lord!
These nations that are valued as nothing
rule over us and devour us, 58 while we, your
people, whom you have called your oldest
offspring, your one and only child, those
who are zealous for you, your dearest ones,
are handed over to them. 59 If the world was
created for our sake, why don't we possess
our world as an inheritance? How long will
this situation last?"

7 When I finished speaking these words,
the angel who had been sent to me on
the previous nights was sent to me again.
2 He said to me, "Rise, Ezra, and hear the
words I have come to speak to you."

3 I said, "Speak, my Lord."

He said to me: "A certain sea is set in a
spacious place so that it can be deep and
vast, 4 but its entrance is set in a narrow
place, like a river. 5 If anyone wants to go
to the sea to see it or to rule over it, how
can he come into the broad place unless
he passes through the narrow? 6 Another
instance: A city is built and positioned on
a broad plain, full of all good things. 7 Its
entrance, however, is narrow and located

[s] Lat *from you* [t] Syr, Eth; Lat *two souls* [u] Lat *world*

on a precipice so that there is fire on the
right and deep water on the left. [8]There is a
single path located between them, between
the fire and the water, and the path has only
room for human footprints. [9]If that city is
given to someone as an inheritance, if the
heir doesn't pass through the danger, how
will the heir receive the inheritance?"

[10]I said, "Indeed, Lord."

He said to me: "So also is Israel's portion. I indeed made the world on account
of them. [11]When Adam transgressed my ordinances, what had been made was judged,
[12]and the entrances of this world were
made narrow, sorrowful, and troublesome.
They are few and bad, full of dangers and
involving people in great hardships. [13]The
entrances of the greater world, however,
are spacious and secure, and they generate
the fruit of immortality. [14]If those who live
don't enter these narrow and empty places,
they can't receive the things that are in
store. [15]Therefore, why are you disturbed,
being corruptible, and why are you upset,
being mortal? [16]Why haven't you focused
your mind on what is still to come, rather
than on what is present?"

[17]I answered: "Supreme Lord, you ordained in your Law that the just will inherit
these things, but the impious will perish.
[18]The just then can tolerate the narrow,
hoping for the spacious, but those who
have acted impiously endure the narrow
and won't see the spacious."

[19]He said to me: "You aren't a higher
judge than God, nor more intelligent than
the Most High. [20]Better that many of those
now alive should perish than that the Law
of God, which is laid out before them, be
disregarded. [21]God commanded those who
come into the world, after they came, what
they needed to do to live, and what laws
they should observe to avoid punishment.
[22]But they weren't persuaded and opposed
him. They filled their heads with worthless
thoughts, [23]and they invented excuses for
their sins. They emphatically denied that
the Most High exists, and they didn't learn
his ways. [24]They despised his Law and rejected his covenants. They weren't faithful to his statutes, and didn't perform the
works he prescribed. [25]Therefore, Ezra,
empty things are for the empty and full
things for the full.

[26]"Look! The time is coming when the
signs appear that I told you about in advance, and the city will appear, appearing
as a bride, and the land that is now hidden
will be openly displayed. [27]Everyone who is
rescued from the evils foretold will see my
wonders. [28]My Son the anointed one[v] will
be revealed along with those who are with
him, and those who remain will rejoice for
four hundred years.

[29]"After these years, my Son the anointed
one and all who have human breath will die.
[30]The world will be turned back to primeval
silence for seven days, as in the earliest beginnings so that no one is left alive. [31]After
seven days, the world that isn't yet awake
will be roused, and the corrupt world will die.
[32]The earth will give back those who sleep,
and the dust will give back in silence those
who dwell in it, and the resting places will
give back the souls that have been entrusted
to them. [33]The Most High will be revealed on
the throne of judgment, and mercy will pass
away. Patience will be withdrawn, [34]and only
judgment will remain. Truth will arise, faith
will recover strength, [35]and works will have
their consequences. Reward will come about,
righteous deeds will awake, and unrighteous
deeds won't sleep.

[36]"The lake[w] of torment will appear, and
across from it will be the place of rest. Hell's[x]
furnace will be displayed and across from it
the delightful paradise. [37]Then the Most
High will speak to the nations that have
been raised: 'Look and understand whom
it is you have denied, whom you haven't
served, and whose ordinances you have
despised. [38]Look to one side and the other:
Here is delight and rest, and over there are
fire and torments.' He will say these things
to them on the Judgment Day, [39]a day that
has no sun or moon or stars, [40]no cloud or

[v]Lat *Jesus;* other versions *anointed one* or *messiah* [w]Lat manuscripts read *place* (*locus* instead of *lacus*).
[x]Lat *Gehennae*

thunder or lightning, no wind or water or air, no darkness or evening or morning, [41]no summer or spring or heat, no winter or frost or cold, no hail or rain or dew, [42]no noon or night or early dawn, no shining or brightness or light, but only the splendor of the light of the Most High. All will then begin to see what things are in store for them. [43]It will take a period of about a week of years. [44]This is my judgment and the arrangements made for it. I have shown this to you alone."

[45]I replied: "I said before, Lord, and I say now: Privileged are those now living who observe what you have commanded. [46]But what of those who were the subject of my prayer? Who is there of all the living who hasn't sinned, or who among those who have been born hasn't transgressed your covenant? [47]Now I see that the world to come will bring delight to few but torment to many. [48]The inclination to do evil[y] grew in us. It alienated us and led us into corruption and the paths that lead to death. It showed us the way to damnation and removed us far from life—and this happened not to a few people but to nearly all who were created."

[49]He replied to me: "Listen to me, and I will instruct you and will advise you yet again. [50]Because of this the Most High made not one world but two. [51]Regarding what you said about the just being not many but few and the wicked being numerous, think about this: [52]If you have very few choice stones, will you add lead and clay to their number?"[z]

[53]I said, "Lord, who would do such a thing?"

[54]He said to me, "Not only this, but ask the earth and it will inform you; flatter it and it will tell you. [55]Say to it: You create gold, silver, bronze, iron, and also lead and clay. [56]But silver is more numerous than gold, and bronze than silver, and iron than bronze, lead than iron, and clay than lead. [57]Decide yourself then which things are precious and desirable, what is abundant or what is rare."

[58]I said, "Supreme Lord, that which is abundant is cheaper, because what is more rare is valuable."

[59]He replied to me: "Reflect on what you have thought. One who has what is scarce rejoices more than one who has what is abundant. [60]So also will be the judgment[a] I have promised. I will rejoice over the few who will be saved, because they are the ones who made my honor to prevail now and through whom my reputation is celebrated. [61]I will have no regrets over the multitude who perish, for they are even now like vapor, the equivalent of flame or smoke; they burn and flare up and are quenched."

[62]I replied: "Earth, what have you brought to birth? If consciousness is made of dust like other creatures, [63]it would have been better that the dust itself had never been born, so that consciousness shouldn't be made from it. [64]But now consciousness grows with us, and due to this we are tortured, because we perish and are aware of the fact. [65]Let the human race lament and let the wild beasts rejoice. Let all people who are born lament, but let four-footed animals and flocks be happy! [66]It is much better for them than for us. They don't expect judgment. They don't know about either the torments or the deliverance that you promise after death. [67]But what does it profit us that we will be preserved, only to be tortured with torments? [68]All who are born are mixed up with violations, full of sins, and weighed down with crimes. [69]If we were not to come into judgment after death, it would perhaps have been better for us."

[70]He replied to me: "When the Most High made the world and Adam and all who are descended from him, he first prepared the judgment and the things that pertain to the judgment. [71]Now understand on the basis of your own words—because you said, 'Consciousness grows with us.' [72]Those who sojourn on earth will be tormented precisely because, although they were aware, they committed violations. Although they received the commandments, they didn't

[y]Lat *evil heart* [z]Lat *lead and clay abound* [a]Syr, Eth; Lat *creation*

keep them. When they did follow the Law,
they falsified its contents. 73What will they
have to say in the judgment? How will they
respond in the last times? 74How long a
time the Most High has put up with those
who inhabit the world! But this wasn't for
their sakes; rather for the sake of the sched-
ule that he has established for the unfold-
ing of the times."

75I replied: "If I have found favor with you,
Lord, show this also to your servant: After
death, as soon as each person gives up his or
her soul, will we be kept asleep until the time
comes for you to begin to renew creation, or
will we be tormented right away?"

76He replied to me: "I will show you this
too. But don't associate yourself with those
who have shown contempt, and don't count
yourself among those who are tormented.
77You have a treasure of works stored up
with the Most High, but it won't be shown
to you until the last times.

78"Now a word about death: When the
final sentence goes forth from the Most
High that a person should die, when the
spirit recedes from the body so that it may
be sent again to him who gave it, the first
thing is to stand in awe before the glory of
the Most High. 79If the spirit belonged to
one of those who showed contempt and
didn't keep the Most High's way, if it was
one of those who despised his Law and who
hates those who fear God, 80these spirits
don't go into their dwellings but will immediately wander about in torments. They
will constantly grieve and be sorrowful for
seven reasons:[b]

81The first reason—because they despised the Law of the Most High.

82The second reason—because they
can't now effectively change their hearts
and lives so that they might live.

83The third reason—because they will
see the reward laid up for those who have
believed the Most High's testimonies.

84The fourth reason—because they
will consider the torment laid up for
themselves in the last days.

85The fifth reason—because they will
see the dwelling places of others, guarded
by angels in great silence.

86The sixth reason—because they see
the torment coming upon them from
now on.[c]

87The seventh reason, which is
greater than all the previously mentioned reasons—because they will melt
away in confusion and be consumed in
disgrace.[d]

"They will wither in fear when they see
the glory of the Most High, before whom
they sinned when they were alive and before whom they are to be judged in the last
times.

88"The arrangement for those who kept
God's ways is this when they begin to be
separated from the corruptible body.[e] 89In
the time of their exile here they labored
hard to serve the Most High. Every hour
they endured danger so that they might
keep the Law of the lawgiver perfectly.
90Therefore, this is the word about them:
91First, they will see with great joy the glory
of him who receives them. They will have
rest on account of seven orders:

92The first order—because they have
struggled hard to overcome the evil
thought fashioned within them so that
it wouldn't lead them astray from life to
death.

93The second order—because they
see the panic in which the souls of the
wicked wander and the punishment that
awaits them.

94The third order—seeing the testimony that their maker has testified on
their behalf, because when they were
alive, they kept the Law that was given
through faith.

95The fourth order—understanding
the peaceful rest that they now enjoy,
gathered in their resting chambers,
guarded by angels in deep silence, and
understanding the glory that awaits
them in their last days.

96The fifth order—rejoicing at how

[b]Lat *ways* [c]Syr and other versions; Lat *they see that torment is passing away from them*, that is, from those the angels guard. [d]Lat uncertain and reads *in honors*, omitting the negative prefix [e]Or *vessel*

they have now escaped the corruptible and how they will have a future inheritance; moreover, seeing the narrow space, full of labor, from which they have been freed, and the spacious place they are about to receive and enjoy, now that they are immortal.

97 The sixth order—when they are shown how their face begins to shine like the sun and how they begin to be like the stars, as beings of incorruptible light.

98 The seventh order, which is greater than all those mentioned—because they will rejoice with confidence and will trust without being disappointed and will rejoice without fear; for they hasten to see the face of him whom they served when they were alive and from whom they are about to receive a reward now that they are glorified.

99 "This is the order of the souls of the just, as is announced immediately, and those previously mentioned are the ways of torment that those who paid no heed will suffer."

100 I answered: "Will time, therefore, be given to souls after they are separated from the bodies to see what you told me?"

101 He said to me: "They will be free for seven days so that they may see in those seven days the things[f] that have been foretold. After this, they will be gathered in their dwelling places."

102 I answered: "If you look on me with favor, show your servant further whether on the Judgment Day the just will be able to seek mercy for the wicked or intercede for them with the Most High. 103 Will parents be allowed to intercede[g] for children, children for parents, siblings for each other, relatives for those close to them, faithful ones for those most dear to them?"

104 He replied to me: "Because I do indeed favor you, I will also show you this. The Judgment Day is decisive.[h] It reveals the seal of truth to all. Even in the here and now a parent doesn't send a child, or a child the parent, or a master his servant, or a faithful friend a dear confidant, so that the one should understand or sleep or eat or be taken care of in the other person's place. 105 Just so, no one will ever intercede for another; everyone will then bear his or her own deeds of justice or injustice."

106 I answered: "How then do we find that Abraham first interceded for the people of Sodom; and Moses for our ancestors who sinned in the desert; 107 and Joshua, who came after him, for Israel, in the days of Achan; 108 and Samuel in the days of Saul;[i] and David for the plague;[j] and Solomon for those in the sanctuary; 109 and Elijah for those who received the rain, and for a dead person that he might live; 110 and Hezekiah for the people in the days of Sennacherib, and many for many people? 111 If, therefore, the just prayed for the wicked when corruption had increased and injustice had multiplied, why won't it be the same then?"

112 He answered me: "The present world isn't the end. Glory does not[k] continuously remain in it, and so those who were able prayed for the weak. 113 But the Judgment Day will be the end of this time and the beginning of the future, endless time in which decay is no more, 114 indulgence is undone, unbelief is cut off, but justice is fully grown, and truth arisen. 115 Therefore, no one will then be able to have mercy on someone who has been condemned in the judgment, nor to overwhelm one who has conquered."

116 I answered: "This is my first and last word: It would have been better if the earth hadn't brought forth Adam, or when it had brought him forth, that it had forced him not to sin. 117 What does it benefit everyone to live in sadness during the present time, and when dead to expect punishment? 118 Adam, what have you done?! If you sinned, the downfall wasn't yours alone but also ours who are descended from you. 119 What benefit is it to us that we are promised an immortal time, but we have done works that bring death? 120 What good is it to us that everlasting hope has been predicted for us, but we have utterly

[f] Lat *words*, a Hebraism [g] Versions lack *can intercede*. [h] Eth *sudden* [i] Syr, Eth; Lat omits *in the days of Saul*.
[j] Lat *breach* or *rupture* [k] Syr, Eth; Lat omits *not*.

failed? 121 What good is it that safe and
healthy dwelling places are reserved, but
we have behaved badly? 122 What good is
it that the glory of the Most High will protect those who have conducted themselves
decently, but we have conducted ourselves
indecently? 123 What good is it that paradise
will be revealed, whose fruit remains uncor-
rupted, in which there is plenty and healing, 124 but we won't enter it, for we have
visited unseemly places? 125 What good
is it that the faces of those who practiced
abstinence will shine brighter than stars
when our faces are blacker than darkness?
126 While we were alive and doing evil, we
didn't think about what we would suffer
after death."

127 He answered: "These are the rules
for the contest in which everyone born on
earth takes part: 128 Those who are defeated
will suffer what you said, but those who
conquer will receive what I say. 129 This is
the path that Moses declared when he was
alive, speaking to the people, *Choose life*
for yourself . . . so that you may live.[l] 130 But
they didn't believe him or the prophets who
came after him. They didn't even believe
me when I spoke to them. 131 There won't
be sadness over their destruction, as there
will be joy over those for whom salvation is
sure."

132 I answered: "I know, Lord, that the
Most High is now called merciful, since he
has mercy on those who haven't yet come
into the world. He is called 133 gracious,
since he has mercy on those who convert to
his Law, 134 and patient, because he shows
patience to those who have sinned, since
they are his own creation. 135 I know that
he is called generous, because he wants to
give gifts rather than demand them, 136 and
very merciful, because he multiplies mercies more and more to those now alive and
those who went before and those who are to
come in the future. 137 If, indeed, he hadn't
multiplied them, the world with those
who live in it would not now exist. 138 He is
called[m] giver, because if he didn't give out
of his own goodness some relief from their
sins to people who committed sins, not one
ten-thousandth part of humanity could
live. 139 He is called judge, because unless
he forgave those created by his word and
wiped out the multitude of their offenses,
140 perhaps only a very few would be left
from the innumerable multitude."

8 He answered me: "The Most High made
this world for the sake of many but the
future world for the sake of few. 2 But I will
tell you a parable, Ezra. Just as when you
ask the earth and it tells you that it provides much clay to make earthenware, but
little dust from which gold comes to be, so
the present world also works. 3 Many indeed
are created, but few will be saved."

4 I replied: "Therefore, take delight[n] in
understanding, my soul, and drink your fill
of knowledge.[o] 5 You came into the world[p]
unwillingly,[q] and against your will you depart, and you are given but a little while
to live. 6 Lord above us—if you will permit
your servants to pray before you—give us
seed for the heart and cultivation for the
understanding that there may be fruit from
which every mortal who bears the form of
a human being may live. 7 You alone exist,
and we are your handiwork, as you have
said. 8 Because you give life to the body that
is now fashioned in the womb and give it
members, your creation is preserved in fire
and water. For nine months the womb you
have fashioned endures what is created in
it. 9 But both the container and its contents
will be conserved by your care. And when
the womb at last gives forth what is created
in it, 10 you have commanded that from
the members themselves; that is, from
the breasts, milk (the fruit of the breasts)
should be provided. 11 By this means, that
which is fashioned may be nourished for
a time, and afterward you will dispose of
this person in your mercy. 12 You nourished him with your justice, tutored him
in your Law, and reproved him in your
wisdom.[r] 13 You will cause him to die as your
creation and give him life as your work.

[l]Deut 30:19 [m]Versions omit *he is called.* [n]Syr and other versions; Lat *dismiss* [o]Syr and other versions; Lat *let the soul feed on what it knows* [p]Versions lack *into the world.* [q]Versions; Lat misread the Gk. [r]Syr; Lat *intelligence*

14 If, therefore, you will destroy with a simple command one who was fashioned at your command with so much labor, why was he made? 15 Now I will surely speak: You know best about the sum total of humanity, but what about your people who grieve me, 16 and about your inheritance because of which I lament, and about Israel, on whose account I am sad, and about the seed of Jacob because of which I am disturbed? 17 Therefore, I will pray before you for myself and for them, because I see the defects of we who live on earth, 18 but I have heard of the swiftness of the judgment that is to come. 19 Therefore, hear my voice and consider my words, and I will speak before you."

20 The beginning of the words of Ezra's prayer before he was taken up.[s] He said:

Lord, you live in eternity.[t] The highest heavens are yours, and your upper chambers are in the air. 21 Your authority[u] is beyond estimation, and your glory is beyond our power to comprehend. The armies of angels wait on in fear, 22 and at your command they are changed into wind and fire. Your word is true, and what you say lasts forever. 23 Your command is powerful, and your precept is fearsome. Your gaze dries up the deeps, and your threat makes mountains melt. Your truth is acknowledged. 24 Hear your servant's voice and listen to my request, the request of one whom you formed, and listen to my words. 25 But me! I will speak as long as I live, and while I still have understanding, I will respond.

26 Don't pay attention to your people's sins but to those who have served you in truth. 27 Don't consider those who do evil by sinning but those who have kept your covenants in the midst of torments. 28 Don't think about those who have conducted themselves wickedly in your presence but of those who have made it their purpose to know what it means to revere you. 29 Don't set your mind to destroy those who have lived as mindlessly as cows,[v] but look on those who showed forth your glorious Law. 30 Don't be angry at those who are esteemed lower than animals, but love those who have constantly hoped to honor you.

31 We and those before us have followed ways that lead to death, but it's on account of us sinners that you are said to be merciful. 32 If you desire to have pity on us who have no good deeds to our credit, then you will be called compassionate. 33 The righteous who have many works laid up with you will receive a reward for their own works. 34 What are human beings that you should be angry with them, or a corrupt race that you should be irate with them? 35 In truth, no one born has not violated your commands, and no one who grew up has not sinned. 36 But this shows your goodness, Lord, when you have pity on those who have no stockpile of good works.

37 He answered me: "You have said some things correctly, and according to your words it will be done. 38 Indeed, I won't think about the formation of sinners or their death or judgment or damnation, 39 but I will rejoice over the creation of the righteous, their journey also, and their deliverance and receipt of a reward. 40 As I've said, then so it is. 41 Just as a farmer sows many seeds on the land, but in time not all seeds that are sown will be saved nor will all the planted things take root, so also not all of those who are sown in the world will be saved."

42 I answered: "If I have found favor with you, let me speak, 43 because the farmer's seed doesn't grow up, perhaps because it didn't receive your rain in season; or if it was spoiled by abundance of rain, it perishes. 44 But human beings, who are shaped by your hands and named in your image, because they are made in your likeness, for whom you created all things—have you compared them to a farmer's seeds? 45 No, Lord above us, but spare your people and have mercy on your inheritance, for you have mercy on your own creation."

46 He answered me: "The present things

[s]Lat text has two forms for 8:30-38, with minor differences between them. [t]Lat *live forever* [u]Lat *throne*
[v]Lat *had the ways of cattle*

are for those who now are, and the future
things for the future. 47 You are a long way
from loving my creation more than I do. But
you have often associated yourself with the
wicked. Never do so! 48 But even in this respect the Most High will admire you, 49 because you have humbled yourself, as befits
you, and didn't count yourself among the
righteous so that you may be glorified the
more. 50 Many miseries will afflict those who
inhabit the world in the last times because
they will walk in great pride. 51 But think of
yourself and ask about the glory of those
like you. 52 For you, paradise is opened, the
tree of life is planted, the future time is prepared, abundance is made ready, the city
is built, rest is appointed, goodness is perfected, and wisdom is perfected in advance.
53 The root of evil[w] is sealed off from you,
weakness is abolished from you, and death
is hidden; the netherworld[x] and decay have
fled into oblivion. 54 Sorrows have passed,
and the treasure of immortality is displayed
to the end. 55 Therefore, don't continue to
ask about the great many who perish.
56 They also received freedom, but they despised the Most High, spoke ill of his Law,
and abandoned his ways. 57 Moreover, they
also trampled his righteous ones. 58 They
said in their heart that there is no God,
even though they knew that they would
have to die. 59 Just as the things that are
predicted will receive you, so also the thirst
and torment that are prepared will receive
them. The Most High didn't intend for
human beings to be destroyed, 60 but those
who were themselves created defiled the
name of their creator and were ungrateful
to him who prepared life for them. 61 Therefore, my judgment draws close, 62 which I
haven't disclosed to all, except to you and
to a few like you."

63 I answered, "Look now, Lord, you have
shown me a multitude of signs that you
are about to perform in the last times, but
you haven't shown me when they will take
place."

9 He answered me: "Measure carefully
within yourself, and when you see that a
certain part of the signs that were predicted
have passed, 2 then you will understand that
the time has come in which the Most High
will begin to visit the world that he made.
3 When the movement of places, tumult of
peoples, plotting of nations, inconstancy of
leaders, and confusion of princes appear in
the world, 4 then you will understand that it
was about these things that the Most High
spoke from former days, from the beginning. 5 Just as with everything that has happened in the world, the beginning is known
from the end,[y] and the end comes to be seen,
6 so also are the times of the Most High.
The beginnings are manifest in prodigies
and mighty works, and the end is evident
in deeds and in signs. 7 All this—who will be
saved, who will be able to escape through
their works or through the faith with which
they believe—8 will survive the predicted
dangers and will see my salvation in my
land and within my borders, which I have
made holy for myself for a long time. 9 Then
whoever has now abused my ways will be
astonished, and whoever rejected them in
contempt will linger in agony. 10 Those who
didn't acknowledge me when they were
alive, even though they received benefits;
11 those who despised my Law while they
were enjoying freedom 12 and didn't come
to their senses but continued to scoff while
the opportunity for a changed life was still
open to them—these people must acknowledge me in torment after death. 13 But don't
be curious any longer about how the wicked
will be tortured. Instead, inquire how and
when the righteous, to whom the world belongs and because of whom the world exists, will be saved."

14 I answered, 15 "I said before and now
will say again that those who perish are
more numerous than those who are saved,
16 just as a wave is greater than a drop."

17 He answered me: "As the field is, so is
the seed; and as the flowers, so also the colors; as the labor, so also the product;[z] and as
the farmer, so the threshing floor. 18 There
was a time in this world—when I was preparing for those who now are, before the

[w]Versions lack *of evil.* [x]Lat *infernum* [y]Syr *its beginning is known* [z]Other versions *judgment*

world in which they would dwell was made for them—no one opposed me, because no one existed yet. 19Now, however, those who have been created in this world—a world furnished with both an inexhaustible table and an endless pasture[a]—have become corrupt in their habits. 20I considered the earth—and, observe, it was ruined. I considered my world, and, observe, it was in danger because of the intrigues of those who had come into it. 21I saw and spared them with great difficulty; I saved for myself one grape out of a cluster and one plant out of a great forest.[b] 22Therefore, let the multitude that was born without purpose perish, and let my grape and my plant be preserved, because I perfected these with much effort. 23But let seven more days pass. Don't fast during this time, 24but go into a field of flowers, where no house is built, and eat only of the flowers of the field. Don't taste meat, and don't drink wine, but eat only flowers. 25Pray to the Most High without pause, and I will come and talk to you."

Vision of the woman in mourning

26I went out as he told me into the field that is called Ardat. I sat there among the flowers, I ate of the plants of the field, and their food satisfied me. 27After seven days I was lying on the grass, and my heart was disturbed again as before. 28My mouth was opened and I began to say before the Most High: 29"Lord, you revealed yourself to us, to our ancestors in the wilderness, when they were going out from Egypt and when they were coming into the desert that no one crossed and that bore no fruit. You said: 30Listen to me, Israel! Offspring of Jacob, pay attention to what I say! 31Look, I am sowing my Law in you, and it will bear fruit in you, and you will be glorified in it forever. 32Though our parents received the Law, they didn't keep it and didn't observe what was lawful. The fruit of the Law didn't perish, nor could it, since it was yours. 33Yet those who received it perished, not keeping what was sown in them. 34Normally, when the ground receives seed or the sea a ship or some other container food or drink, and when it happens that what was sown or what was sent or what was received is destroyed, 35those things themselves are destroyed, but the containers remain. But this hasn't been so in our case. 36We who received the Law sinned and will perish, along with our hearts that received it; 37yet the Law doesn't perish but remains in its glory."

38While I was saying these things in my heart, I looked with my eyes and saw a woman to my right. She was lamenting and crying with a loud voice, and she was experiencing deep grief. Her clothes were torn, and there were ashes on her head. 39I dismissed my own thoughts, turned to her, and said, 40"Why are you weeping, and why do you grieve so deeply?"

41She said to me, "Leave me alone, sir, so that I may weep for myself and continue in my grief, because I am very bitter inside, and I am depressed."

42I said to her, "What have you suffered? Tell me!"

43She said to me: "I, your servant, was infertile, and I hadn't given birth, although I had a husband for thirty years. 44Hour after hour and day after day during these thirty years I pleaded with the Most High by night and day. 45After thirty years God heard your servant and saw how dejected I was. He attended to my distress and gave me a son. I rejoiced greatly over him, as did my husband and all my fellow citizens, and we greatly honored the mighty one. 46I nourished my son with much labor, 47and when he grew up, I came to take a wife for him and set the day of the marriage feast.

10 "But it happened that when my son went into his wedding chamber, he fell down and died. 2We extinguished all our lamps, and all my fellow citizens rose to console me. I was quiet until the next day, until nightfall. 3But when all ceased consoling me so that I would be quiet, I got up at night and fled, and I came into this field, as you see. 4Now I plan not to return to the city but to stay here, and I will neither eat

[a]Lat *law*, misreading Gk [b]Syr, Eth; Lat *tribe*

nor drink but lament and fast without ceasing, until I die."

[5]I abandoned the thoughts that had preoccupied me and responded to her in anger: [6]"Most foolish of all women, don't you see our grief and what has befallen us? [7]Zion the mother of us all is afflicted in sadness and utterly dejected. Grieve mightily [8]now because we all grieve, and be sorrowful because we are all sorrowful. But you are mourning only for one son![c] [9]Ask the earth, and she will tell you that she is the one who should mourn, since so many have sprouted upon her. [10]From her, from the beginning, all have been born and others will come. Look, nearly all go to ruin, and their multitude is doomed to destruction. [11]Who then ought to mourn the more? Shouldn't she who has lost such a great multitude rather than you, who grieve for one? [12]Perhaps you say to me, 'My lamentation isn't like that of the earth, because I lost the fruit of my womb, which I bore with pains and brought forth with sorrows. [13]The earth, however, is just following the way of the earth; the multitude that is present on it goes as it came.' [14]I would then say to you, 'As you gave birth with grief, so also from the beginning the earth yielded its fruit, humanity, to him who made it.' [15]Therefore, keep your grief to yourself, and bear valiantly whatever misfortunes befall you. [16]If you declare the decree of God to be just, you will receive your son back in due time and also be praised among women. [17]Therefore, go into the city to your husband."

She said to me, [18]"I will not, and I will not go into the city, but I will die here."

[19]I spoke again to her: [20]"Don't say this, but let yourself be persuaded because of Zion's fate and be consoled because of Jerusalem's grief. [21]You see that our sanctuary is laid waste, our altar is demolished, our temple is destroyed, [22]our harp is brought low, our hymnody has been silenced, our joy is undone, the light of our lampstand is extinguished, the chest containing our covenant has been taken as plunder, our holy things have been defiled, and the name that is invoked over us has been dishonored. Our free citizens[d] have suffered abuse, our priests have been burned to death, our Levites have gone into captivity, our virgins have been defiled, our wives have been raped, our righteous men have been snatched away, our little ones have been given over, our youths have been enslaved, and our strong men have been deprived of strength. [23]Even more than all this, the seal of Zion (for she has now loosed the seal of her glory) is handed over to those who hate us. [24]Shake off your great sadness then, and put away the multitude of your sorrows so that the mighty one may show you favor and the Most High may give you peace and rest from your labors."

[25]While I was speaking to her, look! Suddenly her face shone brightly and her countenance became a flashing splendor. I became afraid of her, and I wondered what was happening. [26]Without warning she let out a noise, a great voice full of fear, so that the earth itself shook with the sound. [27]I watched, and she no longer appeared to me as a woman, but there was a city built, and a place with great foundations appeared. I was afraid, and I shouted with a great voice, [28]"Where's the angel Uriel, who came to me from the beginning? He's the one who's brought me to the end of my wits! My end has turned into decay and my prayer into a reproach."

[29]While I was saying these things, the angel who had come to me in the beginning came to me again and looked at me. [30]I was laid out like a dead man, and I had lost my mind. He held my strong hand, comforted me, set me on my feet, and said to me, [31]"What has happened to you? Why are you agitated? Why are your mind, your intellect, and your understanding all in turmoil?"

I said, [32]"Because you abandoned me. I followed your instructions, and I went out into the field, and look here, I saw and see what I can't describe."

He said to me, [33]"Stand up like a man, and I'll remind you."

I said, [34]"Speak, my Lord, only don't

[c]Syr adds *but we, the whole world, for our mother.* [d]Lat *children*

abandon me so that I may not die for nothing. 35 I can't make sense out of what I saw, and I don't understand what I've heard. 36 Or is my mind deceived and my soul dreaming? 37 Now then I beg you to explain this bewildering sight to your servant."

38 He answered me: "Listen to me. Let me teach you, and I will speak to you about what you fear, for the Most High has revealed many mysteries to you. 39 He saw that you walk the straight way, because you grieve for your people without ceasing and you mourn greatly over Zion.

40 "Here then is the meaning of the vision. This is the explanation of the woman who appeared to you a little while ago, 41 whom you saw mourning and whom you began to console 42 (though now you don't see a woman, but a fully constructed city has appeared to you), 43 and who told you about the fate of her son. 44 This woman whom you saw is Zion, whom you now see built as a city. 45 As for what she said to you, that she was infertile for thirty years, it is because there were three thousand[e] years in the world when offerings weren't yet made in her. 46 After three thousand[f] years, Solomon built the city and made offerings. That is when the infertile woman bore a son. 47 As for what she said to you, that she nourished him with labor, this was the time that Jerusalem was inhabited. 48 And as for what she said to you, that her son came into his wedding chamber and died and that misfortune happened to her, this is the destruction that happened to Jerusalem. 49 Indeed, you saw her likeness, how she mourns her son, and you began to console her over these things that had happened. (These things were to be shown to you.[g]) 50 Now the Most High, seeing that you are sincerely saddened and that you suffer for her with all your heart, has shown you the splendor of her glory and the beauty with which she is adorned. 51 For this reason I told you to remain in the field where no house is built: 52 I knew that the Most High was about to show you these things. 53 Therefore, I told you to come into the field where there is no building's foundation, 54 for no work of human construction could survive in the place where the city of the Most High was about to be made manifest. 55 Therefore, don't fear, and don't let your heart be afraid. Go inside and see the splendor and greatness of the building, insofar as you are capable of seeing with your eyesight. 56 After this you will hear as much as the hearing of your ears can hear. 57 You are privileged more than many and are called into the presence of the Most High, as few are. 58 Tomorrow night you will remain here, 59 and the Most High will show you in dream visions what the Most High will bring about for those who live on earth in the last days." 60 So I slept that night and the next, as he had told me.

Vision of the eagle and the lion

11 On the second night I had a dream. I saw an eagle, with twelve feathered wings and three heads, rising up from the sea. 2 As I looked, it spread its wings over the whole earth, and all the winds of heaven blew toward it, and the clouds[h] gathered around it. 3 Out of its wings grew opposing wings. These became small, tiny wings. 4 Its heads were at rest. The middle head was larger than the other heads, but it was also at rest with them.

5 I kept looking and saw the eagle flying with its wings to rule over the earth and over those who lived on the earth. 6 I saw how everything under heaven was made to submit to it, and no one opposed it, not a single creature that lives on the earth. 7 I looked and saw the eagle rise on its talons and call out to its wings, saying, 8 "Don't all watch together. Let each one sleep in its place and take turns watching, 9 but the heads will be kept for the end." 10 I looked and saw that the voice didn't come from its heads but from the middle of its body. 11 I counted its opposing wings, and there were eight of them. 12 A wing arose on the right side, and it ruled over the whole earth; 13 and while it was ruling, it came to an end

[e] Lat omits *thousand*. [f] Lat omits *thousand*. [g] Lat; other versions omit *(These things were to be shown to you.)*
[h] Syr and other versions; Lat omits *clouds*.

and disappeared so that its place vanished.
The next one rose up and ruled, and it held
sway a long time. 14While it was exercising
its rule, it came to its end, so that it disappeared like the previous one.
15Then a voice rang out, saying to this
wing, 16"Listen, you who have held sway
over the earth all this time. I announce[i]
this to you before you begin to disappear.
17No one after you will hold sway as long
a time—not even half as long." 18A third
wing raised itself up, and it also exercised
rulership like the previous ones, and it too
disappeared. 19And so it happened to each
of the wings in turn, to come to power and
then never to be seen again. 20I looked, and
indeed the wings that followed on the right
side also rose up in time so that they too
might rule, but some of those who came
to power disappeared immediately, 21while
others of them rose up but didn't succeed
in establishing their rule. 22After all this, I
looked again, and the twelve wings and two
of the little wings had disappeared. 23Noth-
ing remained on the body of the eagle except the three heads that were at rest and
six little wings.
24I looked and noticed that two of the
six little wings were set apart and remained
under the head on the right side, but four
remained in their place. 25I watched as
these little wings plotted to rise up and take
power. 26One was raised up, but it immediately disappeared, 27and then a second, but
this one disappeared more quickly than the
previous one. 28I saw the two that were left
plotting among themselves that they too
should rule, 29and while they were making their plans, one of the heads that had
been at rest, the one in the middle, woke
up. This one was bigger than the other two
heads. 30I saw how it formed a partnership with the two other heads, 31and then
how the head turned with those that were
with it, and it ate the two little wings that
had planned to rule. 32Moreover, this head
gained power over the whole earth and
dominated those who lived on it, inflicting
great distress. It had greater power over
the whole world than all the wings that had
gone before.
33After all this, I watched as the middle
head, just like the wings, suddenly disappeared. 34There were two heads left, however, which also ruled over the earth and
over those who live on it. 35I looked and
watched as the head on the right side devoured the one on the left. 36I heard a voice
saying to me, "Look in front of you and
consider what you see." 37I looked and saw
something like a lion being roused, roaring out of the forest. I heard how he spoke
in a human voice and said to the eagle,
38"Listen, you, and I will speak to you. The
Most High says to you, 39'Aren't you the
last of the four beasts that I made to rule
in my world so that I might bring about
the end of my times through them? 40You,
the fourth that has come, conquered all the
beasts that came before you, ruling over the
world with much terror and over the whole
world with harsh oppression. You have lived
in the world with deceit for so long! 41You
judged the earth, but not in truth, 42for you
have oppressed the meek and injured those
who caused no unrest. You hated those
who spoke the truth and loved liars. You
destroyed the dwellings of those who bore
fruit and tore down the walls of those who
had done you no harm. 43Your insolence
has ascended to the Most High and your
pride to the mighty one. 44The Most High
has reviewed his times. Look! They are finished, and his ages are complete. 45There-
fore, eagle, you must utterly vanish, you
and your terrifying wings, your dreadful
little wings and your evil heads, and your
dreadful talons and all your worthless body.
46Then the whole earth will be refreshed
and restored, set free from your violence,
and will hope for the judgment and mercy
of him who made it.'"

12 While the lion was saying these words
to the eagle, I looked 2and saw that
the head that had prevailed disappeared,
and the two wings that had gone over to it
rose up so that they might rule, but their
rule was weak and chaotic. 3I watched as

[i] Syr

they disappeared, and the whole body of the eagle was burned; the earth was filled with fear.

I woke up because my mind was racing and full of fear. I said to myself, 4Look, you've brought all this on yourself with your probing into the ways of the Most High. 5Look here! I'm emotionally exhausted and barely alive. I don't have even a little strength left in me because of the great fear that has shaken me this night. 6Now, therefore, I will pray to the Most High that he may strengthen me to the end. 7I said, "Supreme Lord, if you do look upon me favorably, if you consider me to be among the more righteous, and if my prayer has indeed risen into your presence, 8strengthen me, and show me, your servant, the interpretation and meaning of this terrible vision. Console my soul, 9since you have thought me worthy to be shown the end of times and the last events of the times."

10He said to me, "This is the interpretation of the vision that you saw. 11The eagle you saw rising from the sea is the fourth kingdom. It appeared in a vision to your brother Daniel, 12but it wasn't interpreted for him as I now interpret it for you or have shown it to you. 13Look, the days are coming when a kingdom will rise on earth that will be more terrifying than all the kingdoms that came before it. 14Twelve kings will rule in it, one after the other. 15The second one to rule will have a longer time than the rest of the twelve. 16This then is the interpretation of the twelve wings that you saw. 17As for the fact that you heard a voice that spoke, coming not from its heads but from the middle of its body, 18this is the interpretation: In the midst of this kingdom's time, great conflicts will arise. It will be in danger of falling; it won't fall then but will be restored again to its beginning.

19"As for the fact that you saw eight little wings clinging to its wings, 20this is the interpretation: Eight kings will arise in it. Their rules will amount to nothing, and their years will be swift. Two of them will perish 21when the middle of the time draws near, but four will be reserved until the time approaches for its end. Two will be preserved until the very end.

22"As for the fact that you saw three heads at rest, 23this is the interpretation: In the last period the Most High will raise up three kings,[j] and he will renew many things in it, and they will rule the earth 24and greatly oppress those who dwell on it, more than all the rest who were before them. Therefore, they are called the heads of the eagle, 25because they will sum up its acts of impiety and complete its last deeds.

26"As for your seeing the biggest head disappear, one of the kings will die on his bed, though in agonies. 27As to the two who are left, the sword will destroy them. 28The sword of one of them will destroy the one who is with him, but he too will fall by the sword in the last days.

29"As for your seeing the two small wings passing over to the head on the right, this is the interpretation: 30The Most High is keeping these for the eagle's end. This rule will be weak and full of upheaval, 31as you saw. The lion whom you saw rousing itself from the forest and roaring and speaking to the eagle and rebuking it for its deeds of injustice, as for all the words that you heard him speaking, 32this is the anointed one. The Most High has kept him for the end of days. He will arise from the line of David, and he will come and speak[k] to them. He will denounce their wicked acts and indict them for their injustice. He will set before them their despicable deeds. 33He will put them on trial while they are still alive, and after he has convicted them, he will destroy them. 34Yet he will mercifully liberate the remaining few from my people who are saved throughout my territory. He will make them joyful until the end comes—the Judgment Day, of which I have spoken to you from the beginning.

35"This is the dream that you saw, and this is its interpretation. 36You alone were counted worthy to know this secret of the Most High. 37Therefore, write all these things that you saw in a scroll and hide it

[j] Lat *kingdoms* [k] Lat omits *of days, who will arise from the line of David, and who will come and speak.*

away. [38]Teach these matters to the wise among your people, whose minds you know can grasp and keep these secrets. [39]But wait here yet another seven days so that you may be shown whatever it pleases the Most High to show you." [40]Then he left me.

When the whole people heard that seven days had passed and I hadn't returned to the city, they all gathered, from the smallest to the biggest. They came and said to me, [41]"How have we sinned against you? What wrong did we do to you that you abandon us and sit in this place? [42]You are the only one of all the prophets left to us, like a cluster of grapes from the vineyard, and like a lamp in a dark place, and like a harbor for a ship saved from a storm. [43]Or are the disasters that have befallen us not enough for us? [44]If you abandon us now, it would have been better for us to have been burned up along with Zion! [45]We are no better than those who died there." They wept with a loud voice.

[46]I answered them: "Have confidence, Israel! Don't be sad, house of Jacob. [47]The Most High keeps you in memory. The mighty one hasn't forgotten you in your struggle. [48]I haven't abandoned you, nor have I gone away from you. I came to this place to pray because of Zion's desolation, in order to seek mercy for the humiliation of your sanctuary. [49]Now go home, each of you, and I will come to you in a few days." [50]So the people went into the city as I told them, [51]but I sat in the field for seven days as he had commanded me,[l] and I ate only the flowers that grew in the field, and plants were my food in those days.

Vision of the man from the sea

13 After seven days, I had a dream during the night. [2]I looked and saw a wind rising from the sea and stirring up all its waves. [3]As I watched, this wind made something like the figure of a man come up out of the heart of the sea.[m] That man was flying among the clouds of heaven. Wherever he turned his face to look, everything that fell under his gaze trembled. [4]Wherever an utterance came from his mouth, all who heard his voice melted as wax melts when it feels the fire.

[5]I kept watching these things, and an innumerable multitude of people came together from the four winds of heaven to fight against the man who had come up from the sea. [6]I watched as he carved a great mountain for himself and flew onto it. [7]I tried to see the region or place from which the mountain was carved, but I couldn't.

[8]After this I looked and I saw that all who had gathered to do battle against him were sorely afraid, yet they dared to fight. [9]When he saw the rush of the multitude coming, he didn't raise his hand or hold a spear or any weapon of war. Rather, I saw [10]something like a wave of fire shoot forth from his mouth, and a breath of flame from his lips, and a storm of sparks from his tongue. All these things—the wave of fire, the breath of flame, and the mighty storm—mixed together [11]and fell upon the crowd that was rushing forward, prepared to fight. It burned them all up so that suddenly nothing was seen of the innumerable mob except the dust of ashes and the smell of smoke. I saw this and was amazed.

[12]After these things I saw the same man coming down from the mountain and calling to himself another crowd—a peaceful one. [13]Many people came to him. Some were rejoicing and some were sad, some were even tied up, while some were bringing other people as an offering.

I woke up in great fear and pleaded with the Most High. I said, [14]"From the beginning you showed your servant these wonders, and you considered me worthy that you should receive my prayer. [15]Now show me also the interpretation of this dream. [16]As I turn it over in my mind, I think: How terrible it will be for those who will be left in those days, and how much worse for those who aren't left! [17]Those who aren't left will be full of sorrow, [18]since they now know what lies in store for the last days, but they won't live to see them. But how terrible it will be also for those who are left, [19]for that

[l]Syr; Lat *as I had commanded* [m]Lat omits *this wind . . . heart of the sea.*

very reason! They will see great dangers, and there will be many kinds of distress, as these dreams show. [20]Yet it is better[n] to encounter these things, even incurring danger, than to pass from the world like a cloud and not see what happens at the end."

[21]He answered me, "I will tell you the interpretation of the dream as well, and I will explain to you the things you spoke about. [22]As to what you said about those who are left, this is the interpretation: [23]He who brings the danger at that time will himself guard those who fall into danger, who have works and faith in the most mighty one. [24]Know, therefore, that those who are left enjoy greater privilege than those who have died. [25]The interpretations of the vision are as follows:

"In that you saw a man going up from the heart of the sea, [26]that is the one whom the Most High has been keeping for many ages. He will liberate God's creation all by himself, and he will put in order those who are left.

[27]"In that you saw something like wind and fire and storm go out of his mouth, [28]and that he didn't hold a spear or weapon of war, yet destroyed the rush of that multitude that had come to fight him, here is the interpretation: [29]Look, the days are coming when the Most High will begin to rescue those who are on the earth. [30]Those who live on earth will go out of their minds. [31]They will plan to wage war against each other, city against city, place against place, nation against nation, and kingdom against kingdom. [32]When these things happen, and the signs that I showed you before take place, then my Son will be revealed, whom you saw as a man rising up. [33]When all the nations hear his voice, then each one will leave its own region and will leave off the wars they were waging against each other. [34]An innumerable mob will be gathered together, as you saw, wanting to come and fight against him. [35]But he will take his stand on the summit of Mount Zion. [36]Zion will come and will appear to all, built and ready, as you saw a mountain carved without hands. [37]My Son himself will indict the assembled nations for their impious deeds—these things were indicated by the storm. He will scold them for their evil plans and reveal the torments with which they are about to be tortured. These things correspond to the flame. [38]He will destroy them without effort by the Law, which was indicated by the fire.

[39]"As to the fact that you saw him collecting to himself another peaceful multitude, [40]these are the ten tribes that were taken captive from their land in the days of King Hoshea, whom King Shalmaneser of the Assyrians took across the river as a captive. They were taken into another land, [41]but they made this plan for themselves: They would leave the multitude of the nations and go into a more remote region, where the human race had never lived. [42]There they would be able to observe their customs, which they hadn't kept in their own region. [43]They went in through the narrow passages of the Euphrates River. [44]Then the Most High gave them signs and stopped the flow of the river until they had passed. [45]They made a long journey through that region for a year and a half, and that region is called Arzareth. [46]They lived there until the last time, and now they begin again to return. [47]The Most High will once again stop the flow of the river so that they can cross. These people make up the multitude gathered in peace, [48]along with those who are left of your people, who are found within my holy boundaries. [49]Then when he begins to destroy the multitude of the nations that are gathered, he will protect the people who have survived. [50]Then he will show them many more signs."

[51]I said, "Supreme Lord, show me why I saw a man rising up from the heart of the sea."

He said to me, [52]"Just as no one can seek out or know what is in the depth of the sea, so no one on earth can see my Son or those who are with him, except in that time when his day has come. [53]This is the interpretation of the dream that you saw, which has enlightened you alone of all people.

[n]Syr; Lat *easier*

54You have abandoned your own affairs
and occupied yourself with mine, and you
have sought out my Law. 55You have given
your life to wisdom, and have called understanding your mother. 56Because of this, I
have shown you these things, for you have
a reward with the Most High. After three
days I will tell you more and explain to you
weighty and wonderful things."
57I went out from there into a large field,
glorifying and praising the Most High for
the wonders he performed over time, 58and
because he governs the times and all that
comes about in its time. I stayed there for
three days.

Ezra renews the scriptures

14 On the third day I was sitting under
an oak tree 2when a voice came out of
a bush opposite me and said, "Ezra, Ezra!"
I said: "I'm here, Lord!" and I got up on
my feet.
He said to me: 3"I revealed myself in a
bush and spoke to Moses when my people
were enslaved in Egypt. 4I sent him and
brought my people out of Egypt, and I led
him to Mount Sinai, and I kept him with
me for many days. 5I told him many wondrous things and showed him the secrets of
the times and the end of the times. I commanded him, saying, 6'You will make these
words public, but you will keep these other
words secret.' 7Now I say to you, 8the signs
that I showed you, the dreams that you saw,
and the interpretations you heard—place
them in your heart! 9You will be taken from
among human beings, and you will associate
from now on with my Son and with those
who are like you until the times are finished.
10The age[o] is no longer young, and the times
are beginning to grow old. 11The age is divided
into twelve parts. Nine[p] parts and half of the
tenth part have already passed. 12Two parts
in addition to half of the tenth part remain.
13Now then put your house in order; give
solemn instruction to your people. Console
the humble among them, and instruct those
who are wise.[q] Renounce now this corruptible
life, 14put away short-lived thoughts, cast off
from yourself human burdens, strip off your
weak nature, push aside the thoughts that
most trouble you, and hasten to depart from
these times. 15As for the evils that you have
now seen happen, people will yet do worse
than these. 16The weaker the world[r] becomes
because of old age, the more will evils multiply upon those who dwell in it. 17Truth will
depart and falsehood will come near. Even
now the eagle, which you saw in your vision,
hastens to come."
18I answered: "I will speak in your presence, Lord! 19Look, I will go as you commanded me and warn the people who are
now living. But who will warn those who
will be born in the future? 20The world is in
darkness. Those who live in it have no light,
21because your Law has been burned, and so
no one knows what things you have done or
what works are about to come to pass. 22If
then I have found favor before you, send a
holy spirit into me, and I will write everything that has happened in the world from
the beginning, the things that were written
in your Law, so that human beings can find
the path, and those who want to live in the
last days may live."
23He replied to me: "Go, gather the
people and say to them that they shouldn't
seek you for forty days. 24Gather up many
writing tablets, and take with you Sarea,
Dabria, Selemia, Ethanus, and Asiel, these
five, who are trained to write fast. 25Come
here, and I will light in your heart the lamp
of understanding. It won't be extinguished
until you have written everything down.
26When you are finished, you will make
some things public, others you will transmit secretly to the wise. You will begin to
write tomorrow at this time."
27I did as he commanded me. I gathered all the people and said, 28"Hear these
words, Israel. 29At first our fathers lived as
strangers in Egypt, and they were liberated
from there. 30They received the Law of life,
but they didn't keep it, and you also transgressed after them. 31You were given land

[o]Lat *world* [p]Correction; Lat and other versions read *ten.* [q]Syr, Eth; Lat lacks *instruct those who are wise.*
[r]Lat *the age*

by allotment in the region of Zion. You and your fathers did evil and didn't keep the ways that the Most High had commanded you. 32Since he is a just judge, in time he took away from you what he granted. 33Now you are here, and your relatives live even farther away.[s] 34If then you will rule your mind and instruct your heart, you will be kept alive, and after death you will attain mercy. 35Judgment comes after death, when we are restored to life, and then the names of the just will appear and the deeds of the wicked will be exposed. 36But let no one approach me now or come looking for me for forty days."

37I took the five men, as he had commanded me, and we went out into the field and remained there. 38So it happened to me on the next day that a voice called me: "Ezra, open your mouth and drink what I give you to drink." 39So I opened my mouth, and a full cup was set before me. It was full of something like water, but its color was like fire. 40I took it and drank, and when I had drunk it my heart poured forth understanding, and wisdom increased in my heart, for my spirit retained memory. 41My mouth was opened and wasn't shut anymore. 42The Most High, moreover, gave understanding to the five men, and they wrote in turns what was dictated, in characters that they didn't know, and they sat for forty days. They wrote by day, 43but by night they ate bread; however, I spoke by day and wasn't silent by night. 44Ninety-four scrolls were written in the forty days. 45Then when the forty days were completed, the Most High said to me, "Make public the ones you wrote first so that the worthy and unworthy may read them. 46But keep the last seventy so that you may transmit them to the wise among your people. 47In these are the fountains of understanding, the source of wisdom, and the river of knowledge." 48And so I did.

A Christian addition

15 [t]Look here, speak in my people's ears the words of the prophecy that I place in your mouth, says the Lord. 2See to it that they are written down on paper, because they are reliable and true. 3Don't be afraid of conspiracies against you, and don't be confused by what unbelievers say, 4because every unbeliever will die in his unbelief.

5Look, I am bringing disasters over the whole earth—the sword, hunger, death, and destruction, says the Lord, 6because wickedness has covered the whole earth, and their deeds are complete. 7Therefore, says the Lord, 8I will no longer be silent about their wicked deeds, which they do in their godlessness, nor will I tolerate any longer the things they do wickedly. Look, innocent and righteous blood calls out to me, and the souls of the just cry out constantly. 9I will surely avenge them, says the Lord, and I will receive all their innocent blood to myself.

10Look, my people are led like sheep to slaughter. I will no longer permit them to live in the land of Egypt, 11but I will bring them out with a great display of my power,[u] and I will strike Egypt with plagues as before, and I will destroy all its land.

12Let Egypt howl from its very foundations because of the plague of beating and punishment inflicted by the Lord. 13Let the farmers who work the ground howl, because they won't have enough seed, and their trees will be devastated by blight, hail, and terrible storms. 14How terrible it will be for the world and those who live in it! 15The sword and distress draw near, and nation will rise against nation to fight with spears in their hands.

16Human beings won't be able to trust each other. As they grow strong against each other, they will pay no respect to their king or to the powerful chief of their great men. 17Someone will want to go into the city and won't be able. 18Cities will be thrown into confusion because of their pride. Houses will be destroyed;[v] people will be afraid. 19People will have no mercy on their neighbors. They will cause their

[s]Latin uncertain; Syr *are farther in than you in the last land* [t]2 Esdras 15–16 = Sixth Ezra. [u]Lat *a mighty hand and an arm upraised* [v]Lat *households will be exposed*

neighbors trouble by breaking into their houses with swords, to pillage their property, because they are hungry for bread and in great distress.

20 Look, says the Lord, I am calling together all the kings of the earth, those from the north and from the south, from the east and from Lebanon. I am stirring them up to make them return and restore whatever my people[w] gave them. 21 As they have done to my chosen ones even to this very day, so I will do to them: they will suffer full payback.[x] This is what the Lord God says: 22 My strong hand won't spare sinners, nor will my sword stop fighting against those who spill innocent blood on earth. 23 God's anger has gone forth like fire to devour the earth's foundations and sinners like kindled straw. 24 How terrible it will be for those who sin and don't keep my laws, says the Lord. 25 I won't spare them. Go away, faithless children! Don't defile my sanctuary!

26 God knows all who sin against him. Therefore, he will hand them over to death and slaughter. 27 Even now disasters have swept over the world, and you will have to endure them. God won't deliver you because you sinned against him.

28 Look! A terrible sight is appearing from the east! 29 The nations of the serpents of Arabia will go out with many chariots. From the day they begin their journey, their hissing will echo over the earth so that all who hear them fear and tremble. 30 The Carmonians will go forth from the forest[y] in furious rage. They will come with great force and engage them in battle, and they will destroy part of the Assyrians' land with their teeth. 31 After this, the serpents will remember their origin and become strong. They will turn, united in great strength, to pursue them. 32 Their enemies[z] will be confused and silent because of their power, and they will turn around and run away. 33 From the Assyrians' land an enemy will attack them in an ambush and will kill one of them. Their army will fall into fear and terror and their kings into indecision.

34 Look! Angry storm clouds from the east and from the north to the south—their appearance is very terrible. 35 They will collide with each other and unleash a mighty tempest on the earth, their own tempest. Blood will flow as high as the belly of a horse, 36 a man's thigh, and a camel's hock because of their swords. Great fear and terror will be on earth. 37 Those who see that wrath will be horrified and seized by fear.

38 After this, the mighty clouds will be moved from the south and the north, and another portion from the west. 39 But the winds from the east will prevail and will stop them, together with the cloud it had stirred up in wrath. The tempest that was to cause destruction will be driven violently from the east to the west. 40 Great, angry storm clouds will be raised up so that they may destroy the whole earth and its inhabitants, and they will unleash over every high and lofty place a terrible tempest—41 fire and hail, flying swords, and much water—so that all the fields and all the streams will be filled with the great quantity of those waters. 42 They will destroy cities, walls, mountains and hills, trees in the forests, grass in the meadows, and their grain. 43 They will proceed steadily to Babylon to destroy it. 44 They will come to it, surround it, and pour out their tempest and all their wrath over it. Dust and smoke will go up to heaven, and all around will mourn it. 45 Those who survive will serve those who destroyed it.

46 You, Asia—you who share in Babylon's splendor and the glory of the mask it wears—47 how terrible it will be for you, wretched one, because you have become like Babylon. You dressed up your daughters for sexual immorality, to please and take pride in your lovers, who have always lusted for you. 48 You have imitated that repulsive one in all her works and devices. Therefore, God says, 49 I will send disasters upon you—widowhood, poverty, hunger, sword, and disease—to desolate your houses, to bring you to devastation and death. 50 Your glorious strength will dry up like a flower when the heat that is sent against you rises. 51 Plagues will leave you weak and impover-

[w] Lat *they* [x] Lat *I will pay it back into their own lap.* [y] Some manuscripts add *like boars.* [z] Lat *they*

ished, wounded by whips, so that you can't receive your powerful lovers. 52 Would I have been so jealous of you, says the Lord, 53 if you hadn't constantly killed my chosen ones, rejoicing, clapping your hands, and talking about their deaths when you were drunk? 54 Make yourself beautiful! 55 The fee due a prostitute is in your lap. Because of this, you will get what's coming to you. 56 As you will do to my chosen ones, says the Lord, so God will do to you and will give you over to disasters. 57 Your children will die of hunger, and you will fall by the sword. Your cities will be laid waste, and all your people will fall by the sword in the open field. 58 Those who are in the mountains will perish by hunger. They will be so hungry for bread and so thirsty for water that they will eat their own flesh and drink their own blood. 59 Already made miserable by the earlier disasters, you will come to suffer even more troubles. 60 As they return from Babylon, passersby will strike the repulsive city and will destroy her. They will destroy another portion of your glory and your land as they return from Babylon. 61 You will be mown down by them like hay, and they will come upon you like fire. 62 They will devour you and your cities, your land, and your mountains. They will burn all your forests and fruit-bearing trees with fire. 63 They will take your children captive, plunder your wealth, and put an end to your beautiful face.

Oracles of doom against the nations

16 How terrible it will be for you, Babylon and Asia! How terrible for you, Egypt and Syria! 2 Dress yourselves in mourning clothes. Howl over your children and grieve for them, because distress has drawn near to you. 3 The sword has been sent against you, and who can turn it away? 4 Fire has been sent against you, and who can extinguish it? 5 Disasters are sent against you, and who can ward them off? 6 Can anyone ward off a hungry lion in the woods? Or put out a fire in dried hay, once it has begun to burn? 7 Or repel an arrow shot by a strong archer? 8 The Lord God sends disasters; who can ward them off? 9 His anger blazes like fire; who can extinguish it? 10 When lightning flashes, who isn't afraid? When it thunders, who doesn't feel fear? 11 The Lord threatens, and who isn't shaken to the core in his presence? 12 The earth and its foundations shake. The sea heaves from the deep; its waves and fish are sent into turmoil when the Lord shows his face and reveals the glory of his power. 13 The one who shoots the arrow is mighty in glory; the tip of the arrow he releases is sharp and won't miss when it's shot to the ends of the earth. 14 Look, disasters are sent forth, and they don't turn back until they fall upon the earth. 15 Fire is lit and not extinguished until it consumes the foundations of the earth. 16 As an arrow that is shot by a powerful archer doesn't turn back, so the disasters that will be unleashed upon the earth won't turn back.

17 I am doomed! I am doomed! Who will save me when those days arrive?

18 The beginning of groaning and an abundance of sighing! The beginning of famine, and many will perish; the beginning of wars, and powerful ones will be afraid; the beginning of disasters, and all will be terrified. 19 What will they do when the disasters come? 20 Look! A plague of famine has been sent out, and the distress it inflicts is like a whip, a punishment for discipline. 21 But in the midst of all these, they won't turn from their sins and won't keep the plagues in mind.

22 Look! In a short time provisions will be so cheap on earth that people will think that peace has been established for them, but then disasters will blossom all over the earth—the sword and famine. 23 They will lack life's necessities, and the sword will scatter those who survive the famine. 24 The dead will be tossed out like dung, and there will be no one to console them, for the earth will be left abandoned, and its cities will be cast down. 25 No farmer will be left to till the ground or to sow seed upon it. 26 Trees will yield fruit, but who will harvest them? 27 Grapes will ripen, but who will gather them? There will be vast, empty wastelands. 28 A person will want to see another human being and hear his voice.

[29]Ten will survive out of an entire city; out
of a field only two who have hidden themselves in dense groves and fissures in the
rocks will be left. [30]As three or four olives
are left on individual trees in an olive orchard, [31]or as in a vineyard that has been
harvested a few clusters are left by those
who diligently search the vineyard, [32]so
in those days three or four will be left by
those who search house to house with the
sword. [33]The earth will be left desolate,
and its fields will be taken over by thornbushes, and its roads and all its paths will
sprout thorns, because sheep won't pass
on them. [34]Virgins will mourn, having no
bridegrooms; women will mourn, having
no husbands; their daughters will mourn,
having no support. [35]Their grooms will be
killed in war, and their husbands will perish
from famine.

Exhortations to God's suffering people

[36]Listen to these things and understand
them, you servants of the Lord. [37]Here
is the Lord's word. Accept it. Don't disbe-
lieve the things that the Lord speaks about.
[38]Look, the disasters are approaching and
won't be delayed. [39]A woman in the ninth
month of pregnancy, when the hour for giving birth arrives, experiences great pains
around her womb for two or three hours
beforehand, but when the infant is ready
to come forth from the womb she doesn't
delay for a moment. [40]In the same way,
these disasters won't delay to come forth on
the earth, but the world will groan and pangs
will envelop it.

[41]Hear the word, my people. Prepare
yourselves for battle, and in the midst of
disasters be like strangers on earth. [42]Let
the person who sells be like a person who is
about to run away, and let the person who
buys be like a person who is about to lose.
[43]Let one who does business be as one who
makes no profit; one who builds as one
who won't get to live in the building; [44]one
who sows as one who will not reap; one who
prunes as one who will not harvest; [45]those
who get married as people who will have
no children; and those who don't marry
as though they were widowed, [46]because
those who toil, toil for no reason. [47]Foreign-
ers will gather their fruits, plunder their
wealth, knock down their houses, and take
their children captive, for in captivity and
hunger they will produce their offspring.
[48]Those who transact business do so only to
be plundered. The longer they adorn their
cities and houses, possessions and persons,
[49]the more I will be enraged against them on
account of their sins, says the Lord. [50]Just
as a proper and good woman is enraged at
a woman who is promiscuous,[a] [51]so justice
will be enraged against sin when it tries to
make itself beautiful, and will accuse it to
its face since he who defends will come,
hunting up sins on the earth. [52]Therefore,
don't be like it or its ways.

[53]Look, just a little longer and sin will
be removed from the earth and justice will
rule over us. [54]Let sinners not deny that
they have sinned, for God will burn coals
of fire over the head of those who say, "I
haven't sinned before God and his glory."
[55]Look, the Lord knows all the works of
humanity, their devices, their plotting,
and their hearts. [56]He said, "Let the earth
be made," and it was made; "Let heaven be
made" and it was made. [57]At his word the
stars were established, and he knows their
number. [58]He examines the abyss and its
treasuries. He measures the sea and its
contents. [59]He shut up the sea in the midst
of the waters and suspended the earth over
the waters by his word. [60]He stretched out
the heaven like a vaulted ceiling and sank
its pillars into the waters. [61]He put springs
of water in the desert and lakes on the tops
of mountains to send forth rivers from on
high so that the earth might drink. [62]He
formed the human being and put a heart in
the middle of his body and gave him spirit,
life, and intelligence [63]and the breath of
God almighty, who made all things and examines the things that are hidden in dark
corners. [64]He certainly knows your designs
and what you think in your hearts.

How terrible it will be for those who sin

[a]Bensly; Bergren *Just as a whore strives very zealously against a dignified and good woman*

and want to hide their sins. 65 The Lord will
certainly examine all their works and will
put you all on parade. 66 You will be put to
shame when your sins are paraded before
people; your own sins will stand up as your
accusers on that day. 67 What will you do?
How will you hide your sins before God and
his glory? 68 Look, God is judge. Fear him.
Stop sinning and forget your wicked practices, never again to commit them. Then
God will lead you out and deliver you from
all tribulation.

69 Look, the rage of a large crowd will be
stirred up against you. They will take some
of you and try to feed you meat that was
sacrificed to idols. 70 Those who consent to
this will be mocked and disgraced by them
and trampled underfoot. 71 There will be
great uprisings against those who fear the
Lord in many places and in neighboring cities. 72 People will be like maniacs on account
of their own distress. They will spare no
one, seeking to plunder and destroy those
who still fear the Lord. 73 They will destroy
and rob their possessions and throw them
out of their own homes. 74 In that time, the
genuine commitment of my chosen ones
will be shown, as gold that is tested by fire.

75 Listen, my chosen ones, says the Lord,
the days of distress are at hand, and I will
deliver you from these. 76 Don't fear or
hesitate, for God is your leader. 77 You who
keep my commandments and precepts,
says the Lord God, don't let your sins drag
you down, and don't let wickedness get the
upper hand over you. 78 How terrible it will
be for those who are choked by their sins
and covered over by their iniquities, as a
field is choked by overgrowth and its paths
are covered over by thorns so that a human
being can't pass through. It is shut off and
consigned to destruction by fire.

4 MACCABEES

The principle of clear thinking

1 I'm about to prove a most important philosophical principle: godly thinking[a] is supreme over emotions and desires. I would be giving you good advice then to pay close attention to philosophy. [2]This principle is essential for knowing what to do in every situation, and it also includes the praise of the highest moral trait—I'm talking about good judgment. [3]Therefore, if clear thinking is shown to control the emotions that prevent self-control, such as the tendency to overeat and rampant desire, [4]then it is clear that it also rules the emotions that prevent us from acting in a just way, such as ill will, and those emotions that prevent us from acting with courage, such as anger, fear, and pain.

[5]Perhaps some people would object: "If clear thinking can control emotions, why doesn't it do away with memory loss and ignorance?" But that's just ridiculous. [6]The mind doesn't have control over such things, but it controls the emotions and desires that resist justice, courage, and self-control. And it does this so that we won't surrender to the emotions, not in order to destroy them.

[7]I could show you that clear thinking has power over emotions and desires in any number of ways. [8]However, I can do this best by showing you the heroic courage of those who died to preserve their moral character: Eleazar, the seven brothers, and their mother. [9]By ignoring their pain to the point of death, all of these persons showed that clear thinking had complete control of their emotions. [10]On the anniversary of these events, it is appropriate for me to praise the moral achievements of those who died along with their mother to preserve their virtuous character. I would also call them fortunate because of the honor in which they are held. [11]All people, including the ones who tortured them, were amazed at their courage and patient endurance. What's more, they caused the defeat of the tyranny that had oppressed their nation. They conquered the tyrant by their endurance. As a result, their homeland was purged of its filth through their actions. [12]I will say more about this shortly. First I will begin with my main point, as is my custom, and then I will return to their story, giving glory to God, who possesses all wisdom.

Definition of terms

[13]So we are exploring the question of whether clear thinking has full power over the emotions. [14]We need to define what careful reasoning is, what we mean by emotion, how many different kinds of emotions there are, and whether clear thinking has full power over all these things. [15]Clear thinking then is the mind-set that uses plain logic to choose the life of wisdom. [16]Next, wisdom is the knowledge of divine and human behavior and what causes the behavior. [17]This knowledge in turn comes from the instruction provided by the Law, through which we learn about divine matters reverently and human matters to our advantage. [18]The different kinds of wisdom are good judgment, justice, courage, and self-control. [19]Good judgment is the ruler among these kinds of wisdom, because clear thinking controls the emotions with it. [20]There are two general categories of emotions: pleasure and pain. Each of these shows up in different ways in the body and in the soul.

[21]Several other emotions accompany pleasure and pain. [22]Desire comes before pleasure, and joy follows it. [23]Fear comes before pain, and grief follows it. [24]Anger is a mixture of both pleasure and pain, as anyone who thinks about the experience would agree. [25]With pleasure there is a tendency to form bad habits, and this is the most varied of the emotions. [26]In the soul, bad habits show up as pride, love of money, thirst for honor, delight in conflict, and envy. [27]In the body, they show up as eating anything and everything, the tendency to overeat, and

[a] Or *pious reason*

indulging in binge eating in private. 28 Just as pleasure and pain are two plants growing from the body and the soul, so there are many branches shooting off from each of these plants. 29 But clear thinking, like an expert gardener, pulls out the weeds, trims, supports, waters, and cares for the plants in every way. So it tames the jungle of habits and emotions. 30 Clear thinking is the guide of moral character, but it has full power over the emotions.

Clear thinking and the Law

Consider first the way in which clear thinking shows that it is supreme over the emotions through the exercise of self-control. 31 Self-control means having control over your desires. 32 Some desires come from the inner person, and others come from the body. Clear thinking obviously has control over both. 33 Otherwise, how is it that when we are attracted by foods that we aren't allowed to eat, we can walk away from the pleasure that we would get from them? Isn't it because clear thinking is in control over our desires? I think so. 34 We keep our distance when we crave any of the foods that are forbidden to us by the Law, whether it is seafood, birds, animals, or anything else, because of the self-control that comes from clear thinking. 35 The sensible mind curbs the drives of the appetite, keeping them in check, and clear thinking silences the impulses of our bodies.

2 So why is it surprising when the soul's desire to join with something beautiful is defeated? 2 Joseph, an example of self-control, is praised for this very thing. He had full control over his sexual desire through mental effort. 3 Although he was a young man in his sexual prime, he defeated his sexual urges[b] with clear thinking. 4 Clear thinking isn't just being able to have control over strong sexual urges but over every other desire as well. 5 So the Law says, "You will not desire your neighbor's wife or anything that belongs to your neighbor." 6 Since the Law commanded us not to desire, I should be able to convince you even more that clear thinking is able to control desires.

This also proves true in the case of emotions that prevent justice. 7 It is obvious that clear thinking is in charge of the emotions—otherwise, how could someone who always indulges in binge eating in private, or a person who tends to overeat, or a person who tends to get drunk, learn a better way? 8 As soon as people who love money decide to live according to the Law, they are forced to change their way of life, lending to those who ask without charging interest and canceling all debts in the seventh year. 9 If people are greedy, they are forced by the Law through clear thinking, so they don't pick up the grain in the field that they missed the first time or go back through the vineyard to pick the last clusters of grapes.

In every other matter we can also see that clear thinking controls the emotions. 10 The Law even controls affection for parents so that a person does not desert moral values because of them. 11 It exercises control over a husband's love for his wife so that he corrects her if she ignores the Law. 12 It rules love for children by punishing them when they do wrong. 13 It comes before the affection for friends, and it challenges them if they are doing evil. 14 Don't think it's strange that clear thinking should have control over hatred between enemies. Because of the Law, we don't cut down an enemy's orchard in war, but instead we try to keep an enemy's property safe from destruction and help rebuild what has fallen down.

15 Clear thinking even keeps the more violent emotions in check, like the thirst for power, desire for glory, pride, self-importance, and jealousy. 16 The sensible mind rejects these destructive emotions, along with anger, because it rules over that emotion as well. 17 When Moses was angry at Dathan and Abiram, he didn't act against them in anger. Instead, he controlled his anger with clear thinking. 18 The sensible mind, as I have said, is able to get the upper hand over the emotions, transforming some

[b] Or *he swatted the gadfly of his urges*

and defeating others. [19]If this were not the case, why did Jacob our wise ancestor denounce the households of Simeon and Levi for the unreasonable killing of the whole nation of Shechem, saying, "Their anger is cursed"? [20]If clear thinking couldn't control anger, he wouldn't have said this. [21]When God formed human beings, God planted emotions and character traits inside them. [22]At that time, God also set the mind on the throne in the middle of the senses, to function as a holy governor over them all. [23]God gave the Law to the mind. Whoever lives in line with the Law will rule over a kingdom that is self-controlled, just, good, and courageous.

Clarification about godly thinking

[24]Someone might say, "Then why doesn't clear thinking control memory loss and ignorance, if it is in charge of the emotions?"

3 But that argument is completely ridiculous. Clear thinking doesn't appear to have control over its own tendencies, but it does control those emotions that come from the body. [2]None of us can eliminate that kind of emotion, but clear thinking makes it possible for us not to be slaves to our emotions. [3]None of you can eliminate anger from your soul, but clear thinking can help you deal with your anger. [4]None of you can completely eliminate meanness, but clear thinking can fight alongside you so that you don't have to give in to your cruel tendencies. [5]Clear thinking does not uproot the emotions, but it is their opponent.

Example of King David

[6]This can be shown more clearly by the story of when King David was thirsty. [7]David had been attacking the enemy[c] all day long, and he had killed many of them with the help of his nation's soldiers. [8]When it was evening, he returned to his royal tent, dripping with sweat and completely exhausted. The whole army of our ancestors was camped around it, [9]and all the others were eating dinner. [10]However, the king was extremely thirsty. Even though there were plenty of water springs in the camp, he couldn't quench his thirst with them. [11]Instead, he was obsessed with an unreasonable desire for water from the enemy's camp. [12]His guards began to complain bitterly about the king's desire. Then two strong young soldiers, embarrassed because of the king's craving, put on their armor, grabbed a pitcher, and went behind the enemy lines. [13]They sneaked past the guards at the gate and began searching through the whole camp. [14]They found the spring and courageously brought the king a drink. [15]But even though he was on fire with thirst, David understood the terrible danger that this drink posed to his soul. It had equal value to the blood of the men who risked their lives to fetch it.[d] [16]So he pitted clear thinking against his desire, and he poured out the drink as an offering to God. [17]The sensible mind can overcome the pressures of the emotions and put out the flames of undisciplined desires. [18]It can overcome the most intense pain in the body and reject the emotions' attempts at gaining control with the dignified character of clear thinking.

Setting: a lesson from history

[19]But the present occasion invites us to give an illustration from history that demonstrates the power of self-controlled clear thinking. [20]Our ancestors were enjoying peace and success because of their obedience to the Law. Even Seleucus Nicanor, king of Asia, set apart money to help support the temple worship and recognized the Jewish constitution. [21]At that time, certain people attempted to overthrow the government. They upset the nation's harmony and caused a lot of trouble.

4 A man named Simon was a political opponent of Onias, who held the office of high priest for life. Onias was an honorable and good man. Simon was unable to injure Onias, even though he falsely accused him of all kinds of crimes, pretending to act on the nation's behalf. He went into exile and planned to betray his nation. [2]So Simon

[c]Or *the foreigners* [d]Gk omits *of the men who risked their lives to fetch it.*

came to Apollonius, the governor of Syria, Phoenicia, and Cilicia, and said, [3]"Since I am devoted to the king's interests, I have come here to report that several tons of silver[e] in private funds have been deposited in the temple treasuries. These funds are not temple property but belong to King Seleucus." [4]When Apollonius learned these things, he praised Simon for watching out for the king. Then Apollonius went to Seleucus to tell him about the stash of treasure.

[5]When Apollonius received authority to take action, he quickly advanced into our nation, bringing along the villain Simon and heavily armed troops. [6]He said that he was commanded by the king to come and confiscate the private funds that were stored in the treasury. [7]The people angrily protested. They thought it would be terrible if the people who had deposited money in trust in the sacred treasury were robbed. They did whatever they could to prevent it.

[8]However, Apollonius went on to the temple, making threats. [9]The priests stood in the temple, together with their wives and children, begging God to protect the holy place that was being treated so shamefully. [10]While Apollonius was approaching with armed soldiers to seize the money, angels on horseback appeared from heaven with flashing weapons. Apollonius and his soldiers were shaking with fear. [11]Apollonius fell down half dead in the temple court that was open to people of every nation and lifted his hands up to heaven. With tears, he begged the Hebrews to pray for him and to intervene with the heavenly army. [12]He admitted that he had committed a sin for which he deserved to die, but he promised that, if he were spared, he would tell people everywhere about the divine favor that shelters the holy place.

[13]The high priest Onias was touched by these words, but he was also aware that King Seleucus might assume that Apollonius was killed by human plots rather than by God's justice. Therefore, Onias prayed for him. [14]When he was unexpectedly delivered from danger, Apollonius left and told the king everything that happened.

Antiochus begins to oppress the Jews

[15]After King Seleucus died, his son Antiochus Epiphanes came to power. He was a proud and horrible man. [16]Antiochus removed Onias from the office of high priest and installed Onias' brother Jason in his place. [17]Jason had agreed to pay the king 208,602 pounds of silver every year if he were made high priest. [18]So Antiochus appointed Jason to the office of high priest and made him the ruler of the nation. [19]Jason changed the nation's culture and the government so that they completely contradicted the Law. [20]He constructed a Greek school and athletic complex in the heart of the city and abandoned the care of the temple.

[21]God's sense of justice was provoked by these things, so God caused Antiochus himself to start a war against the nation. [22]While Antiochus was at war with Ptolemy in Egypt, he heard that the people in Jerusalem had celebrated when they heard a rumor about his death. So Antiochus rushed off to attack them. [23]After he had defeated them, he gave an order that anyone who was caught following the traditional Jewish Law should be put to death. [24]However, his orders had no effect on the people's commitment to keep the Law. He saw that they simply ignored his threats and punishments. [25]Even women were thrown down from a cliff headfirst along with their infants because they continued to circumcise their sons, though they were fully aware that they would suffer the consequences. [26]When Antiochus saw how his orders were despised, he himself tried to use torture to force each and every person in the nation to give up Judaism by eating foods that were unacceptable to Jews.

Antiochus challenges Eleazar

5 The tyrant Antiochus was sitting in a high place surrounded by his advisors

[e] Gk *talantas*

and armed guards. [2]He ordered his soldiers to bring the Hebrews forward one by one and to force them to eat pork and meat from animals sacrificed to idols. [3]If anyone refused to eat the forbidden meat, they were supposed to be tortured to death by being stretched on a wheel. [4]When they rounded up many people, the guards dragged Eleazar forward as the first from the herd to stand in front of the king. He was a man from a priestly family, a legal expert, and quite old. He was known to many in the tyrant's court because he had been around for so long.

[5]Antiochus looked at him and said, [6]"Old man, before I begin to have you tortured, I would advise you to eat the pork and save yourself. [7]I respect your old age. Even though you have had gray hair for a long time, you don't seem to have a mature understanding of things, since you observe the Jewish religion. [8]Why are you disgusted by eating this animal's delicious meat? It's a gift that nature has given to us. [9]It's stupid not to enjoy pleasant things that aren't shameful, and it's wrong to refuse nature's gifts. [10]I will think that you are even more stupid if you continue to disobey me to your own disadvantage for the sake of your brainless ideas about the truth. [11]Come on! Wake up from your silly philosophy, and get rid of your brainless thinking! Adopt an attitude that is more appropriate for a mature person, and adopt a philosophy that is to your advantage! [12]Take pity on your old age, and respect my generous advice. [13]Think about this: if there is some power watching over you and your religion, it will excuse you for any action against the Law if you are compelled to do it."

Eleazar's defense

[14]When the tyrant had finished pressuring Eleazar to eat forbidden food, Eleazar asked to say something. [15]Antiochus gave him permission, and Eleazar began to give the following speech:

[16]"Antiochus, we are persuaded to live our lives in line with the divine Law! We think that nothing is more compelling than our obedience to the Law. [17]That's why we don't think it's right to disobey the Law under any circumstances.

[18]"Even if, as you assume, our Law were not truly divine and we were wrong to think it is divine, even then it would be wrong for us to ruin our reputation for our godly way of life.[f] [19]So don't think it's a minor sin for us to eat forbidden foods. [20]Whether we disobey the Law in a small matter or a big one, it is equally important, [21]because we are showing equal contempt for the Law itself.

[22]"You look down on our way of life as though living this way were unreasonable. [23]However, our way of life teaches us self-control, so that we can have control over any pleasure or desire. It trains us to be brave, so that we willingly bear any suffering. [24]It educates us about justice, so that it is always our custom to treat everyone fairly. It educates us in the godly way of life, so that we worship with due respect the only God who really exists.

[25]"So we don't eat forbidden foods. We believe that God gave us the Law. The creator of the cosmic order has shown us compassion by giving us the Law in accordance with nature. [26]He has allowed us to eat what is most appropriate for our lives, but he has forbidden us to eat meat that would interfere with our welfare. [27]You are acting like a tyrant, trying not only to force us to break our Law but you are trying also to make us eat forbidden food that we hate just so you can make fun of us. [28]You won't have a chance to laugh at me. [29]I'm not going to break the sacred promises my ancestors made to keep the Law, [30]not even if you dig out my eyes and set my guts on fire. [31]I'm not so old and cowardly that I can't exhibit youthful strength in my mind out of respect for God. [32]Get your torture devices ready, and build up the fires to make them burn hotter. [33]I don't pity my old age so much that I will tear down the Law of my ancestors by my actions. [34]I won't prove disloyal to the Law that made me who I am today.

[f]Or *religion*

I won't renounce the virtue of self-control that I value so dearly. [35]I won't put my own philosophical principle to shame, nor renounce the honor of my priestly office or my knowledge of the Law. [36]But as for you, King, you won't pollute my mouth that I have kept pure all of my life nor my long life of living under the Law. [37]My ancestors will welcome me as pure: as a person who isn't afraid of your violence, even to the point of death. [38]You may intimidate a person who has no sense of God, but you won't dominate my religious principles with either your words or your actions!"

Eleazar endures torture

6 When Eleazar had answered the tyrant's arguments, the soldiers who were standing by hauled him off to the instruments used for torture. [2]First they tore off the old man's clothes, though he was still decently dressed by his respect for God. [3]They tied his arms behind him and began to whip him from both sides [4]while an official kept calling out, "Obey the king's orders!" [5]But Eleazar was dignified and generous. He experienced the truth of his name[g] and seemed like a person being tortured only in a dream. He didn't change his resolve in any way. [6]The old man kept his eyes raised toward heaven while the whips tore into his flesh, ripped his sides, and made his blood flow. [7]His body fell to the ground because it couldn't stand the pain, but he kept his thinking upright and unbending. [8]One of the cruel guards rushed up to him and started kicking him in his side to make him stand up again. [9]But Eleazar endured the pain, ignored the agony, and put up with the suffering. [10]Like an honorable athlete in the games, the old man defeated his torturers while they were beating him up. [11]His face dripping with sweat and gasping for breath, he amazed even the torturers with his courage.

[12]Some members of the king's staff were moved by Eleazar's situation, partly out of pity for his old age, [13]partly because of their previous relationship with him, and partly out of admiration for his endurance. These people came to him and said, [14]"Eleazar, why are you throwing your life away so thoughtlessly in the midst of these torments? [15]We will set some cooked meat in front of you. Save yourself by pretending that it is pork and eat it."

[16]Eleazar screamed out as if this advice were even more painful than the whips: [17]"May we who are Abraham's children never think so wickedly that we would pretend to act this inappropriately because we are cowards! [18]To change our ways now would be the truly thoughtless thing to do. We have lived in line with God's truth well into old age and earned a reputation for keeping the Law. [19]We would become an example of ungodly behavior for the younger people, and pave the way for them to eat forbidden food. [20]It would be a disgrace for us to become a joke for our lack of courage, just to survive a little longer. [21]This tyrant would look down on us as cowards because we weren't willing to defend the divine Law to the point of death. [22]For all these reasons, children of Abraham, die well for the sake of showing God proper respect! [23]As for you, soldiers of the tyrant, what are you waiting for?"

[24]When the king's advisors saw that he remained confident in the face of torture and didn't appreciate their compassion, the guards carried him to the fire. [25]They burned his body with diabolical devices, and then they threw him on the ground and poured disgusting liquids into his nostrils. [26]Eleazar was now burned down to his bones and on the edge of death. He raised his eyes toward God and said, [27]"God, you know that I could have saved myself; instead, I am being burned and tortured to death for the sake of your Law. [28]Have mercy on your people. Make our punishment sufficient for their sake. [29]Purify them with my blood, and take my life in exchange for theirs." [30]When he said this, the holy man died with dignity from the torture. By thinking clearly, he resisted even while facing the pains of death for the sake of the Law.

[g]Eleazar means *God helps*.

Eleazar is praised as an example

31 So without question, godly thinking rules over the emotions. 32 If the emotions had overpowered clear thinking in these events, we would have given evidence of their superior strength. 33 But as it is, since clear thinking conquered the emotions, we are correct to affirm its authority to rule. 34 It's only right for us to affirm that clear thinking has greater power when it has gained control over the response to physical pain. It would be ridiculous to say anything else. 35 So I am showing that clear thinking maintains control not only in the face of physical pain but also in the face of pleasure, without giving way to any of these things.

7 Our father Eleazar's godly thinking was like a skilled captain, steering the ship of godly living over the sea of the emotions. 2 Although the tyrant's storms beat against the ship and the powerful waves of torture crashed over its decks, 3 Eleazar kept the rudder of godly living straight until he sailed into the harbor of immortal victory. 4 No city under siege and attacked by every kind of cleverly devised machine has ever held out like that completely holy man did. Torture and racks ravaged his holy soul, but he conquered his opponents by using godly thinking to protect his commitment to godliness. 5 Our father Eleazar made his mind up so it was like an overhanging cliff that broke the raging waves of the emotions.

6 Eleazar, you are a priest who is worthy of the office. You didn't pollute your teeth; you didn't contaminate your stomach by eating the forbidden foods. Your stomach had room only for godly behavior and purity. 7 How you were in harmony with the Law and a philosopher of the divine life! 8 Whoever has the occupation of administering public affairs in line with the Law should be a person like you. They should protect the Law with their own blood and with genuine tears, and suffer to the point of death! 9 Father, you confirmed our commitment to obey the Law through your endurance that brought you honor. You didn't desert the holy way of life that you had praised so sincerely. Your actions made your words about divine philosophy convincing. 10 Old man, you had greater force than torture! Elder, you are more powerful than fire! Eleazar, you are supreme ruler over passions! 11 Our father Aaron ran into the midst of the people, armed with a container of burning incense, and had the victory over a fiery angel. 12 In the same way, Aaron's descendant Eleazar, though eaten up by fire, kept his thinking straight. 13-14 The most remarkable thing is that he became young again in spirit through clear thinking, though he was an old man whose body was no longer hard and strong—his muscles were soft, and his joints were weak. He made the many devices of torture ineffective with clear thinking, such as Isaac had shown. 15 How honorable is old age, respected gray hair, and a law-abiding life that the faithful seal of death made complete!

16 So if an old man thought nothing of being tortured to death for the sake of showing God proper respect, without question godly thinking is the commander of the emotions. 17 Some people might object, "Not everyone has command of the emotions, since not everyone uses wisdom." 18 But the people who are fully committed to give God proper respect from the heart are alone able to control the sensations of the body. 19 This is because they believe that they don't die to God but rather continue to live for God like the ancestors of our nation, Abraham, Isaac, and Jacob. 20 So there is no contradiction in the fact that some people seem to be completely controlled by their emotions because of weak thinking. 21 If a person lives by the complete rule of philosophy, trusts God, 22 and knows that it is a privilege to suffer anything for the sake of their moral character, that person will be able to control the emotions through godly practice. 23 Only the wise and courageous rule their emotions.

Antiochus confronts the seven brothers

8 By following a philosophy consistent with godly thinking, young boys have held out against even more cruel instruments of torture. 2 When the tyrant was publicly defeated in his first attempt by failing to force an old man to eat polluting food, he was overwhelmed by a violent rage and ordered other Hebrew prisoners to be dragged forward. Anyone who ate the polluting meat would be released, but anyone who refused would be tortured even more severely. [3]After the tyrant had given these instructions, seven brothers together with their mother were brought before him. These young men were handsome, modest, well-born, and charming in every way.

[4]The tyrant looked at them as they stood grouped around their mother like a chorus, and was pleased with them. He was struck by their physical appearance and obvious dignified character, and so he smiled at them and invited them to come closer. He said, [5]"Young men, I feel nothing but admiration and favor for each and every one of you, and I have great respect for the size and beauty of your family. Not only would I counsel you not to express the same insanity as that old man who was just tortured, but I would encourage you to obey me now and so enjoy the privileged life[h] I can offer you.[6]I can be generous to those who obey me in the same way as I can punish those who disobey me. [7]Trust me! Abandon your traditional way of life, and I will give you positions in my government. [8]Enjoy your youth by changing your customs and adopting the Greek way of life. [9]However, if you disobey me and make me angry, you will force me to destroy each and every one of you with terrible punishments and tortures. [10]So take pity on yourselves, since I feel sympathy for your youth and handsome appearance even though I am your enemy. [11]Bear in mind that if you disobey, you have nothing to look forward to except to die on these devices of torture!"

[12]As he said these things, he gave orders for the instruments to be brought forward in order to frighten them into eating the polluting food. [13]The guards laid out the instruments in front of them: wheels and machines for pulling joints apart, racks, clubs, and instruments for applying heavy tension, grills and extremely large frying pans, tools to crush fingers, iron claws, wedges, and burning coals. The tyrant continued: [14]"Young men, be afraid. Whatever justice you respect will have mercy on you, since you are being forced to break the Law."

The brothers' response to the tyrant

[15]The brothers heard the promises and saw the terrible instruments, but they weren't afraid. Instead, they resisted the tyrant's arguments with their own philosophy and defeated the power of his tyranny through clear thinking. [16]But let's think about what arguments they might have used if they had been cowardly and unmanly. Wouldn't they have argued like this? [17]"What pitiful and stupid people we must be! When the king has invited and urged us to accept his favor, [18]why are we happy to make useless resolutions? Why should we dare to disobey when death will be the outcome? [19]Men and brothers, shouldn't we be afraid of what these instruments can do and carefully consider the threats of torture? We should run away from our useless beliefs and from our pride that will lead to our destruction! [20]Let's have compassion on our youth, and show pity for our mother's old age as well. [21]Let's take seriously the fact that, if we disobey, we are dead men! [22]Divine justice will not blame us because we were afraid of the king and his power over us. [23]So why should we deprive ourselves of this pleasant life and cheat ourselves out of this sweet world? [24]Let's not fight against fate or take hollow pride in being tortured. [25]The Law itself would have difficulty giving us the death penalty since we sin out of fear of these instruments. [26]Why are we eager to fight a losing battle or so interested in being stubborn when we know it will kill us? We can enjoy a trouble-free life if we just obey the king!"

[27]Even though these young men were about to be tortured, they didn't say or even think about such things. [28]They held their emotions in check and had full control over their pain. [29]Therefore, as soon as the tyrant finished giving them advice

[h]Or *friendship*

about eating the forbidden food, they said together with one voice and with the same mind:

9 [1]"What are you waiting for, tyrant? We are ready to die rather than sin against the commandments handed down by our ancestors! [2]We would be a disgrace to our parents if we didn't maintain our commitment to the Law and to Moses our chief advisor. [3]You, tyrant, advise lawless behavior. In your hatred for us, don't pity us more than we pity ourselves! [4]We consider your pity, which offers safety at the cost of breaking our Law, to be more bitter than death. [5]You are trying to frighten us with threats of torture and death as if you've learned nothing from Eleazar just a short while ago. [6]If the old men among the Hebrews fulfilled their duty toward God by enduring torture for the sake of godly character, it would be even more appropriate for us who are young to die with contempt for the same torture that our aged teacher defeated. [7]So put us to the test, tyrant! Even if you are able to kill us because of our godly character, don't think that you can truly harm us by these tortures. [8]We will gain the awards of moral character through this suffering, and we will be with God, for whose sake we suffer. [9]You, however, will be tortured forever by divine justice, as your cruel thirst for blood deserves."

The first brother's torture and response

[10]When they had said these things, the tyrant was not only upset by their disobedience but was also infuriated by their ungratefulness. [11]He gave the word, and the soldiers brought the oldest brother forward. They tore off his clothing and tied his arms and hands on each side with leather straps. [12]The soldiers beat him with whips until they were completely tired out, without accomplishing anything. So they tied him to the wheel. [13]They stretched the honorable young man around this instrument until all his limbs were pulled out of joint. [14]Although every part of his body was broken, he spoke out against the tyrant, saying, [15]"You blood-stained tyrant, you are an enemy of divine justice, and you have the mind of a savage! You don't abuse me like this because I have murdered someone or acted in a way that wasn't godly but because I protect God's Law!"

[16]The guards said, "Say that you will eat pork so that you can be set free from these tortures!"

[17]But he replied, "You dirty thugs! The wheel is not stretched tight enough to choke off my mind! Keep cutting my limbs, burning my flesh, and twisting my joints. [18]Through all of this suffering, I will persuade you that the Israelites alone can't be defeated when it comes to moral character!" [19]While he was still saying these words, they spread fiery coals below him. They fanned the flames and tightened the wheel even more. [20]By this point, the wheel was covered in blood, the burning coals were being put out by the gory drippings, and chunks of flesh were falling off parts of the machine. [21]Even with all the ligaments of his bones severed, the dignified son of Abraham didn't cry out loud. [22]Instead, he endured the torture with honor, as if he were transformed by the fire into a life without end. He said, [23]"Imitate me, brothers. Don't desert your post in this contest or deny the courage we share as brothers! [24]Fight the holy and dignified battle for our godly way of life. The just providence that watched over our ancestors might become merciful toward our nation and might punish this cursed tyrant through that battle!" [25]After he had said these words, the devout youth died.[i]

The second brother's torture and response

[26]While everyone was still in awe over the oldest son's strong will, the guards dragged forward the next-oldest son. They put on iron gloves with sharp claws and tied the young man to the torture device. [27]Before they began to torture him, they asked if he would eat pork. When they heard his courageous answer, [28]they acted like wild leopards. They ripped out his

[i]Or *snapped the thread of life*

muscles with their iron claws, tore his flesh all the way up to his chin, and tore his scalp off. He bore the pain with difficulty and said: [29]“Any kind of death is sweet for the sake of the godly way of life of our ancestors!” Then he said to the tyrant, [30]“You are the most barbaric tyrant of all. Don’t you think that you are being tortured worse than I am, since you are seeing the proud logic of tyranny defeated by our endurance for the sake of our godly way of life? [31]I ease my pain with the pleasure that comes from godly character. [32]But you are tortured by the threats that hang over your head, because you have no respect for God. You bloodstained tyrant, you won’t escape the revenge of divine wrath!”

The third brother’s torture and response

10 When the second brother had also endured a heroic death, the third brother was brought forward. Many people urged him again and again to taste the pork in order to save himself. [2]He shouted out in response: “Don’t you know that I come from the same father as those who have just died, that the same mother gave birth to me, and that I was raised with the same teaching? [3]I won’t deny these dignified family ties!”[j] [5]The guards were furious at his bold speech. They used their instruments to pull his hands and feet out of joint, and dislocated his arms and legs. [6]Then they broke his fingers, arms, legs, and elbows. [7]In spite of this, they weren’t strong enough to break his will, so they put away their tools and tore off his scalp the way the Scythians do it—they used their fingernails. [8]Then they dragged him to the wheel. As they were pulling his spine apart, he saw his own flesh falling off his bones and his blood pouring out. [9]When he was on the edge of death, he said, [10]“You bloodstained tyrant, we are suffering these things because of our godly training and moral character. [11]But you will endure endless torture because of your lack of respect for God and your cruel thirst for blood!”

The fourth brother’s torture and response

[12]After he died like a true brother, they dragged the fourth one forward. They said, [13]“Don’t show the same craziness as your brothers. Obey the king and save yourself!”

[14]He replied, “You don’t have a fire hot enough to turn me into a coward. [15]I swear by the privileged deaths my brothers have suffered, by the eternal curse that will come on the tyrant, and by the everlasting life of those who love God: I will not deny my ties with my dignified brothers! [16]Think up some new tortures, you tyrant, so that you can learn that I am a brother of those you have already tortured!”

[17]When Antiochus heard this, the bloodsucking, murderous, and completely disgusting man ordered them to cut out the man’s tongue.

[18]But he said, “Tear out my tongue! God still hears those who are silent. [19]See? Here’s my tongue! Cut it off. You won’t make my mind quiet by doing that! [20]For God’s sake we gladly allow our bodies to be cut to pieces. [21]God will quickly hunt you down for this, because you are cutting out a tongue that has been musical when it praised God with hymns!”

The fifth brother’s torture and response

11 When the fourth brother had died from cruel torture, the fifth rushed forward and said, [2]“I’m not about to refuse to be tortured for the sake of moral character, you tyrant! [3]I’ve come forward of my own free will so that by killing me, you will receive even more severe punishment at the hands of God’s justice for more crimes! [4]Enemy of moral character! Enemy of the human race! For what crime are you destroying us in this way? [5]For honoring the creator of all things and living according to his moral Law? [6]Such things deserve honor, not torture!”[k] [9]While he was still speaking, the guards tied him up and dragged him to the catapult. [10]They forced him down onto his knees, bound him

[j]Some manuscripts add 10:4 *Apply whatever torture devices you have to my body; you can’t reach my will, no matter how much you wish.* [k]Some manuscripts add 11:7-8 *If you had feeling for your fellow human beings and any hope of salvation from God—but as it is you are a stranger to God and mistreat God’s servants.*

to the machine, and placed iron clamps on his thighs. They began to work the wheel, drawing him backward around a wedge until he was curled back all the way like a scorpion. With all his bones pulled out of joint, [11]gasping for air and racked by pain in his body, [12]he said: "Tyrant, you are doing us a huge favor without intending to, because you are giving us the chance to show our firm commitment to the Law through this honorable suffering."

The sixth brother's torture and response

[13]After he had died, the sixth brother, still just a boy, was brought forward. The tyrant asked him if he was willing to eat pork and so be set free. [14]He replied, "I may be younger than my brothers in age, but I'm their equal in understanding. [15]We were born and raised to live by these principles, so we should die together for their sake. [16]If you think torturing me for not eating polluting food is the right thing to do, then torture away!" [17]When he said this, they marched him up to the wheel. [18]They stretched him tight until his back broke, and they roasted him from underneath with fire. [19]They ran sharp spits, which they had heated in the fire, through his ribs and burned through his guts. [20]In the middle of this torture he said, "This contest is suitable for our godly way of life. So many of us brothers have been called to an arena of suffering because we respect God and we remain undefeated! We haven't been defeated in this contest! [21]Godly knowledge can never be beaten, you tyrant. [22]I will die with my brothers also because I'm fully armed with moral character. [23]I myself will call for an avenger to come against you. You invent new ways to torture people, and you are an enemy of those who are truly devout! [24]The six of us boys have brought your tyranny to an end. [25]You haven't been able to make us change our minds or to force us to eat polluting food. Isn't this a sign that your rule of tyranny is over? [26]Your hot fires feel cold to us; your catapults are painless; your violence has no real power. [27]The guards of the divine Law are set over us, not the guards of a tyrant. Because of this, our clear thinking remains undefeated."

The seventh brother's response and death

12 When the sixth brother also died a privileged death after being thrown into a burning-hot kettle, the seventh and youngest of all came forward. [2]When he saw that the boy was already in chains, the tyrant felt pity for him, despite the verbal abuse he had endured from the boy's brothers. He called the boy closer and tried to encourage him, saying, [3]"You see the result of your brothers' lack of sense. They died in terrible pain because they disobeyed. [4]If you don't obey me, you too will experience horrible torture and die long before your time. [5]But if you listen to me, you will be my friend, and you will be put in charge over the affairs of the kingdom." [6]After giving his advice, Antiochus sent for the boy's mother to take pity on her after she had lost so many sons and so she could persuade her remaining son to obey and save himself.

[7]After his mother encouraged him in Hebrew (as we will discuss later), [8]he said, "Let me go. I want to speak to the king and all his friends." [9]They were very happy with the boy's announcement, so they quickly let him go. [10]He ran to the nearest container of burning coal [11]and said, "You unholy tyrant! Of all evil people, you are the farthest from God! You received your kingdom and all good things from God. So why have you felt no shame for murdering God's servants and torturing the champions of the godly way of life? [12]For these actions, justice is waiting for you with a stronger and everlasting fire and torture, from which you will never, ever be released! [13]As a human being weren't you ashamed? You are a wild animal! You cut out the tongues and abuse and torture people who have feelings just like you and who are made of the same flesh and blood as you. [14]By dying honorably, they fulfilled their religious duty to God. You, however, will howl bitterly for killing without reason these champions of the godly way of life." [15]Then, since he also was about to die, he said, [16]"I'm

not going to desert the good example of my brothers. [17]I call on the God of our ancestors to show mercy to our nation. [18]On you, however, he will take revenge both now while you are alive and after you are dead." [19]After praying against the tyrant, he threw himself into the container of burning coal and so gave back his life.

Praise for the brothers' achievements

13 So if the seven brothers rose above suffering to the point of death, everyone should recognize that godly thinking is supreme over the emotions. [2]If they had shown that they were slaves to their emotions by eating the polluting food, we would have admitted that they were conquered by the emotions. [3]But it didn't turn out that way at all. Instead, they dominated the emotions through the kind of clear thinking that deserves praise in God's opinion. [4]We can't fail to notice the mind's leadership because they had power over both emotions and pain. [5]How can anyone not recognize the ability of good thinking to govern the emotions in such people as these, since they didn't turn away from the severe pain of fire?

[6]The towers at the entrance of harbors hold back the crashing waves and make a calm place for sailors entering the harbor. [7]In the same way, these youths' ability to reason correctly was seven towers beating back the storm of the emotions and defending the harbor of their godly way of life. [8]Standing together like a holy chorus of the godly way of life, they encouraged each other, saying, [9]"Brothers, let's die together like brothers for the sake of the Law! Let's imitate the three young men in Assyria who refused to back down when facing the same fiery test. [10]Let's not be cowards when we are called to demonstrate religious devotion to God."

[11]One said, "Have courage, brother!" Another said, "Keep going with honor!" [12]Still another reminded them, "Remember where you came from. Remember the father by whose hand Isaac was ready to be killed because of his devotion to God!" [13]All of them were looking at each other with faces that were bright and full of courage, and said, "Let's set ourselves apart for God with all our hearts. He gave us our lives, so let's use our bodies as guards around the Law. [14]Let's not be afraid of the one who wants to kill us; [15]because the soul's contest is great, the danger of eternal punishment prepared for those who break God's command is severe. [16]So then, let's arm ourselves fully with the power that clear thinking gives for the control of the emotions. [17]If we die this way, Abraham, Isaac, and Jacob will give us a warm welcome, and all the ancestors will praise us." [18]The brothers who were left behind were calling out to each one as he was being dragged away, "Don't let us down, brother, or be disloyal to the brothers who have died before us!"

Love between siblings

[19]No doubt you are aware of the powerful love that exists between brothers and sisters. Divine and wise providence gives this kind of love through the father and plants it in the mother's womb. [20]These brothers all spent the same length of time in the same womb. They were formed over the same period of time. They grew from the same blood, and they were brought to full term with the same life. [21]They were born after the same amount of time, and drank milk from the same fountains. The same fond embraces nurtured brotherly love in their souls. [22]They grew more fervent as they were brought up together enjoying each other's company day after day, and being shaped by the same education, particularly their training in God's Law.

[23]So it is clear, when such mutual sympathy and love for each other had been established, these seven brothers had even more sympathy for each other. [24]They loved each other so much because they had been educated in the same Law, held the same moral values, and were raised together to live a life that is just. [25]Their affection for each other and harmony grew even more because they shared a common passion for good character and conduct. [26]Family love for each other was made even more desirable to them by their godly behavior. [27]Still, even though nature, custom, and good

habits made their love toward their brothers stronger, the brothers who were left alive put up with seeing their brothers tortured to death because of their godly way of

14 life. 1More than this, they encouraged them to put up with abuse, not only ignoring their own pain but also controlling the feelings of brotherly love.

2How clear thinking is more royal than a king, and it is freer than a free person! 3How holy and harmonious was the symphony of the seven brothers for the sake of their godly way of life! 4None of the seven boys gave in to fear or hesitated in the face of death. 5Instead, all of them rushed to face death by torture, as if they were running a race toward immortality. 6They were like our hands and feet that move together in harmony, led by the mind. So also these holy boys moved together in harmony toward death as if they were moved by the spirit of respect for God that lasts forever. They were moved to make an agreement with death for the sake of that life.

7How holy was this group of seven, these brothers in harmony! They were like the seven days of creation that danced together around the godly way of life. 8So also these boys surrounded and destroyed their fear of torture when they danced in a circle of seven.

9Now we tremble when we hear about the trials of these young men. They not only saw what was going on but heard the threats directed against them and had to bear the suffering, and this included the pain of being burned by fire. 10What could possibly be more painful than this? The power of fire is strong and fast. It destroys bodies quickly.

The mother is the best example

11Don't think it's surprising that clear thinking had full control over these men during their torture, since even a woman's mind held contempt for even more varied suffering. 12The mother of these seven young men endured the torture of each one of her children.

13You see how a mother's love for her children is a very complex feeling. Everything is focused on a sympathy that she feels for them deep down inside. 14Even animals without understanding have sympathy and love for their young, just as human beings do. 15For example, birds do this. The tame ones protect their young by building their nests on the roof of a house. 16Other birds build their nests on mountain peaks, in steep canyons, and in the holes of trees or treetops, so they can hatch the baby birds and stop anything from coming too close. 17If they can't stop something from coming too close, they do whatever they can to help their young. They fly in circles around their young driven by anguished love, warning their young with their calls. 18But why is it necessary to demonstrate the fact that animals without understanding have sympathy for their young? 19When it is time to build their hive, even the bees defend themselves against those who come too close. They sting like an iron dart anyone who comes near the hive, and fight even to the death. 20But the young men's mother wasn't moved by sympathy for her children. She had the same heart as Abraham.

15 How the clear thinking of these children was a tyrant over their emotions and how respecting God was more precious to the mother than her own children! 2The mother had two options in front of her: the godly way of living, and saving her seven sons for a while, as the tyrant promised. 3She preferred the path of respect for God, saving her sons for eternal life, as God promised.

4How can I describe the emotions of parents who love their children? We stamp a remarkable similarity in heart and in appearance on the character of small children. This is especially true of mothers, who have even more sympathy than fathers toward the feelings of their children because they gave birth to them in great pain. 5To the extent that mothers are weaker and give birth to many, that's how much more they love their children. 6And this mother of seven loved her children more than any other mother. Through seven pregnancies, she planted profound love toward them within herself. 7She was forced to have sympathy for each one through the multiple pains of giving birth. [8]Yet she ignored her concern for her children's temporary safety because of her respect for God. [9]Not only that, but the character and conduct her sons showed in the way they were ready to obey the Law only increased her profound love toward them. [10]They showed themselves to be just, self-controlled, brave, high-minded, and devoted to each other. Moreover, they showed how much they loved their mother as they obeyed her by staying true to God's commands even to the point of death.

[11]Though so many forces were pulling against the mother to feel her children's pain out of her love for them, none of the many tortures they suffered were strong enough to undermine her clear thinking. [12]Rather, the mother urged them individually and all of them together to a death for the sake of their godly way of life.

[13]Sacred nature, a love spell cast over parents, devotion to children, tender care, and the unyielding passion that mothers show—how powerful they are! [14]Even though this mother watched her children tortured and burned up one after another, she kept her resolve firm for the sake of their godly way of life. [15]She watched as the fire devoured her children's flesh, their fingers and toes scattered all over the ground, the flesh of their faces torn off like masks down to their chins.

[16]How the mother was tested by pains far worse than the labor pains she suffered for them! [17]How the woman gave birth alone to such perfect devotion! [18]You didn't change your direction when your oldest son took his last breath, or when your second son was in torment and looked at you pitifully, or when the third son died. [19]You didn't cry out loud when you looked into each one's eyes, gripped by their own pain, or when you saw on the faces the signs of death approaching. [20]You didn't burst into tears when you saw the burned flesh of one child piling up on the burned flesh of the others, severed hands on severed hands, severed heads beside severed heads, bodies piled up on bodies, or when you saw the place filling with many spectators of their torture.

[21]The children's voices calling out to their mother from the midst of their torture held her attention more strongly than the Sirens' singing or the song of swans captures the attention of those who hear them. [22]How great was the pain that this mother suffered while her sons were being tortured by wheels and hot irons! [23]However, godly thinking strengthened her to ignore her natural love for her children. Clear thinking created in her a masculine courage in the middle of this suffering. [24]Even though she saw the destruction of seven children and the various devices of torture, the excellent mother ignored all these things because of her faithfulness toward God. [25]Her life was like a courtroom, and many powerful voices were speaking out—nature, family, a parent's love, and the instruments of torture set out for her children. [26]This mother held two ballots in her hand: the first sentenced her children to death; the second rescued them. [27]She chose not to seek the kind of rescue that would keep her seven sons safe for a short time. [28]This daughter of devout Abraham remembered her ancestor's endurance.

[29]You are the mother of the whole nation. You stood up for the Law, defended the godly way of life, and won the contest that was raging deep inside you. [30]You were better than men when it came to determination, and braver than men when it came to endurance! [31]Noah's ark, which carried the future of the whole world inside of it during the flood that swallowed up creation, steadily endured the waves. In the same way, you, the guardian of the Law, endured the storms honorably for the sake of the godly way of life, [32]though you were battered from every side by the flood of the emotions and by the strong winds of your children's torture.

16 So if a woman who was an elderly mother of seven sons put up with seeing her children tortured to death, then without question godly thinking is the master of the emotions. [2]I have shown that not only men have control over their emotions but also a woman scorned the greatest torture. 3The lions that surrounded Daniel weren't as wild, and Mishael's fiery furnace wasn't as burning hot as this mother's natural love for her children. Her love was stirred up inside her as she saw her seven sons tortured in so many ways. 4But the mother put out the fire of her feelings that were so many and so strong with clear thinking.

5Think about this too: If this woman, even though she was a mother, had been weak-spirited, she would have mourned for them. Maybe she would have said something like this:

6"Look at how miserable I am with one sorrow piled on another! I gave birth to seven children, and now I'm nobody's mother!

7"Look at how I gave birth seven times all for nothing! Seven pregnancies, without anything to show for it! Years of fruitless childcare and years of miserable nursing! 8My sons, I bore the long pains of labor for you and even more stress in raising you for no reason!

9"Look at my children! Some aren't married, others are married, but none of them have children! Now I will never see your children or have the pleasure of being a grandmother. 10I had so many and such beautiful children, and now I'm a widow and left all alone in my many sorrows. 11When I die, I won't have any of my sons to bury me."

12But this holy and devout mother didn't cry for any of her sons with funeral songs. She didn't try to talk any of them out of dying, and she didn't grieve for those who were already dying. 13Instead, she had a mind that was as tough as nails.[1] She gave all of her sons a second birth into a life without end. She encouraged them, urging them on to death for the sake of respect for God.

14Mother, you were a soldier for God in the cause of the godly way of life, though you were old and a woman! You even conquered a tyrant with your resolution. You have proved to be stronger than a man in both speech and action! 15When you and your sons had been arrested and you were watching Eleazar being tortured, you began to say to your children in the Hebrew language:

16"My sons, you have been summoned to an honorable contest, in which you will give evidence that will prove your nation's worth. Compete willingly for the Law of our ancestors. 17It would really be a disgrace if you young men lost your nerve in the face of this torture after an old man endured so much suffering out of respect for God. 18Remember that you have had a place in this world and enjoyed life only because of God. 19Because of this, you owe it to God to put up with any distress for his sake. 20This is why our father Abraham moved quickly to sacrifice Isaac his son, who was supposed to become the father of a nation. Isaac also didn't shrink back when he saw the sword in his father's hand bearing down on him. 21Daniel, that righteous man, was thrown to the lions and Hananiah, Azariah, and Mishael were flung into the blazing furnace and endured it for God. 22So you must show the same faithfulness toward God and not be angry. 23After all, it isn't logical for people who truly know and serve God to not hold out against pain."

24By encouraging them with these words, the mother of the seven brothers persuaded each one of her sons to die rather than disobey God's commandment. 25They knew very well that those who die for God will also live in God's presence, just like Abraham, Isaac, Jacob, and all the ancestors of the nation.

17 Some of the guards reported that, just as they were about to grab the mother and put her to death as well, she threw herself into the fire before anyone could touch her body.

2Mother, together with your seven sons, you made the tyrant's violence look like nothing! You defeated his evil plans, and displayed dignity and bravery by your faithfulness. 3You were set with honor like a roof on top of seven pillars, your sons.

[1]Or *as firm as adamant*

You held them firm without moving as you endured the earthquake of their torture. 4So therefore be confident, holy-minded mother! Keep firm that hope in God that fueled your endurance. 5The moon that is in heaven with the stars is not as royal as you. You lit the path of respect for God for your seven sons who are like stars, and you now stand in front of God in honor, firmly set in heaven along with them. 6Your sons were true descendants of our father Abraham! 7If we had the skill of an artist to paint a picture showing the story of your commitment to God, wouldn't those who viewed the painting tremble to see a mother enduring the experience of seven children being tortured to death in so many ways?

The martyrs' achievements

8What would be an appropriate message that could be carved on their tomb to remind our nation's people? Perhaps these words:

9HERE LIE BURIED AN OLD PRIEST, AN OLD WOMAN, AND SEVEN CHILDREN BECAUSE OF THE VIOLENCE OF A TYRANT WHO WISHED TO DESTROY THE HEBREW WAY OF LIFE.

10THEY WON JUSTICE FOR THEIR NATION BY FIXING THEIR EYES ON GOD AND ENDURING TORTURE TO THE POINT OF DEATH.

11The competition in which they were engaged was truly divine. 12Moral character itself handed out awards that day, having proved their worth through their endurance. Victory brought immortality through an endless life. 13Eleazar was the first competitor. The mother of the seven children and the brothers competed also. 14The tyrant was the opponent, and the world and the human race were the audience. 15Respect for God won the day and crowned its champions. 16Who wasn't amazed at the athletes who were competing in the name of the divine Law? Who wasn't astonished?

17The tyrant himself, along with all his political advisors, was amazed at their resistance, 18for which they now stand in front of God's throne and live a blessed life forever. 19Moses says, "All those who have set themselves apart for you are in your care." 20These people who have dedicated themselves to God are honored, therefore, not only with this privilege but also because they kept our enemies from ruling our nation. 21The tyrant was punished, and our nation was cleansed through them. They exchanged their lives for the nation's sin. 22Divine providence delivered Israel from its former abuse through the blood of those godly people. Their deaths were a sacrifice that finds mercy[m] from God.

23When he saw their extraordinary courage and their commitment in the face of torture, the tyrant Antiochus held up their endurance as an example to his own soldiers. 24This made them dignified and brave when they fought battles or destroyed villages, and so they conquered and raided all of their enemies.

18 Israelite children, all you who are descended from Abraham, obey this Law and worship God in every situation. 2Don't doubt that godly thinking rules over the emotions. This includes not only desires and the feelings that come from the inside but also the suffering that comes from the outside. 3Because of this, those who gave up their bodies to suffering for the sake of the godly way of life not only won human admiration but were also judged to be worthy of a divine reward. 4The nation was at peace again because of them. Once obedience to the Law had been revived across the nation, they slaughtered their enemies. 5The tyrant Antiochus was punished on earth, and he continues to be punished after death. By no means could he force the Israelites to adopt a foreign way of life and to change the customs of their ancestors in any way, and so he left Jerusalem and marched out against Persia.

The mother's moral principles

6The mother of the seven sons also shared these moral principles with her

m Or *a propitiation*

children: [7]"I was a virgin who was sexually pure: I didn't go outside of my father's house, but I carefully took care of the body that was formed from a rib. [8]No man who takes advantage of women ever tempted me to have sex in an isolated field. The destructive, lying snake didn't ruin my innocence either. [9]When I was in my prime, I lived with my husband. He died when my children had grown up. He was privileged to have lived his life enjoying good children, and to have been spared the pain of losing them. [10]While he was still with you, he used to teach you the Law and the Prophets. [11]He read to you about Abel, who was killed by Cain, and about Isaac, who was offered as an entirely burned sacrifice, and about Joseph in prison. [12]He used to tell you about Phinehas' total commitment, and to teach you about Hananiah, Azariah, and Mishael in the fire. [13]He used to praise Daniel in the lions' den—he called Daniel privileged. [14]He kept reminding you about the scripture in Isaiah that says, *Even if you go through fire, the flame will not burn you up.*[n] [15]He used to sing to you the songs of David the psalmist, who said, *The righteous person is bothered by many trials.*[o] [16]He used to quote Solomon's proverb: *There is a tree that gives life for those who do what God wants.*[p] [17]He reinforced the truth of Ezekiel, where it says, *Will these dry bones live?*[q] [18]And he didn't forget to teach you the song that Moses taught, which says, [19]*I kill and I bring things to life: this is your life and the length of your days.*"[r]

Conclusion

[20]How that day was bitter and yet not bitter! That was when the bitter Greek tyrant smothered fire with more fire in his cruel copper pots. That was when he dragged those seven sons of that daughter of Abraham back and forth in his furious anger between the catapult and other torture devices. [21]That was when he skewered their eyes through the pupils, cut out their tongues, and put them to death with all kinds of torture. [22]Because of these acts, divine justice pursued and will pursue the cursed tyrant. [23]The sons of Abraham together with their prizewinning mother have been joined with the chorus of their ancestors and have been given pure and immortal souls by God, [24]to whom belongs the glory forever and always. Amen.

[n]Isa 43:2 [o]Ps 37:16 [p]Prov 3:18 [q]Ezek 37:3-5 [r]Deut 32:39-40

NEW TESTAMENT

MATTHEW

Genealogy of Jesus

1 A record of the ancestors of Jesus Christ,
son of David, son of Abraham:
2 Abraham was the father of Isaac.
Isaac was the father of Jacob.
Jacob was the father of Judah and
his brothers.
3 Judah was the father of Perez and Zerah,
whose mother was Tamar.
Perez was the father of Hezron.
Hezron was the father of Aram.
4 Aram was the father of Amminadab.
Amminadab was the father of Nahshon.
Nahshon was the father of Salmon.
5 Salmon was the father of Boaz, whose
mother was Rahab.
Boaz was the father of Obed, whose
mother was Ruth.
Obed was the father of Jesse.
6 Jesse was the father of David the king.
David was the father of Solomon,
whose mother had been the wife
of Uriah.
7 Solomon was the father of Rehoboam.
Rehoboam was the father of Abijah.
Abijah was the father of Asaph.
8 Asaph was the father of Jehoshaphat.
Jehoshaphat was the father of Joram.
Joram was the father of Uzziah.
9 Uzziah was the father of Jotham.
Jotham was the father of Ahaz.
Ahaz was the father of Hezekiah.
10 Hezekiah was the father of Manasseh.
Manasseh was the father of Amos.
Amos was the father of Josiah.
11 Josiah was the father of Jechoniah
and his brothers.
This was at the time of the exile to
Babylon.
12 After the exile to Babylon: Jechoniah
was the father of Shealtiel.
Shealtiel was the father of Zerubbabel.
13 Zerubbabel was the father of Abiud.
Abiud was the father of Eliakim.
Eliakim was the father of Azor.
14 Azor was the father of Zadok.
Zadok was the father of Achim.
Achim was the father of Eliud.
15 Eliud was the father of Eleazar.
Eleazar was the father of Matthan.
Matthan was the father of Jacob.
16 Jacob was the father of Joseph, the
husband of Mary—of whom Jesus was
born, who is called the Christ.
17 So there were fourteen generations
from Abraham to David, fourteen generations from David to the exile to Babylon,
and fourteen generations from the exile to
Babylon to the Christ.

Birth of Jesus

18 This is how the birth of Jesus Christ took
place. When Mary his mother was engaged
to Joseph, before they were married, she became pregnant by the Holy Spirit. 19 Joseph
her husband was a righteous man. Because
he didn't want to humiliate her, he decided
to call off their engagement quietly. 20 As he
was thinking about this, an angel from the
Lord appeared to him in a dream and said,
"Joseph son of David, don't be afraid to take
Mary as your wife, because the child she carries was conceived by the Holy Spirit. 21 She
will give birth to a son, and you will call him
Jesus, because he will save his people from
their sins." 22 Now all of this took place so
that what the Lord had spoken through the
prophet would be fulfilled:
23 *Look! A virgin will become pregnant and*
give birth to a son,
And they will call him, Emmanuel.[a]
(*Emmanuel* means "God with us.")
24 When Joseph woke up, he did just as
an angel from God commanded and took
Mary as his wife. 25 But he didn't have sexual relations with her until she gave birth to
a son. Joseph called him Jesus.

Coming of the magi

2 After Jesus was born in Bethlehem in
the territory of Judea during the rule
of King Herod, magi came from the east to
Jerusalem. 2 They asked, "Where is the newborn king of the Jews? We've seen his star
in the east, and we've come to honor him."

[a] Isa 7:14

3 When King Herod heard this, he was
troubled, and everyone in Jerusalem was
troubled with him. 4 He gathered all the
chief priests and the legal experts and
asked them where the Christ was to be
born. 5 They said, "In Bethlehem of Judea,
for this is what the prophet wrote:

6 *You, Bethlehem, land of Judah,*
by no means are you least
among the rulers of Judah,
because from you will come
one who governs,
who will shepherd my people Israel."[b]

7 Then Herod secretly called for the magi
and found out from them the time when
the star had first appeared. 8 He sent them
to Bethlehem, saying, "Go and search carefully for the child. When you've found him,
report to me so that I too may go and honor
him." 9 When they heard the king, they
went; and look, the star they had seen in
the east went ahead of them until it stood
over the place where the child was. 10 When
they saw the star, they were filled with
joy. 11 They entered the house and saw the
child with Mary his mother. Falling to their
knees, they honored him. Then they opened
their treasure chests and presented him
with gifts of gold, frankincense, and myrrh.
12 Because they were warned in a dream not
to return to Herod, they went back to their
own country by another route.

Escape to Egypt

13 When the magi had departed, an angel
from the Lord appeared to Joseph in a
dream and said, "Get up. Take the child and
his mother and escape to Egypt. Stay there
until I tell you, for Herod will soon search
for the child in order to kill him." 14 Joseph
got up and, during the night, took the child
and his mother to Egypt. 15 He stayed there
until Herod died. This fulfilled what the
Lord had spoken through the prophet: *I
have called my son out of Egypt.*[c]

Murder of the Bethlehem children

16 When Herod knew the magi had fooled
him, he grew very angry. He sent soldiers
to kill all the children in Bethlehem and
in all the surrounding territory who were
two years old and younger, according to the
time that he had learned from the magi.
17 This fulfilled the word spoken through
Jeremiah the prophet:

18 *A voice was heard in Ramah,*
weeping and much grieving.
Rachel weeping for her children,
and she did not want to be comforted,
because they were no more.[d]

Return from Egypt

19 After King Herod died, an angel from
the Lord appeared in a dream to Joseph in
Egypt. 20 "Get up," the angel said, "and take
the child and his mother and go to the land
of Israel. Those who were trying to kill the
child are dead." 21 Joseph got up, took the
child and his mother, and went to the land
of Israel. 22 But when he heard that Arche-
laus ruled over Judea in place of his father
Herod, Joseph was afraid to go there. Having been warned in a dream, he went to the
area of Galilee. 23 He settled in a city called
Nazareth so that what was spoken through
the prophets might be fulfilled: He will be
called a Nazarene.

Ministry of John the Baptist

3 In those days John the Baptist appeared
in the desert of Judea announcing,
2 "Change your hearts and lives! Here comes
the kingdom of heaven!" 3 He was the one
of whom Isaiah the prophet spoke when
he said:

The voice of one shouting
in the wilderness,
"Prepare the way for the Lord;
make his paths straight."[e]

4 John wore clothes made of camel's hair,
with a leather belt around his waist. He ate
locusts and wild honey.

5 People from Jerusalem, throughout
Judea, and all around the Jordan River came
to him. 6 As they confessed their sins, he
baptized them in the Jordan River. 7 Many
Pharisees and Sadducees came to be baptized by John. He said to them, "You children

[b] Mic 5:2; 2 Sam 5:2 [c] Hos 11:1 [d] Jer 31:15 [e] Isa 40:3

of snakes! Who warned you to escape from the angry judgment that is coming soon? 8 Produce fruit that shows you have changed your hearts and lives. 9 And don't even think about saying to yourselves, Abraham is our father. I tell you that God is able to raise up Abraham's children from these stones. 10 The ax is already at the root of the trees. Therefore, every tree that doesn't produce good fruit will be chopped down and tossed into the fire. 11 I baptize with water those of you who have changed your hearts and lives. The one who is coming after me is stronger than I am. I'm not worthy to carry his sandals. He will baptize you with the Holy Spirit and with fire. 12 The shovel he uses to sift the wheat from the husks is in his hands. He will clean out his threshing area and bring the wheat into his barn. But he will burn the husks with a fire that can't be put out."

Baptism of Jesus

13 At that time Jesus came from Galilee to the Jordan River so that John would baptize him. 14 John tried to stop him and said, "I need to be baptized by you, yet you come to me?"

15 Jesus answered, "Allow me to be baptized now. This is necessary to fulfill all righteousness."

So John agreed to baptize Jesus. 16 When Jesus was baptized, he immediately came up out of the water. Heaven was opened to him, and he saw the Spirit of God coming down like a dove and resting on him. 17 A voice from heaven said, "This is my Son whom I dearly love; I find happiness in him."

Temptation of Jesus

4 Then the Spirit led Jesus up into the wilderness so that the devil might tempt him. 2 After Jesus had fasted for forty days and forty nights, he was starving. 3 The tempter came to him and said, "Since you are God's Son, command these stones to become bread."

4 Jesus replied, "It's written, *People won't live only by bread, but by every word spoken by God.*"[f]

5 After that the devil brought him into the holy city and stood him at the highest point of the temple. He said to him, 6 "Since you are God's Son, throw yourself down; for it is written, *I will command my angels concerning you, and they will take you up in their hands so that you won't hit your foot on a stone.*"[g]

7 Jesus replied, "Again it's written, *Don't test the Lord your God.*"[h]

8 Then the devil brought him to a very high mountain and showed him all the kingdoms of the world and their glory. 9 He said, "I'll give you all these if you bow down and worship me."

10 Jesus responded, "Go away, Satan, because it's written, *You will worship the Lord your God and serve only him.*"[i] 11 The devil left him, and angels came and took care of him.

Move to Galilee

12 Now when Jesus heard that John was arrested, he went to Galilee. 13 He left Nazareth and settled in Capernaum, which lies alongside the sea in the area of Zebulun and Naphtali. 14 This fulfilled what Isaiah the prophet said:

15 *Land of Zebulun and land of Naphtali,*
alongside the sea, across the Jordan,
Galilee of the Gentiles,
16 *the people who lived in the dark*
have seen a great light,
and a light has come upon those
who lived in the region
and in shadow of death.[j]

17 From that time Jesus began to announce, "Change your hearts and lives! Here comes the kingdom of heaven!"

Calling of the first disciples

18 As Jesus walked alongside the Galilee Sea, he saw two brothers, Simon, who is called Peter, and Andrew, throwing fishing nets into the sea, because they were fishermen. 19 "Come, follow me," he said, "and I'll show you how to fish for people." 20 Right away, they left their nets and followed him. 21 Continuing on, he saw another set of brothers, James the son of Zebedee and his brother John. They were

[f] Deut 8:3 [g] Ps 91:11-12 [h] Deut 6:16 [i] Deut 6:13 [j] Isa 9:1-2

in a boat with Zebedee their father repairing their nets. Jesus called them and
22 immediately they left the boat and their
father and followed him.

Ministry to the crowds

23 Jesus traveled throughout Galilee,
teaching in their synagogues. He announced
the good news of the kingdom and healed
every disease and sickness among the
people. 24 News about him spread throughout Syria. People brought to him all those
who had various kinds of diseases, those in
pain, those possessed by demons, those
with epilepsy, and those who were paralyzed, and he healed them. 25 Large crowds
followed him from Galilee, the Decapolis,
Jerusalem, Judea, and from the areas
5 beyond the Jordan River. 1 Now when
Jesus saw the crowds, he went up a
mountain. He sat down and his disciples
came to him. 2 He taught them, saying:

Happy people

3 "Happy are people who are hopeless,
because the kingdom of heaven is theirs.
4 "Happy are people who grieve, because
they will be made glad.
5 "Happy are people who are humble,
because they will inherit the earth.
6 "Happy are people who are hungry and
thirsty for righteousness, because they
will be fed until they are full.
7 "Happy are people who show mercy,
because they will receive mercy.
8 "Happy are people who have pure
hearts, because they will see God.
9 "Happy are people who make peace,
because they will be called God's children.
10 "Happy are people whose lives are
harassed because they are righteous,
because the kingdom of heaven is
theirs.

11 "Happy are you when people insult you
and harass you and speak all kinds of bad and
false things about you, all because of me. 12 Be
full of joy and be glad, because you have a great
reward in heaven. In the same way, people harassed the prophets who came before you.

Salt and light

13 "You are the salt of the earth. But if salt
loses its saltiness, how will it become salty
again? It's good for nothing except to be
thrown away and trampled under people's
feet. 14 You are the light of the world. A city
on top of a hill can't be hidden. 15 Neither do
people light a lamp and put it under a basket.
Instead, they put it on top of a lampstand,
and it shines on all who are in the house.
16 In the same way, let your light shine before
people, so they can see the good things you
do and praise your Father who is in heaven.

Jesus and the Law

17 "Don't even begin to think that I have
come to do away with the Law and the
Prophets. I haven't come to do away with
them but to fulfill them. 18 I say to you very
seriously that as long as heaven and earth
exist, neither the smallest letter nor even the
smallest stroke of a pen will be erased from
the Law until everything there becomes
a reality. 19 Therefore, whoever ignores one
of the least of these commands and teaches
others to do the same will be called the lowest in the kingdom of heaven. But whoever
keeps these commands and teaches people
to keep them will be called great in the
kingdom of heaven. 20 I say to you that unless your righteousness is greater than the
righteousness of the legal experts and the
Pharisees, you will never enter the kingdom of heaven.

Law of murder

21 "You have heard that it was said to
those who lived long ago, *Don't commit
murder*,[k] and all who commit murder will
be in danger of judgment. 22 But I say to
you that everyone who is angry with their
brother or sister will be in danger of judgment. If they say to their brother or sister,
'You idiot,' they will be in danger of being
condemned by the governing council. And
if they say, 'You fool,' they will be in danger of fiery hell. 23 Therefore, if you bring
your gift to the altar and there remember
that your brother or sister has something

[k] Exod 20:13

against you, [24]leave your gift at the altar and go. First make things right with your brother or sister and then come back and offer your gift. [25]Be sure to make friends quickly with your opponents while you are with them on the way to court. Otherwise, they will haul you before the judge, the judge will turn you over to the officer of the court, and you will be thrown into prison. [26]I say to you in all seriousness that you won't get out of there until you've paid the very last penny.

Law of adultery

[27]"You have heard that it was said, *Don't commit adultery.*[l] [28]But I say to you that every man who looks at a woman lustfully has already committed adultery in his heart. [29]And if your right eye causes you to fall into sin, tear it out and throw it away. It's better that you lose a part of your body than that your whole body be thrown into hell. [30]And if your right hand causes you to fall into sin, chop it off and throw it away. It's better that you lose a part of your body than that your whole body go into hell.

Law of divorce

[31]"It was said, 'Whoever divorces his wife must *give her a divorce certificate.*'[m] [32]But I say to you that whoever divorces his wife except for sexual unfaithfulness forces her to commit adultery. And whoever marries a divorced woman commits adultery.

Making solemn pledges

[33]"Again you have heard that it was said to those who lived long ago: *Don't make a false solemn pledge, but you should follow through on what you have pledged to the Lord.*[n] [34]But I say to you that you must not pledge at all. You must not pledge by heaven, because it's God's throne. [35]You must not pledge by the earth, because it's God's footstool. You must not pledge by Jerusalem, because it's the city of the great king. [36]And you must not pledge by your head, because you can't turn one hair white or black. [37]Let your *yes* mean yes, and your *no* mean no. Anything more than this comes from the evil one.

Law of retaliation

[38]"You have heard that it was said, *An eye for an eye and a tooth for a tooth.*[o] [39]But I say to you that you must not oppose those who want to hurt you. If people slap you on your right cheek, you must turn the left cheek to them as well. [40]When they wish to haul you to court and take your shirt, let them have your coat too. [41]When they force you to go one mile, go with them two. [42]Give to those who ask, and don't refuse those who wish to borrow from you.

Law of love

[43]"You have heard that it was said, *You must love your neighbor*[p] and hate your enemy. [44]But I say to you, love your enemies and pray for those who harass you [45]so that you will be acting as children of your Father who is in heaven. He makes the sun rise on both the evil and the good and sends rain on both the righteous and the unrighteous. [46]If you love only those who love you, what reward do you have? Don't even the tax collectors do the same? [47]And if you greet only your brothers and sisters, what more are you doing? Don't even the Gentiles do the same? [48]Therefore, just as your heavenly Father is complete in showing love to everyone, so also you must be complete.

Showy religion

6 "Be careful that you don't practice your religion in front of people to draw their attention. If you do, you will have no reward from your Father who is in heaven.

[2]"Whenever you give to the poor, don't blow your trumpet as the hypocrites do in the synagogues and in the streets so that they may get praise from people. I assure you, that's the only reward they'll get. [3]But when you give to the poor, don't let your

[l]Exod 20:14; Deut 5:18 [m]Deut 24:1 [n]Lev 19:12; Num 30:2; Deut 23:21 [o]Exod 21:24; Lev 24:20; Deut 19:21
[p]Lev 19:18

left hand know what your right hand is doing 4so that you may give to the poor in secret. Your Father who sees what you do in secret will reward you.

Showy prayer

5"When you pray, don't be like hypocrites. They love to pray standing in the synagogues and on the street corners so that people will see them. I assure you, that's the only reward they'll get. 6But when you pray, go to your room, shut the door, and pray to your Father who is present in that secret place. Your Father who sees what you do in secret will reward you.

Proper prayer

7"When you pray, don't pour out a flood of empty words, as the Gentiles do. They think that by saying many words they'll be heard. 8Don't be like them, because your Father knows what you need before you ask. 9Pray like this:

Our Father who is in heaven,
 uphold the holiness of your name.
10Bring in your kingdom
 so that your will is done on earth
 as it's done in heaven.
11Give us the bread we need for today.
12Forgive us for the ways
 we have wronged you,
 just as we also forgive those
 who have wronged us.
13And don't lead us into temptation,
 but rescue us from the evil one.

14"If you forgive others their sins, your heavenly Father will also forgive you. 15But if you don't forgive others, neither will your Father forgive your sins.

Showy fasting

16"And when you fast, don't put on a sad face like the hypocrites. They distort their faces so people will know they are fasting. I assure you that they have their reward. 17When you fast, brush your hair and wash your face. 18Then you won't look like you are fasting to people, but only to your Father who is present in that secret place. Your Father who sees in secret will reward you.

Earthly and heavenly treasures

19"Stop collecting treasures for your own benefit on earth, where moth and rust eat them and where thieves break in and steal them. 20Instead, collect treasures for yourselves in heaven, where moth and rust don't eat them and where thieves don't break in and steal them. 21Where your treasure is, there your heart will be also.

Seeing and serving

22"The eye is the lamp of the body. Therefore, if your eye is healthy, your whole body will be full of light. 23But if your eye is bad, your whole body will be full of darkness. If then the light in you is darkness, how terrible that darkness will be! 24No one can serve two masters. Either you will hate the one and love the other, or you will be loyal to the one and have contempt for the other. You cannot serve God and wealth.

Worry about necessities

25"Therefore, I say to you, don't worry about your life, what you'll eat or what you'll drink, or about your body, what you'll wear. Isn't life more than food and the body more than clothes? 26Look at the birds in the sky. They don't sow seed or harvest grain or gather crops into barns. Yet your heavenly Father feeds them. Aren't you worth much more than they are? 27Who among you by worrying can add a single moment to your life? 28And why do you worry about clothes? Notice how the lilies in the field grow. They don't wear themselves out with work, and they don't spin cloth. 29But I say to you that even Solomon in all of his splendor wasn't dressed like one of these. 30If God dresses grass in the field so beautifully, even though it's alive today and tomorrow it's thrown into the furnace, won't God do much more for you, you people of weak faith? 31Therefore, don't worry and say, 'What are we going to eat?' or 'What are we going to drink?' or 'What are we going to wear?' 32Gentiles long for all these things. Your heavenly Father knows that you need them. 33Instead, desire first and foremost God's kingdom and God's righteousness, and all these things will be given to you as well. 34Therefore, stop

worrying about tomorrow, because tomorrow will worry about itself. Each day has
enough trouble of its own.

Judging

7 "Don't judge, so that you won't be judged.
2You'll receive the same judgment you
give. Whatever you deal out will be dealt out
to you. 3Why do you see the splinter that's in
your brother's or sister's eye, but don't notice the log in your own eye? 4How can you
say to your brother or sister, 'Let me take the
splinter out of your eye,' when there's a log
in your eye? 5You deceive yourself! First take
the log out of your eye, and then you'll see
clearly to take the splinter out of your brother's or sister's eye. 6Don't give holy things to
dogs, and don't throw your pearls in front
of pigs. They will stomp on the pearls, then
turn around and attack you.

Asking, seeking, knocking

7"Ask, and you will receive. Search, and
you will find. Knock, and the door will be
opened to you. 8For everyone who asks, receives. Whoever seeks, finds. And to everyone who knocks, the door is opened. 9Who
among you will give your children a stone
when they ask for bread? 10Or give them a
snake when they ask for fish? 11If you who
are evil know how to give good gifts to your
children, how much more will your heavenly
Father give good things to those who ask
him. 12Therefore, you should treat people in
the same way that you want people to treat
you; this is the Law and the Prophets.

Narrow gate

13"Go in through the narrow gate. The
gate that leads to destruction is broad and
the road wide, so many people enter through
it. 14But the gate that leads to life is narrow
and the road difficult, so few people find it.

Tree and fruit

15"Watch out for false prophets. They come
to you dressed like sheep, but inside they
are vicious wolves. 16You will know them by
their fruit. Do people get bunches of grapes
from thorny weeds, or do they get figs from
thistles? 17In the same way, every good tree
produces good fruit, and every rotten tree
produces bad fruit. 18A good tree can't produce bad fruit. And a rotten tree can't produce
good fruit. 19Every tree that doesn't produce
good fruit is chopped down and thrown into
the fire. 20Therefore, you will know them by
their fruit.

Entrance requirements

21"Not everybody who says to me, 'Lord,
Lord,' will get into the kingdom of heaven.
Only those who do the will of my Father
who is in heaven will enter. 22On the Judgment Day, many people will say to me,
'Lord, Lord, didn't we prophesy in your
name and expel demons in your name and
do lots of miracles in your name?' 23Then I'll
tell them, 'I've never known you. Get away
from me, you people who do wrong.'

Two foundations

24"Everybody who hears these words of
mine and puts them into practice is like
a wise builder who built a house on bedrock. 25The rain fell, the floods came, and
the wind blew and beat against that house.
It didn't fall because it was firmly set on
bedrock. 26But everybody who hears these
words of mine and doesn't put them into
practice will be like a fool who built a house
on sand. 27The rain fell, the floods came, and
the wind blew and beat against that house.
It fell and was completely destroyed."

Crowd's response

28When Jesus finished these words, the
crowds were amazed at his teaching 29because
he was teaching them like someone with
authority and not like their legal experts.

A man with a skin disease

8 Now when Jesus had come down from
the mountain, large crowds followed
him. 2A man with a skin disease came,
kneeled before him, and said, "Lord, if you
want, you can make me clean."

3Jesus reached out his hand and touched
him, saying, "I do want to. Become clean." Instantly his skin disease was cleansed. 4Jesus
said to him, "Don't say anything to anyone.
Instead, go and show yourself to the priest

and offer the gift that Moses commanded. This will be a testimony to them."

Healing of the centurion's servant

[5]When Jesus went to Capernaum, a centurion approached, [6]pleading with him, "Lord, my servant is flat on his back at home, paralyzed, and his suffering is awful."

[7]Jesus responded, "I'll come and heal him."

[8]But the centurion replied, "Lord, I don't deserve to have you come under my roof. Just say the word and my servant will be healed. [9]I'm a man under authority, with soldiers under me. I say to one, 'Go,' and he goes, and to another, 'Come,' and he comes. I say to my servant, 'Do this,' and the servant does it."

[10]When Jesus heard this, he was impressed and said to the people following him, "I say to you with all seriousness that even in Israel I haven't found faith like this. [11]I say to you that there are many who will come from east and west and sit down to eat with Abraham and Isaac and Jacob in the kingdom of heaven. [12]But the children of the kingdom will be thrown outside into the darkness. People there will be weeping and grinding their teeth." [13]Jesus said to the centurion, "Go; it will be done for you just as you have believed." And his servant was healed that very moment.

Healing of many people

[14]Jesus went home with Peter and saw Peter's mother-in-law lying in bed with a fever. [15]He touched her hand, and the fever left her. Then she got up and served them. [16]That evening people brought to Jesus many who were demon-possessed. He threw the spirits out with just a word. He healed everyone who was sick. [17]This happened so that what Isaiah the prophet said would be fulfilled: *He is the one who took our illnesses and carried away our diseases.*[q]

Discussions about following

[18]Now when Jesus saw the crowd, he ordered his disciples to go over to the other side of the lake. [19]A legal expert came and said to him, "Teacher, I'll follow you wherever you go."

[20]Jesus replied, "Foxes have dens, and the birds in the sky have nests, but the Human One[r] has no place to lay his head."

[21]Another man, one of his disciples, said to him, "Lord, first let me go and bury my father."

[22]But Jesus said to him, "Follow me, and let the dead bury their own dead."

Calming a storm

[23]When Jesus got into a boat, his disciples followed him. [24]A huge storm arose on the lake so that waves were sloshing over the boat. But Jesus was asleep. [25]They came and woke him, saying, "Lord, rescue us! We're going to drown!"

[26]He said to them, "Why are you afraid, you people of weak faith?" Then he got up and gave orders to the winds and the lake, and there was a great calm.

[27]The people were amazed and said, "What kind of person is this? Even the winds and the lake obey him!"

Jesus frees demon-possessed men

[28]When Jesus arrived on the other side of the lake in the country of the Gadarenes, two men who were demon-possessed came from among the tombs to meet him. They were so violent that nobody could travel on that road. [29]They cried out, "What are you going to do with us, Son of God? Have you come to torture us before the time of judgment?" [30]Far off in the distance a large herd of pigs was feeding. [31]The demons pleaded with him, "If you throw us out, send us into the herd of pigs."

[32]Then he said to the demons, "Go away," and they came out and went into the pigs. The whole herd rushed down the cliff into the lake and drowned. [33]Those who tended the pigs ran into the city and told everything that had happened to the demon-possessed men. [34]Then the whole city came out and met Jesus. When they saw him, they pleaded with him to leave their region.

[q]Isa 53:4 [r]Or *Son of Man*

Healing of a man who was paralyzed

9 Boarding a boat, Jesus crossed to the other side of the lake and went to his own city. 2People brought to him a man who was paralyzed, lying on a cot. When Jesus saw their faith, he said to the man who was paralyzed, "Be encouraged, my child, your sins are forgiven."

3Some legal experts said among themselves, "This man is insulting God."

4But Jesus knew what they were thinking and said, "Why do you fill your minds with evil things? 5Which is easier—to say, 'Your sins are forgiven,' or to say, 'Get up and walk'? 6But so you will know that the Human One[s] has authority on the earth to forgive sins"—he said to the man who was paralyzed—"Get up, take your cot, and go home." 7The man got up and went home. 8When the crowds saw what had happened, they were afraid and praised God, who had given such authority to human beings.

Calling of Matthew

9As Jesus continued on from there, he saw a man named Matthew sitting at a kiosk for collecting taxes. He said to him, "Follow me," and he got up and followed him. 10As Jesus sat down to eat in Matthew's house, many tax collectors and sinners joined Jesus and his disciples at the table.

11But when the Pharisees saw this, they said to his disciples, "Why does your teacher eat with tax collectors and sinners?"

12When Jesus heard it, he said, "Healthy people don't need a doctor, but sick people do. 13Go and learn what this means: *I want mercy and not sacrifice.*[t] I didn't come to call righteous people, but sinners."

Question about fasting

14At that time John's disciples came and asked Jesus, "Why do we and the Pharisees frequently fast, but your disciples never fast?"

15Jesus responded, "The wedding guests can't mourn while the groom is still with them, can they? But the days will come when the groom will be taken away from them, and then they'll fast.

16"No one sews a piece of new, unshrunk cloth on old clothes because the patch tears away the cloth and makes a worse tear. 17No one pours new wine into old wineskins. If they did, the wineskins would burst, the wine would spill, and the wineskins would be ruined. Instead, people pour new wine into new wineskins so that both are kept safe."

A ruler's daughter and the woman who touched Jesus' clothes

18While Jesus was speaking to them, a ruler came and knelt in front of him, saying, "My daughter has just died. But come and place your hand on her, and she'll live." 19So Jesus and his disciples got up and went with him. 20Then a woman who had been bleeding for twelve years came up behind Jesus and touched the hem of his clothes. 21She thought, If I only touch his robe I'll be healed.

22When Jesus turned and saw her, he said, "Be encouraged, daughter. Your faith has healed you." And the woman was healed from that time on.

23When Jesus went into the ruler's house, he saw the flute players and the distressed crowd. 24He said, "Go away, because the little girl isn't dead but is asleep"; but they laughed at him. 25After he had sent the crowd away, Jesus went in and touched her hand, and the little girl rose up. 26News about this spread throughout that whole region.

Healing of two blind men

27As Jesus departed, two blind men followed him, crying out, "Show us mercy, Son of David."

28When he came into the house, the blind men approached him. Jesus said to them, "Do you believe I can do this?"

"Yes, Lord," they replied.

29Then Jesus touched their eyes and said, "It will happen for you just as you have believed." 30Their eyes were opened. Then Jesus sternly warned them, "Make sure nobody knows about this." 31But they went out and spread the word about him throughout that whole region.

[s]Or *Son of Man* [t]Hos 6:6

Healing of a man unable to speak

32 As they were leaving, people brought to him a man who was demon-possessed and unable to speak. 33 When Jesus had thrown out the demon, the man who couldn't speak began to talk. The crowds were amazed and said, "Nothing like this has ever been seen in Israel."

34 But the Pharisees said, "He throws out demons with the authority of the ruler of demons."

Compassion

35 Jesus traveled among all the cities and villages, teaching in their synagogues, announcing the good news of the kingdom, and healing every disease and every sickness. 36 Now when Jesus saw the crowds, he had compassion for them because they were troubled and helpless, like sheep without a shepherd. 37 Then he said to his disciples, "The size of the harvest is bigger than you can imagine, but there are few workers. 38 Therefore, plead with the Lord of the harvest to send out workers for his harvest."

Mission of the Twelve

10 He called his twelve disciples and gave them authority over unclean spirits to throw them out and to heal every disease and every sickness. 2 Here are the names of the twelve apostles: first, Simon, who is called Peter; and Andrew his brother; James the son of Zebedee; and John his brother; 3 Philip; and Bartholomew; Thomas; and Matthew the tax collector; James the son of Alphaeus; and Thaddaeus; 4 Simon the Cananaean;[u] and Judas, who betrayed Jesus.

Commissioning of the Twelve

5 Jesus sent these twelve out and commanded them, "Don't go among the Gentiles or into a Samaritan city. 6 Go instead to the lost sheep, the people of Israel. 7 As you go, make this announcement: 'The kingdom of heaven has come near.' 8 Heal the sick, raise the dead, cleanse those with skin diseases, and throw out demons. You received without having to pay. Therefore, give without demanding payment. 9 Workers deserve to be fed, so don't gather gold or silver or copper coins for your money belts to take on your trips. 10 Don't take a backpack for the road or two shirts or sandals or a walking stick. 11 Whatever city or village you go into, find somebody in it who is worthy and stay there until you go on your way. 12 When you go into a house, say, 'Peace!' 13 If the house is worthy, give it your blessing of peace. But if the house isn't worthy, take back your blessing. 14 If anyone refuses to welcome you or listen to your words, shake the dust off your feet as you leave that house or city. 15 I assure you that it will be more bearable for the land of Sodom and Gomorrah on Judgment Day than it will be for that city.

Response to harassment

16 "Look, I'm sending you as sheep among wolves. Therefore, be wise as snakes and innocent as doves. 17 Watch out for people—because they will hand you over to councils and they will beat you in their synagogues. 18 They will haul you in front of governors and even kings because of me so that you may give your testimony to them and to the Gentiles. 19 Whenever they hand you over, don't worry about how to speak or what you will say, because what you can say will be given to you at that moment. 20 You aren't doing the talking, but the Spirit of my Father is doing the talking through you. 21 Brothers and sisters will hand each other over to be executed. A father will turn his child in. Children will defy their parents and have them executed. 22 Everyone will hate you on account of my name. But whoever stands firm until the end will be saved. 23 Whenever they harass you in one city, escape to the next, because I assure that you will not go through all the cities of Israel before the Human One[v] comes.

24 "Disciples aren't greater than their teacher, and slaves aren't greater than their master. 25 It's enough for disciples to be like their teacher and slaves like their master. If they have called the head of the house Beelzebul, it's certain that they will

[u] Or *zealot* [v] Or *Son of Man*

call the members of his household by even
worse names.

Whom to fear

26“Therefore, don’t be afraid of those
people because nothing is hidden that won’t
be revealed, and nothing secret that won’t be
brought out into the open. 27What I say to
you in the darkness, tell in the light; and
what you hear whispered, announce from
the rooftops. 28Don’t be afraid of those who
kill the body but can’t kill the soul. Instead,
be afraid of the one who can destroy both
body and soul in hell. 29Aren’t two sparrows sold for a small coin? But not one of
them will fall to the ground without your
Father knowing about it already. 30Even the
hairs of your head are all counted. 31Don’t
be afraid. You are worth more than many
sparrows.

Confessing Christ to people

32“Therefore, everyone who acknowledges
me before people, I also will acknowledge before my Father who is in heaven. 33But everyone who denies me before people, I also will
deny before my Father who is in heaven.

Trouble in the family

34“Don’t think that I’ve come to bring
peace to the earth. I haven’t come to bring
peace but a sword. 35I’ve come to turn a
man *against his father, a daughter against*
her mother, and a daughter-in-law against her
mother-in-law. 36*People’s enemies are mem-*
bers of their own households.[w]

37“Those who love father or mother more
than me aren’t worthy of me. Those who
love son or daughter more than me aren’t
worthy of me. 38Those who don’t pick up
their crosses and follow me aren’t worthy
of me. 39Those who find their lives will lose
them, and those who lose their lives because of me will find them.

Rewards

40“Those who receive you are also receiving me, and those who receive me are receiving the one who sent me. 41Those who
receive a prophet as a prophet will receive a
prophet’s reward. Those who receive a righteous person as a righteous person will receive a righteous person’s reward. 42I assure
you that everybody who gives even a cup of
cold water to these little ones because they
are my disciples will certainly be rewarded.”

Ministry to the people

11 When Jesus finished teaching his
twelve disciples, he went on from there
to teach and preach in their cities.

Question from John the Baptist

2Now when John heard in prison about
the things the Christ was doing, he sent
word by his disciples to Jesus, asking, 3“Are
you the one who is to come, or should we
look for another?”

4Jesus responded, “Go, report to John
what you hear and see. 5*Those who were*
blind are able to see. Those who were crippled are walking. People with skin diseases
are cleansed. Those *who were deaf now hear.*
Those who were dead are raised up. The poor
have good news proclaimed to them.[x] 6Happy
are those who don’t stumble and fall because of me.”

Appeal of John’s ministry

7When John’s disciples had gone, Jesus
spoke to the crowds about John: “What
did you go out to the wilderness to see? A
stalk blowing in the wind? 8What did you
go out to see? A man dressed up in refined
clothes? Look, those who wear refined
clothes are in royal palaces. 9What did you
go out to see? A prophet? Yes, I tell you,
and more than a prophet. 10He is the one
of whom it is written: *Look, I’m sending my*
messenger before you, who will prepare your
way before you.[y]

Significance of John’s ministry

11“I assure you that no one who has ever
been born is greater than John the Baptist. Yet whoever is least in the kingdom of
heaven is greater than he. 12From the days
of John the Baptist until now the kingdom

[w]Mic 7:6 [x]Isa 35:5-6; 61:1 [y]Mal 3:1

of heaven is violently attacked as violent
people seize it. 13 All the Prophets and the
Law prophesied until John came. 14 If you
are willing to accept it, he is Elijah who is to
come. 15 Let the person who has ears, hear.

This generation

16 "To what will I compare this generation? It is like a child sitting in the marketplaces calling out to others, 17 'We played the
flute for you and you didn't dance. We sang
a funeral song and you didn't mourn.' 18 For
John came neither eating nor drinking, and
they say, 'He has a demon.' 19 Yet the Human
One[z] came eating and drinking, and they
say, 'Look, a glutton and a drunk, a friend
of tax collectors and sinners.' But wisdom is
proved to be right by her works."

Condemnation of Bethsaida and Capernaum

20 Then he began to scold the cities where
he had done his greatest miracles because
they didn't change their hearts and lives.
21 "How terrible it will be for you, Chorazin!
How terrible it will be for you, Bethsaida!
For if the miracles done among you had
been done in Tyre and Sidon, they would
have changed their hearts and lives and
put on funeral clothes and ashes a long
time ago. 22 But I say to you that Tyre and
Sidon will be better off on Judgment Day
than you. 23 And you, Capernaum, will you
be honored by being raised up to heaven?
No, you will be thrown down to the place
of the dead. After all, if the miracles that
were done among you had been done in
Sodom, it would still be here today. 24 But I
say to you that it will be better for the land
of Sodom on the Judgment Day than it will
be for you."

The Father and the Son

25 At that time Jesus said, "I praise you,
Father, Lord of heaven and earth, because
you've hidden these things from the wise
and intelligent and have shown them to
babies. 26 Indeed, Father, this brings you
happiness.

27 "My Father has handed all things over
to me. No one knows the Son except the
Father. And nobody knows the Father except the Son and anyone to whom the Son
wants to reveal him.

28 "Come to me, all you who are struggling hard and carrying heavy loads, and I
will give you rest. 29 Put on my yoke, and
learn from me. I'm gentle and humble. And
you will find rest for yourselves. 30 My yoke
is easy to bear, and my burden is light."

Working on the Sabbath

12 At that time Jesus went through the
wheat fields on the Sabbath. His disciples were hungry so they were picking
heads of wheat and eating them. 2 When
the Pharisees saw this, they said to him,
"Look, your disciples are breaking the Sabbath law."

3 But he said to them, "Haven't you read
what David did when he and those with
him were hungry? 4 He went into God's
house and broke the law by eating the
bread of the presence, which only the priests
were allowed to eat. 5 Or haven't you read
in the Law that on the Sabbath the priests
in the temple treat the Sabbath as any other
day and are still innocent? 6 But I tell you
that something greater than the temple is
here. 7 If you had known what this means,
I want mercy and not sacrifice,[a] you wouldn't
have condemned the innocent. 8 The Human
One[b] is Lord of the Sabbath."

Healing on the Sabbath

9 Jesus left that place and went into their
synagogue. 10 A man with a withered hand
was there. Wanting to bring charges against
Jesus, they asked, "Does the Law allow a
person to heal on the Sabbath?"

11 Jesus replied, "Who among you has a
sheep that falls into a pit on the Sabbath
and will not take hold of it and pull it out?
12 How much more valuable is a person than
a sheep! So the Law allows a person to do
what is good on the Sabbath." 13 Then Jesus
said to the man, "Stretch out your hand."
So he did and it was made healthy, just like

[z] Or *Son of Man* [a] Hos 6:6 [b] Or *Son of Man*

the other one. 14 The Pharisees went out and
met in order to find a way to destroy Jesus.

Healing the crowd

15 Jesus knew what they intended to do, so
he went away from there. Large crowds followed him, and he healed them all. 16 But he
ordered them not to spread the word about
him, 17 so that what was spoken through Isaiah the prophet might be fulfilled:

18 *Look, my Servant whom I chose,*
the one I love,
in whom I find great pleasure.
I'll put my Spirit upon him,
and he'll announce judgment
to the Gentiles.
19 *He won't argue or shout,*
and nobody will hear his voice
in the streets.
20 *He won't break a bent stalk,*
and he won't snuff out a smoldering wick,
until he makes justice win.
21 *And the Gentiles will put their hope in his*
name.[c]

22 They brought to Jesus a demon-
possessed man who was blind and unable
to speak. Jesus healed him so that he could
both speak and see. 23 All the crowds were
amazed and said, "This man couldn't be the
Son of David, could he?"

24 When the Pharisees heard, they said,
"This man throws out demons only by the
authority of Beelzebul, the ruler of the
demons."

25 Because Jesus knew what they were
thinking, he replied, "Every kingdom involved in civil war becomes a wasteland.
Every city or house torn apart by divisions
will collapse. 26 If Satan throws out Satan,
he is at war with himself. How then can his
kingdom endure? 27 And if I throw out demons by the authority of Beelzebul, then
by whose authority do your followers throw
them out? Therefore, they will be your
judges. 28 But if I throw out demons by the
power of God's Spirit, then God's kingdom
has already overtaken you. 29 Can people
go into a house that belongs to a strong
man and steal his possessions, unless they
first tie up the strong man? Then they can
rob his house. 30 Whoever isn't with me is
against me, and whoever doesn't gather
with me scatters.

Insulting the Holy Spirit

31 "Therefore, I tell you that people will be
forgiven for every sin and insult to God. But
insulting the Holy Spirit won't be forgiven.
32 And whoever speaks a word against the
Human One[d] will be forgiven. But whoever
speaks against the Holy Spirit won't be
forgiven, not in this age or in the age that
is coming.

Trees and fruits

33 "Either consider the tree good and its
fruit good, or consider the tree rotten and
its fruit rotten. A tree is known by its fruit.
34 Children of snakes! How can you speak
good things while you are evil? What fills
the heart comes out of the mouth. 35 Good
people bring out good things from their
good treasure. But evil people bring out
evil things from their evil treasure. 36 I tell
you that people will have to answer on
Judgment Day for every useless word they
speak. 37 By your words you will be either
judged innocent or condemned as guilty."

Request for a sign

38 At that time some of the legal experts and the Pharisees requested of
Jesus, "Teacher, we would like to see a sign
from you."

39 But he replied, "An evil and unfaithful
generation searches for a sign, but it won't
receive any sign except Jonah's sign. 40 Just
as *Jonah was in the whale's belly for three days*
and three nights,[e] so the Human One[f] will be
in the heart of the earth for three days and
three nights. 41 The citizens of Nineveh will
stand up at the judgment with this generation and condemn it as guilty, because they
changed their hearts and lives in response
to Jonah's preaching. And look, someone
greater than Jonah is here. 42 The queen of
the South will be raised up by God at the
judgment with this generation and condemn

[c]Isa 42:1-4 [d]Or *Son of Man* [e]Jonah 1:17 [f]Or *Son of Man*

it because she came from a distant land to
hear Solomon's wisdom. And look, someone greater than Solomon is here.

Unclean spirit seeking a home

43“When an unclean spirit leaves a person, it wanders through dry places looking
for a place to rest. But it doesn't find any.
44Then it says, ‘I'll go back to the house I
left.’ When it arrives, it finds the place va-
cant, cleaned up, and decorated. 45Then it
goes and brings with it seven other spirits
more evil than itself. They go in and make
their home there. That person is worse off
at the end than at the beginning. This is the
way it will be also for this evil generation.”

Jesus' family

46While Jesus was speaking to the
crowds, his mother and brothers stood outside trying to speak with him. 47Someone
said to him, “Look, your mother and brothers are outside wanting to speak with you.”
48Jesus replied, “Who is my mother? Who
are my brothers?” 49He stretched out his hand
toward his disciples and said, “Look, here are
my mother and my brothers. 50Whoever
does the will of my Father who is in heaven
is my brother, sister, and mother.”

Setting for the parables

13 That day Jesus went out of the house
and sat down beside the lake. 2Such
large crowds gathered around him that
he climbed into a boat and sat down. The
whole crowd was standing on the shore.

Parable of the soils

3He said many things to them in parables:
“A farmer went out to scatter seed. 4As he
was scattering seed, some fell on the path,
and birds came and ate it. 5Other seed fell
on rocky ground where the soil was shallow. They sprouted immediately because the
soil wasn't deep. 6But when the sun came
up, it scorched the plants, and they dried
up because they had no roots. 7Other seed
fell among thorny plants. The thorny plants
grew and choked them. 8Other seed fell on
good soil and bore fruit, in one case a yield of
one hundred to one, in another case a yield
of sixty to one, and in another case a yield of
thirty to one. 9Everyone who has ears should
pay attention.”

Why Jesus speaks in parables

10Jesus' disciples came and said to him,
“Why do you use parables when you speak
to the crowds?”
11Jesus replied, “Because they haven't
received the secrets of the kingdom of
heaven, but you have. 12For those who have
will receive more and they will have more
than enough. But as for those who don't
have, even the little they have will be taken
away from them. 13This is why I speak to
the crowds in parables: although they see,
they don't really see; and although they
hear, they don't really hear or understand.
14What Isaiah prophesied has become completely true for them:

You will hear, to be sure,
but never understand;
and you will certainly see but never
recognize what you are seeing.
15*For this people's senses*
have become calloused,
and they've become hard of hearing,
and they've shut their eyes
so that they won't see with their eyes
or hear with their ears
or understand with their minds,
and change their hearts and lives
that I may heal them.[g]

16“Happy are your eyes because they see.
Happy are your ears because they hear. 17I assure you that many prophets and righteous
people wanted to see what you see and hear
what you hear, but they didn't.

Explanation of the parable of the farmer

18“Consider then the parable of the
farmer. 19Whenever people hear the word
about the kingdom and don't understand it,
the evil one comes and carries off what was
planted in their hearts. This is the seed that
was sown on the path. 20As for the seed

[g]Isa 6:9-10

that was spread on rocky ground, this refers
to people who hear the word and immediately receive it joyfully. 21 Because they have
no roots, they last for only a little while.
When they experience distress or abuse
because of the word, they immediately fall
away. 22 As for the seed that was spread
among thorny plants, this refers to those
who hear the word, but the worries of this
life and the false appeal of wealth choke the
word, and it bears no fruit. 23 As for what
was planted on good soil, this refers to those
who hear and understand, and bear fruit and
produce—in one case a yield of one hundred
to one, in another case a yield of sixty to one,
and in another case a yield of thirty to one."

Parable of the weeds

24 Jesus told them another parable: "The
kingdom of heaven is like someone who
planted good seed in his field. 25 While
people were sleeping, an enemy came and
planted weeds among the wheat and went
away. 26 When the stalks sprouted and bore
grain, then the weeds also appeared.

27 "The servants of the landowner came
and said to him, 'Master, didn't you plant
good seed in your field? Then how is it that
it has weeds?'

28 "'An enemy has done this,' he answered.

"The servants said to him, 'Do you want
us to go and gather them?'

29 "But the landowner said, 'No, because
if you gather the weeds, you'll pull up the
wheat along with them. 30 Let both grow
side by side until the harvest. And at harvesttime I'll say to the harvesters, "First gather
the weeds and tie them together in bundles
to be burned. But bring the wheat into
my barn."'"

Parable of the mustard seed

31 He told another parable to them: "The
kingdom of heaven is like a mustard seed
that someone took and planted in his field.
32 It's the smallest of all seeds. But when
it's grown, it's the largest of all vegetable
plants. It becomes a tree so that the birds in
the sky come and nest in its branches."

Parable of the yeast

33 He told them another parable: "The
kingdom of heaven is like yeast, which a
woman took and hid in a bushel of wheat
flour until the yeast had worked its way
through all the dough."

Purpose of parables to the crowds

34 Jesus said all these things to the
crowds in parables, and he spoke to them
only in parables. 35 This was to fulfill what
the prophet spoke:

I'll speak in parables;
I'll declare what has been hidden
since the beginning of the world.[h]

Explanation of the parable of the weeds

36 Jesus left the crowds and went into the
house. His disciples came to him and said,
"Explain to us the parable of the weeds in
the field."

37 Jesus replied, "The one who plants the
good seed is the Human One.[i] 38 The field is
the world. And the good seeds are the followers of the kingdom. But the weeds are
the followers of the evil one. 39 The enemy
who planted them is the devil. The harvest
is the end of the present age. The harvesters
are the angels. 40 Just as people gather weeds
and burn them in the fire, so it will be at the
end of the present age. 41 The Human One[j]
will send his angels, and they will gather out
of his kingdom all things that cause people
to fall away and all people who sin. 42 He will
throw them into a burning furnace. People
there will be weeping and grinding their
teeth. 43 Then the righteous will shine like
the sun in their Father's kingdom. Those
who have ears should hear."

Parable of the treasure

44 "The kingdom of heaven is like a treasure
that somebody hid in a field, which someone
else found and covered up. Full of joy, the
finder sold everything and bought that field.

Parable of the merchant

45 "Again, the kingdom of heaven is like a
merchant in search of fine pearls. 46 When

[h] Ps 78:2 [i] Or *Son of Man* [j] Or *Son of Man*

he found one very precious pearl, he went
and sold all that he owned and bought it.

Parable of the net

47“Again, the kingdom of heaven is like
a net that people threw into the lake and
gathered all kinds of fish. 48When it was
full, they pulled it to the shore, where they
sat down and put the good fish together
into containers. But the bad fish they threw
away. 49That’s the way it will be at the end
of the present age. The angels will go out
and separate the evil people from the righteous people, 50and will throw the evil ones
into a burning furnace. People there will be
weeping and grinding their teeth.

Treasures new and old

51“Have you understood all these things?”
Jesus asked.

They said to him, “Yes.”

52Then he said to them, “Therefore,
every legal expert who has been trained as
a disciple for the kingdom of heaven is like
the head of a household who brings old and
new things out of their treasure chest.”

Jesus in his hometown

53When Jesus finished these parables, he
departed. 54When he came to his hometown,
he taught the people in their synagogue.
They were surprised and said, “Where did he
get this wisdom? Where did he get the power
to work miracles? 55Isn’t he the carpenter’s
son? Isn’t his mother named Mary? Aren’t
James, Joseph, Simon, and Judas his brothers? 56And his sisters, aren’t they here with
us? Where did this man get all this?” 57They
were repulsed by him and fell into sin.

But Jesus said to them, “Prophets are
honored everywhere except in their own
hometowns and in their own households.”
58He was unable to do many miracles there
because of their disbelief.

Death of John the Baptist

14 At that time Herod the ruler[k] heard
the news about Jesus. 2He said to his
servants, “This is John the Baptist. He’s been
raised from the dead. This is why these miraculous powers are at work through him.”
3Herod had arrested John, bound him, and
put him in prison because of Herodias, the
wife of Herod’s brother Philip.

4That’s because John told Herod, “It’s
against the law for you to marry her.”

5Although Herod wanted to kill him, he
feared the crowd because they thought John
was a prophet. 6But at Herod’s birthday
party Herodias’ daughter danced in front
of the guests and thrilled Herod. 7Then he
swore to give her anything she asked.

8At her mother’s urging, the girl said,
“Give me the head of John the Baptist here
on a plate.” 9Although the king was upset,
because of his solemn pledge and his guests
he commanded that they give it to her.
10Then he had John beheaded in prison.
11They brought his head on a plate and gave
it to the young woman, and she brought it
to her mother. 12But John’s disciples came
and took his body and buried it. Then they
went and told Jesus what had happened.

Feeding the five thousand

13When Jesus heard about John, he
withdrew in a boat to a deserted place by
himself. When the crowds learned this,
they followed him on foot from the cities. 14When Jesus arrived and saw a large
crowd, he had compassion for them and
healed those who were sick. 15That evening
his disciples came and said to him, “This is
an isolated place and it’s getting late. Send
the crowds away so they can go into the
villages and buy food for themselves.”

16But Jesus said to them, “There’s no
need to send them away. You give them
something to eat.”

17They replied, “We have nothing here
except five loaves of bread and two fish.”

18He said, “Bring them here to me.” 19He
ordered the crowds to sit down on the grass.
He took the five loaves of bread and the two
fish, looked up to heaven, blessed them and
broke the loaves apart and gave them to his
disciples. Then the disciples gave them to
the crowds. 20Everyone ate until they were

[k] Or *tetrarch*, which refers to a prince over a small region

full, and they filled twelve baskets with the
leftovers. 21About five thousand men plus
women and children had eaten.

Walking on the water

22Right then, Jesus made the disciples get
into the boat and go ahead to the other side
of the lake while he dismissed the crowds.
23When he sent them away, he went up onto
a mountain by himself to pray. Evening came
and he was alone. 24Meanwhile, the boat,
fighting a strong headwind, was being battered by the waves and was already far away
from land. 25Very early in the morning he
came to his disciples, walking on the lake.
26When the disciples saw him walking on the
lake, they were terrified and said, "It's a ghost!"
They were so frightened they screamed.

27Just then Jesus spoke to them, "Be encouraged! It's me. Don't be afraid."

28Peter replied, "Lord, if it's you, order
me to come to you on the water."

29And Jesus said, "Come."

Then Peter got out of the boat and was
walking on the water toward Jesus. 30But
when Peter saw the strong wind, he became
frightened. As he began to sink, he shouted,
"Lord, rescue me!"

31Jesus immediately reached out and
grabbed him, saying, "You man of weak
faith! Why did you begin to have doubts?"
32When they got into the boat, the wind
settled down.

33Then those in the boat worshipped
Jesus and said, "You must be God's Son!"

Healing the sick

34When they had crossed the lake, they
landed at Gennesaret. 35When the people
who lived in that place recognized him, they
sent word throughout that whole region,
and they brought to him everyone who
was sick. 36Then they begged him that they
might just touch the edge of his clothes. Everyone who touched him was cured.

Rules from the elders

15 Then Pharisees and legal experts
came to Jesus from Jerusalem and
said, 2"Why are your disciples breaking the
elders' rules handed down to us? They don't
ritually purify their hands by washing before they eat."

3Jesus replied, "Why do you break the
command of God by keeping the rules
handed down to you? 4For God said, *Honor
your father and your mother,*[l] and *The person
who speaks against father or mother will certainly be put to death.*[m] 5But you say, 'If you
tell your father or mother, "Everything I'm
expected to contribute to you I'm giving to
God as a gift," then you don't have to honor
your father.' 6So you do away with God's
Law for the sake of the rules that have been
handed down to you. 7Hypocrites! Isaiah really knew what he was talking about when
he prophesied about you, 8*This people honors
me with their lips, but their hearts are far away
from me.* 9*Their worship of me is empty since
they teach instructions that are human rules.*"[n]

10Jesus called the crowd near and said to
them, "Listen and understand. 11It's not what
goes into the mouth that contaminates a
person in God's sight. It's what comes out of
the mouth that contaminates the person."

12Then the disciples came and said to
him, "Do you know that the Pharisees were
offended by what you just said?"

13Jesus replied, "Every plant that my
heavenly Father didn't plant will be pulled
up. 14Leave the Pharisees alone. They are
blind people who are guides to blind people.
But if a blind person leads another blind
person, they will both fall into a ditch."

15Then Peter spoke up, "Explain this
riddle to us."

16Jesus said, "Don't you understand
yet? 17Don't you know that everything that
goes into the mouth enters the stomach
and goes out into the sewer? 18But what
goes out of the mouth comes from the
heart. And that's what contaminates a person in God's sight. 19Out of the heart come
evil thoughts, murders, adultery, sexual
sins, thefts, false testimonies, and insults.
20These contaminate a person in God's
sight. But eating without washing hands
doesn't contaminate in God's sight."

[l]Exod 20:12; Deut 5:16 [m]Exod 21:17; Lev 20:9 [n]Isa 29:13

Canaanite woman

21From there, Jesus went to the regions of
Tyre and Sidon. 22A Canaanite woman from
those territories came out and shouted,
"Show me mercy, Son of David. My daughter is suffering terribly from demon possession." 23But he didn't respond to her at all.
His disciples came and urged him, "Send
her away; she keeps shouting out after us."
24Jesus replied, "I've been sent only to
the lost sheep, the people of Israel."
25But she knelt before him and said,
"Lord, help me."
26He replied, "It is not good to take the
children's bread and toss it to dogs."
27She said, "Yes, Lord. But even the dogs
eat the crumbs that fall off their masters'
table."
28Jesus answered, "Woman, you have
great faith. It will be just as you wish." And
right then her daughter was healed.

Healing of many people

29Jesus moved on from there along the
shore of the Galilee Sea. He went up a mountain and sat down. 30Large crowds came to
him, including those who were paralyzed,
blind, injured, and unable to speak, and
many others. They laid them at his feet, and
he healed them. 31So the crowd was amazed
when they saw those who had been unable
to speak talking, and the paralyzed cured,
and the injured walking, and the blind seeing. And they praised the God of Israel.

Feeding the four thousand

32Now Jesus called his disciples and said,
"I feel sorry for the crowd because they have
been with me for three days and have nothing to eat. I don't want to send them away
hungry for fear they won't have enough
strength to travel."
33His disciples replied, "Where are we
going to get enough food in this wilderness
to satisfy such a big crowd?"
34Jesus said, "How much bread do you
have?"
They responded, "Seven loaves and a few
fish."
35He told the crowd to sit on the ground.
36He took the seven loaves of bread and the
fish. After he gave thanks, he broke them
into pieces and gave them to the disciples,
and the disciples gave them to the crowds.
37Everyone ate until they were full. The
disciples collected seven baskets full of
leftovers. 38Four thousand men ate, plus
women and children. 39After dismissing the
crowds, Jesus got into the boat and came to
the region of Magadan.

Demand for a sign

16 The Pharisees and Sadducees came to
Jesus. In order to test him they asked
him to show them a sign from heaven.
2But he replied, "At evening you say,
'It will be nice weather because the sky is
bright red.' 3And in the morning you say,
'There will be bad weather today because
the sky is cloudy.' You know how to make
sense of the sky's appearance. But you are
unable to recognize the signs that point to
what the time is. 4An evil and unfaithful
generation searches for a sign. But it won't
receive any sign except Jonah's sign." Then
he left them and went away.

Yeast of the Pharisees and Sadducees

5When the disciples arrived on the other
side of the lake, they had forgotten to bring
bread. 6Jesus said to them, "Watch out and
be on your guard for the yeast of the Pharisees and Sadducees."
7They discussed this among themselves
and said, "We didn't bring any bread."
8Jesus knew what they were discussing
and said, "You people of weak faith! Why
are you discussing among yourselves the
fact that you don't have any bread? 9Don't
you understand yet? Don't you remember
the five loaves that fed the five thousand
and how many baskets of leftovers you
gathered? 10And the seven loaves that fed
the four thousand and how many large baskets of leftovers you gathered? 11Don't you
know that I wasn't talking about bread? But
be on your guard for the yeast of the Pharisees and Sadducees." 12Then they understood that he wasn't telling them to be on
their guard for yeast used in making bread.
No, he was telling them to watch out for the
teaching of the Pharisees and Sadducees.

Peter's declaration about Jesus

[13]Now when Jesus came to the area of Caesarea Philippi, he asked his disciples, "Who do people say the Human One[o] is?"

[14]They replied, "Some say John the Baptist, others Elijah, and still others Jeremiah or one of the other prophets."

[15]He said, "And what about you? Who do you say that I am?"

[16]Simon Peter said, "You are the Christ, the Son of the living God."

[17]Then Jesus replied, "Happy are you, Simon son of Jonah, because no human has shown this to you. Rather my Father who is in heaven has shown you. [18]I tell you that you are Peter.[p] And I'll build my church on this rock. The gates of the underworld won't be able to stand against it. [19]I'll give you the keys of the kingdom of heaven. Anything you fasten on earth will be fastened in heaven. Anything you loosen on earth will be loosened in heaven." [20]Then he ordered the disciples not to tell anybody that he was the Christ.

First prediction of Jesus' death and resurrection

[21]From that time Jesus began to show his disciples that he had to go to Jerusalem and suffer many things from the elders, chief priests, and legal experts, and that he had to be killed and raised on the third day. [22]Then Peter took hold of Jesus and, scolding him, began to correct him: "God forbid, Lord! This won't happen to you." [23]But he turned to Peter and said, "Get behind me, Satan. You are a stone that could make me stumble, for you are not thinking God's thoughts but human thoughts."

Saving and losing life

[24]Then Jesus said to his disciples, "All who want to come after me must say no to themselves, take up their cross, and follow me. [25]All who want to save their lives will lose them. But all who lose their lives because of me will find them. [26]Why would people gain the whole world but lose their lives? What will people give in exchange for their lives? [27]For the Human One[q] is about to come with the majesty of his Father with his angels. And then he will repay each one for what that person has done. [28]I assure you that some standing here won't die before they see the Human One[r] coming in his kingdom."

Jesus' transformation

17 Six days later Jesus took Peter, James, and John his brother, and brought them to the top of a very high mountain. [2]He was transformed in front of them. His face shone like the sun, and his clothes became as white as light.

[3]Moses and Elijah appeared to them, talking with Jesus. [4]Peter reacted to all of this by saying to Jesus, "Lord, it's good that we're here. If you want, I'll make three shrines: one for you, one for Moses, and one for Elijah."

[5]While he was still speaking, look, a bright cloud overshadowed them. A voice from the cloud said, "This is my Son whom I dearly love. I am very pleased with him. Listen to him!" [6]Hearing this, the disciples fell on their faces, filled with awe.

[7]But Jesus came and touched them. "Get up," he said. "Don't be afraid." [8]When they looked up, they saw no one except Jesus.

[9]As they were coming down the mountain, Jesus commanded them, "Don't tell anybody about the vision until the Human One[s] is raised from the dead."

[10]The disciples asked, "Then why do the legal experts say that Elijah must first come?"

[11]Jesus responded, "Elijah does come first and will restore all things. [12]In fact, I tell you that Elijah has already come, and they didn't know him. But they did to him whatever they wanted. In the same way the Human One[t] is also going to suffer at their hands." [13]Then the disciples realized he was telling them about John the Baptist.

Healing of a boy who was demon-possessed

[14]When they came to the crowd, a man met Jesus. He knelt before him, [15]saying, "Lord, show mercy to my son. He is epileptic and suffers terribly, for he often falls

[o]Or *Son of Man* [p]Peter means *rock.* [q]Or *Son of Man* [r]Or *Son of Man* [s]Or *Son of Man* [t]Or *Son of Man*

into the fire or the water. 16I brought him to
your disciples, but they couldn't heal him."
17Jesus answered, "You faithless and
crooked generation, how long will I be with
you? How long will I put up with you? Bring
the boy here to me." 18Then Jesus spoke
harshly to the demon. And it came out of the
child, who was healed from that time on.
19Then the disciples came to Jesus in private and said, "Why couldn't we throw the
demon out?"
20"Because you have little faith," he said.
"I assure you that if you have faith the size of
a mustard seed, you could say to this mountain, 'Go from here to there,' and it will go.
There will be nothing that you can't do."[u]

Second prediction of Jesus' death and resurrection

22When the disciples came together in Galilee, Jesus said to them, "The Human One[v] is
about to be delivered over into human hands.
23They will kill him. But he will be raised on
the third day." And they were heartbroken.

Paying the temple tax

24When they came to Capernaum, the
people who collected the half-shekel temple
tax came to Peter and said, "Doesn't your
teacher pay the temple tax?"
25"Yes," he said.
But when they came into the house, Jesus
spoke to Peter first. "What do you think,
Simon? From whom do earthly kings collect
taxes, from their children or from strangers?"
26"From strangers," he said.
Jesus said to him, "Then the children
don't have to pay. 27But just so we don't offend them, go to the lake, throw out a fishing line and hook, and take the first fish you
catch. When you open its mouth, you will
find a shekel coin. Take it and pay the tax
for both of us."

Greatest in the kingdom

18 At that time the disciples came to
Jesus and asked, "Who is the greatest
in the kingdom of heaven?"
2Then he called a little child over to sit
among the disciples, 3and said, "I assure
you that if you don't turn your lives around
and become like this little child, you will
definitely not enter the kingdom of heaven.
4Those who humble themselves like this little child will be the greatest in the kingdom
of heaven. 5Whoever welcomes one such
child in my name welcomes me.

Falling into sin

6"As for whoever causes these little ones
who believe in me to trip and fall into sin,
it would be better for them to have a huge
stone hung around their necks and be
drowned in the bottom of the lake. 7How
terrible it is for the world because of the
things that cause people to trip and fall
into sin! Such things have to happen, but
how terrible it is for the person who causes
those things to happen! 8If your hand or
your foot causes you to fall into sin, chop
it off and throw it away. It's better to enter
into life crippled or lame than to be thrown
into the eternal fire with two hands or two
feet. 9If your eye causes you to fall into sin,
tear it out and throw it away. It's better to
enter into life with one eye than to be cast
into a burning hell with two eyes.

Parable of the lost sheep

10"Be careful that you don't look down on
one of these little ones. I say to you that their
angels in heaven are always looking into the
face of my Father who is in heaven.[w] 12What
do you think? If someone had one hundred
sheep and one of them wandered off, wouldn't
he leave the ninety-nine on the hillsides and
go in search for the one that wandered off?
13If he finds it, I assure you that he is happier
about having that one sheep than about the
ninety-nine who didn't wander off. 14In the
same way, my Father who is in heaven doesn't
want to lose one of these little ones.

Sinning brother or sister

15"If your brother or sister sins against
you, go and correct them when you are alone

[u]17:21 is omitted in most critical editions of the Gk New Testament *This kind doesn't come out except through prayer and fasting.* [v]Or *Son of Man* [w]18:11 is omitted in most critical editions of the Gk New Testament *For the Human One has come to save the lost.*

together. If they listen to you, then you've
won over your brother or sister. 16 But if
they won't listen, take with you one or two
others so that *every word may be established*
by the mouth of two or three witnesses.[x] 17 But
if they still won't pay attention, report
it to the church. If they won't pay attention even to the church, treat them as you
would a Gentile and tax collector. 18 I assure
you that whatever you fasten on earth will
be fastened in heaven. And whatever you
loosen on earth will be loosened in heaven.
19 Again I assure you that if two of you agree
on earth about anything you ask, then my
Father who is in heaven will do it for you.
20 For where two or three are gathered in my
name, I'm there with them."

Parable of the unforgiving servant

21 Then Peter said to Jesus, "Lord, how
many times should I forgive my brother or
sister who sins against me? Should I forgive
as many as seven times?"

22 Jesus said, "Not just seven times, but
rather as many as seventy-seven times.[y]
23 Therefore, the kingdom of heaven is like
a king who wanted to settle accounts with
his servants. 24 When he began to settle accounts, they brought to him a servant who
owed him ten thousand bags of gold.[z] 25 Because the servant didn't have enough to pay
it back, the master ordered that he should
be sold, along with his wife and children
and everything he had, and that the proceeds should be used as payment. 26 But the
servant fell down, kneeled before him, and
said, 'Please, be patient with me, and I'll pay
you back.' 27 The master had compassion on
that servant, released him, and forgave
the loan.

28 "When that servant went out, he found
one of his fellow servants who owed him
one hundred coins.[a] He grabbed him around
the throat and said, 'Pay me back what you
owe me.'

29 "Then his fellow servant fell down and
begged him, 'Be patient with me, and I'll
pay you back.' 30 But he refused. Instead,
he threw him into prison until he paid back
his debt.

31 "When his fellow servants saw what
happened, they were deeply offended. They
came and told their master all that happened. 32 His master called the first servant
and said, 'You wicked servant! I forgave you
all that debt because you appealed to me.
33 Shouldn't you also have mercy on your
fellow servant, just as I had mercy on you?'
34 His master was furious and handed him
over to the guard responsible for punishing
prisoners, until he had paid the whole debt.

35 "My heavenly Father will also do
the same to you if you don't forgive your
brother or sister from your heart."

Teaching about divorce

19 When Jesus finished saying these
things, he left Galilee and came to the
area of Judea on the east side of the Jordan.
2 Large crowds followed him, and he healed
them. 3 Some Pharisees came to him. In order
to test him, they said, "Does the Law allow a
man to divorce his wife for just any reason?"

4 Jesus answered, "Haven't you read that
at the beginning the creator *made them male*
and female?[b] 5 *And God said, 'Because of this a*
man should leave his father and mother and be
joined together with his wife, and the two will
be one flesh.'[c] 6 So they are no longer two but
one flesh. Therefore, humans must not pull
apart what God has put together."

7 The Pharisees said to him, "Then why
did Moses command us to *give a divorce cer-*
tificate and divorce her?"[d]

8 Jesus replied, "Moses allowed you to
divorce your wives because your hearts
are unyielding. But it wasn't that way from
the beginning. 9 I say to you that whoever
divorces his wife, except for sexual unfaithfulness, and marries another woman commits adultery."

10 His disciples said to him, "If that's the
way things are between a man and his wife,
then it's better not to marry."

11 He replied, "Not everybody can accept
this teaching, but only those who have

[x] Deut 19:15 [y] Or *seventy times seven* [z] Or *ten thousand talanta*, an amount equal to the wages for sixty million days [a] Or *one hundred denaria*, an amount equal to the wages for one hundred days [b] Gen 1:27; 5:2 [c] Gen 2:24 [d] Deut 24:1

received the ability to accept it. [12]For there are eunuchs who have been eunuchs from birth. And there are eunuchs who have been made eunuchs by other people. And there are eunuchs who have made themselves eunuchs because of the kingdom of heaven. Those who can accept it should accept it."

Jesus blesses children

[13]Some people brought children to Jesus so that he would place his hands on them and pray. But the disciples scolded them. [14]"Allow the children to come to me," Jesus said. "Don't forbid them, because the kingdom of heaven belongs to people like these children." [15]Then he blessed the children and went away from there.

A rich man's question

[16]A man approached him and said, "Teacher, what good thing must I do to have eternal life?"

[17]Jesus said, "Why do you ask me about what is good? There's only one who is good. If you want to enter eternal life, keep the commandments."

[18]The man said, "Which ones?"

Then Jesus said, "*Don't commit murder. Don't commit adultery. Don't steal. Don't give false testimony.* [19]*Honor your father and mother,*[e] and *love your neighbor as you love yourself*."[f]

[20]The young man replied, "I've kept all these. What am I still missing?"

[21]Jesus said, "If you want to be complete, go, sell what you own, and give the money to the poor. Then you will have treasure in heaven. And come follow me."

[22]But when the young man heard this, he went away saddened, because he had many possessions.

Teaching about giving up things

[23]Then Jesus said to his disciples, "I assure you that it will be very hard for a rich person to enter the kingdom of heaven. [24]In fact, it's easier for a camel to squeeze through the eye of a needle than for a rich person to enter God's kingdom."

[25]When his disciples heard this, they were stunned. "Then who can be saved?" they asked.

[26]Jesus looked at them carefully and said, "It's impossible for human beings. But all things are possible for God."

[27]Then Peter replied, "Look, we've left everything and followed you. What will we have?"

[28]Jesus said to them, "I assure you who have followed me that, when everything is made new, when the Human One[g] sits on his magnificent throne, you also will sit on twelve thrones overseeing the twelve tribes of Israel. [29]And all who have left houses, brothers, sisters, father, mother, children, or farms because of my name will receive one hundred times more and will inherit eternal life. [30]But many who are first will be last. And many who are last will be first.

Workers in the vineyard

20
"The kingdom of heaven is like a landowner who went out early in the morning to hire workers for his vineyard. [2]After he agreed with the workers to pay them a denarion,[h] he sent them into his vineyard.

[3]"Then he went out around nine in the morning and saw others standing around the marketplace doing nothing. [4]He said to them, 'You also go into the vineyard, and I'll pay you whatever is right.' [5]And they went.

"Again around noon and then at three in the afternoon, he did the same thing. [6]Around five in the afternoon he went and found others standing around, and he said to them, 'Why are you just standing around here doing nothing all day long?'

[7]"'Because nobody has hired us,' they replied.

"He responded, 'You also go into the vineyard.'

[8]"When evening came, the owner of the vineyard said to his manager, 'Call the workers and give them their wages, beginning with the last ones hired and moving on finally to the first.' [9]When those who were hired at five in the afternoon came,

[e]Exod 20:12-16; Deut 5:16-20 [f]Lev 19:18 [g]Or *Son of Man* [h]A denarion was a typical day's wage.

each one received a denarion. 10 Now when
those hired first came, they thought they
would receive more. But each of them also
received a denarion. 11 When they received
it, they grumbled against the landowner,
12 'These who were hired last worked one
hour, and they received the same pay as we
did even though we had to work the whole
day in the hot sun.'

13 "But he replied to one of them, 'Friend,
I did you no wrong. Didn't I agree to pay
you a denarion? 14 Take what belongs to you
and go. I want to give to this one who was
hired last the same as I give to you. 15 Don't
I have the right to do what I want with
what belongs to me? Or are you resentful
because I'm generous?' 16 So those who are
last will be first. And those who are first will
be last."

Jesus predicts his death and resurrection

17 As Jesus was going up to Jerusalem, he
took the Twelve aside by themselves on the
road. He told them, 18 "Look, we are going
up to Jerusalem. The Human One[i] will be
handed over to the chief priests and legal
experts. They will condemn him to death.
19 They will hand him over to the Gentiles to
be ridiculed, tortured, and crucified. But he
will be raised on the third day."

Request from James and John's mother

20 Then the mother of Zebedee's sons
came to Jesus along with her sons. Bowing
before him, she asked a favor of him.

21 "What do you want?" he asked.

She responded, "Say that these two sons
of mine will sit, one on your right hand and
one on your left, in your kingdom."

22 Jesus replied, "You don't know what
you're asking! Can you drink from the cup
that I'm about to drink from?"

They said to him, "We can."

23 He said to them, "You will drink from
my cup, but to sit at my right or left hand
isn't mine to give. It belongs to those for
whom my Father prepared it."

24 Now when the other ten disciples heard
about this, they became angry with the two
brothers. 25 But Jesus called them over and
said, "You know that those who rule the
Gentiles show off their authority over them
and their high-ranking officials order them
around. 26 But that's not the way it will be
with you. Whoever wants to be great among
you will be your servant. 27 Whoever wants
to be first among you will be your slave—
28 just as the Human One[j] didn't come to be
served but rather to serve and to give his
life to liberate many people."

Healing of two blind men

29 As Jesus and his disciples were going
out of Jericho a large crowd followed
him. 30 When two blind men sitting along
the road heard that Jesus was passing by,
they shouted, "Show us mercy, Lord, Son
of David!"

31 Now the crowd scolded them and told
them to be quiet. But they shouted even
louder, "Show us mercy, Lord, Son of David!"

32 Jesus stopped in his tracks and called
to them. "What do you want me to do for
you?" he asked.

33 "Lord, we want to see," they replied.

34 Jesus had compassion on them and
touched their eyes. Immediately they were
able to see, and they followed him.

Entry into Jerusalem

21 When they approached Jerusalem and
came to Bethphage on the Mount of
Olives, Jesus gave two disciples a task. 2 He
said to them, "Go into the village over there.
As soon as you enter, you will find a donkey
tied up and a colt with it. Untie them and
bring them to me. 3 If anybody says anything
to you, say that the Lord needs it." He sent
them off right away. 4 Now this happened to
fulfill what the prophet said, 5 *Say to Daughter
Zion, "Look, your king is coming to you, humble
and riding on a donkey, and on a colt the donkey's offspring."*[k] 6 The disciples went and
did just as Jesus had ordered them. 7 They
brought the donkey and the colt and laid
their clothes on them. Then he sat on them.

[i] Or *Son of Man* [j] Or *Son of Man* [k] Isa 62:11; Zech 9:9

8 Now a large crowd spread their clothes on the road. Others cut palm branches off the trees and spread them on the road. 9 The crowds in front of him and behind him shouted, "*Hosanna* to the Son of David! *Blessings on the one who comes in the name of the Lord!*[l] *Hosanna* in the highest!" 10 And when Jesus entered Jerusalem, the whole city was stirred up. "Who is this?" they asked. 11 The crowds answered, "It's the prophet Jesus from Nazareth in Galilee."

Cleansing the temple

12 Then Jesus went into the temple and threw out all those who were selling and buying there. He pushed over the tables used for currency exchange and the chairs of those who sold doves. 13 He said to them, "It's written, *My house will be called a house of prayer.*[m] But you've made it a hideout for crooks."

14 People who were blind and lame came to Jesus in the temple, and he healed them. 15 But when the chief priests and legal experts saw the amazing things he was doing and the children shouting in the temple, "*Hosanna* to the Son of David!" they were angry. 16 They said to Jesus, "Do you hear what these children are saying?"

"Yes," he answered. "Haven't you ever read, *From the mouths of babies and infants you've arranged praise for yourself?*"[n] 17 Then he left them and went out of the city to Bethany and spent the night there.

Cursing the fig tree

18 Early in the morning as Jesus was returning to the city, he was hungry. 19 He saw a fig tree along the road, but when he came to it, he found nothing except leaves. Then he said to it, "You'll never again bear fruit!" The fig tree dried up at once.

20 When the disciples saw it, they were amazed. "How did the fig tree dry up so fast?" they asked.

21 Jesus responded, "I assure you that if you have faith and don't doubt, you will not only do what was done to the fig tree. You will even say to this mountain, 'Be lifted up and thrown into the lake.' And it will happen. 22 If you have faith, you will receive whatever you pray for."

Jesus' authority questioned

23 When Jesus entered the temple, the chief priests and elders of the people came to him as he was teaching. They asked, "What kind of authority do you have for doing these things? Who gave you this authority?"

24 Jesus replied, "I have a question for you. If you tell me the answer, I'll tell you what kind of authority I have to do these things. 25 Where did John get his authority to baptize? Did he get it from heaven or from humans?"

They argued among themselves, "If we say 'from heaven,' he'll say to us, 'Then why didn't you believe him?' 26 But we can't say 'from humans' because we're afraid of the crowd, since everyone thinks John was a prophet." 27 Then they replied, "We don't know."

Jesus also said to them, "Neither will I tell you what kind of authority I have to do these things.

Parable of two sons

28 "What do you think? A man had two sons. Now he came to the first and said, 'Son, go and work in the vineyard today.'

29 "'No, I don't want to,' he replied. But later he changed his mind and went.

30 "The father said the same thing to the other son, who replied, 'Yes, sir.' But he didn't go.

31 "Which one of these two did his father's will?"

They said, "The first one."

Jesus said to them, "I assure you that tax collectors and prostitutes are entering God's kingdom ahead of you. 32 For John came to you on the righteous road, and you didn't believe him. But tax collectors and prostitutes believed him. Yet even after you saw this, you didn't change your hearts and lives and you didn't believe him.

Parable of the tenant farmers

33 "Listen to another parable. There was a landowner who planted a vineyard. He put

[l] Ps 118:26 [m] Isa 56:7; Jer 7:11 [n] Ps 8:3 LXX

a fence around it, dug a winepress in it, and
built a tower. Then he rented it to tenant
farmers and took a trip. 34When it was time
for harvest, he sent his servants to the tenant farmers to collect his fruit. 35But the
tenant farmers grabbed his servants. They
beat some of them, and some of them they
killed. Some of them they stoned to death.
36"Again he sent other servants, more
than the first group. They treated them in
the same way. 37Finally he sent his son to
them. 'They will respect my son,' he said.
38"But when the tenant farmers saw the
son, they said to each other, 'This is the
heir. Come on, let's kill him and we'll have
his inheritance.' 39They grabbed him, threw
him out of the vineyard, and killed him.
40"When the owner of the vineyard
comes, what will he do to those tenant
farmers?"
41They said, "He will totally destroy those
wicked farmers and rent the vineyard to
other tenant farmers who will give him the
fruit when it's ready."
42Jesus said to them, "Haven't you ever
read in the scriptures, *The stone that the
builders rejected has become the cornerstone.
The Lord has done this, and it's amazing in
our eyes?*[o] 43Therefore, I tell you that God's
kingdom will be taken away from you and
will be given to a people who produce its
fruit. 44Whoever falls on this stone will be
crushed. And the stone will crush the person it falls on."
45Now when the chief priests and the
Pharisees heard the parable, they knew
Jesus was talking about them. 46They were
trying to arrest him, but they feared the
crowds, who thought he was a prophet.

Parable of the wedding party

22 Jesus responded by speaking again
in parables: 2"The kingdom of heaven
is like a king who prepared a wedding party
for his son. 3He sent his servants to call
those invited to the wedding party. But
they didn't want to come. 4Again he sent
other servants and said to them, 'Tell those
who have been invited, "Look, the meal is
all prepared. I've butchered the oxen and
the fattened cattle. Now everything's ready.
Come to the wedding party!"' 5But they
paid no attention and went away—some to
their fields, others to their businesses. 6The
rest of them grabbed his servants, abused
them, and killed them.
7"The king was angry. He sent his soldiers to destroy those murderers and set
their city on fire. 8Then he said to his servants, 'The wedding party is prepared, but
those who were invited weren't worthy.
9Therefore, go to the roads on the edge of
town and invite everyone you find to the
wedding party.'
10"Then those servants went to the roads
and gathered everyone they found, both
evil and good. The wedding party was full
of guests. 11Now when the king came in and
saw the guests, he spotted a man who wasn't
wearing wedding clothes. 12He said to him,
'Friend, how did you get in here without
wedding clothes?' But he was speechless.
13Then the king said to his servants, 'Tie
his hands and feet and throw him out into
the farthest darkness. People there will be
weeping and grinding their teeth.'
14"Many people are invited, but few
people are chosen."

Question about taxes

15Then the Pharisees met together to
find a way to trap Jesus in his words. 16They
sent their disciples, along with the supporters of Herod, to him. "Teacher," they said,
"we know that you are genuine and that
you teach God's way as it really is. We know
that you are not swayed by people's opinions, because you don't show favoritism.
17So tell us what you think: Does the Law
allow people to pay taxes to Caesar or not?"
18Knowing their evil motives, Jesus replied, "Why do you test me, you hypocrites?
19Show me the coin used to pay the tax."
And they brought him a denarion. 20"Whose
image and inscription is this?" he asked.
21"Caesar's," they replied.
Then he said, "Give to Caesar what belongs to Caesar and to God what belongs

[o]Ps 118:22-23

to God." [22]When they heard this they were astonished, and they departed.

Question about resurrection

[23]That same day Sadducees, who deny that there is a resurrection, came to Jesus. [24]They asked, "Teacher, Moses said, *If a man who doesn't have children dies, his brother must marry his wife and produce children for his brother.*[p] [25]Now there were seven brothers among us. The first one married, then died. Because he had no children he left his widow to his brother. [26]The same thing happened with the second brother and the third, and in fact with all seven brothers. [27]Finally, the woman died. [28]At the resurrection, which of the seven brothers will be her husband? They were all married to her."

[29]Jesus responded, "You are wrong because you don't know either the scriptures or God's power. [30]At the resurrection people won't marry nor will they be given in marriage. Instead, they will be like angels from God. [31]As for the resurrection of the dead, haven't you read what God told you, [32]*I'm the God of Abraham, the God of Isaac, and the God of Jacob?*[q] He isn't the God of the dead but of the living." [33]Now when the crowd heard this, they were astonished at his teaching.

Great commandment

[34]When the Pharisees heard that Jesus had left the Sadducees speechless, they met together. [35]One of them, a legal expert, tested him. [36]"Teacher, what is the greatest commandment in the Law?"

[37]He replied, "*You must love the Lord your God with all your heart, with all your being,*[r] and with all your mind. [38]This is the first and greatest commandment. [39]And the second is like it: *You must love your neighbor as you love yourself.*[s] [40]All the Law and the Prophets depend on these two commands."

Question about David's son

[41]Now as the Pharisees were gathering, Jesus asked them, [42]"What do you think about the Christ? Whose son is he?"

"David's son," they replied.

[43]He said, "Then how is it that David, inspired by the Holy Spirit, called him Lord when he said, [44]*The Lord said to my lord, 'Sit at my right side until I turn your enemies into your footstool'?*[t] [45]If David calls him Lord, how can he be David's son?" [46]Nobody was able to answer him. And from that day forward nobody dared to ask him anything.

Ways of the legal experts and the Pharisees

23 Then Jesus spoke to the crowds and his disciples, [2]"The legal experts and the Pharisees sit on Moses' seat. [3]Therefore, you must take care to do everything they say. But don't do what they do. [4]For they tie together heavy packs that are impossible to carry. They put them on the shoulders of others, but are unwilling to lift a finger to move them. [5]Everything they do, they do to be noticed by others. They make extra-wide prayer bands for their arms and long tassels for their clothes. [6]They love to sit in places of honor at banquets. [7] They love to be greeted with honor in the markets and to be addressed as 'Rabbi.'

[8]"But you shouldn't be called *Rabbi,* because you have one teacher, and all of you are brothers and sisters. [9]Don't call anybody on earth your father, because you have one Father, who is heavenly. [10]Don't be called *teacher,* because Christ is your one teacher. [11]But the one who is greatest among you will be your servant. [12]All who lift themselves up will be brought low. But all who make themselves low will be lifted up.

Condemnation of the legal experts and the Pharisees

[13]"How terrible it will be for you legal experts and Pharisees! Hypocrites! You shut people out of the kingdom of heaven. You don't enter yourselves, and you won't allow those who want to enter to do so.[u]

[15]"How terrible it will be for you, legal experts and Pharisees! Hypocrites! You travel over sea and land to make one convert. But

[p]Deut 25:5 [q]Exod 3:6, 15-16 [r]Deut 6:5 [s]Lev 19:18 [t]Ps 110:1 [u]Most critical editions of the Gk New Testament omit 23:14 *How terrible it will be for you legal experts and Pharisees! Hypocrites! You eat up widows' houses and make a show of praying long prayers. Therefore, you will receive greater judgment.*

when they've been converted, they become twice the child of hell you are.

16"How terrible it will be for you blind guides who say, 'If people swear by the temple, it's nothing. But if people swear by the gold in the temple, they are obligated to do what they swore.' 17You foolish and blind people! Which is greater, the gold or the temple that makes the gold holy? 18You say, 'If people swear by the altar, it's nothing. But if they swear by the gift on the altar, they are obligated to do what they swore.' 19You blind people! Which is greater, the gift or the altar that makes the gift holy? 20Therefore, those who swear by the altar swear by it and by everything that's on it. 21Those who swear by the temple swear by it and by everything that's part of it. 22Those who swear by heaven swear by God's throne and by the one who sits on it.

23"How terrible it will be for you legal experts and Pharisees! Hypocrites! You give to God a tenth of mint, dill, and cumin, but you forget about the more important matters of the Law: justice, peace, and faith. You ought to give a tenth but without forgetting about those more important matters. 24You blind guides! You filter out an ant but swallow a camel.

25"How terrible it will be for you legal experts and Pharisees! Hypocrites! You clean the outside of the cup and plate, but inside they are full of violence and pleasure seeking. 26Blind Pharisee! First clean the inside of the cup so that the outside of the cup will be clean too.

27"How terrible it will be for you legal experts and Pharisees! Hypocrites! You are like whitewashed tombs. They look beautiful on the outside. But inside they are full of dead bones and all kinds of filth. 28In the same way you look righteous to people. But inside you are full of pretense and rebellion.

29"How terrible it will be for you legal experts and Pharisees! Hypocrites! You build tombs for the prophets and decorate the graves of the righteous. 30You say, 'If we had lived in our ancestors' days, we wouldn't have joined them in killing the prophets.' 31You testify against yourselves that you are children of those who murdered the prophets. 32Go ahead, complete what your ancestors did. 33You snakes! You children of snakes! How will you be able to escape the judgment of hell? 34Therefore, look, I'm sending you prophets, wise people, and legal experts. Some of them you will kill and crucify. And some you will beat in your synagogues and chase from city to city. 35Therefore, upon you will come all the righteous blood that has been poured out on the earth, from the blood of that righteous man Abel to the blood of Zechariah the son of Barachiah, whom you killed between the temple and the altar. 36I assure you that all these things will come upon this generation.

Crying over Jerusalem

37"Jerusalem, Jerusalem! You who kill the prophets and stone those who were sent to you. How often I wanted to gather your people together, just as a hen gathers her chicks under her wings. But you didn't want that. 38Look, your house is left to you deserted. 39I tell you, you won't see me until you say, *Blessings on the one who comes in the Lord's name.*"[v]

The temple's fate

24 Now Jesus left the temple and was going away. His disciples came to point out to him the temple buildings. 2He responded, "Do you see all these things? I assure you that no stone will be left on another. Everything will be demolished."

Beginning of troubles

3Now while Jesus was sitting on the Mount of Olives, the disciples came to him privately and said, "Tell us, when will these things happen? What will be the sign of your coming and the end of the age?"

4Jesus replied, "Watch out that no one deceives you. 5Many will come in my name, saying, 'I'm the Christ.' They will deceive many people. 6You will hear about wars and reports of wars. Don't be alarmed. These

[v]Ps 118:26

things must happen, but this isn't the end yet. 7Nations and kingdoms will fight against each other, and there will be famines and earthquakes in all sorts of places. 8But all these things are just the beginning of the sufferings associated with the end. 9They will arrest you, abuse you, and they will kill you. All nations will hate you on account of my name. 10At that time many will fall away. They will betray each other and hate each other. 11Many false prophets will appear and deceive many people. 12Because disobedience will expand, the love of many will grow cold. 13But the one who endures to the end will be delivered. 14This gospel of the kingdom will be proclaimed throughout the world as a testimony to all the nations. Then the end will come.

The great suffering

15"When you see the disgusting and destructive thing that Daniel talked about standing in the holy place (the reader should understand this), 16then those in Judea must escape to the mountains. 17Those on the roof shouldn't come down to grab things from their houses. 18Those in the field shouldn't come back to grab their clothes. 19How terrible it will be at that time for women who are pregnant and for women who are nursing their children. 20Pray that it doesn't happen in winter or on the Sabbath day. 21There will be great suffering such as the world has never before seen and will never again see. 22If that time weren't shortened, nobody would be rescued. But for the sake of the ones whom God chose, that time will be cut short.

23"Then if somebody says to you, 'Look, here's the Christ,' or 'He's over here,' don't believe it. 24False christs and false prophets will appear, and they will offer great signs and wonders in order to deceive, if possible, even those whom God has chosen. 25Look, I've told you ahead of time. 26So if they say to you, 'Look, he's in the desert,' don't go out. And if they say, 'Look, he's in the rooms deep inside the house,' don't believe it. 27Just as the lightning flashes from the east to the west, so it will be with the coming of the Human One.[w] 28The vultures gather wherever there's a dead body.

Coming of the Human One

29"Now immediately after the suffering of that time the sun will become dark, and the moon won't give its light. The stars will fall from the sky and the planets and other heavenly bodies will be shaken. 30Then the sign of the Human One[x] will appear in the sky. At that time all the tribes of the earth will be full of sadness, and they will see *the Human One*[y] *coming in the heavenly clouds*[z] with power and great splendor. 31He will send his angels with the sound of a great trumpet, and they will gather his chosen ones from the four corners of the earth, from one end of the sky to the other.

A lesson from the fig tree

32"Learn this parable from the fig tree. After its branch becomes tender and it sprouts new leaves, you know that summer is near. 33In the same way, when you see all these things, you know that the Human One[a] is near, at the door. 34I assure you that this generation won't pass away until all these things happen. 35Heaven and earth will pass away, but my words will certainly not pass away.

Day and hour

36"But nobody knows when that day or hour will come, not the heavenly angels and not the Son. Only the Father knows. 37As it was in the time of Noah, so it will be at the coming of the Human One.[b] 38In those days before the flood, people were eating and drinking, marrying and giving in marriage, until the day Noah entered the ark. 39They didn't know what was happening until the flood came and swept them all away. The coming of the Human One[c] will be like that. 40At that time there will be two men in the field. One will be taken and the other left. 41Two women will be grinding

[w]Or *Son of Man* [x]Or *Son of Man* [y]Or *Son of Man* [z]Dan 7:13 *I suddenly saw one like a human being* (Aram *kebar enash) coming with the heavenly clouds.* [a]Or *Son of Man* [b]Or *Son of Man* [c]Or *Son of Man*

at the mill. One will be taken and the other
left. 42Therefore, stay alert! You don't know
what day the Lord is coming. 43But you understand that if the head of the house knew
at what time the thief would come, he would
keep alert and wouldn't allow the thief to
break into his house. 44Therefore, you also
should be prepared, because the Human
One[d] will come at a time you don't know.

Faithful and unfaithful servants

45"Who then are the faithful and wise
servants whom their master puts in charge
of giving food at the right time to those
who live in his house? 46Happy are those
servants whom the master finds fulfilling
their responsibilities when he comes. 47I
assure you that he will put them in charge
of all his possessions. 48But suppose those
bad servants should say to themselves, My
master won't come until later. 49And suppose they began to beat their fellow servants and to eat and drink with the drunks?
50The master of those servants will come
on a day when they are not expecting him,
at a time they couldn't predict. 51He will cut
them in pieces and put them in a place with
hypocrites. People there will be weeping
and grinding their teeth.

Parable of the ten young bridesmaids

25 "At that time the kingdom of heaven
will be like ten young bridesmaids
who took their lamps and went out to meet
the groom. 2Now five of them were wise,
and the other five were foolish. 3The foolish ones took their lamps but didn't bring
oil for them. 4But the wise ones took their
lamps and also brought containers of oil.
5"When the groom was late in coming,
they all became drowsy and went to sleep.
6But at midnight there was a cry, 'Look, the
groom! Come out to meet him.'
7"Then all those bridesmaids got up
and prepared their lamps. 8But the foolish
bridesmaids said to the wise ones, 'Give us
some of your oil, because our lamps have
gone out.'
9"But the wise bridesmaids replied, 'No,
because if we share with you, there won't be
enough for our lamps and yours. We have
a better idea. You go to those who sell oil
and buy some for yourselves.' 10But while
they were gone to buy oil, the groom came.
Those who were ready went with him into
the wedding. Then the door was shut.
11"Later the other bridesmaids came and
said, 'Lord, lord, open the door for us.'
12"But he replied, 'I tell you the truth, I
don't know you.'
13"Therefore, keep alert, because you don't
know the day or the hour.

Parable of the valuable coins

14"The kingdom of heaven is like a man
who was leaving on a trip. He called his servants and handed his possessions over to
them. 15To one he gave five valuable coins,[e]
and to another he gave two, and to another
he gave one. He gave to each servant according to that servant's ability. Then he
left on his journey.
16"After the man left, the servant who
had five valuable coins took them and
went to work doing business with them.
He gained five more. 17In the same way, the
one who had two valuable coins gained two
more. 18But the servant who had received
the one valuable coin dug a hole in the
ground and buried his master's money.
19"Now after a long time the master of
those servants returned and settled accounts with them. 20The one who had received five valuable coins came forward
with five additional coins. He said, 'Master,
you gave me five valuable coins. Look, I've
gained five more.'
21"His master replied, 'Excellent! You are
a good and faithful servant! You've been
faithful over a little. I'll put you in charge of
much. Come, celebrate with me.'
22"The second servant also came forward
and said, 'Master, you gave me two valuable
coins. Look, I've gained two more.'
23"His master replied, 'Well done! You
are a good and faithful servant. You've been
faithful over a little. I'll put you in charge of
much. Come, celebrate with me.'

[d]Or *Son of Man* [e]Or *talantas* (talents)

24“Now the one who had received one
valuable coin came and said, ‘Master, I
knew that you are a hard man. You harvest
grain where you haven’t sown. You gather
crops where you haven’t spread seed. 25So
I was afraid. And I hid my valuable coin in
the ground. Here, you have what’s yours.’

26“His master replied, ‘You evil and lazy
servant! You knew that I harvest grain
where I haven’t sown and that I gather crops
where I haven’t spread seed? 27In that case,
you should have turned my money over to
the bankers so that when I returned, you
could give me what belonged to me with
interest. 28Therefore, take from him the
valuable coin and give it to the one who
has ten coins. 29Those who have much will
receive more, and they will have more than
they need. But as for those who don’t have
much, even the little bit they have will be
taken away from them. 30Now take the
worthless servant and throw him outside
into the darkness.’

“People there will be weeping and grinding their teeth.

Judgment of the nations

31“Now when the Human One[f] comes in
his majesty and all his angels are with him,
he will sit on his majestic throne. 32All the
nations will be gathered in front of him. He
will separate them from each other, just as
a shepherd separates the sheep from the
goats. 33He will put the sheep on his right
side. But the goats he will put on his left.

34“Then the king will say to those on his
right, ‘Come, you who will receive good
things from my Father. Inherit the kingdom that was prepared for you before the
world began. 35I was hungry and you gave me
food to eat. I was thirsty and you gave me a
drink. I was a stranger and you welcomed
me. 36I was naked and you gave me clothes
to wear. I was sick and you took care of me.
I was in prison and you visited me.’

37“Then those who are righteous will
reply to him, ‘Lord, when did we see you
hungry and feed you, or thirsty and give
you a drink? 38When did we see you as a
stranger and welcome you, or naked and
give you clothes to wear? 39When did we
see you sick or in prison and visit you?’

40“Then the king will reply to them, ‘I assure you that when you have done it for one
of the least of these brothers and sisters of
mine, you have done it for me.’

41“Then he will say to those on his left,
‘Get away from me, you who will receive
terrible things. Go into the unending fire
that has been prepared for the devil and
his angels. 42I was hungry and you didn’t
give me food to eat. I was thirsty and you
didn’t give me anything to drink. 43I was a
stranger and you didn’t welcome me. I was
naked and you didn’t give me clothes to
wear. I was sick and in prison, and you
didn’t visit me.’

44“Then they will reply, ‘Lord, when did
we see you hungry or thirsty or a stranger or
naked or sick or in prison and didn’t do anything to help you?’ 45Then he will answer, ‘I
assure you that when you haven’t done it for
one of the least of these, you haven’t done it
for me.’ 46And they will go away into eternal
punishment. But the righteous ones will go
into eternal life.”

Plot to kill Jesus

26 When Jesus finished speaking all
these words, he said to his disciples,
2“You know that the Passover is two days
from now. And the Human One[g] will be
handed over to be crucified.”

3Then the chief priests and elders of the
people gathered in the courtyard of Caiaphas the high priest. 4They were plotting
to arrest Jesus by cunning tricks and to kill
him. 5But they agreed that it shouldn’t happen during the feast so there wouldn’t be
an uproar among the people.

A woman pouring perfume on Jesus

6When Jesus was at Bethany visiting the
house of Simon, who had a skin disease, 7a
woman came to him with a vase made of alabaster containing very expensive perfume.
She poured it on Jesus’ head while he was
sitting at dinner. 8Now when the disciples

[f]Or *Son of Man* [g]Or *Son of Man*

saw it they were angry and said, "Why this waste? [9]This perfume could have been sold for a lot of money and given to the poor."

[10]But Jesus knew what they were thinking. He said, "Why do you make trouble for the woman? She's done a good thing for me. [11]You always have the poor with you, but you won't always have me. [12]By pouring this perfume over my body she's prepared me to be buried. [13]I tell you the truth that wherever in the whole world this good news is announced, what she's done will also be told in memory of her."

Judas betrays Jesus

[14]Then one of the Twelve, who was called Judas Iscariot, went to the chief priests [15]and said, "What will you give me if I turn Jesus over to you?" They paid him thirty pieces of silver. [16]From that time on he was looking for an opportunity to turn him in.

Passover with the disciples

[17]On the first day of the Festival of Unleavened Bread, the disciples came to Jesus and said, "Where do you want us to prepare for you to eat the Passover meal?"

[18]He replied, "Go into the city, to a certain man, and say, 'The teacher says, "My time is near. I'm going to celebrate the Passover with my disciples at your house."'" [19]The disciples did just as Jesus instructed them. They prepared the Passover.

[20]That evening he took his place at the table with the twelve disciples. [21]As they were eating he said, "I assure you that one of you will betray me."

[22]Deeply saddened, each one said to him, "I'm not the one, am I, Lord?"

[23]He replied, "The one who will betray me is the one who dips his hand with me into this bowl. [24]The Human One[h] goes to his death just as it is written about him. But how terrible it is for that person who betrays the Human One![i] It would have been better for him if he had never been born."

[25]Now Judas, who would betray him, replied, "It's not me, is it, Rabbi?"

Jesus answered, "You said it."

Last supper

[26]While they were eating, Jesus took bread, blessed it, broke it, and gave it to the disciples and said, "Take and eat. This is my body." [27]He took a cup, gave thanks, and gave it to them, saying, "Drink from this, all of you. [28]This is my blood of the covenant, which is poured out for many so that their sins may be forgiven. [29]I tell you, I won't drink wine again until that day when I drink it in a new way with you in my Father's kingdom." [30]Then, after singing songs of praise, they went to the Mount of Olives.

Predictions about disciples leaving Jesus

[31]Then Jesus said to his disciples, "Tonight you will all fall away because of me. This is because it is written, *I will hit the shepherd, and the sheep of the flock will go off in all directions.*[j] [32]But after I'm raised up, I'll go before you to Galilee."

[33]Peter replied, "If everyone else stumbles because of you, I'll never stumble."

[34]Jesus said to him, "I assure you that, before the rooster crows tonight, you will deny me three times."

[35]Peter said, "Even if I must die alongside you, I won't deny you." All the disciples said the same thing.

Jesus in prayer

[36]Then Jesus went with his disciples to a place called Gethsemane. He said to the disciples, "Stay here while I go and pray over there." [37]When he took Peter and Zebedee's two sons, he began to feel sad and anxious. [38]Then he said to them, "I'm very sad. It's as if I'm dying. Stay here and keep alert with me." [39]Then he went a short distance farther and fell on his face and prayed, "My Father, if it's possible, take this cup of suffering away from me. However—not what I want but what you want."

[40]He came back to the disciples and found them sleeping. He said to Peter, "Couldn't you stay alert one hour with me? [41]Stay alert and pray so that you won't give in to temptation. The spirit is eager, but

[h]Or *Son of Man* [i]Or *Son of Man* [j]Zech 13:7

the flesh is weak." 42 A second time he went away and prayed, "My Father, if it's not possible that this cup be taken away unless I drink it, then let it be what you want."

43 Again he came and found them sleeping. Their eyes were heavy with sleep. 44 But he left them and again went and prayed the same words for the third time. 45 Then he came to his disciples and said to them, "Will you sleep and rest all night? Look, the time has come for the Human One[k] to be betrayed into the hands of sinners. 46 Get up. Let's go. Look, here comes my betrayer."

Arrest

47 While Jesus was still speaking, Judas, one of the Twelve, came. With him was a large crowd carrying swords and clubs. They had been sent by the chief priests and elders of the people. 48 His betrayer had given them a sign: "Arrest the man I kiss." 49 Just then he came to Jesus and said, "Hello, Rabbi." Then he kissed him.

50 But Jesus said to him, "Friend, do what you came to do." Then they came and grabbed Jesus and arrested him.

51 One of those with Jesus reached for his sword. Striking the high priest's slave, he cut off his ear. 52 Then Jesus said to him, "Put the sword back into its place. All those who use the sword will die by the sword. 53 Or do you think that I'm not able to ask my Father and he will send to me more than twelve battle groups[l] of angels right away? 54 But if I did that, how would the scriptures be fulfilled that say this must happen?" 55 Then Jesus said to the crowds, "Have you come with swords and clubs to arrest me, like a thief? Day after day, I sat in the temple teaching, but you didn't arrest me. 56 But all this has happened so that what the prophets said in the scriptures might be fulfilled." Then all the disciples left Jesus and ran away.

Jesus before the council

57 Those who arrested Jesus led him to Caiaphas the high priest. The legal experts and the elders had gathered there. 58 Peter followed him from a distance until he came to the high priest's courtyard. He entered that area and sat outside with the officers to see how it would turn out.

59 The chief priests and the whole council were looking for false testimony against Jesus so that they could put him to death. 60 They didn't find anything they could use from the many false witnesses who were willing to come forward. But finally they found two 61 who said, "This man said, 'I can destroy God's temple and rebuild it in three days.'"

62 Then the high priest stood and said to Jesus, "Aren't you going to respond to the testimony these people have brought against you?"

63 But Jesus was silent.

The high priest said, "By the living God, I demand that you tell us whether you are the Christ, God's Son."

64 "You said it," Jesus replied. "But I say to you that from now on you'll see *the Human One*[m] *sitting on the right side of the Almighty*[n] *and coming on the heavenly clouds.*"[o]

65 Then the high priest tore his clothes and said, "He's insulting God! Why do we need any more witnesses? Look, you've heard his insult against God. 66 What do you think?"

And they answered, "He deserves to die!" 67 Then they spit in his face and beat him. They hit him 68 and said, "Prophesy for us, Christ! Who hit you?"

Peter's denial

69 Meanwhile, Peter was sitting outside in the courtyard. A servant woman came and said to him, "You were also with Jesus the Galilean."

70 But he denied it in front of all of them, saying, "I don't know what you are talking about."

71 When he went over to the gate, another woman saw him and said to those who were there, "This man was with Jesus, the man from Nazareth."

[k]Or *Son of Man* [l]Or *legions* (of the Roman army, about five thousand soldiers each) [m]Or *Son of Man* [n]Or *the Power* [o]Dan 7:13

72 With a solemn pledge, he denied it
again, saying, "I don't know the man."
73 A short time later those standing there
came and said to Peter, "You must be one of
them. The way you talk gives you away."
74 Then he cursed and swore, "I don't
know the man!" At that very moment the
rooster crowed. 75 Peter remembered Jesus'
words, "Before the rooster crows you will
deny me three times." And Peter went out
and cried uncontrollably.

Jesus before Pilate

27 Early in the morning all the chief
priests and the elders of the people
reached the decision to have Jesus put to
death. 2 They bound him, led him away, and
turned him over to Pilate the governor.

Judas' death

3 When Judas, who betrayed Jesus, saw
that Jesus was condemned to die, he felt
deep regret. He returned the thirty pieces
of silver to the chief priests and elders, and
4 said, "I did wrong because I betrayed an innocent man."

But they said, "What is that to us? That's
your problem." 5 Judas threw the silver
pieces into the temple and left. Then he
went and hanged himself.
6 The chief priests picked up the silver
pieces and said, "According to the Law it's
not right to put this money in the treasury.
Since it was used to pay for someone's life,
it's unclean." 7 So they decided to use it to
buy the potter's field where strangers could
be buried. 8 That's why that field is called
"Field of Blood" to this very day. 9 This fulfilled the words of Jeremiah the prophet:
And I took the thirty pieces of silver, the price
for the one whose price had been set by some
of the Israelites, 10 *and I gave them for the pot-*
ter's field, as the Lord commanded me.[p]

Questioned by Pilate

11 Jesus was brought before the governor. The governor said, "Are you the king of
the Jews?"

Jesus replied, "That's what you say."
12 But he didn't answer when the chief
priests and elders accused him.
13 Then Pilate said, "Don't you hear the
testimony they bring against you?" 14 But
he didn't answer, not even a single word. So
the governor was greatly amazed.

Death sentence

15 It was customary during the festival for
the governor to release to the crowd one prisoner, whomever they might choose. 16 At that
time there was a well-known prisoner named
Jesus Barabbas. 17 When the crowd had come
together, Pilate asked them, "Whom would
you like me to release to you, Jesus Barabbas
or Jesus who is called Christ?" 18 He knew
that the leaders of the people had handed
him over because of jealousy.
19 While he was serving as judge, his wife
sent this message to him, "Leave that righteous man alone. I've suffered much today
in a dream because of him."
20 But the chief priests and the elders persuaded the crowds to ask for Barabbas and
kill Jesus. 21 The governor said, "Which of
the two do you want me to release to you?"

"Barabbas," they replied.
22 Pilate said, "Then what should I do
with Jesus who is called Christ?"

They all said, "Crucify him!"
23 But he said, "Why? What wrong has he
done?"

They shouted even louder, "Crucify him!"
24 Pilate saw that he was getting nowhere
and that a riot was starting. So he took
water and washed his hands in front of the
crowd. "I'm innocent of this man's blood,"
he said. "It's your problem."
25 All the people replied, "Let his blood be
on us and on our children." 26 Then he released
Barabbas to them. He had Jesus whipped,
then handed him over to be crucified.

Soldiers mocking Jesus

27 The governor's soldiers took Jesus into
the governor's house, and they gathered the
whole company[q] of soldiers around him.
28 They stripped him and put a red military coat on him. 29 They twisted together

[p] Zech 11:12-13; Jer 32:6-9 [q] Or *cohort* (approximately six hundred soldiers)

a crown of thorns and put it on his head.
They put a stick in his right hand. Then they
bowed down in front of him and mocked
him, saying, "Hey! King of the Jews!"
[30]After they spit on him, they took the
stick and struck his head again and again.
[31]When they finished mocking him, they
stripped him of the military coat and put
his own clothes back on him. They led him
away to crucify him.

Crucifixion

[32]As they were going out, they found
Simon, a man from Cyrene. They forced
him to carry his cross. [33]When they came
to a place called Golgotha, which means
Skull Place, [34]they gave Jesus wine mixed
with vinegar to drink. But after tasting
it, he didn't want to drink it. [35]After they
crucified him, they divided up his clothes
among them by drawing lots. [36]They sat
there, guarding him. [37]They placed above
his head the charge against him. It read,
"This is Jesus, the king of the Jews." [38]They
crucified with him two outlaws, one on his
right side and one on his left.

[39]Those who were walking by insulted
Jesus, shaking their heads [40]and saying,
"So you were going to destroy the temple
and rebuild it in three days, were you? Save
yourself! If you are God's Son, come down
from the cross."

[41]In the same way, the chief priests, along
with the legal experts and the elders, were
making fun of him, saying, [42]"He saved others, but he can't save himself. He's the king
of Israel, so let him come down from the
cross now. Then we'll believe in him. [43]He
trusts in God, so let God deliver him now
if he wants to. He said, 'I'm God's Son.'"
[44]The outlaws who were crucified with him
insulted him in the same way.

Death

[45]From noon until three in the afternoon
the whole earth was dark. [46]At about three
Jesus cried out with a loud shout, "*Eli, Eli,
lama sabachthani*," which means, "My God,
my God, why have you left me?"[r]

[47]After hearing him, some standing
there said, "He's calling Elijah." [48]One of
them ran over, took a sponge full of vinegar, and put it on a pole. He offered it to
Jesus to drink.

[49]But the rest of them said, "Let's see if
Elijah will come and save him."

[50]Again Jesus cried out with a loud
shout. Then he died.

[51]Look, the curtain of the sanctuary was
torn in two from top to bottom. The earth
shook, the rocks split, [52]and the bodies
of many holy people who had died were
raised. [53]After Jesus' resurrection they
came out of their graves and went into
the holy city where they appeared to many
people. [54]When the centurion and those
with him who were guarding Jesus saw the
earthquake and what had just happened,
they were filled with awe and said, "This
was certainly God's Son."

[55]Many women were watching from a
distance. They had followed Jesus from Galilee to serve him. [56]Among them were Mary
Magdalene, Mary the mother of James and
Joseph, and the mother of Zebedee's sons.

Burial

[57]That evening a man named Joseph
came. He was a rich man from Arimathea
who had become a disciple of Jesus. [58]He
came to Pilate and asked for Jesus' body.
Pilate gave him permission to take it. [59]Jo-
seph took the body, wrapped it in a clean
linen cloth, [60]and laid it in his own new
tomb, which he had carved out of the rock.
After he rolled a large stone at the door of
the tomb, he went away. [61]Mary Magdalene
and the other Mary were there, sitting in
front of the tomb.

Guard at the tomb

[62]The next day, which was the day after
Preparation Day, the chief priests and the
Pharisees gathered before Pilate. [63]They
said, "Sir, we remember that while that
deceiver was still alive he said, 'After three
days I will arise.' [64]Therefore, order the
grave to be sealed until the third day. Oth-

[r]Ps 22:1

erwise, his disciples may come and steal the body and tell the people, 'He's been raised from the dead.' This last deception will be worse than the first."

65 Pilate replied, "You have soldiers for guard duty. Go and make it as secure as you know how." 66 Then they went and secured the tomb by sealing the stone and posting the guard.

Resurrection

28 After the Sabbath, at dawn on the first day of the week, Mary Magdalene and the other Mary came to look at the tomb. 2 Look, there was a great earthquake, for an angel from the Lord came down from heaven. Coming to the stone, he rolled it away and sat on it. 3 Now his face was like lightning and his clothes as white as snow. 4 The guards were so terrified of him that they shook with fear and became like dead men. 5 But the angel said to the women, "Don't be afraid. I know that you are looking for Jesus who was crucified. 6 He isn't here, because he's been raised from the dead, just as he said. Come, see the place where they laid him. 7 Now hurry, go and tell his disciples, 'He's been raised from the dead. He's going on ahead of you to Galilee. You will see him there.' I've given the message to you."

8 With great fear and excitement, they hurried away from the tomb and ran to tell his disciples. 9 But Jesus met them and greeted them. They came and grabbed his feet and worshipped him. 10 Then Jesus said to them, "Don't be afraid. Go and tell my brothers that I am going into Galilee. They will see me there."

Guards' report

11 Now as the women were on their way, some of the guards came into the city and told the chief priests everything that had happened. 12 They met with the elders and decided to give a large sum of money to the soldiers. 13 They told them, "Say that Jesus' disciples came at night and stole his body while you were sleeping. 14 And if the governor hears about this, we will take care of it with him so you will have nothing to worry about." 15 So the soldiers took the money and did as they were told. And this report has spread throughout all Judea to this very day.

Commissioning of the disciples

16 Now the eleven disciples went to Galilee, to the mountain where Jesus told them to go. 17 When they saw him, they worshipped him, but some doubted. 18 Jesus came near and spoke to them, "I've received all authority in heaven and on earth. 19 Therefore, go and make disciples of all nations, baptizing them in the name of the Father and of the Son and of the Holy Spirit, 20 teaching them to obey everything that I've commanded you. Look, I myself will be with you every day until the end of this present age."

MARK

Beginning of good news

1 The beginning of the good news about Jesus Christ, God's Son, 2 happened just as it was written about in the prophecy of Isaiah:

Look, I am sending my messenger
before you.
He will prepare your way,
3 *a voice shouting in the wilderness:*
"Prepare the way for the Lord;
make his paths straight."[a]

John's preaching

4 John the Baptist was in the wilderness calling for people to be baptized to show that they were changing their hearts and lives and wanted God to forgive their sins. 5 Everyone in Judea and all the people of Jerusalem went out to the Jordan River and were being baptized by John as they confessed their sins. 6 John wore clothes made of camel's hair, with a leather belt around his waist. He ate locusts and wild honey.

[a] Isa 40:3; Mal 3:1; Exod 23:20

7He announced, "One stronger than I am
is coming after me. I'm not even worthy to
bend over and loosen the strap of his sandals. 8I baptize you with water, but he will
baptize you with the Holy Spirit."

Jesus is baptized and tempted

9About that time, Jesus came from Nazareth of Galilee, and John baptized him in
the Jordan River. 10While he was coming up
out of the water, Jesus saw heaven splitting
open and the Spirit, like a dove, coming
down on him. 11And there was a voice from
heaven: "You are my Son, whom I dearly
love; in you I find happiness."
12At once the Spirit forced Jesus out into
the wilderness. 13He was in the wilderness
for forty days, tempted by Satan. He was
among the wild animals, and the angels
took care of him.

Jesus' message

14After John was arrested, Jesus came
into Galilee announcing God's good news,
15saying, "Now is the time! Here comes
God's kingdom! Change your hearts and
lives, and trust this good news!"

Jesus calls disciples

16As Jesus passed alongside the Galilee Sea, he saw two brothers, Simon and
Andrew. They were fisherman, so they
were throwing fishing nets into the sea.
17"Come, follow me," he said, "and I'll show
you how to fish for people." 18Right away,
they left their nets and followed him.
19After going a little farther, he saw James
and John, Zebedee's sons, in their boat repairing the fishing nets. 20At that very moment he called them. They followed him,
leaving their father Zebedee in the boat
with the hired workers.

Jesus throws a demon out

21Jesus and his followers went into
Capernaum. Immediately on the Sabbath
Jesus entered the synagogue and started
teaching. 22The people were amazed by his
teaching, for he was teaching them with
authority, not like the legal experts. 23Sud-
denly, there in the synagogue, a person
with an evil spirit screamed, 24"What have
you to do with us, Jesus of Nazareth? Have
you come to destroy us? I know who you
are. You are the holy one from God."
25"Silence!" Jesus said, speaking harshly
to the demon. "Come out of him!" 26The unclean spirit shook him and screamed, then
it came out.
27Everyone was shaken and questioned
among themselves, "What's this? A new
teaching with authority! He even commands unclean spirits and they obey him!"
28Right away the news about him spread
throughout the entire region of Galilee.

Jesus heals Simon's mother-in-law

29After leaving the synagogue, Jesus,
James, and John went home with Simon
and Andrew. 30Simon's mother-in-law was
in bed, sick with a fever, and they told Jesus
about her at once. 31He went to her, took
her by the hand, and raised her up. The
fever left her, and she served them.

Jesus' ministry spreads

32That evening, at sunset, people
brought to Jesus those who were sick or
demon-possessed. 33The whole town gathered near the door. 34He healed many who
were sick with all kinds of diseases, and
he threw out many demons. But he didn't
let the demons speak, because they recognized him.
35Early in the morning, well before sunrise, Jesus rose and went to a deserted
place where he could be alone in prayer.
36Simon and those with him tracked him
down. 37When they found him, they told
him, "Everyone's looking for you!"
38He replied, "Let's head in the other
direction, to the nearby villages, so that I
can preach there too. That's why I've come."
39He traveled throughout Galilee, preaching in their synagogues and throwing out
demons.

A man with a skin disease

40A man with a skin disease approached
Jesus, fell to his knees, and begged, "If you
want, you can make me clean."

41 Incensed,[b] Jesus reached out his hand,
touched him, and said, "I do want to. Be
clean." 42 Instantly, the skin disease left
him, and he was clean. 43 Sternly, Jesus sent
him away, 44 saying, "Don't say anything to
anyone. Instead, go and show yourself to
the priest and offer the sacrifice for your
cleansing that Moses commanded. This will
be a testimony to them." 45 Instead, he went
out and started talking freely and spreading the news so that Jesus wasn't able to
enter a town openly. He remained outside
in deserted places, but people came to him
from everywhere.

Healing and forgiveness

2 After a few days, Jesus went back to
Capernaum, and people heard that he
was at home. 2 So many gathered that there
was no longer space, not even near the
door. Jesus was speaking the word to them.
3 Some people arrived, and four of them
were bringing to him a man who was paralyzed. 4 They couldn't carry him through
the crowd, so they tore off part of the roof
above where Jesus was. When they had
made an opening, they lowered the mat on
which the paralyzed man was lying. 5 When
Jesus saw their faith, he said to the para-
lytic, "Child, your sins are forgiven!"
6 Some legal experts were sitting there,
muttering among themselves, 7 "Why does
he speak this way? He's insulting God. Only
the one God can forgive sins."
8 Jesus immediately recognized what they
were discussing, and he said to them, "Why
do you fill your minds with these questions?
9 Which is easier—to say to a paralyzed person, 'Your sins are forgiven,' or to say, 'Get
up, take up your bed, and walk'? 10 But so
you will know that the Human One[c] has
authority on the earth to forgive sins"—he
said to the man who was paralyzed, 11 "Get
up, take your mat, and go home."
12 Jesus raised him up, and right away he
picked up his mat and walked out in front
of everybody. They were all amazed and
praised God, saying, "We've never seen
anything like this!"

Eating with sinners

13 Jesus went out beside the lake again.
The whole crowd came to him, and he began
to teach them. 14 As he continued along, he
saw Levi, Alphaeus' son, sitting at a kiosk
for collecting taxes. Jesus said to him, "Follow me." Levi got up and followed him.
15 Jesus sat down to eat at Levi's house.
Many tax collectors and sinners were eating
with Jesus and his disciples. Indeed, many
of them had become his followers. 16 When
some of the legal experts from among the
Pharisees saw that he was eating with sinners and tax collectors, they asked his disciples, "Why is he eating with sinners and
tax collectors?"
17 When Jesus heard it, he said to them,
"Healthy people don't need a doctor, but
sick people do. I didn't come to call righteous people, but sinners."

When to fast

18 John's disciples and the Pharisees had
a habit of fasting. Some people asked Jesus,
"Why do John's disciples and the Pharisees'
disciples fast, but yours don't?"
19 Jesus said, "The wedding guests can't
fast while the groom is with them, can
they? As long as they have the groom with
them, they can't fast. 20 But the days will
come when the groom will be taken away
from them, and then they will fast.
21 "No one sews a piece of new, unshrunk
cloth on old clothes; otherwise, the patch
tears away from it, the new from the old, and
makes a worse tear. 22 No one pours new wine
into old leather wineskins; otherwise, the
wine would burst the wineskins and the wine
would be lost and the wineskins destroyed.
But new wine is for new wineskins."

Scripture and the Sabbath

23 Jesus went through the wheat fields
on the Sabbath. As the disciples made their
way, they were picking the heads of wheat.
24 The Pharisees said to Jesus, "Look! Why
are they breaking the Sabbath law?"
25 He said to them, "Haven't you ever
read what David did when he was in need,

[b] Most critical editions of the Gk New Testament read *filled with compassion.* [c] Or *Son of Man*

when he and those with him were hungry?
26 During the time when Abiathar was high
priest, David went into God's house and ate
the bread of the presence, which only the
priests were allowed to eat. He also gave
bread to those who were with him." 27 Then
he said, "The Sabbath was created for humans; humans weren't created for the Sabbath. 28 This is why the Human One[d] is Lord
even over the Sabbath."

Healing on the Sabbath

3 Jesus returned to the synagogue. A
man with a withered hand was there.
2 Wanting to bring charges against Jesus,
they were watching Jesus closely to see if
he would heal on the Sabbath. 3 He said to
the man with the withered hand, "Step up
where people can see you." 4 Then he said to
them, "Is it legal on the Sabbath to do good
or to do evil, to save life or to kill?" But they
said nothing. 5 Looking around at them
with anger, deeply grieved at their unyielding hearts, he said to the man, "Stretch out
your hand." So he did, and his hand was
made healthy. 6 At that, the Pharisees got
together with the supporters of Herod to
plan how to destroy Jesus.

Healing and throwing demons out

7 Jesus left with his disciples and went
to the lake. A large crowd followed him because they had heard what he was doing.
They were from Galilee, 8 Judea, Jerusalem,
Idumea, beyond the Jordan, and the area
surrounding Tyre and Sidon. 9 Jesus told his
disciples to get a small boat ready for him
so the crowd wouldn't crush him. 10 He had
healed so many people that everyone who
was sick pushed forward so that they could
touch him. 11 Whenever the evil spirits saw
him, they fell down at his feet and shouted,
"You are God's Son!" 12 But he strictly ordered them not to reveal who he was.

Jesus appoints twelve apostles

13 Jesus went up on a mountain and
called those he wanted, and they came
to him. 14 He appointed twelve and called
them apostles. He appointed them to be
with him, to be sent out to preach, 15 and to
have authority to throw out demons. 16 He
appointed twelve: Peter, a name he gave
Simon; 17 James and John, Zebedee's sons,
whom he nicknamed Boanerges, which
means "sons of Thunder"; 18 and Andrew;
Philip; Bartholomew; Matthew; Thomas;
James, Alphaeus' son; Thaddaeus; Simon
the Cananaean;[e] 19 and Judas Iscariot, who
betrayed Jesus.

Misunderstandings about Jesus

20 Jesus entered a house. A crowd gathered again so that it was impossible for
him and his followers even to eat. 21 When
his family heard what was happening, they
came to take control of him. They were saying, "He's out of his mind!"
22 The legal experts came down from
Jerusalem. Over and over they charged,
"He's possessed by Beelzebul. He throws
out demons with the authority of the ruler
of demons."
23 When Jesus called them together he
spoke to them in a parable: "How can Satan
throw Satan out? 24 A kingdom involved in
civil war will collapse. 25 And a house torn
apart by divisions will collapse. 26 If Satan
rebels against himself and is divided, then
he can't endure. He's done for. 27 No one
gets into the house of a strong person and
steals anything without first tying up the
strong person. Only then can the house be
burglarized. 28 I assure you that human beings will be forgiven for everything, for all
sins and insults of every kind. 29 But whoever insults the Holy Spirit will never be
forgiven. That person is guilty of a sin with
consequences that last forever." 30 He said
this because the legal experts were saying,
"He's possessed by an evil spirit."
31 His mother and brothers arrived. They
stood outside and sent word to him, calling
for him. 32 A crowd was seated around him,
and those sent to him said, "Look, your
mother, brothers, and sisters are outside
looking for you."
33 He replied, "Who is my mother? Who

[d] Or *Son of Man* [e] Or *zealot*

are my brothers?" 34Looking around at
those seated around him in a circle, he
said, "Look, here are my mother and my
brothers. 35Whoever does God's will is my
brother, sister, and mother."

Parable of the soils

4 Jesus began to teach beside the lake
again. Such a large crowd gathered that
he climbed into a boat there on the lake. He
sat in the boat while the whole crowd was
nearby on the shore. 2He said many things
to them in parables. While teaching them,
he said, 3"Listen to this! A farmer went out
to scatter seed. 4As he was scattering seed,
some fell on the path; and the birds came
and ate it. 5Other seed fell on rocky ground
where the soil was shallow. They sprouted
immediately because the soil wasn't deep.
6When the sun came up, it scorched the
plants; and they dried up because they had
no roots. 7Other seed fell among thorny
plants. The thorny plants grew and choked
the seeds, and they produced nothing.
8Other seed fell into good soil and bore
fruit. Upon growing and increasing, the
seed produced in one case a yield of thirty
to one, in another case a yield of sixty to
one, and in another case a yield of one hundred to one." 9He said, "Whoever has ears
to listen should pay attention!"

Jesus explains his parable

10When they were alone, the people
around Jesus, along with the Twelve, asked
him about the parables. 11He said to them,
"The secret of God's kingdom has been
given to you, but to those who are outside
everything comes in parables. 12This is
so that they can look and see but have no
insight, and they can hear but not understand. Otherwise, they might turn their
lives around and be forgiven.

13"Don't you understand this parable?
Then how will you understand all the parables? 14The farmer scatters the word. 15This
is the meaning of the seed that fell on
the path: When the word is scattered and
people hear it, right away Satan comes and
steals the word that was planted in them.
16Here's the meaning of the seed that fell
on rocky ground: When people hear the
word, they immediately receive it joyfully.
17Because they have no roots, they last for
only a little while. When they experience
distress or abuse because of the word, they
immediately fall away. 18Others are like the
seed scattered among the thorny plants.
These are the ones who have heard the
word; 19but the worries of this life, the false
appeal of wealth, and the desire for more
things break in and choke the word, and
it bears no fruit. 20The seed scattered on
good soil are those who hear the word and
embrace it. They bear fruit, in one case a
yield of thirty to one, in another case sixty
to one, and in another case one hundred
to one."

Parables about lamps and measures

21Jesus said to them, "Does anyone bring
in a lamp in order to put it under a basket
or a bed? Shouldn't it be placed on a lampstand? 22Everything hidden will be revealed,
and everything secret will come out into the
open. 23Whoever has ears to listen should
pay attention!"

24He said to them, "Listen carefully! God
will evaluate you with the same standard
you use to evaluate others. Indeed, you will
receive even more. 25Those who have will
receive more, but as for those who don't
have, even what they don't have will be
taken away from them."

More parables about God's kingdom

26Then Jesus said, "This is what God's
kingdom is like. It's as though someone
scatters seed on the ground, 27then sleeps
and wakes night and day. The seed sprouts
and grows, but the farmer doesn't know
how. 28The earth produces crops all by itself, first the stalk, then the head, then the
full head of grain. 29Whenever the crop is
ready, the farmer goes out to cut the grain
because it's harvesttime."

30He continued, "What's a good image
for God's kingdom? What parable can I use
to explain it? 31Consider a mustard seed.
When scattered on the ground, it's the
smallest of all the seeds on the earth; 32but
when it's planted, it grows and becomes the

largest of all vegetable plants. It produces such large branches that the birds in the sky are able to nest in its shade."

33 With many such parables he continued to give them the word, as much as they were able to hear. 34 He spoke to them only in parables, then explained everything to his disciples when he was alone with them.

Jesus stops a storm

35 Later that day, when evening came, Jesus said to them, "Let's cross over to the other side of the lake." 36 They left the crowd and took him in the boat just as he was. Other boats followed along.

37 Gale-force winds arose, and waves crashed against the boat so that the boat was swamped. 38 But Jesus was in the rear of the boat, sleeping on a pillow. They woke him up and said, "Teacher, don't you care that we're drowning?"

39 He got up and gave orders to the wind, and he said to the lake, "Silence! Be still!" The wind settled down and there was a great calm. 40 Jesus asked them, "Why are you frightened? Don't you have faith yet?"

41 Overcome with awe, they said to each other, "Who then is this? Even the wind and the sea obey him!"

Jesus frees a demon-possessed man

5 Jesus and his disciples came to the other side of the lake, to the region of the Gerasenes. 2 As soon as Jesus got out of the boat, a man possessed by an evil spirit came out of the tombs. 3 This man lived among the tombs, and no one was ever strong enough to restrain him, even with a chain. 4 He had been secured many times with leg irons and chains, but he broke the chains and smashed the leg irons. No one was tough enough to control him. 5 Night and day in the tombs and the hills, he would howl and cut himself with stones. 6 When he saw Jesus from far away, he ran and knelt before him, 7 shouting, "What have you to do with me, Jesus, Son of the Most High God? Swear to God that you won't torture me!"

8 He said this because Jesus had already commanded him, "Unclean spirit, come out of the man!"

9 Jesus asked him, "What is your name?"

He responded, "Legion is my name, because we are many." 10 They pleaded with Jesus not to send them out of that region.

11 A large herd of pigs was feeding on the hillside. 12 "Send us into the pigs!" they begged. "Let us go into the pigs!" 13 Jesus gave them permission, so the unclean spirits left the man and went into the pigs. Then the herd of about two thousand pigs rushed down the cliff into the lake and drowned.

14 Those who tended the pigs ran away and told the story in the city and in the countryside. People came to see what had happened. 15 They came to Jesus and saw the man who used to be demon-possessed. They saw the very man who had been filled with many demons sitting there fully dressed and completely sane, and they were filled with awe. 16 Those who had actually seen what had happened to the demon-possessed man told the others about the pigs. 17 Then they pleaded with Jesus to leave their region.

18 While he was climbing into the boat, the one who had been demon-possessed pleaded with Jesus to let him come along as one of his disciples. 19 But Jesus wouldn't allow it. "Go home to your own people," Jesus said, "and tell them what the Lord has done for you and how he has shown you mercy." 20 The man went away and began to proclaim in the Ten Cities all that Jesus had done for him, and everyone was amazed.

Jesus heals two people

21 Jesus crossed the lake again, and on the other side a large crowd gathered around him on the shore. 22 Jairus, one of the synagogue leaders, came forward. When he saw Jesus, he fell at his feet 23 and pleaded with him, "My daughter is about to die. Please, come and place your hands on her so that she can be healed and live." 24 So Jesus went with him.

A swarm of people were following Jesus, crowding in on him. 25 A woman was there who had been bleeding for twelve years. 26 She had suffered a lot under the care of many doctors, and had spent everything she had without getting any better. In fact, she had gotten worse. 27 Because she had

heard about Jesus, she came up behind him
in the crowd and touched his clothes. 28She
was thinking, If I can just touch his clothes,
I'll be healed. 29Her bleeding stopped immediately, and she sensed in her body that
her illness had been healed.

30At that very moment, Jesus recog-
nized that power had gone out from him.
He turned around in the crowd and said,
"Who touched my clothes?"

31His disciples said to him, "Don't you
see the crowd pressing against you? Yet you
ask, 'Who touched me?' " 32But Jesus looked
around carefully to see who had done it.

33The woman, full of fear and trembling,
came forward. Knowing what had happened to her, she fell down in front of Jesus
and told him the whole truth. 34He responded, "Daughter, your faith has healed
you; go in peace, healed from your disease."

35While Jesus was still speaking with
her, messengers came from the synagogue
leader's house, saying to Jairus, "Your
daughter has died. Why bother the teacher
any longer?"

36But Jesus overheard their report and
said to the synagogue leader, "Don't be
afraid; just keep trusting." 37He didn't allow
anyone to follow him except Peter, James,
and John, James' brother. 38They came
to the synagogue leader's house, and he
saw a commotion, with people crying and
wailing loudly. 39He went in and said to
them, "What's all this commotion and crying about? The child isn't dead. She's only
sleeping." 40They laughed at him, but he
threw them all out. Then, taking the child's
parents and his disciples with him, he went
to the room where the child was. 41Taking
her hand, he said to her, "*Talitha koum*,"
which means, "Young woman, get up."
42Suddenly the young woman got up and
began to walk around. She was 12 years old.
They were shocked! 43He gave them strict
orders that no one should know what had
happened. Then he told them to give her
something to eat.

Jesus in his hometown

6 Jesus left that place and came to his
hometown. His disciples followed him.
2On the Sabbath, he began to teach in the
synagogue. Many who heard him were surprised. "Where did this man get all this?
What's this wisdom he's been given? What
about the powerful acts accomplished
through him? 3Isn't this the carpenter?
Isn't he Mary's son and the brother of
James, Joses, Judas, and Simon? Aren't his
sisters here with us?" They were repulsed by
him and fell into sin.

4Jesus said to them, "Prophets are honored everywhere except in their own hometowns, among their relatives, and in their
own households." 5He was unable to do
any miracles there, except that he placed
his hands on a few sick people and healed
them. 6He was appalled by their disbelief.

Sending out the disciples

Then Jesus traveled through the surrounding villages teaching.

7He called for the Twelve and sent them
out in pairs. He gave them authority over
unclean spirits. 8He instructed them to
take nothing for the journey except a
walking stick—no bread, no bags, and no
money in their belts. 9He told them to wear
sandals but not to put on two shirts. 10He
said, "Whatever house you enter, remain
there until you leave that place. 11If a place
doesn't welcome you or listen to you, as you
leave, shake the dust off your feet as a witness against them." 12So they went out and
proclaimed that people should change their
hearts and lives. 13They cast out many demons, and they anointed many sick people
with olive oil and healed them.

Death of John the Baptist

14Herod the king heard about these things,
because the name of Jesus had become well-
known. Some were saying, "John the Baptist
has been raised from the dead, and this is
why miraculous powers are at work through
him." 15Others were saying, "He is Elijah."
Still others were saying, "He is a prophet like
one of the ancient prophets." 16But when
Herod heard these rumors, he said, "John,
whom I beheaded, has been raised to life."

17He said this because Herod himself had
arranged to have John arrested and put

in prison because of Herodias, the wife of Herod's brother Philip. Herod had married her, [18]but John told Herod, "It's against the law for you to marry your brother's wife!" [19]So Herodias had it in for John. She wanted to kill him, but she couldn't. [20]This was because Herod respected John. He regarded him as a righteous and holy person, so he protected him. John's words greatly confused Herod, yet he enjoyed listening to him.

[21]Finally, the time was right. It was on one of Herod's birthdays, when he had prepared a feast for his high-ranking officials and military officers and Galilee's leading residents. [22]Herod's daughter Herodias[f] came in and danced, thrilling Herod and his dinner guests. The king said to the young woman, "Ask me whatever you wish, and I will give it to you." [23]Then he swore to her, "Whatever you ask I will give to you, even as much as half of my kingdom."

[24]She left the banquet hall and said to her mother, "What should I ask for?"

"John the Baptist's head," Herodias replied.

[25]Hurrying back to the ruler, she made her request: "I want you to give me John the Baptist's head on a plate, right this minute." [26]Although the king was upset, because of his solemn pledge and his guests, he didn't want to refuse her. [27]So he ordered a guard to bring John's head. The guard went to the prison, cut off John's head, [28]brought his head on a plate, and gave it to the young woman, and she gave it to her mother. [29]When John's disciples heard what had happened, they came and took his dead body and laid it in a tomb.

Jesus feeds five thousand people

[30]The apostles returned to Jesus and told him everything they had done and taught. [31]Many people were coming and going, so there was no time to eat. He said to the apostles, "Come by yourselves to a secluded place and rest for a while." [32]They departed in a boat by themselves for a deserted place.

[33]Many people saw them leaving and recognized them, so they ran ahead from all the cities and arrived before them. [34]When Jesus arrived and saw a large crowd, he had compassion on them because they were like sheep without a shepherd. Then he began to teach them many things.

[35]Late in the day, his disciples came to him and said, "This is an isolated place, and it's already late in the day. [36]Send them away so that they can go to the surrounding countryside and villages and buy something to eat for themselves."

[37]He replied, "You give them something to eat."

But they said to him, "Should we go off and buy bread worth almost eight months' pay[g] and give it to them to eat?"

[38]He said to them, "How much bread do you have? Take a look."

After checking, they said, "Five loaves of bread and two fish."

[39]He directed the disciples to seat all the people in groups as though they were having a banquet on the green grass. [40]They sat down in groups of hundreds and fifties. [41]He took the five loaves and the two fish, looked up to heaven, blessed them, broke the loaves into pieces, and gave them to his disciples to set before the people. He also divided the two fish among them all. [42]Everyone ate until they were full. [43]They filled twelve baskets with the leftover pieces of bread and fish. [44]About five thousand had eaten.

Jesus walks on water

[45]Right then, Jesus made his disciples get into a boat and go ahead to the other side of the lake, toward Bethsaida, while he dismissed the crowd. [46]After saying goodbye to them, Jesus went up onto a mountain to pray. [47]Evening came and the boat was in the middle of the lake, but he was alone on the land. [48]He saw his disciples struggling. They were trying to row forward, but the wind was blowing against them. Very early in the morning, he came to them, walking on the lake. He intended to pass by them. [49]When they saw him walking on the lake, they thought he was a ghost and they screamed. [50]Seeing him was

[f] Or *the daughter of Herodias herself*; Gk uncertain [g] Or *two hundred denaria*; a denarion was a typical day's wage.

terrifying to all of them. Just then he spoke to them, "Be encouraged! It's me. Don't be afraid." 51He got into the boat, and the wind settled down. His disciples were so baffled they were beside themselves. 52That's because they hadn't understood about the loaves. Their hearts had been changed so that they resisted God's ways.

Healings at Gennesaret

53When Jesus and his disciples had crossed the lake, they landed at Gennesaret, anchored the boat, 54and came ashore. People immediately recognized Jesus 55and ran around that whole region bringing sick people on their mats to wherever they heard he was. 56Wherever he went—villages, cities, or farming communities—they would place the sick in the marketplaces and beg him to allow them to touch even the hem of his clothing. Everyone who touched him was healed.

What contaminates a life?

7 The Pharisees and some legal experts from Jerusalem gathered around Jesus. 2They saw some of his disciples eating food with unclean hands. (They were eating without first ritually purifying their hands through washing. 3The Pharisees and all the Jews don't eat without first washing their hands carefully. This is a way of observing the rules handed down by the elders. 4Upon returning from the marketplace, they don't eat without first immersing themselves. They observe many other rules that have been handed down, such as the washing of cups, jugs, pans, and sleeping mats.) 5So the Pharisees and legal experts asked Jesus, "Why are your disciples not living according to the rules handed down by the elders but instead eat food with ritually unclean hands?"

6He replied, "Isaiah really knew what he was talking about when he prophesied about you hypocrites. He wrote,

This people honors me with their lips,
but their hearts are far away from me.
7*Their worship of me is empty*
since they teach instructions
that are human words.[h]

8You ignore God's commandment while holding on to rules created by humans and handed down to you." 9Jesus continued, "Clearly, you are experts at rejecting God's commandment in order to establish these rules. 10Moses said, *Honor your father and your mother,*[i] and *The person who speaks against father or mother will certainly be put to death.*[j] 11But you say, 'If you tell your father or mother, "Everything I'm expected to contribute to you is *corban* (that is, a gift I'm giving to God)," 12then you are no longer required to care for your father or mother.' 13In this way you do away with God's word in favor of the rules handed down to you, which you pass on to others. And you do a lot of other things just like that."

14Then Jesus called the crowd again and said, "Listen to me, all of you, and understand. 15Nothing outside of a person can enter and contaminate a person in God's sight; rather, the things that come out of a person contaminate the person."[k]

17After leaving the crowd, he entered a house where his disciples asked him about that riddle. 18He said to them, "Don't you understand either? Don't you know that nothing from the outside that enters a person has the power to contaminate? 19That's because it doesn't enter into the heart but into the stomach, and it goes out into the sewer." By saying this, Jesus declared that no food could contaminate a person in God's sight. 20"It's what comes out of a person that contaminates someone in God's sight," he said. 21"It's from the inside, from the human heart, that evil thoughts come: sexual sins, thefts, murders, 22adultery, greed, evil actions, deceit, unrestrained immorality, envy, insults, arrogance, and foolishness. 23All these evil things come from the inside and contaminate a person in God's sight."

An immigrant's daughter is delivered

24Jesus left that place and went into the region of Tyre. He didn't want anyone

[h]Isa 29:13 [i]Exod 20:12; Deut 5:16 [j]Exod 21:17; Lev 20:9 [k]7:16 is omitted in most critical editions of the Gk New Testament *Whoever has ears to listen should pay attention!*

to know that he had entered a house, but he couldn't hide. [25]In fact, a woman whose young daughter was possessed by an unclean spirit heard about him right away. She came and fell at his feet. [26]The woman was Greek, Syrophoenician by birth. She begged Jesus to throw the demon out of her daughter. [27]He responded, "The children have to be fed first. It isn't right to take the children's bread and toss it to the dogs."

[28]But she answered, "Lord, even the dogs under the table eat the children's crumbs."

[29]"Good answer!" he said. "Go on home. The demon has already left your daughter." [30]When she returned to her house, she found the child lying on the bed and the demon gone.

A deaf man is healed

[31]After leaving the region of Tyre, Jesus went through Sidon toward the Galilee Sea through the region of the Ten Cities. [32]Some people brought to him a man who was deaf and could hardly speak, and they begged him to place his hand on the man for healing. [33]Jesus took him away from the crowd by himself and put his fingers in the man's ears. Then he spit and touched the man's tongue. [34]Looking into heaven, Jesus sighed deeply and said, *"Ephphatha,"* which means, "Open up." [35]At once, his ears opened, his twisted tongue was released, and he began to speak clearly.

[36]Jesus gave the people strict orders not to tell anyone. But the more he tried to silence them, the more eagerly they shared the news. [37]People were overcome with wonder, saying, "He does everything well! He even makes the deaf to hear and gives speech to those who can't speak."

Jesus feeds four thousand people

8 In those days there was another large crowd with nothing to eat. Jesus called his disciples and told them, [2]"I feel sorry for the crowd because they have been with me for three days and have nothing to eat. [3]If I send them away hungry to their homes, they won't have enough strength to travel, for some have come a long distance."

[4]His disciples responded, "How can anyone get enough food in this wilderness to satisfy these people?"

[5]Jesus asked, "How much bread do you have?"

They said, "Seven loaves."

[6]He told the crowd to sit on the ground. He took the seven loaves, gave thanks, broke them apart, and gave them to his disciples to distribute; and they gave the bread to the crowd. [7]They also had a few fish. He said a blessing over them, then gave them to the disciples to hand out also. [8]They ate until they were full. They collected seven baskets full of leftovers. [9]This was a crowd of about four thousand people! Jesus sent them away, [10]then got into a boat with his disciples and went over to the region of Dalmanutha.

Looking for proof

[11]The Pharisees showed up and began to argue with Jesus. To test him, they asked for a sign from heaven. [12]With an impatient sigh, Jesus said, "Why does this generation look for a sign? I assure you that no sign will be given to it." [13]Leaving them, he got back in the boat and crossed to the other side of the lake.

Understanding about the bread

[14]Jesus' disciples had forgotten to bring any bread, so they had only one loaf with them in the boat. [15]He gave them strict orders: "Watch out and be on your guard for the yeast of the Pharisees as well as the yeast of Herod."

[16]The disciples discussed this among themselves, "He said this because we have no bread."

[17]Jesus knew what they were discussing and said, "Why are you talking about the fact that you don't have any bread? Don't you grasp what has happened? Don't you understand? Are your hearts so resistant to what God is doing? [18]Don't you have eyes? Why can't you see? Don't you have ears? Why can't you hear? Don't you remember? [19]When I broke five loaves of bread for those five thousand people, how many baskets full of leftovers did you gather?"

They answered, "Twelve."

20 “And when I broke seven loaves of bread
for those four thousand people, how many
baskets full of leftovers did you gather?”
They answered, “Seven.”
21 Jesus said to them, “And you still don’t
understand?”

A blind man is healed

22 Jesus and his disciples came to Bethsaida. Some people brought a blind man
to Jesus and begged him to touch and heal
him. 23 Taking the blind man’s hand, Jesus
led him out of the village. After spitting on
his eyes and laying his hands on the man,
he asked him, “Do you see anything?”
24 The man looked up and said, “I see
people. They look like trees, only they are
walking around.”
25 Then Jesus placed his hands on the
man’s eyes again. He looked with his eyes
wide open, his sight was restored, and he
could see everything clearly. 26 Then Jesus
sent him home, saying, “Don’t go into the
village!”

Jesus predicts his death

27 Jesus and his disciples went into the
villages near Caesarea Philippi. On the way
he asked his disciples, “Who do people say
that I am?”
28 They told him, “Some say John the
Baptist, others Elijah, and still others one
of the prophets.”
29 He asked them, “And what about you?
Who do you say that I am?”
Peter answered, “You are the Christ.”
30 Jesus ordered them not to tell anyone
about him.
31 Then Jesus began to teach his disciples:
“The Human One[l] must suffer many things
and be rejected by the elders, chief priests,
and the legal experts, and be killed, and
then, after three days, rise from the dead.”
32 He said this plainly. But Peter took hold
of Jesus and, scolding him, began to correct
him. 33 Jesus turned and looked at his disciples, then sternly corrected Peter: “Get behind me, Satan. You are not thinking God’s
thoughts but human thoughts.”

34 After calling the crowd together with
his disciples, Jesus said to them, “All who
want to come after me must say no to themselves, take up their cross, and follow me.
35 All who want to save their lives will lose
them. But all who lose their lives because of
me and because of the good news will save
them. 36 Why would people gain the whole
world but lose their lives? 37 What will people
give in exchange for their lives? 38 Whoever
is ashamed of me and my words in this unfaithful and sinful generation, the Human
One[m] will be ashamed of that person when
he comes in the Father’s glory with the holy
9 angels.” 1 Jesus continued, “I assure you
that some standing here won’t die before
they see God’s kingdom arrive in power.”

Jesus transformed

2 Six days later Jesus took Peter, James,
and John, and brought them to the top of a
very high mountain where they were alone.
He was transformed in front of them, 3 and
his clothes were amazingly bright, brighter
than if they had been bleached white. 4 Elijah and Moses appeared and were talking
with Jesus. 5 Peter reacted to all of this by
saying to Jesus, “Rabbi, it’s good that we’re
here. Let’s make three shrines—one for
you, one for Moses, and one for Elijah.” 6 He
said this because he didn’t know how to respond, for the three of them were terrified.
7 Then a cloud overshadowed them, and a
voice spoke from the cloud, “This is my Son,
whom I dearly love. Listen to him!” 8 Suddenly, looking around, they no longer saw
anyone with them except Jesus.
9 As they were coming down the mountain, he ordered them not to tell anyone
what they had seen until after the Human
One[n] had risen from the dead. 10 So they
kept it to themselves, wondering, “What’s
this ‘rising from the dead’?” 11 They asked
Jesus, “Why do the legal experts say that
Elijah must come first?”
12 He answered, “Elijah does come first to
restore all things. Why was it written that
the Human One[o] would suffer many things
and be rejected? 13 In fact, I tell you that Elijah

[l] Or *Son of Man* [m] Or *Son of Man* [n] Or *Son of Man* [o] Or *Son of Man*

has come, but they did to him whatever they wanted, just as it was written about him."

A demon-possessed boy

14 When Jesus, Peter, James, and John approached the other disciples, they saw a large crowd surrounding them and legal experts arguing with them. 15 Suddenly the whole crowd caught sight of Jesus. They ran to greet him, overcome with excitement. 16 Jesus asked them, "What are you arguing about?"

17 Someone from the crowd responded, "Teacher, I brought my son to you, since he has a spirit that doesn't allow him to speak. 18 Wherever it overpowers him, it throws him into a fit. He foams at the mouth, grinds his teeth, and stiffens up. So I spoke to your disciples to see if they could throw it out, but they couldn't."

19 Jesus answered them, "You faithless generation, how long will I be with you? How long will I put up with you? Bring him to me."

20 They brought him. When the spirit saw Jesus, it immediately threw the boy into a fit. He fell on the ground and rolled around, foaming at the mouth. 21 Jesus asked his father, "How long has this been going on?"

He said, "Since he was a child. 22 It has often thrown him into a fire or into water trying to kill him. If you can do anything, help us! Show us compassion!"

23 Jesus said to him, " 'If you can do anything'? All things are possible for the one who has faith."

24 At that the boy's father cried out, "I have faith; help my lack of faith!"

25 Noticing that the crowd had surged together, Jesus spoke harshly to the unclean spirit, "Mute and deaf spirit, I command you to come out of him and never enter him again." 26 After screaming and shaking the boy horribly, the spirit came out. The boy seemed to be dead; in fact, several people said that he had died. 27 But Jesus took his hand, lifted him up, and he arose.

28 After Jesus went into a house, his disciples asked him privately, "Why couldn't we throw this spirit out?"

29 Jesus answered, "Throwing this kind of spirit out requires prayer."

Jesus predicts his death

30 From there Jesus and his followers went through Galilee, but he didn't want anyone to know it. 31 This was because he was teaching his disciples, "The Human One[p] will be delivered into human hands. They will kill him. Three days after he is killed he will rise up." 32 But they didn't understand this kind of talk, and they were afraid to ask him.

33 They entered Capernaum. When they had come into a house, he asked them, "What were you arguing about during the journey?" 34 They didn't respond, since on the way they had been debating with each other about who was the greatest. 35 He sat down, called the Twelve, and said to them, "Whoever wants to be first must be least of all and the servant of all." 36 Jesus reached for a little child, placed him among the Twelve, and embraced him. Then he said, 37 "Whoever welcomes one of these children in my name welcomes me; and whoever welcomes me isn't actually welcoming me but rather the one who sent me."

Recognize your allies

38 John said to Jesus, "Teacher, we saw someone throwing demons out in your name, and we tried to stop him because he wasn't following us."

39 Jesus replied, "Don't stop him. No one who does powerful acts in my name can quickly turn around and curse me. 40 Whoever isn't against us is for us. 41 I assure you that whoever gives you a cup of water to drink because you belong to Christ will certainly be rewarded.

42 "As for whoever causes these little ones who believe in me to trip and fall into sin, it would be better for them to have a huge stone hung around their necks and to be thrown into the lake. 43 If your hand causes you to fall into sin, chop it off. It's better for you to enter into life crippled than to go away with two hands into the

[p] Or *Son of Man*

fire of hell, which can't be put out.[q] [45]If your foot causes you to fall into sin, chop it off. It's better for you to enter life lame than to be thrown into hell with two feet.[r] [47]If your eye causes you to fall into sin, tear it out. It's better for you to enter God's kingdom with one eye than to be thrown into hell with two. [48]That's a place *where worms don't die and the fire never goes out.*[s] [49]Everyone will be salted with fire. [50]Salt is good; but if salt loses its saltiness, how will it become salty again? Maintain salt among yourselves and keep peace with each other."

Divorce and remarriage

10 Jesus left that place and went beyond the Jordan and into the region of Judea. Crowds gathered around him again and, as usual, he taught them. [2]Some Pharisees came and, trying to test him, they asked, "Does the Law allow a man to divorce his wife?"

[3]Jesus answered, "What did Moses command you?"

[4]They said, "Moses allowed a man to write a divorce certificate and to divorce his wife."

[5]Jesus said to them, "He wrote this commandment for you because of your unyielding hearts. [6]At the beginning of creation, *God made them male and female.*[t] [7]*Because of this, a man should leave his father and mother and be joined together with his wife,* [8]*and the two will be one flesh.*[u] So they are no longer two but one flesh. [9]Therefore, humans must not pull apart what God has put together."

[10]Inside the house, the disciples asked him again about this. [11]He said to them, "Whoever divorces his wife and marries another commits adultery against her; [12]and if a wife divorces her husband and marries another, she commits adultery."

Jesus blesses children

[13]People were bringing children to Jesus so that he would bless them. But the disciples scolded them. [14]When Jesus saw this, he grew angry and said to them, "Allow the children to come to me. Don't forbid them, because God's kingdom belongs to people like these children. [15]I assure you that whoever doesn't welcome God's kingdom like a child will never enter it." [16]Then he hugged the children and blessed them.

A rich man's question

[17]As Jesus continued down the road, a man ran up, knelt before him, and asked, "Good Teacher, what must I do to obtain eternal life?"

[18]Jesus replied, "Why do you call me good? No one is good except the one God. [19]You know the commandments: *Don't commit murder. Don't commit adultery. Don't steal. Don't give false testimony.* Don't cheat. *Honor your father and mother.*"[v]

[20]"Teacher," he responded, "I've kept all of these things since I was a boy."

[21]Jesus looked at him carefully and loved him. He said, "You are lacking one thing. Go, sell what you own, and give the money to the poor. Then you will have treasure in heaven. And come, follow me." [22]But the man was dismayed at this statement and went away saddened, because he had many possessions.

[23]Looking around, Jesus said to his disciples, "It will be very hard for the wealthy to enter God's kingdom!" [24]His words startled the disciples, so Jesus told them again, "Children, it's difficult to enter God's kingdom! [25]It's easier for a camel to squeeze through the eye of a needle than for a rich person to enter God's kingdom."

[26]They were shocked even more and said to each other, "Then who can be saved?"

[27]Jesus looked at them carefully and said, "It's impossible with human beings, but not with God. All things are possible for God."

[28]Peter said to him, "Look, we've left everything and followed you."

[29]Jesus said, "I assure you that anyone who has left house, brothers, sisters, mother, father, children, or farms because of me and because of the good news [30]will receive one hundred times as much now

[q]9:44 is omitted in most critical editions of the Gk New Testament *where worms don't die and the fire never goes out.* [r]9:46 is omitted in most critical editions of the Gk New Testament *where worms don't die and the fire never goes out.* [s]Isa 66:24 [t]Gen 1:27 [u]Gen 2:24 [v]Exod 12:16; Deut 16:20

in this life—houses, brothers, sisters, mothers, children, and farms (with harassment)—and in the coming age, eternal life. 31 But many who are first will be last. And many who are last will be first."

Jesus predicts his death and resurrection

32 Jesus and his disciples were on the road, going up to Jerusalem, with Jesus in the lead. The disciples were amazed while the others following behind were afraid. Taking the Twelve aside again, he told them what was about to happen to him. 33 "Look!" he said. "We're going up to Jerusalem. The Human One[w] will be handed over to the chief priests and the legal experts. They will condemn him to death and hand him over to the Gentiles. 34 They will ridicule him, spit on him, torture him, and kill him. After three days, he will rise up."

A request from James and John

35 James and John, Zebedee's sons, came to Jesus and said, "Teacher, we want you to do for us whatever we ask."

36 "What do you want me to do for you?" he asked.

37 They said, "Allow one of us to sit on your right and the other on your left when you enter your glory."

38 Jesus replied, "You don't know what you're asking! Can you drink the cup I drink or receive the baptism I receive?"

39 "We can," they answered.

Jesus said, "You will drink the cup I drink and receive the baptism I receive, 40 but to sit at my right or left hand isn't mine to give. It belongs to those for whom it has been prepared."

41 Now when the other ten disciples heard about this, they became angry with James and John. 42 Jesus called them over and said, "You know that the ones who are considered the rulers by the Gentiles show off their authority over them and their high-ranking officials order them around. 43 But that's not the way it will be with you. Whoever wants to be great among you will be your servant. 44 Whoever wants to be first among you will be the slave of all, 45 for the Human One[x] didn't come to be served but rather to serve and to give his life to liberate many people."

Healing of blind Bartimaeus

46 Jesus and his followers came into Jericho. As Jesus was leaving Jericho, together with his disciples and a sizable crowd, a blind beggar named Bartimaeus, Timaeus' son, was sitting beside the road. 47 When he heard that Jesus of Nazareth was there, he began to shout, "Jesus, Son of David, show me mercy!" 48 Many scolded him, telling him to be quiet, but he shouted even louder, "Son of David, show me mercy!"

49 Jesus stopped and said, "Call him forward."

They called the blind man, "Be encouraged! Get up! He's calling you."

50 Throwing his coat to the side, he jumped up and came to Jesus.

51 Jesus asked him, "What do you want me to do for you?"

The blind man said, "Teacher, I want to see."

52 Jesus said, "Go, your faith has healed you." At once he was able to see, and he began to follow Jesus on the way.

Jesus enters Jerusalem

11 When Jesus and his followers approached Jerusalem, they came to Bethphage and Bethany at the Mount of Olives. Jesus gave two disciples a task, 2 saying to them, "Go into the village over there. As soon as you enter it, you will find tied up there a colt that no one has ridden. Untie it and bring it here. 3 If anyone says to you, 'Why are you doing this?' say, 'Its master needs it, and he will send it back right away.'"

4 They went and found a colt tied to a gate outside on the street, and they untied it. 5 Some people standing around said to them, "What are you doing, untying the colt?" 6 They told them just what Jesus said, and they left them alone. 7 They brought the colt to Jesus and threw their clothes upon

[w] Or *Son of Man* [x] Or *Son of Man*

it, and he sat on it. [8]Many people spread out their clothes on the road while others spread branches cut from the fields. [9]Those in front of him and those following were shouting, "*Hosanna! Blessings on the one who comes in the name of the Lord!*[y] [10]Blessings on the coming kingdom of our ancestor David! Hosanna in the highest!" [11]Jesus entered Jerusalem and went into the temple. After he looked around at everything, because it was already late in the evening, he returned to Bethany with the Twelve.

Fig tree and the temple

[12]The next day, after leaving Bethany, Jesus was hungry. [13]From far away, he noticed a fig tree in leaf, so he went to see if he could find anything on it. When he came to it, he found nothing except leaves, since it wasn't the season for figs. [14]So he said to it, "No one will ever again eat your fruit!" His disciples heard this.

[15]They came into Jerusalem. After entering the temple, he threw out those who were selling and buying there. He pushed over the tables used for currency exchange and the chairs of those who sold doves. [16]He didn't allow anyone to carry anything through the temple. [17]He taught them, "Hasn't it been written, *My house will be called a house of prayer for all nations*?[z] But you've turned it into *a hideout for crooks*."[a] [18]The chief priests and legal experts heard this and tried to find a way to destroy him. They regarded him as dangerous because the whole crowd was enthralled at his teaching. [19]When it was evening, Jesus and his disciples went outside the city.

Power, prayer, and forgiveness

[20]Early in the morning, as Jesus and his disciples were walking along, they saw the fig tree withered from the root up. [21]Peter remembered and said to Jesus, "Rabbi, look how the fig tree you cursed has dried up."

[22]Jesus responded to them, "Have faith in God! [23]I assure you that whoever says to this mountain, 'Be lifted up and thrown into the sea'—and doesn't waver but believes that what is said will really happen—it will happen. [24]Therefore I say to you, whatever you pray and ask for, believe that you will receive it, and it will be so for you. [25]And whenever you stand up to pray, if you have something against anyone, forgive so that your Father in heaven may forgive you your wrongdoings."[b]

Controversy over authority

[27]Jesus and his disciples entered Jerusalem again. As Jesus was walking around the temple, the chief priests, legal experts, and elders came to him. [28]They asked, "What kind of authority do you have for doing these things? Who gave you this authority to do them?"

[29]Jesus said to them, "I have a question for you. Give me an answer, then I'll tell you what kind of authority I have to do these things. [30]Was John's baptism of heavenly or of human origin? Answer me."

[31]They argued among themselves, "If we say, 'It's of heavenly origin,' he'll say, 'Then why didn't you believe him?' [32]But we can't say, 'It's of earthly origin.'" They said this because they were afraid of the crowd, because they all thought John was a prophet. [33]They answered Jesus, "We don't know."

Jesus replied, "Neither will I tell you what kind of authority I have to do these things."

Parable of the tenant farmers

12 Jesus spoke to them in parables. "A man planted a vineyard, put a fence around it, dug a pit for the winepress, and built a tower. Then he rented it to tenant farmers and took a trip. [2]When it was time, he sent a servant to collect from the tenants his share of the fruit of the vineyard. [3]But they grabbed the servant, beat him, and sent him away empty-handed. [4]Again the landowner sent another servant to them, but they struck him on the head and treated him disgracefully. [5]He sent another one; that one they killed. The landlord sent many other servants, but the tenants beat some

[y]Ps 118:26 [z]Isa 56:7 [a]Jer 7:11 [b]11:26 is omitted in most critical editions of the Gk New Testament *And if you don't forgive, neither will your Father in heaven forgive you your wrongdoings.*

and killed others. 6 Now the landowner had
one son whom he loved dearly. He sent him
last, thinking, They will respect my son. 7 But
those tenant farmers said to each other, 'This
is the heir. Let's kill him, and the inheritance
will be ours.' 8 They grabbed him, killed him,
and threw him out of the vineyard.

9 "So what will the owner of the vineyard
do? He will come and destroy those tenants
and give the vineyard to others. 10 Haven't you
read this scripture, *The stone that the builders
rejected has become the cornerstone.* 11 *The Lord
has done this, and it's amazing in our eyes?*"[c]

12 They wanted to arrest Jesus because
they knew that he had told the parable
against them. But they were afraid of the
crowd, so they left him and went away.

A question about taxes

13 They sent some of the Pharisees
and supporters of Herod to trap him in
his words. 14 They came to him and said,
"Teacher, we know that you're genuine and
you don't worry about what people think.
You don't show favoritism but teach God's
way as it really is. Does the Law allow people to pay taxes to Caesar or not? Should
we pay taxes or not?"

15 Since Jesus recognized their deceit,
he said to them, "Why are you testing me?
Bring me a coin. Show it to me." 16 And they
brought one. He said to them, "Whose
image and inscription is this?"

"Caesar's," they replied.

17 Jesus said to them, "Give to Caesar
what belongs to Caesar and to God what
belongs to God." His reply left them overcome with wonder.

A question about the resurrection

18 Sadducees, who deny that there is a
resurrection, came to Jesus and asked,
19 "Teacher, Moses wrote for us that *if a
man's brother dies*, leaving a widow *but no
children, the brother must marry the widow
and raise up children for his brother.*[d] 20 Now
there were seven brothers. The first one
married a woman; when he died, he left no
children. 21 The second married her and died
without leaving any children. The third did
the same. 22 None of the seven left any children. Finally, the woman died. 23 At the resurrection, when they all rise up, whose wife
will she be? All seven were married to her."

24 Jesus said to them, "Isn't this the
reason you are wrong, because you don't
know either the scriptures or God's power?
25 When people rise from the dead, they
won't marry nor will they be given in marriage. Instead, they will be like God's angels.
26 As for the resurrection from the dead,
haven't you read in the scroll from Moses,
in the passage about the burning bush, how
God said to Moses, *I am the God of Abraham,
the God of Isaac, and the God of Jacob?*[e] 27 He
isn't the God of the dead but of the living.
You are seriously mistaken."

God's most important command

28 One of the legal experts heard their dispute and saw how well Jesus answered them.
He came over and asked him, "Which commandment is the most important of all?"

29 Jesus replied, "The most important
one is *Israel, listen! Our God is the one Lord,*
30 *and you must love the Lord your God with
all your heart, with all your being, with all
your mind, and with all your strength.*[f] 31 The
second is this, *You will love your neighbor
as yourself.*[g] No other commandment is
greater than these."

32 The legal expert said to him, "Well
said, Teacher. You have truthfully said
that God is one and there is no other besides him. 33 And to love God with all of the
heart, a full understanding, and all of one's
strength, and to love one's neighbor as oneself is much more important than all kinds
of entirely burned offerings and sacrifices."

34 When Jesus saw that he had answered
with wisdom, he said to him, "You aren't
far from God's kingdom." After that, no one
dared to ask him any more questions.

Jesus corrects the legal experts

35 While Jesus was teaching in the temple,
he said, "Why do the legal experts say that
the Christ is David's son? 36 David himself,

[c]Ps 118:22-23 [d]Deut 25:5; Gen 38:8 [e]Exod 3:6, 15-16 [f]Deut 6:4-5 [g]Lev 19:18

inspired by the Holy Spirit, said, *The Lord said*
to my lord, 'Sit at my right side until I turn your
enemies into your footstool.'[h] 37 David himself
calls him 'Lord,' so how can he be David's son?"
The large crowd listened to him with delight.
38 As he was teaching, he said, "Watch
out for the legal experts. They like to walk
around in long robes. They want to be
greeted with honor in the markets. 39 They
long for places of honor in the synagogues
and at banquets. 40 They are the ones who
cheat widows out of their homes, and to
show off they say long prayers. They will be
judged most harshly."

A poor widow's contribution

41 Jesus sat across from the collection
box for the temple treasury and observed
how the crowd gave their money. Many
rich people were throwing in lots of money.
42 One poor widow came forward and put
in two small copper coins worth a penny.[i]
43 Jesus called his disciples to him and said,
"I assure you that this poor widow has put
in more than everyone who's been putting
money in the treasury. 44 All of them are giving out of their spare change. But she from
her hopeless poverty has given everything
she had, even what she needed to live on."

The temple's fate

13 As Jesus left the temple, one of his
disciples said to him, "Teacher, look!
What awesome stones and buildings!"
2 Jesus responded, "Do you see these enormous buildings? Not even one stone will be
left upon another. All will be demolished."
3 Jesus was sitting on the Mount of
Olives across from the temple. Peter,
James, John, and Andrew asked him privately, 4 "Tell us, when will these things
happen? What sign will show that all these
things are about to come to an end?"

Keep watch!

5 Jesus said, "Watch out that no one
deceives you. 6 Many people will come in
my name, saying, 'I'm the one!' They will
deceive many people. 7 When you hear of
wars and reports of wars, don't be alarmed.
These things must happen, but this isn't
the end yet. 8 Nations and kingdoms will
fight against each other, and there will be
earthquakes and famines in all sorts of
places. These things are just the beginning
of the sufferings associated with the end.
9 "Watch out for yourselves. People will
hand you over to the councils. You will be
beaten in the synagogues. You will stand before governors and kings because of me so
that you can testify before them. 10 First, the
good news must be proclaimed to all the nations. 11 When they haul you in and hand you
over, don't worry ahead of time about what
to answer or say. Instead, say whatever is
given to you at that moment, for you aren't
doing the speaking but the Holy Spirit is.
12 Brothers and sisters will hand each other
over to death. A father will turn in his children. Children will rise up against their parents and have them executed. 13 Everyone
will hate you because of my name. But whoever stands firm until the end will be saved.
14 "When you see the disgusting and destructive thing standing where it shouldn't
be (the reader should understand this), then
those in Judea must escape to the mountains. 15 Those on the roof shouldn't come
down or enter their houses to grab anything.
16 Those in the field shouldn't come back to
grab their clothes. 17 How terrible it will be at
that time for women who are pregnant and
for women who are nursing their children.
18 Pray that it doesn't happen in winter. 19 In
those days there will be great suffering such
as the world has never before seen and will
never again see. 20 If the Lord hadn't shortened that time, no one would be rescued.
But for the sake of the chosen ones, the ones
whom God chose, he has cut short the time.
21 "Then if someone says to you, 'Look,
here's the Christ,' or 'There he is,' don't believe it. 22 False christs and false prophets
will appear, and they will offer signs and
wonders in order to deceive, if possible,
those whom God has chosen. 23 But you,

[h] Ps 110:1 [i] Or two *lepta* (the smallest Greek copper coin, each worth 1/128 of a single day's pay), that is, a *kodrantes* (the smallest Roman coin, equal in value to two *lepta*)

watch out! I've told you everything ahead of time.

24“In those days, after the suffering of that time, the sun will become dark, and the moon won't give its light. 25The stars will fall from the sky, and the planets and other heavenly bodies will be shaken. 26Then they will see the Human One[j] coming in the clouds with great power and splendor. 27Then he will send the angels and gather together his chosen people from the four corners of the earth, from the end of the earth to the end of heaven.

A lesson from the fig tree

28“Learn this parable from the fig tree. After its branch becomes tender and it sprouts new leaves, you know that summer is near. 29In the same way, when you see these things happening, you know that he's near, at the door. 30I assure you that this generation won't pass away until all these things happen. 31Heaven and earth will pass away, but my words will certainly not pass away.

32“But nobody knows when that day or hour will come, not the angels in heaven and not the Son. Only the Father knows. 33Watch out! Stay alert! You don't know when the time is coming. 34It is as if someone took a trip, left the household behind, and put the servants in charge, giving each one a job to do, and told the doorkeeper to stay alert. 35Therefore, stay alert! You don't know when the head of the household will come, whether in the evening or at midnight, or when the rooster crows in the early morning or at daybreak. 36Don't let him show up when you weren't expecting and find you sleeping. 37What I say to you, I say to all: Stay alert!”

Preparation for burial

14 It was two days before Passover and the Festival of Unleavened Bread. The chief priests and legal experts through cunning tricks were searching for a way to arrest Jesus and kill him. 2But they agreed that it shouldn't happen during the festival; otherwise, there would be an uproar among the people.

3Jesus was at Bethany visiting the house of Simon, who had a skin disease. During dinner, a woman came in with a vase made of alabaster and containing very expensive perfume of pure nard. She broke open the vase and poured the perfume on his head. 4Some grew angry. They said to each other, “Why waste the perfume? 5This perfume could have been sold for almost a year's pay[k] and the money given to the poor.” And they scolded her.

6Jesus said, “Leave her alone. Why do you make trouble for her? She has done a good thing for me. 7You always have the poor with you; and whenever you want, you can do something good for them. But you won't always have me. 8She has done what she could. She has anointed my body ahead of time for burial. 9I tell you the truth that, wherever in the whole world the good news is announced, what she's done will also be told in memory of her.”

Passover meal

10Judas Iscariot, one of the Twelve, went to the chief priests to give Jesus up to them. 11When they heard it, they were delighted and promised to give him money. So he started looking for an opportunity to turn him in.

12On the first day of the Festival of Unleavened Bread, when the Passover lamb was sacrificed, the disciples said to Jesus, “Where do you want us to prepare for you to eat the Passover meal?”

13He sent two of his disciples and said to them, “Go into the city. A man carrying a water jar will meet you. Follow him. 14Wherever he enters, say to the owner of the house, ‘The teacher asks, “Where is my guest room where I can eat the Passover meal with my disciples?”’ 15He will show you a large room upstairs already furnished. Prepare for us there.” 16The disciples left, came into the city, found everything just as he had told them, and they prepared the Passover meal.

[j]Or *Son of Man* [k]Or *three hundred denaria*; a denarion was equivalent to a day's pay.

17 That evening, Jesus arrived with the Twelve. 18 During the meal, Jesus said, "I assure you that one of you will betray me—someone eating with me."

19 Deeply saddened, they asked him, one by one, "It's not me, is it?"

20 Jesus answered, "It's one of the Twelve, one who is dipping bread with me into this bowl. 21 The Human One[l] goes to his death just as it is written about him. But how terrible it is for that person who betrays the Human One![m] It would have been better for him if he had never been born."

22 While they were eating, Jesus took bread, blessed it, broke it, and gave it to them, and said, "Take; this is my body." 23 He took a cup, gave thanks, and gave it to them, and they all drank from it. 24 He said to them, "This is my blood of the covenant, which is poured out for many. 25 I assure you that I won't drink wine again until that day when I drink it in a new way in God's kingdom." 26 After singing songs of praise, they went out to the Mount of Olives.

Predictions about disciples leaving Jesus

27 Jesus said to them, "You will all falter in your faithfulness to me. It is written, *I will hit the shepherd, and the sheep will go off in all directions.*[n] 28 But after I'm raised up, I will go before you to Galilee."

29 Peter said to him, "Even if everyone else stumbles, I won't."

30 But Jesus said to him, "I assure you that on this very night, before the rooster crows twice, you will deny me three times."

31 But Peter insisted, "If I must die alongside you, I won't deny you." And they all said the same thing.

Jesus in prayer

32 Jesus and his disciples came to a place called Gethsemane. Jesus said to them, "Sit here while I pray." 33 He took Peter, James, and John along with him. He began to feel despair and was anxious. 34 He said to them, "I'm very sad. It's as if I'm dying. Stay here and keep alert." 35 Then he went a short distance farther and fell to the ground. He prayed that, if possible, he might be spared the time of suffering. 36 He said, "Abba, Father, for you all things are possible. Take this cup of suffering away from me. However—not what I want but what you want."

37 He came and found them sleeping. He said to Peter, "Simon, are you asleep? Couldn't you stay alert for one hour? 38 Stay alert and pray so that you won't give in to temptation. The spirit is eager, but the flesh is weak."

39 Again, he left them and prayed, repeating the same words. 40 And, again, when he came back, he found them sleeping, for they couldn't keep their eyes open, and they didn't know how to respond to him. 41 He came a third time and said to them, "Will you sleep and rest all night? That's enough! The time has come for the Human One[o] to be betrayed into the hands of sinners. 42 Get up! Let's go! Look, here comes my betrayer."

Arrest

43 Suddenly, while Jesus was still speaking, Judas, one of the Twelve, came with a mob carrying swords and clubs. They had been sent by the chief priests, legal experts, and elders. 44 His betrayer had given them a sign: "Arrest the man I kiss, and take him away under guard."

45 As soon as he got there, Judas said to Jesus, "Rabbi!" Then he kissed him. 46 Then they came and grabbed Jesus and arrested him.

47 One of the bystanders drew a sword and struck the high priest's slave and cut off his ear. 48 Jesus responded, "Have you come with swords and clubs to arrest me, like an outlaw? 49 Day after day, I was with you, teaching in the temple, but you didn't arrest me. But let the scriptures be fulfilled." 50 And all his disciples left him and ran away. 51 One young man, a disciple, was wearing nothing but a linen cloth. They grabbed him, 52 but he left the linen cloth behind and ran away naked.

[l] Or *Son of Man* [m] Or *Son of Man* [n] Zech 13:7 [o] Or *Son of Man*

A hearing before the Sanhedrin

53 They led Jesus away to the high priest, and all the chief priests, elders, and legal experts gathered. 54 Peter followed him from a distance, right into the high priest's courtyard. He was sitting with the guards, warming himself by the fire. 55 The chief priests and the whole Sanhedrin were looking for testimony against Jesus in order to put him to death, but they couldn't find any. 56 Many brought false testimony against him, but they contradicted each other. 57 Some stood to offer false witness against him, saying, 58 "We heard him saying, 'I will destroy this temple, constructed by humans, and within three days I will build another, one not made by humans.'" 59 But their testimonies didn't agree even on this point.

60 Then the high priest stood up in the middle of the gathering and examined Jesus. "Aren't you going to respond to the testimony these people have brought against you?" 61 But Jesus was silent and didn't answer. Again, the high priest asked, "Are you the Christ, the Son of the blessed one?"

62 Jesus said, "I am. And you will see the Human One[p] sitting on the right side of the Almighty[q] and coming on the heavenly clouds."

63 Then the high priest tore his clothes and said, "Why do we need any more witnesses? 64 You've heard his insult against God. What do you think?"

They all condemned him. "He deserves to die!"

65 Some began to spit on him. Some covered his face and hit him, saying, "Prophesy!" Then the guards took him and beat him.

Peter denies Jesus

66 Meanwhile, Peter was below in the courtyard. A woman, one of the high priest's servants, approached 67 and saw Peter warming himself by the fire. She stared at him and said, "You were also with the Nazarene, Jesus."

68 But he denied it, saying, "I don't know what you're talking about. I don't understand what you're saying." And he went outside into the outer courtyard. A rooster crowed.

69 The female servant saw him and began a second time to say to those standing around, "This man is one of them." 70 But he denied it again.

A short time later, those standing around again said to Peter, "You must be one of them, because you are also a Galilean."

71 But he cursed and swore, "I don't know this man you're talking about." 72 At that very moment, a rooster crowed a second time. Peter remembered what Jesus told him, "Before a rooster crows twice, you will deny me three times." And he broke down, sobbing.

Trial before Pilate

15 At daybreak, the chief priests—with the elders, legal experts, and the whole Sanhedrin—formed a plan. They bound Jesus, led him away, and turned him over to Pilate. 2 Pilate questioned him, "Are you the king of the Jews?"

Jesus replied, "That's what you say." 3 The chief priests were accusing him of many things.

4 Pilate asked him again, "Aren't you going to answer? What about all these accusations?" 5 But Jesus gave no more answers, so that Pilate marveled.

6 During the festival, Pilate released one prisoner to them, whomever they requested. 7 A man named Barabbas was locked up with the rebels who had committed murder during an uprising. 8 The crowd pushed forward and asked Pilate to release someone, as he regularly did. 9 Pilate answered them, "Do you want me to release to you the king of the Jews?" 10 He knew that the chief priests had handed him over because of jealousy. 11 But the chief priests stirred up the crowd to have him release Barabbas to them instead. 12 Pilate replied, "Then what do you want me to do with the one you call king of the Jews?"

13 They shouted back, "Crucify him!"

[p] Or *Son of Man* [q] Or *the Power*

14 Pilate said to them, "Why? What wrong has he done?"

They shouted even louder, "Crucify him!"

15 Pilate wanted to satisfy the crowd, so he released Barabbas to them. He had Jesus whipped, then handed him over to be crucified.

Jesus is tortured and killed

16 The soldiers led Jesus away into the courtyard of the palace known as the governor's headquarters,[r] and they called together the whole company of soldiers.[s] 17 They dressed him up in a purple robe and twisted together a crown of thorns and put it on him. 18 They saluted him, "Hey! King of the Jews!" 19 Again and again, they struck his head with a stick. They spit on him and knelt before him to honor him. 20 When they finished mocking him, they stripped him of the purple robe and put his own clothes back on him. Then they led him out to crucify him.

21 Simon, a man from Cyrene, Alexander and Rufus' father, was coming in from the countryside. They forced him to carry his cross.

22 They brought Jesus to the place called Golgotha, which means Skull Place. 23 They tried to give him wine mixed with myrrh, but he didn't take it. 24 They crucified him. They divided up his clothes, drawing lots for them to determine who would take what. 25 It was nine in the morning when they crucified him. 26 The notice of the formal charge against him was written, "The king of the Jews." 27 They crucified two outlaws with him, one on his right and one on his left.[t]

29 People walking by insulted him, shaking their heads and saying, "Ha! So you were going to destroy the temple and rebuild it in three days, were you? 30 Save yourself and come down from that cross!"

31 In the same way, the chief priests were making fun of him among themselves, together with the legal experts. "He saved others," they said, "but he can't save himself. 32 Let the Christ, the king of Israel, come down from the cross. Then we'll see and believe." Even those who had been crucified with Jesus insulted him.

33 From noon until three in the afternoon the whole earth was dark. 34 At three, Jesus cried out with a loud shout, *"Eloi, eloi, lama sabachthani,"* which means, "My God, my God, why have you left me?"

35 After hearing him, some standing there said, "Look! He's calling Elijah!" 36 Someone ran, filled a sponge with sour wine, and put it on a pole. He offered it to Jesus to drink, saying, "Let's see if Elijah will come to take him down." 37 But Jesus let out a loud cry and died.

38 The curtain of the sanctuary was torn in two from top to bottom. 39 When the centurion, who stood facing Jesus, saw how he died, he said, "This man was certainly God's Son."

40 Some women were watching from a distance, including Mary Magdalene and Mary the mother of James (the younger one) and Joses, and Salome. 41 When Jesus was in Galilee, these women had followed and supported him, along with many other women who had come to Jerusalem with him.

Jesus' burial

42 Since it was late in the afternoon on Preparation Day, just before the Sabbath, 43 Joseph from Arimathea dared to approach Pilate and ask for Jesus' body. (Joseph was a prominent council member who also eagerly anticipated the coming of God's kingdom.) 44 Pilate wondered if Jesus was already dead. He called the centurion and asked him whether Jesus had already died. 45 When he learned from the centurion that Jesus was dead, Pilate gave the dead body to Joseph. 46 He bought a linen cloth, took Jesus down from the cross, wrapped him in the cloth, and laid him in a tomb that had been carved out of rock. He rolled a stone against the entrance to the tomb. 47 Mary Magdalene and Mary the mother of Joses saw where he was buried.

[r] Or *praetorium* [s] Or *cohort* (approximately six hundred soldiers) [t] 15:28 is omitted in most critical editions of the Gk New Testament *The scripture was fulfilled, which says, He was numbered among criminals.*

Empty tomb

16 When the Sabbath was over, Mary
Magdalene, Mary the mother of
James, and Salome bought spices so that
they could go and anoint Jesus' dead body.
2 Very early on the first day of the week,
just after sunrise, they came to the tomb.
3 They were saying to each other, "Who's
going to roll the stone away from the entrance for us?" 4 When they looked up, they
saw that the stone had been rolled away.
(And it was a very large stone!) 5 Going
into the tomb, they saw a young man in
a white robe seated on the right side; and
they were startled. 6 But he said to them,
"Don't be alarmed! You are looking for
Jesus of Nazareth, who was crucified.[u] He
has been raised. He isn't here. Look, here's
the place where they laid him. 7 Go, tell his
disciples, especially Peter, that he is going
ahead of you into Galilee. You will see him
there, just as he told you." 8 Overcome
with terror and dread, they fled from the
tomb. They said nothing to anyone, because they were afraid.[v]

Endings Added Later

[9 They promptly reported all of the
young man's instructions to those who
were with Peter. Afterward, through
the work of his disciples, Jesus sent
out, from the east to the west, the sacred and undying message of eternal
salvation. Amen.]
[[9 After Jesus rose up early on the first
day of the week, he appeared first to
Mary Magdalene, from whom he had
cast out seven demons. 10 She went and
reported to the ones who had been with
him, who were mourning and weeping.
11 But even after they heard the news,
they didn't believe that Jesus was alive
and that Mary had seen him.
12 After that he appeared in a different
form to two of them who were walking along in the countryside. 13 When
they returned, they reported it to the
others, but they didn't believe them.
14 Finally he appeared to the eleven
while they were eating. Jesus criticized their unbelief and stubbornness because they didn't believe those
who saw him after he was raised up.
15 He said to them, "Go into the whole
world and proclaim the good news to
every creature. 16 Whoever believes
and is baptized will be saved, but
whoever doesn't believe will be condemned. 17 These signs will be associated with those who believe: they will
throw out demons in my name. They
will speak in new languages. 18 They
will pick up snakes with their hands.
If they drink anything poisonous, it
will not hurt them. They will place
their hands on the sick, and they will
get well."
19 After the Lord Jesus spoke to them,
he was lifted up into heaven and sat
down on the right side of God. 20 But
they went out and proclaimed the
message everywhere. The Lord worked
with them, confirming the word by the
signs associated with them.]]

[u] Or *the Crucified One* [v] In most critical editions of the Gk New Testament, the Gospel of Mark ends at 16:8.

LUKE

Luke's purpose

1 Many people have already applied themselves to the task of compiling an account
of the events that have been fulfilled among
us. [2]They used what the original eyewit-
nesses and servants of the word handed
down to us. [3]Now, after having investigated
everything carefully from the beginning, I
have also decided to write a carefully ordered
account for you, most honorable Theophilus.
[4]I want you to have confidence in the sound-
ness of the instruction you have received.

John the Baptist's birth foretold

[5]During the rule of King Herod of Judea
there was a priest named Zechariah who
belonged to the priestly division of Abijah. His wife Elizabeth was a descendant
of Aaron. [6]They were both righteous before
God, blameless in their observance of all
the Lord's commandments and regulations.
[7]They had no children because Elizabeth
was unable to become pregnant and they
both were very old. [8]One day Zechariah
was serving as a priest before God because
his priestly division was on duty. [9]Follow-
ing the customs of priestly service, he was
chosen by lottery to go into the Lord's sanctuary and burn incense. [10]All the people
who gathered to worship were praying outside during this hour of incense offering.
[11]An angel from the Lord appeared to him,
standing to the right of the altar of incense.
[12]When Zechariah saw the angel, he was
startled and overcome with fear.

[13]The angel said, "Don't be afraid, Zechariah. Your prayers have been heard. Your
wife Elizabeth will give birth to your son
and you must name him John. [14]He will be a
joy and delight to you, and many people will
rejoice at his birth, [15]for he will be great in
the Lord's eyes. He must not drink wine and
liquor. He will be filled with the Holy Spirit
even before his birth. [16]He will bring many
Israelites back to the Lord their God. [17]He
will go forth before the Lord, equipped with
the spirit and power of Elijah. He will turn
the hearts of fathers[a] back to their children,
and he will turn the disobedient to righteous
patterns of thinking. He will make ready a
people prepared for the Lord."

[18]Zechariah said to the angel, "How can I
be sure of this? My wife and I are very old."

[19]The angel replied, "I am Gabriel. I stand
in God's presence. I was sent to speak to you
and to bring this good news to you. [20]Know
this: What I have spoken will come true at
the proper time. But because you didn't
believe, you will remain silent, unable to
speak until the day when these things
happen."

[21]Meanwhile, the people were waiting
for Zechariah, and they wondered why he
was in the sanctuary for such a long time.
[22]When he came out, he was unable to
speak to them. They realized he had seen
a vision in the temple, for he gestured to
them and couldn't speak. [23]When he completed the days of his priestly service, he
returned home. [24]Afterward, his wife Elizabeth became pregnant. She kept to herself
for five months, saying, [25]"This is the Lord's
doing. He has shown his favor to me by removing my disgrace among other people."

Jesus' birth foretold

[26]When Elizabeth was six months pregnant, God sent the angel Gabriel to Nazareth, a city in Galilee, [27]to a virgin who was
engaged to a man named Joseph, a descendant of David's house. The virgin's name
was Mary. [28]When the angel came to her,
he said, "Rejoice, favored one! The Lord is
with you!" [29]She was confused by these
words and wondered what kind of greeting
this might be. [30]The angel said, "Don't be
afraid, Mary. God is honoring you. [31]Look!
You will conceive and give birth to a son,
and you will name him Jesus. [32]He will be
great and he will be called the Son of the
Most High. The Lord God will give him the
throne of David his father. [33]He will rule
over Jacob's house forever, and there will
be no end to his kingdom."

[a]Or *parents*

34 Then Mary said to the angel, "How will
this happen since I haven't had sexual relations with a man?"

35 The angel replied, "The Holy Spirit will
come over you and the power of the Most
High will overshadow you. Therefore, the
one who is to be born will be holy. He will
be called God's Son. 36 Look, even in her old
age, your relative Elizabeth has conceived a
son. This woman who was labeled 'unable
to conceive' is now six months pregnant.
37 Nothing is impossible for God."

38 Then Mary said, "I am the Lord's servant. Let it be with me just as you have
said." Then the angel left her.

Mary visits Elizabeth

39 Mary got up and hurried to a city in
the Judean highlands. 40 She entered Zechariah's home and greeted Elizabeth. 41 When
Elizabeth heard Mary's greeting, the child
leaped in her womb, and Elizabeth was filled
with the Holy Spirit. 42 With a loud voice she
blurted out, "God has blessed you above all
women, and he has blessed the child you
carry. 43 Why do I have this honor, that the
mother of my Lord should come to me? 44 As
soon as I heard your greeting, the baby in
my womb jumped for joy. 45 Happy is she
who believed that the Lord would fulfill the
promises he made to her."

Mary praises God

46 Mary said,
"With all my heart I glorify the Lord!
47 In the depths of who I am
I rejoice in God my savior.
48 He has looked with favor
on the low status of his servant.
Look! From now on, everyone
will consider me highly favored
49 because the mighty one
has done great things for me.
Holy is his name.
50 He shows mercy to everyone,
from one generation to the next,
who honors him as God.
51 He has shown strength with his arm.
He has scattered those with arrogant
thoughts and proud inclinations.
52 He has pulled the powerful
down from their thrones
and lifted up the lowly.
53 He has filled the hungry
with good things
and sent the rich away empty-handed.
54 He has come to the aid
of his servant Israel,
remembering his mercy,
55 just as he promised to our ancestors,
to Abraham and to Abraham's
descendants forever."

56 Mary stayed with Elizabeth about three
months, and then returned to her home.

57 When the time came for Elizabeth to
have her child, she gave birth to a boy. 58 Her
neighbors and relatives celebrated with her
because they had heard that the Lord had
shown her great mercy. 59 On the eighth day,
it came time to circumcise the child. They
wanted to name him Zechariah because that
was his father's name. 60 But his mother replied, "No, his name will be John."

61 They said to her, "None of your relatives have that name." 62 Then they began
gesturing to his father to see what he
wanted to call him.

63 After asking for a tablet, he surprised
everyone by writing, "His name is John."
64 At that moment, Zechariah was able to
speak again, and he began praising God.

65 All their neighbors were filled with
awe, and everyone throughout the Judean
highlands talked about what had happened. 66 All who heard about this considered it carefully. They said, "What then will
this child be?" Indeed, the Lord's power was
with him.

Zechariah's prophecy

67 John's father Zechariah was filled with
the Holy Spirit and prophesied,
68 "Bless the Lord God of Israel
because he has come to help
and has delivered his people.
69 He has raised up a mighty savior for us
in his servant David's house,
70 just as he said through the mouths
of his holy prophets long ago.
71 He has brought salvation
from our enemies
and from the power
of all those who hate us.

72 He has shown the mercy promised
to our ancestors,
and remembered his holy covenant,
73 the solemn pledge he made
to our ancestor Abraham.
He has granted 74 that we would be rescued
from the power of our enemies
so that we could serve him without fear,
75 in holiness and righteousness
in God's eyes,
for as long as we live.
76 You, child, will be called a prophet
of the Most High,
for you will go before the Lord
to prepare his way.
77 You will tell his people how to be saved
through the forgiveness of their sins.
78 Because of our God's deep compassion,
the dawn from heaven
will break upon us,
79 to give light to those
who are sitting in darkness
and in the shadow of death,
to guide us on the path of peace."
80 The child grew up, becoming strong in
character. He was in the wilderness until he
began his public ministry to Israel.

Jesus' birth

2 In those days Caesar Augustus declared
that everyone throughout the empire
should be enrolled in the tax lists. 2 This first
enrollment occurred when Quirinius governed Syria. 3 Everyone went to their own
cities to be enrolled. 4 Since Joseph belonged
to David's house and family line, he went up
from the city of Nazareth in Galilee to David's
city, called Bethlehem, in Judea. 5 He went
to be enrolled together with Mary, who was
promised to him in marriage and who was
pregnant. 6 While they were there, the time
came for Mary to have her baby. 7 She gave
birth to her firstborn child, a son, wrapped
him snugly, and laid him in a manger, because
there was no place for them in the guestroom.

Announcement to shepherds

8 Nearby shepherds were living in the
fields, guarding their sheep at night. 9 The
Lord's angel stood before them, the Lord's
glory shone around them, and they were
terrified.
10 The angel said, "Don't be afraid! Look!
I bring good news to you—wonderful, joyous news for all people. 11 Your savior is
born today in David's city. He is Christ the
Lord. 12 This is a sign for you: you will find
a newborn baby wrapped snugly and lying
in a manger." 13 Suddenly a great assembly
of the heavenly forces was with the angel
praising God. They said, 14 "Glory to God in
heaven, and on earth peace among those
whom he favors."
15 When the angels returned to heaven,
the shepherds said to each other, "Let's
go right now to Bethlehem and see what's
happened. Let's confirm what the Lord has
revealed to us." 16 They went quickly and
found Mary and Joseph, and the baby lying
in the manger. 17 When they saw this, they
reported what they had been told about this
child. 18 Everyone who heard it was amazed
at what the shepherds told them. 19 Mary
committed these things to memory and
considered them carefully. 20 The shepherds
returned home, glorifying and praising God
for all they had heard and seen. Everything
happened just as they had been told.

Jesus' circumcision, naming, and temple presentation

21 When eight days had passed, Jesus'
parents circumcised him and gave him the
name Jesus. This was the name given to
him by the angel before he was conceived.
22 When the time came for their ritual
cleansing, in accordance with the Law from
Moses, they brought Jesus up to Jerusalem
to present him to the Lord. (23 It's written
in the Law of the Lord, "Every firstborn
male will be dedicated to the Lord.") 24 They
offered a sacrifice in keeping with what's
stated in the Law of the Lord, *A pair of turtledoves or two young pigeons*.[b]

Simeon's response to Jesus

25 A man named Simeon was in Jerusalem. He was righteous and devout. He

[b] Lev 12:8; 5:11 LXX

eagerly anticipated the restoration of Israel, and the Holy Spirit rested on him. 26 The Holy Spirit revealed to him that he wouldn't die before he had seen the Lord's Christ. 27 Led by the Spirit, he went into the temple area. Meanwhile, Jesus' parents brought the child to the temple so that they could do what was customary under the Law. 28 Simeon took Jesus in his arms and praised God. He said,

29 "Now, master, let your servant go in
peace according to your word,
30 because my eyes have seen your
salvation.
31 You prepared this salvation in the
presence of all peoples.
32 It's a light for revelation to the Gentiles
and a glory for your people Israel."

33 His father and mother were amazed by what was said about him. 34 Simeon blessed them and said to Mary his mother, "This boy is assigned to be the cause of the falling and rising of many in Israel and to be a sign that generates opposition 35 so that the inner thoughts of many will be revealed. And a sword will pierce your innermost being too."

Anna's response to Jesus

36 There was also a prophet, Anna the daughter of Phanuel, who belonged to the tribe of Asher. She was very old. After she married, she lived with her husband for seven years. 37 She was now an 84-year-old widow. She never left the temple area but worshipped God with fasting and prayer night and day. 38 She approached at that very moment and began to praise God and to speak about Jesus to everyone who was looking forward to the redemption of Jerusalem.

Jesus as a child in Nazareth

39 When Mary and Joseph had completed everything required by the Law of the Lord, they returned to their hometown, Nazareth in Galilee. 40 The child grew up and became strong. He was filled with wisdom, and God's favor was on him.

Jesus in the temple at Passover

41 Each year his parents went to Jerusalem for the Passover Festival. 42 When he was 12 years old, they went up to Jerusalem according to their custom. 43 After the festival was over, they were returning home, but the boy Jesus stayed behind in Jerusalem. His parents didn't know it. 44 Supposing that he was among their band of travelers, they journeyed on for a full day while looking for him among their family and friends. 45 When they didn't find Jesus, they returned to Jerusalem to look for him. 46 After three days they found him in the temple. He was sitting among the teachers, listening to them and putting questions to them. 47 Everyone who heard him was amazed by his understanding and his answers. 48 When his parents saw him, they were shocked.

His mother said, "Child, why have you treated us like this? Listen! Your father and I have been worried. We've been looking for you!"

49 Jesus replied, "Why were you looking for me? Didn't you know that it was necessary for me to be in my Father's house?" 50 But they didn't understand what he said to them.

51 Jesus went down to Nazareth with them and was obedient to them. His mother cherished every word in her heart. 52 Jesus matured in wisdom and years, and in favor with God and with people.

John the Baptist's message

3 In the fifteenth year of the rule of the emperor Tiberius—when Pontius Pilate was governor over Judea and Herod was ruler[c] over Galilee, his brother Philip was ruler[d] over Ituraea and Trachonitis, and Lysanias was ruler[e] over Abilene, 2 during the high priesthood of Annas and Caiaphas—God's word came to John son of Zechariah in the wilderness. 3 John went throughout the region of the Jordan River, calling for people to be baptized to show that they were changing their hearts and lives and wanted God to forgive their sins.

[c] Or *tetrarch* [d] Or *tetrarch* [e] Or *tetrarch*

4 This is just as it was written in the scroll of
the words of Isaiah the prophet,
A voice crying out in the wilderness:
"Prepare the way for the Lord;
make his paths straight.
5 *Every valley will be filled,*
and every mountain and hill
will be leveled.
The crooked will be made straight
and the rough places made smooth.
6 *All humanity will see God's salvation."*[f]
7 Then John said to the crowds who came
to be baptized by him, "You children of
snakes! Who warned you to escape from
the angry judgment that is coming soon?
8 Produce fruit that shows you have changed
your hearts and lives. And don't even think
about saying to yourselves, Abraham is our
father. I tell you that God is able to raise up
Abraham's children from these stones. 9 The
ax is already at the root of the trees. Therefore, every tree that doesn't produce good
fruit will be chopped down and tossed into
the fire."
10 The crowds asked him, "What then
should we do?"
11 He answered, "Whoever has two shirts
must share with the one who has none, and
whoever has food must do the same."
12 Even tax collectors came to be baptized. They said to him, "Teacher, what
should we do?"
13 He replied, "Collect no more than you
are authorized to collect."
14 Soldiers asked, "What about us? What
should we do?"
He answered, "Don't cheat or harass anyone, and be satisfied with your pay."

Responses to John

15 The people were filled with expectation, and everyone wondered whether
John might be the Christ. 16 John replied
to them all, "I baptize you with water, but
the one who is more powerful than me is
coming. I'm not worthy to loosen the strap
of his sandals. He will baptize you with the
Holy Spirit and fire. 17 The shovel he uses
to sift the wheat from the husks is in his
hands. He will clean out his threshing area
and bring the wheat into his barn. But he
will burn the husks with a fire that can't be
put out." 18 With many other words John
appealed to them, proclaiming good news
to the people.
19 But Herod the ruler had been criticized harshly by John because of Herodias,
Herod's brother's wife, and because of all
the evil he had done. 20 He added this to the
list of his evil deeds: he locked John up in
prison.

Jesus' baptism

21 When everyone was being baptized,
Jesus also was baptized. While he was pray-
ing, heaven was opened 22 and the Holy
Spirit came down on him in bodily form like
a dove. And there was a voice from heaven:
"You are my Son, whom I dearly love; in you
I find happiness."

Jesus' genealogy

23 Jesus was about 30 years old when he
began his ministry. People supposed that
he was the son of Joseph son of Heli 24 son
of Matthat son of Levi son of Melchi son of
Jannai son of Joseph 25 son of Mattathias
son of Amos son of Nahum son of Esli son
of Naggai 26 son of Maath son of Mattathias
son of Semein son of Josech son of Joda
27 son of Joanan son of Rhesa son of Zerubbabel son of Shealtiel son of Neri 28 son of
Melchi son of Addi son of Cosam son of
Elmadam son of Er 29 son of Joshua son
of Eliezer son of Jorim son of Matthat son
of Levi 30 son of Simeon son of Judah son of
Joseph son of Jonam son of Eliakim 31 son
of Melea son of Menna son of Mattatha
son of Nathan son of David 32 son of Jesse
son of Obed son of Boaz son of Sala son
of Nahshon 33 son of Amminadab son of
Admin son of Arni son of Hezron son of
Perez son of Judah 34 son of Jacob son
of Isaac son of Abraham son of Terah son
of Nahor 35 son of Serug son of Reu son of
Peleg son of Eber son of Shelah 36 son of
Cainan son of Arphaxad son of Shem son of
Noah son of Lamech 37 son of Methuselah

[f] Isa 40:3-5

son of Enoch son of Jared son of Mahalalel
son of Cainan 38 son of Enos son of Seth son
of Adam son of God.

Jesus' temptation

4 Jesus returned from the Jordan River
full of the Holy Spirit, and was led by the
Spirit into the wilderness. 2 There he was
tempted for forty days by the devil. He ate
nothing during those days and afterward
Jesus was starving. 3 The devil said to him,
"Since you are God's Son, command this
stone to become a loaf of bread."

4 Jesus replied, "It's written, *People won't
live only by bread*."[g]

5 Next the devil led him to a high place
and showed him in a single instant all the
kingdoms of the world. 6 The devil said, "I
will give you this whole domain and the
glory of all these kingdoms. It's been entrusted to me and I can give it to anyone I
want. 7 Therefore, if you will worship me, it
will all be yours."

8 Jesus answered, "It's written, *You will
worship the Lord your God and serve only him*."[h]

9 The devil brought him into Jerusalem
and stood him at the highest point of the
temple. He said to him, "Since you are God's
Son, throw yourself down from here; 10 for
it's written: *He will command his angels
concerning you, to protect you* 11 and *they will
take you up in their hands so that you won't
hit your foot on a stone*."[i]

12 Jesus answered, "It's been said, *Don't
test the Lord your God*."[j] 13 After finishing
every temptation, the devil departed from
him until the next opportunity.

Jesus announces good news to the poor

14 Jesus returned in the power of the
Spirit to Galilee, and news about him
spread throughout the whole countryside.
15 He taught in their synagogues and was
praised by everyone.

16 Jesus went to Nazareth, where he had
been raised. On the Sabbath he went to the
synagogue as he normally did and stood up
to read. 17 The synagogue assistant gave him
the scroll from the prophet Isaiah. He un-
rolled the scroll and found the place where
it was written:

18 *The Spirit of the Lord is upon me,*
because the Lord has anointed me.
He has sent me to preach good news
to the poor,
to proclaim release to the prisoners
and recovery of sight to the blind,
to liberate the oppressed,
19 *and to proclaim the year of the Lord's favor.*[k]

20 He rolled up the scroll, gave it back
to the synagogue assistant, and sat down.
Every eye in the synagogue was fixed on
him. 21 He began to explain to them, "Today,
this scripture has been fulfilled just as you
heard it."

22 Everyone was raving about Jesus, so
impressed were they by the gracious words
flowing from his lips. They said, "This is Joseph's son, isn't it?"

23 Then Jesus said to them, "Undoubtedly,
you will quote this saying to me: 'Doctor,
heal yourself. Do here in your hometown
what we've heard you did in Capernaum.' "
24 He said, "I assure you that no prophet is
welcome in the prophet's hometown. 25 And
I can assure you that there were many widows in Israel during Elijah's time, when it
didn't rain for three and a half years and
there was a great food shortage in the land.
26 Yet Elijah was sent to none of them but
only to a widow in the city of Zarephath in
the region of Sidon. 27 There were also many
persons with skin diseases in Israel during
the time of the prophet Elisha, but none of
them were cleansed. Instead, Naaman the
Syrian was cleansed."

28 When they heard this, everyone in the
synagogue was filled with anger. 29 They rose
up and ran him out of town. They led him to
the crest of the hill on which their town had
been built so that they could throw him off
the cliff. 30 But he passed through the crowd
and went on his way.

Jesus in Capernaum

31 Jesus went down to the city of Capernaum in Galilee and taught the people each
Sabbath. 32 They were amazed by his teach-

[g] Deut 8:3 [h] Deut 6:13 [i] Ps 91:11-12 [j] Deut 6:16 [k] Isa 61:1-2; 58:6

ing because he delivered his message with
authority.
33A man in the synagogue had the spirit
of an unclean demon. He screamed, 34"Hey!
What have you to do with us, Jesus of
Nazareth? Have you come to destroy us?
I know who you are. You are the holy one
from God."
35"Silence!" Jesus said, speaking harshly
to the demon. "Come out of him!" The demon
threw the man down before them, then came
out of him without harming him.
36They were all shaken and said to each
other, "What kind of word is this, that he
can command unclean spirits with authority and power, and they leave?" 37Reports
about him spread everywhere in the surrounding region.
38After leaving the synagogue, Jesus went
home with Simon. Simon's mother-in-law
was sick with a high fever, and the family
asked Jesus to help her. 39He bent over her
and spoke harshly to the fever, and it left her.
She got up at once and served them.
40When the sun was setting, everyone
brought to Jesus relatives and acquaintances with all kinds of diseases. Placing
his hands on each of them, he healed them.
41Demons also came out of many people.
They screamed, "You are God's Son." But he
spoke harshly to them and wouldn't allow
them to speak because they recognized
that he was the Christ. 42When daybreak
arrived, Jesus went to a deserted place. The
crowds were looking for him. When they
found him, they tried to keep him from
leaving them. 43But he said to them, "I
must preach the good news of God's kingdom in other cities too, for this is why I was
sent." 44So he continued preaching in the
Judean synagogues.

Jesus calls disciples

5 One day Jesus was standing beside Lake
Gennesaret when the crowd pressed in
around him to hear God's word. 2Jesus saw
two boats sitting by the lake. The fishermen had gone ashore and were washing
their nets. 3Jesus boarded one of the boats,
the one that belonged to Simon, then
asked him to row out a little distance from
the shore. Jesus sat down and taught the
crowds from the boat. 4When he finished
speaking to the crowds, he said to Simon,
"Row out farther, into the deep water, and
drop your nets for a catch."
5Simon replied, "Master, we've worked
hard all night and caught nothing. But because you say so, I'll drop the nets."
6So they dropped the nets and their
catch was so huge that their nets were
splitting. 7They signaled for their partners
in the other boat to come and help them.
They filled both boats so full that they were
about to sink. 8When Simon Peter saw
the catch, he fell at Jesus' knees and said,
"Leave me, Lord, for I'm a sinner!" 9Peter
and those with him were overcome with
amazement because of the number of fish
they caught. 10James and John, Zebedee's
sons, were Simon's partners and they were
amazed too.
Jesus said to Simon, "Don't be afraid.
From now on, you will be fishing for people." 11As soon as they brought the boats to
the shore, they left everything and followed
Jesus.

A man with a skin disease

12Jesus was in one of the towns where
there was also a man covered with a skin
disease. When he saw Jesus, he fell on his
face and begged, "Lord, if you want, you can
make me clean."
13Jesus reached out his hand, touched
him, and said, "I do want to. Be clean." Instantly, the skin disease left him. 14Jesus
ordered him not to tell anyone. "Instead,"
Jesus said, "go and show yourself to the
priest and make an offering for your cleansing, as Moses instructed. This will be a
testimony to them." 15News of him spread
even more and huge crowds gathered to
listen and to be healed from their illnesses.
16But Jesus would withdraw to deserted
places for prayer.

Jesus heals a paralyzed man

17One day when Jesus was teaching,
Pharisees and legal experts were sitting
nearby. They had come from every village
in Galilee and Judea, and from Jerusalem.

Now the power of the Lord was with Jesus to heal. [18]Some men were bringing a man who was paralyzed, lying on a cot. They wanted to carry him in and place him before Jesus, [19]but they couldn't reach him because of the crowd. So they took him up on the roof and lowered him—cot and all—through the roof tiles into the crowded room in front of Jesus. [20]When Jesus saw their faith, he said, "Friend, your sins are forgiven."

[21]The legal experts and Pharisees began to mutter among themselves, "Who is this who insults God? Only God can forgive sins!"

[22]Jesus recognized what they were discussing and responded, "Why do you fill your minds with these questions? [23]Which is easier—to say, 'Your sins are forgiven,' or to say, 'Get up and walk'? [24]But so that you will know that the Human One[l] has authority on the earth to forgive sins"—Jesus now spoke to the man who was paralyzed, "I say to you, get up, take your cot, and go home." [25]Right away, the man stood before them, picked up his cot, and went home, praising God.

[26]All the people were beside themselves with wonder. Filled with awe, they glorified God, saying, "We've seen unimaginable things today."

Jesus calls a tax collector

[27]Afterward, Jesus went out and saw a tax collector named Levi sitting at a kiosk for collecting taxes. Jesus said to him, "Follow me."

[28]Levi got up, left everything behind, and followed him. [29]Then Levi threw a great banquet for Jesus in his home. A large number of tax collectors and others sat down to eat with them. [30]The Pharisees and their legal experts grumbled against his disciples. They said, "Why do you eat and drink with tax collectors and sinners?"

[31]Jesus answered, "Healthy people don't need a doctor, but sick people do. [32]I didn't come to call righteous people but sinners to change their hearts and lives."

The old and the new

[33]Some people said to Jesus, "The disciples of John fast often and pray frequently. The disciples of the Pharisees do the same, but your disciples are always eating and drinking."

[34]Jesus replied, "You can't make the wedding guests fast while the groom is with them, can you? [35]The days will come when the groom will be taken from them, and then they will fast."

[36]Then he told them a parable. "No one tears a patch from a new garment to patch an old garment. Otherwise, the new garment would be ruined, and the new patch wouldn't match the old garment. [37]Nobody pours new wine into old wineskins. If they did, the new wine would burst the wineskins, the wine would spill, and the wineskins would be ruined. [38]Instead, new wine must be put into new wineskins. [39]No one who drinks a well-aged wine wants new wine, but says, 'The well-aged wine is better.'"

Activities on the Sabbath

6 One Sabbath, as Jesus was going through the wheat fields, his disciples were picking the heads of wheat, rubbing them in their hands, and eating them. [2]Some Pharisees said, "Why are you breaking the Sabbath law?"

[3]Jesus replied, "Haven't you read what David and his companions did when they were hungry? [4]He broke the Law by going into God's house and eating the bread of the presence, which only the priests can eat. He also gave some of the bread to his companions." [5]Then he said to them, "The Human One[m] is Lord of the Sabbath."

[6]On another Sabbath, Jesus entered a synagogue to teach. A man was there whose right hand was withered. [7]The legal experts and the Pharisees were watching him closely to see if he would heal on the Sabbath. They were looking for a reason to bring charges against him. [8]Jesus knew their thoughts, so he said to the man with the withered hand, "Get up and stand in front of everyone." He got up and stood there. [9]Jesus said to the

[l]Or *Son of Man* [m]Or *Son of Man*

legal experts and Pharisees, "Here's a question for you: Is it legal on the Sabbath to do good or to do evil, to save life or to destroy it?" [10]Looking around at them all, he said to the man, "Stretch out your hand." So he did and his hand was made healthy. [11]They were furious and began talking with each other about what to do to Jesus.

Jesus chooses apostles

[12]During that time, Jesus went out to the mountain to pray, and he prayed to God all night long. [13]At daybreak, he called together his disciples. He chose twelve of them whom he called apostles: [14]Simon, whom he named Peter; his brother Andrew; James; John; Philip; Bartholomew; [15]Matthew; Thomas; James the son of Alphaeus; Simon, who was called a zealot; [16]Judas the son of James; and Judas Iscariot, who became a traitor.

Jesus' popularity increases

[17]Jesus came down from the mountain with them and stood on a large area of level ground. A great company of his disciples and a huge crowd of people from all around Judea and Jerusalem and the area around Tyre and Sidon joined him there. [18]They came to hear him and to be healed from their diseases, and those bothered by unclean spirits were healed. [19]The whole crowd wanted to touch him, because power was going out from him and he was healing everyone.

Happy people and doomed people

[20]Jesus raised his eyes to his disciples and said:

"Happy are you who are poor,
because God's kingdom is yours.
[21]Happy are you who hunger now,
because you will be satisfied.
Happy are you who weep now,
because you will laugh.

[22]Happy are you when people hate you, reject you, insult you, and condemn your name as evil because of the Human One.[n] [23]Rejoice when that happens! Leap for joy because you have a great reward in heaven. Their ancestors did the same things to the prophets.

[24]But how terrible for you who are rich,
because you have already received your comfort.
[25]How terrible for you who have plenty now,
because you will be hungry.
How terrible for you who laugh now,
because you will mourn and weep.
[26]How terrible for you when all speak well of you.
Their ancestors did the same things to the false prophets.

Behaving as God's children

[27]"But I say to you who are willing to hear: Love your enemies. Do good to those who hate you. [28]Bless those who curse you. Pray for those who mistreat you. [29]If someone slaps you on the cheek, offer the other one as well. If someone takes your coat, don't withhold your shirt either. [30]Give to everyone who asks and don't demand your things back from those who take them. [31]Treat people in the same way that you want them to treat you.

[32]"If you love those who love you, why should you be commended? Even sinners love those who love them. [33]If you do good to those who do good to you, why should you be commended? Even sinners do that. [34]If you lend to those from whom you expect repayment, why should you be commended? Even sinners lend to sinners expecting to be paid back in full. [35]Instead, love your enemies, do good, and lend expecting nothing in return. If you do, you will have a great reward. You will be acting the way children of the Most High act, for he is kind to ungrateful and wicked people. [36]Be compassionate just as your Father is compassionate.

[37]"Don't judge, and you won't be judged. Don't condemn, and you won't be condemned. Forgive, and you will be forgiven. [38]Give, and it will be given to you. A good portion—packed down, firmly shaken, and overflowing—will fall into your lap. The

[n]*Or Son of Man*

portion you give will determine the portion
you receive in return."

Avoiding self-deception

39 Jesus also told them a riddle. "A
blind person can't lead another blind person, right? Won't they both fall into a
ditch? 40 Disciples aren't greater than their
teacher, but whoever is fully prepared will
be like their teacher. 41 Why do you see the
splinter in your brother's or sister's eye
but don't notice the log in your own eye?
42 How can you say to your brother or sister,
'Brother, Sister, let me take the splinter out
of your eye,' when you don't see the log in
your own eye? You deceive yourselves! First
take the log out of your eye, and then you
will see clearly to take the splinter out of
your brother's or sister's eye.
43 "A good tree doesn't produce bad fruit,
nor does a bad tree produce good fruit.
44 Each tree is known by its own fruit. People
don't gather figs from thorny plants, nor do
they pick grapes from prickly bushes. 45 A
good person produces good from the good
treasury of the inner self, while an evil person produces evil from the evil treasury of
the inner self. The inner self overflows with
words that are spoken.
46 "Why do you call me 'Lord, Lord' and
don't do what I say? 47 I'll show what it's
like when someone comes to me, hears my
words, and puts them into practice. 48 It's
like a person building a house by digging
deep and laying the foundation on bedrock. When the flood came, the rising water
smashed against that house, but the water
couldn't shake the house because it was well
built. 49 But those who don't put into practice
what they hear are like a person who built a
house without a foundation. The floodwater
smashed against it and it collapsed instantly.
It was completely destroyed."

A servant is healed

7 After Jesus finished presenting all his
words among the people, he entered
Capernaum. 2 A centurion had a servant
who was very important to him, but the
servant was ill and about to die. 3 When the
centurion heard about Jesus, he sent some
Jewish elders to Jesus to ask him to come
and heal his servant. 4 When they came to
Jesus, they earnestly pleaded with Jesus.
"He deserves to have you do this for him,"
they said. 5 "He loves our people and he
built our synagogue for us."
6 Jesus went with them. He had almost
reached the house when the centurion
sent friends to say to Jesus, "Lord, don't be
bothered. I don't deserve to have you come
under my roof. 7 In fact, I didn't even consider myself worthy to come to you. Just
say the word and my servant will be healed.
8 I'm also a man appointed under authority,
with soldiers under me. I say to one, 'Go,'
and he goes, and to another, 'Come,' and he
comes. I say to my servant, 'Do this,' and
the servant does it."
9 When Jesus heard these words, he was
impressed with the centurion. He turned
to the crowd following him and said, "I tell
you, even in Israel I haven't found faith like
this." 10 When the centurion's friends returned to his house, they found the servant
restored to health.

Jesus raises a widow's son

11 A little later Jesus went to a city called
Nain. His disciples and a great crowd traveled with him. 12 As he approached the city
gate, a dead man was being carried out. He
was his mother's only son, and she was a
widow. A large crowd from the city was with
her. 13 When he saw her, the Lord had compassion for her and said, "Don't cry." 14 He
stepped forward and touched the stretcher
on which the dead man was being carried.
Those carrying him stood still. Jesus said,
"Young man, I say to you, get up." 15 The
dead man sat up and began to speak, and
Jesus gave him to his mother.
16 Awestruck, everyone praised God. "A
great prophet has appeared among us," they
said. "God has come to help his people."
17 This news about Jesus spread throughout
Judea and the surrounding region.

John the Baptist and Jesus

18 John's disciples informed him about all
these things. John called two of his disciples 19 and sent them to the Lord. They were

to ask him, "Are you the one who is coming,
or should we look for someone else?"
20 When they reached Jesus, they said,
"John the Baptist sent us to you. He asks,
'Are you the one who is coming, or should
we look for someone else?'"
21 Right then, Jesus healed many of their
diseases, illnesses, and evil spirits, and he
gave sight to a number of blind people.
22 Then he replied to John's disciples, "Go,
report to John what you have seen and
heard. *Those who were blind are able to see.*
Those who were crippled now walk. People
with skin diseases are cleansed. Those *who
were deaf now hear. Those who were dead are
raised up. And good news is preached to the
poor.*[o] 23 Happy is anyone who doesn't stumble along the way because of me."
24 After John's messengers were gone,
Jesus spoke to the crowds about John.
"What did you go out into the wilderness
to see? A stalk blowing in the wind? 25 What
did you go out to see? A man dressed up in
refined clothes? Look, those who dress in
fashionable clothes and live in luxury are
in royal palaces. 26 What did you go out to
see? A prophet? Yes, I tell you, and more
than a prophet. 27 He is the one of whom
it's written: *Look, I'm sending my messenger
before you, who will prepare your way before
you.*[p] 28 I tell you that no greater human
being has ever been born than John.
Yet whoever is least in God's kingdom is
greater than he." 29 Everyone who heard
this, including the tax collectors, acknowledged God's justice because they had been
baptized by John. 30 But the Pharisees and
legal experts rejected God's will for themselves because they hadn't been baptized
by John.
31 "To what will I compare the people of
this generation?" Jesus asked. "What are
they like? 32 They are like children sitting in
the marketplace calling out to each other,
'We played the flute for you and you didn't
dance. We sang a funeral song and you
didn't cry.' 33 John the Baptist came neither eating bread nor drinking wine, and
you say, 'He has a demon.' 34 Yet the Human
One[q] came eating and drinking, and you
say, 'Look, a glutton and a drunk, a friend
of tax collectors and sinners.' 35 But wisdom
is proved to be right by all her descendants."

Forgiveness and gratitude

36 One of the Pharisees invited Jesus to
eat with him. After he entered the Pharisee's home, he took his place at the table.
37 Meanwhile, a woman from the city, a sinner, discovered that Jesus was dining in the
Pharisee's house. She brought perfumed
oil in a vase made of alabaster. 38 Standing behind him at his feet and crying, she
began to wet his feet with her tears. She
wiped them with her hair, kissed them, and
poured the oil on them. 39 When the Pharisee who had invited Jesus saw what was
happening, he said to himself, If this man
were a prophet, he would know what kind
of woman is touching him. He would know
that she is a sinner.
40 Jesus replied, "Simon, I have something to say to you."
"Teacher, speak," he said.
41 "A certain lender had two debtors.
One owed enough money to pay five hundred people for a day's work.[r] The other
owed enough money for fifty. 42 When they
couldn't pay, the lender forgave the debts
of them both. Which of them will love
him more?"
43 Simon replied, "I suppose the one who
had the largest debt canceled."
Jesus said, "You have judged correctly."
44 Jesus turned to the woman and said to
Simon, "Do you see this woman? When I entered your home, you didn't give me water
for my feet, but she wet my feet with tears
and wiped them with her hair. 45 You didn't
greet me with a kiss, but she hasn't stopped
kissing my feet since I came in. 46 You didn't
anoint my head with oil, but she has poured
perfumed oil on my feet. 47 This is why I tell
you that her many sins have been forgiven;
so she has shown great love. The one who is
forgiven little loves little."
48 Then Jesus said to her, "Your sins are
forgiven."

[o] Isa 35:5-6; 61:1 [p] Mal 3:1 [q] Or *Son of Man* [r] Or *five hundred denaria*

49 The other table guests began to say
among themselves, "Who is this person
that even forgives sins?"
50 Jesus said to the woman, "Your faith
has saved you. Go in peace."

Women who followed Jesus

8 Soon afterward, Jesus traveled through
the cities and villages, preaching and
proclaiming the good news of God's kingdom. The Twelve were with him, 2 along
with some women who had been healed
of evil spirits and sicknesses. Among them
were Mary Magdalene (from whom seven
demons had been thrown out), 3 Joanna
(the wife of Herod's servant Chuza), Susanna, and many others who provided for
them out of their resources.

Parable of the soils

4 "When a great crowd was gathering and
people were coming to Jesus from one city
after another, he spoke to them in a parable:
5 "A farmer went out to scatter his seed. As
he was scattering it, some fell on the path
where it was crushed, and the birds in the
sky came and ate it. 6 Other seed fell on rock.
As it grew, it dried up because it had no moisture. 7 Other seed fell among thorny plants.
The thorns grew with the plants and choked
them. 8 Still other seed landed on good soil.
When it grew, it produced one hundred
times more grain than was scattered." As he
said this, he called out, "Everyone who has
ears should pay attention."
9 His disciples asked him what this parable meant. 10 He said, "You have been given
the mysteries of God's kingdom, but these
mysteries come to everyone else in parables
so that *when they see, they can't see, and
when they hear, they can't understand.*[s]
11 "The parable means this: The seed is
God's word. 12 The seed on the path are those
who hear, but then the devil comes and
steals the word from their hearts so that
they won't believe and be saved. 13 The seed
on the rock are those who receive the word
joyfully when they hear it, but they have no
root. They believe for a while but fall away
when they are tempted. 14 As for the seed
that fell among thorny plants, these are
the ones who, as they go about their lives,
are choked by the concerns, riches, and
pleasures of life, and their fruit never matures. 15 The seed that fell on good soil are
those who hear the word and commit themselves to it with a good and upright heart.
Through their resolve, they bear fruit.

Sharing the light

16 "No one lights a lamp and then covers it
with a bowl or puts it under a bed. Instead,
they put it on top of a lampstand so that those
who enter can see the light. 17 Nothing is hidden that won't be exposed. Nor is anything
concealed that won't be made known and
brought to the light. 18 Therefore, listen carefully. Those who have will receive more, but
as for those who don't have, even what they
seem to have will be taken away from them."

Jesus' family

19 Jesus' mother and brothers came to
him but were unable to reach him because
of the crowd. 20 Someone told him, "Your
mother and brothers are standing outside,
wanting to see you."
21 He replied, "My mother and brothers are
those who listen to God's word and do it."

Jesus calms the sea

22 One day Jesus and his disciples boarded
a boat. He said to them, "Let's cross over to
the other side of the lake." So they set sail.
23 While they were sailing, he fell asleep.
Gale-force winds swept down on the lake.
The boat was filling up with water and they
were in danger. 24 So they went and woke
Jesus, shouting, "Master, Master, we're
going to drown!" But he got up and gave
orders to the wind and the violent waves.
The storm died down and it was calm.
25 He said to his disciples, "Where is your
faith?"

Filled with awe and wonder, they said
to each other, "Who is this? He commands
even the winds and the water, and they
obey him!"

[s] Isa 6:9

Jesus frees a demon-possessed man

[26]Jesus and his disciples sailed to the Gerasenes' land, which is across the lake from Galilee. [27]As soon as Jesus got out of the boat, a certain man met him. The man was from the city and was possessed by demons. For a long time, he had lived among the tombs, naked and homeless. [28]When he saw Jesus, he shrieked and fell down before him. Then he shouted, "What have you to do with me, Jesus, Son of the Most High God? I beg you, don't torture me!" [29]He said this because Jesus had already commanded the unclean spirit to come out of the man. Many times it had taken possession of him, so he would be bound with leg irons and chains and placed under guard. But he would break his restraints, and the demon would force him into the wilderness.

[30]Jesus asked him, "What is your name?"

"Legion," he replied, because many demons had entered him. [31]They pleaded with him not to order them to go back into the abyss.[t] [32]A large herd of pigs was feeding on the hillside. The demons begged Jesus to let them go into the pigs. Jesus gave them permission, [33]and the demons left the man and entered the pigs. The herd rushed down the cliff into the lake and drowned.

[34]When those who tended the pigs saw what happened, they ran away and told the story in the city and in the countryside. [35]People came to see what had happened. They came to Jesus and found the man from whom the demons had gone. He was sitting at Jesus' feet, fully dressed and completely sane. They were filled with awe. [36]Those people who had actually seen what had happened told them how the demon-possessed man had been delivered. [37]Then everyone gathered from the region of the Gerasenes asked Jesus to leave their area because they were overcome with fear. So he got into the boat and returned across the lake. [38]The man from whom the demons had gone begged to come along with Jesus as one of his disciples. Jesus sent him away, saying, [39]"Return home and tell the story of what God has done for you." So he went throughout the city proclaiming what Jesus had done for him.

Jesus heals two women

[40]When Jesus returned, the crowd welcomed him, for they had been waiting for him. [41]A man named Jairus, who was a synagogue leader, came and fell at Jesus' feet. He pleaded with Jesus to come to his house [42]because his only daughter, a twelve-year-old, was dying.

As Jesus moved forward, he faced smothering crowds. [43]A woman was there who had been bleeding for twelve years. She had spent her entire livelihood on doctors, but no one could heal her. [44]She came up behind him and touched the hem of his clothes, and at once her bleeding stopped.

[45]"Who touched me?" Jesus asked.

When everyone denied it, Peter said, "Master, the crowds are surrounding you and pressing in on you!"

[46]But Jesus said, "Someone touched me. I know that power has gone out from me."

[47]When the woman saw that she couldn't escape notice, she came trembling and fell before Jesus. In front of everyone, she explained why she had touched him and how she had been immediately healed.

[48]"Daughter, your faith has healed you," Jesus said. "Go in peace."

[49]While Jesus was still speaking, someone came from the synagogue leader's house, saying to Jairus, "Your daughter has died. Don't bother the teacher any longer."

[50]When Jesus heard this, he responded, "Don't be afraid; just keep trusting, and she will be healed."

[51]When he came to the house, he didn't allow anyone to enter with him except Peter, John, and James, and the child's father and mother. [52]They were all crying and mourning for her, but Jesus said, "Don't cry. She isn't dead. She's only sleeping."

[53]They laughed at him because they knew she was dead.

[54]Taking her hand, Jesus called out, "Child, get up." [55]Her life returned and she got up at once. He directed them to give

[t]Or *underworld*

her something to eat. 56 Her parents were beside themselves with joy, but he ordered them to tell no one what had happened.

The Twelve sent out

9 Jesus called the Twelve together and he gave them power and authority over all demons and to heal sicknesses. 2 He sent them out to proclaim God's kingdom and to heal the sick. 3 He told them, "Take nothing for the journey—no walking stick, no bag, no bread, no money, not even an extra shirt. 4 Whatever house you enter, remain there until you leave that place. 5 Wherever they don't welcome you, as you leave that city, shake the dust off your feet as a witness against them." 6 They departed and went through the villages proclaiming the good news and healing people everywhere.

Herod's confusion

7 Herod the ruler[u] heard about everything that was happening. He was confused because some people were saying that John had been raised from the dead, 8 others that Elijah had appeared, and still others that one of the ancient prophets had come back to life. 9 Herod said, "I beheaded John, so now who am I hearing about?" Herod wanted to see him.

Jesus feeds the five thousand

10 When the apostles returned, they described for Jesus what they had done. Taking them with him, Jesus withdrew privately to a city called Bethsaida. 11 When the crowds figured it out, they followed him. He welcomed them, spoke to them about God's kingdom, and healed those who were sick.

12 When the day was almost over, the Twelve came to him and said, "Send the crowd away so that they can go to the nearby villages and countryside and find lodging and food, because we are in a deserted place."

13 He replied, "You give them something to eat."

But they said, "We have no more than five loaves of bread and two fish—unless we go and buy food for all these people." 14 (They said this because about five thousand men were present.)

Jesus said to his disciples, "Seat them in groups of about fifty." 15 They did so, and everyone was seated. 16 He took the five loaves and the two fish, looked up to heaven, blessed them, and broke them and gave them to the disciples to set before the crowd. 17 Everyone ate until they were full, and the disciples filled twelve baskets with the leftovers.

Following Christ

18 Once when Jesus was praying by himself, the disciples joined him, and he asked them, "Who do the crowds say that I am?"

19 They answered, "John the Baptist, others Elijah, and still others that one of the ancient prophets has come back to life."

20 He asked them, "And what about you? Who do you say that I am?"

Peter answered, "The Christ sent from God."

21 Jesus gave them strict orders not to tell this to anyone. 22 He said, "The Human One[v] must suffer many things and be rejected—by the elders, chief priests, and the legal experts—and be killed and be raised on the third day."

23 Jesus said to everyone, "All who want to come after me must say no to themselves, take up their cross daily, and follow me. 24 All who want to save their lives will lose them. But all who lose their lives because of me will save them. 25 What advantage do people have if they gain the whole world for themselves yet perish or lose their lives? 26 Whoever is ashamed of me and my words, the Human One[w] will be ashamed of that person when he comes in his glory and in the glory of the Father and of the holy angels. 27 I assure you that some standing here won't die before they see God's kingdom."

Jesus transformed

28 About eight days after Jesus said these things, he took Peter, John, and James, and went up on a mountain to pray. 29 As he was

[u] Or *tetrarch* [v] Or *Son of Man* [w] Or *Son of Man*

praying, the appearance of his face changed and his clothes flashed white like lightning. 30 Two men, Moses and Elijah, were talking with him. 31 They were clothed with heavenly splendor and spoke about Jesus' departure, which he would achieve in Jerusalem. 32 Peter and those with him were almost overcome by sleep, but they managed to stay awake and saw his glory as well as the two men with him.

33 As the two men were about to leave Jesus, Peter said to him, "Master, it's good that we're here. We should construct three shrines: one for you, one for Moses, and one for Elijah"—but he didn't know what he was saying. 34 Peter was still speaking when a cloud overshadowed them. As they entered the cloud, they were overcome with awe.

35 Then a voice from the cloud said, "This is my Son, my chosen one. Listen to him!" 36 Even as the voice spoke, Jesus was found alone. They were speechless and at the time told no one what they had seen.

Jesus heals a boy

37 The next day, when Jesus, Peter, John, and James had come down from the mountain, a large crowd met Jesus. 38 A man from the crowd shouted, "Teacher, I beg you to take a look at my son, my only child. 39 Look, a spirit seizes him and, without any warning, he screams. It shakes him and causes him to foam at the mouth. It tortures him and rarely leaves him alone. 40 I begged your disciples to throw it out, but they couldn't."

41 Jesus answered, "You faithless and crooked generation, how long will I be with you and put up with you? Bring your son here." 42 While he was coming, the demon threw him down and shook him violently. Jesus spoke harshly to the unclean spirit, healed the child, and gave him back to his father. 43 Everyone was overwhelmed by God's greatness.

Jesus warns about his arrest

While everyone was marveling at everything he was doing, Jesus said to his disciples, 44 "Take these words to heart: the Human One[x] is about to be delivered into human hands." 45 They didn't understand this statement. Its meaning was hidden from them so they couldn't grasp it. And they were afraid to ask him about it.

Jesus corrects the disciples

46 An argument arose among the disciples about which of them was the greatest. 47 Aware of their deepest thoughts, Jesus took a little child and had the child stand beside him. 48 Jesus said to his disciples, "Whoever welcomes this child in my name welcomes me. Whoever welcomes me, welcomes the one who sent me. Whoever is least among you all is the greatest."

49 John replied, "Master, we saw someone throwing demons out in your name, and we tried to stop him because he isn't in our group of followers."

50 But Jesus replied, "Don't stop him, because whoever isn't against you is for you."

Jesus sets out for Jerusalem

51 As the time approached when Jesus was to be taken up into heaven, he determined to go to Jerusalem. 52 He sent messengers on ahead of him. Along the way, they entered a Samaritan village to prepare for his arrival, 53 but the Samaritan villagers refused to welcome him because he was determined to go to Jerusalem. 54 When the disciples James and John saw this, they said, "Lord, do you want us to call fire down from heaven to consume them?" 55 But Jesus turned and spoke sternly to them, 56 and they went on to another village.

Following Jesus

57 As Jesus and his disciples traveled along the road, someone said to him, "I will follow you wherever you go."

58 Jesus replied, "Foxes have dens and the birds in the sky have nests, but the Human One[y] has no place to lay his head."

59 Then Jesus said to someone else, "Follow me."

He replied, "Lord, first let me go and bury my father."

[x] Or *Son of Man* [y] Or *Son of Man*

60 Jesus said to him, "Let the dead bury their own dead. But you go and spread the news of God's kingdom."

61 Someone else said to Jesus, "I will follow you, Lord, but first let me say good-bye to those in my house."

62 Jesus said to him, "No one who puts a hand on the plow and looks back is fit for God's kingdom."

Seventy-two sent out

10 After these things, the Lord commissioned seventy-two others and sent them on ahead in pairs to every city and place he was about to go. 2 He said to them, "The harvest is bigger than you can imagine, but there are few workers. Therefore, plead with the Lord of the harvest to send out workers for his harvest. 3 Go! Be warned, though, that I'm sending you out as lambs among wolves. 4 Carry no wallet, no bag, and no sandals. Don't even greet anyone along the way. 5 Whenever you enter a house, first say, 'May peace be on this house.' 6 If anyone there shares God's peace, then your peace will rest on that person. If not, your blessing will return to you. 7 Remain in this house, eating and drinking whatever they set before you, for workers deserve their pay. Don't move from house to house. 8 Whenever you enter a city and its people welcome you, eat what they set before you. 9 Heal the sick who are there, and say to them, 'God's kingdom has come upon you.' 10 Whenever you enter a city and the people don't welcome you, go out into the streets and say, 11 'As a complaint against you, we brush off the dust of your city that has collected on our feet. But know this: God's kingdom has come to you.' 12 I assure you that Sodom will be better off on Judgment Day than that city.

Judgment against cities that reject Jesus

13 "How terrible it will be for you, Chorazin. How terrible it will be for you, Bethsaida. If the miracles done among you had been done in Tyre and Sidon, they would have changed their hearts and lives long ago. They would have sat around in funeral clothes and ashes. 14 But Tyre and Sidon will be better off at the judgment than you. 15 And you, Capernaum, will you be honored by being raised up to heaven? No, you will be cast down to the place of the dead. 16 Whoever listens to you listens to me. Whoever rejects you rejects me. Whoever rejects me rejects the one who sent me."

The seventy-two return

17 The seventy-two returned joyously, saying, "Lord, even the demons submit themselves to us in your name."

18 Jesus replied, "I saw Satan fall from heaven like lightning. 19 Look, I have given you authority to crush snakes and scorpions underfoot. I have given you authority over all the power of the enemy. Nothing will harm you. 20 Nevertheless, don't rejoice because the spirits submit to you. Rejoice instead that your names are written in heaven."

21 At that very moment, Jesus overflowed with joy from the Holy Spirit and said, "I praise you, Father, Lord of heaven and earth, because you've hidden these things from the wise and intelligent and shown them to babies. Indeed, Father, this brings you happiness. 22 My Father has handed all things over to me. No one knows who the Son is except the Father, or who the Father is except the Son and anyone to whom the Son wants to reveal him." 23 Turning to the disciples, he said privately, "Happy are the eyes that see what you see. 24 I assure you that many prophets and kings wanted to see what you see and hear what you hear, but they didn't."

Loving your neighbor

25 A legal expert stood up to test Jesus. "Teacher," he said, "what must I do to gain eternal life?"

26 Jesus replied, "What is written in the Law? How do you interpret it?"

27 He responded, "*You must love the Lord your God with all your heart, with all your being, with all your strength, and with all your mind, and love your neighbor as yourself.*"[z]

[z] Deut 6:5; Lev 19:18

28 Jesus said to him, "You have answered
correctly. Do this and you will live."
29 But the legal expert wanted to prove
that he was right, so he said to Jesus, "And
who is my neighbor?"
30 Jesus replied, "A man went down from
Jerusalem to Jericho. He encountered
thieves, who stripped him naked, beat him
up, and left him near death. 31 Now it just so
happened that a priest was also going down
the same road. When he saw the injured
man, he crossed over to the other side of
the road and went on his way. 32 Likewise,
a Levite came by that spot, saw the injured
man, and crossed over to the other side of
the road and went on his way. 33 A Samaritan, who was on a journey, came to where
the man was. But when he saw him, he was
moved with compassion. 34 The Samaritan
went to him and bandaged his wounds,
tending them with oil and wine. Then he
placed the wounded man on his own donkey, took him to an inn, and took care of
him. 35 The next day, he took two full days'
worth of wages and gave them to the inn-
keeper. He said, 'Take care of him, and
when I return, I will pay you back for any
additional costs.' 36 What do you think?
Which one of these three was a neighbor to
the man who encountered thieves?"
37 Then the legal expert said, "The one
who demonstrated mercy toward him."
Jesus told him, "Go and do likewise."

Jesus visits Martha and Mary

38 While Jesus and his disciples were
traveling, Jesus entered a village where a
woman named Martha welcomed him as
a guest. 39 She had a sister named Mary,
who sat at the Lord's feet and listened to
his message. 40 By contrast, Martha was
preoccupied with getting everything ready
for their meal. So Martha came to him and
said, "Lord, don't you care that my sister
has left me to prepare the table all by myself? Tell her to help me."
41 The Lord answered, "Martha, Martha,
you are worried and distracted by many
things. 42 One thing is necessary. Mary has
chosen the better part. It won't be taken
away from her."

Teaching the disciples to pray

11 Jesus was praying in a certain place.
When he finished, one of his disciples
said, "Lord, teach us to pray, just as John
taught his disciples."
2 Jesus told them, "When you pray, say:
'Father, uphold the holiness of your
name.
Bring in your kingdom.
3 Give us the bread we need for today.
4 Forgive us our sins,
for we also forgive everyone who has
wronged us.
And don't lead us into temptation.'"
5 He also said to them, "Imagine that one
of you has a friend and you go to that friend
in the middle of the night. Imagine saying, 'Friend, loan me three loaves of bread
6 because a friend of mine on a journey has
arrived and I have nothing to set before
him.' 7 Imagine further that he answers
from within the house, 'Don't bother me.
The door is already locked, and my children
and I are in bed. I can't get up to give you
anything.' 8 I assure you, even if he wouldn't
get up and help because of his friendship,
he will get up and give his friend whatever
he needs because of his friend's brashness.
9 And I tell you: Ask and you will receive.
Seek and you will find. Knock and the door
will be opened to you. 10 Everyone who asks,
receives. Whoever seeks, finds. To everyone
who knocks, the door is opened.
11 "Which father among you would give a
snake to your child if the child asked for a
fish? 12 If a child asked for an egg, what father would give the child a scorpion? 13 If
you who are evil know how to give good
gifts to your children, how much more will
the heavenly Father give the Holy Spirit to
those who ask him?"

Controversy over Beelzebul

14 Jesus was throwing out a demon that
causes muteness. When the demon was
gone, the man who couldn't speak began to
talk. The crowds were amazed. 15 But some
of them said, "He throws out demons with
the authority of Beelzebul, the ruler of demons." 16 Others were testing him, seeking
a sign from heaven.

17 Because Jesus knew what they were thinking, he said to them, "Every kingdom involved in civil war becomes a wasteland, and a house torn apart by divisions will collapse. 18 If Satan is at war with himself, how will his kingdom endure? I ask this because you say that I throw out demons by the authority of Beelzebul. 19 If I throw out demons by the authority of Beelzebul, then by whose authority do your followers throw them out? Therefore, they will be your judges. 20 But if I throw out demons by the power[a] of God, then God's kingdom has already overtaken you. 21 When a strong man, fully armed, guards his own palace, his possessions are secure. 22 But as soon as a stronger one attacks and overpowers him, the stronger one takes away the armor he had trusted and divides the stolen goods.

23 "Whoever isn't with me is against me, and whoever doesn't gather with me, scatters. 24 When an unclean spirit leaves a person, it wanders through dry places looking for a place to rest. But it doesn't find any. Then it says, 'I'll go back to the house I left.' 25 When it arrives, it finds the house cleaned up and decorated. 26 Then it goes and brings with it seven other spirits more evil than itself. They go in and make their home there. That person is worse off at the end than at the beginning."

On seeking signs

27 While Jesus was saying these things, a certain woman in the crowd spoke up: "Happy is the mother who gave birth to you and who nursed you."

28 But he said, "Happy rather are those who hear God's word and put it into practice."

29 When the crowds grew, Jesus said, "This generation is an evil generation. It looks for a sign, but no sign will be given to it except Jonah's sign. 30 Just as Jonah became a sign to the people of Nineveh, so the Human One[b] will be a sign to this generation. 31 The queen of the South will rise up at the judgment with the people of this generation and condemn them, because she came from a distant land to hear Solomon's wisdom. And look, someone greater than Solomon is here. 32 The people of Nineveh will rise up at the judgment with this generation and condemn it, because they changed their hearts and lives in response to Jonah's preaching—and one greater than Jonah is here.

33 "People don't light a lamp and then put it in a closet or under a basket. Rather, they place the lamp on a lampstand so that those who enter the house can see the light. 34 Your eye is the lamp of your body. When your eye is healthy, your whole body is full of light. But when your eye is bad, your whole body is full of darkness. 35 Therefore, see to it that the light in you isn't darkness. 36 If your whole body is full of light—with no part darkened—then it will be as full of light as when a lamp shines brightly on you."

Jesus condemns Pharisees and legal experts

37 While Jesus was speaking, a Pharisee invited him to share a meal with him, so Jesus went and took his place at the table. 38 When the Pharisee saw that Jesus didn't ritually purify his hands by washing before the meal, he was astonished.

39 The Lord said to him, "Now, you Pharisees clean the outside of the cup and platter, but your insides are stuffed with greed and wickedness. 40 Foolish people! Didn't the one who made the outside also make the inside? 41 Therefore, give to those in need from the core of who you are and you will be clean all over.

42 "How terrible for you Pharisees! You give a tenth of your mint, rue, and garden herbs of all kinds, while neglecting justice and love for God. These you ought to have done without neglecting the others.

43 "How terrible for you Pharisees! You love the most prominent seats in the synagogues and respectful greetings in the marketplaces.

44 "How terrible for you! You are like unmarked graves, and people walk on them without recognizing it."

[a] Or *finger* [b] Or *Son of Man*

45 One of the legal experts responded,
"Teacher, when you say these things, you
are insulting us too."
46 Jesus said, "How terrible for you legal
experts too! You load people down with
impossible burdens and you refuse to lift a
single finger to help them.
47 "How terrible for you! You built memorials to the prophets, whom your ancestors killed. 48 In this way, you testify
that you approve of your ancestors' deeds.
They killed the prophets, and you build
memorials! 49 Therefore, God's wisdom has
said, 'I will send prophets and apostles to
them and they will harass and kill some of
them.' 50 As a result, this generation will be
charged with the murder of all the prophets
since the beginning of time. 51 This includes
the murder of every prophet—from Abel
to Zechariah—who was killed between the
altar and the holy place. Yes, I'm telling you,
this generation will be charged with it.
52 "How terrible for you legal experts!
You snatched away the key of knowledge.
You didn't enter yourselves, and you stood
in the way of those who were entering."
53 As he left there, the legal experts and
Pharisees began to resent him deeply and
to ask him pointed questions about many
things. 54 They plotted against him, trying
to trap him in his words.

Warnings to Jesus' friends

12 When a crowd of thousands upon
thousands had gathered so that they
were crushing each other, Jesus began to
speak first to his disciples: "Watch out for
the yeast of the Pharisees—I mean, the
mismatch between their hearts and lives.
2 Nothing is hidden that won't be revealed,
and nothing is secret that won't be brought
out into the open. 3 Therefore, whatever you
have said in the darkness will be heard in
the light, and whatever you have whispered
in the rooms deep inside the house will be
announced from the rooftops.
4 "I tell you, my friends, don't be terrified by those who can kill the body but after
that can do nothing more. 5 I'll show you
whom you should fear: fear the one who,
after you have been killed, has the authority to throw you into hell. Indeed, I tell you,
that's the one you should fear. 6 Aren't five
sparrows sold for two small coins?[c] Yet not
one of them is overlooked by God. 7 Even
the hairs on your head are all counted.
Don't be afraid. You are worth more than
many sparrows.

Acknowledging the Human One

8 "I tell you, everyone who acknowledges
me before humans, the Human One[d] will
acknowledge before God's angels. 9 But the
one who rejects me before others will be
rejected before God's angels. 10 Anyone who
speaks a word against the Human One[e] will
be forgiven, but whoever insults the Holy
Spirit won't be forgiven. 11 When they bring
you before the synagogues, rulers, and authorities, don't worry about how to defend
yourself or what you should say. 12 The Holy
Spirit will tell you at that very moment
what you must say."

Warning against greed

13 Someone from the crowd said to him,
"Teacher, tell my brother to divide the inheritance with me."
14 Jesus said to him, "Man, who appointed me as judge or referee between you
and your brother?"
15 Then Jesus said to them, "Watch out!
Guard yourself against all kinds of greed.
After all, one's life isn't determined by one's
possessions, even when someone is very
wealthy." 16 Then he told them a parable: "A
certain rich man's land produced a bountiful
crop. 17 He said to himself, What will I do? I
have no place to store my harvest! 18 Then he
thought, Here's what I'll do. I'll tear down
my barns and build bigger ones. That's
where I'll store all my grain and goods. 19 I'll
say to myself, You have stored up plenty
of goods, enough for several years. Take it
easy! Eat, drink, and enjoy yourself. 20 But
God said to him, 'Fool, tonight you will die.
Now who will get the things you have prepared for yourself?' 21 This is the way it will

[c]Or *two assaria*—that is, 1/8 of a day's wage [d]Or *Son of Man* [e]Or *Son of Man*

be for those who hoard things for themselves and aren't rich toward God."

Warning about worry

22 Then Jesus said to his disciples, "Therefore, I say to you, don't worry about your life, what you will eat, or about your body, what you will wear. 23 There is more to life than food and more to the body than clothing. 24 Consider the ravens: they neither plant nor harvest, they have no silo or barn, yet God feeds them. You are worth so much more than birds! 25 Who among you by worrying can add a single moment to your life?[f] 26 If you can't do such a small thing, why worry about the rest? 27 Notice how the lilies grow. They don't wear themselves out with work, and they don't spin cloth. But I say to you that even Solomon in all his splendor wasn't dressed like one of these. 28 If God dresses grass in the field so beautifully, even though it's alive today and tomorrow it's thrown into the furnace, how much more will God do for you, you people of weak faith! 29 Don't chase after what you will eat and what you will drink. Stop worrying. 30 All the nations of the world long for these things. Your Father knows that you need them. 31 Instead, desire his kingdom and these things will be given to you as well.

32 "Don't be afraid, little flock, because your Father delights in giving you the kingdom. 33 Sell your possessions and give to those in need. Make for yourselves wallets that don't wear out—a treasure in heaven that never runs out. No thief comes near there, and no moth destroys. 34 Where your treasure is, there your heart will be too.

Warning about being prepared

35 "Be dressed for service and keep your lamps lit. 36 Be like people waiting for their master to come home from a wedding celebration, who can immediately open the door for him when he arrives and knocks on the door. 37 Happy are those servants whom the master finds waiting up when he arrives. I assure you that, when he arrives, he will dress himself to serve, seat them at the table as honored guests, and wait on them. 38 Happy are those whom he finds alert, even if he comes at midnight or just before dawn.[g] 39 But know this, if the homeowner had known what time the thief was coming, he wouldn't have allowed his home to be broken into. 40 You also must be ready, because the Human One[h] is coming at a time when you don't expect him."

41 Peter said, "Lord, are you telling this parable for us or for everyone?"

42 The Lord replied, "Who are the faithful and wise managers whom the master will put in charge of his household servants, to give them their food at the proper time? 43 Happy are the servants whom the master finds fulfilling their responsibilities when he comes. 44 I assure you that the master will put them in charge of all his possessions.

45 "But suppose that these servants should say to themselves, My master is taking his time about coming. And suppose they began to beat the servants, both men and women, and to eat, drink, and get drunk. 46 The master of those servants would come on a day when they weren't expecting him, at a time they couldn't predict. The master will cut them into pieces and assign them a place with the unfaithful. 47 That servant who knew his master's will but didn't prepare for it or act on it will be beaten severely. 48 The one who didn't know the master's will but who did things deserving punishment will be beaten only a little. Much will be demanded from everyone who has been given much, and from the one who has been entrusted with much, even more will be asked.

Conflicts brought by Jesus

49 "I came to cast fire upon the earth. How I wish that it was already ablaze! 50 I have a baptism I must experience. How I am distressed until it's completed! 51 Do you think that I have come to bring peace to the earth? No, I tell you, I have come instead to bring division. 52 From now on, a household of five will be divided—three against

[f] Or *eighteen inches to your height* [g] Or *in the second or third watch* [h] Or *Son of Man*

two and two against three. 53Father will
square off against son and son against father; mother against daughter and daughter against mother; and mother-in-law
against daughter-in-law and daughter-in-
law against mother-in-law."

Learning and practicing good judgment

54Jesus also said to the crowds, "When
you see a cloud forming in the west, you immediately say, 'It's going to rain.' And indeed
it does. 55And when a south wind blows,
you say, 'A heat wave is coming.' And it does.
56Hypocrites! You know how to interpret
conditions on earth and in the sky. How is
it that you don't know how to interpret the
present time? 57And why don't you judge for
yourselves what is right? 58As you are going
to court with your accuser, make your best
effort to reach a settlement along the way.
Otherwise, your accuser may bring you before the judge, and the judge hand you over
to the officer, and the officer throw you into
prison. 59I tell you, you won't get out of
there until you have paid the very last cent."[i]

Demand for genuine change

13 Some who were present on that occasion told Jesus about the Galileans
whom Pilate had killed while they were offering sacrifices. 2He replied, "Do you think
the suffering of these Galileans proves that
they were more sinful than all the other
Galileans? 3No, I tell you, but unless you
change your hearts and lives, you will die
just as they did. 4What about those eighteen people who were killed when the tower
of Siloam fell on them? Do you think that
they were more guilty of wrongdoing than
everyone else who lives in Jerusalem? 5No,
I tell you, but unless you change your hearts
and lives, you will die just as they did."
6Jesus told this parable: "A man owned
a fig tree planted in his vineyard. He came
looking for fruit on it and found none. 7He
said to his gardener, 'Look, I've come looking for fruit on this fig tree for the past
three years, and I've never found any. Cut
it down! Why should it continue deplet-
ing the soil's nutrients?' 8The gardener responded, 'Lord, give it one more year, and
I will dig around it and give it fertilizer.
9Maybe it will produce fruit next year; if
not, then you can cut it down.'"

Healing on a Sabbath

10Jesus was teaching in one of the synagogues on the Sabbath. 11A woman was
there who had been disabled by a spirit
for eighteen years. She was bent over and
couldn't stand up straight. 12When he
saw her, Jesus called her to him and said,
"Woman, you are set free from your sickness." 13He placed his hands on her and she
straightened up at once and praised God.
14The synagogue leader, incensed that
Jesus had healed on the Sabbath, responded, "There are six days during which
work is permitted. Come and be healed on
those days, not on the Sabbath day."
15The Lord replied, "Hypocrites! Don't
each of you on the Sabbath untie your ox
or donkey from its stall and lead it out to
get a drink? 16Then isn't it necessary that
this woman, a daughter of Abraham, bound
by Satan for eighteen long years, be set free
from her bondage on the Sabbath day?"
17When he said these things, all his opponents were put to shame, but all those in
the crowd rejoiced at all the extraordinary
things he was doing.

Growth of God's kingdom

18Jesus asked, "What is God's kingdom
like? To what can I compare it? 19It's like
a mustard seed that someone took and
planted in a garden. It grew and developed
into a tree and the birds in the sky nested
in its branches."
20Again he said, "To what can I compare
God's kingdom? 21It's like yeast, which a
woman took and hid in a bushel of wheat
flour until the yeast had worked its way
through the whole."

Who will be saved?

22Jesus traveled through cities and
villages, teaching and making his way to

[i] Or *leptos* (1/128 of a day's wages)

Jerusalem. [23]Someone said to him, "Lord, will only a few be saved?"

Jesus said to them, [24]"Make every effort to enter through the narrow gate. Many, I tell you, will try to enter and won't be able to. [25]Once the owner of the house gets up and shuts the door, then you will stand outside and knock on the door, saying, 'Lord, open the door for us.' He will reply, 'I don't know you or where you are from.' [26]Then you will begin to say, 'We ate and drank in your presence, and you taught in our streets.' [27]He will respond, 'I don't know you or where you are from. *Go away from me, all you evildoers!*'[j] [28]There will be weeping and grinding of teeth when you see Abraham, Isaac, Jacob, and all the prophets in God's kingdom, but you yourselves will be thrown out. [29]People will come from east and west, north and south, and sit down to eat in God's kingdom. [30]Look! Those who are last will be first and those who are first will be last."

Sorrow for Jerusalem

[31]At that time, some Pharisees approached Jesus and said, "Go! Get away from here, because Herod wants to kill you."

[32]Jesus said to them, "Go, tell that fox, 'Look, I'm throwing out demons and healing people today and tomorrow, and on the third day I will complete my work. [33]However, it's necessary for me to travel today, tomorrow, and the next day because it's impossible for a prophet to be killed outside of Jerusalem.'

[34]"Jerusalem, Jerusalem, you who kill the prophets and stone those who were sent to you! How often I have wanted to gather your people just as a hen gathers her chicks under her wings. But you didn't want that. [35]Look, your house is abandoned. I tell you, you won't see me until the time comes when you say, *Blessings on the one who comes in the Lord's name.*"[k]

Healing on the Sabbath

14 One Sabbath, when Jesus went to share a meal in the home of one of the leaders of the Pharisees, they were watching him closely. [2]A man suffering from an abnormal swelling of the body was there. [3]Jesus asked the lawyers and Pharisees, "Does the Law allow healing on the Sabbath or not?" [4]But they said nothing. Jesus took hold of the sick man, cured him, and then let him go. [5]He said to them, "Suppose your child or ox fell into a ditch on the Sabbath day. Wouldn't you immediately pull it out?" [6]But they had no response.

Lessons on humility and generosity

[7]When Jesus noticed how the guests sought out the best seats at the table, he told them a parable. [8]"When someone invites you to a wedding celebration, don't take your seat in the place of honor. Someone more highly regarded than you could have been invited by your host. [9]The host who invited both of you will come and say to you, 'Give your seat to this other person.' Embarrassed, you will take your seat in the least important place. [10]Instead, when you receive an invitation, go and sit in the least important place. When your host approaches you, he will say, 'Friend, move up here to a better seat.' Then you will be honored in the presence of all your fellow guests. [11]All who lift themselves up will be brought low, and those who make themselves low will be lifted up."

[12]Then Jesus said to the person who had invited him, "When you host a lunch or dinner, don't invite your friends, your brothers and sisters, your relatives, or rich neighbors. If you do, they will invite you in return and that will be your reward. [13]Instead, when you give a banquet, invite the poor, crippled, lame, and blind. [14]And you will be blessed because they can't repay you. Instead, you will be repaid when the just are resurrected."

[15]When one of the dinner guests heard Jesus' remarks, he said to Jesus, "Happy are those who will feast in God's kingdom."

[16]Jesus replied, "A certain man hosted a large dinner and invited many people. [17]When it was time for the dinner to begin, he sent his servant to tell the invited guests,

[j]Ps 6:9 LXX [k]Ps 118:26

‘Come! The dinner is now ready.’ [18]One by
one, they all began to make excuses. The
first one told him, ‘I bought a farm and
must go and see it. Please excuse me.’ [19]An-
other said, ‘I bought five teams of oxen, and
I’m going to check on them. Please excuse
me.’ [20]Another said, ‘I just got married, so
I can’t come.’ [21]When he returned, the servant reported these excuses to his master.
The master of the house became angry and
said to his servant, ‘Go quickly to the city’s
streets, the busy ones and the side streets,
and bring the poor, crippled, blind, and
lame.’ [22]The servant said, ‘Master, your instructions have been followed and there is
still room.’ [23]The master said to the servant,
‘Go to the highways and back alleys and
urge people to come in so that my house
will be filled. [24]I tell you, not one of those
who were invited will taste my dinner.’ ”

Discipleship’s demands

[25]Large crowds were traveling with Jesus.
Turning to them, he said, [26]“Whoever
comes to me and doesn’t hate father and
mother, spouse and children, and brothers and sisters—yes, even one’s own life—
cannot be my disciple. [27]Whoever doesn’t
carry their own cross and follow me cannot
be my disciple.

[28]“If one of you wanted to build a tower,
wouldn’t you first sit down and calculate
the cost, to determine whether you have
enough money to complete it? [29]Other-
wise, when you have laid the foundation
but couldn’t finish the tower, all who see
it will begin to belittle you. [30]They will say,
‘Here’s the person who began construction and couldn’t complete it!’ [31]Or what
king would go to war against another king
without first sitting down to consider
whether his ten thousand soldiers could
go up against the twenty thousand coming against him? [32]And if he didn’t think he
could win, he would send a representative
to discuss terms of peace while his enemy
was still a long way off. [33]In the same way,
none of you who are unwilling to give up all
of your possessions can be my disciple.

[34]“Salt is good. But if salt loses its flavor,
how will it become salty again? [35]It has no
value, neither for the soil nor for the manure pile. People throw it away. Whoever
has ears to hear should pay attention.”

Occasions for celebration

15 All the tax collectors and sinners were
gathering around Jesus to listen to
him. [2]The Pharisees and legal experts were
grumbling, saying, “This man welcomes
sinners and eats with them.”

[3]Jesus told them this parable: [4]“Suppose
someone among you had one hundred
sheep and lost one of them. Wouldn’t he
leave the other ninety-nine in the pasture
and search for the lost one until he finds
it? [5]And when he finds it, he is thrilled and
places it on his shoulders. [6]When he arrives
home, he calls together his friends and
neighbors, saying to them, ‘Celebrate with
me because I’ve found my lost sheep.’ [7]In
the same way, I tell you, there will be more
joy in heaven over one sinner who changes
both heart and life than over ninety-nine
righteous people who have no need to
change their hearts and lives.

[8]“Or what woman, if she owns ten silver
coins and loses one of them, won’t light a
lamp and sweep the house, searching her
home carefully until she finds it? [9]When
she finds it, she calls together her friends
and neighbors, saying, ‘Celebrate with me
because I’ve found my lost coin.’ [10]In the
same way, I tell you, joy breaks out in the
presence of God’s angels over one sinner
who changes both heart and life.”

[11]Jesus said, “A certain man had two
sons. [12]The younger son said to his father,
‘Father, give me my share of the inheritance.’ Then the father divided his estate between them. [13]Soon afterward, the younger
son gathered everything together and took
a trip to a land far away. There, he wasted
his wealth through extravagant living.

[14]“When he had used up his resources, a
severe food shortage arose in that country
and he began to be in need. [15]He hired himself out to one of the citizens of that country, who sent him into his fields to feed pigs.
[16]He longed to eat his fill from what the pigs
ate, but no one gave him anything. [17]When
he came to his senses, he said, ‘How many

of my father's hired hands have more than
enough food, but I'm starving to death! [18]I
will get up and go to my father, and say to
him, "Father, I have sinned against heaven
and against you. [19]I no longer deserve to be
called your son. Take me on as one of your
hired hands."' [20]So he got up and went to
his father.

"While he was still a long way off, his
father saw him and was moved with compassion.
His father ran to him, hugged him,
and kissed him. [21]Then his son said, 'Father,
I have sinned against heaven and against
you. I no longer deserve to be called your
son.' [22]But the father said to his servants,
'Quickly, bring out the best robe and put it
on him! Put a ring on his finger and sandals
on his feet! [23]Fetch the fattened calf and
slaughter it. We must celebrate with feasting
[24]because this son of mine was dead
and has come back to life! He was lost and
is found!' And they began to celebrate.

[25]"Now his older son was in the field.
Coming in from the field, he approached
the house and heard music and dancing.
[26]He called one of the servants and asked
what was going on. [27]The servant replied,
'Your brother has arrived, and your father
has slaughtered the fattened calf because
he received his son back safe and sound.'
[28]Then the older son was furious and didn't
want to enter in, but his father came out
and begged him. [29]He answered his father,
'Look, I've served you all these years, and
I never disobeyed your instruction. Yet
you've never given me as much as a young
goat so I could celebrate with my friends.
[30]But when this son of yours returned,
after gobbling up your estate on prostitutes,
you slaughtered the fattened calf for
him.' [31]Then his father said, 'Son, you are
always with me, and everything I have is
yours. [32]But we had to celebrate and be glad
because this brother of yours was dead and
is alive. He was lost and is found.'"

Faithfulness with money

16 Jesus also said to the disciples, "A
certain rich man heard that his
household manager was wasting his estate.
[2]He called the manager in and said to him,
'What is this I hear about you? Give me a
report of your administration because you
can no longer serve as my manager.'

[3]"The household manager said to himself,
What will I do now that my master is
firing me as his manager? I'm not strong
enough to dig and too proud to beg. [4]I know
what I'll do so that, when I am removed
from my management position, people will
welcome me into their houses.

[5]"One by one, the manager sent for each
person who owed his master money. He
said to the first, 'How much do you owe
my master?' [6]He said, 'Nine hundred gallons
of olive oil.'[l] The manager said to him,
'Take your contract, sit down quickly, and
write four hundred fifty gallons.' [7]Then the
manager said to another, 'How much do
you owe?' He said, 'One thousand bushels
of wheat.'[m] He said, 'Take your contract and
write eight hundred.'

[8]"The master commended the dishonest
manager because he acted cleverly. People
who belong to this world are more clever
in dealing with their peers than are people
who belong to the light. [9]I tell you, use
worldly wealth to make friends for yourselves
so that when it's gone, you will be
welcomed into the eternal homes.

[10]"Whoever is faithful with little is also
faithful with much, and the one who is dishonest
with little is also dishonest with
much. [11]If you haven't been faithful with
worldly wealth, who will trust you with true
riches? [12]If you haven't been faithful with
someone else's property, who will give you
your own? [13]No household servant can serve
two masters. Either you will hate the one and
love the other, or you will be loyal to the one
and have contempt for the other. You cannot
serve God and wealth."

Jesus responds to Pharisees

[14]The Pharisees, who were money-lovers,
heard all this and sneered at Jesus.
[15]He said to them, "You are the ones who
justify yourselves before other people, but

[l] Or *one hundred jugs* (approximately nine gallons each) [m] Or *eighty measures* (ten to twelve bushels each)

God knows your hearts. What is highly valued by people is deeply offensive to God.
16Until John, there was only the Law and
the Prophets. Since then, the good news of
God's kingdom is preached, and everyone
is urged to enter it. 17It's easier for heaven
and earth to pass away than for the smallest stroke of a pen in the Law to drop out.
18Any man who divorces his wife and marries another commits adultery, and a man
who marries a woman divorced from her
husband commits adultery.

19"There was a certain rich man who
clothed himself in purple and fine linen,
and who feasted luxuriously every day. 20At
his gate lay a certain poor man named Lazarus who was covered with sores. 21Lazarus
longed to eat the crumbs that fell from the
rich man's table. Instead, dogs would come
and lick his sores.

22"The poor man died and was carried
by angels to Abraham's side. The rich man
also died and was buried. 23While being tormented in the place of the dead, he looked
up and saw Abraham at a distance with
Lazarus at his side. 24He shouted, 'Father
Abraham, have mercy on me. Send Lazarus
to dip the tip of his finger in water and cool
my tongue, because I'm suffering in this
flame.' 25But Abraham said, 'Child, remember that during your lifetime you received
good things, whereas Lazarus received
terrible things. Now Lazarus is being
comforted and you are in great pain.
26Moreover, a great crevasse has been fixed
between us and you. Those who wish to
cross over from here to you cannot. Neither
can anyone cross from there to us.'

27"The rich man said, 'Then I beg you,
Father, send Lazarus to my father's house.
28I have five brothers. He needs to warn
them so that they don't come to this place
of agony.' 29Abraham replied, 'They have
Moses and the Prophets. They must listen
to them.' 30The rich man said, 'No, Father
Abraham! But if someone from the dead
goes to them, they will change their hearts
and lives.' 31Abraham said, 'If they don't listen to Moses and the Prophets, then neither will they be persuaded if someone rises
from the dead.'"

Faithful service

17 Jesus said to his disciples, "Things
that cause people to trip and fall into
sin must happen, but how terrible it is for
the person through whom they happen. 2It
would be better for them to be thrown into
a lake with a large stone hung around their
neck than to cause one of these little ones
to trip and fall into sin. 3Watch yourselves!
If your brother or sister sins, warn them to
stop. If they change their hearts and lives,
forgive them. 4Even if someone sins against
you seven times in one day and returns to
you seven times and says, 'I am changing
my ways,' you must forgive that person."

5The apostles said to the Lord, "Increase
our faith!"

6The Lord replied, "If you had faith the
size of a mustard seed, you could say to this
mulberry tree, 'Be uprooted and planted in
the sea,' and it would obey you.

7"Would any of you say to your servant,
who had just come in from the field after
plowing or tending sheep, 'Come! Sit down
for dinner'? 8Wouldn't you say instead, 'Fix
my dinner. Put on the clothes of a table
servant and wait on me while I eat and
drink. After that, you can eat and drink'?
9You won't thank the servant because the
servant did what you asked, will you? 10In
the same way, when you have done everything required of you, you should say, 'We
servants deserve no special praise. We have
only done our duty.'"

Jesus heals a Samaritan

11On the way to Jerusalem, Jesus traveled along the border between Samaria and
Galilee. 12As he entered a village, ten men
with skin diseases approached him. Keeping their distance from him, 13they raised
their voices and said, "Jesus, Master, show
us mercy!"

14When Jesus saw them, he said, "Go,
show yourselves to the priests." As they left,
they were cleansed. 15One of them, when he
saw that he had been healed, returned and
praised God with a loud voice. 16He fell on
his face at Jesus' feet and thanked him. He
was a Samaritan. 17Jesus replied, "Weren't
ten cleansed? Where are the other nine?

[18]No one returned to praise God except this foreigner?" [19]Then Jesus said to him, "Get up and go. Your faith has healed you."

The kingdom is coming

[20]Pharisees asked Jesus when God's kingdom was coming. He replied, "God's kingdom isn't coming with signs that are easily noticed. [21]Nor will people say, 'Look, here it is!' or 'There it is!' Don't you see? God's kingdom is already among you."

[22]Then Jesus said to the disciples, "The time will come when you will long to see one of the days of the Human One,[n] and you won't see it. [23]People will say to you, 'Look there!' or 'Look here!' Don't leave or go chasing after them. [24]The Human One[o] will appear on his day in the same way that a flash of lightning lights up the sky from one end to the other. [25]However, first he must suffer many things and be rejected by this generation.

[26]"As it was in the days of Noah, so it will be during the days of the Human One.[p] [27]People were eating, drinking, marrying, and being given in marriage until the day Noah entered the ark and the flood came and destroyed them all. [28]Likewise in the days of Lot, people were eating, drinking, buying, selling, planting, and building. [29]But on the day Lot left Sodom, fire and sulfur rained down from heaven and destroyed them all. [30]That's the way it will be on the day the Human One[q] is revealed. [31]On that day, those on the roof, whose possessions are in the house, shouldn't come down to grab them. Likewise, those in the field shouldn't turn back. [32]Remember Lot's wife! [33]Whoever tries to preserve their life will lose it, but whoever loses their life will preserve it. [34]I tell you, on that night two people will be in the same bed: one will be taken and the other left. [35]Two women will be grinding grain together: one will be taken and the other left."[r]

[37]The disciples asked, "Where, Lord?"

Jesus said, "The vultures gather wherever there's a dead body."

Justice for the faithful

18 Jesus was telling them a parable about their need to pray continuously and not to be discouraged. [2]He said, "In a certain city there was a judge who neither feared God nor respected people. [3]In that city there was a widow who kept coming to him, asking, 'Give me justice in this case against my adversary.' [4]For a while he refused but finally said to himself, I don't fear God or respect people, [5]but I will give this widow justice because she keeps bothering me. Otherwise, there will be no end to her coming here and embarrassing me." [6]The Lord said, "Listen to what the unjust judge says. [7]Won't God provide justice to his chosen people who cry out to him day and night? Will he be slow to help them? [8]I tell you, he will give them justice quickly. But when the Human One[s] comes, will he find faithfulness on earth?"

The Pharisee and the tax collector

[9]Jesus told this parable to certain people who had convinced themselves that they were righteous and who looked on everyone else with disgust: [10]"Two people went up to the temple to pray. One was a Pharisee and the other a tax collector. [11]The Pharisee stood and prayed about himself with these words, 'God, I thank you that I'm not like everyone else—crooks, evildoers, adulterers—or even like this tax collector. [12]I fast twice a week. I give a tenth of everything I receive.' [13]But the tax collector stood at a distance. He wouldn't even lift his eyes to look toward heaven. Rather, he struck his chest and said, 'God, show mercy to me, a sinner.' [14]I tell you, this person went down to his home justified rather than the Pharisee. All who lift themselves up will be brought low, and those who make themselves low will be lifted up."

Jesus blesses children

[15]People were bringing babies to Jesus so that he would bless them. When the disciples saw this, they scolded them. [16]Then

[n]Or *Son of Man* [o]Or *Son of Man* [p]Or *Son of Man* [q]Or *Son of Man* [r]Critical editions of the Gk New Testament do not include 17:36 *Two will be in a field: one will be taken and the other left.* [s]Or *Son of Man*

Jesus called them to him and said, "Allow the children to come to me. Don't forbid them, because God's kingdom belongs to people like these children. [17]I assure you that whoever doesn't welcome God's kingdom like a child will never enter it."

A rich man's question

[18]A certain ruler asked Jesus, "Good Teacher, what must I do to obtain eternal life?"

[19]Jesus replied, "Why do you call me good? No one is good except the one God. [20]You know the commandments: *Don't commit adultery. Don't murder. Don't steal. Don't give false testimony. Honor your father and mother.*"[t]

[21]Then the ruler said, "I've kept all of these things since I was a boy."

[22]When Jesus heard this, he said, "There's one more thing. Sell everything you own and distribute the money to the poor. Then you will have treasure in heaven. And come, follow me." [23]When he heard these words, the man became sad because he was extremely rich.

[24]When Jesus saw this, he said, "It's very hard for the wealthy to enter God's kingdom! [25]It's easier for a camel to squeeze through the eye of a needle than for a rich person to enter God's kingdom."

[26]Those who heard this said, "Then who can be saved?"

[27]Jesus replied, "What is impossible for humans is possible for God."

[28]Peter said, "Look, we left everything we own and followed you."

[29]Jesus said to them, "I assure you that anyone who has left house, husband, wife, brothers, sisters, parents, or children because of God's kingdom [30]will receive many times more in this age and eternal life in the coming age."

Jesus predicts his death and resurrection

[31]Jesus took the Twelve aside and said, "Look, we're going up to Jerusalem, and everything written about the Human One[u] by the prophets will be accomplished. [32]He will be handed over to the Gentiles. He will be ridiculed, mistreated, and spit on. [33]After torturing him, they will kill him. On the third day, he will rise up." [34]But the Twelve understood none of these words. The meaning of this message was hidden from them and they didn't grasp what he was saying.

A blind man is healed

[35]As Jesus came to Jericho, a certain blind man was sitting beside the road begging. [36]When the man heard the crowd passing by, he asked what was happening. [37]They told him, "Jesus the Nazarene is passing by." [38]The blind man shouted, "Jesus, Son of David, show me mercy." [39]Those leading the procession scolded him, telling him to be quiet, but he shouted even louder, "Son of David, show me mercy."

[40]Jesus stopped and called for the man to be brought to him. When he was present Jesus asked, [41]"What do you want me to do for you?"

He said, "Lord, I want to see."

[42]Jesus said to him, "Receive your sight! Your faith has healed you." [43]At once he was able to see, and he began to follow Jesus, praising God. When all the people saw it, they praised God too.

A rich tax collector

19 Jesus entered Jericho and was passing through town. [2]A man there named Zacchaeus, a ruler among tax collectors, was rich. [3]He was trying to see who Jesus was, but, being a short man, he couldn't because of the crowd. [4]So he ran ahead and climbed up a sycamore tree so he could see Jesus, who was about to pass that way. [5]When Jesus came to that spot, he looked up and said, "Zacchaeus, come down at once. I must stay in your home today." [6]So Zacchaeus came down at once, happy to welcome Jesus.

[7]Everyone who saw this grumbled, saying, "He has gone to be the guest of a sinner."

[8]Zacchaeus stopped and said to the Lord, "Look, Lord, I give half of my possessions

[t]Deut 5:16-20; Exod 20:12-16 [u]Or *Son of Man*

to the poor. And if I have cheated anyone, I repay them four times as much."

9 Jesus said to him, "Today, salvation has come to this household because he too is a son of Abraham. 10 The Human One[v] came to seek and save the lost."

Faithful service

11 As they listened to this, Jesus told them another parable because he was near Jerusalem and they thought God's kingdom would appear right away. 12 He said, "A certain man who was born into royalty went to a distant land to receive his kingdom and then return. 13 He called together ten servants and gave each of them money worth four months' wages.[w] He said, 'Do business with this until I return.' 14 His citizens hated him, so they sent a representative after him who said, 'We don't want this man to be our king.' 15 After receiving his kingdom, he returned and called the servants to whom he had given the money to find out how much they had earned. 16 The first servant came forward and said, 'Your money has earned a return of one thousand percent.' 17 The king replied, 'Excellent! You are a good servant. Because you have been faithful in a small matter, you will have authority over ten cities.'

18 "The second servant came and said, 'Master, your money has made a return of five hundred percent.' 19 To this one, the king said, 'You will have authority over five cities.'

20 "Another servant came and said, 'Master, here is your money. I wrapped it up in a scarf for safekeeping. 21 I was afraid of you because you are a stern man. You withdraw what you haven't deposited and you harvest what you haven't planted.' 22 The king replied, 'I will judge you by the words of your own mouth, you worthless servant! You knew, did you, that I'm a stern man, withdrawing what I didn't deposit, and harvesting what I didn't plant? 23 Why then didn't you put my money in the bank? Then when I arrived, at least I could have gotten it back with interest.'

24 "He said to his attendants, 'Take his money and give it to the one who has ten times as much.' 25 'But Master,' they said, 'he already has ten times as much!' 26 He replied, 'I say to you that everyone who has will be given more, but from those who have nothing, even what they have will be taken away. 27 As for my enemies who don't want me as their king, bring them here and slaughter them before me.' "

28 After Jesus said this, he continued on ahead, going up to Jerusalem.

Procession into Jerusalem

29 As Jesus came to Bethphage and Bethany on the Mount of Olives, he gave two disciples a task. 30 He said, "Go into the village over there. When you enter it, you will find tied up there a colt that no one has ever ridden. Untie it and bring it here. 31 If someone asks, 'Why are you untying it?' just say, 'Its master needs it.' " 32 Those who had been sent found it exactly as he had said.

33 As they were untying the colt, its owners said to them, "Why are you untying the colt?"

34 They replied, "Its master needs it." 35 They brought it to Jesus, threw their clothes on the colt, and lifted Jesus onto it. 36 As Jesus rode along, they spread their clothes on the road.

37 As Jesus approached the road leading down from the Mount of Olives, the whole throng of his disciples began rejoicing. They praised God with a loud voice because of all the mighty things they had seen. 38 They said,

"Blessings on the king who comes in the
name of the Lord.
Peace in heaven and glory in the
highest heavens."

39 Some of the Pharisees from the crowd said to Jesus, "Teacher, scold your disciples! Tell them to stop!"

40 He answered, "I tell you, if they were silent, the stones would shout."

Jesus predicts Jerusalem's destruction

41 As Jesus came to the city and observed it, he wept over it. 42 He said, "If only you knew on this of all days the things that lead to peace. But now they are hidden from

[v] Or *Son of Man* [w] Or *he divided ten minas among them*

your eyes. 43 The time will come when your
enemies will build fortifications around
you, encircle you, and attack you from all
sides. 44 They will crush you completely, you
and the people within you. They won't leave
one stone on top of another within you, because you didn't recognize the time of your
gracious visit from God."

Jesus clears the temple

45 When Jesus entered the temple, he
threw out those who were selling things
there. 46 He said to them, "It's written, *My
house will be a house of prayer, but you have
made it a hideout for crooks.*"[x]
47 Jesus was teaching daily in the temple.
The chief priests, the legal experts, and the
foremost leaders among the people were
seeking to kill him. 48 However, they couldn't
find a way to do it because all the people
were enthralled with what they heard.

Controversy over authority

20 On one of the days when Jesus was
teaching the people in the temple
and proclaiming the good news, the chief
priests, legal experts, and elders approached
him. 2 They said, "Tell us: What kind of authority do you have for doing these things?
Who gave you this authority?"
3 He replied, "I have a question for you.
Tell me: 4 Was John's baptism of heavenly or
of human origin?"
5 They discussed among themselves, "If
we say, 'It's of heavenly origin,' he'll say,
'Why didn't you believe him?' 6 But if we
say, 'It's of human origin,' all the people
will stone us to death because they are
convinced that John was a prophet." 7 They
answered that they didn't know where it
came from.
8 Then Jesus replied, "Neither will I tell
you what kind of authority I have to do
these things."

Parable of the tenant farmers

9 Jesus told the people this parable: "A
certain man planted a vineyard, rented it to
tenant farmers, and went on a trip for a long
time. 10 When it was time, he sent a servant
to collect from the tenants his share of the
fruit of the vineyard. But the tenants sent
him away, beaten and empty-handed. 11 The
man sent another servant. But they beat
him, treated him disgracefully, and sent
him away empty-handed as well. 12 He sent
a third servant. They wounded this servant
and threw him out. 13 The owner of the vineyard said, 'What should I do? I'll send my
son, whom I love dearly. Perhaps they will
respect him.' 14 But when they saw him, they
said to each other, 'This is the heir. Let's kill
him so the inheritance will be ours.' 15 They
threw him out of the vineyard and killed
him. What will the owner of the vineyard do
to them? 16 He will come and destroy those
tenants and give the vineyard to others."
When the people heard this, they said,
"May this never happen!"
17 Staring at them, Jesus said, "Then what
is the meaning of this text of scripture: *The
stone that the builders rejected has become the
cornerstone?*[y] 18 Everyone who falls on that
stone will be crushed. And the stone will
crush the person it falls on." 19 The legal experts and chief priests wanted to arrest him
right then because they knew he had told
this parable against them. But they feared
the people.

An attempt to trap Jesus

20 The legal experts and chief priests
were watching Jesus closely and sent spies
who pretended to be sincere. They wanted
to trap him in his words so they could
hand him over to the jurisdiction and authority of the governor. 21 They asked him,
"Teacher, we know that you are correct in
what you say and teach. You don't show
favoritism but teach God's way as it really
is. 22 Does the Law allow people to pay taxes
to Caesar or not?"
23 Since Jesus recognized their deception, he said to them, 24 "Show me a coin.[z]
Whose image and inscription does it have
on it?"
"Caesar's," they replied.
25 He said to them, "Give to Caesar what

[x] Isa 56:7; Jer 7:11 [y] Ps 118:22 [z] Or *denarion*

belongs to Caesar and to God what belongs to God." [26]They couldn't trap him in his words in front of the people. Astonished by his answer, they were speechless.

Question about the resurrection

[27]Some Sadducees, who deny that there's a resurrection, came to Jesus and asked, [28]"Teacher, Moses wrote for us that *if a man's brother dies* leaving a widow *but no children, the brother must marry the widow and raise up children for his brother.*[a] [29]Now there were seven brothers. The first man married a woman and then died childless. [30]The second [31]and then the third brother married her. Eventually all seven married her, and they all died without leaving any children. [32]Finally, the woman died too. [33]In the resurrection, whose wife will she be? All seven were married to her."

[34]Jesus said to them, "People who belong to this age marry and are given in marriage. [35]But those who are considered worthy to participate in that age, that is, in the age of the resurrection from the dead, won't marry nor will they be given in marriage. [36]They can no longer die, because they are like angels and are God's children since they share in the resurrection. [37]Even Moses demonstrated that the dead are raised—in the passage about the burning bush, when he speaks of the Lord as *the God of Abraham, the God of Isaac, and the God of Jacob.*[b] [38]He isn't the God of the dead but of the living. To him they are all alive."

[39]Some of the legal experts responded, "Teacher, you have answered well." [40]No one dared to ask him anything else.

[41]Jesus said to them, "Why do they say that the Christ is David's son? [42]David himself says in the scroll of Psalms, *The Lord said to my lord, 'Sit at my right side* [43]*until I make your enemies a footstool for your feet.'*[c] [44]Since David calls him 'Lord,' how can he be David's son?"

Jesus condemns the legal experts

[45]In the presence of all the people, Jesus said to his disciples, [46]"Watch out for the legal experts. They like to walk around in long robes. They love being greeted with honor in the markets. They long for the places of honor in the synagogues and at banquets. [47]They are the ones who cheat widows out of their homes, and to show off they say long prayers. They will be judged most harshly."

A poor widow's offering

21 Looking up, Jesus saw rich people throwing their gifts into the collection box for the temple treasury. [2]He also saw a poor widow throw in two small copper coins worth a penny.[d] [3]He said, "I assure you that this poor widow has put in more than them all. [4]All of them are giving out of their spare change. But she from her hopeless poverty has given everything she had to live on."

The temple's fate

[5]Some people were talking about the temple, how it was decorated with beautiful stones and ornaments dedicated to God. Jesus said, [6]"As for the things you are admiring, the time is coming when not even one stone will be left upon another. All will be demolished."

[7]They asked him, "Teacher, when will these things happen? What sign will show that these things are about to happen?"

[8]Jesus said, "Watch out that you aren't deceived. Many will come in my name, saying, 'I'm the one!' and 'It's time!' Don't follow them. [9]When you hear of wars and rebellions, don't be alarmed. These things must happen first, but the end won't happen immediately."

[10]Then Jesus said to them, "Nations and kingdoms will fight against each other. [11]There will be great earthquakes and widescale food shortages and epidemics. There will also be terrifying sights and great signs in the sky. [12]But before all this occurs, they will take you into custody and harass you because of your faith. They will hand you over to synagogues and prisons, and you will be brought before kings and governors

[a]Deut 25:5; Gen 38:8 [b]Exod 3:6, 15-16 [c]Ps 110:1 [d]Or *two lepta*

because of my name. [13]This will provide you with an opportunity to testify. [14]Make up your minds not to prepare your defense in advance. [15]I'll give you words and wisdom that none of your opponents will be able to counter or contradict. [16]You will be betrayed by your parents, brothers and sisters, relatives, and friends. They will execute some of you. [17]Everyone will hate you because of my name. [18]Still, not a hair on your heads will be lost. [19]By holding fast, you will gain your lives.

[20]"When you see Jerusalem surrounded by armies, then you will know that its destruction is close at hand. [21]At that time, those in Judea must flee to the mountains, those in the city must escape, and those in the countryside must not enter the city. [22]These are the days of punishment, when everything written will find its fulfillment. [23]How terrible it will be at that time for women who are pregnant or for women who are nursing their children. There will be great agony on the earth and angry judgment on this people. [24]They will fall by the edge of the sword and be taken away as captives among all nations. Jerusalem will be plundered by Gentiles until the times of the Gentiles are concluded.

[25]"There will be signs in the sun, moon, and stars. On the earth, there will be dismay among nations in their confusion over the roaring of the sea and surging waves. [26]The planets and other heavenly bodies will be shaken, causing people to faint from fear and foreboding of what is coming upon the world. [27]Then they will see the Human One[e] coming on a cloud with power and great splendor. [28]Now when these things begin to happen, stand up straight and raise your heads, because your redemption is near."

A lesson from the fig tree

[29]Jesus told them a parable: "Look at the fig tree and all the trees. [30]When they sprout leaves, you can see for yourselves and know that summer is near. [31]In the same way, when you see these things happening, you know that God's kingdom is near. [32]I assure you that this generation won't pass away until everything has happened. [33]Heaven and earth will pass away, but my words will certainly not pass away.

[34]"Take care that your hearts aren't dulled by drinking parties, drunkenness, and the anxieties of day-to-day life. Don't let that day fall upon you unexpectedly, [35]like a trap. It will come upon everyone who lives on the face of the whole earth. [36]Stay alert at all times, praying that you are strong enough to escape everything that is about to happen and to stand before the Human One."[f]

[37]Every day Jesus was teaching in the temple, but he spent each night on the Mount of Olives. [38]All the people rose early in the morning to hear him in the temple area.

Plot to kill Jesus

22 The Festival of Unleavened Bread, which is called Passover, was approaching. [2]The chief priests and the legal experts were looking for a way to kill Jesus, because they were afraid of the people. [3]Then Satan entered Judas, called Iscariot, who was one of the Twelve. [4]He went out and discussed with the chief priests and the officers of the temple guard how he could hand Jesus over to them. [5]They were delighted and arranged payment for him. [6]He agreed and began looking for an opportunity to hand Jesus over to them—a time when the crowds would be absent.

Disciples prepare for the Passover

[7]The Day of Unleavened Bread arrived, when the Passover had to be sacrificed. [8]Jesus sent Peter and John with this task: "Go and prepare for us to eat the Passover meal."

[9]They said to him, "Where do you want us to prepare it?"

[10]Jesus replied, "When you go into the city, a man carrying a water jar will meet you. Follow him to the house he enters. [11]Say to the owner of the house, 'The teacher says to you, "Where is the guestroom where I can eat the Passover meal with my disciples?"' [12]He will show you a large upstairs room,

[e]Or *Son of Man* [f]Or *Son of Man*

already furnished. Make preparations there." [13]They went and found everything just as he had told them, and they prepared the Passover meal.

The Passover meal

[14]When the time came, Jesus took his place at the table, and the apostles joined him. [15]He said to them, "I have earnestly desired to eat this Passover with you before I suffer. [16]I tell you, I won't eat it until it is fulfilled in God's kingdom." [17]After taking a cup and giving thanks, he said, "Take this and share it among yourselves. [18]I tell you that from now on I won't drink from the fruit of the vine until God's kingdom has come." [19]After taking the bread and giving thanks, he broke it and gave it to them, saying, "This is my body, which is given for you. Do this in remembrance of me." [20]In the same way, he took the cup after the meal and said, "This cup is the new covenant by my blood, which is poured out for you.

[21]"But look! My betrayer is with me; his hand is on this table. [22]The Human One[g] goes just as it has been determined. But how terrible it is for that person who betrays him." [23]They began to argue among themselves about which of them it could possibly be who would do this.

The disciples debate greatness

[24]An argument broke out among the disciples over which one of them should be regarded as the greatest.

[25]But Jesus said to them, "The kings of the Gentiles rule over their subjects, and those in authority over them are called 'friends of the people.' [26]But that's not the way it will be with you. Instead, the greatest among you must become like a person of lower status and the leader like a servant. [27]So which one is greater, the one who is seated at the table or the one who serves at the table? Isn't it the one who is seated at the table? But I am among you as one who serves.

[28]"You are the ones who have continued with me in my trials. [29]And I confer royal power on you just as my Father granted royal power to me. [30]Thus you will eat and drink at my table in my kingdom, and you will sit on thrones overseeing the twelve tribes of Israel.

Peter's denial predicted

[31]"Simon, Simon, look! Satan has asserted the right to sift you all like wheat. [32]However, I have prayed for you that your faith won't fail. When you have returned, strengthen your brothers and sisters."

[33]Peter responded, "Lord, I'm ready to go with you, both to prison and to death!"

[34]Jesus replied, "I tell you, Peter, the rooster won't crow today before you have denied three times that you know me."

Call for preparedness

[35]Jesus said to them, "When I sent you out without a wallet, bag, or sandals, you didn't lack anything, did you?"

They said, "Nothing."

[36]Then he said to them, "But now, whoever has a wallet must take it, and likewise a bag. And those who don't own a sword must sell their clothes and buy one. [37]I tell you that this scripture must be fulfilled in relation to me: *And he was counted among criminals.*[h] Indeed, what's written about me is nearing completion."

[38]They said to him, "Lord, look, here are two swords."

He replied, "Enough of that!"

Jesus in prayer

[39]Jesus left and made his way to the Mount of Olives, as was his custom, and the disciples followed him. [40]When he arrived, he said to them, "Pray that you won't give in to temptation." [41]He withdrew from them about a stone's throw, knelt down, and prayed. [42]He said, "Father, if it's your will, take this cup of suffering away from me. However, not my will but your will must be done." [43]Then a heavenly angel appeared to him and strengthened him. [44]He was in anguish and prayed even more earnestly. His sweat became like drops of blood falling on the ground. [45]When he got up from

[g]Or *Son of Man* [h]Isa 53:12

praying, he went to the disciples. He found them asleep, overcome by grief. 46He said to them, "Why are you sleeping? Get up and pray so that you won't give in to temptation."

Jesus' arrest

47While Jesus was still speaking, a crowd appeared, and the one called Judas, one of the Twelve, was leading them. He approached Jesus to kiss him.

48Jesus said to him, "Judas, would you betray the Human One[i] with a kiss?"

49When those around him recognized what was about to happen, they said, "Lord, should we fight with our swords?" 50One of them struck the high priest's servant, cutting off his right ear.

51Jesus responded, "Stop! No more of this!" He touched the slave's ear and healed him.

52Then Jesus said to the chief priests, the officers of the temple guard, and the elders who had come to get him, "Have you come with swords and clubs to arrest me, as though I were a thief? 53Day after day I was with you in the temple, but you didn't arrest me. But this is your time, when darkness rules."

Peter denies knowing Jesus

54After they arrested Jesus, they led him away and brought him to the high priest's house. Peter followed from a distance. 55When they lit a fire in the middle of the courtyard and sat down together, Peter sat among them.

56Then a servant woman saw him sitting in the firelight. She stared at him and said, "This man was with him too."

57But Peter denied it, saying, "Woman, I don't know him!"

58A little while later, someone else saw him and said, "You are one of them too."

But Peter said, "Man, I'm not!"

59An hour or so later, someone else insisted, "This man must have been with him, because he is a Galilean too."

60Peter responded, "Man, I don't know what you are talking about!" At that very moment, while he was still speaking, a rooster crowed. 61The Lord turned and looked straight at Peter, and Peter remembered the Lord's words: "Before a rooster crows today, you will deny me three times." 62And Peter went out and cried uncontrollably.

Jesus taunted

63The men who were holding Jesus in custody taunted him while they beat him. 64They blindfolded him and asked him repeatedly, "Prophesy! Who hit you?" 65Insulting him, they said many other horrible things against him.

Jesus before the Jerusalem leadership

66As morning came, the elders of the people, both chief priests and legal experts, came together, and Jesus was brought before their council.

67They said, "If you are the Christ, tell us!"

He answered, "If I tell you, you won't believe. 68And if I ask you a question, you won't answer. 69But from now on, *the Human One*[j] *will be seated on the right side of the power of God*."[k]

70They all said, "Are you God's Son, then?"

He replied, "You say that I am."

71Then they said, "Why do we need further testimony? We've heard it from his own lips."

Jesus before Pilate

23 The whole assembly got up and led Jesus to Pilate and 2began to accuse him. They said, "We have found this man misleading our people, opposing the payment of taxes to Caesar, and claiming that he is the Christ, a king."

3Pilate asked him, "Are you the king of the Jews?"

Jesus replied, "That's what you say."

4Then Pilate said to the chief priests and the crowds, "I find no legal basis for action against this man."

5But they objected strenuously, saying, "He agitates the people with his teaching throughout Judea—starting from Galilee all the way here."

[i]Or *Son of Man* [j]Or *Son of Man* [k]Ps 110:1

Jesus before Herod

6 Hearing this, Pilate asked if the man
was a Galilean. 7 When he learned that Jesus
was from Herod's district, Pilate sent him
to Herod, who was also in Jerusalem at that
time. 8 Herod was very glad to see Jesus, for
he had heard about Jesus and had wanted
to see him for quite some time. He was hoping to see Jesus perform some sign. 9 Herod
questioned Jesus at length, but Jesus didn't
respond to him. 10 The chief priests and the
legal experts were there, fiercely accusing Jesus. 11 Herod and his soldiers treated
Jesus with contempt. Herod mocked him
by dressing Jesus in elegant clothes and
sent him back to Pilate. 12 Pilate and Herod
became friends with each other that day.
Before this, they had been enemies.

Jesus and Barabbas

13 Then Pilate called together the chief
priests, the rulers, and the people. 14 He said
to them, "You brought this man before me as
one who was misleading the people. I have
questioned him in your presence and found
nothing in this man's conduct that provides
a legal basis for the charges you have brought
against him. 15 Neither did Herod, because
Herod returned him to us. He's done nothing that deserves death. 16 Therefore, I'll have
him whipped, then let him go."[l]

18 But with one voice they shouted,
"Away with this man! Release Barabbas
to us." (19 Barabbas had been thrown into
prison because of a riot that had occurred
in the city, and for murder.)

20 Pilate addressed them again because
he wanted to release Jesus.

21 They kept shouting out, "Crucify him!
Crucify him!"

22 For the third time, Pilate said to them,
"Why? What wrong has he done? I've found
no legal basis for the death penalty in his
case. Therefore, I will have him whipped,
then let him go."

23 But they were adamant, shouting
their demand that Jesus be crucified. Their
voices won out. 24 Pilate issued his decision
to grant their request. 25 He released the
one they asked for, who had been thrown
into prison because of a riot and murder.
But he handed Jesus over to their will.

On the way to the cross

26 As they led Jesus away, they grabbed
Simon, a man from Cyrene, who was coming in from the countryside. They put the
cross on his back and made him carry it
behind Jesus. 27 A huge crowd of people followed Jesus, including women, who were
mourning and wailing for him. 28 Jesus
turned to the women and said, "Daughters
of Jerusalem, don't cry for me. Rather, cry
for yourselves and your children. 29 The
time will come when they will say, 'Happy
are those who are unable to become pregnant, the wombs that never gave birth,
and the breasts that never nursed a child.'
30 Then *they will say to the mountains, 'Fall on
us,' and to the hills, 'Cover us.'*[m] 31 If they do
these things when the tree is green, what
will happen when it is dry?"

Jesus on the cross

32 They also led two other criminals to be
executed with Jesus. 33 When they arrived
at the place called The Skull, they crucified
him, along with the criminals, one on his
right and the other on his left. 34 Jesus said,
"Father, forgive them, for they don't know
what they're doing." They drew lots as a way
of dividing up his clothing.

35 The people were standing around
watching, but the leaders sneered at him,
saying, "He saved others. Let him save himself if he really is the Christ sent from God,
the chosen one."

36 The soldiers also mocked him. They
came up to him, offering him sour wine
37 and saying, "If you really are the king of
the Jews, save yourself." 38 Above his head
was a notice of the formal charge against
him. It read "This is the king of the Jews."

39 One of the criminals hanging next to
Jesus insulted him: "Aren't you the Christ?
Save yourself and us!"

[l] Critical editions of the Gk New Testament do not include 23:17 *He had to release one prisoner for them because of the festival.* [m] Hos 10:8

40Responding, the other criminal spoke
harshly to him, “Don't you fear God, seeing that you've also been sentenced to die?
41We are rightly condemned, for we are receiving the appropriate sentence for what
we did. But this man has done nothing
wrong.” 42Then he said, “Jesus, remember
me when you come into your kingdom.”
43Jesus replied, “I assure you that today
you will be with me in paradise.”

Jesus' death

44It was now about noon, and darkness
covered the whole earth until about three
o'clock, 45while the sun stopped shining.
Then the curtain in the sanctuary tore
down the middle. 46Crying out in a loud
voice, Jesus said, “Father, *into your hands
I entrust my life.*”[n] After he said this, he
breathed for the last time.
47When the centurion saw what happened, he praised God, saying, “It's really
true: this man was righteous.” 48All the
crowds who had come together to see this
event returned to their homes beating their
chests after seeing what had happened.
49And everyone who knew him, including
the women who had followed him from
Galilee, stood at a distance observing these
things.

Jesus' burial

50Now there was a man named Joseph
who was a member of the council. He was a
good and righteous man. 51He hadn't agreed
with the plan and actions of the council. He
was from the Jewish city of Arimathea and
eagerly anticipated God's kingdom. 52This
man went to Pilate and asked for Jesus'
body. 53Taking it down, he wrapped it in a
linen cloth and laid it in a tomb carved out
of the rock, in which no one had ever been
buried. 54It was the Preparation Day for
the Sabbath, and the Sabbath was quickly
approaching. 55The women who had come
with Jesus from Galilee followed Joseph.
They saw the tomb and how Jesus' body
was laid in it, 56then they went away and
prepared fragrant spices and perfumed oils.
They rested on the Sabbath, in keeping with
the commandment.

The empty tomb

24 Very early in the morning on the
first day of the week, the women
went to the tomb, bringing the fragrant
spices they had prepared. 2They found
the stone rolled away from the tomb, 3but
when they went in, they didn't find the
body of the Lord Jesus. 4They didn't know
what to make of this. Suddenly, two men
were standing beside them in gleaming
bright clothing. 5The women were frightened and bowed their faces toward the
ground, but the men said to them, “Why
do you look for the living among the dead?
6He isn't here, but has been raised. Remember what he told you while he was still
in Galilee, 7that the Human One[o] must be
handed over to sinners, be crucified, and
on the third day rise again.” 8Then they
remembered his words. 9When they returned from the tomb, they reported all
these things to the eleven and all the others. 10It was Mary Magdalene, Joanna,
Mary the mother of James, and the other
women with them who told these things
to the apostles. 11Their words struck the
apostles as nonsense, and they didn't believe the women. 12But Peter ran to the
tomb. When he bent over to look inside, he
saw only the linen cloth. Then he returned
home, wondering what had happened.

Encounter on the Emmaus road

13On that same day, two disciples were
traveling to a village called Emmaus, about
seven miles from Jerusalem. 14They were
talking to each other about everything that
had happened. 15While they were discussing these things, Jesus himself arrived and
joined them on their journey. 16They were
prevented from recognizing him.
17He said to them, “What are you talking
about as you walk along?” They stopped,
their faces downcast.
18The one named Cleopas replied, “Are
you the only visitor to Jerusalem who is

[n]Ps 31:5 [o]Or *Son of Man*

unaware of the things that have taken place there over the last few days?"

[19]He said to them, "What things?"

They said to him, "The things about Jesus of Nazareth. Because of his powerful deeds and words, he was recognized by God and all the people as a prophet. [20]But our chief priests and our leaders handed him over to be sentenced to death, and they crucified him. [21]We had hoped he was the one who would redeem Israel. All these things happened three days ago. [22]But there's more: Some women from our group have left us stunned. They went to the tomb early this morning [23]and didn't find his body. They came to us saying that they had even seen a vision of angels who told them he is alive. [24]Some of those who were with us went to the tomb and found things just as the women said. They didn't see him."

[25]Then Jesus said to them, "You foolish people! Your dull minds keep you from believing all that the prophets talked about. [26]Wasn't it necessary for the Christ to suffer these things and then enter into his glory?" [27]Then he interpreted for them the things written about himself in all the scriptures, starting with Moses and going through all the Prophets.

[28]When they came to Emmaus, he acted as if he was going on ahead. [29]But they urged him, saying, "Stay with us. It's nearly evening, and the day is almost over." So he went in to stay with them. [30]After he took his seat at the table with them, he took the bread, blessed and broke it, and gave it to them. [31]Their eyes were opened and they recognized him, but he disappeared from their sight. [32]They said to each other, "Weren't our hearts on fire when he spoke to us along the road and when he explained the scriptures for us?"

[33]They got up right then and returned to Jerusalem. They found the eleven and their companions gathered together. [34]They were saying to each other, "The Lord really has risen! He appeared to Simon!" [35]Then the two disciples described what had happened along the road and how Jesus was made known to them as he broke the bread.

Jesus appears to the disciples

[36]While they were saying these things, Jesus himself stood among them and said, "Peace be with you!" [37]They were terrified and afraid. They thought they were seeing a ghost.

[38]He said to them, "Why are you startled? Why are doubts arising in your hearts? [39]Look at my hands and my feet. It's really me! Touch me and see, for a ghost doesn't have flesh and bones like you see I have." [40]As he said this, he showed them his hands and feet. [41]Because they were wondering and questioning in the midst of their happiness, he said to them, "Do you have anything to eat?" [42]They gave him a piece of baked fish. [43]Taking it, he ate it in front of them.

[44]Jesus said to them, "These are my words that I spoke to you while I was still with you—that everything written about me in the Law from Moses, the Prophets, and the Psalms must be fulfilled." [45]Then he opened their minds to understand the scriptures. [46]He said to them, "This is what is written: the Christ will suffer and rise from the dead on the third day, [47]and a change of heart and life for the forgiveness of sins must be preached in his name to all nations, beginning from Jerusalem. [48]You are witnesses of these things. [49]Look, I'm sending to you what my Father promised, but you are to stay in the city until you have been furnished with heavenly power."

Ascension of Jesus

[50]He led them out as far as Bethany, where he lifted his hands and blessed them. [51]As he blessed them, he left them and was taken up to heaven. [52]They worshipped him and returned to Jerusalem overwhelmed with joy. [53]And they were continuously in the temple praising God.

JOHN

Story of the Word

1 In the beginning was the Word
and the Word was with God
and the Word was God.
2 The Word was with God in the beginning.
3 Everything came into being
through the Word,
and without the Word
nothing came into being.
What came into being
4 through the Word was life,[a]
and the life was the light for all people.
5 The light shines in the darkness,
and the darkness doesn't
extinguish the light.
6 A man named John was sent from God.
7 He came as a witness to testify concerning the light, so that through him everyone would believe in the light. 8 He himself
wasn't the light, but his mission was to testify concerning the light.
9 The true light that shines on all people
was coming into the world.
10 The light was in the world,
and the world came into being
through the light,
but the world
didn't recognize the light.
11 The light came to his own people,
and his own people didn't welcome him.
12 But those who did welcome him,
those who believed in his name,
he authorized to become
God's children,
13 born not from blood
nor from human desire or passion,
but born from God.
14 The Word became flesh
and made his home among us.
We have seen his glory,
glory like that of a father's only son,
full of grace and truth.
15 John testified about him, crying out,
"This is the one of whom I said, 'He who
comes after me is greater than me because
he existed before me.' "
16 From his fullness we have all received
grace upon grace;
17 as the Law was given through Moses,
so grace and truth came into being
through Jesus Christ.
18 No one has ever seen God.
God the only Son,
who is at the Father's side,
has made God known.

John's witness

19 This is John's testimony when the Jewish leaders in Jerusalem sent priests and
Levites to ask him, "Who are you?"
20 John confessed (he didn't deny but
confessed), "I'm not the Christ."
21 They asked him, "Then who are you?
Are you Elijah?"
John said, "I'm not."
"Are you the prophet?"
John answered, "No."
22 They asked, "Who are you? We need to
give an answer to those who sent us. What
do you say about yourself?"
23 John replied,
"I am a voice crying out in the wilderness,
Make the Lord's path straight,[b]
just as the prophet Isaiah said."
24 Those sent by the Pharisees 25 asked,
"Why do you baptize if you aren't the
Christ, nor Elijah, nor the prophet?"
26 John answered, "I baptize with water.
Someone greater stands among you, whom
you don't recognize. 27 He comes after me, but
I'm not worthy to untie his sandal straps."
28 This encounter took place across the Jordan
in Bethany where John was baptizing.
29 The next day John saw Jesus coming toward him and said, "Look! The Lamb of God
who takes away the sin of the world! 30 This
is the one about whom I said, 'He who comes
after me is really greater than me because he
existed before me.' 31 Even I didn't recognize
him, but I came baptizing with water so that
he might be made known to Israel." 32 John
testified, "I saw the Spirit coming down

[a] Or *Everything came into being through the Word,/and without the Word / nothing came into being that came into being.* 4 *In the Word was life* [b] Isa 40:3

from heaven like a dove, and it rested on him. [33]Even I didn't recognize him, but the one who sent me to baptize with water said to me, 'The one on whom you see the Spirit coming down and resting is the one who baptizes with the Holy Spirit.' [34]I have seen and testified that this one is God's Son."

Jesus calls disciples

[35]The next day John was standing again with two of his disciples. [36]When he saw Jesus walking along he said, "Look! The Lamb of God!" [37]The two disciples heard what he said, and they followed Jesus.

[38]When Jesus turned and saw them following, he asked, "What are you looking for?"

They said, "Rabbi (which is translated *Teacher*), where are you staying?"

[39]He replied, "Come and see." So they went and saw where he was staying, and they remained with him that day. It was about four o'clock in the afternoon.

[40]One of the two disciples who heard what John said and followed Jesus was Andrew, the brother of Simon Peter. [41]He first found his own brother Simon and said to him, "We have found the Messiah" (which is translated *Christ*[c]). [42]He led him to Jesus.

Jesus looked at him and said, "You are Simon, son of John. You will be called Cephas" (which is translated *Peter*).

[43]The next day Jesus wanted to go into Galilee, and he found Philip. Jesus said to him, "Follow me." [44]Philip was from Bethsaida, the hometown of Andrew and Peter.

[45]Philip found Nathanael and said to him, "We have found the one Moses wrote about in the Law and the Prophets: Jesus, Joseph's son, from Nazareth."

[46]Nathanael responded, "Can anything from Nazareth be good?"

Philip said, "Come and see."

[47]Jesus saw Nathanael coming toward him and said about him, "Here is a genuine Israelite in whom there is no deceit."

[48]Nathanael asked him, "How do you know me?"

Jesus answered, "Before Philip called you, I saw you under the fig tree."

[49]Nathanael replied, "Rabbi, you are God's Son. You are the king of Israel."

[50]Jesus answered, "Do you believe because I told you that I saw you under the fig tree? You will see greater things than these! [51]I assure you that you will see heaven open and God's angels going up to heaven and down to earth on the Human One."[d]

Wedding at Cana

2 On the third day there was a wedding in Cana of Galilee. Jesus' mother was there, and [2]Jesus and his disciples were also invited to the celebration. [3]When the wine ran out, Jesus' mother said to him, "They don't have any wine."

[4]Jesus replied, "Woman, what does that have to do with me? My time hasn't come yet."

[5]His mother told the servants, "Do whatever he tells you." [6]Nearby were six stone water jars used for the Jewish cleansing ritual, each able to hold about twenty or thirty gallons.

[7]Jesus said to the servants, "Fill the jars with water," and they filled them to the brim. [8]Then he told them, "Now draw some from them and take it to the headwaiter," and they did. [9]The headwaiter tasted the water that had become wine. He didn't know where it came from, though the servants who had drawn the water knew.

The headwaiter called the groom [10]and said, "Everyone serves the good wine first. They bring out the second-rate wine only when the guests are drinking freely. You kept the good wine until now." [11]This was the first miraculous sign that Jesus did in Cana of Galilee. He revealed his glory, and his disciples believed in him.

[12]After this, Jesus and his mother, his brothers, and his disciples went down to Capernaum and stayed there for a few days.

Jesus in Jerusalem at Passover

[13]It was nearly time for the Jewish Passover, and Jesus went up to Jerusalem. [14]He found in the temple those who were selling cattle, sheep, and doves, as well as

[c]Or *Anointed One* [d]Or *Son of Man*

those involved in exchanging currency sitting there. 15He made a whip from ropes and chased them all out of the temple, including the cattle and the sheep. He scattered the coins and overturned the tables of those who exchanged currency. 16He said to the dove sellers, "Get these things out of here! Don't make my Father's house a place of business." 17His disciples remembered that it is written, *Passion for your house consumes me.*[e]

18Then the Jewish leaders asked him, "By what authority are you doing these things? What miraculous sign will you show us?"

19Jesus answered, "Destroy this temple and in three days I'll raise it up."

20The Jewish leaders replied, "It took forty-six years to build this temple, and you will raise it up in three days?" 21But the temple Jesus was talking about was his body. 22After he was raised from the dead, his disciples remembered what he had said, and they believed the scripture and the word that Jesus had spoken.

23While Jesus was in Jerusalem for the Passover Festival, many believed in his name because they saw the miraculous signs that he did. 24But Jesus didn't trust himself to them because he knew all people. 25He didn't need anyone to tell him about human nature, for he knew what human nature was.

Jesus and Nicodemus

3 There was a Pharisee named Nicodemus, a Jewish leader. 2He came to Jesus at night and said to him, "Rabbi, we know that you are a teacher who has come from God, for no one could do these miraculous signs that you do unless God is with him."

3Jesus answered, "I assure you, unless someone is born anew,[f] it's not possible to see God's kingdom."

4Nicodemus asked, "How is it possible for an adult to be born? It's impossible to enter the mother's womb for a second time and be born, isn't it?"

5Jesus answered, "I assure you, unless someone is born of water and the Spirit, it's not possible to enter God's kingdom. 6Whatever is born of the flesh is flesh, and whatever is born of the Spirit is spirit. 7Don't be surprised that I said to you, 'You must be born anew.' 8God's Spirit[g] blows wherever it wishes. You hear its sound, but you don't know where it comes from or where it is going. It's the same with everyone who is born of the Spirit."

9Nicodemus said, "How are these things possible?"

10Jesus answered, "You are a teacher of Israel and you don't know these things? 11I assure you that we speak about what we know and testify about what we have seen, but you don't receive our testimony. 12If I have told you about earthly things and you don't believe, how will you believe if I tell you about heavenly things? 13No one has gone up to heaven except the one who came down from heaven, the Human One.[h] 14Just as Moses lifted up the snake in the wilderness, so must the Human One[i] be lifted up 15so that everyone who believes in him will have eternal life. 16God so loved the world that he gave his only Son, so that everyone who believes in him won't perish but will have eternal life. 17God didn't send his Son into the world to judge the world, but that the world might be saved through him. 18Whoever believes in him isn't judged; whoever doesn't believe in him is already judged, because they don't believe in the name of God's only Son.

19"This is the basis for judgment: The light came into the world, and people loved darkness more than the light, for their actions are evil. 20All who do wicked things hate the light and don't come to the light for fear that their actions will be exposed to the light. 21Whoever does the truth comes to the light so that it can be seen that their actions were done in God."

John's final witness

22After this Jesus and his disciples went into Judea, where he spent some time with them and was baptizing. 23John was baptizing at Aenon near Salem because there

[e]Ps 69:9 [f]Or *from above* [g]Or *wind* [h]Or *Son of Man* [i]Or *Son of Man*

was a lot of water there, and people were coming to him and being baptized. (24 John hadn't yet been thrown into prison.)

25 A debate started between John's disciples and a certain Jew about cleansing rituals. 26 They came to John and said, "Rabbi, look! The man who was with you across the Jordan, the one about whom you testified, is baptizing and everyone is flocking to him."

27 John replied, "No one can receive anything unless it is given from heaven. 28 You yourselves can testify that I said that I'm not the Christ but that I'm the one sent before him. 29 The groom is the one who is getting married. The friend of the groom stands close by and, when he hears him, is overjoyed at the groom's voice. Therefore, my joy is now complete. 30 He must increase and I must decrease. 31 The one who comes from above is above all things. The one who is from the earth belongs to the earth and speaks as one from the earth. The one who comes from heaven is above all things. 32 He testifies to what he has seen and heard, but no one accepts his testimony. 33 Whoever accepts his testimony confirms that God is true. 34 The one whom God sent speaks God's words because God gives the Spirit generously. 35 The Father loves the Son and gives everything into his hands. 36 Whoever believes in the Son has eternal life. Whoever doesn't believe in the Son won't see life, but the angry judgment of God remains on them."

Jesus leaves Judea

4 Jesus learned that the Pharisees had heard that he was making more disciples and baptizing more than John (2 although Jesus' disciples were baptizing, not Jesus himself). 3 Therefore, he left Judea and went back to Galilee.

Jesus in Samaria

4 Jesus had to go through Samaria. 5 He came to a Samaritan city called Sychar, which was near the land Jacob had given to his son Joseph. 6 Jacob's well was there. Jesus was tired from his journey, so he sat down at the well. It was about noon.

7 A Samaritan woman came to the well to draw water. Jesus said to her, "Give me some water to drink." 8 His disciples had gone into the city to buy him some food.

9 The Samaritan woman asked, "Why do you, a Jewish man, ask for something to drink from me, a Samaritan woman?" (Jews and Samaritans didn't associate with each other.)

10 Jesus responded, "If you recognized God's gift and who is saying to you, 'Give me some water to drink,' you would be asking him and he would give you living water."

11 The woman said to him, "Sir, you don't have a bucket and the well is deep. Where would you get this living water? 12 You aren't greater than our father Jacob, are you? He gave this well to us, and he drank from it himself, as did his sons and his livestock."

13 Jesus answered, "Everyone who drinks this water will be thirsty again, 14 but whoever drinks from the water that I will give will never be thirsty again. The water that I give will become in those who drink it a spring of water that bubbles up into eternal life."

15 The woman said to him, "Sir, give me this water, so that I will never be thirsty and will never need to come here to draw water!"

16 Jesus said to her, "Go, get your husband, and come back here."

17 The woman replied, "I don't have a husband."

"You are right to say, 'I don't have a husband,'" Jesus answered. 18 "You've had five husbands, and the man you are with now isn't your husband. You've spoken the truth."

19 The woman said, "Sir, I see that you are a prophet. 20 Our ancestors worshipped on this mountain, but you and your people say that it is necessary to worship in Jerusalem."

21 Jesus said to her, "Believe me, woman, the time is coming when you and your people will worship the Father neither on this mountain nor in Jerusalem. 22 You and your people worship what you don't know; we worship what we know because salvation is from the Jews. 23 But the time is coming—and is here!—when true worshippers will worship in spirit and truth. The Father looks for those who worship him this way. 24 God is spirit, and it is necessary to worship God in spirit and truth."

25 The woman said, "I know that the Messiah is coming, the one who is called the Christ. When he comes, he will teach everything to us."

26 Jesus said to her, "I Am—the one who speaks with you."[j]

27 Just then, Jesus' disciples arrived and were shocked that he was talking with a woman. But no one asked, "What do you want?" or "Why are you talking with her?" 28 The woman put down her water jar and went into the city. She said to the people, 29 "Come and see a man who has told me everything I've done! Could this man be the Christ?" 30 They left the city and were on their way to see Jesus.

31 In the meantime the disciples spoke to Jesus, saying, "Rabbi, eat."

32 Jesus said to them, "I have food to eat that you don't know about."

33 The disciples asked each other, "Has someone brought him food?"

34 Jesus said to them, "I am fed by doing the will of the one who sent me and by completing his work. 35 Don't you have a saying, 'Four more months and then it's time for harvest'? Look, I tell you: open your eyes and notice that the fields are already ripe for the harvest. 36 Those who harvest are receiving their pay and gathering fruit for eternal life so that those who sow and those who harvest can celebrate together. 37 This is a true saying, that one sows and another harvests. 38 I have sent you to harvest what you didn't work hard for; others worked hard, and you will share in their hard work."

39 Many Samaritans in that city believed in Jesus because of the woman's word when she testified, "He told me everything I've ever done." 40 So when the Samaritans came to Jesus, they asked him to stay with them, and he stayed there two days. 41 Many more believed because of his word, 42 and they said to the woman, "We no longer believe because of what you said, for we have heard for ourselves and know that this one is truly the savior of the world."

Jesus arrives in Galilee

43 After two days Jesus left for Galilee. (44 Jesus himself had testified that prophets have no honor in their own country.) 45 When he came to Galilee, the Galileans welcomed him because they had seen all the things he had done in Jerusalem during the festival, for they also had been at the festival.

Jesus' second miraculous sign in Galilee

46 He returned to Cana in Galilee where he had turned the water into wine. In Capernaum there was a certain royal official whose son was sick. 47 When he heard that Jesus was coming from Judea to Galilee, he went out to meet him and asked Jesus if he would come and heal his son, for his son was about to die. 48 Jesus said to him, "Unless you see miraculous signs and wonders, you won't believe."

49 The royal official said to him, "Lord, come before my son dies."

50 Jesus replied, "Go home. Your son lives." The man believed the word that Jesus spoke to him and set out for his home.

51 While he was on his way, his servants were already coming to meet him. They said, "Your son lives!" 52 So he asked them at what time his son had started to get better. And they said, "The fever left him yesterday at about one o'clock in the afternoon." 53 Then the father realized that this was the hour when Jesus had said to him, "Your son lives." And he and his entire household believed in Jesus. 54 This was the second miraculous sign Jesus did while going from Judea to Galilee.

Sabbath healing

5 After this there was a Jewish festival, and Jesus went up to Jerusalem. 2 In Jerusalem near the Sheep Gate in the north city wall is a pool with the Aramaic name Bethsaida. It had five covered porches, 3 and a crowd of people who were sick, blind, lame, and paralyzed sat there.[k]

[j] Or *It is I, the one who speaks with you.* [k] Critical editions of the Gk New Testament do not include the following addition *waiting for the water to move.* 4 *Sometimes an angel would come down to the pool and stir up the water. Then the first one going into the water after it had been stirred up was cured of any sickness.*

[5]A certain man was there who had been sick for thirty-eight years. [6]When Jesus saw him lying there, knowing that he had already been there a long time, he asked him, "Do you want to get well?"

[7]The sick man answered him, "Sir,[l] I don't have anyone who can put me in the water when it is stirred up. When I'm trying to get to it, someone else has gotten in ahead of me."

[8]Jesus said to him, "Get up! Pick up your mat and walk." [9]Immediately the man was well, and he picked up his mat and walked. Now that day was the Sabbath.

[10]The Jewish leaders said to the man who had been healed, "It's the Sabbath; you aren't allowed to carry your mat."

[11]He answered, "The man who made me well said to me, 'Pick up your mat and walk.'"

[12]They inquired, "Who is this man who said to you, 'Pick it up and walk'?" [13]The man who had been cured didn't know who it was, because Jesus had slipped away from the crowd gathered there.

[14]Later Jesus found him in the temple and said, "See! You have been made well. Don't sin anymore in case something worse happens to you." [15]The man went and proclaimed to the Jewish leaders that Jesus was the man who had made him well.

[16]As a result, the Jewish leaders were harassing Jesus, since he had done these things on the Sabbath. [17]Jesus replied, "My Father is still working, and I am working too." [18]For this reason the Jewish leaders wanted even more to kill him—not only because he was doing away with the Sabbath but also because he called God his own Father, thereby making himself equal with God.

Work of the Father and the Son

[19]Jesus responded to the Jewish leaders, "I assure you that the Son can't do anything by himself except what he sees the Father doing. Whatever the Father does, the Son does likewise. [20]The Father loves the Son and shows him everything that he does. He will show him greater works than these so that you will marvel. [21]As the Father raises the dead and gives life, so too does the Son give life to whomever he wishes. [22]The Father doesn't judge anyone, but he has given all judgment to the Son [23]so that everyone will honor the Son just as they honor the Father. Whoever doesn't honor the Son doesn't honor the Father who sent him.

[24]"I assure you that whoever hears my word and believes in the one who sent me has eternal life and won't come under judgment but has passed from death into life.

[25]"I assure you that the time is coming—and is here!—when the dead will hear the voice of God's Son, and those who hear it will live. [26]Just as the Father has life in himself, so he has granted the Son to have life in himself. [27]He gives the Son authority to judge, because he is the Human One.[m] [28]Don't be surprised by this, because the time is coming when all who are in their graves will hear his voice. [29]Those who did good things will come out into the resurrection of life, and those who did wicked things into the resurrection of judgment. [30]I can't do anything by myself. Whatever I hear, I judge, and my judgment is just. I don't seek my own will but the will of the one who sent me.

Witnesses to Jesus

[31]"If I testify about myself, my testimony isn't true. [32]There is someone else who testifies about me, and I know his testimony about me is true. [33]You sent a delegation to John, and he testified to the truth. [34]Although I don't accept human testimony, I say these things so that you can be saved. [35]John was a burning and shining lamp, and, at least for a while, you were willing to celebrate in his light.

[36]"I have a witness greater than John's testimony. The Father has given me works to do so that I might complete them. These works I do testify about me that the Father sent me. [37]And the Father who sent me testifies about me. You have never even heard his voice or seen his form, [38]and you don't have his word dwelling with you because you don't believe the one whom he has sent.

[l]Or *Lord* [m]Or Son of Man

39 Examine the scriptures, since you think that in them you have eternal life. They also testify about me, 40 yet you don't want to come to me so that you can have life.

41 "I don't accept praise from people, 42 but I know you, that you don't have God's love in you. 43 I have come in my Father's name, and you don't receive me. If others come in their own name, you receive them. 44 How can you believe when you receive praise from each other but don't seek the praise that comes from the only God?

45 "Don't think that I will accuse you before the Father. Your accuser is Moses, the one in whom your hope rests. 46 If you believed Moses, you would believe me, because Moses wrote about me. 47 If you don't believe the writings of Moses, how will you believe my words?"

Feeding of the five thousand

6 After this Jesus went across the Galilee Sea (that is, the Tiberias Sea). 2 A large crowd followed him, because they had seen the miraculous signs he had done among the sick. 3 Jesus went up a mountain and sat there with his disciples. 4 It was nearly time for Passover, the Jewish festival.

5 Jesus looked up and saw the large crowd coming toward him. He asked Philip, "Where will we buy food to feed these people?" 6 Jesus said this to test him, for he already knew what he was going to do.

7 Philip replied, "More than a half year's salary[n] worth of food wouldn't be enough for each person to have even a little bit."

8 One of his disciples, Andrew, Simon Peter's brother, said, 9 "A youth here has five barley loaves and two fish. But what good is that for a crowd like this?"

10 Jesus said, "Have the people sit down." There was plenty of grass there. They sat down, about five thousand of them. 11 Then Jesus took the bread. When he had given thanks, he distributed it to those who were sitting there. He did the same with the fish, each getting as much as they wanted. 12 When they had plenty to eat, he said to his disciples, "Gather up the leftover pieces, so that nothing will be wasted." 13 So they gathered them and filled twelve baskets with the pieces of the five barley loaves that had been left over by those who had eaten.

14 When the people saw that he had done a miraculous sign, they said, "This is truly the prophet who is coming into the world." 15 Jesus understood that they were about to come and force him to be their king, so he took refuge again, alone on a mountain.

Jesus walks on water

16 When evening came, Jesus' disciples went down to the lake. 17 They got into a boat and were crossing the lake to Capernaum. It was already getting dark and Jesus hadn't come to them yet. 18 The water was getting rough because a strong wind was blowing. 19 When the wind had driven them out for about three or four miles, they saw Jesus walking on the water. He was approaching the boat and they were afraid. 20 He said to them, "I Am.[o] Don't be afraid." 21 Then they wanted to take him into the boat, and just then the boat reached the land where they had been heading.

22 The next day the crowd that remained on the other side of the lake realized that only one boat had been there. They knew Jesus hadn't gone with his disciples, but that the disciples had gone alone. 23 Some boats came from Tiberias, near the place where they had eaten the bread over which the Lord had given thanks. 24 When the crowd saw that neither Jesus nor his disciples were there, they got into the boats and came to Capernaum looking for Jesus. 25 When they found him on the other side of the lake, they asked him, "Rabbi, when did you get here?"

Bread of life

26 Jesus replied, "I assure you that you are looking for me not because you saw miraculous signs but because you ate all the food you wanted. 27 Don't work for the food that doesn't last but for the food that endures for eternal life, which the Human One[p] will give you. God the Father has confirmed him as his agent to give life."

[n] Or *two hundred denaria* [o] Or *It is I.* [p] Or *Son of Man*

28 They asked, "What must we do in order
to accomplish what God requires?"
29 Jesus replied, "This is what God requires,
that you believe in him whom God sent."
30 They asked, "What miraculous sign
will you do, that we can see and believe
you? What will you do? 31 Our ancestors ate
manna in the wilderness, just as it is written,
He gave them bread from heaven to eat."[q]
32 Jesus told them, "I assure you, it wasn't
Moses who gave the bread from heaven to
you, but my Father gives you the true bread
from heaven. 33 The bread of God is the one
who comes down from heaven and gives
life to the world."
34 They said, "Sir,[r] give us this bread all
the time!"
35 Jesus replied, "I am the bread of life.
Whoever comes to me will never go hungry,
and whoever believes in me will never be
thirsty. 36 But I told you that you have seen
me and still don't believe. 37 Everyone whom
the Father gives to me will come to me, and
I won't send away anyone who comes to me.
38 I have come down from heaven not to do
my will, but the will of him who sent me.
39 This is the will of the one who sent me, that
I won't lose anything he has given me, but
I will raise it up at the last day. 40 This is my
Father's will: that all who see the Son and
believe in him will have eternal life, and I
will raise them up at the last day."
41 The Jewish opposition grumbled about
him because he said, "I am the bread that
came down from heaven."
42 They asked, "Isn't this Jesus, Joseph's
son, whose mother and father we know?
How can he now say, 'I have come down
from heaven'?"
43 Jesus responded, "Don't grumble
among yourselves. 44 No one can come to me
unless they are drawn to me by the Father
who sent me, and I will raise them up at the
last day. 45 It is written in the Prophets, And
they *will all be taught by God.*[s] Everyone who
has listened to the Father and learned from
him comes to me. 46 No one has seen the
Father except the one who is from God. He
has seen the Father. 47 I assure you, whoever
believes has eternal life. 48 I am the bread of
life. 49 Your ancestors ate manna in the wilderness and they died. 50 This is the bread
that comes down from heaven so that whoever eats from it will never die. 51 I am the
living bread that came down from heaven.
Whoever eats this bread will live forever,
and the bread that I will give for the life of
the world is my flesh."
52 Then the Jews debated among themselves, asking, "How can this man give us
his flesh to eat?"
53 Jesus said to them, "I assure you, unless you eat the flesh of the Human One[t]
and drink his blood, you have no life in
you. 54 Whoever eats my flesh and drinks
my blood has eternal life, and I will raise
them up at the last day. 55 My flesh is true
food and my blood is true drink. 56 Whoever
eats my flesh and drinks my blood remains
in me and I in them. 57 As the living Father
sent me, and I live because of the Father,
so whoever eats me lives because of me.
58 This is the bread that came down from
heaven. It isn't like the bread your ancestors ate, and then they died. Whoever eats
this bread will live forever." 59 Jesus said
these things while he was teaching in the
synagogue in Capernaum.
60 Many of his disciples who heard this said,
"This message is harsh. Who can hear it?"
61 Jesus knew that the disciples were
grumbling about this and he said to them,
"Does this offend you? 62 What if you were to
see the Human One[u] going up where he was
before? 63 The Spirit is the one who gives life
and the flesh doesn't help at all. The words I
have spoken to you are spirit and life. 64 Yet
some of you don't believe." Jesus knew from
the beginning who wouldn't believe and the
one who would betray him. 65 He said, "For
this reason I said to you that none can come
to me unless the Father enables them to do
so." 66 At this, many of his disciples turned
away and no longer accompanied him.
67 Jesus asked the Twelve, "Do you also
want to leave?"
68 Simon Peter answered, "Lord, where
would we go? You have the words of eternal

[q]Ps 78:24 [r]Or *Lord* [s]Isa 54:13 [t]Or *Son of Man* [u]Or *Son of Man*

life. 69We believe and know that you are
God's holy one."
70Jesus replied, "Didn't I choose you
twelve? Yet one of you is a devil." 71He was
speaking of Judas, Simon Iscariot's son,
for he, one of the Twelve, was going to
betray him.

Jesus goes to Jerusalem

7 After this Jesus traveled throughout
Galilee. He didn't want to travel in Judea,
because the Jewish authorities wanted to
kill him. 2When it was almost time for the
Jewish Festival of Booths, 3Jesus' brothers said to him, "Leave Galilee. Go to Judea
so that your disciples can see the amazing
works that you do. 4Those who want to be
known publicly don't do things secretly.
Since you can do these things, show yourself to the world." 5His brothers said this
because even they didn't believe in him.
6Jesus replied, "For you, anytime is fine.
But my time hasn't come yet. 7The world
can't hate you. It hates me, though, because
I testify that its works are evil. 8You go up
to the festival. I'm not going to this one
because my time hasn't yet come." 9Having
said this, he stayed in Galilee. 10However,
after his brothers left for the festival, he
went too—not openly but in secret.
11The Jewish leaders were looking for
Jesus at the festival. They kept asking,
"Where is he?" 12The crowds were murmuring about him. "He's a good man," some said,
but others were saying, "No, he tricks the
people." 13No one spoke about him publicly,
though, for fear of the Jewish authorities.

Jesus teaches in the temple

14Halfway through the festival, Jesus went
up to the temple and started to teach. 15As-
tonished, the Jewish leaders asked, "He's
never been taught! How has he mastered
the Law?"
16Jesus responded, "My teaching isn't
mine but comes from the one who sent
me. 17Whoever wants to do God's will can
tell whether my teaching is from God or
whether I speak on my own. 18Those who
speak on their own seek glory for themselves. Those who seek the glory of him
who sent me are people of truth; there's
no falsehood in them. 19Didn't Moses give
you the Law? Yet none of you keep the Law.
Why do you want to kill me?"
20The crowd answered, "You have a
demon. Who wants to kill you?"
21Jesus replied, "I did one work, and you
were all astonished. 22Because Moses gave
you the commandment about circumcision
(although it wasn't Moses but the patriarchs), you circumcise a man on the Sabbath. 23If a man can be circumcised on the
Sabbath without breaking Moses' Law, why
are you angry with me because I made an
entire man well on the Sabbath? 24Don't
judge according to appearances. Judge with
right judgment."
25Some people from Jerusalem said,
"Isn't he the one they want to kill? 26Here
he is, speaking in public, yet they aren't saying anything to him. Could it be that our
leaders actually think he is the Christ? 27We
know where he is from, but when the Christ
comes, no one will know where he is from."
28While Jesus was teaching in the temple, he exclaimed, "You know me and where
I am from. I haven't come on my own. The
one who sent me is true, and you don't
know him. 29I know him because I am from
him and he sent me." 30So they wanted to
seize Jesus, but they couldn't because his
time hadn't yet come.
31Many from that crowd believed in Jesus.
They said, "When the Christ comes, will he do
more miraculous signs than this man does?"
32The Pharisees heard the crowd whispering
such things about Jesus, and the chief priests
and Pharisees sent guards to arrest him.
33Therefore, Jesus said, "I'm still with you
for a little while before I go to the one who
sent me. 34You will look for me, but you won't
find me, and where I am you can't come."
35The Jewish opposition asked each other,
"Where does he intend to go that we can't
find him? Surely he doesn't intend to go
where our people have been scattered and
are living among the Greeks! He isn't going
to teach the Greeks, is he? 36What does he
mean when he says, 'You will look for me, but
you won't find me, and where I am you can't
come'?"
37On the last and most important day of
the festival, Jesus stood up and shouted,

"All who are thirsty should come to me!
38 All who believe in me should drink!
As the scriptures said concerning me,[v]
Rivers of living water will flow out from
within him."
39 Jesus said this concerning the Spirit.
Those who believed in him would soon
receive the Spirit, but they hadn't experienced the Spirit yet since Jesus hadn't yet
been glorified.
40 When some in the crowd heard these
words, they said, "This man is truly the
prophet." 41 Others said, "He's the Christ." But
others said, "The Christ can't come from Galilee, can he? 42 Didn't the scripture say that the
Christ comes from David's family and from
Bethlehem, David's village?" 43 So the crowd
was divided over Jesus. 44 Some wanted to arrest him, but no one grabbed him.
45 The guards returned to the chief
priests and Pharisees, who asked, "Why
didn't you bring him?"
46 The guards answered, "No one has ever
spoken the way he does."
47 The Pharisees replied, "Have you too
been deceived? 48 Have any of the leaders
believed in him? Has any Pharisee? 49 No,
only this crowd, which doesn't know the
Law. And they are under God's curse!"
50 Nicodemus, who was one of them and
had come to Jesus earlier, said, 51 "Our Law
doesn't judge someone without first hearing
him and learning what he is doing, does it?"
52 They answered him, "You are not from
Galilee too, are you? Look it up and you will
see that the prophet doesn't come from
Galilee."

Pharisees test Jesus

53 They each went to their own homes,
8 1 and Jesus went to the Mount
of Olives. 2 Early in the morning
he returned to the temple. All the
people gathered around him, and
he sat down and taught them. 3 The
legal experts and Pharisees brought a
woman caught in adultery. Placing her
in the center of the group, 4 they said
to Jesus, "Teacher, this woman was
caught in the act of committing adultery. 5 In the Law, Moses commanded
us to stone women like this. What do
you say?" 6 They said this to test him,
because they wanted a reason to bring
an accusation against him. Jesus bent
down and wrote on the ground with
his finger.
7 They continued to question him, so he
stood up and replied, "Whoever hasn't
sinned should throw the first stone."
8 Bending down again, he wrote on the
ground. 9 Those who heard him went
away, one by one, beginning with the elders. Finally, only Jesus and the woman
were left in the middle of the crowd.
10 Jesus stood up and said to her,
"Woman, where are they? Is there no
one to condemn you?"
11 She said, "No one, sir."[w]
Jesus said, "Neither do I condemn
you. Go, and from now on, don't sin
anymore."[x]

Jesus continues to teach in the temple

12 Jesus spoke to the people again, saying, "I am the light of the world. Whoever
follows me won't walk in darkness but will
have the light of life."
13 Then the Pharisees said to him, "Because you are testifying about yourself,
your testimony isn't valid."
14 Jesus replied, "Even if I testify about
myself, my testimony is true, since I know
where I came from and where I'm going.
You don't know where I come from or where
I'm going. 15 You judge according to human
standards, but I judge no one. 16 Even if I do
judge, my judgment is truthful, because I'm
not alone. My judgments come from me and
from the Father who sent me. 17 In your Law
it is written that the witness of two people is
true. 18 I am one witness concerning myself,
and the Father who sent me is the other."
19 They asked him, "Where is your Father?"

[v] Or *Whoever is thirsty should come to me and drink.* 38 *Whoever believes in me, just as the scriptures said,* rivers of living water will flow out from within them. [w] Or *Lord* [x] Critical editions of the Gk New Testament do not contain 7:53–8:11.

Jesus answered, "You don't know me and you don't know my Father. If you knew me, you would also know my Father." 20 He spoke these words while he was teaching in the temple area known as the treasury. No one arrested him, because his time hadn't yet come.

21 Jesus continued, "I'm going away. You will look for me, and you will die in your sin. Where I'm going, you can't come."

22 The Jewish leaders said, "He isn't going to kill himself, is he? Is that why he said, 'Where I'm going, you can't come'?"

23 He said to them, "You are from below; I'm from above. You are from this world; I'm not from this world. 24 This is why I told you that you would die in your sins. If you don't believe that I Am, you will die in your sins."

25 "Who are you?" they asked.

Jesus replied, "I'm exactly who I have claimed to be from the beginning. 26 I have many things to say in judgment concerning you. The one who sent me is true, and what I have heard from him I tell the world." 27 They didn't know he was speaking about his Father. 28 So Jesus said to them, "When the Human One[y] is lifted up,[z] then you will know that I Am.[a] Then you will know that I do nothing on my own, but I say just what the Father has taught me. 29 He who sent me is with me. He doesn't leave me by myself, because I always do what makes him happy." 30 While Jesus was saying these things, many people came to believe in him.

Children of Abraham

31 Jesus said to the Jews who believed in him, "You are truly my disciples if you remain faithful to my teaching. 32 Then you will know the truth, and the truth will set you free."

33 They responded, "We are Abraham's children; we've never been anyone's slaves. How can you say that we will be set free?"

34 Jesus answered, "I assure you that everyone who sins is a slave to sin. 35 A slave isn't a permanent member of the household, but a son is. 36 Therefore, if the Son makes you free, you really will be free. 37 I know that you are Abraham's children, yet you want to kill me because you don't welcome my teaching. 38 I'm telling you what I've seen when I am with the Father, but you are doing what you've heard from your father."

39 They replied, "Our father is Abraham."

Jesus responded, "If you were Abraham's children, you would do Abraham's works. 40 Instead, you want to kill me, though I am the one who has spoken the truth I heard from God. Abraham didn't do this. 41 You are doing your father's works."

They said, "Our ancestry isn't in question! The only Father we have is God!"

42 Jesus replied, "If God were your Father, you would love me, for I came from God. Here I am. I haven't come on my own. God sent me. 43 Why don't you understand what I'm saying? It's because you can't really hear my words. 44 Your father is the devil. You are his children, and you want to do what your father wants. He was a murderer from the beginning. He has never stood for the truth, because there's no truth in him. Whenever that liar speaks, he speaks according to his own nature, because he's a liar and the father of liars. 45 Because I speak the truth, you don't believe me. 46 Who among you can show I'm guilty of sin? Since I speak the truth, why don't you believe me? 47 God's children listen to God's words. You don't listen to me because you aren't God's children."

48 The Jewish opposition answered, "We were right to say that you are a Samaritan and have a demon, weren't we?"

49 "I don't have a demon," Jesus replied. "But I honor my Father and you dishonor me. 50 I'm not trying to bring glory to myself. There's one who is seeking to glorify me, and he's the judge. 51 I assure you that whoever keeps my word will never die."

Abraham and Jesus

52 The Jewish opposition said to Jesus, "Now we know that you have a demon. Abraham and the prophets died, yet you say, 'Whoever keeps my word will never die.' 53 Are you greater than our father Abra-

[y] Or *Son of Man* [z] Or *exalted* [a] Or *that I am he*

ham? He died and the prophets died, so who do you make yourself out to be?"

54Jesus answered, "If I glorify myself, my glory is meaningless. My Father, who you say is your God, is the one who glorifies me. 55You don't know him, but I do. If I said I didn't know him, I would be like you, a liar. But I do know him, and I keep his word. 56Your father Abraham was overjoyed that he would see my day. He saw it and was happy."

57"You aren't even 50 years old!" the Jewish opposition replied. "How can you say that you have seen Abraham?"

58"I assure you," Jesus replied, "before Abraham was, I Am." 59So they picked up stones to throw at him, but Jesus hid himself and left the temple.

Jesus heals a blind man

9 As Jesus walked along, he saw a man who was blind from birth. 2Jesus' disciples asked, "Rabbi, who sinned so that he was born blind, this man or his parents?"

3Jesus answered, "Neither he nor his parents. This happened so that God's mighty works might be displayed in him. 4While it's daytime, we must do the works of him who sent me. Night is coming when no one can work. 5While I am in the world, I am the light of the world." 6After he said this, he spit on the ground, made mud with the saliva, and smeared the mud on the man's eyes. 7Jesus said to him, "Go, wash in the pool of Siloam" (this word means *sent*). So the man went away and washed. When he returned, he could see.

Disagreement about the healing

8The man's neighbors and those who used to see him when he was a beggar said, "Isn't this the man who used to sit and beg?"

9Some said, "It is," and others said, "No, it's someone who looks like him."

But the man said, "Yes, it's me!"

10So they asked him, "How are you now able to see?"

11He answered, "The man they call Jesus made mud, smeared it on my eyes, and said, 'Go to the Pool of Siloam and wash.' So I went and washed, and then I could see."

12They asked, "Where is this man?"

He replied, "I don't know."

13Then they led the man who had been born blind to the Pharisees. 14Now Jesus made the mud and smeared it on the man's eyes on a Sabbath day. 15So Pharisees also asked him how he was able to see.

The man told them, "He put mud on my eyes, I washed, and now I see."

16Some Pharisees said, "This man isn't from God, because he breaks the Sabbath law." Others said, "How can a sinner do miraculous signs like these?" So they were divided. 17Some of the Pharisees questioned the man who had been born blind again: "What do you have to say about him, since he healed your eyes?"

He replied, "He's a prophet."

Conflict over the healing

18The Jewish leaders didn't believe the man had been blind and received his sight until they called for his parents. 19The Jewish leaders asked them, "Is this your son? Are you saying he was born blind? How can he now see?"

20His parents answered, "We know he is our son. We know he was born blind. 21But we don't know how he now sees, and we don't know who healed his eyes. Ask him. He's old enough to speak for himself." 22His parents said this because they feared the Jewish authorities. This is because the Jewish authorities had already decided that whoever confessed Jesus to be the Christ would be expelled from the synagogue. 23That's why his parents said, "He's old enough. Ask him."

24Therefore, they called a second time for the man who had been born blind and said to him, "Give glory to God. We know this man is a sinner."

25The man answered, "I don't know whether he's a sinner. Here's what I do know: I was blind and now I see."

26They questioned him: "What did he do to you? How did he heal your eyes?"

27He replied, "I already told you, and you didn't listen. Why do you want to hear it again? Do you want to become his disciples too?"

28They insulted him: "You are his disciple, but we are Moses' disciples. 29We know

that God spoke to Moses, but we don't
know where this man is from."
30 The man answered, "This is incredible! You don't know where he is from, yet
he healed my eyes! 31 We know that God
doesn't listen to sinners. God listens to anyone who is devout and does God's will. 32 No
one has ever heard of a healing of the eyes
of someone born blind. 33 If this man wasn't
from God, he couldn't do this."
34 They responded, "You were born completely in sin! How is it that you dare to
teach us?" Then they expelled him.

Jesus finds the man born blind

35 Jesus heard they had expelled the man
born blind. Finding him, Jesus said, "Do
you believe in the Human One?"[b]
36 He answered, "Who is he, sir?[c] I want
to believe in him."
37 Jesus said, "You have seen him. In fact,
he is the one speaking with you."
38 The man said, "Lord,[d] I believe." And he
worshipped Jesus.

Jesus teaches the Pharisees

39 Jesus said, "I have come into the world
to exercise judgment so that those who
don't see can see and those who see will become blind."
40 Some Pharisees who were with him
heard what he said and asked, "Surely we
aren't blind, are we?"
41 Jesus said to them, "If you were blind,
you wouldn't have any sin, but now that you
10 say, 'We see,' your sin remains. 1 I assure you that whoever doesn't enter
into the sheep pen through the gate but
climbs over the wall is a thief and an outlaw.
2 The one who enters through the gate is the
shepherd of the sheep. 3 The guard at the
gate opens the gate for him, and the sheep
listen to his voice. He calls his own sheep
by name and leads them out. 4 Whenever
he has gathered all of his sheep, he goes
before them and they follow him, because
they know his voice. 5 They won't follow a
stranger but will run away because they
don't know the stranger's voice." 6 Those
who heard Jesus use this analogy didn't understand what he was saying.

I am the gate

7 So Jesus spoke again, "I assure you that
I am the gate of the sheep. 8 All who came
before me were thieves and outlaws, but
the sheep didn't listen to them. 9 I am the
gate. Whoever enters through me will be
saved. They will come in and go out and find
pasture. 10 The thief enters only to steal, kill,
and destroy. I came so that they could have
life—indeed, so that they could live life to
the fullest.

I am the good shepherd

11 "I am the good shepherd. The good
shepherd lays down his life for the sheep.
12 When the hired hand sees the wolf coming,
he leaves the sheep and runs away. That's
because he isn't the shepherd; the sheep
aren't really his. So the wolf attacks the
sheep and scatters them. 13 He's only a hired
hand and the sheep don't matter to him.
14 "I am the good shepherd. I know my
own sheep and they know me, 15 just as the
Father knows me and I know the Father. I
give up my life for the sheep. 16 I have other
sheep that don't belong to this sheep pen. I
must lead them too. They will listen to my
voice and there will be one flock, with one
shepherd.
17 "This is why the Father loves me: I give
up my life so that I can take it up again. 18 No
one takes it from me, but I give it up because
I want to. I have the right to give it up, and I
have the right to take it up again. I received
this commandment from my Father."
19 There was another division among the
Jewish opposition because of Jesus' words.
20 Many of them said, "He has a demon
and has lost his mind. Why listen to him?"
21 Others said, "These aren't the words of
someone who has a demon. Can a demon
heal the eyes of people who are blind?"

Jesus at the Festival of Dedication

22 The time came for the Festival of Dedication[e] in Jerusalem. It was winter, 23 and

[b] Or *Son of Man* [c] Or *Lord* [d] Or *Sir* [e] Hanukkah

Jesus was in the temple, walking in the
covered porch named for Solomon. 24The
Jewish opposition circled around him and
asked, "How long will you test our patience?
If you are the Christ, tell us plainly."
25Jesus answered, "I have told you, but
you don't believe. The works I do in my
Father's name testify about me, 26but you
don't believe because you don't belong to
my sheep. 27My sheep listen to my voice.
I know them and they follow me. 28I give
them eternal life. They will never die, and
no one will snatch them from my hand.
29My Father, who has given them to me,
is greater than all, and no one is able to
snatch them from my Father's hand. 30I
and the Father are one."
31Again the Jewish opposition picked
up stones in order to stone him. 32Jesus
responded, "I have shown you many good
works from the Father. For which of those
works do you stone me?"
33The Jewish opposition answered, "We
don't stone you for a good work but for insulting God. You are human, yet you make
yourself out to be God."
34Jesus replied, "Isn't it written in your
Law, *I have said, you are gods?*"[f] 35Scripture
calls those to whom God's word came *gods*,
and scripture can't be abolished. 36So how
can you say that the one whom the Father
has made holy and sent into the world insults God because he said, 'I am God's Son'?
37If I don't do the works of my Father, don't
believe me. 38But if I do them, and you
don't believe me, believe the works so that
you can know and recognize that the Father
is in me and I am in the Father." 39Again,
they wanted to arrest him, but he escaped
from them.

Jesus at the Jordan

40Jesus went back across the Jordan to
the place where John had baptized at first,
and he stayed there. 41Many people came to
him. "John didn't do any miraculous signs,"
they said, "but everything John said about
this man was true." 42Many believed in
Jesus there.

Lazarus is ill

11 A certain man, Lazarus, was ill. He was
from Bethany, the village of Mary and
her sister Martha. (2This was the Mary who
anointed the Lord with fragrant oil and
wiped his feet with her hair. Her brother
Lazarus was ill.) 3So the sisters sent word
to Jesus, saying, "Lord, the one whom you
love is ill."
4When he heard this, Jesus said, "This illness isn't fatal. It's for the glory of God so that
God's Son can be glorified through it." 5Jesus
loved Martha, her sister, and Lazarus. 6When
he heard that Lazarus was ill, he stayed where
he was. After two days, 7he said to his disciples, "Let's return to Judea again."
8The disciples replied, "Rabbi, the Jewish
opposition wants to stone you, but you want
to go back?"
9Jesus answered, "Aren't there twelve
hours in the day? Whoever walks in the day
doesn't stumble because they see the light of
the world. 10But whoever walks in the night
does stumble because the light isn't in them."
11He continued, "Our friend Lazarus is
sleeping, but I am going in order to wake
him up."
12The disciples said, "Lord, if he's sleeping, he will get well." 13They thought Jesus
meant that Lazarus was in a deep sleep, but
Jesus had spoken about Lazarus' death.
14Jesus told them plainly, "Lazarus has
died. 15For your sakes, I'm glad I wasn't there
so that you can believe. Let's go to him."
16Then Thomas (the one called Didymus)
said to the other disciples, "Let us go too so
that we may die with Jesus."

Jesus with Martha and Mary

17When Jesus arrived, he found that
Lazarus had already been in the tomb for
four days. 18Bethany was a little less than
two miles from Jerusalem. 19Many Jews
had come to comfort Martha and Mary
after their brother's death. 20When Martha heard that Jesus was coming, she went
to meet him, while Mary remained in the
house. 21Martha said to Jesus, "Lord, if you
had been here, my brother wouldn't have

[f] Ps 82:6

died. 22 Even now I know that whatever you ask God, God will give you."

23 Jesus told her, "Your brother will rise again."

24 Martha replied, "I know that he will rise in the resurrection on the last day."

25 Jesus said to her, "I am the resurrection and the life. Whoever believes in me will live, even though they die. 26 Everyone who lives and believes in me will never die. Do you believe this?"

27 She replied, "Yes, Lord, I believe that you are the Christ, God's Son, the one who is coming into the world."

28 After she said this, she went and spoke privately to her sister Mary, "The teacher is here and he's calling for you." 29 When Mary heard this, she got up quickly and went to Jesus. 30 He hadn't entered the village but was still in the place where Martha had met him. 31 When the Jews who were comforting Mary in the house saw her get up quickly and leave, they followed her. They assumed she was going to mourn at the tomb.

32 When Mary arrived where Jesus was and saw him, she fell at his feet and said, "Lord, if you had been here, my brother wouldn't have died."

33 When Jesus saw her crying and the Jews who had come with her crying also, he was deeply disturbed and troubled. 34 He asked, "Where have you laid him?"

They replied, "Lord, come and see."

35 Jesus began to cry. 36 The Jews said, "See how much he loved him!" 37 But some of them said, "He healed the eyes of the man born blind. Couldn't he have kept Lazarus from dying?"

Jesus at Lazarus' tomb

38 Jesus was deeply disturbed again when he came to the tomb. It was a cave, and a stone covered the entrance. 39 Jesus said, "Remove the stone."

Martha, the sister of the dead man, said, "Lord, the smell will be awful! He's been dead four days."

40 Jesus replied, "Didn't I tell you that if you believe, you will see God's glory?" 41 So they removed the stone. Jesus looked up and said, "Father, thank you for hearing me. 42 I know you always hear me. I say this for the benefit of the crowd standing here so that they will believe that you sent me." 43 Having said this, Jesus shouted with a loud voice, "Lazarus, come out!" 44 The dead man came out, his feet bound and his hands tied, and his face covered with a cloth. Jesus said to them, "Untie him and let him go."

45 Therefore, many of the Jews who came with Mary and saw what Jesus did believed in him. 46 But some of them went to the Pharisees and told them what Jesus had done.

Caiaphas prophesies

47 Then the chief priests and Pharisees called together the council[g] and said, "What are we going to do? This man is doing many miraculous signs! 48 If we let him go on like this, everyone will believe in him. Then the Romans will come and take away both our temple and our people."

49 One of them, Caiaphas, who was high priest that year, told them, "You don't know anything! 50 You don't see that it is better for you that one man die for the people rather than the whole nation be destroyed." 51 He didn't say this on his own. As high priest that year, he prophesied that Jesus would soon die for the nation—52 and not only for the nation. Jesus would also die so that God's children scattered everywhere would be gathered together as one. 53 From that day on they plotted to kill him.

The Passover draws near

54 Therefore, Jesus was no longer active in public ministry among the Jewish leaders. Instead, he left Jerusalem and went to a place near the wilderness, to a city called Ephraim, where he stayed with his disciples.

55 It was almost time for the Jewish Passover, and many people went from the countryside up to Jerusalem to purify themselves through ritual washing before the Passover. 56 They were looking for Jesus. As they spoke to each other in the temple, they said, "What do you think? He won't

[g] Or *Sanhedrin*

come to the festival, will he?" 57The chief priests and Pharisees had given orders that anyone who knew where he was should report it, so they could arrest him.

Mary anoints Jesus' feet

12 Six days before Passover, Jesus came to Bethany, home of Lazarus, whom Jesus had raised from the dead. 2Lazarus and his sisters hosted a dinner for him. Martha served and Lazarus was among those who joined him at the table. 3Then Mary took an extraordinary amount, almost three-quarters of a pound,[h] of very expensive perfume made of pure nard. She anointed Jesus' feet with it, then wiped his feet dry with her hair. The house was filled with the aroma of the perfume. 4Judas Iscariot, one of his disciples (the one who was about to betray him), complained, 5"This perfume was worth a year's wages![i] Why wasn't it sold and the money given to the poor?" (6He said this not because he cared about the poor but because he was a thief. He carried the money bag and would take what was in it.)

7Then Jesus said, "Leave her alone. This perfume was to be used in preparation for my burial, and this is how she has used it. 8You will always have the poor among you, but you won't always have me."

9Many Jews learned that he was there. They came not only because of Jesus but also to see Lazarus, whom he had raised from the dead. 10The chief priests decided that they would kill Lazarus too. 11It was because of Lazarus that many of the Jews had deserted them and come to believe in Jesus.

Jesus enters Jerusalem

12The next day the great crowd that had come for the festival heard that Jesus was coming to Jerusalem. 13They took palm branches and went out to meet him. They shouted,

"Hosanna!
Blessings on the one who comes
in the name of the Lord![j]
Blessings on the king of Israel!"

14Jesus found a young donkey and sat on it, just as it is written,

15*Don't be afraid, Daughter Zion.*
Look! Your king is coming,
sitting on a donkey's colt.[k]

16His disciples didn't understand these things at first. After he was glorified, they remembered that these things had been written about him and that they had done these things to him.

17The crowd who had been with him when he called Lazarus out of the tomb and raised him from the dead were testifying about him. 18That's why the crowd came to meet him, because they had heard about this miraculous sign that he had done. 19Therefore, the Pharisees said to each other, "See! You've accomplished nothing! Look! The whole world is following him!"

Jesus teaches about his death

20Some Greeks were among those who had come up to worship at the festival. 21They came to Philip, who was from Bethsaida in Galilee, and made a request: "Sir, we want to see Jesus." 22Philip told Andrew, and Andrew and Philip told Jesus.

23Jesus replied, "The time has come for the Human One[l] to be glorified. 24I assure you that unless a grain of wheat falls into the earth and dies, it can only be a single seed. But if it dies, it bears much fruit. 25Those who love their lives will lose them, and those who hate their lives in this world will keep them forever. 26Whoever serves me must follow me. Wherever I am, there my servant will also be. My Father will honor whoever serves me.

27"Now *I am deeply troubled.*[m] What should I say? 'Father, save me from this time'? No, for this is the reason I have come to this time. 28Father, glorify your name!"

Then a voice came from heaven, "I have glorified it, and I will glorify it again."

29The crowd standing there heard and said, "It's thunder." Others said, "An angel spoke to him."

30Jesus replied, "This voice wasn't for my

[h]Or *a litra,* a Roman pound, approximately twelve ounces [i]Or *three hundred denaria* [j]Ps 118:26 [k]Zech 9:9 [l]Or *Son of Man* [m]Ps 6:2

benefit but for yours. 31 Now is the time for
judgment of this world. Now this world's
ruler will be thrown out. 32 When I am lifted
up[n] from the earth, I will draw everyone to
me." (33 He said this to show how he was
going to die.)

34 The crowd responded, "We have heard
from the Law that the Christ remains forever.
How can you say that the Human One[o] must
be lifted up? Who is this Human One?"[p]

35 Jesus replied, "The light is with you for
only a little while. Walk while you have the
light so that darkness doesn't overtake you.
Those who walk in the darkness don't know
where they are going. 36 As long as you have
the light, believe in the light so that you
might become people whose lives are determined by the light." After Jesus said these
things, he went away and hid from them.

Fulfillment of prophecy

37 Jesus had done many miraculous signs
before the people, but they didn't believe
in him. 38 This was to fulfill the word of the
prophet Isaiah:

Lord, who has believed through our message?
To whom is the arm of the Lord
fully revealed?[q]

39 Isaiah explains why they couldn't
believe:

40 *He made their eyes blind*
and closed their minds
so that they might not see with their eyes,
understand with their minds,
and turn their lives around—
and I would heal them.[r]

41 Isaiah said these things because he saw
Jesus' glory; he spoke about Jesus. 42 Even
so, many leaders believed in him, but they
wouldn't acknowledge their faith because
they feared that the Pharisees would expel
them from the synagogue. 43 They believed,
but they loved human praise more than
God's glory.

Summary of Jesus' teaching

44 Jesus shouted, "Whoever believes in
me doesn't believe in me but in the one who
sent me. 45 Whoever sees me sees the one
who sent me. 46 I have come as a light into
the world so that everyone who believes in
me won't live in darkness. 47 If people hear
my words and don't keep them, I don't judge
them. I didn't come to judge the world but to
save it. 48 Whoever rejects me and doesn't receive my words will be judged at the last day
by the word I have spoken. 49 I don't speak on
my own, but the Father who sent me commanded me regarding what I should speak
and say. 50 I know that his commandment is
eternal life. Therefore, whatever I say is just
as the Father has said to me."

Foot washing

13 Before the Festival of Passover, Jesus
knew that his time had come to leave
this world and go to the Father. Having
loved his own who were in the world, he
loved them fully.

2 Jesus and his disciples were sharing
the evening meal. The devil had already
provoked Judas, Simon Iscariot's son, to
betray Jesus. 3 Jesus knew the Father had
given everything into his hands and that
he had come from God and was returning
to God. 4 So he got up from the table and
took off his robes. Picking up a linen towel,
he tied it around his waist. 5 Then he poured
water into a washbasin and began to wash
the disciples' feet, drying them with the
towel he was wearing. 6 When Jesus came
to Simon Peter, Peter said to him, "Lord, are
you going to wash my feet?"

7 Jesus replied, "You don't understand
what I'm doing now, but you will understand later."

8 "No!" Peter said. "You will never wash
my feet!"

Jesus replied, "Unless I wash you, you
won't have a place with me."

9 Simon Peter said, "Lord, not only my
feet but also my hands and my head!"

10 Jesus responded, "Those who have
bathed need only to have their feet washed,
because they are completely clean. You disciples are clean, but not every one of you."
11 He knew who would betray him. That's
why he said, "Not every one of you is clean."

[n] Or *exalted* [o] Or *Son of Man* [p] Or *Son of Man* [q] Isa 53:1 [r] Isa 6:10

12 After he washed the disciples' feet, he put on his robes and returned to his place at the table. He said to them, "Do you know what I've done for you? 13 You call me 'Teacher' and 'Lord,' and you speak correctly, because I am. 14 If I, your Lord and teacher, have washed your feet, you too must wash each other's feet. 15 I have given you an example: Just as I have done, you also must do. 16 I assure you, servants aren't greater than their master, nor are those who are sent greater than the one who sent them. 17 Since you know these things, you will be happy if you do them. 18 I'm not speaking about all of you. I know those whom I've chosen. But this is to fulfill the scripture, *The one who eats my bread has turned against me.*[s]

19 "I'm telling you this now, before it happens, so that when it does happen you will believe that I Am. 20 I assure you that whoever receives someone I send receives me, and whoever receives me receives the one who sent me."

Announcement of the betrayal

21 After he said these things, Jesus was deeply disturbed and testified, "I assure you, one of you will betray me."

22 His disciples looked at each other, confused about which of them he was talking about. 23 One of the disciples, the one whom Jesus loved, was at Jesus' side. 24 Simon Peter nodded at him to get him to ask Jesus who he was talking about. 25 Leaning back toward Jesus, this disciple asked, "Lord, who is it?"

26 Jesus answered, "It's the one to whom I will give this piece of bread once I have dipped into the bowl." Then he dipped the piece of bread and gave it to Judas, Simon Iscariot's son. 27 After Judas took the bread, Satan entered into him. Jesus told him, "What you are about to do, do quickly." 28 No one sitting at the table understood why Jesus said this to him. 29 Some thought that, since Judas kept the money bag, Jesus told him, "Go, buy what we need for the feast," or that he should give something to the poor. 30 So when Judas took the bread, he left immediately. And it was night.

Love commandment

31 When Judas was gone, Jesus said, "Now the Human One[t] has been glorified, and God has been glorified in him. 32 If God has been glorified in him, God will also glorify the Human One[u] in himself and will glorify him immediately. 33 Little children, I'm with you for a little while longer. You will look for me—but, just as I told the Jewish leaders, I also tell you now—'Where I'm going, you can't come.'

34 "I give you a new commandment: Love each other. Just as I have loved you, so you also must love each other. 35 This is how everyone will know that you are my disciples, when you love each other."

Announcement of Peter's denial

36 Simon Peter said to Jesus, "Lord, where are you going?"

Jesus answered, "Where I am going, you can't follow me now, but you will follow later."

37 Peter asked, "Lord, why can't I follow you now? I'll give up my life for you."

38 Jesus replied, "Will you give up your life for me? I assure you that you will deny me three times before the rooster crows.

The way, the truth, and the life

14 "Don't be troubled. Trust in God. Trust also in me. 2 My Father's house has room to spare. If that weren't the case, would I have told you that I'm going to prepare a place for you? 3 When I go to prepare a place for you, I will return and take you to be with me so that where I am you will be too. 4 You know the way to the place I'm going."

5 Thomas asked, "Lord, we don't know where you are going. How can we know the way?"

6 Jesus answered, "I am the way, the truth, and the life. No one comes to the Father except through me. 7 If you have really known me, you will also know the Father. From now on you know him and have seen him."

8 Philip said, "Lord, show us the Father; that will be enough for us."

9 Jesus replied, "Don't you know me, Philip, even after I have been with you all

[s] Ps 41:9 [t] Or *Son of Man* [u] Or *Son of Man*

this time? Whoever has seen me has seen the Father. How can you say, 'Show us the Father'? 10 Don't you believe that I am in the Father and the Father is in me? The words I have spoken to you I don't speak on my own. The Father who dwells in me does his works. 11 Trust me when I say that I am in the Father and the Father is in me, or at least believe on account of the works themselves. 12 I assure you that whoever believes in me will do the works that I do. They will do even greater works than these because I am going to the Father. 13 I will do whatever you ask for in my name, so that the Father can be glorified in the Son. 14 When you ask me for anything in my name, I will do it.

I won't leave you as orphans

15 "If you love me, you will keep my commandments. 16 I will ask the Father, and he will send another Companion,[v] who will be with you forever. 17 This Companion is the Spirit of Truth, whom the world can't receive because it neither sees him nor recognizes him. You know him, because he lives with you and will be with you.

18 "I won't leave you as orphans. I will come to you. 19 Soon the world will no longer see me, but you will see me. Because I live, you will live too. 20 On that day you will know that I am in my Father, you are in me, and I am in you. 21 Whoever has my commandments and keeps them loves me. Whoever loves me will be loved by my Father, and I will love them and reveal myself to them."

22 Judas (not Judas Iscariot) asked, "Lord, why are you about to reveal yourself to us and not to the world?"

23 Jesus answered, "Whoever loves me will keep my word. My Father will love them, and we will come to them and make our home with them. 24 Whoever doesn't love me doesn't keep my words. The word that you hear isn't mine. It is the word of the Father who sent me.

25 "I have spoken these things to you while I am with you. 26 The Companion,[w] the Holy Spirit, whom the Father will send in my name, will teach you everything and will remind you of everything I told you.

27 "Peace I leave with you. My peace I give you. I give to you not as the world gives. Don't be troubled or afraid. 28 You have heard me tell you, 'I'm going away and returning to you.' If you loved me, you would be happy that I am going to the Father, because the Father is greater than me. 29 I have told you before it happens so that when it happens you will believe. 30 I won't say much more to you because this world's ruler is coming. He has nothing on me. 31 Rather, he comes so that the world will know that I love the Father and do just as the Father has commanded me. Get up. We're leaving this place.

I am the true vine

15 "I am the true vine, and my Father is the vineyard keeper. 2 He removes any of my branches that don't produce fruit, and he trims any branch that produces fruit so that it will produce even more fruit. 3 You are already trimmed because of the word I have spoken to you. 4 Remain in me, and I will remain in you. A branch can't produce fruit by itself, but must remain in the vine. Likewise, you can't produce fruit unless you remain in me. 5 I am the vine; you are the branches. If you remain in me and I in you, then you will produce much fruit. Without me, you can't do anything. 6 If you don't remain in me, you will be like a branch that is thrown out and dries up. Those branches are gathered up, thrown into a fire, and burned. 7 If you remain in me and my words remain in you, ask for whatever you want and it will be done for you. 8 My Father is glorified when you produce much fruit and in this way prove that you are my disciples.

Love each other

9 "As the Father loved me, I too have loved you. Remain in my love. 10 If you keep my commandments, you will remain in my love, just as I kept my Father's commandments and remain in his love. 11 I have said these things to you so that my joy will be in

[v] Or *Advocate* [w] Or *Advocate*

you and your joy will be complete. [12]This is
my commandment: love each other just as
I have loved you. [13]No one has greater love
than to give up one's life for one's friends.
[14]You are my friends if you do what I command you. [15]I don't call you servants any
longer, because servants don't know what
their master is doing. Instead, I call you
friends, because everything I heard from
my Father I have made known to you. [16]You
didn't choose me, but I chose you and appointed you so that you could go and produce fruit and so that your fruit could last.
As a result, whatever you ask the Father in
my name, he will give you. [17]I give you these
commandments so that you can love each
other.

If the world hates you

[18]"If the world hates you, know that
it hated me first. [19]If you belonged to the
world, the world would love you as its own.
However, I have chosen you out of the
world, and you don't belong to the world.
This is why the world hates you. [20]Remem-
ber what I told you, 'Servants aren't greater
than their master.' If the world harassed
me, it will harass you too. If it kept my
word, it will also keep yours. [21]The world
will do all these things to you on account of
my name, because it doesn't know the one
who sent me.

[22]"If I hadn't come and spoken to the
people of this world, they wouldn't be sinners. But now they have no excuse for their
sin. [23]Whoever hates me also hates the
Father. [24]If I hadn't done works among
them that no one else had done, they
wouldn't be sinners. But now they have
seen and hated both me and my Father.
[25]This fulfills the word written in their Law,
They hated me without a reason.[x]

[26]"When the Companion[y] comes, whom
I will send from the Father—the Spirit of
Truth who proceeds from the Father—he
will testify about me. [27]You will testify
too, because you have been with me from
the beginning. 16 [1]I have said these
things to you so that you won't fall
away. [2]They will expel you from the synagogue. The time is coming when those who
kill you will think that they are doing a
service to God. [3]They will do these things
because they don't know the Father or me.
[4]But I have said these things to you so that
when their time comes, you will remember
that I told you about them.

I go away

"I didn't say these things to you from
the beginning, because I was with you. [5]But
now I go away to the one who sent me. None
of you ask me, 'Where are you going?' [6]Yet
because I have said these things to you, you
are filled with sorrow. [7]I assure you that it
is better for you that I go away. If I don't go
away, the Companion[z] won't come to you.
But if I go, I will send him to you. [8]When
he comes, he will show the world it was
wrong about sin, righteousness, and judgment. [9]He will show the world it was wrong
about sin because they don't believe in
me. [10]He will show the world it was wrong
about righteousness because I'm going to
the Father and you won't see me anymore.
[11]He will show the world it was wrong about
judgment because this world's ruler stands
condemned.

I still have many things to say

[12]"I have much more to say to you, but
you can't handle it now. [13]However, when
the Spirit of Truth comes, he will guide you
in all truth. He won't speak on his own, but
will say whatever he hears and will proclaim
to you what is to come. [14]He will glorify me,
because he will take what is mine and proclaim it to you. [15]Everything that the Father
has is mine. That's why I said that the Spirit
takes what is mine and will proclaim it to
you. [16]Soon you won't be able to see me;
soon after that, you will see me."

I will see you again

[17]Some of Jesus' disciples said to each
other, "What does he mean: 'Soon you
won't see me, and soon after that you
will see me' and 'Because I'm going to the

[x]Pss 35:19; 69:4 [y]Or *Advocate* [z]Or *Advocate*

Father'? 18 What does he mean by 'soon'? We don't understand what he's talking about."

19 Jesus knew they wanted to ask him, so he said, "Are you trying to find out from each other what I meant when I said, 'Soon you won't see me, and soon after that you will see me'? 20 I assure you that you will cry and lament, and the world will be happy. You will be sorrowful, but your sorrow will turn into joy. 21 When a woman gives birth, she has pain because her time has come. But when the child is born, she no longer remembers her distress because of her joy that a child has been born into the world. 22 In the same way, you have sorrow now; but I will see you again, and you will be overjoyed. No one takes away your joy. 23 In that day, you won't ask me anything. I assure you that the Father will give you whatever you ask in my name. 24 Up to now, you have asked nothing in my name. Ask and you will receive so that your joy will be complete.

I have conquered the world

25 "I've been using figures of speech with you. The time is coming when I will no longer speak to you in such analogies. Instead, I will tell you plainly about the Father. 26 In that day you will ask in my name. I'm not saying that I will ask the Father on your behalf. 27 The Father himself loves you, because you have loved me and believed that I came from God. 28 I left the Father and came into the world. I tell you again: I am leaving the world and returning to the Father."

29 His disciples said, "See! Now you speak plainly; you aren't using figures of speech. 30 Now we know that you know everything and you don't need anyone to ask you. Because of this we believe you have come from God."

31 Jesus replied, "Now you believe? 32 Look! A time is coming—and is here!—when each of you will be scattered to your own homes and you will leave me alone. I'm not really alone, for the Father is with me. 33 I've said these things to you so that you will have peace in me. In the world you have distress. But be encouraged! I have conquered the world."

Jesus prays

17 When Jesus finished saying these things, he looked up to heaven and said, "Father, the time has come. Glorify your Son, so that the Son can glorify you. 2 You gave him authority over everyone so that he could give eternal life to everyone you gave him. 3 This is eternal life: to know you, the only true God, and Jesus Christ whom you sent. 4 I have glorified you on earth by finishing the work you gave me to do. 5 Now, Father, glorify me in your presence with the glory I shared with you before the world was created.

6 "I have revealed your name to the people you gave me from this world. They were yours and you gave them to me, and they have kept your word. 7 Now they know that everything you have given me comes from you. 8 This is because I gave them the words that you gave me, and they received them. They truly understood that I came from you, and they believed that you sent me.

9 "I'm praying for them. I'm not praying for the world but for those you gave me, because they are yours. 10 Everything that is mine is yours and everything that is yours is mine; I have been glorified in them. 11 I'm no longer in the world, but they are in the world, even as I'm coming to you. Holy Father, watch over them in your name, the name you gave me, that they will be one just as we are one. 12 When I was with them, I watched over them in your name, the name you gave to me, and I kept them safe. None of them were lost, except the one who was destined for destruction, so that scripture would be fulfilled. 13 Now I'm coming to you and I say these things while I'm in the world so that they can share completely in my joy. 14 I gave your word to them and the world hated them, because they don't belong to this world, just as I don't belong to this world. 15 I'm not asking that you take them out of this world but that you keep them safe from the evil one. 16 They don't belong to this world, just as I don't belong to this world. 17 Make them holy in the truth; your word is truth. 18 As you sent me into the world, so I have sent them into the world. 19 I made myself holy

on their behalf so that they also would be
made holy in the truth.

20“I’m not praying only for them but also
for those who believe in me because of their
word. 21I pray they will be one, Father, just
as you are in me and I am in you. I pray that
they also will be in us, so that the world will
believe that you sent me. 22I’ve given them
the glory that you gave me so that they can
be one just as we are one. 23I’m in them and
you are in me so that they will be made perfectly one. Then the world will know that
you sent me and that you have loved them
just as you loved me.

24“Father, I want those you gave me to be
with me where I am. Then they can see my
glory, which you gave me because you loved
me before the creation of the world.

25“Righteous Father, even the world
didn’t know you, but I’ve known you, and
these believers know that you sent me.
26I’ve made your name known to them and
will continue to make it known so that your
love for me will be in them, and I myself will
be in them.”

Arrest in the garden

18 After he said these things, Jesus went
out with his disciples and crossed
over to the other side of the Kidron Valley.
He and his disciples entered a garden there.
2Judas, his betrayer, also knew the place
because Jesus often gathered there with
his disciples. 3Judas brought a company of
soldiers[a] and some guards from the chief
priests and Pharisees. They came there
carrying lanterns, torches, and weapons.
4Jesus knew everything that was to happen
to him, so he went out and asked, “Who are
you looking for?”

5They answered, “Jesus the Nazarene.”

He said to them, “I Am.”[b] (Judas, his betrayer, was standing with them.) 6When he
said, “I Am,” they shrank back and fell to
the ground. 7He asked them again, “Who
are you looking for?”

They said, “Jesus the Nazarene.”

8Jesus answered, “I told you, ‘I Am.’[c] If
you are looking for me, then let these people go.” 9This was so that the word he had
spoken might be fulfilled: “I didn’t lose anyone of those whom you gave me.”

10Then Simon Peter, who had a sword,
drew it and struck the high priest’s servant,
cutting off his right ear. (The servant’s
name was Malchus.) 11Jesus told Peter, “Put
your sword away! Am I not to drink the cup
the Father has given me?” 12Then the company of soldiers, the commander, and the
guards from the Jewish leaders took Jesus
into custody. They bound him 13and led him
first to Annas. He was the father-in-law of
Caiaphas, the high priest that year. (14Caia-
phas was the one who had advised the Jewish leaders that it was better for one person
to die for the people.)

Peter denies Jesus

15Simon Peter and another disciple followed Jesus. Because this other disciple
was known to the high priest, he went
with Jesus into the high priest’s courtyard. 16However, Peter stood outside near
the gate. Then the other disciple (the one
known to the high priest) came out and
spoke to the woman stationed at the gate,
and she brought Peter in. 17The servant
woman stationed at the gate asked Peter,
“Aren’t you one of this man’s disciples?”

“I’m not,” he replied. 18The servants and
the guards had made a fire because it was
cold. They were standing around it, warming themselves. Peter joined them there,
standing by the fire and warming himself.

Jesus testifies

19Meanwhile, the chief priest questioned
Jesus about his disciples and his teaching.
20Jesus answered, “I’ve spoken openly to
the world. I’ve always taught in synagogues
and in the temple, where all the Jews
gather. I’ve said nothing in private. 21Why
ask me? Ask those who heard what I told
them. They know what I said.”

22After Jesus spoke, one of the guards
standing there slapped Jesus in the face.
“Is that how you would answer the high
priest?” he asked.

[a]Or *cohort* (approximately six hundred soldiers) [b]Or *It is I* [c]Or *It is I*

23 Jesus replied, "If I speak wrongly, testify about what was wrong. But if I speak correctly, why do you strike me?" 24 Then Annas sent him, bound, to Caiaphas the high priest.

Peter denies Jesus again

25 Meanwhile, Simon Peter was still standing with the guards, warming himself. They asked, "Aren't you one of his disciples?"

Peter denied it, saying, "I'm not."

26 A servant of the high priest, a relative of the one whose ear Peter had cut off, said to him, "Didn't I see you in the garden with him?" 27 Peter denied it again, and immediately a rooster crowed.

Trial before Pilate

28 The Jewish leaders led Jesus from Caiaphas to the Roman governor's palace.[d] It was early in the morning. So that they could eat the Passover, the Jewish leaders wouldn't enter the palace; entering the palace would have made them ritually impure.

29 So Pilate went out to them and asked, "What charge do you bring against this man?"

30 They answered, "If he had done nothing wrong, we wouldn't have handed him over to you."

31 Pilate responded, "Take him yourselves and judge him according to your Law."

The Jewish leaders replied, "The Law doesn't allow us to kill anyone." (32 This was so that Jesus' word might be fulfilled when he indicated how he was going to die.)

Pilate questions Jesus

33 Pilate went back into the palace. He summoned Jesus and asked, "Are you the king of the Jews?"

34 Jesus answered, "Do you say this on your own or have others spoken to you about me?"

35 Pilate responded, "I'm not a Jew, am I? Your nation and its chief priests handed you over to me. What have you done?"

36 Jesus replied, "My kingdom doesn't originate from this world. If it did, my guards would fight so that I wouldn't have been arrested by the Jewish leaders. My kingdom isn't from here."

37 "So you are a king?" Pilate said.

Jesus answered, "You say that I am a king. I was born and came into the world for this reason: to testify to the truth. Whoever accepts the truth listens to my voice."

38 "What is truth?" Pilate asked.

Release of Barabbas

After Pilate said this, he returned to the Jewish leaders and said, "I find no grounds for any charge against him. 39 You have a custom that I release one prisoner for you at Passover. Do you want me to release for you the king of the Jews?"

40 They shouted, "Not this man! Give us Barabbas!" (Barabbas was an outlaw.)

Jesus is whipped and mocked as king

19 Then Pilate had Jesus taken and whipped. 2 The soldiers twisted together a crown of thorns and put it on his head, and dressed him in a purple robe. 3 Over and over they went up to him and said, "Greetings, king of the Jews!" And they slapped him in the face.

4 Pilate came out of the palace again and said to the Jewish leaders, "Look! I'm bringing him out to you to let you know that I find no grounds for a charge against him." 5 When Jesus came out, wearing the crown of thorns and the purple robe, Pilate said to them, "Here's the man."

6 When the chief priests and their deputies saw him, they shouted out, "Crucify, crucify!"

Pilate told them, "You take him and crucify him. I don't find any grounds for a charge against him."

7 The Jewish leaders replied, "We have a Law, and according to this Law he ought to die because he made himself out to be God's Son."

Pilate questions Jesus again

8 When Pilate heard this word, he was even more afraid. 9 He went back into the residence and spoke to Jesus, "Where are you from?" Jesus didn't answer. 10 So Pilate said, "You won't speak to me? Don't you

[d] Or *praetorium*

know that I have authority to release you and also to crucify you?"

11 Jesus replied, "You would have no authority over me if it had not been given to you from above. That's why the one who handed me over to you has the greater sin." 12 From that moment on, Pilate wanted to release Jesus.

However, the Jewish leaders cried out, saying, "If you release this man, you aren't a friend of the emperor! Anyone who makes himself out to be a king opposes the emperor!"

13 When Pilate heard these words, he led Jesus out and seated him on the judge's bench at the place called Stone Pavement (in Aramaic, *Gabbatha*). 14 It was about noon on the Preparation Day for the Passover. Pilate said to the Jewish leaders, "Here's your king."

15 The Jewish leaders cried out, "Take him away! Take him away! Crucify him!"

Pilate responded, "What? Do you want me to crucify your king?"

"We have no king except the emperor," the chief priests answered. 16 Then Pilate handed Jesus over to be crucified.

Crucifixion

The soldiers took Jesus prisoner. 17 Carrying his cross by himself, he went out to a place called Skull Place (in Aramaic, *Golgotha*). 18 That's where they crucified him—and two others with him, one on each side and Jesus in the middle. 19 Pilate had a public notice written and posted on the cross. It read "Jesus the Nazarene, the king of the Jews." 20 Many of the Jews read this sign, for the place where Jesus was crucified was near the city and it was written in Aramaic, Latin, and Greek. 21 Therefore, the Jewish chief priests complained to Pilate, "Don't write, 'The king of the Jews' but 'This man said, "I am the king of the Jews."'"

22 Pilate answered, "What I've written, I've written."

23 When the soldiers crucified Jesus, they took his clothes and his sandals, and divided them into four shares, one for each soldier. His shirt was seamless, woven as one piece from the top to the bottom. 24 They said to each other, "Let's not tear it. Let's cast lots to see who will get it." This was to fulfill the scripture,

They divided my clothes among themselves,
and they cast lots for my clothing.[e]

That's what the soldiers did.

25 Jesus' mother and his mother's sister, Mary the wife of Clopas, and Mary Magdalene stood near the cross. 26 When Jesus saw his mother and the disciple whom he loved standing nearby, he said to his mother, "Woman, here is your son." 27 Then he said to the disciple, "Here is your mother." And from that time on, this disciple took her into his home.

28 After this, knowing that everything was already completed, in order to fulfill the scripture, Jesus said, "I am thirsty." 29 A jar full of sour wine was nearby, so the soldiers soaked a sponge in it, placed it on a hyssop branch, and held it up to his lips. 30 When he had received the sour wine, Jesus said, "It is completed." Bowing his head, he gave up his life.

Witness at the cross

31 It was the Preparation Day and the Jewish leaders didn't want the bodies to remain on the cross on the Sabbath, especially since that Sabbath was an important day. So they asked Pilate to have the legs of those crucified broken and the bodies taken down. 32 Therefore, the soldiers came and broke the legs of the two men who were crucified with Jesus. 33 When they came to Jesus, they saw that he was already dead so they didn't break his legs. 34 However, one of the soldiers pierced his side with a spear, and immediately blood and water came out. 35 The one who saw this has testified, and his testimony is true. He knows that he speaks the truth, and he has testified so that you also can believe. 36 These things happened to fulfill the scripture, *They won't break any of his bones.*[f] 37 And another scripture says, *They will look at him whom they have pierced.*[g]

Jesus' body is buried

38 After this Joseph of Arimathea asked Pilate if he could take away the body of

[e] Ps 22:18 [f] Exod 12:46 [g] Zech 12:10

Jesus. Joseph was a disciple of Jesus, but a secret one because he feared the Jewish authorities. Pilate gave him permission, so he came and took the body away. [39]Nicodemus, the one who at first had come to Jesus at night, was there too. He brought a mixture of myrrh and aloe, nearly seventy-five pounds in all.[h] [40]Following Jewish burial customs, they took Jesus' body and wrapped it, with the spices, in linen cloths. [41]There was a garden in the place where Jesus was crucified, and in the garden was a new tomb in which no one had ever been laid. [42]Because it was the Jewish Preparation Day and the tomb was nearby, they laid Jesus in it.

Empty tomb

20 Early in the morning of the first day of the week, while it was still dark, Mary Magdalene came to the tomb and saw that the stone had been taken away from the tomb. [2]She ran to Simon Peter and the other disciple, the one whom Jesus loved, and said, "They have taken the Lord from the tomb, and we don't know where they've put him." [3]Peter and the other disciple left to go to the tomb. [4]They were running together, but the other disciple ran faster than Peter and was the first to arrive at the tomb. [5]Bending down to take a look, he saw the linen cloths lying there, but he didn't go in. [6]Following him, Simon Peter entered the tomb and saw the linen cloths lying there. [7]He also saw the face cloth that had been on Jesus' head. It wasn't with the other clothes but was folded up in its own place. [8]Then the other disciple, the one who arrived at the tomb first, also went inside. He saw and believed. [9]They didn't yet understand the scripture that Jesus must rise from the dead. [10]Then the disciples returned to the place where they were staying.

Jesus appears to Mary

[11]Mary stood outside near the tomb, crying. As she cried, she bent down to look into the tomb. [12]She saw two angels dressed in white, seated where the body of Jesus had been, one at the head and one at the foot. [13]The angels asked her, "Woman, why are you crying?"

She replied, "They have taken away my Lord, and I don't know where they've put him." [14]As soon as she had said this, she turned around and saw Jesus standing there, but she didn't know it was Jesus.

[15]Jesus said to her, "Woman, why are you crying? Who are you looking for?"

Thinking he was the gardener, she replied, "Sir, if you have carried him away, tell me where you have put him and I will get him."

[16]Jesus said to her, "Mary."

She turned and said to him in Aramaic, "Rabbouni" (which means *Teacher*).

[17]Jesus said to her, "Don't hold on to me, for I haven't yet gone up to my Father. Go to my brothers and sisters and tell them, 'I'm going up to my Father and your Father, to my God and your God.'"

[18]Mary Magdalene left and announced to the disciples, "I've seen the Lord." Then she told them what he said to her.

Jesus appears to the disciples

[19]It was still the first day of the week. That evening, while the disciples were behind closed doors because they were afraid of the Jewish authorities, Jesus came and stood among them. He said, "Peace be with you." [20]After he said this, he showed them his hands and his side. When the disciples saw the Lord, they were filled with joy. [21]Jesus said to them again, "Peace be with you. As the Father sent me, so I am sending you." [22]Then he breathed on them and said, "Receive the Holy Spirit. [23]If you forgive anyone's sins, they are forgiven; if you don't forgive them, they aren't forgiven."

Jesus appears to Thomas and the disciples

[24]Thomas, the one called Didymus,[i] one of the Twelve, wasn't with the disciples when Jesus came. [25]The other disciples told him, "We've seen the Lord!"

[h]Or *one hundred litra*; that is, one hundred Roman pounds [i]Or *the twin*

But he replied, "Unless I see the nail
marks in his hands, put my finger in the
wounds left by the nails, and put my hand
into his side, I won't believe."
[26]After eight days his disciples were
again in a house and Thomas was with
them. Even though the doors were locked,
Jesus entered and stood among them. He
said, "Peace be with you." [27]Then he said
to Thomas, "Put your finger here. Look at
my hands. Put your hand into my side. No
more disbelief. Believe!"
[28]Thomas responded to Jesus, "My Lord
and my God!"
[29]Jesus replied, "Do you believe because
you see me? Happy are those who don't see
and yet believe."
[30]Then Jesus did many other miraculous
signs in his disciples' presence, signs that
aren't recorded in this scroll. [31]But these
things are written so that you will believe
that Jesus is the Christ, God's Son, and that
believing, you will have life in his name.

Jesus appears again to the disciples

21 Later, Jesus himself appeared again
to his disciples at the Sea of Tiberias.
This is how it happened: [2]Simon Peter,
Thomas (called Didymus[j]), Nathanael from
Cana in Galilee, Zebedee's sons, and two
other disciples were together. [3]Simon Peter
told them, "I'm going fishing."
They said, "We'll go with you." They set
out in a boat, but throughout the night
they caught nothing. [4]Early in the morning, Jesus stood on the shore, but the disciples didn't realize it was Jesus.
[5]Jesus called to them, "Children, have
you caught anything to eat?"
They answered him, "No."
[6]He said, "Cast your net on the right side
of the boat and you will find some."
So they did, and there were so many fish
that they couldn't haul in the net. [7]Then
the disciple whom Jesus loved said to Peter,
"It's the Lord!" When Simon Peter heard
it was the Lord, he wrapped his coat around
himself (for he was naked) and jumped into
the water. [8]The other disciples followed
in the boat, dragging the net full of fish, for
they weren't far from shore, only about one
hundred yards.
[9]When they landed, they saw a fire
there, with fish on it, and some bread.
[10]Jesus said to them, "Bring some of the
fish that you've just caught." [11]Simon Peter
got up and pulled the net to shore. It was
full of large fish, one hundred fifty-three of
them. Yet the net hadn't torn, even with so
many fish. [12]Jesus said to them, "Come and
have breakfast." None of the disciples could
bring themselves to ask him, "Who are
you?" They knew it was the Lord. [13]Jesus
came, took the bread, and gave it to them.
He did the same with the fish. [14]This was
now the third time Jesus appeared to his
disciples after he was raised from the dead.

Jesus and Peter

[15]When they finished eating, Jesus
asked Simon Peter, "Simon son of John, do
you love me more than these?"
Simon replied, "Yes, Lord, you know I
love you."
Jesus said to him, "Feed my lambs."
[16]Jesus asked a second time, "Simon son of
John, do you love me?"
Simon replied, "Yes, Lord, you know I
love you."
Jesus said to him, "Take care of my
sheep." [17]He asked a third time, "Simon son
of John, do you love me?"
Peter was sad that Jesus asked him a third
time, "Do you love me?" He replied, "Lord,
you know everything; you know I love you."
Jesus said to him, "Feed my sheep. [18]I assure you that when you were younger you
tied your own belt and walked around wherever you wanted. When you grow old, you
will stretch out your hands and another will
tie your belt and lead you where you don't
want to go." [19]He said this to show the kind of
death by which Peter would glorify God. After
saying this, Jesus said to Peter, "Follow me."

Jesus and the disciple whom he loved

[20]Peter turned around and saw the disciple whom Jesus loved following them. This

[j]Or *the twin*

was the one who had leaned against Jesus at the meal and asked him, "Lord, who is going to betray you?" [21]When Peter saw this disciple, he said to Jesus, "Lord, what about him?"

[22]Jesus replied, "If I want him to remain until I come, what difference does that make to you? You must follow me." [23]Therefore, the word spread among the brothers and sisters that this disciple wouldn't die. However, Jesus didn't say he wouldn't die, but only, "If I want him to remain until I come, what difference does that make to you?" [24]This is the disciple who testifies concerning these things and who wrote them down. We know that his testimony is true. [25]Jesus did many other things as well. If all of them were recorded, I imagine the world itself wouldn't have enough room for the scrolls that would be written.

ACTS OF THE APOSTLES

The risen Jesus with his disciples

1 Theophilus, the first scroll I wrote concerned everything Jesus did and taught from the beginning, [2]right up to the day when he was taken up into heaven. Before he was taken up, working in the power of the Holy Spirit, Jesus instructed the apostles he had chosen. [3]After his suffering, he showed them that he was alive with many convincing proofs. He appeared to them over a period of forty days, speaking to them about God's kingdom. [4]While they were eating together, he ordered them not to leave Jerusalem but to wait for what the Father had promised. He said, "This is what you heard from me: [5]John baptized with water, but in only a few days you will be baptized with the Holy Spirit."

[6]As a result, those who had gathered together asked Jesus, "Lord, are you going to restore the kingdom to Israel now?"

[7]Jesus replied, "It isn't for you to know the times or seasons that the Father has set by his own authority. [8]Rather, you will receive power when the Holy Spirit has come upon you, and you will be my witnesses in Jerusalem, in all Judea and Samaria, and to the end of the earth."

[9]After Jesus said these things, as they were watching, he was lifted up and a cloud took him out of their sight. [10]While he was going away and as they were staring toward heaven, suddenly two men in white robes stood next to them. [11]They said, "Galileans, why are you standing here, looking toward heaven? This Jesus, who was taken up from you into heaven, will come in the same way that you saw him go into heaven."

Jesus' followers in Jerusalem

[12]Then they returned to Jerusalem from the Mount of Olives, which is near Jerusalem—a sabbath day's journey away. [13]When they entered the city, they went to the upstairs room where they were staying. Peter, John, James, and Andrew; Philip and Thomas; Bartholomew and Matthew; James, Alphaeus' son; Simon the zealot; and Judas, James' son—[14]all were united in their devotion to prayer, along with some women, including Mary the mother of Jesus, and his brothers.

A replacement for Judas

[15]During this time, the family of believers was a company of about one hundred twenty persons. Peter stood among them and said, [16]"Brothers and sisters, the scripture that the Holy Spirit announced beforehand through David had to be fulfilled. This was the scripture concerning Judas, who became a guide for those who arrested Jesus. [17]This happened even though he was one of us and received a share of this ministry." ([18]In fact, he bought a field with the payment he received for his injustice. Falling headfirst, he burst open in the middle and all his intestines spilled out. [19]This became known to everyone living in Jerusalem, so they called that field in their own language Hakeldama, or "Field of Blood.") [20]"It is written in the Psalms scroll,

Let his home become deserted and let
there be no one living in it;[a]
and
Give his position of leadership to another.[b]
21 "Therefore, we must select one of those
who have accompanied us during the whole
time the Lord Jesus lived among us, 22 beginning from the baptism of John until the
day when Jesus was taken from us. This
person must become along with us a witness to his resurrection." 23 So they nomi-
nated two: Joseph called Barsabbas, who
was also known as Justus, and Matthias.
24 They prayed, "Lord, you know everyone's deepest thoughts and desires. Show
us clearly which one you have chosen from
among these two 25 to take the place of
this ministry and apostleship, from which
Judas turned away to go to his own place."
26 When they cast lots, the lot fell on Matthias. He was added to the eleven apostles.

Pentecost

2 When Pentecost Day arrived, they were
all together in one place. 2 Suddenly a
sound from heaven like the howling of a
fierce wind filled the entire house where
they were sitting. 3 They saw what seemed
to be individual flames of fire alighting
on each one of them. 4 They were all filled
with the Holy Spirit and began to speak in
other languages as the Spirit enabled them
to speak.
5 There were pious Jews from every nation under heaven living in Jerusalem.
6 When they heard this sound, a crowd gathered. They were mystified because everyone
heard them speaking in their native languages. 7 They were surprised and amazed,
saying, "Look, aren't all the people who
are speaking Galileans, every one of them?
8 How then can each of us hear them speaking in our native language? 9 Parthians,
Medes, and Elamites; as well as residents
of Mesopotamia, Judea, and Cappadocia,
Pontus and Asia, 10 Phrygia and Pamphylia,
Egypt and the regions of Libya bordering
Cyrene; and visitors from Rome (both Jews
and converts to Judaism), 11 Cretans and
Arabs—we hear them declaring the mighty
works of God in our own languages!" 12 They
were all surprised and bewildered. Some
asked each other, "What does this mean?"
13 Others jeered at them, saying, "They're
full of new wine!"
14 Peter stood with the other eleven
apostles. He raised his voice and declared,
"Judeans and everyone living in Jerusalem!
Know this! Listen carefully to my words!
15 These people aren't drunk, as you suspect; after all, it's only nine o'clock in the
morning! 16 Rather, this is what was spoken
through the prophet Joel:
17 *In the last days, God says,*
I will pour out my Spirit on all people.
Your sons and daughters will prophesy.
Your young will see visions.
Your elders will dream dreams.
18 *Even upon my servants, men and women,*
I will pour out my Spirit in those days,
and they will prophesy.
19 *I will cause wonders to occur in the*
heavens above
and signs on the earth below,
blood and fire and a cloud of smoke.
20 *The sun will be changed into darkness,*
and the moon will be changed into blood,
before the great and spectacular day of
the Lord comes.
21 *And everyone who calls on the name of the*
Lord will be saved.[c]
22 "Fellow Israelites, listen to these
words! Jesus the Nazarene was a man
whose credentials God proved to you
through miracles, wonders, and signs,
which God performed through him among
you. You yourselves know this. 23 In accordance with God's established plan and
foreknowledge, he was betrayed. You, with
the help of wicked men, had Jesus killed by
nailing him to a cross. 24 God raised him up!
God freed him from death's dreadful grip,
since it was impossible for death to hang on
to him. 25 David says about him,
I foresaw that the Lord
was always with me;
because he is at my right hand
I won't be shaken.

[a] Ps 69:25 [b] Ps 109:8 [c] Joel 2:28-32

26 *Therefore, my heart was glad*
and my tongue rejoiced.
Moreover, my body will live in hope,
27 *because you won't abandon me*
to the grave,
nor permit your holy one
to experience decay.
28 *You have shown me the paths of life;*
your presence will fill me with happiness.[d]
29 "Brothers and sisters, I can speak confidently about the patriarch David. He died
and was buried, and his tomb is with us to
this very day. 30 Because he was a prophet,
he knew that God promised him with a solemn pledge to seat one of his descendants
on his throne. 31 Having seen this beforehand, David spoke about the resurrection
of Christ, that *he wasn't abandoned to the*
grave, nor did his body experience decay.[e]
32 This Jesus, God raised up. We are all witnesses to that fact. 33 He was exalted to
God's right side and received from the Father the promised Holy Spirit. He poured
out this Spirit, and you are seeing and
hearing the results of his having done so.
34 David didn't ascend into heaven. Yet he
says,
The Lord said to my Lord,
'Sit at my right side,
35 *until I make your enemies*
a footstool for your feet.'[f]
36 "Therefore, let all Israel know beyond
question that God has made this Jesus,
whom you crucified, both Lord and Christ."
37 When the crowd heard this, they were
deeply troubled. They said to Peter and
the other apostles, "Brothers, what should
we do?"
38 Peter replied, "Change your hearts and
lives. Each of you must be baptized in the
name of Jesus Christ for the forgiveness
of your sins. Then you will receive the gift
of the Holy Spirit. 39 This promise is for
you, your children, and for all who are far
away—as many as the Lord our God invites." 40 With many other words he testified to them and encouraged them, saying,
"Be saved from this perverse generation."
41 Those who accepted Peter's message were
baptized. God brought about three thousand people into the community on that
day.

Community of believers

42 The believers devoted themselves to
the apostles' teaching, to the community, to
their shared meals, and to their prayers. 43 A
sense of awe came over everyone. God performed many wonders and signs through the
apostles. 44 All the believers were united and
shared everything. 45 They would sell pieces
of property and possessions and distribute
the proceeds to everyone who needed them.
46 Every day, they met together in the temple and ate in their homes. They shared food
with gladness and simplicity. 47 They praised
God and demonstrated God's goodness to
everyone. The Lord added daily to the community those who were being saved.

Healing of a crippled man

3 Peter and John were going up to the
temple at three o'clock in the afternoon,
the established prayer time. 2 Meanwhile, a
man crippled since birth was being carried
in. Every day, people would place him at the
temple gate known as the Beautiful Gate so
he could ask for money from those entering
the temple. 3 When he saw Peter and John
about to enter, he began to ask them for a
gift. 4 Peter and John stared at him. Peter
said, "Look at us!" 5 So the man gazed at
them, expecting to receive something from
them. 6 Peter said, "I don't have any money,
but I will give you what I do have. In the
name of Jesus Christ the Nazarene, rise up
and walk!" 7 Then he grasped the man's right
hand and raised him up. At once his feet
and ankles became strong. 8 Jumping up, he
began to walk around. He entered the temple with them, walking, leaping, and praising God. 9 All the people saw him walking
and praising God. 10 They recognized him as
the same one who used to sit at the temple's Beautiful Gate asking for money. They
were filled with amazement and surprise at
what had happened to him.
11 While the healed man clung to Peter

[d] Ps 16:8-11 [e] Ps 16:10 [f] Ps 110:1

and John, all the people rushed toward them at Solomon's Porch, completely amazed. [12]Seeing this, Peter addressed the people: "You Israelites, why are you amazed at this? Why are you staring at us as if we made him walk by our own power or piety? [13]The God of Abraham, Isaac, and Jacob—the God of our ancestors—has glorified his servant Jesus. This is the one you handed over and denied in Pilate's presence, even though he had already decided to release him. [14]You rejected the holy and righteous one, and asked that a murderer be released to you instead. [15]You killed the author of life, the very one whom God raised from the dead. We are witnesses of this. [16]His name itself has made this man strong. That is, because of faith in Jesus' name, God has strengthened this man whom you see and know. The faith that comes through Jesus gave him complete health right before your eyes.

[17]"Brothers and sisters, I know you acted in ignorance. So did your rulers. [18]But this is how God fulfilled what he foretold through all the prophets: that his Christ would suffer. [19]Change your hearts and lives! Turn back to God so that your sins may be wiped away. [20]Then the Lord will provide a season of relief from the distress of this age and he will send Jesus, whom he handpicked to be your Christ. [21]Jesus must remain in heaven until the restoration of all things, about which God spoke long ago through his holy prophets. [22]Moses said, *The Lord your God will raise up from your own people a prophet like me. Listen to whatever he tells you.* [23]*Whoever doesn't listen to that prophet will be totally cut off from the people.*[g] [24]All the prophets who spoke—from Samuel forward—announced these days. [25]You are the heirs of the prophets and the covenant that God made with your ancestors when he told Abraham, *Through your descendants, all the families on earth will be blessed.*[h] [26]After God raised his servant, he sent him to you first—to bless you by enabling each of you to turn from your evil ways."

Peter and John questioned

4 While Peter and John were speaking to the people, the priests, the captain of the temple guard, and the Sadducees confronted them. [2]They were incensed that the apostles were teaching the people and announcing that the resurrection of the dead was happening because of Jesus. [3]They seized Peter and John and put them in prison until the next day. (It was already evening.) [4]Many who heard the word became believers, and their number grew to about five thousand.

[5]The next day the leaders, elders, and legal experts gathered in Jerusalem, [6]along with Annas the high priest, Caiaphas, John, Alexander, and others from the high priest's family. [7]They had Peter and John brought before them and asked, "By what power or in what name did you do this?"

[8]Then Peter, inspired by the Holy Spirit, answered, "Leaders of the people and elders, [9]are we being examined today because something good was done for a sick person, a good deed that healed him? [10]If so, then you and all the people of Israel need to know that this man stands healthy before you because of the name of Jesus Christ the Nazarene—whom you crucified but whom God raised from the dead. [11]This Jesus is the stone you builders rejected; he has become the cornerstone! [12]Salvation can be found in no one else. Throughout the whole world, no other name has been given among humans through which we must be saved."

[13]The council was caught by surprise by the confidence with which Peter and John spoke. After all, they understood that these apostles were uneducated and inexperienced. They also recognized that they had been followers of Jesus. [14]However, since the healed man was standing with Peter and John before their own eyes, they had no rebuttal. [15]After ordering them to wait outside, the council members began to confer with each other. [16]"What should we do with these men? Everyone living in Jerusalem is aware of the sign performed through them. It's obvious to everyone and

[g]Deut 18:15, 19 [h]Gen 22:18; 26:4

we can't deny it. [17]To keep it from spreading further among the people, we need to warn them not to speak to anyone in this name." [18]When they called Peter and John back, they demanded that they stop all speaking and teaching in the name of Jesus.

[19]Peter and John responded, "It's up to you to determine whether it's right before God to obey you rather than God. [20]As for us, we can't stop speaking about what we have seen and heard." [21]They threatened them further, then released them. Because of public support for Peter and John, they couldn't find a way to punish them. Everyone was praising God for what had happened, [22]because the man who had experienced this sign of healing was over 40 years old.

The believers pray

[23]After their release, Peter and John returned to the brothers and sisters and reported everything the chief priests and elders had said. [24]They listened, then lifted their voices in unison to God, "Master, you are the one who created the heaven, the earth, the sea, and everything in them. [25]You are the one who spoke by the Holy Spirit through our ancestor David, your servant:

Why did the Gentiles rage,
and the peoples plot in vain?
[26]*The kings of the earth took their stand*
and the rulers gathered together as one
against the Lord and against his Christ.[i]

[27]Indeed, both Herod and Pontius Pilate, with Gentiles and Israelites, did gather in this city against your holy servant Jesus, whom you anointed. [28]They did what your power and plan had already determined would happen. [29]Now, Lord, take note of their threats and enable your servants to speak your word with complete confidence. [30]Stretch out your hand to bring healing and enable signs and wonders to be performed through the name of Jesus, your holy servant." [31]After they prayed, the place where they were gathered was shaken. They were all filled with the Holy Spirit and began speaking God's word with confidence.

Sharing among the believers

[32]The community of believers was one in heart and mind. None of them would say, "This is mine!" about any of their possessions, but held everything in common. [33]The apostles continued to bear powerful witness to the resurrection of the Lord Jesus, and an abundance of grace was at work among them all. [34]There were no needy persons among them. Those who owned properties or houses would sell them, bring the proceeds from the sales, [35]and place them in the care and under the authority of the apostles. Then it was distributed to anyone who was in need.

[36]Joseph, whom the apostles nicknamed Barnabas (that is, "one who encourages"), was a Levite from Cyprus. [37]He owned a field, sold it, brought the money, and placed it in the care and under the authority of the apostles.

Pretenders of sharing

5 However, a man named Ananias, along with his wife Sapphira, sold a piece of property. [2]With his wife's knowledge, he withheld some of the proceeds from the sale. He brought the rest and placed it in the care and under the authority of the apostles. [3]Peter asked, "Ananias, how is it that Satan has influenced you to lie to the Holy Spirit by withholding some of the proceeds from the sale of your land? [4]Wasn't that property yours to keep? After you sold it, wasn't the money yours to do with whatever you wanted? What made you think of such a thing? You haven't lied to other people but to God!" [5]When Ananias heard these words, he dropped dead. Everyone who heard this conversation was terrified. [6]Some young men stood up, wrapped up his body, carried him out, and buried him.

[7]About three hours later, his wife entered, but she didn't know what had happened to her husband. [8]Peter asked her, "Tell me, did you and your husband receive this price for the field?"

She responded, "Yes, that's the amount."

[9]He replied, "How could you scheme with each other to challenge the Lord's Spirit?

[i]Or *anointed one;* Ps 2:1-2

Look! The feet of those who buried your husband are at the door. They will carry you out too." 10At that very moment, she dropped dead at his feet. When the young men entered and found her dead, they carried her out and buried her with her husband. 11Trepidation and dread seized the whole church and all who heard what had happened.

Responses to the church

12The apostles performed many signs and wonders among the people. They would come together regularly at Solomon's Porch. 13No one from outside the church dared to join them, even though the people spoke highly of them. 14Indeed, more and more believers in the Lord, large numbers of both men and women, were added to the church. 15As a result, they would even bring the sick out into the main streets and lay them on cots and mats so that at least Peter's shadow could fall on some of them as he passed by. 16Even large numbers of persons from towns around Jerusalem would gather, bringing the sick and those harassed by unclean spirits. Everyone was healed.

The Jerusalem Council harasses the apostles

17The high priest, together with his allies, the Sadducees, was overcome with jealousy. 18They seized the apostles and made a public show of putting them in prison. 19An angel from the Lord opened the prison doors during the night and led them out. The angel told them, 20"Go, take your place in the temple, and tell the people everything about this new life." 21Early in the morning, they went into the temple as they had been told and began to teach.

When the high priest and his colleagues gathered, they convened the Jerusalem Council, that is, the full assembly of Israel's elders. They sent word to the prison to have the apostles brought before them. 22However, the guards didn't find them in the prison. They returned and reported, 23"We found the prison locked and well-secured, with guards standing at the doors, but when we opened the doors we found no one inside!" 24When they received this news, the captain of the temple guard and the chief priests were baffled and wondered what might be happening. 25Just then, someone arrived and announced, "Look! The people you put in prison are standing in the temple and teaching the people!" 26Then the captain left with his guards and brought the apostles back. They didn't use force because they were afraid the people would stone them.

27The apostles were brought before the council where the high priest confronted them: 28"In no uncertain terms, we demanded that you not teach in this name. And look at you! You have filled Jerusalem with your teaching. And you are determined to hold us responsible for this man's death."

29Peter and the apostles replied, "We must obey God rather than humans! 30The God of our ancestors raised Jesus from the dead—whom you killed by hanging him on a tree. 31God has exalted Jesus to his right side as leader and savior so that he could enable Israel to change its heart and life and to find forgiveness for sins. 32We are witnesses of such things, as is the Holy Spirit, whom God has given to those who obey him."

33When the council members heard this, they became furious and wanted to kill the apostles. 34One council member, a Pharisee and teacher of the Law named Gamaliel, well-respected by all the people, stood up and ordered that the men be taken outside for a few moments. 35He said, "Fellow Israelites, consider carefully what you intend to do to these people. 36Some time ago, Theudas appeared, claiming to be somebody, and some four hundred men joined him. After he was killed, all of his followers scattered, and nothing came of that. 37Afterward, at the time of the census, Judas the Galilean appeared and got some people to follow him in a revolt. He was killed too, and all his followers scattered far and wide. 38Here's my recommendation in this case: Distance yourselves from these men. Let them go! If their plan or activity is of human origin, it will end in ruin. 39 If it originates with God, you won't be able to stop them. Instead, you would actually find yourselves fighting God!" The council was convinced by his reasoning. 40 After calling the apostles back, they had them beaten. They ordered them not to speak in the name of Jesus, then let them go. 41 The apostles left the council rejoicing because they had been regarded as worthy to suffer disgrace for the sake of the name. 42 Every day they continued to teach and proclaim the good news that Jesus is the Christ, both in the temple and in houses.

Selection of seven to serve

6 About that time, while the number of disciples continued to increase, a complaint arose. Greek-speaking disciples accused the Aramaic-speaking disciples because their widows were being overlooked in the daily food service. 2 The Twelve called a meeting of all the disciples and said, "It isn't right for us to set aside proclamation of God's word in order to serve tables. 3 Brothers and sisters, carefully choose seven well-respected men from among you. They must be well-respected and endowed by the Spirit with exceptional wisdom. We will put them in charge of this concern. 4 As for us, we will devote ourselves to prayer and the service of proclaiming the word." 5 This proposal pleased the entire community. They selected Stephen, a man endowed by the Holy Spirit with exceptional faith, Philip, Prochorus, Nicanor, Timon, Parmenas, and Nicolaus from Antioch, a convert to Judaism. 6 The community presented these seven to the apostles, who prayed and laid their hands on them. 7 God's word continued to grow. The number of disciples in Jerusalem increased significantly. Even a large group of priests embraced the faith.

Arrest and murder of Stephen

8 Stephen, who stood out among the believers for the way God's grace was at work in his life and for his exceptional endowment with divine power, was doing great wonders and signs among the people. 9 Opposition arose from some who belonged to the so-called Synagogue of Former Slaves. Members from Cyrene, Alexandria, Cilicia, and Asia entered into debate with Stephen. 10 However, they couldn't resist the wisdom the Spirit gave him as he spoke. 11 Then they secretly enticed some people to claim, "We heard him insult Moses and God." 12 They stirred up the people, the elders, and the legal experts. They caught Stephen, dragged him away, and brought him before the Jerusalem Council. 13 Before the council, they presented false witnesses who testified, "This man never stops speaking against this holy place and the Law. 14 In fact, we heard him say that this man Jesus of Nazareth will destroy this place and alter the customary practices Moses gave us." 15 Everyone seated in the council stared at Stephen, and they saw that his face was radiant, just like an angel's.

7 The high priest asked, "Are these accusations true?"

2 Stephen responded, "Brothers and fathers, listen to me. Our glorious God appeared to our ancestor Abraham while he was still in Mesopotamia, before he settled in Haran. 3 God told him, 'Leave your homeland and kin, and go to the land that I will show you.'[j] 4 So Abraham left the land of the Chaldeans and settled in Haran. After Abraham's father died, God had him resettle in this land where you now live. 5 God didn't give him an inheritance here, not even a square foot of land. However, God did promise to give the land as his possession to him and to his descendants, even though Abraham had no child. 6 God put it this way: *His descendants will be strangers in a land that belongs to others, who will enslave them and abuse them for four hundred years.*[k] 7 *And I will condemn the nation they serve as slaves,* God said, *and afterward they will leave*[l] that land and serve me in this place. 8 God gave him the covenant confirmed through circumcision. Accordingly, eight days after Isaac's birth, Abraham circumcised him. Isaac did the same with Jacob, and Jacob with the twelve patriarchs.

[j] Gen 12:1 [k] Gen 15:13 [l] Gen 15:14

9“Because the patriarchs were jealous of Joseph, they sold him into slavery in Egypt. God was with him, however, 10and rescued him from all his troubles. The grace and wisdom he gave Joseph were recognized by Pharaoh, king of Egypt, who appointed him ruler over Egypt and over his whole palace. 11A famine came upon all Egypt and Canaan, and great hardship came with it. Our ancestors had nothing to eat. 12When Jacob heard there was grain in Egypt, he sent our ancestors there for the first time. 13During their second visit, Joseph told his brothers who he was, and Pharaoh learned about Joseph’s family. 14Joseph sent for his father Jacob and all his relatives—seventy-five in all—and invited them to live with him. 15So Jacob went down to Egypt, where he and our ancestors died. 16Their bodies were brought back to Shechem and placed in the tomb that Abraham had purchased for a certain sum of money from Hamor’s children, who lived in Shechem.

17“When it was time for God to keep the promise he made to Abraham, the number of our people in Egypt had greatly expanded. 18But then *another king rose to power over Egypt who didn’t know anything about Joseph.*[m] 19He exploited our people and abused our ancestors. He even forced them to abandon their newly born babies so they would die. 20That’s when Moses was born. He was highly favored by God, and for three months his parents cared for him in their home. 21After he was abandoned, Pharaoh’s daughter adopted and cared for him as though he were her own son. 22Moses learned everything Egyptian wisdom had to offer, and he was a man of powerful words and deeds.

23“When Moses was 40 years old, he decided to visit his family, the Israelites. 24He saw one of them being wronged so he came to his rescue and evened the score by killing the Egyptian. 25He expected his own kin to understand that God was using him to rescue them, but they didn’t. 26The next day he came upon some Israelites who were caught up in an argument. He tried to make peace between them by saying, ‘You are brothers! Why are you harming each other?’ 27The one who started the fight against his neighbor pushed Moses aside and said, *‘Who appointed you as our leader and judge? 28Are you planning to kill me like you killed that Egyptian yesterday?’*[n] 29When Moses heard this, he fled to Midian, where he lived as an immigrant and had two sons.

30“Forty years later, an angel appeared to Moses in the flame of a burning bush in the wilderness near Mount Sinai. 31Enthralled by the sight, Moses approached to get a closer look and he heard the Lord’s voice: 32*‘I am the God of your ancestors, the God of Abraham, Isaac, and Jacob.’*[o] Trembling with fear, Moses didn’t dare to investigate any further. 33The Lord continued, *‘Remove the sandals from your feet, for the place where you are standing is holy ground. 34I have clearly seen the oppression my people have experienced in Egypt, and I have heard their groaning. I have come down to rescue them. Come! I am sending you to Egypt.’*[p]

35“This is the same Moses whom they rejected when they asked, ‘Who appointed you as our leader and judge?’ This is the Moses whom God sent as leader and deliverer. God did this with the help of the angel who appeared before him in the bush. 36This man led them out after he performed wonders and signs in Egypt at the Red Sea and for forty years in the wilderness. 37This is the Moses who told the Israelites, *‘God will raise up for you a prophet like me from your own people.’*[q] 38This is the one who was in the assembly in the wilderness with our ancestors and with the angel who spoke to him on Mount Sinai. He is the one who received life-giving words to give to us. 39He’s also the one whom our ancestors refused to obey. Instead, they pushed him aside and, in their thoughts and desires, returned to Egypt. 40They told Aaron, *‘Make us gods that will lead us. As for this Moses who led us out of Egypt, we don’t know what’s happened to him!’*[r] 41That’s when they made an idol in the shape of a calf, offered a sacrifice to it, and began to celebrate what they

[m]Exod 1:8 [n]Exod 2:14 [o]Exod 3:6 [p]Exod 3:5, 7 [q]Deut 18:15 [r]Exod 32:1

had made with their own hands. 42 So God turned away from them and handed them over to worship the stars in the sky, just as it is written in the scroll of the Prophets:

Did you bring sacrifices and offerings to me
for forty years in the wilderness,
house of Israel?
43 *No! Instead, you took*
the tent of Moloch with you,
and the star of your god Rephan,
the images that you made
in order to worship them.
Therefore, I will send you far away,
farther than Babylon.[s]

44 "The tent of testimony was with our ancestors in the wilderness. Moses built it just as he had been instructed by the one who spoke to him and according to the pattern he had seen. 45 In time, when they had received the tent, our ancestors carried it with them when, under Joshua's leadership, they took possession of the land from the nations whom God expelled. This tent remained in the land until the time of David. 46 God approved of David, who asked that he might provide a dwelling place for the God of Jacob.[t] 47 But it was Solomon who actually built a house for God. 48 However, the Most High doesn't live in houses built by human hands. As the prophet says,

49 *Heaven is my throne,*
and the earth is my footstool.
'What kind of house will you build for me,'
says the Lord,
'or where is my resting place?
50 *Didn't I make all these things*
with my own hand?'[u]

51 "You stubborn people! In your thoughts and hearing, you are like those who have had no part in God's covenant! You continuously set yourself against the Holy Spirit, just like your ancestors did. 52 Was there a single prophet your ancestors didn't harass? They even killed those who predicted the coming of the righteous one, and you've betrayed and murdered him! 53 You received the Law given by angels, but you haven't kept it."

54 Once the council members heard these words, they were enraged and began to grind their teeth at Stephen. 55 But Stephen, enabled by the Holy Spirit, stared into heaven and saw God's majesty and Jesus standing at God's right side. 56 He exclaimed, "Look! I can see heaven on display and the Human One[v] standing at God's right side!" 57 At this, they shrieked and covered their ears. Together, they charged at him, 58 threw him out of the city, and began to stone him. The witnesses placed their coats in the care of a young man named Saul. 59 As they battered him with stones, Stephen prayed, "Lord Jesus, accept my life!" 60 Falling to his knees, he shouted, "Lord, don't hold this sin against them!" Then he died. **8** 1 Saul was in full agreement with Stephen's murder.

The church scatters

At that time, the church in Jerusalem began to be subjected to vicious harassment. Everyone except the apostles was scattered throughout the regions of Judea and Samaria. 2 Some pious men buried Stephen and deeply grieved over him. 3 Saul began to wreak havoc against the church. Entering one house after another, he would drag off both men and women and throw them into prison.

Philip in Samaria

4 Those who had been scattered moved on, preaching the good news along the way. 5 Philip went down to a city in Samaria[w] and began to preach Christ to them. 6 The crowds were united by what they heard Philip say and the signs they saw him perform, and they gave him their undivided attention. 7 With loud shrieks, unclean spirits came out of many people, and many who were paralyzed or crippled were healed. 8 There was great rejoicing in that city.

9 Before Philip's arrival, a certain man named Simon had practiced sorcery in that city and baffled the people of Samaria. He claimed to be a great person. 10 Everyone, from the least to the greatest, gave him

[s] Amos 5:25-27 [t] Critical editions of the Gk New Testament read *house of Jacob*. [u] Isa 66:1-2 [v] Or *Son of Man*
[w] Or *the city of Samaria*

their undivided attention and referred to
him as "the power of God called Great." [11]He
had their attention because he had baffled
them with sorcery for a long time. [12]After
they came to believe Philip, who preached
the good news about God's kingdom and
the name of Jesus Christ, both men and
women were baptized. [13]Even Simon himself came to believe and was baptized.
Afterward, he became one of Philip's supporters. As he saw firsthand the signs and
great miracles that were happening, he was
astonished.

[14]When word reached the apostles in Jerusalem that Samaria had accepted God's
word, they commissioned Peter and John to
go to Samaria. [15]Peter and John went down
to Samaria where they prayed that the new
believers would receive the Holy Spirit.
([16]This was because the Holy Spirit had
not yet fallen on any of them; they had
only been baptized in the name of the Lord
Jesus.) [17]So Peter and John laid their hands
on them, and they received the Holy Spirit.

[18]When Simon perceived that the Spirit
was given through the laying on of the
apostles' hands, he offered them money.
[19]He said, "Give me this authority too so
that anyone on whom I lay my hands will
receive the Holy Spirit."

[20]Peter responded, "May your money be
condemned to hell along with you because
you believed you could buy God's gift with
money! [21]You can have no part or share in
God's word because your heart isn't right
with God. [22]Therefore, change your heart
and life! Turn from your wickedness! Plead
with the Lord in the hope that your wicked
intent can be forgiven, [23]for I see that your
bitterness has poisoned you and evil has
you in chains."

[24]Simon replied, "All of you, please, plead
to the Lord for me so that nothing of what
you have said will happen to me!" [25]After
the apostles had testified and proclaimed
the Lord's word, they returned to Jerusalem, preaching the good news to many
Samaritan villages along the way.

Philip and the Ethiopian eunuch

[26]An angel from the Lord spoke to
Philip, "At noon, take[x] the road that leads
from Jerusalem to Gaza." (This is a desert
road.) [27]So he did. Meanwhile, an Ethiopian
man was on his way home from Jerusalem,
where he had come to worship. He was a
eunuch and an official responsible for the
entire treasury of Candace. (Candace is the
title given to the Ethiopian queen.) [28]He
was reading the prophet Isaiah while sitting
in his carriage. [29]The Spirit told Philip, "Approach this carriage and stay with it."

[30]Running up to the carriage, Philip
heard the man reading the prophet Isaiah.
He asked, "Do you really understand what
you are reading?"

[31]The man replied, "Without someone
to guide me, how could I?" Then he invited
Philip to climb up and sit with him. [32]This
was the passage of scripture he was reading:

Like a sheep he was led to the slaughter
and like a lamb before its shearer is silent
so he didn't open his mouth.
[33]*In his humiliation*
justice was taken away from him.
Who can tell the story of his descendants
because his life was taken
from the earth?[y]

[34]The eunuch asked Philip, "Tell me,
about whom does the prophet say this? Is
he talking about himself or someone else?"
[35]Starting with that passage, Philip proclaimed the good news about Jesus to him.
[36]As they went down the road, they came
to some water.

The eunuch said, "Look! Water! What
would keep me from being baptized?"[z] [38]He
ordered that the carriage halt. Both Philip
and the eunuch went down to the water,
where Philip baptized him. [39]When they
came up out of the water, the Lord's Spirit
suddenly took Philip away. The eunuch
never saw him again but went on his way
rejoicing. [40]Philip found himself in Azotus. He traveled through that area, preaching the good news in all the cities until he
reached Caesarea.

[x]Or *travel south along* [y]Isa 53:7-8 [z]Critical editions of the Gk New Testament do not include 8:37 *Philip said to him, "If you believe with all your heart, you can be." The eunuch answered, "I believe that Jesus Christ is God's Son."*

Saul encounters the risen Jesus

9 Meanwhile, Saul was still spewing out
murderous threats against the Lord's
disciples. He went to the high priest, 2seek-
ing letters to the synagogues in Damascus.
If he found persons who belonged to the
Way, whether men or women, these letters
would authorize him to take them as prisoners to Jerusalem. 3During the journey, as
he approached Damascus, suddenly a light
from heaven encircled him. 4He fell to the
ground and heard a voice asking him, "Saul,
Saul, why are you harassing me?"

5Saul asked, "Who are you, Lord?"

"I am Jesus, whom you are harassing,"
came the reply. 6"Now get up and enter the
city. You will be told what you must do."

7Those traveling with him stood there
speechless; they heard the voice but saw
no one. 8After they picked Saul up from the
ground, he opened his eyes but he couldn't
see. So they led him by the hand into
Damascus. 9For three days he was blind and
neither ate nor drank anything.

10In Damascus there was a certain disciple named Ananias. The Lord spoke to him
in a vision, "Ananias!"

He answered, "Yes, Lord."

11The Lord instructed him, "Go to Judas'
house on Straight Street and ask for a man
from Tarsus named Saul. He is praying. 12In
a vision he has seen a man named Ananias
enter and put his hands on him to restore
his sight."

13Ananias countered, "Lord, I have heard
many reports about this man. People say he
has done horrible things to your holy people in Jerusalem. 14He's here with authority
from the chief priests to arrest everyone
who calls on your name."

15The Lord replied, "Go! This man is the
agent I have chosen to carry my name before Gentiles, kings, and Israelites. 16I will
show him how much he must suffer for the
sake of my name."

17Ananias went to the house. He placed
his hands on Saul and said, "Brother Saul,
the Lord sent me—Jesus, who appeared to
you on the way as you were coming here.
He sent me so that you could see again and
be filled with the Holy Spirit." 18Instantly,
flakes fell from Saul's eyes and he could see
again. He got up and was baptized. 19After
eating, he regained his strength.

He stayed with the disciples in Damascus for several days. 20Right away, he began
to preach about Jesus in the synagogues.
"He is God's Son," he declared.

21Everyone who heard him was baffled.
They questioned each other, "Isn't he the
one who was wreaking havoc among those
in Jerusalem who called on this name?
Hadn't he come here to take those same
people as prisoners to the chief priests?"

22But Saul grew stronger and stronger.
He confused the Jews who lived in Damascus by proving that Jesus is the Christ.

23After this had gone on for some time,
the Jews hatched a plot to kill Saul. 24How-
ever, he found out about their scheme. They
were keeping watch at the city gates around
the clock so they could assassinate him.
25But his disciples took him by night and
lowered him in a basket through an opening in the city wall.

26When Saul arrived in Jerusalem, he
tried to join the disciples, but they were all
afraid of him. They didn't believe he was
really a disciple. 27Then Barnabas brought
Saul to the apostles and told them the story
about how Saul saw the Lord on the way and
that the Lord had spoken to Saul. He also
told them about the confidence with which
Saul had preached in the name of Jesus in
Damascus. 28After this, Saul moved freely
among the disciples in Jerusalem and was
speaking with confidence in the name of
the Lord. 29He got into debates with the
Greek-speaking Jews as well, but they tried
to kill him. 30When the family of believers
learned about this, they escorted him down
to Caesarea and sent him off to Tarsus.

31Then the church throughout Judea,
Galilee, and Samaria enjoyed a time of
peace. God strengthened the church, and
its life was marked by reverence for the
Lord. Encouraged by the Holy Spirit, the
church continued to grow in numbers.

Peter heals and raises the dead

32As Peter toured the whole region, he
went to visit God's holy people in Lydda.

33 There he found a man named Aeneas who
was paralyzed and had been confined to
his bed for eight years. 34 Peter said to him,
“Aeneas, Jesus Christ heals you! Get up and
make your bed.” At once he got up. 35 Everyone who lived in Lydda and Sharon saw him
and turned to the Lord.

36 In Joppa there was a disciple named
Tabitha (in Greek her name is Dorcas). Her
life overflowed with good works and compassionate acts on behalf of those in need.
37 About that time, though, she became so ill
that she died. After they washed her body,
they laid her in an upstairs room. 38 Since
Lydda was near Joppa, when the disciples
heard that Peter was there, they sent two
people to Peter. They urged, “Please come
right away!” 39 Peter went with them. Upon
his arrival, he was taken to the upstairs
room. All the widows stood beside him,
crying as they showed the tunics and other
clothing Dorcas made when she was alive.

40 Peter sent everyone out of the room,
then knelt and prayed. He turned to the
body and said, “Tabitha, get up!” She
opened her eyes, saw Peter, and sat up. 41 He
gave her his hand and raised her up. Then
he called God’s holy people, including the
widows, and presented her alive to them.
42 The news spread throughout Joppa, and
many put their faith in the Lord. 43 Peter
stayed for some time in Joppa with a certain tanner named Simon.

Peter, Cornelius, and the Gentiles

10 There was a man in Caesarea named
Cornelius, a centurion in the Italian
Company.[a] 2 He and his whole household
were pious, Gentile God-worshippers. He
gave generously to those in need among
the Jewish people and prayed to God constantly. 3 One day at nearly three o’clock in
the afternoon, he clearly saw an angel from
God in a vision. The angel came to him and
said, “Cornelius!”

4 Startled, he stared at the angel and replied, “What is it, Lord?”

The angel said, “Your prayers and your
compassionate acts are like a memorial offering to God. 5 Send messengers to Joppa
at once and summon a certain Simon,
the one known as Peter. 6 He is a guest of
Simon the tanner, whose house is near the
seacoast.” 7 When the angel who was speaking to him had gone, Cornelius summoned
two of his household servants along with a
pious soldier from his personal staff. 8 He
explained everything to them, then sent
them to Joppa.

9 At noon on the following day, as their
journey brought them close to the city, Peter
went up on the roof to pray. 10 He became
hungry and wanted to eat. While others
were preparing the meal, he had a visionary
experience. 11 He saw heaven opened up and
something like a large linen sheet being lowered to the earth by its four corners. 12 Inside
the sheet were all kinds of four-legged animals, reptiles, and wild birds.[b] 13 A voice told
him, “Get up, Peter! Kill and eat!”

14 Peter exclaimed, “Absolutely not, Lord!
I have never eaten anything impure or
unclean.”

15 The voice spoke a second time, “Never
consider unclean what God has made pure.”
16 This happened three times, then the object was suddenly pulled back into heaven.

17 Peter was bewildered about the meaning of the vision. Just then, the messengers
sent by Cornelius discovered the where-
abouts of Simon’s house and arrived at the
gate. 18 Calling out, they inquired whether
the Simon known as Peter was a guest there.

19 While Peter was brooding over the vision, the Spirit interrupted him, “Look!
Three people are looking for you. 20 Go
downstairs. Don’t ask questions; just go
with them because I have sent them.”

21 So Peter went downstairs and told
them, “I’m the one you are looking for. Why
have you come?”

22 They replied, “We’ve come on behalf of
Cornelius, a centurion and righteous man,
a God-worshipper who is well-respected by
all Jewish people. A holy angel directed him
to summon you to his house and to hear
what you have to say.” 23 Peter invited them
into the house as his guests.

[a] Or *cohort* (approximately six hundred soldiers) [b] Or *birds in the sky*

The next day he got up and went with
them, together with some of the believers
from Joppa. [24]They arrived in Caesarea the
following day. Anticipating their arrival,
Cornelius had gathered his relatives and
close friends. [25]As Peter entered the house,
Cornelius met him and fell at his feet in
order to honor him. [26]But Peter lifted him
up, saying, "Get up! Like you, I'm just a
human." [27]As they continued to talk, Peter
went inside and found a large gathering of
people. [28]He said to them, "You all realize
that it is forbidden for a Jew to associate
or visit with outsiders. However, God has
shown me that I should never call a person
impure or unclean. [29]For this reason, when
you sent for me, I came without objection.
I want to know, then, why you sent for me."

[30]Cornelius answered, "Four days ago at
this same time, three o'clock in the afternoon, I was praying at home. Suddenly a
man in radiant clothing stood before me.
[31]He said, 'Cornelius, God has heard your
prayers, and your compassionate acts are
like a memorial offering to him. [32]There-
fore, send someone to Joppa and summon
Simon, who is known as Peter. He is a guest
in the home of Simon the tanner, located
near the seacoast.' [33]I sent for you right
away, and you were kind enough to come.
Now, here we are, gathered in the presence
of God to listen to everything the Lord has
directed you to say."

[34]Peter said, "I really am learning that
God doesn't show partiality to one group of
people over another. [35]Rather, in every nation, whoever worships him and does what
is right is acceptable to him. [36]This is the
message of peace he sent to the Israelites by
proclaiming the good news through Jesus
Christ: He is Lord of all! [37]You know what
happened throughout Judea, beginning in
Galilee after the baptism John preached.
[38]You know about Jesus of Nazareth,
whom God anointed with the Holy Spirit
and endowed with power. Jesus traveled
around doing good and healing everyone
oppressed by the devil because God was
with him. [39]We are witnesses of everything
he did, both in Judea and in Jerusalem.
They killed him by hanging him on a tree,
[40]but God raised him up on the third day
and allowed him to be seen, [41]not by everyone but by us. We are witnesses whom God
chose beforehand, who ate and drank with
him after God raised him from the dead.
[42]He commanded us to preach to the people
and to testify that he is the one whom God
appointed as judge of the living and the
dead. [43]All the prophets testify about him
that everyone who believes in him receives
forgiveness of sins through his name."

[44]While Peter was still speaking, the
Holy Spirit fell on everyone who heard the
word. [45]The circumcised believers who had
come with Peter were astonished that the
gift of the Holy Spirit had been poured out
even on the Gentiles. [46]They heard them
speaking in other languages and praising
God. Peter asked, [47]"These people have
received the Holy Spirit just as we have.
Surely no one can stop them from being
baptized with water, can they?" [48]He directed that they be baptized in the name
of Jesus Christ. Then they invited Peter to
stay for several days.

Jerusalem church questions Peter

11 The apostles and the brothers and sisters throughout Judea heard that even
the Gentiles had welcomed God's word.
[2]When Peter went up to Jerusalem, the circumcised believers criticized him. [3]They accused him, "You went into the home of the
uncircumcised and ate with them!"

[4]Step-by-step, Peter explained what had
happened. [5]"I was in the city of Joppa praying when I had a visionary experience. In
my vision, I saw something like a large linen
sheet being lowered from heaven by its four
corners. It came all the way down to me.
[6]As I stared at it, wondering what it was,
I saw four-legged animals—including wild
beasts—as well as reptiles and wild birds.[c]
[7]I heard a voice say, 'Get up, Peter! Kill and
eat!' [8]I responded, 'Absolutely not, Lord!
Nothing impure or unclean has ever entered
my mouth.' [9]The voice from heaven spoke a

[c]Or *birds in the sky*

second time, 'Never consider unclean what God has made pure.' 10This happened three times, then everything was pulled back into heaven. 11At that moment three men who had been sent to me from Caesarea arrived at the house where we were staying. 12The Spirit told me to go with them even though they were Gentiles. These six brothers also went with me, and we entered that man's house. 13He reported to us how he had seen an angel standing in his house and saying, 'Send to Joppa and summon Simon, who is known as Peter. 14He will tell you how you and your entire household can be saved.' 15When I began to speak, the Holy Spirit fell on them, just as the Spirit fell on us in the beginning. 16I remembered the Lord's words: 'John will baptize with water, but you will be baptized with the Holy Spirit.' 17If God gave them the same gift he gave us who believed in the Lord Jesus Christ, then who am I? Could I stand in God's way?"

18Once the apostles and other believers heard this, they calmed down. They praised God and concluded, "So then God has enabled Gentiles to change their hearts and lives so that they might have new life."

The Antioch church

19Now those who were scattered as a result of the trouble that occurred because of Stephen traveled as far as Phoenicia, Cyprus, and Antioch. They proclaimed the word only to Jews. 20Among them were some people from Cyprus and Cyrene. They entered Antioch and began to proclaim the good news about the Lord Jesus also to Jews who spoke Greek. 21The Lord's power was with them, and a large number came to believe and turned to the Lord.

22When the church in Jerusalem heard about this, they sent Barnabas to Antioch. 23When he arrived and saw evidence of God's grace, he was overjoyed and encouraged everyone to remain fully committed to the Lord. 24Barnabas responded in this way because he was a good man, whom the Holy Spirit had endowed with exceptional faith. A considerable number of people were added to the Lord. 25Barnabas went to Tarsus in search of Saul. 26When he found him, he brought him to Antioch. They were there for a whole year, meeting with the church and teaching large numbers of people. It was in Antioch where the disciples were first labeled "Christians."

27About that time, some prophets came down from Jerusalem to Antioch. 28One of them, Agabus, stood up and, inspired by the Spirit, predicted that a severe famine would overtake the entire Roman world. (This occurred during Claudius' rule.) 29The disciples decided they would send support to the brothers and sisters in Judea, with everyone contributing to this ministry according to each person's abundance. 30They sent Barnabas and Saul to take this gift to the elders.

Herod imprisons Peter

12 About that time King Herod began to harass some who belonged to the church. 2He had James, John's brother, killed with a sword. 3When he saw that this pleased the Jews, he arrested Peter as well. This happened during the Festival of Unleavened Bread. 4He put Peter in prison, handing him over to four squads of soldiers, sixteen in all, who guarded him. He planned to charge him publicly after the Passover. 5While Peter was held in prison, the church offered earnest prayer to God for him.

6The night before Herod was going to bring Peter's case forward, Peter was asleep between two soldiers and bound with two chains, with soldiers guarding the prison entrance. 7Suddenly an angel from the Lord appeared and a light shone in the prison cell. After nudging Peter on his side to awaken him, the angel raised him up and said, "Quick! Get up!" The chains fell from his wrists. 8The angel continued, "Get dressed. Put on your sandals." Peter did as he was told. The angel said, "Put on your coat and follow me." 9Following the angel, Peter left the prison. However, he didn't realize the angel had actually done all this. He thought he was seeing a vision. 10They passed the first and second guards and came to the iron gate leading to the city. It opened for them by itself. After leaving the prison, they proceeded the length of one street, when abruptly the angel was gone.

[11]At that, Peter came to his senses and
remarked, "Now I'm certain that the Lord
sent his angel and rescued me from Herod
and from everything the Jewish people expected." [12]Realizing this, he made his way
to Mary's house. (Mary was John's mother;
he was also known as Mark.) Many believers had gathered there and were praying.
[13]When Peter knocked at the outer gate, a female servant named Rhoda went to answer.
[14]She was so overcome with joy when she recognized Peter's voice that she didn't open the
gate. Instead, she ran back in and announced
that Peter was standing at the gate.

[15]"You've lost your mind!" they responded. She stuck by her story with such
determination that they began to say, "It
must be his guardian angel." [16]Meanwhile,
Peter remained outside, knocking at the
gate. They finally opened the gate and saw
him there, and they were astounded.

[17]He gestured with his hand to quiet
them down, then recounted how the Lord
led him out of prison. He said, "Tell this to
James and the brothers and sisters." Then
he left for another place.

[18]The next morning the soldiers were
flustered about what had happened to
Peter. [19]Herod called for a thorough search.
When Peter didn't turn up, Herod interrogated the guards and had them executed.
Afterward, Herod left Judea in order to
spend some time in Caesarea.

[20]Herod had been furious with the people of Tyre and Sidon for some time. They
made a pact to approach him together,
since their region depended on the king's
realm for its food supply. They persuaded
Blastus, the king's personal attendant, to
join their cause, then appealed for an end
to hostilities. [21]On the scheduled day Herod
dressed himself in royal attire, seated himself on the throne, and gave a speech to the
people. [22]Those assembled kept shouting,
over and over, "This is a god's voice, not the
voice of a mere human!" [23]Immediately an
angel from the Lord struck Herod down,
because he didn't give the honor to God. He
was eaten by worms and died.

[24]God's word continued to grow and
increase. [25]Barnabas and Saul returned to
Antioch from Jerusalem[d] after completing
their mission, bringing with them John,
who was also known as Mark.

Barnabas and Saul sent to minister

13 The church at Antioch included prophets and teachers: Barnabas, Simeon
(nicknamed Niger), Lucius from Cyrene,
Manaen (a childhood friend of Herod the
ruler), and Saul. [2]As they were worshipping
the Lord and fasting, the Holy Spirit said,
"Appoint Barnabas and Saul to the work I
have called them to undertake." [3]After they
fasted and prayed, they laid their hands on
these two and sent them off.

Serving in Cyprus

[4]After the Holy Spirit sent them on their
way, they went down to Seleucia. From
there they sailed to Cyprus. [5]In Salamis
they proclaimed God's word in the Jewish
synagogues. John was with them as their
assistant. [6]They traveled throughout the island until they arrived at Paphos. There they
found a certain man named Bar-Jesus, a Jew
who was a false prophet and practiced sorcery. [7]He kept company with the governor
of that province, an intelligent man named
Sergius Paulus. The governor sent for Barnabas and Saul since he wanted to hear God's
word. [8]But Elymas the sorcerer[e] (for that's
what people understood his name meant)
opposed them, trying to steer the governor
away from the faith. [9]Empowered by the
Holy Spirit, Saul, also known as Paul, glared
at Bar-Jesus and [10]said, "You are a deceiver
and trickster! You devil! You attack anything
that is right! Will you never stop twisting the
straight ways of the Lord into crooked paths?
[11]Listen! The Lord's power is set against you.
You will be blind for a while, unable even to
see the daylight." At once, Bar-Jesus' eyes
were darkened, and he began to grope about
for someone to lead him around by the hand.
[12]When the governor saw what had taken
place, he came to believe, for he was astonished by the teaching about the Lord.

[d]Critical editions of the Gk New Testament read *returned to Jerusalem.* [e]Or *magician* (Gk *magos*)

Paul and Barnabas in Pisidian Antioch

[13]Paul and his companions sailed from Paphos to Perga in Pamphylia. John deserted them there and returned to Jerusalem. [14]They went on from Perga and arrived at Antioch in Pisidia. On the Sabbath, they entered and found seats in the synagogue there. [15]After the reading of the Law and the Prophets, the synagogue leaders invited them, "Brothers, if one of you has a sermon for the people, please speak."

[16]Standing up, Paul gestured with his hand and said, "Fellow Israelites and Gentile God-worshippers, please listen to me. [17]The God of this people Israel chose our ancestors. God made them a great people while they lived as strangers in the land of Egypt. With his great power, he led them out of that country. [18]For about forty years, God put up with them in the wilderness. [19]God conquered seven nations in the land of Canaan and gave the Israelites their land as an inheritance. [20]This happened over a period of about four hundred fifty years.

"After this, he gave them judges until the time of the prophet Samuel. [21]The Israelites requested a king, so God gave them Saul, Kish's son, from the tribe of Benjamin, and he served as their king for forty years. [22]After God removed him, he raised up David to be their king. God testified concerning him, '*I have found* David, Jesse's son, *a man who shares my desires.*[f] Whatever my will is, he will do.' [23]From this man's descendants, God brought to Israel a savior, Jesus, just as he promised. [24]Before Jesus' appearance, John proclaimed to all the Israelites a baptism to show they were changing their hearts and lives. [25]As John was completing his mission, he said, 'Who do you think I am? I'm not the one you think I am, but he is coming after me. I'm not worthy to loosen his sandals.'

[26]"Brothers, children of Abraham's family, and you Gentile God-worshippers, the message about this salvation has been sent to us. [27]The people in Jerusalem and their leaders didn't recognize Jesus. By condemning him they fulfilled the words of the prophets that are read every Sabbath. [28]Even though they didn't find a single legal basis for the death penalty, they asked Pilate to have him executed. [29]When they finished doing everything that had been written about him, they took him down from the cross[g] and laid him in a tomb. [30]But God raised him from the dead! [31]He appeared over many days to those who had traveled with him from Galilee to Jerusalem. They are now his witnesses to the people.

[32]"We proclaim to you the good news. What God promised to our ancestors, [33]he has fulfilled for us, their children, by raising up Jesus. As it was written in the second psalm, *You are my son; today I have become your father.*[h]

[34]"God raised Jesus from the dead, never again to be subjected to death's decay. Therefore, God said, *I will give to you the holy and firm promises I made to David.*[i] [35]In another place it is said, *You will not let your holy one experience death's decay.*[j] [36]David served God's purpose in his own generation, then he died and was buried with his ancestors. He experienced death's decay, [37]but the one whom God has raised up didn't experience death's decay.

[38]"Therefore, brothers and sisters, know this: Through Jesus we proclaim forgiveness of sins to you. From all those sins from which you couldn't be put in right relationship with God through Moses' Law, [39]through Jesus everyone who believes is put in right relationship with God. [40]Take care that the prophets' words don't apply to you:

[41]*Look, you scoffers,*
marvel and die.
I'm going to do work in your day —
a work you won't believe
even if someone told you."[k]

[42]As Paul and Barnabas were leaving the synagogue, the people urged them to speak about these things again on the next Sabbath. [43]When the people in the synagogue were dismissed, many Jews and devout converts to Judaism accompanied Paul and

[f]Tg 1 Sam 13:14 [g]Or *tree* [h]Ps 2:7 [i]Isa 55:3 [j]Ps 16:10 [k]Hab 1:5

Barnabas, who urged them to remain faithful to the message of God's grace.

[44]On the next Sabbath, almost everyone in the city gathered to hear the Lord's word. [45]When the Jews saw the crowds, they were overcome with jealousy. They argued against what Paul was saying by slandering him. [46]Speaking courageously, Paul and Barnabas said, "We had to speak God's word to you first. Since you reject it and show that you are unworthy to receive eternal life, we will turn to the Gentiles. [47]This is what the Lord commanded us:

I have made you a light for the Gentiles,
so that you could bring salvation
to the end of the earth."[l]

[48]When the Gentiles heard this, they rejoiced and honored the Lord's word. Everyone who was appointed for eternal life believed, [49]and the Lord's word was broadcast throughout the entire region. [50]However, the Jews provoked the prominent women among the Gentile God-worshippers, as well as the city's leaders. They instigated others to harass Paul and Barnabas, and threw them out of their district. [51]Paul and Barnabas shook the dust from their feet and went to Iconium. [52]Because of the abundant presence of the Holy Spirit in their lives, the disciples were overflowing with happiness.

Paul and Barnabas in Iconium

14 The same thing happened in Iconium. Paul and Barnabas entered the Jewish synagogue and spoke as they had before. As a result, a huge number of Jews and Greeks believed. [2]However, the Jews who rejected the faith stirred up the Gentiles, poisoning their minds against the brothers. [3]Nevertheless, Paul and Barnabas stayed there for quite some time, confidently speaking about the Lord. And the Lord confirmed the word about his grace by the signs and wonders he enabled them to perform. [4]The people of the city were divided—some siding with the Jews, others with the Lord's messengers. [5]Then some Gentiles and Jews, including their leaders, hatched a plot to mistreat and stone Paul and Barnabas. [6]When they learned of it, these two messengers fled to the Lycaonian cities of Lystra and Derbe and the surrounding area, [7]where they continued to proclaim the good news.

Healing a crippled man in Lystra

[8]In Lystra there was a certain man who lacked strength in his legs. He had been crippled since birth and had never walked. Sitting there, he [9]heard Paul speaking. Paul stared at him and saw that he believed he could be healed.

[10]Raising his voice, Paul said, "Stand up straight on your feet!" He jumped up and began to walk.

[11]Seeing what Paul had done, the crowd shouted in the Lycaonian language, "The gods have taken human form and come down to visit us!" [12]They referred to Barnabas as Zeus and to Paul as Hermes, since Paul was the main speaker. [13]The priest of Zeus, whose temple was located just outside the city, brought bulls and wreaths to the city gates. Along with the crowds, he wanted to offer sacrifices to them.

[14]When the Lord's messengers Barnabas and Paul found out about this, they tore their clothes in protest and rushed out into the crowd. They shouted, [15]"People, what are you doing? We are humans too, just like you! We are proclaiming the good news to you: turn to the living God and away from such worthless things. He *made the heaven, the earth, the sea, and everything in them.*[m] [16]In the past, he permitted every nation to go its own way. [17]Nevertheless, he hasn't left himself without a witness. He has blessed you by giving you rain from above as well as seasonal harvests, and satisfying you with food and happiness." [18]Even with these words, they barely kept the crowds from sacrificing to them.

[19]Jews from Antioch and Iconium arrived and won the crowds over. They stoned Paul and dragged him out of the city, supposing he was dead. [20]When the disciples surrounded him, he got up and entered the

[l]Isa 49:6 [m]Ps 146:6

city again. The following day he left with
Barnabas for Derbe.

Returning to Antioch

[21]Paul and Barnabas proclaimed the good
news to the people in Derbe and made many
disciples. Then they returned to Lystra, Iconium, and Antioch, where [22]they strengthened the disciples and urged them to remain
firm in the faith. They told them, "If we
are to enter God's kingdom, we must pass
through many troubles." [23]They appointed
elders for each church. With prayer and
fasting, they committed these elders to the
Lord, in whom they had placed their trust.
[24]After Paul and Barnabas traveled
through Pisidia, they came to Pamphylia.
[25]They proclaimed the word in Perga, then
went down to Attalia. [26]From there they
sailed to Antioch, where they had been entrusted by God's grace to the work they had
now completed. [27]On their arrival, they
gathered the church together and reported
everything that God had accomplished
through their activity, and how God had
opened a door of faith for the Gentiles.
[28]They stayed with the disciples a long time.

The Jerusalem Council

15 Some people came down from Judea
teaching the family of believers, "Unless you are circumcised according to the
custom we've received from Moses, you
can't be saved." [2]Paul and Barnabas took
sides against these Judeans and argued
strongly against their position.

The church at Antioch appointed Paul,
Barnabas, and several others from Antioch
to go up to Jerusalem to set this question
before the apostles and the elders. [3]The
church sent this delegation on their way.
They traveled through Phoenicia and Samaria, telling stories about the conversion
of the Gentiles to everyone. Their reports
thrilled the brothers and sisters. [4]When
they arrived in Jerusalem, the church, the
apostles, and the elders all welcomed them.
They gave a full report of what God had accomplished through their activity. [5]Some
believers from among the Pharisees stood
up and claimed, "The Gentiles must be circumcised. They must be required to keep
the Law from Moses."
[6]The apostles and the elders gathered to
consider this matter. [7]After much debate,
Peter stood and addressed them, "Fellow believers, you know that, early on, God chose
me from among you as the one through
whom the Gentiles would hear the word
of the gospel and come to believe. [8]God,
who knows people's deepest thoughts and
desires, confirmed this by giving them the
Holy Spirit, just as he did to us. [9]He made
no distinction between us and them, but
purified their deepest thoughts and desires
through faith. [10]Why then are you now
challenging God by placing a burden on the
shoulders of these disciples that neither we
nor our ancestors could bear? [11]On the contrary, we believe that we and they are saved
in the same way, by the grace of the Lord
Jesus."
[12]The entire assembly fell quiet as they
listened to Barnabas and Paul describe all
the signs and wonders God did among the
Gentiles through their activity. [13]When
Barnabas and Paul also fell silent, James
responded, "Fellow believers, listen to me.
[14]Simon reported how, in his kindness, God
came to the Gentiles in the first place, to
raise up from them a people of God. [15]The
prophets' words agree with this; as it is
written,
[16]*After this I will return,*
and I will rebuild David's fallen tent;
I will rebuild what has been torn down.
I will restore it
[17]*so that the rest of humanity*
will seek the Lord,
even all the Gentiles who belong to me.
The Lord says this,
the one who does these things[n]
[18]known from earliest times.
[19]"Therefore, I conclude that we shouldn't
create problems for Gentiles who turn to
God. [20]Instead, we should write a letter,
telling them to avoid the pollution associated with idols, sexual immorality, eating

[n]Amos 9:11-12

meat from strangled animals, and consuming blood. 21After all, Moses has been proclaimed in every city for a long time, and is read aloud every Sabbath in every synagogue."

Letter to the Gentile believers

22The apostles and the elders, along with the entire church, agreed to send some delegates chosen from among themselves to Antioch, together with Paul and Barnabas. They selected Judas Barsabbas and Silas, who were leaders among the brothers and sisters. 23They were to carry this letter:

> The apostles and the elders, to the Gentile brothers and sisters in Antioch, Syria, and Cilicia. Greetings! 24We've heard that some of our number have disturbed you with unsettling words we didn't authorize. 25We reached a united decision to select some delegates and send them to you along with our dear friends Barnabas and Paul. 26These people have devoted their lives to the name of our Lord Jesus Christ. 27Therefore, we are sending Judas and Silas. They will confirm what we have written. 28The Holy Spirit has led us to the decision that no burden should be placed on you other than these essentials: 29refuse food offered to idols, blood, the meat from strangled animals, and sexual immorality. You will do well to avoid such things. Farewell.

30When Barnabas, Paul, and the delegates were sent on their way, they went down to Antioch. They gathered the believers and delivered the letter. 31The people read it, delighted with its encouraging message. 32Judas and Silas were prophets, and they said many things that encouraged and strengthened the brothers and sisters. 33Judas and Silas stayed there awhile, then were sent back with a blessing of peace from the brothers and sisters to those who first sent them.[o] 35Paul and Barnabas stayed in Antioch, where, together with many others, they taught and proclaimed the good news of the Lord's word.

Paul and Barnabas part company

36Some time later, Paul said to Barnabas, "Let's go back and visit all the brothers and sisters in every city where we preached the Lord's word. Let's see how they are doing." 37Barnabas wanted to take John Mark with them. 38Paul insisted that they shouldn't take him along, since he had deserted them in Pamphylia and hadn't continued with them in their work. 39Their argument became so intense that they went their separate ways. Barnabas took Mark and sailed to Cyprus. 40Paul chose Silas and left, entrusted by the brothers and sisters to the Lord's grace. 41He traveled through Syria and Cilicia, strengthening the churches.

Paul adds Timothy

16 Paul reached Derbe, and then Lystra, where there was a disciple named Timothy. He was the son of a believing Jewish woman and a Greek father. 2The brothers and sisters in Lystra and Iconium spoke well of him. 3Paul wanted to take Timothy with him, so he circumcised him. This was because of the Jews who lived in those areas, for they all knew Timothy's father was Greek. 4As Paul and his companions traveled through the cities, they instructed Gentile believers to keep the regulations put into place by the apostles and elders in Jerusalem. 5So the churches were strengthened in the faith and every day their numbers flourished.

Vision of the Macedonian

6Paul and his companions traveled throughout the regions of Phrygia and Galatia because the Holy Spirit kept them from speaking the word in the province of Asia. 7When they approached the province of Mysia, they tried to enter the province of Bithynia, but the Spirit of Jesus wouldn't let them. 8Passing by Mysia, they went down to Troas instead. 9A vision of a man from Macedonia came to Paul during the night. He stood urging Paul, "Come over to Macedonia and help us!" 10Immediately after he saw the vision, we prepared to leave for the

[o] Critical editions of the Gk New Testament do not include 15:34 *Silas decided to remain there.*

province of Macedonia, concluding that God had called us to proclaim the good news to them.

Lydia's conversion

[11]We sailed from Troas straight for Samothrace and came to Neapolis the following day. [12]From there we went to Philippi, a city of Macedonia's first district and a Roman colony. We stayed in that city several days. [13]On the Sabbath we went outside the city gate to the riverbank, where we thought there might be a place for prayer. We sat down and began to talk with the women who had gathered. [14]One of those women was Lydia, a Gentile God-worshipper from the city of Thyatira, a dealer in purple cloth. As she listened, the Lord enabled her to embrace Paul's message. [15]Once she and her household were baptized, she urged, "Now that you have decided that I am a believer in the Lord, come and stay in my house." And she persuaded us.

Paul and Silas in prison

[16]One day, when we were on the way to the place for prayer, we met a slave woman. She had a spirit that enabled her to predict the future. She made a lot of money for her owners through fortune-telling. [17]She began following Paul and us, shouting, "These people are servants of the Most High God! They are proclaiming a way of salvation to you!" [18]She did this for many days.

This annoyed Paul so much that he finally turned and said to the spirit, "In the name of Jesus Christ, I command you to leave her!" It left her at that very moment.

[19]Her owners realized that their hope for making money was gone. They grabbed Paul and Silas and dragged them before the officials in the city center. [20]When her owners approached the legal authorities, they said, "These people are causing an uproar in our city. They are Jews [21]who promote customs that we Romans can't accept or practice." [22]The crowd joined in the attacks against Paul and Silas, so the authorities ordered that they be stripped of their clothes and beaten with a rod. [23]When Paul and Silas had been severely beaten, the authorities threw them into prison and ordered the jailer to secure them with great care. [24]When he received these instructions, he threw them into the innermost cell and secured their feet in stocks.

[25]Around midnight Paul and Silas were praying and singing hymns to God, and the other prisoners were listening to them. [26]All at once there was such a violent earthquake that it shook the prison's foundations. The doors flew open and everyone's chains came loose. [27]When the jailer awoke and saw the open doors of the prison, he thought the prisoners had escaped, so he drew his sword and was about to kill himself. [28]But Paul shouted loudly, "Don't harm yourself! We're all here!"

[29]The jailer called for some lights, rushed in, and fell trembling before Paul and Silas. [30]He led them outside and asked, "Honorable masters, what must I do to be rescued?"

[31]They replied, "Believe in the Lord Jesus, and you will be saved—you and your entire household." [32]They spoke the Lord's word to him and everyone else in his house. [33]Right then, in the middle of the night, the jailer welcomed them and washed their wounds. He and everyone in his household were immediately baptized. [34]He brought them into his home and gave them a meal. He was overjoyed because he and everyone in his household had come to believe in God.

[35]The next morning the legal authorities sent the police to the jailer with the order "Release those people."

[36]So the jailer reported this to Paul, informing him, "The authorities sent word that you both are to be released. You can leave now. Go in peace."

[37]Paul told the police, "Even though we are Roman citizens, they beat us publicly without first finding us guilty of a crime, and they threw us into prison. And now they want to send us away secretly? No way! They themselves will have to come and escort us out." [38]The police reported this to the legal authorities, who were alarmed to learn that Paul and Silas were Roman citizens. [39]They came and consoled Paul and Silas, escorting them out of prison and begging them to leave the city.

40 Paul and Silas left the prison and made their way to Lydia's house where they encouraged the brothers and sisters. Then they left Philippi.

More troubles for Paul

17 Paul and Silas journeyed through Amphipolis and Apollonia, then came to Thessalonica, where there was a Jewish synagogue. 2 As was Paul's custom, he entered the synagogue and for three Sabbaths interacted with them on the basis of the scriptures. 3 Through his interpretation of the scriptures, he demonstrated that the Christ had to suffer and rise from the dead. He declared, "This Jesus whom I proclaim to you is the Christ." 4 Some were convinced and joined Paul and Silas, including a larger number of Greek God-worshippers and quite a few prominent women.

5 But the Jews became jealous and brought along some thugs who were hanging out in the marketplace. They formed a mob and started a riot in the city. They attacked Jason's house, intending to bring Paul and Silas before the people. 6 When they didn't find them, they dragged Jason and some believers before the city officials. They were shouting, "These people who have been disturbing the peace throughout the empire have also come here. 7 What is more, Jason has welcomed them into his home. Every one of them does what is contrary to Caesar's decrees by naming someone else as king: Jesus." 8 This provoked the crowd and the city officials even more. 9 After Jason and the others posted bail, they released them.

10 As soon as it was dark, the brothers and sisters sent Paul and Silas on to Beroea. When they arrived, they went to the Jewish synagogue. 11 The Beroean Jews were more honorable than those in Thessalonica. This was evident in the great eagerness with which they accepted the word and examined the scriptures each day to see whether Paul and Silas' teaching was true. 12 Many came to believe, including a number of reputable Greek women and many Greek men.

13 The Jews from Thessalonica learned that Paul also proclaimed God's word in Beroea, so they went there too and were upsetting and disturbing the crowds. 14 The brothers and sisters sent Paul away to the seacoast at once, but Silas and Timothy remained at Beroea. 15 Those who escorted Paul led him as far as Athens, then returned with instructions for Silas and Timothy to come to him as quickly as possible.

16 While Paul waited for them in Athens, he was deeply distressed to find that the city was flooded with idols. 17 He began to interact with the Jews and Gentile God-worshippers in the synagogue. He also addressed whoever happened to be in the marketplace each day. 18 Certain Epicurean and Stoic philosophers engaged him in discussion too. Some said, "What an amateur! What's he trying to say?" Others remarked, "He seems to be a proclaimer of foreign gods." (They said this because he was preaching the good news about Jesus and the resurrection.) 19 They took him into custody and brought him to the council on Mars Hill. "What is this new teaching? Can we learn what you are talking about? 20 You've told us some strange things and we want to know what they mean." (21 They said this because all Athenians as well as the foreigners who live in Athens used to spend their time doing nothing but talking about or listening to the newest thing.)

22 Paul stood up in the middle of the council on Mars Hill and said, "People of Athens, I see that you are very religious in every way. 23 As I was walking through town and carefully observing your objects of worship, I even found an altar with this inscription: 'To an unknown God.' What you worship as unknown, I now proclaim to you. 24 God, who made the world and everything in it, is Lord of heaven and earth. He doesn't live in temples made with human hands. 25 Nor is God served by human hands, as though he needed something, since he is the one who gives life, breath, and everything else. 26 From one person God created every human nation to live on the whole earth, having determined their appointed times and the boundaries of their lands. 27 God made the nations so they would seek him, perhaps even reach out to him and find him. In fact, God isn't far away from any of us.

28 In God we live, move, and exist. As some of your own poets said, 'We are his offspring.'

29 "Therefore, as God's offspring, we have no need to imagine that the divine being is like a gold, silver, or stone image made by human skill and thought. 30 God overlooks ignorance of these things in times past, but now directs everyone everywhere to change their hearts and lives. 31 This is because God has set a day when he intends to judge the world justly by a man he has appointed. God has given proof of this to everyone by raising him from the dead."

32 When they heard about the resurrection from the dead, some began to ridicule Paul. However, others said, "We'll hear from you about this again." 33 At that, Paul left the council. 34 Some people joined him and came to believe, including Dionysius, a member of the council on Mars Hill, a woman named Damaris, and several others.

Paul in Corinth

18 After this, Paul left Athens and went to Corinth. 2 There he found a Jew named Aquila, a native of Pontus. He had recently come from Italy with his wife Priscilla because Claudius had ordered all Jews to leave Rome. Paul visited with them. 3 Because they practiced the same trade, he stayed and worked with them. They all worked with leather. 4 Every Sabbath he interacted with people in the synagogue, trying to convince both Jews and Greeks. 5 Once Silas and Timothy arrived from Macedonia, Paul devoted himself fully to the word, testifying to the Jews that Jesus was the Christ. 6 When they opposed and slandered him, he shook the dust from his clothes in protest and said to them, "You are responsible for your own fates! I'm innocent! From now on I'll go to the Gentiles!" 7 He left the synagogue and went next door to the home of Titius Justus, a Gentile God-worshipper. 8 Crispus, the synagogue leader, and his entire household came to believe in the Lord. Many Corinthians believed and were baptized after listening to Paul.

9 One night the Lord said to Paul in a vision, "Don't be afraid. Continue speaking. Don't be silent. 10 I'm with you and no one who attacks you will harm you, for I have many people in this city." 11 So he stayed there for eighteen months, teaching God's word among them.

12 Now when Gallio was the governor of the province of Achaia, the Jews united in their opposition against Paul and brought him before the court. 13 "This man is persuading others to worship God unlawfully," they declared.

14 Just as Paul was about to speak, Gallio said to the Jews, "If there had been some sort of injury or criminal behavior, I would have reason to accept your complaint. 15 However, since these are squabbles about a message, names, and your own Law, deal with them yourselves. I have no desire to sit in judgment over such things." 16 He expelled them from the court, 17 but everyone seized Sosthenes, the synagogue leader, and gave him a beating in the presence of the governor. None of this mattered to Gallio.

18 After Paul stayed in Corinth for some time, he said good-bye to the brothers and sisters. At the Corinthian seaport of Cenchreae he had his head shaved, since he had made a solemn promise. Then, accompanied by Priscilla and Aquila, he sailed away to Syria. 19 After they arrived in Ephesus, he left Priscilla and Aquila and entered the synagogue and interacted with the Jews. 20 They asked him to stay longer, but he declined. 21 As he said farewell to them, though, he added, "God willing, I will return." Then he sailed off from Ephesus. 22 He arrived in Caesarea, went up to Jerusalem and greeted the church, and then went down to Antioch.

23 After some time there he left and traveled from place to place in the region of Galatia and the district of Phrygia, strengthening all the disciples.

Apollos and his ministry

24 Meanwhile, a certain Jew named Apollos arrived in Ephesus. He was a native of Alexandria and was well-educated and effective in his use of the scriptures. 25 He had been instructed in the way of the Lord and spoke as one stirred up by the Spirit. He taught accurately the things about Jesus, even though he was aware only of the bap-

tism John proclaimed and practiced. [26]He began speaking with confidence in the synagogue. When Priscilla and Aquila heard him, they received him into their circle of friends and explained to him God's way more accurately. [27]When he wanted to travel to Achaia, the brothers and sisters encouraged him and wrote to the disciples so they would open their homes to him. Once he arrived, he was of great help to those who had come to believe through grace. [28]He would vigorously defeat Jewish arguments in public debate, using the scriptures to prove that Jesus was the Christ.

Paul in Ephesus

19 While Apollos was in Corinth, Paul took a route through the interior and came to Ephesus, where he found some disciples. [2]He asked them, "Did you receive the Holy Spirit when you came to believe?"

They replied, "We've not even heard that there is a Holy Spirit."

[3]Then he said, "What baptism did you receive, then?"

They answered, "John's baptism."

[4]Paul explained, "John baptized with a baptism by which people showed they were changing their hearts and lives. It was a baptism that told people about the one who was coming after him. This is the one in whom they were to believe. This one is Jesus." [5]After they listened to Paul, they were baptized in the name of the Lord Jesus. [6]When Paul placed his hands on them, the Holy Spirit came on them, and they began speaking in other languages and prophesying. [7]Altogether, there were about twelve people.

[8]Paul went to the synagogue and spoke confidently for the next three months. He interacted with those present and offered convincing arguments concerning the nature of God's kingdom. [9]Some people had closed their minds, though. They refused to believe and publicly slandered the Way. As a result, Paul left them, took the disciples with him, and continued his daily interactions in Tyrannus' lecture hall. [10]This went on for two years, so that everyone living in the province of Asia—both Jews and Greeks—heard the Lord's word.

[11]God was doing unusual miracles through Paul. [12]Even the small towels and aprons that had touched his skin were taken to the sick, and their diseases were cured and the evil spirits left them.

[13]There were some Jews who traveled around throwing out evil spirits. They tried to use the power of the name of the Lord Jesus against some people with evil spirits. They said, "In the name of the Jesus whom Paul preaches, I command you!" [14]The seven sons of Sceva, a Jewish chief priest, were doing this.

[15]The evil spirit replied, "I know Jesus and I'm familiar with Paul, but who are you?" [16]The person who had an evil spirit jumped on them and overpowered them all with such force that they ran out of that house naked and wounded. [17]This became known to the Jews and Greeks living in Ephesus. Everyone was seized with fear and they held the name of the Lord Jesus in the highest regard.

[18]Many of those who had come to believe came, confessing their past practices. [19]This included a number of people who practiced sorcery. They collected their sorcery texts and burned them publicly. The value of those materials was calculated at more than someone might make if they worked for one hundred sixty-five years.[p] [20]In this way the Lord's word grew abundantly and strengthened powerfully.

[21]Once these things had come to an end, Paul, guided by the Spirit, decided to return to Jerusalem, taking a route that would carry him through the provinces of Macedonia and Achaia. He said, "After I have been there, I must visit Rome as well." [22]He sent two of his assistants, Timothy and Erastus, to Macedonia, while he remained awhile in the province of Asia.

[23]At that time a great disturbance erupted about the Way. [24]There was a silversmith named Demetrius. He made silver models of Artemis' temple, and his busi-

[p] Or *fifty thousand silver drachmen* (a drachme is equivalent in value to a denarion, a typical day's wage).

ness generated a lot of profit for the craftspeople. 25He called a meeting with these
craftspeople and others working in related
trades and said, "Friends, you know that
we make an easy living from this business.
26And you can see and hear that this Paul
has convinced and misled a lot of people,
not only in Ephesus but also throughout
most of the province of Asia. He says that
gods made by human hands aren't really
gods. 27This poses a danger not only by dis-
crediting our trade but also by completely
dishonoring the great goddess Artemis. The
whole province of Asia—indeed, the entire civilized world—worships her, but her
splendor will soon be extinguished."
28Once they heard this, they were beside
themselves with anger and began to shout,
"Great is Artemis of the Ephesians!"
29The city was thrown into turmoil. They
rushed as one into the theater. They seized
Gaius and Aristarchus, Paul's traveling companions from the province of Macedonia.
30Paul wanted to appear before the assembly,
but the disciples wouldn't allow him. 31Even
some officials of the province of Asia, who
were Paul's friends, sent word to him, urging him not to risk going into the theater.
32Meanwhile, the assembly was in a state
of confusion. Some shouted one thing, others shouted something else, and most of the
crowd didn't know why they had gathered.
33The Jews sent Alexander to the front, and
some of the crowd directed their words toward him. He gestured that he wanted to offer
a defense before the assembly, 34but when
they realized he was a Jew, they all shouted in
unison, "Great is Artemis of the Ephesians!"
This continued for about two hours.
35The city manager brought order to the
crowd and said, "People of Ephesus, doesn't
everyone know that the city of Ephesus
is guardian of the temple of the great Artemis and of her image, which fell from
heaven? 36Therefore, since these facts are
undeniable, you must calm down. Don't be
reckless. 37The men you brought here have
neither robbed the temple nor slandered
our goddess. 38Therefore, if Demetrius and
the craftspeople with him have a charge
against anyone, the courts are in session
and governors are available. They can press
charges against each other there. 39Addi-
tional disputes can be resolved in a legal
assembly. 40As for us, we are in danger of
being charged with rioting today, since we
can't justify this unruly gathering." 41After
he said this, he dismissed the assembly.

Paul visits Macedonia and Greece

20 When the riot was over, Paul sent
for the disciples, encouraged them,
said good-bye, and left for the province
of Macedonia. 2He traveled through that
region with a message of encouragement.
When he came to Greece, 3he stayed for
three months. Because the Jews hatched
a plot against Paul as he was about to sail
for Syria, he decided instead to return
through Macedonia. 4He was accompanied by Sopater, Pyrrhus' son from Beroea,
Aristarchus and Secundus from Thessalonica, Gaius from Derbe, Timothy, and
Tychicus and Trophimus from the province
of Asia. 5They went on ahead and waited
for us in Troas. 6We sailed from Philippi
after the Festival of Unleavened Bread and
met them five days later in Troas, where we
stayed for a week.

Meeting with believers in Troas

7On the first day of the week, as we gathered together for a meal, Paul was holding a discussion with them. Since he was
leaving the next day, he continued talking
until midnight. 8There were many lamps in
the upstairs room where we had gathered.
9A young man named Eutychus was sitting in the window. He was sinking into a
deep sleep as Paul talked on and on. When
he was sound asleep, he fell from the third
floor and died. 10Paul went down, fell on
him and embraced him, then said, "Don't
be alarmed. He's alive!" 11Then Paul went
back upstairs and ate. He talked for a long
time—right up until daybreak—then he
left. 12They took the young man away alive
and they were greatly comforted.

Farewell to the Ephesian leaders

13We went on to the ship and sailed for
Assos, where we intended to take Paul on

board. Paul had arranged this, since he
intended to make his way there by land.
[14]When he met us at Assos, we took him
aboard and went on to Mitylene. [15]The next
day we sailed from there and arrived opposite Chios. On the day after, we sailed to
Samos, and on the following day we came
to Miletus. [16]Paul had decided to sail past
Ephesus so that he wouldn't need to spend
too much time in the province of Asia. He
was hurrying to reach Jerusalem, if possible, by Pentecost Day.

[17]From Miletus he sent a message to Ephesus calling for the church's elders to meet
him. [18]When they arrived, he said to
them, "You know how I lived among you
the whole time I was with you, beginning
with the first day I arrived in the province
of Asia. [19]I served the Lord with great humility and with tears in the midst of trials
that came upon me because of the Jews'
schemes. [20]You know I held back nothing
that would be helpful so that I could proclaim to you and teach you both publicly
and privately in your homes. [21]You know I
have testified to both Jews and Greeks that
they must change their hearts and lives as
they turn to God and have faith in our Lord
Jesus. [22]Now, compelled by the Spirit, I'm
going to Jerusalem. I don't know what will
happen to me there. [23]What I do know is
that the Holy Spirit testifies to me from
city to city that prisons and troubles await
me. [24]But nothing, not even my life, is more
important than my completing my mission.
This is nothing other than the ministry I received from the Lord Jesus: to testify about
the good news of God's grace.

[25]"I know that none of you will see me
again—you among whom I traveled and
proclaimed the kingdom. [26]Therefore,
today I testify to you that I'm not responsible for anyone's fate. [27]I haven't avoided
proclaiming the entire plan of God to you.
[28]Watch yourselves and the whole flock, in
which the Holy Spirit has placed you as supervisors, to shepherd God's church, which
he obtained with the death of his own Son.[q]
[29]I know that, after my departure, savage
wolves will come in among you and won't
spare the flock. [30]Some of your own people
will distort the word in order to lure followers after them. [31]Stay alert! Remember that
for three years I constantly and tearfully
warned each one of you. I never stopped
warning you! [32]Now I entrust you to God
and the message of his grace, which is able
to build you up and give you an inheritance among all whom God has made holy.
[33]I haven't craved anyone's silver, gold, or
clothing. [34]You yourselves know that I have
provided for my own needs and for those of
my companions with my own hands. [35]In
everything I have shown you that, by working hard, we must help the weak. In this
way we remember the Lord Jesus' words:
'It is more blessed to give than to receive.' "

[36]After he said these things, he knelt
down with all of them to pray. [37]They cried
uncontrollably as everyone embraced and
kissed Paul. [38]They were especially grieved
by his statement that they would never see
him again. Then they accompanied him to
the ship.

Paul travels to Jerusalem

21 After we tore ourselves away from
them, we set sail on a straight course
to Cos, reaching Rhodes the next day, and
then Patara. [2]We found a ship crossing over
to Phoenicia, boarded, and put out to sea.
[3]We spotted Cyprus, but passed by it on our
left. We sailed on to the province of Syria
and landed in Tyre, where the ship was to
unload its cargo. [4]We found the disciples
there and stayed with them for a week.
Compelled by the Spirit, they kept telling
Paul not to go to Jerusalem. [5]When our
time had come to an end, we departed. All
of them, including women and children, accompanied us out of town where we knelt
on the beach and prayed. [6]We said good-bye
to each other, then we boarded the ship and
they returned to their homes.

[7]Continuing our voyage, we sailed from
Tyre and arrived in Ptolemais. We greeted
the brothers and sisters there and spent a
day with them. [8]The next day we left and

[q]Or *with the death of his own*, or *with his own death*

came to Caesarea. We went to the house of
Philip the evangelist, one of the Seven, and
stayed with him. [9]He had four unmarried
daughters who were involved in the work of
prophecy. [10]After staying there for several
days, a prophet named Agabus came down
from Judea. [11]He came to us, took Paul's
belt, tied his own feet and hands, and said,
"This is what the Holy Spirit says: 'In Jerusalem the Jews will bind the man who owns
this belt, and they will hand him over to the
Gentiles.' " [12]When we heard this, we and
the local believers urged Paul not to go up
to Jerusalem.

[13]Paul replied, "Why are you doing this?
Why are you weeping and breaking my
heart? I'm ready not only to be arrested but
even to die in Jerusalem for the sake of the
name of the Lord Jesus."

[14]Since we couldn't talk him out of it, the
only thing we could say was, "The Lord's will
be done."

[15]After this, we got ready and made our
way up to Jerusalem. [16]Some of the disciples from Caesarea accompanied us and
led us to Mnason's home, where we were
guests. He was from Cyprus and had been
a disciple a long time. [17]When we arrived
in Jerusalem, the brothers and sisters welcomed us warmly.

Meeting the Jerusalem church leaders

[18]On the next day Paul and the rest of
us went to see James. All of the elders were
present. [19]After greeting them, he gave
them a detailed report of what God had
done among the Gentiles through his ministry. [20]Those who heard this praised God.
Then they said to him, "Brother, you see
how many thousands of Jews have become
believers, and all of them keep the Law passionately. [21]They have been informed that
you teach all the Jews who live among the
Gentiles to reject Moses, telling them not
to circumcise their children nor to live according to our customs. [22]What about this?
Without a doubt, they will hear that you
have arrived. [23]You must therefore do what
we tell you. Four men among us have made
a solemn promise. [24]Take them with you, go
through the purification ritual with them,
and pay the cost of having their heads
shaved. Everyone will know there is nothing to those reports about you but that you
too live a life in keeping with the Law. [25]As
for the Gentile believers, we wrote a letter about what we decided, that they avoid
food offered to idols, blood, the meat from
strangled animals, and sexual immorality."
[26]The following day Paul took the men with
him and went through the purification
ritual with them. He entered the temple
and publicly announced the completion of
the days of purification, when the offering
would be presented for each one of them.

Paul seized by the people

[27]When the seven days of purification
were almost over, the Jews from the province of Asia saw Paul in the temple. Grabbing him, they threw the whole crowd into
confusion by shouting, [28]"Fellow Israelites!
Help! This is the man who teaches everyone
everywhere against our people, the Law,
and this place. Not only that, he has even
brought Greeks into the temple and defiled
this holy place." ([29]They said this because
they had seen Trophimus the Ephesian in
the city with him earlier, and they assumed
Paul had brought him into the temple.)
[30]The entire city was stirred up. The people
came rushing, seized Paul, and dragged him
out of the temple. Immediately the gates
were closed. [31]While they were trying to
kill him, a report reached the commander
of a company of soldiers that all Jerusalem was in a state of confusion. [32]With-
out a moment's hesitation, he took some
soldiers and officers and ran down to the
mob. When the mob saw the commander
and his soldiers, they stopped beating Paul.
[33]When the commander arrived, he arrested Paul and ordered him to be bound
with two chains. Only then did he begin to
ask who Paul was and what he had done.

[34]Some in the crowd shouted one thing,
others shouted something else. Because of
the commotion, he couldn't learn the truth,
so he ordered that Paul be taken to the military headquarters. [35]When Paul reached
the steps, he had to be carried by the soldiers in order to protect him from the vio-

lence of the crowd. 36 The mob that followed
kept screaming, "Away with him!"
37 As Paul was about to be taken into the
military headquarters, he asked the commander, "May I speak with you?"
He answered, "Do you know Greek?
38 Aren't you the Egyptian who started a
revolt and led four thousand terrorists into
the desert some time ago?"
39 Paul replied, "I'm a Jew from Tarsus in
Cilicia, a citizen of an important city. Please,
let me speak to the people." 40 With the commander's permission, Paul stood on the
steps and gestured to the people. When they
were quiet, he addressed them in Aramaic.

Paul's defense before his accusers

22 "Brothers and fathers, listen now
to my defense." 2 When they heard
him address them in Aramaic, they became
even more quiet. 3 Paul continued, "I'm a
Jew, born in Tarsus in Cilicia but raised in
this city. Under Gamaliel's instruction, I
was trained in the strict interpretation of
our ancestral Law. I am passionately loyal
to God, just like you who are gathered here
today. 4 I harassed those who followed this
Way to their death, arresting and delivering both men and women into prison. 5 The
high priest and the whole Jerusalem Council can testify about me. I received letters
from them, addressed to our associates in
Damascus, then went there to bring those
who were arrested to Jerusalem so they
could be punished.
6 "During that journey, about noon, as I
approached Damascus, suddenly a bright
light from heaven encircled me. 7 I fell to
the ground and heard a voice asking me,
'Saul, Saul, why are you harassing me?' 8 I
answered, 'Who are you, Lord?' 'I am Jesus
the Nazarene, whom you are harassing,'
he replied. 9 My traveling companions saw
the light, but they didn't hear the voice of
the one who spoke to me. 10 I asked, 'What
should I do, Lord?' 'Get up,' the Lord replied, 'and go into Damascus. There you will
be told everything you have been appointed
to do.' 11 I couldn't see because of the brightness of that light, so my companions led me
by the hand into Damascus.
12 "There was a certain man named Ananias. According to the standards of the Law,
he was a pious man who enjoyed the respect of all the Jews living there. 13 He came
and stood beside me. 'Brother Saul, receive
your sight!' he said. Instantly, I regained
my sight and I could see him. 14 He said, 'The
God of our ancestors has selected you to
know his will, to see the righteous one, and
to hear his voice. 15 You will be his witness
to everyone concerning what you have seen
and heard. 16 What are you waiting for? Get
up, be baptized, and wash away your sins as
you call on his name.'
17 "When I returned to Jerusalem and
was praying in the temple, I had a visionary experience. 18 I saw the Lord speaking
to me. 'Hurry!' he said. 'Leave Jerusalem
at once because they won't accept your
testimony about me.' 19 I responded, 'Lord,
these people know I used to go from one
synagogue to the next, beating those who
believe in you and throwing them into
prison. 20 When Stephen your witness was
being killed, I stood there giving my approval, even watching the clothes that
belonged to those who were killing him.'
21 Then the Lord said to me, 'Go! I will send
you far away to the Gentiles.' "
22 The crowd listened to Paul until he said
this. Then they shouted, "Away with this
man! He's not fit to live!" 23 As they were
screaming, throwing off their garments,
and flinging dust into the air, 24 the commander directed that Paul be taken into
the military headquarters. He ordered that
Paul be questioned under the whip so that
he could find out why they were shouting at
him like this.
25 As they were stretching him out and
tying him down with straps, Paul said to
the centurion standing there, "Can you legally whip a Roman citizen who hasn't been
found guilty in court?"
26 When the centurion heard this, he
went to the commander and reported it. He
asked, "What are you about to do? This man
is a Roman citizen!"
27 The commander went to Paul and demanded, "Tell me! Are you a Roman citizen?"
He said, "Yes."

[28]The commander replied, "It cost me a lot of money to buy my citizenship."

Paul said, "I'm a citizen by birth." [29]At once those who were about to examine him stepped away. The commander was alarmed when he realized he had bound a Roman citizen.

Paul appears before the Jewish council

[30]The commander still wanted to know the truth about why Paul was being accused by the Jews. Therefore, the next day he ordered the chief priests and the entire Jerusalem Council to assemble. Then he took Paul out of prison and had him stand before them.

23 Paul stared at the council and said, "Brothers, I have lived my life with an altogether clear conscience right up to this very day." [2]The high priest Ananias ordered those standing beside Paul to strike him in the mouth. [3]Then Paul said to him, "God is about to strike you, you whitewashed wall! You sit and judge me according to the Law, yet disobey the Law by ordering that I be struck."

[4]Those standing near him asked, "You dare to insult God's high priest?"

[5]Paul replied, "Brothers, I wasn't aware that he was the high priest. It is written, *You will not speak evil about a ruler of your people*."[r]

[6]Knowing that some of them were Sadducees and the others Pharisees, Paul exclaimed in the council, "Brothers, I'm a Pharisee and a descendant of Pharisees. I am on trial because of my hope in the resurrection of the dead!"

[7]These words aroused a dispute between the Pharisees and Sadducees, and the assembly was divided. [8]This is because Sadducees say that there's no resurrection, angel, or spirit, but Pharisees affirm them all. [9]Council members were shouting loudly. Some Pharisees who were legal experts stood up and insisted forcefully, "We find nothing wrong with this man! What if a spirit or angel has spoken to him?" [10]The dispute became so heated that the commander feared they might tear Paul to pieces. He ordered soldiers to go down and remove him by force from their midst. Then they took him back to the military headquarters.

[11]The following night the Lord stood near Paul and said, "Be encouraged! Just as you have testified about me in Jerusalem, so too you must testify in Rome."

A murder plot discovered

[12]The next morning some Jewish leaders formulated a plot and solemnly promised that they wouldn't eat or drink until they had killed Paul. [13]More than forty people were involved in the conspiracy. [14]They went to the chief priests and elders and said, "We have solemnly promised to eat nothing until we have killed Paul. [15]You and the council must explain to the commander that you need Paul brought down to you. Pretend that you want to examine his case more closely. We're prepared to kill him before he arrives."

[16]Paul's sister had a son who heard about the ambush and he came to the military headquarters and reported it to Paul. [17]Paul called for one of the centurions and said, "Take this young man to the commander because he has something to report to him."

[18]He took him to the commander and said, "The prisoner Paul asked me to bring this young man to you. He has something to tell you."

[19]The commander took him by the hand and withdrew to a place where they could speak privately. He asked, "What do you have to report to me?"

[20]He replied, "The Jewish leaders have conspired to ask that you bring Paul down to the council tomorrow. They will pretend that they want to investigate his case more closely. [21]Don't fall for it! More than forty of them are waiting to ambush him. They have solemnly promised not to eat or drink until they have killed him. They are ready now, awaiting your consent."

[22]The commander dismissed the young man, ordering him, "Don't tell anyone that you brought this to my attention."

[r]Exod 22:28

[23]The commander called two centurions and said, "Prepare two hundred soldiers, seventy horsemen, and two hundred spearmen to leave for Caesarea at nine o'clock tonight. [24]Have horses ready for Paul to ride, so they may take him safely to Governor Felix." [25]He wrote the following letter:

> [26]Claudius Lysias, to the most honorable Governor Felix: Greetings. [27]This man was seized by the Jews and was almost killed by them. I was nearby with a unit of soldiers, and I rescued him when I discovered that he was a Roman citizen. [28]I wanted to find out why they were accusing him, so I brought him to their council. [29]I discovered that they were accusing him about questions related to their Law. I found no charge deserving of death or imprisonment. [30]When I was informed of a conspiracy against his life, I sent him to you at once and ordered his accusers to bring their case against him before you.

[31]Following their orders, the soldiers took Paul during the night and brought him to Antipatris. [32]The following day they let the horsemen continue on with Paul while they returned to the military headquarters in Jerusalem. [33]The horsemen entered Caesarea, delivered the letter to the governor, and brought Paul before him. [34]After he read the letter, he asked Paul about his home province. When he learned that he was from Cilicia, [35]the governor said, "I will hear your case when your accusers arrive." Then he ordered that Paul be kept in custody in Herod's palace.

Paul's trial before Felix

24 Five days later the high priest Ananias came down with some elders and a lawyer named Tertullus. They pressed charges against Paul before the governor. [2]After the governor summoned Paul, Tertullus began to make his case against him. He declared, "Under your leadership, we have experienced substantial peace, and your administration has brought reforms to our nation. [3]Always and everywhere, most honorable Felix, we acknowledge this with deep gratitude. [4]I don't want to take too much of your time, so I ask that you listen with your usual courtesy to our brief statement of the facts. [5]We have found this man to be a troublemaker who stirs up riots among all the Jews throughout the empire. He's a ringleader of the Nazarene faction [6]and even tried to defile the temple. That's when we arrested him.[s] [8]By examining him yourself, you will be able to verify the allegations we are bringing against him." [9]The Jews reinforced the action against Paul, affirming the truth of these accusations.

[10]The governor nodded at Paul, giving him permission to speak.

He responded, "I know that you have been judge over this nation for many years, so I gladly offer my own defense. [11]You can verify that I went up to worship in Jerusalem no more than twelve days ago. [12]They didn't find me arguing with anyone in the temple or stirring up a crowd, whether in the synagogue or anywhere else in the city. [13]Nor can they prove to you the allegations they are now bringing against me. [14]I do admit this to you, that I am a follower of the Way, which they call a faction. Accordingly, I worship the God of our ancestors and believe everything set out in the Law and written in the Prophets. [15]The hope I have in God I also share with my accusers, that there will be a resurrection of both the righteous and the unrighteous. [16]On account of this, I have committed myself to maintaining a clear conscience before God and with all people. [17]After an absence of several years, I came to Jerusalem to bring gifts for the poor of my nation and to offer sacrifices. [18]When they found me in the temple, I was ritually pure. There was no crowd and no disturbance. [19]But there were some Jews from the province of Asia. They should be here making their accusations, if indeed they have something against me. [20]In their absence, have these people who are here declare what crime they found

[s]Critical editions of the Gk New Testament do not include *We wanted to put him on trial according to our Law, [7] but Lysias the commander arrived and took him from our hands with great force. [8] Then he ordered his accusers to appear before you.*

when I stood before the Jerusalem Council. 21 Perhaps it concerns this one statement that I blurted out when I was with them: 'I am on trial before you today because of the resurrection of the dead.' "

22 Felix, who had an accurate understanding of the Way, adjourned the meeting. He said, "When Lysias the commander arrives from Jerusalem, I will decide this case." 23 He arranged for a centurion to guard Paul. He was to give Paul some freedom, and his friends were not to be hindered in their efforts to provide for him.

Paul in custody

24 After several days, Felix came with his wife Drusilla, who was Jewish, and summoned Paul. He listened to him talk about faith in Christ Jesus. 25 When he spoke about upright behavior, self-control, and the coming judgment, Felix became fearful and said, "Go away for now! When I have time, I'll send for you." 26 At the same time, he was hoping that Paul would offer him some money, so he often sent for him and talked with him.

27 When two years had passed, Felix was succeeded by Porcius Festus. Since Felix wanted to grant a favor to the Jews, he left Paul in prison.

Paul appeals to Caesar

25 Three days after arriving in the province, Festus went up to Jerusalem from Caesarea. 2 The chief priests and Jewish leaders presented their case against Paul. Appealing to him, 3 they asked as a favor from Festus that he summon Paul to Jerusalem. They were planning to ambush and kill him along the way. 4 But Festus responded by keeping Paul in Caesarea, since he was to return there very soon himself. 5 "Some of your leaders can come down with me," he said. "If he's done anything wrong, they can bring charges against him."

6 He stayed with them for no more than eight or ten days, then went down to Caesarea. The following day he took his seat in the court and ordered that Paul be brought in. 7 When he arrived, many Jews who had come down from Jerusalem surrounded him. They brought serious charges against him, but they couldn't prove them. 8 In his own defense, Paul said, "I've done nothing wrong against the Jewish Law, against the temple, or against Caesar."

9 Festus, wanting to put the Jews in his debt, asked Paul, "Are you willing to go up to Jerusalem to stand trial before me concerning these things?"

10 Paul replied, "I'm standing before Caesar's court. I ought to be tried here. I have done nothing wrong to the Jews, as you well know. 11 If I'm guilty and have done something that deserves death, then I won't try to avoid death. But if there is nothing to their accusations against me, no one has the authority to hand me over to them. I appeal to Caesar!"

12 After Festus conferred with his advisors, he responded, "You have appealed to Caesar. To Caesar you will go."

King Agrippa informed about Paul

13 After several days had passed, King Agrippa and Bernice arrived in Caesarea to welcome Festus. 14 Since they were staying there for many days, Festus discussed the case against Paul with the king. He said, "There is a man whom Felix left in prison. 15 When I was in Jerusalem, the Jewish chief priests and elders brought charges against him and requested a guilty verdict in his case. 16 I told them it is contrary to Roman practice to hand someone over before they have faced their accusers and had opportunity to offer a defense against the charges. 17 When they came here, I didn't put them off. The very next day I took my seat in the court and ordered that the man be brought before me. 18 When the accusers took the floor, they didn't charge him with any of the crimes I had expected. 19 Instead, they quibbled with him about their own religion and about some dead man named Jesus, who Paul claimed was alive. 20 Since I had no idea how to investigate these matters, I asked if he would be willing to go to Jerusalem to stand trial there on these issues. 21 However, Paul appealed that he be held in custody pending a decision from His Majesty the emperor,

so I ordered that he be held until I could send him to Caesar."

[22]Agrippa said to Festus, "I want to hear the man myself."

"Tomorrow," Festus replied, "you will hear him."

[23]The next day Agrippa and Bernice came with great fanfare. They entered the auditorium with the military commanders and the city's most prominent men. Festus then ordered that Paul be brought in. [24]Festus said, "King Agrippa and everyone present with us: You see this man! The entire Jewish community, both here and in Jerusalem, has appealed to me concerning him. They've been calling for his immediate death. [25]I've found that he has done nothing deserving death. When he appealed to His Majesty, I decided to send him to Rome. [26]I have nothing definite to write to our lord emperor. Therefore, I've brought him before all of you, and especially before you, King Agrippa, so that after this investigation, I might have something to write. [27]After all, it would be foolish to send a prisoner without specifying the charges against him."

Paul's defense before Agrippa

26 Agrippa said to Paul, "You may speak for yourself."

So Paul gestured with his hand and began his defense. [2]"King Agrippa, I consider myself especially fortunate that I stand before you today as I offer my defense concerning all the accusations the Jews have brought against me. [3]This is because you understand well all the Jewish customs and controversies. Therefore, I ask you to listen to me patiently. [4]Every Jew knows the way of life I have followed since my youth because, from the beginning, I was among my people and in Jerusalem. [5]They have known me for a long time. If they wanted to, they could testify that I followed the way of life set out by the most exacting group of our religion. I am a Pharisee. [6]Today I am standing trial because of the hope in the promise God gave our ancestors. [7]This is the promise our twelve tribes hope to receive as they earnestly worship night and day. The Jews are accusing me, King Agrippa, because of this hope! [8]Why is it inconceivable to you that God raises the dead?

[9]"I really thought that I ought to oppose the name of Jesus the Nazarene in every way possible. [10]And that's exactly what I did in Jerusalem. I locked up many of God's holy people in prison under the authority of the chief priests. When they were condemned to death, I voted against them. [11]In one synagogue after another—indeed, in all the synagogues—I would often torture them, compelling them to slander God. My rage bordered on the hysterical as I pursued them, even to foreign cities.

[12]"On one such journey, I was going to Damascus with the full authority of the chief priests. [13]While on the road at midday, King Agrippa, I saw a light from heaven shining around me and my traveling companions. That light was brighter than the sun. [14]We all fell to the ground, and I heard a voice that said to me in Aramaic, 'Saul, Saul, why are you harassing me? It's hard for you to kick against a spear.'[t] [15]Then I said, 'Who are you, Lord?' The Lord replied, 'I am Jesus, whom you are harassing. [16]Get up! Stand on your feet! I have appeared to you for this purpose: to appoint you as my servant and witness of what you have seen and what I will show you. [17]I will rescue you from your own people and from the Gentiles. I am sending you [18]to open their eyes. Then they can turn from darkness to light and from the power of Satan to God, and receive forgiveness of sins and a place among those who are made holy by faith in me.'

[19]"So, King Agrippa, I wasn't disobedient to that heavenly vision. [20]Instead, I proclaimed first to those in Damascus and Jerusalem, then to the whole region of Judea and to the Gentiles. My message was that they should change their hearts and lives and turn to God, and that they should demonstrate this change in their behavior. [21]Because of this, some Jews seized me in the temple and tried to murder me. [22]God

[t]Or *goads*

has helped me up to this very day. Therefore, I stand here and bear witness to the lowly and the great. I'm saying nothing more than what the Prophets and Moses declared would happen: 23 that the Christ would suffer and that, as the first to rise from the dead, he would proclaim light both to my people and to the Gentiles."

24 At this point in Paul's defense, Festus declared with a loud voice, "You've lost your mind, Paul! Too much learning is driving you mad!"

25 But Paul replied, "I'm not mad, most honorable Festus! I'm speaking what is sound and true. 26 King Agrippa knows about these things, and I have been speaking openly to him. I'm certain that none of these things have escaped his attention. This didn't happen secretly or in some out-of-the-way place. 27 King Agrippa, do you believe the prophets? I know you do."

28 Agrippa said to Paul, "Are you trying to convince me that, in such a short time, you've made me a Christian?"

29 Paul responded, "Whether it is a short or a long time, I pray to God that not only you but also all who are listening to me today will become like me, except for these chains."

30 The king stood up, as did the governor, Bernice, and those sitting with them. 31 As they left, they were saying to each other, "This man is doing nothing that deserves death or imprisonment."

32 Agrippa said to Festus, "This man could have been released if he hadn't appealed to Caesar."

Paul's voyage to Rome

27 When it was determined that we were to sail to Italy, Paul and some other prisoners were placed in the custody of a centurion named Julius of the Imperial Company.[u] 2 We boarded a ship from Adramyttium that was about to sail for ports along the coast of the province of Asia. So we put out to sea. Aristarchus, a Macedonian from Thessalonica, came with us. 3 The next day we landed in Sidon. Julius treated Paul kindly and permitted him to go to some friends so they could take care of him. 4 From there we sailed off. We passed Cyprus, using the island to shelter us from the headwinds. 5 We sailed across the open sea off the coast of Cilicia and Pamphylia, and landed in Myra in Lycia. 6 There the centurion found an Alexandrian ship headed for Italy and put us on board. 7 After many days of slow and difficult sailing, we arrived off the coast of Cnidus. The wind wouldn't allow us to go farther, so we sailed under the shelter of Crete off Salmone. 8 We sailed along the coast only with difficulty until we came to a place called Good Harbors,[v] near the city of Lasea.

9 Much time had been lost, and the voyage was now dangerous since the Day of Reconciliation had already passed. Paul warned them, 10 "Men, I see that our voyage will suffer damage and great loss, not only for the cargo and ship but also for our lives." 11 But the centurion was persuaded more by the ship's pilot and captain than by Paul's advice. 12 Since the harbor was unsuitable for spending the winter, the majority supported a plan to put out to sea from there. They thought they might reach Phoenix in Crete and spend the winter in its harbor, which faced southwest and northwest.

13 When a gentle south wind began to blow, they thought they could carry out their plan. They pulled up anchor and sailed closely along the coast of Crete. 14 Before long, a hurricane-strength wind known as a northeaster swept down from Crete. 15 The ship was caught in the storm and couldn't be turned into the wind. So we gave in to it, and it carried us along. 16 After sailing under the shelter of an island called Cauda, we were able to control the lifeboat only with difficulty. 17 They brought the lifeboat aboard, then began to wrap the ship with cables to hold it together. Fearing they might run aground on the sandbars of the Gulf of Syrtis, they lowered the anchor and let the ship be carried along. 18 We were so battered by the violent storm that the next day the men began throwing cargo overboard. 19 On the third day, they picked up

[u] Or *cohort* (approximately six hundred soldiers) [v] Or *Fair Havens*

the ship's gear and hurled it into the sea. 20 When neither the sun nor the moon appeared for many days and the raging storm continued to pound us, all hope of our being saved from this peril faded.

21 For a long time no one had eaten. Paul stood up among them and said, "Men, you should have complied with my instructions not to sail from Crete. Then we would have avoided this damage and loss. 22 Now I urge you to be encouraged. Not one of your lives will be lost, though we will lose the ship. 23 Last night an angel from the God to whom I belong and whom I worship stood beside me. 24 The angel said, 'Don't be afraid, Paul! You must stand before Caesar! Indeed, God has also graciously given you everyone sailing with you.' 25 Be encouraged, men! I have faith in God that it will be exactly as he told me. 26 However, we must run aground on some island."

27 On the fourteenth night, we were being carried across the Adriatic Sea. Around midnight the sailors began to suspect that land was near. 28 They dropped a weighted line to take soundings and found the water to be about one hundred twenty feet deep. After proceeding a little farther, we took soundings again and found the water to be about ninety feet deep. 29 Afraid that we might run aground somewhere on the rocks, they hurled out four anchors from the stern and began to pray for daylight. 30 The sailors tried to abandon the ship by lowering the lifeboat into the sea, pretending they were going to lower anchors from the bow. 31 Paul said to the centurion and his soldiers, "Unless they stay in the ship, you can't be saved from peril." 32 The soldiers then cut the ropes to the lifeboat and let it drift away.

33 Just before daybreak, Paul urged everyone to eat. He said, "This is the fourteenth day you've lived in suspense, and you've not had even a bite to eat. 34 I urge you to take some food. Your health depends on it. None of you will lose a single hair from his head." 35 After he said these things, he took bread, gave thanks to God in front of them all, then broke it and began to eat. 36 Everyone was encouraged and took some food. (37 In all, there were two hundred seventy-six of us on the ship.) 38 When they had eaten as much as they wanted, they lightened the ship by throwing the grain into the sea.

39 In the morning light they saw a bay with a sandy beach. They didn't know what land it was, but they thought they might possibly be able to run the ship aground. 40 They cut the anchors loose and left them in the sea. At the same time, they untied the ropes that ran back to the rudders. They raised the foresail to catch the wind and made for the beach. 41 But they struck a sandbar and the ship ran aground. The bow was stuck and wouldn't move, and the stern was broken into pieces by the force of the waves. 42 The soldiers decided to kill the prisoners to keep them from swimming to shore and escaping. 43 However, the centurion wanted to save Paul, so he stopped them from carrying out their plan. He ordered those who could swim to jump overboard first and head for land. 44 He ordered the rest to grab hold of planks or debris from the ship. In this way, everyone reached land safely.

On the Island of Malta

28 After reaching land safely, we learned that the island was called Malta. 2 The islanders showed us extraordinary kindness. Because it was rainy and cold, they built a fire and welcomed all of us. 3 Paul gathered a bunch of dry sticks and put them on the fire. As he did, a poisonous snake, driven out by the heat, latched on to his hand. 4 When the islanders saw the snake hanging from his hand, they said to each other, "This man must be a murderer! He was rescued from the sea, but the goddess Justice hasn't let him live!" 5 Paul shook the snake into the fire and suffered no harm. 6 They expected him to swell up with fever or suddenly drop dead. After waiting a long time and seeing nothing unusual happen to him, they changed their minds and began to claim that he was a god.

7 Publius, the island's most prominent person, owned a large estate in that area. He welcomed us warmly into his home as his guests for three days. 8 Publius' father was bedridden, sick with a fever and dys-

entery. Paul went to see him and prayed. He placed his hand on him and healed him. 9Once this happened, the rest of the sick on the island came to him and were healed. 10They honored us in many ways. When we were getting ready to sail again, they supplied us with what we needed.

Paul makes it to Rome

11After three months we put out to sea in a ship that had spent the winter at the island. It was an Alexandrian ship with carvings of the twin gods Castor and Pollux as its figurehead. 12We landed in Syracuse where we stayed three days. 13From there we sailed to Rhegium. After one day a south wind came up, and we arrived on the second day in Puteoli. 14There we found brothers and sisters who urged us to stay with them for a week. In this way we came to Rome. 15When the brothers and sisters there heard about us, they came as far as the Forum of Appius and the Three Taverns to meet us. When Paul saw them, he gave thanks to God and was encouraged. 16When we entered Rome, Paul was permitted to live by himself, with a soldier guarding him.

Paul meets Jewish leaders in Rome

17Three days later, Paul called the Jewish leaders together. When they gathered, he said, "Brothers, although I have done nothing against our people or the customs of our ancestors, I'm a prisoner from Jerusalem. They handed me over to the Romans, 18who intended to release me after they examined me, because they couldn't find any reason for putting me to death. 19When the Jews objected, I was forced to appeal to Caesar. Don't think I appealed to Caesar because I had any reason to bring charges against my nation. 20This is why I asked to see you and speak with you: it's because of the hope of Israel that I am bound with this chain."

21They responded, "We haven't received any letters about you from Judea, nor have any of our brothers come and reported or said anything bad about you. 22But we think it's important to hear what you think, for we know that people everywhere are speaking against this faction."

23On the day scheduled for this purpose, many people came to the place where he was staying. From morning until evening, he explained and testified concerning God's kingdom and tried to convince them about Jesus through appealing to the Law from Moses and the Prophets. 24Some were persuaded by what he said, but others refused to believe. 25They disagreed with each other and were starting to leave when Paul made one more statement: "The Holy Spirit spoke correctly when he said to your ancestors through Isaiah the prophet,

26*Go to this people and say:*
You will hear, to be sure,
but never understand;
and you will certainly see but never
recognize what you are seeing.
27*This people's senses have become calloused,*
and they've become hard of hearing,
and they've shut their eyes
so that they won't see with their eyes
or hear with their ears
or understand with their minds,
and change their hearts and lives
that I may heal them.[w]

28"Therefore, be certain of this: God's salvation has been sent to the Gentiles. They will listen!"[x]

Paul's ministry in Rome

30Paul lived in his own rented quarters for two full years and welcomed everyone who came to see him. 31Unhindered and with complete confidence, he continued to preach God's kingdom and to teach about the Lord Jesus Christ.

[w]Isa 6:9-10 [x]Critical editions of the Gk New Testament do not include 28:29 *After he said this, the Jews left, debating among themselves.*

ROMANS

Greeting

1 From Paul, a slave of Christ Jesus, called to be an apostle and set apart for God's good news. [2–3]God promised this good news about his Son ahead of time through his prophets in the holy scriptures. His Son was descended from David. [4]He was publicly identified as God's Son with power through his resurrection from the dead, which was based on the Spirit of holiness. This Son is Jesus Christ our Lord. [5]Through him we have received God's grace and our appointment to be apostles. This was to bring all Gentiles to faithful obedience for his name's sake. [6]You who are called by Jesus Christ are also included among these Gentiles.

[7]To those in Rome who are dearly loved by God and called to be God's people.

Grace to you and peace from God our Father and the Lord Jesus Christ.

Thanksgiving and Paul's plans to visit

[8]First of all, I thank my God through Jesus Christ for all of you, because the news about your faithfulness is being spread throughout the whole world. [9]I serve God in my spirit by preaching the good news about God's Son, and God is my witness that I continually mention you [10]in all my prayers. I'm always asking that somehow, by God's will, I might succeed in visiting you at last. [11]I really want to see you to pass along some spiritual gift to you so that you can be strengthened. [12]What I mean is that we can mutually encourage each other while I am with you. We can be encouraged by the faithfulness we find in each other, both your faithfulness and mine.

[13]I want you to know, brothers and sisters, that I planned to visit you many times, although I have been prevented from coming until now. I want to harvest some fruit among you, just as I have done among the other Gentiles. [14]I have a responsibility both to Greeks and to those who don't speak Greek, both to the wise and to the foolish.

God's righteousness is revealed

[15]That's why I'm ready to preach the gospel also to you who are in Rome. [16]I'm not ashamed of the gospel: it is God's own power for salvation to all who have faith in God, to the Jew first and also to the Greek. [17]God's righteousness is being revealed in the gospel, from faithfulness[a] for faith,[b] as it is written, *The righteous person will live by faith.*[c]

Gentiles are without excuse

[18]God's wrath is being revealed from heaven against all the ungodly behavior and the injustice of human beings who silence the truth with injustice. [19]This is because what is known about God should be plain to them because God made it plain to them. [20]Ever since the creation of the world, God's invisible qualities—God's eternal power and divine nature—have been clearly seen, because they are understood through the things God has made. So humans are without excuse. [21]Although they knew God, they didn't honor God as God or thank him. Instead, their reasoning became pointless, and their foolish hearts were darkened. [22]While they were claiming to be wise, they made fools of themselves. [23]They exchanged the glory of the immortal God for images that look like mortal humans: birds, animals, and reptiles. [24]So God abandoned them to their hearts' desires, which led to the moral corruption of degrading their own bodies with each other. [25]They traded God's truth for a lie, and they worshipped and served the creation instead of the creator, who is blessed forever. Amen.

[26]That's why God abandoned them to degrading lust. Their females traded natural sexual relations for unnatural sexual relations. [27]Also, in the same way, the males traded natural sexual relations with

[a]Or *faith* [b]Or *faithfulness* [c]Hab 2:4

females, and burned with lust for each other. Males performed shameful actions with males, and they were paid back with the penalty they deserved for their mistake in their own bodies. 28 Since they didn't think it was worthwhile to acknowledge God, God abandoned them to a defective mind to do inappropriate things. 29 So they were filled with all injustice, wicked behavior, greed, and evil behavior. They are full of jealousy, murder, fighting, deception, and malice. They are gossips, 30 they slander people, and they hate God. They are rude and proud, and they brag. They invent ways to be evil, and they are disobedient to their parents. 31 They are without understanding, disloyal, without affection, and without mercy. 32 Though they know God's decision that those who persist in such practices deserve death, they not only keep doing these things but also approve others who practice them.

Jews are without excuse

2 So every single one of you who judge others is without any excuse. You condemn yourself when you judge another person because the one who is judging is doing the same things. 2 We know that God's judgment agrees with the truth, and his judgment is against those who do these kinds of things. 3 If you judge those who do these kinds of things while you do the same things yourself, think about this: Do you believe that you will escape God's judgment? 4 Or do you have contempt for the riches of God's generosity, tolerance, and patience? Don't you realize that God's kindness is supposed to lead you to change your heart and life? 5 You are storing up wrath for yourself because of your stubbornness and your heart that refuses to change. God's just judgment will be revealed on the day of wrath. 6 *God will repay everyone based on their works.*[d] 7 On the one hand, he will give eternal life to those who look for glory, honor, and immortality based on their patient good work. 8 But on the other hand, there will be wrath and anger for those who obey wickedness instead of the truth because they are acting out of selfishness and disobedience. 9 There will be trouble and distress for every human being who does evil, for the Jew first and also for the Greek. 10 But there will be glory, honor, and peace for everyone who does what is good, for the Jew first and also for the Greek. 11 God does not have favorites.

12 Those who have sinned outside the Law will also die outside the Law, and those who have sinned under the Law will be judged by the Law. 13 It isn't the ones who hear the Law who are righteous in God's eyes. It is the ones who do what the Law says who will be treated as righteous. 14 Gentiles don't have the Law. But when they instinctively do what the Law requires they are a Law in themselves, though they don't have the Law. 15 They show the proof of the Law written on their hearts, and their consciences affirm it. Their conflicting thoughts will accuse them, or even make a defense for them, 16 on the day when, according to my gospel, God will judge the hidden truth about human beings through Christ Jesus.

Jews will be judged as well

17 But,
if you call yourself a Jew;
if you rely on the Law;
if you brag about your relationship to God;
18 if you know the will of God;
if you are taught by the Law
so that you can figure out
the things that really matter;
19 if you have persuaded yourself that you
are:
a guide for the blind;
a light to those who are in darkness;
20 an educator of the foolish;
a teacher of infants (since you have
the full content of knowledge and
truth in the Law);
21 then why don't you who are teaching
others teach yourself?
If you preach, "No stealing," do you steal?
22 If you say, "No adultery," do you commit
adultery?
If you hate idols, do you rob temples?

[d] Ps 62:12; Prov 24:12

23 If you brag about the Law, do you
shame God by breaking the Law? 24 As it is
written: *The name of God is discredited by
the Gentiles because of you.*[e]
25 Circumcision is an advantage if you
do what the Law says. But if you are a
person who breaks the Law, your status
of being circumcised has changed into not
being circumcised. 26 So if the person who
isn't circumcised keeps the Law, won't
his status of not being circumcised be
counted as if he were circumcised? 27 The
one who isn't physically circumcised but
keeps the Law will judge you. You became
a lawbreaker after you had the written
Law and circumcision. 28 It isn't the Jew
who maintains outward appearances who
will receive praise from God, and it isn't
people who are outwardly circumcised on
their bodies. 29 Instead, it is the person
who is a Jew inside, who is circumcised
in spirit, not literally. That person's praise
doesn't come from people but from God.

God's faithfulness and justice

3 So what's the advantage of being a Jew?
Or what's the benefit of circumcision?
2 Plenty in every way. First of all, the Jews
were trusted with God's revelations. 3 What
does it matter, then, if some weren't faithful? Their lack of faith won't cancel God's
faithfulness, will it? 4 Absolutely not! God
must be true, even if every human being is
a liar, as it is written:

So that it can show
that you are right in your words;
and you will triumph when you are judged.[f]

5 But if our lack of righteousness confirms God's justice, what will we say? That
God, who brings wrath upon us, isn't just
(I'm speaking rhetorically)? 6 Absolutely
not! If God weren't just, how could he judge
the world? 7 But if God's truth is demonstrated by my lie and it increases his glory,
why am I still judged as a sinner? 8 Why
not say, "Let's do evil things so that good
things will come out of it"? (Some people
who slander us accuse us of saying that, but
these people deserve criticism.)

All are under the power of sin

9 So what are we saying? Are we better
off? Not at all. We have already stated the
charge: both Jews and Greeks are all under
the power of sin. 10 As it is written,

There is no righteous person, not even one.
11 *There is no one who understands.*
There is no one who looks for God.
12 *They all turned away.*
They have become worthless together.
There is no one who shows kindness.
There is not even one.[g]
13 *Their throat is a grave that has been opened.*
They are deceitful with their tongues,
and the poison of vipers is under their lips.[h]
14 *Their mouths are full of cursing*
and bitterness.[i]
15 *Their feet are quick to shed blood;*
16 *destruction and misery are in their ways;*
17 *and they don't know the way of peace.*[j]
18 *There is no fear of God*
in their view of the world.[k]

19 Now we know that whatever the Law
says, it speaks to those who are under the
Law, in order to shut every mouth and
make it so the whole world has to answer
to God. 20 It follows that no human being
will be treated as righteous in his presence
by doing what the Law says, because the
knowledge of sin comes through the Law.

God's righteousness through faithfulness of Christ

21 But now God's righteousness has been
revealed apart from the Law, which is confirmed by the Law and the Prophets. 22 God's
righteousness comes through the faithfulness of Jesus Christ for all who have faith
in him. There's no distinction. 23 All have
sinned and fall short of God's glory, 24 but all
are treated as righteous freely by his grace
because of a ransom that was paid by Christ
Jesus. 25 Through his faithfulness, God displayed Jesus as the place of sacrifice where
mercy is found by means of his blood. He
did this to demonstrate his righteousness
in passing over sins that happened before,
26 during the time of God's patient tolerance.
He also did this to demonstrate that he is

[e] Isa 52:5 LXX [f] Ps 51:4 [g] Ps 14:1-3 [h] Ps 5:9 [i] Ps 10:7 [j] Isa 59:7-8 [k] Ps 36:1

righteous in the present time, and to treat the one who has faith in Jesus as righteous.

27 What happens to our bragging? It's thrown out. With which law? With what we have accomplished under the Law? 28 No, not at all, but through the law of faith. We consider that a person is treated as righteous by faith, apart from what is accomplished under the Law. 29 Or is God the God of Jews only? Isn't God the God of Gentiles also? Yes, God is also the God of Gentiles. 30 Since God is one, then the one who makes the circumcised righteous by faith will also make the one who isn't circumcised righteous through faith. 31 Do we then cancel the Law through this faith? Absolutely not! Instead, we confirm the Law.

Abraham's faith was credited as righteousness

4 So what are we going to say? Are we going to find that Abraham is our ancestor on the basis of genealogy? 2 Because if Abraham was made righteous because of his actions, he would have had a reason to brag, but not in front of God. 3 What does the scripture say? *Abraham had faith in God, and it was credited to him as righteousness.*[l] 4 Workers' salaries aren't credited to them on the basis of an employer's grace but rather on the basis of what they deserve. 5 But faith is credited as righteousness to those who don't work, because they have faith in God who makes the ungodly righteous. 6 In the same way, David also pronounces a blessing on the person to whom God credits righteousness apart from actions:

7 Happy are those whose actions
outside the Law are forgiven,
and whose sins are covered.
8 Happy are those whose sin isn't counted
against them by the Lord.[m]

9 Is this state of happiness only for the circumcised or is it also for those who aren't circumcised? We say, "Faith was credited to Abraham as righteousness." 10 So how was it credited? When he was circumcised, or when he wasn't circumcised? In fact, it was credited while he still wasn't circumcised, not after he was circumcised. 11 He received the sign of circumcision as a seal of the righteousness that comes from the faith he had while he still wasn't circumcised. It happened this way so that Abraham could be the ancestor of all those people who aren't circumcised, who have faith in God, and so are counted as righteous. 12 He could also be the ancestor of those circumcised people, who aren't only circumcised but who also walk in the path of faith, like our ancestor Abraham did while he wasn't circumcised.

Abraham's promise is received through faith

13 The promise to Abraham and to his descendants, that he would inherit the world, didn't come through the Law but through the righteousness that comes from faith. 14 If they inherit because of the Law, then faith has no effect and the promise has been canceled. 15 The Law brings about wrath. But when there isn't any law, there isn't any violation of the law. 16 That's why the inheritance comes through faith, so that it will be on the basis of God's grace. In that way, the promise is secure for all of Abraham's descendants, not just for those who are related by Law but also for those who are related by the faith of Abraham, who is the father of all of us. 17 As it is written: *I have appointed you to be the father of many nations.*[n] So Abraham is our father in the eyes of God in whom he had faith, the God who gives life to the dead and calls things that don't exist into existence. 18 When it was beyond hope, he had faith in the hope that he would become the father of many nations, in keeping with the promise God spoke to him: *That's how many descendants you will have.*[o] 19 Without losing faith, Abraham, who was nearly 100 years old, took into account his own body, which was as good as dead, and Sarah's womb, which was dead. 20 He didn't hesitate with a lack of faith in God's promise, but he grew strong in faith and gave glory to God. 21 He was fully convinced that God was able to do what he promised. 22 Therefore, it was credited to him as righteousness.

[l] Gen 15:6 [m] Ps 32:1-2 [n] Gen 17:5 [o] Gen 15:5

23But the scripture that says *it was cred-
ited to him[p] wasn't written only for Abraham's sake. 24It was written also for our sake,
because it is going to be credited to us too. It
will be credited to those of us who have faith
in the one who raised Jesus our Lord from
the dead. 25He was handed over because of
our mistakes, and he was raised to meet the
requirements of righteousness for us.

Therefore, we have peace with God

5 Therefore, since we have been made
righteous through his faithfulness combined with our faith,[q] we have peace with
God through our Lord Jesus Christ. 2We
have access by faith into this grace in which
we stand through him, and we boast in the
hope of God's glory. 3But not only that! We
even take pride in our problems, because
we know that trouble produces endurance,
4endurance produces character, and character produces hope. 5This hope doesn't put
us to shame, because the love of God has
been poured out in our hearts through the
Holy Spirit, who has been given to us.

6While we were still weak, at the right
moment, Christ died for ungodly people.
7It isn't often that someone will die for a
righteous person, though maybe someone
might dare to die for a good person. 8But
God shows his love for us, because while
we were still sinners Christ died for us. 9So,
now that we have been made righteous by
his blood, we can be even more certain that
we will be saved from God's wrath through
him. 10If we were reconciled to God through
the death of his Son while we were still enemies, now that we have been reconciled,
how much more certain is it that we will
be saved by his life? 11And not only that: we
even take pride in God through our Lord
Jesus Christ, the one through whom we
now have a restored relationship with God.

Grace now rules

12So, in the same way that sin entered the
world through one person, and death came
through sin, so death spread to all human
beings with the result that all sinned.
13Although sin was in the world, since there
was no Law, it wasn't taken into account
until the Law came. 14But death ruled from
Adam until Moses, even over those who
didn't sin in the same way Adam did—Adam
was a type of the one who was coming.

15But the free gift of Christ isn't like Adam's failure. If many people died through
what one person did wrong, God's grace is
multiplied even more for many people with
the gift—of the one person Jesus Christ—
that comes through grace. 16The gift isn't
like the consequences of one person's sin.
The judgment that came from one person's
sin led to punishment, but the free gift that
came out of many failures led to the verdict
of acquittal. 17If death ruled because of one
person's failure, those who receive the multiplied grace and the gift of righteousness
will even more certainly rule in life through
the one person Jesus Christ.

18So now the righteous requirements necessary for life are met for everyone through
the righteous act of one person, just as judgment fell on everyone through the failure
of one person. 19Many people were made
righteous through the obedience of one person, just as many people were made sinners
through the disobedience of one person.
20The Law stepped in to amplify the failure,
but where sin increased, grace multiplied
even more. 21The result is that grace will
rule through God's righteousness, leading to
eternal life through Jesus Christ our Lord,
just as sin ruled in death.

Our new life in Christ

6 So what are we going to say? Should we
continue sinning so grace will multiply?
2Absolutely not! All of us died to sin. How
can we still live in it? 3Or don't you know
that all who were baptized into Christ Jesus
were baptized into his death? 4Therefore,
we were buried together with him through
baptism into his death, so that just as
Christ was raised from the dead through
the glory of the Father, we too can walk in
newness of life. 5If we were united together
in a death like his, we will also be united

[p]Gen 15:6 [q]Or *faith*

together in a resurrection like his. [6]This is
what we know: the person that we used to
be was crucified with him in order to get rid
of the corpse that had been controlled by
sin. That way we wouldn't be slaves to sin
anymore, [7]because a person who has died
has been freed from sin's power. [8]But if we
died with Christ, we have faith that we will
also live with him. [9]We know that Christ
has been raised from the dead and he will
never die again. Death no longer has power
over him. [10]He died to sin once and for all
with his death, but he lives for God with
his life. [11]In the same way, you also should
consider yourselves dead to sin but alive for
God in Christ Jesus.

[12]So then, don't let sin rule your body,
so that you do what it wants. [13]Don't
offer parts of your body to sin, to be used
as weapons to do wrong. Instead, present
yourselves to God as people who have been
brought back to life from the dead, and
offer all the parts of your body to God to
be used as weapons to do right. [14]Sin will
have no power over you, because you aren't
under Law but under grace.

Freedom from sin

[15]So what? Should we sin because we
aren't under Law but under grace? Absolutely not! [16]Don't you know that if you
offer yourselves to someone as obedient
slaves, that you are slaves of the one whom
you obey? That's true whether you serve
as slaves of sin, which leads to death, or as
slaves of the kind of obedience that leads
to righteousness. [17]But thank God that
although you used to be slaves of sin, you
gave wholehearted obedience to the teaching that was handed down to you, which
provides a pattern. [18]Now that you have
been set free from sin, you have become
slaves of righteousness. [19](I'm speaking
with ordinary metaphors because of your
limitations.) Once, you offered the parts of
your body to be used as slaves to impurity
and to lawless behavior that leads to still
more lawless behavior. Now, you should
present the parts of your body as slaves to
righteousness, which makes your lives holy.
[20]When you were slaves of sin, you were
free from the control of righteousness.
[21]What consequences did you get from
doing things that you are now ashamed
of? The outcome of those things is death.
[22]But now that you have been set free from
sin and become slaves to God, you have the
consequence of a holy life, and the outcome
is eternal life. [23]The wages that sin pays are
death, but God's gift is eternal life in Christ
Jesus our Lord.

Freedom from the Law

7 Brothers and sisters, I'm talking to you
as people who know the Law. Don't you
know that the Law has power over someone
only as long as he or she lives? [2]A married
woman is united with her husband under
the Law while he is alive. But if her husband
dies, she is released from the Law concerning her husband. [3]So then, if she lives with
another man while her husband is alive,
she's committing adultery. But if her husband dies, she's free from the Law, so she
won't be committing adultery if she marries someone else. [4]Therefore, my brothers and sisters, you also died with respect
to the Law through the body of Christ, so
that you could be united with someone else.
You are united with the one who was raised
from the dead so that we can bear fruit for
God. [5]When we were self-centered, the sinful passions aroused through the Law were
at work in all the parts of our body, so that
we bore fruit for death. [6]But now we have
been released from the Law. We have died
with respect to the thing that controlled
us, so that we can be slaves in the new life
under the Spirit, not in the old life under
the written Law.

The function of the Law

[7]So what are we going to say? That the
Law is sin? Absolutely not! But I wouldn't
have known sin except through the Law. I
wouldn't have known the desire for what
others have if the Law had not said, *Don't
desire to take what others have.*[r] [8]But sin

[r]Exod 20:17; Deut 5:21

seized the opportunity and used this commandment to produce all kinds of desires
in me. Sin is dead without the Law. 9I used
to be alive without the Law, but when the
commandment came, sin sprang to life,
10and I died. So the commandment that
was intended to give life brought death.
11Sin seized the opportunity through the
commandment, deceived me, and killed
me. 12So the Law itself is holy, and the commandment is holy, righteous, and good.

Living under the Law

13So did something good bring death
to me? Absolutely not! But sin caused my
death through something good so that
sin would be exposed as sin. That way sin
would become even more thoroughly sinful through the commandment. 14We know
that the Law is spiritual, but I'm made of
flesh and blood, and I'm sold as a slave to
sin. 15I don't know what I'm doing, because
I don't do what I want to do. Instead, I do
the thing that I hate. 16But if I'm doing the
thing that I don't want to do, I'm agreeing
that the Law is right. 17But now I'm not the
one doing it anymore. Instead, it's sin that
lives in me. 18I know that good doesn't live
in me—that is, in my body. The desire to
do good is inside of me, but I can't do it.
19I don't do the good that I want to do, but
I do the evil that I don't want to do. 20But
if I do the very thing that I don't want to do,
then I'm not the one doing it anymore. Instead, it is sin that lives in me that is doing it.

21So I find that, as a rule, when I want to
do what is good, evil is right there with me.
22I gladly agree with the Law on the inside,
23but I see a different law at work in my
body. It wages a war against the law of my
mind and takes me prisoner with the law
of sin that is in my body. 24I'm a miserable
human being. Who will deliver me from
this dead corpse? 25Thank God through
Jesus Christ our Lord! So then I'm a slave
to God's Law in my mind, but I'm a slave to
sin's law in my body.

Set free by the Spirit

8 So now there isn't any condemnation
for those who are in Christ Jesus. 2The
law of the Spirit of life in Christ Jesus has
set you free from the law of sin and death.
3God has done what was impossible for the
Law, since it was weak because of selfishness. God condemned sin in the body by
sending his own Son to deal with sin in the
same body as humans, who are controlled
by sin. 4He did this so that the righteous
requirement of the Law might be fulfilled
in us. Now the way we live is based on the
Spirit, not based on selfishness. 5People
whose lives are based on selfishness think
about selfish things, but people whose lives
are based on the Spirit think about things
that are related to the Spirit. 6The attitude
that comes from selfishness leads to death,
but the attitude that comes from the Spirit
leads to life and peace. 7So the attitude that
comes from selfishness is hostile to God.
It doesn't submit to God's Law, because it
can't. 8People who are self-centered aren't
able to please God.

9But you aren't self-centered. Instead
you are in the Spirit, if in fact God's Spirit
lives in you. If anyone doesn't have the
Spirit of Christ, they don't belong to him.
10If Christ is in you, the Spirit is your life
because of God's righteousness, but the
body is dead because of sin. 11If the Spirit
of the one who raised Jesus from the dead
lives in you, the one who raised Christ from
the dead will give life to your human bodies
also, through his Spirit that lives in you.

12So then, brothers and sisters, we have
an obligation, but it isn't an obligation to
ourselves to live our lives on the basis of
selfishness. 13If you live on the basis of selfishness, you are going to die. But if by the
Spirit you put to death the actions of the
body, you will live. 14All who are led by God's
Spirit are God's sons and daughters. 15You
didn't receive a spirit of slavery to lead
you back again into fear, but you received
a Spirit that shows you are adopted as his
children. With this Spirit, we cry, "Abba,
Father." 16The same Spirit agrees with our
spirit, that we are God's children. 17But if
we are children, we are also heirs. We are
God's heirs and fellow heirs with Christ, if
we really suffer with him so that we can also
be glorified with him.

Our suffering and our hope

18 I believe that the present suffering is nothing compared to the coming glory that is going to be revealed to us. 19 The whole creation waits breathless with anticipation for the revelation of God's sons and daughters. 20 Creation was subjected to frustration, not by its own choice—it was the choice of the one who subjected it—but in the hope 21 that the creation itself will be set free from slavery to decay and brought into the glorious freedom of God's children. 22 We know that the whole creation is groaning together and suffering labor pains up until now. 23 And it's not only the creation. We ourselves who have the Spirit as the first crop of the harvest also groan inside as we wait to be adopted and for our bodies to be set free. 24 We were saved in hope. If we see what we hope for, that isn't hope. Who hopes for what they already see? 25 But if we hope for what we don't see, we wait for it with patience.

26 In the same way, the Spirit comes to help our weakness. We don't know what we should pray, but the Spirit himself pleads our case with unexpressed groans. 27 The one who searches hearts knows how the Spirit thinks, because he pleads for the saints, consistent with God's will. 28 We know that God works all things together for good for the ones who love God, for those who are called according to his purpose. 29 We know this because God knew them in advance, and he decided in advance that they would be conformed to the image of his Son. That way his Son would be the first of many brothers and sisters. 30 Those who God decided in advance would be conformed to his Son, he also called. Those whom he called, he also made righteous. Those whom he made righteous, he also glorified.

31 So what are we going to say about these things? If God is for us, who is against us? 32 He didn't spare his own Son but gave him up for us all. Won't he also freely give us all things with him?

33 Who will bring a charge against God's elect people? It is God who acquits them. 34 Who is going to convict them? It is Christ Jesus who died, even more, who was raised, and who also is at God's right side. It is Christ Jesus who also pleads our case for us.

35 Who will separate us from Christ's love? Will we be separated by trouble, or distress, or harassment, or famine, or nakedness, or danger, or sword? 36 As it is written,

We are being put to death all day long for your sake.
We are treated like sheep for slaughter.[s]

37 But in all these things we win a sweeping victory through the one who loved us. 38 I'm convinced that nothing can separate us from God's love in Christ Jesus our Lord: not death or life, not angels or rulers, not present things or future things, not powers 39 or height or depth, or any other thing that is created.

The tragedy of Israel's unbelief

9 I'm speaking the truth in Christ—I'm not lying, as my conscience assures me with the Holy Spirit: 2 I have great sadness and constant pain in my heart. 3 I wish I could be cursed, cut off from Christ if it helped my brothers and sisters, who are my flesh-and-blood relatives. 4 They are Israelites. The adoption as God's children, the glory, the covenants, the giving of the Law, the worship, and the promises belong to them. 5 The Jewish ancestors are theirs, and the Christ descended from those ancestors. He is the one who rules over all things, who is God, and who is blessed forever. Amen.

Israel and God's choice

6 But it's not as though God's word has failed. Not all who are descended from Israel are part of Israel. 7 Not all of Abraham's children are called Abraham's descendants, but instead *your descendants will be named through Isaac.*[t] 8 That means it isn't the natural children who are God's children, but it is the children from the promise who are counted as descendants. 9 The words in the promise were: *A year from now I will return, and Sarah will have a son.*[u]

[s] Ps 44:22 [t] Gen 21:12 [u] Gen 18:10, 14

[10]Not only that, but also Rebecca conceived children with one man, our ancestor Isaac. [11]When they hadn't been born yet and when they hadn't yet done anything good or bad, it was shown that God's purpose would continue because it was based on his choice. [12]It wasn't because of what was done but because of God's call. This was said to her: *The older child will be a slave to the younger one.*[v] [13]As it is written, *I loved Jacob, but I hated Esau.*[w]

[14]So what are we going to say? Isn't this unfair on God's part? Absolutely not! [15]He says to Moses, *I'll have mercy on whomever I choose to have mercy, and I'll show compassion to whomever I choose to show compassion.*[x] [16]So then, it doesn't depend on a person's desire or effort. It depends entirely on God, who shows mercy. [17]Scripture says to Pharaoh, *I have put you in this position for this very thing: so I can show my power in you and so that my name can be spread through the entire earth.*[y] [18]So then, God has mercy on whomever he wants to, but he makes resistant whomever he wants to.

[19]So you are going to say to me, "Then why does he still blame people? Who has ever resisted his will?" [20]You are only a human being. Who do you think you are to talk back to God? *Does the clay say to the potter, "Why did you make me like this?"*[z] [21]Doesn't the potter have the power over the clay to make one pot for special purposes and another for garbage from the same lump of clay? [22]What if God very patiently puts up with pots made for wrath that were designed for destruction, because he wanted to show his wrath and to make his power known? [23]What if he did this to make the wealth of his glory known toward pots made for mercy, which he prepared in advance for glory? [24]We are the ones God has called. We don't come only from the Jews but we also come from the Gentiles.

[25]As it says also in Hosea,

I will call "my people" those
who aren't my people,
and the one who isn't well loved,
I will call "loved one."[a]

[26]And in the place where it was said to them,

"You aren't my people,"
there they will be called
"the living God's children."[b]

[27]But Isaiah cries out for Israel,

Though the number of Israel's children
will be like the sand of the sea,
only a remaining part will be saved,
[28]*because the Lord does what he says*
completely and quickly.[c]

[29]As Isaiah prophesied,

If the Lord of the heavenly forces
had not left descendants for us,
we would have been like Sodom,
and we would have become
like Gomorrah.[d]

Israel and God's righteousness

[30]So what are we going to say? Gentiles who weren't striving for righteousness achieved righteousness, the righteousness that comes from faith. [31]But though Israel was striving for a Law of righteousness, they didn't arrive. [32]Why? It's because they didn't go for it by faith but they went for it as if it could be reached by doing something. They have tripped over a stumbling block. [33]As it is written:

Look! I'm putting a stumbling block in Zion,
which is a rock that offends people.
And the one who has faith in him
will not be put to shame.[e]

10 Brothers and sisters, my heart's desire is for Israel's salvation. That's my prayer to God for them. [2]I can vouch for them: they are enthusiastic about God. However, it isn't informed by knowledge. [3]They don't submit to God's righteousness because they don't understand his righteousness, and they try to establish their own righteousness. [4]Christ is the goal of the Law, which leads to righteousness for all who have faith in God.

[5]Moses writes about the righteousness that comes from the Law: *The person who does these things will live by them.*[f] [6]But the righteousness that comes from faith talks

[v]Gen 25:23 [w]Mal 1:2-3 [x]Exod 33:19 [y]Exod 9:16 [z]Isa 29:16; 45:9 [a]Hos 2:23 [b]Hos 1:10 [c]Isa 10:22-23 LXX [d]Isa 1:9 [e]Isa 28:16; 8:14 [f]Lev 18:5

like this: *Don't say in your heart, "Who will*
go up into heaven?"[g] (that is, to bring Christ
down) 7or *"Who will go down into the re-*
gion below?"[h] (that is, to bring Christ up
from the dead). 8But what does it say? *The*
word is near you, in your mouth and in your
heart[i] (that is, the message of faith that we
preach). 9Because if you confess with your
mouth "Jesus is Lord" and in your heart
you have faith that God raised him from the
dead, you will be saved. 10Trusting with the
heart leads to righteousness, and confessing with the mouth leads to salvation. 11The
scripture says, *All who have faith in him*
won't be put to shame.[j] 12There is no distinction between Jew and Greek, because the
same Lord is Lord of all, who gives richly
to all who call on him. 13*All who call on the*
Lord's name will be saved.[k]

14So how can they call on someone they
don't have faith in? And how can they have
faith in someone they haven't heard of?
And how can they hear without a preacher?
15And how can they preach unless they are
sent? As it is written, *How beautiful are the*
feet of those who announce the good news.[l]

16But everyone hasn't obeyed the good
news. As Isaiah says, *Lord, who has had*
faith in our message?[m] 17So, faith comes
from listening, but it's listening by means
of Christ's message. 18But I ask you, didn't
they hear it? Definitely! *Their voice has gone*
out into the entire earth, and their message
has gone out to the corners of the inhabited
world.[n] 19But I ask you again, didn't Israel
understand? First, Moses says, *I will make*
you jealous of those who aren't a people, of a
people without understanding.[o] 20And Isaiah
even dares to say, *I was found by those who*
didn't look for me; I revealed myself to those
who didn't ask for me.[p] 21But he says about
Israel, *All day long I stretched out my hands*
to a disobedient and contrary people.[q]

Israel and God's faithfulness

11 So I ask you, has God rejected his
people? Absolutely not! I'm an Israelite, a descendant of Abraham, from the
tribe of Benjamin. 2God hasn't rejected his
people, whom he knew in advance. Or don't
you know what the scripture says in the case
of Elijah, when he pleads with God against
Israel? 3Lord, *they have killed your prophets,*
and they have torn down your altars. I'm the
only one left, and they are trying to take my
life.[r] 4But what is God's reply to him? *I have*
kept for myself seven thousand people who
haven't bowed their knees to Baal.[s] 5So also
in the present time there is a remaining
group by the choice of God's grace. 6But if it
is by grace, it isn't by what's done anymore.
If it were, God's grace wouldn't be grace.

7So what? Israel didn't find what it was
looking for. Those who were chosen found
it, but the others were resistant. 8As it is
written, *God gave them a dull spirit, so that*
their eyes would not see and their ears not
hear, right up until the present day.[t] 9And
David says,

Their table should become a pitfall
and a trap,
a stumbling block and payback to them
for what they have done.
10*Their eyes should be darkened*
so they can't see,
and their backs always bent.[u]

11So I'm asking you: They haven't stumbled so that they've fallen permanently,
have they? Absolutely not! But salvation
has come to the Gentiles by their failure, in
order to make Israel jealous. 12But if their
failure brings riches to the world, and their
defeat brings riches to the Gentiles, how
much more will come from the completion of their number! 13I'm speaking to you
Gentiles. Considering that I'm an apostle to
the Gentiles, I publicize my own ministry
14in the hope that somehow I might make
my own people jealous and save some of
them. 15If their rejection has brought about
a close relationship between God and the
world, how can their acceptance mean anything less than life from the dead?

16But if part of a batch of dough is offered
to God as holy, the whole batch of dough
is holy too. If a root is holy, the branches

[g]Deut 9:4; 30:12 [h]Deut 30:13 [i]Deut 30:14 [j]Isa 28:16 [k]Joel 2:32 [l]Isa 52:7; Nah 1:15 [m]Isa 53:1 [n]Ps 19:4 [o]Deut 32:21 [p]Isa 65:1 [q]Isa 65:2 [r]1 Kgs 19:10, 14 [s]1 Kgs 19:18 [t]Deut 29:4; Isa 29:10 [u]Ps 69:22-23

will be holy too. 17 If some of the branches
were broken off, and you were a wild olive
branch, and you were grafted in among the
other branches and shared the root that
produces the rich oil of the olive tree, 18 then
don't brag like you're better than the other
branches. If you do brag, be careful: it's
not you that sustains the root, but it's the
root that sustains you. 19 You will say then,
"Branches were broken off so that I could
be grafted in." 20 Fine. They were broken off
because they weren't faithful, but you stand
only by your faithfulness.[v] So don't think
in a proud way; instead be afraid. 21 If God
didn't spare the natural branches, he won't
spare you either. 22 So look at God's kindness and harshness. It's harshness toward
those who fell, but it's God's kindness for
you, provided you continue in his kindness;
otherwise, you could be cut off too. 23 And
even those who were cut off will be grafted
back in if they don't continue to be unfaithful, because God is able to graft them
in again. 24 If you were naturally part of a
wild olive tree and you were cut off from
it, and then, contrary to nature, you were
grafted into the cultivated olive tree, won't
these natural branches stand an even better chance of being grafted back onto their
own olive tree?

All Israel will be saved

25 I don't want you to be unaware of this
secret,[w] brothers and sisters. That way you
won't think too highly of yourselves. A part
of Israel has become resistant until the full
number of the Gentiles comes in. 26 In this
way, all Israel will be saved, as it is written:

The deliverer will come from Zion.
He will remove ungodly behavior
from Jacob.
27 *This is my covenant with them,*
when I take away their sins.[x]

28 According to the gospel, they are enemies for your sake, but according to God's
choice, they are loved for the sake of their
ancestors. 29 God's gifts and calling can't be
taken back. 30 Once you were disobedient to
God, but now you have mercy because they
were disobedient. 31 In the same way, they
have also been disobedient because of the
mercy that you received, so now they can
receive mercy too. 32 God has locked up all
people in disobedience, in order to have
mercy on all of them.

33 God's riches, wisdom, and knowledge
are so deep! They are as mysterious as his
judgments, and they are as hard to track as
his paths!

34 *Who has known the Lord's mind?*
Or who has been his mentor?[y]
35 *Or who has given him a gift*
and has been paid back by him?[z]
36 All things are from him and through him
and for him.
May the glory be to him forever. Amen.

Living sacrifice and transformed lives

12 So, brothers and sisters, because of
God's mercies, I encourage you to
present your bodies as a living sacrifice that
is holy and pleasing to God. This is your
appropriate priestly service. 2 Don't be conformed to the patterns of this world, but be
transformed by the renewing of your minds
so that you can figure out what God's will
is—what is good and pleasing and mature.

Transformed relationships

3 Because of the grace that God gave me,
I can say to each one of you: don't think
of yourself more highly than you ought to
think. Instead, be reasonable since God has
measured out a portion of faith to each one
of you. 4 We have many parts in one body,
but the parts don't all have the same function. 5 In the same way, though there are
many of us, we are one body in Christ, and
individually we belong to each other. 6 We
have different gifts that are consistent with
God's grace that has been given to us. If
your gift is prophecy, you should prophesy
in proportion to your faith. 7 If your gift is
service, devote yourself to serving. If your
gift is teaching, devote yourself to teaching.
8 If your gift is encouragement, devote yourself to encouraging. The one giving should
do it with no strings attached. The leader

[v] Or *faith* [w] Or *mystery* [x] Isa 59:20-21; 27:9; Jer 31:33-34 [y] Isa 40:13 [z] Job 41:11

should lead with passion. The one showing
mercy should be cheerful.
9 Love should be shown without pretending. Hate evil, and hold on to what is good.
10 Love each other like the members of your
family. Be the best at showing honor to
each other. 11 Don't hesitate to be enthusiastic—be on fire in the Spirit as you serve the
Lord! 12 Be happy in your hope, stand your
ground when you're in trouble, and devote
yourselves to prayer. 13 Contribute to the
needs of God's people, and welcome strangers into your home. 14 Bless people who
harass you—bless and don't curse them.
15 Be happy with those who are happy, and
cry with those who are crying. 16 Consider
everyone as equal, and don't think that
you're better than anyone else. Instead,
associate with people who have no status.
Don't think that you're so smart. 17 Don't
pay back anyone for their evil actions with
evil actions, but show respect for what everyone else believes is good.
18 If possible, to the best of your ability,
live at peace with all people. 19 Don't try to
get revenge for yourselves, my dear friends,
but leave room for God's wrath. It is written, *Revenge belongs to me; I will pay it back,
says the Lord.*[a] 20 Instead, *If your enemy is
hungry, feed him; if he is thirsty, give him
a drink. By doing this, you will pile burning
coals of fire upon his head.*[b] 21 Don't be defeated by evil, but defeat evil with good.
13 Every person should place themselves
under the authority of the government. There isn't any authority unless it
comes from God, and the authorities that
are there have been put in place by God.
2 So anyone who opposes the authority
is standing against what God has established. People who take this kind of stand
will get punished. 3 The authorities don't
frighten people who are doing the right
thing. Rather, they frighten people who
are doing wrong. Would you rather not
be afraid of authority? Do what's right,
and you will receive its approval. 4 It is
God's servant given for your benefit. But
if you do what's wrong, be afraid because
it doesn't have weapons to enforce the law
for nothing. It is God's servant put in place
to carry out his punishment on those who
do what is wrong. 5 That is why it is necessary to place yourself under the government's authority, not only to avoid God's
punishment but also for the sake of your
conscience. 6 You should also pay taxes for
the same reason, because the authorities
are God's assistants, concerned with this
very thing. 7 So pay everyone what you owe
them. Pay the taxes you owe, pay the duties you are charged, give respect to those
you should respect, and honor those you
should honor.
8 Don't be in debt to anyone, except for
the obligation to love each other. Whoever
loves another person has fulfilled the Law.
9 The commandments, *Don't commit adultery, don't murder, don't steal, don't desire
what others have,*[c] and any other commandments, are all summed up in one word: *You
must love your neighbor as yourself.*[d] 10 Love
doesn't do anything wrong to a neighbor;
therefore, love is what fulfills the Law.

The day is near

11 As you do all this, you know what time
it is. The hour has already come for you to
wake up from your sleep. Now our salvation
is nearer than when we first had faith. 12 The
night is almost over, and the day is near. So
let's get rid of the actions that belong to the
darkness and put on the weapons of light.
13 Let's behave appropriately as people who
live in the day, not in partying and getting
drunk, not in sleeping around and obscene
behavior, not in fighting and obsession.
14 Instead, dress yourself with the Lord
Jesus Christ, and don't plan to indulge your
selfish desires.

Welcoming each other like Christ

14 Welcome the person who is weak
in faith—but not in order to argue
about differences of opinion. 2 One person
believes in eating everything, while the
weak person eats only vegetables. 3 Those
who eat must not look down on the ones

[a] Deut 32:35 [b] Prov 25:21-22 [c] Exod 20:13-15, 17; Deut 5:17-19, 21 [d] Lev 19:18

who don't, and the ones who don't eat must not judge the ones who do, because God has accepted them. 4 Who are you to judge someone else's servants? They stand or fall before their own Lord (and they will stand, because the Lord has the power to make them stand). 5 One person considers some days to be more sacred than others, while another person considers all days to be the same. Each person must have their own convictions. 6 Someone who thinks that a day is sacred, thinks that way for the Lord. Those who eat, eat for the Lord, because they thank God. And those who don't eat, don't eat for the Lord, and they thank the Lord too. 7 We don't live for ourselves and we don't die for ourselves. 8 If we live, we live for the Lord, and if we die, we die for the Lord. Therefore, whether we live or die, we belong to God. 9 This is why Christ died and lived: so that he might be Lord of both the dead and the living. 10 But why do you judge your brother or sister? Or why do you look down on your brother or sister? We all will stand in front of the judgment seat of God. 11 Because it is written,

As I live, says the Lord,
every knee will bow to me,
and every tongue will give praise to God.[e]

12 So then, each of us will give an account of ourselves to God.

13 So stop judging each other. Instead, this is what you should decide: never put a stumbling block or obstacle in the way of your brother or sister. 14 I know and I'm convinced in the Lord Jesus that nothing is wrong to eat in itself. But if someone thinks something is wrong to eat, it becomes wrong for that person. 15 If your brother or sister is upset by your food, you are no longer walking in love. Don't let your food destroy someone for whom Christ died. 16 And don't let something you consider to be good be criticized as wrong. 17 God's kingdom isn't about eating food and drinking but about righteousness, peace, and joy in the Holy Spirit. 18 Whoever serves Christ this way pleases God and gets human approval.

19 So let's strive for the things that bring peace and the things that build each other up. 20 Don't destroy what God has done because of food. All food is acceptable, but it's a bad thing if it trips someone else. 21 It's a good thing not to eat meat or drink wine or to do anything that trips your brother or sister. 22 Keep the belief that you have to yourself—it's between you and God. People are blessed who don't convict themselves by the things they approve. 23 But those who have doubts are convicted if they go ahead and eat, because they aren't acting on the basis of faith. Everything that isn't based on faith is sin.

15 We who are powerful need to be patient with the weakness of those who don't have power, and not please ourselves. 2 Each of us should please our neighbors for their good in order to build them up. 3 Christ didn't please himself, but, as it is written, *The insults of those who insulted you fell on me.*[f] 4 Whatever was written in the past was written for our instruction so that we could have hope through endurance and through the encouragement of the scriptures. 5 May the God of endurance and encouragement give you the same attitude toward each other, similar to Christ Jesus' attitude. 6 That way you can glorify the God and Father of our Lord Jesus Christ together with one voice.

7 So welcome each other, in the same way that Christ also welcomed you, for God's glory. 8 I'm saying that Christ became a servant of those who are circumcised for the sake of God's truth, in order to confirm the promises given to the ancestors, 9 and so that the Gentiles could glorify God for his mercy. As it is written,

Because of this I will confess you
among the Gentiles,
and I will sing praises to your name.[g]

10 And again, it says,

Rejoice, Gentiles, with his people.[h]

11 And again,

Praise the Lord, all you Gentiles,
and all the people should sing his praises.[i]

12 And again, Isaiah says,

There will be a root of Jesse,

[e]Isa 45:23 [f]Ps 69:9 [g]Ps 18:49 [h]Deut 32:43 [i]Ps 117:1

who will also rise to rule the Gentiles.
The Gentiles will place their hope in him.[j]
[13]May the God of hope fill you with all
joy and peace in faith so that you overflow
with hope by the power of the Holy Spirit.

Paul's ministry to the Gentiles

[14]My brothers and sisters, I myself am
convinced that you yourselves are full of
goodness, filled with all knowledge, and are
able to teach each other. [15]But I've written to
you in a sort of daring way, partly to remind
you of what you already know. I'm writing
to you in this way because of the grace that
was given to me by God. [16]It helps me to be
a minister of Christ Jesus to the Gentiles.
I'm working as a priest of God's gospel so
that the offering of the Gentiles can be acceptable and made holy by the Holy Spirit.
[17]So in Christ Jesus I brag about things that
have to do with God. [18]I don't dare speak
about anything except what Christ has done
through me to bring about the obedience
of the Gentiles. He did it by what I've said
and what I've done, [19]by the power of signs
and wonders, and by the power of God's
Spirit. So I've completed the circuit of
preaching Christ's gospel from Jerusalem
all the way around to Illyricum. [20]In this
way, I have a goal to preach the gospel
where they haven't heard of Christ yet, so
that I won't be building on someone else's
foundation. [21]Instead, as it's written, *Those
who hadn't been told about him will see, and
those who hadn't heard will understand.*[k]

Travel plans to visit Rome

[22]That's why I've been stopped so many
times from coming to see you. [23]But now,
since I don't have any place to work in these
regions anymore, and since I've wanted to
come to see you for many years, [24]I'll visit
you when I go to Spain. I hope to see you
while I'm passing through. And I hope you
will send me on my way there, after I have
first been reenergized by some time in your
company.
[25]But now I'm going to Jerusalem, to
serve God's people. [26]Macedonia and Achaia
have been happy to make a contribution for
the poor among God's people in Jerusalem.
[27]They were happy to do this, and they are
actually in debt to God's people in Jerusalem. If the Gentiles got a share of the Jewish people's spiritual resources, they ought
to minister to them with material resources.
[28]So then after I have finished this job and
have safely delivered the final amount of
the Gentiles' offering to them, I will leave
for Spain, visiting you on the way. [29]And I
know that when I come to you I will come
with the fullest blessing of Christ.
[30]Brothers and sisters, I urge you,
through our Lord Jesus Christ and through
the love of the Spirit, to join me in my
struggles in your prayers to God for me.
[31]Pray that I will be rescued from the people
in Judea who don't believe. Also, pray that
my service for Jerusalem will be acceptable
to God's people there [32]so that I can come
to you with joy by God's will and be reenergized with your company. [33]May the God of
peace be with you all. Amen.

Introduction to Phoebe

16 I'm introducing our sister Phoebe to
you, who is a servant[l] of the church in
Cenchreae. [2]Welcome her in the Lord in a
way that is worthy of God's people, and give
her whatever she needs from you, because
she herself has been a sponsor of many
people, myself included.

Greetings to Roman Christians

[3]Say hello to Prisca and Aquila, my coworkers in Christ Jesus, [4]who risked their
own necks for my life. I'm not the only
one who thanks God for them, but all
the churches of the Gentiles do the same.
[5]Also say hello to the church that meets
in their house. Say hello to Epaenetus, my
dear friend, who was the first convert[m] in
Asia for Christ. [6]Say hello to Mary, who
has worked very hard for you. [7]Say hello
to Andronicus and Junia, my relatives and
my fellow prisoners. They are prominent
among the apostles, and they were in Christ
before me. [8]Say hello to Ampliatus, my dear

[j]Isa 11:10 [k]Isa 52:15 [l]Or *deacon* [m]Or *is the firstfruits*

friend in the Lord. [9]Say hello to Urbanus, our coworker in Christ, and my dear friend Stachys. [10]Say hello to Apelles, who is tried and true in Christ. Say hello to the members of the household of Aristobulus. [11]Say hello to my relative Herodion. Say hello to the members of the household of Narcissus who are in the Lord. [12]Say hello to Tryphaena and Tryphosa, who are workers for the Lord. Say hello to my dear friend Persis, who has worked hard in the Lord. [13]Say hello to Rufus, who is an outstanding believer, along with his mother and mine. [14]Say hello to Asyncritus, Phlegon, Hermes, Patrobas, Hermas, and the brothers and sisters who are with them. [15]Say hello to Philologus and Julia, Nereus and his sister, and Olympas, and all the saints who are with them. [16]Say hello to each other with a holy kiss. All the churches of Christ say hello to you.

Warning against divisions

[17]Brothers and sisters, I urge you to watch out for people who create divisions and problems against the teaching that you learned. Keep away from them. [18]People like that aren't serving the Lord. They are serving their own feelings. They deceive the hearts of innocent people with smooth talk and flattery. [19]The news of your obedience has reached everybody, so I'm happy for you. But I want you to be wise about what's good, and innocent about what's evil. [20]The God of peace will soon crush Satan[n] under your feet. The grace of our Lord Jesus Christ be with you.

Greetings from Paul's coworkers

[21]Timothy my coworker says hello to you, and Lucius, Jason, and Sosipater, my relatives. [22]I'm Tertius, and I'm writing this letter to you in the Lord—hello! [23]Gaius, who is host to me and to the whole church, says hello to you. Erastus the city treasurer says hello to you, along with our brother Quartus.[o]

Final prayer

[25]May the glory be to God who can strengthen you with my good news and the message that I preach about Jesus Christ. He can strengthen you with the announcement of the secret[p] that was kept quiet for a long time. [26]Now that secret is revealed through what the prophets wrote. It is made known to the Gentiles[q] in order to lead to their faithful obedience based on the command of the eternal God. [27]May the glory be to God, who alone is wise! May the glory be to him through Jesus Christ forever! Amen.

1 CORINTHIANS

Greeting

1 From Paul, called by God's will to be an apostle of Jesus Christ, and from Sosthenes our brother.

[2]To God's church that is in Corinth:

To those who have been made holy to God in Christ Jesus, who are called to be God's people.

Together with all those who call upon the name of our Lord Jesus Christ in every place—he's their Lord and ours!

[3]Grace to you and peace from God our Father and the Lord Jesus Christ.

Thanksgiving for the Corinthians

[4]I thank my God always for you, because of God's grace that was given to you in Christ Jesus. [5]That is, you were made rich through him in everything: in all your communication and every kind of knowledge, [6]in the same way that the testimony about Christ was confirmed with you. [7]The result is that you aren't missing any spiritual gift while you wait for our Lord Jesus Christ to be revealed. [8]He will also confirm your testimony about Christ until the end so that you will be blameless on the day of our Lord Jesus Christ. [9]God is faithful, and you were

[n]Or *the Adversary* [o]Critical editions of the Gk New Testament do not include 16:24 *The grace of our Lord Jesus Christ be with you.* [p]Or *mystery* [q]Or *all the Gentiles*

called by him to partnership with his Son,
Jesus Christ our Lord.

Rival groups in Corinth

[10]Now I encourage you, brothers and sisters, in the name of our Lord Jesus Christ:
Agree with each other and don't be divided
into rival groups. Instead, be restored with
the same mind and the same purpose. [11]My
brothers and sisters, Chloe's people gave me
some information about you, that you're
fighting with each other. [12]What I mean is
this: that each one of you says, "I belong
to Paul," "I belong to Apollos," "I belong
to Cephas," "I belong to Christ." [13]Has Christ
been divided? Was Paul crucified for you, or
were you baptized in Paul's name? [14]Thank
God that I didn't baptize any of you, except
Crispus and Gaius, [15]so that nobody can say
that you were baptized in my name! [16]Oh, I
baptized the house of Stephanas too. Otherwise, I don't know if I baptized anyone
else. [17]Christ didn't send me to baptize but
to preach the good news. And Christ didn't
send me to preach the good news with
clever words so that Christ's cross won't be
emptied of its meaning.

Human wisdom versus the cross

[18]The message of the cross is foolishness
to those who are being destroyed. But it is
the power of God for those of us who are
being saved. [19]It is written in scripture:
I will destroy the wisdom of the wise, and I
will reject the intelligence of the intelligent.[a]
[20]Where are the wise? Where are the legal
experts? Where are today's debaters?
Hasn't God made the wisdom of the world
foolish? [21]In God's wisdom, he determined
that the world wouldn't come to know
him through its wisdom. Instead, God was
pleased to save those who believe through
the foolishness of preaching. [22]Jews ask for
signs, and Greeks look for wisdom, [23]but
we preach Christ crucified, which is a scandal to Jews and foolishness to Gentiles.
[24]But to those who are called—both Jews
and Greeks—Christ is God's power and
God's wisdom. [25]This is because the foolishness of God is wiser than human wisdom,
and the weakness of God is stronger than
human strength.
[26]Look at your situation when you were
called, brothers and sisters! By ordinary
human standards not many were wise, not
many were powerful, not many were from
the upper class. [27]But God chose what the
world considers foolish to shame the wise.
God chose what the world considers weak
to shame the strong. [28]And God chose what
the world considers low-class and low-
life—what is considered to be nothing—to
reduce what is considered to be something
to nothing. [29]So no human being can brag
in God's presence. [30]It is because of God
that you are in Christ Jesus. He became
wisdom from God for us. This means that
he made us righteous and holy, and he delivered us. [31]This is consistent with what
was written: *The one who brags should brag*
in the Lord![b]

2 When I came to you, brothers and sisters, I didn't come preaching God's secrets to you like I was an expert in speech
or wisdom. [2]I had made up my mind not
to think about anything while I was with
you except Jesus Christ, and to preach
him as crucified. [3]I stood in front of you
with weakness, fear, and a lot of shaking.
[4]My message and my preaching weren't
presented with convincing wise words but
with a demonstration of the Spirit and of
power. [5]I did this so that your faith might
not depend on the wisdom of people but on
the power of God.

Definition of wisdom

[6]What we say is wisdom to people who
are mature. It isn't a wisdom that comes
from the present day or from today's leaders
who are being reduced to nothing. [7]We talk
about God's wisdom, which has been hidden
as a secret. God determined this wisdom in
advance, before time began, for our glory.
[8]It is a wisdom that none of the present-
day rulers have understood, because if they
did understand it, they would never have
crucified the Lord of glory! [9]But this is

[a]Isa 29:14 [b]Jer 9:24

precisely what is written: *God has prepared things for those who love him that no eye has seen, or ear has heard, or that haven't crossed the mind of any human being.*[c] 10 God has revealed these things to us through the Spirit. The Spirit searches everything, including the depths of God. 11 Who knows a person's depths except their own spirit that lives in them? In the same way, no one has known the depths of God except God's Spirit. 12 We haven't received the world's spirit but God's Spirit so that we can know the things given to us by God. 13 These are the things we are talking about—not with words taught by human wisdom but with words taught by the Spirit—we are interpreting spiritual things to spiritual people. 14 But people who are unspiritual don't accept the things from God's Spirit. They are foolishness to them and can't be understood, because they can only be comprehended in a spiritual way. 15 Spiritual people comprehend everything, but they themselves aren't understood by anyone. 16 *Who has known the mind of the Lord, who will advise him?*[d] But we have the mind of Christ.

Wisdom applied to divisions in the church

3 Brothers and sisters, I couldn't talk to you like spiritual people but like unspiritual people, like babies in Christ. 2 I gave you milk to drink instead of solid food, because you weren't up to it yet. 3 Now you are still not up to it because you are still unspiritual. When jealousy and fighting exist between you, aren't you unspiritual and living by human standards? 4 When someone says, "I belong to Paul," and someone else says, "I belong to Apollos," aren't you acting like people without the Spirit? 5 After all, what is Apollos? What is Paul? They are servants who helped you to believe. Each one had a role given to them by the Lord: 6 I planted, Apollos watered, but God made it grow. 7 Because of this, neither the one who plants nor the one who waters is anything, but the only one who is anything is God who makes it grow. 8 The one who plants and the one who waters work together, but each one will receive their own reward for their own labor. 9 We are God's coworkers, and you are God's field, God's building.

10 I laid a foundation like a wise master builder according to God's grace that was given to me, but someone else is building on top of it. Each person needs to pay attention to the way they build on it. 11 No one can lay any other foundation besides the one that is already laid, which is Jesus Christ. 12 So, whether someone builds on top of the foundation with gold, silver, precious stones, wood, grass, or hay, 13 each one's work will be clearly shown. The day will make it clear, because it will be revealed with fire—the fire will test the quality of each one's work. 14 If anyone's work survives, they'll get a reward. 15 But if anyone's work goes up in flames, they'll lose it. However, they themselves will be saved as if they had gone through a fire. 16 Don't you know that you are God's temple and God's Spirit lives in you? 17 If someone destroys God's temple, God will destroy that person, because God's temple is holy, which is what you are.

18 Don't fool yourself. If some of you think they are worldly-wise, then they should become foolish so that they can become wise. 19 This world's wisdom is foolishness to God. As it's written, *He catches the wise in their cleverness.*[e] 20 And also, *The Lord knows that the thoughts of the wise are silly.*[f] 21 So then, no one should brag about human beings. Everything belongs to you—22 Paul, Apollos, Cephas, the world, life, death, things in the present, things in the future—everything belongs to you, 23 but you belong to Christ, and Christ belongs to God.

Paul's role as an apostle

4 So a person should think about us this way—as servants of Christ and managers of God's secrets. 2 In this kind of situation, what is expected of a manager is that they prove to be faithful. 3 I couldn't care less if I'm judged by you or by any human court; I don't even judge myself. 4 I'm not

[c] Isa 64:4 [d] Isa 40:13 [e] Job 5:13 [f] Ps 94:11

aware of anything against me, but that doesn't make me innocent, because the Lord is the one who judges me. [5]So don't judge anything before the right time—wait until the Lord comes. He will bring things that are hidden in the dark to light, and he will make people's motivations public. Then there will be recognition for each person from God.

[6]Brothers and sisters, I have applied these things to myself and Apollos for your benefit. I've done this so that you can learn what it means not to go beyond what has been written and so none of you will become arrogant by supporting one of us against the other. [7]Who says that you are better than anyone else? What do you have that you didn't receive? And if you received it, then why are you bragging as if you didn't receive it? [8]You've been filled already! You've become rich already! You rule like kings without us! I wish you did rule so that we could be kings with you! [9]I suppose that God has shown that we apostles are at the end of the line. We are like prisoners sentenced to death, because we have become a spectacle in the world, both to angels and to humans. [10]We are fools for Christ, but you are wise through Christ! We are weak, but you are strong! You are honored, but we are dishonored! [11]Up to this very moment we are hungry, thirsty, wearing rags, abused, and homeless. [12]We work hard with our own hands. When we are insulted, we respond with a blessing; when we are harassed, we put up with it; [13]when our reputation is attacked, we are encouraging. We have become the scum of the earth, the waste that runs off everything, up to the present time.

[14]I'm not writing these things to make you ashamed but to warn you, since you are my loved children. [15]You may have ten thousand mentors in Christ, but you don't have many fathers. I gave birth to you in Christ Jesus through the gospel, [16]so I encourage you to follow my example. [17]This is why I've sent Timothy to you; he's my loved and trusted child in the Lord; he'll remind you about my way of life in Christ Jesus. He'll teach the same way as I teach everywhere in every church. [18]Some have become arrogant as if I'm not coming to see you. [19]But, if the Lord is willing, I'll come to you soon. Then I won't focus on what these arrogant people say, but I'll find out what power they possess. [20]God's kingdom isn't about words but about power. [21]Which do you want? Should I come to you with a big stick to punish you, or with love and a gentle spirit?

Confronting sexual immorality in the church

5 Everyone has heard that there is sexual immorality among you. This is a type of immorality that isn't even heard of among the Gentiles—a man is having sex with his father's wife! [2]And you're proud of yourselves instead of being so upset that the one who did this thing is expelled from your community. [3]Though I'm absent physically, I'm present in the spirit and I've already judged the man who did this as if I were present. [4]When you meet together in the name of our Lord Jesus, I'll be present in spirit with the power of our Lord Jesus. [5]At that time we need to hand this man over to Satan to destroy his human weakness so that his spirit might be saved on the day of the Lord.

[6]Your bragging isn't good! Don't you know that a tiny grain of yeast makes a whole batch of dough rise? [7]Clean out the old yeast so you can be a new batch of dough, given that you're supposed to be unleavened bread. Christ our Passover lamb has been sacrificed, [8]so let's celebrate the feast with the unleavened bread of honesty and truth, not with old yeast or with the yeast of evil and wickedness.

[9]I wrote to you in my earlier letter not to associate with sexually immoral people. [10]But I wasn't talking about the sexually immoral people in the outside world by any means—or the greedy, or the swindlers, or people who worship false gods—otherwise, you would have to leave the world entirely! [11]But now I'm writing to you not to associate with anyone who calls themselves "brother" or "sister" who is sexually immoral, greedy, someone who worships false gods, an abu-

sive person, a drunk, or a swindler. Don't
even eat with anyone like this. 12What do I
care about judging outsiders? Isn't it your
job to judge insiders? 13God will judge outsiders. *Expel the evil one from among you!*[g]

Confronting lawsuits in the church

6 When someone in your assembly has a
legal case against another member, do
they dare to take it to court to be judged
by people who aren't just, instead of by
God's people? 2Or don't you know that
God's people will judge the world? If the
world is to be judged by you, are you incompetent to judge trivial cases? 3Don't
you know that we will judge angels? Why
not ordinary things? 4So then if you have
ordinary lawsuits, do you appoint people as
judges who aren't respected by the church?
5I'm saying this because you should be
ashamed of yourselves! Isn't there one
person among you who is wise enough to
pass judgment between believers? 6But instead, does a brother or sister have a lawsuit against another brother or sister, and
do they do this in front of unbelievers? 7The
fact that you have lawsuits against each
other means that you've already lost your
case. Why not be wronged instead? Why
not be cheated? 8But instead you are doing
wrong and cheating—and you're doing it to
your own brothers and sisters.

9Don't you know that people who are unjust won't inherit God's kingdom? Don't be
deceived. Those who are sexually immoral,
those who worship false gods, adulterers,
both participants in same-sex intercourse,[h]
10thieves, the greedy, drunks, abusive people, and swindlers won't inherit God's kingdom. 11That is what some of you used to be!
But you were washed clean, you were made
holy to God, and you were made right with
God in the name of the Lord Jesus Christ
and in the Spirit of our God.

Avoid sexual immorality

12I have the freedom to do anything,
but not everything is helpful. I have the
freedom to do anything, but I won't be
controlled by anything. 13Food is for the
stomach and the stomach is for food, and
yet God will do away with both. The body
isn't for sexual immorality but for the Lord,
and the Lord is for the body. 14God has
raised the Lord and will raise us through
his power. 15Don't you know that your bodies are parts of Christ? So then, should I
take parts of Christ and make them a part
of someone who is sleeping around?[i] No
way! 16Don't you know that anyone who is
joined to someone who is sleeping around
is one body with that person? The scripture
says, *The two will become one flesh.*[j] 17The
one who is joined to the Lord is one spirit
with him. 18Avoid sexual immorality! Every
sin that a person can do is committed outside the body, except those who engage in
sexual immorality commit sin against their
own bodies. 19Or don't you know that your
body is a temple of the Holy Spirit who is
in you? Don't you know that you have the
Holy Spirit from God, and you don't belong
to yourselves? 20You have been bought and
paid for, so honor God with your body.

Marriage and celibacy

7 Now, about what you wrote: "It's good
for a man not to have sex with a woman."
2Each man should have his own wife, and
each woman should have her own husband
because of sexual immorality. 3The husband
should meet his wife's sexual needs, and the
wife should do the same for her husband.
4The wife doesn't have authority over her
own body, but the husband does. Likewise,
the husband doesn't have authority over his
own body, but the wife does. 5Don't refuse
to meet each other's needs unless you both
agree for a short period of time to devote
yourselves to prayer. Then come back together again so that Satan might not tempt
you because of your lack of self-control.
6I'm saying this to give you permission; it's
not a command. 7I wish all people were like
me, but each has a particular gift from God:
one has this gift, and another has that one.

[g]Deut 17:7; 19:19; 22:21, 24; 24:7 [h]Or *submissive and dominant male sexual partners* [i]Or *a prostitute;* commonly, women who sell their bodies to multiple sex partners but includes those who are sexually immoral [j]Gen 2:24

8 I'm telling those who are single and
widows that it's good for them to stay
single like me. 9 But if they can't control
themselves, they should get married, because it's better to marry than to burn
with passion. 10 I'm passing on the Lord's
command to those who are married: A wife
shouldn't leave her husband, 11 but if she
does leave him, then she should stay single
or be reconciled to her husband. And a man
shouldn't divorce his wife.

12 I'm telling everyone else (the Lord
didn't say this specifically): If a believer has
a wife who doesn't believe, and she agrees to
live with him, then he shouldn't divorce her.
13 If a woman has a husband who doesn't believe and he agrees to live with her, then she
shouldn't divorce him. 14 The husband who
doesn't believe belongs to God because of
his wife, and the wife who doesn't believe
belongs to God because of her husband.
Otherwise, your children would be contaminated by the world, but now they are spiritually set apart. 15 But if a spouse who doesn't
believe chooses to leave, then let them leave.
The brother or sister isn't tied down in these
circumstances. God has called you to peace.
16 How do you know as a wife if you will save
your husband? Or how do you know as a
husband if you will save your wife?

17 Nevertheless, each person should live
the kind of life that the Lord assigned when
he called each one. This is what I teach in
all the churches. 18 If someone was circumcised when called, he shouldn't try to
reverse it. If someone wasn't circumcised
when he was called, he shouldn't be circumcised. 19 Circumcision is nothing; not being
circumcised is nothing. What matters is
keeping God's commandments. 20 Each person should stay in the situation they were
in when they were called. 21 If you were a
slave when you were called, don't let it
bother you. But if you are actually able to
be free, take advantage of the opportunity.
22 Anyone who was a slave when they were
called by the Lord has the status of being
the Lord's free person. In the same way,
anyone who was a free person when they
were called is Christ's slave. 23 You were
bought and paid for. Don't become slaves
of people. 24 So then, brothers and sisters,
each of you should stay with God in the
situation you were in when you were called.

25 I don't have a command from the Lord
about people who have never been married,[k]
but I'll give you my opinion as someone
you can trust because of the Lord's mercy.
26 So I think this advice is good because of
the present crisis: Stay as you are. 27 If you
are married, don't get a divorce. If you are
divorced, don't try to find a spouse. 28 But
if you do marry, you haven't sinned; and
if someone who hasn't been married gets
married, they haven't sinned. But married
people will have a hard time, and I'm trying
to spare you that. 29 This is what I'm saying,
brothers and sisters: The time has drawn
short. From now on, those who have wives
should be like people who don't have them.
30 Those who are sad should be like people
who aren't crying. Those who are happy
should be like people who aren't happy.
Those who buy something should be like
people who don't have possessions. 31 Those
who use the world should be like people
who aren't preoccupied with it, because this
world in its present form is passing away.

32 I want you to be free from concerns. A
man who isn't married is concerned about
the Lord's concerns—how he can please
the Lord. 33 But a married man is concerned
about the world's concerns—how he can
please his wife. 34 His attention is divided.
A woman who isn't married or who is a virgin is concerned about the Lord's concerns
so that she can be dedicated to God in both
body and spirit. But a married woman is
concerned about the world's concerns—
how she can please her husband. 35 I'm saying this for your own advantage. It's not to
restrict you but rather to promote effective
and consistent service to the Lord without
distraction.

36 If someone thinks he is acting inappropriately toward an unmarried woman
whom he knows, and if he has strong feelings and it seems like the right thing to

[k] Or *virgins*

do, he should do what he wants—he's not
sinning—they should get married. 37But
if a man stands firm in his decision, and
doesn't feel the pressure, but has his own
will under control, he does right if he decides in his own heart not to marry the
woman. 38Therefore, the one who marries
the unmarried woman does right, and the
one who doesn't get married will do even
better. 39A woman is obligated to stay in
her marriage as long as her husband is alive.
But if her husband dies, she is free to marry
whomever she wants, only it should be a
believer in the Lord. 40But in my opinion,
she will be happier if she stays the way she
is. And I think that I have God's Spirit too.

Meat sacrificed to false gods

8 Now concerning meat that has been
sacrificed to a false god: We know that
we all have knowledge. Knowledge makes
people arrogant, but love builds people up.
2If anyone thinks they know something,
they don't yet know as much as they should
know. 3But if someone loves God, then they
are known by God.

4So concerning the actual food involved
in these sacrifices to false gods, we know
that a false god isn't anything in this world,
and that there is no God except for the one
God. 5Granted, there are so-called "gods,"
in heaven and on the earth, as there are
many gods and many lords. 6However, for
us believers,

There is one God the Father.
All things come from him, and we
belong to him.
And there is one Lord Jesus Christ.
All things exist through him, and we
live through him.

7But not everybody knows this. Some
are eating this food as though it really is
food sacrificed to a real idol, because they
were used to idol worship until now. Their
conscience is weak because it has been
damaged. 8Food won't bring us close to
God. We're not missing out if we don't eat,
and we don't have any advantage if we do
eat. 9But watch out or else this freedom of
yours might be a problem for those who
are weak. 10Suppose someone sees you (the
person who has knowledge) eating in an
idol's temple. Won't the person with a weak
conscience be encouraged to eat the meat
sacrificed to false gods? 11The weak brother
or sister for whom Christ died is destroyed
by your knowledge. 12You sin against Christ
if you sin against your brothers and sisters
and hurt their weak consciences this way.
13This is why, if food causes the downfall of
my brother or sister, I won't eat meat ever
again, or else I may cause my brother or sister to fall.

Waiving rights for the gospel

9 Am I not free? Am I not an apostle?
Haven't I seen Jesus our Lord? Aren't
you my work in the Lord? 2If I'm not an
apostle to others, at least I am to you! You
are the seal that shows I'm an apostle. 3This
is my defense against those who criticize
me. 4Don't we have the right to eat and drink?
5Don't we have the right to travel with a wife
who believes like the rest of the apostles,
the Lord's brothers, and Cephas? 6Or is it
only I and Barnabas who don't have the
right to not work for our living? 7Who joins
the army and pays their own way? Who
plants a vineyard and doesn't eat its fruit?
Who shepherds a flock and doesn't drink
its milk? 8I'm not saying these things just
based on common sense, am I? Doesn't the
Law itself say these things? 9In Moses' Law
it's written: *You will not muzzle the ox when
it is threshing.*[1] Is God worried about oxen,
10or did he say this entirely for our sake?
It was written for our sake because the
one who plows and the one who threshes
should each do so with the hope of sharing
the produce. 11If we sowed spiritual things
in you, is it so much to ask to harvest some
material things from you?

12If others have these rights over you,
don't we deserve them all the more? However, we haven't made use of this right, but
we put up with everything so we don't put
any obstacle in the way of the gospel of
Christ. 13Don't you know that those who

[1] Deut 25:4

serve in the temple get to eat food from the temple, and those who serve at the altar share part of what is sacrificed on the altar? [14]In the same way, the Lord commanded that those who preach the gospel should get their living from the gospel. [15]But I haven't taken advantage of this. And I'm not writing this so that it will be done for me. It's better for me to die than to lose my right to brag about this! [16]If I preach the gospel, I have no reason to brag, since I'm obligated to do it. I'm in trouble if I don't preach the gospel. [17]If I do this voluntarily, I get rewarded for it. But if I'm forced to do it, then I've been charged with a responsibility. [18]What reward do I get? That when I preach, I offer the good news free of charge. That's why I don't use the rights to which I'm entitled through the gospel.

[19]Although I'm free from all people, I make myself a slave to all people, to recruit more of them. [20]I act like a Jew to the Jews, so I can recruit Jews. I act like I'm under the Law to those under the Law, so I can recruit those who are under the Law (though I myself am not under the Law). [21]I act like I'm outside the Law to those who are outside the Law, so I can recruit those outside the Law (though I'm not outside the law of God but rather under the law of Christ). [22]I act weak to the weak, so I can recruit the weak. I have become all things to all people, so I could save some by all possible means. [23]All the things I do are for the sake of the gospel, so I can be a partner with it.

[24]Don't you know that all the runners in the stadium run, but only one gets the prize? So run to win. [25]Everyone who competes practices self-discipline in everything. The runners do this to get a crown of leaves that shrivel up and die, but we do it to receive a crown that never dies. [26]So now this is how I run—not without a clear goal in sight. I fight like a boxer in the ring, not like someone who is shadowboxing. [27]Rather, I'm landing punches on my own body and subduing it like a slave. I do this to be sure that I myself won't be disqualified after preaching to others.

Warning from the wilderness generation

10 Brothers and sisters, I want you to be sure of the fact that our ancestors were all under the cloud and they all went through the sea. [2]All were baptized into Moses in the cloud and in the sea. [3]All ate the same spiritual food, [4]and all drank the same spiritual drink. They drank from a spiritual rock that followed them, and the rock was Christ. [5]However, God was unhappy with most of them, and they were struck down in the wilderness. [6]These things were examples for us, so we won't crave evil things like they did. [7]Don't worship false gods like some of them did, as it is written, *The people sat down to eat and drink and they got up to play.*[m] [8]Let's not practice sexual immorality, like some of them did, and twenty-three thousand died in one day. [9]Let's not test Christ, like some of them did, and were killed by the snakes. [10]Let's not grumble, like some of them did, and were killed by the destroyer. [11]These things happened to them as an example and were written as a warning for us to whom the end of time has come. [12]So those who think they are standing need to watch out or else they may fall. [13]No temptation has seized you that isn't common for people. But God is faithful. He won't allow you to be tempted beyond your abilities. Instead, with the temptation, God will also supply a way out so that you will be able to endure it.

Avoid false gods to glorify God

[14]So then, my dear friends, run away from the worship of false gods! [15]I'm talking to you like you are sensible people. Think about what I'm saying. [16]Isn't the cup of blessing that we bless a sharing in the blood of Christ? Isn't the loaf of bread that we break a sharing in the body of Christ? [17]Since there is one loaf of bread, we who are many are one body, because we all share the one loaf of bread. [18]Look at the people of Israel. Don't those who eat the sacrifices share from the altar? [19]What am I saying then? That food sacrificed to a false god is

[m]Exod 32:6

anything, or that a false god is anything?
[20]No, but this kind of sacrifice is sacrificed
to demons and not to God. I don't want you
to be sharing in demons. [21]You can't drink
the cup of the Lord and the cup of demons;
you can't participate in the table of the
Lord and the table of demons. [22]Or should
we make the Lord jealous? We aren't stronger than he is, are we?

[23]Everything is permitted, but everything isn't beneficial. Everything is permitted, but everything doesn't build others
up. [24]No one should look out for their own
advantage, but they should look out for
each other. [25]Eat everything that is sold in
the marketplace, without asking questions
about it because of your conscience. [26]*The
earth and all that is in it belong to the Lord.*[n]
[27]If an unbeliever invites you to eat with
them and you want to go, eat whatever is
served, without asking questions because
of your conscience. [28]But if someone says to
you, "This meat was sacrificed in a temple,"
then don't eat it for the sake of the one who
told you and for the sake of conscience.
[29]Now when I say "conscience" I don't mean
yours but the other person's. Why should
my freedom be judged by someone else's
conscience? [30]If I participate with gratitude,
why should I be blamed for food I thank God
for? [31]So, whether you eat or drink or whatever you do, you should do it all for God's
glory. [32]Don't offend either Jews or Greeks,
or God's church. [33]This is the same thing
that I do. I please everyone in everything I
do. I don't look out for my own advantage,
but I look out for many people so that they
11 can be saved. [1]Follow my example, just
like I follow Christ's.

Appropriate dress in worship

[2]I praise you because you remember all
my instructions, and you hold on to the
traditions exactly as I handed them on to
you. [3]Now I want you to know that the head
of every man is Christ, and the head of the
woman is the man, and the head of Christ
is God. [4]Every man who prays or prophesies with his head covered shames his
head. [5]Every woman who prays or prophesies with her head uncovered disgraces
her head. It is the same thing as having her
head shaved. [6]If a woman doesn't cover her
head, then she should have her hair cut off.
If it is disgraceful for a woman to have short
hair or to be shaved, then she should keep
her head covered. [7]A man shouldn't have his
head covered, because he is the image and
glory of God; but the woman is man's glory.
[8]Man didn't have his origin from woman,
but woman from man; [9]and man wasn't
created for the sake of the woman, but
the woman for the sake of the man. [10]Be-
cause of this a woman should have authority over her head, because of the angels.
[11]However, woman isn't independent from
man, and man isn't independent from
woman in the Lord. [12]As woman came from
man so also man comes from woman. But
everything comes from God. [13]Judge for
yourselves: Is it appropriate for a woman
to pray to God with her head uncovered?
[14]Doesn't nature itself teach you that if a
man has long hair, it is a disgrace to him;
[15]but if a woman has long hair, it is her
glory? This is because her long hair is given
to her for a covering. [16]But if someone
wants to argue about this, we don't have
such a custom, nor do God's churches.

The community meal

[17]Now I don't praise you as I give the following instruction because when you meet
together, it does more harm than good.
[18]First of all, when you meet together as
a church, I hear that there are divisions
among you, and I partly believe it. [19]It's
necessary that there are groups among you,
to make it clear who is genuine. [20]So when
you get together in one place, it isn't to eat
the Lord's meal. [21]Each of you goes ahead
and eats a private meal. One person goes
hungry while another is drunk. [22]Don't you
have houses to eat and drink in? Or do you
look down on God's churches and humiliate those who have nothing? What can I say
to you? Will I praise you? No, I don't praise
you in this.

[n]Ps 24:1

23 I received a tradition from the Lord, which I also handed on to you: on the night on which he was betrayed, the Lord Jesus took bread. 24 After giving thanks, he broke it and said, "This is my body, which is for you; do this to remember me." 25 He did the same thing with the cup, after they had eaten, saying, "This cup is the new covenant in my blood. Every time you drink it, do this to remember me." 26 Every time you eat this bread and drink this cup, you broadcast the death of the Lord until he comes.

27 This is why those who eat the bread or drink the cup of the Lord inappropriately will be guilty of the Lord's body and blood. 28 Each individual should test himself or herself, and eat from the bread and drink from the cup in that way. 29 Those who eat and drink without correctly understanding the body are eating and drinking their own judgment. 30 Because of this, many of you are weak and sick, and quite a few have died. 31 But if we had judged ourselves, we wouldn't be judged. 32 However, we are disciplined by the Lord when we are judged so that we won't be judged and condemned along with the whole world. 33 For these reasons, my brothers and sisters, when you get together to eat, wait for each other. 34 If some of you are hungry, they should eat at home so that getting together doesn't lead to judgment. I will give directions about the other things when I come.

Spiritual gifts

12 Brothers and sisters, I don't want you to be ignorant about spiritual gifts. 2 You know that when you were Gentiles you were often misled by false gods that can't even speak. 3 So I want to make it clear to you that no one says, "Jesus is cursed!" when speaking by God's Spirit, and no one can say, "Jesus is Lord," except by the Holy Spirit. 4 There are different spiritual gifts but the same Spirit; 5 and there are different ministries and the same Lord; 6 and there are different activities but the same God who produces all of them in everyone. 7 A demonstration of the Spirit is given to each person for the common good. 8 A word of wisdom is given by the Spirit to one person, a word of knowledge to another according to the same Spirit, 9 faith to still another by the same Spirit, gifts of healing to another in the one Spirit, 10 performance of miracles to another, prophecy to another, the ability to tell spirits apart to another, different kinds of tongues° to another, and the interpretation of the tongues to another. 11 All these things are produced by the one and same Spirit who gives what he wants to each person.

12 Christ is just like the human body—a body is a unit and has many parts; and all the parts of the body are one body, even though there are many. 13 We were all baptized by one Spirit into one body, whether Jew or Greek, or slave or free, and we all were given one Spirit to drink. 14 Certainly the body isn't one part but many. 15 If the foot says, "I'm not part of the body because I'm not a hand," does that mean it's not part of the body? 16 If the ear says, "I'm not part of the body because I'm not an eye," does that mean it's not part of the body? 17 If the whole body were an eye, what would happen to the hearing? And if the whole body were an ear, what would happen to the sense of smell? 18 But as it is, God has placed each one of the parts in the body just like he wanted. 19 If all were one and the same body part, what would happen to the body? 20 But as it is, there are many parts but one body. 21 So the eye can't say to the hand, "I don't need you," or in turn, the head can't say to the feet, "I don't need you." 22 Instead, the parts of the body that people think are the weakest are the most necessary. 23 The parts of the body that we think are less honorable are the ones we honor the most. The private parts of our body that aren't presentable are the ones that are given the most dignity. 24 The parts of our body that are presentable don't need this. But God has put the body together, giving greater honor to the part with less honor 25 so that there won't be division in the body and so the parts might have mutual concern for each other. 26 If one part

°Or *ecstatic speech* or *languages* could be used for *tongues* or *tongue* throughout chaps 12–14.

suffers, all the parts suffer with it; if one part gets the glory, all the parts celebrate with it. 27 You are the body of Christ and parts of each other. 28 In the church, God has appointed first apostles, second prophets, third teachers, then miracles, then gifts of healing, the ability to help others, leadership skills, different kinds of tongues. 29 All aren't apostles, are they? All aren't prophets, are they? All aren't teachers, are they? All don't perform miracles, do they? 30 All don't have gifts of healing, do they? All don't speak in different tongues, do they? All don't interpret, do they? 31 Use your ambition to try to get the greater gifts. And I'm going to show you an even better way.

Love: the universal spiritual gift

13 If I speak in tongues of human beings and of angels but I don't have love, I'm a clanging gong or a clashing cymbal. 2 If I have the gift of prophecy and I know all the mysteries and everything else, and if I have such complete faith that I can move mountains but I don't have love, I'm nothing. 3 If I give away everything that I have and hand over my own body to feel good about what I've done but I don't have love, I receive no benefit whatsoever.

4 Love is patient, love is kind, it isn't jealous, it doesn't brag, it isn't arrogant, 5 it isn't rude, it doesn't seek its own advantage, it isn't irritable, it doesn't keep a record of complaints, 6 it isn't happy with injustice, but it is happy with the truth. 7 Love puts up with all things, trusts in all things, hopes for all things, endures all things.

8 Love never fails. As for prophecies, they will be brought to an end. As for tongues, they will stop. As for knowledge, it will be brought to an end. 9 We know in part and we prophesy in part; 10 but when the perfect comes, what is partial will be brought to an end. 11 When I was a child, I used to speak like a child, reason like a child, think like a child. But now that I have become a man, I've put an end to childish things. 12 Now we see a reflection in a mirror; then we will see face-to-face. Now I know partially, but then I will know completely in the same way that I have been completely known. 13 Now faith, hope, and love remain—these three things—and the greatest of these is love.

Spiritual gifts and church order

14 Pursue love, and use your ambition to try to get spiritual gifts but especially so that you might prophesy. 2 This is because those who speak in a tongue don't speak to people but to God; no one understands it—they speak mysteries by the Spirit. 3 Those who prophesy speak to people, building them up, and giving them encouragement and comfort. 4 People who speak in a tongue build up themselves; those who prophesy build up the church. 5 I wish that all of you spoke in tongues, but I'd rather you could prophesy. Those who prophesy are more important than those who speak in tongues, unless they are able to interpret them so that the church might be built up. 6 After all, brothers and sisters, if I come to you speaking in tongues, how will I help you unless I speak to you with a revelation, some knowledge, a prophecy, or a teaching? 7 Likewise, things that aren't alive like a harp or a lyre can make a sound, but if there aren't different notes in the sounds they make, how will the tune from the harp or the lyre be recognized? 8 And if a trumpet call is unrecognizable, then who will prepare for battle? 9 It's the same way with you: If you don't use language that is easy to understand when you speak in a tongue, then how will anyone understand what is said? 10 It will be as if you are speaking into the air! There are probably many language families in the world, and none of them are without meaning. 11 So if I don't know the meaning of the language, then I will be like a foreigner to those who speak it, and they will be like foreigners to me. 12 The same holds true for you: since you are ambitious for spiritual gifts, use your ambition to try to work toward being the best at building up the church.

13 Therefore, those who speak in a tongue should pray to be able to interpret. 14 If I pray in a tongue, my spirit prays but my mind isn't productive. 15 What should I do? I'll pray in the Spirit, but I'll pray with my mind too; I'll sing a psalm in the Spirit,

but I'll sing the psalm with my mind too.
[16]After all, if you praise God in the Spirit,
how will the people who aren't trained in
that language say "Amen!" to your thanksgiving, when they don't know what you are
saying? [17]You may offer a beautiful prayer
of thanksgiving, but the other person is not
being built up. [18]I thank God that I speak in
tongues more than all of you. [19]But in the
church I'd rather speak five words in my
right mind than speak thousands of words
in a tongue so that I can teach others.

[20]Brothers and sisters, don't be like children in the way you think. Well, be babies
when it comes to evil, but be adults in your
thinking. [21]In the Law it is written: *I will
speak to this people with foreign languages
and foreigners' lips, but they will not even
listen to me this way,*[p] says the Lord. [22]So
then, tongues are a sign for those who
don't believe, not for those who believe.
But prophecy is a sign for believers, not for
those who don't believe. [23]So suppose that
the whole church is meeting and everyone
is speaking in tongues. If people come in
who are outsiders or unbelievers, won't
they say that you are out of your minds?
[24]But if everyone is prophesying when an
unbeliever or outsider comes in, they are
tested by all and called to account by all.
[25]The secrets of their hearts are brought to
light. When that happens, they will fall on
their faces and worship God, proclaiming
out loud that truly God is among you!

[26]What is the outcome of this, brothers and sisters? When you meet together,
each one has a psalm, a teaching, a
revelation, a tongue, or an interpretation.
All these things must be done to build up
the church. [27]If some speak in a tongue,
then let two or at most three speak, one
at a time, and someone must interpret.
[28]However, if there is no interpreter, then
they should keep quiet in the meeting. They
should speak privately to themselves and to
God. [29]In the case of prophets, let two or
three speak and have the rest evaluate what
is said. [30]And if some revelation comes to
someone else who is sitting down, the first
one should be quiet. [31]You can all prophesy
one at a time so that everyone can learn
and be encouraged. [32]The spirits of prophets are under the control of the prophets.
[33]God isn't a God of disorder but of peace.
Like in all the churches of God's people,
[34]the women should be quiet during the
meeting. They are not allowed to talk. Instead, they need to get under control, just
as the Law says. [35]If they want to learn
something, they should ask their husbands
at home. It is disgraceful for a woman to
talk during the meeting.

[36]Did the word of God originate with
you? Has it come only to you? [37]If anyone
thinks that they are prophets or "spiritual
people," then let them recognize that what
I'm writing to you is the Lord's command.
[38]If someone doesn't recognize this, they
aren't recognized. [39]So then, brothers and
sisters, use your ambition to try to get the
gift of prophecy, but don't prevent speaking in tongues. [40]Everything should be
done with dignity and in proper order.

The resurrection

15 Brothers and sisters, I want to call
your attention to the good news that
I preached to you, which you also received
and in which you stand. [2]You are being saved
through it if you hold on to the message I
preached to you, unless somehow you believed it for nothing. [3]I passed on to you as
most important what I also received: Christ
died for our sins in line with the scriptures,
[4]he was buried, and he rose on the third day
in line with the scriptures. [5]He appeared to
Cephas, then to the Twelve, [6]and then he
appeared to more than five hundred brothers and sisters at once—most of them are
still alive to this day, though some have
died. [7]Then he appeared to James, then to all
the apostles, [8]and last of all he appeared to
me, as if I were born at the wrong time. [9]I'm
the least important of the apostles. I don't
deserve to be called an apostle, because I
harassed God's church. [10]I am what I am
by God's grace, and God's grace hasn't been
for nothing. In fact, I have worked harder

[p]Isa 28:11-12

than all the others—that is, it wasn't me but the grace of God that is with me. [11]So then, whether you heard the message from me or them, this is what we preach and this is what you have believed.

[12]So if the message that is preached says that Christ has been raised from the dead, then how can some of you say, "There's no resurrection of the dead"? [13]If there's no resurrection of the dead, then Christ hasn't been raised either. [14]If Christ hasn't been raised, then our preaching is useless and your faith is useless. [15]We are found to be false witnesses about God, because we testified against God that he raised Christ, when he didn't raise him if it's the case that the dead aren't raised. [16]If the dead aren't raised, then Christ hasn't been raised either. [17]If Christ hasn't been raised, then your faith is worthless; you are still in your sins, [18]and what's more, those who have died in Christ are gone forever. [19]If we have a hope in Christ only in this life, then we deserve to be pitied more than anyone else.

[20]But in fact Christ has been raised from the dead. He's the first crop of the harvest[q] of those who have died. [21]Since death came through a human being, the resurrection of the dead came through one too. [22]In the same way that everyone dies in Adam, so also everyone will be given life in Christ. [23]Each event will happen in the right order: Christ, the first crop of the harvest,[r] then those who belong to Christ at his coming, [24]and then the end, when Christ hands over the kingdom to God the Father, when he brings every form of rule, every authority and power to an end. [25]It is necessary for him to rule until *he puts all enemies under his feet.*[s] [26]Death is the last enemy to be brought to an end, [27]since he has brought everything under control under his feet. When it says that everything has been brought under his control, this clearly means everything except for the one who placed everything under his control. [28]But when all things have been brought under his control, then the Son himself will also be under the control of the one who gave him control over everything so that God may be all in all.

[29]Otherwise, what are those who are getting baptized for the dead doing? If the dead aren't raised, then why are they being baptized for them? [30]And what about us? Why are we in danger all day every day? [31]Brothers and sisters, I swear by the pride I have in you in Christ Jesus our Lord, I'm facing death every day. [32]From a human point of view, what good does it do me if I fought wild animals in Ephesus? If the dead aren't raised, *let's eat and drink because tomorrow we'll die.*[t] [33]Don't be deceived, bad company corrupts good character. [34]Sober up by acting like you should and don't sin. Some of you are ignorant about God—I say this because you should be ashamed of yourselves!

[35]But someone will say, "How are the dead raised? What kind of body will they have when they come back?" [36]Look, fool! When you put a seed into the ground, it doesn't come back to life unless it dies. [37]What you put in the ground doesn't have the shape that it will have, but it's a bare grain of wheat or some other seed. [38]God gives it the sort of shape that he chooses, and he gives each of the seeds its own shape. [39]All flesh isn't alike. Humans have one kind of flesh, animals have another kind of flesh, birds have another kind of flesh, and fish have another kind. [40]There are heavenly bodies and earthly bodies. The heavenly bodies have one kind of glory, and the earthly bodies have another kind of glory. [41]The sun has one kind of glory, the moon has another kind of glory, and the stars have another kind of glory (but one star is different from another star in its glory). [42]It's the same with the resurrection of the dead: a rotting body is put into the ground, but what is raised won't ever decay. [43]It's degraded when it's put into the ground, but it's raised in glory. It's weak when it's put into the ground, but it's raised in power. [44]It's a physical body when it's put into the ground, but it's raised as a spiritual body.

If there's a physical body, there's also a

[q]Or *firstfruits* [r]Or *firstfruits* [s]Ps 110:1 [t]Isa 22:13

spiritual body. 45 So it is also written, *The first human, Adam, became a living person,*[u] and the last Adam became a spirit that gives life. 46 But the physical body comes first, not the spiritual one—the spiritual body comes afterward. 47 The first human was from the earth made from dust; the second human is from heaven. 48 The nature of the person made of dust is shared by people who are made of dust, and the nature of the heavenly person is shared by heavenly people. 49 We will look like[v] the heavenly person in the same way as we have looked like the person made from dust.

50 This is what I'm saying, brothers and sisters: Flesh and blood can't inherit God's kingdom. Something that rots can't inherit something that doesn't decay. 51 Listen, I'm telling you a secret: All of us won't die, but we will all be changed—52 in an instant, in the blink of an eye, at the final trumpet. The trumpet will blast, and the dead will be raised with bodies that won't decay, and we will be changed. 53 It's necessary for this rotting body to be clothed with what can't decay, and for the body that is dying to be clothed in what can't die. 54 And when the rotting body has been clothed in what can't decay, and the dying body has been clothed in what can't die, then this statement in scripture will happen:

Death has been swallowed up by a victory.[w]
55 *Where is your victory, Death?*
Where is your sting, Death?[x]

(56 Death's sting is sin, and the power of sin is the Law.) 57 Thanks be to God, who gives us this victory through our Lord Jesus Christ! 58 As a result of all this, my loved brothers and sisters, you must stand firm, unshakable, excelling in the work of the Lord as always, because you know that your labor isn't going to be for nothing in the Lord.

Collection for Jerusalem

16 Concerning the collection of money for God's people: You should do what I have directed the churches in Galatia to do. 2 On the first day of the week, each of you should set aside whatever you can afford from what you earn so that the collection won't be delayed until I come. 3 Then when I get there, I'll send whomever you approve to Jerusalem with letters of recommendation to bring your gift. 4 If it seems right for me to go too, they'll travel with me.

Plans to visit

5 I'll come to you after I go through Macedonia, and because I'm going through Macedonia, 6 I may stay with you or even spend the winter there in Corinth so that you can send me on my way to wherever I'm off to next. 7 I don't want to make a quick visit to you, since I hope to spend some time with you if the Lord lets it happen. 8 I'll stay here in Ephesus until the Festival of Pentecost. 9 In spite of the fact that there are many opponents, a big and productive opportunity has opened up for my mission here.

10 If Timothy comes to you, be sure that he has no reason to be afraid while he's with you, because he does the work of the Lord just like I do. 11 So don't let anyone disrespect him, but send him on in peace so he can join me. I'm waiting for him along with the brothers and sisters. 12 Concerning Apollos our brother: I strongly encouraged him to visit you with the brothers and sisters, but he didn't want to go now. He'll come when he has an opportunity.

Final greeting

13 Stay awake, stand firm in your faith, be brave, be strong. 14 Everything should be done in love.

15 Brothers and sisters, I encourage you to do something else. You know that the people in Stephanas' household were the first crop of the harvest to come from the mission to Achaia. They have dedicated themselves to the service of God's people. 16 So accept the authority of people like them and of anyone who cooperates and works hard. 17 I'm so happy that Stephanas, Fortunatus, and Achaicus have arrived; they've made up for my missing you. 18 Indeed they've provided my spirit and yours with a much-needed rest. Therefore, give them proper recognition.

[u] Gen 2:7 [v] Or *bear the image of* [w] Isa 25:8 [x] Hos 13:14

[19]The churches in the province of Asia
greet you. Aquila and Prisca greet you
warmly in the Lord, together with the church
that meets in their house. [20]All the brothers and sisters greet you. You in turn should
greet each other with a holy kiss. [21] Here
is my greeting in my own handwriting—
Paul.
[22]A curse on anyone who doesn't love
the Lord. Come, Lord! [23]The grace of the
Lord Jesus be with you. [24]My love is with
all of you in Christ Jesus.

2 CORINTHIANS

Greeting

1 From Paul, an apostle of Christ Jesus
by God's will, and Timothy our brother.
To God's church that is in Corinth, along
with all of God's people throughout
Achaia.
[2]Grace to you and peace from God our
Father and from our Lord Jesus Christ.

God's comfort in trouble

[3]May the God and Father of our Lord
Jesus Christ be blessed! He is the compassionate Father and God of all comfort. [4]He's
the one who comforts us in all our trouble
so that we can comfort other people who
are in every kind of trouble. We offer the
same comfort that we ourselves received
from God. [5]That is because we receive so
much comfort through Christ in the same
way that we share so many of Christ's
sufferings. [6]So if we have trouble, it is to
bring you comfort and salvation. If we are
comforted, it is to bring you comfort from
the experience of endurance while you go
through the same sufferings that we also
suffer. [7]Our hope for you is certain, because
we know that as you are partners in suffering, so also you are partners in comfort.
[8]Brothers and sisters, we don't want you
to be unaware of the troubles that we went
through in Asia. We were weighed down
with a load of suffering that was so far beyond our strength that we were afraid we
might not survive. [9]It certainly seemed to
us as if we had gotten the death penalty.
This was so that we would have confidence
in God, who raises the dead, instead of
ourselves. [10]God rescued us from a terrible
death, and he will rescue us. We have set our
hope on him that he will rescue us again,
[11]since you are helping with your prayer for
us. Then many people can thank God on
our behalf for the gift that was given to us
through the prayers of many people.

Paul explains his change of plans

[12]We have conducted ourselves with godly
sincerity and pure motives in the world, and
especially toward you. This is why we are
confident, and our conscience confirms this.
We didn't act with human wisdom but we
relied on the grace of God. [13]We don't write
anything to you except what you can read
and also understand. I hope that you will
understand totally [14]since you have already
understood us partly. Understand that in
the day of our Lord Jesus, we will make you
proud as you will also make us proud.
[15]Because I was sure of this, I wanted
to visit you first so that you could have a
second opportunity to see me. [16]I wanted
to visit you on my way to Macedonia, and
then come to you again on my way back
from Macedonia, at which point I was hoping you would help me on my way to Judea.
[17]So I wasn't unreliable when I planned
to do this, was I? Or do I make decisions
with a substandard human process so that
I say "Yes, yes" and "No, no" at the same
time? [18]But as God is faithful, our message
to you isn't both yes and no. [19]God's Son,
Jesus Christ, is the one who was preached
among you by us—through me, Silvanus,
and Timothy—he wasn't yes and no. In him
it is always yes. [20]All of God's promises have
their yes in him. That is why we say Amen
through him to the glory of God.
[21]God is the one who establishes us with
you in Christ and who anointed us. [22]God
also sealed us and gave the Spirit as a down
payment in our hearts. [23]I call on God as my
witness—I didn't come again to Corinth be-

cause I wanted to spare you. 24 It isn't that we are trying to control your faith, but we are working with you for your happiness, because

2 you stand firm in your faith. 1 So I decided that, for my own sake, I wouldn't visit you again while I was upset. 2 If I make you sad, who will be there to make me glad when you are sad because of me?

Paul's former letter

3 That's why I wrote this very thing to you, so that when I came I wouldn't be made sad by the ones who ought to make me happy. I have confidence in you, that my happiness means your happiness. 4 I wrote to you in tears, with a very troubled and anxious heart. I didn't write to make you sad but so you would know the overwhelming love that I have for you.

5 But if someone has made anyone sad, that person hasn't hurt me but all of you to some degree (not to exaggerate). 6 The punishment handed out by the majority is enough for this person. 7 This is why you should try your best to forgive and to comfort this person now instead, so that this person isn't overwhelmed by too much sorrow. 8 So I encourage you to show your love for this person.

9 This is another reason why I wrote you. I wanted to test you and see if you are obedient in everything. 10 If you forgive anyone for anything, I do too. And whatever I've forgiven (if I've forgiven anything), I did it for you in the presence of Christ. 11 This is so that we won't be taken advantage of by Satan, because we are well aware of his schemes.

Paul's ministry

12 When I came to Troas to preach Christ's gospel, the Lord gave me an opportunity to preach. 13 But I was worried because I couldn't find my brother Titus there. So I said good-bye to them and went on to Macedonia.

14 But thank God, who is always leading us around through Christ as if we were in a parade. He releases the fragrance of the knowledge of him everywhere through us. 15 We smell like the aroma of Christ's offering to God, both to those who are being saved and to those who are on the road to destruction. 16 We smell like a contagious dead person to those who are dying, but we smell like the fountain of life to those who are being saved.

Who is qualified for this kind of ministry? 17 We aren't like so many people who hustle the word of God to make a profit. We are speaking through Christ in the presence of God, as those who are sincere and as those who are sent from God.

3 Are we starting to commend ourselves again? We don't need letters of introduction to you or from you like other people, do we? 2 You are our letter, written on our hearts, known and read by everyone. 3 You show that you are Christ's letter, delivered by us. You weren't written with ink but with the Spirit of the living God. You weren't written on tablets of stone but on tablets of human hearts.

4 This is the confidence that we have through Christ in the presence of God. 5 It isn't that we ourselves are qualified to claim that anything came from us. No, our qualification is from God. 6 He has qualified us as ministers of a new covenant, not based on what is written but on the Spirit, because what is written kills, but the Spirit gives life.

Ministers of the new covenant

7 The ministry that brought death was carved in letters on stone tablets. It came with such glory that the Israelites couldn't look for long at Moses' face because his face was shining with glory, even though it was a fading glory. 8 Won't the ministry of the Spirit be much more glorious? 9 If the ministry that brought condemnation has glory, how much more glorious is the ministry that brings righteousness? 10 In fact, what was glorious isn't glorious now, because of the glory that is brighter. 11 If the glory that fades away was glorious, how much more glorious is the one that lasts!

12 So, since we have such a hope, we act with great confidence. 13 We aren't like Moses, who used to put a veil over his face so that the Israelites couldn't watch the end of what was fading away. 14 But their minds were closed. Right up to the present day the same veil remains when the old covenant

is read. The veil is not removed because
it is taken away by Christ. 15 Even today,
whenever Moses is read, a veil lies over their
hearts. 16 But whenever someone turns back
to the Lord, the veil is removed. 17 The Lord
is the Spirit, and where the Lord's Spirit is,
there is freedom. 18 All of us are looking
with unveiled faces at the glory of the Lord
as if we were looking in a mirror. We are
being transformed into that same image
from one degree of glory to the next degree
of glory. This comes from the Lord, who is
the Spirit.

4 This is why we don't get discouraged,
given that we received this ministry in
the same way that we received God's mercy.
2 Instead, we reject secrecy and shameful
actions. We don't use deception, and we
don't tamper with God's word. Instead,
we commend ourselves to everyone's conscience in the sight of God by the public
announcement of the truth. 3 And even if
our gospel is veiled, it is veiled to those who
are on the road to destruction. 4 The god
of this age has blinded the minds of those
who don't have faith so they couldn't see
the light of the gospel that reveals Christ's
glory. Christ is the image of God.

5 We don't preach about ourselves. Instead, we preach about Jesus Christ as
Lord, and we describe ourselves as your
slaves for Jesus' sake. 6 God said that light
should shine out of the darkness. He is the
same one who shone in our hearts to give
us the light of the knowledge of God's glory
in the face of Jesus Christ.

Physical bodies and eternal glory

7 But we have this treasure in clay pots so
that the awesome power belongs to God and
doesn't come from us. 8 We are experiencing
all kinds of trouble, but we aren't crushed.
We are confused, but we aren't depressed.
9 We are harassed, but we aren't abandoned. We are knocked down, but we aren't
knocked out.

10 We always carry Jesus' death around
in our bodies so that Jesus' life can also be
seen in our bodies. 11 We who are alive are always being handed over to death for Jesus'
sake so that Jesus' life can also be seen in
our bodies that are dying. 12 So death is at
work in us, but life is at work in you.

13 We have the same faithful spirit as
what is written in scripture: *I had faith, and
so I spoke.*[a] We also have faith, and so we
also speak. 14 We do this because we know
that the one who raised the Lord Jesus will
also raise us with Jesus, and he will bring
us into his presence along with you. 15 All
these things are for your benefit. As grace
increases to benefit more and more people,
it will cause gratitude to increase, which results in God's glory.

16 So we aren't depressed. But even if our
bodies are breaking down on the outside,
the person that we are on the inside is
being renewed every day. 17 Our temporary
minor problems are producing an eternal
stockpile of glory for us that is beyond all
comparison. 18 We don't focus on the things
that can be seen but on the things that
can't be seen. The things that can be seen
don't last, but the things that can't be seen
are eternal.

5 We know that if the tent that we live
in on earth is torn down, we have a
building from God. It's a house that isn't
handmade, which is eternal and located
in heaven. 2 We groan while we live in this
residence. We really want to dress ourselves
with our building from heaven—3 since we
assume that when we take off this tent,
we won't find out that we are naked. 4 Yes,
while we are in this tent we groan, because we are weighed down. We want to
be dressed not undressed, so that what is
dying can be swallowed up by life. 5 Now the
one who prepared us for this very thing is
God, and God gave us the Spirit as a down
payment for our home.

6 So we are always confident, because we
know that while we are living in the body,
we are away from our home with the Lord.
7 We live by faith and not by sight. 8 We are
confident, and we would prefer to leave the
body and to be at home with the Lord. 9 So
our goal is to be acceptable to him, whether

[a] Ps 116:10 (115:1 LXX)

we are at home or away from home. [10]We all must appear before Christ in court so that each person can be paid back for the things that were done while in the body, whether they were good or bad.

Ministry of reconciliation

[11]So we try to persuade people, since we know what it means to fear the Lord. We are well known by God, and I hope that in your heart we are well known by you as well. [12]We aren't trying to commend ourselves to you again. Instead, we are giving you an opportunity to be proud of us so that you could answer those who take pride in superficial appearance, and not in what is in the heart.

[13]If we are crazy, it's for God's sake. If we are rational, it's for your sake. [14]The love of Christ controls us, because we have concluded this: one died for the sake of all; therefore, all died. [15]He died for the sake of all so that those who are alive should live not for themselves but for the one who died for them and was raised.

[16]So then, from this point on we won't recognize people by human standards. Even though we used to know Christ by human standards, that isn't how we know him now. [17]So then, if anyone is in Christ, that person is part of the new creation. The old things have gone away, and look, new things have arrived!

[18]All of these new things are from God, who reconciled us to himself through Christ and who gave us the ministry of reconciliation. [19]In other words, God was reconciling the world to himself through Christ, by not counting people's sins against them. He has trusted us with this message of reconciliation.

[20]So we are ambassadors who represent Christ. God is negotiating with you through us. We beg you as Christ's representatives, "Be reconciled to God!" [21]God caused the one who didn't know sin to be sin for our sake so that through him we could become
6 the righteousness of God. [1]Since we work together with him, we are also begging you not to receive the grace of God in vain. [2]He says, *I listened to you at the right time, and I helped you on the day of salvation.*[b] Look, now is the right time! Look, now is the day of salvation!

[3]We don't give anyone any reason to be offended about anything so that our ministry won't be criticized. [4]Instead, we commend ourselves as ministers of God in every way. We did this with our great endurance through problems, disasters, and stressful situations. [5]We went through beatings, imprisonments, and riots. We experienced hard work, sleepless nights, and hunger. [6]We displayed purity, knowledge, patience, and generosity. We served with the Holy Spirit, genuine love, [7]telling the truth, and God's power. We carried the weapons of righteousness in our right hand and our left hand. [8]We were treated with honor and dishonor and with verbal abuse and good evaluation. We were seen as both fake and real, [9]as unknown and well known, as dying—and look, we are alive! We were seen as punished but not killed, [10]as going through pain but always happy, as poor but making many rich, and as having nothing but owning everything.

Call to relationship and holiness

[11]Corinthians, we have spoken openly to you, and our hearts are wide open. [12]There are no limits to the affection that we feel for you. You are the ones who placed boundaries on your affection for us. [13]But as a fair trade—I'm talking to you like you are children—open your hearts wide too.

[14]Don't be tied up as equal partners with people who don't believe. What does righteousness share with that which is outside the Law? What relationship does light have with darkness? [15]What harmony does Christ have with Satan?[c] What does a believer have in common with someone who doesn't believe? [16]What agreement can there be between God's temple and idols? Because we are the temple of the living God. Just as God said, *I live with them, and I will move among them. I will be their God, and they will be my people.*[d] [17]Therefore, *come out*

[b]Isa 49:8 [c]Or *Beliah* [d]Lev 26:11-12

from among them and be separated, says the
Lord. Don't touch what is unclean. Then I will
welcome you.[e] [18]*I will be a father to you, and*
you will be my sons and daughters, says the
7 *Lord Almighty.*[f] [1]My dear friends, since
we have these promises, let's cleanse
ourselves from anything that contaminates
our body or spirit so that we make our holiness complete in the fear of God.
[2]Make room in your hearts for us. We
didn't do anything wrong to anyone. We
didn't ruin anyone. We didn't take advantage of anyone. [3]I'm not saying this to
make you feel guilty. I've already said that
you are in our hearts so that we die and live
together with you. [4]I have every confidence
in you. I'm terribly proud of you. I'm filled
with encouragement. I'm overwhelmed
with happiness while in the middle of our
problems.

Titus' good report

[5]Even after we arrived in Macedonia,
we couldn't rest physically. We were surrounded by problems. There was external
conflict, and there were internal fears.
[6]However, God comforts people who are
discouraged, and he comforted us by Titus'
arrival. [7]We weren't comforted only by his
arrival but also by the comfort he had received from you. He told us about your
desire to see me, how you were sorry, and
about your concern for me, so that I was
even happier.
[8]Even though my letter hurt you, I don't
regret it. Well—I did regret it just a bit because I see that that letter made you sad,
though only for a short time. [9]Now I'm
glad—not because you were sad but because you were made sad enough to change
your hearts and lives. You felt godly sadness
so that no one was harmed by us in any
way. [10]Godly sadness produces a changed
heart and life that leads to salvation and
leaves no regrets, but sorrow under the influence of the world produces death. [11]Look
at what this very experience of godly sadness has produced in you: such enthusiasm,
what a desire to clear yourselves of blame,
such indignation, what fear, what purpose,
such concern, what justice! In everything
you have shown yourselves to be innocent
in the matter.
[12]So although I wrote to you, it wasn't
for the sake of the one who did wrong, or
for the sake of the one who was wronged,
but to show you your own enthusiasm for
us in the sight of God. [13]Because of this
we have been encouraged. And in addition
to our own encouragement, we were even
more pleased at how happy Titus was. His
mind has been put at rest by all of you. [14]If
I've bragged about you to him in any way,
I haven't been embarrassed. Instead, our
bragging to Titus has also been proven to
be true, just like everything we said to you
was true. [15]His devotion to you is growing
even more as he remembers how all of you
were obedient when you welcomed him
with fear and trembling. [16]I'm happy, because I can completely depend on you.

Encouragement to give generously

8 Brothers and sisters, we want to let
you know about the grace of God that
was given to the churches of Macedonia.
[2]While they were being tested by many
problems, their extra amount of happiness
and their extreme poverty resulted in a surplus of rich generosity. [3]I assure you that
they gave what they could afford and even
more than they could afford, and they did it
voluntarily. [4]They urgently begged us for
the privilege[g] of sharing in this service for
the saints. [5]They even exceeded our expectations, because they gave themselves to
the Lord first and to us, consistent with
God's will. [6]As a result, we challenged Titus
to finish this work of grace with you the
way he had started it.
[7]Be the best in this work of grace in the
same way that you are the best in everything, such as faith, speech, knowledge,
total commitment, and the love we inspired in you. [8]I'm not giving an order, but
by mentioning the commitment of others,
I'm trying to prove the authenticity of your
love also. [9]You know the grace of our Lord

[e]Isa 52:11; Ezek 20:34, 41 [f]2 Sam 7:14 [g]Or *grace*

Jesus Christ. Although he was rich, he became poor for our sakes, so that you could become rich through his poverty.

10I'm giving you my opinion about this. It's to your advantage to do this, since you not only started to do it last year but you wanted to do it too. 11Now finish the job as well so that you finish it with as much enthusiasm as you started, given what you can afford. 12A gift is appreciated because of what a person can afford, not because of what that person can't afford, if it's apparent that it's done willingly. 13It isn't that we want others to have financial ease and you financial difficulties, but it's a matter of equality. 14At the present moment, your surplus can fill their deficit so that in the future their surplus can fill your deficit. In this way there is equality. 15As it is written, *The one who gathered more didn't have too much, and the one who gathered less didn't have too little.*[h]

Plans for the Collection

16But thank God, who put the same commitment that I have for you in Titus' heart. 17Not only has he accepted our challenge but he's on his way to see you voluntarily, and he's excited. 18We are sending the brother who is famous in all the churches because of his work for the gospel along with him.

19In addition to this, he is chosen by the churches to be our traveling companion in this work of grace, which we are taking care of for the sake of the glory of the Lord himself, and to show our desire to help. 20We are trying to avoid being blamed by anyone for the way we take care of this large amount of money. 21We care about doing the right thing, not only in the Lord's eyes but also in the eyes of other people.

22We are sending our brother with them. We have tested his commitment in many ways and many times. Now he's even more committed, because he has so much confidence in you. 23If there is any question about Titus, he is my partner and coworker among you. If there is any question about our brothers, they are the churches' apostles and an honor to Christ. 24So show them the proof of your love and the reason we are so proud of you, in such a way that the churches can see it.

9 It's unnecessary for me to write to you about this service for God's people. 2I know about your willingness to help. I brag about you to the Macedonians, saying, "Greece has been ready since last year," and your enthusiasm has motivated most of them.

3But I'm sending the brothers so that our bragging about you in this case won't be empty words, and so that you can be prepared, just as I keep telling them you will be. 4If some Macedonians should come with me and find out that you aren't ready, we (not to mention you) would be embarrassed as far as this project goes.

5This is why I thought it was necessary to encourage the brothers to go to you ahead of time and arrange in advance the generous gift you have already promised. I want it to be a real gift from you. I don't want you to feel like you are being forced to give anything. 6What I mean is this: the one who sows a small number of seeds will also reap a small crop, and the one who sows a generous amount of seeds will also reap a generous crop.

7Everyone should give whatever they have decided in their heart. They shouldn't give with hesitation or because of pressure. God loves a cheerful giver. 8God has the power to provide you with more than enough of every kind of grace. That way, you will have everything you need always and in everything to provide more than enough for every kind of good work. 9As it is written, *He scattered everywhere; he gave to the needy; his righteousness remains forever.*[i]

10The one who supplies seed for planting and bread for eating will supply and multiply your seed and will increase your crop, which is righteousness. 11You will be made rich in every way so that you can be generous in every way. Such generosity produces

[h]Exod 16:18 [i]Ps 112:9

thanksgiving to God through us. 12 Your ministry of this service to God's people isn't only fully meeting their needs but it is also multiplying in many expressions of thanksgiving to God. 13 They will give honor to God for your obedience to your confession of Christ's gospel. They will do this because this service provides evidence of your obedience, and because of your generosity in sharing with them and with everyone. 14 They will also pray for you, and they will care deeply for you because of the outstanding grace that God has given to you. 15 Thank God for his gift that words can't describe!

Paul's personal request for obedience

10 I, Paul, make a personal request to you with the gentleness and kindness of Christ. I'm shy when I'm with you, but I'm bossy when I'm away from you! 2 I beg you that when I'm with you in person, I won't have to boss you around. I'm afraid that I may have to use that kind of behavior with those people who think we live by human standards. 3 Although we live in the world, we don't fight our battles with human methods. 4 Our weapons that we fight with aren't human, but instead they are powered by God for the destruction of fortresses. They destroy arguments, 5 and every defense that is raised up to oppose the knowledge of God. They capture every thought to make it obedient to Christ. 6 Once your obedience is complete, we are ready to punish any disobedience.

7 Look at what is right in front of you! If anyone is sure about belonging to Christ, that person should think again. We belong to Christ just like that person. 8 Even if I went on to brag about our authority, I wouldn't be ashamed of it. The Lord gave us that authority to build you up and not to destroy you.

9 I don't want it to seem like I'm trying to intimidate you with my letters. 10 I know what some people are saying: "His letters are severe and powerful, but in person he is weak and his speech is worth nothing." 11 These people need to think about this—that when we are with you, our actions will show that we are the same as the words we wrote when we were away from you. 12 We won't dare to place ourselves in the same league or to compare ourselves with some of those who are promoting themselves. When they measure themselves by themselves, and compare themselves with themselves, they have no understanding.

13 We won't take pride in anything more than what is appropriate. Let's look at the boundaries of our work area that God has assigned to us. It's an area that includes you. 14 We aren't going out of bounds, as if our work area doesn't extend as far as you. We were the first ones to travel as far as Corinth with the gospel of Christ. 15 We don't take pride in what other people do outside of our boundaries. We hope that our work will be extended even more by you as your faith grows, until it expands fully (within the boundaries, of course). 16 We hope that our work grows even to the point of the gospel being preached in places beyond Corinth, without bragging about what has already been done in another person's work area. 17 But, *the one who brags should brag in the Lord.*[j] 18 It isn't the person who promotes himself or herself who is approved but the person whom the Lord commends.

Confrontation of the super-apostles

11 I hope that you will put up with me while I act like a fool. Well, in fact, you are putting up with me! 2 I'm deeply concerned about you with the same concern that God has. As your father, I promised you in marriage to one husband. I promised to present you as an innocent virgin to Christ himself. 3 But I'm afraid that your minds might be seduced in the same way as the snake deceived Eve with his devious tricks. You might be unable to focus completely on a genuine and innocent commitment to Christ.

4 If a person comes and preaches some other Jesus than the one we preached, or if you receive a different Spirit than the one you had received, or a different gospel than the one you embraced, you put up with it so

[j] Jer 9:24

easily! [5]I don't consider myself as second-rate in any way compared to the "super-apostles." [6]But even if I'm uneducated in public speaking, I'm not uneducated in knowledge. We have shown this to you in every way and in everything we have done. [7]Did I commit a sin by humbling myself to give you an advantage because I preached the gospel of God to you free of charge? [8]I robbed other churches by taking a salary from them in order to serve you! [9]While I was with you, I didn't burden any of you even though I needed things. The believers who came from Macedonia gave me everything I needed. I kept myself from being a financial drain on you in any way, and I will continue to keep myself from being a burden.

[10]Since Christ's truth is in me, I won't stop telling the entire area of Greece that I'm proud of what I did. [11]Why? Is it because I don't love you? God knows that I do! [12]But I'm going to continue to do what I'm doing. I want to contradict the claims of the people who want to be treated like they are the same as us because of what they brag about. [13]Such people are false apostles and dishonest workers who disguise themselves as apostles of Christ. [14]And no wonder! Even Satan disguises himself as an angel of light. [15]It is no great surprise then that his servants also disguise themselves as servants of righteousness. Their end will be what their actions deserve.

Paul defends himself

[16]I repeat, no one should take me for a fool. But if you do, then allow me to be a fool so that I can brag like a fool for a bit. [17]I'm not saying what I'm saying because the Lord tells me to. I'm saying it like I'm a fool. I'm putting my confidence in this business of bragging. [18]Since so many people are bragging based on human standards, that is how I'm going to brag too. [19]Because you, who are so wise, are happy to put up with fools. [20]You put up with it if someone enslaves you, if someone exploits you, if someone takes advantage of you, if someone places themselves over you, or if someone hits you in the face. [21]I'm ashamed to say that we have been weak in comparison! But in whatever they challenge me, I challenge them (I'm speaking foolishly).

[22]Are they Hebrews? So am I. Are they Israelites? So am I. Are they descendants of Abraham? So am I. [23]Are they ministers of Christ? I'm speaking like a crazy person. What I've done goes well beyond what they've done. I've worked much harder. I've been imprisoned much more often. I've been beaten more times than I can count. I've faced death many times. [24]I received the "forty lashes minus one" from the Jews five times. [25]I was beaten with rods three times. I was stoned once. I was shipwrecked three times. I spent a day and a night on the open sea. [26]I've been on many journeys. I faced dangers from rivers, robbers, my people, and Gentiles. I faced dangers in the city, in the desert, on the sea, and from false brothers and sisters. [27]I faced these dangers with hard work and heavy labor, many sleepless nights, hunger and thirst, often without food, and in the cold without enough clothes.

[28]Besides all the other things I could mention, there's my daily stress because I'm concerned about all the churches. [29]Who is weak without me being weak? Who is led astray without me being furious about it? [30]If it's necessary to brag, I'll brag about my weaknesses. [31]The God and Father of the Lord Jesus, the one who is blessed forever, knows that I'm not lying. [32]At Damascus the governor under King Aretas was guarding the city of Damascus in order to capture me, [33]but I got away from him by being lowered in a basket through a window in the city wall.

Paul's visions and revelations from the Lord

12 It is necessary to brag, not that it does any good. I'll move on to visions and revelations from the Lord. [2]I know a man in Christ who was caught up into the third heaven fourteen years ago. I don't know whether it was in the body or out of the body. God knows. [3-4]I know that this man was caught up into paradise and that he heard unspeakable words that were things no one is allowed to repeat. I don't know whether it was in the body or apart from the body. God knows. [5]I'll brag about this

man, but I won't brag about myself, except
to brag about my weaknesses.
6 If I did want to brag, I wouldn't make
a fool of myself because I'd tell the truth.
I'm holding back from bragging so that no
one will give me any more credit than what
anyone sees or hears about me. 7 I was given
a thorn in my body because of the outstanding revelations I've received so that
I wouldn't be conceited. It's a messenger
from Satan sent to torment me so that I
wouldn't be conceited.
8 I pleaded with the Lord three times for it
to leave me alone. 9 He said to me, "My grace
is enough for you, because power is made
perfect in weakness." So I'll gladly spend
my time bragging about my weaknesses so
that Christ's power can rest on me. 10 Therefore, I'm all right with weaknesses, insults,
disasters, harassments, and stressful situations for the sake of Christ, because when
I'm weak, then I'm strong.
11 I've become a fool! You made me do it.
Actually, I should have been commended by
you. I'm not inferior to the super-apostles in
any way, even though I'm a nonentity. 12 The
signs of an apostle were performed among
you with continuous endurance through
signs, wonders, and miracles. 13 How were
you treated worse than the other churches,
except that I myself wasn't a financial burden on you? Forgive me for this wrong!

Paul's plans to visit and a warning

14 Look, I'm ready to visit you a third time,
and I won't be a burden on you. I don't want
your things; I want you. It isn't the children's
responsibility to save up for their parents
but parents for children. 15 I will very gladly
spend and be spent for your sake. If I love
you more, will you love me less?
16 We all know that I didn't place a burden
on you, but in spite of that you think I'm a
con artist who fooled you with a trick. 17 I
haven't taken advantage of you through any
of the people I sent to you, have I? 18 I strongly
encouraged Titus to go to you and sent the
brother with him. Titus didn't take advantage
of you, did he? Didn't we live by the same
Spirit? Didn't we walk in the same footsteps?
19 Have you been thinking up to now that
we are defending ourselves to you? Actually, we are speaking in the sight of God and
in Christ. Dear friends, everything is meant
to build you up. 20 I'm afraid that maybe
when I come you will be different from the
way I want you to be, and that I'll be different from the way you want me to be. I'm
afraid that there might be fighting, obsession, losing your temper, competitive opposition, backstabbing, gossip, conceit, and
disorderly conduct. 21 I'm afraid that when I
come again, my God may embarrass me in
front of you. I might have to go into mourning over all the people who have sinned before and haven't changed their hearts and
lives from what they used to practice: moral
corruption, sexual immorality, and doing
whatever feels good.

13 This is the third time that I'm coming
to visit you. Every matter is settled
on the evidence of two or three witnesses.
2 When I was with you on my second visit, I
already warned those who continued to sin.
Now I'm repeating that warning to all the
rest of you while I'm at a safe distance: if
I come again, I won't spare anyone. 3 Since
you are demanding proof that Christ speaks
through me, Christ isn't weak in dealing with you but shows his power among
you. 4 Certainly he was crucified because
of weakness, but he lives by the power of
God. Certainly we also are weak in him, but
we will live together with him, because of
God's power that is directed toward you.
5 Examine yourselves to see if you are in
the faith. Test yourselves. Don't you understand that Jesus Christ is in you? Unless,
of course, you fail the test. 6 But I hope that
you will realize that we don't fail the test.
7 We pray to God that you don't do anything
wrong, not because we want to appear to
pass the test but so that you might do the
right thing, even if we appear to fail.
8 We can't do anything against the truth
but only to help the truth. 9 We are happy
when we are weak but you are strong. We
pray for this: that you will be made complete. 10 This is why I'm writing these things
while I'm away. I'm writing so that I won't
need to act harshly when I'm with you by
using the authority that the Lord gave me.

He gave it to me so that I could build you
up, not tear you down.

Final greeting

11Finally, brothers and sisters, good-bye.
Put things in order, respond to my encouragement, be in harmony with each other,
and live in peace—and the God of love and
peace will be with you.
12Say hello to each other with a holy
kiss.[k] All of God's people say hello to you.
13The grace of the Lord Jesus Christ, the
love of God, and the fellowship of the Holy
Spirit be with you all.

GALATIANS

Greeting

1 From Paul, an apostle who is not sent
from human authority or commissioned through human agency, but
sent through Jesus Christ and God
the Father who raised him from the
dead; 2and from all the brothers and
sisters with me.
To the churches in Galatia.
3Grace and peace to you from God the
Father and the Lord Jesus Christ. 4He
gave himself for our sins, so he could
deliver us from this present evil age,
according to the will of our God and
Father. 5To God be the glory forever
and always! Amen.

The gospel challenged in Galatia

6I'm amazed that you are so quickly deserting the one who called you by the grace
of Christ to follow another gospel. 7It's not
really another gospel, but certain people
are confusing you and they want to change
the gospel of Christ. 8However, even if we
ourselves or a heavenly angel should ever
preach anything different from what we
preached to you, they should be under a
curse. 9I'm repeating what we've said before: if anyone preaches something different from what you received, they should be
under a curse!

Paul's leadership

10Am I trying to win over human beings
or God? Or am I trying to please people?
If I were still trying to please people, I
wouldn't be Christ's slave. 11Brothers and
sisters, I want you to know that the gospel
I preached isn't human in origin. 12I didn't
receive it or learn it from a human. It came
through a revelation from Jesus Christ.
13You heard about my previous life in
Judaism, how severely I harassed God's
church and tried to destroy it. 14I advanced
in Judaism beyond many of my peers, because I was much more militant about the
traditions of my ancestors. 15But God had
set me apart from birth and called me
through his grace. He was pleased 16to reveal his Son to me, so that I might preach
about him to the Gentiles. I didn't immediately consult with any human being. 17I
didn't go up to Jerusalem to see the men
who were apostles before me either, but I
went away into Arabia and I returned again
to Damascus. 18Then after three years I
went up to Jerusalem to visit Cephas and
stayed with him fifteen days. 19But I didn't
see any other of the apostles except James
the brother of the Lord. 20Before God, I'm
not lying about the things that I'm writing
to you! 21Then I went into the regions of
Syria and Cilicia, 22but I wasn't known personally by the Christian churches in Judea.
23They only heard a report about me: "The
man who used to harass us now preaches
the faith that he once tried to destroy." 24So
they were glorifying God because of me.

Confirmation of Paul's leadership

2 Then after fourteen years I went up to
Jerusalem again with Barnabas, and I
took Titus along also. 2I went there because
of a revelation, and I laid out the gospel
that I preach to the Gentiles for them. But
I did it privately with the influential lead-

[k] 2 Cor 13:12-13 is in some versions equivalent to 13:12-14.

ers to make sure that I wouldn't be working or that I hadn't worked for nothing. [3]However, not even Titus, who was with me and who was a Greek, was required to be circumcised. [4]But false brothers and sisters, who were brought in secretly, slipped in to spy on our freedom, which we have in Christ Jesus, and to make us slaves. [5]We didn't give in and submit to them for a single moment, so that the truth of the gospel would continue to be with you.

[6]The influential leaders didn't add anything to what I was preaching—and whatever they were makes no difference to me, because God doesn't show favoritism. [7]But on the contrary, they saw that I had been given the responsibility to preach the gospel to the people who aren't circumcised, just as Peter had been to the circumcised. [8]The one who empowered Peter to become an apostle to the circumcised empowered me also to be one to the Gentiles. [9]James, Cephas, and John, who are considered to be key leaders, shook hands with me and Barnabas as equals when they recognized the grace that was given to me. So it was agreed that we would go to the Gentiles, while they continue to go to the people who were circumcised. [10]They asked only that we would remember the poor, which was certainly something I was willing to do.

The Jewish-Gentile controversy

[11]But when Cephas came to Antioch, I opposed him to his face, because he was wrong. [12]He had been eating with the Gentiles before certain people came from James. But when they came, he began to back out and separate himself, because he was afraid of the people who promoted circumcision. [13]And the rest of the Jews also joined him in this hypocrisy so that even Barnabas got carried away with them in their hypocrisy. [14]But when I saw that they weren't acting consistently with the truth of the gospel, I said to Cephas in front of everyone, "If you, though you're a Jew, live like a Gentile and not like a Jew, how can you require the Gentiles to live like Jews?"

[15]We are born Jews—we're not Gentile sinners. [16]However, we know that a person isn't made righteous by the works of the Law but rather through the faithfulness of Jesus Christ. We ourselves believed in Christ Jesus so that we could be made righteous by the faithfulness of Christ and not by the works of the Law—because no one will be made righteous by the works of the Law. [17]But if it is discovered that we ourselves are sinners while we are trying to be made righteous in Christ, then is Christ a servant of sin? Absolutely not! [18]If I rebuild the very things that I tore down, I show that I myself am breaking the Law. [19]I died to the Law through the Law, so that I could live for God. [20]I have been crucified with Christ and I no longer live, but Christ lives in me. And the life that I now live in my body, I live by faith, indeed, by the faithfulness of God's Son, who loved me and gave himself for me. [21]I don't ignore the grace of God, because if we become righteous through the Law, then Christ died for no purpose.

Works versus the Spirit

3 You irrational Galatians! Who put a spell on you? Jesus Christ was put on display as crucified before your eyes! [2]I just want to know this from you: Did you receive the Spirit by doing the works of the Law or by believing what you heard? [3]Are you so irrational? After you started with the Spirit, are you now finishing up with your own human effort? [4]Did you experience so much for nothing? I wonder if it really was for nothing. [5]So does the one providing you with the Spirit and working miracles among you do this by you doing the works of the Law or by you believing what you heard?

Abraham: an example of righteousness

[6]Understand that in the same way that Abraham *believed God and it was credited to him as righteousness,*[a] [7]those who believe are the children of Abraham. [8]But when it saw ahead of time that God would make the Gentiles righteous on the basis of faith, scripture preached the gospel in advance to Abraham:

[a]Gen 15:6

All the Gentiles will be blessed in you.[b] 9There-
fore, those who believe are blessed together
with Abraham who believed.
10All those who rely on the works of the
Law are under a curse, because it is written, *Everyone is cursed who does not keep
on doing all the things that have been written in the Law scroll.*[c] 11But since no one is
made righteous by the Law as far as God is
concerned, it is clear that *the righteous one
will live on the basis of faith.*[d] 12The Law isn't
based on faith; rather, *the one doing these
things will live by them.*[e] 13Christ redeemed
us from the curse of the Law by becoming a
curse for us—because it is written, *Everyone who is hung on a tree is cursed.*[f] 14He redeemed us so that the blessing of Abraham
would come to the Gentiles through Christ
Jesus, and that we would receive the promise of the Spirit through faith.
15Brothers and sisters, I'll use an example
from human experience. No one ignores or
makes additions to a validated will. 16The
promises were made to Abraham and to his
descendant. It doesn't say, "and to the descendants," as if referring to many rather
than just one. It says, "and to your descendant," who is Christ. 17I'm saying this: the
Law, which came four hundred thirty years
later, doesn't invalidate the agreement that
was previously validated by God so that it
cancels the promise. 18If the inheritance
were based upon the Law, it would no longer
be from the promise. But God has given it
graciously to Abraham through a promise.

The Law's origin and purpose

19So why was the Law given? It was
added because of offenses, until the descendant would come to whom the promise had
been made. It was put in place through angels by the hand of a mediator. 20Now the
mediator does not take one side; but God
is one. 21So, is the Law against the promises of God? Absolutely not! If a Law had
been given that was able to give life, then
righteousness would in fact have come
from the Law. 22But scripture locked up all
things under sin, so that the promise based
on the faithfulness of Jesus Christ might
be given to those who have faith. 23Before
faith came, we were guarded under the Law,
locked up until faith that was coming would
be revealed, 24so that the Law became our
custodian until Christ so that we might be
made righteous by faith.

God's children are heirs in Christ

25But now that faith has come, we are no
longer under a custodian.
26You are all God's children through faith
in Christ Jesus. 27All of you who were baptized into Christ have clothed yourselves
with Christ. 28There is neither Jew nor
Greek; there is neither slave nor free; nor is
there male and female, for you are all one in
Christ Jesus. 29Now if you belong to Christ,
then indeed you are Abraham's descendants, heirs according to the promise.
4 I'm saying that as long as the heirs are
minors, they are no different from slaves,
though they really are the owners of everything. 2However, they are placed under trust-
ees and guardians until the date set by the
parents. 3In the same way, when we were
minors, we were also enslaved by this world's
system. 4But when the fulfillment of the
time came, God sent his Son, born through
a woman, and born under the Law. 5This was
so he could redeem those under the Law so
that we could be adopted. 6Because you are
sons and daughters, God sent the Spirit
of his Son into our hearts, crying, "Abba,
Father!" 7Therefore, you are no longer a slave
but a son or daughter, and if you are his child,
then you are also an heir through God.

Paul's concern for the Galatians

8At the time, when you didn't know God,
you were enslaved by things that aren't gods
by nature. 9But now, after knowing God (or
rather, being known by God), how can you
turn back again to the weak and worthless
world system? Do you want to be slaves to
it again? 10You observe religious days and
months and seasons and years. 11I'm afraid
for you! Perhaps my hard work for you has
been for nothing.

[b]Gen 12:3 [c]Deut 27:26 [d]Hab 2:4 [e]Lev 18:5 [f]Deut 21:23

12I beg you to be like me, brothers and
sisters, because I have become like you! You
haven't wronged me. 13You know that I first
preached the gospel to you because of an
illness. 14Though my poor health burdened
you, you didn't look down on me or reject
me, but you welcomed me as if I were an
angel from God, or as if I were Christ Jesus!
15Where then is the great attitude that you
had? I swear that, if possible, you would have
dug out your eyes and given them to me.
16So then, have I become your enemy by telling you the truth? 17They are so concerned
about you, though not with good intentions.
Rather, they want to shut you out so that
you would run after them. 18However, it's
always good to have people concerned about
you with good intentions, and not just when
I'm there with you. 19My little children, I'm
going through labor pains again until Christ
is formed in you. 20But I wish I could be with
you now and change how I sound, because
I'm at a loss about you.

Slave versus free

21Tell me—those of you who want to
be under the Law—don't you listen to the
Law? 22It's written that Abraham had two
sons, one by the slave woman and one by
the free woman. 23The son by the slave
woman was conceived the normal way, but
the son by the free woman was conceived
through a promise. 24These things are an
allegory: the women are two covenants.
One is from Mount Sinai, which gives birth
to slave children; this is Hagar. 25Hagar is
Mount Sinai in Arabia, and she corresponds
to the present-day Jerusalem, because the
city is in slavery with her children. 26But
the Jerusalem that is above is free, and she
is our mother. 27It's written:

Rejoice, barren woman, you who
have not given birth.
Break out with a shout, you who
have not suffered labor pains;
because the woman who has been deserted
will have many more children
than the woman who has a husband.[g]

28Brothers and sisters, you are children
of the promise like Isaac. 29But just as it
was then, so it is now also: the one who
was conceived the normal way harassed the
one who was conceived by the Spirit. 30But
what does the scripture say? *Throw out the*
slave woman and her son, because the slave
woman's son won't share the inheritance with
the free woman's son.[h] 31Therefore, brothers
and sisters, we aren't the slave woman's
children, but we are the free woman's
children. 5 1Christ has set us free for freedom. Therefore, stand firm and don't
submit to the bondage of slavery again.

Arguments against being circumcised

2Look, I, Paul, am telling you that if you
have yourselves circumcised, having Christ
won't help you. 3Again I swear to every man
who has himself circumcised that he is required to do the whole Law. 4You people
who are trying to be made righteous by the
Law have been estranged from Christ. You
have fallen away from grace! 5We eagerly
wait for the hope of righteousness through
the Spirit by faith. 6Being circumcised or
not being circumcised doesn't matter in
Christ Jesus, but faith working through
love does matter.

7You were running well—who stopped
you from obeying the truth? 8This line of
reasoning doesn't come from the one who
calls you. 9A little yeast works through the
whole lump of dough. 10I'm convinced about
you in the Lord that you won't think any
other way. But the one who is confusing you
will pay the penalty, whoever that may be.
11Brothers and sisters, if I'm still preaching
circumcision, why am I still being harassed?
In that case, the offense of the cross would
be canceled. 12I wish that the ones who are
upsetting you would castrate themselves!

13You were called to freedom, brothers
and sisters; only don't let this freedom be an
opportunity to indulge your selfish impulses,
but serve each other through love. 14All the
Law has been fulfilled in a single statement:
Love your neighbor as yourself.[i] 15But if you
bite and devour each other, be careful that
you don't get eaten up by each other!

[g]Isa 54:1 [h]Gen 21:10 [i]Lev 19:18

Two different ways of living

16I say be guided by the Spirit and you
won't carry out your selfish desires. 17A
person's selfish desires are set against the
Spirit, and the Spirit is set against one's
selfish desires. They are opposed to each
other, so you shouldn't do whatever you
want to do. 18But if you are being led by the
Spirit, you aren't under the Law. 19The actions that are produced by selfish motives
are obvious, since they include sexual immorality, moral corruption, doing whatever
feels good, 20idolatry, drug use and casting spells, hate, fighting, obsession, losing
your temper, competitive opposition, conflict, selfishness, group rivalry, 21jealousy,
drunkenness, partying, and other things
like that. I warn you as I have already
warned you, that those who do these kinds
of things won't inherit God's kingdom.

22But the fruit of the Spirit is love, joy,
peace, patience, kindness, goodness, faithfulness, 23gentleness, and self-control. There
is no law against things like this. 24Those
who belong to Christ Jesus have crucified
self with its passions and its desires.

25If we live by the Spirit, let's follow the
Spirit. 26Let's not become arrogant, make
each other angry, or be jealous of each other.

Caring and sharing

6 Brothers and sisters, if a person is
caught doing something wrong, you
who are spiritual should restore someone
like this with a spirit of gentleness. Watch
out for yourselves so you won't be tempted
too. 2Carry each other's burdens and so
you will fulfill the law of Christ. 3If anyone thinks they are important when they
aren't, they're fooling themselves. 4Each
person should test their own work and be
happy with doing a good job and not compare themselves with others. 5Each person
will have to carry their own load.

6Those who are taught the word should
share all good things with their teacher.
7Make no mistake, God is not mocked. A
person will harvest what they plant. 8Those
who plant only for their own benefit will
harvest devastation from their selfishness,
but those who plant for the benefit of the
Spirit will harvest eternal life from the
Spirit. 9Let's not get tired of doing good,
because in time we'll have a harvest if we
don't give up. 10So then, let's work for the
good of all whenever we have an opportunity, and especially for those in the household of faith.

Final greeting

11Look at the large letters I'm making
with my own handwriting! 12Whoever
wants to look good by human standards
will try to get you to be circumcised, but
only so they won't be harassed for the cross
of Christ. 13Those who are circumcised
don't observe the Law themselves, but they
want you to be circumcised, so they can
boast about your physical body.[j]

14But as for me, God forbid that I should
boast about anything except for the cross of
our Lord Jesus Christ. The world has been
crucified to me through him, and I have
been crucified to the world. 15Being circumcised or not being circumcised doesn't
mean anything. What matters is a new creation. 16May peace and mercy be on whoever follows this rule and on God's Israel.

17From now on, no one should bother
me because I bear the marks of Jesus on my
body.

18Brothers and sisters, may the grace of
our Lord Jesus Christ be with your spirit.
Amen.

[j] In Gk the word traditionally rendered as *flesh* is rendered here as *physical body*, but it has a wide range of meaning. Gal 5:13-25; 6:8, 12 contain nine close occurrences of the same word in Gk, but it is rendered as *selfish* in regard to impulses, desires, motives, or benefit, and *human standards* in 6:12.

EPHESIANS

Greeting

1 From Paul, an apostle of Christ Jesus by God's will.

To the holy and faithful people in Christ Jesus in Ephesus.[a]

2 Grace and peace to you from God our Father and our Lord Jesus Christ.

The believers' blessings

3 Bless the God and Father of our Lord Jesus Christ! He has blessed us in Christ with every spiritual blessing that comes from heaven. 4 God chose us in Christ to be holy and blameless in God's presence before the creation of the world. 5 God destined us to be his adopted children through Jesus Christ because of his love. This was according to his goodwill and plan 6 and to honor his glorious grace that he has given to us freely through the Son whom he loves. 7 We have been ransomed through his Son's blood, and we have forgiveness for our failures based on his overflowing grace, 8 which he poured over us with wisdom and understanding. 9 God revealed his hidden design[b] to us, which is according to his goodwill and the plan that he intended to accomplish through his Son. 10 This is what God planned for the climax of all times:[c] to bring all things together in Christ, the things in heaven along with the things on earth. 11 We have also received an inheritance in Christ. We were destined by the plan of God, who accomplishes everything according to his design. 12 We are called to be an honor to God's glory because we were the first to hope in Christ. 13 You too heard the word of truth in Christ, which is the good news of your salvation. You were sealed with the promised Holy Spirit because you believed in Christ. 14 The Holy Spirit is the down payment on our inheritance, which is applied toward our redemption as God's own people, resulting in the honor of God's glory.

Paul's prayer for the Ephesians

15 Since I heard about your faith in the Lord Jesus and your love for all God's people, this is the reason that 16 I don't stop giving thanks to God for you when I remember you in my prayers. 17 I pray that the God of our Lord Jesus Christ, the Father of glory, will give you a spirit of wisdom and revelation that makes God known to you. 18 I pray that the eyes of your heart will have enough light to see what is the hope of God's call, what is the richness of God's glorious inheritance among believers, 19 and what is the overwhelming greatness of God's power that is working among us believers. This power is conferred by the energy of God's powerful strength. 20 God's power was at work in Christ when God raised him from the dead and sat him at God's right side in the heavens, 21 far above every ruler and authority and power and angelic power, any power that might be named not only now but in the future. 22 God put everything under Christ's feet and made him head of everything in the church, 23 which is his body. His body, the church, is the fullness of Christ, who fills everything in every way.

Saved from sin to life

2 At one time you were like a dead person because of the things you did wrong and your offenses against God. 2 You used to live like people of this world. You followed the rule of a destructive spiritual power. This is the spirit of disobedience to God's will that is now at work in persons whose lives are characterized by disobedience. 3 At one time you were like those persons. All of you used to do whatever felt good and whatever you thought you wanted so that you were children headed for punishment just like everyone else.

4-5 However, God is rich in mercy. He brought us to life with Christ while we were dead as a result of those things that we did

[a]The location of Ephesus was added in some later manuscripts, probably to make the opening of this letter similar to the others in the collection of Paul's letters. [b]Or *mystery* [c]Or *the fullness of times*

wrong. He did this because of the great love that he has for us. You are saved by God's grace! 6And God raised us up and seated us in the heavens with Christ Jesus. 7God did this to show future generations the greatness of his grace by the goodness that God has shown us in Christ Jesus.

8You are saved by God's grace because of your faith.[d] This salvation is God's gift. It's not something you possessed. 9It's not something you did that you can be proud of. 10Instead, we are God's accomplishment, created in Christ Jesus to do good things. God planned for these good things to be the way that we live our lives.

The reconciliation of God's people

11So remember that once you were Gentiles by physical descent, who were called "uncircumcised" by Jews who are physically circumcised. 12At that time you were without Christ. You were aliens rather than citizens of Israel, and strangers to the covenants of God's promise. In this world you had no hope and no God. 13But now, thanks to Christ Jesus, you who once were so far away have been brought near by the blood of Christ.

14Christ is our peace. He made both Jews and Gentiles into one group. With his body, he broke down the barrier of hatred that divided us. 15He canceled the detailed rules of the Law so that he could create one new person out of the two groups, making peace. 16He reconciled them both as one body to God by the cross, which ended the hostility to God.

17When he came, he announced the good news of peace to you who were far away from God and to those who were near. 18We both have access to the Father through Christ by the one Spirit. 19So now you are no longer strangers and aliens. Rather, you are fellow citizens with God's people, and you belong to God's household. 20As God's household, you are built on the foundation of the apostles and prophets with Christ Jesus himself as the cornerstone. 21The whole building is joined together in him, and it grows up into a temple that is dedicated to the Lord. 22Christ is building you into a place where God lives through the Spirit.

Paul, apostle to the Gentiles

3 This is why I, Paul, am a prisoner of Christ for you Gentiles.

2You've heard, of course, about the responsibility to distribute God's grace, which God gave to me for you, right? 3God showed me his secret plan[e] in a revelation, as I mentioned briefly before (4when you read this, you'll understand my insight into the secret plan[f] about Christ). 5Earlier generations didn't know this hidden plan that God has now revealed to his holy apostles and prophets through the Spirit. 6This plan is that the Gentiles would be coheirs and parts of the same body, and that they would share with the Jews in the promises of God in Christ Jesus through the gospel. 7I became a servant of the gospel because of the grace that God showed me through the exercise of his power.

8God gave his grace to me, the least of all God's people, to preach the good news about the immeasurable riches of Christ to the Gentiles. 9God sent me to reveal the secret plan[g] that had been hidden since the beginning of time by God, who created everything. 10God's purpose is now to show the rulers and powers in the heavens the many different varieties of his wisdom through the church. 11This was consistent with the plan he had from the beginning of time that he accomplished through Christ Jesus our Lord. 12In Christ we have bold and confident access to God through faith in him.[h] 13So then, I ask you not to become discouraged by what I'm suffering for you, which is your glory.

Paul's prayer for the Ephesians

14This is why I kneel before the Father. 15Every ethnic group in heaven or on earth is recognized by him. 16I ask that he will strengthen you in your inner selves from the riches of his glory through the Spirit. 17I ask that Christ will live in your hearts through

[d]Or *through his faithfulness* [e]Or *mystery* [f]Or *mystery* [g]Or *mystery* [h]Or *through his faithfulness*

faith. As a result of having strong roots in love, 18I ask that you'll have the power to grasp love's width and length, height and depth, together with all believers. 19I ask that you'll know the love of Christ that is beyond knowledge so that you will be filled entirely with the fullness of God.

20Glory to God, who is able to do far beyond all that we could ask or imagine by his power at work within us; 21glory to him in the church and in Christ Jesus for all generations, forever and always. Amen.

Unity of the body of Christ

4 Therefore, as a prisoner for the Lord, I encourage you to live as people worthy of the call you received from God. 2Conduct yourselves with all humility, gentleness, and patience. Accept each other with love, 3and make an effort to preserve the unity of the Spirit with the peace that ties you together. 4You are one body and one spirit, just as God also called you in one hope. 5There is one Lord, one faith, one baptism, 6and one God and Father of all, who is over all, through all, and in all.

7God has given his grace to each one of us measured out by the gift that is given by Christ. 8That's why scripture says, *When he climbed up to the heights, he captured prisoners, and he gave gifts to people.*[i]

9What does the phrase "he climbed up" mean if it doesn't mean that he had first gone down into the lower regions, the earth? 10The one who went down is the same one who climbed up above all the heavens so that he might fill everything.

11He gave some apostles, some prophets, some evangelists, and some pastors and teachers. 12His purpose was to equip God's people for the work of serving and building up the body of Christ 13until we all reach the unity of faith and knowledge of God's Son. God's goal is for us to become mature adults—to be fully grown, measured by the standard of the fullness of Christ. 14As a result, we aren't supposed to be infants any longer who can be tossed and blown around by every wind that comes from teaching with deceitful scheming and the tricks people play to deliberately mislead others. 15Instead, by speaking the truth with love, let's grow in every way into Christ, 16who is the head. The whole body grows from him, as it is joined and held together by all the supporting ligaments. The body makes itself grow in that it builds itself up with love as each one does its part.

The old and new life

17So I'm telling you this, and I insist on it in the Lord: you shouldn't live your life like the Gentiles anymore. They base their lives on pointless thinking, 18and they are in the dark in their reasoning. They are disconnected from God's life because of their ignorance and their closed hearts. 19They are people who lack all sense of right and wrong, and who have turned themselves over to doing whatever feels good and to practicing every sort of corruption along with greed.

20But you didn't learn that sort of thing from Christ. 21Since you really listened to him and you were taught how the truth is in Jesus, 22change the former way of life that was part of the person you once were, corrupted by deceitful desires. 23Instead, renew the thinking in your mind by the Spirit 24and clothe yourself with the new person created according to God's image in justice and true holiness.

25Therefore, after you have gotten rid of lying, *Each of you must tell the truth to your neighbor*[j] because we are parts of each other in the same body. 26*Be angry without sinning.*[k] Don't let the sun set on your anger. 27Don't provide an opportunity for the devil. 28Thieves should no longer steal. Instead, they should go to work, using their hands to do good so that they will have something to share with whoever is in need.

29Don't let any foul words come out of your mouth. Only say what is helpful when it is needed for building up the community so that it benefits those who hear what you say. 30Don't make the Holy Spirit of God

[i]Ps 68:18 [j]Zech 8:16 [k]Ps 4:4

unhappy—you were sealed by him for the day of redemption. [31]Put aside all bitterness, losing your temper, anger, shouting, and slander, along with every other evil. [32]Be kind, compassionate, and forgiving to each other, in the same way God forgave you in Christ.

5 Therefore, imitate God like dearly loved children. [2]Live your life with love, following the example of Christ, who loved us and gave himself for us. He was a sacrificial offering that smelled sweet to God.

[3]Sexual immorality, and any kind of impurity or greed, shouldn't even be mentioned among you, which is right for holy persons. [4]Obscene language, silly talk, or vulgar jokes aren't acceptable for believers. Instead, there should be thanksgiving. [5]Because you know for sure that persons who are sexually immoral, impure, or greedy—which happens when things become gods—those persons won't inherit the kingdom of Christ and God.

Be children of light

[6]Nobody should deceive you with stupid ideas. God's anger comes down on those who are disobedient because of this kind of thing. [7]So you shouldn't have anything to do with them. [8]You were once darkness, but now you are light in the Lord, so live your life as children of light. [9]Light produces fruit that consists of every sort of goodness, justice, and truth. [10]Therefore, test everything to see what's pleasing to the Lord, [11]and don't participate in the unfruitful actions of darkness. Instead, you should reveal the truth about them. [12]It's embarrassing to even talk about what certain persons do in secret. [13]But everything exposed to the light is revealed by the light. [14]Everything that is revealed by the light is light. Therefore, it says, *Wake up, sleeper!*[l] *Get up from the dead,*[m] *and Christ will shine on you.*[n]

Be filled with the Spirit

[15]So be careful to live your life wisely, not foolishly. [16]Take advantage of every opportunity because these are evil times. [17]Because of this, don't be ignorant, but understand the Lord's will. [18]Don't get drunk on wine, which produces depravity. Instead, be filled with the Spirit in the following ways: [19]speak to each other with psalms, hymns, and spiritual songs; sing and make music to the Lord in your hearts; [20]always give thanks to God the Father for everything in the name of our Lord Jesus Christ; [21]and submit to each other out of respect for Christ. [22]For example, wives should submit to their husbands as if to the Lord. [23]A husband is the head of his wife like Christ is head of the church, that is, the savior of the body. [24]So wives submit to their husbands in everything like the church submits to Christ. [25]As for husbands, love your wives just like Christ loved the church and gave himself for her. [26]He did this to make her holy by washing her in a bath of water with the word. [27]He did this to present himself with a splendid church, one without any sort of stain or wrinkle on her clothes, but rather one that is holy and blameless. [28]That's how husbands ought to love their wives—in the same way as they do their own bodies. Anyone who loves his wife loves himself. [29]No one ever hates his own body, but feeds it and takes care of it just like Christ does for the church [30]because we are parts of his body. [31]*This is why a man will leave his father and mother and be united with his wife, and the two of them will be one body.*[o] [32]Marriage is a significant allegory,[p] and I'm applying it to Christ and the church. [33]In any case, as for you individually, each one of you should love his wife as himself, and wives should respect[q] their husbands.

6 As for children, obey your parents in the Lord, because it is right. [2]The commandment *Honor your father and mother* is the first one with a promise attached: [3]*so that things will go well for you, and you will live for a long time in the land.*[r] [4]As for parents, don't provoke your children to anger, but raise them with discipline and instruction about the Lord.

[5]As for slaves, obey your human masters with fear and trembling and with sincere

[l]Isa 26:19; 51:17; 52:1; 60:1 [m]Isa 26:19 [n]Isa 60:1 [o]Gen 2:24 [p]Or *mystery* [q]Or *fear* [r]Exod 20:12; Deut 5:16

devotion to Christ. 6Don't work to make yourself look good and try to flatter people, but act like slaves of Christ carrying out God's will from the heart. 7Serve your owners enthusiastically, as though you were serving the Lord and not human beings. 8You know that the Lord will reward every person who does what is right, whether that person is a slave or a free person. 9As for masters, treat your slaves in the same way. Stop threatening them, because you know that both you and your slaves have a master in heaven. He doesn't distinguish between people on the basis of status.

Put on the armor of God

10Finally, be strengthened by the Lord and his powerful strength. 11Put on God's armor so that you can make a stand against the tricks of the devil. 12We aren't fighting against human enemies but against rulers, authorities, forces of cosmic darkness, and spiritual powers of evil in the heavens. 13Therefore, pick up the full armor of God so that you can stand your ground on the evil day and after you have done everything possible to still stand. 14So stand with the belt of truth around your waist, justice as your breastplate, 15and put shoes on your feet so that you are ready to spread the good news of peace. 16Above all, carry the shield of faith so that you can extinguish the flaming arrows of the evil one. 17Take the helmet of salvation and the sword of the Spirit, which is God's word.

18Offer prayers and petitions in the Spirit all the time. Stay alert by hanging in there and praying for all believers. 19As for me, pray that when I open my mouth, I'll get a message that confidently makes this secret plan[s] of the gospel known. 20I'm an ambassador in chains for the sake of the gospel. Pray so that the Lord will give me the confidence to say what I have to say.

Final greeting

21Tychicus, my loved brother and faithful servant of the Lord, can inform you about my situation and what I'm doing. 22I've sent him for this reason—so that you will know about us. He can reassure you.

23May there be peace with the brothers and sisters as well as love with the faith that comes from God the Father and the Lord Jesus Christ. 24May grace be with all those who love our Lord Jesus Christ forever.

PHILIPPIANS

Greeting

1 From Paul and Timothy, slaves of Christ Jesus.

To all those in Philippi who are God's people in Christ Jesus, along with your supervisors[a] and servants.[b]

2May the grace and peace from God our Father and the Lord Jesus Christ be with you.

Thanksgiving and prayer

3I thank my God every time I mention you in my prayers. 4I'm thankful for all of you every time I pray, and it's always a prayer full of joy. 5I'm glad because of the way you have been my partners in the ministry of the gospel from the time you first believed it until now. 6I'm sure about this: the one who started a good work in you will stay with you to complete the job by the day of Christ Jesus. 7I have good reason to think this way about all of you because I keep you in my heart. You are all my partners in God's grace, both during my time in prison and in the defense and support of the gospel. 8God is my witness that I feel affection for all of you with the compassion of Christ Jesus.

9This is my prayer: that your love might become even more and more rich with knowledge and all kinds of insight. 10I pray this so that you will be able to decide what really matters and so you will be sincere and blameless on the day of Christ. 11I pray that

[s]Or *mystery* [a]Or *overseers, bishops* [b]Or *deacons*

you will then be filled with the fruit of righteousness, which comes from Jesus Christ,
in order to give glory and praise to God.

Priority of the gospel

12 Brothers and sisters, I want you to
know that the things that have happened
to me have actually advanced the gospel.
13 The whole Praetorian Guard and everyone else knows that I'm in prison for
Christ. 14 Most of the brothers and sisters
have had more confidence through the
Lord to speak the word boldly and bravely
because of my jail time. 15 Some certainly
preach Christ with jealous and competitive
motives, but others preach with good motives. 16 They are motivated by love, because they know that I'm put here to give
a defense of the gospel; 17 the others preach
Christ because of their selfish ambition.
They are insincere, hoping to cause me
more pain while I'm in prison.
18 What do I think about this? Just this:
since Christ is proclaimed in every possible
way, whether from dishonest or true motives, I'm glad and I'll continue to be glad.
19 I'm glad because I know that this will result in my release through your prayers and
the help of the Spirit of Jesus Christ. 20 It
is my expectation and hope that I won't be
put to shame in anything. Rather, I hope
with daring courage that Christ's greatness will be seen in my body, now as always,
whether I live or die. 21 Because for me, living serves Christ and dying is even better.
22 If I continue to live in this world, I get
results from my work. 23 But I don't know
what I prefer. I'm torn between the two because I want to leave this life and be with
Christ, which is far better. 24 However, it's
more important for me to stay in this world
for your sake. 25 I'm sure of this: I will stay
alive and remain with all of you to help your
progress and the joy of your faith, 26 and to
increase your pride in Christ Jesus through
my presence when I visit you again.

Live worthy of the gospel

27 Most important, live together in a
manner worthy of Christ's gospel. Do this,
whether I come and see you or I'm absent
and hear about you. Do this so that you
stand firm, united in one spirit and mind as
you struggle together to remain faithful to
the gospel. 28 That way, you won't be afraid
of anything your enemies do. Your faithfulness and courage are a sign of their coming
destruction and your salvation, which is
from God. 29 God has generously granted
you the privilege, not only of believing in
Christ but also of suffering for Christ's
sake. 30 You are having the same struggle
that you saw me face and now hear that I'm
still facing.

Imitate Christ

2 Therefore, if there is any encouragement
in Christ, any comfort in love, any sharing in the Spirit, any sympathy, 2 complete
my joy by thinking the same way, having
the same love, being united, and agreeing
with each other. 3 Don't do anything for
selfish purposes, but with humility think of
others as better than yourselves. 4 Instead
of each person watching out for their own
good, watch out for what is better for others.
5 Adopt the attitude that was in Christ Jesus:

6 Though he was in the form of God,
he did not consider being equal
with God something to exploit.
7 But he emptied himself
by taking the form of a slave
and by becoming like human beings.
When he found himself
in the form of a human,
8 he humbled himself by becoming
obedient to the point of death,
even death on a cross.
9 Therefore, God highly honored him
and gave him a name above all names,
10 so that at the name of Jesus everyone
in heaven, on earth,
and under the earth might bow
11 and every tongue confess
that Jesus Christ is Lord,
to the glory of God the Father.

Carry out your salvation

12 Therefore, my loved ones, just as you
always obey me, not just when I am present
but now even more while I am away, carry
out your own salvation with fear and trembling. 13 God is the one who enables you

both to want and to actually live out his good purposes. 14 Do everything without grumbling and arguing 15 so that you may be blameless and pure, innocent children of God surrounded by people who are crooked and corrupt. Among these people you shine like stars in the world 16 because you hold on to the word of life. This will allow me to say on the day of Christ that I haven't run for nothing or worked for nothing. 17 But even if I am poured out like a drink offering upon the altar of service for your faith, I am glad. I'm glad with all of you. 18 You should be glad about this in the same way. Be glad with me!

Sending Timothy and Epaphroditus

19 I hope in the Lord Jesus to send Timothy to see you soon so that I may be encouraged by hearing about you. 20 I have no one like him. He is a person who genuinely cares about your well-being. 21 All the others put their own business ahead of Jesus Christ's business. 22 You know his character, how he labors with me for the gospel like a son works with his father. 23 So he is the one that I hope to send as soon as I find out how things turn out here for me. 24 I trust in the Lord that I also will visit you soon.

25 I think it is also necessary to send Epaphroditus to you. He is my brother, co-worker, and fellow soldier; and he is your representative who serves my needs. 26 He misses you all, and he was upset because you heard he was sick. 27 In fact, he was so sick that he nearly died. But God had mercy on him—and not just on him but also on me, because his death would have caused me great sorrow. 28 Therefore, I am sending him immediately so that when you see him again you can be glad and I won't worry. 29 So welcome him in the Lord with great joy and show great respect for people like him. 30 He risked his life and almost died for the work of Christ, and he did this to make up for the help you couldn't give me.

Values and priorities

3 So then, my brothers and sisters, be glad in the Lord. It's no trouble for me to repeat the same things to you because they will help keep you on track. 2 Watch out for the "dogs." Watch out for people who do evil things. Watch out for those who insist on circumcision, which is really mutilation. 3 We are the circumcision. We are the ones who serve by God's Spirit and who boast in Christ Jesus. We don't put our confidence in rituals performed on the body, 4 though I have good reason to have this kind of confidence. If anyone else has reason to put their confidence in physical advantages, I have even more:

5 I was circumcised on the eighth day.
I am from the people of Israel and the tribe of Benjamin.
I am a Hebrew of the Hebrews.
With respect to observing the Law, I'm a Pharisee.
6 With respect to devotion to the faith, I harassed the church.
With respect to righteousness under the Law, I'm blameless.

7 These things were my assets, but I wrote them off as a loss for the sake of Christ. 8 But even beyond that, I consider everything a loss in comparison with the superior value of knowing Christ Jesus my Lord. I have lost everything for him, but what I lost I think of as sewer trash, so that I might gain Christ 9 and be found in him. In Christ I have a righteousness that is not my own and that does not come from the Law but rather from the faithfulness of Christ. It is the righteousness of God that is based on faith. 10 The righteousness that I have comes from knowing Christ, the power of his resurrection, and the participation in his sufferings. It includes being conformed to his death 11 so that I may perhaps reach the goal of the resurrection of the dead.

12 It's not that I have already reached this goal or have already been perfected, but I pursue it, so that I may grab hold of it because Christ grabbed hold of me for just this purpose. 13 Brothers and sisters, I myself don't think I've reached it, but I do this one thing: I forget about the things behind me and reach out for the things ahead of me. 14 The goal I pursue is the prize of God's upward call in Christ Jesus. 15 So all of us who are spiritually mature should think this way, and if anyone thinks differently,

God will reveal it to him or her. [16]Only let's live in a way that is consistent with whatever level we have reached.

Imitate Paul

[17]Brothers and sisters, become imitators of me and watch those who live this way—you can use us as models. [18]As I have told you many times and now say with deep sadness, many people live as enemies of the cross. [19]Their lives end with destruction. Their god is their stomach, and they take pride in their disgrace because their thoughts focus on earthly things. [20]Our citizenship is in heaven. We look forward to a savior that comes from there—the Lord Jesus Christ. [21]He will transform our humble bodies so that they are like his glorious body, by the power that also makes him able to subject all things to himself.

Stand firm in the Lord

4 Therefore, my brothers and sisters whom I love and miss, who are my joy and crown, stand firm in the Lord.

Loved ones, [2]I urge Euodia and I urge Syntyche to come to an agreement in the Lord. [3]Yes, and I'm also asking you, loyal friend, to help these women who have struggled together with me in the ministry of the gospel, along with Clement and the rest of my coworkers whose names are in the scroll of life.

[4]Be glad in the Lord always! Again I say, be glad! [5]Let your gentleness show in your treatment of all people. The Lord is near. [6]Don't be anxious about anything; rather, bring up all of your requests to God in your prayers and petitions, along with giving thanks. [7]Then the peace of God that exceeds all understanding will keep your hearts and minds safe in Christ Jesus.

[8]From now on, brothers and sisters, if anything is excellent and if anything is admirable, focus your thoughts on these things: all that is true, all that is holy, all that is just, all that is pure, all that is lovely, and all that is worthy of praise. [9]Practice these things: whatever you learned, received, heard, or saw in us. The God of peace will be with you.

Paul's thanks for gifts

[10]I was very glad in the Lord because now at last you have shown concern for me again. (Of course you were always concerned but had no way to show it.) [11]I'm not saying this because I need anything, for I have learned how to be content in any circumstance. [12]I know the experience of being in need and of having more than enough; I have learned the secret to being content in any and every circumstance, whether full or hungry or whether having plenty or being poor. [13]I can endure all these things through the power of the one who gives me strength. [14]Still, you have done well to share my distress.

[15]You Philippians know from the time of my first mission work in Macedonia how no church shared in supporting my ministry except you. [16]You sent contributions repeatedly to take care of my needs even while I was in Thessalonica. [17]I'm not hoping for a gift, but I am hoping for a profit that accumulates in your account. [18]I now have plenty and it is more than enough. I am full to overflowing because I received the gifts that you sent from Epaphroditus. Those gifts give off a fragrant aroma, an acceptable sacrifice that pleases God. [19]My God will meet your every need out of his riches in the glory that is found in Christ Jesus. [20]Let glory be given to God our Father forever and always. Amen.

Final greeting

[21]Greet all God's people in Christ Jesus. The brothers and sisters with me send you their greeting. [22]All God's people here, especially those in Caesar's household, send you their greeting. [23]The grace of the Lord Jesus Christ be with your spirits.

COLOSSIANS

Greeting

1 From Paul, an apostle of Christ
Jesus by God's will, and Timothy our
brother.

[2] To the holy and faithful brothers and
sisters in Christ in Colossae.

Grace and peace to you from God our
Father.

Thanksgiving and prayer for the Colossians

[3] We always give thanks to God, the Father of our Lord Jesus Christ, when we pray
for you. [4] We've done this since we heard of
your faith in Christ Jesus and your love for
all God's people. [5] You have this faith and
love because of the hope reserved for you
in heaven. You previously heard about this
hope through the true message, the good
news, [6] which has come to you. This message has been bearing fruit and growing
among you since the day you heard and
truly understood God's grace, in the same
way that it is bearing fruit and growing in
the whole world. [7] You learned it from Epaphras, who is the fellow slave we love and
Christ's faithful minister for your sake. [8] He
informed us of your love in the Spirit.

[9] Because of this, since the day we heard
about you, we haven't stopped praying for
you and asking for you to be filled with the
knowledge of God's will, with all wisdom
and spiritual understanding. [10] We're praying this so that you can live lives that are
worthy of the Lord and pleasing to him in
every way: by producing fruit in every good
work and growing in the knowledge of God;
[11] by being strengthened through his glorious might so that you endure everything
and have patience; [12] and by giving thanks
with joy to the Father. He made it so you
could take part in the inheritance, in light
granted to God's holy people. [13] He rescued
us from the control of darkness and transferred us into the kingdom of the Son he
loves. [14] He set us free through the Son and
forgave our sins.

Hymn about Christ's work

[15] The Son is the image
of the invisible God,
the one who is first over all creation,[a]

[16] Because all things were created by him:
both in the heavens and on the earth,
the things that are visible
and the things that are invisible.
Whether they are thrones or powers,
or rulers or authorities,
all things were created
through him and for him.

[17] He existed before all things,
and all things are held together
in him.

[18] He is the head of the body, the church,
who is the beginning,
the one who is firstborn
from among the dead[b]
so that he might occupy
the first place in everything.

[19] Because all the fullness of God
was pleased to live in him,
[20] and he reconciled all things to himself
through him—
whether things on earth
or in the heavens.
He brought peace
through the blood of his cross.

[21] Once you were alienated from God and
you were enemies with him in your minds,
which was shown by your evil actions. [22] But
now he has reconciled you by his physical
body through death, to present you before
God as a people who are holy, faultless, and
without blame. [23] But you need to remain
well established and rooted in faith and not
shift away from the hope given in the good
news that you heard. This message has been
preached throughout all creation under
heaven. And I, Paul, became a servant of
this good news.

[a] Or *firstborn of all creation* [b] Or *first over the dead*

Paul's service for the church

24Now I'm happy to be suffering for you. I'm completing what is missing from Christ's sufferings with my own body. I'm doing this for the sake of his body, which is the church. 25I became a servant of the church by God's commission, which was given to me for you, in order to complete God's word. 26I'm completing it with a secret plan[c] that has been hidden for ages and generations but which has now been revealed to his holy people. 27God wanted to make the glorious riches of this secret plan[d] known among the Gentiles, which is Christ living in you, the hope of glory. 28This is what we preach as we warn and teach every person with all wisdom so that we might present each one mature in Christ. 29I work hard and struggle for this goal with his energy, which works in me powerfully.

2 I want you to know how much I struggle for you, for those in Laodicea, and for all who haven't known me personally. 2My goal is that their hearts would be encouraged and united together in love so that they might have all the riches of assurance that come with understanding, so that they might have the knowledge of the secret plan[e] of God, namely Christ. 3All the treasures of wisdom and knowledge are hidden in him. 4I'm telling you this so that no one deceives you with convincing arguments, 5because even though I am absent physically, I'm with you in spirit. I'm happy to see the discipline and stability of your faith in Christ.

Error threatening the church

6So live in Christ Jesus the Lord in the same way as you received him. 7Be rooted and built up in him, be established in faith, and overflow with thanksgiving just as you were taught. 8See to it that nobody enslaves you with philosophy and foolish deception, which conform to human traditions and the way the world thinks and acts rather than Christ. 9All the fullness of deity lives in Christ's body. 10And you have been filled by him, who is the head of every ruler and authority. 11You were also circumcised by him. This wasn't performed by human hands—the whole body was removed through this circumcision by Christ. 12You were buried with him through baptism and raised with him through faith in the power of God, who raised him from the dead. 13When you were dead because of the things you had done wrong and because your body wasn't circumcised, God made you alive with Christ and forgave all the things you had done wrong. 14He destroyed the record of the debt we owed, with its requirements that worked against us. He canceled it by nailing it to the cross. 15When he disarmed the rulers and authorities, he exposed them to public disgrace by leading them in a triumphal parade.

16So don't let anyone judge you about eating or drinking or about a festival, a new moon observance, or sabbaths. 17These religious practices are only a shadow of what was coming—the body that cast the shadow is Christ. 18Don't let anyone who wants to practice harsh self-denial and worship angels rob you of the prize. They go into detail about what they have seen in visions and have become unjustifiably arrogant by their selfish way of thinking. 19They don't stay connected to the head. The head nourishes and supports the whole body through the joints and ligaments, so the body grows with a growth that is from God.

20If you died with Christ to the way the world thinks and acts, why do you submit to rules and regulations as though you were living in the world? 21"Don't handle!" "Don't taste!" "Don't touch!" 22All these things cease to exist when they are used. Such rules are human commandments and teachings. 23They look like they are wise with this self-made religion and their self-denial by the harsh treatment of the body, but they are no help against indulging in selfish immoral behavior.

Your life hidden in Christ

3 Therefore, if you were raised with Christ, look for the things that are above where Christ is sitting at God's right side. 2Think about the things above and not

[c]Or *mystery* [d]Or *mystery* [e]Or *mystery*

things on earth. 3You died, and your life is hidden with Christ in God. 4When Christ, who is your life, is revealed, then you also will be revealed with him in glory.

5So put to death the parts of your life that belong to the earth, such as sexual immorality, moral corruption, lust, evil desire, and greed (which is idolatry). 6The wrath of God is coming upon disobedient people because of these things. 7You used to live this way, when you were alive to these things. 8But now set aside these things, such as anger, rage, malice, slander, and obscene language. 9Don't lie to each other. Take off the old human nature with its practices 10and put on the new nature, which is renewed in knowledge by conforming to the image of the one who created it. 11In this image there is neither Greek nor Jew, circumcised nor uncircumcised, barbarian, Scythian, slave nor free, but Christ is all things and in all people.

12Therefore, as God's choice, holy and loved, put on compassion, kindness, humility, gentleness, and patience. 13Be tolerant with each other and, if someone has a complaint against anyone, forgive each other. As the Lord forgave you, so also forgive each other. 14And over all these things put on love, which is the perfect bond of unity. 15The peace of Christ must control your hearts—a peace into which you were called in one body. And be thankful people. 16The word of Christ must live in you richly. Teach and warn each other with all wisdom by singing psalms, hymns, and spiritual songs. Sing to God with gratitude in your hearts. 17Whatever you do, whether in speech or action, do it all in the name of the Lord Jesus and give thanks to God the Father through him.

18Wives, submit to your husbands in a way that is appropriate in the Lord. 19Husbands, love your wives and don't be harsh with them. 20Children, obey your parents in everything, because this pleases the Lord. 21Parents, don't provoke your children in a way that ends up discouraging them.

22Slaves, obey your masters on earth in everything. Don't just obey like people pleasers when they are watching. Instead, obey with the single motivation of fearing the Lord. 23Whatever you do, do it from the heart for the Lord and not for people. 24You know that you will receive an inheritance as a reward. You serve the Lord Christ. 25But evildoers will receive their reward for their evil actions. There is no discrimination.

4 Masters, be just and fair to your slaves, knowing that you yourselves have a master in heaven.

2Keep on praying and guard your prayers with thanksgiving. 3At the same time, pray for us also. Pray that God would open a door for the word so we can preach the secret plan[f] of Christ—which is why I'm in chains. 4Pray that I might be able to make it as clear as I ought to when I preach. 5Act wisely toward outsiders, making the most of the opportunity. 6Your speech should always be gracious and sprinkled with insight so that you may know how to respond to every person.

Final greeting

7Tychicus, our dearly loved brother, faithful minister, and fellow slave in the Lord, will inform you about everything that has happened to me. 8This is why I sent him to you, so that you'll know all about us and so he can encourage your hearts. 9I sent him with Onesimus, our faithful and dearly loved brother, who is one of you. They will let you know about everything here.

10Aristarchus, my fellow prisoner, says hello to you. So does Mark, Barnabas' cousin (you received instructions about him; if he comes to you, welcome him). 11Jesus, called Justus, also says hello. These are my only fellow workers for God's kingdom who are Jewish converts. They have been an encouragement to me. 12Epaphras, who is one of you, says hello. He's a slave of Christ Jesus who always wrestles for you in prayers so that you will stand firm and be fully mature and complete in the entire will of God. 13I can vouch for him that he has worked hard for you and for those in Laodicea and Hierapolis. 14Luke, the dearly loved physician, and Demas say hello.

Or *mystery*

15Say hello to the brothers and sisters
in Laodicea, along with Nympha and the
church that meets in her house. 16After this
letter has been read to you publicly, make
sure that the church in Laodicea reads it
and that you read the one from Laodicea.
17And tell Archippus, "See to it that you
complete the ministry that you received in
the Lord."

18I, Paul, am writing this greeting personally. Remember that I'm in prison.
Grace be with you.

1 THESSALONIANS

Greeting

1 From Paul, Silvanus, and Timothy.
To the Thessalonians' church that is
in God the Father and the Lord Jesus
Christ.

Grace and peace to all of you.

Thanksgiving to God

2We always thank God for all of you
when we mention you constantly in our
prayers. 3This is because we remember your
work that comes from faith,[a] your effort
that comes from love, and your persever-
ance that comes from hope in our Lord
Jesus Christ in the presence of our God and
Father. 4Brothers and sisters, you are loved
by God, and we know that he has chosen
you. 5We know this because our good news
didn't come to you just in speech but also
with power and the Holy Spirit and with
deep conviction. You know as well as we do
what kind of people we were when we were
with you, which was for your sake. 6You became imitators of us and of the Lord when
you accepted the message that came from
the Holy Spirit with joy in spite of great
suffering. 7As a result you became an example to all the believers in Macedonia and
Achaia. 8The message about the Lord rang
out from you, not only in Macedonia and
Achaia but in every place. The news about
your faithfulness to God has spread so that
we don't even need to mention it. 9People
tell us about what sort of welcome we had
from you and how you turned to God from
idols. As a result, you are serving[b] the living
and true God, 10and you are waiting for his
Son from heaven. His Son is Jesus, who is
the one he raised from the dead and who is
the one who will rescue us from the coming
wrath.

Paul's ministry in Thessalonica

2 As you yourselves know, brothers and
sisters, our visit with you wasn't a
waste of time. 2On the contrary, we had
the courage through God to speak God's
good news in spite of a lot of opposition,
although we had already suffered and were
publicly insulted, as you know. 3Our appeal isn't based on false information, the
wrong motives, or deception. 4Rather
we have been examined and approved by
God to be trusted with the good news, and
that's exactly how we speak. We aren't trying to please people, but we are trying to
please God, who continues to examine our
hearts. 5As you know, we never used flattery, and God is our witness that we didn't
have greedy motives. 6We didn't ask for
special treatment from people—not from
you or from others—7although we could
have thrown our weight around as Christ's
apostles. Instead, we were gentle with you
like a nursing mother caring for her own
children. 8We were glad to share not only
God's good news with you but also our very
lives because we cared for you so much.
9You remember, brothers and sisters, our
efforts and hard work. We preached God's
good news to you, while we worked night
and day so we wouldn't be a burden on any
of you. 10You and God are witnesses of how
holy, just, and blameless we were toward
you believers. 11Likewise, you know how
we treated each of you like a father treats
his own children. 12We appealed to you, encouraged you, and pleaded with you to live

[a]Or *faithfulness* [b]Or *to become slaves of*

lives worthy of the God who is calling you
into his own kingdom and glory.

How the Thessalonians received God's message

13 We also thank God constantly for this:
when you accepted God's word that you
heard from us, you welcomed it for what it
truly is. Instead of accepting it as a human
message, you accepted it as God's message,
and it continues to work in you who are believers. 14 Brothers and sisters, you became
imitators of the churches of God in Judea,
which are in Christ Jesus. This was because
you also suffered the same things from your
own people as they did from the Jews. 15 They
killed both the Lord Jesus and the prophets
and drove us out. They don't please God, and
they are hostile to the entire human race
16 when they try to stop us from speaking
to the Gentiles so they can be saved. Their
sins are constantly pushing the limit.[c] God's
wrath has caught up with them in the end.

Paul's desire to visit

17 Brothers and sisters, we were separated
from you for a while physically but not in
our hearts. We made every effort in our
desire to see you again face-to-face. 18 We
wanted to come to you—I, Paul, tried over
and over again—and Satan stopped us.
19 What is our hope, joy, or crown that we
can brag about in front of our Lord Jesus
when he comes? Isn't it all of you? 20 You are
our glory and joy!

3 So when we couldn't stand it any longer,
we thought it was a good idea to stay on
in Athens by ourselves, 2 and we sent you
Timothy, who is our brother and God's coworker in the good news about Christ. We
sent him to strengthen and encourage you in
your faithfulness. 3 We didn't want any of you
to be shaken by these problems. You know
very well that we were meant to go through
this. 4 In fact, when we were with you, we
kept on predicting that we were going to face
problems exactly like what happened, as you
know. 5 That's why I sent Timothy to find
out about your faithfulness when I couldn't
stand it anymore. I was worried that the
tempter might have tempted you so that our
work would have been a waste of time.

Paul's prayer for the Thessalonians

6 Now Timothy has returned to us from
you and has given us good news about your
faithfulness and love! He says that you always have good memories about us and that
you want to see us as much as we want to
see you. 7 Because of this, brothers and sisters, we were encouraged in all our distress
and trouble through your faithfulness. 8 For
now we are alive if you are standing your
ground in the Lord. 9 How can we thank God
enough for you, given all the joy we have
because of you before our God? 10 Night and
day, we pray more than ever to see all of you
in person and to complete whatever you still
need for your faith. 11 Now may our God and
Father himself guide us on our way back to
you. 12 May the Lord cause you to increase
and enrich your love for each other and for
everyone in the same way as we also love
you. 13 May the love cause your hearts to be
strengthened, to be blameless in holiness
before our God and Father when our Lord
Jesus comes with all his people. Amen.

Living that pleases God

4 So then, brothers and sisters, we ask
and encourage you in the Lord Jesus
to keep living the way you already are and
even do better in how you live and please
God—just as you learned from us. 2 You
know the instructions we gave you through
the Lord Jesus. 3 God's will is that your lives
are dedicated to him.[d] This means that you
stay away from sexual immorality 4 and
learn how to control your own body in a
pure[e] and respectable way. 5 Don't be controlled by your sexual urges like the Gentiles who don't know God. 6 No one should
mistreat or take advantage of their brother
or sister in this issue. The Lord punishes
people for all these things, as we told you
before and sternly warned you. 7 God didn't
call us to be immoral but to be dedicated
to him.[f] 8 Therefore, whoever rejects these

[c] Or *They constantly fill up the measure of their sin.* [d] Or *holy, sanctified* [e] Or *holy, sanctified* [f] Or *holy, sanctified*

instructions isn't rejecting a human authority. They are rejecting God, who gives his Holy Spirit to you.

9You don't need us to write about loving your brothers and sisters because God has already taught you to love each other. 10In fact, you are doing loving deeds for all the brothers and sisters throughout Macedonia. Now we encourage you, brothers and sisters, to do so even more. 11Aim to live quietly, mind your own business, and earn your own living, just as I told you. 12That way you'll behave appropriately toward outsiders, and you won't be in need.

Believers who have died

13Brothers and sisters, we want you to know about people who have died[g] so that you won't mourn like others who don't have any hope. 14Since we believe that Jesus died and rose, so we also believe that God will bring with him those who have died in Jesus. 15What we are saying is a message from the Lord: we who are alive and still around at the Lord's coming definitely won't go ahead of those who have died. 16This is because the Lord himself will come down from heaven with the signal of a shout by the head angel and a blast on God's trumpet. First, those who are dead in Christ will rise. 17Then, we who are living and still around will be taken up together with them in the clouds to meet with the Lord in the air. That way we will always be with the Lord. 18So encourage each other with these words.

The Lord's coming

5 We don't need to write to you about the timing and dates, brothers and sisters. 2You know very well that the day of the Lord is going to come like a thief in the night. 3When they are saying, "There is peace and security," at that time sudden destruction will attack them, like labor pains start with a pregnant woman, and they definitely won't escape. 4But you aren't in darkness, brothers and sisters, so the day won't catch you by surprise like a thief. 5All of you are children of light and children of the day. We don't belong to night or darkness. 6So then, let's not sleep like the others, but let's stay awake and stay sober. 7People who sleep sleep at night, and people who get drunk get drunk at night. 8Since we belong to the day, let's stay sober, wearing faithfulness and love as a piece of armor that protects our body[h] and the hope of salvation as a helmet. 9God didn't intend for us to suffer his wrath but rather to possess salvation through our Lord Jesus Christ. 10Jesus died for us so that, whether we are awake or asleep, we will live together with him. 11So continue encouraging each other and building each other up, just like you are doing already.

Final instructions and blessing

12Brothers and sisters, we ask you to respect those who are working with you, leading you, and instructing you. 13Think of them highly with love because of their work. Live in peace with each other. 14Brothers and sisters, we urge you to warn those who are disorderly. Comfort the discouraged. Help the weak. Be patient with everyone. 15Make sure no one repays a wrong with a wrong, but always pursue the good for each other and everyone else. 16Rejoice always. 17Pray continually. 18Give thanks in every situation because this is God's will for you in Christ Jesus. 19Don't suppress the Spirit. 20Don't brush off Spirit-inspired messages, 21but examine everything carefully and hang on to what is good. 22Avoid every kind of evil. 23Now, may the God of peace himself cause you to be completely dedicated to him; and may your spirit, soul, and body be kept intact and blameless at our Lord Jesus Christ's coming. 24The one who is calling you is faithful and will do this.

Final greeting

25Brothers and sisters, pray for us. 26Greet all the brothers and sisters with a holy kiss. 27By the Lord's authority, I order all of you to have this letter read aloud to all the brothers and sisters. 28The grace of our Lord Jesus Christ be with all of you.

[g]Or *fallen asleep* [h]Or *breastplate*

2 THESSALONIANS

Greeting

1 From Paul, Silvanus, and Timothy:
To the church of the Thessalonians,
which is in God our Father, and in the
Lord Jesus Christ.
[2]Grace and peace to all of you from God
our Father and the Lord Jesus Christ.

Thanksgiving and encouragement

[3]Brothers and sisters, we must always
thank God for you. This is only right because your faithfulness is growing by leaps
and bounds, and the love that all of you
have for each other is increasing. [4]That's
why we ourselves are bragging about you in
God's churches. We tell about your endurance and faithfulness in all the harassments
and trouble that you have put up with.
[5]This shows that God's judgment is right,
and that you will be considered worthy of
God's kingdom for which you are suffering.
[6]After all, it's right for God to pay back the
ones making trouble for you with trouble
[7]and to pay back you who are having trouble with relief along with us. This payback
will come when the Lord Jesus is revealed
from heaven with his powerful angels. [8]He
will give justice with blazing fire to those
who don't recognize God and don't obey
the good news of our Lord Jesus. [9]They will
pay the penalty of eternal destruction away
from the Lord's presence and away from
his mighty glory. [10]This will happen when
he comes on that day to receive honor from
his holy people and to be admired by everyone who has believed—and our testimony
to you was believed.

[11]We are constantly praying for you for
this: that our God will make you worthy of
his calling and accomplish every good desire and faithful work by his power. [12]Then
the name of our Lord Jesus will be honored
by you, and you will be honored by him,
consistent with the grace of our God and
the Lord Jesus Christ.

Day of the Lord

2 Brothers and sisters, we have a request for
you concerning our Lord Jesus Christ's
coming and when we are gathered together
to be with him. [2]We don't want you to be
easily confused in your mind or upset if you
hear that the day of the Lord is already here,
whether you hear it through some spirit, a
message, or a letter supposedly from us.
[3]Don't let anyone deceive you in any way.
That day won't come unless the rebellion
comes first and the person who is lawless
is revealed, who is headed for destruction.
[4]He is the opponent of every so-called god
or object of worship and promotes himself over them. So he sits in God's temple,
displaying himself to show that he is God.
[5]You remember that I used to tell you
these things while I was with you, don't
you? [6]Now you know what holds him back
so that he can be revealed when his time
comes. [7]The hidden plan to live without any
law is at work now, but it will be secret only
until the one who is holding it back is out
of the way. [8]Then the person who is lawless
will be revealed. The Lord Jesus will destroy
him with the breath from his mouth. When
the Lord comes, his appearance will put an
end to him. [9]When the person who is lawless comes, it will happen through Satan's
effort, with all kinds of fake power, signs,
and wonders. [10]It will happen with every
sort of wicked deception of those who are
heading toward destruction because they
have refused to love the truth that would
allow them to be saved. [11]This is why God
will send them an influence that will mislead them so that they will believe the lie.
[12]The result will be that everyone will be
judged who is not convinced by the truth
but is happy with injustice.

Prayer of thanks and encouragement

[13]But we always must thank God for you,
brothers and sisters who are loved by God.
This is because he chose you from the beginning to be the first crop of the harvest. This
brought salvation, through your dedication
to God by the Spirit and through your belief
in the truth. [14]God called all of you through
our good news so you could possess the
honor of our Lord Jesus Christ. [15]So then,

brothers and sisters, stand firm and hold on
to the traditions we taught you, whether we
taught you in person or through our letter.
16 Our Lord Jesus Christ himself and God our
Father loved us and through grace gave us
eternal comfort and a good hope. 17 May he
encourage your hearts and give you strength
in every good thing you do or say.

Prayer request

3 Finally, brothers and sisters, pray for us
so that the Lord's message will spread
quickly and be honored, just like it happened with you. 2 Pray too that we will be
rescued from inappropriate and evil people
since everyone that we meet won't respond
with faith. 3 But the Lord is faithful and will
give you strength and protect you from the
evil one. 4 We are confident about you in
the Lord—that you are doing and will keep
doing what we tell you to do. 5 May the Lord
lead your hearts to express God's love and
Christ's endurance.

Discipline for the undisciplined

6 Brothers and sisters, we command you
in the name of our Lord Jesus Christ to stay
away from every brother or sister who lives
an undisciplined life that is not in line with
the traditions that you received from us.
7 You yourselves know how you need to imitate us because we were not undisciplined
when we were with you. 8 We didn't eat anyone's food without paying for it. Instead,
we worked night and day with effort and
hard work so that we would not impose on
you. 9 We did this to give you an example
to imitate, not because we didn't have a
right to insist on financial support. 10 Even
when we were with you we were giving you
this command: "If anyone doesn't want to
work, they shouldn't eat." 11 We hear that
some of you are living an undisciplined life.
They aren't working, but they are meddling
in other people's business. 12 By the Lord
Jesus Christ, we command and encourage
such people to work quietly and put their
own food on the table. 13 Brothers and sisters, don't get discouraged in doing what
is right. 14 Take note of anyone who doesn't
obey what we have said in this letter.
Don't associate with them so they will be
ashamed of themselves. 15 Don't treat them
like enemies, but warn them like you would
do for a brother or sister.

Final greeting

16 May the Lord of peace himself give you
peace always in every way. The Lord be with
all of you. 17 I, Paul, am writing this greeting with my own hand. This verifies that the
letter is from me, as in every letter of mine.
This is how I write. 18 The grace of our Lord
Jesus Christ be with all of you.

1 TIMOTHY

Greeting

1 From Paul, who is an apostle of Jesus Christ by the command of God our savior and of Christ Jesus our hope.
2To Timothy, my true child in the faith.
Grace, mercy, and peace from God the Father and from Christ Jesus our Lord.

Timothy's purpose in Ephesus

3When I left for Macedonia, I asked you to stay behind in Ephesus so that you could instruct certain individuals not to spread wrong teaching. 4They shouldn't pay attention to myths and endless genealogies. Their teaching only causes useless guessing games instead of faithfulness to God's way of doing things. 5The goal of instruction is love from a pure heart, a good conscience, and a sincere faith. 6Because they missed this goal, some people have been distracted by talk that doesn't mean anything. 7They want to be teachers of Law without understanding either what they are saying or what they are talking about with such confidence. 8Now we know that the Law is good if used appropriately. 9We understand this: the Law isn't established for a righteous person but for people who live without laws and without obeying any authority. They are the ungodly and the sinners. They are people who are not spiritual, and nothing is sacred to them. They kill their fathers and mothers, and murder others. 10They are people who are sexually unfaithful, and people who have intercourse with the same sex. They are kidnappers,[a] liars, individuals who give false testimonies in court, and those who do anything else that is opposed to sound teaching. 11Sound teaching agrees with the glorious gospel of the blessed God that has been trusted to me.

Thanksgiving

12I thank Christ Jesus our Lord, who has given me strength because he considered me faithful. So he appointed me to ministry 13even though I used to speak against him, attack his people, and I was proud. But I was shown mercy because I acted in ignorance and without faith. 14Our Lord's favor poured all over me along with the faithfulness and love that are in Christ Jesus. 15This saying is reliable and deserves full acceptance: "Christ Jesus came into the world to save sinners"—and I'm the biggest sinner of all. 16But this is why I was shown mercy, so that Christ Jesus could show his endless patience to me first of all. So I'm an example for those who are going to believe in him for eternal life. 17Now to the king of the ages, to the immortal, invisible, and only God, may honor and glory be given to him forever and always! Amen.

Importance of faith and a good conscience

18Timothy, my child, I'm giving you these instructions based on the prophecies that were once made about you. So if you follow them, you can wage a good war 19because you have faith and a good conscience. Some people have ruined their faith because they refused to listen to their conscience, 20such as Hymenaeus and Alexander. I've handed them over to Satan so that they can be taught not to speak against God.

Prayer for everyone

2 First of all, then, I ask that requests, prayers, petitions, and thanksgiving be made for all people. 2Pray for kings and everyone who is in authority so that we can live a quiet and peaceful life in complete godliness and dignity. 3This is right and it pleases God our savior, 4who wants all people to be saved and to come to a knowledge of the truth. 5There is one God and one mediator between God and humanity, the human Christ Jesus, 6who gave himself as a payment to set all people free. This was a testimony that was given at the right time. 7I was appointed to be a preacher and apostle of this testimony—I'm telling the

[a]Or *slave dealers*

truth and I'm not lying! I'm a teacher of the
Gentiles in faith and truth.

Instructions for men and women

8 Therefore, I want men to pray everywhere by lifting up hands that are holy,
without anger or argument. 9 In the same
way, I want women to enhance their appearance with clothing that is modest and
sensible, not with elaborate hairstyles, gold,
pearls, or expensive clothes. 10 They should
make themselves attractive by doing good,
which is appropriate for women who claim
to honor God.

11 A wife[b] should learn quietly with complete submission. 12 I don't allow a wife[c] to
teach or to control her husband.[d] Instead,
she should be a quiet listener. 13 Adam was
formed first, and then Eve. 14 Adam wasn't
deceived, but rather his wife[e] became the
one who stepped over the line because she
was completely deceived. 15 But a woman[f]
will be kept safe through childbirth[g] provided she continues in faith, love, and holiness, combined with self-control.

Supervisors in God's household

3 This saying is reliable: if anyone has a
goal to be a supervisor[h] in the church,
they want a good thing. 2 So the church's
supervisor must be without fault. They
should be faithful to their spouse, sober,
modest, and honest. They should show
hospitality and be skilled at teaching. 3 They
shouldn't be addicted to alcohol or a bully.
Instead, they should be gentle, peaceable,
and not greedy. 4 They should manage their
own household well—they should see that
their children are obedient with complete
respect, 5 because if they don't know how
to manage their own household, how can
they take care of God's church? 6 They
shouldn't be new believers so that they
won't become proud and fall under the
devil's spell. 7 They should also have a good
reputation with those outside the church
so that they won't be embarrassed and fall
into the devil's trap.

Servants in God's household

8 In the same way, servants[i] in the church
should be dignified, not two-faced, heavy
drinkers, or greedy for money. 9 They should
hold on to the faith that has been revealed
with a clear conscience. 10 They should also
be tested and then serve if they are without
fault. 11 In the same way, women who are
servants[j] in the church should be dignified
and not gossip. They should be sober and
faithful in everything they do. 12 Servants[k]
must be faithful to their spouse and manage their children and their own households well. 13 Those who have served well
gain a good standing and considerable confidence in the faith that is in Christ Jesus.

Leading God's household

14 I hope to come to you quickly. But I'm
writing these things to you so that 15 if I'm
delayed, you'll know how you should behave
in God's household. It is the church of the
living God and the backbone and support of
the truth. 16 Without question, the mystery
of godliness is great: he was revealed as a
human, declared righteous by the Spirit,
seen by angels, preached throughout the
nations, believed in around the world, and
taken up in glory.

4 The Spirit clearly says that in latter
times some people will turn away from
the faith. They will pay attention to spirits
that deceive and to the teaching of demons.
2 They will be controlled by the pretense of
lying, and their own consciences will be
seared. 3 They will prohibit marriage and
eating foods that God created—and he intended them to be accepted with thanksgiving by those who are faithful and have come
to know the truth. 4 Everything that has
been created by God is good, and nothing
that is received with thanksgiving should
be rejected. 5 These things are made holy by
God's word and prayer. 6 If you point these
things out to the believers, you will be a
good servant of Christ Jesus who has been
trained by the words of faith and the good
teaching that you've carefully followed.

[b] Or *a woman* [c] Or *a woman* [d] Or *a man* [e] Or *the woman* [f] Or *a wife* [g] Or *saved through childbearing* [h] Or *bishop, overseer* [i] Or *deacons* [j] Or *wives*, omit *who are servants* [k] Or *deacons*

7But stay away from the godless myths that are passed down from the older women.

Practices of spiritual leadership

Train yourself for a holy life! 8While physical training has some value, training in holy living is useful for everything. It has promise for this life now and the life to come. 9This saying is reliable and deserves complete acceptance. 10We work and struggle for this: "Our hope is set on the living God, who is the savior of all people, especially those who believe." 11Command these things. Teach them. 12Don't let anyone look down on you because you are young. Instead, set an example for the believers through your speech, behavior, love, faith, and by being sexually pure. 13Until I arrive, pay attention to public reading, preaching, and teaching. 14Don't neglect the spiritual gift in you that was given through prophecy when the elders laid hands on you. 15Practice these things, and live by them so that your progress will be visible to all. 16Focus on working on your own development and on what you teach. If you do this, you will save yourself and those who hear you.

Caring for God's family

5 Don't correct an older man, but encourage him like he's your father; treat younger men like your brothers, 2treat older women like your mother, and treat younger women like your sisters with appropriate respect.

3Take care of widows who are truly needy. 4But if a particular widow has children or grandchildren, they should first learn to respect their own family and repay their parents, because this pleases God. 5A widow who is truly needy and all alone puts her hope in God and keeps on going with requests and prayers, night and day. 6But a widow who tries to live a life of luxury is dead even while she is alive. 7Teach these things so that the families[l] will be without fault. 8But if someone doesn't provide for their own family, and especially for a member of their household, they have denied the faith. They are worse than those who have no faith.

9Put a widow on the list who is older than 60 years old and who was faithful to her husband. 10She should have a reputation for doing good: raising children, providing hospitality to strangers, washing the feet of the saints, helping those in distress, and dedicating herself to every kind of good thing. 11But don't accept younger widows for the list. When their physical desires distract them from Christ, they will want to get married. 12Then they will be judged for setting aside their earlier commitment. 13Also, they learn to be lazy by going from house to house. They are not only lazy, but they also become gossips and busybodies, talking about things they shouldn't. 14So I want younger widows to marry, have children, and manage their homes so that they won't give the enemy any reason to slander us. (15Some have already turned away to follow Satan.) 16If any woman who is a believer has widows in her family, she should take care of them and not burden the church, so that it can help other widows who are truly needy.

Instructions for elders

17Elders who lead well should be paid double, especially those who work with public speaking and teaching. 18The scripture says, *Don't put a muzzle on an ox while it treads grain*,[m] and *Workers deserve their pay*.[n] 19Don't accept an accusation made against an elder unless it is confirmed by two or three witnesses. 20Discipline those who are sinning in front of everyone so that all the others will be afraid. 21I charge you before God and Christ Jesus and the elect angels to follow these practices without bias, and without playing favorites. 22Don't rush to commission anyone to leadership, and don't participate in the sins of others. Keep yourself morally pure.

23Don't drink water anymore, but use a little wine because of your stomach problems and your frequent illnesses. 24The sins of some people are obvious, and the sins are

[l]Or *they* [m]Deut 25:4 [n]Luke 10:7

judged before the people must face judgment, but the sins of other people show up
later. [25]In the same way, the good that people do is also obvious and can't be hidden.

Conduct of Christian slaves

6 Those who are under the bondage of
slavery should consider their own masters as worthy of full respect so that God's
name and our teaching won't get a bad
reputation. [2]And those who have masters
who are believers shouldn't look down on
them because they are brothers. Instead,
they should serve them more faithfully,
because the people who benefit from your
good service are believers who are loved.
Teach and encourage these things.

Warning about false teachers

[3]If anyone teaches anything different and
doesn't agree with sound teaching about
our Lord Jesus Christ and teaching that is
consistent with godliness,[4]that person is
conceited. They don't understand anything
but have a sick obsession with debates and
arguments. This creates jealousy, conflict,
verbal abuse, and evil suspicions. [5]There is
constant bickering between people whose
minds are ruined and who have been robbed
of the truth. They think that godliness is a
way to make money! [6]Actually, godliness is
a great source of profit when it is combined
with being happy with what you already
have. [7]We didn't bring anything into the
world and so we can't take anything out of
it: [8]we'll be happy with food and clothing.
[9]But people who are trying to get rich fall
into temptation. They are trapped by many
stupid and harmful passions that plunge
people into ruin and destruction. [10]The
love of money is the root of all kinds of evil.
Some have wandered away from the faith
and have impaled themselves with a lot of
pain because they made money their goal.

[11]But as for you, man of God, run away
from all these things. Instead, pursue righteousness, holy living, faithfulness, love,
endurance, and gentleness. [12]Compete in
the good fight of faith. Grab hold of eternal
life—you were called to it, and you made
a good confession of it in the presence of
many witnesses. [13]I command you in the
presence of God, who gives life to all things,
and Christ Jesus, who made the good confession when testifying before Pontius
Pilate. [14]Obey this order without fault or
failure until the appearance of our Lord
Jesus Christ. [15]The timing of this appearance is revealed by God alone, who is the
blessed and only master, the King of kings
and Lord of lords. [16]He alone has immortality and lives in light that no one can come
near. No human being has ever seen or is
able to see him. Honor and eternal power
belong to him. Amen.

Wealth of good works

[17]Tell people who are rich at this time
not to become egotistical and not to place
their hope on their finances, which are uncertain. Instead, they need to hope in God,
who richly provides everything for our enjoyment. [18]Tell them to do good, to be rich
in the good things they do, to be generous,
and to share with others. [19]When they do
these things, they will save a treasure for
themselves that is a good foundation for
the future. That way they can take hold of
what is truly life.

Protect the tradition

[20]Timothy, protect what has been given
to you in trust. Avoid godless and pointless
discussions and the contradictory claims of
so-called "knowledge." [21]When some people
adopted this false knowledge, they missed
the goal of faith.

May grace be with you all.

2 TIMOTHY

Greeting

1 From Paul, an apostle of Christ Jesus
by God's will, to promote the promise
of life that is in Christ Jesus.
2 To Timothy, my dear child.
Grace, mercy, and peace from God the
Father and Christ Jesus our Lord.

Thanksgiving and prayer

3 I'm grateful to God, whom I serve with a
good conscience as my ancestors did. I constantly remember you in my prayers day and
night. 4 When I remember your tears, I long
to see you so that I can be filled with happiness. 5 I'm reminded of your authentic faith,
which first lived in your grandmother Lois
and your mother Eunice. I'm sure that this
faith is also inside you. 6 Because of this, I'm
reminding you to revive God's gift that is in
you through the laying on of my hands. 7 God
didn't give us a spirit that is timid but one
that is powerful, loving, and self-controlled.

Don't be ashamed of the testimony

8 So don't be ashamed of the testimony
about the Lord or of me, his prisoner. Instead,
share the suffering for the good news, depending on God's power. 9 God is the one who saved
and called us with a holy calling. This wasn't
based on what we have done, but it was based
on his own purpose and grace that he gave us
in Christ Jesus before time began. 10 Now his
grace is revealed through the appearance of
our savior, Christ Jesus. He destroyed death
and brought life and immortality into clear
focus through the good news. 11 I was appointed a messenger, apostle, and teacher of
this good news. 12 This is also why I'm suffering the way I do, but I'm not ashamed. I know
the one in whom I've placed my trust. I'm convinced that God is powerful enough to protect
what he has placed in my trust until that day.
13 Hold on to the pattern of sound teaching
that you heard from me with the faith and
love that are in Christ Jesus. 14 Protect this
good thing that has been placed in your trust
through the Holy Spirit who lives in us.
15 You know that everyone in Asia has
turned away from me, including Phygelus
and Hermogenes. 16 May the Lord show
mercy to Onesiphorus' household, because
he supported me many times and he wasn't
ashamed of my imprisonment. 17 After I arrived in Rome, he quickly looked for me and
found me. 18 May the Lord allow him to find
his mercy on that day (and you know very
well how much he served me in Ephesus).

Pass on the message and share suffering

2 So, my child, draw your strength from
the grace that is in Christ Jesus. 2 Take
the things you heard me say in front of
many other witnesses and pass them on
to faithful people who are also capable of
teaching others.
3 Accept your share of suffering like a
good soldier of Christ Jesus. 4 Nobody who
serves in the military gets tied up with ci-
vilian matters, so that they can please the
one who recruited them. 5 Also in the same
way, athletes don't win unless they follow
the rules. 6 A hardworking farmer should
get the first share of the crop. 7 Think about
what I'm saying; the Lord will give you understanding about everything.
8 Remember Jesus Christ, who was
raised from the dead and descended from
David. This is my good news. 9 This is the
reason I'm suffering to the point that I'm in
prison like a common criminal. But God's
word cannot be imprisoned. 10 This is why
I endure everything for the sake of those
who are chosen by God so that they too
may experience salvation in Christ Jesus
with eternal glory. 11 This saying is reliable:

"If we have died together,
we will also live together.
12 If we endure, we will also rule together.
If we deny him, he will also deny us.
13 If we are disloyal, he stays faithful"
because he can't be anything else
than what he is.

Speak, instruct, and act correctly

14 Remind them of these things and warn
them in the sight of God not to engage in
battles over words that aren't helpful and

only destroy those who hear them. 15 Make
an effort to present yourself to God as a
tried-and-true worker, who doesn't need to
be ashamed but is one who interprets the
message of truth correctly. 16 Avoid their
godless discussions, because they will lead
many people into ungodly behavior, 17 and
their ideas will spread like an infection. This
includes Hymenaeus and Philetus, 18 who
have deviated from the truth by claiming
that the resurrection has already happened.
This has undermined some people's faith.

19 God's solid foundation is still standing
with this sign: *The Lord knows the people who
belong to him,*[a] and *Everyone who confesses
the Lord's name must avoid wickedness.*[b] 20 In
a mansion, there aren't just gold and silver
bowls but also some bowls that are made of
wood and clay. Some are meant for special
uses, some for garbage.[c] 21 So if anyone washes
filth off themselves, they will be set apart as a
"special bowl." They will be useful to the owner
of the mansion for every sort of good work.

Avoid conflict with opponents

22 Run away from adolescent cravings.
Instead, pursue righteousness, faith, love,
and peace together with those who confess the Lord with a clean heart. 23 Avoid
foolish and thoughtless discussions, since
you know that they produce conflicts.
24 God's slave shouldn't be argumentative
but should be kind toward all people, able
to teach, patient, 25 and should correct opponents with gentleness. Perhaps God will
change their mind and give them a knowledge of the truth. 26 They may come to their
senses and escape from the devil's trap that
holds them captive to do his will.

Avoid people like this

3 Understand that the last days will be
dangerous times. 2 People will be selfish
and love money. They will be the kind of
people who brag and who are proud. They
will slander others, and they will be disobedient to their parents. They will be ungrateful, unholy, 3 unloving, contrary, and
critical. They will be without self-control
and brutal, and they won't love what is
good. 4 They will be people who are disloyal, reckless, and conceited. They will love
pleasure instead of loving God. 5 They will
look like they are religious but deny God's
power. Avoid people like this. 6 Some will
slither into households and control immature women who are burdened with sins
and driven by all kinds of desires. 7 These
women are always learning, but they can
never arrive at an understanding of the
truth. 8 These people oppose the truth in
the same way that Jannes and Jambres opposed Moses. Their minds are corrupt and
their faith is counterfeit. 9 But they won't
get very far. Their foolishness will become
obvious to everyone like those others.

Take Paul as your model

10 But you have paid attention to my
teaching, conduct, purpose, faithfulness, patience, love, and endurance. 11 You have seen
me experience physical abuse and ordeals in
places such as Antioch, Iconium, and Lystra.
I put up with all sorts of abuse, and the Lord
rescued me from it all! 12 In fact, anyone who
wants to live a holy life in Christ Jesus will
be harassed. 13 But evil people and swindlers
will grow even worse, as they deceive others
while being deceived themselves.

14 But you must continue with the things
you have learned and found convincing. You
know who taught you. 15 Since childhood
you have known the holy scriptures that
help you to be wise in a way that leads to salvation through faith that is in Christ Jesus.
16 Every scripture is inspired by God and is
useful for teaching, for showing mistakes,
for correcting, and for training character,
17 so that the person who belongs to God can
be equipped to do everything that is good.

Timothy's commission and Paul's departure

4 I'm giving you this commission in the
presence of God and of Christ Jesus, who
is coming to judge the living and the dead,
and by his appearance and his kingdom.
2 Preach the word. Be ready to do it whether

[a] Num 16:5 LXX [b] Possibly modeled on Isa 26:13 [c] Or *dishonorable purposes*

it is convenient or inconvenient. Correct, confront, and encourage with patience and instruction. 3There will come a time when people will not tolerate sound teaching. They will collect teachers who say what they want to hear because they are self-centered. 4They will turn their back on the truth and turn to myths. 5But you must keep control of yourself in all circumstances. Endure suffering, do the work of a preacher of the good news, and carry out your service fully.

6I'm already being poured out like a sacrifice to God, and the time of my death is near. 7I have fought the good fight, finished the race, and kept the faith. 8At last the champion's wreath that is awarded for righteousness[d] is waiting for me. The Lord, who is the righteous[e] judge, is going to give it to me on that day. He's giving it not only to me but also to all those who have set their heart on waiting for his appearance.

Final instructions

9Do your best to come to me quickly. 10Demas has fallen in love with the present world and has deserted me and has gone to Thessalonica. Crescens has gone to Galatia, and Titus has gone to Dalmatia. 11Only Luke is with me. Get Mark, and bring him with you. He has been a big help to me in the ministry. 12I sent Tychicus to Ephesus. 13When you come, bring along the coat I left with Carpus in Troas. Also bring the scrolls and especially the parchments. 14Alexander, the craftsman who works with metal, has really hurt me. The Lord will pay him back for what he has done. 15But watch out for him, because he opposes our teaching.

16No one took my side at my first court hearing. Everyone deserted me. I hope that God doesn't hold it against them! 17But the Lord stood by me and gave me strength, so that the entire message would be preached through me and so all the nations could hear it. I was also rescued from the lion's mouth! 18The Lord will rescue me from every evil action and will save me for his heavenly kingdom. To him be the glory forever and always. Amen.

Final greetings

19Say hello to Prisca and Aquila and the household of Onesiphorus. 20Erastus stayed in Corinth, and I left Trophimus in Miletus because of his illness. 21Try hard to come to me before winter. Eubulus, Pudens, Linus, Claudia, and all the brothers and sisters say hello.

22The Lord be with your spirit. Grace be with you all.

TITUS

Greeting

1 From Paul, a slave of God and an apostle of Jesus Christ. I'm sent to bring about the faith of God's chosen people and a knowledge of the truth that agrees with godliness.

2Their faith and this knowledge are based on the hope of eternal life that God, who doesn't lie, promised before time began. 3God revealed his message at the appropriate time through preaching, and I was trusted with preaching this message by the command of God our savior.

4To Titus, my true child in a common faith.

Grace and peace from God the Father and Christ Jesus our savior.

Appointing elders

5The reason I left you behind in Crete was to organize whatever needs to be done and to appoint elders in each city, as I told you. 6Elders should be without fault. They should be faithful to their spouse,[a] and have faithful children who can't be accused of self-indulgence or rebelliousness. 7This is because supervisors[b] should be without fault as God's managers: they shouldn't be stubborn, irritable, addicted to alcohol, a bully, or greedy. 8Instead, they should show

[d]Or *justice* [e]Or *just* [a]Or *they should be a one-woman man.* [b]Or *overseers*

hospitality, love what is good, and be reasonable, ethical, godly, and self-controlled. [9]They
must pay attention to the reliable message as
it has been taught to them so that they can
encourage people with healthy instruction
and refute those who speak against it.

Correcting rebellious people

[10]In fact, there are many who are rebellious people, loudmouths, and deceivers,
especially some of those who are Jewish
believers.[c] [11]They must be silenced because
they upset entire households. They teach
what they shouldn't to make money dishonestly. [12]Someone who is one of their
own prophets said, "People from Crete are
always liars, wild animals, and lazy gluttons."
[13]This statement is true. Because of this,
correct them firmly, so that they can be
healthy in their faith. [14]They shouldn't pay
attention to Jewish myths and commands
from people who reject the truth. [15]Every-
thing is clean to those who are clean, but
nothing is clean to those who are corrupt
and without faith. Instead, their mind and
conscience are corrupted. [16]They claim to
know God, but they deny God by the things
that they do. They are detestable, disobedient, and disqualified to do anything good.

Teaching all people how to be godly

2 But you should talk in a way that is consistent with sound teaching. [2]Tell the
older men to be sober, dignified, sensible,
and healthy in respect to their faith, love,
and patience.

[3]Likewise, tell the older women to be
reverent in their behavior, teaching what is
good, rather than being gossips or addicted
to heavy drinking. [4]That way they can mentor young women to love their husbands
and children, [5]and to be sensible, morally
pure, working at home, kind and submissive to their own husbands, so that God's
word won't be ridiculed. [6]Likewise, encourage the younger men to be sensible [7]in
every way. Offer yourself as a role model of
good actions. Show integrity, seriousness,
[8]and a sound message that is above criticism when you teach, so that any opponent
will be ashamed because they won't find
anything bad to say about us.

[9]Tell slaves to submit to their own masters and please them in everything they do.
They shouldn't talk back [10]or steal. Instead,
they should show that they are completely
reliable in everything so that they might
make the teaching about God our savior attractive in every way.

[11]The grace of God has appeared, bringing
salvation to all people. [12]It educates us so
that we can live sensible, ethical, and godly
lives right now by rejecting ungodly lives
and the desires of this world. [13]At the same
time we wait for the blessed hope and the
glorious appearance of our great God and
savior Jesus Christ. [14]He gave himself for us
in order to rescue us from every kind of lawless behavior, and cleanse a special people
for himself who are eager to do good actions.

[15]Talk about these things. Encourage
and correct with complete authority. Don't
3 let anyone disrespect you. [1]Remind
them to submit to rulers and authorities. They should be obedient and ready to
do every good thing. [2]They shouldn't speak
disrespectfully about anyone, but they
should be peaceful, kind, and show complete courtesy toward everyone. [3]We were
once foolish, disobedient, deceived, and
slaves to our desires and various pleasures
too. We were spending our lives in evil behavior and jealousy. We were disgusting,
and we hated other people. [4]But "when God
our savior's kindness and love appeared,
[5]he saved us because of his mercy, not because of righteous things we had done. He
did it through the washing of new birth and
the renewing by the Holy Spirit, [6]which God
poured out upon us generously through
Jesus Christ our savior. [7]So, since we have
been made righteous by his grace, we can
inherit the hope for eternal life." [8]This saying is reliable. And I want you to insist on
these things, so that those who have come
to believe in God might give careful attention to doing good. These things are good
and useful for everyone.

[c]Or *from the circumcision*

Final instructions and greetings

9 Avoid stupid controversies, genealogies, and fights about the Law, because they are useless and worthless. 10 After a first and second warning, have nothing more to do with a person who causes conflict, 11 because you know that someone like this is twisted and sinful—so they condemn themselves.

12 When I send Artemas or Tychicus to you, try to come to me in Nicopolis, because I've decided to spend the winter there. 13 Help Zenas the lawyer and Apollos on their journey with enthusiasm so that they won't need anything. 14 But our people should also learn to devote themselves to doing good in order to meet pressing needs so they aren't unproductive.

15 Everyone with me greets you; greet those who love us faithfully.

Grace be with all of you.

PHILEMON

Greeting

1 From Paul, who is a prisoner for the cause of Christ Jesus, and our brother Timothy.

To Philemon our dearly loved coworker, 2 Apphia our sister, Archippus our fellow soldier, and the church that meets in your house.

3 May the grace and peace from God our Father and the Lord Jesus Christ be with you.

Paul's prayer for Philemon

4 Philemon, I thank my God every time I mention you in my prayers 5 because I've heard of your love and faithfulness, which you have both for the Lord Jesus and for all God's people. 6 I pray that your partnership in the faith might become effective by an understanding of all that is good among us in Christ. 7 I have great joy and encouragement because of your love, since the hearts of God's people are refreshed by your actions, my brother.

Paul's appeal for Onesimus

8 Therefore, though I have enough confidence in Christ to command you to do the right thing, 9 I would rather appeal to you through love. I, Paul—an old man, and now also a prisoner for Christ Jesus—10 appeal to you for my child Onesimus. I became his father in the faith during my time in prison. 11 He was useless to you before, but now he is useful to both of us. 12 I'm sending him back to you, which is like sending you my own heart. 13 I considered keeping him with me so that he might serve me in your place during my time in prison because of the gospel. 14 However, I didn't want to do anything without your consent so that your act of kindness would occur willingly and not under pressure. 15 Maybe this is the reason that Onesimus was separated from you for a while so that you might have him back forever—16 no longer as a slave but more than a slave—that is, as a dearly loved brother. He is especially a dearly loved brother to me. How much more can he become a brother to you, personally and spiritually in the Lord!

17 So, if you really consider me a partner, welcome Onesimus as if you were welcoming me. 18 If he has harmed you in any way or owes you money, charge it to my account. 19 I, Paul, will pay it back to you (I'm writing this with my own hand). Of course, I won't mention that you owe me your life.

20 Yes, brother, I want this favor from you in the Lord! Refresh my heart in Christ. 21 I'm writing to you, confident of your obedience and knowing that you will do more than what I ask. 22 Also, one more thing—prepare a guest room for me. I hope that I will be released from prison to be with you because of your prayers.

Final greeting

23 Epaphras, who is in prison with me for the cause of Christ Jesus, greets you, 24 as well as my coworkers Mark, Aristarchus, Demas, and Luke.

25 May the grace of the Lord Jesus Christ be with your spirit.

HEBREWS

The Son is God's ultimate messenger

1 In the past, God spoke through the prophets to our ancestors in many times and many ways. [2]In these final days, though, he spoke to us through a Son. God made his Son the heir of everything and created the world through him. [3]The Son is the light of God's glory and the imprint of God's being. He maintains everything with his powerful message. After he carried out the cleansing of people from their sins, he sat down at the right side of the highest majesty. [4]And the Son became so much greater than the other messengers, such as angels, that he received a more important title than theirs.

Speaking to the Son and angels

[5]After all, when did God ever say to any of the angels:

You are my Son.
Today I have become your Father?[a]

Or, even,

I will be his Father,
and he will be my Son?[b]

[6]But then, when he brought his firstborn into the world, he said,

All of God's angels must worship him.[c]

[7]He talks about the angels:

He's the one who uses the spirits
for his messengers
and who uses flames of fire as ministers.[d]

[8]But he says to his Son,

God, your throne is forever
and your kingdom's scepter
is a rod of justice.
[9]*You loved righteousness*
and hated lawless behavior.
That is why God, your God,
has anointed you with oil
instead of your companions.[e]

[10]And he says,

You, Lord, laid the earth's foundations
in the beginning,
and the heavens are made by your hands.
[11]*They will pass away,*
but you remain.
They will all wear out like old clothes.
[12]*You will fold them up like a coat.*
They will be changed
like a person changes clothes,
but you stay the same,
and the years of your life
won't come to an end.[f]

[13]When has he ever said to any of the angels,

Sit at my right side
until I put your enemies
under your feet like a footstool?[g]

[14]Aren't all the angels ministering spirits who are sent to serve those who are going to inherit salvation?

Listen to the Son's message

2 This is why it's necessary for us to pay more attention to what we have heard, or else we may drift away from it. [2]If the message that was spoken by angels was reliable, and every offense and act of disobedience received an appropriate consequence, [3]how will we escape if we ignore such a great salvation? It was first announced through the Lord, and then it was confirmed by those who heard him. [4]God also vouched for their message with signs, amazing things, various miracles, and gifts from the Holy Spirit, which were handed out the way he wanted.

Jesus is the enthroned human being

[5]God didn't put the world that is coming (the world we are talking about) under the angels' control. [6]Instead, someone declared somewhere,

What is humanity
that you think about them?
Or what are the human beings
that you care about them?
[7]*For a while you made them lower*
than angels.
You crowned the human beings
with glory and honor.
[8]*You put everything*
under their control.[h]

[a]Ps 2:7 [b]2 Sam 7:14; 1 Chron 17:13 [c]Deut 32:43 and Ps 97:7 LXX [d]Ps 104:4 [e]Ps 45:6-7 [f]Ps 102:25-27 [g]Ps 110:1 [h]Ps 8:4-6

When he puts everything under their control, he doesn't leave anything out of control. But right now, we don't see everything under their control yet. [9]However, we do see the one who was made lower in order than the angels for a little while—it's Jesus! He's the one who is now crowned with glory and honor because of the suffering of his death. He suffered death so that he could taste death for everyone through God's grace.

Qualified to be a high priest

[10]It was appropriate for God, for whom and through whom everything exists, to use experiences of suffering to make perfect the pioneer of salvation. This salvation belongs to many sons and daughters whom he's leading to glory. [11]This is because the one who makes people holy and the people who are being made holy all come from one source. That is why Jesus isn't ashamed to call them brothers and sisters when he says,

[12]*I will publicly announce your name*
to my brothers and sisters.
I will praise you in the middle
of the assembly.[i]

[13]He also says,
I will rely on him.[j]
And also,
Here I am with the children
whom God has given to me.[k]

[14]Therefore, since the children share in flesh and blood, he also shared the same things in the same way. He did this to destroy the one who holds the power over death—the devil—by dying. [15]He set free those who were held in slavery their entire lives by their fear of death. [16]Of course, he isn't trying to help angels, but rather he's helping Abraham's descendants. [17]Therefore, he had to be made like his brothers and sisters in every way. This was so that he could become a merciful and faithful high priest in things relating to God, in order to wipe away the sins of the people. [18]He's able to help those who are being tempted, since he himself experienced suffering when he was tempted.

We are Jesus' house

3 Therefore, brothers and sisters who are partners in the heavenly calling, think about Jesus, the apostle and high priest of our confession. [2]Jesus was faithful to the one who appointed him just like Moses was faithful in God's house. [3]But he deserves greater glory than Moses in the same way that the builder of the house deserves more honor than the house itself. [4]Every house is built by someone, but God is the builder of everything. [5]Moses was faithful in all God's house as a servant in order to affirm the things that would be spoken later. [6]But Jesus was faithful over God's house as a Son. We are his house if we hold on to the confidence and the pride that our hope gives us.

Respond to Jesus' voice now

[7]So, as the Holy Spirit says,
Today, if you hear his voice,
[8]*don't have stubborn hearts*
as they did in the rebellion,
on the day when they tested me
in the desert.
[9]*That is where your ancestors*
challenged and tested me,
though they had seen my work
for forty years.
[10]*So I was angry with them.*
I said, "Their hearts always go off course,
and they don't know my ways."
[11]*Because of my anger I swore:*
"They will never enter my rest!"[l]

[12]Watch out, brothers and sisters, so that none of you have an evil, unfaithful heart that abandons the living God. [13]Instead, encourage each other every day, as long as it's called "today," so that none of you become insensitive to God because of sin's deception. [14]We are partners with Christ, but only if we hold on to the confidence we had in the beginning until the end.

[15]When it says,
Today, if you hear his voice,
don't have stubborn hearts
as they did in the rebellion.[m]

[16]Who was it who rebelled when they heard his voice? Wasn't it all of those who were

[i]Ps 22:22 [j]Isa 8:17 LXX [k]Isa 8:18 [l]Ps 95:7-11 [m]Ps 95:7-8

brought out of Egypt by Moses? [17]And with whom was God angry for forty years? Wasn't it with the ones who sinned, whose bodies fell in the desert? [18]And against whom did he swear that they would never enter his rest, if not against the ones who were disobedient? [19]We see that they couldn't enter because of their lack of faith.

Enter the rest

4 Therefore, since the promise that we can enter into rest is still open, let's be careful so that none of you will appear to miss it. [2]We also had the good news preached to us, just as the Israelites did. However, the message they heard didn't help them, because they weren't united in faith with the ones who listened to it. [3]We who have faith are entering the rest. As God said,

And because of my anger I swore:
"They will never enter into my rest!"[n]

And yet God's works were completed at the foundation of the world. [4]Then somewhere he said this about the seventh day of creation: *God rested on the seventh day from all his works.*[o] [5]But again, in the passage above, God said, *They will never enter my rest!*[p] [6]Therefore, it's left open for some to enter it, and the ones who had the good news preached to them before didn't enter because of disobedience. [7]Just as it says in the passage above, God designates a certain day as "today," when he says through David much later,

Today, if you hear his voice,
don't have stubborn hearts.[q]

[8]If Joshua gave the Israelites rest, God wouldn't have spoken about another day later on. [9]So you see that a sabbath rest is left open for God's people. [10]The one who entered God's rest also rested from his works, just as God rested from his own.

First summary of the message

[11]Therefore, let's make every effort to enter that rest so that no one will fall by following the same example of disobedience, [12]because God's word is living, active, and sharper than any two-edged sword. It penetrates to the point that it separates the soul from the spirit and the joints from the marrow. It's able to judge the heart's thoughts and intentions. [13]No creature is hidden from it, but rather everything is naked and exposed to the eyes of the one to whom we have to give an answer.

[14]Also, let's hold on to the confession since we have a great high priest who passed through the heavens, who is Jesus, God's Son; [15]because we don't have a high priest who can't sympathize with our weaknesses but instead one who was tempted in every way that we are, except without sin.

[16]Finally, let's draw near to the throne of favor with confidence so that we can receive mercy and find grace when we need help.

Introduction to a deeper teaching

5 Every high priest is taken from the people and put in charge of things that relate to God for their sake, in order to offer gifts and sacrifices for sins. [2]The high priest is able to deal gently with the ignorant and those who are misled since he himself is prone to weakness. [3]Because of his weakness, he must offer sacrifices for his own sins as well as for the people. [4]No one takes this honor for themselves but takes it only when they are called by God, just like Aaron.

[5]In the same way Christ also didn't promote himself to become high priest. Instead, it was the one who said to him,

You are my Son.
Today I have become your Father,

[6]as he also says in another place,

You are a priest forever,
according to the order of Melchizedek.[r]

[7]During his days on earth, Christ offered prayers and requests with loud cries and tears as his sacrifices to the one who was able to save him from death. He was heard because of his godly devotion. [8]Although he was a Son, he learned obedience from what he suffered. [9]After he had been made perfect, he became the source of eternal salvation for everyone who obeys him. [10]He was appointed by God to be a high priest according to the order of Melchizedek.

[n]Ps 95:11 [o]Gen 2:2 [p]Ps 95:11 [q]Ps 95:7-8 [r]Ps 110:4

11We have a lot to say about this topic,
and it's difficult to explain, because you
have been lazy and you haven't been listening. 12Although you should have been
teachers by now, you need someone to
teach you an introduction to the basics
about God's message. You have come to the
place where you need milk instead of solid
food. 13Everyone who lives on milk is not
used to the word of righteousness, because
they are babies. 14But solid food is for the
mature, whose senses are trained by practice to distinguish between good and evil.

Let's press on to maturity

6 So let's press on to maturity, by moving on from the basics about Christ's
word. Let's not lay a foundation of turning
away from dead works, of faith in God, 2of
teaching about ritual ways to wash with
water, laying on of hands, the resurrection
from the dead, and eternal judgment—all
over again. 3We're going to press on, if God
allows it.

4Because it's impossible to restore people
to changed hearts and lives who turn away
once they have seen the light, tasted the
heavenly gift, become partners with the
Holy Spirit, 5and tasted God's good word
and the powers of the coming age. 6They are
crucifying God's Son all over again and exposing him to public shame. 7The ground receives a blessing from God when it drinks up
the rain that regularly comes and falls on it
and yields a useful crop for those people for
whom it is being farmed. 8But if it produces
thorns and thistles, it's useless and close to
being cursed. It ends up being burned.

Make your hope sure

9But we are convinced of better things in
your case, brothers and sisters, even though
we are talking this way—things that go together with salvation. 10God isn't unjust so
that he forgets your efforts and the love
you have shown for his name's sake when
you served and continue to serve God's
holy people. 11But we desperately want each
of you to show the same effort to make
your hope sure until the end. 12This is so
you won't be lazy but follow the example of
the ones who inherit the promises through
faith and patience.

Our hope in Jesus' priesthood

13When God gave Abraham his promise,
he swore by himself since he couldn't swear
by anyone greater. 14He said, *I will certainly
bless you and multiply your descendants.*[s] 15So
Abraham obtained the promise by show-
ing patience. 16People pledge by something
greater than themselves. A solemn pledge
guarantees what they say and shuts down
any argument. 17When God wanted to further demonstrate to the heirs of the promise
that his purpose doesn't change, he guaranteed it with a solemn pledge. 18So these
are two things that don't change, because
it's impossible for God to lie. He did this
so that we, who have taken refuge in him,
can be encouraged to grasp the hope that
is lying in front of us. 19This hope, which
is a safe and secure anchor for our whole
being, enters the sanctuary behind the curtain. 20That's where Jesus went in advance
and entered for us, since he became a high
priest according to the order of Melchizedek.

7 This Melchizedek, who was king of
Salem and priest of the Most High God,
met Abraham as he returned from the defeat of the kings, and Melchizedek blessed
him. 2Abraham gave a tenth of everything
to him. His name means first "king of righteousness," and then "king of Salem," that
is, "king of peace." 3He is without father or
mother or any family. He has no beginning
or end of life, but he's like God's Son and
remains a priest for all time.

A priest like Melchizedek

4See how great Melchizedek was! Abraham, the father of the people, gave him a
tenth of everything he captured. 5The descendants of Levi who receive the office
of priest have a commandment under the
Law to collect a tenth of everything from
the people who are their brothers and sisters, though they also are descended from

[s] Gen 22:17

Abraham. 6 But Melchizedek, who isn't related to them, received a tenth of everything from Abraham and blessed the one who had received the promises. 7 Without question, the less important person is blessed by the more important person. 8 In addition, in one case a tenth is received by people who die, and in the other case, the tenth is received by someone who continues to live, according to the record. 9 It could be said that Levi, who received a tenth, paid a tenth through Abraham 10 because he was still in his ancestor's body when Abraham paid the tenth to Melchizedek.

11 So if perfection came through the levitical office of priest (for the people received the Law under the priests), why was there still a need to speak about raising up another priest according to the order of Melchizedek rather than one according to the order of Aaron? 12 When the order of the priest changes, there has to be a change in the Law as well. 13 The person we are talking about belongs to another tribe, and no one ever served at the altar from that tribe. 14 It's clear that our Lord came from the tribe of Judah, but Moses never said anything about priests from that tribe. 15 And it's even clearer if another priest appears who is like Melchizedek. 16 He has become a priest by the power of a life that can't be destroyed, rather than a legal requirement about physical descent. 17 This is confirmed:

You are a priest forever,
according to the order of Melchizedek.[t]

Able to save completely

18 On the one hand, an earlier command is set aside because it was weak and useless 19 (because the Law made nothing perfect). On the other hand, a better hope is introduced, through which we draw near to God. 20 And this was not done without a solemn pledge! The others have become priests without a solemn pledge, 21 but this priest was affirmed with a solemn pledge by the one who said,

The Lord has made a solemn pledge
and will not change his mind:
You are a priest forever.[u]

22 As a result, Jesus has become the guarantee of a better covenant. 23 The others who became priests are numerous because death prevented them from continuing to serve. 24 In contrast, he holds the office of priest permanently because he continues to serve forever. 25 This is why he can completely save those who are approaching God through him, because he always lives to speak with God for them.

26 It's appropriate for us to have this kind of high priest: holy, innocent, incorrupt, separate from sinners, and raised high above the heavens. 27 He doesn't need to offer sacrifices every day like the other high priests, first for their own sins and then for the sins of the people. He did this once for all when he offered himself. 28 The Law appoints people who are prone to weakness as high priests, but the content of the solemn pledge, which came after the Law, appointed a Son who has been made perfect forever.

Meeting tents, sacrifices, and covenants

8 Now the main point of what we are saying is this: We have this kind of high priest. He sat down at the right side of the throne of the majesty in the heavens. 2 He's serving as a priest in the holy place, which is the true meeting tent that God, not any human being, set up. 3 Every high priest is appointed to offer gifts and sacrifices. So it's necessary for this high priest also to have something to offer. 4 If he was located on earth, he wouldn't be a priest because there are already others who offer gifts based on the Law. 5 They serve in a place that is a copy and shadow of the heavenly meeting tent. This is indicated when Moses was warned by God when he was about to set up the meeting tent: *See that you follow the pattern that I showed you on the mountain in every detail.*[v] 6 But now, Jesus has received a superior priestly service just as he arranged a better covenant that is enacted with better promises.

7 If the first covenant had been without fault, it wouldn't have made sense to expect a second. 8 But God did find fault with them, since he says,

[t] Ps 110:4 [u] Ps 110:4 [v] Exod 25:40

Look, the days are coming, says the Lord,
when I will make a covenant
with the house of Israel,
and I will make a new covenant
with the house of Judah.
9 *It will not be like the covenant*
that I made with their ancestors
on the day I took them by the hand
to lead them out of the land of Egypt,
because they did not continue
to keep my covenant,
and I lost interest in them,
says the Lord.
10 *This is the covenant that I will make*
with the house of Israel
after those days, says the Lord.
I will place my laws in their minds,
and write them on their hearts.
I will be their God,
and they will be my people.
11 *And each person*
won't ever teach a neighbor
or their brother or sister, saying,
"Know the Lord,"
because they will all know me,
from the least important of them
to the most important;
12 *because I will be lenient*
toward their unjust actions,
and I won't remember
their sins anymore.[w]

13 When it says new, it makes the first
obsolete. And if something is old and out-
dated, it's close to disappearing.

Christ's service in the heavenly meeting tent

9 So then the first covenant had regulations for the priests' service and the
holy place on earth. 2 They pitched the first
tent called the holy place. It contained the
lampstand, the table, and the loaves of
bread presented to God. 3 There was a tent
behind the second curtain called the holy
of holies. 4 It had the gold altar for incense
and the chest containing the covenant,
which was covered with gold on all sides.
In the chest there was a gold jar containing
manna, Aaron's rod that budded, and the
stone tablets of the covenant. 5 Above the
chest there were magnificent winged creatures[x] casting their shadow over the seat of
the chest, where sin is taken care of. Right
now we can't talk about these things in
detail. 6 When these things have been prepared in this way, priests enter the first tent
all the time as they perform their service.
7 But only the high priest enters the second
tent once a year. He never does this without blood, which he offers for himself and
for the sins the people committed in ignorance. 8 With this, the Holy Spirit is showing that the way into the holy place hadn't
been revealed yet while the first tent was
standing. 9 This is a symbol for the present
time. It shows that the gifts and sacrifices
that are being offered can't perfect the conscience of the one who is serving. 10 These
are superficial regulations that are only
about food, drink, and various ritual ways
to wash with water. They are regulations
that have been imposed until the time of
the new order.

11 But Christ has appeared as the high
priest of the good things that have happened. He passed through the greater and
more perfect meeting tent, which isn't
made by human hands (that is, it's not a
part of this world). 12 He entered the holy
of holies once for all by his own blood, not
by the blood of goats or calves, securing our
deliverance for all time. 13 If the blood of
goats and bulls and the sprinkled ashes of
cows made spiritually contaminated people
holy and clean, 14 how much more will the
blood of Jesus wash our consciences clean
from dead works in order to serve the living
God? He offered himself to God through the
eternal Spirit as a sacrifice without any flaw.

Christ's death and the new covenant

15 This is why he's the mediator of a new
covenant (which is a will): so that those
who are called might receive the promise of
the eternal inheritance on the basis of his
death. His death occurred to set them free
from the offenses committed under the
first covenant. 16 When there is a will, you

[w] Jer 31:31-34 [x] Heb *cherubim*

need to confirm the death of the one who made the will. 17This is because a will takes effect only after a death, since it's not in force while the one who made the will is alive. 18So not even the first covenant was put into effect without blood. 19Moses took the blood of calves and goats, along with water, scarlet wool, and hyssop, and sprinkled both the Law scroll itself and all the people after he had proclaimed every command of the Law to all the people. 20While he did it, he said, *This is the blood of the covenant that God established for you.*[y] 21And in the same way he sprinkled the meeting tent and also all the equipment that would be used in the priests' service with blood. 22Almost everything is cleansed by blood, according to the Law's regulations, and there is no forgiveness without blood being shed.

23So it was necessary for the copies of the heavenly things to be cleansed with these sacrifices, but the heavenly things had to be cleansed with better sacrifices than these. 24Christ didn't enter the holy place (which is a copy of the true holy place) made by human hands, but into heaven itself, so that he now appears in God's presence for us. 25He didn't enter to offer himself over and over again, like the high priest enters the earthly holy place every year with blood that isn't his. 26If that were so, then Jesus would have to suffer many times since the foundation of the world. Instead, he has now appeared once at the end of the ages to get rid of sin by sacrificing himself. 27People are destined to die once and then face judgment. 28In the same way, Christ was also offered once to take on himself the sins of many people. He will appear a second time, not to take away sin but to save those who are eagerly waiting for him.

Christ's once-for-all sacrifice

10 The Law is a shadow of the good things that are coming, not the real things themselves. It never can perfect the ones who are trying to draw near to God through the same sacrifices that are offered continually every year. 2Otherwise, wouldn't they have stopped being offered? If the people carrying out their religious duties had been completely cleansed once, no one would have been aware of sin anymore. 3Instead, these sacrifices are a reminder of sin every year, 4because it's impossible for the blood of bulls and goats to take away sins.

5Therefore, when he comes into the world he says,

You didn't want a sacrifice or an offering,
but you prepared a body for me;
6*you weren't pleased with entirely burned*
offerings or a sin offering.
7*So then I said,*
"Look, I've come to do your will, God.
This has been written about me
in the scroll."[z]

8He says above, *You didn't want* and *you weren't pleased with a sacrifice or an offering* or *with entirely burned offerings or a purification offering,*[a] which are offered because the Law requires them. 9Then he said, *Look, I've come to do your will.*[b] He puts an end to the first to establish the second. 10We have been made holy by God's will through the offering of Jesus Christ's body once for all.

11Every priest stands every day serving and offering the same sacrifices over and over, sacrifices that can never take away sins. 12But when this priest offered one sacrifice for sins for all time, he sat down at the right side of God. 13Since then, he's waiting until his enemies are made into a footstool for his feet, 14because he perfected the people who are being made holy with one offering for all time.

15The Holy Spirit affirms this when saying,

16*This is the covenant*
that I will make with them.
After these days, says the Lord,
I will place my laws in their hearts
and write them on their minds.
17*And I won't remember their sins*
and their lawless behavior anymore.[c]

18When there is forgiveness for these things, there is no longer an offering for sin.

[y]Exod 24:8 [z]Ps 40:6-8 [a]Ps 40:6 [b]Ps 40:7-8 [c]Jer 31:33-34

Second summary of the message

19 Brothers and sisters, we have confidence that we can enter the holy of holies by
means of Jesus' blood, 20 through a new and
living way that he opened up for us through
the curtain, which is his body, 21 and we have
a great high priest over God's house.
22 Therefore, let's draw near with a genuine heart with the certainty that our faith
gives us, since our hearts are sprinkled
clean from an evil conscience and our bodies are washed with pure water.
23 Let's hold on to the confession of our
hope without wavering, because the one
who made the promises is reliable.
24 And let us consider each other carefully for the purpose of sparking love and
good deeds. 25 Don't stop meeting together
with other believers, which some people
have gotten into the habit of doing. Instead, encourage each other, especially as
you see the day drawing near.

Judgment for intentional sin

26 If we make the decision to sin after we
receive the knowledge of the truth, there
isn't a sacrifice for sins left any longer.
27 There's only a scary expectation of judgment and of a burning fire that's going to
devour God's opponents. 28 When someone
rejected the Law from Moses, they were put
to death without mercy on the basis of the
testimony of two or three witnesses. 29 How
much worse punishment do you think is
deserved by the person who walks all over
God's Son, who acts as if the blood of the
covenant that made us holy is just ordinary
blood, and who insults the Spirit of grace?
30 We know the one who said,

Judgment is mine; I will pay people back.[d]

And he also said,

The Lord will judge his people.[e]

31 It's scary to fall into the hands of the living God!

Confidence and faith to endure

32 But remember the earlier days, after
you saw the light. You stood your ground
while you were suffering from an enormous
amount of pressure. 33 Sometimes you
were exposed to insults and abuse in public. Other times you became partners with
those who were treated that way. 34 You
even showed sympathy toward people in
prison and accepted the confiscation of
your possessions with joy, since you knew
that you had better and lasting possessions.
35 So don't throw away your confidence—it
brings a great reward. 36 You need to endure
so that you can receive the promises after
you do God's will.

37 *In a little while longer,*
the one who is coming will come
and won't delay;
38 *but my righteous one will live by faith,*
and my whole being won't be pleased
with anyone who shrinks back.[f]

39 But we aren't the sort of people who
timidly draw back and end up being destroyed. We're the sort of people who have
faith so that our whole beings are preserved.

Description of faith

11 Faith is the reality of what we hope for,
the proof of what we don't see. 2 The
elders in the past were approved because
they showed faith.

Acts of faith by God's people

3 By faith we understand that the universe has been created by a word from God
so that the visible came into existence from
the invisible.
4 By faith Abel offered a better sacrifice to
God than Cain, which showed that he was
righteous, since God gave approval to him
for his gift. Though he died, he's still speaking through faith.
5 By faith Enoch was taken up so that
he didn't see death, and *he wasn't found*
because God took him up.[g] He was given approval for having pleased God before he
was taken up. 6 It's impossible to please God
without faith because the one who draws
near to God must believe that he exists and
that he rewards people who try to find him.
7 By faith Noah responded with godly
fear when he was warned about events he

[d] Deut 32:35 [e] Deut 32:36; Ps 135:14 [f] Hab 2:3-4 [g] Gen 5:24

hadn't seen yet. He built an ark to deliver
his household. With his faith, he criticized
the world and became an heir of the righteousness that comes from faith.
8 By faith Abraham obeyed when he was
called to go out to a place that he was going
to receive as an inheritance. He went out
without knowing where he was going.
9 By faith he lived in the land he had
been promised as a stranger. He lived in
tents along with Isaac and Jacob, who were
coheirs of the same promise. 10 He was looking forward to a city that has foundations,
whose architect and builder is God.
11 By faith even Sarah received the ability
to have a child, though she herself was
barren and past the age for having children, because she believed that the one
who promised was faithful. 12 So descendants were born from one man (and he
was as good as dead). They were as many
as the number of the stars in the sky and
as countless as the grains of sand on the
seashore. 13 All of these people died in faith
without receiving the promises, but they
saw the promises from a distance and
welcomed them. They confessed that they
were strangers and immigrants on earth.
14 People who say this kind of thing make
it clear that they are looking for a homeland. 15 If they had been thinking about
the country that they had left, they would
have had the opportunity to return to it.
16 But at this point in time, they are longing for a better country, that is, a heavenly
one. Therefore, God isn't ashamed to be
called their God—he has prepared a city
for them.
17 By faith Abraham offered Isaac when
he was tested. The one who received the
promises was offering his only son. 18 He
had been told concerning him, *Your legitimate descendants will come from Isaac.*[h] 19 He
figured that God could even raise him from
the dead. So in a way he did receive him
back from the dead.
20 By faith Isaac also blessed Jacob and
Esau concerning their future.
21 By faith Jacob blessed each of Joseph's
sons as he was dying and *bowed in worship
over the head of his staff.*[i]
22 By faith Joseph recalled the exodus of
the Israelites at the end of his life, and gave
instructions about burying his bones.
23 By faith Moses was hidden by his parents for three months when he was born, because they saw that the child was beautiful
and they weren't afraid of the king's orders.
24 By faith Moses refused to be called the
son of Pharaoh's daughter when he was
grown up. 25 He chose to be mistreated with
God's people instead of having the temporary pleasures of sin. 26 He thought that the
abuses he suffered for Christ were more
valuable than the treasures of Egypt, since
he was looking forward to the reward.
27 By faith he left Egypt without being
afraid of the king's anger. He kept on going
as if he could see what is invisible.
28 By faith he kept the Passover and
the sprinkling of blood, in order that the
destroyer could not touch their firstborn
children.
29 By faith they crossed the Red Sea as if
they were on dry land, but when the Egyptians tried it, they were drowned.
30 By faith Jericho's walls fell after the
people marched around them for seven days.
31 By faith Rahab the prostitute wasn't
killed with the disobedient because she welcomed the spies in peace.
32 What more can I say? I would run out
of time if I told you about Gideon, Barak,
Samson, Jephthah, David, Samuel, and the
prophets. 33 Through faith they conquered
kingdoms, brought about justice, realized
promises, shut the mouths of lions, 34 put
out raging fires, escaped from the edge of
the sword, found strength in weakness,
were mighty in war, and routed foreign
armies. 35 Women received back their dead
by resurrection. Others were tortured and
refused to be released so they could gain a
better resurrection.
36 But others experienced public shame
by being taunted and whipped; they were
even put in chains and in prison. 37 They
were stoned to death, they were cut in

[h] Gen 21:12 [i] Gen 47:31 LXX

two, and they died by being murdered with swords. They went around wearing the skins of sheep and goats, needy, oppressed, and mistreated. 38The world didn't deserve them. They wandered around in deserts, mountains, caves, and holes in the ground.

39All these people didn't receive what was promised, though they were given approval for their faith. 40God provided something better for us so they wouldn't be made perfect without us.

Let's also run the race

12 So then let's also run the race that is laid out in front of us, since we have such a great cloud of witnesses surrounding us. Let's throw off any extra baggage, get rid of the sin that trips us up, 2and fix our eyes on Jesus, faith's pioneer and perfecter. He endured the cross, ignoring the shame, for the sake of the joy that was laid out in front of him, and sat down at the right side of God's throne.

Run the race with discipline

3Think about the one who endured such opposition from sinners so that you won't be discouraged and you won't give up. 4In your struggle against sin, you haven't resisted yet to the point of shedding blood, 5and you have forgotten the encouragement that addresses you as sons and daughters:

My child, don't make light
of the Lord's discipline
or give up when you are corrected by him,
6 *because the Lord disciplines*
whomever he loves,
and he punishes every son or daughter
whom he accepts.[j]

7Bear hardship for the sake of discipline. God is treating you like sons and daughters! What child isn't disciplined by his or her father? 8But if you don't experience discipline, which happens to all children, then you are illegitimate and not real sons and daughters. 9What's more, we had human parents who disciplined us, and we respected them for it. How much more should we submit to the Father of spirits and live? 10Our human parents disciplined us for a little while, as it seemed best to them, but God does it for our benefit so that we can share his holiness. 11No discipline is fun while it lasts, but it seems painful at the time. Later, however, it yields the peaceful fruit of righteousness for those who have been trained by it.

12So strengthen your drooping hands and weak knees! 13Make straight paths for your feet so that if any part is lame, it will be healed rather than injured more seriously. 14Pursue the goal of peace along with everyone—and holiness as well, because no one will see the Lord without it. 15Make sure that no one misses out on God's grace. Make sure that no root of bitterness grows up that might cause trouble and pollute many people. 16Make sure that no one becomes sexually immoral or ungodly like Esau. He sold his inheritance as the oldest son for one meal. 17You know that afterward, when he wanted to inherit the blessing, he was rejected because he couldn't find a way to change his heart and life, though he looked for it with tears.

Priestly service in heavenly Jerusalem

18You haven't drawn near to something that can be touched: a burning fire, darkness, shadow, a whirlwind, 19a blast of a trumpet, and a sound of words that made the ones who heard it beg that there wouldn't be one more word. 20They couldn't stand the command, *If even a wild animal touches the mountain, it must be stoned.*[k] 21The sight was so frightening that Moses said, "I'm terrified and shaking!"

22But you have drawn near to Mount Zion, the city of the living God, heavenly Jerusalem, to countless angels in a festival gathering, 23to the assembly of the God's firstborn children who are registered in heaven, to God the judge of all, to the spirits of the righteous who have been made perfect, 24to Jesus the mediator of the new covenant, and to the sprinkled blood that speaks better than Abel's blood.

25See to it that you don't resist the one who is speaking. If the people didn't escape when they refused to listen to the one

[j]Prov 3:11-12 [k]Exod 19:12-13

who warned them on earth, how will we escape if we reject the one who is warning from heaven? 26His voice shook the earth then, but now he has made a promise: *Still once more I will shake not only the earth but heaven also.*[l] 27The words "still once more" reveal the removal of what is shaken—the things that are part of this creation—so that what isn't shaken will remain. 28Therefore, since we are receiving a kingdom that can't be shaken, let's continue to express our gratitude.[m] With this gratitude, let's serve[n] in a way that is pleasing to God with respect and awe, 29because our God really is a consuming fire.

Our acts of service and sacrifice

13 Keep loving each other like family. 2Don't neglect to open up your homes to guests, because by doing this some have been hosts to angels without knowing it. 3Remember prisoners as if you were in prison with them, and people who are mistreated as if you were in their place. 4Marriage must be honored in every respect, with no cheating on the relationship, because God will judge the sexually immoral person and the person who commits adultery. 5Your way of life should be free from the love of money, and you should be content with what you have. After all, he has said, *I will never leave you or abandon you.*[o] 6This is why we can confidently say,

The Lord is my helper,
and I won't be afraid.
What can people do to me?[p]

7Remember your leaders who spoke God's word to you. Imitate their faith as you consider the way their lives turned out. 8Jesus Christ is the same yesterday, today, and forever!

9Don't be misled by the many strange teachings out there. It's a good thing for the heart to be strengthened by grace rather than by food. Food doesn't help those who live in this context. 10We have an altar, and those who serve as priests in the meeting tent don't have the right to eat from it. 11The blood of the animals is carried into the holy of holies by the high priest as an offering for sin, and their bodies are burned outside the camp. 12And so Jesus also suffered outside the city gate to make the people holy with his own blood.

13So now, let's go to him outside the camp, bearing his shame. 14We don't have a permanent city here, but rather we are looking for the city that is still to come.

15So let's continually offer up a sacrifice of praise through him, which is the fruit from our lips that confess his name. 16Don't forget to do good and to share what you have because God is pleased with these kinds of sacrifices.

Closing greeting and blessing

17Rely on your leaders and defer to them, because they watch over your whole being as people who are going to be held responsible for you. They need to be able to do this with pleasure and not with complaints about you, because that wouldn't help you. 18Pray for us. We're sure that we have a good conscience, and we want to do the right thing in every way. 19I'm particularly asking you to do this so that I can be returned to you quickly.

20May the God of peace,
who brought back
the great shepherd of the sheep,
our Lord Jesus,
from the dead by the blood
of the eternal covenant,
21equip you with every good thing
to do his will,
by developing in us what pleases him
through Jesus Christ.
To him be the glory forever and always.
Amen.

22I urge you, brothers and sisters, to put up with this message of encouragement, since I've only written a short letter to you! 23You should know that our brother Timothy has been set free. If he comes soon, we will travel together to see you.

24Greet your leaders and all of God's holy people. The group from Italy greets you.

25May grace be with all of you.

[l]Exod 19:18 [m]Or *hold on to grace* [n]Or *offer priestly service* [o]Deut 31:6; Gen 28:15 [p]Ps 118:6

JAMES

Greeting

1 From James, a slave of God and of the
Lord Jesus Christ.
To the twelve tribes who are scattered
outside the land of Israel.
Greetings!

Stand firm

2 My brothers and sisters, think of the
various tests you encounter as occasions
for joy. 3 After all, you know that the testing
of your faith produces endurance. 4 Let this
endurance complete its work so that you
may be fully mature, complete, and lacking
in nothing. 5 But anyone who needs wisdom
should ask God, whose very nature is to
give to everyone without a second thought,
without keeping score. Wisdom will certainly be given to those who ask. 6 Whoever
asks shouldn't hesitate. They should ask in
faith, without doubting. Whoever doubts is
like the surf of the sea, tossed and turned
by the wind. 7 People like that should never
imagine that they will receive anything
from the Lord. 8 They are double-minded,
unstable in all their ways.
9 Brothers and sisters who are poor
should find satisfaction in their high status.
10 Those who are wealthy should find satisfaction in their low status, because they will
die off like wildflowers. 11 The sun rises with
its scorching heat and dries up the grass so
that its flowers fall and its beauty is lost.
Just like that, in the midst of their daily
lives, the wealthy will waste away. 12 Those
who stand firm during testing are blessed.
They are tried and true. They will receive
the life God has promised to those who love
him as their reward.

Our cravings versus God's gifts

13 No one who is tested should say, "God
is tempting me!" This is because God is
not tempted by any form of evil, nor does
he tempt anyone. 14 Everyone is tempted
by their own cravings; they are lured away
and enticed by them. 15 Once those cravings
conceive, they give birth to sin; and when
sin grows up, it gives birth to death.
16 Don't be misled, my dear brothers and
sisters. 17 Every good gift, every perfect gift,
comes from above. These gifts come down
from the Father, the creator of the heavenly lights, in whose character there is no
change at all. 18 He chose to give us birth by
his true word, and here is the result: we are
like the first crop from the harvest of everything he created.

Welcoming and doing the word

19 Know this, my dear brothers and sisters: everyone should be quick to listen,
slow to speak, and slow to grow angry.
20 This is because an angry person doesn't
produce God's righteousness. 21 Therefore,
with humility, set aside all moral filth and
the growth of wickedness, and welcome the
word planted deep inside you—the very
word that is able to save you.
22 You must be doers of the word and
not only hearers who mislead themselves.
23 Those who hear but don't do the word are
like those who look at their faces in a mirror. 24 They look at themselves, walk away,
and immediately forget what they were like.
25 But there are those who study the perfect
law, the law of freedom, and continue to do
it. They don't listen and then forget, but
they put it into practice in their lives. They
will be blessed in whatever they do.
26 If those who claim devotion to God don't
control what they say, they mislead themselves. Their devotion is worthless. 27 True
devotion, the kind that is pure and faultless
before God the Father, is this: to care for orphans and widows in their difficulties and to
keep the world from contaminating us.

Don't show favoritism

2 My brothers and sisters, when you show
favoritism you deny the faithfulness of
our Lord Jesus Christ, who has been resurrected in glory. 2 Imagine two people coming into your meeting. One has a gold ring
and fine clothes, while the other is poor,
dressed in filthy rags. 3 Then suppose that
you were to take special notice of the one
wearing fine clothes, saying, "Here's an

excellent place. Sit here." But to the poor person you say, "Stand over there"; or, "Here, sit at my feet." 4Wouldn't you have shown favoritism among yourselves and become evil-minded judges?

5My dear brothers and sisters, listen! Hasn't God chosen those who are poor by worldly standards to be rich in terms of faith? Hasn't God chosen the poor as heirs of the kingdom he has promised to those who love him? 6But you have dishonored the poor. Don't the wealthy make life difficult for you? Aren't they the ones who drag you into court? 7Aren't they the ones who insult the good name spoken over you at your baptism?

8You do well when you really fulfill the royal law found in scripture, *Love your neighbor as yourself.*[a] 9But when you show favoritism, you are committing a sin, and by that same law you are exposed as a lawbreaker. 10Anyone who tries to keep all of the Law but fails at one point is guilty of failing to keep all of it. 11The one who said, *Don't commit adultery*, also said, *Don't commit murder.*[b] So if you don't commit adultery but do commit murder, you are a lawbreaker. 12In every way, then, speak and act as people who will be judged by the law of freedom. 13There will be no mercy in judgment for anyone who hasn't shown mercy. Mercy overrules judgment.

Showing faith

14My brothers and sisters, what good is it if people say they have faith but do nothing to show it? Claiming to have faith can't save anyone, can it? 15Imagine a brother or sister who is naked and never has enough food to eat. 16What if one of you said, "Go in peace! Stay warm! Have a nice meal!"? What good is it if you don't actually give them what their body needs? 17In the same way, faith is dead when it doesn't result in faithful activity.

18Someone might claim, "You have faith and I have action." But how can I see your faith apart from your actions? Instead, I'll show you my faith by putting it into practice in faithful action. 19It's good that you believe that God is one. Ha! Even the demons believe this, and they tremble with fear. 20Are you so slow? Do you need to be shown that faith without actions has no value at all? 21What about Abraham, our father? Wasn't he shown to be righteous through his actions when he offered his son Isaac on the altar? 22See, his faith was at work along with his actions. In fact, his faith was made complete by his faithful actions. 23So the scripture was fulfilled that says, *Abraham believed God, and God regarded him as righteous.*[c] What is more, Abraham was called God's friend. 24So you see that a person is shown to be righteous through faithful actions and not through faith alone. 25In the same way, wasn't Rahab the prostitute shown to be righteous when she received the messengers as her guests and then sent them on by another road? 26As the lifeless body is dead, so faith without actions is dead.

Taming the tongue

3 My brothers and sisters, not many of you should become teachers, because we know that we teachers will be judged more strictly. 2We all make mistakes often, but those who don't make mistakes with their words have reached full maturity. Like a bridled horse, they can control themselves entirely. 3When we bridle horses and put bits in their mouths to lead them wherever we want, we can control their whole bodies.

4Consider ships: they are so large that strong winds are needed to drive them. But pilots direct their ships wherever they want with a little rudder. 5In the same way, even though the tongue is a small part of the body, it boasts wildly.

Think about this: a small flame can set a whole forest on fire. 6The tongue is a small flame of fire, a world of evil at work in us. It contaminates our entire lives. Because of it, the circle of life is set on fire. The tongue itself is set on fire by the flames of hell.

7People can tame and already have tamed every kind of animal, bird, reptile, and fish.

[a]Lev 19:18 [b]Exod 20:13, 15 LXX (English: 20:13-14); Deut 5:17-18 [c]Gen 15:6

8 No one can tame the tongue, though. It is a restless evil, full of deadly poison. 9 With it we both bless the Lord and Father and curse human beings made in God's likeness. 10 Blessing and cursing come from the same mouth. My brothers and sisters, it just shouldn't be this way!

11 Both fresh water and salt water don't come from the same spring, do they? 12 My brothers and sisters, can a fig tree produce olives? Can a grapevine produce figs? Of course not, and fresh water doesn't flow from a saltwater spring either.

Wisdom from above

13 Are any of you wise and understanding? Show that your actions are good with a humble lifestyle that comes from wisdom. 14 However, if you have bitter jealousy and selfish ambition in your heart, then stop bragging and living in ways that deny the truth. 15 This is not the wisdom that comes down from above. Instead, it is from the earth, natural and demonic. 16 Wherever there is jealousy and selfish ambition, there is disorder and everything that is evil. 17 What of the wisdom from above? First, it is pure, and then peaceful, gentle, obedient, filled with mercy and good actions, fair, and genuine. 18 Those who make peace sow the seeds of justice by their peaceful acts.

Conflict with people and God

4 What is the source of conflict among you? What is the source of your disputes? Don't they come from your cravings that are at war in your own lives? 2 You long for something you don't have, so you commit murder. You are jealous for something you can't get, so you struggle and fight. You don't have because you don't ask. 3 You ask and don't have because you ask with evil intentions, to waste it on your own cravings.

4 You unfaithful people! Don't you know that friendship with the world makes you an enemy of God? 5 Or do you suppose that scripture is meaningless? Doesn't God long for our faithfulness in[d] the life he has given to us?[e] 6 But he gives us more grace. This is why it says, *God stands against the proud, but favors the humble.*[f] 7 Therefore, submit to God. Resist the devil, and he will run away from you. 8 Come near to God, and he will come near to you. Wash your hands, you sinners. Purify your hearts, you double-minded. 9 Cry out in sorrow, mourn, and weep! Let your laughter become mourning and your joy become sadness. 10 Humble yourselves before the Lord, and he will lift you up.

11 Brothers and sisters, don't say evil things about each other. Whoever insults or criticizes a brother or sister insults and criticizes the Law. If you find fault with the Law, you are not a doer of the Law but a judge over it. 12 There is only one lawgiver and judge, and he is able to save and to destroy. But you who judge your neighbor, who are you?

Warning the proud and wealthy

13 Pay attention, you who say, "Today or tomorrow we will go to such-and-such a town. We will stay there a year, buying and selling, and making a profit." 14 You don't really know about tomorrow. What is your life? You are a mist that appears for only a short while before it vanishes. 15 Here's what you ought to say: "If the Lord wills, we will live and do this or that." 16 But now you boast and brag, and all such boasting is evil. 17 It is a sin when someone knows the right thing to do and doesn't do it.

5 Pay attention, you wealthy people! Weep and moan over the miseries coming upon you. 2 Your riches have rotted. Moths have destroyed your clothes. 3 Your gold and silver have rusted, and their rust will be evidence against you. It will eat your flesh like fire. Consider the treasure you have hoarded in the last days. 4 Listen! Hear the cries of the wages of your field hands. These are the wages you stole from those who harvested your fields. The cries of the harvesters have reached the ears of the Lord of heavenly forces. 5 You have lived a self-satisfying life on this earth, a life of luxury. You have stuffed your hearts in preparation for the day of slaughter.

[d] Or *jealously longs for* [e] Or *Doesn't the spirit that God placed in us have jealous desires?* [f] Prov 3:34

6You have condemned and murdered the righteous one, who doesn't oppose you.

Courageous patience

7Therefore, brothers and sisters, you must be patient as you wait for the coming of the Lord. Consider the farmer who waits patiently for the coming of rain in the fall and spring, looking forward to the precious fruit of the earth. 8You also must wait patiently, strengthening your resolve, because the coming of the Lord is near. 9Don't complain about each other, brothers and sisters, so that you won't be judged. Look! The judge is standing at the door!

10Brothers and sisters, take the prophets who spoke in the name of the Lord as an example of patient resolve and steadfastness. 11Look at how we honor those who have practiced endurance. You have heard of the endurance of Job. And you have seen what the Lord has accomplished, for the Lord is full of compassion and mercy.

Final instructions

12Most important, my brothers and sisters, never make a solemn pledge—neither by heaven nor earth, nor by anything else. Instead, speak with a simple "Yes" or "No," or else you may fall under judgment.

13If any of you are suffering, they should pray. If any of you are happy, they should sing. 14If any of you are sick, they should call for the elders of the church, and the elders should pray over them, anointing them with oil in the name of the Lord. 15Prayer that comes from faith will heal the sick, for the Lord will restore them to health. And if they have sinned, they will be forgiven. 16For this reason, confess your sins to each other and pray for each other so that you may be healed. The prayer of the righteous person is powerful in what it can achieve. 17Elijah was a person just like us. When he earnestly prayed that it wouldn't rain, no rain fell for three and a half years. 18He prayed again, God sent rain, and the earth produced its fruit.

19My brothers and sisters, if any of you wander from the truth and someone turns back the wanderer, 20recognize that whoever brings a sinner back from the wrong path will save them from death and will bring about the forgiveness of many sins.

1 PETER

Greeting

1 Peter, an apostle of Jesus Christ,
To God's chosen strangers in the world of the diaspora, who live in Pontus, Galatia, Cappadocia, Asia, and Bithynia.
2God the Father chose you because of what he knew beforehand. He chose you through the Holy Spirit's work of making you holy and because of the faithful obedience and sacrifice of Jesus Christ.
May God's grace and peace be multiplied to you.

Thanksgiving

3May the God and Father of our Lord Jesus Christ be blessed! On account of his vast mercy, he has given us new birth. You have been born anew into a living hope through the resurrection of Jesus Christ from the dead. 4You have a pure and enduring inheritance that cannot perish—an inheritance that is presently kept safe in heaven for you. 5Through his faithfulness, you are guarded by God's power so that you can receive the salvation he is ready to reveal in the last time.

6You now rejoice in this hope, even if it's necessary for you to be distressed for a short time by various trials. 7This is necessary so that your faith may be found genuine. (Your faith is more valuable than gold, which will be destroyed even though it is itself tested by fire.) Your genuine faith will result in praise, glory, and honor for you when Jesus Christ is revealed. 8Although you've never seen him, you love him. Even though you don't see him now, you trust him and so rejoice with a glorious joy that is too much for words. 9You

are receiving the goal of your faith: your
salvation.
10 The prophets, who long ago foretold
the grace that you've received, searched
and explored, inquiring carefully about this
salvation. 11 They wondered what the Spirit
of Christ within them was saying when he
bore witness beforehand about the suffering
that would happen to Christ and the glory
that would follow. They wondered what sort
of person or what sort of time they were
speaking about. 12 It was revealed to them
that in their search they were not serving
themselves but you. These things, which
even angels long to examine, have now been
proclaimed to you by those who brought you
the good news. They did this in the power of
the Holy Spirit, who was sent from heaven.

Response of obedience

13 Therefore, once you have your minds
ready for action and you are thinking clearly,
place your hope completely on the grace that
will be brought to you when Jesus Christ is revealed. 14 Don't be conformed to your former
desires, those that shaped you when you were
ignorant. But, as obedient children, 15 you
must be holy in every aspect of your lives, just
as the one who called you is holy. 16 It is written, *You will be holy, because I am holy.*[a] 17 Since
you call upon a Father who judges all people
according to their actions without favoritism,
you should conduct yourselves with reverence during the time of your dwelling in a
strange land. 18 Live in this way, knowing that
you were not liberated by perishable things
like silver or gold from the empty lifestyle you
inherited from your ancestors. 19 Instead, you
were liberated by the precious blood of Christ,
like that of a flawless, spotless lamb. 20 Christ
was chosen before the creation of the world,
but was only revealed at the end of time. This
was done for you, 21 who through Christ are
faithful to the God who raised him from the
dead and gave him glory. So now, your faith
and hope should rest in God.
22 As you set yourselves apart by your
obedience to the truth so that you might
have genuine affection for your fellow believers, love each other deeply and earnestly.
23 Do this because you have been given new
birth—not from the type of seed that decays but from seed that doesn't. This seed is
God's life-giving and enduring word.
24 Thus,

All human life on the earth is like grass,
and all human glory
is like a flower in a field.
The grass dries up and its flower falls off,
25 *but the Lord's word endures forever.*[b]

This is the word that was proclaimed to
you as good news.

Your identity as believers

2 Therefore, get rid of all ill will and all
deceit, pretense, envy, and slander. 2 Instead, like a newborn baby, desire the pure
milk of the word. Nourished by it, you will
grow into salvation, 3 since you have tasted
that the Lord is good.
4 Now you are coming to him as to a living stone. Even though this stone was rejected by humans, from God's perspective
it is chosen, valuable. 5 You yourselves are
being built like living stones into a spiritual temple. You are being made into a holy
priesthood to offer up spiritual sacrifices
that are acceptable to God through Jesus
Christ. 6 Thus it is written in scripture,
Look! I am laying a cornerstone in Zion, cho-
sen, valuable. The person who believes in him
will never be shamed.[c] 7 So God honors you
who believe. For those who refuse to believe, though, the stone the builders tossed
aside has become the capstone. 8 This is
a stone that makes people stumble and a
rock that makes them fall. Because they refuse to believe in the word, they stumble.
Indeed, this is the end to which they were
appointed. 9 But you are a chosen race, a
royal priesthood, a holy nation, a people
who are God's own possession. You have
become this people so that you may speak
of the wonderful acts of the one who called
you out of darkness into his amazing light.
10 Once you weren't a people, but now you
are God's people. Once you hadn't received
mercy, but now you have received mercy.

[a]Lev 19:2 [b]Isa 40:6-8 [c]Isa 28:16

Life as strangers in the world

11 Dear friends, since you are immigrants
and strangers in the world, I urge that you
avoid worldly desires that wage war against
your lives. 12 Live honorably among the
unbelievers. Today, they defame you, as if
you were doing evil. But in the day when God
visits to judge they will glorify him, because
they have observed your honorable deeds.
13 For the sake of the Lord submit to every
human institution. Do this whether it means
submitting to the emperor as supreme ruler,
14 or to governors as those sent by the emperor. They are sent to punish those doing
evil and to praise those doing good. 15 Submit to them because it's God's will that by
doing good you will silence the ignorant talk
of foolish people. 16 Do this as God's slaves,
and yet also as free people, not using your
freedom as a cover-up for evil. 17 Honor everyone. Love the family of believers. Have
respectful fear of God. Honor the emperor.
18 Household slaves, submit by accepting the authority of your masters with all
respect. Do this not only to good and kind
masters but also to those who are harsh.
19 Now, it is commendable if, because of
one's understanding of God, someone
should endure pain through suffering unjustly. 20 But what praise comes from enduring patiently when you have sinned and are
beaten for it? But if you endure steadfastly
when you've done good and suffer for it,
this is commendable before God.
21 You were called to this kind of endurance, because Christ suffered on your behalf. He left you an example so that you
might follow in his footsteps. 22 He committed no sin, nor did he ever speak in ways
meant to deceive. 23 When he was insulted,
he did not reply with insults. When he suffered, he did not threaten revenge. Instead,
he entrusted himself to the one who judges
justly. 24 He carried in his own body on the
cross the sins we committed. He did this so
that we might live in righteousness, having
nothing to do with sin. By his wounds you
were healed. 25 Though you were like straying sheep, you have now returned to the
shepherd and guardian of your lives.

3 Wives, likewise, submit to your own
husbands. Do this so that even if some
of them refuse to believe the word, they may
be won without a word by their wives' way
of life. 2 After all, they will have observed
the reverent and holy manner of your lives.
3 Don't try to make yourselves beautiful on
the outside, with stylish hair or by wearing gold jewelry or fine clothes. 4 Instead,
make yourselves beautiful on the inside, in
your hearts, with the enduring quality of a
gentle, peaceful spirit. This type of beauty
is very precious in God's eyes. 5 For it was
in this way that holy women who trusted
in God used to make themselves beautiful, accepting the authority of their own
husbands. 6 For example, Sarah accepted
Abraham's authority when she called him
master. You have become her children when
you do good and don't respond to threats
with fear.
7 Husbands, likewise, submit by living
with your wife in ways that honor her,
knowing that she is the weaker partner.
Honor her all the more, as she is also a co-
heir of the gracious care of life. Do this so
that your prayers won't be hindered.
8 Finally, all of you be of one mind, sym-
pathetic, lovers of your fellow believers,
compassionate, and modest in your opinion of yourselves. 9 Don't pay back evil for
evil or insult for insult. Instead, give blessing in return. You were called to do this so
that you might inherit a blessing. 10 For

those who want to love life
and see good days
should keep their tongue from evil speaking
and their lips from speaking lies.
11 *They should shun evil and do good;*
seek peace and chase after it.
12 *The Lord's eyes are on the righteous*
and his ears are open to their prayers.
But the Lord cannot tolerate
those who do evil.[d]

13 Who will harm you if you are zealous
for good? 14 But happy are you even if you
suffer because of righteousness! Don't be
terrified or upset by them. 15 Instead, regard
Christ as holy in your hearts. Whenever

[d] Ps 34:12-16

anyone asks you to speak of your hope,
be ready to defend it. 16Yet do this with
respectful humility, maintaining a good
conscience. Act in this way so that those who
malign your good lifestyle in Christ may be
ashamed when they slander you. 17It is better to suffer for doing good (if this could possibly be God's will) than for doing evil.

18Christ himself suffered on account
of sins, once for all, the righteous one on
behalf of the unrighteous. He did this in
order to bring you into the presence of God.
Christ was put to death as a human, but
made alive by the Spirit. 19And it was by the
Spirit that he went to preach to the spirits
in prison. 20In the past, these spirits were
disobedient—when God patiently waited
during the time of Noah. Noah built an ark
in which a few (that is, eight) lives were rescued through water. 21Baptism is like that. It
saves you now—not because it removes dirt
from your body but because it is the mark
of a good conscience toward God. Your salvation comes through the resurrection of
Jesus Christ, 22who is at God's right side.
Now that he has gone into heaven, he rules
over all angels, authorities, and powers.

4 Therefore, since Christ suffered as a
human, you should also arm yourselves
with his way of thinking. This is because
whoever suffers is finished with sin. 2As a result, they don't live the rest of their human
lives in ways determined by human desires
but in ways determined by God's will. 3You
have wasted enough time doing what unbelievers desire—living in their unrestrained
immorality and lust, their drunkenness and
excessive feasting and wild parties, and their
forbidden worship of idols. 4They think it's
strange that you don't join in these activities
with the same flood of unrestrained wickedness. So they slander you. 5They will have to
reckon with the one who is ready to judge
the living and the dead. 6Indeed, this is the
reason the good news was also preached to
the dead. This happened so that, although
they were judged as humans according to
human standards, they could live by the
Spirit according to divine standards.

7The end of everything has come. Therefore, be self-controlled and clearheaded so
you can pray. 8Above all, show sincere love
to each other, because love brings about
the forgiveness of many sins. 9Open your
homes to each other without complaining.
10And serve each other according to the gift
each person has received, as good managers of God's diverse gifts. 11Whoever speaks
should do so as those who speak God's
word. Whoever serves should do so from
the strength that God furnishes. Do this
so that in everything God may be honored
through Jesus Christ. To him be honor and
power forever and always. Amen.

Stand firm in the last times

12Dear friends, don't be surprised about
the fiery trials that have come among you
to test you. These are not strange happen-
ings. 13Instead, rejoice as you share Christ's
suffering. You share his suffering now so
that you may also have overwhelming joy
when his glory is revealed. 14If you are
mocked because of Christ's name, you are
blessed, for the Spirit of glory—indeed, the
Spirit of God—rests on you.

15Now none of you should suffer as a
murderer or thief or evildoer or rebel. 16But
don't be ashamed if you suffer as one who
belongs to Christ. Rather, honor God as
you bear Christ's name. Give honor to God,
17because it's time for judgment to begin
with God's own household. But if judgment
starts with us, what will happen to those
who refuse to believe God's good news?
18If the righteous are barely rescued, what
will happen to the godless and sinful? 19So
then, those who suffer because they follow
God's will should commit their lives to a
trustworthy creator by doing what is right.

5 Therefore, I have a request for the elders
among you. (I ask this as a fellow elder
and a witness of Christ's sufferings, and as
one who shares in the glory that is about to
be revealed.) I urge the elders: 2Like shepherds, tend the flock of God among you.
Watch over it. Don't shepherd because you
must, but do it voluntarily for God. Don't
shepherd greedily, but do it eagerly. 3Don't
shepherd by ruling over those entrusted
to your care, but become examples to the
flock. 4And when the chief shepherd ap-

pears, you will receive an unfading crown of glory.

5 In the same way, I urge you who are younger: accept the authority of the elders. And everyone, clothe yourselves with humility toward each other. God stands against the proud, but he gives favor to the humble.

6 Therefore, humble yourselves under God's power so that he may raise you up in the last day. 7 Throw all your anxiety onto him, because he cares about you. 8 Be clear-headed. Keep alert. Your accuser, the devil, is on the prowl like a roaring lion, seeking someone to devour. 9 Resist him, standing firm in the faith. Do so in the knowledge that your fellow believers are enduring the same suffering throughout the world. 10 After you have suffered for a little while, the God of all grace, the one who called you into his eternal glory in Christ Jesus, will himself restore, empower, strengthen, and establish you. 11 To him be power forever and always. Amen.

Final greeting

12 I have written and sent these few lines to you by Silvanus. I consider him to be a faithful brother. In these lines I have urged and affirmed that this is the genuine grace of God. Stand firm in it. 13 The fellow-elect church in Babylon greets you, and so does my son Mark. 14 Greet each other with the kiss of love. Peace to you all who are in Christ.

2 PETER

Greeting

1 From Simon Peter, a slave and apostle of Jesus Christ.

To those who received a faith equal to ours through the justice of our God and savior Jesus Christ.

2 May you have more and more grace and peace through the knowledge of God and Jesus our Lord.

Christian life in outline

3 By his divine power the Lord has given us everything we need for life and godliness through the knowledge of the one who called us by his own honor and glory. 4 Through his honor and glory he has given us his precious and wonderful promises, that you may share the divine nature and escape from the world's immorality that sinful craving produces.

5 This is why you must make every effort to add moral excellence to your faith; and to moral excellence, knowledge; 6 and to knowledge, self-control; and to self-control, endurance; and to endurance, godliness; 7 and to godliness, affection for others; and to affection for others, love. 8 If all these are yours and they are growing in you, they'll keep you from becoming inactive and unfruitful in the knowledge of our Lord Jesus Christ. 9 Whoever lacks these things is shortsighted and blind, forgetting that they were cleansed from their past sins.

10 Therefore, brothers and sisters, be eager to confirm your call and election. Do this and you will never ever be lost. 11 In this way you will receive a rich welcome into the everlasting kingdom of our Lord and savior Jesus Christ.

Reminder of the Christian life

12 So I'll keep reminding you about these things, although you already know them and stand secure in the truth you have. 13 I think it's right that I keep stirring up your memory, as long as I'm alive. 14 After all, our Lord Jesus Christ has shown me that I am about to depart from this life. 15 I'm eager for you always to remember these things after my death.

Christ's return is true

16 We didn't repeat crafty myths when we told you about the powerful coming of our Lord Jesus Christ. Quite the contrary, we witnessed his majesty with our own eyes. 17 He received honor and glory from God the Father when a voice came to him from the magnificent glory, saying, "This is my dearly

loved Son, with whom I am well-pleased."
18 We ourselves heard this voice from heaven
while we were with him on the holy mountain. 19 In addition, we have a most reliable
prophetic word, and you would do well to
pay attention to it, just as you would to a
lamp shining in a dark place, until the day
dawns and the morning star rises in your
hearts. 20 Most important, you must know
that no prophecy of scripture represents
the prophet's own understanding of things,
21 because no prophecy ever came by human
will. Instead, men and women led by the
Holy Spirit spoke from God.

Appearance of false teachers

2 But false prophets also arose among the
people. In the same way, false teachers
will come among you. They will introduce
destructive opinions and deny the master
who bought them, bringing quick destruction on themselves. 2 Many will follow
them in their unrestrained immorality, and
because of these false teachers the way of
truth will be slandered. 3 In their greed they
will take advantage of you with lies. The
judgment pronounced against them long
ago hasn't fallen idle, nor is their destruction sleeping.

Active judgment of God

4 God didn't spare the angels when they
sinned but cast them into the lowest level
of the underworld and committed them
to chains of darkness, keeping them there
until the judgment. 5 And he didn't spare
the ancient world when he brought a
flood on the world of ungodly people, even
though he protected Noah, a preacher of
righteousness, along with seven others.
6 God condemned the cities of Sodom and
Gomorrah to total destruction, reducing
them to ashes as a warning to ungodly
people. 7 And he rescued righteous Lot, who
was made miserable by the unrestrained
immorality of unruly people. (8 While that
righteous man lived among them he felt
deep distress every day on account of the
immoral actions he saw and heard.) 9 These
things show that the Lord knows how to
rescue the godly from their trials, and how
to keep the unrighteous for punishment on
the Judgment Day. 10 This is especially true
for those who follow after the corrupt cravings of the sinful nature and defy the Lord's
authority.

Evil character of the false teachers

These reckless, brash people aren't afraid
to insult the glorious ones, 11 yet angels,
who are stronger and more powerful, don't
use insults when pronouncing the Lord's
judgment on them. 12 These false teachers are like irrational animals, mere creatures of instinct, born to be captured and
destroyed. They slander what they don't
understand and, like animals, they will be
destroyed. 13 In this way, they will receive
payment for their wrongdoing.

They even enjoy unruly parties in broad
daylight. They are blots and blemishes,
taking delight in their seductive pleasures
while feasting with you. 14 They are always
looking for someone with whom to commit
adultery. They are always on the lookout
for opportunities to sin. They ensnare people whose faith is weak. They have hearts
trained in greed. They are under God's
curse. 15 Leaving the straight path, they
have gone off course, following the way of
Balaam son of Bosor, who loved the payment of doing wrong. 16 But Balaam was rebuked for his wrongdoing. A donkey, which
has no voice, spoke with a human voice and
put a stop to the prophet's madness.

17 These false teachers are springs without water, mists driven by the wind. The
underworld has been reserved for them.
18 With empty, self-important speech, they
use sinful cravings and unrestrained immorality to ensnare people who have only just
escaped life with those who have wandered
from the truth. 19 These false teachers promise freedom, but they themselves are slaves
of immorality; whatever overpowers you,
enslaves you. 20 If people escape the moral
filth of this world through the knowledge
of our Lord and savior Jesus Christ, then
get tangled up in it again and are overcome
by it, they are worse off than they were before. 21 It would be better for them never to
have known the way of righteousness than,

having come to know it, to turn back from the holy commandment entrusted to them. 22They demonstrate the truth of the proverb: “A dog returns to its own vomit, and a washed sow wallows in the mud.”

Delay of Christ's coming in judgment

3 My dear friends, this is now my second letter to you. I have written both letters to stir up your sincere understanding with a reminder. 2I want you to recall what the holy prophets foretold as well as what the Lord and savior commanded through your apostles. 3Most important, know this: in the last days scoffers will come, jeering, living by their own cravings, 4and saying, “Where is the promise of his coming? After all, nothing has changed—not since the beginning of creation, nor even since the ancestors died.”

5But they fail to notice that, by God's word, heaven and earth were formed long ago out of water and by means of water. 6And it was through these that the world of that time was flooded and destroyed. 7But by the same word, heaven and earth are now held in reserve for fire, kept for the Judgment Day and destruction of ungodly people.

8Don't let it escape your notice, dear friends, that with the Lord a single day is like a thousand years and a thousand years are like a single day. 9The Lord isn't slow to keep his promise, as some think of slowness, but he is patient toward you, not wanting anyone to perish but all to change their hearts and lives. 10But the day of the Lord will come like a thief. On that day the heavens will pass away with a dreadful noise, the elements will be consumed by fire, and the earth and all the works done on it will be exposed.

11Since everything will be destroyed in this way, what sort of people ought you to be? You must live holy and godly lives, 12waiting for and hastening the coming day of God. Because of that day, the heavens will be destroyed by fire and the elements will melt away in the flames. 13But according to his promise we are waiting for a new heaven and a new earth, where righteousness is at home.

Preparing for Christ's coming in judgment

14Therefore, dear friends, while you are waiting for these things to happen, make every effort to be found by him in peace—pure and faultless. 15Consider the patience of our Lord to be salvation, just as our dear friend and brother Paul wrote to you according to the wisdom given to him, 16speaking of these things in all his letters. Some of his remarks are hard to understand, and people who are ignorant and whose faith is weak twist them to their own destruction, just as they do the other scriptures.

Final instruction

17Therefore, dear friends, since you have been warned in advance, be on guard so that you aren't led off course into the error of sinful people, and lose your own safe position. 18Instead, grow in the grace and knowledge of our Lord and savior Jesus Christ. To him belongs glory now and forever. Amen.

1 JOHN

Announcement about the word of life

1 We announce to you what existed from the beginning, what we have heard, what we have seen with our eyes, what we have seen and our hands handled, about the word of life. 2The life was revealed, and we have seen, and we testify and announce to you the eternal life that was with the Father and was revealed to us. 3What we have seen and heard, we also announce it to you so that you can have fellowship with us. Our fellowship is with the Father and with his Son, Jesus Christ. 4We are writing these things so that our joy can be complete.

The message: God is light

5This is the message that we have heard from him and announce to you: “God is light and there is no darkness in him at all.” 6If we claim, “We have fellowship with him,” and live in the darkness, we are lying and do not act truthfully. [7]But if we live in the light in the same way as he is in the light, we have fellowship with each other, and the blood of Jesus, his Son, cleanses us from every sin. [8]If we claim, "We don't have any sin," we deceive ourselves and the truth is not in us. [9]But if we confess our sins, he is faithful and just to forgive us our sins and cleanse us from everything we've done wrong. [10]If we claim, "We have never sinned," we make him a liar and his word is not in us.

Living in the light

2 My little children, I'm writing these things to you so that you don't sin. But if you do sin, we have an advocate with the Father, Jesus Christ the righteous one. [2]He is God's way of dealing with our sins, not only ours but the sins of the whole world. [3]This is how we know that we know him: if we keep his commandments. [4]The one who claims, "I know him," while not keeping his commandments, is a liar, and the truth is not in this person. [5]But the love of God is truly perfected in whoever keeps his word. This is how we know we are in him. [6]The one who claims to remain in him ought to live in the same way as he lived.

[7]Dear friends, I'm not writing a new commandment to you, but an old commandment that you had from the beginning. The old commandment is the message you heard. [8]On the other hand, I am writing a new commandment to you, which is true in him and in you, because the darkness is passing away and the true light already shines. [9]The one who claims to be in the light while hating a brother or sister is in the darkness even now. [10]The person loving a brother and sister stays in the light, and there is nothing in the light that causes a person to stumble. [11]But the person who hates a brother or sister is in the darkness and lives in the darkness, and doesn't know where to go because the darkness blinds the eyes.

Motivations for writing

[12]Little children, I'm writing to you because your sins have been forgiven through Jesus' name. [13]Parents, I'm writing to you because you have known the one who has existed from the beginning. Young people, I'm writing to you because you have conquered the evil one. [14]Little children, I write to you because you know the Father. Parents, I write to you because you have known the one who has existed from the beginning. Young people, I write to you because you are strong, the word of God remains in you, and you have conquered the evil one.

Warning about the world

[15]Don't love the world or the things in the world. If anyone loves the world, the love of the Father is not in them. [16]Everything that is in the world—the craving for whatever the body feels, the craving for whatever the eyes see and the arrogant pride in one's possessions—is not of the Father but is of the world. [17]And the world and its cravings are passing away, but the person who does the will of God remains forever.

Remaining in the truth

[18]Little children, it is the last hour. Just as you have heard that the antichrist is coming, so now many antichrists have appeared. This is how we know it is the last hour. [19]They went out from us, but they were not really part of us. If they had been part of us, they would have stayed with us. But by going out from us, they showed they all are not part of us. [20]But you have an anointing from the holy one, and all of you know the truth. [21]I don't write to you because you don't know the truth but because you know it. You know that no lie comes from the truth. [22]Who is the liar? Isn't it the person who denies that Jesus is the Christ? This person is the antichrist: the one who denies the Father and the Son. [23]Everyone who denies the Son does not have the Father, but the one who confesses the Son has the Father also.

[24]As for you, what you heard from the beginning must remain in you. If what you heard from the beginning remains in you, you will also remain in relationship to the Son and in the Father. [25]This is the promise that he himself gave us: eternal life. [26]I write these things to you about those who

are attempting to deceive you. 27 As for you, the anointing that you received from him remains on you, and you don't need anyone to teach you the truth. But since his anointing teaches you about all things (it's true and not a lie), remain in relationship to him just as he taught you.

Remaining until Jesus appears

28 And now, little children, remain in relationship to Jesus, so that when he appears we can have confidence and not be ashamed in front of him when he comes. 29 If you know that he is righteous, you also know that every person who practices righteousness is born from him.

3 See what kind of love the Father has given to us in that we should be called God's children, and that is what we are! Because the world didn't recognize him, it doesn't recognize us.

2 Dear friends, now we are God's children, and it hasn't yet appeared what we will be. We know that when he appears we will be like him because we'll see him as he is. 3 And everyone who has this hope in him purifies himself even as he is pure. 4 Every person who practices sin commits an act of rebellion, and sin is rebellion. 5 You know that he appeared to take away sins, and there is no sin in him. 6 Every person who remains in relationship to him does not sin. Any person who sins has not seen him or known him.

Practicing sin or righteousness

7 Little children, make sure no one deceives you. The person who practices righteousness is righteous, in the same way that Jesus is righteous. 8 The person who practices sin belongs to the devil, because the devil has been sinning since the beginning. God's Son appeared for this purpose: to destroy the works of the devil. 9 Those born from God don't practice sin because God's DNA[a] remains in them. They can't sin because they are born from God. 10 This is how God's children and the devil's children are apparent: everyone who doesn't practice righteousness is not from God, including the person who doesn't love a brother or sister. 11 This is the message that you heard from the beginning: love each other. 12 Don't behave like Cain, who belonged to the evil one and murdered his brother. And why did he kill him? He killed him because his own works were evil, but the works of his brother were righteous.

Loving each other

13 Don't be surprised, brothers and sisters, if the world hates you. 14 We know that we have transferred from death to life, because we love the brothers and sisters. The person who does not love remains in death. 15 Everyone who hates a brother or sister is a murderer, and you know that no murderer has eternal life residing in him. 16 This is how we know love: Jesus laid down his life for us, and we ought to lay down our lives for our brothers and sisters. 17 But if a person has material possessions and sees a brother or sister in need and that person doesn't care—how can the love of God remain in him?

18 Little children, let's not love with words or speech but with action and truth. 19 This is how we will know that we belong to the truth and reassure our hearts in God's presence. 20 Even if our hearts condemn us, God is greater than our hearts and knows all things. 21 Dear friends, if our hearts don't condemn us, we have confidence in relationship to God. 22 We receive whatever we ask from him because we keep his commandments and do what pleases him. 23 This is his commandment, that we believe in the name of his Son, Jesus Christ, and love each other as he commanded us. 24 The person who keeps his commandments remains in God and God remains in him; and this is how we know that he remains in us, because of the Spirit that he has given to us.

Testing the spirits

4 Dear friends, don't believe every spirit. Test the spirits to see if they are from God because many false prophets have gone into the world. 2 This is how you know if a spirit comes from God: every spirit that

[a] Or *genetic character*

confesses that Jesus Christ has come as a
human[b] is from God, [3]and every spirit that
doesn't confess Jesus is not from God. This
is the spirit of the antichrist, which you
have heard is coming and is now already
in the world. [4]You are from God, little children, and you have defeated these people
because the one who is in you is greater
than the one who is in the world. [5]They
are from the world. So they speak from the
world's point of view and the world listens
to them. [6]We are from God. The person who
knows God listens to us. Whoever is not
from God doesn't listen to us. This is how
we recognize the Spirit of truth and the
spirit of error.

Love and God

[7]Dear friends, let's love each other, because love is from God, and everyone who
loves is born from God and knows God. [8]The
person who doesn't love does not know God,
because God is love. [9]This is how the love
of God is revealed to us: God has sent his
only Son into the world so that we can live
through him. [10]This is love: it is not that we
loved God but that he loved us and sent his
Son as the sacrifice that deals with our sins.

[11]Dear friends, if God loved us this way,
we also ought to love each other. [12]No one
has ever seen God. If we love each other,
God remains in us and his love is made perfect in us. [13]This is how we know we remain
in him and he remains in us, because he has
given us a measure of his Spirit. [14]We have
seen and testify that the Father has sent
the Son to be the savior of the world. [15]If
any of us confess that Jesus is God's Son,
God remains in us and we remain in God.
[16]We have known and have believed the
love that God has for us.

God is love, and those who remain in love
remain in God and God remains in them.
[17]This is how love has been perfected in
us, so that we can have confidence on the
Judgment Day, because we are exactly the
same as God is in this world. [18]There is no
fear in love, but perfect love drives out fear,
because fear expects punishment. The person who is afraid has not been made perfect
in love. [19]We love because God first loved
us. [20]If anyone says, I love God, and hates
a brother or sister, he is a liar, because the
person who doesn't love a brother or sister
who can be seen can't love God, who can't
be seen. [21]This commandment we have
from him: Those who claim to love God
ought to love their brother and sister also.

5 Everyone who believes that Jesus is the
Christ has been born from God. Whoever loves someone who is a parent loves
the child born to the parent. [2]This is how
we know that we love the children of God:
when we love God and keep God's commandments. [3]This is the love of God: we
keep God's commandments. God's commandments are not difficult, [4]because everyone who is born from God defeats the
world. And this is the victory that has defeated the world: our faith. [5]Who defeats
the world? Isn't it the one who believes that
Jesus is God's Son?

Testimony about Jesus

[6]This is the one who came by water and
blood: Jesus Christ. Not by water only but
by water and blood. And the Spirit is the
one who testifies, because the Spirit is
the truth. [7]The three are testifying—[8]the
Spirit, the water, and the blood—and the
three are united in agreement. [9]If we receive human testimony, God's testimony
is greater, because this is what God testified: he has testified about his Son. [10]The
one who believes in God's Son has the testimony within; the one who doesn't believe
God has made God a liar, because that one
has not believed the testimony that God
gave about his Son. [11]And this is the testimony: God gave eternal life to us, and this
life is in his Son. [12]The one who has the Son
has life. The one who doesn't have God's
Son does not have life.

Confidence in prayer

[13]I write these things to you who believe in
the name of God's Son so that you can know
that you have eternal life. [14]This is the confi-

[b]Or *come in the flesh*

dence that we have in our relationship with
God: If we ask for anything in agreement with
his will, he listens to us. [15]If we know that he
listens to whatever we ask, we know that we
have received what we asked from him. [16]If
anyone sees a brother or sister committing a
sin that does not result in death, they should
pray, and God will give life to them—that is,
to those who commit sins that don't result in
death. There is a sin that results in death—I'm
not saying that you should pray about that.
[17]Every unrighteous action is sin, but there is
a sin that does not result in death.

Be on guard

[18]We know that everyone born from
God does not sin, but the ones born from
God guard themselves,[c] and the evil one
cannot touch them. [19]We know we are
from God, and the whole world lies in the
power of the evil one. [20]We know that
God's Son has come and has given us understanding to know the one who is true.
We are in the one who is true by being in
his Son, Jesus Christ. This is the true God
and eternal life. [21]Little children, guard
yourselves from idols!

2 JOHN

Greeting

[1]From the elder.

To the chosen gentlewoman and her children, whom I truly love (and I am not the only one, but also all who know the truth), [2]because of the truth that remains with us and will be with us forever.

[3]Grace, mercy, and peace from God the Father and from Jesus Christ, the Son of the Father, will be ours who live in truth and love.

Love each other

[4]I was overjoyed to find some of your
children living in the truth, just as we had
been commanded by the Father. [5]Now, dear
friends, I am requesting that we love each
other. It's not as though I'm writing a new
command to you, but it's one we have had
from the beginning. [6]This is love: that we
live according to his commands. This is the
command that you heard from the beginning: live in love.

Reject false teachers

[7]Many deceivers have gone into the
world who do not confess that Jesus Christ
came as a human being. This kind of person
is the deceiver and the antichrist. [8]Watch
yourselves so that you don't lose what
we've worked for but instead receive a full
reward. [9]Anyone who goes too far and does
not continue in the teaching about Christ
does not have God. Whoever continues in
this teaching has both the Father and the
Son. [10]Whoever comes to you who does
not affirm this teaching should neither be
received nor welcomed into your home,
[11]because welcoming people like that is the
same thing as sharing in their evil actions.

Plans to visit

[12]I have a lot to tell you. I don't want to use paper and ink, but I hope to visit you and talk with you face-to-face, so that our joy can be complete.

Final greeting

[13]Your chosen sister's children greet you.

[c]Or *but the one who is born from God guards him from sin*

3 JOHN

Greeting

[1]From the elder.
To my dear friend Gaius, whom I truly
love.
[2]Dear friend, I'm praying that all is well
with you and that you enjoy good
health in the same way that you prosper spiritually.

Encouragement for Gaius

[3]I was overjoyed when the brothers and
sisters arrived and spoke highly of your
faithfulness to the truth, shown by how
you live according to the truth. [4]I have no
greater joy than this: to hear that my children are living according to the truth. [5]Dear
friend, you act faithfully in whatever you do
for our brothers and sisters, even though
they are strangers. [6]They spoke highly of
your love in front of the church. You all
would do well to provide for their journey
in a way that honors God, [7]because they
left on their journey for the sake of Jesus
Christ without accepting any support from
the Gentiles. [8]Therefore, we ought to help
people like this so that we can be coworkers
with the truth.

Criticism of Diotrephes

[9]I wrote something to the church, but
Diotrephes, who likes to put himself first,
doesn't welcome us. [10]Because of this, if I
come, I will bring up what he has done—
making unjustified and wicked accusations
against us. And as if that were not enough,
he not only refuses to welcome the brothers
and sisters but stops those who want to do
so and even throws them out of the church!
[11]Dear friend, don't imitate what is bad but
what is good. Whoever practices what is
good belongs to God. Whoever practices
what is bad has not seen God.

Approval of Demetrius

[12]Everyone speaks highly of Demetrius,
even the truth itself. We also speak highly
of him, and you know that what we say
is true.

Final greeting

[13]I have a lot to say to you, but I don't
want to use pen and ink. [14]I hope to see you
soon, and we will speak face-to-face.
[15]Peace be with you. Your friends here
greet you. Greet our friends there by name.

JUDE

Greeting

[1]Jude, a slave of Jesus Christ and brother
of James.
To those who are called, loved by God
the Father and kept safe by Jesus
Christ.
[2]May you have more and more mercy,
peace, and love.

Certain judgment of the false teachers

[3]Dear friends, I wanted very much to
write to you concerning the salvation we
share. Instead, I must write to urge you to
fight for the faith delivered once and for all
to God's holy people. [4]Godless people have
slipped in among you. They turn the grace
of our God into unrestrained immorality
and deny our only master and Lord, Jesus
Christ. Judgment was passed against them
a long time ago.
[5]I want to remind you of something you
already know very well. The Lord, who once
saved a people out of Egypt, later destroyed
those who didn't maintain their faith. [6]I remind you too of the angels who didn't keep
their position of authority but deserted
their own home. The Lord has kept them
in eternal chains in the underworld until
the judgment of the great day. [7]In the same
way, Sodom and Gomorrah and neighboring towns practiced immoral sexual relations and pursued other sexual urges. By
undergoing the punishment of eternal fire,
they serve as a warning.

8 Yet, even knowing this, these dreamers in the same way pollute themselves, reject authority, and slander the angels. 9 The
archangel Michael, when he argued with the
devil about Moses' body, did not dare charge
him with slander. Instead, he said, "The Lord
rebuke you!" 10 But these people slander
whatever they don't understand. They are
destroyed by what they know instinctively,
as though they were irrational animals.

Prophecies about the false teachers

11 They are damned, for they follow in
the footsteps of Cain. For profit they give
themselves over to Balaam's error. They are
destroyed in the uprising of Korah. 12 These
people are like jagged rocks just below the
surface of the water waiting to snag you
when they join your love feasts. They feast
with you without reverence. They care
only for themselves. They are waterless
clouds carried along by the winds; fruitless autumn trees, twice dead, uprooted;
13 wild waves of the sea foaming up their
own shame; wandering stars for whom the
darkness of the underworld is reserved
forever.
14 Enoch, who lived seven generations
after Adam, prophesied about these people
when he said, "See, the Lord comes with his
countless holy ones, 15 to execute judgment
on everyone and to convict everyone about
every ungodly deed they have committed
in their ungodliness as well as all the harsh
things that sinful ungodly people have
said against him." 16 These are faultfinding
grumblers, living according to their own desires. They speak arrogant words and they
show partiality to people when they want a
favor in return.
17 But you, dear friends, remember the
words spoken beforehand by the apostles of
our Lord Jesus Christ. 18 They said to you, "In
the end time scoffers will come living according to their own ungodly desires." 19 These
people create divisions. Since they don't
have the Spirit, they are worldly.

A strategy for the faithful

20 But you, dear friends: build each other
up on the foundation of your most holy
faith, pray in the Holy Spirit, 21 keep each
other in the love of God, wait for the mercy
of our Lord Jesus Christ, who will give you
eternal life. 22 Have mercy on those who
doubt. 23 Save some by snatching them
from the fire. Fearing God, have mercy on
some, hating even the clothing contaminated by their sinful urges.

Blessing

24 To the one who is able
to protect you from falling,
and to present you blameless
and rejoicing
before his glorious presence,
25 to the only God our savior,
through Jesus Christ our Lord,
belong glory, majesty, power,
and authority,
before all time, now and forever.
Amen.

REVELATION

Greetings

1 A revelation of Jesus Christ, which
God gave him to show his servants
what must soon take place. Christ
made it known by sending it through
his angel to his servant John, 2 who
bore witness to the word of God and
to the witness of Jesus Christ, including all that John saw. 3 Favored is
the one who reads the words of this
prophecy out loud, and favored are
those who listen to it being read, and
keep what is written in it, for the time
is near.
4 John, to the seven churches that are
in Asia:
Grace and peace to you from the one
who is and was and is coming, and
from the seven spirits that are before God's throne, 5 and from Jesus
Christ—the faithful witness, the
firstborn from among the dead, and
the ruler of the kings of the earth.
To the one who loves us and freed us

from our sins by his blood, 6 who
made us a kingdom, priests to his
God and Father—to him be glory and
power forever and always. Amen.
7 Look, he is coming with the clouds!
Every eye will see him, including those
who pierced him, and all the tribes of the
earth will mourn because of him. This is so.
Amen. 8 "I am the Alpha and the Omega,"
says the Lord God, "the one who is and was
and is coming, the Almighty."

Christ appears to John

9 I, John, your brother who shares with
you in the hardship, kingdom, and endurance that we have in Jesus, was on the island called Patmos because of the word of
God and my witness about Jesus. 10 I was in
a Spirit-inspired trance on the Lord's day,
and I heard behind me a loud voice that
sounded like a trumpet. 11 It said, "Write
down on a scroll whatever you see, and
send it to the seven churches: to Ephesus,
Smyrna, Pergamum, Thyatira, Sardis, Philadelphia, and Laodicea."
12 I turned to see who was speaking to me,
and when I turned, I saw seven oil lamps
burning on top of seven gold stands. 13 In
the middle of the lampstands I saw someone
who looked like the Human One.[a] He wore a
robe that stretched down to his feet, and he
had a gold sash around his chest. 14 His head
and hair were white as white wool—like
snow—and his eyes were like a fiery flame.
15 His feet were like fine brass that has been
purified in a furnace, and his voice sounded
like rushing water. 16 He held seven stars in
his right hand, and from his mouth came a
sharp, two-edged sword. His appearance was
like the sun shining with all its power.
17 When I saw him, I fell at his feet like a
dead man. But he put his right hand on me
and said, "Don't be afraid. I'm the first and
the last, 18 and the living one. I was dead,
but look! Now I'm alive forever and always.
I have the keys of Death and the Grave. 19 So
write down what you have seen, both the
scene now before you and the things that are
about to unfold after this. 20 As for the mystery of the seven stars that you saw in my
right hand and the seven gold lampstands,
here is what they mean: the seven stars are
the angels of the seven churches, and the
seven lampstands are the seven churches.

Message to Ephesus

2 "Write this to the angel of the church
in Ephesus:
These are the words of the one who holds
the seven stars in his right hand and walks
among the seven gold lampstands: 2 I know
your works, your labor, and your endurance.
I also know that you don't put up with those
who are evil. You have tested those who say
they are apostles but are not, and you have
found them to be liars. 3 You have shown endurance and put up with a lot for my name's
sake, and you haven't gotten tired. 4 But I
have this against you: you have let go of the
love you had at first. 5 So remember the high
point from which you have fallen. Change
your hearts and lives and do the things you
did at first. If you don't, I'm coming to you.
I will move your lampstand from its place if
you don't change your hearts and lives. 6 But
you have this in your favor: you hate what
the Nicolaitans are doing, which I also hate.
7 If you can hear, listen to what the Spirit is
saying to the churches. I will allow those who
emerge victorious to eat from the tree of life,
which is in God's paradise.

Message to Smyrna

8 "Write this to the angel of the church
in Smyrna:
These are the words of the one who is the
first and the last, who died and came back
to life: 9 I know your hardship and poverty
(though you are actually rich). I also know
the hurtful things that have been spoken about you by those who say they are
Jews (though they are not, but are really
Satan's synagogue). 10 Don't be afraid of
what you are going to suffer. Look! The
devil is going to throw some of you into
prison in order to test you. You will suffer hardship for ten days. Be faithful even
to the point of death, and I will give you

[a]Or *Son of Man*

the crown of life. 11If you can hear, listen to what the Spirit is saying to the churches. Those who emerge victorious won't be hurt by the second death.

Message to Pergamum

12"Write this to the angel of the church in Pergamum:

These are the words of the one who has the sharp, two-edged sword: 13I know that you are living right where Satan's throne is. You are holding on to my name, and you didn't break faith with me even at the time that Antipas, my faithful witness, was killed among you, where Satan lives. 14But I have a few things against you, because you have some there who follow Balaam's teaching. Balaam had taught Balak to trip up the Israelites so that they would eat food sacrificed to idols and commit sexual immorality. 15In the same way, you have some who follow the Nicolaitans' teaching. 16So change your hearts and lives. If you don't, I am coming to you soon, and I will make war on them with the sword that comes from my mouth. 17If you can hear, listen to what the Spirit is saying to the churches. I will give those who emerge victorious some of the hidden manna to eat. I will also give to each of them a white stone with a new name written on it, which no one knows except the one who receives it.

Message to Thyatira

18"Write this to the angel of the church in Thyatira:

These are the words of God's Son, whose eyes are like a fiery flame, and whose feet are like fine brass. 19I know your works, your love and faithfulness, your service and endurance. I also know that the works you have done most recently are even greater than those you did at first. 20But I have this against you: you put up with that woman, Jezebel, who calls herself a prophet. You allow her to teach and to mislead my servants into committing sexual immorality and eating food sacrificed to idols. 21I gave her time to change her heart and life, but she refuses to change her life of prostitution. 22Look! I'm throwing her onto a sickbed. I am casting those who have committed adultery with her into terrible hardship—if they don't change their hearts from following her practices—23and I will even put her children to death with disease. Then all the churches will know that I'm the one who examines minds and hearts, and that I will give to each of you what your actions deserve. 24As for the rest of you in Thyatira—those of you who don't follow this teaching and haven't learned the so-called "deep secrets" of Satan—I won't burden you with anything else. 25Just hold on to what you have until I come. 26To those who emerge victorious, keeping my practices until the end, I will give authority over the nations—27to rule the nations with an iron rod and smash them like pottery—28just as I received authority from my Father. I will also give them the morning star. 29If you can hear, listen to what the Spirit is saying to the churches.

Message to Sardis

3 "Write this to the angel of the church in Sardis:

These are the words of the one who holds God's seven spirits and the seven stars: I know your works. You have the reputation of being alive, and you are in fact dead. 2Wake up and strengthen whatever you have left, teetering on the brink of death, for I've found that your works are far from complete in the eyes of my God. 3So remember what you received and heard. Hold on to it and change your hearts and lives. If you don't wake up, I will come like a thief, and you won't know what time I will come upon you. 4But you do have a few people in Sardis who haven't stained their clothing. They will walk with me clothed in white because they are worthy. 5Those who emerge victorious will wear white clothing like this. I won't scratch out their names from the scroll of life, but will declare their names in the presence of my Father and his angels. 6If you can hear, listen to what the Spirit is saying to the churches.

Message to Philadelphia

7"Write this to the angel of the church in Philadelphia:

ine, disease, and the wild animals of the
earth.
[9]When he opened the fifth seal, I
saw under the altar those who had been
slaughtered on account of the word of God
and the witness they had given. [10]They
cried out with a loud voice, "Holy and
true Master, how long will you wait before you pass judgment? How long before
you require justice for our blood, which
was shed by those who live on earth?"
[11]Each of them was given a white robe, and
they were told to rest a little longer, until
their fellow servants and brothers and
sisters—who were about to be killed as
they were—were finished.
[12]I looked on as he opened the sixth seal,
and there was a great earthquake. The sun
became black as funeral clothing, and the
entire moon turned red as blood. [13]The
stars of the sky fell to the earth as a fig tree
drops its fruit when shaken by a strong
wind. [14]The sky disappeared like a scroll
being rolled up, and every mountain and
island was moved from its place. [15]Then the
kings of the earth, the officials and the generals, the rich and the powerful, and everyone, slave and free, hid themselves in caves
and in the rocks of the mountains. [16]They
called to the mountains and the rocks, "Fall
on us and hide us from the face of the one
seated on the throne and from the Lamb's
wrath! [17]The great day of their wrath has
come, and who is able to stand?"

One hundred forty-four thousand sealed

7 After this I saw four angels standing at
the four corners of the earth. They held
back the earth's four winds so that no wind
would blow against the earth, the sea, or
any tree. [2]I saw another angel coming up
from the east, holding the seal of the living
God. He cried out with a loud voice to the
four angels who had been given the power
to damage the earth and sea. [3]He said,
"Don't damage the earth, the sea, or the
trees until we have put a seal on the foreheads of those who serve our God."
[4]Then I heard the number of those
who were sealed: one hundred forty-four
thousand, sealed from every tribe of the
Israelites:

[5]From the tribe of Judah,
twelve thousand were sealed;
from the tribe of Reuben,
twelve thousand;
from the tribe of Gad,
twelve thousand;
[6]from the tribe of Asher,
twelve thousand;
from the tribe of Naphtali,
twelve thousand;
from the tribe of Manasseh,
twelve thousand;
[7]from the tribe of Simeon,
twelve thousand;
from the tribe of Levi,
twelve thousand;
from the tribe of Issachar,
twelve thousand;
[8]from the tribe of Zebulun,
twelve thousand;
from the tribe of Joseph,
twelve thousand;
from the tribe of Benjamin,
twelve thousand were sealed.

The great crowd and seventh seal

[9]After this I looked, and there was a
great crowd that no one could number.
They were from every nation, tribe, people,
and language. They were standing before
the throne and before the Lamb. They wore
white robes and held palm branches in their
hands. [10]They cried out with a loud voice:

"Victory belongs to our God
who sits on the throne,
and to the Lamb."

[11]All the angels stood in a circle around
the throne, and around the elders and the
four living creatures. They fell facedown
before the throne and worshipped God,
[12]saying,

"Amen! Blessing and glory
and wisdom and thanksgiving
and honor and power and might
be to our God forever and always.
Amen."

[13]Then one of the elders said to me,
"Who are these people wearing white robes,
and where did they come from?"

14 I said to him, "Sir, you know."
Then he said to me, "These people have
come out of great hardship. They have
washed their robes and made them white
in the Lamb's blood. 15 This is the reason
they are before God's throne. They worship
him day and night in his temple, and the
one seated on the throne will shelter them.
16 They won't hunger or thirst anymore. No
sun or scorching heat will beat down on
them, 17 because the Lamb who is in the
midst of the throne will shepherd them. He
will lead them to the springs of life-giving
water,[d] and God will wipe away every tear
8 from their eyes." 1 Then, when the Lamb
opened the seventh seal, there was silence in heaven for about half an hour.

The first four trumpet plagues

2 Then I saw the seven angels who stand
before God, and seven trumpets were given
to them. 3 Another angel came and stood at
the altar, and he held a gold bowl for burning incense. He was given a large amount
of incense, in order to offer it on behalf of
the prayers of all the saints on the gold altar
in front of the throne. 4 The smoke of the
incense offered for the prayers of the saints
rose up before God from the angel's hand.
5 Then the angel took the incense container
and filled it with fire from the altar. He
threw it down to the earth, and there were
thunder, voices, lightning, and an earthquake.
6 Then the seven angels who held the
seven trumpets got ready to blow them.
7 The first angel blew his trumpet, and hail
and fire mixed with blood appeared, and
was thrown down to the earth. A third of
the earth was burned up. A third of the
trees were burned up. All the green grass
was burned up. 8 Then the second angel
blew his trumpet, and something like
a huge mountain burning with fire was
thrown down into the sea. A third of the sea
became blood, 9 a third of the creatures living in the sea died, and a third of the ships
were destroyed. 10 Then the third angel blew
his trumpet, and a great star, burning like a
torch, fell from heaven. It fell on a third of
the rivers and springs of water. 11 The star's
name is Wormwood, and a third of the waters became wormwood, and many people
died from the water, because it became
so bitter. 12 Then the fourth angel blew his
trumpet, and a third of the sun was struck,
and a third of the moon, and a third of the
stars so that a third of them became dark.
The day lost a third of its light, and the
night lost a third of its light too.
13 Then I looked and I heard an eagle flying high overhead. It said with a loud voice,
"Horror, horror, oh! The horror for those
who live on earth because of the blasts of
the remaining trumpets that the three angels are about to blow!"

The fifth and sixth trumpet plagues

9 Then the fifth angel blew his trumpet,
and I saw a star that had fallen from
heaven to earth, and he was given the key
to the shaft of the abyss. 2 He opened the
shaft of the abyss; and smoke rose up from
the shaft, like smoke from a huge furnace.
The sun and air were darkened by the smoke
from the shaft. 3 Then locusts came forth
from the smoke and onto the earth. They
were given power like the power that scorpions have on the earth. 4 They were told not
to hurt the grass of the earth or any green
plant or any tree. They could only hurt the
people who didn't have the seal of God on
their foreheads. 5 The locusts weren't allowed
to kill them, but only to make them suffer
for five months—and the suffering they inflict is like that of a scorpion when it strikes
a person. 6 In those days people will seek
death, but they won't find it. They will want
to die, but death will run away from them.
7 The locusts looked like horses ready for
battle. On their heads were what seemed
to be gold crowns. Their faces were like
human faces, 8 their hair was like women's
hair, and their teeth were like lions' teeth.
9 In front they had what seemed to be iron
armor upon their chests, and the sound
of their wings was like the sound of many
chariots and horses racing into battle.

[d] Or *the water of life*

[10]They also have tails with stingers, just like
scorpions; and in their tails is their power
to hurt people for five months. [11]Their king
is an angel from the abyss, whose Hebrew
name is Abaddon,[e] and whose Greek name
is Apollyon.[f]

[12]The first horror has passed. Look! Two
horrors are still coming after this.

[13]Then the sixth angel blew his trumpet,
and I heard a voice from the four horns of
the gold altar that is before God. [14]It said
to the sixth angel, who had the trumpet,
"Release the four angels who are bound at
the great river Euphrates." [15]Then the four
angels who had been made ready for that
hour, day, month, and year were released to
kill a third of humankind. [16]The number of
cavalry troops was two hundred million. I
heard their number. [17]And this is the way
I saw the horses and their riders in the vision: they had breastplates that were fiery
red, dark blue, and yellow as sulfur. The
horses' heads were like lions' heads, and
out of their mouths came fire, smoke, and
sulfur. [18]By these three plagues a third of
humankind was killed: by the fire, smoke,
and sulfur coming out of their mouths.
[19]The horses' power is in their mouths and
their tails, for their tails are like snakes
with heads that inflict injuries.

[20]The rest of humankind, who weren't
killed by these plagues, didn't change their
hearts and lives and turn from their handiwork. They didn't stop worshipping demons and idols made of gold, silver, bronze,
stone, and wood—idols that can't see or
hear or walk. [21]They didn't turn away from
their murders, their spells and drugs, their
sexual immorality, or their stealing.

John receives the open scroll

10 Then I saw another powerful angel
coming down from heaven. He was
robed with a cloud, with a rainbow over
his head. His face was like the sun, and
his feet were like fiery pillars. [2]He held an
open scroll in his hand. He put his right
foot on the sea and his left foot on the land.
[3]He called out with a loud voice like a lion
roaring, and when he called out, the seven
thunders raised their voices. [4]When the
seven thunders spoke, I was about to write,
but I heard a voice from heaven say, "Seal
up what the seven thunders have said, and
don't write it down."

[5]Then the angel I saw standing on the
sea and on the land raised his right hand
to heaven. [6]He swore by the one who lives
forever and always, who created heaven
and what is in it, the earth and what is in it,
and the sea and what is in it, and said, "The
time is up. [7]In the days when the seventh
angel blows his trumpet, God's mysterious purpose will be accomplished, fulfilling
the good news he gave to his servants the
prophets."

[8]Then the voice I heard from heaven
spoke to me again and said, "Go, take the
opened scroll from the hand of the angel
who stands on the sea and on the land." [9]So
I went to the angel and told him to give me
the scroll. He said to me, "Take it and eat it.
It will make you sick to your stomach, but
sweet as honey in your mouth." [10]So I took
the scroll from the angel's hand and ate it.
And it was sweet as honey in my mouth,
but when I swallowed it, it made my stomach churn. [11]I was told, "You must prophesy
again about many peoples, nations, languages, and kings."

Two witnesses

11 Then I was given a measuring rod,
which was like a pole. And I was told,
"Get up and measure God's temple, the
altar, and those who worship there. [2]But
don't measure the court outside the temple.
Leave that out, because it has been given to
the nations, and they will trample the holy
city underfoot for forty-two months.

[3]"And I will allow my two witnesses to
prophesy for one thousand two hundred
sixty days, wearing mourning clothes.
[4]These are the two olive trees and the two
lampstands that stand before the Lord of the
earth. [5]If anyone wants to hurt them, fire
comes out of their mouth and burns up their
enemies. So if anyone wants to hurt them,

[e]Destruction [f]Destroyer

they have to be killed in this way. 6 They have the power to close up the sky so that no rain will fall for as long as they prophesy. They also have power over the waters, to turn them into blood, and to strike the earth with any plague, as often as they wish.

7 "When they have finished their witnessing, the beast that comes up from the abyss will make war on them, gain victory over
them, and kill them. 8 Their dead bodies will lie on the street of the great city that is spiritually called Sodom and Egypt, where also
their Lord was crucified. 9 And for three and a half days, members of the peoples, tribes, languages, and nations will look at their dead bodies, but they won't let their dead
bodies be put in a tomb. 10 Those who live on earth will rejoice over them. They will celebrate and give each other gifts, because these two prophets had brought such pain to those who live on earth.

11 "But after three and a half days, the breath of life from God entered them, and they stood on their feet. Great fear
came over those who saw them. 12 Then they heard a loud voice from heaven say to them, 'Come up here.' And they went up to heaven in a cloud, while their enemies
watched them. 13 At that hour there was a great earthquake, and a tenth of the city fell. Seven thousand people were killed by the earthquake, and the rest were afraid and gave glory to the God of heaven."

14 The second horror is over. The third horror is coming soon.

Seventh trumpet

15 Then the seventh angel blew his trumpet, and there were loud voices in heaven saying,

"The kingdom of the world has become
the kingdom of our Lord and his Christ,
and he will rule forever and always."

16 Then the twenty-four elders, who were seated on their thrones before God, fell on
their faces and worshipped God. 17 They said,

"We give thanks to you,
Lord God Almighty,
who is and was,
for you have taken your great power
and enforced your rule.
18 The nations were enraged,
but your wrath came.
The time came for the dead to be judged;
The time came to reward your servants,
the prophets and saints,
and those who fear your name,
both small and great,
and to destroy those
who destroy the earth."

19 Then God's temple in heaven was opened, and the chest containing his covenant appeared in his temple. There were lightning, voices, thunder, an earthquake, and large hail.

A woman, her child, and the dragon

12 Then a great sign appeared in heaven: a woman clothed with the sun, with the moon under her feet and a crown of
twelve stars on her head. 2 She was pregnant, and she cried out because she was
in labor, in pain from giving birth. 3 Then
another sign appeared in heaven: it was a great fiery red dragon, with seven heads and ten horns, and seven royal crowns
on his heads. 4 His tail swept down a third of heaven's stars and threw them to the earth. The dragon stood in front of the woman who was about to give birth so that when she gave birth, he might devour
her child. 5 She gave birth to a son, a male child who is to rule all the nations with an iron rod. Her child was snatched up to
God and his throne. 6 Then the woman fled into the desert, where God has prepared a place for her. There she will be taken care of for one thousand two hundred sixty days.

Michael and the dragon

7 Then there was war in heaven: Michael and his angels fought the dragon. The
dragon and his angels fought back, 8 but they did not prevail, and there was no lon-
ger any place for them in heaven. 9 So the great dragon was thrown down. The old snake, who is called the devil and Satan, the deceiver of the whole world, was thrown down to the earth; and his angels were
thrown down with him. 10 Then I heard a loud voice in heaven say,

"Now the salvation and power
and kingdom of our God,
and the authority of his Christ
have come.
The accuser
of our brothers and sisters,
who accuses them day and night
before our God,
has been thrown down.
11 They gained the victory over him
on account of the blood of the Lamb
and the word of their witness.
Love for their own lives
didn't make them afraid to die.
12 Therefore, rejoice, you heavens
and you who dwell in them.
But oh! The horror for the earth and sea!
The devil has come down to you
with great rage,
for he knows that he only has
a short time."

The dragon pursues the woman

13 When the dragon saw that he had been
thrown down to the earth, he chased the
woman who had given birth to the male
child. 14 But the woman was given the two
wings of the great eagle so that she could
fly to her place in the desert. There she
would be taken care of—out of the snake's
reach—for a time and times and half a time.
15 Then from his mouth the snake poured a
river of water after the woman so that the
river would sweep her away. 16 But the earth
helped the woman. The earth opened its
mouth and swallowed the river that the
dragon poured out of his mouth. 17 So the
dragon was furious with the woman, and
he went off to make war on the rest of her
children, on those who keep God's commandments and hold firmly to the witness
of Jesus.

The beast from the sea

18 Then the dragon stood on the seashore,
13 1 and I saw a beast coming up out of
the sea. It had ten horns and seven
heads. Each of its horns was decorated with
a royal crown, and on its heads were blasphemous names. 2 The beast I saw was like
a leopard. Its feet were like a bear's, and its
mouth was like a lion's mouth. The dragon
gave it his power, throne, and great authority. 3 One of its heads appeared to have
been slain and killed, but its deadly wound
was healed. So the whole earth was amazed
and followed the beast. 4 They worshipped
the dragon because it had given the beast
its authority. They worshipped the beast
and said, "Who is like the beast, and who
can fight against it?"

5 The beast was given a mouth that spoke
boastful and blasphemous things, and it
was given authority to act for forty-two
months. 6 It opened its mouth to speak
blasphemies against God. It blasphemed
God's name and his dwelling place (that is,
those who dwell in heaven).

7 It was also allowed to make war on
the saints and to gain victory over them.
It was given authority over every tribe,
people, language, and nation. 8 All who live
on earth worshipped it, all whose names
hadn't been written—from the time the
earth was made—in the scroll of life of
the Lamb who was slain. 9 Whoever has
ears must listen: 10 If any are to be taken
captive, then into captivity they will go. If
any are to be killed by the sword, then by
the sword they will be killed. This calls for
endurance and faithfulness on the part of
the saints.

The beast from the land

11 Then I saw another beast coming up
from the earth. It had two horns like a
lamb, but it was speaking like a dragon.
12 It exercises all the authority of the first
beast in its presence. It also makes the
earth and those who live in it worship the
first beast, whose fatal wound was healed.
13 It does great signs so that it even makes
fire come down from heaven to earth in the
presence of the people. 14 It deceives those
who live on earth by the signs that it was
allowed to do in the presence of the beast.
It told those who live on earth to make an
image for the beast who had been wounded
by the sword and yet came to life again. 15 It
was allowed to give breath to the beast's
image so that the beast's image would even
speak and cause anyone who didn't wor-

ship the beast's image to be put to death. 16 It forces everyone—the small and great, the rich and poor, the free and slaves—to have a mark put on their right hand or on their forehead. 17 It will not allow anyone to make a purchase or sell anything unless the person has the mark with the beast's name or the number of its name. 18 This calls for wisdom. Let the one who understands calculate the beast's number, for it's a human being's number. Its number is six hundred sixty-six.

The Lamb and the one hundred forty-four thousand

14 Then I looked, and there was the Lamb, standing on Mount Zion. With him were one hundred forty-four thousand who had his name and his Father's name written on their foreheads. 2 I heard a sound from heaven that was like the sound of rushing water and loud thunder. The sound I heard was like that of harpists playing their harps. 3 They sing a new song in front of the throne, the four living creatures, and the elders. And no one could learn the song except the one hundred forty-four thousand who had been purchased from the earth. 4 They weren't defiled with women, for these people who follow the Lamb wherever he goes are virgins. They were purchased from among humankind as early produce for God and the Lamb. 5 No lie came from their mouths; they are blameless.

Messages of three angels

6 Then I saw another angel flying high overhead with eternal good news to proclaim to those who live on earth, and to every nation, tribe, language, and people. 7 He said in a loud voice, "Fear God and give him glory, for the hour of his judgment has come. Worship the one who made heaven and earth, the sea and springs of water."

8 Another angel, a second one, followed and said, "Fallen, fallen is Babylon the great! She made all the nations drink the wine of her lustful passion."

9 Then another angel, a third one, followed them and said in a loud voice, "If any worship the beast and its image, and receive a mark on their foreheads or their hands, 10 they themselves will also drink the wine of God's passionate anger, poured full strength into the cup of his wrath. They will suffer the pain of fire and sulfur in the presence of the holy angels and the Lamb. 11 The smoke of their painful suffering goes up forever and always. There is no rest day or night for those who worship the beast and its image, and those who receive the mark of its name."

12 This calls for the endurance of the saints, who keep God's commandments and keep faith with Jesus.

13 And I heard a voice from heaven say, "Write this: Favored are the dead who die in the Lord from now on."

"Yes," says the Spirit, "so they can rest from their labors, because their deeds follow them."

Two harvests of the earth

14 Then I looked, and there was a white cloud. On the cloud was seated someone who looked like the Human One.[g] He had a gold crown on his head and a sharp sickle in his hand. 15 Another angel came out of the temple, calling in a loud voice to the one seated on the cloud: "Use your sickle to reap the harvest, for the time to harvest has come, and the harvest of the earth is ripe." 16 So the one seated on the cloud swung his sickle over the earth, and the earth was harvested.

17 Then another angel came out of the temple in heaven, and he also had a sharp sickle. 18 Still another angel, who has power over fire, came out from the altar. He said in a loud voice to the one who had the sharp sickle, "Use your sharp sickle to cut the clusters in the vineyard of the earth, because its grapes are ripe." 19 So the angel swung his sickle into the earth, and cut the vineyard of the earth, and he put what he reaped into the great winepress of God's passionate anger. 20 Then the winepress was tram-

[g] Or *Son of Man*

pled outside the city, and the blood came
out of the winepress as high as the horses'
bridles for almost two hundred miles.[h]

Song of Moses and the Lamb

15 Then I saw another great and awe-
inspiring sign in heaven. There were
seven angels with seven plagues—and
these are the last, for with them God's
anger is brought to an end. 2 Then I saw
what appeared to be a sea of glass mixed
with fire. Those who gained victory over
the beast, its image, and the number of its
name were standing by the glass sea, holding harps from God. 3 They sing the song of
Moses, God's servant, and the song of the
Lamb, saying,

"Great and awe-inspiring
are your works,
Lord God Almighty.
Just and true are your ways,
king of the nations.
4 Who won't fear you, Lord,
and glorify your name?
You alone are holy.
All nations will come and fall down
in worship before you,
for your acts of justice
have been revealed."

Seven bowl plagues

5 After this I looked, and the temple in
heaven—that is, the tent of witness—was
opened. 6 The seven angels, who have the
seven plagues, came out of the temple. They
were clothed in pure bright linen and had
gold sashes around their waists. 7 Then one
of the four living creatures gave the seven
angels seven gold bowls full of the anger of
the God who lives forever and always. 8 The
temple was filled with smoke from God's
glory and power, and no one could go into
the temple until the seven plagues of the
seven last angels were brought to an end.

16 Then I heard a loud voice from the
temple say to the seven angels, "Go
and pour out the seven bowls of God's
anger on the earth." 2 So the first angel
poured his bowl on the earth, and a nasty
and terrible sore appeared on the people
who had the beast's mark and worshipped
its image. 3 The second angel poured his
bowl into the sea, and the sea turned into
blood, like the blood of a corpse, and every
living thing in the sea died. 4 The third angel
poured his bowl into the rivers and springs
of water, and they turned into blood. 5 Then
I heard the angel of the waters say,

"You are just, holy one, who is and was,
because you have given these
judgments.
6 They poured out the blood
of saints and prophets,
and you have given them blood
to drink. They deserve it!"

7 And I heard the altar say,

"Yes, Lord God Almighty,
your judgments are true and just."

8 The fourth angel poured his bowl on
the sun, and it was allowed to burn people
with fire. 9 The people were burned by intense heat, and they cursed the name of the
God who had power over these plagues. But
they didn't change their hearts and lives
and give him glory. 10 The fifth angel poured
his bowl over the beast's throne, and
darkness covered its kingdom. People bit
their tongues because of their pain, 11 and
they cursed the God of heaven because of
their pains and sores; but they didn't turn
away from what they had done.

12 Then the sixth angel poured his bowl
on the great river Euphrates. Its water was
dried up so that the way was ready for the
kings from the east. 13 Then I saw three
unclean spirits, like frogs, come from the
dragon's mouth, the beast's mouth, and
the mouth of the false prophet. 14 These
are demonic spirits that do signs. They
go out to the kings of the whole world, to
gather them for battle on the great day of
God the Almighty. (15 Look! I'm coming like
a thief! Favored are those who stay awake
and clothed so that they don't go around
naked and exposed to shame.) 16 The spirits
gathered them at the place that is called in
Hebrew, Harmagedon.[i]

17 Then the seventh angel poured his

[h] Or *one thousand six hundred stades* [i] Or *Armageddon*

bowl into the air, and a loud voice came out from the temple, from the throne, saying, "It is done!" [18]There were lightning strikes, voices, and thunder, and a great earthquake occurred. The earthquake was greater than any that have occurred since there have been people on earth. [19]The great city split into three parts, and the cities of the nations fell. God remembered Babylon the great so that he gave her the wine cup of his furious anger. [20]Every island fled, and the mountains disappeared. [21]Huge hailstones weighing about one hundred pounds came down from heaven on the people. They cursed God for the plague of hail, because the plague was so terrible.

Babylon and the beast

17 Then one of the seven angels who had the seven bowls spoke with me. "Come," he said, "I will show you the judgment upon the great prostitute, who is seated on deep waters. [2]The kings of the earth have committed sexual immorality with her, and those who live on earth have become drunk with the wine of her whoring."

[3]Then he brought me in a Spirit-inspired trance to a desert. There I saw a woman seated on a scarlet beast that was covered with blasphemous names. It had seven heads and ten horns. [4]The woman wore purple and scarlet clothing, and she glittered with gold and jewels and pearls. In her hand she held a gold cup full of the vile and impure things that came from her activity as a prostitute. [5]A name—a mystery—was written on her forehead: "Babylon the great, the mother of prostitutes and the vile things of the earth." [6]I saw that the woman was drunk on the blood of the saints and the blood of Jesus' witnesses. I was completely stunned when I saw her.

[7]Then the angel said to me, "Why are you amazed? I will tell you the mystery of the woman and the seven-headed, ten-horned beast that carries her. [8]The beast that you saw was and is not, and is about to come up out of the abyss and go to destruction. Those who live on earth, whose names haven't been written in the scroll of life from the time the earth was made, will be amazed when they see the beast, because it was and is not and will again be present. [9]This calls for an understanding mind. The seven heads are seven mountains on which the woman is seated. They are also seven kings. [10]Five kings have fallen, the one is, and the other hasn't yet come. When that king comes, he must remain for only a short time. [11]As for the beast that was and is not, it is itself an eighth king that belongs to the seven, and it is going to destruction. [12]The ten horns that you saw are ten kings, who haven't yet received royal power. But they will receive royal authority for an hour, along with the beast. [13]These kings will be of one mind, and they will give their power and authority to the beast. [14]They will make war on the Lamb, but the Lamb will emerge victorious, for he is Lord of lords and King of kings. Those with him are called, chosen, and faithful."

[15]Then he said to me, "The waters that you saw, where the prostitute is seated, are peoples, crowds, nations, and languages. [16]As for the ten horns that you saw, they and the beast will hate the prostitute. They will destroy her and strip her bare. They will devour her flesh and burn her with fire [17]because God moved them to carry out his purposes. That is why they will be of one mind and give their royal power to the beast, until God's words have been accomplished. [18]The woman whom you saw is the great city that rules over the kings of the earth."

Babylon's fall

18 After this I saw another angel coming down from heaven. He had great authority, and the earth was filled with light because of his glory. [2]He called out with a loud voice, saying, "Fallen, fallen is Babylon the great! She has become a home for demons and a lair for every unclean spirit. She is a lair for every unclean bird, and a lair for every unclean and disgusting beast [3]because all the nations have fallen[j] due to the wine of her lustful passion. The kings

[j]Critical editions of the Gk New Testament read *have drunk*.

of the earth committed sexual immorality
with her, and the merchants of the earth
became rich from the power of her loose
and extravagant ways."
4 Then I heard another voice from heaven
say, "Come out of her, my people, so that you
don't take part in her sins and don't receive
any of her plagues. 5 Her sins have piled up
as high as heaven, and God remembered her
unjust acts. 6 Give her what she has given
to others. Give her back twice as much for
what she has done. In the cup that she has
poured, pour her twice as much. 7 To the extent that she glorified herself and indulged
her loose and extravagant ways, give her
pain and grief. In her heart she says, 'I sit
like a queen! I'm not a widow. I'll never see
grief.' 8 This is why her plagues will come in a
single day—deadly disease, grief, and hunger. She will be consumed by fire because
the Lord God who judges her is powerful.
9 "The kings of the earth, who committed
sexual immorality with her and shared her
loose and extravagant ways, will weep and
mourn over her when they see the smoke
from her burning. 10 They will stand a long
way off because they are afraid of the pain
she suffers, and they will say, 'Oh, the horror!
Babylon, you great city, you powerful city! In
a single hour your judgment has come.'
11 "The merchants of the earth will weep
and mourn over her, for no one buys their
cargoes anymore—12 cargoes of gold, silver,
jewels, and pearls; fine linen, purple, silk,
and scarlet; all those things made of scented
wood, ivory, fine wood, bronze, iron, and
marble; 13 cinnamon, incense, fragrant ointment, and frankincense; wine, oil, fine flour,
and wheat; cattle, sheep, horses, and car-
riages; and slaves, even human lives. 14 "The
fruit your whole being craved has gone from
you. All your glitter and glamour are lost to
you, never ever to be found again.'
15 "The merchants who sold these things,
and got so rich by her, will stand a long way
off because they fear the pain she suffers.
They will weep and mourn, and say, 16 'Oh,
the horror! The great city that wore fine
linen, purple, and scarlet, who glittered
with gold, jewels, and pearls—17 in just one
hour such great wealth was destroyed.'
"Every sea captain, every seafarer, sailors, and all who make their living on the
sea stood a long way off. 18 They cried out as
they saw the smoke from her burning and
said, 'What city was ever like the great city?'
19 They threw dust on their heads, and they
cried out, weeping and mourning. They said,
'Oh, the horror! The great city, where all who
have ships at sea became so rich by her prosperity—in just one hour she was destroyed.
20 Rejoice over her, heaven—you saints,
apostles, and prophets—because God has
condemned her as she condemned you.' "
21 Then a powerful angel picked up a
stone that was like a huge millstone and
threw it into the sea, saying, "With such
violent force the great city of Babylon will
be thrown down, and it won't be found anymore. 22 The sound of harpists and musicians, of pipers and trumpeters, will never
be heard among you again. No craftsman
of any kind will ever be found among you
again. The sound of the hand mill will never
be heard among you again. 23 The light of
a lamp will never shine among you again.
The sound of a bridegroom and bride will
never be heard among you again because
your merchants ran the world, because all
the nations were deceived by the spell you
cast, and because 24 the blood of prophets,
of saints, and of all who have been slaughtered on the earth was found among you."[k]

Celebration in heaven

19 After this I heard what sounded like a
huge crowd in heaven. They said,
"Hallelujah! The salvation and glory and
power of our God!
2 His judgments are true and just,
because he judged the great prostitute,
who ruined the earth by her whoring,
and he exacted the penalty
for the blood of his servants
from her hand."
3 Then they said a second time,
"Hallelujah! Smoke goes up
from her forever and always."

k Or *her*

4 The twenty-four elders and the four living creatures fell down and worshipped God, who is seated on the throne, and they said, "Amen. Hallelujah!"

5 Then a voice went out from the throne and said,

"Praise our God, all you his servants,
and you who fear him,
both small and great."

6 And I heard something that sounded like a huge crowd, like rushing water and powerful thunder. They said,

"Hallelujah! The Lord our God,
the Almighty,
exercised his royal power!
7 Let us rejoice and celebrate,
and give him the glory,
for the wedding day of the Lamb
has come,
and his bride has made herself ready.
8 She was given fine, pure white linen
to wear,
for the fine linen
is the saints' acts of justice."

9 Then the angel said to me, "Write this: Favored are those who have been invited to the wedding banquet of the Lamb." He said to me, "These are the true words of God." 10 Then I fell at his feet to worship him. But he said, "Don't do that! I'm a servant just like you and your brothers and sisters who hold firmly to the witness of Jesus. Worship God! The witness of Jesus is the spirit of prophecy!"

Christ defeats the beast

11 Then I saw heaven opened, and there was a white horse. Its rider was called Faithful and True, and he judges and makes war justly. 12 His eyes were like a fiery flame, and on his head were many royal crowns. He has a name written on him that no one knows but he himself. 13 He wore a robe dyed[l] with blood, and his name was called the Word of God. 14 Heaven's armies, wearing fine linen that was white and pure, were following him on white horses. 15 From his mouth comes a sharp sword that he will use to strike down the nations. He is the one who will rule them with an iron rod. And he is the one who will trample the winepress of the Almighty God's passionate anger. 16 He has a name written on his robe and on his thigh: King of kings and Lord of lords.

17 Then I saw an angel standing in the sun, and he called out with a loud voice and said to all the birds flying high overhead, "Come and gather for God's great supper. 18 Come and eat the flesh of kings, the flesh of generals, the flesh of the powerful, and the flesh of horses and their riders. Come and eat the flesh of all, both free and slave, both small and great." 19 Then I saw that the beast and the kings of the earth and their armies had gathered to make war against the rider on the horse and his army. 20 But the beast was seized, along with the false prophet who had done signs in the beast's presence. (He had used the signs to deceive people into receiving the beast's mark and into worshipping the beast's image.) The two of them were thrown alive into the fiery lake that burns with sulfur. 21 The rest were killed by the sword that comes from the mouth of the rider on the horse, and all the birds ate their fill of their flesh.

Satan confined

20 Then I saw an angel coming down from heaven, holding in his hand the key to the abyss and a huge chain. 2 He seized the dragon, the old snake, who is the devil and Satan, and bound him for a thousand years. 3 He threw him into the abyss, then locked and sealed it over him. This was to keep him from continuing to deceive the nations until the thousand years were over. After this he must be released for a little while.

The saints rule with Christ

4 Then I saw thrones, and people took their seats on them, and judgment was given in their favor.[m] They were the ones who had been beheaded for their witness to Jesus and God's word, and those who hadn't worshipped the beast or its image, who hadn't received the mark on their forehead or hand.

[l] Critical editions of the Gk New Testament read *dipped* or *covered with*. [m] Or *to them*

They came to life and ruled with Christ for one thousand years. 5 The rest of the dead didn't come to life until the thousand years were over. This is the first resurrection. 6 Favored and holy are those who have a share in the first resurrection. The second death has no power over them, but they will be priests of God and of Christ, and will rule with him for one thousand years.

Satan's defeat

7 When the thousand years are over, Satan will be released from his prison. 8 He will go out to deceive the nations that are at the four corners of the earth—Gog and Magog. He will gather them for battle. Their number is like the sand of the sea. 9 They came up across the whole earth and surrounded the saints' camp, the city that God loves. But fire came down from heaven and consumed them. 10 Then the devil, who had deceived them, was thrown into the lake of fire and sulfur, where the beast and the false prophet also were. There painful suffering will be inflicted upon them day and night, forever and always.

Final judgment

11 Then I saw a great white throne and the one who is seated on it. Before his face both earth and heaven fled away, and no place was found for them. 12 I saw the dead, the great and the small, standing before the throne, and scrolls were opened. Another scroll was opened too; this is the scroll of life. And the dead were judged on the basis of what was written in the scrolls about what they had done. 13 The sea gave up the dead that were in it, and Death and the Grave gave up the dead that were in them, and people were judged by what they had done. 14 Then Death and the Grave were thrown into the fiery lake. This, the fiery lake, is the second death. 15 Then anyone whose name wasn't found written in the scroll of life was thrown into the fiery lake.

New heaven and new earth

21 Then I saw a new heaven and a new earth, for the former heaven and the former earth had passed away, and the sea was no more. 2 I saw the holy city, New Jerusalem, coming down out of heaven from God, made ready as a bride beautifully dressed for her husband. 3 I heard a loud voice from the throne say, "Look! God's dwelling is here with humankind. He will dwell with them, and they will be his peoples. God himself will be with them as their God. 4 He will wipe away every tear from their eyes. Death will be no more. There will be no mourning, crying, or pain anymore, for the former things have passed away." 5 Then the one seated on the throne said, "Look! I'm making all things new." He also said, "Write this down, for these words are trustworthy and true." 6 Then he said to me, "All is done. I am the Alpha and the Omega, the beginning and the end. To the thirsty I will freely give water from the life-giving spring. 7 Those who emerge victorious will inherit these things. I will be their God, and they will be my sons and daughters. 8 But for the cowardly, the faithless, the vile, the murderers, those who commit sexual immorality, those who use drugs and cast spells, the idolaters and all liars—their share will be in the lake that burns with fire and sulfur. This is the second death."

New Jerusalem

9 Then one of the seven angels who had the seven bowls full of the seven last plagues spoke with me. "Come," he said, "I will show you the bride, the Lamb's wife." 10 He took me in a Spirit-inspired trance to a great, high mountain, and he showed me the holy city, Jerusalem, coming down out of heaven from God. 11 The city had God's glory. Its brilliance was like a priceless jewel, like jasper that was as clear as crystal. 12 It had a great high wall with twelve gates. By the gates were twelve angels, and on the gates were written the names of the twelve tribes of Israel's sons. 13 There were three gates on the east, three gates on the north, three gates on the south, and three gates on the west. 14 The city wall had twelve foundations, and on them were the twelve names of the Lamb's twelve apostles.

15 The angel who spoke to me had a gold measuring rod with which to measure the

city, its gates, and its wall. 16 Now the city
was laid out as a square. Its length was the
same as its width. He measured the city with
the rod, and it was fifteen hundred miles.[n]
Its length and width and height were equal.
17 He also measured the thickness of its wall.
It was two hundred sixteen feet[o] thick, as
a person—or rather, an angel—measures
things. 18 The wall was built of jasper, and
the city was pure gold, like pure glass. 19 The
city wall's foundations were decorated with
every kind of jewel. The first foundation was
jasper, the second was sapphire, the third
was chalcedony, and the fourth was emerald.
20 The fifth was sardonyx, the sixth was carnelian, the seventh was chrysolite, and the
eighth was beryl. The ninth was topaz, the
tenth was chrysoprase, the eleventh was jacinth, and the twelfth was amethyst. 21 The
twelve gates were twelve pearls; each one of
the gates was made from a single pearl. And
the city's main street was pure gold, as transparent as glass.

22 I didn't see a temple in the city, because its temple is the Lord God Almighty
and the Lamb. 23 The city doesn't need the
sun or the moon to shine on it, because
God's glory is its light, and its lamp is the
Lamb. 24 The nations will walk by its light,
and the kings of the earth will bring their
glory into it. 25 Its gates will never be shut
by day, and there will be no night there.
26 They will bring the glory and honor of the
nations into it. 27 Nothing unclean will ever
enter it, nor anyone who does what is vile
and deceitful, but only those who are registered in the Lamb's scroll of life.

22 Then the angel showed me the river
of life-giving water,[p] shining like crystal, flowing from the throne of God and the
Lamb 2 through the middle of the city's main
street. On each side of the river is the tree
of life, which produces twelve crops of fruit,
bearing its fruit each month. The tree's leaves
are for the healing of the nations. 3 There will
no longer be any curse. The throne of God
and the Lamb will be in it, and his servants
will worship him. 4 They will see his face, and
his name will be on their foreheads. 5 Night
will be no more. They won't need the light of
a lamp or the light of the sun, for the Lord
God will shine on them, and they will rule
forever and always.

Jesus is coming soon

6 Then he said to me, "These words are
trustworthy and true. The Lord, the God of
the spirits of the prophets, sent his angel
to show his servants what must soon take
place.

7 "Look! I'm coming soon. Favored is the
one who keeps the words of the prophecy
contained in this scroll."

8 I, John, am the one who heard and saw
these things. When I heard and saw them, I
fell down to worship at the feet of the angel
who had shown them to me. 9 But he said
to me, "Don't do that! I'm a servant just
like you and your brothers and sisters, the
prophets, and those who keep the words
of this scroll. Worship God!" 10 Then he
said to me, "Don't seal up the words of the
prophecy contained in this scroll, because
the time is near. 11 Let those who do wrong
keep doing what is wrong. Let the filthy still
be filthy. Let those who are righteous keep
doing what is right. Let those who are holy
still be holy.

12 "Look! I'm coming soon. My reward is
with me, to repay all people as their actions
deserve. 13 I am the alpha and the omega, the
first and the last, the beginning and the end.
14 Favored are those who wash their robes
so that they may have the right of access to
the tree of life and may enter the city by the
gates. 15 Outside are the dogs, the drug users
and spell-casters, those who commit sexual
immorality, the murderers, the idolaters,
and all who love and practice deception.

16 "I, Jesus, have sent my angel to bear
witness to all of you about these things for
the churches. I'm the root and descendant
of David, the bright morning star. 17 The
Spirit and the bride say, 'Come!' Let the one
who hears say, 'Come!' And let the one who
is thirsty come! Let the one who wishes receive life-giving water[q] as a gift."

18 Now I bear witness to everyone who

[n] Or *twelve thousand stades* [o] Or *one hundred forty-four pechon* (cubits) [p] Or *the water of life* [q] Or *the water of life*

hears the words of the prophecy contained in this scroll: If anyone adds to them, God will add to that person the plagues that are written in this scroll. [19]If anyone takes away from the words of this scroll of prophecy, God will take away that person's share in the tree of life and the holy city, which are described in this scroll.

[20]The one who bears witness to these things says, "Yes, I'm coming soon." Amen. Come, Lord Jesus!

[21]The grace of the Lord Jesus be with all.